ISBN 978-0-260-82720-3
PIBN 10974114

FB &c Ltd, Dalton House, 60 Windsor Avenue, London, SW19 2RR.
Company number 08720141. Registered in England and Wales.

For support please visit www.forgottenbooks.com

INDEX TO VOLUME 118

MINING AND SCIENTIFIC PRESS

January to June, 1919

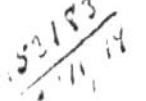

A

F

G

H

I

H

I

N

O

Q

R

T

U

W

PRESIDENT WILSON has received an enthusiastic welcome in England, as was to have been expected. It is amusing to read the sub-heading in one of our San Francisco papers saying that the reception was "the greatest ever accorded to a foreign citizen," as if the President would feel himself a 'foreigner' in a land in which his native language is spoken, in which his mother was born, and from which his grandfather came. There are three kinds of people in the world Americans, British, and foreigners.

ALREADY the workers are returning from military service to their places at the mines. Juneau reports a turn in the tide of migration that at one time threatened to paralyze local industry. Similar news comes from other mining districts. We hope and believe that there will be no hesitation in giving the 'boys' their old jobs, if not better ones. All the talk in the world in the way of praise to our young men for their patriotic service will not compensate for their having to wait for the work they are willing to resume. This applies to the technical staffs of the mines, mills, and smelters. The returning soldiers and sailors must be given first consideration. They deserve it, having proved themselves good citizens. Most of them will have benefitted from the intensive education of military service and should prove to be not only as good as before but better. Make room for the soldier boys!

DURING November the American production of copper, including that from mines controlled by American capital in South America, was 148,763,000 pounds, or about 6,000,000 pounds less than in October. The decrease is not remarkable, having regard to the holidays, which include not only Thanksgiving but the day of the Armistice. It is estimated that 800,000,000 pounds of copper is in transit, awaiting refining, and in surplus stocks. The total output for 1918 will be about equal to that of 1917. The demand for the metal is being withheld pending a decrease in price, which is inevitable. At London sellers offered metal at £100 and buyers quoted only £62 immediately after the withdrawal of Government control, this meaning that whereas sellers asked 21 cents per pound the buyers offered only 13⅜ cents. No business was done; which is typical of the situation. In the United States the supply of labor is improving appreciably, but no effort is being made to cut wages, so that no radical reduction in cost is likely for the present. The existing scale of wages is based upon a 26c. price for copper. Smelter purchases are being made now on a preliminary settlement at 15 cents per pound. This hiatus cannot continue indefinitely.

PRISONERS of war released by the Germans are furnishing damning testimony to the inhumanity of the Huns. American officers writing home tell about the terrible condition of the poor fellows whom they are succoring as soon as they reach the zone occupied by the troops of the Allied Armies; they tell how abominably the prisoners have been treated and how the miserably small allowance of food was cut down as against American prisoners. British soldiers returning from captivity are in a horrible condition, many of them having to be sent either to a hospital or an asylum immediately on their arrival in England. The Germans have a black account to settle and all the whining, accompanying the kamerad act, should not obscure the need for settling the account on terms of stern justice. As Cardinal Mercier has said, "There is no Christian justice without charity and no charity without justice."

IN this issue we publish the findings of the committee appointed in July 1918 by the Secretary of the Interior "to investigate the gold-mining situation in the United States." This committee consisted of Messrs. Hennen Jennings, chairman, J. H. Mackenzie, and Charles Janin, all of the U. S. Bureau of Mines, with H. D. McCaskey and F. L. Ransome of the U. S. Geological Survey. Their report is dated October 30. The style of publication indicates the fact that there was much difficulty in expediting the issuance of the report owing to the enormous demands on the capacity of the Public Printer at Washington. We give the findings of this committee because they will interest many of our readers and because we have a large measure of respect for the gentlemen who prepared it, but we are frank to say that it throws no new light on the subject. All the data in the report that are of any consequence have appeared already in various issues of our paper and the suggestions of the committee call for no fresh comment. We believe that the gold 'situation', meaning the unfortunate economic status of the metal during the War and the effect of it upon mining operations will be remedied automatically by the conclusion of peace, when the nations will have to resume the settlement of their balances by the transfer of gold bullion and by lifting the embargoes on the shipment of the metal in trade. We take pleasure in reproducing a table prepared by Mr. Charles Janin, who acted as secretary to the committee. This table is well worthy of close study, and criticism; it gives the cost of producing a dollar's worth of gold during the three years 1913, 1917, and 1918, showing how this has risen from 57 to 70 cents, such increase however being due apparently to the decline in the yield of gold per ton of ore rather than to any increase in the cost of recovery. Comparisons are vitiated by the decrease of development and the stoping of ore previously made accessible. The effect of higher wages and dearer supplies has been to curtail exploratory work and to prompt the extraction of ore ready to hand. Any statistics that show a decrease in the total cost of gold mining are certain to be wrong.

MR. HOOVER'S reply to Baron von der Lancken and Dr. Reith was keenly appreciated, especially by those who remembered that the name of the first is associated with the killing of Nurse Cavell, whereas the second was born in Belgium and is for that reason particularly detested as an agent of German tyranny. They wired to Mr. Walter L. Brown, an American mining engineer now director for the Commission for Relief in Belgium, whose article on 'Rotterdam, the distributing centre for the C. R. B.' appeared in our issue of September 21. In their telegram these two German officers notified Mr. Brown of their appointment to negotiate with Mr. Hoover for food supplies, whereupon he telegraphed to Mr. Brown saying: "You can describe two and a half years of arrogance toward ourselves and cruelty to the Belgians in any language you may select, and tell the pair personally to go to hell with my compliments. If I do have to deal with Germans it will not be with that pair." This may be shirt-sleeve diplomacy, but there are times when it has more dignity than the insincerities of conventional diplomacy. To Mr. Hoover there must have been much satisfaction in sending that message, and we share his satisfaction.

ON another page we publish a letter giving some interesting details concerning the Arctic Coal Company's operations on one of the islands of the Spitzbergen group. It will be noted that this American company sold out to a Norwegian company in April 1916. Apparently the British expedition that made a landing upon Spitzbergen on August 30 was organized by the Northern Exploration Company, which sent the 'Ella', in charge of the famous Arctic explorer, Sir Ernest Shackleton, accompanied by Captain Frank Wild and two mining engineers, Messrs. Arthur and Bertram Maugham, father and son. Two convoying vessels were torpedoed by German submarines before Tromsö, in Norway, was reached. The Norwegian press was full of threats against the expedition. Sir Ernest Shackleton was recalled by the War Office and Captain Wild took command of the 'Ella', which reached her destination on Lowe Sound without further mishap. It is reported that iron deposits of great value were discovered, besides coal measures, but the report concerning the iron is not convincing. Remains of a Zeppelin base established by the Germans were found and destroyed at Ebeltoft Haven. A fully equipped party of miners was landed at Davis City to exploit the "vast coalfields" of the Northern Exploration Company, so it is said. No mention, curiously enough, is made of the Arctic Coal Company's operations and establishment, although these must be far the most important on the island. The 'Ella' returned safely after having "defeated the German aim to establish a coaling, submarine, and Zeppelin base within 38 hours' steam of Great Britain," so says the London 'Graphic', from which we quote. It looks to us as if the Northern Exploration Company has acquired the Norwegian rights to the Arctic Coal Company's property and that the description refers to the workings and plant of that former American venture. The photographs and the mention of an aerial tramway alike suggest this inference.

WE publish the text of the brief presented to Congress in behalf of the chrome producers. This was prepared by Mr. De Kalb, who has spent the last three months at Washington in behalf of the Chrome Producers' Association. The 'Mining and Scientific Press' was glad to give his services in an effort to assist the cause of our Western miners and to rectify what seemed to us to be a public wrong. Even those wholly detached from the mining of chromite will find the brief interesting, on account of the information it contains and the lucid statement of the case that it presents. We regret being unable to give space for the various exhibits, but their character is fairly well indicated. A good deal of bitterness is felt in the West against Mr. Hugh W. Sanford personally as the official chiefly responsible for issuing misleading advices and as one whose actions favored the buyers of chromite rather than the industry itself. His letter to Mr. N. J. Sinnott and his telegrams to Messrs. W. F. Berger and F. J. Koster will be printed in our next issue. Although the Geological Survey and the Bureau of Mines must take some share of the blame for inciting the miners to a production for which no adequate market was forthcoming, it must be conceded that these bureaus were misled by the group of buyers to whose benefit the scheme seems to have inured. The entire control of the chromite industry appears to have been vested in the Ferro-Alloys Committee, which consisted entirely of buyers and their representatives. On another page we give the text of the bill that has been presented to Congress in order to give relief to those injured by the chrome fiasco. In our next issue we shall give our readers a detailed account of the meeting on December 16 called by the American Mining Congress to discuss this subject at Washington.

The Copper Export Association

Details concerning the Copper Export Association, organized by the principal producers of copper, will be found in this issue. The directorate is a 'Who's Who' in the copper world, for it includes representatives of all the 'big interests', as they are called by the financial reporter. Mr. Simon Guggenheim is chairman of the Board, the representative of the Anaconda is president, and the representatives of the Phelps Dodge and Calumet & Hecla groups respectively are the vice-presidents. Mr. Joseph C. Clendenin, of the American Smelting & Refining Company, is chairman of the selling committee. His office for the present will be at 42 Broadway, New York. Mr. John D. Ryan, speaking for the Association, made a number of remarks all of which will be read with keen interest. The idea is to establish a collective selling agency for the marketing of copper abroad, thereby avoiding the handicap under which formerly the producers of copper in this country were placed when dealing with the combination of buyers in Europe. An eye has been kept on the Federal Trade Commission; in the first place, the organization is made in conformity with the Webb Act legalizing combinations for the regulation of export trade; next, the small producers are invited to join the big fellows, so that none need feel that he has been left out in the cold. Nominal brokerage fees are to be charged and something additional to pay expenses. It is stated that the War Industries Board sent representatives to Europe before the armistice was signed in order to determine the copper requirements for 1919 and that they reported a probable demand for a billion pounds of the metal, to be increased by half a billion more if Germany regains a normal financial footing. It is estimated that Great Britain will take 200,000 long tons, France 145,000, and Italy 85,000 tons. Meanwhile, of course, the meetings of this Export Association enable the producers to discuss other subjects, such as the weather and the domestic production of copper. It is understood that a general reduction of output is to be made forthwith, beginning with a cut of 15% per month, until the supply of copper ceases to be in excess of the demand. The copper producers, like others engaged in mining the metals needed for the War, have been rushing production in response to the urgent solicitation of the Government and now like other metal producers they find themselves with unsold stocks since the Government ceased to buy on December 20. Costs are high, particularly labor, and no immediate reduction is practicable so long as the cost of living remains where it is. Therefore the policy will be to stop all over-time, to discharge inefficient men, and to reduce the output until Europe resumes buying of copper on a large scale. When an over-supply of labor becomes available, the rate of wages will be lowered in accordance with the equity of the case, for the existing pay is based upon copper at 26 cents. Some re-sales have taken place, it is rumored, at a price as low as 19 cents, and all signs point to something like 20 cents as the price to prevail during the period of reconstruction.

After the War

The new year dawns rich in promise. Behind us the thunder-clouds of war retreat sullenly while in front the glad sun of peace is rising over a battle-scarred world. The talk of reconstruction almost drowns the conversations of the peacemakers, although until peace is formally ratified and the system of war-controls expires we shall not feel the full force of the new conditions amid which we are to live henceforth; nevertheless every engineer and every manufacturer is already appraising the probabilities becoming discernible. The mining profession has come out of the War comparatively unscathed and with added self-respect. Our engineers responded promptly to the national call and if they suffered fewer casualties at the front than from the influenza at home it was not for lack of willingness to go wherever duty called them. As against a very small number of casualties there is set their inspiring experience of service in the Army and Navy, and the widening of their intellectual horizon. Ample reasons exist for optimism, despite the great destruction of life and capital in Europe during the four years of battle, murder, and sudden death. The United States, as compared with the other belligerents, has suffered little from loss of life or of capital; indeed, the increased efficiency of the living brought about by the stimulus of a great emergency has made this country industrially stronger, and the waste of capital in the materials of warfare has been largely compensated by the big purchases made in the United States by the Allied governments both before and after our own participation in the conflict. The War leaves America richer not only in money but in character. The stock of money in the United States has increased from $34 per capita in 1914 to $56 per capita at the present time. It is true, the National Debt has been increased by some twenty-five billions of dollars, but the bonds are held by our own people and the interest on them remains at home. Even though taxes are heavier, they are paid to the Treasury, which returns the money to the bondholders, who are also the taxpayers. No national impoverishment is involved in the transaction. The United States has lent 8½ billions to the Allied governments, and private investors in this country have lent fully 2 billions more, so that we shall be receiving some 500 million dollars per annum as income from Europe, whereas before the War we were remitting 20 million dollars per annum on the 5 billions of American securities held abroad, of which three-quarters has been repurchased during the War, reducing the interest correspondingly. Besides remittances to Europe on this account we paid freights for transporting goods in foreign bottoms, insurance in foreign companies, and the money spent by our people as tourists in Europe, so that the annual merchandise trade-balance of 500 million dollars was almost entirely offset. Now that a tremendous tonnage of foodstuffs will be shipped to Europe, besides a great mass of materials for reconstruction, the balance in our favor will be at least a billion dollars per annum.

which added to the half a billion income on loans to the Allies will yield $1,500,000,000 payable annually from abroad to the United States. These favorable financial conditions should last at least three years. From a debtor we have changed to a creditor nation. As soon as the work of rehabilitation and reconstruction begins in the countries devastated by war there will be a demand first for food, then for clothing, then for steel and the other metals of manufacture. The immediate demand will be for raw materials. The food sent to Europe will be paid for, at good prices, for there is no reason to suppose that any of it, least of all to the enemy countries, will be gratuitous. We shall send 20,000,000 tons of food to Europe this year. The farmer is assured a splendid market for his products. The lack of clothing in Europe will create a strong demand for cotton and wool. The Southern States should be rendered prosperous thereby. An insistent call for metals is inevitable; the miners of the West will benefit from the consumption consequent upon the rebuilding and re-equipment necessitated by German frightfulness. There are 4000 tons of machinery and tools waiting for shipment in New York harbor and orders for $10,000,000 worth of mining machinery for the French coalfields have been placed already. A statistical comparison demonstrates the commanding position of the United States in its possession of a preponderating share of the raw materials of civilization.

	Coal	Iron	Copper	Gold	Petroleum
	%	%	%	%	%
United States	52	63	56	19	64
British Empire	23	18	11	63	2
Germany and Austria	6	2	3	..	2
France, Belgium, and Italy	1	2	..	..	..
All other countries	18	15	30	18	32

An immense quantity of the materials of construction is needed in Europe. Mr. William C. Redfield, the Secretary of Commerce, states that materials for building more than a million houses will be required in Belgium and France, but even such a statement fails to suggest the amount of reconstruction necessitated by the destruction of cities, railways, roads, bridges, factories, foundries, with their contents of machinery and tools, not only in Belgium and France, but in the devastated regions of eastern and south-eastern Europe. Much of this material, particularly the machine-tools and other elements of skillful manufacture requiring the consumption of metals, must be provided by the United States. It is proper to add that difference of opinion exists as to the prospects of supplying Europe. Mr. C. W. Barron thinks that not much will be required in the devastated areas because local brick and mortar, reinforced by timber, will suffice for the villages of France and Belgium, and he seems to belittle the need of steel and other metals in the cities that have been shelled and looted. Judge Gary expects to see an expansion of the trade in steel products with South America and South Africa, rather than with Europe, but he predicts confidently that "the next five years in this country will be the most progressive, prosperous, and successful in its history." In the past a large part of the metal production of this country and of the overseas dominions of Great Britain was in the control of German combinations having their headquarters at Frankfort. The Alien Property Custodian has broken the German hold on the American metal trade and has thereby offered new opportunities for the distribution of the miner's products abroad and new chances of American participation in the exploration and exploitation of foreign mineral regions. Here we come to a fundamental consequence of the financial change caused by the War. This country cannot expect either to increase its exports or even to collect the interest due on its loans abroad except by the further extension of credit. As Mr. George E. Roberts of the National City Bank insists, we shall have to capitalize the interest payments and re-invest them abroad. If we want to sell goods to our foreign customers, we shall have to buy their bonds and stocks. We shall have to increase our investments abroad. On that point every intelligent economist agrees. This conclusion is of immediate interest to the mining profession. Just as England before the War was the great creditor nation and had to find an outlet for her capital by adventure in foreign lands, so now the United States will find a logical consequence of her creditor position in the urge to use her surplus income and surplus energy in foreign enterprise, including mining. A beginning, a handsome beginning, has been made in copper mines in South America. A large amount of capital had been placed in Mexican mines before the European war and before the Mexican revolution; there will be a hearty resumption of American activities in Mexico as soon as political conditions improve south of the Rio Grande. By the way, it is fairly obvious that one of the first results of the Peace Conference at Versailles, a consequence both complementary and complimentary, will be a polite suggestion to Uncle Sam that he ought to clean up his backyard. Turning to other parts of the world, in Siberia the American participation in mining development has been less important in money than in men, for a considerable number of our best engineers have taken part in the work, mainly financed at London and Paris. Siberia is a continental area of large and varied mining potentialities; we expect to see an increased American interest in that direction and the growth of trade in machinery between San Francisco and Vladivostok. Even in South Africa, more distant as it may seem, it is noteworthy that during the period of the War there has been a considerable investment of American money on the part of some of our cleverest financiers in the development of mines on the Rand. We refer to the Anglo-American Corporation of South Africa, with which several American engineers are closely identified. Again, in the country of our good neighbors the Canadians, it is noteworthy that most of the important metal-mining enterprises of British Columbia are controlled by citizens of the United States. This we take to be a sign of the times. The American engineer never was parochially minded, he must enlarge his horizon and prepare to apply his home experience to regions farther afield. This we believe will be the salient feature of American mining enterprise *après la guerre*.

DISCUSSION

The American Supply of Potash

The Editor:

Sir—Under late dates the newspapers have quoted some remarks by Secretary Lane of the Interior Department, regarding the increased potash production of this country that to people conversant with the actual conditions may seem somewhat misleading. A few words in criticism may not be out of place. Referring to the strangle-hold that Germany had upon the potash market of the world prior to the War, the Secretary announces that "within two years the United States can become entirely independent of Germany through the development of our own resources, and by the use of processes devised by persons connected with the Department of the Interior."

From these words it would naturally be inferred that the authorities at Washington had played a great part in the up-building of this indispensable industry and fully expected to have finished the work about the end of the Wilsonian regime, two years hence. The facts, however, are entirely at variance with these claims, as will be shown in this brief résumé of the industry, which depends wholly upon private enterprise for whatever measure of success has attended it since the beginning of the War. If the Government has given it any practical assistance that fact has not yet been pointed out. I might go further and assert, without much fear of being controverted, that the Government has opposed rather than assisted the industry. At least I can say truthfully that it has opposed, through its agents, every large attempt to make potash. I take it, therefore, that the honorable Secretary either is misinformed on the subject, or that he was indulging in political camouflage. It will be worth while to examine briefly the economic aspects of potash-making.

Potash is mined, manufactured, and marketed in a variety of forms, which for discussion are ordinarily brought into statistics in the single form of the oxide of potassium, K_2O. In a normal year the country consumes the various products to the extent of 260,000 tons of oxide. The gross weight of all the compounds in such a year is well over a million tons. Nearly nine-tenths of the whole goes into artificial fertilizers, potash being, as is well known, an important, if not indispensable, element of fertility. The remaining tenth is taken for the manufacture of chemicals, soap, glass, matches, explosives, and a multitude of other necessary and common articles. The farmers, therefore, were the principal customers of Germany, which, before the War, supplied the United States with nine-tenths of all the potash used. Germany, by virtue of her enormous deposits of potash-bearing minerals, cheaply mined, was under-selling the world, and rapidly becoming rich. Our potash production virtually ceased, wrecking what, with judicious encouragement, would have become of national importance. But the free-trade proclivities of the Washington authorities had done their work and we were left helpless when the War began. Since that date imports have ceased, the land has received no potash, the crops in some regions have sunk far below the normal, and the question of proper fertilization is rapidly coming to the front. The price of potash compounds had risen within a year or two from ten to thirteen times the pre-war prices, and the small amount produced had to be devoted only to those manufactures which could afford to pay such prices. Chloride of potassium, which in its crude form sold at New York in the spring of 1914 for $38 per ton, brought in 1917 as much as $400 per ton, and still brings almost as much, in spite of the great efforts that have been and still are being made to produce it. The production of potash now, after four years of energetic work and the expenditure of much money, is still small, as we shall see. To show its actual extent, after four years of struggle, I append the following table, prepared from the U. S. Government statistics. By this it will be seen that we produced last year about one-eighth the normal requirements of the country, the content in potassium oxide being only 32,366 tons, valued at $13,791,972 at the points of production, which is a gratifying increase over the production of the preceding year, namely, a little short of 10,000 tons.

Potash Produced in the United States in 1917

Sources	Number of producers	Total, tons	K_2O contents, tons	K_2O, %	Total Value of shipping-point
Natural brines	10	79,876	20,652	55	$8,200,490
Alunite	3	7,150	2,402	33	892,763
Cement-dust	8	13,582	1,621	11.9	700,000
Blast-furnace dust ...	3	2,133	185	8.7	68,841
Kelp	10	11,306	3,572	31.6	2,134,815
Distillery refuse	4	8,580	2,846	33.1	1,130,907
Wood-ash	36	706	424	60	406,836
Sugar-refinery refuse..	5	2,593	359	13.8	143,436
Wool-washings, etc. ..	3	645	305	47	113,875
Total	82	126,580	32,366	...	$13,791,972

This table is interesting, not only as exhibiting the commercial aspects of the business, but as showing the diversity of the materials from which potash is being extracted. The sources are mainly old; and the methods, while improvement is rife, are in the main old also. While disposed to give ample credit to the young men of the Secretary's staff who may have had their attention called to this industry, I am unable to discover more than a single case in which their investigations, discoveries, or patents have been of significant utility. I much suspect that the honorable Secretary is occasionally given to obeying the precept, "magnify thine office".

The passing year has seen an expansion of potash manufacture, and, so far as we may judge from immature statistics, the output for 1918 will probably reach the equivalent of 55,000 tons of the oxide. The increase is mainly due to the activity of Californian producers, who have led the way in the development of the industry, and have put out by far the greater part of the domestic supply. California, in fact, is the greatest producer, and seems destined to remain so, in view of the immense supplies and great diversity of substances from which potash may be won.

Under the stimulus of war prices, and by the expenditure of fully $35,000,000, we have reached an annual production of 55,000 tons, or one-fifth the normal requirements. Should prices hold up there will undoubtedly be a large increase of production in 1919 and again in 1920, at which time, the Secretary informs us, the normal of 260,000 tons will be reached. But I see no reason for believing that any such quantity will be produced in either year. I doubt much if we reach 80,000 tons next year, and while prophesying in this as in other matters is dangerous, I venture to say that even if prices were to hold up we can scarcely extract more than 100,000 tons in the succeeding year, and we would be likely to fall far below it. This is on the assumption that prices will hold. However, all the probabilities are against the assumption, for, as the supply increases and the imperative demands of the chemical manufacturer and others are more fully met, the price is certain to fall, thereby destroying the strong incentive to increased production. Many of the smaller producers, who have all along regarded the business as a war-baby, and who are only able to carry it on when the margin is wide, will naturally cease production. These concerns have extemporized plants, for the most part gotten up cheaply and quickly for a temporary purpose, and are in no condition to fight to a finish, though for the present they are struggling with might and main to swell their output. Now that the War has reached a sudden end they feel generally that their circumstances are precarious, to say the least, and are unanimously hoping that Congress will take such action, in the form of a protective tariff, as will ensure a period of at least some profit. It is probable that the re-introduction of German potash would drive out of business fully four-fifths of the 80-odd producers in the preceding table, and, of course, would reduce the profits of the remainder to a very low figure. There are probably no more than four or five concerns in the whole country that could keep going at pre-war prices, and their situation would not be any too enviable. This is tantamount to saying that the greater part of the $35,000,000 lately invested in the industry will be practically lost if a strong protective tariff be not adopted at once. If free trade prevails foreign potash will be imported in vast quantities, the price will fall, our industry, built up with so much care and expenditure, will succumb, Germany will again be enriched with American money, and later, perhaps, the whole cycle of events will be repeated.

In common with other persons I have used the expression "normal supply of potash", as if it were only necessary to reach the pre-war basis of supply in order to satisfy commercial demands; but the term 'normal' has become meaningless in this connection. There was strictly no 'normal', since the demands of agriculture especially had been growing with the greatest rapidity; fertilizing the soil was becoming more and more a matter of course, and there were some important crops that could not be raised without manuring. Whereas in 1913, 200,000 tons of potassium oxide would have covered the requirements of agriculture, perhaps 300,000 might have been needed in 1918, through the growth of the fertilizing habit. But, as I have before remarked, the land has received no potash for four years, during which time the crops, such as they have been, have continued to draw upon the fast diminishing stores buried by nature in the ground. This draft must be made up some time, the sooner the better. It will require the addition of an immense quantity of potash, which must somehow be provided. Thus, for some years to come an extra amount will have to be supplied, in addition to the habitual amounts, as dictated by the apparent needs of the growing plants, thus calling for a vastly increased quantity in all. The time will surely come when the farmers will require, not 200,000 tons per year, but half a million tons or, more probably, twice that; and the demands, in the nature of things, will increase, the fertilizing habit having taken root to an amazing extent. The potash industry, then, is not a thing of today but of all time. It should therefore have the fostering care of the Government, and not be left to the chance devices of tariff-tinkerers as heretofore. I have said that in the past the authorities at Washington have acted adversely to the potash industry. I will cite cases to show as much. Some ten years since a well-directed effort was made by private parties to develop the potash deposits in Wyoming, and a good deal of money was spent by them in working out a process and in securing rights. Immediately attention had been attracted to their efforts the Government proceeded to withdraw the lands in question from location, and cutting them up into small tracts offered them for lease. Under these conditions the new company would have had to be at the expense of working out its process, apply it, build the necessary roads to make the deposit accessible, and undergo the pains and risks of a new enterprise—in fact, perform all the public services of the pioneer—at the end of which it would naturally find itself in competition with whomever might be incited to imitate its methods. This it naturally declined to do, and those promising sources of national wealth remain unworked. Again, when British capital became interested in the Searles Lake potash-soda deposit the attitude of Washington was far from friendly, and the regulations of the Land Office were invoked to hinder this most meritorious enterprise. It is most regrettable that these, and other concerns, were not encouraged to proceed, the effect of which would have been to relieve the great dearth of potash that has since been experienced. In view of the large amount of money required to establish a potash enterprise on a workable scale the governmental idea of leasing (not selling) small tracts of potash-bearing land is absurd. This policy does not, and cannot, harmonize with the views of those investors who alone have the means to carry out successfully the comprehensive plans necessary. Meantime the industry remains in a precarious position, the more so as the farmers, who will have a great deal to say in the matter of tariffs, clamor for cheap potash, regardless of its source. Under these circumstances it will be well for the industry to take up the question of extracting a supply of potash from minerals, such as feldspar, that contain other valuable materials besides, and obtain the potash concurrently with other saleable salts. This opens an avenue for more enduring enterprise, less affected by accident and by tariff changes.

HERBERT LANG.

Oakland, California, December 8.

Spitzbergen

The Editor:

Sir—Referring to the article in your issue of November 2 and the letter in your issue of December 21, I am glad to give you the following information.

The coal seams on the island of West Spitzbergen were first called to the attention of John M. Longyear, of Marquette, one of the subsequent backers of a mining enterprise there, in the summer of 1901, when he landed at Advent bay in the Ice fiord from a Hamburg-American liner then making an Arctic excursion.

In 1904 and 1905 the iron fields of Sydvaranger at the north tip of Norway, near the Russian line, were offered to Mr. Longyear and his associates, and he had engineers there for about one year and a half examining these deposits. Mr. Longyear's instructions to his engineers were to investigate the iron and at the same time to look at Spitzbergen for a possible source of coal. The results of the investigations were that the iron deposits were shown to be too low-grade to be of interest to Lake Superior mining people, but that the coalfields of West Spitzbergen, in the vicinity of Advent bay, were extensive, and the coal of excellent quality. The Americans dropped the iron-mining operations, but the coal-mining possibilities looked too good to be abandoned, so Frederick Ayer of Boston and Mr. Longyear formed the Arctic Coal Co. to open and equip coal mines on a fairly large scale.

The mines lay at a latitude of 79° 13′ N., a little over 700 miles from the North Pole, and 825 miles north of the north tip of Iceland. Iceland lies entirely south of the Arctic Circle. The mines were 1200 miles from the nearest railroad that could be of service to them, and 600 miles north of the island of Tromsö, which has been the headquarters of the Arctic Coal Co. in Norway.

As you know, Spitzbergen was uninhabited; although the area of the Spitzbergen archipelago is something like 32,000 square miles, it was supposed that no one could live there; of course, the Eskimo never inhabited this place. Occasionally whaling parties had been shipwrecked on the island and forced to winter there, and a few small hunting parties had spent the winter months trapping white and blue fox and polar bears and shooting reindeer and seals.

Spitzbergen is recognized by all the Great Powers as a *terra nullius* and is thus subject to the jurisdiction of no government or court; as no international commission had ever been appointed to govern it or deal with it, no form of government existed there, nor was any code of laws applicable.

The Americans staked four tracts of land known as the Cape Boheman, Sassen Bay, Green Harbor, and Advent Bay tracts, comprising about 600 square miles and covering the best of the coalfields; in fact, there is practically no mineable coal outside there areas. Maps and location notices showing areas and boundaries were sent to Washington and to the Foreign Offices of the Scandinavian and Russian Powers.

In addition to building docks, roads, railways, tramways, and a complete city with electric light and water system, the Arctic Coal Co. explored for coal on a big scale and eventually developed a large tonnage of semi-bituminous coal of Tertiary age. Our engineers' estimate of coal, all classes, assured, probable, and possible, in the one best seam under the portion of the area controlled by the American people, was about 700,000,000 tons. Run-of-mine averaged 3.8% ash, and the heat-value was over 14,400 B.t.u. The Arctic Coal Co. maintained a force of from two to six hundred men on the Island; many women spent the winters there at various times and more than a dozen children were born there during the American occupation. Dogs, horses, cows, pigs, and chickens were raised there, the pigs doing exceptionally well.

The problem of policing and administrating justice on the Island inhabited by so many men of the rougher type was solved by the Arctic Coal Co. by framing a simple code of laws, which code was largely written into the contract covering the employment of the individual by the company. It was found that one American to about fifty Scandinavians was the necessary proportion to maintain law and order. All men were transported to and from Norway on ships operated by the company, because no other regular means of transportation existed. Before leaving Norway the luggage and belongings of the employees were searched and all fire-arms, weapons, and liquor were confiscated and their possession or use forbidden on the Island according to the terms of the contract.

The only backing that the Americans in charge of the work had, was the questionable backing of the State Department at Washington. Its potency was never put to test, but every year a statement of the affairs and operations of the company was filed with the Secretary of State, and notices of such filing were sent to the Ministers of Foreign Affairs of Norway and Russia, through the American Ministers at Christiania and Petrograd. Under the guise of this slim protection the American flag was hoisted on this foreign soil and American rights were successfully maintained, although there were a few narrow escapes in this regard.

An attempt was made by the American owners to have what is known as the Guano Act, covering the protection of American interests in uninhabited islands, extended to read "Guano and other minerals and products." I believe this passed the Senate, but at Mr. Longyear's request was side-tracked in committee, as the State Department thought it would interfere with negotiations the Department was then carrying on with others of the Great Powers for recognition of American claims on the Island and possibly for the creation of an international commission to administer the affairs of the Island. The latter point was also a concession on the part of the Arctic Coal Co., as it was apparent that the affairs of the Island, the inhabitants, and the company could better be administered by the officials of the Arctic Coal Co. than by any international commission. Various meetings were held in Europe attended by representatives of Norway, Sweden, Denmark, Russia, and Germany, and various proposals for handling the Spitzbergen situation were made, all of which were rejected by the U. S. State Department at the request of the Arctic Coal Company.

In the summer of 1914 a meeting of representatives of eleven of the Great Powers was called in Christiania and this convention was in session all through July 1914. The Arctic Coal Co.'s interests were represented by officials of the company, by a representative of the State Department sent from Washington, by the American Minister in Norway, and by a diplomatic expert sent from France. Toward the end of July 1914 ten of the Great Powers (all except Russia) had verbally agreed to a recognition of the American claims and had assented to a scheme of government, and complete possession by the Arctic Coal Co. of land covered by original location notices. The entire matter would have been closed, settled, and signed by the end of the first week in August, if Emperor William had not mistakenly supposed that he could whip the world. On July 29 the various representatives at Christiania got telegrams from their respective governments instructing them to sign nothing and to come home quickly. So this whole thing will have to be gone over again, although the proceedings of the convention, as stenographically reported verbatim, have been printed and are in the archives at Washington and in the possession of the officials of the Arctic Coal Co. The proceedings, of course, were in the French language and this report is printed in French.

The European War made labor, supplies, and shipping-bottoms difficult to get, so it was decided to sell the property. In 1915 Scott Turner, the manager of the Arctic Coal Co., went to Petrograd to sell the mines to the Czar, in order to ensure a coal-supply reaching Alexandrovsk, the terminus of the railroad being built northward to secure a port free from ice all the year. He was to do business direct with the Czar and his Cabinet, but the German advance on Riga frightened these gentlemen away from Petrograd, and the highest he could reach in the political scale were a few dukes, so nothing resulted. He then went back to Christiania and met representatives of 42 of the largest banks in Norway, working through the Norwegian Prime Minister and the State Bank of Norway, and finally sold all the holdings of the Arctic Coal Co. to the Norwegians, the deal being closed in April 1916.

The new Norwegian company, called the Store Norske Kulcompani, has encountered many operating difficulties and in the two years that it has operated, in spite of great efforts and increased expenditures, it has succeeded in mining less than the normal eight-months' winter output under American administration. Labor has been troublesome and in 1917 Norwegian soldiers had to land at Advent Bay and ship the strikers back to Norway.

Houghton, Michigan, December 22. R. W. B.

Radium and Meso-Thorium

Radium luminous paint has been used in the War for a number of purposes, more particularly on the dials of instruments used in airplanes, so that these instruments can be read at night; for electric push-buttons, door numbers, and small images for shrines, etc. The paint is permanently luminous in the dark and contains from 0.1 to 0.25 milligrammes of radium element to 1 gramme of zinc sulphide. A luminous watch face usually has from 10 to 20 cents of radium on it. An excellent substitute for radium for certain purposes is meso-thorium. This is a radio-active element found in monazite sand and other thorium minerals. When first extracted it is not in a satisfactory condition for luminous paint, but must be allowed to 'ripen' for several months or even a year before it can be used. During this time the alpha radiation, which is required for luminous paint, becomes sufficiently strong. On the other hand, the beta and gamma radiation of meso-thorium grows rapidly and it can be used for medical purposes within a few days after preparation. Radium has a long life, half of it decaying in approximately 1600 years; meso-thorium, on the other hand, has a short life, 5 or 6 years being its useful life for luminous paint purposes. The price in the past has varied from 40 to 60% of that of radium, the comparison being on products of equal activity. For medical purposes, therefore, it cannot compete with radium as long as there is plenty of the latter; for luminous paint, to be used on objects that themselves have a short life, it is an excellent substitute for radium and will tend toward the saving of radium for medical purposes, according to the U. S. Bureau of Mines. The newspaper reports some time ago greatly exaggerated the future of meso-thorium.

Report of the Committee on Gold

Relief Measures Proposed by Gold-Mining Industry in Responses to Questionnaire

*The following nine items cover briefly the different measures of relief asked for by the gold-mining industry in response to the questionnaire sent out by the Committee:

1. Payment by the Government of a bonus on all the newly mined gold. This was qualified by some of the operators who asked that it apply only to primary gold mines, that is, to gold produced at mines where gold is the principal metal and not a by-product. The amount of bonus advocated ranges from $10 to $20 per ounce, $10 being the amount nearly always suggested.
2. Exemption from draft of necessary employees and the placing of labor for gold mines in the deferred class.
3. The assistance of the United States Employment Service in securing and maintaining a sufficient supply of labor.
4. Furnishing of supplies to gold mines by the Government at prices more nearly in keeping with pre-war figures.
5. The abolishment of the excess-profit tax; to this some added the demand that a larger allowance for depletion for ore extracted should be permitted by Treasury officials in computing tax-charges on profits.
6. Preferred classification for railroad freight, a reduction of the advance in freight-charges for supplies to gold mines and on ore shipments.
7. In California the activities of the Debris Commission are said to cause hardships at some mines.
8. Preferred classification for electric power.
9. Allowance of free export and sale to industry of new gold.

Discussion of Proposed Relief Measures

Gold miners believe that their industry is entitled to consideration of Government aid more than any other industry that may have suffered financially through conditions brought about by the War, because other industries can and do raise the prices of their goods while the purchasing power of gold is proportionately decreased. They urge that it is vital from an economic standpoint that the gold reserve be increased and the production of gold be maintained at approximately normal pre-war figures, or be stimulated beyond such amounts. If these premises be accepted, then it is necessary to find what measures can be best taken in order to accomplish these ends and to maintain as large a production of gold as is justifiable on economic grounds.

*Part of the 'Report of the Committee appointed by the Secretary of the Interior to study the Gold Situation', October 30, 1918.

Bonus

Payment by the Government of a bonus on all newly mined gold, in order to stimulate the production of gold, has been strongly advocated by some miners and has been approved by some bankers. The amount suggested as allowable for this purpose as agreed upon at different conferences held by the representatives of the gold-mining industry is $10 per ounce. To what extent a bonus of $10 per ounce would increase the production of gold is questionable, but naturally a bonus would have a stimulating effect on the industry; it would cause renewed activity at operating mines, the re-opening of a number of mines that have recently closed, and would encourage the search for new mines, unless some restrictions were put in force. By way of qualifications, it has been suggested that the bonus apply:

1. Only at those mines at which gold is the principal metal.
2. Only to mines at present operating or which were operating up to the war period and were obliged to close on account of increasing costs.
3. Only on the amount of gold produced at a mine in excess of 1917 production.
4. That the bonus apply only during the war period and cease soon after the War ends.[1]

The following also is of interest in this connection:

"To stimulate the gold industry it would seem that the most practical relief to the producer would be for the Government to pay a fixed sum for every ounce of new gold sold to the Mint in addition to the price of $20.6718, at which liquidations are now made. While I cannot speak from the viewpoint of a mining man, I have received convincing statements from reliable sources which lead me to believe that such relief during the War, and perhaps prolonged for a year or two after peace, would be the best and most effective plan for maintaining and encouraging the production of gold in this country."[2]

It is obvious that with the restrictions mentioned the production of gold for the next two or three years would not be greatly increased over the amount produced for the year 1917. Assuming that the production of 1917 might be maintained for a few years by granting a bonus to new gold produced, a matter for consideration is to determine to what level would the production of gold fall without such a bonus. With the adjustment of economic conditions after peace is declared, and the return to industry of soldiers and laborers engaged in war-work, it is to be expected that the shortage of labor will be at least partly relieved. Wages may be expected to fall, but

[1]Speech at meeting in Spokane, September 15, by George Greenwood, Old National Bank.

[2]John Clausen, vice-president, Crocker National Bank, San Francisco.

prices of supplies will probably continue at high level for some time, or until industry is readjusted to nearly normal conditions as compared to the pre-war period. With the return of conditions comparable to the pre-war period the gold situation would be automatically re-adjusted.

If scarcity of labor, high wages, and high costs of materials should continue for two years the annual production of gold in the United States may fall to $60,000,000 or less. On the assumption that a difference of $25,000,-000 in the gold production would result from the payment of a bonus by the Government on new gold produced and that a bonus of $10 per ounce or approximately 50% of the present value of gold would need to be paid for all gold produced in order to obtain an increased output of $25,000,000, it is apparent that the cost of securing this $25,000,000 would be the normal cost of $25,000,000 plus a bonus, or approximately $42,500,000, on the total annual production of $85,000,000, making a total extra cost to the Government of $67,500,000, in order to increase the gold production $25,000,000. The suggestion that a bonus apply only to the amount of gold produced at a mine in excess of the production of that mine for 1917 would give preferential treatment to a few well-known mines, and would be of little benefit to the majority of gold mines in the United States. Sound business judgment would be against the bonus at this time.

In connection with the proposed bonus on gold it is interesting to note that the matter has had recent attention in South Africa and Australia and is now under discussion in England. The South African and Australian governments ruled against the payment of a bonus on gold.

In October 1918 the British Treasury appointed a strong commission representative of the leading financial interests of the empire to investigate into the effects of the War on gold production in the British empire. The personnel of this commission includes Lord Inchcape, chairman, Sir Thomas Elliott, Sir Charles Addis, and W. H. Goshen. William Frechville, mining engineer, advises on technical mining problems. This commission is making a sweeping inquiry into the conditions at gold mines and possible measures of relief. Especial attention is being given to the desirability of granting the demands of the gold producers for a revision of the selling price of their products to compensate for the increase in cost of labor and supplies, to means of encouraging the mining of low-grade ores, and of stimulating the production of gold in general.

The producers of South Africa and Australia have requested the Treasury to contract for all gold mined by them for a term of ten years at a price calculated to ensure maximum production. The seriousness of the situation in those countries is reflected in a statement by A. E. Waller, chairman of the Transvaal Chamber of Mines, to the effect that out of 46 companies operating in the Transvaal, 6 were running at a loss and 15 were barely paying expenses. Confirmation of this statement is given by Sir Lionel Phillips, who says, according to an article published in September 1918, that a large number of the mines on the Rand will have to shut down unless some relief can be obtained.

Exemption from Military Service

The exemption from draft of necessary employees and the placing of labor for gold mines in the deferred class, has been granted to a certain extent by recent rulings of the War Department; gold mining has been declared an essential industry and the matter is one for local draft-boards to decide whether individual men are necessary to the industry.

Assistance of United States Employment Service

The assistance of the United States Employment Service in securing and maintaining a sufficient labor supply is asked. The United States Employment Service can, if authorized by proper Government action, assist the gold miners in the returning to the mines experienced men who have gone into other war industries for patriotic or other reasons. It can also transfer men now employed in less essential industries. Some advertising could properly be undertaken by the gold mines to impress upon labor that gold mining is regarded as an essential war industry and that men necessary to that industry are subject to deferred classification by the local draft-boards. The Director of the Bureau of Mines, as certifying officer to the War Department on industrial furloughs for metal mining and metallurgical industries, can aid greatly in the rehabilitation of the labor-supply of the gold mines. Negotiations are now under way whereby men returned from France for recuperation may be used to some extent in industry where their health would be benefited during the period of their recuperation; this would release more able-bodied men for the more arduous tasks, such as mining.

Allotment of labor to mines must be guided by intimate knowledge of the gold mines requesting assistance, otherwise labor might be wasted on unimportant projects. Because of this fact, and the fact that wages are higher in other industries, and on account of the isolated location of many of the gold mines, it is difficult for the United States Employment Service to recruit labor for gold mines. Relief through the War Department would not be hampered by these objections since no man is to be furloughed unless willing. The men would be properly cared for and paid at some wage fixed by the Government. It is the opinion of this committee that the labor situation is the most serious problem confronting the gold miner and that this should be given consideration by the proper Government agency. It is only through Government action as above outlined or through the importation of laborers as discussed elsewhere, that the labor situation during the War and the readjustment period after the War can be greatly improved.

Furnishing supplies to gold miners by the Government at prices more nearly comparable with pre-war figures than now paid would cause great dissatisfaction at mines producing other metals and in other important industries, and it is not considered feasible. A central purchasing agency for buying supplies would give some relief to the small miner as suggested elsewhere.

Abolishment of Taxes

Excess profits were imposed at few gold mines in 1917. The total amount paid as reported by mines answering questionnaires was under $500,000, though some disputes for additional amounts are still unsettled between companies and tax officials. Proper allowances should be given mines for depreciation of plant and depletion of ore by tax officials; much remains to be done to educate tax officials to appreciation of the proper rate of such allowances. Should a small group of miners or prospectors form a small company, of say, $10,000 to $100,000 capital, and expend the entire capital but strike it rich and take out as net profit an amount equal or more than the capital put in, in such case they would be obliged to turn over to the Government nearly half of their profits. Under such conditions the search for new gold deposits is greatly discouraged by the tax. The elimination of all excess-profit taxes on gold mining and the encouraging of maximum outputs might in reality bring in greater revenue to the Government than the tax, for larger dividends paid to shareholders would mean greater revenue from individuals.

Preferred Classification for Freight

Gold mining has been declared an essential industry and given a Class C rating. As such it is entitled to receive priority orders for freight, etc. The reduction of freight-charges on ore shipments where there has been a recent advance, as in Colorado, is a measure that should be allowed. The cost of freight on shipments of materials to gold mines is but a small part of the total cost of mining.

Debris Commission (California)

This applies to California only. The Committee has received many general statements to the effect that the Commission has been especially active and that their orders for expensive construction are causing great hardship at some of the lode mines at this time, when costs are high and profits from gold mining are abnormally low.

Preferred Classification for Electric Power

In California there was a shortage of power caused by lack of mains and the action of the State Power Administration in discriminating against gold-dredging caused general dissatisfaction. It was rightly felt that other forms of power consumption, such as amusements, excess lighting facilities, etc., could be curtailed with far less loss to industry. The gold mines should have a high-class rating with regard to power consumption, and power should be curtailed only when there is great necessity for such action.

Free Export and Sale of Gold

Gold has been sold in England at 115 shillings per ounce as against 85 shillings per ounce paid by the Bank of England for coinage purposes and the Government found it necessary to prohibit the melting of coins. Gold, under present conditions, could be also sold at a premium in this country for use in industrial arts, and if a free sale of gold were now permitted a certain amount could be absorbed at a considerable premium. A study of the market for gold shows that for the last four years about 45 millions per annum, approximateley one-half the amount produced in the United States, went into manufactures. Dentists use a large part of this gold and could pay a higher price for it, as could also jewelers. The amount of old material, jewelry, etc., that is consumed in manufactures in the United States has been approximately $8,000,000 worth per annum, and new gold to the value of approximately 37 millions per annum is consumed in this manner. The amount that could be absorbed at a premium is not known and would depend to some extent upon psychological conditions. If it were thought that the price of gold would go higher, quantities would be bought for speculative purposes, unless restrictions were imposed. The following is of interest in regard to the sale of gold in the open market:

"It seems to have been overlooked by many that the Mint price for gold (85 shillings, or $20.67) is quite different from the market-value or exchange-value of the metal. Gold, as a commodity, has had this last month in England a value some 35% in excess of the Mint price; the 'Annalist' tells us that minted coins have been at a high premium because of profiteering by labor. Workers are receiving wages higher than ever before in their experience and there is a demand for jewelry which exhausts the supply of gold, the commodity. An ounce of gold in a jeweler's hands will make four rings, for which he will get at least $30; in consequence, the market-price of gold, in those countries in which gold has been commandeered, is nearly 50% above the Mint price. This is the fact that has led Sir Lionel Phillips and his committee to approach the British government for permission to sell the gold produced by their mines in the 'open market', that is, sell it as a commodity."[3]

Further Suggestions

In addition to the matter discussed above it is the opinion of this Committee that gold should be placed under authority of the War Materials Administrator. In that way Government assistance can be given gold mines where desirable as provided for in the War Minerals bill for the other important metals included therein.

It is also suggested that a thorough study be made of the gold-mining industry with a view to improving mining and metallurgical conditions and also to go thoroughly into the labor situation.

It seems feasible for the Government, through the Bureau of Mines, to assist in improving methods of mining and metallurgy, particularly the latter, in the treatment of complex ores and those of low gold-content. A number of technical problems requiring solution may be mentioned. Among these are the regeneration of cyanide

[3]Bulletin, Canadian Mining Institute, October 1918.

solution, the treatment of complex and refractory ores, the cheaper production of cyanide, and the recovery of by-products from tailings. The practical solution of a few of these problems might easily bridge the gap between failure and success in the operation of low-grade properties. That particular field of work has been almost untouched by the Government and the present action may be particularly opportune for planning adequate work in that field.

Efforts should also be made to extend co-operative buying of supplies by mining companies. A central agency could be established in each State or district for co-operating with those elsewhere and thus reduce costs. This would ensure not only the best prices, but the greatest consideration from firms dealing in mining supplies. It would naturally prove more beneficial to the smaller mines that do not maintain purchasing departments, and would to some extent ensure the larger mines better prices than they now obtain.

Besides securing better prices great benefits would result from the distribution of knowledge, based on the experience of the larger users, as to the most satisfactory material to use for different kinds of work. Information of this kind could be properly discussed in a report on the gold mining industry by the Bureau of Mines.

Conclusion

There is no doubt that the output of the gold mines of the United States is seriously falling off, and under present economic conditions still smaller returns must be looked for in the future. The cause of the decrease is not wholly due to war conditions, but also to the fact that some of the most productive lode and placer mining deposits are showing exhaustion without equivalent new discoveries taking their places.

War conditions are a serious burden and bear with special weight on the gold-mining industry, in that as the prices of other commodities advance the purchasing power of gold necessarily decreases. The prohibition of exports of gold and the limitation of the circulation and internal trade in gold are injurious to the gold miner and justly entitle him to special consideration.

The different aids that have been suggested are outlined in detail. The granting of a bonus, or bounty, has the greatest advocacy from the mine operators, but seemingly such a measure would net the Government only a very small percentage of increase in its present great gold reserve, and then only at great cost. The principle of the bonus appears to be in general economically unsound and its application might result in serious abuses.

As a result of the War the United States has been transformed from a debitor nation into the great creditor nation of the world, and has the greatest gold reserve and best gold cover for its paper currency. Its credit, while undoubtedly the soundest, is still probably in need of gold backing for the reconstruction period, if this country is to make use of its advantage as a world power in trade. It must be remembered that we control only about one-fifth of the current output of the gold mines of the world and peace conditions may not prove so favorable for our holding our premiership as a creditor nation. The Liberty Loan bonds, with pledges for redemption on a gold basis, may amount to several times the total gold reserves of the world, and some provision must be made from time to time to pay at least a portion of them in gold as they fall due at the option of the holders.

The various measures of relief asked for by the gold-mining industry, with the exception of No. 1, 4, and 6, could easily be granted by executive action without additional legislation. As the profit of a gold mine, no matter how large, cannot be ascribed to war conditions, and, in fact, is seriously handicapped on that account, the remission of this tax is a logical and just demand, and might well be considered. The free export and sale of new gold should be permitted not only because it will help the miner but also because it gives freedom of movement, thus preventing inflation.

Intelligent relief to the most struggling and deserving of the gold mines might be obtained by amending the War Minerals Act to include gold mining and at the same time voting an appropriation that would be at the disposal of the Administrator to encourage gold discovery and aiding in the re-opening of mines shut down on account of adverse economic conditions. This we have pleasure in recommending.

Comparative Statement Showing Details of Operations at Most Important Gold Mines in the United States, Grouped by States

Dredging Operations Combined in One Group

(Compiled by Charles Janin)

1913

State	Tons treated	Total recovery	Operating cost	Per ton: Recovery	Per ton: Cost	Per ton: Cost per dollar
Oregon	......	....	....	...	...	...
California	697,606	4,464,755	2,430,748	6.31	3.48	0.54
Alaska	1,361,604	3,598,334	1,767,295	2.34	1.30	0.49
Colorado	741,067	6,544,823	4,207,105	8.83	5.68	0.64
So. Dakota	1,540,961	6,184,421	4,576,654	4.01	2.97	0.74
Nevada*	797,228	11,954,534	5,597,082	15.00	7.02	0.47
Arizona	151,891	1,823,234	1,172,509	12.00	7.72	0.64
Montana	44,726	414,594	247,335	9.27	5.53	0.60
Total	5,335,083	34,986,695	19,998,728	6.56	3.75	0.57
Total dredging	51,405,333	5,518,942	2,683,084	0.106	0.062	0.49

*Recovery given for Nevada mines includes silver value, 1913, $4,828,824.

1917

State	Tons treated	Total recovery	Operating cost	Per ton: Recovery	Per ton: Cost	Per ton: Cost per dollar
Oregon	31,893	311,410	215,950	9.76	6.77	0.69
California	939,131	6,140,530	4,003,673	6.54	4.26	0.65
Alaska	3,153,364	3,724,191	3,375,104	1.18	1.07	0.91
Colorado	1,152,714	8,037,218	5,425,392	6.97	4.71	0.68
So. Dakota	1,677,623	6,609,442	5,016,098	3.94	2.99	0.76
Nevada*	866,983	8,498,658	5,960,538	9.80	6.88	0.70
Arizona	166,204	2,429,872	1,251,178	1.46	7.52	0.52
Montana	79,047	939,866	492,300	9.29	6.19	0.67
Total	8,087,550	36,691,187	25,687,233	4.51	3.18	0.70
Total dredging	65,654,228	7,645,103	3,459,077	0.114	0.052	0.45

*Recovery given for Nevada mines includes silver value, 1917, $5,003,824.

1918 (6 months)

State	Tons treated	Total recovery	Operating cost	Per ton: Recovery	Per ton: Cost	Per ton: Cost per dollar
Oregon	14,785	145,206	131,358	9.82	8.88	0.90
California	328,587	3,347,126	2,144,000	10.20	6.52	0.64
Alaska	1,304,000	1,700,000*	1,600,000	1.30	1.22	0.94
Colorado	616,604	3,367,633	2,449,821	5.46	3.97	0.72
So. Dakota	827,104	3,300,000	2,572,672	3.99	3.11	0.78
Nevada†	184,594	2,135,386	1,748,570	11.60	9.47	0.82
Arizona	87,130	1,409,147	762,209	16.20	8.74	0.54
Montana	36,277	392,574	256,109	10.80	7.06	0.65
Total	3,399,081	15,997,072	11,660,790	4.71	3.43	0.70
Total dredging	29,074,604	3,140,733	1,733,542	0.111	0.59	0.55

*Partly estimated.

†Recovery given for Nevada mines includes silver value, 1918, $1,235,000, estimated.

Figures for 1918 not given by some mines reporting for previous years.

Brief on the Status of the Chrome Industry

PREPARED BY COURTENAY DE KALB

ELEMENTS OF THE CASE. For war-equipment the Government required supplies that could not be produced without chrome.

The need of ships for military purposes cut off the supplies from abroad on which this country previously had depended.

The contractors under obligation to use chrome in their operations for supplying war-material to the Government demanded Government co-operation in securing a domestic output in lieu of imported chrome.

The Government, through its Departments and War-Boards, responded by issuing circulars, bulletins, and letters urging the people to search for, to mine, and to deliver chrome ore.

It introduced into Congress a bill to protect all parties concerned, to-wit: to protect the producers by a remunerative market; to protect the consumers by a domestic supply; and to protect the Government in an adequate supply of chrome-ore, ferro-chrome, and chemicals prepared from chrome.

It undertook, until the bill should be passed, to protect the miners by embargoes; to protect the contractors by import licenses for supplementing any deficiencies in domestic deliveries; to protect the Government by insisting that mine-owners should operate their properties, or permit them to be operated, in order to produce chrome.

Importations amounting to 90,456 tons, made to a large extent in defiance of the regulations of the Government, broke the market.

The miners, most of whom are men of small means, will be ruined unless relief be extended immediately. Their aggregate losses will be not less than $1,000,000.

The Pacific Coast Chrome Producers Association demands that relief be extended through the Minerals Control Act, or by such other means as can be made effective at once, in order to save the producer from ruin.

They insist that a moral responsibility exists which must be fulfilled in order to uphold the honor of the Government, and they petition the Government to take instant measures in their behalf.

PRE-WAR CONDITIONS. The average consumption formerly was about 45,000 long tons per annum. Practically the whole of this was imported.

The consumption has been increasing with the normal progress of the metal industry; it had risen to 65,000 tons in the year 1913.

WAR CONDITIONS. Consumption, as indicated by domestic production and imports, rapidly augmented.

Total Chrome Available

	Long tons
1914	75,277
1915	79,736
1916	162,980
1917	115,788

Consumption in 1918, as determined by the U. S. Geological Survey, amounts to 104,000 tons. The decrease in 1918 was due to restrictions upon consumption in fear of shortage.

A summary of the situation is given in a memorandum prepared for Pope Yeatman, dated October 26, 1918, attached hereto as Exhibit A.

Domestic Output of Chromite

Year	Long tons	Average price per ton at shipping-point
1908	359	$20.14
1909	598	13.88
1910	205	13.31
1911	120	13.58
1912	201	13.70
1913	255	11.19
1914	591	14.75
1915	3,281	14.50
1916	47,035	17.00
1917	43,725	....
1918	60,000	....

The foregoing table shows that an increased use in 1908 stimulated the price and the production. The response to a price of $20 per ton that year exceeded the demand, and the price promptly fell to $13, after which production almost ceased for four years. The consumption had so far increased by 1913 as to again stimulate domestic production, with a slight gain in price. The demand for war-uses in Europe acted as a great stimulant to chrome mining in this country.

Properties near transportation facilities were thus brought into production. Each increase in price made it possible to develop properties more remote from the railroad. At a price of about 50 cents per unit, for 40% ore, a production of about 40,000 tons yearly was made feasible. This fact was recognized by the consumers, and it was on their suggestion to Government officials that an increase of production was attempted by raising the price. This meant that the cost of long local hauls to the railroad could be overcome. The price was raised from 85c. to $1.25 per unit for 38% ore by the chief consumer, being equivalent to $47.50 per ton at the shipping-point. This extended the radius of operations to a distance of about 70 miles from the railroad, the local haul absorbing as much as $25 or more of this price.

The result was to increase the number of domestic chrome miners from a few who had mines near the railroad to more than 450 in 1918. Of these, 365 were in California, 59 in Oregon, and the remainder scattered through other States. Of the above number, approximately 200 shipped ore. The majority were making ready for production by developing their properties, establishing camps, and building roads when the armistice was signed.

OFFICIAL ESTIMATES OF DOMESTIC PRODUCTION. The U. S. Geological Survey's estimate, made in May 1918, indicated a probable domestic output of 50,000 tons for the year. This was a conservative estimate as shown by the fact that the actual output reached 65,000 tons, being only 15,000 tons in excess of the forecast. The Survey evidently had not anticipated such a great increase in price as was made by the California Chrome Co. This resulted in preparations for production that would have brought approximately 100,000 tons into the market in 1919.

In making the forecast for supplying the consumers it was assumed that 140,000 tons would be needed in 1918. The officials of the Government cut this down to 130,000 tons. As domestic production grew, and as shipping space became more urgently needed for military purposes, importations were further restricted, and an absolute embargo was placed against imports by sea, effective on June 15, 1918.

Reduction in the consumption, through severe economy in the use of chromite, coupled with large importations, to a considerable extent in violation of the embargo, swamped the market. Large tonnages were brought in over the embargo, and much of this reached American ports unannounced and without license. This can be confirmed by C. K. Leith.

Illustrative of the activities of the importers, who were importing for the consumers, the following table is important.

Chromite Imports

Origin	Sept. 1918 tons	Oct. 1918 tons
Canada	2,064	3,070
Australia (originating in New Caledonia)	2,778	64
French Oceania (New Caledonia)	748	....
Brazil	534	....
Cuba	2,170	2,500
Portuguese Africa	5,000	....
British Oceania	....	523
British South Africa	....	521
Total	13,834	7,120

The total imports, according to estimates of the Geological Survey, will amount to 90,456 tons, based on 50% ore, for the year 1918.

For a further review of these conditions, and for confirmation of the effect of raising the price, see pages 39 and 40 of the report on 'Chromite', by J. S. Diller, constituting part of the 'Mineral Resources' for the year 1918, attached hereto as Exhibit B. The circumstances under which the price was raised are therein stated.

One of the advertisements of the California Chrome Co. is also attached as Exhibit C.

Government Stimulation of Chrome Mining. The great response to the needs of the country for more chrome ore was the direct result of the insistent call of various Government Departments and War Boards through circulars and statements issued to the people and the press. Examples of these urgent requests for patriotic effort in providing these minerals are contained in Exhibit D. This has nine items, which constitute but a few of the many that were sent out. Not only were the people reached in this way, but the Committee on Public Information issued circulars urging the production of chrome and manganese.

Special attention is directed to the circular from the Committee on Mineral Imports and Exports of the U. S. Shipping Board, dated May 4, 1918, shown in Exhibit D. In this the people are reminded that the War Minerals Bill, to control the mineral industries, is pending in Congress, but they are urged not to wait until every detail is settled before beginning operations, and they are assured that it is a "safe assumption that the absolutely necessary things will be done in time," this referring to Government protection.

Equally important is the letter from the Chemical and Explosives Section of the War Industries Board, dated March 4, 1918, also appearing in Exhibit D. This announces a general policy of the War Industry Board, as follows: "It is the desire and intention of the War Industries Board that all properties containing valuable deposits of chromite, that can be reasonably operated, shall be developed at an early date, and we are willing that properties should be leased which are of value to the country, and should neither be operated by the leasor or leased by him to another operator."

Attitude of the Chrome Miners. There was hesitancy on the part of many miners to open up mines of chromite until they had received further assurances as to the needs of the Government and as to a dependable price, since chrome mining was recognized as a particularly speculative operation. They were not seeking an extremely high price. The prevalent feeling is summed up in the testimony by Pope Yeatman at the hearings before the Committee on Mines and Mining, U. S. States Senate, 65th Congress, 2nd Session, on the Bill H. R. 11259, on May 10 (see pages 200 and 201):

"The Chairman. Do you feel that it is necessary to provide for price fixing in this bill?

"Mr. Yeatman. I do; yes, sir.

"The Chairman. Why?

"Mr. Yeatman. I do, for this reason, that in every conference that we have ever had the producers have always asked for that, and the reason they have asked for price fixing has been that they wanted to know, they wanted to feel that the business was more or less stabilized; they wanted to feel that if they started in new—as many of them would have to do—they were going to be able to count on some regular price, and such a price as would be made regular by the Government fixing it.

"Senator Shafroth. Does not that apply, however, to the fixing of a minimum price only?

"Mr. Yeatman. Not necessarily, no; even if it is a maximum price. If it is a maximum price, it is a price beyond which they cannot go, but at the same time they feel that something is fixed. They would all prefer a minimum price, but many of them feel that even with a maximum price a great benefit would result."

It must be emphasized that a great part of the injury done to the chrome miners came from an unwise establishment of a price by a private corporation, the California Chrome Co., acting with the consent of the Government, whereby an unjustifiably high price was applied as a minimum, without being regularly fixed and made permanent by the Price-Fixing Board. Accordingly the price did not affect the entire market, but only the domestic end, and the consumers succeeded in bringing in ore at lower rates while the miners in this country were left without protection.

Restrictions imposed upon the refractories companies limited their freedom to buy ores that they otherwise would have accepted. Originally they were restricted to ore of 38% grade. This was changed later to 43%, and was held at that figure until November 1. That was long after the market had been broken by large importations. As late as September 25, A. A. Fowler (secretary of the sub-committee of the Ferro Alloys Committee of the American Iron & Steel Institute, co-ordinated with the War Industries Board for control of the non-ferrous alloys), stated that the restrictions had not been removed, but that, in cases of error, when ore received proved to exceed the 43% limit, an adjustment would be allowed "if there were no valid reasons to the contrary."

That these restrictions were continued to the detriment of the domestic chrome producers is shown by the admission in the circular letter of the American Iron & Steel Institute of November 1, signed by James T. McCleary, that, while the steel-makers had not permitted the reduced consumption of chrome ore to interfere seriously with the quality or output of steel, "we note, however, in some of the replies, that a reduced life of the furnaces resulted from cutting down the use of chrome ore, and that indirectly some loss of production has occurred. Also that, in some cases, the use of magnesite as a substitute has increased costs."

Government Responsibility. Provision of the war material covered by the output of the war minerals, divides into two parts:

1. The Producers. These were scattered, and to a large extent not personally known. With these a blanket-order for output was the only possible means of securing a supply.

2. The Consumers. These were known in advance, and contracts were made, or were being made, for products dependent upon the supplies derived from the producers. Prices were based on the cost of raw material, with a large differential, especially in the case of ferro-chrome, so that the market for raw material might vary within wide limits without extinguishing the manufacturers' profit.

Production was undertaken for the benefit of those known to the Government and with whom it was possible to directly make contracts.

Production was made in this country at the urgent request of consumers, through the Government acting for them, in order that the contracts might not fail to be fulfilled.

Production was urged by the Government through its various Departments, War Boards, the Shipping Board, and the Committee on Public Information.

Producers were urged not to wait for confirmation of guarantees, but to begin production at once, while the War Minerals Bill was pending for definite control of production and market. It was also announced officially as the intention of the War Industries Board that properties would not be allowed to remain unexploited for the public welfare, and producers were warned of this purpose in cases where it was thought that they were hesitating to produce.

For continuation of the above, see Exhibit D, giving quotations from official Government circulars, bulletins, and letters, urging energetic production of chrome and other war minerals, containing ten items.

The Analogy Between Blanket Orders of this kind and orders by word of mouth and by telephone, but without formal written contract, is such as to put them in the same class. In the case of the latter verbal orders, agreed prices were part of the transactions, while the price for war minerals is a matter of adjustment under the operation of the Minerals Control Act, if the Act be used for the protection of the war-minerals industry. The War Department has taken steps to protect those who were operating under verbal orders.

How the Government Carried Out Its Obligations. The chrome industry was intended to be protected, until Congressional action could be taken, by means of an embargo against imports. This was supplemented by licenses for importation as a means of protecting the consumer, so as to give him surety of obtaining raw materials from abroad, so far as the circumstances of shipping-space permitted. By a combination of embargo to protect the producer, and of licenses to protect the consumer, a fair and equitable arrangement was aimed at. Important official rulings in regard to these matters are annexed hereto as Exhibit E, consisting of eight items.

Violation of these rulings by importers resulted in further accumulation of stocks of chrome ore in this country. Part of these imports were made under sanction of the Ship Control Committee of the Shipping Board of New York, which is said to have exceeded its authority. This, however, is not the cause of the bulk of the unlicensed importations.

Acceptance by Government officials of the proposal of consumers to raise the price of chrome 40c. per unit, as a means for stimulation of the production, has done great damage to the producers by leading them to develop properties remote from transportation lines, and to erect concentration works to treat low-grade ores, all of which would never have been done except for such stimulation, and except it had been understood that the chief consumer was acting on behalf of the Government. The suggestion of Mr. Yeatman should have been followed, and the whole market controlled by a fixed Government price. Failure to do this has proved disastrous.

Continued Inducement by Government Officials to produce chrome after the market had gone wrong, and when it was known to Government officials that large stocks had been accumulated and thereby had made the market weak, led to persistence of production, and to a continued outlay in preparation therefore, which otherwise would have been stopped. The public should have been informed officially to cease development and production rather than encouraged to believe that "it is the present intention of the War Industries Board to arrange for continued chromite production in the United States for the first half of 1919 at a rate proportionate to the rate of 1918." On the same day (September 28, 1918) the same official, in charge of these matters for the War Industries Board, sent out communications, in one case giving doubtful encouragement to producers, and holding out the prospect of being able to dispose of output for producers; in the second case giving positive encouragement to believe that a market would be available for the remainder of the year at the California Chrome Co.'s schedule and that the output for the first half of 1919 would be absorbed by the consumers; and in the third case announcing that the market had been weakened by large accumulations of stocks in the hands of consumers, and he further pointed out that the consumption by the makers of ferro-chrome and by the chemical trade had declined one-third, although he had advised other producers on the same day that the chemical trade was a likely buyer. These are examples of communications that have done serious damage to producers by encouraging them to continue, because they believed that information from the Government boards could be relied upon. This group of communications constitutes Exhibit F.

The list of chrome buyers and the California Chrome Co.'s schedule of prices, which is at least semi-official, is given in Exhibit G. Recognition of the attitude of the Government toward this schedule will be found in the Geological Survey's bulletin, constituting Exhibit B, pp. 39 and 40.

Further Encouragement to Produce was given by the same party who wrote the communications in Exhibit F, in a communication to Senator Chamberlain, on the strength of which that gentleman committed himself to constituents (A. E. Reames and George Putnam, Medford, Oregon) by wire, dated September 24, 1918, quoting Hugh W. Sanford as his authority, as follows: "New survey chromite situation indicates tonnage domestic chromite produced balance this year can be sold at average price prevailing this summer."

As late as October 2, after having acknowledged in one letter that stocks were large and consumption greatly reduced, the same party sent a letter of encouragement for chrome production to Representative N. J. Sinnott of Oregon, causing him to mislead his constituents and allow them to proceed with expenditures that would not have been made had the facts been correctly represented.

See copy of letter to Mr. Sinnott, Exhibit H.

Control of Production and Market for the Government was vested primarily in a committee of the American Iron & Steel Institute, known as the Ferro-Alloys Committee, acting officially for the War Industries Board, in conjunction with the Chemical Division, Ferro-Alloys Section, of the War Industries Board, Hugh W. Sanford, chief. The Ferro-Alloys Committee consisted of the following persons:

J. A. Farrell, chairman, U. S. Steel Corporation.
E. F. Price, Electro-Metallurgical Co.
F. W. White, Mutual Chemical Co.
E. J. Lavino, broker and dealer in chrome, etc.
Frank Samuel, broker and dealer in chrome, etc.
C. A. Buck, Bethlehem Steel Corporation.
E. A. S. Clarke, Lackawana Steel Co.
A. D. Ledoux, Rogers, Brown & Co.
D. G. Kerr, Carnegie Steel Co.

H. C. Dubois was also for a time on the Chemical Division, Ferro-Alloys Section, of the War Industries Board. He was an employee of E. J. Lavino & Co. Mr. Sanford was of the firm of Sanford & Day of Knoxville, Tennessee, and a consumer of ferro-chrome, which is produced by the Electro-Metallurgical Company.

Not a single producer nor representative of the producers was on any of the committees in charge of this matter.

A group of producers prepared a memorandum regarding this phase of the case, which has the merit of showing how it appears to the man in the field, and for this reason is valuable as presenting a point of view that prevails widely among producers. Whether wholly capable of substantiation or not, it reveals a situation that is unfortunate, and which the Government can remedy only by wise and prompt action for the future welfare of the wronged producers, in compensation for the errors and injuries of the past. This opinion of producers constitutes Exhibit I.

Outlook for a Chrome Industry. The development undertaken through the inspiration of the Government has shown that the domestic mines can supply the total output needed in this country. Much of the chrome discovered is of high grade, and still larger deposits of low-grade ores have been revealed. These can be concentrated in increasing quantity if the industry persists. The product of the concentration mills will be peculiarly adapted to use by the ferro-chrome makers and in the chemical trade. The refractories makers find some difficulties with concentrates, but there is a sufficiency of raw ore available that is suitable for their needs.

There is no need of reliance upon foreign resources if our domestic mines are sustained. They will employ profitably several millions of capital.

The industry will give employment to large numbers of workers, the aggregate needed for the war-minerals, if sustained as an American industry, running into the thousands, and resulting in a distribution of wages earned amounting to many millions of dollars annually.

If not sustained as an American industry our chrome supply will depend upon the output of low-priced labor in Oceania, Brazil, Cuba, and Africa, causing a loss of opportunity to American workmen who need the advantage of every source of profitable employment during this period of reconstruction.

Remedies for the Injured Chrome Miners. Three methods seem to be advisable:

1. To use the War Minerals Act (Public 220). It was passed, as shown, to cover the blanket-orders given, and to better regulate production, in the interest of the Government, that depended upon the fulfilment of its contracts with the consumers.

It is the opinion of eminent attorneys that it can be applied if construed according to the strict wording of the statute, considering that we are technically at war until a treaty of peace is proclaimed.

The title of the Act indicates its purpose, and the following abstract from a letter written by the Director of the U. S. Geological Survey cites important court decisions regarding the significance of the title of a statute:

The excerpt is from a letter of Director George Otis Smith, U. S. G. C., to Hugh W. Sanford, October 29, 1918, as follows: "I realize your legal forebodings, but common sense is one mental function to be used in construing law. You and I understand pretty well the purpose of the mineral control law, and I know the temper of Congress in passing it. The minerals listed, whose production is to be encouraged, are 'those which have formerly been largely imported' and now needed as war necessaries. My quotation from the title of the Act is justified by the well recognized rules of construction that "where the mind labors to discover the design of the legislature, it siezes everything from which aid can be derived; and in such case the title claims a degree of notice, and will have its due share of consideration.' (United States v. Fisher), and that 'The intention of the lawmaker is the law. . . . Where doubt exists as to the meaning of a statute the title may be looked to for aid in its construction.' (Smythe v. Piske)."

Director Smith adds: "The need of ensuring the new producer that his prospective output if not at once needed would be purchased by the Government is part and parcel of the need of ensuring the nation against a prospective inadequacy of supply."

It is admitted that, as regards chrome, manganese, and potash, there is no shortage of supply if we continue to draw upon foreign resources. The manganese market has dropped out altogether, as has the market for chrome, and the potash producers cannot sell their stocks on hand because the consumers are so confident of being able to secure cheaper supplies from Germany that they will not buy. In none of these cases, however, is there a sufficient domestic supply available without definitely protecting the producer, so that he may continue to develop his properties and prepare for marketing his output.

These industries are vital to the security of the country in the event of trouble that should again cut off or threaten our access to foreign sources of supply.

Application of the Minerals Act would therefore fulfil the obligation of the Government toward those to whom it gave blanket-orders to produce ore: and it would also perform a duty to the whole nation in keeping it in a strong position so that it will be less assailable from a military standpoint or by intimidation through diplomatic negotiations. Difficulties of the latter sort are matters of recent history in connection with our supply of nitrates.

2. It has also been suggested that a bounty might be paid, but it is recognized that this principle is not popular with the American people.

3. The last resort is Congressional relief. If this were asked it should be taken speedily, as many of the chrome miners are operating on leases that will expire unless work persists, and they are so encumbered with debts at the banks that they will be ruined and unable to resume operations unless relief is given at a very early date.

The chrome producers ask, if none of these be the proper remedy, how does the Government propose to proceed for their relief? They understand that the Government has repeatedly confirmed its sense of responsibility involved. They are ready to co-operate with the Government in effecting a practical solution of the problem that will become operative in time to save those who are now threatened with early ruin as a result of their entry into the production of chrome at the request of the Government.

Note. Later figures show that importations under license since July 1, 1918, have amounted to 45,360 tons, of which 13,000 tons came from New Caledonia. The total illicit entries are said to have been about 7000 tons, this figure being subject to revision. The licenses, made for the protection of consumers, allowed entry of far more ore than events prove to have been necessary, and they have worked great harm to the producers. As late as the middle of October the War Boards were figuring on having to meet demands from consumers for 1919 at the estimated rate of consumption for 1918, and they had allowed in their forecast for importing about 50,000 tons from Canada, Cuba, and Brazil, keeping in mind that consumers have always insisted on having reserve stocks, as a margin of safety, to the extent of 60,000 tons.

The responsibility of the Government is thus shown to be even greater than would appear from other statements in this brief, because it was encouraging further production for the national security long after the stocks of chrome in the hands of consumers in this country were so large as to weaken and break the market, which fact was known to the officials of the Government.

A wire hoisting-cable at the Canadian Western Fuel Co.'s mine, B. C., snapped on September 10 last, resulting in the death of 16 miners. A careful investigation was made at the mine, also tests at McGill University, Montreal. According to W. Fleet Robertson, Provincial mineralogist, the failure of the rope was entirely due to the oxidizing of the wires, chiefly internally, caused by apparent lack of internal lubrication, leaving the wires exposed to the action of a more than normally corrosive water and a humid atmosphere. The internal hemp core, which under a sufficiently effective lubricating system would serve as a reservoir of oil to keep the wires oiled and protected from corrosion, not being supplied with oil, became a reservoir of moisture and so hastened corrosion of the wires. Apropos of this, a recent test of a 1¼-in. cable from a Sudbury, Ontario, mine was made at McGill. It broke at 58,600 lb., whereas the new rope had a breaking strength of 128,000 lb. Internal corrosion was the cause, although the wires showed little deterioration externally. At some mines oil is allowed to drop on the ropes from a feeder above the sheaves.

A Non-Drowning Pump-Station

By C. ERB WUENCH

During the unwatering operations at the Yak mine, in the Leadville district, it was noticed that in the backs of several old stopes air-pockets had been formed. Even though the water had risen considerably above the highest points in these stopes, the small cavities in the back were entirely unwetted. Such air-pockets have saved the lives of miners. This suggested to me the possibility of designing underground pumping-stations utilizing the principle of the hydraulic 'diving-bell'.

In the history of a great many mines that have been drowned it is on record that if only an hour or two more time could have been had in which to make the necessary repairs thousands of dollars of expense in unwatering might have been saved. In the Yak mine, owing to a sudden inflow of acid water that corroded the pumps of an intermediate pumping-station and caused an excessive flow to be handled by the pumps at the bottom, the motors burnt out. The sudden flow of acid water was due to the Moyer mine, an adjoining property, having been abandoned. There being no underground connection at depth the water, which was formerly handled by the Moyer pumps, backed up through the old stopes and took into solution the sulphates of iron and zinc formed by the exposure of sulphides to oxidation for a number of years, and then the waters charged with these sulphates found their way into the Yak mine and corroded the intermediate pumps.

By referring to the accompanying sketch, the general design of this style of pumping-station can be readily comprehended. The station is cut out so that the area at the back will be contracted as shown in the sketch. A raise will be driven from the back of the station to the level above. Through this raise an air-line and a water-gauge line and the wires to the auxiliary starting-box will pass. There will also be a ladder-way. At the bottom of this raise there will be two air-tight doors forming an air-lock. When everything is running smoothly, these doors will be open and the heated air, which is usually present in the back of a pump-station owing to the heat from the motors, will pass up the raise and fresh air come in at the bottom. This will have the minor advantage of having the electric motors working in a cooler atmosphere. In case anything happens to the motors or pumps, the lower air-tight door is closed, and as the water rises in the mine sufficient air will be admitted through the air-tight door to balance the water-pressure due to the rising water. The air may either be obtained from the mine air-line, or, if this is out of order also, the small amount of air necessary can be forced down through a hand air-pump as shown. Two gauges are provided: one, a water-gauge to measure the hydrostatic pressure of the water in the mine, and the other, to measure the pressure of the air that is forced into the pump-station to balance this hydrostatic pressure.

At the bottom of this raise is an air-lock. Men can go down the raise to the top of the pump-station, close the upper air-tight door, and by releasing the valve in the lower air-tight door they can gradually become accustomed to the pressure; then they open the lower air-tight door and pass into the station to make the necessary repairs. It can be seen that the men can work for a considerable time before the pressure will become too

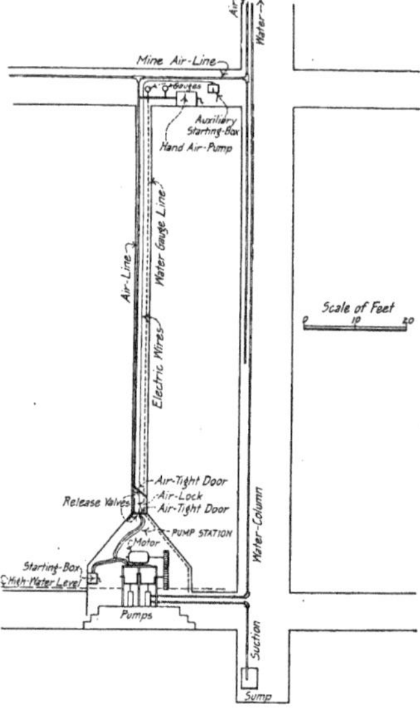

great for their lungs. The raise can be made large enough so that the various parts of machinery can be hoisted in and out of the pump-station.

When men are working in the pump-station under pressure, caustic soda (sodium hydrate) should be placed about the station to absorb the carbon di-oxide that is exhaled.

An auxiliary starter is shown in the sketch on the same level as the hand air-pump. This is merely used to start the motor to obviate going down the manway, passing through the air-lock, and thence entering the pump-station, in order to start the motors when the shut-down was due to power trouble.

Simple Tests of Economic Minerals

By HERBERT LANG

The old-time prospector, intent only on the discovery of paying deposits of gold, or of silver, did well to confine himself thus narrowly, because in his day there was little local demand for anything else. But nowadays, when the necessities of the world embrace such diverse things, the old methods are outgrown, and the modern prospector, when he shall come on the scene, will find a much larger outlook and will need a greater range of knowledge. There is needed a class of painstaking men that will make it their business to look up deposits of any kind that possess present or even future economic value, and to go over a comparatively restricted area with a vigilant eye for everything in the way of minerals. Almost any mineral now has value, either actual or potential, and even the soil and common rocks are worth careful inspection. There are fortunes in this kind of prospecting if properly performed, but to do it properly requires more knowledge and adaptability than are ordinarily possessed. On the whole I do not think that a trained mineralogist is precisely the right man to tackle such work. Many expert 'rock-sharps' have tried it, but I cannot think of many that have made a success of it, either for themselves or for the State. Probably the reason is that they undertook too much and covered too much ground. Success will be achieved by the careful scrutiny of a comparatively limited area, taking account of every mineral exposure, no matter how insignificant, and leaving nothing for the next man to find out.

It would naturally be supposed that all the resources of a complete laboratory would be required in such a pursuit; but such is not necessarily the case. No one need be discouraged because he cannot take a great store of apparatus into the field, because a good deal may be extemporized and all the rest done without. This is especially true in the examination of simple minerals, for which primitive methods of determination are almost always possible. No doubt some analytical work must eventually be done; yet the prospector may remain away from the chemical laboratory indefinitely and still find plenty to do in the field.

To identify a mineral offhand is frequently difficult to an expert, and may prove impossible to the prospector in the mountains. Aggregations and mixtures of minerals, of course, are still more difficult, requiring from the first the assistance of chemical analysis. This is especially true when quantitative results are desired instead of qualitative, when 'how much' takes the place of 'what'. Naturally the first thing done is to note its color, its hardness, and its crystalline form (provided that it be a simple mineral), and the finder anxiously 'hefts' it, knowing that as a rule the heavier rocks are more valuable than the lighter. This is so certain that no prospector should pass over a specimen that is strikingly heavy without a close investigation into its character. This may require the services of a skilled chemist; but in default of such aid the intelligent prospector may do a good deal to inform himself of the nature of his find, by homely and extemporized means. Some would advise the searcher to take along this and that piece of apparatus, thus loading him down with articles of which he can make no present use. A scale of hardness, embracing at least eight fragments of stone is often prescribed; but the indications thus got invariably have to be taken in connection with other tests, more difficult, perhaps, to carry out, and even then certainly may not be reached. The prospector must at least take his magnifying glass, his pocket-knife, and his horn or pan, and I will suppose him to be also provided with a small glass-stoppered bottle of sulphuric acid, and a test-tube or two. In default of the test-tube he can make use of a glass tumbler. A small cast-iron mortar and pestle come handy, but in lieu of them an anvil or the smooth surface of some weatherworn boulder may answer quite well. It is surprising how much may be found out by means of these simple tools.

The taste of some soluble minerals serves to identify them at once. Common salt, saltpetre, epsom salts, and the sulphates of iron and zinc cannot be mistaken. The prospector who intends to go into the desert regions of this State will do well to familiarize himself beforehand with the taste of some of the more common chemicals found in the dry lakes there. Some other substances, like clays, have also a smell of their own. Clay, by the way, is worth looking for. First-rate clays, suited to the manufacture of firebrick, pottery, and porcelain, are scarce, and will well repay the finder. In testing clay it should be moistened and rubbed between the fingers, when it will generally, but not always, form a sticky or plastic mass, which is a good feature. A piece molded into brick-form may be heated as hot as possible in the camp-fire, to ascertain if it cracks on drying, as most so-called 'fat' clays do. This is no injury to its quality. If it burns red or black it betrays the presence of iron or manganese, which render the material useless for making firebrick or porcelain, although it may still be of use in making common brick or cheap pottery. Try a sample in the blacksmith's forge, to find if it fuses. If so, let it alone.

The desert salts are now being sought for with avidity, especially those of potash and soda. It would materially assist those that go to look for them to familiarize themselves with the crystal form of the principal of those salts, such as borax, the chlorides, and nitrates, which they can do easily enough by purchasing a nickel's worth of each, and taking a few crystals along. In default of this, a few simple tests will serve. Borax is detected by dissolving a little of the suspected substance in a saucer in the least possible water, adding a few drops of sulphuric acid, then some alcohol or strong whiskey, and setting the latter on fire. A bright-green flame proves that borax, or at least boric acid, is present. The nitrates are also easily distinguished. Mix the suspected substances with some combustible material and set it on fire. It will add to the amusement of camp-life if somebody's tobacco pipe is surreptitiously charged with a mixture of Virginia's weed and some native salt-petre, and the unsuspecting owner induced to smoke it. A miniature volcano results, and there is much surprise and a good deal of fun.

To get really satisfactory results it is necessary to re-crystallize the usually impure and mixed salts, which may be done by a simple process of evaporation in a glass, or even an iron dish, taking plenty of time, and removing the crystals as soon as they form on the sides. Then compare them with the samples that have been brought. The nitrates are especially impure, much of the stuff supposed to be saltpetre not containing above 5 to 10% of the pure nitrate. However, it is easily purified, all the impurities being left in the mother liquor after the nitrate has deposited.

It is a pity that there is no rough-and-ready way to discriminate between soda and potash in the field. But to do so requires the use at least of the blowpipe, and a sheet of blue glass, which the prospector might object to carrying.

It would appear that the old-time prospector was invariably baffled when it came to telling tin ore. The fact is that tin is one of the easiest metals to detect. Its ore, the oxide (cassiterite) is usually black, or nearly so, and is quite heavy. It looks so much like magnetic iron that many have thought they had a tin mine when it was only an iron prospect. Take a piece of the suspected ore, powder it, mix it with charcoal powder, and heat it in the blacksmith's fire, and you will get globules of tin—maybe. But do not set too much store by globules said to have been melted out in the forge, for the most of those shown came from tin-cans. After you have got the globules, hammer one out flat like a silver dime, hold it to your ear, and listen for the 'cry' that all tin makes when bent.

It is not everybody who can tell molybdenite from graphite. In fact, the ability to tell them apart seems to stamp one as an expert. It is easy. Just rub a little on your thumb-nail. Molybdenite stains it gray or green; graphite stains it black.

There may be people that do not know iron ore when they see it. If such there be they can easily learn. First, powder a little of the suspected rock and apply the magnet (note: all minerals should be powdered before applying the magnet); if it lifts the grains the ore is magnetite, the prevailing iron ore in California. If it does not lift them, it may be hematite or limonite. Throw a chunk into the camp-fire and cover it with hot coals and leave it for an hour or two. Scrape the outside of the chunk, powder the product, and try the magnet again. If iron, it will have been reduced to the magnetic form and will be lifted. To tell hematite from limonite, powder the ore finely. Powdered hematite is red; powdered limonite is brown or yellow. Weigh a chunk of iron ore on the scales at the nearest grocery, and burn it in the camp-fire. Magnetite will lose no weight; hematite will lose a trifle, but not enough to be told on the scales; limonite will lose a great deal, sometimes as much as one-seventh.

The carbonates are a numerous and important class; they are the stumbling-block to the miner, who generally lumps them together as 'lime'. Yet they are easily told apart. There are carbonates of lime, magnesia, lead, iron, manganese, baryta, and others, all of which are valuable in their places. Throw a piece into the camp-fire. It is a good thing to 'burn' an ore or rock, especially if you don't know what else to do. If the fire is hot enough they lose their carbonic acid and fall to pieces. If the residue is white, taste it. If lime it will prove very hot in the mouth. If magnesia it will be disagreeably bitter. If iron or manganese it will have turned dark, and you may tell whether iron or manganese by applying the magnet, provided that the fire has been hot enough to make the iron magnetic. Manganese, of course, has no effect on the magnet. However, carbonates are more than likely to be a mixture, iron with manganese, lime, or magnesia, lime almost always with magnesia, etc. The burnt lime will slake. Mix it with a little water and it will get hot. Magnesia will not, and slakes slowly. Lead carbonate needs no testing other than heating in the camp-fire, when lead is quickly reduced, long before the other carbonates would have been affected at all. Besides, it is heavy, which gives the clue to its composition. The acid-bottle is handy now, for all carbonates effervesce with acids, the most of them freely with even vinegar or lemon-juice. Always pulverize the mineral before testing with acid.

The carbonate of baryta is both rare and valuable: there is but one mine of it in America, and that, naturally, is in this State. It would be a better mine if there were no sulphate of baryta in it. The sulphate, however, is useful and profitable in some countries. Over here it is frequently mistaken for scheelite, the favorite ore of tungsten, which it somewhat resembles. To tell which is which throw a piece into the camp-fire or onto a hot stove. Heavy spar (baryta) has a tendency to decrepitate (fly to pieces) on heating; scheelite does not. Both are otherwise unaltered at this heat. Barite (heavy spar) is about as hard as limestone, and about as heavy as iron ore. Scheelite is both harder and heavier. There is sulphur in barite, none in scheelite. The sulphur test should be learned and applied. Powder the mineral, mix a trifle with soda (baking-powder or washing-soda will answer), add a drop of water, and place on a piece of charcoal. Using a candle if you have no proper lamp, blow with the blowpipe until you are tired. Then place the melted mass, which should be as big as a buckshot, on a cleaned silver coin, add a drop of water, and let it alone for a time. On removing it, if sulphur had been present, a black stain will show on the coin. It will be well to make a blank assay beforehand, to ensure the absence of sulphur from the water and soda used, for both these may contain it. This test reveals sulphur, no matter what form it may have been in, and should be fully mastered by the investigator. It depends on the reduction of the sulphur by carbon to the form of sulphide of sodium, which is soluble, and in its turn is decomposed by metallic silver, forming the black sulphide of silver.

Zinc ores have been much sought after of late, the carbonate especially. Prospectors have often been much puzzled about the lime carbonate intermixed with the zinc carbonate, and quite unable to tell them apart by the looks. Having recourse to the acid-bottle, add a little sulphuric acid to the powdered ore and wait until all the gas has gone off. If lime is present a heavy white powder (gypsum) will be left in the bottom of the glass. If zinc, the sulphate will have been formed, but it will dissolve in water. Both may be present. Add water, pour off the solution after it has settled, and add a little baking-powder or washing-soda previously dissolved in water, when a heavy white precipitate of zinc carbonate will fall.

Zinc-blende, which some miners call by the stupid name of 'black jack,' is harder to identify, but it often has to be done. If the color of its powder—white to brown, according to the amount of impurity—is not enough, throw a piece in the fire and let it heat a long time, smelling it occasionally to detect sulphur. After a while a coating of oxide will form; this is nearly white when cold. It generally serves to identify the mineral, but if not considered satisfactory, the oxide may be dissolved in a little sulphuric acid, plus water, and the baking-powder test applied, getting a white precipitate as before.

Diatomaceous earth (infusorial earth, or kieselguhr) should not be overlooked, especially if near a railway or seaport. This and a similar rock, tripoli, which results from the decomposition of silicious limestone, are frequently mistaken for clay, though so much lighter in weight. Unlike most clays, they do not form a plastic mass with water, so they cannot be stuck together in brick form and hardened by heat.

Quicksilver ore is generally known by the red color of the cinnabar. To make certain, pulverize some ore finely and wash it out in the horn or pan, and save the concentrate. Cinnabar is brittle, and you cannot save more than a small part of it. Put the red particles on a clean sheet of iron and heat over the camp-fire, when they, if cinnabar, pass off in gray smoke. This is conclusive.

The commoner ores of manganese are dark, quite black in most cases, their powder is also dark and has the property of soiling the hands. The di-oxide, the prevailing ore, may be discovered thus: Powder it and mix with an equal amount of salt. Place in a tea-cup and add sulphuric acid. Chlorine will be set free, a greenish-yellow gas which will fill the cup and may be smelled (very cautiously, since it injures the lungs). It has a strong and disagreeable smell, which cannot be forgotten. It comes from the salt, not the manganese. Why then use the manganese? Let the reader supply the answer.*

These rough-and-ready tests, which might be multiplied by hundreds, so as to embrace all the minerals in the field, are only intended to show what can be done with apparently inadequate means. Still, it would seem to be much to the advantage of the prospector to prepare himself for more systematic and far-reaching examination of what he finds, which he can only do by learning the use of the blowpipe. This takes time and labor, which few would care to expend upon so apparently trivial an instrument. Some use it as a matter of course; but most practitioners tend to advance beyond blowpipe practice and take up analysis in the wet way, and become chemists. The most progress is made and the best results are got by those that practice in both ways, but men of this sort rarely find the time for any prolonged investigations in the field.

Flotation of Zinc-Lead Tailing in Idaho

During the quarter ended September 30, 1918, the Consolidated Interstate-Callahan company's mill near Wallace, Idaho, treated old tailing only, by flotation. Results are as under:

Tailing concentrated, tons	42,661
Zinc content, per cent	11.13
Lead content, per cent	2.05
Silver content, ounces	0.81
Recovery, per cent	85.63
Zinc in concentrate, per cent	47.19
Zinc in concentrate, pounds	8,117,806
Lead in concentrate, per cent (also 12.20% zinc)	66.00
Lead in concentrate, pounds	62,222
Silver in lead, ounces	990
Cost of making one ton of concentrate, at shipping point	$8.068

THE WAR TRADE BOARD announces that, in addition to the General license PBF No. 14, covering the importation of iron ore from Sweden and Spain, when coming as ballast in ships returning from these countries, licenses may be issued for the importation of a maximum total from all sources of 70,000 tons of low-phosphorous iron ore from Spain, Sweden, Norway, and North Africa, provided the said ore be imported and entered prior to July 1, 1919. By low-phosphorous iron ore is meant that which contains the proportion of not more than 0.012% of phosphorus to 50% of metallic iron. The total amount of low-phosphorous iron ore so permitted to come forward will be allocated by the Bureau of Imports.

EXPORTATION OF PLATINUM is to be taxed and limited in Colombia, the Chamber of Deputies authorizing the Government until July 20, 1919.

*Why so secretive, Mr. Lang? The manganese carries the oxygen that combines with the acid to release the chlorine gas.—Editor.

Electrostatic Precipitation

By R. B. RATHBUN

*While the engineer should carefully weigh the merits of the various types of equipment, he must bear in mind that the object of his plant is the recovery of suspended solids, and a thing is unimportant except as it contributes to this end, other engineering principles being duly considered. The controversy regarding the use of synchronous motor-driven rectifiers by which the power for the treater is taken directly from the mains of the local power system, rather than the motor-generator rectifier giving each treater unit its own isolated electric system, has led many to think that on the type of rectifier depends the success of the plant. It is in fact a relatively unimportant part of the plant, and represents a small fraction of the investment; the recoveries in dust and fume are practically the same in each case. One large smelting concern has adopted the motor-generator type for all of its plants after years of experience with the synchronous-motor type. Its reasons are practically the same as those set down by Mr. Eschholz for his preference. Given more in detail they are:

1. An independent electric system prevents outside power-line conditions, like voltage fluctuations, from interfering with the operation of the Cottrell plant and eliminates the possibility of the Cottrell plant causing trouble for the power company. The latter, while not very probable, must be considered, for it is sometimes difficult to convince the transmission engineer that the make and break of the synchronous switch, which is the rectifier, does not introduce destructive voltage transients into his system like the well-known phenomena attending high-tension switching. It is not surprising that the power company hesitates to take any chances for the small amount of load acquired.

2. An isolated electric system for each treater prevents the possibility of any disturbance in one treater being communicated to the other treaters through the transformers and rectifiers.

3. By means of the generator-field and the exciter-field regulations, the treater potential may be maintained very close to the critical disruptive value. This is considered essential for good work and can only be equaled when using a synchronous-motor type method by the use of an induction regulator with remote electric control, which is more complicated than a simple rheostat control in the generator field.

4. The motor-generator is free from all the drawbacks to which the synchronous motor is subject, such as falling out of step and hunting.

Against these things is urged a slightly smaller first cost and approximately 86% power efficiency, as compared with a 76% efficiency of the motor-generator set. In addition, if the synchronous-motor method is used, the large power system will tend to absorb the surges, while the small generator circuit will tend to reflect and magnify any wave distortions that may be present. But if there are no wave irregularities, this function of a large power system is not necessary. Oscillograms taken on a large motor-generator Cottrell plant in Utah showed the treater and transformer circuits to be remarkably free from these surges. In this case, however, the generator wave was a true sine without any irregularities. Oscillograms taken on a large plant at Coram, California, where synchronous-motor rectifiers and induction regulators were used, showed that steep wave-fronts and surges were present to a marked degree, in spite of the absorbing qualities of a large power system. Oscillograms taken on three plants recently constructed, where motor-generators were used, showed that under certain conditions of the load voltage transients in the high-tension side of the transformer circuit became troublesome. In these plants the voltage wave was not a true sine, a number of small peaks or harmonics being apparent in the wave. The small peak that occurs just at the point of breaking contact is seen in the oscillogram to be manifest in the wave on the high side of the transformer greatly magnified, due to the steep wave-front in the primary wave. From the foregoing it is a fair assumption that if the voltage wave of the generator is a true sine, with no steep wave-fronts, there is no disadvantage due to surges in motor-generator rectifiers. This method, then, should not be condemned on account of a defect in a particular type of generator used. It seems better to correct the defect in the generator, although this defect has not proved as detrimental as might be supposed, for in every case known to the writer this surge, which makes itself manifest by arcing across a protective spark-gap placed across the high-potential terminals of the transformer, decreases so as to be negligible as soon as the gas is in a state permitting good precipitation with either method. There are electrical remedies that often prove beneficial, such as absorbing this oscillating energy by inserting ballast resistance in the primary and secondary circuits, or by shunting condensers across the primary circuit. Sometimes the inductive reactance of the circuit may be changed to advantage; and, too, the critical frequency of the system may be changed by changing the rectifier to contact to only one alternation per cycle without any loss in precipitation in the treater.

*Discussion of papers of O. H. Eschholz, presented at the Colorado meeting A. I. M. E., September 1918.

LEAD PIGMENTS sold in the United States during 1917 amounted to 87,331 tons of white lead in oil, 27,869 tons dry, 25,478 tons of red lead and orange mineral, and 44,102 tons of litharge. The total value was $36,663,923. This value is 18% above that of 1916, but 3% less in quantity.

THE PLATINUM (20,923 oz.) brought from Russia to the United States in January 1918 was refined at the New York Assay Office to a fineness of 999 and above. It yielded 17,640 oz. of platinum, 65 oz. of palladium, 182 oz. of iridium, and 49 oz. of rhodium.

Copper Export Association

The new association of American copper producers (organization of which has been under way since passage of the Webb-Pomerene bill in the last Congress held) elected the following officers and directors: Chairman of the board, Simon Guggenheim; president, John D. Ryan; first vice-president, Walter Douglas; second vice-president, R. L. Agassiz; and secretary and treasurer, C. W. Welch.

Directors: Murray Guggenheim, Simon Guggenheim, and F. H. Brownell, American Smelting & Refining Co.; John D. Ryan, Cornelius F. Kelley, and Benjamin B. Thayer, Anaconda Copper Mining Co. and Inspiration Consolidated Copper Co.; W. D. Thornton, Greene-Cananea Copper Co.; Charles Hayden, Charles M. MacNeill, and D. C. Jackling, Utah Copper Co., Nevada Consolidated Copper Co., Ray Consolidated Copper Co., and Chino Copper Co.; Walter Douglas and James McLean, Phelps Dodge Corporation; R. L. Agassiz and James MacNaughton, Calumet & Hecla Mining Co.; Stephen Birch, Kennecott Copper Corporation; William A. Clark, United Verde Copper Co.; Archibald Douglas, United Verde Extension Mining Co., Adolph Lewisohn, Miami Copper Co.; and Gordon R. Campbell, Calumet & Arizona Mining Company.

An executive committee was chosen consisting of: Chairman of the board, president, first vice-president, second vice-president, and the following directors: James McLean, Murray Guggenheim, Cornelius F. Kelley, William A. Clark, James MacNaughton, Adolph Lewisohn. The executive committee will choose a selling committee, in whose hands actual conduct of the business will be placed. The executive committee will, under the board of directors, determine policies with regard to the export trade of the association.

John D. Ryan, chairman of Anaconda Copper Mining Co., speaking for the new association, gave out the following statement:

"All the important copper producers of the country are represented in the directorate. The plan adopted by the association is purely a mutual one. Only a nominal capital is proposed. Two hundred fifty thousand dollars of preferred will be offered pro rata to all producers and each producer will be entitled to one share of common stock, with cumulative voting power, based upon his production of copper. Common stock will have no par and no market value, as it is provided that no earnings shall be divided among the common shareholders, and any profit made, after providing for dividends or a retirement of the preferred, will be credited to the producers in proportion to their export sales.

"Every producer, large and small, in the country, will be invited to join the association on precisely the same basis as the larger interests; that is, all representation, voting rights, and other privileges are based upon the proportion of production and export of each member of the association.

"Prices will be averaged over monthly periods and each producer will receive identically the same price at the seaboard for his product.

"It is believed that the plan being a purely mutual one, and providing for no advantage on account of the size or location of any contributing organization, will fulfill the expectations of its promotors and firmly unite all American exporters of copper.

"The production of American smelters and refineries was, before the War, fully 70% of that of the whole world. It is believed now to be 85%. About 60% of the pre-war production was exported. It is expected that proportion will continue to hold good. The Federal Trade Commission, in its investigation of the copper trade, found that by combination of buyers in European countries and manipulation of markets for futures the foreign consumer had been enabled to obtain his copper from American producers, over a period of years, for about 1 cent per pound less than the American consumer has paid. It is believed that the Export Association will remedy this situation, and, without interfering with the domestic trade, will not permit the foreign combinations to secure such undue advantage.

"The fact that every producer, large and small, in the country, has been or will be invited to join, and the door will not only be open, but will be kept open for any who desire to come in, will undoubtedly satisfy every possible requirement of public policy and it is the belief of all the copper people that the organization is formed along ideal lines to commend itself favorably to the Federal Trade Commission or other governmental agencies having to do with the regulation of export trade."

Mr. Ryan explained that every producer who signs an agency agreement will receive one share of common stock, which is without par value and without market value. Each share of common stock will represent one vote for each 500 tons produced in the 12 months preceding the time when the vote is taken. The 7% preferred shares have a par of $100.

"In the past," said Mr. Ryan, "copper exports have approximated 60% of production. This is running at the rate of 2,500,000,000 pounds a year, and if the 60% ratio holds good this country will export 1,500,000,000 pounds of copper a year. If foreign selling agencies have been able to make one cent a pound out of the copper we sold them, it means that they have taken out of our pockets $15,000,000 annually. We would like to keep that $15,000,000 here," said Mr. Ryan, "and spend it in this country."

Every copper interest of any importance is in this movement. The metal will be sold at a net price f.o.b. New York. All details of the association have been submitted to the Federal Trade Commission. It has been incorporated under laws of Delaware. The total issue of common stock will depend upon how many producers come into the association. Five hundred shares of no par value have been authorized.

"It would seem," said Mr. Ryan, "as if Europe had been milking the copper industry in this country for about $20,000,000 a year for twenty years."

EVIEW

RENO, NEVADA

Copper Mines and Effect of

of copper metal

in this State

been presented

of the demoralized

many

their utmost efforts

which the War

following the

Instances are known

paying demurrage on cars

anything from their

that they will be unable

ceased nearly everywhere

copper mine near

700 tons monthly, has

100 miners.

Purchasing Co.,

ores, says that the

for copper on the

remaining

RENO, NEVADA

Copper Mines and Effect of L er Prices.

Producers of copper metal and of co er, manganese, and tungsten ores in this State are fac:n difficulties greater than have been presented even during he war period, by reason of the demoralized state of th metal market. In recent months many prospectors anc claim-owners have devoted their utmost efforts to develc ing and marketing ores for which the War created a dem d. The collapse of the market, following the armistice, h left these men in

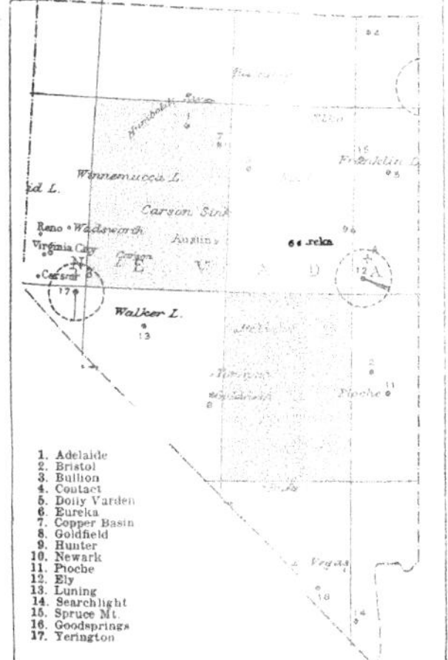

MAP SHOWING COPPER DISTRICTS OF NEVA. SMELTERS ARE AT ELY AND THOMPSON. (U. S3.8)

a serious plight. Instances are knov of men having ore in transit, paying demurrage on cars, nd with no prospect of realizing anything from their prodct. Others have incurred debts that they will be unabl to meet. Ore shipments have ceased nearly everywhei in the State. The Wall Street copper mine near Luning, iipments from which have averaged 700 tons monthly, hasbeen closed and has dismissed over 100 miners. F. M. Mason, manager for the Western Ore Purchasing Co., which eceives the bulk of Nevadan custom ores, says that the sm ters are making preliminary settlement for copper on theasis of 11 cents per pound, the remaining payment to be de when a market is established. Samuel Newhouse of Utah, who has been here, said this figure, 11 cents, had been established on an estimated basis of 6 cents below the market, making a theoretical market value for copper of 17 cents, but offering no assurance of any fixed price to producers. It is said that only large companies, able to carry their metal stocks or possessing funds to carry on development work, can avoid closing down if the existing chaotic situation continues for any appreciable time. Production of the Nevada Consolidated Copper Co. at Ely has not been affected, according to late reports. The Mason Valley Mines Co. maintains a normal output of copper matte from its smelter at Thompson. Copper ore has been exposed in considerable volume in the Jumbo Copper Mountain property, north-east of Luning and west of Rawhide, and a mill is to be built as soon as it can be operated at a reasonable expense. Confidence in the future demand for copper is stimulating the search for this metal by prospectors. Several companies are being organized for the purpose of intensive prospecting over wide areas. Each company will have several prospecting parties in the field, under the direction of an engineer and equipped with field assaying outfits. It is designed by this means to bridge the gap between the prospector and the development company.

DENVER, COLORADO

A Little Wyoming History.—Also a Boulder County Affair.

In the recent death at Los Angeles of Willis George Emerson, there terminated a human career as dramatic as that of the fictitious J. Rufus Wallingford. The recent prominence of this financier has been in connection with the notorious Emerson Motors Co., but the country at large has reason to remember him better through his remarkable manipulations, two decades ago, in southern Wyoming. The history of his project reads more like fiction than reality. It is difficult for anybody now, in retrospect, to believe that an individual could accomplish the things he did, 'get away with it', remain within the law, and evade all serious consequences.

About 1896 a Wyoming sheepherder named Ed Haggerty located a group of claims covering the outcrop of a strong lode showing heavy indications of copper, in Carbon county, Wyoming. An interest in the claims was soon acquired by a man named Ferris, and the property thereafter was spoken of as the Ferris-Haggerty mine, although it was located as the Rudefeha group. The two owners succeeded in organizing a company to which they sold the property for $40,000. About this time, Emerson, a Kansas banker with some available capital and plenty of influence, appeared in Wyoming and soon seized upon the Ferris-Haggerty as the nucleus of a gigantic chain of promotions. In those days, Wyoming law did not permit a corporation to secure a charter to do business in more than one special branch. This fitted Emerson's schemes to a T. He and associates are said, upon good authority, to have bought out the company then owning the mine by actually paying a million dollars; the property thereby going into the possession of the new North American Copper Co. As the mine was devoid of all transportation and treatment facilities, it was essential that it be provided

Bill of Relief for Miners

On December 15 Senator Henderson introduced the following bill for the relief of miners and mining companies that had suffered loss while responding to the Government's urgent solicitation to promote chromite, manganese, and other war minerals.

A Bill to supplement an Act of Congress approved October fifth, nineteen hundred and eighteen (public, numbered two hundred and twenty), and to authorize the Secretary of the Interior, from the funds appropriated by said Act, to determine, adjust, and pay losses sustained by investments preparatory to production of war minerals mentioned in said act.

Be it enacted by the Senate and House of Representatives of the United States of America in Congress assembled, That the Secretary of the Interior be, and hereby is, authorized and directed to ascertain and determine the amount or amounts of money heretofore invested or contracted to be invested and obligations incurred by any and all persons and investors for producing or acquiring property for producing, within the United States, to supply the urgent, published, and evident needs of the Nation during the war, any ores, metals, minerals, or mineral substances mentioned and enumerated in an Act of Congress approved October fifth, nineteen hundred and eighteen (public, numbered two hundled and tweuty), entitled "An Act to provide further for the national security and defense by encouraging the production, conserving the supply, and controlling the distribution of those ores, metals, and minerals which have formerly been largely imported, or of which there is or may be an inadequate supply;" and that said Secretary ascertain, determine, adjust, liquidate, and out of the moneys provided and appropriated by said Act pay to the parties entitled thereto the amount of such losses and damages as he, the said Secretary, shall find and determine have been sustained and suffered or are likely to be sustained and suffered, by reason of having made such investments for said purposes or having produced surplus stocks of such materials; and that in each case he shall make such determination, provision, settlement, advancement, or final payment, and by agreement with owners and claimants make such other adjustment or take such other action as he shall find and determine to be just, equitable, reasonable, and expedient; and that he make such provisions as he may deem necessary, advisable, and reasonable to prevent further losses pending final decision, settlement, and disposition in any case or cases; that the payments herein authorized be made to the claimant or claimants the said Secretary shall find to be morally, equitably, and justly entitled thereto; that in ascertaining and determining the losses and damages sustained or to be sustained, and the adjustments, settlements, payments, and provisions to be made, the said Secretary shall consider the prices and conditions existing at the time of each investment and the prices and conditions existing prior to the war, as well as those existing at the time of such determination, adjustment, and settlement, together with all of the circumstances and conditions of each case; that the final determination, decision, provision, disposition, and action of said Secretary in each case shall be conclusive and final; that all payments shall be made and all expenses incurred by the Secretary paid from the funds and appropriations provided and appropriated by said Act of October fifth, nineteen hundred and eighteen (public, numbered two hundred and twenty), and that said funds and appropriations shall continue to be available for said purposes until such time as the said Secretary shall have fully exercised the authority hereby granted and performed and completed the duties hereby provided and imposed.

Sec. 2. That a report of all operations under this Act, including receipts and disbursements, shall be made to Congress on or before the first Monday in December of each year.

Sec. 3. That nothing in this Act shall be construed to confer jurisdiction upon any court to entertain a suit against the United States.

An Oil Flotation Patent

The following interesting patent has been called to our attention. It is U. S. No. 744,171, dated November 17, 1903, application filed on December 1, 1902, granted to Henry Tadwell Davis and Ernest Perrett, of Lewisham, England, assignors to Davis-Perrett, Limited, of London, England. It is called a 'Method of Separating Oily or Similar Impurities from Water'.

Among other claims are these:

1. The method of separating oily and similar particles from water containing the same in emulsive condition, which consists in passing an electric current through the emulsified water for the purpose of *causing the oily particles therein to unite with metallic particles and float on the surface of the liquid* and separating the supernatant product, substantially as described.

2. The method of separating oily and similar particles from water containing the same in emulsive condition, which consists in mixing with the liquid a suitable electrically conductive liquid, and causing the oily particles to unite with a suitable metal and become disengaged from said water by electrolyzing the mixture between metallic electrodes, substantially as described.

3. The method of separating oily and similar particles from water containing the same in emulsive condition, which consists in passing an electric current through the emulsified water for the purpose of causing the oily particles to unite with iron, substantially as described.

4. The method of separating oily and similar particles from water containing the same in emulsive condition, which consists in mixing therewith a suitable conductive liquid and electrolyzing the mixture between iron electrodes, thereby causing iron to unite with the oil and removing the supernatant product thus formed, substantially as described.

REVIEW OF MINING

RENO, NEVADA

Copper Mines and Effect of Lower Prices.

Producers of copper metal and of copper, manganese, and tungsten ores in this State are facing difficulties greater than have been presented even during the war period, by reason of the demoralized state of the metal market. In recent months many prospectors and claim-owners have devoted their utmost efforts to developing and marketing ores for which the War created a demand. The collapse of the market, following the armistice, has left these men in a serious plight. Instances are known of men having ore in transit, paying demurrage on cars, and with no prospect of realizing anything from their product. Others have incurred debts that they will be unable to meet. Ore shipments have ceased nearly everywhere in the State. The Wall Street copper mine near Luning, shipments from which have averaged 700 tons monthly, has been closed and has dismissed over 100 miners. F. M. Manson, manager for the Western Ore Purchasing Co., which receives the bulk of Nevadan custom ores, says that the smelters are making preliminary settlement for copper on the basis of 11 cents per pound, the remaining payment to be made when a market is established. Samuel Newhouse of Utah, who has been here, said this figure, 11 cents, had been established on an estimated basis of 6 cents below the market, making a theoretical market value for copper of 17 cents, but offering no assurance of any fixed price to producers. It is said that only large companies, able to carry their metal stocks or possessing funds to carry on development work, can avoid closing down if the existing chaotic situation continues for any appreciable time. Production of the Nevada Consolidated Copper Co. at Ely has not been affected, according to late reports. The Mason Valley Mines Co. maintains a normal output of copper matte from its smelter at Thompson. Copper ore has been exposed in considerable volume in the Jumbo Copper Moun'ain property, north-east of Luning and west of Rawhide, and a mill is to be built as soon as it can be operated at a reasonable expense. Confidence in the future demand for copper is stimulating the search for this metal by prospectors. Several companies are being organized for the purpose of intensive prospecting over wide areas. Each company will have several prospecting parties in the field, under the direction of an engineer and equipped with field assaying outfits. It is designed by this means to bridge the gap between the prospector and the development company.

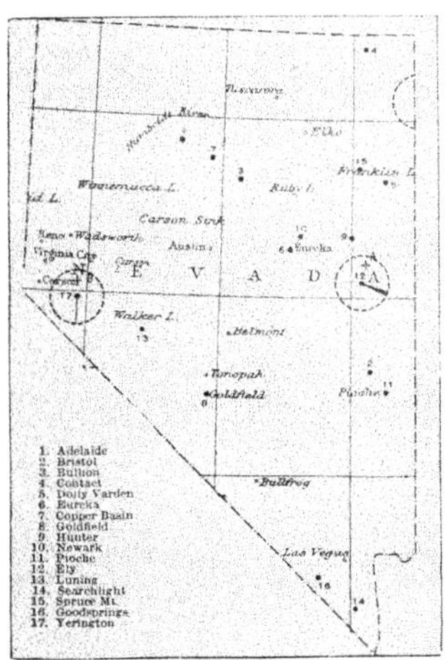

MAP SHOWING COPPER DISTRICTS OF NEVADA. SMELTERS ARE AT ELY AND THOMPSON. (U. S. G. S)

DENVER, COLORADO

A Little Wyoming History.—Also a Boulder County Affair.

In the recent death at Los Angeles of Willis George Emerson, there terminated a human career as dramatic as that of the fictitious J. Rufus Wallingford. The recent prominence of this financier has been in connection with the notorious Emerson Motors Co., but the country at large has reason to remember him better through his remarkable manipulations, two decades ago, in southern Wyoming. The history of his project reads more like fiction than reality. It is difficult for anybody now, in retrospect, to believe that an individual could accomplish the things he did, 'get away with it', remain within the law, and evade all serious consequences.

About 1896 a Wyoming sheepherder named Ed Haggerty located a group of claims covering the outcrop of a strong lode showing heavy indications of copper, in Carbon county, Wyoming. An interest in the claims was soon acquired by a man named Ferris, and the property thereafter was spoken of as the Ferris-Haggerty mine, although it was located as the Rudefeha group. The two owners succeeded in organizing a company to which they sold the property for $40,000. About this time, Emerson, a Kansas banker with some available capital and plenty of influence, appeared in Wyoming and soon seized upon the Ferris-Haggerty as the nucleus of a gigantic chain of promotions. In those days, Wyoming law did not permit a corporation to secure a charter to do business in more than one special branch. This fitted Emerson's schemes to a T. He and associates are said, upon good authority, to have bought out the company then owning the mine by actually paying a million dollars, the property thereby going into the possession of the new North American Copper Co. As the mine was devoid of all transportation and treatment facilities, it was essential that it be provided with its own smelting plant. The nearest suitable site for a smelter was at a point on the North Platte river, fully 16 miles from the mine. A smelting company was floated. To convey ore to the plant it was logical to incorporate a tramway company and to erect what was then the longest aerial tram in the world. Inasmuch as a smelter must not be isolated from sources of supply and market for its products, the Saratoga & Encampment Railroad Co. was incorporated and the road built. Such a great project being unable to operate without homes for employees and officials, the townsite of Grand Encampment came in for another big promotion. The city grew like magic and substantial stores, banks, hotels, and homes were erected. Other corporations were chartered to build and operate water-works and to furnish electric light and power to the city and the smelter. Coal mines were purchased and placed in the ownership of a new coal-mining company. An irrigation project was framed to add agricultural features to the district. Stocks in the many companies were sold readily throughout the country. Altogether some $20,000,000 was put into Emerson's schemes. To his credit it must be said that he made a pretty good showing, spending money liberally in every individual project and putting in first-class equipment. The mine was systematically developed, the tramway worked well, the smelter was a model of its period, and the railroad was complete. Things boomed along for a time; there were regular activities by every link in the chain; there were shipments of bar copper frequently. Yet the shareholders—perhaps Emerson himself—failed to perceive that an unjust burden had been put upon an out-of-the-way copper mine by requiring it to support so many thousands of people, to pay liberal salaries to officials, to carry the overhead on $20,000,000, and to furnish dividends. Before the inevitable crash came, Emerson had time to get from under, although he has always since claimed he was frozen out. At any rate he avoided prosecutions and appeared as the injured victim of "the Standard Oil crowd," in his own words. He must have emerged from the whole bubble well financed, as his subsequent life was one of leisure and comfort. He was something of a litterateur and wrote several interesting books on Western life, some of them vividly portraying the exciting times at Grand Encampment. Nothing but desolation and decay remains of the Ferris-Haggerty mine, the tramway, the city, or the smelter. There are engineers who assert that the mine has merit and could yet be made to pay under rational operation.

Boulder county has a reputation for springing surprises on the mining fraternity. Every few years the county comes forward with disclosures of unsuspected but valuable metals or non-metallic minerals. Jimtown was long and favorably known as a gold district. About a year ago, when it was decidedly dull, a sudden revival occurred in the discovery that hitherto neglected fluorspar veins could be profitably worked. Two abandoned gold mills were rehabilitated to concentrate the crude fluorspar before its shipment to Eastern steel plants. On ordinary tables, by skillful manipulation, most of the silica, pyrite, and other impurities can be eliminated from the Jimtown fluorspar. During the dressing of this ore, a millman observed a tiny streak of particularly heavy black mineral, which his curiosity caused him to save, his hope being that he had discovered platinum. Good money was being made from the sale of the fluorspar, but the recovery of platinum, even in small amount, would be velvet. He took a small quantity of the heavy concentrate to the U. S. Bureau of Mines station at Golden. Tests for platinum there proved negative. However, while handling the tiny sample, one of the Bureau chemists identified pitchblende, and made as careful a test for radio-activity as the quantity of material would permit. It seems that the millman declined to tell the chemists the source of the sample, either as to district or preparation. The Bureau possibly exceeded its function in giving out a statement that the sample showed 0.1% U_3O_8. Soon thereafter the Denver dailies appeared with full-page advertisements of the Colorado Pitchblende Co., which claimed to own an area one mile wide and two miles long, embracing the heart of Jimtown's fluorspar belt. The company has a fluent press agent, who has supplemented the advertisements with stories about the solid mountains of fluorspar carrying wonderful quantities of magic radium, etc. It is rather unusual for any mining community to dispute the claims of its own people to valuable strikes, but, in this instance the Boulder County Metal Mining Association and the Boulder Commercial Association promptly took issue with the promoters of this stock-selling concern, and caused an investigation of the matter to be made by such men as R. D. George, State geologist, and J. B. Ekeley, professor of chemistry in the State

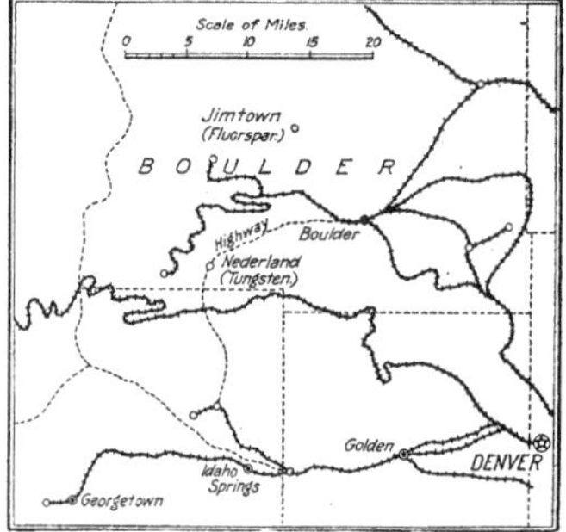

PART OF COLORADO. SHOWING BOULDER COUNTY

University. Their findings were sufficient to discourage further attention to this affair, but the promoters immediately came back with full-page advertisements severely criticizing the investigators and simultaneously laying stress upon the analyses of their ore made by a chemist who had long been connected with the Government, not one of the chemists at Golden. The promoters likewise insisted upon an unbiased investigation by one or more of Denver's civic organizations. It was the purpose of the company to sell stock in Denver, but this would be precluded by Denver's blue-sky ordinance unless some such authoritative favorable report were secured. In consequence, the Denver Civic and Commercial Association and the Denver Manufacturers' Association has each selected an engineer who is personally supervising the mining, milling, and assay of ore taken from the company's holdings at Jimtown. Dr. Lind of the U. S. Bureau of Mines insists that unfair use was made of the information given out by him, and he believes that his low result was secured from a sample representing a concentration of raw ore in a ratio of at least 1200 to 1. Be that as it may, the world is full of 0.1% uranium material, and no value attaches to this excitement. Your correspondent predicts a negative report from M. S. MacCarthy and James M. McClave, the two engineers now making the official investigation. [The prospectus of the Colorado Pitchblende Co. was unfavorably commented upon editorially in the 'Press' of December 28.—Editor.]

The Colorado Metal Mining Association and American Mining Congress met at Denver on January 2 and 4.

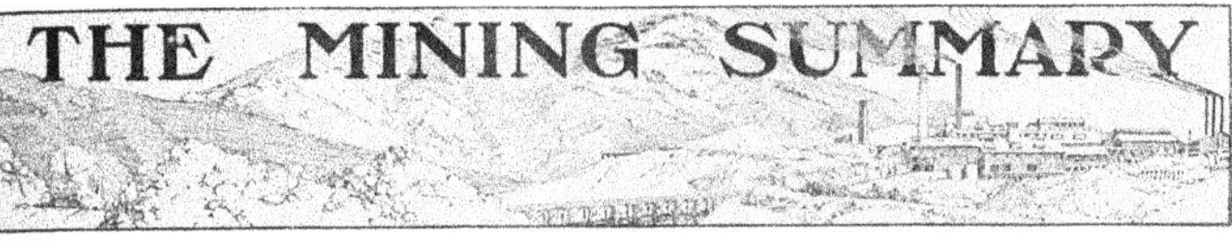

ARIZONA

Hayden.—The Lavell Gold Mining Co., with A. H. Parker as engineer in charge, has erected a 50-ton mill. This includes a crusher, Quinner pulverizer, amalgamating plates, concentrators, and a 120-hp. Fairbanks-Morse engine and dynamo. A 4-mile road is being constructed between the mine and mill. A large quantity of high-grade gold-silver-lead ore is said to be blocked out. The mine is 8 miles from Hayden.

Jerome.—Returns from the first shipment of ore from the Shea mine to the United Verde Extension smelter yielded 9.56% copper, 191.34 oz. silver, and 0.26 oz. gold per ton. A little less than 13 tons was shipped and netted the company $2800. When making arrangements for treatment the following samples were submitted to the U. V. X. Co.: (1) Gold 0.17 oz., silver 424 oz., copper 22.7%, silica 30.4%, iron 2.6%; (2) 0.09 oz., 186 oz., 9.6%, 15.8%, 9.2%; (3) 0.10 oz., 258 oz., 13.3%, 45.6%, 9%; and (4) 0.99 oz., 150 oz., 8.1%, 44%, 15.6%, respectively. The shipment was made from ore mined and sorted from the drift running west from the bottom of the 350-ft. incline shaft.

Mayer.—W. W. Elliott is superintending erection of a reduction plant at the old Peck mine in the Bradshaw mountains. This mill is designed to treat $20 silver ore.

CALIFORNIA

The U. S. Geological Survey has surveyed and sign-posted a great area of the most dangerous desert region of the United States. The thirty-ninth Annual Report of the topographic division of the Survey, just made public, describes the method employed of making the desert safe to the unwary traveler. The region surveyed occupies about 60,000 square miles in southern California and south-western Arizona. In California it includes the southern part of Death Valley and the region between this valley and the Mexican border; in Arizona it includes the region west of Tucson and Phoenix and south of Wickenburg and Parker. This region was selected because it it the driest, hottest, and least explored part of the desert region, and also because of the strategic importance of obtaining information on the water supplies along the 350 miles of national frontier that it includes. The field work was done by four parties, each of which consisted of one geologist and one non-technical assistant outfitted with an automobile and light camping equipment. Practically all watering-places in the region were examined, about 160 samples of water were collected and shipped to the water-resources laboratory at Washington for analysis, and a general exploration was made of the geography, geology, and ground-water conditions of the region. The maps prepared and the data obtained were made available to the Army engineers for incorporation in the progressive military map of the United States. Guides with maps are being prepared for publication.

Signs directing travelers to water were erected at 167 localities in California and 138 in Arizona. The sign-posts are galvanized iron, 1.9 in. outside diameter and 12 ft. long. Each post is anchored in the ground with two redwood blocks. The signs are 18-gauge steel, galvanized, are white, with dark-blue letters, and are substantially bolted to the posts. They are of two sizes, 18 by 20 in. and 9 by 20 in. Most of the larger signs, of which 470 were erected, give the names, distances, and directions to four watering places; most of the smaller signs, 165 of which were erected, give the names, distances, and directions to two watering-places. The work done last year is a part of a comprehensive plan for mapping and marking the watering-places in the entire arid region lying east of the Sierra Nevada and Cascade mountains, and west of a line running approximately from eastern Oregon through Salt Lake City and Santa Fe to the mouth of Pecos river.

Grass Valley.—The Idaho-Maryland mine is to be re-opened by Bulkeley Wells, of Colorado, and others.

Idria.—New Idria Quicksilver Co. paid 25 cents per share on January 1. This is equal to $25,000. Previous distributions were $50,000. Word from Hollister states that the New Idria is to electrify its plant. Rights-of-way papers for the King City-New Idria power-line have been filed by the Coast Valleys Gas & Electrical Co. and work will begin shortly. The proposed line will cost $85,000. At present the company generates its power with Diesel engines using crude oil. The oil is hauled in from Mendota and is a source of heavy expense and inconvenience, being handled by truck.

Martinez.—The new electrolytic works of the Butters company are in full operation at Peyton, employing 30 men.

Redding.—The Arps Copper Co. of Copper City has given an option to John A. Rice of San Francisco on the Arps, Reno, Sacramento, and Black Oak groups of mines—37 claims. The option expires on July, 1921, and calls for the aggregate payment of $200,000, to be made in installments of $50,000.

Victorville.—The United Tungsten-Copper Mines of New York and Los Angeles, whose tungsten properties are in the Morongo district, San Bernardino mountains, has completed purchase of the remainder of the machinery for the tungsten mill. As soon as weather permits, the heavy machinery will be trucked from Victorville. By a sluicing process heretofore employed, the company has been able to produce a high-grade concentrate—above 70% WO_3. This concentrate takes the form of translucent crystals. Smith-Emery & Co. of Los Angeles states that this is the highest grade of concentrate that has yet been brought to its office for analysis.

COLORADO

Aspen.—The Newman Leasing Co. paid a dividend of 25%, equal to $12,500, during December. An old property was re-opened and is being worked profitably.

Breckenridge.—The Farncomb Hill Gold Dredging Co. paid a 5% dividend early in December. This is equal to $15,000 on the $300,000 capital. R. W. Foote is president. Several years ago, when the Tonopah Placers Co.'s No. 2 dredge reached the upper boundary of the ground owned by the Farncomb Hill in Swan valley, the Tonopah company made a contract with the Farncomb Hill to dredge its ground— paying a royalty on the net proceeds of the gold recovered by the Tonopah company from the leased ground. The arrangement proved satisfactory and has enabled the Farncomb Hill to pay dividends without having to operate the property itself.

Idaho Springs.—The old North American sampling-works have been re-modeled by the Clear Creek-Gilpin Ore Co. Ralph Chase, for years with the Chamberlain sampler at Black Hawk, is assayer; W. E. Passmore is manager.—— M. T. Chestnut was recently at Idaho Springs, examining property in Virginia canyon.

IDAHO

Boise.—The State inspector of mines, Robert N. Bell, gives the following approximate metal output of the State for 1918: lead, 275,000,000 lb.; zinc, 45,000,000 lb.; and silver, 9,000,000 oz. In 1917 the respective figures were 375,000,000 lb., 95,000,000 lb., and 12,000,000 ounces.

Burke.—The Hecla company in November sent 200 tons of zinc ore daily from the Oro-or-no-go vein to its leased mill, and 600 tons of lead-silver ore to the Gem mill. From 35 to 45 tons of high-grade lead-silver ore is also mined daily. Between 500 and 550 men are employed. Driving is progressing on the 2000-ft. level alongside the vein, where it is valueless. By this means timber will be saved.

Mullan.—Profit of the Federal M. & S. Co. during the quarter ended October 31 was $371,972. In the two previous periods the figures were $323,309 and $62,945.

Wallace.—Agents of powder companies in the Coeur d'Alene have announced a cut in prices. This reduction is not large, but it is expected to be followed by others. Those grades of powder that have been $28.50 per 100 lb. have been reduced to $26.50; the pre-war price was $14.50. Grades that have sold for $35 are reduced to $31; this sold for $18.50 before the War.

The Success company reports having 2000 tons of ore broken on the 700-ft. level stope. At 1400 ft. the stope is 50 ft. long, at 1500 ft., 110 ft. long, while at 1600 ft. stoping is to start on a shoot 80 ft. long and 3 to 7 ft. wide. This is the richest lead-zinc orebody opened so far. While the mine was closed for four months the cost of maintenance was $21,000. An assessment of 2 cents per share has been levied.

A vocational school for miners, giving practical instruction in rock-breaking, use of powder, timbering, pumping, and other underground work will be established at Wallace, as part of the short course offered by the University of Idaho at Moscow. An eight weeks term will be held, most of the time being spent in one of the big mines. Lieutenant Frank H. Skeels, engineer and practical miner, has been placed in charge of the vocational school. He recently returned from a military training camp to take this work. The course is being established by the university under the recent Smith-Hughes act by which the Government furnishes half the money for such a course and the State the other half. If the course proves the success that is expected, Idaho will be asked for an additional appropriation for enlarging the work.

MICHIGAN

Houghton.—Champion Copper Co. pays $6.40 per share on January 15. During 1918 there was $19.20 paid, against $44.80 in 1917, $60.14 in 1916, and $31 in 1915.

St. Mary's Mineral Land Co. pays $2 on January 15. This makes $7 for 1918, just half of the distribution in 1917.

MISSOURI

Joplin.—Production of the Tri-State region last week was as under.

State	Blende tons	Calamine tons	Lead tons	Value
Kansas	278	...	61	$17,668
Missouri	1,080	590	580	......
Oklahoma	4,986	...	858	289,124
Average per ton.....	$44	$37	$80	......

Over 10,000 tons was sold. The price of blende declined $2.50 per ton.

A 250-ton (in 10 hours) mill has just been erected by the Henryetta Lead & Zinc Co. at Smelter Hill. Bessemer gas-engines will drive the plant, also an air-compressor. Three shafts have opened ore, shown by 22 drill-holes. M. G. Brady is in charge.

MONTANA

Anaconda.—The new smoke-stack at the Anaconda Copper company's Washoe Reduction Works is 585 ft. 1½ in. high, according to the 'Butte Miner'. Removal of the scaffolding from the interior of the chimney is finished, and construction of the connecting flues is in progress. The stack was built in 142 days. It has an octagonal base 86 ft. high, above which it is circular, with five different tapers. The thickness of the walls varies from 60 to 22½ in. Outside

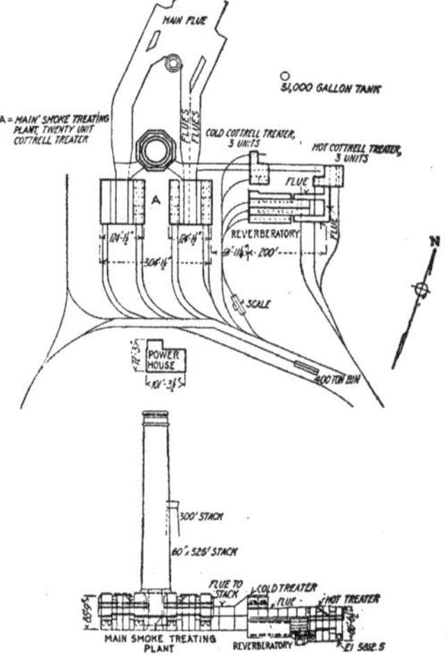

PLAN AND ELEVATION OF NEW STACK AT WASHOE WORKS, ANACONDA, MONTANA. (DRAWING FROM 'POWER').

dimensions are 86 ft. across the base and 63¾ ft. at the base of the cap. The chimney-blocks (17,000 tons) used in construction are the Custodis type. They are made in five different lengths, 4, 5, 7½, 8⅜, and 10¾ in., and vary in width from 6½ to 6⅜ in., but are of the standard thickness of 4⅜ in. The blocks are all laid in a mortar of cement, fire-clay, and sand (10,350 bbl., 1850 tons, and 2700 cu. yd., respectively). The cap for protection of the top of the chimney from weather and gases is of special terra-cotta blocks, with interlocking joints. To protect the chimney from lightning, two down-leading copper cables are fixed on opposite sides of the stack. These cables are connected with an intersecting cable near the top of the chimney, to which are attached 20 copper rods, each 8 ft. long and tipped with platinum. To protect the copper from the action of gases, the 20-point rods, winding cable, 50 ft. of the two down-leading cables and anchor, are coated with lead ⅛ in. thick. The chimney has an outside ladder from base to cap which is provided with body-guards. The radial blocks used throughout the construction were manufactured by the Anaconda company and delivered to the site on flat-cars. The blocks were made from slime-flotation tailing, mixed with sand. The brick machines of the American Clay Machine Co., type No. 290, which has a capacity of 100 tons per eight hours, were used in making the bricks. The blocks were burned in an Oregon kiln of 26 chambers to a temperature of 1800°F. The Alphonse Custodis Chimney Construction Co. designed and erected the chimney.

Butte.—Anaconda Copper has declared a dividend of $1.50 per share, equal to 6% per annum. Previous distributions were $2 per quarter.

Neihart.—The Ripple Consolidated Mining Co. has been incorporated in Montana with James H. Rowe, president, James A. Canty, vice-president, and H. A. Frank, secretary and treasurer. The property is six miles from Neihart, Cascade county, and consists of 10 claims, including the Ripple and Black Diamond groups. The ore carries silver and lead, and it is the intention of the company to erect a 100-ton mill as soon as arrangements can be made.

NEVADA

Auburn.—The White Pine Copper Co. has been organized at Salt Lake City with a capital of 1,000,000 shares, $1 par value. G. T. Hansen is manager. The 9 claims are 24 miles south of Ray, on the Nevada Northern. Tunnels and cross-cuts have opened 5% copper and 3-oz. silver ore. Equipment includes a 325-cu. ft. air-compressor, 1000-ft. aerial tram, and camp.

Dayton.—The Dayton Placer Recovery Co. is now cyaniding 175 tons daily of old Comstock mill tailing extracted from the Carson River valley. Gold, silver, copper, and mercury is saved. G. T. Hansen is general manager and C. I. Sherwood manager.

Goodsprings.—According to the 'Gazette', the Hoosier mine has just been examined for the new owner, the Galena Canyon Mining Co.——The Manse claim of the Boss group is yielding some good copper ore for the lessee.——The Copper Chief, Bill Nye, Columbia, Dawn, and Anchor mines are all producing.——The Bullion and others are opening encouragingly.

The Yellow Pine Mining Co. paid 12 cents per share on December 16. This amounts to $120,000, and makes $300,-000 for 1918.

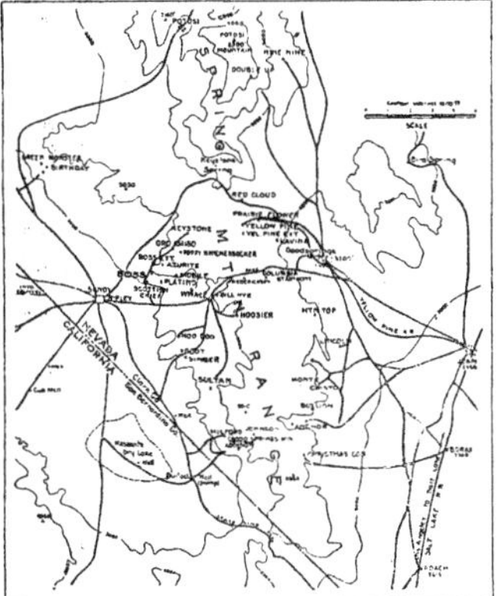

Map of Goodsprings District, Nevada

NEW MEXICO

Petaca.—A large mica deposit is being opened in this district of Rio Arriba county by L. M. Stiles and J. C. Miller They report that during 15 months they have mined over 40,000 lb. of 'black' mica, which is cleaned and stored, and over 150,000 lb. of cleaned 'scrap' mica. The deposit was worked as early as 1852 by Mexicans.

OKLAHOMA

Picher.—Production of the various centres last week totaled 4986 tons of blende and 858 tons of lead, valued at $289,124.

TEXAS

Orla.—Development of the large sulphur deposit of the West Texas Sulphur Co., in Culberson county, about 15 miles from Orla, will be started on an extensive scale soon, according to W. H. Beard, general manager. The company has finished construction of a mill and refining plant.

UTAH

Alta.—Columbus-Rexall paid 2½ cents per share, equal to $14,659, on December 30. This is the only company in the Alta district that distributed anything during 1918.

Green River.—The Shinntown and Needles manganese companies have suspended mining, while the May Dew is working on a small scale.

Marysvale.—The potash plant of the Florence company resumed treatment of alunite last week, after being closed for over two months. There is about 400 tons of ore to be treated. After this the mill is to handle ore from the Nebraska-Utah Potash Company.

Tintic.—The Liberty Manganese Co. in the West Tintic district has suspended operations on account of the state of the market. A few carloads of ore was shipped. The property is well equipped for a large output.

WASHINGTON

Leadpoint.—The Electric Point Mining Co. distributed 5 cents per share, $39,675, for Christmas. This makes a total of $253,785 in two years. Ore has been sent to the U. S. S. R. & M. Co.'s smelter at Midvale, Utah, as the smelter at Trail, B. C., is not receiving foreign lead ore. The Northport smelter, Washington, is reducing a carload daily.

CANADA

British Columbia

The Provincial government proposes opening up the Duncan River district, which is highly mineralized, by granting financial assistance for construction of a wagon-road. The minerals of the area, which has been handicapped in development by lack of transportation facilities, include gold, silver, copper, lead, and zinc, occurring in promising conditions.

Anyox.—Granby Consolidated pays $2.50 per share, equal to $374,962, on February 1. The November output was 1,970,027 lb. of copper from the Hidden Creek mines and 177,378 lb. from the Phoenix mines, a total of 2,886,489 lb. This is the lowest yield for 1918, save that of 2,580,288 lb. in February.

Rossland.—Conditions are improving in this gold-producing centre, due to resumption of work by the Consolidated M. & S. Co. Up to the end of November the War Eagle-Centre Star-Le Roi group sent 88,934 tons of ore to the smelter at Trail.

PERSONAL

Note. The Editor invites members of the profession to send particulars of their work and appointments. The information is interesting to our readers.

Fred J. Pope of New York is in Nevada.

H. Hardy Smith has left London for Osaka, Japan.

J. E. Smith of Ketchikan, Alaska, is at the Manx hotel.

F. H. Skeel has returned from Camp Humphreys to Wallace, Idaho.

Eugene A. H. Tays is now stationed at San Blas, in Sinaloa, Mexico.

Morton Webber is at Butte. He is expected shortly in San Francisco.

Charles E. Prior, Captain in the Motor Transport Corps, is still in France.

F. M. Hartman, of Tucson, Arizona, is spending the holidays in San Francisco.

C. A. Burdick has become general manager to the Nechako River Mines in British Columbia.

Robert T. Hill has opened an office at Dallas, Texas, in addition to the one at Los Angeles.

Gilmour E. Brown is consulting engineer for the Mentoukou Coal Mining Co. near Peking, China.

Maxwell W. Atwater has been appointed general manager for the Davis-Daly Copper Co., at Butte, Montana.

Algernon Del Mar is erecting a concentrator for the Montezuma Mining Co., near Big Pine, California.

F. W. Libbey, Lieutenant in the Army, at Camp Humphreys, Virginia, has received his discharge and has returned to Phoenix, Arizona.

A. J. Eveland, of the American Zinc, Lead & Smelting Co., has recently gone to Mexico City, where he will make his headquarters for several months.

John W. Sherman, recently manager for the West End and other mines at Tonopah, has been appointed manager for the Trona Corporation at Searles Lake, California.

Lucien Eaton, Captain of Engineers, honorably discharged, has returned to his former position as superintendent in the Ishpeming district for the Cleveland Cliffs Iron Co., at Ishpeming, Michigan.

Maurice Altmayer, Captain in the French Artillery, representing the Franco-American Department of War Co-operation, is expected shortly in San Francosco. He is engaged in studying the latest mining and metallurgical practice in behalf of French consumers of the base metals.

J. C. Haas was elected chairman of the Columbia section A. I. M. E. at the annual session held at Spokane last week. William J. Hall, of the Federal Mining & Smelting Co., Wallace, Idaho, was elected vice-chairman, and L. K. Armstrong was re-elected secretary-treasurer.

A meeting to organize a local chapter of the American Mining Congress will be held in San Francisco on January 15.

Obituary

In the death of Ernest H. Simonds from influenza in Oakland on December 26 the mining profession loses a valuable member. From the days when he was instructor in mining under Professor Christy at Berkeley, to the laboratory he established in San Francisco, about 1898, and more recently to the metallurgical operations on the Mother Lode, where he successfully handled tailings that were, previous to his experiments, thought too low-grade for profitable treatment, all who came in contact with Simonds were impressed by the thoroughness of the man's work, his close attention to detail, and his modest unassuming ways. Those of us who in the old days had occasion to send samples to Simonds' laboratory for analysis always had complete and comfortable confidence in the results obtained by him. What he undertook to do he did well.—C. J.

Alfred McLean Hamilton, who died on November 25, was born at Montreal, Canada, in 1879. He was educated at the Montreal high-school and graduated B. Sc. in mining and metallurgy from McGill University in 1905. While at the University he captained the football team, winning the Canadian intercollegiate championship. During his summer vacations he worked in smelters in Mexico and at Anaconda, taking his dinner-pail and his "chances with the boys". In 1905 he obtained a position at the Washoe smelter, Anaconda. In 1906 he went to Mexico and since then he has been in the employ of the American Smelting & Refining Co. in various capacities, his last being that of manager of the smelters at Velardeña and Aguas Calientes. He rose rapidly under most trying conditions of revolutions and counter-revolutions with the accompanying murders, 'executions', and hold-ups by bands of brigands. On one occasion he went late at night into the little town and destroyed all the whiskey and got up about 1 a.m. and made another round and destroyed the new supply that had already made its appearance. During the successive revolutions a great many men were killed in and around his plants. On one occasion six nice young well educated Mexicans were stood against his wall and shot after the 'general' instructed his men "We don't take prisoners." Men were hung to telegraph poles in and around the plant—one pole having six men hung to it at one time. He pitied the under dog. On one occasion he hid the defeated Mexican 'general' under the bed while he entertained the victorious 'general'. His greatest troubles were the bandits, who rode into the plant drunk, holding him up many times, and with pistols on each side of him and behind marched him to open the safe. On one occasion when some one else had the key he was subjected to a great deal of abuse and he thought he was going to lose his life. On other occasions he considered that his life was saved by calling on some one to bring the camera and he got the bandits to mount their horses and pose for a picture. Sometimes the camera had neither plates nor films. He lost all of his belongings when his house was burned by the Mexicans. His difficulties and worries were increased by his struggles to 'carry on' while unable to communicate with his company, which tried to support him. He left Mexico for a time and started a smelter at Sasco, Arizona. About two years ago he went back to Mexico and again started up the smelters at Velardeña and later at Aguas Calientes. The trouble of getting the smelting plants repaired and started in operation was enough for most men, but he found the people starving and so made efforts to get corn planted to feed them. It was found that the Mexican railways were unable to handle the necessary supplies of ore, coke, etc., for the smelters on account of the revolutionists having burned the cars and blown up the locomotives, so he undertook to re-build 500 cars and a great number of locomotives in the smelter-shops. The Mexican government then levied prohibitive taxes on the company and this greatly worried him, though subsequently the taxes were cut down considerably. About a year ago while in Mexico City he had an attack of ptomaine poisoning. It was thought he would die at the time, but he seemed to be getting over it and returned to his work at the smelter, but finally he had a hemorrhage and it was found that he had heart and lung trouble and he was carried out of Mexico completely broken down, very weak, and suffering from nervous prostration. He died at San Antonio, Texas, on November 25, 1918, in his 39th year. He is survived by his widow, who was Miss Freda Harms of Illinois, and by his mother, five brothers, and three sisters.—E. H. H.

THE METAL MARKET

METAL PRICES

San Francisco, December 31

Aluminum-dust, large and small lots, cents per lb.	66—70
Antimony (wholesale), cents per pound	10.00
Copper, electrolytic, cents per pound, in carload lots	26.00
Copper, electrolytic, cents per pound, in small quantities	27.35
Lead, pig, cents per pound	6.25—6.75
Platinum, per ounce	$108
Quicksilver, per flask of 75 lb.	$110
Spelter, cents per pound	9.50
Zinc-dust, cents per pound	16.00

ORE PRICES

December 31

Chrome, no definite quotations available.

Fluorspar, 85% CaF_2, f.o.b. shipping point, or San Francisco, per ton	$22—$30
Manganese, domestic, 35 to 54%, f.o.b. South Chicago, per unit (Government price, effective May 29)	$0.86—$1.30
Manganese, domestic, 35 to 45%, f.o.b. east of South Chicago per unit (Government price, effective May 29)	$1.01—$1.15
(Manganese, domestic, penalty of 50c. to $1 per ton for 8% and up to 25% silica, and bonus of 50c. to $1 for less than 8 and 5%.)	
Molybdenite, per lb., 90% MoS_2	$0.85
Pyrite, per unit of sulphur, cents	28—32
Tungsten, 60% WO_3, per unit	$17—$23

EASTERN METAL MARKET

(By wire from New York)

December 31.—Copper is inactive and lower at 23 cents from December 26. Lead is dull and lower. Speller is stagnant and falling.

SILVER

Below are given official (not Government) quotations, in cents per ounce, of silver 999 fine. In order to make prompt settlements with smelters and brokers, producers allow a discount from the maximum fixed price of $1.01½, hence the lower price. The Government has not fixed the general market price at $1, but will pay this price (as from April 23, 1918) for all silver purchased by it. The equivalent of dollar silver (1000 fine) in British currency is 46.65 pence per ounce (925 fine), calculated at the current rate of exchange. On August 15, 1918, the Treasury announced that the maximum price was fixed at $1.01½ per ounce. The British government fixed its maximum at 49½ pence, on September 2, but on November 12 this was changed to 48¾ pence, due to a drop in price.

Date		New York	London
Dec.	25 Holiday		
"	26	101.12	48.75
"	27	101.12	48.75
"	28	101.12	48.75
"	29 Sunday		
"	30	101.12	48.75
"	31	101.12	48.75

Average week ending		
Nov.	19	101.12
"	26	101.12
Dec.	3	101.12
"	10	101.12
"	17	101.12
"	24	101.12
"	31	101.12

Monthly averages

	1916	1917	1918
Jan.	56.76	75.14	88.72
Feb.	56.74	77.54	85.79
Mch.	57.89	74.13	88.11
Apr.	64.37	72.51	95.35
May	74.27	74.61	99.50
June	65.04	76.44	99.50
July	63.06	78.92	99.62
Aug.	66.07	85.40	100.31
Sept.	68.51	100.73	101.12
Oct.	67.86	87.38	101.12
Nov.	71.60	85.97	101.12
Dec.	75.70	85.97	101.12

COPPER

On September 21, 1917, the Government fixed copper prices at 23.50c. per lb. for large lots, and 24.67½c. for small lots, effective until June 1, 1918. On this date the prices were re-fixed until August 15; but on July 2 the price was increased to 26c. and 27.35c., respectively, until August 15. On August 7 the current rates were again fixed until November 1, which have since been extended to January 1, 1919, prices to be effective on the day of shipment, not the day of sale. Quotations in cents per pound are as under:

Date		
Dec.	25 Holiday	
"	26	26.00
"	27	26.00
"	28	26.00
"	29 Sunday	
"	30	26.00
"	31	26.00

Average week ending		
Nov.	19	26.00
"	26	26.00
Dec.	3	26.00
"	10	26.00
"	17	26.00
"	24	26.00
"	31	26.00

Monthly averages

	1916	1917	1918
Jan.	24.30	29.53	23.50
Feb.	26.62	34.57	23.50
Mch.	26.65	36.00	23.50
Apr.	28.02	33.16	23.50
May	29.02	31.69	23.50
June	27.47	32.57	23.50
July	25.66	29.67	26.00
Aug.	27.03	27.42	26.00
Sept.	28.28	25.11	26.00
Oct.	28.50	23.50	26.00
Nov.	31.95	23.50	26.00
Dec.	32.89	23.50	26.50

Copper production of twenty of the largest properties in North and South America during November totaled 148,763,177 lb., against 154,708,552 lb. in October. The total for 11 months is 1,620,345,326 lb., compared with 1,480,926,956 in 1917.

The London copper market is again open. Standard metal has been offered at 19 cents, but no business followed.

The sliding-scale for copper miners' wages is likely to come into effect again. Many are now being paid on the basis of 30-cent metal, but will be reduced to a 23-cent basis.

LEAD

Lead is quoted in cents per pound, New York delivery. Early in July, producers agreed to fix prices at 8.05c. per lb., New York. This was reduced to 7.05c. on December 2. On the 21st all restrictions were removed from lead, the market now being free.

Date		
Dec.	25 Holiday	
"	26	6.50
"	27	6.00
"	28	6.00
"	29 Sunday	
"	30	6.00
"	31	6.00

Average week ending		
Nov.	19	8.05
"	26	8.05
Dec.	3	7.85
"	10	7.05
"	17	7.05
"	24	6.45
"	31	6.10

Monthly averages

	1916	1917	1918
Jan.	5.95	7.64	6.83
Feb.	6.23	9.10	7.07
Mch.	7.26	10.07	7.26
Apr.	7.70	9.38	6.99
May	7.38	10.29	6.88
June	6.88	11.74	7.58
July	6.40	10.93	8.03
Aug.	6.28	10.75	8.05
Sept.	6.86	9.07	8.05
Oct.	7.02	6.97	8.05
Nov.	7.07	6.38	8.05
Dec.	7.55	6.49	6.90

ZINC

Zinc is quoted as spelter, standard Western brands, New York delivery, in cents per pound. On May 25, 1918, the Government fixed prices until September for grade A spelter at 12c. per lb. for itself and the open market. This is to be continued until January 1, 1919, the price at point of delivery to be at East St. Louis plus freight. Lower grades can make their own prices as usual. Sheet-zinc is fixed at 15c., and plate at 14c. per pound.

Date		
Dec.	25 Holiday	
"	26	8.30
"	27	8.20
"	28	8.10
"	29 Sunday	
"	30	8.05
"	31	8.00

Average week ending		
Nov.	19	8.62
"	26	8.61
Dec.	3	8.67
"	10	8.61
"	17	8.58
"	24	8.45
"	31	8.13

Monthly averages

	1916	1917	1918
Jan.	18.21	9.75	7.87
Feb.	19.09	10.45	7.97
Mch.	18.40	10.78	7.67
Apr.	18.62	10.20	7.04
May	16.01	9.41	7.29
June	12.85	9.63	7.92
July	9.90	8.98	8.72
Aug.	9.03	8.58	8.87
Sept.	9.18	8.33	9.58
Oct.	9.92	8.32	9.11
Nov.	11.81	7.76	8.75
Dec.	11.26	7.84	8.49

QUICKSILVER

The primary market for quicksilver is San Francisco, California being the largest producer. The price is fixed in the open market, according to quantity. The Government was taking 40% of the United States quicksilver output, paying therefor $105 per flask, and will continue to pay this until contracts are completed. Outside of this business the competitive market can make any price as usual. Prices, in dollars per flask of 75 pounds.

Date		
Dec.	3	120.00
"	10	120.00
Dec.	17	110.00
"	24	110.00
"	31	110.00

Monthly averages

	1916	1917	1918
Jan.	222.00	81.00	128.06
Feb.	295.00	126.25	118.00
Mch.	219.00	113.75	112.00
Apr.	141.60	114.50	115.00
May	90.00	104.00	110.00
June	74.70	85.50	112.00
July	81.20	102.00	120.00
Aug.	74.50	115.00	120.00
Sept.	75.00	112.00	120.00
Oct.	78.20	102.00	120.00
Nov.	79.50	102.50	120.00
Dec.	80.00	117.42	115.00

TIN

Prices in New York, in cents per pound. The monthly averages in 1918 are nominal. Under the international agreement, the United States is to get 66% of the world's supply of tin; but this control ends on January 1, 1919. On December 3 the War Industries Board fixed the price to consumers and jobbers at 72½c. f.o.b. Chicago and Eastern points, and 71¼c. on the Pacific Coast.

Monthly averages

	1916	1917	1918
Jan.	41.76	44.10	85.13
Feb.	42.60	51.47	85.00
Mch.	50.50	54.27	85.00
Apr.	51.49	55.63	88.53
May	49.10	63.21	100.91
June	42.07	61.93	91.00
July	38.37	62.60	93.00
Aug.	38.88	62.53	91.33
Sept.	36.66	61.54	80.40
Oct.	41.10	62.24	78.82
Nov.	44.12	74.18	73.67
Dec.	42.55	85.00	72.50

ORES (New York)

Manganese: It is reported that as low as 80c. per unit has been offered for high-grade ore, but no transactions are recorded. There have been no developments in manganese alloys. The domestic output of ferro in November was 36,300 tons, the largest ever recorded.

Molybdenum: The market is nominal at 75c. to $1 per lb., with small sales reported at 85 cents.

Tungsten: No developments are recorded in the ore situation, nor are any sales heard of as representative of the ideas of buyers and sellers. This is also true of ferro-tungsten.

All British metal regulations have been revoked, according to a Consular cable from London on December 18. The Ministry of Munitions announces the following stocks of imported metals (exclusive of old metal and scrap) in Great Britain and in possession of Ministry of Munitions on December 1: copper, 27,530; spelter (g.o.b.), 18,768; spelter, refined, 6544; aluminum, 10,215; soft pig lead, 49,111; nickel, 1735; antimony regulus, 3303 tons. Official orders controlling dealings in chrome ore, tin, copper, brass, cupro-nickel, scrap spelter, and lead are revoked.

Eastern Metal Market

New York, December 24.

Actual buying of any of the metals is negligible. Open markets are assured for nearly every metal by January 1 or before.

The copper market is to be an open one after January 1. Re-sale metal is reported offered already under the official price.

Conditions in the tin market are unchanged.

The lead market has been officially released from control and prices have fallen.

The zinc market is dead with the tendency of prices downward.

The antimony market is unchanged.

The official announcement of the formation of a new export company was made in the last week. It is to be known as the North American Steel Products Corporation, and at its head will be E. A. S. Clarke, now president of the Lackawanna Steel Co. The new company will have its headquarters in New York and will commence business on January 2, 1919. It will have representatives in all parts of the world. A new form of contract has been agreed upon by the contract committee of the American Iron and Steel Institute, which is intended to prevent both over-selling and over-buying, to bind both buyer and seller, and to be strong enough to resist all attempts at cancellation. There is very little buying at the lower level of prices and the market will probably remain dull until some time in January.

COPPER

As expected for some little time, copper will be a free and open market after January 1. This was officially announced after a meeting at Washington last Friday between the copper producers and the War Industries Board. It was a foregone conclusion in the light of the events in steel. The official price continues to exist and will obtain until January 1 at 26c. per lb. for both Lake and electrolytic. No business is reported; demand is absolutely flat. Reports of re-sale offerings are heard, but no confirmation of any sales are obtainable. Some of these are said to have been offered as low as 22 to 23c. per lb. It is also stated that some interests using copper in their products are making sales for future delivery based on a price of copper of 23.50c. In the absence of any business we quote the market as nominal at 26c. Casting copper is still quoted as low as 21c. por lb. An interesting development is the official announcement of the formation of an export company to control and handle export sales of copper. What is to be known as the Copper Export Association has been incorporated and in its make-up are all the principal copper producers. It is expected that this new organization will handle 50% of the output of the companies interested. The undertaking is regarded as decidedly important and as likely to act as a stabilizing influence on the domestic market. [Extended reference to this Association appears on page 23 of this issue.] There seems to be no line on the future price of copper and the outcome is eagerly and in some cases anxiously awaited.

TIN

Developments in the tin situation have been few in the past week. Fundamental conditions are much as they were a week ago. The market is extremely dull. It appears that consumers are sending in very few orders to the United States Steel Products Co. for the tin that it has been allocated by the International Tin Executive to distribute at cost. Present prospects seem to point to a control of the market of indefinite duration, especially if Bolivian concentrates are allowed to continue to be imported without restriction. This importation enables American smelters to operate at a good profit and still sell under the U. S. Steel Products Co.'s fixed price of 72.50c. per lb., New York and Chicago, thus introducing competition in the domestic market and prolonging the time in which the allocated material may be disposed, and hence the period of control. In this connection it is now estimated that the output of American smelters has reached about 1500 tons per month, or nearly one-third the annual consumption. An interesting suggestion has been made which might settle the complicated tin question and give general satisfaction. As it is now consumers know that in a free market tin could be bought for future shipment as low as 56 to 58c. per lb. They argue why should they be obliged to continue to pay high prices because what some regard as a mistake was made in instituting the present arrangement. The suggestion is that the Government stand whatever loss there may be involved in the allocated tin by throwing the market in the open in every respect, the same as in wool or other materials. This may happen yet. The London and world markets are free again. Arrivals thus far this month have been 1600 tons at Pacific with 80 tons at Atlantic ports.

LEAD

Quite unexpectedly the lead market is the first one to be thrown entirely open. After a meeting Saturday, December 21, the Lead Producers' Committee announced that from that date it would cease to act as the exclusive selling agent and that producers are at liberty to quote individually and that there would be no restrictions as to re-sale metal. This comes as a surprise, but is a pleasant one. One dealer expressed the opinion that the lead market would find itself and return to normal conditions sooner than any and this probably within two weeks, due largely to the fact that the war situation has been handled with practically no blundering.' On Monday came another surprise: The American Smelting & Refining Co. announced a reduction in the price of lead to 6.50c., New York, which compares with the former official price of 7.05c., New York, or the re-sale price of 6.75c., New York. This again is another step in the return to normal conditions, as it inaugurates the old two-market situation—the Trust price and the outside market price. Buyers are few and far between. We quote the market at 6.50c., New York, or 6.20c., St. Louis.

ZINC

The zinc market continues extremely dull with demand lighter than in many weeks; some say it is the dullest period in many months. One cause is the large buying that immediately followed the armistice. Then came the prospect of lower prices for steel, which unsettled the prospects of the galvanized market, resulting in a complete holding off in this department of the business. Of course, brass-makers have been out of the market for some time. December and prime Western are generally conceded to be scarce, but January and first-quarter zinc is easier to obtain, particularly from the smaller producers. Either the larger producors are well sold up or they are trying to support the market, as they are not free offerers of this delivery at any concession. The market for early or 30-day delivery seems quotable at about 8.05c., St. Louis, or 8.40c., New York, with first quarter at about 7.80 to 7.90c., St. Louis, or 8.15 to 8.25c., New York.

ANTIMONY

The market is unchanged from last week, with wholesale lots for early delivery held at 8 to 8.25c., New York, duty paid.

Book Reviews

Quicksilver Resources of California. With a section on 'Metallurgy and Ore-Dressing'. By Walter W. Bradley. Pp. 389, ill., plans, charts, maps, index. Bulletin No. 78 of California State Mining Bureau, Ferry building, San Francisco, from where copies are obtainable.

New publications on quicksilver have been few and far between, likewise articles in the technical press. Between Becker's 'Geology of the Quicksilver Deposits of the Pacific Slope', Monograph XIII of the U. S. Geological Survey in 1888, and Forstner's 'Quicksilver Resources of California', Bulletin 27 of the State Mining Bureau in 1903, there was a lapse of 15 years; while between the latter and Bradley's 'Quicksilver Resources of California', Bulletin 78 in 1918, there is another period of 15 years. A perusal of the excellent 9-page bibliography in the new book shows that, while in the aggregate a good deal has been written on mercury during the present century, the matter of real merit is inconsiderable. In fact, it would seem that it is only within the last four years that there have been discussions of practical value to the quicksilver industry. Until recently there has been little advance in the metallurgy of the metal for 40 years. Bulletin 78 must not be considered another edition of No. 27; it is something quite new, save for certain excerpts from Forstner. The author has had it in preparation for about three years, during which time he made many field and original laboratory investigations. Quicksilver men knew that the work was in preparation, and now they have available a volume that brings the subject down to the latest improvement, more especially metallurgy.

As California yields approximately 70% of the United States output of quicksilver (1917 figures), this work is particularly opportune for local interests. This State has produced 2,137,728 flasks since 1850, valued at over $101,000,000. A production and price-chart shows that the two highly-productive periods—1861-1869 and 1875-1883—were accompanied by low prices, though each was immediately preceded by a sudden increase in price. The increased output at present is responding, in a measure, to the stimulus of the higher prices of the past three years, yet not fully. A graph of prices during the war period is instructive, the speculation during early 1916 being most prominent; also the subsequent drop. Government action in 1918 practically stabilized the price. Chapter II briefly discusses the general geology of the Californian deposits and theories of ore deposition. The cinnabar is found at or near the contact of sandstone or serpentine in the Coastal Ranges. Prefacing the notes on mercury minerals, there being 20 species of which only three are of commercial importance, are three natural-color reproductions of cinnabar. In chapter IV we find 175 pages covering Californian quicksilver districts, mines, and works, scattered through 39 counties. Inserted are 18 geologic maps (some colored) and plans of underground openings of the principal mines; also 40 illustrations depicting various operations. Being on coated paper these are well reproduced, as are all the 77 photos in the book. The new matter pertaining to producing properties is of considerable interest.

The most valuable part of this text-book is the metallurgical section of 147 pages, with 37 photos and 20 drawings. It is all new, including Mr. Bradley's own experiments on concentration, those of the U. S. Bureau of Mines on losses, and those of the staffs of certain mines. This will remain a standard of reference for many years. There is little literature on this phase of the industry. Quicksilver metallurgy is simple. Producers have been satisfied with the recovery, and up to 1916 little sampling and assaying had been done to determine the percentage obtained. No systematic investigation in concentration was done until 1913. For calcining ore, the D-retort is useful only for high-grade ore and concentrate. The Scott furnace was designed in 1875, and may be styled the standard in California. It has its advantages and defective points. The cost of operating the Scott furnace is from 50 to 75c. per ton, plus 25 to 50c. for other charges. The recovery from one ore, assaying from 0.26 to 0.36% mercury, was 91.3%, at another, under careful supervision, treating 0.66% ore, it was 86.6%; but Mr. Bradley has publicly (meeting of A. I. M. E.) stated that it was doubtful whether over 75% has been recovered by average furnace practice in California. There follow descriptions, operations, costs, and pictures of the Johnson-McKay pipe-retorts, Livingston furnaces, Lander's continuous-feed retort, Exell, Knox-Osborne, Neate, and Hüttner-Scott furnaces; also the latest adaptation—the

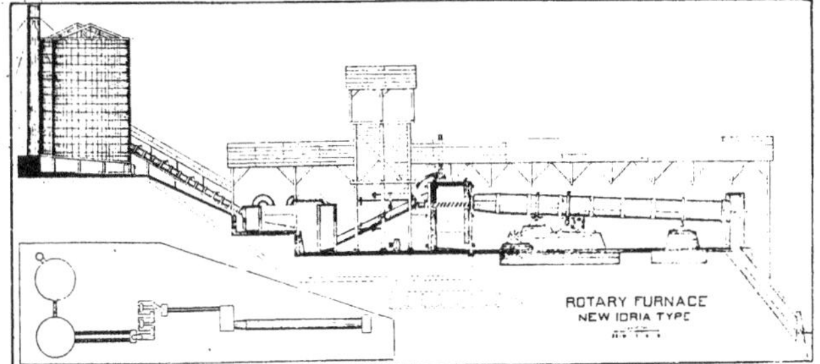

The furnace is fed by screw-feeder from the ore-bin. The fuel is oil, and the air is heated by passing over the hot ore-tailing. The mercurial fume then passes through dust chambers, tile headers, brick condensers, junction-boxes, cast-iron condensers, tile headers, and tank-type condensers of wood. The fan shown above the dust chambers is for blowing cold air into the condensing system. (Plan from State Mining Bureau Bulletin 78.)

rotary-kiln furnace, as at the New Idria mine. In multiple-hearth furnaces, such as the Herreshoff, dust is a nuisance, but with the Cottrell precipitator this is avoided. At Almaden one of these furnaces is now at work. Condensers have been constructed of brick, but wood is preferable, as it does not absorb mercury. Condensing methods have been erratic in the past. The vertical circular wooden tank seems to be the best condenser. It is necessary that the fume be cooled as soon as possible after leaving the furnace. The introduction of cooled air is advantageous.

There seem to be great possibilities for the revolving type of calcining-furnace. These cost $250 per ton of capacity against $1000 for the Scott type, the consumption of fuel is one-third to one-half that of the Scott, labor is one-fifth to one-fourth, and the furnace is automatic. It is more flexible than the Scott, the ore passes through in 15 to 30 minutes, and there is no mercury left in the ore-tailing. There are no absorption losses in the furnaces, as all the brick is hot. There is no personal element attached to the rotary, as the discharge is automatic, whereas in the Scott this is irregular. The furnace now working at New Idria is 4 by 50 ft.; it makes from 1½ to 4 r.p.m., and treats up to 96 tons of 1½-in. ore daily. No salivation of the workmen is possible on account of the joints at each end of the furnace. Four others, 5 by 56 ft., have been erected. A sectional view of the plant accompanies this review.

The assay of cinnabar is either by distillation or solution. Nine pages are devoted to the various methods, particularly the Whitton apparatus. New Idria uses a combination of distillation and solution.

In the concluding 68 pages, those who have conducted tests in the milling of cinnabar, will find a fund of real practical value. Tests made at the University of California showed that in wet concentration of cinnabar the feed must be classified before passing to tables. 'Paint' cinnabar cannot be collected by tables, but the native metal can. By flotation, paint and slime ore can be collected. The flotation results are highly interesting. The specific gravity of cinnabar is 8, yet quicksilver miners considered concentration impracticable. Concentrate must be roasted, but if the mercury content is too high, that is, as much as 40%, this product packs in the furnace. A wet plant would cost half as much as a furnace plant. Brief notes are given on ore-dressing at a number of mines. Summarizing his metallurgical investigations, Mr. Bradley considers that furnace treatment will continue to be the method used for recovering mercury from ore. Concentration may serve as an adjunct to some existing plants, to increase their capacity; while at others concentration or the sodium sulphide method can be economically adopted, depending on the nature of the ore and gangue.

It would have been well if a little more care had been given to the editing of the text. The adoption of the number sign for No., the use of dashes for the minus sign, the irregular employment of the prefix Mr. before the names of those cited, and erratic spelling (such as sulphide and sulfide) might have been avoided.

It might be added that this useful Bulletin is not free, but the charge is a nominal one, simply to cover the cost of publication. The State Mining Bureau will advise further as to the price.

M. W. vB.

Metallurgy of Lead. By H. O. Hofman. Pp. 664, ill., plans, index. McGraw-Hill Book Co., New York, 1918. For sale by Mining and Scientific Press. Price, $6.

By the use of thinner paper, the author of this new edition has been able to add 105 pages of new matter, and yet the publishers made a book of 664 pages a half-inch thinner than the previous one of 559 pages. In addition to this, the margins are narrower, so that in all the present work is fully 25% larger than the last one, which was mostly re-written. The author is a well-known authority on lead; since 1892 he has reviewed annually in 'The Mineral Industry' the progress made in the metallurgy of this metal; and he visits the principal reduction works in North America from time to time. Comparing the new chapters with the previous edition, we find that the historical and statistical introduction is much better. The 'Properties of Lead' has been condensed by giving the compounds separate treatment, yet enhanced in value by half-tones of several forms of the metal. The chapters, 'Lead of Commerce' and 'Industrial Alloys' are new. Discussion of 'Lead Ores' includes their occurrence, distribution, and purchase; in the previous volume these were in separate chapters, rather the better arrangement. The former 38 pages on sampling are omitted. The advent of blast-roasting of lead-sulphide ores has resulted in the smelting of these in reverberatories becoming obsolete, yet the treatment of the intermediary products of a refinery in these furnaces has grown in importance, therefore the chapter covering the subject is retained. Recent plans and actual results from certain plants make the chapter on smelting in the ore-hearth much more valuable. Chapter IX, 'Smelting Lead Ores in the Blast-Furnace', occupies half of the book—330 pages—and is a considerable expansion on the former section on this subject. The reactions in roasting sulphides are given, followed by descriptions of furnaces, details of blast-roasting (Huntington-Heberlein, Carmichael-Bradford, Savelsberg, and Dwight-Lloyd, the last in detail at the new Bunker Hill & Sullivan smelter in Idaho), plans of modern blast-furnaces and accessories, ore-bins, fuels, calculation of charges, flue-dust and flues, etc. The remainder of the book is occupied by the desilverization of lead bullion, giving the processes in vogue and their products. A short chapter on lead poisoning, an important subject, completes a complete work on lead. A feature of the new edition is the large number of references.

Structural Service Book. Pp. 138, index. The Journal of the American Institute of Architects, Washington, D. C. For sale by 'Mining and Scientific Press', San Francisco. Price, $3.50.

The fact that no book resembling this one except in a general way has ever been published makes it difficult to write an adequate review. In substance the book is a revised reprint of 12 articles that appeared in the Journal of the American Institute of Architects during 1917. Each article deals with a particular aspect of building construction, the titles being as follows: Research and general standardization, foundational requirements, damp-proofing, cement and concrete, iron and steel; lime, sand and gravel, stone masonry, stone, and slate; clay products and fire-resistive construction; fire-prevention and protection; timber, lumber, and wood construction; electricity; gas; construction by the Government; plumbing and public health; metal, plastic, and other products; paints and painting, glass and glazing. Each number comprises a sort of combined index and bibliography concerning the subjects discussed. This in turn is indexed and cross-referenced by a unique system, which might be described as a cross between the Dewey decimal system and a set of football signals. A general index of subjects, alphabetically arranged, gives references that, just as a handbook is a summary of data on various allied subjects, so this book is a summary of the sources of data on the subjects listed. There is a good deal of repetition, and the book is generally in need of re-arrangement. Nevertheless, it will be of considerable value to anyone engaged either in the design or the construction of buildings, provided that he also has access to a good reference library.

INDUSTRIAL PROGRESS

INFORMATION FURNISHED BY MANUFACTURERS

POWER AND PUMPING EQUIPMENT FOR THE YAKIMA PROJECT, WASHINGTON

The plant for the Grandview irrigation district, Sunnyside unit, is at the head of the Mabton feeder canal, two miles from the town of Grandview, on the Sunnyside main canal. It contains one direct-connected turbine-driven pumping unit, and two motor-driven units. All three units receive water from the Sunnyside canal.

The net power-head under which the turbine operates is 21 ft., while the working-head against which the pump operates is 78 ft. The water is discharged through 6000 ft. of 40-in. inside diameter wood-stave pipe, the maximum velocity in the pipe being 3 ft. per second. The horizontal centre-line of the turbine unit is placed 7 ft. above tail-water and 4 ft. below the floor of the pump-house. The turbine is installed in a closed concrete scroll and discharges through a concrete elbow-shaped draft-tube. The turbine consists of a vertical shaft 30-in. type 'O' Smith wicket-gate unit, which under 21-ft. head develops 214 b-hp. at 225 r.p.m. The maximum discharge of the turbine is 110 cu. ft. per second, but at a point of best efficiency it discharges 95 cu. ft. The design of the turbine is such as to give unusually high efficiency over the complete range of gate from half to full opening.

Most of the submerged wearing parts of the turbine and pumps are protected from the action of sharp silt that comes with the water at certain seasons. This design includes the use of a cast-iron speed-ring or guide-ring, imbedded in the concrete scroll. This ring has stationary guide vanes that direct the water in toward the turbine-runner. Inside this speed-ring are placed the top and bottom plates between which are the wicket-gates of the turbine. These top and bottom plates are provided with removable steel wearing-plates, which can be easily renewed. The wicket-gates are of cast steel, and the gate stems or spindles are cast integral with the wickets, and the gate spindles move in bronze-bushed bearings in the top and bottom plates. The gate stems on the upper end extend through stuffing-boxes in the top plate, and all the gate mechanism is on the top plate, where it is in plain view of the operator for inspection and lubrication. This design leaves practically no movable part of the turbine in the water except the cast-steel wickets, and the turbine runner. There is no step bearing in connection with the turbine unit, as it is of the suspended type, and the weight of the rotating element including the turbine runner, the turbine shaft, and the downward thrust of the turbine, as well as the rotating parts of the pump are supported by means of an oil-bath thrust-bearing placed on top of the pump unit, the turbine and pump being so designed as to support this bearing and the load that it carries. The gate operating mechanism of the turbine consists of hand-wheel and worm-gear so arranged that the turbine gates can only be moved very slowly, thus giving fine adjustment and avoiding water-hammer due to the long discharge-line.

The pump is of the vertical shaft four-stage type, with 20-in. diameter intake and discharge openings. It has a capacity of 7500 g.p.m. against 78 ft. total head, and requires 212 hp. maximum. The general design and construction of the four-stage pump consists of four individual cases substantially bolted together, and extends 16 ft. above the floor. The intake connection is made at the bottom, and the discharge at the top of the pump. The three initial or lower stages contain suitable guide-vanes, which guide the water in a continuous stream through the pump. These guide-vanes form a part of the pump casting. The upper

HYDRAULIC TURBINE AND PUMP SET

stage or discharge-case of the pump is of spiral or volute form, increasing to 20-in. diameter where it connects to the discharge-line, an outside screw rising-stem 20-in. gate-valve being fitted between the discharge-flange of the pump and the pipe-line.

The hydraulic turbine and accessories, together with designs of the concrete scroll and concrete draft-tube, were supplied to the Government by the S. Morgan Smith Co., of York, Pennsylvania, while the pump unit was made by the Byron Jackson Iron Works, Inc., San Francisco, California. The accompanying illustration shows the combined unit.

A similar combined unit is now in course of construction by the two companies mentioned for installation at the Price Stub pumping-plant of the Grand Valley project of the U. S. Reclamation Service in Colorado. Here the net head on the turbine is 17 ft., and the water is supplied to the turbine through a 60-in. diameter penstock 150 ft. long.

HOW RADIUM-BEARING ORE IS MINED

By Wallace T. Roberts

*Of the world's radium supply, 95% is mined in Colorado. In Montrose county, in south-western Colorado, extending through the Paradox valley over into Utah, are large deposits of carnotite, encircling the base of the La Sal mountains.

About six companies have holdings in the Colorado and Utah fields, but all of these are not operating. The largest is the Standard Chemical Co., with general offices at Pittsburgh and head offices at Coke Ovens in Montrose county, about four miles from the town of Naturita, which in turn is about 40 miles from Placerville, the nearest railroad point. The company's property extends over some 400 square miles of rather desolate country characteristic of this part of the State. The Radium Company of Colorado, Inc., is another operating company.

The Standard Chemical Co. employs two methods of prospecting, both by means of drills. The first of these employs the diamond core-drill. A series of holes is first planned, covering a given acreage, at intervals of 25 ft. If one of the holes indicates the presence of ore, a secondary series is then drilled around it, sometimes only a few feet apart. With the diamond-drill holes 40 to 50 ft. in depth are commonly put in, this being as stated, the limit of occurrence of this ore below the surface.

SULLIVAN BRAVO DRILL, BELTED FROM GASOLINE ENGINE. THE OVERHEAD FRAME SUPPORTS A CANVAS WEATHER COVER.

The rig most used, of which a number have been in the district for several years past, is the Sullivan 'Bravo' machine, operated by a belt from a gasoline engine. The drill, engine, and pump for forcing water down the rods are mounted on heavy timbers with low wheels, so that moving from hole to hole is an easy matter. The great number of prospects and their shallowness makes this a handy arrangement. In this formation the rate of progress is perhaps 30 ft. per shift. The cost is low because of this high speed and because the wear of diamonds is slight. At first borts were used in the bits, but later black diamonds or carbon are employed, such as are used in all hard mineral formations in these drills. While the initial cost is more, the cost per foot of drilling is much less. Substitutes for the diamond-drill have been tried, but the combination described above has proved most economical. The drills are operated by a crew of two men with a general foreman in charge of several machines.

Another method of prospecting, still more widely used, employs Sullivan air-tube rotater hammer-drills, weighing 39 lb. each and operated by one man. These machines are used for the shallower holes, seldom exceeding 30 ft. in depth. They employ hollow drill-steel in two-foot changes. A jet of live air, carried down the steel to the bits, acts to blow the cuttings to the surface in spite of such obstacles as clay seams, which are frequently encountered. The powerful rotation of the drill is a factor in enabling it to work successfully to such a depth. Light steel tripods are used to lift the longer lengths of steel. At intervals, or if trouble with dust arises, the steel is withdrawn and a blowpipe used to clean the hole.

BURROS CARRYING WATER FOR DIAMOND-DRILLS.

These Sullivan hammer-drills are operated by gasoline engine driven air-compressors of the Sullivan WG-3 type, one of which is shown in the accompanying picture.

The carnotite mines in a technical sense are seldom 'mines' of much size or elaborateness, owing to the limited extent of the ore deposits. When a body has been sufficiently mapped out and when production is desired from it, a slope is driven and the mining is accomplished with the air-tube rotators described above. Mining is done in the ore under the sandstone strata, on a specialized room and pillar system. The slope is so driven that the tracks are lower than the mining floor. The ore is carried from the face in wheel-barrows and dumped from these into the cars. These cars are of small capacity, and are hauled up the slope by a windless or a small air-hoist. They are then dumped onto a canvas or platform where the ore is sorted by hand. Little of the carnotite ore runs above 5% in grade. The value consists of uranium oxide (U_3O_8), varying in grade from ½ to 7%. Ore that must be milled is sent to a concentrator 12 miles from the offices at Coke Ovens, and from 4 to 25 miles from the various camps. Shipping-ore, including that above 2½%, is sent to the company's works in Pennsylvania. All ore is placed in sacks, weighing 100 lb. each, as it is sorted, owing to its great value. John I. Mullen is in charge of the Standard Chemical Co.'s property, and has overcome many difficulties.

GASOLINE-ENGINE DRIVEN COMPRESSOR-PLANT

*Abstract from 'Mine and Quarry'.

EDITORIAL

THEODORE ROOSEVELT is dead! The loss of so vital a personality will be a shock to men in every part of the world. The news comes as we go to press; we hope next week to pay proper tribute to his life and character. So passes a great American.

IN 1918 the United States produced nearly two billion dollars worth of metallic products, the total value of mineral products being estimated at $5,160,000,000, or about $50,000,000 more than in 1917. These figures bear eloquent testimony to the importance of our mining industry.

VARIOUS suggestions have been made for the disposal of the German submarines, now interned at Harwich and other British ports. It seems to us that a good use to make of them would be to scrap them and make structural steel for the rebuilding of the bridges and railways that the Germans destroyed in Belgium.

BONDS to the amount of $25,000,000 at 6% and for a term of 10 years are being issued by the Anaconda Copper Mining Company in order to furnish working capital for the development of its South American properties, more particularly the Andes and Portrerillos mines. This is a notable example of the foreign expansion of American mining activities.

HOPE of better days in Mexico is revived by the recent meeting of representative men at El Paso and the organization of the Union de Los Mexicanos to promote peace and the repatriation of political exiles. It is announced that delegates are to be sent to Paris in order to plead the cause of Mexico at the Peace Congress and to bespeak the assistance of the nations in restoring order in the distracted country south of the Rio Grande. While the United States is aiding in the rehabilitation of distressful Europe it will be proper to invite European co-operation in quieting Mexico.

GOLD production in the United States last year decreased to 3,313,000 ounces, worth $68,493,000, as against $83,750,700 in 1917 and $101,035,700 in 1915. The output in 1918 was the lowest in 20 years. California continues to be the leading gold-producing State, the preliminary official estimate showing 932,389 ounces, valued at $17,207,000, as against $20,929,400 in 1917. Colorado is again second with an output of $12,853,000, as against $15,974,500 in 1917. The silver production of this country in 1918 amounted to 67,879,000 fine ounces, the smallest output since 1913 and 3,861,000 ounces below that of 1917. Montana is the leading producer of silver, yielding 15,341,000 ounces, and Utah is second, with 13,439,000 ounces, the latter scoring a slight gain on 1917. Even the enhanced price of silver, which stood at the Government quotation of $1 during the year, failed to stimulate production to a higher level, owing to the excessive costs of mining.

IMPATIENCE is being expressed in the press on both sides of the Atlantic at the delay in the meeting of the Peace Conference. Preliminary conversations are useful and necessary, of course, and they seem to have taken place with fairly satisfactory results, so far as one can learn, but the world is becoming eager to have its affairs settled before anarchy takes a firm grip. Political and industrial conditions in Central Europe continue in a state of flux and it is about time for concerted action to crush bolshevism, otherwise any effort to call Germany and Austria to account will be frustrated and the completion of a settlement postponed indefinitely. Every week of delay accentuates the disorder in the conquered territories and increases the sufferings of the civilian population, while hindering the conquering nations in the immense task of restoration and rehabilitation in the regions devastated by warfare. Moreover, both in this country and in England there is a growing demand for the demobilization of the armies and the return of our young men to the works of peace.

LABOR adjustments menace many industries, simply because any attempt at adjustment in accordance with the declining market-price of the products resulting from the use of labor threatens to provoke strikes. This, of course, is a serious defect in our economic system. We note that the General Petroleum Corporation, under the leadership of its president, Capt. John Barneson, has announced to its employees that "there will be no reduction by the Company in the present scale of wages for a period of at least two years from this date," also that "all employees who left to join the colors will be re-employed upon their return if they so desire," and that "present employees who have taken the places of those who left to join the colors, and who perform their duties to the satisfaction of their department heads, will be continued in the Company's service." This seems to us to be an eminently sagacious policy and quite in accord with the reputation that Capt. Barneson enjoys in this community. Presumably the market for the Petroleum Corporation's products will be good for the next two or three years, presumably also the corporation's employees will render better service if they know that the current rate of wages is established for a long period, and, lastly, they and their friends will appreciate the display of proper consideration for those that have served their country at the front. We commend this as an example to those that can afford to imitate it.

TO the older men in the profession the passing of Fraser & Chalmers is a notable event. This pioneer firm used to be easily first in the manufacture of mining machinery, and Mr. William J. Chalmers, still, we are glad to say, alive and well, was a personality of the first rank in the world of Western mining fully thirty years ago. When the firm was absorbed by the Allis-Chalmers Company, in 1904, it was still perpetuated by the English subsidiary company, which meanwhile had gained in importance, largely through the business done by its branch-office at Johannesburg. As Mr. Chalmers was identified with the American firm, so Mr. Walter McDermott was the personification of the British business. A public-spirited man of rare sagacity and good sense, he occupied a position second to none in the mining community of London and when he resigned as managing director not long ago, the event marked the changes that had supervened in the machinery business. The manufacturing plant at Erith, on the Thames, has been sold to the General Electric Company and negotiations are pending for the sale of the assets of the remaining branches in Canada, Australia, and the Malay States. This is likely to be followed by the liquidation of the company.

LAST week we quoted the latest casualty estimates, as published at Berlin and at Petrograd. We had hardly gone to press when new figures appeared in dispatches from Europe. The 'Cologne Gazette' stated that up to October 25 the German casualties were 6,066,769 and the dead about 2,000,000. The loss in officers alone namely, 140,760, of whom 44,700 were killed—exceeded the total casualties of Germany in the war of 1870. Our disbelief in the low figure of 659,000 Germans killed is amply confirmed. The latest Russian estimate gives 9,150,000 casualties, including 1,700,000 dead, 1,450,000 permanently crippled, 3,500,000 wounded, and 2,500,000 taken prisoner. These figures are merely approximations, but they appear nearer the truth than the 3,000,000 given as 'dead' in the earlier report. The French are stated, in the Chamber of Deputies, to have lost 1,400,000 killed in the War. This appears probable; it may be compared with the British loss of 1,000,000 dead, not the 658,704 "killed in action", which did not include those reported missing who actually lost their lives, nor those that died at the front from disease. There is a wide difference between the various phrases used to express casualties. A later estimate gives 1,071,300 as the French killed in action, besides 760,300 deceased, prisoners, and missing, so that the total casualties, including the wounded, must be fully 3,500,000. The Italians claim 500,000 killed or died of wounds, out of a total of 2,000,000 casualties. The later total of 2,800,000 includes those taken prisoner. The Austro-Hungarian armies are reported to have suffered 4,000,000 casualties, of whom 800,000 were killed. This looks correct. The various countries have different methods of compiling these mortuary statistics, so that comparisons are difficult. In any event the loss of life tabulated by them does not begin to include all those that died on account of injury in battle and in the trenches, because many soldiers that have been invalided home have succumbed subsequently either to the direct consequences of their wounds or to the indirect results of an enfeebled vitality when attacked by minor diseases. The horror of war is not all on the battlefield nor even at the base hospital. The Central Empires appear to have lost about 3,000,000 in dead and 10,000,000 in total casualties, as against 4,500,000 dead and nearly 20,000,000 casualties of all kinds on the side of the four Allied powers, not including the United States, Belgium, Serbia, Rumania, and Greece. Apparently the Germans killed and wounded many more than their proportion, owing to the fact that they started the War so much better equipped in death-dealing weapons, although it is more than likely that their casualties are under-stated in order to placate domestic sentiment, now aroused to the criminal folly of their military enterprise. In any event, their responsibility for the great calamity is appalling. Germany and Austria face a terrible indictment at the bar of human justice.

Rossiter Worthington Raymond

On the last day of 1918 there died, at Brooklyn, New York, the most notable figure in the history of mining in America. Others may have directed bigger mining and metallurgical operations, others may have achieved a greater share of the success that is measured by money, others may have invented or designed a larger number of the methods or processes used in the winning of metals, but no man exerted so great an influence for so long a period of time as Rossiter Worthington Raymond—'the Doctor', as he was familiarly and affectionately known to the profession. In the adult portion of his 78 years of life he saw the development of the American mining industry from a mere beginning to a majestic maturity; and in that development he played a notable part by the help and stimulus that he gave to two generations of men. He was the comrade of Clarence King, J. D. Whitney,

James D. Hague, S. F. Emmons, and that earlier generation of scientific men to whom we owe the application of geology to mining and the systematic exploration of the continental area that was thrown open to the prospector as soon as the railroad joined the East with the West. He was the guide, philosopher, and friend of the generation that followed, of many of the young men now directing the big enterprises of this country. He influenced the men that now influence others. When he was born, in 1840, the mining industry of the United States had made a feeble start; when he went to Freiberg in 1860 there was no mining school in this country; when he served in the Union army the discoveries of gold in California and of silver in Nevada had laid the foundation for the mineral development of the West; and when he was Commissioner of Mining Statistics, from 1868 to 1876, he gave a lead to the application of science to the art of mining in America. Long the dean of the mining profession, he has been its spokesman from a time as early as most of us can remember. In him a profession usually inarticulate found an eloquent exponent; through him the public learned to appreciate the breadth of culture that is required by an accomplished engineer. From his father, the editor of the New York 'Times', he inherited his ability as a writer and an expositor, an ability that he developed to an effectiveness unmatched in our profession, not only as a public speaker, but in the more systematic duties of lecturer on economic geology and of editor of two mining journals, notably the 'Engineering and Mining Journal', on which he collaborated for many years with Richard P. Rothwell. His abilities, however, were put to their maximum usefulness when he became Secretary to the American Institute of Mining Engineers in 1884. As editor, as organizer, as permanent executive, he managed the affairs of the Institute until his retirement in 1910, and so successfully that it became a national institution of the first rank. He brought his vivid personality so actively into play, he marked the Institute so strongly with his own identity, that for 25 years it might with truth and credit have been known as the Raymond Institute. This condition had the defect of its qualities and eventually called forth the need for reorganization, to which he objected so strenuously that the last decade of his life was clouded by a controversy in the course of which he became estranged from several of his best friends. But that disagreement is now placed in its true perspective and is remembered only as the manifestation of an exuberant egoism not uncommon in great men. He was a great man, an inspiring figure of a man. We like to think of him at the meetings of the Institute; how he would rise and look about him, then speak clearly, incisively, and humorously, making the rest of us seem a blundering lot of incompetents. He was the mainspring of those meetings; he saved the dullest from being a failure; he was ready for any exigency. This is not the occasion for touching upon the many other facets of his character: his legal career, for he was admitted to the bar; his church work, for he was superintendent of the sunday-school, teacher of a bible-class, and preacher at Plymouth Church; of his skill in many ways, from playing chess to writing stories—he was amazingly versatile; these aspects of his many-sided personality demand more considered treatment than is permissible here. He had the gift of leadership, winning the devotion of old and young, of men and women alike; he was kind to those in distress and generous to those needing help, whether mentally or financially; he was religious in a glad and unaffected way; he was a maker of fun and of happy hours; he was an inspiring companion and a beloved comrade. It is likely that many of his friends will desire to pay a tribute to his memory; we invite them to do so in our pages, which could be put to no more interesting or stimulating purpose. For ourselves we tender to his memory the homage of a fellow journalist, the respect of a fellow engineer, and the affectionate remembrance of a friend.

Potash

In our issue of December 7 we published a comprehensive article on potash by Mr. F. W. Brown, and in our last issue we printed a letter on the same subject by Mr. Herbert Lang, who knows how to write interestingly on many phases of mining and metallurgical activity. He finds fault with the attitude of the Government toward the potash industry and lays emphasis on the fact that our domestic production represents a small fraction of the consumption, which is growing rapidly and continually. Even the stimulus given by war prices and war industry failed to bring forth anything like the quantity required. Since the cessation of hostilities the quotations for potash have dropped to $4 per unit on a 35% K_2O product, as against a maximum of $6 last year and a price of 80 cents per unit, or $38.40 per ton, for German potash before the War. In regard to the Searles Lake operations, we are glad to think that the American Trona Corporation has begun to justify the expectation of its promoters. There are two plants at work at Trona, that of the Boro-Solvay Company, about which we have no definite knowledge, and that of the Trona Corporation, which during 1918 will have shipped 23,000 tons of crude salts, containing about 13,000 tons of potassium chloride, as the first fruits of an investment of between two and three million dollars. The seaweed idea is dead already, the cost of harvesting being prohibitive. It is unlikely that the deposits of leucite and alunite, in Wyoming and Utah, for example, will prove important sources of potash, because it it impracticable to extract both the aluminum and the potash from the same ore. It may seem simple to roast an alunite ore at a temperature sufficiently high to reduce the aluminum sulphate to alumina, leaving the potash as a soluble sulphate, and then to dissolve and separate the potash from the alumina. In practice, however, it is found that it is impossible to recover all the potassium sulphate, leaving enough to render the alumina of no value commercially. Apparently the exploitation of leucite ore presents similar difficulties. On the other hand, recent experience indicates that the recovery of potash as a by-product from cement works will afford an important source of supply, more particularly when the clay from which the cement is manufactured contains decomposed feldspars. It might be suggested that alunite be used as part of the mixture in cement manufacture, but when this is done, owing to the high temperature used in the burning of cement, the small particles containing the potash are not caught on the filters but pass through the stack. Much useful research has been done in response to the demands created by the cessation of imports during the War and the foundations of a valuable domestic industry have been laid, but it is obvious that if the German products are again permitted to enter this country free, after the treaty of peace has been signed, there will be no chance of a survival of our potash industry. Is it not advisable to render this country independent of the Kali Syndicate?

Alaska

Alaska is a beautiful country and the photographs that we publish in this issue bear testimony to the fact. Alaska is also a health-giving country, as those who have sojourned there know full well. The interior, or 'inside', beyond the coast range, enjoys a comparatively dry and extraordinarily vitalizing climate. In days to come this part of the world will be recognized as a sanitarium for those in need of a tonic. To be in Alaska is to feel that "the world is young and life an epic." We are glad therefore to endorse the suggestion of the writer of the article on the Kennecott district and to commend this region to the attention of the young men of the profession, especially those returning from the War and unwilling to resume the humdrum existence of ordinary routine. To the young man with a little money, some knowledge of mining, and a lot of energy there is no better occupation today than exploratory work in the North. The official statistics show that in 1918 the mines of Alaska produced $28,900,000, thus the output was $12,000,000 less than in 1917, but it is not due to exhaustion of resources but to the adverse effects of the War, chiefly shortage of labor and shipping. The production of gold was only $10,000,000, as against $14,671,-400 in 1917, and of last year's yield $6,100,000 came from the placer mines. Copper is the principal product of Alaska at this time, the output having been 69,426,000 pounds, worth $17,180,000 during 1918. We note that the tin production was valued at $90,000, this serving as a reminder of one of Alaska's potentialities. Since 1880 Alaska has produced $302,000,000 in gold and $105,800,-000 in copper. The figures are impressive. For this territory the United States paid Russia the sum of $7,200,-000 in 1867. It is an enormous region, not less than 514,700 square miles, with a population of barely 50,000, most of whom are collected in a number of small communities, leaving large tracts uninhabited and hardly explored, although any mention of exploration prompts instant recognition of the splendid work done by the U. S. Geological Survey under the leadership of Mr. Alfred H. Brooks, whose many reports and bulletins are of the utmost practical value to those engaged in the search for deposits of ore. Anybody going to Alaska can obtain maps and other information of the most helpful kind simply by writing to the Director of the Geological Survey at Washington. No mining region has been so well served in the matter of geological reconnaissances and reports, all of which are available either gratis or at a nominal price. Besides giving this geologic aid the Government has undertaken to build a railroad, which will traverse the coast range and reach the interior through the Broad Pass. We publish an article by Mr. F. LeRoy Thurmond detailing mining activities in the vicinity of this mountain pass and showing the district to be rich in minerals, including stibnite. It covers a portion of the line of contact between the sedimentary rocks and the granite intrusions along which the orebodies of Alaska and British Columbia are chiefly distributed. The Government Railroad has its principal terminus at Anchorage, on Cook Inlet, although the outer rail-head is at the harbor of Seward, on the Gulf of Alaska. It taps the Matanuska coalfield, the Kenai, Willow Creek, and Talkeetna goldfields; it will serve the Nenana coalfield, as well as the gold-mining districts and the agricultural tracts in the Tanana valley. This railway will afford direct entry into the heart of Alaska, instead of necessitating the roundabout journey either down the Yukon from White Horse or up that river from St. Michael. Another article, reviewing the mineral development of Alaska during 1918, by Mr. J. L. McPherson, affords an excellent idea of the various mining activities now in progress. The finding of palladium in copper ore near Ketchikan and of platinum on the Seward peninsula emphasizes the possibilities of this remote part of the continent and should provoke further search for the rare metals. The exploitation of tungsten and chrome deposits has been stimulated by the War and may lead to something permanent in case the ore is rich enough to overcome lower prices for the ferro-alloys. Juneau has suffered by the closing down of the Treadwell group, except the Ready Bullion mine, owing to the caving of the surface and the drowning of the workings. Another blow to the Juneau district has been the failure of the Alaska Gold and Alaska Juneau enterprises, although there is good reason to believe that, thanks to the courage and persistence of Mr. F. W. Bradley, the latter failure may yet be retrieved. One of Alaska's chief assets is its coal, the exploitation of which has been hindered by political and other troubles, but is destined to prove an important factor in the industrial development of the Pacific Coast. We are glad therefore to note the recent work done on the Nenana, Bering River, and Matanuska coalfields because it appears to indicate a renewed effort to develop these resources. Any consideration of Alaskan mining makes clear the great variety of mineral deposits distributed over this enormous region and justifies our drawing attention at this time to a part of the world for which, by reason of personal experience, we have a warm spot in our heart.

The War Minerals Meeting at Washington

By COURTENAY DE KALB

The problems of the producers of war minerals has assumed a new phase. The War Minerals Act (Public 220) still stands on the statute books unused, and the Secretary of the Interior has definitely stated that it could be employed, but that he will not do so without the express direction of Congress. This admission was made to a committee from the meeting of the manganese, chrome, pyrite, and magnesite producers assembled in Washington under the auspices of the American Mining Congress on December 16. The committee consisted of W. L. Gazzam of Seattle, J. A. Edwards of Los Angeles, and Nelson Franklin of Denver. Secretary Lane expressed sympathy with the producers in their predicament, and said that while the Act was, in his opinion, technically and legally effective, he felt that further authorization to apply it was needed to warrant his taking such steps as administrator. He had not consulted the Attorney General, but the matter seemed clear without soliciting his advice. If Congress should direct that he administer the Act he would welcome the opportunity, although he would prefer to make use of the appropriation granted in the Act for the purpose of liquidating the losses incurred by the producers. He was willing to express these opinions to senators and representatives who might confer with him.

The Act would have to be amended to enable the appropriation to be utilized in that manner. It is well understood that no new appropriations relating to war-work can be passed at this Congress. At least a decided change in congressional opinion will have to come about if such legislation can be secured. The Chairman of the Appropriations Committee of the Senate, Thomas S. Martin, has set his face determinedly against any further appropriations, owing to the critical attitude of the Republican members. Therefore any effort at relief must take advantage of appropriations already made. The fact that the Minerals Control Act carries an appropriation of $50,000,000 makes it available if it can be suitably amended. It is assumed, on the strength of statements made by many members of the Senate and the House, that this will not be extremely difficult to accomplish, since there is a growing sense that the Government must find means for relieving those who have suffered by reason of unfulfilled contracts that were entered into before the armistice was arranged. The War Department has taken the initiative in providing for payments on the so-called verbal contracts, which the Comptroller of the Treasury declared could not be settled legally under existing laws. At the instance of Secretary Baker the Department put itself squarely on record through a letter to Chairman S. H. Dent of the Committee on Military Affairs of the House, in which he said: "The signing of the armistice has left numerous persons and corporations engaged in supplying or preparing to supply the war needs of the United States at the request of the War Department, without contracts covering the service to be rendered by them executed in the manner required by law. . . . Yielding to the exigencies of the war situation, such contractors put the work of production ahead of the work of negotiation, and have often put themselves in a position where their only reliance was the good faith and fairness of the Government in finally fixing the terms of the agreement. . . . Under all the foregoing classes of cases the contractors have, at the request of the United States and in response to the needs of the war emergency, made expenditures and incurred obligations in preparing, or actually entering upon, the task of supplying the war needs of the country. They have a part, and in many cases an essential part, of their working capital tied up in the expenditures they have made in preparing to begin work, in the creation of facilities, in actual materials purchased, wages paid to labor employed, or in work in process. In order that this working capital may be returned to them so that they may as speedily as possible go into commercial work, it is essential that there be a prompt adjustment under these informal or implied agreements. In this matter time is of the essence. To effect such adjustment . . . it is necessary . . . to secure the remedial legislation now proposed. Contractors who have had formal written contracts should not be penalized for the reason that it now develops that the Chief of the Procurement Division of Ordnance could not deputize his principal assistants to sign a contract. Nor should the patriotism be penalized of those who in the exigencies of the war have gone ahead to produce instead of waiting to bargain. It is true that such persons have nothing to rely on except the good faith of the United States, but surely there should be no more solid ground for reliance than that good faith."

In accordance with this representation to Congress the Dent Bill (H. R. 13,274) was introduced and has been reported from the Committee favorably, on December 19, and is expected to become law within a short time. Friends of the mineral producers have not been slow to see in this bill the full recognition of the moral principles involved in the Government requests for chrome, manganese, and other materials coming under the provisions of Public 220, and while a separate measure for the relief of the minerals producers will be introduced* without delay, it is certain that the Dent Bill will not be per-

*This has been done. We gave the text of the bill in our last issue.

mitted to pass without being amended so as to include the implied contracts in the case of the miners of chrome, manganese, and other materials, unless the amendment to the War Minerals Act should be passed first.

The meeting of the American Mining Congress for the benefit of the producers of the war minerals was largely attended. Fifty-five representatives of the interests involved were present, coming from 22 States. They held credentials from over 1000 producers, employing in the aggregate about 200,000 workmen. A permanent War Minerals Division of the American Mining Congress was organized, and an executive committee was appointed consisting of the following persons: Theodore Swan of Alabama, A. J. Edwards of Arkansas and California, W. W. Pettis of Montana, and J. C. Jensen of Utah, representing manganese; W. L. Gazzam of Washington and Oregon and Courtenay De Kalb of California, representing chrome; N. P. Pratt of Georgia, representing pyrite; Nelson Franklin of Colorado, representing tungsten; and H. F. Wierum of Washington, representing magnesite. On the return of Mr. Gazzam to Seattle his place was taken on the committee by Walter H. Denison of Arkansas, acting as a substitute. This committee has been active since the adjournment of the convention in framing the desired amendment to the War Minerals Act, and in arranging to have it introduced into Congress through the Committees on Mines of both houses. It will be noted that the potash industry is not represented, and in fact no potash representatives were invited, but provision was made by a motion carried by the convention for increasing the executive committee by additions to its membership consisting of the representatives of other interests affected, and thus the alliance of the potash producers is made possible. As they are equally injured, and as they represent large investments, their addition is of great importance for adding strength to the petition to Congress.

The convention adopted the following resolution:

WHEREAS, on October 5, 1918, H. R. 11,259 (Public 220), was approved by the President, and

WHEREAS, on November 11, 1918, the day on which the armistice was signed, the administration of this Act, with the exception of the imposing of duties, was turned over to the Secretary of the Department of the Interior by the President of the United States, thereby indicating his intent to have the provisions of the Act carried out, and

WHEREAS, up to the present time none of the provisions of the Act have been carried into effect, and

WHEREAS, American producers of the minerals specified therein, who were induced to invest large sums of money for the purpose of producing such minerals under the implied protection of the Act, have suffered serious losses, and will continue to do so, and in many cases will be financially ruined by reason of the non-enforcement of said Act; now therefore be it

Resolved, by this convention of mineral producers, constituting the War Minerals Division of the American Mining Congress, assembled in the City of Washington, December 16 and 17, 1918, that the Congress of the United States be and hereby is requested to take such legislative action at its present session as it may deem proper to enforce the carrying out of the purpose and spirit of the aforesaid Act so that justice may be done.

It is evident from the foregoing resolution that the sense of the convention was that the Act as it stands ought to be administered. The addresses of delegates from all over the country distinctly maintained the importance of doing more than to merely redeem the losses incurred. They felt that they had made a contribution to the welfare of the country that should not end with the fulfilment of their duty in providing necessaries for the national emergency just passed, but that the purpose and spirit of the Act should be broadly interpreted as meaning that the production of the minerals mentioned therein should be continued "to provide further for the national security and defence." They felt that the United States, having once been caught in a dangerous position because of our reliance upon imported minerals, it was our duty to make ourselves secure for the future by sustaining these new industries as part of a rational and necessary program of preparedness, both from an industrial and a military standpoint. It may be said that the opinion is growing rapidly that the academic position of the Democratic party with regard to free trade must yield, and that the leaders of the party are beginning to perceive that a change of policy is necessitated. This opinion is spreading, without reference to sectional lines, and the Southern delegates to the mineral convention were as emphatic in their declaration for protection to the chrome and manganese industries as were those from other parts of the country. The producers of pyrite, magnesite, and tungsten insisted that, while liquidation would be accepted, they believed that protection should be accorded to comply with the true spirit of the Act which was passed for their benefit. Mr. Wierum showed that this country now had developed sufficient deposits of magnesite to supply domestic needs for years to come, and that if the industry should be allowed to languish, this material would be supplied again, as in the past, from the mines of Austria. Over two millions of dollars had been expended in preparing the magnesite mines of this country for production, and more than 2000 workmen had been employed until recently. J. C. Jensen also held that it was our duty to maintain the industrial independence of America with regard to pyrite, and N. P. Pratt pointed out that the Chestatee mine in Lumpkin county, Georgia, had enormous resources of pyrite developed, at a cost of $850,000, which was superior in quality to the Spanish ores. The Chestatee pyrite is entirely free from arsenic, averages 46% sulphur, and contains in addition approximately 1.75% copper, and $2 in gold per ton. Theodore Swan of Alabama, representing the Primos Chemical Co., called attention to the fact that the chief difficulty experienced in the maintenance of an American manganese industry lay in the competition from England. The English makers of ferro-manganese have been accustomed to supply this market to a large extent, and can deliver the ferro-alloy at $60 per ton. This is made possible by the fact that manganese ore coming from India in ballast can be laid down at British ports at about $3 to $4 per long ton. The costs of labor and reduction in this country make it impossible to produce the ferro-alloy for less than about $150 to $160 per ton. The conversion cost in the electric furnace, he asserted, was about $100 per ton of ferro, with the volatilization and slag losses averaging close to 20%. At the present time, he estimated, there were stocks of ferro-manganese in the hands of the steel-makers sufficient for three to four months, and the total stocks in the country were adequate for eight months. With the ores now available it would be possible to go through another year without having to buy a single ton of ore. Dr. C. K. Leith estimated that the supply might be sufficient for even 14 months. Mr. Swan said that his company "had a lucky hunch some time ago," so that its stocks of manganese will be exhausted by next February. He did not explain how nor where this "hunch" was obtained. Frank D. Brown described the conditions of manganese mining at Philipsburg, Montana. He and many of his friends had been induced to embark in the production of manganese after conferences with Government representatives who gave them assurance of Government protection. In the beginning they experienced difficulties on account of their newness in the business, and losses were met through failure to adhere to the specifications of the buyers. Heavy penalties were imposed, in one case as much as $900 being paid for excess silica on one carload. These problems were solved, and concentration supplemented careful hand sorting. The work of development and the erection of plant absorbed all the profits in the Philipsburg mines, so that the signing of the armistice left them just ready to realize some fair return for their money. They were, consequently, serious sufferers, and not only did the operators feel that they were entitled to consideration, but large numbers of miners who had been attracted by the new enterprise at Philipsburg were left without work at the beginning of winter, and many of these would undergo severe hardships unless the work were permitted to go on.

A ringing address was given by W. H. Denison of Cushman, Arkansas, which produced a profound impression, not only upon the delegates to the convention, but, by their own confession, upon the senators and representatives present, who had come to gather a better idea of the situation of the producers of the war minerals. He had been called to Washington when a shortage of manganese was feared, and was induced to develop his properties and to persuade others to enter into the business. As a result a total of $1,038,000 had been expended in one district alone, of which $263,000 had gone into plant for dressing the ores. Only 4830 tons had been shipped when the market fell, but 60,000 tons is in sight ready for delivery next year. The closure of the mines in his district had thrown 1400 men out of employment. While the miners of Arkansas had lost nearly their entire capital, the shippers of Brazilian manganese had paid in export-duties to that government $1,500,000, and their profits were estimated at $30,000,000. If the American producers had been permitted, by proper protection, to produce so as to make that much profit, they would have paid to our Government in taxes $18,000,000, in addition to providing our steel furnaces with their requirements and giving remunerative employment to thousands of workmen. If the American producer was not to be protected in the industry that he was encouraged to initiate, he was at least entitled to have been warned of the growing stocks of manganese so that he might have ceased operation and have saved the waste of his capital. Now that the damage has been done there is but one way to do justice and that is to discharge the obligations of the Government even if it should cost as much as to have fought on through two more years of war.

As a matter of fact the estimates of the amount required to liquidate all the producers of the war minerals is variously placed at from $15,000,000 to $25,000,000. It is understood that the estimate of the Bureau of Mines is as low as $5,000,000. This is undoubtedly short of the truth. Chrome will absorb as much as $1,000,000 for liquidation; manganese is stated by prominent producers to require for this purpose at least $7,000,000; pyrite will take about $1,000,000; magnesite $2,000,000; tungsten as much more; and potash probably $4,000,000. These are crude estimates, but beyond doubt the sums needed will be so large that it would appear sounder as a national policy to frankly accept the plan of protecting and encouraging the industries for the general good of the country. In effecting any settlements under a plan for liquidation it has been pointed out that the Government will necessarily demand the right to make salvage as far as possible. This will raise the question of disposal of equipment and of ores acquired in the process, which in turn will lead to a consideration of disposal. The Act as it stands provides for this under protection of the price, and it is an interesting problem as to how liquidation can be made without calling into action the provisions of the measure as originally passed. These are details that must be taken into consideration by Congress.

The convention of mineral producers has resulted in giving impetus to the movement for Congressional action to relieve the distress occasioned by the failure of the Government to put the Act into effect at the proper time. In view of the situation that arose during the autumn, and considering the fact that the War was still in progress after the break in the market for chrome and manganese occurred, and that the Minerals Control Bill was signed by the President on October 5, delay to utilize it then, when there could have been no question as to propriety of doing so, increases the responsibility of the Government through negligence to do what Congress had intended for the protection of these industries.

Silver melted in a Rennerfelt electric furnace at the Philadelphia Mint during the fiscal year 1917-'18 amounted to 10,031,101 oz. It takes 60 minutes to melt 1000 lb. (12,000 oz.), consuming 198 kw-hr. per net ton.

Minerals Separation Litigation

Two new petitions have been presented to the United States Supreme Court by the Minerals Separation North American Corporation in its litigation against the Butte & Superior Mining Co. One of them constitutes a motion to advance the case, while the other seeks to restrain the Butte & Superior company from disposing of its assets pending action in the matter.

In motioning that the case be assigned for argument at an early day the Minerals Separation company says that "this suit not only involves a patent which has been heretofore passed upon by this (Supreme) Court but the respondent, Butte & Superior, carried on in its mill, by its employees, with its own ore and for its own profit, the acts formerly adjudicated by this court to be infringements. . . ."

The petition then says that the Butte & Superior Co. varied its procedure and process in an immaterial respect, after the Supreme Court rendered its decision in the Hyde case; that the District Court on the basis of that decision, held the variation immaterial and that the infringement had continued; and that the Circuit Court of Appeals reversed this holding as to continuing infringement, on the sole basis of its different interpretation of the Supreme Court decision in the Hyde case. This, the petitioner charges, voided and rendered practically nugatory and valueless, the invention which the Supreme Court pronounced to be patentable, thereby opening the way for the use and enjoyment of the invention without liability to the owners.

"The point at issue," charges Minerals Separation, "is whether the decision of this (Supreme) Court in the Hyde case, properly interpreted, permits such a limitation to be given the patent as to enable the respondent, Butte & Superior Mining Co., to obtain the benefit of the patented invention and escape infringement."

In asking for an injunction restraining the disposition of assets and payments of dividends Minerals Separation claims that from reports formerly filed with the District Court by the Butte & Superior, that company's operations from November 1, 1913, to and including December 31, 1916, show that "in these admitted and adjudged infringing operations the total value of concentrates recovered was $18,970,876, the total cost of the operation of the flotation plant was $1,136,452 and that therefore the profit of the infringing operations was $17,834,423, or about $18,000,000." Dividends paid total $16,940,258.

The Butte & Superior company has deposited with the District Court as security for the Minerals Separation, a surety bond for $75,000 and $100,000 in Liberty bonds against $18,000,000 of profit "made by the defendant in operations unquestionably infringing the patent in suit," the total security being less than 1% of the profit.

As another reason for desiring a restraining order preventing the dissipation of assets, the Minerals Separation company refers to two diverse decisions against Butte & Superior secured by Elm Orlu Mining Co. in its litigation for title to a "substantial portion of its mine."

The Passing of a War-Industry

By F. H. MASON

The notice by the Hercules Powder Co. to its employees that its plant at Chula Vista, near San Diego, will be dismantled gradually brings to a close an exceedingly interesting piece of chemical research. After a futile endeavor to find a market for its output at post-war prices the company has decided to close the plant. The fact that in the month since the signing of the armistice the prices of the principal products, acetone and potash, have dropped respectively from $15 to 75c. per gallon and from $400 to $100 per ton shows clearly that the company had no alternative in its decision.

The plant was designed and built in order to fill a contract that the company had made with the British government for a large quantity of cordite, the understanding being that in filling this order the company should not compete against the British government in the purchase of acetone derived from the then existing sources of supply of that material. In other words, the company should find some new source from which to derive its acetone to fill the order. Cordite, it may be mentioned in passing, is the principal propellant used in the British army. It is a mixture of 65% gun-cotton and 30% trinitro-glycerine blended by the common solvent acetone. Five per cent of vaseline is added to stabilize the explosive and lubricate the guns, and then the acetone is made to volatilize in heated rooms.

The Hercules Powder Co. turned to the kelp fields off the coast of southern California for its supply of acetone. The kelp was cut and macerated and stored in huge harvesters that were kept continuously at work, barges being in attendance to take the kelp from the hold of the harvesters to the works. From the barges the kelp is pumped to 50,000-gal. redwood tanks, of which there are 150, where it is maintained at the proper temperature for fermentation by steam pipes and agitated by compressed air. Fermentation proceeds for 10 to 14 days, the products being acetic, butyric, and other organic acids, which are converted into calcium salts by the addition of lime. The undigested kelp is screened from the solution, containing the calcium salts, together with potassium chloride, iodide, and other salts that have been released from the kelp by fermentation. The solution is filtered, evaporated, and the various salts separated by fractional crystallization and other means. The acetone, of course, is derived from the calcium acetate.

Such is a brief outline of an industry made possible only by the exigencies of war. It represents a capitalization of $5,000,000, and it steadily employed from 1000 to 1500 men, while it retained from 15 to 20 chemists on the research staff to solve difficulties that were continually arising. The plant was started in the fall of 1916, so, by the time it is closed, it will have run, perhaps, two and a half years. During the last year, it has cut and treated on an average 24,000 tons of kelp per month. Besides acetone and potassium chloride, a number of by-products were made, all of which were in good demand.

MOTOR-ROAD TO STRELNA

THE KENNECOTT MILL

Alaska's Mineral Development During 1918

By J. L. McPHERSON

INTRODUCTION. The arrival of 135 ounces of platinum, valued at $13,577, from Alaska, during November of this year, marks not only the first shipment of that metal from the Northland but anticipates the opening of a new and promising industry for the territory. The platinum comes from widely separated localities; five ounces from the Salt Chuck mine in the Ketchikan district; six ounces from Slate creek in the upper Copper River region; and 22 ounces from Dime creek on the Seward peninsula. The first shipment was from a lode deposit; the second, from a placer.

Despite the shortage of labor and transportation, the high cost of materials and supplies, prohibitive to the mining of low-grade deposits, mining development in Alaska, during 1918, showed material progress in the opening of many new properties and the enlargement of plant and equipment.

The most striking instances of new development include the opening of the molybdenite property by the Alaska Treadwell company on the northern end of Prince of Wales island; the starting of a tunnel to connect the workings of the world-famous Bonanza mine with the Mother Lode property and the enlargement of the Kennecott plant for the treatment of tailings; the completion of an auto-truck road, 20 miles long, connecting the mining property of the Alaska Copper Mining Co. at Nugget Creek with the Copper River & Northwestern railroad at Strelna; the erection of a mill on the gold-mining property of the North Midas Copper Co. on the Kuskulana river; increased production in the Willow Creek quartz-mining district, which had its most prosperous year; and the discovery that the minerals in this district carry platinum.

SOUTH-EASTERN ALASKA. The molybdenite deposit at Shakan is being extensively developed by the Alaska Treadwell Mining Co., which has installed a 20-stamp mill and has a 4000-ft. tramway under construction to connect the mine with the wharf. It is reported that 100,000 tons of ore is in reserve. The company has erected at Treadwell a Heroult electric furnace for making ferro-molybdenum.

The Pacific Gypsum Co. has re-organized with sufficient capital to operate its holdings at Gypsum on a large scale. Dockage facilities will also be added to accommodate Japanese freighters.

The Salt Chuck mine at Kasaan has been operating successfully, the first copper concentration plant to be installed in the Ketchikan district. The plant has a capacity of 60 tons per day and consists of a Blake crusher, ball-mill, drag classifier, followed by flotation rougher and cleaner cells.

The Rush, Brown, Sulzer, and It mines are shipping steadily and supplying considerable ore to the smelters.

The Alaska-Endicott Mining & Milling Co. has constructed approximately 800 ft. of tunnel and has cross-cut an 18-ft. vein on the property. A strong vein of ore continues in line with the tunnel. The Jualin gold mine, situated about 60 miles from Juneau, will resume operations at capacity with the opening of the 1919 season. It is estimated that 100 men will be employed. The mine has not been operated since 1917.

The first consignment of copper ore was shipped from the Rainy Hollow district this fall, when Kennedy, Conway, and Burnham sent 26 tons of bornite south from the Maid of Erin mine by way of Haines.

Other operations in the south-eastern part of the Territory include the construction of a plant for the treatment of a complex copper-zinc-lead ore by the J. L. Harper syndicate at Moira Sound; the discovery of a free gold and galena deposit at Windham bay; and the operations of the Alaska Copper Co., which has sunk 200 ft. below sea-level at Port Esterly, cross-cutting a vein of shipping and milling ore for 15 ft. The ore carries copper, silver, and lead. Development work has continued on the nickel properties on Chichagof island. Exploration underground is progressing on the Alex group at McLeans Arm.

The Alaska Treadwell Mining Co. is hoisting ore from the 2800-ft. level of the Ready Bullion mine on Douglas island. This is the lowest level ever attained in Alaska. The Alaska Gastineau, at Thane, has undertaken no new development work this year on account of the shortage of labor and the high cost of operation. During September the mine produced 47,850 tons of $1.247 ore, or just half the August tonnage. At the end of the second quarter, the estimate of broken ore in the stopes was 1,901,394 tons. The Alaska Gastineau added a second shift during November and contemplates operating three shifts in the near future.

F. W. Bradley, president of the Alaska Juneau Gold Mining Co., states that the company is preparing to operate 45 drills on this property next year, which means a greatly increased output, for the handling of which plans are now being completed.

COPPER RIVER. The Kennecott Copper Corporation has been employing about 550 men at the highest wages ever paid by quartz or lode properties in the Territory. Still, they have been obliged to work short-handed. This company has been operating the Jumbo and Bonanza mines and recently acquired the controlling interest of the Mother Lode property. To connect the Bonanza and Mother Lode workings, a tunnel 1400 ft. long is under construction, through which ore from the Mother Lode will be brought to the Kennecott mill, resulting in a great saving in transportation from the present system of hauling by auto-truck from the mine to McCarthy on the Copper River & Northwestern Railroad, a distance of 12 miles. The Kennecott company is enlarging its plant for the treatment of the tailing by an ammonia process perfected by E. H. Stannard, manager for the Kennecott Corporation.

Important discoveries of silver, lead, gold, and a large body of low-grade copper ore have been made during the year in the Chitina region. The North Midas Copper Co. has constructed a cyanide mill for the treatment of its gold-bearing ore. This property is situated on the Kuskulana river about 14 miles from Strelna on the Copper River & Northwestern Railroad.

The Slate Creek placer district, which has been a steady producer for the last 18 years, had its most successful season in 1918. Through the receding of a glacier in this district, a gold-quartz vein about four and a half feet wide, and carrying rich ore, has been exposed for several hundred feet.

The Alaska Copper Corporation has developed its bornite deposit on Nugget creek in the Kuskulana valley to a depth of 300 ft. A 50-ton experimental concentrating mill has been constructed this season and will be enlarged next year. Ore will be transported by auto-trucks over a new road, 20 miles long, constructed by the company from the mine to Strelna, on the railroad.

PRINCE WILLIAM SOUND. The copper mines in Prince William Sound district have all been greatly handicapped by lack of transportation facilities, due to the governmental order requiring steamship companies to care first for fish products. The Granby Consolidated Co. has constructed an aerial tram, 28,360 ft. long, from the Midas mine to tide-water on Valdez bay. This is the longest tramway in Alaska. It is divided into six sections with 77 towers. The longest span is 3080 ft. The cable for the loaded skips is 1⅛ in. diam., and for empties, ⅞ inch. Eighty buckets of 1000-lb. capacity each are in use. The cost complete was $3.66 per foot; cost of operation, 0.328 cents per ton. The company produced 11,860,679 lb. of copper during the first quarter of 1918.

At Harriman Fiord, in the Port Wells district, the Free Gold Mining Co. has carried on considerable development work including a 500-ft. adit, and has installed a small Gibson mill and an air-compressor. The company has handled some rich free-milling ore this year.

SUSITNA VALLEY AND KENAI PENINSULA. Discovery of platinum on a tributary of Squentna river, the development of chrome ore properties at Port Chatham, the operations of the Cache Creek dredge, and general activity in the Willow Creek district characterize the mining season in the Susitna valley and Kenai peninsula this year. Platinum is believed by Dr. Herschel Parker to be available in commercial quantity in the Susitna valley.

Whitney and Lass are making regular shipments of chrome ore from their properties at Port Chatham. Geologists of the U. S. Geological Survey report the Red Mountain chrome deposits to be the best in the United States.

In the Yentna district, the Cache Creek Dredging Co. employed 45 men and had a successful season. The dredge was operated with coal secured from a near-by mine belonging to the company.

The Willow Creek quartz district has experienced the most successful season of its history, the yield this year exceeding that of last by about $100,000. The Miller-Straub people have erected a stamp-mill and have made a test-run, which was successful. The mills of the Gold Bullion, Alaska Free Gold Mining Co., and the Mable have operated at a profit during the past year. A small crew of men is mining free-milling ore at the Chase property on Turnagain Arm, where Mr. Chase is arranging for the erection of a prospecting mill to enable him to give the ore a thorough test.

The Valdez Placer Mining Co. has completed a large hydraulic plant on Valdez creek near the headwaters of the Susitna river and is prepared to begin active operations at the opening of next season. W. W. Woodward is installing a dredge in the Kachitna district. C. H. Packard is prospecting a graphite deposit at Red Bluff, on Seldovia bay. Extensive deposits of magnetic ore have been discovered by Henry Emard at Snug Harbor.

ESKA MINE, IN THE MATANUSKA COALFIELD

LOADING COPPER ORE AT KENNECOTT

FAIRBANKS. In spite of labor shortage, about $1,000,-000 in placer gold is predicted as the output from the Tolovana this year. At least 30 plants are at work, employing between 250 and 300 men. New gold-placer strikes have been reported at Takotna, on Crooked creek, George river, and Holitna river. Molybdenite has been discovered about 100 miles from Fairbanks in the Delta country. The mining season at Fairbanks bids fair to equal, if not surpass, the output of last year.

One hundred tons of ore from the Smith-McGone mine, recently milled at Eva creek, yielded $1875 in gold. The company has an additional 250 tons of the ore to mill and expects to operate all winter. Recent arrivals from Brooks report a quiet stampede to Washington creek, nine miles from Olnes. Thirty tons of silver-lead ore shipped from the head of Cleary creek averaged $45 per ton. Ground yielding better than $1 per foot in placer gold and carrying a considerable quantity of placer tin has been discovered on lower Patterson, about 22 miles from Hot Springs, which is 40 miles from Nenana.

Numerous strikes are reported from various parts of the district. Vaughn and Fox are reported to have made a copper strike near the head of the Maclaren river in the Susitna watershed. Smith Brothers have struck a new vein on their quartz property on Easter creek. J. C. Murphy has been working his tungsten property at the head of Pearl creek. U. G. McDowell and L. J. McCarty have taken a lease on the McCarty quartz property on Fairbanks creek and expect to treat their ore at the Gilmore mill.

UPPER YUKON, KOYUKUK. Production in the Koyukuk and Upper Yukon is not expected to equal that of former years. In the vicinity of Circle and Eagle several hydraulic plants are in operation or are completing development work, preparatory to hydraulicking next season. Circle, Alaska's old reliable placer camp, has had one of the most prosperous seasons of its history; several new hydraulic plants have been started in the district; the six-mile ditch on Dome creek has been enlarged and a new dam completed.

KUSKOKWIM. Gravel richer than $1 per foot is said to have been uncovered at Greenestone on the Tolatna. $80,000 was taken out of Flat creek in the Iditarod district this season. Boland and Hansen on Wetketchum creek report better than average pay, while Arndt and Nelson on the same creek, report as high as $5 per foot. 'Smiling' Albert is said to have struck it rich on Nixon fork, a tributary of the Takotna, by uncovering $1 pans from six feet of gravel in a 60-ft. hole. Good pay is also reported from Moore creek in the Kuskokwim. News of a good strike was reported early in the year by a native named Wattemuse (or Watermouse) in the Good News Bay district. Later reports state that pay was found on only three claims. Six outfits are operating approximately 125 men on Willow creek in the Marshall district.

SEWARD PENINSULA. Shortage of water has been keenly felt by the operators in this region. The introduction of the Miles system of thawing to replace the old steam method, was tried effectively by the Alaska Mines Corporation in the Candle section this year. Tin-dredging has been carried on successfully in the Port Clarence section on Lost river. Sixty tons of ore was recently shipped from the tin mines at York to the States. Dime creek has been one of the most active mining centres in this district. Olaf Nelson reports a gold strike with uniform pay on California creek, which is in the Shungnak section of the upper Kobuk and within the well-known gold-bearing areas of that river and its tributaries. H. L. Stull has bought a Keystone drill and will prospect for old pay-channels in the Immachuk district. Chandler and Dawson, from New York, have been drilling on the Immachuk properties of the Fairhaven Ditch Company.

COAL DEVELOPMENT. The first shipment of coal, a small consignment from Lignite creek, reached Nenana from the Nenana coalfield early in February. The Alaska Anthracite Railroad, under construction from Controller bay to the coal property of the Alaska Petroleum & Coal Co., was completed to tide-water at Bering river on October 7, and will permit of the shipment of high-grade bituminous and anthracite coal. It is planned to extend this railroad seven miles from Okalee channel on Controller bay, which will allow of direct loading onto ocean carriers. The Bering Coal Co. has taken a lease on the Bering coalfield and has a large force engaged in extensive development work. In the Matanuska field. the Alaska Engineering Commission is employing 150 men at the Eska mine, which is producing 100 tons daily for use locally. Forty men are employed at the Chickaloon mine in development work. The Chickaloon Coal Co. is pushing drilling and other exploratory work on its leases, which are adjacent to Chickaloon. The Alaska Engineering Commission recently let contracts to R. E. Burns & Co. for the delivery of 5000 tons of Nenana coal, to be mined from a deposit 49 miles south of Nenana; and to W. J. Lynn, for 1000 tons from a deposit 29 miles south of Nenana. This marks the beginning of real development of Alaska's great interior coalfields.

The Shakan Molybdenite Mine

Near the north-west end of Prince of Wales island, at a navigable distance of 180 miles from Treadwell, Douglas island, Alaska, the Alaska Treadwell company is developing the Shakan mine.

The vein on this property outcrops for a length of over 500 ft., with an average width of 5 ft., and an average assay of 1% molybdenite. A tunnel being driven on the strike of the vein has now advanced a distance of 320 ft., and has developed the vein for an average width of 7.7 ft., with an average assay of 1.89% MoS_2. The average of the surface and underground showings is a width of 5.85 ft., assaying 1.58% MoS_2, indicating 100,000 tons, of which 6270 tons is positively blocked-out with an average of 2.28% MoS_2. This block alone should eventually yield sufficient profit to more than repay the whole cost of the operation. The average ore should yield 15 lb. molybdenum per ton, which, at the average price for the molybdenum content of molybdenite concentrate for the seven pre-war years—1908-1914 inclusive—would mean a recovery of $15 per ton of run-of-mine ore.

At the time the option on this property was secured, there was considerable demand for molybdenite concentrate at a high price; but war prices afterward so stimulated production that the company has not yet been able to contract for an output of either molybdenite concentrate or for an output of ferro-molybdenum, a product planned to be made in the 2-ton Heroult electric-furnace at Treadwell. While war prices have resulted in overloading the market for the time being, the expectation is that the intensified advances forced by the War in metallurgy and in manufacturing, will eventually create a sufficient demand to absorb all the molybdenum production that is now in sight.

The Shakan ore is not only twice as high grade as that mined from the Climax molybdenum property situated at an elevation of 12,200 ft. above sea-level in Colorado, but it also promises to yield the metal vanadium and soluble phosphorous salts as by-products.—Excerpt from report of F. W. Bradley, October 1918.

Refining Gold Bullion With Chlorine Gas and Air

By R. R. KAHAN

*At the Royal Mint, Perth, Western Australia, a modification of the Miller chlorine process and Rose's method for toughening gold bullion by means of oxygen, gas, or air, is used.

It is a common experience for the refiner using Miller's process to notice that, with various classes of bullion, which contain only gold and silver, the final stages of the refining process occupy only a short time; whereas, with bullion which contains, besides gold and silver, varying quantities of certain base metals, such as lead, antimony, etc., the final stages of the refining process take a considerable time. It is in the final stages of the chlorine process that the major portion of the losses of gold occur. In the literature of refining bullion by chlorine gas, only brief mention is made of the stage of the operation when the losses of gold occur. Most of the losses of gold take place in the final stages of the refining process.

Various methods were experimented with to attain this object, the most successful being as follows: Two clay pipe-stems are introduced into the refining crucible. One is connected to an air-compressor delivering at a pressure of 6 or 7 lb. per sq. in., and the other to the chlorine generator. At the beginning of the refining operation the maximum amount of air is used, so much as will just avoid the globules of metal being projected through the borax cover, and a slow stream of chlorine. As the operation progresses the volume of air used is diminished, and that of the chlorine is increased, until finally, the air-pipe is removed and chlorine alone is used. The principle governing the regulation of the air and the chlorine is that fumes should be prevented from leaving the borax cover; if the fumes become too voluminous more air must be used and less chlorine.

When using this method it is found an advantage to mix the brittle bullion with the bullion containing the most silver. If the refining does not appear to be progressing satisfactorily, it is beneficial to remove the borax cover, and replace it with fresh borax.

Extracting Sulphur From Pyrite

At Queenstown, Tasmania, the Mt. Lyell company continues its work in this connection. The experiments have been hampered by slow delivery of materials. Coal-dust firing was applied to the rotary distillation furnace, but success was frustrated or delayed by the failure of the locally-obtainable refractory materials. Tests are now being made with gas-fired retort-furnaces.

THE COST OF MELTING the most refractory alloy—cupro-nickel—used at the Philadelphia Mint, in a Rennerfelt 1000-lb. electric furnace, is $9.45 per ton. This is 50% less than the cost with gas or crucible-furnace melting.

*Abstract from Bull. 170, Inst. Min. & Met., Nov. 1918.

UPPER—
The Kennecott Mill and the Glacier

LOWER—
The Green Prospect

KENNECOTT, ALASKA

THE CHUGACH RANGE

Baird Canyon, Copper River

Chitina, Alaska

COPPER RIVER & NORTH-WESTERN RAILWAY

MCCARTHY, OR SHUSHANNA JUNCTION

Mining Copper at Kennecott, Alaska

BY AN OCCASIONAL CORRESPONDENT

It is well known that the Kennecott Copper Corporation is operating successfully and is, in fact, obtaining brilliant results today in Alaska. This property has the advantage of handling large bodies of the highest known grades of copper ore, beginning at the outcrop. The actual tonnage handled has not been large, and the cost, even under war conditions, is not over 8 cents per pound.

The entire region in the neighborhood of this property has been thoroughly mapped and reported on by the U. S. Geological Survey.* All of this information is easily accessible. Anyone studying this mass of information will agree, after careful reflection, that this region offers many attractions to any development company that has no unreasonable hope of finding a bonanza without expending a proper amount of time, skill, and money, all of which are as much, but no more, required in this

*See 'Mining in the Lower Copper Basin', by F. H. Moffit. M. & S. P., June 8, 1918.

U. S. GEOLOGICAL SURVEY BULLETIN 662 PLATE XI

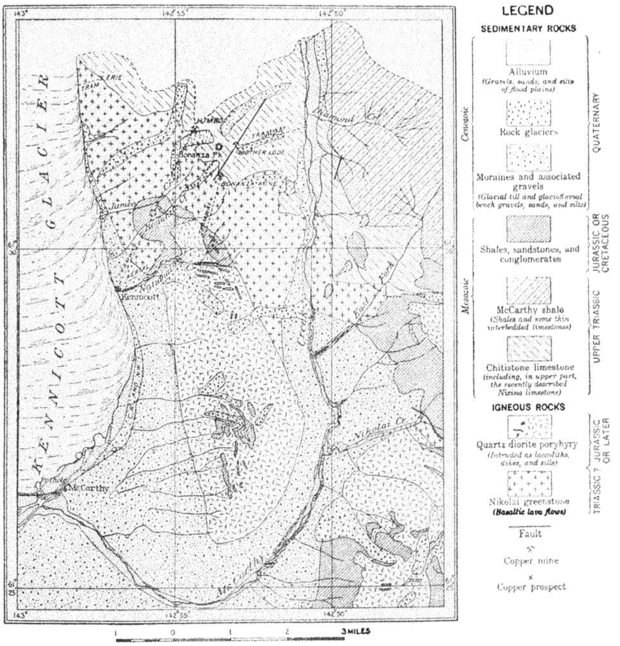

LEGEND

SEDIMENTARY ROCKS

Alluvium (Gravels, sands, and silts of flood plains)

Rock glaciers

Moraines and associated gravels (Glacial till and glaciofluvial bench gravels, sands, and silts)

Shales, sandstones, and conglomerates

McCarthy shale (Shales and some thin interbedded limestones)

Chitistone limestone (including, in upper part, the recently described Nizina limestone)

IGNEOUS ROCKS

Quartz diorite porphyry (Intruded as laccoliths, dikes, and sills)

Nikolai greenstone (Basaltic lava flows)

Fault

Copper mine

Copper prospect

SKETCH MAP OF VICINITY OF McCARTHY AND KENNECOTT

Alaskan district as in any other part of the world.

Of course, all prospecting work will be necessarily done under extravagantly expensive conditions and without the usual facilities for obtaining supplies and labor. Costs will vary greatly, but after the work is centralized and systematized, they will be made reasonable. The large gold mines in the neighborhood of Juneau have not shown unreasonably high costs, but they have had their difficulties in obtaining sufficient labor and in recovering the gold in their low-grade ores.

If anyone asks the point-blank question, "What is Alaska like?", it is as difficult to give an enlightening reply as it is to describe Africa or Russia in a few words. There are as many different local conditions of climate and topography as there are in any other large country. It is hard to convince some people that it is at all practicable to work throughout the year. On the other hand, one very capable Arizonan operator believes that mining costs over an extended period should not be higher on the average in Alaska than in many other localities where copper mining is being conducted profitably.

In the already prospected regions of Alaska there are no easily recognized surface indications of large bodies of primary ore, such as, for instance, the mountain of oxidized material at Ajo, Arizona, where with very little overburden, large acreages of oxidized material lay absolutely exposed to all prospectors. As one clever traveler in Alaska has said, many of the mountainous regions in Alaska literally "rain rocks". This part of the world, of course, is subject to great fluctuations of freezing and melting, so that the forces of erosion are naturally very active. This has its effect on the ore and is the cause of the great concentration in fissures and along contacts.

One of the accompanying photographs shows the Kennecott mill at the foot of the tramway from the mines and close to the Kennecott glacier. Right above the mill is an island or peak, which, as can be seen, is capped with limestone above the greenstone. The orebodies here lie, as in the Bonanza mine, along the contact, which dips sharply. The snow-capped peaks are Mount Blackburn and Mount Regal.

The following description of the Bonanza mine is borrowed from Mr. Moffit:

The Bonanza mine is in the mountains between the Kennecott glacier and McCarthy creek, at an elevation of 6000 ft. The first large orebodies found were in the magnesian limestone, so that at one time it was supposed that this rock had controlled the ore deposition and work was conducted accordingly. This supposition had to be given up, however, as the work proceeded, for ore was found in both the magnesian and the non-magnesian limestone. In the early days a great deal of talk was heard of the "favorable" lime, by which was meant the magnesian lime. Also, a great deal of talk is heard locally about bedding-planes. The bedding-planes, or flat faults, indicate the movement of one limestone bed on another, or movement along a plane parallel or approximately parallel to the planes of bedding. Bedding-plane faults occur in the lower part of the Chitistone limestone at many places and at least four are recognized in the Bonanza mine. The ore is dominantly chalcocite. The great orebodies belong primarily to the vertical fault system and have been found at the intersection of the vertical with the flat faults. They lie above the flat fault and terminate sharply against the underlying limestone. The exposures at the surface of the Bonanza mine show no more oxidized ore than those in some of the lower levels. Oxidized ore continues to the 700-ft. level. All small veins in stringers must be closely followed for many of them develop into valuable bodies of ore within short distances.

The copper deposits of the Jumbo mine resemble in most respects those of the Bonanza. The mine is in the Chitistone limestone, just above the contact with the underlying greenstone. The width of the ore-bearing ground worked is not less than 240 ft., yet the limits of the ore have not yet been reached. In form the orebodies are like those of the Bonanza, large tabular masses of

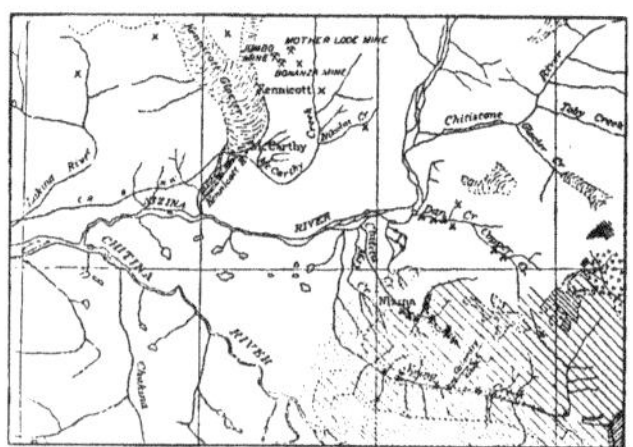

THE COPPER RIVER DISTRICT

chalcocite replacing limestone along the north-easterly faults. Ore was deposited in great quantities at the intersection of the vertical and bedding-plane faults, between the 400 and 600-ft. levels.

The great orebody lay for the most part above the bedding-plane fault between it and the magnesian limestone. It extended from a point a short distance above the 600-ft. level to a point 30 ft. above the 400-ft. level. In projection on a horizontal plane it had a length of 400 ft. A horizontal section of the orebody at the 500-ft. level is shown. This great mass of ore was practically solid chalcocite, with which was mixed an almost insignificant quantity of included limestone. It has yielded 50,000 tons of copper ore, much of which ran 76%. This is the largest single body of this grade of copper ore ever mined.

The Eric mine is a little more than 3½ miles north of Kennecott and less than ½ mile from the glacier. The ore so far uncovered is much more oxidized than that of the Bonanza and Jumbo mines. At least one well-defined bedding-fault was encountered. This mine is equipped with an aerial tram 2700 ft. long, running between the lateral moraine of the Kennecott glacier and

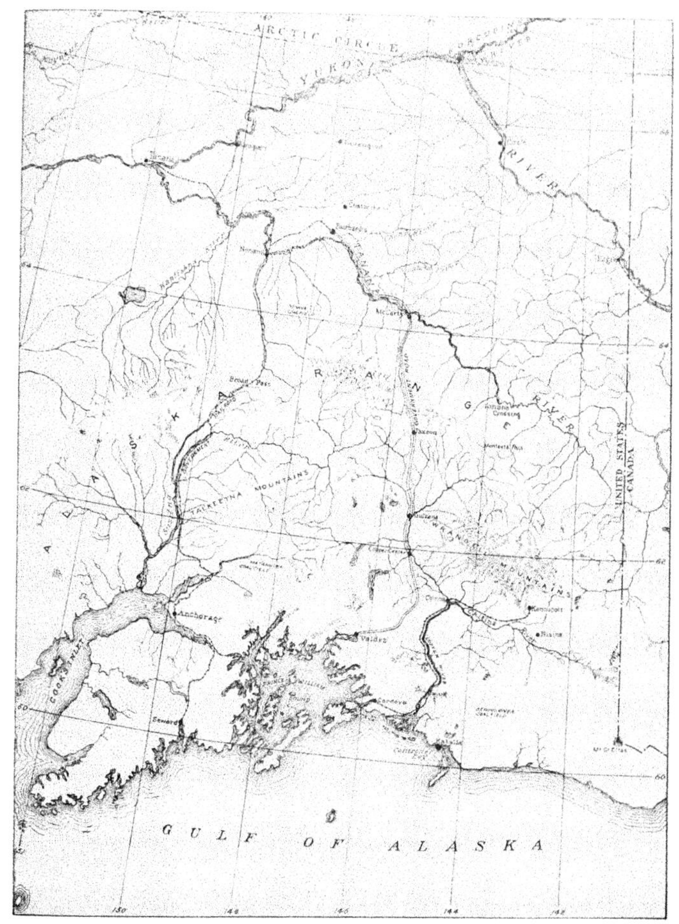

PART OF SOUTH-EASTERN ALASKA, SHOWING THE GOVERNMENT RAILROAD AND SOME OF THE PRINCIPAL MINING CENTRES the upper adit. Most of the ore shipped from Kennecott is of high grade and requires no concentration. Part of it, however, is concentrated in the mill, the tailing from which is treated in the leaching-plant with ammonia, which dissolves the copper carbonate. By this process 65 to 72% of the copper content is recovered from the tailing. The loss is probably due to the fact that fine particles of chalcocite are not attacked by the ammonia. Much experimental work is being done to perfect the leaching-plant. The difficulties encountered have been mechanical rather than chemical.

The Mother Lode mine is situated north-east of the Bonanza mine. Since 1913 it has made shipments of ore each winter. This property has just been purchased by the Kennecott Copper Corporation. The ore is chiefly chalcocite; besides copper, it carries silver in the ratio of one ounce to each 4% of copper.

The deposits so far exposed are high above the limestone-greenstone contact, and in this respect differ from the orebodies of the Bonanza and Jumbo mines, which are near the contact. The mine is equipped with a tramway having a length of slightly more than 5000 feet.

Another photograph shows a prospecting tunnel on the Green group of claims driven on a fissure, in which stringers and veins of high-grade ore have been found. This working is connected by an aerial tram with the bed of McCarthy creek, 2700 ft. away, and the operations are prompted by the supposition that a similar geological formation should contain similar ore to that of the Kennecott group.

The showing of copper, in the form of patches and lenses of bornite in the limestone above and near its contact with the greenstone, is of a most inviting character, because among reasons the ore is so high-grade as to remind one more of precious-metal mining than the conventional disseminated copper deposit.

The purpose of this sketchy description of the district by one that knows it well is to suggest that it offers reasonable chances to the adventurous prospector, particularly to the young men returning from the War and previously possessed of some knowledge of mining.

NOTE. In 1917 the Kennecott mine produced 265,579 tons of ore assaying 13.78% copper. Of this 206,253 tons, averaging 8.92%, was treated in the mill for a yield of 29,559 tons of concentrate averaging 53.52% copper. The recovery was 85.98%. At the leaching plant a total of 98,075 tons of tailing averaging 0.9% copper, was treated, for a yield of 1,244,200 pounds of copper. The aggregate shipments to the smelter came to 89,799 tons averaging 38.57% per ton. The ore contains silver and gold. During 1917 a total of 933,573 ounces of silver was recovered, with 78,211,429 lb. copper. It is rumored that ore rich in gold has been struck recently in the lower workings. The Kennecott Corporation has absorbed the Braden Copper Mines and other mining property, so that the exact performance of the Kennecott mine is now obscured. Production averages 6,000,000 lb. of copper per month.

The Magnesite Industry

Magnesite production of California and Washington during the first nine months of 1918 was as under, in tons, according to the U. S. Geological Survey:

State	First quarter	Second quarter	Third quarter	Total
California	25,000	28,000	16,500	69,500
Washington	22,000	23,500	45,000	90,500
	47,000	51,500	61,500	160,000

The combined output of these two States in the fourth quarter will be about 65,000 tons, making the total for the year 225,000 tons. This is a large decrease—30%—from the output of 1917, when California produced 211,000 tons, and Washington, 105,000 tons.

Two Californian mines—the White Rock mine in Napa county, and that of the Refractory Magnesite Co. in Sonoma county—yield a product that contains more iron than other Californian magnesite. It is dead-burned and sold as grain magnesite and brick for use as refractory material by steel manufacturers in the Western States. These two mines, which have been steadily producing this material and will probably continue to do so, are now making a large part of the total output of the State. All the small mines in the State are closed, and the few larger mines that remain in operation are producing at a rate representing only 25 to 50% of their capacity.

In the State of Washington only two companies are operating. They have spent large sums during the last two years in developing quarries and building plants, and are now able to produce raw and calcined magnesite in large quantities. Each company can turn out more than 10,000 tons of raw magnesite per month. The Northwest Magnesite Co. is making several thousand tons of ferro-magnesite per month in a large plant which it has erected at Chewelah, 60 miles north of Spokane. The plant includes five rotary-kilns, each 120 ft. long, which are fired with pulverized coal. The machinery is driven by electricity furnished by the Stevens County Power & Light Co. Two 300-hp. gas engines, together generating 400 hp., have been installed at the plant for additional power. The American Mineral Production Co. ships several thousand tons of raw magnesite per month from Valley to Irvin, 8 miles east of Spokane, where it is converted into ferro-magnesite in the plant of the International Portland Cement Co. It is reported that the output of ferro-magnesite from this plant in October, 1918, was about 150 tons daily.

NICHROME MUFFLES are now used in the cupellation furnaces of the New York Assay Office. In evenness of temperature and freedom from cracks the new material is much superior to the best of clay muffles. It is anticipated that the life of a nichrome muffle will be not less than a year. Nichrome plates, holding 16 cupels, are used, permitting the whole to be inserted and removed from the furnace at one time, according to the recently-published annual report of the Director of the Mint. Nichrome is mainly an alloy of nickel and chromium. Wire made of this is worth about $35 per ounce.

Broad Pass, Alaska

By F. Le ROI THURMOND

Broad Pass is a wide glaciated valley between the head of the Chulitna river and a tributary of the Nenana, named Jack river. It is commonly regarded as one of the passes through the Alaska range, but in reality it is part of an east-west valley connecting the heads of the Susitna and Chulitna rivers.

The Broad Pass region, as the term is here used, includes the headwater tributaries of the Chulitna and Nenana rivers and the heads of some streams flowing into the Susitna.*

The vicinity of Broad Pass was first visited by Government exploring parties in 1898, when G. H. Eldridge and Robert Muldrow of the U. S. Geological Survey, accompanied by five others, ascended the Susitna river as far as Indian river, whence they proceeded on foot, packing their suppiles on their backs. In 1902, Alfred Brooks led an exploring party across the Alaska range, starting from Tyonek on Cook's Inlet, crossing the range at Rainy pass, then along the flanks of the range to the Nenana river, and thence to the Tanana and the Yukon. This party, while visiting only the borders of the Broad Pass region, collected a great deal of valuable information, which has been published by the Survey.†

In 1902-1903 a reconnaisance survey was made through the Pass by the promoters of the Alaska Northern Railroad, which was designed to extend from Seward on Resurrection bay to a point on the Tanana river. It was at this time that mineral deposits were discovered in the Broad Pass region by prospectors attracted thither by the prospect of an early completion of the railroad. When the railroad failed, however, the claims were abandoned. In 1910, John Coffee, Frank Wells, and Lon Wells re-discovered promising prospects on the west fork of the Chulitna river about 12 miles from its junction with the middle fork. Other prospects were found on Costello and Colorado creeks, tributary to the west fork.

In 1914 and 1915, when it became generally known that Broad Pass had been selected as the route of the Government railroad, there was a considerable rush of prospectors to the region, attracted by reports of large orebodies and rich assays. Many of the assays reported were fictitious, being the work of an unscrupulous assayer who sought to profit from the excitement caused by reporting high values. While there was some disappointment resulting from the failure of the facts to measure up to expectations, mining prospects of merit were discovered. More recent exploration has further enlarged the known mineralized area, which extends from the middle fork near Caribou pass, in a south-westerly direction to the Chulitna glacier.

The rocks of the region are mainly sedimentary, consisting of slate and graywacke, limestone, chert, and cherty conglomerate, and andesitic tuffs, belonging for the most part to pre-Devonian periods. They have been

*'The Broad Pass Region, Alaska'. Fred H. Moffit, U. S. G. S., Washington, 1915.

†Professional Paper No. 70, 'Mt. McKinley Region, Alaska'. Alfred H. Brooks, Washington, 1911.

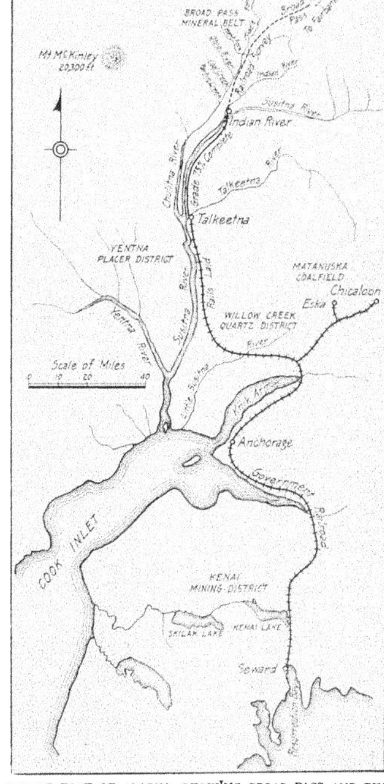

MAP OF PART OF ALASKA, SHOWING BROAD PASS AND THE GOVERNMENT RAILROAD

tilted, in the uplift of the Alaska range, and intruded with granitic and rhyolitic dikes and stocks. Ultra-acid magmatic phases are present as 'alaskite'. Metamorphism is local, being confined to the borders of intrusions. Mineralization followed the intrusions, in places being confined to fissures, but in others, impregnating whole masses of intrusive rock, as at the Golden Zone group of claims on the west fork, owned by John Coffee and the Wells brothers. Here an acidic dike invading cherty conglomerate has been mineralized with pyrite, chalcopyrite, arseno-pyrite, gold, and silver. High average values have been reported from trench-samples over widths exceeding a hundred feet. This property was under bond to the Guggenheims in 1915, but they released it without doing sufficient work to determine its real value.

About a mile from this property is the Riverside group, located by the same parties and held by a Spokane corporation, which proposes to exploit the ground when transportation conditions shall have made such a course advisable. Gold and silver are contained in an acidic dike invading chert and limestone. Arsenopyrite and chalcopyrite are the common sulphide minerals. A cross-cut tunnel, 80 ft. long, is not through the mineralized zone.

On Long creek, about a mile from the Golden Zone, is a promising copper prospect owned by the Bouker brothers. The ore is chalcopyrite and high-grade, and is said to occur in a large body.

Southward in the zone on the Ohio river is a group of claims owned by Dr. McCallie, Howard Wilmoth, and associates, of Anchorage. This property has recently been bonded. It was examined by me during the summer of 1918. The formation is limestone and tuff invaded by dikes of granite and alaskite. The ore contains galena, pyrite, chalcopyrite, and arsenopyrite, with silver and gold in fissure-veins, of which there are a number in parallel.

A typical analysis from an outcrop eight feet wide shows: silver 25 oz. per ton, gold 0.04 oz., copper 1.5%, lead 6.8%, iron 22%, silica 30%, and sulphur 12.9%. A sample from another vein shows more chalcopyrite and assayed as follows: silver 15 oz. per ton, gold 0.2 oz., copper 3%, iron 12.5%, silica 55%, and sulphur 6.8%.

About ten miles from the Ohio River location, on Partin creek, are a number of large copper-bearing veins in limestone. High assays in gold and silver have been obtained by me, and from the meager data at hand the prospects appear to be promising.

At a locality near the head of Coal creek there occurs a body of zinc-blende associated with pyrrhotite in a granite-slate contact. The orebody is exposed for a width of 20 ft. where the moss has been stripped off. Copper float found in large masses near-by indicates more extensive and varied mineralization.

The genesis of the ore deposits is undoubtedly connected with the invasions of the sedimentary rocks by the granite and other acid intrusives. Discussing the mineral resources in Professional Paper No. 70, Mr. Brooks says:

"Large masses of intrusive granites and grano-diorites cut the Tordrillo formation and older sedimentary rocks of the province. These intrusive rocks are believed to be for the most part of Mesozoic age and were probably injected chiefly during latter Jurassic time. Lithologically and in time of intrusion, they correspond to the great batholiths of granite which form the Coast range of south-eastern Alaska and British Columbia. It has been shown by Spencer, the Wrights, and others, that in south-eastern Alaska there is a close association and a genetic relation of the orebodies and the granitic intrusive rocks. As the granites of the Alaskan range are similar in character to those of the Coast range, it is plausible to consider that they may also be agencies of mineralization."

From a consideration of data obtained in the field, I am convinced of the truth of the above-quoted conclusion. In every instance where orebodies were seen, a granite or other acidic igneous rock was found near-by, in one instance giving indisputable evidence of the genetic relationship of dike to vein.

The fact that in south-eastern Alaska, where similar conditions exist, there are known to occur many large and valuable orebodies, together with the evidence of extensive mineralization in the area under discussion, and the prospect of an early completion of the Government railroad, places this region favorable for exploration.

Power-Plant on a Philippine Dredge

A radical innovation is the motive power designed for the Mambuloa dredge in Ambos Camarines in the Philippines, according to Charles Janin in 'Gold Dredging'. A steam turbo-generator was placed on the dredge to provide the electric current, being the first instance of such a plant being used for gold dredging. The dredge plant consists of a 300-hp. wood-burning boiler with condenser and a 625-kva. (500 kw. at 80% power-factor) turbo-generator running at 3600 r.p.m., 440-volt, alternating-current, three-phase, 60-cycle, with direct-connected exciter. The main drive motor is 150 hp. with reversible speed-controller, which will reduce full speed one-third. The other motors are as follows: main winch, 20 hp.; high-pressure pump, 120; low-pressure pump, 75; screen drive, 40; and stacker, 40 hp. In addition to the main power-plant there is an auxiliary steam engine of 20 hp. which can operate the winch and move the dredge in case of accident to the turbo-generator, during a storm or other emergency. This engine is used for lighting the dredge when the main plant is shut-down, and can also be used to take the place of the exciter in the generator should that get out of order. The water for the boilers comes through a special pipe-line from a fresh-water spring in the hills. This plan was adopted to obviate the possibility of damage from salt water in the river, which caused serious boiler trouble on one of the dredges in the Paracale district.

A Letter From Garcia, on Returning From the War

From Placedio Garcia on arrival at Ellis Island, N. Y., to his cousin at Santa Rita, N. M. From the 'Chino News.'

Dear Cousin:

Much would be your cousin's pleasure if this letter would find you in good health, in companionship of my dear aunt and the rest of the family. The present leaves your cousin in good health, living a good and gay life. Thanks to God.

Cousin, after much suffering, I have come back to the U. S. A. with good health, but a cripple, and I think that I will be such for life. Four of the bones are missing from my right foot, which is enough so that I will not be able to walk again as I used to. I have completed two months since I left my crutches, and yet I cannot straighten my foot. But I don't care; the pleasure that was left me is that I was not the victim of my enemies. Thanks to God for everything. He is the one who took care of me in all dangers and in all my sufferings and pain. Last of all, He brought me back to my idolized country, for which I would die, and for which I fought, and while doing so was left thrown, at the blackest and most dangerous place of the battle.

The hours in which without water and without food for two days, I fought desperately, so desperately that I sought death and could not find it. It was a dark and sad night where only pain and things that looked like hills or piles could be seen at a distance. These were the bodies of those who only a day and a half before had lost their lives and sent their last sigh and breathed their last breath for their dear mothers—their unfortunate mothers who had not even the pleasure of seeing their beloved sons for the last time. It is cruel, my dear cousin. At first it strikes with terror those who decide whether to win or die. The first few days you cannot get accustomed to it, but after the third or fourth day you have made up your mind to win or die, and you don't even give a snap for death or thoughts of it. I thought that never in my life I would or could support a similar blow, but I was able to support it. Not like the bravest of my company, but like a good soldier and not a coward.

It was about eleven at night when we had to make the first attack. The command was given and we marched to the trenches. We had not gone half a mile when a bullet passed over my head and went through the heart of an unfortunate one who was coming behind me. He lifted his arms in the air, gave a heavy sigh, and died. This was the first death that I saw. We covered his face and went forward, but we had not taken twenty steps when we were overtaken by the grapeshot. We were suddenly flung to a rivulet and could do no more than fall into any hole that we might be able to find.

"From where are they firing?" This was a question asked me by an American who had his head in a hole and the rest of his body out where ten or more bullets could have passed through his body. I said, "Take your head out of the hole; if death pursues us in this battle it will continue no matter where you hide; this is no time to hide, the enemy is about to come upon us; let us take a good position." He turned around and with trembling hands filled his rifle, which he had not filled yet, and placed himself by my side to observe and wait for the command from our captain to advance. The command came and forward we went again. No sooner had we started than the grapeshot from a distant battery overtook us again with all the force possible. All of a sudden we were lying on the ground on our stomachs with our eyes fixed to the place where we thought the grapeshot came from, but we could see nothing but darkness. That is how we passed the night. It was the night of the 27th of July.

On the 28th, at dawn, we were overtaken by the aeroplanes, which threw bombs very fast, but they did nothing to us. I do not deny, cousin, I was perishing of hunger and thirst. We went forward until we came to a forest very near the enemy, and had just gotten into position when the German artillery at one side, the grapeshot at another, and the areoplanes above, overtook us. Our company was almost destroyed, only a few were left. We ran as the command was given, taking holes for refuge. I ran and looked hard for a hole, and I said within me "Good-bye world." It had not been three minutes after I left the hole where I was protecting myself when a high explosive fell and tore it to pieces, making of said place a hole about 12 ft. long and 12 ft. wide, and at the time that it exploded the sand that was blown by the act fell over me, covering my entire body, only leaving my head a little uncovered. I began to move it a little, until desperate as I was from lack of breath I was able to uncover my eyes and nostrils. I began to breathe little by little until, at last, with heavy breaths, I was able to blow the sand and uncover my mouth. Then it was different. This is how I passed three hours of that night until one of my companions discovered me and helped me out. The enemy was retiring. We ran ahead to catch our company and joined them, and I began to work hard with my little rifle. I soon found a hole for myself big enough for two persons. I sat down and started to clean my rifle, when all of a sudden, just as a cat jumps upon a mouse, an American companion fell into my hole. We soon began to make a noise. He had a slice of bread and some water, so he gave me half of what he had and we started to converse and to laugh and chatter. He was the first American that I had seen laughing since I had been in battle. He showed me the picture of his mother, and also the picture of his sweetheart, and told me that if he died first for me to send his things to his folks and that if I died first he would do likewise. That is what he was saying when he thought he would like to make the hole larger and began to work with his little shovel, but on one of the times that he straightened up to rest he fell to the bottom of the hole with a horrible groan. This struck me with terror. I placed my arms around him and talked to him, asking him questions, but he would not answer. What he said was only this: "Take care of yourself, my dear friend." and he breathed his last and was gone. I said to myself "Goodnight", may God take him to Glory, and for the first time while in battle tears were running from my eyes, to see that as soon as I would get a good companion to laugh and chatter with he was taken from me.

I took my rifle and examined it and found it perfect. I saw ahead of me through a little hole, and through the weeds and dust. Bullets passed fast over my head to stop on the body of some one else, and God only knows who were the unfortunates. I soon discovered the head of a German who was working hard with his elbows to take possession of the hole I had. This unfortunate German thought that he had killed the only occupant of the hole, but seeing the muzzle of my rifle very near his head he threw down his rifle and lifting his hands cried with all his might "Kamerad!" I did not give him time to say more, but answered him with a bullet that passed through his head. At that time I heard the command to advance. I took my rifle, ran ahead, and found another very good hole. Just behind me an Indian came in, and he was as unfortunate as my unlucky American companion, but nothing happened to me, thanks to God. No sooner had he come in when a German killed him. This German also thought that he had killed the proprietor of the hole. He worked hard with his elbows until he was about five feet from my hole, when I saw him. He gave me time only to take my rifle and receive him with my bayonet. Because my magazine was empty I had to use my bayonet, which I ran into his breast making him fall dead at my feet. The command came again, and we advanced a little more. A high explosive fell near me and sent a piece of iron into the lower part of my foot, throwing me about five feet from the ground at the same time. That was enough to put me in bed for quite a long time. I was taken to the base hospital, No. 3, and here you have me now, full of life and happiness, hoping to see you soon.

Give my best regards to my auntie and to all my cousins, and you receive your cousin's sincere love. I remain.

PLACEDIO GARCIA.

PHOTOGRAPHY eventually is expected to reduce the cost of topographic surveys and lessen the time required for them. Alaska contains a greater proportion of mountains favorable for photo-topographic surveying than the United States proper. The panoramic camera is the instrument used. This camera has been highly developed for topographic mapping in Austria, France, and Germany; while large areas have been so mapped in Canada.

Minerals Separation and the Federal Trade Commission

The aggregate tonnage of ore milled and in part treated under upward of 100 licenses issued in the United States by the Minerals Separation North American Corporation runs in excess of 28,000,000 tons annually. That its licenses have tended to encourage the mining industry rather than stifle it through recovering from ores formerly dumped important values; and that the company uses no coercion in the use of its inventions are statements made by the Minerals Separation Co. in answering the recent charges of the Federal Trade Commission. General denials to the Commission's allegation of monopoly and unfair discrimination are made.

In citing the one-time business relations of the Minerals Separation companies with Beer, Sondheimer & Co., the former state that the firm "acted as agents for Minerals Separation American Syndicate, Ltd., between 1910 and 1913 and . . . for Minerals Separation American Syndicate (1913) Ltd. from September 1913 to on or about August 3, 1914, when at the outbreak of the European war, the agreement . . . was canceled and the agency terminated." The citation further disclaims knowledge as to whether Beer, Sondheimer & Co., Inc., a New York corporation, acts as agent or representative of the German firm of similar name.

Minerals Separation North American Corporation is now and for more than a year has been, the answer cites, engaged in issuing licenses for the treatment of certain ores and dumps in accordance "with inventions, patents, processes, and apparatus described and claimed in letters patent . . ." It denies, however, doing an interstate commerce or trade. It also denies competition, but "alleges on the contrary that said Minerals Separation North American Corporation is the sole beneficial owner of certain letters patent of the United States of America and of certain processes and inventions covered by such patents relating to the separation and concentration of ores and that its business is limited to the granting and administration of licenses . . . and to lawful enforcement of . . . rights . . . and that no one is lawfully entitled to engage in said business in competition with this respondent." Minerals Separation denies entering into or enforcing or attempting to enforce agreements for purpose of stifling and suppressing competition.

Minerals Separation alleges that "this commission is without any jurisdiction to pass upon the reasonableness of any royalty charged . . ." On two occasions were special terms granted, the respondent admits, one being the license granted to the Anaconda-Inspiration group and the other to the Colusa Parrot Milling Co. The former assured Minerals Separation a large sum of money regardless of what the Supreme Court decision in the Hyde case might be; the other because of "the quality of its dumps, the low recovery and the narrow margin of profit of which to said company made it equitable at the time . . ."

LEWISTOWN, MONTANA

Mining in Central Montana During 1918.

Mining in central Montana has not been as active in 1918 as usual. There was a shortage of labor resulting from the draft, high wages in other industries, and volunteers for the engineering corps. Litigation and disagreements between stockholders caused some mines and prospects to remain idle. The owners of other properties, especially those producing gold, await the return of normal conditions before commencing development work or re-opening their mines. Influenza seriously affected many mines during the last three months.

In the Little Rocky Mountains in Phillips county the Ruby Gulch company was the only operator. Its properties are at Whitcomb, a few miles from Zortman. About 200 men are employed and the output is $30,000 per month. The ore contains only $1 to $3 worth of gold per ton, but occurs in a wide lode of altered porphyry, and such cheap methods of mining are possible as to permit the company to make a good profit. The August mine at Landusky was closed in 1918, but some encouraging development work was done on prospects near-by. The mines near Zortman are about 50 miles from Dodson and 60 miles from Malta, the nearest railroad points.

The Barnes-King Development Co. operated its North Moccasin mine at Kendall, in Fergus county, regularly and its production will be nearly $200,000 in gold for the year. The production came from the old orebodies, from which $8 to $10 gold per ton was recovered by the cyanide process. Unless new ore-shoots are discovered the outlook for a long life for this property is not encouraging. The Barnes-King has produced about $4,000,000 from its Kendall properties. The gold occurs as a replacement of limestone and was probably derived from laccolithic intrusions, although no igneous rock is found in the mine itself. The orebody is in part composed of altered porphyry. The Kendall mine has been operated by lessees the last three years, and an output of several thousand dollars per month has been maintained. The ore comes entirely from an open-cut, which permits of cheap mining. The mine seems to be worked out in depth. Very little prospecting has been done in the North Moccasins during 1918.

Mining in the Judith mountains has been at a low ebb. During 1916 and 1917 the Maginness, Spotted Horse, and Cumberland mines at Maiden were all operated under lease and produced a large amount of gold, but this year the Spotted Horse was closed because of difficulty in renewing the lease, the lessees of the Cumberland joined the army, and the Maginness operated only a short time. It is expected that the return of normal conditions will cause the mines at Maiden to be operated as usual. Bardwell and Pittman of Lewistown are opening a copper prospect in Alpine gulch. Several men were prospecting near Giltedge, but no good orebodies were discovered. Development work was done on the Sutter copper claims on Armell's creek, but litigation prevented the sale of ore. S. P. Williams of Lewistown reports some good assays from his claims. E. B. Coolidge built a small cyanide mill at Giltedge to re-treat the tailing from an old mill.

Several mines were active at Neihart in the Little Belt mountains. A new mill was built and considerable ore was developed. The valuable metals are zinc and silver. The ore goes to Great Falls and East Helena for treatment. Butte and Eastern capital have invested in the Neihart mines. Very little production came from the lead-silver and copper mines of the northern and eastern parts of the Little Belts. The sapphire mines at Yogo have been closed most of the time since the War began, but it is planned to resume operations in 1919.

Prospecting was done in the Castle mountains in Meagher county for copper, lead, silver, and manganese, but the production will be small.

Oil and gas prospecting, the leasing of structurally favorable ground, and the formation of new companies characterized the oil industry in central Montana in 1918, but no important discoveries have been made. Drilling was done on an immense dome near Bowdoin in northern Montana. In Fergus county two companies are drilling in the Winifred field, a well was drilled near Piper, another north of Grass Range, and a fifth south of Winnett in Devil's Basin. Drilling was also in progress in Woman's Pocket in the Musselshell valley, and in Elk's Basin, west of Harlowton. Several hundred thousand acres of domes, anticlines, terraces, and faults have been leased in central Montana and several dozen companies are organized for business. Gas was found in commercial volume at Havre a few years ago, and has been found in small amounts elsewhere. No producing oil-well has yet been brought in. Prospecting and drilling will continue actively in 1919, although the poor crops in some sections make it difficult to raise funds for drilling.

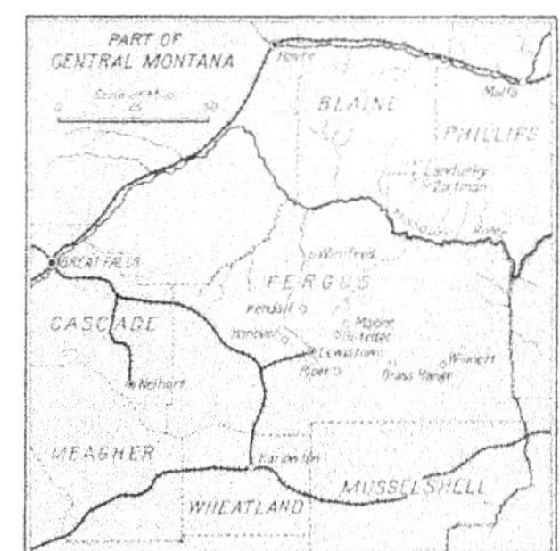

The Barnes-King properties at Kendall are among the chief gold producers of Montana. The Southern Cross mine at Georgetown, from which iron ore is mined, was the third largest producer during 1918.

CRIPPLE CREEK, COLORADO

Drainage-Tunnel Developments.—Production in 1918.

The Portland cross-cut from the Roosevelt drainage-tunnel was on December 14, seventy feet distant from its objective point under No. 2 shaft, and the shaft had been sunk to a depth of 2113 ft., or 20 ft. above the tunnel-level. The work is estimated to be completed and connection made by the end of the year.——The Cresson company's main shaft has been connected with the tunnel cross-cut at a depth of 1950 ft., and the station and shaft have been timbered. Production from the two orebodies under development at the tunnel-level, however, will be carried on through the Elkton shaft.

The Roosevelt tunnel may now be considered completed, as work has ceased with the heading in the centre of the Hawkeye claim of the Portland company. The total length of the tunnel from portal to breast is 24,355 ft., or 4.6 miles, and it is one of the longest in the United States. The Roosevelt tunnel has taken 11 years to drive and its cost has been $812,000. This sum includes sinking of an intermediate shaft 700 ft., and a raise of 160 ft. to connect with the Elkton main shaft, through which the tunnel is now operated. The average cost has been $33.30 per foot. The saving in pumping costs alone is conservatively estimated at $3,000,000. In 1918 two long drifts were driven from the tunnel, one of 1720 ft. to connect with the Cresson shaft; the other 2000 ft. connecting with the Portland No. 2 shaft, at a depth of 2133 ft. The flow from the tunnel has varied from 17,000 gal. per min. in 1906 to the present flow of 2500 gal. The district has been effectively drained, as not a mine is pumping.

The Lincoln Mines & Reduction Co. is making progress with construction of the concentrating plant on its Ironclad Hill holdings. The concrete retaining walls and foundations for machinery have been laid, and 200,000 ft. of lumber has been contracted for. The plant is to make use of the Gasche air-concentrating process. It should be ready for a trial within 90 days.

Christmas dividends will be passed this year by the regular dividend-paying companies, but while shareholders are overlooked employees will be remembered. The Cresson and Golden Cycle companies paid their regular monthly dividends on December 10, and on Christmas Day their employees were given bonds and thrift stamps. Those in service the longest will receive bonds and larger gifts. The Portland company, paying quarterly dividends, will give every miner in its service prior to October 1, a $5 bill, and those since that date $2.50. Other companies and lessees will also remember their employees in substantial form.

A reduction of from 1 to 2 cents in powder, according to grade, has been put in effect by dealers in explosives.

Frank Kurie, former superintendent for the Portland company, who has been absent for a long period in Government service, will resume operations after January 1. He has secured a lease option on blocks 215-216 of the Stratton estate on Bull hill. The ground covers the Shurtloff holding of the estate, and Kurie some years ago mined a good grade of ore from the Hawk shaft on the property. The blocks are directly over the Basket and Luce discovery at the 1500-ft. level of the American Eagle shaft, and Kurie is confident that with sinking he will open the vein nearer the surface.

The Golden Cycle company's protest against the increase in rates for electric light and power, put in effect by the Colorado Springs Light & Power Co., came up for hearing before the State Utilities Commission at Denver during the past week and has been taken under advisement.

The output of Cripple Creek during 1918 is over $2,000,000 below the 1917 total. The tonnage reported as treated by mills and smelters is 1,087,029, valued at $10,509,705 gross. The average value, due to large tonnage of dump ore treated, is low, $9.47 per ton.

Five companies paid dividends totaling $2,380,000—Cresson, $1,464,000; Golden Cycle, $540,000; Portland, $300,000; Vindicator, $60,000; and Granite, $16,500. The distribution of close corporations and the division of profits by lessees and leasing companies is conservatively estimated to add $250,000.

Properties of 65 companies, including dumps, were in operation during 1918. Many discoveries were made at and near the surface and at a great depths. The more important were those made in the Cresson, Rose Nicol, and Portland mines, at depths of 1950 ft. in the Cresson to 2133 ft. in the Portland. These discoveries were made on the Roosevelt tunnel-level.

ELY, NEVADA

Silver, Tungsten, Manganese, and Copper Notes.

There is considerable activity at the old camp of Cherry Creek, 50 miles north of Ely. J. W. Walker took hold of the Mary Ann property, a mile west of town, last February, with practically no capital. His first three cars of ore assayed 25 oz. of silver per ton, putting him on his feet; he has been shipping continuously since. Recently he sold to prominent New York people, who are providing a capital of $100,000 for development. They have purchased a small ranch in the canyon, which has some water, for milling purposes. The Black Metals mine, 5 miles north of Cherry Creek, from which Fletcher and son-in-law have shipped 13 cars during the past six months, has been taken over by Walker, and will be developed; also the Mother Lode, a large contact vein, adjoining. Walker also has an option on the old Exchequer silver mine adjoining the Star mine, which is being examined for New York interests. They will also examine the old Egan mines in Egan canyon, 5 miles south of Cherry Creek.

The Delker copper mines, 25 miles west of Currie and 70 miles north of Ely, is also under option and examination. Two years ago Ames shipped a dozen or more carloads of 7% copper ore from this property. The vein faulted and was lost.

Salt Lake City people are developing the Lucky Deposit copper mine, at Aurum, 30 miles east of Cherry Creek on the Spring Valley side of the range. Many shipments were made from this until climatic conditions interfered. East of this 25 miles, O. E. Roodhouse, who was superintendent for the U. S. Tungsten Co., 12 miles south of Osceola, two years ago, and shipped a quantity of concentrate, is developing the Shepherd tungsten mine.

W. Stewart and Millick brothers' tungsten property, 25 miles south of Osceola, which has been under development by Los Angeles people during the past year, recently have completed a 100-ton mill. The price of tungsten is the question that is worrying the management.

A. B. Witcher is finishing his contract on his manganese shipments from the property 9 miles south of Ely. This has been a profitable mine, having shipped 2500 tons of 42% ore. Holmquist & Bowen, adjoining, shut-down some time ago. Both of these mines have large bodies of good-grade ore. Witcher has over 1000 tons blocked out. The future is problematical.

It is reported by officials of the Consolidated Coppermines Co. that they will close their Pilot Knob mill within the next 60 days, operations not being profitable. The grade of ore from the Morris shaft is reported at present to be less than 1% copper. The Alpha workings, at the Giroux shaft, on the 1200-ft. level are in good ore, carload shipments carrying 7 to 14% copper. There are large bodies of 5% ore. Development is proceeding on the 1300-ft. level, which shows high-grade ore.

A review of mining in the Western States, prepared by the U. S. Geological Survey, appears on the last three pages of this issue.

ARIZONA

Bisbee.—Shattuck-Arizona pays 50c. per share, equal to $175,000, on January 20.

Humboldt.—Consolidated Arizona Smelting Co. reports as follows for nine months of 1918, and corresponding data for the same period of 1917 and 1916:

	1918	1917	1916
Ore mined, tons	137,342	107,077	80,420
Concentrator treated ore and tailing, tons	82,270	76,713	60,054
Smelter treated:			
Company ore and concentrate, tons	79,412	59,900	38,456
Custom ore and concentrate, tons	41,262	42,537	33,370
Total smelted, tons	120,674	102,437	71,826
Copper produced, pounds	15,500,000	13,930,000	7,101,000
Silver produced, ounces	349,237	175,530	97,116
Gold produced, ounces	11,067	6,815	4,355
Profit from operations	$705,087	$685,779	$566,724
Average price of copper, cents	24.002	28.474	26,400

The company produced 1,030,000 lb. of copper during November. There has been a decrease since March, when the output was 2,270,000 pounds.

Kingman.—Discovery of wulfenite has been made by R. O. Pierson, 20 miles east of Kingman. The ore carries considerable silver.

The Yucca Tungsten Co. has recently put in two K & K flotation machines, enabling the company to clean-up a large tonnage of copper-tungsten ore on dumps. It is said that a carload each of copper and tungsten concentrates can be shipped monthly.

The mill that was constructed by contract for the Standard Minerals Co. has been completed and turned over to the company. This plant will treat 50 tons of molybdenum ore daily.

Metcalf.—The store management of the Shannon Copper Co. has advertised its intention of closing, and from this rumors are current that the company will shut-down early in 1919.

Miami.—Inspiration Consolidated pays $2 per share, equal to $2,363,934, on January 27.

Oatman.—In the 'Press' of December 14 it was stated that ore from the Carter mine was being treated in the United Eastern mill. This was incorrect, the mill having been worked continuously at capacity on United Eastern ore since the plant started on January 4, 1917.

Patagonia.—It is rumored that the Magma Copper Co. is completing arrangements for purchase of the Three R mine.

Prescott.—The old Zonia copper mine, 10 miles from Kirkland in the Placeritas district, is again active after being idle over 25 years. Nine men are employed in development at present.

San Simon.—The Hilltop company, in the Chiricahua mountains, has found ore 1900 ft. in the lower level tunnel, which is being driven 300 ft. below the upper workings.

Superior.—It is reported that the Fortuna Consolidated Mining Co. has made a final payment of $18,000 on its holdings.

Silver Bell. The Stump mine, so-called because the copper-silver ore outcrop was uncovered when a Mexican dislodged a stump when gathering fuel, has been sold by G. H Daily to C. H. Behr of New York for $75,000. A wide vein is said to be exposed to a depth of 75 feet.

CALIFORNIA

Grass Valley.—There are about 1150 men employed in this district. The operating mines are the Allison Ranch, Empire, Golden Center, North Star, Sultana, and Union Hill By next summer 350 additional men could be employed.

Placerville.—Charles Wachter and Fred Husler are operating a chrome lease on Webber creek, seven miles due west of Placerville. On their leased property they have driven a tunnel more than 100 ft. and sunk a vertical shaft 50 ft., and have opened a large body of high-grade chromite About mid-December they shipped a 60-ton car of 43% ore The property is developed so that regular carload shipments can be made for many months. The deposit is a vast kidney-shaped lens within the wide serpentine dike that trends across El Dorado county on a course west of north. The ore is hauled by auto-truck six miles south and shipped from the Shingle railroad station.

Some rich gravel has been opened in the Rising Hope deep-gravel mine, three miles east of Placerville. The channel has been cross-cut for 115 ft., without finding the opposite side of the 'rim'. The thickness is 15 ft. A barrel-gravel mill is recovering $10 per ton. G. W. Engelhardt is manager, C. M. Henson mine superintendent, and G. O Perry millman.

COLORADO

Georgetown.—The Colorado Central mill is treating 500 tons of ore daily. A steam-shovel is working on the dump.

Lessees at the Capital, Onondaga, Santiago, and Jo Reynolds mines are working on good ore.

IDAHO

Wallace.—The Consolidated Interstate-Callahan company's mill is now concentrating 500 tons of ore daily. C. W. Newton is general manager.

Dividends paid by Coeur d'Alene companies during 1918 were about $3,200,000 less than in 1917, according to the 'Miner'.

MONTANA

Elkhorn.—The Boston & Montana Development Co., through Boston brokers, is offering $400,000 first-mortgage 6% gold coupon bonds of the Montana Southern Railway Co. This line is 39 miles long, between Divide and the Elkhorn mines of the B. & M. company. About 95% of the grading is finished. Rails and rolling-stock have been purchased, and rail laying is in progress. Up to December 1, 1918, there has been spent $478,000, but the total cost will be $700,000. To a depth of 1000 ft. in the mines, the report says, from 600,000 to 800,000 tons of $20 copper-silver-gold-lead ore has been developed. The output is to be 500 tons daily for a start, to be increased to 2000 tons within 18 months.

NEVADA

Ely.—Consolidated Coppermines Co. produced 1,278,116

lb. of copper during November. This is up to the average for the previous months.

Goldfield.—In Tule canyon, 35 miles south of here, lessees are to sink the Ingalls shaft from 300 to 400 ft. Some good ore has been opened, and the dump is expected to supply the 20-ton mill for a year. This plant consists of a crusher, Huntington mill, Wilfley tables, amalgamating-plates, and gas-engine. A. Borcherding, P. J. McDermitt, and F. Hill are the operators.

Tonopah.—Production of the district last week totaled 7381 tons of ore, valued at $125,477. For the year 1918 the yield is estimated at $9,000,000, the product of 500,000 tons. The total to date is $118,000,000. Dividends last year amounted to $1,371,140, paid by the West End, Belmont, Tonopah Mining, Jim Butler, and Extension, ranking in the order given, according to 'The Tonopah Miner'.

In the Divide district, the Tonopah Divide company has opened 6 to 12 ft. of $150 ore. Shares immediately responded, rising to over $2.

NEW JERSEY

Franklin Furnace.—The New Jersey Zinc Co. pays $4 per share, equal to $1,400,000, on February 10.

OREGON

Portland.—The hills of the Coast Range in Clatsop and Tillamook counties contain some valuable mineral ores, according to H. Gilmore Price, who has just finished a mineralogical survey of that region. Two years has been spent in an exhaustive unofficial survey, the report of which will be forwarded soon to the Secretary of the Interior. A large number of samples of gold, silver, lead, and quicksilver ore are to be sent East for analysis.

UTAH

Dividends paid by Utah mining companies during 1918 were as follows, as tabulated by the 'Deseret Evening News' of Salt Lake City:

Company	Per share, 1918	Total in 1918	Grand total
Bingham Mines	$2.00	$288,000	$536,250
Cardiff	0.20	100,000	725,000
Chief Consolidated	4.45	397,900	1,234,871
Daly Mining	0.50	75,000	3,060,000
Dragon Consolidated	0.04	75,000	150,000
Eagle & Blue Bell	0.30	270,000	1,161,089
Grand Central	0.12	72,000	1,808,750
Horn Silver	0.05	17,400	5,729,400
Iron Blossom	0.07½	75,000	3,175,000
Judge M. & S.	0.50	240,000	2,310,000
Ontario-Silver	1.50	225,000	15,187,500
Pacific	0.01	4,000	12,000
Silver King Consolidated	0.10	70,000	1,559,000
Tintic Standard	0.27	317,230	400,480
Utah Apex	0.50	265,000	1,188,000
Utah Consolidated	1.50	450,000	13,417,000
Utah Copper	10.00	16,245,000	91,861,000
Western Utah Copper	0.07½	37,000	37,000
Total		$19,221,530	$143,550,340

Gold Hill.—The Western Utah Copper Co., in the Deep Creek district, has its new 50-ton mill ready to start early in 1919. The plant is at Salt Springs, 18 miles from Wendover. Duncan MacVichie is manager.

Moab.—The Big Indian Copper Co.'s mine and mill have been leased to the Metallurgic Improvement Association for three years. J. E. Barlow of Havana, Cuba, is head of the latter concern, which states that it has devised a process for extracting copper from carbonate ore.

Park City.—The Silver King Coalition company has lost its appeal to the Circuit Court of Appeals, in which judgment of the District Court was in favor of the Conkling Mining Co. The Conkling company was joint-owner of some property adjoining the Silver King Coalition, and alleged that the latter extracted ore worth $500,000 from the jointly-owned property without the knowledge of the Conkling. The judgment rendered was for $542,000, which, with accrued interest, would be about $600,000. The ground in question was worked through the Coalition company's shaft. The defense is to take the case to the U. S. Supreme Court.

Salt Lake City.—In the tax suit in this State between the Utah Copper Co. and 19 others against the State Treasurer, protesting against the collection of the occupation mine tax and seeking an injunction restraining the Treasurer from selling the properties for the alleged delinquent taxes, it was decided to submit the case on its merits to Judge Johnson on January 6.

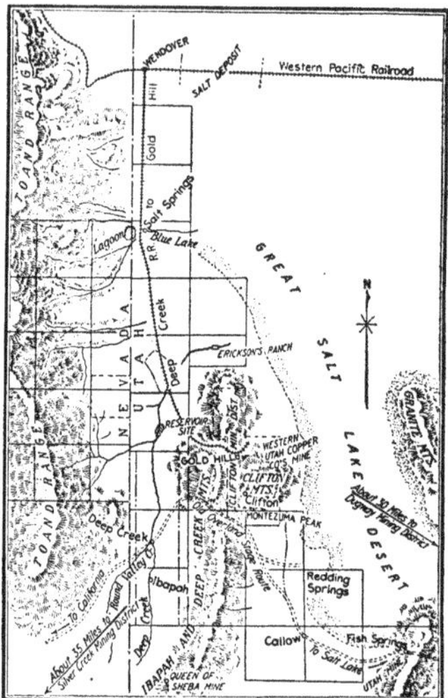

SKETCH OF THE DEEP CREEK DISTRICT, UTAH

Later advice states that the State Treasurer has answered the complaint of the mining companies, and asks that the proceedings be dismissed, on the ground that the sums involved in the aggregate do not exceed $3000, therefore the matter is not within the jurisdiction of the United States Court. He also asks that he be allowed to collect the taxes.

WASHINGTON

Chewelah.—The United Copper Mining Co. proposes to increase its capital, deepen and extend its workings, and double the capacity of its mills. A plan of expansion will be laid before the directors by Raymond Guyer, consulting engineer. Ore above 1000 ft. is not so good as that at 1200 ft., so mining will be concentrated at depth. Recent diamond-drilling from the 1000-ft. level has been disappointing. The two mills, of 225 tons capacity each, are a quarter-mile apart.

Colville.—The Tulare Mining Co. of California is now shipping 700 tons of calcined dolomite per month. Two kilns are in blast. The product is consumed by the Crown-Willamette paper mills in this State and in Oregon.

Republic.—The Quilp Gold Mining Co. is reported to have resumed work after being stopped for several years. To a depth of 600 ft. about 6000 ft. of development was done. The output was $492,843 from 39,653 tons of ore. Unwatering is in progress, while ore is being extracted from the upper levels. W. G. C. Lanskail is in charge.

The Lone Pine-Surprise company is to sink its Last Chance shaft from 550 to 700 ft. Ore shipments will be started again early in February, according to C. P. Robbins, the manager.

The Knob Hill company shipped five cars of ore to smelters during December.

CANADA

British Columbia

Britannia.—The Howe Sound Co. pays 5c. per share on January 15. This amounts to $99,207.

The Bowena Copper Co., whose property is situated on Howe sound, is constructing a concentrating plant with a daily capacity of 100 tons. It is being erected by T. A. Walsh & Co., Ltd., of Vancouver.

Slocan.—The Rambler-Cariboo Mines Co. made a net profit of $20,000 during 1918, according to estimates of its president, A. F. McClaine. Gross returns were $80,000. No dividends were declared in 1918, but the profits have increased the surplus of the company to approximately $50,000.

AMERICAN MINING CONGRESS

The following is a tentative program for organization meeting of the California Chapter, American Mining Congress, January 15 and 16, Palace hotel, San Francisco:

January 15

10:00 a.m.: Address by J. F. Callbreath, Secretary American Mining Congress, Washington, D. C. Subject: Aims, History, and Future of the American Mining Congress.

11:00 a.m.: Address by a Senator or Representative to be selected later. Subject: Relation of American Mining Congress to National Legislation.

12:00 m: Luncheon. Address by James K. Lynch, Governor Federal Reserve Bank. Subject: Relation of Mining to the Banking and Financial Interests of the Country.

2:00 p.m.: Organization meeting.

3:30 p.m.: Address by Thomas Thorkildsen, of Los Angeles. Subject: Non-Metallic Mining Industry of California.

7:00 p.m.: Dinner. Address by Bulkeley Wells. Subject: the American Mining Congress from the standpoint of an operator. Address by H. Foster Bain, Assistant to the Director of the U. S. Bureau of Mines. Subject: The American Mining Congress and the Bureau of Mines. Address by T. A. Rickard, Editor 'Mining and Scientific Press'. Subject: The Effect of Publicity upon Mining.

January 16

10:00 a.m.: Address by Honorable Emmett Boyle, Governor of Nevada. Subject: The American Mining Congress as I saw it in Washington.

10:45 a.m.: Address by David M. Folsom, Ex-Federal Oil Director for Pacific Coast. Subject: Valuation of Oil Lands for Purpose of Federal Taxation.

11:30 a.m.: Business meetings.

12:00 m.: Luncheon. Address by Judge John F. Davis. Subject: The Necessity for a Secretary of Mines as a Member of the Cabinet. Address by Frank B. Anderson, President of Bank of California. Subject: The Attitude of Bankers Toward Mining Investments.

2:00 p.m.: Business meeting.

PERSONAL

Note. The Editor invites members of the profession to send particulars of their work and appointments. The information is interesting to our readers.

E. M. Rabb is at Tonopah.

Jackson A. Pearre has gone to Dayton, Nevada.

Walter Broadbridge is on his way back to London from San Francisco.

Pomeroy & Hamilton have moved from San Francisco to Tulsa, Oklahoma.

C. F. Sherwood, of Salt Lake City, was here this week on his way to Dayton, Nevada.

William S. Evans is now in the engineering department of the Tennessee Copper Co., at Copperhill, Tennessee.

Ott F. Heizer has resigned as superintendent of the Sheep Ranch mine, in Calaveras county, California, and will re-open the Dead Horse mine at Tuolumne, California.

W. D. B. Motter, Jr., has resigned as manager for the Benson Mines Co. to join the staff, as assistant consulting mining engineer, of Guggenheim Brothers, with headquarters at 120 Broadway, New York.

K. B. Thomas has resigned as superintendent of the sulphuric acid department of the Calumet & Arizona Mining Co. to become general superintendent for the Standard Chemical & Oil Co., at Troy, Alabama.

M. H. McLean, for years general manager of the Detroit copper mines of the Phelps Dodge Corporation, has resigned and will make his home in California. He will be succeeded by J. P. **Hodgson**, who has been with the Copper Queen at Bisbee.

John C. Greenway, who went from Arizona to France as a Major, has been promoted a second time and is now Colonel. He has been awarded the Croix de Guerre for valor in action. Just before the armistice he was gassed and from the effects of it he is slowly recovering. He has done just as his friends confidently expected.

Obituary

Rossiter W. Raymond died on December 31 at his home in Brooklyn, New York, at the age of 78. He was born at Cincinnati in 1840 and after graduating from the Brooklyn Polytechnic Institute he went to Germany, where he was a student successively at Munich, Heidelberg, and Freiberg. He served for three years in the Civil War and attained the rank of captain. Afterward he opened an office as consulting engineer in New York. From 1868 to 1876 he was U. S. Commissioner of Mining Statistics, publishing annual reports that contained technical information of great value to the young mining industry of this country. For 12 years, 1870-1882, he was lecturer on economic geology at Lafayette College. In 1867 he began his career as an editor by conducting the 'American Journal of Mining', which was the forerunner of the 'Engineering & Mining Journal', with which he was connected as editor for several years and as special contributor for the rest of his life. One of the organizers of the American Institute of Mining Engineers, he served as secretary from 1884 to 1911, after having been president in 1872, 1873, and 1874. In 1911 he retired, becoming secretary emeritus. He published a large number of books and pamphlets on a variety of subjects, including poems, children's stories, biblical tales, glossaries, and obituaries, all marked by an incisive style and a broad human interest. We publish an editorial appreciation on another page.

THE METAL MARKET

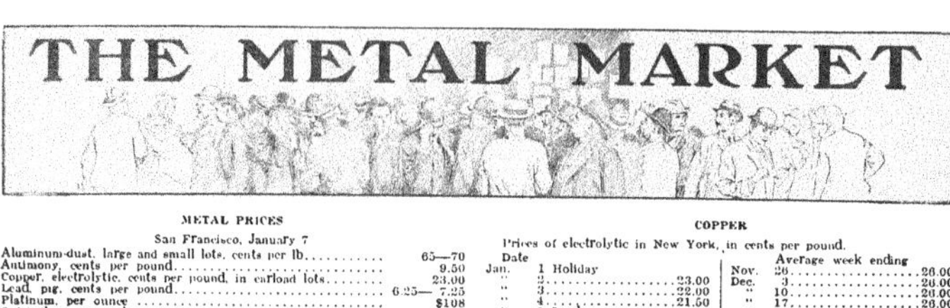

METAL PRICES

San Francisco, January 7

Aluminum-dust, large and small lots, cents per lb.	65—70
Antimony, cents per pound	9.50
Copper, electrolytic, cents per pound, in carload lots	23.00
Lead, pig, cents per pound	6.25— 7.25
Platinum, per ounce	$108
Quicksilver, per flask of 75 lb.	$110
Spelter, cents per pound	9.50
Zinc-dust, cents per pound	16.00

ORE PRICES

January 7

Chrome, no definite quotations available.	
Fluorspar, 85% CaF_2, f.o.b. shipping point, or San Francisco, per ton	$22—$30
Manganese, domestic, 35 to 54%, f.o.b. South Chicago, per unit (Government price, effective May 29)	$0.86—$1.30
Manganese, domestic, 35 to 45%, f.o.b. east of South Chicago, per unit (Government price, effective May 29)	$1.01—$1.45
(Manganese, domestic, penalty of 50c. to $1 per ton for 8% and up to 25% silica, and bonus of 50c. to $1 for less than 8 and 5%.)	
Molybdenite, per lb., 90% MoS_2	$0.75—$1.00
Pyrite, per unit of sulphur, cents	28—32
Tungsten, 60% WO_3, per unit	$17—$23

EASTERN METAL MARKET

(By wire from New York)

January 7.—Copper is inactive and lower. Lead is dull and easy. Spelter is stagnant and prices are nominal.

SILVER

Below are given official (not Government) quotations, in cents per ounce, of silver 999 fine. In order to make prompt settlements with smelters and brokers, producers allow a discount from the maximum fixed price of $1.01½, hence the lower price. The Government has not fixed the general market price at $1, but will pay this price (as from April 23, 1918) for all silver purchased by it. The equivalent of dollar silver (1000 fine) in British currency is 46.65 pence per ounce (925 fine), calculated at the current rate of exchange. On August 15, 1918, the Treasury announced that the maximum price was fixed at $1.01½ per ounce. The British government fixed its maximum at 49½ pence, on September 2, but on November 12 this was changed to 48¾ pence, due to a drop in price.

Date		New York	London		Average week ending	
Jan.	1 Holiday			Nov.	26	101.12
"	2	101.12	48.75	Dec.	3	101.12
"	3	101.12	48.75	"	10	101.12
"	4	101.12	48.75	"	17	101.12
"	5 Sunday			"	24	101.12
"	6	101.12	48.75	"	31	101.12
	7	101.12	48.75	Jan.	7	101.12

Monthly averages

	1916	1917	1918		1916	1917	1918
Jan.	56.76	75.14	88.72	July	63.06	78.92	99.62
Feb.	56.74	77.54	85.79	Aug.	66.07	85.40	100.31
Mch.	57.80	74.13	88.11	Sept.	68.51	100.73	101.12
Apr.	64.37	72.51	95.35	Oct.	67.86	87.38	101.12
May	74.27	74.61	99.50	Nov.	71.60	85.97	101.12
June	65.04	76.44	99.50	Dec.	75.70	85.97	101.12

QUICKSILVER

The primary market for quicksilver is San Francisco, California being the largest producer. The price is fixed in the open market, according to quantity. Prices, in dollars per flask of 75 pounds:

Date					
Dec.	10	120.00	Dec.	24	110.00
	17	110.00	"	31	110.00
			Jan.	7	110.00

Monthly averages

	1916	1917	1918		1916	1917	1918
Jan.	222.00	81.00	128.06	July	81.20	102.00	120.00
Feb.	295.00	126.25	118.00	Aug.	74.50	115.00	120.00
Mch.	219.00	113.75	112.00	Sept.	75.00	112.00	120.00
Apr.	141.60	114.50	115.00	Oct.	78.20	102.00	120.00
May	90.00	104.00	110.00	Nov.	79.50	102.50	120.00
June	74.70	85.50	112.00	Dec.	80.00	117.42	115.00

TIN

Prices in New York, in cents per pound. The monthly averages in 1918 are nominal. On December 3 the War Industries Board fixed the price to consumers and jobbers at 72½c. f.o.b. Chicago and Eastern points, and 71½c. on the Pacific Coast. This will continue for some months.

Monthly averages

	1916	1917	1918		1916	1917	1918
Jan.	41.76	44.10	85.13	July	38.37	62.60	93.00
Feb.	42.60	51.47	85.00	Aug.	38.88	62.53	91.33
Mch.	50.50	54.27	85.00	Sept.	36.66	61.54	80.40
Apr.	51.49	55.63	88.53	Oct.	41.10	62.24	78.82
May	49.10	63.21	100.01	Nov.	44.12	74.18	73.67
June	42.07	61.03	91.00	Dec.	42.55	85.00	71.52

The War Trade Board announces that the restrictions hitherto existing on the exportation of tin and tin-plate have been removed, as the necessity for strict conservation of tin and its products no longer exists. If, therefore, applicants will re-file applications for which licenses have been hitherto refused, these will be given immediate consideration.

COPPER

Prices of electrolytic in New York, in cents per pound.

Date				Average week ending	
Jan.	1 Holiday		Nov.	26	26.00
"	2	23.00	Dec.	3	26.00
"	3	22.00	"	10	26.00
"	4	21.50	"	17	26.00
"	5 Sunday		"	24	26.00
"	6	21.50	"	31	26.00
"	7	21.00	Jan.	7	21.80

Monthly averages

	1916	1917	1918		1916	1917	1918
Jan.	24.30	29.53	23.50	July	25.66	29.67	26.00
Feb.	26.62	34.57	23.50	Aug.	27.03	27.42	26.00
Mch.	26.65	36.00	23.50	Sept.	28.28	25.11	26.00
Apr.	28.02	33.16	23.50	Oct.	28.50	23.50	26.00
May	29.02	31.69	23.50	Nov.	31.95	23.50	26.00
June	27.47	32.57	23.50	Dec.	32.89	23.50	26.00

Domestic copper production in 1918 totaled 1,910,000,000 lb., a gain of 24,000,000 lb. over that of 1917. Metal from all sources amounted to 2,450,000,000 lb., an increase of 88,000,000 pounds.

Standard copper, three months, has been sold in London at £88 per ton, equivalent to 18⅝ cents per pound.

The War Trade Board announces that the regulations governing the importation of copper ore and copper concentrates, announced October 4, 1918, have been modified, and that henceforth they will consider applications for license to import copper ore and copper concentrates. There is no restriction upon the importation of copper matte or blister copper.

LEAD

Lead is quoted in cents per pound, New York delivery.

Date				Average week ending	
Jan.	1 Holiday		Nov.	26	8.05
"	2	6.00	Dec.	3	7.85
"	3	5.75	"	10	7.05
"	4	5.75	"	17	7.05
"	5 Sunday		"	24	6.45
"	6	5.75	"	31	6.10
"	7	5.75	Jan.	7	5.80

Monthly averages

	1916	1917	1918		1916	1917	1918
Jan.	5.95	7.64	6.85	July	6.40	10.93	8.03
Feb.	6.23	9.10	7.07	Aug.	6.28	10.75	8.05
Mch.	7.26	10.07	7.26	Sept.	6.86	9.07	8.05
Apr.	7.70	9.38	6.99	Oct.	7.02	6.97	8.05
May	7.38	10.29	6.88	Nov.	7.07	6.38	8.05
June	6.88	11.74	7.58	Dec.	7.55	6.49	6.90

Lead production of the United States last year was 563,000 tons, against 651,156 tons in 1917.

ZINC

Zinc is quoted as spelter, standard Western brands, New York delivery, in cents per pound.

Date				Average week ending	
Jan.	1 Holiday		Nov.	26	8.61
"	2	7.95	Dec.	3	8.67
"	3	7.95	"	10	8.61
"	4	7.95	"	17	8.58
"	5 Sunday		"	24	8.45
"	6	7.90	"	31	8.13
"	7	7.90	Jan.	7	7.93

Monthly averages

	1916	1917	1918		1916	1917	1918
Jan.	18.21	9.75	7.87	July	9.90	8.98	8.72
Feb.	19.99	10.45	7.97	Aug.	9.03	8.58	8.87
Mch.	18.40	10.78	7.67	Sept.	9.18	8.33	9.58
Apr.	18.62	10.20	7.04	Oct.	9.92	8.32	9.11
May	16.01	9.41	7.29	Nov.	11.81	7.76	8.75
June	12.85	9.63	7.02	Dec.	11.26	7.84	8.49

Domestic spelter production in 1918 was 502,300 tons, a decrease of 82,297 tons when compared with 1917. The apparent consumption was 440,000 tons, an increase of 26,000 tons. Stocks at the end of the year amounted to 30,000 tons. There were 123,033 retorts in blast at the end of November.

COPPER PRODUCTION IN 1918

The U. S. Geological Survey gives the following estimates:

Arizona produced about 777,000,000 lb., compared with 712,000,000 lb. in 1917.

The mines of Montana produced 328,000,000 lb., against 274,000,000 lb. in 1917.

Michigan produced 225,000,000 lb., compared with 268,000,000 lb. produced in 1917.

Utah produced 233,000,000 lb., compared with 245,000,000 lb. in 1917.

Nevada produced 105,000,000 lb., compared with 122,000,000 lb. produced in 1917.

Alaska, with a production of about 60,000,000 lb. showed a large decrease from the previous year.

New Mexico produced 98,000,000 lb., compared with 105,000,000 lb. in 1917.

The production of California was considerably above the 48,000,000 lb. produced in 1917.

The production in Tennessee was about 14,500,000 pounds.

Eastern Metal Market

New York, December 31.

The new year opens with all the metal markets unrestricted, except tin and aluminum. Interest in the major metals is becoming keen, and future developments are expected to present many interesting market phases.

The Copper Export Association has set a price of 23c. per lb. for export sales of Lake and electrolytic, and producers are offering the domestic trade at the same level. No sales or demand are heard of.

The tin market continues dull, with offerings of Straits metal at 71.50c., or 1c. under the fixed price.

Lead has again been reduced, but buyers still refrain from the market.

Zinc continues to weaken gradually with demand light.

Antimony is slightly lower.

ALUMINUM

The Government maximum prices are to prevail until March 1, 1919, according to a ruling of the War Industries Board. For virgin metal or for scrap there are 35c. per lb. for 50-ton lots, 33.10c. per lb. for 15 to 50-ton lots, and 33.20 per lb. for 1 to 15-ton lots.

ANTIMONY

Demand is reported as light and quotations have fallen slightly to 7.62½c., New York, duty paid.

COPPER

The interesting development of the last week of the year is the announcement by the Copper Export Association, the new organization to control and promote copper exports, of a 23c. price on Lake and electrolytic copper, or 3c. under the Government maximum price which has been in effect since August 2. No business is reported to have been booked at the new level. The producers are also offering both Lake and electrolytic at 23c. to domestic buyers, with no transactions reported. The market is extremely dull with demand almost entirely absent. Re-sale electrolytic is reported as being offered as low as 22c. in small quantities. We quote the market for both Lake and electrolytic at 23c. nominal for early delivery. It remains to be seen whether the new price will attract either foreign or domestic buyers, or whether, as in the case of lead, still further reductions will be necessary. The estimated domestic output for 1918, reported by the U. S. Geological Survey, is 1,910,000,000 lb., against 1,886,000,000 lb. in 1917. Copper imports are believed to have made a record in 1918 at 566,720,000 lb., against 556,000,000 lb. in 1917. Exports did not make a record in 1918, according to estimates, having been 694,000,000 lb., which is less than the 1917, 1916, and 1914 output, but larger than that of 1915.

It is reported that an organization is being formed by brass manufacturers to control the export trade in their business, similar to that of the Copper Association.

IRON AND STEEL

First evidences of slackening activity characterizes the steel trade as the new year opens. There have been shut-downs for repairs, and the prospects are that a further slowing-down may appear. Buying for emergency is plainly not equal to the replacement of what has been lost, though it has been more than was expected by some. Prediction as to rollings for the first quarter range from 75% to somewhat less. Pig-iron producers are trying to hold to the old prices, but there is some indication that $3 will be conceded on new business, with the prospect that some furnaces will have to shut-down. The annual statistics of 'The Iron Age' show that 44 new open-hearth furnaces were completed and put in operation in 1918 with an annual capacity of 1,945,000 tons, against 4,326,000 tons per year for that added in 1917. New steel capacity projected for 1919, as now under construction, represents only 1,130,000 tons per year. Eight blast-furnaces were completed in 1918, with seven building at present.

LEAD

Lead has experienced another drop. On December 27 the American Smelting & Refining Co. reduced its price for the third time to 6c., New York, or 5.70c., St. Louis, a reduction of ¼c. per lb. This was in order to meet the outside market, which had fallen on the 26th to 6c. Re-sale metal is also being offered at these levels. Uncertainty prevails as to whether the bottom has been reached. Some expect no further reduction, with a steady market from now on. Others think it may fall to 5.50c., New York, or until the law of supply and demand is in operation. Dealers are apparently well supplied and consumers heavily stocked.

TIN

Dulness continues to pervade the market, and market developments have been insignificant. The chief of the tin section of the War Industries Board last week asked the secretary of the Tin Importers' Association how much of the tin, allocated to the United States Steel Products Co. and now said to be 10,000 tons, the Association would be willing to take over at cost (72.50c. per lb.) in lieu of an open market. The directors of the Association replied that they were unwilling to consider such a proposition, which would mean a loss to them. It is believed that the orders coming into the U. S. Steel Products Co. for tin are few. Straits tin has been offered in the last week often at 71.50c., New York, which we quote as the market, but buyers have been uninterested. American tin continues to be offered at a concession from the fixed price. All these facts points to a long period of control unless there is some unlooked for and unusual change in the situation. This control will probably be assumed by the War Trade Board after January 1, as the War Industries Board goes out of existence on that date. Arrivals of tin to date for the month total 2530 tons, of which 2450 tons came through Pacific ports.

ZINC

The market has continued to decline, largely because of lack of demand. Inquiry is reported as very light. While large producers do not seem to be pressing the sale of their product, offerings by others have caused quotations to decline, at least nominally, until today prime Western for early or January delivery is held at 7.60c., St. Louis, or 7.95c., New York, with prompt delivery rather scarce and quoted at 7.90c., St. Louis, or 8.25c., New York. The statistical position of the metal is not favorable, according to the weekly reports of the Government as to stocks and output.

ORES

Manganese Alloys: The market continues devoid of activity with prices problematical. Some re-sale ferro is appearing, but no quotation is put on it. It is stated that producers will quote on inquiries $225 per ton, delivered, for 70% alloy, or $3 per unit, making 80% alloy about $240 per ton.

Tungsten: There have been no developments in this market. Prices are really unknown, and there are no quotations obtainable. It is understood that the committee of the trade has ended its labors, its efforts at Washington to obtain relief having been unavailing.

Western States Metal Production in 1918

The following preliminary reports are from the U. S. Geological Survey:

ALASKA

The mines of Alaska yielded in 1918 products worth $28,900,000, according to G. C. Martin. Although Alaskan mining was so adversely affected by shortage of labor and shipping and by the high cost of supplies, that though the value of the output fell nearly $12,000,000 from 1917 the production was still far greater than in any year before 1915. Alaska's chief mineral product is copper, of which 69,426,000 lb., valued at $17,180,000, was mined in 1918. The gold output, worth $10,000,000, of which placers yielded $6,100,000, was $4,650,000 less than in 1917, and was the smallest since 1904. The mining of 77,000 tons of coal, worth $435,000, is significant as the only marked advance over the production of 1917, as by far the largest coal output in Alaskan mining, and as the probable beginning of a substantial coal industry. Alaska also produced silver worth $870,000; tin, $90,000; lead, $85,000; chromite, tungsten, palladium, platinum, and antimony aggregating $117,000; and petroleum, marble, gypsum, lime, and bricks aggregating $120,000.

ARIZONA

The output of gold, silver, copper, lead, and zinc from Arizonan mines in 1918, according to the estimate of Victor C. Heikes, had a total value of $205,500,000, an increase of $3,800,000. There were decided increases in both the copper and the gold of Arizona during the year. The silver output was close to the production of 1917, but the lead was only half as much, and the zinc fell to a small production.

The production of gold gained from $5,068,193 in 1917 to $5,551,000 in 1918.

The mine output of silver decreased slightly, from 6,983,913 oz. in 1917 to 6,787,000 oz. in 1918.

The output of copper increased from 712,166,891 lb. to nearly 777,000,000 lb., but the value decreased from $194,421,561 in 1917 to a little over $192,000,000 in 1918, as the average price of copper decreased from 27.3 to 24.75 cents per pound.

Production of lead decreased from 23,465,445 to less than 13,000,000 lb., and the value decreased from $2,018,028 to $985,000.

The output of recoverable zinc decreased from 20,984,860 lb. in 1917 to about 1,800,000 lb. in 1918. The value decreased from over $2,000,000 to $151,000.

CALIFORNIA

The metal mines of California made an output of gold, silver, copper, lead, and zinc valued at $32,223,500 in 1918, compared with $37,685,985 in 1917, according to Charles G. Yale of San Francisco. This is a decrease of $5,462,500, or 14%.

The output of gold for 1917 was $20,087,504, while the estimate for 1918 indicates a yield of $17,242,400. The deficit is, perhaps, less than had been expected. The number of mines in the State producing gold was 585 fewer at the end of 1917 than at the end of 1912, a loss of 59.7% In the same period the number of productive quartz mines has fallen off 69%; hydraulic mines, 49%; dredges, 15%; drift mines, 63%; and surface placers, 55%. It must suffice to say that the decrease in number of productive gold mines in California cannot be attributed to war conditions alone.

The silver output from Californian mines in 1918 is estimated at 1,533,000 oz., valued at $1,483,000, compared with 1,775,431 oz. in 1917, valued at $1,462,955. The silver was derived mainly from the copper and lead ores.

The estimated mine yield of copper is 48,538,000 lb., valued at $12,013,000, compared with 48,153,139 lb., and $13,145,807 in 1917. Shasta continues to be the most productive copper county.

The output of lead in 1917 was 21,868,626 lb., valued at $1,880,702; the estimated yield for 1918 is 14,655,800 lb., valued at $1,099,000.

The estimated zinc output of the State in 1918 is 4,697,900 lb., valued at $385,200, compared with 10,872,716 lb., valued at $1,109,017 in 1917.

COLORADO

The mine output of gold, silver, copper, lead, and zinc in Colorado for the first 11 months of 1918 and the estimated output for December, according to data compiled by Charles W. Henderson, amounted to $12,950,000 in gold, 7,120,000 oz. of silver, 64,300,000 lb. of lead, 6,450,000 lb. of copper, and 85,200,000 lb. of zinc, having a total value of $33,260,000; compared with $15,849,302, 7,304,350 oz., 67,990,000 lb., 8,122,000 lb., and 118,200,000 lb., respectively, having a total value of $41,988,935, in 1917.

As predicted in the Survey's six months' review issued in July, the production of Cripple Creek fell from $10,394,847 in 1917 to $8,294,000 in 1918.

IDAHO

The value of the gold, silver, copper, lead, and zinc mined in Idaho in 1918, according to the estimate of C. N. Gerry, was $38,140,000, a decided decrease of $16,700,000 from the value in 1917. The decrease was marked in all the metals but gold, as well as in the total value of the output. Even the value of the silver, which increased in price during the year, was less by more than $600,000.

The gold yield increased from $804,809 in 1917 to $867,000 in 1918.

The output of silver decreased from 12,029,338 to 9,595,000 oz., an unusual decline of nearly 20%, and the value from $9,912,175 to $9,286,000.

The output of copper decreased from 7,827,574 to 5,195,000 lb., and the value from $2,136,928 to $1,286,000.

The output of lead, which is the most abundant metal in Idaho, decreased from 393,559,521 lb. in 1917 to 300,274,000 lb. in 1918. The average price was somewhat lower, and the value of the output decreased from $33,846,119 to $22,760,000.

The output of recoverable zinc decreased from 79,854,136 to 47,000,000 lb. One of the main decreases was made by the largest zinc producer—the Interstate-Callahan.

OREGON

A preliminary estimate of the production of metals in Oregon in 1918, compiled by Charles G. Yale, of the San Francisco office of the Survey, shows a decrease only in the yield of gold, with an increase in that of silver, copper, and lead. The output of gold in 1917 was $1,491,798, and the estimated output in 1918 is $1,270,300. The silver output in 1917 was 125,656 oz., valued at $103,541, while in 1918 it was 148,200 oz., worth $143,500. The yield of copper in 1917 was 2,474,487 lb., valued at $675,535, and in 1918 it was 2,935,000 lb., valued at $726,400.

MONTANA

The value of the gold, silver, copper, lead, and zinc mined in Montana in 1918, according to the estimate of C. N. Gerry, was more than $122,000,000, an increase of $12,000,000. There was a decided decrease in the gold output, but increases in all other metals.

The value of the gold output decreased from $3,517,253

in 1917 to $3,177,000 in 1918, in spite of the fact that gold from copper ores probably increased. One of the main reasons for this difference was the decreased output from the Conrey dredges in Alder gulch, Madison county. Gold from the mines of the Barnes-King company was also much less than in 1917, though the company is still one of the chief gold producers in the State. The Southern Cross mine, at Georgetown, from which iron ore is shipped, was the third largest gold producer of Montana. Some rich ore came from the Scratch Gravel mine, in Lewis and Clark county.

The output of silver increased from 13,128,142 to 16,000,000 oz., and the value from $10,817,589 to $16,600,000. This makes Montana the leading silver producer of the United States.

The output of copper increased from 274,462,574 lb. in 1917 to 328,000,000 lb. in 1918. This represents a gain of nearly 54,000,000 lb. in quantity and over $6,000,000 in value. However, the increase was unusual, as the year 1917 was not a normal one, the main properties being idle several months.

The production of lead increased from 21,951,220 lb. in 1917 to 35,000,000 lb. in 1918, the value increasing from $1,887,805 to $2,668,000.

The output of recoverable zinc in Montana increased from 186,259,331 to 210,000,000 lb. The value increased from $18,998,452 to $19,551,000. The three main zinc producers of Montana were the Butte & Superior, the Anaconda, and the Elm Orlu.

Dividends paid by Montana companies for the first 11 months of 1918 amounted to $19,745,870. The principal dividend-payers were the Anaconda, North Butte, Butte Copper & Zinc, Davis-Daly, and Barnes-King.

NEVADA

The value of the gold, silver, copper, lead, and zinc mined in Nevada in 1918 was over $45,000,000, according to preliminary figures compiled by Victor C. Heikes. This is a decrease of over $9,000,000 from the output of 1917, when the mines produced $54,424,580. The decrease was general, and in point of value the largest drop was that in copper, amounting to over $7,000,000.

The gold output decreased from $6,959,468 in 1917 to $6,700,000 in 1918. This is a comparatively small decrease when the isolation of the fields and the excessive costs are considered. Gold from the Tonopah district was also decidedly lower, amounting to $1,200,000. Gold producers of the State that had an output of more than $200,000 each were the Nevada Consolidated from copper ore, Aurora Consolidated, White Caps at Manhattan, Elko Prince, Olympic in Mineral county, Union Consolidated at Virgina City, and the Rochester Mines at Rochester. Other notable gold producers were the Round Mountain, Nevada Wonder, Dahl placer, Consolidated Virginia, Comstock Leasing, and Consolidated Coppermines. There was a decided decrease in gold from the Seven Troughs district and from Churchill county. As a result of developments at depth on the Comstock lode, that district produced more than $400,000 in gold.

The mine production of silver decreased from 12,269,969 oz. to 10,000,000 oz. in 1918. The value of the output, however, increased from $9,286,454 to $9,687,000. The largest output of silver, or about 5,800,000 oz., was from the Tonopah district.

The output of copper decreased from 122,794,704 to 105,000,000 lb., and the value from $33,522,954 to $26,000,000.

The output of lead decreased from 27,677,928 to 20,600,000 lb., and the value from $2,380,302 to $1,567,000. One of the largest lead producers in the State was the Prince Consolidated, at Pioche, which shipped iron-manganese ore containing gold, silver, and lead. From the Yellow Pine district of Clark county considerable high-grade lead ore was shipped.

The output of recoverable zinc decreased from 22,307,868 lb. in 1917 to 15,000,000 lb. in 1918. The value of the output declined from $2,275,402 to $1,267,000. Nearly all of the output came from the Yellow Pine district, though there was a distinct decrease from this region.

Dividends declared by Nevadan mining companies for the first 11 months of 1918 amounted to $7,374,458. The principal contributors were the Tonopah Belmont, Tonopah Mining, Nevada Consolidated, West End, Boss, Jim Butler, Union Consolidated, Yellow Pine, Nevada Wonder, Rochester Mines, Tonopah Extension, and Nevada Packard.

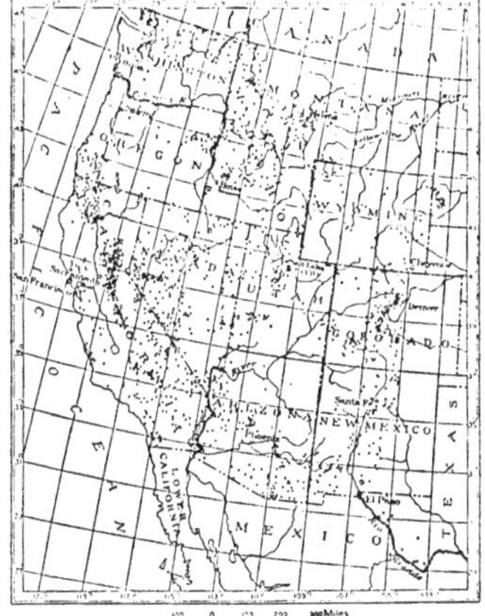

MAP OF WESTERN STATES, SHOWING GENERAL DISTRIBUTION OF MINING DISTRICTS. (U. S. G. S.)

NEW MEXICO

The output of the mines of New Mexico for the first 11 months of 1918 and the estimated output for December, as reported by Charles W. Henderson, amounted to $681,000 in gold, 868,000 oz. of silver, 9,250,000 lb. of lead, 98,620,000 lb. of copper, and 25,000,000 lb. of recoverable zinc, valued in all at $28,625,000; compared with $1,067,969, 1,453,454 oz., 9,501,000 lb., 105,568,000 lb., and 30,200,000 lb., respectively, with a total value of $34,986,765, in 1917. These preliminary figures thus show decreases of $387,000 in gold, 585,000 oz. in silver, 251,000 lb. in lead, 7,000,000 lb. in copper, and 5,200,000 lb. in zinc.

The decreased output of gold and silver was general throughout the State. Mills of the Mogollon district, Socorro county, yielded $115,948 in gold and 312,000 oz. of silver, compared with $258,620 in gold and 722,644 oz. in silver in 1917. This district in 1916 yielded $373,068 in gold and 1,008,483 oz. of silver.

Copper, the principal metal product of New Mexico, is produced in several districts, the greater part of the output coming from Chino Copper Co.'s deposit at Santa Rita. The

Burro Mountain Copper Co.'s operations at Tyrone were continuous.

Lead ores were shipped from the Central and Steeplerock districts, Grant county, and the Cooks Peak and Victorio districts, Luna county.

Decreased shipments of zinc carbonate and zinc sulphide ores were made in 1918. At Kelly, Socorro county, the principal producing mines were the Kelly, Graphic, and Juanita. The Ozark mill was operated steadily, but the Kelly mill was not in operation. At Hanover, zinc-carbonate ores were shipped from the Empire zinc mines and others, and zinc-sulphide concentrates were shipped from the Hanover magnetic-separation mill. The Cleveland magnetic-separation mill, at Pinos Altos, was operated steadily but at a reduced yield. In September, the Carlisle mill, in the Steeplerock district, Grant county, was again set in operation; the lead concentrates were shipped, but the zinc concentrates were stored.

SOUTH DAKOTA

The mines of South Dakota produced in 1918 gold worth \$6,853,000, compared with \$7,364,233 in 1917, and 164,000 oz. of silver, compared with 186,765 oz. in 1917. In addition, 67,000 lb. of lead and 90,000 lb. of copper were produced from smelting ores shipped. These are preliminary estimates, reported by Charles W. Henderson.

The yield from the Homestake mills fell off approximately \$400,000. For several years the Homestake mine has been supplying ore to its stamp-mills—numbering 1020 stamps—without interruption, but in October 1918 this company was forced to shut-down 100 or more stamps. Of the other important properties the Golden Reward mines and cyanidation mill were closed in the spring of 1918, owing to advances in cost and low-grade ores. The Wasp No. 2 mill was dismantled; the New Reliance was idle; the Bismarck mill was operated for a short period only; the Mogul mine continued operation on custom ore. The Trojan mill and mines were active. Small shipments of lead-silver ore were made from Galena and of copper ore from Roubaix and Hill City.

Placer mines in Custer, Lawrence, and Pennington counties were not actively worked.

TEXAS

The Presidio silver mine, in Texas, was in continuous operation during the year 1918, according to Charles W. Henderson. Desultory mining was also carried on in the Van Horn and Sierra Blanca districts, and several shipments of copper ore were made from deposits in the 'red beds' of Foard and Knox counties. The result was a small output of copper and lead, and an output of silver of 590,000 ounces.

UTAH

The output of gold, silver, copper, lead, and zinc from the mines of Utah in 1918, according to Victor C. Heikes, had a value of \$87,600,000, which represents a decrease of nearly \$12,000,000 from the value in 1917. Except in silver, the production of which increased slightly, there were decreases in all five of the metals produced. The industry in general was greatly hampered by the scarcity of labor and the unusually high cost of materials and supplies.

The four smelting-plants of the State were active throughout the year, on both Utah and custom ores, but they were not run at full capacity during the entire year and no records were made.

The production of gold dropped from \$3,355,156 in 1917 to approximately \$3,000,000 in 1918, a decrease of nearly 10%. Most of the gold came from copper, lead, and zinc ores treated at smelting-plants. No great quantity of ore was either amalgamated or cyanided.

The output of silver increased from 13,479,133 oz., valued at \$11,106,806, in 1917 to about 13,680,000 oz., valued at \$13,200,000, in 1918. Although this is not a large increase in quantity, it is rather surprising that the output was upheld, inasmuch as there were decided decreases in all the other metals.

The production of copper decreased from 246,674,153 lb. in 1917 to 233,000,000 lb. in 1918.

The output of lead declined from 178,521,958 lb. in 1917 to 162,000,000 lb. in 1918, a decrease of over 9%.

There was a decrease of 20% in the production of recoverable zinc. The mine output decreased from 21,286,871 lb. in 1917 to 17,500,000 lb. and the value of the output from \$2,171,261 to \$1,454,000.

In 1918 the mines of Utah produced approximately 14,606,000 tons of ore, a decrease from 15,358,481 tons in 1917. Of this total, the Bingham district yielded 13,978,000 tons, against 14,150,394 tons in 1917. There was a decrease in the Tintic district, where 41 mines produced 344,000 tons of ore, exclusive of iron ore, against 392,386 tons in 1917. Shipments of ore and concentrate from the Park City region in 1918 amounted to 90,000 tons, a decrease from 96,516 tons in 1917. Tabulation of the important mines gave an estimated output for the district of \$77,395 in gold, 2,626,000 oz. of silver, 918,000 lb. of copper, 24,064,000 lb. of lead, and 2,650,000 lb. of recoverable zinc. The decrease was general, but the largest decline was in lead. Tooele county mines produced 99,000 tons in 1918, against 132,048 tons in 1917. About 39,000 tons of ore was shipped from the Big Cottonwood, Little Cottonwood, and American Fork districts, against a total of 51,813 tons in 1917. In Beaver county, shipments increased from 64,532 tons in 1917 to 67,000 tons in 1918. This included the large amount of low-grade lead tailings shipped by the Caldo Mining Company.

WASHINGTON

The value of gold, silver, copper, and lead mined in Washington in 1918, according to the estimate of C. N. Gerry, was \$1,654,000, a decrease of \$635,000. There were slight increases in both silver and copper, but decided decreases in gold, lead, and zinc. The copper output in the Chewelah district, Stevens county, was not greatly changed, but there was a marked decrease in the shipments of silicious ore from the Republic district, in Ferry county. Washington mines suffered from the general scarcity of men and high cost of operation. The price of silver was considerably higher, but the average prices of copper, lead, and zinc were less than those of 1917. The copper smelter and refinery at Tacoma and the lead plant at Northport were both active throughout the year, but toward the end the Northport plant was not operated at full capacity.

The output of gold decreased from \$492,324 in 1917 to \$341,000 in 1918, a decrease of nearly 31%. The greater part of the gold came from the Republic district, but there was a distinct decrease in ores amalgamated throughout the State.

The output of silver increased from 282,320 oz. to 320,000 oz. and the value from \$232,632 to \$310,000. About half the silver came from copper ores, and most of the remainder from Republic ores.

The copper output increased from 2,199,518 to 2,322,000 pounds.

The mine output of lead decreased from 9,789,687 lb. to 5,600,000 lb. Most of the product came from the Electric Point mine, near Northport, in Stevens county.

Washington mines made no shipments of zinc ore or concentrate during the year, although in 1917 they produced over 1,000,000 lb. of spelter.

The only dividend paid by Washington mines during the first 11 months of 1918 was that of the Electric Point company.

INDEX to Volume 117 is now ready and can be obtained by asking for it.

THE Supreme Court of the United States has denied the Minerals Separation company's motion for an order restraining the Butte & Superior Mining Company from disposing of its assets pending the decision in the main case, which is set for hearing on March 3.

CALCREOSE, the remedy for influenza described on another page, is made by the Maltbie Chemical Company, at Newark, New Jersey, as we note from the bottle sent to us by a friend in New York. We have used it successfully at home. The writer of the article is Dr. Baldwin.

GOVERNOR BOYLE of Nevada has taken a hand in the labor trouble at Ely. Mr. Emmet D. Boyle was a good mining engineer before he proved himself a capable State executive and we have high hopes that he will be successful in adjusting the dispute between the Nevada Consolidated Copper Company and its employees.

HERMYINGUI is the name of the premier wolfram mine in the world. It is in the Tavoy district of Burma. In 1917 the owners of the mine, Marshall Cotterell & Company, shipped 1063 tons of concentrate; in August 1918 the Hermyingui—we linger on this charming name—produced 120 tons of wolfram concentrate, containing about 65% tungstic oxide.

SPEAKING of returning soldiers, we venture to ask for suitable employment in behalf of a young man that served for three years with the Canadian Expeditionary Force and was so badly gassed that he must live in a warm and dry climate. He held the rank of sergeant major and is well fitted for the post of store-keeper or a similar job. Will some friend in Arizona, New Mexico, or southern California give him a chance?

FROM Boston comes the suggestion that the Panama Canal be re-named in honor of Theodore Roosevelt. The idea is a good one. The Canal was a big thing, done in a big way, under the leadership of a big man. To President Roosevelt we owe the pushing of the work and the completion of the water-way. It was a thoroughly American feat of engineering and it should be worthily linked with the memory of the greatest American of this generation.

IN our issue of December 21 we published an editorial on the proposed merger of the two mining-engineering societies. The information came to us in the form of a circular, and we had no inkling that it was of a confidential character, but we are informed now that the circular was confidential, and that our editorial comment was untimely. We regret if, even unwittingly, we contributed to a breach of confidence, and hope that the incident will in no way interfere with the completion of the merger.

THE question is still asked, 'Who killed Cock Robin?' and the scribes of the daily press are perspiring in their efforts to answer the conundrum. Some of them, in their patriotic fervor, see only one conqueror of the Huns, as if the job had not required several hands, and as if there were not credit enough to go around. To them we commend the statement issued by the British War Office on November 11: "After fifty-two months of war, France with the aid of her allies has succeeded in defeating the enemy."

FRANKLIN K. LANE has been mentioned in connection with the presidency of the University of California. Those who care for the welfare and usefulness of that splendid institution will welcome the suggestion that the present Secretary of the Interior be invited by the regents to become its chief executive. Mr. Lane has all the qualities needed for the position. He is a man of constructive ability, large vision, and engaging personality. He is an alumnus of the University, a citizen of commanding experience in big affairs, in touch with the main currents of thought, and peculiarly fitted to act as an interpreter of university ideals and activities to the public. Such a man would be a sympathetic link between the University and the people of the State.

IT is reported that for 11 months of 1918 more than 325,000 men and women in California alone secured employment through the Employment Service of the United States Department of Labor. This help is rendered by the Government free to both employee and employer. Every kind of occupation is included, manual and professional. We are glad to give what aid we can to this excellent work, the importance of which will be greatly emphasized during the demobilization of our military forces. The managers of mines, mills, and smelters in need of help of any kind may secure for themselves the benefit of this service either through this paper or by communicating direct with the Employment Service of the United States Department of Labor, 806 Claus Spreckels Building, San Francisco.

SAN FRANCISCO exported silver to the value of $200,918,373, or 203,143,247 ounces, during the past year. Of this amount no less than 161,295,559 ounces went to British India, 'the sink for silver', as it has been called by economists. China took only 22,752,279 ounces, but an increased absorption by that country of teeming millions may be anticipated as the natives develop a taste for the luxuries of a more complex mode of living. To the missionaries the miner is under great obligation, for it is owing to their teachings and the consequent enlightenment of the natives that we owe the expansion of the market for silver. Our friends at the mines ought to contribute cheerfully to the foreign missions and to similar beneficent organizations for converting the heathen. The danger of any accumulation of surplus silver in the United States is gone, the Orient will take all that our West can produce. No metal is in so assured a position as silver is today.

WE venture to tell a Roosevelt story that we have not yet seen in print. When the ex-President was passing through London in 1910, a luncheon in his honor was arranged by the late Ambassador, Walter Hines Page, whose son, Mr. Ralph Page, is our authority for the story. Mr. Roosevelt was asked to suggest those whom he would like to meet; he prepared a list of twenty names, comprising men of naval and military distinction, publicists, politicians, and others, among whom were included two persons whom the embassy people were with difficulty able to find, namely, a Hebrew scholar and an expert on moths. When the hour of the luncheon arrived, the younger Mr. Page went down the line of guests, introducing each in turn to Mr. Roosevelt. He greeted each person cordially and engaged in a short conversation with him, discussing his own special subject, although the "discussion" consisted chiefly in Mr. Roosevelt telling them something they ought to know. He told the naval man something new about naval strategy, he corrected the military expert in something he had written, he told the politicians what errors England had made in Egypt or India, and then he came to the two men last on the list. Turning to the Hebrew scholar, he asked him how he would translate a certain passage in the Hebrew scripture. The learned man told him. "You are entirely wrong," said Roosevelt, "it ought to be done in this way." He explained his reasons for preferring his own version, and the professor felt impelled to express his polite acquiescence. Finally, he set eyes on the lepidopterist, a seedy-looking individual, with moth-eaten clothes; "Have you ever seen the Catacola Fraxini [or some other scientific name]?" "No, I never have; it is exceedingly rare, and is only reported from the upper reaches of the Amazon [or some other remote locality]." Thereupon Roosevelt beamed triumphantly and told him that he had seen it, he described it minutely, to the delight of the other fellow. The encyclopedic range of information and the amazing mental agility of the Colonel astonished all those present.

REPRESENTATIVE ELSTON'S resolution in Congress advocating the purchase of Lower California and of contiguous territory in northern Mexico is nothing new, for in February 1916 Representative Randall, another Californian Congressman, introduced a resolution to the same effect. The proposed 'purchase' appears, however, to be a parliamentary camouflage for making Mexico pay for the expedition to Vera Cruz and the chase of Villa in Chihuahua, besides the loss of life and property to Americans during the Mexican revolutions. A reckoning with Mexico must come some day, we presume, and when it does come the cession of Lower California would be one way of adjusting the account. Lower California covers 58,328 square miles; it is an arid region, not without mineral resources, for in the Boleo copper mine and the Progresso silver mine it has two notable sources of metallic wealth, but it is a little amusing to read a newspaper description that credits this desert country with the climate of Italy. Under Señor Esteban Cantu's strong governorship this part of Mexico has been spared the vicissitudes of government under the various 'istas and peace has persisted throughout the period of Mexican misrule. The transfer of Baja California to the United States would stimulate mining on the peninsula. We note the opening, a few days ago, of the new highway between Tiajuana, on the border of this State, and Mexicali, the capital of Lower California.

Theodore Roosevelt

The flag flies at half-mast; and well it may, for one who stood for all that the flag symbolizes has passed from the stage of human action. The sudden death of a man so intensely vital was a shock in more than the conventional sense; even to a world grown callous to the sight of the dying it was a blow to think of Theodore Roosevelt as quiet in the sleep that knows no waking. We had learned to think of him as a dynamic element in American life and some of us were still hoping that he might be spared for official leadership in national affairs; we regarded him as a tonic to jaded politics, as a stimulant to robust patriotism, as a spur to independent thinking. Now the great silence has laid hold upon him, the strong voice is hushed, the vigorous arms lie folded, the ardent spirit is quenched, and the mighty hunter has crossed that range from which no traveler returns.

"A great American" they call him; all of them say that—his friends and his enemies; presidents and kings, statesmen and politicians, editors and scholars. Indeed he was "a great American". His greatness lay in the bigness of his heart and the catholicity of his mind; he knew not fear, physical or moral; to him a lion in the path or a great wrong in the community were alike an object of the chase, to be vanquished single-handed if no help offered; whether other enemies lay in wait for him in the jungle of either Africa or politics he cared not at all, he would attend to them in due course with unconquerable ardor and conviction. Mankind loves a brave man. As a cowboy in North Dakota, as a legislator in New York, as Police Commissioner of Manhattan, as Colonel of the Rough Riders, as President, he faced any odds joyously. Even in his retirement he was irrepressible, and when the critical hour came at the beginning of the War he did not hesitate to take sides for the right, nor, as soon as his country drew the sword, did he delay to offer either his own services or those of his gallant sons. Although the supreme honor of leading American soldiers in battle with the Hun was denied to him, he lived long enough to see his four sons 'make good'—an American phrase that fits exactly. When one of them died fighting and another was wounded in action, he received the sad news as Theodore Roosevelt should. History will record the fact to his credit that he foresaw our participation in the War and that he urged preparedness for it; he had the gift of statesmanship: to foresee the event. He preached Americanism and he lived it. His last public utterance, which was read at a meeting of the American Defense Society the night before his death, was an eloquent plea that there might be "no sagging back in the fight for Americanism merely because the War is over." He was American in his faults as in his virtues. Outspoken, expansive, impulsive, careless of precedent, supremely egoistic, sometimes offensively belligerent, he may have had English blood, Dutch blood, French blood, even German blood, in his veins, but it had long ceased to be a mechanical mixture; it was that chemical compound we call American because it is different from any of the ingredients of which it was composed. His chief fault was in subordinating his heart to his head, his feelings to his reason. For differences of opinion he had a large tolerance, for diversity of feelings he had no charity whatever; hence his violence in controversy. He was not self-opinionated to his friends; on the contrary, he was willing to listen to advice and to follow it. As President he availed himself of such aid continually, particularly in law and economics, for neither of which he had any liking. His wide vision and keen idealism were controlled by a large stock of common-sense, as well as bed-rock morality. Thomas B. Reed, the Speaker of the House, said, "Roosevelt has discovered the Ten Commandments," meaning that he had taken them out of the Sunday-school into the political arena. He enriched American literature not only by his writings, which were the unaffected expression of himself and therefore in good style, but by the words and phrases that he coined. Even if he had never been President or Colonel of the Rough Riders his fame would be preserved in our language by such phrases as 'the big stick', 'the strenuous life', and 'the square deal', or by such terms as 'mollycoddle', 'pussy-footer', and 'muck-raker'. He had a capacity for making enemies, but it was as nothing compared to his gift for friendship. The devotion of his followers was a reproach to the cynics. He had the kingly faculty for remembering those that had done him the slightest good turn; when he became famous and powerful he delighted to recognize the humbler comrades of the ranch and the camp; to them he was 'Teddy' and 'the Colonel' until the very end. He was as beloved by the staff at the White House as he was by his fellow-townsmen at Oyster Bay, and in the telegrams of condolence showered upon his sorrowing wife were as many from the simple and the unknown as from the rulers of the nations. His was a happy lot; he was fortunate in his birth and education, in his wealth and health, in finding a field for his activities, in achieving the highest political ambition, in winning the affection of millions, and in dying before he was old. Every part that was assigned to him he played with undiluted sincerity; he was a devoted husband, a good father, an upright citizen, a just magistrate, a brave soldier, a fearless hunter, and an honest politician. As President Wilson has said, in a tribute of singular felicity, "his private life was characterized by a simplicity, a virtue, and an affection worthy of all admiration and emulation by the people of America." He was an elemental figure, a complete man. Under all the obvious traits there was strong character, sound common-sense, and an intellectual moderation that guided him in the far-reaching changes introduced by him in his efforts toward social reform. The torch that he held over the corrupt places of internal politics was grasped by the firm hand of a high-minded patriot, not the feverish fingers of an anti-social incendiary. "Put out the light, please," were his last words. The light is extinguished at last and deep is the gloom in which it leaves his fellow-citizens, but the whole world is the brighter for the presence of his vivid personality. America has been ennobled for all time by the tradition of his manliness, and the steps of human progress have been illumined by the torch-bearer who has gone now through the open door into the night. "He was a man; take him for all in all, we shall not see his like again."

Mr. Lane and Americanization

On another page we publish a part of the annual report of the Secretary of the Interior. Such an official paper might be expected to be dull, probably statistical, and almost certainly out-of-date. Our readers will be undeceived as soon as they read the first paragraph, which strikes a vibrant note of human interest. We are glad, even in a technical periodical, to give so much space to this discussion on Americanization by the Secretary of the Interior, because Mr. Lane is held in affectionate regard by Californians and in great respect both in his own State and throughout the country. That respect will be heightened by his treatment of a vital subject, namely, the making of Americans out of the immigrants that seek shelter and a home in this country. He asserts truly that in challenging the world to political idealism we have incurred the responsibility of proving to the world that we know how to develop the character of our own democracy. We must be purposeful at home as well as abroad. Our destiny depends chiefly upon the development of the character of the individuals that make the nation. The War has taught the value of national spirit and of co-operative effort. In organizing for war we used the draft for mobilizing our man-power and in so doing we discovered an extraordinary number of young men who were unable to speak our language. Ability to speak English—to think in it—is a condition precedent to Americanism. Mr. Lane gives some startling figures to show how far that condition is lacking. One fact that he mentions deserves to be underlined; he says that the average teacher's salary is less than that of the average day-laborer. A democracy that pays its school-teachers less than its hod-carriers is making a fundamental blunder. The fact that men and women will accept the work of teaching for small pay does not excuse us for giving such pay as attracts only second-rate people to become teachers. The instructors and educators in a democratic scheme of living ought to be among the best paid of public officials because their work is of basic importance. Inadequate instruction and ineffective education are the deadly enemies of representative government, particularly in communities in which a meretricious and ignorant press becomes the principal source of information and suggestion to the average man or woman. More especially is it our duty and opportunity to see that the ignorant immigrants from overseas are trained for American citizenship so that they can be absorbed into the body politic without causing a fit of political dyspepsia. The existence of a large mass of unassimilated aliens in the United States does impair the good health of this commonwealth, by affording facilities for the cultivation of the noxious germs of anti-social ideas. The immigrant may be an economic asset if he works, but he is a political liability if he remains alien. The rampant anarchy of the I. W. W. and the irreconcilable elements in the Socialist party are largely the result of our failure to exclude the undesirables of Europe and of our dereliction of responsibility for those that land at our ports. Restriction of immigration, which should have been taken in hand long ago, has gone only so far as to exclude those likely to be a public charge, those obviously insane, epileptic, afflicted with contagious diseases, or otherwise seriously defective, also those known to be criminals, prostitutes, or procurers, together with such as acknowledge themselves to be anarchists or polygamists. In 1916 we deported or debarred 21,773 of the unfit, but no anarchists were turned away. Such sifting of immigration was begun too late, and, whatever may be done to restrict entry in the future, there remains the task of making the most of those already admitted. Of the white population of this country, 45% is foreign-born or of foreign parentage. In the mining regions entire communities are foreign in speech and in ideas. Mining engineers can testify that they have walked for miles on the Mesabi range before meeting a man that could tell them the way in English; they have been in parts of the South-West where Spanish only is spoken, in parts of Wisconsin where German is the common tongue, and in parts of Minnesota where Swedish is the dominant language. Such conditions are deadly to the growth of an American spirit. As Theodore Roosevelt said, in his last public utterance: "We have room for but one language here and that is the English language, for we intend to see that the crucible turns our people out as Americans of American nationality and not as dwellers in a polyglot boarding-house." An American may be compounded of many racial stocks, as the great ex-President was, but he must fuse them into one if he is to be a real American, and of all the fluxes that will melt unlike racial ingredients into the good metal of pure nationalism there is none like the flux of language. The most remarkable democracy of the ancient world was that of Athens; it was a success because, among other reasons, it was only a town and all the Athenians spoke Greek. The United States is a continent and its very bigness renders solidarity more difficult to attain unless all its citizens speak the same language. By means of it we can achieve a common understanding; by aid of it we can teach the immigrant the essentials of citizenship. Lack of national unity gave the Bolshevists the chance to destroy the Russian attempt at democracy; let us see to it that, through carelessness, we do not become the victims of the anti-social element that is constantly threatening to undermine the development of the democratic idea in this country. One of the first steps toward the Americanization of our foreign laborers is to start classes in English in our mining communities. Now that men work for eight hours only, it should be practicable to make arrangements with the local Board of Education for ensuring that every foreigner may have at least an hour's lesson in English every day. Another aid to the same purpose would be to employ educated English-speaking foreigners on the staff of mines and mills, so that the foreign element may be represented, thereby promoting a better understanding between the management and the foreign workmen, and arousing a proper ambition among the more intelligent of them. As Mr. Charles M. Schwab said recently: "The thing that we have got to do is teach, not patronize." The War has awakened the American people to a keen realization of the necessity for assimilating our alien people, not by naturalization only, but by teaching them the English language and by inoculating them with American ideas, which is the first requisite to real citizenship. To quote again the stalwart American just gone from us: "There must be no sagging back in the fight for Americanism merely because the War is over. There can be no divided allegiance; we have room for but one soul-loyalty."

International Control of Minerals

By COURTENAY DE KALB

It is creditable to the Administration that, though tardy in realizing the significance of economics as a basis for making peace and maintaining peace, it seems at last to have grasped the fact that economics is a rock and that politics is a quicksand. It is to be hoped that the evidence of an awakening to a wiser view of international relationships does in truth mean that such a realization has come to the men who are now guiding our destinies, for good or ill, through the difficulties of a world-conference for the re-writing of international law to make feasible a closer association under a modern *jus gentium*.

The original party of peace delegates that went abroad was wholly political, diplomatic, and legal. It is said that Colonel House of Texas had been directing an elaborate historical research by State Department officials, to serve as a basis for dealing with the problems of the European re-association of nations. This was, of course, useful and necessary. Knowledge of the intricate aspirations, grievances, and propensities of the many States in Europe was needed in order to deal intelligently with the demands that will be made, and to comprehend the influences that will subtly work at cross-purposes to the superficial current of peace when the delegates begin their deliberations. The political side of the problem is not to be ignored; it is, indeed, of vital import, and in the end will prove to be the side that determines most of what the Peace Congress will accomplish. This, however, does not prevent a clear vision of the fact that a political adjustment will have the defect of a structure built on the sands, and that it might have been founded on the rock of economics had all parties been so minded. A recent despatch from Paris assures us that the new spirit will be that of a concert of nations, rather than the maintenance of the balance of power. This may mean progress, for the old balance was not a compensated mechanism, and disaster followed; but there was a period when Europe tried the principle of a concert also, especially as regarded Mediterrean affairs, and after the last appearance of the players on the Greek stage at the time of the Cretan trouble, it was universally admitted that the European concert was a dead failure.

A new conception has now dawned, and it may lead to better things in course of time. Instead of starting with an economic basis as the determinant of the political relations that should exist between the nations, it is now proposed to admit economic considerations in designing the framework of an association of nations. Accordingly three men have been called to Paris, each of whom is specially equipped to render useful service in economics. These men are Bernard M. Baruch, representing productive industry, Vance McCormick, representing international trade, and C. K. Leith, representing international control of minerals. The lessons of the War, which were lessons in mobilizing resources, have developed surer knowledge of the interdependence of nations upon fundamental raw materials. So far as minerals are concerned, this experience in war has accumulated in the hands of Dr. Leith a fund of new knowledge, which he has outlined in a bulletin just off the press, to appear ultimately as part of the 'Mineral Resources' for 1917, when issued shortly by the U. S. Geological Survey. Some of the leading statements in this bulletin will set many minds thinking upon things that will soon be reflected in the utterances from Versailles. Dr. Leith states that the annual world production of minerals is approximately 1,700,000,000 tons, over 90% of which is coal and iron. Of this amount one-third figures in international trade. The world movement is characterized by a remarkable degree of concentration. For instance "manganese moves from three principal sources and converges at four or five consuming centres; chromite moves from two principal sources; tungsten also from two. The world movement of coal is controlled by the United States, England, and Germany." He draws the following general conclusion: "The convergence of these materials toward a few consuming centres indicates concentration of coal production necessary to smelting, high development of manufacturing, large per capita use, concentration of facilities, strong financial control and, not least, a large element of enterprise which has taken advantage of more or less favorable conditions."

The pre-war movement of minerals was hindered by tariffs, trade-control, and various types of monopoly. It conformed to the law of supply and demand as determined and influenced by artificial efforts at concentration for control and stimulated industrial effort at certain points. The net result was enterprise from which the principle of equality of opportunity was excluded. The War wrought great changes. The total annual imports of mineral commodities into the United States were reduced by 1,200,000 tons. The flow of manganese from India and Russia ceased abruptly, and we turned to Brazil and to our own resources to supply the deficiency. Curtailment of chrome imports led to the development of a domestic supply. Pyrite was no longer available from Spain, and this gave a great impulse to the operation of our own mines of pyritic ores and of sulphur.

One important result of the changed conditions was the creation of an Inter-Allied Purchasing Committee, with branches in London and Paris, to agree on the distribution and price of nitrate, tin, tungsten, platinum, and many other minerals and metals. Thus new problems of concerted action for world-allocation became part of the business of the nations. Dr. Leith presents the deduction from experience obtained during the War in these words: "We now face the immediate and pressing question whether the centralized international control required by the War shall be retained or extended as a means of furthering the aims of a league of nations. When such a league was first proposed emphasis was placed mainly on political and military considerations. It now seems to be recognized that these are so closely interlocked with economic considerations that any league of nations, to be effective as a means of minimizing future international discord, must make provision for some degree of international or supernational control of business. Recent statements by officials of Great Britain and France seem to indicate a definite purpose to urge such control."

The concrete conceptions of the international need for mineral control are set forth in the succeeding paragraphs:

1. Equitable distribution of certain minerals, such as gold, tungsten, vanadium, and platinum, of which there may be a world shortage.

2. Ensuring equality of opportunity in regard to basic raw materials, as against the national monopolies now existing with reference to some mineral commodities.

3. To reach an agreement for a division of the market for iron, steel, coal, and some other vital necessaries.

4. To maintain an equilibrium of price.

5. To centralize control over the restraint of trade that is now accomplished through tariffs and other means for national monopoly.

The proposals for international agreement on principles of world economics, as outlined in the paper by Dr. Leith, enter into details of general application, and represent ideas that mainly originated in America. That they will be strongly modified in contact with the delegates from France, England, and Italy is indubitable, but it is significant of the point of view that is being carried to Paris, not only by Dr. Leith, but by his close associates, Messrs. Baruch and McCormick, as the expression of a conception with which America will be assumed to be in accord. What this is may be seen from his following statement: "Extension of international control of minerals seems to offer possibilities of loss and gain—loss through a considerable sacrifice of national trade and a narrowing of the field for private initiative in trade; gain through the possibility of attaining certain ends which are attainable only by international agreement, such as an allocation of supplies. The interests of conservation clearly require international control. Moreover, the lesson of the War points to the necessity of overhauling old international understandings and machinery, even though such a task would encounter great difficulties, not the least of which lie in the persistence of human habits and inertia. . . . The mineral industry should fully understand that, with international control, efforts to promote export will need to be modified and curtailed; that expansion of our trade in many lines will mean equivalent loss of trade to other nations; that the almost universal conception that expansion of foreign trade is a meritorious aim and end in itself, without regard to its effect on other countries, will need revision."

With the intent of developing the ideas presented in this brief bulletin, by collecting further information relative to the world requirements and movements of minerals, a plan is now being perfected for the transfer of the special mineral activities of the War Boards to the Bureau of Mines and the Geological Survey. It is also recommended that "the American Institute of Mining Engineers and our technical publications have the same reason for extending their current surveys of mineral conditions to cover the world."

The invitation to co-operation by extra-governmental organs of influence will not be neglected. The issues involved are so vast, so vital, and in some respects so revolutionary, that every serious person will urge immediate response. The MINING AND SCIENTIFIC PRESS has persistently swept far beyond the confines of our single country, in its criticism and efforts for the welfare of the mining world. The Iron and Steel Institute has been drawn into close association with the Government, in an advisory, and partly in an administrative capacity. The American Institute of Mining Engineers has performed useful functions of an advisory character, and has cooperated helpfully in mobilizing the mining engineers for military service, and its experience as a body of representative managers of industry should be made available for the constructive work that is now, in some degree, to be undertaken in giving an economic platform to the league of nations.

A platform designed chiefly by men whose business is politics is a dangerous construction, albeit they may employ some practical artisans in the work of erection. A platform is always liable to collapse, and the multitude is then found considerably injured in the débris. The dominant note that has been struck so often by the apostles of the League of Nations, considered as a political institution, also vibrates through Dr. Leith's paper on the problem of mineral control. There is wisdom in it, as a broad theory, and sincerity of purpose. No criticism of idealism is valid except as the ideal is competent to function as a force in itself rather than to promote evolution of the body politic. The idealists, represented primarily by the President, have been warning the people of the need for economic sacrifices as an international discipline, and this has been done in the face of very definite statements from France and England of a practical sort, such as one would meet in the banking house rather than at a conference of government ministers. The security of the world's peace is an economic question, and acquiescence in the control established between the nations will depend upon the economic advantages it may offer. The Administration, through many of its agencies, has revealed insufficiency of constructive thinking upon economics by its frequent announcement of the sacrifices that must be made to achieve the international ideal. The true bond would be one that made it economically advantageous to sustain a new order of international unity, and equally disadvantageous economically to secede from the league. The object of a closer linking of the nations must be for an uplift of mankind, and that means the maintenance of the higher standards of living. This does not call for sacrifice, because sacrifice of economic effort means sacrifice of earning capacity, which is retrogression. The measure of prosperity is found in the ratio between productivity and consuming power. As Dr. Leith indicates, this does not necessarily depend upon the balance of foreign trade for or against a people; but progress requires that the ratio be not unity, but rather an over-weighting of the productive factor. Without that the re-absorption of capital into the invested form for betterment and expansion is not feasible, and a condition of balance therefore is toppling toward decline and weakness. Aside from accumulations for insurance and to cover accidental wastage and loss, a balance may be the ideal; it assuredly is the ideal of the conservationist school of thought to which Dr. Leith belongs. In the end, which, speaking in terms of the life of the race, may be remote, the principle of the economic balance may rule. On the way to a realization of such an ideal, however, another type of conservation must be upheld, which is the preservation of the standard of living of the most highly evolved nation, and that necessitates the leading upward of those less highly developed, taking the average of all classes into account, to the more elevated plane. The industrially successful, the well-requited of the industry in which they work, are those that first and last achieve the broader, happier, and more wholesome conception of life and duty. We would prefer to risk opening new mines in America to provide the means for more and happier homes here in our own country than to suppress the industry that lies nearest to the hands of willing workers, on the chance that in some corner of the globe a man who could produce the same metals a little cheaper might find it possible to divert his labor from something else to competition with the men in our own land of high development and high achievement.

THAT GOLD has been sold recently at a premium is well known, so it is of interest to note that the Oriental Consolidated in its statement for October says, "The above bullion [$91,856] was shipped to the Imperial Japanese Mint at Osaka for refining, after which it will be turned over to E. H. Hunter & Co. of Osaka, who pays us a 2% premium on the gold. Last month we included the premium in the clean-up figures, but we have now decided to discontinue this system, as such a 'falsification' of the bullion figures reacts throughout all our ore valuation and extraction data, and would render them inaccurate. The premium will from now on be included among 'other receipts'."

ANTIMONY MINING in Alaska has almost ceased owing to the low price of the metal.

Californian Mineral Output in 1918

The statistical division of the State Mining Bureau, under the direction of Fletcher Hamilton, State Mineralogist, estimates the mineral production of California for the year 1918 at a total of $191,100,000. This is a conservative figure, and includes all products, metallic and non-metallic, being in advance of the actual figures which will be available later after the complete returns are received from the various producers. The continued increased value over the 1917 total of $161,202,962 is due mainly to the greatly enhanced prices of all grades of crude oil, coupled with an increase of approximately 5,000,000 bbl. in quantity. Reports to hand indicate a decrease of nearly $3,000,000 in gold output, and considerable decreases also for lead and zinc. Copper apparently increased slightly in quantity, but decreased in value. Quicksilver dropped off 2000 flasks in quantity, but with a higher price per flask, so that the total value of $2,310,000 showed a relatively smaller loss.

Of the so-called 'war minerals,' chromite had a large output up to the latter part of September, when the market collapsed. Otherwise, California's 1918 shipments bade fair to eclipse the record output of 52,379 short tons in 1917, worth $1,130,298. The actual tonnage finally shipped was probably about the same as the 1917 total, but with a greater value per ton. Shipments of manganese ores are estimated to have reached a total of 25,000 tons, worth $1,125,000, a considerable increase over the 15,515 tons and $396,659 in 1917. Magnesite apparently dropped off to about 90,000 tons, or only 40% of the previous year's yield, on account of the competition of the cheaper iron-bearing Washington magnesite and the curtailing of construction work that utilizes high-grade magnesite for plastic purposes.

The date of publication of the final and complete report on the mineral production for the year is dependent upon the promptness of the replies from operators. But for the delayed replies of less than 10% of the operators, partly carelessness, the complete report could be compiled inside of three months after the close of the calendar year, instead of at least six months usually taken. The law requires that reports must be made to the State Mining Bureau, and should be complied with promptly. Details of the individual returns are held confidential.

The estimated quantities and values for 1918 are tabulated as follows:

Substance	Quantity	Value
Gold	....	$17,250,000
Silver, ounces	1,500,000	1,450,000
Tungsten concentrates, tons	2,300	3,000,000
Copper, pounds	49,000,000	12,000,000
Lead, pounds	15,000,000	1,100,000
Zinc, pounds	4,500,000	375,000
Quicksilver, flasks	22,000	2,310,000
Antimony, iron, molybdenite, platinum	....	90,000
Petroleum, barrels	100,000,000	123,000,000
Chromite, tons	52,000	2,000,000
Manganese ore, tons	25,000	1,125,000
Magnesite, tons	90,000	900,000
Natural gas	....	3,000,000
Brick, cement, stone, rock, etc.	....	10,000,000
Salines (borax, soda, salt, potash)	....	12,000,000
Sundry industrial minerals	....	1,500,000
Total Value		$191,100,000

Minerals in the Disputed Chile-Peru Territory

The region of Tacna and Arica, which is the cause of the acute frontier controversy between Chile and Peru, is, in itself, of comparatively small economic value. The Province of Tacna, as organized by the Government of Chile, has an area of 8688 square miles, mostly lying among the western foothills of the Andes. Like most of the contiguous coastal regions, it is arid, except where it can be irrigated from the scanty and intermittent streams that rise in the Andes.

The most important feature in the industrial life of the region is the Arica-La Paz railway, rather than the

THE DISPUTED REGION IS NORTH AND SOUTH OF THE ARICA-LA PAZ RAILROAD

relatively small intrinsic resources of the Province. This line furnishes the shortest route from the plateau to the coast, and is the natural gateway for the foreign trade of the most of Bolivia. The railway is a Chilean State property, though Chile agreed to transfer the Bolivian section of the line to that nation in 1928. Opened in 1913, its traffic has increased rapidly, from 47,000 tons in the first year of operation to 105,000 tons in 1917. It has, however, been hampered by inadequate rolling-stock and by the lack of port facilities at Arica. Efforts have been made to remedy the shortage of rolling-stock by purchases in the United States, and the Chilean government has ratified projects for the improvement of the port works. This railway supplies the principal channel for the increasing Chilean economic activity in Bolivia. Chileans are heavily interested in the Corocoro copper field, the Llalagua tin mines, the Socavón tin mines near Oruro, and the large properties of the Compañía Minera y Agrícola Oploca, in the Province of South Chichas, Department of Potosi. Chilean capital is also interested in the development of the petroleum field in the Santa Cruz country of eastern Bolivia, and in the possibilities of Bolivia as a market for the surplus product of Chile's expanding manufacturing industries.

The topography of the Province bears, in the main, a resemblance to that of the contiguous coastal regions. Most of its area is occupied by the western foothills of the Andes, whose continuity is, however, broken by the existence of barren and relatively level pampas. These are crossed from east to west by several quebradas, or narrow closed valleys, which serve as beds for the scanty and intermittent streams that rise in the Andes.

In 1916 the mineral production of the Province of Tacna was valued at ₱1,687,563 (exchange-rate, 1 peso = 30 cents) compared with ₱143,724,951 for Tarapaca, and ₱250,658,239 for Antofagasta. Thus the mineral production of Tacna amounted to only a little more than a third of 1% of the total production of all Chile for that year.

The mineral product of 1916 was classified as follows, with its quantity and value:

Gold (dust), 9340 grammes	₱11,049
Copper ore, 722 metric tons	171,373
Ores containing gold, silver, and copper, 906,261 kilogrammes	193,950
Ores containing molybdenum, 1652 kilogrammes	16,520
Ores containing tungsten, 102 kilogrammes	140
Gold contained in copper ore, 2165 grammes	1,949
Silver contained in copper ore, 144,315 grammes	5,772
Sulphur, 8579 tons	1,201,060
Salt, 2450 tons	85,750

The total value in U. S. currency is approximately $550,000.

Contrary to the current impression, Tacna is not one of the nitrate provinces, as this industry is largely confined to Tarapaca and Antofagasta, the two Provinces to the south.

Sulphur comprises about 71.2% of the total value of the mineral production of Tacna for 1916. It is in fact the most valuable single resource of the region. The solfataras of Tacora are among the most important in the world. The deposits are estimated to hold from 10,000,000 to 45,000,000 tons of sulphur. The exploitation of these vast beds has been greatly hindered by lack of capital and proper transportation facilities.

A distinction must be drawn in considering the traffic of the port of Arica between the specifically Chilean trade and the Bolivian transit trade. As at both Mollendo and Antofagasta, the Bolivian government maintains at the port a customs agent, who takes charge of goods destined for Bolivia, and expedites their transportation across Chile. Bolivian exportations through Arica for 1915 can be classified as follows:

Antimony	₱66,800
Bismuth	7,220
Copper:	
Barillas (concentrate)	7,189,703
Minerales de cobre (ores containing copper)	6,657,189
Silver:	
Cemento de plata	1,065,152
Minerales	50,529
Sulphur of molybdenum	4,500
Tin:	
Barillas	12,708,000
Barras	870
Wolfram:	
Barillas	2,300,384
Minerales	4,500
Lead: Minerales	14,500
Total	30,181,931

The total value in U. S. currency is approximately $9,000,000.

The above notes are abstracted from 'Commerce Reports'.

The Salesman

By CHARLES T. HUTCHINSON

WHEN Eve disposed of the apple to Adam, she qualified as the first salesman, or perhaps, saleslady would be better. Indeed, the apple proved to have been a lemon, as the ills to which all flesh has been heir ever since will bear abundant testimony. The serpent was the first advertising man, whose full-cap headlines and masterful composition so forcibly sold the apple idea to Eve, and then to Adam, that selling, with all its ramifications, lights, and shades has been an inseparable part of our scheme of existence ever since.

From then on, through the time when Noah was compelled to tie up at Ararat on account of tire troubles, the science of salesmanship grew and grew. The first expense account for entertaining is found in the sad case of Esau, who sold his birthright for a mess of pottage. This handy adjunct to salesmanship, the psychology of the full stomach as a first-aid to the persuasiveness of the glib-tongued salesman, is just as much a part of the game as the wise old serpent of advertising and the sales talk of Eve.

From the sonorous tomes of the Old Testament to the slang of the cities, at heart it is the same old story repeated in never-ending variety and cadence. The men who go out on the job with quips, knights of the grip-sack, armed cap-a-pie with price-book, order-blanks, and a pocket full of cigars, move the output of the world of factory and farm, and do it well.

The drummer, in the eyes of those who know not, lives a charmed life. He is a hail-fellow—well-met with everybody. He fairly exudes optimism and good nature. His pockets are always full of cigars—good ones too—and his first words are, "What are you going to take?" He travels everywhere, knows everything, and, rumor has it, all expenses are paid, actually PAID, and gladly, by a complaisant boss, who loves his little drummer, and cares for him as he would a rare exotic in the conservatory of hired men. This genial, rather stout, red-faced young man, in clothes like the collar 'ad' in the magazines, is the favorite of the gods, and takes off his hat to no man. "What a cinch!" thinks Rollo, the high-school freshman, who then and there decides that, come what may, he will be a salesman when he grows to man's estate.

There are salesmen and salesmen. There is the vendor of peanuts on the street corner, whose plaintive piping steam-whistle is as significant of his calling as the striped pole that proclaims the barber. The beautifully tailored exquisite with the air of Lord Cholmondeley, who, with raised eyebrows expresses his contempt when you inquire for the fifty-cent counter at the fashionable jewelers, and the man who barks "Where to," when you approach the ticket-window at the railroad depot, all seem, in a way, to absorb a certain atmosphere from the nature of their calling. Their varying attitudes toward those they serve, from haughty disdain to servile adulation, are an index to the amount of competition they must face.

These are all salesmen, so called, but really, salesmen for such worthies is a gross libel upon an honorable and intricate calling. They are order-takers, not order-getters, and there is a vast difference between the two. Again, there is the new profession, that of sales-engineering, wherein the sales engineer is a creator, a builder, and must have, not only a highly trained technical and commercial brain, but the sales temperament as well, a quality as rare as that of music, art, or any of the other gifts not to be acquired from books.

Each particular kind of selling is a specialty in itself. The successful vendor of delicatessen would not make much of a job at selling ball-mills to a copper mine, and vice versa. However, it is not with delicatessen, ready-to-wear garments, or breakfast food that this article will deal. Let us talk of something of which we know, the mining machinery salesman. Solomon, with all his wives, had no problems such as his.

There is no fixed method by which the ability of any

salesman may be determined before a trial, nor is there any physical peculiarity by which any man may be said to be, literally, a born salesman. There are almost as many types as men. There are fat ones and lean ones, loquacious ones and monosyllabic ones. Some achieve such sartorial eminence as to be worthy of the appellation, 'swell dressers', while others are downright shabby, and neglect the occasional shoe-shine and haircut. Nevertheless, in each, somewhere, there is that indefinable something that produces the signature on the dotted line.

Employment managers, psychologists, phrenologists, and other intellectual highlights have promulgated innumerable fads and fancies whereby the round and square pegs may be classified and placed in exactly the kind of holes for which they are temperamentally fitted, but none of these handy formulas for the solution of the human equation amount to much where the selection of salesmen is concerned. Some years ago a young man, then heralded as an advanced intellectual genius, and since determined to have been little other than a disgusting German propagandist, used to determine the ability and adaptability of prospective employees by running $\frac{1}{32}$ contours all around their craniums and calculating the distance between their medulla oblongata and their pneumogastric nerve, and saying, when the answer was found, "My boy, you are a born machinist's helper, the fish-oil for yours." But, when you want to hire a salesman, test him by seeing whether he can sell himself to you. If he can, let him try to sell something to your customers. Your sales report will tell the story; your bank account will furnish the answer.

The salesman of mining machinery is a reflection of those with whom he deals. It could not be otherwise. As he gets deeper and deeper into the toils, he assimilates the viewpoint of the mine manager, in some cases even aping his picturesque manner of expression and characteristic taste in dress. Once upon a time, there was a young man called Smith (which was not his name). Said Smith found for himself a job with a local manufacturer of mining machinery. As he progressed from job to job, his superiors thought they discerned in him the spark of genius as a salesman. Smith, naturally imitative, took to aping the bluff heartiness, the superior swagger, and debonair bearing of the road salesmen, who, back from their trips, filled his head with their Munchausen tales of glorious accomplishment, and how they 'put it over' their envious rivals.

It was not long before he became so efficient an understudy that the boss decided to give him a chance 'on his own'. The great news told, Smith, beside himself with joy, rushed out to the nearest outfitter in order to prepare himself, not merely to be, but to look a mining machinery salesman. The next morning he put in his appearance at the office and nearly caused a riot. He was, like the 'Sassy Six' automobile, fully equipped with

A four-dent Stetson nearly three feet wide,

A pair of knee-length lace-boots,

A pair of flowing brown corduroy trousers, coyly tucked into said lace-boots, and, last, but not least,

A benzine-tainted breath, as a symptom of his acquisition of an expense account.

Smith got fired, which, in a way, was not quite fair to Smith, whose imaginative temperament caused him to mistake the Dare-devil-Dick dime-novelistic yarns of the salesmen for the real literature of salesmanship.

Shakespeare once wrote something about the garb proclaiming the man, which may account for the paper cap and pile of shavings used so frequently by the cartoonist in depicting a horny-handed son of toil, yet, many an excellent mechanic comes to work in a cut-away coat and a hard-boiled hat of the derby variety. Every mine manager does not attend receptions in lace-boots and a khaki shirt worn decolleté, and every salesman does not rely upon John Barleycorn as his chief talking-point, nor camouflage his expense account. As a matter of fact, the best salesmen, those who have the analytical faculty and regard nothing as sold until it is in satisfactory operation, look like other humans and act like them.

John Barleycorn, as a first-aid toward making sales, is fast coming into disrepute in well-ordered business establishments. Time was, not so many years ago either, when no salesman could get away with his job without being able to load himself well below the Plimsoll mark, and still get home under his own power.

The mining man, a type quite distinct from the mining engineer, after having spent months in the waste places trying to find the elusive pay-shoot, came to town to buy a mill, incidentally, and to quaff deep of the distractions offered by the city as a major duty. The fortunate salesman who saw him first took extraordinary precautions to keep his 'game' out of the bags of his rivals, all of which was both the out and in-door pastime in the mining machinery district. Extraordinary strategy by the general staff was resorted to, wherein closed carriages, hotels of a kind, unlimited credit at the bar, and rides in the park were the order of the day, and night. Relays of salesmen doing eight-hour shifts were in constant attendance, while in the office, specifications and contracts were being rapidly typed in preparation for the psychological moment when the signature might be appended to the dotted line.

When the mining man reached that state of satiety when nothing looked so good as a pitcher of ice-water and a cold compress, the contract was produced, wearily signed, and the used-up conqueror of the desert and the mountains journeyed back to pure air, flapjacks and

bacon, to await the coming of the mill that would demonstrate the existance either of a mine or of just another hole in the ground.

The best thing about such methods, and the salesmen that went with them, is that they are gone. Gradually, better business morality grew, not merely with the vendor but also with the vendee of mining machinery. The American passion for efficiency expressed itself with the summary curtailment of the expense account privilege, whereby close scrutiny by a cold-blooded person known as an auditor eliminated such items as 'sundries', under the cloak of which many indiscretions were formerly hidden. The cause of all this betterment is, of course, education, a more intelligent conception of responsibilities. The mine manager of today is a trained man, usually a university graduate, and so is the mining machinery salesman. Practice is applied with the logic of the thinker to the solution of the problem at hand, whether that problem be one of ore deposits and metallurgical treatment, or design and manufacture of apparatus. One large manufacturer of mine supplies exacts from his employees a signed pledge to abstain from alcoholic liquors during the period of their employment. Commercial hospitality, such of it as still remains, takes the innocuous form of an occasional lunch, dinner, or theatre party. The old-time orgies no longer have place; in fact, the easiest way to put the salesman out of the running would be to try and put over something of this kind.

There is a certain amount of regret, that in the passing of the old methods, and old salesmen, is also going the general practitioner. Ten or fifteen years ago, the mining machinery salesman was the whole show. He was expected to handle the job from soup to nuts, from caviare to demi-tasse. He could diagnose ore, draw up the specifications for the plant, both machinery and building material; prepare, unaided, the complete construction estimates as well as the cost of the machinery; go out and get the contract signed in competition with a lot of rivals; come home with the scalp of the mine manager under his belt and a check for the first payment; see the job through the shop, and, if necessary, take charge of erection of the machinery; turn the completed plant over in running order, and then, last but not least, come home, tired but happy, with a formal acceptance and a check for the final payment.

The tendency toward specialization to the *n*th degree has revolutionized the methods of the manufacturer of machinery and of his selling force. In the old days, the mining machinery manufacturer used to make everything in sight, not merely milling, concentrating, and smelting machinery but the power equipment, engines, boilers, compressors, rock-drills, in fact, nearly everything that went to make milling or smelting plants as they were in those days. Now practically everything in a modern mill or smelter is manufactured by a specialist, and sold by a specialist salesman.

Great establishments for specialized manufacture have been built up, international in their scope, whose selling organization and trade connections penetrate the far corners of the earth. In the old time sense of the word, there are very few manufacturers of mining machinery any more, but instead there are manufacturers of air-compressors, hoisting-engines, ball-mills, concentrators, transmission machinery, power apparatus of each kind, and so forth. In the equipment for a modern mine will be found the product of dozens of specialty manufacturers, and many dozens more, when such details as belting, hose, pipe, valves, and fittings are taken into account.

The same transition has produced the specialized salesman, who knows air-compressors, but not ball-mills, concentrators, but not internal-combustion engines. One objection to this specialization lies in the divided responsibility. No one contractor can guarantee the performance of the plant as a whole. On the other hand, the highly developed concentration upon one piece of apparatus has resulted in an infinitely superior product than that turned out by the old-time jack-of-all-trades. A firm of consulting engineers, purchasing equipment a few years ago for a plant of considerable magnitude, interviewed some two hundred manufacturers' representatives before deciding upon the equipment that would be used. Under the old order of things, half-a dozen bidders would have sufficed.

The salesman is himself a specialist, a sales engineer in fact. He has a concentrated knowledge of his own apparatus in many cases far superior to that of the consulting engineer, who, himself, is a general practitioner, whose duty it is to co-ordinate all the various units into one efficient plant. As a result, the sales engineer is consulted with respect by the consulting engineer, and has a large voice in the selection of the apparatus; in fact, there are lots of consulting engineers whose reports would lack much without the sound knowledge imparted by the sales engineer.

The sales engineer gets no fee for professional services. He is supposed to be a sordid commercial person, who, by reason of the fact that he has something to sell, has his advice and counsel used, but not paid for. The consulting engineer collects the fee. If the sales engineer lands the order for his principals, well and good. If not, he turns to other prospects.

Many of the larger manufacturing establishments, appreciating the increasing responsibilities developing upon the sales engineer, have given much thought to his training. Young graduates in engineering courses from the universities are taken into the manufacturing establishment and put through a regular course of training, and are paid for their time as well. Generally two years are devoted to shop practice in various departments, supplemented by lectures in the evening by department heads on pertinent subjects. During the training period, the candidate absorbs a thorough practical knowledge of the manufacturer's product, and what is even more important, the spirit of the institution, morale, in other words: the inspiration without which no sales engineer can put heart into his work.

The observance of rigid standards of personal conduct are insisted upon; representatives, not mis-representatives, are wanted by the modern business establishment. Of the many cases of business turpitude and unfair competition investigated by the Federal Trade Commission during the period of the War, it is noteworthy that, of the offenders designated as such by the Board, comparatively few were American concerns, and further, that it was found that unfair competition, graft, bribery of officials, and other forms of business dishonesty were characteristic business methods of the Germans wherever they hung out their signs.

A few reactionary narrow-minded persons are prone to sneer at modern methods of sales promotion as a developer of natural resources because, forsooth, the motive inspiring the salesman is commercial rather than altruistic. This viewpoint is the sheerest nonsense. Things to be successful must be profitable, morally or financially. Things, schemes, and ideas must be able to withstand the acid test of practical application; they must pay; if they do not, they are failures. The salesman too must be made to pay. He cannot be made to pay, without, in turn, paying those with whom, and for whom, he deals. A salesman who introduces a piece of apparatus that renders good service to the user and a profit to the maker is doing a real constructive service; he is doing his bit toward making the world a better place for the rest of mankind.

ORGANIC CHEMISTRY is the chemistry of the compounds of carbon. The number of compounds that contain carbon is extraordinarily large. The only other elements that enter into the composition of any large number of substances are hydrogen and oxygen. Carbon is the dominant element, remaining intact in many of the chemical changes that occur, while hydrogen and oxygen are added, subtracted, or exchanged for other elements or groups of elements. Most of the compounds of carbon are decomposed at temperatures below a red heat. The majority of organic substances are practically insoluble in water, while compounds are more sensitive to light and air than are the inorganic. Most organic substances are practically insoluble in water, which is the solvent of so many inorganic compounds.—J. T. Stoddard in 'Introduction to Organic Chemistry'.

THE TERM 'MANGANESE ORE' is used to denote ore that contains 35% or more of metallic manganese, and 'ferruginous-manganese ore' to denote ore that contains 35 to 10% of metallic manganese and 10 to 40% of iron. Ore containing less than 10% of metallic manganese is known as 'manganiferous-iron ore.'

The Oil-Shale Industry in Colorado

By R. L. CHASE

I had the good fortune to spend two months in the oil-shale country of Colorado this fall and found many things of interest that are worth noting, especially as so many wild stories have been circulated in regard to the shale. The district I covered is reached from Grand Valley, a station on the Denver & Rio Grande railroad, thence by good motor-road up Parachute creek to its forks as shown on the map, which also shows the line of outcrop of the shale cliffs.

All the available shale has been covered by placer locations in this district, those claims having cliff-faces being the most valuable on account of offering the best and cheapest working conditions. A supply of water and timber is necessary, especially the water, as large quantities are used in retorting the shale.

No. 1. Looking down Parachute creek, all the bottom-land being taken up by prosperous ranchers. The mesas measure the extent of oil-shale, the valley being practically at the bottom of the formation, then 1500 ft. of oil-shale, the top of the mesas being capped by a huff-colored sandstone in places several hundred feet thick.

No. 2. Mountains of oil-shale showing the weathering, which goes on very fast, the cliffs breaking down into the talus-slopes. Rock falls from the cliffs daily.

No. 3. This shows the banding of the horizontal beds of poor and rich shale. The rich shale forms the darker bands and resists weathering longer. The lower part of the formation is interbedded with considerable amounts of sandstone and is not workable.

No. 4. The talus-slopes represent a vertical height of about 800 ft. and the cliffs 500 ft. Heavy pine-timber can be seen growing on the shady slope. The workable bed of oil-shale, from 8 to 30 ft. thick, occurs near the bottom of these cliffs. Some narrow beds run as high as 90 gallons to the ton of shale.

No. 5. Showing the rough character of the tops of the mesas. This forms grazing land for thousands of cattle.

All of the shale carries some oil, the range being from 10 to 90 gallons per ton of shale. The richer shale is dark-brown to black on a freshly broken surface, the very rich shale having a glossy satiny lustre and a curling banding, somewhat resembling the banding of gneiss. This rich shale is exceedingly light in weight, some running 20 cu. ft. to the ton. The richer the shale the lighter the weight. It is very tough, a hammer bouncing back from it is though from rubber. A freshly broken piece gives off a peculiar petroleum-like odor. Some of the rich shale can be lighted with a match and makes a very hot fire. The beds vary from massive to 'paper' shale, showing the structure implied. In one district a paper shale will form the rich beds, in another the massive.

The mining will be underground, following a horizontal bed from 8 to 20 ft. thick, and will probably closely follow the methods used in the lead districts of Missouri. The shale is exceedingly tough and rubbery and should form a good roof.

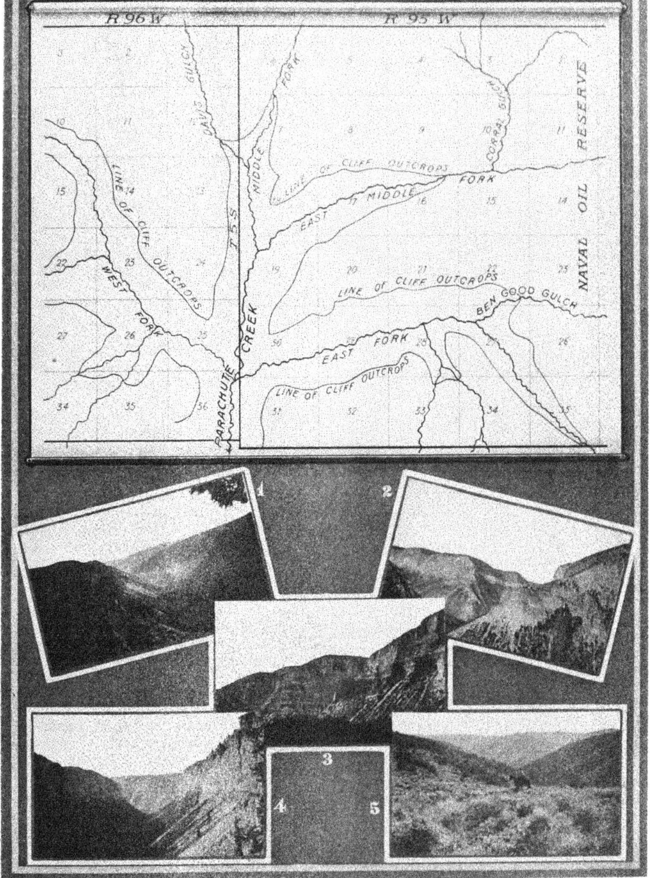

AN OIL-SHALE DISTRICT IN COLORADO

Americanization

By FRANKLIN K. LANE, Secretary of the Interior

INTRODUCTION. America threw the world into a daring maze of possibilities by its entrance into this war upon lines more idealistic than any other national venture in history. And in doing this we challenged the world to a contest for supremacy, not upon the field of battle but in the much larger field of intellectual, moral, and social leadership. Whether we can make good before the world depends upon our willingness and our ability to see the problems that we must meet and our will to meet them forehandedly. For clearly our right to world leadership in the new day is not to be measured by the number of men who have gone to France or the things they have done, but by the use we now and from this time forward make of the freedom we have secured for ourselves and others.

The world has taken us at our word. We said that the institutions which we enjoyed were those which the world should enjoy, for they were based upon rights inherent in man. We announced ourselves as coming to the rescue of imperiled democracies, and as the War progressed we came to the point where we would discuss peace only with those whose government, like our own, came from the people. Beaten upon land and frustrated upon sea, those sole surviving autocracies with which we fought broke into fragments before the mandate of an idea, and the map of Europe changed more in a few days than it had changed in centuries. The aggregating process which had gone on throughout many hundreds of years, and which had been deemed essential to national self-protection, was not only stayed but set at naught, and nations fell into pieces like a child's picture-puzzle, to be re-placed in the general picture along lines of racial desire and a common culture. This is an unprecedented thing in history. Enemy nations came to an 'about face', professing themselves converts to the new faith, willing pupils in a new school. Thus out of an international struggle which we entered upon unwillingly we find ourselves emerging with a greater burden of national responsibility and a larger sense of the meaning of America—America as a leader in a world of democracies, if not a world democracy.

NEW RESPONSIBILITIES. What change in national policies is involved in this world-change? Who are these re-born racial groups who now come forward to their places at the family table? What is our duty toward them and upon what are they to live? What economic independence is essential to national existence? To what extent are we trustees for other peoples? What national purposes have we that should be made secure by international pact or union? Such questions go deep into problems to which even the ripest statesmen have in the past given little thought. And how much less the great body of the people! Yet now it is the duty of the American citizen to know of these things; to talk of them, as a process of whipping his own chaotic notions into shape; to project himself into a world where all horizons are new. While yet we may hardly be said to have learned to think nationally, we are compelled to give serious concern to the affairs of people of whom we had not heard four years ago. Most removed and isolated of all nations, living on and to ourselves, America has overnight moved into the centre of the world's stage and become subject to every scrutinizing and critical eye. This is a test for all that we have dignity and wisdom.

A wholesale challenge has been given as a result of our own idealism—how now may we meet it? Clearly we must set about making ourselves adequate to think in the larger terms of this greater life. Yet we must hold fast to that which makes possible any such broad conception—the ability of men and women to live together under the proved form of our own Government. To think in terms of many democracies or of mankind, we must work in terms of America. For all thought of making good in a greater sphere must be checked, qualified, and limited by our capacity to prove ourselves first of all strong and capable and purposeful at home. Our international value depends upon our strength, unity, and vision. And this in turn must in a democracy rest upon the intelligence, the capabilities, and the character of the individuals who make the Nation.

Now, the question that we must put to ourselves is: Are we doing all that can be done to develop these?

Our war experience has taught us, among many things, the value of a strong national spirit, the vital importance of national ideals, the impotence of ignorance, the dependence of this modern world upon skilled men and organizing ability, the need for and the possibilities that lie in the extension of co-operative effort of all kinds. Are we making full use of the facilities that we have for the promotion of these ends? Are we making out of America as a growing crop all that might reasonably be expected or that is demanded by our position in the world?

AMERICA IN 1918. The vitality of this question was put strongly to the Nation during the past year in a form that was not altogether agreeable. For the draft revealed the astonishing percentage of those in this country who were unable to speak our language or to read or write any language. Yet, I take it, there is no one thing so supremely essential in a government such as

*Excerpt from the Annual Report of the Secretary of the Interior.

ours, where decisions of such importance must be made by public opinion, as that every man and woman and child shall know one tongue—that each may speak to every other and that all shall be informed.

There can be neither national unity in ideals or in purpose unless there is some common method of communication through which may be conveyed the thought of the Nation. All Americans must be taught to read and write and *think* in one language; this is a primary condition to that growth which all nations expect of us and which we demand of ourselves.

What should be said of a world-leading democracy wherein 10% of the adult population cannot read the laws which they are presumed to know?

What should be said of a democracy which sends an army to preach democracy wherein there was drafted out of the first 2,000,000 men a total of 200,000 men who could not read their orders or understand them when delivered, or read the letters sent them from home?

What should be said of a democracy which calls upon its citizens to consider the wisdom of forming a league of nations, of passing judgment upon a code which will insure the freedom of the seas, or of sacrificing the daily stint of wheat or meat for the benefit of the Rumanians or the Jugo-Slavs when 18% of the coming citizens of that democracy do not go to school?

What should be said of a democracy in which one of its sovereign States expends a grand total of $6 per year per child for sustaining its public-school system?

What should be said of a democracy which is challenged by the world to prove the superiority of its system of government over those discarded, and yet is compelled to reach many millions of its people through papers printed in some foreign language?

What should be said of a democracy which expends in a year twice as much for chewing-gum as for school-books, more for automobiles than for all primary and secondary education, and in which the average teacher's salary is less than that of the average day laborer?

What should be said of a democracy which permits tens of thousands of its native-born children to be taught American history in a foreign language—the Declaration of Independence and Lincoln's Gettysburg speech in German and other tongues?

What should be said of a democracy which permits men and women to work in masses where they seldom or never hear a word of English spoken?

Yet, this is all true of the United States of America in this year of grace 1918, wherein was fought the second Battle of the Marne and the Battle of the Argonne Forest.

These figures and facts look discouraging. They seem to present a picture that bodes ill for the Republic. But in reality they present an outlook that is far from disturbing, and that is the one cheering thing about such a Government as ours, wherein we can do as we will. And our will to do is never wanting when we see clearly the difficulty and know the way out. Already there have been devised methods by which these conditions may be remedied in large part, and these methods have been worked out practically by experiment and in no little detail.

A NATIONAL CONCERN. If once we realize that education is not solely a State matter but a national concern, the way is open. And what argument that could be advanced would be more persuasive that education deserves and must have the consideration of the central Government than the figures that are given?

If men cannot be converted readily into soldiers, but must be held in camp while they receive a primary education, surely no one can hold that this is a matter deserving of merely State attention. The Nation's life may not have been imperiled by the presence in the Army of a considerable percentage of men who could not be equipped for service promptly, but this is the minor part of the reason why this humiliating condition should not obtain in this country. The greater reason is that we cannot govern ourselves while in ignorance. We cannot have a small portion of our population unable to sense the movement of our times save through the gossip of the corner and altogether unable to check the idle rumor and the slogans of demagogues, without putting at hazard the success of our system of government. And if we lag others will lead. The American must be the exemplar of democracy.

We are training boys and men to be farmers out of Federal funds, preparing to advance vocational education on a large scale, promoting the construction of solid highways within the States as part of an inter-state system, subjecting the packer, the canner, and the banker to Federal supervision; surely without violation of our fundamental law we can find a way by which the Nation can know that all of its people are able to talk and read our own language. I do not suggest Federal control, but I would strongly urge Federal co-operation with the States toward definite ends.

A little money, the co-operation of the States, and of the industries of the country—and both can be had—a little money, perhaps as much in a year as we have gloriously spent in five hours in France, and the work could be done. It could be done without coercion, without trenching on the prerogatives of the State in the slightest. If we could offer help to those willing to accept it, the end would be accomplished. Make the same kind of an offer to the States for the education of their illiterates that we make to them for the construction of roads, and in five years there would be few, if any, who could not read and write in this country. It may be worth while to consider some of the groups that, taken together, constitute the problem.

NATIVE-BORN WHITES. Adult illiteracy in the less-developed sections of our country is not a proud matter of which to talk, but it is present. Men who speak in the language of Shakespeare—and this is literally true, for their ancestors came here in his time bringing the language of Shakespeare and the King James version of the Bible on their tongues—tens of thousands of these men and women are today, after three centuries in this country, unable to read one line of Shakespeare or to sign their names. And yet they have fought for this country through every war and have died as heroes for a land that did not concern itself enough about them to see that they were educated. These people have not had their chance. Their condition is a reproach to a republic. And it is not that they are unwilling to take instruction, or that they feel superior to it. For the experiment has been made; and, day after day, old gray-bearded men and eager-eyed women went to the mountain schools when given the opportunity, and their letters tell of the delight that is theirs because the world has been opened to them.

And the children of these American-born people of Anglo-Saxon stock—what of them? Are they to be left to burrow their way through the darkness—one out of a thousand, perhaps, emerging to the opportunities of a railroad brakeman or a skilled mechanic after a splendid struggle against the handicap of early ignorance? These boys are expected to vote, and to vote wisely for those who shape not only the destinies of their own land, but, as we now see, for those who are to mold the lives of many peoples. Are they to vote without knowing that such new nations exist—without the ability to read the names on a map or the text of a treaty? This would seem to be challenging too strongly the protecting hand of a patient Providence.

THE NEGRO. Then, we must consider the negro. For him and his condition we are responsible as for no one else. He came here without exercising his own will. He was made a citizen without discrimination and in a large out-of-hand way. The Indian we feel we are responsible for as a Nation, and we give him an education—a most practical one. But the negro, who is a charge upon the American conscience and whose education, I believe, should long ago, in some part, at least, have been a charge upon the American pocket, is slowly, very slowly, coming into that knowledge which is his one chance of developing into a growing national asset—the knowledge of the way of making a living. When one looks into the effort that is being made to give the negro the right sort of an education, he finds a much more cheerful picture than he had thought. The Southern States, for instance, are meeting with no little eagerness the offers that come to them to give some direction to the education of the negro. The problem is basically one of money. The way has been found to give our colored citizen an education that will strengthen his fibre, widen his vision, and at the same time make him happy in achieving a useful place in society. There are no more inspiring and promising reports written in this country than those of the various foundations which are promoting the right method of educating the negro. Not only is the response from the States encouraging, but experience has gone far enough forward by this time to demonstrate that with guidance, oversight, and the bearing of only a part of the financial burden, this whole problem of lifting a backward people onto a level more compatible with our hopes for them and with their status as citizens can be realized. Still, this Nation may learn what education will do for an undeveloped race by the study of its own work in the far-off Philippine Islands.

THE FOREIGN-BORN. The next grand division of those who need education, inspiration, and outlook, and for whom we are responsible, is the foreign-born. Our responsibility arises out of our generosity. These sons and daughters of all the world have been drawn here by the generosity of our laws; the open hand has been extended across the seas. We have said to them that coming clean they would be welcome. This was the land of their heart's desire, where men could be their own masters and rise according to the quality that they had. Here was youth with which they could identify themselves, land which they could own, society of which they could become an integral part, political life which they could help to shape and in which they would have satisfied that world-long yearning for recognition. The man could here be developed, the full man, for schools were here and a sympathetic environment; others were climbing, too, with whom they could measure their progress. This was a fair picture surely. And they came, some for economic reasons, desiring their chance at the good things spread on this rich table that Columbus found. Others came that they might have the larger satisfaction of an independent, unhampered, unmastered growth as men among equals. They came in no apologetic humor, for they brought something from the older lands which they felt would be a contribution to a new civilization—their art, literature, their far-reaching historical perspective, their fervor for the opportunity to experiment, to adventure, to give a cast to this new world's life.

Here was an opportunity. We met them at the gate with a truly American welcome, which most of them could not understand: "Enter and make a place for yourself." This had been the greeting we ourselves had received. There was to be coddling here. This was a man's land, a place of test. The art that was most needed was the art of getting on. If literature and science and experiment were to come they must be founded upon the solid rock of a self-sustained, unpatronized people. Dreams of ease and long debate must be cast aside until the right to dream was earned. The American was to be a journeyman, doing his bit at the making of the land. If this was not a worth-while job, then there was no place for the stranger. We had mines to dig, wells to drill, buildings to erect, railroads to construct, farms to plow, sewers to lay, machines to build, and when one had done his share of these there might come the singing. The Lord had laid on us the responsibility of reclaiming for mankind a large slice of this lost land, and all else could wait in life till this end was reached. In this steady drive we made ourselves. We were impatient with those who called out to stop or go slow. The pace that we set was that which must be kept. "All men are born free and equal," we called to the newcomer, and went on, forgetful that he was not free, for he had still the limitations of his old life, nor equal, for many reasons. Manifestly a man without tools is not the equal of the man with, and those here already were men who knew the language of the new land, who knew its spirit and the way to meet it and run with it, who had access to the heart of a people and knew what its call was. Things did not lie obvious before the eye like a seam of coal on a naked hillside. This new land was a hunting ground, and those who knew the favorite cover and could blend most quietly into the landscape found themselves best at the game.

THE NEWCOMER'S DILEMMA. So this is America! A scramble for a living! Much to see, but no one to interpret it all. So thought this new American. Then the padrone came forward as a savior. Life was not to go out anyway. And, with others in like situation, possibly from his own country, equally ignorant, equally handicapped, the new American starts his life. It takes a brave and a very ambitious man to lift himself out of such an environment. Easily he becomes a victim to the shrewd, predatory padrone or boss. He falls into debt and becomes mortgaged to ignorance and squalor for years. His ideal of America has suffered a change. "And is this freedom?" he says to himself, as with tired back he bends to his work, without hope that the burden will be lighter tomorrow. He cannot read the signs which warn him of danger. He cannot read of the opportunities which city and country offer. In his own land perhaps he had no chance to learn in his own tongue. In this new land he is too tired, too hesitant to learn this strange difficult tongue. Is it any wonder if to this dissatisfied stranger the voice of one who speaks to him in the language of home has authority and carries far? And if this voice preaches discontent, and violent discontent, as the one sure path to better days, is it strange that he should listen? Who are the men who master this new world? Plainly the ones he knows, from whom he has suffered. Do these same men control everything; are there no sweet places of refuge? He can find no one to make him see the greater America. The whole of this continent is to him the cramped apartment, the dirty street, and the sweatshop or the factory. To the sweep of the great land and its many beckonings his eyes are closed. And in his isolation and ignorance and disappointment there is fruitful nesting place for all the hurtful microbes that attack society.

REASONS FOR AMERICANIZATION. This man is our charge. He needs and deserves care, solicitude, thoughtful consideration. Ignobly put—it will pay. More manfully said—it is our duty. Worthily—it is our opportunity.

Economically that man is a potential asset which we should not waste. Give him a glimpse into the philosophy which underlies our struggle and he will turn into a cheerful, strong fellow worker in the making of America, as have all the rest who have preceded him. It is money in our pockets that he should be able to care for himself; that he should know our language; that his body shall be well nourished and his mind hopeful. So much for the purely selfish side.

As to our duty, it grows out of our loyalty to ourselves. *noblesse oblige*. But we may look beyond these and find a finer reason for doing all in our power to reveal America to this man. He is a human being whom we can help to a truer view of that which we have said before the world was the most stimulating, invigorating, developing of all atmospheres, that of freedom. And the test of our democracy is in our ability to absorb that man and incorporate him into the body of our life as an American. He will learn to play the game, to stand to the challenge that makes Americans; the unfostered self-sufficiency of the man who knows his way and has learned it by fighting for it will yet be his. And we will learn from him the viewpoint of those peoples who now are wrestling with all their new-found strength and weakness to realize long-nurtured hopes. If we are to deal wisely in this larger day we must get within that man and look out with his eyes not only upon this country but upon the land from which he came, for has not America become as a foster mother to these struggles?

METHODS. First of all, the hand of friendship for that new American, the voice of a friend who shall be an unselfish adviser, a guide in this strange land of troubles, small and large, but equally incomprehensible. Then the school, the night school, or if not that, the shop school. And with these the community centre, the gathering place that represents all America.

This is a program that has been well thought out. It has been tried out in a small way and found successful. It needs but nurturing to develop into a plan that will make the word 'Americanization' one of exceptional pride. For this plan the great cities of the country, where mostly our foreign born have congregated, are ready. For it the industries, the business men, are ready. I am warranted in the statement that all the largest industries in the land will from their own time offer an opportunity for an elementary education to every foreign-born man or woman in their employ. Some are willing to furnish the teacher if one competent for this class of work can be found. If the Government will shape the policy and undertake to make the propaganda for this definite end of giving a first insight into American words, newspapers, politics, life, that which has been regarded as the work of generations can be started in a very short time and men put on their way toward real citizenship.

I am not urging the absurdity that men can be transformed into Americans by a course in school. This is but a beginning. Knowledge of our language is but a tool. America is the expression of a spirit, an attitude toward men and material things, an outlook, and a faith. Our strange and successful experiment in the art of making a new people is the result of contact, not of caste, of living together, working together for a living, each one interpreting for himself and for his neighbors his conception of what kind of social being man should be, what his sympathies, standards, and ambitions should be. Now, this cannot be taught out of a book. It is a matter of touch, of feeling, like the growth of friendship. Each man is approachable in a different way, appealed to by very contradictory things. One man reaches America through a baseball game, another through a church, a saloon, a political meeting, a woman, a labor union, a picture gallery, or something new to eat. The difficulty is in finding the meeting place where there is no fear, no favor, no ulterior motives, and, above all, no soul-insulting patronage of poor by rich, of black by white, of younger by elder, of foreign born by native born, of the unco' bad by the unco' good. To meet this need the schoolhouse has been turned into a community centre. It is a common property, or should be. All feel entitled to its use. When we were younger this kind of machinery was not necessary, for we were fewer in number, lived in smaller communities, and felt a common interdependence which made each one a trumpet blowing herald of democracy. Today, however, there must be some thought given and some money expended in even having an opportunity to touch the hand of a fellow man.

I believe that more and more thought will be given to our school system as the most serviceable instrumentality we possess for the development of a better America. It has been, we must confess, a very much taken-for-granted institution. It is probably of all our inventions the one of which we are most proud, and like other of our inventions we have not realized the greatness of its possibilities. We have become accustomed to hearing it spoken of as the heart of the Nation. But this figure must be taken with very definite limitations. It is the beginning of things for the boys and girls, but to the man and the woman it is almost a thing outside of life. This should not be so, for it may be the very centre of the social, the intellectual, and in smaller places of the economic life. This is so, in fact, in Switzerland and in Denmark, and is becoming so in many places in our country.

To the necessity for more thorough education of the people all countries have become keenly alive. One large part of England's grand plan of reconstruction is the founding and conducting of a great national school system out of which will come more men and women of trained minds and trained hands.

As we move further and further from the War we will discover much that we do not now see. But this one thing stands out more plainly than ever before, that this world is to belong to the workers, those who do and those who direct the doing. Not merely to those who drive the nail or lay the brick, but also to those who have come to a higher capacity through education and larger experience, the men of scientific knowledge, of skill in the arts, of large organizing capacity. Ease, sheltered repose, will come only to those who themselves have earned it. This is the inevitable tendency of democracy.

This thought is not new to America, it is American, for here we have climbed the rough road of experience together, each jostling the other and pushing the weak ones aside. To the swift and to the strong there will always come the premiums, but to the cunning and to the greedy there will be given less and less opportunity.

The test is to be in peace as it was in the time of war. Are you fitted for the fight? The man who knew how knowledge could be converted into power was the man for whom there was unlimited call. So it is increasingly to be. To be useful is to be the test that society will put. Each man's rights are to be measured not by what he has but by what he does with what he has. The honors—the *croix de paix*—the richest rewards will go to the capables, those who are not standardized into 'men-machines', those who dare to venture and learn to lead. But all must work, and this duty to work and respect for work should be the earliest lesson learned. And it should be taught in the school, not as a homily but in a living way, by tieing work with instruction, making the thing learned to apply to something done. I should like to see the day when every child learned a trade while at school, trained his mind and his hand together, lifted labor into art by the application of thought.

To be useful is the essence of Americanism, and against the undeveloped resources, whether if be land or man, the spirit of this country makes protest.

An Annealing Furnace for Crucibles

The ideal annealing-furnace consists of two chambers, the size depending upon the number of crucibles used. A firm that buys crucibles by the car-load has built a modern annealing-plant. It consists of two rooms side by side, each large enough to contain a carload of crucibles. The heating in this case is done by steam-pipes around the walls, sufficient to raise the temperature in the room gradually to 300°. When a new lot of crucibles is received they are put in one of these rooms. The heat is turned on and gradually raised until at the end of a week or 10 days it has reached the 300° point and eliminated all the moisture from the crucibles. They are kept in this atmosphere until they are all used. In the meantime, when another lot of crucibles comes in, they are put in the second room—the reason for this being that if they were to put the fresh lot in with some of the seasoned ones, the moisture in the new ones would counteract all the good effect that the previous heat had done.

After it is taken into consideration that a crucible which comes out of the Dixon kilns contains as little as 0.25% moisture, as soon as it cools and comes in contact with the atmosphere it is liable to gather as much as 6%. This would mean that in a crucible weighing 100 lb. there would be nearly one gallon of water absorbed, so if this 'green' crucible is placed in an oven where the dry ones are, the result can readily be seen.

Furthermore, it is necessary that some ventilation be arranged in an annealing-oven of this kind. One opening at the top on one side of the oven and another at the bottom in the opposite side allows for the circulation of air necessary to carry the moisture away. What has been said in regard to a plant to take care of a carload of crucibles is equally true in regard to a smaller quantity. The principle involved is the same, and the increased life of crucibles will certainly pay the expense involved in erecting this kind of a plant. A. C. Sorenson in 'Graphite,' December 1918.

Concentration of Lead-Zinc-Silver Ore at the Zinc Corporation's Mine

By GEORGE C. KLUG

*The methods employed in the Broken Hill practice of concentration apply the principle of gravity concentration by jigging and tabling for the production of a high-grade lead concentrate: a ziney tailing is also produced, and this is either treated direct by flotation for the separation of a mixed lead and zinc concentrate that is afterward separated into a high-grade zinc concentrate and a leady concentrate by ordinary tabling methods, or the tailing is treated by preferential flotation methods for the separation of galena and blende to produce lead and zinc concentrates respectively. The flotation methods employed are those of Minerals Separation, De Bavay, and Delprat.

The slime produced in the crushing and grinding of the ore is treated by preferential or selective flotation, whereby the galena and blende contents are separated into lead and zinc concentrates. In this section of the work are employed the processes of Lyster, Owen, Bradford, and Seale-Shellshear.

A recent innovation has been the introduction of the Seale-Shellshear method of cascading as modified by Lyster and Hebbard for the purpose of selectively separating the galena from the mill-pulp. The tailing from this de-leading process is further treated by cascading in an acid circuit for the separation of the blende as a zinc concentrate. This system of cascading has been further improved upon by the Wallaroo company in connection with the flotation of copper ores. The latter modification is now being tested by the Sulphide Corporation, which company has in its milling practice already displaced a large number of Wilfley tables by cascade flotation. While this cascading method is certainly attractive and undoubtedly effects a saving in power, it is a debatable point whether it offers a more profitable scheme than that of tabling followed by a selective process such as the Lyster. For a company designing a new mill, it would be well to test both systems experimentally before deciding the point.

Where the ore is of a calcitic nature, the elimination of the acid-consuming mineral, calcite, by gravity methods producing a tailing of low metal content and a zinc middling containing about 16% zinc, is a more profitable practice than treating the whole of the tailing by flotation methods such as can be successfully carried out on an ore having a silicious or rhodonitic gangue.

The concentration practice adopted by the Zinc Corporation at the South Blocks mine is typical of that which obtains when dealing with an ore containing an appreciable amount of calcite, and this is described in the following notes and accompany flow sheet.

The treatment aims at separating the ore into the following products:

1. Lead concentrate assaying 66% lead, by jigging and tabling.

2. The elimination of as much of the calcitic gangue as possible in the form of a sand, which assays 5% zinc, 0.6 oz. silver, and 1.6% lead, and which is used for filling underground.

3. Collection of all the slime for preferential flotation treatment in the slime unit.

4. The balance forms a zinc middling, which is treated at the zinc concentrator.

The lead mill, which has a capacity of 26 tons of crude ore per hour, is situated on the south side of the main hauling-shaft. The ore is raised from underground in self-dumping skips, with a capacity of 2.5 tons, and is automatically tipped into the breaker-bin, the capacity of which is 200 tons, of which 150 tons is live. The rough ore (up to 10 in. maximum dimension) is fed from the bin on to a 36-in. belt-conveyor, traveling at 50 ft. per minute, and any large pieces of waste are picked off this belt by hand. This conveyor delivers the ore to a Bigelow jaw-breaker, 12 by 30 in., running at 215 r.p.m., set to break at 4-in. gauge. The ore from this breaker is conveyed by a short 18-in. belt to a bar-grizzly 6 ft. long with 1¼-in. openings, the oversize falling into the No. 2 breaker and the undersize joining the product from the No. 2 breaker. This breaker, of similar size as the previous one, is set to break to 2-in. gauge. The broken ore is conveyed by 18-in. belt-conveyors over a Blake-Denison continuous weigher, and is delivered either to the mill-bin or the crude-ore storage-bin. The former bin has a capacity of 300 tons, and the latter 1200 tons. The crude-ore storage-bin has a chinaman chute running longitudinally along its bottom, and the ore, when required, is delivered to the mill-bin by an 18-in. conveyor under the chinaman.

The average sizing of the ore at this point is:

	%
On 1 in. square aperture	51.1
On 7/16 in. square aperture	21.7
On 7/32 in. square aperture	7.9
On 3 mm. round aperture	3.8
Through 3 mm. round aperture	15.5

From the mill-bin the ore is fed by means of two shaking screens. These screens are 7 ft. 9 in. long by 2 ft. wide, 1¼ in. stroke, run at 240 strokes per minute, and fitted with punched-screen plates with 3-mm. holes. The

*From 'The Mining Magazine', of November, 1918.

oversize from these screens passes to two sets of Cornish rolls 32 by 18 in., running at 20 r.p.m., the undersize going to No. 2 elevator and thence to the jig-screens. The crushed ore from each set of rolls goes to a bucket-elevator (12 in. by 8-ply rubber belt, traveling at 320 ft. per minute) and portion of it is delivered to the Raff screens, the balance going to the shaking screen feeding the rolls. The Raff screens are of the ordinary revolving type, clothed with 7 by 7 by 18 gauge wooven steel wire, running at 11 r.p.m. The oversize is returned to the rolls, and the undersize is elevated to the jig-screens. There are four of these, clothed with 25 by 25 by 25 gauge woven brass wire. The oversize goes to the jigs, of which there are two, and the undersize, which contains about 19% lead, after it is thickened, is fed to the north row of primary Wilfley tables.

The jigs are of the May type, with only three hutches, using punched-plate screens of 4 mm. diam. and 3½ mm. diam. holes on No. 1 and 2 hutches, respectively. The concentrate from the two hutches averages about 66% lead, and the tailing 6% lead. The latter product is elevated and laundered to seven revolving screens, clothed with 20-mesh Tyler brass ton-cap screening, the undersize from which forms the feed for the south row of primary Wilfley tables. The oversize from these screens is distributed between twelve 5-ft. grinding-pans, fitted for a central feed and negative discharge. The jig-tailing amounts to about 1.25 tons per pan per hour, and the returned oversize from the pan-discharge brings the total feed per pan to about 3 tons per hour. This type of pan produces a minimum amount of slime, and, before the introduction of flotation methods, when the mineral in the slime was practically unrecoverable, had much to recommend it. In view, however, of recent developments in selective flotation, the slime is no longer a bugbear, and any new installation would probably embody tube-mills for secondary grinding. The discharge from the pans joins the jig-tailing, and the oversized material is returned again to the pans.

The primary tables are arranged in two rows of 8 tables each. The northern row treats the undersize from the jig-screens, and the other row treats the re-ground jig-tailing. The feed for each row is thickened in 8-ft. Callow settlers, the slime-overflow from which is sent to the Dorr thickeners. These tables (No. 5 Wilfley, run at 280 r.p.m.) make three products:

1. Finished lead concentrate assaying 68% lead, which joins the concentrate from the jigs, and is laundered to No. 8 elevator which delivers to the concentrate-collecting vats, four in number, each having a capacity of 300 tons, and each fitted with filter-bottoms. The concentrate is distributed in the vat by means of a Butters distributer, which is mounted on a trolley and serves each vat as required. The overflow from these vats goes to the Dorr thickeners. The concentrate, after being drained by means of a vacuum-pump, whereby the moisture is reduced to about 4%, is loaded, through bottom-discharge doors, into trucks for dispatch to the smelters.

2. A middling, which is elevated, and after being thickened, is sent to eight secondary Wilfley tables for re-treatment. These tables reduce the lead content to 2 to 3%, and the residual zinc middling, now assaying 15.5% zinc and 4.2% lead, and representing 28% by weight of the crude ore, is elevated, collected, and drained in steel vats. This product is sent to the zinc concentrator for recovery of metals in the form of zinc and lead concentrates. Experiments have demonstrated that this material is amenable to preferential galena flotation, followed by Bradford's copper-sulphate method for flotation of the blende in an alkaline circuit, and this process will ultimately replace the ordinary flotation-acid method.

3. Tailing. This is elevated and separated by cones into (a) coarse sand, (b) fine sand, (c) slime. (a) and (b) are re-treated on five and three tables respectively, whereby small quantities of lead concentrate and zinc middling are recovered, and a residue sand produced assaying 0.6 oz. silver, 5% zinc, and 1.6% lead. The last mentioned product, representing 40% by weight of the crude ore, is dewatered on a draining-belt, and conveyed to the residue dump. The slime is sent to the Dorr thickeners.

All overflows from cone thickeners, etc., are fed to two Dorr thickeners (25 ft. diam. and 30 ft. diam. respectively). The clear water from these flows to a sump and balance tanks having a capacity of 25,000 gallons. From these tanks the water is elevated 40 ft. to the head service tank (14,000 gal.) by three 6-in. centrifugal pumps, one of which is kept as a stand-by. The slime from the Dorr thickeners is elevated and fed to the head of the 10-compartment lead-flotation unit, at a consistence of about 33% solid.

The flotation box, which is fitted with the vertical hollow spindles, is of the single-level type, each compartment being 24 in. square by 4 ft. deep. The impellers are of 10 in. diam. by 2 in. deep, shrouded on the upper surface, and are driven at 700 r.p.m. and set ¾ in. from the bottom of the box. The 10-compartment unit, including counter-shaft, requires 21 hp. Air is drawn in through the vertical hollow spindle, and the float overflows from the surface of the mixing-compartment. Cast-iron baffles are used in the lower 2 ft. of the boxes, and upper 18 in. is crowded toward the adjustable overflow-lip. A mixture of eucalyptus oil and tar oil, in equal parts (about 0.2 lb. per ton of slime) is added at the launder between the elevator and the head of the box. The lead concentrate passes to thickening-cones, and is periodically run into dams on the lead-drying floor.

The tailing from the lead-flotation unit is elevated and fed to a 14-compartment unit similar to the lead unit, except that phosphor-bronze impellers are used. About 0.6 lb. of copper sulphate per ton of slime is added to the pulp at the exit from the lead unit, and about 0.3 lb. of eucalyptus oil per ton of slime is added just before the pulp enters the flotation unit. This treatment, from 10 of the boxes, yields a float product assaying about 39% zinc, and a tailing assaying 2% zinc, 0.5 oz. silver, and 0.5% lead, which latter is sent to the residue-dam. The floated product is re-treated, without further reagents, in

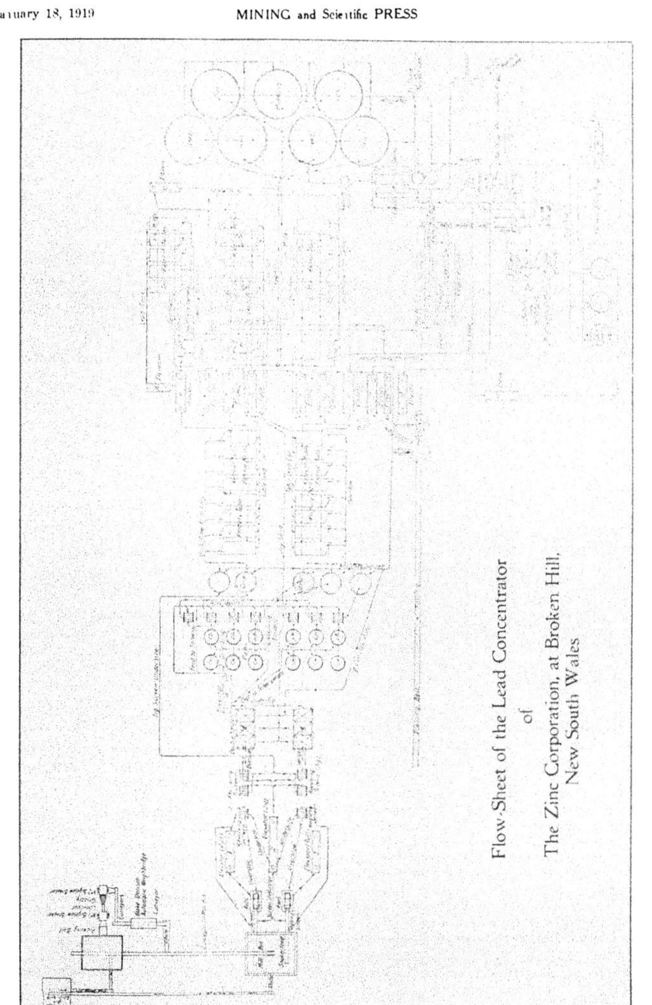

Flow-Sheet of the Lead Concentrator
of
The Zinc Corporation, at Broken Hill,
New South Wales

the remaining four boxes, to remove a further quantity of gangue, and the resultant float assays 42 to 43% zinc.

This mill is effecting an average recovery of 85% lead and 68.2% silver, from an ore containing 14.3% lead, 2.6 oz. silver, and 9.2% zinc. A further recovery of 2% lead is made from the treatment of the zinc middling at the zinc concentrator. The percentage of zinc recovered in the form of zinc middling is 60%. This, on re-treatment, produces 50% zinc in the form of zinc concentrate.

The Lyster process is used for the preferential flotation of the galena from the blende and other minerals in the slime. This was the first preferential flotation process to be successfully applied to Broken Hill ores, and, although the machines used by other mines differ considerably, the process is still used more than any other for preferential flotation work on crude ore along the Broken Hill lode. The process depends on the presence of certain salts, notably calcium and magnesium sulphates, in the circuit-water, which act as a modifier on oil-frothing media. The water pumped from the underground workings contains a sufficient quantity of suitable salts, and the mill-circuit water is made up from this source. The addition of a soluble copper salt, according to the Bradford copper sulphate process, causes the blende to float, and advantage is taken of this to lift the blende after the slime has been de-leaded by the Lyster process. The above results are obtained in a neutral circuit, and the presence of the calcite, therefore, presents no difficulties.

Besides the Lyster, two other preferential flotation methods are being widely used at the present time. These are the Bradford hyposulphite or sulphurous acid, and the Seale-Shellshear processes. The Bradford hyposulphite process depends on the wetting of the blende in the presence of SO_2 liberated from $Na_2S_2O_3$ in a faintly acid circuit: this prevents the blende from floating, and, when the galena has been floated, the SO_2 is expelled by heat, air, or acid, and then the blende is lifted in the ordinary way. This method is especially applicable to dump-slime that has become partly oxidized, but, being an acid process, the cost of the reagent renders it too expensive for very calcitic material.

The Seale-Shellshear cascade system is, strictly speaking, only a system to reduce the power usually employed for agitation in flotation machines. The pulp flows from the bottom of each box to the one immediately below it, through an injector which draws in air, and the air mixing with the pulp causes the mineral to float in the lower box. When used for preferential galena flotation, such results are undoubtedly due to the Lyster conditions being present. The only power required for this system is that necessary to elevate the pulp to the first box. The method is applied to the de-leading of fine sandy material and, as previously stated, has taken the place of tables in one of the mills. Judging from observation, however, the tailing obtained by this method is not as clean as that from some of the other types of machines.

[Other articles on flotation practice at Broken Hill appeared in our issues of September 21 and 28, 1918.—EDITOR.]

Notes on Powdered Coal

By A. V. ADAMSON

*The experience of users of pulverized fuel in metallurgical work, particularly for open-hearth furnaces, has demonstrated that high ash and sulphur in the fuel are a detriment. The sulphur in the coal enters into the finished product, hence, in this class of work it is extremely important, when powdered coal is to be used, that it be selected with care, and only those having low percentages of sulphur be used in combination with proper means for combustion.

It has been found that no general rule can be laid down as to either fineness or dryness; for some uses a wide range is permissible in both factors, while some classes of fuel require different treatment than others.

Ash, slag, and clinker are a real problem; to prevent their formation on tubes, checker-work, and furnace-walls, is absolutely essential. Methods of combustion, and furnace design are of vital importance. Scientific analysis of the difference in heat transmission due to radiant fuel and ash in suspension has offered a real opportunity for research. None of these items can be disregarded; yet the beaten highway of cement practice has offered no answer because in long-flame rotary-kilns, such as are used in cement work, these questions are of no importance.

Four years' practical operating experience on locomotives, heating-furnaces, and boilers, have definitely settled the following factors:

1. Pulverized coal is not suitable for all purposes, and the character of the fuel available is one of the factors causing the necessity for separately considering each proposed installation.

2. Honeycomb and ash on tubes, and slag on walls and furnace-floor, can be controlled.

3. Flame velocity must be reduced to a minimum.

4. No continuous operating efficiency or continuous good results can be obtained with pressure for combustion, even if only $\frac{3}{8}$-oz. pressure is used; and the more nearly a furnace approximates a balanced-draft condition, the better the operating results.

5. The incoming fuel must be mechanically mixed with the air-conveying medium to prevent a pulsating flame and the formation of coke due to lumps of pulverized coal in the feed.

6. In general, the future for the use of coal in pulverized form for steam generating, metallurgical, and chemical work, offers a real opportunity for fuel economy and increased production; it is the one way by which shortage of oil, gas, and coal, together with transportation and labor difficulties can be overcome. Due consideration, however, must be given to the difficulties inherent in and the troubles incident to improper design and erection. Each installation requires special development.

*Abstract of discussion of the paper of H. R. Collins, presented at the Colorado and Milwaukee meetings of the A. I. M. E., Sept. and Oct., 1918.

The Treatment of Influenza

By A PHYSICIAN

During and since the epidemic of 1889-'90 I have been a strong believer in active treatment against infective colds, influenza, and pneumonia. Practising in Rome, Italy, during that epidemic gave a good opportunity to discuss and compare methods of treatment with Italian, English, French, and German physicians. It was then generally conceded that those who treated influenza cases actively had fewer cases of pneumonia and in their cases of pneumonia had fewer fatalities. The salicylates when well borne and benzoate of soda in large doses otherwise was the favorite active treatment. Creosote was looked upon with favor in pneumonia. The symptomatic and sustaining remedies were, of course, used when indicated. Nitro-glycerine was held important. Dr. A. A. Smith of New York advocated nitro-glycerine to effect regardless of dosage in cyanosis. I believe he was sound in that, and many have forgotten it to their cost.

The various methods of treatment advocated I have studied with respectful interest, while looking for something immediately available for the general public. Having experimented with a chemical compound of lime and creosote, alleged to be non-poisonous, in various infectious diseases, and observed it to be effective against several toxic diseases, including ptomaine poisoning, I believed it to promise some usefulness against influenza. Being sensitive to this infection and believing that I would not survive another epidemic unless something was found effective as a cure and prophylactic, I used this aqueous solution of lime and creosote on myself rather recklessly. To my surprise I experienced no untoward results but was improved in several particulars. Premonitory symptoms of influenza were remarkably cleared up, such as coryza, muscular pains, general debility, and loss of appetite. My influenza patients began to make such good recoveries that I soon decided that this solution was acting as a true specific against the infection. After further convincing observations I decided that it was my duty to give the remedy to the public as widely as possible, especially to our Army and Navy. Subsequent observations have convinced me that the solution is also effective against the toxemia of pneumonia.

Here we have a colossal infection and the toxemia is what kills the patient. In the present epidemic the toxemia is variously manifested. Notably in both bronchial and lobar pneumonia, severe cyanosis, and oedema of the lungs. To meet the toxemia my dependence is upon the aqueous solution of lime and creosote. To relieve the cyanosis I depend upon adequate doses of nitro-glycerine given frequently enough for a sustained effect. I believe the charts of cases will adequately illustrate this treatment among physicians. I have repeatedly seen cyanosis clear up, and oedema of the lungs as well, under this treatment.

We first observe the blueness of the nails, then the gradual spread of this to the skin and lips, then the feeling in the patient of impending suffocation, the coarse bubbling rales of the chest, sometimes called the death rattle, then the gray pallor of death. Having repeatedly seen severe cyanosis and oedema of the lungs, with a sense of impending suffocation, yield to nitro-glycerine and the solution, I am bold enough to state as my belief that in Calcreose solution we have a remedy against even the toxemia of pneumonia.

I have with me the charts and histories of six cases of pneumonia, some of them having been examples of extreme cyanosis and even of commencing oedema of the lungs. In my practice I have had no death from pneumonia during this epidemic, though my cases range from four months to 75 years of age. Also I have had the pleasure of seeing several recoveries in desperate cases, seen in consultations.

Several cases of pneumonia have been without nursing or adequate care and have made good recoveries with the aid of the Calcreose solution and what little attention I could give at long intervals.

Now I beg your indulgence while I relate quite from memory a case that seems to me remarkable. A young lady of 28 called me on Saturday. I found her with pneumonia involving the lower lobe of the right lung and a temperature of 105°. The pulse was 138. As no nurse was obtainable, I was obliged to depend upon a married sister with no training. I was obliged to teach her the use of the thermometer. As the young woman had a loud obstructive mitral murmur from an attack of rheumatism some years previously, I was doubtful about the outcome. By Thursday morning things had progressed so favorably that I thought convalescence was near. The temperature had dropped to 99½° and resolution seemed begun. Thursday noon the temperature suddenly shot up to 105° and the patient became cyanotic with a sense of impending suffocation. The condition I found was sufficiently grave to dismay me. Fine crepitant rales at the base of the left lung and coarse bubbling rales over the whole upper chest were indicative of oedema. The patient declared she was dying, that the medicine had disagreed with her, and that she would take no more of it. She also declared that every time her heart beat it pulled her over. As the pulse was 160 that alone seemed serious. I persuaded her that the disease instead of the medicine was at fault, doubled the dose of Calcreose solution and administered 1/50 gr. of nitro-glycerine every hour for three doses. Then things were so far relieved that I left the nitro-glycerine to be administered by mouth at two-hour intervals, 1/100 grain.

At four-hour intervals I administered a pill containing 4 m. tr. digitalis 2 m. tr. stropanthus and 1/60 gr. strychnine. The patient took at this time four teaspoonfuls of Calcreose solution every two hours. She has made a good recovery, though she still has the mitral murmur.

The youngest case of broncho-pneumonia was four months of age. Her sister, four years of age, also had broncho-pneumonia and five other children had severe influenza. A young man 27 years old hoarding in the family had pneumonia at the base of the right lung. All made good recoveries, though no care was available save that given by the mother of the family. The treatment was simple. For the most part consisting of milk, Calcreose solution, and clay poultices to the cases of pneumonia. The question was put to me recently, "Would you advocate the use of Calcreose solution by the general public as a prophylactic?" I replied, "Yes, let the public substitute it for aspirin, in my opinion a dangerous heart depressant far too prevalently used."

Two months ago, having sent this treatment to Cripple Creek and other mining centres in Colorado, the six physicians there have reported remarkable results in pneumonia cases even in those high altitudes. On the strength of this report I have recently been asked to send the treatment to the copper mines of the Anaconda company at Butte, Montana.

In closing a word about the scope of what may be reasonably expected of the solution. It does not immunize. It is rapidly excreted. It simply kills the germs and I believe also exerts a favorable action against the toxemia. Prolonged use does not seem at all injurious. It can be pushed to any necessary extent in an emergency. Its use in pneumonia requires the services of a skilled physician. However, the nature of the remedy is such that the public can scarcely abuse it.

When we have classified the various germs, including the local rascals that have joined the aliens, we can label them and possibly write an epitaph, after the manner of certain cowboys in a frontier town. There was a bad man called Jake Deadeye who had killed several men. Finally he killed some one under such circumstances as to send the sheriff and a posse after him. He declared he would not be taken alive. The sheriff and posse surrounded his hiding-place, and finally, to the dismay of the posse, they saw the sheriff deliberately approach Jake. Jake for a few moments was like a flaming torch with his 45, shooting from the hip. Then the sheriff calmly lifted his gun and shot once. Jake crumpled up and fell forward with a bullet between the eyes. The posse rushed up upbraiding the sheriff for his apparent callousness. "Pshaw! boys," said he, "I always figured none of them hip-shooters could hit a barn-door beyond 15 or 20 paces, so I waited at 50 paces and let him have it." Certain qualities of Jake seemed to impress his fellow-citizens, so they voted him a monument with an epitaph reading as follows: "Here lies the body of Jake Deadeye. He done his damndest. Angels could do no more."

The non-poisonons nature of Calcreose solution was demonstrated by an accident. An elderly woman with a severe attack of influenza took four ounces of the solution at one dose and undiluted Her attendant was instructed to give her a glass of milk and during the remainder of the night to give fluids freely. No bad effect resulted from this large dose.

German Sabotage

A statement has just been issued by the Société des Hauts Fourneaux Forges et Aciéries de Denain et d'Anzin (Denain and Auzin Blast Furnaces Forges and Steel Foundries Company), in Northern France, as to the methods by which their vast establishments were destroyed by the Germans. The buildings, blast-furnaces, foundries, and work-shops of the company occupied an area three miles long by a mile and a half wide. The Germans having captured the district in September 1914 the works were closed down on September 15 owing to lack of labor and raw material. The general manager was asked several times by the Germans to re-start his works to meet German military requirements, they offering to provide labor and materials and also engineers if required. The manager, however, refused to work for the Germans, and the works were taken possession of at the end of 1914 by Captain Bocking, of the German 'Removals' Department. Captain Bocking, who is himself in civilian life an important German ironmaster, proceeded to make a complete inventory of the works. Numerous gangs of German workmen, helped by 3000 Russian prisoners of war, proceeded to remove the whole of the ore, castings, together with all intermediary and finished products, as well as machinery and plant. The main buildings were demolished under the guidance of a man named Dryer, a German subject, who had formerly been employed as chief foreman by the French Homécourt Foundries Company. By means of threats he succeeded in getting possession of 80 tons of bronze, of the cages of the flattening and rolling-mills, frames, and all other machinery not already removed. All these goods were dispatched to competitors in Germany, the names and addresses of which are in the hands of the representatitves of the plundered company who succeeded in retaining possession of the railway consignment notes. Finally, when everything removable had been taken away, the Demolition Department at Metz sent a squad of men who blew up with dynamite the offices and all other remaining buildings. Seven or eight sheds were, however, allowed to remain as storehouses for wood for the German armies. When the German retreat took place recently these storehouses, filled with wood, were fired so that they should not fall into the hands of the Allies. The entire establishment of the company, one of the largest in France, has thus been entirely destroyed, and it will require several years to reconstruct the works. —'Financial Times.'

JOPLIN, MISSOURI

Review of the Zinc-Lead Region During 1918, and Present Conditions.

The month of December saw a radical readjustment set in for the ore markets of the Tri-State region. It was not unexpected in time, but the degree was not only not greater than expected, but was an astonishing one for an industry that has been producing on a losing basis for the last six months. The readjustment has been paralyzing in its intensity, and the industry shows signs of weakness among even its strongest units.

With the end of the War came an end of the agreement price for high-grade zinc concentrates, so that once more these are practically on the open market. They are still being allocated by a board, but on a much lower price. High-grade zinc concentrate is now selling freely at $45 to $55 per ton, while second grades are being bought readily at $40 to $45. Some undesirable product is as low as $37.50. The amount of high-grade material sold during December was small, so that the average for the period dropped perceptibly. The average for all grades of zinc-blende was $44.60, compared with $56.20 in the previous month. The quantity sold amounted to 26,300 tons, against 26,915 in November. This does not represent all the ores sold, as the buyers have a large tonnage in bins as yet unloaded. Surplus stocks of blende decreased to 25,000 tons during the month, compared with 27,270 at the end of November. This was due mainly to the greatly lowered production when the month saw a decreased market.

Calamine remained steadier and sold at $25 to $38 per ton. The average price for all grades of this class of ores was $33.86. The average shipment per week was 448 tons, while the average shipment of blende reached 6575 tons.

Lead fell at the beginning of December to $80 per ton, after holding steadily to the $100 mark for months. The closing month of the year saw still another radical reduction, reaching a minimum of $65, or a 35% decrease in 30 days. That this reduction hurt the industry became apparent immediately when mill after mill closed down during the holidays, and offered no hope of re-opening unless there was a cut in the cost of supplies and labor. There has been a small reduction in the price of powder and steel, but in no other supplies. This week sees the announcement of wage-scale revision downward. This cut in wages amounts to 50 cents on the day for day men, and 2 cents per can or 4 cents per ton for the piece-work men, who are the shovelers and who make the largest wage in the district. Often this class of laborer makes a larger weekly salary than the superintendent. The new wage-scale is to take effect beginning in the first week of 1919.

It is difficult to forecast the production for the next few weeks or months; that it will be lower is generally agreed. Producers are making every effort to adjust themselves to new conditions, but, even so, many mines cannot hope to operate during the reconstruction period, if ever again. Labor is plentiful now; in fact there is a huge surplus arising from the returning soldiers and the number of men laid off from mines closed down or put on single shift or on minimum development. Prospecting by drilling is also generally at a standstill and little new work can be anticipated for a number of months. If the district maintains a semblance of its former activity it can produce 8000 tons easily, but where it will find a market for it remains to be shown. Surplus stocks have lowered to 25,000 tons, which is 2200 tons above the weekly average for the year. On the other hand, there is in this surplus stock a considerable tonnage of sold concentrate, which cannot be moved on account of the roads. Had this been shipped as it normally would have been with good weather, it is doubtful if the surplus would have been over 15,000 tons at the end of the year.

The year 1918 started with what has proved to be an average month's surplus stock of zinc concentrate. While the market for zinc ores ranged from $50 to $65 per ton, lead ores sold at $80. Calamine held steadily at $30 to $45 during the early months. With the exception of an advance in lead to $85, the ore markets remained stationary until the middle of March, when zinc began a sharp decline, immediately threatening to demoralize the entire industry if not checked. Spelter remained fairly firm, and zinc-sheets, into which a large part of the district's output was entering, had been sold to the Government on a fixed price which should have maintained an ore market at $80 to $90 per ton. It was at this juncture that the ore producers' woes were

TYPICAL SCENE IN THE WEBB CITY DISTRICT, MISSOURI

carried to Washington before the War Industries Board, resulting in an agreement being made between the sheet-zinc manufacturers and the high-grade zinc ore producer, to fix concentrate at $75 as long as the Government sheet-zinc price was maintained. This agreement was reached in the latter part of April, by which time blende prices had declined to $40 to $45. Lead ore had also dropped to $80 base at this time. The increase in the base price for high-grade zinc ore helped to stabilize the market, and through an allocation board sales were made. The first allocation amounted to 1300 tons weekly, and was made in the first week of May, and continued unchanged for 33 weeks. During that period 38,052 tons of high-grade blende had been sold on the $75 market, compared with an open market for the same class of ores ranging from $40 to $65. The gain to the field by the arrangement during the war period amounted to approximately $750,000. A maximum of 45 mining companies participated in the allocation of the tonnage, while the average reached 29 for the entire period. The proportionate share allocated to the producer ranged from 30 to 46% of the output of high-grade product. The end of the War brought an end to the agreement and the market dropped at the end of November. The range for the last month of the year was $37.50 to $45, except for 600 tons of high-grade which sold at $55. Calamine held its own much better throughout the year, the base range being from $25 to $35 most of the time.

The lead-ore market also began to move upward in June and by the middle of July had reached $100, at which price it held steadily till the first week of December, when it was cut 20%, the last week of the year seeing the base for 80% lead going down to $85. The average price of blende for the year was $51.68, of calamine $23.70, and of lead $88.72 per ton.

The decrease in tonnage was large for both blende and calamine. The former decrease over 1917 was 34,137 and calamine 15,127 tons. In value the decrease amounted to $9,038,505 for blende and $677,062 for calamine, when compared with 1917. Lead ore showed an increase in tonnage of 3421, but a decrease in valuation due to lower prices. The difference in the average price of lead ore was in favor of 1917 by $7.89 per ton.

Summarizing the shipments during 1918 we get the following:

Product	Tons	Average price per ton	Total value	Average surplus tons
Blende	278,856	$51.68	$14,380,482	22,830
Calamine	15,032	23.70	506,561	.....
Lead	68,738	88.72	6,106,062	2,102

GOLDFIELD, NEVADA

Work in the Spearhead, Merger, Crackerjack, Great Bend, and Lone Star.

The new development in the Spearhead continues to create interest. The ground is highly mineralized and has every indication of making into a big orebody. In this mineralized mass are bunches of rich ore. At present a raise is being driven to the shale contact while driving continues on the ore to determine its extent. The cross-cut is still in ore.

The Merger company has an excellent showing and has shipped several cars of ore lately. There is 6 ft. of ore, averaging $34 per ton, on the 1350-ft. level. A winze is contemplated at this point. The raise continues promising.

The Crackerjack company has secured a lease on the Florence. Work has been started and a good shoot has been discovered.

Work at the Great Bend is progressing, and the management is highly pleased with results. A carload of ore was shipped lately.

Work at the Lone Star is well under way. The hoist and other equipment has been overhauled, and in a few days cross-cutting and driving will commence on the 250-ft. level of the Nelligan shaft. Work on other parts of the property will be started either by the company or responsible lessees as soon as equipment can be brought onto the ground. Gerald B. Hartley, vice-president and superintendent of the company, arrived here from Mazuma, Humboldt county, last month. The property consists of 15 patented claims, on the south slope of Vindicator mountain. It lies immediately east of the Spearhead, Blue Bell, and Grandma; and north of the Merger, Blue Bull, and Commonwealth mines. Considerable work has been done, and in the early days of Goldfield several carloads of high-grade ore was shipped from the ground now accessible to the Nelligan shaft. Two other shafts are each 300 ft. deep. The management will undertake extensive development of what is regarded as promising ground, in which there is every likelihood of finding orebodies similar to those just discovered in the Merger, Spearhead, and Blue Bull.

RENO, NEVADA

Notes from Scattered Mining Centres.

The Panama Canal Mining Co., owning the only mining property that has operated in Ormsby county in recent times, has shipped a 50-ton carload of silver ore and has shut-down for the winter. The mine is in the Voltaire district.

A Christmas dividend of one cent was paid by the Fairview Round Mountain Mining Co., the third since September. The mine, situated at Round Mountain, in Nye county, produced $28,000 gross in October, and is said to be maintaining that output. As the gold is all free, recovery is by amalgamation. Louis D. Gordon, president of the Round Mountain Mining Co. and manager of the Cerro Gordo mine in California, is at the head of the company.

The Como Consolidated mine, near Virginia City, is said to have a large quantity of high-grade milling ore and is treating it in a modern cyanide plant.

Development is progressing on several properties in the Peavine district, a short distance from Reno.

Mines and leases in the National district, in the northern end of Humboldt county, are producing small quantities of rich ore. Lessees at the Buckskin National have made a shipment and declare that some of their product is worth $50 per pound. Miners from the district say that a large tonnage of good milling ore has been exposed in opening the high-grade.

Two mills in the Gold Circle district are treating ore from several mines. The Elko Prince is the largest producer, and its rather narrow but rich vein has been opened at a depth of over 800 feet.

At the old camp of Candelaria, the Lucky [illegible] mine, owned by the Candelaria Consolidated Mines Co., is shipping 200 tons weekly, the product containing from 20 to 25 oz. of silver per ton. The same company has the old Mt. Diablo and Argentum mines, once large producers, and is blocking out a large tonnage of ore with a view to providing a mill and treating both the ore from these mines and the large amount of tailing from early-day amalgamation mills.

At Pioneer, miners with supplies and powder have arrived at the Consolidated Mayflower property, control of which has been acquired by a group of mining men including J. H. Miller of Hawthorne; F. M. M[illegible] of Reno, manager of the Western Ore Purchasing Co.; W. E. Tobin, president of the Reorganized Pioneer Mines Co.; R. H. O'Neil, stockman and mine operator of Los Angeles; and J. B. Kendall, former superintendent for the Goldfield Consolidated company. Mr. Kendall is president and manager of the Mayflower company and has assumed charge at the mine. The 15-stamp mill is to be remodeled and enlarged to more than double its present capacity.

Samuel Newhouse of Utah, while at Reno recently, said

that the Louisiana Consolidated mine at Tybo would resume work in the near future. He expressed confidence in the future of the property.

Goldfield miners have exposed some good ore in working a lease on the Life Preserver group at Tolicha, 50 miles southeast of Goldfield. The claims are owned by J. Jordan and 'Jumbo' Yeiser, and were worked last year under a short-term option by men in the employ of George Wingfield and Zeb Kendall, when some milling ore was exposed in prospect shafts.

Frank Hertzer and Dan O'Keefe of Goldfield have opened two feet of good silver-gold ore on leased ground near Railroad Springs, 20 miles south-west of Goldfield.

Exhaustive tests in shale-oil extraction have been conducted here at the Mackay School of Mines, connected with the University of Nevada. The men doing this work have experimented with shale found near Elko and in Utah. Results are said to have been satisfactory, but incomplete; a detailed statement covering the work is promised shortly.

Treatment of mill tailing by the Goldfield Consolidated Mines Co. has been discontinued for the winter. The Lidgerwood radial cableway has been delivering 700 tons of tailing daily to the cyanide department of the 1000-ton mill. Freezing of the water supply and wet tailing, with plant breakage due to cold and the necessity of employing a larger working force, prompted the decision to close down during the winter. The mill continues to treat approximately 6000 tons of ore monthly, divided equally between flotation and cyanidation, and 300 tons weekly of ore from the Tonopah Divide mine is received in the cyanide department.

DURANGO, COLORADO

Present Conditions in the San Juan Region.

The San Juan region is rapidly recovering from the epidemic of influenza that swept over it, and development has been resumed at many properties. However, production of ore during the winter will be materially reduced, as a number of smaller operators have ceased for the season. The Red Mountain railroad has been closed owing to the heavy snowfall.

Ouray.—The McClellan-Dunmore tungsten claims are under lease and option to De Golyer, who plans extensive development. A small force is engaged on preliminary work, and the Gold Crown mill is being re-modeled to dress both tungsten and other ores.

High-grade ore has been discovered in the Hidden Treasure, some samples carrying over 300 oz. of silver per ton.

Silverton.—The outlook is encouraging for a busy and prosperous season during 1919. Extensive work is under way by the Sunnyside M. & M. Co., Gold King Extension Co., Caledonian M. & M. Co., Mayflower Leasing Co., Henrietta Copper Co., and the Red Mountain Mines Co., and will make heavy and continuous shipments.

The Sunnyside company, after an idleness of over a month, resumed milling on December 26. The acute labor shortage is being relieved by the continuous arrival of common labor, but machine-men and skilled miners are still in great demand.

The Pride of the West, one of the leading producers of the district, closed for the winter, owing to scarcity of labor and high operating costs.

The Mayflower will continue to operate during the winter and is shipping heavily at present. The Mayflower had a successful season, having continued work with hardly any interruption, except while the Iowa-Tiger mill was shut-down.

Development continues at the Buffalo Boy, including the driving of a cross-cut tunnel 50 ft. long to cut a vein.

The Caledonian is now in the producing class, and a large number of men are employed at both mine and mill. Preliminary mill runs gave satisfactory returns.

The Henrietta company is doing extensive work, in addition to shipping high-grade copper ore. The outlook for heavy shipments during 1919 is promising.

The long tunnel being driven to cut the main vein in the workings of the Ariadne is almost completed, and the mine is being prepared for shipping.

Telluride.—This district has continued to ship heavily, although the Belmont Wagner company has closed the Alta mine and mill owing to heavy snow and scarcity of labor.

The Tomboy continues to ship iron concentrates.

The Smuggler Union is shipping all classes of ore.

The Liberty Bell has cut down the force at the mill.

A group of vanadium claims is under development by the Colorado Vanadium Co. Equipment includes a compressor and pipe-lines for drills. A two-bucket tram is being constructed to carry ore from the workings to rail. The ore will be treated at the Primos Chemical Co.'s plant.

Rico.—The outlook for this district is promising, better than for years past. Numerous new developments are under way, and the leading producers are installing electric motors and compressed-air drills. The heavy snow that has fallen insures an abundance of water-power during the coming year. Supplies and fuel are now being hauled to many of the properties in anticipation of a continued winter campaign.

The outside work at the alunite field is being hurried before the heavy snow falls, as the elevation is 12,000 to 13,000 feet.

The Rico Mining Co., known as the Syndicate Mining Co., is developing the Group and Syndicate tunnels. Compressors and electric power are being installed, and work will continue during the winter, with the prospects of light shipments. The virgin ground near the Vestal shaft of the Group tunnel gives promise of good orebodies.

The Marmatite M. & M. Co., is now sending out 300 tons of ore per month, and at present is the only shipper from the district. A number of other properties in addition to the Rico Argentine are under development by this company, and power-lines are being built to all of these holdings, also compressed-air lines for drilling. As the labor shortage is relieved this company will gradually increase its output of ore.

The lawsuit between the Rico Consolidated Mining Co. and the Rico Argentine company has tied up a large body of good ore. The former claims trespass, while the latter claims apex rights.

The Rico-Wellington has discontinued operations for the winter.

PORCUPINE, ONTARIO

The new president of the Dome Mines, in place of the late Captain De Lamar, is Jules S. Bache, of the firm of J. S. Bache & Co., brokers of New York, and a director of many prominent corporations. It is intimated that one result of the change may be in the direction of greater publicity concerning the mine, about which little official information has lately been forthcoming. It is generally anticipated that the mill will resume operations early in the new year.

The Dome Lake has appointed Charles A. Randall as manager in place of A. H. Brown, who resigned. The shaft will be put down to 600 feet.

The Davidson is now operated by electric power. An orebody of high grade has been opened from the 400 to the 500-ft. level. There has been some trouble from water, necessitating installation of additional pumps.

Operations will be resumed at the Sovereign mine, the president, C. W. Moodie, having underwritten 100,000 shares at 25c. each to raise the necessary funds.

carried to Washington before the War Industries Board, resulting in an agreement being made between the sheet-zinc manufacturers and the high-grade zinc ore producer, to fix concentrate at $75 as long as the Government sheet-zinc price was maintained. This agreement was reached in the latter part of April, by which time blende prices had declined to $40 to $45. Lead ore had also dropped to $80 base at this time. The increase in the base price for high-grade zinc ore helped to stabilize the market, and through an allocation board sales were made. The first allocation amounted to 1300 tons weekly, and was made in the first week of May, and continued unchanged for 33 weeks. During that period 38,052 tons of high-grade blende had been sold on the $75 market, compared with an open market for the same class of ores ranging from $40 to $65. The gain to the field by the arrangement during the war period amounted to approximately $750,000. A maximum of 45 mining companies participated in the allocation of the tonnage, while the average reached 29 for the entire period. The proportionate share allocated to the producer ranged from 30 to 46% of the output of high-grade product. The end of the War brought an end to the agreement and the market dropped at the end of November. The range for the last month of the year was $37.50 to $45, except for 600 tons of high-grade which sold at $55. Calamine held its own much better throughout the year, the base range being from $25 to $35 most of the time.

The lead-ore market also began to move upward in June and by the middle of July had reached $100, at which price it held steadily till the first week of December, when it was cut 20%, the last week of the year seeing the base for 80% lead going down to $65. The average price of blende for the year was $51.68, of calamine $33.70, and of lead $89.73 per ton.

The decrease in tonnage was large for both blende and calamine. The former decrease over 1917 was 34,137 and calamine 15,137 tons. In value the decrease amounted to $9,038,505 for blende and $677,062 for calamine, when compared with 1917. Lead ore showed an increase in tonnage of 3431, but a decrease in valuation due to lower prices. The difference in the average price of lead ore was in favor of 1917 by $7.89 per ton.

Summarizing the shipments during 1918 we get the following:

Product	Tons	Average price per ton	Total value	Average surplus, tons
Blende	374,956	$51.68	$19,380,482	22,830
Calamine	15,032	33.70	506,581	.....
Lead	68,738	80.73	6,168,062	2,102

GOLDFIELD, NEVADA

Work in the Spearhead, Merger, Crackerjack, Great Bend, and Lone Star.

The new development in the Spearhead continues to create interest. The ground is highly mineralized and has every indication of making into a big orebody. In this mineralized mass are bunches of rich ore. At present a raise is being driven to the shale contact, while driving continues on the ore to determine its extent. The cross-cut is still in ore.

The Merger company has an excellent showing and has shipped several cars of ore lately. There is 6 ft. of ore, averaging $30 per ton, on the 1350-ft. level. A winze is contemplated at this point. The raise continues promising.

The Crackerjack company has secured a lease on the Florence. Work has been started and a good shoot has been discovered.

Work at the Great Bend is progressing, and the management is highly pleased with results. A carload of ore was shipped lately.

Work at the Lone Star is well under way. The hoist and other equipment has been overhauled, and in a few days cross-cutting and driving will commence on the 250-ft. level of the Nelligan shaft. Work on other parts of the property will be started either by the company or responsible lessees as soon as equipment can be brought onto the ground. Gerald B. Hartley, vice-president and superintendent of the company, arrived here from Mazuma, Humboldt county, last month. The property consists of 15 patented claims, on the south slope of Vindicator mountain. It lies immediately east of the Spearhead, Blue Bell, and Grandma; and north of the Merger, Blue Bull, and Commonwealth mines. Considerable work has been done, and in the early days of Goldfield several carloads of high-grade ore was shipped from the ground now accessible to the Nelligan shaft. Two other shafts are each 300 ft. deep. The management will undertake extensive development of what is regarded as promising ground, in which there is every likelihood of finding orebodies similar to those just discovered in the Merger, Spearhead, and Blue Bull.

RENO, NEVADA

Notes from Scattered Mining Centres.

The Panama Canal Mining Co., owning the only mining property that has operated in Ormsby county in recent times, has shipped a 50-ton carload of silver ore and has shut-down for the winter. The mine is in the Voltaire district.

A Christmas dividend of one cent was paid by the Fairview Round Mountain Mining Co., the third since September. The mine, situated at Round Mountain, in Nye county, produced $28,000 gross in October, and is said to be maintaining that output. As the gold is all free, recovery is by amalgamation. Louis D. Gordon, president of the Round Mountain Mining Co. and manager of the Cerro Gordo mine in California, is at the head of the company.

The Como Consolidated mine, near Virginia City, is said to have a large quantity of high-grade milling ore and is treating it in a modern cyanide plant.

Development is progressing on several properties in the Peavine district, a short distance from Reno.

Mines and leases in the National district, in the northern end of Humboldt county, are producing small quantities of rich ore. Lessees at the Buckskin National have made a shipment and declare that some of their product is worth $50 per pound. Miners from the district say that a large tonnage of good milling ore has been exposed in opening the high-grade.

Two mills in the Gold Circle district are treating ore from several mines. The Elko Prince is the largest producer, and its rather narrow but rich vein has been opened at a depth of over 800 feet.

At the old camp of Candelaria, the Lucky Hill mine, owned by the Candelaria Consolidated Mines Co., is shipping 200 tons weekly, the product containing from 20 to 35 oz. of silver per ton. The same company has the old Mt. Diablo and Argentum mines, once large producers, and is blocking out a large tonnage of ore with a view to providing a mill and treating both the ore from these mines and the large amount of tailing from early-day amalgamation mills.

At Pioneer, miners with supplies and powder have arrived at the Consolidated Mayflower property, control of which has been acquired by a group of mining men including J. H. Miller of Hawthorne; F. M. Manson of Reno, manager of the Western Ore Purchasing Co.; W. J. Tobin, president of the Reorganized Pioneer Mines Co.; P. H. O'Neil, stockman and mine operator of Los Angeles; and J. B. Kendall, former superintendent for the Goldfield Consolidated company. Mr. Kendall is president and manager of the Mayflower company and has assumed charge at the mine. The 15-stamp mill is to be remodeled and enlarged to more than double its present capacity.

Samuel Newhouse of Utah, while at Reno recently, said

that the Louisiana Consolidated mine at Tybo would resume work in the near future. He expressed confidence in the future of the property.

Goldfield miners have exposed some good ore in working a lease on the Life Preserver group at Tolicha, 50 miles southeast of Goldfield. The claims are owned by J. Jordan and 'Jumbo' Yeiser, and were worked last year under a short-term option by men in the employ of George Wingfield and Zeb Kendall, when some milling ore was exposed in prospect shafts.

Frank Hertzer and Dan O'Keefe of Goldfield have opened two feet of good silver-gold ore on leased ground near Railroad Springs, 20 miles south-west of Goldfield.

Exhaustive tests in shale-oil extraction have been conducted here at the Mackay School of Mines, connected with the University of Nevada. The men doing this work have experimented with shale found near Elko and in Utah. Results are said to have been satisfactory, but incomplete; a detailed statement covering the work is promised shortly.

Treatment of mill tailing by the Goldfield Consolidated Mines Co. has been discontinued for the winter. The Lidgerwood radial cableway has been delivering 700 tons of tailing daily to the cyanide department of the 1000-ton mill. Freezing of the water supply and wet tailing, with plant breakage due to cold and the necessity of employing a larger working force, prompted the decision to close down during the winter. The mill continues to treat approximately 6000 tons of ore monthly, divided equally between flotation and cyanidation, and 300 tons weekly of ore from the Tonopah Divide mine is received in the cyanide department.

DURANGO, COLORADO

Present Conditions in the San Juan Region.

The San Juan region is rapidly recovering from the epidemic of influenza that swept over it, and development has been resumed at many properties. However, production of ore during the winter will be materially reduced, as a number of smaller operators have ceased for the season. The Red Mountain railroad has been closed owing to the heavy snowfall.

Ouray.—The McClellan-Dunmore tungsten claims are under lease and option to De Golyer, who plans extensive development. A small force is engaged on preliminary work, and the Gold Crown mill is being re-modeled to dress both tungsten and other ores.

High-grade ore has been discovered in the Hidden Treasure, some samples carrying over 300 oz. of silver per ton.

Silverton.—The outlook is encouraging for a busy and prosperous season during 1919. Extensive work is under way by the Sunnyside M. & M. Co., Gold King Extension Co., Caledonian M. & M. Co., Mayflower Leasing Co., Henrietta Copper Co., and the Red Mountain Mines Co., and will make heavy and continuous shipments.

The Sunnyside company, after an idleness of over a month, resumed milling on December 26. The acute labor shortage is being relieved by the continuous arrival of common labor, but machine-men and skilled miners are still in great demand.

The Pride of the West, one of the leading producers of the district, closed for the winter, owing to scarcity of labor and high operating costs.

The Mayflower will continue to operate during the winter and is shipping heavily at present. The Mayflower had a successful season, having continued work with hardly any interruption, except while the Iowa-Tiger mill was shut-down.

Development continues at the Buffalo Boy, including the driving of a cross-cut tunnel 50 ft. long to cut a vein.

The Caledonian is now in the producing class, and a large number of men are employed at both mine and mill. Preliminary mill runs gave satisfactory returns.

The Henrietta company is doing extensive work, in addition to shipping high-grade copper ore. The outlook for heavy shipments during 1919 is promising.

The long tunnel being driven to cut the main vein in the workings of the Ariadne is almost completed, and the mine is being prepared for shipping.

Telluride. This district has continued to ship heavily, although the Belmont Wagner company has closed the Alta mine and mill owing to heavy snow and scarcity of labor.

The Tomboy continues to ship iron concentrates.

The Smuggler Union is shipping all classes of ore.

The Liberty Bell has cut down the force at the mill.

A group of vanadium claims is under development by the Colorado Vanadium Co. Equipment includes a compressor and pipe-lines for drills. A two-bucket tram is being constructed to carry ore from the workings to rail. The ore will be treated at the Primos Chemical Co.'s plant.

Rico.—The outlook for this district is promising, better than for years past. Numerous new developments are under way, and the leading producers are installing electric motors and compressed-air drills. The heavy snow that has fallen insures an abundance of water-power during the coming year. Supplies and fuel are now being hauled to many of the properties in anticipation of a continued winter campaign.

The outside work at the alunite field is being hurried before the heavy snow falls, as the elevation is 12,000 to 13,000 feet.

The Rico Mining Co., known as the Syndicate Mining Co., is developing the Group and Syndicate tunnels. Compressors and electric power are being installed, and work will continue during the winter, with the prospects of light shipments. The virgin ground near the Vestal shaft of the Group tunnel gives promise of good orebodies.

The Marmatite M. & M. Co., is now sending out 300 tons of ore per month, and at present is the only shipper from the district. A number of other properties in addition to the Rico Argentine are under development by this company, and power-lines are being built to all of these holdings, also compressed-air lines for drilling. As the labor shortage is relieved this company will gradually increase its output of ore.

The lawsuit between the Rico Consolidated Mining Co. and the Rico Argentine company has tied up a large body of good ore. The former claims trespass, while the latter claims apex rights.

The Rico-Wellington has discontinued operations for the winter.

PORCUPINE, ONTARIO

The new president of the Dome Mines, in place of the late Captain De Lamar, is Jules S. Bache, of the firm of J. S. Bache & Co., brokers of New York, and a director of many prominent corporations. It is intimated that one result of the change may be in the direction of greater publicity concerning the mine, about which little official information has lately been forthcoming. It is generally anticipated that the mill will resume operations early in the new year.

The Dome Lake has appointed Charles A. Randall as manager in place of A. H. Brown, who resigned. The shaft will be put down to 600 feet.

The Davidson is now operated by electric power. An orebody of high grade has been opened from the 460 to the 500-ft. level. There has been some trouble from water, necessitating installation of additional pumps.

Operations will be resumed at the Sovereign mine, the president, C. W. Moodie, having underwritten 100,000 shares at 25c. each to raise the necessary funds.

carried to Washington before the War Industries Board, resulting in an agreement being made between the sheet-zinc manufacturers and the high-grade zinc ore producer, to fix concentrate at $75 as long as the Government sheet-zinc price was maintained. This agreement was reached in the latter part of April, by which time blende prices had declined to $40 to $45. Lead ore had also dropped to $80 base at this time. The increase in the base price for high-grade zinc ore helped to stabilize the market, and through an allocation board sales were made. The first allocation amounted to 1300 tons weekly, and was made in the first week of May, and continued unchanged for 33 weeks. During that period 38,052 tons of high-grade blende had been sold on the $75 market, compared with an open market for the same class of ores ranging from $40 to $65. The gain to the field by the arrangement during the war period amounted to approximately $750,000. A maximum of 45 mining companies participated in the allocation of the tonnage, while the average reached 29 for the entire period. The proportionate share allocated to the producer ranged from 30 to 46% of the output of high-grade product. The end of the War brought an end to the agreement and the market dropped at the end of November. The range for the last month of the year was $37.50 to $45, except for 600 tons of high-grade which sold at $55. Calamine held its own much better throughout the year, the base range being from $25 to $35 most of the time.

The lead-ore market also began to move upward in June and by the middle of July had reached $100, at which price it held steadily till the first week of December, when it was cut 20%, the last week of the year seeing the base for 80% lead going down to $65. The average price of blende for the year was $51.68, of calamine $33.70, and of lead $89.73 per ton.

The decrease in tonnage was large for both blende and calamine. The former decrease over 1917 was 34,137 and calamine 15,137 tons. In value the decrease amounted to $9,038,565 for blende and $677,062 for calamine, when compared with 1917. Lead ore showed an increase in tonnage of 3431, but a decrease in valuation due to lower prices. The difference in the average price of lead ore was in favor of 1917 by $7.89 per ton.

Summarizing the shipments during 1918 we get the following:

Product	Tons	Average price per ton	Total value	Average surplus, tons
Blende	371,950	$51.68	$10,380,482	22,830
Calamine	15,032	33.70	506,581	.....
Lead	68,738	89.73	6,168,062	2,162

GOLDFIELD, NEVADA

Work in the Spearhead, Merger, Crackerjack, Great Bend, and Lone Star.

The new development in the Spearhead continues to create interest. The ground is highly mineralized and has every indication of making into a big orebody. In this mineralized mass are bunches of rich ore. At present a raise is being driven to the shale contact, while driving continues on the ore to determine its extent. The cross-cut is still in ore.

The Merger company has an excellent showing and has shipped several cars of ore lately. There is 6 ft. of ore, averaging $30 per ton, on the 1350-ft. level. A winze is contemplated at this point. The raise continues promising.

The Crackerjack company has secured a lease on the Florence. Work has been started and a good shoot has been discovered.

Work at the Great Bend is progressing, and the management is highly pleased with results. A carload of ore was shipped lately.

Work at the Lone Star is well under way. The hoist and other equipment has been overhauled, and in a few days cross-cutting and driving will commence on the 250-ft. level of the Nelligan shaft. Work on other parts of the property will be started either by the company or responsible lessees as soon as equipment can be brought onto the ground. Gerald B. Hartley, vice-president and superintendent of the company, arrived here from Mazuma, Humboldt county, last month. The property consists of 15 patented claims, on the south slope of Vindicator mountain. It lies immediately east of the Spearhead, Blue Bell, and Grandma; and north of the Merger, Blue Bull, and Commonwealth mines. Considerable work has been done, and in the early days of Goldfield several carloads of high-grade ore was shipped from the ground now accessible to the Nelligan shaft. Two other shafts are each 300 ft. deep. The management will undertake extensive development of what is regarded as promising ground, in which there is every likelihood of finding orebodies similar to those just discovered in the Merger, Spearhead, and Blue Bull.

RENO, NEVADA

Notes from Scattered Mining Centres.

The Panama Canal Mining Co., owning the only mining property that has operated in Ormsby county in recent times, has shipped a 50-ton carload of silver ore and has shut-down for the winter. The mine is in the Voltaire district.

A Christmas dividend of one cent was paid by the Fairview Round Mountain Mining Co., the third since September. The mine, situated at Round Mountain, in Nye county, produced $28,000 gross in October, and is said to be maintaining that output. As the gold is all free, recovery is by amalgamation. Louis D. Gordon, president of the Round Mountain Mining Co. and manager of the Cerro Gordo mine in California, is at the head of the company.

The Como Consolidated mine, near Virginia City, is said to have a large quantity of high-grade milling ore and is treating it in a modern cyanide plant.

Development is progressing on several properties in the Peavine district, a short distance from Reno.

Mines and leases in the National district, in the northern end of Humboldt county, are producing small quantities of rich ore. Lessees at the Buckskin National have made a shipment and declare that some of their product is worth $50 per pound. Miners from the district say that a large tonnage of good milling ore has been exposed in opening the high-grade.

Two mills in the Gold Circle district are treating ore from several mines. The Elko Prince is the largest producer, and its rather narrow but rich vein has been opened at a depth of over 800 feet.

At the old camp of Candelaria, the Lucky Hill mine, owned by the Candelaria Consolidated Mines Co., is shipping 200 tons weekly, the product containing from 20 to 35 oz. of silver per ton. The same company has the old Mt. Diablo and Argentum mines, once large producers, and is blocking out a large tonnage of ore with a view to providing a mill and treating both the ore from these mines and the large amount of tailing from early-day amalgamation mills.

At Pioneer, miners with supplies and powder have arrived at the Consolidated Mayflower property, control of which has been acquired by a group of mining men including J. H. Miller of Hawthorne; F. M. Manson of Reno, manager of the Western Ore Purchasing Co.; W. J. Tobin, president of the Reorganized Pioneer Mines Co.; P. H. O'Neil, stockman and mine operator of Los Angeles; and J. B. Kendall, former superintendent for the Goldfield Consolidated company. Mr. Kendall is president and manager of the Mayflower company and has assumed charge at the mine. The 15-stamp mill is to be remodeled and enlarged to more than double its present capacity.

Samuel Newhouse of Utah, while at Reno recently, said

that the Louisiana Consolidated mine at Tybo would resume work in the near future. He expressed confidence in the future of the property.

Goldfield miners have exposed some good ore in working a lease on the Life Preserver group at Tolicha, 50 miles southeast of Goldfield. The claims are owned by J. Jordan and 'Jumbo' Yeiser, and were worked last year under a short-term option by men in the employ of George Wingfield and Zeb Kendall, when some milling ore was exposed in prospect shafts.

Frank Hertzer and Dan O'Keefe of Goldfield have opened two feet of good silver-gold ore on leased ground near Railroad Springs, 20 miles south-west of Goldfield.

Exhaustive tests in shale-oil extraction have been conducted here at the Mackay School of Mines, connected with the University of Nevada. The men doing this work have experimented with shale found near Elko and in Utah. Results are said to have been satisfactory, but incomplete; a detailed statement covering the work is promised shortly.

Treatment of mill tailing by the Goldfield Consolidated Mines Co. has been discontinued for the winter. The Lidgerwood radial cableway has been delivering 700 tons of tailing daily to the cyanide department of the 1000-ton mill. Freezing of the water supply and wet tailing, with plant breakage due to cold and the necessity of employing a larger working force, prompted the decision to close down during the winter. The mill continues to treat approximately 6000 tons of ore monthly, divided equally between flotation and cyanidation, and 300 tons weekly of ore from the Tonopah Divide mine is received in the cyanide department.

DURANGO, COLORADO

Present Conditions in the San Juan Region.

The San Juan region is rapidly recovering from the epidemic of influenza that swept over it, and development has been resumed at many properties. However, production of ore during the winter will be materially reduced, as a number of smaller operators have ceased for the season. The Red Mountain railroad has been closed owing to the heavy snowfall.

Ouray.—The McClellan-Dunmore tungsten claims are under lease and option to De Golyer, who plans extensive development. A small force is engaged on preliminary work, and the Gold Crown mill is being re-modeled to dress both tungsten and other ores.

High-grade ore has been discovered in the Hidden Treasure, some samples carrying over 300 oz. of silver per ton.

Silverton.—The outlook is encouraging for a busy and prosperous season during 1919. Extensive work is under way by the Sunnyside M. & M. Co., Gold King Extension Co., Caledonian M. & M. Co., Mayflower Leasing Co., Henrietta Copper Co., and the Red Mountain Mines Co., and will make heavy and continuous shipments.

The Sunnyside company, after an idleness of over a month, resumed milling on December 26. The acute labor shortage is being relieved by the continuous arrival of common labor, but machine-men and skilled miners are still in great demand.

The Pride of the West, one of the leading producers of the district, closed for the winter, owing to scarcity of labor and high operating costs.

The Mayflower will continue to operate during the winter and is shipping heavily at present. The Mayflower had a successful season, having continued work with hardly any interruption, except while the Iowa-Tiger mill was shut-down.

Development continues at the Buffalo Boy, including the driving of a cross-cut tunnel 50 ft. long to cut a vein.

The Caledonian is now in the producing class, and a large number of men are employed at both mine and mill. Preliminary mill runs gave satisfactory returns.

The Henrietta company is doing extensive work, in addition to shipping high-grade copper ore. The outlook for heavy shipments during 1919 is promising.

The long tunnel being driven to cut the main vein in the workings of the Ariadne is almost completed, and the mine is being prepared for shipping.

Telluride.—This district has continued to ship heavily, although the Belmont Wagner company has closed the Alta mine and mill owing to heavy snow and scarcity of labor.

The Tomboy continues to ship iron concentrates.

The Smuggler Union is shipping all classes of ore.

The Liberty Bell has cut down the force at the mill.

A group of vanadium claims is under development by the Colorado Vanadium Co. Equipment includes a compressor and pipe-lines for drills. A two-bucket tram is being constructed to carry ore from the workings to rail. The ore will be treated at the Primos Chemical Co.'s plant.

Rico.—The outlook for this district is promising, better than for years past. Numerous new developments are under way, and the leading producers are installing electric motors and compressed-air drills. The heavy snow that has fallen insures an abundance of water-power during the coming year. Supplies and fuel are now being hauled to many of the properties in anticipation of a continued winter campaign.

The outside work at the alunite field is being hurried before the heavy snow falls, as the elevation is 12,000 to 13,000 feet.

The Rico Mining Co., known as the Syndicate Mining Co., is developing the Group and Syndicate tunnels. Compressors and electric power are being installed, and work will continue during the winter, with the prospects of light shipments. The virgin ground near the Vestal shaft of the Group tunnel gives promise of good orebodies.

The Marmatite M. & M. Co., is now sending out 300 tons of ore per month, and at present is the only shipper from the district. A number of other properties in addition to the Rico Argentine are under development by this company, and power-lines are being built to all of these holdings, also compressed-air lines for drilling. As the labor shortage is relieved this company will gradually increase its output of ore.

The lawsuit between the Rico Consolidated Mining Co. and the Rico Argentine company has tied up a large body of good ore. The former claims trespass, while the latter claims apex rights.

The Rico-Wellington has discontinued operations for the winter.

PORCUPINE, ONTARIO

The new president of the Dome Mines, in place of the late Captain De Lamar, is Jules S. Bache, of the firm of J. S. Bache & Co., brokers of New York, and a director of many prominent corporations. It is intimated that one result of the change may be in the direction of greater publicity concerning the mine, about which little official information has lately been forthcoming. It is generally anticipated that the mill will resume operations early in the new year.

The Dome Lake has appointed Charles A. Randall as manager in place of A. H. Brown, who resigned. The shaft will be put down to 600 feet.

The Davidson is now operated by electric power. An orebody of high grade has been opened from the 460 to the 500-ft. level. There has been some trouble from water, necessitating installation of additional pumps.

Operations will be resumed at the Sovereign mine, the president, C. W. Moodie, having underwritten 100,000 shares at 25c. each to raise the necessary funds.

SAN ANTONIO, TEXAS

Conditions in Mexico, as Seen by Reliable Authorities.

According to L. H. Coley, manager in Mexico for the Ingersoll-Rand Co., with headquarters in the City of Mexico, industrial conditions in that country are showing material improvement since the armistice was signed. He said:

"There is still some interference from the lawless elements in the western districts, but not nearly so bad as for the last few years. Nearly all the mines are being worked, especially those owned by large foreign companies. Ores are being accumulated with a view to supplying the smelters with the quantity and variety of ores needed to make continuous operation possible, and the great smelters are being put in the best possible condition in anticipation of heavy business. The administration has decided that it is unprofitable for the mines to remain idle, as the taxes are needed by the Government, therefore the railroads to the mines are kept in as good condition as possible, supplies are transported with but little delay, and they are doing

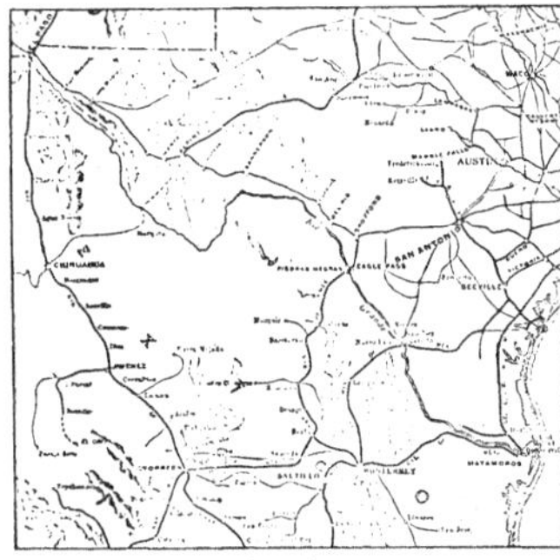

NORTH-EASTERN MEXICO AND TEXAS.

what they can to further production. I travel to all parts of Mexico and have not been delayed, hampered, or even insulted during all my journeys. Since the signing of the armistice there has been a wonderful change in the attitude of the masses, and there is no anti-American spirit in evidence. Americans are now wanted and welcomed. There is a complete alignment of allies in Mexico as there is in Europe at this time, and the Mexican masses expect that their affairs will brighten after the peace compact has been signed, believing that Uncle Sam will be their good friend, and that they will get a square deal from all foreign nations in the future. There is considerable activity among the largest foreign mining companies in the acquisition of desirable mining properties, and any good prospect promptly receives careful examination. The British are notably active in this regard, and I take it to be a sign that they are convinced that their investments will be safe and profitable. Common laborers in the mines now receive P1.50 per day and the higher class of operatives get from P3 to P5 per day. They are spending money freely, and business is good with the merchants near the mines and reduction works. That is, with all but German dealers, who are beginning to feel the pinch of the voluntary discrimination against everything German. Their young men find it difficult to obtain employment, and in various ways they are now reaping what they sowed so recklessly to the very last. What the Mexican people want now is plenty of work at fair pay, and they will be contented and happy; they have had their fill of war and want no more of it. The influenza greatly interfered with mining and there is still a shortage of labor in many localities, but those who were frightened away are gradually returning. The question most frequently heard is: 'When is Uncle Sam going to help Mexico as he has helped all other countries?' "

Miss Elisa Cortez of San Antonio, who has just returned from Mexico, where she investigated the possibilities of extending the activities of the Y. W. C. A., said:

"Mexico is clamoring for the benefits of our work as the girls and women are now employed in all sorts of occupations—just as they have been in the United States during the War. The women say this aid is essential to the hoped for reconstruction of social conditions in the Republic, and they will welcome with open arms the presence of a branch of the organization that shall have a wide scope of operations throughout the industrial districts, especially. The people of the City of Mexico also are highly desirous for an extension of Young Men's Christian Association activities, having been greatly pleased by the workings of the Association thus far. Business seems to be nearer the normal than I had supposed. At San Rafael the paper-mills, which will give employment to 1800 people, are about to start operation, and many other large factories will soon resume work on a large scale. The railway line from the City of Mexico to Nuevo Laredo is maintaining its scheduled service. There is a noticeably large number of Americans at the capital, having mining and other interests of importance, and the talk is all favorable to a steady restoration of old-time prosperity. People do not hesitate to walk along the streets of the city at night without guards, which has not been the case for a long time previously. All thoughts of the masses are centred on the peace conference at Paris, and you would think they were parties to the negotiations, so eager are they for news. They seem to feel that good is coming to Mexico from the final outcome. The people are more industrious and more eager for employment than I can remember, and there are not nearly so many idle ones."

CRIPPLE CREEK, COLORADO

Operations of the Smaller Properties.

Operations have been resumed by the Blue Flag company on Raven hill. The shaft is being sunk from 1227 to 1400 ft. A raise is also being driven from the 1100 to the 800-ft. level for ventilation. Cross-cutting is proposed to prospect ground east of the shaft toward the Cresson mine.

The Victory company shipped 1226 tons, worth $13,872, from the Howard shaft of the Mary McKinney company on Gold hill during the nine months following acquisition at the end of April 1918. The company also shipped 394 tons valued at $3886 during the year.

The Anona company has leased its property, adjoining the Victor mine on Bull cliffs, for a five-year term to Math Korff, lessee of the Victor. The lessees propose to prospect this undeveloped ground—26 acres—from the 1000-ft. level of the Victor shaft.

The December output of the United company totaled 760 tons, averaging $17.50 per ton.

The Modoc company has commenced heavy production and is dispatching two cars per day during the ensuing week. The ore is coming from two ore-shoots on the 1200-ft. level. These shoots are on distinct veins. The ore will average $30 per ton.

Oregon timber has commenced to arrive for the Lincoln Mines & Reduction Co. for use in construction of its concentrating plant on Ironclad hill. The concrete foundations are ready for the machinery.

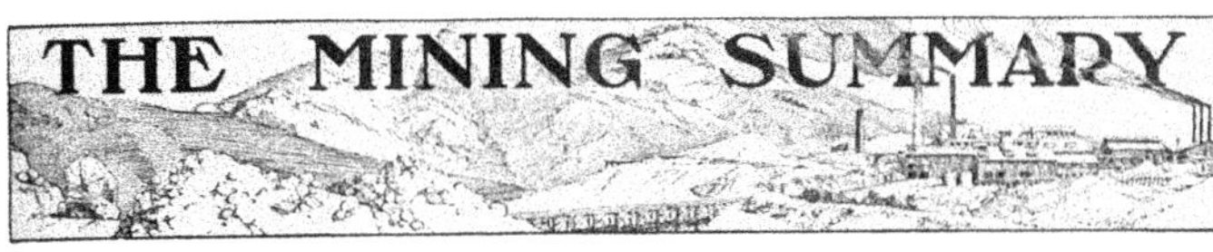

ALASKA

Nome.—According to G. C. Martin, of the U. S. Geological Survey, Seward Peninsula yielded gold worth $1,140,000 during 1918, against $2,747,000 in 1917. Nome contributed $455,000; Council, $293,000; Fairbanks, $118,000; Koyukuk, $145,000; Solomon, $62,000; and Kougarok, $60,000. Twenty dredges were operated, eight less than in 1917. They yielded 40% of the gold from the Peninsula. The 28 underground mines yielded 25%, 24 hydraulic mines 23%, and 55 open-cut mines 12%. About 56 oz. of platinum was recovered from all placers.

ARIZONA

Benson.—It is reported that the old smelting plant here, which includes a 250-ton copper stack never used, is to be blown-in within the next three months. The plant has been taken over by the recently incorporated Arizona Smelting & Power Co., of which C. E. Goetz is president. The company has an old slag dump of what is said to be good fluxing material, and it expects to draw ores from Patagonia, Johnson, Helvetia, and other districts.

Bisbee.—Phelps Dodge mines yielded 12,563,000 lb. of copper during December. There has been almost a general decline each month since the 20,815,110 lb. in March.

Douglas.—The Copper Queen smelter management announces that it is in the market for custom ore and will pay 16 cents per pound for copper pending a settled market price.

Globe.—The general manager, W. G. McBride, has announced that the Old Dominion smelter has adopted a 15-cent payment for copper, settlements in excess of that price from copper sold going to the shipper of custom ore when sale is made. The Old Dominion produced 2,686,000 lb. of copper in December, the highest yield since the 3,368,000 lb. in June.

Owing to a bolt destroying the coils of a 200-hp. motor in the Old Dominion flotation plant, about 1500 men in this district are out of work. As the spare motors were also damaged in some manner, the shut-down is indefinite. The damage is said to have been done purposely.

A 50-ton cyanide mill is to be built by the Gila Monster Mining Co. for its Richmond Basin property, 7 miles north of Globe. According to the superintendent, W. H. Séamon, there is 30,000 tons of 15-oz. silver ore on the dump; also some rich ore in the mine.

Miami.—Copper output of the Miami company in December was 4,989,435 lb. The average during 1918 was 4,850,000 lb. per month. The company pays $1 per share on February 15. This is equal to $747,114.

Inspiration Consolidated produced 7,350,000 lb. of copper during December. This is the lowest yield since February.

Patagonia.—It is now announced that the well-known Three R mine has been purchased by the Gunn-Thompson interests through the Magma Copper Co. for $750,000. This property has been under inspection for some time.

Ray.—Copper output of Ray Consolidated in December was 5,800,000 lb., the lowest yield for the year. In May it was 8,120,000 pounds.

Superior.—A 30-ton ball-mill and flotation plant is now working at the Silver King mine. Five tons of concentrate sent to El Paso assayed $1500 per ton, mostly in silver. There is said to be 10,000 tons of $20 ore developed.

The Magma Chief has purchased the Sombrero Butte property.

CALIFORNIA

Blythe.—The Chamber of Mines and Oil of Los Angeles recently received the following letter from P. H. Bray, a leading manganese producer in Riverside county: "Herewith is a brief description of the manganese mining situation in the Ironwood Mountain district, Riverside county, California. This district contains a great many unusually large deposits of manganese ore—probably the best quality obtainable in the United States, as it contains but a small perpentage of silica and is easily handled. Prior to the middle of November there were eight producing properties in this district. Since that time, however, six of these have been forced to close—including the Talbot, Grose, Parsons, Maybery, Perkins, and Nicholas properties—as they were unable to obtain a market for their ore at any price. Two of the larger properties—the Black Jack and the Bray—were fortunate enough to have contracts with the Western Ore Purchasing Co. for the account of the U. S. Steel Corporation, which contracts will run for about seven months longer. Both of these properties are well developed, and at the present time have practically 100 carloads (40-ton cars) of ore blocked-out. The Bray property has a 100-ft. shaft and about 250 ft. of drifts on the lead, which ranges from 3 to 9 ft. in width. The various manganese properties in this district could easily produce 25 or 30 carloads of ore per month with their present equipment if a market could be found for same. It is a deplorable condition that the properties, which have been forced to close, had been extensively developed at the specific request of Government representatives, and at great expense to the operators. Practically all the owners or lessees of these properties are poor men who have put all the money they had, or could raise, into the development of these mines. Also, the money which has been taken out during the past year in nearly every instance has been put back into the properties in the form of machinery and other operating equipment, as it was the general opinion that the demand for manganese ore would continue indefinitely. When the market closed all these operators had large quantities of ore mined; in fact, one man had the ore loaded on the car, when the order for same was cancelled. As these men were working without contracts, they were unable, in many cases, to even pay their workmen or other operating expenses in connection with mining the ore. It is needless to say that the present condition of affairs is a matter of great discouragement to the miners. . . ."

Daggett.—The Ord copper mine in San Bernardino county, formerly known as the Osborn, 12 miles south of this place, is being developed by New York people, who agreed to do 300 shifts of work per month. The ore is said to occur in wide contact veins between different eruptives, and carries up to 4% copper and $4 gold per ton.

Grass Valley.—During 1918 the North Star Mines Co. distributed $100,000 in dividends. This was on June 29, and amounted to 20 cents per share. The total to date is $5,437,040.

Madera.—It is reported that the old California copper mine, 12 miles from this town, has been leased to W. T. Perry of Fresno. The workings have been flooded for 20 years, and the water is considered to carry copper. Dumps amounting to over 20,000 tons are to be treated by simple water leaching.

Placerville.—A 2-ft. pay-shoot of good-grade gold quartz between well-defined slate walls and more than 100 ft. long is being mined and milled at the Burger mine, within the city limits of Placerville. The vein trends west of north and dips slightly to the east. The present working-shaft, now down 70 ft., is an incline on the foot-wall. About 300 ft. north of this rich shoot recent work has disclosed another larger shoot of similar rich quartz in the same formation. The quartz is the well-known 'blue ribbon rock' of the Mother Lode, showing free gold along the ribbon seams, which also contain high-value sulphides. The mine has been under development for the last three months, under lease and bond, by N. H. Burger of Placerville, A. L. Conger of Berkeley, and T. B. McLane of Seattle. A No. 3 Gibson quartz-mill and concentrator, handling 8 tons daily, has been used to sample the ore as work progressed. Both the mine and the plant have been so satisfactory that a No. 1 Gibson mill and concentrator of 30-ton capacity, an electric hoist, mine pump, and other improvements are to be made. After the new equipment is erected the mine will be operated continuously.

Plymouth.—The Plymouth Consolidated pays 24 cents per share, $57,600, on January 31. Results during October and November are as under:

	October	November
Ore treated, tons	10,550	8,600
Gold yield	$55,700	$51,000
Working expense	36,000	33,600
Development	4,500	3,600
Surplus	15,200	13,800

On the 2450-ft. level, the north foot-wall drift is out 378 ft., assaying $7.10 per ton across 67 inches.

COLORADO

Cripple Creek.—The Portland Gold Mining Co. pays 2 cents per share, equal to $60,000, on January 20. This makes a total of $11,317,080.

Cresson Consolidated pays 10 cents per share on January 10. This is equal to $122,000, and makes $7,271,163 to date.

Kokomo.—The Mutual Co-operative Mining Co. during 1918 shipped 1280 tons of ore from its Golden Queen mine.

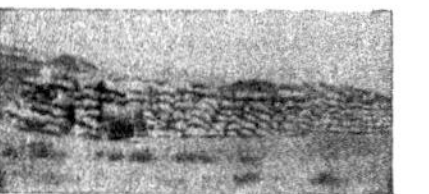

ORE READY FOR TRANSPORT TO RAIL IN THE SAN JUAN REGION

settlements totaling $20,018. The Silver Queen is reported to be developing well. The Gold Hill mine may be sold. The tungsten mine at Lee Hill, Boulder county, is closed and is for sale.

Red Cliff.—A mill is being erected at the Alpine mine, which is owned by Lincoln, Nebraska, people.

The Empire Zinc Co. has acquired additional property at Red Cliff. Daily shipments of concentrate amount to 16 carloads, sent to smelters at Canon City and East St. Louis. A long tunnel is to be driven to facilitate mining the ore.

Telluride.—The Primos Chemical Co. has a good many men working at its mines up Leopard creek, near the old town of Placerville. Buildings, tramway, compressor station, and other equipment are being constructed. Ore was formerly carried on mules over a mile to rail at Placerville, from where it was sent to Vanadium, in San Miguel county, for concentration. The new tramway will dispense with mules.

MICHIGAN

Houghton.—On December 28 a rush shipment of copper, amounting to 3,136,000 lb., was sent by rail from here to New York. During the previous 30 days no metal was moved, excepting small lots.

In the Seneca company's shaft the Kearsarge lode was cut at 1625 ft. The ore carries 1½% copper. Sinking was started on February 13, 1918. The new head-frame is finished. W. J. Uren is superintendent.

Mohawk pays $2 per share on February 1.

MISSOURI

Joplin.—Production of the Tri-State region last week was as under:

State	Blende, tons	Calamine, tons	Lead, tons	Value
Kansas	148	..	173	$17,040
Missouri	944	45	168	52,456
Oklahoma	4,231	..	392	209,684

Average prices were $44, $38, and $60 per ton, respectively. The surplus stock of concentrate has been reduced to 9000 tons.

MONTANA

Butte.—Operations in this district have been curtailed somewhat owing to the unsettled metal markets.

The Original and Leonard mines of the Anaconda company were closed on January 3 for alterations, and will remain so for several months. The Original has a two-compartment shaft, but a pump compartment will be added during the shut-down.

The Butte & Superior company allowed its option on the Germania mine to lapse on January 1. All machinery and supplies have been taken away.

Manganese producers have not much chance of getting Government aid, according to Lieutenant-Governor W. W. McDowell, who recently returned from Washington. A tariff of $20 per ton would be necessary to protect the domestic industry from foreign ore. Steel works are said to have large stocks of manganese. While production of manganese ore has ceased at Butte, it is at half capacity in the Philipsburg district.

Anaconda pays $1.50 per share, $3,496,875, on February 24. The general manager, John Gillie, estimates the 1917 production of metals as 298,000,000 lb. of copper, 74,700,000 lb. of zinc, 10,700,000 oz. of silver, and 64,500 oz. of gold, valued at $93,998,700. The red metal output was 11% less than in 1916. Comparison with 1917 is unsuitable, owing to the labor troubles during that year.

Anaconda produced 21,900,000 lb. of copper during December. The average monthly output in 1918 was 24,800,000 lb. May was the highest with 28,400,000 pounds.

As the company has suspended treatment of custom zinc ore the Butte & Superior is reported to have reduced operations by half.

NEVADA

Ely.—Nevada Consolidated produced 5,800,000 lb. in December, the lowest return for 1918. The average for the previous 11 months was 6,660,000 pounds.

NEW MEXICO

Santa Rita.—Chino Copper yielded 5,507,635 lb. during December, the lowest for the year, save August.

OKLAHOMA

Commerce.—The Lennan Lead & Zinc Co. is to move its mills to the Oka lease, near Picher.

Picher.—Production of Oklahoma mines last week was 4231 tons of blende and 392 tons of lead, valued at $209,-684.

UTAH

Bingham.—The apex dispute between the Utah Metal and Utah Consolidated companies has been settled. Apex rights of the former, as well as any claims it may have against the Utah-Apex company, are transferred to the Utah Consolidated, which concedes to Utah Metal certain rights to work in its ground.

The Utah Copper Co. laid-off between 500 and 600 men at its mine and mills last week, according to reports from Salt Lake City. The company produced 13,835,000 lb. during December. This is the lowest since February, but the winter months always show a decline. In August the yield was 19,920,947 pounds.

Gold Hill.—A 40-ton shipment of ore from the Western Utah Extension mine to the smelter averaged 60 cents gold, 4 oz. silver, and 7.15% copper, equal to $25 per ton. This mine is now 450 ft. deep. A. E. Custer is manager.

WASHINGTON

Chewelah.—The United Copper Mining Co., operating near here, is the first of the big mining companies so far reported that has cut wages since the end of the War. The reduction is a substantial one, as follows: Miners, skip-tenders, timber-men and hoist-men, from $5 per day to $4.25; shovelers and motormen, from $4.50 to $3.75; blacksmiths, from $5.50 to $4.75; blacksmiths helpers, from $4.50 to $3.75; and millmen and carpenters, from $4.50 to $4. "We worked in 1918 for the men and the Government, but this year we will operate for the benefit of the stockholders," explained the president, Conrad Wolfle. "We made about $45,000 last year, but had a hard struggle to do it. The best part of it is that after explaining the situation to the men they see the justice of our position and of 75 men employed only five left."

CANADA

British Columbia

Nelson.—The first session of the committee appointed to investigate the rates charged British Columbian mine operators for treatment of their ore by the Consolidated Mining & Smelting Co. at Trail will be held January 21 at Nelson. The personnel of this committee is S. S. Fowler of Riondel, Ivan de Lashmutt of Silverton, and James Anderton of Kaslo. The Provincial government will be represented by A. G. Langley, resident engineer with headquarters at Revelstoke.

Trail.—The Consolidated M. & S. Co.'s smelter here produced metals and by-products worth over $12,500,000 during 1918. The products were 40,662,704 lb. of lead, 25,405,-797 lb. of spelter, 9,951,781 lb. of copper, $2,000,476 of silver, $1,444,000 of gold, 3926 tons of sulphuric acid, 174,-178 lb. of bluestone, and 75 tons of lead pipe.

Vancouver.—An international mining convention will be held at Vancouver some time during March. It had been proposed that this gathering should be called for January, but a postponement to the latter date has been agreed on by members of the Vancouver Chamber of Mines. The convention has the sanction of Hon. William Sloan, Minister of Mines, and the resident mining engineers of the various mining districts of the Province are expected to take an active part. The proceedings are likely to be of special importance.

PERSONAL

Note. The Editor invites members of the profession to send particulars of their work and appointments. The information is interesting to our readers.

Francis Drake is at Monte Video.

George Crerar is at San Luis Potosi, Mexico.

Morton Webber is on his way back to New York.

J. S. Morgan of Juneau, Alaska, is at the Stewart hotel

Bulkeley Wells is president of the American Mining Congress.

H. H. Knox, of Knox & Allen, has returned to New York from Mexico.

E. M. Hamilton has gone to Parral, Mexico, where he will be about two months.

Arthur L. Pearse has gone from New York to London, intending to return shortly.

H. J. Sheafe, Captain in the Engineers, has returned from France to Saratoga, California.

Morris P. Kirk is now manager for the Yellow Pine Mining Co., at Goodsprings, Nevada.

W. G. Devereux, Lieutenant-Colonel of the 144th Field Artillery, has returned from France.

F. W. Bradley is making one of his periodical visits to the Bunker Hill & Sullivan mine at Kellogg, Idaho.

A. D. Nicholas has been appointed comptroller for the Calumet & Hecla and its subsidiary corporations.

Hugh F. K. Picard, of Sulman & Picard, is president-elect of the Institution of Mining & Metallurgy, London.

William H. Landers, Major in the U. S. Army, has secured his discharge and will be in San Francisco about February 1.

Robert Hawxhurst, Jr., has resigned as manager for the Eden Mining Co., in Nicaragua, and is now in San Francisco.

W. D. B. Motter, Jr., until recently manager for the Benson Mines Co., has joined the headquarters staff of Guggenheim Brothers.

Maurice Altmayer, Captain in the French Artillery, is here as a representative of the Department of Franco-American War Co-operation.

F. D. Baker, lately chief engineer to the Colorado department of the A. S. & R. Co., has retired, to engage in consulting practice with his sons at Denver.

Owen F. Brinton, formerly at Butte, has been appointed manager for the Western Utah Copper Co., on the resignation of Duncan MacVichie, who becomes consulting engineer to the company.

Alfred C. North has been granted a leave of absence from his duties as engineer for the Eden Mining Co. in the Pis Pis district of Nicaragua, and is now on his way to the United States with his family for a vacation.

E. H. Dickenson, formerly with the Mond Nickel Co., Bruce Mines, Ontario, Beatson Copper Co., La Touche, Alaska, and Nevada Consolidated, Ely, Nevada, has recently been appointed general manager of mines for the Tata Iron & Steel Co., at Sakchi, India.

F. H. Hawkins, who for several years past has held the position of chief assayer for the Standard-Silver Lead Mining Co. of Silverton, B. C., has gone to Anyox, B. C., to accept an appointment with the Granby Consolidated Mining & Smelting Co. Thomas Brown will succeed him at the Silverton assay-office.

The annual meeting of the Canadian Mining Institute will be held at Montreal on March 5, 6, and 7.

THE METAL MARKET

METAL PRICES

San Francisco, January 14

Aluminum-dust, large and small lots, cents per lb	65—70
Antimony, cents per pound	8.00
Copper, electrolytic, cents per pound, in carload lots	23.00
Lead, pig, cents per pound	6.25— 7.25
Platinum, per ounce	$108
Quicksilver, per flask of 75 lb	$105
Spelter, cents per pound	9.50
Zinc-dust, cents per pound	16.00

EASTERN METAL MARKET

(By wire from New York)

January 14.—Copper is quiet and easy. Lead is dull though steady. Spelter is inactive and weak.

SILVER

Below are given official (not Government) quotations, in cents per ounce, of silver 999 fine. In order to make prompt settlements with smelters and brokers, producers allow a discount from the maximum fixed price of \$1.01¼, hence the lower price. The Government has not fixed the general market price at \$1, but will pay this price (as from April 23, 1918) for all silver purchased by it. The equivalent of dollar silver (1000 fine) in British currency is 46.65 pence per ounce (925 fine), calculated at the current rate of exchange. On August 15, 1918, the Treasury announced that the maximum price was fixed at \$1.01½ per ounce. The British government fixed its maximum at 49½ pence, on September 2, but on November 12 this was changed to 48¾ pence, due to a drop in price.

Date		New York	London	Average week ending		
Jan.	8	101.12	48.75	Dec.	3	101.12
"	9	101.12	48.75	"	10	101.12
"	10	101.12	48.75	"	17	101.12
"	11	101.12	48.75	"	24	101.12
"	12 Sunday			"	31	101.12
"	13	101.12	48.75	Jan.	7	101.12
"	14	101.12	48.75	"	14	101.12

Monthly averages

	1916	1917	1918		1916	1917	1918
Jan.	56.76	75.14	88.72	July	63.06	78.92	99.62
Feb.	56.74	77.54	85.79	Aug.	66.07	85.40	100.31
Mch.	57.89	74.13	88.11	Sept.	68.51	100.73	101.12
Apr.	46.37	72.51	95.35	Oct.	67.86	87.38	101.12
May	74.27	74.61	99.50	Nov.	71.60	85.97	101.12
June	65.04	76.44	99.50	Dec.	75.70	85.97	101.12

COPPER

Prices of electrolytic in New York, in cents per pound.

Date			Average week ending		
Jan.	8	21.00	Dec.	3	26.00
"	9	21.00	"	10	26.00
"	10	21.00	"	17	26.00
"	11	20.50	"	24	26.00
"	12 Sunday		"	31	26.00
"	13	20.50	Jan.	7	21.80
"	14	20.50	"	14	20.75

Monthly averages

	1916	1917	1918		1916	1917	1918
Jan.	24.30	29.53	23.50	July	25.66	29.67	26.00
Feb.	26.62	34.57	23.50	Aug.	27.03	27.42	26.00
Mch.	26.65	36.00	23.50	Sept.	28.28	25.11	26.00
Apr.	28.02	33.16	23.50	Oct.	28.50	23.50	26.00
May	29.02	31.69	23.50	Nov.	31.95	23.50	26.00
June	27.47	32.57	23.50	Dec.	32.89	23.50	26.00

LEAD

Lead is quoted in cents per pound, New York delivery.

Date			Average week ending		
Jan.	8	5.75	Dec.	3	7.85
"	9	5.75	"	10	7.05
"	10	5.75	"	17	7.05
"	11	5.75	"	24	6.45
"	12 Sunday		"	31	6.10
"	13	5.75	Jan.	7	5.80
"	14	5.75	"	14	5.75

Monthly averages

	1916	1917	1918		1916	1917	1918
Jan.	5.95	7.64	6.85	July	6.40	10.93	8.03
Feb.	6.23	9.10	7.07	Aug.	6.28	10.75	8.05
Mch.	7.26	10.07	7.26	Sept.	6.86	9.07	8.05
Apr.	7.70	9.38	6.99	Oct.	7.02	6.97	8.05
May	7.38	10.29	6.88	Nov.	7.07	6.38	8.05
June	6.88	11.74	7.58	Dec.	7.55	6.49	6.90

TIN

Prices in New York, in cents per pound. The monthly averages in 1918 are nominal. On December 3 the War Industries Board fixed the price to consumers and jobbers at 72½c. f.o.b. Chicago and Eastern points, and 71½c. on the Pacific Coast. This will continue for some months.

Monthly averages

	1916	1917	1918		1916	1917	1918
Jan.	41.76	44.10	85.13	July	38.37	62.60	93.00
Feb.	42.60	51.47	85.00	Aug.	38.88	62.53	91.33
Mch.	50.50	54.27	85.00	Sept.	36.66	61.54	80.40
Apr.	51.49	55.63	88.53	Oct.	41.10	62.24	78.82
May	49.10	63.21	100.01	Nov.	44.12	74.18	73.07
June	42.07	61.93	91.00	Dec.	42.55	85.00	71.52

ZINC

Zinc is quoted as spelter, standard Western brands, New York delivery, in cents per pound.

Date			Average week ending		
Jan.	8	7.85	Dec.	3	8.67
"	9	7.80	"	10	8.61
"	10	7.75	"	17	8.58
"	11	7.70	"	24	8.45
"	12 Sunday		"	31	8.13
"	13	7.65	Jan.	7	7.93
"	14	7.60	"	14	7.72

Monthly averages

	1916	1917	1918		1916	1917	1918
Jan.	18.21	9.75	7.87	July	9.90	8.98	8.72
Feb.	19.99	10.45	7.97	Aug.	9.03	8.58	8.87
Mch.	18.40	10.78	7.67	Sept.	9.18	8.33	9.58
Apr.	18.62	10.20	7.04	Oct.	9.92	8.32	9.11
May	16.01	9.41	7.29	Nov.	11.81	7.76	8.75
June	12.85	9.63	7.92	Dec.	11.26	7.84	8.49

QUICKSILVER

The primary market for quicksilver is San Francisco, California being the largest producer. The price is fixed in the open market, according to quantity. Prices, in dollars per flask of 75 pounds:

Date					
Dec.	17	110.00	Dec.	31	110.00
"	24	110.00	Jan.	7	110.00
			"	14	105.00

Monthly averages

	1916	1917	1918		1916	1917	1918
Jan.	222.00	81.00	128.06	July	81.20	102.00	120.00
Feb.	295.00	126.25	118.00	Aug.	74.50	115.00	120.00
Mch.	219.00	113.75	112.00	Sept.	75.00	112.00	120.00
Apr.	141.60	114.50	115.00	Oct.	78.20	102.00	120.00
May	90.00	104.00	110.00	Nov.	79.50	102.50	120.00
June	74.70	85.50	112.00	Dec.	80.00	117.42	115.00

LEAD AND ZINC IN 1918

The mine output of lead and zinc in the United States declined greatly in 1918, according to a statement compiled by C. E. Siebenthal of the U. S. Geological Survey from reports and estimates by producers and from the records of the Bureau of Foreign and Domestic Commerce. The output of soft lead by mines of the Mississippi Valley and Eastern States was 250,000 short tons, and that of argentiferous lead by mines of the Western States was 313,000 tons, a total of 563,000 tons, compared with 273,046 tons and 378,110 tons, respectively, and a total of 651,156 tons in 1917, a decrease of nearly 100,000 tons. The decrease in output of domestic lead was partly made up by an increase in imports of lead in ore and bullion, particularly from Canada and Mexico, which are estimated at 14,100 tons and 78,600 tons, respectively, against 5867 tons and 62,891 tons in 1917.

The recoverable zinc content of ore mined in 1918 was about 627,000 tons, compared with 711,192 tons in 1917. The output of the Eastern States was 127,000 tons, of the Central States 297,000 tons, and of the Western States 203,000 tons, compared with 155,169, 310,471, and 245,552 tons by those divisions in 1917. The output of the Central States fell off proportionately less than that of the other sections. Montana apparently had the largest output, with 105,000 tons, and New Jersey and Oklahoma were next, with 100,000 tons each. Imports of zinc in ore fell off from 72,470 tons in 1917 to 24,000 tons in 1918. The zinc content of imports from Mexico decreased from 45,697 tons in 1917 to 18,000 tons in 1918.

The production of primary domestic desilverized lead in 1918 was about 284,000 tons, of soft lead 210,500 tons, and of desilverized soft lead 47,000 tons, making a total output from domestic ores of 541,500 tons of refined lead, compared with 549,895 tons in 1917, made up of 303,679 tons of desilverized lead, 187,735 tons of soft lead, and 58,481 tons of desilverized soft lead. The output of lead smelted and refined from foreign ore and bullion was 96,500 tons, compared with 62,319 tons in 1917. The total of lead smelted or refined in the United States was thus 638,000 tons, compared with 612,214 tons in 1917. The production of antimonial lead was 22,000 tons, against 18,647 tons in 1918. Exports of lead of foreign origin were 38,000 tons and of lead of domestic origin 64,500 tons, compared with 41,160 tons and 56,209 tons, respectively, in 1917. The quantity of lead available for consumption in this country was 540,000 tons, compared with 515,258 tons in 1917. In both years some of the available lead was shipped abroad for use of the American Expeditionary Force, but such shipments are not recorded as exports. The average price of lead at New York was 7.6 cents per pound, compared with an average value of 8.6 cents in 1917.

The production of primary spelter from domestic ores in 1918 was 502,300 tons, and from foreign ores 23,300 tons, a total of 525,600 tons, compared with 584,597 tons and 84,976 tons, respectively, and a total of 669,573 tons in 1917. Of the output of domestic spelter over 29,000 tons consisted of electrolytic spelter, including some that was refined from prime Western metal. Exports of spelter made from foreign ores were 24,400 tons, and of spelter from domestic ores 78,600 tons, compared with 66,288 tons of foreign and 153,455 tons of domestic spelter in 1917. Stocks of spelter at smelters and in warehouses at the end of the year are estimated at 36,000 tons, and the apparent consumption during the year was 440,000 tons, compared with 413,984 tons in 1917. The decrease in exports and the increase in apparent consumption are accounted for by the shipments for use of the American Expeditionary Force, which are not recorded as exports and hence appear as domestic consumption.

At the end of November, 123,033 retorts were in operation at plants having a total of 166,060 retorts. The average quotation for prime Western spelter at St. Louis was 8 cents per pound, compared with 8.9 cents in 1917.

Eastern Metal Market

New York, January 8.

Demand for all metals is light and the markets are all lifeless; they are now entirely unrestricted except tin.

Copper demand is small, with the tendency of prices downward.

The tin market is extremely quiet, with underlying conditions very unsatisfactory.

The lead market may be considered as practically stabilized, with demand better.

Zinc buying is of small proportion, and quotations are nominally lower.

Antimony is dull and unchanged.

ANTIMONY

The market is devoid of demand and is nominally unchanged at 7.62½ to 7.75c., New York, duty paid, for wholesale lots for early delivery.

COPPER

The copper situation is mixed and full of uncertainty. There are few buyers—this is an outstanding fact. Leading producers continue to insist that their price for not only foreign but for domestic business is not less than 23c. for both Lake and electrolytic, yet some of them admit that copper has been sold as low as 21c. for January delivery. It develops that these sales do not represent large quantities, but only such orders as a few consumers here and there must place. These orders are being filled, it is understood, by a few producers who are not included in the export company, or by some re-sale or second-hand metal available from those having more than they can use. These sales are made at 21c., New York. We therefore quote the market as nominal at that level. The group of producers referred to are not acting in concert with those that formed the Copper Export Association. As to foreign demand, as far as can be learned there is very little of this. The large governments are well provided with metal, and it is the opinion of some producers here that it may be the second quarter before foreign demand makes itself felt. It is generally conceded that American production of crude copper is being curtailed decidedly, some putting it at not more than 90% of what it was in the last year of the War.

IRON AND STEEL

New steel business in the first week of the new year has increased slightly, but it is not significant. Some steel companies are operating at 85% of capacity, but the general average is 65%; the present rate, however, is equivalent to 90% of the capacity of four years ago. Consumers and producers are settling down to a contest to tire each other out, the former being convinced that prices must go lower, the latter claiming it would be disastrous if they did unless labor declines in value also. The pig-iron output for 1918, according to the blast-furnace reports of 'The Iron Age', was 38,506,249 tons, compared with 38,185,981 tons in 1917 and 39,039,356 tons in 1916. The December output was 3,433,617 tons, or 110,762 tons per day.

LEAD

As was predicted in this letter some weeks ago, based on the opinion of a lead broker, the lead market has regained its feet quicker than any of the other non-ferrous markets; the market seems to have scraped bottom. Early last week some business was done as low as 5.25c., New York, but the market soon reacted to 5.50c. and then to 5.75c., New York, which is now the quotation for early or January delivery. There has been a good inquiry during the past week and some business has been done, but the volume was not large. For spot delivery the quotation is 6c., New York. It is not believed that there is much metal available below these levels. The market may be regarded as firm and quiet. The American Smelting & Refining Co. still holds at 6c., New York.

TIN

It is not surprising that consumers of tin are gradually becoming dissatisfied with the present situation. Those desiring the metal can obtain it only at high levels, or at 72.50c., New York, if they buy from the United States Steel Products Co., or slightly under this fixed price if they purchase outside. This fact is emphasized by the appearance this week of offerings of future shipments of Straits tin from the East at 53c. c.i.f., New York, importations of which are prohibited. The market is decidedly quiet, and there is almost no activity. Small quantities held by outsiders are still being offered but they are not being absorbed. Consumers are also well provided with supplies, all of which makes it seem probable that the U. S. Steel Products Co. is not getting rid of its allotment very fast, and that the period of control may be long drawn out. Consumers are buying only when forced to. December deliveries of tin were 4050 tons, of which 3950 tons came through Pacific ports. The quantity in stocks and landing on December 31 was 185 tons. Imports of tin in 1918 were 58,027 tons, compared with 54,867 tons in 1917. Straits tin made up 34,243 tons of the 1918 imports.

ZINC

The market continues to sag and is now quoted, nominal largely, at 7.50c., St. Louis, or 7.85c., New York, for prime Western for early delivery. What little business is being done is taken by some of the smaller producers, the larger ones asking 7.65c., St. Louis, or 8c. for the same position and are disinclined to press the market. The output of spelter from domestic and foreign ore was 525,600 tons in 1918, as compared with 669,573 tons in 1917, according to the U. S. Geological Survey. The apparent domestic consumption was 440,000 tons, against 413,984 tons in 1917.

ORES

Manganese Alloys: The market for both ferro and spiegel is dead. Quotations are nominal at $225 per ton, delivered, for 70% ferro or $3 per unit with no sales reported. A carload or two of spiegel has been sold at $65 to $70, furnace, but a large order would bring a lower price, possible $60, furnace.

Tungsten: Appraisal of prices is difficult owing to the absence of demand and sales. One dealer says that high-grade ore is now offered at $15 per unit of 60% concentrate. There is no quotation on ferro-tungsten.

OIL PRODUCTION DURING 1918

According to John D. Northrop of the U. S. Geological Survey, the past two years' output was as under, in barrels:

Field	1917	1918
Appalachian	24,932,205	25,300,000
Lima-Indiana	3,670,293	3,100,000
Illinois	15,776,860	13,300,000
Oklahoma-Kansas	155,043,596	139,600,000
Central and North Texas	10,900,048	15,000,000
North Louisiana	8,561,963	13,000,000
Gulf Coast	26,087,587	21,700,000
Rocky Mountain	9,199,310	12,000,000
California	93,877,549	101,300,000
Alaska and Michigan	10,300	....
Total	335,315,601	345,500,000

Company Reports

CONSOLIDATED MINING & SMELTING CO. OF CANADA, LTD.

Property: about 20 mines in the Rossland, Kimberley, Ainsworth, Nelson, Sandon, Silverton, and Greenwood districts of British Columbia; also at Republic, Washington; also large smelter and refinery at Trail.

Operating Officials: J. J. Warren, managing director; S. G. Blaylock, assistant general manager; W. M. Archibald, manager of mines, and staff consisting of F. S. Peters at Rossland, E. G. Montgomery at Sullivan and St. Eugene, L. W. Oughtred at Highland, John Cannon at Number One, Ronald Stonier at Molly Gibson, Dan Matheson at Ottawa and Rock Candy, Edward Nordman at Emma, D. M. Tattrie at Lucky Thought, W. Clancy with Coast Copper, and G. H. Kilburn at Blue Grouse; (field operations under direction of M. E. Purcell, R. M. Macaulay, J. K. Cram, and G. H. Kilburn); T. W. Bingay, comptroller; James Buchanan, smelter superintendent, G. E. Murray, assistant; B. A. Stimmel, assistant manager of zinc plant; J. K. Batchelder, superintendent of refineries, F. E. Beasley, assistant; R. W. Diamond, superintendent of concentration and testing; G. F. Chapman, construction engineer; W. E. Jones, mechanical engineer; A. L. MacCallum, superintendent of acid plants; F. E. Lee, W. H. Hannay, and R. K. Blois, research engineers; R. Vaughan, F. S. Willis, H. Woodburn, and R. G. S. Anthony, department superintendents in zinc plant; R. H. Hatchett, chief chemist.

Financial Statement: during the year ended September 30, 1918, sales of smelter product realized $9,780,565. The total revenue, including ore and metals on hand $2,828,416, and dividends from the West Kootenay Power company $160,000, was $12,784,985. The profit, after deducting depreciation $408,557, and allowing for ore purchased, taxes, etc., was $867,259. After paying dividends, the balance was $2,148,123, against $2,360,275 at the end of the previous year. Debenture bonds of $3,000,000, at 7%, are to be issued for extensions to plant. Bank loans and overdrafts total $2,809,071.

Dividends: the rate is 10% per annum, and four absorbed $1,047,745. Another distribution was paid on October 1, amounting to $261,936, and one on January 1, 1919.

Development: at 17 mines there was a total of 16,122 ft. of exploration accomplished, also 21,174 ft. of diamond-drilling. Over 100 miles of workings have now been opened. Notwithstanding heavy shipments from all the mines, ore-reserves are equal to those at the beginning of the year under review. Owing to metallurgical improvements in treating the complex ore (zinc-lead) of the Sullivan mine, many years have been added to its life. This is a valuable mine. A fluorspar mine was acquired to supply the lead refinery with acid; the Coast Copper Co.'s property is developing well; and the San Poil mine at Republic was purchased to ensure a supply of silicious ore.

Production: the smelter reduced (in 10 months actual work) a total of 374,889 tons of company and custom ores, yielding 52,917 oz. of gold, 1,708,692 oz. of silver, 38,844,946 lb. of lead, 7,982,903 lb. of copper, and 21,800,932 lb. of spelter, valued at $10,533,367. This makes a total since 1894 of 5,554,196 tons of ore, 1,831,838 oz. of gold, 28,714,042 oz. of silver, 497,171,470 lb. of lead, 83,030,313 lb. of copper, and 44,857,928 lb. of spelter, valued at $104,849,121.

From 1914 to October 1918 the company supplied the British government with 6831 tons of copper, 39,606 tons of lead, and 22,356 tons of zinc. The $700,000 advance from the Imperial Munitions Board toward extension of the zinc plant was repaid in full during the year.

Reduction Works: the financial year began under unfavorable conditions, both as to costs, metal contracts, and labor. The plant was eventually closed for six weeks on account of a strike. At the copper smelter, operation was intermittent; but metallurgical work gave improved gold recovery. The lead smelter worked unprofitably for a time, due to metal recoveries not being as high as the quantities paid for. Metal losses were lower than for years. Previously each unit of lead cost the company from 40 to 50 cents, while in 1917-'18 the same amount cost as much as $2.20. Smelting rates were therefore advanced in February 1918. The copper refinery is to be increased in capacity from 20 to 50 tons daily, at a cost of $250,000; and a rod mill is to be built costing $75,000. The sulphuric and hydro-fluosilicic acid plants were in operation all the year. Important changes were made in the zinc plant and mill.

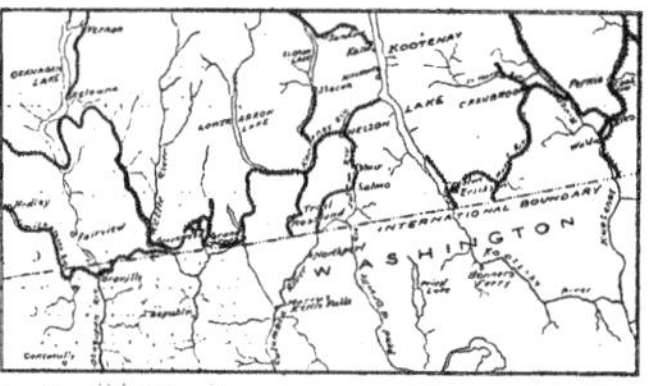

PART OF BRITISH COLUMBIA, SHOWING CENTRES CONTIGUOUS TO TRAIL.

Power: the revenue-producing load of the West Kootenay Power & Light Co. was 22,360 hp., a slight decrease due to the unsettled conditions. A line to supply 1500 hp. to the Northport smelter in Washington was completed, and work is under way on the line to supply 5000 hp. to the Canada Copper Corporation at Copper Mountain.

BENDIGO AMALGAMATED GOLDFIELDS

Property: this is a consolidation of the mines of about 40 companies at Bendigo, Victoria, Australia. Eight lines of 'reef' are included in the area, ranging from 4500 to 22,000 ft. in length, totaling 93,900 ft. Most of the shafts are over 2000 ft. deep, some being over 3000 ft., from which, in the aggregate, a great deal of work has been done and ore extracted. The concentration of development at certain points and operation on modern lines is the fixed policy.

Operating Officials: E. C. Dyason, managing director; A. H. P. Moline, superintendent.

Financial Statement: during the year ended July 2, 1918, receipts were £161,907 ($777,000) from gold, other items making a total of £165,789 ($797,000). Wages absorbed £108,032 ($518,000). Including the previous balance of £58,841 ($283,000) expenditures used up the total revenue.

Development: there was carried out 22,555 ft. of prospecting and development, and 3737 ft. of drilling (shot and diamond). Fifty faces were being followed. Continuous geologic examination is made, as the structure of the field is complex. A number of minor discoveries were made, but no high-grade shoots of any extent were found. Tributors are at work in certain parts of the mines.

Production: the mills crushed a total of 132,351 tons for the company, yielding, with concentrates, gold worth £134,390 ($643,000); and for tributors 14,418 tons for £27,517 ($136,000). Ore treatment—stamps, amalgamation, and concentration—is not difficult, and tailings assay only from 24 to 56 cents per ton. The report gives considerable details of underground work and drilling.

INFORMATION FURNISHED BY MANUFACTURERS

ELECTRICAL EQUIPMENT FOR MINE PUMPS

The most essential requirements of mine pumps are that they run continuously and take as little power as possible. These points are met by a complete line of Westinghouse motors and control built for all sizes and commercial circuits, either alternating or direct-current. In addition to

UNDERGROUND PUMPING UNIT

these, the advantage of lower first cost and maintenance expense, greater compactness, flexibility, and ease of control inherent with electric drive are obtained. Simplicity and ruggedness of the type CS squirrel-cage motor is especially adapted to mine-pump service, as it is built largely

UNDERGROUND PUMPING UNIT

of steel and has nothing to wear except the bearings, which are large, well lubricated, and require little attention. These motors may be started at the motor or at a distance. When started at the motor those smaller than 7½ hp. use a simple fused knife-switch and the larger ones require hand-operated auto-starters. When started from a distance an automatic starter is used of the resistor or auto-transformer type, which gives thorough protection operating at high-efficiency at both speeds. Only a simple double-throw switch is required to change from one speed to the other. If the power source is limited or a speed reduction is at times desired, the wound-rotor type CW motor, with the same general mechanical characteristics as the type CS motor, is furnished. With this motor also, either hand-operated control at the motor or automatic control at a distance may be used.

Many mines have only direct current available; for these, type SK motors having the same, simple, strong, and reliable construction, steel frame, and rugged bearings are used. These motors are built self-starting as large as 20 hp., so that they may be thrown directly on the line from any desired point. For pumping from a sump, a float-switch in connection with an automatic controller will start and stop the motor at the desired limits. An especially handy outfit and an efficient arrangement of pumping equipment is obtained by mounting a motor-driven pump on a truck or mine-car. This will enable quick transportation of the pump to any desired point.

COMMERCIAL PARAGRAPHS

It has always been impossible, according to the du Pont company, to obtain a satisfactory covering for concentrating tables. In lieu of a better material, linoleum has been largely used, but the abrasive action of ore and, in the case of mine water containing sulphuric acid, the corrosive action soon destroys the linseed-oil content of linoleum and necessitates its frequent replacement. 'Minefab' is the name of a new material that has been specially developed to meet the requirements demanded of a table covering. A recent testing program, carried on simultaneously in a number of mining districts, proved conclusively that all objectives have been attained. Minefab will give longer and more efficient service than any other material. Minefab is made with a heavy fabric base, coated on both sides with an extremely tough, flexible, protective film of pyroxylin, which ruggedly resists abrasion and is highly immune to sulphuric acid. The coldest weather does not affect its flexibility, and it is absolutely water-proof. Being white in color, the contrast between it and the ore increases the opportunity of recovering a maximum of the metallic content from the sludge.

Zelnicker's Bulletin No. 250 of 84 pages contains long lists of second-hand machinery, such as rails, locomotives, cars, cranes, tanks, power-plants, machine-tools, wire rope, hoists, etc.

Camphuis, Rives & Gordon, Inc., exporters and importers, inform us that their New York office at 81 New street is now fully organized for this business. The president, W. D. Gordon, and secretary-treasurer, L. G. Unzueta, have been connected with this class of trade for 20 and 15 years, respectively.

The Waugh drill-steel punching-machine, model 110, is briefly described in Bulletin 10-V of the **Denver Rock Drill Manufacturing Co.** The machine will open the hole (in hollow steel) in a bit or shank in one-twentieth the time required to do this by hand. All gauges of steel can be handled without changing the dies.

Although Book No. 333 of the **Link-Belt Co.** of Chicago contains 88 pages on equipment for the handling and preparation of coal at the mine, metal companies will find therein a great deal of information, thoroughly illustrated. Besides the operation of conveyors, screens, chutes, rolls, silent-chain drives, and the 3-compartment car-dumps are described.

Manganese-steel sand and gravel pumps of large size are discussed in a new bulletin of the **American Manganese Steel Co.** of Chicago Heights, Illinois. When excavation is necessary, and there is plenty of water, the centrifugal pump is an economical efficient means for moving loose material. Cutter-heads of careful construction are important, also a rock-ejector in the suction-pipe. This firm makes special pipe, and renewable parts of manganese steel.

Steam mine hoists and accessories are illustrated and described in Bulletin 19 of the **Lidgerwood Manufacturing Co.** This is a well-prepared publication. The hoists shown are the single fixed-drum reversible gear type, single-friction drum, band-friction drum, incline haulage engine, double friction drum reversible, double tanden-friction drum, belt hoist, prospecting hoist, and other types. A few notes are given on cages, sheaves, buckets, and indicators.

The 'Giant' semi-Diesel fuel-oil engine is discussed by the **Chicago Pneumatic Tool Co.** in Bulletin 34-W. This engine is considered to differ from all others in its horizontal position, the use of a cross-head, and the use of a hot plate instead of a hot ball or electric ignition. A horizontal engine means easier accessibility. The crank is counter-balanced. Oil used may be any distillate of 28 to 40°B. Some crude oils can be used. All the parts are illustrated and described.

The Green Engineering Co. of East Chicago has issued a booklet on its 'materials transfer and storage-hopper', showing the stages in its construction. The supporting structure is built of standard steel sections, cut and punched ready for erection. After this, cast-iron plate supports are hooked to the angle struts of the steel frame, and into the recesses in the sides of these supports are slipped the cast-iron side plates and corner plates. The whole assembling requires no skilled labor.

'Superior' McCully crushers are described in Bulletin PM-50 of the **Worthington Pump & Machinery Corporation.** These machines are made by the Power & Mining Machinery Works of Cudahy, Wisconsin. Sectional views and list of parts makes the parts easily understood. Lubrication of eccentric and gear is a feature of this design. Chilled iron or manganese steel are used in the crushing head. Sizes manufactured vary from the laboratory crusher with each feed opening 2½ by 10 in. to No. 36 of 36 by 126 in. Some notes are given on revolving screens and elevators.

H. W. Clarke, who until December 15 has been connected with the advertising department of the McGraw-Hill Book Co. at Chicago, has been appointed manager of advertising for the Chicago Pneumatic Tool Co., Chicago, Illinois. Mr. Clarke has been identified with the engineering advertising field for several years. Prior to his connection with the McGraw-Hill publications he was eight years with the Westinghouse Electric & Mfg. Co., East Pittsburgh, Pennsylvania, part of the time as a member of the sales and publicity department and later as Western publicity representative with headquarters at Chicago.

Horace N. Trumbull, who recently received his discharge from the Engineers Officers' Training School at Camp A. A. Humphreys, Virginia, has been appointed advertising manager of the **Wellman-Seaver-Morgan Co.** of Cleveland, Ohio. Before entering the service he acted in a similar capacity for the SKF Ball Bearing Co. of Hartford, Connecticut. The Wellman-Seaver-Morgan Co. has opened a San Francisco office at 415 Rialto building, in charge of Norman S. Ross. Business originating from California, Nevada west of the 115th meridian, and the counties of Josephine, Jackson, and Klamath in Oregon, will receive the attention of Mr. Ross.

The A. H. Simpson Co. of 633 Stevenson street, San Francisco, has established a high prestige as dealers, purchasing and selling-agents in new and second-hand machinery of every description. Efforts have been directed toward the establishing of business along sound lines. Every piece of used equipment sold by them carries with it definite guarantees of what it will do. During the last year, when new machinery was hard to secure, many mines found the company a reliable clearing-house in which to get what they needed. A. H. Simpson and Irving Thyle are looking forward to greatly increased business during 1919. Their yards and warehouse are stocked with a large and varied line of both new and second-hand machinery. It will pay any mine manager or superintendent to consult them when in need of equipment.

Of unusual interest to mining men is the announcement that the well-known Congress, Alvarado, and Rincorn mills at Congress Junction, Arizona, are to be dismantled immediately. The Congress plant has been in operation only a short time and the machinery is said to be in perfect condition. **Rosenburg & Co.**, of Los Angeles, have purchased the entire plant, including the railroad, and will sell the equipment of all three mines. According to one of the officials of the company, nothing will be reserved and everything will be sold as rapidly as possible. Among the large list of materials to be disposed of will be 6 miles of standard-gauge, 45 and 55-lb. rails, 75 tons of 8 and 10-lb. re-laying rails, 100-stamp mill complete, railroad gondolas, donkey engines, hoists, air-compressors, 9 miles of riveted pipe, 3 miles of 4-in. standard pipe, 5 miles of other standard pipe, ore and timber cars, boilers, machine-shop equipment, including lathes, drill-presses, and planers, tanks, cable, pulleys, belting, pipe fittings, tools, etc. The Rosenburg company has already begun the dismantling of the mills and all of the goods are open to inspection at Congress Junction, Arizona.

Oxwelding and Cutting: Manual of Instruction. **Pp. 124,** ill., index. The Oxweld Acetylene Co., Chicago. Price, 50 cents.

The oxy-acetylene process, like so many other important innovations, has suffered from the belief that almost any one could use it successfully without instruction, while, as a matter of fact, the work requires highly-skilled labor with special training. The present volume aims to supply this instruction. After a brief and non-technical explanation of the various physical and chemical laws upon which work with the oxy-acetylene torch depends, the general subject of welding with the torch is considered. Next comes a discussion of the properties of the various metals that are welded. Then generators and other apparatus used in the work are considered. The remainder of the book is devoted to practical problems in welding and cutting—60 in all. The text is supplemented by a number of line drawings. Any one having to do with oxy-acetylene welding or cutting will find the book invaluable.

Oil production of the United States during 1918 amounted to 345,500,000 barrels. This is a gain of 3% over the output of 1917.

IN a recent issue we referred to Dr. Raymond as the son of an editor of the New York 'Times'; this was an error; he was editor of the 'Free Democrat', in 1852, and then, until 1854, of the 'Evening Chronicle', both newspapers published at Syracuse, New York. His father was also Professor of English in the Brooklyn Polytechnic Institute.

PRESIDENT POINCARE, in the speech that opened the proceedings of the Peace Conference, mentioned the fact that this meeting at Versailles began its work on the very same day—January 18—as that on which 48 years ago, at the same place, the German empire was proclaimed by a German army of invasion. Thus does "Time bring in his revenges".

AMONG the agencies established for aiding re-employment of those returning from the War, we may mention the Engineering Societies Employment Bureau at 29 West 39th street, New York. This bureau is under the management of the secretaries of the four engineering societies, namely, the American Society of Civil Engineers, the American Institute of Mining Engineers, the American Society of Mechanical Engineers, and the American Institute of Electrical Engineers. Employers are invited to write to the Bureau and specify the type of men whom they desire to engage.

UNDER 'Discussion' this week we publish a number of interesting letters. Mr. R. T. Walker replies to Mr. G. A. Duncan, and contributes a scholarly account of legislation regulating the ownership of water in Nevada. It is a good-tempered and informing rejoinder. The Alaska Engineering Commission is defended by Mr. William Gerig. The chrome scandal and the pitchblende promotion are the subjects of two notes. Mr. Herbert T. Lacey suggests a corrective for the abnormal status of gold. To Mr. Arthur L. Pearse we are indebted for timely information on the oil-shale industry, with which he is in close touch. Finally, Mr. H. R. Chartran, recently in Siberia, writes to advise intervention.

HOW unrepentant the Germans remain is suggested by a recent public utterance of Dr. Alfred Zimmermann, the Foreign Minister whose Mexican scheming was one of the causes that drew this country into the War. Speaking for publication on January 16 he said that he feared other nations did not desire freedom of the seas and a league of nations "as much as Germany desires them because we want justice and protection from oppression." They want exactly what they refused to give to other nations, particularly those unable, like Belgium and Serbia, to withstand their depredations. He objected to the blockade maintained by the British navy as being against the law of nations, as if a German official could appeal to "the law of nations" without being ridiculous or impertinent, because the nation that attacked Belgium without warning under the blatant slogan of 'Necessity knows no law' outlawed itself by the act. Dr. Zimmermann also says that but for the blockade Germany "would perhaps have won the War." Then we say, thank God for the blockade!

WE note that a group of editors and publishers of American trade journals, recently on a visit of observation to the former battlefields of France, has sent a letter to President Wilson urging the punishment of the German leaders and agents responsible for acts "of piracy, murder, and pillage." This letter is signed by Mr. Horace M. Swetland of New York, the chairman of the delegation. We know Mr. Swetland well as an able, honorable, and enterprising publisher; we know him to be a man of kindly nature and broad sympathies; in short, he is well worthy of representing the enlightened public opinion of the United States. Therefore we feel respect for his stand in this matter and confidence in his judgment. He, in his representative capacity, insists that the devastation and ruin wrought by the German armies "are not the work of one man or a group of men" but "of a system, the policies of which have been executed with thoroughness by a willing people." He proceeds to emphasize the fact that "the laws of nations that civilization has so painfully built up through the centuries have been wantonly violated for four long years. To fail to enforce these laws now would be tacitly to concede the power of repeal by the criminals themselves. These laws must be re-established."

BOLSHEVISM, says President Poincare, is a microbe that attacks defeated countries, not victorious ones. It is a germ that finds lodgment in decaying organisms and feeds on ferment. Germany's bitterest pill is that her vaunted political and industrial organizations should have succumbed to the germ with which the German himself poisoned the illiterate Russian, proving that kultur, after all, was but a degenerate system. Bolshevism is thriving on the ruins of autocracy, but it threatens democracy quite as much. Most of our people are looking upon the Bolshevist campaign as if it were a Villa raid or a Yaqui uprising in Sonora: it is far more sinister than that. It is a formidable barrier to the successful issue of the Peace Conference and threatens the very basis of European civilization. As yet the Bolshevist campaign has gained no headway in this country, where it is identified properly with I. W. W. insanity, but if it prospers on the other side of the Atlantic it is sure to affect us also. If the old Russian term Nihilism were used as a synonym for Bolshevism, as it should be, we would recognize its tendencies more vividly. No more dangerous blunder can be made than to regard it as an extreme phase of Socialism; it is as opposed to Socialism as to any other scheme of organized and orderly society, it is distinctly anti-social, a reversion to the ape-and-tiger stage of human existence.

CONVICTION of 43 Industrial Workers of the World after trial at Sacramento brings before the public the seriousness of American bolshevism. Their "silent defence" was interrupted just before the Court pronounced judgment by an orgy of frothy oratory in the course of which several of the defendants defied the Government and the community that they had outraged. It is noteworthy that the Judge, wisely, we think, allowed them free scope for utterance, because the reckless expression of their anarchism is calculated to open the eyes of the public to the danger of their perverted ideas. The I. W. W. recognize no country; they respect no flag except the red one; they would pull down the structure of civilization on which centuries of human labor have been spent; they ignore the differences in men and would reward the stupid or incompetent equally with the wise and capable; they are the negation of human advancement. To them "the uniform of the United States soldier is the livery of the scab," so they seek to bring us to the level of Russia. They assert that "sabotage is a sign of courage," so they throw a bomb into a haystack and take great pains to be a hundred miles away before the bomb ignites. They try to undermine, degrade, or destroy the institutions of a country that to most of them has offered either an asylum of refuge or the chances of an honorable career. They are the bubonic rats of civilization, carrying with them the fleas of the political diseases from which this and other progressive countries try so hard to rid themselves. Bolshevism has brought eastern Europe to ruin; let us see to it that it gets no foothold on this continent.

ASHANTI is a name made familiar to some of us when we were boys by George Henty's story of 'The March to Koomassie', founded on the romance of Wolseley's campaign in the West African blackamoor country then called and spelled Ashantee. To our readers it will be interesting as the name of a great gold-mining enterprise, the Ashanti Goldfields Corporation. We make mention of it because it has just come 'of age', having been started in 1897. The first prospecting expedition to go into Ashanti arrived at Obuasi on Christmas Eve of that year. At that time Obuasi was a small village in an almost impenetrable jungle. Now it is a well organized town, with a population of 16,000, governed by a committee appointed jointly by the Government and the mining company. Bush-tracks have been superseded by a railway, the fever has been controlled by scientific sanitation, the natives have been taught many handicrafts, and the sun of civilization has pierced the miasma of the forest primeval. The mine is 124 miles from the coast and for five years everything had to be carried on the heads—not backs—of natives at an average cost of $300 per ton. Obuasi is now the seat of government for the Southern Province of Ashanti. All of this is well worthy of mention, but the original purpose of the white man's intrusion was to win gold. During the 21 years the Ashanti Corporation has produced £5,523,749, or $26,890,182 worth of gold, of which £1,867,014 or $9,055,018 has been net profit and 94.3% of it has gone into the pockets of the shareholders, leaving 5.7% to credit in the profit and loss account. For the success of its technical operations the company is indebted to Mr. W. R. Feldtmann, whose writings on cyanidation have made him known in this country.

ONE of our local organs of misinformation recently published an article on the Aurora Consolidated mines, in Nevada, and stated that an attempt to unwater this group of old mines had been dropped after spending a million dollars. The flood of water was so great, it was said, that the pumps had failed to lower the water-level. From this was drawn the major premise that gold mining is exceedingly hazardous, special emphasis being placed on "the essentially gambling nature of all mining." These mines, it was said, had produced ore that was "exceedingly rich," but all of it had been removed before they were abandoned by their former owners. The facts are these: the workings of the Aurora Consolidated were reached through an adit, so that all the water, only a few thousand gallons per day, gravitated into the storage-tanks at the mill. This supply of water from the mine was insufficient for the milling of the ore, so that it had to be supplemented by a spring two miles distant. The veins are big quartz-filled fissures in andesite. The quartz contains enough gold to bring it under the category of low-grade ore, the physical and economic conditions being favorable to cheap mining and milling. In consequence, the Goldfield Consolidated Mines Company acquired 87% of the 685,500 shares in the old company during 1913 and started to re-open the mines in June 1914, at which time it was estimated that a reserve of 600,000 tons of ore assaying $4.81 was available. The property, including a 500-ton mill, was valued at $877,000. During 1915 an output of 180,529 tons, averaging $4.14 per ton, was made, and from this a yield of $3.55

per ton was obtained, at a cost of $3.56 per ton, exclusive of interest, current construction, and royalties. In 1916 the output was 173,270 tons, averaging $3.32 per ton, from which $2.89 per ton was extracted at a cost of $2.46 per ton, showing a profit of 43 cents per ton. In 1917 the output was 175,447 tons, averaging $2.82, from which $2.32 was obtained at a cost of $2.42, showing a loss of 10 cents per ton. In 1918, up to September, the output was 104,086 tons, averaging $3.41 per ton, from which $2.83 was obtained at a cost of $3.48 per ton, showing a loss of 65 cents per ton. Evidently the rising rate of wages and the advancing price of supplies caused the curves of recovery and cost to cross each other during 1917, without any immediate prospect of a reversal of their fateful relations; therefore operations ceased in October 1918. These facts may be useful in days to come when the Aurora Consolidated again invites resuscitation.

The Peace Conference

Apparently the success of the Peace Conference depends upon an amicable adjustment of the claims of France for reparation as against the idealistic proposals embodied in the Fourteen Points, on which, as a basis for peace, the armistice was accepted by the principal belligerents. At the opening ceremony President Poincare took pains to emphasize the fact that he represented "a country which more than any other has endured the sufferings of war, of which entire provinces have been transformed into a vast battlefield and have been systematically laid waste by the invader. France has borne these enormous sacrifices although she has not the slightest responsibility for the frightful catastrophe that has overwhelmed the world." The French, naturally, want to be ensured against another such experience, they consider that they are entitled to the fullest measure of protection, at the expense of the beaten enemy; therefore Marshal Foch and others have suggested the Rhine as the natural barrier against German aggression. France says that England is protected by the Channel and America by the Atlantic, why then should she not avail herself of a natural barrier? France insists that she has twice felt the heel of the predatory German, whereas America knows nothing of the horrors of invasion and England suffered only from air-raids. "France," says Marshal Foch, "has a right to effective measures of protection after the formidable efforts she put forth to save civilization. The natural frontier which will protect civilization is the Rhine." This suggestion is incompatible with President Wilson's policy and is opposed to the understanding on which the German armies capitulated. To make the Rhine the north-eastern frontier of France and to compel Germany to cede all the rich and thickly populated region west of the river would be to create another Alsace-Lorraine, another festering sore in the body politic of Europe. England, however sympathetic with France in her sufferings through the War, will support the United States in objecting firmly to a settlement that would inevitably stimulate a war of revenge on the part of Germany as soon as she regained her strength, as undoubtedly she will. The Allies, and the Associate, have committed themselves to the doing of justice, which means reparation and restitution, but not depredation. It remains to reconcile these acutely divergent views. No league of nations can be founded on such an act as the partition of Germany and the annexation of the Rhineland; it would stultify all the idealism that President Wilson has endeavored so strenuously to inject into international politics. Moreover, as we have suggested in a previous issue, it is at least doubtful whether a river like the Rhine would prove an effective barrier to invasion, having regard to the possibilities of attack from the air and the rapidly increasing range of modern artillery. England, we believe, will be willing to pool her claim for indemnities, chiefly for air-raid damages and losses of shipping, with those of her Allies; she will not, we hope, present any such claim, for compensation for the cost of the war, as Mr. Lloyd George suggested in a reckless election speech. On the contrary, we feel confident that England will establish a good working agreement with the United States, looking to a settlement that will stand, not one that will sow the seed of another internecine struggle for world dominion. Even the 'freedom of the seas' will prove no source of friction as between the two English-speaking peoples, because England's trade depends upon giving to all nations a complete access to the sea, including the creation of 'corridors' for those physiographically detached from the water, such as Switzerland, and possibly Hungary. Undoubtedly Mr. George and the other British representatives see the splendid opportunity afforded at this time for establishing, not an alliance, but a friendly understanding between Great Britain and the United States. This ought to be one of the chief gains of the War to both countries, but it need not diminish the friendship either of France for England or of the United States for France; on the contrary, the Anglo-French *entente cordiale* should join with the historic Franco-American friendship in uniting the three great democracies for the safeguarding of civilization and the advancement of human progress. In that peaceful association lies the hope of the world, pending the day when nations will behave like good citizens and forego the appeal to arms every time either their honor is hurt or their business is menaced. If the individual will abate his assertiveness for the general good, and if we can compel him to do so when he refuses to behave, then the time must come when a recalcitrant nation will likewise be called to order by the superior power of social combination. It is not the least remarkable outcome of the recent European calamity that the anti-social instincts of the human brute should have asserted themselves at the very time when intelligent men are doing their utmost to curb the aggressive individualism of the nations by a pact for the establishment of mutually beneficial relations. The cosmic process, as Huxley pointed out, fights continually against the ethical process. The history of civilization is the construction of "an artificial world within the cosmos." Thinking man found it necessary for his own happiness to modify the cosmic process of animal evolution by the discipline of ethical principles. "The intelligence which has converted the brother of the wolf into the faithful guardian of the flock ought to be able to do something toward curbing the instincts of savagery in civilized man." So said Huxley. To this we may add that the intelligence that drove the Barbary pirates off the Mediterranean, that suppressed the slave-traders on the Atlantic, and that stultified duelling, will be competent not only to check German submarine piracy and the German attempt to enslave subject peoples but to compel Germany and every other nation to live in accord with the international laws that mankind has been trying, not without success, to establish for the benefit of all the countries of the world, whether small or large, whether poor or rich, whether weak or strong. As members of a family compelled to live on a small planet we have made a pitiful mess of our opportunities, we have behaved like the lawless members of a frontier community, we have acted like a mutinous crew in peril of shipwreck. It should be the aim of the fateful conference at Versailles to correct these blunders, not to make new ones nearly as bad; it should be the purpose of the delegates to act on the principle of 'Live and let live' within the bounds of the law.

The American Mining Congress

During the past week a Californian chapter of the American Mining Congress has been organized under the auspices of the California Metal Producers Association of San Francisco and the Chamber of Mines and Oil of Los Angeles. The meetings on January 15 and 16 in San Francisco proved an unqualified success, as was assured from the start because the affair had the whole-hearted backing of the best men in our mining community. A report of the proceedings appears on page 128 of this issue. In due course we hope to publish the text of the principal addresses, which dealt with subjects of national interest. Mr. Albert Burch, the chairman of the Metal Producers Association, presided over the sessions with conspicuous success, due in no small degree to the esteem with which he is held by the fraternity of Western mining men. The Congress in recent years has been fortunate in its presidents; Mr. Walter Douglas has been succeeded by Mr. Bulkeley Wells, who was present and added largely to the interest of the occasion by the appropriately prominent part he took in the discussions. Mr. J. F. Callbreath, the Secretary and chief organizer of the Congress, and to whom the success of its political activities at Washington are largely due, gave a most informing history of the organization, and, of course, took a guiding part in the business meetings. Our friends in the South were worthily represented by Messrs. G. M. Swindell, who acted as local secretary, and by Mr. T. A. O'Donnell, whose speech on the part that petroleum played in the War was the chief feature of the dinner on Wednesday evening. One consequence of the convention was the new start given to agitation in favor of creating a Federal Department of Mines with a Secretary in the Cabinet. The campaign for this purpose was launched in an eloquent address by Mr. John F. Davis, a distinguished lawyer not without experience of mining. We hope to publish this address at an early date. Another important utterance was that of Mr. Frank B. Anderson, the President of the Bank of California, who explained the attitude of bankers toward mining enterprise in a weighty speech that was heard with eager attention and that our readers will find stimulating to serious thought. This brief summary of the convention will indicate to those not present that the proceedings were well organized and unusually informing. One fact was unmistakable, namely, that this gathering of mine operators and mining engineers was thoroughly tired of being regulated, controlled, and disciplined by the halo-batted gentlemen at Washington. While willing to submit to the unpleasantness during war-time, they were looking forward to their accustomed freedom of initiative. Every expression of protest against unnecessary regulation after the War elicited prompt approval and any reference to the necessity for giving the customary scope to individual effort evoked loud applause. This fact is one that sagacious politicians—not to mention statesmen—will not disregard, for we believe it to be no mere local manifestation of feeling. In this as in other matters the American Mining Congress is representative of the mining community in the nation. The experience of the War period has shown the mining community that it needs to be protected at Washington against ill-digested legislation, whether on the score of taxes and embargoes, or of regulations devised sometimes by persons in control of the market. The committees sent to the national capital to protest against sundry eccentricities of legislation have been assisted by Mr. Callbreath and his colleagues in a manner for which they have reason to feel grateful. Until recently the Mining Congress has been supported mainly by the small operators, but now the large companies have decided to co-operate. For instance, in Arizona the copper companies have agreed to contribute 10 cents per $1000 of annual production, the contribution being limited to a maximum of $6000 and a minimum of $60 per company. This financial assistance is given without representation on the board of management, so that there is no danger of the big interests exercising undue control. The vote is still restricted to individual membership. It is now proposed to enlarge the activities of the Mining Congress by organizing eight statistical and technical divisions, but we trust that the mistake of duplication already being made by the Geological Survey and the Bureau of Mines will not be imitated. If the Mining Congress should fail it will be by branching out unduly and trespassing on the preserves of the official agencies. We believe that the Mining Congress has a useful function to perform on behalf of the mining industry, and we trust that it will not endanger its effectiveness by undertaking to do too much.

Water Laws of Nevada

The Editor:

Sir—In your issue of December 21, there was published, under the caption of 'Water Laws of Nevada', a letter from Mr. G. A. Duncan relative to recent water litigation in the Eldorado Canyon mining district of southern Nevada, which he used as a text for criticism of the existing water laws of the State, concluding with a plea for corrective action at the approaching session of the legislature.

As the superintendent of the defendant company at the time the action referred to was tried, I desire an opportunity to reply, partly because the circumstances of the case have not been fully stated in Mr. Duncan's letter, and partly because I consider that the legislation urged by Mr. Duncan would be highly detrimental to the welfare of the mining industry of this State.

The case was rather unusual in several respects, and a brief summary of the salient features will be desirable to illuminate the legal point involved. The climate of the Eldorado Canyon district is very arid; the annual precipitation averages about six inches, and the surface-drainage channels retain water only briefly after the infrequent storms. The rocks of the district, which are entirely of igneous origin, are firm, hard, and practically impermeable, and the ground-water of the district, from which the permanent supply for mining, milling, and domestic purposes is obtained, is confined chiefly to three intersecting systems of post-mineral faults, which form a network of faults traversing the igneous complex. During the years 1915, 1916, and 1917, the effective precipitation (by which reference is made to storms of sufficient intensity to contribute to the stock of ground-water) was very small; and the result was promptly felt in a materially diminished flow of ground-water into all mine-workings throughout the district. The defendants, needing a supplementary supply of water for their cyanide mill, sank a shaft to intersect at some depth one of the strongest faults of the district, at a point where it crossed a deep gulch in the vicinity of their property; and their enterprise was rewarded by a considerable flow of water from the fault, when it was encountered by the shaft. A pumping-plant and pipe-line were installed, and the water was pumped to their mill, a mile and a half distant. The plaintiffs, whose property was situated about a mile down the same gulch, protested against the use of this water by the defendants, on the score that it was diminishing materially the amount of ground-water entering their mine, and which they used for milling purposes. The plaintiffs' orebody occurs in a porphyry dike, one wall of which is followed by a post-mineral fault, from which the ground-water entering their mine is largely supplied; and it was claimed by them that this dike with its accompanying fault passed through the "water-shaft", which the defendants had sunk, and that the latter, consequently, were intercepting ground-water that otherwise would eventually have reached the plaintiffs' mine by flowing along the subterranean conduit formed by the fault accompanying their "water-bearing dike". The defendants pointed out that, at several places in the intervening distance, the plaintiffs' "water-bearing dike" was faulted for considerable distances by cross-faults of later age than the fault accompanying the dike, thereby interrupting any continuous channel that might once have existed; that, further, a pronounced difference in the chemical analyses of the water from the defendants' "water-shaft" and the water from the plaintiffs' mine, which could not reasonably be explained by chemical reactions in transit, pointed to the conclusion that there could be no immediate connection between the ground-water at the two places; and that, finally, the decrease in the amount of ground-water entering the plaintiffs' mine could reasonably be accounted for, in part by the prevailing drouth from the effects of which the entire district was suffering, and in part as the natural consequence of the depletion of the accumulation of ground-water in the vicinity of the plaintiffs' property, resulting from their several years constant pumping from their mine—a common and, in fact, almost universal experience in mining. The defendants further contended that the water, which they were pumping from their water-shaft, was "percolating water", under the definition of the term in the Nevada statutes, and as such appertained to the land upon which it was developed, and that title to it could not be claimed by outside parties. Nevertheless, the plaintiffs—fortified by a unique water-right, issued by the Nevada State Engineer, which granted them priority of use of the ground-water entering their mine from the "water-bearing dike"—brought suit to restrain the defendants from pumping water from their "water-shaft"; and the case was tried in 1917 before the Tenth District Court of Nevada. As the defendants were able to prove that they had not commenced pumping from their water-shaft until a number of weeks after the date established by the plaintiffs as the time when the decrease in their water supply first became noticeable, and as the defendants were further able to show that the total amount of water pumped by them was only a fraction of the total decrease in the plaintiffs' water supply, the plaintiffs were unable to establish any significant relationship between the decrease in their water supply and the action of the defendants in pumping from the water-shaft, and the case was decided against the plaintiffs for this reason; but no decision was rendered by the Court as to the validity of the water-right issued by the State Engineer, or in regard to the point as to whether water, flowing along a fault-plane, entirely enclosed in rock, is or is not 'percolating' water and as such not subject to appropriation under the Nevada laws.

The Nevada statutes provide that only water "flowing along a well-defined channel" in a definite and constant direction is subject to appropriation by means of a water-right: and previous interpretation of the phrase has confined the application of the law either to surface streams or to water permeating the gravel-filled channels of surface streams. While it is recognized that there is considerable movement of water in subterranean rock-enclosed channels, as is evidenced by the occurrence of springs issuing from hillsides and by existence of underground streams in limestone regions, the practical impossibility in most cases of determining the course of such streams has prevented any attempt to subject them to the application of the same laws which govern the disposition of the water of surface streams, and consequently they have been classified, in common with ground-water in a passive state, as 'percolating water', and as such have been held to be unsuitable for appropriation for purposes of individual usage by means of water-rights. It is Mr. Duncan's recommendation, I understand, that water moving along subterranean rock-enclosed conduits with somewhat definite boundaries, such as faults, fracture-zones, joints, bedding-planes, etc., be declared to occupy "well-defined channels" within the legal definition of the term, and as such be subject to appropriation in accordance with the usual procedure.

Before attempting to point out the impracticability and danger of such a law, a brief consideration of the nature of ground-water is necessary. The commonly used expression of 'a sea of ground-water', which suggests the idea of complete saturation of the rocks below water-level and of rather free communicability of such water, is misleading. Some conglomerates and sandstones, volcanic agglomerates and tuffs, etc., are sufficiently porous to permit the free passage of water; but mining operations have demonstrated that most rocks both of sedimentary and igneous origin, are 'dry' when unfractured: that is to say, such water as they contain is so small in amount as not to produce the condition of moistness, and the majority of it is contained in openings of capillary or sub-capillary size, where it is immobilized by molecular attraction. The greater part of all mobile water, encountered in underground workings, is contained in faults, fracture-zones, slips, joints, and other cavities that have been produced in the rocks by dynamic action after their formation. The bulk of the ground-water is undoubtedly in a passive condition or in a state of circulation too slow to be measured by instruments.

From the preceding, the differences between surface-water systems and ground-water and the difficulty of applying the same laws to both are apparent. Surface-water systems may be considered chiefly in terms of two dimensions; but in the ground-water the third dimension is also of importance. Surface-water systems are always arborescent in plan, with well-defined trunk and branches; but ground-water systems, on the other hand, have no uniform type of arrangement, but are usually complexly net-like. In surface-water systems the direction of flow, which is dependent upon the topography, is readily perceptible, is always in a constant and definite direction, and is irreversible. Ground-water systems are governed chiefly by the geologic structure, and are influenced to a much less extent by the surface topography. Hence the latter affords no positive clue to the direction of movement of ground-water, which is usually entirely unpredictable except in a general way. The direction of movement of ground-water is also subject to deflection or reversal to a considerable extent, through the interposition of current geological forces or through human agencies. It is rarely possible to determine with certainty the natural direction of flow (if such has previously existed) of the ground-water encountered in underground workings, for the reason that any artificial excavation always profoundly modifies the subterranean drainage in that vicinity, new directions of flow toward the underground workings being instituted. Even the case where the water enters underground workings chiefly from one direction does not afford conclusive evidence that the previous flow of the ground-water was from that direction, since the same situation would result from the penetration of the underground workings into a subterranean accumulation of stationary ground-water, close to one boundary of the 'reservoir', so that the flow of water from one direction might soon terminate, but might continue from the other direction, in which the bulk of the accumulated water was situated, for so much longer a period as to create an illusory appearance of a natural flow in a constant direction.

In the case where ground-water is confined to a certain definite, constant, and readily identifiable formation, as is artesian-water basins, there are possibilities for the equitable apportionment of such water to consumers under State or National control; and there is a distinct tendency in this direction, in certain States, which appears worthy of encouragement, provided the proper limitations of such control are recognized and suitable safeguards against its abuse are provided. But where, as in most mining districts, the ground-water occurs in an inconceivably complex maze of faults, fissures, joints, fracture-zones, and erratic areas of permeable rocks, any attempt at a similar control of distribution would be attended with endless difficulties and certain to result in trouble. Most mineral veins contain water, and are so permeable that the removal of water at one point of the vein affects the water-level elsewhere along the vein. The first mining locator on such a vein, using the water therefrom for mining or milling purposes, and having taken out a water-right thereupon under the application of the law proposed by Mr. Duncan, would be able to prevent subsequent locators on other portions of the same vein, or on branch or cross-veins, from using the water for their own mining requirements, or might even enjoin the removal of any water, such as would be necessary for the prosecution of underground development, on the ground that it would deprive the original locator of water that he required for his operations and had appropriated for that purpose. In most mining districts, indeed, the ground-water of the whole district is, through the influence of communicating faults or veins, more or less affected by the operations of any single mine; and hence a mine, strategically located, might conceivably dominate an entire mining district, and either prohibit its development or place it under tribute. The opportunity that would be afforded for litigation and blackmail, under such conditions, is obvious.

A law of the nature recommended by Mr. Duncan, in fact, would practically amount to granting extra-lateral ground-water rights, and, as a legal sand-bag in the hands of the unscrupulous, would be a fit consort of the present apex law. Like the latter, it might seem to be required, in certain cases, to protect the original locator and to assure him the full rewards of his toil and enterprise; but the practical application of such a statute would soon demonstrate that it could be used as easily to defeat the ends of justice as to defend them, that it would prove a ready weapon for those who seek to profit by the labor of others and to reap where they have not sown, and that it would place a heavy tax on the mining industry in litigation and blackmail. Like many other refinements of procedure, exact and absolute justice usually costs more than it is worth; and for purposes of practical utility, it is best to have laws that are simple, plain, and common-sense, and which require no expensive legal machinery to interpret and apply them, even if it is necessary to sacrifice the interests of a few individuals for the sake of the general welfare. Therefore, in mining districts, at least, ground-water rights as well as mineral rights are, for practical working purposes, best confined to the ground included between vertical planes passing through the surface boundaries of the mining claims.

R. T. WALKER.

Pioche, Nevada, December 27.

The Chrome Scandal

The Editor:

Sir—In your issue of December 28 Mr. Justice F. Grugan, chief engineer to the Suffern company here, states a typical case of grief resulting from mine development and machinery installation because of present conditions.

I make the suggestion that the Government buy and store at the mines such ores and mine-products as will result from such conditions as are referred to by Mr. Grugan. I am thinking not only of chromite but of manganese, these two being the best examples of malnutrition among the war-babies of the mining world. Fifty millions or more spent in hundreds of piled and labeled and branded U. S. ORE PILES would steady conditions not a little. Regulations for the gradual sale of such ore, in emergencies, could be made, but I think that a reserve of 500,000 tons of manganese ore and perhaps a tenth as much chromite would be a national asset equal to the gold back of a billion dollars worth of our paper money. It would certainly be of more value than some of the houses being constructed for projects that have stopped, although I am not criticizing such construction, as it is relieving someone.

Tens of thousands of tons of American-owned minerals were mined in foreign countries for patriotic and personal motives. Such stocks are usually in strong hands and need no aid, though logically entitled to it. Since returning from South America in November, I am shocked to note that Government officials and the Government are often referred to as something apart from ourselves. Is it not up to us to make our public servants see what is for the greatest good to the most—miners?

W. H. S.

New York, January 3.

Alaskan Engineering Commission

The Editor:

Sir—In your issue of November 9 there appears a letter from Henry Legin, of Talkeetna, Alaska, charging the Alaskan Engineering Commission, which is building the Government railroad from Seward to Fairbanks, with pro-Germanism. The article declares that the Commission, in hiring labor, discriminates against loyal Americans, and gives preference to alien-enemy Germans and Austrians, draft-slacker Swedes, and other disloyal foreigners. This accusation, ostensibly, is based by the person making it on what purports to be his observation and experience in the Talkeetna district, where, in at least one camp, No. 221, he says "all Americans were fired, to be replaced by aliens."

This charge of Mr. Legin was brought to the attention of the Alaskan Engineering Commission last fall, and was found to be false, and he was invited to the head offices of the Commission at Anchorage. In a talk with me he admitted his charge was based on misinformation, and he made the same admission to the Anchorage Council of National Defense. Mr. Legin had been led and encouraged into making his baseless charge by personal grievances of his own and a few other persons against one or two of the employing officials of the Commission in the Talkeetna district. Also as he is very excitable and French, many things were said in his presence in jest, which he took as the truth.

The Alaskan Engineering Commission is, and always has been, loyal to the core. One of the former members of the Commission and hundreds of its former employees are now in the United States Army in France. No pro-German, if his sentiments were known, could hold a job with us for a minute. Every division and every district has supported in the most praiseworthy manner every one of the war activities of the Government. And of all the districts, one of the best records in these war activities has been made by Talkeetna. Its subscriptions to Liberty bonds, and its donations to Red Cross and military hospital funds, exceed, considering the number of employees, all the districts. I enclose the figures now available relative to subscriptions to Liberty bonds, donations to the Red Cross, the Washington Hospital for Wounded Soldiers at Neuilly, France, and to the Department of Interior War Relief Association. Of course, there were donations to many other causes, such as Syrian and Armenian Relief, care of French and Belgian orphans, food and clothing for destitute Serbians, etc., but no record at all of these was kept. In the figures available you can see that the employees of the Commission always subscribed more than their allotment of bonds and were generous in all their various donations and that the employees in the Talkeetna district subscribed or donated a higher average for every war activity than the employees of the division. Their loyalty, like that of all workers in the Government Railroad, cannot be subjected to honest criticism.

WILLIAM GERIG,
Anchorage, December 16. Engineer in Charge.

[We take much pleasure in publishing this letter. The accompanying tabulated statement shows that the employees in the Talkeetna district averaged $144.84 per man to the Fourth Liberty Loan, $8.10 to the Red Cross drive, and $5.79 (in 1917 and 1918) to the Neuilly bed.—EDITOR.]

Radium in Fluorspar

The Editor:

Sir—After many years of sleeping, the old camp of Jamestown, in Colorado, has awakened, and the reason is radium. Although originally a gold-mining community Jamestown has for some months past been devoting its whole attention to fluorspar. This spar was mined mainly by lessors and sold to the nearest mill. The mill crushed the ore and ran it over tables, taking out most of the silica and making, besides the fluorspar, a gold-silver-lead-iron concentrate.

At one of these mills, the Golden Age, a black streak was noted above the lead streak on the tables. This indicated the presence of some material of a higher specific gravity than lead and in all probability a rare metal. This material was taken to the laboratory for a 100% analysis. Various tests were tried and it was believed to be one of the platinum group of metals, as it came down as the general group precipitate. It failed to give any results, however, on separate tests for the individual members of the group, and it was soluble in simple acid, proving it not to be platinum itself. The fact that it was uranium in the form of pitchblende was finally determined. The Curie photographic experiment was then performed and a picture of a lead key obtained, showing radio-activity.

The uranium content of the crude ore is from 0.12 to 0.2% and the amount of radium is proportional to that of the uranium. When the uranium is concentrated up to 2% it is worth $3 per pound; to 3%, $4.50 per pound, and to 10%, $6 per pound.

Pitchblende does not occur in all the fluorspar of the district, and where it does occur it is in the spotted formation so typical of Boulder county. There is about two square miles of territory in this vicinity covered with fluorspar, but I doubt if one-tenth of it contains pitchblende. However, rare-metal experts consider this a great find and an unlimited amount of investment capital is pouring into the district.

RICHARD G. PLACE.
Pasadena, California, December 28.

[We referred to the wildcatting of the Colorado Pitchblende Company in our issue of December 28. The discovery is most interesting, but the public should be extremely careful in placing their money in such schemes. —EDITOR.]

The Status of Gold

The Editor:

Sir—I have read the letters appearing in your paper concerning the present-day gold question, and have obtained therefrom much information, but it seemed to me that in some of them, the most profound and erudite of them all, the chief point of the whole question was missed, resulting in a hopeless confusion of ideas and tending to paralyze all efforts to remedy the difficulty.

Soon after the War started in 1914 the banks made a show of slipping a few gold-notes into currency paid over the counter, but every recipient of such payments knew instinctively that he could not on demand get it all, or even a considerable part, in gold or gold-notes. I noticed this at Washington, and out of curiosity wrote to a broker in New York to see if he could get me a small sum in gold or gold-notes. His reply was in the negative. The simple fact was the country was no longer on a gold basis, although the custom of paying out a little in gold-notes was continued for a considerable period.

Then followed the period of tremendous imports of gold, on which in a vague and uncertain sort of way was predicated an immense expansion of credits and currency, but still there was no gold paid out, and there was no definite or published relation between the gold and the credit expansion as a whole. As a result of the expansion and the insistent demand, labor and many commodities advanced 100 and even 200%. On top of this situation came the entry of the U. S. into the War. Gold imports ceased, and all thought of any relation between our huge expanding credits and gold was lost sight of completely. The transition from a precautionary suspension of the gold basis, or payments, at the beginning of the War to a real and necessary suspension through an excessive expansion of credits took place so gradually that hardly a thought was given to it.

It is worth while to narrate these well-known facts

merely to show that we are not on a gold basis, and have not been since 1914, although during much of the time the suspension was purely voluntary and precautionary. The letters which have been referred to as being obscure and confusing ignore this fact. The writers of them, in an unconscious effort to reconcile a double standard, namely, a gold standard and a paper-currency standard (medium of exchange), naturally fall into confusion. There is no harm in the paper-currency basis so long as it is frankly recognized, and preparations are made accordingly. The people have faith in themselves and in the country and in the banks and in the Government, and therefore have faith in the currency, but it is not gold. It will probably be several years before the currency bears the same relation to gold that it did previous to July 1914.

When one admits the facts in regard to present-day currency the gold question becomes a perfectly simple one to understand, for it is then seen that gold at present is a commodity like everything else. When embargoes against gold shipments are raised, and Government control of foreign exchance ceases it will soon be seen whether gold is worth $20 an ounce or $40 an ounce in the accepted 'medium of exchange' or 'standard of value,' that is to say, in our present-day currency. It is clear, however, that these forces cannot operate to determine the value of gold in terms of our present-day currency if and so long as our Government pays it out freely across the counter at $20.67 per ounce.

The situation is one that should be regarded with equanimity by gold miners and gold-mine owners. It is a case where the other man will 'do the walking.' Embargoes on gold shipments and control of foreign exchanges must be given up before international trade is resumed on a considerable scale, and gold cannot be commandeered in times of peace. Furthermore it is not likely that the Government will give up to a hungry world any large part of its stores of gold for less than a fair equivalent in value.

The following is suggested as a temporary expedient to bridge over the period of transition to the new order of things financial: Let the Government, through the Federal banks, name from time to time, as advisable, prices at which it is willing either to buy or to sell both gold and silver, thus fixing prices to exporters and importers, and to miners. The first prices could be arrived at by a consideration of the prices of commodities and labor, and thereafter by experience and by the state of foreign exchange. Under such a plan it would be impossible to use gold as money (except as token money, as silver is used today), but the Government could hold gold reserves against the currency, the proportion of reserve to be stated from time to time. When the financial affairs of the world have settled down and become stable it would be but a step to the resumption of a gold standard and gold payments.

HERBERT D. LACEY.

New York, December 31, 1918.

Oil-Shale

The Editor:

Sir—From time to time you have published interesting notes on the prospective oil-shale industry, dealing principally with the geology, extent, and mode of occurrence of the potential beds in Colorado, Utah, and Wyoming. Two years ago this industry was in its beginning and very little was really known of it; it is now growing rapidly.

The facts regarding the position of well-oil production and reserves are becoming known and the need for supplementing the output of oil is being appreciated. The method of handling shale is better understood and the certainty that it can be a highly profitable industry is clearer. The wild-cat element, so vicious a few months ago, is moribund, investigations are showing more clearly the real status of the shale deposits both from scientific and economic standpoints, and a solid basis is being established. This appeals to investors. Many people and companies are making serious investigations and enquiries.

The simplest form of the industry means the production of high-grade gasoline, lubricating oil, paraffine-wax, ammonium sulphate, and a residue which it is claimed has value as a rubber filler and binder for briquettes, for the Colorado shale is gilsonitic. All these products have a ready market; one of the pressing needs today is lubricating oil, while the other products speak for themselves. I deprecate much some of the statements that are circulated even now, claiming shale as the best basis for dyes, explosives, and a long list of medicines and salts; this is not true, for all such can better be obtained from carbonaceous material and more cheaply. The prime products from shale above mentioned are enough in themselves.

The treatment of shale is an old industry; both in France and Scotland. It has been successfully done for a century and it is quite well understood. As applied to Colorado it involves: mining, and mining too of a high class; coal mining most closely approximates it; shale however lends itself better to the long-wall system and the plentiful use of high explosives is to be preferred, which is not the case with coal, and it should consequently be more cheaply mined. One hears of steam-shovel schemes, and perhaps, but solely for the reason that it will be possible to work low-grade or mixed shale economically, which hitherto has been difficult.

The shale has to be crushed finely; in the Scotch system it is reduced to two inches; in others and the most modern plants it is broken to one-quarter inch. Shale is tough and hard to reduce and special machines will be required.

The retorting is the most difficult operation; it is the crux of the treatment. The Scottish system has been successful. It has made good, but present-day requirements are much advanced. There are more retorts in Scotland today than shale to supply them and no retort improvements have been called for. The carbonization of coal in various forms of retorts, especially the continuous vertical, has led to much improvement in the art, for such undoubtedly it is. One prime object is a better arrangement to drive the heat-units to the centre of the charge or otherwise cook the molecule of coal or shale, and the other is better care of the gas immediately after it has been evolved. Mass carbonization has disadvantages, for as the heat passes from the wall of the retort the very act of carbonization sets up a heat screen. The carbonized material is a good non-conductor and the greater the thickness of the material the more costly does the heat become, and then the gas evolved in a mass of material has either to stagger its way out through temperatures that either involve 'cracking' it or it is condensed and falls back again for re-evolution at its critical temperature.

Much time and work have been spent on this question, both here and in England, where the work of treating hydrocarbon materials is being fostered by both the Government and private enterprise, with a large degree of success. It is possible to say that the latest form of retort deals effectively with the two points I have mentioned; it is comparatively inexpensive, will handle most forms of hydrocarbon material effectively, including shale, for which it was primarily designed; it has a large output, from one to three tons per hour; it is flexible, easy of access and repair, and as the carbonization is good and the gas drawn off nearly as and when evolved, the quantity and quality of the products are the best yet. From what I know of it, I expect it will be the most useful form of retort for reducing the sulphur contents of some of the shales.

The condensation of the gas and watery vapor is simple and either of the well-known systems are good according to circumstances and the water-supply. This condensation results in oil, ammoniacal liquor, and a certain amount of uncondensed gas. This last will be 'scrubbed' for its ammonia and light oil, leaving a non-condensable scrubbed gas that is to be used in heating the retort, apropos of which I would say that a well-balanced plant should produce enough of this gas for all the heating requirements. Hence no extraneous fuel is required.

The refining of the oil presents too many angles for me to discuss, except to remark that an acceptable proposal is to take off the natural gasoline, crack the gas-oil and lighter fractions, and refine the rest for lubricants and wax. The residue, if the shale is good and if it has been properly retorted, will be small, but still of some value as before-mentioned—again we have to depend on the proper retorting.

It will be understood, of course, that all these notes refer to low-temperature carbonization, a high temperature or one mid-high would produce a totally different series of products of less value and more costly. The results of the treatment of an average Colorado shale yielding a barrel of oil per ton of shale and carrying 0.5% of nitrogen, should be 16 to 18 gal. of gasoline, 16 to 18 gal. of lubricating oil, 16 lb. of paraffine-wax, and 25 lb. ammonium sulphate. Of course, Colorado shale, like every other shale, varies in different strata, both in its yield of oil and of ammonia. I know of shale that will yield 65 gal. over considerable areas and I have seen analyses showing over 1.15% of nitrogen. I have taken the figures for yield as representing what I believe will be the practice from a general average of many tests over large areas.

It is easy to figure out the value of the above products; today's prices would show a return of $9 per ton or more. The costs will vary according to economics, location, and the tonnage treated. On the basis of a 1000-ton plant with railroad facilities, water, and sulphuric acid at $18 per ton, and the shale mined and delivered to the plant for $1 per ton, including depreciation and all overhead charges, the cost will not exceed $4 to $4.25 per ton, which figure is based on actual cost elsewhere adjusted to local conditions. With the erection of large plants many improvements are bound to be introduced, so that any change is likely to be downward, even including labor, which surely cannot be worse than it is; but after making all allowances, there is still a good margin for the venture.

A word of warning: some people have thought that if they had a good area of good shale it was enough; there are other conditions just as important, such as plenty of water, dump-room, cheap acid, and, last but not least, good railroad facilities. Present knowledge on the subject has only come through years of patient and sometimes disappointing work. There is much to be solved in every locality, and many adjustments will be necessary. It is a difficult art and one too that requires a large investment of money, but if properly handled it has proved itself elsewhere the basis for a sound remunerative industry.

ARTHUR L. PEARSE.

New York, January 6.

Russia

The Editor:

Sir—I have just read in your issue of December 28, a very interesting article on Russia. Coming myself from the Lena goldfield where I prospected for two years, having also been in Irkutsk during the revolution, and seeing how anarchy reigns everywhere, I realize how absolutely necessary it is for the Allies to send forces to fight Bolshevism and Germans. American and French papers contain articles stating that Russia will get along without us. Such a policy is simply to leave Russia wide open to the Germans, who swarm there under Russian names.

May your magazine take an active part in the matter and do as much propaganda as possible to have the Allies make that country a decent place in which to work and live.

H. R. CHARTRAN.

Winthrop, California, January 1.

GRAVEL on Potato creek, Seward Peninsula, Alaska, carries cassiterite (black tin); and Moran creek, a tributary of the Molozi river, has gravel containing 2½ lb. of tin and 10 cents of gold to the cubic yard.

Mr. Roosevelt at Oxford

From the MINING and Scientific PRESS of July 9, 1910

By T. A. RICKARD

On Tuesday, June 7, Mr. Theodore Roosevelt delivered the Romanes lecture at Oxford University. It is an event so significant and so interesting as to warrant description even in a technical journal. I was privileged to be present and enjoyed the episode so greatly that I venture to record my impressions.

A week earlier Mr. Roosevelt had received the freedom of the City of London and no sooner had he been made a burgess than he exercised the right of citizenship by offering counsel to the British administrators in Egypt. It was a magnificent indiscretion, but a friendly act. After a year spent in Africa, in four spheres of British rule, he was well fitted to give both intelligent praise and salutary warning. He was as generous in emphasizing the beneficence of the work the British are doing in the Sudan, East Africa, and Uganda as he was outspoken in condemning the Egyptian nationalists who "treat assassination as a corner-stone of government" and the officials who are timorous in extinguishing violence, for "of all broken reeds, sentimentality is the most broken reed on which righteousness can lean." Fortunately his criticisms were well received. Englishmen have a sense of humor, not too evident, but it does save the day occasionally. Moreover, the administration of Egypt is now under the control of a Liberal government, hence the Conservatives, with their daily press and their social influence, were tickled to hear strictures upon the policy of their opponents and amused to see Roosevelt, under providence, embarrass those in authority. If the Government of the day had been Tory, the speech at the Guildhall would have proved less palatable, for instance, at Oxford, where the Chancellor, Lord Curzon, was able to refer to it approvingly and even gleefully.

The American ex-President himself was amused at the sensation caused by his speech in the City and did not scruple to refer to the "engaging frankness" of it. This was at the luncheon given in his honor by the American Club just before the Romanes lecture. The Club is composed of Rhodes scholars and other American students in residence at Oxford. The chairman was F. P. Griffiths, who made an admirable speech, in the course of which he dropped the particularly apt remark: "Good sermons are rare.' He referred, of course, to the lay sermons on sociology delivered by the guest of the occasion. Mr. Roosevelt does indeed sermonize, but with what tremendous effect! Ordinarily the sermon in church is delivered by a man whose opinion on the weather we would scarcely value, but the preaching of Roosevelt is that of a man who has done things, a governor of men, a hunter of lions, a foe of corruption, and a prophet of good.

He responded to the chairman's speech and to the enthusiastic welcome of those present by making a few happy observations, chiefly in appreciation of the Rhodes gift and the hospitality of Oxford to American students. He speaks with extreme slowness, and clearly; he has a good voice, tending to hoarseness; he is emphatic, with an accent that a Britisher calls American and a Bostonian would term Philadelphian. When speaking he has neither the cultivated ease nor the oratorical charm that mark the best American speakers, but the slowness and distinctness of his utterance are decidedly impressive as evincing deliberate thought and strong conviction.

The Romanes lecture was founded twenty years ago by J. G. Romanes, a biologist, who desired to see instituted at Oxford a lectureship similar in kind to that of the Rede foundation at Cambridge. The founder insisted that the lecturers should be selected irrespective of nationality, and that neither politics nor religion should be made a part of the subject-matter. The first lecture was delivered by Gladstone in 1892, the second by Huxley in 1893, the third by Weismann. Last year the lecturer was Arthur J. Balfour. An honorarium of £25 is paid to each lecturer. Gladstone modestly called his address 'An Academic Sketch', but it culminated in a magnificent burst of eloquence and concluded with the words that are near every Oxford man's heart: *Dominus illuminatio mea*. The 'Evolution and Ethics' of Huxley was one of his finest expositions of the development of civilization amid the welter of the struggle for existence and it illustrated the illuminating quality of a highly trained scientific imagination when applied to the profoundest problems of existence. In many ways this lecture was a superb preface to Roosevelt's, although it would be unfair to compare the latter's treatment of his subject with that of the greatest expositor of the nineteenth century. Yet Huxley would have appreciated Roosevelt, for he, too, had an intensely virile strain; intellectually he repeatedly proved the possession of an essential manliness, strong to meet the blows of fate and circumstance, and a self-mastery as striking, and far more touching, than that of the Colonel of Rough Riders. The last words of the second Romanes lecture were curiously in accord with Rooseveltian sentiment, for Huxley said:

> "'We are grown men, and must play the man, strong in will
> To strive, to seek, to find, and not to yield,'
>
> cherishing the good that falls in our way, and bearing the evil, in and around us, with stout

hearts set on diminishing it. So far, we all may
strive in one faith towards one hope:
'It may be that the gulfs will wash us down,
It may be we shall touch the Happy Isles,
...... but something ere the end,
Some work of noble note may yet be done'."

Roosevelt at Oxford! The association of names provokes a contrast between the old and the new, between ideas and ideals so unlike that the difference excites humor, between the romantic and the practical, between thought and action. It was delicious to think of the Strenuous One lecturing the dons of the university, to hear the Rough Rider in the home of ecclesiastic romance, to see the ex-President of the United States facing the ex-Viceroy of India.

It happened to be a lovely summer day, smiling in sunshine, dropping the tear of a shower only to freshen the wealth of flowers, shrubs, and trees that softens the architectural beauty of the long line of noble colleges. "Beautiful city! so venerable, so lovely, so unravaged by the fierce intellectual life of our century, so serene!" No wonder Matthew Arnold wrote rapturously concerning "the home of lost causes and forsaken beliefs, of unpopular names and impossible loyalties." Her ineffable charm is as potent, nay more, in this restless era of telegraphs and telephones, of motorists and airmen, than fifty years ago when Arnold thus apostrophized her. She still "whispers the last enchantments of the Middle Ages," but she is no longer withdrawn from the flowing river of the nation's intellectual life; on the contrary, to Oxford largely is given the task of training the rulers of empire. She may not be an incubator for engineers nor a nursery for financiers, but pre-eminently it is her task to train the men who become pro-consuls and administrators, the just and wise rulers over those alien races that live in peace under the British flag. Selborne, Milner, and Curzon typify the Oxford product. The noble traditions, the philosophic teaching, the aristocratic *milieu*, the historic associations, the reality of greatness, all afford fit environment wherein to teach young Englishmen to act worthily as the representatives of a dominant race when exercising imperial sway; but it may well be questioned whether Oxford affords the atmosphere in which to educate the leaders of a democracy, even under the shelter of a limited monarchy. Of social snobbery there is none worth mentioning, the students take rank on their merits as men, they work and they play under ideal conditions; the bank balance does not count; they discover that life is good if you know how to live it; they are happy! The learning is disinterested, for no commercial purpose is in view; the play is not made a business, it is just enjoyed for itself. Oxford is not a training-ship nor a hot-house: youth learns to live and to think there. Her windows are Gothic but through them is seen the wide world of today.

The Romanes lecture is always delivered in the Sheldonian theatre, which was the first public building designed by Sir Christopher Wren, the architect of St. Paul's cathedral. In this university theatre the Duke of Wellington was installed as Chancellor, amid great enthusiasm, in 1833; here Disraeli declared: "I prefer to be on the side of the Angels." Here, in the previous century, Handel conducted the performance of his oratorio 'Athalia'. It is not a large building and it was full to overflowing long before the proceedings began. The audience numbered about four thousand. In the galleries were the undergraduates, in the side aisles were such of the general public as had been fortunate enough to secure tickets, and the floor of the theatre was wholly occupied by graduates, wearing gowns with their distinctive hoods; the white ermine of the Bachelor of Arts and the magenta satin of the Master of Arts. Facing the entrance was the 'throne' of the Chancellor and below him were two curving tiers of seats left vacant for the learned doctors who would come in procession escorting the distinguished man about to be numbered with them.

At three o'clock the academic procession entered. Through the window I could see them leave the School of Divinity, where they robed and where they had performed the formalities preliminary to conferring an honorary degree. They crossed the short space between the two buildings and entered the theatre, led by the marshal, followed by the bedels, with their rods of office, the Chancellor of the University (Lord Curzon of Kedleston), the Vice-Chancellor, the heads of Colleges, and then a long line of doctors in scarlet hoods, among whom I recognized Andrew Lang and Rudyard Kipling. The two representatives of Oxford in Parliament (Sir William Anson and Lord Hugh Cecil) had already taken their seats. The train of the gorgeous robes worn by the Chancellor was borne by a younger son of the Earl of Selborne, recently High Commissioner in South Africa.

The audience being technically seated, although hundreds stood for lack of accommodation, the Chancellor addressed the Convocation in Latin, asking them if it were their pleasure that the honorary degree of Doctor of Civil Law be conferred on "the Honorable Theodore Roosevelt, ex-President of the United States of North America, and that the long-expected Romanes lecture may be delivered by him, etc." Cries of '*placet*' followed. Whereupon the bedels were sent to bring the honorable gentleman, and the Chancellor turned to the Vice-Chancellor and said, in Latin, what can be freely translated thus:

"Behold, Vice-Chancellor, the promised wight
Before whose coming comets turned to flight,
And all the startled mouths of sevenfold Nile took fright!"

The audience laughed appreciatively, and as Mr. Roosevelt entered a mighty burst of applause greeted him. Walking to the foot of the steps leading to the Chancellor's chair, he halted, and was addressed (still in Latin) by Henry Goudy, the Regius Professor of Civil Law. In a felicitous speech, heard only by those that were near, the orator referred to the principal events of Roosevelt's life, especially how "with unrivaled energy and tenacity of purpose he had combined lofty ideals with a sincere devotion to the practical needs not only of his fellow-countrymen, but of humanity at large." This presentation speech being ended, the Chancellor spoke; and at the first word there was a roar of laughter, for he said: "*Strenuissime, insignissime civium toto urbe terrae hodie agentium.*" And the Most Strenuous One enjoyed it, as he did the references that followed, especially the "*hominum domitor, beluarum ubique vastator.*" This short speech ended with the words that conferred the degree. The recipient allowed himself to be robed in a scarlet gown, and then shook hands with the Chancellor. The latter directed the bedels to conduct "the honorable Doctor to the lectern," whereupon Roosevelt, amid further applause, took his place, ready to begin the lecture.

Before he began, however, he had to listen to another speech, this time in English, by the Chancellor. Lord Curzon, a tall and imposing figure in gorgeous gilded robes, stood facing him. It was worth coming a long way to see these two men *vis à vis*, each playing a great part in an impressive performance. Curzon spoke excellently, in cultivated accents, easily, with a touch of humor, an obvious friendliness, and with the superb confidence of a practised orator addressing a chosen audience. The nobleman, the statesman, the ex-Viceroy of India paid his compliments to the citizen, the leader of the greatest democracy in history, the ex-President of the United States, and it must be confessed that the phrasing was worthy of both men. It thrilled me through and through that so fine an appreciation could be uttered, and yet be true. The Chancellor said that he had just had the pleasure of addressing Mr. Roosevelt in a language which, of course, he would recognize as the habitual medium of intellectual intercourse in the university to which they now both belonged. It now fell to him to say a few words of welcome to Dr. Roosevelt, in a language of which in its most picturesque and forcible idioms he was an acknowledged master. The invitation to deliver the Romanes lecture had served as a nucleus around which had been built "that wonderful progress of his through the countries of Europe, a triumphal progress such as had been enjoyed but by few even among conquerors and kings." He then went on to say: "And yet I doubt whether in all the countries he has visited Mr. Roosevelt has anywhere received a warmer welcome than that which has been given him in this ancient seat of learning, for we greet him not merely as a great ruler of men, the most conspicuous figure in America's history since Abraham Lincoln, not simply as a sincere and outspoken friend of his country, though from all his utterances we knew that he was, but also as a student of many forms of knowledge, a writer of books, a fearless preacher of robust and manly faith, a relentless foe of conventions and shams, and, above all things, in all that he says and does he is what Browning said of Clive, 'pre-eminently a man'."

It may be that the Chancellor was a trifle too facetious; at least some of the audience thought so, but I confess to having enjoyed his witty touches, because they gave relief to the general tone of handsome eulogy. It was a delightful speech, delivered perfectly.

All the while the subject of it stood quietly at the lectern, with his sheets of manuscript ready to read. An astonishingly young-looking man, not within ten years of his real age. A head covered with short thick ruddy brown hair and a stalwart figure, he looked anything but academic. The back of his head seemed that of a man in the thirties and belligerent in every line of it: not domed, but flat on top; it bespoke action rather than contemplation. Obviously he was in splendid health and brim-full of vitality. When Gladstone delivered the Romanes lecture he was 83, Huxley was 68, Roosevelt was 52. Such physical well-being is a great factor in the career of a political reformer. Roosevelt is pre-eminently the eupeptic hero of our day: May he outlive all his enemies!

When he began to deliver the lecture his accent was strongly marked. Perhaps a touch of nervousness affected his enunciation: as he proceeded this defect was less evident, although in some words the pronunciation was persistently provincial, by which I mean that he did not speak the English language as it is spoken by the most cultivated Americans, for instance, at his alma mater, Harvard. Whether life in the West or association with politicians in the East of America be the cause, the fact remains that Mr. Roosevelt speaks English with an eccent no purer than that of many Britishers. However, this detail is not material. It was lost in the broad effect.

The subject was 'Biological Analogies in History.' He began with a graceful compliment to local associations and to memories that "are living realities in the minds of scores of thousands of men who have never seen" Oxford. Such associations, he said, "are no stronger in the men of English stock than in those who are not. My people have been for eight generations in America, but in one thing I am like the Americans of tomorrow rather than like the Americans of today, for I have in my veins the blood of men who came from many different European races." This reference to his own "ethnic make-up" and to that of his fellow countrymen was apt; it enabled him to emphasize an understanding sympathy superior to biological antecedents. Loud applause punctuated the statement that ended the introduction when he said: "Common heirship in the things of the spirit makes a closer bond than common heirship in the things of the body."

Next he discoursed on the study of history, laying stress on the necessity for treating such a study not only as a science but as literature. "We need a literature of science that shall not only be read but shall be readable." Many of those present must have thought of the great biologist who delivered the second Romanes lecture and who in the work of his life illustrated to perfection the application of literary treatment to scientific knowledge. I wondered why Roosevelt omitted the chance to refer to Huxley. He proceeded to point out that the proper study of mankind is man in a biological sense and that the historian must avail himself of "the science of evolution, which is inseparably connected with the great name of Darwin." He confessed himself as impressed by the parallelism between the cycles of animal life and those of national life; but not without a warning against false analogies. "As knowledge increases our wisdom is often turned into foolishness." Terms must be defined lest we fall into the error of hasty generalization. We talk of a 'new species', yet no living thing can really belong to a new species. Similarly, the 'extinction of species' may mean either of two things: that the species has literally died out; or that it has so changed as to be no longer recognizable.

Then followed a sketch of the biological history of South America. As soon as the southern continent became joined, by the elevation of the isthmus, with the northern regions, the animals of North America passed over the land bridge and invaded South America. A riot of life ensued. The conquering type developed enormous bulk and complete armor protection. The indigenous creatures that survived also grew in size and power according to their needs. Events such as these are matched in the history of man. Nations go under and disappear; others survive and are regenerated into a 'new' nation, in which the remnants of the old are perpetuated.

In this first portion of his address Mr. Roosevelt discussed fundamental biological principles without saying anything new. Remembering Huxley's lecture on 'Evolution and Ethics,' remembering that in biology Roosevelt was the veriest amateur, I felt that he was on the edge of a fiasco, and the feeling oppressed me keenly. But when he got off this treacherous ground and began to touch on matter in which he could show a clearer insight, I realized that the early part of the lecture laid the foundation for what was to follow. He drew analogies between the fate befalling the forms of animal life and the destiny of the great artificial civilizations, such as Babylon and Nineveh, Greece and Rome. "The growth of soft luxury, after it has reached a certain point, becomes a national danger patent to all. If the homely commonplace virtues die out, if strength of character vanishes in graceful self-indulgence, then the nation has lost what no material prosperity can offset." There he struck a characteristic chord. Holland furnished another example. "Her fatal weakness was that so common in rich peace-loving societies, where men hate to think of war as possible, and try to justify their own reluctance to face it either by high-sounding moral platitudes or else by a philosophy of short-sighted materialism." But Holland and Italy taught us how races that fall may rise again. "When the Roman Empire went down in ruin, it was one of the greatest cataclysms of history, but it was not all mere destruction. Not only did Rome leave a vast heritage of language, culture, law, ideas to all the modern world, but the people of Italy kept the old blood as the chief strain in their veins. In a few centuries came a wonderful new birth of Italy." Italy rose and fell again, more than once. Spain and Portugal also had their day. "Their flowering time was as brief as it was wonderful. When the first brilliant period of the leadership of the Iberian peoples was drawing to a close, at the other end of Europe, in the land of the melancholy steppe and forest, the Slav turned in his troubled sleep and stretched out his hand to grasp dominion."

The memories of men are short and the supremacy of races is brief. "More than a century passed after the voyages of Columbus before the mastery of war began to pass from the Asiatic to the European." Then "the European advance gathered momentum, until at the present time peoples of European blood hold dominion over all America and Australia and the islands of the sea, over most of Africa, and the major half of Asia." The various nations of Europe in turn sought "a place in the movement of expansion, but for the last three centuries the great phenomenon of mankind has been the growth of the English-speaking peoples and their spread over the world's waste spaces."

Here he entered the third phase of the lecture; he now held the sympathy of his audience and frequent applause punctuated his speech. Unfortunately so much time had been given to the preliminaries and to his own introductory observations that, realizing the inadequacy of time, he began to discard sheets of typewritten manuscript without reading them. As the newspapers had received advance copies of the lecture several weeks earlier, the reporters had an easy task and the frequent rustling of leaves as they followed his utterances indicated the omission of long paragraphs. Another result followed, for the evening papers, and even some of those appearing next morning, quoted portions of the lecture omitted by the lecturer and offered comment on matters of which he had not spoken. He held the sheets in his left hand and used his right for an occasional gesture, raising his hand with the index finger erect to emphasize a point. But there were no oratorical flourishes; he spoke as a man careless of everything except the desire to convince.

Thus he came to the comparison between Britain and Rome, and between the British empire and the American democracy. "England has peopled continents with her children, has swayed the destinies of teeming myriads of alien races, has ruled ancient monarchies, and wrested from all comers the right to the world's waste spaces, while at home she has held her own before nations each of military power comparable to Rome at her zenith." Rome fell by attack from without, because of domestic ills. He pushed the analogy: "We should be vigilant against foes from without, yet we need never really fear them so long as we safeguard ourselves against the enemies within our own households; and those enemies are our own passions and follies." Americans and Englishmen alike must keep in mind that the success of a great democracy depends on self-knowledge and self-mastery. "In the last analysis the all-important factor in national greatness is national character." What was to be our destiny? Were we as nations soon "to come under the rule of that great law of death which is itself but part of the law of life"? None could tell. The growth of luxury, the love of ease, the taste for vapid and frivolous excitement were both evident and unhealthy. The ominous sign was the decline in the birth-rate. But "no man is more apt to be mistaken than the prophet of evil." It was "strange indeed to look back at Carlyle's prophecies, and then think of the teeming life of achievement, the life of conquest of every kind, and of noble effort crowned by success which has been ours for the two generations since Carlyle complained to High Heaven that all the tales had been told and all the songs sung, and that all the deeds really worth doing had been done." "Come what might we belonged to people "who have not yielded to the craven fear of being great." Moreover, while freely admitting all the follies and weaknesses of our day, it is yet mere perversity to refuse to realize the incredible advance that has been made in ethical standards. He was no pessimist. He had scant patience with "the silly cynicism which insisted that kindliness of character only accompanies weakness of character." On the contrary, he held that "rugged strength and courage would go hand in hand with a lofty scorn of doing wrong to others." Each nation had problems of its own and must solve them in its own fashion, in a spirit of broad humanity, free from weakness and sentimentality. "As in war to pardon the coward was to do cruel wrong to the brave man whose life his cowardice jeopardized, so in civil affairs it was revolting to every principle of justice to give to the lazy, the vicious, or even the feeble or dull-witted, a reward which was really the robbery of what braver, wiser, abler men had earned." In dealing with social problems "the one prime necessity was to remember that though hardness of heart is a great evil, it is no greater an evil than softness of head." Each man was entitled to be treated on his worth as a man. "To more than such just treatment no man is entitled, and less than such just treatment no man should receive." Thus he harped on that noble string from which the American makes the sweetest music known to humanity.

He spoke at length in this strain and I select from his concluding remarks the following sentences: "The only effective way to help any man is to help him to help himself; and the worst lesson to teach him is that he can be permanently helped at the expense of some one else. True liberty shows itself to best advantage in protecting the rights of others, and especially of minorities. Privilege should not be tolerated because it is to the advantage of a minority; nor yet because it is to the advantage of a majority. No doctrinaire theories of vested rights or freedom of contract can stand in the way of cutting out abuses from the body politic. Just as little can we afford to follow the doctrinaires of an impossible—and incidentally of a highly undesirable—social revolution, which in destroying individual rights—including property rights—and the family would destroy the two chief agents in the advance of mankind, and the two chief reasons why either the advance or the preservation of mankind is worth while."

When he finished, the theatre resounded with hearty applause. The audience had listened with the closest attention; contrary to precedent, even the undergraduates in the gallery had forborn to chaff; it was evident that the academic gathering was deeply touched, sympathetically appreciative, and finally heartily enthusiastic. In its strong points, as in its weak ones; in its general tone of outspoken virility, unsophisticated reasoning, and cheerful optimism, the lecture was representative of the lay sermonizing for which the lecturer is now famous. He spoke as one who reads the classics in the intervals of lion-hunting, and studies history while fighting monopolies. He is as downright as he is upright, as broad in his ideas as he is deep in his convictions. It may be that his sayings do not apply the stimulus of novelty to a cultivated mind, but the same may be said of many lectures delivered at Oxford, and elsewhere. He makes plain things obvious and gives a new life to platitudes. He dresses the eternal verities in the garments of his own manly sincerity so that they seem endowed with the freshness of a new day instead of the staleness of forgotten ideas. He came to Oxford a man on horseback, a Rough Rider in a cathedral, a practical man among scholars, a radical among reactionaries, but he left it vibrating to the glad optimism, sound common-sense, and inspiring invocation of his thoughtful utterances. He forged another golden link between the two English-speaking peoples and proved indeed that "common heirship in the things of the spirit makes a closer bond than common heirship in the things of the body."

Gold and Silver Production in 1918

The Bureau of the Mint and the U. S. Geological Survey have issued the following joint preliminary estimate of the production of gold and silver in the United States during the calendar year 1918:

State or territory	Gold		Silver	
	Fine oz.	Value	Fine oz.	Value*
Alaska	440,622	$9,108,500	796,836	$796,836
Alabama	36	700	2	2
Arizona	278,647	5,760,200	6,771,490	6,771,490
California	832,389	17,207,000	1,555,417	1,555,417
Colorado	621,791	12,853,500	6,982,313	6,982,313
Georgia	169	3,500	41	41
Idaho	30,764	636,000	10,188,056	10,188,056
Illinois	......	....	8,939	8,939
Maryland	......	....	164	164
Michigan	......	....	491,939	491,939
Missouri	10	200	40,948	40,948
Montana	153,375	3,170,000	15,341,793	15,341,793
Nevada	322,276	6,662,000	10,113,405	10,113,405
New Mexico	30,871	638,200	763,758	763,758
North Carolina	38	800	9	9
Oregon	60,951	1,260,000	150,207	150,207
Philippine Islands	44,202	913,700	12,597	12,597
South Dakota	328,305	6,786,700	165,865	165,865
Tennessee	263	5,400	131,931	131,931
Texas	5	100	612,436	612,436
Utah	152,018	3,142,500	13,439,811	13,439,811
Vermont	47	800	5,117	5,117
Virginia	20	400	2,967	2,967
Washington	16,556	342,300	302,446	302,446
Wyoming	18	400	719	719
	3,313,373	$68,493,500	67,879,206	$67,879,206

*Valued at the Government buying price of $1 per ounce.

These figures, compared with those showing the production in 1917—gold, $83,750,700; silver, 71,740,362 oz.—indicate a reduction in the output of gold of $15,257,200 and in that of silver of 3,861,156 oz. The output of gold in 1918 was the smallest in 20 years and that of silver was the lowest since 1913.

Topography and Geology of Dredging Areas—III

By CHARLES JANIN

COLORADO. *The principal dredging areas in Colorado are near Breckenridge, in Summit county, where the gravel occupies the bottoms of existing valleys. The greatest known thickness, about 90 ft., is near the Gold Pan pit at Breckenridge.† Along French creek the depth to bedrock in the main channel, from Nigger gulch down, is 45 to 50 ft. Along the Blue river, between Braddocks and the mouth of the Swan, the depth in the old channel is 55 to 60 ft., and along the Swan, from Galena gulch down, the maximum thickness is 40 to 50 ft. The width of the gravel-filled valley bottoms is 600 to 3000 ft. along the Blue, 500 to 1200 ft. along the Swan, and 700 to 1500 ft. in French gulch.

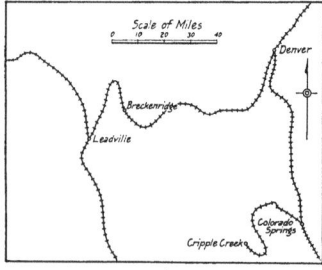

THE COLORADO DREDGES ARE NEAR BRECKINRIDGE AND LEADVILLE

In general, the gravels are loose and the readiness with which they crumble when undercut by the buckets facilitates dredging. Those on the lower Swan cave more easily than those on French creek. The gravels are generally coarse and contain hard well-rounded boulders. Along the Blue these boulders range in diameter from a maximum of about 6 ft. near Breckenridge to 4 ft. near Valdoro. In French gulch the large boulders rarely exceed 3 ft. in greatest diameter and are not so well rounded as those on the Blue. On the Swan, below Galena gulch, the gravel is more uniform and contains fewer large boulders than that along the Blue or in French gulch. Drilling and dredging show that the rock-bottoms of the channels are smooth as a whole, but at a few places where the streams have cut into quartzite the auriferous surface of the bedrock is rough and hard enough to tax the dredge machinery severely. Shales generally are so soft as to be easily excavated by the buckets; and the porphyries, owing to more or less decomposition, also constitute a tractable bottom material.

*Abstract from Bull. 127, U. S. Bureau of Mines.

†Ransome, F. L., 'Geology and Ore Deposits of the Breckenridge District, Colorado': U. S. Geol. Survey Prof. Paper 75, 1911, 187 pp.

MONTANA. The most important dredging operations in Montana are on Alder creek, in Madison county, at Ruby. In fact, this is the only field, except for early work at Bannack, where gold dredging has been successful in this State.

Alder creek rises on the northern slopes of Old Baldy mountain, at the south end of the Tobacco Root mountains, and flows north-west in an irregular curve to the Ruby river at Laurin. The prevailing rocks in the Tobacco Root range are schist and gneiss, with limestone and quartzite in places. The auriferous gravels at Ruby lie on volcanic ash beds that form a smooth false bedrock that shows only gentle undulations and slopes regularly to the west. In the gulch itself occasional spurs of the true or original bedrock are struck in dredging and are in part responsible for some of the ensuing repairs.

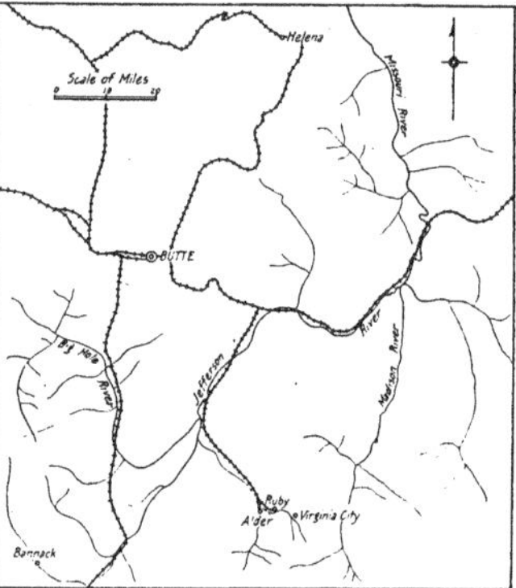

THE ONLY DREDGING IN MONTANA IS AT RUBY

Auriferous gravel extends at least 16 miles along Alder gulch, but the area known to be profitable for dredging is probably only about six or seven miles long, and contains about 1750 acres of proved dredging ground.

Although not as cemented nor as hard as the hardest ground in the Oroville district or the deep gravel at Folsom, the gravel has a clay matrix that makes it rather tenacious, especially near the false bedrock. The gold grains vary in coarseness; the average size increasing up the gulch. In the dredging ground 40 to 50% of the gold passes a 60-mesh screen, and 15 to 30% passes a 100-mesh screen. The gold varies in fineness also, that from the dredge farthest up the gulch running about 0.836 fine and that from the lowest dredge, about two miles below, being about 0.873 fine.

IDAHO AND OREGON. In Idaho the placer deposits are largely confined to the large area of deeply eroded granite in the central part of the State. Most of the placer gold has been derived from the gold-bearing

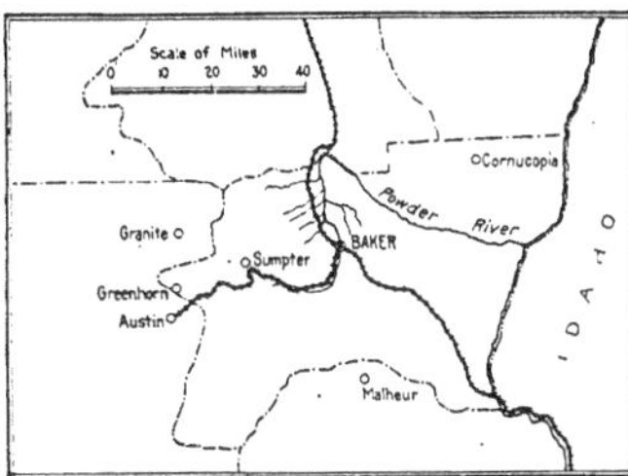

IN OREGON, DREDGING IS LIMITED TO THE POWDER RIVER DISTRICT

quartz veins with which the districts are invariably ribbed.‡ The most important placer district in Idaho is Boise Basin, where the Boston & Idaho Dredging Co. has been at work a number of years.

In this basin, the ground is light and easily handled; the gravel is about 30 ft. deep; and at times a dredging face 1300 ft. wide has been carried. Before dredging started there had been extensive hydraulic mining in the vicinity and much of the material handled by the dredges is tailing from the old workings. The dredges usually work through the year, but on account of severe weather they shut down in January and February, 1915. There is a great deal of sand in the ground and it is often necessary to run the top material dry through the screens.

Other dredging operations in Idaho have been carried on at Kirtley Creek and Bohannan Bar near Salmon City, in Lemhi county, and minor operations at Moose creek, also in Lemhi county; Pierce City, in Clearwater county; and at Elk City.

In Oregon the only profitable dredging enterprise as yet developed is that of the Powder River Dredging Co. near Sumpter. The Powder river drains the richest mineral district in eastern Oregon. The ground may be characterized as a medium-size dredging gravel, being somewhat larger than the average Californian gravel

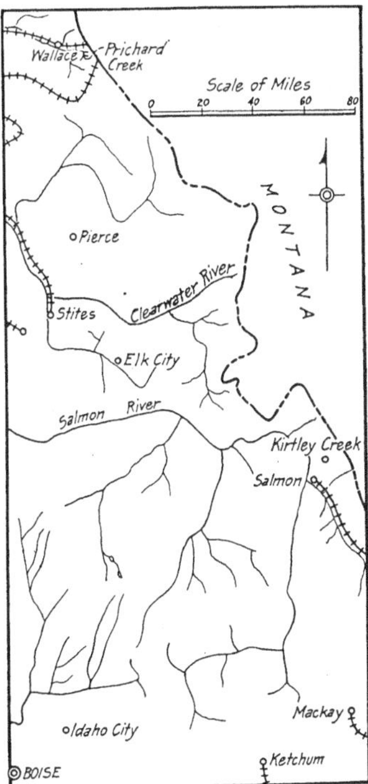

DREDGING IN IDAHO IS MAINLY NEAR IDAHO CITY. A NEW BOAT IS WORKING ON PRICHARD CREEK IN THE COEUR D'ALENE. ELK CITY, KIRTLEY CREEK, PIERCE, AND SALMON HAVE BEEN DREDGING AREAS.

and containing some large boulders. It is 12 to 25 ft. deep, the average depth being about 16 ft. and 300 to 1500 ft. wide. A few ledges of hard country rock are occasionally encountered. The gold content is mostly in the lower beds and on or near the soft decomposed bedrock, which is known to the dredgemen as 'clay webfoot.'

‡Bell, R. N., State Inspector of Mines, Boise, Idaho.

The Position of Copper

By CHARLES HAYDEN

The following interesting review by Mr. Hayden, of Hayden, Stone & Co., appeared recently in the New York 'Times'.

This is one of the most interesting times in the copper situation that one can imagine. Starting with the beginning of the world war in 1914, which, due to the interruption of the commerce of peace, led to a general demoralization in this country financially and commercially, and which compelled a curtailment of production at the copper mines to about 50% of normal, we have seen the demands of war cause a steady increase of production up to the point of forcing the same, so that the mines of this country during the last year universally pushed production to the limit.

Although the demand for copper for actual consumption in manufactures was still at its height last spring and summer, a peculiar series of events occurred which are now making themselves felt, at least temporarily, in a most marked way. By reason of the exceedingly cold weather around New Year's a year ago and the difficulties of transportation due to the heavy war-manufacturing business and other reasons, although copper was being outputted from the mines at an enormous rate, the refineries, owing to delays in transportation, were not running at nearly full capacity, as the blister copper was not arriving at the refineries from the West. The summer months, because of the intense heat, are always months of low output in a copper refinery. Then early this fall came the Gillespie explosion close to the refineries, which demoralized the situation for a week. After that came the Spanish influenza, which, coupled with the labor difficulties the entire year due to the high wages paid by the shipyards and the acute labor shortage, has meant that regardless of output from the mines the refineries have not been able to refine all of their product, so that a very substantial accumulation of unrefined copper was on hand when the armistice came.

While this copper could easily have been delivered had it been refined as produced, there is now naturally a let-up in the commercial demand, due to the readjustment which we are going through from a war basis to a peace basis. Immediately after luncheon one does not eat another meal, but one is invariably hungry by dinner-time, and so we should be unreasonable were we to expect a big consumptive demand for copper at the moment. But that is no reason for the producers to be stampeded and think there is never going to be a demand again, for as soon as the reconstruction which accompanies peace begins a very substantial demand will again spring up. And in the meantime the copper companies are all very strong in cash and cash assets, and there is no more reason why they should not carry a substantial amount of copper than there is that a dry goods company should not always have a substantial stock of goods in its store.

While costs remain high the consumer must expect the price of copper to remain up, as it is certainly not to the interest of the country at large, whose natural resources should be conserved, nor to the interest of the stockholders of the companies, that their copper, which is their principal, should be depleted by being taken out of the ground without profit.

Now as to a few statistics of the last year. It is undoubtedly true that this fall the amount of unrefined copper in process between the mine and the market was some 400,000,000 lb. greater than it was on January 1, 1914, and that accumulation is due to the conditions previously mentioned. The stock of refined copper, of course, has not only not increased since January 1, 1918, but actually decreased and is substantially smaller than it has been any year since the War began. The production for the year 1918 (December estimated) was about 2,400,000,000 lb. It is estimated that the consumption was 2,300,000,000 pounds.

As previously stated, the production does not mean the amount of copper refined, but what is mined from the properties, and the excess of production over consumption is not fully measured by the increased stock on hand. There is no doubt that while the stock of copper in process in this country is larger than in former times, it is also a fact of equal importance that the large stocks which were formerly carried all over Europe, not only in warehouses, but in transit and in the plants of consumers, do not now exist. What stocks there are in Europe today are all practically in the hands of the governments under their control and are relatively small compared to previous times.

It may be interesting to look back to the conditions existing in the first half of 1914. At that time consumption and production were about equal, namely, 140,000,000 lb. per month, and that production was consumed about as follows:

	Pounds per month
Germany and Austria	46,000,000
England	14,000,000
France	14,000,000
Italy	4,000,000
Other European countries	2,000,000
Total Europe	80,000,000
United States	60,000,000
Grand total	140,000,000

For the 10 to 15 years preceding the War, both production and consumption showed a steady average increase from year to year of about 7%, and had there been no war a continuation of this increase would have given us a consumption at the present time of about 190,000,000 lb. per month, whereas consumption has been during 1918 about 200,000,000 lb. per month. But as I expect production from now on will be substantially less than 190,000,000 lb. per month, it is very evident that consumption will very quickly outrun the reduced production, so that next spring there will undoubtedly be necessary another increase in production.

The Smelting and Refining of Cobalt Silver Ore

By SYDNEY B. WRIGHT

*The ore received at the Deloro Reduction Co.'s works from the shippers of the Cobalt and Gowganda districts, consists of silver-cobalt ore in lump form, jig and table concentrate, and residues such as those produced by the Nipissing Mining Co. and the Mining Corporation.

For sampling purposes the ore is ball-milled to about a 20-mesh product, a 14% cut being drawn by a Snyder disc-machine as the bulk sample. After a second Snyder cut, the sample, now constituting about 2% of the original ore, is transferred to the sampling-floor, where after thorough mixing it is coned and quartered into two samples that are then quartered down separately.

Reserve samples of these original pulps are sealed and retained for umpire purposes, until settlement has been made for the shipment. The control-samples are ground to pass a 100-mesh screen, scales being separated as usual for assay purposes. The requisite number of assay-samples is drawn for the shipper, smelter, and independent assayer, the certificate of the last governs in settlement for the shipment.

Metallics or nuggets are removed from the ball-mill after the carload or lot has been crushed, and are melted down to base bullion in an oil-fired crucible-furnace. The silver content as shown by assay, is added to the total silver contained in the milled pulp, and settlement made accordingly.

After the ore is sampled it is transferred to bins, from which it is charged to the blast-furnace. The charge is so calculated as to furnish a practically neutral slag and, on account of the large quantity of fine present, the furnace is run generally at a blast-pressure of only 6 to 8 oz. It was considered probable that by briquetting the fine the capacity of the furnace would be increased, but the test-runs made on these lines did not produce the desired metallurgical results. The ore, and reverts from other sections of the plant, are therefore mixed wet and charged to the furnace in the form of a stiff mortar; this sinters fairly well before the smelting zone is reached, the actual flue-dust produced amounting to about 6% of the ore and slime charged. The products of the smelting operation are speiss (from which a quantity of base silver is liquated in the case of high-grade runs) slag, and arsenic fume, which is collected in bag-houses of the regular type.

The speiss produced contains approximately:

	%
Co	22 to 25
Ni	16 to 18
As	25
Fe	18
S	7
Cu	1
Ag	1000 to 1200 oz. per ton

*Abstracted from the Canadian Mining Institute Bulletin, December 1918.

This speiss product is ground in a ball-mill until the whole passes a 40-mesh screen. The ground material is then roasted until it contains only 10% of arsenic. The roasting is done in a furnace of the reverberatory type equipped with a mechanical rabble having water-cooled arms. The chloridizing is done in a Bruckner cylinder.

The chloridized speiss is washed with water and then agitated for one hour with a cyanide solution containing the equivalent of 20 lb. KCN per ton. The silver is precipitated from the solutions by means of aluminum dust, one part of which deposits about eight parts of silver in our practice. In is interesting to note that the cyanide actually regenerated in this precipitation is practically equal to the theoretical quantity formerly present in the double silver salt.

The precipitate now goes to the silver refinery and the desilverized speiss residues to the oxide plant.

The base silver, liquated in the form of bottoms from pots of speiss, averages about 800 fine, the balance consisting of arsenic and antimony, with some cobalt, nickel, iron, copper, and bismuth.

This bullion is refined by melting it in an oil-fired Schwartz furnace, which is equipped as a small converter. As soon as the charge is in a molten state the furnace is tilted backward into blowing position and the metal is blown for about three hours. During the first half-hour of this period the oil is shut off from the burner, the heat of the reaction being sufficient to keep the metal molten for that length of time. After a short further heating up the charge is poured into ingot molds.

The silver bullion thus obtained averages from 992 to 995 fine, and is brought up to commercial grade (996 and better) by re-melting with silver precipitate from the cyanide plant; this operation is performed in a second Schwartz furnace. The gases from these furnaces are drawn through coolers and passed to a small bag-house. The fume is rich in silver, carrying about 800 oz. per ton, and consists essentially of arsenious oxide with some antimony and bismuth oxides. All bullion-slags and this fume are eventually re-charged to the blast-furnace.

The gases from the blast-furnaces, the roasters, and chloridizers are drawn through flues and coolers before reaching the bag-houses, which collect the crude arsenious oxide. The temperature of the gases entering the bag-houses is regulated at a maximum of 250°F. by means of a thermostat operating a damper in the main flue; when the temperature rises to 250°F. cool air is immediately drawn in, reducing the temperature.

The crude arsenic collected in the bag-houses is sent to refining furnaces, which are coke-fired reverberatory-hearths. The arsenious oxide is volatilized and condensed in chambers that are emptied at intervals of ten to fourteen days. The products from these chambers are pulverized and packed in barrels by means of a Raymond pulverizer, a system that certainly deserves the admiration and gratitude of the packer and his employer when handling such materials as arsenious oxide.

The clinker or slag drawn from the refining-hearth contains all the silver that was formerly present in the crude arsenic; this slag goes back to the blast-furnace.

It is necessary now to return to the de-silverized speiss residue, which contains the cobalt and nickel of the ore. The metals in this material are present principally in the form of oxides, so the first treatment is that of sulphatizing in order to render the cobalt and nickel soluble as sulphates. The sulphatized speiss is charged to vats in which the mass is agitated with hot water and the sulphates dissolved. The liquors thus obtained are then freed from copper and iron before passed to the precipitation vats, first freeing them from the copper and iron contained.

The cobalt and nickel are separated by fractional precipitation with hypochlorite solutions, the nickel being finally precipitated as hydroxide by means of milk of lime. The hydroxides of cobalt and nickel thus obtained are filter-pressed, washed, and dried, after which treatment the oxides are either pulverized and packed for the market, or are transferred to the metals department for reduction to the metallic state.

For the purpose of reducing the oxides they are mixed with charcoal and reduced to rough metal in oil-fired furnaces. After separation from excess carbon by means of a magnetic separator, the rough metal is melted in electric furnaces and converted into shot form by pouring into water. The 50-kw. electric furnaces used are of the single-phase, top and bottom electrode type, lined with magnesite, and have a capacity of 100 lb. of cobalt or nickel metal per hour.

TUNGSTEN ORE sent from Hongkong to America during the first nine months of 1918 was 3323 tons, valued at $2,852,913. In October the exports rose to 1265 tons. The United States Consul General at Hongkong, writing on November 7, states that the fall in price of the ore in America, apparently due to unusual supplies and an overstocked market, has resulted in a reduction of the output of the Chinese mines, and there is likely to be more or less irregularity of production until the situation in the consuming countries resolves itself into a more stable condition. Local mining engineers, however, are of the opinion that whatever may be the situation in the United States, China will be called upon for all the tungsten it can produce, for the simple reason that under normal conditions and notwithstanding the Chinese government 'military' tax of $15 per picul of 133⅓ lb. (which works out to about $25 in actual practice), the ore can be produced more cheaply in this field than in any other part of the world. A fall in the exchange-value of silver to a more ordinary level will reduce materially the cost of production of the ore in terms of gold. It is thought, therefore, that there is a great future for the trade despite the uncertainty of the present moment. Exports to Europe continue at about the volume that has moved so far during 1918, but the bulk of the exports have been to the United States.

Copper Output

Production of copper in the United States during 1918 was slightly in excess of the output of the mines during the previous year, according to advance figures on the year's tonnage given out by the U. S. Geological Survey. At an average price of 24.75 cents per pound the production of the mines was $473,000,000, compared with $510,000,000 in 1917 and $190,000,000 in 1913.

These figures represent the actual output of the companies for the first 11 months of the year and the estimated output for December. Production of blister and Lake copper from domestic ores was 1,910,000,000 lb. last year as against 1,886,000,000 lb. in 1917 and 1,224,000,000 in 1913. The supply of refined copper from primary sources for the year, including both domestic and foreign figures, is estimated at 2,450,000,000 lb., compared with 2,362,000,000 lb. in 1917 and 1,615,000,000 lb. in 1913. The production was thus distributed over the country: Arizona produced 777,000,000 lb. against 712,000,000 in 1917; Montana 328,000,000 against 274,000,000; Michigan 225,000,000 against 268,000,000; Utah 233,000,000 against 245,000,000; Nevada 105,000,000 against 122,000,000; Alaska 69,000,000, a heavy decrease; New Mexico 98,000,000 against 105,000,000. California is estimated at considerably above the 48,000,000 lb. that was produced in 1917. The output in Tennessee was about 14,500,000 pounds.

Imports for the first 11 months of the year were 535,868,000 lb., compared with 556,000,000 lb. for the 12 months of 1917. Exports of copper, including pigs, ingots, bars, plates, sheets, rods, wire and products, for the first 11 months of the year were 692,759,000 pounds.

At beginning of 1918 about 114,000,000 lb. of refined was in stock in the United States. Adding this to refinery output shows total available supply about 2,564,000,000 lb. Subtracting exports for 11 months and estimated exports for last month shows, on assumption there was no change in stocks, that supply available for domestic consumption in 1918 was considerably more than 1,316,000,000 lb. available in 1917.

EXPLOSIVES in most common use in quarries are black blasting-powder, granulated powder containing a small percentage of nitro-glycerine, dynamite containing 15 to 60% nitro-glycerine, ammonia dynamite, and blasting gelatin. The choice depends mainly on the nature of the material to be broken.

THE HOLLINGER, at Porcupine, Ontario, is the richest gold mine on this continent. In 1918 it produced $6,250,000 worth of gold and paid $1,230,000 in dividends.

TONOPAH, NEVADA

Important Developments in the Divide District.

In the Tonopah Divide mine, six miles south of Tonopah in the Divide district, a cross vein has been found in exploring what has been known as the main silver vein on the 370-ft. level. The newly-opened shoot is said to be the older fissure and the source of enrichment of the ore-channel that has been opened for a length of over 300 ft. The shaft was sunk for the purpose of cutting, on its dip to the north, a vein that crops near the high summit to the south and that had produced rich ore from surface workings. A cross-cut south on the 165-ft. level penetrated the silver vein 140 ft. from the shaft. This vein outcrops boldly in places, but shows little of value at the surface. The shaft was continued to the 370-ft. level, and cross-cuts were driven to the silver vein on the 265 and 370-ft. levels. A cross-cut extended south on the 265-ft. level cut the gold vein 580 ft. from the shaft, and a drift east on this vein exposed gold ore assaying from $40 to $80 per ton, varying from 2 to 4 ft. wide. Drifts on the silver vein were extended both ways from the cross-cuts on three levels, and at 50-ft. intervals raises and cross-cuts have been driven to block-out the ore for a distance of over 300 ft. along the vein, showing a mean width of 25 ft. of ore. On the 370-ft. level the south-east foot-wall drift, at a point 250 ft. from the shaft cross-cut, exposed the foot-wall of the new vein. This wall, like that of the silver vein, stands nearly vertical, with a slight south-east dip. The silver vein has a south-east strike, the new vein north-east, and the gold vein almost due east. High-grade ore was found at the foot-wall of the new vein, the faces for several days here assaying from $150 to $300 per ton. A drift was started south-west along the foot-wall of the new vein and a cross-cut through the latter, back of the foot-wall of the silver vein. The rock between these faces was broken down to the point where a 12-ft. face was exposed. Of this ore, a width of 5 ft. assayed $236 and 7 ft. sampled $87; car samples averaged $177 per ton. The cross-cut was continued 31 ft. before the hanging wall

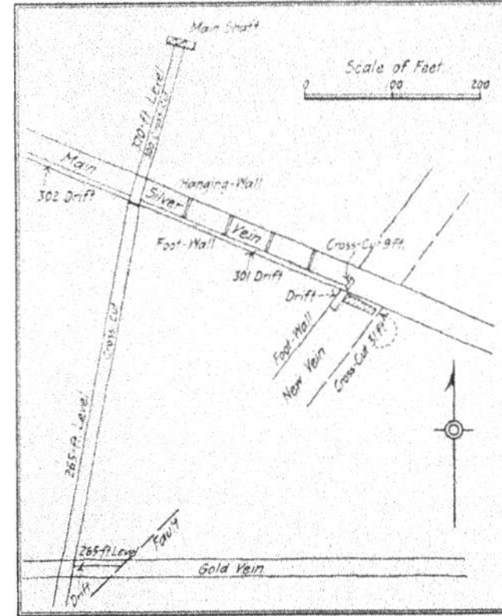

UNDERGROUND WORKINGS OF THE TONOPAH DIVIDE MINE

TONOPAH DIVIDE MINE, LOOKING NORTH-WEST

appeared. At 22 ft. the face assay dropped to $48, but after the next round of shots it was $68 per ton. A cross-cut here back into the silver vein gave an average of $265 for a length of 9 ft. The area about the point of junction of the two walls is greatly crushed and contains seams and masses of kaolin, filled with particles and sheets of glassy horn silver. Large pieces of this ore have been found, containing 1000 oz. of silver per ton. At other points native silver is present. The main shaft is being sunk below the 370-ft. level by means of auxiliary hoisting equipment, and is down 465 ft. Sinking will continue to water-level, estimated to be not less than 700 ft., and stations will be cut at 100-ft. intervals. The property is owned chiefly by J. C. Brougher of Tonopah and George Wingfield of Reno; William Watters is superintendent, and A. I. D'Arcy is consulting engineer and has directed all development. Mr. D'Arcy's analysis of the district geology shows the mountain to be composed of a series of rhyolites, the upper strata being a hard, fine-grained, and glassy rhyolite showing distinct phenocrystals of quartz. Below this is a thin bed of fine-grained rhyolite breccia and below this a series of fine-grained rhyolites, the distinguishing features of which are the stratifications due to the floor structure of this series. The lowest rock exposed on the mountain is a rather coarse-grained rhyolite breccia. The silver vein was found in the rhyolite breccia, but the gold vein was found on the 265-ft. level encased in the upper rhyolite, owing to fault action that has brought this rhyolite down to the level of the breccia, and the opinion is expressed that only at and below the 465-ft. level will this vein be found encased in the breccia that forms the casing of the other ore-channels. Ore from the Tonopah Divide mine is now being hauled to the MacNamara mill at Tonopah, and an early increase in production is probable. Shipments have been at the rate of 300 tons weekly, and until recently most of this ore went to the Goldfield Consolidated mill.

Exploration at adjacent properties has been in progress for several months. On the Brougher Divide, adjoining the

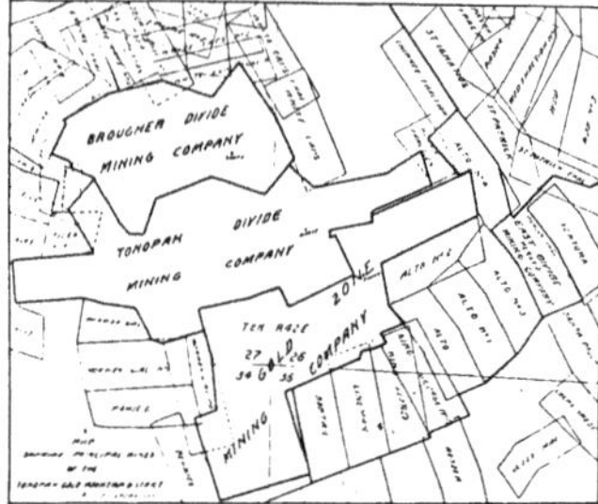

Tonopah Divide mine on the north-west, drifts have been advanced for a considerable distance in the Divide vein on the 177-ft. level, but no pay-ore has been found. The shaft is being sunk deeper; it is now below the 375-ft. point and lateral work is to be resumed at the 400-ft. level.

The Gold Zone, adjoining the Tonopah Divide on the south-east, explored the main silver vein on its 295-ft. level and had a full face of $11 ore near the Divide boundary. Sinking was resumed and the vein has just been cut on the 500-ft. level, not far from the Divide end-line.

The Tonopah Dividend, adjoining the Brougher on the north-west, has been exploring on the 300-ft. level and has cross-cut the main silver vein, known in this territory as the Brougher vein, securing some good assays. Drifts are now being started both ways in this vein, which is over 40 ft. wide in this territory.

The Divide Extension has a shaft down over 150 ft. but has not been working for some time. It is announced that sinking will be resumed at once.

The East Divide, east of the Gold Zone, is sinking with good equipment near a prominent blow-out where the vein cropping yields assays up to $5 in gold. The shaft, down 175 ft., is in the breccia typical of the Tonopah Divide mine and cross-cuts will be driven at the 200-ft. level.

The Hasbrouck is driving a long tunnel, and has cut good ore in it and in the shaft workings. It has produced shipping ore in considerable quantity.

The Sutherland Divide, situated over 2000 ft. north of the Divide, has a 400-ft. incline shaft, and has produced shipping ore from this shaft and from surface workings. It is to be equipped for lateral work on the 300 and 400-ft. levels, and a cross-cut is now being driven at 300 feet.

The Gold Reef group, south-east of the central properties, and the Gold Seam, south of the Gold Reef, show good vein croppings and are to be developed at depth.

The Rosetta Divide has had some good surface assays, and is preparing for work on a substantial scale. Several other properties in the district will soon be under development, stimulated by the results of work in the Tonopah Divide mine, and the district now promises to become the most active in Nevada during the next few months.

SAN FRANCISCO, CALIFORNIA

The American Mining Congress in California.

On January 15 and 16, a total of 160 mining and oil-men attended the convention called by the California Metal Producers Association of San Francisco and the Chamber of Mines and Oil of Los Angeles to organize a California chapter of the American Mining Congress. Albert Burch presided, with G. M. Swindell as secretary.

Mining politics is the special business of the American Mining Congress, according to the secretary, J. F. Callbreath, whose address we shall publish at an early date.

The history of the American Mining Congress was briefly covered by H. Foster Bain, Assistant Director of the Bureau of Mines. The origin of the Congress was in Gilpin county, Colorado. The dominant idea was to have a member—a Secretary of Mines—of the President's Cabinet who would look after the mining industry. Conventions were held. J. J. Holmes of Carolina was one of the active members, he eventually becoming director of the U. S. Bureau of Mines. The present Mining Congress is vastly different from that of the early days. Several coal-mine explosions resulted in investigations being made for the safety of miners, when the Mining Congress saw its opportunity, and in 1910 the Bureau of Mines was created. The scope of the Bureau has enlarged greatly. The War showed that the mining industry was not in concentrated hands, and the formation of a mining department has recently come up again. Franklin K. Lane, head of the U. S. Bureau of Mines and Geological Survey, would make a good Secretary of Mines. A representative mining organization will always receive attention at Washington.

The president of the American Mining Congress, Bulkeley Wells, general manager of the Smuggler Union mine, Telluride, Colorado, said that for years the American Mining Congress was Mr. Callbreath, and Mr. Callbreath was the American Mining Congress. At one time he was owed over $15,000. The present scope of the activities of the head office at Washington is more extensive than realized. Committees sent to the Capital to watch mining legislation have no entré, therefore the Mining Congress guides them to the right quarters. One important function of the head office is to advise Government bureaus on certain phases of mining under consideration. Until 18 months ago the Mining Congress consisted mainly of small operators, the larger people thinking that they could fight their troubles alone. Since then the latter have come in, seeing that co-operation is best.

The War Minerals Relief Bill—to give aid to chrome, magnese, pyrite, and other products—would not have received attention unless the Mining Congress had been behind it. Another accomplishment of the Congress was in fighting taxation, and when the Gold Commission in November 1918 was heard by the Treasury Department at Washington, the gold crisis was fully discussed. Unfortunately the end of the War relieved the urgent need of relief to producers. Mr. Wells thinks that eventually aid will be given, probably through operation of the Revenue Bill.

Regarding the labor situation, Mr. Wells considered that it would be folly to reduce wages until the cost of living is changed. If this were forced there would be disaster.

The active support of members of the Mining Congress is urged; officers should be backed vigorously and promptly. Mr. Wells hoped that the Mining Congress was here to stay.

Mr. Burch followed Mr. Wells by saying that until a year ago he knew nothing of the American Mining Congress, but when at Washington he saw the valuable work being done by this organization. An instance was the aid given the silver producers who eventually received $1 per ounce, mainly through the Congress.

Regarding the Revenue Bill for 1918 and gold producers, Mr. Callbreath here added that if passed by Congress, it would mean that companies producing gold from a gold mine and gold from a base-metal mine would be relieved of taxation to the amount of such production.

Few mining projects have ever been financed by banks, according to Albert Burch when introducing J. K. Lynch, Governor of the Federal Reserve Bank to the mining men assembled at lunch on the 15th. Mr. Lynch said that civilization and mining have gone hand in hand; metals are necessary for such a state of living. He briefly traced the use of metals. The world is dependent on iron for progress; electricity is dependent on copper mining. The most interesting metals to the miner are gold and silver. No market has to be found; it is always available with cash. When a $20 piece is given for groceries or the like, a barter has taken place, there being received value for value. Credit, the clearing-house, and paper all reduced the amount of gold needed to be handled; then came the Federal Reserve Bank to further reduce the quantity held by banks. Gold and silver production has not increased as fast as the credit of the world, and gold is still the medium of settlement of balances. Mr. Lynch thinks that there will be a drop in the price of silver later.

From the banker's standpoint, mining may be divided into four stages: (1) prospecting, (2) exploration, (3) development, and (4) production. When a mine is ready for production it may be considered a manufacturing business; until this stage is reached the banker is not interested. The bank is only lending other people's money and must be careful, and will not lend until the property is scientifically developed and equipped for production. Most mining today is not for the poor man, it is one for capital.

The gold reserve in Federal Reserve Banks on January 3, 1919, was $2,092,000,000, about 33% of the gold in the country; but estimates of the total gold are generally doubtful, due to unknown quantities hoarded. The ratio of gold to credit in this country at June 30, 1918, was 1:5; at the end of the next fiscal year it is estimated at 1:12½. Only for the Federal Reserve Bank the country would have been bankrupt during the War; the gold was concentrated in this bank from other banks.

'The Attitude of Bankers Toward Mining Investments' was the important topic covered by Frank B. Anderson, president of the Bank of California at San Francisco, at the second day's luncheon. This speech will be published in another issue.

Accomplishments of the American oil industry during the War were discussed at considerable length by T. A. O'Donnel, formerly assistant to the oil director of the U. S. Fuel Administration, in charge of production. He considered that every phase of the conflict was dependent upon petroleum, which mostly came from the United States. The Government here did not force the oil producers to do anything, but when asked to do what they could there was a ready response by spending large sums in additional equipment, much of which will be useless after the War. In spite of everything, the oil output in 1918 was 3% greater than in 1917.

In discussing the effect of publicity upon mining, T. A. Rickard, editor of the 'Mining and Scientific Press', dwelt upon the general good results that come from the public and employees knowing what is being done by a mining company; how a little judicious advertising and writing aids engineers; and how the American Mining Congress can be benefited by publicity. The War brought home to Americans the great importance of mining, about which they would otherwise have remained comparatively ignorant.

One of the desires of the American Mining Congress is the appointment of a Secretary of Mines, to be a member of the President's Cabinet. This phase was discussed by Judge John F. Davis, who has graduated, so to speak, from mining to law. His address will be reproduced in the 'Press' later.

The War has shown the fundamental relationship and dependencies of industry upon fuel; peace has not altered this, according to D. M. Folsom. He referred specially to oil-fuel, particularly in the Pacific Coast region. This paper will also be published later on.

DENVER, COLORADO

American Mining Congress and Colorado Metal Miners Association Meet.

The first important event of the new year for Colorado's mining industry was the joint meeting of the Colorado Chapter of the American Mining Congress and the Colorado Metal Miners Association during three days at the Brown Palace hotel, Denver. The sessions on January 2, 3, and 4 were well attended. It was noticeable that the mining men of the State are finally getting together in a worth-while way, this meeting displaying more enthusiasm and concerted opinion than has been manifested at any meetings heretofore. Until within the past two or three years the main support of these organizations has remained with a relatively few small-mine operators, who usually held discordant views regarding ways of securing relief from their hardships. During discussions in former sessions it often seemed that there existed a wide gap between the interests of operators of small mines on one hand and of large mining companies on the other, and that co-operation between the two classes could not be expected to bring back to Colorado the same degree of universal interest in metal mining that prevailed some years ago. However this wrong point of view has been removed through the efforts of the officers in these two organizations, with the result that successful large-scale operators of the State are prominent in the affairs of both the Mining Association and the local Mining Congress chapter. Harmony now prevails, and the small miner feels that his general interests are identical, in most respects, with those of the large mining corporations.

Taking all things into consideration no meetings in Colorado in recent years have been more harmonious or portended greater benefits to the State's metal-mining industry.

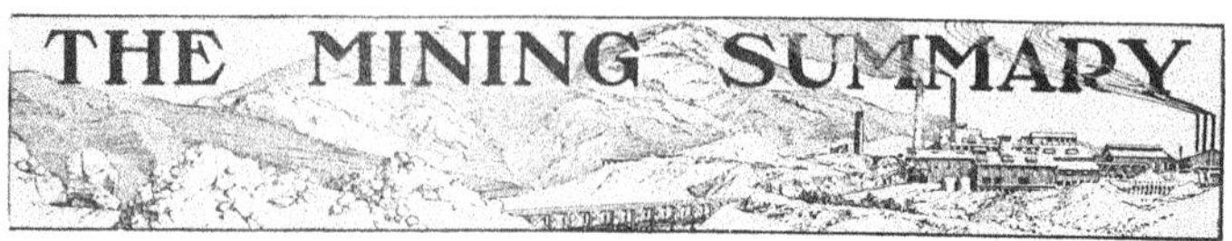

ALASKA

Juneau.—Alaska Gastineau in December produced 117,310 tons of 98.3-cent ore, recovering 80.57%. The past two years compare as under:

Month	1918 Tons	1918 Value	1917 Tons	1917 Value
January	170,300	$0.903	173,300	$1.240
February	140,305	0.934	150,000	1.350
March	150,093	1.114	217,700	1.090
April	125,435	1.148	212,200	1.090
May	101,200	1.114	227,900	1.787
June	82,600	1.250	202,490	1.102
July	74,830	1.319	166,988	0.985
August	96,250	1.367	179,150	0.994
September	47,850	1.247	177,828	1.064
October	75,870	0.995	191,610	1.069
November	94,395	0.968	175,960	1.080
December	117,310	0.983	165,131	1.036

McKinley.—According to a circular of the bondholders committee, the Valdez Creek Placer Mines company has defaulted in the payment of interest on its bonds ($500,000) and notes ($731,481) and defaulted in part in the payment of principal. The company is to be reorganized as the McKinley Placers, after the post-office at Valdez Creek. Present bondholders are to get $560,000 in 8% preferred stock in exchange for their bonds and coupons thereon up to January 1, 1919; in exchange for notes held it is proposed to issue a second 8% preferred stock; and holders of shares are to get one share of common stock, $5 par, for every five shares of Valdez Creek stock now held. Henry A. Cutter of Nashua, New Hampshire, is counsel.

ARIZONA

Ajo.—New Cornelia produced 4,248,000 lb. of copper in December, one of the largest outputs since starting in June 1917.

Bisbee.—Shattuck-Arizona produced in December, 506,332 lb. of copper, 401,593 lb. of lead, 21,506 oz. of silver, and 86 oz. of gold.

The lead-flotation plant of the Shattuck-Arizona company was closed last week, 85 men being laid off.

Calumet & Arizona yielded 3,904,000 lb. of copper in December.

Clifton.—The mines of the Shannon Copper Co. were closed on January 4. The company has operated at a loss during the past six months, partly due to the increased freight rates of 25%, increase in wages, and a stagnant market. Mr. Bennie, the general manager, is to remain at Clifton for the present, and the resumption of operations will depend upon the future copper market.

Arizona Copper Co. produced 3,600,000 lb. during December.

Metcalf.—The Shannon company produced 688,000 lb. of copper in December. There has been almost a general decline since the 972,000 lb. in January last.

Phoenix.—A six-inch vein of almost pure cinnabar has been opened at the Jeter and Larson mine in the Phoenix mountains, north of Phoenix.

Ray.—The Ray Hercules is producing about 300,000 lb. of copper monthly. The mill has treated as much as 1100 tons per day, recovering 87%. The ore has been as low as 1% copper, no sorting being done. It is said that the company is considering erection of a smelter, jointly with the Magma Copper Company.

ARKANSAS

Yellville.—Zinc-ore production in northern Arkansas last year totaled 1730 tons, also 70 tons of lead. The district of Zinc contributed 1000 tons, Rush 345 tons, and Yellville 105 tons. Except at the first-named centre nearly all the mines were closed since last spring. The Bald Hill company at St. Joe is said to have 750 tons of ore in bins; other mines also have large stocks. A better demand for carbonate ore has resulted in the re-opening of several properties.

COLORADO

Boulder.—It is reported that the Colorado Pitchblende Co. recently paid $10,000 as final settlement for properties acquired at Jimtown. The president, J. F. Barnhill, announced that the company will construct a railway to Jimtown, also a mill.

Breckenridge.—The Wellington Mines Co. has just paid a dividend of 10%, equal to $100,000. This makes a total of $1,850,000. The company's cash resources are $407,894. This mine produces zinc ore.

Salida.—The Ohio & Colorado Smelting Co. at Salida reports the following ore receipts during 1918:

Counties	Ore, tons	Gold, oz.	Silver, oz.	Lead, lb.	Copper, lb.
Chaffee	4,028	2,493	30,312	896,032	......
Custer	4,003	205	95,860	292,917	52,010
Dolores	140	....	1,124	54,233	86
Eagle	10,809	920	189,965	146,134	387,445
Gunnison	1,486	479	7,178	20,365	73,599
Hinsdale	1,119	294	14,704	693,400	14,815
Lake	58,730	3,004	556,283	1,708,106	188,198
Ouray	7,137	2,813	382,692	2,614,219	79,902
Saguache	1,774	129	84,360	134,579	131,291
San Juan	3,905	1,967	63,500	2,683,478	277,525
San Miguel	516	85	16,019	210,773	32,589
Summit	1,658	71	12,600	148,853	3,893
Colorado total	95,305	12,460	1,454,597	9,603,089	1,241,353
Idaho	19,459	....	537,931	16,460,972	41,971
Oklahoma (zinc residues)	23,198	3,776	790,872	3,132,349	501,517
Mexico	218	....	3,733	197,493	1,100
Grand total	138,180	16,236	2,787,133	29,393,903	1,785,941

IDAHO

Salmon.—The manager for the Harmony Mines Co., E. F. Nieman, estimates that reserves amount to 60,000 tons, so a concentrating plant is to be erected for the copper ore.

At the Big Dyke mine a Koering cyanide process plant is being erected in charge of C. W. Sherwood. A hydro-electric plant is also under construction.

MISSOURI

Joplin.—Production of the Tri-State region last week was:

State	Blende, tons	Calamine, tons	Lead, tons	Total value
Kansas	98	...	106	$16,170
Missouri	1,130	470	150	81,689
Oklahoma	5,076	...	885	276,144
Average price per ton	$45	$38	$90	......

MICHIGAN

Houghton.—Calumet & Hecla and subsidiaries now are using 42 storage-battery locomotives for ore haulage—12 at Isle Royale, 12 at Ahmeek, 5 at North Kearsarge, and 13 at the Calumet & Hecla. Five more have been ordered for the last named. They are working quite satisfactorily. The Allouez is using all trolley locomotives.

CALIFORNIA

Almaden.—It is reported from San Jose that a quarter interest in the New Guadalupe Mining Co. has been sold by J. L. Stubbs to H. C. Davey for $100,000. Extensive improvements are to be made. The total recorded output to the end of 1917 was 105,772 flasks of quicksilver. The 1918 yield was about 1000 flasks.

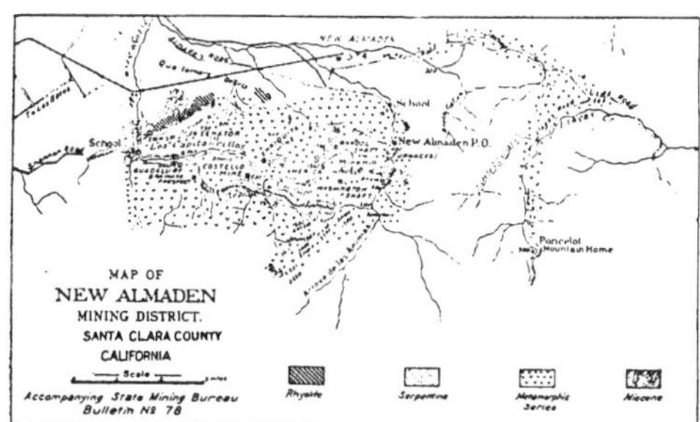

Copperopolis.—Calaveras county in 1918 yielded 6,480,-000 lb. of copper, a decrease of 1,250,000 lb. when compared with 1917, but as large as any previous year save 1910. The Calaveras Copper and Penn Mining were the principal contributors.

Engelmine.—During 1918, Plumas county copper mines produced about 11,700,000 lb., against 7,463,000 lb. in 1917, 4,933,000 lb. in 1916, 3,165,000 lb. in 1915, and 150,000 lb. in 1914. The Engels company is the largest producer, its figures for the last and previous periods being, according to M. E. Dittmar of Redding:

Year	Ore tons	Copper, lb.
1915	59,741	2,893,133
1916	168,712	4,312,408
1917	157,423	5,940,741
1918	275,000	9,100,000

Two flotation mills are at work, one of up to 500 and the other up to 600 tons capacity.

Another good copper producer in Plumas is the Walker, near Portola.

Forbestown.—The old Denver mine here is reported to have been purchased from C. L. Falck by San Francisco people for $40,000. The workings are to be unwatered.

Kennett.—Copper production of Shasta county last year was about 24,680,000 lb., 4,000,000 lb. less than in 1917, and 15,000,000 lb. less than in 1916. The Mammoth, Balaklala, Mountain Copper, Afterthought, Bully Hill, and other mines contributed. Some important developments were reported from the Crystal and Oak Run copper mines.

Placerville.—James Nutley, field superintendent for the Linscott Drilling Co., of San Francisco, with a crew of 10 men, is drilling five holes with Keystone machines, to the depth of 60 ft. to sample the Rocky Bar gravel mine, situated on the middle fork of the Consumnes river, 14 miles due north-east of Placerville.

Sacramento.—One of the bills introduced to the Legislature Assembly on January 15 was that of Mr. McColgan, to compel underground mining companies to pay employees from the time they enter the mine until they reach the surface.

A joint resolution endorsing the National Congressional proposal to reimburse various individuals and corporations for losses sustained in producing war minerals such as chrome was introduced to the Assembly by Senator Rigdon on the 15th.

San Luis Obispo.—A. H. Simpson, who was managing a group of chromite producing properties in El Dorado county for the Union Chrome Co., now has charge of a manganese mine for the Manganese Company of California, seven miles from this place. The daily output is 10 tons of high-grade di-oxide ore.

Sutter Creek.—At the Old Eureka the shaft is down 2880 ft., with 270 ft. to go.

The Central Eureka is increasing work on its 3500-ft. level. Good ore has been opened at 3450 ft., from which it is sent to the mill.

MONTANA

Butte.—Anaconda is reported to have reduced operations by over 25%, due to the metal markets.

The Pennsylvania mine of the Anaconda group was closed indefinitely on January 10. The daily output was 1200 tons of ore, employing 750 men.

Butte & Superior produced 10,600,000 lb. of spelter and 220,000 oz. of silver during December. The average for 1918 was 11,500,000 lb. per month, the range being from 6,850,000 to 14,300,000 pounds.

East Butte produced 1,929,720 lb. of copper in December, nearly up to the average.

North Butte yielded in December 2,230,507 lb. of copper and 97,443 oz. of silver.

Davis-Daly produced 977,015 lb. of copper and 37,972 oz. of silver in December. This is the largest return for 1918, save 1,013,521 lb. in January.

Missoula.—The main plant of the lumber department of the Anaconda company at Bonner, seven miles east of this place, was totally destroyed by fire on the 16th. The damage probably will amount to $500,000.

NEVADA

Ely.—Labor troubles of the Nevada Consolidated were settled last week. Little change was made in conditions of employment.

Tonopah.—Production of the district last week totaled 7450 tons of ore, valued at $126,650. Nine mines contributed, including the Tonopah Divide with 225 tons.

December yelds were as under:

Mine	Tons	Silver, oz.	Gold, oz.	Profit
Tonopah Belmont	8,937	113,115	1,080	$57,227
Tonopah Extension	9,617	122,248	1,107	57,703
Jim Butler	...	......	....	5,555

West End pays 5 cents per share, equal to $89,424, on February 18.

OKLAHOMA

Picher.—The Great Premier company paid a dividend of $20,000 late in 1918, and another on January 1 of $50,000. The surplus is $30,000. A. M. Gains is in charge.

Production of Oklahoma fields last week totaled 5076 tons of blende and 880 tons of lead, valued at $276,144.

UTAH

Alta.—The Wasatch Mines Co.'s tunnel is now in 3300

ft., directly under the Columbus-Rexall dump. Two shifts are driving up to 8 ft. daily.

Columbus-Rexall paid 2½ cents per share last week, the sum of $14,600. A restraining order of the Monetaire company had held up the disbursement until the District Court declined further to allow this.

Bingham.—Utah Copper Co. closed its Boston Consolidated property on the 17th, dispensing with 400 men.

The Utah-Apex company has laid-off 300 men.

Eureka.—The Centennial Eureka is sinking a winze in good ore below water-level—1900 ft. depth. The present flow is 250 gal. per min. This is pumped to the 1800, 1200, and 600-ft. levels, in three lifts. Additional pumps will give a capacity of 1250 gallons per minute.

At a depth of 2200 ft. the Iron Blossom company has cut a promising stringer of lead ore. Rich copper ore is being followed below the 1100-ft. level.

The Iron King company's new shaft is down 1300 ft., with encouraging indications. This shaft is to prospect for an extension of the orebody from the Tintic Standard adjoining.

The new drainage-tunnel of the Jesse Knight company is in 1500 ft. This will drain several mines in the eastern and southern parts of the district. Henry Barney is in charge.

Provo.—Iron Blossom pays 2½ cents per share on January 25. This is equal to $25,000, and makes the total $3,200,000.

Tintic.—Chief Consolidated pays 12½ cents per share on February 1. This amounts to $110,529, and brings the total to $1,345,399. The cash surplus is $194,280, plus $505,482 of Liberty Bonds, etc.

The Copper Leaf company's shaft is down 1060 ft., and it has been decided to continue to 1200 ft., and drive at 1000 ft. Machinery to cost $2000 is to be purchased. Cash on hand amounts to $19,000. J. W. Taylor is superintendent.

WASHINGTON

Keller.—At the Walla Walla mine, 500 ft. of air pipe is being hung to permit of extending the adit to the Handspike vein. If as rich ore is found as in the upper workings the company will erect a mill. J. E. Leonard is in charge.

CANADA

Ontario

Boston Creek.—The Allied Gold Mines has been organized by Detroit, Michigan, people to work the O'Donald and Cutler-Renaud claims here. Diamond-drilling is under way. R. W. Norrington is in charge.

Cobalt.—Trethewey paid a dividend of 5% on January 2. This amounts to $50,000, and makes a total of $1,211,999.

MEXICO

Durango

Guanacevi.—At the Anita mine, E. F. Knotts of El Paso, Texas, is erecting a 50-ton flotation plant, including ball-mill and revolving filter.

Sonora

Cananea.—Owing to the uncertain copper market about 2500 men have been laid off by companies in this district.

Greene-Cananea produced 5,100,000 lb. of copper and 174,900 oz. of silver during December. The total for 1918 was 53,270,000 lb. and 1,549,672 oz., compared with 30,260,000 lb. and 807,217 oz. in 1917. Trouble with the Government caused a shut-down in mid-1917.

Hermosillo.—According to advices received at Monterrey, the United States Graphite Co. has resumed extensive development at its property. Regular shipments of 80 tons daily of high-grade graphite are now being made. The mineral is obtained mostly from open-cuts and is hauled to rail, a distance of 20 miles, by motor-trucks. The company is composed of Grand Rapids, Michigan, men. The crude graphite is shipped to the company's refinery in the East.

PERSONAL

Note. The Editor invites members of the profession to send particulars of their work and appointments. The information is interesting to our readers.

Askin M. Nicholas is at Globe, Arizona.

W. P. Lass has returned to Seattle from Juneau, Alaska.

Howland Bancroft, of Denver, was in San Francisco last week.

G. W. Miller has opened an office as consulting engineer at Los Angeles.

W. H. Blackburn, of Tonopah, has been elected president of the Nevada Mine Operators Association.

T. O. McGrath, secretary of the Shattuck-Arizona Copper Co., has returned to Bisbee from a visit to Chicago.

Lafayette Hanchett has been retained as consulting engineer to the Silver King Coalition Mines Co., of Park City, Utah.

H. Foster Bain represented the Bureau of Mines at the recent meeting, in San Francisco, of the American Mining Congress.

Charles H. White has received his discharge from the Army and is returning to resume his practice as mining geologist in San Francisco.

J. W. Sherwin has not resigned as general manager for the West End Mining Co., but his office has been moved from Tonopah to Oakland, California.

Fergus L. Allan, manager of the Mexico mine at El Oro, and **Hedley D. Crowder**, manager for the Mexican Exploration Co., have been taking a holiday in California.

Selwyn G. Blaylock, assistant general manager for the Consolidated Mining & Smelting Co. of Canada, was married to Miss Kathleen Riddle on December 31 at Calgary, Alberta.

Russell R. Bryan has resigned as hydro-metallurgist with the U. S. Bureau of Mines to accept the position as metallurgist with the Sunnyside Mining & Milling Co., at Eureka, Colorado.

Edgar Rickard, **Millard K. Shaler**, and **Walter L. Brown** have received the honor of being made Chevaliers of the Legion of Honor in recognition, by the French government, of their work in behalf of the Belgian Relief Commission in the invaded territories.

C. F. Kelley of the Anaconda, **Joseph R. Clendenin** and **Murray Guggenheim** of the A. S. & R., and **R. L. Agassiz** of the Calumet & Hecla sailed from New York to Europe on January 20 in order to confer with the foreign metal consumers on behalf of the Copper Export Association.

A. T. Thomson, assistant to the president of the Phelps Dodge Corporation, Copper Queen branch, and **John S. Williams, Jr.**, general manager for the Moctezuma Copper Co., at Nacozari, were at Bisbee last week in conference with **G. H. Dowell**, general manager of the Copper Queen branch.

The California Chapter of the American Mining Congress announces the following members elected on January 16:

Directors for one-year term: Andrew Carrigan, L. D. Gordon, M. H. Whittier, K. R. Kingsbury, and Clifford G. Dennis.

Directors for two-year term: Albert Burch, George W. Metcalfe, W. J. Loring, E. L. Doheney, and John Barneson.

Directors for three-year term: F. W. Bradley, T. A. Rickard, J. H. Mackenzie, L. P. St. Clair, and H. R. Gallagher.

Mr. Rickard has declined the honor, believing that he can be more useful as a detached critic and friend of the Congress.

THE METAL MARKET

METAL PRICES

San Francisco, January 21

Aluminum-dust, large and small lots, cents per lb	65—70
Antimony, cents per pound	8.00
Copper, electrolytic, cents per pound, in carload lots	[illegible]
Lead, pig, cents per pound	5.75—6.75
Platinum, per ounce	$108
Quicksilver, per flask of 75 lb	$100
Spelter, cents per pound	9.00
Zinc-dust, cents per pound	16.00

EASTERN METAL MARKET

(By wire from New York)

January 21.—Copper is inactive. Lead is dull. Speller is lifeless.

SILVER

Below are given official (not Government) quotations, in cents per ounce, of silver 999 fine. In order to make prompt settlements with smelters and brokers, producers allow a discount from the maximum fixed price of $1.01¼, hence the lower price. The Government has not fixed the general market price at $1, but will pay this price (as from April 23, 1918) for all silver purchased by it. The equivalent of dollar silver (1000 fine) in British currency is 48.65 pence per ounce (925 fine), calculated at the current rate of exchange. On August 15, 1918, the Treasury announced that the maximum price was fixed at $1.01½ per ounce. The British government fixed its maximum at 49½ pence, on September 2, but on November 12 this was changed to 48¾ pence, and on December 13 to 48 7/16 pence.

Date	New York	London		Average week ending	
Jan. 15	101.12	48.44	Dec.	10	101.12
16	101.12	48.44	"	17	101.12
17	101.12	48.44	"	24	101.12
18	101.12	48.44	"	31	101.12
19 Sunday			Jan.	7	101.12
20	101.12	48.44	"	14	101.12
21	101.12	48.44	"	21	101.12

Monthly averages

	1916	1917	1918		1916	1917	1918
Jan.	56.76	75.14	88.72	July	63.06	78.92	99.62
Feb.	56.74	77.54	85.79	Aug.	66.07	85.40	100.31
Mch.	57.89	74.13	88.11	Sept.	68.51	100.73	101.12
Apr.	46.37	72.51	95.35	Oct.	67.86	87.38	101.12
May	74.27	74.61	99.50	Nov.	71.60	85.97	101.12
June	65.04	76.44	99.50	Dec.	75.70	85.97	101.12

COPPER

Prices of electrolytic in New York, in cents per pound.

Date			Average week ending	
Jan. 15	20.50	Dec.	10	26.00
16	20.50	"	17	26.00
17	20.50	"	24	26.00
18	20.50	"	31	26.00
19 Sunday		Jan.	7	21.80
20	20.50	"	14	20.75
21	20.50	"	21	20.50

Monthly averages

	1916	1917	1918		1916	1917	1918
Jan.	24.30	29.53	23.50	July	25.66	29.67	26.00
Feb.	26.62	34.57	23.50	Aug.	27.03	27.42	26.00
Mch.	26.65	36.00	23.50	Sept.	28.28	25.11	26.00
Apr.	28.02	33.16	23.50	Oct.	28.50	23.50	26.00
May	29.02	31.69	23.50	Nov.	31.95	23.50	26.00
June	27.47	32.57	23.50	Dec.	32.89	23.50	26.00

LEAD

Lead is quoted in cents per pound, New York delivery.

Date			Average week ending	
Jan. 15	5.62	Dec.	10	7.05
16	5.62	"	17	7.05
17	5.62	"	24	6.45
18	5.62	"	31	6.10
19 Sunday		Jan.	7	5.80
20	5.62	"	14	5.75
21	5.62	"	21	5.62

Monthly averages

	1916	1917	1918		1916	1917	1918
Jan.	5.95	7.64	6.85	July	6.40	10.93	8.03
Feb.	6.23	9.10	7.07	Aug.	6.28	10.75	8.05
Mch.	7.26	10.07	7.26	Sept.	6.86	9.07	8.05
Apr.	7.70	9.38	6.99	Oct.	7.02	6.97	8.05
May	7.38	10.29	6.88	Nov.	7.07	6.38	8.05
June	6.88	11.74	7.38	Dec.	7.55	6.49	6.90

TIN

Prices in New York, in cents per pound. The monthly averages in 1918 are nominal. On December 3 the War Industries Board fixed the price to consumers and jobbers at 72½c. f.o.b. Chicago and Eastern points, and 71¼c. on the Pacific Coast. This will continue for some months.

Monthly averages

	1916	1917	1918		1916	1917	1918
Jan.	41.76	44.10	85.13	July	38.37	62.60	93.00
Feb.	42.60	51.47	85.00	Aug.	38.88	62.53	91.33
Mch.	50.50	54.27	85.00	Sept.	36.66	61.54	80.40
Apr.	51.49	55.63	88.53	Oct.	41.10	62.24	78.82
May	49.10	63.21	100.01	Nov.	44.12	74.18	73.67
June	42.07	61.93	91.00	Dec.	42.55	85.00	71.52

ZINC

Zinc is quoted as spelter, standard Western brands, New York delivery, in cents per pound.

Date			Average week ending	
Jan. 15	7.60	Dec.	10	8.61
16	7.60	"	17	8.58
17	7.60	"	24	8.45
18	7.45	"	31	8.13
19 Sunday		Jan.	7	7.93
20	7.45	"	14	[illegible]
21	7.45	"	21	[illegible]

Monthly averages

	1916	1917	1918		1916	1917	1918
Jan.	18.21	9.75	7.87	July	9.90	8.98	8.72
Feb.	19.99	10.45	7.97	Aug.	9.03	8.58	8.87
Mch.	18.40	10.78	7.67	Sept.	9.18	8.33	9.58
Apr.	18.62	10.20	7.04	Oct.	9.92	8.32	9.11
May	16.01	9.41	7.29	Nov.	11.81	7.76	8.75
June	12.85	9.63	7.92	Dec.	11.26	7.84	8.49

QUICKSILVER

The primary market for quicksilver is San Francisco, California being the largest producer. The price is fixed in the open market, according to quantity. Prices, in dollars per flask of 75 pounds:

Date				
Dec. 24	110.00	Jan.	7	110.00
31	110.00	"	14	105.00
		"	21	100.00

Monthly averages

	1916	1917	1918		1916	1917	1918
Jan.	222.00	81.00	128.00	July	81.20	102.00	120.00
Feb.	295.00	126.25	118.00	Aug.	74.50	115.00	120.00
Mch.	219.00	113.75	112.00	Sept.	75.00	112.00	120.00
Apr.	141.60	114.50	115.00	Oct.	78.20	102.00	120.00
May	90.00	104.00	110.00	Nov.	79.50	102.50	120.00
June	74.70	85.50	112.00	Dec.	80.00	117.42	115.00

UNITED STATES CONTROL OF MINERALS

The United States is more nearly self-sustaining in regard to mineral commodities as a whole than any other country on the globe, according to C. K. Leith of the U. S. Geological Survey. The following statement summarizes qualitatively our position:

1. Minerals of which there is an adequate supply or exportable surplus in the United States:

A. Minerals of which our exportable surplus dominates the world situation: Copper and petroleum.

B. Minerals of which our exportable surplus constitutes an important but not a dominant factor in the world trade: Sulphur, phosphate, silver, iron and steel, coal, cement, uranium, and radium.

C. Minerals of which our exportable surplus is not an important factor in world trade. Small amounts of most of these minerals have been and will doubtless continue to be imported because of special grades, back-haul, or cheaper sources of foreign supply, but these imports are for the most part incidental: Lead, zinc, aluminum and bauxite, gold, tungsten, molybdenum, asphalt and bitumen, pyrite, barite, fluorspar, building-stone (except Italian marble), cadmium, gypsum, lime, tripoli and diatomaceous earth, mineral paints (except umber, sienna, and ochre from France and Spain), pumice, garnet, salt (except special classes), talc, arsenic, bismuth, bromine, artificial abrasives, corundum, and emery (except naxos emery), fuller's earth, and mercury.

2. Minerals for which the United States demand must continue to be met by imports:

A. Minerals for which the United States must depend almost entirely on other countries: Tin, nickel, platinum and metals of the platinum group.

B. Minerals for which the United States will depend on foreign sources for a considerable fraction of the supply: Antimony, vanadium, zirconium, mica, monazite, graphite, asbestos, ball clay and kaolin, chalk, cobalt, naxos emery, and grinding-pebbles.

3. Minerals normally imported into the United States which in future can be largely produced from domestic sources if it seems desirable:

A. The following minerals were mainly imported before the War, but under war conditions the domestic resources have been developed to such an extent that the United States can become self-sustaining if desirable, though at so great a cost that a protective tariff will be necessary if these industries are to survive: Nitrates (except potassium nitrates), potash, manganese, chromite, and magnesite.

Eastern Metal Market

New York, January 15.

All markets are decidedly inactive, and the price tendency is downward.

Antimony is changed but little.

Copper has sold as low as 20c. per pound for first-quarter delivery.

Lead has become inactive again, with lower prices possible.

Tin continues stagnant with fundamental conditions unchanged.

Zinc demand is light, and quotations are lower.

ALUMINUM

Market conditions are governed by the Government maximum prices which are left effective until March 1 for No. 1 virgin metal and for scrap. They are 33c. per lb. for 50-ton lots, 33.10c. for 15 to 50-ton lots, and 33.20c. for 1 to 15-ton lots.

ANTIMONY

The market is quiet and steady, perhaps a little stronger. Quotations are 7.75 to 8c., duty paid, New York, for wholesale lots for prompt and early delivery.

COPPER

Almost each day since the first of January has seen the copper market seeking lower levels. While some think that 20c. is the low mark, others expect as low as 18c. before the turn comes or before bottom is reached. Little is now heard of 23c. copper, excepting for export, which is the quotation still of the Copper Export Association. Both electrolytic and Lake copper are now quoted at from 20 to 21c., New York, for delivery in the next 30 to 90 days, or the first quarter. Some sales have been made at these prices, but no large quantities have changed hands. Nevertheless a fair business has been done and we quote the market at 20.50c., New York, for early delivery. Some producers have made sales at 23c. with the price to be paid ruling at the time of shipment. No sales have been made for foreign shipment, despite statements of buying by Italy. The large foreign countries have big stocks estimated to be sufficient to last two to three months, and it is not expected that buying from this source will materialize before the end of that period. England is officially reported to have had 36,000 long tons in stock on January 1. A few representatives of the Copper Export Association will soon sail for Europe to investigate the copper market and its prospects, and perhaps attempt to make sales. Domestic output has shrunk decidedly in the last few weeks, estimated by some to be only 60% of what it was previous to the end of the War.

IRON AND STEEL

The week has been devoid of features, and the market is quiet. Incomplete surveys indicate that the aggregate of peace-time buying is larger than generally supposed, but no attempt is made to express it in figures. Producers generally describe conditions as better than expected. The trade has been used so long to full-steam operation that it is not yet accustomed to the present low demand. A surplus of labor has already appeared at steel plants with offers to work at lower than existing wage-scales. Estimates of the 1918 output of steel ingots show it to have been 42,212,000 tons, according to statistics compiled by the American Iron & Steel Institute, from reports submitted by 29 companies which made 85.1% of the 1917 output.

LEAD

The market has again turned dull and the quickened demand, evident last week, has disappeared. Quotations are unchanged at 6c., New York, or 5.70c., St. Louis, from the American Smelting & Refining Co., with the outside market at 5.75c., New York. The outside St. Louis quotation for some reason is 5.50c. and not 5.45c. as might be expected, based on the freight differential. There is, however, no demand and no business at these levels. The opinion is expressed that the market may have to seek lower levels before there is any revival of interest. Stocks of lead in Great Britain on January 1 are officially given as 62,852 long tons.

TIN

The market is extremely dull and there seems to be no prospect of its improving soon—not until the restricted conditions are removed. The re-sale or second-hand offerings, mentioned last week, are still unabsorbed and this fact reinforces the assumption that the United States Steel Products Co. is not getting rid of its allocated tin which it holds at the fixed Government price of 72.50c., New York, because the cheaper lots would be taken first. These are held at about 71.50c., New York, which we quote as the nominal market. Tin from American smelters, 99% pure, is offered at 67.50c., New York, while at last accounts metal for shipment from the East is offered at 53c. delivered. These contrasts in price with the fixed one are a source of discontent in the trade. The Tin Importers Association is receiving many responses from tin consumers to its circulars setting forth these facts and pointing out the harm being done to the trade in all its phases by the continuance of this control, and urging a campaign among Congressmen looking to legislation to open the market again as soon as possible. In London, spot Straits tin is quoted at £225 10s. per ton.

ZINC

The market is again lower and the tendency has been downward nearly each day. There has been no improvement in demand, but there has been competition by some interests for the little business going each day. Prime Western for January and early delivery is quoted at 7.25c., St. Louis, or 7.60c., New York, with the leading producers uninterested and refraining from quoting. For February and March delivery, quotations are about 7.12½ and 7c., St. Louis, respectively. An increase in stocks of all grades is shown by the weekly Government report for the week ended January 4; this fact is not a bull factor. England's stocks of zinc on hand January 1 were 22,273 long tons.

ORES

Antimony: No developments in this ore.

Chrome: The War Trade Board announces that applications for licenses to import chromite will be considered, provided shipments were actually in transit on November 11.

Manganese Alloys: It has been officially announced that any British ferro-manganese sold to American consumers prior to April 6, 1917, will be allowed to be imported. It is estimated that 25,000 to 27,000 tons is involved, most of which was sold at from $164 to $185 per ton, seaboard. There is no demand for domestic 70% ferro for which $225 per ton, delivered, is asked.

Molybdenum: There has been more activity, particularly in small lots, which have sold at 80c. per pound of MoS_2 in 90% material. Quotations range from 75c. to $1 per pound.

Tungsten: Buyers are still awaiting developments and the market continues dead. Quotations are entirely absent because of the lack of even an inquiry to test the market. The same is true of ferro-tungsten. Consumers of both concentrate and alloy are apparently fully supplied.

Quicksilver Production in 1918

The domestic output of quicksilver in 1918, according to statistics compiled by F. L. Ransome, of the United States Geological Survey, was 33,432 flasks of 75 lb. each, valued at the average quoted market price at San Francisco ($117.92 a flask) at $3,942,301. Compared with the output in 1917 of 36,159 flasks, valued at $3,808,266, this shows a decrease in quantity of 2727 flasks but an increase in value of $134,035.

The productive States were California, Texas, Nevada, Oregon, and Idaho, named in the order of decreasing importance.

The production of California was 23,231 flasks, against 23,938 flasks in 1917, a decrease of 707 flasks. As usual of late years, the New Idria mine, with which is included the San Carlos mine, yielded nearly half of the total output of the State. Its product was greater than in 1917, and exceeded that of any other year in its history except 1867 and 1868. No other old quicksilver mine in California has so well sustained in recent years a production comparable with that of those early years when quicksilver mining in California was in its prime. Only one other mine in the State, the New Almaden (which includes the Senator mine), produced over 2000 flasks in 1918. New Almaden has produced to date 1,124,100 flasks, and in 1865 alone yielded 48,138 flasks from ore that yielded 11.3% of quicksilver. In total production, New Idria, with 315,434 flasks to the end of 1918, ranks second, and Oat Hill (Napa Consolidated), with 140,000 flasks, comes third. The New Guadalupe, Oceanic, Sulphur Bank, Aetna, and Cloverdale mines each produced over 1000 flasks in 1918; and the St. Johns over 500 flasks. Other mines that yielded less than 500 but more than 100 flasks are the Great Eastern, Socrates, Culver-Baer, Helen, Big Chief, Patriquin, and Cuddeback.

Sulphur Bank nearly trebled its output of the previous year and probably would have made still larger gains were it not for the fact that the high sulphur content of the ore renders furnace treatment and condensation difficult. The Rutherford mine, in Napa county, formerly known as the Bella Union, became productive in 1918 after a period of idleness. A rotary furnace is being put up near-by, and this mine should increase its output in 1919. The Big Chief, near Anderson Springs, Lake county, is a new mine, opened on a body of ore that was discovered at the beginning of the year. The ore extracted has been reduced in the retorts of the neighboring Big Injun mine. The Patriquin mine (formerly the Cholame), in Monterey county, after a period of successful operation with retorts, has been for the time abandoned, and the operations of the Patriquin Mining Co. have been transferred to a hitherto undeveloped deposit about 2 miles from the 20-ton Scott furnace formerly operated by the Kings Quicksilver Mining Co., in Kings county. To this furnace, which is reported to be in excellent condition, the ore from the new mine is hauled in motor-trucks. Prospecting at the Oat Hill mine was carried on during the year, but no quicksilver was produced. The Cloverdale mine, under new management and in spite of an unsatisfactory furnace, notably increased its output in 1918.

In general, quicksilver mining in California maintained fairly well during the year the revival of activity due to the War, as indicated by comparison of the output (33,432 flasks) with the production of 11,303 flasks in 1914. A large number of mines that were formerly productive have remained idle, however, and with the gradual return to normal conditions other mines are likely to revert to this class.

The output of quicksilver in Texas was 8475 flasks, against 10,791 flasks in 1917. The Ellis mine, near McKinney Springs, considerably increased its output; and the Mariposa mine also made a small gain. The output of the Chisos mine, however, declined, and that of the Big Bend showed a still larger falling off. The Big Bend has been nearly exhausted down to the level of the underground water, so that pumping and additional development will be necessary if any considerable output is to be maintained. Prospecting has been continued by the Rainbow Mining Co. on the westward continuation of the Chisos ore-zone, and some ore is reported to have been found.

Nevada produced 1023 flasks, the greater part of which was obtained by the Mercury Mining Co., operating near Ione, in Nye county. The remainder came from small mines in Mineral county, particularly in the Pilot mountains east of Mina and on Mount Montgomery. No output was made by the Goldbanks Quicksilver Co., in Humboldt county. As the production of Nevada in 1917 was 997 flasks, the yield for 1918 shows a small increase.

Oregon produced 673 flasks in 1918, chiefly from the Black Butte mine, but also from the Ranier mine, in Jackson county, which was not in operation in 1917.

No production was reported from Arizona or Washington.

When, in 1917, the Government requisitioned 40% of the output of the principal mines at the price of $105 per flask, an agreement was reached with the producers that quicksilver would not be sold in the open market at more than $125 per flask. The average quotation in San Francisco was $128.06 in January 1918, but declined to $118 in February and $112 in March. It rose to $115 in April, but fell to $110, the lowest monthly average for the year, in May. In June the average quotation was $112, and from July on it has stood at $120.

Quicksilver imported for consumption in the United States for the six months ended June 30, 1918, amounted to 261,879 lb., or 3491 flasks, valued at $365,930. In the 11 months ended November 30, 1918, the exports amounted to 216,770 lb., or 2890 flasks, valued at $313,272.

With the return of peace and a decrease in the Government demand for quicksilver for military purposes, the quicksilver-mining industry, faced with uncertainty as to the future, already shows signs of declining, and unless prices are kept up by some Government action or unless there is a decided fall in the cost of labor and supplies, this decline will probably be rapid in 1919. The exigencies of war have failed to bring to light any large new sources of supply, and it is clear that the output of 36,159 flasks in 1917 marks the maximum response of which the known deposits are capable, even under the unusually stimulating conditions of that and the immediately preceding year.

Arsenic Production in 1918

There was available for consumption in the United States during 1918 approximately 12,000 short tons of arsenic, which quantity about equals the estimated demand and is 3850 tons greater that the average yearly supply (8150 tons) for the period 1911-1916, inclusive.

The domestic production of arsenic in 1918, as estimated from the known production during 11 months, was about 6395 short tons and was made by four companies. This quantity is 10% greater than that produced in 1917. The value of the output in 1918 at a price fixed at 9c. per pound was $1,151,100, but the actual value was probably slightly greater, as that price was not fixed until February 1918. Owing to the lower price fixed under governmental regulation this value is lower by $150,000 that the value of the 5826 tons produced in 1917, according to J. M. Hill.

The imports of arsenic for the first 11 months in 1918 were 5048 short tons, 3480 tons of which came from Mexico, 1566 tons from Canada, and the rest from England and Australia. The total imports for the year will be 5600 tons.

Book Reviews

Topographic Stadia Surveying. By C. E. Grunsky. Pp. 95, ill., index. D. Van Nostrand Co., New York. For sale by 'Mining and Scientific Press', San Francisco. Price, $2.

This book comprises a discussion of the theory and practice of stadia surveying together with reduction tables for both horizontal and vertical distances and a reduction chart. The surveyor that wishes the data on this subject in a compact form with no additional matter will find the book of value.

Introduction to Organic Chemistry. By J. T. Stoddard. Second edition, revised. Pp. 423, index. P. Blakiston's Son & Co., Philadelphia, 1918. For sale by 'Mining and Scientific Press'. Price, $1.50.

Organic chemistry is the chemistry of the compounds of carbon. The number of compounds that contain carbon is very large, and those who wish to get an insight into the C-H-O series will find everything discussed in this work. Their study is naturally rather highly technical. Cyanide and flotation men will find notes on cyanides and oils, these substances being compounds of carbon.

Mill and Cyanide Handbook. By A. W. Allen. Pp. 128, charts, index. Charles Griffin & Co., London, and J. B. Lippincott Co., Philadelphia, 1918. For sale by 'Mining and Scientific Press'. Price, $2.

The author of this little work has had considerable experience in gold and silver ore treatment in Africa, Australia, Mexico, and South America. Along with much research, he has been particularly observant and kept copious notes, many of which appear in the book before us. While essentially a compilation—there being no discussions of methods—the mill operator will find the comparative data he needs in short tables, a somewhat unusual arrangement. Some of these cover lime and caustic soda, oxidizing agents, conversion factors, decimal equivalents, capacity of leaching and solution tanks, screens, testing for alkali and cyanide, crushers, stamp, ball, and tube-mills, filtration, recovery of precious metals, and the conveyance of ore, pulp, and solution. The 21 pages of treatment flow-sheets give as many process from ore to bullion, from pulp to bullion, and from precipitate to bullion. These are very clear, the important points in the charts being in capitals. The next 19 pages consist of report forms of all departments in mills. A new glossary of mill and laboratory terms completes a reliable and practical handbook for the millman's desk.

Handbook of Mathematics for Engineers. By Edward V. Huntington and Louis A. Fischer. Pp. 186, ill., index. McGraw-Hill Book Co., Inc., New York. For sale by 'Mining and Scientific Press', San Francisco. Price, $1.50.

This is a re-print of sections 1 and 2 of Marks' 'Mechanical Engineers' Handbook'. The first section contains mathematical tables, such as squares and square roots, cubes and cube roots, areas and volumes, logarithms, radians, trigonometric functions, reciprocals, hyperbolic logarithms and other hyperbolic functions, and interest and annuity tables. It also contains tables of weights and measures, both common and metric, work and energy units, Baume degrees, and miscellaneous conversion tables. While some of the tables are not arranged in the manner most familiar to engineers, a little practice should make anyone accustomed to them. The second is devoted to mathematics, the various divisions being arithmetic, geometry and mensuration, algebra including determinants, trigonometry, analytical geometry, differential and integral calculus, graphical representation of functions, and vector analysis. In the small space that is available, little except rules and formulas can be given, there being little room for explanations. This part of the book is therefore of value mainly as a reference book for the engineer who has forgotten only part of his college mathematics, rather than for the man that has forgotten all, or nearly all of them. The book's principal value lies in the fact that all the material it contains is not available elsewhere in this convenient pocketbook form.

Handbook of Machine-Shop Electricity. By C. E. Clewell. Pp. 447, ill., index. McGraw-Hill Book Co., New York. For sale by 'Mining and Scientific Press', San Francisco. Price, $3.

The use of electricity in the machine-shop both for lighting and for power has become so general that there is need for a convenient handbook for the use of managers and foremen. This need is met by the present volume. The language is as non-technical as is possible for a book of this character, and, while it could hardly be used as a text-book, the book will be serviceable to men of relative little technical education along these particular lines. The divisions of the book are as follows: Abbreviations, Terminology, and Units; Circuits, which includes wiring for both direct and alternating current; Costs, mainly pre-war, but some of them, unfortunately, are not dated; Communication and Distant Control; Current Supply, Generators, and Transformers; Electro-chemical, Soldering, and Welding; Heating and Magnetic Apparatus; Lamps and Shop-Lighting; Measuring Instruments and Measurements; Motors.

SALE OF GOVERNMENT EQUIPMENT

Ten million dollars worth of equipment owned by the United States Spruce Production Corporation, with headquarters at Portland, Oregon, is to be sold, and sealed bids for the same will be received by the sales in the Yeon building in that city up to and including February 15. Members of the sales board, appointed by Brigadier-General Brice P. Disque, commanding officer of the corporation, are Major Watson Eastman, president, Captain I. D. Wolf, Captain H. C. Eustis, and Lieutenant Louis P. Pink, the last being recorder. This great organization during its operations directed the activities of 130,000 men.

The equipment, which consisted of everything from picks and shovels to complete railroads and mills, capable of producing stock from the huge tree in the forest to the finished plank ready for shipment to the airplane factory, is in excellent condition and much of it was never used because of the abrupt ending of the War. The plant has been stored at Vancouver, Washington, where it may be inspected by interested persons, upon proper certification by the board in the Yeon building at Portland.

MINING DECISION

Mining Option—Effect of Failure in Payments

A contract to convey mining claims that binds the holder thereof neither to make the specified payments nor to do or perform any of the acts stipulated therein to be performed by him except during the life of the agreement, and that expressly gives him the option either to comply with its terms or forfeit the 'option', is merely an option contract. The holder is not a purchaser but merely the owner of an option. If he does not live up to the terms of his option in making payments, the owner of the claims may not only repossess himself of the property, but may also enforce the right to retain the mining machinery and equipment placed thereon by the delinquent purchaser if such right was given him under the option. The owner does not have to rescind the contract in order to sue the option holder for such recovery.

Smith v. Beebe (Idaho), 174 Pacific, 608. June 26, 1918.

EDITORIAL

LAST year the Rand produced 8,416,000 fine ounces of gold, worth $173,958,720. This is the lowest output since 1914 and compares with 9,022,263 ounces in 1917 and 9,295,538 ounces in 1916. An epidemic of influenza affected production adversely during the last quarter of 1918.

THE 119th meeting of the American Institute of Mining Engineers will be held at New York on February 17 and 18. One joint session will be held with the American Institute of Electrical Engineers and two joint sessions with the Canadian Mining Institute. A delegation of Canadian engineers is expected and it is proposed to emphasize the fraternization of the two neighboring and neighborly peoples in dealing with after-the-war problems.

MOLYBDENITE has been found at a depth of 1320 feet in the Silver Pick mine at Goldfield. Mr. G. F. Dyer, the superintendent, informs us that the molybdenite occurs in quartz veins traversing the alaskite and has been followed for 135 feet in depth, a thickness of 72 feet, and a length of 100 feet. The average content is 2% molybdenite, and with it are found gold and silver, up to $75 in value, but sporadically. It remains to be ascertained, by exploration, whether this is an orebody or a mineralogic eccentricity.

WE note a paragraph in a local paper praising the work done by the geologists of California under the auspices of the State Council of Defense in finding supplies of chrome, manganese, and other war-minerals. Reference is made to the survey of our State resources made by Mr. George D. Louderback, professor of geology in the University of California. We happen to know how conscientiously and effectively he labored in the good cause, co-operating with the Bureau of Mines and the Geological Survey in a manner and with a spirit that do him infinite credit.

MINERALS SEPARATION, in trying to enjoin the Butte & Superior from disposing of its assets pending action on the mandate of the U. S. Supreme Court, followed the old tactics of claiming everything in sight, namely, the $18,000,000 of total profit made during the 12 years in which the Butte & Superior company has been engaged in mining and milling operations. More than once Minerals Separation has tried to collect royalty on all the ore that goes to a mill, even when only a fraction of it is subjected to flotation. They have tried to levy toll on ore that has been hand-picked, jigged, concentrated on tables, and so forth. It is this greedy policy, plus attempts to bulldoze the profession, that has developed a general dislike of them and of the incubus they hope to place permanently on the mining industry.

PLATINUM on the Pacific Coast is associated with chromite, ilmenite, magnetite, and various silicious minerals, the aggregate constituting what is known as 'black sands'. The U. S. Bureau of Mines, through one of its staff, Mr. R. R. Hornor, has recently investigated some of the more promising localities in Coos, Curry, and Josephine counties of Oregon, and in Del Norte county, California, to ascertain whether the deposits were valuable enough to exploit for platinum and gold. The Bureau now reports, in Technical Paper 196, that "in general the black-sand deposits are disappointing in both value and quantity; they rarely contain enough gold and platinum or occur in adequate quantity to be exploited at a profit. There are, it is true, a few favored places where small areas of the black sand show some precious-metal content, and these may become the site of small operations . . . The chief difficulties in the profitable exploitation of these deposits are: first, lack of uniformity in occurrence and metallic content, and, second, the high cost of mining and treating the material. . . ." This conclusion should once and for all settle—*pace* Dr. David T. Day—the many reports of rich black sand along the coast of California and Oregon.

ENGINEERING knows no boundaries, natural or strategic. It is interesting to note that a San Francisco firm of engineers, Bradley, Bruff & Labarthe, has been retained by the Penarroya Mining & Metallurgical Company to design a complete smelting and refining plant for the company's properties at Penarroya, in Spain. The company itself is French and has its headquarters at Paris. In our issue of October 12 we published a summary of the annual report of this famous enterprise, which in 1917 marketed 7,715,354 ounces of silver, 330,708,400 pounds of lead, and 3,740,600 pounds of zinc. The company owns large coal mines and a fleet of cargo-vessels; it is operating a new smelter at Marseilles and is engaged in mining and metallurgical operations in Algeria and in Tunis. In 1917 it distributed $2,350,000 in dividends to its shareholders. We are informed that the new smelting equipment will include the usual crushing and sampling machinery, multiple-hearth roasters and Dwight-Lloyd sintering machines, four large blast-furnaces for smelting lead ore and one blast-furnace for copper ore, also a lead-copper matte-converting plant, a complete zinc desilverizing lead refinery, and lead manufacturing machinery. The furnaces will be fired with pulverized coal. We hope to publish a detailed description of this smelter at a later date.

SEVERAL telegrams and letters have come to us in regard to the preventive of influenza, namely Calcreose, the use of which was described in our issue of January 18. As we have stated in an editorial note appearing in the same issue, this prophylactic can be obtained from the Maltbie Chemical Company, of Newark, New Jersey. We find now that Wakelee's Pharmacies in San Francisco have it in stock, for instance, at 58 Market Street. The author of the article is Dr. C. T. Baldwin, of New York. Calcreose can be obtained in tablets, but the better form is in powder, from which any druggist can prepare the medicine in 24 hours, in the proportion of one pound of Calcreose to one gallon of water. The dose is one teaspoonful in a wine-glass of water every four hours as a preventive, and two to four teaspoonfuls every two hours for influenza or pneumonia. The No. 2 tablets contain four grains of Calcreose powder, with a little iron, arsenic, and strychnine, as a tonic for use during convalescence. Dr. Baldwin says he is "increasingly sure that the solution is an efficient prophylactic against influenza. It enables the physician to control the septic conditions not only in severe influenza but even after pneumonia has developed it so modifies the infection and toxemia as to enable the physician to treat pneumonia successfully."

Another Gold Report

We have received a copy of the report of the committee, under the chairmanship of Lord Inchcape, appointed to advise the British government on the policy of aiding the production of gold. The terms of reference were as follows: "To consider and report upon the effect of the War upon the gold production of the British empire, with reference more particularly to the treatment of low-grade ores, and how far it may be of importance to the national interests to secure the continuance of the treatment of such ores and generally how to stimulate the production of gold." The report can be summarized in one word: No. The committee answers in the negative to every suggestion embodied in the terms of reference. It finds that the production of gold in the Empire did not decline during the period of the War, as compared with the corresponding period immediately preceding. The lessened output of the Transvaal in 1917 was due, it is stated, to a shortage of explosives, although shortage of labor was a contributory factor, but this was not due "to any large extent" to the War. The tonnage of low-grade ore treated in the Transvaal has not been diminished by the War. The decreased exploitation of low-grade ore, in favor of richer ore, "will not within any measurable period reduce the output of the Empire" and the continued working of low-grade mines therefore is not "of any great importance to the national interests." The decline in Australasia was "normal and due in the main to natural causes" aggravated by increased costs and deficiency of labor caused by the War. The report concludes by refusing to recommend "any bounty or subsidy for the purpose of stimulating the gold output; gold being the standard of value, no more can properly be paid for it than its value in currency." These findings will disappoint the mining community in London, at Johannesburg, and at Melbourne, because they seem to ignore several fairly obvious facts, such as the fluid price of gold in terms of paper currency. Moreover, whereas normally the commodity value of gold is regulated by the laws of supply and demand, it is patent that the War introduced abnormal conditions, of which the most unfortunate was the lavish issue of paper money, in the form of notes and bonds, by the belligerent governments. This interfered directly with the demand for gold, even in countries where gold was not immediately commandeered. Opportunity for further argument remains, especially in regard to the working of low-grade mines. Even a mine that yields no profit is beneficial to the community, and to the nation, because it affords employment and furnishes training to those connected with it; moreover, whether the gold produced be won at a profit or not, it vitalizes the arteries of commerce. The Committee, we venture to say, shows a narrow imagination and possibly lack of knowledge in dismissing the low-grade mines so bluntly. With one of the Committee's incidental observations we agree: "The gold producers have argued that the unavoidable expansion of currency by the issue of currency notes has raised prices against them unduly as against the producers of other commodities who have been able to obtain higher prices for their products, but it is to be remembered that the gold producers have always had the advantage of the standard price of their product during the periods when the price of other commodities has fallen." That is true, and in the backward swing of the pendulum the gold miner will find, we trust, a corrective for the disadvantage under which he has had to labor during the last four years; always provided that the swing of the pendulum is not checked by artificial restraints, such, for example, as the proposed international pool for obviating the necessity for shipping gold from country to country whenever trade-balances have to be settled. The Committee was assisted by the technical advice of Mr. William Frecheville, Professor of Mining in the Royal School of Mines. His review of gold mining in the British empire is given in an appendix to the report and we shall publish it at the earliest opportunity.

Mining v. Bolshevism in Russia

The impact of Bolshevism on mining in Siberia was described recently in London by the chairman of the Irtysh Corporation when addressing the annual meeting of the shareholders. This holding company, formed soon after the commencement of the War, is an outgrowth of the Russo-Asiatic Corporation, which, in 1912, acquired the Ridder concession, covering 1600 square miles, and the Ekibastus coalfield in the Altai region of Siberia. As Mr. Leslie Urquhart, the chairman of this company, said, at the meeting, with pardonable pride, there has been built a great industry, in spite of many difficulties, so that at the end of 1916 an output of finished metals was being made from the ores mined at Ridder and smelted at Ekibastus, these two points being joined by a broad-gauge railroad 90 miles long. In March 1917 the revolution in Russia created troubles exceeding those arising from the War, yet the company completed its plant for extracting the lead, silver, and gold in its ore, so that it is now prepared to deliver zinc, lead, silver, gold, and copper on the market. Under normal conditions this enterprise would have reached the productive stage earlier, but late in 1917 the deleterious effects of Bolshevist activity among the workers was apparent and the interference with operations became a severe handicap. The management decided to curtail operations gradually without exciting too much attention from the Soviets. Not until 1918, however, did the Red Guards of the Bolshevist regime obtain control of the Trans-Siberian Railway. Then by aid of the German and Austrian prisoners of war they seized this continental artery of transport, but by that time the policy of closing-down had been carried out both at the metal and coal mines. In May the Bolshevists attempted unsuccessfully to work the Ekibastus collieries. The company's workmen, particularly the Kirgiz, who are the Turkomans, of pastoral and nomadic habits, refused to work for the Bolshevists. In order, however, to prevent the scattering of skilled labor, a portion of the staff remained on the ground and employed a force sufficient to operate the machine-shops, foundries, and the company's branch railways, one 75 miles long to Ust Kamenogorsk, on the Irtysh river, and the other 90 miles long, to Ekibastus, in the province of Semipalatinsk. This prevented theft and sabotage. The Bolshevists were in power for only a few months in Siberia, from February to May, by which time bands of Czecho-Slovak prisoners of war, aggregating 50,000, broke away from the mob of anarchists and joined the opposition. By the end of June these Czecho-Slovaks, aided by Cossacks and others, had driven the Bolshevist forces out of western Siberia. They joined the Russians under Semenoff and their own compatriots in eastern Siberia, so that by August the whole country from the Volga to the Pacific was rid of Bolshevist domination. In August the company resumed the production of coal at Ekibastus and in November coke was being made once more. Owing to the high local prices then prevailing this production proved extremely remunerative. The lead plant is about to be re-started, because the demand for shot is acute and this branch of the company's business should also be highly profitable. It is deemed inopportune to make zinc at present, owing to the closing of outlets to the markets for that metal. The mill at Ridder will treat the old dumps and also the gold ore from the Sokolni mine, but the Ridder mine itself will not be unwatered just now. The company's steamers on the river Irtysh are being overhauled preparatory to navigation this spring and when again in operation this traffic should yield a substantial revenue. In short, the policy of the management has been to feel its way and to start such departments as can be made immediately remunerative. The labor question is crucial. A persistent effort has been made by the company to provide for the comfort of the workmen and their families. Colonies of dwellings, with proper sanitary arrangements and an adequate supply of water, fuel, and light, have been provided; likewise co-operative stores, vegetable gardens supplying their products at cost-price, schools, churches, clubs, and hospitals have been established. This has been done both at Ridder, where the metal mines are, and at Ekibastus, on the coalfield. The company has introduced labor-saving appliances and pays comparatively high wages. This liberal policy has attracted good workers and created cordial relations between the management and the men, as is proved by the fact that the latter continued to work for four months without wages, asking only to be provided with food, and they refused to work for the Bolshevists. At the coal mines 80% of the men are Kirgiz; they are intelligent and tractable. The Russian managers and chiefs of staff have proved loyal and capable during the times of stress. The metal mines are estimated to contain 3,534,000 tons of ore in reserve; from this a profit of $65,000,000 is anticipated. At Ridder a concentrating mill and sulphuric acid works are in operation. The coal mines are producing 150,000 tons per annum. At the collieries are the smelters, with a capacity of 15,000 tons of refined lead and 5000 tons of refined spelter per annum, and with more than ample capacity for extracting the accompanying precious metals. Evidently this is a large, diversified, and exceedingly interesting enterprise. Messrs. R. Gilman Brown, Thomas J. Jones, and William C. Madge are the engineers to whom the credit for the technical work is due, but the big task of organization and direction is largely in the hands of Mr. Urquhart, who knows Russia intimately and has been at the back of the more important part of recent British mining undertakings in Siberia. The Kyshtim and Tanalyk corporations, two enterprises with which Mr. H. C. Hoover was connected at the start, were more exposed to Bolshevist misrule because their properties are nearer European Russia. In December 1917 the Kyshtim plant was 'nationalized' by decree of the Soviet; it was operated by a Workmen's Committee until May 1918, when the Czecho-Slovaks routed the Bolshevist forces near the town of Kyshtim. The Provisional Government re-started operations and later placed one of the company's general managers in charge, the works themselves not having been damaged during the interregnum. The establishment is now being re-organized and the company resumes, as regards title, its former status. After such an orgy of disorder it is difficult to restore former conditions, but as the new government of Siberia becomes strengthened it will be easier to repair the normal economic life of the country. This is now being done in places. The new government, according to Mr. C. J. Cater Scott, the chairman of the Kyshtim Corporation, "has gained the support of experienced public men in the country who have hitherto been reluctant to join any of the experimental administrations." Among them are men in whom he and his co-directors have unlimited confidence. It is important to note that the Siberian government "has recognized its liability for damages and financial expropriation or loss caused by the Bolshevist regime, and when the proper time comes a claim will be preferred by the company for restitution of materials and funds expropriated by the Bolshevists." We quote Mr. Cater Scott, who also stated that the Kyshtim enterprise is capable of producing from 12,000 to 15,000 tons of copper per annum. It has a sulphuric acid works of 8000 tons capacity per annum, a dynamite plant of 1200 tons capacity, and a plant to produce 4000 tons of copper sulphate annually. At the Tanalyk mines, which are in the Ural region, the production of copper, gold, and silver proceeded profitably, thanks largely to the premium obtainable in Russia for all metals, until the close of 1917, when the Bolshevists seduced the younger men among the Russians employed, but failed to mislead the Bashkirs, Mussulmans of Tartar origin, who constitute the native population and the main supply of labor in this region. It is from them that the Tanalyk properties are held under a lease of 76 years, and to them that the company pays a royalty. In March 1918, thanks to the Bashkirs, the mines were freed of the anarchists and later the representatives of the provisional government of the Bashkir community-lands, with headquarters at Orenburg, established an office at Tanalyk. These agents of the new government have shown the most friendly and helpful attitude to the company. Owing to the difficulty of obtaining supplies, such as mercury and cyanide for the mill and coke for the smelter, it is not practicable to resume operations on the maximum scale, but productive work is in progress and the opportunity is being taken to push the construction of a branch railway to connect with the main line. The ore in reserve is valued at $5,000,000. At the Tanalyk meeting Mr. Urquhart recorded his conviction that Russia will soon recover herself, if only the Allies will give a helping hand. He protested against the irresponsible scaremongering that was causing the world to exaggerate the resources of the Bolshevist regime, he pointed to signs of a healthy reaction, and expressed a confident hope that the influence of civilization would assert itself before long. It seems worth while to give this authentic information concerning the experience of typical foreign enterprises in Siberia because it affords direct light on the industrial conditions obtaining there. We note with pleasure that the San Francisco Chamber of Commercial Activities is endeavoring to keep in touch with Russian business. This is useful work, for we look forward to the re-establishment, on a broader basis, of trade between San Francisco and the Russian republic—or republics.

Independence in Minerals

On another page we publish an article on a most timely subject by Mr. George Otis Smith, Director of the U. S. Geological Survey. This article, we believe, is intended as a preface to the forthcoming volume of the 'Mineral Resources'. It is well worthy of the chief of a scientific bureau to which the mining industry has been indebted for aid and guidance since it was first organized by Clarence King in 1879. He reviews the market for mineral products during the War and shows how it reacted to economic laws, creating new demands to which the industry responded. He gives several striking illustrations of the unexpected economic value discovered in scientific researches that at the time they were made seemed to serve no utilitarian purpose. Recent experience has proved how the geologist has developed—how he had to develop—from the academic student of Lyell's and Murchison's time to a pioneer of commerce; he has been required to submit his work to the test of economic usefulness, and he has succeeded triumphantly; he has become a real partner to the engineer and the capitalist, and they appreciate his comradeship. Together they study the conditions governing the exploitation of mineral deposits. We like Mr. Smith's analysis of the various factors influencing successful mining. He utters a timely warning when he says, "a nation that robs its domestic consumers so as to have an exportable surplus or to sell that surplus at a price below cost will be copying a German blunder in economics." Our home market should always be given precedence, not only on plainly patriotic grounds but out of regard for the welfare of the mining industry itself. Although before the War we were producing a third of the world's output of essential minerals, as soon as international trade was disorganized we had to face an unexpected shortage of many minerals for which theretofore we had looked abroad. The list of such minerals is comparatively small and of some of them we have developed a supply under the spur of necessity. It remains for us to appreciate the strategic value of being wholly independent of foreign supplies and to stimulate the development of the deposits of such minerals as are lacking for our national industries. A survey of the elements of this problem is needed at once, in order to guide possible legislation. The matter must be placed in trustworthy hands, for the experience of war-time has shown how the market for certain mineral products is controlled by small groups having many of the unpleasant features of a selfish monopoly. Such control of the market is today the chief menace to independent activity in exploring for the few minerals inadequately produced in this country.

The Status of Gold

The Editor:

Sir—In this and other periodicals I have read some dozens of articles dealing with the gold situation. It would seem that the need for a greater gold supply is so clearly apparent that no further argument on that score should be necessary. Thus far I have failed to see in any of these articles a clear statement as to the extent to which the gold supply could be increased. This may be due to the fact that it would be extremely difficult to make such a statement with any degree of accuracy. So many factors would have to be taken into consideration that even the most skillful of statisticians would be hard put to it to arrive at anything more than an approximation.

It may be said that the three principal uses for gold are (1) to lend stability to government obligations, (2) to back up currency, (3) to adjust trade balances, internationally and infra-nationally. Obligations have been increased tenfold and new currency has been issued freely, while trade balances have been dealt with in so unheard of a manner that we shall not know just how they stand for some time to come.

The fact is that at this time we have dependable information only as to the extent of national obligations, and about the only way in which a conclusion that will be at all illuminating can be arrived at is to strike a ratio between gold-supply and government obligations as the same existed prior to the War, and apply it to present conditions. Thus we find that in 1914 the total indebtedness of all the nations that subsequently engaged in the War was approximately $28,000,000,000, and that the total gold-supply which these governments could lay hand to at that time was something more than $9,000,000,000. The ratio of gold-supply to indebtedness, therefore, was just about 1:3. The total indebtedness of belligerent nations, figured to the end of 1918, will exceed $160,000,000,000. Assuming that the $9,000,000,000 pre-war gold-supply remains intact, and that every ounce of gold produced in the world during 1915-'16-'17-'18 is added, the total available gold-supply is now $10,720,000,000. This allows $380,000,000 for the 1918 production. The ratio, then, between gold-supply and indebtedness is now 1:15, instead of 1:3. There is to be superadded to this $160,000,000,000, probably $120,000,000,000 which Germany must pay to the Allies, bringing the total national debts of belligerent nations to the neat sum of $280,000,000,000, and fixing the ratio at 1:26.

As a side-light, look at the accumulated interest. The $160,000,000,000 is payable, principal and interest, in gold. Interest at 4% is $6,400,000,000 annually. On the $280,000,000,000 it would be $11,200,000,000 per year. The world's annual gold production is less than $400,000,000, or 6¼% of the interest payable on the $160,000,000,000 and little more than 3½% of the interest on the $280,000,000,000.

To place the nations on a pre-war basis as regards gold-supply and indebtedness we would require a reserve of $53,000,000,000, and an annual production of $2,400,000,000 when we limit the obligations to $160,000,000,000, or a reserve of $93,000,000,000 and an annual production of more than $4,000,000,000 if we take these obligations to be $280,000,000,000. On its face the foregoing may appear to be a *reductio ad absurdum*, but it serves a purpose. It shows that, no matter how ingenious the financing, it is going to be most difficult to stretch our present gold-supply sufficiently to meet all requirements. It must be borne in mind that legislation cannot bring gold into existence. The world has been quite thoroughly prospected and the outlook for the discovery of new goldfields of importance is not particularly encouraging. Hard-headed financiers can scarcely proceed upon the assumption that such discoveries will be made when the fact is that existing gold mines are being exhausted much faster than new ones are being found. We must also remember that gold disappears. Possibly the total production of fifty years past might be accounted for, but the world has been producing gold for thousands of years. It seems reasonable to believe that, at the low rate of production now obtaining, about as much gold will, for all practical purposes, become non-existent as is brought into existence. This would leave us with some 500,000,000 ounces, which must back all national obligations and all currency, supply the requirements of trade and the arts, and generally act as the standard of measurement for all wealth. It would certainly appear that the superstructure of credit that must be built upon this small supply, figured at its present monetary value, might be in danger of becoming top-heavy.

Possibly, if this $10,000,000,000 in gold were held solely as a reserve to protect government obligations, some color of stability might be lent such obligations. But governments cannot hold all of the gold in reserve. In order to do so every nation which has any gold must place a strict embargo on its export. During war-time such an embargo may be enforced because trade is not following the usual channels but in times of peace such an embargo would mean no trade. That would spell general ruin, regardless of whether a nation were or were not well supplied with gold. The ability of the world to rid itself of its enormous burden of debt depends upon unrestricted commerce. Large gold-shipments have always heretofore been necessary in order to adjust credits, both foreign and domestic. Gold is so used because it has a standard value throughout the world, and because such value is great in proportion to its bulk and weight; in fact, this is the most important of the three principal uses for gold, and if commerce is denied this convenience in the future it will be most seriously crippled.

All of these conditions considered together seem to imply that either the monetary value of gold must be increased, or gold must take a partner, or else that both of these things must be brought about. If it is at all possible to make a change in our monetary standards, now is the accepted time. That it is possible seems proved by the fact that, in 1812, England alone did arbitrarily declare the price of gold to be 85 shillings an ounce, and that the world accepted her valuation. The net result of the world-war has been to seat the English-speaking peoples firmly in control of world policies. Great Britain and the United States of America hold absolute control of all gold, whether mined or unmined. Together they command all avenues of trade and can aid or ruin other peoples at their will. We may all be truly thankful that such unlimited power rests with nations which may be trusted to work out the rehabilitations of the world. Surely what England, alone and unaided, accomplished a century ago, can now be done by England and the United States together.

Three things these two must do. They must see to it that the integrity of the obligations of *all* nations is guaranteed. Being themselves the heaviest creditors, it particularly behooves them to do so. They must be certain that currency is backed by an ample supply of standardized metal. They must provide commerce with a supply of gold commensurate with the volume it is sure to attain. To go about it in a manner which is but a temporary makeshift is lacking in dignity and does not discharge the duty which we owe to present and future generations. A subsidy on newly-mined gold may relieve the gold-miner of an unjustly sustained burden and it may increase production a few percentages, but the increment will be slow and of future value, while our needs are present and imeprative. With all due diffidence toward those who now have the matter in band. I would venture to suggest the following:

1. That all gold be called in and paid for at $20.6718 per ounce, and that all silver be called in and paid for at $1.015 per ounce. The manner of payment is inconsequential, but it might be made by the issuance of Treasury certificates payable at a certain date in legal tender as provided at that date.

2. That the monetary value of gold be fixed at double the present, that is, at $41.3436 per fine ounce, and at the same time that silver be standardized at a ratio of 20 : 1 or at $2.06718 per fine ounce.

3. That all newly-mined gold and silver be paid for at the newly established prices.

4. That all metal so accumulated be coined as needed, that not required for coinage to be retained in bar form.

5. That all coin be released freely as called for from any quarter of the globe.

As a matter of course proper precautions should be taken against fraud, both as regards retention of metal called in and as regards proof or origin of newly-mined metal. It is no more difficult to do this than it is to prevent other frauds that are constantly being attempted. Special provisions might be made to apply to articles of sentimental or useful value.

Some may consider the increases in price above suggested too great, but are they? We might count on an accumulation of 600,000,000 oz. of gold, which, in round numbers, would have a value of $25,000,000,000. We might also count on 5,000,000,000 oz. of silver, which would have a value of $10,000,000,000. The value of all standardized metal would then be $35,000,000,000. The annual production, allowing for an augmented supply, would be approximately $1,000,000,000 in gold and $400,000,000 in silver. This would be a real help, but yet it would not have nearly met the indicated requirements.

Some others may agree that a doubled price on gold is reasonable, but that $2.067 per ounce is too much for silver. The only reason that silver is now selling at greatly less than $2 per ounce is because England and the United States have fixed a maximum price on it. Even in the face of this maximum, China offers 20 cents per ounce premium. If the lid were taken off for India and for all other countries under British rule the bids would rise by leaps and bounds. Silver has the disappearing habit to a greater extent than gold. Fully one-half of the silver that is annually coined is retained by India alone. China hoards another big fraction and other Orientals take some more.

No doubt the loudest outcry against standardizing silver would come from those who bow down to the proposition of the inviolability of the gold standard. This is a numerous retinue, but I venture to assert that the personnel of the same consists largely of individuals who have, by force of a habit, contracted some twenty years ago, become addicted to fits at the mere mention of 'bimetalism'. At the time that Bryan advocated the double standard there was no need for it. The only excuse for dragging it in then was that there was an astonishing dearth of real live political issues. The Bryan fiasco was an episode of the last generation, and should not influence this one. Emerson, in his 'Essay on Self-Reliance', says: "A foolish consistency is the hobgoblin of little minds, adored by little statesmen and philosophers and divines. With consistency a great soul has simply nothing to do. He may as well concern himself with his shadow on the wall. Out upon your guarded lips! Sew them up with pack thread, do. Else if you would be a man, speak what you think today in words as hard as cannon-balls, and tomorrow speak what tomorrow thinks in hard words again, though it contradict everything you said today.'' Surely, if ever there was a time when we need a generation of "great souls" it is now. I should hate to be a little statesman leading the hobgoblin bimetallism around always trembling lest it break loose.

What if the United States of America had retained the shibboleths of the past, so that our attitude toward Great Britain as it existed during the first 40 years of our national existence remained unaltered to this day! Would we have allied ourselves with Britain, and would the emancipation of humanity which we now foresee have been possible? I take it that the present generation holds itself unfettered by any of the propaganda of the past, and especially so when that propaganda was conceived without reason. What we are to serve are the needs of today and what, in our best judgment, appear to be the needs of the future. If a man owns a garden-plot he would be foolish to throw away his spade and acquire a gang-plow and a tractor, but if he is to farm a thousand acres he would be equally foolish to retain the spade and curse the tractor as an invention of the devil. With all due respect to some of our hoary statesmen, I think their attitude toward silver places them quite on a par with the supposititious man I have mentioned. The world's need for more standardized metal is so great and so immediate that it is beyond possibility to meet that need in an adequate manner with gold alone. Even now the call of the Orient for coin, not paper, is being answered with silver, and that call is becoming more insistent than ever. The monetary demands of three-quarters of the earth's population can be satisfied with silver.

Many able men have advocated an increase in the monetary value of gold and the standardization of silver. Among all the criticisms of these suggestions I find none that does not admit that such steps would effectually rectify the faults of our monetary system. Mainly the critics state that, first, it would be impossible to make such changes, since to do so would require the consent of all nations, and, second, that it would be undesirable because the result would be to cheapen money by making it more plentiful, and thus would be brought about an unwelcome increase in wages and prices. I assert that both of these claims are unfounded. As to impossibility, the most timorous will admit that the joint power of the United States and Great Britain is unlimited. In view of the remarkable identity of their interests, an agreement between these two should be easily effected. The rest of the world will gladly accept their decision as a boon. As to the undesirability, none exists. That high wages and high prices are not due to a plentiful money supply is proved by the fact that the scale was on the ascendant long before the War began, and it has continued to climb ever since. These conditions have been developed at a time when gold money was never more scarce. It is an immutable law of evolution that as a need becomes existent a power is developed to cope with that need. This law is responsible for the development of the reasoning power in man and for many other things less sublime. In a vague way the demands to be made upon our resources were recognized years before the whys and wherefores were known. Wealth was multiplied manyfold, wages increased, and prices sky-rocketed. Once our conception of dollars in money was limited to seven figures. Even before the War our minds could compass ten, and now it takes more than twelve to stagger us.

What has happened is that our scale of living has been magnified. Not only is material wealth increased in acres of productive land, tons of metal, and bushels of wheat, but the value of each unit measures more dollars. Do we not all recall the time when all attempts to diagnose the situation failed? Now we can do it. The law I have spoken of was at work, and values were being created against the time of need. These are conditions which have been thrust upon us without our volition, and we are just about as able to alter them as we are to change the pattern of the firmament. Labor will not submit to material reduction in wages, and a corrolary of high wages is high prices. Furthermore, I say that the man who engages to readjust these conditions by decreasing the scale of living is a fool. He assumes to accomplish the impossible, and even were it possible the accomplishment would be an injury instead of a benefit. Assume that our country has a debt of $30,000,000,000 to pay, and assume that we are now in position to pay it with 15,000,000,000 bushels of wheat at $2 per bushel. Are we rendering any service to ourselves and to posterity by forcing the price of wheat down to $1 per bushel, and thereby making 30,000,000,000 bushels requisite for the payment of our debt? By so doing are we not obliging ourselves to raise double the quantity of wheat, and does that not double our work?

It is a deluded mind that advocates a decrease in the dollar-value of each unit of effort in order to re-establish the former ratio between value as measured in dollars and the dollars on hand with which to measure. To decrease the value of all effort would be unwise if it were not impossible, while to increase the number of dollars with which to measure the value is not difficult and is the wise course to pursue.

Not long ago I had what I now believe to be a mistaken conception of our needs and of the manner in which they were to be met. It seemed to me that a great injustice was being perpetrated upon both gold and silver miners, and I felt that a bonus on gold and the maintenance of a higher price on silver would eliminate the cause for complaint. This view of the situation is from the point of the miner alone, and is altogether too narrow. The need has assumed such proportions and reaches to such limits that the question is one for statesmen. As is set out in the report of our own committee on gold "the principle of the bonus appears to be in general economically unsound." Apparently the governments of other gold-producing countries view it in the same light. Suppose that, by means of a bonus of $10 per ounce, the annual world production were increased from 20,000,000 oz. to

25,000,000 oz. This 25,000,000 oz. would still, for all monetary purposes, be worth but $500,000,000, while it would have cost $750,000,000. Would not the bonus, instead of ministering to our ills, involve us still further in financial decrepitude? But an increase in the monetary value of gold and the standardization of silver is a means which may be adopted without cost to anyone and with great gain to us all. The nation enhances its wealth to the extent of the increased value accorded to gold and silver. The nation benefits, therefore we benefit because we are the nation. Some people cannot see it that way because they look upon the nation as a seperate entity and clothe it with all the base attributes which they themselves possess. The place for the man who chronically looks upon his government as a wicked power, inimical to him, is a blank wall at sunrise.

The situation in which we find ourselves is this: Although it takes no more effort now to elevate one pound one foot, we must pay more dollars to hire that effort; although it now takes no more bread to sustain life, we must pay more dollars to acquire that bread. Thus the total value of all the labor that may be hired, the total value of all commodities that are purchasable, and the total value of all securities that are outstanding is measured by many more dollars than was the case prior to the War. This is as it should be. Taxes alone will pay the world's debts. The greater the dollar-measure of wealth, the greater the dollar-measure of taxes, and, consequently, the more quickly will the debts be paid. It is far more fitting that we devise a means whereby the supply of dollars is increased to meet conditions, than that we attempt to alter conditions so as to correspond with our supply of dollars.

In answer to those who may claim that the increase in existing dollars will decrease the value of the securities they hold, let me say this: The only way in which these securities will be affected will be that, when interest and principal are paid, payment will be made with a coin half the size of the one now used. The buying power of the income from these securities is already fixed at a new level. We have already adjusted ourselves to this condition. A readjustment of our monetary standards merely rectifies a ratio that has become out of proportion. To increase the buying power of the income from securities is highly dangerous. It would mean that the securities would gravitate to those with money to invest. Eventually a few would hold all the evidences of indebtedness, while the many would be sweating to pay them tribute. One can imagine what this would lead to. Are there not Bolshevists enough?

This generation has imposed an enormous burden of debt, not only upon itself, but upon generations to follow. It is the duty of this generation to devise means whereby the burden may be minimized. I claim that the only way in which this can be effectually accomplished is by maintaining a high scale of prices, and I assert that an essential to maintaining this scale is a complete reorganization of our monetary standards.

San Francisco, January 6. EDW. S. VAN DYCK.

The Market Price of Copper

The Editor:

Sir—In order to set forth the recent dilemma of small mine-owners in disposing of copper ores, I would say that on November 15, 1918, Mr. Bernard M. Baruch, chairman of the War Industries Board, conferred with a committee of the copper industry of America, among which were the following:

Daniel Guggenheim, of the American Smelting & Refining Co.,

C. F. Kelley, of the Anaconda Copper Mining Co.,

Daniel C. Jackling, of the Utah Copper Co.,

R. L. Agassiz, of the Calumet & Hecla Mining Co.

This meeting developed the following decisions, which were to remain effective until January 1, and then be subject to renewal or revision, as already agreed upon. Of these the first two only will be quoted as being pertinent to the subject-matter of this letter, namely:

"1. The present rate of production is to be maintained in the mines, smelters, and refineries, continuous employment being thus insured during the first period of the transition from a war to a peace basis.

2. The present level of prices of the metal and the wage-scale of labor are to be preserved."

You may well imagine my surprise therefore when the Garfield smelter people wrote me on December 16 as follows:

"At the present time the 'Engineering and Mining Journal' is not making any quotations for copper and any ore which we might receive from you will have to be settled for on a basis of a provisional price of 11c. for copper, the balance to be determined when the 'Journal' again makes quotations for copper. In any event, some of the balance would have to be paid on quotation 120 days after settlement of assays."

In the face of the fixed price of 26c. for copper until January 1, such action is unaccountable. On the other hand, the Phelps Dodge Corporation, as in other years of crises in the price of copper, issued a circular letter on December 31, notifying their customers of the dissolution of the fixed price on January 1, and stating that during the period of readjustment, in order to keep their customers going, they would pay 16c. per pound for copper upon sampling, the remainder to be paid from their selling-price 90 days thereafter. This method of settlement, as compared with A. S. & R. quotation mentioned, means to many small shippers the difference between continuance and closing-down, but unhappily Nevadan shippers are not all tributary to the Bisbee smelter, in fact, but a small proportion.

Personally, I am not interested pecuniarily in this matter, but I want to see justice be done for those that are struggling in building up the mining industry. I am personally acquainted with the officers of the Garfield Smelting Co., and know that men of more charming personality do not exist, but even they are compelled to obey the edicts that issue from the New York office.

No really large copper organization with whom I have ever dealt has, to my knowledge, attempted the rank deductions that the A. S. & R. people have made in the purchase of copper ores. In recent years, when copper was quoted around 20c., that company paid but ¾c. for each one cent above 14c., and when copper quotations continued to advance to around 30c., there was paid but ¾c. for each one cent above 17c. per pound for copper. Inasmuch as the regular deduction of 3½c. per lb. was also made, and, in addition, on extremely low-grade ores, a deduction of three-quarters of one per cent (later increased to 1%) was made from the assay-value, which latter sometimes meant a deduction of as much as 40 to 50% of the copper content, instead of the customary 10%, it seems to me that the A. S. & R. Co., and all those concerns that have pursued similar methods, should be compelled to reimburse their customers for the above-mentioned extraordinary deduction of ¼c. per pound, which has been simply taken away from them without any apparent reason whatever during the past three years: the only excuse given me, at the time of its inception, being that the copper market might drop rapidly at any moment, thus leaving them with an enormous stock of high-priced metal on hand, although they were selling their former stock evidently as rapidly as the market advanced. Upon calling their attention to the fact that they might readjust their enforced quotations and deductions after they had marketed their copper, they refused to discuss it further.

The use of copper quotations furnished by any mining magazine for the purpose of settlements would appear to be erroneous, for, however fair it might desire to be, many sellers would consider it to be more or less controlled by the smelters, and it is hardly within the province of any magazine's staff to obtain the average price, which should be based upon the total sales that are made. The 'Engineering & Mining Journal', published in New York, our central mart, has established a notable record for its endeavor to give fair quotations of copper, based, of course, upon actual sales insofar as its staff was able to obtain. The forming of the Copper Export Association recently is designed to save fifteen to twenty millions of dollars annually to the exporters of that metal. Now the question arises, how many millions annually would the domestic ore-sellers save if a proper commission were established, with Government authority, to ascertain the actual price of the metal sold by the Copper Export Association?

Searchlight, Nevada, January 13. W. W. WISHON.

INJURIES IN QUARRIES are mostly the result of falling, rolling, or flying objects. It is therefore necessary to pay more than casual attention to proper methods for removing the danger of falls of overburden or of rocks into the quarry pit. Constant watch must be kept and at frequent intervals tests for scale and loose rock should be made. The walls as well as the roofs of quarry tunnels should be inspected and tested, and also the walls in undercut or open workings. One means of preventing such dangers is to make overburden walls less steep and to strip some distance ahead of quarry operations.

Tungsten and Molybdenum in 1918

The total value of the tungsten marketed in this country, coming from domestic sources, during the year 1918, is estimated by F. L. Hess of the U. S. Geological Survey at $2,557,400. This represents an output of 5020 tons of 60% ore and concentrate. The most productive State was Colorado, which delivered 1910 tons of ferberite; California came next with 1781 tons of scheelite, estimated on the standard basis of 60% WO_3. Nevada was third on the list, having marketed 885 tons, this also being scheelite. The production of Arizona amounted to 213 tons, consisting of mixed wolframite and huebnerite. Practically the whole of the remainder, amounting to 231 tons, was derived from South Dakota, with small quantities from Washington and Utah. The largest single producer of ferro-tungsten in the country was the Vanadium Alloy Steel Co., of Latrobe, Pennsylvania, followed closely by the Primos Chemical Co., of Primos (Philadelphia). Other important reducers of tungsten are the York Metal & Alloy Co., of York, Pennsylvania, the Latrobe Electric Steel Co., through its subsidiary the Hudson Reduction Co., the Capitol Chemical Co. and the Chemical Products Co., both of Washington, D. C. The Black Metals Reduction Co., and the Tungsten Products Co. of Boulder, in Colorado, make ferro-tungsten at the works of the Tungsten Products Co., at Baltimore, Maryland. The Electro-Metallurgical Co., a subsidiary of the Union Carbide Co., at its works at Niagara Falls, New York, smelts tungsten exclusively for E. J. Lavino & Co., of Philadelphia. The Lavino firm also owns the Tungsten Metals Corporation at Boulder, Colorado, which is a mining company under the management of George Teal. The largest consumer of tungsten, in the finished product, is the Crucible Steel Co., of Pittsburgh. This concern likewise maintains a large electric smelter for the reduction of tungsten to the ferro-alloy.

Molybdenum was used in considerable quantity for a time, but the end of the War has caused a decrease in the consumption. It was employed in the crank-shafts and in the connecting-rods of the Liberty motors, these requiring about 250 pounds for the two pieces in each machine. The steel used for this purpose consisted of an alloy with 1% of metallic molybdenum. Steel of that composition could be readily forged, and showed superior strength, especially in resistance to torsional strains. This material was made by the United Alloys Steel Co. at Canton, Ohio, a concern owned or controlled by Garford & Timkin, which is closely associated with the Ford Motor Co. The latter company was preparing to produce thin armor plate containing approximately 1% of molybdenum. This steel gave excellent results in test pieces, and would have been produced in large quantities for use in armoring tanks had the War continued. The armor was made one inch thick, and while not directly specified by the Government, it would have been accepted for the reason that the steel conformed to the tests required by the regulations of the War Department.

The Economic Limits to Domestic Independence of Minerals

By GEORGE OTIS SMITH

The war demands placed upon the United States created many new problems in connection with the supply of raw materials. Not only were former sources of supply cut off by the war's interference with commerce, but the large industrial expansion due to the world's larger need of American manufactured products caused in turn increased consumption of raw materials; the net result was an unprecedented and a too largely unexpected call upon the basal industries of the country—agriculture, forestry, and mining.

Already the United States had become more nearly independent than any other industrial nation in the production of minerals; our output in 1913 was 36% of the total for the world and included even larger percentages of the mineral fuels and copper, aluminum, zinc, and sulphur. Yet there were on the other side of the Nation's ledger notable deficiencies in tin, platinum, nickel, manganese, chrome, potash, and nitrates, and the domestic supply of some of these minerals continues to be hopelessly inadequate. To meet the war demand for every mineral raw material was the larger task set before the mineral industry, and the degree of success attained and its cost are the basal facts in any inquiry as to the economic limits that must be recognized in developing the domestic supply.

The conditions presented in the four years of war have been novel and have changed from month to month. Yet in no sense have these changing conditions been outside the realm of economic law. Premises previously unthought of because they involved facts outside former experience, such as destruction of cargo ships or shortage of freight cars, have formed the basis for action incredible in its novelty, yet so necessary that the term 'war times' was used to express the excuse for every act seemingly in violation of both business sense and economic law. In fact, however, both economic law and business sense were being applied to new problems and in new ways in obtaining the raw materials for a nation's expanded industry.

Under these special conditions of supply and demand some minerals have taken on new values—indeed, certainty of supply has had larger significance than price. These new values may persist for varying periods, but for some products they must be recognized as only temporary.

It is enlightening, however, to note how large a family of inventions and improvisations can be credited to necessity, and how these substitutes born in time of need develop into lively competitors with the older commodities. Thus, certain potassium salts may never recover the industrial fields that were temporarily (it was thought) given over to the equivalent salts of sodium, and sintered dolomite already competes with magnesite, even though a domestic supply of magnesite is now assured and the imported magnesite may be again available as shipping conditions become normal.

The peace readjustment of the mineral industry requires immediate consideration, involving as it does the future of war-born infant industries but first of all the recalculation of the country's needs. It may be only suggested here that the real issue is to what extent it is of national benefit that this or that new industry should be continued, and that national benefit is to be measured in terms of the premise that industry is the basis of social welfare, not an end unto itself or an opportunity for profit to the few. So it becomes a debatable economic question how much influence can be properly exercised on the natural course of commercial evolution. American experience has shown that some industries soon outgrow the need of governmental fostering but that others never grow up. An all-important element in the problem is whether the product meets an essential need of the country.

In speaking of the expected war demands for raw materials the present writer earlier made the statement that "the mineralogic curiosity of one decade may become the valuable ore of the next." As the years of war have passed many illustrations of this truth have come to the notice of the Survey's investigators. Perhaps no better example can be cited than that of the Leucite Hills, in Wyoming. The Government geologist who was classifying the public coal-lands in that vicinity desired to add to our knowledge of this unique occurrence of interesting rock-types, and before the Survey could publish his scientific contribution the world potash situation gave potential economic value to his field-study. His quantitative estimates of possibly available potash-content are now the incentive to large expenditures in working out extraction processes on a commercial scale, and quarry-sites have been selected where he mapped this peculiar rock. The latest example of an unforeseen use of scientific data is the connection that has recently been developed between the shipping program and the Survey's investigations of the quality of water. These studies of the surface-waters of the United States were begun years ago, and their basis has been geologic as well as chemical. The practical usefulness of the results has, of course, been realized from the start, in connection with steam-making and other industrial uses of river-water, but recently it was found that with a supply of brass tubes sufficient only for the condensers of the naval and merchant vessels under construction, steel tubes must be substituted wherever possible in other condenser installations, and the extent of this substitution, as ordered by the War Industries Board, was conditioned by the quality-of-water data furnished by the Survey.

The war program, with its reaction upon industry, has opened the eyes of many to old facts. Mineral raw materials have won a recognition based upon the new realization of their value. De Launay's recent and apt characterization of coal and iron as the two "grand seigneurs" of the mineral world is in strong contrast with the ancient idea of nobility among metals. The new measure of value is usefulness.

Economic geology is useful geology—the theoretical science applied to meet the material needs of man. These human needs as presented in the last four years have demanded a specialized type of geology—the application of geology in terms of commerce. Geology to be most useful in these days of world problems must take the world view of values, and we find ourselves working in commercial geology—that is, geology applied in terms of commerce. The world is the field of commerce, and the requirements of commercial geology are simply that the geologic relations of a Nevadan ore deposit, for example, must be observed with an eye trained to see far beyond the Basin range; the geologist needs to compare the quality and quantity of the unmined ore here with similar facts of nature that give value to the ores in other districts, as in Peru or Burma. Whether the investigator is called a geologist, mining engineer, or economist, his vision must take in not simply the ore minerals as they have been deposited, segregated, or enriched by the processes of nature, but also the smelted ore and the refined metal on their way to the markets of the world, where they can serve mankind. Thus to broaden and extend the investigator's view is not to commercialize his science; it is rather to make geology more useful, and in that way to give the science a higher rank.

Geology must needs continue to furnish the basal facts, but the geologist has a call to go further than he has gone heretofore in the interpretation of his facts—not simply by translating his technical words into the language of the market-place, but, more than that, by showing the relation of geology to national life.

In terms of commercial geology, therefore, ore deposits take on competitive relationships, and in terms of national interest there must be a determination of relative worth. The practical question concerns not simply the quantity of metal present in the ore but the quantity that can be won to the profit of mankind. First of all, then, in fixing the economic limits to the utilization of domestic mineral deposits, comes the balancing of cost of production with the value of the product. This requirement, which holds good in any business undertaking, however small, is none the less operative in an industry viewed in its national aspect. Economic profit is attained only by reducing cost or increasing value until the margin appears on the right side of the account.

Into the cost of production enter the items of transportation, investment, and labor. An industrial leader like Mr. Schwab appreciates the "handicap of distance," although with a sportsmanlike spirit he and other industrial leaders regard this handicap as simply another incentive to American ingenuity, not as a plea for preferential freight-rates. The transportation factor has played a noteworthy part in every large production enterprise in the United States, where commonly mine and market are separated by hundreds if not thousands of miles.

Improvement in transportation, whether interstate or international, tends to the equalization of opportunity: the peoples of the world are brought closer together. Artificial rates, however, in either interstate or international commerce will impose burdens rather than confer benefits, and we cannot afford to throw back to the era of rebates. Therefore the facts of transportation must be written into the statement of production costs; the geologist and the engineer must from the start be geographers, for distance cannot be eliminated from any commercial problem. The place-factor enters so largely into the determination of value of mineral raw materials that many a promoter would gladly have the scientific investigator close his eyes to the facts regarding the accessibility of the deposit under examination. Yet the transportation cost is too often the cause of financial disaster, even when the geologic and other engineering facts have been correctly determined and are favorable to success.

Investment and labor costs come less under the purview of the geologic engineer in his study of mineral resources, yet the power element is one that touches both of these items and is not to be overlooked by any student of industrial problems. It becomes more and more evident that the use of power, either steam or water, will become the deciding factor in American industry. The statistics of man power cited by Butler* furnish the most convincing arguments as to the stability of our copper industry and its ability to dominate the world markets. The community of interest between some of the largest mining and power corporations is therefore to be regarded as a natural development along economic lines—not as an artifice in restraint of trade. Whether cheap power is made available for mine use by private initiative or by public control, the result is the same—cheap raw materials for other industries.

During the war period the value of raw materials was in large part due to the emergency demand, and the experience should leave its realization of the exigency element in the determination of value. Under war conditions no one questions the great advantage of domestic independence in raw materials, and then adequate supply rather than low price is all-desirable. Nearness of source of raw materials is advantageous at other times, but the amount that can then be added to the value on that account is less easily determined. The purchasing agent of a large manufacturing plant may favor the

*Butler, B. S. Copper: U. S. Geol. Survey Mineral Resources, 1917, pt. 1 (in preparation).

near-by to the distant source of raw material and the domestic to the foreign producer as a matter of assurance that there will be no interruption to 'keeping the works running'. Yet the spirit of cost accounting leads usually to the cheapest market. Again it happens that when a productive industry so contributes to some larger business or group of industries as to be absolutely essential to their continuance this key industry takes on a larger significance than its size suggests.

In the consideration of any domestic industry the factor of home consumption must not be overlooked; indeed, home consumption is more directly connected with national welfare than exports. Our high per capita consumption of copper, for instance, means more to the Nation than our exportable surplus of the same metal, the true value of which is indirect through the means it furnishes for trade or exchange for imports of other commodities for our own consumption. A nation that robs its domestic consumers so as to have an exportable surplus or to sell that surplus at a price below cost will be copying a German blunder in economics. Increased consumption of metals and mineral fuels means expansion of all industries, which in turn should mean a larger home market for all the things that go with a higher standard of living.

The Mineral Control Act of 1918 furnishes a too long delayed expression of the emergency value of mineral independence. The exigencies of war revealed many deficiencies in industrial preparedness, and although over one-third of the world output in essential minerals was credited to the United States at the beginning of the war period, the largest part of the raw materials found to be inadequately supplied included minerals and their derivatives. Interruption to the importation of a relatively few ores brought immediate realization of the industrial advantages of a domestic supply, and the coincident shortage in rail transportation showed that the disadvantage of an international long haul differs only in degree from that of too long an interstate haul. The premium that industry can afford to pay for the assurance of an uninterrupted supply of raw material provides the answer to this question of the emergency value of either national or local independence.

The proper valuation of national independence in raw materials therefore requires a careful weighing of the emergency factor, which introduces the insurance idea, as well as an estimating of future possibilities of lower costs as the industry develops.

In every business there are elements of value that do not appear on the cost-sheets. The war record of American business will not be complete except as it includes the story of those producers who kept up their output regardless of the losses involved—a type of patriotism not spectacular, but exceedingly helpful. So, too, in time of peace there may be conditions under which, viewed in the larger way, it pays to do business at a loss.

A composite diagram of either current output or future reserves of the essential minerals for the countries of the world would show so large a centralization in North America as to suggest that here is a group of nature-favored nations. This strategic advantage expresses itself in the well-recognized large degree of self-sufficiency of the United States, so that the question of economic limits to domestic independence concerns a relatively small number of minerals and makes our problem quite different from that in other and less favored nations. However, whether the debatable list includes only chromite, manganese, pyrite, and potash or is much longer, clear analysis of the economic problem is needed, for cost keeping on a national scale is the only safeguard against a loss which is real though not at once apparent.

Whether wisest utilization of mineral resources means full utilization is debatable, and every student of natural resources realizes that the time of utilization is often an element in the degree of wisdom shown. It is not necessarily prodigal wastefulness that only the richest ore is mined when a new district is discovered; creation of transportation facilities, construction of smelters and mills, and general advance in technology are the intermediate steps between bonanza exploitation and the highly organized operation of low-grade deposits. Utah had a long history as a mining State and its contributions to the world's wealth were large before Bingham started a new epoch in copper mining. So, too, the re-working of dumps and of tailing-ponds furnishes illustrations of the complete utilization that is evolved in these changing conditions.

The largest degree of national usefulness will be won from our mineral resources only through the highest industrial efficiency, which is in turn secured by engineering advance and the linking up of mechanical power and man power. This means to the end is typically American, but too much emphasis cannot be put upon the importance of governmental action that is constructive in its co-operation with industry. While, unfortunately, public regulation seems to start usually with measures that are wholly restrictive in effect, because too often abuse of privilege has led to the legislative action, yet regulatory measures can be truly promotive, as has been shown in the recent co-operation of business and the Government. Public interest and private interest in the long run are less antagonistic than either the captain of industry or the public servant has suspected. It is true that the measure of economic worth must be the welfare of the individual, the community, and the people of the Nation, and not the dollar of profit to the corporation or the State, yet only a successful industry can be made to serve both owner and workman and the public as well. If the product is not actually worth its whole cost, no camouflage of bounty or tax exemption or import duty will long conceal the inherent weakness of the industry. The basic importance of the raw material resources to the country makes it a prime public duty of citizens generally to know the facts regarding the mineral industry, and to ascertain these facts the intensive study of our own resources is not enough: we must also acquire a comprehension of what minerals other countries contain to supplement what we have at home.

The Flotation of Galena at the Central Mine, Broken Hill

By R. J. HARVEY

*Introduction. The ore is a complex silver-lead-zinc sulphide associated in the main with quartz, rhodonite, rhodochrosite, and some garnet-sandstone. The assay-value is now approximately 11 oz. silver, 14% lead, 15% zinc. The silver accompanies the galena. The lead is present as a good-grade galena and the zinc as a somewhat low-grade blende not assaying much better than 50% zinc. Crushing to 40-mesh has been found necessary to obtain complete freeing of the mineral particles from the matrix and from each other.

In brief, the milling operations prior to the introduction of selective flotation were:

Crushing to ½ inch and jigging.

Re-grinding the jig-tailing to 40-mesh.

Concentration on Card and Wilfley tables, and Weir-Meredith vanners, the former for the grainy material and the latter for the slime.

Flotation for a leady-zinc concentrate that was re-tabled on Wilfley tables and Weir-Meredith vanners produced an improved grade of zinc-concentrate and gave a little more lead-concentrate. See Fig. 1.

The milling results of the above operations were:

	Proportion %	Silver Oz.	Lead %	Zinc %	Recovery Silver %	Recovery Lead %	Recovery Zinc %
Crude ore	100.0	11.6	14.5	16.4	...	...	...
Lead-mill lead concentrate	15.5	32.9	67.6	6.2	43.9	72.1	5.8
De-leading lead concentrate	1.3	46.3	60.6	13.8	5.3	5.5	1.1
					49.2	77.6	...
Zinc concentrate	30.8	16.1	8.3	45.8	42.6	17.7	85.8
Residue	...	2.3	1.8	2.9	...	...	...

Effective lead recovery 77.6%
" zinc " 85.8%
" silver " 49.2%

Tonnage treated: 4000 long tons per week.

In 1902 or 1903 it was a matter of common observation that, wherever there was a splash of pulp with the consequent aeration, bubbles of air were formed carrying galena, and at one period boys were employed to skim off this froth, which was added to the concentrate before shipment.

The introduction of flotation as a commercial process for the recovery of blende caused the matter, however, to be dropped for the time and no more was done in the direction of galena flotation until the middle of 1913, when the first serious attempt to do so was made. This comprised the erection of a plant on the systems devised by F. J. Lyster and T. M. Owen, and involved aeration aided by the use of an essential oil, namely, eucalyptus. This operated on slimes and demonstrated the possibilities of the selective flotation of galena.

About the same time the then mill-superintendent, A. W. Wincey, designed a crowding-hood on a distributing-box that received the discharge of an elevator carrying pulp, and by this means was able to obtain without cost about 15 tons weekly of a float-lead concentrate rich in silver. This further confirmed the feasibility of selective flotation.

Experimental Work. The use of selective flotation and its evident great bearing on the possible profits from

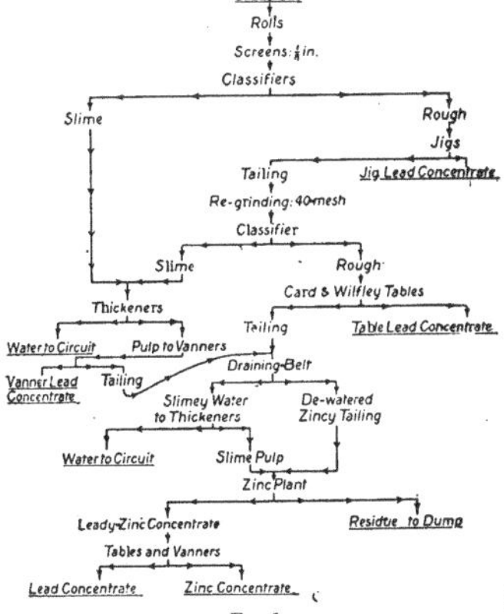

Fig. 1

the company's operations determined the management to erect an experimental laboratory where flotation methods suitable to the ore could be evolved. I was appointed experimentalist in this laboratory. The first important investigation carried out was to determine the possibility of recovering the valuable metals from a large dump of slime, all of which was ten years old. This dump represented the slime accumulated during several years before the flotation process was in use on the mine.

After some experiments, I found it possible to obtain

*A paper read before the Institution of Mining and Metallurgy, London, on November 21, 1918.

a fair recovery of fine argentiferous galena by flotation, using only sulphuric acid as a medium, the results, however, being improved by performing the operation in a flotation circuit (water already used for flotation purposes). This, with the apparatus, was patented in the names of James Hebbard (the manager of the mine) and myself, and assigned to Minerals Separation, Ltd. Following these results an already existing plant was altered to suit the new conditions and commenced operations early in 1914. A description of this plant, the flotation machine of which was the outcome of experi-

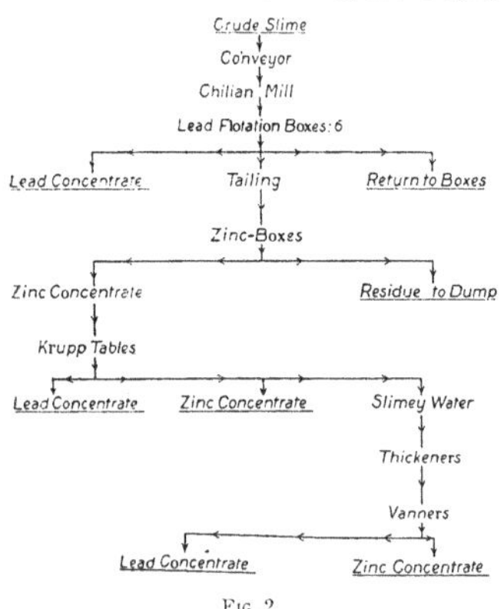

FIG. 2

ments conjointly carried out by the Broken Hill South Silver Mining Co., Amalgamated Zinc (DeBavay's), Ltd., and the Sulphide Corporation, follows later.

While this dump-slime investigation was proceeding, tests were made upon current slime production in the same apparatus, using eucalyptus in place of acid, and indications were obtained of the possibility of future success.

DUMP-SLIME PLANT. It has already been stated that his plant started operations after re-modeling early in 914. Previously it had been used quite successfully to treat the dump-slime making a leady-zinc concentrate, which, however, was not readily marketed, and in consequence in 1909 the plant was stopped and has not since been in operation. The plant lay some distance from the slime-dump; and this involved haulage by rail. Hopper-wagons with bottom-discharge were used. The material was shoveled, after discharge from the wagons, onto a belt-conveyor and fed to a pair of grinding-pans adapted as Chilean mills. After thorough pulping, it was elevated to a set of six mixer-boxes. These boxes, of cast-iron, 3 ft. 6 in. square and 5 ft. deep, were of the under-driven sub-aeration type. The stirrer, which was 18 in. diam. and 3½ in. deep, acted both as agitator and air-pump and ran at a peripheral speed of 2300 ft. per minute.

Immediately before the pulp reached the first box, sulphuric acid was added. Lead-concentrate was removed from the first four boxes, the float from the last two being returned to the feed. Flotation for the remaining valuable metals followed, using acid, eucalyptus, and steam sufficient to raise the pulp to 130° F. The leady-zinc concentrate obtained by this second flotation operation was passed over Krupp tables and Weir-Meredith vanners to induce a further separation of the galena from the blende. It was not expected that the selective flotation would recover all the galena, but that it would catch the finest of the lead unobtainable by ordinary gravity concentration.

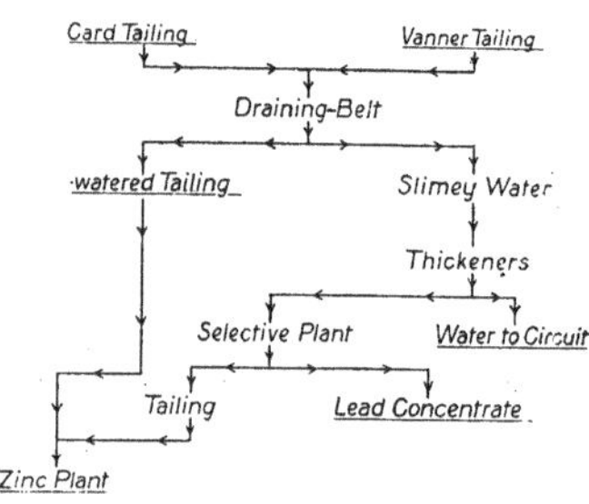

FIG. 3

It must be remembered that the slime being treated was accumulated in days when classification apparatus was not so effective as it is today, and, consequently, quite coarse galena existed in the dump. The pulp would practically all pass 200-mesh, but galena of this size is obtained associated with larger sizes both on a jig and on a table.

This plant (Fig. 2) was in operation with improving results until war broke out in August 1914, when it was once more stopped and has since remained so. The following table shows the work being done immediately prior to closing-down:

	Proportion %	Silver Oz.	Lead %	Zinc %	Recovery Silver %	Recovery Lead %	Recovery Zinc %
Feed	100.0	15.6	17.0	19.1	...	...	...
Lead concentrate by flotation	10.3	53.8	49.9	21.4	35.5	30.1	11.6
Lead concentrate on tables	4.2	35.2	60.4	14.5	9.6	15.0	3.2
Zinc concentrate	30.2	17.5	15.2	41.7	33.9	26.9	65.9
Residue	...	5.0	8.6	6.7	...	...	...

LEAD MILL. It has already been remarked that experiments demonstrated the possibility of recovering galena from the slime produced in the lead-concentrating mill. Early in 1915 it was decided to apply sub-aeration methods to this slime in preference to the Lyster system. For

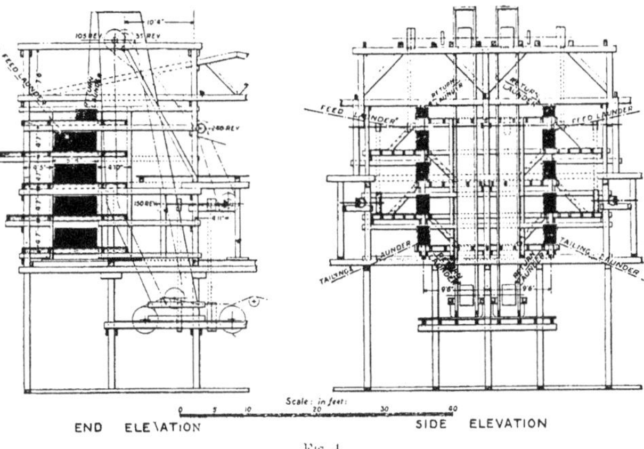

Fig. 4

a start, an 8-box machine was erected. This was similar in design to that used at the dump-slime plant, but smaller. Wooden boxes 24 by 24 in. by 36 in. high were supplied with 10-in. stirrers driven from below at a speed of 1000 r.p.m. The air was drawn by the stirrers through ½-in. pipes supplied with regulating valves. Two horse-power was required per stirrer. To control the rate of feed to the boxes a feed-tank was installed. As this 8-box unit gave satisfactory results, two more similar units were erected, and the 24 boxes were then capable of handling the full output of slime, some 800 tons weekly. This plant used the ordinary mill-circuit, a mixture of mine-water and excess water from the existing zinc-flotation plant, with addition of Broken Hill Water Supply Co.'s water when required.

As flotation media, eucalyptus oil, wood-tar oil, and pine-oil were used, being added to the feed-tank elevator. No definite mixture of these was supplied, the quantity of each being regulated by requirements for the time being. The amount used per ton of slime averaged 0.25 lb., and wood-tar oil predominated.

The following table gives the results obtained by this plant:

	Proportion %	Lead %	Recovery of lead %
Slime feed	100.0	13.3	...
Lead concentrate	13.3	67.1	67.1
Tailing	86.7	5.0	...

So much less fine galena was now going to the zinc-flotation plant and thence to the zinc-concentrate de-leading section that it was possible to put the Weir-Meredith vanners in the latter section out of commission, still, however, retaining the Wilfley tables.

For some time prior to 1915 it was evident that a saving in cost and an enhanced recovery could be obtained by the erection of a new zinc-flotation plant. Work in the experimental plant had demonstrated that sub-aeration methods would be satisfactory, and a plant for this purpose was designed, erected, and in October, 1915, was put into operation. While experimenting, it was found that fine galena could be recovered by flotation from the by-products of the lead-mill. Here it should be mentioned that the flow-sheet then in use did not provide for quite all the slime to go to the selective plant (24 by 24 in. boxes). The Card and vanner tailings were de-watered by means of a draining-belt, the de-watered material containing some settled fine going to the zinc-plant, and the slimy water to thickeners. The settled slime from the latter provided the feed for the selective plant, the tailing from which went to the zinc-plant, which in one section handled the whole of the zincy tailings (coarse and slimes) of the lead-mill, which handled 4000 tons per week of 136 hours. The flow-sheet (Fig. 3) will help to make matters clear. In view of the presence of this recoverable galena in the feed to the zinc-plant it was decided to make the new plant a combined lead and zinc flotation plant, that is, capable of first floating off the galena and subsequently the blende. This dual machine was of the same design as that at the dump-slime plant, with boxes 42 by 42 by 60 in. high. Five boxes were set apart for galena flotation and nine for zinc—14 boxes in all.

The tailing from No. 5 box was re-elevated to No. 6 box, no direct connection existing between No. 5 and 6.

In reality the five lead-boxes formed a trough with five stirrers in it, the divisions between the boxes only existing for 18 in. from the bottom. Stirrers 18 in. long, 3½ in. deep, making 530 r.p.m., were used, taking an average of 12 hp. each. By degrees it was found possible first to discard the vanners in the lead-mill, relying on the selective plant and the five boxes in the new zinc-plant to recover the galena. This was found quite satisfactory and the next step was to drop out the Wilfley tables that were handling the middlings from the Card tables in the lead-mill. This also proved satisfactory. Finally, the selective plant was closed-down and the whole of the galena flotation was done by the five boxes in the zinc-plant. This was the result hoped for by the management, but it was deemed advisable to perform the discarding of plant in stages so that no increased loss of lead in the zinc concentrate should take place unnoticed.

So far, then, it was found that by the use of flotation for galena:

1. An enhanced recovery of lead and silver was obtained.

2. Vanners were unnecessary first in the de-leading plant and subsequently in the lead-mill.

3. Re-treatment of middlings from Card tables was not required.

4. As a result of No. 1 point, less lead was in the zinc-concentrate.

More than this, it was demonstrated that fine galena could be floated out of ordinary mill-pulp without previous classification of the pulp.

The introduction of the above methods increased the recovery of lead from the crude ore by 7% and of silver by 15%.

The fineness of the galena concentrate won by flotation is shown by the following analysis:

Selective Lead Concentrates

I. M. M. screens	Proportion %	Silver Oz.	Lead %	Zinc %
Bulk	...	59.1	60.0	13.3
+ 120	1.2	...	48.8	16.6
− 120 + 150	1.2	...	61.4	12.4
− 150 + 200	3.6	63.4	61.0	12.2
− 200	94.0	56.6	60.4	13.6

The improvement in the grade of the zinc concentrate as a result of the installation of galena flotation is shown by a comparison of the following sizing analyses, the lower assay of lead in the finer sizes being marked.

Sizing Analysis, Zinc Concentrate Before the Installation of Galena Flotation

I. M. M. screens	Proportion %	Silver Oz.	Lead %	Zinc %
Bulk	...	16.8	8.0	46.0
+ 40	6.2	10.0	4.5	46.6
− 40 + 60	20.1	12.4	4.8	47.4
− 60 + 80	19.0	15.2	5.5	49.6
− 80 + 130	3.5	15.6	6.0	49.6
− 130 + 180	6.2	17.0	7.3	48.4
− 180	38.2	21.2	13.0	44.6

Sizing Analysis, Zinc Concentrate After the Installation of Galena Flotation

I. M. M. screens	Proportion %	Silver Oz.	Lead %	Zinc %
Bulk		12.2	4.6	47.3
+ 40	6.7	8.8	3.0	50.2
− 40 + 60	22.0	11.4	4.2	48.4
− 60 + 80	20.0	11.4	4.5	47.6
− 80 + 100	11.6	12.0	5.0	46.6
− 100 + 120	4.2	11.2	3.8	47.0
− 120 + 150	6.2	11.2	3.5	47.2
− 150 + 200	5.0	11.8	4.7	47.4
− 200	24.2	14.2	6.0	45.4

The marked success of the above changes in the milling operations and the evident possibilty of floating the slimed galena naturally led to seeking means of concentration of coarser particles of galena by flotation. Two metallurgists on an adjacent mine, H. V. Seale and W. Shellshear, had utilized the principle of the nozzle for aeration of a flotation pulp, and had designed an apparatus that was capable of floating coarse galena. Their

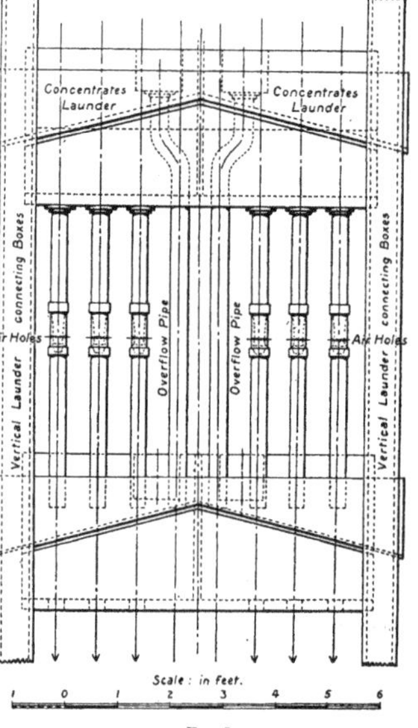

FIG. 5

idea was modified by others on the staff of the Zinc Corporation and was then tried by the management of the Central mine. A plant to treat 2000 tons per week was erected and after experiments a successful design was evolved by the metallurgical staff of the Central mine. So satisfactory was the design and so encouraging were the results obtained that it was decided to erect a plant large enough to handle the whole output of re-ground jig-tailing previously treated on Card tables. This new plant has recently been completed and is now in operation with good results; in fact, it is hoped that in the end it will be possible to discard the five boxes in the zinc-plant that are now used for floating galena. A

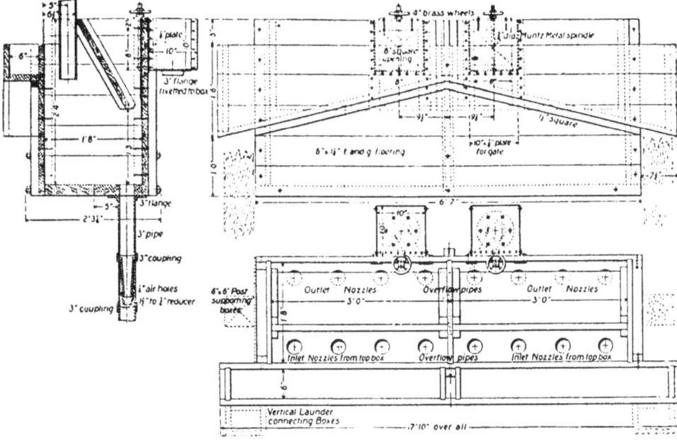

FIG. 6

small quantity, about 2 oz. per ton, of a mixture of coal-tar and eucalyptus is added to the pulp as flotation media.

The following comparative tables show the recovery made by the Card tables and that obtained with the Cascade machines:

	Proportion %	Silver Oz.	Lead %	Zinc %	Recovery Silver %	Recovery Lead %	Recovery Zinc %
By-products from jigs.....	...	10.6	10.0	16.1	...	...	...
Table concentrate	5.4	38.6	63.5	8.0	19.6	34.4	2.7
By-products from tables....	...	9.0	6.9	16.5	...	...	...
By-products from jigs.....	...	9.7	8.9	16.6	...	...	...
Cascade concentrate	6.6	46.2	63.0	11.6	31.4	47.3	4.5
By-products from Cascades..	...	7.1	5.0	17.0	...	...	...

LEAD-CASCADES. This is the name given to the latest galena-flotation plant of the Central mine, which has ousted the Card tables previously in use. The plant is simplicity itself (Fig. 4, 5, and 6). There are no moving parts, no use of compressed air. All that is required is the necessary elevating of prepared pulp. On a suitable site this elevating would not be required. The plant consists of a series of boxes set one above the other, the pulp in descending from box to box passing through nozzles, thereby drawing into itself the air necessary for flotation. The concentrate flows over the lip of each box and the tailing passes to the next in series. The boxes are 36 in. long, 18 in. wide, and 28 in. high. Three nozzles are supplied to each box. The distance between the bottoms of any two boxes is 4 ft. 9 in., and nine boxes of the above size in series form one unit. In order to reduce the height of the plant and bring it on to as few floors as possible, there is an elevator between No. 4 and 5. Two units are in use, the intermediate elevator being common to both. By means of a system of overflows, irregularities in the volume of pulp are checked. This plant has been a complete success, the recovery of the lead and silver being greater than with Card tables, and no Card tables are now in use for concentrating crushed ore. The

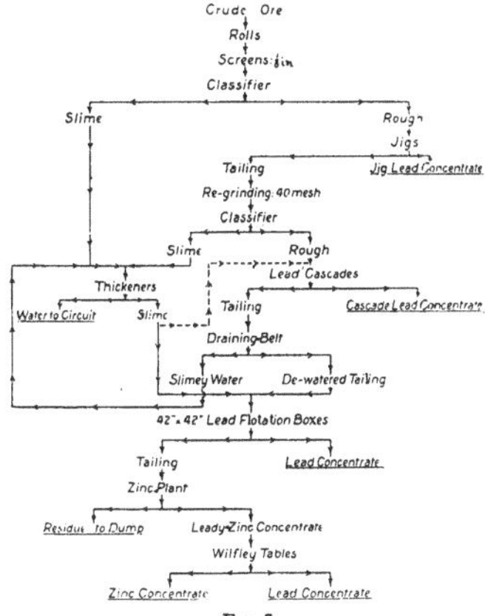

FIG. 7

galena that escapes the Cascades is, if fine, caught by the galena-flotation boxes in the zinc-plant and, if coarse, is removed from the zinc-concentrate by the Wilfley tables in the de-leading plant.

The following shows the milling results for a recent period:

	Proportion %	Silver Oz.	Lead %	Zinc %	Recovery Silver %	Recovery Lead %	Recovery Zinc %
Crude ore	100.0	11.8	14.0	15.0	...	...	...
Lead-mill lead	17.4	40.8	64.6	9.0	60.1	80.2	10.0
De-leading lead	1.3	39.3	58.1	13.8	4.3	5.4	1.1
					64.4	85.6	
Zinc concentrate	27.2	12.8	5.1	47.9	29.4	9.9	83.3
Residue	...	1.3	1.1	1.5	...	...	...

Effective recovery, lead 85.6%, silver 64.4%, and zinc 83.3%.

In conclusion, I may say that the problem is not completely solved, perhaps it never will be, but scientific investigation is proceeding all the time. The substitution of flotation for gravity concentration has meant the discarding of 20 Card tables, 4 Wilfley tables, and 16 Weir-Meredith vanners in the lead mill, and of 14 Weir-Meredith vanners in the de-leading plant, with the necessary attendants and maintenance, and it has simplified the flow-sheet of the Central mill. (Fig. 7).

Screen-analysis of jig-lead concentrate, Card-table lead-concentrate, and Cascade lead-concentrate are appended, as they are instructive and of some interest in conjunction with the foregoing history.

The object of this paper being almost entirely to trace the steps by which flotation has superseded gravity concentration at the Central mine, the various mechanical contrivances tried or adopted have not been elaborated, hence no machine-drawings are appended.

Sizing-Analysis, Jig-Lead Concentrate

I M M screen	Proportion %	Silver Oz.	Lead %	Zinc %
Bulk	...	33.8	64.2	6.5
+ 40	43.8	37.6	68.4	7.3
− 40 + 60	13.4	35.2	70.0	4.0
− 60 + 80	15.0	32.4	66.8	4.3
− 80 + 100	7.5	26.6	60.8	6.0
− 100 + 120	3.4	27.2	58.2	5.8
− 120 + 150	5.9	24.8	51.4	7.4
− 150 + 200	3.1	27.2	55.0	7.9
− 200	7.8	30.2	54.8	9.3

Sizing-Analysis, Card-Table Lead-Concentrate

I M M	Proportion %	Silver Oz.	Lead %	Zinc %
Bulk	...	33.4	63.8	4.6
+ 40	0.5	...	30.6	14.0
− 40 + 60	3.2	56.2	48.6	8.3
− 60 + 80	6.4	39.6	56.6	5.5
− 80 + 100	10.3	35.0	59.2	4.7
− 100 + 120	7.6	32.0	59.4	4.4
− 120 + 150	9.2	30.8	59.4	4.6
− 150 + 200	17.9	30.6	61.2	4.8
− 200	44.9	32.1	69.6	4.0

Sizing-Analysis, Cascade Lead-Concentrate

I M M	Proportion %	Silver Oz.	Lead %	Zinc %
Bulk	...	46.9	61.0	13.3
+ 80	4.2	65.6	39.4	24.3
− 80 + 100	7.1	51.1	50.0	19.1
− 100 + 120	5.0	47.1	52.0	18.1
− 120 + 150	11.6	41.8	55.8	16.3
− 150 + 200	9.6	43.2	60.1	15.1
− 200	62.5	45.8	65.8	11.2

The Sulphide Corporation, owning the Central mine mentioned above, has paid large dividends since 1898, 25% in 1917. The output last year was 41,426 tons of concentrate assaying 40.9 oz. silver, 63.1% lead, and 8.9% zinc, and 55,990 tons containing 12.6 oz., 5.7%, and 47.3%, respectively.

Anaconda and Chile

Copper and financial circles were distinctly surprised at the public offering of $25,000,000 6% 10-year bonds by the Anaconda Copper Mining Co. The bonds are to be a direct obligation of the company and will be additionally secured by specific pledge of stocks of constituent companies valued in excess of $100,000,000. Proceeds of these bonds are to be used toward the equipment of the properties of its two South American subsidiaries, Andes Copper Mining Co. and the Santiago Mining Co. and to replace in current account earnings already invested. Anaconda's Andes project in South America is by far the biggest piece of copper mining development in progress today. Churn-drills have determined an ore-body 1800 ft. long, 900 ft. wide, and 850 ft. deep containing over 32,000,000 tons of ore averaging 1½% copper. In addition to this known body of ore, other ore in the vicinity has been proved up to the extent that the total now exceeds over 100,000,000 tons averaging 1.4% copper. The property is situated at a height of 10,500 ft. in the mountains. Construction of a '70-pound' railroad is in process from Port Charnaral to the mine, the last five miles of which will be through a 75% hard rock tunnel. In addition to building a railroad and steamship terminus at Port Charnaral, a 22,000-kw. steam-turbine electric plant is being installed which will provide power for the mine and mill at 100,000 volts. At the mine a 15,000-ton concentrator is to be erected and plans are being made for a model town of about 5000 inhabitants. Much of this construction has been held up by war conditions and inability to get either raw material or shipping. With the way clear ahead it is the intention to prosecute development work to make Andes Copper Co. a backlog against any possible diminution in output from the Butte mines. The company states that during the period from January 1, 1913, to September 30, 1918, net earnings after interest and all taxes but before depreciation "averaged $28,700,000 per annum, or over the face value of the bonds." In the five years to the first of January, 1918, Anaconda's net after interest but before taxes and depreciation totaled $134,471,916. Estimating the company's 1917 tax bill at $2,000,000, the net total was $132,471,916. On the basis of the company's statement that net averaged $28,700,000 per year for the last six years or a total of $172,200,000, it would seem that earnings for the nine months to September 30, 1918 were approximately $39,728,084 before taxes and depreciation. Anaconda is the largest producer of copper in the world and its mines are located in one of the greatest mineral districts known. During the past 25 years over 16% of the copper production of the world, and over 25% of that of the United States came from the mines now owned by the company.—'Boston News Bureau'.

A Mine Latrine

By WILLIAM W. CORT

*In mines in which the conditions of temperature and humidity underground are suitable for the development of hookworm larvae proper underground latrines are essential for the protection of miners from infection with hookworm disease. This is one of the most difficult problems of sanitation with which the mine operator has to deal. An underground latrine to be successful must be simple, sanitary, of small cost, easy to install, conveniently placed for use, and easy to keep clean. In Special Bulletin No. 28 of the California State Board of Health, 'Sanitation in Mines for the Prevention and Eradication of Hookworm', the general problem of underground sanitation in mines in relation to hookworm is considered and a number of specific suggestions are made in regard to suitable latrines. In that paper a latrine devised by G. F. Williamson and installed in the Belmont Shawmut mine is figured. More recently a number of improvements have been made in this and its utility has been fully demonstrated. A detailed description of this latrine and the sanitary arrangements connected with it may be helpful to mine operators who are considering improvements of this kind. Such a system of underground sanitation as that of the Belmont Shawmut mine, if carefully kept up and backed by definite rules against soil pollution, will prevent hookworm from being introduced into a mine, and will make effective other steps for its eradication in mines already infected.

I wish to thank Mr. Williamson, the superintendent of the Belmont Shawmut mine, for his kindness in permitting me to use the drawings reproduced in this article and for his help in gathering information included.

Drawings of this latrine, including materials and cost of construction, are shown in Fig. 1. Fig. 2 is a photograph of the completed latrine. The low cost, less than ten dollars apiece, is a decided advantage, since it makes possible the use of a large number, which renders them easier to keep clean, since fewer men use each one. It also tends to decrease soil pollution, since the latrines can be placed in places convenient for all. The framework is so light and easily handled that the latrine can be carried down in the skip after being completely constructed above ground: it also can be easily moved from one part of the mine to another when the shifting of the work demands the transfer of the men. The latrines should be placed conveniently in well-lighted well-ventilated places, and a sufficient number placed, so that there will be at least one for every 12 men.

Several features call for mention. Recognizing the importance of keeping the seat clean and the tendency of the miners to stand on the seat, the top of the frame is made so low that it is impossible to stand up. The seat is constructed so that it can be easily removed when badly soiled and a new one substituted. It is suggested that several extra seats be kept constantly on hand. The can is simple in construction with a tight-fitting lid that can be clamped down. For convenience in emptying, a paraffined bag is placed in the can. These bags are water-tight and when the cans are emptied they slip out, leaving the cans entirely clean. The bag must fit closely and should be a little taller than the height of the can

FIG. 2. THE LATRINE

so that the free edges can be turned over to hold it in position. Paraffined paper bags for this purpose were obtained for this purpose at about $25 per hundred. The bags must be carefully packed for shipment and carefully unpacked, because even the slightest break spoils them for use in the cans. The paraffined bags will serve their purposes well. In one case the can was not emptied for two weeks; at the end of this time the bag was still water-tight and slid out without difficulty when the can was emptied. The use of these bags does away with most of the disagreeable features incident to the care of latrines. When a latrine is installed ready for use a layer of sawdust about three inches deep is sprinkled in the bottom of the paper sack. Each man is instructed to throw a little sawdust and lime into the can after using. With a maximum number of 12 men, using one of these latrines, the can should be emptied once a week.

*The author is Consulting Helminthologist to the California State Board of Health.

The care of these underground latrines is a difficult problem. It is hard to get men who are willing to do this type of work and the time involved is an important item of expense. In the Williamson arrangement the disagreeable features and the time involved in emptying the cans are reduced to a minimum. Before emptying, lime is sprinkled into the cans and they are then filled with sawdust. The clamps on the covers make the cans perfectly tight and easily handled in the skips. The actual time necessary to bring five cans from different levels of the Belmont Shawmut mine to the surface and empty them was four hours for one man. Extra cans should be kept and each can immediately replaced when taken out for emptying. The fact that the incinerator in this mine is about half a mile from the mouth of the adit increased the time necessary for this work.

To dispose of the waste material an incinerator was used, drawings of which are shown in Fig. 3. (See opposite page.) Such an incinerator can be used for a number of other purposes. It is not expensive and will last for a long time. In regard to the cost of the incinerator, I quote from a letter from Mr. Williamson:

"We are unable to furnish a very accurate estimate of the cost of building this incinerator and therefore have made no comments. As you doubtless noticed, the one we have is made up of old boiler equipment and scrap material. A cost estimate is hardly worth while, as it can be made up of either an old boiler or other cast-off material usually found around a mine."

The use of an incinerator, especially in mines where hookworm is prevalent, is by far the safest method for disposing of the waste and is recommended as a sanitary precaution.

Blueprints of the Williamson latrine and incinerator will be furnished on request. Communications should be addressed to the Division of Parasitology, California State Board of Health, East Hall, Berkeley, California.

Output of Petroleum

Domestic petroleum requirements in 1918 were almost 400,000,000 barrels, according to the U. S. Geological Survey. Production in this country was 345,500,000 bbl., and the year's needs had to be met by withdrawals from surplus stocks and imports from Mexico.

Production of 345,000,000 bbl., a new high record, compares with 335,000,000 in 1917, a gain of 3%. Output in leading fields, was as follows:

	1918	1917
Appalachian	25,300,000	24,932,205
Lima-Indiana	3,100,000	3,670,293
Illinois	13,300,000	15,776,860
Oklahoma-Kansas	139,600,000	155,043,596
Central and North Texas	15,600,000	10,900,646
North Louisiana	13,000,000	8,561,963
Gulf Coast	21,700,000	26,087,587
Rocky Mountain	12,600,000	9,199,310
California	101,300,000	93,877,549
Alaska and Michigan	....	10,300
Total	345,500,000	335,315,601

The output in 1918 includes 6,500,000 bbl. of crude removed from field-storage, but it excludes drafts aggregating 20,500,000 additional barrels from the stocks of pipe-line companies. The surface reserve of crude held by producers and pipe-line companies in the United States at end of 1918 is estimated at 123,000,000 bbl., compared with 150,000,000 at end of 1917. These figures show that the demand for domestic petroleum in 1918 was about 366,000,000 bbl. Exports of crude, most of it to Canada and north-western Mexico, aggregated about 5,500,000 bbl., leaving 360,500,000 available to supply domestic needs. This was insufficient, however, and about 36,500,000 was imported, nearly all from Mexico, to meet domestic requirements, which amounted in all to about 397,000,000 barrels.

The increase in output was made in response to the steadily growing demand for petroleum, expressed in advancing prices for crude oil, which were stabilized, with Government approval, at record levels during the closing months of the year. The most pronounced response to stimulus of war-time demand was made in Central and North Texas, North Louisiana, Rocky Mountain, and California fields, but the gain of the old Appalachian field, though moderate, is significant.

In California the principal source of new production was the Montebello field, discovered in 1917, in Los Angeles county, which, with the Casmalia district, in Santa Barbara county, and older districts in both San Joaquin Valley and Coastal-Southern divisions apparently succeeded in establishing a new record for production in California, exceeding 100,000,000 barrels.

The gain in the Rocky Mountain field is credited to Wyoming and ascribed in part to the Big Muddy field in the western part of Converse county, in part to drilling of a few new wells of large capacity in the heart of the Salt Creek field.

Momentous developments that affect the future supply of high-grade petroleum in the United States took place in 1918 in Central and North Texas field, after petroleum had been discovered in considerable quantities near Ranger, in Eastland county; near Caddo, in Stephens county; near Brownwood, in Brown county; and near Burkett, in Coleman county, in 1917. About 60 wells were completed during 1918, and at the end of that year the new field was credited with a potential capacity of 50,000 bbl. per day, although its actual capacity, limited by pipe-line facilities, was only about 18,000 barrels.

ALUMINUM DUST burns quietly when in a pile, but if this pile be disturbed in such a manner as to raise a cloud of the dust into the air, the burning takes place with explosive violence. If a dust-cloud already formed that has a density within the explosive limits be ignited, a violent explosion results, according to Alan Leighton of the U. S. Bureau of Mines. Water is worse than useless in extinguishing fire in aluminum dust; it is positively dangerous. The fire may be smothered by sand or oil, carbon tetrachloride being used to put out the oil later on.

COPPER OUTPUT of the Chile Copper Co. during 1918 totaled 102,130,000 lb., against 87,450,000 lb. in 1917 and 44,100,000 lb. in 1916.

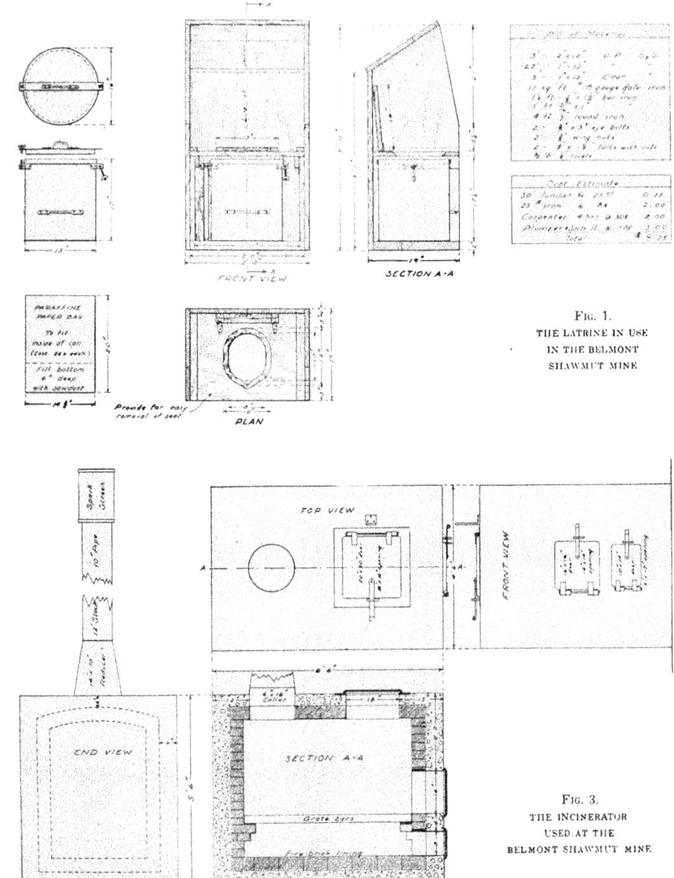

FIG. 1. THE LATRINE IN USE IN THE BELMONT SHAWMUT MINE

FIG. 3. THE INCINERATOR USED AT THE BELMONT SHAWMUT MINE

Social Betterment in Arizona

By A. M. HECKMAN

Metal-mining operations have probably been the most backward of any of the great industries in the recognition of the influence of sociological conditions upon their work, probably due to the fact that the development of large-scale organizations has been so gradual. Mines are not found in the centres of population where recreational and educational facilities are at hand. Most of the big industrial enterprises of the eastern portion of the United States were established after the cities had taken root, and their problem of providing a proper environment for their employees was but to assist in the continuation of those already available. On the contrary, metal mines are found in the wilderness, and the towns grow around them; the welfare work necessary in such a community must start from the ground.

The reason for a comparatively small amount of welfare work in metal-mining communities has been due partly to the fact that everything was subordinated to the winning of the metals. The conditions under which the workmen spend hours per day, their living conditions, their sanitary conditions, their houses, were often thought to be of secondary importance, but recent years have seen a remarkable change, both in the attitude of the mining companies and of the employees.

Not long ago, when mining operations were almost entirely on a small scale, the boss knew every man by his first name, he know whether Johnny or Mary was ill and how they were getting along at school. With the growth of individual operations, however, the time has come when the man at the top deals with the man at the bottom through a series of departments. In such large organizations it is impossible to retain the personal touch that is given to the workman of an earlier period, and this personal touch, enabling the workman to feel that he is really something more than a cog in the machine is the important factor today.

There have been other notable factors, such as the changes in the character of labor and the multiplicity of nationalities coincident with large operations. The larger the number of nationalities, the greater the number of groups or clans.

While undoubtedly there has been an immense financial loss in the numerous strikes that have occurred all over Arizona during the past year, it is believed by many that the ultimate result will be an improvement of conditions. The mine-operator had thought that he had done everything that he could, but when the strikes broke out he began to think whether he really understood the other fellow's side of the controversy.

From the activities that have followed the strikes it is evident that there has been an awakening to the real need for welfare work. It is not a direct result of the strikes, but rather an indirect one; it does not involve giving to the men all the things for which they struck, for when men strike for better conditions they themselves are unable to define what they really want, and it remains for the operator to determine what fairness demands. I do not believe that there is one large operator in Arizona who is so narrow or so prejudiced that he would not immediately grasp any possible suggestions for the improvement of social conditions.

Personnel work is a term recently introduced to cover the great variety of activities in industrial work that deal with the human factor. Much attention has been focused upon individual phases of personnel work, such as accident prevention, sanitation, and reduction in the turnover of labor. In most cases these activities have been carried on as though they were distinct and separate; as a matter of fact, they are only phases of the one fundamental problem of human engineering, and each has important relations with the others. Thus, for example, a high turnover is one of the most important causes of a high accident rate, and unsatisfactory housing conditions are an important cause of labor turnover. In the early stages of the investigation, it was necessary to take each phase separately, the time has now arrived, however, at which it is desirable to consider them as a whole in order to bring them all into the right relation to each other.

A discussion of the importance of personnel work as a means of increasing dividends in industry may be objected to by some as a materialistic way of looking upon work that is humanitarian, but humanitarianism, as such, has no place in industry, and nothing is gained and much is lost by pretending that it has. The only reason why a corporation engages in business is to make a profit, and any activity of the corporation that does not tend either directly or indirectly toward that end is poor business. It is equally poor business to overlook any activities that do tend indirectly to the making of a profit. On this basis, personnel work can be justified as a corporate activity, even if there be no justification whatever for abstract humanitarianism from the business standpoint. One characteristic of the American workman is a high level of intelligence, and it is an insult to intelligence to ask a man to believe that anything so impersonal as a corporation is really desirous of benefiting him without advantage to itself. The inevitable result is suspicion and opposition. On the other hand, it is easy to make clear to the worker that he, as well as the corporation, benefits from personal work; thus his support can be won.

It must be kept in mind, as a major premise of this discussion, that through the rapid increase of invested capital in recent years and the much slower increase of labor supply, most corporations have already passed from the position of buying labor to that of selling employment. The difference needs no emphasis. The majority of important industrial organizations are now in the position where they need more capable men than they can secure, and it has become essential to hold out inducements for capable men to enter their employ and to develop the capabilities of those they can get.

The industrial leaders have learned to recognize one of the greatest needs of the workman, namely, that of a place for recreational and educational purposes—a place to spend the leisure hour. As a result, we have the club and Y. M. C. A. organized for and run by the workmen, although the money for the original investment may have been furnished by the company. The Ray Consolidated Copper Co. has the Ray Con. club at Ray and the Nocyar club at Hayden; the Magma Copper Co. has the Magma club at Superior; the Phelps Dodge Corporation has the Morenci club at Morenci; the Old Dominion Co. has the O. D. library and club-house at Globe. Other companies have gone in the club-house idea through the Y. M. C. A. and commodious Y buildings are to be found at Bisbee, Douglas, Miami, Clifton, and Hayden. A number of the mining camps are providing excellent baseball for their workmen. Bands have been organized and good music is available. Parks are common, although the maintenance of parks often proves very expensive.

Another phase of welfare work, although it is not often regarded as such, has been the introduction of physical examination as a method of preventing illness and accident. There is probably no place where it is more important to prevent the spread of contagious diseases than in the mine. The physical examination has two most excellent results: First, the correct knowledge on the part of the man himself of his physical condition, the knowledge of his capabilities, his dangers, and his possibilities; second, the knowledge of the man's physical condition by the company, enabling them to place him where his work will not be injurious to himself, and in the case of a man having a contagious disease, preventing the spread of that disease among the other workmen.

The introduction of medical and physical examinations of new employees is one of the greatest steps toward placing a premium on health. Take, for instance, a college boy preparing for engineering work; if you let him know that his whole future carreer depends upon his living a clean life, it will do more toward raising the standard of college morality than many reforms that might otherwise be instituted. The Army and Navy require it, so why should not employers, especially in view of the liability of accidents occurring as the result of physical weakness.

Practically every mining district in Arizona has a building and loan association, the object of which is to enable the workman to own his own home; the money is loaned at low rates of interest; in the Warren district it is 6%.

Splendid welfare work is being done in this district, in which are three of the largest companies in the State, the Copper Queen branch of the Phelps Dodge Corporation, the Calumet & Arizona Mining Co., and the Shattuck Arizona Mining Co. Practically everything along recreational and educational lines has been provided by these companies. The Copper Queen has furnished the community with a splendid library, containing some 8000 volumes, and has subscribed for 26 daily papers and 94 magazines. The company buys all the books and pays all the expenses. The companies contribute generously to the Y. M. C. A., one of the most influential organizations in the district. The Y occupies two buildings, and is one of the finest equipped association buildings in the country. Directly outside of the Y building is a swimming pool, which has the greatest attraction for young and old alike. Among the educational activities of this association are the miners' educational courses, which are given with a view to training men for greater efficiency in their work and to qualify them for better positions.

In 1916 there was erected a fine Y. W. C. A. building, equipped with every modern convenience and comfort. This was a gift from the Phelps Dodge Corporation as a memorial to Miss Grace Dodge, who, at the time of her death, was national president of the Y. W. C. A. One member of the staff works entirely among the Mexican girls and women of the city, teaching them home duties, English, conservation, and the use of substitutes. The association has also established a camp in the Huachuca mountains, where the girls may enjoy a vacation at nominal expense.

For a number of years the companies of the Warren district have had a pension system. The benefits of this system apply only to employees who have been 15 years or longer in the service of the company, and who are in either of the following classes: employees who have become mentally or physically disqualified, and those who have attained the age of 70 years. The amount of the annual pension allowed is 2% of the average salary of a man for the three years of active service immediately preceding his retirement, multiplied by the number of years of his service in the employ of the company. The maximum amount is in no case more than 60% of such average salary, nor is it ever more than $1000.

A Benefit Association for health and accident insurance is supported by the companies of this district. The Phelps Dodge plan is as follows: The object of the Association is to provide its members with a certain income when sick, or when killed or disabled by accident suffered on duty, and to pay to their families certain definite sums in case of natural deaths; to create and maintain a fund that belongs to the employees to be used in payments of benefits to them, and to cost them the least money possible, considering the benefits received. The dues of this Association are 1¾% of the daily wages received.

On January 1, 1918, the companies in this district announced a bonus system for tenure of service, and on that day $287,000 was distributed among the workmen of the community, $100 going to each underground man who had been in the employ of the companies for one year and $50 to those that had been employed for six months. Similarly the sums of $60 and $30 were given to surface men. In July the plan was announced as a permanent feature with a few changes. The six months' bonus has been eliminated, but now all employees who have been with the companies for a year will receive $100 on the completion of that year's work, with the addition of $10 for each year of service, $250 being the maximum.

This is a method of recognizing faithfulness in service, for there is no question that the number of men who stay with a company for a year or more are more efficient, they reduce the labor turnover and thereby increase the profit of the company. The distribution of a bonus to these men is but a division of the extra profit derived from their continuity of service.

The latest welfare activity is a new housing scheme, which was announced a short time ago by the Copper Queen branch of the Phelps Dodge Corporation and the Calumet & Arizona Mining Co. This provides that the companies will build houses for their employees on plans provided either by the employees or the companies, and will sell them to the employees on terms of rent, with interest on deferred payments at only 6%. No charge will be made for house-lots. The land set aside for the new homes is in the most attractive residence section of Warren, within easy distance of the mines.

The above are a few of the many things that the mining companies in Arizona are doing to ameliorate the life of their workmen. We can look for immense changes in social conditions, for the operators appreciate that it is an important factor in their success.

GOLD MINING in British Guiana has fallen off considerably since the War began, according to a recent U. S. Consular Report. Foodstuffs, implements, machinery, and labor have been costing so much that the industry has not been profitable. In fact, a gradual decrease in the quantity of gold obtained from the mines has been taking place during the last 25 years. In 1893, which was the best year, 137,629 oz. was won, valued at £512,000 ($2,492,000), whereas the return in 1917 was only 29,538 oz., worth £108,016 ($525,660). The difficulty in obtaining labor for the workings has had perhaps more to do with the decline in the output of gold than any other cause. The sugar and rice lands, near the coast, attract labor rather than the mines, which are in the interior of the colony or at least pretty far inland, and the rate of wages paid on the sugar estates is higher. Labor has also been attracted by the recent boom in bauxite mining, which has reduced that available for gold. There is strong confidence still in the gold industry, which is supported by the Geological Department, and a belief that with the proper opening of the colony a great future is in store for it. At present undoubtedly gold mining must be considered a waning industry. In addition to the labor difficulty it is probable that the machinery and methods employed leave much to be desired, and may account for present conditions.

Gold Situation in Australia

A conference of Australian gold producers was to be held at Melbourne during the third week of January, when the following proposals were to be discussed: (1) That a Gold Producers Association with a central committee be formed to look after the special interests of Australian gold producers. (2) That this Association demand the removal of embargoes on the export of new gold. (3) That the Federal or Imperial governments pay a subsidy on gold production proportionate to the increase in working costs since 1914. (4) That the Repatriation Department subsidize the employment of returned soldiers producing low-grade and otherwise unpayable gold ores. (5) That the Repatriation Department subsidize tribute [lessee] parties composed of returned soldiers. (6) That the Association organize the co-operative buying and distribution of all gold-mining stores. (7) That the Federal government subsidize the State Railway Departments to allow of the carriage of stores at reduced rates. (8) That the Commonwealth government be urged to encourage gold prospecting by (*a*) removal of restrictions on the flotation of gold mining companies; (*b*) subsidies to prospecting parties consisting of returned soldiers in west, north, and central Australia; and (*c*) construction of dams, wells, water-bores, and other means of conserving water in west, north, and central Australia to serve the gold and pastoral industries.

Metal Output of British Columbia

A preliminary review and estimate of production of British Columbia during 1918 has just been prepared by the Department of Mines. The accompanying table shows that the mineral output was valued at $41,083,093, a gain of 11% when compared with 1917.

	1918		1917	
	Quantity	Value	Quantity	Value
Gold, placer, ounces	15,400	$308,000	24,800	$496,000
Gold, lode, ounces...	157,276	3,250,895	114,523	2,367,190
Total gold	172,676	$3,558,895	138,323	$2,863,190
Silver, ounces	2,886,861	2,601,120	2,929,216	2,265,749
Lead, pounds	43,949,661	2,944,627	37,307,465	2,951,020
Copper, pounds	63,387,010	15,681,946	59,007,565	16,038,256
Zinc, pounds	36,149,894	2,501,573	41,848,513	3,166,259
Total metals......	....	$27,288,161	....	$27,284,474
Coal, tons	2,292,068	11,460,340	2,149,975	7,524,913
Coke, tons	190,656	1,334,592	159,905	959,430
Total collieries..	....	$12,794,932	....	$8,484,343
Miscellaneous	....	1,000,000	....	1,241,575
Total production..	....	$41,083,093	....	$37,010,392

The increase in gold output is rather a surprise, yet the yield for 1917 was abnormally low. The Belmont Surf Inlet mine was a large contributor in 1918, yielding 43,000 ounces.

DUTY payable to the government of Siam by tin companies is from 10 to 25.2%, depending on the price of Straits tin. In the Federated Malay States the duty is from 10 to 14¼%, ad valorem.

REVIEW OF MINING

KAMLOOPS, BRITISH COLUMBIA

Three Gold Mines in the Cadwallader District.

One of the promising gold properties of the Cadwallader Creek district, Kamloops mining division, is the Lorne mine. During the past year, owing to abnormal conditions, work has been confined largely to development. This work yielded 380 tons of ore, producing 192 oz. gold and 37 oz. silver.

The Pioneer mine is another gold mine in the Cadwallader district that has been operated steadily during the greater part of the past year. Milling was started on March 10 and ceased July 21. Sinking of a shaft was continued from the latter date, and is now down 280 ft. from the collar. Driving has been carried on at the 280-ft. level for 120 ft. and good ore opened. The head-frame, hoist-house, and blacksmith-shop were destroyed by fire on November 17, but milling is expected to be resumed in a short time. Gold produced during 1918, up to November 16, totals 1925 oz. It is estimated that the output to the end of the year will total 2500 ounces.

At the Ida May mine, also in the Cadwallader district, a reduction plant consisting of a small jaw-crusher, Huntington mill, with a capacity of 10 tons per day, and an amalgamating table, was erected during the past year. Power is supplied by a 10-hp. gasoline engine. A trial run gave 30 oz. of gold. The property is now closed, but is expected to re-commence operations in the spring.

IDA MAY MILL PIONEER MINE LORNE MINE

THESE PROPERTIES ARE IN THE CADWALLADER CREEK DISTRICT OF THE KAMLOOPS MINING DIVISION, BRITISH COLUMBIA

WINNIPEG, MANITOBA

Possibilities of Northern Manitoba.

The Commissioner of northern Manitoba, R. C. Wallace, has issued a statement concerning operations of the Mandy company, a subsidiary of the Tonopah Mining Co., at Schist Lake, north of The Pas. During 1917, the company shipped 3300 tons of ore, containing copper valued at $261,360, gold, $6600, and silver, $6600; a total of $274,560. In 1918 shipments of ore were 6000 tons, containing copper, $624,000; gold, $12,000; and silver, $15,000; a total of $651,000. Production of copper for the two years was 3,588,000 lb. The company has mined 12,000 tons for shipment in 1919, and almost completed the stoping of high-grade ore to the 200-ft. level, and has blocked out 200,000 tons of low-grade ore. It is expected that 15,000 tons will be shipped during the coming summer. Mining men are urging upon the Manitoban government construction of a railway, which would be an extension of the Canadian Northern, to open the copper properties in this region, one of which, the Flin-Flon, has ore blocked out estimated to be worth $200,000,000.

BISBEE, ARIZONA

Stripping Overburden.—Employment.—Bonuses and Living Conditions.

All records for stripping overburden on Sacramento hill were broken by the Copper Queen company on January 8, when in a 16-hour day, 433 carloads of rock was loaded. This amounted to more than 7000 yards, or an average of a trainload of four cars every 9 minutes. The best previous record was 6000 yd. in 16 hours. In an 8-hour shift on January 9 even greater speed was made, an average of a trainload every 5 minutes being maintained. December was the best month on Sacramento hill, a total of 140,314 cu. yd. being moved, or a daily average of 4800 yd. The January record, as indicated by the two days mentioned, should not be far from 180,000 yards.

Enlargement of the C. & C. shaft of the Copper Queen from the surface to the 1000-ft. level has been completed, and work has been started cutting a large pumping-station at the 800-ft. level. Within a short time everything will be ready to start sinking a standard 3½-compartment shaft from the 1500 to the 1800-ft. level. The new head-frame and hoist have been erected.

Contrary to reports, it was announced by the Copper Queen that it was discharging no men at present, aside from the ordinary turnover. The present policy of the company in employment, and it is the same with the Calumet & Arizona company, is to take on only returned soldiers, sailors, or war workers, or men who had been employed by them during the last two years and who had worked for them for two years. The Night Hawk Leasing Co., operating at the lower end of the Warren district, reports that it now is working along the fault on the 450-ft. level with an increasingly good showing. In the raise on the main fault the workings have opened lenses of mineralized ground, carrying streaks of rich copper ore. Indications appear to favor finding an orebody at an early date. The property now is looking better than ever.

The Copper Queen company and the Calumet & Arizona company paid the second annual bonus to employees on the first January pay-day to 1354 men at Bisbee, putting $153,-040 additional money into circulation. The Copper Queen bonus-roll at Bisbee and Douglas included 1400 men, 877 of whom were at Bisbee. Of this number 834 received the second annual bonus of $110, while 43 received the first $100. The Calumet & Arizona bonus-roll at Bisbee was 520 men, 500 of whom received the second-year bonus and 20 the first year's. Under the plan in effect with both companies, the bonus becomes due and payable at the end of the year's employment of each individual employee. However, as the bonus payments began January 1, 1917, the largest single month of the year is January. The men receive a sum ranging from $100 for the first year to $250 at the end of 15 years, at the end of which time they are retired under pension. In conjunction with the payment of the annual bonus, attention was called by the companies to the fact that the Third Addition to Warren, a residential suburb of Bisbee, opened recently for the benefit of employees of the mining division of the Phelps Dodge and C. & A. companies, in conjunction with the bonus, offered a study worth consideration of the men. The annual bonus, intended as a reward for faithful service of the men, is sufficient in amount to cover the interest on the average amount expended on a home in the suburb. The companies, through the Warren company, a joint subsidiary, are loaning money to employees, charging only 6% annual interest, to be expended on homes in the Addition. The principal and interest are to be repaid to the Warren company in 100 monthly payments. Taking $2900 as the average amount expended on a home in the Addition, the first year's interest, roughly figured, without taking into consideration monthly reductions in principal which would affect it, would be $120. Thus the first year's bonus would lack but $20 of paying the interest, while the third year's bonus would cover it. At the end of the eighth year the bonus would have brought to the employee a total of $1160; at the end of 12 years it would have reached a total of $1960, and at the end of the 15th year he will have received $2230, or more than the cost of his home. Eighteen houses have been completed in the tract, or are under construction, but at present the Addition is not being pushed. It is the belief of the company officials that building material and labor, high while the War was on, have passed their highest and soon will be obtainable at more reasonable figures. In the meantime, grading, laying of water and sewer-pipes, erection of electric lights and telephone poles, and other betterments are being pushed. In the houses themselves the conveniences of the wives of employees is being studied; built-in features, sanitary plumbing, and 'step-saving devices' are being installed by the architect in charge. The Addition will be open to none except the men actually employed in the mining division, according to official announcement, although efforts are being made to secure rulings that would permit office-men and employees of subsidiary corporations to enjoy the advantages of the scheme.

CRIPPLE CREEK, COLORADO

Notes on Some of the Small Mines.

A rich strike is reported from the 600-ft. level of the Dante mine, on Bull hill, by Craig and Horn, sub-lessees of the Big Toad company. The core of the 4-ft. vein, a streak 2 to 4 in. wide, is worth 50 cents per pound. The screenings from the entire orebody assay 5 oz. per ton.

Operations will be resumed on the Midget and Bonanza King mines of the Midget Consolidated on Gold hill by the Hackof Leasing Co., of St. Louis, early in February. The property has been closed since December 1917. The old sub-lessees, nine sets, who were in ore when the mine was closed, will return to work.

H. M. Gilbert of Cripple Creek, with Chicago associates, has secured a 3-year lease on a large block in the Index mine of the El Paso Extension Gold Mines Corporation, on the south-western slope of Gold hill, extending from the 600-ft. level to surface. Driving north from the 600-ft. level of the Index shaft to the Anchoria Leland-Index line has been started on the main Index vein. The drift will pass, through undeveloped ground, traversed by three known veins—the Index, Keystone, and Pointer, also the Index basalt dike. All of these veins and the dike have been big producers.

A fifth interest in the Hayes-Cartee lease on the Vindicator company's 1100-ft. level, which has produced $200,-000 since last April, has been sold by Pete Cartee to W. E. Craig for a cash consideration not made public. Cartee has purchased a ranch in Missouri with the profits accruing from his lease.

The properties of the Gold Dollar Consolidated Mining Co., comprising 64 acres on the eastern slope of Beacon hill, will be sold by the Sheriff of Teller county on February 15, under a judgment issued from the District Court, in favor of the First National Bank of Cripple Creek, in the sum of $16,310.45, with interest and costs.

DURANGO, COLORADO

General Notes From the San Juan Region.

Silverton.—The Sunnyside M. & M. Co. has purchased the Gold Prince mill at Animas Forks. The intense cold that has prevailed during the past week caused some delay in starting the plant and mining operations generally.

The North Star mill and mine is under lease to M. De Golyer, the tungsten operator. Men have been at work for several months re-modeling the mill to dress tungsten ore.

Development continues at the Buffalo Boy. The litigation that involved the property, tieing-up operations for a number of years, is practically settled. Plans are under way for a season of heavy production, with a return to the former status. A strong organization is backing the project. Among other exploration is the driving of a tunnel under the present workings, cutting the vein at depth.

The Henrietta company proposes to drive a tunnel from the Cement Creek side to the Joker Tunnel side of Red mountain, cutting through large veins and having two points of shipment, the Gladstone branch, or the Red Mountain railroad.

The D. L. & W. Co. has almost completed the extensive development on the Lackawanna necessary to shipping ore. Re-timbering and driving a cross-cut tunnel to give access to a large area of stoping ground has been done; a tram has been built also. Plans are being drawn for a mill.

The Anvil Leasing Co. is driving a tunnel to cut a large vein on the Emerald lode. Shipments are being resumed from the Diamond lode.

Telluride.—Heavy production continues from the Tomboy and Smuggler Union mines. Although difficulty is being experienced with drifting snow on Lizard Head on the Rio Grande Southern, there has been no serious interference with traffic. The movement of live stock, which has held up ore movement, is now completed.

Ouray.—Ouray Consolidated continues development of its various holdings. Extensive work is now under way in the Guadeloupe, a large body of high-grade copper ore, for which the mine is noted, having been opened. Since the Red Mountain railroad has suspended running, the ore is packed to Ouray by mule-team. A tram will be constructed in the spring to facilitate removal of ore.

Rico.—The Standard Chemical Co., at Naturita, has erected an electric plant to provide light for all workings. A large reservoir has been constructed to provide a continuous supply of good water.

DENVER, COLORADO

Further Notes on the Copper Mines at Encampment, Wyoming, and Possibilities of Their Being Re-opened.

In the 'Press' of January 4, under the above head, was given some details of the Ferris-Haggerty mine in Wyoming, and something of the life at Encampment in 1896 and later. The latest concerning the properties there is that the Morse Bros. Machinery & Supply Co. of Denver has purchased the entire assets of the Penn-Wyoming Copper Co. at Encampment, owners of the Saratoga & Encampment railroad, the Ferris-Haggerty and Doane-Rambler mines at that place. The various subsidiary companies purchased and their respective bond issues are as follows:

Company	Bond issue
Ferris-Haggerty Copper Mining Co.	$1,000,000
Battle Lake Tunnel Site Mining Co.	750,000
Saratoga & Encampment Railroad Co.	750,000
Encampment Smelting Co.	500,000
Encampment Tramway Co.	350,000
Encampment Pipe Line Ditch Co.	100,000
Emerson Electric Light Co.	50,000
Encampment Water Works Co.	50,000
North American Mercantile Co.	22,000
Carbondale Coal Co.	20,000
Encampment Town Lot & Land Co.	8,000
Total	$3,000,000

The capital of the Penn-Wyoming Copper Co. was $10,000,000. This company was the successor of the North American Copper Co., the promotion of W. G. Emerson, who recently died at Los Angeles, California. The Penn-Wyoming company took over the property in 1904, and operated it under the most unfortunate conditions of fire losses and financing of the railroad until 1907 when it was closed. Numerous attempts have been made to reorganize and resume operation. Dissensions arising during the efforts at reorganization, a receiver was appointed, and litigation commenced which only ended in the Court of Appeals, the property sold to the Bondholders Protective Committee and the purchase by the Morse Bros. company from them brings the history to date. The mine produced over 10,000,000 lb. of copper from its discovery in 1898 by E. Haggerty.

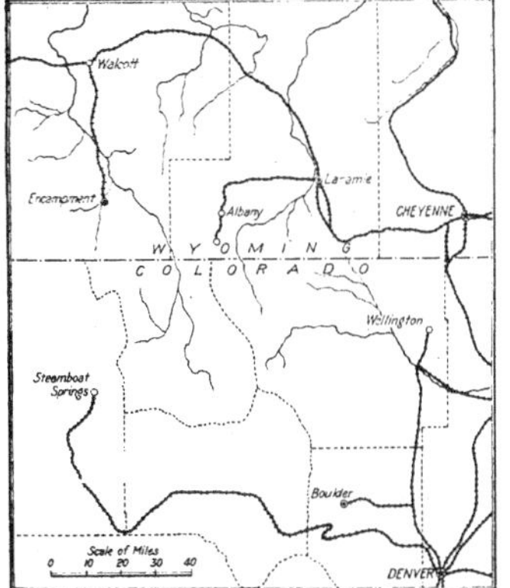

PART OF WYOMING AND COLORADO, SHOWING PLACES MENTIONED IN DENVER LETTER

The records of the Penn-Wyoming Copper Co. show a production of 6,414,011 lb. from 59,000 tons of ore mined, or 107.18 lb. of copper per ton recovered. From 1904 until operation ceased in 1907, the plants worked a total of 372 days during this period. In 1906 the concentrating and power-plant was destroyed by fire and re-built and put in operation the latter part of March 1907, and operated until May 10 of that year, when the smelter and tramway terminal were burned. These plants were re-built and commenced in May 1908, and operated until closed in October of that year owing to financial difficulties occurring through the building of the Saratoga & Encampment railroad, which connected the smelter at Encampment with Walcott, Wyoming, on the main line of the Union Pacific railroad. Previously, all of the coke and supplies were hauled in and the finished product hauled out to Walcott, the nearest railroad point, 47 miles distant.

The tramway connecting the Ferris-Haggerty mine with the smelter at Encampment is one of the longest, if not the longest, aerial tram in the world, the distance being 16¾ miles. It is operated in three sections, with a power-plant for each. There are 304 towers, tension, and anchor stations, 884 buckets, and 63 miles of wire rope. The track cables are 1¼ and 1 in., and the traction cable ¾ and ⅞ in. The cost of operation during the period was 93.47 cents per ton of ore handled.

Twelve cars of ore shipped from the Doane-Rambler mine in 1901 averaged 40.7% copper, and exhibits of ore from this mine at the St. Louis Exposition carried 900 lb. or 45% copper per ton. These ores were bornite and chalcocite. This mine was bought to supplement the production of the Ferris-Haggerty and has been developed to a depth of 665 ft. from the surface. No ore being taken out from the lower levels, as development was in progress at the time of closing. A great deal of the ore from the Ferris-Haggerty was hauled a distance of 60 miles to Walcott, and none of the Doane-Rambler ore was shipped that could not stand this transportation.

The Saratoga & Encampment railroad runs directly south from Walcott to Encampment, which is at the foot of the Continental Divide, at one of the lowest passes in the range. A survey has been made to connect this line with the Moffat road at Steamboat Springs, a distance of 60 miles on a 2% grade and a maximum altitude of 8500 feet.

The geological features of this district, many of which are interesting, are fully described in Professional Paper No. 25, by A. C. Spencer of the U. S. Geological Survey, published in 1904.

An effort will be made by the purchasers to prove the value of the mines, and have them operated if investigation will warrant the expenditures necessary. The smelter and concentrating plants at Encampment will be dismantled and material sold, as mills will be built at the mines and the concentrate transported to Encampment rather than hauling the crude ore, as mill-sites and water-rights are available at both the Ferris-Haggerty and the Doane Rambler mines.

PLATTEVILLE, WISCONSIN

Conditions in the Zinc, Lead, and Pyrite Mines and Markets.

The close of 1918 brought to zinc-mine operators in the Wisconsin fields conditions and prices that were sufficient to unnerve the most courageous. High-grade blende from refining plants, which had been sold for several months under agreement at $75 per ton, gave way to lower figures. Two large smelting firms continued to buy this grade, paying $55 and $50, respectively. On second grades the price at the beginning of December stood at $47.50, from where it fell to $42.50, with demand rather indifferent. Most of the ore was sold at this price, but sales were as low as $40. These figures were unsatisfactory and shut-downs were numerous. Severe weather made production difficult, and roads were so bad that some producers were isolated for a week at a time. There was also a scarcity of cars.

Lead-ore producers were also in a bad way, the price of ore dropping from $80 to $60 per ton. Demand was poor. Production fell off appreciably on account of cold weather.

Pyrite shippers remained out of the market nearly all December, prices and demand being unsatisfactory. The refining plants in the field where much of this class of ore is recovered were fairly well occupied, and there was held in reserve at the end of the year several thousand tons of fine. There are three sulphuric acid plants in the field, but only one is in operation at present.

Satisfactory developments were made during December in the northern districts of the field for the New Jersey Zinc Co. Carbonate of zinc in heavy blanket formations was found at shallow depths permitting cheap mining.

Gross recovery of zinc ore for December totaled 11,281 tons; net deliveries to smelters, including high-grade blende from local refining plants, 4853 tons. Conservative and reliable estimates show a reserve at all points in the field at the close of 1918 totaling 7500 tons of zinc concentrate, all grades; iron pyrite, 3000 tons; and lead, 500 tons.

SUTTER CREEK, CALIFORNIA

Encouraging Reports from the Central Eureka, Old Eureka, and Keystone Mines.

Developments on the lowest level of the Central Eureka mine are most encouraging. The winze sunk below the 3500-ft. level continued for 100 ft. in ore of excellent grade; then the vein turned slightly, and rather than make a bend in the winze, it was decided to cut a station and ore-pocket at that point and begin driving on the ore. This work is new well under way both north and south from the winze. The south drift is out 40 ft. in ore averaging $40 per ton, and the north drift 28 ft. long, in ore averaging $17. The north breast shows 8 ft. of $30 ore, and there are splendid indications of the good value continuing for some distance. These drifts will be extended far enough to ensure ample stoping area from this winze-level. In the meantime the ore extracted from driving is raising the grade of that from stopes above the 3500-ft. level, showing well in the mill. Excepting necessary repairs to the shaft and upper levels all work is confined at present to the 3500-ft. stopes and the two drifts from the winze 100 ft. below. The orebody now being worked on the lowest levels was found to apex on or near the 3425-ft. level. The vein is far less broken than near the point of discovery, and all signs point to persistence. The Central Eureka has had a long hard struggle for many years past—scarcity of labor, excessive costs, and apparent meagre ore-reserves proved most discouraging. The closing of the adjoining South Eureka mine, necessitating the Central company taking over the entire pumping expense for the two properties, added seriously to the maintenance charges, and during the last year in particular, assessments have been levied with heart-breaking regularity. The new development, however, bids fair to soon put the property on its feet; in fact, a fair profit is anticipated for this month's run, and it will be only a short time until sufficient ore is blocked out to warrant dropping the 40 stamps instead of 20 now. Albion S. Howe is superintendent, and W. J. Bryant underground foreman of this mine.

PART OF THE MOTHER LODE IN AMADOR COUNTY, CALIFORNIA

The above developments in the Central Eureka mine have brightened prospects for the Old Eureka adjoining. The new orebody in the Central is 350 ft. below the present bottom of the Old Eureka shaft, and 160 ft. from its boundary-line. The Old Eureka shaft is now down 2900 ft., and is being extended at the rate of about 20 ft. per week. The company now feels encouraged to continue sinking for several hundred feet more, even should the ore opened on the upper levels not come up to expectations. A north drift on the 2100-ft. level is in 480 ft. from the shaft, while the south drift has reached 660 ft. Considerable ore has been found in both directions, that to the north being higher in grade than that in the south. Preparations are also under way for considerable work on the 1200-ft. level, where ore of good grade is showing, and indicating that a large body may be uncovered. With these levels to draw from and the more persistent orebodies that the history of neighboring mines lead the owners to expect when greater depth is attained, a bright future for Hetty Green's old mine seems assured. The Old Eureka company has already spent a large sum in equipping and re-opening this old producer, and the faith in the property is evidenced by the substantial character, of all construction. A cross-cut is being driven at this time on the 500-ft. level to prospect an old ore-zone, and the intention is to construct an emergency dam at that point later; other improvements are contemplated. T. C. Gorrie is general manager of the Old Eureka and T. J. Donovan has charge of underground work. The recent improvement in the labor situation means much to the Old Eureka, and better progress will be made from now on.

During the past six months the old Keystone Mines at Amador City have kept up the struggle against adverse conditions, and added over $100,000 to the gold supply. On ore the gross value of which was less than $2.52 per ton this mine not only paid expenses but added something to its sinking-fund. Forty stamps of the mill were steadily operated during the six months, during which time there was crushed 44,322 tons of ore, producing $4652 in bullion and $106,860 in concentrates. Freight and smelter charges reduced the total to $85,516. While a small amount of ore was hoisted during the half-year from the 1000 and 2100-ft. levels, most of it came from the 1200, 1400, and 1800-ft. levels. Operations at 900, 1000, and 1200 ft. have been discontinued until more extensive prospecting can be done. On the 1400-ft. level, the south drift has been in ore for 45 ft., with several feet of milling ore in the face. Stoping is in progress at two points in the north workings. Some stoping is also under way on the 1500-ft. level. At 2100 ft. the east cross-cut has been advanced 543 ft. east of the shaft. At 360 and 468 ft. from the shaft ore has been found. Carlton R. Downs is managing this property, which has been in constant operation since its discovery in 1851; B. I. Hoxsie is supervising underground operations.

THE MINING SUMMARY

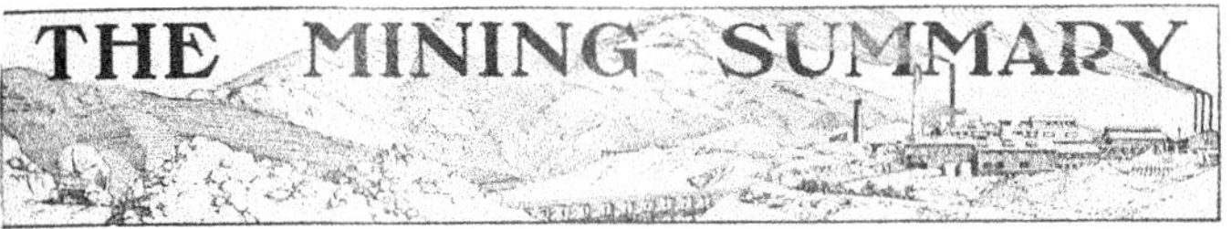

ALASKA

A joint resolution by Senator Jones of Washington, suspending assessment work on mining claims in Alaska for four years beginning with 1917, was passed by the Senate at Washington on January 20 and sent to the House. It also would extend to mining claims of Alaska the provisions of the acts suspending for two years the requirement that $100 worth of work be performed each year on claims, and exempting from the requirement those who served in the War.

ARIZONA

Humboldt.—Consolidated Arizona Smelting produced 1,060,000 lb. of copper in December. The monthly average in 1917 was 1,550,000 pounds.

Jerome.—The Jerome-Portland company has been reorganized as the Jerome-Bisbee. The receiver has been discharged. George Brookshire is president and L. H. Beyerle is secretary. A 500-ft. shaft has been sunk and 2800 ft. of other work done.

Mayer.—The Arizona Binghampton Copper Co. recently issued a report detailing the director's meeting and including the examination of the property by Horace V. Winchell. In over two years the flotation plant has concentrated 90,000 tons of ore, while 922 tons of high-grade was sent to smelter, the total being nearly 5,000,000 lb. This is equal to 3% ore. As low as 2½% was treated profitably. Reserves are estimated by Mr. Winchell as 100,000 tons of 3% ore and 150,000 tons of lower grade, all above the 600-ft. level. The total length of the ore-zone is 1400 ft. A new shaft is being sunk to 750 ft. depth, to be finished by June. The mill may be enlarged to 300 tons daily capacity, or double the present size. Generally, the possibilities of this mine are considered attractive.

The Big Bug company has erected a gasoline hoist and has sunk its shaft 75 of the 300 ft. contemplated. Some rich copper glance has been opened.

The Little Egypt is extracting enough ore to pay for development expenses. The old shaft is to be sunk to 500 ft. when the tunnel connection is made.

Ore has been found at 600 ft. in the Kay mine, probably an extension of the shoot worked at 500 feet.

Oatman.—United Eastern paid 5 cents per share, equal to $68,150, on January 27.

Superior.—Magma Copper Co. produced 1,049,783 lb. during December. The average for 1918 was 900,000 lb. per month, ranging from 560,000 to 1,169,000 pounds.

CALIFORNIA

Oil production during December amounted to 275,596 bbl. daily from 8606 wells. There were 41 wells completed during the month. In 1918, according to the Standard Oil Co., the total output was 101,637,870 bbl., equal to 278,460 bbl. per day. Stocks declined 407,542 bbl. to the present total of 32,042,923 barrels.

Angels.—The W. J. Loring interests have purchased the old Morgan mine, on the north-east slope of Carson hill, 4 miles south of Angels. The option was completed after considerable exploration was done. From 1898 to 1914 this mine, part of the estate of J. K. Fair of San Francisco, was idle. Some famous pockets of gold ore were found in the early days, one being worth $300,000. The ore is free-milling, and will be sent to the Melones mill.

Keswick.—The Mountain Copper Co.'s enlarged flotation plant at Minnesota station, midway between Keswick and Iron Mountain, is now in operation.

Cima.—The Piute silver-lead mine at Cima, San Bernardino county, has been acquired by the Nevada Mine Leasing & Holding Co. During 1917 this property was the largest silver-lead producer in the district, but the owners became financially involved in the latter part of that year and until the present time. The financial difficulties have been cleared, the new owners have started rehabilitating the old workings. The property is a regular producer and will shortly commence shipping again. The mine is developed by shaft and 2000 ft. of workings.

Coram.—The First National Copper Co., controlling the Balaklala mines, pays a dividend of 15 cents per share on February 25. This amounts to $90,000.

St. Louis.—Hydraulicking to be started here next spring will result in the ground upon which the town stands being washed away by the Loftus company. To restrain the gravel the company has a concrete dam across Slate creek.

COLORADO

Boulder.—J. G. Clark, general manager for the Boulder Tungsten Production Company, expresses confidence in a revival in the tungsten industry during the current year, and is especially optimistic of the re-establishment of his company on a producing basis. He is not only ready to announce plans upon which he has been working to put the company on its feet financially for work in the mines and the extension of a tunnel which is nearing the mineral-bearing zone, but is at this time confident that the plans will work out successfully in a short time.

Georgetown.—The Wide West Mining Co. has driven its tunnel a distance of 3000 ft.; it is also driving on several veins. A 24-in. track of 40-lb. rails and a 4-in. air pipe-line were laid. This tunnel is to explore the Colorado Central 1000 ft. below present workings. G. W. Hall is superintendent.

Idaho Springs.—During 1918 the Argo mill treated 19,700 tons of ore, settling with producers for a total of $328,348.

IDAHO

Kellogg.—Caledonia pays a dividend of 1 cent per share, equal to $26,050, on February 5. The total is now $3,725,150.

Leadore.—The Sunset M. & M. Co.'s new 40-ton concentrating plant is working well. Concentrate assays 44% lead and 36 oz. silver per ton. By adding more tables the capacity is to be increased to 80 tons. W. Van Wagenen is manager, with W. Fagregreen as mill superintendent.

KANSAS

Baxter Springs.—The Chanute Spelter Co., in charge of W. H. Eardley, has four pumps with a capacity of 3000 gal. per min. drawing water from drill-holes, and as the water is lowered a shaft is sunk. The shaft is going down in limestone, following a dry hole. Much interest is being taken in this method.

MICHIGAN

Houghton.—It is reported that copper production in this district is to be curtailed as in other parts of the country.

Copper outputs of the Calumet & Hecla group in December were as follows: Ahmeek, 1,761,823 lb.; Allouez, 543,988; C. & H., 5,533,690; Centennial, 195,021; Isle Royale, 1,601,244; La Salle, 130,670; Osceola, 253,254; Superior, 109,875; and White Pine, 410,141, a total of 10,539,706 pounds.

MISSOURI

Joplin.—Production of the Tri-State region last week was:

State	Blende, tons	Calamine, tons	Lead, tons	Value
Kansas	965	...	12	$44,328
Missouri	497	59	145	32,957
Oklahoma	5,363	...	830	280,409
Average price	$45	$34	$60	......

MONTANA

Kendall.—Barnes-King Development Co. pays 10 cents per share, equal to $40,000, on February 15. This makes a total of $300,000. The December gold yield was $45,400, from 4627 tons of ore. The labor situation is much improved.

NEVADA

Carson.—The biennial report of the State inspector of mines, A. J. Stinson, for 1917-'18, has just been published. In the 96 pages are statistics of production, warnings to certain mining companies, accidents, and a list of properties in the various counties. There were 26 fatalities during the year ended November 30, 1918. The average number of men employed in mines last year was 6295, an increase of 204 compared with the 1917 total. Expenditures of the Inspector's department in 1918 totaled $12,442.

Ely.—The old Taylor mine in the Ward district, 15 miles south of this place, is to be re-opened by the W. S. Bennett of Cody, Wyoming, representing Wyoming and South Dakotan people. The copper ore is said to carry a good deal of silver. A mill may be put up to treat dumps.

Goldfield.—The Goldfield Consolidated was to close its mines and mill on February 1, but it is proposed to re-open all of the mines on a leasing system.

Kimberly.—The Consolidated Coppermines Co. states that the note in the 'Press' of January 11 to the effect that the Pilot-Knob mill is to be shut-down on account of unprofitable operation, and that the mill-heads have been running less than 1% copper, is incorrect. The plant on Pilot Knob was re-modeled as an experimental mill to determine a flow-sheet for design of a larger unit. On account of its position, design, and the water condition obtaining at Kimberly it was never intended that the Pilot Knob be run over any protracted time. Owing to the present condition of the copper market, and also that it is no longer necessary to operate this unit for testing purposes, it was deemed expedient to stop this work. During the last three months of 1918 the mill-heads averaged 1.29% copper, while at the time the plant stopped the ore carried 1.5%. H. S. Munroe is general manager.

Pioneer.—The Consolidated Mayflower Mines Co., in charge of J. B. Kendall of Goldfield, will soon be in the market for a ball-mill, to be used in its plant at Pioneer.

Thompson.—Mason Valley produced 1,273,176 lb. of copper during December, well up to the average.

Tonopah.—Production of the district last week was 7168 tons of ore valued at $121,856.

Tonopah Mining Co. in December treated 6514 tons for 101,605 oz. of silver and 1135 oz. of gold, and a profit of $38,000.

A geological description of the Divide district has been prepared by A. H. Elftman for the Rosetta Divide Mining Co. The rock formations are, he says, a continuation of some of those found in Tonopah mines. The character of the veins and conditions of mineralization in the two districts are somewhat different. The Divide breccia, in which the main ore deposits occur, have not been extensively explored at Tonopah.

'The Genesis of the Ores at Tonopah, Nevada', is the title of Professional Paper 104, just issued by the U. S. Geological Survey, written by E. S. Bastin and F. B. Laney. An abstract of this report will be given in the 'Press' later.

NEW MEXICO

Mogollon.—The old Little Dry Creek gold-silver district, 20 miles south of here and 60 miles north-west of Silver City, is said to be receiving attention again. Several parties have uncovered good ore.

Santa Rita.—A company has been organized by C. A. Petterson of this place, and Chicago people, to take over the Log Cabin mine. A recent shipment of ore assayed high in lead, silver, and copper. Fourteen men are employed.

TENNESSEE

Deposits of manganese ores in eastern Tennessee have been examined recently by G. W. Stose and F. C. Schrader, geologists of the U. S. Geological Survey, in co-operation with W. A. Nelson, State geologist, and Arthur McFarlan, assistant State geologist, of Tennessee. The deposits were studied systematically with a view to determining their relation to the underlying rocks and to the surface features and their probable extent and content of ore. The studies of the geologists and the exploratory work of the mining companies have revealed the existence in the State of fairly large reserves of ore of good grade. Many of the deposits are being worked, much prospecting preparatory to mining has been done, and new deposits have recently been discovered.

The deposits occur in a belt about 10 miles wide and 220 miles long, extending diagonally across eastern Tennessee from the Virginia State line at the north-east corner of the State south-westward to the Georgia State line near Cleveland, 20 miles east of Chattanooga. This belt follows the north-west foot of the Appalachian mountains, lying in the adjoining lowlands known as the Great Valley, or the Valley of East Tennessee, and in minor inter-montane valleys. It is traversed from north-east to south-west by the Tennessee river, which drains practically the whole of eastern Tennessee. Elizabethton, Johnson City, Newport, Morristown, Knoxville, Marysville, Sweetwater, Athens, and Cleveland, the largest towns within the manganese area, are served by the Bristol-Chattanooga line of the Southern Railway and its seven branches and by ten other smaller independent lines.

The manganese deposits are exposed at 119 mines and prospects, most of which were visited by the Survey's geologists, and are distributed through 16 counties, which, named in order, beginning at the north-east, are Johnson, Carter, Unicoi, Greene, Cocke, Hamblen, Grainger, Jefferson, Sevier, Knox, Anderson, Blount, Loudon, Monroe, McMinn, and Bradley.

Most of the ore is shipped to the Southern Manganese Corporation at Anniston, Alabama, and the Tennessee Coal, Iron & Railroad Co. at Birmingham, Alabama. Some, however, is shipped to the Carnegie Steel Co. at Pittsburgh, the Seaboard Steel & Manganese Co. at Temple, and the Miami Metals Co. at South Chicago.

Most manganese ore that contains over 35% metallic

manganese is made into forro-manganese; ferruginous manganese are that contains 10 to 35% of metallic manganese is made into spiegeleisen.

The available ore-reserves at the mines that were examined is estimated to be 85,000 tons, of which 75,000 tons is manganese ore and 10,000 tons is ferruginous manganese ore. These estimates are undoubtedly moderate or low; the reserves may be more than twice as great, possibly 200,000 tons.

TEXAS

Austin.—In the mandamus suit of C. D. Greene of Wichita Falls versus J. T. Robinson, State Land Commissioner, the former demands a permit to prospect for and acquire the oil and gas on 320 acres of land in Wilbarger county in the oil-field. The Commissioner is of the opinion that the State owns the minerals in this land, but the State Attorney-General having given him an opinion to the contrary he declined to issue the permit in order that a mandamus suit could be brought and the matter finally adjudicated by the Supreme Court. The application of Greene for a mineral permit was filed in 1915. At the term of Court last fall the arguments were submitted, and now all parties are anxiously awaiting a decision.

El Paso.—According to the 'Herald', S. H. Worrell, dean of the Texas School of Mines here, and chairman of the committee appointed by the mining circle of the University club, and the rest of the committee-men had their first meeting on the 12th to draft a new mining law to be submitted to the Texas Legislature. It was generally agreed to follow the general law of the United States, leaving out the feature regarding extra-lateral rights, as it is the cause of a great deal of litigation. It was stated by a member of the committee that it is probable that a provision will be made to pay the State a royalty on production, but it will be made free from ambiguity. The consensus of opinion of the members is that if it is finally determined to put in a royalty provision to make it on the net production, say, take the selling price of the product and then deduct all transportation charges at least. There is a disposition to leave out the United States provisions regarding tunnel-sites. This part of the laws is complex, and as the topography of Texas is different and the land laws different from the other States, it appears to be the opinion of the committee to leave this out and leave it for future action if found necessary.

UTAH

Alta.—The Woodlawn Mining Co., in the Little Cottonwood district, has opened 4½ ft. of high-grade lead-silver carbonate ore. W. J. Lawrence is manager.

Marysvale.—The Florence mill started again treating alunite for potash last week.

OKLAHOMA

Douthat.—The Tar Creek Mining Co., leasing south of this place, has two hand-jigs worked by one man. An unusual class of formation is being treated.

Hockerville.—The St. Louis Smelting & Refining Co. is erecting a hand-jig plant on a new lease on the Weiss land, south of here. A crusher and rolls will be part of the machinery.

Quapaw.—At the Gander mine 16 hand-jigs are to be installed by the Thelma Jane company, composed of O. A. Dunn and B. F. Routh of Tar River, and others. A carload of blende weekly is expected from these machines.

HAND-JIGGING PLANT IN JOPLIN DISTRICT, MISSOURI

WASHINGTON

Loon Lake.—The Loon Lake Copper Co. has started erecting a 100-ton flotation plant. Estimates give reserves amounting to 30,000 tons. W. L. Zeigler is in charge of construction.

Oroville.—Mining is said to be more active here than for some time. The Oroville Copper Co. is driving a tunnel on its vein, extracting good ore.—Arkins & Smith are erecting a 50-ton mill near Nighthawk to treat silver-lead ore.— — The Copper World Extension is erecting an aerial tram.

CANADA

British Columbia

Princeton.—The Canada Copper Corporation has contracted with the Consolidated Mining & Smelting Co. at Trail to smelt its concentrate and refine its copper. Accommodation is being made here for 150 men by the Consolidated M. & S. Co. This work is understood to be preliminary to commencement of development of the property known as Voight's claims, which have been taken over by the company. This property adjoins that of the Canada Copper Corporation, near Princeton, on which extensive work has been under way for several years, and which will soon be ready for production on a large scale.

Quesnel.—About three years ago, gold was discovered by E. L. Armstrong on Proserpine mountain, just south of Barkerville. On his Independence claims Armstrong has since uncovered a 14-ft. orebody showing free gold. Sixteen samples taken by J. D. Galloway, government district engineer, averaged $61.50 per ton. On the Imperial claims, Tregillus, Carey, and others, nearby, uncovered this vein, where it was 9 ft. wide, with free gold. Assay from several points are reported to have yielded from $6.10 to $231.60 per ton. A 20-in. cross-vein, highly mineralized, was also opened. This assayed $16 gold and $8.30 silver. Sulphides appear at shallow depth.

Vancouver.—A statement of the gold deposited at the Dominion Assay Office here, shows that the year 1918 established a new record. The value of the bullion deposited was $4,080,185; in 1917 it was $3,257,221; and in 1916, $2,828,240. During the latter part of the season 189 assays of platinum-hearing ores and sands were made and 77 deposits of platinum metals received. The purchase of these metals has been discontinued, but assays of platinum-bearing material will be continued.

Ontario

Dividends paid by Ontario mines during 1918 are as under, according to 'The Daily Nugget' of Cobalt:

Cobalt:	
Nipissing, 25%	$1,500,000
Mining Corporation, 85¼ cents per share	1,244,731
Kerr Lake, 20%	600,000
Coniagas, 12½%	500,000
Buffalo Mines (capital reduction)	250,000
Temiskaming, 3%	75,000
McKinley-Darragh, 12%	269,712
Penn-Canadian, 3%	40,491
La Rose, 2%	30,000
Total	$4,509,934
Porcupine:	
Hollinger Con., 5%	$1,230,000
McIntyre-Porcupine, 15%	541,542
Total	$1,771,542
Kirkland Lake:	
Lake Shore, 5%	$ 100,000
Grand total	$6,381,477

Cobalt.—Kerr Lake pays 25 cents per share, equal to $150,000, on March 15.

Cobalt.—The Coniagas company paid 2½% on February 1. This amounted to $100,000, and makes $9,340,000 to date.

Nipissing produced silver worth $254,118 during December, from 182 tons of high and 6700 tons of low-grade ores. The total for 1918 was $3,544,790, an increase of $155,322 over 1917.

Kirkland Lake.—The Lake Shore company distributed $100,000 during 1918. On December 10 the last dividend was $50,000.

Sudbury.—The Mond Nickel Co., which has mines and a smelter here, and a refinery at Swansea, Wales, will largely increase its output. It is offering a new stock issue of £1,520,000 to raise funds for extension of its refining works and provide for an increased volume of business, anticipating an expansion of 50%.

MEXICO

Chihuahua

Chihuahua.—Manganese mining in this district is practically at a standstill, owing to the absence of any market in the United States.

Santa Eulalia.—Villa has been active again in this part, raiding the town on January 22. He looted the safes and stores of the mining companies, hanging the mayor, capturing Federal soldiers, and telling the mine managers that they must increase wages and shorten the hours of labor.

Sonora

Cananea.— Greene-Cananea pays $1.50 per share on February 24. The previous quarterly rate was $2, during 1918, 1917, and 1916.

PERSONAL

Note. The Editor invites members of the profession to send particulars of their work and appointments. The information is interesting to our readers.

Morton Webber is at Butte.

F. A. Beauchamp is visiting Sonora, California, this week.

Nicholas Troweek, of Salt Lake City, was in San Francisco last week.

Walter Broadbridge sailed for London from New York on January 22.

A. T. Thomson, P. G. Beckett, and **W. D. Hanbridge** were at Bisbee on January 18.

Courtenay De Kalb, associate editor of the M. & S. P., has returned to San Francisco.

Scott Turner has received his discharge from the Navy and is now at Lansing, Michigan.

C. E. Hoffman, manager for the Democrata Mining Co., at Cananea, was in Bisbee last week.

L. E. Porter, secretary and vice-president of the Tungsten Reef Mining Co., was in Bisbee last week.

Michael H. Loveman has opened an office at 32 Broadway, New York, for the practice of mining geology.

Isakichi Takenouchi, of the Sumitomo Beshi Copper mine, in Japan, is visiting the copper districts of Arizona.

V. H. Smith, of the Canada Copper Corporation, operating at Princeton, B. C., has been here on his wedding trip.

Frank H. Probert has been appointed member of a U. S. Government commission to study mining and metallurgical conditions in Europe.

T. C. Gorrie is general manager of the Old Eureka mine, at Sutter Creek, California, with **T. J.** Donovan as underground superintendent.

W. D. Thornton, Frederick Laist, William Wraith, W. N. Tanner, M. B. Gentry, A. G. Parsons, and **L. D. Ricketts** have been visiting Bisbee, Cananea, Ajo, and Miami.

Edwin Higgins has resigned as engineer to the California Metal Producers Association and is succeeded by **C. H. Fry**. Mr. Higgins has joined the staff of Bulkeley Wells in San Francisco.

Daniel Guggenheim has retired as president of the A. S. & R., and is succeeded by his younger brother **Simon Guggenheim. Edgar L. Newhouse** becomes chairman of the board of directors.

R. A. Conrads has resigned his position as metallurgical engineer for the Nevada Consolidated Copper Co. to take a position on the Federal Board for Vocational Education, with headquarters at Salt Lake City.

Obituary

E. M. Rabb, superintendent of the Ajax mine at Victor, Colorado, died from influenza at Tonopah, Nevada, on January 16.

T. J. Curran, well known in California and Mexico, died in San Francisco on January 15 from pneumonia following influenza. He was 55 years of age and was a native of Maryland. He was president of the American Magnesite Co. of Porterville, California.

The American Mining Congress and the American Zinc Institute formed local chapters at Joplin, Missouri, on January 28. Victor Rakowsky was chairman of the meeting.

At a joint meeting of the San Francisco branches of the national engineering societies last week the subject of 'Engineering Education' was discussed. The principal speakers were **J. W. Beckman, John A. Britton, C. L. Cory, C. D. Marx,** and **T. A. Rickard. James M. Hyde** led the discussion that followed.

THE METAL MARKET

METAL PRICES

San Francisco, January 28

Aluminum-dust, large and small lots, cents per lb	65—70
Antimony, cents per pound	8.00
Copper, electrolytic, cents per pound, in carload lots	22.00
Lead, pig, cents per pound	5.75— 6.75
Platinum, per ounce	$108
Quicksilver, per flask of 75 lb	$100
Spelter, cents per pound	9.00
Zinc-dust, cents per pound	16.00

Aluminum-dust consumers will find a number of points of interest in 'The Inflammability of Aluminum-Dust,' by Alan Leighton, in Technical Paper 152 of the U. S. Bureau of Mines.

The War Trade Board announces that the restriction upon the importation of manganese ore or manganese di-oxide from Asia and Australia has been removed, and that licenses will now be issued, when the applications therefor are otherwise in order, for the importation of manganese ore or manganese di-oxide from any country.

EASTERN METAL MARKET

(By wire from New York)

January 28.—Copper is quiet. Lead is inactive. Spelter is weak.

SILVER

Below are given official (not Government) quotations, in cents per ounce, of silver 999 fine. In order to make prompt settlements with smelters and brokers, producers allow a discount from the maximum fixed price of $1.01½, hence the lower price. The Government has not fixed the general market price at $1, but will pay this price (as from April 23, 1918) for all silver purchased by it. The equivalent of dollar silver (1000 fine) in British currency is 46.65 pence per ounce (925 fine), calculated at the current rate of exchange. On August 15, 1918, the Treasury announced that the maximum price was fixed at $1.01½ per ounce. The British government fixed its maximum at 49½ pence, on September 2, but on November 12 this was changed to 48¾ pence, and on December 13 to 48 7/16 pence.

Date		New York	London		Average week ending	
Jan.	22	101.12	48.44	Dec.	17	101.12
"	23	101.12	48.44	"	24	101.12
"	24	101.12	48.44	"	31	101.12
"	25	101.12	48.44	Jan.	7	101.12
"	26	Sunday		"	14	101.12
"	27	101.12	48.44	"	21	101.12
"	28	101.12	48.44	"	28	101.12

Monthly averages

	1916	1917	1918		1916	1917	1918
Jan.	56.76	75.14	88.72	July	63.06	78.92	99.62
Feb.	56.74	77.54	85.79	Aug.	66.07	85.40	100.31
Mch.	57.89	74.13	88.11	Sept.	68.51	100.73	101.14
Apr.	46.37	72.51	95.35	Oct.	67.86	87.38	101.12
May	74.27	74.61	99.50	Nov.	71.60	85.97	101.12
June	65.04	76.44	99.50	Dec.	75.70	85.97	101.12

The Mint has not purchased any silver in the open market since July 1918. The price ($1 per oz.) of silver is likely to remain at that point for some time to come, as the Mint has power to purchase the same equivalent to the number of ounces resulting from the melting of silver dollars at that rate.

Weather conditions in India, which always influence the silver market, have been good. Silver coinage by the two Indian Mints has been on a large scale, as shown by the following output in August last, valued at 55,279,290 rupees ($17,689,373):

Whole rupees (silver)	51,500,024
Half rupees (silver)	993,666
Quarter rupees (silver)	1,132,488
Two-anna (nickel)	957,112
One-anna (nickel)	619,000
Single pice (bronze)	47,900
Pie pieces (bronze)	29,000

As the average speed of coining is estimated at 2600 coins a minute in Calcutta and at 1600 in Bombay, the velocity of the output per second equals 70 coins, worth an average of 46 rupees ($14.70).

A reduction in the size of 50-sen, 20-sen, and 10-sen silver coins has been announced by a Japanese ordinance, the reason being, not only that the silver coins in use at present are rather inconvenient to carry, but because of the practice of melting them into bullion on account of the appreciation in the market price of silver. The new silver coins will be smaller in size by about 1/100 of an inch than the preceding coins, and will contain a smaller quantity of silver. The Government intends to mint Y20,000,000 ($10,000,000) in the three denominations during the current fiscal year, and gradually to withdraw the old coins from circulation.

TIN

Prices in New York, in cents per pound. The monthly averages in 1918 are nominal. On December 3 the War Industries Board fixed the price to consumers and jobbers at 72½c. f.o.b. Chicago and Eastern points, and 71¼c. on the Pacific Coast. This will continue until the U. S. Steel Products Co.'s stock is consumed.

Monthly averages

	1916	1917	1918		1916	1917	1918
Jan.	41.76	44.10	85.13	July	38.37	62.60	93.00
Feb.	42.60	51.47	85.00	Aug.	38.88	62.53	91.33
Mch.	50.50	54.27	85.00	Sept.	39.00	61.54	80.40
Apr.	51.49	55.63	88.53	Oct.	41.10	62.24	78.82
May	49.10	63.21	100.01	Nov.	44.12	74.18	73.07
June	42.07	61.93	91.00	Dec.	42.55	85.00	71.52

COPPER

Prices of electrolytic in New York, in cents per pound.

Date				Average week ending	
Jan.	22	20.00	Dec.	17	26.00
"	23	20.00	"	24	26.00
"	24	20.00	"	31	26.00
"	25	19.75	Jan.	7	21.80
"	26 Sunday		"	14	20.75
"	27	19.75	"	21	20.50
"	28	19.75	"	28	19.87

Monthly averages

	1916	1917	1918		1916	1917	1918
Jan.	24.30	29.53	23.50	July	25.66	29.67	26.00
Feb.	26.62	34.57	23.50	Aug.	27.03	27.42	26.00
Mch.	26.65	36.00	23.50	Sept.	28.28	25.11	26.00
Apr.	28.02	33.16	23.50	Oct.	28.50	23.50	26.00
May	29.02	31.69	23.50	Nov.	31.05	23.50	26.00
June	27.47	32.57	23.50	Dec.	32.89	23.50	26.00

The War Trade Board announces that the restriction upon the importation of copper ore and copper concentrates has been removed, and that license will now be issued, when the applications therefor are otherwise in order, for the importation from any country of copper ore and copper contrates, regardless of the copper content thereof.

LEAD

Lead is quoted in cents per pound, New York delivery.

Date				Average week ending	
Jan.	22	5.50	Dec.	17	7.05
"	23	5.50	"	24	6.45
"	24	5.50	"	31	6.10
"	25	5.50	Jan.	7	5.80
"	26 Sunday		"	14	5.75
"	27	5.50	"	21	5.62
"	28	5.50	"	28	5.50

Monthly averages

	1916	1917	1918		1916	1917	1918
Jan.	5.95	7.64	6.85	July	6.40	10.93	8.03
Feb.	6.23	9.10	7.07	Aug.	6.28	10.75	8.05
Mch.	7.26	10.07	7.26	Sept.	6.86	9.07	8.05
Apr.	7.70	9.38	6.99	Oct.	7.02	6.97	8.05
May	7.38	10.29	6.88	Nov.	7.07	6.38	8.05
June	6.88	11.74	7.58	Dec.	7.55	6.49	6.90

ZINC

Zinc is quoted as spelter, standard Western brands, New York delivery, in cents per pound.

Date				Average week ending	
Jan.	22	7.35	Dec.	17	8.58
"	23	7.30	"	24	8.45
"	24	7.20	"	31	8.13
"	25	7.15	Jan.	7	7.93
"	26 Sunday		"	14	7.72
"	27	7.10	"	21	7.52
"	28	7.10	"	28	7.20

Monthly averages

	1916	1917	1918		1916	1917	1918
Jan.	18.21	9.75	7.87	July	9.80	8.98	8.72
Feb.	19.99	10.45	7.97	Aug.	9.03	8.58	8.87
Mch.	18.40	10.78	7.67	Sept.	9.18	8.33	9.58
Apr.	18.62	10.20	7.04	Oct.	9.92	8.32	9.11
May	16.01	9.41	7.29	Nov.	11.81	7.76	8.75
June	12.85	9.63	7.92	Dec.	11.26	7.84	8.49

Zinc ore (60% metal basis) had a lower tendency at Joplin, Missouri, last week, and was sold as low as $42.50 per ton.

QUICKSILVER

The primary market for quicksilver is San Francisco, California being the largest producer. The price is fixed in the open market, according to quantity. Prices, in dollars per flask of 75 pounds:

Date					
Dec.	31	110.00	Jan.	14	105.00
Jan.	7	110.00	"	21	100.00
			"	28	100.00

Monthly averages

	1916	1917	1918		1916	1917	1918
Jan.	222.00	81.00	128.00	July	81.20	102.00	120.00
Feb.	295.00	126.25	118.00	Aug.	74.50	115.00	120.00
Mch.	219.00	113.75	112.00	Sept.	75.00	112.00	120.00
Apr.	141.60	114.50	115.00	Oct.	78.20	102.00	120.00
May	90.00	104.00	110.00	Nov.	79.50	102.50	120.00
June	74.70	85.50	112.00	Dec.	80.00	117.42	115.00

Eastern Metal Market

New York, January 21.

Prices have a downward tendency, with copper selling at 20c. or lower and all markets inactive. No business of any importance is being done in tin. The price of lead has been reduced ½c. per lb. by the leading interests (A. S. & R. Co.) Prices of spelter are weak as a result of over-production.

ALUMINUM

Dealers are offering virgin metal at 32c. per lb. and it is not at all unlikely that this price could be shaded. The Government price, which will continue in force until March 1, is 33c. per lb. for 50-ton lots, 33.10c. for 15 to 50-ton lots, and 33.20c. for smaller quantities.

ANTIMONY

Antimony is weaker, and 5-ton or larger lots can be bought at 7.50 to 7.75c. per lb. The prices for smaller lots are higher, the quotations being 8.25 to 8.50c. On last Monday a 50-ton lot of Chinese antimony was sold on the New York Metal Exchange. The price paid was 5.95c. in bond, equivalent to approximately 7c. per lb., duty paid.

COPPER

The copper market is noticeably easy, and the sales that have been made during the past week were at prices ranging from 20c. per lb. downward. In fact, it is not at all unlikely that business can be done at 19 or 19.50c. While copper producers are still quoting the 23c. price, it is considered doubtful if much business is being placed on that basis, in spite of the fact that consumers will be protected by the producers against their own price declines. The point has been raised as to how long producers will maintain the higher quotation, especially as there is barely enough business to keep the people busy who are willing to sell at 19.50 or 20c. Cabled reports from England stating that there is 36,000 tons of copper in that country had a markedly depressing tendency upon the New York market, it being considered not likely that there would be any demand from England for some time to come. It is also believed that there is a large supply of this metal in France, bought for war purposes but not used. The demand for copper in the first two weeks of this year was fairly good. About 10,000,000 to 20,000,000 lb. changed hands in that time, but the market then relaxed into extreme dullness. This prevailed until last Monday, when some renewed interest in February shipments was observed.

LEAD

Dullness and quiet characterize the lead market which is decidedly easier. The output is being curtailed by the producers to stabilize the situation. On Tuesday the American Smelting & Refining Co. reduced its price from 6 to 5.50c., New York, and in the outside market 5.37½ to 5.50c. is being quoted. In spite of this, little business is being done.

TIN

Tin is still quoted at 71.50c. per lb., New York, which is the same as last week. The market is dull. An effort is being made by the Tin Section of the War Trade Board to sell the allotment of tin bought for this country, but consumers cannot see why they should pay 72.50c. per lb. when the metal can be imported for about 20c. per lb. less. They consider that the Government should take this tin as a war measure, and sell it at the present market value, accepting the loss as part of the fortunes of war. It is probable that many of the consumers will take the tin from the Government, although they do not regard its plan favorably, as they consider it their patriotic duty to do so. The London quotation for spot Straits today was £250.

ZINC

Spelter production is noticeably in excess of demand, and the market is weak. Prime Western is being quoted at 6.75 to 6.82½c., New York, and at St. Louis the quotation for high-grade spelter is approximately 8.50c. For the week ended January 11, production increased 380 tons and stocks increased 2684 tons, according to the Government's report.

COPPER NOTES

A conference between employees of copper companies of Utah, Montana, and Arizona and the Department of Labor, to discuss the present labor situation, was called by the Secretary of Labor for January 31 at Washington. The formal announcement reads:

"In view of the curtailment of the copper output following the signing of the armistice and the consequent reduction of the working forces, the Secretary of Labor has invited the grievance committee of the employees of all the copper companies operating in Arizona and representatives of labor in Utah and Montana to send delegates here to confer with him Friday next to co-operate in obtaining the best possible working conditions during the readjustment period."

Twenty of the principal copper producers of North and South America yielded a total of 1,763,668,637 lb. during 1918, an increase of nearly 90,000,000 lb. when compared with the previous year; but during 1917 there were many labor troubles in the United States, resulting in shut-downs. Since last December there has been a general curtailment of operations ranging from 25 to 50% of capacity. The much expected demand for copper from Europe has not materialized, there being large stocks in England, France, and Italy. Exports during 1918 were as under:

Month	Pounds	Month	Pounds
January	81,058,000	August	42,300,000
February	56,324,000	September	71,220,000
March	62,370,000	October	22,400,000
April	47,622,000	November	18,000,000
May	61,586,000	December	11,000,000
June	63,582,000		
July	64,673,000	Total	602,041,000

According to Daniel Guggenheim, retiring president of the A. S. & R. Co., the finances of this company are in excellent condition: "As to the immediate future," he said, "because of problems of reconstruction confronting the whole world, some difficult months may be expected; but I am a great optimist as to the future, based upon the enormous demand that must be made for raw materials. These demands will be felt as soon as the various business interests realize that prices and supplies are at a low ebb. For many years, the senior members of Guggenheim brothers have been the dominant factors in affairs of A. S. & R. Co. and American S. S. Co. They feel that, if these companies are to retain and improve their business positions, it is advisable to turn over the management and control to younger and more aggressive men. It has been decided that three of the older members of Guggenheim Brothers should retire, so that the important offices of president, chairman of executive committee, and chairman of finance committee may be filled by others. Those succeeding to our positions are contemplating putting into effect many excellent plans, which will be of prime importance, and which will, I believe, ensure their signal success in directing affairs of the companies. During the years of my presidency, many important reforms in the business have been inaugurated, and none more important, in my judgment, than permitting its important managing and operating officials and employees a participation in profits of the companies. . . ."

INFORMATION FURNISHED BY MANUFACTURERS

RE-BUILDING USED MACHINERY

The purchase, overhaul, and re-sale of used machinery of all descriptions is a specialty of Buttress & McClellan of 205 N. Los Angeles St., Los Angeles, California. The business has expanded to the present large ground-floor store and upper floors, a shop completely equipped for the re-building and overhauling of used machinery; also two warehouses where equipment is stocked for sale.

Following the course of a piece of machinery as it goes through the shop, we find the procedure to be: Supposing an engine or compressor is purchased in the field: When it enters the shop it is immersed in a bath of lye; a specially-constructed vat has been provided for this purpose, and it will take anything intact up to a fair size piece. All grease, dirt, and even what is left of the original paint is cleaned off in this way. This makes possible a thorough inspection. The engine is then dismantled, the different parts going to various departments in the shop fitted to do any special work necessary. When this is completed, the engine is re-assembled, thoroughly tested, re-painted, and ready to go out, backed by the firm's guarantee. The same is true of other equipment purchased and re-sold by them. Mine managers and those purchasing for mines are invited to inspect their shop when in Los Angeles. The firm is also building several types of new machines in its shops. Among these is the small hoist illustrated. They also manufacture an impact screen. A competent engineering staff is maintained ready to advise concerning the erection of any equipment sold. Many complete mine and mill plants have been built under their direction. Many problems have been worked out. During 1918, when new equipment was at a premium and deliveries were uncertain, Buttress & McClellan filled many orders with judgment and dispatch.

A HOIST FOR SMALL MINE

This firm is also in the market for used machinery. Anyone about to dismantle plant would do well to communicate with them.

INTERIOR VIEW OF WAREHOUSE, SHOWING MACHINERY READY FOR SHIPMENT

REMOVING A PECULIAR OVERBURDEN FROM IRON ORE

Stripping overburden on the iron ranges of Lake Superior frequently is handicapped by the presence of a vegetal matter known as muskeg. When dry, this material burns like peat, and when wet, runs like mercury. The latter characteristic is being taken advantage of on the Gogebic range in northern Michigan. Muskeg is prevalent near the Plymouth mine at Verona. One dump has been set aside for handling this material exclusively. A stream of water

SHOWING HOW MUSKEG DUMPS SLIDE

plays upon the dump continually, pumped from a near-by water-hole, as shown in the illustration. The result is that when the stripping train arrives and discharges its load of muskeg, the wet material on the dump slips out under the weight and flows down the slope into the field below. Using this method, cars can be dumped at the same spot for two or three weeks without shifting the track.

The equipment used for stripping the 85 ft. of overburden consists of a 225-B Bucyrus shovel, with 6-yard dipper, loading into Western 20-yard automatic compression-lock air-dump cars. These cars were developed on the Mesabi

SHOVEL FILLING DUMP-CARS AT A HIGH LEVEL

range for handling the heavy overburden at the U. S. Steel Corporation's properties. A stripping average of 125 20-yd. cars in a 10-hour shift has been maintained, and a maximum of 204 cars in the day shift has been reached. On the Cuyuna range, 100 miles west of Duluth, Minnesota, there is a layer of muskeg at the surface that has been burning for a number of years. The smoldering fire leaves a hot ash, which has the appearance of solid ground. Since a workman sank into it up to his hips in trying to make a short-cut, the men keep to the beaten paths. Last August the Gordon Mining Co. at Crosby began stripping the Portsmouth mine, one of the Coates & Tweed properties. The ground had the appearance of a smoldering volcano, with puffs of smoke arising in all directions. Using an equipment, consisting of a Bucyrus 85 shovel, with 5-yard dipper, loading into Western 12-yard air-dump cars, the company succeeded in clearing most of its 40 acres of muskeg before the freeze-up. The remainder of the overburden, being of a sandy nature, can be handled easily in winter.

Cuyuna is the youngest developed of the Lake Superior iron ranges. There are 34 mines in operation on the range; most of them underground, although there are several open pits. Cuyuna ore has attracted much attention on account of its manganese content. There is 75 ft. of overburden to be taken off, in case of steam-shovel operation. Ordinarily, steam-shovels and Western dump-cars are used in stripping, but the John A. Savage Co. is to try hydraulicking.

PORTABLE-LAMP GUARDS

A new departure in portable-lamp guards is shown in the illustration of the Flexco split-handle, which can be quickly attached to the well-known Flexco expanded-steel lamp-guards made by the Flexible Steel Lacing Co. of Chicago. This portable successfully fills a demand for a substantial handle guard which does not need to be wired. The halves of the guard, including the handle itself, open wide from the hinge at the bottom of the guard, and can be closed instantly and locked around the socket at the end of any extension cord. The cord runs through grooves in the handle. The convenience of this new product will be appreciated in factories, mills, or warehouses, and by the motorist in his garage, because it permits light to be safely carried to dark corners. Danger from fire is avoided, and lamp users will readily see the advantage and economy, as the modest cost of the guard is soon repaid through prevention of breakage.

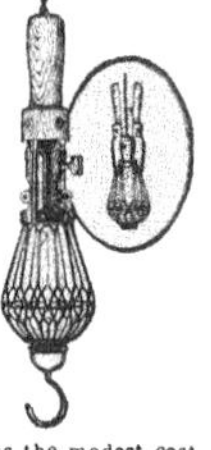

CARBON AND COMMUTATOR WEAR

According to R. E. Hellmund, of the Westenghouse Electric & Mfg. Co., carbon manufacturers, as well as makers of dynamos, have made numerous tests to determine contact resistances, friction losses, etc., of various carbons. While such tests are of interest, they contribute little toward the real practical need; namely, a carbon that can stand high-current densities and high-sparking voltages with small wear. In order to develop such carbons, it would seem essential to first make tests determining how the carbon wear is affected by current density, sparking voltage, and peripheral speed. Present indications are that with many commercial carbons appreciable densities can be used if there is no sparking voltage, while such up to 15 or even 20 volts across the brush cause little wear at certain speeds, if the current density is low enough.

The General Briquetting Co., 25 Broad street, New York, is erecting new demonstration and custom briquetting plant at 57th street and 12th avenue. Provisions have been made to demonstrate on a commercial scale modern methods of briquetting ores and concentrates of all kinds, as well as metal, coal, lignite, and flue-dust. The installation includes a type FE rotary 12-mold toggle-press; a type A 325-ton hydraulic-metal briquetting-press, adaptable to various kinds of metal scrap; Belgian roll coal-briquetting machinery; masticators, annealing ovens, dryers, elevator and conveyor system, and power-plant. It will commence operations about February 1, 1919, having cost $200,000. H. K. Schoch, chemist, late of the National Bureau of Standards, at Washington, and George R. Cowan, briquetting engineer, late of Ellington Field, Texas, have resumed their positions with the General Briquetting Company.

OUR friends the silver miners will be pleased with the statistics of exportation as given by the Department of Commerce. During 1918 the exports of silver amounted to $253,000,000 as compared with $84,000,000 in 1917. During last year the imports were small, only $71,000,000, as compared with $53,000,000 the year before.

UPON December 18 the medical correspondent of the London 'Times' estimated that 6,000,000 had died from influenza and its sequelæ in the preceding 12 weeks; if that be so, it is safe to estimate that fully 10,000,000 have succumbed to the epidemic by this time. India alone was credited with 3,000,000 deaths nearly two months ago.

HEARST is publishing a series of letters by Shaw. It is in Hearst's papers that one would expect to see Shaw's neatly insinuating, subtly corrosive, lucubrations. We know George Bernard Shaw. He is a blue-faced baboon with his fingers to his nose, making faces at all that is of good report, all that is worth while. He is a disintegrating factor in modern life and it is fitting that his sneering affectations should be printed by the bubonic rat of American journalism.

KEEN satisfaction will be felt by those interested in the oil industry of California at the agreement by the conference of the House and Senate to pass the Oil-Leasing Bill, which will go far to settle a long and bitter controversy. The Bill provides that persons holding claims on the Naval Reserves may lease the land from the Government on payment of one-eighth royalty, but no new wells may be drilled; on the other hand, it will permit development work to be resumed on existing wells on the Naval Reserves and will encourage extensive exploration in disputed oilfields outside the Reserves.

WHAT systematic and persistent propaganda can accomplish has been proved by the success of the prohibition policy and also by the German effort to influence and mislead public opinion in this and in other countries. The one propaganda has achieved its purpose; the other is still insidiously at work. If the vintners and the temperate users of wine as a wholesome beverage had not left the saloon-keepers to oppose the intemperate policy of prohibition the result would have been far different. We might have agreed to close the saloons and check the debauchery of the young by alcoholism without foregoing the sane use of one of Nature's best gifts. If we leave the defence against German propaganda merely to the opponents of Hearst and Shaw, we shall invite a like regrettable consequence.

CHAIRMAN GARY of the United States Steel Corporation strikes no uncertain note. At a time when hesitation and timidity characterize the general attitude of business men, it is pleasant to read his confident assertion that this country is "in an era of prosperity undreamed of." "What we need to do," he says, "is simply to get to work and not talk about unemployment. Psychology has a good deal to do with it. Pessinistic talk will do more to bring about unemployment than it will do to prevent it. This season of the year is always clean-up time. As for the steel industry, we are not thinking of any depression." These are brave words.

AMERICAN rights in Mexico have been made the subject of a national association that includes representatives of a number of industrial enterprises. The personnel of the executive committee of this National Association for Protection of American Rights in Mexico has not been disclosed, but Mr. E. L. Doheny is one of them and he has been deputed to go to Paris in order to present the legitimate grievances of American business-men operating in Mexico before the Peace Conference. It is estimated that $2,500,000,000 of foreign capital is invested in Mexico; of this $1,000,000,000 is American money, $700,000,000 is English, $500,000,000 is French, and $300,000,000 is Canadian. As the 'Boston News Bureau' suggests, if bolshevism in Eastern Europe is to engage the attention of the Conference at Paris, why not the bolshevism in Mexico? Is Lenine to be censured and Carranza to be immune? Hence another judgment of Paris. Who is to play the part of Venus?

ANACONDA is never behindhand in public-spirited action. We note with pleasure that the Anaconda Copper Mining Company—to give the full name of this great enterprise—has cancelled the lease given on the Florence hotel at Butte and has transferred the building, which has accommodation for 500, to the use of returned soldiers and sailors lacking a home and unable to support themselves until employment is forthcoming. Everything is to be free, and this includes a gymnasium, a poolroom, and a library. The company supplies all the attendance and restores the S in the word hotel, making it a real guest-house. This gift represents $15,000 per month, but it is worth much more than that in good-will and in the example it sets.

MANY of our readers are aware that the proposed merger of the Mining and Metallurgical Society with the Institute was not put into effect, owing to a difference of opinion that developed at the last moment. The delay has been fortunate on two counts: in the first place, the president, Mr. Walter R. Ingalls, was enabled to deliver a timely and interesting presidential address, a portion of which we take pleasure in reproducing on another page. Secondly, the Society has been enabled, with dignity, to award its annual gold medal to Mr. P. H. Schneider of the Creusot steel works, the plant responsible for making and improving the celebrated 75-millimetre gun. The medal was transmitted through Mr. E. Gybbon Spilsbury, who is in France. Speaking of the Society, we are in receipt of a letter from Messrs. C. R. Corning and George C. Stone correcting the statement we made regarding the removal of the constitutional provision against the participation of the Institute in public affairs and emphasizing the fact that the Society would lose its freedom in this respect if it were to be merged with the older organization. We mention this because the letter from our friends in New York arrived too late for publication in this issue. It will appear next week.

RAILROAD freight-rates differ from any other kind of rates in one important particular, namely, they have no bearing on the cost of the service. In this issue Mr. N. H. Emmons 2nd suggests a rate-making scheme that defies all precedent in that the cost of the service is taken into consideration. If any dyed-in-the-wool traffic-man should read this article he will pour the vials of his wrath on the head of our author, for the railroad people resent furiously any curiosity, however innocent, on the part of the mere layman, into the mysteries of rate-fixing. From the famous truism "all the traffic will bear", attributed to the late Collis P. Huntington, to the motto "the public be damned", enunciated by William H. Vanderbilt, there have been evolved various hypotheses according to which freight-rates, by laborious economic evolution, have been developed to a complexity that would lead even a twin-six expert into a maze of confusion and contradiction if subjected to skilful cross-examination. The railroad-builder was one of our pioneers. He built miles of steel highways into the waste places of this continent, he risked the chance of being repaid by the communities that were to benefit by the improved transportation he brought to them or created in advance of them. If the luck was with him, he, like the dog, had his day and gathered the shekels with one hand while using the other to ward off the federal commissions, chambers of commerce, and merchants' associations that threatened to interfere with his prosperity. The one rule that established the rate was the cost of whatever competitive service was available. What the outcome of the present Government control will be, nobody knows. For ourselves, judging from a limited experience, we would rather take our chance under normal competition, despite all its self-evident sins, than be in the hands of a paternal department at Washington.

PRODUCERS of zinc ore, especially those in the Tri-State region of Kansas, Missouri, and Oklahoma, also the New Jersey Zinc Co., have been urging the greater use of spelter and have been investigating how consumption of the metal could be increased. With interest we learn that the New Jersey Zinc Company, pressed for room in its quarters in the National City Bank on Wall street, has moved into its new seven-story building on Front street. Zinc has been used here in many ways, on the exterior and interior, including flashings, gutters, and all other outside work, all of which are made of rolled zinc, instead of copper. The doors of the vestibule are of zinc sheets rolled on wood. The knobs and locks are of zinc-plate throughout the building. The hinges are made of zinc alloy. The inside walls of the elevators and doors are of this material, and all the window-fittings are manufactured from zinc-plate. Interior fixtures, trimmings, and fittings are of zinc materials. All low-tension work in the electric equipment and lighting fixtures are of zinc-plate; and the frames for the illuminating lamps are spun from rolled zinc-sheets. Ornaments throughout the building are cast from zinc. Paints, enamels, and tints that compose the interior decorations include zinc oxide and lithopone. Thus the New Jersey Zinc Company furnishes an object lesson for its propaganda on the larger use of spelter.

THE attraction of Mexico, like 'the call of the wild', is one to which every mining engineer surrenders if once he has lived in the southern land. Hence we are asked at intervals whether conditions in Mexico are improving and whether it is safe to return thither. To that we would reply that such information as comes to us indicates that the Carranza government is settling in the saddle and is steadily establishing its ascendancy, owing, in part, as was to be expected, to the lavish use of graft. For example, the Mexican army boasts some 300 generals, who, thanks to their pay and their gorgeous uniform, have been won to the support of the de facto government. Mining is taxed 10% on the gross output, but the cheapness of labor and the high price of silver mitigate the affliction. At El Oro, Pachuca, and other old centres of activity the unsettled state of the country does not hinder operations, partly because the Government needs the metals produced and the revenue derived from the English and American companies. On the West Coast there is increased activity and also news of highly satisfactory developments underground. On the East Coast the oil companies are paying tribute to Pelaez, but that does not excuse them from being mulcted by Carranza. In due course we may hope that President Wilson, having aided so usefully in arranging European affairs, will join with his friends at Versailles in cleaning up things in Mexico. Americans in that country are entitled to protection. Of course, we are aware of the Administration's policy of washing its hands free of responsibilty for our nationals in Mexico, but that is a doctrine not yet accepted by the people, and least of all by the mining community. During the War the Government has not scrupled to collect income-tax from Americans in Mexico, nor has it hesitated to call upon them to give military service. It is a poor rule that does not work both ways. If it be the duty of an American resident in a foreign country to pay taxes to his home government and to enlist in his country's military forces in time of war, then, it seems to us, any reasonable notion of reciprocity or fair play requires his government to protect him in the exercise of legitimate industry wherever he may be, at home or abroad.

The Relief Bill

Our attention has been called to an editorial in the issue of the 'Engineering and Mining Journal' of January 18 on 'Aid for War-Minerals Producers'. We had not noticed it, but several of our friends in the West express keen irritation against the sneering attitude assumed by our contemporary toward the producers of chrome, manganese, and tungsten because they ask to be compensated for loss caused by reason of their effort to comply with the urgent requests of representatives of the Government who made an insistent demand for sundry secondary minerals essential to the successful waging of the War. Our own views on the controversy have been expressed frankly and frequently; we think that the chrome producers, for example, are entitled to redress, and we gave the services of Mr. Courtenay De Kalb in an effort to induce some measure of relief at Washington. The result is a bill introduced by Senator Henderson on December 15, as duly chronicled in our issue of January 4. Since then Senator Henderson, after conferring with the Secretary of the Interior, has re-introduced his bill as an amendment to the Dent-Chamberlain bill. In order to restrict the application of relief to the genuine sufferers a clause has been inserted limiting liability to claims filed "on or before three months from and after the approval of this act." and the recipients of the relief are described as those exploiting minerals "the production of which was in pursuance of a request or demand of the War Industries Board, the Shipping Board, the Department of the Interior, or other authorized agency of the Government." On January 30 the amendment was passed, with the Dent-Chamberlain bill for validating war contracts, but it was altered so as to apply only to those that received personal requests for production. We hope that this latest proviso will be deleted because it seems picayune. A Government does not make requests in person when it is in need of material, it uses its agencies of publicity, and whether the request comes direct from one of its agents or is made effective by a circular or other duly authorized printed statement makes no difference, if it be the intention to deal honorably by those that complied with its solicitations. We expect, therefore, that this restrictive proviso will be omitted when the Bill goes into conference of the two houses of Congress, so that a public wrong may be righted without more delay. The gentleman in New York thinks otherwise. He says the amendment ought to be worded as follows: "A bill to create endless work for the Interior Department; and a cemetery for the blasted hopes of those who, at one time, classed themselves as patriots." That is not even clever; it is merely insulting, and will be so regarded by a large number of worthy men, who were not seeking any dollar-halo but did use their experience, time, and money to produce the minerals for which the agents of the Government, in circulars and in letters, were clamoring. The gentleman in New York uses the pontifical "we" in order to identify himself with the very persons he is so reckless in maligning. "We are not harder hit than thousands who are not miners." "We went after chrome and manganese ores because the prices for these ores were high and we believed that we could get in and make money." "We were certainly led to believe, etc. etc." *ad nauseam*. What warrant, may we ask, has the editor in New York for identifying himself with the Western miners of chrome and manganese? His sense of humor must be curiously awry if he supposes that those whom he ridicules will appreciate this attempt to identify himself with them. He says that "not one good American but would say that he was glad to see it [the War] stop the day it did," thereby intimating that the producers of chrome and manganese might have wished the War to continue in the hope of profiting from the sale of their products. It would have been much better if the gentleman in New York had foreborne to lecture and to ridicule; and if instead he had made an inquiry into the reasons underlying the misinformation of the agents of the Government; and if he had directed some of his jaundiced sarcasm at the real profiteers, at those that controlled the consumption of chrome and manganese in this country and succeeded in bamboozling both the War Industries and Shipping boards.

American Mining Congress

In this issue we publish a considerable part of the address delivered recently by Mr. J. F. Callbreath, the Secretary of the Mining Congress. Mr. Callbreath is the key-man of that organization and its principal spokesman; therefore anything he says in public is sure to interest our readers. We are glad to give publicity to his remarks because we consider that every mine-operator and manager of a mining company should join the Mining Congress, which is an organization dedicated to the protection and furtherance of the political interests of the mining industry of the United States. Mr. Callbreath reviews the history of the organization and shows how much it has accomplished already by influencing good legislation and by opposing that which might prove injurious. He says, frankly, it has "mining politics" for its special business. He insists, rightly, that every good citizen must be a politician, that is, he must show an intelligent interest in the government of his country and in the laws enacted by his representatives at Washington. The mining industry—likewise the mining profession—has suffered by too much detachment from political matters, leaving such vital business to men it took but little interest in electing and still less interest in advising and checking. With all this we are in entire accord; and believing as we do that the American Mining Congress has a distinctly useful function to perform we venture again to criticise the proposal to expand its activities in a wrong direction. We refer to the proposal to establish eight divisions for the collection of statistics and technical data concerning the various branches of mining and metallurgical work. Each division is to be headed by a thoroughly competent man. In the first place, that will involve a large expense, for competent men are not cheap. Next, the proposed scheme will traverse the ground now covered by the U. S. Bureau of Mines and the Geological Survey, whose energies already are in danger of wastage by reason of duplication of effort. This duplication is a manifest blunder. For example, when information was needed by the Government on the question of an adequate supply of mercury, for war purposes, an inquiry was made in triplicate, by Mr. Hennen Jennings for the Bureau of Mines, by Mr. F. L. Ransome for the Survey, and by Mr. William Forstner for the War Industries Board, besides the investigation made by the State Mineralogist of California. Similar overlappings involving waste of time, money, and service, marked the campaign organized at Washington to stimulate the production of chrome and manganese. There should be no excuse for repeating such mistakes. If Mr. Callbreath or any other director of the American Mining Congress is in want of trustworthy data on any phase of mining or metallurgy, and if they cannot obtain such information from the existing Federal bureaus, then the latter are failing to justify their expensive existence; and of such delinquency there is no evidence whatever. Therefore we hope that, rather than start another costly organization for collecting information, the Mining Congress will make use of the offices already available and that it will co-operate with them in the friendly manner that has always characterized its relations with both the U. S. Bureau of Mines and the Geological Survey.

Emigration After the War

Doubts are being expressed as to the trend of popular migration after the War, which we must remember is not yet ended, and until it is finished by the signing of peace the conditions of normal international communication will not be restored. Mr. Frederic C. Howe, who has recently returned from Europe, where he studied the subject of emigration from his vantage point of Commissioner of Immigration at the port of New York, says that an emigration of large volume from this country to Europe will ensue as soon as the barriers to travel are removed. These departing guests will be prompted by diverse motives; some of them just want to go home, others are dissatisfied with the menial position they occupy in the American community, others again are anxious to take part in the political changes now in progress in their native land; many feel that they must go in order to ascertain what has happened to their relatives; a few seek inheritances left to them by the decease of those victimized by the War; others are attracted by the prospect of acquiring the land released by revolution, and so forth. It is said that immigrants from neutral countries, such as Holland and Scandinavia, resent the rough treatment to which they have been, in their opinion, subjected in this country during the War. The agents of steamship companies report that during the past four years 1,250,000 applied for passage home; they estimate that now twice as many are awaiting the chance to leave. It looks as if we were to lose a large number of European sojourners. Italy is prosperous and organized industrially as never before; she is in a position to welcome her sons home and promise them good pay. The breakdown of the autocracies of Central Europe has created opportunities that will attract many from here. The American Jew may shy at the chances offered in the new Zion of rehabilitated Palestine, but the poorer Jews of Russia and Germany may go thither, making so much more room for American repatriates. Apparently the legislation already introduced in Congress to prohibit immigration for four years following the signing of the treaty of peace is based on wrong information. It is said that one of the purposes of the proposed embargo is to exclude Bolshevists and other anarchists. Unfortunately these enemies to society are not labeled or readily recognized; they arrive not uncommonly in the guise of suckling lambs, and it is only after they are domiciled with us that they assume their real character of political wolves. The first thing to do is to deport any of them that are not already protected by naturalization. The representatives of organized labor are said to be urging the bill now before Congress. On the other hand, representative workers in Europe object to the erection of any such barriers to the movements of the laboring populations. One would imagine off-hand that the spirit of democracy now aroused in Europe would resent any restriction on the citizen's choice of a place to work or to live, and we see in this difference of opinion one of the many obstacles to the international solidarity of the working class. This is not to be regretted, for an alignment of citizens on the basis of class would stultify the basic principle of democracy and give us an internationalism of labor based on the predatory ideas of bolshevism instead of the ideals for which President Wilson, for example, is striving at Versailles. One consolation we may take to ourselves: if there should be an emigration to Europe on the part of the alien folk in this country, it would consist mostly of un-Americanized foreigners, of those that have failed to assimilate. The result would be a shortage of labor, perhaps, but a strengthening and a purifying of the national spirit.

Leasehold v. Fee-Simple Tenure for Mineral Land

The Editor:

Sir—Although I find much to approve in the editorial entitled 'Mining Law' in your issue of October 5, 1918, I feel obliged to dissent from its approval of Van Wagenen's preference for fee-simple titles on the ground of democracy. The German autocracy under the astute guidance of Prince Bismarck in the 'eighties adopted many measures to improve the economic well-being of the masses, such as compulsory education, state insurance, and factory legislation for hours, wages, and sanitation. These measures were largely copied from the experience of England, which had found them necessary to restrain the national degeneration caused by the unregulated adoption of the machine-factory system in the later 18th century. While the purpose of Bismarck was to steal the Socialists' thunder and meanwhile develop brighter and stronger soldiers for the Kaiser, that does not make his social legislation undemocratic, for anything tending to sharpen the wits and improve the physique of the masses must ultimately tend to increase their influence in the State as the present German revolution demonstrates.

Similarly, the fact that Germany leases her mineral lands and operates her publicly-owned railroads does not denote that either practice is, *per se*, autocratic; for otherwise Australia would be the most undemocratic of the British dominions since she owns her railways and every State, except Queensland, leases her mineral lands.[1] The State ownership of mines and public utilities cannot be oppressive to Demos provided that Demos controls the State. Bureaucracies, being merely creatures of the government, are equally as harmless for individualism wherever the people own the government.

My observation of the fee-simple system for mineral land in the United States and Canada, and of the leasehold system in Latin America, has convinced me that the latter system is much easier to control in the public interest, either from the standpoint of an equitable division of mineral wealth, or from that of equality of opportunity for the individual to acquire mining property or development.

If one holds the democratic theory that every citizen has equal rights, it is evident that this means not only political rights but economic rights; in other words, as the chief economic possession of a modern nation is its territory, every citizen should enjoy an equal share in its natural resources. This does not mean a share of *gross* output but of the residual output—called 'land rent', 'mineral royalty', etc.—remaining after the necessary living wages for the labor and capital expended in production have been expended. For urban, agricultural, and pastoral lands the land rent can be garnered equitably by land-value taxation, as shown by Shearman[2], assessed against either the rent or the selling-value (capitalized rent). Although many classes of mineral land—such as those of petroleum and the non-ferrous metals—cannot usually be evaluated until developed for production, the public's share in their exploitation can still be obtained by assessing the royalty-value of their output, as I have elsewhere eexplained in detail.[3] Still, none of our States now collect from our developed—and still less from our undeveloped—richer mineral lands anything like the taxes which the above democratic criterion would require. And they are not as liable to do so under fee-simple as under leasehold, simply because the former system tends to mask the special nature of landed possessions, which cannot, like true capital (labor products) be ever considered in a consistent democracy as absolute private property.[4]

To attain and maintain my second criterion—equality of opportunity for development—the leasehold system's superiority to fee-simple is noteworthy. The ideal condition for the prospective miner is to find all mineral land in the public domain and freely open to exploration except those areas either under exploitation or to be exploited within this generation. To secure this ideal, the possession of mineral land by speculators, who will wait indefinitely to get rich without mining, or by monopolists, who will idly bestride a whole mineral range to keep out competitors, must be prevented.

Unfortunately, the fee-simple tenure of our Eastern States has encouraged both speculation and monopoly on a vast scale. A new district is hardly found when it is covered by paper titles, as witness the Mesabi iron range and the Connellsville coke-field, in the 'nineties, and the coalfields of West Virginia and the South within the present century, without mentioning the anthracite lands of Pennsylvania and the copper and iron ranges of Michigan which were cornered by the last generation. The West, outside California, was hardly feasible for mining

[1] 'Mining Laws of Australasia', by A. C. Veatch, Bulletin U. S. G. S., No. 505.

[2] 'Natural Taxation', by T. G. Shearman.

[3] 'Natural Taxation of Mineral Land', 'M. & S. P.', Oct. 29, 1915.

[4] 'Progress and Poverty', by Henry George, Book II.

until the completion of the Union Pacific railway in 1869, yet where is the metallic mineral district that is not plastered with locations in every direction, whose owners will do everything but dig? Where these locations have been patented they have fee-simple titles that imply no further obligation than the payment of State taxes, which are absurdly low in the case of undeveloped land; where they are 'claims' under the Federal law of 1872 they imply obligatory development at the rate of $100 per 20 acres annually, yet, owing to the mere local inspection this obligation can be, and often is, evaded by perjury. Had it not been for the conservation measures, which, a decade ago, stopped further sequestering of the Federal coal, oil, and phosphate lands of the West, it is probable that these too would have long ago followed their Eastern counterparts into the hands of speculators and monopolists.

Under the Diaz law of 1892, which abolished the ancient obligatory development and allowed large mineral areas to be held simply by paying an areal tax of ₱3 per hectare (60 cents per acre) annually, the leasehold system of Mexico became as favorable for speculators as our fee-simple tenure, and by 1910 every likely district was covered with idle locations. Under the new policy of Carranza conditions have improved for the working prospector, because under an annual areal tax varying from ₱6 per hectare, for areas of under 5 hectares, up to ₱18 for areas exceeding 100 hectares, coupled with the obligation of mining activity, large numbers of idle holdings are rapidly reverting to the public domain. Had the paper-money plague and the continual civil war not disorganized finance and transportation, the new legislation would undoubtedly stimulate an unprecedented mining development in this country.

It is important for the individual that he be protected against avoidable accidents and diseases when engaged in mining and for that reason all civilized states attempt to control underground operations in these items by public inspectors. It is evidently easier to incorporate the proper standards for mine operations in leasing contracts than to proceed against recalcitrant mine-owners in the courts, a method inevitable with fee-simple tenure. Under the latter system, too, a mine-owner has the right to exclude from his property even the Federal scientist studying geology for the public benefit, and this right has been exercised for many years in the case of a great mine in the South-West.

Mines are akin to public utilities, like railways, in that they would often be benefitted by having the right of eminent domain to acquire extensive stretches of adjacent surface-rights for reduction works, tramways, pipe-lines, etc. In countries handling mineral deposits, under the Napoleonic code, as subsoil property distinct from the surface, it is easy to grant mine-lessees the right of condemnation for surface needs. By such leaseholds, too, the extra-lateral right, which has caused so much costly litigation in the West, could be abolished with the least disturbance of vested interests, at least such is the opinion of Colby,[6] who says:

"By reserving minerals from agricultural lands and allowing the miner the right of entry for purposes of prospecting under restrictions, with the added requirement that the surface proprietor be compensated for damage, the interests of both the miner and the agriculturist would be conserved. In all the important mining countries of the world, this segregation has taken place, and this is the reason why in such countries the extra-lateral principle is not essential, whereas, in the United States, without such segregation or severance of minerals from the surface, the extra-lateral right has a most powerful additional reason for existence. With severance of minerals and segregation of agricultural and mineral interests, the element of discovery also, now so vital in the mining laws of the United States, would assume secondary importance. Discovery instead of being of prime importance, as of necessity it must be under existing law where no segregation of minerals from the surface exists, could be made a secondary requisite, only required after the mineral locator had plenty of time in which to make a discovery, taking into consideration the difficulty of so doing in particular cases. If the principle of severance is incorporated in a revised public-land law, a vertical boundary system for the acquisition of mineral lands could be simultaneously adopted without resulting in great hardship to the miner, for the agricultural surface claimant could no longer claim the underlying minerals * * * The severance of surface title from the underlying minerals would also discourage speculators and blackmailers who now fraudulently seek to acquire title to surface lands under agricultural laws in order to levy tribute upon the bona-fide mining operator."

Finally, I believe in leasehold tenures for mineral land because it means the socialization of our natural resources, a necessary step, not for Marxian socialism or the public ownership of all means of production, but for the preservation of individualism. As long as there was plenty of government land 'out West' to be had for the asking, the aristocratic tendencies of unrestricted private-land ownership were little in evidence, for the discontented in the settled districts could move to the frontier and become land-owners. But this happy condition passed with the 19th century and the doubling of American farmland-values between 1900 and 1910 marked the end of accessible fertile lands for homesteaders. As only 25% of the arable land was being cultivated in 1910, the remainder evidently was being held for speculation—in order to profit by the unearned increment created by the growth of population and business.

Similarly the profiteers from the forestalling of mineral deposits are in evidence in every productive district and render it hopeless to attempt to moralize industry and put in practice the principle that 'industrial rewards should be in proportion to service rendered'. Until we are willing to become consistent democrats and boldly moralize industry by the socialization of all natural re-

[6]'Extralateral Right', by W. E. Colby, Cal. Law Review, 1917, pp. 324-26.

sources we have really little beyond physical weapons for defence against the ignorant excesses of labor-unionism and the criminal violence of Bolshevism. The restriction of private property in land along the lines suggested would inevitably abolish the undue concentration of unearned wealth and its host of attendant evils. The happy ending of the European conflict seems a propitious time for thoughtful Americans to attempt to reconstruct their property laws on a truly democratic basis before it is too late.

R. B. BRINSMADE.

Ixmiquilpan, Mexico, December 22, 1918.

Justice v. Sympathy

The Editor:

Sir—I have been an interested reader of the various articles appearing in the 'Press' relative to the present manganese and war metals muddle, and thoroughly appreciate and approve the stand you have taken in the matter. I also have been one of the well-meaning, if misguided, individuals that cast patriotism into the manganese balance, at the urgent behest of our Government, and, with many others, view with dismay an apparent inclination of the Government officials to discount both commodities now that the demand for each has subsided to normal. I say 'demand' with full knowledge of the fact that both patriotism and manganese, as well as the other war metals, were not only requested, but were actually commanded to be produced by authentic communications emanating from the various governmental sources responsible for the supply of those essential war-winning commodities.

You have published several articles in your journal from parties representing, or purporting to represent, the consuming end of the manganese industry, but their arguments embody not a single logical reason for the destruction of a valuable domestic industry by unrestricted imports of foreign-mined war metals, and none of them attempt to justify the Government's threatened failure to keep faith with the miners it induced to enter a patent unprofitable industry under pre-war conditions. The miners of the war metals have the Government's solemn assurance that their patriotic investment of time, money, and labor will be amply safeguarded against loss, and it was accepted and acted upon by them in absolute good faith. To arbitrarily rescind such an agreement and thereby cause the large majority of this volunteer corps of industrial patriots to lose their all would be equally as culpable as for the Government to summarily suspend or reduce the guaranteed interest rate on its Liberty Bonds. To repudiate the former and sustain the latter is to make a distinction without a difference and arbitrarily creates fish of the one and flesh of the other obligation in a flagrant ex parte manner. We cannot picture to ourselves any such policy by *our* Government; it smacks too much of the "scrap of paper" episode of the late unlamented German empire, and satirically recalls the old adage of "when the Devil was sick, the Devil a saint would be, but when the Devil was well, the devil of a saint was he."

It is quite evident that none of the opponents to the Government fulfilling its contract with the war-metal miners have the slightest conception of the obstacles, both physical and financial, that had to be surmounted by the mining fraternity in answering their Government's appeal for the prompt production of these metals; otherwise their pens would not have so smoothly glided along in their course of objecting to justice being done to these men. It is well to add here that the appeal to search out and produce these metals was made directly to the *only* class that *could* produce them. Theirs was the province of specialists in prospecting, mining, and engineering. They alone possessed the ability and knowledge required to obtain the desired results, and to do it upon the spur of the moment. Very few of the opponents of the guaranteed remuneration for their efforts have the ability or knowledge to mine and move a ton of these ores to market, if left to their own devices, and their attitude in the matter can only be ascribed to a complete ignorance of the difficulties and expense accompanying the extraction and transportation of the larger part of the tonnage mined, or else to the fact that "there are none so blind as those that will not see."

They do not realize that the large majority of the manganese, chrome, and other war-metal deposits, occupy the most inaccessible portions of our country, and require the heaviest expense to get in supplies and equipment and the ore out to the railroad. Personally, I am packing ore on mules along a rough mountain trail; thence it is pulled down to the valley on a sled or 'stone-boat', and from there it has to be hauled 26 miles through the mountains over a rough rocky road to the railroad—and all of the trails and part of the road had to be made. Consequently it costs considerably more just to transport the ore to the railroad from where it is mined in the majority of instances than it can be laid down duty-paid on the Atlantic seaboard, at pre-war prices by foreign exporters. Yet our eminent and fair-minded critics assure us—after we have been induced to invest our capital in the enterprise—that this is as it should be, and we should close up shop, charge off our investment of time, money, and labor to a misdirected patriotism and go blithely forth (broke) to evils yet unknown! We are adjured to take our loss calmly and as a matter of course, as all pertaining to the vicissitudes of mining, despite the fact that if under normal peace conditions any mining man with the slightest adumbration of intellect should take on the herculean task of developing mineral in places where his transportation costs alone more than balances the delivered price of cheaply mined imported ore he would have no logical excuse for being at large.

Money is frequently lost in mining, as 'A Miner' succinctly advances as balm to our ruffled feelings, but his sapient conclusion does not apply to the specific case under discussion. True enough, money is lost in mining—as well as made—and chiefly under three heads, to wit: by miscalculation of the quantity and grade of ore in depth from surface prospects, by mismanagement, and through plain deceit and misrepresentation. The first catches all alike, both layman and miner, but is smallest in the case of the highly trained and experienced mining engineer, and while disappointing, it yet leaves no regrets or hard feeling in its wake. Nature has simply proved false to promise; but undismayed, we strive to secure a toe-hold upon her anatomy in some other favorable locality. Mismanagement, and its entrained monetary mining loss, is usually caused by the lack of a competent engineer at the operating end of the enterprise. The third cause of financial regrets in mining can be ascribed to downright fraud and misrepresentation concerning the entire venture. These are perpetrated by a noisy swarm of irresponsible promoters, whom we jail as fast as we can fasten the shackles of the law upon them.

But we can't jail the Government for its failure to carry out its covenant with the producers of the war metals, for indeed, the struggling producers of these metals, as free and law-abiding citizens of our great country, are a component part of the Government, of which they ask but justice, and have given far more as a class toward winning the War than they have ever thought of or expected any recompense from. And it is a grievous mistake of their critics in the present controversy to assume that they are asking for government charity in their present distress. All that they request is the protection they were guaranteed on their investment in a precarious but necessary industry and they will work out their own salvation by their individual energies. Most certainly they do not believe that their Government, after inducing them to invest their all in the creation of a vital industry, which may have to be drawn upon heavily again, will place them on a par with the foreign exporter of cheaply produced ores, that never lifted a finger or ventured a dime toward winning our fight for liberty and justice.

Our conception of plighted troth and good faith does not consist of patting a man on the back and calling him a good fellow, and the next day kicking the props from under him, the while admonishing him to "light easy." We, as a whole, put our shoulder to the martial wheel to secure justice to mankind throughout the entire world, and our worthy President thought it such an imperative desideratum that he felt it incumbent upon him to go across the seas to see the job well done. This is, perhaps, as it should be, but it is well to remark that justice, like charity, should become a household virtue before being bestowed promiscuously beyond the three-mile limit, and plain justice, as embodied in solemn covenants by our Government officials, to protect and sustain the war-metal markets, is what is urgently needed by domestic producers of those metals just now.

F. H. MITCHELL.

Hot Springs, Arkansas, January 13.

THE man in charge of a mine store holds a responsible position; storekeeping problems are of vital importance in the economics of a mining company.

Hoisting Accidents

The biennial report of A. J. Stinson, State Inspector of Mines for Nevada, contains the following:

"A perusal of the list of accidents will show that a number of fatalities have occurred as a result of being thrown from a bucket or cage while being hoisted to the surface. In the majority of such cases I find that the hoisting engine-man has had little previous experience as such, or the particular hoist is new to him; and most astonishing of all the engine-man has not secured a license as provided by law. This is the element of human fallibility that always must be faced in controlling accidents. It is perhaps the most difficult of all sources of accident to face. In this connection I made a recommendation in my last biennial report, suggesting that a new and comprehensive law be enacted covering the method of issuing licenses, and I am again making this recommendation. At the present time licenses are issued by the Board of County Commissioners to anybody, upon application, whom they have reason to believe is qualified to operate a hoist.

The law itself suggests that an applicant shall have had one year's experience as a hoisting engineer as a pre-requisite to the issuance of a license, but even that is not necessary according to the interpretation of the Attorney-General. As a result of years of experience I am convinced that fewer accidents will occur if engine-men are required to obtain licenses that mean something, and when once issued carry the dignity and recommendation that a man is a first-class mechanic insofar as the operation of a hoist is concerned. The majority of hoisting-men with whom I have discussed the matter are in favor of such a law. In nearly every walk of life where the lives of men are entrusted to a single individual—as railroad engine-men and steamship pilots—standards of qualification are prescribed, and usually some credentials are required before they are entrusted with the lives of other men. It is my recommendation that all engine-men who are required to hoist men be required to obtain licenses before undertaking such work, and that operators be prohibited from employing men in such capacity unless a license is exhibited. The licenses should be issued, without limit as to number, by a board who shall examine the applicants in detail and give practical tests before passing upon the qualifications. The board should be composed of a technical man, a practical man, and at least one other conversant with mining. Such a law can be put into effect without great expense and without unduly upsetting the existing scheme of affairs of the present operating engineers. Provision can be made for the issuance of temporary licenses upon practical tests in the event of emergency so as not to work a hardship upon the men who must earn a living that way, or upon the operators who may at times require the service of a hoisting-man in an emergency. However, this would be only at the commencement of the working of the act, for in a short time all engine-men would provide themselves with licenses."

The Middlemarch Mine and Mill

By B. M. SNYDER

The Middlemarch mine is situated nine miles west of Pearce, Arizona, in the Dragoon mountains; it is one of the old copper mines of Arizona and was first operated about twenty years ago by Richard Gird and others. They built a small water-jacket furnace and made black copper from the oxidized ore of the Missouri claim, but when the low-grade sulphide ore was encountered at shallow depth, smelting was discontinued. Later they erected a small concentrating plant to treat the sulphide ore, but owing to the high specific gravity of the gangue (mainly garnet and epidote) and the tendency of the copper minerals to float, this mill proved a failure. The extraction was low and the concentrate contaminated with the heavy gangue-minerals. Later an attempt was made to operate the property as a shipping proposition and about 70 carloads of ore were shipped to the smelters at Douglas, for the most part at a loss.

In the early part of 1917 the Arizona Middlemarch Copper Co. took over the property and now owns or controls a total of 43 claims, with an area of over 860 acres. This company is controlled by Los Angeles business-men. They have erected a flotation mill of 125 tons daily capacity, and have demonstrated that the ore is readily amenable to this treatment. Shortage of water, owing to several dry seasons, has prevented the mill running more than a small part of the time, but sinking to reach water at depth is now under way.

The geologic formation consists of a series of Paleozoic sedimentaries that have been extensively intruded by granitic stocks and porphyry dikes. The sedimentary rocks have been so metamorphosed as to obliterate any fossils they may have contained. By correlation with formations the age of which is known, it is believed that the sedimentaries are largely Cambrian. They consist of quartzite, lime-shale, silicious limestone, and clay-slate.

The intrusive granite occurs in stocks of considerable area and along the contacts of such intrusives with the sedimentaries are found altered zones within which orebodies occur. The latter are also found as veins on one or both sides of the strong rhyolite-porphyry (or quartz-porphyry) dikes that cut both the sedimentaries and the granite. There are three strong dikes running the full length of the property and most of the orebodies are found between two of these, or along their contact.

The orebodies are fairly typical contact-metamorphic deposits and are plainly the result of the action of vapors and solutions given off by the intrusives. On the upper end of the property the gossan is found along the contact of the granitic stock with slate and limestone. This gossan shows some copper carbonates and oxides with specular hematite, garnet, epidote, and pyroxene. A tunnel on the Cobreloma vein exposes a vein along the contact of granite and slate, from two to six feet wide, and showing commercial ore in places. This ore carries chalcopyrite, pyrite, and specular hematite, and several carloads of such ore have been shipped to the smelter.

The Missouri orebody is a contact-metamorphic deposit in calcareous quartzite, the shape of the ore being that of a chimney or pipe. On the fifth level this pipe has an area of over 2000 sq. ft., with an oval section and

a dip of about 45°. The ore is made up largely of finely crystallized garnet and epidote, with calcite and a little quartz, the metallic minerals being pyrite, chalcopyrite, and zinc-blende. The ore is low-grade, running from 0.5 to 4% copper and averaging, as delivered at the mill, about 2% copper. This is primary ore, showing no sign of enrichment or leaching below a depth of about 75 ft. The residual carbonate ores above this horizon were enriched somewhat and were smelted on the ground.

The Missouri workings reach a depth of about 250 ft. below the surface, and the orebody has been proved to the sixth level. At about 50 to 60 ft. below the sixth level, the inclined shaft passes through a crushed zone (fault-breccia) and below this fault it passes into aplitic granite. At 100 ft. below the sixth level, a station will be cut and a cross-cut driven to the orebody on this level.

The ore has been mined heretofore in large open stopes by milling or similar methods, but a shrinkage stope is now being opened on the sixth level. The ore is drawn off through chutes and trammed to a pocket below the sixth level, and any large boulders are broken on a grizzley over this pocket. A measuring pocket is used to fill the one-ton skip and the latter delivers into a bin on the adit-level, from which the ore is trammed to the mill-bins.

The mill was designed and erected by me. It is a straight flotation mill of the simplest type possible, as shown by the flow-sheet. The ore is drawn to a Telsmith No. 5 gyratory crusher, set to deliver a 1½-in. maximum product. The crushed ore is elevated by a Telsmith bucket-elevator to the fine-ore bin, from which it is fed by a plunger-feeder to a Colorado Iron Works 6 by 6-ft. ball-mill. The balls used are of 2 in. and 2½ in. diam., larger balls having been found unnecessary.

The ball-mill is in closed circuit with an Akins 45-in. classifier, and the pulp discharged by it is elevated by a Byron Jackson 3-in. sand-pump to two launder (or Crerar) pneumatic flotation machines. The froth from these machines goes to a standard K & K flotation machine for cleaning. The finished concentrate from the latter is carried by launders to ponds outside the mill-building. When a pond is full, the concentrate is allowed to drain and dry for about two weeks. It is then trammed to a loading-pocket, from which it is drawn by gravity into motor-trucks for transportation to the railroad, nine miles distant. If the collodial gangue is eliminated thoroughly in the flotation cells, no trouble is found in getting a concentrate dry enough to handle during nine months of the year. During the wet season, this method is not satisfactory.

The tailings from the K & K machine are returned to the roughers for re-treatment, and the rougher tailing goes to a 24 by 8-ft. Dorr thickener for settling and recovery of water. The underflow of the thickener carries 55 to 70% solid, and the clear overflow is pumped back to the head of the mill by a 2-in. centrifugal sump-pump, which also returns all drainage of mill-floors, concentrate-pond overflow, etc. By such means the consumption of water is kept down to an average of 200 gal. per ton of ore treated.

The flotation reagents used are coal-tar. No. 5 pine-oil (General Naval Stores), and coal-tar creosote. Coal-tar makes up 80% or more of the mixture. No acid is used, and the pulp is not heated. A little lime is added occasionally to assist settling in the Dorr thickener and this keeps the pulp slightly alkaline. No changes in the flow-sheet as originally designed have been found necessary, except the substitution of the Dorr thickener for settling-ponds, to recover water more completely.

The following results are averages for the past four months:

1918	Mill-heading %	Tailing %	Extraction %	Solid thickener-discharge %
August	1.49	0.14	91.07	62.8
September	1.64	0.185	89.60	64.8
October	1.92	0.215	89.73	62.8
November	1.64	0.152	91.57	63.0

Ball consumption. 1.23 lb. per ton ore
Flotation reagents. 0.86 lb. per ton ore

The following typical screen-analyses of tailings are given to show that the principal losses are in the coarser sizes, and that by still finer grinding and closer classification the extraction could be brought up to 95% or more. It is doubtful, however, if it would pay to make this addi-

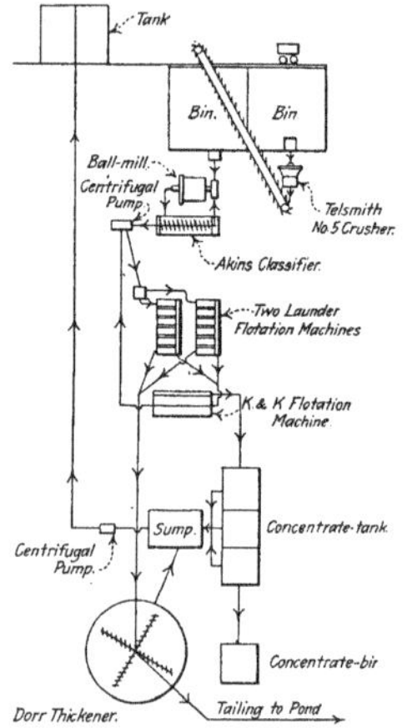

FLOW-SHEET OF MIDDLEMARCH MILL

tional recovery at the expense of reduced capacity and increased grinding costs.

	Tailings weight %	Copper %	Tailings weight %	Copper %
On 65 mesh......	3.46	0.77	0.66	0.66
" 100 "	16.26	0.22	6.88	0.19
" 150 "	16.48	0.11	16.31	0.15
" 200 "	19.50	0.04	13.50	0.16
Through 200 "	44.30	0.04	62.65	0.04

Tyler standard screens were used in above analyses.

The concentrate is marketed under contract with the Copper Queen smelter, at Douglas, 60 miles south of the property. As showing its quality, the following assays of shipments are given:

Lot number	Moisture %	Silver oz.	Copper %	Silica %	Alumina %	Iron %	Lime %
33	10.9	5.30	17.63	13.8	1.2	21.6	4.6
34	9.2	5.78	16.90	14.6	6.5	22.8	4.5
35	12.0	6.30	15.62	15.2	7 1	21.4	3.8
36	13.2	7.30	15.05	13.0	7.8	21.6	3.1
37	11.7	6.34	14.96	18.0	6.9	21.6	3.6
38	16.0	6.12	13.20	15.2	8 2	17.0	5.7
39	13.8	8.20	18.08	7.8	4 6	21.4	3.3

Technical Writing: Naturalness

By T. A. RICKARD

*The key-note of good writing, as of good manners, is *B natural*. Sincerity is the first requisite for effective writing. When a man says what he knows or believes, he is likely to be interesting, because each human being possesses an individuality, a point of view, or a range of sympathy that makes him different from his fellows. To say or to write what you do not think, for the mere sake of talking or writing, is a cerebral exercise that must be performed with extraordinary skill if it is to be attractive. Affectations are rarely attractive, rarely effective. To be natural is to be yourself, not a *poseur*; to give the reader the best of yourself, instead of re-warming the baked-meats of yesterday. Quotations—which are second-hand thoughts—will serve occasionally when the thing you want to say has been said so well by another that it would be waste of energy to try to say it better; but, as a rule, the utterance of the writer himself is more interesting than the quotation, because the writer brings something of himself to bear on the subject and for the moment is more in touch with the reader than any dear departed author. Therefore, say things as best you can in your own way, neither in borrowed words nor in the phraseology that mimics another. Write as if you were speaking to a person whom you are anxious to persuade or convince. You will then write better than you speak, because, in the first place, you can be more deliberate, and secondly, you can revise what you have written.

Speaking and writing are similar mental acts, with a difference: the difference between eating food raw and eating it cooked. Some kinds of food gain nothing by being cooked; likewise some kinds of utterance are not bettered by being written down first; but most expressions of thought, especially those that deal with complex ideas, must undergo preparation before they may be digested comfortably. The transactions of engineering societies are overburdened with half-baked chunks of knowledge that provoke mental dyspepsia. How palatable, on the other hand, is the carefully prepared article that has been seasoned with Attic salt, served with a *sauce piquante*, and dressed with the parsley of pleasant fancy—like the writings of Rossiter Raymond or of Clarence King.

Composition, however, is less natural than speaking. The pen or the pencil intervenes between the thought and the expression, introducing an element of artificiality, as well as one of deliberation. The spoken word cannot be recalled; the written word can be erased. Yet it is unwise to criticize your writing as it proceeds, for such self-criticism tends to embarrassment or self-consciousness. Revise the work carefully after it is done, not before, so as to avoid chilling the warmth of composition by cold analysis. You have heard of the centipede that was too much aware of his many legs, and became hopelessly entangled. Inopportune self-criticism will cripple writing, just as self-consciousness prevents most men from becoming satisfactory after-dinner speakers.

To be natural in writing, you must have something to say: something concerning which you feel impelled to write. To have something to say is the first requisite for effective speaking or writing. Most speeches and many writings are ineffective, if not worse, because, like an unhappy golfer, the speaker or writer does not see the object of his aim; he does not "keep his eye on the ball." Wait until you have something definite to tell. Only a fool talks for the sake of talking; that is why so many speeches fall flat. It is unnatural for a man to write for the sake of exercising his index finger and thumb; that is why so much writing is a weariness of the flesh. Make sure that you have something to say; then say it; and when you have said it, stop. "The best spoke in the wheel is the fittest, not the longest."

The story is told that President Wilson, when a boy, used to read to his father whatever he wrote. Whereupon his father would ask, "What do you mean by that?" He would explain. "Then write it," was the advice. If, after writing something you will ask yourself 'What do I mean?' you may discover that you have not written what you meant to say.

The student while at college, and for some time afterward, is occupied mainly with the effort to acquire knowledge. To write is to convey information to others, which is the reverse of the normal youthful attitude; it involves a pose difficult to assume gracefully or effectively without practice; but such practice should be encouraged, because the effort to record thought involves the mobilization and marshalling of ideas, a disciplinary effort highly beneficial to the student's mind. Therefore it were well if some exercise in writing could be taken during the early process of acquiring knowledge.

To write naturally, you must exercise the faculty of writing until it becomes flexible and strong. The best way to learn how to swim is to plunge into the water. Most of those that write well have written a good deal, but you may be sure that they have not published all of it. Do your preliminary cantering in the paddock, not on the race-course. Good writers obtained their reputation by being wise enough to keep their preliminary trials to themselves; meanwhile, they noted the results obtained from the methods used by others. Ben Jonson said. "For a man to write well there are three neces-

*A chapter from a forthcoming book on Technical Writing to be published by John Wiley & Sons, New York.

saries: to read the best authors, observe the best speakers, and much exercise of his own style.' Naturalness comes from exercise, not lack of care.

Aristotle said, long ago: "Naturalness is persuasive and artificiality the reverse; for people take offence at an artificial speaker, as if he were practising a design upon them, in the same way as they take offence at mixed wines."†

Some technical writers, aiming to be natural, succeed only in being sloppy.

(1) "If it is inconvenient to keep the *muck* [waste rock] drawn off, tap the *dirt-way* [ore-chute] a few feet up, on the opposite side of the man-way."

The writer is describing a method of mining and uses the language of an uneducated laborer, perhaps with the idea that it sounds 'practical'. Here are two more examples:

(2) "With the *advent* [completion] of the new mill, which has a capacity of over 100 tons per day, the haulage problem becomes *one for careful consideration* [important]."

Advent means the season before the Nativity; it is also used when referring to an important arrival, not the starting of a stamp-mill. The last sentence in the quotation exemplifies the use of an abstract phrase instead of a concrete word. The language is 'natural' to a semi-literate promoter but not to an educated engineer. Do not mistake vulgarity for ease, nor inaccuracy for freedom.

(3) "The process is said to have done such satisfactory work that other *plants* [operators] have been *contemplating* [considering] the *installation* [adoption] of *the process* [it]."

This also illustrates an uncouthness that simulates naturalness. The writer, a graduate of a university, has fallen into the style of those about him in a mining community. The 'contemplation' of plans, the 'installation' of plants, the 'inauguration' of methods, and the 'prosecution' of developments are the stock-in-trade of local reporters and of the equally illiterate persons that play the mining 'game' on the frontiers of industry. The imitation of them should be beneath an educated engineer.

Young men, when about to describe a mine or explain a metallurgical process, are prone to start with the idea that they must indulge in 'fine' writing; meaning thereby a style pitched several tones higher than is habitual to them. When they prepare matter that is to be printed, they affect a vocabulary and a phraseology foreign to them; like the queer persons that have 'society' manners as distinguished from their behavior at home. There are public occasions, of course, when an added dignity of hearing is befitting. For similar reasons, it is proper that the irresponsibility and ease of ordinary talk should give place to deliberate thoughtfulness when one is making a business statement or preparing matter for print; but the extra effort should not entail a pomposity that smothers the subject in verbiage. The attempt to write in a key higher than that of conversation need not provoke insincerity or affectation. It requires only more care and more deliberation. Write as if you were addressing an honored senior in your own profession to whom you wished to convey information; do not try to impress him with your skill as a stylist, but make yourself perfectly clear, so that he may have the benefit of any facts or ideas that you can place at his service. As a warning, I quote the following description of the Mount Morgan lode, in Australia:

(4) "It may be considered as consisting of a network of veins, traversing on the one hand a metamorphic matrix of a somewhat argillo-arenaceous composition and on the other hand what appears to be a feldspathic tufaceous igneous rock."

This is metamorphosed English pseudomorphic after flapdoodle. Much of the geologic description that poses as profundity is rhetorical rot. Similarly the technical terms needlessly used by half-educated writers remind one "of the French that is spoken by those who do not speak French."

A Tasmanian geologist described an ore deposit as due to "the effects of a reduction in temperature of the hitherto liquefied hydro-plutonic solutions, and their consequent regular precipitation. These ascended in the form of metallic super-heated vapors which combined eventually with ebullient steam to form other aqueous solutions, causing geyser-like discharges at the surface, aided by subterranean and irrepressible pressure. What can you make of this "geyser-like discharge" of language? You will find, if you take the trouble to translate the pretentious terms, that the description conveys a minimum of information with a maximum of sound: "Full of sound and fury, signifying nothing;" or as Ruskin has said, "Great part of the supposed scientific knowledge of the day is simply bad English, and vanishes the moment you translate it."

Here is another sentence written by a young man who also mistook sound for sense :

(5) "Since the installation of their air-compressor, a new campaign of development has been inaugurated, operations have been extensively prosecuted, more particularly in the Carboniferous limestone, which is usually so prolific of values, due to the well recognized leaching of mineral solutions emanating from the plutonic magma."

Many of these words are out of place; a bishop is installed, a president is inaugurated, a criminal is prosecuted, a rabbit is prolific. Incidentally, it may be noted that the water that leached the limestone probably came from above, not from below; originating in rain-fall, not from the depths. These grandiose words, being inappropriate, fail to convey a definite meaning; they only make a confusing noise. Probably he meant to say:

"The use of the new compressor has greatly expedited operations, particularly in the Carboniferous limestone, which has been enriched by mineral solutions."

This, however, is not satisfactory, because the sentence

†'The Rhetoric of Aristotle'. Translated by J. E. C. Welldon. 1886.

contains discrete ideas, wholly unrelated; therefore they should be separated, thus:

"The use of the new compressor has greatly expedited operations, particularly in the Carboniferous limestone. This is important, because the limestone has been enriched by mineral solutions and therefore is a likely place to find ore."

Samuel Johnson exclaimed: "Witness the immense pomposity of sesquipedalian verbiage;" and we know how he himself sinned in that way. George Meredith, a master of words, recorded his objection to "conversing in tokens not standard coin," which is what 'prosecute', 'install', and 'prolific' are in such a context; they are not legal tender in the forum of technology; they are like Canadian quarters, British shillings, or French francs tendered to a merchant at Chicago or Denver, legal though they be at Montreal, Manchester, or Marseilles. As you know, I hold that the use of words of Latin origin, usually of more than one syllable, is helpful, if not indeed unavoidable in expressing ideas current in technology, but writing becomes incoherent when words are used because of their sound rather than their sense. Such usage bespeaks a snobbishness of mind, the aping of erudition, a mere pretence. If a man knows what a thing really is, he describes it as black or white; if he does not know what it is, he masks his ignorance by saying in long words that it partakes of the general quality of grayness. The young writers that clothe meagre observation in elaborate words soon fall into the habit of using terms that they do not understand, and therefore fail to make themselves understood, if indeed they do not convey information that is positively false. The employment of words that are unfamiliar to the writer, and that therefore are inconsistent with his own way of saying things, serves but to cripple his power of expression. He may get into a tangle by dragging strange words from afar. When he does find himself thus entangled he should cut loose, stating things in his own way, that is, in plain words that he understands thoroughly. Again I say: REMEMBER THE READER. If you do, you will win respect as a writer. The man with only a smattering of his subject splashes all over it with words of learned sound and unlearned meaning, because the ability to make such a noise is more easily acquired than the reality of knowledge. Huxley said that if a man really knows his subject, "he will be able to speak of it in an easy language and with the completeness of conviction with which he talks of an every-day matter. If he does not, he will be afraid to wander beyond the limits of the technical phraseology which he has got up."‡ In his lectures to working-men Huxley showed how the fundamental truths of science could be stated in the simplest and most illuminating speech, without loss of accuracy. Indeed, the ability to explain scientific or technical matters to the unlearned is a test of the thoroughness of a teacher's understanding of his subject. If, for example, you care to test your grasp of engineering or geology, try to impart what you know to a younger brother or sister. That is a good test of your understanding and of your use of language.

‡The concluding phrase illustrates how a great writer may lapse into poor English.

No Platinum in the Grand Canyon

Platinum has been reported for many years as occurring in the Grand Canyon, Arizona, near Grand Canyon station. From time to time the supposed presence of platinum ore in this region has received new advertisement, and recently stock in a company organized to exploit the alleged deposits was offered for sale in an alluring prospectus wherein were published assays of the so-called ore that showed as much as 2.4 oz. of platinum per ton. It has been asserted that the platinum occurs in a colloidal state, and that this explains the failure of standard methods of assay to show its presence. The claims referred to in the prospectus mentioned are near Indian Garden, a locality well known to visitors to the Canyon as a point on the Bright Angel trail, about 3250 ft. below the brink of the canyon and visible from El Tovar. Considerable prospecting has been done in this vicinity on both sides of the trail by means of open-cuts and short tunnels, according to the U. S. Geological Survey. The supposed platinum-bearing deposits are beds of green and red ferruginous sandstone that constitute a subordinate part of the geologic formation known as the Bright Angel shale, of Cambrian age. In 1911, F. L. Ransome, while examining certain supposed copper deposits in the Grand Canyon, had his attention called to the alleged platinum ore near Indian Garden, and collected a sample that was afterward carefully assayed for platinum by the Bureau of the Mint. The results were negative. In 1915, H. G. Ferguson was detailed by the Survey to examine and sample the claims near Indian Garden that were being held as platinum-bearing ground. The sampling was done with great care, and about 30 samples were assayed specially for platinum by Ledoux & Co. of New York. As a check, portions of five of these samples were assayed by E. E. Burlingame & Co. of Denver. None of the assays showed any platinum. In the summer of 1918, Mr. Ransome again examined the supposed platinum deposits in company with the geologist who had been engaged by the exploiting company to report on them. He took additional samples, and two of these, selected as representative of the alleged ore, were divided into three portions. One portion of each was submitted for assay to the Bureau of the Mint, one portion of each to the U. S. Bureau of Standards, and one portion of each to the laboratory of the Survey. The nature of the problem was outlined, and the chemists were requested to take all possible precautions to discover any platinum present. None was found. As a result of these investigations it may be safely stated that the supposed platinum deposits in the Grand Canyon do not contain platinum—certainly not enough to be of any value. The claim that the platinum is present in some form that would prevent its detection is an absurdity. Even if the platinum were in a colloidal condition it would give the reactions characteristic of that metal.

The American Mining Congress

By J. F. CALLBREATH, Secretary

*The American Mining Congress was organized in the city of Denver in the year 1896. Its purpose, and at that time its sole purpose, was to secure Federal aid for the mining industry. Its aim at that time was that it should secure the creation of a Department of Mines, with its head a member of the President's cabinet. For several years thereafter it held annual conventions, some of which were important gatherings. They discussed matters of mining in a general way, but took no action except to pass resolutions. At that time it would have been very easy for us, had we created the proper force in an effective way and gone to Washington, to have secured the creation of a Department of Mines; but as time went on there seemed to be a feeling that the President's cabinet was already too large; and when the American Mining Congress in the year 1905 and 1906, at the time it decided to create permanent headquarters and establish permanent work and put a permanent secretary in charge, a feeling had grown up that there should be no new members of the Cabinet. At that time the board of directors met in Denver, and instructed me to go to Washington to find out what could be done. I went to Washington, and after a careful talk with a number of people I came to the conclusion that the effort to secure the creation of a Department of Mines was futile at that time. At the Joplin meeting my report was made to the members of the Congress; and it was then decided after much misgiving and discussion that we should ask for the creation of a Bureau of Mines. Many of our Western people had the notion that there was no mining except in the Rocky Mountain States, and they could not conceive of the fact that we must have Eastern support in order to accomplish our purposes. But at that meeting it was decided to work for the creation of a Bureau of Mines. I was then sent to Washington again to take that matter up. One of the first men that I talked with was the Secretary of the Interior, James Garfield. Mr. Garfield gave no approval to the plan. He did not believe that it was essential or wise, and he thought any effort in that direction would prove futile. Later I had the pleasure of taking the matter up with that distinguished statesman, then President of the United States, who has recently passed beyond, Theodore Roosevelt. Mr. Roosevelt was the first man in an official position to give encouragement to the idea, and said to me that if Congress should see fit to pass a bill creating a Bureau of Mines he would be glad to give it his endorsement. From that time on the fight began for the Bureau of Mines; and in the year 1910 a Bureau of Mines bill was passed, but that bill was so emasculated from the original provisions that it had nothing whatever to do with Western mining; in fact, the words which made it cover the Western mines had been deliberately taken from its provisions; so we were immediately forced to work for an amendment to the bill, and it took another year before the law in its present form was passed by which the Bureau of Mines was given some power to take a hand in the development of Western mines.

As a part of the history of the American Mining Congress it might be well to say that during the first year of the incumbency of the present secretary we had $1100 with which to carry on the work of the organization. During the second year that had grown to $2200. During the year 1910, when the Bureau of Mines bill was first enacted, we had $5600; and at that time while our support had been entirely from the West from a financial standpoint, after that the West seemed to think that the Mining Congress had served its purpose and they had no further use for it, and the support thereafter given to the Mining Congress from the West was practically nothing. In the meantime the coal people saw in the Bureau of Mines bill an agency by which they could get some aid, and the coal industry came to the relief of the Mining Congress, and was its principal support for three or four years after 1910. In the meantime, having secured the creation of the Bureau of Mines, as well as having done some excellent work in other directions, the Mining Congress still felt that it had a mission to perform. It had first to see that the Bureau of Mines got proper support before Congress, and while bureaus are inclined to grow by their own power, it is necessary in order that a bureau of this character shall receive public support that somebody educate Congress to the necessity of the work. In the beginning and when the Bureau of Mines was created its sole purpose, so far as those who passed it (and they were coal people of the East) knew, was that it should make investigations toward decreasing the loss of life in mining operations. Having accomplished that many people thought the Bureau of Mines had done all that could be expected of it. Since then the work of the Mining Congress and its aims have greatly expanded. As conditions arose requiring action at Washington we have tried as best we could to meet those requirements. During the last few years there has been a strong trend toward concentration of power in the Federal government. Whether we like it or not we have to face in the future a strong tendency in that direction. During the period of the War that tendency has increased with untold strength and rapidity. Hereafter we must expect that the national government is going to

*An address delivered before the California chapter of the American Mining Congress on January 15, 1919.

control in many matters with which heretofore it has had nothing whatever to do. Personally I do not know whether it is proper to make the statement at this time, but I feel that one of the things in which this organization should take a part is in opposition to the trend of government which has for its purpose the taking away of those rights and powers and duties which the Constitution put upon the several States. This morning's 'Chronicle' had an extended article on the oil industry, and makes reference to the plan of the Federal government to create a bill for the leasing of the power resources of the West. As you gentlemen know, the West stood as a unit against the whole principle of leasing. It believed that each State should control the development of its own resources. It believed that each State should have the benefit of those natural resources. It believed that each State should have the power to tax its own wealth, because it was required under the Constitution to provide and enforce and support a republican form of government, and it did not seem fair that half of the territory of the State should be free from the taxing power of the State while the State within itself was bound to support and protect and enforce the law over that total area. More than half the land west of a north and south line drawn through the eastern border of Colorado is still in Federal ownership. If the West is to be called upon to support the law and enforce the law over that additional half of her territory, she has also the right to tax that territory in order to support the development of that law. The West is expected to build roads; it is expected to maintain its charitable institutions; it is expected to maintain as good, if not a better, educational system in proportion to its population than any other section of the United States; and because of that it is the belief of many men that the principle of the leasing system, which puts the power to tax that property entirely and forever beyond the taxing power of the State, is wrong, and that it cannot work out to the advantage of the country. Just to the extent that the Federal government has the power to tax the resources in your Western States, she is creating a double system of taxation: a system which is not certain; it contravenes that principle of the constitution which says that taxation shall be certain; that we have a right to know the taxes that we have to pay, and that tax depends upon the royalties and the development of our resources. If the conditions are such that the highest development may be secured, then the tax will be large which goes to the Federal government.

This question is not new. So far as I was able for a number of years in Washington I fought that principle and talked against it whenever I had the opportunity. You will find a record of that in many a hearing before different committees in Congress, of the expression of something of the views that I have just expressed to you. However, we had not the power to educate the people of the East. We could not go to Boston with $3000 or $4000 annual income, and demonstrate to the Boston Chamber of Commerce the fact that the harbor was just as much a part of the property of the United States as the water-power in your State. We could not say to them, "If you will consent to the use of this harbor for the benefit of all the people, we are willing that you should have the water-power of California for all the people." We could not say to them, "If you are willing that every vessel that comes into your harbor shall pay a tax to the Federal government for the benefit of all the States, then we are willing that you should collect a royalty from the water-powers of California." I believe that if we had taken that story to the people of the East, they would have seen, first, that it was unfair that this special rule should apply to the Western States and not to the East; and, second, that the centralization of power in the Federal government tended to the destruction of those principles laid down in the Constitution of the United States when the separate States were organized, each with its own powers, and retaining all of those powers except those which were given under the constitution to the central government. I still believe that the principle involved is wrong; and yet after years of fighting against this provision, and after forcing Congress to put liberal provisions into that leasing law, we then got out of the way, and said, "All right. It is the law. We will make no further objection." More than two years have elapsed since the West surrendered its opposition to the principle and said, "Now that you have created a fair leasing bill, which if it were in the hands of the States rather than in the nation would be extremely desirable; now that you have created a fair leasing bill, go ahead and pass it; we object no further." In the meantime this centralization of power idea to which we objected has developed itself; and right now we have the pitiable spectacle from the standpoint of a republican government, that three members of the President's cabinet are quarreling among themselves as to what they will permit the legislative body to do. Secretary Lane has stood for the West. His statement and his position with reference to the leasing bill are fair to the West. Secretary Daniels and Attorney General Gregory are saying, "We won't permit you to pass that bill." I cannot help but feel that if this Government is to be maintained in the future as a republican form of government there will need to be a more careful defining of the rights and powers of the several departments of government. I do not believe that the executive power can say to the legislative power, "You can pass only such a law," and, following that up, tell the Congress how they should construe that law, and still maintain a republican form of government as laid down by the constitution. And therefore I believe that the present situation is one filled with danger.

Now if I were to say what I think ought to be done, I would say to the conference committee, which for months and months has been wrangling over the provisions of the bill to which they may agree after it has been passed by both houses of Congress, and its members taking their advice from the executive department of the Government, I would say to those gentlemen, "You will either pass that bill before the 4th day of March, and if you fail the West will again take up its cudgel against the whole principle of leasing, and you will have to fight if you ever pass a leasing bill.''

That is one of the things which the American Mining Congress has been endeavoring to do, to see if a leasing bill were passed that it should contain this provision which should enable it to operate fairly, and under which the resources of the West might be developed. The War has taught us among other lessons the great importance of the mining industry. Never before have we realized that as a nation, without the development of the mining industry, without its operation in the hands of those who understand the business, the nation could not carry on its work. We have been brought face to face as a nation now with the importance of mining. We have discovered another thing, namely, to the extent that those operations were interfered with by people who had no knowledge of the business disaster was sure to follow.

I want before I leave the leasing bill proposition to say a word on another matter. Alaskan coal was available, and should have been poured into your industries along the Coast long ago in unlimited quantities to the full extent of your needs; but because of the desire for a leasing bill in Alaska the coal could not be mined. The story is long: I will only touch upon it. A leasing bill was finally enacted. It seemed to be within the province of the Federal government, owning Alaska as a Territory without any State duties put upon its people, that a leasing bill there might apply. The leasing bill was passed. Until the present year there has been no production under the law. Alaska had coal which the tests showed conclusively was better, if there was a difference, than the Pocahontas coal for the use of the Navy; and yet last year, at a time when this nation was girding up its loins to meet the great emergency of the War, and when coal was needed by all the Western industries, when the railroads were overburdened with the carrying of the coal to the industrial centres of the East, at that time railroad trains were starting from West Virginia with coal to be carried away across the continent to deliver to the Pacific Coast navy—one of the fruits of the interference of the Federal government with the development of Western resources.

The American Mining Congress has for its duty to look after matters of interest to the mining industry in different parts of the country. These matters are partly national matters. I have sometimes been reprimanded somewhat for using a term which has grown to be somewhat out of repute with many people, but not with me, because I believe that the man who says that he is not a politician is not a good citizen. I believe that every citizen in the United States should be a politician and take part in the carrying out of his responsibility to the Government; and I believe that wherever there have been failures in our governmental policy it is because individuals have not been politicians. Therefore I say that the American Mining Congress has for its special business mining politics. We are not afraid to say to Congress, either Democrats or Republicans, "It is not good politics or bad politics, but it is the business of mining that we want you to consider. It has peculiar problems that you do not understand. We know you will be fair to us if you understand our conditions;" and we know that having 36 members of Congress west of the Missouri river. I have insisted for years that the West was that section of country where two different systems of law prevail; where the doctrine of riparian rights has been set aside absolutely and the doctrine of appropriation of water has taken its place; where the side-line theory of ownership has been set aside and where the doctrine of extra-lateral rights prevails for mining. I am not arguing as to the advantage of this. I am saying that where that system of law prevails is a country which has conditions entirely different from those understood by people in the East; and therefore we need to present to those people the conditions under which, and under which alone, we can develop the Western country as it needs to be developed, and therefore that we ought to be in a position personally to appeal to every man where it is essential to improve conditions hindering the mining industry. Therefore we are anxious to so extend the work of the American Mining Congress that it shall have one man at the head of its several departments of mining who can be better posted on that subject than anyone else can hope to be. Heretofore the Mining Congress has staggered along with a Secretary that has tried to keep himself posted as to chrome and manganese and oil and coal and gold and silver and all of the various branches of mining, and jumping from one subject to another. While he may, because of the justice of his cause, have made some success, he has never been able to do the work as it ought to have been done. During recent days there has been a development which looks toward a great extension of our work. We are proposing that there shall be eight divisions of the mining industry; that the precious or rare metals shall constitute one division; that the ferro-iron and the ferro-metals shall constitute another division; that the base metals, lead and zinc, shall constitute one division. The plan is to appeal to the mining men of the country to create new funds in order that we may have at the head of each one of these divisions some one man who may put in his time in equipping himself upon that and be accounted as the authority in the United States on that subject. This cannot be done in a day. At the Arizona meeting the day before yesterday they adopted a plan of support of this organization. The plan was first to ask each industry to contribute a fund composed of 10 cents of each thousand dollars of its production. It may be that in future years that assessment will not be sufficient. It is barely possible it may be too much now. We do not know. But we want at the head of each one of these departments a man who not only has the knowledge of the business, who can visit your plant and know exactly the conditions of your production, and be almost as able to present your case as you could yourself, but in addition to that, may inform himself as to all the avenues of approach through which the plain justice of your demand may be presented to the proper authorities. We believe that such a man will be consulted by Congress when it wants to know about these things. We want that man capable of going to the President, if the occasion requires it, of going to anyone wherever he may be, and be recognized as the representative of that branch of the industry.

The most important question which faces the American people is the relation of labor and capital. It comes vitally home to the mining industry as it does to every other industry. There was a time when individual employers each worked by himself, and as time went on we found that organized labor was acting as a unit. It is no criticism of organized labor when we say that in many instances it gained advantages which it was not entitled to, because they acted for their best interest, and they had a right to press their cause. Upon the other hand, the employers of labor were entirely disorganized. In a recent questionnaire which was sent from our office I received one peculiar answer with reference to this question from the President of the 5th and 9th Coal Districts of Illinois. He said if he had his way no man should be permitted to have a job who did not belong to the union; and no employer should be permitted to carry on his business unless he joined the association of others in that business, so that there should be perfect mutuality. He said that the danger in the labor world was the professional agitator; that if you forced people to join the union you did away with the necessity for agitators. Whether that is true or not, I do not agree with the principle, but it is worth considering. This thing is true: in the future there is going to be a different relation between employers and employees. I believe that the employers should undertake an educational campaign, and should themselves endorse the principle that the workmen should receive the highest wage which it is possible for the industry to pay. You employers should fight for the maximum wage, not the minimum wage. Right now we are faced with a peculiar condition, and it is up to us now to show our good faith in the matter. We cannot, when work is scarce, when men are being turned loose without employment, say, "Wages have been high. Now we are going to starve you. You must take the minimum wage." No, the employers of this country are not going to take that position, but there are many men who think we take that position unless we show that our desire is to pay the maximum wage possible. Now a maximum wage may not be maximum if we get a proper service for it. In the inquiry which I sent out with reference to the gold industry, practically all of the replies were to the effect that they were paying 25 or 35% more wages, and receiving 35 to 50% less in efficiency. If we can say to the working men, "We are going to pay you every dollar that this industry will bear, and upon the other hand we expect from you the best service which you can render; we want from you the highest efficiency; we are willing to pay for it," then I think we can go further, and point out to the employee that out of the total product of his own and his fellow workmen the production is to give the luxuries which he enjoys. In other words, one principle which organized labor has advocated, and which I believe is wrong, is to the effect that you must not do too much work, for if you do there won't be jobs enough to go around. That I believe to be intrinsically and fundamentally wrong; and if we expect to increase the luxuries of the laboring men we must increase his production, we must increase his efficiency, because out of the total sum of production these luxuries come. If we produce more the excess supply in the market will depress prices; that is one of the natural rules; and as a result the wages which you pay him will go further and their wages are worth more to them. I believe that a campaign of education along this line will do much to bring more harmonious relations between capital and labor; it will convince the laboring man that we want to be fair to him, but that if we pay him so much that the cost of goods is so high that the market won't use them, the lack of use will come back, and there will be no demand and no production and no work. A few years ago I made a study of production, and I found that when we shipped 5% of our goods to foreign markets we have pretty poor times in this country; when we ship 7½% we have fairly good times; when we ship 10% we have flush business conditions. So we must ship from 7 to 10% to foreign markets to keep the men employed and the capital at work. If that is true, that 10% must be produced cheaply enough to find a market in competition with more cheaply produced material there. I am not of those who think that the amount of dollars you pay for a day's wage is the whole criterion. It is a question of efficiency; and when we can instill into our workmen the belief that they are working squarely with us in order to increase production, and make that production as cheaply as possible to the consumer, and because of the cheaper production there will be an increased demand for work, and we have thus brought about the right condition, and when we have done that we can hope that the laboring man, no longer feeling that his employer is opposed to his interest, will join in making a hand in hand fight together to develop the best interests of the industry in which they are both engaged.

Gold output of the Rand last year was 8,416,000 oz. In 1917 it was 9,022,263 oz., 9,295,538 oz. in 1916, 9,093,671 oz. in 1915, and 8,394,320 oz. in 1914. A diamond weighing 388½ carats (1231 grains, or 2.56 ounces) was found at the Jagersfontein mine in Orange River Colony, adjoining the Transvaal, last week. The famous Cullinan diamond, found in the Premier mine near Pretoria, Transvaal, weighs 3025 carats, or over 1¼ pounds.

Sinking at the Seneca copper mine in Michigan cost $305 per foot. The 3-compartment shaft was vertical to a depth of 1450 ft., after which it curved slightly to 1629 ft., where the Kearsarge lode was cut. The shaft is lined with steel and is therefore fireproof. The above cost includes all shaft work and surface equipment, the latter equal to $100 per foot.

The Economic Duties of the Engineer

By W. R. INGALLS

*What engineer is there who does not know that the essential assumption of pure democracy as applied to industry—that production should be controlled by the people themselves—is in direct antithesis to the fact that in modern industrial life efficiency of production has increased as the efforts of the many have been directed and organized by the talents of the few? Must not every engineer of experience in leadership agree with Mallock, the great philosopher, that the oligarchic principle is as dominant in industry as it is in political democracy?

But superior to all industrial and political principles are economic laws, for it is those laws, which are laws of nature, that create and determine principles and practices. One of the greatest of economic laws is that of the survival of the fittest, which exhibits itself in competition, and from that is derived the classic economic doctrine that labor is the residual claimant upon the produce of industry. After the shares of the State, the landlord, the capitalist, and the entrepreneur have been deducted, all the rest goes to labor, and here is what is mystifying to many, to wit, rent, interest, and profits are limited by competition, and of them the laborer can get neither the share of the landlord nor of the entrepreneur by any economic means, while, as for interest, the residual claimant is benefited by every payment on account of capital used in the production of wealth, and is better off when a high rate of interest is being paid than when a low rate is paid. We may apply the principles to the concrete case of the United States.

The wealth of the United States at the end of 1916 was estimated at about $250,000,000,000. The production of things was about $50,000,000,000. These are very rough figures, as they are bound to be. Estimates relating to this subject vary considerably. I have mentioned the highest that I have seen. There is reason to suppose that the higher figures are more nearly correct than the lower. Anyhow, I am going to use the highest only to give an approximate idea of proportions. This was before the United States entered the War, and, according to the United States Bureau of Labor, we had 4,000,000 workers. Let us assume that rent, interest, and profits averaged 4% of the wealth of the nation, which would hardly be extravagant. That would account for $10,000,000,000 out of the total produce, leaving $40,000,000,000 for labor, or $1000 per worker. We have already seen that 2,000,000 railway workers and 250,000 iron and steel workmen received about that sum. Those figures are specific expressions of two whole industries. The workmen in some other industries earned more; in some they earned less. However, there is considerable evidence that the general average was about that figure, or something near it, and, anyhow, whatever error in statement there may be will not invalidate my following argument.

That labor does not get increased wages at the expense of capital (unless capital be confiscated, in which event the increased wages will not long endure) is illustrated by the experience with the railways in Great Britain and America. The governments guaranteed the bond and stockholders their average return for a series of pre-war years. In the United States this was $1,000,000,000 per annum, or just about 5% on the capital as reported by the Interstate Commerce Commission. The increase of $800,000,000 in wages has been paid by the public in higher freight and passenger rates. To have left the roads in private hands, compelling them to pay higher wages without permission to make higher charges, would have resulted, first, in impaired service and finally in the State having to take over the lines and supply the deficit in order to have any service at all, just as has happened with some of the street railway lines in Massachusetts. Thus, what is virtual confiscation aids the wage-earner only slightly and only temporarily.

But apart from confiscation, the winning of increased wages by one group of labor is obtained only at the expense of other groups. The inequality in the distribution of wealth is not between the capitalist and the laborer, but rather is it among laborers themselves. There is ample ground for the surmise that the professional, clerical, shop-tending, and similar classes, and the salaried classes generally, have suffered especially at the hands of the railway operators, mechanics, artisans, builders, and miners, but the farmers and the factory folk have not been immune.

I am not going to enter upon any fine analysis of the very rough statistical data that I have given, and shall point out merely that after the State, the landlord, the capitalist, and the entrepreneur have got their taxes, rent, interest, and profits, of which the last three are severely limited by competition, labor gets all the rest, and what it gets is what it produces. The only way it can get more is to produce more.

It is unfortunate that the only way of expressing production is in terms of money. If it were possible to express it in terms of goods, there would be less misunderstanding. However, it is clear that if the total goods and the total population remained the same, it would not matter if the money value of the goods fell from $50,000,000,000 to $30,000,000,000, that is, it would not matter at all if money wages fell from $1000 per annum to $600, as, indeed, they would fall inevitably. On the other hand, if commodity prices remained the same, and the value of products should rise from $30,000,000,000 to $50,000,000,000, labor would get so much more, for it would be producing more goods. This is the only way that the war scale of wages can be maintained, and it is a problem of capital, labor, and talent to co-operate in accomplishing it, for only by co-operation can it be done.

This is no preaching of capitalism as commonly understood, but is simply classic and proved economic doctrine.

*Abstract from presidential address before the Mining & Metallurgical Society of America, January 14, 1919.

One Phase of the Railroad Problem

By N. H. EMMONS 2nd

The railroad freight rate is the one question in connection with our whole transportation scheme that cannot have said of it that it is based on actual work performed. From the railroad owners' standpoint the question of earning interest on the capital invested is the first consideration. The second question is the return to labor for work done. The public is interested in these two, but is more interested in the efficient and economical movement of people and material.

Whether the railroads are operated by the Government or by private owners is largely a question of whether the public be allowed to choose their own investments or whether they all be forced to own a part of all the railroads. Operation by the Government means that if there is a loss the Government pays it and takes it from the whole people in the form of taxes. Government operation and ownership mean that instead of a group of interested owners electing their representatives to operate their road, the general election for President of the country will be the basis of deciding who will operate the railroads, and each time the Government changes its head there will be a new secretary of transportation, who, of course, will need new men under him.

Before the War people were satisfied to pay an average of two and one-half cents per mile for passenger service. Special or lower rates were made for various reasons. There was mileage, or rates based upon a great deal of traveling; there was commutation, or rates based upon a large number of people traveling a short distance daily; there were through rates, to cover long trips; and there were party rates, whereby a number of people made a trip from one station to another as a party. The public was satisfied and made selection of localities to live in and roads to be traveled over according to the advantages offered.

Express, which may be considered a branch of the freight service, was paid on the basis of value of goods, weight or bulk of the goods, size of shipment, and distance between point of origin and destination. The essential difference between freight and express service is the time element. There does not seem to be any basic reason why the railroads should not handle the express business of the country. Our railroad business has been built up by private ownership. It is the most efficient transportation in the world and it would seem a good policy to let well enough alone.

But the question causing continual irritation between the railroads and the public is that of railroad freight-rates. The public is willing to pay for service rendered, but wants to know what the basis of the charges is. It has often been said, and is probably very near the truth, that rates are based on the principle of charging all the traffic will bear. There is no justice in this. How are rates arrived at? A shipper goes to the railroad and asks for a rate on a new movement. The railroad makes a thorough investigation of all conditions, ascertains as nearly as possible the cost of production, the selling-price of the commodity at the market end, advises the shipper what it thinks should be the rate, and proposes to the Interstate Commerce Commission this rate. If the party asking for the rate happens to be familiar with the system he puts in a brief to the Commission independent of the railroad; if not, there is but one side of the question offered for the Commission's enlightenment, and the rate is granted. After the shipper has become more familiar with his market he finds that competitors have better rates than he has and goes before the Commission asking relief. This is a most unscientific, unsatisfactory, and irritable way of adjusting rates; and yet on account of custom it is considered the only way to make them.

Here we are with prices of commodities that were never dreamed of before, with railroad rates higher than ever before, with business conditions unsettled by the idleness of many plants, and with a complete new start in many things facing us. Now would be the time, if ever, to make an adjustment to new conditions. We are entering a period when capital must begin to go into new industries, when the rates being paid to labor are more nearly equal all over the country, thus eliminating the question of unequal wages, and when the establishment of manufacturing concerns should be located with reference to nearness to market and short railroad haul rather than to labor market.

There should be a railroad freight-rate commission appointed by Congress to study the question and propose a new order of things promptly.

The purpose of this article is to suggest a method of making rates based on service rendered, forgetting the old system and the old divisions of territory, and looking at the question broadly and with an eye to the future.

What is the service rendered by railroads in handling freight? First there is the cost of receiving goods. Second, the transportation of these goods. Third, the delivery of the goods at the destination. If the first and the third are considered as fixed quantities, as they do not depend on the distance between origin and destination, a fixed sum can be charged for this service. The transfer from one railroad system to another involves extra cost for work done and special accounting, and a charge for this should be made. The main variable is the transportation. This variable contains several points that should be recognized in basing rates. They are distance hauled, value of shipment per unit of weight or bulk, and quantity handled. There should be an inducement offered to railroads to originate traffic and to take especial care of its section of the country. The following suggestion for basing rates is offered at this time for serious consideration by the American public.

First, allow a charge for receiving, transfer, and delivery of freight, these charges to be added to the charge for hauling.

The hauling charge should be made up with two main variables, distance hauled, and value of material hauled, and two lesser variables, size of shipment, and section of the country traversed.

The first variables can be dealt with as follows. Establish a base rate depending on the value of the material, and allow a discount for length of haul.

The base rate should be made up somewhat as follows:

Value of commodity per ton or 80 cu. ft.	Base-rate per ton-mile, cents	Value of commodity per ton or 80 cu. ft.	Base-rate per ton-mile, cents
Up to $1.00	0.20	$100.01 to $200.00	1.50
$1.01 " 5.00	0.30	200.01 " 500.00	2.00
5.01 " 10.00	0.40	500.01 " 1000.00	3.00
10.01 " 20.00	0.50	1000.01 " 2000.00	4.00
20.01 " 50.00	0.75	2000.01 up	5.00
50.01 " 100.00	1.00		

The variable for distance hauled starts with the base rate and allows a discount for length of haul. For the first 100 miles or fraction thereof, charge the base rate for distance hauled. Thus on the fourth classification of 0.5c. base.

For 100 miles the rate would be	0.50c.
For the next 100 miles 10% off, or	0.45
100 " 5% " "	0.4275
100 " 5% " "	0.4061
100 " 5% " "	0.3858
100 " 5% " "	0.3670
200 " 5% " "	0.3487
200 " 5% " "	0.3313
500 " 5% " "	0.3147
500 " 5% " "	0.2990
1000 " 5% " "	0.2840
All above 3000 " 5% " "	0.2698

On this basis a haul of 3000 miles would be at an average rate of 0.3268c. per ton-mile, or $9.80 per ton for a commodity worth between $10 and $20. One ton of copper falling between $200 and $500 in value would cost $39.18 to haul 3000 miles and a ton of lumber $9.80 for the same haul. To these rates should be added the receiving, delivery, and transfer charges.

The value of one ton of copper, on a pre-war basis, was $280 (ten-year average) and the freight-rate from Montana to the Atlantic seaboard was $10.50. The value of lumber in Idaho was around $30 per 1000 feet, or somewhere between $15 and $20 per ton, and the freight-rate was $15 per ton, or from $22.50 to $30 per 1000 feet for the same haul.

QUANTITY. It costs a great deal more to handle small shipments, that is, less than a carload, and an increase of perhaps 25% should be allowed for less than carload shipments with a receiving and delivery charge added. It costs less to handle a train-load than a car from one station to another, and a discount should be allowed for train-load shipments.

LOCALITY. The country has been divided into three sections for the purpose of rate-making. The North, which meant north of the Potomac and Ohio rivers, and east of the Mississippi; the South, which was south of the Potomac and Ohio rivers and east of the Mississippi; and the West, all west of the Mississippi. The country has grown since this division was made and a new arrangement is needed, perhaps allowing the classification by value to be moved up one mill, on points west of a new western line or covering what may be known as the Rocky Mountain section.

Our present system of rates has favored certain manufacturing districts and has congested certain lines to the limit. Many localities could be built up if rates were equalized to a greater extent. Such a system as the one outlined will have that tendency. Everyone will say at the first glance that this is impossible or impracticable, but looking deeply into the question will show that this idea will give the greatest benefit to the greatest number of our American people.

THE ROCK, chiefly flint, in the Joplin zinc-lead region of Missouri, is hard and brittle, and rapidly wears the cutting edge of drill-bits, but because of its brittleness it is more easily fractured by the concussion of the drill. In some of the mines the gangue-rock is tough, so that the footage per shift is less, whereas in other deposits it is more or less soft and the footage for the same amount of time consumed in drilling is much greater than the average. The average footage for drilling in sheet-ground is 20 to 50 ft. per 8-hour shift for each drill, varying with the character of the ground and the skill of the drill-man. Changes every two ft. are often necessary. —U. S. Bureau of Mines Bulletin 154.

FLOTATION of galena at Broken Hill, New South Wales, was discussed by the Institution of Mining and Metallurgy on November 21, when V. F. S. Low said, "taking Broken Hill as an instance in which, along a very short line of lode, there were such great variations in the ore treatment methods of the several companies concerned—variations which were in great part due to the difference in the ores mined—the engineer who contemplated undertaking selective or other flotation would be well advised to first put up an experimental unit and thoroughly test the treatment of his ore before finally committing himself to any finished design."

DREDGING FOR TIN by the Tongkah Harbour Tin Dredging Co. in Siam, during the year ended September 30, 1918, cost 10 cents per cubic yard. This is exclusive of depreciation. In 1917 the cost was 8.8 cents. Five boats worked 34,346 hours, during which they dug 3,383,250 cu. yd. The average yield was 0.87 lb. of tin per yard, equal to 31.4 cents. The total tin oxide recovered was 1314 tons, equal to 69.34 to 73.34% metal. This is an Australian company that pays regular dividends.

DURING 1918 the Brazilian Minister of Finance arranged with the St. John del Rey and Ouro Preto mining companies, both British corporations, that the Government acquire the whole gold output of these properties, owing to the embargo on exportation of the precious metals. Up to the end of 1916 all gold from Brazil went to England. Exports in 1915 totaled 142,000 ounces.

PIONEER, NEVADA

Resuscitation of an Old Gold District.

Some interesting work is now in progress at Pioneer, five miles north of Rhyolite and 60 miles south of Goldfield. It had a memorable boom in 1908, and is again the most active mining centre in the region south of Goldfield. Plans are being made to start work on several other properties in the district, besides those described in the following notes:

On December 26 work was resumed at the property of the Consolidated Mayflower Mines Co. with sufficient men to work two shifts, under direction of J. B. Kendall, president and manager. Prior to this the 500-ft. main incline shaft and some of the drifts had been re-timbered. All mine and shaft timbering was destroyed by fire in January 1912. Repairs to shaft and surface eequipment were completed within a few days, and drills of the Waugh 'turbo' type were brought in by express. Drills are breaking ground rapidly on four levels—the 200, 300, 400, and 500—and five working faces in good milling ore, assaying from $12 to $35 per ton. The ore is oxidized and free-milling down to the 500-ft. level; water-level is at 510 ft. Records of former production are incomplete, but show a net profit of $158,000 from 11,053 tons. During this period, mining costs averaged $2 and milling $3.53 per ton. Development had been confined for the most part to the 300-ft. level, where a stope was opened 300 ft. long, yielding 10,000 tons of $14 ore. A smaller stope on the 400-ft. level produced ore of higher grade. A pumping station on the 500-ft. level was the only work at this depth.

Surface equipment was found to be in good condition. The Ingersoll-Sergeant compressor will operate 15 of the new drills and is driven by a 90-hp. Western distillate engine. A 32-hp. Fairbanks-Morse engine is used for hoisting and a similar engine provides power for the mill, a 6-hp. engine of the same make driving the solution pumps. This machinery was put in and used for a short time before an electric power-line was extended to the district. Power service was discontinued in 1916 and the engines, accorded good care, are as good as new. The 15-stamp mill is to be re-modeled and increased by the addition of a ball-mill. Formerly, coarse crushing resulted in heavy metallurgical loss, and a large part of the impounded tailing assays from $3 to $6 gold per ton. Water for milling is pumped from below the 500-ft. level of the mine. The ore is trammed 100 ft. from the collar of the incline shaft, over a Fairbanks scale, to a grizzley, the fine falling to the ore-bin and the coarse passing to a 9 by 14-in. Blake jaw-crusher; thence to the ore-bin, and fed to the batteries by Challenge feeders of the Joshua Hendy type. After passing 40-mesh screens the pulp flowed over 4 by 12-ft. silvered copper plates, where a recovery of 50% of the gold content was made by amalgamation. The pulp was then elevated to a Dorr classifier, the sand passing to ten 5 by 16 leaching vats for cyanidation, the slime being impounded below the mill. It is said that the available power will be adequate with the added ball-mill, and it is proposed to complete these changes at an early date.

The geology is described as a readily distinguished series of rhyolite flows, in part brecciated and with strata, varying greatly in width, of red volcanic mud. A number of fault-planes are observed, but displacement is negligible. The ore-channel is a fissure striking N. 55° W. and dipping SW. from 60 to 70°, and averages 5 ft. in width. The Starlight incline shaft, 1400 ft. north-west of the main shaft, was sunk 93 ft. in ore of milling grade, and a hanging-wall cross-cut on the 85-ft. level, out 30 ft., exposed 6 ft. of $12 ore in a parallel vein. Near this shaft the vein was sampled for 60 ft. by 3-ft. cuts at 3-ft. intervals, giving an average of $51 per ton. A winze from the 400-ft. level of the main shaft was sunk 80 ft. in ore assaying from $12 to $25 per ton. The vein was cut recently on the 500-ft. level, where it was 12 ft. wide, with 18 in. of ore on the hanging wall assaying $30 per ton. Winzes are to be sunk from the 500-ft. level to determine the character of the ore below water-level.

The main shaft of the Reorganized Pioneer Mines Co., formerly the Pioneer Consolidated Mines Co., has been re-timbered to the bottom—400 ft.—and sinking is again in progress. The shaft will be sunk at least to 800 ft., following recommendations of J. K. Turner, the consulting engineer. His report points out that the orebodies found on

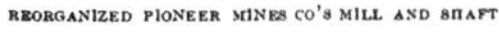

REORGANIZED PIONEER MINES CO'S MILL AND SHAFT.

CONSOLIDATED MAYFLOWER MINES CO PROPERTY AT PIONEER.

existing levels are broken masses of quartz, with no semblance of vein formation, and he holds that these quartz-zones may be found at depth to assume the form of veins. He sees no geologic reason why enrichment should not be found to persist in depth. The mine has produced nearly $600,000 from ore and bullion shipments, the famous Bonanza stope, opened above the 200-ft. level, yielding over $300,000 in shipping ore, and breaking a $100 product across 30 ft. The 10-stamp amalgamation and cyanide mill operated continuously for several years, with costs lower than those of any plant in southern Nevada, but was closed as a result of the withdrawal of electric power service.

BISBEE, ARIZONA

Exploration in the C. & A. Mines.—Labor and Employment.—Warehouses and Change-houses.—Demand for Copper.—Tungsten Mining.—Cananea, Sonora.

While no statement has been given out by either of the large operating companies here—Calumet & Arizona and Phelps Dodge Corporation—it is known that development of the class styled as 'pioneering' is retarded to some extent by the failure of several hundred skilled miners now in the army to return here. Only a small proportion of the men enlisted in army, navy, or war work has arrived in Bisbee since demobilization began. All of these are being given positions upon application, either their old ones or others of equal grade. The C. & A. service flag contains 447 stars, of which about 400 were miners, and that of the Copper Queen branch of Phelps Dodge more than 600. A change in the rule of employment by the companies has been made, as this is now offered only to returning soldiers and sailors. Formerly soldiers, sailors, and men who had worked for the companies for two years and within two years, were employed.

Built along fire-resisting lines the Copper Queen supply warehouse on the site of the one destroyed by fire on October 31 is now ready for business. Floors are of concrete, and a sprinkler system has been installed.

Drifts from the Junction shaft of the Calumet & Arizona, leading east toward the Denn-Arizona company's western line, have not yet reached their objective, which is the rich orebodies opened by the Denn between the 1000 and 1600-ft. levels. However, the Junction workings are in favorable looking ground, particularly at 1600 ft. The other drift is at 1400 ft. Driving toward the Denn, particularly on the lower level, has been tedious and costly. The problem of ventilation has been difficult, while the distance material had to be brought from the surface has been another handicap. The Denn orebody extended directly up to the eastern line of the Junction, so the one feature the C. & A. has to look to in its exploration of this ground is to ascertain how far it extends into its property. The drifts when completed will be 2000 ft. long. This is the largest amount of strictly development work in the C. & A. properties in new territory, just at present.

A party of engineers from the Anaconda at Butte and others recently visited Bisbee. Among them was Dr. L. D. Ricketts, who said that nobody could predict anything for copper at present as there was no demand, not even a reliable quotation for the metal. Reduction both in forces and output to avoid tying up great quantities of unsaleable bullion is the policy observable throughout the industry, he said.

Work has been started on a new change-house at the Lowell shaft of the Copper Queen, built along the same modern lines as those recently completed at the Czar and Holbrook mines. A change-room is to be erected at the Gardner as soon as that at the Lowell is finished, giving employees of Phelps Dodge every comfort. The locker system allows wet clothes to be hoisted on pullies to the roof of the building, where free circulation of air soon dries them, doing away with much of the discomfort experienced under old conditions. The change-houses are scientifically heated and supplied with baths.

Closing of the lead concentrating plant of the Shattuck-Arizona took place on the afternoon of January 15; 40 men employed were laid-off, as were 45 engaged in mining lead-silver ore. This step was taken because of the low price of lead and unsatisfactory mining conditions. The Shattuck mill was completed less than six months ago, and included a flotation process evolved for treating this ore after long experimentation. Recovery was said to be very high. No reduction at present is contemplated in the copper mining forces of the company.

Deep snows in the Huachuca mountains, 40 miles southwest of Bisbee, preclude operations of the Tungsten Reef Mining Co., exceping on construction of a mill for concentration of ore from three large blanket veins. The crusher for the plant already has arrived on the ground, also the boilers. The ore is said to contain a high percentage of tungsten, also some gold. A pipe-line to supply the mill with water is being laid from springs in the mountains near-by. A. J. Clark of Montana is president and treasurer, L. E. Porter vice-president and secretary, and G. D. Kislingbury superintendent. It is expected to re-open the mining about mid-February.

Though fully 1500 employees of the Cananea Consolidated Copper Co. at Cananea, the Democrata Mining Co., and Calumet & Sonora have been discharged during the last few weeks, there have been no disorders in the camp, and few of the men have remained. Most of them with their full families have gone to southern Sonora, where less rigorous weather and cheaper food have offered inducement. According to mining men arriving at Bisbee the total output of Cananea will be cut from a third to a half.

DEADWOOD, SOUTH DAKOTA

Position of Gold Mining in the Black Hills.

Mining men recently met here to discuss the gold production of the Black Hills. The principal speaker was H. W. Seaman, president of the Trojan Mining Co. He covered government regulations, cost of supplies, the fixed price and cost of producing gold, the embargo on gold exports and premiums paid for the metal in foreign countries, and the cost of cyanide. He was not in favor of the proposed premium for gold, but thought that if the Government made an open market for it there would be a remedy for present conditions.

The following resolutions were adopted on January 10 by the Black Hills Mining Men's Association:

Resolved, That the Legislature of the State of South Dakota be, and it is hereby respectfully petitioned and urged to memorialize the Congress of the United States to take, as promptly as possible, such appropriate action as may be effective to grant the fullest relief to the gold-mining industry of the Nation, including (1) a removal of all restriction upon the sale of bullion, either in domestic or foreign markets; (2) a more liberal allowance for depreciation, including exhaustion of mines; (3) a substantial release from the payment of taxes occasioned by the War, inasmuch as the gold industry was a sacrifice for the Government during the period of the War, and wholly subordinated to the winning of the War, and was during that period and still is being operated at a loss, we only ask for a square deal and an even break; (4) the good offices of the Government in securing for us reasonable prices for the machinery and supplies necessary for the successful operation of the gold-mining industry, and in aiding and abetting all endeavors to increase the production of 'new' gold; and (5) any direct assistance given the gold miner as a prospector or producer during the period of reconstruction which will as much or more than any other measure be instrumental in stabilizing the markets of the world in all other commodities, as gold is the bedrock foundation of all national and international transactions.

JEROME, ARIZONA

Operations Curtailed at the Big Mines.—Developments at the Small Mines.

On account of the copper market both the United Verde Copper Co. and the United Verde Extension Mining Co. are cutting-down their working forces and lessening production of the red metal. About 300 men have been laid-off at Jerome, Clarkdale, and Verde, and the U. V. Copper Co. has closed one blast-furnace, while the Extension is working only one furnace and on lower-grade ore than usual. Due to the lay-off and the fact that returning soldiers are being put to work, there is a large surplus of labor in the district at present, and notices have been posted at the outside railroad station warning those seeking employment that there is no chance of securing work at the present time in the Verde district.

Prospecting by diamond-drilling is again being done at the Calumet & Jerome, a contract for three or four holes, comprising over 2000 ft., having been let to the Diamond Drilling Company.

A small force is at work at the Shea mine extracting and sorting the ore from the west drift on the 350-ft. level. Sufficient is now ready for a second shipment to the U. V. X. smelter at Verde. The first shipment of 13 tons netted about $2800.

The superintendent of the Pittsburgh-Jerome, Charles Arata, is still awaiting the arrival of certain compressor parts necessary for the starting of the machinery before work can be resumed on a large scale.

A depth of over 1275 ft. has now been reached in the shaft at Verde Combination, and it will take two weeks more to attain the 1300-ft. level and allow for a sump below that point. For the first 100 ft. below the 1080-ft. level the shaft was in a well-mineralized bluish-black schist. The formation from 1200 ft. down and up to the last few rounds is a hard diorite and jasper. Recently the shaft has been passing through a hard silicious quartz, and the last round has broken into a soft schist, fairly well mineralized in pyrite and chalcopyrite, and showing some specks of bornite. The formation all appears to dip toward the north-west.

At the Gadsden, under development by Calumet & Arizona, the cross-cut being run north-west on the 1200-ft. level recently cut through a water-course 900 ft. from the shaft, exposing several small pockets of native copper. No driving was done on this formation and the heading is being continued on toward the north and south fault, a distance of 1800 ft. from the shaft. The heading has now gone 1050 ft. passing through a quartz-schist. The last few rounds are showing a soft decomposed schist. Occasionally evidences of chalcopyrite are to be seen in the formation.

Extraction from the Maintop orebody of the Jerome Verde continues at the rate of over 20 tons per day, and shipments are still being made to the smelter at Humboldt. The value of the ore remains at around 9%.

Driving both ways on the contact on the 900-ft. level from the Dorothy May shaft of the Green Monster is still being done at this property, and while nothing of an important nature has been opened in the work so far, there have been occasional evidences of mineralization.

The Jerome Bisbee Copper Co. was recently organized to take over the defunct Jerome Portland Mining Co. Late last year the properties of the latter were bid-in at a receivership sale for $14,000, by parties interested in the welfare of that company, and an option has been given the new company that will permit of the purchase of the property at the same figure. The Jerome Bisbee is capitalized at 1,500,000 shares, 50 cents par. The property, which has been grossly mismanaged in the past, is well thought of as a prospect, and lies adjacent to the Copper Chief, Shea, Green Monster, Equator, and Jerome St. Louis, and 3½ miles south-east from the town of Jerome.

Grand island has been attracting more than the usual attention during the past few weeks, not only locally, but in various outside quarters as well, where the demand for the shares has been brisk. The 500-ft. level has been reached, with 30 ft. below for a sump, and a station is being cut. This work should take from 10 to 12 days, after which a cross-cut will be run north-east to cut the vein. It is estimated that a distance of only a little over 100 ft. will have to be driven. However, as there are three distinct veins showing on the surface near the shaft, one of which is said to be the rich Shea vein, other lateral development will be initiated later on. In the meantime, ore is being extracted from the drift run from the bottom of the 40-ft. shaft, and will be shipped to the smelter. The vein now shows a width of 3 ft., and contains good value in copper.

DENVER, COLORADO

Further Notes on Meeting of American Mining Congress.—Drainage-Tunnels.

At the meeting of the Congress held here on January 2, topics were: 'Advantages of Co-operation with U. S. Employment Service', 'Freight Rates', 'The State Metal Mining Fund', 'The Colorado Mining Situation', 'County Organization', 'Modern Mine Promotion', 'State Legislation and the Mining Industry', 'Proposed Blue-Sky Legislation', 'National Legislation and the American Mining Congress', 'The American Gold Conference', 'National Aid for the Metal Mining Industry', 'Relief for Producers of War Minerals', and 'Colorado War Minerals'. Lively discussions were elicited by some of these papers, especially the one proposing a blue-sky law as drafted and presented to the meeting by one of Denver's prominent brokers. One critic believed that Denver bond-dealers do not, under any circumstances, assist in financing new mining ventures, no matter how legitimate they may be; but that they devote their efforts to knocking metal mining and to trading in bonds and securities of companies in other lines or industry, usually of Eastern origin. The majority of speakers on this subject felt that the greatest good to all concerned would result by passing State legislation requiring stock-selling concerns of all sorts to publish complete figures and facts relative to their businesses. The effectiveness of straight publicity in squelching illegitimate promotions was amply proved in Denver last year in the application of a new and simple ordinance. This provided for the appointment of a commission whose duty it was to investigate personally all new oil and other promotions and to publish their findings in the local press. The commission was given no authority to bring action of any other sort against guilty promoters, but it did its assigned work. The results were not only effectual but prompt, all questionable concerns quickly scampering to cover.

The secretary of the American Mining Congress, J. F. Callbreath, outlined his plans for enlarging the usefulness of the organization this coming year by the establishment of eight departments in his Washington office, each in personal charge of a capable man, to deal with all sorts of legislative and legal matters arising in the several branches of the mining industry. It is planned to grant free service to all mining men of the country who may, at any time, require special information or assistance at Washington.

At times the sessions were enlivened by humorous remarks and stories. For instance: when U. S. Senator-elect

Lawrence C. Phipps, well known nationally as a steel magnate, spoke informally, he surprised the audience somewhat by his frank ignorance on mining and his statement that he had never put any money into metal mining. Upon the conclusion of his address, Bulkeley Wells, the president, announced his intention of appointing a committee of five to immediately sell Mr. Phipps a gold mine; whereupon the senator arose and solemnly explained that his wife had warned him in advance that somebody at the meeting would try to do that very thing and he had promised to refrain from any such purchase.

Because many large mining tunnel projects in Colorado had proved failures, the opinion prevailed a few years ago that enterprises of this nature were risky from the investor's standpoint. There are, indeed, scattered about the State abandoned large development or drainage-adits of this kind offering mute emphasis to this opinion. Some of these projects absorbed considerable expenditure of money without attaining any measure of success. There had been a period when tunnel-sites were a popular subject in every rugged mining region.

There have been a few decidedly successful tunnel enterprises. Among these there was one great project holding undoubted promise from the moment of its inception, that has been in process of excavation for about 11 years and that has finally attained its predestined goal: the Roosevelt deep drainage-tunnel at Cripple Creek, 24,225 ft. long, is finished. [An article describing the work will be published in the 'Press' in the near future.—Editor.]

TORONTO, ONTARIO

Canadian Metal Output.—Dividends From Ontario Mines.

The total value of the mineral production of Canada during 1918 is estimated by the Canadian Department of Mines at $220,000,000, compared with $189,646,821 in 1917. The production of the more important metals was as follows: gold, $14,750,000; silver, 20,800,000 oz.; copper, 117,000,000 lb.; nickel, 91,500,000 lb.; zinc, 36,000,000 lb.; pig-iron, 1,182,000 tons; and steel ingots and castings, 1,010,000 tons. Coal production was 15,180,000 tons, against 14,046,759 tons in 1917.

During the past year, twelve of the gold and silver-mining companies of northern Ontario paid dividends, nine being silver and three gold producers. The dividend-payers during 1917 number twenty in all, fifteen of them silver and five gold mines. The aggregate amount paid in dividends in 1918 was $6,381,477, not including the profits of private corporations, which would bring the total up to over $7,000,000. Dividends paid in 1917, including private concerns, amounted to $7,726,843. Total dividends paid since the beginning of mining in northern Ontario to the end of 1918 amount to $91,065,110.

PORCUPINE, ONTARIO

Labor Available and Re-opening of Mines.

Since the closing of munition plants in Canada a large number of the men released have gone to northern Ontario in search of employment. Most of them have been absorbed by lumber companies, and the pulp and paper mills, but many have obtained work at the mines. The shortage prevailing at Cobalt has almost been made up, although the working forces at Porcupine and other goldfields are being steadily increased, there is still a great demand for men. It is estimated that the present requirements of Porcupine alone, without making any allowance for new development, could give employment to 2000 more men.

At the Dome Mines the staff has been largely increased. New supplies are being purchased for the mill, and preparations are being made for the resumption of ore treatment as soon as an adequate working force can be secured.

It is officially announced that mining will be resumed at the West Dome Consolidated in the spring.

The Davidson, which has opened extensive orebodies of fair milling grade, is expected to become a large producer in 1919. The company has obtained control of the Bilsky property adjoining.

The Porcupine Crown will resume operations when sufficient men can be secured. The workings have been kept unwatered, while the mill is in good condition.

Kirkland Lake.—Interest is increasing in the southern section of this field, the leading prospects of which are the Ontario-Kirkland, Canadian-Kirkland, and Hunton-Kirkland. At the Ontario an electrically-driven mining plant, costing $15,000, is being put up. The shaft will be sunk from its present depth of 100 ft., to 300 ft. The Drummond interests of Montreal are negotiating for control of the Canadian-Kirkland, consisting of approximately 150 acres, on which a number of large and well-mineralized veins have been found. Should the deal go through a large amount of money will be expended.

Boston Creek.—The Miller Independence has been encouraged by the exceedingly favorable developments to proced with the construction of a new mill several times larger than the 40-ton plant now in operation. It has been decided to increase the capital from $500,000 to $700,000, also to provide for electric power and other improvements.

On the Campbell claims, in a direct line with what is considered to be the strike of the main vein of the Miller Independence, a strong vein has been opened containing free gold and tellurides.

Porquis Junction.—The Alexo Nickel Co. is steadily producing nickel ore, which is shipped to the Mond Nickel Co. plant at Coniston in the Sudbury district, for treatment. During the week ended November 22, the company shipped 137 tons. It is the only nickel producer in Canada outside the Sudbury district. The grade of the ore is high, and as mining is principally done from an open-cut, costs are low.

CRIPPLE CREEK, COLORADO

New Work at Some Small Mines.

Lessees of the El Paso Consolidated, operating on the C. K. & N. vein from the Roosevelt tunnel-level, are mining ore that averages between $30 and $40 per ton. The tunnel connects with El Paso No. 1 shaft at a depth of 1300 ft. The ore is being mined by raise 80 ft. above the tunnel. The shoot under development has been proved to the eighth level of the shaft, 1150 ft. from surface.

The Phoenix Mining Co., C. W. Howbert manager, is re-timbering the Conundrum incline where shaft-timbers were burned out recently. The timbers were destroyed to a depth of 200 ft. below the collar. The incline is 1500 ft. deep vertically. This is the deepest working on Gold hill.

Operations have been resumed on the Kalamazoo on Bull hill, by lessees of the Elmohar Gold Mining Co., who are unwatering the shaft. The property was originally owned by the Alert Gold Mining Co., W. H. Reynolds of New York president. The new company was formed on the expiration by limitation of the Alert charter.

Kissell & Phelps, lessees of block 8 of school section 16, have commenced to break and hoist ore from the main shaft on the eastern slope of Bull hill. This is the only property on school land in the district that has paid royalties to the State.

The output of the Vindicator mines for 1918, it is reported, closely approximates the present market price of shares. The annual report is now with printer. The company paid a 1-cent dividend—$15,000—on January 25.

ALASKA

Juneau.—Telegraphic advice states that Territorial officials issued a warning on January 27 to laborers to stay away from Alaska for at least two months. On account of the reduction of copper-mining operations several hundred experienced men are now out of employment, and more will be out by February 1. All the largest mine operators are taking returning soldiers back to former positions, and these, in view of the number of men let out, will fill all vacancies likely to exist for some time, it is said. Work at the canneries and placer fields of the interior will not be available before April 1.

ARIZONA

Ajo.—A school is to be erected here costing $129,000. Plans were prepared by Lescher & Kibbey of Phoenix, while the lowest bid, as above, was by Edwards & Wilder of Los Angeles.

Chloride.—Campbell & Scott are reported to have taken an option on the Argyle and Elkhart mines here.

Dragoon.—J. T. Long, manager of the Arizona United Copper Co., in the Johnson district, is authority for the statement that practically all shipments of copper from the district have ceased.

Globe.—One hundred and twenty-five employees of the Iron Cap Copper Co. recently received a $50 Liberty Bond each as a bonus for six months' steady work. The Iron Cap in 1918 produced 57,291 tons of smelting and 27,399 tons of milling ore, yielding 9,441,000 lb. of copper and 153,585 oz. of silver. The surplus at the end of the year was $334,170, a gain of $47,668. The Iron Cap shaft was sunk 111 ft. to 1126 ft. depth. An electric 3-ton skip hoist is to be installed. The Williams shaft is down 1200 ft., and is connected with the Iron Cap.

It is reported that J. D. Coplen has given a 30-day option to the Development Company of America to examine the Porphyry and Barney mines, which adjoin the Inspiration.

Oatman.—At a recent meeting of the Arizona Mossback Mining Co.'s shareholders it was decided to issue $400,000 in bonds, to be used in construction of a mill and for other improvements.

Wickenburg.—The Bullard mine has been bonded to B. C. Wilson, W. Douglas, and E. Bemdurant. It is claimed that the mine contains 300,000 tons of 4% copper and $5 gold ore. A leaching-plant may be erected at Aguila on the Parker cut-off, also 8 miles of railway.

CALIFORNIA

Idria.—New Idria Quicksilver company is laying off 40 men daily (to total 240) owing to the condition of the quicksilver market. The operating force will then amount to between 110 and 150.

Porterville.—Erection of additional machinery, costing $20,000, at the plant of the Porterville Magnesite Co. is practically finished.

The magnesite industry of this district is steadily returning to the condition of pre-war days. Daily shipments out of Porterville at present average two carloads. The building of the McKnight Fire Brick Co.'s plant in this city is expected to further stimulate the magnesite business. This company, controlled by Los Angeles people, is to erect a plant here for magnesite, chrome, silica, and clay brick. The corporation has secured, through the Porterville Chamber of Commerce, a five-acre tract in the south part of the city at the junction of the Santa Fe railroad and the Southern Pacific's branch line. The first of six units will have a capacity of 10,000 magnesite brick monthly.

Redding.—The 'Courier-Free Press', edited by W. H. Fink, has issued a Prosperity Edition. Among the interesting reviews we find illustrated descriptions of the Bully Hill and Mammoth copper mines, dredging on Clear creek, and the Noble Electric Steel Co.'s reduction works.

San Francisco.—The State Mining Bureau has issued the following circular:

The various industries and the people of California are almost entirely dependent upon petroleum for power and

fuel. They must be assured that all possible precautions conducive to a stable and long-continued supply are being taken. The question of whether or not their interests in this regard are to be protected is now definitely before the State Legislature. A bill introduced by Senator Thompson and Assemblyman Argabrite provides for serving the public interest and that of all the industries dependent upon oil, either through its consumption or production. The bill is based upon the result of the intimate study and investigation made by the State Mining Bureau in the oilfields during the past four years, and combines all the best features developed during the enforcement of the present law. It provides regulations requiring that all oil-wells, even those belonging to powerful but careless concerns, shall be drilled and maintained in such a manner that the oil deposits will not be ruined merely to obtain quick profits to a short-sighted operator. The interests of oil operators are safe-guarded through sure and speedy action of the Superior Courts by injunction proceedings against possible error or abuse of power by the State officers. No change in the present general policy of co-operating with and providing for the interests of oil operators is contemplated. Certain oil-producing concerns who have never recognized that the public is vitally interested in the preservation of the oilfields, and have always opposed adequate State supervision, have introduced other bills. Realizing that absolute repeal of a conservative measure would not meet with public approval, their ultimate object is concealed by provisions that would leave merely the skeleton of an impotent law on the statute books. In order to allow no possibility that even a skeleton law might be operative, they further propose to put the enforcement of the law into the hands of a few large oil producers.

COLORADO

Caribou.—In the old Caribou mine near Boulder, J. G. Clark, the owner, with some lessees, has opened a shoot assaying up to 3000 oz. of silver per ton. Two carloads of rich ore was shipped last week.

Leadville.—The Mt. Champion gold mine in Half Moon gulch, above Twin Lakes, will probably be re-opened at an early date. It was closed in May last.

IDAHO

Bonners Ferry.—The Cyanide Gold Mining Co. has been incorporated with a capital of 3,000,000 $1 shares to operate the Deer Creek Gold Mining Co.'s property 20 miles east of this place. A cyanide plant is to be built at once. J. B. Ellis, G. R. Caustin, G. and J. La Fountain, and F. Lafear are largely interested.

Kellogg.—On Pine creek the Nabob Consolidated is erecting a concentrating plant to cost $50,000.

The Coeur d'Alene Antimony Mining Co. recently re-elected M. E. Jolley as president. C. M. Powell of Kellogg is secretary. The mine has considerable ore-reserves, and the new concentrating plant awaits a favorable market.

Wallace.—The mining position in the Couer d'Alene district remains unchanged, according to the 'Miner'. The reduced price and lack of demand for lead has re-acted on production, causing curtailment generally; and, with the exception of two mines that have closed down, this reduction in output is being accomplished without reducing working forces to any great extent so far.

The Big Creek Mining Co.'s compressor building was destroyed by fire last week. Included were a motor, compressor, machine-drills, shop tools, etc., valued at $2500. This was covered by insurance. The plant is to be renewed.

MICHIGAN

Houghton.—Mass Consolidated has reduced miners' wages to $4, and trammers and unskilled workers to $3.75 per day, 75 cents less than the scale in force since October 1918. There are 318 men employed, against 450 in normal times. The men will work 6 days a week.

The Victoria company has also lowered wages 15%.

Copper Range will neither reduce wages nor production, as it is already at only 75% capacity.

Wolverine and Mohawk are producing at less than 70%.

Lake Copper Co. suspended work indefinitely on February 1. The output in 9 weeks was about 900,000 pounds.

Quincy has reduced operations by 25%.

The Franklin president frankly told employees last week that they must revert to the old wage-scale, with elimination of the 20% bonus, or else have the mine closed. The men have accepted the inevitable.

After January 20, Calumet & Hecla and subsidiaries are to work four days one week and five the next, alternately, equal to 75% capacity.

MISSOURI

Joplin.—Production of the Tri-State region last week was as under:

State	Blende, tons	Calamine, tons	Lead, tons	Value
Kansas	1,009	..	126	$51,956
Missouri	1,077	30	121	47,235
Oklahoma	6,801	..	1,100	351,642
Average price	$42	$30	$60	......

The Mining Edition of the 'Joplin Globe' for January 26 contains a section of especial interest on mining and milling methods.

NEW MEXICO

Socorro.—The New Mexico State School of Mines has issued Bulletin No. 2, 'Manganese in New Mexico,' by E. H. Wells. This is a well-arranged book of 85 pages, with map. In the 'Press' of November 23, 1918, we gave an abstract of this report, as published by the U. S. Geological Survey.

TEXAS

Houston.—The recent incorporation, with headquarters here, of the Universal Sulphur Products Co., with a paid-up capital of $12,000,000, marks the addition of large financial interests to the sulphur mining and manufacturing industry of this State. W. C. Hardcastle of Houston, representing New York and Boston men, holds most of the capital of the company. Others interested are Henry Oliver of Pittsburgh and E. F. Simms, H. T. Staiti, John Hamman, F. P. Phair, C. H. Lane, and S. A. Millican, all of Houston. The company owns a 7000-acre tract at Damon Mound, near the mouth of the Brazos river, which is largely underlaid by a sulphur bed, as proved by drillings. Prospecting the land for sulphur has been in progress for some time, and it is reported that a great tonnage already has been found. This sulphur is in the same section of the Gulf Coast region as the big producing property of the Freeport Sulphur Co. It is announced that the Universal company will spend a large sum in plant for extracting the sulphur from the ground, refining it, and manufacturing sulphuric acid.

Orla.—The West Texas Sulphur Co. of Philadelphia has placed in operation three furnaces of its new refining plant near here. These units have a total capacity of five tons of sulphur per day. It is planned to enlarge greatly the capacity of the plant.

Valentine.—Extensive exploration is being made of nitrate deposits south of here near the Rio Grande. They are owned by the Capote Nitrate Co. of San Antonio, of which Guy C. Simpson is president. The work is under direction of Carl Halter, formerly of Chihuahua.

UTAH

Eureka.—Chief Consolidated during 1918 yielded 2,354,797 oz. of silver, 4099 oz. of gold, and 8,019,454 lb. of lead, against 1,534,907 oz., 9175 oz., and 10,780,540 lb., respectively, also 600,360 lb. of zinc, in 1917. Ore shipments totaled 66,019 tons. Walter Fitch is manager.

Morrissey.—The Utah Sulphur Corporation has two retorts yielding 40 tons of refined sulphur daily. Another shift being added is expected to double the output. When the three new retorts are finished, each of the five will treat 105 tons of ore per day. On this property is a large dump of old tailing, said to carry 42% sulphur. According to the general manager, M. P. Morrissey, if this material averages 31% sulphur, it will be treated in a machine of his own design.

WASHINGTON

Spokane.—Provision for the regulation of mining companies, while avoiding the 'vicious' features of the blue sky laws, is the object of a plan now being worked out by the Northwest Mining Association, which discussed the problem at a recent session here.

OREGON

Homestead.—Of the $2,100,000 of gold and other metals produced in this State during 1918, the largest proportion came, as usual, from Baker county, which produces annually 90% of the gold mined. One of the properties is the Iron Dike, in the Homestead district, at the terminus of a branch line from Huntington. This mine is controlled by Goodrich Rubber Co. interests, under the name of the Iron Dyke Copper Co. The mine is opened by shaft and tunnels. The 150-ton mill includes a ball-mill, tables, and flotation plant. Concentrates assay around 15% copper, 8 oz. silver, and $8 gold per ton. Up to 100 men are employed in charge of E. F. Gilligan. The company pays considerable attention to the social life of its employees.

MILL OF THE IRON DYKE COPPER CO. AT HOMESTEAD, BAKER COUNTY, OREGON

CANADA

British Columbia

Kaslo.—The Gibson Mining Co. is laying a spiral-riveted pipe 2200 ft. long to carry water under a head of 825 ft. This will drive a generator, compressor, etc. A mill may be erected to concentrate the lead-silver and zinc ores. A. C. Brintnall is in charge of the new plant being erected.

Three Forks.—The Rambler-Cariboo company pays a dividend of 1 cent per share on February 15. This is equal to $17,500, and makes $560,000 to date. The surplus is $55,000. A large snowslide recently covered the flume carrying water to the mill, resulting in a short shut-down. W. A. Cameron is manager of this lead-zinc mine in the Slocan district.

Trail.—The Mine Owners Association of the Province will not recognize the Committee that has been authorized by the Dominion government to investigate the rates charged for ore treatment by the Consolidated Mining & Smelting Co. at Trail, according to a statement issued by C. F. Caldwell, president of the association.

Manitoba

The Commissioner for northern Manitoba, R. C. Wallace, in a review of mining in the Province during 1918, published in 'The Daily Nugget', says that steady progress was made, and that with construction of a railway and a smelter a large copper industry is assured. At the Flin-Flon, diamond-drilling continued until July, when preliminary work in mapping-out the orebody was finished. A large tonnage is available of $10 ore, remarkably uniform in value. The Mandy mine sent 6300 tons to Trail, B. C. Duluth people were drilling at the Chica claims near the mouth of the Pine-root river. On the north-east of Lake Athapapuskow is some promising copper ore. The Rex mine at Wekusko lake yielded gold worth $21,550 from May to October. Operating conditions are not favorable so the result is good. The mill includes a 30-ton Lane mill, two amalgamating plates, two Deister-Overstrom tables, a 60-hp. engine, two 60-hp. boilers, and a 320-cu. ft. air-compressor. The Pas Consolidated Mines acquired the Dauphin-Elizabeth mine.

Ontario

Cobalt.—The Adanac company is to send 50 or more tons of ore to the Temiskaming mill. In the new vein being opened there is 6 to 8 in. of ore, much of it carrying from 2000 to 4000 oz. of silver per ton. The formation is the Keewatin.

MEXICO

The United States Ambassador to Mexico, Henry P. Fletcher, while at St. Louis on January 29 on his way to Washington, said conditions in Mexico are rapidly improving, avenues of commerce are opening, and when restrictions against trading are removed the United States can resume business relations with Mexico on a larger scale than ever before. The principal barrier, he said, is the condition of Mexican railroads, and until equipment is supplied from America it will be difficult to carry on business. He termed as false reports that large numbers of Germans crossed the border into Mexico when the United States declared war.

Formal announcement of the organization of the National Association for the Protection of American Rights in Mexico with a membership representing 41 concerns in the oil, mining, smelting, agricultural, land, cattle, rubber, banking, and other fields in that country, was made at New York on January 29, by Frank J. Silsbee of Los Angeles, its secretary. Declaring that "gross injustices have been committed in Mexico to American citizens and American property rights," the Association plans to make "a thorough study of the Mexican situation from historical, legal, and economic standpoints," and to furnish from time to time to the United States and Mexican governments "accurate information regarding foreign industries and enterprises, decrees and other developments affecting American rights, with a view to removing causes of friction." Among the concerns represented in the new association are the Mexican Petroleum Co., Standard Oil Co., the Texas Company, Panuco Boston Oil Co., Greene-Cananea Copper Co., Phelps Dodge Corporation, Guaranty Trust Co., National City Bank, J. P. Morgan & Co.,

National Bank of Commerce, Chase National Bank, Bankers' Trust Company of New York, the Yaqui Delta Land & Water Co., the California-Mexican Land & Cattle Co., and the Inter-Continental Rubber Company.

Information reaching Washington states that Carranza had reorganized the Mexican army to a considerable extent, obtained sufficient arms and equipment, and had started a new campaign against the rebels and bandits operating in different parts of the republic. Several bands of rebels surrendered unconditionally with their commanders, the reports said, and other groups dispersed, the men promising to return home, while the leaders either fled or were captured. The States of Jalisco and Guerrero have been cleared of rebels, according to these advices, together with the extermination of the band under Pedro Zamona, with headquarters near Autlan. Zamona was wounded and later captured.

General Barcenas, one of Zapata's commanders, was reported to have surrendered unconditionally with his force to the Government army in the State of Guerrero, this being the last armed band in the State opposing the Government. The rebels also have been suppressed in the State of Morelos, it was stated, while the forces in Pueblo and Tlaxcala laid down their arms. General Aguilar has been placed in command of the reorganized Government force sent against Diaz. The advices reported that five generals, with other officers of lesser rank, had been ordered to Chihuahua for a new campaign against Villa.

In an address before the Investment Bankers' Association of America at Atlantic City on December 10, George E. Roberts of the National City Bank of New York said: "If conditions in Mexico were as favorable to the employment of capital there as on this side of the line, there would be a great flow of capital into Mexico and quick leveling of living conditions there to what they are in this country. And, finally, the development of Mexico and of her now idle resources would react beneficially upon this country."

Chihuahua

Chihuahua.—The Mines Company of America is to be reorganized by the sale of its assets to the Dolores Esperanza Corporation, which will have 864,802 shares, as in the old company. Upon payment of $2 and the deposit of one share of existing stock, the Mines company's shareholders may subscribe for one share of the new corporation. Hayden, Stone & Co. are behind the arrangement. Ore-reserves in the various mines are valued at over $6,000,000, based on silver at $1 per ounce.

Hidalgo

Pachuca.—Santa Gertrudis reports for the quarter ended September 30, 1918, that the working profit was £74,914 ($360,000). The mill treated 70,272 tons of ore, yielding silver and gold worth £204,135 ($979,000). The crushing rate was 70% of capacity. By the addition of two Merrill filter-presses the rate has been increased to 90%. The ore is now of a more colloidal nature, so the settling area is being increased by rearrangement of tanks and addition of tanks from the Guadalupe mill. An 8-ft. by 48-in. Hardinge ball-mill has been ordered. Aluminum-dust has replaced zinc-dust permanently. Development amounted to 1699 ft., of which 429 ft. was in pay-ore. In El Bordo mine there was 896 ft. of work accomplished, mostly short cross-cuts to determine widths of veins. These were as under:

Level	Width, ft.	Silver, oz.	Gold, dwt.
415	23.2	10.1	0.81
430	9.9	10.4	0.92
450	21.3	10.3	1.42
465	36.2	49.9	1.86
490	5.5	10.6	1.08
490	8.7	24.5	2.40
500	5.1	27.0	3.33
525	5.5	43.0	4.13
525	7.8	43.2	4.33

In another issue an editorial will discuss Santa Gertrudis.

PERSONAL

Note. The Editor invites members of the profession to send particulars of their work and appointments. The information is interesting to our readers.

J. Morgan Clements is at Peking.

David T. Day is at the Palace hotel.

F. W. Bradley has returned from Idaho.

D. M. Riordan was in Shasta county last week.

Percy A. Robbins is living at the Claremont hotel, Berkeley.

E. H. Clausen, recently Captain of Engineers, has returned to Berkeley, California.

D'Arcy Weatherbe has been in China recently and is expected in San Francisco next week.

J. S. Bradford, manager for the Chiksan Gold Mining Co. in Korea, has returned to the mine.

Allen H. Rogers and **Sydney H. Ball** are examining the Ray Hercules copper mine in Arizona.

William J. Millard has received an honorable discharge from the Army and is now at Tulsa, Oklahoma.

F. C. French, who, as Major of the 79th Engineers, has been honorably discharged, is now at Salt Lake City.

E. P. Mathewson, **E. L. Doheny**, and **John C. Howard** are the new directors of the American Mining Congress.

C. W. Purington has opened an office at Vladivostok, as eastern director of the Far Eastern Development Co., Ltd.

Alex. M. Boyle and **Weldon B. Morris** have formed a partnership, as consulting engineers, with headquarters at Reno, Nevada.

Thomas F. **Cole** has resigned as president of the North Butte Mining Co., and is succeeded by **Robert Linton**, the first vice-president.

E. E. Barker has been transferred to the Morococha mines of the Cerro de Pasco Copper Corporation as superintendent of those properties.

The Colorado Scientific Society held its annual dinner on January 24 at the University Club, Denver. The officers for 1919 are: **Lewis B. Skinner**, president; **L. G. Carpenter**, first vice-president; **John B. Ekeley**, second vice-president; **Charles W. Henderson**, treasurer; and **Harry Wolf**, secretary. These, with **Marmaduke B. Hall** and **George O. Argall**, comprise the excutive committee.

The Montana Section of the A. I. M. E. held its sixth annual meeting at the Silver Bow Club at Butte, on February 7. At the technical session there were read two papers: 'The Metallurgy of Aluminum and Magnesium,' by **H. B. Pulsifer**, professor of metallurgy in the Montana State School of Mines; and 'The Manufacture of High Explosives and Their Use in Metal Mining,' by J. C. Horgan, of the Du Pont Powder Co. In the discussion on the relation of the engineering profession to public welfare, led by **C. D. Demond**, the Engineering Council and human engineering and co-operation were the principal topics.

Obituary

John T. Milliken, chemist, banker, railroad director, and mining and oil operator, died at his home at St. Louis on January 31, from pneumonia, at the age of 66 years. He was prominently connected with Cripple Creek mines, also in developing an old property near the Homestake in South Dakota.

THE METAL MARKET

METAL PRICES

San Francisco, February 4

Aluminum-dust, large and small lots, cents per lb.	65—70
Antimony, cents per pound	8.00
Copper, electrolytic, cents per pound, in carload lots	22.00
Lead, pig, cents per pound	5.50— 6.50
Platinum, per ounce	$108
Quicksilver, per flask of 75 lb.	$95
Spelter, cents per pound	9.00
Zinc-dust, cents per pound	16.00

EASTERN METAL MARKET

(By wire from New York)

February 4.—Copper is quiet. Lead is inactive and weak. Spelter is dull and lower.

SILVER

Below are given official (not Government) quotations, in cents per ounce, of silver 999 fine. In order to make prompt settlements with smelters and brokers, producers allow a discount from the maximum fixed price of $1.01½, hence the lower price. The Government has not fixed the general market price at $1, but will pay this price (as from April 23, 1918) for all silver purchased by it. The equivalent of dollar silver (1000 fine) in British currency is 46.65 pence per ounce (925 fine), calculated at the current rate of exchange. On August 15, 1918, the Treasury announced that the maximum price was fixed at $1.01½ per ounce. The British government fixed its maximum at 49½ pence, on September 2, but on November 12 this was changed to 48¾ pence, and on December 13 to 48 7/16 pence.

Date		New York	London
Jan.	29	101.12	48.44
"	30	101.12	48.44
"	31	101.12	48.44
Feb.	1	101.12	48.44
"	2 Sunday		
"	3	101.12	48.44
"	4	101.12	48.44

Average week ending		
Dec.	24	101.12
"	31	101.12
Jan.	7	101.12
"	14	101.12
"	21	101.12
"	28	101.12
Feb.	4	101.12

Monthly averages

	1917	1918	1919		1917	1918	1919
Jan.	75.14	88.72	101.12	July	78.92	99.62	....
Feb.	77.54	85.79	....	Aug.	85.40	100.31	....
Mch.	74.13	88.11	....	Sept.	100.73	101.12	....
Apr.	72.51	95.35	....	Oct.	87.38	101.12	....
May	74.61	99.50	....	Nov.	85.97	101.12	....
June	76.44	99.50	....	Dec.	85.97	101.12	....

COPPER

Prices of electrolytic in New York, in cents per pound.

Date		
Jan.	29	19.50
"	30	19.50
"	31	19.25
Feb.	1	19.25
"	2 Sunday	
"	3	19.00
"	4	18.75

Average week ending		
Dec.	24	26.00
"	31	26.00
Jan.	7	21.80
"	14	20.75
"	21	20.50
"	28	19.87
Feb.	4	19.21

Monthly averages

	1917	1918	1919		1917	1918	1919
Jan.	29.53	23.50	20.43	July	29.67	26.00	....
Feb.	34.57	23.50	....	Aug.	27.42	26.00	....
Mch.	36.00	23.50	....	Sept.	25.11	26.00	....
Apr.	33.16	23.50	....	Oct.	23.50	26.00	....
May	31.60	23.50	....	Nov.	23.50	26.00	....
June	32.57	23.50	....	Dec.	23.50	26.00	....

Copper miners' wages in Arizona are to be reduced to the old scale, or based on 20-cent metal. This will also apply to Montana and Utah. At the conference at Washington, the Secretary of Labor met 33 union delegates from the various copper centres.

The American Brass Co., the largest consumer of copper in America, made profits totaling $55,247,000 during the past six years. Dividends absorbed $17,325,000 of this. Depreciation and taxes accounted for a large sum, also $20,824,000 for improvements. The surplus stands at $21,447,000.

The U. S. Shipping Board has fixed 1 cent per pound as the freight-rate on copper from the United States to Great Britain. This is a decrease from the recent rates of 3 and 4¾ cents. Normal rates are 0.17 cents.

ZINC

Zinc is quoted as spelter, standard Western brands, New York delivery.

Date		
Jan.	29	7.00
"	30	6.90
"	31	6.85
Feb.	1	6.80
"	2 Sunday	
"	3	6.75
"	4	6.70

Average week ending		
Dec.	24	8.45
"	31	8.13
Jan.	7	7.93
"	14	7.72
"	21	7.52
"	28	7.20
Feb.	4	6.83

Monthly averages

	1917	1918	1919		1917	1918	1919
Jan.	9.75	7.87	7.44	July	8.98	8.72	....
Feb.	10.45	7.97	....	Aug.	8.58	8.87	....
Mch.	10.78	7.97	....	Sept.	8.33	9.58	....
Apr.	10.20	7.04	....	Oct.	8.32	9.11	....
May	9.41	7.29	....	Nov.	7.76	8.75	....
June	9.63	7.92	....	Dec.	7.84	8.49	....

Zinc-blende was in good demand at Joplin, Missouri, last week, buying ranging from $40 to $42 per ton, basis 60% metal.

LEAD

Lead is quoted in cents per pound, New York delivery.

Date		
Jan.	29	5.50
"	30	5.40
"	31	5.30
Feb.	1	5.25
"	2 Sunday	
"	3	5.25
"	4	5.25

Average week ending		
Dec.	24	6.46
"	31	6.10
Jan.	7	5.80
"	14	5.75
"	21	5.62
"	28	5.50
Feb.	4	5.32

Monthly averages

	1917	1918	1919		1917	1918	1919
Jan.	7.64	6.85	5.60	July	10.93	8.03	....
Feb.	9.10	7.07	....	Aug.	10.75	8.05	....
Mch.	10.07	7.26	....	Sept.	9.07	8.05	....
Apr.	9.38	6.99	....	Oct.	6.97	8.05	....
May	10.29	6.88	....	Nov.	6.38	8.05	....
June	11.74	7.58	....	Dec.	6.49	6.90	....

The A. S. & R. Co. reduced its price on lead last week from 5½ to 5¼ cents.

The president of the National Lead Co., E. J. Cornish, stated in Philadelphia recently that large quantities of lead were held by manufacturers having contracts with the Government. This surplus spot lead is the bear influence on the market. In a month, prices declined from 8 to 5½ cents per pound. The price of white lead must also drop accordingly.

Important lead-producing interests of the Coeur d'Alene region, Idaho, held a meeting at Spokane last week. Particulars are not available, but the matters discussed are said to have included the wage question and curtailment of production to meet market depression.

QUICKSILVER

The primary market for quicksilver is San Francisco, California being the largest producer. The price is fixed in the open market, according to quantity. Prices, in dollars per flask of 75 pounds:

Date					
Jan.	7	110.00	Jan.	21	100.00
"	14	105.00	"	28	100.00
			Feb.	4	95.00

Monthly averages

	1917	1918	1919		1917	1918	1919
Jan.	81.00	128.06	103.75	July	102.00	120.00	....
Feb.	126.25	118.00	....	Aug.	115.00	120.00	....
Mch.	113.75	112.00	....	Sept.	112.00	120.00	....
Apr.	114.50	115.00	....	Oct.	102.00	120.00	....
May	104.00	110.00	....	Nov.	102.50	120.00	....
June	85.50	112.00	....	Dec.	117.42	115.00	....

TIN

Prices in New York, in cents per pound. The monthly averages in 1918 are nominal. On December 3 the War Industries Board fixed the price to consumers and jobbers at 72½c. f.o.b. Chicago and Eastern points, and 71¼c. on the Pacific Coast. This will continue until the U. S. Steel Products Co.'s stock is consumed.

Monthly averages

	1917	1918	1919		1917	1918	1919
Jan.	44.10	85.13	71.50	July	62.60	93.00	....
Feb.	51.47	85.00	....	Aug.	62.53	91.33	....
Mch.	54.27	85.00	....	Sept.	61.54	80.40	....
Apr.	55.63	88.53	....	Oct.	62.24	78.82	....
May	63.21	100.01	....	Nov.	74.18	73.67	....
June	61.93	91.00	....	Dec.	85.90	71.52	....

ORES (New York)

Manganese Alloys: The market is devoid of any transactions and quotations are uncertain. As low as $185 and $200 is heard as asked for 80% ferro. There is an inquiry for several hundred tons of spiegel, which it is certain can be bought for not more than $60 per ton, delivered.

'Production of Ferro-Manganese in Blast-Furnaces' is the title of the U. S. Bureau of Mines War Minerals Investigation Series No. 5, by P. H. Royster. It consists of 31 pages, and tells how such furnaces are operated in making the alloy.

Molybdenum: A fair inquiry is reported, but no business has resulted. Quotations are nominal at 75c. to $1 per lb. of MoS_2 in 90% concentrates.

Tungsten: Some dealers report more inquiry, but as a whole the market is unchanged. Quotations are impossible (although $17 to $18 has been mentioned) in the face of an absence of testing prices. The output of tungsten ores in the United States in 1918 was about 5065 tons of 60% concentrates, according to the U. S. Geological Survey.

Eastern Metal Market

New York, January 29.

All the metal markets are waiting, and buying is only of a spasmodic character of small proportions.

Antimony is lifeless and unchanged.

Copper has sold as low as 20c. and perhaps 19c., but in small quantities.

Lead continues to fall with limited buying.

The tin market is absolutely dead and disorganized.

Zinc is weak, and demand is only to meet absolute needs.

ANTIMONY

The market is unchanged and stagnant. Wholesale lots for prompt and early delivery can be purchased at 7.50c., New York, duty paid.

COPPER

The entire market is a waiting one, and is marking time like nearly every branch of industry. Demand is of small proportions. Consumers are buying only what they absolutely need, and in view of the slackened pace of industry in general these needs are small. Copper has been sold in this limited scope as low as 20c. per lb., which we quote as the market. It is stated that it can be bought as low as 19c. for early delivery, but no sales under 20c. have been confirmed. As long as stocks of both crude and refined copper remain as large as they are, buying interest will continue small. There is also to be considered the large quantities of scrap copper which must be disposed of, some of it of good quality. Copper exports in December were about 20,000 tons. It is possible that complete Government reports may show the 1918 exports to be as large as the record outgo for 1917.

IRON AND STEEL

There have been no developments in the week, and the market is marking time. Domestic business is slow and export business is not developing promptly. Ship freights in competition with Great Britain are a handicap. An American mill has sold tin-plates to Japan in open competition. The British fixed price is $43 per ton higher than the Pittsburgh quotation, and a lower freight differential was all that was necessary to turn the order to the United States.

LEAD

There is little inquiry and the market is slow; it might be characterized as spotty. Demand is of such small proportions that it is not able to sustain the market and quotations have as a consequence fallen to 5.30c., New York, or 5c., St. Louis. There are more sellers than buyers and little business has been done. It is probable that this market is readjusting itself faster than any other, and that rock-bottom prices will be reached soon, if they have not already. The American Smelting & Refining Co. reduced its price to 5.50c., New York, last week, Tuesday, the 21st, and it still remains at this level.

TIN

Extreme dullness continues to pervade this market. There is absolutely no demand and conditions in general are chaotic. Consumers are still being importuned to absorb the large quantity of tin allocated to the United States Steel Products Co. for which they are expected to pay 72.50c. per lb., but they are generally assuming the attitude that they do not want to take any more of this metal than possible when they can buy for less. They realize that American tin can be bought in fair quantities at under 69c. and that, were imports permitted and the market free of control, the metal could be bought for shipment from the Far East at nearly 20c. per lb. less than the controlled price. Efforts to induce the babbitt and solder manufacturers to absorb their share of the allocated tin are understood to have failed last week. There are also rumors that the operations and sales of the American tin smelters are to be restricted. Tin arrivals to date in January have been 2375 tons, all through Pacific ports.

ZINC

The zinc market continues to drag and prices to fall. Demand is of the hand-to-mouth character, consumers buying only what they must and for early delivery at that. None are purchasing into the future. Prime Western for early delivery is quoted at 6.75c., St. Louis, or 7.10c., New York, with March and April positions 10 to 15 points under this level. It is claimed by some that 6.75c., St. Louis, is under the present cost of production.

LEAD NOTES

A year or more may elapse before mining and other conditions return to a pre-war level, or some level above it, is the belief of F. W. Bradley, president of the Bunker Hill & Sullivan Mining & Concentrating Co., at Kellogg, Idaho, recently interviewed at Spokane, Washington, by the 'Spokesman-Review'. The leveling may be gradual, as conditions are ironed out, but an improvement is expected in the meantime. Too much of a shock would be suffered in an abrupt flattening to a pre-war level, although it would not be unwelcome to the gold miner.

He said that "the lead market is unstable and inactive, and but for the silver in its ore the Bunker Hill & Sullivan would be in bad shape. If a property operated under these conditions was owned by an individual or two it would be a policy of business to shut it down and wait for better conditions, but the condition is different with a great many stockholders and a community that is dependent upon its operations. At Kellogg we have a community that has stood by us and did not run off to the shipyards, so it is no more than fair that we should stand by it now. We are up against a condition. The question of wages is not involved in the situation, because the cost of living is as much above the pre-war condition as the wages, so far as the married man is concerned. Of course the single man is far ahead on the increase. There has been no profiteering by the local merchants. The increase has not come from them. They are paying a higher price for goods than they have raised the price to the consumer. If there is any profiteering at all on foods it is behind the wholesalers and jobbers. Railroad rates have eaten deeply into the cost of lead. The price of lead today is below the average of the last 11 years. Railroad rates are up, and it looks as if they would have to be put up again. Railroad rates have been material in raising costs, and it doesn't seem as if there was to be any relief from that source. The shipper has already stood for a 25% increase and other burdens, including sidings. This means that for several years some things will be higher than before the War. We will re-employ all of our soldiers, of whom 238 are on the honor-roll at Kellogg. Room will be made for them by letting go those who proved inefficient. The lead we produced in December, when the market failed, is stored, but our current production is moving to consumers, including automobile and tire manufacturers, locomotive works, and paint manufacturers. All consumers are taking some. We are completing and co-ordinating the different parts of the smelter so that it will have a capacity of 200 tons of lead by the middle of this year. More depth is being attained in the mine. This has necessitated the establishment of additional hoisting, pumping, and ventilating machinery, by which our operation cost is increased."

FOREIGN loans in the United States on January 1 are given, by the Guaranty Trust Company of New York, as $9,483,327,330, and even this does not include subscriptions to foreign internal loans, with the exception of the French fives of 1931 and the Russian five and a halfs of 1926.

SOME of our friends, led by that indefatigable propagandist for simplefyde spellin, Mr. W. H. Shockley, are bombarding the Secretary of the Institute with requests to introduce sundry unpleasant and unnecessary changes in the style of spelling used in the bulletins and transactions, despite the fact that the Committee on Papers and Publications has declined to make them. We hope that the members of the Institute will be slow to support these efforts to disfigure our language in the manner of the 'Bad Boy's Diary' and that they will leave such matters to the Committee on Publications, which is thoroughly representative and quite competent to act in the best interests of our official language.

SEVERAL interesting mining transactions concluded recently appear to indicate a revival of initiative. For example, the old Idaho-Maryland mines have been consolidated with the Union Hill group in the name of the Gold Point Consolidated Mines by Mr. Bulkeley Wells and his associates, who include such well-known men as Messrs. Errol MacBoyle, Rufus Thayer, F. W. McNear, John McCrossen, Roy H. Elliott, and Edwin Letts Oliver. The venture should prove a good one, for it is in the hands of capable men and is based upon a promising portion of one of the best gold-mining districts in the West. Another promising consolidation has been completed in the Rochester district of Nevada, where the five important properties—the Rochester Mines, Rochester Combined Mines, Nenzel Crown Point, Elda Fina, and Rochester Merger—have been united in order to terminate litigation both pending and threatened. The papers were signed at Reno on February 3 by the principals, Messrs. L. A. Friedman, H. G. Humphrey, and Joseph Nenzel. Two of the mines in the consolidation—the two first mentioned—own well equipped mills, capable of treating a total of 500 tons per day. From Goldfield comes the news that the old—in our Western sense—Goldfield Consolidated Mines, credited with a production of $70,000,000 since 1905, has passed into the hands of a new corporation to be known as the Goldfield Mining Company, organized by Mr. H. G. MacMahon, of Goldfield, who is associated with a group of experienced Californian and Nevadan operators. Some of the property is taken over by purchase and the remainder is leased for a period of five years. It is the intention of the new controllers to establish a new system of leases, enabling large areas of the property to be re-exploited and re-developed. Many applications for leases indicate a general renewal of activity.

AMERICAN rights in Mexico are to be amply safeguarded by the Mexican government, says our Ambassador to Carranza's court. This is interesting, as also is the further declaration by Mr. Henry P. Fletcher that the feeling toward this country has become more friendly since Von Eckhardt, the German minister, was recalled. Evidently the latter was a person of large 'influenza' in Mexico. We are further informed that President Carranza "has accomplished a great work in preparing for development and reconstruction, and has made such headway that the various bandit leaders are now without real influence." Another press dispatch asserts that President Carranza intends to call a special session for the purpose, among others, of legislation devised to protect American oil-holdings in Mexico, and it is hoped that "ultimately" a law will be passed recognizing title to oil-lands acquired by American citizens in good faith in accordance with the laws of the country, this being done without trespassing upon "the sovereign rights of Mexico in respect of taxation and regulation of property." Now comes the milk in the cocoanut, the nigger in the woodpile, and the fly in the amber. Señor Carranza has no intention of appealing to the Peace Conference at Versailles; he is opposed to "any foreign meddling in the adjustment of Mexico's internal affairs." He sees the shadow of a portentous event. Finally, it is stated that the Mexican government is "contemplating steps looking to a refunding of the public debt and might in the near future send a representative to the United States to study the possibility of making financial adjustments." In short, Don Venus is about to 'touch' Uncle Sam, and prepares for that delicate operation by being good. So much the better; we are just as anxious as Señor Carranza to see the Mexican house put in order and the ground cleared for peaceful industry, including mining.

A Victory of Americanization at Seattle.

Bolshevism reached out a feeler to try the firmness of that true democracy which is the United States. It chose a city rich, flourishing, notable as a great port, a stopping place on one of the principal highways of international trade, and yet detached from the crowded centres of American life. The leaders hoped that measures of suppression at such a place would be less vigorous, because there would be a less insistent call from neighboring communities to extinguish the threatening flame of anarchy. The point was well chosen; Seattle afforded strategic advantages for an experiment in substituting the principle of the soviet for the administration of justice by a representative government. Had insubordination desolated Seattle, had civil strife developed there into a human horror, the evil of Bolshevism might have spread in the United States, as the friends of Trotsky, Lenine, Hindenburg, and Bernstorff desired. The attempt has failed and Americanism has stood the test. Seattle deserves honor of the country. Her people did not lose their heads; they did not trifle with a grave danger; they and their Mayor, Mr. Ole Hanson, and the Citizens' Committee, headed by Mr. A. J. Rhodes, cowed the bullies by simple manhood, resorting to no foolish display of futile bulldozing by the police, nor seeking to come to a compromise with the instigators of disorder. They branded the 'general strike' as "revolution" and issued a statement that, unless the strikers should yield by a certain date and hour, they would face the power of the United States Army. Mr. Hanson knew how to employ the forceful persuasion of an ultimatum so that the would-be Bolshevists recognized that he had in truth given them his last word. Democracy, sanity, the government of the people, by the people and for the people, has been vindicated at Seattle. Through this the winning of world-peace has been made still more sure.

Already we see how the disturbing I. W. W. organization has weakened at Butte. An outbreak was ripe to follow any symptom of success by the Bolshevists at Seattle, and the flames might then have run like fire in dry grass. No one denies that many workers in America have some cause for complaint. So have they in England. The collapse of stimulated and special industry, without pre-arranged plans for financial re-adjustment, necessarily has reduced production, and that has thrown numbers of men out of employment. Business men are doing all they can to rehabilitate industry and lessen the burdens of the people. The copper companies have undertaken to do a gracious thing in this direction that must win wide approval. Despite the fact that copper is a drug on the market, that no important European demand has appeared, that nearly the whole of the present output must go into storage, the operation of the mines is being continued on as slightly reduced a basis as possible, and with wages cut only in accordance with the sliding scale upon which they had been advanced during the period of high prices. This is a service to humanity, and it is to be hoped that the workers will appreciate the financial sacrifice entailed by such action. It means that the millions paid as wages, which stand between the miner and destitution in the hard months of winter, are largely borrowed millions on which the producers are paying interest at six per cent, while the copper itself that has been produced is costing money for storage each day that it lies unsold. It cannot be said that this yields a wholly compensating benefit to the corporations. Every intelligent man knows that it is uneconomical to close a mine and to suffer an organization to become disintegrated, but there is a limit to this, for the workers themselves realize that the value of an organization lies in the efficient nucleus. Operations may be trimmed very close to that nucleus before serious damage is involved either for the mine, the smelting plant, or the refinery. The copper companies have not cut their forces anywhere near to the narrow limit of that skilled and capable minimum. They are serving the people in a way that deserves the loyal recognition they are receiving from sensible workingmen who are declining to follow the red agitators whose maniac voice would lead into the valley of disaster, hideous with murder and famine. It must not be overlooked that the victory of good sense at Seattle was the fruit of conservative thought among the workers themselves. Hesitant in the face of the possible subversion of law and order, fearing to be exposed to the vengeance of a momentarily dominant mob, which brings swifter violence upon the non-conformist laboring man than upon his employer, this large body of rational men only needed a strong leader. The heart of the people is always sound; the excesses of the multitude grow out of infection from masses wrongly led. The plain people, rightly generalled, stand on the side of law and order. This has been proved again at Seattle.

The Bolshevists, alien in spirit and mind, may as well give up their hope of corrupting the sound principles of democracy in America. This country is not yet ready to abandon its high ideals of government or the high standard of living that gives opportunity to save against the stringencies of old age and to push forward the children of each generation to larger achievement. America is not disposed to plunge into the abyss with disordered Russia, nor to clamor against the bewildering financial difficulties of reconstruction as an injustice to be resisted by destroying industry. Troubled employers of labor, trying to find their way back to normal business, need the trusting co-operation of labor, just as labor needs the guidance of the managers of industry, in order that all concerned may be saved from hardship and suffering. Mr. Samuel Gompers has said wisely that all must pull together, and that employers should organize to meet organized labor, so as to eliminate cut-throat competition and to stabilize industry. After the failure of the demons of destruction in their attempt at Seattle, we may look forward confidently to constructive efforts between workers and employers. There must now be an end to disorder, and a turning more determinedly than ever to that hearty co-operation of all Americans which is the glory of our democracy. In that spirit we won the War, and in the same spirit will we establish peace.

A Post-Mortem

Prolongation of the life of a mining enterprise by purchase of new property has become an acceptable method of company finance. When, in 1910, the Camp Bird mine, in Colorado, showed signs of approaching exhaustion, the English company, which had acquired it ten years earlier from the late Thomas F. Walsh, bought the control of the Santa Gertrudis mine, at Pachuca, in Mexico. When the Santa Gertrudis, in turn, began to exhibit loss of vitality, the company decided to acquire rights to the El Bordo group, also in the Pachuca district. This transaction was closed recently. It is estimated that the El Bordo has an assured reserve of 253,000 tons of ore, from which a profit of $2,142,000 is anticipated. The report was made by Mr. Hugh Rose, the manager of the Santa Gertrudis. In this case, we believe, the company did not have to pay a large commission to its own engineers, as it did in the Santa Gertrudis deal, from which Mr. J. Hays Hammond, who was then consulting engineer to the Camp Bird company, drew a commission of $600,000—cut down from an original demand for $1,000,000. Indeed the directors themselves, except Mr. W. F. Fisher, all drew profits from underwriting and trading of various kinds. It is a marvel that the British public took these proceedings so tamely after the chairman, Mr. Arthur M. Grenfell, had gone bankrupt and had involved the Camp Bird and other companies in difficulties. That was in the early part of 1914. It is interesting now to make a post-mortem inquiry into the Santa Gertrudis business, if it be not brutal to conduct an autopsy upon an enterprise that is still alive. According to the latest report of the subsidiary company operating the Santa Gertrudis, the ore in reserve amounts to 880,433 tons, from which a profit of $3,750,000 is expected. The mine has yielded dividends aggregating £731,250 on a capital of £1,500,000, of which the Camp Bird company owns 81%. If we place 81% of the estimated remaining profit to the credit of that company and add 81% to the dividends distributed, we get the sum of just about $6,000,000 as the realizable money to be obtained by the Camp Bird company on the operation. On the other side, the Camp Bird company paid £922,131, or $4,481,550, for the 81% interest. Thus the principal will be returned plus about 25%. A silver mine should pay at least 10% per annum to warrant the risk incurred; in eight years the company should have received 80%; it will take three years more to exhaust the ore resources; thus 30% more is needed. The mine should have yielded at the end of 11 years at least twice the amount of money paid for it, that is 200%, instead of 125%, disregarding the refinements of amortization. It was expected to do much more than it has done. The estimate, at the time of flotation, stated that the ore in reserve amounted to 1,150,000 tons, from which a profit of £1,650,000, or $7,019,000, was assured, with undefined prospects of finding more ore and winning more profit. Evidently the mine will yield the amount of profit estimated as being assured when it was acquired, but no more. In short, the expectation of favorable development in depth has not been fulfilled. It was likely to be falsified by reason of the conditions under which the mine was appraised. An appraisal that will stand the test of time is unlikely when the engineers reporting upon a mine are participating heavily in the promotion profits. Even honorable men are biased by self-interest. It is true, the working of the Santa Gertrudis has been impeded by the revolutions in Mexico, but that has prolonged its life and postponed the closing of the account with the submissive shareholders. Moreover, silver stood at 54 cents per ounce in 1910, when the mine was acquired, and the price of the metal is now nearly twice as much. Experience teaches; we need more post-mortems of this kind to guide and warn speculators against paying excessive prices for mines and overburdening them with the undue profits of promotion.

A Mining Geologist

In these days when we review, with sadness and affection, the career of Dr. Raymond and go back to the beginning of scientific mineral exploration in this country, it is brought home to us how recent has been the use of geology as an economic instrument of industry. In the days of the founders of geology, of such men as Lyell and Murchison, for example, the study of geology was an amateur's hobby, which feared the taint of commercialism and deemed itself gentlemanly so long as it abstained from helping people to make money. We have traveled far from that aristocratic idea; we cherish the democratic ideal of using geology, as any other science, for furthering the welfare of man; we have discarded the old-fashioned notion that any science loses caste by becoming utilitarian. In this country Clarence King and his comrades led the way by their work in the Fortieth Parallel exploration and by founding the U. S. Geological Survey in 1879. At that time the geologist was retained by the Federal Government for the purpose of guiding the development of the national mineral domain, but he had not yet become a distinctly professional man with a regular practice among private clients. That phase of geologic study did not ensue until the beneficial consequences of official examinations and reports became manifest in the actual search for ore on the surface and underground. As soon as this fact was appreciated the enterprising owner of mines, whether an individual or a company, turned to the geologist as a regular consultant. Thus a new specialist was evolved. We publish an interview with an honored representative of this branch of the mining profession, for he belongs more to the practical side than to the scientific, or, rather, he is a successful compound, having learned that the object of mining is to make money and not to prove or disprove hypotheses, while yet retaining a genuine love for scientific research. We are glad to publish the interview with Mr. Horace V.

A Victory of Americanization at Seattle.

Bolshevism reached out a feeler to try the firmness of that true democracy which is the United States. It chose a city rich, flourishing, notable as a great port, a stopping place on one of the principal highways of international trade, and yet detached from the crowded centres of American life. The leaders hoped that measures of suppression at such a place would be less vigorous, because there would be a less insistent call from neighboring communities to extinguish the threatening flame of anarchy. The point was well chosen; Seattle afforded strategic advantages for an experiment in substituting the principle of the soviet for the administration of justice by a representative government. Had insubordination desolated Seattle, had civil strife developed there into a human horror, the evil of Bolshevism might have spread in the United States, as the friends of Trotsky, Lenine, Hindenburg, and Bernstorff desired. The attempt has failed and Americanism has stood the test. Seattle deserves honor of the country. Her people did not lose their heads; they did not trifle with a grave danger; they and their Mayor, Mr. Ole Hanson, and the Citizens' Committee, headed by Mr. A. J. Rhodes, cowed the bullies by simple manhood, resorting to no foolish display of futile bulldozing by the police, nor seeking to come to a compromise with the instigators of disorder. They branded the 'general strike' as "revolution" and issued a statement that, unless the strikers should yield by a certain date and hour, they would face the power of the United States Army. Mr. Hanson knew how to employ the forceful persuasion of an ultimatum so that the would-be Bolshevists recognized that he had in truth given them his last word. Democracy, sanity, the government of the people, by the people and for the people, has been vindicated at Seattle. Through this the winning of world-peace has been made still more sure.

Already we see how the disturbing I. W. W. organization has weakened at Butte. An outbreak was ripe to follow any symptom of success by the Bolshevists at Seattle, and the flames might then have run like fire in dry grass. No one denies that many workers in America have some cause for complaint. So have they in England. The collapse of stimulated and special industry, without pre-arranged plans for financial re-adjustment, necessarily has reduced production, and that has thrown numbers of men out of employment. Business men are doing all they can to rehabilitate industry and lessen the burdens of the people. The copper companies have undertaken to do a gracious thing in this direction that must win wide approval. Despite the fact that copper is a drug on the market, that no important European demand has appeared, that nearly the whole of the present output must go into storage, the operation of the mines is being continued on as slightly reduced a basis as possible, and with wages cut only in accordance with the sliding scale upon which they had been advanced during the period of high prices. This is a service to humanity, and it is be hoped that the workers will appreciate the financi sacrifice entailed by such action. It means that the mill ns paid as wages, which stand between the miner and estitution in the hard months of winter, are largely borowed millions on which the producers are paying irerest at six per cent, while the copper itself that ha been produced is costing money for storage each day hat it lies unsold. It cannot be said that this yields a holly compensating benefit to the corporations. Every ntelligent man knows that it is uneconomical to close mine and to suffer an organization to become disintærated, but there is a limit to this, for the workers themslves realize that the value of an organization lies in he efficient nucleus. Operations may be trimmed very lose to that nucleus before serious damage is involved ther for the mine, the smelting plant, or the refinery The copper companies have not cut their forces anywere near to the narrow limit of that skilled and capat minimum. They are serving the people in a way tht deserves the loyal recognition they are receiving fro sensible workingmen who are declining to follow the ed agitators whose maniac voice would lead into the valley of disaster, hideous with murder and famine. t must not be overlooked that the victory of good sens at Seattle was the fruit of conservative thought amng the workers themselves. Hesitant in the face of te possible subversion of law and order, fearing to be xposed to the vengeance of a momentarily dominant mob, which brings swifter violence upon the non-confonist laboring man than upon his employer, this large bdy of rational men only needed a strong leader. The hart of the people is always sound; the excesses of the mtitude grow out of infection from masses wrongly led. The plain people, rightly generalled, stand on the side of law and order. This has been proved again at eattle.

The Bolshevists, aen in spirit and mind, may as well give up their hoe of corrupting the sound principles of democracy in America. This country is not yet ready to abandon it high ideals of government or the high standard of livig that gives opportunity to save against the stringencs of old age and to push forward the children of each generation to larger achievement. America is not dispsed to plunge into the abyss with disordered Russia, nc to clamor against the bewildering financial difficulties c reconstruction as an injustice to be resisted by destroing industry. Troubled employers of labor, trying to fin their way back to normal business, need the trusting c-operation of labor, just as labor needs the guidance o the managers of industry, in order that all concerned my be saved from hardship and suffering. Mr. Samuel Gompers has said wisely that all must pull together, nd that employers should organize to meet organized lbor, so as to eliminate cut-throat competition and to sibilize industry. After the failure of the demons of desruction in their attempt at Seattle, we may look forwar confidently to constructive efforts between workers and employers. There must now be a end to disorder, and a turning more determinedly th ever to that hearty co-operation of ... iericans which is the glory of our democracy. In th... rit we won the War, and in the same spirit will we es... sh peace.

A Post-Mortem

Prolongation of the life of a m... enterprise by purchase of new property has bee... an acceptable method of company finance. When, in 1910, the Camp Bird mine, in Colorado, showed si... f approaching exhaustion, the English company, wh... ad acquired it ten years earlier from the late Thomas ... Walsh, bought the control of the Santa Gertrudis mi... at Pachuca, in Mexico. When the Santa Gertrudis, in turn, began to exhibit loss of vitality, the company de...ded to acquire rights to the El Bordo group, also in ... Pachuca district. This transaction was closed rece...ly. It is estimated that the El Bordo has an assure... reserve of 253,000 tons of ore, from which a profit ... $2,142,000 is anticipated. The report was made by ...r. Hugh Rose, the manager of the Santa Gertrudis. ... this case, we believe, the company did not have to p... a large commission to its own engineers, as it did i... the Santa Gertrudis deal, from which Mr. J. Hays Ha...mond, who was then consulting engineer to the Camp Bird company, drew a commission of $600,000—cut ...own from an original demand for $1,000,000. Inde... the directors themselves, except Mr. W. F. Fisher, ... drew profits from underwriting and trading of vario... kinds. It is a marvel that the British public took thes... proceedings so tamely after the chairman, Mr. Arthur ... Grenfell, had gone bankrupt and had involved the ...amp Bird and other companies in difficulties. That ...s in the early part of 1914. It is interesting now ... make a post-mortem inquiry into the Santa Gertru... business, if it be not brutal to conduct an autopsy up... an enterprise that is still alive. According to the lat... report of the subsidiary company operating the Sant... Gertrudis, the ore in reserve amounts to 880,433 tons, fr... which a profit of $3,750,000 is expected. The mine has ...lded dividends aggregating £731,250 on a capital of £1,...0,000, of which the Camp Bird company owns 81%. If ...e place 81% of the estimated remaining profit to the cr... it of that company and add 81% to the dividends dis...ibuted, we get the sum of just about $6,000,000 as the ...alizable money to be obtained by the Camp Bird compa...y on the operation. On the other side, the Camp Bi... company paid £922,131, or $4,481,550, for the 81% in...rest. Thus the principal will be returned plus about ...%. A silver mine should pay at least 10% per annu... to warrant the risk incurred; in eight years the comp...y should have received 80%; it will take three years ...ore to exhaust the ore resources; thus 30% more is needed. The min... should have yielded at the end of 11 years at l... twice the amount of money paid for i... that is 2... instead of 125%, disregarding the refin...nents of ...tization. It was expected to do much ...ore tha... done. The estimate, at the time of flot...on, st... the ore in reserve amounted to 1,150,000 ...ns, f... a profit of £1,650,000, or $7,019,000, w... a... undefined prospects of finding more ore and winning more profit. Evidently the mine will yield the amount of profit estimated as being assured when it was acquired, but no more. In short, the expectation of favorable development in depth has not been fulfilled. It was likely to be falsified by reason of the conditions under which the mine was appraised. An appraisal that will stand the test of time is unlikely when the engineers reporting upon a mine are participating heavily in the promotion profits. Even honorable men are biased by self-interest. It is true, the working of the Santa Gertrudis has been impeded by the revolutions in Mexico, but that has prolonged its life and postponed the closing of the account with the submissive shareholders. Moreover, silver stood at 54 cents per ounce in 1910, when the mine was acquired, and the price of the metal is now nearly twice as much. Experience teaches; we need more post-mortems of this kind to guide and warn speculators against paying excessive prices for mines and overburdening them with the undue profits of promotion.

A Mining Geologist

In these days when we review, with sadness and affection, the career of Dr. Raymond and go back to the beginning of scientific mineral exploration in this country, it is brought home to us how recent has been the use of geology as an economic instrument of industry. In the days of the founders of geology, of such men as Lyell and Murchison, for example, the study of geology was an amateur's hobby, which feared the taint of commercialism and deemed itself gentlemanly so long as it abstained from helping people to make money. We have traveled far from that aristocratic idea; we cherish the democratic ideal of using geology, as any other science, for furthering the welfare of man; we have discarded the old-fashioned notion that any science loses caste by becoming utilitarian. In this country Clarence King and his comrades led the way by their work in the Fortieth Parallel exploration and by founding the U. S. Geological Survey in 1879. At that time the geologist was retained by the Federal Government for the purpose of guiding the development of the national mineral domain, but he had not yet become a distinctly professional man ...ly a regular practice among private clients. The ... the geologic study did not ensue until the benefi... of the quences of official examinations and reports ... and fest in the actual search for ore on the surfa... were ground. As soon as this fact was apprecia... duction of prising owner of mines, whether an ind... ouraged by pany, turned to the geologist as a ... patriotism, ... ved. W... ...as necessary for ...ilities in each in... in foreign coun...ia, chrome from ... should say the ...oth the miner ... profit by his ... should be guar-

Winchell because he is a distinctly American product, both as an individual and as an example of the type of geologist that has done so much for the systematic exploration of our mineral resources. He comes of a family of geologists and illustrates the technical evolution to which we have referred, both his father and uncle having been professors of geology and State geologists, so that in his family we see the progression from the academic to the official geologist, and from the latter to the practitioner. He was lucky in being born in an atmosphere so favorable to the incubation of the talent for which a demand was developing in the mining world. As a boy he showed a thirst for exact, as distinguished from vague, information. He determined early to become not an academic geologist but a practitioner, and he told his chum, Mr. John A. Blair, of this ambition. In 1887, when only 22 years old, while assistant State Geologist of Minnesota, he told Mr. Blair that he had ascertained the existence of an enormous iron deposit on the Mesabi range. As he says, it was "the practical side of geology" that attracted him from the start, when he was fortunate in serving his apprenticeship with two such capable field-geologists as the brothers N. H. and Alexander Winchell. Almost at the beginning of his career Mr. Winchell scored both a scientific and an economic success. He suggested the now accepted explanation for the origin of the Lake Superior iron ores and he predicted the future tremendous importance of the Mesabi range as a source of iron ore. In the treatment he received from the U. S. Geological Survey he was by no means unique; unfortunately the reputation of the Survey for generosity in giving credit to the mining engineers and unofficial geologists who have done pioneer work is quite in accord with the Mesabi story. We are in entire sympathy with Mr. Winchell in the criticism that he implies. Besides his auspicious start as a mining geologist, Mr. Winchell was fortunate in acquiring early in life an ability to write on his subject. To the articles that he wrote for sundry technical periodicals and transactions he owes his capacity for clear exposition, a capacity that he was enabled to put to profitable and honorable use when serving as an expert witness in mining litigation, a branch of mining geology in which he has earned a reputation second to none. His success in this work was due mainly to his thorough preparation as a geologist, in his grasp of the points involved, and in his direct application of scientific theory. The splendid library that he established in his office at Butte, as a part of the organization of a geological department for the Amalgamated Copper Company, enabled him to acquire an unrivaled command of information. At the same time he developed a system of underground maps, useful not only for litigation but for finding ore, which, it must be insisted, is the primary purpose of mining geology. He succeeded in that as he did in the courts of law. His name is linked with the discovery of the genetic principle we call secondary enrichment. Here again the geologists of the Survey took to themselves the lion's share of credit, mainly because Mr. Winchell's lips were sealed by the exigencies of a fierce litigation at Butte, so that he could not burst into print at the time when the gentlemen at Washington were thriling the mining profession with their inductions and deductions. In later years Mr. Winchell came before the public as a protestant against the cancellation of the Cunningham coal-claims in Alaska, an enterprise in which he personally was interested and the killing of which, by an arbitrary act of the Government, aroused his bitter resentment. He made a plucky fight, in which he took with him the sympathy of many. The incident served to accentuate his dislike of the mining law and the administration of it. He led a powerful propaganda for the amendment of the regulations controlling the exploitation of the public domain and he consistently attacked the manifest defects of the so-called apex law. In these and other matters he has proved himself a fearless leader of men and a citizen of unquestioned public spirit. In him the mining profession, usually so inarticulate, has found an effective spokesman. It is not surprising therefore that he has recently been elected the president of the American Institute of Mining Engineers, an honor that he has earned and a position for which he is well fitted. The present writer has found himself in disagreement with Mr. Winchell more than once, as is likely between men so ready to express positive opinions, but we recognize not only the possibility of his being right and of our being wrong, but, what is more important, the sincerity of his purpose and the highmindedness of his motives. In the interview he outlines what he deems to be the main function of the Institute, namely, service to the profession. We feel sure that during his term of office he will further that concept and do something noteworthy in enabling the profession to play its proper part in the era of reconstruction bequeathed by the War. As for the more personal aspects of Mr. Winchell's character, we know several kind stories, of which the most memorable is that of a former partner, who testifies to his generosity in the early days of their practice at Minneapolis. The partner—it was Mr. F. F. Sharpless—did the assaying of iron ores while Mr. Winchell did the field-work. After the panic of 1893 the assay business went to pieces and prospects were black. Mr. Winchell made a sale of some iron-land, a deal entirely outside the partnership, and telegraphed to his discouraged associate that he was credited with a half-share of the commission. Blessed is the man with such a partner. Another friend tells us that he was a serious boy, whose chief enthusiasm was for music. Another likes to remember how this taste for music was manifested during the litigation at Butte when Mr. Winchell added to the jollity of the evening by singing 'Dunderberg's Sausage Machine', a song suggesting that his boyhood seriousness was not invincible. He has left a bright trail of good-fellowship and warm-heartedness wherever he has been, and that means much of the map; he has proved himself not only an untiring investigator and an exact thinker but a cheery companion and a loyal friend—in other words, a highly civilized man. We wish him every success in his year of office as the standard-bearer of the mining profession.

The M. & M. Society and the Merger

The Editor:

Sir—On December 21 an interesting editorial appeared in your paper concerning the suggestion that the Mining & Metallurgical Society of America merge with the American Institute of Mining Engineers. The general tone of the article is apt to cause a misconception regarding the Mining & Metallurgical Society, its functions, and its scope of action under the law. The Society has wide rights, including that of expressing its opinion as a body on all matters of public as well as private interest—a much valued and important privilege.

One particular point which it is well to call attention to at the present time refers to such privileges and is represented by the following sentence in your article:

"Another difference, namely, the constitutional provision prohibiting the Institute from taking part in the discussion of public affairs, was removed five years ago."

This statement is inaccurate.

The Institute is incorporated under the general law of the State of New York which sanctions such organizations and permits to them a wide scope of activity, unless the incorporators choose to limit their activity in their certificate of incorporation, which is the underlying and life-giving document to all such organizations. That the Institute recognized these limitations is clear from the fact that it was thought to abrogate them by amending the Constitution so as to permit expression of opinion on public questions by the membership as a body.

The certificate of incorporation of the Institute does so limit the activities of the association, where in paragraph five it reads:

"That the purposes for which this corporation is to be formed are: To promote the arts and sciences connected with the economic production of the useful minerals and metals and the welfare of those employed in these industries by means of meetings for social intercourse and the reading and discussion of professional papers, and to circulate by means of publications among its members the information thus obtained: and to establish and maintain a place of meeting for its members and a hall for the reading of papers and delivery of addresses, and a library of books relating to subjects cognate to the sciences and arts of mining and metallurgy."

This is the only authoritative definition of the purposes of the Institute; it distinctly sets forth what these purposes are; and for that reason the functions of the organization are limited. Under this certificate of incorporation it has consequently no right as a body to take part in the public discussion of affairs as is erroneously stated in the editorial mentioned above. Not having the right to discuss public affairs, because of the limitation of powers fixed in these articles of incorporation, it cannot of course legally acquire such right by changing its constitution alone, a document deriving its own powers and value from the certificate of incorporation, nor can it validly, through any of its representatives, exercise such a right until such time as it may have modified its articles of incorporation which govern both its constitution and its by-laws. Unless consequently the Mining & Metallurgical Society of America is disposed to forego the unquestioned right of public expression of its opinion, it seems ill advised that it join the American Institute of Mining Engineers, whose right to such expression of opinion, to say the least, is very obscure.

There has been so much loose thinking and so much verbiage during the War that it would seem advisable to try and relieve misconceptions and false understandings regarding important matters in the difficult times now approaching. It is for this reason we are taking the liberty of addressing this argument to your paper in the hopes that it may go far toward correcting an erroneous impression which surely was conveyed entirely inadvertently.

C. R. Corning.
Geo. C. Stoke.

New York, January 28.

Wheat and Chromite

The Editor:

Sir—To watch our Government shoulder a billion dollar loss and refuse to fairly meet a moral responsibility one one million dollars is quite interesting, to say the least. Such, however, appears to be the outcome of the relationship of the Government to the wheat-raiser and the chrome-producer. Both wheat and chromite were of vital importance in winning the War. Production of each was stimulated by higher prices and encouraged by our Government by solicitation, appeals to patriotism, and constant urging.

Increase in domestic production was necessary for the same reason: lack of shipping facilities in each instance. Both could have been obtained in foreign countries; wheat from Australasia and India, chrome from New Caledonia and Rhodesia. No one should say the miner is less patriotic than the farmer. Both the miner and the farmer expected, or expects, to profit by his endeavors. Who then will tell why one should be guaranteed a large profit and the other entail a comparatively great loss?

Government reports show the fall-wheat crop to be promising a good yield. The outlook for a large acreage of spring wheat is evident. All of which is excellent. But why the Government should pay $2.26 per bushel for wheat when it can be brought to our door for $1 to $1.25 per bushel and will no doubt be sold to the Government for the latter figures—meaning a loss of a billion dollars or more—can only be answered in one way, namely, to keep faith with the domestic producer. This is only paying the farmer what he justly deserves, as he has founded his production and figured his venture on a promise made by the most reliable of governments.

Government reports will also show that there is and was ample chromite available in our country to meet the demands necessary to successfully prosecute the War. No one conversant with the reports of the consumers of chrome ore as to amounts on hand and with the quantities now opened up and available in 1918 and still awaiting a market can dispute the ability of the domestic producer to meet all requirements placed upon him. Nevertheless branches of our Government at Washington permitted foreign ore to be brought to our ports and unloaded, through issuing illicit licenses and against orders which, if they had been obeyed, would have given the domestic producer of chromite a market for all he could have produced during the year 1918 at least. Statistics show this conclusively. What is the result? The domestic producer of chromite found himself last fall with ore on hand and opened up, properties just made available for production by building roads and installing machinery at mines and mills, and no market in sight. A large majority of the producers have lost money and some a snug fortune owing to this condition.

It has been reliably estimated that one million dollars will cover the loss of the chromite producer. This is but one-thousandth part of the billion dollars the country will lose in buying the entire wheat crop next fall at $2.26 per bushel. It seems reasonable then that the chromite-producer should expect to be taken care of to the extent of at least getting even, when the wheat-raiser will not only get even but make hundreds of millions of dollars. Each industry needed stimulation and a resultant increase of production in order that we be assured of winning the War. We got the assurance and have the increased production and why not pay the premium and back up the moral obligations and promises now the War is won?

We are seriously considering cancelling the indebtedness of our Allies, which is over eight and one-half billions of dollars. If we can do that much for our Allies we should be able to re-imburse our own patriots to the extent of the existant moral obligation now so generally admitted. There are many ways to do this which can be successfully worked out during this term of Congress. Our legislative servants should be importuned till the chromite-producer is assured recompense for capital properly invested and capably managed.

Much has been accomplished in ascertaining where the responsibility rests for the condition of the chromite patriot. This is gratifying but not sufficient. From a world-wide economic standpoint, perhaps, it is just that the foreign ore now take the place of our domestic ore, inasmuch as it can be produced much cheaper. This does not lessen the responsibility of our Government in taking care of a dead war-baby and giving it fit and proper interment.

GEO. S. BARTON.

Grants Pass, Oregon, January 31.

The Future of Copper

The Editor:

Sir—Copper is under strong discussion at the present time. With the demand and consumption of two billion and a half pounds per year and increasing at the rate of 7% per annum—which increase will most likely be larger in the future—is there not the possibility that we will be strong importers of copper in twenty years instead of an exporter, and are we not selling something that later we will have to buy back at an advanced price? This country with its immense resources and stability will increase in foreign population in the next few years as never before. My opinion is that the copper people of this country are making a mistake in selling so much copper to foreign countries, especially at a price less than copper can be imported into this country at a later date.

ALEX. F. ESKE.

Oakland, California, January 26.

[Our correspondent's fears are, we think, unfounded. The copper resources of this country are not within sight of exhaustion; moreover, those owning the deposits of copper ore are desirous of turning them into money, which is the prime purpose of mining, while the market is favorable. It must be remembered that a substitute for copper, such as cheap aluminum, may spoil the demand that now obtains. The miner cares little for posterity.—EDITOR.]

Copper Production in Mexico

The Editor:

Sir—Referring to 'Copper Production in Mexico' in your issue of December 21, 1918, I note that statement is made that production of copper in Nuevo Leon for 1917 was 31,089,484 kilo. This must, of course, refer to the amount smelted in Nuevo Leon, as the mines of that State could not have produced any such amount. The table for production of copper in the 'Boletin Minero' would appear to me to have some inaccuracies. From the list given therein I must infer that only smelter production is intended to be made, and if that be the case in one instance at least there must be an error. The smelters that were operating in the States mentioned were as follows:

Aguascalientes—American Smelting & Refining Co.

Baja California—Compagnie du Boleo.

Coahuila—American Metal Co., at Torreon; and Mazapil Copper Co., at Saltillo.

Nuevo Leon—American Smelting & Refining Co., at Monterrey; Monterrey Mining, Smelting & Refining Co., at Monterrey; and American Metal Co., at Villaldama.

Sonora—Cananea Con. Copper Co.

San Luis Potosi—American Smelting & Refining Co., at Matehuala; and Cia. Metalurgica Mexicana, at San Luis Potosi.

Zacatecas—Mazapil Copper Co., at Concepcion del Oro.

The production for Coahuila at the Torreon and Saltillo plants was probably not great, as most of the ore smelted was lead ore. Only the copper collected in matte at Saltillo would have been produced from that smelter. The actual production of copper from Coahuila mines was probably not much greater than 300,000 kilogrammes.

Copper produced in Nuevo Leon smelters was almost entirely from mines outside that State. All of the plants mentioned are principally lead smelters, although a small tonnage of copper ore was treated at the Monterrey plant of the A. S. & R.

Presumably the ore exported from the Moctezuma Copper property at Nacozari was included in the production for Sonora.

The San Luis Potosi smelters must have produced much in excess of 565,000 kg. of copper. Possibly matte shipped from one smelter to another for converting in a different State was not included. It is probable that the copper produced from one mine alone in San Luis Potosi was four times as great as that noted in the table, and this was smelted in one of the smelters of that State.

S. F. Shaw.

Charcas, S. L. P., January 11.

Water Laws of Nevada

The Editor:

Sir—In your issue of January 25 there is a letter by Mr. R. T. Walker in reply to a letter by Mr. G. A. Duncan published in your issue of December 21 under the caption of 'Water Laws of Nevada'. These letters pertain to the laws governing the ownership of subterranean water in the arid mining regions, a topic of great importance to the mining industry.

Preliminary to being one of the witnesses who testified concerning the water-governing conditions in Eldorado canyon, in the trial of the case cited by Mr. Duncan, it was necessary for me to make a thorough study of the region involved, and I deem this subject of sufficient general importance to warrant my asking a portion of your space for an effort to clear a simple palpable regional structure enforcing a watercourse in Eldorado canyon, from the intricacies and beclouding elaboration enshrouding it in Mr. Walker's article; and for the reason that the mining district and trial used by Mr. Duncan as an illustration furnish marked examples of the possibility of unrighteous judgment under the construction of the laws as advocated by Mr. Walker.

Your editorial of December 21 wisely recognizes the fact that, as to water-rights, "the courts have yet to adjudicate in special cases." Mr. Walker's proposition to dispose of the whole question by limiting water-ownership between "vertical planes passing through the surface boundaries of the mining claims" is as impossible of application as it is opposed to equity and the decisions of the higher courts.

Mr. Walker claims that all the water of Eldorado canyon is contained in a network of fractures, and that the water in question is percolating water, and for that reason not subject to appropriation under Nevada laws, and he makes the general statement that underground waters cannot be said to flow in any given direction.

All students of hydrology agree that, as a rule, ground-water conforms to the topography, and that there is a more or less constant movement of this ground-water from the higher to the lower elevations, finding outlet frequently in springs in depressions or formation fractures. This movement takes place in so-called trunk channels fed by many tributaries, as in the case of surface streams. These tributaries, coming in from both sides of the trunk channel, form part of the watercourse, and would be so treated in disputes arising over surface-flowing streams. The water of a given region, flowing underground or contained within the rocks, gravitates toward the section of lowest altitude for that region. This is not alone true of the surface run-off, but of the ground-water as well, as is clearly shown by C. R. Van Hise, whose work on underground flowage is regarded as authoritative.

Eldorado canyon is the lowest or deepest canyon in its vicinity, and toward it all water accumulations in the rocks on either side will gravitate, particularly as these rocks stand high above the bottom of the canyon on either side. Eldorado canyon is marked for its entire length by a strong porphyry dike of exceptional alignment and almost unbroken continuity, a condition giving rise not only to the canyon itself, but to the water-bearing fracture referred to by Mr. Walker, which fracture is fed chiefly by the great mass of water-bearing 'malpais' along the summit of the river range, and, to a lesser degree, by the meeting under the canyon-floor of the water conducted there from either side, and the water of the region flows within this channel down the canyon into the Colorado river, at its mouth maintaining, in times of low water, a small area of clear water in the surrounding muddy water of the river.

We have here all the simple palpable features of a stream. The direction and movement of this water and the channel conducting it are alike obvious. Water movement in any other direction would encounter the resistance of a constantly increasing head. As water cannot flow toward its pressure-head, but must flow away from it, the water in the region in question must flow toward the axis of Eldorado canyon. The many shafts, cross-cuts, tunnels, and drifts on both sides of Eldorado canyon demonstrate an almost complete absence of water from the rocks, the rainfall not resting there but quickly finding its way to the natural drainage channel of the region, as is the case with surface-stream maintenance.

The above conditions, all plainly open to observation, of common knowledge in the region, and easy of comprehension from testimony, unquestionably establish Eldorado canyon and its accompanying dike-fracture as a watercourse whose boundaries and direction of flow can be determined.

Mr. Walker advances the idea that cross-faults necessarily cut off underground water-flow. This statement is in error; as faults, or even dikes crossing a master regional line of weakness are generally subject to fracture by frequent movements along the greater fault. A fault might divert the water for a distance, just as would a dam in a stream, but the flow would continue where some movement had opened a way, and again seek its old channel. Mr. Walker's naive theory of a network of fractures, if applied in this instance, would scarcely comport with his claim of interruptions of flow by cross-faults.

The fault mentioned by Mr. Walker, in which he sank his shaft, is merely a tributary to the main trunk channel in the canyon. The water-shaft was sunk at the junction of the fault with the main channel of the canyon and may owe much of its water to the main channel supply, but such water as the shaft operations exhaust from the fault constitutes a diversion of appropriated water from its normal channel in the same way that water taken from the tributary of a surface stream would, if permanently diverted, affect the flow of the main channel.

It is certainly highly significant that for almost the entire water-supply needed by Mr. Walker, even for domestic use, he found it necessary to leave his own gulch and go a mile and a half over the mountain into Eldorado canyon, and to the dike in the canyon-bottom to get his supply. Certainly, if his theory that a network of fractures induces a general percolation of water in the region is valid, a well sunk anywhere in that vicinity should have found water.

The structural features of Eldorado canyon not only establish beyond a reasonable doubt the fact of a well-defined subterranean watercourse along its dike-fracture, in which water is always found, but positive proof is added by the universal dryness of the many shafts and tunnels in Eldorado canyon on both sides of this main trunk channel.

The water flowing in this channel was granted to the plaintiff mentioned by filing and appropriation under the laws of Nevada, his priority and clearness of title being beyond question. Upon the basis of the possession of this water an excellent mill was built, and mining and milling operations successfully entered upon, only to be presently stopped by the diversion of the water-supply. A great wrong has been done here, and there has been established a dangerous precedent, in the confirmation by the Court of the diversion of that appropriated and beneficially used water from its natural channel.

May not these wrongs be perpetrated otherwhere in Nevada?

Evidently there is need of the correction of Nevada water laws, or of their interpretation.

EDWARD W. BROOKS.

Los Angeles, February 1.

Rossiter W. Raymond

The Editor:

Sir—Having read with interest your editorial comments on the life and achievements of Dr. R. W. Raymond, I take the liberty of sending you this brief communication, hoping that it will be of some interest to those who knew him, and they are many.

I was associated with him, in the years 1870 and '71, in editing the 'Engineering & Mining Journal' in New York, and went with him to Wilkes-Barre to attend a meeting of engineers which had been called with a view to forming an association of men whose chief interests were in mining and metallurgy. Our first meeting was held in the office of Richard P. Rothwell in that city.

Your tribute to Raymond is accurate and well-founded, and I fully agree with your judgment of his merits and abilities. I would, however, call your attention to one inaccuracy. His father was not Henry J. Raymond, the founder, and for many years, editor of the New York 'Times', but Dr. Robert R. Raymond, president of the Packer Institute in Brooklyn, a fine courteous old gentleman whom I frequently met.

For some years past Dr. Raymond, Dr. H. S. Drinker, and I were the only survivors of the founders of the A. I. M. E., and now the number is reduced to two. The second meeting was held at Bethlehem, Pennsylvania, at which so many new members were taken in that the success of the Institute was assured, especially as a large number of these came from all over the country, whereas the original members, with the exceptions I have mentioned, and of J. H. Bramwell, were all, as I remember it, connected with the anthracite mining in Pennsylvania. Anton Eilers and Dr. Thomas M. Drown, who was for many years Secretary, were among the new members. Martin Coryell was the first secretary, Drown the second, and he was succeeded by Raymond, in the most important office of the Institute, and it is largely to them that its success is due.

WILLARD P. WARD.

Savannah, Georgia, January 30.

[We were wrong, as Mr. Ward says, about Dr. Raymond's father; he was editor of the 'Free Democrat' and the 'Evening Chronicle', at Syracuse, New York, from 1852 to 1854. We are glad to publish Mr. Ward's letter and invite other reminiscences of Dr. Raymond for publication.—EDITOR.]

THE 'Times of India' on hoarding bullion says "India should not expect a full arbitration in bullion at present, because, owing to the War, gold and silver are not parted with by the leading nations of the world. * * * Gold and silver lying in the houses of our farmers have no economic value, and it only obstructs the financial growth of India and cripples its money power."

THE efficiency of graphite crucibles is expressed as so many heats per crucible. This also applies to clay crucibles.

ANACONDA HILL, BUTTE

Horace V. Winchell, Mining Geologist

AN INTERVIEW, BY T. A. RICKARD

Mr. Winchell, you were born in Montana?

No, sir; in Michigan, in 1865.

Were your parents of New England origin?

My father was born in New York State and my mother in Vermont.

What was your early education?

I attended the public schools of Minneapolis and the University of Minnesota and finished at the University of Michigan, graduating in the class of 1889. I went there to study with my uncle, Alexander Winchell, who was then Professor of Geology in the University of Michigan.

Your family has been conspicuous in geology, has it not?

My uncle, Alexander Winchell, was one of the early State Geologists of Michigan and Professor of Geology for many years at the State university. My father, Newton H. Winchell, a younger brother of Alexander, was, for a quarter of a century, State Geologist of Minnesota, and Professor of Geology in the University of that State for many years. These two brothers with others established and my father edited and published during its entire existence of 18 years 'The American Geologist', which was the first monthly geological journal published on this continent.

So you were brought up in an atmosphere kindly to mining? You intended when a boy to become a mining engineer or geologist?

I did, my interest has always been in the practical side of geology and in connection with the application of that science to the art of mining. I have never been interested in the other branches of geology, such as paleontology or stratigraphy.

After graduation at the University of Michigan, what did you do?

Prior to graduation even I was engaged in geological work with the field-parties of the Minnesota survey, assisting my uncle, who was engaged in that work for two or three years, and my father, in the study of the iron-ore regions of northern Minnesota. Immediately after graduation I began work as an assistant on the Minnesota survey and made a special study of the Mesabi iron range.

What was the result of this work?

The first result of this geological investigation was a joint report by my father, N. H. Winchell, and myself upon the iron ores of Minnesota, a volume of 430 pages, published in 1891, a year before the first production of ore from the Mesabi range. The geological map that

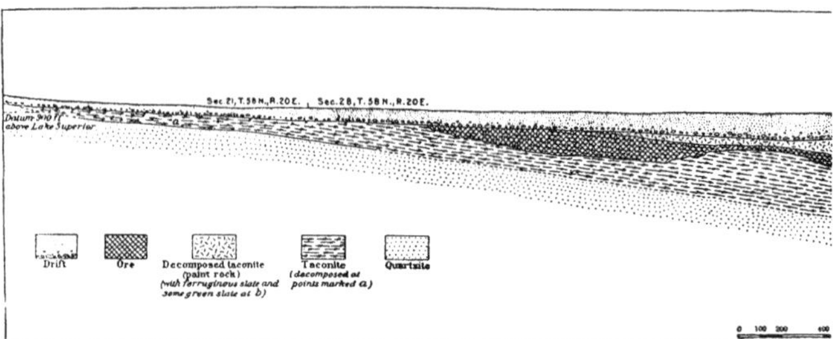

NORTH-SOUTH CROSS-SECTION THROUGH IRON-BEARING BIWABIK

accompanies this report was prepared and printed in 1890 and upon this map was shown for the first time the approximate location and extent of the Mesabi range. I was so convinced at that time of the importance of the Mesabi, although it had not yet been explored, that in that report we made the prediction that its production would exceed that of the Gogebic range in Michigan, which at that time was one of the wonders of the world and produced much the largest amount of high-grade iron ore mined in any one district.

What has been the production of the Mesabi range since then?

The Mesabi range, since its first shipment of ore in 1892, has produced approximately five hundred million tons representing nearly three hundred million tons of pig-iron. It now produces more than 50% of all the iron ore mined in the United States; and if it were not for this supply, it is perhaps not too much to say that it would be a physical impossibility for the United States to play its part in the present war.

Having accomplished this geological reconnaissance, what did you do next?

The general report upon the iron ores of Minnesota was followed in 1892 by a report of my own upon the Mesabi range. This was the first report upon this region describing its extent, its geology, the character of its ores, and attempting to estimate the cost of production and its relative importance in the iron industry. This report was re-published a number of times* and was used by all of the prospectors on the iron range for several years. Its conclusions were confirmed by monograph LII published some 15 years later by the U. S. Geological Survey, by Charles R. Van Hise and Charles K. Leith.

Were you given proper credit for your earlier work?

Not at all: my report was barely mentioned. By the way, that reminds me that, in 1890, I wrote an article in the 'American Journal of Science' suggesting the origin of the Lake Superior iron ores by chemical oceanic precipitation. This theory, which was ridiculed at the time, has later been adopted holus-bolus by the Lake Superior geologists of the U. S. Geological Survey as their fundamental concept, likewise without reference to the first presentation of the idea.

So you became thoroughly familiar with the geology of the iron deposits?

The fact that I was optimistic regarding the Mesabi range, led to my employment early in 1893 by the Minnesota Iron Company, which was at that time the largest producer of iron ore in the world, under the direction of Mr. Don H. Bacon, subsequently in charge of the operations of the Tennessee Coal & Iron Co. and now residing at New York, where I saw him a few days ago. My association with Mr. Bacon was one of the pleasant experiences of my career. He was always stimulating, sympathetic, and appreciative, and was easily brought to a belief in the importance of the Mesabi range at a time when other iron men were unbelieving. If Mr. Bacon's plans had been adopted, the control and management of the best deposits of that region would be vastly different today.

What objection was there to the development of these iron resources?

It will be remembered that there was a period of financial depression in 1893; at that time there was not a great demand for iron ore; those who were interested in the iron mines were also interested in steel plants, and they believed that if the Mesabi possessed such vast deposits as were indicated by my report, iron ore would have very little value. For that reason they were dilatory in buying the lands which I recommended and which Mr. Bacon urged them to purchase. The result was that other interests, notably John D. Rockefeller, acting on the advice of W. J. Olcott, and appreciating their value, acquired various properties almost as rapidly as they were developed and soon controlled many of the largest

*Trans. A. I. M. E., 1893, Vol. XXI, p. 644.

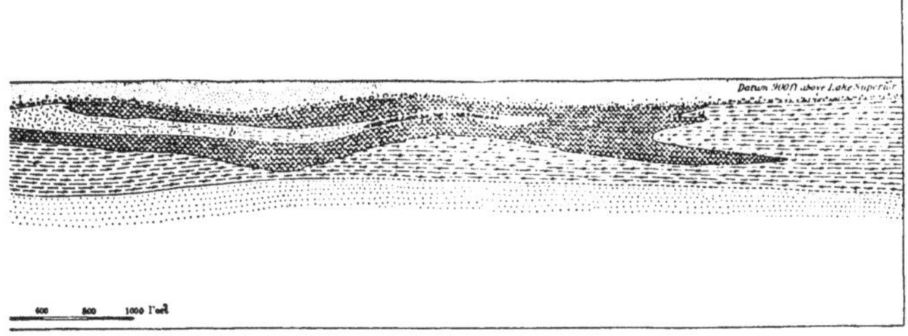

FORMATION, MESABI DISTRICT, MINNESOTA. U. S. GEOLOGICAL SURVEY.

deposits. At that time I used to write an occasional unsigned editorial for the 'Iron Trade Review' of Cleveland, the recognized organ of the iron-ore industry. In one of these editorials, I remember analyzing the consumption of iron ore and pointed out the fact, which in a short time became evident, that all the ore of the Mesabi range would soon be needed to keep up with a greatly expanding industry, and that, instead of a calamity, it was a blessing to the country, because it became available in the nick of time.

Can you quote from that editorial?

In the 'Iron Trade Review' for February 16, 1893, under the caption 'Is There a Shortage of Bessemer Ore?' I called attention to the dwindling of supplies, and reached the conclusion expressed above, stating that "there is most decidedly a shortage, amounting almost to a famine, in the visible supply of Bessemer ore. The day of more general utilization of the basic process of steel-making may be nearer at hand than is generally supposed."

Observing that the information contained in articles regarding the reserves of iron ore in the United States, published in England and abroad, were, in most cases years behind-hand, I prepared for the North of England Institute of Mining and Mechanical Engineers, a paper upon the Lake Superior iron-ore region. This won for me the annual medal awarded for the best contribution to the transactions of that technical society in that year, and in that paper I made what was then considered the wild guess that the Mesabi might produce five hundred million tons of iron ore.

When was this?

In 1896.

How long were you engaged in your work on the iron region of Minnesota?

The financial depression of 1893 brought about a cessation of exploratory work by the Minnesota Iron Co. in 1894. I then engaged in general practice and, in connection with it, established a chemical laboratory at Minneapolis in partnership with F. F. Sharpless. This laboratory starved through a precarious existence for less than two years. My professional connections from that time became more and more diverted to the Western mining districts.

To which districts in the West did you go first?

My first examination of mining property in the West was made for James J. Hill in 1894; he sent me to the State of Washington to examine iron ore and coal deposits. I also recall examining gold mines at Murray, Idaho, and in the Black Hills of South Dakota, in 1894 and 1895. Later, in 1898 I went to Butte at the instance of Mr. David W. Brunton, to study the Anaconda mine, in connection with apex litigation in which Senator W. A. Clark was plaintiff and the Anaconda Copper Mining Co. was defendant.

How did you meet Brunton?

I met Brunton at a meeting of the American Institute of Mining Engineers in Minnesota in 1897. I prepared a little hand-book for that meeting, descriptive of the various iron mines, and acted as a kind of guide to the members on their visit to the iron ranges, pointing out the interesting features and describing the geology in little talks on the spot. My next meeting with Brunton was on a train in Colorado, early in the following year, on which occasion he broached the idea of the Butte engagement. I promptly declined, saying that I had assured my wife that there was one place in the world where she never would have to live, namely, Butte, but Brunton's persuasive arguments induced me rashly to make a proposition, which I had no idea would be accepted. The result was a telegram from Marcus Daly, saying "When can you be here?" I agreed to spend one year at Butte, but actually spent eight. During this time I was engaged in the organization of a geological department for the Amalgamated Copper Co., which was organized after I began my residence at Butte, about the year 1900.

I remember meeting you at Butte in 1898 and being im-

pressed by the spacious room all lined with books in which you had your office and remarking the fact that you were able to do your writing amid thoroughly congenial surroundings.

That was in 1901, I think. My early efforts as an author impressed upon me the necessity for books of reference. When writing the volume on 'The Iron Ores of Minnesota', I prepared a bibliography and found it necessary to send East to borrow many books of reference. Libraries in the West at that time were and perhaps even now are incomplete; hence with the library of my uncle, Alexander Winchell, as a nucleus, I began spending all my spare cash in the purchase of books. This resulted in the collection of an excellent library upon the subjects in which I was interested.

So you began to participate in apex litigation?

The particular lawsuit which brought me to Butte lasted more than one year and was settled finally in favor of the Anaconda company by a court decision that was based entirely upon geological structure. It was in this case that the existence of the so-called Blue veins of Butte was first announced. These veins have proved to be some of the richest and most important in the Butte district.

When was your attention first drawn to the theory of secondary enrichment of copper ores?

In studying the ore deposits of Butte, I had the invaluable assistance and co-operation of Clarence King, N. S. Shaler, R. W. Raymond, Louis Janin, J. P. Iddings, W. H. Wiley, and others. King's interest in the subject, his breadth of mind, his wide experience, were most helpful. He was one of the most delightful and interesting men with whom I have ever been associated and his memory has always been a source of inspiration. In connection with the solution of our problems it was important to be able, if possible, to distinguish clearly between the old Anaconda vein and the later Blue vein; both of them contain rich copper ore and yet one is clearly later than the other. It was necessary to show in what respects their mineralogy differed. The occurrence of the chalcocite suggested to me, freshly from the study of the iron-ore deposits of the Lake Superior region, where descending waters have done all the work, that the formation of at least a portion of this chalcocite might be due to the action of descending waters. This idea had not, so far as I know, ever been suggested or discussed previously. In order to test the possibility of such chalcocite deposition, I secured permission to establish a chemical laboratory in which to conduct the necessary research. My chemist was C. F. Tolman, Jr. Chemically, our difficulty lay in finding the reducing agent that would reduce cupric sulphate to cuprous sulphide. The only chalcocite and bornite recognized as secondary, and mentioned in chemical literature up to that time, was that found upon the bronze coins discovered in the hot springs at Bourbonne-les-Bains, in southern France. The French chemists attributed the formation of these minerals to the reducing action of organic matter. My first experiments, therefore, were with the use of all sorts of organic compounds. The invariable result, however, was not the formation of any sulphide of copper, but the native metal. Its formation in such a manner is illustrated in the fire-zone of the mines at Butte and in other districts where the mine-waters have penetrated charred timbers and deposited scales and particles of native copper to their very core.

May I suggest also the deposits characteristic of the Permian sandstone in western Siberia and in the Ural region, where native copper is deposited on fossil remains, particularly those of plants?

Yes; I think this is characteristic of the Permian in many parts of the world, such also as Texas and the Mansfeld district in Germany. I remember finding in the bottom of a shaft at Butte an old tarred manila rope that when unwound disclosed a mass of native copper, several inches thick, encrusting the rope. Finding that organic matter did not produce sulphide minerals, we experimented with hydrogen, and with hydrogen and ammonium sulphides, and the sulphides of the alkalies, inasmuch as the rock minerals contain soda and potash, but here the result was not chalcocite (Cu_2S) but covellite (CuS). In connection with the study of the processes of oxidation we discovered that cupriferous iron sulphide produced sulphurous acid, whereupon we thought that this might be the long-sought reducing agent. Using therefore mine-waters of known composition and jig-concentrates from the Parrot mill, and a solution saturated with SO_2 in jars sealed from the air with paraffine, we were gratified at finding in a few months that all the copper previously in solution had been deposited as crystallized chalcocite, coating the fragments of primary ore. This was the first time that chalcocite had been produced synthetically and it was a demonstration of the possibility of its formation from descending sulphide solutions; in other words, this was the starting point for the theory of secondary sulphide enrichment, subsequently elaborated by Emmons, Weed, and Van Hise. It is interesting to note that Van Hise's conclusion was based entirely upon deduction from chemical principles, whereas my conclusion was based upon experimental research.

When did your research culminate in this discovery?

In 1899 or 1900.

Then it was a pure coincidence that Van Hise's deductions appeared on the same date as the announcement of your results?

Oh, no; my announcement was not made until two or three years later in a communication to the Geological Society of America. My lips were still sealed and I was unable to do any writing for publication during the progress of the litigation at Butte. It was thought that if I promulgated a theory which could by any possible means have a bearing upon the litigation, that if my theory seemed to favor the side I represented, I should be accused of attempting to frame a case in advance; if, on the contrary, it could by any interpretation be made

THE SHENANGO IRON MINE, ON THE MESABI RANGE. U. S. GEOLOGICAL SURVEY

to favor the other side, it would be used against us. The date of the experiment and of the discovery, as given just now, is stated in the proceedings of the Geological Society of America, Vol. 14, page 269.

To what did you turn next?

During the next eight years, that is, until 1906, I was in charge of the Geological Department of the Amalgamated Copper Co. and the results obtained by regular systematic recording of observations underground were so satisfactory that many other mining companies followed suit and established departments of geology. This was one of the earliest experiments along this line and such pioneer work seems to have been well justified. A large part of my work was in connection with the Heinze litigation, but there were also many outside investigations and examinations of mines all over the West and in Mexico, for the Amalgamated. When the Heinze troubles were settled in 1906, I left Butte and became Chief Geologist for the Great Northern Railway Co., a position that I occupied for about two years, with headquarters at St. Paul. During this time, I explored iron-ore properties in Minnesota and large coal deposits in Wyoming, Montana, and British Columbia, and purchased lands containing hundreds of millions of tons of both coal and iron.

When did you go to Alaska?

I have made ten trips to Alaska; my first extended trip was in 1903. During the summer of that year, I spent several months in the examination of copper mines both along the coast and in the interior, particularly in the Copper River region. My examination was made for H. H. Rogers, John Hays Hammond, and their associates. It was part of my duty to look into the question of railroad construction in that region and to report upon the general prospects for the development of valuable mines. No law at that time had been passed by Congress for the location of coal in Alaska. This was first permitted under the law of February 1904. On the occasion of this visit, I had an amusing experience with Stephen Birch. Mr. Birch was in charge of what is now known as the Kennecott mine; he had been instructed by telegram, which was taken overland more than a hundred miles by an Indian, under no circumstances to let me see this property. He carried out his instructions faithfully, although it was the Fourth of July, and we were regaled with Scotch and cigars, his military force to the number of nine men being each provided with a loaded rifle and a bottle of whiskey wherewith they successfully repelled invasion. Since leaving the employ of the Great Northern Railway in 1908, I have been engaged in general practice with an office in Minneapolis and during that time have visited most of the mining regions in North America, besides others in South America, Europe, and Asia.

When did you get into the controversy over the Cunningham claims in Alaska?

My first intimation of the existence of coal in Alaska came from Mr. H. T. Burls, an engineer associated with Sir Boverton Redwood. I met Burls on my Alaska trip in 1903. He was then on his way to examine an oilfield near Cold Bay, west of Kodiak island, and I accompanied him. Burls told me that he had twice before examined and sampled high-grade coal outcropping in thick seams back of Controller bay. He told me that a large tract of land had been staked by an English company in this district and that the quality of the coal was superior to that of any to be found elsewhere on the Pacific Coast. As already said, there was no law providing for the location of coal in Alaska and although the English company at a considerable expense long maintained their operations and possession of their properties, and did considerable development work, yet the lands were taken from them by the United States government. Some years later, in 1909, I learned from M. K. Rodgers, lately deceased, that a number of claims had been located under the law of 1908 by Clarence Cunningham and 32 associates. Rodgers brought samples of this coal to St. Paul and showed them to Mr. Hill and myself. He was then in charge of the construction of a railroad from Katalla to the Kennecott mine for the Guggenheim interests. This railroad was never completed. There was not a good harbor and the winter storms destroyed the breakwaters and harbor improvements, which had been constructed at the cost of more than $1,000,000. Becoming somewhat interested and believing that there was great need for first-class coking-coal on the Pacific Coast, I looked up Mr. Cunningham and investigated the status of his claims. I found that he and his friends had located 33 claims in one group and that their claims had been developed in accordance with the terms of the act of Congress and that they had been approved for patent and the requisite payment, amounting to $52,800, made to the General Land Office, and that these various claims were held by the original locators. Acting under the advice of competent lawyers, I proceeded to acquire some of these claims, before patent, but after the issuance of a receipt from the Commissioner of the General Land Office. I visited these claims myself in 1910, in company with competent geologists and coal-mining engineers, notably, Frank C. Greene, of Cleveland, and my brother Prof. A. N. Winchell of the University of Wisconsin. On the way to Alaska we were shipwrecked in the middle of the night and our vessel, the 'Ohio', went to the bottom with all our equipment. This made it necessary for us to return to Seattle in order to procure new supplies, instruments, and other outfit, so that our examination of the properties was delayed. This was not the first time that Mr. Cunningham, in attempting to acquire and develop in Alaska an important industrial product for the Pacific Coast, had been shipwrecked. The property was difficult of access and the hardships he underwent and the undoubted good faith he displayed in that entire unfortunate affair deserved a better fate than was accorded to him by the conservation-mad administration at Washington. The action of the Government in confiscating these claims, and in retaining the money paid for them, is to my mind one of the black spots on our national escutcheon and comparable only to similar happenings which have come under my own observation in Russia and the Argentine. In spite of the fact that the special Commissioner appointed to look into the charges against these Cunningham locators found nothing whatever against their integrity or honesty, and in spite of the fact that two subsequent Commissioners recommended the issuance of patents, still under the slanders and foul insinuations of Gifford Pinchot and one Glavis, the Secretary of the Interior arbitrarily cancelled these claims, blackening the reputation of the good citizens who had located them in pursuance of the invitation contained in an act of Congress, after subjecting them to great expense in sending attorneys to all parts of the world—London, Rome, and Paris—to take the testimony of every living locator, and even kept the money that had been paid the United States government for them. This was followed by an ingenious act of Congress withholding from patent forever the coal-lands of Alaska and setting aside as a reserve for naval purposes these particular Cunningham claims, thus making it impossible for the claimants ever to get into Court and have their rights vindicated.

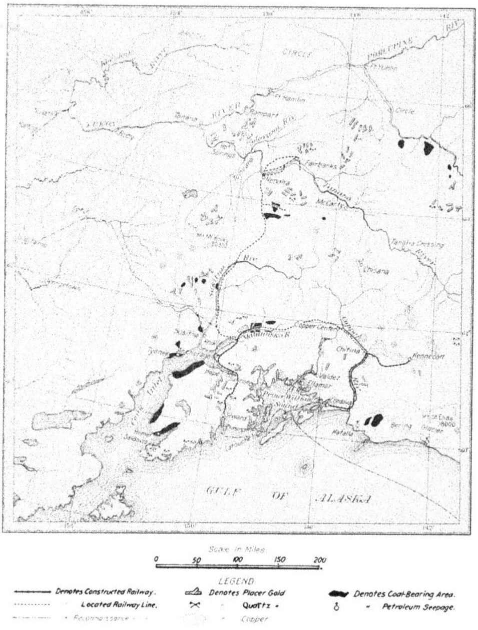

MAP OF PART OF ALASKA SHOWING COALFIELDS

So you devoted a good many years to this bitter controversy and to your attempt to obtain justice?

Yes, it was somewhat difficult for a time for me to feel the deep sense of pride and warm patriotism which should be in the heart of every American. It was a bitter pill to me.

When did you go to the Argentine?

In 1912 I made the acquaintance in England of a prominent Argentino, Dr. Julio Pueyrredon, the brother of the present Minister for Foreign Affairs in that country, who handed the notorious Dr. Luxburg of 'spurlos versenkt' fame his walking-papers. By Señor Julio Pueyrredon I was invited to go to the Argentine and acquire petroleum lands in Patagonia, near the port of Comodoro Rivadavia. This oilfield is the most important in the Argentine; it was discovered by the Bureau of Geology and Hydrography while sinking an artesian well on a desert coast for water. The oil is not of high grade but it is of considerable value in the absence of coal mines. The land was located under the Argentine mining law and the title was supposed to be good. I went down there early in 1913; I found an interesting district and had a pleasant excursion. Before I left the property, however, the President of the Argentine Republic, imitating the action of the United States in a similar case already referred to, issued an order cancelling all the locations, creating a Government reserve 40 miles square, and instructing the Administrator of Public Works to proceed to develop the land by drilling wells, to make harbor improvements, and to build an oil-refinery. When I returned to Buenos Ayres and expressed my willingness to complete the purchase of these properties, I found that title could not be obtained. I was told that the Argentine law specifically forbade the Government to engage in any mining operations, which appeared to be true, as I discovered by translating into English the entire Codigo Mineria, which manuscript I still possess; and although I was further advised that the President had no authority to cancel the locations made validly under the law, nevertheless these locations were cancelled and I am informed that the Government controls the entire oilfield today. Such arbitrary acts are not only manifestly unjust, but so weaken the confidence of those having money to invest in the development of mines that in many cases important mineral districts remain idle and unproductive. What a boon it would now be to our country if Alaska were producing several thousand tons of coal per day! It is there in abundance, safely 'conservated' for future generations instead of being developed and used at a most critical period.

You have been in Russia recently, Mr. Winchell, and you have formed some idea of the present condition of the country, particularly with regard to participation of America in the exploitation of mineral deposits in Siberia?

I spent six months in Russia in 1917. During a portion of this time I was accompanied by Messrs. Charles Janin and Ira B. Joralemon. We arrived in Petrograd the Sunday following the revolution, and found the people of that metropolis in a strangely exalted and ecstatic frame of mind. Although sub-zero weather prevailed the people were parading the streets in groups discussing the form of government which they intended to establish. The poor misguided uninformed people had an idea that the millenium had arrived and that they were thenceforth, without delay and without undergoing any period of adjustment or reconstruction, to live in idleness and luxury. Having no idea of the problems of government nor of the organization needed in carrying on the business of the nation, they looked upon themselves as the most wonderful creators of new schemes of existence that the world had ever seen. It was perfectly apparent that disappointments and trouble were in store and that idleness such as they evidently contemplated could lead to nothing but misery.

H. V. WINCHELL, ON HIS RANCH AT GRASS VALLEY. ESTIMATING THE SEASON'S GROWTH.

The resources of Russia and Siberia are so varied and so vast that it is impossible within the limits of this interview to enter into any discussion of them. In many lines there should be opportunity for development: forestry, agriculture, mining, and manufacturing may be successfully developed and there will some day certainly be an opportunity for the business men and the engineers of the United States to play an active part in the work. I fear, however, that the Russian people have not yet seen the bottom of the grade. They are rapidly sliding downhill into a condition of anarchy and degradation which has already and will still cause the loss of many lives and the destruction of a great deal of property. It is too soon to expect the establishment of a stable government and the restoration of conditions under which the investment of foreign capital and resumption of commerce and industry will be possible. I have constantly since my return endeavored to impress upon the people of the United States a feeling of their moral responsibility toward Russia. It seems incredible that this great nation could so long stand aside and refrain from assisting the better elements of Russia in their program of rehabilitation. Without our assistance it must be years before Russia is again habitable in the modern way; with it, and the co-operation of the Allies in this present war, stable conditions may be restored rapidly. At the present time there is no safety for life or property and titles are insecure. It is my belief that there will naturally be a certain amount of disintegration, but that there will eventually emerge a Russian nation whose system of political economy will incorporate many advanced socialistic ideas, some of which may perhaps be an improvement upon anything the world has heretofore known.

You have taken a leading part in arousing public interest in the defects of our mining laws, particularly those based upon the so-called law of the apex. Will you please state definitely your attitude in the matter?

An overwhelming majority of the mining men of the United States are opposed to our present Federal Mining Law. It is only here and there that some theoretical and ultra-conservative student of the subject expresses himself as in favor of the retention of the law of the apex. This unfortunate provision of our laws is a constant source of expensive litigation and is a handicap to the mining industry.

There are several other features of the present laws that do not adequately protect the prospector in searching for and developing our mineral resources. There is no provision under our present system for opening to exploration by the public at large those vast tracts of land which have passed out of the Government ownershp into the hands of private individuals. Most countries have retained some jurisdiction over their mineral resources and make it possible for the prospector to enter upon any lands, whether owned by the government or by individuals, under provisions which safeguard the rights of the individual owner, and to sink shafts, drive tunnels, or explore by drilling for underground orebodies. The time is approaching when all the public domain will have passed into the hands of private owners, and in many cases these lands will thus be not only withdrawn from the field of the prospector, but foreclosed against his operations by the unwillingness of the private owner to permit mining and prospecting work. The inevitable result will be a decline in the mining industry. It is well known to all of us that mines do not live forever. As you, Mr. Rickard, have well said, "even Methuselah died"; and the production of ores in such an active country as the United States can only be maintained over long periods by the discovery of new mines. For this reason I have advocated the incorporation of some provision in our statutes providing for the development of mines upon all lands sold by the Government to private individuals. I believe it may even be necessary, in view of the court decisions upon this matter, for us some day to adopt an amendment to the National Constitution declaring the mining industry paramount and making it possible for mines to be developed wherever they may be found, regardless of the wishes of the owner of the surface, but at the same time making a suitable provision for recompensing him for surface ground actually occupied and for damage to crops and improvements.

Do you think that there is any prospect of amending the mining laws in the near future?

There is not only a prospect that the laws will be amended, but they are actually being amended and not always under the advice of competent and experienced mining men nor in ways best calculated to promote the general interest of the industry and the country at large. There is a great deal of inconsistency in the present laws as applied to the various classes of mineral products, and there is frequently a conflict between the clashing interest of the agriculturist, the stock-grower, the lumberman, and the miner. The subject is one that should be submitted to careful analysis and study by representatives of the interests involved, and the laws should be given a thorough revision so as to make them as simple as possible and at the same time productive of the best results. I see no immediate prospect for such a revision as this. It has been recommended time and again by the Secretaries of the Interior and by Presidents in messages in Congress without eliciting any general response. What is everybody's business is nobody's business, and this subject which affects in many ways every individual in the country is understood by few and neglected by all.

You have taken prominent part in the work of the American Institute of Mining Engineers. I would like to ask you what you consider to be the principal functions of the Institute as an organization of Mining Engineers?

The existence of such an organization rests primarily upon and can only be justified by its usefulness to its members, and the industry which they represent. I should say the underlying concept is that of service; service, first, to its members by furnishing them with some means of becoming acquainted with each other, by giving them in published form the results of the latest discoveries and developments in their chosen field of work, and by providing a forum for the discussion of questions upon which different opinions are entertained; service to the industry at large and to the communities in which such industries are operated; service to the country by increasing its productivity and efficiency and in supplying the minerals needed in commerce, manufacturing, and in all the manifold requirements of an industrial nation.

These are days of organization; of co-operation and of

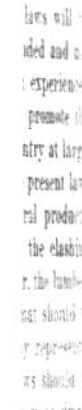

GUANAJUATO, MEXICO

joint effort. No man is sufficient unto himself alone; the best results in all lines are achieved by a combination of minds and of efforts. It is my belief that the attention of the American Institute of Mining Engineers should be directed to every branch of political economy and national life with which the production of minerals and their utilization is even remotely connected. I believe that the engineer in the past has been too secluded; too much engrossed with his own particular and individual problems, and that his services and information have not always been as fully utilized for the general public good as their real importance justifies. Nothing has made this idea more emphatic than the events of the past few years. It should be the effort of every engineer in the period of reconstruction to take an intelligent and active part in the problems which are now arising for solution, recognizing, as he must, the fact that the achievements of

engineers and the production of our mines have made it possible for us to play our part in the world conflict now coming to a close. We must realize further the great field of expansion which lies just ahead. It is a source of pride to every member of the Institute to know that its policy is now so shaped as to enable it to take its part in the work.

The mining industry must and will be expanded. We are on the eve of important developments and are entirely confident in the ability and the intention of the American engineer to take a prominent rôle both at home and abroad.

MAKING A LANDING IN THE ARGENTINE

SPOUTING OIL-WELL IN THE ARGENTINE

Gold Production in the British Dominions

By WILLIAM FRECHEVILLE

*In making a review of the world's gold production during the twenty years from 1897 to 1915, both included (1915 being the last year for which figures are available), it is seen that it has increased from 43 millions sterling in 1897 to 98 millions in 1915. In examining the statistics given annually in the American publication 'Mineral Industry', it is seen, for instance in those given for 1915, that 44 different countries contributed to the world's total, and attention may be drawn to the fact that the large number of different countries contributing to the supply, gives a certain amount of stability to the total output.

The British empire is the largest contributor.

The following details are given in the above statistics for 1915:

Transvaal	£38,679,918
Australasia	9,890,446
Canada	3,896,498
Rhodesia	3,891,770
British India	2,369,670
West Coast of Africa	1,708,580
British Borneo	271,400
British Guiana	215,288
Malay States	72,330
United Kingdom	3,964
Total	£60,999,862

The production of the British empire increased from 26 millions sterling, forming 60½% of the world's production, in 1897, to 61 millions, given in detail above, and forming 62¼% of the total, in 1915.

On looking at the yearly figures during this period in Table A, it is seen that the increase has, on the whole, been gradual and persistent, except during the Transvaal war, when the proportion of the world's production contributed by the British empire fell to 47% in 1901.

This feature of steady increase applies to the world generally, as well as to the British empire; in both cases, although there are decreasing sources of supply, this feature is more than made up by increases in other directions.

In connection with the decreasing sources of supply, it may be pointed out that the constant improvements in method and appliances tend to make the exhaustion of the older districts slower than may be calculated on the data available at any given time, and, on the other hand, the periodical discovery of new districts makes it impossible to forecast with any degree of accuracy what increases the future may have in store.

On looking at the discoveries of new districts made during the last 40 years, it is found that they certainly show a tendency to occur periodically. This is illustrated by the following table of dates:

Pilgrim's Rest, Leydenburg, Transvaal	1873
Indian Gold Mines (Mysore)	1880
Witwatersrand, Transvaal	1886
Western Australia, Kalgoorlie	1893
Klondyke (Yukon), Canada	1897
Porcupine (Ontario), Canada	1909

The periodicity of the discoveries is no doubt due to the gradual extension of the area prospected. Considering the large areas, both in the British empire and in other parts of the world, still to be examined, it is exceedingly unlikely that a line should be drawn now, and that this phase of exploration and discovery can be considered to have ended.

In connection with this aspect of the subject, attention may be drawn to recent reports regarding the Belgian Congo. It has been known for some time that gold existed in the Kilo district, north-west of Lake Albert Nyanza, and shipments of gold have been made from there for some years. Sir Alfred Sharpe traveled through those parts recently, and an interview with him was published in 'The African World' on July 7 of last year, in which he is reported as saying that the discoveries are assuming great importance and give the impression that a large goldfield exists there, which is awaiting development, but that up to the present time it has been the policy of the Belgian government to reserve the deposits, which are both alluvial and reef, as a Government monopoly.

It may be pointed out that in the case of the discovery of payable gold mines in the working of which British companies can take part in regions outside the British empire—particularly if the neighboring country is not in an advanced stage of industrial development—the machinery and stores required by these British companies will, to a great extent, be purchased in the British empire, and the gold they win will be sent there to be realized. On the other hand, in this particular instance one can well understand that there may be, for several reasons, reluctance to admit outside capital or outside white population.

The six principal gold-producing countries in the British empire are the Transvaal, Australasia, Rhodesia, Canada, British India, and the West Coast of Africa, and the figures of yearly production in each of these countries for the 20 years ending with 1915 are given in Table B.

THE TRANSVAAL. The increase from 11½ millions sterling in 1897 to 38½ millions in 1912 was large and continuous if the period of the Transvaal war is omitted.

After 1912 the figures fluctuate somewhat, but show no decided tendency, either upward or downward. The

*Appendix to the Inchcape Commission's Report on the Status of Gold. Owing to the fluctuations in exchange it is impracticable to convert pounds into dollars; it can be done roughly by taking the ratio of 1:5. The current rate is \$4.75 for a pound sterling.

TABLE A.

Year	Gold Production of the world for the 20 years ending 1916 (taken from the American publication "Mineral Industry") dollars being converted into sterling at the rate of £1=$4·86.	Gold Production of the *British Empire* for the 20 years ending 1916.	Per cent. of the total production of the world.
	£	£	
1897	42,934,976	26,011,277	60·6
1898	59,120,953	32,065,913	54·2
1899	64,095,874	38,481,522	60·0
1900	53,257,140	*25,777,743	48·4
1901	53,678,483	25,191,803	46·9
1902	61,484,052	31,642,175	51·4
1903	67,793,292	38,924,444	57·4
1904	71,828,867	41,828,230	58·2
1905	77,862,501	46,829,500	60·1
1906	83,446,712	49,831,584	59·7
1907	85,617,571	50,862,342	59·4
1908	91,225,402	53,613,966	58·8
1909	94,325,938	54,195,034	57·5
1910	93,367,596	53,359,177	57·1
1911	95,544,546	54,651,847	57·2
1912	97,599,256	59,670,024	62·1
1913	95,199,498	59,068,755	62·0
1914	93,760,617	57,407,283	61·2
1915	97,985,185	60,999,862	62·3
1916	96,090,535	—	—

* British occupied Johannesburg June, 1900.

TABLE B.

Yearly gold production of the six principal gold producing regions in the British Empire, for the 20 Years 1897–1916.

Year.	Transvaal.	Australasia.	Canada.	Rhodesia.	India.	West Coast of Africa.
	£	£	£	£	£	£
1897	11,653,725	10,800,674	1,240,127	—	1,501,966	205,690
1898	16,240,630	12,817,794	2,818,930	89,235	1,597,903	148,199
1899	15,452,025	16,204,809	4,331,220	231,928	1,943,750	144,512
1900	1,481,412	15,176,198	5,742,418	337,500	2,180,577	154,321
1901	1,096,051	15,879,479	5,033,379	632,661	1,938,859	127,593
1902	7,304,501	16,569,612	4,390,261	735,354	1,992,551	82,305
1903	12,628,057	18,355,296	3,877,282	858,953	2,305,988	300,961
1904	16,028,883	17,950,959	3,374,485	991,815	2,369,000	403,256
1905	20,854,440	17,689,461	2,980,830	1,482,277	2,453,561	705,319
1906	24,606,336	16,946,133	2,474,060	1,985,099	2,233,034	818,202
1907	27,400,992	15,606,862	1,724,852	2,178,886	2,126,756	1,154,679
1908	29,973,115	15,085,323	2,025,124	2,526,006	2,204,596	1,182,474
1909	30,987,650	14,605,516	1,930,500	2,651,323	2,444,742	918,610
1910	31,973,123	13,218,869	2,099,966	2,568,201	2,202,827	755,985
1911	35,041,485	12,000,570	2,012,567	2,672,791	2,242,748	1,071,613
1912	38,711,581	11,212,428	2,602,633	2,710,712	2,274,611	1,451,747
1913	37,372,949	10,860,396	3,415,416	2,934,433	2,294,745	1,636,718
1914	35,656,814	10,270,645	3,288,685	3,584,997	2,341,242	1,729,354
1915	38,628,437	9,890,146	3,896,496	3,891,770	2,369,672	1,708,580
1916	39,489,522	8,311,255	3,912,798	3,891,358	2,294,856	1,617,466

TABLE C.

WITWATERSRAND GOLD MINES.

ESTIMATE OF FUTURE DECREASES IN OUTPUT.

Closing down.			Opening up or Increasing.			Date.	Increase or Decrease.	Running Increase or Decrease on Annual Tonnage.
Date.	Annual Tons.	Running Tons.	Date.	Annual Tonnage.	Running Tonnage.			
1918 ...	410,000	410,000	1918 ...	620,000	620,000	1918 ...	+ 210,000	+ 210,000
1919 ...	1,570,000	1,980,000				1919 ...	— 1,570,000	— 1,360,000
1920 ...	2,020,000	4,000,000				1920 ...	— 2,020,000	— 3,380,000
1921 ...	650,000	4,650,000	1921 ...	130,000	750,000	1921 ...	— 520,000	— 3,900,000
1922 ...	1,100,000	5,750,000	1922 ...	1,850,000	2,600,000	1922 ...	+ 750,000	— 3,150,000
1923 ...	420,000	6,170,000	1923 ...	720,000	3,320,000	1923 ...	+ 300,000	— 2,850,000
1924 ...	1,280,000	7,450,000	1924 ...	1,440,000	4,760,000	1924 ...	+ 160,000	— 2,690,000
1925 ...	1,020,000	8,470,000				1925 ...	— 1,020,000	— 3,710,000
1926 ...	1,100,000	9,570,000	1926 ...	1,400,000	6,160,000	1926 ...	+ 300,000	— 3,410,000
1927 ...	680,000	10,250,000				1927 ...	— 680,000	— 4,090,000
1928 ...	780,000	11,030,000	1928 ...	360,000	6,520,000	1928 ...	— 420,000	— 4,510,000
1929 ...	360,000	11,390,000	1929 ...	360,000	6,880,000	1929 ...	——	— 4,510,000
1930 ...	520,000	11,910,000	1930 ...	500,000	7,380,000	1930 ...	— 20,000	— 4,530,000
1933 ...	450,000	12,360,000	1933 ...	450 000	7,830,000	1933 ...	——	— 4,530,000
								Decreasing rapidly thereafter (probably at the rate of 1,000,000 tons or over p.a., for several years).

Notes:—1. Where possible the estimates are based on official estimates of life and dates of commencement of milling.
2. Estimates are based on pre-war conditions. If costs continue at present level the rate of decrease will be *much more rapid*.
3. The estimates of new mines opening up (exclusively Far East Rand Mines) are, in my opinion, on the liberal side.
4. Far East Rand Mines lying outside the Central Zone are excluded.

general consensus of opinion appears to be that on the basis of present conditions, production has about reached its zenith, and from now on a gradual falling off may be anticipated. It is true large new areas in the far Eastern Rand are being developed and equipped, but the new production from this source, on the basis of what is at present known, is not expected to make good the deficiencies caused by old mines closing down.

In order to throw some further light on this subject, I have had a statement prepared, dealing with the next 10 or 12 years (see Table C). This statement is in the nature of an account in which the new tonnage to be crushed is taken on one side, and the probable loss of tonnage due to mines closing down, on the other, and the balance is shown in the last column. From this table it appears that on balance a reduction of over one million tons is indicated in 1919, equivalent to 27s. per ton to £1,350,000. The loss of tonnage rising to over three million tons in 1920, and that then for the following 7 years the further anticipated losses and gains very nearly neutralize each other, but that after that further reduction is indicated.

This estimate, however, must be taken for what it is, namely, an attempt to get some approximate figures based on what is known. The problem is complicated by the fact that the ore for the new stamps in the Far Eastern Rand is likely to be somewhat better than that at the old mines closing down; also by the fact that experience in the past shows that the operation of actually exhausting one of the old mines generally takes longer than originally anticipated, and further, by the uncertainty as to possible extensions of the ore-bearing beds beyond their present known limits. It will be noticed that all these factors operate against the calculated fall of production.

AUSTRALASIA. During the first part of the period of 20 years under review, the production increased from about 11 millions sterling in 1897 to at little over 18 millions in 1903, owing to the growing output of Western Australia. After 1903, however, there was a steady decline, and in 1916 the output of gold had shrunk to 8¾ millions sterling.

The present indications are that this decline will continue, unless new goldfields are opened out, of which there are as yet no indications. An examination of a map of Australia on which the goldfields are marked, will, however, I think, justify a hopeful view with regard to the future. It will be seen that the goldfields are fairly well scattered over the known coastal regions, and the idea appears to be justified that probably when the central and northern parts have been traveled over, and properly prospected, other goldfields will be found.

CANADA. The gold production amounted to 1¼ million sterling, in 1897, and increased to 5¾ millions in 1900, owing to the yield of the Yukon. These deposits, however, proved to be only alluvial, and a falling off soon took place, and in consequence, the gold production of Canada declined to 2 millions sterling in 1909. In that year two or three rich quartz veins were discovered at Porcupine in the northern part of the province of Ontario, and since then the yield of Canada has again taken an upward turn, and in 1916 amounted to 4 millions sterling. Since then the production of these mines has been seriously curtailed, owing to scarcity of labor, but the position of the gold-mining industry of Canada points to an expansion in the future. It is true the production of the Yukon is likely to continue to decrease, but this should be more than counterbalanced by the position in northern Ontario, where the older mines are in a sound position, and small new producers are being discovered from time to time. An important factor in the future possibilities of Canada, as a gold-producing country, lies in the large expanse of unexplored country, which stretches up north from the comparatively narrow occupied belt extending from the Atlantic to the Pacific.

RHODESIA. The production shows a gradual and continuous increase from nothing in 1897, to just under 4 millions sterling in 1916. The gold derived from a number of quartz mines, worked on modern lines, with considerable reserves of ore, and although one or two mines are known to be failing, there is no reason to apprehend any sudden change.

INDIA. The principal producers are the quartz mines in Mysore, which have been very considerable and consistent producers for the last 30 years, worked on sound lines, with good reserves of ore opened out ahead of immediate requirements, and nothing is known to indicate any considerable change in the position, or of any distinct signs of failing. On the other hand, they are becoming very deep, and in the ordinary course of events, a falling off in production would seem to be probable in the not far distant future, unless new mines are opened up. So far there are no reports or suggestions of new gold discoveries in India, but some of the country north of it has been reported by travelers to be gold-bearing.

WEST COAST OF AFRICA. The production has increased slowly from £200,000 in 1897 to a little over £1,500,000 in 1916. No doubt, if it were not for the climate, the production would have been much greater. Nothing is generally known to indicate that any serious falling off is looming ahead. The climate, as already remarked, has been the great drawback to the industry.

GENERAL CONCLUSIONS. Assuming that gold mines will soon be able to work again under normal conditions, and that the effect of the War will be limited to an increase of working costs in some cases of as much as two shillings per ton, it does not appear to me likely that such a rise would have a serious effect on the production of gold.

On the above assumption that the industry will go on in its normal course, and in the light of what is known about the principal gold-producing districts of the Empire, it appears that a falling off may be expected in the Transvaal, and in Australasia, but an increase in Canada, and that there is no very plain indication as to the probable course of events in other directions.

Setting the probable increase in Canada against the decrease in Australasia, there remains the anticipated falling off in the Transvaal and a consequent probable decrease of about 4 millions sterling annually in the total gold production of the Empire in the near future.

Against this must be set the possibility of unexpected increases and of new discoveries—two factors of such an uncertain nature that it would be idle to attempt to appraise them accurately.

There is so much unprospected territory in the Empire that, personally, I look forward to further discoveries, sooner or later, with a good deal of confidence.

BOARDING-HOUSES operated by mining companies are often operated at a loss, due to a low charge made for food, also to certain fixed charges. In isolated districts a company house is of great benefit to employees, they responding by being more content and giving better efficiency. The Alaska Treadwell group boarding-house generally ran at a loss. A recent instance is that of the Snowstorm Mines Consolidated at Troy, Montana, where during 1918 the house loss was $4868. Company stores are also a great convenience, both to employees and the public.

Graphics of Gold and Silver

By M. W. von BERNEWITZ

Amid the instructive matter that we published last year on the precious metals, many calculations and tables were given, yet, with the exception of H. N. Lawrie, the graphic method was not used. To make up for the lack of such records I have prepared the accompanying graphs.

A table of yearly outputs leaves much to be considered, but a chart showing causes and effects of certain movements briefly explained thereon makes the problem easier understood. While preparing these curves, it was quite interesting to note that frequently when one country had reached the apex of production and declined rapidly, another country took up the running, as it were. I have followed the progress of gold and silver for 25 years, and hope that some fresh causes will soon arise to move the curves diagonally upward.

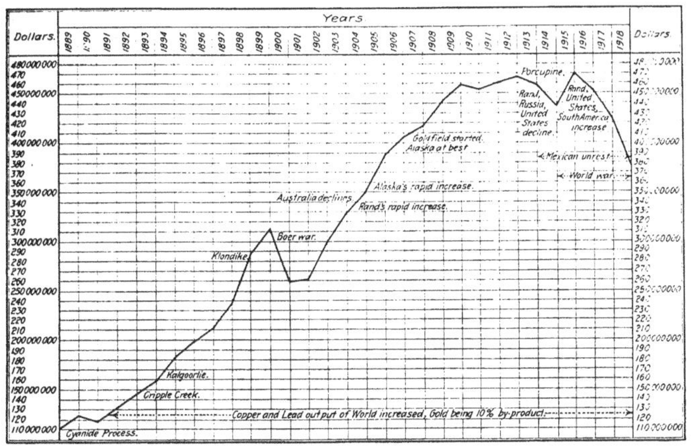

Graph Showing Gold Production of World For 30 Years.

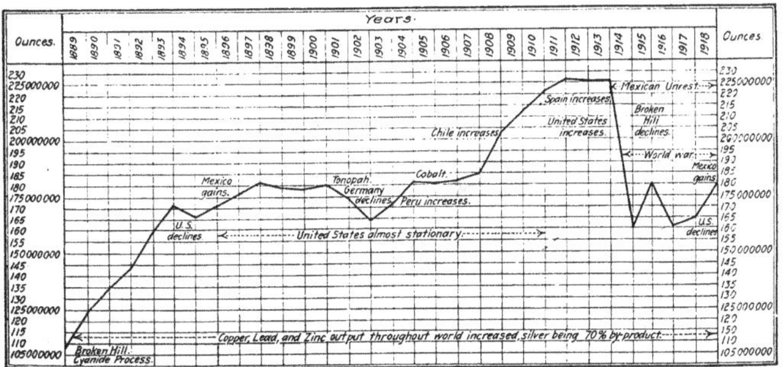

Graph Showing Silver Production of World For 30 Years.

Staff of the War Minerals Investigation Committee, U. S. Bureau of Mines

Reading from left to right:

A. G. White—In charge of the sulphur resources, also administrative assistant to the executive of the War Minerals Investigation; mine economist for the Bureau of Mines; secretary of War Minerals Committee.

J. E. McGuire—In charge of the War Minerals Investigations of chrome and tungsten.

J. C. Orchard—Assistant mine economist for the Bureau of Mines. In charge of the editing and publication of a series of confidential reports on the political and commercial control of the world's mineral resources.

W. C. Phalen—Mineral technologist for the Bureau of Mines; field-work on manganese for the War Minerals Investigations.

G. J. Salmon—In charge of labor problems connected with the metal and non-metalliferous mining industry; member of committee on mechanical labor-saving devices as applied to mining. Also in charge of matters related to industrial furlough from the Army in co-operation with the War Department.

A. W. Stockett—In charge of the War Minerals Investigations for potash resources. Also a member of the committee of the Bureau of Mines appointed to advise the Capital Issues Committee on mining and related applications.

J. E. Spurr—Executive of the War Minerals Investigations of the Bureau of Mines. Formerly a member of committee on Mineral Imports of the Shipping Board.

H. S. Mudd—In charge of the War Minerals Investigation of graphite, antimony, and bismuth; assistant-secretary to the War Minerals Committee; member of the committee of the Bureau of Mines appointed to advise the Capital Issues Committee on mining and related applications; representative of the Bureau on Joint Information Board for minerals and derivatives.

A. E. Wells—In charge of sulphuric acid works for the Bureau of Mines in co-operation with the War Industries Board and the Chemical Alliance.

H. C. Morris—In charge of the War Minerals Investigations of various metals, and member of the committee to advise the Capital Issues Committee on mining.

C. M. Weld—In charge of War Minerals Investigation of manganese, iron ore, ferro-silicon, and later chrome; representative of Bureau of Mines on ferrous section of the War Industries Board; now assistant-executive of the Minerals Investigation.

F. H. Probert—Engaged in special field-work for the War Minerals Investigations; dean of the Mining Department of the University of California; consulting engineer to the Bureau of Mines.

H. A. Buehler—In charge of the War Minerals Investigations of pyrite; also State Geologist of Missouri.

HOUGHTON, MICHIGAN

Stocks of Copper at Smelters Growing.

Accumulations of copper at Michigan smelting plants are commencing to attract attention. Stocks of finished copper on hand here are smaller than normal for February. Up to the year 1915 it was the custom for the smelters to store metal in January, and continue to pile it up until the opening of navigation, in April or May. The question of freight charges from Michigan to New York cut such an important figure in the total cost of production that the difference between the cost of freight by rail and by water was a factor that had always to be reckoned with. However, when the war demands sent the selling price of copper above 20 cents, shipments by rail to New York became common. In fact, the demand for the metal was so urgent that express shipments were made frequently in order to facilitate transportation to catch certain fast boats crossing the Atlantic. For the past four winters, then, there has been no smelter accumulation of copper and the output has been forwarded, either to war munition plants operating in this country or to the order of war departments of foreign governments at New York. Now that the copper stocks are coming in evidence again they are attracting a good deal of attention, producing as they do concrete and positive evidence of the unsatisfactory condition of the metal market as a whole.

CRIPPLE CREEK, COLORADO

Gold Output, Dividends, and General Development.

Gold production of the district in January was again below normal. The treatment plants reported 82,510 tons, worth $735,151 gross. The average value of all grades treated was low, $8.90 per ton. Compared with the December output, a decrease is shown of 4650 tons and $80,870.

The reported outputs were as under:

Works	Tons	Average value
Golden Cycle	25,500	$8.90
Portland	39,010	2.07
Vindicator	16,000	2.15
Smelters	2,000	55.00

Dividends paid during January totaled $242,000, as follows: Portland, $60,000; Vindicator, $15,000; Golden Cycle, $45,000; and Cresson, $122,000.

Another rich discovery has been made at the Roosevelt tunnel-level at a depth of 2131 ft. on No. 5 Lee vein of the Portland company. Commenting on the discovery, Irving Howbert, chairman of the Portland directors, said: "Some of the ore is as good as anything I ever saw come out of the mine. The sylvanite is sprinkled all through the rock instead of the seams as usually occurs."

Development on an extensive scale is projected by the Granite company for its Battle mountain properties. A large quantity of ore is reported available. Work will be started at the Dillon shaft, now 1500 ft. deep.

Work was resumed during the week last past by the Midget company's lessee, the Backoff Leasing Co. of St. Louis. Nine sets of lessees who were with the company when the mine was closed in December 1917 have resumed work on their respective blocks.

A promising discovery has been made by J. L. Wilson in the Anaconda tunnel penetrating Gold hill from the south. He has opened an orebody on the junction of the Virginia M and Work veins at a short distance from the portal of the tunnel and will shortly commence production.

The Vindicator Consolidated, in a letter to shareholders accompanying dividend checks of January 25, announced the resumption of development on its Bull Hill estate.

DENVER, COLORADO

Mining Situation in the State.—Good Ore at Depth at Cripple Creek.—Labor and Wages.—A Mining Survey for the State.—Wyoming Copper and Boulder County Oil.

In Denver one hears contradictory prophecies regarding the metal-mining outlook in Colorado; some persons express pessimistic opinions, but the majority of mining men speak hopefully. There is unanimity, however, in one attitude of metal miners who feel that they would discontinue operations for most of the metals if obliged to face the conditions that prevailed during the past two years. The statement made by the U. S. Geological Survey to the effect that the 1919 output of gold in this State was the least in 20 years, while that of silver was the smallest since 1913, fixes in one's mind the status of these metals. Colorado, the 'silver State', stands fifth in silver production, although occupying second place in the yield of gold. Leadville had a disappointing year in many ways. The districts decreased output of gold, silver, copper, and zinc ore was, to some measure, compensated by increases in manganese and pyrite. That centre endeavors, with more or less right, to claim the molybdenite deposits at Climax on the crest of the Continental Range a few miles north of Leadville, coming forward in 1918 with a large production. Boulder county suffered from the set-back given tungsten; so, while

SOURCE OF WATER SUPPLY OF COLORADO POWER CO. AT NEDERLAND. THE GENERATING PLANT FURNISHES POWER TO MINES IN BOULDER COUNTY AND TO DENVER.

the market for this product was low, miners turned their attention to the districts in which silver had proved attractive in former years, with the result that several encouraging discoveries of this metal were made in the county.

The persistence of good ore at depth is proved in all cases of deep exploitation within the Cripple Creek district. The latest proof of such is on the 21st level of the Portland mine, in the Lee claim. Here, a bulk sample taken across 5-ft. vein, assayed 14 oz. gold per ton. In this instance it was found that, on screening the same ore, the fine carried much less than the crude, or a little better than 4 oz. gold per ton. The present condition of this district warrants optimism.

Speaking of labor conditions, the public was, early in January, informed by the press that the Colorado Fuel & Iron Co., one of the largest employers in this State, would immediately reduce wages because the War is over. J. F. Welborn, president of the company, has announced that no reduction in wages has been contemplated, that his company hopes wages will remain at their present level and that, if there is a general tendency to lower wages in the country, this company will not act in such a reduction without a conference with its employees' representatives.

Feeling that the metal-mining industry of Colorado has not been receiving the support it deserves from the State as a whole, the Colorado Metal Mining Association and the Colorado Chapter of the American Mining Congress are endeavoring to stimulate more interest therein by a bill introduced in both houses of the Legislature calling for the creation of a mining survey. For years past it seems that the agricultural and manufacturing interests of the State have dominated in the passage of legislative acts, and have been awarded an undue amount of State support, at the neglect of the primary industry of Colorado. If these new bills become law we shall have a metal-mining survey organized, this to be in charge of a commission of men directly interested in mining, but who will serve without compensation. It is provided that no appropriations will be required from the treasury, but that the survey will be maintained by the levy of a tax (one-half of 1% has been proposed) on the gross proceeds of all metalliferous ores mined, this tax to be collected by county commissioners and turned over by them to the Treasurer who will act simply as agent or custodian of the funds. The income from such a tax will be bountiful, and will be utilized to make "investigations regarding the prospecting for, mining, production, transportation, buying, selling and treatment or reduction of metalliferous ores as well as economic conditions relating thereto. * * * The directors shall have power and authority to examine all books and records of all producers, dealers or ore-purchasing agencies insofar as they relate to production, sale, transfer or purchase of ore."

In the 'Press' of January 4, a brief history of great things projected years ago in the Encampment region of southern Wyoming was published. It is rumored here that the publicity given by this description is responsible for an effort being made to secure from bondholders the assets of the several related defunct companies by Denver interests that propose either to junk the numerous plants, aerial tram, and town, or to rehabilitate the projects and place them in operation. [Details were given in our issue of February 1. —Editor.]

Right on the heels of disheartening news that two large oil companies had drilled deep holes at Boulder, and had pulled up their outfits with a view of permanent abandonment of the field, comes the news that two other large companies are moving rigs into a wildcat region in T. 11 N., R. 69 W., which is close to the Wyoming line in Larimer county, where geologists have outlined a well-defined structure in which oil may exist at a depth of from 1200 to 1400 ft. Maybe we shall yet discover another oilfield in Colorado.

COBALT, ONTARIO

Developments in the Silver Mines.

The most important development at Cobalt for some time has been the opening of a new and rich vein recently discovered on the 200-ft. level of the Crown Reserve. For 100 ft. it maintains an average width of 3 in. and carries 3000 oz. per ton. A large quantity has been sacked.

The McKinley-Darragh continues to produce sufficient silver to maintain the quarterly dividend of 3%. At the flotation mill, which is closed for the winter, better equipment is being erected.

At the Adanac, high-grade ore is being broken in a raise driven above the 310-ft. level. The mineralized section of the vein is 2 ft. wide.

In the Nipissing, a new stope, which will have a length of 125 ft., is being started on a vein on the 4th level near 98 shaft. On January 2 the company had cash assets totaling $3,898,711. Cash amounted to $2,545,063.

The annual report of the Coniagas for the year ended October 31 shows an output of 974,264 oz. of silver, compared with 1,344,267 oz. during the preceding year. The combined sales of ore and profits of the Reduction company aggregated $4,099,490, against $4,256,597 in 1917. The profits were $470,164. The president, R. W. Leonard, reports that the future output depends more than ever on the low-grade ore concentrated in the mill, and estimates that a three years' supply of this will be available.

The Temiskaming was obliged to lay-off a large number of men owing to a shortage in the power supply. This also affected some other mines at which large auxiliary compressor plants were put in operation.

At the Violet property of La Rose Consolidated an orebody opened at the 470-ft. level shows considerable enrichment over the silver content at the 370-ft. level.

At Gowganda a cobalt-diabase vein with good silver content has been cut on the 350-ft. level of the Castle mine, which is under option to the Trethewey of Cobalt.

Gowganda.—Companies operating in this silver district want transportation facilities improved. A railway from Elk Lake would solve the problem and reduce charges. Coal sells at $14 per ton at rail, but when hauled to Gowganda the price is $44. If nothing is done, then only the richest ore can be shipped, thus retarding development.

LEADVILLE, COLORADO

Notes on the Carbonate of Zinc Ores.

The oxidized zinc ores of Leadville are discussed by G. F. Loughlin in Bulletin 681 of the U. S. Geological Survey. The discovery of these deposits in 1910 and the reason why they had been overlooked so long is covered in the introduction. Most of this ore has come from a body in Carbonate hill, extending through claims controlled by the Western Mining Co. and a few adjoining claims. From 1910 to 1916, inclusive, there was mined a total of 651,492 tons of oxide and 840,243 tons of sulphide ores, carrying much the same percentage of zinc, say from 21 to 31%. The mineralogy and occurrence is then fully discussed, concluding with a note on prospecting. The area covered by the numerous and extensive oxidized lead-silver stopes in the district, extending from the western edge of the Down Town section eastward to Ball mountain, and from Fryer hill southward to Rock hill, is legitimate prospecting ground for oxidized zinc ores; but it remains for those most familiar with the details of individual mines or claims to formulate the best methods of prospecting. Furthermore, especially where ground has been abandoned for a long time and detailed knowledge of it is slight, prospectors should be ever on the lookout for new and unexpected evidence, and should modify their methods accordingly.

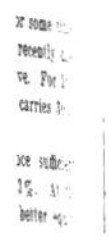

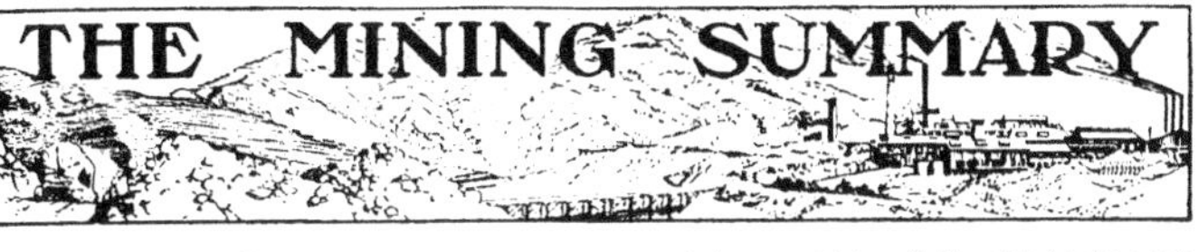

ALASKA

Anchorage.—On February 8, the Secretary of the Interior at Washington asked Congress for $13,800,000 to complete the Government railroad. It will take three years to complete the line, according to the Alaskan Engineering Commission. The total cost will be $44,800,000, instead of the original estimate of $35,000,000. At present there is plenty of labor and rails available. The chairman of the Commission, W. C. Edes, states that it is desirable that the line be completed as early as possible. Agriculture and mining in the Tanana and Yukon valleys will be greatly stimulated and the settlement of the country advanced. The prospector will be afforded easier access to the great undeveloped country in the Broad Pass and adjacent regions. Access to Mt. McKinley National Park will be easy. The through freight and passenger travel from Seward to the interior will undoubtedly be one of the main sources of revenue to the railroad. The great interior of Alaska, which has produced so much gold and minerals in the past, and which will undoubtedly produce much more in the future when the working expenses are reduced, is entitled to cheaper and more reliable transportation, and the completion of the railroad will afford this according to Mr. Edes.

Juneau.—Alaska Gastineau in January treated 151,515 tons of 78.7-cent ore. The recovery was 76.87%, leaving 18.2 cents in the tailing. In December the output was 117,310 tons of 98.3-cent ore.

ARIZONA

Douglas.—Copper output of the Phelps Dodge properties in January totaled 11,818,733 lb. A year ago it was 21,766,836 pounds.

Globe.—The Cole-Goodwin mine near here, formerly operated by the Cole Development Co., and recently examined by G. M. Butler, dean of the College of Mines at Tucson, is being equipped for extensive development of the large bodies of low-grade copper ores disclosed.

Humboldt.—The Consolidated Arizona Smelting Co. has started to reduce its force at the Humboldt plant. The Blue Bell and DeSoto mines are not affected so far.

Jerome.—United Verde Copper Co. paid a dividend of $1.50 per share, equal to $450,000, last week. This is the first distribution since July 1918.

Following the reduction of wages in this centre a general strike has been started.

Miami.—Copper output of the Miami Copper Co. in January was 5,273,260 lb., an increase of nearly 300,000 lb. over December. This company, with the Inspiration Consolidated, have reduced wages from $5.90 to $5.15 per day, based on 20-cent copper. If the price is 18 cents, wages will be lowered to the minimum of $4.90. The Old Dominion company at Globe has acted similarly.

Ray.—Copper output of Ray Consolidated in January was 4,470,000 lb., a decrease of 1,330,000 pounds.

Superior.—The Silver King is to start sinking a 1000-ft. shaft as soon as machinery can be placed and other arrangements made.

Tucson.—A five-year lease and option on the El Tiro mine in the Silver Bell district has been taken by Percy Williams, who has operated it profitably and is forming a leasing company to work it. The property was recently purchased from the receiver by Mr. Williams as trustee for the bondholders. A good part of the funds for this purchase was derived from royalties paid for shipments made during the past year. Approximately $95,000 was received from the Sasco and Hayden smelters for copper ore taken out during development in 1918. As the property is on the railroad and is well equipped, it has been in a position to produce copper at a much lower cost than most other small producers. Mr. Williams' plans for development under the new company include the completion of a haulage tunnel by driving 550 feet.

It is reported that the Twin-Buttes Extension Mining Company is arranging to start extensive drilling of its property, which adjoins the Magnate property in the Twin-Buttes district.

Wickenburg.—The mining and milling machinery of the Alvarado, Congress, and Rincon mills, valued at more than $1,000,000, is being dismantled for auction.

CALIFORNIA

Kennett.—The Mammoth Copper Co. has not yet reduced its output or wages. The general manager, George W. Metcalfe, said last week: "We have not made any move to reduce production, but there is one thing certain: the company is not making money under present conditions. The cost of production is as great as ever. There has been no market since December 6, and on that date copper was selling at 26 cents. I received the first quotation since that date on February 7 in a telegram from New York. The quotation was 18¾ cents. When copper was going up, the company made several advances in wages paid to its employees. The present wage-scale was adjusted on a basis of 30 cents for copper. The company is up against a hard proposition. What will be done I cannot prophesy."

The Shasta King mine, one of the Mammoth's producing properties, will be closed down in a few days. This mine employed 100 men a few months ago, but for the last month employed only thirty.

Oroville.—It is reported here that the north fork of the Feather river is being investigated at Big Bend. This part of the river is 13 miles long, and it is proposed, as has been suggested for years, to divert the river and recover the gold from the bed. Negotiations are to be made with the Great Western Power Co., which controls some of the land there.

Plymouth.—The Plymouth Consolidated during December treated 10,800 tons of ore, yielding gold worth $60,900. Operations cost $37,900, equal to $3.51 per ton. The net profit, after paying for other charges, was $12,900. On the 2450-ft. level the north foot-wall drift is out 389 ft., the last 9 ft. assaying $10.20 per ton across 8 ft. A south drift of east north foot-wall drift assays $4.61 across 4 ft. A raise yields $12 for a width of 7 feet.

Redding.—The deed transferring 107 acres of dredging ground across the river from Redding to the American Gold Dredging Co. was filed for record last week. Mrs. Rhoda B. Menzel received $107,000, or $1000 per acre. The deal was made a year ago, but the final payment has just been made. The company has been operating a boat on the ground for six months.

COLORADO

Cripple Creek.—Cresson Consolidated paid dividend No. 76, of 10 cents per share, equal to $122,000, on February 10. This makes $244,000 for 1919, and $7,353,163 to date.

Telluride.—This district shipped 5250 tons of ore and concentrate during December. Of this, the Tomboy accounted for 1400 tons. A circular issued by the company in London on January 10 states that an oil-flotation plant is to be erected at once, to cost $150,000. It is estimated that at least $1 per ton more can be saved, giving an additional profit of $12,500 per month.

IDAHO

Boise.—In a bill before the Legislature it is proposed to establish a State bureau of mines and geology at the University of Idaho at Moscow. An appropriation of $30,000 is asked, $15,000 for co-operation with the U. S. Bureau of Mines, $10,000 for co-operation in topography and hydrography with the U. S. Geological Survey, and $5000 for an economic and geologic investigation of the mineral resources of the State. F. A. Hanson, dean of the School of Mines at Moscow, has great hopes of the measure passing this session.

The Idaho Mining Association met here on February 11, well representing the mining industry of the State. Some first-aid contests were held, and interesting addresses were read and discussed.

Mullan.—The National Copper company's mill is concentrating 300 tons of ore daily. During January, 13 cars of concentrates was dispatched, assaying 15% copper and 40 oz. silver per ton.

MICHIGAN

Houghton.—The Hancock mine was closed on February 7, letting out 200 men. It costs this company 22 cents per pound to produce copper, which results in a loss at present prices.

The Winona has also suspended operations. About 200 were employed.

MISSOURI

Bonne Terre.—The St. Louis correspondent of 'The American Metal Market' recently wrote as follows: The lead market continues dull and featureless, with offerings light, but the demand is so small that the feeling continues weak. Producers continue to reduce their output, and the Desloge Consolidated Lead Co. is seriously considering the idea of closing down its plants altogether. The labor situation is no longer acute and weather conditions are favorable to a large output of ore, but many mines are closed down, and others are on part time, keeping production low. Some of the producers say that they are running at a loss, but others deny this, and say that they still are able to operate at a profit, although the present profit is small as compared with their war time profits. The movement is light, but is larger than it was a year ago. Receipts of lead at St. Louis last week were 18,760 pigs, compared with 39,010 pigs for the preceding week, and 8740 pigs for the corresponding week last year. Shipments for the week were 43,850 pigs, against 59,200 pigs for the preceding week, and 19,770 pigs a year ago.

The St. Joseph Lead Co., the largest producer in America, has reduced mining and treatment operations to 60% of capacity.

Joplin.—Production of the Tri-State region last week totaled 7839 tons of blende and 995 tons of lead, averaging $41 and $55 per ton, respectively.

It is proposed to organize a community drilling corporation to develop lands in the Webb City-Carterville, Duenweg, Oronogo, and Neck City districts. It is proposed that royalties payable to the land-owners shall be based on mill recovery alone, that is, if 3, 4, 5, or 6% is recovered the royalty will equal those figures.

NO. 3 MILL OF THE ST. JOSEPH LEAD CO., AT ELVINS, MISSOURI

MONTANA

Butte.—Wages at Butte were reduced $1 per shift on February 7. This includes the reduction works at Anaconda and Great Falls. This is the outcome of the conference of Union delegates and the Secretary of Labor at Washington.

Anaconda produced only 15,900,000 lb. of copper in

January, a reduction of six million pounds from December.

On February 7 two mass-meetings called by the I. W. W. were attended by several thousand miners, who adopted prepared resolutions calling for a general strike at Butte. Speakers who addressed the meetings declared that the recently announced wage cut of $1 per day was a challenge to the "workers to start the class war." It was announced that an attempt would be made immediately to close all industries in the city, including restaurants, theatres, stores, and barber shops. Another mass-meeting of miners was called for the 8th. A committee appointed on the previous day drafted demands to be made on the mining companies, and to be presented to the strikers on the following day. While the day shifts showed almost full forces, except at the Elm Orlu mine, where 250 men walked out on the 7th, the evening reports show that 1400 men of the Anaconda alone failed to go underground and several mines are virtually closed. The men who quit work were for the most part Finns. No other properties in the district were affected and all of these mines report normal shifts at work. None of the companies as yet has received demands from trade unions affected by the wage reduction. A few men who gathered at the collar of the Elm Orlu shaft at 8 o'clock on the 8th with the evident intention of working, were jeered by the strikers and not permitted to go on the job. There was no disorder at the mines and no arrests have been made or guards stationed.

By Saturday night there was almost a general strike at Butte. According to a statement from the secretary of the local I. W. W. organization, the demands of the strikers also include a six-hour day with pay at the rate of $1 per hour, and abolition of the rustling card system, and the I. W. W. is in sympathy with the Seattle strike.

The new wage is $4.75 for miners, which is 50 cents above the schedule in existence at Butte for years. Shaft-men are reduced to $5.25, and mechanics to $5.50.

The East Butte company yielded 2,291,950 lb. of copper in January, a gain of 370,000 lb. over December.

Troy.—The Snowstorm Mines Consolidated in 1918 made an operating profit of $129,792 and a net profit of $47,314, after deducting taxes, insurance, boarding-house loss, interest, and exploration. Current assets total $42,562 and liabilities $101,581. The mill dressed 65,342 tons of ore, yielding the following:

Lead concentrate, tons	5,093
Lead content, pounds	5,864,174
Silver, ounces	126,077
Gold, ounces	561
Zinc concentrate, tons	3,644
Zinc, pounds	2,474,969
Lead, pounds	1,196,310
Silver, ounces	38,528

The Snowstorm mill is treating ore at the rate of 6000 tons per month. The new tunnel is in 1200 ft. Plenty of miners are available.

NEVADA

Belmont.—In charge of Jay A. Carpenter, the old Monitor Belmont silver mine is being re-opened for the Nevada Wonder company. Air-lifts and bailers have lowered the water in the workings to 400 ft. below the collar of the vertical shaft. The vein has a dip of 45°, so a large area is opened for exploration. There were no plans of the mine, parts of which have been flooded for 50 years. Drifts are blocked with cave-ins. The old-timers extracted the ore fairly well, but had to leave faces that are ore today. It is hoped that enough ore will be found to justify altering the mill.

Ely.—Nevada Consolidated produced 4,400,000 lb. of copper in December, a drop of 1,400,000 pounds.

Goldfield.—The Goldfield Consolidated Mines Co.'s property has been taken over by lease and purchase by the Goldfield Mining Co., represented by H. G. MacMahon of Goldfield, and San Francisco people. A new system of leasing is to be announced. The new company will operate the surface equipment, pumps, etc.

Rochester.—An agreement to consolidate five of the six principal properties in this district, thus terminating litigation pending and threatening, was signed at Reno on February 3 by L. A. Friedman, H. G. Humphrey, and Joseph Nenzel. The companies to be merged are the Rochester Mines, Rochester Combined Mines, Nenzel Crown Point, Elda Fina, and Rochester Merger. Two of these—the sec-

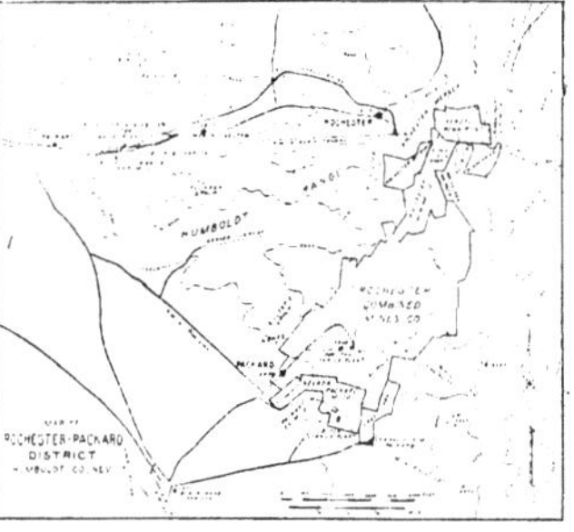

ond and third named—are equipped with modern mills. The combined area measures over two miles in length and a mile in width, containing considerable silver deposits. The respective owners of the companies have been at cross-purposes for the past two or three years. The agreement provides for dismissal of an apex suit and attachment proceedings against the Rochester Mines, for settlement of terms by February 12, and for reorganization by April 15. The new corporation probably will be known as the Rochester Nevada Silver Mining Co. The agreement was signed through the mediating efforts of Frank M. Manson, of the Western Ore Purchasing Co., who, with Judge French of Reno, is named as a trustee to handle the funds of the companies pending reorganization and to pay off an indebtedness of the Rochester Mines Co. amounting to $60,000.

NEW MEXICO

Santa Rita.—Chino Copper produced 4,421,000 lb. in January, a decrease of 1,201,000 pounds.

TEXAS

Austin.—On February 4, Senator R. M. Dudley of El Paso introduced into the Senate a bill providing for a comprehensive mining law designed to encourage the development of mining in the State. The bill pertains exclusively to mining and eliminates oil, coal, and gas, and makes provision for the sale and operation of mineral deposits. It was patterned largely after the Federal mining law, and was drawn up by several mining engineers of west Texas with the co-operation of the Commissioner of the General Land Office.

UTAH

Bingham.—The Utah Metal & Tunnel Co. has issued a circular explaining settlement of the apex dispute with the Utah Consolidated. The former company has the unrestricted right to follow all beddings of fissures that may be found on the western part of the Bingham-New Haven ground downward extra-laterally, in and under the Utah Con. ground without regard to how the apexes of such lime beddings or fissures lie on the Utah Metal. To the east of the Occidental fault, Utah Metal has full mining rights in a strip of ground within the Utah Con., without royalty or any charge, and with privilege of using the workings of Utah Con. in carrying on development and mining. Wherever they appear in this area, Utah Metal transfers to Utah Con. all apex-rights and releases them from any claim for damages that it may have by reason of the Utah Con. extracting ore from the two lime-beddings in the past.

Last week the Utah Consolidated began suit against the Utah-Apex to settle the matter of title to fissure-veins which apex, according to the complaint, in the Keepapitchinin and Rattlesnake claims. The dip of the veins is to the north, passing through the property of the Utah-Apex, adjoining that of the Utah Consolidated. It is alleged in the complaint that by means of tunnels, cross-cuts, and drifts the Utah-Apex has entered the veins at depth and has extracted ore to the approximate value of $500,000 from each of the veins in dispute. It is claimed by the plaintiff that the alleged ownership of the veins by the Utah-Apex is groundless, and casts a cloud on the title claimed by the Utah Consolidated. In addition to asking that the title to the veins in dispute be established by court, the Utah Consolidated asks for an accounting for the ore alleged to have been illegally extracted. Last October the Utah-Apex brought suit against the Utah Consolidated based on the same grounds as the suit filed last week. This suit was finally compromised.

Utah-Apex has laid-off about 300 men, due to the drop in price of lead.

Utah Copper produced only 10,500,000 lb. in January, a falling-off of 3,335,000 lb. On February 6, wages were reduced 75 cents per shift.

The Bingham Mines and Ohio Copper companies have also made a cut in wages.

The Montana-Bingham mine has suspended work until the metal markets are better. C. G. Ballantine is manager.

Tintic.—Twenty-one mines and leases shipped a total of 667 cars of ore during January, an increase of 133 cars over December. The Dragon dispatched 139, Chief Con. 96, Tintic Standard 92, Iron Blossom 53, and Centennial-Eureka 52.

WASHINGTON

Chewelah.—Stevens county is endeavoring to obtain an appropriation of $150,000 from the Legislature to improve roads into the mining regions. The Columbia section of the A. I. M. E. is backing the request.

The United Copper mine is estimated to contain 123,700 tons of ore below the 1000-ft. level, all of which was developed during 1918. The assay is 1.6% copper and 4.35 oz. silver per ton. Silver increases with depth. It is intended to sink the shaft 700 ft. to the 2000-ft. level.

Leadpoint.—The Electric Point Mining Co. in 1918 shipped 146 cars of ore to Trail, B. C., and 70 cars to Northport. This is a lead-carbonate ore. The income was $242,538, expenses $272,704, and net loss $25,917. Dividends amounted to $87,312. Current assets total $173,541, of which half is cash.

Republic.—The Knob Hill company made a loss of $9216 during 1918. Ore shipments realized $33,933. January shipments were 9 cars of 40 tons each.

CANADA

British Columbia

Silverton.—The superintendent of the Silver-Standard mine, W. G. Norrie-Lowenthal, in announcing the temporary shutting-down of the mine, says: "Our reason for closing

THE UTAH-APEX LEAD MINE, BINGHAM DISTRICT, UTAH

down the mine and the mill at this time is purely one of freight-rates and the value of Silver Standard ore and concentrates. The railways, chiefly on the American side where the zinc is shipped, have been altering their rates to such an extent that smelter people are unable to make a settlement until the rates are adjusted. The matter has been up for two or three months, the Silver Standard people hoping all the time that the rates would be satisfactorily adjusted and operations continued at the mine. As yet nothing has been accomplished and it may take another two or three months. The position of the Silver Standard is very simple: They have not yet received a dollar for all the zinc concentrates sent to the smelter on the other side, and no chance of getting any until the rates are adjusted, either for what has been shipped or for what is on hand. To continue operations under the circumstances is out of the question. As for the mine itself, it never was in better shape. There are several shoots of high-grade ore recently opened up. Work at both the mine and the mill has been running satisfactorily. There are on hand 100 tons of zinc concentrates and 72 tons of lead concentrates."

The Standard company reports a surplus of $317,565 at the end of 1918, an increase of $20,000 when compared with November 30.

Ontario

Kirkland Lake.—The Lake Shore Mines, Limited, during the year ended November 30, 1918, made a net profit of $144,978, of which $100,000 was paid in dividends. Milling started in March. The plant treated 14,948 tons of ore averaging $24.76 per ton, yielding gold worth $370,128. In the mine, 80% of all driving was in ore of milling grade. Work is conducted to a depth of 400 ft. R. C. Coffey is manager.

The Teck Hughes Gold Mines produced 2035 tons of $10.12 ore during December.

Porcupine.—The Dome Mines company, after considerable silence, has issued a report covering 9 months ended Devember 31, 1918. Current assets total $601,089, and liabilities only $11,238. The labor position is much better and will improve. A station was cut on No. 9 level, but no other work has been done there; also one on No. 10, and a loading-station 50 ft. below No. 10, or 1150-ft. level. A drift east was driven at this depth to explore for the zone cut by No. 9 drill-hole. Since December 20 this and three drill stations have been cut along the drift, from which more drilling will be done. Drilling 1435 ft. from No. 8 level resulted in nothing definite. Ore-reserves remain as in the last annual report, namely, 1,950,000 tons worth $5.10 per ton.

Sudbury.—The International Nickel Co. has closed its Crean Hill mine, laying off 800 men. The high-grade ore of the Creighton mine will supply the reduction works.

MEXICO

Mexico City.—Influenza caused the death of 436,200 persons in Mexico during 1918, according to data published by 'El Universal'. This figure is believed to be conservative, according to the paper, as several States were unable to supply figures on the mortality. In others, it is added, the epidemic still prevails. In Morelos, in particular, few families escaped illness. In fact, the influenza is credited with having destroyed the power of Emiliano Zapata, long the rebel ruler of that State.

Chihuahua.—Advices from Mexico City state that more than 300 mining properties confiscated since 1913 are to be returned to their owners, who will be obliged to work them and pay the corresponding taxes under penalty of losing them. Only the properties of ex-governor Creel, of General Tarrazas and sons, and the mine owned in Cusihuiriachic by the late General Orozco are to continue confiscated.

PERSONAL

Note The Editor invites members of the profession to send particulars of their work and appointments The information is interesting to our readers

S. J. Speak is in Rhodesia.

T. A. Rickard is in New York.

L. D. Ricketts is at Chandler, Arizona.

L. H. Duschak, of the U. S. Bureau of Mines, is at Washington.

P. N. Nissen, now Lieutenant-Colonel, has returned from France to London.

Norman C. Stines was in London recently, on his way from Russia to France.

Frederick G. Cottrell has been awarded the Perkin medal of the Society of Chemical Industry.

J. P. Hutchins sailed from New York on February 17 on his way to the Black Sea region of Russia.

William W. Mein sailed from San Francisco on February 11, on his way from New York to Nicaragua.

John A. Fulton has been appointed superintendent of the Idaho-Maryland property at Grass Valley, California.

John M. Nicol has returned to San Francisco from a lengthy investigation of mining properties in Honduras.

J. M. Wadsworth has resigned from the U. S. Bureau of Mines to enter the employ of the Empire Gas & Fuel Co., with headquarters at Bartlesville, Oklahoma.

J. C. Farrant, London representative of the Hardinge Conical Mill company, has returned to England after having been a prisoner of war in Germany for four years.

Judd Stewart, for 36 years identified with smelting operations in this country, and long connected with the American Smelting & Refining Co., of which he was a director, has tendered his resignation effective March 1.

E. W. Wagy, of the U. S. Bureau of Mines, is investigating the Texas, Louisiana, and Mid-Continent oilfields for the purpose of making a special study of methods used in those districts in the matter of perforating casing and setting screen-pipe.

Obituary

James Cumming, a pioneer of the Canadian West, died at Vancouver, B. C., on December 3. He was prominent in the Cariboo gold rush in 1862.

T. Walter Beam, well known in the West, and more recently from his connection with the re-opening of the Old Eureka mine at Suttor Creek, California, died at Denver on February 1. He was born in Ohio in 1854, going to Colorado in 1871. He leaves a wife, one daughter, and one son.

Alan Fraser McCormick died of pneumonia at El Paso, Texas, on December 23, 1918. He was born in the Province of Ontario, Canada, 43 years ago, and at the time of his death was assistant-superintendent of the El Paso Smelting Works. He began his career in the smelting business about twenty years ago at the smelter at Trail, B. C. From Trail he went with the Granby Consolidated M., S. & P. Co., and subsequently was connected with mining companies in Montana. When the Nevada Consolidated Copper Co.'s smelter was blown-in, Mr. McCormick was assistant to Walter G. Perkins, who was in charge of smelting operations. In 1911 he went to the El Paso Smelting Works as assistant-superintendent in charge of copper reverberatory smelting and converting operations, where he remained until the time of his death.

THE METAL MARKET

METAL PRICES

San Francisco, February 11

Aluminum-dust, large and small lots, cents per lb.	65—70
Antimony, cents per pound	8.00
Copper, electrolytic, cents per pound, in carload lots	18.25
Lead, pig, cents per pound	5.25—6.25
Platinum, per ounce	$108
Quicksilver, per flask of 75 lb.	$95
Spelter, cents per pound	9.00
Zinc-dust, cents per pound	16.00

EASTERN METAL MARKET

(By wire from New York)

February 11.—Copper is quiet and lower. Lead is dull though steady. Spelter is inactive but firmer.

SILVER

Below are given official (not Government) quotations, in cents per ounce, of silver 999 fine. In order to make prompt settlements with smelters and brokers, producers allow a discount from the maximum fixed price of $1.01½, hence the lower price. The Government has not fixed the general market price at $1, but will pay this price (as from April 23, 1918) for all silver purchased by it. The equivalent of dollar silver (1000 fine) in British currency is 46.65 pence per ounce (925 fine), calculated at the current rate of exchange. On August 15, 1918, the Treasury announced that the maximum price was fixed at $1.01½ per ounce. The British government fixed its maximum at 49½ pence, on September ?, but on November 12 this was changed to 48¾ pence, and on December 13 to 48 7/16 pence.

Date		New York	London	Average week ending		
Feb.	5	101.12	48.44	Dec.	31	101.12
"	6	101.12	48.44	Jan.	7	101.12
"	7	101.12	48.44	"	14	101.12
"	8	101.12	48.44	"	21	101.12
"	9 Sunday			"	28	101.12
"	10	101.12	48.44	Feb.	4	101.12
"	11	101.12	48.44	"	11	101.12

Monthly averages

	1917	1918	1919		1917	1918	1919
Jan.	75.14	88.72	101.12	July	78.92	99.62	....
Feb.	77.54	85.79	....	Aug.	85.40	100.31	....
Mch.	74.13	88.11	....	Sept.	100.73	101.12	....
Apr.	72.51	95.35	....	Oct.	87.38	101.12	....
May	74.61	99.50	....	Nov.	85.97	101.12	....
June	76.44	99.50	....	Dec.	85.97	101.12	....

The Annual Bullion Letter of Samuel Montagu & Co. of London is to hand. It contains a great deal of interesting matter on silver, to be published in this journal later.

In January there was some activity in trade demand for silver in London, but not of sufficient size to incommode the market, deprived, as it has been for some time, of competition from abroad, owing to export restrictions which remain in force.

Silver worth $14,000,000 was sent to the Orient by the 'Colusa' on Saturday, the 8th.

COPPER

Prices of electrolytic in New York, in cents per pound.

Date			Average week ending		
Feb.	5	18.75	Dec.	31	26.00
"	6	18.50	Jan.	7	21.80
"	7	18.50	"	14	20.75
"	8	18.25	"	21	20.50
"	9 Sunday		"	28	19.87
"	10	18.00	Feb.	4	19.21
"	11	18.00	"	11	18.33

Monthly averages

	1917	1918	1919		1917	1918	1919
Jan.	29.53	23.50	20.43	July	29.67	26.00	....
Feb.	34.57	23.50	....	Aug.	27.42	26.00	....
Mch.	36.00	23.50	....	Sept.	25.11	26.00	....
Apr.	33.16	23.50	....	Oct.	23.50	26.00	....
May	31.00	23.50	....	Nov.	23.50	26.00	....
June	32.57	23.50	....	Dec.	23.50	26.00	....

It is reported in Boston that a large copper producer recently refused 19 cents per pound for several million pounds.

Standard copper is selling in England at £79 10s. per ton, equal to 18¾ cents per pound.

ZINC

Zinc is quoted as spelter, standard Western brands, New York delivery.

Date			Average week ending		
Feb.	5	6.70	Dec.	31	8.13
"	6	[illegible]	Jan.	7	7.93
"	7	[illegible]	"	14	7.72
"	8	[illegible]	"	21	7.52
"	9 Sunday		"	28	7.20
"	10	6.70	Feb.	4	6.83
"	11	[illegible]	"	11	6.68

Monthly averages

	1917	1918	1919		1917	1918	1919
Jan.	9.75	7.87	7.44	July	8.98	8.72	....
Feb.	10.45	7.97	....	Aug.	8.58	8.87	....
Mch.	10.78	7.67	....	Sept.	8.33	9.58	....
Apr.	10.20	7.04	....	Oct.	8.32	9.11	....
May	9.41	7.29	....	Nov.	7.76	8.75	....
June	9.63	7.92	....	Dec.	7.84	8.49	....

Demand for zinc ore at Joplin, Missouri, was better last week, but the price moved only slightly to $41 per ton, basis 60% metal.

LEAD

Lead is quoted in cents per pound, New York delivery.

Date			Average week ending		
Feb.	5	5.10	Dec.	31	6.10
"	6	5.00	Jan.	7	5.80
"	7	5.00	"	14	5.75
"	8	5.00	"	21	5.62
"	9 Sunday		"	28	5.50
"	10	5.00	Feb.	4	5.32
"	11	5.00	"	11	5.02

Monthly averages

	1917	1918	1919		1917	1918	1919
Jan.	7.64	6.85	5.60	July	10.93	8.03	....
Feb.	9.10	7.07	....	Aug.	10.75	8.05	....
Mch.	10.07	7.26	....	Sept.	9.07	8.05	....
Apr.	9.38	6.99	....	Oct.	6.97	8.05	....
May	10.29	6.88	....	Nov.	6.38	8.05	....
June	11.74	7.58	[illegible]	Dec.	6.49	6.90	....

Lead ore, basis 80% metal, fell from $60 to $55 per ton last week, following the drop in the metal.

QUICKSILVER

The primary market for quicksilver is San Francisco, California being the largest producer. The price is fixed in the open market, according to quantity. Prices, in dollars per flask of 75 pounds:

Date					
Jan.	14	105.00	Jan.	28	100.00
"	21	100.00	Feb.	4	95.00
			"	11	95.00

Monthly averages

	1917	1918	1919		1917	1918	1919
Jan.	81.00	128.06	103.75	July	102.00	120.00	....
Feb.	126.25	118.00	....	Aug.	115.00	120.00	....
Mch.	113.75	112.00	....	Sept.	112.00	120.00	....
Apr.	114.50	115.00	....	Oct.	102.00	120.00	....
May	104.00	110.00	....	Nov.	102.50	120.00	....
June	85.50	112.00	....	Dec.	117.42	115.00	....

TIN

Prices in New York, in cents per pound. The monthly averages in 1918 are nominal. On December 3 the War Industries Board fixed the price to consumers and jobbers at 72½c. f.o.b. Chicago and Eastern points, and 71½c. on the Pacific Coast. This will continue until the U. S. Steel Products Co.'s stock is consumed.

Monthly averages

	1917	1918	1919		1917	1918	1919
Jan.	44.10	85.13	71.50	July	62.60	93.00	....
Feb.	51.47	85.00	....	Aug.	62.53	91.33	....
Mch.	54.27	85.00	....	Sept.	61.54	80.40	....
Apr.	55.63	88.53	....	Oct.	62.24	78.82	....
May	63.21	100.01	....	Nov.	74.18	73.67	....
June	61.93	91.00	....	Dec.	85.00	71.52	....

ORES (New York)

Manganese Alloys: It is the opinion of a leading ore-dealer that there is at present in the United States enough manganese ore and ferro to supply the country's needs for 14 months. The output of ferro in America in December was 23,907 tons, bringing the total for 1918 to 345,300 tons, a record for any year. Demand for ferro or spiegel is light. Only a few carloads of the former have been sold at $175 to $200 per ton delivered. It was nearly all re-sale material. Spiegel is nominal at $60 delivered, for 16 to 18% alloy and $65 for the 19 to 21% material. It can be bought under those levels.

Molybdenum.—The market is regarded as firm at about 90c. to $1 per lb. of 90% concentrate, but it is not active. One statement is to the effect that transactions in January involved about 40 tons.

Tungsten: There has been no change, and quotations are not available in the absence of any test of the market. It is stated that some ferro-tungsten sold at $2 per lb. of contained tungsten.

The War Trade Board announced on January 25 that it received official information from the French High Commission in the United States to the effect that France will be unable, at least until April, to ship potash from the mines of Alsace. Also for the next few months practically the entire potash output of the Alsatian mines will be urgently required for agricultural purposes in France. It is the view of the Board, based upon this information, that even under the most favorable circumstances, no potash from Alsace could be available in the United States for agricultural uses before June 1919, and that, therefore, it will be necessary that this country rely entirely upon its domestic potash production for the coming spring season.

Eastern Metal Market

New York, February 5.

All the markets are stagnant and entirely lacking in interest; demand and buying is only spasmodic.

On small sales the copper market continues to decline.

There is no activity in tin, and the market is still held down by restrictions.

The lead market continues to slide, and lower levels have been reached with light buying.

Zinc is still declining on a small volume of transactions, and the position is not strong.

Antimony is slightly easier.

ANTIMONY

Demand is poor and the market is quiet. Prices are a little lower with wholesale lots for early delivery quoted at 7.37½ to 7.50c., duty paid, New York.

COPPER

Copper buying has been and still is on a small scale; this is generally admitted. One statement is to the effect that not more than two days' production of copper has been sold since the armistice (November 11). Another holds that the sales in January have not been over 24,000,000 lb., and that there is not any market in the broad sense. Production has been curtailed decidedly, an illustration being that for Anaconda in January which fell off about 6,000,000 lb. from that in December—the lowest month's output since September 1917. On small sales and a fair demand the market has gradually eased off until electrolytic copper for early delivery has sold as low as 18.75c., New York. There are numerous sellers at this level, which we quote as the market. Lake copper is slightly higher and nominal at 19.50c., New York. Considerable interest attaches to the outcome of the conference with miners at Washington as to a resumption of the sliding-scale of wages. [In The Mining Summary will be found what is happening at all the principal copper centres.]

IRON AND STEEL

There are still no signs of any buying movement from domestic or foreign sources. Further moderate reductions in ocean freights are an aid in the export field, but transportation costs are still four to five times the former normal charges. According to cable information from London the German steel output in 1918 was about 16,500,000 metric tons, nearly the same as that in 1917. The pig-iron output of the United States in January was 3,302,260 tons, which establishes a record for that month, although there were 27 less furnaces in blast at the end than at the beginning of the month. The daily output was 106,525 tons, against 110,762 tons in December. The combined output of manganese alloys in January was 32,787 tons, compared with 49,435 tons in December; it was the smallest of any month since February 1917, when it was 26,114 tons.

LEAD

The lead market continues to decline and it is uncertain yet whether the bottom has been reached. Last Friday, January 31, the American Smelting & Refining Co. reduced its price from 5.50 to 5.25c. per lb., New York, or to 4.95c., St. Louis. It has thus far been of little avail. Independents have met this and gone one better until today lead is quoted at 5.05c., New York, or 4.75c., St. Louis, for early delivery. As low as 5c., New York, has been done, but it was of a special nature. The market is generally quotable at 5.05c., New York, or 4.75c., St. Louis, with demand light. Some regard the price as attractive, and feel that though it may go lower the turn in the market is likely any day. Considerable depends on demand from all other consumers of lead who have been slow to assert themselves. At present levels more interest is reported as being shown by buyers, and a good demand is regarded as possible.

TIN

With the War over nearly three months, and with all other markets free and open in every respect, the tin market continues under restrictions. No imports nor buying for future delivery are possible, although the metal is purchasable at about 20c. under the present controlled price. How long such a condition is to prevail is disconcerting. The market is demoralized, slow and stale, and there is no buying except for the direst needs. It is understood that only about one-third of the metal allocated to the United States Steel Products Co. has been absorbed. The price for this is 72.50c., New York. American tin (from foreign ore) can be bought at 67 to 68c. per lb., New York. An interesting rumor is to the effect that purchasing for shipment from the Far East may be attempted on the assumption that by the time such shipments could reach the United States import restrictions may have been lifted; if not, such metal could be held in England until it could be imported into this country. The arrivals of tin in January were only 1900 tons, of which 1850 tons came through Pacific ports. In January 1918 there were 4912 tons.

ZINC

On one or two occasions recently it has been thought that the bottom of the market had been reached, but the decline has continued another week until today prime Western for early delivery is quoted at 6.35c., St. Louis, or 6.70c., New York, at which level sales of small quantities have been made. The market is very slow, and the present price level regarded as under the cost of production. Some producers are either not quoting or are taking what loss is necessary and contemplating shutting-down at the same time. The report of the Government for the week ended January 18 shows stocks of all grades of zinc to have increased nearly 2900 tons, with a decrease in output of 150 tons. Weekly reports of stocks will no longer be issued, as certain companies refuse to give further returns; the reports of output may continue.

COPPER NOTES

Copper stocks in this country, according to a statement issued by the conference of Union representatives at Washington last week, amount to 1,000,000,000 lb., that is, in all stages from mill to refinery. In addition to this are the large quantities held by manufacturers and the various Allied governments, perhaps a total of 400,000,000 lb. Sales for 75 days did not amount to 5% of the output. Production in 1918 averaged 200,000,000 lb. per month, against 125,000,000 lb. in the pre-war years.

The following comparison of war basis of wages as recently paid with the normal sliding-scale, was prepared at the conference:

Price and place	War basis	Sliding scale
26-cent copper at Butte	$5.75	$5.00
20-cent copper at Butte	5.00	4.50
18-cent copper at Butte	4.75	4.25
26-cent copper at Clifton	5.00	4.00
20-cent copper at Clifton	4.25	3.25
18-cent copper at Clifton	4.00	3.00
26-cent copper at Globe, Miami, and Jerome	5.90	5.15
20-cent copper at Globe, Miami, and Jerome	5.15	4.40
18-cent copper at Globe, Miami, and Jerome	4.90	4.15
26-cent copper at Bisbee	6.05	5.30
20-cent copper at Bisbee	5.25	4.50
18-cent copper at Bisbee	5.00	4.25

Book Reviews

American Highway Engineers' Handbook. Arthur H. Blanchard, editor-in-chief. Pp. 1579, ill., index. John Wiley & Sons, Inc., New York. For sale by 'Mining and Scientific Press', San Francisco. Price, $5.

This is by far the most complete handbook that has been published on this relatively new subject. The treatment is in fact so complete that it might almost be used as a text-book. The book is divided into 29 sections, each written by a specialist on the particular subjects treated. At the end of each section is a bibliography. The first section is devoted to definitions, most of them based on accepted standards, and constituting a complete dictionary of highway engineering. The second section treats briefly mathematics, mechanics, and the structural materials used in highway work. The third section, on engineering geology, covers rocks, soils, physical geology, the use of maps, and quarrying. Preliminary plans and surveys are considered in the next four sections, the special titles being preliminary investigations, surveys and office practice, planning of roads and road systems, and planning of streets and street systems. The section of surveys contains a number of tables, including some curve-tables arranged particularly for use in highway work. The next section deals with grading, drainage, and foundations. The various types of roads and road surfaces are then discussed in detail, earth and sand-clay roads, gravel roads, broken-stone roads, bituminous materials, dust prevention, bituminous surfaces, bituminous-macadam pavements, bituminous-concrete pavements, sheet-asphalt and rock-asphalt pavements, wood-block pavements, stone-block pavements, brick pavements, and cement-concrete pavements, each being given a section. The remaining sections are devoted to various miscellaneous subjects, including street cleaning, collection and disposal of waste, and snow removal; car-tracks and pipe systems; comparison of types of roads and pavements; sidewalks, curbs, gutters, and highway signs; highway bridges, culverts, retaining-walls, foundations, and guard-rails; preservation of materials used in highway structures; financing of highway improvements; and organization and administration of highway departments. In their zeal to make the book comprehensive, the authors and the editor have occasionally erred on the side of being prolix, and there is also considerable repetition, most of it unavoidable if the general plan of the book were to be followed. Nevertheless, the book will be of great value to highway engineers and others engaged in street and road construction.

Heaton's Annual for 1919. Pp. 512, ill., index. Heaton's Agency, Toronto, Ontario, 1919. For sale by 'Mining and Scientific Press.' Price, $1.50.

The fifteenth edition of Heaton's Annual—Commercial Handbook of Canada—has been received. As usual we notice important new features: The clear-cut commercial maps of each Province are new and add greatly to the value of the descriptions of towns. A complete educational guide with illustrated announcements of the leading universities and schools of Canada is interesting and valuable; but this edition is chiefly remarkable for the section on Natural Resources, covering agriculture, fisheries, forest products, fur trade, mining, and water-power, with cross references to the special Government publications from which complete information can be obtained. This section alone is worth the price of the book. A chapter on the war record of Canada will be useful for all time. The Annual is known as the standard authority on the customs tariffs and regulations. There is a valuable set of exchange and commercial tables at the end of the book. The clear side-heads and alphabetical arrangements make this a valuable book of reference.

American Methods in Foreign Trade. A guide to export selling policy. By George C. Vedder. Pp. 204, index. McGraw-Hill Book Co., New York, 1919. For sale by 'Mining and Scientific Press'. Price, $2.

This is one of the latest American publications dealing with foreign business and contains many suggestions of value to exporters, especially to those just beginning to enter foreign markets. The author, with a knowledge gained from practical experience, has briefly set forth what he considers the fundamentals of export policies. While many experienced exporters will not agree with some of his conclusions, all will agree that he has succeeded in placing clearly before the reader many suggestions of real practical value. Much of the information contained in his book can be found elsewhere, but most of it is worthy of reiteration, especially when presented in such an attractive style. The author is firm in his convictions and his style is vigorous and pleasing. He has divided the subject into chapters that are crisp, brief, and to the point. Altogether it is a book that offers many helpful suggestions to the established exporter and is at the same time full of valuable advice to the beginner. H. S.

Electric Welding. By Douglas T. Hamilton and Erik Oberg. Pp. 283, ill., index. The Industrial Press, New York. For sale by 'Mining and Scientific Press', San Francisco. Price, $2.50.

Although the first experiments in resistance-welding were made in 1886 by Elihu Thomson, the great development in both types of electric welding is a matter of the past few years, and particularly of the past year because of the tremendous activity in shipbuilding, where electric welding seems likely to supplant riveting to a considerable extent, if not entirely. The present volume is the most complete on the subject that has yet appeared. Two chapters are devoted to butt-welding including a discussion of special machines and processes. Spot-welding is next considered, and it will be a surprise to many people to learn that plates ⅞ in. thick have been spot-welding. Seam-welding and riveting are compared in the next chapter. Percussion welding and electric soldering are then considered in turn. The last three chapters are devoted to electric-arc welding and cutting, including a comparison with similar work done by the oxy-acetylene torch. The book will be of value to anyone interested in welding, electric or otherwise.

Practical Oil Geology. By Dorsey Hager. Third edition. Pp. 243, ill., index. McGraw-Hill Book Co., Inc., New York. For sale by 'Mining and Scientific Press', San Francisco. Price, $2.50.

An edition every two years seems to be the settled rule for this useful handbook. The present edition has been thoroughly revised and considerable new material added to bring it up to date. The general arrangement, however, is the same as in the earlier editions. The chapter-headings are: Origin and Accumulation of Petroleum; Physical and Chemical Properties; Stratigraphy; Structural Geology; Prospecting and Mapping; Locating Drill-Hole Sites; Oil-Well Drilling; Oil Production; Water; Gas; Oil-Shales; Geological Field Methods and Instruments. The book will be of value to anyone interested in the oil business, from prospecting to production.

'**The Genesis of the Ores at Tonopah, Nevada**,' is the title of Prof. Paper 104 of the Geological Survey.

INDUSTRIAL PROGRESS

INFORMATION FURNISHED BY MANUFACTURERS

POWDERED COAL AS A SUBSTITUTE FOR FUEL-OIL

For most of the past two or three years, the consumption of Californian fuel-oil has exceeded production to an alarming extent. Recently, consumption has decreased slightly, partly because a number of former users of fuel-oil have adopted coal, and partly because many of the less essential industries have been compelled to get along on reduced deliveries of oil. At the same time, the flush output of one new field has increased production. The result has been that, for the time being at least, production and consumption are approximately equal. However, the less-essential industries cannot be expected meekly to take what is given to them after peace is declared. At the same time the demand for Californian lubricants is increasing rapidly, and the refineries are taking an increasingly large amount of the oil formerly burned in a crude state. Users of Californian fuel-oil must expect higher prices in the future and increased difficulty of obtaining supplies, and it behooves them to investigate other possible fuels.

The lignites and semi-bituminous coals of California and other Pacific Coast States are poor fuels when burned in the lump state. Experiments with powdered fuel were made more than thirty years ago, both in the West and in other parts of the country, but the early results were not satisfactory. The processes now in use, however, are economical and efficient. The greatest advance in the use of powdered coal has been made in the cement industry. At the present time nearly 90% of the cement produced in the United States is made with powdered coal. Powdered coal is also being employed in metallurgical work and many other uses, and has even been tried with good results for firing locomotives, and, in one case, for ship propulsion.

The estimated available supply of lignite 'in sight' in California is 35,000,000 tons, divided as follows: Stone Canyon, 6,000,000; Tesla, 10,000,000; Ione, 10,000,000; Dos Rios, 6,000,000; and miscellaneous sources, 3,000,000 tons. It is probable that the total that can be obtained is considerably more than this amount. With the co-operation of officials of the Bureau of Mines, and of J. M. Wadsworth, of the Federal Fuel Administration, R. N. Buell, one of the patentees of the Buell-Santmyer system for using powdered coal, has been making some experiments with Western lignites, employing a disused boiler-plant at 330 Eleventh street, San Francisco. These experiments indicate that, at the present prices of both fuels, powdered coal is at least 10% cheaper than oil on the basis of pounds of water evaporated.

Lignite from Ione, California, is one of the fuels used in these experiments. The following analysis is a fair sample:

	As received	Dry
Moisture	22.44%	0.00%
Ash	14.78%	19.08%
Volatile matter	42.37%	54.60%
Fixed carbon	20.41%	26.32%
Sulphur	2.98%	3.85%
B.t.u. per pound	9322	12,016

The fuel is dried in a Ruggles drier. While good results can be obtained with as much as 6% moisture, it is better to reduce the moisture to 3%. A Williams crusher and a Raymond pulverizer are used to bring the coal to such a fineness that 90% will pass a 200-mesh sieve. Fineness of grinding is desirable, since it assists combustion. The pulverized coal is then transported in closed receptacles to the storage-bunker at the furnaces. No trouble has been experienced either here or at Seattle with explosives or spontaneous combustion. It is advisable, however, to see

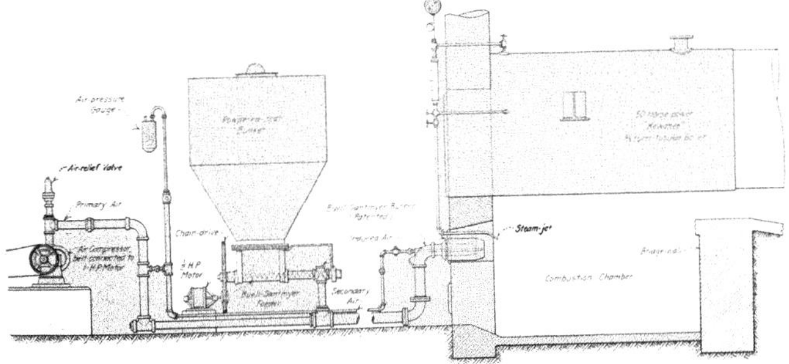

GENERAL LAY-OUT OF EXPERIMENTAL PLANT USING BUELL-SANTMYER SYSTEM

that the temperature of the coal is kept low, and that no conveying or other apparatus be used such that friction might create a spark.

Several good-sized commercial plants using the Buell-Santmyer system are in operation at Seattle, the largest being the Western Avenue plant of the Puget Sound Tramway Co. with a capacity of several thousand horse-power. There is also a 2500-hp. plant at a coal mine near Seattle, which supplies electric energy to several nearby industries. In all about 100 boilers, ranging from 100 to 600 hp., in Seattle are fired by powdered coal. Most of these plants used fuel-oil formerly.

The general lay-out of the experimental plant at San Francisco, which is typical of any plant using this system, is shown in the accompanying sketch. The fuel supply is regulated by a screw-feed. The combination of the coal and air takes place in a specially designed mixing-chamber. If desired, the bunker and mixing-chamber may be placed at a considerable distance from the boiler, and the fuel conveyed by means of a 'booster' service, without danger of separation or of clogging the pipes. In all, about 15% of excess air over that required for complete combustion is used. Where maximum combustion and consequently minimum length of flame is required, about 40% of the air is forced and the remainder induced. These proportions can be altered so as to give almost any length of flame desired.

At the San Francisco plant, using Ione lignite and similar fuels, an evaporation per pound of coal burned of 8.5 to 9.5 lb. of water from and at 212° F. has been obtained. The furnace temperature was 2000° F., the temperature of waste gases, 470° F. The CO_2 reading was 14.4%. The proportion of CO was negligible. Better results than these could probably be obtained with a new plant.

The owner of a small plant will probably find it more economical to purchase his fuel in a pulverized form. Where this is done, the cost of altering an oil-burning plant of two 150-hp. boilers to use pulverized coal will be about $1200, other sizes in proportion. For the larger plants, it would probably be better to construct an entire crushing and drying works. Such an outfit, for a plant using 100 tons per day, would cost, exclusive of building, from $25,000 to $30,000. The cost per ton used would decrease with the capacity of the plant. Thus a plant for preparing 200 tons per day would cost, exclusive of building, $35,000 to $40,000. The cost of processing, from freight car to furnace, will vary from $0.50 to $0.90 per ton. Another way of using the coal is to construct a steam-electric plant at the mine itself and burn the coal there.

A test was conducted at the San Francisco experimental plant on December 5 in the presence of a number of engineers from the San Francisco Bay district. On December 16, at a meeting held at the Engineers' Club under the auspices of the local section of the American Society of Mechanical Engineers, the subject of powdered fuel was discussed by M. C. M. Hatch, of the Locomotive Pulverized Fuel Co., by Mr. Buell, and by several others.—'Metal Trades'.

IMPROVED MINE TELEPHONES

The entrance of the Klaxon Company, makers of 'Klaxon' auto-horns, into the field of inter-communication equipment is of special interest to mine, mill, and smelter operators, since it will afford an improvement over the ordinary mine-telephone for many purposes.

The Stentor Electric Mfg. Co., makers of 'Stentor' loud-speaking telephones, has recently been taken over by the Klaxon Company which will manufacture and distribute the Stentor products in connection with the Klaxon industrial signals through its industrial division with offices in New York. During the War, all of the inter-communication apparatus manufactured by this company was required by the United States government, and announcement of the change was withheld until individual concerns could be supplied. To meet the requirements of our Navy for inter-communication equipment that withstands all weather conditions and can be heard in noisy places, this company developed a transmitter and a receiver that can be heard even under gunfire.

The inter-communication apparatus for mines is fitted with these improved transmitters and receivers. The instruments are enclosed in sturdy, practically unbreakable, weather-proof housings. These need not be opened, as the Klaxon-Stentor loud-speaking telephone transmits messages in so loud and clear a tone that they can be heard at a distance from the instrument itself without the use of ear receivers.

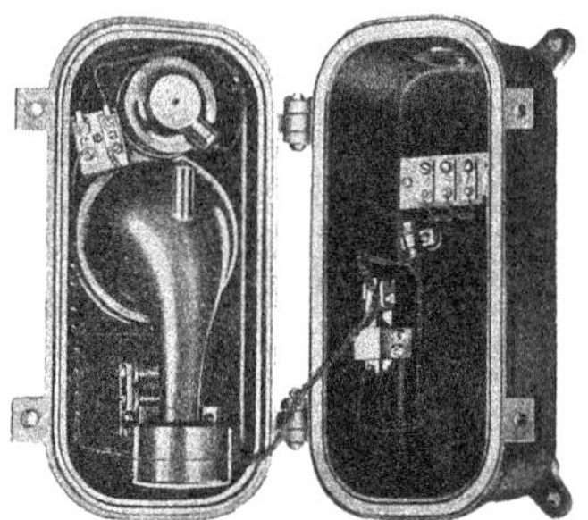

LOUD-SPEAKING MINE TELEPHONE IN CASE

The Klaxon Company was a pioneer in sound reproducing engineering. Klaxon industrial signals are in wide use not only for fire-alarms but also for replacing electric gongs, which must operate under extremely noisy conditions. The Klaxon signal gives a peculiarly raucous far-reaching sound which is readily heard above all the noise of concentrators or stamps and ball-mills.

While the tones of Klaxon-Stentor loud-speaking telephones are in no sense similar to the saw-tooth sounds of Klaxon horns, still their carrying power is developed along the same lines and is equally effective for their purpose.

TELEPHONE CASE CLOSED

The Klaxon Company has aggressively entered the inter-communication equipment field, extending its laboratory facilities for experimental research work and engaging several engineers of wide experience in this field to that end. It has employed one of the foremost authorities on telephony and sound reproduction in the United States, and the inventor of the Stentor loud-speaking telephones will devote all his time to development work on inter-communication apparatus. This should be useful in machine-shops.

SPEAKING of Germany's financial resources we note a letter in the 'Financial Times', of London, from Mr. F. Faithfull Begg, an authority on company finance, at least. He says truly that Germany cannot pay if the Allies ruin her, but he concludes, from careful investigation, that revenues to the amount of 1300 million dollars should be available for the purpose, for which Germany should be called upon to issue indemnity bonds.

OUR Spokane contemporary, the 'Spokesman-Review', has something kind to say concerning the management of the Bunker Hill & Sullivan company, and we are glad to read it. The company has decided not to cut the existing rate of wages, although this was fixed during war-time, when the price of lead was high; nor is the company making any large reduction in its force of workmen, although a suspension of operations might seem justified by the temporary collapse of the metal market. It appears that whereas wages were increased 50% during the War and the wholesale price of living supplies was raised 67%, the local storekeepers have absorbed 10% of this, selling at retail on an increase of 57%. Thus the miners absorb 7% and the retailers 10% of the difference created by the profiteers. In short, the local community shows a fine spirit, justifying the statement made by Mr. F. W. Bradley, the president of the company, "At Kellogg we have a community that stood by us and did not run off to the shipyards, so it is not more than fair that we should stand by it now." We are glad to learn that the Bunker Hill brand of lead is finding a ready market throughout the country.

COMPLAINT is general among those interested in the mines and oilfields of California, that a movement should have been started at Sacramento to re-organize the State government so as to include the administration of minerals along with fish, game, land-settlement, the animal industry, and State fairs, which latter comprise, among other things, jellies, jams, and pumpkin pies. We suppose the close connection between fish and the mineral industry is found in the character of the prospectuses issued by certain promoters, though we were under the impression that the 'blue-sky' laws had required such literature to be written, not in the form of romances, but in a dry statistical style. The relation to deer, ducks, and other undomesticated creatures sought after by the Nimrods is obvious, for who is there in California that has not pursued the mining game? The seemingly incongruous association of jellies, gold mines, wild ducks, copper smelters, hogs, tungsten, and rock cod is not as peculiar as some of our miners seem to think. The war-minerals relief bill, on being introduced recently into the House of Representatives, was referred to the Fisheries Committee, which would indicate some essential connection that the plain man of the hills has failed to grasp. The ways of politicians are past finding out, though there sometimes may be sound reason for their apparent anomalies. It is not many years ago that the legislature of Missouri lumped the State School of Mines with the State Asylum for the Insane in a committee-appointment for investigation. We are glad to know that the California Metal Producers' Association is sending representatives to Sacramento to see to it that the administration of the mineral industry shall be controlled in a manner commensurate with the magnitude of the interests involved. The value of the metal output of California last year exceeded $32,000,000, and that of oil and other substances included among the mineral resources of the State reached $159,000,000.

THE article on the possibilities of re-dredging the gravels of the Oroville district, in California, by Mr. Charles H. Thurman, which we publish this week, will create wide interest. Oroville witnessed the pioneer efforts at gold recovery by this method; many of the problems of dredge-construction for that particular service were there worked out, and the lessons, which have benefited other areas, were in many cases too late for application to the field where they were learned. Mr. Thurman is superintendent of gold dredges in the Feather River Division of the Natomas company's operations, so he speaks from fulness of knowledge. He shows that the earlier work was in many ways imperfect: that the old type of dredge often failed to dig all the gravel available, and that the recovery of gold was below the efficiency now attainable. There are other reasons given for not winning all that might be obtained from the gravels of the Feather River fan. He estimates that considerable portions of the ground may be dredged again, with modern equipment, and made to yield a profit. This will lead to scrutiny of other dredged areas. Incidentally, it is worth while to note that even the latest practice is still wanting in that degree of efficiency which practical men think should be realized, and that serious investigations are under way to correct the heavy losses that are known to take place. It is not unlikely that gold-dredging practice ten years hence will be as far in advance of that now followed as the present methods are superior to those of a decade ago. Despite all the sampling done, it appears that the content of gravel deposits has never yet been accurately determined, although the sampling methods have given results in fairly close accord with the results secured in dredging. No art ever reaches a state of final perfection, and gold-dredging standards change like every other.

Explosives

It is a pleasure to publish in this issue an article on explosives by Mr. Robert S. Lewis. With his customary thoroughness he presents a survey of all the leading explosive compounds now in general industrial and military use. It is a little compendium on the subject. The discussion is most timely on account of the interest in these materials awakened by the War. Important developments have taken place through the creation of new explosives, and it is nearly certain that the progress made will re-act upon the industrial application for blasting operations. A more extended use of tri-nitro-toluene is highly probable, as it is an exceptionally safe explosive, and the growth of by product coking will furnish the basic ingredients in larger amounts than heretofore. It is safe to assume that T.N.T., as it is commonly called, will play a more important rôle in future, despite the fact that the large quantities left in the hands of the Government at the close of the War proved so serious an embarrassment that it was proposed to dump thousands of tons of it into the sea. Actually about 5000 tons, which had been ordered by the French government but not yet shipped, was disposed of in that manner.

Mr. Lewis offers some valuable suggestions regarding the proper application of explosives in blasting, although this phase of the subject might be extended greatly. In the larger operations, especially in the great open-cast 'porphyry' mines, explosives are employed in a highly scientific manner by men of special training. Blasting under such conditions is no longer a matter of mere experience in rule-of-thumb methods; it is a question of the application of mechanical principles to utilize in the most effective manner the work developed by the explosive used under the conditions of the blast. In smaller mines, however, the older rude empirical methods still prevail, and the average miner and foreman, fixed in the habits handed down to them by their predecessors, persistently misapply the giant forces placed in their hands by the manufacturers of explosives. In no department of mining today is a greater waste of energy tolerated than in blasting in the way it is practised in the majority of small and medium-sized mines. Not only is this wastage the result of improper preparation of primers, wrong methods of loading holes, weak exploders, and incorrect ways of adjusting the cap to the fuse, but in an improper estimation of the amount, grade, and rapidity of action of the explosives loaded in order to secure the best results. Hints regarding these points may be gleaned from the instructive article by Mr. Lewis, which we hope will be elaborated later to cover more specifically the problems indicated. We may point out that the manufacturers of explosives themselves are not without a selfish interest in the economical application of their products. One of the great items of cost in mining is the powder used in blasting. If it is judiciously applied to loosen the maximum possible amount of ore or rock it is facilitating the expansion of enterprise; if wrongly, that is, uneconomically used, it is retarding enterprise.

The Business Outlook

In the last five years business has received two hard jolts, one on August 2, 1914, and the other on November 11, 1918. Business as usual, was unprepared. No one anticipated war when it burst without warning upon a stricken world, and no one anticipated peace when Germany's backbone broke with a crash in November last. The two crises are analogous, both in their psychological and physical aspects. The swing of the business pendulum in one direction in the first instance indicates the direction and character of the return swing in the second. In the solution of a mathematical problem, the task is to obtain the expression of an unknown quantity in terms of the known. In this case, the phenomena manifested in the transition from peace to war are the known quantity. These phenomena indicate the probable trend of business as the world gradually assumes a normal aspect. It will be remembered that a tremendous slump occurred during the first months of the War. Shock succeeded shock, and, as a realization of the enormity of the catastrophe broke through the crust of man's understanding, the confidence, the credit, and the actuating power that propelled the wheels of business seemed to dissolve. The slough of despond was filled to overflowing. When Lord Kitchener, in his famous interview with an American journalist, placed three years as the minimum duration of the War, a shudder followed by loud cries of incredulity burst forth from millions of throats. Judge Gary said that the War could not last more than six months, probably more for the purpose of allaying the panic that seized American business than as a real expression of his own mature judgment. It remained for Mr. James Farrell, himself an expert steel-maker and not a financier, to make the prediction that the War would bring about a business boom in the United States. Remember what happened, and the conditions that preceded. From the utter disruption of commercial business outside the United States, the collapse of all commercial export trade, the slump in industrials and mining securities, and no buying in consequence, to the meteoric career of the 'war babies' on Wall Street and the creation of that new species, the munitions millionaire, are all a matter of contemporaneous history, too recent to have been forgotten, crowded as the last four years have been with exciting events. It becomes increasingly evident, as we study the present situation, how strikingly similar the two periods of depression are, the pre-war and post-war periods. There is this difference, however, that while the necessities of war were immediate and resulted in an abnormal pressure to secure production of everything at unheard of speed, the pressure due to the return of commercial business will be less violent, but insistent nevertheless. The rate of increased activity will be steady: it will not produce those overload peaks in the curve; it will be rather a steady ascending line that means economical results as well as increasing quantity production. American industry has been heaving with all its might and main against the stone wall of Germanic military organization for nearly two years. Suddenly that wall collapsed, and we all fell forward in a heap; some of us even barked our shins and skinned our noses. Just now, we are picking ourselves up, dusting our clothes, and taking account of damages, still a little rattled at the suddenness of it all. The Government had just gotten into tune with industry; production of everything was under way at an abnormal rate. Now, the Government is trying to dam the stream it created. Industry is lopping off as fast as it reasonably can, in order that it may get its breath and readjust itself to meet the new conditions. The miners of the base metals, threatened with the two bugbears of business, an overstock and a falling market, are curtailing their output. They know perfectly that the need of metals for reconstruction will be enormous, but just when that demand will manifest itself, they don't know, and until they do the program is to mark time. Before the demand will begin to show in real earnest, order must be re-established in Europe, ocean transport must be resumed, war export and import restrictions must be removed, banking and credit machinery must be re-established, and the traveling salesman must again become a familiar figure in the smoking-rooms of ocean greyhounds and the capitals of the old world. The labor situation in one way is not reassuring, and in another way it is. Labor, carried away with the ease with which it put over the most exorbitant demands during the War, drunk with power, seems to have forgotten that on November 11 last the War ceased. The unions of Seattle, in flagrant disregard of all contracts, agreements, and everything else, temporarily succeeded in shutting-down a great city from one end to the other. A similar attempt in San Francisco has already cost millions of dollars in cancelled ship-contracts, and millions in wages to the workmen. One of the elementary rules of barter and trade lies in the fact that when one desires to sell something that is not actually essential at the time, it is well to be circumspect in one's conduct toward the buyer. The labor of the shipbuilder is no longer so essential as it was a few months ago. The action of the strikers will simply dry up the source of wages; that is all. The exorbitant rates of pay and the deliberate restriction of output are in a fair way to destroy themselves through the overmastering greed of the men. Profiteering in time of War is despicable; in times of peace it simply can't be done. No one wants a low wage-rate; no one wants to lower the scale of living for the American workman. A fair return for the dollar paid is essential, or the world's business will seek other sources of supply. We shall no longer be able to compete; the United States will sink to a second-rate power. The labor unions, however, show unmistakable signs of a return to reason. San Francisco is having strikes, but of comparatively minor importance compared with the great walk-out at Seattle. Attempts of Bolshevist agitators to stampede the unions into reckless action have met with scant success. A steady hand at the wheel is all that is needed for the successful passage of the rapids. All this instability, this uncertainty, which is just as present in the minds of those directing business affairs as in those of the rank and file, is but a stage in the transition from the collapse of the military mobilization of industry to the re-mobilization of peaceful commerce. England is in the throes of labor troubles worse than ours. It is a condition not confined to any geographic boundaries. In time, not so long a time either, these premonitory symptoms will pass. The transition will be gradual, perhaps imperceptible, but nevertheless positive. Within less than a year the product of American mines and factories will again find normal outlets, blocked for nearly two years. Look at the list of 'non-essential' industries, non-essential for war perhaps, but most essential in peace. They are waking from their long sleep and clamoring for recognition. Again we hear of good roads, new buildings, power projects, reclamation, irrigation, municipal improvements, and all sorts of development enterprises that have been quiescent for so many months. Europe's stock of metals has been worse than depleted, South America is waiting for American goods, the Orient beckons to the enterprise of American capital and energy. Buyers, who are holding off hungrily, waiting for the time when they think the falling markets have reached low water, will perforce soon be compelled to come through. Then the starter will work, a snort or two will come from under the hood, the black smoke from the exhaust will become colorless, indicating perfect combustion, the business motor of the United States will be shooting on all six.

The Banker and Mining

One of the most interesting addresses delivered before the recent meeting of the American Mining Congress in San Francisco was that of Mr. Frank B. Anderson, the president of the Bank of California. To those engaged in mining an address on the subject of the banker's relation to mining enterprise was bound to have a piquant interest when coming from the party of the first part, in this instance a financier of the highest reputation, not only in California but farther afield. We give the address on another page of this issue. The function of the banker in a young and growing commonwealth is outlined; it is more closely related to the commercial life of a Western community than is the case in the older communities on the Atlantic coast or on the other side of the same body of turbulent water. The banker is a more important person here than there because he plays a bigger part in the economic life of the region. He is expected to stimulate enterprise and to foster it when started; he plays the benevolent part of the right kind of uncle to a lively school-boy. Mr. Anderson is quick to draw the line at risky escapades; these the good uncle cannot sanction. He delegates the fostering of prospective ventures to syndicates and companies organized for that purpose—to exploration companies. He thinks the Pacific Coast has lacked the help of this type of organization, although he is aware that sundry small groups have done the same kind of work, namely, of selecting prospects and developing them into productive mines. That may be; but California has not entirely escaped the attention of exploration companies established in Boston and New York, in London and Paris. "Venturesome capital" has been available and it is still available, for the United States Smelting, Refining & Mining Company, the New England Exploration Company, the Goldfield Consolidated Mines Company, and Mr. D. C. Jackling—to mention a few—maintain offices in San Francisco for the purpose of investigating promising prospects. A market exists here, and it protects the banker from the importunities of the miner. Not until the enterprise has character, that is, dependability, and not unless the men in control have character, does the banker care to be drawn into the business. That seems proper, for no man—least of all a banker, who is a trustee—should use other people's money in a hazardous venture. Mining should not be done with borrowed money. That is a sound business axiom. We are referring here to working capital, the money that is risked in the effort to ascertain first the value of a mineral deposit and then to bring it to the productive stage. We might go a step further and say that a wise man would use in prospecting only the money that he could afford to lose. At least, no man unversed in mining should do so; let him leave such hazardous, but useful, ventures first to those having the experience required to minimize the risk and preferably to those who have made it their vocation to search for the plums in earth's great pudding. In drawing a distinction between the prospect and the dividend-paying mine Mr. Anderson made a slip; he talked about a "manufacturing proposition". No mining enterprise comes under that category. It is a phrase beloved of persons whom the banker abominates, the reckless promoter. A manufacturer buys raw material and converts it into a finished product; the miner's chief task is to find his own raw material and it is the uncertainty of the finding and the uncertainty as to the quantity of it when found that gives both zest and risk to his work. Mining is always risky; risk is inherent. It is neither a 'gamble', as some say, nor an 'investment', as others assert; at best, it is a sane speculation, in which the risk of great loss is balanced by the chances of exceptional gain. On that we have insisted in these columns many a time. Mr. Anderson quotes the Natomas and Anaconda flotations as examples of the friendly attitude of the banks toward mining. The Natomas was no ordinary mining deal; in that enterprise two phases of business were made complementary, namely, the wasting asset of gold-dredging ground and the accruing asset of land undergoing reclamation. It was expected that the exhaustion of the gold-bearing gravel would keep pace with the winning of cultivable land, but the progress of the two engineering processes did not quite connect, so that further financing became necessary, and it was done, but not without heart-burnings and sacrifices. Likewise the Anaconda Copper Mining Company's issue of bonds for its South American ventures cannot be regarded as a typical transaction, because the Anaconda's proved assets and the proved character of the men behind those assets placed that issue of bonds, for new properties concerning which ample and substantial information was available, on a plane far above that of ordinary mining finance. Mr. Anderson did not refer to a fact, which must have been in the minds of many of the older men listening to him, namely, that the old Bank of California came to grief in 1875 through the speculation of its president, William Ralston, in Comstock shares, notably those of the Ophir mine. We like, however, his insistence upon the basic value of the moral element—of reputation, of the known truthfulness and integrity of a man—as the decisive factor in loaning money, whether for mining or any other purpose. Let us revert to our axiom. Mining is neither an investment nor a gamble; an investment is held for the income that will accrue therefrom, the safety of the principal being deemed sure; a gamble is a game with chance, it bears no relation to business, because it depends upon luck, not sagacity. The test of an investment is to be willing to lock it in a safe for five years; no wise man would do that with mining stock. Speculation is the use of money on the expectation that the principal will enhance in value quickly; to the speculator the dividend is important, not as income or interest on his money, but as an indication of a rise in the market-price of his speculation. The simple-minded buy mining shares for income, the sagacious buy them to sell at a profit; the former are many, the latter are few. Speculation is based on judgment; a gamble is based on hazard. An investment supposes a minimum of risk and a small income return; a speculation involves a large risk, fully compensated by the possibility of a big gain. Risk is implicit in mining; that is why the banker, even if he knew more about it, would properly be wary of participation, as a lender of money; but the risk is no disgrace to mining; on the contrary, it is its chief attraction to those willing to use their money speculatively or adventurously, giving that word its fine old meaning. The sane speculation, after all, may prove not only more profitable than the wild gamble of the reckless and ignorant, but it often proves more profitable than the supposedly safe investment of the timid, for not even the gilt-edged security is immune from loss. A large risk for a large gain makes mining attractive to the adventurous.

The Trust Price of Copper

The Editor:

Sir—The above headline is due to the reading, in your issue of February 1, of the illuminating letter from W. W. Wishon. The caption you give his article is: 'The Market Price of Copper'.

Philosophers inform us that knowledge is limited by experience. Front the encomiums passed on the Phelps Dodge Corporation by Mr. Wishon, and from his vivid exposition of the 'rank cussedness' of the A. S. & R. Co., I judge his experience has been limited largely to the latter concern. Certainly our own experience with both these corporations has conveyed the knowledge that the difference between them is precisely the same that exists between tweedledum and tweedledee.

Last April, when issuing the annual report of his company, Daniel Guggenheim took the Government of the United States to task for "interfering with the supply-and-demand price of copper," which late in 1917 had been fixed at 23½c. per pound. Irrefragable history, however, teaches us that on March 14, 1916, all copper producers subject to custom smelters—or in other words, the Little Fellows who were subject to the Big Fellows—awoke to the fact that the supply-and-demand price of copper, which had reached about 28c. per pound, would thenceforth be settled for on the basis of 14c. plus ¾c. for each cent additional that the said public market showed. This meant that the Big Fellows had entered into a brazen conspiracy to grab off the cream of the high prices induced by the World War. This "rank deduction" (note the mildness of the language of one of the victims) put a clear profit of 3½c. per pound in the pockets of the custom smelters *before* they began their usual and long-endured exactions, deductions, and hold-outs. The only excuse advanced by these price-fixers was that the high market might drop before they had sold what they had bought. It was a 'sure thing' deal. In *their* business they had discovered a way to eliminate business chances. The buck was successfully passed to the Little Fellows. The coup was so simple and resulted in such a harvest of profit on copper that the Big Fellows put over the same deal, within a few months, on silver and on lead. They 'fixed' the price of silver at 60c. per ounce and the price of lead at 4½c. per pound.

When this grab on copper occurred Mr. Wishon advises us: "Upon calling their attention to the fact that they might readjust their enforced quotations and deductions after they had marketed their copper, they refused to discuss it further." Certainly, there was nothing to discuss. And so, some of us in southern Arizona (who were "unhappily tributary to the Bisbee smelter," as well as to those of the A. S. & R.) determined to invoke the aid of the law. The situation and the records were submitted to the Federal Trade Commission at Washington. This was in September 1917. The hold-up had been going on for a year and a half. In January 1918 the Government sent a corps of examiners to Arizona to investigate. The chief examiner spent nearly two months in Tucson as headquarters. His whereabouts and personality were unknown to the Big Fellows (or supposed to be unknown). In the meantime the Government had stepped in (October 1917) and fixed the price of copper at 23½c. per pound. This action absolutely cut out the excuse given by the Big Fellows in March 1916, but they still withheld their quarter cent deduction, which on a fixed price of 23½c. amounted to almost 2½c. per pound.

While the Government's chief examiner was hard at his labors in Tucson, the Copper Queen smelter suddenly advised all the Little Fellows whose shipping contracts were expiring that they would accept no more of their ores unless they agreed to sign up for either three or five years. The contracts were signed under duress, hence they are voidable.

Upon completion of his work in Tucson the Government's chief examiner remarked: "From all I had seen and heard before reaching Arizona, I had expected to encounter evidence of unfairness and injustice on the part of the custom smelters, but what I have found amazes me. It is the rottenest record I have ever investigated."

Well, what happened? Some of the Little Fellows—those who meet death with their backs facing the wall—concluded to endeavor to lilliputianize our smelter profiteers. In March 1918, I was sent to Washington to confer with the Government's representative, who had finally determined the price of copper at 23½c. per pound. It was soon apparent that this representative knew little or nothing of the small producers' problems and hardships. He was weighted down with smelter 'dope'. Small producers had to journey three thousand miles to present their case. Smelter 'experts' were thick in Washington and New York. After replying to several stereotyped questions and remarks on the copper situation, I turned and asked some pertinent questions of said Government representative. One of the very first replies was: "I'll admit I haven't seen a producer in three months." When crowded on another phase of the matter the response was: "What am I to do when the smelter experts come here and tell me that out in Arizona you have all sorts and varieties of ore that necessitate all sorts and varieties of treatment, which means all sorts and varieties of price schedules?" The reply to that outbreak was: "I'll name you half a dozen mining men in southern Arizona and if you will confront any one of them with your smelter experts he will make 50% of what they have been telling you spell bunk."

On June 1, 1918, with "about the rottenest record ever investigated" in the hands of the Government, the Little Fellows fully anticipated that the contemplated action at Washington on copper would be favorable; that it would result not only in a rise of price but in the elimination of that arbitrary deduction based on 14c. copper. But June 1 came and went without any change whatever. Evidently the lid was diminutive and Barney Baruch was heavy. The lid failed to lift. Late in June the fighters went over Baruch's head and submitted the crucial points to the President. On July 2 (whatever the real reason) the price of copper was unexpectedly announced at 26c. per pound. No reference was made to the arbitrary deduction theretofore by custom smelters—and so the smelters continued to profiteer. Encouraged with the half-victory, the Little Fellows hitched up their pants and took another crack at the Big Fellows. It again resulted in a partial victory. The smelters were permitted to deduct 3½c. per pound instead of their old former basis of 2½c. from the New York price. They died hard and it took months to make them live up to this agreement. They hated to quit on any of their graft.

In March 1918, I had told the authorities at Washington that it would be a futile act, so far as the interests of the Little Fellows were concerned, to raise the price of copper and to shake the custom smelters loose from their 14c. basis steal, unless the other hand of the smelters was also tied. It was pointed out that unless specifically restrained, the custom smelters would equalize the situation again in their favor by raising treatment charges, increasing insoluble deductions, and raising the minimum copper deduction.

Within 48 hours after the Government action on July 2nd last, the custom smelters had issued new *printed* contract-schedules. They raised treatment charges a minimum of one dollar per ton. They raised the minimum deduction of the copper content in ores to 20 pounds from 12. With one stroke these smelters killed the production of any copper carrying less than 5% by the Little Fellows; and if there happened to be any considerable haul to reach a railroad station (as there usually is in the case of said Little Fellows, who cannot construct railroads or smelters) then such arbitrary action likewise killed off 5%, 6%, and even 7% copper ores. But as this would tend to reduce the quantity of copper produced, so much the better for the Big Fellows, who owned all the big copper mines. Not content with those two knockout punches, the smelters soon raised the insoluble deduction from a maximum of 10c. per unit to 18c. per unit. In the refined phrase of modern days: "Can you beat it?"

Yes, the smelters can still beat it. Listen. Mr. Wishon tells us that at the memorable meeting of the Big Fellows in Washington on November 15, 1918, with our old friend Barney presiding, the following decision was recorded: "The present level of prices of the metal and the wage-scale of labor are to be preserved." Just 30 days later the Copper Queen smelter notified the Little Fellows that they would settle for copper at 16c. per pound less that 3½c. deduction—or at 12½c. (and less, of course, treatment charges, insoluble deductions, minimum copper deductions, etc.), and no satisfaction was given as to when the arbitrarily withheld 7c. per pound would be refunded. So once again the Big Fellows are placing *their* business on a sure-thing foundation. Little pickings are not to be sneezed at, and the use of the other fellow's money, when interest rates are high and money all powerful, is worth, it seems, the Big Fellows' while."

But, I regret to admit, that is not the end or the whole of the Little Fellows' story. You can kick a man for falling, after you have knocked him down, or you can keep beating a dog after it has died—on the theory that the lesson may be learned that there is such a thing as punishment after death. The Copper Queen smelter, in the face of that "decision" of November 15, 1918, "to preserve the present level of prices and the wage-scale of labor," coolly advised its little clients that the aforesaid reduced price settlement would be retroactive to December 1. Can you beat *that*? No. And so the Little Fellows have quit. They are mostly busy re-paying the local banks what they had drawn against car shipments from December 1, on the basis of their *contracts* with the Big Fellows. And what has become of all their laborers? Why their wages were *not* "preserved"—they were ruthlessly slaughtered. They are seeking jobs now from the Big Fellows *at reduced wages*. And so, you see, the Big Fellows killed two birds with a single throw. They reduced the production of copper and they increased the mine-labor supply. To the greed and crafty cunning thus displayed we are compelled to doff hats, but to such an exhibition of humanity and wisdom—well, we shall pause for a right decision. Can this nation go on indefinitely raising, side by side, patriots and profiteers?

But if this story be true—if these statements can be verified—then most assuredly a public outrage has been committed. Why do not Arizona newspapers exploit it? Why not unsheath that deadly weapon, pitiless publicity? Alack and alas! The newspapers of Arizona (those that really know these conditions) are like its United States senators—they lack either guts or freedom, or both. Why does the Copper Queen smelter own or control a string of newspapers in southern Arizona? Why does it own the 'Daily Morning Star' of Tucson? Who would you guess is the original sower of the national seeds that bloom into the scarlet flowers of sansculottism, bolshevism, and I. W. W.-ism? Does American law recognize a distinction between the wicked poor and the wicked rich?

BEN HENEY.

Tucson, Arizona, February 4.

[We publish this letter as expressing the feelings of the small-scale producer toward the smelting companies. Our readers will appreciate further enlightenment on both sides of the question.—EDITOR.]

The Position of Copper Analyzed

The present condition of the copper industry is clearly given in a statement issued by the Federal government on February 4, said Robert C. Gemmell, general manager for the Utah Copper Co., on February 8, according to the Salt Lake 'Tribune'. The official statement follows:

"No market since the armistice was signed. Sales for last 75 days do not amount to 5% of output. Copper stocks on hand at mill, smelter, in transit, and at refineries about 1,000,000,000 lb., representing over $175,000,000 tied-up in stock.

The seriousness of this surplus stock of 1,000,000,000 lb. of copper is the fact that it was all produced on the maximum basis of cost with the expectation of realizing 26c. per pound.

For every cent less than 26c. the producers will lose $10,000,000, so that 18-cent copper means a loss of $80,000,000, which is a very serious factor of demoralization apart from practically no sales for the last 90 days, and little in sight.

Copper production in 1918 averaged 200,000,000 lb. per month, or about 2,500,000,000 lb. for the year, against a pre-war production of 1,500,000,000 pounds.

Normal consumption before the War was about 125,000,000 lb. per month, divided nearly equally between home and export trade.

When peace is proclaimed and the necessary foreign credits are established in this country to finance foreign sales, the normal sales may be recovered and even exceeded, to say 150,000,000 lb. per month.

The problem now before us is how best to safeguard the industry to ensure continued operations and a living wage. Terms of the various sliding-scales automatically regulate wages according to the market price.

Current prices for January 1919 on the terms of the sliding-scale are paid on basis of 30-cent and 32-cent copper, although the December market price for copper was 26 cents, as fixed by the War Industries Board, but no sales.

Wages are therefore 50 to 75 cents higher on the war-basis than they would have been on a peace-basis, according to the sliding-scale.

The absence of any market necessitates reduced production.

Only the most favored operations could continue operations on the 18-cent copper at present cost, and then only if a market can be found for production, as all have reached the limit of their ability in carrying surplus stocks.

It must be realized that the end of the War destroyed the principal consuming market. The building-up of the peace market is being pushed as rapidly as possible, but necessarily requires a little time.

On the signing of the armistice the following conditions existed:

First—the copper producers had very little copper held ahead, as the needs of our Government and of the Allies, which were taking close to 80% of the entire production, were being supplied monthly as required.

Second—at the request of the War Industries Board, the mines continued to run from the middle of November until the end of the year at a fairly high production in order to keep the labor employed awaiting developments.

Third—there now exists an unsold stock of copper in process from the mine to the refinery or in finished form at the refinery of approximately 1,000,000,000 lb. This copper, it must be borne in mind, has been produced on a scale of wages of a 26-cent price, and none of it has been marketed or can be marketed at that price or anywhere near it.

Fourth—a stock of copper is found to be on hand in France, England, and Italy which, while small for war consumption, is a considerable amount in peace times. Amounts of scrap metals are for sale in connection with the cancellation of munitions manufacturing program.

Fifth—foreign governments having purchased their copper at 23 to 26 cents are re-marketing under Government control the stocks bought at those prices, and meanwhile are discouraging and in some cases prohibiting imports of new stocks.

Sixth—in the domestic market manufacturing industry finds itself suddenly cut-off from its business on account of the cancellation of the munitions programs. The renewal of peace industry takes time to bring about and a gap in the business is the result.

Seventh—the combination of the cessation of export trade and the interval required to turn war industries into peace industries has brought about declining prices in copper as well as other commodities, and, while prices are falling, buyers lack courage to purchase."

Commenting upon the evidence, Mr. Gemmell said:

"This is the summing-up of the conditions which have brought about the existing situation, but the present and future interests use even more than the past. It appears that:

First—the using-up of accumulated stocks is progressing, even though it may be slowly, in Europe and in America.

Second—with the coming of peace, northern neutrals and central empires, as well as the rest of the world, will need copper and the manufactured forms in which copper is an important part.

Third—telephone and telegraph companies have a large amount of postponed construction work which must soon be placed.

Fourth—with the coming of spring, considerable construction work may be expected and orders will undoubtedly be placed which require copper.

Fifth—with the better understanding of the very

great increase in the cost of production that has occurred in the last five years, confidence will be restored to buyers and they will, accordingly, come into the market, probably at present level of prices.

Sixth—giving credits to foreigners for exports will greatly facilitate marketing of copper and other American products. This is now being considered."

The conference between the copper producers and labor delegates, under the auspices of the Department of Labor, also adopted the following resolution:

"Whereas, the copper industry in peace times has always depended upon export trade for over half its product; and

"Whereas, it appears upon reliable authority that foreign countries have great difficulty at the present time in financing purchases of the products of our country; and

"Whereas, we deem it to the best interest of labor and industry in this country to help remedy this temporary breakdown of the machinery of international trade; therefore, be it

"Resolved, that this meeting of representatives of the labor of the copper industry do urge and recommend that Congress pass such legislation authorizing Government aid as well as furnishing the necessary long-term credits to facilitate the resumption of our export trade in raw materials, agricultural products, and manufactured goods."

"In the light of the foregoing," said Mr. Gemmell, "it is apparent that we cannot continue to produce and finance the production of copper which we cannot now sell at any price. It was therefore imperative to reduce production, which action necessarily carries with it an increased production cost. In other words, as the production tonnage decreases, the cost per pound of copper increases. It should also be borne in mind that our costs have recently been and are now such, that even if there was a demand for our output at present prices, which there is not, I doubt very much that we would be doing any more than 'swapping' dollars, when the cost of permanent upkeep of the property is considered, and entirely regardless of the fact that these high production costs do not include anything in the way of return of investment for the copper in the ground, which we have paid for in the purchase and improvement of our property.

All these factors considered, it is an indisputable and irrefutable fact that true economy of operation, or what might be termed selfish interest, calls for the closing down of the property until the restoration of normal conditions. This we have no thought of doing, and sincerely hope that such action will not be necessary.

At Bingham we are continuing stripping operations, rather than lay-off men. Stripping means the removal of the overburden or waste rock to expose the ore. This work is always kept several years ahead of ore production, and the true economy of present operations demands its cessation.

At Magna we are operating the mill on a 50% capacity. Inasmuch as all of the ore now being produced could be treated at the Arthur mill, true economy of operations calls for the closing down of the Magna mill. It must be clear that it costs practically as much to operate the Magna mill on a 50% capacity as it does on a full capacity. The cost of treatment is greatly increased by this limited production distributed to the two mills, when one mill could treat the entire tonnage now being produced. Should we close the Magna mill it would mean one of two things, to wit: either no work for the entire working force at Magna, or consolidating the Magna force with the Arthur force and providing half-time work for the consolidated force. This will not be done unless stern necessity compels such action.

It is a matter of keen regret to me that a wage reduction was necessary at this time. I hope I have made it plain that conditions in no way controlled by the management forced such action. In this connection it should be borne in mind that the Utah Copper Co. voluntarily made seven wage increases between August 1, 1914, and July 1, 1918. The fourth increase was made on December 1, 1916, and was based on a selling price of copper at 27½ cents or more per pound. Although the price subsequently fixed by the Government was below 27½ cents per pound, three wage increases were made since December 1, 1916, to wit: July 1, 1917, February 1, 1918, and July 1, 1918, respectively. These three wage increases, amounting to $1 per day for skilled labor and 85 cents per day for unskilled labor, were based, not upon an advance in the price of copper, but in recognition of the increased cost of living expenses, and these three increases still remain in effect. In short, the present wages are based on the sliding-scale, assuming a quotation of 20 cents per pound for copper, and to the wages based upon 20-cent copper there is added the three wage increases aggregating $1 per day for skilled labor and 85 cents per day for unskilled labor in recognition of the increased cost of living. The outstanding fact is that our present wage schedule is today in excess of the schedule which became effective December 1, 1916, based on copper quoted at 27½ cents or more per pound.

The problem before the copper industry today is the preservation of its existence. It is fighting for its very life as an industry. I always have been, and always will be, an optimist as regards the industrial life of our nation; I have no fear of the ultimate results, but in the light of the facts presented, it must be apparent to every sane and reasonable person that until peace terms are definitely known and normal industrial conditions re-established upon a sound foundation, the ad interim period presents grave and perplexing problems. Calm judgment and mutual sacrifices are necessary to tide over this critical period and bring about a restoration of satisfactory and prosperous industrial conditions.

This matter has been the subject of much correspondence between D. C. Jackling, the managing director, and myself, and I may say that, in expressing the views herein stated, I do so with the knowledge and approval of Mr. Jackling."

Explosives

By ROBERT S. LEWIS

INTRODUCTION. Explosives are divided into two classes: low explosives, such as gunpowder and blasting-powder, characterized by a relatively low rate of detonation and slow pushing effect upon the substances with which they come in contact, and high explosives, such as nitroglycerine, dynamite, and nitrotoluene, characterized by a very rapid rate of detonation and a sharp shattering effect upon the substances they touch.

In general, the energy of explosives is considered to be very great, yet, compared with fuels, explosives are costly and uneconomical sources of energy. Thus the

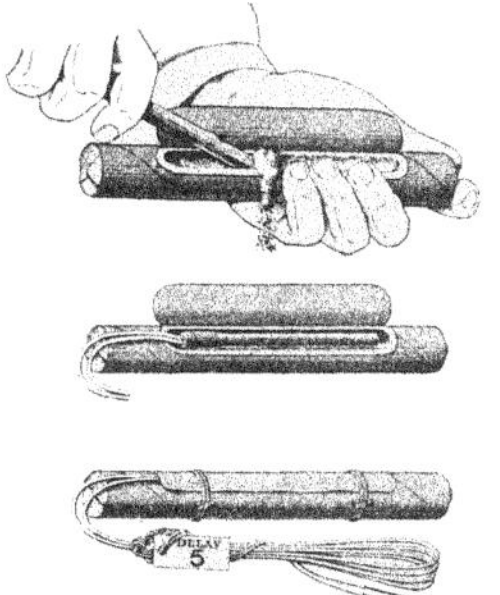

STAGES IN PREPARING PRIMER FOR ELECTRIC BLAST
(HERCULES POWDER CO.)

energy furnished by one kilogramme of petroleum in burning to carbon dioxide and water is about 12,000 calories; for coal, about 8000 calories; and for dry wood, from 3500 to 4000 calories. The energy furnished by nitroglycerine is about 1580 calories; by gun-cotton, 1100; and for 75% dynamite, about 1290 calories. The great value of explosives is found in the fact that they liberate all their energy instantly. However, the full force of explosives will not be obtained unless they are properly detonated. Combustion, explosion, and detonation represent three steps of explosive reaction, increasing in violence in the order named. This may apply to high explosives. Dynamite will simply burn if sticks are ignited in the open air. The use of a weak cap or primer may cause dynamite to explode, but only detonation by a primer of suitable strength will bring into action its full explosive force. Nitrotoluene, used as a shell-filler and for demolitions in war, can be detonated only by the use of a very strong cap.

BLACK POWDER is a low explosive. It is also called a progressive, or propelling, explosive. The composition of a good military black powder is 75 parts pulverized potassium nitrate, 15 parts pulverized charcoal, and 10 parts pulverized sulphur. The black charcoal used is

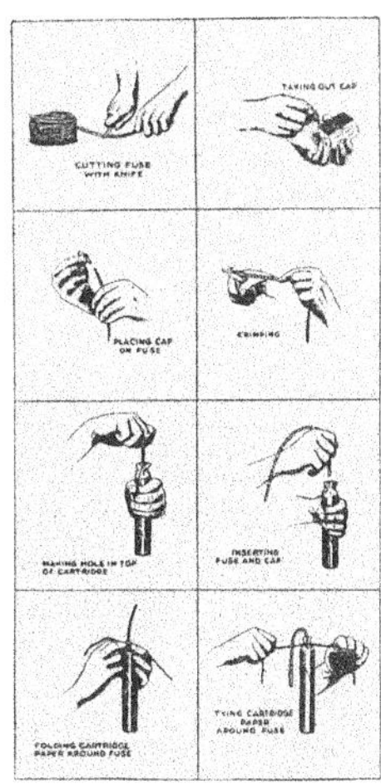

STAGES IN PREPARING PRIMER FOR ORDINARY BLAST
(HERCULES POWDER CO.)

made from wood thoroughly charred at about 350°C., and has a composition of 76% C, 4% H, 19% O, and 1% ash.

All the ingredients are separately ground, sifted to ensure the desired fineness, and are then weighed out carefully into 50-lb. lots, in the relative proportions given above. Three lots at one time are run through a mechanical mixing-machine, after which the material goes to another grinding-machine, called the incorporating mill. Here, the ingredients must be most carefully and thoroughly blended to ensure that the powder will be satisfactory. The resultant product, called mill-cake, is placed in open tubs and exposed to the action of the air until the content of moisture is equalized throughout the entire mass. From 2 to 3% moisture should remain in the cake, when it is broken into lumps of approximately uniform size. This material is now pressed into solid and compact cakes. A granulating machine, fitted with toothed cylinders, breaks the press-cake into grains, the size of which is regulated by the length of the teeth and the apertures of the screens placed beneath the machine. The sharp corners of the grains are worn off and the adhering dust is removed in a revolving cylindrical framework covered with coarse canvas, called a dusting machine. If desired, the grains are glazed by revolving them in a barrel-like receptacle in which is placed a small amount of pulverized graphite. Glazing protects the grains to a certain extent from the action of moisture in the air and renders the powder less likely to form dust during storage and transportation. The final step in manufacture is to remove all excess moisture by drying for 16 to 18 hours at 130°F. in shallow canvas-bottomed trays. After drying, the powder is packed in containers holding 100 pounds.

A good black powder should be of even grain, of suitable hardness and density, and free from dust. A small quantity should leave little or no dust when poured upon the back of the hand. Little water should be absorbed from the air, and 10 grains flashed on a copper plate should leave no head or excessive residue.

Perfect combustion of black powder would give carbon dioxide, nitrogen, and potassium sulphide as products, but in practice combustion is always more or less incomplete. Peele gives the following reaction for the combustion of black powder:

$$20KNO_3 + 30C + 10S = 6K_2CO_3 + K_2SO_4 + 3K_2S_3 + 14CO_2 + 10CO + 10N_2$$

On account of incomplete combustion, carbon monoxide, hydrogen sulphide, nitrate and hyposulphite of potassium may be given off. These products are poisonous when breathed and render it dangerous to carry open lights into the fume.

Military black powders are made only from potassium nitrate, but sodium nitrate, owing to its cheapness, is often used for the manufacture of commercial blasting-powders. It has the disadvantage of readily absorbing moisture, thereby causing rapid deterioration of the powder. Such powders have a composition of 73% sodium nitrate, 16% charcoal, and 11% sulphur. They are made in the following sizes:

Size of grains	Through round holes	On round holes
CCC	40/64 in.	32/64 in.
CC	36/64	24/64
C	27/64	18/64
F	20/64	12/64
FF	14/64	7/64
FFF	9/64	3/64
FFFF	5/64	2/64

The smaller sizes burn more quickly than the coarser grains, and are used for blasting rock and hard material. The larger sizes are used for blasting coal, shale, and especially for earthwork. Military powder, or gunpowder, is generally smaller in size than blasting-powder except that for large guns balls of powder two inches in diameter may be used. Fuse-powder is a finely granulated (—40 to 100 mesh) black powder having potassium nitrate as the oxidizing agent.

The advantages of black powder are cheapness, non-freezing character, comparative safety for shipping, easy explosion by ignition, and slow action. Its disadvantages are that it requires much tamping, it is easily spoiled by moisture (the nitrate is readily soluble in water), it has a long flame, it yields harmful gases, and it can be easily exploded by blows or friction, especially of iron on iron.

Brown powder is made from under-charred rye-straw. The ingredients are proportioned approximately as follows: potassium nitrate 80 parts, charcoal 16 parts, sulphur 3 parts, and moisture 1 part. This mixture burns more slowly than black powder. Though no longer used as a service powder by the United States, it is interesting to note that the shape of the grains of modern smokeless cannon-powders was evolved from a long series of experiments on brown powder. The fundamental idea involved was to so control the combustion of a charge of powder that there would be a uniformly increasing evolution of gas. As a result, the projectile would be started from rest under a minimum pressure, with the quantity of gas evolved in consecutive instants of time gradually increasing until the projectile reached a certain point in the bore of the gun. The pressure in the gun increases to a maximum soon after the projectile is started, and then falls regularly. The velocity increases to a maximum at a point just beyond the muzzle. Slow combustion was obtained by increasing the density and the size of the grains. The rate of evolution of gas was controlled by perforating the grains. Thus, from the interior outward, the powder burns on an increasing surface, giving for this portion of the grain increasing quantities of gas in successive intervals of time. Uniformity of rate of burning was obtained by molding grains in hexagonal form and producing a higher density on the surface than at the interior. The form of grain most generally used is that of a right hexagonal prism with seven perforations, one opposite each angle and one in the centre. The portion of the grain between the perforations is called the web. Its thickness is the determining factor in the time of combustion.

Nitro-cellulose Powders. When substances containing cellulose, such as cotton, flax, and wood fibre, are treated with nitric and sulphuric acids the product is called nitro-cellulose. This is an explosive material that may be considered the base of all forms of smokeless powders. By varying the composition and concentration of the acid mixtures a series of nitro-cellulose can be obtained. Those of highest nitration, having a nitrogen content about 13% or over, are called 'guncottons' and are characterized by their insolubility in a mixture of ether and alcohol. They are soluble in acetone and glacial acetic acid. The nitro-celluloses of lower nitration are called collodion cottons, pyro-collodions, or pyro-celluloses, and are soluble in ether-alcohol solutions. Vielle, as a result of extended research carried out in

1883, concluded that there were eight varieties of nitro-cellulose. He wrote the formula for cellulose $C_{24}H_{40}O_{20}$, quadrupling the common formula $C_6H_{10}O_5$ to account for the amount of NO_2 given by the products of his experiments. He named the different nitro-celluloses as follows:

Cellulose tetra-nitrate,	$C_{24}H_{36}O_{20}(NO_2)_4$,	having	6.76%	nitrogen.	
penta-	$C_{24}H_{35}O_{20}(NO_2)_5$	"	8.02	"	
hexa-	$C_{24}H_{34}O_{20}(NO_2)_6$	"	9.15	"	Slightly attacked by ether-alcohol
hepta-	$C_{24}H_{33}O_{20}(NO_2)_7$	"	10.18	"	Becomes gelatinous in ether-alcohol
octo-	$C_{24}H_{32}O_{20}(NO_2)_8$	"	11.11	"	Soluble in ether-alcohol.
ennea-	$C_{24}H_{31}O_{20}(NO_2)_9$	"	11.96	"	Highly soluble in ether-alcohol.
deca-	$C_{24}H_{30}O_{20}(NO_2)_{10}$	"	12.75	"	Highly soluble in ether-alcohol
endeca-	$C_{24}H_{29}O_{20}(NO_2)_{11}$	"	13.47	"	Insoluble in ether-alcohol.

A FACE IN A MASCOT, TENNESSEE, ZINC MINE PREPARED FOR BLASTING (DU PONT CO.)

The French chemist Bruly has made what is undoubtedly the most complete investigation of the nitration of cellulose. He states that the various grades of nitro-cellulose have given rise to many varied uses such as photographic films, celluloid, artificial silk, smokeless powder, and guncotton. As ordinarily made nitro-cellulose is not a single definite chemical compound but is a mixture of guncottons (endeca and deca-nitrates), collodions (ennea, octo, and hepta-nitrates), and friable cottons (penta and tetra-nitrates). One class predominates according to the composition of the nitrating acid-mixture. Since the nitro-celluloses have different properties and are used for various purposes, his experiments had for their object the determination of a method by which any desired degree of nitration could be obtained. He gives the necessary composition of the nitrating mixture to obtain a desired result, and classifies the nitro-celluloses according to their nitrogen content, thus:

Guncottons.	Nitrogen content over 12.9%.
Higher colloids.	Nitrogen content between 12 and 12.9%.
Inferior colloids.	Nitrogen content between 10 and 12%.

Nitro-cellulose has the important property of being soluble in certain liquids in which it was not soluble as cellulose. The most important of these liquids are, as stated above, acetone and a mixture of two parts of ether to one part of alcohol. If an excess of the solvent is used a true solution is formed. Evaporation of the liquid leaves the nitro-cellulose in a horn-like mass called a colloid. No evidence of the cellular structure of the cellulose remains. Acetone dissolves nitro-cellulose of highest nitration, but gives colloids that are brittle and consequently not desirable for gunpowders. The shock of explosion would cause the grains to disintegrate and the rate of combustion would be greatly increased, causing excessive pressures in the gun. The ether-alcohol solution colloids are characterized by their toughness and elasticity. Most smokeless powders are made from this class of colloids, but some satisfactory powders are made from a mixture of the two colloids.

For making military powders short-fibered and clean cotton is generally used. It is stated that the Germans have discovered that wood-pulp gives a higher nitrification and forms a better base for smokeless powder than cotton. The details of making the various grades of smokeless powder vary, but a brief general outline will be given to show the complexity of the process.

Baled cotton is picked apart in a carding machine, boiled in a caustic soda solution to remove grease, and is then bleached in a solution of calcium hypochlorate to remove lignine substances, as these form unstable nitrates. The cotton is then rolled into felt-like sheets, is again picked apart, and is dried at 105° to 110°C. It is now nitrated with the acid mixture in a centrifugal machine. The nitrated cotton does not appear to the eye to have undergone any change, but its weight has increased from 150 to 165%, depending upon the degree of nitration. After boiling in water, the nitro-cellulose is pulped in a machine similar to those used by paper manufacturers. The pulp goes to 'poachers', or large deep tanks, where it is subjected to several boilings (some sodium carbonate being added to the water), stirrings, and washings with cold water. Certain nitro-celluloses receive as many as ten washings with cold water. It is in these poachers that various nitro-celluloses may be mixed or blended to give a product of any desired nitrogen content. After poaching, the material is screened to remove knots, large fibres, sticks, and dirt. It is then dried in a centrifugal wringer. Dehydration is accomplished in a press, in which the nitro-cellulose is first subjected to a pressure of about 3000 lb. per square inch to squeeze out most of the water. Alcohol is then forced in to drive out the remaining water. The cakes are removed from the press, weighed, and immediately placed in tight cans to stop evaporation of the alcohol, enough of which remains in the cake to bring about colloidization when the necessary amount of ether is added in the next step in the process. The resultant colloid is pressed into small cylindrical blocks and then goes to the macaroni press, so called because it gives out its product in long perforated strings. The dies of the press impart the proper size and shape to the strings, which are then cut into suitable lengths to make the grains of powder. This now goes to the solvent-recovery house, where warm air carries off most of the ether and alcohol as vapors. These are condensed on refrigerating-coils. The grains are then 'wet dried' in water at 65°C. This serves to remove the remaining alcohol and ether. After passing through a drying-house the grains are given a coating of trinitrotoluene, which greatly improves the powder. Another wet drying is necessary to remove the solvent used in coating. The final step, before packing and sealing, is to coat the grains with graphite. This protects the grains from sudden shock and also forms a protecting skin to carry off the static electricity caused by friction of the grains against each other.

A pure colloid powder as described above may have other substances added to it for the purpose of obtaining a better ballistic effect. The English cordite originally contained 37% guncotton (acetone colloided), 58% nitro-glycerine, and 5% vaseline. Nitro-glycerine has an excess of oxygen, while guncotton does not contain sufficient oxygen to burn all its carbon to carbon dioxide. The high temperature of the explosion caused rapid erosion of guns, and cordite was replaced by a powder having about 38% nitro-glycerine. The French 'poudre BN' contains 38.67% of guncotton, 33.23% of nitro-cellulose, 18.74% of barium nitrate, 5.54% of potassium nitrate, 3.65% of sodium carbonate, and 1.29% of solvents. The powder for American army and navy guns is a pure nitro-cellulose of not less than 12.6% nitrogen. The well-known E.C. sporting powder contains 26% guncotton, 28% of nitro-cellulose, 4% of cellulose, 38% of potassium nitrate, 2% of camphor, and 2% volatile matter.

GUNCOTTON is a nitro-cellulose of high nitration and contains more than 12.9% nitrogen. The nitro-cellulose is taken from the poacher to the stuff chest, a large vat with an air-tight top. Feathered paddles mounted on a vertical shaft keep the pulp evenly suspended in the liquid. From the stuff chest the pulp is drawn into the molding-press. This makes blocks for the next and final pressing during which operation a maximum pressure of 7000 lb. per square inch is attained. Even then the blocks as they come from the press contain about 15% moisture. Before being placed in storage or put in service they should be soaked in pure water until they contain about 35% moisture. After nitrating, but before pulping, guncotton retains the complete cotton structure, even when viewed under the microscope. The density of the pulp is 0.8 and compressed blocks 1.2.

Nitro-glycerine will not dissolve guncotton, but both guncotton and nitro-glycerine are soluble in acetone, and a combined colloid can be made in this way. Nitro-cellulose soluble in alcohol-ether is partly soluble in nitro-glycerine. The manufacture of blasting gelatine and gelatine dynamites is based upon this property of nitro-cellulose.

Guncotton is used for filling shells, for charging torpedoes, and for various kinds of demolitions. It is pressed into the requisite form in wet state, in which condition it is safe to handle, requiring a powerful primer or a small piece of dry guncotton to effect its detonation. It will keep almost indefinitely when thoroughly purified, and will withstand temperatures as high as 200°F. for a long time, if stored under water or in a damp magazine.

Sodium carbonate in small amount is generally contained in guncotton used for demolitions. It is used to neutralize any free acid that may form in storage and thus prevents decomposition. However, it is not used in finished smokeless powders, as it would cause some smoke and would increase the solid residue in guns.

Cold has no effect on dry guncotton, but wet guncotton when frozen is less compact than dry guncotton owing to the expansion of the mass of the block. Unpulped dry guncotton burns with great rapidity. A small quantity can be burned on top of black powder without igniting it, or in the open hand without injury. Berthelot writes the reaction for guncotton exploded in a closed vessel, as in torpedoes, thus :

$$C_{24}H_{18}O_9(HNO_3)_{11} = 24CO + 24CO_2 + 17H_2 + 12H_2O + 11N_2$$

The value of guncotton as a disrupting agent is due to the fact that it has great force, yet is safe to manufacture, handle, and store. Burning guncotton can be extinguished with water. Wet guncotton cannot be ignited by a flame. A wet disk will dry on the surface and then burn. This process will continue through the whole disk. As much as a ton of guncotton has been safely burned in this way. It has been estimated that the explosion of guncotton in its own volume will give a pressure of 160 tons per square inch. The rate of propagation of explosion in rigid tubes is from 16,000 to 19,000 ft. per second. The violence of the explosion is increased by confinement or tamping. A torpedo does little damage if it explodes against the side of a ship at the water-line.

Nitro-glycerine. The process of making nitro-glycerine is comparatively simple. Well purified glycerine is treated with about 8 parts of nitric acid and 14 parts of sulphuric acid. The time required for nitrating is about one hour. Only a small quantity of nitro-glycerine is made at one time, otherwise it would be impossible to keep the temperature within safe limits because the reaction is very energetic and much heat is produced. Jets of compressed air are used for cooling. The temperature must be held between 60° and 86° F. After nitration, the nitro-glycerine is washed first with cold water, and then with a dilute alkaline solution to remove all remaining traces of acid.

Commercial nitro-glycerine has a yellowish color, but pure nitro-glycerine is a water-white oily liquid and is without odor at ordinary temperatures. It has a slightly sweetish taste and is highly poisonous. A small quantity absorbed through the mouth, nose, or skin will produce symptoms of giddiness and a severe headache. Nitro-glycerine freezes at from 37° to 46° F., and does not melt from the frozen condition until at about 51° F. It is soluble in alcohol of 90% strength and over, ether, chloroform, benzene, methyl and amyl, alcohol, carbolic acid, acetone, and olive oil, but it is insoluble in cold water, 50% alcohol, caustic soda solution, and kerosene. The freezing of nitro-glycerine makes it less sensitive to shock. When frozen it should never be thawed over a naked flame, as such a procedure is likely to cause an explosion. Thawing should be done over steam-pipes at a temperature not above 122° F. or in water-tight vessels at the same temperature. If not pure, nitro-glycerine will decompose spontaneously, changing into a greenish gelatinous substance composed chiefly of oxalic acid, ammonia, and water. A mass of nitro-glycerine will explode if struck by a bullet. Heating it to 356° F. or above will also cause an explosion. The explosive reaction is

$$2C_3H_5O_3(NO_2)_3 = 6CO_2 + 5H_2O + 3N_2 + O$$

It should be noted that no poisonous gases are formed. Nitro-glycerine is about eight times more powerful than gunpowder, weight for weight. When exploded in its own volume it gives a pressure of about 165 tons per square inch. It can be shipped in safety by dissolving it in 15 to 20% wood-alcohol whereupon it loses its explosive properties. The addition of from six to eight times its volume of water to the solution will precipitate the nitro-glycerine. Outside of 'shooting' oil-wells, nitro-glycerine is seldom used in its pure state. It is too dangerous to handle in this form. Its chief use is in the manufacture of dynamites and some smokeless powders. When used in compositions, it has the disadvantage of liquefying at moderately high temperatures and evaporates from explosive substances when they are exposed to a continually varying temperature and a moist atmosphere at the same time. When necessary, nitro-glycerine can be destroyed by chemical action. Any alkaline sulphide solution is satisfactory. An excellent solution is made by dissolving flowers of sulphur in a solution of sodium carbonate.

Picric Acid is obtained by the nitration of carbolic acid. Equal quantities of sulphuric and carbolic acids are heated to from 212° to 259° F. in an iron vessel until the mixture becomes readily soluble in cold water. The resultant phenol-sulphuric acid is then treated with nitric acid. After the rather violent action has subsided and the solution has cooled, the picric acid settles out as bright-yellow crystalline flakes. It is purified and dried at 95° F. Picric acid is sparingly soluble in cold water. It dissolves in hot water and benzene and is easily soluble in alcohol. It melts at 252.5° F. without decomposing, and this characteristic is taken advantage of in filling shells and explosive bombs, though picric acid alone is not so much used as are some of its derivatives and mixtures with other substances. The Austrian ecrasite, the English lyddite, the French melinite, the Japanese shimose, the American explosive D, and one form of rackarock are derivatives of picric acid. Experiments have shown that picric acid coming in contact with some metals or their oxides or nitrates, such as lead, iron,

A COYOTE BLAST IN SOUTHERN CALIFORNIA. 95,950 LB. OF TROJAN POWDER BROKE 897,000 TONS OF LIMESTONE

strontium, or potassium, is quite likely to form sensitive explosive salts. Many accidents in handling shells are presumed to be due to red or white lead being used to seal the threads of shell-plugs. The explosive reaction is

$$2C_6H_2(NO_2)_3OH = CO_2 + H_2O + 11CO + 2H_2 + 3N_2$$

TRI-NITRO-TOLUENE, tri-nitro-methyl-benzene, or T. N. T., for short, is made by nitrating toluene, a by-product from the manufacture of illuminating gas or obtained by 'cracking' or distilling petroleum. The nitration is done in stages, mono-nitro-toluene and di-nitro-toluene being intermediate products. T. N. T. behaves in a stable manner when exposed to the air under varying conditions of temperature. It is not affected by contact with metals and forms no sensitive compounds with them. Though a powerful explosive when detonated, it cannot be exploded by flame or a blow. A rifle-bullet may be fired through it without effect. Its ignition point is 356° F. Upon being exposed to a flame, the explosive melts, takes fire, and burns with a heavy black smoke. Because of these advantages, T. N. T. is now largely used as a shell-filler and for demolitions, for which use it is cast into blocks, which are then copper-plated to protect the corners. Pure T. N. T. is a slightly yellow fine crystalline powder. It melts at about 177° F. Its explosive force is somewhat less than that of guncotton, nitro-glycerine, or the picrates. Its chemical formula is $C_6H_2CH_3(NO_2)_3$ and the products of its explosion are much like those of picric acid and nitro-celluloses of low nitration.

BLASTING GELATINE is a yellow or light-brown elastic mixture. It is made by mixing from 5 to 7 parts of soluble nitro-cellulose with from 93 to 95 parts of nitro-glycerine. These two materials are agitated in troughs by means of wooden paddles. When too hard to work with the paddles, the mixture is kneaded by hand until it has a smooth and even consistence. It is then allowed to cool, when the mass becomes a firm compact jelly-like substance soft enough to be easily cut with a knife. It is forced through a circular opening by a screw-conveyor forming a rope or cable that is cut into definite lengths and then wrapped in paraffined paper like ordinary dynamite cartridges. Theoretically it is the most powerful explosive known. From a chemical standpoint more complete combustion takes place with the mixture than with either ingredient. The nitro-glycerine has an excess of oxygen and this supplies the deficiency of oxygen in the nitro-cellulose, causing all the carbon to burn to carbon dioxide instead of to carbon monoxide. Heated slowly to 400° F. blasting gelatine will explode, but small quantities can be burned in the air without exploding.

Blasting gelatine differs from common dynamite in that ordinary pressure does not cause the nitro-glycerine to exude, and it is not affected by the action of water, except at the surface, where it turns white due to the dis-

SAME AS OPPOSITE, AFTER THE DUST HAD SETTLED, SHOWING ROCK BROKEN (TROJAN POWDER CO.)

placement of the nitro-glycerine in the outer layer. At ordinary temperatures it is much less sensitive than common dynamite. However, when frozen it is very sensitive to shock, and, in this respect, is the opposite of common dynamite. If from 1 to 4% of camphor is added to blasting gelatine, it is rendered insensitive to ordinary shock and friction, and requires a very powerful primer for detonation. Owing to its violent action, blasting gelatine is usually mixed with other substances in order to deaden the violence or prolong the duration of the explosive force.

GRANULATED NITRO-GLYCERINE POWDER. The composition of this powder is somewhat similar to that of black blasting powder, but the grains are formed by first melting the ingredients and then forcing the mass through a fine mesh screen. This method of manufacture produces a hard and porous grain. The nitro-glycerine is then added; part of it remains on the surface and part is taken into the pores of the grains. The rate of detonation of this powder is about double that of black blasting powder, and hence it is more suitable for use in rock that is soft and full of seams.

Analysis of a Typical Granulated Nitro-glycerine Powder

	%
Nitro-glycerine	5
Combustible (sulphur, coal, and resin)	35
Sodium nitrate	60

DYNAMITES are a means of utilizing the powerful explosive force of nitro-glycerine and at the same time of avoiding the handling of that substance in its dangerous liquid form by absorbing it in some porous material. The absorbing medium is called a dope. A dope may be inactive as infusiorial earth, or it may be active, as wood pulp, flour, or even black powder, in which case it takes part in the explosion of the dynamite.

Composition of Typical Straight Dynamites

	15%	20%	25%	30%	35%	40%	45%	50%	55%	60%
Nitro-glycerine	15	20	25	30	35	40	45	50	55	60
Combustible*	20	19	18	17	16	15	14	14	15	16
Sodium nitrate	64	60	56	52	48	44	40	35	29	23
Calcium or magnesium carbonate	1	1	1	1	1	1	1	1	1	1

*Wood pulp, flour, and sulphur for grades below 40%; wood pulp only for others.

The combustible material is the absorbing dope. The principal function of the sodium nitrate is to supply oxygen for burning the combustible. The alkali carbonates are for the purpose of neutralizing any traces of acid that might be present, and which would affect the keeping qualities of the nitro-glycerine. These dynamites are powerful explosives. In fact from a practical standpoint they are the strongest of any of the dynamites. Their action is a quick shattering one, making them suitable for very tough or hard rock. The rate of detonation of 30% dynamite is 14,920 ft. per second and of 64% dynamite 20,490 ft. per second.

AMMONIA DYNAMITES. In this type of dynamite, ammonium nitrate is used to replace part of the nitro-glycerine of the straight dynamites. Upon explosion the ammonium nitrate forms a large amount of water and thus lowers the temperature of the products of explosion. Such a dynamite has a slower rate of detonation and is weaker than straight dynamite. Its great disadvantage is found in the tendency of the ammonium nitrate to absorb moisture from the air. For this reason ammonia dynamites should never be stored in damp or wet places.

Composition of Typical Ammonia Dynamites

	30%	35%	40%	50%	60%
Nitro-glycerine	15	20	22	27	35
Ammonium nitrate	15	15	20	25	30
Sodium nitrate	51	48	42	36	24
Combustible	18	16	15	11	10
Calcium carbonate or zinc oxide	1	1	1	1	1

LOW-FREEZING DYNAMITES. The nitro-glycerine in straight dynamites crystallizes or freezes at a temperature of about 52° F. Once frozen, dynamite should be carefully thawed before using. It has been found that the addition of certain substances, called nitro-substitution compounds, will lower the freezing point to 35° F. or less. These compounds are formed by the action of nitric acid on products derived from coal tar, and all form explosives when mixed with oxidizing agents such as ammonium nitrate, sodium nitrate, or potassium chlorate. Common nitro-substitution compounds are picric acid and derivatives, nitro-toluene, nitro-benzene, and nitro-naphthalene.

Composition of Typical Low-Freezing Dynamites

	30%	35%	40%	45%	50%	55%	60%
Nitro-glycerine	23	26	30	34	38	41	45
Nitro-substitution compounds	7	9	10	11	12	14	15
Combustible	17	16	15	14	14	15	16
Sodium nitrate	52	48	44	40	35	29	23
Calcium or magnesium carbonate	1	1	1	1	1	1	1

Low-freezing dynamites also have a slower rate of detonation than straight dynamites. Their action is more of a simple propulsion or pushing effect, and they are used where the action of straight dynamite would be too violent.

Composition of Low-Freezing Ammonia Dynamites

	30%	35%	40%	50%	60%
Nitro-glycerine	13	17	17	21	27
Nitro-substitution compounds	3	4	4	5	6
Ammonium nitrate	15	15	20	25	30
Sodium nitrate	53	49	45	36	27
Combustible	15	14	13	12	9
Calcium carbonate, or zinc oxide	1	1	1	1	1

GELATINE DYNAMITES. Because of their imperviousness to moisture and the relatively small quantity of poisonous gases produced by their detonation, gelatine dynamites are commonly used in wet or submarine blasting and for blasting in many mines and tunnels. Theoretically gelatine dynamites are the most powerful of dynamites, but practically they are not the equal of straight dynamites in explosive force. This is probably due to the difficulty of securing complete detonation, and also because they are more or less elastic and consequently cannot well be made to completely fill a drill hole.

Composition of Typical Gelatine Dynamites

	30%	35%	40%	50%	55%	60%	70%
Nitro-glycerine	23.0	28.0	33.0	42.0	46.0	50.0	60.0
Nitro-cellulose	0.7	0.9	1.0	1.5	1.7	1.9	2.4
Sodium nitrate	62.3	58.1	52.0	45.5	42.3	38.1	29.6
Combustible*	13.0	12.0	13.0	10.0	9.0	9.0	7.0
Calcium carbonate	1.0	1.0	1.0	1.0	1.0	1.0	1.0

*Wood pulp in 60 and 70% grades; flour, wood pulp, and, in some makes, resin, and sulphur in the other grades.

POISONOUS GASES. Practically all dynamites and blasting powders give off poisonous gases upon exploding. The most important of these gases are carbon monoxide and hydrogen sulphide. The following table shows the results of some tests carried out by the U. S. Bureau of Mines:

	Carbon monoxide, %	Hydrogen sulphide, %
Granulated nitro-glycerine powder	2.7	15.7
Black blasting powder	10.8	8.7
Straight dynamite	26.9 to 34.6	not determined
Low-freezing dynamite	47.5	not determined
Ammonia dynamite	3.8	5.4
Gelatine dynamite	3.0	4.1

Fatal accidents due to breathing these fumes have occurred in mines and tunnels. Gelatine dynamite produces the least amount of harmful gases, but even this quantity is dangerous. Workings should be thoroughly ventilated after blasting before men are allowed to return to work. If explosives are not in good condition or are not fully detonated very great quantities of poisonous gases will be evolved.

STRENGTH OF VARIOUS EXPLOSIVES. The following table gives the potential energy and disruptive and propulsive effects of dynamites and blasting powders. These are given in percentages and in all cases 40% straight dynamite is taken as unity or 100%.

	Potential strength	Disruptive effect	Propulsive effect
30% straight dynamite	93.1	84.1	96.8
40% " "	100.0	100.0	100.0
50% " "	111.0	109.2	107.4
60% " "	104.0	119.8	114.9
60% low-freezing dynamite	60.2	93.5	91.2
40% ammonia dynamite	101.8	67.9	99.1
40% gelatine dynamite	105.7	78.4	95.8
5% granulated nitro-glycerine powder	67.6	21.6	53.3
Black blasting powder	71.6	6.8	58.6

Potential energy is determined in the bomb calorimeter and represents the maximum energy that can be produced by the explosive. However, the useful work done by the explosive is a small fraction of this theoretical maximum, consequently a knowledge of the potential energy of an explosive is of little help as a guide in selecting a suitable explosive. The disruptive effect, which is closely related to the shattering force of an explosive, is determined by a rate of detonation apparatus and the expansion of lead blocks from the detonation of internal charges of explosives. The propulsive effect corresponds to the heaving or pushing force of the explosives, and is found by means of pressure gauges and the arc through which a heavy pendulum is swung by the explosion of a definite charge of the explosive. The two latter characteristics are useful guides for comparing the practical value of explosives.

The Du Pont Co. gives the following table for getting the number of cartridges of any given strength required to equal one cartridge of any other strength.

One cartridge, %	60%	50%	45%	40%	35%	30%	25%	20%	15%
60	1.00	1.12	1.20	1.28	1.38	1.50	1.63	1.80	2.08
50	0.89	1.00	1.07	1.14	1.23	1.34	1.45	1.60	1.85
45	0.83	0.93	1.00	1.07	1.16	1.25	1.36	1.50	1.73
40	0.78	0.87	0.94	1.00	1.08	1.17	1.27	1.40	1.59
35	0.72	0.81	0.87	0.93	1.00	1.09	1.18	1.30	1.50
30	0.67	0.75	0.80	0.85	0.92	1.00	1.09	1.20	1.38
25	0.61	0.69	0.74	0.78	0.85	0.92	1.00	1.10	1.27
20	0.55	0.62	0.67	0.71	0.77	0.83	0.90	1.00	1.15
15	0.48	0.54	0.58	0.61	0.66	0.72	0.78	0.86	1.00

Thus 2.08 cartridges of 15% strength would equal 1

cartridge of 60% strength and 1.38 cartridges of 15% would be equivalent to 1 cartridge of 30% strength. The table is, of course, an approximately accurate one, and should be used in connection with some actual tests on the rock to be blasted, in which case it will enable the blaster to select an explosive that will do the work efficiently and satisfactorily.

Unfortunately the trade names of different kinds of dynamites does not truly represent their comparative strengths. A 60% straight dynamite and a 60% low-freezing dynamite will not have the same strength. The potential energy of 40% ammonia dynamite and 40% gelatine dynamite is greater than that of 40% straight dynamite, but the useful work that can be done, represented by the propulsive and disruptive effects, is less. The strength of 60% low-freezing dynamite is not quite equal to that of 40% straight dynamite.

The writer is indebted to the publications listed below for much of the information presented in this article. The subject matter is so arranged that it is impractical to give detailed credit. All the tables but one have been taken from the Bulletins of the U. S. Bureau of Mines.

'Military Explosives', Weaver.

'Explosives', Munroe and Kibler.

'The Nitration of Toluene', E. J. Hoffman, 'Met. & Chem. Eng.', May 1, 1916.

'Chemical Engineering in Nitrocellulose Manufacture', S. L. Stadelman, 'Met. & Chem. Eng.', June 1914.

'Mining Engineers' Handbook', Peele.

Bulletin 12, U. S. Bureau of Mines, 'A Primer on Explosives for Coal Miners', Munroe and Hall.

Bulletin 48, U. S. Bureau of Mines, 'The Selection of Explosives Used in Engineering and Mining Operations', Hall and Howell.

Bulletin 80, U. S. Bureau of Mines, 'A Primer on Explosives for Metal Miners and Quarrymen', Munroe and Hall.

Dressing Bismuthinite-Molybdenite Ore

At the Kingsgate mine, New South Wales, Australia, a mill to dress 25 tons daily of sorted Bi_2S_3-MoS_2 ore is being erected, to be ready early in April.

The ore occurs as small 'pipes' scattered through a large area of ground, making mining costs rather high. Out of every 100 tons of material mined, sorting reduces this to 40 tons for the concentrating plant.

The power-plant consists of two 100-hp. multitubular boilers, 160-hp. cross-compound engine driving the mill and 14 by 12-in. Ingersoll-Rand compressor, 4 jack-hammers, 1 stope-hammer, Little Tugger hoist for hauling ore from the various deposits, and pumps.

The mill flow-sheet is as follows:

The ore passes over a timber-bridge roadway to an elevated ore-paddock, thence through a No. 1 Dodge breaker into a 50-ton ore-bin. A Challenge ore-feeder (water is added at this point) feeds a pair of 25 by 14-in. rolls. An 8-in. balata belt bucket-elevator delivers to 14 by 14-in. rolls, followed by a shaking-screen, 14 by 14-in. rolls, another 8-in. elevator, May brothers' 2-hutch jig, 2 sets of 14 by 14-in. rolls, and 3 Wilfley tables. This comprises the coarse concentrating portion of the plant. The pulp then flows on to two 5-ft. Forwood-Down grinding-pans, being reduced to 30 or 40-mesh, then over 1 Wilfley table and 2 Frue vanners. This completes the bismuth recovery. Spitzkasten are used throughout for classification. The molybdenite is recovered by the latest type Minerals Separation 8-cell sub-aeration machine. The first concentrate is raised to 80% MoS_2 or over, by means of a single-cell sub-aerator.

Manganese Ore in Uruguay

*Manganese is found in practically all parts of Uruguay. Numerous small and some larger deposits have been examined by, or are known to, the Bureau of Geology, and are mentioned in a report on the mineral resources of the country published in 1916. Most of the deposits are too small or too poor in quality to make exploitation worth while. In other cases, lack of transportation and timber stand in the way of successful operation.

One of the principal deposits is found in the Department of Rivera, near the Arroyo Zapucay. Here there are two hills almost entirely of ore, and it is estimated that 80,000,000 tons could be extracted by open-cuts. The deposit is covered by nine concessions extending over 22,000 acres, and is the property of the Uruguay Manganese Co. Analysis shows an average content of 34.8% iron, 22.7% manganese, 9% silica, 0.03% phosphorus, and 0.05% sulphur. The Uruguay Manganese Co. was formed at Montevideo several years ago, the capital being subscribed largely in Great Britain. It was planned to build a 75-mile branch of the Central Uruguay railroad to the deposit, and the venture aroused much interest. Little development has been done, however, and the deposit is not being worked. There are at present no transportation facilities, and the necessary fuel and timber for such a manganiferous-iron property are lacking. The same difficulties stand in the way of working a similar deposit at Caraguatá, in the Department of Tucuarembó.

There are a number of smaller deposits of manganese in other departments. One of these is at Carrasco, 9 miles east of Montevideo on the coast. It has been examined by representatives of British and German interests, and is being worked at present on a small scale, the ore being used by glass factories. The outcrops are small and scattered, and the deposit appears to extend north and south from 500 to 650 ft., with a width of 165 ft. The ore is stated to contain from 30 to 40% manganese.

As far as is known, the only manganese in Uruguay being worked on any scale at present is a 16-ft. vein composed of small stringers at the Pantanoso, in the immediate vicinity of Montevideo. The owners, who are Argentines, claim to have invested $100,000. Ore is being extracted at a depth of 90 ft. Most of the ore is hand-picked.

*U. S. Consular Report from Montevideo.

The Banker and Mining

By FRANK B. ANDERSON

*Your chairman has given me two suggestions—one the duty of the banks, and the other the duty of the clients of the banks. The banks in a locality are charged with the duty of seeing that the resources of that locality are financed in some way. Whether or not it is possible for the banks to directly engage in that financing is another question. We are living in a comparatively young country—in a comparatively young section of that country. We are living under a democracy, and sometimes I think of the story that was once told me of the discussions of, I think, the Constitutional Convention, when there seemed to be so much doubt as to the nature of the different classes of government. One of the delegates from New England got up and made a speech on the subject of what constituted a monarchy, and what constituted a limited monarchy, and finally what constituted a democracy. He said that a monarchy was like a great ship that plowed across a smooth ocean, lights burning, bands playing and the passengers all happy, and struck a rock and went down; that a democracy was like a raft: you could not sink it, but your feet were in the water all the time. That applies as well to the banking business of the United States in the past. We have in this country about 28,000 banks. Unfortunately we are a few shy of 28,000 bankers. The prime duty of the men sitting at the head of those banks is to keep their institutions in such shape that they can respond to the demands of the people whose money they are loaning. Their prime duty is to keep their investment in such liquid form that they will be able to respond to the demands of the community, the demands of their depositors, and so that they will not bring about a failure on their part which will be reflected in every walk of life in that particular community.

The banks of a city like San Francisco have a peculiar duty, as the reserves of all the country banks are entrusted to the city banks, and their duty to keep their funds in liquid shape is a much sterner duty than the duty of the country banker, who has no such obligation to perform. I was brought up in that wicked street called Wall Street. I came to California in 1903. In looking over the banking situation it was perfectly clear to me that the banks were called upon to do a great deal of financing which was not proper financing for commercial banks to do. At the same time they had to do it in order to perform the duty that your chairman speaks of, and that is to bring to a high point of development the resources of this territory. The Coast lacked a number of different pieces of financial machinery: the bond-broker, the note-broker, for instance. We induced those men to come out to the Coast. We told them of the opportunity there was on this Coast. They came; and I remember with some amusement that some of the bankers rather resented this foreign money being brought into this territory for the purpose of competing with their money. The answer seemed to me to be perfectly obvious, that if their money came into these fields, and plowed any of these fields, I get my share of the worms. You gentlemen know that these different agencies have brought into the community many hundreds of millions of dollars, and you know that these dollars, working, seeking the reward that they were after, have aided in building up a great many of the industries of the Coast. This Coast has never had anything in the nature of an exploration company. It has always needed something in the nature of an exploration company, a company formed by men whose character was high, whose capital was large, whose capital was subscribed for the purpose of taking risks, subscribed for the purpose of investigating prospects, bringing them into being, and bringing them to a point where the banks were justified in making loans, and bringing them to a point where they were justified in offering the securities to the public. There have been small groups on this Coast who have taken those risks as individuals. There have been large groups that have come from the older parts of the country—New England, for instance. There have been large groups that have come from England and from France; but the mining industry, beginning at the point of development, is one that has got to be carried on by venturesome capital. It finally passes that stage, and it gets to a point where it is nothing but a manufacturing proposition, a question of whether or not intelligence is used in directing the enterprise, and whether the costs are kept down, and whether there is character sufficient to keep enough of the reserve back of you so that you can continue to conduct your enterprise when your ore is pinching out. The attitude of the bank that I happen to represent toward the mining industry is practically the same that it is toward any other industry. If there is character back of the management, if the men have the reputation of being experts, if they have the reputation of being honest—in other words, if they have character—the bank that I represent has aided those men, and the other banks in the city of San Francisco have aided many of them. I can think of instances where the banks, traveling along the line of least resistance, when mining enterprises have gotten into difficulties, would have exercised a banker's lien, taken the deposit that happened to be there, to cancel the loan and say, "We are sorry. Go ahead and work yourself out." I have known of several instances where

*An address delivered before the California chapter of the American Mining Congress at San Francisco on January 16.

the banks have refrained from doing that, and have put their shoulders to the wheel, and have carried the undertaking to a sound reorganization. Most people think that the banks lend against collateral entirely. That is a false idea. The commercial banks, very few of them, lend against collateral. The banks loan against the statement of men in whom they have gained confidence and whom they trust.

So far as the duty of the client goes, I do not know that I can blame all bankers, Mr. Chairman, for measuring every line of effort with the same yard-stick. There are few business men who realize the value of one asset that they have got. Their are very few of them that will take the trouble to educate their banker in their particular line of business, and by educating him unconsciously make him become interested in their problems. A number of people resent even the questions that their bankers ask. I don't know exactly why; but there is no more valuable asset that any business man has, I will say over again, than that of forcing his banker to know his business and to unconsciously become interested in his problems. So much for the duty of the client.

The banks of the country have recently given evidence of their attitude toward mining in the large flotation of the bonds by the Anaconda. The banks of this community have given evidence of their attitude toward mining investments in connection with such companies as the Natomas Company and the General Petroleum Corporation. The type of mine that my friend over here represents, if it ever needed money, would have no difficulty in getting it; and the type of mine that all of you gentlemen represent, if you run along the same lines. You never had any difficulty in getting money from your bankers, and you never will; but the banker cannot loan its funds to exploit or develop a mining enterprise, whether it be gold or oil or what it may be; but the individual who wants to exploit that particular prospect, if those individuals are known to have the expert knowledge, if they have formed a habit of telling the truth and keeping their word, they can be helped, and they have been helped in the past; and there are men in this room who can testify to the fact.

The problem that confronts us in the future is a difficult one. I have no solution for it. It is extremely interesting to me to sit down and listen to the guesses of the men who have solutions for them. They are no better than guesses. Some of them are fascinating guesses. The situation in which we stand today is one where we have got to pick up each day as it comes and solve the problems of that day, and to keep our heads, keep our courage, and exercise our usual common-sense. We have successfully solved the problems of the past: we may have made a good deal of noise about it and made a lot of waste, but we have solved them, and I think we will solve the problems of the future in the same way. I hope and pray that men who have the influence that you gentlemen have will make it known in no uncertain terms that this country was made through personal initiative, and we want to get back to personal initiative as quickly as we can. The demands on the Government for all sorts of expenditures and commissions for reconstruction problems are insistent: some of them sound logical; some of them should be undertaken; but the Government has got to be made to understand that it has got to live inside of its income, and live inside of an income that the business man can contribute without paralyzing his business. You gentlemen are interested in the thing that interests the whole people, and that is to see the dollar get back to its purchasing power. The expenditures of the Government during the War have exceeded the amount that can be raised by taxation or by loans from the actual savings of the people. The expenditures have been upon a scale that has never yet been attempted; necessarily so; and because the object that we were trying to attain was so high up—hung up so high that everybody could see it and understand it—the population got back of it, and had no patience with the theorist or the politician or anyone who objected or tried to work against it. The people could see the object and they went for it. But we were forced into a position where we had to spend money in a year and a half a lot of which we ought to have been spending over the last twenty or twenty-five or forty years. The father of every generation in this country since the foundation of the country has either had to put the uniform on his back or he has had to sit by and look at a war. There is no doubt there are men in this room who can go back to their family record and find that the father of every generation has had to put the uniform on his back. There are men sitting in this room that have seen this country in three wars, and yet there has been no sentiment whatever to make any preparation, or to give any of the young men growing up any teaching that would aid them to carry out the duties that were going to be thrust upon them as it was thrust upon their fathers. Necessarily we had to spend a great deal more money than would have been necessary if we had thought ahead a little.

Now that is not only true in regard to the question of preparedness. It is true in regard to practically everything that we have to undertake. We have been busy during all these generations settling and developing a great big, vast, rich territory. The rewards for that development right under our nose were more attractive than the rewards from the outside. We were too busy to care very much about the character of people that were elected to office, many of them earnest men, but men whose knowledge was confined to the needs of their own localities; and practically all the laws that we have on the statute-books are laws which were put there by brains and minds that understood local problems only. We have reached a point where, in order to keep our great manufacturing institutions going, to keep up the purchasing power of the people that have been built up around those great manufacturing institutions, we have got to seek the trade of the world, and we have got to go out and compete with peoples who have spent hundreds of years and thousands of lives and millions of dollars in entrenching themselves in strategical points (from the commercial standpoint) and we have to compete with them with laws that practically make it impossible for us to compete. We have got to get that thing hung up so that the population can see and understand it, and then sweep aside the theorist and demand laws that will allow us to compete successfully.

To go back a minute, I said that the Government had exceeded the amount that could be raised by taxation or by loans from the actual savings of the people, necessitating the creation of credits with the banks direct, and through the people with the banks, to enable them to carry out their duty in purchasing these new credits, with the result that the purchasing power created has exceeded the purchasable goods and services, resulting in competition for those goods and services between the Government and its own people, and consequently driving up prices, which has created a hardship for the people of the country, and particularly for the gold-mining industry, whose product is at a fixed price. A sound permanent cure can come only through an absorption of that credit which has been created, by actual savings, by a cessation of borrowing on the part of the Government as soon as it is practicable, and by an understanding on the part of the Government that it must reduce its activities to a point where it can live within its income, and within an income, as I said before, that can be collected without paralyzing every line of effort. The situation can only be cured, as I said, through genuine savings. Continued borrowing beyond the power of the people to absorb will only retard the return to normal prices and aggravate the situation that exists at present. Abnormal taxation, such taxation as we have today, will kill initiative and paralyze business. I know of institutions which, if they could liquidate today, would be in a much better position than if they continue to do the business because of the fact that the day is coming that they will have to liquidate their high-priced assets at declining prices. The quick solution of the problem, again, I say, is economy on the part of the nation and the people; and to the extent that this is observed the purchasing power of the dollar will be restored. To the extent that it is ignored the purchasing power of the dollar will decline. Mere creation of money and credits will not solve the problem. The bills of the past have got to be paid by goods and services, and the nation that works the hardest, that produces the most, and that consumes the least, will be the nation that gets out of its problems the quickest.

THE December bulletin of the National Bank of New York, in the course of some interesting remarks anent the great accumulation of gold in the United States, contains the following: There are people who will listen with amazement to the suggestion that we ought to get rid of some of our gold. It seems altogether inconsistent with our embargo, still in effect, under which we forbid the exportation of gold even to pay our legitimate debts. But it was pointed out two years ago when the heavy importations were made that they involved an after-the-war problem. The perils of having more than our rightful share of the world's gold were pointed out at that time. They exist in the fact that in the long run there is a relationship between the gold reserves, the state of credit, and the level of prices. Gold does not lie indefinitely idle. While it is idle it is harmless, but when it is used in excess it works mischief. Nothing but a condition of industrial activity and level of prices approximating that which we have been experiencing during the War can keep this stock of gold employed, and at this level of prices it is very doubtful whether we can sell anything abroad after Europe has resumed production at the normal rate. In other words, this stock of gold seems likely to be either idle on our hands, in which case it is dead capital, or, if in use as the basis of credit, the means of elevating us to a trade position so far above the rest of the world outside that it will be untenable.

Analysis of Graphite Ore

*The method of analyzing graphite products or ores has never been standardized to the extent of defining volatile and fixed carbon in a manner acceptable to all analysts. Accurate methods used in determining carbon in graphite products are tedious. Work recently done by the Pittsburgh Experiment Station of the U. S. Bureau of Mines on the chemical analysis of graphite products had in view the devising of a rapid, accurate, and simple method of analysis with a fair degree of accuracy.

A sample, weighing 0.2 to 1 gramme, depending upon the relative amount of graphitic carbon, is placed in a 100-cc. evaporating dish with 25 cc. of 1 to 1 HCl, heated over a hot plate for 15 minutes, filtered through a filter of ignited asbestos, and washed with hot water until free from chlorides. The filter and the residue are then transferred to a porcelain or platinum boat, and dried on the hot plate. The boat containing the residue is transferred to the tube of a combustion furnace and burned in a stream of oxygen gas, the CO_2 formed being collected in a potash bulb with a 30% KOH solution, and the amount of CO_2 weighed. The combustion tube should contain some fused lead chromate to retain any sulphur that may be present.

Concentrates are likely to contain flotation oils, which must, of course, be removed before combustion, or too high results will be obtained for graphitic carbon. This may be done by placing a sample weighing 0.2 to 0.5 gramme in a small Erlenmeyer flask, adding 25 cc. of ether, corking loosely, and allowing to stand for about a half hour, shaking at intervals. This mixture is filtered onto asbestos in a Gootch crucible, the asbestos having previously been washed with hydrochloric acid and ignited. The residue on the filter is then washed with alcohol and finally with distilled water; it is then ready to be treated with acid for the removal of possible carbonates, as is done in the treatment of ores.

*Abstract from U. S. Bureau of Mines publication 'Preparation of Crucible Graphite', by G. C. Dub.

Possibilities of Dredging in the Oroville District, California

By CHARLES H. THURMAN

The possibility of re-dredging profitably the Oroville field has been the subject of much interest to gold miners, especially those who were active in the district during its early days.

There were three reasons why the earlier type of dredge did not recover all of the gold:

1. Inability to dig all of the gold-bearing gravel from any given area.
2. Inadequate gold-saving appliances.
3. Limited storage for tailing at the rear of the dredge on account of short sluices and stackers.

On account of the light weight of the digging-ladder on the older dredges they could not dig efficiently at a greater depth than 22 ft. below water-level. In many cases the constant danger of running the bucket-line off the lower tumbler prevented digging to a greater depth. Where the dredge was set stationary and the buckets were lowered straight down, the gravel was excavated to a depth of 30 ft. Then the buckets would be raised and the dredge moved sideways the width of the bucket-line, becoming chored in a stationary position once more while the operation of 'chopping down' was continued.

In stiff ground this did not work well, because the hubs of the lower tumbler would ride on the side of the gravel-bank. This had a tendency to cause the digging-ladder to slip sideways into the cut out of which it had just been moved. In such cases it became necessary to move sideways more than the width of the bucket-line, which resulted in leaving ridges or peaks of un-dredged ground between 'settings'. These ridges had a height of from 1 to 10 ft., with a corresponding width at the base. This condition was noticeable in 106 acres that were re-dredged from September 1916 to date. The same results were produced with both the dipper type of dredge and the continuous bucket-line type, the latter of which then dug on a head-line instead of a spud.

Many of the head-line dredges endeavored to clean-up the bottom by the side-swinging method, as now practised on newer dredges, but, on account of the light digging-ladders in use at that time, and the limited distance that the dredge could swing on account of the head-line, it was impossible to clean-up the bedrock thoroughly.

All the gold-bearing material brought up by the bucket-lines did not reach the gold-saving devices, as the flat-shaped buckets of the open-link type spilled much of the gravel back into the pond in the first 30 ft. of travel up the ladder.

Another great waste occurred when the buckets began to turn on the upper tumbler. The shape of the buckets allowed the gravel to spill too soon, and the receiving end of the hopper was set so far aft that considerable material fell back into the pond. This spill in the well-hole was excessive at times, filling up the pond until the hull of the dredge became grounded. Usually only sufficient overburden was removed to float the dredge, in some cases not over 10 ft. in depth. These abandoned strips of ground varied in size from 20 to 30 ft. wide to the full length of the hull, which was approximately 100 feet.

Much ground was left undredged on account of short tail-sluices, which dumped the fine so close to the hull that the dredges were crowded ahead before the bedrock was cleaned-up. Short stacking-conveyors for heavy gravel were another cause of abandoned ground. These conveyors fouled against the high tailing-piles in the rear and necessitated the moving of the dredge ahead before all of the ground was cleaned-up. On the modern dredges there is a drip-pan that extends the full length of the digging-ladder. This carries the spilled material back to the face of the cut, where the buckets can pick it up again. At the receiving-hopper the bucket-idler below the upper tumbler holds the slack of the bucket-line in order that the receiving-hopper can be built out far enough under the buckets to catch material with as little spill as possible. Furthermore, the newer dredges have a much more elaborate 'save-all' than the earlier ones; also, spray nozzles to wash out gold-bearing material that might stick to the inside or outside of the buckets after they have dumped. It may be well at this point to state that enough gold is caught in the 'save-all' alone to pay for the power required to operate the modern dredge. This furnishes an idea of the gold lost at this point alone on the earlier dredges.

On the old dredges the screens for separating sand and gold from the gravel were adequate, but the gold-saving riffles were inefficient on two different counts:

1. The system for the distribution of water and fine allowed 75% of the fine to flow out of the first two riffle-sluices on the tables, while it should have been distributed equally between 16 riffle-sluices. In many cases, this caused the fine sediment to collect to a depth of three inches and the fine gold had little chance to settle on the quicksilver in the riffles.

2. The fine passed over only from 30 to 50 ft. of gold-saving riffles, whereas, by actual test made on the Oroville property of the Natomas company, in 1915, it was proved that the fine should pass over not less than 90 ft. of gold-saving riffles in order to save the major portion of the fine gold.

This last point was demonstrated by me several years

ago with a 6-ft. Bucyrus dredge that had a very efficient digging apparatus but a length of riffle insufficient to treat the fine sediment. After this dredge had been operated ten years at a profit, riffles were put in a drop-extension tail-sluice and an average of $125 per month was saved during the remaining life of the dredging operation.

Another waste of ground was caused in some instances by crowding the dredge-masters and winch-men for heavy yardages. This had a tendency to cause careless winch-men to move ahead without thoroughly cleaning up the bedrock, often leaving several feet of the best gravel on the bottom. Areas dredged in this manner may be detected easily today by the unevenness of the tailing-piles, showing that the maximum depth was reached in some places only every 25 ft., as the dredge advanced.

The main reason why it appears possible to re-dredge successfully in certain portions of the Oroville district is the fact that 106 acres have been re-dredged since September 1916 by the Natomas company. In this work there were used two 7½-ft. dredges and a satisfactory profit was made. There can be little doubt that there remains a large area of the same character of tailing.

In the re-dredging operations of the Natomas company, ground has been found untouched and in the condition indicated in previous paragraphs. The net profit from re-dredging is much less than was won at the first dredging, but it has been proved that the tailing can be re-dredged at a cost 33⅓% less than the work in virgin ground, and that 99% of the remaining gold can be saved with riffle-sluices that are ample in length.

It should not be difficult to determine what part of the Oroville area would yield a profit from re-dredging, for the first ground dredged was close to the mouth of the cañyon and this was the richest in gold and principally worked by the type of dredge that could not recover all of the gravel nor save all of the gold. The decision of the proper type of dredge to re-dredge this ground is easily made. It should be the Hopfield type, which leaves the ground level and would make it possible to derive some revenue from the reclaimed land.

SHORTAGE of potash during the War demonstrated the fact that extremely injurious effects are produced by the want of a suitable quantity of this material available in the soil for plant food. Despite the efforts that have been made to produce potash in this country, which will probably result in the continuance of the industry under some proper form of protection, the possibilities of releasing more potash from the mineral constituents of the soil by proper treatment has also assumed a new importance. This subject was recently discussed by D. K. Tressler in 'Soil Science'. He found that calcium sulphate in solution increases the solubility of K_2O in some soils. It is more marked in clay than in silt or sand. Certain silt-loam soils showed a higher degree of solubility for potash in the presence of large amounts of CO_2 and $CaCO_3$. Sodium salts are very active in dissolving K_2O from the soil minerals.

The Crushing of Steel Caps

By A. C. STODDARD

At the Inspiration Consolidated Copper Co. there was a main haulage-drift into one side of which there holed a branch haulage-drift; also, from this main haulage-drift there was another branch haulage-drift that was on the same line as the one first-mentioned. This arrangement threw one pair of raises into the main haulage-drift and made a train go to this one pair instead of drawing from them in succession; therefore, it was decided to drive

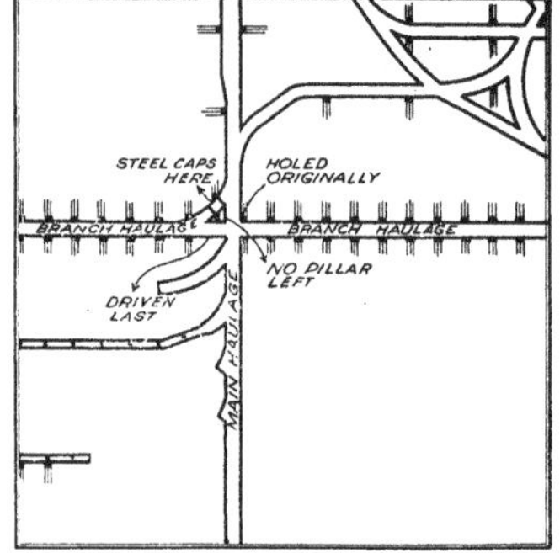

DIAGRAM SHOWING AREA OF HEAVY PRESSURES

through from the drift that holed into the main haulage to another branch haulage. When this was done it was found that there was no pillar left, this was due to a number of causes, which, in detail, were:

The size of the drifts left a very small area standing; almost immediately over this area a cross-cut had been driven on the first level above, and on the second level above there had been a pillar left in stoping, which allowed the weight to be transferred to the haulage and branch-haulage levels. This weight was almost straight down and it was found that it could not be held by wooden caps. It was decided, therefore, to use steel caps, and wooden 12 by 12-in. posts. The posts were framed flat on the top and a steel bearing-plate was put on the surface. The caps were made of 12-in. I-beams that had a riveted shoulder of 2½ by 2½-in. angles on them. These caps were put in place on the bearing-plates, and, although they deformed, they took and held the weight. The posts, owing to the bearing-plates, had their whole area in compression and did not fail, although the plates pushed down into them. The sets were put in about June 1916, took the weight immedately, and have stood ever since.

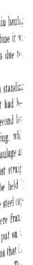

WOODEN POSTS WITH STEEL CAPS REPLACING ORE-PILLARS

DETAIL-VIEW SHOWING POST WITH WHOLE AREA UNDER COMPRESSION

Graphical Analysis of Accounting

By WALTER E. GABY

While recently reviewing texts on accounting, I hit upon a scheme of representing somewhat in the form of a flow-sheet the elements of double-entry book-keeping. Engineering and mining geology hardly fit one to offer an instructive article on such a subject, but as the chart here given may help others to a firmer grasp of some of the principles of accounting, it is presented with this hope.

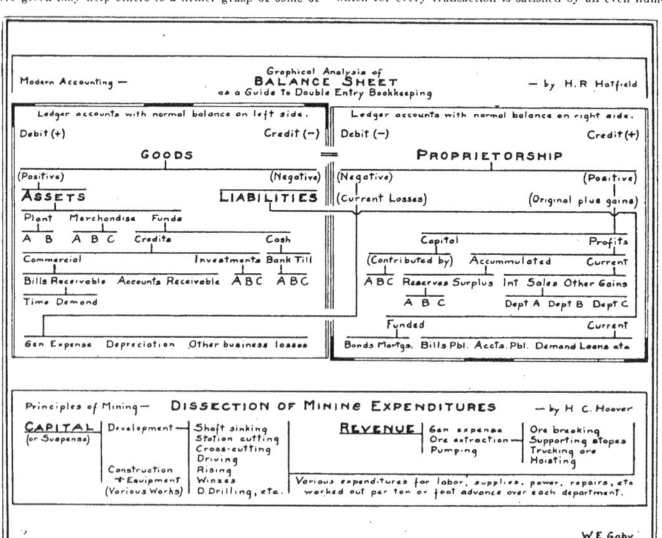

Industrial accounting is based on the indicated system, in which there is a constant balancing of the equation:

Goods = Proprietorship

By following the lines of the diagram it will also be seen that there are positive and negative goods (assets and liabilities), and positive and negative proprietorship (represented by items showing worth). The algebraic sum of goods is equal to proprietorship or net worth, and is the equation shown by the balance-sheet. Transpositions of the negative accounts being made as indicated in order to avoid subtractions. For the purpose of securing a balance, it is obvious that a negative proprietorship account is equivalent to a positive goods account, and hence is listed on the same side of the balance-sheet.

The sub-titles in the diagram are the names of the various customary accounts or classes thereof. When all ledger entries are properly made these accounts normally divide themselves according to the above principles, one division with balances on the left (debit) side and the other with balances on the right (credit) side. The confusion often experienced by the novice in using the terms 'debit' and 'credit' may be avoided if it is remembered that they are merely the names of sides of an equation, which for every transaction is satisfied by an even number (four) of equivalent balanced entries in the ledger. With a clear conception of how every item should enter into the balance-sheet, and why, there should be little difficulty in handling accounts in the ledger. This is the logic—the secret—of double-entry book-keeping.

Questions sometimes arise as to the classification of expenditures, and for the convenience of those desiring something definite on these points in the mining industry there has been added such an authoritative dissection of mining costs.

SLIME from the Balaghat, Champion Reef, Mysore, Nundydroog, and Ooregum mills on the Kolar goldfield, India, is now utilized in the manufacture of brick of excellent quality. A plant was erected by the principal companies, the product being used at the mines.

BUTTE, MONTANA

Strike Notes.—A. I. M. E. Meeting.—Boston & Montana Development Company.

The strike at Butte has reached serious proportions; operations at the mines are at a standstill therefrom. The striking miners are picketing all roads and trails leading to the mines, and were successful in stopping the street-car service entirely throughout the city, thus making it practically impossible for loyal men to go to work. None of the other unions have voted on the strike, but many of their members are out in sympathy with the miners. In hand-bills, which the I. W. W. strikers are circulating, they demand a six-hour day—from collar to collar—with $6 as minimum pay; but so far they have not made any formal demands on the companies. Major A. M. Jones is here with part of the 44th U. S. Infantry, and while martial law has not been declared, the soldiers are assisting local authorities in preventing lawlessness. [Further notes on the strike will be found in The Mining Summary.]

The sixth annual meeting of the Montana Section of the A. I. M. E. was held at the Silver Bow club on February 7. The following officers were elected for the ensuing year: Frederick Laist, president; F. W. Bacon, vice-chairman; E. B. Young (re-elected), secretary-treasurer; C. H. Clapp and C. D. Demond, additional members of executive committee. H. B. Pulsifer, professor in the Montana School of Mines at Butte, then read a paper on the 'Metallurgy of Aluminum and Magnesium'; and J. C. Horgan, of the Du Pont Powder Co. read a paper on the manufacture of 'High Explosives and Their Use in Metal Mining'. J. J. Carrigan, in discussion of Mr. Horgan's paper, told how the Anaconda had saved many thousands of dollars through 'propaganda', inducing the miners to make proper use of tamping.

The Boston & Montana Development Co. is designing a 500-ton concentrator for its property near the head of Wise river in the Elkhorn district, Beaverhead county. Construction will start as soon as practicable in the spring. The Montana-Southern railway, connecting the company's property with the Oregon Short Line at Divide, will be completed early in the spring. Part of the equipment is already on the ground. Work has also been started on the transmission-line from the Montana Power Co.'s plant on the Big Hole river. The mine and mill are to be electrically equipped.

BISBEE, ARIZONA

General Exploration.—Treatment of Mineral Water.—Work at Tombstone.—Placer Gold in Ash Canyon.—California District.—Pearce and Middlemarch.

The shaft of the Denn-Arizona Copper Co. has passed the 1800-ft. level, which, with the exception of a sump 30 ft. deep, is the bottom for the present. Stations are to be cut at 1700 and 1800 ft., and exploration drifts started on both levels. It is confidently expected that the orebodies partly developed between the 1000 and 1600-ft. levels will be found at this depth. Results are being watched with great interest by the Warren district, as through this property alone can the ground in the extreme north-eastern zone be explored.

At the Shattuck Arizona copper production for January was a trifle less than that for December, antl it is rumored that there is likelihood of further decrease for February. Operations are now more limited than during December or in early January, owing to the cessation of extraction of lead-silver ores, closing of the flotation plant, antl the discharge of men employed in this division.

As a result of the recent flooding of the shaft of the Great Western mine at Courtland, when so heavy a head of water was encountered between the 200 and 300-ft. levels that it could not be handled by the pumping equipment, the property is now practically closed. In the meantime engineers

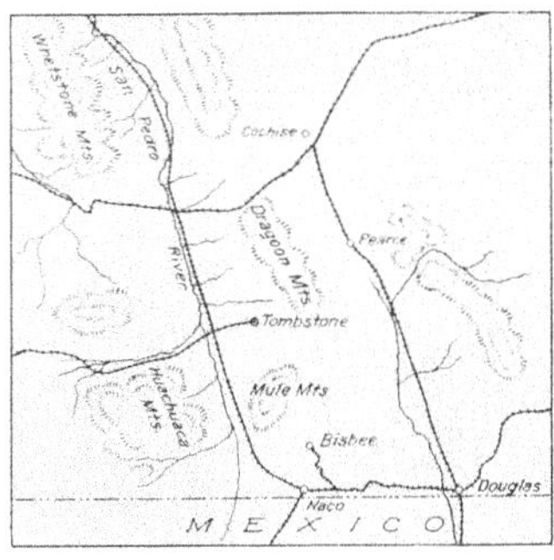

PART OF SOUTHERN ARIZONA.

have investigated the position, and more pumps may be put in. So strong is the head of water that a well at the foot of the slope in which the shaft was sunk, in which the water formerly stood a number of feet below the surface, has developed a considerable artesian flow. The shaft is a new one, upon which antl its equipment the company is reported to have expended considerable money.

One of the most interesting developments in the Warren district was the starting of a Reisert water-treating plant by the Phelps Dodge Corporation, Copper Queen branch, late in January. The water, obtained from the Junction mine of the Calumet & Arizona company, when treated, will be used in the steam-shovels and locomotives on Sacramento hill. Treatment of the water consists of the use of barium carbonate and lime which precipitate the soluble sulphates, the scale-forming constituents of the water in its natural state. Scaling of boiler tubing and its consequent short life in service has been a problem of more than ordinary vexation to the mining companies of Bisbee. Its elimination will mean a great saving. No announcement as to results from the plant have been made.

The Night Hawk Leasing Co., composed of Bisbee capital, shipped a carload of ore from its property near Don Luis in the south-eastern corner of the Warren district, to the Copper Queen smelter at Douglas last week. This is the third lot of ore sent from development, which has been encouraging.

Reports from Tombstone state that a number of Bisbee miners, presumably anticipating a long lull in copper activity, with possible reduction in mining forces, have made inquiries of the management of the Bunker Hill company relative to leases on portions of its ground. In part these inquiries are attributed to the high price of silver and the fact that several small deposits of good-grade ore are known to be on the Bunker Hill near the surface.

The Hershel Mining Co. at Tombstone is about to start work at its mill, the machinery having been overhauled and put in shape for a run by the manager, Douglas Gray.

One effect of the cessation of the copper boom has been to send many miners to the hills between Tombstone and the old camp of Charleston. At the latter several prospectors are working old silver-lead mines in a small way.

An effort to develop a sufficient head of water for sluicing operations, by which it is believed gold could be recovered in Ash canyon in the Huachuca mountains, 40 miles from Bisbee and 14 miles south-west of Hereford, is now being made by A. R. Bergquist, Dan Leedy, and Charles Morgan of Bisbee. A few men are driving a tunnel. For some time Ash canyon has been known to contain placer gold, several nuggets having been picked up in the bed of the small stream flowing through it. However, the sand was too wet for dry washing, while the water was insufficient for sluicing. A number of Bisbee people hold placer or lode claims in the canyon or on the hills surrounding it.

In the California mining district, surrounding Paradise in the eastern part of Cochise county, near the New Mexico border, several mines are working successfully. The Hill Top Metal Mines Co., a Kansas City corporation, has cut a vein in its second tunnel on the south side of the Chiricahua mountains, at a distance of 200 ft. from the mouth. Indications are favorable for a large body of ore to be developed by further driving in the lower tunnel, which has a total vertical depth of 900 ft. The orebody already has been proved from the upper tunnel, which extends entirely through the mountain, to the second tunnel 400 ft. down the mountain side. The third tunnel is in 1350 ft. and must be driven approximately 3000 ft. before finding the ore, which is dipping away from the tunnel mouth. The middle tunnel has developed a fine flow of water, making 1000 gal. per min. Approximately $750,000 has been spent on the property of which J. O. Fife is manager. Good wagon-roads have been built by the company to Rodeo, New Mexico, its present shipping point. It is currently reported that a railroad is to be built by the company, but whether it will tap the El Paso & Southwestern at Rodeo, or the Southern Pacific at Dos Cabezos, is not known. The company also is reported to be considering a smelter. Machinery, including a large engine of the Diesel type and a compressor, were installed some time ago. There is ample timber in the hills close-by for general use. The ore carries copper, lead, and silver. About 30 men are employed.

At the Hill Top Extension, adjoining the Hill Top, under the management of John Blumberg, the tunnel is in 750 ft. on the vein. At present a carload of lead-silver carbonates, carrying 60% lead and 50 oz. silver, it awaiting shipment, but recent heavy snows froze the ore in bins, delaying matters.

The King Copper mine, operated by C. E. Welch, a merchant of Paradise, is driving on the 300-ft. level on the main vein. A good grade of copper ore has been opened for 80 feet.

The old surface workings of the Commonwealth company at Pearce, Cochise county, are being exploited by lessees under the direction of A. Y. Smith, manager for the Commonwealth. Approximately 750 tons of highly silicious ore is shipped each month to the C. & A. smelter at Douglas, where it is ground and used mostly for converter lining.

The Middlemarch Copper Co. has finished sinking its new shaft, according to arrivals at Bisbee, who say the present intention is to drive on the lower levels to the contact where ore has been developed on upper levels. The shaft was sunk both to develop ore and bring in a supply of water, if possible, for the mill. A lack of water has been felt keenly in the past. The flotation mill has operated with unusual success as far as recovery is concerned, it is reported. E. L. Elson is manager. The mill was described in the 'Press' of February 8, 1919.

PLATTEVILLE, WISCONSIN

Zinc, Lead, and Pyrite During January.

January as a rule is not responsible for large production in the zinc-lead districts, and this year a combination of restrictive influences preclude the possibility of even a fair showing. Prices for ores declined. Local mining exchanges, ordinarily looked to for current weekly quotations, deliberately avoided publishing figures in the first two weeks of the month. Buying was restricted, two prominent smelter companies, locally represented, withdrew for a time. Operating costs have become unendurable, and since no relief is being afforded through lower costs of mine and mill supplies, many consistent low-grade producers have shut-down. Some are gradually working off enough surplus product to keep mines dewatered and plants ready in case of an improvement. The spring-like weather experienced through the month, in one of the mildest winters this field has known in 30 years, offered sufficient incentive for a large yield; but operators were content to go along as conservatively as circumstances would permit, and both recoveries and shipments were exceptionally light when compared with previous records. Physically, the industry is better organized than in a great many years, and new high outputs are possible under fairly normal conditions.

Lead-ore producers suffered adversity, prices declining abruptly at times, bringing quotations down to $55 per ton, base, 80% lead, with a poor demand. The mild weather has enabled small operators to continue gophering through shallow and surface diggings, with the result that at the end of the month a fair surplus was held in bins.

Carbonate of zinc producers enjoyed a fair month, the price holding at about $25 to $35 per ton, 40% metal, all the month. New strikes made in the northern districts of the field, in virgin soil, of more than ordinary importance, give better prospects of an increased output. The outlet too, is of a more substantial nature, the ore going almost entirely to the Mineral Point Zinc Co. for the manufacture of zinc oxide. Prices for the latter rule high, and until white lead makes a sufficient fall to make inroads here it is believed that mining will be conducted at maximum capacity. More miners were taken on, and no attempt was made at any point, in the field, in fact, to reduce wages.

Shippers of pyrite, although regaled with high prices for sulphuric acid, found the markets for this ore entirely to their dislike and not a pound of ore of this class was marketed during the month, something that has not occurred in the field in a dozen years. A fair reserve has accumulated, held, mainly, at refinery plants engaged in zinc-ore separation.

Deliveries of zinc ore from mines to refining plants in the field, and from mines direct to smelter for January amounted to 12,826 tons; and of lead ore, 331 tons. Refiners delivered to smelters 3659 tons of blende. The Mineral Point Zinc Co.'s output and purchases totaled 5227 tons.

TELLURIDE, COLORADO

General Conditions in This Part of the San Juan.

The sharp decline in the price of lead and copper will not affect this district as seriously as adjoining ones, owing to the nature of the ores, which carry high gold and silver contents, and comparatively small low quantities of base metals. During the past month there has been a steady influx of labor, both common and skilled, due to the shut-down in the Rico district, the laying-off of miners in Arizona, and the return of soldiers. Although the labor supply now exceeds the demand, the present wage-scale will be maintained until such a time as the lower cost of living permits less wages. The relieving of the acute labor shortage is shown by heavier production and development work.

The Tomboy Gold Mines Co. is now shipping 50 cars of concentrate per month, and as the ore carries mainly gold and silver, the drop in other metal prices will not seriously affect earnings of this company. Work on the new flotation plant is to be started as soon as snow conditions permit. The plant will recover the zinc in the ore, which hitherto has been lost.

The Smuggler Union company is producing larger quantities, as all properties are working. The Black Bear is shipping 5 cars per week; the Humboldt, 5 cars; the Colorado Superior, 13 cars; and the Caruthers Lease, operated by Inamo & Perino, 1 car.

The Belmont-Wagner company continues extensive development at the Alta mine, and is rapidly getting the mine in condition for the season's run. As there is now plenty of labor to draw upon, the mine and mill will be operated at full capacity as soon as snow conditions permit resumption of outside work.

The Mt. Blaine Oil Shale Co. has everything ready to resume operations in the spring. An abundant supply of good water is now assured at the plant, as a large tank has been constructed of 7000-gal. capacity, water being piped thereto from a nearby creek.

VICTORIA, BRITISH COLUMBIA

Smelter Investigation.—Work at Trail.—Ladysmith Smelter.—Mining Convention.—Closed Towns.—Mine-Rescue Apparatus.

At the opening session of the committee appointed to inquire into the fairness or otherwise of the treatment rates charged on custom ores by the Consolidated Mining & Smelting Co. at Trail it was explained by S. S. Fowler, the chairman, that evidence either in the nature of criticism or suggestion would be heard from anyone. Such evidence might be given orally or in writing. It had been decided that, where witnesses made the request, their testimony would be heard en camera and would be treated confidentially. Members of the committee, after taking the evidence of one witness behind closed doors, decided that they would visit the Trail smelter and meet representatives of the company in order that necessary arrangements might be made for investigation into operation of the plant.

Notwithstanding the present unsettled condition of the metal markets, the smelter of the Consolidated M. & S. Co. is as busy now as it was some months ago and has more men on its payroll. The explanation of this is briefly that the management is preparing for the time, expected soon, when there will be a big demand for the products of the plant. One of the most important projects is the construction of a concentrating plant in connection with the zinc plant for dressing the tailing of the Sullivan mine and other silver-lead-zinc ores after they have passed through the electrolytic process. There is an immense quantity of this residue, which has been accumulating ever since the electric process was started, because there was no known practical method of extracting the lead. This problem has been solved by the company's chemists.

Progress is being made in development of the fluorspar property of the Consolidated M. & S. Co. near Grand Forks. Eighty-two men are employed there. The tram-line being built to convey ore from the mine to bunkers for shipment is nearly completed. At the bunkers a mill is being erected to grind the ore before shipment. The mill-site is to be connected with the Kettle Valley railway by a branch line, which is under construction.

There is a prospect that the Ladysmith smelter will be in operation again before long. W. J. Watson, in charge of the plant, has just returned from a conference with F. A. Seiberling, of Akron, Ohio, and associates. He states that it is Mr. Seiberling's intention to commence, without delay, the development of several good mining properties. One of these is on Latouche island. Other first-class prospects have been secured and will be opened as fast as possible.

The president of the Associated Boards of Trade of eastern British Columbia, Fred A. Starkey, has announced that the Northwest International Mining Convention will be held at Nelson this year.

Legislation is proposed by the Hon. T. D. Pattullo, Minister of Lands for British Columbia, that will affect the policy of the Granby Consolidated M. & S. Co., as well as other mining and manufacturing companies, of maintaining what are termed 'closed towns' in those areas near their plants where homes are provided for officials and employees. The companies' explanation for their course in this regard is that it is in the interest of their business that agitators, idlers, and people with no particular business, shall be kept out of such centres. On the other hand, the Minister of Lands takes the position that the right of any private corporation to arbitrarily prohibit intercourse between the members of its particular community with the outside world is questionable, that it results in the restraint of free competitive trade, and is an unjustifiable interference with the freedom of the subject. It is not proposed by the Government, however, to place any law on the statutes that will force the companies to throw open their towns to the same extent as are the usual run of municipal corporations. The Lieutenant-Governor-in-Council will be given power to declare certain communities company towns, within the limits of which the public shall have free right of ingress and egress over the ways and roads used by the companies as avenues of traffic, but it is not intended that the ways immediately adjacent to the works themselves and used solely in connection with actual industrial operations shall be deemed avenues of traffic. In other words the prohibition will be lifted as regards avenues of traffic that are in the townsite proper and on which are located the various public offices, public buildings, etc. Provision also will be made for wharf accommodation for public traffic and use in cases of those towns where water transportation is the only means of approach.

Notice has been posted at the Grand Forks smelter of the Granby Consolidated to the effect that it proposes to reduce wages of its employees.

The mining companies of the Golden and Windermere districts are organizing the Northwest Kootenay Mining Association, the object of which will be to encourage mining in that region.

Mining men and citizens generally of the Canadian West propose once more to ask the Dominion government to secure the passage of legislation placing a bounty of 50c. per ton on the production of pig-iron in Canada.

Acting on instructions from the Minister of Mines, the Chief Inspector of Mines has arranged for a series of practical tests of the Gibbs mine-rescue apparatus and the Paul breathing apparatus. These began on January 28 at the Government mine-rescue station at Nanaimo.

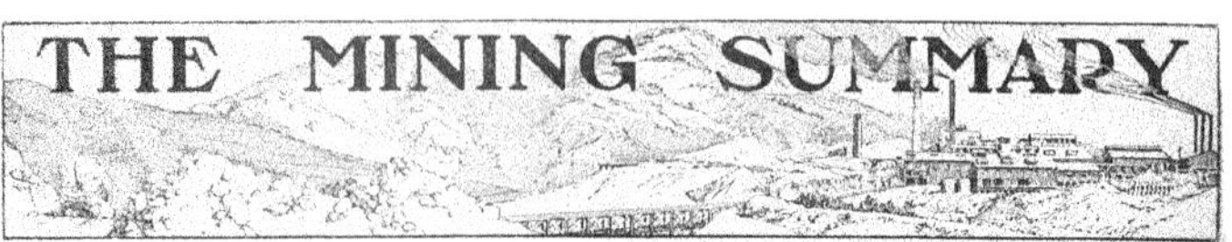

ALASKA

Jualin.—Work will be resumed at once on the property of the Jualin Alaska Mines Co. at Jualin. This property was taken over in 1912 by the Algunican Development Co., a Belgian and French company with head office at Brussels, Belgium. At the time a 7800-ft. tunnel was started, intended to cross-cut the vein system at a lower depth, also to drain the mine. This tunnel, which had advanced 2000 ft., was discontinued when war broke out, attention being confined to the actual production of the mine. All work was suspended in November 1917, owing to labor shortage and extreme operating conditions. During the last year of its operations the mine produced nearly $200,000 of gold from a 10-stamp mill. It is now proposed to complete the tunnel, at the same time carry out extensive development from the present workings. Until the tunnel is completed no ore except that obtained from the development will be milled. Jean Vanophem, Brussels, Belgium, is president, and Charles G. Titus, Juneau, Alaska, is general manager.

Kennecott.—Copper production of the Kennecott company has been reduced by about 50%.

ARIZONA

Ajo.—New Cornelia produced 4,318,000 lb. of copper in January, an increase of 70,000 pounds.

Bisbee.—The Oliver shaft of the Calumet & Arizona Copper Co. has been closed for an indefinite period. This shaft was opened at the commencement of the War. The ore extracted was low-grade, however. The January output was 2,284,000 lb., a reduction of 620,000 pounds.

Globe.—Old Dominion produced 2,812,000 lb. of copper in January, a gain of 130,000 pounds.

Jerome.—Charles H. Moyer, president of the Industrial Union of Mine, Mill, and Smelter Workers, in a statement made at Denver on the 11th on the action of miners in the Jerome copper district in striking as a result of a cut in wages, said: "These men are members of the I. W. W., and are in no manner connected with the Mine Workers' Union. Our men in the Jerome district are satisfied with their contract with the mine-owners, and have been expecting a wage reduction. The men responsible for the disturbances at Jerome are members of the same branch of the I. W. W. that has created all of the trouble in Butte."

Several I. W. W.'s were arrested on the 12th and 13th. The United Verde Copper and United Verde Extension mines and works were closed indefinitely during the week.

Miami.—The Miami Copper Co. has so far not reduced its scale of operations.

Inspiration produced 6,500,000 lb. in January, a drop of 850,000 lb. from December.

Tombstone.—A few men are at work at the Hershal mine opening lead-silver ore. Shipments are expected to be started in the near future. In the past, ore valued at $5000 per car has been shipped from this property.

The high price of silver is encouraging prospecting in the old Charleston district.

Wenden.—Officers of the Black Reef Copper Co., operating near here, have been requested by the Arizona Corporation Commission to make explanation of the alleged sale of shares after the expiration of its selling-permit of July 1, 1917.

CALIFORNIA

Crescent.—Mention was made editorially in the issue of February 1 of the views of R. R. Horner in Technical Paper

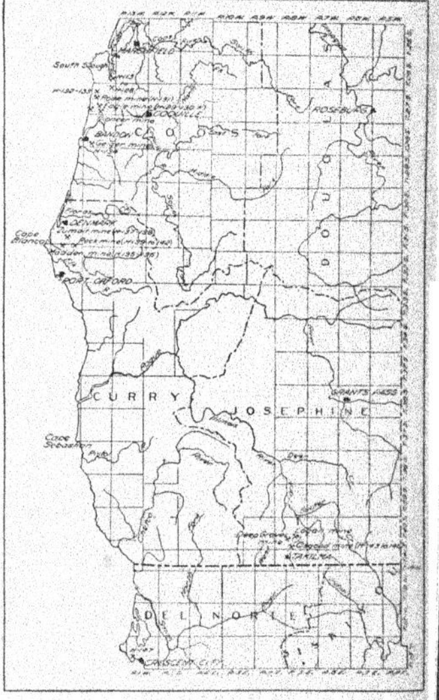

MAP OF PART OF OREGON AND PART OF CALIFORNIA, SHOWING SITUATION OF BLACK SAND DEPOSITS SAMPLED.

196 of the U. S. Bureau of Mines on platinum in the black-sand deposits of northern California and southern Oregon, wherein he considered that this metal did not exist in payable quantities, save in a few spots, so now a map is appended to show where the investigations were made. The chief difficulties in the profitable exploitation of the sand is lack of uniformity in occurrence and metallic content, and the high cost of mining and treating the minerals.

Engelmine.—The Engels Copper Mining Co. held its annual meeting at San Francisco on the 11th. Gross earnings totaled $1,781,637, of which $479,173 was profit. Dividends totaled $269,979. Improvements and investments in Liberty bends amounted to $424,560. The general manager, E. E. Paxton, estimates reserves in the mine as 2,275,000 tons, a large increase; while drilling has disclosed much more, so that 5,000,000 tons is confidently expected in 1919. The mill treated 265,000 tons of ore, yielding 9,500,000 lb. of copper. Recovery was 78%. The total production cost was 19.58c. per lb., but this is now 16½ cents. "Electric power, rail transportation, and tailing disposal having been provided, three of our big problems have been solved," says Mr. Paxton. "The company is now fully equipped for successful and economical operation, and with mill additions to be made in 1919 we will rank among the country's largest producers of the red metal. With the natural advantages of timber and water-supply, and attractive living conditions on the property, results of the company's operations should compare favorably with any of the large mines of the country."

Grass Valley.—After months of negotiation a merger of the Idaho-Maryland and Union Hill companies and several lesser claims have been united in one corporation known as the Gold Point Consolidated Mines. The land involved extends over two miles in length on the Idaho-Maryland lode, and embraces an extensive vein system, the greater part of which is virgin ground. A new vertical shaft is to be sunk at some central point. Prior to the War, Errol MacBoyle and associates took over the Union Hill mine. Later the Gold Point company absorbed all interests and elected Bulkeley Wells as president with the following directorate: Bulkeley Wells, Edwin L. Oliver, F. W. McNear, John McCrossen, Roy H. Elliott, Rufus Thayer, and Errol MacBoyle. No change in the present operations at Union Hill is contemplated, but the trend of the new development will be toward the Idaho-Maryland ground. To Mr. MacBoyle is due the credit of bringing the various interests together.

Kennett.—On February 14 the Mammoth Copper and Balaklala Copper companies posted notices that on February 16 wages would be reduced 50 cents per day all around. The Mammoth employs 550 men, the Balaklala 170. The present wage-scale base on 30-cent copper gives miners $4.50, shovelers $4, and common laborers $3.52 per shift. The Mountain Copper Co. has not made any announcement so far.

Redding.—A contour survey is being made of the Greenborn group of copper mines near Tower House, under the direction of the general manager, Albert Hanford. There are 10 full claims, 2 fractions, and 260 acres outside of the mining ground. Fifteen men are employed underground on development. No attempt is being made to extract and ship ore.

Weaverville.—High water in the Trinity river carried away the levee protecting the Valdor dredge on the Heurtevant claim below Junction City. No damage was done to the dredge, further than that it was left high on the sand, and a rubber belt costing $1800 was swept away. It will take 10 days to re-build the levee and sluice away the sand around the boat.

COLORADO

Boulder.—The Colorado Pitchblende Co., in full-page advertisements in Denver papers, states that the Jimtown radium and uranium find is vindicated, according to the report of M. S. MacCarthy, who was appointed by an outside association to make an examination. With a 1000-ton plant, a daily profit of $9140 is expected. This matter will be discussed editorially in another issue of the 'Press'. People are now advised by the company to buy shares, and make each dollar invested earn an indicated $3.29 per annum.

A company is being formed at Boulder to purchase the Chamberlin sampler, the purchase-price being $10,000. Employment will be given to 75 men.

A rich 'voin' of platinum is reported from Pandora mountain, near Caribou. J. I. Elsberry and E. E. Smith are part owners with Denver people. Assays from 10 in. of ore returned $350 silver, $20 gold, some lead, and $8 to $15.80 per ton in platinum.

Central City.—The Fairfield mine, at the head of Russell gulch, recently unwatered after being unworked for over 10 years, is being opened by J. Thouvenell for Eastern people. Some rich gold ore is being extracted.

The 'Gilpin Observer' is rather pessimistic about gold, and said in part: "There is no use of our trying to reason that things in a mining way will be any better during the coming year than they have been in 1918, unless there is a re-adjustment of conditions to a pre-war basis. . . ."

Durango.—The local smelter is working three shifts. According to the manager, R. P. Raynolds, in 1918 there was received 470,256 tons of ore, yielding 132,253 oz. of gold, 9,236,058 oz. of silver, 86,575,999 lb. of lead, and 6,169,057 lb. of copper, Colorado ores accounting for 126,927 oz., 5,239,318 oz., 54,131,063 lb., and 5,350,094 lb., respectively.

Leadville.—The Down Town Mines Co. in 1918 produced 70,000 tons of ore, valued at $755,000. There was a great variety of ores marketed, the Penrose shaft yielding silver-lead carbonate, zinc carbonate, silver-copper-lead carbonate, silver-copper-lead sulphide, manganese and silver-iron; and contained seven metals; gold, silver, lead, copper, zinc, manganese, and iron. A fair tonnage, which is included in the company total, was extracted through the Bohn, Hibschle, Grey Eagle, and P. O. S. shafts, where small syndicates operated sub-leases.

IDAHO

Mullan.—The Copper King M. & S. Co. has optioned its property to Tacoma and other people, represented by J. M. Jackson, for $250,000, on terms. Certain development is to be done, also a 50-ton mill erected. H. W. Ingalls is secretary of the Copper King.

Wallace.—The Success has been closed, pumps were withdrawn, and the workings will be allowed to fill with water, until the lead and zinc markets improve. About 75 men are affected. A new orebody has been opened for over 100 ft. on the 1400, 1500, and 1600-ft. levels. An assessment of 2 cents per share was levied recently.

MISSOURI

Joplin.—In Bulletin 154 of the U. S. Bureau of Mines, mining and milling of lead and zinc ores in the Missouri-Kansas-Oklahoma zine district is fully described by Clarence A. Wright, who co-operated with the Missouri Bureau of Mines and Geology. The publication covers 134 pages and is well illustrated.

Production of the Tri-State region last week was as under:

State	Blende, tons	Calamine, tons	Lead, tons	Value
Kansas	1,744	...	350	$93,242
Missouri	2,707	398	131	88,209
Oklahoma	7,012	...	764	343,536
Average price	$42	$25	$54	......

MONTANA

Anaconda.—By the probable construction of a highway from Anaconda to Hamilton, the old Moose Lake mining district will be re-opened; also the Frog Pond district, immediately south. The ore carries gold.

Butte.—A summary of events in the labor dispute last week includes the following:

Early in the week troops arrived to maintain order if necessary.

Practically no ore is being sent to the Washoe and Great Falls reduction works.

The Anaconda company's acid plant was stopped on the 12th, dispensing with 50 men.

Open warfare on the high cost of living was declared by the mining companies, when a committee from the mine-owners visited local merchants and asked that they make some move to reduce the price of merchandise, rents, and other necessities. Unwillingness to do so on the part of Butte dealers will probably mean that either the local mines will announce an indefinite closing of the properties or that stores will be opened for the sale of goods at cost to all employees. This action was determined upon by mine operators after they had met with Major A. M. Jones of the 44th Infantry.

The strike was declared off on the 17th.

Zinc output of Butte & Superior in January was 9,450,000 lb., also 178,000 oz. of silver. This is a reduction of 1,200,000 lb. when compared with December.

NEVADA

Ely.—Nevada Consolidated reduced wages 75 cents per day last week. The notice posted by C. B. Lakenan, the general manager, includes the following wage reductions when copper is under 26 cents per pound:

	Over $4.35 per shift	Under $4.35 per shift
Between 26 and 25 cents......	12.5c.	12.5c.
" 25 " 24 "	12.5c.	12.5c.
" 24 " 23 "	12.5c.	12.5c.
" 23 " 22 "	12.5c.	12.5c.
" 22 " 21 "	12.5c.	7.5c.
" 21 " 20 "	12.5c.	7.5c.
" 20 " 19 "	12.5c.	7.5c.
" 19 " 18 "	12.5c.	7.5c.

The above scale takes into account the present cost of living, and is subject to revision as living costs decrease. When copper sells below 18 cents there will be a further consideration of the wage-scale.

Goldfield.—An agreement between the Spearhead and Booth companies, whereby the latter receives 250,000 shares of the former in consideration of surrendering all extra-lateral and apex rights, was signed in Reno on the 13th. The Spearhead followed the example of the Jumbo Extension, Merger Mines, Kewanas, and others which made share settlements rather than engage in apex litigation.

The new company taking over the Goldfield Consolidated properties is the Goldfield Development Co. A charter under the name of the Goldfield Mining Co. was refused by the Secretary of State because of the former existence of a company with a similar name. Officers and directors are Corrin Barnes, president; A. I. D'Arcy, vice-president and manager; H. G. McMahon, secretary and treasurer; with A. H. Howe and Ben J. Henley.

Tonopah.—The East Divide company has acquired the Alto claims in the Divide district. R. G. Williams was the owner, while the buyers were C. S. Sprague and others. The Alto claims are around the east end of the Gold Zone property. The ground is considered to have good possibilities.

Production of the district last week was 7229 tons of ore valued at $122,893. Of this, 210 tons came from the Tonopah Divide.

The Belmont in January treated 9290 tons for 1130 oz. of gold and 114,998 oz. of silver, giving a profit of $57,092.

The Tonopah Mining Co. sent 4925 tons to the Belmont mill, yielding 950 oz. of gold and 85,300 oz. of silver, and a profit of $42,000.

The Extension is preparing to sink its Victor Shaft below 1760 feet.

The Jim Butler is also to sink deeper, starting at the 800-ft. level.

OKLAHOMA

Picher.—While a good number of mines are closed, there are still many at work. Stocks of concentrate are rapidly decreasing.

Tailing from the Netta mine here is now delivered into railroad cars by a flume, erected by the Independent Gravel Co. The daily shipment is 23 carloads from the flume, and two from the conveying system. The tailing (flint or chert) is used as ballast, in concrete, and on highways.

OREGON

Bandon.—From this place in Coos county small quantities—300 to 500 lb.—of chromite are being sent to San Francisco by H. M. Axtell, superintendent of the black-sand plant at Camp Day. The chromite is separated from the black sand. David T. Day of the U. S. Geological Survey is said to be owner of the plant.

TEXAS

Austin.—The new mining bill before the Legislature is expected to pass. It provides for the location of minerals on all State land or lands on which the mineral rights have been reserved by the State. All placers, veins, lodes, or any rocks, or aqueous solutions carrying metallic or non-metallic substances of value, except oil, natural gas, coal, and lignite, can be located under the provisions of this act. The size of claims is placed at 1500 ft. in length by 600 ft. in width as the maximum. The extra-lateral rights are excluded, saving the endless litigation under the United States law.

UTAH

Alta.—The Emma Consolidated and Old Emma Mines companies are to be amalgamated. The latter and the Emma Copper Co. were controlled by Emma Consolidated, which arrangement tended to oppress the others, the only remedy being to eliminate the holding company. A new company with 5,000,000 shares is suggested.

The South Hecla Mining Co. had net current assets amounting to $113,363 at the end of 1918. Ore production was 6912 tons, valued at $180,021, of which $69,849 was profit. The metal contents were 104 oz. of gold, 89,173 oz. of silver, 111,616 lb. of lead, 502,924 lb. of copper, 71,560 lb. of zinc, and 3,961,781 lb. of iron. Lessees produced 2322 tons of ore, worth $35,472, of which the company's share was $3855.

Bingham.—The Utah Copper Co. continues to strip over-burden, in spite of the fact that the work is a long way ahead of ore extraction.

Morrissey.—The Utah Sulphur Co. is to construct a railway to its property here, according to M. S. Morrissey, general manager. More equipment is to be added.

Park City.—Production of this district in January totaled 10,880 tons of ore and concentrate, compared with 8468 tons in December. The producers were: Judge M. & S., 2880 tons; Ontario-Silver, 2779; Silver King Coalition, 2220; Daly, 1012; Daly Mining, 700; Naildriver, 360; Silver King Con., 185; and miscellaneous 500 tons.

WASHINGTON

Spokane.—The blue sky law presented to the State Legislature by Representatives from Chehalis county has been condemned by the Northwest Mining Association. "The bill contains some points that are good," said F. C. Bailey, secretary of the Association, "also it contains some that are vicious. It would permit me to dispose of 1000 shares of personal stock for a personal benefit, but would deny me the right to sell 100,000 shares for the benefit of the mine and its stockholders, unless I submitted to a burdensome and expensive investigation."

Keller.—Geology and mineral deposits of the Colville Indian reservation in Okanogan and Ferry counties are discussed by J. T. Pardee in Bulletin 677 of the U. S. Geological Survey. The total metal output, excepting placer gold, up to 1912 was not over $25,000. The placers are of relatively little economic importance. The metal-bearing lodes are those of most interest at present. Silver is the principal constituent in most of the veins and shear-zones. As a rule, lead is associated with the silver, in some deposits of equal value. Zinc is almost as widely distributed as lead, but at present it is commonly penalized by smelters. Copper is present in many deposits, but save in some shear-zones and disseminated deposits it is of little value. Gold occurs sparingly in most of the lodes, but in few does it add materially to the value of the ores. Antimony and molybdenum are possibly important in exceptional localities. The Nespelem, Park City, Sanpoil (Keller), and Covada (Enterprise) district possibilities are described in detail in this 186-page publication.

MAP SHOWING COLVILLE INDIAN RESERVATION, WASHINGTON.

CANADA

British Columbia

Ainsworth.—The Florence Silver Mining Co. pays 14 cents per share, equal to $16,500, on March 20. It is expected that from now on monthly disbursements will be made. The mill produces lead-silver-zinc concentrate.

Anyox.—Mine operators and prospectors interested in the Alice Arm district were pleased to read a recent Toronto press dispatch regarding the ownership of the Dolly Varden mine that reads as follows: "The shareholders of the Temiskaming Mining Co. at their annual meeting yesterday (February 4) consented to the proposal of the directors to extend the operations of the company by taking over the Dolly Varden and Wolf silver mines in British Columbia. These mines have been handicapped for some time owing to lack of finances and the Temiskaming company has entered into an agreement whereby operations will be resumed. The purchase price of the properties is $900,000, but the obligation to the former holders of the mines is only $450,000, because of the liabilities the Temiskaming company has to assume." The railroad from the beach at Alice Arm to the Dolly Varden mine was practically re-built and nearing completion when the construction company went into liquidation, with the result that most of the mining properties and prospects of the district were tied-up. Hopes were entertained, however, that an early adjustment of the railroad difficulties would be arranged and negotiations to that end were started. The Dolly Varden Mines Co.'s mine is 18 miles from tidewater, on the west bank of the Kitsault river, while the Wolf mine is two miles farther up on the east bank of the Kitsault. The former has been extensively opened underground, and is therefore in condition to start shipping at any time. The orebodies have been exposed by much diamond-drilling. At the Wolf a tunnel proves the orebody for a width of 60 ft., with neither wall in sight. Several thousand feet of diamond-drilling has been done showing ore to be of good milling grade.

PERSONAL

Note. The Editor invites members of the profession to send particulars of their work and appointments. The information is interesting to our readers.

G. C. Bateman, of Cobalt, Ontario, was in San Francisco last week.

D'Arcy Weatherbe returned from China on February 12, and has gone to London.

John Wellington Finch was here on his way from China, and has gone to New York.

James B. Pearce has been appointed engineer with the Inspiration Copper Co., at Inspiration, Arizona.

Chester B. Neiswender is connected with the concentrator of the Inspiration Copper Co., at Inspiration, Arizona.

Jerome J. Day, of Moscow, was elected president of the State Mining Association to succeed Stanly Easton on February 12.

Horace F. Lunt has been honorably discharged from the Engineer Corps of the Army and has returned to Colorado Springs.

J. W. Crowdus, First Lieutenant of Engineers, has received his discharge and has returned to his consulting practice at El Paso, Texas.

S. J. Kidder has resumed the management of the Mogollon Mines Co., at Mogollon, New Mexico, having completed his work with the Engineer Corps.

E. W. Bullard, Lieutenant in the U. S. Army since the beginning of the War, has returned from France, and will take up his old position with his father, E. D. Bullard, in the mine lamp and mine safety supply business.

J. H. McMillan, Provincial District Inspector of Mines for the Prince Rupert district, has resigned in order to become general manager for the Jasper Park Collieries, Ltd., operating in the Province of Alberta, with headquarters at Pocahontas.

The Utah Society of Engineers held its regular meeting February 19 when there was given a symposium on potash. The papers were: 'The General Potash Situation,' by F. L. Cameron, U. S. Bureau of Soils; 'Recovery of Potash at the Ogden Portland Cement Plant,' by O. C. Hart; 'Potash from Leucite Rock,' by Guy Sterling; Nebraska Potash Brines,' by Dr. W. D. Bonner; 'Potash from Alunite,' by Mr. Cohen, chemist for Mineral Products Co.; 'Agricultural Uses of Potash,' by E. M. Ledyard, agricultural director for U. S. Smelting Co.; 'Potash from the Great Lakes,' by H. A. Margetts, superintendent for the Solvay Process Co.; 'Proposed Government Syndicate,' by A. E. Wells, U. S. Bureau of Mines; 'Recovery of Potash from Blast-Furnaces by the Cottrell Process,' also 'The Possibilities of Getting Potash as a By-Product from Other Industries,' by other speakers.

Obituary

D. T. Leonard, metallurgist in Rhodesia, died in November from pneumonia.

Dennis Reardon, prominent in the Coeur d'Alene, Idaho, district, died at Los Angeles on February 1. His wife died two weeks previously.

Sherman H. Boright, mining engineer at the Lonely Reef mine, Rhodesia, died from pneumonia last November. He was born in Canada in 1881, receiving his education at McGill University.

Elmer Higginbotham, mill superintendent at the Oronogo Circle mine, near Joplin, Missouri, for 10 years, died from pneumonia on February 9. He was born in Illinois in 1879. He leaves a wife and four children.

THE METAL MARKET

METAL PRICES

San Francisco, February 18

Aluminum-dust, large and small lots, cents per lb	65—70
Antimony, cents per pound	8.00
Copper, electrolytic, cents per pound, in carload lots	17.50
Lead, pig, cents per pound	5.25— 6.25
Platinum, per ounce	$108
Quicksilver, per flask of 75 lb	$90
Speiter, cents per pound	9.00
Zinc-dust, cents per pound	16.00

EASTERN METAL MARKET

(By wire from New York)

February 18.—Copper is quiet and lower. Lead is dull though steady. Speiter is inactive and weak.

SILVER

Below are given official (not Government) quotations, in cents per ounce, of silver 999 fine. In order to make prompt settlements with smelters and brokers, producers allow a discount from the maximum fixed price of $1.01½, hence the lower price. The Government has not fixed the general market price at $1, but will pay this price(as from April 23, 1918) for all silver purchased by it. The equivalent of dollar silver (1000 fine) in British currency is 40.65 pence per ounce (925 fine), calculated at the current rate of exchange. On August 15, 1918, the Treasury announced that the maximum price was fixed at $1.01½ per ounce. The British government fixed its maximum at 49½ pence, on September 2, but on November 12 this was changed to 48¾ pence, and on December 13 to 48 7/16 pence.

Date		New York	London	Average week ending		
Feb.	12 Holiday			Jan.	7	101.12
"	13	101.12	48.44	"	14	101.12
"	14	101.12	48.44	"	21	101.12
"	15	101.12	48.44	"	28	101.12
"	16 Sunday			Feb.	4	101.12
"	17	101.12	48.44	"	11	101.12
"	18	101.12	48.44	"	18	101.12

Monthly averages

	1917	1918	1919		1917	1918	1919
Jan.	75.14	88.72	101.12	July	78.92	99.62	....
Feb.	77.54	85.79	....	Aug.	85.40	100.31	....
Mch.	74.13	88.11	....	Sept.	100.73	101.12	....
Apr.	72.51	95.35	....	Oct.	87.38	101.12	....
May	74.61	99.50	....	Nov.	85.97	101.12	....
June	76.44	99.50	....	Dec.	85.97	101.12	....

The A. S. & R. Co. has had no difficulty in marketing all of the silver it recovers. It is considered that an open market would send silver upward.

COPPER

Prices of electrolytic in New York, in cents per pound.

Date			Average week ending		
Feb.	12 Holiday		Jan.	7	21.80
"	13	18.00	"	14	20.75
"	14	17.75	"	21	20.50
"	15	17.50	"	28	19.87
"	16 Sunday		Feb.	4	19.21
"	17	17.25	"	11	18.33
"	18	17.00	"	18	17.50

Monthly averages

	1917	1918	1919		1917	1918	1919
Jan.	20.53	23.50	20.43	July	29.67	26.00	....
Feb.	34.57	23.50	....	Aug.	27.42	26.00	....
Mch.	30.00	23.50	....	Sept.	25.11	26.00	....
Apr.	33.16	23.50	....	Oct.	23.50	26.00	....
May	31.60	23.50	....	Nov.	23.50	26.00	....
June	32.57	23.60	....	Dec.	23.50	26.00	....

The A. S. & R. Co.'s output of copper is only 50% of normal.

ZINC

Zinc is quoted as speiter, standard Western brands, New York delivery.

Date			Average week ending		
Feb.	12 Holiday		Jan.	7	7.93
"	13	6.85	"	14	7.72
"	14	6.75	"	21	7.52
"	15	6.70	"	28	7.20
	16 Sunday		Feb.	4	6.83
	17	6.70	"	11	6.68
"	18	6.70	"	18	6.74

Monthly averages

	1917	1918	1919		1917	1918	1919
Jan.	9.75	7.87	7.44	July	8.98	8.72	....
Feb.	10.45	7.97	....	Aug.	8.58	8.87	....
Mch.	10.78	7.67	....	Sept.	8.33	9.58	....
Apr.	10.20	7.04	....	Oct.	8.32	9.11	....
May	9.41	7.29	....	Nov.	7.76	8.75	....
June	9.63	7.92	....	Dec.	7.84	8.49	....

The price of sheet-zinc has been reduced 2 cents per pound to the basis of 11c. for sheets and 10c. for plates, subject to extras and discounts. The market is now 4c. below the official price ruling when the War ended. Extreme annual fluctuations for the past 10 years are as under, in cents:

	High	Low		High	Low
1919	13.00	11.00	1914	8.75	7.00
1918	19.00	15.00	1913	9.00	7.00
1917	21.00	19.00	1912	9.00	8.00
1916	25.50	15.00	1911	8.50	7.25
1915	33.00	9.00	1910	7.75	7.50

LEAD

Lead is quoted in cents per pound, New York delivery.

Date			Average week ending		
Feb.	12 Holiday		Jan.	7	5.80
"	13	5.00	"	14	5.75
"	14	5.00	"	21	5.63
"	15	5.00	"	28	5.50
"	16 Sunday		Feb.	4	5.32
"	17	5.00	"	11	5.02
"	18	5.00	"	18	5.00

Monthly averages

	1917	1918	1919		1917	1918	1919
Jan.	7.64	6.85	5.60	July	10.93	8.03	....
Feb.	9.10	7.07	....	Aug.	10.75	8.05	....
Mch.	10.07	7.26	....	Sept.	9.07	8.05	....
Arp.	9.38	6.99	....	Oct.	6.97	8.05	....
May	10.29	6.88	....	Nov.	6.38	8.05	....
June	11.74	7.58	....	Dec.	6.49	6.90	....

The A. S. & R. Co.'s output of lead is only 50% of normal.

QUICKSILVER

The primary market for quicksilver is San Francisco, California being the largest producer. The price is fixed in the open market, according to quantity. Prices, in dollars per flask of 75 pounds:

Date					
Jan.	21	100.00	Feb.	4	95.00
"	28	100.00	"	11	95.00
			"	18	90.00

Monthly averages

	1917	1918	1919		1917	1918	1919
Jan.	81.00	128.06	103.75	July	102.00	120.00	....
Feb.	126.25	118.00	....	Aug.	115.00	120.00	....
Mch.	113.75	112.00	....	Sept.	112.00	120.00	....
Apr.	114.50	115.00	....	Oct.	102.00	120.00	....
May	104.00	110.00	....	Nov.	102.50	120.00	....
June	85.50	112.00	....	Dec.	117.42	115.00	....

TIN

Prices in New York, in cents per pound. The monthly averages in 1918 are nominal. On December 3 the War Industries Board fixed the price to consumers and jobbers at 72½c. f.o.b. Chicago and Eastern points, and 71¼c. on the Pacific Coast. This will continue until the U. S. Steel Products Co.'s stock is consumed.

Monthly averages

	1917	1918	1919		1917	1918	1919
Jan.	44.10	85.13	71.50	July	62.60	93.00	....
Feb.	51.47	85.00	....	Aug.	62.53	91.33	....
Mch.	54.27	85.00	....	Sept.	61.54	80.40	....
Apr.	55.63	88.53	....	Oct.	62.24	78.82	....
May	63.21	100.01	....	Nov.	74.18	73.07	....
June	61.93	91.00	....	Dec.	85.00	71.52	....

The War Trade Board announced on February 1 that licenses for the importation of wolfram will be issued freely when the applications therefor are otherwise in order.

Announcement was made in Washington on the 17th that it had been decided to throw on the market surplus stocks of copper, brass, and lead held by the War Department. This decision was reached at meetings attended by officials of the Director of Sales' office, representatives of the lead and copper industries and officials of the U. S. Geological Survey. This will be done gradually, however, in order that prices may not be affected. Details of the plan for marketing the surplus metal stocks will be worked out later in a series of conferences at which producers will have full representation.

Eastern Metal Market

New York, February 11.

The markets all continue to be inactive, with consumers playing the waiting game. As bearing on the American situation, it is interesting to note that, taking the three major metals—copper, spelter, and lead—England today has stocks equal to over 66% of its annual pre-war imports of copper, over three times its normal import of lead, and over 110% of its imports of spelter.

Antimony is lower with demand light.

Copper continues to sell at lower prices on small transactions.

Lead is believed to have reached bottom, but demand is still light.

Tin market is dead and demoralized.

Zinc is a little firmer, but sales are not large.

ALUMINUM

The market is quiet. While Government maximum prices are to continue until March 1, the metal is obtainable at about 1c. per lb. under those levels, which were from 33 to 33.50c. per lb. in lots of 50 tons to 1 ton. This applies to No. 1 virgin metal and scrap.

ANTIMONY

The market is quiet with wholesale lots, duty paid, obtainable at 7 to 7.12½c. per lb., New York, for early delivery.

COPPER

Fundamentally the copper position is regarded by many as better. This is so because at the meeting at Washington last week virtually all the bad news came out. The worst is therefore unknown, and the situation is somewhat clarified. Representatives of producers and others laid their cards on the table, and showed the miners that among other things not more than 5% of the net output had been sold in the preceding 75 days, and at falling prices; also that there was probably 1,000,000,000 lb. of copper at smelters, refineries, in transit and otherwise, representing a sum of over $175,-000,000. This has been interpreted as meaning that the cost to produce this was about 17.50 cents per lb. A further inference has been that this is an irreducible minimum as to selling-price. A billion pounds is said to represent over eight months' domestic consumption and export. The result of this meeting has been that miners' wages will be put on a sliding-scale with copper at 18c. During the last week the market has fallen further on sales of small amounts. The quantity disposed of would not be regarded by some as sufficient to make a market in normal times. Today, electrolytic copper is quoted at 18c., New York, and this could probably be shaded. Lake copper is nominal at 18.50c., New York. It is the opinion of some that the market has nearly if not quite reached a stable basis. Copper stocks in Great Britain on February 1 were 41,882 tons, an increase of 5882 tons over those on January 1.

LEAD

It appears not improbable that the lead market has reached the bottom, or close to it. Many regard the present level as attractive, and some consumers are displaying more interest than for some time. On Friday of last week, February 7, the American Smelting & Refining Co. again reduced its price to the level of the outside market or to 5c., New York, or 4.70c., St. Louis. The Independents have not cut this price, and the market is generally quotable at 5c., New York, or 4.70c., St. Louis, for early delivery. A buying movement is expected by some in the near future. If the market holds, buying is probable, if it goes down, it is also likely to start. One difficulty is the slow sales of lead products. Stocks of lead in Great Britain on February 1 were 76,493 tons, an increase of 13,641 tons over January 1.

IRON AND STEEL

Buyers still remain only indifferently interested, and it is being admitted that a further lowering of prices may be necessary to kindle a purchasing interest. There has been a lack of inquiry for about nine weeks, this being explained by some as due to the maintenance of too high a level of prices. How to get labor to recognize its share in any such readjustment is a problem. Steel ingot output in January, as estimated by the American Iron and Steel Institute, was 3,082,427 tons, or 90,000 tons more than in December. The January output was at the rate of 43,047,585 tons per year. Unfilled orders of the United States Steel Corporation on January 31 were 694,884 tons less than on December 31. The total was 6,684,268 tons, or the lowest for any month since October 1915.

TIN

There is no tin market, nor is any possible under present Government restricted conditions. Tin enjoys (?) the distinction of being the only metal still under control. If a rumor that is current proves true, there will be still less trading. It is to the effect that the authorities at present restricting the tin market may decide or have decided that there will be no further trading in outside lots by dealers, importers, or American smelters, until the unabsorbed allocated metal is disposed of. If this should be so, some predict violent opposition. It is stated that already purchase licenses for lots of over five tons of American 99% tin have been refused. The market is dull and devoid of interest. Straits tin is quoted at 72.50c., New York, the fixed price, as practically all the metal outside of the allocated tin has been sold. American tin, at least in small lots, under five tons possibly, is obtainable at 66 to 67c., New York. So far in February only 50 tons has arrived. Straits tin in London was quoted yesterday at £225 10s. for spot delivery.

ZINC

The market is a little firmer than a week ago, with prime Western quoted at 6.50c., St. Louis, or 6.85c., New York, for early delivery. The better tone is not particularly significant, although some think the market has touched bottom. The slightly higher level is attributed to the failure of a speculative movement late last week when spelter was sold as low as 6.25c., St. Louis, and also to a somewhat better inquiry from galvanizers. Grade A spelter is in poor demand, but is probably obtainable at 8 to 8.50c., base, compared with the former Government maximum price of 12c. The British stocks of ordinary spelter on February 1 were 23,905 tons, an increase of 1732 tons over those on January 1.

ORES

Antimony: No developments or quotations.

Manganese Alloys: Ferro is still quoted by producers at $225 per ton delivered, but carload lots of re-sale material are going now and then at $175 to $200 for early delivery. Small lots of spiegel have been sold in the past week at about $60 delivered for early shipment.

Molybdenum: Quotations continue nominal at 80c. to $1 per lb. of MoS_2 in 90% material.

Tungsten: There have been no developments, and quotations are absent because of no testing of the market. It is stated that ferro-tungsten can probably be bought as low as $1.50 per lb. of contained tungsten. If this is so, high-grade ore would sell at about $15 to $17 per unit in 60% concentrate.

INFORMATION FURNISHED BY MANUFACTURERS

INSPECTION OF METALLIC-ELECTRODE ARC-WELDS

By O. S. Escholz*

Determining the character of welded joints is of prime importance. The lack of a satisfactory method, more than any other factor, has been responsible for the hesitancy met with among the engineering profession toward the extensive adoption of arc-welding.

The four factors that determine the physical characteristics of metallic electrode arc-welds are: fusion, slag content, porosity, and crystal structure. Some of the other important methods that have been suggested and used for indicating these characteristics are:

1. Examination of the weld by visual means to determine: (a) Finish of the surface as an index to workmanship; (b) length of deposits, which indicates the frequency of breaking arc, and therefore, the ability to control the arc; (c) uniformity of the deposits, as an indication of the faithfulness with which the filler metal is placed in position: (d) fusion of deposited metal to bottom of weld scrap as shown by appearance of under side of welded joint; and (e) predominance of surface porosity and slag.

2. The edges of the deposited layers chipped with a cold chisel or calking-tool to determine the relative adhesion of deposit.

3. Penetration tests to indicate the linked unfused zones, slag-pockets, and porosity by: (a) X-ray penetration; (b) rate of gas penetration; and (c) rate of liquid penetration.

4. Electric tests (as a result of incomplete fusion, slag inclusions, and porosity), showing variations in: (a) electric conductivity; and (b) magnetic induction.

These tests, if used to the best advantage, would involve their application to each layer of deposited metal as well as to the finished weld. This, excepting in unusual instances, would not be required by commercial practice in which a perscribing welding process is carried out.

Of the above methods, the visual examination is of more importance than generally admitted. Together with it, the chipping and calking tests are of particular usefulness. The latter test serves to indicate gross neglect by the operator of the cardinal welding principles, due to the fact that only a very poor joint will respond to the tests. The most reliable indication of the soundness of the weld is offered by the penetration tests. Obviously, the presence of unfused oxide surfaces, slag deposits, and blow-holes will offer a varying degree of penetration. Excellent results in the testing of small samples are made possible by the use of the X-ray. However, due to the nature of the apparatus, the amount of time required, and the difficulty of manipulating and interpreting results, it can hardly be considered at the present time as a successful means to be used on the large scale production.

Kerosene, of the various liquids that may be applied, has marked advantages, due to its availability, low volatility, and high surface-tension. Sprayed on a welded surface it is rapidly drawn into any capillaries produced by incomplete fusion between deposited metal and weld scarf, or between succeeding deposits, slag inclusions, gas pockets, etc., penetrating through the weld and showing the existence of an unsatisfactory structure by a stain on the emerging side. A bright red stain can be produced by dissolving suitable oil soluble dyes in the kerosene. By the means of this test, the presence of faults have been found that could not be detected with hydraulic pressure or other methods. By the kerosene penetration, a sequence of imperfect structures linked through the weld, which presents the greatest hazard in welded joints, could be found immediately. This method is not applicable to the detection of isolated slag or gas pockets, nor small disconnected unfused areas. It has been shown by various tests, however, that a weld may contain a considerable amount of distributed small imperfections,

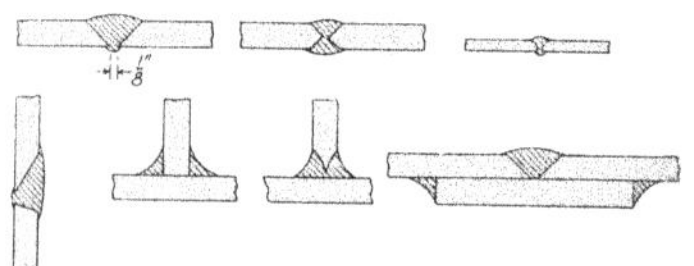

COMMON TYPES OF ARC-WELD SCARFS

without affecting, to a great extent, its characteristics. If a bad fault is betrayed by the kerosene test, it is advisable to burn out the metal with a carbon arc before re-welding under proper supervision. By means of the sand-blast, steam, gasolene, etc., large quantities of kerosene are preferably removed. No difficulty, however, has been encountered on welding over a thin film of the liquid.

Electric test methods by which the homogeneity of welds are determined, are still in the evolutionary stages.

The inspector of metallic-arc electrode welds may consider that through the proper use of visual, chipping, and penetrating tests, a more definite appraisal of the finished joint may be secured than is possible in either riveting or concrete construction. The operation may be still further safeguarded by rigid adherence to a specified process.

Regardless of the metal welded with the arc, the cardinal in welding steps are: (1) Preparation of weld; (2) electrode selection; (3) arc-current adjustment; (4) arc-length maintenance; and (5) heat treatment.

*Research engineer with Westinghouse Electric & Mfg. Company.

The Holt Manufacturing Co., of Stockton, California, announces the appointment of Sutherland G. Taylor, Jr., as export manager. He assumed his duties at the Peoria plant on January 1. For several years he was vice-president and New York manager of Cyrus Robinson & Co., engineers and exporters of New York and London. Ever since the winter of 1914 the Holt plant has worked on British war contracts.

CONGRESS is still squabbling over the distinction between the Government's moral obligation toward the producers of chrome and manganese and toward those who supplied other materials without formal contract. The hair-splitters come chiefly from Missouri, Pennsylvania, and Ohio. The distinction depends upon whose ox is gored.

WHILE we hear so much about the increased cost of producing copper, it is refreshing to note that during 1918 the Engels Copper Mining Co. in California reduced its operating charges from 19.58 cents per pound to 16.50 cents on an output of over 9,000,000 pounds. This mine is one of great possibilities, where much interesting work is being done under the management of Mr. E. E. Paxton.

TUNGSTEN producers in this country will be interested to learn that the Burmese miners admit that ninety per cent of their output would cease if the price should fall below £3 per unit for 60% ore. The Portuguese mines continue in operation because of their long-time contracts with the French government at a price of £4 10s. per unit. The Burmese production comes almost wholly from the detrital deposits, the lodes having proved expensive to work. The opinion of foreign producers is that tungsten would become scarce if an attempt were made to reduce the price below the present level.

GEORGES CLEMENCEAU still lives! Let the world be thankful! To have lost the grand old man of France at this moment, when his clear understanding and sound philosophy are required to help restore an aching world to health and strength, would have been one of the calamities of the ages. He, in his own person, is the expression of France, of her mourning for those lost in the struggle for the survival of civilization, of her yearning for a safe and durable peace, of her indestructible faith in mankind to build better in the future. He also expresses more than that, for he is the needed coadjutor to help our own statesmen frame a universal democratic society of nations. Through his eyes are seen, as few others can see them, the political perils of Europe, for Clemenceau has grappled with them in the flesh for decades. It is with a feeling that Providence is guiding our destinies that we behold the great Premier laughing at his wounds, and returning with unclouded intellect to the paramount problems of peace.

IT is pleasing to note that the Bureau of Mines objected to the removal of restrictions upon the importation of graphite, thus displaying proper concern for an American industry which was created largely in response to the needs of the country in time of war. It appears that the War Trade Board disregarded this objection. The result will be helpful to foreign countries in the recuperation of their business. A circular issued by the Bureau of Mines says that large stocks of graphite had accumulated in France. Shipments of Ceylon graphite are also available. Our friends in Alabama and Pennsylvania would like to know what reciprocity arrangements are pending to cover the damage that is done to their investments for the production of graphite.

ON November 11 last year a truce was signed, and the nations rested on their arms, save for those that Germany had to deliver to the Entente Powers as an earnest of good faith. Meanwhile questions of internationalization have been discussed and an informal draft of a platform for a new body of international law has been read to the Peace Congress in Paris. Now the great question of a treaty of peace will come forward for discussion, and it is to be hoped that some progress in that direction soon may be assured. The future of business is deeply concerned with the extent and character of competition and demand that will follow the determination of future trade relations. These will come through the ratification of a peace treaty, putting an end to the War and giving a firmer basis for commercial and political reconstruction.

FOREIGN trade is assuming increased importance in American industry. The National Foreign Trade Council, which will hold its sixth convention in Chicago beginning April 24, is an expression of the conviction among business men throughout the country that a struggle for markets abroad is essential to our national welfare. The drift of population to manufacturing centres has been intensified during the War. This means that a surplus of labor is available for manufacturing, and that the domestic demand cannot absorb the output of the workers. That is the situation, reduced to its simplest terms. Business at home is tending toward a normal volume because the stocks of general commodities are low. It is the surplus production for which a market must be found. The National Foreign Trade Convention will discuss this problem, and seek a practical solution. The chairman, Mr. James A. Farrell, who is president of the United States Steel Corporation, will bring to the debate the ripened thought of a man in a position to judge the needs of big business, and to estimate at their true value the opportunities for expansion into foreign fields. Every manufacturer of mining machinery is concerned in these efforts, and should contribute to the deliberations.

AMONG the papers read before the recent meeting of the Californian chapter of the American Mining Congress was one, by Mr. David M. Folsom, on the oil industry. We take pleasure in publishing it, because the writer is particularly well qualified on the subject, having been Professor of Mining in Stanford University and Oil Director for the Pacific Coast for the Fuel Administration before he became assistant to the president of the General Petroleum Company of California. Mr. Folsom makes clear the important part played by oil in our industrial system, for the economic welfare of the Pacific Coast is dependent upon an ample supply of cheap fuel-oil. He deplores the disadvantages to which the development of oil-lands is subjected and arraigns the administrative policy under which such development has been blocked during recent years. Since he spoke the Minerals Leasing Bill has been pushed nearly to enactment and it is hoped that many of the anomalies and handicaps crippling work on the oilfields of California will be removed. His objection to Government ownership was heartily applauded. Undoubtedly the mining community is extremely anxious to be relieved from the attentions of the halo-batted gentlemen at Washington. The spirit of the pioneers is not dead; the sons of the frontiersmen resent the impact of paternalism. They want to be let alone to proceed on their own initiative, under the law, as their fathers did, and they are heartily tired of the policy of repression that hinders the legitimate play of that individualism to which the West owes its economic existence.

MR. JULIUS KAHN, who will be chairman of the Military Affairs Committee of the House in the Sixty-sixth Congress, has announced his firm belief in the need of universal military training. It is impossible, when writing on Washington's birthday, not to recall that we owe to our first President the slogan "In time of peace prepare for War." America has learned anew the value of that advice, and it is encouraging to know that eminent leaders in Congress are disposed to follow it. The disturbed conditions in American life today, the hardships of industrial re-adjustment, the taxes that will oppress the people for years to come, are partly the result of failure to adhere to the doctrines pronounced by George Washington in his great address of political warning. Had we been ready to defend our rights, and determined to preserve world peace by forceful persuasion if necessary, had we shown it in our dealings with irresponsible revolutionaries in Mexico and elsewhere, it is almost certain that the German madness would have been restrained by considerations of prudence. Even in designing the league for peace it was recognized in the course of debate that this country must maintain a military establishment larger than we had ever seriously considered in the days before the War, all which indicates that we do well to apply the old lessons for the maintenance of happy international relations, uncontaminated by peace, and undisfigured by war.

PRODUCERS of silver will be interested in the Annual Bullion Letter of Samuel Montagu & Co. of London. The concluding paragraph should please our friends in Colorado, Idaho, Montana, Nevada, and Utah. It says: "Although the output [of the world] may be accelerated, the needs of India and China, the obligation of the United States government to re-purchase, and the cumulated demand for the trade will ensure a high level of prices for some time." We note that Mr. Edward Brush, vice-president of the American Smelting & Refining Company, which recovers more than 60,000.000 ounces of silver annually at its refineries, recently took a favorable view of the future of silver, although he considered it doubtful if England would continue to purchase "dollar coins" for any great time. Neither did he think it probable that the United States Mint would complete the purchase of 200,000,000 ounces of silver for many years to come. Mr. Brush estimates an annual shortage of silver amounting to 170,000.000 ounces. These factors point to the continuance of high prices for that metal. On the other hand, Mr. J. K. Lynch, governor of the Federal Reserve Bank at San Francisco, recently stated as his opinion that when all embargoes on gold are removed there would be a drop in price. At present most of the silver for the Orient is shipped across the Pacific. This is the result of war. Now that the danger of losing shipments is past, and that England's control of India is confirmed, the metal may resume its movement to London and thence to the Far East. Four times since September last the price was reduced there, the latest being last week, when it was lowered to 47¾ pence, equal to 95 cents. However, the immediate future for producers of silver appears to be bright. This view is substantiated by the fact that the output of silver in the United States during 1918 was 68,000,000 ounces, notwithstanding the stimulus afforded by an increased price and the extraordinary output of by-product silver, caused by the abnormal production of copper and lead. About 70% of the total silver marketed in the United States has been derived from the refining of these two metals. The politico-economic emergency in India, which prompted the call from England that resulted in special legislation in this country to release large quantities of silver for export, has passed, but there remain large balances in favor of the Orient to be settled.

Exporting the Alien Firebrands

Bolshevik agitators by the carload are being shipped to the Atlantic seaboard for re-export. We have no equipment in this country for utilizing such raw material, and it displayed poor business judgment on the part of the Russians to ship it here. The American laboring man is not a cut-throat and a firebrand; he is an industrial worker, a gentleman in a good old uncorrupted sense of that word, the father of children who still, as in the days of Jefferson, Madison, Jackson, and Buchanan, become trained in the duties of honorable citizenship, with the thought encouraged in their minds that before them leads, as the reward of industry and culture, the ascending highway through local offices to the opportunity of serving their country in the highest positions within the gift of the people. It was in no jesting spirit that the poorest little ragamuffins were told that they might aspire to the presidency. They believed it; they aimed at it; and they achieved it. It was an inspiration, in the month of February, when we celebrated the man who made and that other who saved the United States of America, to contrast the alien doctrine howled at our laboring men from the harsh throats of the crazed fiends of anarchy, with those uplifting principles upon which this country has been nourished and which endure vitally today in the hearts of all who are in deed and in truth Americans. Every citizen feels the dignity of partnership in a nation that enabled a Millard Fillmore, the 'bound-boy', to buy his freedom to enter a lawyer's office from which he should rise to the seat of the Chief Executive, or that recognized a master in Andrew Jackson after he had, by his own native intelligence, pulled himself out of the obscurity of Waxhaw, or that discerned the power in that self-made giant, Abraham Lincoln, who labored with axe and plough without counting the hours, and then studied by the light of the fat-pine on the hearth in preparation for a work that proved to be the rescue of these United States from rupture and disaster.

Of such men is the galaxy of American heroes constituted; of laboring men, of workers, who cultivated and strengthened both hand and brain that they might devote them to the service and protection of their countrymen. That has ever been the way of the true American. He is constructive, not destructive; he is a citizen, not a pillaging carpet-bagger; he accepts civic responsibility and is found always with the forces that sustain law and order. The times have not changed, save in the imagination of some who are confused with the disorders of a world that has suffered restrictions, in political privilege and material resources, such as we cannot experience in America if we hold to the birthright God has given us. It is a corrupted view, an alien conception, that opportunity here has narrowed, and that simple ability cannot win, as in the days when every man regarded his daily wage merely as the stepping-stone to a business of his own. We have but to look at our captains of industry to find refutation. Were they not workers, laborers with their own hands? Was not Mr. Charles M. Schwab reared as a humble boy serving in a Pennsylvanian livery stable? Did he not select as his chief of staff Mr. E. G. Grace, who had to work his way through Lehigh University? Did not Mr. F. A. Vanderlip earn his bread in the sweat of his brow before he became the great figure that he is, a leader in the broadening of America's banking and financial relations to cover the whole wide world?

The wholesome days of the individualists, who believed in their own personal capability to rise, and who held fast to their Government as the safeguard of their sacred rights to political protection, are not ended. They have been clouded at times by dark teachings brought to us from abroad, but bright ideals have come also with crowds of immigrants who recognized the possibilities of free America for the uplift of men. America has been generous in admitting the hordes of Europe; they were welcomed as home-seekers, and lavishly the lands of a continent were given to them, but when they come as destroyers of home and industry they must be treated as the firebrand has ever been. The instigators of riot in Seattle prove to have been professional foreign agitators; the outlaws at Butte were mostly aliens of a type that should have been barred at Ellis Island and never permitted to contaminate a democracy by their presence. The peaceful miners at Jerome, though complaining because of reduced pay, were prevented from going to work by the mob of alien I. W. W. miscreants, who made it impossible for the mines safely to continue in operation. It is evident that the time has come to safeguard America by drastic restriction of immigration. There is no fear of those who have received benefit from the liberal opportunities accorded them to make money in America; the peril of the hour is in revolution taught by the Russian tools of the German 'imperial republic', encouraged for the purpose of crippling American industry so as to make easier the new commercial war that the Germans are preparing. Bolshevism is now the weapon with which the Teuton seeks to crush those whom he failed to conquer on the battlefield. Let no one for a single moment confound the propaganda of the Bolshevist I. W. W. with the honest purposes of the American laboring man.

An International Gold Reserve

Proposals, offered tentatively by the Federal Reserve Board, for the establishment of an international gold fund, to be used for balancing the credits and debits between the nations without the actual exchange of bullion, is another of the interesting idealistic suggestions that give so peculiar a flavor to the politics of the period. The first reason for creating such an international gold reserve is that losses are thereby obviated; not alone the losses that take place in minting, melting, and handling, but those arising from the cost of transportation also. On similar grounds the rationality of creating national gold reserves as a basis for currency issues has resulted finally in driving gold coin out of general circulation. To extend the idea to international exchange is, therefore, but to take the next logical step. That was foreseen many years ago. It is a familiar conception, but hitherto regarded as only another of the brilliant Utopian dreams that no one expected would take form and substance in a world of hard reality. It had been discussed as a fanciful trust for a new order of St. John, laboring for the safety of the world in what concerned its vital commercial needs, that is, its need to be fed and clothed, as the Knights of Malta defended the citadel of Valetta from which the Christian world once made good its commands of peaceful intercourse on the Mediterranean. An international gold reserve would require a body of custodians, trusted, authorized, sustained, by the common need and faith of all nations, in short, a new method of finance. How might their sacred responsibility be assured? Where should be the monetary Valetta, and what nation or group of nations should supply the defensive equipment competent to exert an effective offensive against a would-be aggressor? Will England consent that we hold the treasure of the world, or that France guard it, or will we surrender our own expectations of becoming, in this newer fashion, the world's banker? We initiated something suggestive of this custodianship during the War, when we held gold deposits for the credit of the Argentine against which she issued currency at home; but will the world accept our guardianship of the universal stock of gold? It is not in levity that we ask these questions, but the mere asking of them turns the proposal into a jest. Sober sense teaches that, if gold have any use as a basis for exchange, and thereby have any command over the resources and products of the world, the jealousies of self-determined separate nations will not agree upon any custodian possessed of actual power in commerce and in population. If they should agree upon a lesser nation, a petty internationalized Malta, then the centre of imminent international political vulcanism would surely be found at that spot. In practice it might prove possible to accomplish nearly the same thing on the principle of our own distributed gold reserve, where bullion in San Francisco, under control of the Federal Reserve Bank, may be considered for financial purposes as being in New York, merely by crediting it to the account of that branch. Similarly, gold in Ottawa has been treated by the British government as if on deposit in the Bank of England. This would be one way of solving the question of custody, but it would not alter the relations of gold to the currency employed by the man in the street. The conception involves one more step in financial evolution. Just as soon as an international treasury for an international gold reserve should become established, gold would cease to be the real basis of exchange. Its present function would of necessity automatically cease. Adjustments then would be in terms of the so-called market-gauge dollar, for if an agreement for an internationalized gold-reserve could be reached between the nations, the qualities of density, indestructibility, and the rest, that so long have marked gold as the acceptable medium of exchange, would cease to be important. It would instantly appear that the settlement of balances was actually being effected on the basis of the ratios subsisting in commerce from day to day or from week to week between the volumes of production and consumption of essential commodities. The Federal Reserve officials, East and West, are developing a new cult; they tell us that gold more and more is being pushed into the background. Such indeed is the tendency of the moment, and it should not be obscured that this is a fact. It concerns deeply the business man, the investor of savings, and all those who still entertain sufficient doubt concerning the eternal wisdom of law-makers and law-making at this stage of the world's progress as to insist upon writing into bonds and contracts the time-honored phrase, "payable in gold." It is of vital moment likewise to the gold miner, for he has been counting upon the need of that metal as a basis for currency-expansion by the treasuries of this or other countries. The Government was his market, but the logical outcome of the new financial policy proposed would be to dispense with gold as a basis for credit-money. The single consideration that serves to convert gold in the Treasury into a basis on which paper money may be put into circulation is the fact that the paper is a warrant with which the holder may draw out its nominal equivalent in the metallic money with the ring to it that has made seductive music down the ages. Except for that, currency would stand on a political basis, and the value of the certificates of service, or whatsoever they might be called, would depend on acts of Congress, national or international. With gold held as a trust in a world treasury, it would be practically as if it had disappeared from the face of the earth, and then the miner's market would be the public, at advanced rates, for hoarding, unless the governments should commandeer the output.

Idealism often presents the defect of perfection that destroys adaptability to the unbalanced and indeterminate conditions of mundane affairs. As long as human nature remains inferior to the lofty plans that the human brain can evolve, and until the schemes for a society of nations gain the assurance of survival through long-continued practical test, the attempt to concentrate the world's gold in the vaults of an international custodian will be fruitless. To undertake it would mean the frank acceptance of credit-money as the sole medium for commercial transactions. Until confidence in such credits should become established by decades of proof that society was firmly planted on the new foundation, this inevitably would check the expansion of those forms of enterprise that are characteristic of modern civilization. It would once again divert men from the mechanic arts to the ancient solid basis for existence that is found in agriculture, but a new set of industrial conditions also would follow, tending, for good or ill, to bring back the land baron as a dominant factor in human society. Despite the fanciful notion of a gold-reserve league to match a league of nations, the world will long cling to the feeling of safety that the individuals in it cherish when their currency reads as a promise to pay on demand in the yellow coin of the realm.

DISCUSSION

In Behalf of the Prospector

The Editor:

Sir—Your paper, with other mining journals, has given much space to discussions about prospecting and of the causes leading to its decline. Nearly all the articles have regretted the passing of the prospector, and not a few have touched upon one or more valid reasons for his disappearance as a class. But it seems to me that no mention has been made of one of the most vital points of the subject, which, to put it briefly, is that the prospector's domain is being taken away from him by such adverse legislation as the 640-acre stock-raising homestead law. In other words, no new mining discoveries are being made for the all-sufficient reason that the territory wherein they might be made is rapidly being patented to stockmen and put under fence. And you know, and I know, and every man raised in the West who has had any dealings with prospectors knows, that they will not go inside a fence to prospect.

This is a fact of human nature Congress did not take into consideration when it framed that law. It presumed that it was amply protecting the miner when it reserved the minerals to the Government. Such reservation is valueless from a practical standpoint. Why? Because the Government is not going to mine the reserved minerals and no one else will. The result is that thousands of acres of prospectively valuable mineral land is being patented to some cattle or sheep man—as to surface at least; and that means all of it from a practical standpoint.

To illustrate: Jones is an American-born miner. He has a high-school education and is observant, intelligent, and studious. He has worked in the Bisbee mines for several years and has supplemented his work by considerable study of geology, mineralogy, and the theory of ore deposition. He takes a prospecting trip north of Bisbee in the vicinity of Gleeson. He notes that the limestones are of relatively the same age as those at Bisbee, and that the known orebodies are closely allied to the granite-porphyry intrusions as at Bisbee. He locates three claims, upon each of which is some showing of copper carbonates. For several years he does his annual work as required by law, realizing that he must have more capital ere he can undertake to explore his outcrop for any depth.

Meanwhile, the 640-acre homestead law is passed with its reservation of the minerals of the entered land to the Government. The Bar Z Cattle Co., by reason of settlement of the Sulphur Spring valley below Gleeson, finds itself crowded for range. Wherefore, several of its cowpunchers enter 640-acre homesteads, one of which includes and covers Jones's unpatented mining claims.

Under our system of land laws the U. S. Land Office has no record of unpatented mining claims. The land they cover is, so far as the Land Office records are concerned, public land until such claims have been surveyed for patent and patent application duly filed (I am speaking here of lode-claims). Consequently, when the Bar Z's cowpunchers file their 640-acre homesteads over Jones's three lode-claims the Land Office allows such filing simply because it knows nothing of Jones's prior title to a portion of the land.

Jones has held these three claims for several years. He has expended thereon \$100 per claim per year, which money went to the community. He has not sought to patent them, because, being a wage-earner, he hasn't had the money—for it costs about \$1000 to patent a lode-claim nowadays. But he has felt secure in his title under the mining laws, having a valid discovery of "mineral in place" and having each year done and recorded his statutory work. But now he sees his claims inside a cattle-fence. And when he consults the law (Act of December 29, 1916) he is confronted with the astonishing fact that he, with his prior and better title, must actually give a bond to the homesteader if he wishes to work his claims. Knowing the Bar Z outfit, and being an intelligent man, he realizes that insofar as realizing anything from his claims he might as well 'forget it'. If he sought to enjoin them, or if he protested to the Land Office and ask for a hearing, they will swear him out of court by a preponderance of witnesses—most of whom will be other cowpunchers and know nothing whatever about geology or minerals. Soon a fence is around the claims, Jones gives up in disgust, and thus are some promising claims taken from the domain of the prospector.

The above illustration is founded on facts. True, the names are fictitious but the places and facts are not. And not alone in Arizona, where most of the orebodies are deep-seated, is this very thing happening, but likewise all over the West.

It seems to me that mining men as a body should take cognizance of this situation. If they inquire closely into the law they will see that they have much on their side, although it has not been presented or threshed out. Section 2322, Revised Statutes, says, in express words, that mining locators "shall have the exclusive right of possession and enjoyment of all the surface included within the lines of their locations * * *"

Now the stock-raising homestead law, the Act of December 29, 1916, states that such homestead shall be filed only upon "unappropriated, unreserved public lands."

Land has ceased to be "unappropriated" or "unreserved" when there has been a valid mining location made on that land. If the locator has a discovery of "mineral in place" he has a title second to none that can be initiated under our public-land laws, as, I think, our courts have pretty well decided. Hence, any homestead filed over mining locations made and held in good faith, even though those locations have not been surveyed for patent, is not made in accordance with the spirit or intent of the law.

But the ugly fact remains that it is being done every day, just as I have herein illustrated. Wherefore, as I said at the first, prospectors as a class are disappearing simply because their domain has disappeared; taken from them largely by legislation like this 640-acre law, which, the records show, was fathered, fostered, and lobbied through by the cattle interests. And yet in all the West the prospector has preceded the farmer and stockman, and has generally made possible their coming.

Strange, is it not, that such legislation should be passed at the very time when the War boards, papers, mining journals, Bureau of Mines, etc., were making appeals in the public print to develop our mineral resources! And the old prospector who has done so much for the progress and comfort of the American nation through his patient search and uncovering of mineral deposits cannot but feel that Congress says to him, by the 640-acre law:

"Yes, you are a good fellow all right. But for you we would not have been able to make the wonderful industrial progress we have, simply because man cannot multiply his power through his use of agricultural products as with the metals and coal and the minerals to harden and temper his tools. You have braved the terrors of the desert heat and thirst, conquered its difficulties, scaled its mountains, bridged its barrenness, and, in the end, wrested from it its age-long secrets and its hidden hoards. But your day of usefulness is over, and in place of affording you a chance to develop a second Bisbee we are going to turn your claims over to the stockman that their scanty browsing may furnish subsistence to a few more head of scrawny Mexican cattle."

It's not that bad you say? Try it once; or try to hold a mining claim within the thousands of acres in our national forests!

Again I say that all prospecting needs is the land to prospect!

J. E. Bush.

Phoenix, Arizona, January 31.

[This is a matter that deserves the urgent attention of the American Mining Congress.—Editor.]

The Status of Gold

The Editor:

Sir—I read the article in the 'Mining and Scientific Press' on the 'Status of Gold', by E. S. Van Dyck and had the same re-published in the Deadwood 'Pioneer Times'. In the discussion of the article various ideas were expressed, and one point particularly has been challenged. The author states that the world has been quite thoroughly prospected, and that the outlook for the discovery of new goldfields of importance is not particularly encouraging. In case his plan should be considered as feasible and the intrinsic value of gold doubled, there would be vast deposits of $2 to $3 gold ore containing probably a half to one ounce of silver, which could be prospected and developed. There are here in the Black Hills such deposits, both in the shales and quartzites as well as in the schists, lying idle at the present time. Innumerable veins were disclosed in cross-cuts and not followed for the reason that the contents were not sufficiently large to warrant further exploration. Whether the veins might have developed into deposits of ore that could be handled economically under present conditions has never been determined. It stands to reason that deposits of the grade mentioned above, if Mr. Van Dyck's plan were accepted, will be developed, and under those conditions new goldfields of importance will more than likely be discovered.

A. T. Roos.

Deadwood, S. D., February 10.

Costs of Mine Supplies

The Editor:

Sir—The following table, showing the relative cost of the ten chief commodities entering into our [the Mogollon Mines Co.] operations, will be of interest, and may bring out comparative data of value from other operators.

Unit. f. o. b.	July 1, 1914	January 1, 1919	Increase, %
Powder, cwt., Silver City	$12.50	25.50	104.0
Fuse, case, Silver City	21.00	43.69	108.0
Caps, M, Denver	6.79	18.20	168.0
Drill steel, cwt., Silver City	7.25	14.55	100.1
Battery steel, cwt., El Paso	4.70	10.50	123.4
Cyanide, cwt., New York	20.70	30.00	44.9
Lead acetate, cwt., Mogollon	10.20	19.615	92.3
Sheet zinc, cwt., La Salle, Ill	6.44	13.00	101.9
Belting, ft., El Paso	0.095	0.194	104.2
Fuel oil, bbl., Silver City	1.55	3.45	122.6

The prices, as of January 1, 1919, represent practically the peak of the cost of supplies. There have already been some decreases, notably in the price of powder. Taking the normal prices as given on July 1, 1914, it will be noted that the average advance has been 106.9%. On January 1, 1918, the advance in the cost of the same supplies averaged 96.5%, and on January 1, 1917, 56.74%. It is interesting to observe that the smallest advance was that in the price of cyanide, namely, 44.9%. This commodity, of course, is all furnished by the Roessler & Hasslacher Company.

S. J. Kidder.

Mogollon, New Mexico, February 8.

Latin American commerce has been growing enormously, with the balance of trade strongly in its favor. The imports to the United States from Latin America in 1918 were valued at $1,046,943,000, and our exports in return amounted to $668,240,000. Money is easy in the southern countries at present, and extensive developments of mining enterprises, irrigation schemes, and further hydro-electric plants are said to be in contemplation.

Leaching of Lead From Carbonate Ores

By DORSEY A. LYON and OLIVER C. RALSTON

*At the time the experimental work on lead carbonate ores was initiated little was known of the solubility of lead chloride or of lead sulphate in strong brines, and hence the first work done was to endeavor to convert the lead of the ore into lead chloride, which is known to be soluble in hot water.

The solubility of lead chloride, as given by Landolt and Börnstein,[1] is shown in Table 1. A curve plotted from the figures given in Table 1 is shown in Fig. 1.

If a cheap method of conversion of lead carbonate into lead chloride can be found, as well as a cheap source of heat for heating water, the number of tons of solution necessary per ton of ore to leach out the lead from most of the ores tabulated would not be large.

PRELIMINARY TESTS. With this possibility in view, some of the ores were treated with dilute solutions of hydrochloric acid, followed by washing with hot water. Only small quantities of ore were treated in these tests, 35 grammes being the usual amount. It was found that the lead could be extracted in this way. The next step was to use brine to which sulphuric acid had been added in order to generate hydrochloric acid, although it was felt that this would be a failure, as the sodium sulphate resulting from the reaction of sulphuric acid on sodium chloride should precipitate lead sulphate, if no soluble double salts are formed. However, the brines leached out the lead in spite of their containing sulphates in solution. As the final leaching solution to be adopted was a saturated solution of sodium chloride, the results of these tests are briefly summarized in Table 2 following.

The ore treated was from the May Day mine of the Tintic district, Utah, and contained about 5% lead, and some silver.

In the first series of tests shown in this table two variables are involved—the concentration of the acid used, and the amount of acid relative to the weight of ore. The time of contact with the material was of sufficient length to obliterate any effect of the acid concentration. Thus the results of this series of tests show the effect of the relative amount of acid on the extraction of the lead and on the acid efficiency. By acid efficiency is meant the amount of acid theoretically needed to convert all of the lead to chloride, compared to the amount of acid actually consumed. In other words, if one equivalent of lead is extracted by an expenditure of acid equivalent to twice that amount of lead, the acid efficiency is 50%. The acid efficiency was calculated in each test by observing the number of grammes of lead extracted, and also the number of grammes of acid used up by the ore. One gramme of lead theoretically requires 0.3125 gm. HCl to convert it to chloride. If twice that amount of acid was consumed by the ore for every gramme of lead extracted, the acid efficiency was (0.3125 ÷ 0.6150) × 100 = 50%.

The first series of tests (series A) showed that hardly enough acid had been used. Series B was run with slightly more acid, and the time of contact of the acid with the ore was varied from 1 hour to 48 hours. The results of this series of tests shows that a fairly good extraction can be obtained in a few hours, but that the acid efficiency increases slowly. This latter result is difficult to interpret, as it seems to indicate that after 48 hours more acid is left in the solution than after 24 hours from identical charges. Regeneration of acid is not probable. There is no method of determining accurately the acid content of a solution containing metals such as iron and lead, and it is probable that in the longer tests more of the material that affected the end point in

Per cent Pb in solution.	Per cent $PbCl_2$ in solution.	Temperature, °C.	Per cent Pb in solution.	Per cent $PbCl_2$ in solution.	Temperature, °C.
0.475	0.637	0.0	1.156	1.550	45.00
.518	.695	8.0	1.550	2.080	65.00
.716	.961	19.95	1.892	2.540	80.00
.767	1.030	25.00	2.382	3.200	100.00

TABLE 1

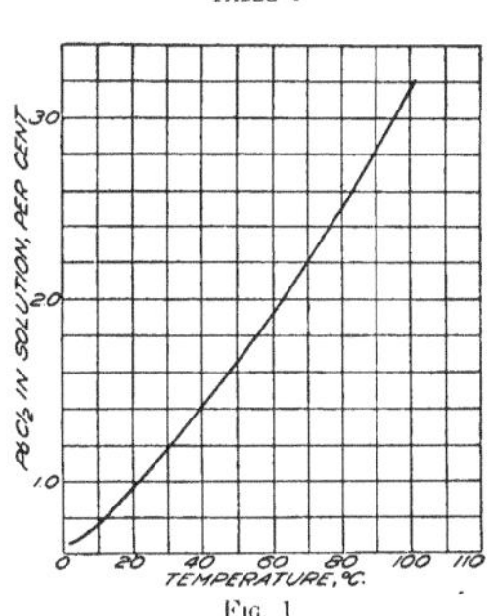

FIG. 1

*Experiments by C. Y. Pfoutz, C. L. Larson, M. J. Udy, H. C. Neeld, C. E. Sims, G. J. Holt, F. G. Moses, J. F. Cullen, C. E. Williams, and O. C. Ralston. Abstracted from 'Innovations in the Metallurgy of Lead, Bulletin 157, U. S. Bureau of Mines.

[1]Landolt, H. H., Landolt-Börnstein, physikalische-chemische Tabellen, 1905, 3rd ed., p. 564.

titrating the acid had gone into solution. As much more important and more nearly commercial results were obtained shortly afterward with the use of brine for leaching, this point was not investigated further.

In the third series of tests, series C, the same weight of acid relative to the weight of ore was used, but was diluted with different amounts of water and the concentration of the acid varied accordingly. Seemingly the more dilute acid converted a greater proportion of the lead to chloride and with a greater efficiency of acid.

The discovery that the brine solutions used in one or more tests were more efficient solvents of lead chloride was coincident with several other lines of evidence learned of at about the same time. The mills of the Holt-Dern Co. at Park City, the Knight-Christensen Co. at Silver City, and of the Bunker Hill & Sullivan Co. at Kellogg, Idaho, were visited. In each of them the use of brine solutions for other purposes had revealed the fact that the lead chloride formed in the particular processes used was soluble in brine solutions to a greater extent than in water. At the Bunker Hill plant it had been found that the sulphate of lead was likewise soluble in brine. About the same time Demassieux[2] published the results of measurements of the solubility of lead chloride in solutions of salt. His results are given in the curves of Fig. 2.

Sample No.	Time of leaching.	Volume of solution used.	Concentrated acid used.	Acid efficiency.	Lead extraction.
	Hours.	*C.c.*	*Per cent.*	*Per cent.*	*Per cent.*
A 1	48	100	1.88	30.9	52
A 2	48	100	2.82	33.2	63
A 3	48	100	3.76	36.7	71
B 1	1	100	4.00	15.4	40
B 2	2	100	4.00	26.8	82
B 3	4	100	4.00	28.6	87
B 4	24	100	4.00	23.6	98
B 5	48	100	4.00	45.7	98
C 1	24	100	3.58	23.4	50
C 2	21	150	2.39	41.4	69.7
C 3	24	200	1.79	51.0	70.3

TABLE 2

The curves show that the solubility of lead chloride in water is at first decreased by small additions of sodium chloride, owing to the well-known 'common ion'' effect, but that after about 5% of sodium chloride has been added, the solubility of the lead chloride begins to increase within the range of temperatures shown (0° to 100° C.), to the point of saturation of the solution with both $PbCl_2$ and NaCl, and finally falls to zero again with a solution saturated with NaCl. The increase in solubility in such solutions is usually ascribed to the formation of a double salt of the two substances involved. No attempt was made to determine the formula of this double salt, as the increased solubility is the important fact in these experiments, the character of the compound formed being chiefly of scientific interest.

[2]Demassieux, N., Equilibrium between lead chloride and sodium chloride in aqueous solutions; Chem. Abs., vol. 8, 1914, p. 1899.

The curves in Fig. 2 show that at any temperature between 0° and 100° C., the solubility of the lead chloride is greatest in the solutions that are more concentrated in sodium chloride. Consequently all brines used as leaching solutions in further experiments were made nearly saturated.

USE OF ACIDIFIED BRINE. To verify the fact that lead chloride was soluble in saturated brine, three different carbonate-of-lead ores were treated with brine to which had been added either sulphuric or hydrochloric acid. Five tests of each ore were made. In the first three tests of each ore increasing amounts of sulphuric acid were

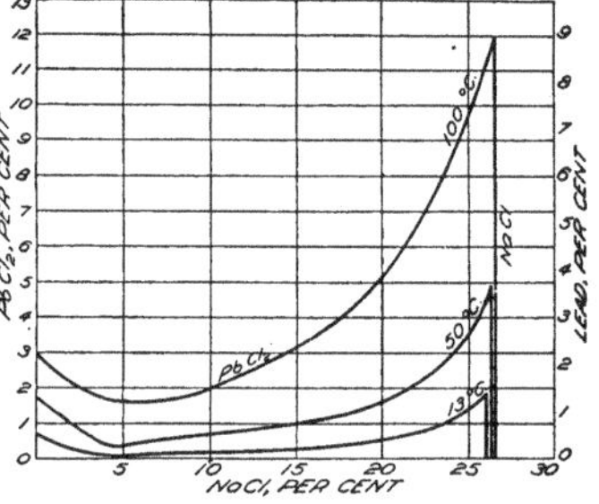

FIG. 2

added to the brine; the other two tests were with hydrochloric acid. Sulphuric acid reacts with the brine to form hydrochloric acid and sodium sulphate, and it was thought that the sodium sulphate would decrease the solubility of the lead chloride by tending to precipitate insoluble lead sulphate. It was found that sodium sulphate has no such effect unless a considerable proportion is present, and later tests of the solubility of lead sulphate in brines showed that as a rule the addition of sodium sulphate in proportions ranging up to about 2% of the weight of the solution tended to increase the solubility of the lead sulphate. This is a curious chemical anomaly.

As all of the ores tested contained more or less silver, and some of it was known to be present as chloride, the leaches were tested for that metal. The results showed that some silver was being leached.

In each charge 100 gm. of 10-mesh ore and 1000 cc. of saturated brine (1210 gm.), into which the acid was measured, were used. The charges were agitated in 2.5-litre acid bottles for 24 hours. In the first three tests with each ore the theoretical, three times the theoretical, and five times the theoretical amount of sulphuric acid, respectively, needed to convert the lead carbonate to sulphate were used. In the fourth and the fifth tests the theoretical and five times the theoretical amount of hydrochloric acid needed, respectively, to convert the lead carbonate to lead chloride were used.

The results are shown in Table 3. Excellent extraction of the lead is possible if sufficient acid is applied, but only part of the silver is extracted. The efficiency of the acid is lowest with the ores that contain the largest amount of soluble gangue materials, such as lime, alumina, and iron. The best acid efficiency obtained with the Chief Consolidated ore was 24.6%, that is, of all the acid consumed only 24.6% did useful work in leaching lead, the rest of the acid being wasted on gangue materials.

As regards the action of hydrochloric acid and that of sulphuric acid, there did not seem to be any great difference except in a few instances. Thus tests No. 1 and 4 on the ore from the May Day mine apparently showed that a high extraction of lead was possible with one equivalent of hydrochloric acid, whereas one equivalent of sulphuric acid gave only a low extraction. With five equivalents of acid present the action seemed to be the same. Considerable care was taken in making up the samples, but it is possible that some error crept into one of these determinations, as there is no such marked discrepancy in the other results. Former experiments by Ralston and Gartside[3] had shown definitely that there was no difference in the action of the two acids in the leaching of zinc from oxidized ores. Most of the data in Table 3 tend to show the same result for the lead carbonate ores, although there seems to be some minor differences, probably due to errors in the analytical work.

SECOND SERIES OF TESTS. As these tests showed that it was possible to leach most of the lead from all three ores tested, and with encouraging consumptions of acid for two of them, a number of other ores from different localities were tested to determine whether they would respond in like manner. The results are shown in Table 4.

[3]Ralston, O. C., and Gartside, A. E., Leaching a zinc-lime ore with acids; Met. & Chem. Eng., vol. 13, 1915, pp. 151-155.

Ore.[b]	Weight of material.		Lead.			Silver.			Acid.			
	Ore in charge.	Tailing.	In charge.	In tailing.	Extraction.	In charge.	In tailing.	Extraction.	Quantity applied.	Quantity remaining.	Quantity consumed.	Acid efficiency.
	Gm.	Gm.	Per cent.	Per cent.	Per cent.	Oz. p. ton.	Oz. p. ton.	Per cent.	Gm.	Gm.	Gm.	Per cent.
May Day:												
No. 1[b]	100	98.2	4.29	3.41	20.5	2.50	2.54	......	1.99	......	1.99	20.9
No. 2	100	94.0	2.29	.18	96.0	......	2.40	5	5.97	1.10	4.87	40.1
No. 3	100	93.7	4.29	.12	97.4	......	2.04	23	9.95	5.37	4.58	43.0
No. 4	100	97.5	4.29	.63	85.4	......	2.00	25	1.42	......	1.42	9.1
No. 5	100	93.1	4.29	.10	97.9	......	2.18	16	7.20	4.87	2.33	63.2
Chief Consolidated:												
No. 1	100	97.9	3.10	2.83	8.7	6.88	9.44	......	1.48	......	1.48	8.6
No. 2	100	93.4	3.10	1.74	33.0	......	8.02	......	4.44	......	4.44	14.5
No. 3	100	91.9	3.10	.10	97.0	......	4.82	30	7.40	......	7.40	24.6
No. 4	100	97.1	3.10	2.42	22.0	......	5.70	17	1.42	......	1.42	16.8
No. 5	100	89.0	3.10	.20	93.5	......	3.94	43	7.20	......	7.20	14.2
Scranton:												
No. 1	100	93.5	9.02	5.4	44.0	1.36	1.08	20.6	4.29	......	4.29	43.9
No. 2	100	87.5	9.02	.55	94.6	......	1.00	26	12.9	4.39	7.51	53.9
No. 3	100	89.4	9.02	.98	90.2	......	1.12	18	21.45	11.45	10.00	39.5
No. 4	100	92.0	9.02	5.97	39.2	......	1.32	3	3.18	......	3.18	39.1
No. 5	100	84.7	9.02	1.26	88.1	......	1.82	......	15.90	10.60	5.30	52.5

TABLE 3

In each test a pulp consisting of 1000 cc. of brine to 100 gm. of ore was prepared. The leaches were agitated all night and on the next day were filtered for analysis. The temperature at which these experiments were run was that of the laboratory, about 20° C. The extractions of lead from the Daly Judge carbonate ore were not as high as was expected. Later tests showed that it was difficult to get more than 1% of lead into solution in a brine at the laboratory temperatures, hence the use of 10 volumes of solution to 1 weight of ore was slightly below the requirements for the proportion of lead in this ore. Only one type of ore, Iron Blossom No. 10, gave discouragingly low extractions. This ore was really a silver ore containing a small amount of lead. In all of the materials tested the silver content was disregarded for the time being, as the object was to study the lead in as many different ores as possible. As regards acid efficiency, the ore from the Scranton mine and the tailings from the Wilbert and the Horn Silver dumps seemed to use less acid per unit of lead extracted than the other samples, and further tests were therefore made with these materials.

The amount of acid used in each test is expressed as an equivalent to the lead. That is, one pound of lead is equivalent to 0.474 lb. of sulphuric acid (anhydrous), or, roughly, one-half pound, so that in general one pound of sulphuric acid should convert two pounds of lead to a soluble form, provided some of the acid is not used up by other constituents of the ore. The data in Table 4 were used in preparing the curves in Fig. 3, except that the results have been converted to the number of pounds of acid that gave an extraction of a definite number of pounds of lead from a ton of ore. This is the information that is needed in any calculations as to the financial possibilities of such a process.

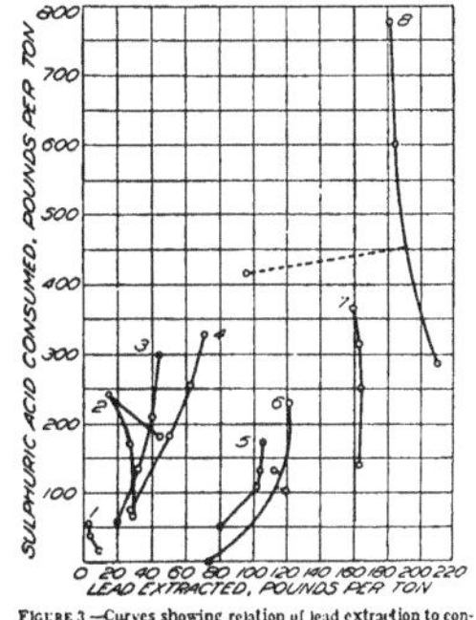

FIGURE 3.—Curves showing relation of lead extraction to consumption of acid in first series of leaching tests with acidified brine. 1, Iron Blossom No. 10 ore; 2, Iron Blossom No. 3 ore; 3, Chief Consolidated ore; 4, American Flag ore; 5, tailing from Wilbert dump; 6, tailing from Horn Silver dump; 7, Scranton ore; 8, Daly Judge ore.

From these curves it is evident that with some of the ores the amount of lead extracted after adding more than two equivalents of acid is actually smaller than with less acid. The result is probably due to the excess of sulphate radical present that tends to re-precipitate lead sulphate from the solution. The materials that acted in this way are the ones that did not contain noteworthy amounts of acid-consuming constituents, and hence gave high acid efficiencies. Down to the limit of the amount of acid necessary to convert the lead carbonate to a soluble form it is best not to use any more acid than such material seems to require. With some of the other materials the addition of more acid always resulted in the extraction of a little more lead.

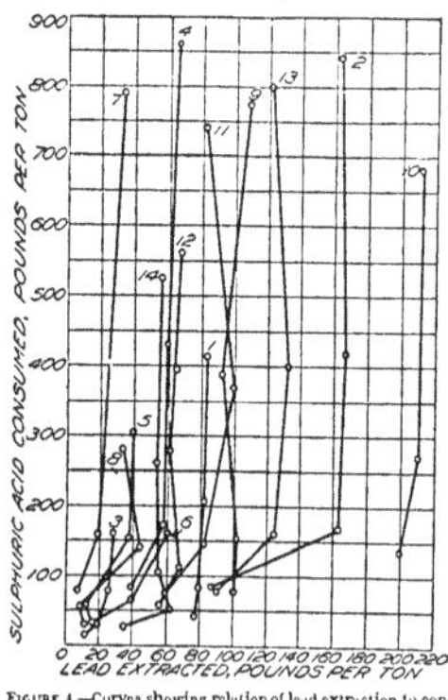

FIGURE 4.—Curves showing relation of lead extraction to consumption of acid in second series of leaching tests with acidified brine. *1*, tailing from Ontario dump; *2*, tailing from Bullionville dump; slimes from Eureka Hill dump; *4* to *7*, Michigan-Utah ores; *8*, Chief Consolidated ore; *9*, slimes from Copper Queen dump; *10*, Shattuck ore; *11*, tailing from Dry Valley dump; *12*, tailing from Daly West dump; *13*, slimes from Bullion Beck dump; *14*, Nevada United ore.

THIRD SERIES OF TESTS. Another set of argentiferous lead carbonate ores was treated in the same way. The data on the lead extraction from these ores have been calculated and plotted in Fig. 4, to make the results comparable with those in Fig. 3. Although the various ores tested vary widely in lead content, it is a strange coincidence that in only a few ores will the use of more than 150 lb. of sulphuric acid per ton of ore give a higher extraction of lead than is obtainable with that amount of acid. In those experiments, however, the main consideration governing the amount of acid used was the possible extraction of the silver in the ore. Therefore the data on the lead extractions are only of technical interest.

TESTS OF TAILING. Two of the samples that seemed to give the best acid efficiencies were the Wilbert tailing and the Scranton ore. These were chosen for further experimentation. It was necessary to know the minimum time required to extract the lead and the minimum amount of brine that would hold it in solution. It also seemed possible that the application of stronger acid solutions would dissolve the lead faster than weaker acid solutions containing the same weight of acid in a greater volume of brine. All of these points were tested on a sample of the Wilbert tailing. The charges consisted of 100 gm. of ore, usually with 1000 cc. of saturated brine unless otherwise stated. The material was placed in ordinary 2.5-litre acid-bottles, which were placed on their sides on a cyanide agitator and rolled over about once every two seconds. After agitation, the contents were filtered on suction-filters consisting of a pump, flask, and a Büchner porcelain funnel.

Material tested.	Pb.	Equivalents of acid.[a]		Efficiency of acid.	Lead extraction.	Time of leaching.
		Applied.	Consumed.			
	Per cent.			*Per cent.*	*Per cent.*	*Hours.*
Ore, Chief Consolidated mine	2.81	2.0	2.0	18.2	36.0	16
Do.	2.81	5.0	5.0	12.7	69.5	16
Do.	2.81	8.1	7.8	9.5	71.0	16
Do.	2.81	11.6	11.2	7.3	78.5	16
Ore, American Flag mine	3.83	2.0	2.0	17.3	37.3	16
Do.	3.83	5.0	5.0	12.3	66.5	16
Do.	3.83	7.0	7.0	10.7	81.0	16
Do.	3.83	10.0	8.95	10.2	93.0	16
Tailings dump, Wilbert mine	5.51	1.0	1.0	63.0	73.0	24
Do.	5.51	2.0	2.0	42.0	92.0	24
Do.	5.51	3.0	2.47	31.4	94.6	24
Do.	5.51	5.0	3.2	27.4	95.2	24
Tailings dump, Horn Silver mine	7.16	2.0	1.49	53.5	83.0	16
Do.	7.16	5.0	1.97	38.6	79.0	16
Do.	7.16	7.0	1.91	39.0	78.0	16
Do.	7.16	10.0	3.35	22.2	84.5	16
Do.	7.16	None.	None.	....	51.6	16
No. 10 ore, Iron Blossom mine	1.94	2.0	.34	5.4	9.7	20
Do.	1.94	5.0	.52	14.6	16.0	20
Do.	1.94	7.0	2.14	.7	5.5	20
Do.	1.94	10.0	2.83	.7	5.6	20
No. 3 ore, Iron Blossom mine	3.63	2.0	2.00	14.3	38.6	18
Do.	3.63	5.0	5.00	7.8	39.4	18
Do.	3.63	7.0	6.98	2.0	20.2	18
Do.	3.63	10.0	5.26	7.8	61.5	18
Ore, Daly Judge mine	15.33	2.0	1.95	33.0	70.0	20
Do.	15.33	5.0	2.82	16.9	31.4	20
Do.	15.33	7.0	4.12	13.9	60.0	20
Do.	15.33	10.0	5.34	10.2	59.0	20
Ore, Scranton mine	8.64	2.0	1.7	53.0	94.0	20
Do.	8.69	5.0	3.06	29.0	94.0	20
Do.	8.64	7.0	3.86	23.0	93.8	20
Do.	8.64	10.0	4.4	20.0	92.5	20

[a] 1 equivalent of H_2SO_4=0.474 pound per pound of lead.

TABLE 4

These data are presented in Table 5. Some of the results are plotted in Fig. 5. The curves showing the effect of time on the acid efficiency represent two series of tests, one of solutions containing two equivalents of acid, and one of solutions containing four equivalents of acid. The curve showing the percentage extraction of the lead represents the series of tests of solutions containing two equivalents of acid. The corresponding curve for the results with solutions containing four equivalents of acid would practically coincide with this curve, and was not plotted. The percentage of efficiency of the acid when four equivalents are used is considerably lower than when two equivalents are used, so both efficiency curves were plotted. The curves show that there is no advantage to be gained by prolonging a leach for more than two hours, either on the score of lead extraction or of acid efficiency. In fact, after two hours both the lead extraction and the acid efficiency fall off to some extent. One would expect that any excess of acid, on long standing, would gradually waste itself on other constituents of the ore, hence, the fall in efficiency of the acid is easy to understand. It may be that on long standing certain other constituents of the ore would also precipitate some lead, as lead is a metal that might be easily precipitated from solution by finely divided iron or particles of other minerals such as zinc oxide or zinc sulphide.

As these tests showed that two hours of leaching was sufficient, it was thought that a series of leaches of varying acidity might reveal the most advantageous concentration of acid to use. However, the percentage of extraction of lead and the acid efficiency seemed to be unaffected, or at least were not affected in two-hour leaches, of acid and the other with solutions containing 1.5. The leaches containing less brine, therefore, had higher concentrations of acid, although the total amount of acid was either 2 or 1.5 equivalents in every test. As the results of the previous series of tests had shown little or no effect due to acid concentration, any effects shown by these two series were probably due to causes other than acid concentration. Leaches were successful down to the point where 400 cc. of brine to 100 gm. of tailing was used, when the lead extraction fell off slightly in the series containing 1.5 equivalents of acid. The acid efficiency was not affected. These solutions contained almost 1.2% lead. Therefore 1% lead was chosen as the probable maximum in practical work at temperatures of about 20° C., and many of the later experiments were so planned that there would always be 1 volume of cold

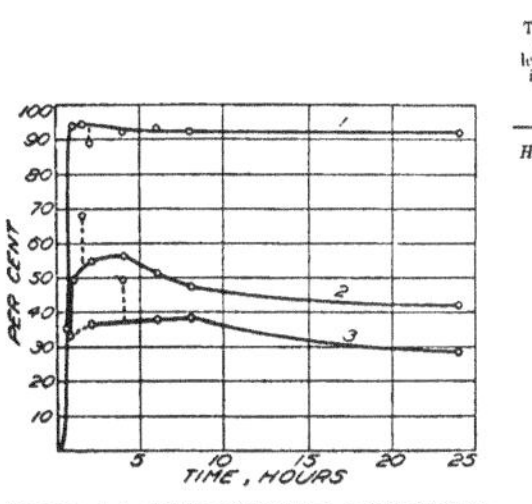

FIGURE 5.—Curve showing effects of time on lead extraction and acid efficiency in leaching Wilbert tailing with acidified brine.

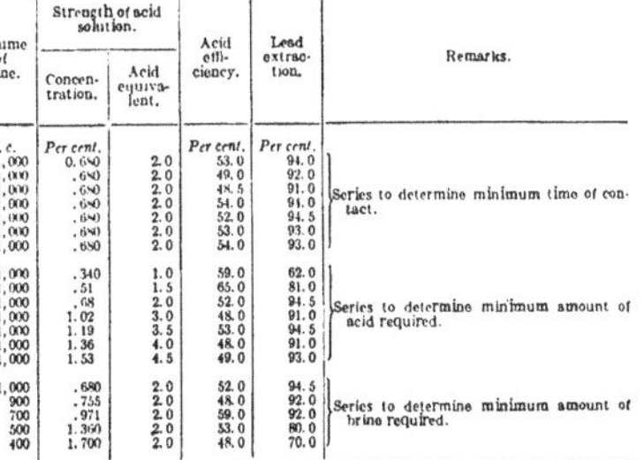

Time of leaching.	Volume of brine.	Strength of acid solution.		Acid efficiency.	Lead extraction.	Remarks.
		Concentration.	Acid equivalent.			
Hours.	*C. c.*	*Per cent.*		*Per cent.*	*Per cent.*	
20	1,000	0.680	2.0	53.0	94.0	Series to determine minimum time of contact.
8	1,000	.680	2.0	49.0	92.0	
6	1,000	.680	2.0	48.5	91.0	
4	1,000	.680	2.0	54.0	91.0	
2	1,000	.680	2.0	52.0	94.5	
1	1,000	.680	2.0	53.0	93.0	
½	1,000	.680	2.0	54.0	93.0	
2	1,000	.340	1.0	59.0	62.0	Series to determine minimum amount of acid required.
2	1,000	.51	1.5	65.0	81.0	
2	1,000	.68	2.0	52.0	94.5	
2	1,000	1.02	3.0	48.0	91.0	
2	1,000	1.19	3.5	53.0	94.5	
2	1,000	1.36	4.0	48.0	91.0	
2	1,000	1.53	4.5	49.0	93.0	
2	1,000	.680	2.0	52.0	94.5	Series to determine minimum amount of brine required.
2	900	.755	2.0	48.0	92.0	
2	700	.971	2.0	59.0	92.0	
2	500	1.360	2.0	53.0	80.0	
2	400	1.700	2.0	48.0	70.0	

TABLE 5

The strength of the acid solution may possibly have some effect on the extraction or on the acid efficiency in leaches of less than two hours' time. This point was not investigated, as the results of the former series of tests, with two of the extremes of acid concentration used, showed that about two hours of contact between the solution and the ore was needed to get the most satisfactory extraction.

The solubility curves for lead chloride in brines (Fig. 2) indicate that at ordinary room temperatures (about 20° C.), solutions containing as much as 1.5% lead when saturated with respect to lead can be obtained. Such a concentration could not be expected in practice, but it might be possible to get solutions containing considerably more than 1% of lead. Hence a series of tests was run to determine the minimum amount of brine, of a given strength, necessary to leach the lead from the Wilbert tailing, as in the previous tests leaches consisting of 1000 cc. of brine to 100 gm. of ore that contained only 5.5% of lead had been used. With complete extraction of the lead such a leaching solution would contain only 0.5% of lead.

Two series of tests with decreasing amounts of brine were tried—one with solutions containing 2 equivalents

brine for each 1% of lead in the ore. Thus the Wilbert tailing, containing 5.5% lead, could be leached with about 550 cc. of brine for every 100 gm. of ore. As the brine had a specific gravity of about 1.2 at room temperatures this rule will give, roughly, solutions containing somewhat less than 1% of lead. Hence a pulp ratio slightly less than that given by the rule will still have a large factor of safety. In counter-current decantation it would probably be safe to use pulp ratios that would give solutions more nearly saturated with lead.

TESTS OF MATERIAL FROM SCRANTON MINE. The results of a series of tests on the Scranton ore, similar to the series on the Wilbert tailing, are recorded in Table 6. Unlike the results with Wilbert tailing, as good an extraction of the lead was made in one half-hour as in 24 hours, and the efficiency of the acid was the same throughout the series. This indicates that practically all of the chemical reactions liable to take place had been completed during the first half-hour. As there are few types of modern agitating or leaching machinery that will receive and discharge the ore to be leached in less than a half-hour, no tests were made for a shorter length of time. The acid requirements of this ore are such that they must be used before the maximum extraction of lead is possible. The brine requirements of the ore are shown in the third series of tests to be about 700 cc. of brine to a solution containing more than 1.5 equivalents of acid every 100 gm. of ore. As the ore contains 8.65% lead,

Time.	Volume of brine.	Strength of acid solution.		Acid efficiency.	Extraction of lead.	Remarks.
		Concentration.	Acid equivalent.			
Hours.	*Cubic centimeters.*	*Per cent.*		*Per cent.*	*Per cent.*	
24	1,000	0.442	2.0	42.0	92.5	Two series, to determine minimum time necessary.
8	1,000	.442	2.0	47.5	92.0	
6	1,000	.442	2.0	51.6	93.0	
4	1,000	.442	2.0	57.0	92.	
2	1,000	.442	2.0	54.5	88.	
1.5	1,000	.442	2.0	68.0	94.	
1	1,000	.442	2.0	49.0	94.0	
0.5	1,000	.442	2.0	34.0	35.0	
24	1,000	.884	4.0	28.4	91.	
8	1,000	.884	4.0	38.2	93.	
6	1,000	.884	4.0	38.0	93.	
4	1,000	.884	4.0	49.7	93.0	
2	1,000	.884	4.0	37.2	91.0	
2	1,000	.442	2.0	54.5	88.5	Series to determine effect of strength of acid in short-time leaches.
2	1,000	.552	2.5	50.0	91.0	
2	1,000	.663	3.0	46.5	89.5	
2	1,000	.774	3.5	51.3	91.5	
2	1,000	.884	4.0	37.2	91.0	
2	1,000	.994	4.5	49.0	92.5	
2	1,000	.442	2.0	54.5	88.5	Series to determine minimum amount of brine for ore.
2	900	.49	2.0	62.0	97.0	
2	700	.631	2.0	48.5	91.0	
2	500	.884	2.0	50.0	92.5	
2	400	1.102	2.0	64.5	91.5	
2	1,000	.332	1.5	58.0	87.5	
2	900	.369	1.5	59.0	98.0	
2	700	.475	1.5	58.0	98.	
2	500	.665	1.5	61.0	97.0	
2	400	.830	1.5	58.0	82.0	

TABLE 6

the leaching solutions could be built up to a strength of 1.03% lead under conditions that would give a maximum extraction of lead.

Iron Ore in 1918

Statistics and estimates of the production of iron ore in 1918, compiled under the direction of Ernest F. Burchard, of the U. S. Geological Survey, show a moderate decrease in output compared with the high records of 1916 and 1917. The estimated quantity of iron ore mined in the United States in 1918 amounted to 69,712,000 tons, compared with 75,288,851 tons in 1917, a decrease of 7.4%. The estimated shipments of ore from the mines in 1918 were 72,192,000 tons, valued at $246,043,000, compared with 75,573,207 tons, valued at $238,260,444 in 1917, a decrease in quantity of 4.5% but an increase in value of 3.3%. The average selling-value of the ore per ton at the mines for the whole United States in 1918 was $3.41, compared with $3.15 in 1917. The stocks of iron ore at the mines apparently decreased from 10,628,908 tons in 1917 to 8,139,000 tons in 1918, or 23.4%.

About 86% of the iron ore mined and shipped in 1918 came from the Lake Superior district, in which 60,092,000 tons were mined and 62,285,000 tons were shipped in 1918, compared with 63,666,068 tons mined and 63,854,752 tons shipped in 1917, representing decreases of 5.6% and 2.5%, respectively, in 1918. The average selling price of iron ore at the mines in the Lake Superior district in 1918 was $3.50 per ton compared with $3.28 in 1917.

In the Western States—Colorado, New Mexico, Utah, and Wyoming—there were mined 750,000 tons, compared with 837,673 tons in 1917, a decrease of 10%. The shipments in 1918 amounted to 740,000 tons, compared with 832,056 tons in 1917, a decrease of 11%. The average selling-value of the ore in this group of States in 1918 was $1.72 per ton, compared with $1.39 in 1917.

BEARING-METAL should possess the following properties, according to G. H. Clamer: (1) It should be sufficiently rigid to support the load or resist the impact, but yet not so brittle that it will easily crack; (2) it should have as yielding or plastic a nature as is consistent with its ability to support the load or resist the impact without deformation of the bearing as a whole; (3) the ideal structure combines a hard matrix to support the load and a softer metal or alloy contained within such matrix, to permit the bearing surface to adjust itself to irregularities of the surface; (4) it should be easy to handle in the foundry and machine-shop; (5) it should be capable of being re-melted without deterioration; (6) for use in babbitt-lined bearings, it should be capable of being tinned, so that the babbitt can be applied thereto; (7) it should have good heat-conducting power in order to dissipate the heat generated by friction. Alloys have been made carrying as high as 30% lead with 3% tin and 2% antimony; also alloys of 65% copper, 30% lead, 2% tin, and 3% antimony; also with the 5% tin replaced entirely with antimony. Car-bearings, 4½ by 8 in., made from the same pattern and subjected to a breaking stress applied longitudinally at the middle of the back bearing and throughout its entire length, broke at the following average loads: with 2% antimony substituted, 60,000 lb.; with 3%, 62,000 lb.; with total substitution, 52,000 lb.; as compared with a breaking load of 67,000 lb. for the alloy of copper 65, tin 5, and lead 30. The castings produced with each of the three alloys mentioned are not so satisfactory as those made with the straight tin alloys, being rather rough, and showing slight globules of lead on the surface. The hardening effect of antimony is obtained at the sacrifice of ductility. A certain amount of nickel can be used for replacing tin with very satisfactory results. The castings produced when zinc is substituted for a certain amount of tin are decidedly unsatisfactory. The substitution of alumina for tin is entirely impractical, and such castings are worthless. The substitution of any other metals for tin in the Cu-Sn-Pb alloys can be made only by sacrificing its quality.

Concentration of Graphite Ore

By GEORGE D. DUB

*Ceylon and Madagascar have supplied 70% of the total graphite imported into the United States. Of this amount, 90% was used in the manufacture of crucibles. The use of domestic graphite before 1915 was confined largely to lubricants. In the past two years, imports of graphite were eight times the domestic output. The War Minerals Investigations last year made a survey of present mining, milling, refining, sampling, and analyzing methods; did experimental work in concentrating and refining to improve present practice; and made various tests in crucible manufacture. The graphite-producing States are Alabama, New York, Pennsylvania, and Texas.

At the present time there are 39 plants in the three graphite-producing counties of Alabama—Clay, Coosa, and Chilton. Early in October 1918, four of these plants were in course of erection, and fourteen were temporarily closed because of changes in method of treatment or because of plant fires. Thus, a little over half of the plants were then operating and only six were on full time. Even if the market required an expansion, it is doubtful whether labor would be available to enable all of the mills to operate two shifts per day. It should be noted that this industry has seen its greatest development during the past two years. It is natural therefore that operating difficulties should still cause considerable trouble.

Graphite occurs in the Talladega schist accompanied by quartz, feldspar, mica, and other accessory minerals and alteration products. At present only the upper 30 to 60 ft. of the graphitic schist is being mined. This consists of the decomposed and weathered part of the schist, and is normally rather soft and easily broken. For this reason operators are loath to work the unaltered 'blue rock'. Alabaman ore contains, as far as is known, no amorphous graphite. All of the operating companies have open-pit workings. With a single exception, all drilling is done by means of a 'jumper' drill, holes being put down 8 to 30 ft. All blasting is done with black powder. The deeper holes are chambered with dynamite or blasting gelatine. The ore is covered with 1 to 6 ft. of overburden, which carries some graphite. However, it contains so much clay and vegetal matter that it is removed and disposed of as waste to obviate milling difficulties caused by the presence of these materials. The overburden is removed by plows, scrapers, and wheelbarrows, this operation not involving much labor or expense. Machine-drills are employed at only one mine. At this mine self-rotating hammer-drills of the jack-hammer type are used to drill holes 15 ft. in depth.

*Abstract from War Minerals Investigation Series No. 3, U. S. Bureau of Mines.

The ore in Alabama averages about 2½% graphitic carbon. From this is obtained in general three products: No. 1 crucible flake, No. 2 flake, and dust. The aim in concentrating is to recover as much as possible of the No. 1 flake, analyzing 85% graphitic carbon and remaining on a No. 8 silk cloth of 86-mesh. No. 2 flake, analyzing 75 to 80% carbon and of finer size than the No. 1, is a by-product for which the market is limited. Dust analyzes 30% or more carbon and is a greater drug on the market than the No. 2. In view of these facts the problem of ore-dressing is obviously complicated by the necessity of recovering as much as possible of the graphite in the ore in such form as to be marketable as No. 1 flake. The measure of efficiency therefore in graphite milling is not the percentage of extraction, but the number of pounds of No. 1 flake recovered per ton of ore. Unfortunately graphite plants do not make a practice of analyzing their mill-heads, and it is impossible, because of this fact, to establish a relation between the total graphite in the ore and the amount recovered as No. 1 flake. The by-product grades can readily be used in the manufacture of lubricating flake, paint stock, foundry

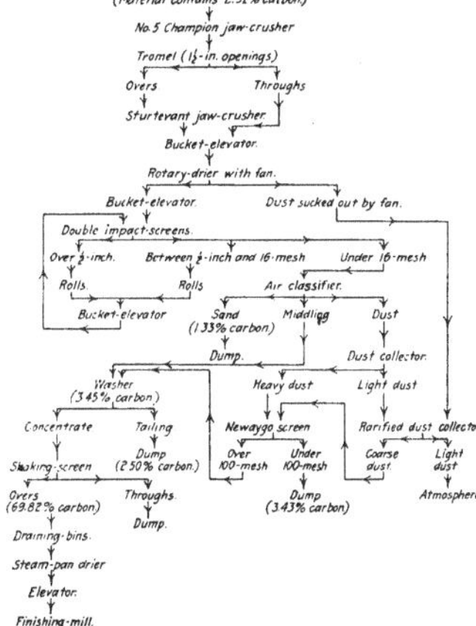

FIG. 1. FLOW-SHEET OF SKIN-FLOTATION SYSTEM

facings, stove polish, etc., but seemingly the demand for these manufacturing branches are not great, with the result that this market does not readily absorb all the No. 2 flake and dust produced.

Many different crushing machines and combinations are used in Alabama in the preparation of graphite ore. The coarse breaker most commonly used is a jaw-crusher of the Blake or Dodge type, which reduces the ore to 1½ inch. In some plants, a toothed impact-roll is used for coarse crushing. In plants where dry material is crushed fine, rolls, dry-mullers, or Symons disc-crushers are used to reduce the material to final-treatment size, which is about 1/16 or 3/32 in. For fine crushing in plants in which an oil-froth flotation method of concentration is used, coarse crushing is followed by some type of rotating mill, ball-mill, pebble-mill, or rod-mill. These machines are sometimes preceded by a Symons disc-crusher.

In general there are four methods of concentrating graphite ores, with several modifications, as described in the following notes:

In the water 'skin-flotation' system, a typical flow-sheet of which is shown in Fig. 1, the ore is crushed dry to 1/16 or 3/32 inch. It is then passed through a rotary-drier, screened, and passed over an air-separator, which classifies the material into three products—'scalping' or tailing, which goes to the waste dump; middling, which forms the 'washer' feed; and fine, which is generally treated on a separate group of 'washers'. The middling plus the fine, which form 50 to 65% of the crude ore, go to a bin for fine ore, from which the material drops to 'surface-tension' washers. In this machine, the graphite and some of the mica are floated off, on the surface film of water, while the gangue minerals are wet by the water and sink to the hutch of the washer which discharges to the tailing launder. The rough graphite concentrate is then dewatered on a trommel or shaking-screen, which also removes both the graphite too fine to make No. 1 flake and the fine sand that has been carried over into the concentrate by the film formed by the graphite on the surface of the water. The dewatered concentrate, a dry sample of which assays 40 to 60% graphitic carbon, is then dried in a rotary or steam-pan drier and sent to the finishing plant. Average figures for the amount of rough concentrate recovered per ton of ore are not available.

The variations in detail of this system are many and often unusual. Crushing differences have been noted above. There is quite as wide a variation in the types of screening and air-classifying apparatus used. For screening, Newaygo and 'whip-tap' screens are most popular; but other types of impact and shaking-screens are used, as well as hexagonal trommels. Most of the air-classifying apparatus is individually designed and erected, and gives results that seem to be efficient. Practically no work has been done to check the work of this class of machine, its operation being judged entirely by looking at the products without having even the 'scalpings' analyzed. So far as is known, no tests have been made on the 'scalpings' to determine whether, by regrinding, a sufficient additional quantity of No. 1 flake would be recovered to justify the additional treatment.

There are three types of 'skin-flotation' washers sufficiently distinct in principle to permit individual description. The sketches (Fig. 2 and 3) are given simply to illustrate the underlying principles in design, and the dimensions given are estimates and not actual measurements.

The Munro washer is a rectangular tank in which the

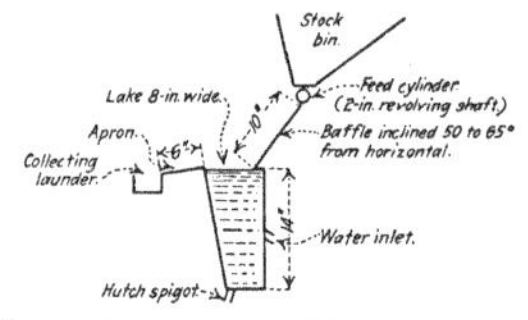

FIG. 2. SECTION THROUGH ORIGINAL MUNRO WASHER. THESE ARE BUILT IN UNITS 4 FT. LONG, PLACED END TO END AND BACK TO BACK. DIMENSIONS ARE APPROXIMATE.

feed drops from the feed cylinder to an inclined flat baffle, thence to the water-film, which carries the graphite to the collecting launder and permits the gangue to sink to the hutch.

The Colmer washer is a circular tank with a conical feed-baffle. The ore falls from the baffle on a revolving circular disc with ribs cast on it. The tangential motion thus imparted to the ore is intended to assist in carrying off the graphite, by reducing the tendency of the falling

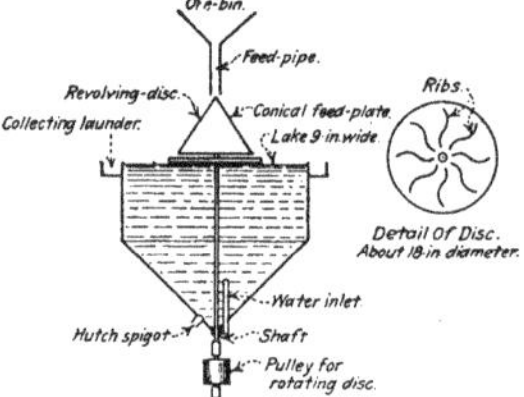

FIG. 3. SECTION THROUGH COLMER WASHER NOT DRAWN TO SCALE

particles to rupture the surface film of water. Some operators claim that better results are obtained with this washer by keeping the disc stationary, relying on the disc solely to change the direction of travel of the particles of ore. It was claimed by these operators that the tangential motion given by the revolving disc produced a lower-grade concentrate than was obtained by maintaining the disc stationary. As shown in Fig. 3, the washer is about 42 in. diameter.

The new Munro washer, which also is circular in shape, is 6 to 12 in. larger in diameter than the Colmer, most of this increase in size being taken up by increasing the width of the 'lake'. In this apparatus the treatment water is forced through an anular opening formed by placing a cast-iron cover over a bell-mouth casting attached to the feed-water pipe. This washer does away with the mechanical motion in the Colmer type. It is difficult, however, to keep an unobstructed flow of water through the annular opening.

In the treatment of graphite ores by the pneumatic process, pneumatic apparatus is used throughout. A typical flow-sheet for this system is not given, because it has been successful in only one mill. The details of the operation of this plant cannot be made public.

A typical flow-sheet of the log-washer process is shown in Fig. 4. In this method of treatment the crude ore is crushed and screened without drying. It is then treated in log-washers, kerosene being added to the water in the apparatus. The concentrate is screened, washed on a cement floor, drained, and dried. This system eliminates the expensive preliminary drying of the crude ore, necessary with the water skin-flotation. The simplicity and effectiveness of this plant are clear to the observer. The grade of rough concentrate made is excellent, and the only loss of any extent occurs in the coarse-sand tailing, which, with re-grinding, might be made to yield considerably more flake graphite. A test of the coarse-sand tailing in the same way that has been suggested under the discussion above with reference to the scalping of air-classifiers, would determine the feasibility of re-grinding. The fine-sand tailing is remarkably free from detached flakes of graphite.

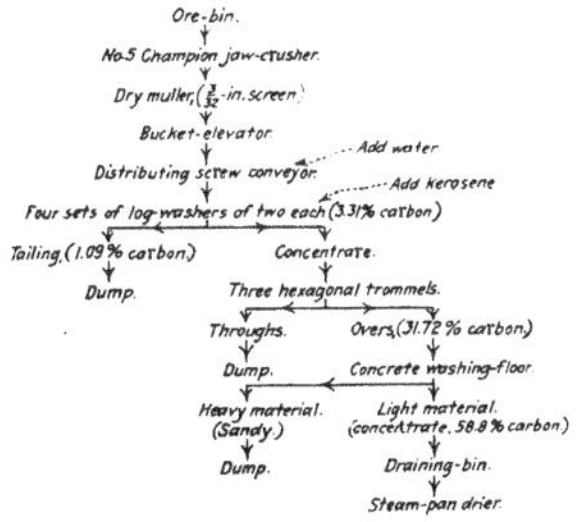

Ore-bin.
No.5 Champion jaw-crusher.
Dry muller, ($\frac{3}{32}$-in. screen)
Bucket-elevator.
Add water
Distributing screw conveyor.
Add kerosene
Four sets of log-washers of two each (3.31% carbon)
Tailing, (1.09% carbon)
Dump.
Concentrate.
Three hexagonal trommels.
Throughs.
Dump.
Overs, (31.72% carbon)
Concrete washing-floor.
Heavy material. (Sandy.)
Dump.
Light material. (concentrate, 58.8% carbon)
Draining-bin.
Steam-pan drier.

FIG. 4. FLOW-SHEET OF LOG-WASHER PROCESS

The extent to which these various processes are used in Alabama is as follows, the figures including plants that are contemplating putting in systems under which they have been classified: (1) The skin-flotation washer system is used in 12½ plants, one of them consisting of two units, one of which is the Minerals Separation system; (2) the pneumatic system is used in three plants; and (3) the log-washer system is used in two plants.

The majority of companies in Alabama have installed some type of oil-froth flotation cell. Thus, 8 plants have put in the Callow pneumatic cells; four the Simplex type; 3½ (a two-unit plant has one skin-flotation washer system) have Minerals Separation cells; and 6 plants have or intend to have home-made cells or washers combining some of the principles of the above-enumerated processes.

The chief difficulty with an oil-froth flotation system seems to be in the loss of the large flakes. In recovering this, so low grade a concentrate is obtained that an added burden is placed on the finishing plant. There is no difficulty in obtaining a high recovery of high-grade dust, but there is at present no ready market for this material. The best results in the district are now being obtained from the home-made cells or washers mentioned.

In both the Minerals Separation and the Callow systems, fine crushing is accomplished by Marcy, Lehigh, Marathon, or Hardinge ball and pebble-mills. Water classifiers of the Deister or Gemmell type are used in practically all of the plants in which these two systems have been installed. In two plants Dorr classifiers are in use. As rough concentrate dewatering devices, vacuum-filters of the Portland or Oliver type are generally used rather than shaking-screens.

A typical flow-sheet of the Callow pneumatic system is shown in Fig. 5. This system has received greater development in the Alabama district than any other oil-froth flotation system. At one plant the tailing from the Callow cells are now being treated in a washer of home-made construction, with highly satisfactory recovery.

The Simplex system includes a method of crushing as well as concentration. The crushing apparatus has no particular advantage over other crushing machinery, but the concentration method appears to be efficient. In this system, the pulp comes unclassified to the centre of an elliptical washer on the surface of which jets of water, with flotation oils, are forced at a pressure as high as 40 lb. per square inch. The jet of water entrains air, and a froth is formed which floats the graphite over the side of the washer, while the gangue drops to the hutch. A sketch through the washer is shown in Fig. 6.

At the present time in various mills in Alabama, Wilfley and Deister tables are being installed to raise the grade of the rough concentrate and to remove gangue from the feed to the finishing plant. The gangue wears the surfaces of the buhr stones, necessitating their more frequent dressing, an operation that is both tedious and expensive. At one of the plants, concentrate from a table is being treated in an improvised pebble-mill. The dust is then removed and the material is passed through a series of screens, producing No. 1 flake ready for market. The most vital question to be considered in connection with the use of concentrating tables is their capacity. Unfortunately, experiments have not proceeded sufficiently to permit the presentation of any data as to the success of this new departure in Alabama.

The rough concentrate as it comes from the concentrating plants contains a minimum of 40% graphitic carbon. In some cases this crude concentrate is as high as 75% carbon, although the usual proportion is 40 to 60%. The impurities consist of quartz, mica, wood fibre, etc. Material of this character is not readily marketable except at prices far below those obtained for No. 1 flake. Moreover, the market for crude concentrate is limited. These facts therefore necessitate the refining of crude concentrate to No. 1 flake, containing 85% carbon and remaining on a No. 8 silk cloth of 86-mesh. Under the microscope the flakes are found to consist of thin laminæ

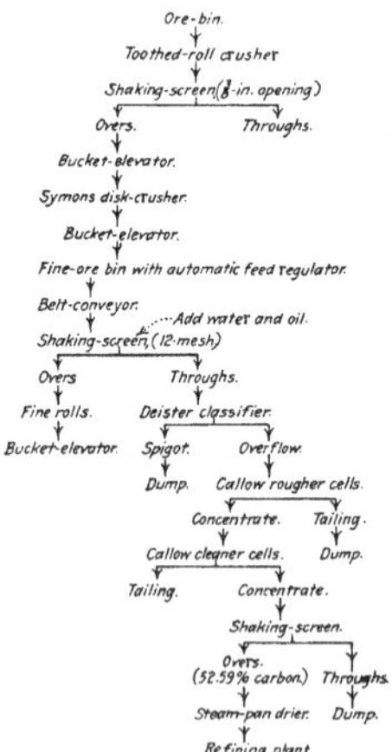

FIG. 5. FLOW-SHEET OF PLANT USING CALLOW SYSTEM

of graphite, between which occur the minerals, chiefly quartz and mica, which must be eliminated to raise the grade.

There are two general methods of refining, as follows: (1) If the crude concentrate comes to the finishing plant with most of the impurities inter-laminated or attached to the graphite, the crude concentrate must be subjected to grinding in a pebble or buhr-mill in order to separate the graphite laminæ or to free attached particles of the graphite, and (2) if, on the other hand, the crude concentrate comes to the finishing plant with the larger part of impurities as detached particles of quartz and mica, refining can be done pneumatically or with electrostatic machines. Where the latter methods are employed, crushing in the concentrating plant has been of such a character as to accomplish what is usually done in the finishing plant with the buhr or pebble-mill. The first method is the one most generally used; the second method is used by only two plants.

The average final products in Alabama are No. 1 flake containing 87% carbon, No. 2 flake with 77%, and dust with 30% carbon. A ton of ore yields, respectively, 19 lb., 5 lb., and 3 lb. of these grades. The recovery of the three grades totals 42.56%, leaving 54.44% in the tailing.

The cheapest plant to erect is the log-washer type, which is probably the cheapest to operate. No figures are available as to either initial or operating costs for a plant of this kind. For a plant capable of treating 10 tons per hour, the initial cost ranges from $35,000 to $60,000 erected, not including the cost of a finishing plant, which would add $5000 to $10,000 more.

Operating costs in the United States range from 6 to 14c., with an average of 10c. per pound of No. 1 flake. No allowance has been made in these costs for depletion and depreciation, which would add 1 to 2c. to the costs

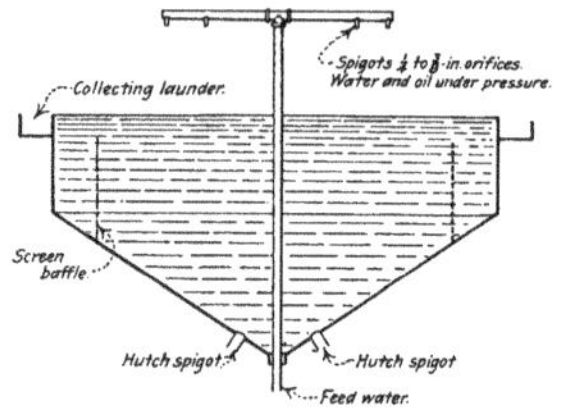

FIG. 6. SECTION OF SIMPLEX WASHER. NOT DRAWN TO SCALE

stated. In these costs the production of No. 1 flake has been charged with all operating expenses, and credited with the miscellaneous income derived from the sale of No. 2 flake and dust. The great variation in cost is due to difference in efficiency and in the grade of ore treated.

THE GREENE electrolytic furnace is of the rolling-cylinder arc-type. The 3-ton furnace at Seattle has two 5-inch graphite electrodes requiring from 500 to 600 kw. 2-phase, 100 to 110 volts. A 3-ton charge of scrap-steel is melted in 2 to 3 hours. The scrap is de-oxidized by the Greene slag-process, the slag being composed of sand, clay, or lime. The slag dissolves the iron oxides, which are in turn reduced by adding powdered coke or ferro-silicon to the charge. The elimination of iron oxides obviates imperfect castings caused by blow-holes. The newer type of 3-ton furnace has three electrodes, uses a 3-phase current and a 400-kva. transformer. The shell of the furnace is made of ¾-inch boiler-plate.

IN a patent recently granted to G. H. Clevenger, (U. S. 1,283,077) cobalt is removed from $ZnSO_4$ electrolytes containing manganese by neutralizing the electrolyte with CaO or ZnO and then precipitating the Co by the addition of an oxidizing agent such as $KMnO_4$. Another patent (U. S. 1,283,078) specifies the addition of β-naphthol, $NaNO_2$, and acid to the electrolyte, forming nitroso-β-naphthol which precipitates the Co.

The Ores of Tonopah, Nevada

By EDSON S. BASTIN and FRANCIS B. LANEY

*DEPTH OF OXIDATION. General oxidation is characteristic only of the upper portions of the few veins that crop out. In the upper portions of the veins that do not crop out and in the deeper portions of the out-cropping veins oxidation is local only. Such local oxidation was noted in some of the deepest workings near cross-fractures that intersect the veins. It is well shown, for example, on the 770-ft. level of the Tonopah Extension mine, the deepest level reached by the workings connected with the main shaft, where fractured ore and wall-rock just above the Rainbow fault are much more oxidized than those at a distance from the fault. On the 600-ft. level of this mine the Extension north vein is cut and offset by the Rainbow fault; for over 100 ft. west of the fault-plane proper the ore is much shattered and is considerably more oxidized than the less shattered ore farther west. Slight oxidation near fractures was noted in ore of the Belmont vein on the 1500-ft. level of the Tonopah Belmont mine. In the workings on the Murray vein slight oxidation was noted on the 1170-ft. level, but not on the 1260-ft. or deepest level.

OXIDATION AT SEVERAL PERIODS. At a number of localities in Tonopah there is evidence of oxidation connected not with the present surface but with ancient land-surfaces now deeply buried. The most striking evidence of this sort is found at several points near the 300 and 400-ft. levels of the West End mine, where the ore of the West End vein is capped for short spaces by the Fraction dacite-breccia. In the vicinity of the West End mine the Fraction dacite-breccia is the surface rock; its base appears to have a general south-westerly dip of about 30° and truncates the Midway andesite, the Mizpah trachyte, and in a few places the West End vein. The general structural relations are shown in Fig. 1.

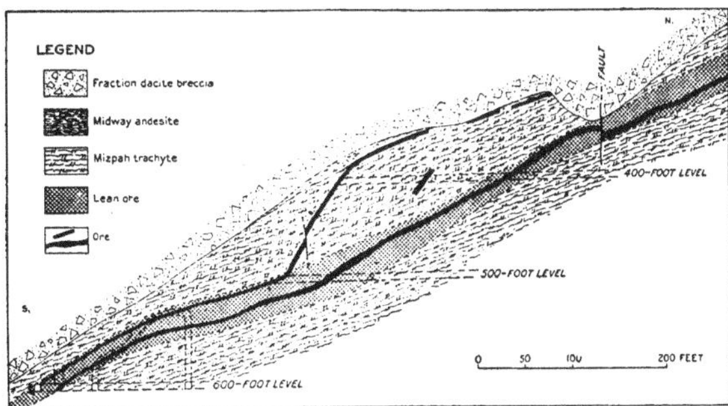

FIG. 1

The dacite-breccia is, at least in large part, a volcanic tuff, which, like the other volcanic rocks of the region, is believed by Spurr to be of Tertiary age. Its tuffaceous nature is suggested by its appearance to the unaided eye, but is especially evident under the microscope as shown in Fig. 2. The specimen studied microscopically and figured in this illustration was obtained near station 1447 on the 300-ft. level of the West End mine. It contains rock fragments irregularly angular in form and of various sizes and kinds; most of them are so much altered that their original character cannot be determined: some show plagioclase phenocrysts in a finely granular ground-mass. In addition, there are numerous fragments of quartz and feldspar phenocrysts, as shown in the illustration. The feldspar crystals are mostly andesine. A few of the feldspar crystals are perfect, but most of them are mere fragments, and many are very angular and irregular in form. Some are much fractured, not along cleavage planes but very irregularly; the fractures do not extend into the inclosing matrix. One feldspar crystal may be much fractured and another very close to it may be unfractured, indicating that the

*Abstracted from Professional Paper 104, U. S. Geological Survey.

fracturing took place before the crystals became embedded in their present matrix. Under high magnification (240 diameters) the matrix still appears fragmental and the fragments show diversity of size and shape. The smallest fragments are isotropic and are possibly volcanic glass. The alterations include part calcitization of the plagioclase, some secondary enlargement of quartz fragments, and the development of chlorite in certain rock fragments.

That the breccia is younger than the ore of the West End vein is shown by the presence of a number of fragments of ore and pyritized wall-rock in the breccia near its contacts with the vein.

Where the relations are not complicated by faulting the breccia appears to have been deposited directly upon the ore; in places it shows an obscure stratification parallel to the contact. Oxidation of the breccia near its contact with the vein is not general, but is usually confined to the vicinity of fractures, as shown in Fig. 3. Breccia in immediate contact with the vein may be wholly free from oxides of iron. The ore underlying the breccia, on the other hand, is as highly oxidized as much of the ore found at the present surface and carries iron oxides in mammillary and botryoidal forms. Some of the quartzose ore next to the contact is porous from part solution of its constituents.

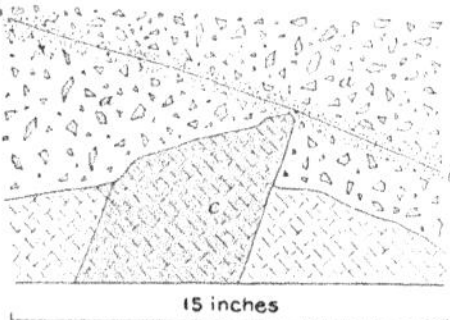

FIG. 3

The high degree of oxidation in the ore, the unoxidized condition of much of the breccia in contact with the ore, and the local inclusion of oxidized fragments of ore in unoxidized breccia indicate that much of the oxidation of this ore took place before the deposition of the breccia.

Other evidence leading to the same conclusion consists in the presence of coatings of calcite, barite, crystalline quartz, and, rarely, pyrite on the hydrous iron oxides of the ore just below the breccia contact. In ore from stope 484, not far above the 400-ft. level of the West End mine, a coating of crystals of a carbonate of iron and calcium is deposited on hydrous iron oxides. Some barite is intergrown with the carbonate. On top of the carbonate occur well-formed crystals of clear quartz. Locally, quartz has replaced the exterior of scalenohedral crystals of calcite which rest on iron oxide. Ore from stope 400A shows thin coatings of pyrite on hydrous oxides of iron. These associations, except that of quartz, constitute mineral misalliances, for the minerals of the coatings are not normally formed during the oxidation of a sulphide ore. Their presence is, therefore, indicative of a change in the physical and chemical conditions surrounding this ore. The structural relations indicate that this change was brought about by the burial of an ancient, probably Tertiary, gossan under a great thickness of volcanic tuffs, inducing a return from superficial to deeper-seated conditions.

Spurr[1] calls attention to the probability of a still earlier period of denudation and oxidation between the deposition of the Mizpah trachyte and that of the Midway andesite. He says: "Most likely the earlier andesite [Mizpah trachyte] was deeply eroded and the veins were exposed before the later andesite [Midway andesite] was poured out." The contact between these two formations is in most exposures a fault contact, so that conclusive evidence of oxidation during this period could not be obtained.

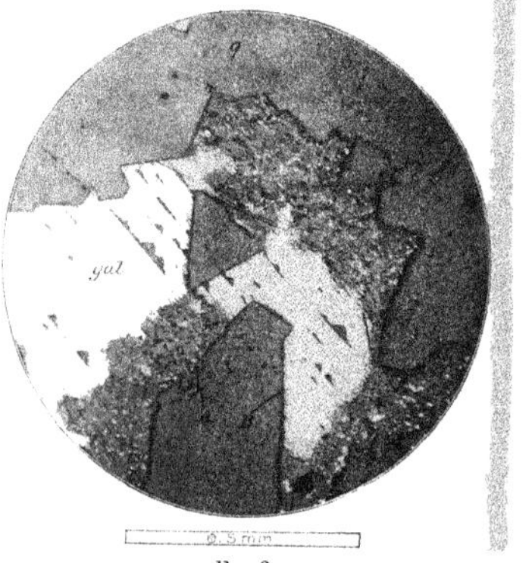

FIG. 2

From the evidence above set forth it may be concluded that although a part of the oxidation, even in those veins which do not crop out, is certainly recent, some is to be correlated with ancient, probably Tertiary, land-surfaces. As downward enrichment has been an accompaniment of the recent oxidation, it is logical to suppose that it was also an accompaniment of the ancient oxidation, and that there have, therefore, been several periods of downward enrichment.

GROUND-WATER. The common textbook diagram in which the water-table is shown as a subdued counterpart of the land-surface is applicable in a general way to regions, such as the Mississippi Valley, characterized by moderate humidity and flat-lying strata through which lateral circulation of ground-water is easy, but it does

[1]Spurr, J. E. 'Geology of the Tonopah Mining District, Nevada', U. S. Geol. Survey Prof. Paper 42, p. 35, 1905.

not at all express the relations at Tonopah. In the Tonopah mines the active ground-water circulation is practically confined to zones of fracturing: copious flows are limited to a few such zones and usually to their more open parts. Other fractures have, for considerable periods at least, and to great depths, been sufficiently free from water to permit extensive oxidation through the agency of the atmosphere. These relations were emphasized by Spurr,[2] who says:

"No general body of ground-water has been encountered, although the rocks are extremely fractured: yet along certain steeply inclined fracture-zones water is found sometimes quite near the surface and occasionally in considerable quantity. This water is cool, is sufficiently non-mineral to be fair drinking-water, and is undoubtedly the storage of precipitation."

Spurr cites much evidence found in the sinking of shafts and driving of drifts illustrating the localization of the ground-water in fractures. Observations from later mining experience, reported to the writers, are wholly similar in their import and need not be enumerated here.

Ore-Storage Warehouses

By JAMES McNICHOLAS

Progress in construction of warehouses for the storage of zinc and lead concentrates in the Tri-State region of Missouri-Kansas-Oklahoma has been chronicled from time to time in the 'Mining and Scientific Press'. The Oklahoma Ore Storage Association of Picher, with an authorized capital of $500,000, is responsible for the work now under way. One building at Picher is finished, while one is being erected at Cardin and one at Century.

The warehouse at Picher is 200 ft. long and 36 ft. wide and has a bin capacity of 14,000 tons of concentrate. The building when finally completed is to be 600 ft. long, or three times the present capacity. These warehouses are 1½ miles apart. They are all built on the same plan as the Picher warehouse.

In order fully to understand the necessity for these warehouses, it might be advisable to explain the conditions pertaining to ore-buying in this region. First, the area in which these warehouses are built, comprising not over 50 square miles, contributes 40% of the entire zinc output of the United States. The production, as concentrates, amounts to 9000 tons per week. The concentrates consist of sulphide of zinc, averaging 60% metal. The smelters buying these concentrates are small, of 60, 70, and 100 tons daily capacity, yet there is a sufficient number of them in the aggregate to handle the output of this field. Now, the smelters supplied by this field are not custom works, in other words, the producers here are not privileged to send concentrates to the smelters after milling, but they must await the arrival of an ore-buyer who buys direct from the mills. Under the present system the price of spelter in New York in no way affects the price of ore here. The ore-buyers decide what price they shall pay and the amount they shall take each week, and that is the fixed price of the ores.

During the War, spelter prices have been higher than at any time known, while the price of zinc concentrates has been lower than at any time before. Of course the logical solution of our problems here would be the building of custom smelters with a fixed tariff on smelting. However, that condition does not exist, and the warehouse scheme was proposed as a missing-link in the present system of ore-buying and selling between smelters and producers.

The idea is to issue bonded warehouse receipts to the producers, and to permit them to borrow from the banks during periods of depression until such time as the price of ore is satisfactory to the producers. The bankers of the district have all met in general session and have endorsed the scheme. They appointed a committee to get the endorsement of the Federal Reserve Bank of Kansas City. This endorsement has been secured, and upon this encouragement producers have organized themselves into an association, have selected five bankers of the district to act as officers and directors of the Association, and are now building warehouses situated in the field for the purpose of making a central depository for the ore and issuing bonded receipts to the producers. This arranges the collateral for the banks who are willing to loan on the ores. Similar warehouses could be erected for other ores in other parts of the country.

On Kruger mountain, Washington, within a few miles of each other are two lakes, one on each side of the international boundary, from which large amounts of natural epsom salts have been mined and shipped. Photographs of the lakes, made in connection with a study of the occurrence by Olaf P. Jenkins, suggest a snow-covered field with dark areas, nearly circular, and occupying about half the total area. The dark spots are shallow pools of brine, immediately beneath which are solid rock-like masses of epsomite. The areas between the spots are white and consist of efflorescent salts resting on black mud. During the rainy season the rise of water in the lakes causes the spotted appearance to vanish. The smaller of the lakes is in Washington, and contains nearly pure $MgSO_4$. The Canadian lake contains Na_2SO_4 mixed with $MgSO_4$. Other lakes in the vicinity show a predominance of Na_2SO_4. Rocks in the vicinity contain pyrite and pyrrhotite. These may, upon oxidation, have produced sulphates, which reacted with the magnesia and lime of the rocks. This view is supported by the fact that between the epsomite and the underlying metamorphic rocks is a thin layer of gypsum. A point of much interest is the expansive force with which a saturated solution of $MgSO_4$ crystallizes upon a sudden drop in the temperature. This was sufficient to split a 3-inch iron pipe from end to end. It was also found that crystallizing salts could not be kept in wooden tanks, as the solution would work into the cracks and upon crystallization would open the joints. Such tanks had to be lined with metal.

Oil and Oil-Lands in Time of Peace

By DAVID M. FOLSOM

*The title assigned to this paper is, in a sense, a misnomer, since it implies that the conditions surrounding oil-lands and the problems of the operating companies are different in times of peace from the conditions and problems of war. In actual fact the oil industry is facing conditions which are fundamental and are in no way related to war, although the War emphasized certain phases of the industry and the return of peace has removed this emphasis and restored normal aspects to the industry.

One fact which has been clearly demonstrated by the War is the inter-dependence of all industries and the fundamental relationship between fuel and the manufacturing and transportation facilities of the country. This is a relationship which is not changed by peace, although the extreme emergency conditions and fuel shortage of last winter were largely due to the War.

Oil may be considered from various viewpoints. Taking the broadest view, in considering petroleum and its products as a national asset, the products of the oil-well are as essential to the industrial and commercial life of our country as wheat is to our very existence. Fuel-oil means transportation, since it operates the railroads of the western and south-western States. Fuel-oil operates a great part of our shipping both in the Atlantic and in the Pacific; and both the Navy and the United States Shipping Board are committed to the future use of liquid fuel as the only practical means of propelling modern ocean vessels. Oil on land means power, light, and heat, since all of the Pacific Coast public utilities are, in part, dependent on steam stations. California points with pride to her hydro-electric power development in the streams of the Sierras; but the very heart of these power systems is the stand-by stations maintained by fuel-oil, and the installed capacity of steam-stations is greater than the installed capacity of hydro-electric plants. The artificial-gas plants of California, Oregon, and Arizona are dependent on oil, and this dependence of the public-utility companies on oil brings the wells in the field very close to the welfare and daily life of every individual on the Coast.

The widespread use of oil in industry connects the fortunes of the oil companies with the prospertiy of all mining enterprises; and the chemist, the metallurgist, and the miner on the Pacific Coast must find the problems of his own business intimately connected with the problems of the oil industry.

To summarize this preamble: Oil is not a 'war-baby'. The market for oil was not immediately affected by the declaration of war nor by the signing of the armistice. The industrial life of the Pacific Coast has been developed on fuel-oil, and the welfare of all commercial enterprises on the Coast is dependent on oil.

A question of interest to this Congress is the attitude of the administrative and legislative departments of the National Government toward oil and the development of oil-lands. I think this attitude can best be illustrated by a hypothetical case, a case, however, based on the actual experience of Californian companies. Assume a company with strong financial backing and organized in 1916 for the legitimate purpose of developing and operating petroleum land. Members of this American Mining Congress might have so organized and incorporated a holding company, under the name of the American Development Company, with the idea of developing national resources and providing an additional source of power and of wealth to the nation. Roughly speaking, there are three methods by which such a company can acquire prospective oil territory:

(1) By location and discovery upon public land;

(2) By leasing patented land from the owners and paying a royalty in oil or in money and, possibly, a cash bonus in addition to this royalty; and

(3) By the direct purchase of patented land.

Let us assume that the American Development Company, as a holding company, follows all three methods through subsidiary operating companies. Following the first method, the company, upon the recommendation of geologists, and acting with legal advice, locates a number of oil claims on public lands in a western State. This must be absolutely a wild-cat venture, since all land of probable value has long been withdrawn from entry and the property may be 50 miles from a railroad, in territory undeveloped and unknown.

The mining laws of the United States are, supposedly, intended to encourage such development and framed to reward the successful prospector. Judging by the history of recent years, the operating company, however, would have this experience: A test well, drilled to a depth of 3000 ft., representing an initial investment of over \$100,000, might discover oil. Immediately, the President of the United States, acting on the recommendation of the Department of the Interior, would withdraw from mineral entry all the public land around the discovery-well except 160 acres, which would go with the discovery-well.

The first withdrawal of public land from mineral entry, made by President Taft on September 27, 1909, contained the following language:

*An address delivered before the California chapter of the American Mining Congress at San Francisco on January 15.

"In aid of proposed legislation affecting the use and disposition of the petroleum deposits on the public domain, all public lands in the accompanying lists are hereby temporarily withdrawn from all forms of location, settlement, selection, filing, entry, or disposal under the mineral or non-mineral public land laws."

The intent of this first withdrawal was, apparently, to protect the legitimate operator, and to provide legislation which would enable the petroleum fields of the West to be most efficiently and effectively developed for the good of the nation. In nine years and a half, however,

LAYING AN 8-INCH OIL PIPE-LINE

administrative departments of the National Government have successfully blocked all legislation aimed at the development of public lands. As a result of this administrative policy, the American Development Company, with one well upon 160 acres, shut off from the acquisition of additional territory, would suddenly find its property a liability and not an asset. Instead of reward the company would actually pay a forfeit for its success and be penalized for adding a new oil-pool to the known national resources.

The theory which has been held by some Congressmen that oil-land can and should be developed by small companies with small land-holdings is based on an absolute misconception of the nature of the oil industry. Efficient development and operation of oil-land can be had only on areas which are large enough to justify the organization and equipment required to prevent waste and to insure economy of operation. Furthermore, the value of oil is dependent on its availability, and extensive pipe-line construction is warranted only where a large volume of oil is to be handled. The operating company would have no outlet for its production and would probably be forced to shut down and to abandon all operations. One venture of the American Development Company would be a failure although oil was discovered.

Carrying our assumption still further: If our holding company had acquired, through a second subsidiary, patented land on lease, paying a small cash bonus, and through successful development had brought in a substantial production of oil which the company was able to market at a profit, it would today be penalized for its prosperity, under the excess-profit tax, since the property was acquired since March 1, 1913, and the land-holdings under lease could not be capitalized. All production will be treated as income and a 60 to 80% tax collected on the net return.

In view of the risks incident to the oil business, and in view of the gradual exhaustion of oil and, therefore, of capital with each month's production of oil, the American Development Company would find itself paying taxes upon the profit without adequate return for the hazard taken, even with successful development upon patented land. To emphasize this point we have only to assume that upon the patented land acquired either by lease or by purchase no oil is found. In which case, the company stands the entire loss, although paying into the Federal Treasury the greater part of its profit for the one successful venture. The second venture of the company returns to the stockholders a small profit.

In the case of land acquired by the third method—direct purchase of patented land—the cost of the land can be taken as capital investment and written off in depreciation over a period of years. The most serious injustice to the individual stockholder or to a holding corporation from the present tax laws comes in the case of a man who may have an investment in several oil companies. Only one of these companies may be successful and that company pays an 80% profit tax to the Government with correspondingly small return to the stockholder, who at the same time loses his investment in other operations. In other words, the Government takes the lion's share of the profits without assuming any share of the risks of an extremely speculative and hazardous industry. It should be a recognized principle that no tax

CRUDE OIL FLOWING FROM WELL

should be so burdensome as to extinguish its source.

Yet the case I have sketched is typical of many operating companies, and of the individual investor behind these companies, and illustrates the difficulty under which oil corporations are operating. In justification of the withdrawal of all public land the Federal Government takes the position that the oil resources of the nation must be saved for future generations: but, at the same time, the only substitute for oil on the Pacific Coast —the development of natural water-power—is also handicapped by equally prohibitive legislation.

There is no justification for the proposed features of the excess-profit tax except the great need for money and the unsympathetic attitude of many members of Congress toward private development of the public domain. I believe that the financial sacrifice and national debt assumed by the United States in the emergency of war can be met only by aggressive development of our natural resources and that the problems of the oil industry are so fundamental to the national prosperity of all industries as to require immediate and intelligent solution.

The United States is now committed to a government-owned merchant marine, and to the expansion of international commerce. What products are these ships to carry unless power is provided for manufacturing? And where are these boats to obtain fuel unless oil development and power development is encouraged?

The Government, apparently, is trying to turn the wheels by hand when all the brakes are set hard and fast. I believe that with these brakes released the machine of national industry would run and run smoothly and noiselessly of its own momentum under the initiative and guidance of private, not public, ownership. I imagine someone saying, as various individuals inside and outside official Washington have said in the past: "Why not public ownership? Why not develop these oil-lands by the Government itself? Why allow private individuals or private corporations to control national resources?" To my mind there are many good and sound reasons why the Government should not attempt the nationalization of any industry; but I shall only mention two reasons.

To begin with, I question the possibility of Government success in the actual operation of any industry as many-sided and as sensitive as the oil industry. Nothing that the Government has done either before the War or during the War has indicated that Uncle Sam is as good a business manager or even a fair success as an industrial executive. Over and above that fact, however, as an argument against Government ownership is the fundamental character of the American people. If we have any national trait worth enlarging and worth preserving it is our initiative and our individuality.

America has developed as a nation of pioneers. The frontier line has never quite faded away and the race which has grown up on this continent has acquired its character and its liberty of action and its self-reliance as a result of the free opportunity given to the individual. This is so fundamental that I only emphasize it here because of the socialistic winds which blow through the world.

The will o' the wisp of nationalism, of paternalism, and of public ownership may tempt the dreamers and inspire the demagogue even in our own country, but, in their elusive visions of a Utopia, the dreamers forget that the human race has risen from the stone age through the acquisition of property and the human quality of selfishness. All human experience and all human wisdom points to national development through the opportunity for development given to individual initiative. I do not believe it is necessary before this Congress further to defend the best traditions of our nation.

In the past, each industry which has attempted to secure favorable legislation from Congress has had to work alone. The result has been that each industry has immediately and directly been accused of lobbying to its own interest and has been discredited before the committees of the National Congress in every attempt to obtain relief or justice from the legislative branch of the Federal Government. In turn, various groups of mining men, representing companies producing certain metals, attorneys for oil companies, and executives of power companies have appeared in Washington; have carefully and patiently explained to various committees the need of constructive legislation; and in regular rotation bills have been introduced in one or both houses of Congress only to die in committee or in conference. From time to time promises of legislation have been made, and Presidential messages have been written, in regard to the development of power and the release of withdrawn lands. But the temporary withdrawals still stand and the producer of power from water and the producer of power from oil are both prevented from developing the resources of the nation. This policy of repression was inconsistent and unfair before the War. It was almost fatal to the prosecution of the War and if continued will certainly be fatal to the development of a national constructive program for peace. I believe that the American Mining Congress or a similar organization, general in character, and representative of all Western industries, instead of a single interest, should direct its best efforts to creating in Congress a recognition of the national importance of legislation which will make public lands in America available for development by American citizens.

THE LARGEST REFINERY IN THE WORLD AT RICHMOND, CALIFORNIA

(Photos courtesy of Standard Oil Co.)

Silver: Market Factors and Future

*The position of the silver market at the beginning of 1918 was overshadowed by difficulties connected with the Indian currency. The prospects of any amelioration in then existing conditions were remote, and each return of the Indian currency showed a shrinkage in the holding of coined rupees, despite the volume of silver continually imported on account of the Mint. Events pointed toward the assumption of Government control in some form or other over the distribution and disposal of production—a comparatively easy measure to enforce in view of the large proportion of the world's supplies that is derived from America.

The quotation on the first working day—January 2—was 43½ pence, as it had been on the concluding day of 1917. Owing doubtless to the approach of the Chinese New Year (due on February 11), supplies were scanty, and an advance soon began which by January 5 had carried the quotation to 45½d., at which figure it remained until the middle of the month. From this point a decline set in, which, without a reaction, carried the price to 42½d. on February 22. It remained at this figure until March 8. During the whole period, a constant inquiry was maintained from Holland and France, mostly on account of coinage.

By this time the stock of coined rupees in the Indian currency reserve had reached a low ebb. On March 7 the total was returned as 1271 lacs (1 lac = $32,000), against 1905 on the eve of the year. Within the next month, the total fell to 1044 lacs, the low-water mark, not only for 1918, but also for eight years past. The issue of 1 and 2½ rupee notes (introduced last year with a view to easing the situation), did not make much impression. On February 15, for instance, not more than 5% of the total note issue was represented by notes below five rupees.

Attempts were made to induce Mexico to release a portion of its output, hitherto retained for local coinage. With this end, the United States government undertook to furnish Mexico with £1,000,000 in gold on condition that the latter relaxed its restrictions upon the export of silver. This, however, was only palliative in effect. The situation was aggravated by the firmness of the Chinese exchanges, with a corresponding demand for silver.

In these circumstances, some drastic action in America became necessary in order to cope with the keen coinage demand from India, evidenced by the drain of coined rupees from Indian currency reserves, and to minimize the efforts of China to replenish its silver stocks up-country, seriously depleted by the heavy shipments previously made to India. The United States, owing to the difficulty in obtaining remittances to India, had a direct interest in easing the situation. Hence it was decided to introduce a bill into Congress authorizing the realization of some portion of the reserve of 460,000,000 silver dollars, held by the United States Treasury as security for silver certificates to that value.

Meanwhile the price began to rise rapidly, accelerated doubtless by rumors as to the precise nature of the action which the American government was likely to adopt. Impelled by such considerations, the quotation reached 46d. on March 23. After remaining for a fortnight between that figure and 45¾d., the quotation again hardened, moving sharply, on April 11, from the last-named figure to 46¼ pence.

The announcement that a bill was being introduced into the United States Senate, providing for the melting and sale of silver dollars above-mentioned, coincided with an announcement by the Indian Council that its drawing rate would be raised one penny—that is to say, from 1s.5d. to 1s.6d. (34 to 36 cents) per rupee for telegraphic transfers, and for other descriptions of drawing in proportion. At the minimum rate at which the United States government ultimately received power to sell the melted dollars, namely, $1 per fine ounce, and at the rate of exchange then obtaining between Great Britain and the United States, the cost of providing the silver contents of a rupee worked out at 1s.5.335d. (34.67 cents), to which shipping expenses, etc., from the United States to India had to be added.

The Bill granted power to melt 350,000,000 silver dollars (about 271,000,000 fine ounces) and to dispose of the bullion at not less than $1 per fine ounce. Immediately upon sale of the melted coin, the Director of the United States Mint was to be instructed to purchase in the United States, of the product of mines and reduction works in the United States, an equivalent amount of silver for each dollar so dealt with, at the fixed price of $1 per fine ounce. Purchases were to continue until the equivalent of the melted or broken-up dollars was acquired. As a result of this legislation, by means of which the United States placed itself in a position to obtain such rupee remittances as it required, the needs of the Indian government as to currency could be supplied also for a considerable time to come.

As a consequence of this Government action, the price of silver in America rose to about $1 per ounce. The quotation in this country (England) followed suit, and 49¼d. was fixed on April 24. Since that date fluctuations have been slight, never exceeding 13/16d. below and ¼d. above. The price of silver practically became stabilized, and subsequent fluctuations represented little more than alterations in the cost of transit (war risk, insurance, etc.) from America to London.

The supply of silver coin in the United Kingdom

*Abstract from Annual Bullion Letter of Samuel Montagu & Co., London.

gradually became deficient, partly owing to the unsettled political condition of Ireland. Considerable consignments of newly-minted and other silver coin were sent to that island in order to provide currency in lieu of coin set aside in hoards. As a consequence, a Defence of the Realm regulation, published on May 21, made it illegal for a person to retain current silver coins in excess of the amount reasonably required for his domestic and business concerns. Further, it was made an offence to sell or purchase, or offer to do so, any current coin in excess of its face value.

Owing to the regulation forbidding shipment of silver without a license, and to the extreme difficulty of obtaining the necessary permission, neutral countries were in great straits to provide this metal either for coinage or industry. Indeed, so great did the scarcity become, that it was reported that in Holland current silver coin was being melted down in order to keep manufactories at work.

In the early part of June, the China exchanges developed great firmness, and in the next month this country acquired eagerly such American supplies as came into the open market. In consequence of the competition thus evoked, the export of silver from America, except under license, was officially forbidden. Whereupon export eventually came to a standstill, and the Shanghai exchange was quoted considerably above the parity of silver.

A Treasury Order dated August 9, 1918, published on the 13th, fixed the minimum price for silver in the United Kingdom at $48\frac{13}{16}$d. per standard ounce, at which figure it had remained since July 2. After having been quoted at $48\frac{13}{16}$ for 42 successive working days, the maximum price was raised to $49\frac{1}{2}$d. on August 21. This movement was caused by the fixation of an official minimum of $101\frac{1}{2}$ cents per ounce in the United States. As the demand was constant and active, the London quotation naturally rose at once to correspond.

The rise in the Chinese exchanges having been so pronounced as to cause grave embarrassment to trade with that country, and there being no check to the figure to which they could advance, now that it had become impossible to obtain imports of silver, the Chinese government decided to conserve the stock in that country by forbidding exports. This ameliorated the situation.

The fixing of official maxima in the United Kingdom and in the United States of America naturally deprived the market of animation, though trade demand in this country was well sustained, stimulated by the impracticability of securing sufficient gold for jewelry and like purposes. On September 11 the American gold and silver administrator met silver dealers in New York and obtained a promise that they would confine the supply to their old customers, and only to an extent of not more than 75% of their former requirements.

The French Commission on the stability of exchange asserted as follows: "The early establishment and permanent security of the gold exchange standard in countries now upon the silver standard would be materially aided by stability in the price of silver bullion. Stability in the price of silver bullion would be promoted by reasonable regularity in the purchase of silver required by each Government for actual coinage purposes." Any combination of nations, to ensure more or less continuous purchases of silver for the purpose of coinage, could hardly fail to draw India, the chief silver-using country, within its orbit.

The coinage of silver at the Indian Mints during the fiscal year 1917-'18 amounted to 23,87,07,287 rupees, compared with 30,77,07,326 rupees during the preceding financial year.

With the exception of 1,26,76,902 rupees re-coined from uncurrent and withdrawn coin, the silver was provided from purchases. The amount thus acquired and applied was therefore about 77,500,000 fine ounces.

In October, unsatisfactory climatic conditions caused a cessation of demand for Indian remittances and induced the India Council to offer sterling drafts on London to the extent of £1,000,000 per week. The all-important place in the destiny of India occupied by the monsoon, which has been described as the jugular vein of Indian trade, was thus again demonstrated. In normal times the reversal of the flow of remittances would have been reflected in the price of silver. Such, however, has been, and is still likely to be, the need for Indian metallic currency, that this check, possibly temporary, to the steady advance of Indian prosperity does not as yet relieve the Indian government from feeding its mints with fresh purchases of silver.

Although the India Council eventually raised the amount of sterling drafts on London offered in India for disposal by tender to £2,000,000 per week, the Indian note issue continued to increase, and the demand for metallic currency showed no sign of abatement. Therefore, while Government restrictions upon the export of certain goods were removed, owing to the great change in the aspect of military affairs, silver remained under a ban, except for articles manufactured wholly or partly of the metal. In America, about 2,000,000 oz. purchased for China some months back, but licenses for which were refused, were released for export, and were shipped from San Francisco.

The signing of the armistice, which brought hostilities to an end on November 11, had some effect upon the silver market. The quotation had remained at $49\frac{1}{2}$d. for 71 successive working days—a record duration in living memory—but the withdrawal of submarine activity at once reduced the rates of war-risk insurance. This substantially lowered the cost of bringing silver from America, and the price fell on November 12, $\frac{3}{4}$d. to $48\frac{3}{4}$d. (the new official maximum). Much variation cannot be expected so long as the value of silver in New York is maintained about $1 per ounce. The cost of insurance from America having been reduced to an almost normal figure, the quotation was lowered to $48\frac{7}{16}$d. on December 6, after remaining at $48\frac{3}{4}$d. for 21 working days. The official maximum was also reduced to $48\frac{7}{16}$. Notwithstanding this reduction, the closing quotation exceeded the average for the year. We append the annual averages for the last four years: 1915, $23\frac{11}{16}$d.; 1916, $31\frac{5}{16}$d.; 1917, $40\frac{3}{4}$d.; 1918, $47\frac{9}{16}$d.

It is an interesting fact that the first-named is the lowest and the last-named the highest annual average for more than a quarter of a century. In 1909 the annual average was the same as in 1915, namely, $23\frac{11}{16}$ pence.

The return of erstwhile soldiers and war-workers to peaceful occupations will afford more labor for the mining industry, and, in so doing, increase the output of silver. Mexico, that great reservoir of precious metal, is setting her house in order, and will substantially swell the total.

As long as the United States government is pledged to re-purchase at $1 per ounce the bullion, composed of melted United States coin, which it placed at the disposal of the Indian Mint (at present amounting to 115,000,000 oz.), the price cannot fall much, if at all, below 46d. (allowing for the return of the American exchange to a normal figure). If there were external competition with the United States government, the re-purchase of this bullion, together with local trade requirements, would absorb probably two years' production of that country.

Trade all over the world has felt the lack of silver; hence a good and continuous demand may be expected from many quarters. As to coinage demand generally, no positive views can be expressed, for currency arrangements are now in a state of flux, rendering future policy as to the precious metals uncertain. In view of the shortage of gold that may prevail for many years to come, large supplies of silver for currency reserves may be considered desirable in other quarters. It must not be forgotten that many millions of medals will be struck.

Indian coinage operations will depend on the harvests. As gold may be scarce for some years, the onus of supplying India with currency will fall upon silver. Should unfavorable conditions (such as recently have obtained) continue, there may eventually ensue a redundancy of silver coin in India. At the present sterling value of the rupee (1s. 6d.), full-weight rupees would be worth about $48\frac{1}{2}$d. per ounce standard (exclusive of cost of bringing to market here in a marketable condition). Similarly if the sterling value of the rupee reverted to 1s. 4d., the worth would be about 43d. per ounce standard.

The deduction from the preceding remarks is, that although output may be accelerated, the needs of India and China, the obligation of the United States government to re-purchase, and the cumulated demand for the trade, will ensure a high level of prices for some time.

The table below gives the average price of silver for each year since 1860:

Year	Per oz.	Year	Per oz.	Year	Per oz.	Year	Per oz.
1860	$1.352	1875	$1.242	1890	$1.046	1905	$0.610
1861	1.333	1876	1.164	1891	0.988	1906	0.676
1862	1.346	1877	1.201	1892	0.871	1907	0.661
1863	1.345	1878	1.153	1893	0.780	1908	0.534
1864	1.345	1879	1.123	1894	0.634	1909	0.520
1865	1.338	1880	1.145	1895	0.654	1910	0.540
1866	1.339	1881	1.132	1896	0.675	1911	0.539
1867	1.328	1882	1.135	1897	0.604	1912	0.614
1868	1.326	1883	1.108	1898	0.590	1913	0.604
1869	1.325	1884	1.110	1899	0.601	1914	0.553
1870	1.328	1885	1.065	1900	0.620	1915	0.518
1871	1.326	1886	0.994	1901	0.595	1916	0.686
1872	1.322	1887	0.979	1902	0.527	1917	0.875
1873	1.297	1888	0.939	1903	0.542	1918	0.968
1874	1.278	1889	0.935	1904	0.578		

Prevention of Illness Among Mine Employees

By A. J. LANZA

*This subject is especially important in view of the magnitude of metal mining, the unsettled conditions of labor, which emphasize the economic necessity for conservation of labor, and for humanitarian reasons. The burden of chronic illness is altogether unwarranted and unnecessary. If the industry is to maintain its labor supply in an efficient manner and keep the standard high, it is essential that it make every effort to keep its labor in good physical condition.

The first step in the prevention of illness lies in securing employees who are in sound health and free from organic disease. I do not mean that all men who go underground should be physically perfect, but they should be free from defects of the heart, lungs, and other organs; or from anatomical defects which would markedly increase their liability to accident. The number of men underground in this country whose physical condition totally unfits them for such work presents a condition that should not be allowed to continue, which I believe is not equalled in any other industry in the country. There is but one way to secure men who come up to the required standard, and that is by a thorough physical examination before employment. I am fully aware of the objections felt toward such a procedure by many employers and employees. There is much to be said on both sides, but to any one who is at all familiar with the mining industry as it is today, and who approaches the matter with an unbiased mind, there can be no doubt as to the necessity for such an examination. As a purely logical idea this is self-evident, but there remains the further necessity of placing these examinations on such a basis that they can be administered in a just and equitable manner, free from the abuses and suspicions to which they have been subject in the past. The best way of administering this work would be to have them conducted by properly constituted authorities of the various States. I believe that the time has come for the American Institute of Mining Engineers to consider seriously the necessity and the means for carrying out physical examinations and to take a definite stand.

The second requisite for the prevention of illness among employees is the maintenance of working conditions underground on a high plane of sanitation and efficiency, so that sickness arising therefrom may be held at a fair minimum. The greatest needed improvement is the elimination of dry drilling in hard-rock mines. Ventilation and temperature are not what they should be, and have never received the attention in metal mines that they have in coal mines.

The third requisite consists of adequate provision for medical and surgical service, so that minor illness and injuries may be promptly treated and not become of major importance.

*Abstract from Bull. 146 of the A. I. M. E.

Sulphuric Acid Forecast for 1919

In a report recently issued by the Chemical Alliance a forecast of the output of sulphuric acid in 1919 was presented, this having been prepared by Arthur E. Wells, metallurgist of the U. S. Bureau of Mines. He shows that, on January 1 of this year, the total manufacturing capacity of the United States for sulphuric acid was 427,000 tons per month, on a basis of 100% H_2SO_4, or 8,200,000 tons per year, on a basis of 50° B., of which 29% was at contact-acid plants. On November 1 of this year, the total manufacturing capacity of the country was 500,000 tons per month, on a basis of 100% H_2SO_4, or 9,600,000 tons per year, on the basis of 50°B. Of this total capacity 40% was at contact-acid plants. This capacity was divided among: (1) the Government; (2) explosives companies; (3) all others, including commercial manufacturers and by-product manufacturers, as follows:

	Capacity: In tons per month, 100% H_2SO_4	Capacity: In tons per year, 50° B.
1. At Government plants	54,000	1,040,000
2. At plants of explosives manufacturers	58,000	1,120,000
3. All others	388,000	7,440,000
	500,000	9,600,000

Inasmuch as the acid market conditions in the inter-mountain and Pacific coast districts are quite distinct from those in the East, and as very little, if any, disturbance has been brought about in those districts, except possibly for some slight disturbance in the San Francisco district, it is not necessary to include the figures for these in the discussions regarding Eastern conditions. The total capacity east of the Mississippi river, including the plant at Argentine, Kansas, and the plants in Louisiana and Arkansas, is as follows:

	Tons per month as 100% H_2SO_4
1. At Government plants	54,000
2. At plants of explosives companies	50,000
3. All others	350,000
Total	454,000

Assuming that the Government plants and the contact-plants, which were built by the explosives companies primarily to supply acid for munitions, are not operated in 1919, or, if operated at all, the production will be utilized only for munitions, and thus will not be placed on the market, there remains a total capacity to be considered in the eastern part of the United States amounting to 365,000 tons per month, on a basis of 100% H_2SO_4, or 7,000,000 tons per year, on a basis of 50° B. During the first nine months of 1918 the actual rate of production was only about 90% of the rated maximum capacity, although many plants were operating much above the rated capacities. Therefore, it is fair to conclude that the probable maximum output from these plants during the year 1919 cannot be greater than 90% of the rated capacity, or in other words, the maximum output could be only about 328,000 tons per month, on a basis of 100% H_2SO_4, or 6,300,000 tons per year, on a basis of 50° B. During the months of June, July, and August 1918 the following industries in the eastern part of the United States consumed approximately the following tonnages of acid:

Industries	Tons per month basis 100% H_2SO_4
1. Domestic explosives	7,500
2. Fertilizers	109,400
3. Chemicals and drugs, including nitric acid, hydrochloric acid, and ammonium sulphate	37,600
4. Oil refining	28,700
5. Steel pickling and galvanizing	36,200
6. Fabrics, textiles, tanning, rubber, paper, and bleaching	5,100
7. Paints, lithopone, dyes, glue, glycerine, and alcohol	7,200
8. Storage batteries, metallurgical work	4,700
9. Miscellaneous and unknown	3,600
Total	240,000

This is equivalent to 4,600,000 tons per year on a basis of 50° B.

It is believed that the consumption of acid in the various industries during the period given above offers a better basis for estimating the future consumption during 1919 than any reference to the figures for 1914, but it may be stated by way of comparison that in the eastern half of the United States there was consumed in 1914 about 3,500,000 tons of acid, on a basis of 50° B., according to the figures compiled by the Geological Survey. From these it is evident that, between the years 1914 and 1918, there was an increase in the requirements of acid for industries, other than munitions, amounting to about 1,000,000 tons, on the basis of 50° B. The consumption of acid for fertilizers will undoubtedly be greater in 1919 than in 1918, and will probably average at least 130,000 tons of 100% acid per month, or 2,500,000 tons per year, 50° B. Thus, with business conditions favorable, the average monthly consumption of acid in the above industries in the eastern part of the country during the year 1919 should not be less than 260,000 tons per month, on a basis of 100% H_2SO_4, or 5,000,000 tons per year, 50° B. This would require operating all the plants at about 71% of the rated maximum capacity, if the business were distributed proportionately to the manufacturing capacity in the various districts. As a matter of fact, the Southern fertilizer plants will probably operate to full capacity, while the plants in the Boston, New York, Philadelphia, and Baltimore districts may average less than 70% of the rated capacity.

The production and consumption of acid in the western half of the United States will probably be about 500,000 tons per year, 50° B., so that the probable total production for the whole country will be about 5,500,000 tons in 1919.

Copper Selling Agencies

According to the 'Boston News Bureau', many important changes have taken place in selling agency affiliations. The following table gives the principal selling interests, and their 1918 totals, in pounds:

American Smelting & Refining Co	743,000,000
American Metal Co	54,000,000
Calumet & Hecla and subsidiaries	140,000,000
Lewisohn & Sons	70,900,000
Mohawk Mining Co. (direct)	10,700,000
Phelps Dodge Corporation	353,000,000
Todd. W. Parsons	82,000,000
United Metals Selling Co	566,000,000
United Smelting Co.	24,000,000
United Verde Copper Co. (direct)	60,000,000
Wolverine Mining Co. (direct)	4,200,000

REVIEW OF MINING

RENO, NEVADA

Silver From Candelaria and Unionville.—Leasing at Goldfield.

Silver ore carrying from 20 to 40 oz. per ton is being shipped to smelter from properties operated by the Candelaria Mines Co., at the old camp of Candelaria, near the boundary between Esmeralda and Mineral counties. The Argentum and Mt. Diablo mines were worked in the late seventies, and were among the largest of Nevada silver producers in that period. The district was then known as the Columbus. The adjoining Lucky Hill property, also owned by the Candelaria Mines Co., is being worked through a tunnel and shaft. Stopes on the 100 and 200-ft. levels are breaking from 8 to 11 ft. of shipping ore, and a large tonnage of milling ore has been exposed. The first-named properties have a large quantity of impounded tailing from the old mills that is said to be valuable. Four carloads of smelting ore was shipped during the last week of January. Ore is shipped at a rate sufficient only to pay for development and leave a moderate surplus. A. J. Jarmuth is manager.

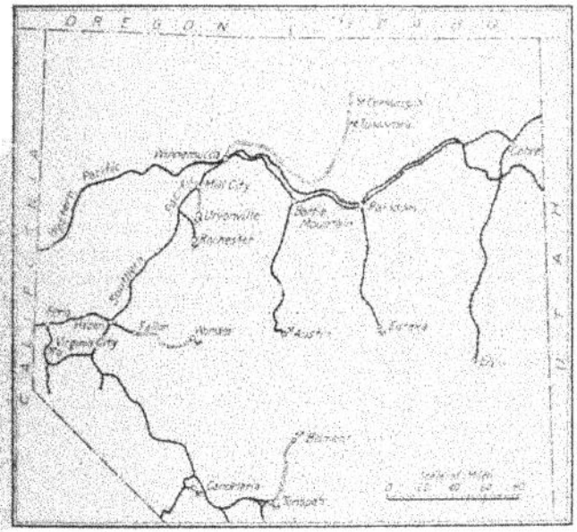

PART OF NEVADA

A flotation mill has been completed at Unionville, in southern Humboldt county, to treat ore from the once famous Arizona silver mine, owned by the Sunset Mining & Development Co. Connection with the old mine workings has been made by a 390-ft. tunnel, giving access to the ore-channel below any point reached before. The ore, a straight silver sulphide, is found in a wide bedded zone, lying nearly horizontal and worked in earlier operations to a depth of only 250 ft. The mine is said to have produced $5,000,000 in the 'sixties, the high-grade ore having been shipped to Wales by way of Sacramento. It was located in 1862, and the richest ore was freighted to the Coast before the railroad came to Nevada. E. S. Van Dyck, vice-president, is now at the mine. He says that a relatively small part of the ore-channel has been prospected. F. W. Lockman is superintendent. The ore has been tested for flotation, and is said to be well adapted to that process.

The new leasing policy of the Goldfield Development Co. will give longer lease terms, with no restrictions on profits, and ample time for the removal of ore extracted. It is expected, together with operations planned by the new company, to result in a more energetic and more venturesome policy of mining in this area, a large part of which has not been prospected. The company will furnish equipment, air, timber, and supplies to the lessees at about cost, and its own work is designed to produce ore for company account and to open the properties for leasing. The manager, H. G. McMahon, reports over 100 applications for leases already in hand. It is not likely that lessees will for the present undertake work on deep levels, as the product contains copper and the Consolidated company is opposed to resuming the operation of its flotation plant until the copper market is stabilized.

In a report on the Atlanta property, the manager, A. I. D'Arcy, says that a considerable quantity of milling ore has been exposed, and the east cross-cut on the 1900-ft. level, driven to cut the Atlanta vein, has lately shown several seams of good ore, assaying as high as $59 per ton in gold and copper. While the lens-shape of the deposits renders it impossible to estimate the tonnage, he believes sufficient ore will be available soon to warrant leasing or building a mill.

DURANGO, COLORADO

Conditions and Operations in the San Juan.

Silverton.—The decline in lead and copper and present high costs are handicapping operations of smaller producers, as the average ores of the district carry the greatest value in these metals. Despite the fall in metal prices, there is a spirit of optimism prevailing and development continues. The present miner's and operator's agreement continues in force until July 1, 1919, and the present wage-scale will prevail until that date, when it is expected that there will be a re-adjustment. Health conditions here are excellent. The labor supply is growing rapidly, owing to the importation of men from outside points by the Sunnyside M. & M. Co., and the closing of the Rico mines. If operating costs permit, there are a number of mines ready to ship during the coming season, but until the metal market is better no decided change may be expected.

The Sunnyside M. & M. Co. now has 350 men employed and is increasing the number. As soon as more are at work underground the mill will be increased to full capacity. At the present time lead concentrate is shipped at the rate of one car daily, and zinc concentrate at the rate of 10 tons. A shortage of expert machine-men is being relieved as a result of extensive advertising, the present scale is $5.25; board is still furnished at $1. The low prices for lead and copper seriously affect the company, and if there is no betterment, the extensive production planned for the current year may be curtailed.

The Gold King Extension Co. is hurrying preliminary work. Delay in receiving milling machinery has postponed operations somewhat, so that the date of the opening run is postponed until the latter part of April. The Gladstone branch of the Silverton Northern railroad continues to run, no difficulty having been experienced with slides. A number of new Card concentrating tables have been ordered. Although the mill may not be running until the time mentioned, a little will be shipped for testing, and there will be a small quantity put through the stamp-mill during early spring.

The Dives Leasing Co. is now shipping much high-grade silver ore, and it is expected that the Dives will shortly resume its place as one of the foremost producers of the district.

Red Mountain.—This district will be seriously affected by the recent fall in copper, as the ores of the district carry the highest value in this metal. At present there are two mines shipping ore. King, Lovingood & Co. are handicapped in getting ore from the Congress, as it is hauled to the Silverton station of the D. & R. G., so that in addition to the high railroad freight, there is a haulage charge of $6 per ton. The roads are in good condition, and the operators are getting out large quantities of ore. Klang & Carlson are leasing the St. Paul mine and are hauling ore to Silverton by sled.

The Radiant Mining & Reduction Co. has taken over the holdings of the Ruby Mining Co., comprising 450 acres and 50-ton mill. A few men have been employed for some time, and the mine is now to produce. Officers of the new company are H. M. Kingsley, A. B. McClave, and O. L. Keen, all local men.

After a period of low production, due to shortage of labor, the Mayflower mine is again on the shipping list, concentrate amounting to 2 cars per day.

The D. L. & W. M. & R. Co. continues to open the Lackawanna. The double-compartment raise between levels is finished, permitting easier handling of ore from both levels, also improving ventilation. A vein of $20 ore has been cut on No. 2 level, ore from 8 to 10 ft. wide, and a drift 60 ft. along the vein shows the quality and width not lowered. On No. 1 level, driving operations continue, a distance of 200 ft. having been made into a good grade of milling ore. A large quantity of ore is blocked out and ready for shipment. At a recent election of officers the following were chosen: George Harris, president; Fred Free, vice-president; Hugh Dealy, secretary-treasurer; E. Dealy, general manager; and E. W. Walter, consulting engineer.

Rico.—The rapid decline in copper has caused an almost complete shut-down here. The Rico Argentine has ceased and the Rico-Marmatite has only 20 men employed. Little ore will be produced from the Marmatite holdings until operating costs and metal prices permit of a profit being made. As the ores of this district carry copper, the uncertain condition of the market has stopped development on a number of promising properties, in addition to this, health conditions have become bad, so that the district is now having a trying period. However, the Rico Mining Co. continues to develop its orebodies. The Resolute company has run into a body of high-grade silver ore on the Telegraph vein, and the Syndicate company is to continue operations.

Placerville.—The New Era vein is being worked by D. H. Donegan, who has shipped vanadium ore in large quantities to the reduction plant at Vanadium.

Development on the old Placerville property held by the Primos Chemical Co. is now completed, compressed air is piped to the machine-drills in the workings, a two-bucket tram conveys ore to a dumping-bin alongside of a newly-constructed railroad switch, and the ore is moved to the reduction plant of the company at Vanadium from the workings with a minimum of expense and labor.

Interest is directed toward the Cashin copper mine in Paradox valley, as a new company has been organized to operate it and contemplates its purchase. Large bodies of copper ore are known to be exposed. Numerous attempts have been made to secure a lease on this property by local mining men, but without success.

Telluride.—Exploration was to be resumed in the old Calumet during February, after a shut-down since the beginning of the year.

De Beque.—With the near completion of the tramway from the shale-beds to the retorts, the Mt. Logan Oil Shale Co. expects to be producing oil within a few days. The retorts have a capacity of 60 tons per day of shale, and the first runs are awaited with keen interest.

WASHINGTON, D. C.

Provisions of the Revenue Bill for Income-Tax.—Potash.

The Commissioner of Internal Revenue has issued the following notes:

The income-tax provisions of the Act reach the pocket-book of every single person in the United States whose net income for 1918 was $1000 or more, and of every married person whose net income was $2000 or more. Persons whose net income equalled or exceeded these amounts, according to their marital status, must file a return of income with the collector of internal revenue for the district in which they live on or before March 15.

Penalties are as follows:

Failure to file a return on time entails a fine of not more than $1000 and an additional assessment of 25% of the amount of tax due. For wilfully refusing to make a return on time, a fine not exceeding $10,000, or not exceeding one year's imprisonment, or both. For making a false or fraudulent return, a fine of not more than $10,000, or imprisonment for not more than one year, or both, together with an additional assessment of 50% of the amount of tax evaded. For failure to pay the tax on time, a fine of not more than $1000 and an additional assessment of 5% of the amount of tax unpaid, plus 1% interest for each full month during which it remains unpaid.

In addition to the $1000 and $2000 personal exemptions, taxpayers are allowed an exemption of $200 for each person dependent upon them for chief support if such person is under 18 years of age and incapable of self-support. Under the 1917 Act, this exemption was allowed only for each dependent child. The head of a family—one who supports one or more persons closely connected with him by blood relationship, relationship by marriage, or by adoption—is entitled to all exemptions allowed a married person.

The normal rate of tax under the new act is 6% of the first $4000 of net income above the exemptions, and 12% of the net income in excess of $4000. Incomes in excess of $5000 are subject also to a surtax ranging from 1% of the amount of the net income between $5000 and $6000, to 65% of the net income above $1,000,000.

Payment of the tax may be made in full at the time of filing return or in four installments, on or before March 15, on or before June 15, on or before September 15, and on or before December 15.

Revenue officers will visit every county in the United States to aid taxpayers in making out their returns. The date of their arrival and the location of their offices may be ascertained by inquiring at offices of collectors of internal revenue, post offices, and banks. Failure to see these officers, however, does not relieve the taxpayer of his obligation to file his return and pay his tax within the time specified by law. In this case taxpayers must seek the Government, not the Government the taxpayer.

In the bill of Senator Henderson of Nevada to protect American potash producers, the maximum price for the first year is $2.50 per unit, and for the second year $2. Imports would be regulated thereby.

ARIZONA

Bisbee.—Shattuck Arizona pays 25 cents per share on April 19. The amount is $87,500 and makes $262,500 for the current year and $7,348,000 to date.

A report issued by a committee claimed to represent the I. W. W. announces that no strike is contemplated in the Bisbee district.

Mayer.—It is reported that J. C. Rankin of Kingman has purchased the McCabe and Gladstone mines. The former mine was worked extensively about 20 years ago.

The England and France claims have been taken over by the Arizona Binghampton Copper Company.

Patagonia.—Grading is under way at the Hardshell mine, preparing for the surface plant and new shaft which is to be sunk to the 350-ft. level.

Prescott.—The U. S. Consolidated Mining Co., which is operating the Homestead mine in the Walker district, is to put in a new hoist, air-compressor, and an 80-hp. boiler. The 150-ft. shaft is to be sunk another 300 ft. Fifteen hundred feet of development work has been done on this property so far with encouraging results.

Superior.—Magma Copper Co. produced 900,000 lb. in January, a drop of 149,000 pounds.

Wickenburg.—The Towers ranch has been leased to Brooklyn, New York, people, who have commenced work on the Green Mountain mine, on the ranch. It is one of the oldest properties in Arizona, and has produced considerable gold and silver in the past.

CALIFORNIA

Bakersfield.—Oil production of all fields in January totaled 277,363 bbl. per day, from 8617 wells, according to the Standard Oil Co. Fifty-two new wells were completed, yielding 17,375 bbl. Stocks at the end of the month were 32,299,589 bbl., an increase of 256,666 barrels.

Twelve wells were reported to the State oil and gas supervisor, R. P. McLaughlin, as ready to drill during the week ended February 15. This makes a total of 80 wells reported since the first of the year, against 112 for the same period of 1918, and 144 for the same period in 1917. This indicates a continued decline in drilling activity. It is certain that such a condition cannot continue for any length of time without a noticeable decline in State production. The flush yield of the no longer new Montebello and Casmalia fields masked this condition temporarily. However, the history of oilfield development, even if present production data of the Montebello and Casmalia fields were not available, should warn operators against counting too heavily upon initial productive conditions. Rapid decline of gas pressure and improper drilling, with respect to protection from water, are two of the principal causes which prevent oilfields from maintaining their brilliant initial records. Gas pressures can be controlled to a large extent, and their expulsive powers conserved by the proper drilling and preparation of wells for production. However, the supervisor has on a number of occasions directed popular attention to the fact that even the new fields of the State have not been drilled in a manner best to conserve the petrolum resources and protect them from water. One example of such operations in the Montebello field should suffice to quiet any claims to the contrary. One well in the Montebello field drilled by one of the largest companies produced 70.3% of all water produced during the fiscal year ended June 1918. The average water production for all other wells was 3%. The average daily production of oil was 722 barrels.

Keswick.—The Mountain Copper Co. has reduced wages from $4.50 to $4, and from $4 to $3.50 per shift. The three principal copper companies in Shasta county are now paying at the same rate.

COLORADO

Boulder.—The latest concerning the Colorado Pitchblende Co. is that it has started suit against the mining bureau of the Denver Civic and Commercial Association, alleging conspiracy, the Association withholding a report made on the company's property. The bureau states that the report will be issued in due time, and that it will not be bulldozed in the matter.

In a full-page advertisement in the 'Denver Times' of February 20, the Colorado Pitchblende Co. states that J. M. McClave's report on its property at Jamestown more than substantiates that of M. S. MacCarthy. McClave estimates that with a 1000-ton plant a daily net profit of $11,850 is probable, or $4,266,000 per year. MacCarthy estimated $9140 per day.

Central City.—W. O. Jenkins, representative in the State Legislature, sent a copy of the new 'blue sky' law to the local chapter of the Colorado Metal Miners' Association for criticism. In its reply this body said in part: "We have given this bill a careful scrutiny, and came to the conclusion that it contains several very objectionable features."

Golden.—In the School of Mines Quarterly for October last, Colorado's future as an oil producer is discussed by Victor Ziegler, professor of geology and mineralogy in the School. In his conclusions, he says that Colorado lacks persistent sands capable of acting as reservoirs. Those present are either very thin or very much restricted laterally. While there are a number of large and well-defined structures in the State, it is unfortunately true that the more promising horizons of the Cretaceous are eroded off the surface, or are absent, or are so deeply buried as to be out of reach of the drill. Large fields need, therefore, not be expected in Colorado. The chances are bright of finding a few widely-scattered fields with wells of small capacity, yielding a high-grade oil.

IDAHO

The State Senate has passed a memorial asking Congress to appropriate $500,000 with which to construct a highway up the south fork of the Clearwater river in central Idaho. According to I. L. Jones of Elk City, "the great region of north-central Idaho has been served by a mountain road not worthy of the name of road, which commences at a point 1240 ft. above sea-level, ascends to 6500 ft., then descends 2700 ft. into a valley, and ascends to 6700 ft. altitude before dropping down into Elk City basin, which has an altitude of 3900 ft., and is considered the trading centre of the district. The entire trip is made either through a sea of mud or over an uneven rock road-bed, which four and six horse-teams are ever struggling to negotiate, a distance of 52 miles in three days. This is the only way the miner, the farmer, and the stockman has of getting in and out. The proposed water-grade road up the south fork of the Clearwater river would open districts tributary to having good bench lands upon which clover and grasses grow in abundance, and upon which farms have been cut out of the forest. The pastures of many of these farms are filled with cattle and hogs which will compare with any raised in the most favored districts of the North-West. Farming has extended into the Red River district, which is one of the tributaries of the south fork. This development is being done by the same pioneer stock that blazed the way through the West and many of them have prospered abundantly. Large numbers of outside cattle graze there, and last year 60,000 head of sheep were pastured in the district. The water-grade road would pass through some good timber lands, and along its course scenic conditions are excellent. The river and its tributaries abound in fish. Central Idaho has produced in round numbers $150,000,000 in gold from its placer mines. Under modern methods placer mining has some good districts to be developed. For several years quartz mining has been carried on in the face of great handicaps created by the lack of transportation, but notwithstanding that there are at least 50 gold mines in the district having a good deal of development, and many of them equipped with mills. Some have a depth of 500 ft. or more with ore in quantity and quality which precludes any question as to their merit. There are also prospects, good, bad, and indifferent galore. Much of this work has been done in the last five years. The entire territory lies in the National Forest Reserve, which Department is trying to attract homesteaders. The lack of a general understanding by the public of the Forest Reserve law is being removed. . . ."

Porthill.—Lessees (Klockmann brothers) of the Idaho-Continental lead-silver mine near here paid the company $173,283 in royalties during the past 2½ years. The lessees spent $248,699 on improvements, and were credited with this sum on royalty account. There was mined 12,579 tons of ore during the period, and the mill worked 560 full days out of 892 possible. The orebody has been proved for 1450 ft. in length, and reserves are now 250,000 tons, an increase of 100,000 tons. No profit has been drawn by the lessees so far, and owing to the low price of lead they will either have to close the mine or have a reduction in the royalty, which is 30% of smelter returns. The new aerial tram across the river was recently completed. James Wilson is superintendent.

Wallace.—Tamarack & Custer shareholders were to decide on acquiring control of the Sherman Lead Co. on February 26. A 51% interest will cost $150,000. The purchase would give T. & C. two claims and fractions containing a large orebody, also 4000 tons of ore on dumps. A 49% interest in the Sherman is held by James F. Callahan, Charles McKinnis, Harry R. Allen, Alex Swan, Ed. Doyle of Denver, and Mrs. James Leonard. The chief holders of the Tamarack & Custer are the Day brothers of Wallace.

The Sunshine Mining Company has taken over the Sunset-Banner Mining Co.'s six claims, making a compact group of twenty on Beaver creek. The deal was on a share basis. Tunnels have been driven, No. 5 being in 1100 ft. D. L. McGrath is president and manager.

The Consolidated Interstate-Callahan is to move its main office from New York to Wallace. According to the president, J. A. Percival, the mine is in fine condition.

KANSAS

Baxter Springs.—The Federal Mining & Smelting Co., a subsidiary of the A. S. & R. Co., is operating the Lucky O. K. mine, just north of Hockerville, Oklahoma. A mill is working one shift. P. W. George is manager.

The Delaware Zinc Co. put down 30 drill-holes west of this place, none of them recording blanks. Ore in some was cut at a depth of 55 ft., the face being 45 ft. deep, of good grade.

MICHIGAN

Houghton.—So far no labor agitators have turned up in the Copper Country, consequently there is no talk of strikes. The local smelters continue to pile up copper, as is usual during the winter.

The Copper Range company pays $1 per share on March 15. This is a reduction of 50 cents per quarter.

Production of the Calumet & Hecla group was as follows in January: Ahmeek, 1,928,305 lb.; Allouez, 486,708 lb.; C. & H., 5,588,051 lb.; Isle Royale, 1,514,220 lb.; Osceola, 1,405,898 lb.; and White Pine, 404,000 pounds.

MISSOURI

Annapolis.—The Annapolis Lead Co. has been organized with a capital of $2,500,000, head office at St. Louis, to develop holdings in Iron county. It is said that $50,000 has already been spent in exploration. F. M. Strickland and J. A. Nolan are largely interested.

Joplin.—Production of the Tri-State region last week was as under.

State	Blende, tons	Calamine, tons	Lead, tons	Value
Kansas	1708	..	328	$88,582
Missouri	1390	32	238	70,274
Oklahoma	4146	..	510	195,996
Average price	$41	$28	$51	

The total value is a decrease of $170,135 when compared with the previous week.

MONTANA

Anaconda.—The Washoe Reduction Works is operating at 60% of capacity. Only the concentrating section was stopped during the labor troubles at Butte.

Butte.—Mining companies here are reported to have decided to employ only Americans or those that have declared their intention of becoming citizens. This resulted in a rush to take out naturalization papers last week.

Concerning the Butte Central Mining & Milling Co., controlled by the Butte-Detroit Copper & Zinc Co., a circular dated at Boston, December 14, 1918, says in part, the bonds of this company, which amount to $300,000, have been defaulted by non-payment of interest. The value of the mine has not been thoroughly established but it seems clear that the personal property must be worth $100,000, and that the real estate has important value in connection with adjoining mining property, the owner of which can use the shaft and other property, should be worth upward of $100,000—a total of more than $200,000, outside of any value which it may have as a mine. From this sum the old underlying attachment on the real estate (aggregating with some other charges about $65,000) would have to be deducted in estimating the present value of the bonds, and the $80,000 of bonds pledged should be deducted from the total of bonds to be liquidated. It is thought by many that the property has great value as a mine.

Davis-Daly reports for the last quarter of 1918 a net profit of $129,936, an increase of $20,000 compared with the previous term. There was smelted 15,191 tons of 7.80% ore, yielding 2,432,010 lb. of copper and 100,050 oz. of silver. Quick assets on December totaled $503,660. The 2100-ft. level was opened during the term, a fine orebody being exposed. Improvement in ventilation continues. Production is to be curtailed on account of the market. M. W. Atwater is now general manager. Davis-Daly produced 1,018,889 lb. of copper and 39,093 oz. of silver in January, a gain of 40,000 pounds.

NEVADA

Austin.—Ground-water in the Reese River basin and adjacent parts of Humboldt River basin is discussed by G. A. Waring in Water-Supply Paper 425-D of the U. S. Geological Survey. The climate of the area is arid, annual rainfall at Battle Mountain being 7 and at Austin 12½ inches. Between these two places is a railway 103 miles long. The water from dug wells in the region contains more of the alkalies and less calcium and magnesium than water not concentrated by evaporation and transpiration, the processes at work here. The water from springs are not so highly mineralized as those from wells. Water from drilled wells is only fair for domestic use, and could not be used satisfactorily in boilers. Austin is supplied by a spring.

VIEW SHOWING EXTENT OF OLD WORKINGS AT AUSTIN, NEVADA

Carson.—A bill prohibiting aliens from locating or holding mining claims in Nevada has been introduced to the State Legislature by Senator Chandler. The measure specifies that only American citizens may locate or hold mineral lands.

Eureka.—The Eureka district seems to be taking on new life, and the following items may be of interest:

J. S. Bagg has begun development on the Silver Connor group, four miles south-west of Eureka on Prospect mountain. The property has a tunnel 2300 ft. long that cuts the orebodies at a depth of over 800 ft. A gasoline compressor will be installed. This mine was worked in the early days when water for the hoist had to be carried on horses at a cost of 25 cents per gallon.

D. States, manager for the Nevada Eureka Mining Co., has opened a large body of shipping ore on the Licid Tufa property, also has several lessees in the different parts of the mine, all extracting shipping ore. This class of ore assays better than $25, generally from $40 to $60 per ton.

The Hope Consolidated company of Ruby hill has been driving a tunnel several hundred feet long, and is now in promising ground.

Charles Wittenburg of Tonopah, owner of the Cyanide mine on Adams hill, has purchased a new compressor and machinery, and will soon begin operations.

Charles Mau is opening a promising prospect in Newark valley, near the old Bay State mine, 20 miles north-east of Eureka.

Mason.—In Professional Paper 114, of 68 pages, of the U. S. Geological Survey, by Adolph Knopf, the geology and ore deposits of the Yerington district are discussed. An abstract of this will be published at a later date. From 1912 to the end of 1917 the copper output of the region totaled 61,200,000 lb. The average tenor of the ores has ranged from 2.75 to 6.00%. All of the mines are described, and numerous illustrations are given.

The Bluestone Mining & Smelting Co.'s flotation plant stopped work indefinitely on February 19, while the mine and other operations will cease on March 1. A general clean-up has been made, so everything will be left in good order for resumption. With the shutting down of the smelter at Thompson there remained no outlet for the oxide ore. Plans had been made for another unit to the mill, and it is generally understood that this will be built before commencing milling again. The K & K machine recently put in did good work.

Rochester.—The Rochester Nevada Silver Mining Co. was finally organized this week. Full details will be given next week.

Thompson.—The Mason Valley Copper Co. produced 1,100,000 lb. in January, a decrease of 160,000 pounds.

The company's smelter is expected to suspend work at any time.

Tonopah.—Production of the district last week totaled 7130 tons of ore valued at $121,210.

The Jim Butler, from 905 tons, made a profit of $5900.

At the West End last week fire damaged the engine-house to the extent of $20,000.

NEW JERSEY

Franklin Furnace.—The New Jersey Zinc Co. in the last quarter of 1918 reports a net surplus of $2,313,969, compared with $3,926,428 a year ago, and $7,297,051 in 1916. A dividend of $1,400,000 left a balance of $913,969.

NEW MEXICO

Pinos Altos.—The Calumet-New Mexico company has nearly finished its 50 to 125-ton concentrating plant at this place. The zinc-copper-gold-silver ore is refractory, and needs careful treatment.

OKLAHOMA

Picher.—Owing to the hoist getting beyond control, four men at the Picher company's No. 9 mine were dropped 270 ft. on February 14. About 40 ft. from the bottom of the shaft the hoist-man regained control, but a brake bolt broke, and although the fall was partly broken the bucket struck the bottom. Injuries received were serious but not fatal.

TEXAS

El Paso.—The A. S. & R. smelter here has reduced wages by 50 cents for those receiving $2.50 or more, those between $2.50 and $2 will get $2, and laborers getting $2 will be paid $1.75.

UTAH

Bingham.—The Bingham Amalgamated Copper Co. is succeeded by the United Bingham Mining Co., with a capital of 1,000,000 shares.

Dugway.—The Metal States Mining & Milling Co. has been organized with a capital of $100,000 to develop copper-gold claims in this district. J. F. Cannon of Salt Lake City is president. E. S. Fisher is secretary, also engineer and geologist.

Oasis.—The old Detroit Copper Mining Co., which has a lease on the Ibex Gold Mining Co.'s property in Millard county, about 35 miles north-east of this place on the Salt Lake Route, was reorganized at Salt Lake City last week. Joshua Greenwood is president. The ore carries gold and copper, dumps being valued at $300,000.

Park City.—The Three Kings mine has been examined by E. L. Zalinski. The shaft is down 700 ft., and at 500 ft. a cross-cut entered ore-bearing limestone and quartzite. Samples assay 3% lead and 4 oz. silver per ton. Further work is recommended in the Ontario limestone, where is the No. 4 fissure.

Tintic.—Wages were reduced by $1 per shift at the Mammoth mine last week, the forerunner of a general cut of 75 cents.

The Tintic Paymaster Mines Co. has been incorporated with a capital of 2,000,000 shares, 50 cents par. W. I. Snyder is president, and William Knight vice-president. The property is a consolidation of 1700 acres. A fair amount of exploration has already been done.

WASHINGTON

Leadpoint.—The Electric Point company has suspended operations for the present on account of the lead market. Tests are to be made on concentration of the carbonate ore; if successful, a mill is to be built. The surplus at the end of 1918 was $175,000.

Northport.—It is reliably stated that the smelter here is to close indefinitely at an early date.

Spokane.—The annual mining convention, which is usually held here in February, but which was postponed owing to influenza, has been definitely abandoned; and Spokane will do what it can to make the Vancouver and Nelson meetings successful. Vancouver's first convention will be held March 17, 18, and 19. The Nelson convention will be held some time in June, when the Kootenay country is at its best.

CANADA

British Columbia

Anyox.—The British Columbian Legislature has before it a petition relative to the 18-mile railway that has been constructed from Alice Arm nearly to the Dolly Varden mine. This is of special interest in view of the recent announcement that the Temiskaming Mining Co. has secured possession of the Dolly Varden and Wolf silver mines. The petition sets out that the Taylor Engineering Co. spent $425,000 on the line, almost completing it, without being repaid by the owners of Dolly Varden.

Sandon.—The Roseberry Surprise mill is closed, and the ore treated there will be sent to the Roseberry mill. To Sandon this is a decided set-back, as it constituted one of its chief industries and employed a large number of residents, mostly men with families, who will be without work.

Invermere.—Snowslides have caused some trouble and not a little damage so far in this district. The Paradise Mines road was blocked for several days by a slide. On December 4 a slide at the Lead Queen carried down the foreman and a miner. The former was dug out from 10 ft. of snow after being buried two hours; he was uninjured. The miner has not been found. On the morning of January 19 a slide carried away the tram and the tunnel-house at the Trojan mine; no one was injured and the damage was nominal. The tram will be repaired at once, and will be in operation again shortly.

The Sitting Bull Mining Co. has built 8 miles of wagon-road up Boulder creek at a cost of $15,000. This enables it and others to get ore out and necessary supplies in. The Sitting Bull has 90 tons of ore sacked that will average 132 oz. silver and 29% lead. The orebody is opened on 5 levels, and a tunnel will be driven this spring to cut the shoots at depth. E. D. Smith is superintendent.

The Trojan Copper Mines Corporation on Boulder creek has erected a 3-drill Ingersoll-Rand compressor, and a jig-back tram across the creek to the ore-bunkers. High-grade copper ore is being hauled to rail at Athalmer. The ore is chiefly chalcopyrite in a quartz gangue, averaging 20% copper, 6 oz. silver, and from 50 cents to $2 gold per ton. There is about 600 tons of shipping ore on the dump. A raise from No. 2 to No. 1 level shows 7 ft. of rich ore. There is from 18 to 25 in. of concentrating ore carrying from 4 to 6% copper and some precious metals. The company expects to erect a 50-ton mill during 1919. E. D. Smith is superintendent.

The Paradise Mines Co. on Toba creek has driven a raise from No. 4 to No. 3 level, and is constructing a surface 3-rail jig-back tram, and in future will work the mine through No. 4 level. The ore is a carbonate, and occurs as chamber deposits in a crushed zone, it evidently being a replacement of the crushed areas in the limestone. Several teams are hauling ore to rail at Invermere.

The Lead Queen on No. 2 creek was bonded to Seattle people, who took out two carloads of ore during November, but it has been shut-down since December 4. Mr. Denhart, the manager, is expected back from Seattle, and it is reported work will be resumed soon.

Kimberly.—At the Consolidated M. & S. Co.'s Sullivan zinc-lead mine the two-mile tunnel has reached ore. The output in the last 10 days of January was 4690 tons of zinc and 1405 tons of lead ore.

Princeton.—The Canada Copper Corporation finished laying track from Princeton to the millsite at Allenby on January 31. A spur will next be laid to the mine. Machinery can now be hauled to the 2000-ton mill, the building of which will be ready for the equipment.

Stewart.—The Missouri gold-silver-copper-lead mine at the head of Portland canal has been re-purchased by Sir Donald Mann. Diamond-drilling is to be undertaken. The new owner formerly had an option in 1910.

Vancouver.—The Vancouver Chamber of Mines has decided to change its title to that of the British Columbia Chamber of Mines. This step has been decided in order that the influence of the organization may be extended to include the whole Province. At the last election of officers a selection was made of some representative mining men outside of Vancouver, it being felt that, if the Chamber of Mines is to make its work beneficial to the industry, it must be understood to be a body belonging, not to any particular locality or community, but to the whole of the Province. Good progress is being made in preparations for the International Mining Convention to be held in March.

Manitoba

Resources and characteristics of northern Manitoba are further described in the February 'Granby News', published by the Granby Consolidated of British Columbia, by C. M. Campbell. In this illustrated article the rivers and railway are covered.

The Pas.—A reconnaissance of the proposed railway from The Pas to the copper fields of Flin Flon, Schist, and Athapapuskow lakes has been made by J. P. Gordon, whose report has been submitted to the authorities. The main line is about 75 miles long.

Ontario

Cobalt.—The Nipissing mills treated 178 tons of ore for $106,586 and 5959 tons for $121,350, in January, a total of $227,936.

The Wettlaufer Lorrain Silver Mines company during 1918 leased its mine to the Pittsburgh Lorrain Syndicate, which paid royalties totaling $2209. No important developments were recorded. The surplus on January 1, 1919, was $103,342.

Haileybury.—The ore-dressing laboratory of the Haileybury School of Mines is in operation, in charge of D. A. Mutch of the Coniagas mine. The school board consists of F. D. Reid of the Coniagas, J. J. Denny of the Nipissing, M. F. Fairlie of the Mining Corporation, and E. A. Collins, formerly mining inspector here. The plant is well arranged.

including jaw-crusher, 3 stamps, amalgamating plate, classifiers, tube-mill, concentrators, agitators, thickeners, and flotation apparatus; also assay-office. According to the Cobalt 'Nugget', seven processes may be used on ores, namely: (1) Straight gravity concentration test, by crushing to the desired size in stamp-battery and tube-mill and concentrating the crushed product on jigs and tables. (2) Combination of concentration, followed by cyanidation. (3) Straight cyanidation in which provision is made for all-sliming and agitating process, or leaching the sand and agitating the slime. Provision is also made to precipitate precious metals from the solution by sodium sulphide, zinc-dust, or aluminum dust. (5) Amalgamation followed by concentration. (6) Amalgamation followed by cyanidation. (7) Amalgamation followed by a combination of concentration, cyanidation, or flotation. This school is contiguous to Cobalt, Porcupine, Gowganda, Kirkland Lake, and other centres.

Kirkland Lake.—The Kirkland Lake Proprietary late in January issued the following circular to shareholders: The directors announce that a scheme of amalgamation and absorption by the Kirkland Lake Proprietary, Ltd., of the properties and assets of the Tough Oakes Gold Mines, Ltd., Burnside Gold Mines, Ltd., Sylvanite Gold Mines, Ltd., Sudbury Syndicate, Ltd., and an important Cobalt company, has now been provisionally agreed. It is subject to the confirmation of their respective valuations by H. H. Johnson, consulting engineer for the Kirkland Lake Proprietary, and will only be submitted to the shareholders of the various companies for approval after his report has been received. Mr. Johnson was expected to arrive in Canada during February, and the detailed proposals should be ready for the consideration of shareholders some time in March. The amalgamation, as previously agreed, should prove advantageous to all the mining companies concerned, as well as to the Kirkland Lake Proprietary, which holds a controlling interest in most of them, as well as a considerable area of further claims. The absorbing company will own a continuous and compact block of claims aggregating over 600 acres in extent, situated in the centre of the Kirkland Lake goldfield, and it is believed that the results already obtained at several points on the various properties warrant the erection of a large central installation, which will ensure quicker and more effective development, with much lower working costs than have hitherto been possible. Active operations are in progress on the Cobalt property and good developments are reported.

The Teck Hughes mill treated 2459 tons of $8.62 gold ore during January.

Porcupine.—The Hollinger Consolidated in 1918 treated 578,755 tons of ore, yielding gold worth $5,752,370. In 1917 the output was $4,261,938, and $5,073,401 in 1916. Ore-reserves are valued at $41,080,005, a slight decrease. The Hollinger pays a dividend of 5 cents per share on February 25, equal to $246,000.

The Schumacher mine is expected to resume milling shortly, after being closed since July last.

MEXICO

Chihuahua

Chihuahua.—According to arrivals at El Paso, Texas, on account of raids and threats by bandits, the A. S. & R. and other mining companies may shut-down their properties. Both Carranza and Villa's men are collecting taxes, and the companies refuse to pay this.

Sonora

Cananea.—Greene-Cananea in January produced 3,000,000 lb. of copper and 106,480 oz. of silver, a decrease of 2,100,000 lb. and 68,000 oz. when compared with December. For 1918 the total was 53,270,000 lb. and 1,549,672 ounces.

PERSONAL

Note The Editor invites members of the profession to send particulars of their work and appointments. The information is interesting to our readers.

Frederick G. Cottrell and **George S. Rice** sailed for France on February 22.

L. V. Cummins, mining and electrical engineer, has gone to Yokohama, Japan.

Jasper T. Robertson has opened an engineering office in the Hobart building, San Francisco.

Errol MacBoyle has moved his offices from the Crocker building to the Hobart building, San Francisco.

M. J. Conover, manager of the Valley View mine at Lincoln, California, was in San Francisco last week.

S. E. Bretherton, Jr., has returned from Burma and is occupying offices in the Mills building, San Francisco.

B. C. Austin and **Walter V. Wilson** have opened an engineering office in the Santa Marina building, San Francisco.

Sydney J. Jennings has gone to Mexico City to confer with the Mexican division of the A. I. M. E. regarding problems of mining engineers in that country.

Charles F. Williams, formerly with the Tonopah Belmont Development Co., who has been in France for over a year with the 30th Engineers, has received his discharge.

William Brandt and **F. A. Voorhees** are returning to the Bacis G. & S. M. Co.'s property in Durango, Mexico, by way of Mazatlan, Sinaloa. The works have been shut-down for six years.

George H. Parsons has received his discharge from the Gas Defense Service, and has returned to his position as chief chemist for the Ray Consolidated Copper Co. at Hayden, Arizona.

John R. Van Fleet, who was with the California Chrome Co. in San Luis Obispo county, California, has been in the Black Lake chrome district of Quebec, and is now at Niagara Falls, New York.

Chester Naramore, who succeeded **W. A. Williams** as chief petroleum technologist, Bureau of Mines, has resigned from the Bureau to engage in commercial work. **J. O. Lewis**, superintendent of the Petroleum Station of the Bureau of Mines, at Bartlesville, Oklahoma, has been appointed to fill Mr. Naramore's position, and **W. P. Dykema**, petroleum engineer, has been appointed as superintendent of the Petroleum Station to succeed Mr. Lewis.

G. S. Crouse, general foreman of the McDougall furnace department at the Anaconda company's Great Falls plant, died of pneumonia recently. He had been employed at the plant for 24 years.

The International Mining Convention will be held at Vancouver, B. C., on March 17, 18, and 19. The Chamber of Mines is making arrangements.

The annual meeting of the Colorado Section of the A. I. M. E. was held at Denver on February 8, 53 members attending the dinner. The following were elected officers: Chairman, R. J. Grant; vice-chairman, W. H. Leonard; secretary-treasurer, Robert M. Keeney; and executive committee, S. I. Ionides and Robert Hursh.

The California Chapter of the American Mining Congress held its first meeting on February 13 in the offices of the California Metal Producers' Association, Merchants' National Bank building, and elected the following officers: George W. Starr, governor; Albert Burch, first vice-governor; L. P. St. Clair, second vice-governor; K. R. Kingsbury, third vice-governor; P. C. Knapp, secretary.

THE METAL MARKET

METAL PRICES

San Francisco, February 18

Aluminum-dust, large and small lots, cents per lb	65—70
Antimony, cents per pound	8.00
Copper, electrolytic, cents per pound, in carload lots	17.00
Lead, pig, cents per pound	5.35— 6.35
Platinum, per ounce	$100
Quicksilver, per flask of 75 lb	$85
Spelter, cents per pound	9.00
Zinc-dust, cents per pound	15.00

The Union Trust Co. of Pittsburgh has purchased from the Aluminum Company of America $12,000,000 6% serial notes. Heavy inventories and expansion program necessitated this financing.

ORES

Monthly reports on minerals investigations are now being issued by the U. S. Bureau of Mines at Washington. In the first issue are given the names of the minerals and the officer in charge of the respective work. The following subjects are briefly covered: tin, cost-keeping methods for small mines, pyrite and sulphur, tungsten, political and commercial control of minerals, iron ores, copper, gold, silver, magnesite, potash, chalk, stone, manganese, chrome, lead, zinc, antimony, and graphite. The report covers 30 pages. All interested in these minerals should arrange to get copies of these regular bulletins.

Concentration of domestic low-grade manganese ore is the subject of War Minerals Investigations Series No. 9 of the Bureau of Mines, by Edmund Newton. The deposits, ores, requirements of the steel industry, mining and marketing, factors affecting treatment, methods, and costs are discussed.

EASTERN METAL MARKET

(By wire from New York)

February 25.—Copper is inactive and lower. Lead is quiet but firm. Spelter is dull though steady.

SILVER

Below are given official (not Government) quotations, in cents per ounce, of silver 999 fine. In order to make prompt settlements with smelters and brokers, producers allow a discount from the maximum fixed price of $1.01½, hence the lower price. The Government has not fixed the general market price at $1, but will pay this price (as from April 23, 1918) for all silver purchased by it. The equivalent of dollar silver (1000 fine) in British currency is 46.65 pence per ounce (925 fine), calculated at the current rate of exchange. On August 15, 1918, the Treasury announced that the maximum price was fixed at $1.01½ per ounce. The British government fixed its maximum at 49½ pence, on September 2, but on November 12 this was changed to 48¾, on December 13 to 48 7/16, and in February to 47¾ pence.

Date		New York	London		Average week ending	
Feb.	19	101.12	47.75	Jan.	14	101.12
"	20	101.12	47.75	"	21	101.12
"	21	101.12	47.75	"	28	101.12
	22 Holiday			Feb.	4	101.12
	23 Sunday			"	11	101.12
	24	101.12	47.75	"	18	101.12
	25	101.12	47.75	"	25	101.12

Monthly averages

	1917	1918	1919		1917	1918	1919
Jan.	75.14	88.72	101.12	July	78.92	99.62	....
Feb.	77.54	85.79	....	Aug.	85.40	100.31	....
Mch.	74.13	88.11	....	Sept.	100.73	101.12	....
Apr.	72.51	95.35	....	Oct.	87.38	101.12	....
May	74.61	99.50	....	Nov.	85.97	101.12	....
June	76.44	99.50	....	Dec.	85.97	101.12	....

Writing on January 30, Samuel Montagu & Co. of London said that no change had taken place in the price of silver, but one might occur at any moment on account of reduced freights from America to England. The text above the price table shows that this took place in February. On the editorial pages will be found a brief summary of the silver position.

COPPER

Prices of electrolytic in New York, in cents per pound.

Date				Average week ending	
Feb.	19	17.00	Jan.	14	20.75
"	20	16.75	"	21	20.50
"	21	16.50	"	28	19.87
"	22 Holiday		Feb.	4	19.21
	23 Sunday		"	11	18.33
"	24	16.00	"	18	17.50
"	25	15.75	"	25	16.40

Monthly averages

	1917	1918	1919		1917	1918	1919
Jan.	29.53	23.50	20.43	July	29.67	26.00	....
Feb.	34.57	23.50	....	Aug.	27.42	26.00	....
Mch.	36.00	23.50	....	Sept.	25.11	26.00	....
Apr.	33.16	23.50	....	Oct.	23.50	26.00	....
May	31.69	23.50	....	Nov.	23.50	26.00	....
June	32.57	23.50	....	Dec.	23.50	26.00	....

The American Brass Co. has dropped its base price for finished goods to a 17-cent copper level, the lowest that has prevailed for several years.

ZINC

Zinc is quoted as spelter, standard Western brands, New York delivery.

Date				Average week ending	
Feb.	19	6.70	Jan.	14	7.72
"	20	6.70	"	21	7.52
"	21	6.70	"	28	7.20
"	22 Holiday		Feb.	4	6.89
	23 Sunday		"	11	6.68
"	24	6.70	"	18	6.74
"	25	6.65	"	25	6.69

Monthly averages

	1917	1918	1919		1917	1918	1919
Jan.	9.75	7.87	7.44	July	8.98	8.72	....
Feb.	10.45	7.97	....	Aug.	8.58	8.87	....
Mch.	10.78	7.67	....	Sept.	8.33	9.58	....
Apr.	10.20	7.04	....	Oct.	8.32	9.11	....
May	9.41	7.29	....	Nov.	7.76	8.75	....
June	9.63	7.92	....	Dec.	7.84	8.49	....

LEAD

Lead is quoted in cents per pound, New York delivery.

Date				Average week ending	
Feb.	19	5.00	Jan.	14	5.75
"	20	5.00	"	21	5.82
"	21	5.00	"	28	5.50
"	22 Holiday		Feb.	4	5.32
	23 Sunday		"	11	5.02
"	24	5.10	"	18	5.00
"	25	5.15	"	25	5.05

Monthly averages

	1917	1918	1919		1917	1918	1919
Jan.	7.64	6.85	5.60	July	10.93	8.03	....
Feb.	9.10	7.07	....	Aug.	10.75	8.05	....
Mch.	10.07	7.26	....	Sept.	9.07	8.05	....
Arp.	9.38	6.99	....	Oct.	6.97	8.05	....
May	10.29	6.88	....	Nov.	6.38	8.05	....
June	11.74	7.58	....	Dec.	6.49	6.90	....

The lead market at St. Louis has been dull and lower, according to the 'American Metal Market,' as despite the attempts of some of the producers to sustain prices there is enough re-selling to keep the market on a downward course. The production is still restricted, but lead is coming out from unexpected sources, and the demand is so limited that a small amount offered is sufficient to cause a decline. The Desloge Lead Co. is refusing to quote a price, but buyers appear to find no difficulty in securing enough lead for their requirements. There have been sales at 4.60 cents.

QUICKSILVER

The primary market for quicksilver is San Francisco, California being the largest producer. The price is fixed in the open market, according to quantity. Prices, in dollars per flask of 75 pounds:

Date					
Jan.	28	100.00	Feb.	11	95.00
Feb.	4	95.00	"	18	90.00
			"	25	85.00

Monthly averages

	1917	1918	1919		1917	1918	1919
Jan.	81.00	128.06	103.75	July	102.00	120.00	....
Feb.	126.25	118.00	....	Aug.	115.00	120.00	....
Mch.	113.75	112.00	....	Sept.	112.00	120.00	....
Apr.	114.50	115.00	....	Oct.	102.00	120.00	....
May	104.00	110.00	....	Nov.	102.50	120.00	....
June	85.50	112.00	....	Dec.	117.42	115.00	....

TIN

Prices in New York, in cents per pound. The monthly averages in 1918 are nominal. On December 3 the War Industries Board fixed the price to consumers and jobbers at 72½c. f.o.b. Chicago and Eastern points, and 71¼c. on the Pacific Coast. This will continue until the U. S. Steel Products Co.'s stock is consumed.

Monthly averages

	1917	1918	1919		1917	1918	1919
Jan.	44.10	85.13	71.50	July	62.60	93.00	....
Feb.	51.47	85.00	....	Aug.	62.53	91.33	....
Mch.	54.27	86.00	....	Sept.	61.54	80.40	....
Apr.	55.63	88.53	....	Oct.	62.24	78.82	....
May	63.21	100.01	....	Nov.	74.18	73.07	....
June	61.93	91.00	....	Dec.	85.00	71.52	....

The Price Fixing Committee of the War Industries Board terminates its duties on March 1.

Eastern Metal Market

New York, February 19.

The markets are all inactive and featureless, although the tendency in some is to be firmer.

Antimony is unchanged.

Copper continues to decline on sales of small tonnages.

Lead is more active, with quotations firm.

Tin is still restricted by governmental control and is stagnant.

Zinc is extremely quiet, but fairly firm.

ALUMINUM

No. 1 virgin aluminum is obtainable now at 31 to 32c. per lb., New York, for early delivery. The maximum Government prices continues in force until March 1, but are nominal and of little significance. They are 33 to 33.20c. per lb. in 50-ton to 1-ton lots.

ANTIMONY

The market is flat and featureless. For early delivery, wholesale lots are obtainable at 7.12½ to 7.25c., duty paid, New York, but demand is light.

COPPER

The market continues to fall, but sales are still of small proportion and insignificant, judged by normal trading. While fair sales have been made for such times as these, the quantities involved would not be regarded as enough to fairly judge the market when conditions are normal. Production continues to be curtailed, and there is no doubt that it is considerably below normal or what it was before the War. The quotation today for electrolytic copper is 17c. per lb., New York, for early delivery, and it is said by some that this could be shaded. Sales of small lots have been made, largely by small producers or second-hands in the last week on a scale down from 18c. until today the metal can be bought at or under the 17c. level. Lake copper is largely nominal at 17.50c., New York, with demand light. The market as a whole may be termed stagnant, with buyers holding off as much as possible. Casting copper is quoted at 16.25 to 16.75c., depending on delivery. The London market has been declining, and is now about £90 for spot and £84 per ton for future electrolytic.

IRON AND STEEL

The situation in the iron and steel trade is better than it was a month ago, only in that there are 30 less days to wait for revised buying, says 'The Iron Age'. Business is almost wholly for necessities. By the end of this week the machinery of the Government price investigating board will be under way, but there is some doubt as to what are by this medium to be regarded as fair prices. The downward marking of prices is proceeding naturally, but it is generally confined to quotations and not to actual transactions. Inquiry for export is in better volume, but high shipping costs retard business in this direction. England had lost a tinplate order to this country at $18.55 c.i.f. Lisbon, which compares with a base price here of $7.35 per box.

LEAD

Inquiry has been much better during the past week, in fact it may be regarded as having been nearly widespread. It is felt by many that the present quotation of both the leading interest and the outside market of 5c., New York, or 4.70c., St. Louis, which has remained firm for nearly two weeks, is bottom, and that an upward turn is near. The American Smelting & Refining Co. is said to be taking most of the business now going at 5c. per lb., but total sales under 5c. by independents have not been large, though a few have been willing to shade this level. Lessening of output continues, and it is predicted by some that the leading interest will advance its quotation in the near future. [This was done late last week, an advance to 5.10 cents.]

TIN

The tin market continues to labor under the restrictions of vital Government control, and there is not much encouragement in sight. The only possible satisfactory feature is the report that the War Trade Board has been refusing import licenses for Bolivian concentrates and ores since February 3. This would mean a shorter period of time in which to dispose of the allocated metal, especially if it were known how much raw material is in stock and en route. It is still impossible to import tin except through the United States Steel Products Co., and it is also therefore impossible to purchase for future shipment from the Far East, despite the report that Straits tin can be bought at less than 47c. per lb. for that position. This contrasts with the fixed price of 72.50c. for Government allocated metal. Straits tin is still nominal at 72.50c., New York, with 99% American tin offered at about 67c. Receipts so far in February have been 615 tons at Pacific ports and 50 tons at Atlantic. Spot Straits in London is quoted at £212 per ton.

ZINC

The market is extremely quiet but firm at 6.35c., St. Louis, or 6.70c., New York, for prime Western for early delivery. Producers do not seem inclined to concede anything to buyers, as present prices are considered under cost of production in most if not all cases. Consumers also are not eager to buy except for immediate needs, and the slightly better inquiry mentioned last week has disappeared. It is believed by some that the bottom has been reached much the same as in lead.

ORES

Manganese Alloys: The market for ferro and spiegel continues quiet, though inquiry for small lots of both are more numerous than in the recent few weeks. The demand is for early delivery. Quotations for ferro range from $175 to $200 for early delivery with $225, delivered, asked by most domestic producers. Spiegel is nominal at about $60 delivered. The ferro output in January was 21,331 tons and spiegel 11,456 tons, according to the blast-furnace reports of 'The Iron Age'.

Molybdenum: Quotations are nominal at 85 to 90 cents per lb. of contained MoS_2, with inquiry reported as better.

Tungsten: The market is stagnant and the situation has not changed during the last week. It is understood that ferro has sold in small amounts at about $1.50 per pound of contained tungsten. This would mean $15 per unit in 60% concentrates for high-grade ore. One trade paper is quoting $14 to $16 per unit for high-grade ore with low grade at $12 to $14.

CONGRESS ACTS ON WAR-MINERALS RELIEF

Just as we go to press a telegram from Washington brings the pleasing news that the House of Representatives has re-considered its action taken on February 14, and has voted to accept the Henderson amendment to the informal War-Contracts bill for reimbursing producers of chrome, manganese, and other war minerals.

INFORMATION FURNISHED BY MANUFACTURERS

CONCENTRATING MOLYBDENUM ORE

In the Hualpai mountains, south of Kingman, Arizona, the Standard Minerals Co., controlled by southern Californians, recently started its 50-ton mill treating molybdenum ore. According to the 'Bulletin' of the Chamber of Mines and Oil of Los Angeles, the process was devised by the resident engineer, R. L. Cornell, the design and erection of plant was done by the Wellman-Lewis Co., and the machine was supplied by Collins & Webb, all of Los Angeles. The accompanying flow-sheet shows the system of dressing the ore.

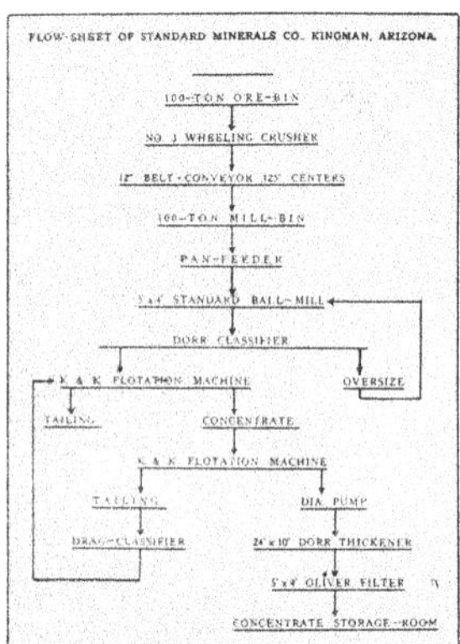

The mine is opened to a depth of 350 ft., and on the 200 and 300-ft. levels is said to be exposed a large quantity of ore assaying 1% MoS_2. At the shaft is a 45-ft. head-frame, 40-hp. hoist, 80-hp. engine driving a 400-cu. ft. Ingersoll-Rand compressor, and a 25-hp. engine for the generator, pumps, and blower. All of the ore passes through a Vezin sampler, which takes a 1/20 cut. The mill is driven by a 120-hp. oil engine. All the gas engines were made by the Western Machinery Co. of Los Angeles. The company is fortunate enough to have a contract for its concentrate.

Officers of the Standard Minerals Co. are: G. M. Simpson, president; Dr. Lee C. Deming, vice-president; C. E. Holcomb, treasurer; and C. C. Randall, secretary. The main office is at Anaheim, California.

Catalogue 'B' of the Southwestern Engineering Co., of Los Angeles, is a handsomely-prepared 32-page publication on the K & K flotation machine. In a part list of companies using this apparatus is 67 names, operators in North, Central, and South America; also in Japan. The K & K has been so often described in this journal that it is unnecessary to do so again. Full details are given in the catalogue, including blue-prints and photos of parts; also reproductions of experimental reports, and various flow-sheets using flotation.

A NEW GAS REVERSING-VALVE

In the operation of any gas-fired furnace it is desirable that the valve controlling the direction of the flow of gas shall operate rapidly and easily. These factors have been kept in mind in designing this new gas reversing-valve, which has just been placed on the market by the Wellman-Seaver-Morgan Co, of Cleveland, Ohio. That the conditions have been ideally met is evidenced by the fact that a 36-in. hand-operated valve can be reversed in from 3 to 7½ seconds, with a pressure of not over 25 lb. This is accomplished by a perfectly balanced hood and counter-weights. An equally important feature is that, in this new design, the operating mechanism is outside of the casing where it is easily accessible and always cool. This new valve is similar in principle to the well-known Forter valve and is interchangeable as to ports and clearances.

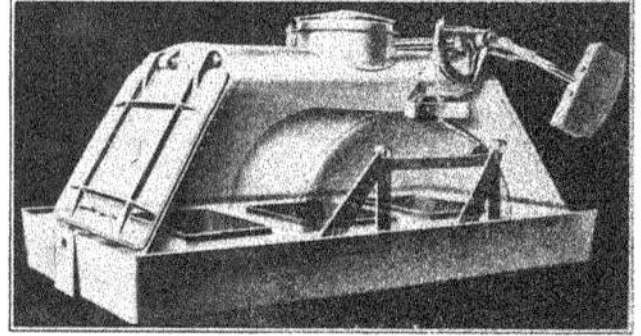

NEW GAS REVERSING-VALVE.

The general design and construction of the W-S-M valve are clearly shown in the phantom view. It consists of an outer casing, a base with three ports, a hood to connect two ports, and the operating mechanism. The centre port is connected with the chimney. Waste gas from the furnace flows from whichever outside port the hood is covering to the chimney port. This leaves a clear passage for the fuel gas or the air entering the casing through the mushroom-valve at the top to pass through the third port to the furnace regenerator. Reversal of the flow of gas or air is accomplished by moving the hood to a position over the centre port and the one previously uncovered. The base of the valve is a cast-iron rectangular pan with three walled circular openings or ports. The hood that covers the centre and one end port is semi-elliptic in form, made of steel plates with angles at the bottom to support a fire-brick lining.

The base-pan holds a quantity of water so that when the

hood is over the ports a water-seal is formed to prevent the escape of gas. The base-pan has a tapped hole at each end for a water-pipe. There is a perforated strainer at the intake-end, and a dam-plate at the other end, to hold the water at such a level as to allow the hood to extend 3 in. into the water forming the seal.

The outer casing is made of steel plate and lined with fire-brick. It has cast-iron door-frames and door at each end through which the hood may be removed or inserted. Each door has a small peek-hole with a swinging cover which enables inspection at any time. On the top of the casing is a cast-iron neck which connects either with the fuel-gas line or the air intake, depending upon the purpose for which the valve is used. The hood is moved by a series of levers and coupling-shafts, which extend through the water under the casing and into sockets on the hood. The shafts move on chilled-iron bearings. The operating mechanism is actuated by a hand lever.

With all hand-operated valves, a special stand is furnished, as well as six sheaves with hangers, clamps, and wire rope. At each side of the valve is a counter-weight attached to an arm and sector over which passes a chain connecting with the supports of the hood. The form of this sector is such that the counter-weights balance the weight of the hood at any position. The W-S-M valve has the following distinct advantages, the combination of which will be found in no other valve used for reversing the gases of melting or heating-furnaces.

The semi-elliptical form of the hood allows free flow of the gas, as there are no abrupt turns or constricted areas in the passage formed by the ports and hood. This feature is important in obtaining maximum efficiency from the stack draft. All leakage or waste of gas is prevented by the water-seal. Such a seal does away with all packing, tightening, and adjusting, the only attention required being the flow of a small quantity of water into the bed-plate to replace the amount evaporated. Due to its compactness, this valve requires comparatively little floor-space, and adapts itself to various arrangements of flues from the regenerator to the stack. The weight of the hood is counter-balanced by the weights of the lever-arm in such a way that the hood is in balance at any position, so to move the hood it is only necessary to exert enough force to overcome friction. This is an important feature in hand-operated valves.

The materials used for each part of the valve are selected to give long life. The hood and casing are lined with fire-brick, and all working joints are protected from the hot gas. Bearings and wearing parts are designed with a high factor of safety. There are chilled bearings in the bed-plate for the rocker-arms and hardened links and pins on the hood supporting arms. Construction of the valve is such that all parts may be easily inspected and removed. The doors at each end of the outer casing are large enough to allow the hood to be removed. The reversing mechanism does not require the removal of bolts or nuts in placing or removing. The levers, links, and pins of the operating mechanism are on the outside, thus permitting oiling and adjustment, and ensuring long life and easy operation.

MOTOR-DRIVEN SHOVELS AND DRAG-LINE EQUIPMENT

As a further means of economy and wherever electric power is available, electrically-driven shovels or drag-lines are used for stripping overburden, mining coal, excavating, dredging, re-loading coal and coke, making railroad cuts, and similar work. The advantages arising from the use of such machinery are as follows: lower operating cost, when fuels are scarce, expensive, and hard to transport; fewer operators are required; fuel is not an essential; there is no water to supply or freeze; no boiler or boiler troubles, no stand-by losses, no smoke, no sparks, no objectionable noises, and more material can be handled. A complete line of this equipment that meets the especially severe service encountered in such work, has been designed by the Westinghouse Electric & Mfg. Co. Simplicity is another feature of the apparatus tending to give it reliability in operation without skilled and frequent attention. Both alternating and direct-current equipments can be furnished, but the former is preferable because it is more economical.

CONSTRUCTION OF K & K FLOTATION MACHINES

All K & K flotation machines have a standard cross-section, the different sizes varying only in length. The standard construction is redwood and cast-iron. It has been

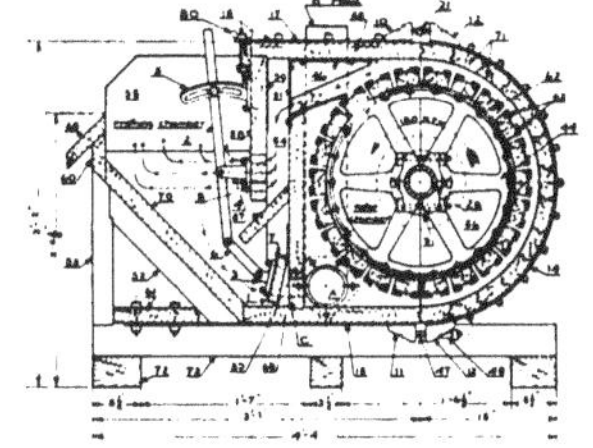

END SECTION OF K & K MACHINE.

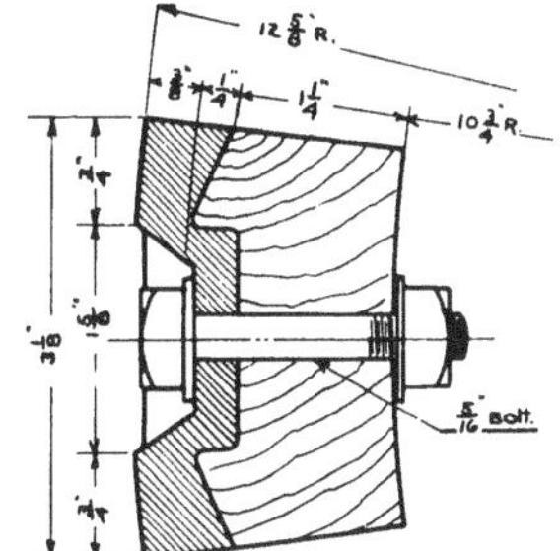

DETAIL OF RIFFLE IN K & K MACHINE.

demonstrated that these materials will give long life with the most severe flotation feeds. All parts of the machine, subject to wear, are provided with cast-iron wearing-plates, which may be cheaply and quickly replaced. Wherever necessary, all parts are accurately machined and are interchangeable.

The riffle (part 63 shown on cut) has proved to be that part of the machine that receives the greatest wear. The maple riffle gives satisfaction in most cases, and is in general use where abrasive action is not severe. The cast riffle is designed to give long life where coarse or sharp feeds are used and is by far the most satisfactory wearing material for this class of work. Machines with wooden riffles can be fitted quickly with cast-iron riffles by simply removing the lagging carrying the wood riffle and replacing with lagging carrying the cast-iron riffles. All parts of the machine are accessible. By operating clamps 80 and turnbuckles 21, the top or cover of the housing, part 68, can be removed for inspection and replaced within a few minutes. For repairs to rotor, the circular back of the housing is easily and quickly removed by releasing turnbuckles 21 and 47.

The diameter of the rotor, which determines the size of the machine in cross-section, is the same for all types of machines, and was determined after experimenting to obtain the maximum aeration with the greatest efficiency. It is built on a $3\frac{7}{16}$ in. diameter hollow shaft of different weight and strength for the various sizes of machines. This shaft carries the cast-iron spiders 44, to which are attached the lagging 62 and riffles 63. The spiders have a split hub, and are securely fastened to the shaft by means of clamping-bolts and two heavy set-screws, which prevent slipping or movement on the shaft. Skimmer plate 77 is cast-iron made in convenient sections for assembling. Wearing plates 50 and 51 are either of cast-iron or of rubber belting, and give full protection to the wood partitions. The South-western Engineering Co. of Los Angeles makes this apparatus.

COMMERCIAL PARAGRAPHS

The **Aspromet Co.**, of Pittsburgh, announces the opening of a sales office in the Schmulbach building, Wheeling, West Virginia, under the direction of E. A. Short.

The **Hammond Iron Works** of Warren, Pennsylvania, announces that George Armstrong has been appointed Pacific Coast representative, with offices in the Hobart building.

The **Cling-Surface Co.**, Buffalo, New York, in more than 20 years of existence considers that it has done much toward conserving fuel and saving belts by eliminating belt-slip. It has made belt-slip and its attendant costs and troubles a special study, resulting in devising a formula for more accurately figuring slip costs.

J. J. Edwards, who for a number of years represented the Sullivan Machinery Co. in Mexico, and has recently been connected with the machinery and engineering material division of the supply department of the Government at Washington, is now manager of the rock-drill department of the Chicago Pneumatic Tool Company.

The **All-Russian Central Union of Co-operative Societies**, representing 30,000 societies containing 20,000,000 members, and which did a gross business of 700,000,000 rubles in 1918, has opened offices at 167 Post street, San Francisco, in charge of Alexander Zelenko. Manufacturers and producers in general desiring to engage in exporting to Russia and Siberia are requested to send in duplicate, catalogues, price-lists, and other information to the office of the Societies.

The **Ingersoll-Rand Co.** has published the following: Form No. 9120, on the Leyner oil furnace No. 3. No. 9010, on the Sergeant ticket-cancelling box, by railroads, toll bridges, ball grounds, race-tracks, lecture-halls, moving-picture theatres, etc. No. 9026, on Ingersoll-Rand high-speed piston-valve steam engine, class FP. No. 9123, on imperial tie-tamping outfits. And No. 9028, on Ingersoll-Rand equipment for sugar factory and refineries, in English and Spanish.

The **Liberty National Bank** of New York announces that it has created an industrial department for the purpose of offering its services, in an advisory capacity, on matters pertaining to manufacturing and industrial problems. It has been the banks' observation in the past that there exists on the part of many manufacturers a distinct feeling that bankers, as a whole, have not appreciated their individual, technical, and commercial problems. This new work will be directed by Donald D. Davis, a man of practical engineering, accounting, and factory executive experience. It is the Bank's desire that customers avail themselves of such service. The department will be in a position to furnish, upon request, general information concerning the trend of industrial conditions, raw materials, labor, and all the other important influences to which a going concern is susceptible.

The **Sullivan Machinery Co.** of Chicago has published the following air-compressor bulletins: No. 75-D, 'Single-Stage Straight-Line Steam-Driven Compressors' (class WA-5); No. 75-E, 'Straight-Line Simple-Steam and Two-Stage Air-Compressors' (class WB-3; this is the familiar two-stage straight-line machine, which the firm has built for a number of years, but which has now been re-designed to incorporate the end-rolling finger or plate-type of valve, improved speed and pressure regulator and steam-valve motion, and other features); No. 75-G, 'Class WG-3 Single-Stage and Class WH-3 Two Stage Belt-Driven Compressor, Standard Pattern'; No. 75-I, 'Underground Mine Car Compressor' (class WK-2, complete with motor, electric fitting, and receiver for operating coal-pick machines, hammer-drills, etc., a popular type in quite general use, especially in coal mines); and No. 72-C, 'Sullivan Drill-Sharpening Machine of the All-Hammer Pattern'. This bulletin includes mention of the newly-designed Sullivan double arc-drill bits, which are fitted with double taper on the wing; together with the adjustable vertical-gauging dies in which this double taperwing is made.

The **Denver Engineering Works Co.**, of Denver, Colorado, reports that it has recently received orders for the reconstruction of 80 stamps at the Gold King Extension Mines Co. at Silverton, Colorado. W. Z. Kinney, general manager, has recently developed new orebodies in the mine and is now making extensive repairs at the old mill, machinery for which was furnished by this Denver firm several years ago. ——The original designer of the Gold King tailing plant was Frank E. Shepard, president of the Denver Engineering Works. One of the first steam-turbine electric-lighting generating plants was installed at the Gold King mill near Gladstone. These improvements at the Gold King Extension promise to greatly increase ore production of Silverton.—— The firm also recently furnished ball-mills and other apparatus for the new mill of the United States Smelting, Refining & Mining Co. at Eureka, Colorado. This new mill was erected on the site of the old Sunnyside mill, which has been a prominent producer at Silverton for many years. ——A contract with the Chinese Ministry of War for a complete tungsten concentrating plant, including the crushing and concentrating machinery, as well as the complete detailed designs of the mill, was recently completed.—— Among recent orders is one for a large electric hoist for the Compania Minera de Penoles, Mapimi, Mexico. One of the first electric hoists used in the republic was manufactured and installed by this company, and during these years the firm has enjoyed the continuous patronage of the Penoles company for electric hoists and smelting machinery.——Recent shipments also include crushing, concentrating, and mine timber-framing machinery for South America.——A Richards jig installation for the concentration of diamond-bearing gravel in South Africa was also furnished.——Another important Richards jig plant is for the concentrating of tin ores in South Dakota.——The firm is now constructing a large electric hoist of 25,000 lb. capacity for the Colorado Fuel & Iron Co. to be used in connection with its furnace plant at Pueblo.——A large number of Hardinge conical mills for distribution to Western mining districts are being built.

OUR compliments to Governor Boyle of Nevada for the spirit shown by him in vetoing the prize-fight bill. It took a mining engineer to show such political courage. Here we take the opportunity of correcting the impression that Mr. George ('Tex') Rickard is in any way connected with this paper; we may promote the belligerency of the pen but not that of the list!

HORACE V. WINCHELL was elected president of the Institute at the 119th meeting, held in New York, on February 17. At the same time it was announced that the proposal to change the name to the American institute of Mining and Metallurgical Engineers had been carried by the vote of the members. This will prevent 'M & M' being used as a 'short' for the Mining and Metallurgical Society of America—another wrong to Ireland!

EVERY time a Californian returns home from the transcontinental journey to the Atlantic coast he wonders why intelligent people live elsewhere. The sudden transition, in crossing the mountains that bortier this State, from a world dead in the grip of winter to the verdant foothills of the Sierra and the fruitful lands of the Sacramento valley is a marvel that is ever new and always joyful. What must it mean to our gallant soldiers at the end of the long and wearisome journey from Europe! We join with them in singing "I love you, California."

HOW difficult it is to obtain reliable information concerning the internal condition of Germany is indicated by two dispatches appearing in the same issue of the daily papers. An Associated Press dispatch states that a group of British officers, who had made a tour of inspection in order to ascertain the need for revictualing Germany, reported that "the country is living on its capital as regards food supplies, and that either famine or bolshevism—or both—will ensue before the next harvest if outside help is not forthcoming." On the other hand, an American correspondent asserts that "such privations as the Germans suffered during the War are rapidly disappearing and the German workmen, comparatively speaking, are prospering." The same writer says that "the Boche on the street believes he is not crushed and that economically Germany doesn't compare unfavorably with the Allies." Before long we shall get the truth, from Mr. Hoover.

BRITISH mining companies are getting rid of enemy-owned shares by arranging to buy those shares, now in the hands of the Public Trustee, who plays the useful part assigned in this country to the Alien Property Custodian. For example, the Consolidated Mines Selection Company, identified with the honored name of Mr. Walter McDermott, has purchased the enemy-owned shares in that company and now offers them to the non-enemy stockholders in the proportion of one 'enemy' share to every three shares already held, the price being the cost to the company after allowing for expenses incurred in the process of acquisition and transfer. After the non-enemy stockholders have had this opportunity to increase their holdings, any remaining 'enemy' shares will be allotted at the discretion of the directors to those making application for them.

MINING conventions are numerous at this season, largely because it is the time of the 'break up'—the melting of the snows and the approach of spring—a period during which mining operations, especially such as are surficial, are in temporary abeyance. We refer to the New York meeting of the American Institute on another page. Last week the Canadian Mining Institute held its annual meeting at Montreal, and we feel certain that under the leadership of its president, Mr. D. B. Dowling, and its efficient secretary, Mr. H. Mortimer-Lamb, the sessions were of unusual interest and usefulness. Coming nearer home, the Idaho Mining Association held its sixth annual meeting at Boise on February 11 and 12, under the presidency of our friend Mr. Stanly A. Easton, the manager for the Bunker Hill & Sullivan company. Several interesting papers were read, notably on 'Human Engineering' by Mr. E. H. Lindley, on 'The Physiography of Idaho' by Professor Douglas C. Livingston, on 'The School of Mines and the State' by Professor Francis A. Thomson, and on 'The Mining Industry of the Coeur d'Alene' by Mr. Walter C. Clark. We note that Mr. Jerome J. Day was elected president for the ensuing year. This association maintained a representative, namely, Mr. Ravenel Macbeth, its secretary, at Washington last year for the purpose of keeping in touch with Federal legislation, co-operating with other agencies of a similar character. Another important meeting is that of the International Northwest Mining Convention to be held at Vancouver on March 17 and the two following days under the auspices of the British Columbia Chamber of Mines. Mr. A. M. Whiteside is the president and Mr. William Sloan, Minister of Mines in the British Columbian government, is honorary president. This gathering, so near our frontier, of Canadian and American mine-operators and engineers promises to be interesting, and, like the meetings at New York and Montreal, will tend further to tighten the links of goodwill between neighboring peoples.

NORTHCLIFFE'S retirement from the management of the London 'Times' is an event of international importance, even if we do not agree with Mr. George Harvey's high appraisement of Lord Northcliffe's services to Britain and to the Cause during the War. While this dynamic newspaper proprietor may have done signal patriotic service during the period of world crisis, we yet regard with dislike and fear the power he exercised by means of his string of publications. Superior as he may be in a hundred ways to Hearst, his ownership of so many mediums of publicity constitutes a danger to the development of the democratic idea in Britain and in the world at large. Hearst is a pestilence, Northcliffe is a menace.

RECENT and revised estimates of the War's holocaust awaken a feeling of horror even in minds calloused by familiarity with the stories of battle and sudden death. The 'Manchester Guardian', a newspaper of the highest character, states that 17,500,000 deaths were caused by the War. This excludes fatalities attributable indirectly to the War, but it does include a mortality of 4,000,000 due to the pneumonia and influenza provoked by war conditions. It is estimated that 4,000,000 Armenians, Syrians, Greeks, and Jews were massacred by the Turks, and that 1,000,000 Serbian civilians died through massacre, hunger, or disease. If justice is to be done, Turkey has yet to expiate her crimes. Her account is overdue. Another estimate, compiled by General March, at Washington, gives 7,354,000 as the total killed in battle or died of wounds. The losses of Russia and Germany are nearly equal, namely, 1,600,000. France comes next with 1,385,000 then Austria-Hungary and England with 750,000 each. These figures are below the official British estimate but they serve to indicate how great was the destruction of life caused by Germany's criminal ambition; she and her partners in the attempt to conquer Europe lost 2,750,000 lives, whereas the defenders of human liberty sacrificed 4,604,000 lives. The account is horribly ill balanced. Germany alone caused 3,250,000 deaths in the Allied armies, as against her total loss of 1,600,000. These figures show how much she gained by her preparedness for the attack and how much less she suffered than her victims. Shall she be given another and a better chance to carry out her fell designs?

posed to set aside an allowance for traveling expenses, so that the selection of representatives will not be confined to men of wealth. In order to prevent this system becoming financially burdensome to the Institute it is expected that the more distant sections will choose men whose business takes them frequently to New York or even Western men temporarily resident in New York. All this indicates the desire to draw closer the bonds of fellowship and to remove even a suspicion that the Institute is dominated by a coterie in the East, as was the case, of course, when Dr. Raymond was in control. In those days the cost, in money and time, of a journey across the continent was an effective obstacle to any such plan of representation. Another recent development of social co-operation between engineers has been the joint meetings of local sections of the various branches of the profession. This feature of engineering activity has proved attractive in San Francisco, for example: it does not weaken the bond that ties each section to its headquarters, usually in New York, whereas it does promote general solidarity and incite the growth of sound ideas on matters vital to engineering as a comprehensive profession. Our readers are aware of the organization, at Chicago, of a society known as the American Association of Engineers. Mr. F. H. Newell was one of the principal promoters of it and we published his propaganda in our issue of October 16, 1915. This new departure is incited by the belief that the engineer's place in society is inadequately recognized, that he is under-paid, and that his scope as a citizen is too restricted. The aim is to establish employment agencies and fix rates of remuneration; also to emphasize the relation of the engineer to the Government and to the public; in short, something not only professional but occupational, something between a scientific society and a labor-union, has been created for the purpose of asserting the rights and dues of the engineer, under which term not only the manager and the consultant, the superintendent and the expert, but all the personnel of a highly diversified business are comprised. No liberal mind will be antagonized by such cooperative activity, least of all the members of our Institute. Here mention must be made of the Mining and Metallurgical Society, which has not been absorbed, as was hoped, by the Institute. This essentially New York organization of a group of men of the highest standing, all members also of the Institute, is disinclined to extinguish itself because it claims to afford a means of public utterance denied to the Institute and necessary to the profession. It is quite clear that this reaching forth for useful service on the part of other organizations does compel the Institute to take stock of its own performance and to consider gravely whether in any way it has been delinquent. We see no reason for dejection or disappointment, but ample cause for stimulation to further useful effort; and that is exactly the view taken by the directors of our Institute; they are facing the position resolutely and cheerfully. Much has been done already by co-operation with the Engineering Council, which is an upper house, as it were, of the engineering parliament, and one well adapted by its selectively representative character to take action for the whole profession whenever required *vis-à-vis* either the public or the Government. It seems to us that the conditions as we have outlined them call mainly for a further expression of loyalty on the part of our membership to the Institute and to the service for which it stands; it remains for the unofficial members to hold up the hands of the president and the directorate, assisting them both with cordial support and with helpful suggestion; in short, to take increased interest in all the activities of the Institute, and thereby to further the best interests of our profession. Let us work together in time of peace with the spirit that we showed during war.

Relief for the Miner

Nothing that the Government has done in recent months will produce so kindly a feeling among the miners of the West as the passage by Congress of the relief bill for the benefit of the producers of chrome, manganese, tungsten, and other war minerals. The effect will reach far beyond those immediately concerned in digging these emergency minerals, for what has been done to reimburse the producers of chrome, manganese, and tungsten is appreciated by the whole brotherhood of prospectors and miners. The Henderson bill, which finally became a greatly modified amendment to the Dent-Chamberlain Informal War-contracts bill, is a democratic measure, keeping faith with the host of small operators instead of being only for the benefit of the rich. It so happens that the men who responded to the call of the Government for a supply of these essentials minerals at a time of crisis were chiefly hard-working miners, men used to handling the pick and shovel in earning their daily bread; they were not of the alien class that so often disturbs the peace; they were real Americans, of the good old sort that made the nation strong in the pioneer days. It would have been a shame, a disgrace, a grave political mistake, to have denied honorable recognition of the right of such patriots to reimbursement of the losses they sustained, seeing that the Government was planning to re-pay the contractors who had done no more, and who, in most cases, had risked far less. It is amazing that men could be found who would oppose settlement of such just obligations, but in spite of such antagonism the Government's good faith has been sustained by the action of both branches of the national Legislature. At this writing the bill has not been signed by the President, but it is inconceivable that he would veto it, as it represents the wish of the Secretary of War in order to settle the obligations of his Department, and it is understood that the Dent bill had the President's cordial endorsement. [The Bill was signed on March 3.]

The full text of the bill will be printed next week. Meanwhile we are able to give a telegraphic summary, which shows that it authorizes the Secretary of the Interior to adjust, liquidate, and pay such net losses incurred by any person in producing or preparing to produce manganese, chrome, tungsten, and pyrite in compliance with the request or demand of the Department of the Interior, or the War-boards, to supply the urgent needs of the Nation in the prosecution of the War; the Secretary of the Interior to make such adjustments and payments as he shall determine to be just, and his decision will be final. The Act appropriates $8,500,000 for liquidation of claims arising within its jurisdiction, and all claims, in order to receive consideration, must be filed within the next three months. No claim will be paid unless the expenditure has been made in good faith for production on property containing mineral in such quantity as reasonably to seem to be 'commercial', and the money expended must have been applied during the War, that is, between April 6, 1917, and November 12, 1918. No profits on the money invested will be allowed, and business for purposes of speculation will be ruled out; moreover, if settlement is made on claims that subsequently prove to be fraudulent the Government is given the right and power to recover. In determining the net losses the value of any ore on hand and possible recovery from salvage of plant will be taken into account. The foregoing admits of reimbursement to everyone equitably entitled to it, so that the miners of these minerals may feel that they have received honorable treatment. The representatives of the people have not forgotten that the Government is operated for the good of the people, and not to play sharp tricks in getting something for nothing. The miners responded with what meant protection to their country, and now the country they helped to defend protects them from loss. Honors are even. The result that has been achieved has come from organization and intelligent direction of the propaganda for informing the officials in Washington of the facts. The first organization to have a representative on the ground was the Pacific Coast Chrome Producers Association, which, in conjunction with the Oregon Chrome Producers Association, asked Mr. Courtenay De Kalb to present their case at Washington. His services were contributed by the 'Mining and Scientific Press' in behalf of the mining industry. The foundation laid in Washington was broad and strong, and subsequently other organizations, under the auspices of the American Mining Congress, led to the creation of a War Minerals division of that body, which carried the fight to a finish. It was a notable achievement, for the time was brief and Congress was crowded with urgent business. The justice of the cause, the able advocacy of those in charge of the propaganda, and the sympathetic and efficient efforts of such men as Senators Chamberlain, Henderson, Johnson, and Poindexter, Mr. Julius Kahn, Mr. Nicholas J. Sinnott, Jr., and in fact the entire delegation from the West Coast States, Messrs. Otis Wingo, William A. Oldfield, William Schley Howard, and Edward S. Denison, who will probably be the next chairman of the House Mines Committee—all these, and many others, struggled from a high sense of duty to see that the Government made good in its moral obligation to the miners. The proper presentation of the claims is a matter of great importance. We understand that the Pacific Coast Chrome Producers Association will arrange to serve as a sort of clearing-house for such claims, giving advice and aid in putting them into shape for submission to the Department of the Interior. Information regarding these matters should be widely disseminated at once through the local papers in the mining districts in order to reach all legitimate claimants in time to enable them to take advantage of the relief now offered.

Mexican Concessions

Several weeks ago the State Department presented to Señor Carranza a demand for protection to the rights of American investors in Mexico. It was curt and direct, but the astute Coahuilense seated in the presidential chair found a clause in the document that served as a loophole. He had been asked, among other things, to protect American lives and property. It was easy to regard that as fundamental, so Carranza singled it out for reply. "Lift the embargo on arms and ammunition," was his plea, "and then I can maintain order." To the uninformed this would appear reasonable and just. Back of it is the black history of years of misrule in Mexico that has ruined the business of her own people and of those who have come from abroad to develop the resources of the southern republic. Of course, Carranza would rejoice to have the embargo lifted; he could then the more readily impose upon the industrious and respectable majority of the Mexicans, who are now powerless because unorganized and without leaders, the will of the petty minority that holds the reins of government. To accede to his request would be to sign the death-warrants of the real democrats that have stood by their constitutionalist principles, which means the constitution of 1857, the defence of which served Carranza as excuse for taking up arms against Huérta. Emboldened by his success in thwarting once more the effort of our Government to compel respect for American rights, he has started a new campaign for dispossessing the 'gringo' of his property in Mexico. This time it is the land concessions that are assailed. Under these grants great areas were being brought under irrigation and subdivided into small farms for sale to actual settlers. This was precisely in line with the spirit of the revolution, which was to give clear title to areas that were of a proper size for cultivation by individual owners. The order for revising land concessions cites examples in Chiapas, Lower California, and Quintana Roo, as if to divert attention from the more important concessions, judged on the basis of development done. A further point of interest is that the application of this principle would establish a precedent capable of being extended to concessions for water-rights, timber-lands, smelting, transportation, and other privileges of vital import to mining companies, which have continued to hope that the Mexican storm sometime might end, permitting the sun of prosperity once more to shine upon them.

Americanization

The Editor:

Sir—The Secretary of the Interior's views on this subject, as published in the MINING AND SCIENTIFIC PRESS of January 18, have given me the temerity to express a point I have considered for some time. Mr. Lane said: "All Americans must be taught to read, write, and think in one language." I would like to add: "and to do their banking business in the same language, namely, in English, the tongue of the United States."

The banks of this country have given freely a great service to the Nation during the War, and I suggest that they continue that service and extend it to include the teaching of Americanization. It is admitted that the habit of the immigrant of forming national communities is detrimental to his early Americanization, and I consider that some of the banks foster and encourage this community feeling.

In this I refer to the foreign named and hyphenated American banks. Among the large commercial banks of this country there are few offenders; but the fault is common with savings institutions. Right there a danger lies, because the immigrant seeks the savings bank at once. He looks among the list and finds the following: the Scandinavian-American Bank, the Italian-American Bank, the German-American Bank, the Hibernian-American Bank, the French-American Bank, the British-American Bank, and the Swiss-American Bank; and still more alluring and deceiving, the Bank of Italy. At one time, in Oakland, California, there was a Bank of Ireland and a Bank of Germany.

There is no good excuse for employing such national names, entirely out of keeping with their business, with no foreign national connection. The majority of our best banks use suitable titles. The only palpable reason that these banks do this is to attract the depositor who has a preference for one of these nations, and in so doing to cater to him as an Italian, German, Oriental, or other **alien.**

These banks do not even encourage the newcomer to learn English; they furnish tellers who speak his language. This sort of thing prevents the assimilation of the future citizen. With the genuine foreign banker it is entirely a different matter, and the two institutions must not be confused. Let the American banks use American names, and draw business because of the service given to their customers, thereby furthering Americanization.

DISCOUNT.

San Francisco, February 13.

Proposed Change in State Insurance

The Editor:

Sir—The Industrial Accident Commission is opposing the passage of Senate Bill No. 603 and Assembly Bill No. 791. These bills propose to take the State Compensation Insurance Fund from the management of the Commission and place it under the jurisdiction of other State officials.

The bills have been prepared and introduced by the private insurance companies, competitors of the State Fund. The employers have shown their confidence in the Fund by patronizing it in such large numbers that fully one-third of California's employers have policies with the Fund against the compensation risk. The employees are in favor of State insurance. The 'Reconstruction Program' of the American Federation of Labor opposes private insurance for profit in the domain of workmen's compensation and strongly advocates State monopoly.

There are excellent reasons why the Industrial Accident Commission should continue to direct the State Compensation Insurance Fund. Ever since January 1, 1914, the Fund has been under the actual management of expert insurance men, selected for their positions because of their ability. The outcome is a well-managed Fund, recognized as the most successful institution of its kind in the United States.

More than \$790,000 has been returned in dividends to policy-holders, thus affording a striking example of mutual insurance under State auspices. The overhead expenses of the Fund are less than 13% of premiums, as against 40% for stock companies. The net surplus on January 1, 1919, was over \$1,000,000. Over \$2,000,000 of assets is invested in United States Liberty bonds and Californian municipal bonds, drawing interest for the benefit of policy-holders. California's employers have been saved an average of over 34% of compensation insurance cost for the years 1914 and 1915 (for which the reserve period has expired), and an initial refund averaging 15% is returned to policy-holders at the end of each year.

Equally important is the State Fund's relation to injured employees. Over \$2,500,000 has been paid by the Fund for medical service and compensation to injured workers and their dependents. In addition, the Fund is holding a loss reserve of over \$1,250,000 for death, permanent and continuing disability cases.

The State Compensation Insurance Fund's policy is liberal. Compensation is paid when morally due. Legal technicalities are avoided. For the fiscal year ended

June 30, 1918, there were 1086 contested cases referred to the Commission for decision, in which insurance carriers were involved. There are approximately 20 compensation insurance carriers in California. Though the State Fund is doing over one-third of the compensation business of the State, only 138 Fund cases were so referred, out of the total of 1086, and the Fund had 18,095 injuries reported during the fiscal year named. That record shows the attitude of the Fund toward claimants under the Commission's administration. The Commission carefully decided each Fund case, as it did each of the 948 contested cases in which the other insurance carriers were interested.

All State Funds in this country are operated by the State Industrial Accident Commissions. This enables these Commissions to so administer the State Funds that they will carry out the intent of compensation laws in setting an example for other insurance carriers in dealing with employers and employees, within the spirit, as well as the letter, of such laws. To divorce the State Fund from the Commission in California would interfere with this vital feature of administration. Not one instance of discrimination against private insurance carriers can be shown. There isn't a practical reason for the divorcement. The idea has been put forward by the avowed enemies of State insurance in California, and that alone should be sufficient to condemn the proposed legislation.

H. L. WHITE, Secretary.

San Francisco, February 21.

Platinum and Government Red-Tape

The Editor:

Sir—Last fall an appeal was made through the public press to the people throughout the United States to surrender their platinum, as the Government was sorely in need of that metal. Being a chemist myself and knowing how essential platinum is in many chemical investigations, I felt that, under the circumstances, it would be unpatriotic to continue to wear a platinum and gold chain, from which a small platinum crucible might easily be made, so I packed up the chain, together with some scrap platinum I happened to have, and sent it to the United States Assay Office at New York, which was the department designated by the Director of the Mint to receive such material. I received an acknowledgment of the receipt of the platinum, dated November 7. A month later, as I had heard nothing further, and thinking a letter might have gone astray in the mail, I wrote to the Assay Office, inquiring if the work had been completed. I received a reply, dated December 16, stating that the work would be finished in about a week. Another notice, dated January 20, informed me that the assay had been completed and the necessary certificate had been forwarded to the Ordnance Department on January 14. A letter, dated January 22, was received from the Ordnance Department, giving the assay and value of the metal, and requesting that an enclosed receipt be signed, when payment would be made. This, though it did not seem to be exactly business, was duly signed and returned on the day it was received, January 28. Finally, a check, dated February 7, was received in settlement for the metal. Thus, it will be seen, it was exactly three months after the receipt of the platinum stock at the United States Assay Office that payment was made by the Ordnance Department.

Though the War, happily, is over, it is evident that platinum is still needed for post-war reconstruction, as appears from the fact that the price of the metal has risen since the Government removed the fixed price of $105 per ounce, but if the Government takes as long to refine the metal as it does to find out its value and settle for it—and it reasonably may be presumed that it takes longer—it is offering little encouragement to the people to contribute platinum, which is now used for ornamental purposes, for such post-war reconstruction.

F. H. MASON.

San Diego, February 12.

Nevada Water Laws

The Editor:

Sir—I realize that we who are permitted to express our views in your columns are mere trespassers upon your space and the time and patience of your readers unless we deliver a message of integrity and service, and that, concerning the discussion between Mr. R. T. Walker and myself touching Nevada water adjudication as exemplified in a certain suit referred to by us, there is no question of general interest involved nor justification for appeal to the judgment and action of your readers, unless it is a fact that there is in Eldorado canyon, in southern Nevada, a continuous water-bearing fracture accompanying the porphyry dike that extends from the Colorado river 11 miles westward to the great mass of 'malpais', which, lying along the summit of the River range, is the only water reservoir of the region: that the water of this subterranean channel was first developed, used, appropriated, and filed upon, and granted by the State to the plaintiff company in the suit mentioned: that the defendants in that suit diverted the water from its natural channel in Eldorado canyon, thereby stopping for the first time in nine years the plaintiff's water-supply and making it necessary to cease its mining and milling operations: that waters flowing in such channels and so used, appropriated, and granted, are subject to the same laws that govern surface streams, and that such reservoirs and such subterranean water-channels developed in mining along the dikes in the impermeable igneous rocks of arid regions frequently comprise the sole water-supply for operating that property, and if not being used by others, it becomes by filing, appropriation, beneficial use, and State grant the property of those who developed it; then, its diversion by later comers to the district should not be confirmed by court decision. I regret the necessity for even briefly supplementing my former letter in an effort to establish the fact of these conditions, but they are basic, and, together with the attitude of the courts toward them, constitute a problem of grave interest to many mine-operators in arid regions.

In Mr. Walker's reply to my former letter, his most plausible opposing contention is that his water-shaft sunk in Eldorado canyon above plaintiff's shaft could not have attacked plaintiff's water-supply, because he did not pump water from the canyon until some weeks after plaintiff complained of the sudden stoppage of its water-flow.

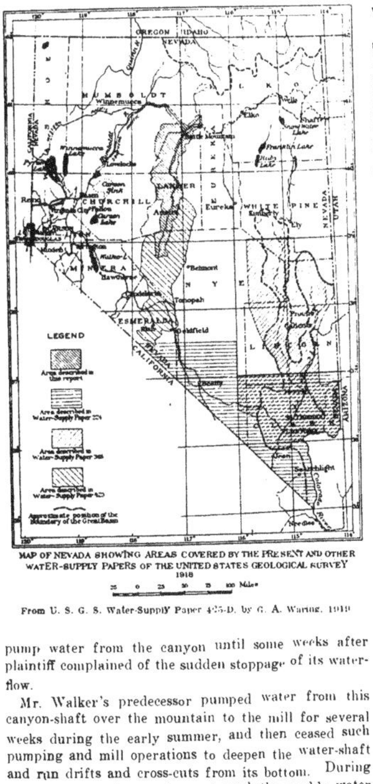

MAP OF NEVADA SHOWING AREAS COVERED BY THE PRESENT AND OTHER WATER-SUPPLY PAPERS OF THE UNITED STATES GEOLOGICAL SURVEY 1916

From U. S. G. S. Water-Supply Paper 425-D, by G. A. Waring, 1919

Mr. Walker's predecessor pumped water from this canyon-shaft over the mountain to the mill for several weeks during the early summer, and then ceased such pumping and mill operations to deepen the water-shaft and run drifts and cross-cuts from its bottom. During this quite extensive development work the muddy water constantly baled from the shaft to permit work was not pumped over the mountain to Mr. Walker's mill, but was dumped into the 'wash', whence it could not return to its subterranean channel and thence into plaintiff's mine workings because the conducting dike-apex is almost continuously above the canyon floor for the short distance between these two openings in the channel. It will therefore be readily seen that the effect of this hourly exhaustion of the water from the dike-fracture as opened by Mr. Walker's water-shaft as effectually cut off plaintiff's water-supply as did his resumption of pumping over the mountain in the fall. The fall is the season of low water in that region. Plaintiff's ten years experience had demonstrated a water-flow of about 9000 gallons per day during this dry season, and up to 20,000 gal. during the wet season of the year.

Shortly after Mr. Walker's resumption of pumping, he told me that he was taking 8000 gal. of water a day from Eldorado canyon, but that he hoped later to reduce that pumping to 5000 gal. At that time plaintiff was getting less than 1000 gal. per day in its shaft, as against the 9000 gal. formerly coming to it during the dry season. Mr. Walker's statement that his water-shaft supply and the water in the dike-fracture a mile farther down the canyon could not be the same, because of difference in analysis, is hardly plausible, because of the chemical changes probable to water in subterranean transit when passing from one enclosing rock to another, as does the water-carrying dike in question; which passes from monzonite to old andesite between Mr. Walker's shaft and the defendant's mine-workings. His suggestion that the water of the region should be treated as percolating water because of the many fractures common to the igneous rocks of the district is not supported by the fact of the absence of water from the miles of drifts, shafts, cross-cuts, and tunnels in the property worked by him, and in other properties, even in Eldorado canyon, whose workings do not open the water-channel. If "the inconceivably complex maze of faults, fissures, joints, fracture-zones, and erratic areas of permeable rocks" as pictured by Mr. Walker, really carried water, the operator's problem would be one of too much water, instead of not enough, and the present conflict could not arise. In Eldorado canyon all these fractures are dry, except the main dike-fracture and its two or three tributaries. I am seeking an adjustment of law to the needs of arid regions, not to localities where all the complex rock-fractures are filled with water.

In view of these facts the question arises, how can a man who invests in the development of his mine and in the building upon it of a mill, basing his operations upon a water-supply and grant of the nature and conditions of the sufferer in the case cited, be protected from ruinous trespass upon his water-supply by later comers to the district?

Several attorneys and judges of special information and experience in water law and decisions in Colorado, Utah, Nevada, and California have stated to me, in effect, that conditions as herein recited set up a water-course and ownership governed by the well-known laws pertaining to surface streams, and that the miner who first develops, uses, and under the laws, files upon and is granted his needed portion of such water, and continues it in beneficial use, stands, in ownership, in the same legal and community relationship to that water as does the farmer to his rightly appropriated and granted water taken from a surface stream. This view will, I believe, commend itself generally to mining men as the most equitable, rational, and simple solution of the problem.

We will admit that care must be exercised by the trial judge to learn whether the ground formation and topography of the section in dispute induce or permit percolation, in the proper meaning of that term; or if the contained water can only move along fractures of the impermeable rock in the manner of the following of depressions upon the surface by streams and their tributaries. This determination is not as difficult as Mr. Walker would have us believe, if the trial judge, after going as far as he can with the testimony and exhibits in the case, will apply "the simple plain common-sense" so ably advocated by Mr. Walker, and make a leisurely personal inspection of the section involved in the suit; taking with him, at the cost of the contestants, his own advisory engineer, if he wishes to do so.

These water cases are well worthy of such personal study by the Court, and during such action the judge may employ various means of satisfying himself as to the questions at issue, and the truth of the testimony presented. For instance: at the close of the trial of the suit cited in this discussion, Judge Horsey, the trial judge in the case, agreed to visit Eldorado canyon and to study its water conditions before rendering his decision. After this, and some months before decision in the case was rendered, the plaintiff succeeded in getting a few gallons of fluorescene, and urged the judge to put this strong coloring, though perfectly harmless, agent in Mr. Walker's water-shaft, and see if the fluorescene color did not presently show in the water-channel openings farther down Eldorado canyon, including the mine-workings of the plaintiff; the latter agreeing to abide by the result of the test. Mr. Walker, through his attorney, refused to consent to this test and Judge Horsey did not visit Eldorado canyon; but the serious results depending upon his decision warranted the proposed effort by him to arrive at the truth, and it may be that Nevada laws, with some modification, would be sufficiently protective if usages sanctioned such aids to the conclusions of the judges.

If necessary, readjustment of court procedure should be made to meet the demands of equity in such cases, and personal inspection and such simple and conclusive evidence as the proposed fluorescene test would disclose should come within the scope of the Coort's study of the case, not to be regarded as prejudicial to either party to the suit, but as a high endeavor to arrive at justice.

G. A. DUNCAN.

Hollywood, California, February 5.

Molybdenum-Steel

The Editor:

Sir—We notice on page 145 of your issue of February 1 an article regarding tungsten and molybdenum in 1918, in which you say with reference to molybdenum steel: "This material was made by the United Alloys Steel Co., at Canton, Ohio, a concern owned and controlled by Garford & Timkin, which is closely associated with the Ford Motor Co."

We would like to call your attention to the fact that we are not owned or controlled by any company. We are at a loss to understand how you could have received this information, and would like to have you correct this mistake if possible.

UNITED ALLOY STEEL CORPORATION.

[The article mentioned was an abstract of a review published by the U. S. Geological Survey, as is stated clearly in the text.—EDITOR.]

GRAPHITE in Texas is found in the silicious pre-Cambrian Packsaddle schist in the central region of the State, between the towns of Llano and Burnet. In many places, the graphite schist has been penetrated and disrupted by granite and pegmatite intrusions. This schist, according to Paige, is a metamorphosed sedimentary, in which the carbonaceous materials have been re-crystalized to form graphite. The ore analyzes 6 to 10% graphite carbon, but the recovery of No. 1 flake is comparatively low because of the presence of amorphous graphite and very small flake in the ore; moreover, the gangue is hard, so that in crushing, a large amount of the flake is destroyed by being ground to finer sizes than are used as No. 1 flake. Three properties are now operating: the Southwestern Graphite Co., 9 miles west of Burnet, and the Burnet-Texas Graphite Co., 7 miles west, have developed open-pits; the Dixie Graphite Co., 4 miles north-east of Llano, is mining underground.

'KISH' consists of graphite, slag, iron oxide, fragments of iron, and other materials that accumulate about a pig-iron casting-ladle, or a Bessemer or open-hearth furnace. The graphite is formed during cooling by the crystallization of excess carbon from molten pig-iron. The kish obtained for refining has contained 8 to 10% of graphitic carbon in the form of a light, thin, and fluffy flake. The method of concentrating and refining kish is similar in many ways to the methods employed with natural graphite. The chief points of difference are that kish is not subjected to crushing, but is carefully screened and passed over magnetic separators. Kish, as a possible source of graphite, should not be overlooked. At the present time, however, it is questionable whether enough of this material can be obtained to interfere or compete seriously with the mining of natural flake graphite.

MAGNETIC SEPARATORS, somewhat similar to those used in the zinc-ore plants of Wisconsin, find a place in foundries for separating sand, coke, and iron. Cupola cinder should be crushed first to free the iron, the larger pieces being ready for re-melting, but the finer particles mixed with slag are passed through the separator. Ordinary floor scrapings and chippings are shoveled directly into the machine. Only direct current can be used.

BATTERIES, CHEMICALS, and kindred industries consume 25,000 tons of high-grade manganese annually, about 1/30 of that used in steel manufacture.

Rossiter W. Raymond: In Memoriam

Addresses by HENRY S. DRINKER and T. A. RICKARD

A memorial service in honor of Dr. Raymond was held on February 17 at New York on the occasion of the annual meeting of the American Institute of Mining Engineers. Dr. Raymond, who was Secretary Emeritus of the Institute, passed away suddenly and peacefully at his home in Brooklyn on the last day of 1918. As the official announcement said, "his passing marks an epoch in mining and metallurgical literature." He is survived by his wife and daughter, both of whom, together with relatives and friends, were present at the memorial service. Sidney J. Jennings, the president of the Institute, presided and opened the meeting with a short and appropriate reference to his great services to the profession of which he had been so long the recognized leader. Addresses were delivered by Dr. Henry S. Drinker, president of Lehigh University and one of the founders of the Institute, and by T. A. Rickard.

Address by HENRY S. DRINKER

A friend, whom we loved, has gone from among us. He was a man who by his genius dominated any assembly in which he stood. He was a teacher of teachers, a leader in all the many lines in which his energetic able personality led him. Of his eminence as an engineer, and of his ability, learning, and surpassing power in argument and presentation as an expert and as a lawyer, I will not speak—the tributes paid him by Mr. Rickard and Mr. Ingalls are so well studied that they should stand as the record of our friend's professional reputation. He was a wonderful man in the absolute absence of pretense in all that he said and did. If Raymond said it, you could rely it was so—and his mind was so encyclopedic—his learning so vast, that association with him was an education, intensive and broad.

It was my privilege to know him for a lifetime. We were associated with the founding of our Institute at Wilkes-Barre in May 1871. I was then a young fellow just stepping out into practice from college training under Rothwell in the Lehigh School of Mines, and Raymond and Rothwell, Coxe and Coryell, the men who organized the first coming together of the Institute, were men in the leadership of the profession, earnest, enthusiastic—early exponents of the profession they dignified and in fact introduced into this country.

From the beginning, Dr. Raymond's trained mind, inexhaustible energy, and wonderful aptitude of expression enhanced by his personal charm of manner, meant everything in the early setting and development of our Institute, which has grown into such a power in the engineering progress of our land.

We all pay tribute to Dr. Raymond's recognized ability and power of leadership—but there are today but few of us left who can personally turn and look back over a half century of actual association with him, a precious privilege tilled with memories of a man of whom it may well be said he was typical of "whatsoever things are true, whatsoever things are honest, whatsoever things are just, whatsoever things are pure, whatsoever things are lovely, whatsoever things are of good report," for he was of virtue—and we may well, in thinking of him, think of these things. Dr. Raymond was generous in his encouragement and aid to younger men. I can personally, with all my heart, echo the words of Ingalls in his recent splendid tribute to Raymond where he speaks of having in his early association with the 'Engineering and Mining Journal' looked on Raymond as "a guide, philosopher, and friend," trite words—but never more aptly or better or more truthfully applied.

Dr. Raymond's history has been recorded, and his engineering record has been and is being given by men far better fitted than I to do technical justice to so large a subject. It is for me as one of Raymond's many friends and admirers, one of his old friends, yet speaking from the standpoint of one younger than he and ever looking up to him as a leader and teacher, to pay tribute to his personal qualities that so endeared him to all who were privileged to know him. I owe a great personal debt to him for encouragement and aid to me as a young man, and I am moved to speak of it only as an instance of what was common to so many, for he was ever ready with counsel and cheering words of uplift and practical suggestion to the younger men who came under his observation, and in this he typified in person what our Institute has done as an Association. Founded as it was by men of large heart and human sympathy, such as Raymond and Eckley B. Coxe, the Institute, particularly in its younger days when our membership was small, and the friendships engendered among members were intimate and common to all, did, and indeed has ever continued to do, a great work in giving to young engineers who came into its fold opportunity for betterment by association with older and eminent men, with an opening for the publication and discussion of their engineering experiences, and theories. In the development of this practice, and as the able Editor for many years of our Transactions, Dr. Raymond ever showed his kindly sympathetic helpful nature, and the men, and their number is legion, whom he so aided, pay tribute today to his memory with loving gratitude and appreciation.

He was a wonderful man in his faculty of doing so well so many different things.

Did his record rest only on his professional work as Mining Engineer, Metallurgist, and Mining Lawyer, his friends might be content, but he was not content with this. Dr. Hillis has told us in his beautiful tribute to our friend, of Dr. Raymond's leadership in religious work in Plymouth Church, and how after Mr. Beecher's death Dr. Raymond was asked to retire from his engineering and editorial work and take up the pastorate of Plymouth Church (and how beautifully his reply reflects Raymond in his sincerity, good judgment, and never-failing humor). Dr. Raymond said, that the Providence of God, through his fathers, had lent him certain gifts, and by His providence guided him into an appointed path, and now that his life journey had been two-thirds fulfilled, he did not believe that the Lord was going to return to the beginning of that path, and reverse Himself, and he would, therefore, follow the way appointed to the end thereof.

And in Plymouth Church and the friendships he made and cherished there, we can see how, while laboring for the good of his fellow-men, and for their souls' good, he yet rested from his professional work, and took pleasure and solace in his touch with the church and sunday-school in which his heart delighted.

His addresses in the church of which many have been published, show a vivid and ever fresh and inspiring flood of wise helpful admonition and teaching—and his annual Christmas stories to the sunday-school children—fifty in all—ending with the one given on Sunday, December 29, only two days before his death on December 31, are a unique and beautiful illustration of the faculty he possessed of using his great gifts for the young. The fiftieth and last of his sunday-school addresses is as vivid in interest as its predecessors, among which those who read them can never forget the delicious talks chronicling the woodchuck who inhabited the Doctor's garden at Washington, Connecticut, and who is introduced with the words—"At our place in the country, where we spend five or six months of the year, we have among other fascinating attractions, a woodchuck of our own. That is nothing very remarkable. The whole region is full of woodchucks, and the difficulty is, *not* to have one. . . . Our garden is not far from his hole on the lawn, yet he never comes into the garden—for which reason we call him Maud, after the lady in Tennyson's poem. That lady did come into the garden; but then she was invited. If the gentleman had sung to her 'Don't come into the garden, Maud', or even if he had never mentioned the garden, I am sure she would have stayed away politely, just as our Maud does"—and then the address goes on with Raymond's never-ending sense of humor, deliciously emphasizing the wise words on current events and international politics that are voiced by the woodchuck in his conference with his host.

As Ingalls has well said, Dr. Raymond was one of the most remarkable cases of versatility that our country has ever seen—sailor, soldier, engineer, lawyer, orator, editor, novelist, story-teller, poet, Biblical critic, theologian, teacher, chess-player—he was superior in each capacity. What he did he always did well.

In his writings and poems his ever-present sense of humor shone out—and yet always there was an adumbration of wise reflection or suggestion—often a direct emphasis of advice on current questions of the day. In his wonderful story of 'The Man in the Moon', published over forty years ago, and doubtless reflecting some of his own personal experiences as an officer in the Civil War, Dr. Raymond recorded in his inimitable way what today may well be read as a prophetic utterance on the folly and the wickedness of the world war, in his account of the way that the opposing soldiers in the ranks come together on Christmas Day—and how a sentiment in favor of peace spread from the ranks to the peoples concerned until the generals in charge of the war, and the governing authorities of the countries concerned, awakened to the folly of the contention in which they had been striving and came together in a peaceful solution.

The story is an immortal one, and those of you who have not read it, have a great treat in store when you find it: 'The Man in the Moon—A War Story.'

Dr. Raymond's home-life was ideally beautiful and loving. On Christmas Day just passed this little poem—so characteristic of him, and so expressive of the love he bore Mrs. Raymond, accompanied his gift to her of a bond:

"'Tis strange, Oh! Lady fair and fond
Of me (as likewise I of you),
That there should be another bond
Between us two!

"You do not need this thing to make
Your life more full of hope and zest;
And yet sometimes you well might take
More interest!

"And there is nothing better serves
For weary hearts and hands to droop on,
And stimulate exhausted nerves
Than a good coupon."

Dr. Raymond suffered a great sorrow in the loss of the son of whom he was so justly proud, a loss that he bore with a man's fortitude, and in which he was upheld by the faith and hope that his life so strikingly exemplified. That he should have been first taken, leaving here the wife to whom he devoted so many years of loving care is a part of that great mystery into which we cannot look, but she at least has the comfort of the memory of her knight as one "without fear and without reproach," a Bayard among warriors, a Sir Percival among knights.

Dr. Raymond belonged to many societies and his abilities received due recognition in many honorary titles from societies, universities, and colleges. Among them it was the pleasure and honor of Lehigh University to confer on Dr. Raymond in June 1906 the first Doctorate of Laws ever granted by the Institution. When in 1905 I was asked by my fellow-alumni of Lehigh to lay aside my professional work and take on the responsibility of the Presidency of Lehigh University, it was to Dr. Raymond I went for advice on my course. He urged me to take it up and during the years since then I have reason to be grateful for his steady counsel and support, and his

ROSSITER W. RAYMOND

visits to speak to our student body have ever been welcome and uplifting.

He and our honored Dr. Drown and I had a close and common bond in the association we all three had with Lehigh, and I know of no words more fittingly applicable to Dr. Raymond than those he spoke of Dr. Drown at the time we laid the foundation of Drown Memorial Hall on our Lehigh campus. Dr. Raymond said: "How well I remember that sunny afternoon at Philadelphia, when in the sacred stillness of 'God's Acre', ringed with the noisy life of the metropolis, we buried in flowers and evergreens the body of our beloved friend, while, overhead, branches like these, waved their solemn murmurous benediction, and all around us white fingers pointed upward, mutely saying, 'He is not here; he is risen!'—and in our ears sounded that deep, dear message of the Spirit, chanting how the blessed dead rest from their labors, while their works do follow them!

"Methinks we do not always perceive the full meaning of that message. Too often we interpret it as saying, 'They depart; they cease from their labors; and the work they have done takes their place, as their only representation on earth, as all that is now left of their fruitful power'. Surely, this is not all. To rest is not to cease; to follow is not to remain behind forever separated from the leader, but rather to abide with the leader, though he be on the march.

"Our human experience is not without interpreting analogies. We know what it is to rest from our labors for a few happy summer weeks, laying upon other shoulders the daily burden and upon other hearts the daily anxiety, yet still in forest solitudes or up shining summits or by the boundless sea, carrying with us in a higher mood our work—weighing it more accurately, because we are not too tired; seeing it more clearly, because we are out of the dust of it; realizing its proportions and purpose, because distance gives us a perspective view; tasting its full sweetness, because its bitter cloudy precipitate has had time to settle; and renewing our high ambitions for it as we renew our strength for it. We rest from our labors, but our work goes with us, inseparably—only now we bear it, not as weight, but as wings.

"So, it seems to me, we are to think of our absent dead; they rest, but do not cease; they go on, and their work goes on with them. Indeed, the interpretation is yet deeper. To my ears, the Spirit says, 'Blessed are they who have labored so earnestly as to deserve the rest of a higher sphere of labor, and who have left behind them works which deserve to follow them, and to receive, even in that higher sphere, their continued remembrance and interest'."

How more fittingly can I close this tribute to the memory of our beloved friend than by these, his own words, spoken of a friend dear to him, and honored by us all—words that today we may cite as a requiem and fitting thought of Rossiter W. Raymond himself, loved by us, whose name will go down in the annals of our Institute as that of a superman of many parts to whom we owe much.

Address by T. A. RICKARD

"Brethren"—it was thus that he addressed us on an occasion that many of you will remember: in 1893, at Chicago, at the closing session of the International Engineering Congress. Other men, representing other nations, had spoken—some of them in poor English—before he was called upon to reply for the arts of mining and metallurgy in America. When he said "Brethren," the audience was startled into lively attention, which was maintained throughout his speech; for then, as always, he knew how to reach the minds of men, and their hearts too. I remember his saying that those present had taken part in numerous scientific discussions, that they had evolved new ideas and had discovered new principles, but that they had done something much better: they had "discovered one another." So saying he had put his finger on the distinctive feature of all such conventions. His mode of salutation also reminded those of us who were his personal friends that he was an evangelist as well as an engineer, and that he could instruct a bible-class in Job or St. Paul with the same power of exposition as he could deliver a lay sermon on mining and metallurgy. Indeed, Rossiter Raymond was a deeply religious man, and no sympathetic understanding of his extraordinarily versatile character is possible without appreciating this fact. He was not only a prominent member of Plymouth Church, Brooklyn, he was superintendent of the sunday-school for 25 years, he led in prayer-meeting and in bible-class, he interpreted the Old Testament during the period when the so-called higher criticism was undermining the faith of the churches, and he aided Henry Ward Beecher in steering his congregation through the storm of biblical exegesis that crossed the Atlantic forty years ago. The eminence that he attained as a religious teacher is measurable by the fact that when Beecher died the trustees asked him "to give up his work as editor, lawyer, and mining engineer, and take the pastorate of Plymouth Church," as recorded by the Rev. Dr. Dwight Hillis. He declined the honor, thinking it better "to give his life and strength to the vocation of an interpreter, chronicler, guide, and assistant to engineers, rather than to that of a creative and constructive leader." I quote the words he himself used at the dinner celebrating his 70th birthday.

Not many in the mining profession knew this phase of his character, although during his journeys through the West he would occasionally take the pulpit in some mining community and surprise a congregation that knew him only as the most distinguished of the experts engaged during the previous week in an important apex litigation. I have spoken of the part he played in the history of Plymouth Church, but his deeply religious nature was never so brought home to me as when his son Alfred died in 1901. He was a son of whom any father might feel proud; gifted and amiable, and on the threshold of a brilliant career. When he died Dr. Raymond proved, if it were necessary, the sincerity of his religious convictions, for his glad way of speaking of his departed son showed his confidence in a future reunion. I never saw a more convincing expression of the belief in immortality than in the attitude of Alfred Raymond's father and mother. It were improper for me therefore on this occasion to speak of the passing of our honored friend in a melancholy strain. I shall speak of his life and career as an inspiring memory to be treasured as a heritage of our profession; and in doing so, I shall abstain from flattery. To extol the honored dead with honeyed words is an impertinence. Rossiter Raymond's career was so rich in performance as to require none of the insincerities of conventional biography.

To the profession. Dr. Raymond's work as Secretary of the American Institute of Mining Engineers was the outstanding feature of his supremely useful life. When the Institute was founded, in 1871, he was elected vice-president, with the understanding that he would perform the duties of president, which David Thomas, by reason of his age, could not discharge. Thus from the beginning Raymond was the real president, and, on the resignation of Thomas, a few months later, he became president, in name as well as in fact; thereafter to be elected again and again, until an amendment to the rules, proposed by himself, provided that no president could serve more than two years. Soon afterward, in 1884, he became Secretary, a post that he held for 28 years—until his retirement from active service in 1912. He was Secretary Emeritus until the end.

The duties of the Secretary included the editing of the Transactions. For this he was well prepared. He had been the writer of successive volumes of the 'Mining Statistics West of the Rocky Mountains'; he had been editor of the 'American Journal of Mining' for one year, in 1867, and for the seven following years the editor of its successor, the 'Engineering and Mining Journal', of which he continued to be associate editor with Richard P. Rothwell until they had a friendly disagreement over the 'silver question' in 1893, after which he withdrew from editorial responsibility, becoming a 'special contributor', in which capacity he assisted the editors that succeeded Rothwell. Thus he played a notable part in the development of technical journalism in this country, but I regard his share in the early editing of the 'Journal' as important chiefly because it was a training for his life-work, that of Secretary of the Institute. It is noteworthy that as the owner of the 'Journal' in its early days he found the work of writing and editing far more to his taste than the management, for in financial affairs he was too kindly to be a shrewd business-man.

As Secretary of the Institute he performed divers duties; he invited written contributions and revised them before publication; he organized the meetings; he was the administrator. In course of time his ebullient personality so dominated the Institute that he was allowed a free hand to do as he thought fit. Presidents came and went; although nominally Secretary, he exercised complete control. The personnel of the board of management, or 'council', of the Institute changed from year to year, but Dr. Raymond managed its affairs, practically without let or hindrance. The Institute became identified with him. For a period longer than a generation he was the mainspring of the activities of the Institute, its presiding genius, its chief spokesman. Those who participated in the meetings of ten or twenty years ago will retain a vivid impression of the way in which Dr. Raymond stamped his individuality on the organization. Courteous and friendly to all, resourceful and tactful in steering the discussions, witty and eloquent whenever he rose to his feet, he was the managing director of the proceedings; he gave point and distinction to them; he infused them with his keen enthusiasm; he lighted them with the brilliance of his mind. His versatility was unlimited. All knowledge was his patrimony and nothing human was alien to his understanding. Whatever the subject of a paper, he could add something to it; nay more, on many occasions when some new phase of geology or engineering was presented for discussion, he would rise to supplement the speaker's remarks and show himself so well informed on the subject as to eclipse the specialist. He did this not unkindly, but out of superabundance of knowledge and sheer exuberance of spirit. On the other hand, no member engaged in preparing a paper for the Transactions failed to obtain his whole-hearted assistance in collecting the necessary data or in hunting for the needed references. When the member's manuscript arrived, the Doctor went through it with painstaking care. Before the use of the typewriting machine came into vogue, and even after, he would send letters in long-hand of as much as ten pages, explaining or suggesting improvements in the text. As a beneficiary of his conscientious industry, I can testify to the instruction in the art of writing that he gave to those who contributed to the Transactions. He was a delightful helper and a stimulating teacher. If any criticism is to be made, I venture to suggest that he over-edited; that is to say, the writings of the inexperienced were so much revised as to be practically re-written by him. He would take the half-baked production of a semi-literate engineer and subject it to the warmth of his intellectual combustion until it emerged a wholesome biscuit. I recall a valuable metallurgical paper, written by a professor now recognized as an authority, that was so full of German idioms that Dr. Raymond had to re-write it. Shortly before the Colorado meeting of 1896 I persuaded a Cornish mining engineer to contribute a paper on the lode-structure of Cripple Creek. He was a keen observer, but a poor writer; when the paper arrived it was quite unsuitable for publication. Dr. Raymond showed it to me and said, "What am I to do with this?" I replied, "Don't accept it." "No," said he, "that would not be fair; we asked him to write it." "Yes," I said, "but I am responsible for asking him; let me lick it into shape." "No," he insisted, "that is my job. I'll see what I can do with it." He did, and he did it so thoroughly that my Cousin Jack friend obtained credit for an informing and well-written contribution to the Transactions. The result of such revision was to lessen the value of the paper as scientific evidence. The authenticity of the testimony, it seems to me, suffered by being given through the mouth of a skilled advocate. On the other hand, this overplus of editorial labor gave the Transactions a level of style that no other technical society could claim either then or since. All technical writing in the English language has felt, and long will continue to feel, the inspiration to excellence that he gave while editor of the reference library that we call the Transactions of the American Institute of Mining Engineers.

He left an enduring mark on the jurisprudence of mining. As a keen observer and a clear expositor, he achieved distinction when he became an expert witness in the litigation arising from attempts to apply the law of the apex, a subject on which he wrote a series of essays that exercised a strong influence on the interpretation given by the highest courts to that Congressional statute. In the first big case in which he took part, the famous Eureka-Richmond lawsuit, he gave the term 'lode' a definition that not only swayed the decision in that controversy, but influenced all later mining litigation. On one occasion he was invited to address the United States Supreme Court on a point of mining law, and his exposition is said to have been accepted by the Court in its subsequent opinion. At that time he was not qualified as a lawyer, but in 1898 he was admitted to practise in both the State and the Federal courts. Five years later he was appointed lecturer on mining law at Columbia University.

As an expert witness, he was, as he said of Clarence King, approvingly, "an honest partisan." He used the gift of exposition with great effect when addressing the jury, under cover of giving evidence. I recall the explanation of the formation of mineral veins with which he began his testimony in the Montana-St. Louis case. Fortunate was the jury that had the opportunity of listening to such a fascinating lecturer. He was not only an able witness in chief and extremely dexterous in circumventing cross-examination, but he was a great general. He was quick to recognize the important features of a case and skilful in marshaling his forces to the discomfiture of the enemy. In forensic duels he displayed characteristic wit and versatility. This legal practice was a source of honor and profit to him, but I venture to say that he helped geology more in other ways.

In 1868, when only 28 years of age, he was appointed U. S. Commissioner of Mining Statistics, and in that capacity he visited the mining districts of the West, which was then at the beginning of an era of widespread exploration. He was quick to appreciate the economic value of geology and to utilize the opportunities for study afforded by his official travels. In 1870 he was appointed lecturer on economic geology at Lafayette College, which appointment he held for twelve years.

When he became Secretary of the Institute he transferred his keen interest in economic geology to the Transactions. As Secretary he persuaded the engineers to record observations made underground and at the same time he induced the officers of the Geological Survey to present their scientific inductions to the Transactions in a form that rendered them attractive to the mining profession. Thus he brought the official geologist into touch with the mine-manager and consulting engineer, greatly to the advantage of all. He also did much to diminish the self-sufficiency of the Survey and to lessen the shyness of the so-called practical man. By his understanding of geology, his knowledge of Western mining conditions, and the zest with which he pursued the application of geology to mining, he aided greatly in exciting intelligent interest in the genesis of ore deposits. The Posepny volume proves that; so does the volume dedicated to the memory of his friend Emmons. In 1893 he translated Posepny's treatise from the German into his own vigorous English, and organized a discussion that enhanced the value of the original paper. By means of another treatise, by Van Hise, presented to the Institute seven years later, in 1900, he gave a fresh impetus to the study of ore deposits, the general result being to make the mining geologists of this country the leaders in a branch of study in which European scientists had theretofore held pre-eminence.

On his skill as a writer it is pleasant to dwell. He wrote out of the fullness of a rich mind, an alert imagination, and an abundant vocabulary, aided by the knowledge of several modern languages. He knew not only how to select *le mot juste*, but also how to weave words into ingenious phrases and to construct balanced sentences, following each other in logical order within well proportioned paragraphs. He liked to number his paragraphs, in order to emphasize points at issue. He wrote with pen or pencil, usually the former, because it is more resilient and therefore less fatiguing to the fingers. He did not like to dictate anything except ordinary correspondence, but he could dictate a long article or legal testimony, punctuation included, with remarkable clearness and continuity. He wrote easily, with all the joy of the practised hand and the disciplined brain. He twitted one of his contributors with having "an inveterate fluent profuseness of speech" and the happy victim protested that the phrase exactly fitted *him*, not the lesser writer. He was fluent and profuse, but not to redundance or verbosity; on the contrary, his style was marked by force and consecutiveness, and, not infrequently, by those "saber thrusts of Saxon speech" that are the delight of the critical.

His literary ability was partly inherited from his father, Robert Raikes Raymond, who was editor successively of the 'Free Democrat' and the 'Evening Chronicle', at Syracuse, New York, from 1852 to 1854, and later Professor of English in the Brooklyn Polytechnic Institute and Principal of the Boston School of Oratory. It is also a safe surmise that Rossiter Raymond owed much of his fine feeling for the language of Shakespeare to his daily draughts from that well of English undefiled, the King James version of the Bible. There is no better schooling in our language than familiarity with The Book. A third aid to the cultivation of a good prose style was his frequent exercise in versification. The expression of simple ideas in verse by means of short words is excellent training for the effective construction of logical sentences in prose; moreover, the sense of rythm incites assonance. On his return from life at the German universities, he brought with him many old folk-songs and student-songs, some of which he adapted to sunday-school use. Thousands of children sang his hymns with delight because he knew how to present pretty thoughts in simple guise. That he could write serious poetry we know; for example, the lines to the Grand Canyon engraved on the silver tray that formed part of the gift presented to him on his 70th birthday. He wrote merry rhymes for our Institute meetings and for other occasions of a similar kind, making good-natured fun for himself and his friends. This playing with words in rhyme and rhythm gave him facility of expression in the more serious business of prose, and also in public speaking.

He was a delightful speaker. Our profession has never had a more eloquent spokesman. He seemed as little at a loss for ideas as for words; his enunciation was clear, he had a resonant voice, and his gestures were natural. Owing to his retentive memory and easy delivery, it was difficult to distinguish a speech that he had written from one that was extempore.

At any gathering he was individual—a distinguished figure. The wearing of a black silk cap and an old-fashioned way of trimming his beard gave him a striking appearance. Clear eyes wide apart, an aquiline nose, and a square chin indicated imagination, perception, and determination. His military training had taught him to stand upright. His pose was that of a captain of men. When he made a humorous hit he would tilt his head and smile, as if eager to share the fun with his audience. He never touched anything without giving it a human interest. He found

"Tongues in trees, books in the running brooks,
Sermons in stones, and good in everything."

Rossiter Raymond exercised an immense influence in his day and generation—nay more, two generations felt the force of his personality. How he stimulated his religius co-workers has been recorded by the successors of Henry Ward Beecher. Both Lyman Abbott and Dwight Hillis have testified to the courage that he imparted to them during the troublous times of Plymouth Church. To the geologists who broke the trail for the scientific investigations of a later day he was a guide, philosopher, and friend. Such men as Clarence King, James D. Hague, and S. F. Emmons have recorded their gratitude for his support and advice. Among his engineering contemporaries were scores to whom he was an ever-ready source of information, a wise counselor, a cheery friend; for them he did many unselfish and kindly things. To those of us who were young when he was at his prime he was the very embodiment of scientific attainments. We looked up to him as the exemplar of effective writing and polished speaking, the pattern of engineering culture, the leader in everything that concerned the welfare of our profession. As Secretary of the Institute we found him a lovable man, full of natural kindness and that helpfulness, without condescension, which the young appreciate so keenly when shown by a senior whom they admire. We—for I was one of them—found him an inspiring leader and a loyal friend. Loyalty—yes, that was one of his qualities. It got him into trouble more than once, for in friendship, as in apex litigation, he was unmistakably partisan. He stuck to his friends through thick and thin; he gave them the benefit of the doubt if they did wrong; he championed them when they were set upon. Lucky was the man on whose side he fought.

He was pre-eminently a publicist and an educator; he declined the pastorate of Plymouth Church to become the pastor of a bigger congregation; he resigned his professorship at Lafayette to be a teacher in a bigger school; he was the dean of the mining profession in the United States. For fifty years the force of his personality was felt among the men that were organizing and directing the mining industry of a continent; for fifty years he did not fail to write a Christmas story for the children of his sunday-school; he was a friend to the old and to the young. Age could not wither him nor custom stale his infinite variety. He influenced those that today are influencing others; his spirit still moves among men. Blessed be his memory!

CUPELS with cement bottoms were found by T. G. Martyn to be satisfactory. The mold is first filled with cement, pressed moderately, then filled up with bone-ash, and pressed as hard as possible. In experiments with crucibles those of coarse texture showed more endurance when fired. When fine-grained and hard-burned they tend to fissure in use. Necessity for repeated re-use has shown the average life to be about 18 fusions per crucible. The life is shortened by basic charges (borax, etc.) or by bedding in glowing fuel. A borax substitute, 'fluxite', is practically pulverized fluorspar, of which 10% less should be used. Martyn believes that in the fusion this forms fluo-silicate, rendering the charge more basic, the reaction being, $2CaF_2 + SiO_2 = SiF_4 + 2CaO$. The SiF_4 forms fluo-silicate. When silver occurs in more than a trace in litharge it is never evenly distributed. For assays of low-grade material such as residues and tailing, the lead button aimed at should be 50 or 60 gm.; 20 gm. is dangerously low. The nitric acid used in parting can be economized by re-distilling. The first run of weak acid might be reserved for cleaning out the still subsequently. Soda ash containing carbonaceous matter is frequently supplied to assay laboratories. Dissolving, filtering, and re-calcining may be necessary for some purposes. The necessary heat for use in parting can be obtained most economically by having an extra muffle-door, which, when heated, can be propped up suitably and made to serve as a hot-plate on which to place an aluminum frying pan carrying the parting capsules.

A SHORTAGE of silver exists at Hongkong, according to a recent Consular Report. There is estimated to be $15,500,000 less metal at present than at the beginning of 1919, despite the prohibition of exports. About $2,000,000 has been smuggled out of the colony.

Grinding and Sizing Diagrams

By ALFRED T. FRY

In making tests of the grinding efficiency of a given machine under varied conditions, the following method of constructing an efficiency curve will be found useful in comparing and using the results obtained.

Suppose, for instance, that during each run we have sampled the feed and product for sizing; that the rate of feed and power consumption have also been determined, together with other data that may be considered important. When the effect of tonnage alteration is being studied, if several tests have been made under identical conditions, except as regards rate of feed, from which the results, shown in the accompanying table, were obtained, then, by drawing a simple graph, in which ordinates represent relative efficiency, and abscissæ represent tonnage, several points may be decided. Obviously not less than three tests should be plotted. See diagram A.

Test	Feed per day, tons	Relative efficiency
1	10	36
2	30	79
3	50	106
4	70	115

Then, by drawing a simple graph, in which ordinates represent relative efficiency, and abscissæ represent tonnage, several points may be decided. Obviously not less than three tests should be plotted.

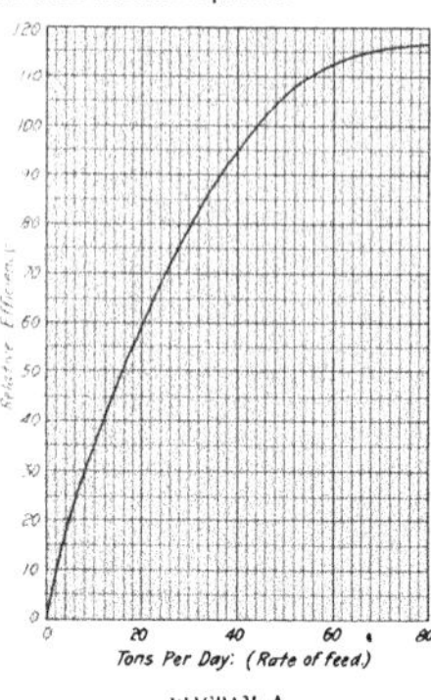

DIAGRAM A

1. If the points lie on a fair curve, it may be inferred that the results include very slight interference, such as: (*a*) error in rate of feed; (*b*) error in sampling; (*c*) error in sizing; and (*d*) error in calculation. Freak results may be recognized and omitted.

2. If the upper end of the curve has attained almost a horizontal direction, it is obviously unnecessary to make further tests at the higher rates of feed. This saves time and expense, besides giving a certainty that the possibilities of the variations observed have been exhausted.

3. The curve shows the efficiency to be expected from any rate of feed of the same sample under the same other conditions in the same machine.

4. The curves resulting from sets of tests (determining the effects of changes such as rate of feed, degree of dilution, speed of machine, change of screens if used, size of feed, size of product) should be plotted together,

ELMORE EXPERIMENTAL SIZING APPARATUS

or to the same scale, on tracing-cloth, so that they may be conveniently compared.

It may be well to remark that curves from a machine of a given size should not be used to predict the performance of other sizes of the same type of machine. Such curves can only suggest the best lines of making tests. for instances are known where the difference in performance of machine bears no apparent relation to the size of the machines. Thus a small single stamp might be more efficient than a large one, owing to the probability of more square inches of screen per pound of ore being presented than in a larger machine. Also, a small tube-mill might be less efficient than one of medium size, owing to the lessened distance of pebble-drop as well as the decreased pressure between the pebble-surfaces resulting from a less height of pebble-load.

It may be of interest to say that I use the method of calculation of grinding efficiency, for which I, and possibly many other silent friends, have to thank H. Stadler. In view of the recent adverse criticism of his method and theories, it is a welcome development to find that in Mr. Stanley's reconciliation of the "warring laws of grinding," is a statement from which a set of sizes may be calculated in such close agreement with the 'grades' originally proposed by Mr. Stadler that these latter may be regarded as confirmed. Thus Mr. Stanley says (Journal of C. M. & M. Soc. of S. Africa, August 1914, page 27): "The work required to reduce a given weight of rock from one size to another is proportional to the log of the $\frac{\text{initial}}{\text{final}}$ diameter."

Taking Stadler's initial 1 in. diam. size, we wish to find such a set of sizes down to his lowest grade 0.00098 in., as will involve the expenditure of equal amounts of work to reduce a given weight of a homogeneous rock from any one size, or grade, to the next. The lowest size mentioned is well beyond the limits of any possible screens, and any error arising from imperfect determination of sizes beyond it will scarcely affect the problems we have to attack.

Taking 1 in. and 0.00098 in. as the limiting sizes in the 31 grades to be determined, the work done in crushing from each grade to the next will be 1/30 of that required to crush from 1 in. to 0.00098 inch.

$$\text{Log } \frac{1}{0.00098} \text{ diam.} = \log \frac{\text{initial}}{\text{final}} \text{ diam.}$$

$$\text{Log } 1020.408 = 3.00877386$$

$$\frac{3.00877386}{30} = 0.100292462 = \text{increment for each grade.}$$

Commencing with 1-in. grade and crushing to the next grade X in., the work is represented by:

$$\text{Log. } \frac{1}{X} = 0.100292462$$

$$\text{Log } 1 - \log X = 0.100292462$$

$$\text{Therefore } \log X = 0 - 0.100292462$$

$$= \bar{1}.899707538$$

Therefore $X = 0.7937$ in. which is Stadler's second grade. Similarly the other sizes may be found. Sizes above 1 in. may be found in this way if they are required. Thus: 1.0 in., 1.2598 in., 1.5870 in., 1.9993 in., 2.5186 in., 3.1739 in., but the difficulty of handling and sampling quantities of such large sizes will in most cases preclude any use being made of these.

I have found the scale herewith a convenience in obtaining the E. U. corresponding to a size of any diameter. Its accuracy is sufficient for ordinary purposes. Its length is about 15 in. Each logarithmic interval is marked off into equal spaces representing 10 E. U. numbers, each being subdivided into 10 parts.

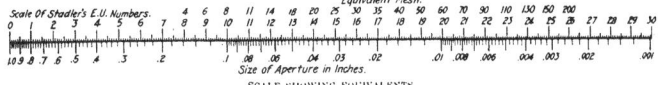

SCALE SHOWING EQUIVALENTS

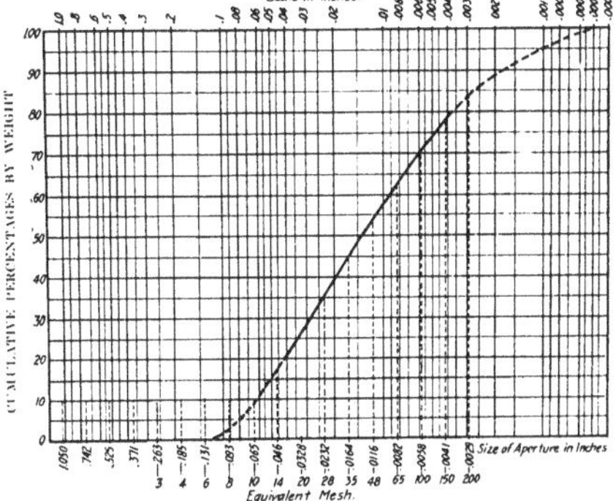

SCREEN ANALYSIS, RATIO 1:1.414

While the relative efficiency figures obtained in tests give a good summary of the grinding, I have often felt the need of a means of graphically emphasizing the change in sizes during a particular grinding operation, and had made several unsatisfactory attempts to devise a method. Then a friend tried to explain a cumulative-per cent diagram by A. O. Gates, but it didn't 'get over the footlights'. Then the W. S. Tyler Screen Co. kindly sent me their booklet describing two cumulative methods, the direct and the logarithmic, but partly through interruptions I did not quite appreciate them, though the cumulative percentage idea took firm root. Finally I made a diagram in this way: A horizontal base-line is divided into 30 equal parts, representing Stadler's grades 0 to 30. At the divisions the corresponding screen apertures are marked. Between these figures the even divisions 1.0, 0.9, 0.8, etc., are inserted. It is found that the resulting scale is logarithmic. Hence the easiest way to make the diagram is to copy a set of divisions from a slide-rule, the slider used upside down, and reduce them to a suitable interval. This is repeated along the base-line as required to get the three intervals. At the left end of the base-line erect a perpendicular divided into 100 parts to represent percentages; draw the horizontal percentage-lines across the diagram; erect perpendiculars from those points in the base-line which represent the apertures of the screens in use. Plot the cumulative percentages, obtained by sizing, on these lines, to plot the sizing curve. It will have been noticed that we have reconstructed the essential portion of the Tyler Screen Co.'s logarithmic diagram; but their diagram looks much more complicated by the inclusion of lines having reference only to their standard screens and by subdivisions whose utility is overshadowed by their confusing appearance. None the less the Tyler company deserves hearty thanks for the assistance they have offered, not only in the diagrams referred to, but in the set standard screens whose apertures are marked on them. Their reminder to "Indicate the screen crushed through and also the first retaining screen" is a good one. As long as the apertures of the screens are known, however, it does not matter whether there is any definite ratio between these apertures. The main thing is to choose the screens at suitable points in the diagram. As an instance that different sets of screens yield the same sizing curve on the same sample, when their apertures are known, I quote the following sizing tests and refer to the accompanying sizing diagram. The sample was Broken Hill ore crushed through rolls to pass a No. 7 mesh screen.

The apertures of the commercial screens had been determined by a microscope with micrometer eye-piece, but the 'I. M. M.' screens were made up and could not be so determined, so I had to assume their apertures to be as quoted.

ROLL-PRODUCT THROUGH 7-MESH

Sized on 'Commercial' Screen

Mesh	Aperture, in.	%	Cumulative, %
12	0.047	10.5	10.5
30	0.0220	19.9	30.4
60	0.01	22.2	58.7
90	0.0063	10.2	68.9
-90	.....	31.1	100.0

Sized on 'I. M. M.' Screens

Mesh	Aperture, in.	%	Cumulative, %
20	0.0250	33.2	33.2
40	0.0125	17.8	51.0
80	0.0063	20.3	71.3
150	0.0063	7.4	78.7
-150	.....	21.3	100.0

It will be observed from the diagrams that the assumed or nominal apertures of the 80 and 150-mesh 'I. M. M.' screens are not borne out by their behavior in this sizing. Variations such as this may be unavoidable in the manufacture of screens, or may have been due to some other accidental cause of which I am unaware. It would be interesting to have the result put on record of sizing a particular sample on, say, a dozen or two of new 100-mesh screens, to determine what concordance in results is to be expected. The test should conclude by re-testing the first one or two screens tried, on the same sample, to see whether the sample is altered appreciably by the repeated sizing. Three ways of ascertaining the apertures are usually available: (1) Measurement with a microscope micrometer, the average of a number of readings in both directions being taken. When a microscope is not at hand, samples cut from the rolls of screen in use can be posted to someone whose equipment is more complete. (2) By another use of the sizing curve, as follows: Get an ore-sample which has been sized on a known set of screens and draw its sizing curve. Size the sample again on the screens whose apertures are required and make the list of cumulative percentages. Where these

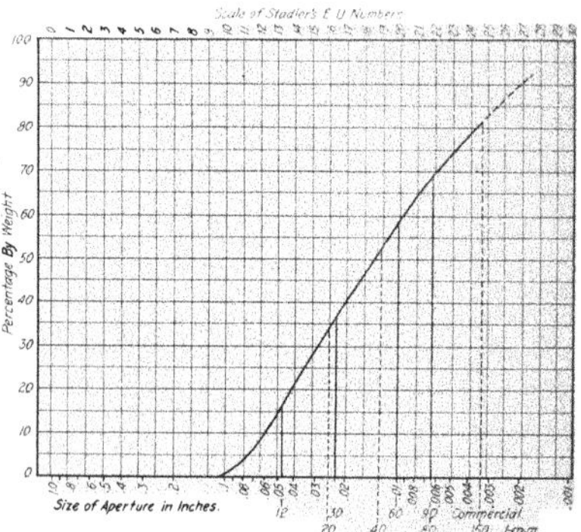

CUMULATIVE SIZING DIAGRAM

percentages cut the sizing curve, drop perpendiculars to the base-line to find the required or corresponding apertures. (3) Count the meshes both ways and gauge both wires. Referring to the standard gauge diameters, the average apertures may be calculated.

A third use of the sizing curve arose in a case where another operator on a check-sample of the product, and using a different set of screens, arrived at a different result in calculation. On drawing his sizing curve beside mine, it was apparent that a serious sampling error had occurred.

A fourth use of the sizing curve lies in cases where, in a mill, for example, it is desired to try some new make of screen without altering the degree of grinding in use. Square-mesh screens may have to be temporarily replaced by slot-wire, round or slot-punched screens. To find whether they are suitable, size the screen-feed, and draw its curve. Size the same sample on the old and new screens, and on marking the plus percentages on the sizing curve it can be seen readily whether the difference between them is likely to be of importance, with reference to the other known properties of the screen. When, however, a change in degree of grinding is contemplated, such as testing the effects on recovery of a finer screen, by making the curve of the screen-feed and marking the percentages retained by the old mill-screen and the proposed new screen, one may get an idea of the extra amount at first put back into the return to the grinders, but it must not be forgotten that there will probably be a partial cumulative effect in that circuit among the fine sizes which the new screen just rejects. This is because practically all grinding machines do less efficient work as the size of the feed decreases. Thus one may have the coarse sizes well ground while the fine sizes may be imperfectly reduced and come back again from the screens. With coarse screens this effect might not be easy to detect, but with fine screens it would be more noticeable.

Bolts and Spikes From Scrap

By LETSON BALLIET

During the War I was employed at one of the shipyards as an efficiency engineer. While so engaged, my mining experience proved of great benefit in several ways. Incidentally the adaption of a mining tool to ship-building work carried the development further, which I think might be profitably used at a mine.

One particular installation and its subsequent development is of interest. I had installed a Sullivan drill-sharpener with which to make bolts. The idea was not wholly new nor original with me, though I designed and made special dies and dollies for special shaped heads needed. Drift-pins were headed, countersunk heads of various sizes and the like were made in large numbers. Then we made ball stanchions, grab-iron ends, rivet dies, and numerous other things that required upsetting; in fact, the drill-sharpener became an upsetting machine of great possibilities.

Heading long rods quickly in three seconds dispensed with the necessity of threading two ends of a rod, and using two nuts. Upsetting the end of a rod to a ball, and then flattening it under the vertical hammer, and punching a hole in the flattened part, did away with drawing a rod out and welding it into an eye-bolt. In some cases this dispensed with expensive turnbuckles. All of these features will have more or less use in building of head-frames, the framework for mill buildings, and possibly in making one side of hanging-bolts, to avoid the upward pointing hook for safety. What appears to me to be of greatest value for a mine is the making of the track-spikes and track-bolts out of the scrap-pile.

Few mines can be found that do not have a lot of old bolts, hanging-rods, and scrap rod-iron lying around. This may be run through the drill-sharpener and made into spikes of any size. They make a better, stronger, and more perfectly formed spike than any that can be bought; they are all uniform because they are in effect a drop-forge spike, and all come from the same die; they can be made by the blacksmith helper or any common laborer because they do not require tempering. A heater boy, who heats rivets, can lay them with the tongs in the die, and throw the lever that operates the machine the machine does the rest. A perfect spike is made in about three seconds from the scrap now wasted. The machine can be so used when it is not engaged in sharpening drills, and it will make easily from 3000 to 4000 spikes in eight hours.

The question arises, why pay from $8 to $10 per 100

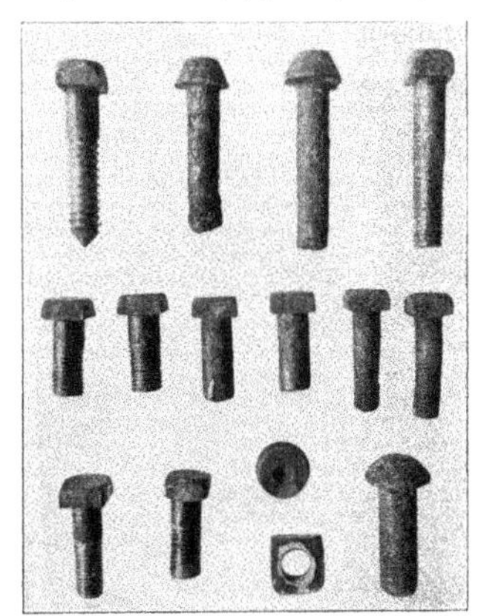

The above shows a lag-screw made from a burnt rivet from the scrap-pile, and a 7/8 by 5-in. bolt made from another rivet. In the centre are two 3/4 by 2-in. bolts made from two bent bolts with stripped threads. On the bottom line is the end of a headed drift-bolt which is 1 by 32 in., and 7/8-in. nut made from a punching from boiler-plate. The nut is partly or imperfectly finished on the outside to retain enough of its rounded corners to show what it originally was.

lb. for 300 or 400 spikes (depending on size) when a man or boy at 50 cents per hour can make them from the scrap-pile in an hour? Any old bolt 3 or 4 in. long will make a track-spike. More than this, the same machine with a change of die, will make all the track-bolts from the same scrap or will make a new bolt out of an old one. The neck and head of every bolt is perfect in size and shape. Naturally they come from the machine without threads, but the threading die can be chucked in a small lathe or drill-press, and a head-holding tool made for the lathe or press. Thus a track-bolt or any other bolt that is costing from $7 to $15 per 100 lb. (depending on size) can be made and threaded for $1 or $1.50. Even the nuts are hot forged from bits of scrap in three seconds time, and the hole punched. They must be tapped, but by using an extension chuck fastened in the lathe, or in a wood-boring machine fastened to a work bench, we tapped them at the rate of 720 per hour.

The Attitude of Employers

By P. B. McDONALD

The outstanding problem in industry seems more and more to be that of labor. Prominent capitalists are directing their thought to get at the fundamentals of the matter in a way that a few years ago would have seemed most extraordinary. The more far-seeing employers recognize that labor unrest such as now impends cannot be quashed by ignoring or throttling it. Many of them are sincerely anxious to adjust things fairly and are striving to compensate for the traditional dilatoriness of their class as regards labor problems by convincing their business associates that a change is necessary. When such a conservative engineer as W. R. Ingalls admits the seriousness of the situation and suggests that employers may be partly to blame, it is evident that the sentiment in the country's financial circles has altered considerably in a few months. Mr. Ingalls said, in his presidential address before the Mining & Metallurgical Society of America, "Probably, on the whole, there is more intelligence among the great corporations than there is among the labor-unions, and a better understanding of economic principles, but there are some labor-unions whose leadership is bright and some corporations whose management is stupid, while of both there are many that are only mediocre."

The same attitude of conciliation is noticeable in England. The master of Balliol College, Oxford, recently presided over a governmental committee that has published an interim report of the Committee on Adult Education, in which the statement is made that "the degradation of human beings to the position of 'mere hands' and the treatment of labor as a commodity to be bought and sold, has created a revolt in the minds of a large section of the community." This same idea has been enunciated by Mr. Gompers, who protests against the ruthlessness with which employers 'hire and fire' labor. The 'Athenaeum', formerly devoted to literary subjects, has turned over a good share of its pages to the discussion of problems of labor and reconstruction. It makes the suggestion that, while wages is the obvious bone of contention, it is not everything. Unrest among workmen, argues this famous London monthly, is due in part to a sneering and condescending attitude of employers based on the premise that capital can do as it pleases in its own factory; and so it can, continues the 'Athenaeum', so long as the factory is empty, but when men enter to work, a responsibility arises that is all the more serious when it is remembered that on such labor are men dependent for the living of themselves and families. As our Secretary of War has pointed out, industry exists for men, not men for industry.

Charles Eliot of Harvard has offered the explanation, in regard to labor troubles, that increases of wages brought by strikes and propaganda do not necessarily bring happiness to the worker, because "happiness is a point of view." Perhaps it can be stated in another way by saying that the habit of mind induced in employees by frequent strikes is fundamentally opposed to being satisfied no matter what monetary conditions are obtained. If, then, the important point is the comparative contentment of the employees, it is probably true that their point of view is dependent on how they are treated by their employers. That is, the latter have the power of inspiring class hatred by their attitude toward the men who work for them. Unfortunately, too many employers have done this. Disraeli portrayed such conditions in his novels of seventy-five years ago, and, although a Conservative, he advocated improving the workman's lot.

In correcting the attitude of employers, such that class hatred will be minimized and democratic practice more nearly prevail, the mistake should not be made of patronizing, or playing to, the grand-stand. Some employers, figuratively speaking, slap an employee on the back and call him brother in a way which they think is particularly comradely, but which, as a matter of fact, is peculiarly irritating. The Y. M. C. A. in France has been criticized for just such affectation and ignorance toward the soldiers.

On the other hand, it is remarkable what a hold and influence for good some emyloyers have over the men who choose to work for them. The employee is not slow in judging character; on the contrary, he is quick to recognize the qualities of a real leader in the boss. Unfortunately, broad-minded leaders are not plentiful. The quality is, perhaps, partly a natural gift, but, for the most part, it varies with the philosophy of life of the individual. A philosophy of life can be cultivated, but to be effective it must ring true. In a general way, it might be said that the men put in charge of important industries are picked too much for showy characteristics of mis-called efficiency or for a disposition to kow-tow before the directors or owners. Such qualities as tolerance, humaneness, and far-sightedness are often disregarded to make room for pushfulness, bossiness, and obviousness. The following extract from a recent number of 'Blackwood's Magazine' is a description of the showy type of business-man as seen by the veteran soldier, Sir C. E. Callwell: "The man of business procedure, when he is placed at the head of a Government department in time of war, is well known. He makes himself master of some gigantic building or some set of buildings. He then sets to work to people the premises with creatures of his own. He then becomes wrapped up in devising employment for the multitudinous personnel that has been got together. . . . While the big men at the top are wrestling with housing problems, the staff are engaged in writing minutes to each other—a process which, when indulged in by anyone else is called 'red tape', but which, when put in force by men of business is called 'push and go'."

The more one notices the signs of the times the more it appears that quick transitions in industry and sociology are near. Pessimists are inclined to compare these present times with the decline of the Roman empire. William James considered what he called the prevalent world-weariness to be analogous to the noisy period of the Sophists in Socrates' time, and he advocated pragmatism as a practical way out. Some optimistic thinkers predict such an awakening and broadening of life as occurred in the days of the Renaissance and of the Romantic movement, the former marked by a disposition to organize into guilds of workmen, the latter distinguished by idealistic schemes for individual freedom. Whatever course things take, few will deny that a menacing tension is in the air, and that in industry much appears to hinge on the attitude of the employers.

Silverado Flotation Concentrator

By W. L. ZEIGLER

The ore in the Silverado mine is minute stringers and grains of galena, gray copper, and pyrite disseminated through a heavy gangue of spathic iron with quartz, all the silver being associated with the galena and gray copper. Gravity or water concentration is not suitable for this ore, as it requires fine grinding to free the mineral particles and the gangue is of nearly the same specific gravity as that of the tetrahedrite.

The flotation mill was built at a cost of $7500 and will treat five tons of ore an hour, making the cost of erection about $62.50 per ton of daily capacity. The mill as a unit is the utmost in simplicity, both in construction and operation, and has no screens, elevators, or pumps.

It was found that grinding to about 40-mesh gave results as good as when all passed 100-mesh. The walls of the vein are barren quartzite, which is much harder than the vein material, so that the coarser particles going to the flotation machines are practically all quartzite.

The following results were compiled from an average:

Screen-test of flotation feed

	%
On 40 mesh	7
" 50 "	10
" 60 "	11
" 100 "	23
" 150 "	13
" 200 "	8
Through 200 "	28

	Feed	Concentrate	Tailing
Lead	2.8%	40.0%	0.1%
Silver	6.0 oz.	83.0 oz.	0.5%
Copper	0.35%	5.4%	Trace

The ratio of concentration is about 15 : 1.

The lead shows an extraction of 97%, the silver 92.2%, with practically all the copper.

The total power is supplied by a 75-hp. induction-motor, which draws 13.5 amperes at 2200 volts, equivalent to about 54 horse-power.

Consumption of water is very small, 75 to 80 gal. per minute being required to bring the pulp to the proper dilution. A small amount is added at the head of the ball-mill and diluted enough for classification at the discharge end.

The ball-mill is of the quick-discharge type using manganese-steel grates in the discharge end, and white-iron step-liners with chilled iron balls. The feed to the mill is delivered by a conveyor, after being crushed to [illegible] in., about 50% of the discharge being returned by the drag-classifier.

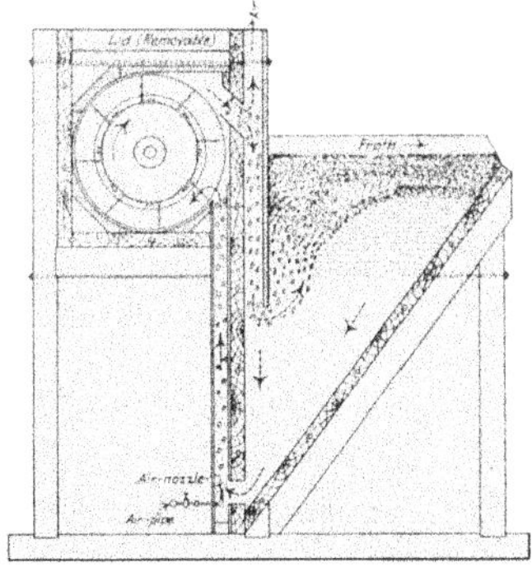

SECTION OF ZEIGLER FLOTATION MACHINE

Two Zeigler flotation machines were installed, but only one is operated at a time, as one handles the feed perfectly. They will treat the sand at 40-mesh with very little wear or trouble with clogging. Only a small amount of compressed air at five pounds pressure is required for the air-lifts, which spray the pulp and air into the atomizing-chamber. After leaving this chamber the greater part of the air passes out the openings at the top, the pulp being so thoroughly aerated that it carries enough air into the frothing-compartment to make a froth that strongly resembles that made by a pneumatic cell.

The agitator is light in weight, yet is made extremely rigid by the angle-iron blades. Angular vanes are bolted to the blades between the cells, which prevent longitudinal flow in the compartment and keep the pulp in the form of a spray. Special water-drip collars, requiring no packing, are used at both ends of the shaft, which prevent leakage. The total power required by the machine is four to five horse-power.

The concentrate flows into tanks where it is drained, and, as the principal part is galena, it settles readily.

A Mining Camp Club

*The accompanying drawings and photograph illustrate the club house built for the employees of the Tennessee Copper Co. at Copperhill in 1909. The building is a wooden structure with shingle exterior; it consists of two stories and basement and has a wide verandah around two sides. On the main floor to the right of the entrance is the billiard-room. To the left is the main hall, which is used for dances and receptions, and at other times as a music and lounging room. The library opens off the main room, thence a pantry, kitchen, etc. The library serves as dining-room when occasion requires.

On the second floor are four bedrooms for the use of directors and other visiting officials.

On the ground-floor are bowling-alleys, swimming-pool, showers, gymnasium, handball court, lockers, and heating plant. Outside of the building the club exercises control over two tennis-courts and trap-shooting grounds.

*From the 'Granby News'.

The organization, which is called the Cowanee Club, started in 1903 from very modest beginnings. For quarters it had a room in the basement of the office-building. Here were pool and billiard tables and an assortment of periodicals. Club dances were given in the dining-room of the company mess-house. All expenses were borne by the club, except heat and light, which the company donated. The need for proper and more commodious quarters was felt and a movement was started to achieve this end. The 40 members of the club subscribed $2000, and with this amount in hand the company was approached for assistance. The response surpassed expectations, making possible a building that cost $15,000.

The club has a State charter and its administration is altogether in the hands of the members. It is not run as a company affair, and while most of the members are on the technical or clerical staff, employment by the company is not a requirement for membership. The ladies of the members' households are accorded the same rights as the men, and the club is open to them at all times, thus taking into account the equal if not greater need of women for recreation and diversion under conditions of mining-camp life. The club house is on the flat below the acid works.

With its new home, the club soon came to be the social centre of the camp. Its design and equipment, proved so successful that the prevailing comment was "How did we ever get along without it?"

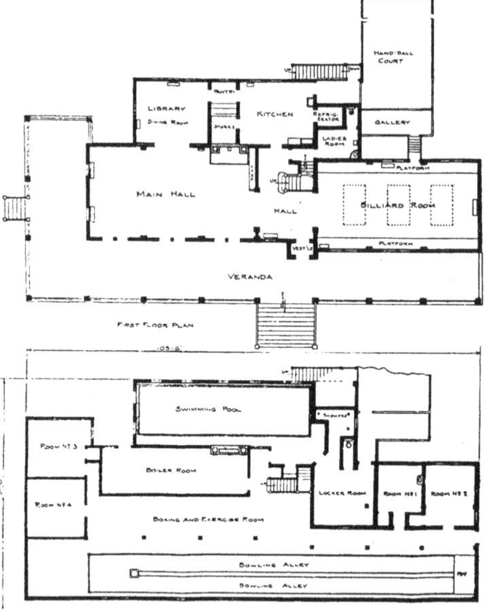

PLAN OF FIRST FLOOR AND BASEMENT OF THE COWANEE CLUB, COPPERHILL.

SUB-ATOMIC studies by Kotaro Hondo show that in the molecules of a solid there are rectilinear vibrations about a mean position, and small dependent rotational vibrations about central nuclei. At fusion, the rotational vibrations become complete revolutions. The latent heat of fusion is shown to consist of the energy of rotation gained during fusion. By experiment he proved that for the elements, except where specific heat is abnormal or a transformation takes place during fusion, the latent heat of fusion consists of the energy of rotation gained by the molecules during fusion. Amorphous substances have little or no latent heat of fusion; they are very viscous liquids and already have the rotational energy characteristic of liquids.

HAVANA, CUBA

Mining Possibilities of the Republic.

In 'The Cuba Review' for November 1918, the mining industry of Cuba is described by Edward I. Montoulieu. To the layman, even to engineers, beyond copper and iron production, the industry is considered unimportant. This idea is incorrect. The Spaniards took great interest in mining from the earliest times. Gold, copper, iron, asphalt, manganese, and chrome was the order in which the minerals were extracted tront buccaneering days until the present.

MAP OF CUBA SHOWING WHERE THE VARIOUS MINERALS ARE MINED.

Mr. Montoulieu then briefly covers the various deposits and properties operating, the accompanying map showing their situation.

CRIPPLE CREEK, COLORADO

Dividends and General Development.—The Vindicator in 1918.—The Cresson Discovers More Rich Ore.

Dividends to the amount of $167,000 were paid on the 10th to shareholders of the Cresson and the Golden Cycle. The Cresson was at the usual monthly rate of 10 cents per share, $122,000, and the Golden Cycle at 3 cents, $45,000.

The Modoc is now shipping 150 tons per week from two orebodies under development on the 1200-ft. level. The No. 1532 or Last Dollar-Modoc ore-shoot is 275 ft. long, and the stope has been carried up 100 ft. so far with good indications. The new vein has been driven on for 130 ft. in length, with the value holding in the north breast. The ore averages $30 per ton.

Rich float has been found in the Petrel, a Squaw mountain property; and the lessee, Gus Nelson, claims to have found its source, a vein in place in the granitic country rock. Samples shown here were plastered with rusty gold. The property is owned by the Petrel G. M. Company.

E. B. Mack is saving ore at the Engineer, a Mineral hill property. Mack is driving on the vein in an adit, and ore in the bins will ship at about 1 oz. per ton. This is the only property on Mineral hill that is active at present.

Darwin T. Mason, lessee of the El Paso Consolidated, has opened a new shoo[illegible] the Tillery vein between the second and fourth levels o[illegible] No. 1 shaft, on the south end of this Beacon Hill estate. The pay-streak, 3 ft. wide, will ship close to 2 oz. per ton for screenings and 1 oz. for coarse rock.

The Backhoff Leasing Co., operating the properties of the Midget Bonanza company on the western slope of Gold hill, has resumed production after a shut-down lasting from December 1917. Ten sets of sub-lessees are at work.

The annual report of the Vindicator Consolidated Gold Mining Co. was presented at the annual meeting last week at Denver, by George A. Stahl, the general manager. The output during 1918 was 230,304 tons of crude ore, from which was shipped to the mill or smelter 21,392 tons of ore valued at $1,166,295 gross. Lessees shipped 24,320 tons worth $463,513, from which the company received $151,285 in royalties. The flotation plant treated 222,626 tons averaging $2.13 per ton. Of this, 176,623 tons of $1.42 ore was rejected by screening and 46,003 tons assaying $4.18 was sent to the flotation plant. There was shipped front the flotation plant 6029 tons of concentrate valued at $206,254 gross, and after marketing $171,037 net. After deduction of all operating costs the net profit from this source was $27,955. The yearly financial statement shows a gross income of $1,175,471, of which $1,167,181 was proceeds of ore sales on company account and royalties. Ore-reserves are estimated at $870,129. The company's property is valued at $1,269,613; mill, $181,286; mine equipment, $287,658; and ferro-alloy plant and equipment at Denver, $68,696. Current assets are given as $574,927, including $279,316 cash, and $50,000 U. S. certificates. Dividends paid during 1918 amounted to $60,000, making a total of $3,772,500.

Another rich discovery is officially reported by the Cresson company. This was made at the 10th level of the main shaft, where a new orebody has been opened, with ore assaying 10 oz. per ton.

Fifty-dollar ore has been exposed in a new vein opened in the Yellow Bird, a Gold hill property, by Martin Colgin, the lessee. The shaft is down but 25 ft., and will be equipped with an electric hoist.

The discovery made by J. L. Wilson in the Anaconda tunnel of the Mary McKinney company on the southern slope of Gold hill persists with development. The vein cut, between 3 and 4 ft. wide, is assaying from $30 to $160 per ton. Shipping commenced last week.

COBALT, ONTARIO

Labor in Plenty.—Boston Creek Developments.

For the first time since the period of labor shortage due to the War set in there is a surplus here. It is now possible for mine managers to select experienced men.

Shareholders of the Ophir company have ratified an agreement giving the Nipissing an option on a two-thirds interest for $150,000. The Nipissing is now in possession of the property, and will carry on development at the contact at a depth of 580 feet.

Production at the Kerr Lake is falling off considerably. The December output was 102,289 oz. of silver, a decrease of about 50% when compared with the monthly average of the last two years.

The annual statement of the Temiskaming showed earnings of $425,014, and profits of $135,394. Current assets amounted to $870,114.

Boston Creek.—The result of sinking the Miller Independence shaft to 500 ft. is a large tonnage of high-grade ore. Plans are being prepared for erection of a 100-ton mill and roasting plant.

At the Cotter property the eastern continuation of the Independence vein has been cut by diamond-drilling at a depth of 600 ft., with high assays.

The Patricia was closed last fall on account of labor shortage and the difficulty of obtaining fuel, but arrangements are being made to resume in March, when the shaft will be sunk.

A 75% interest in the Connell, adjacent to the Independence, has been sold to Dayton people.

VICTORIA, BRITISH COLUMBIA

Engineers to Have Access to all Properties.—Educating Miners.—Gold-Cobalt-Molybdenite Ore.

Engineers in the employ of the Provincial government, of whom there are six, each having charge of one of the mineral districts into which the Province has been divided, have been given authority to make examination of any metalliferous mine, reduction works, or concentrating plant. Non-compliance entails a fine of from $10 to $500. It is not suggested that the engineers have received anything but the most courteous treatment from the mine and smelter operators, but the Minister of Mines proposes that they shall be provided with the fullest authority in carrying out their responsible duties.

Arrangements have been made by the Minister of Mines and Minister of Education for the establishment of a system of instruction by means of correspondence, which will give all miners who are British subjects and resident in British Columbia an opportunity to qualify for positions of trust and responsibility in connection with their chosen vocation. In making this announcement it is pointed out that for some years the Department of Education has been conducting night schools for the benefit of men engaged in the mining industry, with a view to providing that instruction which is necessary for thorough preparation for the examinations set by the Department of Mines for those aspiring to important charges in connection with the operation of mines. The conditions of the shift system under which miners work heretofore has mitigated against the success that is so much desired by both the Mines and the Education departments, and in order to overcome this difficulty and to bring the opportunities of study within reach of a greater number of men the decision has been reached to conduct the classes and disseminate the required knowledge through the medium of correspondence. It is considered probable, although no definite statement has been authorized as yet, that the correspondence will be augmented by personal visits on the part of instructors to the various sections of the Province for the purpose of giving at intervals such guidance and assistance to students as, perhaps, may not readily be obtained through the mail.

The property of the New Hazelton Gold-Cobalt Mines company, situated on the west side of Rocher de Boule mountain and close to the line of the Grand Trunk railway, gives promise of developing into a producer of importance. Returns have been received on a carload of gold-cobalt-molybdenite ore which was shipped last August to the Government ore-testing plant at Ottawa. The gross value of the 26 tons, based on molybdenite at $1 per lb., cobalt at the same, nickel at 50 cents, arsenic at 5 cents, and gold at $20, was $2399. This company some months ago shipped 28 tons to the Anyox smelter that gave returns of $1090 in gold, or $53 net per ton in gold alone after payment of railway and smelter charges. As there is no means at Anyox for saving the other metals they were not considered.

PORCUPINE, ONTARIO

Labor Influx and Accommodation.—Kirkland Lake Producers.—Cobalt Developments.

Porcupine.—A large number of the men laid-off by the International Nickel Co. at Sudbury are seeking employment on the goldfields, in addition to the influx of labor from southern Ontario. The main drawback in the way of the companies increasing their staffs is the lack of house accommodation, which is entirely inadequate. The Hollinger has undertaken the construction of 50 new dwellings for its employees, which, however, will only go a short way toward meeting the difficulty. Until sufficient provision has been made for housing the men the plans of the leading producers for greatly increasing their forces cannot be put into effect.

Kirkland Lake.—At the annual meeting of the Tough Oakes on January 23 it was announced that as the result of litigation, control of the property had been handed over to the directors chosen on January 26, 1916. The number of directors was reduced from seven to five, the following being elected, Harry Oakes, R. J. Robins, John B. Holden, J. Y. Murdoch, and A. Burt. The head office was changed from Haileybury to Toronto, and the sale of unissued shares at a discount of not less than 55% of par value authorized. An investigation will be made by a competent engineer before any program of operation is adopted.

The fifth annual report of the Teck-Hughes shows that operations were carried on under great difficulties, resulting in the mill being closed down in July, having during the previous term of about 10 months treated 15,879 tons of ore averaging $7.87 per ton. The December output however was the highest, 2035 tons of $10.12 ore was treated.

Diamond-drilling results at the Elliott-Kirkland have been encouraging. A large 'break' has been cut in a contact between the conglomerate and porphyry formations, and a belt of conglomerate 400 ft. wide has been passed through.

ROCHESTER, NEVADA

The Rochester Nevada Silver Mining Company.

Controlling stockholders of the five leading Rochester companies have signed an agreement fixing the status upon which these companies are to be consolidated. This supplements the earlier agreement of January 31, which placed the administrative control in the hands of two trustees. The new agreement provides for the immediate incorporation of a holding company, known as the Rochester Nevada Silver Mining Co., to control a majority of the issued shares of the five corporations involved and to bring about a single economical conduct and operation of the properties. The new corporation will have 8,000,000 shares, $1 par, of which 3,000,000 shares will remain in the treasury. Of the remaining 5,000,000 shares, 60% will be issued to owners of shares of the Rochester Mines Co. and Rochester Combined Mining Co. and 40% to holders of the Rochester Merger Mines Co., Rochester Elda Fina Mining Co., and Nenzel Crown Point Mining Co. In the division of the 60%, the Rochester Mines Co. receives 35/60 and the Rochester Combined 25/60, and of the remaining 40% the Rochester Merger receives one-half. Shares of the old companies are to be deposited for exchange in the Reno National Bank, and are to remain in pool until all indebtedness of the constituent companies is paid, but not longer than one year from April 1, 1919, and the pool may be dissolved earlier by resolution of the directors. Judge L. N. French, Frank M. Manson, and Jay H. Clemons are constituted trustees, to act as attorneys and proxies for the stockholders, and are empowered to vote all stock in pool. The directors of all the companies are to resign upon the organization of the new company, and the trustees have power to fix the number and name the members of the new directorate. A majority of the directors are to be selected from holders of the Rochester Mines and Rochester Combined companies. Upon deposit of a majority of the shares, judgments will be entered in favor of the defendant in the suit for $2,272,000 damages, brought by the Elda Fina company against the Rochester Mines Co., without costs to either side. The latter has resumed operating its mine and mill. Engineers report a large quantity of ore available in three of the properties, and under the new management a tram will be built to the Combined mill. The two mills are in good condition, and have a total capacity of 600 tons daily.

DURANGO, COLORADO

Fire Destroys Vanadium Concentrator.—Smuggler Union Closes Part of Mine.

Ouray.—The Ouray Consolidated M. & R. Co. continues to find rich shoots in the Guadeloupe. One carries 29% copper, and pockets that assay high in gold and silver have also been opened.

Placerville.—The reduction plant of the Primos Chemical Co. at Vanadium has been destroyed by fire. The loss is estimated at $100,000, but is covered by insurance. One hundred and fifty men have been thrown out of employment, and this may result in the abandonment of the little town of Vanadium, which has grown up about the plant. The works were built by the Vanadium Alloy Co. The structure was a frame type, with only part fire protection of corrugated iron. The fire started in the drying-room, spreading with great rapidity. The boarding-house, laboratory, and office adjoining escaped. Whether the buildings will be rebuilt is unknown. The large deposits of vanadium ore are now at old Placerville, and it is probable that if the plant is re-built it will be at that point, as the deposits of the Bear Creek section are practically worked out.

Rico.—The Standard Chemical Co. has temporarily closed some of its workings, as its Eastern plant has a surplus of ore on hand. There is a large quantity of ore blocked out. This will be milled as soon as water-power is available.

The Syndicate M. & M. Co. has opened a large body of lead-zinc ore.

Telluride.—An important even in this district is the closing of the Humboldt workings of the Smuggler Union company, due to high operating costs and insufficient profit. While the ore of the Humboldt carries high value in silver, it entails expensive mining and milling methods. Fortunately the closing of this part of the mine will not seriously affect production, as the majority of the men employed on the Humboldt have been placed in the other workings, and the output from these will be doubled. A number of men will be kept on development.

WASHINGTON, D. C.

The Army Gas-Mask Unsuitable for Mines.

A warning against the indiscriminate use of the army gas-mask in the industries and by fire departments as being dangerous to life was issued on February 26 by Van H. Manning, director of the U. S. Bureau of Mines, who said:

"Through the fact that the American army gas-mask proved to be most efficient for the purpose intended, there has grown up a general belief on the part of the public that this type of mask will protect the wearer under all conditions against any gas whatsoever, even in absolutely irrespirable air, to the exclusion of the more cumbersome mine-rescue oxygen-breathing apparatus. This erroneous belief will, no doubt, be further confirmed by millions of discharged soldiers, who have been trained in the use of the gas-mask and have been taught that it gives them absolute protection against all gases used or likely to be used in warfare. These men will not realize that out in the open air of the battlefield the percentage of gas in the atmosphere can never be anywhere near as large as may occur in the confined space of factory operations. A mask may afford complete protection under out-of-door conditions, yet break down at once when used indoors, where a gas-container has burst and filled the room with a greater concentration of gas. It must also be remembered that the absorbent in the army respirator, which filter out the poison gas, are especially designed for the gases used in warfare, and, as a matter of fact, do not protect against the most common industrial gases, as, for example, illuminating, natural, producer, and blast-furnace gases. The army gas-mask should never be used in mines, because of the uncertainty that exists as to the amounts of gases in the atmosphere and the liability of there being insufficient oxygen to support life. Its use in the mines will lead to serious accidents and fatalities. The army gas-mask is by no means the unusual protective appliance that it is popularly believed. It does not afford absolute protection against all gases, nor can it ever be safely used in low-oxygen atmospheres. It furnishes no oxygen to the wearer and can only remove comparatively small percentages of poisonous gas from inhaled air, usually less than 1 or 2%. Higher percentages will immediately penetrate the canister and will gas the wearer. The field of usefulness of the army mask is confined to certain of the chemical industries, around smelters and roasters, where sulphur fumes are given off, and in the industries using chlorine and bleaching powder. The army canister also contains cotton filter-pads which remove irritating and poisonous dusts, which increases its usefulness around smelters where sulphur and arsenic fumes must be removed. The army mask furnishes no protection whatever against carbon monoxide. This is the poisonous constituent of blast-furnace, producer, and illuminating gases, and of mine gases after fires and explosions in coal mines. Carbon monoxide is also likely to be present in ordinary fire-fighting conditions met by fire departments. Moreover, in all of these cases there is likely to be a deficiency of oxygen. Therefore, for adequate protection the oxygen-breathing apparatus must be used, and reliance on the army mask may be fatal.

Owing to the many factors entering into the use of protective respiratory appliances, the importance of competent advice on the selection and use of such appliances cannot be over-estimated. In connection with the Bureau's work in safeguarding the health and safety of miners and workmen in the metallurgical industries, a general investigation of respirators, gas-masks, and breathing-appliances is to be undertaken at the Pittsburgh experiment station of the Bureau. The results of these investigations will be given to the industries promptly."

In the canister of the army gas-mask is charcoal and soda-lime for filtering poisonous gas from inhaled air.

ALASKA

Juneau.—The Alaska Bureau of Publicity has issued its first monthly bulletin. The matter is authorized by the Governor, and is optimistic for the current year. Mining, fishing, lumber, agriculture, stock and reindeer, climate, and business opportunities are discussed. The Territorial Legislature convened on March 3 for a session of 60 days.

Kennecott.—The Kennecott Corporation has borrowed $12,000,000 for one year from March 1 at 6½%. This money is said not to be actually needed, but it was thought advisable to obtain additional funds to carry accumulated metal (over 50,000,000 lb.) without using up cash reserves until the copper market improves, also to continue development.

ARIZONA

Ajo.—Foundations for the new 500-ton experimental flotation plant of the New Cornelia Copper Co. are almost complete. Most of the machinery is on the ground, and it is anticipated that it will be in operation within three months. The company has announced that it will curtail production 40%, with a similar reduction in working force.

It is announced that the Little Ajo company is to have a second drill-hole sunk by the Longyear company. This hole will be put down by diamond-drill instead of churn-drill as was done in the first, which reached a depth of 1750 feet.

Chloride.—Driving in the 900-ft. level of the Tennessee mine, being done by the Schuylkill Mining Co., has opened 6 ft. of ore said to be as good as any ever opened in that mine.

Christmas.—It is reported that the management of the Christmas mine of the Gila Copper & Sulphide Co. has been relinquished by the A. S. & R. Co. The mine will be operated by the receivers of the Gila company.

Clifton.—The Arizona Copper Co. in its last financial year, ended September 30, 1918, paid 3s. (72 cents) per share, against 4s. (96 cents) in the two previous years. The directors state that "in view of the present uncertainty of the copper situation the board considers it prudent to increase the amount to be carried forward, which will be £66,400 ($317,000), against £13,700 ($65,700) at the end of 1916-1917."

Jerome.—The strike has been declared off, but the mining companies will not resume work until all agitators have left the place.

The United Verde Copper Co. in 1918 produced 77,501,-595 lb. of copper, 29,281 oz. of gold, and 1,292,109 oz. of silver. Of the total, 51,431,342 lb. was sold at 24.427 cents per pound. Total sales were $13,902,199.

The United Verde Copper Co. during the next two years contemplates improvements that will double the present output. These consist of steam-shovel mining, erection of three reverberatories, a coal-pulverizing plant, a crushing-plant, a Cottrell precipitator, 12 additional roasting-furnaces, and a new concrete-lined shaft.

Kingman.—A payment of $15,000 to Clack brothers has just been made by the Rico Consolidated Mines Co., this being the first payment on the purchase price of the property.

Ray.—The fourth quarterly statement of Ray Consolidated Copper Co. for 1918 shows a net profit of $408,113, about half of the previous term. Dividends amounted to $1,182,884, thus leaving a deficit of $774,770. The mill dressed 805,600 tons of 1.621% ore, recovering 75.05%. The yield was 19,601,149 lb., making 86,919,270 lb. for 1918, a reduction of 5,300,000 lb. from 1917. The average cost of producing copper was 14.305 cents per pound, a decrease of 0.978 cents.

Tucson.—The Sasco smelter of the American Smelting & Refining Co. has been closed because of lack of sufficient ore. The mines at Silverbell will ship their ore to the El Paso plant.

Managers of the large copper-producing companies of Arizona recently met at Tucson to discuss measures to meet the new operating conditions caused by the fall in the price of copper.

CALIFORNIA

Bakersfield.—At Los Angeles, on the 3rd, the Federal Oil Inspection Board for California announced the new wage-scale for all workers in the oil industry, effective December 1, 1918, and February 1, 1919, for certain classes. Increases were awarded all employees.

Engelmine.—The Engels Copper company has reduced wages by 50 cents per day.

Junction.—The $1800 belt that was swept off the Valdor company's dredge during high water two weeks ago, has been found. Work on the levee protecting the boat is under way, so that digging will be resumed shortly.

Sacramento.—The Senate Mining Committee's only bill was disposed of on February 27. A measure by Senator Boggs proposing an appropriation of $25,000 for the establishment of a mining and metallurgical experiment station at the University of California mining building was ordered favorably reported. It will be re-referred to the Finance Committee.

COLORADO

Creede.—Collins & Wheeler are shipping a carload per day of high-grade silver ore from their lease on the Monon at Sunnyside.——Some shipments are being made by lessees from the Manitoba adjoining the Monon.——Lessees at the Bachelor and Commodore mines are making regular shipments of low-grade ore.——Nothing has been sent out from the Last Chance during the past two months, as road conditions have prevented hauling coal to the hoisting-plant; but the lessees have several carloads stored in stopes to be dispatched shortly.——The Creede Exploration Co. is making regular output from the New York mine. This company has abandoned work below the level of the Nelson tunnel at the Amethyst, as ore in commercial quantities was not found in the drifts from the Berkshire shaft. The 350-ft. level of the Commodore shaft is being driven both ways.——Regular production of a good-grade ore is being made from the Equity mine.——The Solomon has been leased recently. Some ore has been opened and preparations are being made to start the mill.

The fluorspar mine at Wagon Wheel Gap is shipping several carloads per week to various parts of the country.

Leadville.—Silver in the Fryer Hill district is receiving much attention at present, and several lessees are extracting rich ore. Some of it is carbonate, other is iron bearing.

The Dold Mining Co., having a long contract, continues to mine 75 tons of manganese ore daily, employing 65 men.

Ouray.—The American-Nettie group of 14 claims, north of this town, is to be leased for one-year terms, with extension privileges. The royalty basis is 15% on ore valued up to $100 per ton, and 20% on ore over that grade. Previously the royalty was 30% straight. This new arrangement is expected to result in more leases being taken.

Silverton.—The Sunnyside M. & M. Co. will be operating three shifts after March 1, producing two cars of lead concentrate daily and a similar quantity of zinc. The Sunnyside has been working only one shift for some time, a large force of men being engaged at underground development. The fear of contagion had a tendency to restrict the importation of miners from districts where the plague was prevalent.

The Empire State M. & R. Co. has been organized to develop the holdings of the company, which are in the Eureka district, adjoining the Sunnyside properties. The Empire will build a mill similar to that of the Sunnyside company, and anticipates similar results, as the ore carries high zinc content. The first 50-ton unit of the mill will be constructed during the coming season.

IDAHO

Boise.—The annual report of the State Mine Inspector, Robert N. Bell, for 1918 has been issued. It covers 135 pages, is illustrated, and is well indexed. Statistics are given for 21 years. The past two years compare as follows:

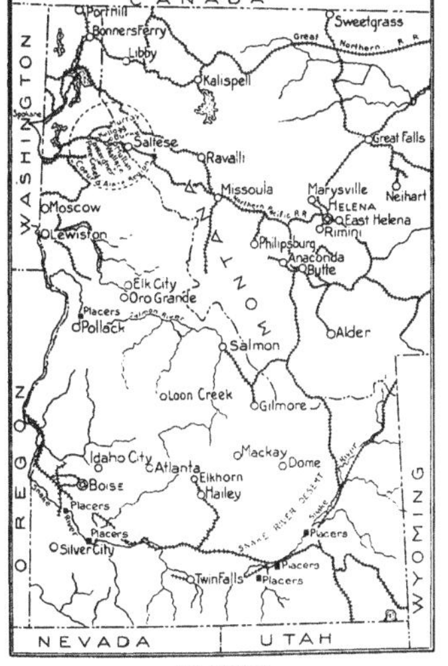

MAP OF IDAHO.

Metal	1918	1917
Copper, pounds	5,240,400	7,282,000
Gold, ounces	36,367	53,000
Lead, pounds	290,818,425	[illegible]
Silver, ounces	9,572,211	12,196,000
Zinc, pounds	51,691,000	96,000,000
Total value	$37,820,000	$56,292,210

There were 4500 full time workers employed at mines and works last year. There were 19 fatalities, a decline of 5 from 1917; also 485 serious and 663 minor injuries. In his usual outspoken, though expert, manner, Mr. Bell discusses all phases of the industry in Idaho, especially in connection with trouble at the Morning mine, mine inspection, and ventilation. Notes on the various mines come under main heads of the metals or minerals they produce. Generally the report is interesting, and has been issued promptly. We will abstract from it in other numbers of the 'Press'.

Forest.—The Deer Creek Mining Co. will start its new 125-ton mill as soon as water power is available. The former plant was burned in August 1916. To recover gold, silver, and copper the process is amalgamation and concentration by tables and flotation. W. J. Orr is manager.

MICHIGAN

Houghton.—The Allouez company has now six electric locomotives. One on No. 19 and one on No. 20 level of No. 1 shaft are of the storage-battery type; four trolley type are operating at No. 2 shaft. Tramming costs and speed have been improved greatly.

A small steam-shovel is being tried in the Quincy mine as an aid to tramming. Calumet & Hecla has had success with this machine. Tramming is the hardest work in the mines. Good men do not remain trammers for long; they fast develop into miners, so that the problem of maintaining a new and constantly shifting supply of trammers always has been the greatest difficulty in this district even with normal labor conditions.

Electric haulage will soon be installed at the No. 6 shaft of the old Osceola. This is a long haul. Two four-ton trolleys will be used. Five storage-battery type will be placed in the North Kearsarge No. 1 and 3. One now is used on the 15th and one on the 16th level, No. 4 North Kearsarge, and are doing efficient work.

At the Calumet & Hecla mine proper, on the Osceola lode, the use of electric haulage has made profitable this low-grade copper ore. The locomotives haul two cars 1000 ft. each trip. Cars hold 3½ tons and dump by air back of the shaft directly into skips.

Ahmeek has 12 locomotives, using them the same as the C. & H. and Isle Royale.

Isle Royale is using four locomotives at each shaft—4, 5, and 6. At this mine the cars carry 5 tons an average distance of 800 ft., each car filling a skip.

Wages were cut 15% by the Calumet & Hecla and subsidiaries on March 1. About 10,000 men are affected.

MISSOURI

Bonne Terre.—St. Joseph Lead Co. in 1918 produced 160,000,000 lb., against 190,000,000 lb. in 1917. The current year's output may be lower than last year on account of the present curtailment. The net surplus at the end of 1918 was $1,823,183, compared with $5,610,273 a year ago.

Joplin.—Production of the Tri-State region last week was as under:

State	Blende, tons	Calamine, tons	Lead, tons	Value
Kansas	1,859	...	382	$100,183
Missouri	1,178	71	44	54,266
Oklahoma	5,541	...	983	283,788
Average price...	$42	$27	$52	......

The total value is $83,000 greater than that of the previous week. The general tone of the ore market was somewhat improved.

MONTANA

Butte.—The fourth quarterly report of the Butte & Superior Mining Co. shows that a net operating profit was made of $96,506, compared with $145,448, $128,386, and $327,981, in the previous periods. The revenue was fairly even for the four terms. The mill concentrated 110,039 tons of ore assaying 15.5% zinc and 6.51 oz. silver. The recovery was 93.78%, yielding 15,997 tons of zinc in concentrate. Costs totaled $11.19 per ton, a reduction 3 cents, but the second quarter's costs were only $9.90. Ore-reserves were increased somewhat. The supply of labor is now plentiful.

In the suit of the Clark-Montana Realty Co. (Elm Orlu Mining Co.) versus the Butte & Superior Copper [Mining] Co., before the Supreme Court at Washington, D. C., on March 3, the plaintiff was awarded the ownership of the Rainbow lode, through prior location of the Elm Orlu claim, of which the lode is a part. The Court restrained Butte & Superior from entering the vein, which lies beneath those worked by it. The decision also awarded the Clark company $178,000 for ore alleged to have been extracted by the defendant from the plaintiff's holdings through secret underground workings.

Helena.—To maintain a State bureau of mines and metallurgy, A. V. Corry has introduced a measure to the Legislature for an appropriation of $20,000. The bureau would be connected with the School of Mines at Butte, similar to the arrangements in other States.

NEVADA

Ely.—The Nevada Consolidated Copper Co. in its last quarter reports a profit of only $10,189, against $1,070,213, $2,372,171, and $470,809 in the previous periods. After paying the dividend, equal to $1,499,592, there was left a deficit of $1,489,403. The surplus for 1918 was reduced to $9,934,361, against $13,180,526 in 1917. The mill treated in the fourth quarter 985,665 tons of 1.51% ore, plus 21,765 tons of custom ore. Operating costs were 19.01 cents per pound, a decrease of 1.69 cents.

Goldfield.—The Goldfield Development Co., successor to the Goldfield Consolidated Mines Co., has elected Corrin Barnes as president, A. I. D'Arcy as vice-president and general manager, H. G. McMahon as secretary and treasurer, with A. H. Howe and B. J. Henley as other directors. The capital is $125,000, shares 5 cents par, of which 1,500,000 shares have been set aside to permit Consolidated holders to have the first opportunity for purchasing shares in the new corporation, their purchases to be limited to one share of Development for each share of Consolidated held. All subscriptions by Consolidated holders must be in the hands of the secretary before March 20. Twenty-six leases have been granted so far.

Manhattan.—The White Caps company has opened the main orebody on No. 6 level.

McGill.—The Nevada Consolidated Copper Co. is to open a new store here and at Ruth, supplying employees with groceries at lower prices than the local firms charge.

Tonopah.—The Extension in January treated 9390 tons for 1324 oz. of gold and 131,549 oz. of silver, and a profit of $65,251.

NEW MEXICO

Santa Rita.—The Chino Copper Co.'s report for the fourth quarter of 1918 shows a net profit of $66,801, compared with $1,030,562 in the third period. Dividends paid were $869,980, leaving a deficit of $803,179. The mill treated 991,400 tons of 1.705% ore. The output was 20,191,391 lb., making 79,340,372 lb. for the year, a decrease of 4,000,000 lb. Costs totaled 18.10 cents per lb., a drop of 0.98 cents.

OKLAHOMA

Bartlesville. The Bartlesville and Lanyon-Starr zinc companies have curtailed smelting operations by 50%, laying off over 200 men. The companies assert that at present prices for spelter they are running at a loss.

Miami.—It is probable that a school of mines will be organized here. The Tri-State Safety and Sanitation Association is behind the movement, and 29 members of the State legislature recently visited Miami and Picher.

TEXAS

Terlingua.—A promising quicksilver district is being exploited in a remote section of the Big Bend region, 50 miles east of this place, according to B. H. Hedrick of San Antonio. Some claims are yielding rich cinnabar, but no furnaces have been erected yet. In the Terlingua district the Chisos, Rainbow, Study Butte, and Texas Almaden properties continue operations.

UTAH

Alta.—The Albion, Alta-Germania, and Mineral Flat properties of 600 acres have been consolidated under the name of Albion Consolidated Mining Co. G. H. Watson is general manager. The Quincy tunnel, now 1½ miles in Albion ground, is to be extended, and it is estimated that 400 ft. should cut the downward extension of lead-silver ore on the surface.

Bingham.—Effective March 1, the Utah Copper Co. has reduced wages of skilled miners another 25 cents and all other labor 20 cents per day. At the mills the cut was from 15 to 25 cents.

The Utah Copper Co. reports a profit of $1,577,138 during the last quarter of 1918. In the previous term it was $4,169,697. Adding other income, there was available the sum of $3,331,728. Dividends absorbed $4,061,225, leaving a deficit of $729,496. The mills concentrated 3,047,400 tons of 1.23% ore, recovering 64.43%. The copper output was 48,303,692 lb., making 197,978,557 lb. for the year, a decrease of 8,000,000 lb., an increase of 1.07 cents.

Garfield.—Up to February 26 a total of 259 men had downed tools at the A. S. & R. smelter here, as a protest against the cut of 75 cents in wages. The Magna mill of the Utah Copper Co. was closed on the 27th.

Heber.—The Glenallen Mining Co.'s 100-ton mill is nearly completed. The property is near that of the Ontario company at Park City, and the ore carries lead, silver, and zinc. J. B. Allen is general manager.

Park City.—The Daly West, Judge, and Ontario companies have reduced wages by 75 cents per shift, effective March 1. This is the first cut made in this district.

Salt Lake City.—The Cardon bill, passed by the House and sent to the Senate, provides for the creation of a State Securities Commission, consisting of the Secretary of State, State Bank Commissioner, and Attorney General. It would be the duty of this Commission to pass upon all proposed issues of stocks, bonds, or other securities by corporations in the State. It would require that persons engaged in the sale of securities be licensed by the board. The issuance or sale of securities not authorized by the Commission would be made a felony.

The joint appropriations committee of the Legislature has not reported favorably on the proposed fund of $12,000 for maintenance of the office of State geologist.

Tintic.— The Tintic Central Mining Co.'s balance-sheet for 1918 shows a deficit of $205. The revenue was $14,351, including an assessment of $9942. Most of the work was carried out on the 1700-ft. level. Part of the property was leased.

MEXICO

Mexico

Mexico City.—The general manager, Felipe Pescador, of National Railways of Mexico, including the old Mexican Central system, has issued a frank statement on the physical and traffic conditions of these lines. He says:

"To pretend that railroad service in Mexico is given with accommodations of former days would be devoid of reflection. Many passenger-coaches are lacking in usual interior equipment; in some the window-glass is broken, in many the seats are worn out, and it is impossible to get prompt repairs. Coaches which have been used in military service are in dilapidated condition. Train-schedules are difficult to maintain, as precautions have been taken against rebel bands. Generally speaking, however, service is normal and accidents not frequent. On the Interoceanic we have not been able to control the situation. Rebels have frequently torn-up the rails and attacked the trains. They have been very bad between Puebla and Jalapa, destroying the road and requiring guards of 100 or more soldiers to protect each repair-gang. Often we find newly repaired track again destroyed before a train can be got over it. The Mexican Central from Mexico City to La Colorado in Zacatecas may be said to be open. North of the latter point repairs have been made only as the military situation would permit work. Between Torreon and Chihuahua City, and north of the latter there have been frequent interruptions by Villa rebels. On the old Mexican Central's Gulf line from Monterrey to Tampico the roadbed is in bad condition, and repair work has been effected only with great difficulty. This is on account of scarcity of laborers and danger from rebels which infest that section. A tri-weekly service is maintained, however, also, tri-weekly trains are run each way between San Luis Potosi and Tampico. This last is also a part of the old Central system. Construction on the projected line from the city of Durango to Mazatlan, Sinaloa, continues; but completion of it is very remote. Laborers and money are needed in large amounts, and are both lacking. Over 100 kilometres of this line is in operation and material trains are being run over it. A part of the revenues of the National Railways is being used to re-build stations and other structures, as well as for renewing rails."

Nuevo Leon

Monterrey.—Preparations are being made by the American Smelting & Refining Co. to resume at an early date operation of its smelter at Asarco. Mechanics have been overhauling it for some time. This plant is in the division of the National Railways of Mexico that runs between Torreon and Durango. Ever since the revolutionary period began more than eight years ago the region around Asarco has been bandit-ridden. That this condition still exists, to some extent at least, is shown by the fact that only a few days ago the 'stub' passenger train that runs from Asarco to Velardena, where connection is made with the main line, was held up by bandits and all the passengers robbed. It is understood that pending restoration of complete tranquillity, the Government will give military protection.

PHILIPPINE ISLANDS

Manila.—The Benguet Consolidated Mining Co., operating in the Benguet district, island of Luzon, during 1918 treated 23,539 tons of ore averaging $21.35 per ton. The residue assayed $2.34 per ton, giving an extraction of 89% of the gold. The loss was made up of 34 cents as dissolved and $2 as undissolved metal. There was shipped 160 bars, weighing 30,012.77 ounces, slightly over one ton. The average fineness was 664.4 in gold and 194.7 in silver, and the Mint value per ounce, $13.73. The total estimated value was $417,611. Added to this was the estimated value of slag produced, $35,400, giving a total production of $453,011 for the year. C. M. Eye is superintendent.

PERSONAL

Note The Editor invites members of the profession to send particulars of their work and appointments. The information is interesting to our readers.

Hennen Jennings is in San Francisco.

Maurice D. Leehey was here last week from Seattle.

Philip Wiseman has returned from New York to Los Angeles.

W. H. Aldridge is president of the Texas Gulf Sulphur Co., of New York.

F. H. Mason was in San Francisco last Saturday on his way from San Diego to Victoria, B. C.

Sergio Bagnara, recently in the Ordnance Department at Washington, is at Santa Rosa, California.

Cecil G. Fennell passed through San Francisco on his way from Arizona to the Pend Oreille region of Idaho.

Louis A. Wright is returning from Chile in the middle of April. His address will be 61 Broadway, New York.

H. Robinson Plate will be in charge of the operating end of the Golden Gate Exploration Co., with offices in the Hobart building.

Joseph H. Playter, manager of the Crown Mines at Golconda, Nevada, has returned to Golconda after professional work in California.

E. H. Nutter, of the Minerals Separation company, is in New York. His assistant, **Albert Roberts**, is now in the North-West and will go shortly to Utah.

Donald McLaughlin has been appointed geologist to the Cerro de Pasco Mining Co., and **H. I. Altshuler** has been appointed his assistant. The latter sails for Peru this week.

Robert D. Adams, well-known chrome and magnesite engineer in this State, who has been in northern Russia for several months with the Canadian forces, has been awarded the D. S. O.

Courtenay De Kalb has gone to Washington, on his way to Spain, as a commissioner appointed by the Department of Commerce to investigate the mining and metallurgical resources of that country.

Livingston Wernecke, geologist of the Alaska Treadwell and Alaska Juneau mines, is giving a course of lectures at the College of Mines, University of Washington, on the mining geology of the Juneau district.

James T. Norton, ore-dressing engineer with the U. S. Bureau of Mines, who has been engaged in work on war minerals at Minneapolis and Colorado Springs, has lately been transferred to Moscow, Idaho, to investigate the differential flotation of lead-zinc ore.

The fourth annual meeting of the American Association of Petroleum Geologists is to be held at Dallas, Texas, on March 13 to 15. W. E. Wrather is secretary.

Obituary

Anthony W. Barnard, who staked the first claim at Butte, Montana, died there on Feburary 27. He was 73 years old.

H. P. Tracy, advertising manager for the Denver Rock Drill Mfg. Co., died on February 18 from pneumonia following influenza.

James S. Austin, president of the Tonopah Mining Co., died suddenly at his home in Ardmore, Pennsylvania, on February 27.

Charles H. Gibbs, for the past few years general manager for the Wasatch Mines Co., Salt Lake City, died on February 18 from the effects of influenza. He leaves his widow and two children.

METAL PRICES

San Francisco, March 4

Aluminum-dust, large and small lots, cents per lb	65—70
Antimony, cents per pound	8.00
Copper, electrolytic, cents per pound, in carload lots	16.00
Lead, pig, cents per pound	5.50— 6.50
Platinum, per ounce	$100
Quicksilver, per flask of 75 lb.	$85
Spelter, cents per pound	9.00
Zinc-dust, cents per pound	15.00

EASTERN METAL MARKET

(By wire from New York)

March 4.—Copper is quiet though steadier. Lead is more active and firm. Spelter is dull but steady.

SILVER

Below are given official (not Government) quotations, in cents per ounce, of silver 999 fine. In order to make prompt settlements with smelters and brokers, producers allow a discount from the maximum fixed price of $1.01½, hence the lower price. The Government has not fixed the general market price at $1, but will pay this price (as from April 23, 1918) for all silver purchased by it. The equivalent of dollar silver (1000 fine) in British currency is 46.65 pence per ounce (925 fine), calculated at the current rate of exchange. On August 15, 1918, the Treasury announced that the maximum price was fixed at $1.01½ per ounce. The British government fixed its maximum at 49½ pence, on September 2, but on November 12 this was changed to 48¾, on December 13 to 48 7/16, and in February to 47¾ pence

Date		New York	London	Average week ending		
Feb.	26	101.12	47.75	Jan	21	101.12
"	27	101.12	47.75	"	28	101.12
"	28	101.12	47.75	Feb.	4	101.12
Mch.	1	101.12	47.75	"	11	101.12
"	2 Sunday			"	18	101.12
"	3	101.12	47.75	"	25	101.12
"	4	101.12	47.75	Mch.	4	101.12

Monthly averages

	1917	1918	1919		1917	1918	1919
Jan	75.14	88.72	101.12	July	78.92	99.62	....
Feb	77.54	85.79	101.12	Aug.	85.40	100.31	....
Mch	74.13	88.11	....	Sept.	100.73	101.12	....
Apr	72.51	95.35	....	Oct.	87.38	101.12	....
May	74.61	99.50	....	Nov.	85.97	101.12	....
June	76.44	99.50	....	Dec.	85.97	101.12	....

The shortage of silver is adversely affecting the general trade situation all over China, but its effects are much more serious in some portions of the country than in others, according to a recent U. S. Consular Report. In the interior districts of northern and central China comparatively good crops and general financial conditions have made the demand for the metal increasingly acute. In southern China, particularly the districts subsidiary to Hongkong, the demand is felt much less commercially, for despite the fact that the export of silver from Hongkong except for government account—even for the protection of Hongkong bank-notes—is prohibited, the Hongkong bank-note issues are always fully protected under the laws of the colony by the banking policy of the institutions issuing them. At times during the past year Hongkong bank-notes have circulated at a discount, because they could be redeemed in silver only in Hongkong, whence no silver could be exported; whereas when native bank-notes were at par they represented silver obtainable on demand, at least theoretically. But with the uncertainty of finances in China generally this condition continued for a short time only. Owing to the increasing discount of Canton notes silver could only be had in small amounts, causing a considerable appreciation in the value of subsidiary coins, and transactions, especially in import and export lines, could be counted upon safely only in Hongkong bank-notes. In some districts in southern China the need of silver has been very acute—for example in the Kotchiu tin mines, where silver for the payment of expenses could only be had from Shanghai at times, and then only on the payment of a considerable premium. In the districts near the Indo-China border there has been continued trouble, due largely to the drain on the stocks of silver in those districts for the benefit of Indo-China. In a general way inter-city trade in the interior has been greatly retarded by a lack of silver, and this has borne particularly heavy upon districts where it was necessary to have silver at any price. The result has been an inflated value of the Shanghai and northern China dollars compared with Hongkong dollars, exchange in favor of Shanghai most of the time. The respective stocks of silver in Shanghai and northern and central China, on the one hand, and in Hongkong territory, on the other, are rather significant.

COPPER

Prices of electrolytic in New York, in cents per pound.

Date			Average week ending		
Feb.	26	[illegible]	Jan.	1	20.50
"	27	[illegible]	"	8	19.87
"	28	[illegible]	Feb.	4	19.21
Mch	1	[illegible]	"	11	18.33
"	2 Sunday		"	18	17.50
"	3	15.00	"	[illegible]	16.40
"	4	15.00	Mch.	[illegible]	15.25

Monthly averages

	1917	1918	1919		1917	1918	1919
Jan.	29.53	23.50	20.43	July	29.67	26.00	....
Feb.	34.57	23.50	17.34	Aug.	27.42	26.00	....
Mch.	36.00	23.50	....	Sept.	25.11	26.00	....
Apr.	33.16	23.50	....	Oct.	23.50	26.00	....
May	31.69	23.50	....	Nov.	23.50	26.00	....
June	32.57	23.50	....	Dec.	23.50	26.00	....

Copper held by the Government, over 100,000,000 lb., is to be sold through the large copper-selling agencies.

Copper for export has been sold at 15 cents per lb., f.o.b.

With the lower price for copper comes a drop in refining charges. These were raised last year when the price was fixed at 26 cents per lb. As much as $35 per ton (1¾ cents per lb.) was paid by some mining companies to the refineries.

Casting copper has been sold at £68 per ton in London, equal to 14¾ cents per pound.

ZINC

Zinc is quoted as spelter, standard Western brands, New York delivery.

Date			Average week ending		
Feb.	26	6.65	Jan.	21	7.52
"	27	6.60	"	28	7.20
"	28	6.60	Feb.	4	6.83
Mch.	1	6.60	"	11	6.98
"	2 Sunday		"	18	6.74
"	3	6.60	"	25	6.60
"	4	6.60	Mch.	4	6.61

Monthly averages

	1917	1918	1919		1917	1918	1919
Jan.	9.75	7.87	7.44	July	8.98	8.72	....
Feb.	10.45	7.97	6.71	Aug.	8.58	8.87	....
Mch.	10.78	7.67	....	Sept.	8.33	9.58	....
Apr.	10.20	7.04	....	Oct.	8.32	9.11	....
May	9.41	7.29	....	Nov.	7.76	8.75	....
June	9.63	7.92	....	Dec.	7.84	8.49	....

LEAD

Lead is quoted in cents per pound, New York delivery.

Date			Average week ending		
Feb.	26	5.25	Jan.	21	5.92
"	27	5.25	"	28	5.50
"	28	5.25	Feb.	4	5.32
Mch.	1	5.25	"	11	5.09
"	2 Sunday		"	18	5.00
"	3	5.25	"	25	5.05
"	4	5.25	Mch.	4	5.25

Monthly averages

	1917	1918	1919		1917	1918	1919
Jan.	7.64	6.85	5.60	July	10.93	8.03	....
Feb.	9.10	7.07	5.13	Aug.	10.75	8.05	....
Mch.	10.07	7.26	....	Sept.	9.07	8.05	....
Arp.	9.38	6.99	....	Oct.	6.97	8.05	....
May	10.29	6.88	....	Nov.	6.38	8.05	....
June	11.74	7.58	....	Dec.	6.49	6.90	....

QUICKSILVER

The primary market for quicksilver is San Francisco, California being the largest producer. The price is fixed in the open market, according to quantity. Prices, in dollars per flask of 75 pounds:

Date					
Feb.	4	95.00	Feb.	18	90.00
"	11	95.00	"	25	85.00
			Mch.	4	85.00

Monthly averages

	1917	1918	1919		1917	1918	1919
Jan.	81.00	128.06	103.75	July	102.00	120.00	....
Feb.	126.25	118.00	90.00	Aug.	115.00	120.00	....
Mch.	113.75	112.00	....	Sept.	112.00	120.00	....
Apr.	114.50	115.00	....	Oct.	102.00	120.00	....
May	104.00	110.00	....	Nov.	102.50	120.00	....
June	85.50	112.00	....	Dec.	117.42	115.00	....

TIN

Prices in New York, in cents per pound. The monthly averages in 1918 are nominal. On December 3 the War Industries Board fixed the price to consumers and jobbers at 72½c. f.o.b. Chicago and Eastern points, and 71½c. on the Pacific Coast. This will continue until the U. S. Steel Products Co.'s stock is consumed.

Monthly averages

	1917	1918	1919		1917	1918	1919
Jan.	44.10	85.13	71.50	July	62.60	93.00	....
Feb.	51.47	85.00	72.44	Aug.	62.53	91.33	....
Mch.	54.27	85.00	....	Sept.	61.54	80.40	....
Apr.	55.63	88.53	....	Oct.	62.24	78.82	....
May	63.21	100.01	....	Nov.	74.18	73.67	....
June	61.93	91.00	....	Dec.	85.00	71.52	....

Eastern Metal Market

New York, February 26.

Demand is light for all metals, but in one or two the price tendency is firmer.

Antimony is inactive and unchanged.

Copper has reached lower levels again on sales of small quantities.

Lead has advanced, and there has been some buying and more inquiry.

Tin is still restricted, and is stale and stagnant.

Zinc is quiet, with the price situation easier.

ALUMINUM

Conditions are unchanged. Government maximum prices are nominally in effect until March 1 at 33 to 33.20c. per lb. for 50 to 1-ton lots, but No. 1 virgin metal, 98 to 99% pure, is obtainable at 31 to 32c. per lb., New York, for early delivery.

ANTIMONY

The market is quiet and demand is light. Wholesale lots are obtainable for future delivery at 7 to 7.12½c., New York, duty paid, with spot delivery at 6.87½ to 7c. per lb. In jobbing lots, quotations range from 7.37½ to 7.50c., New York.

COPPER

The market continues to fall, and there seems to be no bottom to it. On Monday, electrolytic copper had reached 16c., New York, and yesterday it was obtainable at 15.50c. Even this could be shaded by both large and small producers. There is evidently no control possible, and it is probably a question of supply and demand. The seriousness of the entire situation is exemplified, in the opinion of some, by the fact that one large copper company [the Kennecott Copper Corporation] recently borrowed $12,000,000 to carry its copper metal in stock, rather than sell it and take a loss now. Demand now is only hand to mouth and the total turnover is ridiculously small, as judged by normal times. Lake copper is nominal at about 16.25c., New York. As to Government stocks, it is stated that a plan is under consideration whereby producers and consumers or manufacturers may possibly take over this supply on some fixed basis. Copper for export is still held at 23c. The committee of the Copper Export Association, which went abroad some time ago to visit England, France, Italy, and Germany, is expected back about March 15.

IRON AND STEEL

The scheme of the Secretary of Commerce to establish prices on a lower plane is not looked on favorably by steel producers; it is regarded as more than a matter of price that is holding back business. There has been more evidence of price shading recently. In a sale of 3000 tons of plates, part for export to Canada, a cut of $2 per ton was made by three makers. Hard-steel bars have been sold at a concession of $2. There is not much export business so far. An inquiry for 12,000 tons of billets and 1200 tons of sheet-bars has come from Belgium, and a recent order for 50,000 boxes of tin-plate for export is said to have been closed at slightly above the domestic price.

LEAD

The American Smelting & Refining Co. advanced its price last week. On February 21 it announced an increase of 10 points to 5.10c., New York, and yesterday, February 25, one of 15 points more to 5.25c., New York, or 5c., St. Louis. The market has evidently reached bottom. Inquiry is better and a moderate business has been done in the past week at not under 5c., New York. Lead is really the first market to approximate stabilization.

TIN

The only really open market in tin is that in jobbing lots or under five tons. Such quantities can be purchased without a purchase-license from the authorities controlling the larger market. Anything above five tons or more can only be secured from the United States Steel Products Co. at 72.50c., the fixed price, for allocated metal. Of the 10,000 tons allocated by the International Tin Executive to the United States, only about 4000 tons has been disposed of, it is said. This does not portend an early unrestricted market. There is no market now; it is dull, stale, and stagnant, and could hardly be otherwise. American electrolytic tin is obtainable at 69.12½c. per lb., New York, in small lots and at about 68.25c. in wholesale quantities. The 99% metal is quoted at under 67c. per lb., New York. Spot Straits in London is quoted at £213 per ton. Arrivals in February to the 17th were 1190 tons at Pacific and 50 tons at Atlantic ports.

ZINC

After a period of firmness covering several weeks—firm for markets like these—a weakness has developed that is reflected slightly in lower quotations. The market for prime Western for early delivery is down to 6.25c., St. Louis, or 6.60c., New York, today, with demand very light. A fair business for nearby delivery has been done in the last week or so at 6.30 to 6.40c., St. Louis, but the market is now quiet. It is believed that stocks are piling up rather than otherwise, which may explain the lower tendency. Producers generally are supposed by each other to be curtailing output, but it is probably a fact, as suggested by one dealer, that each one is expecting the other to cut his production, and as a result the yield has not been decreased as much as has been estimated.

ORES

Manganese Alloys: Ferro has sold in lots up to 300 tons in all at $150, delivered, establishing a market for the first time in many weeks. These sales include both re-sale material and some 80% alloy by one or two producers. Spiegel is nominal at $50 to $53, delivered, with inquiry light.

Molybdenum: The market is quiet with quotations nominal at 85c. per lb. of MoS_2 in 85 to 90% material.

Tungsten: Prices are not obtainable in the absence of any testing of the market, but the condition has not improved. Ferro is said to be obtainable at less than $1.50 per lb. of contained tungsten, but no definite quotations are available.

Production of fuel briquettes in the United States in 1918 was 477,235 net tons, valued at $3,212,793, an increase, compared with 1917, of 70,379 tons, or 17%, in quantity, and of $978,905, or 44%, in value. The output in 1918, which represented the results of the third successive year of material progress in the industry, was the highest yet recorded. It was more than double that in 1915, according to the U. S. Geological Survey.

Value of the primary aluminum produced in the United States in 1918, as reported by the U. S. Geological Survey, was $41,159,225, a decrease of $4,722,775, or 10% from the value in 1917. The decrease is due largely to a decline in the price of aluminum during 1918, and does not represent a corresponding decline in quantity of output.

Company Reports

BARNES-KING DEVELOPMENT CO.

Property: mines and mills at Kendall and Marysville, Montana.

Operating Official: O. T. McGee, general manager. At the North Moccasin: T. W. Heatherley in the mine, A. E. Worsdell in the mill, C. A. Morgan in the office, E. G. R. Manwaring, mining engineer, and W. A. Young, assaying. At the Piegan-Gloster: J. H. McCormick in the mill, J. W. Johns in the mine, William McClean, mechanical engineer, F. C. Eccles in the office, and Ward Cole, assaying. At the Shannon: J. W. Johns in the mine and J. E. Goyer in the office. At the Kendall: A. B. Fox in the power-plant.

Financial Statement: the operating profit in 1918 was $159,313, less $49,980 for taxes, development of outside claims, etc., leaving $139,333 net. Current assets at December 31, 1918, amounted to $198,246, and liabilities $42,229. Cash at that date was $88,808.

Dividends: four absorbed $160,000, making a total of $260,000.

Development and Production:

Mine	Feet	Tons	Gold	Profit	Cost per ton
Kendall (leased)	....	7,152	$12,873	$657	....
North Moccasin	3384	21,378	178,230	16,926	$7.56
Piegan-Gloster	2890	15,338	141,326	16,941	10.20
Shannon	4359	26,048	349,138	163,110	6.89
Total	10,633	69,916	$681,577	197,634	

In the North Moccasin, exploration on the lowest level was unsatisfactory. Reserves are 5255 tons of $8.90 ore, consisting mainly of pillars. In the Piegan-Gloster, the advance of the 500-ft. level, 937 ft. west, cut four ore-shoots with a combined length of 350 ft. They do not appear to extend far above the level. Reserves are 2835 tons of $7.30 ore in the Shannon, only 100 ft. of the 620 ft. opened on the vein at the 650-ft. level was of milling value. In the 500-ft. level a new shoot was opened for 400 ft. of good value.

Milling Data: the Gloster mill treated 41,386 tons of ore from the Piegan-Gloster and Shannon mines, extracting gold worth $443,513 and silver worth $49,084. The ore assayed $11.56 per ton, of which 95.6% was extracted. The milling cost was $2 per ton. At the North Moccasin the extraction was 93.4%; cyanide and zinc consumption, ¼ lb. each per ton; and lime, 3.4 pounds.

ENGELS COPPER MINING CO.

Property: mines, tramways, mills, and railroad in Plumas county, California; the mining claims covering 3175 acres.

Operating Official: E. E. Paxton, general manager.

Financial Statement: gross earnings in 1918 totaled $1,781,637. Operations cost $1,302,464, leaving $479,173 net. Deducting depreciation, depletion, and compensation liability—$429,249, the balance to profit was $49,925; and adding the balance of $400,210 from 1917, there was available $450,135. After paying dividends the balance at December 31, 1918, was $179,882. Current assets totaled $531,681, and liabilities $324,585. Since operations started, the company has expended $1,165,720 in cash. During 1918, additions to capital investment totaled $489,089 net. The entire property is valued at $960,982, but ore broken in stopes, ready to mill, represents a net value of at least that sum.

Dividends: in 1918 the sum of $269,979 was distributed.

Development: there was a total of 25,181 ft. of work done last year. At the upper, or Engels mine, the three-compartment shaft was driven from the surface to a depth of 400 ft., and is well equipped with a large Nordberg hoist, capable of hauling from 2000 to 3000 tons of ore daily. This shaft is being sunk as rapidly as possible below No. 6 level, and at 200 ft. a new level, No. 7, will be opened. The ore from No. 7 will be hoisted to No. 6, from there transported by rail and aerial tram to the Superior mill. No. 6 tunnel has been extended in the main orebody for a distance of 600 ft. Fifteen cross-cuts have been driven from the main tunnel partly blocking the ore on that level. The main tunnel will be extended at least 200 ft. farther in continuous ore already developed by diamond-drilling. The first ore opened on No. 6 level, 1800 ft. from the portal, is now being opened, and promises a large deposit of chalcocite ore of high-milling grade. As yet this ore is separate from the main body, but may connect with the same at depth. A deep diamond-drill hole, driven at an angle of 58° and cross-cutting the orebody, carried value for a depth of nearly 600 ft., and high-grade ore for nearly 300 ft. below No. 6.

At the Superior mine a large stope, 500 ft. long by an average width of 120 ft., has been opened on the main orebody on No. 1 level. In addition to this two other shoots are also being developed, with stopes from 100 to 300 ft. in length and of varying width, from 10 to 40 ft. The main tunnel, cross-cutting the orebodies in the Superior, is now being driven toward another large deposit disclosed last year by diamond-drill. No. 2 level, 200 ft. below No. 1, is now being opened, and already a large quantity of ore has been developed. The three-compartment shaft at the Superior has been sunk to a depth of 342 ft.; this ultimately will be extended not less than 1000 ft., and is well equipped with hoisting machinery for handling large tonnage at that depth.

During the past two years there has been expended $23,690 on diamond-drilling, but the results have more than justified the cost, as the basis of the value of any mining property depends first, on the amount of probable ore, and second, on the amount of ore blocked and ready for milling. There was also expended during the past year a total of $197,379 on mine development, that is, in driving, raising, and blocking out the ore, which to a considerable extent accounts for the high cost of operation. With the work already accomplished and planned for the coming year (1919) the mines are in good condition for yielding 2000 tons of ore daily.

The tonnage of ore blocked out by the stopes now being excavated, is shown below:

	Engels	Superior	Total
Blocked above stopes, tons	1,400,000	500,000	1,900,000
Broken in stopes, tons	350,000	25,000	375,000
Total	1,750,000	525,000	2,275,000

During the past year 1,200,000 tons of additional reserves have been blocked and 90,000 tons added to broken ore in stopes, the cost of which has been charged to operating expense. In addition to the foregoing blocked reserve, further driving and diamond-drilling in both mines have disclosed probable orebodies of many times the amount actually blocked, already insuring a long life to the property on large-scale operations.

Production: the two mills concentrated, by flotation, a total of 265,888 tons of ore, averaging 2.23% copper. This yielded 9,244,069 lb. of copper, 1108 oz. of gold, and 119,708 oz. of silver. The quantity treated was an increase of 71% over that of 1917. The average recovery was 77.94%, somewhat low due to the inclusion of some carbonate ore. With the 748 tons of crude ore shipped direct to smelter, the output was 9,419,957 lb. of copper, 1131 oz. of gold, and 114,262 oz. of silver. Since 1915, there has been treated 622,485 tons for 22,566,239 lb. The plants were enlarged last year, and additions are under way in 1919.

Costs: operations cost 11.73c., development 2.10c., freight and smelting 5.75c., a total of 19.58c. per lb. of copper. The price received was 24.68c. Reductions have been made so that total charges are now [February 1919] 16.50c., but when normal conditions are prevailing this is expected to be lowered to 11 cents.

Mining Decisions

Mineral Leases of Washington State Lands

Under the laws of the State of Washington mineral leases of State lands may be had in legal sub-divisions upon application by the discoverer of precious minerals therein to the State Commissioner of Public Lands.

State v. Savidge (Washington), 175 Pacific, 568.

Party in Possession—Right to Enjoin Trespass

Where a plaintiff has been in open, peaceable, and notorious possession of land, even though his legal title thereto is not well established, he will be awarded an injunction against the forcible entry of defendant under a claim of legal title made for the purpose of extracting oil from the land.

Collier v. Bartlett (Oklahoma), 175 Pacific, 247.

Miners' Liens—Not Available to Superintendent

The claim of an oil-well superintendent for unpaid salary cannot be made the basis for a miner's lien in California. Such liens are only for the benefit of those who perform manual labor on the property in question. A lien cannot be filed until after the claimant has ceased to labor.

McCreary v. Toronto Midway Oil Co. (California), 175 Pacific, 87.

Severance of Minerals—Adverse Possession

A purchaser of land having notice that the minerals have been severed by deeds from the surface, cannot claim adverse possession of the minerals through adverse possession of the surface. Adverse possession of the minerals can be obtained only by actual working of them or some other act of domain over them showing assertion of title and use in accordance therewith.

Midkiff v. Colton (West Virginia), 252 Federal, 420.

Adverse Possession—What Does Not Constitute

Where there has been severance of title to land and underlying minerals, the owner of the surface, in possession thereof, does not acquire title to the coal by taking from existing openings of the veins coal for his own domestic purposes and occasionally permitting neighbors to take it, or himself digging it and selling it to them for their domestic use. Such evidence does not establish adverse possession of the coal.

Vance v. Clark (West Virginia), 252 Federal, 495.

Mining Location—Abandonment and Re-location

A re-location of a claim located by another admits the validity of the original location. In an action to quiet title to a mining claim, where the complaint set forth an affidavit of assessment work done by defendants at a certain time but alleged that the defendants had abandoned the claim, and the answer denied the allegations of abandonment, a prima facie case was made in favor of the defendants, even though their answer did not aver that they were in actual possession at the commencement of the action.

Betsch v. Umphrey (Alaska), 252 Federal, 573.

Miner's Liens—Owner's Interest

The holder of an option contract to purchase mining claims, with permission, during the life of the option, to occupy and work the same at his own expense, upon condition that he return to the owner a specified portion of the profits, is a lessee during occupancy of the property. The owner's interest in the mining claims is not, under the laws of Idaho, made lienable for work done at the instance of his tenant, unless, by some additional act, understanding or arrangement he causes the work to be done or makes the tenant his agent.

Nicholson v. Smith (Idaho), 174 Pacific, 1008.

Excess Placer Location—Rights of Locators

A placer location, made in good faith, but containing by mistake an excess area, is void as to the excess which may be rejected from such portion as the owner may select after reasonable notice of the mistake in area.

Where a locator attempted to initiate a new location within the limits of such an existing placer claim which contained an excess area, without notifying all of the co-owners of said placer so as to give them an opportunity to cast off the excess, he was a mere trespasser and acquired no rights by his attempted location.

Adams v. Yukon Gold Co. (Alaska), 251 Federal, 226.

Public Lands—Jurisdiction During Patent Proceedings

The public lands being under the control of the Land Department, including a bureau headed by the Commissioner of the General Land Office, to whom, as a special tribunal with quasi judicial powers, Congress has confided the execution of laws for the sale and disposal of public lands, where a patent for mineral oil-lands has been applied for and charges of fraud are under investigation, pending action upon the application, the courts are without jurisdiction to determine the rights of claimants in possession as against the United States. Receivership applied for by the Government refused.

Devils Den Consolidated Oil Co. v. United States (California), 251 Federal, 548.

Injury to Surface Defined

The right of support is vital to the overlying surface and strata. Therefore it is not presumed to have been given up unless expressly or by strong implication. The word "surface" in mining controversies means that part of the earth or geologic section lying over the minerals in question, unless the contract or conveyance otherwise defines it. It is not merely the top of the glacial drift, soil, or the agricultural surface. Clause in the deed granting coal rights, providing that the grantee shall not enter upon or injure the surface construed as prohibiting them from letting down the surface through removal of coal pillars, including the word "surface" plaintiff's cement deposits which overlay defendant's coal seams. Injunction awarded.

Marquette Cement Mining Co. v. Oglesby Coal Co. (Illinois), 253 Federal, 107.

Potash production of the United States last year, according to W. B. Hicks of the U. S. Geological Survey, was as under:

Sources	Number of producers	Production, tons	Available potash (K_2O), tons
Natural brines	21	147,125	39,255
Alunite	4	6,073	2,019
Dust from cement mills	9	11,739	1,420
Kelp	6	14,450	4,292
Molasses distillery waste	4	9,505	3,322
Steffens waste water	5	2,818	761
Wood ashes	26	609	305
Other sources	3	202	92
	78	192,587	52,135

The output in 1918 was almost double that of 1917, and is 22% of normal domestic consumption. The brines of Nebraska yielded 55% of the total.

Graphite (domestic) sales during 1918 totaled 6500 tons, valued at $1,500,000, compared with 5292 tons and $1,094,398 in 1917. About 4400 tons was of the No. 1 and 2 flake grades.

Book Reviews

Steam Engines. By E. M. Shealy. Pp. 286, ill., index. McGraw-Hill Book Co., Inc., New York. For sale by 'Mining and Scientific Press'. Price, $2.50.

The author is associate professor of steam engineering at the University of Wisconsin, and the book is written primarily as a textbook for students, but it will also be of value to the operating engineer who wishes to increase his knowledge of the technical side of the subject. The book is almost entirely devoted to reciprocating engines, turbines being discussed in the last chapter only, and then very briefly. The first chapter considers elementary principles, also the plain slide-valve engine, and this is followed by a discussion of Corliss engines, locomotive engines, and marine engines. The book is well illustrated and is as nearly non-mathematical as is possible, considering the subject.

Organic Compounds of Arsenic and Antimony. By Gilbert T. Morgan. Pp. 376, index, bibliography. Longmans, Green & Co., New York, 1918. For sale by 'Mining and Scientific Press'. Price, $4.80.

The study of organic arsenical and antimonial compounds has extended from early times, and has received the careful attention of chemists for more than 200 years. These substances, apart from the fact that most of them are highly toxic, are of special interest from their therapeutic value. The selective action of many of them permits their use in combating various diseases resulting from protozoal parasites. Atoxyl has proved useful as a remedy in sleeping sickness, and neosalvarsan has supplied a means for combating some of the serious contagious diseases that afflict mankind. The work by Dr. Morgan is a highly-technical discussion of the typical compounds, cacodyl, alipathic arsenicals and antimonials, aromatic arsenicals, atoxyl, salvarsan, neosalvarsan, aromatic antimonials, hydro-aromatic derivatives of arsenic and antimony, heterocyclic rings containing arsenic and antimony, arsenical esters and arsenical lipoid and protein combinations. Methods of preparation and characteristic reactions of the compounds are given in detail.

Storing. Its economic aspects and proper methods. By H. B. Twyford. Pp. 200, ill., index. D. Van Nostrand Co., New York, 1918. For sale by 'Mining and Scientific Press'. Price, $3.50.

The author of this book has also written on a kindred subject, namely 'Purchasing'. He is connected with the Otis Elevator Co., so should be fully conversant with storage methods. From a number of manufacturers of storeroom equipment he has obtained data and illustrations on the subject, so that it would seem as if the work before us should be thorough. In the 12 chapters are covered the economic questions connected with storing material, the location and equipment of storeroom, appliances used, manual and clerical work, the storekeeper, receiving, inspecting, and placing material, and deliveries. A few pertinent remarks from the book are suggestive: "Into every form of commercial activity which involves the retention for long or short periods of materials and supplies is penetrating the new importance of storing." "Every business needs a certain amount of raw material or manufactured articles, or supplies. For successful operation there must be sufficiency, and there must not be lack." "Too often the storekeeper is looked upon as a man whose duties are exclusively physical. He is not supposed to have a thinking job. The position of storekeeper needs better recognition; it needs recognition on a somewhat different basis to that which is usually accorded it. Sufficient consideration has not been given to the potentialities of the keeper of the stores. He is in complete control of a very large proportion of the wealth of many concerns." "Buying and storing, although distinct and separate functions in any business, are closely related in all those cases where the goods do not immediately pass out of the possession of the purchaser." "It is essential that stock in storerooms be properly described and designated." And "Nothing should be permitted to enter the storeroom unaccompanied by some form of advice . . . no material should be allowed to leave the stores without a properly drawn requisition." The many duties of store employees are fully discussed, and the illustrations show how stocks should be arranged, handled, and counted. Many companies will find this book worth-while when on their storekeepers' desks.

Metallurgy of the Non-Ferrous Metals. Second edition, revised and enlarged. By William Gowland. Pp. 588, ill., plates, index. Charles Griffin & Co., London, 1918. For sale by 'Mining and Scientific Press'. Price, $8.50.

Having no copy of the first edition of this work we are unable to make comparisons, but from a preliminary perusal we find the book before us to be one of much value. Alphabetically, the metals considered are aluminum, antimony, arsenic, bismuth, cadmium, cobalt, copper, gold, lead, mercury, nickel, platinum, silver, tin, and zinc. And thinking over the latest metallurgical practice for these metals, we find that the author has as much as is possible to procure on aluminum, although his statistics are rather behind; the notes on antimony include the liquation and the preferred process of volatilizing-roasting and reduction of the oxide to metal; the American system of recovering arsenic, as in the Washoe works at Anaconda, is included; those having bismuth in their ores will find the eight pages of value, as little is available otherwise; as cadmium is a by-product of zinc, and is comparatively rare, the two pages given are sufficient; the new use of cobalt in the alloy 'stellite', and in electro-plating, also its recovery from Cobalt, Ontario, silver ores, is covered; copper is dealt with in 114 pages, wherein is described roasting, smelting, converting, leaching by ammonia and sulphuric acid, and electrolytic refining; the 136 pages on gold cover all phases of milling with the most modern machinery, cyanidation, and refining; in 68 pages lead is considered, including the Bunker Hill & Sullivan and Trail works, but the Morse system of open tops to furnaces, as at El Paso, is rather too recent for inclusion; in the chapter on mercury some of the new work being done at Idria and Almaden and by the State Mining Bureau of California is described, although the rotary type furnace is not mentioned, being rather recent; the complex processes for recovery of nickel as at Sudbury are described; the note on preparation of pure platinum is useful; in the 51 pages on silver we note the latest processes in Ontario, Nevada, and Mexico, although the sodium-sulphide precipitation method is omitted; tin-smelting practice in Cornwall, Germany, New Jersey, the Straits, and Tasmania is detailed, also the recovery of tin from scrap; and lastly zinc includes distillation, electrolytic extraction, and smelting from ores. Besides the metallurgical notes, each metal has its physical and chemical properties stated briefly, also its ores, alloys, and uses. Ahead of all chapters on the metals are 12 pages on refractory materials, 29 pages on roasting principles and furnaces, and 6 pages on fluxes and slags. There are 217 illustrations, mostly of modern plant. The Cottrell precipitator is dismissed rather too briefly, and flotation is hardly mentioned. Statistics are mostly of 1913 or 1914, of course showing normal production, yet later data are available. A few typographical errors and peculiar style for terms are noticeable, but the work is probably the best reference extant on the non-ferrous metals.

M. W. vB.

INFORMATION FURNISHED BY MANUFACTURERS

MINE SECTION-INSULATOR WITH SWITCH

By N. A. Wahlberg

In mines, every cross-entry should have a section-insulator fixed in the cross-entry trolley-wire on tangent as close as possible to the main entry. As most cross-entry trolley-wires are used only a small part of the time, it would increase the safety if the voltage were cut-off when not in use.

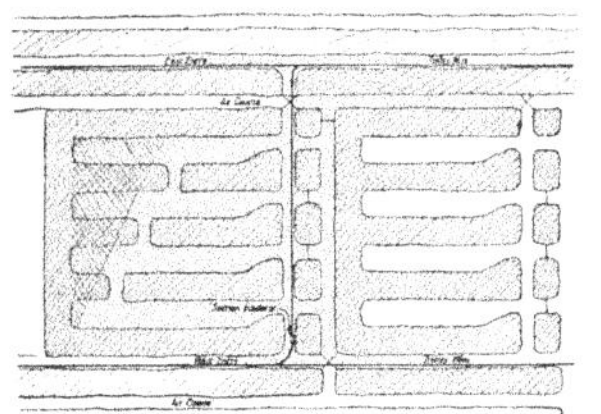

FIG. 1. MINE LAY-OUT WITH SECTION-INSULATOR.

Fig. 1 shows a coal-mine lay-out in line with Eastern practice, with section-insulators at each end of the cross-entry connecting the east entry with the west entry. A common practice is to use a section-insulator similar to Fig. 2. This type of insulator has no switch attachment, and it is necessary to have a knife-switch connected in the circuit so that the cross-entry trolley-wire can be energized, as in Fig. 3. The knife-switch should be mounted in a box to protect same from moisture and dust. It is readily seen that this arrangement requires considerable amount of labor and material. It also has its disadvantages, as the locomotive may get stalled with the trolley-wheel on the insulated part of the section-insulator when the locomotive is pulling a load. Considerable delay will be experienced in case there is insufficient room to turn the trolley-pole, and it is often necessary to detach several cars to enable the locomotive to get over the dead section in the overhead.

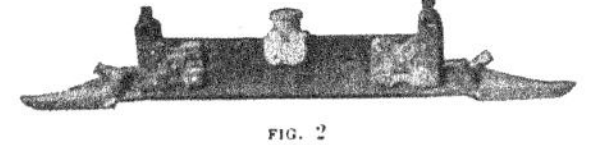

FIG. 2

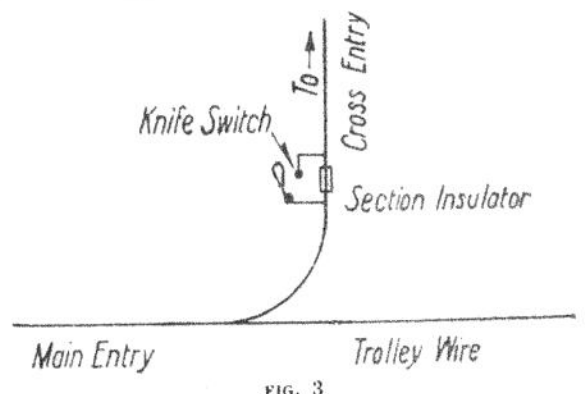

FIG. 3

Mine operators have demanded a combination of section-insulator and knife-switch that would eliminate delays of this nature in their haulage service, and the section-insulators designed by the Westinghouse Electric & Mfg. Co., illustrated in Fig. 4 and 5, have proved successful in a number of installations.

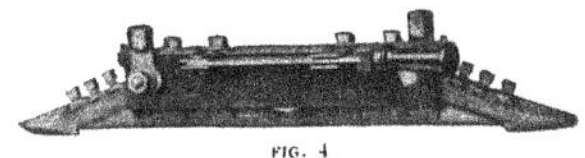

FIG. 4

A section-insulator should not permit of any leakage whatever if the switch is open. Its construction, as a whole, should be mechanically strong, yet not too heavy to add any unnecessary weight in case the local conditions are such that it cannot be supported direct by means of suspensions from the mine-roof. Two supporting lugs with longitudinal adjustment are preferable, as in Fig. 4. Where conditions do not permit of using two supports and space is limited, a swivel-boss in the centre is desirable, as section-insulator can be easily put up without turning the complete section-insulator, as in Fig. 5. The runner of the switch should never obstruct the passage of the trolley-wheel, regardless as to whether switch is open or closed.

FIG. 5

A metallic runner with air insulation has several advantages. It allows uniform wearing and no parts require renewal; for instance, where treated wood or fibre is used, see Fig. 2, considerable arcing when breaking the circuit takes place, eventually increasing to such an extent that the runner parts have to be replaced frequently. The switch should be independent of the runner, and of such section that it will permit a heavy current to pass through without heating the section-insulator at any point, as this may damage the insulation qualities of the section-insulator.

Direction of feeding in a mine varies, and a switch should be made so that it can be opened either right or left hand. Fig. 5 shows a switch that can easily be converted to right or left hand by loosening the machine bolts and interchanging the break-jaws with the hinge-jaws. Changes of this nature can easily be made in the mine. When the switch is open, the break-jaw should always be the live terminal.

this can be accomplished by interchanging the hinge and break-jaws as mentioned above.

A CONTINUOUS TWIN-SCOOP LOADER

After several years of development, the Wellman-Seaver-Morgan company of Cleveland, Ohio, has placed upon the market a mine loading-machine known as the McDermott continuous twin-scoop loader. As its name implies, this machine digs loose ore, dirt, or muck, by a continuous scooping process. The material is picked up by scoops or buckets on an endless chain, elevated and dropped into a hopper, which feeds a conveyor-belt, in turn loading a car. The accompanying illustration shows these points. The scooping mechanism is so pivoted that it can dig to the side as well as in front of the machine. The ore, however, being delivered to the conveyor through the hopper, reaches the car behind the loader, irrespective at what angle the scoop is working. The movement of the scoop is continuous, not reciprocating. The machine is self propelled, and is so designed that it can easily be transferred about a mine. It will load at the rate of over 1 ton per minute, and may be operated by unskilled labor. In designing this machine, the adverse conditions and restricted space underground have been kept in mind, and particular attention has been given to rigidity with minimum weight. While specially designed for underground work, the loader is not limited to this, as it can also be used on the surface for loading coal from piles to cars, removing piles of rock and sand, and similar operations.

THE CONTINUOUS TWIN-SCOOP LOADER.

The loader consists of three main parts, truck, digging-head, and conveyor. These parts can readily be dismounted and as readily re-assembled, permitting ease of handling in getting the machine underground and in moving from level to level. The levers are at one side, in a position convenient for the operator to watch the various movements.

The loader is fitted with motors wound for 230 volts, d.c., providing power for all of the operations. The motors are of the entirely enclosed type. All chains and gears are protected. All chains are provided with take-ups, and the digging-edge of the bucket is filled with renewable tooth sections. The entire frame-work is of steel, the digging-head is mounted on a large ball-bearing, and all parts are protected as much as possible against dirt and water.

The general dimensions of the loader are: Maximum overall length, 15 ft. 9 in.; height, with buckets in lowest position, 5 ft. 6¾ in.; height, when machine is in operation, 6 ft. 7¼ in.; width, 4 ft.; gauge of truck wheels, 24 in.; maximum rated capacity with full buckets, 1.75 tons per min.; average capacity, 45 tons per hour; and weight of complete machine, 8000 pounds.

From the illustration will be seen the difference between this and other mine loading machines.

COMMERCIAL PARAGRAPHS

Catalogue No. 7 of the **Hardinge Conical Mill Co.**, New York, in 5 sections, covers its ball and pebble-mills.

Paint and varnish dealers will be interested in a new pamphlet just issued by the paint and varnish department of the **Du Pont Co.** of Wilmington, Delaware, on mill and mine paints. It describes a line especially designed for the painting and up-keep of machinery, equipment, factory and mill buildings.

The American Manufacturers Export Association has been organized by 1100 of the leading manufacturers of the United States, and will collect and issue news of interest to exporters. The head office is at 160 Broadway, New York, with S. J. Quinn as secretary. Well-known industrial men are among the directorate.

At the annual meeting of the **Wellman-Seaver-Morgan Co.** at Cleveland on February 18, the retiring directors were re-elected. The following officers were elected: Edwin S. Church, president and general manager; S. G. Pitkin, vice-president; G. W. Burrell, second vice-president; and W. H. Cowell, secretary-treasurer. Mr. Burrell has been in the continuous employ of the company for 21 years. He will have entire charge of the works at Cleveland and Akron.

The proper caustic soda to be used with Proto Fleuss self-contained breathing-apparatus is especially prepared for **H. N. Elmer of Siebe, Gorman & Co.,** Chicago, by the Mendleson Corporation. This is put up in 4-lb. cans in 24-can crates, and labeled, and is the only soda, except c. p. stock soda, to be used with the Proto apparatus. The lump caustic soda is sold by the Mendleson Corporation of Albany, New York, at 12 to 15c. per lb. for 2016 to less than 480-lb. lots.

The Material-Handling Machinery-Manufacturers' Association was formed recently at the suggestion of the Department of Commerce and the U. S. Shipping Board, and offices have been opened at 35 West 39th street, New York. The work of the Association will be similar to that of most trade organizations, except that more extensive technical committee work will be required than is usually the custom. There is one aspect of the work that is unusual. Other trade organizations will be asked to appoint material-handling committees which will meet with committees appointed by the new Association to consider the special handling problems of each particular industry. The officers of the Association are Calvin Tomkins, president; J. A. Shepard, vice-president; Zenas W. Carter, secretary and manager; Lucian C. Brown, treasurer; J. A. Shepard, Lucian C. Brown, R. W. Scott, F. W. Hall, William Clark, J. C. Walter, C. M. Watson, and F. Stadelman.

The **Heine Safety Boiler Co.,** of St. Louis, Missouri, has issued the latest edition of its 'Boiler Logic', an 86-page treatise on steam boilers. The following topics are covered:

I. 'Some Fundamental Considerations of Boiler Design': (a) Furnace design requirements: Mixing, time, temperature; (b) heat transmission from fire by radiation; (c) heat transmission by convection; and (d) heat transmission through tubes and to water.

II. 'Practical Baffling of Water-Tube Boilers': (a) Flexibility of design; (b) leakage and cost of repairs and renewals; (c) active and inactive surface; and (d) ease of cleaning soot and ash deposits.

III. 'Heine Boilers for Different Fuels, Firing, and Services': including hand firing with bituminous coal, shavings, and refuse; hand firing with anthracite coal and bagasse (sugar-cane residue); chain-grate and underfeed stokers; oil-fired, gas-fired, waste-heat, and dredge boilers.

IV. 'Overloads'.

V. 'The Boiler as a Pressure Vessel'.

VI. 'Details of Construction of Heine Boilers'.

ALTHOUGH we are passing through a period of re-adjustment, the signs of prosperity are visible to anyone but a confirmed pessimist. Bank clearings are big, the railroads are carrying an enormous tonnage, insolvencies are comparatively few, our foreign trade is beating the record. It is true, food is dear and wages are high, so that the cost of living is excessive, but the dearness of food and labor is due largely to the inefficiency of the latter, not to excessive pay. These matters are being arranged by the incorrigible ratio of supply and demand.

ONE of our local organs of misinformation told its readers a few days ago that the Butte & Superior Mining Company had reduced its working force 50% on account of the over-production of copper. We suppose that the words 'Butte' and 'Superior' suggested copper, but the fact is, as our readers are aware, that the Butte & Superior, although originally organized to mine copper ore and formerly called the Butte & Superior Copper Company, now produces zinc and silver, with a little lead, and we hope that it will continue to produce all of them for many years to come, profitably.

WITH this issue we publish a review of Josiah Royce's book on the early days of California by our friend Mr. Grant H. Smith, himself a native of Sutter Creek, one of California's earliest mining settlements. Mr. Smith is a lawyer by profession, but his boyhood was spent among the mines, so he is able to interpret sympathetically not only Royce but the frontier life of which Royce writes. Here we give ourselves the pleasure of acknowledging that we have found it advantageous, more than once, to make use of Mr. Grant Smith's fine feeling for our language, the language of Shakespeare, of whom he is an affectionate student.

IN the Internal Revenue Act for 1918 is included a stipulation exempting gold-mining enterprises from the excess-profit tax. This may be taken as one result of the good work done by the Committee on Gold, of which Mr. Hennen Jennings was chairman. The idea that mining for gold profited from the War is absurd, of course, because even under ordinary conditions the 'price' of gold would not be directly affected, whereas it is a fact that the abnormal financial conditions produced by world-wide belligerency did have the effect of depreciating the standard metal. If this exemption had not been made the owners of many gold mines, especially those coming into production for the first time during the War, after years of expensive development, would have fared very badly. We are glad therefore to note that the excess-profit tax is not to be added to the burdens of the gold miner. This exemption should draw the attention of legislators and financiers to the peculiar position of gold in world economics and stimulate study of a subject that is of compelling importance.

REPORTS from Europe indicate that there will be a good market for American copper in the near future. Orders from several sources, with France as the principal buyer, are promised. Second-hand and speculative holdings of copper are said to be undergoing rapid reduction through purchases made by domestic consumers, making way for the re-establishment of a normal market. Some of the copper companies may have to borrow money in order to carry their stocks of metal, as, for instance, was done recently by the Kennecott Copper Corporation, which borrowed $12,000,000 to protect the 55,000,000 pounds of copper it was carrying, but this can be done without serious financial injury because of the inherent soundness of the copper-mining business. Conditions will re-adjust themselves slowly. There is no cause for panic.

IT is reported that at the conference of Governors and Mayors held at Washington on March 5 an attempt to invite the meeting to endorse the Government ownership of railroads was defeated by acclamation. This expression of opinion, we believe, represented the feelings of the public at large. Not only is the present administration of the railroads costly and inefficient, as compared with the management of the companies owning the railroads, but most thoughtful citizens will appreciate the great danger of expanding the political machine and aggrandizing the patronage of the party in power at Washington. This refers to both parties, of course. No non-partisan democrat can contemplate without uneasiness the continued growth of bureaucratic organizations at the capital.

THOSE who are concerned with the winning of oil, and everybody desiring to be well informed, will find something to interest them in the article, appearing in this issue, by Mr. J. H. G. Wolf, who has made a special study of the problems, technical and economic, arising from the exploitation of our oil resources. He recites the course of the market for petroleum products during the War and shows how hard this industry was hit by the general dislocation of trade, but the chief feature of his article is a lucid explanation of the manner in which the flow of oil is regulated by the pressure of the gas that constitutes an integral part of such natural deposits. This gas-pressure gives the impulse necessary for collecting and impelling the oil to the surface and it comes into active play just as soon as an opening is made by a bore-hole or well. During periods of non-production, when operations cease for any reason, this valuable force is dissipated, so that the human effort to win the oil has to be increased. This fact should govern the selection of the time and place for drilling new wells, as Mr. Wolf's statistical summary shows conclusively.

EFFORTS are being made to persuade the Secretary of Commerce in the Mexican cabinet to call a general meeting, at Mexico City, of mine operators in the four northern States for the purpose of discussing the welfare of the mining industry and the settlement of important questions arising out of the conditions created both by the European war and the domestic revolution. A scarcity of explosives is said to be crippling mining operations and the imposition of excessive taxes is menacing the stability of the industry. It is hoped that President Carranza, who is seeking financial aid in New York, will realize the need for dealing fairly with those who are engaged legitimately in the production of metals and of oil in Mexico.

WE have received a telegram from Mr. J. E. Spurr, of the War Minerals Investigation Committee of the U. S. Bureau of Mines, stating that the President has signed the War Minerals Relief Act, providing for the adjustment of war claims on account of the production of manganese, chrome, tungsten, and pyrite during the period of the War; and that settlement of such claims is to be made at the discretion of the Secretary of the Interior; therefore it will become necessary to examine a large number of mines in order to ascertain the validity of the claims. The Bureau of Mines invites applications, for appointment as inspectors for this purpose, from mining engineers of the requisite standing, judgment, and experience. Salaries will range from $300 to $400 per month and it is probable that the engagement will cover a number of months. The Bureau would also like to receive applications for appointment as assistant engineers for the same purpose at $150 to $250 per month, the pay depending upon individual experience in the mining of the minerals covered by the Act.

SECRETARY WILSON, of the Department of Labor, told the conference of Governors and Mayors that it was folly to attempt the reduction of wages at this time, because it was possible to lower the cost of living, and of materials generally, without interfering with the existing rates of pay. To this doctrine we shall not demur, for it is not the cost, but the inefficiency of labor, that is the chief handicap of industry in these days. The Government shipyards and the other shipyards and factories engaged in doing Government work have presented a spectacle of inefficiency that is appalling. Profiteering and inefficiency together have sent the price of the necessaries of life skyward and upset both national and domestic economics. Intelligent employers do not object to high wages if it yields efficient labor, but they do protest against being victimized by a service that is both costly and inefficient. We do not overlook the rank imposture of the patriotism of sundry manufacturers who used the War as an excuse for business of a predatory character, raising prices simply because the public was helpless, but we doubt whether anything so glaringly fictitious was presented during the War as the 'patriotism' of the young workers who demanded double wages under cover of 'holding the trenches' at home and of 'backing the soldiers' at the front. They remind us of the man "who fought with Sousa"—and his band at a naval station on Lake Erie. The discontent of Labor is due in part to the reaction from the exorbitant pay and lax supervision of an abnormal period—to a disinclination to return to normal conditions, which include specifically a degree of efficiency that will promote economy. We question whether the copper miners, for example, have profited more from the War, or profited less honorably, than the companies and shareholders by whom they were employed, but we do believe that the mad rush to put men to work at fancy wages on highly profitable ship, munition, and armament contracts has demoralized a large part of the labor population and established a standard of inefficiency that is not to be endured.

The League of Nations

We envy Mr. Taft. It is an eminently gracious act at this time to be able sincerely to support the President in his advocacy of democratic ideals at Paris, and it is particularly fortunate for a Republican ex-President to be able to play this graceful rôle before the world. Certainly he cuts a more dignified figure than sundry senators at Washington whose opposition unfortunately for them appears to be colored by political prejudice. Mr. Taft's tour of the country in company with the president of Harvard university, the ex-ambassador to Turkey, and other distinguished citizens equally earnest in their support of Mr. Wilson s proposals for preventing war, is bound to make a profound impression on public opinion in Europe. It strengthens the President's hands enormously. We would like to be equally enthusiastic in favor of this league "to enforce peace," for any sane man must wish with all his heart and soul to ensure civilization against suicide, but it seems to us that in the hurry to interpret ideals in terms of international compacts there is a failure to take account of the concrete duties ensuing from an acceptance of the abstractions now being ventilated at Versailles. After a journey from San Francisco to New York, in the course of which we read the various newspapers available along the line of the railroad, we detect a lamentable failure on the part of the public to recognize the responsibilities involved in the President's propaganda. He has forced the idea of a League of Nations into the foreground of international politics and he has succeeded in obtaining a general acceptance of that idea, as expressed in the preliminary constitution drafted immediately before his return from Paris. Apparently Mr. Wilson has overcome the opposition of the French delegates, more particularly M. Clemenceau; he has been enabled to impose his wishes upon the Conference by reason of the prestige of the United States, the support of the English delegates, and the enthusiasm that he has evoked among the liberals in every one of the Allied countries. The United States, by its belated but decisive participation in the struggle of the nations and by the obviously disinterested character of its international policy, has occupied a dominating position at Versailles. To the exhausted belligerents in Europe the President of the United States came as the prophet of a new dispensation, to the imperialistic traditions of the old world he brought the promise of a reconstruction based on the democratic ideals of a new world. He was received with acclamation and he was heard with deep respect. If most of the delegates from the other countries listened to him so approvingly, despite the growing anxiety of the French premier and his associates, it was because they believed that Mr. Wilson had a mandate from the United States and that anything he undertook to do would be performed in due course by the great nation whom he represented. Has he such a mandate? At the present time the President is opposed by a large proportion of the Republican party, but he has the enthusiastic backing of all the idealists and pacifists, without respect to party, that is, of the big mass of the people of this country, horrified by the War, eager to prevent a repetition of it, and confident that a means can be evolved to do so. But do the supporters of the League of Nations realize the responsibilities to be incurred, to be accepted and loyally fulfilled, by the United States? We think not; and therein lies a grave danger not only to this nation but to the world at large. The acceptance by us of the League proposal would involve the maintenance of an expeditionary force and of the multitudinous equipment, including transport, required to transfer it for prompt service in Europe, or elsewhere, whenever the safety of the League was jeopardized. Such an expeditionary force would not be one of less than 100,000 men and might be possibly 250,000. Another responsibility implicit in our joining the League would be the acceptance of a mandatory to administer sundry troublous regions, for example, Armenia and Georgia, and possibly to provide a government for Constantinople, the warder of three continents and the gateway of the Near East. America's share in the rehabilitation of Europe will involve burdens not lightly to be considered, much less ignored. Besides soldiers and governments, we shall have to provide large sums of money as our contribution to the cost of so policing and protecting an unquiet world that peace may be preserved. Moreover, if the United States becomes a signatory to the international covenant to preserve peace she may have to forego sundry rights now freely exercised, such as the control of immigration, the expulsion of undesirable aliens, the fortification of the Panama canal, and the regulation of our foreign trade by tariff or embargo. It may not involve the abrogation of the Monroe doctrine as applied to the Americas, but it will involve us in the "entangling alliances" so feared and disliked by our forefathers. Mr. Taft says that "the League of Nations was invented for the purpose of extending the Monroe doctrine to all the nations of the world, and it is proposed that the league stand behind it to see its enforcement." Mr. Taft is a jurist, so his dicta concerning the Monroe doctrine and the constitution are authoritative. He says that the proposed covenant does not conflict with the constitution of the United States, yet we can imagine the conferees at Paris asking each other "what is a constitution between friends" and proceeding to take liberties even with so sacrosanct a body of fundamental principles if thereby they could further the peace of the world. With such a great gain there must be some minor losses. Any international partnership for good work involves some sacrifice of national freedom. Even the relinquishment of some part of the sovereignty of the United States is not terrifying, for every decision of international law involves some surrender of national rights; they are conceded just as the individual citizen foregoes some of his private rights for the sake of the community as a whole. None of these things need intimidate us at this time when so earnest an effort is being made to stabilize international relations; it is worth while to surrender a good deal for the sake of ensuring peace and of saving the world from another hideous calamity such as we have but lately witnessed; but we must know what we are going to do, we must be told just what responsibilities are to be assumed by the United States. The President in his last speech, made the night before he sailed from New York, referred three times to the sacrifices this country will be called upon to make. He said that "we are ready to make the supreme sacrifice for an idea; the supreme sacrifice of throwing in our fortunes with the fortunes of men everywhere." He prayed God that we would not falter, that we might be given "the privilege of knowing that we did it without counting the cost, and because we were true Americans, lovers of liberty and of doing right." We share that pious hope and look forward to the consummation of it, but we venture to suggest, at this critical period of international reorganization, that the people of the United States ought to be told—in the first instance by the President, and secondly by such leaders of public opinion as Mr. Taft—just what the "sacrifice" or the "cost" entails. Before this country is committed to so basic a departure from established policy and before the President affixes his signature, as our representative, to a solemn covenant —not a 'scrap of paper'—binding the United States to many serious obligations, it is imperative that full information be given to the people. If in the enthusiasm of the moment we permit the President to bind this country to membership in the League of Nations and if afterward we shirk the fulfillment of the duties imposed upon us, we shall be stultified, if not indeed dishonored. We intend nothing of the kind, therefore we want to know just what it is to which we are to be committed. For ourselves, we do not fear that these obligations will be too heavy a price to pay for an enduring peace; we pray for the success of the Paris conference: we are in no wise intimidated by the speeches of Senators Reed and Sherman; but we do ask for the information to which every thoughtful citizen is entitled. There is no quick way of ascertaining the will of the nation in such a matter as this; the President comes more near to interpreting the national sentiment, we believe, than most of his noisy opponents at Washington, but he has received no mandate for his actions at Paris, except his election in 1916, the force of which was weakened in the congressional election of last November. All the more therefore he should, we submit, take pains to inform the public concerning the conditions governing the League of Nations, so that our people may have a proper understanding of the tasks we are accepting. Tell us, Mr. President, what we are to do in this matter, and we will face the music manfully.

International Control of Minerals

The underlying motive in the paper by Mr. C. K. Leith, which we reproduce elsewhere in this issue, is to utilize a principle which had developed suddenly in working form under the pressure of war, for the assembling and distribution of minerals more economically than in times past. He asks "whether the centralized international control required by the War shall be retained or extended as a means of furthering the aims of a league of nations." Viewing one aspect of the case, an affirmative answer might be given. If the nations were to be organized into a universal State, if they were to surrender the administration of their economic activities to a central governing body, and if, in place of private initiative and the spontaneous operation of the law of supply and demand, there were to be substituted a controlling board to regulate the production of raw materials and manufactured commodities, giving, in effect, a sort of cartel system, expanded for application to a world-wide highly socialized government, the international control of minerals would follow as a logical necessity. Since the article by Dr. Leith was written the draft of a constitution for the proposed league of nations has been placed before the world, and it is seen to signify a closer association of independent nations, each retaining the right to manage its own affairs in matters of trade and internal development. Therefore the world comes back to the old principle of self-sufficiency for each political entity, so far as that may be attainable, and questions of pure economy must be modified by considerations, on the part of each commonwealth, of the problem of self-preservation. The more elaborate artificial characteristics of the ideal of international control of essential commodities are therefore eliminated, but there were some advantages in the plan suggested by Dr. Leith that may still be retained. Since it is fashionable at the present time to be idealistic, one is in no danger of being suspected of mental errancy by stopping to consider politico-economic theories that are apart from the usual program of hum-drum business. Five years ago a man would have been set down as a dreamer to have recommended international control and 'allocation' of basic supplies; today it puts him into the class of neo-progressives to advocate such reforms. The symbol of this new party has not yet been adopted, but there is no evidence to suggest that the Bull Moose will evolve into a type suitable for the purpose. Seriously, the conception possesses features of merit. Man has always been wasteful, even when not prodigal. The time may be at hand when he should display a wiser sense of responsibility in his use of the products of the earth. Nevertheless, we must beware the error of Babel and not aspire to usurp and surpass the prerogatives of providence, whose scheme of economy seems also to involve waste for the sake of achieving particular ends. While mindful of the conservation of forces, which depends on transmutation of energy, we are also not forgetful of the millions of eggs that go to the making of a single adult codfish. Leaving playful philosophy aside, we urge that problems of conservation be weighed seriously and that suggestions for developing workable plans be not neglected. Among the ideas recently advanced is one that deserves attention, because it seems to offer a practical means for promoting the distribution of raw materials, without introducing the harsh methods of exclusion by rigid protection. This, so far as we know, originated as a proposal by Mr. Franklin K. Lane, the Secretary of the Interior, for the encouragement of potash production in the United States. It would necessitate appropriate legislation requiring that some definite proportion of the domestic output, at a fixed price, be used in conjunction with imported supplies of the same material. It was suggested that the price of the home product be established at $2.50 per unit of K_2O, and that an amount of the American salt corresponding to the ratio that the American output may bear to the total consumption should be employed by all prime users. This method of fomenting a domestic enterprise holds possibilities for wider application. It would conserve the benefit of economic development of the industries that depend upon a particular raw material, without subjecting the country to the burden of abnormally high prices to protect them where their future magnitude and value might be open to doubt. Conservation is a complex problem. It involves not merely getting what is wanted from any part of the world at the lowest possible cost, nor the limitation of output in view of the needs of coming generations, nor the distribution of materials on an ideal basis of economy; it demands consideration also of the need of each nation to become as nearly self-supporting as possible. That is one guarantee of contentment, leading to the elimination of a form of commercial cupidity that is the frequent disturber of international peace.

Buy It Now!

The Editor:

Sir—There is a lot of more or less loose talk going on about reconstruction, rehabilitation, post-war re-adjustment, or whatever you have a mind to call it. In other words, business is most certainly not good, particularly in contrast with the flush industrial conditions and high prices for material and labor that obtained during the period of the War. Nevertheless, business is worse than it should be, and we all of us are responsible for this state of affairs. When will things start up again? The answer is, when you do your part to start them up, and not before. Everybody, from the office boy to the trust magnate, from the mucker to the mine manager, is sitting on his haunches gazing speculatively at the market quotations, his hand on his watch, expecting a sort of low-water-small to enable him to buy what he wants for less than it is worth. That may be business in one sense of the word, but it certainly is not in another. It spells idleness rather than business. You who want a return to 'business as usual', trot out and buy something, and buy it right away. If you have a strike on your hands, or are operating on part-time with a reduced working crew, utilize this opportunity to overhaul your plant equipment, make those changes that have been in your mind for eighteen months. Install that new, more efficient, air-compressor, ball-mill, power-plant, or whatever it may be that will lower your costs when you resume operations. The quicker you get it in, the quicker it will make returns on the investment. If you wait for the rush that will come as people gradually return to their sense of the realities of things, you won't get the delivery you want, and you will have wasted the golden opportunity. The old familiar saying about saving at the spigot and wasting at the bunghole is apt. You might, perhaps, save 5 or even 10% in the purchase price by waiting six months or a year, and even that is questionable. You might also lose the use of this same piece of apparatus, or those supplies just when you want them most, which would make your theoretical saving look like thirty cents compared to the much larger issue of impairment in efficiency, and much greater loss on this account. Then there is the greatest issue of all. We, as a people, are dependent absolutely upon one another. Where there is a tendency so general as now exists to buy nothing, start nothing, and do nothing; where everybody expresses the hope that 'business will pick up soon', and does nothing on his own account to make it pick up, you have begun to raise a crop of hard-time tares for which you yourself are principally responsible. Cut it out! Place your orders! You will inspire confidence in the fellow who gets them, and he, in turn, will pass on the glad tidings that 'business as usual' has returned, and the first thing you know you will have a demand for your overstock of metals.

C. T. HUTCHINSON.

San Francisco, March 4.

Rossiter W. Raymond

The Editor:

Sir—Without the suggestion of yourself and the President of the Institute I would not have thought of intruding in any way between Dr. Rossiter W. Raymond and his work and a mining audience to whom he and it were so familiar and appreciated. Raymond was no office knight, but a chief among men on any occasion, a great artist in his work, performing all duties to the best of his ability.

From 1885 to 1895 I was filled with gratitude for his labors on the Transactions of the Institute, and the 'Engineering and Mining Journal', regarding these publications with those of the U. S. Geological Survey as my alma mater, and he and his brilliant confreres as my generous and enthusiastic professors, and I always felt deeply for myself and other young men how much we owed to himself and associates. Their example probably molded the American mining engineer, by imitation, into the splendid aggregates and individuals who have been called on for such important duties during the War.

In taking charge for the War Eagle and Centre Star mining companies, at Rossland, B. C., I inherited an apex suit, Iron Mask v. Centre Star. Both our mines and those about them were taken under the first lode location law of British Columbia, which followed the American law, with extra-lateral rights. The B. C. law was quickly replaced by the present one of 1500 ft. square locations and vertical boundaries. The idea of digging under another person's property was so alien to the English law, that the only precedent was that of digging in Yorkshire for a hundred feet or so to find a drain. But the Court expressed itself as wishing in decisions and rulings to follow U. S. precedents.

As I disagreed with the depiction of the geology in the preliminary Iron Mask v. Centre Star suits and injunction proceedings, it was necessary to engage new council and witnesses. There was much at stake, for the purchase price of the War Eagle and Centre Star mines by the two companies was $2,700,000; and $500,000 had been spent for equipment.

The legal personnel was organized as follows: Edward P. Davis and Aleck C. Galt, attorneys, with Thomas P. Galt as further counsel and directly representing the Eastern owners. Rossiter W. Raymond, Clarence King, and Waldemar Lindgren, were the leading witnesses, assisted by members of our staff, Walter F. Ferrier on petrography and geology, Theodore Simons and Roy H. Clarke for the maps and models, Arthur A. Cole for assays and analysis, and Henry Kehoe, Joseph J. Taylor, and Guy H. Kirkpatrick, as general assistants, all members of the Institute.

The Iron Mask company was represented by Bodwell and Duff, lawyers, and Louis Janin and W. S. Keyes as leading witnesses. In presenting their view of the geology they had obtained a written opinion from Curtis H. Lindley, and I, with my own view of it, had one from John Forbis. The case was heard before Judge Walkem, at Rossland, in 1899.

On arrival, Raymond took charge of the case, but in doing so he did not detract from the initiative of King and Lindgren. As I went underground with all three, I know that from end to end of the workings exposed, in the ground in conflict, there was no seam or slight differentiation of the rock with which they were not familiar. Raymond was delicate, and husbanded his strength better than the others, by intenser application, satisfying his memory and note-book with fewer trips.

One of our main workings in conflict was a 25° inclined shaft where a continuous streak of pyrrhotite ore, averaging ten inches thick, was claimed. Rossland veins were not remarkable for crustification, and almost any vein might have been excused a lapse of a few inches of continuity in such a sulphide stretch. I had installed comfortable stairs and landings, and electric lights, and water-pipe to wash the whole exposure clean, greatly to the delight of Janin, whose avoidupois matched his fine disposition. I went down the incline with Raymond on his crucial examination. He put the point of his pick on every weak spot, "How about here?" but the continuity always held.

After conclusion of the Raymond, King, and Lindgren testimony the Iron Mask attorneys pleaded the geological version was so different from that in the preliminary suits that they needed a long time to prepare a rebuttal and asked for a year's adjournment, which was granted. The suit did not get into court again.

Next year, not being willing that our case should depend in the mind of the Court on memories twelve months old, I engaged S. F. Emmons, Walter H. Wiley, and Samuel S. Fowler, but these gentlemen did not appear in court, because the Iron Mask consented to our writing the verdict, each side paying its own cost. Our direct cost was $65,000, indirect $60,000 more; the Iron Mask direct cost was $45,000. It is not known whether Janin and Keyes differed from Raymond, King, and Lindgren on the geology; as I have stated, these were the only witnesses heard. Their printed testimony fills a quarto volume, and, coming without revision from the stenographer may be said not to need correction.

It was the first experience of our attorney, Mr. Davis, in mining suits and parlance. After he had patiently mastered volumes of geology and thoroughly digested the maps and models he was taken in state by all hands underground to see what it actually looked like. But presto, all the careful training was gone at once, the flat fault, the co-ordinate fissures, the junction of the veins, etc., were irretrievably mixed in that noisy, dirty darksome hole, so he was quickly hurried to surface and put to bed with Professor Simons' large model on a table by his side. Before the trial began he had entirely recovered. This incident made me wonder about the capability of judges to decide the facts, by visits underground, where differences of opinion exist between highly trained engineers. I am quite confident, however, that, in extra-lateral litigation, if the Nominating Committee of the American Institute of Mining Engineers were requested by the Court to name 25 engineers and from this number three or five were chosen by lottery, the litigants paying fees and expenses in common, the Court would receive such an intelligent and correct version of the facts that a just verdict, according to law, could be rendered.

Sometimes the 'enemy' would dine with us. Janin would tell us plaintively about his California ranch, where his wife was trying to raise chickens, and he a mortgage, or he would complain of our hanging wall with its hinge that allowed a vein to open like a crocodile's maw. Keyes would portray the terrible fate in store for us when they took the stand. Raymond, who had but recently been victorious with Keyes as an opponent, said he could only reply like the Yankee to the irate and threatening Britisher's talk of invasion, "What, again?"

Raymond and King had the common trait of drawing out the best in men, the former technically, and it helped to obtain the valuable contributions with which he filled the Transactions. King was a warm ray of sunshine and the most limpid thoughts of his auditor would creep out to bask in his sympathy. To the amusement of his colleagues, his most enthusiastic reception in Rossland came from a portly colored matron, who, shaking his hand with both of hers, said, "Why, Mr. King, where did you come from? I'se sure glad to see you." Probably either a dinner or a sealskin coat had been shared with herself and babies on a rough trip.

I am sure all present at the Raymond 70th birthday dinner have been looking forward to the 80th one and are sad it is not to be. He sent me greeting from the 1905 Rossland meeting regretting by inability to attend where "We had fought a good fight and a clean fight."

JOHN B. HASTINGS.

Los Angeles, February 4.

Misfires

The Editor:

Sir—There is so much loss of efficiency from misfired caps, and so much danger to life and limb from accidents caused by re-shooting, that a glance at the fundamental causes of misfired blasting caps will not be out of place.

An examination of any misfired blasting cap always shows the surface of the cap marked with burnt carbon; the spit of the fuse has come through and the fire had not been sufficient to accomplish ignition. Potassium nitrate and other chemical ingredients in the fulminate of the cap-charge are exceedingly sensitive to moisture, and

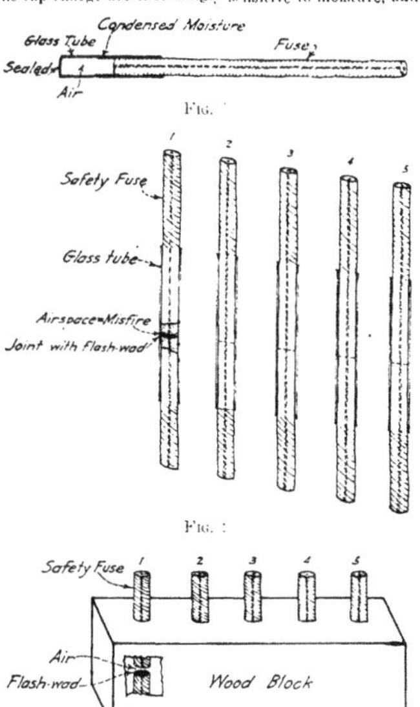

Fig. 1

Fig. 2

Fig. 3

since nature is constantly striving for a balance between elements in opposition, the present method of putting fuse and caps together, is perhaps unwittingly artificial in the light of a fundamental principle. When a railroad train enters a tunnel, the moisture is instantly deposited on the window glass; so also when blowing your breath on a glass surface, or when a glass of ice-cold water is brought into a hot room.

Any plugged receptacle will contain compressed air; a perfect vacuum is secured only by an exact mechanical process; so it is clear that air is caught in the blasting-cap when the fuse is put into it. Moisture is condensed always from the spit of the fuse inserted in a glass tube, and it will be noticed before the fire spits out at the end in the glass that fume precedes the fire. It is a well known principle that 'sparks fly upward', which will answer at times for an insufficiency of heat coming through the fuse causing misfires. When the fuse is spitted, the fire finds a path of least resistance, leaving too little powder at the point of contact with the charge in the cap, and thus it cannot overcome the presence of the air in the space between the charge and the end of the inserted fuse; the result is inevitable. Many tests made with different brands of fuse show extreme differences in the end-spit of the fuse, and in the amount of fire delivered when the fuse spits. The per cent of misfires from the natural spit of the fuse is shown in Fig. 2 where the fuse is held lightly on little squares of magnesium paper, (Eastmen's No. 1 flash sheets) and fired with a shield to protect the hand. In this case double-tape waterproof fuse gave one misfire in five shots.

The proportion of misfires in Fig. 3 is about the same as in actual blasting. The dryness or humidity of the atmosphere has much to do with the results, but this can be corrected and perfect shooting of the blasting caps obtained by the use of a supplemental pinch of meal-powder in the cap, which is then well crimped and sealed with asphaltum paint.

A. J. AVERELL.

Medford, Oregon, January 20.

Stimulation of Gold Mining

The Editor:

Sir—In viewing the situation it must be borne in mind that gold is the standard of value and cannot be changed. It has been established at the fixed valuation of $20.67 per ounce. Should a bonus be paid upon gold production, it simply increases its value. To increase the value of a standard, relatively increases all that is based upon it, and the standard is no longer a standard. The removal of the excess-profit tax will stimulate mining investment by creating in the public mind the idea that the Government recognizes the desirability and necessity of aiding gold mining. Capital will be easy to obtain to float the average gold enterprise, gold stocks will be in demand, and speculation active. It will aid the promoter and increase mining operations; but it is a question whether this is the way to go about it. Will it not injure the gold-mining industry in the long run? It cannot increase actual production to any great extent, there being no profit in the average gold-mining enterprises today, hence an exemption from taxation on excess profit means nothing.

A better plan would be to permit the excess-profit taxes to go into actual underground development, improvement of equipment, and processes of mining, as well as treatment, thus putting more ore-reserves in sight; then, after the excess-profit taxes are removed, the gold miner will reap his reward. Meanwhile gold reserves will be established for future use. The average mine is being worked in a hand to mouth manner, doing only the development work that is forced upon the operators, with little or no exploration work, which is so essential to its life. It must be remembered that mining is a depleting process;

every pound of ore extracted is gone, and can never be produced again. Therefore there can only be two real assets to a mining property, the ore in sight and the money in the treasury. Many instances can be cited in the history of mining, of a mine being on its last legs, when some lucky extension or forced prospecting work disclosed new orebodies and other unknown enrichments, giving it years of profitable life. Systematic exploration work would have shown it long before its actual discovery.

In order to effectually aid the present operator to increase the production at a reasonable profit, it must be approached along an entirely different avenue. It must be broad enough to cover all the conditions, and must effectively reach the production. This must begin at the source, primarily reducing the costs. To do this it is necessary to view the situation as it is, in other words to make a plan, as the efficient architect prepares a careful plan of the structure to be changed, in order to study it, and make the alterations to meet the required conditions, so as to bring out as nearly as possible the desired results with the least disturbance. In order to study the matter intelligently a tabulated plan of the chief items of expense, in their order of size is hereby presented.

MINING

Vein

1. Labor. 2. Munitions (powder, fuse, and caps). 3. Fuel and power. 4. Timber and lumber. 5. Steel (tool-steel and castings).

MILLING

Concentrators and Stamp-Mills

1. Fuel and power. 2. Steel and castings. 3. Lumber. 4. Labor.

Cyanide Mills

1. Fuel and power. 2. Chemicals. 3. Steel and castings. 4. Lumber. 5. Labor.

PLACER MINING

Hydraulic

1. Lumber. 2. Steel and castings. 3. Labor.

Dredging

1. Fuel and power. 2. Steel and castings. 3. Labor. 4. Lumber

SMELTING

1. Fuel and power. 2. Fluxes. 3. Labor. 4. Lumber.

SAMPLING WORKS

1. Fuel and power. 2. Castings and steel. 3. Chemicals (assaying). 4. Labor. 5. Lumber.

The other items of expense cut but little figure and must be left to the economic efficiency of the individual management. A glance at the foregoing plan will at once reveal the fact that labor is the least item of expense in practically all except vein or quartz-mining. By a reduction of all the other items, the item of labor would not have to be disturbed. In vein or quartz-mining, by reducing the cost of powder, more could be used and thereby effect a saving of labor; in other words, use more powder and less labor. The reduction of these items will effectually aid all branches of the industry, individually and collectively, without a disturbance of the standard, taxation, or labor. This reduction could best be brought about by Government supply, resources, and regulation.

To stimulate and increase new production, we must consider:

1. Old sources: Government aid in re-opening well-known old properties and bringing into activity dormant and restricted sources.

2. New sources: stimulate systematic prospecting under supervision and direction, as prospecting is an art requiring trained observation and skill; make geological maps, and assay maps in connection with them; reward for original discovery of new sections; Government aid to open them up; the free use of the working factors and advantages of the Bureau of Mines and the Geological Survey. The needs of the prospector are quick and reliable assaying, especially gold and silver determinations, therefore there should be free Government-assaying of gold and silver. There should be less discouragement and persecution of prospectors and miners by agents of the Land Office and Forest Service; and the opening to prospecting and development of all mineral lands within Indian reservations including those established by executive orders, upon a proper royalty basis.

3. Guarantee: Government control and establishment of sampling-works; Government control-assaying to determine the true and full valuation of all precious metals, ores, and bullion.

4. Control: Government control of the distribution of gold through its mints and by controlling or supervising all refineries.

5. Revival: encourage investors by the advantage of Government aid the use of the Bureau of Mines and Geological Survey; Government aid and encouragement for developing prospects; Government aid in new districts for transportation, milling, and smelting facilities.

In presenting this it is hoped that there will be further discussion and criticism. It requires someone to create, someone to execute, and a multiplicity of brains to attain perfection. Under improved conditions the gold production in the United States would be doubled in a comparatively short period of time, and a supply created for our future needs.

CHARLES A. LAWRENCE GEHRMANN.

Oatman, Arizona, February 14.

THE commercial feasibility of the electric smelting of iron ores in British Columbia is the subject of a report (Bulletin No. 2 of the Department of Mines, Victoria, B. C.) completed by Alfred Stansfield, professor of metallurgy in McGill University, Montreal. He concludes that the problem is perfectly feasible from a metallurgical point of view; that the Province has a sufficient supply of ores of a quality well suited to the process and capable of being converted into high-grade iron or steel; and that there also are available all fluxes wherewith to carry out the process completely. But two difficulties are made clear, namely, the present cost of power and the limited market for the products.

Californian Petroleum and the European War

By J. H. G. WOLF

In an article bearing the same title that I contributed to 'Western Engineering', in October 1915, I traced the course, to that period, of the influence of the War upon the petroleum business of California; the notes here presented will carry the review to the close of the War. The outstanding facts appear to be:

1. On the day that the War started the crude-oil production of California, as well as the consumption in the Pacific region supplied by California, reached the imposing figure of 300,000 barrels per day, a greater quantity than had ever before been steadily produced by any State in the Union, or by any country in the world; the other oilfields of the United States were then producing 500,000 bbl. per day. During the years 1910 to 1912, the crude-oil stocks in California were increased by 28,000,000 bbl., indicating that markets had not yet been found for the surplus production, but the excessive accumulation of stocks ceased with the year 1912, and from January 1913 to June 1914 the surplus was only 4,000,000 bbl., which meant that consumption had about overtaken the rampant production. On January 1 of each succeeding year, from 1910 to June 1914, the consuming market had been absorbing 33,000 bbl. of oil per day more than on the corresponding day of the previous year, while the production, after January 1, 1913, increased at no greater rate than the consumption. The local industry, if not entirely and fundamentally sound, because of the low prices that the product was bringing, was, as a whole, in a flourishing condition on the day when the War started. The great marketing agencies were expanding their facilities in keeping with the demands of trade, and an ultimate output of 400,000 bbl. per day seemed not unreasonable to expect. The great Midway field, covering about 36,000 acres, or 55 square miles of proved oil-land at the southern end of the San Joaquin valley, was still in its first flush of high production under the influence of original high gas-pressures. Flowing wells, gushers of large capacity, ruled in nearly all sections of the newer territory.

2. Then came the holocaust. In common with its effect on all branches of industry the outbreak of the War caused an immediate break in the local oil business. The reason for this is not difficult to understand, for crude petroleum is the sub-structure on which many enterprises are founded. In the multitudinous applications of crude and refined products it lies behind the economic life of the whole Pacific region. That is truer here than elsewhere in the United States because of the lack of other fuels. When the wheels of orderly progress were suddenly arrested, the effect upon this basic staple was instantaneous. There was a break of 70,000 bbl. per day in the consuming power between the high point in June 1914 and the low point in February 1915; and because production could not be curtailed fast enough there ensued a further accumulation of 8,000,000 bbl. of stocks on hand, while the shut-in production, that is, developed but not utilized production, mounted to 28,000 bbl. per day, as reported by the Independent Producers' Agency. The Pacific Coast, being so far removed from the industrial centre of the Nation, did not at any time share conspicuously in the activities engendered essentially by the War, hence business did not receive that temporary artificial stimulus, and recovery in the spring of 1915 came solely as a reaction. Plainly the War proved a heavy blow to the industry, from which in fact it has not recovered, particularly as regards the vital question of output, and such improvement in prices as has occurred is due, if the situation is correctly interpreted, to the lessened available supply. When the business paralysis from the shock of war had passed and the normal demand for fuel-oil had returned, it was seen that the once abundant supply was curtailed, that production could not be brought back for reasons to be stated, whereupon prices began to mount immediately. The lowest prices prevailed in 1912, being 30c. per bbl. for low-gravity oil. There was improvement in the spring of 1913, when it was found that the current consumption had been brought about even with the production.

3. The features of the third phase of the story of the War, as written in this industry, can best be seen or followed on the accompanying graph. The crude stocks reached their apex at 60,000,000 bbl. in the mid-summer of 1915, while the price of low-gravity oil at the well again scraped bottom, or dropped to the ridiculous figure of 33c. per bbl., which meant that fuel consumers on San Francisco bay, 300 miles from the point of origin, got their supply at a price of one-third its economic value. If the atmosphere was hazy at this period, the clouds at most were thin, for, with the return of a semblance of normal conditions, the pre-war rate of expansion in consumption, namely, 33,000 bbl. per day per annum, was again quick to assert itself. This condition prevailed until about January 1917, when new elements appeared halting further progress. Throughout the period of readjustment, while consumption was working back to the previous 300,000 bbl. per day, production lagged, and the best the oilfields could do, when a renewed demand was made, left a deficit of 1,000,000 bbl. per month, so that on 28 months, or by January 1, 1918, stocks dropped to 32,000,000 bbl., which was the amount that had been in storage on January 1, 1919. On the other hand, prices began to move up the moment the draft on the stocks became noticeable, or as soon as it was seen that production no longer responded to the current demand, and the

upward movement in price continued as long as this draft persisted. It stopped only when the drawing ceased, resting at $1.23 per bbl. Major developments do not as a rule flow from single causes, but are the result of many contributing currents and counter-currents, just as the War itself resulted from complex causes. It is therefore difficult to say just what factors govern prices in the local business, but it is obvious that the current available supply, rather than the crude stocks on hand, comes near to being the major consideration; in other words, the first principle in the law of supply and demand governs here as elsewhere.

4. Granting that this diagnosis is correct, and that it is the failure of production to respond which has caused the present unsatisfactory situation, it is desirable to examine briefly the reasons for this condition.

The oilfields of California had, in 1914, developed by easy strides a larger output than was ever recorded in any oil region anywhere. The wells of the State were yielding 50 bbl. per day per well from 6150 wells, as compared with 3.5 bbl. from 200,000 wells for the oilfields of the United States outside of California. The output during June 1912 and 1913, had also been 50 bbl. per well per day. In 1915, when the business equilibrium was re-established, and the demand for crude oil struck its accustomed pace, the valves of throttled wells in the oilfields were again opened, but it was found that the wells did not respond. The 'sleeping potion' had been administered too effectually. Frantic efforts by operators to restore former conditions were unavailing, the virgin gas-pressure had failed, and the flowing wells, with few exceptions, which had at one period painted the desert hills with tawny black (or the 'brown gold' of the oilfield poet) had now become ordinary pumping wells. In these six months of repression the production dropped from 50 to 40 bbl. per well per day, and the reduction since has gone down to 33 bbl. This drop of 20% in the first six months was in spite of the fact that during this period wells of large capacity were completed in one of the Southern fields (Whittier-Fullerton). The 28,000 bbl. of shut-in production, when called upon, proved to be largely mythical; the oil had been held back altogether too successfully! The daily production could not be brought back to as much as 250,000 bbl. per day until the middle of 1916, and an average of 266,000 bbl. per day was not exceeded until July 1917, when the influence of the flush production of a new field in southern California, the Montebello, began to assert itself. New wells to the extent of 40% above the number producing in 1914 have failed to prevent a drop in the yield per well to 33 bbl., which is disquieting, in whatever light it may be viewed.

Why does the failure of production to respond to the demand, despite the fact that California has 85,000 acres of proved oil-lands of which not over 20% are intensively drilled, trace back so directly to the failure of the gas-pressure? What has gas-pressure to do with oil production? It has long been known that there existed a close relationship between output and pressure; that the first wells drilled in a new field usually 'came-in' as flowing wells, but that the subsequent wells in the immediate territory proved only nominal producers. Recent research on this subject brings out the important fact that this close relationship, heretofore recognized but not accurately defined, is susceptible of analysis and definition, and can be expressed satisfactorily in empirical laws and general principles. This research shows that there can be no turning back when once the exploitation of an oil-deposit is begun upon an extended scale, provided, of course, that the maximum output, or the maximum possible recovery of oil, is sought. With a resource so important, and so fixed in volume as crude petroleum, every barrel originally available must be won if broadest interests are to be served best. The reason why the gas-pressure holds the power it does over oil production is found in the principles governing the occurrence and existence of the oil underground. It has only required this tremendous experience, revealed here in this instance at the cost of untold millions of barrels in the ground now rendered unrecoverable, to verify the important technical fact involved. In the briefest possible terms the impulse behind oil production is the natural gas with which it is so intimately associated. Crude petroleum is a mixture of many complex hydrocarbon substances existing in several physical forms, that is, as gases, liquids, and solids, the first and third forms being incorporated or held in suspension in the second. Under certain conditions of pressures and temperatures in the earth, some of the oil that is in the gaseous state becomes liquid, and, again, certain portions existing as liquid may, under changed pressures and temperatures, become gas. In other words, the forms in which certain portions of the oil exist undergo a change with variations in the physical conditions surrounding the deposit. The gaseous part of crude oil constitutes one portion of the natural gas which accompanies the oil. In the ultimate analysis the crude oils from all parts of the world do not vary sensibly from the following proportions: carbon, 84 to 86%; hydrogen, 12 to 16%; together with small percentages of oxygen, nitrogen, and sulphur. However, in the chemical association of these organic elements there is the widest range of combination in every oil, which produces so many different hydrocarbon substances that the world's chemists seem yet to be uncertain as to their number, or as to the number that can be isolated from crude oil. Eighteen different series of component compounds have been isolated, and each of these in turn is composed of many members. In composition, the series conform to the general formula $C_nH_{2n} \pm 2$. The hydrogen component becomes less as the series rises. The first, or paraffine series ($C_nH_{2n} + 2$) which is broadly the predominant one in all crude oils, is also the series of which natural gas is generally almost wholly constituted. Methane, which always exists as a gas under ordinary conditions, is the first member of the paraffine series; it also constitutes from 80 to 90% of the ordinary natural gas of commerce. Here is an explanation and a reason for the intimate association of oil and gas: the former probably does not exist in the natural state without the latter. As a rule oil froths when it issues from the ground, and settles as much as 30% in volume in the receiving tanks, from the release of the low-pressure gases. This is particularly true of the heavy oils. The low-gravity asphalt-base oil is a heavy viscous substance, and in its natural state is locked in the minute pore-spaces between the sand grains, and there must of necessity be some pressure like that of expanding gas to cause much of it to leave the sand-filled chambers. At best a surprisingly small proportion of the oil of this character contained in the sand is won under the most favorable conditions.

All are familiar with the manner in which oil clings to a piece of glass: it does not drain away, and can hardly be removed except by rubbing or by dissolving with distillates. How much more so must it cling in the voids among the sand-grains, which are only particles of silicates, in effect the same as glass, and where the wetted perimeter of each minute chamber is large compared with its volume? Unquestionably, a force like that of expanding gas is required to eject or push the oil from its containers. The force of gravity must be largely ineffectual, for this purpose, for reasons that are obvious. The only conception that will explain how the oil is moved at all, is that it probably exists underground in a finely divided, or possibly emulsified state, in a 'bath' of gas, if that expression be allowable. The ore of a quartz-vein of a mine is a fixed and tangible entity, and can be seen and studied at leisure; the oil in a 'vein' of oil-sand is a fugitive substance; it cannot be seen in place; it alters its form and even its composition on coming into view; and the facts as to its underground state must be studied largely through deductive evidence. There is even the widest diversity of opinion among scientists as to its origin, hence it is not strange that there should be uncertainties as to the facts regarding its physical state and its underground movement; an untraversed field of large area is yet before the investigator.

Analyzing further the conditions of occurrence, the gas being very light and less retarded by friction and capillarity, and being also under compression, travels faster toward the well-opening than does the oil, and the natural tendency is to drop its burden of finely-divided oil with the release of pressure. Oil, being a liquid, is incompressible, and the two substances exhaust themselves at different rates. Hence a well will drain the gas from a wide territory if not suitably controlled, whereas it may at the same time drain but a small part of the oil in its immediate vicinity. It is therefore evident that every cubic foot of gas must be made to do its maximum duty in the work of expelling the oil, and recognition of this fact is of cardinal importance in selecting the time as well as the position for drilling new wells.

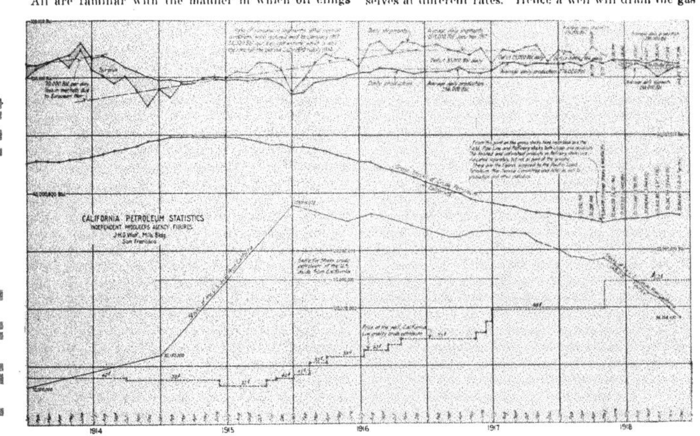

On the foregoing premise, the arrest of development in these oilfields in 1914, undoubtedly allowed the wells then drilled to dissipate pressures over wide areas. When drilling was resumed the agency for expelling the oil was lacking in both volume and pressure, and flowing wells of large capacity, except in some instances, became conspicuous by their absence in regions where big wells had before been common. This is the simplest explanation of the reason why the oilfields could not respond when called upon, and why wells of the character of those brought-in from 1910-'14 can never be duplicated, except when drilled in uninfluenced territory.

This condition is most common in the great Midway-Sunset field which comprises 42% of the known oil-lands of California. Whereas the San Joaquin Valley fields, in which the Midway is situated, yielded 80% of the output of California in 1914, not over 62% is now coming from this area. Without the weight of production that came from the new fields of southern Caliornia, the discrepancy in supply might have grown to alarming proportions.

The aforesaid arrest of development may be attributed to be the major blow struck upon the industry by the War, which means indirectly all industries on the Pacific Coast. As a direct consequence of this loss there are facilities and equipment in the way of storage containers and pipe-lines now idle in California for handling and storing 28,000,000 bbl. of oil, which equipment was provided in the years from 1910 to 1914 by the great marketing agencies, at high cost. Whether or not these facilities will ever again be made to function is a question; the probabilities are they will not, and that the industry as a whole, and more particularly the consuming public, will have to carry not only the capital loss but the interest thereon as well.

A secondary loss attributable to the War was caused by the shunting of raw materials ordinarily used in making well-drilling equipment into munitions-channels. For long periods it was practically impossible to obtain casing, boilers, steel cable and rope, rig-irons, and the like, needed for drilling new wells. Labor costs mounted, and apostles of unrest are still abroad among the operatives in the oilfields to force yet higher costs. These and other ills which flow in the wake of such an unnatural social condition as war, have beset this industry in common with industry in general, but in the oil business, as far as California is concerned, the consequences will be felt for years to come. To speak only of one of the most conspicuous directions in which the ill-effects of this unfortunate situation will be felt: at the moment, it is the avowed purpose of the Government to put the American merchant marine back on the ocean. The Director of Operations of the fleet, now building at a cost of hundreds of millions of dollars, and at a reported cost of 50% above that of foreign-built ships, is reported to have publicly announced that the expectation of maintaining the fleet on the seas in competition with the lower-cost operating ships of other nations, is based on the expectation of having an unlimited supply of crude oil as fuel, because of the wonderful advantages of oil over all other forms of fuel. The great oilfields of Mexico are expected to afford the supply on the Atlantic, and probably will; while California, which has the only oilfields of large importance in the West, or upon the Pacific Ocean, is expected to carry the Pacific part of the burden. Because of the above, it is necessary not only, in the near future, to take care of the demands of normal trade and business as developed in 1914, which so far has not been done, but in addition to assume our part of an added burden, of undefined character and weight, if the reasonable expectations of a new governmental policy concerning ships and shipping are to be realized. The volume of oil in storage in the United States outside of California dropped 23,000,000 bbl. last year. It has dropped steadily for three years, and so have the Californian stocks, the two combined having lost 67,000,000 bbl. This continued descent must be arrested, or the consequences will be felt universally at no distant date.

What the War did, to emphasize in a broad way, to the value of crude petroleum is a subject of fascinating interest, and worthy of separate consideration. Suffice it to say, petroleum has become the most sought after of all raw materials, and at the moment the fight for the control of its sources of supply may be the subject of much maneuvering at the peace table in Paris.

AMMONIA is effectively separated from steam and tar contained in producer gas, and from this clean ammoniacal salts of any acid is obtained by passing the gaseous mixture, after it has been washed at a temperature of about 80° C. in water, which may contain lime, through a tubular or other condenser, arranged to act as reflux condensers, the part of the condenser at which the mixture enters being kept at such a temperature, for example 80° C., that the steam and tar are simultaneously condensed, but any ammonia which condenses with them is immediately volatilized. The other end of the condenser system is kept at such a temperature, for example 40° C., that practically all the steam and tar are condensed but not the producer gas and the ammonia, which are passed through a tar-separator to remove final traces of this material. The ammonia is then converted into any desired salt by passage through an acid, and the gas is left in a pure condition. Ammonia remaining in the condensate from the reflux condenser is volatilized by any known method. Two or more condensers in series or parallel may be used, and free spaces in which the gases and vapors are stated to mix may be arranged between the tube-plates of adjacent condensers. The air-blast for the producer may be heated by the water from the condensers. In one form of heating and saturating this blast with moisture, the blast is passed between two tubes forming the condenser, and the water is used in the form of a film or spray. This method constitutes the basis of a British patent granted to A. H. Lynn and N. E. Rambush (Brit. 119,049).

THE Yukon Gold Co.'s holding in Idaho covers several miles along Prichard creek. It has been sampled by drilling, and carries good value in coarse gold that resisted all former methods of treatment by reason of the flat grade of the creek and the depth of the gravel. It was freely predicted by old-timers that this deposit could not be successfully worked by dredging, on account of the rough bed-rock; but these difficulties have been overcome. The 7-cu. ft. boat is operating successfully. It is electrically driven by six motors, aggregating 300 hp., with current from the Beaver Creek district, 10 miles distant.

International Control of Minerals

By C. K. LEITH

*WORLD MOVEMENT OF MINERALS. The annual world production of minerals approximates 1,700,000,000 tons, over 90% of which consists of coal and iron. Of this amount about two-thirds is used within the countries where the minerals are produced and one-third is shipped to other countries. The mineral production of the United States amounts to about one-third of the total. In the discussion of mineral resources in their international aspects we are concerned primarily with the 33% of the mineral output which moves between countries. It may be assumed that the consumption within the countries of origin is a matter of national rather than international concern.

One of the several interesting facts in this world movement of minerals is that the movement of most of them shows a remarkable concentration. For instance, manganese moves from three principal sources and converges at four or five consuming centres. Chromite moves from two principal sources; tungsten also from two. Even for certain commodities which are widely distributed and move in large amounts the concentration of movement is marked—for instance, the world movement of coal is controlled by the United States, England, and Germany. In other words, although the world movement of mineral commodities is widespread and exhibits many complex features, most of the individual minerals follow two or three salient lines of movement. This means in general that for each mineral there are certain sources of limited geographic extent, which, because of location, grade, relation to transportation, cost—in short, all the factors that enter into availability—are drawn upon heavily for the world's chief demands. The convergence of these materials toward a few consuming centres indicates generally concentration of coal production necessary to smelting, high development of manufacturing, large per capita use, concentration of facilities, strong financial control, and, not least, a large element of enterprise which has taken advantage of more or less favorable conditions.

Another significant fact which emphasizes the interdependence of nations and the importance of international considerations is that no country is entirely self-sustaining in its mineral requirements.

MOVEMENT OF MINERALS. If the world pre-war movement is considered broadly, it may be regarded as conforming essentially to normal trade conditions of supply and demand. There have been barriers to overcome, such as tariffs and trade controls and monopolies of various kinds, but these barriers have not prevented the major movements between the best sources of supply and the principal consuming centres. These movements may be regarded as a more or less spontaneous internationalization of mineral resources by private enterprise. The aim of free trade or unrestricted commerce was equality of trade opportunities, but such conditions of unrestricted competition tended to concentrate trade in the hands of the strongest interests and to prevent equality of opportunity.

The efforts made to promote or hinder international mineral movement by tariffs, bonuses, embargoes, subsidies, transport control, patents, Government management, financial pressure, and other means have been incited mainly by national or imperial self-interest and have thus been to some extent inimical to an internationalization based on the principle of the greatest good to the greatest number. It may be supposed that in any effort to attain supernational or international control, motives and measures based on national self-interest of the sort here mentioned will continue to play an important part. The question to be determined is the extent to which national interest can and will be subordinated to international interest.

CHANGES DUE TO THE WAR. The War wrought fundamental changes in the world movement of minerals. The character and distribution of the demands changed. Customary sources of supply were cut off. Financial disturbances and ship shortage profoundly modified the nature, distribution, and extent of the world movement. Our domestic mineral industry was abruptly brought to a realization of its vital relations with international trade. To illustrate, the large movement of manganese from India and Russia to the United States was abruptly stopped, and we had to develop a source of supply in Brazil. The stoppage of pyrite importations from Spain as a means of saving ships required the development of pyrite and sulphur supplies in the United States. The export of oil from the United States to European countries was greatly stimulated, and the export to other countries was correspondingly decreased. The world movements of coal were vitally affected, principally by the limitation of the coal shipments from England and the United States to South America and the concentration of shipments to European countries. The closing of German coal supplies to near-by countries had far-reaching consequences. The cutting off of the German potash left the world for the time being almost unsupplied with this vital fertilizing ingredient. The Chilean nitrates, on which the world had relied for fertilizer, were diverted

*A paper to form part of 'Mineral Resources', 1917, of the U. S. Geological Survey. Mr. Leith has been serving as mineral adviser to the War Industries and Shipping boards, at Washington.

almost exclusively to the manufacture of powder. The total annual imports of mineral commodities into the United States were reduced by 1,200,000 tons. Our exports, though they continued in large volume, were mainly concentrated in Europe. The story of these disturbances in the world movement of minerals, though highly interesting, is too long to be told here.

INTERNATIONAL CONTROL. Out of these sweeping and rapid changes in the world movement of mineral commodities there arose, partly as cause and partly as effect, international agreements for the allocation of minerals, as a means of insuring the proper proportions of supplies to the different countries for the most effective prosecution of the War. Inter-Allied purchasing committees in London and in Paris found it necessary to make an inter-Allied allocation of the output of Chilean nitrate, because the sum of the demands exceeded the total supply by a considerable fraction, and to agree on distribution and price of the world's supplies of tin, tungsten, and platinum. For many other commodities agreements of various sorts were made. For instance, the United States entered into an agreement with England and France for the purchase of iron ore and molybdenum from Scandinavia to keep it out of Germany. The United States and England agreed as to supplying Canada with ferro-manganese. New problems of world allocation came up almost daily.

We now face the immediate and pressing question whether the centralized international control required by the War shall be retained or extended as a means of furthering the aims of a league of nations. When such a league was first proposed emphasis was placed mainly on political and military considerations. It now seems to be recognized that these are so closely interlocked with economic considerations that any league of nations, to be effective as a means of minimizing future international discord, must make provision for some degree of international or supernational control of business. Recent statements by officials of Great Britain and France seem to indicate a definite purpose to urge such control.

Some of the reasons which have been urged for the international control of the movements of minerals are as follows:

1. To ensure equitable distribution of certain minerals, such as tungsten, vanadium, platinum, and gold, of which there may be a world shortage.

2. To mitigate a world shortage of ships by international allocation of ship space, which would entail limitations on the movement of minerals.

3. To prevent nations which are more advantageously situated in regard to finance, location, and general control of trade from monopolizing the business in any commodity at the expense of other nations—in other words, to ensure equality of opportunity in regard to basic raw materials. The control of many mineral commodities now approaches national monopoly.

4. To reach some agreement as to division of markets for commodities such as iron, steel, and coal, which are available in so great abundance that several of the larger nations have considerable exportable surplus, in order to prevent international difficulties due to unrestricted competition.

5. To maintain equilibrium of price.

6. To ensure common and equitable contribution of supplies for rehabilitation of the devastated countries.

7. To serve as a means of disciplining any nation that will not conform to any code or control established by a league of nations. To many this has been a dominant consideration.

8. In general to prevent economic friction that might vitiate any world political agreements.

9. To replace the crude and cumbersome arrangements for international control through complex treaties and tariffs by a more centralized system.

The foregoing is merely a list of suggestions that have been made; it is not a unit statement of the requirements of the situation.

SPECIFIC PLANS. The various schemes proposed to meet these requirements centre fundamentally about allocation of supplies. There seem to be two main lines of approach to this problem. One leads to equality of economic opportunity through means expressed as follows by the League of Free Nations Association of New York:

(*a*) No State shall accord to one neighbor privileges not accorded to others—this principle to apply to the purchase of raw material as well as to access to markets.

(*b*) States exercising authority in non self-governing territories shall not exercise that power as a means of securing a priveleged economic position for their own nationals; economic opportunity in such territories shall be open to all peoples on equal terms, the peoples of nations possessing no such territories being in the same position economically as those that possess great subject empires. Investments and concessions in backward countries should be placed under international control.

(*c*) Goods and persons of the citizens of all States should be transported on equal terms on international rivers, canals, straits, or railroads.

(*d*) Landlocked States must be guaranteed access to the sea on equal terms both by equality of treatment on communication running through other States, and by the use of seaports.

The other main line of approach to the problem leads to definite international allocation of raw materials as a means of preventing the strong nations from crowding out the weak, an inequity which would be possible under even ideal arrangements for ensuring equal economic opportunities. More specifically it is proposed that the exportable surplus of selected minerals from the countries that enter into a league of nations shall be distributed as may be mutually agreed. This proposal means presumably continuance of Government control of international trade through licenses and ships. It means a curbing of private initiative and a sacrifice of the self-interest of the stronger in favor of the weaker.

The purpose of this paper is to discuss some of the specific relations of this arrangement to the mineral industry of the United States, that we may weigh the advantages and disadvantages of international control.

POSITION OF THE UNITED STATES. The United States is more nearly self-sustaining in regard to mineral commodities as a whole than any other country on the globe. The following statement summarizes qualitatively our position:

1. Minerals of which there is an adequate supply or exportable surplus in the United States:

A. Minerals of which our exportable surplus dominates the world situation:

Copper.
Petroleum.

B. Minerals of which our exportable surplus constitutes an important but not a dominant factor in the world trade:

Sulphur.
Phosphates.
Silver.
Iron and steel.
Coal.
Cement.
Uranium and radium.

C. Minerals of which our exportable surplus is not an important factor in world trade. Small amounts of these minerals have been and will doubtless continue to be imported because of special grades, backhaul, or cheaper sources of foreign supply, but these imports are for the most part incidental:

Lead.
Zinc.
Aluminum and bauxite.
Gold.
Tungsten.
Molybdenum.
Asphalt and bitumen.
Pyrite.
Barite.
Fluorspar.
Building stone (excepting Italian marble).
Cadmium.
Gypsum.
Lime.
Tripoli and diatomaceous earth.
Mineral paints (except umber, sienna, and ocher from France and Spain).
Pumice.
Garnet.
Salt (except special classes).
Talc.
Arsenic.
Bismuth.
Bromine.
Artificial abrasives, corundum, and emery (except naxos emery).
Fuller's earth.
Mercury.

2. Minerals for which the United States demand must continue to be met by imports:

A. Minerals for which the United States must depend almost entirely on other countries:

Tin.
Nickel.
Platinum and metals of the platinum group.

B. Minerals for which the United States will depend on foreign sources for a considerable fraction of the supply :

Antimony.
Vanadium.
Zirconium.
Mica.
Monazite.
Graphite.
Asbestos.
Ball clay and kaolin.
Chalk.
Cobalt.
Naxos emery.
Grinding pebbles.

3. Minerals normally imported into the United States which in future can be largely produced from domestic sources if it seems desirable:

A. The following minerals were mainly imported before the War, but under war conditions the domestic resources have been developed to such an extent that the United States can become self-sustaining if desirable, though at so great a cost that a protective tariff will be necessary if these industries are to survive:

Nitrates (except potassium nitrates).
Potash.
Manganese.
Chromite.
Magnesite.

No attempt will be made here to present the detailed figures on which the above generalizations are based. In view of the present disturbance in production and consumption, any judgment as to future demands or available surplus must take into account several factors which cannot be accurately measured, such as financial control in foreign countries, possible tariffs, and foreign competition. For this reason the above statement should be regarded as only tentative, though it is the result of a rather exhaustive study of conditions in relation to the world control of shipping. The classes named overlap to some extent, and it is to be expected that some of the commodities placed in one class may in the near future be transferred to another.

GENERAL CONCLUSIONS. 1. It is clear that a league of nations offers but little advantage as a means of ensuring adequate supplies for the United States, and that the limitations on the distribution of exportable mineral supplies would probably weigh more heavily on the United States than on any other country. The few minerals for which the United States is dependent on foreign countries are offset by so many in which we have a dominance of supply and our financial position is so strong that it appears certain that the United States does not need the aid of a league of nations to ensure adequate supplies even of these few minerals. In short, in this respect our entrance into a league of nations would not be based on self-interest. We would sacrifice to some extent an independent and dominant position. In our dealings with other nations this fact should give weight to whatever emphasis the United States may wish to put on the desirability of international control of minerals. At the same time it imposes a hard task on the United States to arouse the mineral interests to the support of a measure that involves so much self-sacrifice. The value of our annual potential exportable surplus of minerals approximates a billion dollars: that of our necessary mineral imports about $175,000,000. Our active allies, Great Britain, France, and Italy, together have a maximum annual exportable surplus worth perhaps $325,000,000, and their necessary imports amount to $265,000,000.

2. It seems clear that our effort to make this country entirely self-sustaining in regard to raw materials, which has been especially marked during the War, will need to be modified if we are to adapt ourselves to conditions of international control. Although we may be able to become self-sustaining in respect to essential commodities like manganese, chromite, and potash, by so doing we are cutting off the export market of other countries where these commodities exist in such quantities and grades that they would be, under conditions of free trade, our principal sources of supply. By drawing on such sources we not only get a cheaper and higher grade of product, but we develop a return market for the products in respect to which our natural advantages entitle us to a share in the export trade. The potash situation will illustrate the problem. The War cut off German supplies. We made every possible effort to meet the deficiency. Prices rose tenfold. Now, are we to continue this effort at high cost? Our instinctive answer is, Yes. But suppose at the peace table it is mutually agreed that for the welfare of France and Spain we should absorb a certain part of their output, or even that we should take German potash as an indirect way of collecting indemnity? This question is put for the purpose of making the problem concrete, and no answer is attempted here, though I venture to suggest that the practicable course will be found to lie between the two extreme alternatives.

If all countries take the stand that they must be self-sustaining in regard to natural resources, they can accomplish their purpose only by high artificial barriers to offset inequalities in the factors which determine the availability of the several commodities, with the result that the world movement of raw materials will be greatly lessened. Instead of free circulation of essential basic commodities vitalizing any world agreement there will be a series of compartments in which trade is maintained at different levels, under different pressures and conditions—a situation difficult to maintain and inimical to world agreements based on mutual concessions. It is clear that if each of the States of the United States should adopt the principle of making the State self-sustaining in minerals so far as possible, the result would be to increase largely the chances of interstate friction and to lower efficiency in the United States as a whole.

3. Following President Wilson, the League of Free Nations Association, before quoted, states: "Equality of economic opportunity does not mean the abolition of all tariffs or the abolition of the right of self-governing States to determine whether free trade or protection is to their best interests." If the view expressed in conclusion 2 is correct, it follows that the United States, as a member of a league of nations, would not be free to impose tariffs dictated by national self-interest beyond such minor duties as might tend to equalize the labor element of cost of production. Also, when we remember the remarkable degree to which many of the leading mineral commodities are geographically concentrated, it is clear that a tariff on any particular commodity will usually affect mainly some one or two foreign nations—a result which does not accord with the principle that a State shall not give to one neighbor privileges that it withholds from others.

More might be said for a temporary tariff designed to let down easily, for example, the manganese, chromite, and potash industries, which face large losses because of overdevelopment to meet war needs. The Mineral Act perhaps might be used for this purpose. If this principle were adopted for a few minerals, however, it probably would soon be extended to others and into more general non-mineral fields, thereby presenting a problem of enormous difficulty.

In passing it may be noted that as long as shipping is inadequate, as it may be for some years, high and slowly declining freight rates may serve much the same purpose as a tariff for low-priced commodities of much bulk, like manganese, though not for high-priced commodities like tungsten.

Something might also be paid for tariffs intended to ensure the smelting of ores and their conversion to usable forms within the country of origin, thus reducing the tonnage to be transported and supporting the largest industry within the country; but it must be remembered that the distribution of coal resources and centres of production marks certain world centres of smelting and manufacturing, which are entitled by natural advantage to an unhampered movement of raw materials from other countries.

The question of protective tariffs is becoming acute at present, owing to the release of the restrictions imposed by the War Trade Board as a means of saving ships.

4. The interests of conservation clearly call for an international viewpoint in the handling of our mineral resources. The deposits of most minerals are so highly concentrated in their distribution and general availability that the principal sources for the world are in comparatively few places. When all factors of conservation are taken into account, including labor and efficient use of the product, it would seem that the minerals

should be drawn from these natural sources of supply. To illustrate, the chromite and manganese deposits of the United States are relatively small and of low grade as compared with other sources of supply. Insistence on the use of the domestic material would mean early exhaustion of local supplies, lowered efficiency in use, and higher cost. As cost includes not only the intrinsic value of a product but items for labor and transportation, it appears that the use of these domestic materials means a higher expenditure of human effort than is necessary.

There is perhaps as much need of specializing in mineral output as there is of specializing in manufacturing. The thought that every country on the globe should be self-sustaining in regard to mineral supplies is of somewhat the same order as the thought that every family should produce all its own raw materials rather than take advantage of the more favorable conditions existing elsewhere and so specialize in human effort. If for a certain amount of capital and labor we can produce copper more cheaply than any other country and thus dominate the world's markets, it is not economy to divert this capital and labor to the production of ores of manganese or chromite, which because of natural conditions can be produced much more cheaply elsewhere.

Extension of international control of minerals seems to offer possibilities of loss and gain—loss through a considerable sacrifice of national trade and a narrowing of the field for private initiative in trade; gain through the possibility of attaining certain ends which are attainable only by international agreement, such as an allocation of supplies which will be to the advantage of the greater number of nations rather than to the advantage of the few that are strong enough to dominate the situation and which will in general prevent economic friction from endangering a league of nations based on political and policing considerations.

In a world governed by good-will the effective internationalization of trade might well be gained by leaving trade unrestricted. In proportion as the actual condition may depart from this ideal condition, some sort of international agreement as to control seems justified. Such control would by no means eliminate international rivalries and jealousies; it would transfer them to the international governing body. The duties of such a body would be onerous and perplexing. It might even be supposed that nationalistic aspirations might be so strenuously presented and so firmly backed by national steps in the way of embargoes and protective tariffs that the international control would amount to little. But it may be further supposed that a league of nations whose members enter into it voluntarily and with mutual good faith might control the situation sufficiently to bring recalcitrant members into line. The questions thus suggested are difficult to answer.

6. It is sometimes argued that any attempt to control the movement of raw materials, for whatever purpose, defeats itself because it leads to the automatic development in the restricted area of increased exploration, new sources of supply, substitutions, etc. Restriction unquestionably has this effect, but nevertheless such measures are expensive makeshifts and offset the effects of limitation only in part, as is clearly proved by the experiences of the War.

7. The purpose of this paper is primarily to state the problem of international control of minerals, rather than to present an argument for it. Such control entails difficulties which are especially burdensome on the United States and which at present may be insuperable. The interests of conservation clearly require international control. Moreover, the lesson of the War points to the necessity of overhauling old international understandings and machinery, even though such a task would encounter great difficulties, not the least of which lie in the persistence of human habits and inertia. Whether the time has come to establish a league of nations with economic control can be determined only by our individual and collective answers to the question whether we are willing to make the necessary economic sacrifices, individually and nationally, in the interest of world harmony. The mineral industry should fully understand that with international control efforts to promote export will need to be modified and curtailed; that expansion of our trade in many lines will mean equivalent loss of trade to other nations; that the almost universal conception that expansion of foreign trade is a meritorious aim and end in itself, without regard to its effect on other countries, will need revision. It is necessary only to cite the present movement to create great export associations under the Webb Act to show that present tendencies for definite action do not take into account the possible conflict of such action with the economic requirements of a league of nations.

8. Whatever action may be taken in regard to international control, it is clear that the War has brought the United States into such world relations that it has become imperative for us to study and understand the world mineral situation much more comprehensively than before, in the interest not only of intelligent management of our own industries but of far-sighted handling of international relations. When the European war began we found our mineral industries vitally affected by international developments which we only partly understood. Government mineral organizations, as well as those outside the Government, had given relatively little attention to foreign mineral resources and markets. Information and statistics were scattered and incomplete. Under the stress of war the Government, especially the Geological Survey, the Bureau of Mines, and the several war boards, found it necessary to use extraordinary efforts to obtain even elementary information on the international features of mineral trade. Much progress has been made, but only a start. I would like to make a plea for definite recognition of the necessity of a systematic study of the world's mineral resources from the world's standpoint to supplement the studies made of the domestic resources, both by the mineral industry itself and by governmental and other agencies.

Pioneer Life in California—A Review

By GRANT H. SMITH

"Whoever wants merely an eulogistic story of the glories of the pioneer life of California must not look for it in history, and whoever is too tender-souled to see any moral beauty or significance in events that involve much foolishness, drunkeness, brutality, and lust must find his innocent interests satisfied elsewhere. * * * Early California history is not for babes, nor for sentimentalists; but its manly wickedness is full of the strength that, on occasion, freely converts itself into an admirable moral heroism," says Josiah Royce, in his painstaking and philosophical inquiry into the lives and manners of the early Californians, entitled 'California. A Study of American Character'.

Whoever is interested in that period should read Professor Royce's book; in it he will find the true background for the history of the State. Some of the glamor and romance will be gone, it is true, but the thoughtful reader will have a new and better understanding of California's period of stress and travail, and of American character.

The book was a labor of love to the author and he brought exceptional qualifications to the task. The son of pioneer parents; born and reared in one of the early California mining camps; a graduate of the University of California, and later assistant professor of philosophy there; afterward famous as a professor of philosophy at Harvard—one of the clearest and most original thinkers of his time.

So much unreal and exaggerated stuff has been written of the lives of the Pioneers, that it is a deep satisfaction to find a book on the subject by a rarely competent and sympathetic author, which bears on every page the impress of research, wise discrimination, and a desire to arrive at the truth.

In outlining his picture, Royce says:

"We are to deal with a California that was to be morally and socially tried as no other American community ever has been tried, and that was to show, as we Americans have not elsewhere so completely and in so narrow compass shown, both the true nobility and the true weakness of our national character. All our brutal passions were here to have full sweep, and all our moral strength, all our courage, our patience, our docility, and our social skill were to contend with these our passions."

Of the success of the fortune-hunters we read:

"From that land many of them would indeed return, more or less defeated, poor and broken-spirited; many would die early deaths; the survivors would for the most part stay in the new land as hard toilers and poor men; a few only would reap great fortunes, and of these few only a part would ever again see the old home. The average net income per man throughout the whole mining community, even in the best days, was, in view of the high expenses of living, seldom more than equal to treble the wages of an unskilled day laborer at home, and was usually much less than that."

As a trained sociologist, the author dwells upon the fact, seldom noticed by earlier writers, that the social condition of the camps was, in the successive years and despite all good intentions, largely and almost irresistibly determined by the various successively predominant methods of mining; namely, the pan, the rocker, and the sluice.

Washing gravel with a pan was almost the only method of mining at first. This was slow and tedious and economically wasteful; none but rich and accessible gravel would pay; even when found, such diggings were soon exhausted; men were constantly on the move, and necessary supplies difficult to obtain. Worse still, from a sociological point of view, each man worked for himself and by himself; there was no community of interest. Pan-mining, the author finds, was a social deterrent, because tending to a selfish, roving, hazardous, and irresponsible life. Mining life, on the whole, in 1848, was seriously demoralizing to all concerned in it and remained so until more elaborate methods of mining could be introduced.

In the latter part of 1848, the rocker came into general use. The effect, socially and materially, was remarkable. "Gravels that the pan-miner contemptuously abandoned were well worth working on this plan. Camps that would have been deserted remained and were prosperous. The great thing, however, * * * was that men now began voluntarily, and in an organized way, to work together. The miners' partnership, which grew up in this second stage of mining life, soon became one of the closest of California relationships, and, as such, has been widely and not unjustly celebrated in song and story."

The small partnership and cradle system of mining was the common practice in 1849, and in the early part of 1850. After several improved rockers had been tried with varying success, the 'long tom', a large and efficient rocker, came into general use in 1850; and, a little later, that finely simple invention, the board sluice, revolutionized the whole business of placer-mining.

"The introduction of the sluice, with its various auxiliaries, not only secured the productiveness of California placer mines for many years, but it acted indirectly on society, as a check to the confusion and disorder that began to grow among the miners in 1850 and 1851."

Social life was still further stabilized by the great enterprises that were undertaken in the early 'fifties for building flumes and ditches to bring large volumes of water for long distances to the mines; and by the river-mining enterprises. River-bed mining was early undertaken on a small scale, and on a large scale, but with general disaster, in 1850. The season of 1850-1851 was the dryest in the history of California, the rivers were low and remained so for many months, and river-bed mining became and remained for a number of years a great and fruitful industry.

"It was one of the boldest and most dramatic of the miner's great fights with fortune. He had to organize his little army of laborers, to risk everything, to toil nearly through the summer for the hope of a few weeks at most of hard-earned harvest at the end; and often, at the very moment when victory seemed nearest, an early rain swept everything away, and left absolutely no return. In this type of mining, whose operations have been very frequently described, the object was to turn the course of some one of the greater mountain-streams, by means of a dam and a canal or flume. The bed would thus be left bare, perhaps for miles, while the flume carried along the whole body of the stream, whose impulse was meanwhile used to turn water-wheels in the flume, and so to pump from the stream-bed the surplus water that still interfered with active operations."

Many pages of the book are devoted to an inquiry into 'miners' law' and 'lynch law', which Prof. Royce distinguishes; although he says that of the sharp line of demarcation between the two, the miners themselves seemed at the time to be largely unconscious. 'Miners' law' was open in its methods, liked regularity of procedure, gave the accused a fair chance to defend himself before a jury of his fellows, and was carried out in broad daylight by men publicly chosen. 'Lynch law' needs no definition.

"The California newspapers of 1850, 1851, and 1852 generally defend miners' justice; but they show us two things, first, that the miners' justice was not usually sharply distinguished from mob law, even in the minds of those concerned in it; and secondly, that, in the concrete instances of the use of miners' justice, we can discover all possible gradations from the most formal, calm, and judicial behavior of a healthy young camp, driven by momentary necessity to defend itself against outrage, down to the most abominable exhibitions of brutal popular passion, or even of private vengeance. * * * I wish that the latter class of incidents had been rarer than one actually finds them."

The ill treatment of all foreigners by the miners is most severely criticized by Royce. He says:

"The fearful blindness of the early behavior of the Americans in California towards foreigners is something almost unintelligible. The avaricious thirst for gold among the Americans themselves can alone explain the corruption of heart that induced this blindness."

The American miners deeply resented the presence of foreigners in the diggings, and frequently declared that only citizens of the United States were entitled to own and work mines. Cases were not infrequent where peaceable foreigners were driven from their claims, which were promptly appropriated by the aggressors. The Mexicans, who were numerous in the southern camps, came in for particularly shameful treatment. Apparently they had no rights that anybody was bound to respect, although, until a few short years before, this land had been theirs, and we had taken it from them, in what many fair-minded men believe to have been an unrighteous war.

"The foreigners were often enough degraded wretches; such drank, gambled, stole and sometimes murdered; they were also, often enough, honest fellows, or even men of high character and social positions; and such we tried in our own way to ruin. In all cases they were, as foreigners, unable to form their own government, or to preserve their own order. And so we kept them in fear, and, as far as possible, in misery. * * * We did not massacre them wholesale, as Turks might have massacred them: that treatment we reserved for the defenseless Digger Indians, whose villages certain among our miners used on occasion to regard as targets for rifle-practice, and as subjects for other brutal abominations."

The compiler of these paragraphs, himself the son and the grandson of pioneers, has no desire to rob the early days of their romance, nor reflect upon the character of the men that, on the whole, set a great impress upon the State; but, like the author, he believes that the truth should be told, not only for its own sake but in order that we may have a right understanding of the history and development of this glorious State. As Royce says:

"Everything that has since happened in California, or that ever will happen there, so long as men dwell in the land, must be deeply affected by the forces of local life and society that then took their origin."

The chapter on 'Social Evolution in San Francisco' is particularly interesting and illuminating. Elsewhere the struggle for the cause of progress in California was either in the mining camps or in the rural districts, but upon the success or failure of law and order in San Francisco, the centre of the State's mental and political life, the future of California was dependent.

Necessarily the author deals at length with the two remarkable vigilance committees of San Francisco. Of them he says:

"Not the same judgment, by any means, can be passed upon the San Francisco vigilance committees of 1851 and 1856 as we have already passed upon the popular justice of the miners. In some respects, to be sure, there is an unfortunate likeness. Both in the mines and in San Francisco, carelessness had led to a destructive general license of mischief-makers. In both places the men of sense were forced at last to attend to their social duties. But in the mines there was, for a while, a far too general, a very absurd and wicked, trust in lynch law as the best expression, under the circumstances, of the popular hatred of crime. San Francisco, as a community, never went so far as this. In that city lynch law was, both in 1851 and in 1856, the expression of a pressing desire so to reform the social order that lynch law should no longer be necessary."

"What had made it [the second vigilance committee] inevitable was a long continued career of social apathy, of treasonable public carelessness. What it represented was not so much the dignity of the sovereign people, as the depth and bitterness of popular repentance for the past. What it accomplished was not the direct destruction of a criminal class, but the conversion of honest men to a sensible and devout local patriotism. What it teaches to us now, both in California and elsewhere, is the sacredness of a true public spirit, and the great law that the people who forget the divine order of things have to learn thereof anew some day, in anxiety and pain."

"The great committee [of 1856] was productive of more good than evil only because in the sequel it was not left to its natural tendencies, but was constantly guided by cautious and conscientious men, whose acts were not always wise, but whose purposes were honest and rational. * * * The first real test of the success of the committee in its one true work, which was to agitate for a reform in municipal society and politics, came at the autumn elections, when the people sustained the whole movement by electing city officers to carry on in a legal way the reform which had been begun without the law. And thenceforth, for years, San Francisco was one of the best governed municipalities in the United States.

Determination of Sulphuric Acid

*It is possible to estimate H_2SO_3 and $H_2S_2O_3$ in the presence of each other, by first determining both iodometrically, and then the H_2SO_3 by a method based on the reaction $Na_2S_2 + Na_2SO_3 = Na_2S + Na_2S_2O_3$. This change takes place rapidly near the boiling temperature, and is further accelerated by the addition of NH_4Cl. The persistence of the yellow color of the reagent serves as a satisfactory end-point. To prepare a normal solution of Na_2S_2, saturate 500 cc. normal NaOH with H_2S, remove the excess gas under diminished pressure, add an equal volume of normal NaOH, then dissolve in the cold solution, 16 gm. of sulphur crystallized from CS_2. To the flask containing the solution join a burette by means of a siphon, and connect both with a gas holder of nitrogen for displacing air from the system. Standardize the Na_2S_2 solution gravimetrically. Measure 20 cc. into a solution containing AcONa and a slight excess of AcOH, expel H_2S by boiling in a current of CO_2, collect the sulphur on a filter of tared glass-wool, dry in vacuo over H_2SO_4 and weigh. The small amount of thiosulphate always present in the solution of Na_2S_2 can be determined iodometrically, and the necessary correction applied. The greater the dilution the more rapid is the titration and the more definite is the end point. However, it is not advisable to have more than 100 cc. per 5 cc. of reagent. Under these conditions each 100 cc. should contain 5 cc. twice-normal NH_4Cl and should be slightly alkaline (alkalinity equivalent to 4 cc. normal Na_2CO_3 per 50 cc.). A current of CO_2 should be kept passing over the surface of the liquid during the titration, which should require less than 10 minutes, especially if the approximate titration has been ascertained by previous experiment. If trithionate is present, the situation is more complicated. Trithionate is not acted upon by iodine in the cold but it is converted into thiosulphate by Na_2S, thus: $Na_2S_3O_6 + Na_2S \leftrightarrows 2Na_2S_2O_3$. This reaction is slow in the cold, but is rapid at higher temperatures; in the presence of Na_2S_2, sulphur is precipitated. Heat a dilute solution with a slight excess of Na_2S or Na_2S_2, in presence of NH_4Cl, for several minutes near the boiling point, add AcONa and a slight excess of AcOH; heat for 15 minutes in a current of CO_2, then titrate with tenth normal iodine. Results are good; 0.1785 gm. $K_2S_3O_6$ requires 13.25 cc. tenth normal iodine. In the case of a mixture of sulphite and trithionate, the Na_2S_2 produces both changes simultaneously: $Na_2SO_3 + Na_2S_3O_6 + Na_2S_2 \leftrightarrows 3Na_2S_2O_3$. If trithionate is present in excess, it is shown by a turbidity due to sulphur which appears after the sulphite is consumed. The turbidity does not interfere with the end point, as the yellow color of the reagent is readily observed. A mixture for analysis contained 5 cc. $Na_2S_2O_3$ solution corresponding to 4.80 cc. tenth normal iodine; 2 cc. Na_2SO_3 solution corresponding to 9.19 cc. tenth normal iodine and to 1.84 cc. Na_2S_2; 0.1337 gm. $K_2S_3O_6$ corresponding to 9.88 cc. tenth normal iodine. Titration of this mixture required 1.90 cc. Na_2S_2 and 24.00 cc. tenth normal iodine. An alternative method for trithionate is based on the titration of the residual iodine after heating with excess of iodine under pressure. This follows the titration of sulphite and thiosulphate in the cold. The tetrathionate from the latter is then changed to sulphate, as is the trithionate. The principle appears to be sound, but there are many sources of error. Another procedure for determining trithionate employs the action of heat; $H_2S_3O_6 \leftrightarrows H_2SO_4 + SO_2 + S$. Acidify the solution by adding HCl, heat near the boiling point in a current of CO_2 until SO_2 is all expelled (end of operation being detected by dipping the end of the delivery tube into dilute iodine solution), filter off the sulphur and precipitate the H_2SO_4 with $BaCl_2$. Investigation showed that the precipitate thus obtained contained 97.9–97.5% of the trithionate, which was converted into sulphate. In the presence of H_2SO_3 and $H_2S_2O_3$ the loss is more or less compensated by the unavoidable oxidation of the H_2SO_3. If H_2SO_4 is also present, it is of course precipitated. A known mixture containing 0.3457 gm. K_2SO_4 (1.982 millimols) with 0.1315 gm. $K_2S_3O_6$ (0.486 millimol) also 1.813 millimols of $Na_2S_2O_3$ and 2.445 millimols Na_2SO_3, gave on analysis 2.485 millimols of trithionate and sulphate (100.7% theoretical). In dealing with a mixture of all four acids, oxidize with bromine water, precipitate with $BaCl_2$, and thus obtain total sulphur as sulphate. The determinations outlined above then complete the data for calculation of the four constituents. In titrating trithionate by iodine and Na_2S_2, and determining $H_2SO_4 + H_2S_3O_6$ gravimetrically, H_2SO_4 is thus obtainable by difference. The determination of total sulphur serves as a check.

*O. Billeter and B. Wavre, Helvetia Chim. Acta, 1, 174-80, (1918).

CRIPPLE CREEK, COLORADO

Gold Production, Dividends, and General Notes.

Gold production of the district for the short month of February was curtailed by the weather, deep snow preventing movements of ore, both by team and by rail. The tonnage reported from the treatment plants fell to 75,350, with an average value of $8.46 per ton, and gross bullion value of $647,500, shown as under:

	Tons	Average Value	Gross Value
Golden Cycle mill, Colorado Springs......	23,000	$20.00	$460,000
Portland, Independence mill, Cripple Creek	37,000	2.08	77,250
Vindicator mill	13,000	2.20	28,600
Smelters, Denver and Pueblo............	1,850	55.00	81,750
Total	75,350	$8.46	$647,500

FLOW-SHEET OF GOLDEN CYCLE MILL AT COLORADO SPRINGS, WHERE NOTHING BUT CUSTOM ORE FROM CRIPPLE CREEK IS TREATED. (CHEM. AND MET. ENG.)

Dividends in February totaled $167,000, as follows: Cresson, $122,000; Golden Cycle, $45,000.

The Midget mine on Gold hill, the Blue Bird on Bull hill, and the Rose Nicol on Battle mountain will re-enter the shipping list during March.

Litigation between the El Paso Consolidated and the Kalinka company over extra-lateral rights has been averted by settlement out of court. Operations will now be resumed at the Nichols shaft on the north end of the El Paso estate. Machinery had been removed from the shaft-house but a powerful electric hoist is to take the place of the steam engine.

The 25th annual report of the Portland company, presented to shareholders at the meeting, at which the officials were all re-elected, shows a net profit of $196,598 for 1918. [An abstract of the report appears in another part of this issue.]

Driving on the 11th level of the Cresson shaft for a distance of 100 ft. has exposed a network of veins of high value, according to the general manager, A. L. Blomfield. Driving is also in progress on the 9th and 10th levels, on the same orebody, and assays are 2 oz. per ton from grab-samples.

During the past week the tonnage treated at the mill of the Golden Cycle company at Colorado Springs has averaged 1000 tons daily, compared with 700 tons the last quarter of 1918. The increase is directly due to increased activity, made possible by the return of miners, discharged soldiers, and others to the district, and consequent relief of the labor shortage.

The lessee of the Deerhorn mine of the Stratton company, W. C. Green, has been honorably discharged from the U. S. Army and has resumed work.

Returns from a carload shipment of ore from the recent discovery made by Hamilton and son in the Gold Bond tunnel on Gold Hill gave $17.70 per ton. The lessees report improvement in value as the drift is extended.

The Komat Leasing Co., operating the Victor mine on Bull cliffs, under lease from the Smith-Moffat Mines Co., is shipping from three to four cars per week of milling ore. The January production was 400 tons, averaging $12.50 per ton.

Articles of incorporation have been filed for the Cocks Mining & Leasing Co., with a capital of $10,000. The directors are Frank W. Cocks, Roswell P. Russell, and Henry C. Cassidy of Colorado Springs.

DENVER, COLORADO

The Portland Company.—Potash from Mill Tailing.—Gas in Cripple Creek Mines.—Radium Companies and the Affair at Jimtown.—Colorado School of Mines.

Annual reports of mining companies are interesting mainly in data regarding expenses, production, development, and profits, but the last report of the Portland Gold Mining Co. [detailed on another page of this issue], in addition to such statistical matter, presents several items having a bearing upon the status of the Cripple Creek district. Corroborating what has been said in the press and in public discussion, the troubles of a gold-mining concern last year are effectively exhibited in a comparison of the net profits of this company during the last two years. In 1917 the profit was $663,254, while in 1918 it was only $196,596. This drop of approximately 70% in a single year is significant material for the war economist. The president, Frank G. Peck, hints at re-opening the company's mill at Colorado Springs. He also briefly explains that Federal chemists spent nine months of last year in developing a process for recovering potash from the residue at this same mill. Sampling and measurements show about 2,000,000 tons averaging 7% K_2O. Still another item in this report states that the Portland's share in the cost of the Roosevelt drainage-tunnel was $144,951.

Salvage of potash from gold-mill residue is the object of the International Potash Corporation composed of Omaha and Lincoln capitalists, who have secured a lease from the Morse Bros. Machinery & Supply Co. on the 6,000,000-ton dump at the dismantled mill of the United States Reduction & Refining Co. near Colorado Springs. Chemists have decided that the dumps average 11% potash. Answering an inquiry into the discrepancy between the potash content of the dumps at two mills treating ores from the same district, the explanation has been offered that the United States mill tailing was mostly made at a period when the ore was subjected to different treatment from that subsequently practised in the Portland mill. A new plant, 125 ft. square, costing approximately $100,000, is being erected and is expected to be in commission by May 1. The process is one developed by professors of Johns Hopkins University and goes by the name of that institution.

The peculiar effect of atmospheric conditions upon mining in the Cripple Creek district is again brought to our attention in two fatalities that resulted on February 12 in the Midget mine. During a heavy snowstorm the barometric pressure became so low as to permit an undue amount of the residual nitrogen gas from the extinct volcano to exude into the workings. Such phenomena were discussed by Lindgren and Ransome in Professional Paper 54 of the U. S. Geological Survey, published in 1906.

Denver seems destined to become the centre of the world's supply of radium. This city was selected several years ago as the site for the plant erected and financed by the National Radium Institute, but operated by the U. S. Bureau of Mines. This relationship continued a sufficient time to demonstrate amply the success of a process proposed by the Bureau and to make a total extraction of more than six grams of radium. The plant was closed down when the Bureau moved its Colorado branch from Denver to Golden. Recently this complete plant has been purchased by the Minerals Recovery Co., whose officers are P. H. Chambers, president; W. W. Anderson, vice-president; and William E. Bryan, secretary and general manager; all of Denver. Your correspondent is informed that the company is fully financed and will soon engage in the commercial treatment of four tons of carnotite ore daily.——The name of the established and highly successful Schlesinger Radium Co. has been changed to the Colorado Radium Co. This company is steadily expanding its operations, its gross production last year being in excess of $1,000,000. Its product is assured a constant market in the manufacture, by the subsidiary, the Cold Light Manufacturing Co., of luminous articles.——The Chemical Products Co., incorporated a few years ago by Denver men and occupying the old paper-mills, has changed ownership, but it continues its reduction of radium from carnotite ore.——Finally we come to the project of the widely-advertised Colorado Pitchblende Co. with plans for extensive treatment of uranite-bearing fluorite mined at Jimtown, Colorado, although the milling and concentration of the crude ore will be done near the mines, the refining will probably be done at Denver.

Speaking of the Colorado Pitchblende Co. one finds good reading in newspaper accounts, more or less accurate, of incidents connected with the publicity campaign conducted by the company's officers. The 'Mining and Scientific Press' has published several items regarding this scheme, but the following sketch is offered to bring the story to date:

The first offering of shares in this company was with so much full-page newspaper advertising, and such extravagant statements regarding reserves and grades of ore, that public suspicion was promptly aroused and efforts were made to suppress the company's sales. Subsequently the promoters disclaimed any motive of exaggeration and 'passed the buck' for the flambouyant ads to a local advertising agency which is accustomed to handle publicity matters for new oil companies having few scruples. Last year the Denver City Council passed and enforced an ordinance that accomplished results in eliminating many questionable promotions by conducting official investigations of all concerns offering shares to the public. The bearing of this ordinance upon the project of the Pitchblende company was such that the president and general manager, J. F. Barnhill, personally urged an official investigation of his project, and ceased all efforts at selling shares pending such investigation. At that time the city's mayor was ill with influenza and nothing along this line could be done officially by the city government, so Mr. Barnhill turned his attention to the representative commercial organization of Denver. His attitude was so emphatic and serious that he prevailed upon the Denver Civic and Commercial Association to conduct a thorough examination of his project. The matter was immediately referred to the Manufacturers Association and the Mining Bureau, both sub-divisions of the C. and C. Association. Each subsidiary selected a well-known local mining engineer who went to Jimtown and rendered a professional report at the company's expense. M. S. MacCarthy was the engineer appointed by the Manufacturers Association, while James S. McClave was the choice of the Mining Bureau. These gentlemen co-operated in their work at the mines and mill and during their later experimentation at Denver, but they rendered separate reports which, while in substantial agreement, differed slightly in details. They reported affirmatively. Mr. MacCarthy delivered his report to the chairman of the Manufacturers Association, and it was then promptly handed over successively to the parent association and to the Pitchblende company, thereby directly giving the Association's endorsement to the promotion. However, Richard A. Parker, a prominent mining engineer and chairman of the Mining Bureau, upon his receipt of the McClave report, withheld it for more than a week during which period he not only critically studied it himself but caused it to be discussed in detail by a gathering of some 30 mining engineers. The idea back of this criticism was that the Civic and Commercial Association, particularly its mining branch, should not endorse any promotion until the project could be weighed with the same conscientious consideration that a professional engineer gives to a case for a private client. During this delay the company instituted suit for the possession of the McClave report, but the suit was dropped, with reluctance, Mr. Parker finally relinquished the report to the manager of the main Association, and it thereupon was delivered to the Pitchblende company. Immediately after the company's receipt of each report, large display advertising was resumed in newspapers, the extravagant statements in former space being replaced by I-told-you-so sarcasm. Agreeable to promise, both reports were printed verbatim: without any such promise, the reports would have appeared. The advertisements played up certain paragraphs of the reports in large bold type. The discussion at the gathering of engineers tended to prove that, admitting the tonnages and gross value given in the two reports, the profits to be expected from the contemplated commercial operations of the company were erroneous; that the daily handling of 1000 tons of crude ore would soon flood the nation's fluorspar market; and that the estimated costs of producing radium salts from carnotite ores did not apply to the rather complex ore involved in this project. These criticisms were not directed in any measure at the integrity of the examining engineers, but were proposed as the differing viewpoints of impartial critics. No representative of the company was present at the lengthy session of the engineers, although Mr. McClave was the leading person, and endeavored to explain every question put to him in an absolutely frank manner. No reporters were present, either, but one newspaper presented an account of the meeting, accompanying the account with insinuations that the opposition to the reports emanated from the Boulder Commercial Association which, in turn, was dominated by Prussian interests— an imputation wholly without a vestige of warrant. It is true that the Boulder people, including State Geologist R. D. George and Warren Bleeker, participated in the opposition, but this was purely upon technical grounds. In the Jimtown ore, fluorite, the principal mineral, is associated with very small amounts of gold, silver, lead, and iron, the ore being of sulphide character. During the dressing of the fluorite to raise it to a marketable grade, a streak of mineral heavier than galena was seen on the tables. Investigation proved this thin streak to be pitchblende, but, in practice, it was found next to impossible to effect a clean table separation of this mineral from the sulphides. However, the research conducted at Denver by the examining engineers (Mr. McClave has long been a flotation engineer) upon large samples secured during the mill-runs at Jimtown proved that a clean separation can be effected by oil flotation. It was doubt upon this subject that caused most criticism by various engineers who discussed the report. The reports show that the daily dressing of 1000 tons of crude ore will yield a gross production per ton as follows: gold, silver, and lead, $1.04; fluorspar, $3.81; uranium oxide and radium, $7.09; total $11.94. The operating costs being estimated at $2.80, the profit per ton will be $9.14. Corresponding figuring upon a basis of 100 tons daily gives a profit of $17.27. The wide discrepancy between these estimated profits arises because of assumed different market prices for the fluorspar, the figures on the smaller tonnage being based on present prices around $19 per ton for 85% grade, while the figures on the 1000-ton basis admit a post-war price for fluorspar of only $10 per ton. The affair thus far has consumed two months. It is rumored that the end "is not yet." Your correspondent desires to say here that he was among the most skeptical regarding the merits of this affair at the start. However, he is now disposed to accept the sincerity of the promoters of the company in their belief that they possess what they claim, this much being admitted without acknowledging actual merit to the project. If the promoters are disposed to be positively frank in their advertising, they might now come out with apology for their bald statement that they own mountains of fluorspar, that they have a belt of solid ore one-half mile wide and two miles long, and they might give full publicity to a letter written by Mr. Parker and accompanying the McClave report when he released it. In this letter he says: "Our conclusion is that the business hazards of this enterprise, which we have touched upon briefly in this report, are such that its commercial success is a problem still insufficiently demonstrated, and that upon the present evidence no such profits as are advertised can be expected." The writer is informed by the consulting engineer of the company that its metallurgist has perfected a process for the extraction of radium that will obviate troubles heretofore experienced in treating complex ores. He further says that the company owns extensive deposits of bauxite elsewhere, and is conducting research looking to a large consumption of its fluorspar in the commercial reduction of aluminum from the bauxite.

Troubles at the Colorado School of Mines cannot remain quiet for long. Little has been heard for some months regarding this once-famous school, although it is generally understood that affairs at Golden are in bad shape. A bill pending in the Legislature aims to compel governors of the State to see to it that at least three of the five trustees of the school are alumni, this measure being sufficient, it is presumed by the framer of the bill, to ensure the employment of capable honest presidents in the future. [The bill was killed, due to some clever lobbying.] Steps are being taken by the American Association of University Professors to conduct a thorough investigation of the many charges of disqualification preferred against the present executive.

PLACERVILLE, CALIFORNIA

Mining in Eldorado County.

It is understood that the Manzaneta gold mine, in the Kelsey district, 3½ miles north of Placerville, is developing so well that a company is to be incorporated to equip and operate it on a larger scale. At present a 10-ton daily capacity Bryant mill and a small concentrator are at work. A pay-shoot 700 ft. long and 20 ft. wide has been opened by a tunnel. The vein is incased in a well-defined diabase hanging and slate foot-wall. Five feet of the ore averages $9.17 per ton. Of this, $5.25 is saved on the plates and $3.92 in the concentrate. E. N. Fissler is general manager. C. M. Jackson and D. J. Mathews of Stockton are largely interested.

Six men are busy cleaning-up the Lotus mine, 9 miles north-west of Placerville, putting it in shape for a large mill. A lease and bond was given on the property by county supervisor J. B. Wagner to N. K. Cooper, of San Francisco, about a month ago. The mine is somewhat developed, and contains a well-defined, persistent, and payable vein.

W. E. Jones, of the Aluminum quartz mine, three miles south-east of Placerville, recently took advantage of the

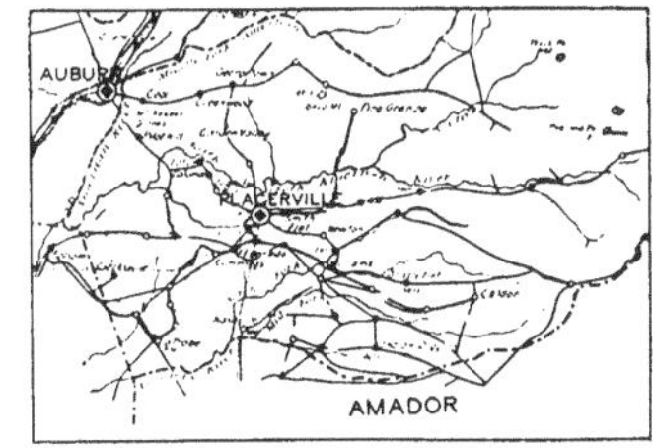

MAP OF ELDORADO COUNTY, CALIFORNIA

heavy rains to ground-sluice a 10-ft. square patch of surface placer ground on his property that was left by early-day miners. He recovered over $90. From another overlooked piece of ground containing two tons of gravel, he obtained $32; one nugget was worth $8. After this ground had been hydraulicked in the 'fifties, an old miner made an average of $3 daily for over six months with a rocker, washing the patches of bedrock that the giant operator missed.

Definite arrangements have been made to procure a new quartz mill and electric hoist at the Burger mine, situated on Coloma street, less than a mile north of the post office, within the city limits of Placerville. T. B. McLane is here from Seattle consulting with his partners A. L. Conger of Berkeley, and N. H. Burger of this town. Two long pay-shoots have been opened in the 5-ft. vein, samples of which give assay of $27 gold per ton.

The recent rain has supplied an abundance of water so that the barrel gravel mill at the Rising Hope deep-gravel mine, three miles east, is now in constant operation washing the large body of cemented deep-channel gravel that was found there last fall. On March 4 the manager brought in about 100 oz., the result of a part clean-up. Charles M. Henson is mine superintendent and George O. Perry is millman.

F. L. Kendall, of Denver, arrived here on March 1. He represents a Colorado company and is examining the Bean Hill gold and platinum placer mine, 12 miles south-east of Placerville. This is the property from which several large pieces of platinum were reported to have been recovered.

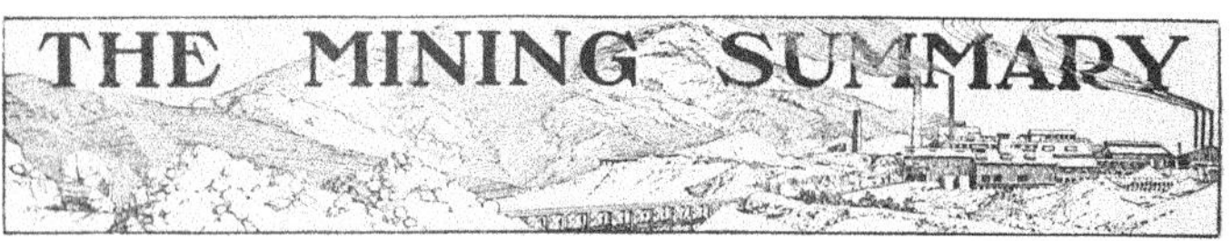

ALASKA

Juneau.—Alaska Gastineau Mining Co. has issued its report for the last quarter of 1918. Results, compared with previous periods, are as under:

	Fourth	Third	Second	First
Tons	287,571	218,930	309,249	469,695
Value per ton......	$0.986	$1.323	$1.164	$0.986
Extraction, per cent.	80.22	82.39	81.96	79.92
Extracted	0.791	1.093	0.954	0.790
Cost per ton.......	1.060	1.140	0.990	0.800
Loss per ton........	0.270	0.050	0.040	0.080

The mine contains 1,718,173 tons of ore broken in stopes, according to the survey at the end of 1917. A re-survey is now being made. No development was done. The year shows an operating loss of $110,290.

The company's gold output in February was 162,400 tons of 83.7c. ore, of which 77.3% was recovered.

ARIZONA

Ajo.—The Ajo-Cornelia Copper Co.'s property, against which the E. J. Longyear Company obtained an injunction for $2000 for diamond-drill work, has been advertised for sale. Shareholders have appealed to the State Corporation Commission for protection, claiming mismanagement by its officers. As soon as the tangle is adjusted shareholders are prepared to pay the debt.

Bisbee.—Calumet & Arizona is to pay $1 per share, equal to $642,462.

Indefinite suspension of operations at the Denn-Arizona has been necessary because of fire. Two hundred men have been laid off.

Globe.—The Arizona Commercial Mining Co. is suing the Iron Cap Copper Co. for alleged illegal extraction of ore, also for refusing to share the expense in draining the ground within its boundary. The Iron Cap property is between two areas of the Commercial. The latter alleges that in the last six years it has spent over $250,000 in draining its ground, which also drained that of the Iron Cap, and claims damages at $150,000 for this work. Regarding the ore mined, the Commercial claims that over 250,000 tons, for which the Iron Cap received $3,000,000, was taken out. The hearing on these actions was to be held at Boston on March 11.

Grand Canyon.—Developments have been so satisfactory in the past eight months at the vanadium property of W. I. Johnson on Cataract creek that a 25-ton mill is to be erected immediately.

Jerome.—It is announced that following the shut-down due to the recent strike here the Green Monster Mining Co. will not resume operations until industrial conditions are more stable.

Ray.—The Ray Consolidated Copper Co. pays 50 cents per share on March 31, equal to $788,589. This is a reduction of 25 cents.

ARKANSAS

Yellville.—The dry concentrating plant for zinc ore erected here some time ago by the Sutton, Steele & Steele company is to be re-started. The process is said to be successful, especially in districts where water is scarce.

CALIFORNIA

Bakersfield.—Delegates from the 14 Oil, Gas and Refinery Workers' locals of California, on the 6th and 7th discussed the wage award made public by the Federal Oil Inspection Board at Los Angeles. Lee Scott, vice-president of the International Oil, Gas and Refinery Workers' Association presided. The Oil Inspection Board announced a wage-scale that the oil-workers are said to consider too low. The demand of the oil-workers submitted last September to the Board was for a $5 per day minimum. The award, individual members of the union say, amounts in effect to about 25 cents per day increase for single men and 50 cents for married men. The majority of the 15,000 members of the California branch of the Oil Workers' Union are said to come under the 25-cent increase or those who earn now from $4 to $4.25. The present minimum wage is $4 for eight hours.

The wage-schedule was accepted, excepting the $4 minimum and 9-hour day for teamsters and truck-drivers. If within 30 days there is no adjustment to the $5 minimum and the 9-hour day, there will be an appeal to the Secretary of Labor.

The oilmen have locals at Bakersfield, Taft, McKittrick, Maricopa, Lost Hills, Los Angeles, Coalinga, Richmond, Rodeo, Brea, Whittier, Santa Maria, Martinez, and El Segundo.

The Standard Oil Co. of California in 1918 produced 22,446,021 bbl., a gain of 23% over the 1917 yield. Stocks at the end of last year were 11,825,598 bbl., a decrease of 19%. The value of sales increased 29%. The earnings were $44,276,582, after deducting operations and marketing. After writing off $3,895,758 for depreciation, $6,022,228 for depletion, and $19,405,462 for excess profits tax, the net profit was $14,953,074. In 1917 the profit was $18,649,630. Dividends in 1918 were $12,421,663, against $9,316,248. Total assets are $145,231,331, an increase of $18,308,171.

Heroult.—The Noble Electric Steel Co.'s smelter has been closed, the company being in financial difficulties.

Keswick.—The Mountain Copper Co. has stopped work at its Iron Mountain mine near this place, also its New Year mine near Coram. The Hornet mine, a mile away, is to be kept open.

Plymouth.—On March 7, the California Exploration Co., controlling the Plymouth Consolidated, paid a dividend of 12 cents per share, equal to $28,000.

San Francisco.—The value of gold, oil, and all other minerals in this State is shown in the following table, prepared by the State Mining Bureau:

Year	Gold	Oil	All minerals
1890	$12,309,793	$384,200	$18,039,666
1900	15,863,355	4,152,928	32,622,945
1910	19,715,440	37,689,542	88,419,079
1915	22,442,296	43,503,837	96,663,369
1916	21,410,741	57,421,334	127,901,610
1917	20,087,504	86,976,209	161,202,962
1918	17,250,000	123,000,000	191,100,000

The Bureau has issued Bulletin '76' 'Manganese and Chromium in California', by W. W. Bradley, Emile Huguenin, C. A. Logan, W. B. Tucker, and C. A. Waring (since deceased). The publication covers 248 pages, is well illustrated with photos and maps, and contains descriptions of every property in the State, and names of buyers of the ores. The accompanying map is abstracted therefrom. Those interested should procure copies. The price of the bulletin is 50 cents.

The State Mining Bureau announces that Bulletin 78, 'Quicksilver Resources of California,' by W. W. Bradley, is now ready for distribution. The price is $1.50. This work was reviewed fully in the 'Press' of January 4, 1919.

Sutter Creek.—The Old Eureka company has finished sinking to 3150 feet.

COLORADO

Alma.—The Louisiana-Colorado Mining Co. in Park county has just finished its 200-ton mill. The flow-sheet is simple, including a ball-mill, Dorr classifier, and flotation plant, the tailing from which pass over a Deister-Overstrom and a rectangular deck-table.

Boulder.—The Colorado Pitchblende Co. is erecting machinery at its fluorspar mine at Jimtown. A contract has been let for hauling concentrate to Boulder.

Breckenridge.—Owing to the mild winter and light snowfall, dredging will be started this season about a month earlier than usual. There are five boats now being overhauled.

Central City.—Lessees at the Becky Sharpe mine in Russell gulch have opened some pockets of rich gold-silver-lead-copper ore. These shoots are 6 to 12 in. wide, but the whole formation is 36 to 60 in. Two cars, 52 tons, of second-class ore sent to the Argo mill at Idaho Springs averaged 4 oz. gold, 8 oz. silver, and 2.85% copper. The ore is easily mined.

IDAHO

Wallace.—As the result of a recent meeting of the principal mine operators of the Coeur d'Alene region, an early announcement of a reduction in wages is expected. A committee was selected to look into the cost of living, and see that all merchants are keeping prices at a minimum. This action is similar to that recently taken at Butte, where operators threatened to open their own stores unless merchants reduced prices. Even if a sharp reduction in wages should be made, no labor trouble is anticipated, as most of the men are said to realize the necessity for such action owing to the present lead market. The radical element in the Coeur d'Alene is greatly in the minority.

The Consolidated Interstate-Callahan mine is to be closed on account of the lead and spelter markets. Fully 300 men will be dismissed.

The Hecla company pays 15c. per share, equal to $150,000, on March 28. This makes $7,405,000 to date.

MICHIGAN

Houghton.—Dividends payable on March 31 are: Allouez, $1, equal to $100,000; Isle Royale, 50 cents, equal to $75,000; and Quincy, $1, equal to $110,000.

Wolverine pays 50 cents per share, equal to $30,000, on April 1. This is a reduction of 50 cents from the previous quarter. The total for 1919 is $1.50 per share.

The Victoria Copper Mining Co. in 1918 made a net profit of $17,046. The surplus—cash, bonds, and copper—totals $238,228. From 106,730 tons of ore the yield was 1,533,536 lb., of which 1,230,230 lb. was sold. The ore averaged 0.72% copper. The cost was 22.2 cents per lb. Development covered 2847 ft. There are over 14 miles of workings in the whole property. Results generally may be termed fairly satisfactory. George Hooper is superintendent.

The 15% cut in wages by the C. & H. is general throughout the Copper Country, affecting 18,000 men.

Copper continues to accumulate at every smelter in the district, and there is more unsold metal on hand here now than at any time within four years. Smelters continue their output without regard to market conditions.

MISSOURI

Joplin.—Production of the Tri-State region last week was as under:

State	Blende, tons	Calamine, tons	Lead, tons	Value
Kansas	1327	...	347	$78,922
Missouri	1428	788	160	92,950
Oklahoma	6348	...	911	330,357
Average value.	$42*	$28†	$62‡	

*60% Zn. †40% Zn. ‡80% Pb.

The total value is $75,000 more than the previous week. The demand was much better last week.

MONTANA

Butte.—East Butte Copper Co. has blown-in its smelter and notified custom producers to that effect.

North Butte Mining Co. has curtailed its ore output from 1200 to 450 tons daily.

Thompson Falls.—The Silver King Mining Co. has been incorporated by Kellogg, Idaho, men, to operate the Silver King mine, near this place. The property was acquired some time ago by Mr. Price and associates, and development has been under way. The mine has a record of nearly $100,000 in shipments of ore carrying high value in silver.

NEVADA

Dayton.—The Dayton Placer Recovery Co., a Utah corporation, has filed a petition in voluntary bankruptcy. Assets total $34,214, and liabilities $48,760. Of the latter, $3314 is due for wages. The cyanide plant was treating gold-silver-mercury tailing from the old Comstock mills.

Ely.—The Boston Ely Mining Co., Smokey Development Co., and Ely Northern Copper Co. have been consolidated by S. H. Williams into the Boston Ely Consolidated Mining Co. The capital is $1,000,000, shares $1 par. About 250,000 shares will be held in the treasury. Cash amounts to $150,000. There are no debts, bonds, or notes. L. E. Whicher of New York has had the properties examined. The Ely Northern is said to have a fine deposit of carbonate ore. Work is to start in the Smokey, on a sulphide vein found in the long cross-cut tunnel.

Nevada Consolidated has reduced operations to 50% of capacity. The mill works five days per week. The smelter is catching up on the accumulation of ore and concentrate.

Nevada Consolidated Copper Co. pays 37½ cents per share, or $749,796, on March 31. This is a reduction of 37½ cents.

Goodsprings.—The Yellow Pine company is storing its zinc concentrate but is shipping lead. The mill is to be altered, and a calcining-plant erected.

Jarbidge.—This centre apparently has a good future. The Elkoro Mines Co., E. A. Austin general manager, started its 200-ton mill on March 1, 1918, and it has continued running ever since. Rolls are used for grinding when the pulp goes to the cyanide plant. A $30 average is said to be maintained. This company owns the Longhike claims, including the Log Cabin, Laurel, O K, and Starlight groups, also a controlling interest in the Jarbidge gold and the North Star claims and several others. The ore being treated is from the Longhike mine.

The owners of the Bluster mine and mill have completed plans, and will erect a cyanide plant as soon as weather conditions permit.

The Jarbidge Nevada Mining Co., of Tacoma, owner of the Legitimate mine, is having 300 lb. of its ore tested at Salt Lake City, with the idea of erecting a flotation plant. The saving by flotation is not as good as that made by cyanidation when treating Jarbidge ores. This may be due to the colloidal nature of the ore.

Tonopah.—On April 1 the Tonopah Extension pays a dividend of 5%, equal to $64,140. This makes $1,980,000 to date.

The Jim Butler company is to resume development in the Desert Queen mine.

The Tonopah Belmont pays a dividend of 10%, equal to $150,000, on April 1. This makes $9,718,063 to date.

Four new companies, making fifteen in all, are operating in the Divide district, namely, the Silver King Divide, Alto Divide Mining, North Divide, and Gold Wedge Divide. All are said to be favorably located and are managed by reliable men.

A brief summary of what is being done in the Divide district is as follows:

The Allied Divide has been organized to develop claims adjoining the East Divide.——The Alto Divide, next to the Allied and East, is sinking. A 1000-ft. electric hoist and 7-drill compressor have been secured.——The Brougher Divide is exploring on the 500-ft. level, and has cut some ore. G. Hanson is in charge.——The Divide Consolidated is sinking. A geologic report has been made by A. H. Elftman.——The Divide Extension is sinking from 150 to 300 ft. Machinery has been purchased from Manhattan. E. Bevis is superintendent.——The East Divide is sinking through favorable ground at 300 ft. depth.——The Gold Wedge is prospecting from a 70-ft. shaft, and is preparing for a head-frame and hoist.——The North Divide is erecting machinery.——The Rosetta is sinking to 100 ft.——The Silver King has started sinking, and has secured machinery at Manhattan.——The Tonopah Divide shaft has reached a depth of 520 ft. The south cross-cut at 475 ft. is out 100 ft. in rhyolite-breccia, similar to that in the levels above, where the rich ore is being mined. At 370 ft., the vein has been opened 350 ft. beyond the south cross-cut, still in ore. Daily shipments to the MacNamara mill at Tonopah are 35 tons. William Watters is superintendent.

The Tonopah Divide sent 245 tons of ore to be milled last week.

Unionville.—The West End Consolidated of Tonopah has purchased the Adamson claims, near the Arizona mine. The ore, which is in rhyolite, carries good value in silver and gold.

NEW MEXICO

Magdalena.—The Graphic, Kelly, and Ozark zinc mines are not doing much work at present. At the Kelly there are 40 or 50 lessees.

Santa Rita.—Chino Copper Co. pays 75 cents per share on March 31, amounting to $652,485. The previous dividend was $1.

OKLAHOMA

Picher.—An oil-flotation machine is to be tried here by the R. W. Johnson Association on local zinc ore.

SOUTH DAKOTA

Lead.—The Homestake Mining Co. distributes 50c. per share, $125,580, on March 25. The total to date is $41,794,444.

UTAH

Bingham.—The Bingham Mines company is to pay 25 cents per share, equal to $37,500.

Utah Copper Co. pays $1.50 per share, equal to $2,436,735, on March 31. This is a decrease of $1.

Eureka.—Rich silver-lead ore is being mined from the bottom—1875 ft.—level of the Eagle & Blue Bell mine. The shoot is continuous from 1700 ft. Exploration is under way at 2000 ft. A dividend of 5 cents per share, equal to $44,657, has been declared.

The Tintic Standard company has arranged for construction of an 11-mile spur track to the mine, connecting with the D. & R. G. This line will also aid the Iron King, Eureka Lily, Eureka Bullion, Provo, and other properties. The new hoist at the Standard is finished.

Park City.—The Silver King Consolidated is holding its lead-zinc concentrate until the market improves or costs drop, or both, to ensure a reasonable profit. The company is offering $200,000 in short-term notes to enable this product to be carried and development continued.

The Ontario Silver Mining Co. during 1918 had a total revenue of $605,859, of which $561,768 was from ore. Cash assets total $554,674. Little profit was made during the past six months owing to abnormal conditions.

WASHINGTON

Chewelah.—The United Copper company is opening 14 in. of 600-oz. silver ore on and below the 1300-ft. level. The remainder of the ore assays 5% copper and 20 oz. silver per ton. Two carloads in February were settled for $3500 each. An electric hoist of 1000-ft. capacity has been ordered.

A chamber of mines is being organized here to look after mining in Stevens county.

Leadpoint.—The Lead Trust company is erecting a 60-hp. boiler, 25-hp. engine, compressor, etc, and is to advance its No. 2 tunnel. The sulphide ore carries lead and silver.

Northport.—The Northport S. & R. Co.'s plant was closed on February 25, for how long, nobody knows. Work has been started on the drossing plant to cost $150,000.

Tacoma.—The A. S. & R. smelter here has only one furnace in blast, compared with three last year. Wages were cut 12½% on March 1, the minimum now being $3.75 per day. A number of mines in British Columbia and others contiguous to the smelter feel the reduction in payment for copper ore.

CANADA

British Columbia

Anyox.—Granby Consolidated, from March 1, is paying wages on a sliding-scale, regulated by the price of copper.

Fire last week damaged the roof of the blast-furnace and converter building.

Britannia.—The Howe Sound company has discharged over 400 men, due to the copper market.

Ontario

Boston Creek.—A depressed diamond-drill hole at the Cotter property, about 720 ft. long, has cut 28 ft. of ore at a depth of 492 ft. The average assay is $12.42 per ton.

Cobalt.—The ore-sampling firm of Compbell & Deyell, here since 1909, has discontinued business. Ore containing 61,000,000 oz. passed through the plant, and metallics weighing 1,200,000 oz. were melted there.

The Trethewey Silver-Cobalt Mines company in 1918 made a net profit of $103,368. The mill treated 24,514 tons at a cost of $2.21 per ton. Silver in ore-reserves is estimated as 159,172 oz., a decrease of 39%. An interest has been acquired in the Castle mine at Gowganda, where conditions are encouraging.

Porcupine.—The Hollinger last week started another 40 stamps crushing. A 1000-hp. hoist and 9000-cu. ft. compressor are to be added to the equipment. The Hollinger pays a dividend of 5 cents per share on February 25, equal to $246,000.

The Porcupine-Crown Mines company made a profit of $4814 last year, against $109,421 in 1917. Operations were only conducted in the first half of the year. The mill treated 10,907 tons of $9.64 ore, extracting 97.09%. The surplus is $271,956. The main vein has been opened to a depth of 1100 ft., reserves being valued at $500,000. A continuation to 1400 ft. is expected. A cave-in carried down three levels, but this will soon be cleared away and mining will be resumed at an early date.

The University of Illinois maintains 14 research graduate assistantships in the Engineering Experiment Station. Two other such positions have been established under the patronage of the Illinois Gas Association. These, for each of which there is an annual stipend of $500 and freedom from all fees, except the matriculation and diploma fees, are open to graduates of approved American and foreign universities and technical schools who are prepared to undertake graduate study in engineering, physics, or applied chemistry.

The Spokane Engineering and Technical Association, composed of nine societies having chapter headquarters at Spokane, held a two-day session last week. L. K. Armstrong was chairman. The membership embraces men actively engaged in eastern Washington, northern Idaho, western Oregon, western Montana, and southern British Columbia. The societies represented are civil, mining, electrical, mechanical, chemical, and electro-chemical engineers, architects, and the society for the promotion of engineering education.

The Colorado Chapter of the American Institute of Mining Engineers enjoyed a splendid dinner, February 8, at the Denver Athletic Club. The affair was enlivened by several surprising cabaret numbers. The following officers were elected for the current year: Robert J. Grant, chairman; W. H. Leonard, vice-chairman; Robert M. Keeney, secretary-treasurer; these, with Stephan Ionides and Robert Hursh, executive committee. Lieut. Horace Wells of Denver informally adressed the gathering upon his part in war aviation, especially his experience as a German prisoner of war. ——At the February meeting of the Denver Teknik Club, Harry J. Wolf spoke at length upon recent research in the treatment of manganiferous-silver ores.——The Colorado Scientific Society held a dinner, February 15, at the Shirley hotel, and was addressed by Stephan Ionides upon H_2SO_4 and M. E. K., this cryptic title covering late developments in the manufacture of war munitions.

PERSONAL

Note. The Editor invites members of the profession to send particulars of their work and appointments. The information is interesting to our readers.

Scott Turner is at Toronto.

W. P. Hammon has returned from Boston.

J. C. Hopper has returned to San Francisco from Silverton, Colorado.

W. H. Woodbury, secretary of the Duluth Engineers Club, was in San Francisco last week.

W. H. Goodchild, who has been to Cuba, has returned to New York on his way to London.

R. T. Schraubstadter, of St. Louis, has been examining a mine in Plumas county, California.

D'Arcy Weatherbe sailed from New York to London on March 15, on his return from China.

W. H. **Weed** was at Tonopah last week, as advisor to the Divide Consolidated Mining Company.

S. M. Levy, superintendent for the Calaveras Copper Co., has returned to Copperopolis, California.

George R. Allen, president of the Chosen Minerals Co., has arrived in San Francisco from Keijyo, Korea.

S. A. Knowles succeeds James Humes as superintendent for the Silver King Coalition, Park City, Utah.

G. H. Edmonds, superintendent of the Conrey dredges in Montana, has been in San Francisco to consult with Hennen Jennings.

Among those decorated by the Belgian government are two mining engineers: Edgar Rickard and E. Coppee Thurston.

Morton **Webber** has arrived here from New York. He has become consulting engineer to the Empire Copper Co., at Mackay, Idaho.

H. C. Dudley has received his discharge as Captain of the 36th Engineers of the Army, and is now in the Landsdale building, at Duluth, Minnesota.

C. M. **Wilson**, until recently engineer for the Garfield Smelting Co., has been appointed chief engineer for the A. S. & R. Co., at El Paso, Texas.

H. C. Hoover is withdrawing from his work as International Food Administrator in July, and will resume his practice and business of mining engineering, with offices at New York.

Lloyd C. **White**, designer and superintendent of the Mountain Copper mill, has joined the firm of Burch, Caetani & Hershey, on the resignation of Gelasio Caetani, who finds it necessary to remain in Italy to look after the property of his family, the head of which is the Duke of Sermoneta.

THE POSITION OF ASSOCIATE EDITOR ON THIS PAPER IS VACANT. APPLICATIONS FOR THE APPOINTMENT ARE INVITED.

Obituary

J. K. Batchelder, superintendent of refineries for the Consolidated M. & S. Co. of Canada, at Trail, B. C., died recently of pneumonia. He was born at Wilton, New Hampshire, in 1890.

James W. Abbott died in February at a sanatarium near Clifton Springs, New York. He had been an invalid for several years. A graduate of the Sheffield Scientific School of Yale University, he took a prominent part in the early mining of the San Juan region in Colorado, living successively at Lake City and at Ouray. He was a public-spirited man and did much to foster the 'good roads' movement, writing many articles on the subject and participating in conventions organized for the purpose.

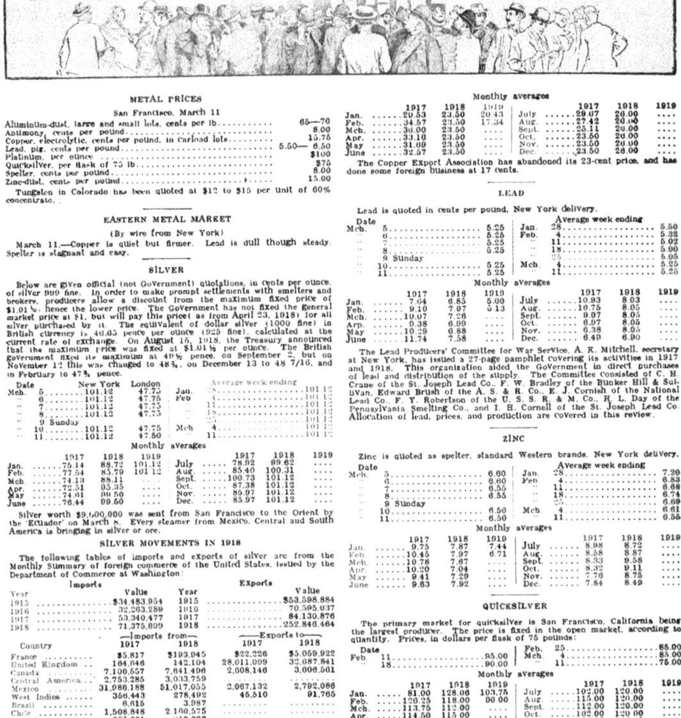

METAL PRICES

San Francisco, March 11

Aluminium-dust, large and small lots, cents per lb	65—70
Antimony, cents per pound	8.00
Copper, electrolytic, cents per pound, in carload lots	15.75
Lead, pig, cents per pound	5.50— 6.50
Platinum, per ounce	$100
Quicksilver, per flask of 75 lb	$75
Spelter, cents per pound	8.00
Zinc-dust, cents per pound	15.00

Tungsten in Colorado has been quoted at $12 to $15 per unit of 60% concentrate.

EASTERN METAL MARKET

(By wire from New York)

March 11.—Copper is quiet but firmer. Lead is dull though steady. Spelter is stagnant and easy.

SILVER

Below are given official (not Government) quotations, in cents per ounce, of silver 999 fine. In order to make prompt settlements with smelters and brokers, producers allow a discount from the maximum fixed price of $1.01½, hence the lower price. The Government has not fixed the general market price at $1, but will pay this price (as from April 23, 1918) for all silver purchased by it. The equivalent of dollar silver (1000 fine) in British currency is 40.65 pence per ounce (925 fine), calculated at the current rate of exchange. On August 15, 1918, the Treasury announced that the maximum price was fixed at $1.01½ per ounce. The British government fixed its maximum at 49½ pence, on September 2, but on November 12 this was changed to 48¾, on December 13 to 48 7/16, and in February to 47¾ pence.

Date		New York	London	Average week ending		
Mch.	5	101.12	47.75	Jan.	28	101.12
"	6	101.12	47.75	Feb	4	101.12
"	7	101.12	47.75	"	11	101.12
"	8	101.12	47.75	"	18	101.12
"	9 Sunday			"	25	101.12
"	10	101.12	47.75	Mch	4	101.12
"	11	101.12	47.50	"	11	101.12

Monthly averages

	1917	1918	1919		1917	1918	1919
Jan.	75.14	88.72	101.12	July	78.92	99.62	....
Feb.	77.54	85.79	101.12	Aug.	85.40	100.31	....
Mch.	74.13	88.11	....	Sept.	100.73	101.12	....
Apr.	72.51	95.35	....	Oct.	87.38	101.12	....
May	74.61	99.50	....	Nov.	85.97	101.12	....
June	76.44	99.50	....	Dec.	85.97	101.12	....

Silver worth $9,600,000 was sent from San Francisco to the Orient by the 'Ecuador' on March 8. Every steamer from Mexico, Central and South America is bringing in silver or ore.

SILVER MOVEMENTS IN 1918

The following tables of imports and exports of silver are from the Monthly Summary of foreign commerce of the United States, issued by the Department of Commerce at Washington:

Imports		Exports	
Year	Value	Year	Value
1915	$34,483,954	1915	$53,598,884
1916	32,263,289	1916	70,595,037
1917	53,340,477	1917	84,130,876
1918	71,375,699	1918	252,846,464

Country	Imports from 1917	Imports from 1918	Exports to 1917	Exports to 1918
France	$5,817	$193,045	$22,226	$5,059,922
United Kingdom	164,646	142,104	28,011,099	32,687,841
Canada	7,100,557	7,641,496	2,608,146	3,006,561
Central America	2,753,285	3,033,759	....	....
Mexico	31,986,188	51,017,055	2,067,132	2,792,086
West Indies	356,443	278,492	46,510	91,765
Brazil	6,615	3,987	....	....
Chile	1,508,848	2,160,575	....	....
Colombia	225,381	210,327	....	....
Peru	7,214,747	5,115,577	....	....
Venezuela	2,981	1,019	....	....
China	10,750	....	12,106,631	23,786,077
East Indies	1,713,117	248,223	....	....
Argentina	....	....	8,695	178,621
India	....	....	24,392,403	163,154,135
Hongkong	....	....	8,612,757	19,322,299
Other countries	291,102	1,329,140	6,256,277	2,107,157
	$53,340,477	$71,375,699	$84,130,876	$252,846,464

COPPER

Prices of electrolytic in New York, in cents per pound.

Date			Average week ending		
Mch.	5	15.00	Jan.	28	19.87
"	6	14.75	Feb.	4	19.21
"	7	14.50	"	11	18.33
"	8	14.75	"	18	17.50
"	9 Sunday		"	25	16.40
"	10	15.00	Mch	4	15.25
"	11	15.00	"	11	14.83

Monthly averages

	1917	1918	1919		1917	1918	1919
Jan.	29.53	23.50	20.43	July	29.07	26.00	....
Feb.	34.57	23.50	17.34	Aug.	27.42	26.00	....
Mch.	36.00	23.50	....	Sept.	25.11	26.00	....
Apr.	33.16	23.50	....	Oct.	23.50	26.00	....
May	31.60	23.50	....	Nov.	23.50	26.00	....
June	32.57	23.50	....	Dec.	23.50	26.00	....

The Copper Export Association has abandoned its 23-cent price, and has done some foreign business at 17 cents.

LEAD

Lead is quoted in cents per pound, New York delivery.

Date			Average week ending		
Mch.	5	5.25	Jan.	28	5.50
"	6	5.25	Feb.	4	5.32
"	7	5.25	"	11	5.02
"	8	5.25	"	18	5.00
"	9 Sunday		"	25	5.05
"	10	5.25	Mch.	4	5.25
"	11	5.25	"	11	5.25

Monthly averages

	1917	1918	1919		1917	1918	1919
Jan.	7.64	6.85	5.60	July	10.93	8.03	....
Feb.	9.10	7.07	5.13	Aug.	10.75	8.05	....
Mch.	10.07	7.26	....	Sept.	9.07	8.05	....
Arp.	9.38	6.99	....	Oct.	6.97	8.05	....
May	10.29	6.88	....	Nov.	6.38	8.05	....
June	11.74	7.58	....	Dec.	6.49	6.90	....

The Lead Producers' Committee for War Service, A. K. Mitchell, secretary at New York, has issued a 27-page pamphlet covering its activities in 1917 and 1918. This organization aided the Government in direct purchases of lead and distribution of the supply. The Committee consisted of C. H. Crane of the St. Joseph Lead Co., F. W. Bradley of the Bunker Hill & Sullivan, Edward Brush of the A. S. & R. Co., E. J. Cornish of the National Lead Co., F. Y. Robertson of the U. S. S. R. & M. Co., H. L. Day of the Pennsylvania Smelting Co., and I. H. Cornell of the St. Joseph Lead Co. Allocation of lead, prices, and production are covered in this review.

ZINC

Zinc is quoted as spelter, standard Western brands, New York delivery.

Date			Average week ending		
Mch.	5	6.60	Jan.	28	7.20
"	6	6.60	Feb	4	6.83
"	7	6.55	"	11	6.68
"	8	6.55	"	18	6.74
"	9 Sunday		"	25	6.69
"	10	6.50	Mch	4	6.61
"	11	6.50	"	11	6.55

Monthly averages

	1917	1918	1919		1917	1918	1919
Jan.	9.75	7.87	7.44	July	8.98	8.72	....
Feb.	10.45	7.97	6.71	Aug.	8.58	8.87	....
Mch.	10.78	7.67	....	Sept.	8.33	9.58	....
Apr.	10.20	7.04	....	Oct.	8.32	9.11	....
May	9.41	7.29	....	Nov.	7.76	8.75	....
June	9.63	7.92	....	Dec.	7.84	8.49	....

QUICKSILVER

The primary market for quicksilver is San Francisco, California being the largest producer. The price is fixed in the open market, according to quantity. Prices, in dollars per flask of 75 pounds:

Date					
Feb.	11	95.00	Feb.	25	85.00
"	18	90.00	Mch.	4	85.00
			"	11	75.00

Monthly averages

	1917	1918	1919		1917	1918	1919
Jan.	81.00	128.06	103.75	July	102.00	120.00	....
Feb.	126.25	118.00	90.00	Aug.	115.00	120.00	....
Mch.	113.75	112.00	....	Sept.	112.00	120.00	....
Apr.	114.50	115.00	....	Oct.	102.00	120.00	....
May	104.00	110.00	....	Nov.	102.50	120.00	....
June	85.50	112.00	....	Dec.	117.42	115.00	....

The quicksilver market is active at the present price. If it goes lower some mines will have to suspend operations, as evidence given before the Federal Tariff Commission here last June showed that costs are from $60 to $75 per flask.

TIN

Prices in New York, in cents per pound. The monthly averages in 1918 are nominal. On December 3 the War Industries Board fixed the price to consumers and jobbers at 72½c. f.o.b. Chicago and Eastern points, and 71¼c. on the Pacific Coast. This will continue until the U. S. Steel Products Co.'s stock is consumed.

Monthly averages

	1917	1918	1919		1917	1918	1919
Jan.	44.10	85.13	71.50	July	62.60	93.00	....
Feb.	51.47	85.00	72.44	Aug.	62.53	91.33	....
Mch.	54.27	85.00	....	Sept.	61.54	80.40	....
Apr.	55.63	88.53	....	Oct.	62.24	78.82	....
May	63.21	100.01	....	Nov.	74.18	73.07	....
June	61.93	91.00	....	Dec.	85.00	71.52	....

Eastern Metal Market

New York, March 5.

There is a tendency for most of the markets to be firm, although prices of some metals have declined further.

Antimony is unchanged.

Copper has reached lower levels, but on small transactions.

Lead is more active in both inquiry and sales, and prices are firm.

Tin has no market, it being still under restrictions that are unnatural and demoralizing.

Zinc is inactive and dead, with prices nominal but fairly steady.

ALUMINUM

No. 1 virgin metal is quoted at 31 to 32c. per lb., New York, for early delivery, but demand is light. An announcement by the War Trade Board is to the effect that the importation of aluminum ingots into the United Kingdom is not prohibited, but that aluminum sheets require an import license.

ANTIMONY

The market is dull with quotations nominal at 7 to 7.12½c. per lb., duty paid, New York, for wholesale lots for early delivery.

COPPER

The market has continued to decline until yesterday electrolytic had sold as low as 15c. per lb., New York, for early delivery. It was stated that this had been or could be shaded, but actual transactions below 15c. have not been confirmed. We therefore quote the market at 15c., New York, for electrolytic, with Lake nominal at about 15.75 to 16c. per lb. Demand, even at these low prices, which are generally admitted as under cost, is very small, and the foregoing quotations are based on small sales in all cases. Large producers generally are meeting the 15c. price, but no lower. The feeling is becoming more evident that bottom has nearly been reached. Export demand is insignificant. An interesting fact in this connection is that on a recent export inquiry it was impossible to obtain quotations from the leading members of the Copper Export Association. A tentative agreement has been made between about 90% of the American producers and a representative of the Ordnance Department whereby the 140,000,000 lb. of copper bought by the Government at 26c. per lb. late in the War will be marketed by producers during the next 15 months, probably at the market price. Reports are conflicting as to whether a minimum price was decided upon. Casting copper is quoted at 14.75c. per lb., New York.

IRON AND STEEL

The need of the steel market is stabilized prices, according to the general feeling of leading steel-makers. There have been such prices for three months now, and producers count on being able to maintain them without Government intervention. Any cut, even a sharp one, which would leave the impression of further recessions in the near future, would not help business now. The February pig-iron output, according to 'The Iron Age,' was 2,940,168 tons, or 105,000 tons per day, which is 1519 tons less than the daily output in January. On March 1 there were 306 furnaces in blast, against 323 on February 1. Better furnace operation, due probably to better coke, is reported.

LEAD

Considerable activity has developed in the lead market, and a fair business has been done in the last week. The market is firm at 5.25 to 5.35c., New York, or 5 to 5.10c., St. Louis, the former prices being those of the leading interest (A. S. & R. Co.), which has probably taken most of the business. All sales in the outside market have been close to 5.35c., New York. All consuming lines have participated in this demand, this being cited to demonstrate the fact that consumers have about realized that the market has reached bottom. Sentiment is approaching the bullish stage, as production has been curtailed decidedly and the labor situation is not helping matters as to output or an accumulation of stocks.

TIN

There is little to be said about this market, which from day to day and from week to week is virtually held by the throat. Dissatisfaction is growing. Restrictions are still in force, the only metal available in wholesale quantities being the allocated metal which is held at 72.50c., New York, a fixed price. In this letter some weeks ago it was reported that it was rumored that further restrictions would be placed on the tin market, or in other words, that the lid would be placed on the sales of all tin, even by jobbers, with the exception of course of the allocated metal. It is now intimated that this plan has been modified, in that the price of American tin will be marked up, ostensibly to lessen the competition with the allocated metal. The originators of this controlled market are surely having a most difficult and sad time. The market is dead, for there is none. Spot Straits is nominal at 72.50c., New York, while American 99% metal can be bought at 67 to 68c. per lb., New York. The only free movement, devoid of restrictions, is in lots of 5 tons and less. Tin arrivals in February were 2450 tons, 2340 tons coming through Pacific ports. The total to March 4, 1919, has been 4366 tons, against 7740 tons to March 1, 1918.

ZINC

Consumers are neither inquiring nor buying, and the market is at a standstill. It is believed that stocks are increasing rather than otherwise, no more. Government reports of stocks and output are not being published, and this is a disappointment to many. The quotation for prime Western is nominal at 6.25c., St. Louis, or 6.60c., New York, for early delivery or even most any delivery. The entire situation is one of marking time.

ORES

Ferro-chrome. Alloy containing 60 to 70% chromium is nominal at 32c. per lb. of contained metal, with light demand.

Manganese. High-grade Indian manganese ore has been offered at seaboard for 80c. per unit, but no sales have been effected, it is said.

Manganese-Iron Alloys.—Producers are generally quoting $200 per ton delivered for 78 to 82% ferro, with $3 deducted for each unit under 78%. Small trading among consumers has been at $150 per ton, delivered. Spiegel is nominal at $50 to $53, delivered. Re-sale 18 to 22% alloy has been offered at $42.50 per ton, point of shipment.

Molybdenum. The market is quiet and nominal at 85c. per lb. of MoS_2 in high-grade concentrate.

Tungsten. There have been no developments and no trading. The market is flat with practically no quotations. It is probable that ferro can be bought under $1.50 per lb. of contained tungsten. If so, this would mean about $14 to $15 per unit for high-grade concentrate.

Company Reports

UNITED VERDE EXTENSION MINING CO.

Property: mine, smelter, and railway at Jerome, Arizona.

Operating Officials: G. Kingdon, general manager; Barry Hogarty, superintendent of smelter.

Financial Statement: the gross revenue in 1918 was $15,-156,716. Operations cost $5,596,485, State and County expenses, $661,244, estimated Federal taxes, $2,000,000, and depletion and depreciation, $3,567,933, leaving $3,331,054 net. After paying dividends the surplus was $1,756,054. Supplies are valued at $740,907; cash, $1,874,646; Liberty Bonds, $3,350,000; due for ore and bullion sold, $852,445; and ore and bullion on hand, $3,477,407.

Dividends: No. 9 and 10 absorbed $1,575,000, making $7,455,000 to date.

Development: underground work totaled 10,919 ft., including 7155 ft. in the haulage-tunnel. No prospecting was done and no new orebody was developed. When the Audrey shaft is finished in April 1919, driving will be started at 1500, 1600, and 1700 ft. depth. It will be necessary to drive 900 ft. to get under the ore. New systems of mining, ventilation, and safety will result in lower costs. Only 1180 ft. remained to be driven in the haulage-level to connect the Texas shaft and the section east of the Audrey. This level will mean no change of ore-cars from mine to works and the disuse of the aerial tram.

Production: the new smelter was blown-in during July, and is a complete success. The company's output (some custom work was done) is shown in the following table:

	Tons	Copper, lb.	Gold, oz.	Silver, oz.
Ore to custom smelters......	62,277	32,261,742	615	224,325
Ore to U. V. X. smelter.....	71,258	23,220,335	2431	279,414
Total	133,535	55,401,077	3046	503,739
Average per ton..................		407 lb. (20.35%)	0.024	4.18

PORTLAND GOLD MINING CO.

Property: mines and mills at Cripple Creek, Colorado.

Operating Officials: G. M. Taylor, general manager; Fred Jones, superintendent at the mine; T. B. Crowe, superintendent at the mill; Luther Lennox, assistant; and Merrill Metallurgical Co., consulting metallurgists.

Financial Statement: the net profit in 1918 was $196,596. The balance from 1917 was $278,383, and that carried to 1919 was $127,622. Current assets total $395,966, and liabilities $14,052.

Dividends: the total last year was $300,000, making $11,-257,080 to date.

Development: there was accomplished 8071 ft., making 63 miles in the Portland mine. The Independence mine has 17 miles of openings. The branch tunnel from the Roosevelt drainage-tunnel to No. 2 shaft of the Portland, at a depth of 2131 ft., was connected during the year. At the end of 1918 the main shaft was sunk to No. 21, or the drainage-level. Development of No. 1 vein will soon be under way. The Lee No. 5 orebody was cut by the tunnel cross-cut, and driving is opening high-grade ore. Generally the outlook is promising.

Production: the Colorado Springs mill was closed on March 31, and the Victor mill on July 30, leaving the Independence in operation. The extraction at the last named was good, but the profit was small. Almost without exception, every improvement devised to reduce costs was immediately offset by some increase in cost of labor or supply entering into the extraction of gold. The output was 53,887 tons (Colorado Springs) valued at $1,120,851, and 522,756 tons (Victor mills) worth $1,071,925. The output to date is 3,949,248 tons, worth $48,773,378 gross.

INFORMATION FURNISHED BY MANUFACTURERS

PULVERIZING AND BLOWING MACHINERY FOR POWDERED COAL

By F. B. Collin

*Electric power is probably used more extensively in the preparation and handling of pulverized fuel, on the basis of kilowatt-hours per ton, than is the case with any other form of fuel. One possible exception is briquetted fuel. In this country, however, the amount of fuel briquetted is small [477,235 tons in 1918]. Electric power is used for the following operations in connection with pulverized fuel:

These pulverizers are a type commonly used for pulverizing coal

Crushing the coal to 1-inch size or less; energizing magnetic separators; rotating the dryer-drums; pulverizing the coal; elevating lump and pulverized coal; driving screw-conveyors; driving feed-screws for burners; driving reciprocating air-compressors for high-pressure air, transport systems, and blast-feed to burners; driving centrifugal air-compressors for supplying air for combustion at a pressure of 1 lb. per square inch; and driving low-pressure blowers for supplying air for combustion at lower pressures, and for conveying coal in suspension through pipes; also for separating the finished product from the unfinished in pulverizing.

No one plant uses power for all of these items, as the list includes the component parts of several different systems for preparing and handling pulverized coal.

The amount of pulverized fuel used in the United States at mid-1918 was 10,000,000 tons, divided by industries approximately as follows: manufacture of cement, 6,000,000 tons; iron and steel industry, 2,000,000 tons; production of copper, 1,500,000 tons; and generation of power, 100,000 to 200,000 tons.

The requirements of one representative system of preparing, conveying, and burning pulverized coal are 35 hp-hr. per ton. With a motor efficiency of 89%, this corresponds to a power consumption of 29.4 kw-hr. per ton.

*Abstract from 'General Electric Review'.

Some systems require less power and others more, according to the methods used in pulverizing and conveying. Air transport systems require more power for their operation than mechanical systems, but have the advantage of greater simplicity and flexibility. Assuming an average consumption of 30 kw-hr. per ton, for the 10,000,000 tons used, the yearly power requirements will be 200,000,000 kw-hr. As many of the furnaces using pulverized coal have to operate fairly continuously, we will assume an average yearly operation of 5000 hours out of 8760. At this load-factor, the average power consumption will be 60,000 kw. If 2.5 lb. of coal are consumed in the power station per kilowatt-hour, this corresponds to 375,000 tons yearly for preparing and handling 10,000,000, or 3.75% of the total.

When burning other fuels there will be a corresponding charge which will vary according to the fuel and the method of firing. When atomizing oil with a steam jet, the amount of steam consumed is from 2 to 3% of the total

Centrifugal air-compressor with capacity of 3300 cu. ft. per min. at 1 lb. per sq. in. This machine is used for blowing pulverized coal into open-hearth steel furnaces.

steam generated in an oil-fired boiler. In addition, power is required for pumping the oil and for the blowers, which maintain the air-blast. This is an extravagant way of burning oil, but requires the least equipment. Pumping oil through mechanical atomizers is a more efficient method of burning. In power-stations, the stokers require power for actuating the fuel-feed, and for the under-grate air-blast. In addition, power is required for crushing and conveying the coal. With pulverized fuel the combustion is more complete and the stack loss is reduced. The result is that the net efficiency is a little better with pulverized coal under test conditions; and taking the human factor into consideration, it should be easier to maintain operating efficiencies which are more nearly comparable to those attained in test. It is evident, therefore, that the power charges against the preparation and handling of pulverized coal are offset by the more efficient utilization of the fuel. By the use of off-peak power for preparing pulverized fuel the comparison can be made still more favorable and a margin provided to absorb other charges, such as labor at the pulverizing plant,

Three-stage centrifugal air-compressor with capacity of 250 to 350 cu. ft. per minute at 1½ lb. per sq. in. This type of machine can supply the primary air to pulverized coal burners at any pressure from ½ to 3¼ lb., by varying the number of stages from 1 to 6. The power required is from 2 to 8.5 horse-power.

when the installation is of sufficient size. If this be the case where the margin is smallest, it must be more marked in the case of metallurgical furnaces where the fuel saving is greater than is possible in a modern boiler-plant. Considerable fuel economies are possible, however, in boiler-plants having old-style stokers or where hand-firing can be superseded.

LIFE AND COST OF SHOVELS

In a valuable paper on shoveling, prepared for the New York meeting of the American Institute of Mining Engineers in February, G. T. Harley had the following to say regarding the wear of shovels: To determine the relative wearing qualities and the cost per ton for supplying the men underground with new shovels, different places in the mine [Burro Mountain copper mine, Tyrone, New Mexico] were equipped with different makes and styles of shovels, and the results carefully noted. At frequent intervals, these shovels were measured to detect the wear of the blade, and checked up to see that all were being used in the proper places underground; the tonnage coming from each place, and the number of shovelers employed were also noted. The table gives the results obtained with the different classes of shovels.

Type of shovel	Used on	Tonnage handled by blades made of — Chrome-nickel steel	Secret composition steel	Common carbon steel	Extra light carbon steel
No. 2 scoop	Iron sheet	1220	950	750	...
No. 2 scoop	Rough bottom	....	...	...	...
No. 2 scoop	Wooden mat	1500	1100	900	...
No. 4 shovel	Iron sheet	990	770	620	250
No. 4 shovel	Rough bottom	1075	870	...	...
No. 4 shovel	Wooden mat	1108	1000	730	340
Gage of steel in blade		15	13	14	16
Cost of shovel per ton handled, cents		0.0015	0.0018	0.0019	0.0026

The shovels made of chrome-nickel and special steel were excellent implements, but the special steel shovel was considerably heavier than the other. Cracks developed along the form line of the chrome-nickel steel blade, on each side, but these did not impair the shovel's usefulness. The blades of the three other shovels bent easily with rough usage, while the blade made of extra-light carbon-steel wore rapidly and the edges curled up almost immediately. The No. 2 scoop was used until its capacity had been reduced 25%, and the No. 4 shovel until its capacity had been reduced 9%. The cost of shovel per ton handled includes the cost of the shovel, freight, supply-house handling, handling new shovels into mine, and disposal of worn shovels. We had hoped to be able to detect a difference in the man efficiency on account of the different styles and weights of shovels in use at this time, but owing to the constantly changing conditions in the working-places selected for the trials, no conclusive evidence was available.

The wearing quality of any shovel used on an iron sheet varies from 74 to 86% of the wearing quality of the same shovel on a wooden mat, the average being 82%. The wearing quality of a shovel on a rough bottom is about 90% of that on a wood mat. These figures are based on about 50 observed shovels underground.

COMMERCIAL PARAGRAPHS

The **Chicago Pneumatic Tool Co.** announces the removal of its Cleveland district office from room 813 to rooms 406-408 Engineers building, effective March 1. Ross Watson, the district manager, will gladly welcome visitors to the new offices.

In Bulletin 180, the **Wood Equipment Co.** of Chicago describes its pneumatic rotary-dump machine for the rapid, safe, and economical unloading of mine-cars. This apparatus has great capacity. Such mines as the Alaska Gastineau, and many coal properties use them.

The **Wyoming Shovel Works**, of Wyoming, Pa., in its Catalogue No. 4, gives some interesting data on its 'Mayari red-edge shovels', which are of chrome-nickel steel. The sole agents in San Francisco are **Harron, Rickard & McCone**. All shapes and sizes and prices are given, besides many illustrations.

The **J. D. Fate Co.** of Plymouth, Ohio, has recently prepared a new catalogue, No. 4. It is a most attractive bulletin and is illustrated profusely with views of both underground and surface operations employing the Plymouth gasoline locomotive. This engine, which has found a wide market in the metal-mining industries, has been most favorably received by numerous companies all over the country, as shown in the present catalogue. It deals with the high efficiency and adaptability of the locomotive to both surface and underground conditions. The new publication will be sent upon request.

'Dixon's Graphite Products' is the title of a new pocket catalogue issued by the **Joseph Dixon Crucible Co.** of Jersey City. While not so complete as the large general catalogue, it gives a good idea of the variety of products made by this old concern. Pages are devoted to lists of articles especially for mills, railroads, automobiles, etc. The descriptions are brief, but the company will gladly send pamphlets dealing in detail with any of the individual members of the line. This new catalogue should be in the file of every purchasing agent, engineer, superintendent, and others who have occasion to use lubricants, paint, or pencils. Ask for Booklet No. 141-KP.

In order to give a practical working idea of what sizes of fuses to use for motors, the **Westinghouse Electric & Mfg. Co.** has prepared a series of tables. These are based on the size of fuse required to stand starting current without blowing. The proper fuse for a motor is only too often obtained by an electrician or a repair-man by haphazard methods. The motor's normal operating current is given by the maker on the name-plate, but fuses are properly selected of a larger capacity to allow for starting and for momentary overloads. Hence it is rather more unusual for the maintenance man to select his fuses by guess, with a view to their permanence in service rather than the safety of the motor they are supposed to protect.

IN this issue we give an abstract of the excellent speech delivered by Judge John F. Davis at the recent meeting of the American Mining Congress. His subject was the need for the creation of a Department of Mines headed by a member of the President's cabinet. As our readers will find, he made a good argument, which, we feel assured, will appeal to all those engaged in mining.

LIKE other minerals, tungsten is suffering from large stocks, imports, and low prices. Although $10 per unit is considered to be about the present price in this country, and $7.20 in England, we have heard of a contract for Oriental wolfram at $14.50. The new mines and plants at Mill City, Nevada, are closed. In our next issue we hope to give an interesting summary of the tungsten industry.

GOLD, as a standard metal, is the subject of two good letters under 'Discussion'. We refer elsewhere to Mr. McPherson's contribution. That from Mr. Percy A. Robbins came to hand after the other matter had gone to press. It will be noted that Mr. Robbins likewise presents the argument based on hoarding and predicts that it will prove an important factor in settling this problem of international finance. As most of our readers are aware, Mr. Robbins has been for many years the general manager of the famous Hollinger mine, in Ontario, the success of which is due largely to his skill and sagacity.

"A boom is on with a vengeance at Divide," writes an engineer from Tonopah, which is six miles from the new silver-gold district. New companies are being organized every week, and more than twenty shafts are being sunk. The only real mine is the Tonopah Divide, in which is blocked out several million dollars worth of high-grade ore at a depth of 375 feet. This mine is producing 35 tons daily of ore averaging $25 per ton. The finding of rich ore at other points in the district will be needed to sustain the boom, which seems to have fostered a litter of young wild-cats. However, much of the work is real mining, generously financed, and under competent advice. In our Mining Summary last week we gave a résumé of what is being done at Divide, and this week we give further news from our local correspondent.

DR. HENRY S. DRINKER, the president of Lehigh University and an engineer needing no introduction to our readers, has issued a reprint of an address made by him in January on the League of Nations, in which he mentions the fact that to Mr. Taft is due the credit for initiating—in June 1915—the movement in behalf of the League to Enforce Peace, which, in the hands of President Wilson, has become the basis for a League of Nations. It was the suggestion of pacifism that caused the words "to enforce peace" to be deleted by the European friends of the movement, so that in England and elsewhere similar organizations are entitled 'League of Nations', this sufficing to indicate the effort of thoughtful men everywhere to stimulate the representatives of the peoples in their striving toward the great consummation.

IN a recent speech Dr. David Starr Jordan pointed at the fact that the capitals of Europe are nearer to Washington today than were the capitals of the thirteen colonies in the early days of American independence. The development of systems of communication has not only brought human beings nearer in point of time but the development of various systems of telegraphy and telephony has annihilated distance. The 3300 odd miles of the Atlantic separates America from Europe today less than the 22 miles of the English Channel used to separate England from France in the days of Napoleon. The aeroplane promises to emphasize the change. Meanwhile there are good prospects that at last a tunnel will be built under the Channel, and there is talk of tunneling Bering Strait, so as to join the American and Asiatic continents, and thereby avoid the need for crossing the Pacific Ocean. Should aerial navigation be developed as is anticipated, the most distant parts of the world will be reached with a speed and an ease that will have an enormous influence in promoting acquaintance and goodwill between the peoples of the earth.

OUR boys in writing from the army of occupation in Germany, express bewilderment on seeing the contrast between "the seemingly unscathed Germany and the devastated regions of France." When the German troops returned home after the Armistice they marched through the towns with heads up, singing, decorated with bunting, and deporting themselves like heroic victors. The people of the German towns occupied by the Allied troops take their shame without a shiver, they even make friendly advances to the soldiers of their enemies. What would happen if German soldiers were in conquering occupation of Sacramento or Denver? We can imagine, and so can our readers. The fact is, the German's mental processes are different from ours; we are unable to understand him. Think of the young aviator that killed Quentin Roosevelt talking about the pleasure he anticipated in going to the United States to live! He vanquished Theodore Roosevelt's gallant son fairly enough, but what real American would look upon him with admiration or affection for having done so? Many German prisoners talk glibly about coming to the United States, and even some of those who left the United States to cross the Atlantic and fight for Germany expect to resume their careers in the country whose hospitality they violated. We hope that they will be compelled to remain where they are and take their part in a kultur that they understand, and we do not. If immigration is to be restricted, it were well to keep an eye on these.

IN a recent appeal made by M. Georges Clemenceau in behalf of France to the United States, he refers to the suggestion of payment for trenches and for the graves of American soldiers in France as "atrocious". It was a vile canard started by some irresponsible journalist, and we are glad to take the opportunity to give this publicity to the denial. France merits our most friendly, respectful, and sympathetic consideration. She has suffered more than any of the Allies, she bore the brunt of the German onslaught, and she still holds the front trench of civilization. The loss of life, the ruin of industry, and the cruelties to her people caused by the German invasion are horrors that weigh heavily on the minds of the French and it is not for us to be impatient if they do not share our own—so much more detached and optimistic—views concerning the settlement of the account with Germany and her dupes.

HEARINGS held before the Mexican committee of the Council on Foreign Relations are said to promise a free ventilation of affairs in Mexico. The committee is thoroughly representative, for it includes Mr. Ole Hanson, the mayor of Seattle, now worthily famous, Judge Ben Lindsey of Denver, Mr. John Bassett Moore, formerly assistant-secretary in the Department of State, Mr. Alton B. Parker, and Mr. Frank P. Walsh. According to Mr. Mark Osmond Prentiss, who is described as the manager, it is intended "to tear the lid off the truth about Mexico and our citizens there." If American citizens are being "deprived of their rights, their property confiscated, and their persons outraged by responsible or irresponsible authorities in Mexico," he says, "we want to know it. On the other hand, if American interests or any other interests are fostering revolution there, we want to know it also." With that we agree; the one thing we deplore is a 'watchful waiting' policy that leads nowhere, but postpones indefinitely the hour of settlement and readjustment, which we, in common with the mining fraternity, have been anticipating year after year, ever since Porfirio Diaz was turned out of office and left Mexico to the free play of the forces of disintegration. If the Mexicans are not denied arms and ammunition, now on sale at many counters in Europe, we may expect further outbreaks of disorder. It is imperative that such imports be withheld not only at our frontier but at Mexican ports, as can be done by the friendly pressure of the Paris Conference, for the sake of the restoration of peaceful conditions in Mexico and for the good of the Mexican people, now harassed, despoiled, and famishing, by reason of continued revolts and vendettas. The committee to which reference has been made is one that will command confidence and it ought to be able to bring its findings effectively before the Foreign Relations Committee of Congress, the State Department, and the President. We wish it success in its useful labors.

IN an effort to bring about a more rapid resumption of business, the Secretary of Commerce has announced the formation of an 'Industrial Board', consisting of six members, whose function will be the stabilization of prices of basic materials. The names of three members of the Board have been announced, namely, George N. Peek, formerly vice-chairman of the War Industries Board, Hugh Frayne, representing labor, and Thomas C. Powell, now director of capital expenditures of the Railroad Administration. It is recognized that the present tendency of buyers to delay purchases in the hope of marked reductions is so general as to seriously paralyze industry. In order to lend governmental aid toward overcoming this condition, conferences are to be held with various leaders of industry in order to determine, as far as possible, fair prices for basic commodities. The first to be considered are iron, steel, lumber, textiles, cement, copper, brick, and other materials of construction. The findings of the Board will be valuable for their psychological effect only, as the Board is not empowered either to fix prices or to enforce them. Nevertheless, the announcement of what may be considered as a 'fair' price for any commodity, cannot help but produce its effect upon the buyers. There is nothing to prevent their buying for either more or less than the price determined upon by the Board if they can. It will be at least a reasonable assumption that little if anything can be gained by holding out for prices less than those determined by the Board.

MR. ROBERT LANSING'S speech on March 11 before the Inter-Allied Press Club in Paris was a weighty utterance and most timely in its frank analysis of the European crisis. Undoubtedly, as he made clear, the anarchy fostered by the Germans in Russia and now reducing Germany herself to a condition of bloody chaos, threatens to spread over western Europe with such violence as to shatter all plans for the restoration of order being devised by the Conference at Paris. The victors in the War are menaced by the consequences of their Enemy's disintegration. How much of it is deliberately planned in order to checkmate the efforts of the Allies to bring Germany to account, nobody knows; but it is evident, as Mr. Lansing says, that if the forces of social disorder are not soon controlled, there will be no organized Germany to bring to the bar of justice, only a mob of terrorists rampant over the ruins of Prussian misrule. When a burglar is injured while being captured by the police, it is usual to send him to a hospital, so that he may be restored to a normal physical condition before appearing in court to stand trial. So we must allow Germany to recover her sanity of mind and body before she will be fit to receive her punishment. Food and peace are the best weapons for killing bolshevism. We must make peace and relax the blockade without delay, not for the sake of the Germans, who are now getting some of their own richly deserved medicine, but in order to check the spread of the red terror and to save civilization, thereby completing the good work done by our armies and navies. Time presses. The representatives of the Allied nations, and their Associate, must act promptly and in unison, for the purpose of concluding the terms of peace, if the spread of this anti-social movement is to be circumvented. The desire to complete the organization of the League of Nations before signing the treaty of peace is causing delays that are dangerous. We realize the enormous complexity of the difficulties faced by the delegates at Paris, but we appreciate the wisdom of the appeal made by Mr. Lansing and we hope that this speech will make an impression in the right quarters.

Flotation Litigation

The hearing of the Minerals Separation v. Butte & Superior case before the Supreme Court of the United States was postponed from March 3 to March 19, on which date the matter came up for final decision. The judgment of the Court is not expected for several months and when it is made known it will not, we believe, be the end of the litigation over the patents covering the technique of the flotation process. Other issues remain to be tried. We have held to the opinion—and we hold to it still—that no single inventor or patentee has rights that give him the control of this branch of metallurgical industry; we believe that the process as now conducted so successfully and on so large a scale is the result of the ideas and efforts of a large number of men during the last twenty years. It would be a public wrong to give any patent-exploiting company the right to impose royalties and to interfere with the metallurgic operations of everybody using this process of concentration. We refuse to believe that a manifest injustice can be upheld for any length of time and we expect therefore, no matter what the ultimate decision may be in this particular case, that further litigation will be initiated with a view to asserting the rights of other patentees. Indeed, as we have remarked on a previous occasion, the opponents of Minerals Separation made a grave blunder in allowing themselves always to be placed in the position of defendants; they ought to have attacked Minerals Separation for infringement of older patents, such as those of Elmore and Wolf. The Elmore vacuum-oil patents of 1904 are now owned in this country and they ought to be asserted, for successful flotation was effected by means of them and by the use of a proportion of oil well within the so-called critical limits. The Wolf patent is not as well known, but it is significant in this connection. We refer to No. 787,814, of J. D. Wolf dated April 18, 1905, for which application was made on May 22, 1903. It may be noted that Mr. Wolf, like the Elmores, had an unpleasant experience with Minerals Separation, culminating in a lawsuit, tried in 1905, in the course of which he claimed that the Minerals Separation metallurgists, Sulman & Picard, employed by him to investigate his process, had used the information obtained thereby and taken out patents in respect of discoveries that they made while in his employ. The Judge held that Sulman & Picard had fulfilled every obligation of their contract. In his patent Mr. Wolf, who is now in New York preparing for battle, describes an aerating mechanism for mixing the oil and the ore, for the production of a mineral-bearing froth, which is withdrawn in a spitzkasten. The use of warm water is specified and the oil is one that has been sulpho-chlorinated. He recommends mineral oil to which a little animal oil has been added before sulpho-chlorinating. We quote the full text of the patent on another page, so that our readers can examine it critically for themselves. This patent was recited in the Hyde case and both parties to that litigation appear to have agreed not to say too much about it, as would appear from the examination and cross-examination of Dr. Samuel P. Sadtler. It looks to us as if this patent might cover the main features of the flotation practice of today. We understand that an intelligent person unacquainted with the manipulation or the technique of the flotation process can obtain an effective mineral-bearing froth by following the description and specifications of this patent. We recommend some of our readers to try it, forgetting for the moment what they already know about flotation. Of course, it is not surprising that either this patent or the Elmore vacuum-oil patents were not cited in the early litigations between Minerals Separation and American mining companies, because the latter feared to establish fresh royalty-hunting enterprises: they did not wish to run the risk of jumping from the frying-pan into the fire, but now that they have had a full taste of Minerals Separation methods any other patent-owner looks friendly. Here we may refer to the Federal Trade Commission's inquiry into the doings of Minerals Separation. The hearing was held on December 31, the immediate result, so far as disclosed, has been to lessen the truculence of the Minerals Separation people, who appear now willing to revise their contracts as regards the manufacture of apparatus. We understand that the American Mining Congress is taking a hand in the matter, and we know of none more worthy of the attention of that organization. Nobody can forecast the opinion of the Supreme Court in the Butte & Superior case; if it sustains the Circuit Court of Appeals, all will be well; if it holds to the restrictive decision in the Hyde case, the outlook will be bad for the mining community. If the result should sustain the contentions of the Minerals Separation company, we advise our readers not to be dismayed and not to be driven into quick surrender. The flotation issue will not necessarily be settled by the decision on patent

No. 835,120. There are other patents, conflicting with this one, that are yet to be asserted, and through them relief may possibly be obtained.

Gold and Credit Money

Discussions concerning gold are of vital moment at this period when sober financiers are willing to consider economic experiments not less at variance with the old order than the freak State constitutions that became epidemic in the West some years ago. We are not now concerned with those legislative anomalies, some but not all of which represented proper and desirable social evolution, but we welcome letters such as that by Mr. John McPherson, in this issue, since they deal with gold, the thing that is fundamental in economics, because it is the basis of exchange. Critics may entertain divergent opinions on details, but Mr. McPherson and every other man who thinks seriously and with conviction on the problems of supply and demand, of production and consumption, of distribution of commodities, and the currency settlements involved, is contributing to the mental poise of the nation at a time when popular theories tend to lead away from the old tried practices. Some economic principles have been established which seem to be as fundamental and certain as biologic laws, but views change, and the physiocrats of one age are superseded by the conservationists of another; we swing from the idealism of individualistic free-traders to dreams of controlled free trade under a system of international 'allocation'. Nevertheless, through all the vicissitudes of social evolution there has been one unchanging economic fact: men have been universally agreed, apart from and above statutes and decrees, that gold in the hand will buy meat for the belly. The reasons why gold was selected as the supremely desirable metal to serve as a token of service with which to command the service of others has been discussed so often that we need not review them. The reason, however, for seeking and employing a metal possessing the well-known monetary attributes is not often brought into prominence. It is simply the fear of political disturbance. Banking is based on confidence. It is not merely reliance on the honor and integrity of the banker, nor belief in the wisdom of the banking laws, but faith in the stability of the Government, that admits of the development of a credit system. Granting such confidence, all manner of conveniences in the facilitation of exchange become possible. A smaller ratio of gold to the volume of business in terms of money then proves to be practicable. It is part of our belief in each other as social beings, as reasonable law-abiding men and women, that makes us content with the credit-paper that society gives its pledge to honor in the wares of daily need. One glance at Russia or Mexico, however, reveals why men insist upon available gold on demand as the basis for exchange.

In days of peace men laugh at tales of buried treasure. It is hard to realize, at a time when peace and security reign, that a preceding generation lived in the midst of alarms and subject to pillage by irresponsible and transitory officials, yet deep in the mind, like the instinct of a wild animal, lies the fear of danger that prompts us to desire the one substance for which men will exchange the food and clothing necessary for existence. It takes a long time to civilize the whirl out of a dog before he lies down; it has not yet been done successfully. Likewise, before the primitive desire for gold as a personal possession is supplanted by satisfaction with a piece of paper as the only representation of a claim on this world's goods as a return for service rendered, it will be necessary that many generations shall have grown so accustomed to the undisturbed enjoyment of the refinements of social organization that they may count upon the stability of the new order as firmly as on the daily rising of the sun.

The significance of this psychology of the demand for gold is that the royal metal will not be retired from its ancient duty as real money. To internationalize the gold reserve would be equivalent to retiring it, but the reaction would be so prompt and so pronounced that the attempt to initiate such a scheme would defeat itself. This, however, does not settle the question that so deeply concerns the gold miner, which is the purchasing power of the bullion produced. If gold mining were to cease, the demand for payment in metallic currency would increase, and a further rise in prices undoubtedly would follow on account of the different esteem on the part of the public for credit-money and for hard cash. This would encourage an outside market for gold where a normal ratio to commodities would assert itself. Ordinarily we would hesitate to offer suggestions of this character, but the time has come, not for ultra-social experiments in finance, but for grappling firmly with the concrete problem of giving to gold such a relation to exchange as will admit of continued profitable production of the metal, so that a reasonable amount may be forthcoming to serve as a safe basis for the currency-expansion required by the increasing population of the earth and the growing magnitude of commercial transactions. Retiring gold into the financial background will not do while the Bolshevists are raging in Russia, while the I. W. W. hamper industry in the United States, and while the Premier of England openly warns his country of the danger of civil war. The best antidote for revolution is the surety of opportunity to make a due amount of money for one's needs by peaceful industry, and to receive payment in something that is convertible into gold on demand. With gold mining on the wane, with the shortage of gold leading financiers to discuss cobweb designs of a frail beauty, it is evident that serious consideration of this problem should not be deferred. In the interest of the public welfare the restoration of gold, as a measure of value compatible with the measure of the effort required to get it, is imperative. This does not mean that we must 'raise the price', or juggle with the standard, but it does mean that we must find a way, without incurring disaster, to bring credit-money back to the level of the real.

The Status of Gold

The Editor:

Sir—The article by Van Dyck entitled 'The Status of Gold', appearing in the 'Mining and Scientific Press' of February 1, 1919, contains so alluring an aspect of feasibility that its pitfalls of fallacy are not immediately apparent. In casting about for a ready solution of the much-discussed gold problem he has hit upon this proposal: 1. That all gold be called in and paid for at $20.6718 per ounce, and that all silver be called in and paid for at $1.015 per ounce. 2. That the monetary value of gold be fixed at double the present, that is, at $41.3436 per fine ounce * * * 3. That all newly-mined gold be paid for at the newly-stabilized price. 4. That all metals so accumulated be coined as needed. 5. That all coin be released freely as called for from any quarter of the globe.

In brief his proposal is that the Government take every gold coin, melt it, and re-stamp it with double its present face value. In this manner the present-day confident face of the 'twenty' would re-appear tomorrow stamped 'forty dollars', without any change in weight or bulk; or perhaps the Government would decide to make two coins of 'twenty' each out of one present twenty. Mr. Van Dyck would thus supplant the printing-press manner of making money by the mint-stamp method; yet he would laugh in reasonable merriment at a Mexican leader or a Bolsheviki ruler who should order the printing presses to start as the nation was running short of money to pay foreign debts, or any debts. "It must be borne in mind," he says, "that legislation cannot bring gold into existence," but he implies that legislation can double its purchasing power.

One might reasonably ask why the Government should waste labor and time in melting every twenty-dollar coin and re-stamping the gold into forty dollars when a quick and handy plan would be to leave the twenty-dollar coin as it is but strike as many brass discs as there are such 'twenty' coins, stamp each brass disc "twenty dollars" and shackle one of these discs to each twenty-dollar coin, thereby making, by Government authority, a twin gold and brass coin of forty-dollar purchasing power? While this method would economize time and labor it would be as powerless as the ounce of gold with the forty-dollar stamp on it to reduce the ratio between paper money and real money, between symbol money and money carrying its value around in its own body. This gold-brass twin coin illustration is given to demonstrate more clearly the fact that one half the coin is real money and the other half symbol money. This is exactly what the present twenty-dollar coin would be when it should have received its new stamped face.

What is this subtle mystery in the process of exchange that prevents any nation from stamping an arbitrary figure or figures representing value on the face of any metal disc, gold included? There is only one thing that prevents it, and that thing is the intrinsic or social value of the given metal. Is there any difference in intrinsic value between a disc of brass stamped 'twenty dollars' by the Government and a twenty-dollar paper note? There is no difference; they are both symbols of value and do not contain within their physical or chemical bodies the value they represent. The gold metal disc, provided it is stamped with its current value on the face, carries always with it, within itself, its own actual value in metal bulk and weight. This actual value is always approximate to that marked on its face. 'Approximate' is used advisedly because there is a constant invisible fluctuation in price of the metal which would be revealed in arithmetical figures in a free market only.

By acting on Mr. Van Dyck's suggestion the gold coin, as if by enchantment, should double in purchasing power at the instantaneous drop of a mint-stamp; where the twenty-dollar gold piece procured but ten bushels of wheat at two dollars per bushel yesterday it would purchase twenty bushels today! If it were possible for any nation to perform such legerdemain as this it would be equally possible to act similarly in regard to the case of the wheat which Mr. Van Dyck gives. He says: "Assume that our country has a debt of $30,000,000,000 to pay, and assume that we are now in a position to pay it with 15,000,000,000 bushels of wheat at two dollars a bushel." The Government could as easily leave gold as it was, and arbitrarily fix the price of wheat at four dollars per bushel, or double the price of any commodity it was sending to pay the debt. What could be more preposterous than this? Fancy the astonishment on the face of the Chinaman or the Japanese, for instance, when he should receive one bushel of wheat instead of the two bushels he expected; or, imagine his protest if he should receive but half an ounce of gold when only the day before there was agreement to pay him a full ounce!

If any nation or group of nations can double the figure on the face of a gold coin, or on the face of an iron coin for that matter, that nation or group of nations can as easily treble it, or quadruple it, or multiply it by tens or by hundreds. There is, however, one obstacle always in the way of this, and that is the intrinsic and social value of the metal itself. This social inherent value is what renders it useful as a measure of the value of all other commodities. Any metal, gold included, derives this value from the amount of social human energy and time expended in its production. It is a fallacy to assert that the law of supply and demand regulates this value. It is true, of course, that supply and demand have the effect of raising or lowering the price of a metal in a free market, but the price does not by any means always indicate its value. The price may be sometimes above, sometimes below, its value according to the social and human circumstances of the occasion. An increase of population with no increase of gold production would undoubtedly have the same effect on price as a corresponding decrease of production with no increase of population.

There is virtually only one buyer for gold and that is the Government: therefore free competition is not seen in its natural action. It is difficult to determine what the price of gold would be if every banking institution were allowed to buy and coin its own metal. Undoubtedly the price would rise for a time at least, but would drop again as the relations between nations became more stabilized and international confidence became more firmly established. Gold is called into active functioning as a monetary metal during war times owing to its being a metal high in actual value in proportion to its weight and bulk, and therefore easily transferred from one country to another. It also carries around with it, in the form of social energy-value, the security necessary to settle payments from nations whose stability is at the moment more or less uncertain. Iron money, brass checks, or paper, do not possess these characteristics, and if gold coin itself were arbitrarily stamped with figures far above its intrinsic value it too would not possess complete security as a measure of value; it would possess its original intrinsic social value and the difference between this and the figures stamped on its face would be fictitious.

JOHN MCPHERSON.

Seattle, Washington, February 14.

The Editor:

Sir—On January 13, 1917, I published in the Toronto 'Saturday Night' an article upon the gold situation, in which article I advanced the argument that the standard of gold should be changed to $30 per ounce. My suggested plan was that the Crown should commandeer all gold, paying for it upon a sliding scale; for a period of 15 years, payment to be made $22.50 per ounce to all mines in operation prior to the enactment of the measure; $25 per ounce to old mines that have been closed down through inability to make profits at the old value of gold; $27.50 to new mines discovered after the enactment of the decree. It was understood that this arrangement would be entered into between Great Britain, France, United States, and Russia, and it was assumed that all coin and plate commandeered would be paid for at $20.67 per ounce.

I submitted the article to both yourself and to Mr.

necessary that some definite base-value of gold in relation to labor should be fixed, for the interest to be paid was to be payable in gold. So it was decided that one ounce of gold should have a monetary value such that the expression £100 would for all time mean the same Troy weight of gold. In 1812, therefore, a man with one-hundred standardized sovereigns was willing to exchange them for a Consol bearing the denomination £100.

After the passing of a century we find that our forbears arrogated too much wisdom and power to themselves; their 'fixed' gold-value no longer holds good. For many years the Bank of England has maintained its reserves in gold and Consols. When gold became scarce, Consols were taken out of the vaults and exchanged for gold. When too much gold was accumulated, it was got rid of by exchanging it for Consols. But the exchange has not always been made upon the same basis. During the Boer war Consols sold down to 85; during the European war they sold as low as 51½; and 59 is about the present value of Consols.

The meaning of this is obvious: the man with one hundred standard sovereigns will no longer exchange them for a Consol bearing the inscription £100. He knows that his golden sovereigns will purchase more labor in other markets. He is not willing to receive such a small annual return from the British empire as his great-grandfather was satisfied with.

Now bear in mind that Consols are not payable in the labor of any particular generation, they are payable in the labor of the present and all future generations, and in fixing the labor equivalent of an ounce of gold Great Britain assumed to do so for all time. The fair equivalent in 1812 was that one hundred sovereigns in gold were worth the future labor pledged in a Consol bearing the inscription £100. The fair equivalent in 1918 is that 80 sovereigns in gold are worth the future labor pledged in a Consol bearing the inscription £100. In other words, the investment value of an ounce of gold in 1918 was 25% greater than it was in 1812. Gold has enhanced 25% in its labor equivalent. The stability of the British empire as a going concern may be questioned; owners of gold may not consider it as stable as it was in 1812. The danger of a political upheaval may cause the extremely cautious to hoard gold, rather than that they hoard Consols.

Gold has always been hoarded, it is as natural for human beings to hoard gold as it is for squirrels to hoard nuts. Through ten thousand years of growth, black, yellow, and white men have learned that under any conditions of life or politics, where men have some commodity to exchange, they will exchange that commodity for gold. The amount of gold demanded may vary, but our fundamental knowledge of finance is that a man with gold can always get something in exchange for it. It is, as Mr. Jennings says, a storage-battery of human energy, and while at times the battery may need re-charging, yet at all times it has been capable of giving out something; it has never yet completely 'run down.'

When a man accumulates wealth, he must have some means of proving that he possesses wealth. He may buy diamonds, automobiles, clothes, and a house, and put all of his wealth into such visible objects. He may exchange his credit for gold and hide the gold: this is done to a large extent throughout the world. The usual method, however, is for him to purchase securities, with the idea that he may at any time convert them into gold or diamonds or automobiles or food, as fancy or need dictate

All securities to be of value must be guaranteed by other men, for a commercial security is a bond upon the productiveness of men, and the holder of a security only has command over that productiveness in so far as other men are prepared to accept that command. A bond of a city is more secure than a bond or note of an individual; and a bond of a nation is more secure than the bond of a city. Among the nations the degree of security is accurately reflected by the interest rates paid for loans by the various governments, and at the present time, the United States presents the greatest security. But at the present time there is great unrest throughout the world, and we are not at all certain that future generations will live up to our present-day guarantee. Our successors may repudiate our promises.

This has happened in Great Britain; the present generation repudiates the relation established in 1812 between labor and gold. The greater the political disquietude, the less secure are the guarantees of political states, and as these guarantees become less secure, the potential value of a hoard of gold becomes greater. The individual looks to the possibility of a disruption of political bonds, when in the state of chaos which will follow, men will barter between themselves for their needs; when the man with gold will be able to get something for it; when securities will be unsaleable or valueless. Therefore for purposes of hoarding, gold has an enhanced value over government securities, for today a man with 81 gold sovereigns will hoard them rather than hoard a British Consol of £100 denomination.

Thus we see that, either as applied to active interest-earning investment, or as a hoard of wealth, gold has a greater labor equivalent than was ascribed to it when the weight of a pound stirling was fixed.

The fixing of the weight of the British sovereign and the issue of Consols constituted a definite appraisal of the value of labor expressed in terms of gold. The value was arrived at by taking the value of an ounce of gold as expressed in terms of monetary nomenclature on the day that act came into effect. Upon the same basis today gold is selling at an enhanced value of 25%.

I maintain that with the present unsettled condition of the world, if gold were demonetized, it would immediately rise in comparative value, this claim being made upon the basis that the possession of gold is an absolute and incontrovertible fact; while the possession of a command over future labor, as guaranteed by government or other securities, is a suppositive possession.

An analysis of the status of British Consols today seems to indicate that clipping 20% from the weight of a soveriegn is not only justifiable but is necessary in order to restore the natural balance between gold and labor, and a further reduction in the weight of the sovereign

No. 835,120. There are other patents, conflicting with this one, that are yet to be asserted, and through them relief may possibly be obtained.

Gold and Credit Money

Discussions concerning gold are of vital moment at this period when sober financiers are willing to consider economic experiments not less at variance with the old order than the freak State constitutions that became epidemic in the West some years ago. We are not now concerned with those legislative anomalies, some but not all of which represented proper and desirable social evolution, but we welcome letters such as that by Mr. John McPherson, in this issue, since they deal with gold, the thing that is fundamental in economics, because it is the basis of exchange. Critics may entertain divergent opinions on details, but Mr. McPherson and every other man who thinks seriously and with conviction on the problems of supply and demand, of production and consumption, of distribution of commodities, and the currency settlements involved, is contributing to the mental poise of the nation at a time when popular theories tend to lead away from the old tried practices. Some economic principles have been established which seem to be as fundamental and certain as biologic laws, but views change, and the physiocrats of one age are superseded by the conservationists of another; we swing from the idealism of individualistic free-traders to dreams of controlled free trade under a system of international 'allocation'. Nevertheless, through all the vicissitudes of social evolution there has been one unchanging economic fact: men have been universally agreed, apart from and above statutes and decrees, that gold in the hand will buy meat for the belly. The reasons why gold was selected as the supremely desirable metal to serve as a token of service with which to command the service of others has been discussed so often that we need not review them. The reason, however, for seeking and employing a metal possessing the well-known monetary attributes is not often brought into prominence. It is simply the fear of political disturbance. Banking is based on confidence. It is not merely reliance on the honor and integrity of the banker, nor belief in the wisdom of the banking laws, but faith in the stability of the Government, that admits of the development of a credit system. Granting such confidence, all manner of conveniences in the facilitation of exchange become possible. A smaller ratio of gold to the volume of business in terms of money then proves to be practicable. It is part of our belief in each other as social beings, as reasonable law-abiding men and women, that makes us content with the credit-paper that society gives its pledge to honor in the wares of daily need. One glance at Russia or Mexico, however, reveals why men insist upon available gold on demand as the basis for exchange.

In days of peace men laugh at tales of buried treasure. It is hard to realize, at a time when peace and security reign, that a preceding generation lived in the midst of alarms and subject to pillage by irresponsible and transitory officials, yet deep in the mind, like the instinct of a wild animal, lies the fear of danger that prompts us to desire the one substance for which men will exchange the food and clothing necessary for existence. It takes a long time to civilize the whirl out of a dog before he lies down; it has not yet been done successfully. Likewise, before the primitive desire for gold as a personal possession is supplanted by satisfaction with a piece of paper as the only representation of a claim on this world's goods as a return for service rendered, it will be necessary that many generations shall have grown so accustomed to the undisturbed enjoyment of the refinements of social organization that they may count upon the stability of the new order as firmly as on the daily rising of the sun.

The significance of this psychology of the demand for gold is that the royal metal will not be retired from its ancient duty as real money. To internationalize the gold reserve would be equivalent to retiring it, but the reaction would be so prompt and so pronounced that the attempt to initiate such a scheme would defeat itself. This, however, does not settle the question that so deeply concerns the gold miner, which is the purchasing power of the bullion produced. If gold mining were to cease, the demand for payment in metallic currency would increase, and a further rise in prices undoubtedly would follow on account of the different esteem on the part of the public for credit-money and for hard cash. This would encourage an outside market for gold where a normal ratio to commodities would assert itself. Ordinarily we would hesitate to offer suggestions of this character, but the time has come, not for ultra-social experiments in finance, but for grappling firmly with the concrete problem of giving to gold such a relation to exchange as will admit of continued profitable production of the metal, so that a reasonable amount may be forthcoming to serve as a safe basis for the currency-expansion required by the increasing population of the earth and the growing magnitude of commercial transactions. Retiring gold into the financial background will not do while the Bolshevists are raging in Russia, while the I. W. W. hamper industry in the United States, and while the Premier of England openly warns his country of the danger of civil war. The best antidote for revolution is the surety of opportunity to make a due amount of money for one's needs by peaceful industry, and to receive payment in something that is convertible into gold on demand. With gold mining on the wane, with the shortage of gold leading financiers to discuss cobweb designs of a frail beauty, it is evident that serious consideration of this problem should not be deferred. In the interest of the public welfare the restoration of gold, as a measure of value compatible with the measure of the effort required to get it, is imperative. This does not mean that we must 'raise the price', or juggle with the standard, but it does mean that we must find a way, without incurring disaster, to bring credit-money back to the level of the real.

The Status of Gold

The Editor:

Sir—The article by Van Dyck entitled, 'The Status of Gold', appearing in the 'Mining and Scientific Press' of February 1, 1919, contains so alluring an aspect of feasibility that its pitfalls of fallacy are not immediately apparent. In casting about for a ready solution of the much-discussed gold problem he has hit upon this proposal: 1. That all gold be called in and paid for at \$20.6718 per ounce, and that all silver be called in and paid for at \$1.015 per ounce. 2. That the monetary value of gold be fixed at double the present, that is, at \$41.3436 per fine ounce * * * 3. That all newly-mined gold be paid for at the newly-stabilized price. 4. That all metals so accumulated be coined as needed. 5. That all coin be released freely as called for from any quarter of the globe.

In brief his proposal is that the Government take every gold coin, melt it, and re-stamp it with double its present face value. In this manner the present-day confident face of the 'twenty' would re-appear tomorrow stamped 'forty dollars', without any change in weight or bulk; or perhaps the Government would decide to make two coins of 'twenty' each out of one present twenty. Mr. Van Dyck would thus supplant the printing-press manner of making money by the mint-stamp method; yet he would laugh in reasonable merriment at a Mexican leader or a Bolsheviki ruler who should order the printing presses to start as the nation was running short of money to pay foreign debts, or any debts. "It must be borne in mind," he says, "that legislation cannot bring gold into existence," but he implies that legislation can double its purchasing power.

One might reasonably ask why the Government should waste labor and time in melting every twenty-dollar coin and re-stamping the gold into forty dollars when a quick and handy plan would be to leave the twenty-dollar coin as it is but strike as many brass discs as there are such 'twenty' coins, stamp each brass disc "twenty dollars" and shackle one of these discs to each twenty-dollar coin, thereby making, by Government authority, a twin gold and brass coin of forty-dollar purchasing power? While this method would economize time and labor it would be as powerless as the ounce of gold with the forty-dollar stamp on it to reduce the ratio between paper money and real money, between symbol money and money carrying its value around in its own body. This gold-brass twin coin illustration is given to demonstrate more clearly the fact that one half the coin is real money and the other half symbol money. This is exactly what the present twenty-dollar coin would be when it should have received its new stamped face.

What is this subtle mystery in the process of exchange that prevents any nation from stamping an arbitrary figure or figures representing value on the face of any metal disc, gold included? There is only one thing that prevents it, and that thing is the intrinsic or social value of the given metal. Is there any difference in intrinsic value between a disc of brass stamped 'twenty dollars' by the Government and a twenty-dollar paper note? There is no difference; they are both symbols of value and do not contain within their physical or chemical bodies the value they represent. The gold-metal disc, provided it is stamped with its current value on the face, carries always with it, within itself, its own actual value in metal bulk and weight. This actual value is always approximate to that marked on its face. 'Approximate' is used advisedly because there is a constant invisible fluctuation in price of the metal which would be revealed in arithmetical figures in a free market only.

By acting on Mr. Van Dyck's suggestion the gold coin, as if by enchantment, should double in purchasing power at the instantaneous drop of a mint-stamp; where the twenty-dollar gold piece procured but ten bushels of wheat at two dollars per bushel yesterday it would purchase twenty bushels today! If it were possible for any nation to perform such legerdemain as this it would be equally possible to act similarly in regard to the case of the wheat which Mr. Van Dyck gives. He says: "Assume that our country has a debt of \$30,000,000,000 to pay, and assume that we are now in a position to pay it with 15,000,000,000 bushels of wheat at two dollars a bushel." The Government could as easily leave gold as it was, and arbitrarily fix the price of wheat at four dollars per bushel, or double the price of any commodity it was sending to pay the debt. What could be more preposterous than this? Fancy the astonishment on the face of the Chinaman or the Japanese, for instance, when he should receive one bushel of wheat instead of the two bushels he expected; or, imagine his protest if he should receive but half an ounce of gold when only the day before there was agreement to pay him a full ounce!

If any nation or group of nations can double the figure on the face of a gold coin, or on the face of an iron coin for that matter, that nation or group of nations can as easily treble it, or quadruple it, or multiply it by tens or by hundreds. There is, however, one obstacle always in the way of this, and that is the intrinsic and social value of the metal itself. This social inherent value is what renders it useful as a measure of the value of all other commodities. Any metal, gold included, derives this value from the amount of social human energy and time expended in its production. It is a fallacy to assert that the law of supply and demand regulates this value. It is true, of course, that supply and demand have the effect of raising or lowering the price of a metal in a free market, but the price does not by any means always indicate its value. The price may be sometimes above, sometimes below, its value according to the social and human circumstances of the occasion. An increase of population with no increase of gold production would undoubtedly have the same effect on price as a corresponding decrease of production with no increase of population.

There is virtually only one buyer for gold and that is the Government; therefore free competition is not seen in its natural action. It is difficult to determine what the price of gold would be if every banking institution were allowed to buy and coin its own metal. Undoubtedly the price would rise for a time at least, but would drop again as the relations between nations became more stabilized and international confidence became more firmly established. Gold is called into active functioning as a monetary metal during war times owing to its being a metal high in actual value in proportion to its weight and bulk, and therefore easily transferred from one country to another. It also carries around with it, in the form of social energy-value, the security necessary to settle payments from nations whose stability is at the moment more or less uncertain. Iron money, brass checks, or paper, do not possess these characteristics, and if gold coin itself were arbitrarily stamped with figures far above its intrinsic value it too would not possess complete security as a measure of value; it would possess its original intrinsic social value and the difference between this and the figures stamped on its face would be fictitious.

JOHN MCPHERSON.

Seattle, Washington, February 14.

The Editor:

Sir—On January 13, 1917, I published in the Toronto 'Saturday Night' an article upon the gold situation, in which article I advanced the argument that the standard of gold should be changed to $30 per ounce. My suggested plan was that the Crown should commandeer all gold, paying for it upon a sliding scale; for a period of 15 years, payment to be made $22.50 per ounce to all mines in operation prior to the enactment of the measure; $25 per ounce to old mines that have been closed down through inability to make profits at the old value of gold; $27.50 to new mines discovered after the enactment of the decree. It was understood that this arrangement would be entered into between Great Britain, France, United States, and Russia, and it was assumed that all coin and plate commandeered would be paid for at $20.67 per ounce.

I submitted the article to both yourself and to Mr. Ingalls of the 'Mining Journal', for comment, but failed to get a 'rise' out of either of you. Inasmuch as both the 'Press' and 'Journal' subsequently published a number of discussions upon the subject of the gold standard, and as their columns reflect current thought, I take it that I erred in being somewhat too early with the suggestion. Later, in May 1917, I published a second article giving further arguments in support of the proposal.

The criticisms aroused by these articles were remarkable for their paucity of ideas, the stock arguments being, "It can't be done" and "if you raise the base of values in gold you will raise the values of everything else." During the past eighteen months many articles have appeared, and everyone interested in the problem is by this time thoroughly conversant with the arguments. The findings of both the American and British committees, being against any adjustment of values, would seem to put a quietus upon further argument, but the excellent letter of Mr. Van Dyck in your issue of February 1 prompts me to again attack the problem.

Mr. Van Dyck points out that before the War the ratio of gold-supply to indebtedness was about 1:3 and at present it is about 1:15. Now, either gold reserve does perform a function or it does not. If the ratio 1:3 was a sound condition before the War, then the ratio 1:15 is unsound. If 1:15 is a sound condition, then we were all wrong in our ideas before the War. I do not see how we are to avoid the conclusion that something is wrong somewhere in our financial standards. Mr. Hennen Jennings used a unique explanation of the function of gold in calling it a storage-battery of human energy; its value represents a certain amount of labor at the command of the possessor of gold.

In 1812 Great Britain determined the quantity of energy so stored in a unit of gold, and gave gold its present nominal valuation. At the time of fixing this value Great Britain needed money for settling war-bills, and she set about raising these funds by issuing Consols,* or government bonds. Her proposition was this: To every person who would give her £100 in gold she would give a piece of paper stamped £100, and forever thereafter the holder of this piece of paper would have a right to a certain amount of the wealth produced per annum by the combined labor of the British empire.

This was collective bargaining. The producers of Great Britain through their government representative said, "We are in debt; we need money; we do not want to borrow money; we do not want to confiscate money, but we must have money; now therefore we make this proposition to you who have money: we will give you a bond upon ourselves and our progeny throughout all generations, and the holder of that bond will forever receive from us a certain amount of the wealth produced by us annually." That is to say, in exchange for immediate gold, the Empire offered the products of future labor.

The holders of gold accepted this offer, but it was

*'Consols' is an abbreviation of 'consolidated annuities'.—Editor.

necessary that some definite base-value of gold in relation to labor should be fixed, for the interest to be paid was to be payable in gold. So it was decided that one ounce of gold should have a monetary value such that the expression £100 would for all time mean the same Troy weight of gold. In 1812, therefore, a man with one-hundred standardized sovereigns was willing to exchange them for a Consol bearing the denomination £100.

After the passing of a century we find that our forbears arrogated too much wisdom and power to themselves: their 'fixed' gold-value no longer holds good. For many years the Bank of England has maintained its reserves in gold and Consols. When gold became scarce, Consols were taken out of the vaults and exchanged for gold. When too much gold was accumulated, it was got rid of by exchanging it for Consols. But the exchange has not always been made upon the same basis. During the Boer war Consols sold down to 85; during the European war they sold as low as 51½; and 59 is about the present value of Consols.

The meaning of this is obvious: the man with one hundred standard sovereigns will no longer exchange them for a Consol bearing the inscription £100. He knows that his golden sovereigns will purchase more labor in other markets. He is not willing to receive such a small annual return from the British empire as his great-grandfather was satisfied with.

Now bear in mind that Consols are not payable in the labor of any particular generation, they are payable in the labor of the present and all future generations, and in fixing the labor equivalent of an ounce of gold Great Britain assumed to do so for all time. The fair equivalent in 1812 was that one hundred sovereigns in gold were worth the future labor pledged in a Consol bearing the inscription £100. The fair equivalent in 1918 is that 80 sovereigns in gold are worth the future labor pledged in a Consol bearing the inscription £100. In other words, the investment value of an ounce of gold in 1918 was 25% greater than it was in 1812. Gold has enhanced 25% in its labor equivalent. The stability of the British empire as a going concern may be questioned; owners of gold may not consider it as stable as it was in 1812. The danger of a political upheaval may cause the extremely cautious to hoard gold, rather than that they hoard Consols.

Gold has always been hoarded, it is as natural for human beings to hoard gold as it is for squirrels to hoard nuts. Through ten thousand years of growth, black, yellow, and white men have learned that under any conditions of life or politics, where men have some commodity to exchange, they will exchange that commodity for gold. The amount of gold demanded may vary, but our fundamental knowledge of finance is that a man with gold can always get something in exchange for it. It is, as Mr. Jennings says, a storage-battery of human energy, and while at times the battery may need re-charging, yet at all times it has been capable of giving out something; it has never yet completely 'run down.'

When a man accumulates wealth, he must have some means of proving that he possesses wealth. He may buy diamonds, automobiles, clothes, and a house, and put all of his wealth into such visible objects. He may exchange his credit for gold and hide the gold; this is done to a large extent throughout the world. The usual method, however, is for him to purchase securities, with the idea that he may at any time convert them into gold or diamonds or automobiles or food, as fancy or need dictate.

All securities to be of value must be guaranteed by other men, for a commercial security is a bond upon the productiveness of men, and the holder of a security only has command over that productiveness in so far as other men are prepared to accept that command. A bond of a city is more secure than a bond or note of an individual; and a bond of a nation is more secure than the bond of a city. Among the nations the degree of security is accurately reflected by the interest rates paid for loans by the various governments, and at the present time, the United States presents the greatest security. But at the present time there is great unrest throughout the world, and we are not at all certain that future generations will live up to our present-day guarantee. Our successors may repudiate our promises.

This has happened in Great Britain; the present generation repudiates the relation established in 1812 between labor and gold. The greater the political disquietude, the less secure are the guarantees of political states, and as these guarantees become less secure, the potential value of a hoard of gold becomes greater. The individual looks to the possibility of a disruption of political bonds, when in the state of chaos which will follow, men will barter between themselves for their needs; when the man with gold will be able to get something for it; when securities will be unsaleable or valueless. Therefore for purposes of hoarding, gold has an enhanced value over government securities, for today a man with 81 gold sovereigns will hoard them rather than hoard a British Consol of £100 denomination.

Thus we see that, either as applied to active interest-earning investment, or as a hoard of wealth, gold has a greater labor equivalent than was ascribed to it when the weight of a pound stirling was fixed.

The fixing of the weight of the British sovereign and the issue of Consols constituted a definite appraisal of the value of labor expressed in terms of gold. The value was arrived at by taking the value of an ounce of gold as expressed in terms of monetary nomenclature on the day that act came into effect. Upon the same basis today gold is selling at an enhanced value of 25%.

I maintain that with the present unsettled condition of the world, if gold were demonetized, it would immediately rise in comparative value, this claim being made upon the basis that the possession of gold is an absolute and incontrovertible fact; while the possession of a command over future labor, as guaranteed by government or other securities, is a suppositive possession.

An analysis of the status of British Consols today seems to indicate that clipping 20% from the weight of a sovereign is not only justifiable but is necessary in order to restore the natural balance between gold and labor, and a further reduction in the weight of the sovereign is justifiable in the light of an analysis of the relation between gold supply and indebtedness. The present weight of the sovereign seems bound to incite private hoarding by individuals and banking interests, and this condition will increase labor troubles. The wealthy man today has every incentive to convert a large part of his wealth into gold, not only on account of the insecurity of investments, but because he can beat the inheritance tax by creating an untraceable hoard of gold, for the benefit of his heirs.

It seems to me that re-coining at one-half or two-thirds of the present weights of gold coins is a matter which merits a continued discussion.

P. A. ROBBINS.

San Francisco, February 11.

Spelling Reform

The Editor:

Sir—I agree in the main with an editorial note in your issue of February 15 regarding simplified spelling, that it is best as far as the A. I. M. E. is concerned to leave these matters to the committee on publications, but if the members can assist the committee toward a decision in favor of certain moderate reforms that is a different matter. I am sure that many spelling reformers do not aim at "unpleasant and unnecessary changes," as some proposed changes make for greater convenience. For instance, the usage is not uniform in dropping the final e of a primitive upon adding a suffix beginning with some consonants, as in 'abridgment' and 'judgement'. The Simplified Spelling Board advises that the final e be dropped in all cases, thus removing an element of doubt and real annoyance to some writers without incommoding or startling anybody except proof-readers.

We should not ignore the fact that good usage in spelling is not fixed but is changing before our very eyes, the virus of rather rapid change having found its way into thousands of schools, a hundred colleges, and the best dictionaries. It was only twenty years ago that the National Educational Association adopted the "twelve words" with the spellings, tho, thru, catalog, etc., but they are now in use by many good publishing houses, and the time will soon come—I believe now is—when these shorter spellings should be regarded as good usage. In the 18th century these and other shorter spellings had the sanction of the highest literary authority and the abandonment of these forms shows that our spelling has been changing, in this instance at least, for the worse.

In the prayer-book Psalter, among other old spellings, occurs the spelling "slipt" for slipped. If you ask a professor of language and literature about this, he will probably say that the shorter spelling is the proper one to use only in elevated metaphor, but the real fact seems to be that in printing successive editions of the Book of Common Prayer the publishers were not allowed to follow the changes of fashion in spelling and for that reason the shorter and strictly phonetic form has been preserved.

I sympathize with your general position in the matter, because no author has a right to distract the attention of his readers from the subject by spellings so unusual as to appear grotesque, but this matter is receiving such earnest attention from educators that it behooves us to walk somewhere within hailing distance of the procession. One well-known university has not endorsed this reform because the dean of the college in which English is taught has no patience with the 'Bad Boy's Diary', but the execrable spelling of his students has driven him to the advocacy of a less practicable scheme, a phonetic alphabet of over 40 letters. That a few of us can spell is beside the point, because we learned spelling at a time when the younger scholars studied very little else. I spelled while I filled the wood-box and fed the chickens and when too young to stand up in school I would spell a hundred times the hard word on which Mary Ann spelled down that up-river school. However, our children are too busy to fill the wood-box, feed the chickens, or even to spell, and the professors say we must make spelling easier. I am inclined to think that some day the idea will be exploded that the word-form containing the most letters is the most dignified.

JOHN RANDALL.

Mogollon, New Mexico, March 1.

[We are not unwilling to publish this reasonable letter, but no further discussion of the subject will be accepted. —EDITOR.]

GOOD ANALYTICAL WEIGHTS are made of three metals: 2 grammes and over of brass, gold plated; 50 to 1000 milligrammes of platinum; and 1 to 20 milligrammes of aluminum, according to H. D. Greenwood of the Chrome, New Jersey, refinery of the U. S. Smelting Co. For the lesser weights, platinum is the best, as it is hard and wears the least; but weights of 1 to 20 mg. made of platinum are so tiny that they slip from the forceps, and the assayer spends too much of his time and patience looking for lost weights. Aluminum being a lighter metal, the weights are larger and easier to handle. It does not wear well, and the constant picking up of the weight with forceps wears off small particles, making the weight lighter than it should be, and a light weight means a high assay. For example, if a weight should wear away 0.02 mg. in the course of a year, the assayer reports 0.02 oz. gold or 40 cents more on every ton of material coming into the plant than is actually in the material, and on a yearly tonnage of 120,000 the loss would be $48,000. Similarly, copper and silver are also affected. Weights are listed by the makers and dealers through 11 stages, from medium accuracy to extremely accurate, with prices to suit. The Chrome laboratory recognizes only the seal and certificate of the Bureau of Standards, for calibration of weights.

MAGNESITE production of Canada fell off last year from 58,090 to 39,365 tons. Quebec is the only Province yielding this mineral. The proportion of calcined and dead-burned clinker is increasing. The latter is sintered in rotary-kilns after being mixed with 5% of iron ore (magnetite). Prices were $9.50 per ton for the crude, $25 for calcined, and $35 to $40 for dead-burned product.

A Federal Department of Mines

By JOHN F. DAVIS

*In California the idea of advocating a Secretary of Mines in the Cabinet is not a new one. I remember when the old California Miners' Association took it up; and back in 1898 I remember hearing Mr. Tirey L. Ford, afterward our Attorney-General, make an address in favor of the creation of a Cabinet position of Mines and Mining. It is not a new idea in other communities. It is true that England has no such Cabinet position; but there are such departments on the Continent. There is a Department of Mines in Canada, in South Africa, and in Australia.

The great trouble in getting a Department of Mines and Mining in the United States has always been among the miners themselves: to get the miners thoroughly to understand the necessity of such a proposition, and to dispel false ideas of what is involved. You will remember that the last time we took it up it was a part of the mining community itself, or rather, of a prominent representative of it, that defeated the proposal. We had it almost within our grasp, and yet the historic fact is that the reason that the campaign for a Cabinet officer of Mines and Mining was not pushed to final success was the attitude of Senator Teller of Colorado, who insisted that the Cabinet of the President had already become top-heavy, too large, and too numerous; and he picked out the very industry in which you would think he ought to have been interested to stop the creation of additional memberships in the Cabinet. The proposal had to be abandoned, and we had to compromise on a Bureau of Mines as a substitute therefor, or a nucleus for future work, and even that Teller opposed.

Now I feel that the very first thing we should do is to dispel any impression that there is any antagonism to the Bureau of Mines involved in the creation of a Cabinet office of Mines and Mining. Nothing is farther from the fact. It is the inspiration that the Bureau of Mines has given us that makes us feel that the time has now come to ask for a Cabinet office. It is the success that the Bureau of Mines has made that encourages us to believe that we may now go to the country and, as it were, ask for the next step in promotion for the industry. It is the Bureau of Mines itself that is back of this very proposition. It finds that it cannot do all that it would like to do; it finds that it cannot do everything with the same ease that other industries have found at their disposal when they advocate some great measure in their industry; it feels that the time is ripe now for the mining industry to be graduated from a Bureau of Mines into a Department of Mines. Instead of its being in antagonism to anything that now exists in defence or in behalf of mining at Washington, this movement is something not only in accord with what we already have there, but it is promoted by the Geological Survey, by the Bureau of Mines, and by the American Mining Congress.

It would be the worst thing in the world if, from anything that was said or done in San Francisco at this session, any false impression should be created that this movement was anything in promotion of Government paternalism; that this movement was anything that was back of a scheme under which the Government might be reaching out to obtain control and ownership of the mines of the United States. Instead, the motive back of this proposition is the diametric opposite, namely, that if the time has come when certain industries will now again be conducted under individualistic control, we find that if the industry of mining is to have an even break with other interests that are already represented in the Cabinet, it must have, like them, its representative in the Cabinet of the President of the United States. And so, instead of this being anything in aid of reaching out for an unfair control, the idea is that mining shall not only be on its own basis, and conducted on its own individual merits by individuals and corporations, but that these individuals and corporations shall have the same aid, or at least have the same opportunity to bring about proper legislation for its protection and its advancement, that agriculture, that commerce, that labor, that any other equally important industry in this country has already. The great trouble is that we have not always realized in America just what the importance of mining is, what constitutes its importance, that is, its relative importance to other industries; and I imagine that much of this feeling throughout the United States has come from the fact that out here in California, until the War, we were mostly interested in gold mining, and, therefore, we partook of a certain isolation in the domain of mining. We had even here built up an idea of a common law of mining that was different from that of any other part of the country; the very tenure of these mines was different; and, at the risk of detaining you I shall read just one paragraph of the Report of Major Powell of the Land Commission of 1880, in which he calls attention to that fact in the most succinct way.

He calls attention, in the first place, to the fact that the gold prospectors out here were in the eyes of the law mere trespassers on the public domain; there was no national law existing over this domain in California at the time. They simply were invaders and trespassers. "Finding themselves far from the legal traditions and restraints of

*Abstract of an address delivered before the California Chapter of the American Mining Congress at San Francisco, on January 16, 1919.

the settled east," he says, "in a pathless wilderness, under the feverish excitement of an industry as swift and full of chance as the throwing of dice, the adventurers of 1849 spontaneously instituted neighborhood or district codes of regulations, which were simply meant to define and protect a brief possessory ownership. The ravines and river bars which held the placer gold were valueless for settlement or homemaking, but were splendid stakes to hold for a few short seasons and gamble with nature for wealth or ruin.

"In the absence of State or Federal laws competent to meet the novel industry, and with the inbred respect for equitable adjustment of right between man and man, which is the inheritance of centuries of English common law, the miners only sought to secure equitable rights and protection from robbery by a simple agreement as to the maximum size of a surface claim, trusting, with a well founded confidence, that no machinery was necessary to enforce their regulations other than the swift rough blows of public opinion. The gold-seekers were not long in realizing that the source of the dust which had worked its way into the sand and bars, and distributed its precious particles over the bedrock of rivers, was derived from solid quartz veins, which were thin sheets of mineral material enclosed in the foundation rocks of the country. Still in advance of any enactments of legislature or congress, the common sense of the miners, which had proved strong enough to govern with wisdom the ownership of placer mines, rose to meet the question of lode claims, and decreed that ownership should attach to the thing of value, namely, the thin sheet-like veins of quartz, and that a claim should consist of a certain horizontal block of the vein, however it might run, but extending indefinitely downward with a strip of surface on or embracing the vein's outcrop, for the placing of necessary machinery and buildings. Under this theory the lode was the property, and the surface became a mere easement.

"This early California theory of a mining claim, consisting of a certain number of running feet of vein with a strip of land covering the surface length of the claim, is the obvious foundation for the federal legislation and present system of public disposition and private ownership of the mineral lands west of the Missouri river. Contrasted with this is the mode of disposition of mineral bearing lands east of the Missouri river, where the common law has been the one rule, and where the surface tract has always carried with it all minerals vertically below it.

"The great coal, iron, copper, lead, and zinc wealth east of the Rocky Mountains, have all passed with the surface titles; and there can be little doubt that if California had been contiguous to the western metallic regions, and its mineral development progressed naturally with the advance of home-making settlements, the power of common law precedent would have governed the whole mining industry. But California was one of those extraordinary historic exceptions that defy precedent, and create original modes of life and law. And since the developers of the great precious emtal mining of the far west have for the most part swarmed out of the California hive, California ideas have not only been everywhere dominant over the field of industry, but have stemmed the tide of Federal land policy, and given us a statute-book with English common law in force over half the land and California common law ruling in the other."

That is the situation, and that is one reason why we were never able, when our industries were confined to gold-mining alone, to get that hearing and that audience to which we felt we were entitled from people who owned mines containing metal of any kind east of the Missouri river. That was the reason why we were never able seemingly to get the co-operation which there is an opportunity to get today.

Now the effect of the lack of standing of gold production, under the inaction that we have had, without that initiative for the benefit of the industry which would come from a Cabinet office of Mines and Mining, was probably well illustrated by what happened in this country not long after we entered the War. You will remember that America had not been long in the War when all of a sudden rumors began to come out of Washington with reference to a question that was mooted in the Priorities Board, whether or not that Board was going to give opportunities for transportation or manufacture to anything except war essentials; and soon men in California, who seemed to be drifting along in gold mining in a blissful inaction that was simply incomprehensible, were amazed to read in the dispatches suggestions that it might be contended in certain quarters in Washington that gold was a non-essential of war. Of course we Californians never for a moment believed that any such theory would gain a hearing anywhere in the United States, for every one of us had read in the history, not of California, but of the United States, that the great crowning glory of California at the time of the Civil War was that this State, though far removed from the scene of the conflict, so far that it could contribute only a small quota in man-power to the conflict, had actually helped to save the day, because in California we had found the gold and had produced the gold that had saved the credit of the United States.

And so, when those first rumors began to come out of Washington, it was impossible for our people to believe that there was anything back of them; and yet they grew apace, so that the first thing we knew we found that not only were the rumors true, but that there was no representative of gold mining on the Priorities Board at all; and it was not long before Mr. Hennen Jennings came out here, palpably aroused, pleading with us to get up some propaganda of reflex action and sentiment to convince Washington that gold actually was a war-essential, and that no such order as was feared must ever be allowed to be made.

Then it was that we began to realize that, by reason of the fact that we had no special representation in any Cabinet office, a great essential industry was in danger of being ignored or even paralyzed. We actually formed a committee on gold, which went out over California and the West, which held hearings, at luncheons and dinners, that committee being composed of Hennen Jennings, John H. Mackenzie, and Charles Janin of the U. S. Bureau of Mines, and F. L. Ransome of the Geological Survey. They formulated a report, which was presented on October 30, 1918, vindicating the production of gold as an essential war measure, twelve days before the Armistice. Of course, long before that the result of their important work was known in Washington, and so the proper order was finally made by the Priority Board. But when you think of the position into which gold production as an industry had fallen, you will realize that there is something wanting in the representation of this industry at Washington.

And if that incident does not convince you of the fact, let me then give you the absolute statistics of the production of gold during this war. Now, the production of gold in the United States, including Alaska, for the year 1915, was $101,035,700; in 1916 it had declined to $91,-307,630; in 1917 it had declined to $83,750,000, and in 1918, to the first day of January 1919, it had declined to $68,493,000. In other words, you cut it nearly in half, when you stop to think that on January 1, 1915, it was nearly $102,000,000, and on January 1, of this year, it had declined to $68,000,000. So it would look as if the familiar reference to gold as the 'royal' metal was in danger of serious revision; and that De Launay, the French author, when he issued his book on mining that has just come out, was not far from the fact when he said that coal and iron are now "the *grand seigneurs* of the mineral world," and that the ancient idea that gold was the royal metal was fast disappearing, and that the new measure of value was the usefulness of a metal. We of California, I think, might be tempted to say to De Launay that he might have added oil to his list.

When you stop to think of what started this world-war, where the seeds were sown, you may well come to the conclusion, not only from the incident that you almost had gold declared a non-essential of war, but from this marked decrease in the production of gold you may begin to realize the tremendous importance of other metals besides gold in the mining world. Away back in 1870 the seeds of this conflict, as far as Germany was concerned, were sown. You will remember that in the peace conference at the end of the Franco-Prussian war the question whether or not they would take Alsace and Lorraine was the great question debated at Versailles: that Bismarck opposed the acquisition of Alsace and opposed the acquisition of Lorraine, whether he intended to be taken seriously or not. At any rate, he opposed it *pro forma* on the score of the race question, and the legacy of *revanche* that would be involved in taking them; and you remember that in that debate Von Moltke and the rest of the General Staff protested, and urged that Alsace must be taken and Lorraine must be taken, because the new German empire then created could not afford to have on its border the two great forts of Metz and Strasburg; and yet we now know that, no matter what was the camouflage of the debate, the real reason was that it would never do to take a chance not to get the iron of Alsace-Lorraine, and that the real reason for the taking of Alsace and Lorraine was the existence of the iron deposits, not the forts of Metz and Strasburg. And who is going to say that when this war was precipitated one of the great reasons why it was precipitated may not have been the opportunity to get the iron mines of Briey, and the coal mines in the Department of the Nord and the Pas-de-Calais, in northern France, and the opportunity to get the oilfields at Baku and the minerals in the Urals?

We begin to realize as part and parcel of the outcome of this war the tremendous significance of the ownership of oil, of iron, and of coal; and it is about time that we began, in California especially, after the experience we have had in the mining of the baser metals during this war, to wake up to a realization of what mining now means, and what economic geology now means to the world. I cannot do better than to quote a very short paragraph from the recent report of George Otis Smith, the head of the Geological Survey at Washington, in which he uses these words:

"Economic geology is useful geology—the theoretical science applied to meet the material needs of man. These human needs as presented in the last four years have demanded a specialized type of geology—*the application of geology in terms of commerce*. Geology to be most useful in these days of world problems must take the world view of values, and we find ourselves working in commercial geology—that is, geology applied in terms of commerce. The world is the field of commerce, and the requirements of commercial geology are simply that the geologic relations of a Nevada ore deposit, for example, must be observed with an eye trained to see far beyond the Basin range; the geologist needs to compare the quality and quantity of the unmined ore here with similar facts of nature that give value to the ores in other districts, as in Peru or Burma. Whether the investigator is called a geologist, mining engineer, or economist, his vision must take in not simply the ore minerals as they have been deposited, segregated, or enriched by the processes of nature, but also the smelted ore and the refined metal on their way to the markets of the world where they can serve mankind. Thus to broaden and extend the investigator's view is not to commercialize his science; it is rather to make geology more useful, and in that way to give the science a higher rank. Geology must needs continue to furnish the basal facts, but the geologist has a call to go further than he has gone heretofore in the interpretation of his facts—not simply by translating his technical words into the language of the market place, but, more than that, by showing *the relation of geology to national life*."

You remember that when the War grew apace we were confronted with the question of enacting a War Minerals bill. If ever there was an illustration of how little representation we had at Washington in comparison with banking, with labor, with commerce, with agriculture, for the obtaining of necessary protection, it was illustrated in the preparation of the War Minerals bill. That bill with all the aid that could be given it by the Geological Survey, by the Bureau of Mines, by the American Mining Congress, by every other authority that got back of it and promoted it, took until the 5th of October, 1918, in order to get enacted into law. The President did not sign the order transferring the operation of it to the Secretary of the Interior until the morning of November 11, and by noon the Armistice had been signed, and it lay there nine days undelivered, and everybody seemed to have forgotten its existence. Would that have happened if we had had a Department of Mines with a Cabinet officer at the President's table? Then, when it came to relieving a crisis that had been created by the Government in its effort to urge the chrome men and the manganese men and the pyrite men and others to speed up and to spend money patriotically borrowed in order to provide the Government with the necessary material to carry on this war, then there was a scramble to see what help, if any, could be obtained from the War Minerals bill. It was submitted to competent authority to find out whether it was possible to stretch its meaning, to twist it into something that would warrant the Government in either continuing embargoes, or doing something to make good to the chrome men and to these other men who had strained or impaired their financial resources on the good faith of the appeal from Washington; and it was found, no matter how hard the legal interpretation was strained, there was nothing in the War Minerals bill that gave any comfort, and that we would have to start all over again to prepare the mining industry for the problems of peace just as we had started before to prepare it for the business of war.

You will remember what Mr. Callbreath told you of the fight that had to be put up to get a modification of the Internal Revenue law with reference to the doctrine of depletion, so that individuals and mining companies paying dividends would not have their business wiped off the earth by taxes. If we had had a Cabinet officer of Mines and Mining, the manifest logic and equity of the miner's contention would have been understood from the beginning. The educational propaganda in its favor would have been given a place at the President's table, and we would not have had the situation that confronted us even when faithful subordinate bureaus of the Government took into hand so plain a proposition as the depletion of ore in a mine. We had to educate a committee in charge of a Revenue bill from the ground up. Why, the first suggestion of the doctrine of depletion in a mine was met almost as if it were the dream of a porch-climber; and I imagine that if the Bureau of Mines and the Geological Survey had not taken it in hand, it would not have had even a respectful hearing at the hands of the promoters of the bill.

Now let us look for a moment at the process of legislation at Washington. In the first place, the Interior Department cannot represent an industry like Mines and Mining. It is unfair to say that any man, unless he happened to be a man who was in the mining industry and was conducting mining operations before he became Secretary of the Interior, should have such detailed knowledge as would make him practically a Cabinet officer of Mines and Mining, though he were named a Secretary of the Interior. But put even an extraordinary man who was not a miner at the head of the Department of the Interior, and load him down with the Irrigation problems, the Reclamation problems, the Indians, Alaska, the disposition of the public domain, and all the other hundred and one problems, and you overwhelm him. Only a man like the present Secretary of the Interior can make any headway. When I think of the work that the Department of the Interior has on hand, it reminds me of the residuary clause at the end of a will: after you have given everything on earth that you think you own, or expect to own by the time you die, to everybody you care anything about, then you put in a dragnet clause at the end of the will. That seems to be the position of the Department of the Interior—the sump at the bottom of the shaft; something that is going to catch everything that any other department has left out. It is impossible to expect that this great industry is going to have the benefit of expert knowledge and proper consideration at the hands of an officer so loaded down as it would have at the hands of a special officer who is a mining man knowing all the dips, spurs, and angles of mining, and whose jurisdiction is confined to mining and the subjects affiliated with it.

Speaking of Congressional relief, I remember once a Congressman who was ready to take almost anything that constituent would give him in the shape of a matter of legislation. He did not stop to ascertain who was the sponsor of the bill. If he could do a favor, or if it appeared right, he would introduce it, let it go to print, and probably never examine it in critical detail until it came back from the printer. That is the attitude of many men when they first go to Congress. They soon learn to act differently. They learn not to land outside the breastworks. They aim to have their names identified with measures that have the backing of the Administration; and after they have been there a number of sessions they become the tamest house-cats you ever saw, and if you go to them with a bill, about the first thing they want to know is whether the particular department in the Cabinet, the department that would have charge of the bill or within whose scope it would be, has done anything or said anything in approval of the bill. Not only must you have, if you can get it, the benefit of the approval of the Department, but no bill will go through without the approval of the department; and once you get the approval of the department there is very little trouble with the bill except in the initial stages.

Under the process of legislation at Washington, there is no comparison between the authority that a Mining Bureau even, or a Geological Survey or any other kind of a survey, can give to a bill—a relief measure, for instance, such as we need right now—and that which would come from the approval of it given by a Cabinet officer who sits at the President's table. And if any controversy comes, under which the President himself might have some idea at variance with the bill, you have a Cabinet officer who can debate the matter with complete data and fair opportunity for such consideration or amendment as will gain his approval.

Mining men will find that henceforth mining is not going to be considered simply with reference to the geological conditions under which mineral can be produced, but from an entirely different aspect, namely, in its international aspect.

You are going to have not only the question of whether you can physically mine, as, for instance, whether you may or may not be allowed to dump something into a river, or any other little local question that may arise, but you are going to have on your hands the question of the production of minerals in the United States in its international aspect; you are going to have that all before you now when you take up the question of conducting mines and mining for the future. And it seems to me that no stronger case can be made than the experience that we have had in this war to demonstrate the utter inadequacy of our present instrumentalities to accomplish what we found we needed to do in a hurry at the beginning of the War and to grapple with the tremendous problems that are now coming before us after the War is over. What was needed then, and what is needed now, is a Cabinet Department of Mines and Mining.

Draining Air-Piping for Pneumatic Tools

*It is important to provide means for effectually separating and draining the water of condensation from the piping system of pneumatic tools.

The 'slugs' of water frequently coming through the pipes, in the general run of plants, not only interfere with the momentary operation of tools, but cut out the valves, cylinders, and wash out the oil, seriously interfering with lubrication. The water cannot be properly taken care of merely by placing drain-cocks at low points in the ordinary piping system, but should be removed by special separation tanks or chambers placed at these points, and near the distributing manifolds. The separators will also serve as collectors of scale and dirt coming through the pipes, and the drain or blow-out valves should be large enough to discharge these matters as well as the water.

The separating-chamber should be large enough to lower the velocity of the air to a point where entrained water or dirt will not be carried through with the air current, and should be fitted with bafflers or connections which will change the direction of flow, so as to precipitate the entrained matter.

While the arrangement of separators will necessarily be governed by the piping lay-out in each individual installation, the accompanying cuts. Fig. 1 and 2, illustrate two types, which in the smaller sizes can readily be made up of standard pipe fittings. Fig. 1 shows a type suitable for vertical risers, while Fig. 2 indicates a type suitable for horizontal distributing lines

An air-piping system should be uniformly graded with

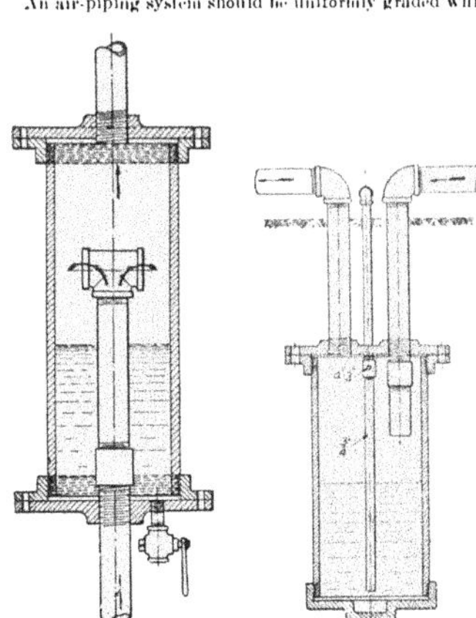

Fig. 1 Fig. 2

the direction of flow, so far as the main runs are concerned, and should always have separators at or near rising points. Sags or pockets without separators for the accumulation of water should never be permitted.

Where it is possible to do so, separators on outdoor lines should be placed in the ground below the frost-line, to prevent freezing, as shown by Fig. 2. The condensation can be blown out through a vertical discharge pipe by the pressure of the air in the separator.

*'Standard Practice Bulletin', Emergency Fleet Corporation.

By-products of the silver ore mined at Cobalt, Ontario, during 1918 were 243,186 lb. of metallic nickel valued at $88,720, and 962,309 lb. of nickel oxide, carbonate, and sulphate valued at $215,277. The total nickel content was 736,005 lb., or 368 tons. The Sudbury district of Ontario produced 45,886 tons of nickel last year

---

Manganese imports last year amounted to 491,303 tons, worth $15,095,867. Brazil supplied 345,877 tons and Cuba 82,974 tons. In 1917 the total amount was 629,972, and 576,321 tons in 1916.

Oil and products exported from the Tampico district, Mexico, to the United States during 1918 amounted to 39,618,121 barrels.

The Wolf Patent on Flotation

No. 787,814. Patented April 18, 1905.
United States Patent Office.
Jacob David Wolf, of London, England.
Separation of Metals from Their Ores.
Specification Forming Part of Letters Patent No. 787,-814, Dated April 18, 1905. Application Filed May 22, 1903. Serial No. 158,346.

To all whom it may concern:

Be it known that I, Jacob David Wolf, a citizen of the United States, residing at London, England, have invented certain new and useful Improvements in the Separation of Metals from Their Ores, of which the following is a specification.

The present invention relates to improvements in obtaining metals from their ores, the object being to separate the valuable and metallic-mineral constituents of an ore from its gangue by the use of oil or grease, particularly oil or grease which has been treated with chlorid of sulfur.

According to this invention the ore-pulps are agitated with oil, preferably mineral oil mixed with viscous animal or vegetable oil and treated with chlorid of sulfur, until the oil has taken up all the metallic-mineral contents with some gangue. The mineral-bearing oil is separated from the pulps, and suspended particles of gangue are removed from the oil by passing it through warm water, the metallic minerals being thereafter separated out from the oil, which can be used again. At the same time oil is recovered from the waste pulps by blowing air through them.

In order to increase the viscosity of certain mineral oils, a small proportion—say five per cent.—of animal oil, such as lard-oil, may be added before sulfo-chlorinating. Vegetable oils—such as rape, castor, or linseed oil—act in a similar manner. With pulps having a large proportion of mineral, as in the case of copper, lead, or zinc ores, the prepared oil should be made thick and viscous to produce the necessary power of flotation; but with pulps in which the percentage of mineral is small, as with gold ores, the oil need not be thickened to the maximum extent. In the same way if the particles of mineral are coarse the oil should be specially viscous, while with fine particles the oil may be relatively thinner.

The accompanying drawing is a diagrammatic sectional view of apparatus suitable for use in carrying out this process.

In the following description it is assumed that the oil is treated with chlorid of sulfur; but it is to be understood that the same process and apparatus would apply to other suitable but untreated oils.

The ore mixed with water is crushed into a pulp and is introduced by a launder A into a mixer B, the oil, preferably treated with chlorid of sulfur, being simultaneously run in from the tank A' through the pipe A^2. The mixing vessel B has a vertical hollow cylinder B' fixed in the middle of it, and below the cylinder is a turbine-wheel B^2 on a vertical shaft B^3, rotatable through the pulley B^4. The mixture of oil and pulps passes into the hollow cylinder B', and the rotation of the turbine-wheel B^2 causes a rapid circulation of the mixture downward within the cylinder and upward between the cylinder and the vessel B. The liquid is continuously discharged from the mixer through the pipe B^5 and passes into a separating-tank or spitzkasten C. Here the sulfo-chlorinated oil adhering to the mineral of the ore floats, while the gangue remaining in admixture with the water sinks and is removed by the waste-pipe C'. The mineral-bearing oil passes off from the surface through the conduit C^2. The mixture is next forced—for example, by means of a rotary pump D—in at the bottom of a vertical cylindrical vessel E, containing warm water and surrounded by a steam or hot-water jacket E'. The vessel is provided with a water-inlet pipe E^2 and a waste-outlet E^3 at the bottom, and an oil-outlet E^4 is also provided near the top of the vessel. The oil mixture carrying particles of gangue in suspension is passed into the vessel E, preferably through a perforated inlet D', to break the oil into thin streams or globules, which rise through the warm water and drop out the gangue in their upward course on account of the decrease in viscosity. If desired, two or more of these vessels may be used in series, the mineral-bearing oil being removed from the surface of each vessel. By the means thus provided for eliminating gangue it is possible to treat ores with such a degree of agitation that the whole of the mineral contents are taken up by the oil, accompanied, however, by a not inconsiderable proportion of gangue; but as practically all this gangue is removable from the oil by a sufficient treatment with hot water much cleaner and sharper concentrates can be obtained than would be the case under any circumstances without such washing. The oil carrying practically only the values is next passed into a receiver F, from which it is forced, by means of a pneumatic forcing apparatus G, into a filter-press H, which may be of any suitable form—for example, of the type now largely used in the treatment of lard, tallow, and similar oils by fullers' earth. The separated oil is received in a tank J and is returned, by means of a pump K, to the oil-supply tank A' to be mixed with fresh quantities of pulps, the process being thus rendered cyclic. The properties of the oil are permanently altered by treatment with chlorid of sulfur; but it may be found advisable to add a further quantity of chlorid of sulfur after the oil has been in use for some time.

The waste pulps removed from the bottom of the settling-tank C are collected in a vessel L. After agitating the pulps with the oil-globules, which from various causes are not completely separated by flotation, but remain in the waste pulps, can be largely separated therefrom and recovered by blowing a current of air or air and steam through jets L' upward through the waste pulps. The oil-globules rise to the surface and break, forming a film which is not liable to sink again and can be recovered by skimming or by surface baffles or the like.

It is to be understood that the form of the apparatus used can be varied without departing from this invention. For example, when separating the suspended gangue from the oil any convenient means may be used for passing the oil through warm water, and in removing the oil from the waste pulps currents of air or steam may be produced in any way. Also any other suitable method separating the values from the oil may be adopted.

What I claim as my invention, and desire to secure by Letters Patent, is—

1. The herein-described process of separating metals from their ores which consists in agitating pulps with oil until the oil has taken up all the metallic-mineral contents with some gangue, separating the mineral-bearing oil from the pulps, removing suspended particles of gangue from the oil by passing it through warm water and separating metallic minerals from the oil.

2. The herein-described process of separating metals from their ores which consists in agitating pulps with oil until the oil has taken up all the metallic-mineral contents with some gangue, separating the mineral-bearing oil from the pulps, removing suspended particles of gangue from the oil by passing it through warm water, separating metallic minerals from the oil which can be used again and recovering oil from the waste pulps by blowing air through them.

3. The herein-described process of separating metals from their ores which consists in agitating pulps with sulfo-chlorinated oil until the oil has taken up all the metallic-mineral contents with some gangue, separating the mineral-bearing oil from the pulps by flotation and removing suspended particles of gangue from the oil by passing the finely-divided oil upward through warm water.

4. The herein-described process of separating metals from their ores which consists in agitating pulps with sulfo-chlorinated oil until the oil has taken up all the metallic-mineral contents with some gangue, separating the mineral-bearing oil from the pulps by flotation, removing suspended particles of gangue from the oil by passing the finely-divided oil upward through warm water and filter-pressing the oil to separate out the metallic minerals from the oil.

5. The herein-described process of separating metals from their ores which consists in agitating pulps with mineral oil mixed with viscous oil and treated with chlorid of sulfur until the oil has taken up all the metallic-mineral contents with some gangue, separating the mineral-bearing oil from the pulps by flotation, removing suspended particles of gangue from the oil by passing it through warm water, and after that the metallic minerals are separated from the oil which can be used again.

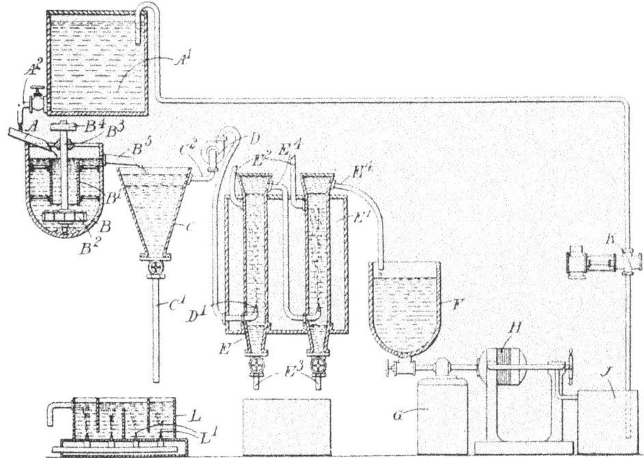

APPARATUS OF WOLF PATENT

6. The herein-described process of separating metals from their ores which consists in agitating pulps with mineral oil mixed with viscous oil and treated with chlorid of sulfur until the oil has taken up all the metallic-mineral contents with some gangue, separating the mineral-bearing oil from the pulps by flotation, removing suspended particles of gangue from the oil by passing the finely-divided oil upward through warm water, filter-pressing the oil to separate out the metallic minerals from the oil and removing oil-globules from the waste pulps by spraying jets of air and steam upward through the pulps and skimming off the oil which floats.

In testimony whereof I have signed my name to this specification in the presence of two subscribing witnesses.

Witnesses: JACOB DAVID WOLF.
CLAUDE MCKENZIE.
H. D. JAMESON.

Concentrating Graphite in New York

By GEORGE D. DUB

*Graphite mining in New York was started 60 years ago. That State, for many years, and until 1915, produced more graphite than any other, but since 1915 has had to relinquish first place to Alabama, where the growth has been remarkably rapid.

The ore in New York averages 4 to 6% graphitic carbon, compared with the 2½% ore of Alabama. There are two important types of graphite deposits in the Adirondack foothills of New York—first, those on the contact of a limestone and pegmatite; and, second, those on the contact of the Hague garnet-sillimanite gneiss and Faxon limestone or Swede-Pond gneiss. In the former occurrence, large flakes of graphite are obtained, but deposits of this nature are extremely pockety, and their development has not been profitable. Present production is obtained from the second type of deposit, in which the ore is nearly regular and of a more uniform grade. The ore is, as a whole, much harder and more silicious than that of Alabama, resembling in many respects the unweathered blue rock of Alabama, which is the original blue-colored Talladega schist.

At the present time, there are only three mines in operation, namely, the mine of the Graphite Products Corporation, three miles north of Saratoga Springs; Hooper brothers mine, four miles west of Whitehall; and the mine of the American Graphite Co., operated by the Joseph Dixon Crucible Co., four miles west of Hague.

Ore is mined in New York both in open pits and underground, the larger part from the latter system. Drilling in all cases is done with machines. Because of the silicious character of the ore, a greater quantity of fine is produced during crushing than is obtained in Alabama. The ore-bearing horizon is usually not over 25 ft. thick, and averages 15 ft. Wherever possible, the open-pit system is used, because of the ease and cheapness of preparing for mining, where there is no excessive amount of overburden requiring stripping. The deposits dip 25 to 35°, so that it soon becomes necessary to go under cover for the ore. This has its advantage in the north, because of the long and severe winters which hamper open-cut operations. The system of underground mining at the largest mine in the district is the room-and-pillar method, with underhand stoping. In new developments, a definite system of mining has not as yet been decided upon.

A flow-sheet of one of the plants in New York is given in the accompanying figure.

As indicated, gravity stamps are used as fine crushers, and 'buddles' as concentrating machines. It is also to be noted that concentrating tables are in use for treating 'buddle' middling, while in Alabama they are to be employed in raising the grade of rough concentrates preparatory to their treatment in the finishing mills.

With crude ore that analyzed 7.95% graphitic carbon,

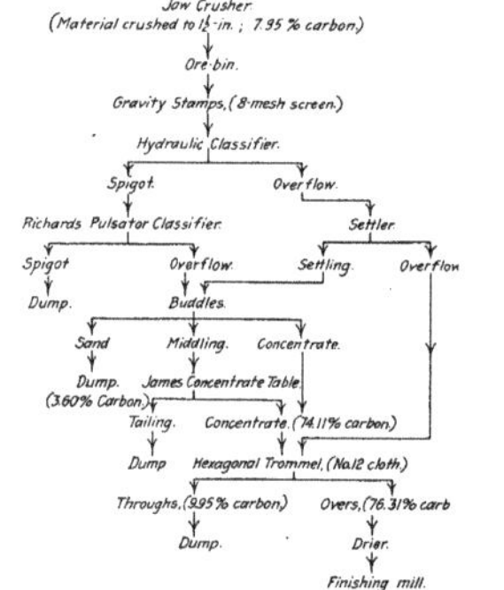

FLOW-SHEET OF A NEW YORK GRAPHITE PLANT

'buddle' tailing analyzed 3.60% C. Tailing from various other machines carried 3.96 to 9.95% C, the latter product consisting of the fine through the rough concentrate trommel. The crude concentrate assayed 76.31%.

Refining methods do not differ greatly from methods employed in Alabama plants. One variation noted was the use of the Hooper air-jig instead of air classification. The chief disadvantage ascribed to the Hooper air-jig is its small capacity. The refinery operated by the American Graphite Co. at Ticonderoga is used in preparing graphite from many sources, foreign as well as domestic, and of both the amorphous and crystalline varieties, for use in the manufacture of commercial articles, such as paints, foundry-facings, pencils, lubricating flake, and boiler compounds.

*Abstract from U. S. Bureau of Mines War Minerals Investigation Series No. 3.

American Institute of Mining and Metallurgical Engineers

Speech of the President, H. V. WINCHELL

*I am told that it is customary on the recurrence of this annual event, for the incoming President to present for your consideration and that of the members at large a few thoughts as to the work of our Institute, and the industry which it is supposed to represent; to sound the keynote of progress for the coming year and to direct attention to the work of the hour.

If this be already a custom, it is something for which neither you nor I can be held responsible, and yet something which neither of us can escape. It is therefore my duty and high privilege to prepare the dose, and yours to take it as gracefully as possible, in the full belief that what is customary is proper, and what the doctor prescribes is beneficial, though not always palatable. In this case I trust it may be both.

It is a trite saying and a true one that we are living in the most wonderful period of history. We are witnessing the evolution of a new order of things. We are participants in movements which are everlasting in their effect and world wide in their scope. Forces and activities now set in motion will have their influence on the human race throughout its entire period of existence, and the lustrum of time of which 1919 is the closing year will be forever marked in red and gold on the pages of history.

It is entirely proper for us to reflect with pride upon the service which our Institute and its members have rendered the cause of humanity in the recent conflict. The names of those who have given their money, their time, their efforts, and in many cases, their lives, will ever be held in honored memory. But it is not sufficient to complacently remember the past. Our work is still ahead, and it is timely for us to consider our relation to our profession, to our country, and to ourselves in the working out of the problems of the future. What part are we able to play in reaping the benefit which should and must accrue from the sacrifices of the world since 1914? Is there any work which the engineer is better qualified than any other class to undertake? Is he now already preparing in true engineering fashion to get 100% efficiency out of himself and his organization? As educated and reasoning citizens of the world's greatest democracy, as trained engineers, as members of the American Institute of Mining and Metallurgical Engineers, what can we as individuals and as an organization do, what are we morally and in a sense of reciprocity obligated to do, under the new conditions with which we are confronted, to improve our own situation and that of all mankind?

The answer depends on the nature of the problem and the conditions with which it is surrounded. Do we fully realize the momentous changes which have already taken place? A nation which was taught by Washington to avoid foreign entanglements has in the interests of self-preservation been forced to take an active part in the settlement of a war in Europe, and is now occupying a prominent seat at the council of nations. Within a single twelve months we have abandoned the policy of our forefathers and become an arbiter and co-administrator of the affairs of all countries. Never again can we pretend to stand aloof and unconcerned while war flames are kindled abroad. No longer can we afford to be provincial. The ocean now is narrower than was the English Channel before the construction of telegraph lines, steamships, submarines, and airplanes. The food supplies, the raw materials, the factories, the mines, the schools, the people of foreign lands are now subjects for our careful study and consideration. We are and shall be impelled to it by motives of every variety, materialistic and humanitarian. The better we understand the world and its problems, the more successful we shall be in our commerce, in the development and handling of our internal affairs, our finances and our labor questions, our crops, our mineral production; everything that concerns our prosperity and welfare.

Then, too, from a nation of borrowers, needing foreign capital to develop our resources and owing vast sums upon which we were paying interest to the bankers of Europe, we have suddenly by fortune of war become a creditor nation. The nations of the world owe us inconceivable sums. The interest on our loans abroad would have paid the entire expense of our national government when we men were youths. This change in our status is of tremendous importance to the engineer, whose field of operations has thus suddenly become widely extended. The first and immediate demand for engineering talent probably lies in connection with the problems of restoration and reconstruction in the devastated areas. To what extent American engineers will be used in this work depends largely upon the supply of materials of construction and of engineers in Europe and upon the ability of our trans-Atlantic neighbors to finance their operations without our aid. In many districts, mines and manufacturing plants have been destroyed: in others, worn out; in most cases on the Continent, production has been pushed to the maximum without stop-

*A speech made at the banquet in New York on February 20.

ping for repairs; railroads and highways have been worn unceasingly, and must need renewing. And in addition to this plant and material exhaustion, it must be remembered that there has been appalling loss of life among the engineers and those of sufficient mentality to make army officers. Increased and intensified demand for materials and a shortage of designing and constructing engineers would seem to create unprecedented opportunities for this country of matchless resources in both. And here is where the advantage of the United States as an opulent and creditor nation becomes doubly accentuated. Now for the first time in our history we have more money than we can spend at home; now the wide world is our field of operations; now we are compelled to search for development enterprises in which our surplus capital may be employed; now we must, in spite of ourselves, become cosmopolitan. And since those very countries which are our debtors are the ones which most need our assistance, it is only by increasing our business with them and our investments there that those debts will ever be paid. By enabling them to re-build, by establishing them again on a prosperous basis we shall at the same time protect the investments and loans already made under the necessities of war. Does this situation not promise work and opportunity for the engineer?

But the War has brought other changes. The employment of man power and materials for the sole purpose of destruction has been so general and widespread as to change living conditions over a large portion of the inhabited globe. Economic laws have been arbitrarily set aside, and the governments have been compelled to establish artificial prices and regulations for the transportation and allocation of labor and materials. The inevitable result has been dissatisfaction, uncertainty, and confusion. The workman who has recently been receiving fifty dollars per week instead of the former twenty-five cannot understand why there should be any reduction now that the War is over. The farmer still wants war price for wheat; the Southern planter wants war price for cotton; and the field hand still desires to work half time and get double wages. On the other hand there is a general desire for a reduction of the cost of the every-day necessities of life. In short, we are faced with a condition of unrest and uncertainty in all quarters of the globe. Every thoughtful person knows that there must be re-adjustment, but no one can foresee its precise trend and effect. Is there not here again a demand for the influence and effort of the intelligent engineer?

Those of us who have watched the spread of Marxian socialism abroad, who have seen its adoption by the Russian Bolsheviki and have seen their poisonous propaganda insidiously inoculating the workingmen of Russia, Austria, Germany, and even England, and who have read the anarchistic publications of their disciples in this country cannot but feel that it is high time something was done to counteract it. Bolshevism is the antithesis of democracy; it is the foe of freedom; it is a rule by a class, and that class the most ignorant and least civilized in the community. It matters not whether it be found in the parlor or in the revolutionary parade, in the poisoned press or on the street platform, bolshevism is an abomination subversive of order and government, and must be opposed by every patriot and loyal citizen, by every influence and power which desires the welfare of mankind.

It has often seemed to me that the engineer is not fully awake to his duties and privileges as a citizen; that he is too engrossed with the details and the mechanism of his profession; that his mind dwells too much on facts and figures and processes; that he is too retiring by training and disposition, too little of a publicist and a humanitarian, and too much of a materialist. I believe that individually and through his organizations he should take an active part in every movement that concerns the good of society; that he should take the initiative in shaping the policies of government: that he should be an aggressive educating and moral force in every community.

On his visit to this country in 1876, at the founding of the Johns Hopkins University at Baltimore, Thomas Huxley addressed us as follows: "Truly America has a great future before her—great in toil, in care and in responsibility, great in true glory if she be guided in wisdom and righteousness, great in shame if she fail. I cannot understand why other nations should envy you or be blind to the fact that it is for the highest interest of mankind that you should succeed; but the one condition of success, your sole safeguard, is the moral and intellectual clearness of the individual citizen."

In all branches of business, in all lines of human endeavor, we have been taught to strive for efficiency. Indeed, so greatly has the idea been stressed that we have been in danger of regarding it as the end in itself. We have forgotten why we are thus striving. We have often had our attention directed to the efficiency of the German people as something well worth imitating. Dr. Nicholas Murray Butler, in a most scholarly address on 'Education after the War,'[1] has given us a timely warning: "The War has taught the lesson that the proper place of efficiency is as the servant of a moral ideal, and that efficiency apart from a moral ideal is an evil and a wicked instrument which in the end can accomplish only disaster. In other words, we should encourage efficiency not for its material results, not simply for the greater amount of wealth in dollars and cents, in bushels of wheat, tons of ore or yards of cloth thereby produced, but for its value in the development of character, and for its aid in the achievement of our ideals and the guidance of the individual and the race in their progress toward fuller self-expression and more complete self-realization."

Now, the only road to efficiency is education. In all departments of life, in business, in government, in commerce and trade, education must precede efficiency, and the broader and more widely disseminated the real education of a people, of a class, of a community, the higher its efficiency. And this brings me down to the suggestions which I wish to make this evening.

[1]'Educational Review', January 1919.

Scarcely a day passes that the newspapers do not contain notices of strikes, of lock-outs, of labor dissatisfaction and disturbances in this or that industry. The strife between the employer and the laboring man is incessant and irritating to both. It is world-wide and apparently everlasting and its cost is beyond calculation. It has received the careful consideration of the world's greatest economists, and is a problem whose solution requires far greater intellect than mine. Nevertheless, it vitally affects the interests of every one of us here tonight, for it contains possibilities which one shudders to contemplate, with the tide of Bolshevism rolling westward, and other forces at work to mold our civilization into new and different and untried forms. Here and now are demanded more than ever before that "moral and intellectual clearness of the individual citizen" referred to by Huxley; now, more than at any period in our history do we appreciate the worth of that poise and stability which are provided and acquired by education; and now do we feel more fully than ever the importance of extending education to those of all classes who are in any way responsible for the industrial turmoil existing and impending.

It has always seemed to me that labor troubles must, in large measure, result from a failure on the part of the protagonists to understand each other's respective situations and motives; from a lack of comprehension of the simple elements of economics on the part of the masses, and the failure on the part of the employer to explain how and why conditions have arisen which have made necessary or inadvisable a readjustment of any accepted or demanded situation. In other words, through lack of education. And here, it seems to me, is an opportunity and a duty for the engineer. He occupies a peculiar relation to the capitalist and the laborer. He is customarily one of the employed; he is, on the other hand, the adviser and trusted representative of capital. He comes into frequent and close contact with the laborer, and is in a position to understand his difficulties, to win his friendship and confidence, and to impart advice and information which would go far to explain the difficulties of any given situation. He is a sort of middle-man, who might easily acquire such influence with those above and below him as to be of very great aid in time of industrial crises. If this be indeed true, then it must follow that in not exercising his privilege, in not performing this service, he is not meeting fully his responsibilities as an engineer and a citizen. As the boys would say: he is not strictly "on his job."

Let us consider for a moment the situation in the average mining camp. A few hundred or a few thousand miners are employed. Here they come, muckers, mule skinners, trammers, nippers, timbermen, machine men, track layers, powder monkeys, station tenders, pipe men, carpenters, electricians, shift bosses, blacksmiths, and helpers, of different nationalities and varying degrees of intelligence and education. They are checked in and checked off by the time keeper: except in case of accident they spend their allotted time on the job and disperse without receiving as much personal attention as the mules underground. When not at work, they spend their time idling around saloons or other shady resorts where they not only learn nothing to their advantage, but spend their substance and sap the foundations of their health and strength, mentally, morally, and physically. Under such conditions they afford fertile and receptive soil for the seeds sown by the demagogic agitator. They attend open or secret meetings of the union and are constantly taught the program of violence and disrespect for law and order. In those camps where club houses are provided and reading matter and forms of amusement furnished, they are seldom visited and cultivated by anyone connected with the mine management. The men are still left to their own devices, and no advantage is taken of the opportunity to gain the friendship and confidence of those who are approachable, to aid those who are worthy and in need of some sort of encouragement or assistance, or to educate those eager for knowledge.

In recent years, it is true, many mining companies have arranged for moving-picture shows two or three times each week; in some States like Nevada, the State educational institutions, such as the College of Mines, have of late years conducted night schools for instruction in scientific and technical subjects; and the Federal Bureau of Mines has sent its car around and taught the men the principles and methods of safety first. In all of these matters, the mining engineers have taken a part and shown sympathetic interest; but it seems to me we have fallen far short of the full measure of our duty and our opportunity. We have failed on the social and humanitarian side; we have done little to counteract the deliberate spread of socialistic and bolshevistic doctrines; we have permitted the raising of a crop of noxious weeds on soil which might well have yielded the fruits of thrift, industry, loyalty, and patriotism.

With the coming of prohibition and the closing of the saloons, those old-time haunts of the miner, we find the men increasingly in need of comfortable recreation quarters, and in better condition to be interested in opportunities for entertainment which shall be at the same time instructive and uplifting. There are many forms of such entertainment, and many methods by which such instruction may be given without the appearance of officiousness or pedantry. I have never yet visited a mining camp where there were not some men of ideas, of travel, of wide experience and observation, of talent in some form of entertaining, where there are not frequent visitors who could be pressed into service for the benefit of the general cause of education and good fellowship. And there are ways and means by which such service could be organized and carried forward. There are national organizations and societies; there are State institutions; there are our own Local Sections; and there are the mining companies themselves which would quickly appreciate the value of such work among their men. It is probable that our Committee on Industrial Organization, with its sub-committee on Education, may be already at work along these lines. But we should not leave it entirely to small committees. It is work for every one of us, to be performed daily and perpetually, wherever we may be. It is not only a moral duty, but is one of the best expedients for making sure of permanent tenure of our positions and the salaries thereto attached. How many of our engineers are now enjoying princely honorariums in Russia? None. How many are at work in Mexico? Very few. What is the fundamental reason in both countries? Illiteracy. How many engineers will be thrown out of employment if bolshevism carries out its declared program in the United States? Untold thousands. Is it not then, in the most literal sense, our job to protect our jobs by dissolving and dispersing the clouds of prejudice and ignorance which threaten the existence of all kinds of employment and the destruction of all industry? Yea, verily.

Nor is the laboring man the only one who needs educating. We need it ourselves; and so do Congress and capitalists, managers, and the general public. The engineer's own education is too often defective in economics and politics, and he suffers thereby. He is wounded in his most sensitive parts by bad mining laws, by wrong principles of taxation, by ill-advised governmental regulation. In the conduct of all these matters he often has a keen sense of defective functioning, but is not sure of the remedy, nor skillful and earnest in urging its adoption; and in his perplexity often decides that he is not the doctor nor the plumber to stop up that particular leak! And when the trouble has grown irritating and chronic and no one provides a cure he is apt to become cynical and to blame society and the government for a situation which he himself should have helped to alleviate.

Now, Brother Engineers, let us have more confidence in the essential fair-mindedness of our fellows; let us believe in the future of our country; let us feel some responsibility for the condition of society; let us individually and through our Institute and kindred organizations cultivate simplicity of analysis, clearness of thought, expression in words of one syllable, and let us seek means by which we may increase our moral efficiency, improve the relations between the citizen and the Government, between the employer and the employed; and so add to the sum of human happiness. The task may appear great, but there are many workers, and there will be an abundant reward in the resultant and well justified consciousness of service rendered, combined with a swelling sense of pride of profession, pride of race, and pride of country.

CYANIDE (sodium) imported into the United States during 1918 amounted to 69,279 lb., valued at $12,615, compared with 1,604,117 lb. and $803,604 in 1917, and 483,811 lb. and $102,663 in 1916. The potash salt imported was 141,808 lb., valued at $47,460, against 104,316 lb. and $76,303 in 1917, and 2705 lb. and $803 in 1916. These figures show that the supply of cyanide for this country is mainly from domestic sources.

TUNGSTEN IMPORTS in 1918 totaled 10,362 tons, valued at $11,409,237. In 1917 the quantity was 4357 tons and value $4,467,608.

Ventilation Methods in Coeur d'Alene Mines

By ROBERT N. BELL

*The metal mines of this State are mostly in high mountain regions. Those of the Coeur d'Alene have their vein outcrops on the mountain-sides, and are developed by adit or cross-cut tunnels to depths varying down to over 2000 ft. This gives ample natural gravity air-pressure circulation that usually affords good ventilation and is easily controlled. The natural advantages of this region in this respect and its deep sedimentary formations are exceptional, but in recent years, in three particular cases, the ore penetration has been developed extensively below the lowest points of surface-drainage entry, involving cross-cut tunnels, three of which are two miles long. In these cases the tunnels are of a minimum size of 7 by 8 ft., and are used for drainage, haulage, and ventilation. They are costly openings to drive, and owing to the uncertainty of results to be found a double-entry tunnel was never warranted as it is in coal mine development, and the further fact that return outlets are invariably provided at high elevations for air circulation.

Above these deep drainage-levels, ventilation by natural gravity air-currents was a simple matter; but each of these mines, and several others in lesser degree, have shown persistence in their orebodies to great depth below these lowest drainage-entries, and the sub-levels thus developed have rapidly expanded in the past few years. This involves a new problem in ventilation, where the long tunnel is depended upon for the main air supply, by reason of the fact that the long electric ore-trains running in these air-courses act as a part piston and resistance when in motion against the air, and materially retard its flow. Sub-level ventilation by natural gravity air, even with these deep drainage advantages and numerous higher outlets, has lately proved inadequate in volume and velocity to fully supply the normal working requirements of the men, and must be assisted by mechanical means. A ventilating system that will simply carry away the smoke and gases from blasting and emanations from men and lights, is a mistaken economy in big mine operation, as the great harm resulting from an insufficient supply of good air is markedly shown in the behavior of the men employed in such a mine. Surliness, discontent, inefficiency, and a general desire to cut work or taper are often directly traceable to poor air, and there is no investment that will pay a bigger return in resulting efficiency of the workers than good ventilation.

The long tunnels of the Morning and Bunker Hill & Sullivan mines, due to the natural wall resistance and moving trains, are incapable of carrying sufficient air to properly ventilate their extensive and rapidly deepening sub-levels without mechanical induction. Fortunately, both have several other outlets in addition to their long tunnels which, while at a much higher level, can be used and are used as additional sources of fresh air, with the return or up-cast directed through still other outlets. These matters have been under discussion for the past four years with the State Mines Department, and the managements of these mines have been entirely willing and anxious to improve their ventilating conditions. To do so, however, in addition to mechanical installations, it involves the driving of several thousand feet of expensive straight-line raise connections, but as labor has been so scarce this work has been decidedly retarded.

In this connection, as men have been available, over 900 ft. of big raises have been driven at the west end of the Bunker Hill mine and are now being extended, to be used exclusively as an air-course, and during my visit to the property in December, a large station was being cut for a recently ordered 60,000-cu. ft. Sirocco fan. This is to take fresh air not only from the Kellogg tunnel, but also from the adjacent Sweeney shaft and other west end outlets, affording an ample supply for all purposes, when mechanically driven and controlled, to the deepest point of the mine within the necessary air-doors and stoppings. Present plans contemplate, if it is found necessary, the installation of another large Sirocco fan near the head of the No. 2 East shaft, which is a natural up-cast, and will afford a permanent circuit through the East end outlets, above the Kellogg tunnel. This is the deepest mine in actual ground penetration in the plane of the vein in the Coeur d'Alene. Its orebodies are entirely in quartzite formation. They vary in size up to 100 ft. in horizontal cross-section and 900 ft. in length. The mined spaces are uniformly timbered with square-sets and closely filled with waste. The levels are 200 ft. apart vertically and 300 ft. on the dip of the vein, which is 40°. The hottest place in the mine is 1500 ft. above the bottom level at the apex of the Cameron stope at the No. 10 level cross-cut connection. This is one of the largest stopes in the mine that has been actively operated for the past 12 years. At this point the temperature is 80°. The humidity reaches dew-point, and is largely due to local faulting, the friction of slowly packing fill, oxidizing timbers of the big stope, and the fact that it is a converging point of return air.

The highest bottom level temperature in the mine at the new 15th level, which is 4800 ft. on the dip of the vein below its highest crest, and 3400 ft. vertically under the mountain, registered only 70°F. This point is 5400 ft. in the pitch of the main ore-channel below discovery

*Abstract from report of State Inspector of Mines for 1918.

cut. The top of the big stopes at No. 13 and 14 levels registered 75°, and the No. 2 shaft-station main return air-course at the 13th level, 70°.

These are comparatively low temperatures for such depths. The mine, however, is damp throughout and the relative humidity is high in all these sub-levels, causing men to perspire freely at work, this giving the impression of much higher temperatures than actually prevails. The only remedy for this humid condition is a greater volume and velocity of fresh air-currents, and the company is making an earnest effort to attain this improved condition, which, I think, will shortly be accomplished.

At the Hercules mine, with a drainage cross-cut tunnel at its lowest point from Canyon creek only a few hundred feet short of two miles in length, the natural ventilation in its new sub-levels is still good. Its new vertical four-compartment shaft from this level is 1400 ft. deep, but only three sub-levels have yet been opened down to the 600-ft. level. The large underground hoisting-stations are completely sealed with tight air-doors. The main shaft in the winter carried 30,000 cu. ft. of fresh air in December, affording ample ventilation for the present levels, by way of the shaft, drifts, stopes, and up-cast through several large rock raises to the No. 4 tunnel outlet, 600 ft. above No. 5, a natural return-circuit in the summer. Stations are now being cut in the new shaft at the 800 and 1000-ft. sub-levels in this mine, where the natural temperatures are slightly under 70° and well ventilated by an exhaust-fan at the 600-ft. station.

The Hecla mine has a natural advantage in ventilation from the fact that its main working shaft starts at the surface, and does not involve the long adit approaches of the other mines mentioned. It is ideally situated for natural gravity-air ventilation, and the management has taken full advantage of this condition. This mine has a drainage-level on the course of its ore-zone several thousand feet, striking directly into the east side of the abrupt slope of Canyon creek, near the main surface shaft-collar. The main shaft now has a maximum depth to its new bottom station of 2000 ft. vertical. The bottom working-level is at 1600 ft., and the lineal distribution of the orebodies are strung out through fully 3000 ft., and duplicated with several parallel shoots of ore with many raises, chutes, and manways at short intervals.

Near the east end of the ore development an expensive straight-line raise, nearly vertical and 1400 ft. high, was put through to the surface from the drainage-tunnel for ventilation purposes. It gives a maximum gravity vertical range to the 1600-ft. level through connecting raises for natural air pressure of 3000 ft., with several other outlets above the drainage-tunnel to relieve the main west stopes. This theoretically presents almost ideal conditions for natural-gravity air circulation.

The main shaft has a large-size idle compartment, and each station drift-entry is provided with an air-door. In December this shaft, acting as a natural down-cast, was distributing 28,000 cu. ft. of fresh air per minute at high velocity through the lower levels, with return through numerous outlets to the surface. The recent rapid expansion and duplication of the operating openings and ore-shoots of this mine, all heavily timbered, develops a heavy resistance to free air circulation, in spite of its extremely high chimney-draft value. It also retards the flow of the return air, which is believed to be due, in part, to lack of proper splits in the west orebody, a condition that the company's engineers are now studying carefully with a view to remedy by additional doors and stoppings. If this is not effective, a powerful Sirocco fan will be put in as an exhaust, probably at the head of the No. 3 tunnel, 1400-ft. raise.

The temperature at the new 2000-ft. station in this mine in December was 70°, with relatively high humidity. Like all the other sub-level mines, the maximum or warmest place tested in this one, due to the same cause of temperature localization as the Bunker Hill & Sullivan and Morning mines, was at the top of an exhausted stope on the 600-ft. level, 1000 ft. above the bottom working-level, which gave a reading of 70°.

It would seem from the foregoing that the temperatures in the deepest mines of the Coeur d'Alene district are comparatively low, and range around ordinary normal summer heat at the surface. There prevails, as previously stated, however, a general dampness of the ground, with the resulting humidity or moisture in the air.

At the Bunker Hill & Sullivan mine, the stoping is all done on day shift; at the other mines most of it is done on day shift, and when two shifts are working in the stopes, the blasting is practically all done at the end of the second shift, which permits 8 to 16 hours' time for the mines to clear of smoke and gas from the blasts. Exhaust-fans are invariably used in dead-ends, and there is no point in the district where the air can be called bad at this time. In several of the properties, at the end of a shift with a big crew of men, it is poor, and can be greatly improved by mechanical means and new connections designed to facilitate the distribution of the currents. I look for a big improvement in these conditions during the coming year [1919] in all these deep mines, and an ultimate full solution of the problems involved, as is possible.

Aside from these growing ventilation problems, all of the great mines of the Coeur d'Alene are otherwise in good physical condition.

Wolfram production of Bolivia in 1917 (the latest figures) totaled 3828 tons of 60% concentrate. This was an increase of 842 tons over 1916, which in turn was 2207 tons greater than the 1915 return.

Chromite imports last year totaled 100,142 tons, valued at $2,891,725, against 72,063 tons and $1,098,659 in 1917, and 115,886 tons and $1,548,402 in 1916.

Graphite ore milled in Canada during 1918 amounted to 19,614 tons, averaging 8.6% graphitic carbon.

Manganese in steel averages 14 lb. per ton.

ROCHESTER, NEVADA

The New Arrangements in This Field.

Organization of the Rochester Nevada Silver Mines Co. will be perfected shortly, upon deposit in the Reno National Bank of a majority of stock in the constituent corporations. Under terms of the agreement brought about by F. M. Manson, executive head of the Western Ore Purchasing Co., the bank will issue certificates of exchange for shares of the new holding company, but this stock is to remain in pool, in possession of the bank, until all indebtedness for the various companies is paid, but not longer than for one year from April 1, 1919. A board of trustees, composed of Mr. Manson, Judge L. N. French, and Jay H. Clemons, will select the directorate of the holding company. Attachments against the property of the Rochester Mines Co. have been released, and that company is again operating its mine and mill. Apex-rights were claimed by the Rochester Elda Fina and Rochester Merger Mines companies involving the principal vein system worked by the Rochester Mines Co. Voluminous reports were prepared in behalf of the apex claimants by O. H. Hershey, H. V. Winchell, Fred Searls, and other engineers and geologists. It was contended that the east vein, mined extensively in Rochester Mines territory, had its apex on the east side of the ridge that trends through those claims of the Elda Fina, Merger, and Nenzel Crown Point adjoining the Rochester Mines on the east, and penetrated by the Friedman and Pitt tunnels. A large amount of development work has been done in this area, and connection has been made from the Rochester tunnel workings with a tunnel debouching east of the ridge. All mine workings excepting the deepest in the Rochester Mines property are in oxidized material, and the geologists agree that there is good promise in the sulphide zone, particularly in the western area, where the veins dip into the Merger ground adjoining the Rochester Mines on the west, toward the town of Rochester. The Rochester Combined mill, with a capacity of 400 tons, is nearly new, and it is proposed to haul ore for this mill from the Merger and Crown Point properties, probably extending the tramway along the east side of the ridge. The Combined property has little ore of commercial grade, and its large area is so lightly regarded that it is referred to by one engineer as "a desert goat ranch." The other properties are regarded as valuable mines, and all have considerable quantities of ore available for milling. The Rochester mill is in good condition and has treated over 200 tons daily. It is now indicated that the new directorate and management will include few, if any, of the men formerly in control of these properties.

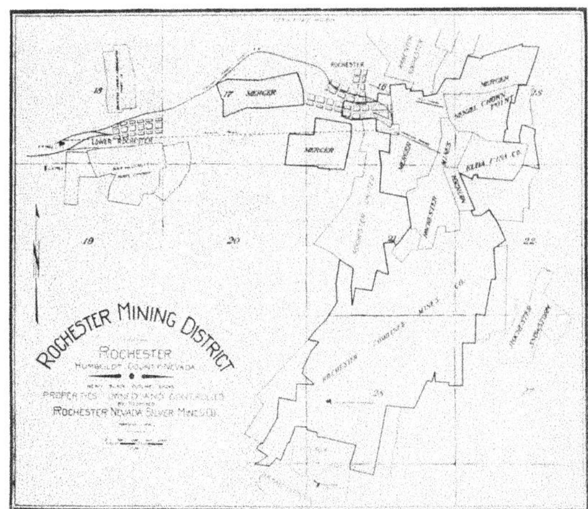

The Nevada Packard continues operating at full capacity.

DIVIDE, NEVADA

What is Being Done in the Divide District.

At least 30 shafts are being sunk at Divide, formerly known as the Tonopah Gold Mountain district, six miles south of here, on the main road to Goldfield. New companies are being formed almost daily and the district is staked for an area many miles in extent, new locations covering both the north and south slopes of Gold mountain.

In the Tonopah Divide mine the south cross-cut from the shaft has been extended to cut the main silver vein on the 465-ft. level. With the aid of an auxiliary hoist the shaft has been sunk 50 ft. below the fourth level, and stations will be cut at 100-ft. intervals. Water-level is estimated to be at 700 ft. When water is developed in the mine a mill is to be built. A contract just signed provides for treatment by the MacNamara mill at Tonopah of a maximum of 60 tons and minimum of 40 tons of ore daily from the Divide mine. The mill has been equipped with additional shallow settling-vats and a Dorr thickener. The Divide ore requires greater settling capacity than Tonopah ore, and the additions will permit the MacNamara company to treat its own ore. The main south-east drift on the third level has been advanced to the 350-ft. point from the shaft cross-cut, and from this point cross-cuts are being driven both ways in good ore. At the 300-ft. point the cross-cuts advanced 40 ft. each way; that to the north-east for the greater part in low-grade material. The ore-shoot is now opened for a length of 430 ft. on the third level. Raises from the second and third levels are nearing the drifts above.

On the 500-ft. level of the Brougher Divide the cross-cut, 75 ft. from the shaft, exposed a two-foot seam of ore assaying $18.85. About 15 ft. farther it passed through a seam of ore assaying $80 per ton. These seams dip from the vein, and were not found in development work on the 177-ft. level.

The Divide Consolidated, adjoining the Brougher on the north-west and said to have the Divide vein, has one of the best surface plants in that region. Vein formation exposed in starting the shaft assayed $9 over its width. The vein has been exposed by open-cuts, yielding assays from $2 to $104 per ton.

The Tonopah Dividend, working on the 300-ft. level, has exposed kaolin in a crushed zone in its main vein, with a small amount of horn-silver. This material resembles the Divide high grade.

The East Divide shaft entered the lower breccia at 300 ft., and will be continued to 400 ft. for cross-cutting.

The Gold Zone has prospected its vein, apparently the Divide lode, up to the latter's boundary, and at this point found two feet of $20 ore. Cross-cuts are being driven to prospect for parallel veins, and a drift is being driven south-east on the 500-ft. level. F. Sommer Schmidt has been made director and consulting engineer of the Gold Zone, which is now said to be controlled by L. E. Whicher of New York and associates.

Divide Extension has the hoisting plant formerly on the Manhattan Morning Glory, and is sinking from the 150-ft. level.

The Sutherland Divide, north of the Tonopah Divide, has a good plant in place at its 400-ft. incline shaft, which will be sunk further 200 ft. while drifts are extended on the 400-ft. level.

The Alto Divide, adjoining the Gold Zone and East Divide, has started its shaft.

The Gold Wedge Divide, Rosetta Divide, Gold Seam, and several others are situated some distance south-east of the Divide mine, on the south slope of the mountain.

The Hasbrouck, farther west, is a relatively old property, having shipped a considerable quantity of ore several years ago. It is working in a 400-ft. shaft and 900-ft. tunnel, and in the latter has developed 3000 tons of shipping ore, which will be sent to Tonopah mills.

New companies that have equipped their ground for deep work, include the Florence Divide, Mohawk Divide, Divide Annex, North Divide, Hennessy Divide, Silver King Divide, and a half-dozen more. All roads are alive with freight-teams, motor-trucks, and touring-cars, bringing in equipment and visitors.

400-TON CYANIDE MILL OF THE ROCHESTER COMBINED MINES, NOW PART OF THE ROCHESTER NEVADA SILVER MINES CO.

A list of companies operating in the Divide district is as under:

Name	Shares	Par value	Development
Tonopah Divide Mining Co.	1,250,000	$1.00	Shaft 520 ft.; ore-reserves $5,000,000; shipping to Tonopah
Brougher Divide Mining Co.	1,000,000	1.00	Shaft 500 ft.; cut Divide vein on 177 and 500-ft. levels
Gold Zone Divide Mining Co.	1,500,000	0.10	Shaft 500 ft.; cut Divide vein on 295 and 500-ft. levels
East Divide Mining Co.	1,500,000	0.10	Shaft 320 ft.
Divide Extension Mining Co.	1,000,000	0.10	Shaft 170 ft.
Tonopah Hasbrouck Min. Co.	1,500,000	1.00	Shaft 400 ft. and tunnel 900 ft.; ore-reserves $50,000
Divide Consolidated Min. Co.	1,500,000	0.10	Started shaft
Tonopah Dividend Mining Co.	1,500,000	0.10	Shaft 300 ft.; cut two wide veins
Alto Divide Mining Co.	1,500,000	0.10	Started shaft
Sutherland Divide Mining Co.	1,500,000	0.10	Incline shaft 400 ft.; two shallower shafts; will sink 200 ft. deeper
High Divide Mining Co.	1,000,000	1.00	Not yet working
Gold Wedge Divide Min. Co.	1,500,000	0.10	Started shaft
Rosetta Divide Mining Co.	1,500,000	0.10	Started shaft
Divide Annex Mining Co.	1,000,000	0.10	Will sink shortly
Allied Divide Mining Co.	1,500,000	0.10	Will sink shortly
Silver King Divide Min. Co.	1,000,000	0.10	Started shaft
North Divide Mining Co.	2,000,000	0.10	Sinking shaft
Florence Divide Mining Co.	1,500,000	0.10	Will start soon
Mohawk Divide Mining Co.	1,500,000	0.10	Ready to sink
Divide City Mining Co.	1,500,000	0.10	Starts shortly
Goldsmith Divide Mining Co.	1,500,000	0.10	Not yet working
Gold Reef Divide Mining Co.	1,500,000	0.10	Starts work soon

A recent meeting of mining men at Divide formally named the place the Divide Mining District. It has no post-office or camp, and mail goes to Tonopah. A townsite is to be organized shortly, on the claims of the Divide City Mining Co., on the main road, just north of the Mammoth claim of the Tonopah Divide group.

GOLDFIELD, NEVADA

Development of the Florence.—The Consolidated in 1918.

Following a recent examination of the Florence Goldfield mine, F. Sommer Schmidt, representing New York interests, reports that with exception of legal details, the shares owned by A. D. Parker and the estate of Thomas G. Lockhart has been sold to them. The deal involved, according to J. W. Dunfee, of Goldfield, who was instrumental in making the sale, 318,650 shares owned by Parker and 314,000 owned by the Lockhart estate. The purchase price is said to have been $100,000. Ample funds for development of the Florence will be provided, without the sale of additional treasury shares. The company proposes to sink the 1200-ft. shaft to the shale-latite contact, and will investigate the possibility of mining a large block of ground by the caving system, as is contemplated by the Goldfield Development Co. on the same vein. It is reported that leases on the upper levels of the Florence will be renewed by the company after expiration on January 1, 1920. One of these leases—the Witt-Brandon-Taylor-Mechlin—has exposed for a distance of 41 ft. on the 400-ft. level, a seam of ore from 6 to 18 in. wide, from which high assays are obtained. Front 4 to 6 ft. of material assaying from $400 to $500 per ton is being broken in a drift on this level. Ten lessees are operating, but the one mentioned is the only one producing regularly. On the same vein, on the 350-ft. level, the Cracker Jack company has a lease, and has started raising through the vein to open the rich shoot exposed in the Witt lease. The Red Hill-Florence, owning adjoining claims and holding a lease on the Florence, is being developed on the 600-ft. level, to the south and on the same vein. The Florence has produced over $7,000,000, and during the period of the receivership, from November 1916 to October 1918, the gross value of ore produced was $225,000.

The report of the Goldfield Consolidated Mines Co. for the year ended December 31, 1918, states that 94,654 tons of ore, worth $1,065,381, was produced. Of this, $921,514 was extracted. Also, 164,121 tons of tailing was treated, from which $116,804 was extracted. Operating charges, including sums paid to lessees, totaled $1,059,696, leaving a net balance of $3433. Development amounted to 4848 ft., performed at a cost of $6.72 per foot. Operation was continuous throughout the year, except for a short period in July; but at the close of the year less than 150 tons of ore was being treated daily. As is well known now, on February 1, 1919, the property was leased to the Goldfield Development Co., and two claims were sold to this company. At the end of the year the Consolidated company had on hand $136,062 in cash. No dividends have been paid since October 30, 1915.

PLATTEVILLE, WISCONSIN

Blende, Carbonate, Lead, and Pyrite Mining and Prices.

The zinc situation in the Wisconsin field for February was bad, to say the least. The Government has, for instance, 1200 tons of spelter at the Hillsboro, Illinois, plant alone, a drug on the market, which speculators believe will be thrown on the market at an early date, and so depress the price of spelter further. Until the stock on hand is worked off, and business conditions improve, it is difficult to expect anything better in the ore business for several months. Leading smelter officials interviewed personally profess to believe that by autumn of this year we ought to be doing better than now, but not before then.

Operating conditions in this field last month were satisfactory to the mine manager, and a fair recovery was obtained, although with greatly reduced working forces. Several low-grade zinc-ore producers shut-down on account of low markets and irregular demand. In the Benton district, the Frontier Mining Co. alone released 200 men and closed three producers. At all points mines suspended operations temporarily, some with bins well stocked with surplus ore. One consistent producer suffered the loss of its surface plant by fire, a score of miners losing their jobs there. Little prospecting is being carried out.

Prices were not regarded as satisfactory by ore sellers. The high-grade product obtained by roasting and electrostatic separation diverted to the uses of sheet-zinc makers held all month on a $45 per ton base, with some premium grade at times realizing prices in advance of this. On second grade, high-lead blende, prices ranged from $40 to $43.50, with the bulk of the sales on a $42.50 base. It was this figure that enabled most operators to continue, otherwise the shut-down might have been more general. The Matthiesen & Hegeler Zinc Co., for 25 years one of the most aggressive as well as liberal buyers of zinc ores of high grade, was practically out of the market. Low-grade producers had an exceedingly bad inning. The reserve of zinc ore in the field at the close of the month showed 7500 tons of all grades.

Producers of lead ore were given severe set-backs during February, and sales and shipments of this class of Wisconsin product were exceedingly light. The price held at $55 at the beginning of the month, but demand was painfully absent and buyers showed no real interest. The price receded to $50, and at one time offerings were made under this figure. Toward the close of the month some competition developed and interest shown by a new lead-smelting concern, at Wauwatosa, Wisconsin, caused prices to take an upward trend. Deliveries agreed upon at the close of the month found the offerings in advance of $60. It was held that improvement in the pig-lead market suggested the advance in the price of ore, which may be true, but competition in ore buying helped materially. The reserve in all at the close of the month was in excess of 1000 tons, all choice high-grade lead concentrate. Shipments out of the field for the month were 240 tons. Producers took advantage of fine weather to invade shallow and surface diggings, making a fair production.

Pyrite was not in good demand at any time, although commercial sulphuric acid ruled high. At Mineral Point, one of the reduction plants was closed, but the McDougall furnace in one of two plants was run on ore separation and for making acid. Fine ore recovered at separating plants, has been accumulating since early last autumn, and there is now in the field a reserve amounting to several thousand tons. It is said the two new Government acid plants, built last year, are for sale, and that local mining corporations are negotiating for their transfer.

Production of carbonate of zinc ore has taken on new impetus in the northern districts of the field, the New Jersey Zinc Co. opening large deposits. Much ground proved by drilling is being exploited. Machinery is being erected, and more miners are being employed, instead of curtailing operations. Prices continue to be satisfactory, as high as $35 per ton being paid for 40% zinc content, but the average for the month was $28. This ore is cheaply mined. During cold weather, concentrating this ore is almost impossible, so it is shipped direct to the oxide furnaces at Mineral Point. It is here converted into the oxide, and packed in 300-lb. barrels. At this time it is said that the Mineral Point Zinc Co. has its warehouses filled with the oxide, in excess of 50,000 barrels.

THE MINING SUMMARY

ALASKA

Kennecott.—The Kennecott Copper Corporation has declared a quarterly dividend of 50 cents per share, half of the previous one.

ARIZONA

Bowie.—The Helen-Dome, a gold-silver-lead mine in the Dos Cabezos, is being operated under bond and lease. Mine machinery and a 25-ton mill are arriving at Bowie.

Copper Hill.—The Superior & Boston Copper Co. has issued a report for the year ended September 30, 1918. A. L. Graham is superintendent. Receipts were $246,158 from ore sold to the El Paso smelter, and $104,828 from calls. Development cost $110,485, and ore extraction $223,896. The balance from 1917 was $141,577, and that carried to 1919 was $129,374. Exploration was mainly in the eastern part of the mine, on the 800 and 1000-ft. levels, also re-opening the 1200-ft. level. Faults were encountered, and the formation on the two upper levels was much leached and oxidized. Work was therefore suspended there and transferred to 1200 ft. to get under this material. A total of 199 ft. of work was done. Above the 800-ft. level, 100 ft., a body of oxide ore was opened, in places 20 ft. wide, carrying 6% copper. Ore shipments totaled 22,751 tons, assaying 3.88% copper and 0.4 oz. silver. A profit of $1.03 per ton was made, but at present costs and prices a loss would result.

Hackberry.—The new mill of the Hackberry Consolidated Mining Co. is ready for operation. The mine is said to be in good condition to supply the mill, there being sufficient ore broken in the stopes to supply the mill for some time.

Mayer.—The Arizona Binghampton Copper Co. has purchased the Hazel and Gold Hill claims for $10,000. These are contiguous to the Binghampton.

Prescott.—The Anderson silver claims in the Thumb Butte district are to be opened within the next 30 days. A little development was carried on during the War.

Ray.—The Ray Hercules in February concentrated 733 tons of 1.427% ore daily, recovering 80.5%. On March 1 the mill treated 1130 tons of 1.705% ore, recovering 88.5%.

Superior.—The Maverick group of 20 claims in the Superstition mountains, owned by Woodbury brothers, have been sold to the Pillsbury interests for a consideration said to be $100,000. The property is to be churn-drilled.

Tucson.—The concentrating and cyanide mill of the El Progresso Mining Co. is ready for operation. This mill will treat 500,000 tons of ore now on the dump.

COLORADO

Breckenridge.—The Juventa Mines Co. has been organized to resume work on the Juventa claims, idle for 18 years. The main tunnel is in 1200 ft. Some deposits of iron-manganese ore have been developed. Possibilities are considered good.

The Gold Belt Mining Co. has been formed to operate a property on Brewery hill, 5 miles east of Breckenridge. It is well developed and heavily timbered.

Lawson.—The Matrix Mines Co. has increased its capital from $30,000 to $95,00. It has a lease on 16 claims, 8 miles from Idaho Springs, on which work has been under way for two years. Some good silver-lead ore has been opened. Shipments are to be started by mid-summer.

Pitkin.—The Pennsylvania Molybdenum Mines Co. has started its new flotation mill. S. G. Fetterman is manager.

IDAHO

Stites.—According to Mr. Roebuck, this town is to construct the first 13 miles of the 52-mile road to the Elk City, Orogrande, and Ten Mile gold districts. At that point the road would enter the forest reserve, after which the Federal government might finish it.

Talache.—At the Armstead Mines property in Bonner county, in charge of D. G. McLachlan during the absence of H. H. Armstead, who was in the Engineers, a 600-ft. raise has connected No. 3 and 2 tunnels, giving an exit through No. 3, which is 4000 ft. long, of 1600 ft. of backs.

Wallace.—Wages in the Coeur d'Alene region were reduced by $1 per day on March 16. Under the sliding-scale in force this is still 50 cents higher than provided for. Miners will now receive $4.25 per shift. Lead is selling at 5.25 cents per lb., and the following schedule shows the wage-bonus paid and the lead prices controlling same:

Price per 100 lb.	Bonus
$5.00 to $5.50	$0.25
$5.50 to $6.00	0.50
$6.00 to $6.50	0.75
Above $6.50	1.00
Above $7.50	1.25
Above $8.00	1.75

The operators are hopeful that lead prices will permit the maintenance of the proposed scale at least until living costs have been reduced or the price of lead substantially raised. If it were not for the high silver price it is safe to say every mine in the district would now be closed. The disquieting part of the present position is the lack of a market for lead. It is perhaps not known generally that there is piled up in the yards at the Bunker Hill, at Kellogg, smelter more than 5000 tons of lead bullion. This has accumulated since November 11, and is sufficient to supply all demands on the Bunker Hill smelter, as they are at present, for the next four or five months. It is generally believed that the proposed cut will be accepted without protest.

KANSAS

Pittsburg.—The Newkirk Smelter Co. is to remove the 8-block, 16-furnace zinc plant of the Pittsburg Zinc Co. to Newkirk, Oklahoma. Instead of coal, gas will be used as fuel.

MISSOURI

Duenweg.—The Coahuila Lead & Zinc Co. has closed its No. 3 mine at Porto Rico. The reasons for this are low prices for zinc ore and excessive water, due to adjoining mines being closed. From 1909 to 1916, the company operated a 900-ton mill (24 hours), after which the new 1400-ton mill was started. In 10 years, 2,040,031 tons of ore was hoisted, 362,506 tons being in 1917. C. S. Smith designed the new plant, which recovered 79%. Total costs were from

$1.16 to $1.25 per ton during the past three years. D. D. Dunkin was in charge recently.

Joplin.—Production of the Tri-State region last week was as under:

State	Blende, tons	Calamine, tons	Lead, tons	Value
Kansas	1350		180	$60,453
Missouri	1057	108	263	60,081
Oklahoma	6293		1002	330,809
Total	8700	108	1445	$450,[illegible]
Average price	$42	$25	$92	

MONTANA

Butte.—The Butte & Superior company produced 4,175,000 lb. of zinc and 78,000 oz. of silver during February. This is only one-third of the same month of last year.

The Tuolumne Copper Mining Co. held its annual meeting here last week. In spite of spending $66,086 on development, and $34,174 on repairs, etc., there was a net balance of $26,843 at the end of 1918. New openings amounted to 6543 ft. The Main Range mine yielded 25,405 tons assaying 2.253% copper, 8.082 oz. silver, and 0.0075 oz. gold. Net smelter returns were $248,221, equal to $10.54 per ton. The Spread Delight vein at 700 and 800 ft. produced this ore. At 800 ft. the shoots are over 500 ft. long, and are from 5 to 35 ft. wide. Until the Main Range has been opened to 1200 ft., and connection made with the Colusa-Leonard, no further work will be done in the latter mine. Production of the Main Range in January, 1919, was 6682 tons, averaging 3.057% copper, 10.235 oz. silver, and 0.01 oz. gold, giving a profit of $17,227; and in February, 2840 tons of 2.18%, 7.03 oz., and 0.0075 oz., and $7684 profit. Paul P. Gow is general manager, H. M. Fay, assistant, and M. Little superintendent.

ELECTRIC TRACTION UNDERGROUND AT BUTTE

Troy.—The Snowstorm Mines Consolidated is treating 6000 tons of ore monthly. The No. 7 tunnel is in over 1500 ft., with 950 ft. to go.

NEVADA

Goldfield.—The Goldfield Development Co. contemplates treating a large quantity of ore from Combination hill. A drift on the 380-ft. level of this mine is to be extended, preparing a block of ground 40 by 1000 ft. to that depth. Over 1000 samples from this area give an average of $5.60 per ton, and milling 1000 tons daily total costs would be $2.50 per ton. The caving system of mining is suggested.

Hilltop.—Three horse-teams are hauling ore from the Kimberly Consolidated mine to Battle Mountain. The mine is 19 miles from rail. It is reported that the company is to build a flotation plant at an early date, also add more mine equipment. Machine-drills were recently installed. The property produces silver-lead and copper ores.

Mina.—Twenty-two miles east of this place is the Simon lead mine, which, under O. E. Schiffner of Tonopah, is said to be developing into a large producer. Machinery includes a 25-hp. Fairbanks-Morse gasoline hoist, and 3-drill Sullivan compressor. The shaft is 300 ft. deep, and is to be sunk further. At 230 ft. is 35 ft. of $25 lead-zinc ore, while at 300 ft. there is similar ore.

Pioche.—The Prince Consolidated Mining & Smelting Co. in 1918 made an operating profit of $78,969, according to the general manager, M. C. Godbe. There was sold 84,137 tons of iron and siliclous ores and concentrates. General results were good. The Prince orebody was proved for over 575 ft. farther to the south than before. Better grade shoots were developed. While the Bullionville mill will not recover what was expected, it can be operated profitably, and when the ore available has passed through, there will be in one pit 100,000 tons of tailing for cyanidation, assaying 8 oz. silver, $1.80 gold, and 3% lead. Two new diamond-drill holes from No. 6 level have cut ore; one passing through 10 ft. of iron-manganese, assaying 25 oz. silver and $3.60 gold; the other 11 ft. of clean sulphide carrying 30% zinc. The mine was examined by F. J. Pack of the University of Utah.

Tonopah.—Net earnings of the Tonopah Mining Co. in 1918 were $782,000, against $825,000 in 1917. Dividends were $375,000, a decrease of $225,000.

TEXAS

Austin.—The 'blue sky' law introduced by Senator Dorrough is not likely to pass the House at this session, although it passed the Senate two weeks ago. Oil interests are said to oppose the measure.

Burkburnett.—Since August last, when the Fowler oil-well was brought-in, this town has grown from 200 to over 15,000 people. A veritable oil-boom is raging here and at Ranger. The first well is only 1700 ft. deep. There are now over 100 producing wells, each said to be yielding 1000 barrels.

UTAH

Alta.—The Wasatch Mines Co.'s tunnel is in 3650 ft., and is being advanced 200 ft. per month. The face is 700 ft. from the Howland ore in the Columbus property. The opening is 7 by 9 ft., and will eventually be the most convenient outlet for the Columbus-Rexall, Emma Consolidated, Sells, Michigan-Utah, South Hecla, and Cardiff properties, such as are in Big Cottonwood, having only a short distance to go to reach the Wasatch tunnel outlet.

Park City.—This district produced 9770 tons of ore in

February, compared with 10,632 tons in January, a longer month. The Silver King Coalition and Ontario Silver produced 2677 tons each, followed closely by the Judge with 2608 tons.

Tintic.—This district produced about 2600 tons of ore during February, which is below the average for January.

WASHINGTON

Chewelah.—The United Copper Mining Co., according to Conrad Wolfle, will not increase its capital as proposed. Developments are very encouraging, and 15 machines are working two shifts. The winze is down 67 ft. below the 1300-ft. level, showing 5 ft. of ore, 2 ft. of which assays 16% copper and 200 oz. silver per ton, the remainder 5% and 20 oz. Emanuel Wolde is assistant manager, Thomas Ferguson, mine superintendent; B. E. Bell, mill superintendent; and P. A. Brady, engineer and assayer.

Olympia.—By a vote of seven to five, the Rules Committee of the House of Representatives on March 5 refused to place the Fawley 'blue sky' bill upon the calendar, thus killing it for this session.

CANADA

British Columbia

Alamo.—The Lucky Jim company is to send 2000 tons of zinc ore to the mill built by Clarence Cunningham for concentrating tests. Another lot will be sent to the General Engineering Co. at Salt Lake City for experiments with the Callow process.

Anyox.—Announcement is made that the employees, 1200 men, of the Granby Consolidated have decided, after deliberating for six days over the company's proposal to return to the sliding-scale of pay, with certain other concessions, to reject such an arrangement for the continuance of the work at the smelter. The vote showed a majority of only 19 in favor of refusing the terms offered. As a result the plant has been shut-down, and the men are losing $7500 daily. There has been no trouble here, and it is hoped that in a few weeks, perhaps by the time the damage caused by the recent fire (damages $50,000) are repaired, an amicable settlement will have been reached.

Grand Forks.—The Granby Consolidated has blown-in another furnace, making three in blast. Wages have been reduced 25 cents per shift, yet they are 50 cents higher than the pre-war rate.

Kaslo.—The Utica Mines company, in charge of W. F. Caldwell, has taken over the Bell and Sunset claims.

Lillooet.—The discovery of copper deposits at the head of Gun creek on Copper mountain in the Mackinnon range is reported, and it is stated that the area has been examined by Charles Camsell, of the Dominion Geological Survey, and who will publish a report shortly. He visited the region last summer, and is said to have formed a favorable opinion.

Nelson.—The Mountain Chief mine has been acquired by a syndicate headed by J. W. Evans. On the reported purchase price of $150,000, a payment of $15,000 has been made.

Sandon.—On No. 10 level of the Silversmith mine there is lead-zinc ore for a length of 325 ft. Crude ore being shipped assays 40% lead and 90 oz. silver per ton.

Trail.—The assistant general manager of the Consolidated M. & S. Co., S. G. Blaylock, in a recent statement asserts that there has been no change in the wage-scale at the Trail smelter since June 1, 1918.

Ontario

Cobalt.—The Mining Corporation pays a dividend of 12½%, equal to $207,455, on March 31. This brings the total to $6,113,400.

The McKinley-Darragh-Savage company's profit in 1918 was $295,662. Dividends absorbed $269,723. The tailing mill (flotation) is to resume work in the spring.

Kirkland Lake.—The new 30-ton mill at the Burnside is in operation. It is proposed to amalgamate this property with that of the Tough-Oakes and Sylvanite.

The Ontario-Kirkland is sinking its shaft 4 ft. daily, the present depth being below 150 feet.

Porcupine.—The Dome Extension property is to be sold to the Dome Mines company for 76,667 shares of the latter.

The Schumacher company is preparing to unwater its mine, which is 700 ft. deep. The 180-ton mill is ready to resume ore treatment.

KOREA

Seoul.—During the past year the Seoul Mining Co. treated 201,151 tons of ore, yielding gold worth 2,892,385 yen, or about $1,446,000.

Unsan.—The Oriental Consolidated cleaned-up gold worth $102,000 in January. In November, 160 stamps crushed 21,326 tons, with the cyanide plants recovering $129,155 of gold. Operating costs, $67,546, and improvements, $75,725, left a deficit of $14,117. In December, 22,181 tons yielded $124,350. While the mills were operating at full capacity, there was a shortage of 350 men underground. Progress on the new power project is good. The February output was $88,000.

MEXICO

Hidalgo

Pachuca.—Santa Gertrudis in January treated 30,970 tons of ore, making a profit of ₱24,720 ($117,000).

Jalisco

Guadalajara.—The Chamber of Mines of Guadalajara has been formed here to assist the development of mining and allied industries in Mexico. The president is Othon Camarena; vice-president, Manuel F. Chavez; and secretary-treasurer, W. J. Pentland. The mining companies in the Chamber are as follows: Amajac Mines Co., Amparo Mining Co., Cinco Minas Co., Castellana Mining Co., Cia. Minera de la Española, Cobre Grande Mining Co., El Carmen y Anexas, El Favor Mining Co., E. R. Downs, Magistral Mining Co., Mezquital Mining Co., Mexican Mines Co., and Navidad Development Company.

Mexico

Mexico City.—According to a dispatch from Washington, D. C., on March 5, mine operators of four Mexican States have united in a request to the Secretary of Commerce, Industry, and Labor of the Mexican cabinet that a general mining congress be called to meet at an early date in Mexico City for discussion of all questions relating to the industry. Official dispatches state that the question of high explosives was one of the chief problems of Mexican operators. National and international restrictions were said to operate so as to prevent securing a sufficient supply.

The National Association for Protection of American Rights in Mexico, with head offices at New York, and backed by influential mining and oil companies, has issued a call for members, saying the well-being of the Mexican people themselves as well as lives and property of foreigners are to be protected from chaotic conditions prevailing. "We wish to emphasize the fact that it is the desire of this Association," the circular states, "not to embarrass our government and not to bring it into conflict with the Mexican government; but its chief aim will be to work with both governments upon a friendly and helpful basis. If such a program can be carried out, the organization can be of great service in assisting to remove causes of friction between the United States and Mexico."

Sonora

Cumpas.—Closing of copper mines and the long drouth has resulted in much depression in this district, 150 miles south of Douglas, Arizona.

Nacozari.—Conditions are practically normal and miners are plentiful in northern Sonora, says J. S. Williams, Jr., general manager for the Moctezuma Copper Co., in a recent communication to Sill & Sill of Los Angeles, according to the Bulletin of the Chamber of Mines and Oil. Mr. Williams gave an interesting analysis of taxation in Sonora, covering State, Federal, and municipal taxes, as follows:

State—2% on the value of all ores, concentrates, and metals exported. Valuation of gold is fixed at ₱1333.33 per kilogramme; valuation of silver is governed by current prices of metals in New York. Thus, the tax for January 1919 would be as follows: gold, 2% on ₱1333.33; silver, 2% on ₱65.025; ₱5 per ₱1000 per annum on value of plant buildings, machinery, and stocks of supplies carried.

Mercantile business is taxed ₱8 per ₱1000 per annum on the value of merchandise stocks carried in stores, plus 60% contribution to the Federal government; 2% on all sales of merchandise, both wholesale and retail, plus 60% contribution to the Federal government.

Federal taxes on mining claims—Pertenencias, with the annual tax on each division, as follows: 1 to 5, ₱6; 6 to 50, ₱9; 51 to 100, ₱12; and 100 or more, ₱18. The tax is payable each third of the year, or every four months, in advance. The progressive rates are applicable provided that the pertenencias belong to a single owner and are in the same mining district.

Eight per cent on the value of the gold and silver when these are exported in the form of mineral rock or earth, concentrates, cyanides, sulphurets, smelter residue, or in any other form in which they are found combined or mixed with substances which are not metals, properly speaking. Seven per cent on the value of the gold and silver exported, these having been treated in the country up to the point where they are not alloyed or mixed, except with other metals and whatever be the assay-value of the product. For the collection of the tax on ores exported, pure gold shall always be considered at the rate of ₱1333.33 per kilogramme, and for silver and other ores the Department of Hacienda shall issue each month a tariff to govern in the following month, taking as a basis the current prices of the metals, metallurgical products or natural ores in New York, and in accordance with the special circumstances of each case. Thus, the tax for January 1919 would be as follows: gold in ores or concentrates, ₱106.67 per kilogramme; in bars (treated in the country), ₱93.33; silver, in ores or concentrates, ₱5.205; in bars (treated in the country), ₱4.561.

Exporters of mixed bars of any assay-value in gold and ores or concentrates of any class, when these contain an assay-value in gold greater than two grammes per ton, shall re-import into the country precisely in coinable gold bars or in Mexican or foreign gold coins an amount equal to that of the gold contained in the bars and products exported.

Exporters of refined or mixed silver and of ores or concentrates of any class when these contain an assay-value of silver greater than 250 grammes per ton, must re-import into the country precisely in coinable gold bars or in Mexican or foreign gold coins, a percentage which periodically and in each case shall be fixed by the Department of Hacienda on the value of the silver contained in the bars, minerals, or concentrates extracted.

The assay-tax is fixed at ₱3 for each lot of 20,000 kg. of ores and concentrates exported.

All receipts given must be stamped as follows: Up to ₱40, 5 centavos; ₱40 to ₱100, 10 c.; and over ₱100, 5c. for each ₱40 or fraction. Stamps must be affixed on all pay-rolls where earnings of salaried men appear, wages of day laborers excepted. The rate is the same as for receipts.

Municipal—Stores from which sales of merchandise or supplies are made pay the following tax: 1st class, ₱100 to ₱800 per month; 2nd class, ₱30 to ₱95; and 3rd class, ₱5 to ₱25. On the above tax, the Federal contribution is 60%.

Note The Editor invites members of the profession to send particulars of their work and appointments. The information is interesting to our readers.

Myron A. Folsom is in the Ranger oilfield of Texas.

H. B. Lowden, of the Colorado Iron Works, was in San Francisco last week.

C. Yen, recently in Michigan and New Mexico, sailed on March 15 for Shanghai.

F. L. Firebaugh, Lieutenant in the A. E. F., has returned to Berkeley from France.

Oscar V. White has resumed his former position as superintendent of the Silver Smith mine, Slocan, B. C.

Wilbert V. Certon has opened an office of information on mines in Central America at Tegucigalpa, Honduras.

Frank Merricks passed through San Francisco on his way from London to China, sailing from here on March 15.

John Linn, of Oakland, has been appointed general superintendent of the Empire copper mine, at Mackay, Idaho.

G. W. Eade has taken the position of chief electrician for the Wolverine and Mohawk mines, succeeding Joseph Mette.

S. K. Dahl, mill superintendent for the Messina Development Co., in the Transvaal, was here and has gone to New York.

C. W. Beauchamp is still with the 28th Engineers, now at St. Maurice in the St. Mihiel sector of the former French front.

Clark G. Mitchell, managing director of the Isabella Mines Co. at Cripple Creek, has resigned. Frank Gunn continues as superintendent.

Charles Camsell, head of the Geological Survey in British Columbia, has gone to Ottawa to arrange for field work for the coming season.

Alan M. Bateman, professor of the Department of Economic Geology, Yale University, has become editor of the 'Journal of Economic Geology'.

R. G. Wayland, formerly general superintendent at the Alaska Treadwell, has been appointed chief engineer to the Homestake Mining Co. in South Dakota.

George R. Tingle, formerly mill superintendent for the Syndicate Mining Co., at Aroroy, Masbate, Philippine Islands, passed through San Francisco this week.

Ernest W. Ellis, Lieutenant in the field artillery of the 13th division, has accepted a position in the experimental metallurgical plant at the Bunker Hill & Sullivan mill.

Donald C. Smith has resigned as metallurgist for the Penn Mining Co. and has accepted a similar position with the Afterthought Copper Co., at Ingot, California.

Herbert C. Enos, formerly manager for the Cia. Minera y Fundidora Internacional, at Matehuala, Mexico, will engage in consulting work with headquarters at San Luis Potosi.

Henry H. Armstead has received his discharge from the Corps of Engineers and has been re-commissioned for five years as Major in the Engineers Reserve Corps. He has returned to Talache, Idaho, to take up again the active direction of the Armstead Mines, Inc., and will also give personal attention to the Utica Mines at Kaslo, British Columbia.

Philip N. Moore, past president of the A. I. M. E., has been appointed by the Secretary of the Interior to serve on the commission to adjust claims growing out of governmental efforts to stimulate production of war minerals. The other members of the commission are J. F. Shafroth, formerly Senator from Colorado, and M. D. Foster, ex-member of Congress from Illinois.

The American Electrochemical Society holds its annual meeting at New York on April 3 to 5.

METAL PRICES

San Francisco, March 18

Aluminum-dust, large and small lots, cents per lb	65—70
Antimony, cents per pound	8.00
Copper, electrolytic, cents per pound, in carload lots	15.00
Lead, pig, cents per pound	5.50— 6.50
Platinum, per ounce	$100
Quicksilver, per flask of 75 lb	$68
Spelter, cents per pound	8.00
Zinc-dust, cents per pound	12.50

EASTERN METAL MARKET

(By wire from New York)

March 18.—Copper is quiet and steady. Lead is inactive but firm. Spelter is dull and unchanged.

SILVER

Below are given official (not Government) quotations, in cents per ounce, of silver 999 fine. In order to make prompt settlements with smelters and brokers, producers allow a discount from the maximum fixed price of $1.01½, hence the lower price. The Government has not fixed the general market price at $1, but will pay this price(as from April 23, 1918) for all silver purchased by it. The equivalent of dollar silver (1000 fine) in British currency is 46.65 pence per ounce (925 fine), calculated at the current rate of exchange. On August 15, 1918, the Treasury announced that the maximum price was fixed at $1.01½ per ounce. The British government fixed its maximum at 49½ pence, on September 2, but on November 12 this was changed to 48¾, on December 13 to 48 7/16, and in February to 47¾ pence.

Date		New York cents	London pence	Average week ending		
Mch.	12	101.12	47.75	Feb.	4	101.12
"	13	101.12	47.75	"	11	101.12
"	14	101.12	47.75	"	18	101.12
"	15	101.12	47.75	"	25	101.12
"	16 Sunday			Mch.	4	101.12
"	17	101.12	47.75	"	11	101.12
"	18	101.12	47.75	"	18	101.12

Monthly averages

	1917	1918	1919		1917	1918	1919
Jan.	75.14	88.72	101.12	July	78.92	99.62	....
Feb.	77.54	85.79	101.12	Aug.	85.40	100.31	....
Mch.	74.13	88.11	....	Sept.	100.73	101.12	....
Apr.	72.51	95.35	....	Oct.	87.38	101.12	....
May	74.61	99.50	....	Nov.	85.97	101.12	....
June	76.44	99.50	....	Dec.	85.97	101.12	....

The conclusion arrived at by the 'Metal World' of London is that a big trade in silver will be done as soon as the markets are free from control, and while high prices may stimulate production, this will not be sufficient to hold the market down for a long time to come.

The silver market in London remains steady, according to Samuel Montagu & Co. The Shanghai exchange has receded to 4s.7½d. ($1.11). Doubtless the easier tendency is owing to the completion of an arrangement by which China will receive a substantial amount of silver from America. The Indian Currency report for 1917-'18 has the following: "The rupee coinage of the year was 2312 lacs (1 lac. = $32,000) and purchases of silver for this coinage amounted to 83,750,000 oz. These were supplemented by local purchases in Bombay and Calcutta of 3,500,000 oz. There were purchased in America 40,000,000, in China 28,000,000, and in Australia 5,000,000 oz., while 1,750,000 oz was obtained from the Bawdwin mines (in Burma). The balance was shipped from London."

COPPER

Prices of electrolytic in New York, in cents per pound.

Date			Average week ending		
Mch.	12	15.00	Feb	4	19.21
"	13	14.87	"	11	18.33
"	14	14.75	"	18	17.50
"	15	14.50	"	25	16.40
"	16 Sunday		Mch	4	15.25
"	17	14.75	"	11	14.83
"	18	14.87	"	18	14.79

Monthly averages

	1917	1918	1919		1917	1918	1919
Jan.	29.53	23.50	20.43	July	29.07	26.00	....
Feb.	34.57	23.50	17.34	Aug.	27.42	26.00	....
Mch.	36.00	23.50	....	Sept.	25.11	26.00	....
Apr.	33.16	23.50	....	Oct.	23.50	26.00	....
May	31.69	23.50	....	Nov.	23.50	26.00	....
June	32.57	23.50	....	Dec.	23.50	26.00	....

Copper production of the large mines in February was as under:

Name	Pounds	Name	Pounds
Anaconda	12,400,000	Miami	4,462,578
Arizona	3,300,000	Nevada Consolidated	4,150,000
Calumet & Arizona	5,028,000	New Cornelia	2,872,000
Calumet & Hecla and subsidiaries	10,263,868	Ohio	395,150
Cerro de Pasco	4,586,000	Phelps Dodge (Copper Queen, Detroit, Burro Mountain, Moctezuma)	9,185,000
Chino	3,552,000	Ray	4,150,000
East Butte	633,560	Shattuck	370,166
Greene-Cananea	3,000,000	Utah	10,335,000
Inspiration	6,000,000		
Kennecott (and Braden)	5,292,000		

According to S. R. Guggenheim and others just returned from Europe, it will be a long time before a large foreign outlet can be expected for American copper. Further curtailment of production is hinted at in this country.

According to D. C. Jackling at Salt Lake City recently, nobody can safely predict the immediate future of copper.

LEAD

Lead is quoted in cents per pound, New York delivery.

Date			Average week ending		
Mch.	12	5.25	Feb.	4	5.32
"	13	5.25	"	11	5.02
"	14	5.25	"	18	5.00
"	15	5.25	"	25	5.05
"	16 Sunday		Mch.	4	5.25
"	17	5.25	"	11	5.25
"	18	5.25	"	18	5.25

Monthly averages

	1917	1918	1919		1917	1918	1919
Jan.	7.64	6.85	5.60	July	10.93	8.03	....
Feb.	9.10	7.07	5.13	Aug.	10.75	8.05	....
Mch.	10.07	7.26	....	Sept.	9.07	8.05	....
Arp.	9.38	6.99	....	Oct.	6.97	8.05	....
May	10.29	6.88	....	Nov.	6.38	8.05	....
June	11.74	7.58	....	Dec.	6.49	6.90	....

ZINC

Zinc is quoted as spelter, standard Western brands, New York delivery.

Date			Average week ending		
Mch	12	6.50	Feb.	4	6.83
"	13	6.50	"	11	6.68
"	14	6.50	"	18	6.74
"	15	6.50	"	25	6.69
"	16 Sunday		Mch.	4	6.61
"	17	6.50	"	11	6.55
"	18	6.50	"	18	6.50

Monthly averages

	1917	1918	1919		1917	1918	1919
Jan.	9.75	7.87	7.44	July	8.98	8.72	....
Feb.	10.45	7.97	6.71	Aug.	8.58	8.87	....
Mch.	10.78	7.67	....	Sept.	8.33	9.58	....
Apr.	10.20	7.04	....	Oct.	8.32	9.11	....
May	9.41	7.29	....	Nov.	7.76	8.75	....
June	9.63	7.92	....	Dec.	7.84	8.49	....

QUICKSILVER

The primary market for quicksilver is San Francisco, California being the largest producer. The price is fixed in the open market, according to quantity. Prices, in dollars per flask of 75 pounds:

Date					
Feb.	18	90.00	Mch.	4	85.00
"	25	85.00	"	11	75.00
			"	18	68.00

Monthly averages

	1917	1918	1919		1917	1918	1919
Jan.	81.00	128.06	103.75	July	102.00	120.00	....
Feb.	126.25	118.00	90.00	Aug.	115.00	120.00	....
Mch.	113.75	112.00	....	Sept.	112.00	120.00	....
Apr.	114.50	115.00	....	Oct.	102.00	120.00	....
May	104.00	110.00	....	Nov.	102.50	120.00	....
June	85.50	112.00	....	Dec.	117.42	115.00	....

TIN

Prices in New York, in cents per pound. The monthly averages in 1918 are nominal. On December 3 the War Industries Board fixed the price to consumers and jobbers at 72½c. f.o.b. Chicago and Eastern points, and 71¼c. on the Pacific Coast. This will continue until the U. S. Steel Products Co.'s stock is consumed.

Monthly averages

	1917	1918	1919		1917	1918	1919
Jan.	44.10	85.13	71.50	July	62.60	93.00	....
Feb.	51.47	85.00	72.44	Aug.	62.53	91.33	....
Mch.	54.27	85.00	....	Sept.	61.54	80.40	....
Apr.	55.63	88.53	....	Oct.	62.24	78.82	....
May	63.21	100.01	....	Nov.	74.18	73.67	....
June	61.93	91.00	....	Dec.	85.00	71.52	....

ORES (New York)

Manganese. It is stated that Indian ore has been offered as low as 45c. per unit, the ore to be shipped in ballast, thus reducing freight charges.

Manganese-iron Alloys. Ferro is selling only in small lots at $150 delivered, mostly re-sale material. Producers quote $200 for 80% alloy with $3 per unit deducted for each per cent under 78%. Spiegel is nominal at $40 to $45 delivered, with no demand. The output of ferro in February was 21,796 tons, compared with 21,331 tons in January, much in excess of needs and of the earlier expectations in the trade. The February production of spiegel was only 6309 tons, against 11,456 tons in January and much higher average per month in 1918.

Molybdenum. The market is devoid of demand and nominal at about 85c. per lb. of MoS_2 in 90% concentrates.

Tungsten. Inquiries are few, and the market is very inactive with practically no test of prices. As low as $9 to $10 per unit is heard of for certain grades, but there is no buying. In the meantime stocks are being consumed and the position is improving to this extent only. No one seems to know what ferro-tungsten could be bought for—certainly at a little less than $1.50 per lb. of contained tungsten.

Eastern Metal Market

New York, March 12.

The markets are all quiet, but the general tone is better, with prices of most metals firm.

Antimony is inactive.

Copper sold at lower levels last week, but it has again advanced and inquiry is better.

Lead is quiet but firm.

Tin is at a standstill, being still under control.

Zinc demand is still light, and the price tendency is lower.

COPPER

After a further recession in prices on small sales to as low as 14.50c. per lb. for electrolytic copper in the last week, the market has turned stronger and is now back to 15c., New York, for early delivery. It is stated that a considerable buying movement, small as compared with normal times but large as judged by recent events, appeared last week, and one producer stated to the writer of this letter tha he has sold copper every day this month at not less than 15c. The feeling is general that a turn has come, but some sellers doubt the endurance of it, one stating that he expects lower prices again. The situation as a whole, however, is brighter than in some weeks. The basis for improvement is not tangible, however. There is little export demand, nor is domestic demand broad. Lake copper is nominal at about 15.75c., New York. It is the understanding that the arrangement reported last week, whereby the producers will sell the Government stocks of copper, has been ratified by the Federal authorities. British stocks of copper on March 1 were 51,379 tons, against 27,530 tons on December 1, 1918.

LEAD

The market has lost its recent activity, and is now quiet but firm. The quotation of the American Smelting & Refining Co. is unchanged at 5.25c., New York, or 5c., St. Louis, with that of the outside market a little easier at 5.30c., New York. The general situation is unchanged, and fundamental conditions are sound. Buyers' wants have been temporarily satisfied. Stocks of lead in Great Britain on March 1 are officially reported as 100,063 tons, compared with 49,111 tons on December 1, 1918.

TIN

The market continues at a standstill, and there is little of interest. Governmental control continues, with Straits tin available at nothing lower than the fixed price of 72.50c., New York. Imports continue prohibited, and there is no free market except in quantities of 5 tons or less. The rumor mentioned last week developed into a certainty in that an attempt was made to increase the price of American tin so as to lessen the competition with the allocated. While this was in progress there was a fair demand for tin, but this has died out. American 99% metal is available at about 68c. per lb., New York. There has been some buying of future tin for shipment to England to be held there until American import restrictions are removed, but it is estimated that this has not exceeded 200 to 250 tons. The tin has probably been bought at from 46 to 54c. per lb. It is calculated that 6000 tons of the 10,000 tons of allocated metal has been disposed of, and that it will be at least two months before the rest is taken up and a free market results. Arrivals thus far in March have been 850 tons, all at Pacific ports. The London market is higher at £243 per ton for spot Straits on March 10.

ZINC

There is no life to the market, and demand continues insignificant. It is hardly enough to establish quotations which have receded slightly in the past week. They are largely nominal at 6.15c., St. Louis, or 6.[illegible]c., New York, for prime Western for early delivery. Consumers are still showing no disposition to buy, and producers are not forcing the market. It is understood that sales last week were made as low as 6.12½c., St. Louis, but that at this level a speculative movement appeared causing the market to grow firm. This has, however, died out.

TEXT OF MINERALS RELIEF BILL

The War Minerals Relief Measure, referring to producers of chrome, manganese, pyrite, and tungsten, is known as Section 5 of the Dent-Chamberlain War Contract Validating Bill, and became law on March 3, 1919. The State Mineralogist, Fletcher Hamilton, desires to call the attention of the Californian mining public to this law, a summary of which follows:

"Sec. 5. That the Secretary of the Interior be, and he hereby is, authorized to adjust, liquidate, and pay such net losses as have been suffered by any person, firm, or corporation by reason of producing or preparing to produce, either manganese, chrome, pyrites, or tungsten in compliance with the request or demand of the Department of the Interior, the War Industries Board, the War Trade Board, the Shipping Board, or the Emergency Fleet Corporation to supply the urgent needs of the Nation in the prosecution of the War. . . .

The said Secretary shall make such adjustments and payments in each case as he shall determine to be just and equitable; that the decision of said Secretary shall be conclusive and final, subject to the limitations hereinafter provided, . . . and provided further that said Secretary shall consider, approve, and dispose of only such claims as shall be made hereunder and filed with the Department of the Interior within three months from and after the approval of this act; and provided further, that no claims shall be paid unless it shall appear to the satisfaction of said Secretary that moneys were invested or obligations were incurred subsequent to April 6, 1917, and prior to November 12, 1918, in a legitimate attempt to produce either manganese, chrome, pyrites, or tungsten for the needs of the Nation for the prosecution of the War, and that no profits of any kind shall be included in the allowance of any claims, and that no investment for merely speculative purposes shall be recognized in any manner by said Secretary; and provided further, that the settlement of any claim arising under the provisions of this section shall not bar the United States Government through any of its duly authorized agencies, or any committee of Congress hereafter duly appointed, from the right of review of such settlement, nor the right to recover any money paid by the Government to any party under and by virtue of the provisions of this section, if the Government has been defrauded, and the right of recovery in all such cases shall extend to the executors, administrators, heirs, and assigns of any party. . . .

That nothing in this section shall be construed to confer jurisdiction upon any court to entertain a suit against the United States; provided further, that in determining the net losses of any claimant the Secretary of the Interior shall, among other things, take into consideration and charge to the claimant the then market value of any ores or minerals on hand belonging to the claimant, and also the salvage or usable value of any machinery or other appliances which may be claimed was purchased to equip said mine for the purpose of complying with the request or demand of the agencies of the Government above mentioned in the manner aforesaid."

Claims must be filed with the Secretary of Interior, before June 3, 1919.

Mining Decisions

Mining Claim—Innocent Purchaser

Persons who purchased a mining claim in good faith and for valuable consideration are not responsible for an accounting to one who had rights as against the former owner and vendor under a grubstake agreement.

Kimball v. Superior Court (California), 177 Pacific, 488. December 23, 1918.

Possessory Actions to Recover Mining Claims—Rule

In possessory actions to recover unpatented mining claims, the rule that usually prevails in ejectment cases, that plaintiff must recover on strength of his own title and not on the weakness of his adversaries', does not apply. In such actions the better title prevails.

Oroville International Salt Co. v. Rayburn (Washington), 176 Pacific, 14. November 13, 1918.

Extra-Lateral Right—Narrow and Undulating Veins

A miner in following his vein extra-laterally is not limited in his operations to the exact area within the walls of the vein where the same narrows down to a width which would make working impracticable, or to the exact course of the vein where the same is undulating in its course and economical mining requires straight drifts. Congress, in granting to the locator the exclusive right of possession and enjoyment of all veins, lodes, and ledges throughout their entire depth, did not exclude narrow or undulating veins, and the word 'enjoyment' must be given such a construction as will make the grant effective, even if it involves widening of the drift beyond the vein-walls to make mining of the vein possible. The surface owner of the claims beneath which such extra-lateral rights of adjoining claims extend holds his title subject to this right of the adjoining claim-owners.

Twenty-One Mining Co. v. Original Sixteen to One Mine, Inc. (California), U. S. Circuit Court of Appeals Decision dated February 3, 1919. Not yet reported.

Improvements on Claim—Pass to Re-locator

When the locator of a mill-site ceases, by reason of abandonment or forfeiture due to non-performance of assessment work, to be the owner of the vein or lode, the right to the associated mill-site is ended also. A re-locator of the claims, after such a forfeiture, obtains the right to possession and use of any buildings or improvements which had been so affixed to the land by the original locator as to become a part of it. The original locator has no time after forfeiture within which he may lawfully remove such fixtures. Consequently he cannot enjoin the re-locator from disposing of them as he sees fit. The estate acquired by a perfected mining location (or re-location) has the attributes of a fee-title so long as the requirements of law with reference to continued development are satisfied.

Watterson v. Cruse (California), 176 Pacific, 870. December 7, 1918.

Excess Claim—Adverse Location Thereon

Where public mineral land is open to location at the time a claim is initiated, the location is valid, though the land is excess ground within staked boundaries of another excessive claim, and though the persons initiating the new location had knowledge thereof. Every competent locator has the right to initiate a lawful claim to unoccupied public land by a peaceable adverse entry upon it while it is in the posession of those who have no superior right to acquire title or hold possession. Generally, where a claim is excessive in length, the claim is valid if the error is innocently made, but the excess is void.

Nelson v. Smith (Nevada), 176 Pacific, 261. December 4, 1918.

Company Reports

ARIZONA COPPER CO.

Property: mines, mills, and smelter at Clifton and Morenci, Arizona.

Operating Official: Norman Carmichael, general manager.

Financial Statement: during the year ended September 30, 1918, sales of copper realized £2,085,112 ($10,008,000). Operations, etc., cost £1,573,445 ($7,540,000). After paying dividends, interest on debentures, etc., the balance carried forward was £60,121, against £13,738 from 1917.

Dividends: preferred shareholders received £2374, and preferred stockholders £22,157; and ordinary shares £227,984 ($1,094,000).

Development: work was curtailed during the year on account of lack of men, but reserves in the Coronado, King, and Pyramid mines were increased. This is milling ore carrying 2% copper. Ground east of the Coronado adit is being drilled to 700 and 1000 ft. depth, but the only mineral is finely-disseminated primary pyrite of low value. The manganese mine a mile from Clifton was opened by 1311 ft. of work, revealing 48,000 tons of 12% Mn ore. This is too low grade for present methods of treatment.

Production: the 11 mines yielded 41,357 tons of smelting (6.38%) and 1,054,211 tons of concentrating ore (2.338%), a total of 1,095,568 tons.

The mills at Clifton and Morenci gave the following results.

Mill	Tons	Copper %	Oxide %	Recovery %
Clifton	113,257	2.13	0.49	71.25
Morenci	1,049,118	2.36	0.35	71.63

Deister tables replaced old vanners at the Clifton plant, and changes were made in the flotation department. At Morenci, the grinding department was improved. Iron balls replaced pebbles in the mills; 12 Allen cones are used for thickening the mill-feed; 12 Dorr classifiers are in close-circuit with Hardinge mills; 8 more Callow cells and several large Dorr thickeners were added. The old crushing plant has been arranged as a sampling and testing mill of 400 tons capacity. It will be used for experimental work on the low-grade ores developed.

The smelter reduced 216,336 tons, 3 furnaces averaging 390 tons each daily. A number of economical improvements were made. The output of copper was 40,468,000 lb., a decrease of about 2,000,000 lb. when compared with 1917.

TECK-HUGHES GOLD MINES, LTD.

Property: gold mine and mill in the Kirkland Lake district, Ontario.

Operating Official: D. L. H. Forbes, general superintendent.

Financial Statement: the gross income during the year ended August 31, 1918, was $107,280. The deficit on operations was $152,415, including interest and discount on bonds, $48,157. The balance at debit is $407,830.

Development: up to July, when the mine was closed on account of labor shortage and cost of supplies, 2540 ft. of work was done in the period under review. The opening of No. 3 vein on No. 4 and 5 levels was the most important work.

Production: the mill treated 15,879 tons of $7.87 ore. On account of unavoidable dilution of waste rock the grade was lower than cut samples. The output in November was 1826 tons of $8.99 ore.

INFORMATION FURNISHED BY MANUFACTURERS

PRESERVATION OF HOT-WATER SUPPLY-PIPE

By F. N. Speller* and R. G. Knowland

†The principles involved in the corrosion of iron and steel have been so frequently discussed during the last few years and so clearly enunciated by various writers that a further attempt may seem a little unnecessary. That the problem is not yet generally understood, however, is apparent from the tendency of some writers to confuse many of its essential facts. Such a confusion is not warranted in view of our present knowledge of the mechanism of corrosion and of the factors controlling it. There are a few broad simple principles applying to every case of corrosion and these will be briefly discussed with particular reference to hot-water supply systems.

With reference to corrosion it is possible to classify any particular water under one of two types which may be distinguished by the terms 'active' and 'inactive'. The quality of activity is not primarily dependent upon the acid, alkaline, or neutral condition of a water; but rather upon certain dissolved substances, which exert a modifying influence upon the universal tendency of even the purest water to initiate the corrosion process. This inherent tendency of pure water to attack metal may be greatly aided in those cases where dissolved gases exist in the liquid; and under such conditions the term 'active' typifies its corrosive qualities. An inactive water is one that is not able to promote in any marked degree the corrosion of iron. The sharp boundary between the behavior of these two types of water furnishes a sufficient reason for thus distinctively classifying them. It is a simple matter to demonstrate the fact that an inactive water, after a few minutes aeration, becomes capable of great damage to iron. Fig. 1 shows the steps in corrosion.

By keeping hot water under pressure in contact with a large surface of iron for sufficient time it is possible to remove and 'fix' the oxygen. It is this process of fixing the O that renders water practically inactive or non-corrosive. A successful adaptation of this method is shown in Fig. 2 and 3. The deactivator or treating tank, consists of a Gurney coal-fired heater, a treating and storage tank, and a filter as shown by Fig. 2. The tank was built with a 42-in. flanged head, thus permitting easy packing of the Cambridge metal-lath with which the tank was filled in horizontal layers from bottom to top. In circulation, as the arrows indicate, the water passes from the heater up into the deactivating tank, where it makes contact with the sheet-metal at a high temperature. It moves through this slowly as cooling currents or water from the cold supply urge it, and back into the heater or off through the building supply-line.

The hot-water house supply-pipe leaves the tank at the top and passes to the filter, part of its contents being shunted off through a coil in the filter-bed. A constant circulation of hot water in this coil makes it impossible for the filter to reach a temperature notably lower than that in the deactivating tank itself. Through a four-way valve at the top of the filter, the water for circulation in the building system passes into the space above the filter bed and down through

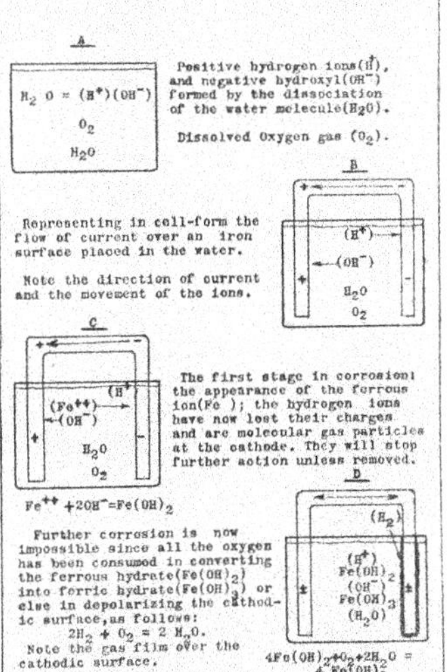

FIG. 1. THE ELECTRO-CHEMICAL MECHANISM OF CORROSION.

the sand into a chamber at the bottom. In this passage, the rust formed in the deactivation of the water is wholly removed. The building supply is withdrawn through the vertical pipe in the centre of the filter, while the gravity return-line entering at the bottom provides for a continuous circulation of water. It is thus apparent that we have three complete and independent systems of circulation: (1) the one between the heater and tank, (2) that between the filter and tank for keeping the former hot, and (3) the building and filter system. This installation was highly successful, whereas previously troubles were many and expensive.

*Metallurgical engineer, National Tube Co., Pittsburgh, Pennsylvania.

†Abstract of paper prepared for the American Society of Heating and Ventilating Engineers, New York.

A notable instance of the successful treatment of hot-water was at the Irene Kaufman Settlement. Pipes were laid on November 22, 1916. On December 24, 1917, the wrought-iron and steel pipe was found to be practically uncorroded; but in duplicate pipes in part of the same hot-water system, unprotected by the deoxidizer, there had been perforation by corrosion. On January 3, 1919—or 2 years

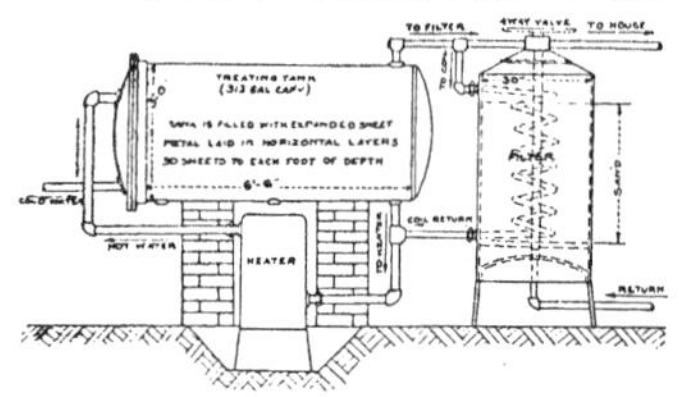

FIG. 2. WATER-HEATER AND DEACTIVATOR FOR BUILDING.

and 42 days service—the pipes in the deactivated hot-water line were again observed, and found to be so good that it was decided to continue the test for at least another year. The pipes showed the same soft black coating as before, but

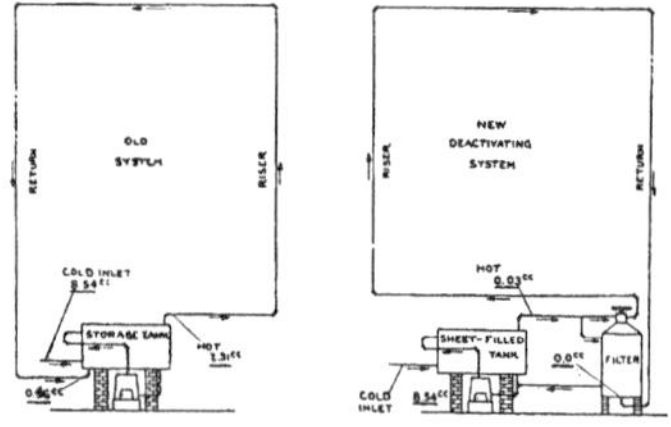

FIG. 3. HOT-WATER SYSTEM IN BUILDINGS SHOWING FREE OXYGEN IN WATER AT VARIOUS POINTS.

there was no evidence of pitting, even where the steel pipe was in contact with a brass union, a condition favorable to rapid corrosion by electrolytic action.

STATUS OF EMPLOYMENT IN UNITED STATES

The U. S. Employment Service has further extended the scope of its work by the establishment of two new zone offices of the professional and special section, in Philadelphia (1518 Walnut street) and Boston (16 Tremont street), and it plans to establish other offices of this section in the near future. The new offices are in addition to the two main offices at New York (16 East 42nd street) and Chicago (62 East Adams street), and will serve the particular zones in which they are.

During the eight weeks ended February 22, the Service received 1,090,124 applications from men and women for jobs. Of this number, 930,029 were referred to opportunities and 679,513 were reported placed in employment. The difference between the number referred to places and the number reported placed is due in a large measure to the failure either of the employee or employer to send in their return cards. Unless these are received, the Service has no record of whether the prospect has received employment or not.

COMMERCIAL PARAGRAPHS

Marine machinery and accessories—steam or gasoline—are described and illustrated in the 104-page catalogue—No. 19—of the **Marine Iron Works** of Chicago.

Walter Fitch, Jr., mining contractor of Eureka, Utah, is sinking two shafts, 16 by 22 ft. and 1200 ft. deep, and driving several thousand feet of tunnels, 7 by 12 ft., for the Susquehanna Collieries Co. in Pennsylvania.

The firm of **Woods, Huddart & Gunn**, 444 Market street, San Francisco, has been incorporated under the new name of Gunn, Carle & Co. Iron and steel products, electric furnaces, cranes, trucks, etc., are supplied, also fluorspar is purchased.

Crucibles, cupels, muffles, and scorifiers, as made by the **Denver Fire Clay Co.**, are the subject of Bulletin 100 of this firm. Capacity, sizes, and prices are given. The company has been manufacturing these clay articles for 40 years. Notes are also appended on laboratory crushers and the Case oil-fired furnace—1, 2, or 3-muffle design. Another bulletin deals with fire-brick, fire-clay, and metallurgical tile.

The Powdered Coal Engineering & Equipment Co. of Chicago announces the following: Capt. A. U. Wetherbee, who recently received his discharge from the Chemical Warfare Branch of the Service, and who was formerly chief engineer and assistant works manager of the Niagara Alkali Co., has accepted a position as chief mechanical engineer, and C. C. Wallace, formerly manager of loading of munitions section of the Stenotype Co., Indianapolis, Indiana, is now director of development and service.

John Herman, well-known assayer and chemist of 514 South Los Angeles street, Los Angeles, has equipped a mill for commercial grinding of both coarse and fine at 55th and Alameda streets. It has a capacity of about 40 tons per day, and orders for the grinding of ores of all kinds are solicited. The Herman screening ball-mill is used. Eventually a complete ore-testing plant will be established, including concentration, oil flotation, amalgamation, and cyanidation. Work on this section of the plant is now under way. Herman's slogan. "I do not guarantee satisfaction—I guarantee accuracy," which has been a feature of his assaying, will be adhered to in this new plant.

C. W. Johnson has been appointed assistant manager of works for the **Westinghouse Electric & Manufacturing Co.** After graduating from the Ohio State University he entered the employ of the Steel Motor Co. of Johnstown. A year later he became associated with the Bullock Electric Co., of Cincinnati, Ohio, and in 1904 was made superintendent of the Allis Chalmers Bullock, Ltd., of Montreal, Canada. In 1907 he entered the employ of the Westinghouse company, later being promoted to general superintendent, in which capacity he has served until his recent appointment. Mr. Johnson is a member of the American Society of Mechanical Engineers, American Institute of Mining Engineers, and Engineers' Society of Western Pennsylvania.

The war-time regulations requiring licenses for the purchase, possession, and use of explosives for reclaiming land, stump blasting, ditching, and other agricultural purposes were revoked on March 15, by the Interior Department. The only qualification is that this revocation does not allow enemy aliens or subjects of a country allied with an enemy of the United States to manufacture, purchase, or sell, use, or possess explosives at any time. This letting-up in the regulations was recommended by Van. H. Manning, Director of the U. S. Bureau of Mines, who has charge of the enforcement of the act, and for the reason that the public safety does not longer require such close regulation. It will be of interest to all farmers and those engaged in reclamation work.

EDITORIAL

ON the way to Vancouver and back the present writer had the pleasure of reading two issues of the 'Oregonian', the paper that has made Portland famous. It was a keen delight to read the editorials in the 'Oregonian' and to note the intelligent handling of the world's news. San Francisco suffers more than it knows from a daily press that is the poorest and meanest in the English language. The Hearst infliction is bad enough, but why have we nothing better?

HIGHER taxes await the citizen. The War Revenue Bill signed by the President immediately after he landed at Boston puts into operation the machinery for collecting $6,000,000,000 of taxes this year. The things affected by this taxation include necessaries as well as luxuries. We need not be appalled by the prospect of paying for a successful war but we must discipline ourselves into habits of thrift. We are an extraordinarily extravagant people, wasteful in ways that shame the democratic ideal.

DIVIDENDS paid by the gold-mining companies of the Rand amounted to £5,330,966 in 1918, as compared with £6,556,188 in 1917 and £8,073,436 in 1914. The yield of distributable profit was the lowest since 1905, in which year the tonnage treated was 11,160,422 and the average yield $9 per ton, as against 24,922,763 tons averaging $6.70 in 1918. In 1918 the Central Rand Methuselah is feeling his age. His friends asserted that he would live forever, disregarding the testimony of the truthful tombstone.

MUCH good will come from such public debates as the one at Boston, on March 19, between Senator Lodge and President Lowell of Harvard. Such debates, if properly reported, serve as a means of educating not only those present but the much larger number that read the proceedings in their morning paper. The two distinguished speakers at Boston performed a public service. We venture to refer to Senator Lodge's objection to allowing "our sons to fight the battles of all the nations of the world." This elicited both applause and dissent. As phrased, it should provoke dissent: but if the Senator meant to appeal to the idea of national detachment from foreign quarrels, he was ignoring the lesson so recently taught by the War in which technically we are still engaged. It is certain that any future European war will again be a general battle of the nations: the world has grown small; if one starts to fight, the others are drawn into the mêlée. Europe and America are too close now to refuse to concern themselves with each other's affairs. If our idea of American isolation had not been taken seriously by Germany, the world would have been saved an untold sacrifice of men and money, of homes and happiness. Whether we like it or not, we have become the neighbors of the European countries and we must take our part now in helping them to arrange their quarrels and in joining them in an effort to prevent another Armageddon, lest we be drawn again into a maelstrom of blood and crime.

RAFAEL NIETTO, the Mexican Minister of Finance, is said to be on his way to Mexico City, after a visit to New York, where he negotiated for a loan from Mr. J. P. Morgan, representing a group of British, French, and American bankers willing to finance Señor Carranza's government on certain conditions, the exact nature of which Señor Nietto will now be able to communicate himself to the President of Mexico. These conditions include evidence of a willingness to pay at least some of the interest due, and over-due, on previous foreign loans incurred by Mexico; also this group of bankers shall control the handling of the new funds to be raised by them, and the Mexican government shall furnish evidence that the country is returning to the normal of peaceful order. It is reported that President Carranza has invited Señor José Ives Limantour to return from France and to resume his former position as Minister of Finance. This is good news, so far as it goes. Evidently Carranza recognizes the fact that he cannot get the money he needs unless he is friendly to the United States and gives assurances that legitimate industry, foreign and domestic, will be protected against brigandage, his own included.

AMERICAN engineers and capital have been particularly successful in their exploitation of gold properties in Korea, or Chosen, as that country is officially styled. We refer especially to the profitable results of the Oriental Consolidated and Seoul mining companies, with which the names of Henry C. Perkins and H. H. Collbran respectively are linked. In this issue will be found an excellent review of the operations of the first named company, by Messrs. H. J. Evans and K. F. Hoefle. We are glad to add that the article was well written, needing little editing, and containing just the essential points worth reading. Since 1896, when operations commenced, the Oriental Consolidated has treated 4.766.270 tons of ore, valued at $29,423,235, from which $7.938,645 was distributed among shareholders as dividends. The mines and mills are scattered over a fairly large concession, necessitating the use of different methods of mining, but costs are fairly uniform. The ore is comparatively low-grade, but its metallurgy is not difficult, and extraction is high. The native labor problem has been solved without serious perplexities, mainly by a close study of the Korean adaptability and industry. In regard to the reported breach between Chosen and Japan, we were told this week by a reliable informant that the Korean is better in every way if under a moderate restraint by others; but perhaps he does not think so himself.

ACCORDING to the law of the Transvaal a mining company has to furnish reasons for ceasing operations, on pain of forfeiting its rights. We note that the Government Mining Engineer, Sir Robert Kotze, has approved of the closing down of the Bantjes mine and has analyzed the conditions justifying such action by the British company controlling the enterprise. Recent development work underground has failed to uncover fresh reserves of ore, that is, of gold-bearing conglomerate sufficiently rich to be exploited profitably. The ore-reserves have been steadily depleted during recent years without the adding of fresh resources adequate to supply the mill, which has a capacity of 360,000 tons per annum. The total cost of operations has risen by reason of the decreased efficiency of labor, from 12.4 to 10.3 tons per month per native laborer; likewise skilled white labor yields only 1.17 fathoms of ore stoped per shift in 1918 as against 1.79 tons in 1916. Recovery in the mill has decreased from 29½ shillings per ton in 1912 to 22¼ shillings in 1917. This is due not only to the declining grade of the ore blocked out, falling from 7.6 to 6 dwt. of gold per ton, but also to the increased admixture of waste-rock. In the nine years to 1914 the company earned a total profit of £202,500, or £22,500 per annum, as against a loss of £30,500 during the succeeding three years. The Government Mining Engineer appears not to state definitely that the lode has become impoverished in depth, but that evidently is the fact.

The Colorado Pitchblende Company

In our issue of December 28 we criticized the prospectus of the Colorado Pitchblende Company, an enterprise organized to exploit fluorspar deposits near Jimtown, in Boulder county, Colorado. These veins of fluorspar have been found to contain pitchblende, an oxide of uranium commonly associated with the occurrence of radium and therefore affording opportunity for embellishing a prospectus with pseudo-scientific statements. The public was told that examinations made by scientific and technical men had "tested and proved the ore," of which there was 20,000,000 tons "worth $85 per ton," thus representing $1,700,000,000, owned by a company capitalized for only $100,000 divided into two million shares, which were offered at $2 apiece. Every $500 of 'investment' would earn $100,000 per annum, it was asserted by the promoters. All of which was deeply interesting, if true. It did not appear true, if experience was a safe guide in such matters. Twenty million tons of ore is a quantity not easily "tested and proved." It is not usual to sell for $2 anything that will earn $400 per annum. The prospectus provoked objection from the Boulder County Metal Mining Association and the Boulder Commercial Association, which appointed a committee of investigation headed by Mr. R. D. George, State Geologist of Colorado, and Dr. J. B. Ekeley, professor of chemistry in the State University. The committee reported unfavorably, but this did not abate the impetuosity of the promoters, who then insisted upon an unbiased investigation by one or more of Denver's civic organizations, as related by our Colorado correspondent in our issue of January 4. The word 'unbiased' is used advisedly, because the promoters, Mr. J. F. Barnhill and his associates, imputed the criticism of their stock-selling scheme to "the activities of certain enemy aliens and pro-German influences, which have prior to, during, and subsequent to our war with Germany been continuously brought to bear against legitimate enterprises in this country for the benefit of certain corporations and individuals friendly to our enemies." They mentioned the names of several Germans connected with a radium company, but not content with that they impugned the good faith and patriotism of the State Geologist and others connected with the Tungsten Products Company, as also of Mr. S. C. Lind, of the U. S. Bureau of Mines, and of Mr. R. W. Gordon, of the Stearns-Roger Manufacturing Company. Messrs. George, Lind, and Gordon need no certificate of good citizenship from us or anybody else. The attack on them is mentioned as one of the humors of the controversy. To return to our story. When the matter was brought to the attention of the mining fraternity in Denver, it was arranged by the mining bureau of the Civic and Commercial Association to start an independent enquiry. Mr. James M. McClave was selected to make an examination, at the expense of the promoters of the Colorado Pitchblende Company, and they agreed to abide by the report. At the same time the Manufacturers Association of Colorado appointed Mr. M. S. MacCarthy to make a similar and separate investigation, also at the expense of the promoters. Both Messrs. McClave and MacCarthy are mining engineers of good repute in Colorado. To the surprise of the mining bureau of the Civic Association, if not to that of the Manufacturers Association, the reports of these two engineers were much alike and both of them were favorable. Thus the gentlemen whose examinations were expected to check the stock-selling operations of the promoters furnished ammunition for the furtherance of their campaign. However, the mining bureau of the Civic Association was not satisfied with the reports and that may have been the reason why it withheld publication of Mr. McClave's report until the Colorado Pitchblende Company brought suit on February 12 in the District Court and filed a complaint in which charges of conspiracy and German influence were made against the Civic Association. In reply, the secretary of the Association stated that the delay was due to the need for studying and analyzing the report, which would be issued—as it was a few days later—with the results of their further enquiry into the commercial phase of the enterprise. The Association's report is published on another page. It appears to be a reasonable and intelligent analysis of the facts. We are inclined to give it weight because it is signed by two engineers whom we know: Mr. Richard A. Parker, the chairman of the Bureau, scarcely needs an introduction to our readers as an honored member of our profession; Mr. George A. Stahl is manager of the Vindicator mine at Cripple Creek and is known as a man of high character. We may add that this last report, or analysis of the business, was not published by the Manufacturers Association, for a reason not difficult to guess: the desire not to discourage local industry. With such a desire we sympathize, up to a point, namely, until it transgresses right dealing with the public. The whole truth about this affair has not yet been disclosed, but we give the facts as we know them at this time. The original prospectus was open to condemnation on account of its wild statements. We regret that the U. S. Bureau of Mines should have become involved through the opinion given by Dr. C. E. Scholl, who forecasted a profit of $45 per ton on 20,000,000 tons of ore. The promoters made the most of this statement by "a chemist of international reputation." A chemist's appraisal of a mine is usually futile; he has rarely had the experience enabling him either to make a correct diagnosis of an ore deposit or an accurate estimate of the quantity and quality of ore available; to do that a mining engineer is required. As a matter of fact, the exploiting and marketing of fluorspar, the recovery of the pitchblende, and the extraction of the radium are matters outside the ken of common experience; all of them call for careful study and thorough scrutiny, such as has been given to them in the later stages of the affair, but not at its inception, when the local press was filled with glaring promises of sudden wealth. Dr. Scholl is not now with the U. S. Bureau of Mines, but he is described in the prospectus as having been "associated with Dr. Lind at the Government radium plant in Denver." Moreover, Dr. Lind, the acting chief of the Rare Metals division of the U. S. Bureau of Mines, was dragged into the controversy through the fact that the recognition of the pitchblende was made in the laboratory of the Experiment Station of which he is superintendent, and he himself stated that the sample of galena concentrate contained "over 2%" of uranium oxide. Later he discounted the commercial significance of this statement by explaining that the sample represented a concentration in the ratio of at least 1200 : 1—whereat the friends of the promoters called him a bold bad man. After the reports of Messrs. McClave and MacCarthy were published, with their respective estimates of a profit of $11.85 and $9.14 per ton on a 1000 tons daily output, the promoters resumed their solicitation of subscriptions for stock, by means of full-page advertisements, and, using the estimates of the two engineers, announced $3,290,400 as the net potential annual profit. They are justified in doing so, for the responsibility now lies on the shoulders of Messrs. McClave and MacCarthy, more particularly Mr. MacCarthy, who states in his report that he had made "no attempt to show the maximum profits which might be expected from operation, but, on the contrary, the lowest grades of ores have been selected and maximum factors of safety and highest costs applied thereto for the purpose, if possible, of arriving at the minimum profits to be expected under the several conditions of operation and production established." This seems to us to detract from the value of his report. If it is based upon the 'selection' of ore, instead of accurate sampling, it stands upon a dangerous foundation. On what principle was the selection made and who was responsible for the selection? Advertisements appearing more than ten days ago state that the 100-ton mill will be in full operation "within ten days," so that the controversy should be settled decisively ere long by the logic of events. It is claimed that 5000 tons of ore is ready for treatment and that this will "net over $50,000 in 50 days." *Qui vivra, verra.* Meanwhile we commend the action taken by the Civic Association and advise our readers to study the statement they have issued. It is a good example of the way in which such projects should be analyzed.

The Vancouver Convention

The British Columbia Chamber of Mines, co-operating with its friends at Seattle, Portland, and Spokane, organized the International Mining Convention which met at Vancouver on March 17 and 18. It was a most successful affair, more than 600 delegates and representatives attending the meetings; it was well organized, and the program was so arranged as to include subjects interesting to the various types of men present, the prospector and the operator, the promoter and the engineer of mines. From the opening speech of Mr. A. M. Whiteside, the president of the British Columbia Chamber of Mines, to the closing words of Mr. Maurice D. Leehey, the toastmaster at the banquet, there was evident an Anglo-American friendliness that fully justified the title "International." Every reference made by successive speakers to the establishment of good-will between those living on the two sides of the unfortified frontier between Canada and the United States evoked instant applause. In that spirit the proceedings were conducted and with that spirit the delegates dispersed homeward, determined to attend the next similar occasion, which will be in February next year, when Seattle will act as host to this neighborly gathering of mining men. It is expected that Spokane will take its turn the year after, and that henceforward these three north-western mining centres—Vancouver, Seattle, and Spokane—in rotation will summon the mining fraternity in annual conclave. Mr.

William Sloan, the Minister of Mines of British Columbia, welcomed the delegates in an interesting speech full of good sense and sane optimism. He was able to report healthy progress in the mining of the Province, an increase of production, and an expansion of activity. His government had expended $207,523 in assisting mining, more particularly in building 98 miles of roads and 75 miles of trails, besides repairing 437 miles of roads and 420 miles of trails. He made the important statement that there was sufficient iron ore proved in British Columbia to supply a blast-furnace plant capable of yielding 250 to 300 tons of pig-iron per day. This served as a text for an enthusiastic speech delivered at the banquet by Mr. M. J. Carrigan of Seattle, who laid emphasis upon the paramount importance of this statement, as forecasting the establishment of an iron and steel industry on the Pacific Coast, tending aiding every manufacture, most particularly that of ship-building. He recited a long list of iron deposits on the Coast and laid stress on the fact that the hope of an iron and steel industry lies in British Columbia on account of its abundant resources in coking-coal. We expect to hear more concerning this vital matter at an early date. A bonus [illegible] per ton is offered on iron produced from British Columbia ores. The Minister of Mines said that the wild-cat was not encouraged in the Province, but the Government aimed to encourage the introduction of new capital. As our readers are aware, most of the big metal mines of British Columbia are operated by American companies such as the Granby Consolidated, the Britannia, Canada Copper Corporation, Hedley, and the newest gold mine—the Belmont, on Surf Inlet, which is owned by the Tonopah Belmont company and last year came into production with an output of a million dollars. At the luncheon, following the first session, 'Industrial Welfare Work' was advocated by Lieutenant-Colonel R. W. Leonard, president of the Canadian Institute of Engineers. He was followed by a Mr. Bellinger, a representative of the Y. M. C. A., who spoke with the eloquence of a man who knows his subject and is fired by enthusiasm for good work. In the afternoon a comprehensive review of mining prospects in British Columbia was given [illegible] by the District Engineers and their chief, Mr. William Fleet Robertson, the Provincial Mineralogist. It is the duty of each Engineer to investigate the [illegible] assigned to his charge and to report progress annually. Each of them was in a position to give exactly the kind of information that the Convention needed and they did it effectively and in succession, beginning with District No. 1 and ending with No. 6. The District Engineers are Messrs. George A. Clothier, John D. Galloway, E. W. Thomson, Philip B. Freeland, A. G. Lang[illegible] William Brewer, the last an old friend of technical journalism and an engineer well known in our [illegible]. These mineral districts are domains of im[illegible] for British Columbia covers 335,835 square [illegible] afford a remarkable diversity of metallic [illegible] wide scattering of mining activity, but [illegible] probably the most attractive because it is traversed, with a part of No. 3 District, from south to north, by the Coast o Alaskan range, whose back-bone of granite is flanked by the schist and other metamorphic rocks in which recent important finds of copper, gold, and silver have been made Nowhere in the world is there a more attractive field fr intelligent prospecting, because this long stretch of mineralized country is penetrated by numerous inlets or sounds, which afford ready access to the very feet of the muntains in which the miner finds the ore. In the ovenir Mr. T. A. Rickard gave an address on 'Mining as a Investment'. This, and other papers presented at th Convention, will be published in later issues of the 'Mining and Scientific Press'. Next day, Mr. H. W. Lawrie gave a paper on 'Gold'; this was illustrated by excellent diagrams and was highly appreciated by a large audince. The subsequent discussion proved the vital interest of the subject. Mr. Sidney Norman of Spokane, the edtor of 'Northwest Mining Truth', made a spirited attack n the smelter monopoly and advocated the Governmen control of smelters. It is a pity that the other side in his controversy was not represented; the reticence of he representatives of the smelting companies—for several such representatives were present—was, it seems o us, a tactical blunder. We commend the sensible attitude of the Granby Consolidated company, which, y means of the reasoned argument offered in Mr. Vantine Quinn's paper, appealed against unfair taxation. Mention must be made of the discussion on prospectin and the prospector, started by Mr. J. P. McConnell's paper on the subject. The effect of prohibition on mineral exploration engaged sympathetic attention. It was asserted that the prospector will keep ahead of prohibition; he will not flourish in an arid region! Many suggestions were made for the instruction of the prospector in technical matters, but Mr. Brewer, who knows the pioneer of mining better than most of us, insisted that it was vain to teach him and that "no government on earth can do it". That seems contradicted by the good work being done at several of our Western mining-schools, where special classes for prospectors are well attended. It is probably true that some of the old-time prospectors are unwilling pupils, but, in a broad way, it is certain that th prospecting of the future will have to be done by men possessed of some measure of scientific knowledge and trained observation. The old haphazard search for minerals will not suffice, now that the more evident exposurs of ore have been located and exploited. The eye of scince is needed, and it will have to be aided not by the pick alone but by the churn-drill or the diamond-bit. It will be noted that the program was of such scope and variety as to cover the chief interests of a diversified gathering of mining men. For this the Convention owes thanks to Dr. Edwin T. Hodge, who was chairman of the Progam Committee, and did much to make the arrangements run smoothly. Two days were devoted to the public sessions and on the third an excursion to the Britannia mine brought the Convention to a close. The success of it augurs well for the meeting at Seattle next year.

Mill-Tests v. Han -Sampling

The Editor:

Sir—Regarding a certain int esting discussion appearing of late in your columns, seems to me that this is hardly well named as 'Mill-T s v. Hand-Sampling'. The issue seems to me rather as whether mill-tests are necessary or desirable as a sup ment to and a check on hand-sampling. I take it t t no serious engineer holds that a deposit should be v ied without hand-sampling. He may believe that mi tests are necessary or desirable as above, but not that ill-tests alone should be used. The latter so obviously uld mean either that very few points in the deposit s uld be represented in the sampling (valuing) or that rther operation would involve a prohibitive cost.

It is well to remember that th aluing of deposits has frequently to be done with lim ed facilities and with limited expenditure and many re to be reported upon under circumstances where mi tests are not feasible. This discussion, therefore, does ot cover all cases, but only those where mill-tests are f sible. Applied to such cases, it deals with the importa e of mill-tests as compared with, and as supplementry to, hand-sampling; also with the manner in which ill-tests should be utilized, in order to provide the m ximum check on hand-sampling, and with the methods f taking the samples.

In all valuing there are thre actors essentially to be kept in mind:

(1) To see that each sample orrectly represents the actual spot it is taken from; tha t does not contain more or less than the proper proport ns of the different sorts of mineral composing the ore t that spot. The old trouble of the tendency to get a unduly big proportion of the softer (especially the mo friable) mineral, is the most common cause of error. T is consideration, in conjunction with (2), should determne the manner in which the actual work of taking the mples must be carried out, including probably the prearation of the faces before sampling.

(2) To take the samples so iat—assuming that each sample accurately represents th spot it is taken from—these, taken on the whole, gi , with what degree of accuracy is feasible, the valu of the faces sampled. This consideration must determne the general plan of the campaign, where the samtes shall be taken, the weight of each, the length of st p to each sample (if the sampling be done in strips), te distance apart of the samples, the manner of taking tem (by moil or blasting or drilling).

(3) The next points to consier are whether the deposit will all be excavate and whether any other rock (wall-rock, 'horses', etc.) will be excavated with it. The former point oes not on the whole affect the gra e, it woul affect the tonnage, of course. The latter point affects both gra e and tonnage. Generally, the former point will be ignore, although it is by no means certain that it shoul be, as ore is certainly lost y some metho s of mining. It is frequently more than compensate y the existence of ore, not in sight at ate of valuing, a ing to the tonnage. This requires serious consi eration. To this matter the engineer must simply apply his experience to a stu y of the walls. If the mine has been partly worke, he shoul e able to get valua le ata from comparisons of previous recor s and from stu y of accessi le stopes. Again, if neigh oring mines have similar characteristics he ought to be able to secure valua le ata regar ing this point from them.

The a ove eing the factors, the question arises, can han -sampling alone—ai e, of course, y experience and o servation—be relie on to give the results? If not, can mill-tests assist in so oing; and if so, what is the est way in which to apply the mill-tests? It is assume here that mill-tests are use only as large (bulk) samples, not as metallurgical gui es.

(1) and (2) if performe correctly will give the average value of the faces sample as accurately as is practica le. Whether the sai faces are representative of the whole eposit (or of the evelope portion of it) is another matter. Sampling results will not eci e that point, although stu y of them in general and in etail may (and pro ably will) help very materially to o tain a fair ju gment on it. It is purely a matter for the engineer to eci e as to the interpretation he will place upon the value of the expose faces as reflecting upon the value of those parts of the eposit some istance from the faces. Anyhow, we can o nothing but sample the expose faces; the rest is a matter of surmise and ju gment, and we must e content with it as such. The likelihoo of the value of the expose faces representing the value of the eposit surroun e y them will, among other things, epen on the reasons that cause the sai faces to be in the places they are.

However, having ma e whatever allowance he thinks fit in this regar, the engineer can take it that, having sample accurately with regar to factors (1) and (2), he has all the ata he can get—so far as sampling is concerne—for his valuation of the eposits as it stan s *in situ*.

In any case mill-tests will not assist in settling the factor (3). The only practical test that will assist here

William Sloan, the Minister of Mines of British Columbia, welcomed the delegates in an interesting speech full of good sense and sane optimism. He was able to report healthy progress in the mining of the Province, an increase of production, and an expansion of activity. His government had expended $207,523 in assisting mining, more particularly in building 98 miles of roads and 75 miles of trails, besides repairing 437 miles of roads and 420 miles of trails. He made the important statement that there was sufficient iron ore proved in British Columbia to supply a blast-furnace plant capable of yielding 250 to 300 tons of pig-iron per day. This served as a text for an enthusiastic speech delivered at the banquet by Mr. M. J. Carrigan, of Seattle, who laid emphasis upon the paramount importance of this statement, as forecasting the establishment of an iron and steel industry on the Pacific Coast, thereby aiding every manufacture, more particularly that of ship-building. He recited a long list of iron deposits on the Coast and laid stress on the fact that the hope of an iron and steel industry lies in British Columbia on account of its abundant resources in coking-coal. We expect to hear more concerning this vital matter at an early date. A bonus of $3 per ton is offered on iron produced from British Columbian ores. The Minister of Mines said that the 'wild-cat' was not encouraged in the Province, but the Government aimed to encourage the introduction of new capital. As our readers are aware, most of the big metal mines of British Columbia are operated by American companies, such as the Granby Consolidated, the Britannia, Canada Copper Corporation, Hedley, and the newest gold mine—the Belmont, on Surf Inlet, which is owned by the Tonopah Belmont company and last year came into production with an output of a million dollars. At the luncheon, following the first session, 'Industrial Welfare Work' was advocated by Lieutenant-Colonel R. W. Leonard, president of the Canadian Institute of Engineers. He was followed by a Mr. Bellinger, a representative of the Y. M. C. A., who spoke with the eloquence of a man who knows his subject and is fired by enthusiasm for good work. In the afternoon a comprehensive account of mining prospects in British Columbia was given seriatim by the District Engineers and their chief, Mr. William Fleet Robertson, the Provincial Mineralogist. It is the duty of each Engineer to investigate the mineral area assigned to his charge and to report progress annually. Each of them was in a position to give exactly the kind of information that the Convention needed and they did it effectively and in succession, beginning with District No. 1 and ending with No. 6. The District Engineers are Messrs. George A. Clothier, John D. Galloway, R. W. Thomson, Philip B. Freeland, A. G. Langley, and William Brewer, the last an old friend of technical journalism and an engineer well known in our South-West. These mineral districts are domains of imperial extent, for British Columbia covers 335,835 square miles; they afford a remarkable diversity of metallic products and a wide scattering of mining activity, but No. 1 District is probably the most attractive because it is traversed, with a part of No. 3 District, from south to north, by the Coast or Alaskan range, whose back-bone of granite is flanked by the schist and other metamorphic rocks in which recent important finds of copper, gold, and silver have been made. Nowhere in the world is there a more attractive field for intelligent prospecting, because this long stretch of mineralized country is penetrated by numerous inlets or sounds, which afford ready access to the very feet of the mountains in which the miner finds the ore. In the evening Mr. T. A. Rickard gave an address on 'Mining as an Investment'. This, and other papers presented at the Convention, will be published in later issues of the 'Mining and Scientific Press'. Next day, Mr. H. W. Lawrie gave a paper on 'Gold'; this was illustrated by excellent diagrams and was highly appreciated by a large audience. The subsequent discussion proved the vital interest of the subject. Mr. Sidney Norman of Spokane, the editor of 'Northwest Mining Truth', made a spirited attack on the smelter monopoly and advocated the Government control of smelters. It is a pity that the other side in this controversy was not represented; the reticence of the representatives of the smelting companies—for several such representatives were present—was, it seems to us, a tactical blunder. We commend the sensible attitude of the Granby Consolidated company, which, by means of the reasoned argument offered in Mr. Valentine Quinn's paper, appealed against unfair taxation. Mention must be made of the discussion on prospecting and the prospector, started by Mr. J. P. McConnell's paper on the subject. The effect of prohibition on mineral exploration engaged sympathetic attention. It was asserted that the prospector will keep ahead of prohibition; he will not flourish in an arid region! Many suggestions were made for the instruction of the prospector in technical matters, but Mr. Brewer, who knows the pioneer of mining better than most of us, insisted that it was vain to teach him and that "no government on earth can do it." That seems contradicted by the good work being done at several of our Western mining-schools where special classes for prospectors are well attended. It is probably true that some of the old-time prospectors are unwilling pupils, but, in a broad way, it is certain that the prospecting of the future will have to be done by men possessed of some measure of scientific knowledge and trained observation. The old haphazard search for minerals will not suffice, now that the more evident exposures of ore have been located and exploited. The eye of science is needed, and it will have to be aided not by the pick alone but by the churn-drill or the diamond-bit. It will be noted that the program was of such scope and variety as to cover the chief interests of a diversified gathering of mining men. For this the Convention owes thanks to Dr. Edwin T. Hodge, who was chairman of the Program Committee, and did much to make the arrangements run smoothly. Two days were devoted to the public sessions and on the third an excursion to the Britannia mine brought the Convention to a close. The success of it augurs well for the meeting at Seattle next year.

Mill-Tests v. Hand-Sampling

The Editor:

Sir—Regarding a certain interesting discussion appearing of late in your columns, it seems to me that this is hardly well named as 'Mill-Tests v. Hand-Sampling'. The issue seems to me rather as to whether mill-tests are necessary or desirable as a supplement to and a check on hand-sampling. I take it that no serious engineer holds that a deposit should be valued without hand-sampling. He may believe that mill-tests are necessary or desirable as above, but not that mill-tests alone should be used. The latter so obviously would mean either that very few points in the deposit should be represented in the sampling (valuing) or that further operation would involve a prohibitive cost.

It is well to remember that the valuing of deposits has frequently to be done with limited facilities and with limited expenditure and many have to be reported upon under circumstances where mill-tests are not feasible. This discussion, therefore, does not cover all cases, but only those where mill-tests are feasible. Applied to such cases, it deals with the importance of mill-tests as compared with, and as supplementary to, hand-sampling; also with the manner in which mill-tests should be utilized, in order to provide the maximum check on hand-sampling, and with the methods of taking the samples.

In all valuing there are three factors essentially to be kept in mind:

(1) To see that each sample correctly represents the actual spot it is taken from; that it does not contain more or less than the proper proportions of the different sorts of mineral composing the ore at that spot. The old trouble of the tendency to get an unduly big proportion of the softer (especially the more friable) mineral, is the most common cause of error. This consideration, in conjunction with (2), should determine the manner in which the actual work of taking the samples must be carried out, including probably the preparation of the faces before sampling.

(2) To take the samples so that—assuming that each sample accurately represents the spot it is taken from—these, taken on the whole, give, with what degree of accuracy is feasible, the value of the faces sampled. This consideration must determine the general plan of the campaign, where the samples shall be taken, the weight of each, the length of strip to each sample (if the sampling be done in strips), the distance apart of the samples, the manner of taking them (by moil or blasting or drilling).

(3) The next points to consider are whether the deposit will all be excavated and whether any other rock (wall-rock, 'horses', etc.) will be excavated with it. The former point does not on the whole affect the grade, it would affect the tonnage, of course. The latter point affects both grade and tonnage. Generally, the former point will be ignored, although it is by no means certain that it should be, as ore is certainly lost by some methods of mining. It is frequently more than compensated by the existence of ore, not in sight at date of valuing, adding to the tonnage. This requires serious consideration. To this matter the engineer must simply apply his experience to a study of the walls. If the mine has been partly worked, he should be able to get valuable data from comparisons of previous records and from study of accessible stopes. Again, if neighboring mines have similar characteristics he ought to be able to secure valuable data regarding this point from them.

The above being the factors, the question arises, can hand-sampling alone—aided, of course, by experience and observation—be relied on to give the results? If not, can mill-tests assist in so doing; and if so, what is the best way in which to apply the mill-tests? It is assumed here that mill-tests are used only as large (bulk) samples, not as metallurgical guides.

(1) and (2) if performed correctly will give the average value of the faces sampled as accurately as is practicable. Whether the said faces are representative of the whole deposit (or of the developed portion of it) is another matter. Sampling results will not decide that point, although study of them in general and in detail may (and probably will) help very materially to obtain a fair judgment on it. It is purely a matter for the engineer to decide as to the interpretation he will place upon the value of the exposed faces as reflecting upon the value of those parts of the deposit some distance from the faces. Anyhow, we can do nothing but sample the exposed faces; the rest is a matter of surmise and judgment, and we must be content with it as such. The likelihood of the value of the exposed faces representing the value of the deposit surrounded by them will, among other things, depend on the reasons that caused the said faces to be in the places they are.

However, having made whatever allowance he thinks fit in this regard, the engineer can take it that, having sampled accurately with regard to factors (1) and (2), he has all the data he can get—so far as sampling is concerned—for his valuation of the deposits as it stands *in situ*.

In any case mill-tests will not assist in settling the factor (3). The only practical test that will assist here is to excavate sufficient ground and watch results. Generally, such a proceeding is quite outside the time and money available for a report. It seems to me, however, that mill-tests may be a most useful check on the results obtained from (1) and (2), more particularly in some deposits (obviously those whose nature render them more open to errors in sampling).

The extent of the mill-tests and the manner of applying them should, of course, depend on the nature of the deposit. In some cases a very few mill-tests might give all the check that is wanted and all that is of practical use. In others, a considerable number might be necessary if the principle of checking by mill-tests is to be safely or consistently utilized. This point (as to the number required) is not one that can be written about. It is purely a matter for individual judgment in each case. Generally speaking, the same might be said concerning the manner of taking the ore for the mill-tests. For ordinary cases the best method seems to me to be to select certain faces—drifts, cross-cuts, winzes, or stopes—selecting these as the ones most representative of the deposit—or the part of the deposit specially in mind—to sample these faces particularly carefully, both as regards the number of points sampled and the actual taking of the samples, and to then take strips—say two feet deep—over the whole area of the faces sampled. The comparison of such bulk-samples with the averages obtained from moiling the faces should give ordinarily about as valuable a check as is obtainable. If the fresh face (two feet back from the original) be also specially carefully sampled, and two face-samplings averaged, the check would be better. In choosing faces for such checking it would seem to me that, if it appeared that the values in the deposit were tending to, so to speak, form a grain in certain directions, faces running across the said 'grain' would constitute better checks than those running with it. This is only applying the principle adopted in cutting strips across vein-formations because these commonly tend to have a 'grain' parallel to the walls. The faces would also be selected as being as closely as possible ones representing the average character of the orebody. In cases where the character of the ore varied in such a way that it was advisable and feasible to obtain different factors of error for the different kinds of ore, they would be selected as being representative of certain portions of the deposit, whether such portions (of varying nature) occurred in large or small masses. For this purpose each face selected would need to be wholly of one kind of ore. Having obtained checks on the sampling of various faces by these means the obvious procedure would be to then correct the results obtained from hand-sampling by the factors of error so discovered. We should have, for the different characters of ore, different factors of error with which to adjust the sampling results, and the adjustments would be applied to the samples according to the character of the ore represented by each. In the event of the different kinds of ore being so mixed that it is impossible to find faces of any length of one character, I would suggest that a number of short lengths of faces of one character could be taken, the strips therefrom be aggregated and the sampling results averaged.

Mr. Morton Webber has put forward a method of checking hand-sampling by means of mill-tests. I cannot say that his method appeals to me, as I understand it. His taking of a bulk-sample from one spot only, this being compared with only two or three hand-samples, is, I believe, insufficient for the purposes of comparison. I submit that it is only by taking a number of hand-samples that a result can be secured for such a comparison. Mr. Webber's method assumes that the two or three hand-samples taken before, intermediate to, and after certain breakings, truly represent the average value of the ore secured by such breaking. This seems to me to be contrary to experience, which indicates that hand-samples individually (taken with care) may accurately represent the actual spot sampled, but do not represent accurately the immediate areas of the faces of ore which they stand for, nor do they even represent accurately an area, say, covering a foot all round the actual sample. A considerable length of face very closely sampled might reasonably be expected, on the law of averages, to fairly accurately represent the value of the ore behind that face to a depth of, say, a foot to two feet. Even this is no certainty, but it is about as much as can reasonably be done to ascertain the factor of error we seek.

I must confess to a considerable doubt on this matter of securing and using factors of error and agree with those who say that the attempt to do it would need great circumspection and judgment, and would, in many hands, introduce a most dangerous element.

My experience has been much more limited than that of Mr. Webber, but so far as it has gone, I know of no deposits where in my opinion his method of dividing the mine up into areas would correctly interpret the facts. If the method is designed to suit variations in the nature of the ore, my experience is that the variation would occur in much too irregular a manner to enable this method to be applied. If the character of the ore is apparently fairly uniform, then I should say that it would be more consistent to average the results of the whole of the hand-samples taken at the places where the bulk-samples are taken, and compare this with the average of the whole of the bulk-samples and establish a general factor of error from this comparison. It may be said that this would result in giving an average result much the same as by Mr. Webber's method of subdivision. In a deposit of no great variation of width it would do so. In cases of great variation it might be far from doing so. In any case, I submit that it would be based on a sounder principle—that of averages. If a sufficient number of bulk-samples were taken in that way, no doubt a fairly correct factor of error could be secured. The greater the number the more accurate would the factor so calculated become. In Mr. Webber's method, supposing in one or more cases the bulk-sampling gave considerably higher results than the hand-sampling, would the calculated factor be added to the values obtained by hand-sampling in that area? To be consistent it should be so.

Personally, I believe that practically all deposits can be better sampled by a number of small samples than by any method of bulk-sampling, which would be within reasonable cost, alone. I believe that bulk-sampling can be used in most, if not all, cases with advantage as a check on the small samples and probably its use may enable factors of error to be obtained that can be applied to the whole of the small samples. In the event of bulk-sampling not being practicable as a check, it may be necessary to take more elaborate care to avoid mistakes in the small samples than if the said check can be used. I believe that where bulk-sampling is used as a check, its method of application must depend entirely on the character of the deposit. A discussion of various methods may, however, give useful ideas in this respect.

In mines that have been worked fairly extensively, if accurate and sufficient records have been kept of treatment results and of mine-sampling and if the methods have been good, the need for mill-tests should disappear. A factor of error should be obtainable from the records. In any case, whether taking bulk-samples or not, all possible information should be obtained from the records, as a further check on sampling results.

In cases where no metallurgical treatment has been done the dumps from development should constitute most useful sources of information, especially if it is possible to identify the ore from various headings. The proper sampling of dumps, of course, implies large samples and brings in again the use of the mill.

With especial regard to the sampling of large low-grade orebodies, I cannot myself see that any special features come into play as compared with the sampling of mines of moderate size. It appears to me generally that, other things being similar, the larger the orebody—or rather the greater the total area of the face that is exposed—the fewer need be the number of samples per unit of area. This simply comes back to the law of averages. Of course, an orebody having variable character of ore, if it is desired to value the different types of ore, would require more samples than would an orebody of equal size and of uniform type of ore.

With regard to the manner of taking the individual samples, whether taken by hammer and moil, by blasting, by drilling (the drillings forming the samples), etc., whether the samples should be taken in the form of parallel sections or at equidistant points, the size of each sample, the distance apart, and so on, it appears to me that no general rule can be laid down. The engineer must decide these points for each case on its merits. In view of the widespread use of the method of cutting parallel sections, I may say that I cannot see any special virtue in the method except where there is reason to suppose a tendency of the values to form 'grains'. Generally speaking, it no doubt suits nearly all vein-formations whose width is small compared with the length and depth. In sampling masses of ore of a schistose or laminated or stratified structure, the method of taking sections across the laminations, etc., would no doubt often be advisable. Certainly one would not take sections along them. Ordinarily in a mass deposit where there is no reason to believe a 'grain' exists, the sampling would more logically be done by taking samples at equidistant spots rather than by parallel sections. The same amount of work should give a more representative result.

The case of valuing deposits where the ore occurs in rich patches (like the quoted plums in a pudding) is often mentioned. It is obviously impossible to value such a deposit accurately by sampling. It cannot be too clearly or often stated that after all sampling is a method only of ascertaining the values of exposed faces. If the faces do not accurately represent the deposit, obviously sampling cannot give the true value of the deposit, even if it gives that of the faces. In such deposits it appears to me that all one can do is to sample the exposed faces by means of small samples taken at short distances apart. Such sampling may be reasonably supposed to indicate the distribution of the rich patches exposed by the faces. These patches can then be sampled with a greater degree of thoroughness, including perhaps some bulk-sampling, and their values estimated separately. The results should give, as closely as work can give it, the value of the faces. Whether the faces truly represent the deposit is another matter. The engineer must either gamble on this or decline the responsibility. The obvious way would be to give the results of the sampling and explain the uncertainty (and the degree thereof) of these truly representing the whole orebody. It is fair to remember in this connection that the faces may indicate a lower value than is really the case. We all know that many mines have turned out better than prospects at one time indicated. All we can do is to value the exposed faces and decide on that whether the deposit is a good mining risk or not.

H. R. SLEEMAN.

Whim Creek, Western Australia, November 5, 1918.

The Editor:

Sir—I have studied Mr. Sleeman's letter above, and in that part of his letter where he criticizes my 'combination method' of mine sampling, it would seem that he has read my views in a superficial way. For example, he says: "I cannot say that his [Webber's] method appeals to me, as I understand it. His taking of a bulk-sample from one spot only, this being compared with only two or three hand-samples, is, I believe, insufficient for the purpose of comparison. I submit it is only by taking a number of hand-samples that a result can be secured for such a comparison."

Regarding the statement about taking "a bulk-sample from one spot only," if Mr. Sleeman will refer to my contribution more carefully, he will read as follows: "I desire to say that in the examination of large ore deposits, I do not consider a mill-test to be representative individually, but only as a link in a chain of mill-tests supplemented by corrected hand-sampling. . . . I contend that a mill-test from a particular part of a large ore deposit will represent only the particular spot from which the ore has been removed." I further stated that "In the majority of cases, in dealing with the sampling of large low-grade ore deposits the estimation of ore-reserves must be based on hand-sampling. This can be corrected by a series of mill-tests employed for the sole purpose as a sampling error indicator. Once this error is obtained for a given place, the mill-test should terminate. A fresh mill-test should be made elsewhere to obtain the sampling error for another zone."

Where does Mr. Sleeman get his authority for the words "two or three," when I say clearly "a reliable estimate can be made of the local sampling error by obtaining the average of successive sampling of the stope-faces as the ore is removed for a mill-test and comparing this result with the recovery plus the tailing loss. Surely the adjective 'successive' cannot be intelligently taken to mean but 'two or three.' This sort of thing suggests the attempt of an attorney to make a case, rather than the constructive criticism of one engineer on the work of another.

The combination method of sampling a large low-grade deposit was not intended to apply to ordinary size mine examinations. This was clearly pointed out in the original contribution. This method, as will be remembered, was intended for the sampling of great low-grade deposits such as the Alaska Gastineau, Alaska Juneau, and others, where a large sum of money is involved, and where a discrepancy of, say, 40 cents per ton between the mine sampling and the mill heads might mean complete financial failure.

Mr. Sleeman states: "I believe that practically all deposits can be better sampled by a number of small samples than by any method of bulk-sampling." I presume by "small samples" he means hand-samples, that is, samples taken by moil or by pneumatic channeler. The Alaska Gastineau case has conclusively proved that hand-sampling alone will not meet the case, nor would a relatively small number of large mill-tests indicate what should be expected from supposed ore-zones considerably remote from the point whence the large mill-test sample came. The mining industry paid about fifteen million dollars to find this out. It was, therefore, a desire to anticipate the recurrence of a similar mistake that led to my combination method, where I divide the area, into a large number of small mill-tests, and fall back on corrected hand-sampling and the law of average to sample the intervening spaces in the "chain of mill-tests." The distance between mill-tests, or, in other words, the size of the area or zone over which the mill-test would control the hand-sampling, as I explained, must depend upon the individual case. R. E. Raymond wrote a valuable contribution on this phase of the subject, which appeared in the 'Press' of November 3, 1917.

After the mine has been sampled by this combination method, or in event of the property being sampled during process of development, the further complication would have to be considered of whether all the ore could be mined clean as sampled without dilution from sloughing or the inclusion of 'horses' that escaped sampling. The latent sampling error common to the great majority of ore deposits and the mechanical dilution owing to sloughing are distinct problems, and should be considered separately. In my experience I know of several cases where it was possible to mine the walls clean, but there was a latent sampling error in the moil channeling of the backs and other parts, always resulting in a discrepancy between the average of the sampling and the mill-head.

The title 'Mill-Tests v. Hand-Sampling' has evidently somewhat confused Mr. Sleeman in his criticism of my views; the title is unfortunate. It had its origin in an article I wrote for the issue of July 28, 1917, entitled 'Mill-Tests v. Hand-Sampling in Valuing Mines.' The title was suitable for the original article, which dealt with three important examinations I had conducted. Later valuable contributions emanated, as a result, from E. P. Spalding, R. E. Raymond, Charles Bennett, F. F. Sharpless, and several other engineers, and the original title was continued—no doubt to identify the series. The combination method of sampling that I devised was a utilization of the important merits of both methods in combination, a description of which appeared in the issue of September 29, 1917.

MORTON WEBBER.

New York, March 10.

MANGANESE EXPORTS from Brazil during the 16 years ended with 1917 are shown in the following table, together with the average price in paper milreis (worth about \$0.25 in United States currency):

Year	Exports Tons	Average price per ton Milreis	Year	Exports Tons	Average price per ton Milreis
1902	157,295	28.388	1911	173,941	22.279
1903	161,926	20.629	1912	154,870	22.250
1904	208,260	29.086	1913	122,300	22.250
1905	224,377	22.673	1914	183,630	25.485
1906	121,131	22.058	1915	288,671	36.477
1907	236,778	33.828	1916	503,130	58.641
1908	166,122	23.708	1917	532,855	107.503
1909	240,774	23.694	1918	....345,877*	117.000
1910	252,958	22.526			

*Tonnage imported into the United States.

When war orders for manganese commenced to be placed in 1915, the price immediately began to rise, but the greatest increase was shown during 1917, when 1916 prices were nearly doubled.—Consular Report.

GOLD-MINING COMPANIES fare under the Revenue Act as follows: Section 304-d—"In the case of any corporation engaged in the mining of gold, the portion of the net income derived from the mining of gold shall be exempt from the tax imposed by this title, and the tax on the remaining portion of the net income shall be the proportion of a tax computed without the benefit of this sub-division which such remaining portion of the net income bears to the entire net income."

MANGANESE MINING has been resumed by four companies at Batesville, Arkansas. Ore of 45% grade is quoted there at 55 cents per unit, equal to \$24.75 per ton. From this basis to 50% the rise is 5 cents per unit. It is evident that these centrally-situated deposits can possibly compete with foreign ores.—W. R. Crane in charge of this division of the U. S. Bureau of Mines.

TRANSPORTATION OF MACHINERY TO THE ORIENTAL CONSOLIDATED MINES

The Unsan Mines, Korea

By H. J. EVANS and K. F. HOEFLE

INTRODUCTION. The mines operated by the Oriental Consolidated Mining Co. are situated in Unsan, one of the north-western districts of Korea, officially known as Chosen, the small peninsula extending south from Manchuria between the Japan and Yellow seas, now a part of the Japanese empire. The mining concession embraces the entire district, an area of approximately 400 square miles, and is familiarly known as 'the Unsan mines'. As it is the pioneer foreign mining company in the country, a short history of the undertaking may be of interest.

Gold mining along primitive lines had been carried on in Korea for centuries, but not until 1895 was foreign capital enlisted in its development. In that year the Emperor granted permission to James R. Morse, an American business man, to work all the mines in the Unsan magistracy for a royalty of 25% of the net profit. During the following year—1896—passports were issued to engineers to proceed to the mines, and more favorable terms were granted by the Emperor. Some development was started on the richer quartz lodes, and a 10-stamp mill was erected to treat the ore from the Chittabalbie mine.

The concessionaire was again granted an extension of 25 years to the lease, free entry for all supplies, release from the royalty, and exemption from taxes. The Chittabalbie mine proved highly profitable, and the promoters procured sufficient capital to ensure success to the venture. The three companies that were interested in the concession during the years previous to 1901 were merged in that year by Leigh S. J. Hunt, one of the largest holders, and the Oriental Consolidated Mining Co. was formed with a capital of $5,000,000. Under the direction of Henry C. Perkins, now president of the company, the undertaking was carried through the critical stage of its life. During the early exploration of the prospects and erection of reduction works, natural obstacles to progress were so numerous that only men of tenacious character and indomitable courage could have carried the work to completion. The absence of roads, scarcity of timber and fuel, remoteness from civilization and sources of supplies, the absence of skilled labor, the Korean's natural disinclination to work for a foreigner, and the not always veiled opposition of the populace constituted a set of problems that might well have discouraged any group of men. The fact that the pioneers not only merely overcame these troubles, but did it in such a way as to establish the company on the sound basis it enjoys today, at the same time winning the goodwill of the people and maintaining amicable relations with a chaotic and unstable government, deserves more than passing mention. With an original investment of less than $100,000, the company was built up from its own profits, until at one time there were five mills operating with a total of 240 stamps.

Unlike most mineral regions, the community presents the appearance of being an agricultural centre rather than one of gold mining. The country has a delightful climate; all seasons being remarkably agreeable and healthy. The mines are 60 miles distant from the main railway, requiring four hours travel by motor-car to reach them. The connecting highway traverses a wide and matured valley depressed between long low ranges overgrown with an abundance of shrubbery and lonely pines.

GENERAL GEOLOGY AND ORE DEPOSITS. Heavy precipitation, warm summers, and cold winters form an ideal combination of eroding agencies, whose action on the granitic formation give the region a rather high and rugged topographic relief.

The structural features of the geological formation

included in this area are comparatively simple. The lodes are typical fissures with filling from 20 to 140 ft. wide, and of unusual vertical persistence. While no detailed study of the entire concession has been made, one formation only has been observed at surface exposures or found in any of the underground workings. This formation has been subjected to intense crushing and faulting. A series of fissures running close to, and more or less parallel with each other, have been developed at various points on the concession, many of them containing substantial orebodies. The following extract, taken from a report made to the company, in 1916, by J.

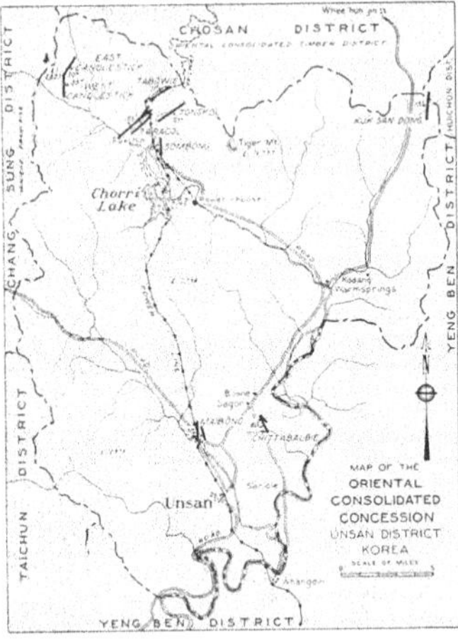

Malcolm Maclaren. concisely describes the formation near the larger mines:

"Two granites differing greatly in age and character, make up the rocks. The older granite, probably Archaean in age—now essentially a gneiss, is the basement rock of the country. Economically, the most important rock is a coarsely-grained grano-diorite which has absorbed a great portion of the older gneiss."

The most prominent lodes are located along the northeastern boundary, near the town of Pukchin. In this section much faulting, subsequent to the period of ore deposition, and the intrusion of dolerite dikes, following the channels of least resistance, are the prominent features noticed in most of the mines. Two parallel fissures, about 500 ft. apart and three miles in length, striking N. 75 E., and one large cross-fracture, striking N. 55 E., with numerous branches of no economic value, on both foot and hanging walls, are of the greatest importance. The later development of a cross-fault displaced the western half of these three lodes about 4000 ft., with a down-throw of possibly 600 ft. The fault-zone is several hundred feet wide, and contains fragments of the disconnected orebody. The dikes, which follow or cross through the veins or along the fault-zone without regularity, vary in thickness from a few inches to 30 ft. On opposite sides of this fault-zone—Tabowie and Taracol—are situated the company's two largest mines. On the Taracol side of the fault, the dike is seldom found in the lode-centre, suggesting much less movement in adjustment of stresses on that side, while in Tabowie mine it follows along or crosses through the ore without rule, and frequently reaches 10 ft. in width. The orebodies occur in the centre and along both walls; the central shoot being the larger and more persistent.

STOPE ON NO. 15 LEVEL OF TABOWIE MINE SHOWING LODE CUT BY THE INTRUSION OF A DOLERITE DIKE

Lode Material and Orebodies. The lode material is quartz containing pyrite, galena, sphalerite, gold, and a small quantity of silver. A predominance of galena is generally accompanied by an increase in gold. The ore is comparatively low-grade, visible gold being rare. Small high-grade pockets do occur in the Taracol mine, some fine specimens having been recently found on the 1230-ft. level. An abundance of graphitic gouge follows along the walls and planes of movement. Graphite in small quantity is distributed through the ore, filling the seams giving the quartz a characteristic banded appearance. The main orebodies appear at or near the junctions, and pitch westward with them. However, substantial oreshoots are found entirely separated from these connections, especially on the hanging-wall side. There is no marked evidence of any secondary enrichment, and the zone of oxidation extends only a short distance below the surface. The ore shows remarkable persistence in depth. An apparently rich zone of secondary sulphides seems to exist between the 10th and 16th levels in the Tabowie mine. The stoping width was uniformly much wider and the value lower above this horizon, while below there was a slight impoverishment. The ends of the orebodies are generally accompanied by large masses of barren quartz, changing to graphitic gouge and altered wall-rock. The present depths of the Tabowie and Taracol mines are 2600 ft. and 1800 ft. respectively. The lowest workings are still in ore.

The Chintui and Nuchadagi mines are on separate orebodies on the same lode, 2000 ft. west of Taracol. Many other lodes within the immediate vicinity have been prospected, but so far only two of these smaller mines—Sambong and Tongkol—situated a short distance south and east of Taracol, have warranted extensive development. The Charabowie mine, near the southern boundary, contains two parallel fissures 80 ft. apart, having the same dip of 70°. Each lode carries an ore-shoot 5 ft. wide and 500 ft. long. Both orebodies pitched at an angle of 45° with the horizon, and persisted to a depth of 1850 ft. before showing any impoverishment. The minerals contained are similar to the other mines. About 80% of the gold content is in a coarse free state. The mine was exhausted and closed during July 1918, after having produced nearly $4,000,000.

The Chittabalbie, in the same locality, the first mine to be operated by the company, yielded much high-grade ore from the oxidized zone near the surface. The company has operated several other mines during the past, all being of similar type.

MINING METHODS. The different sizes of the orebodies, the varying strength of the walls, and widely differing physical characteristics, necessitate the adoption in each mine of different methods of mining. Overhead stoping with or without timber is the general practice. Narrow hard veins or weak walls prohibit the use of any more advanced or cheaper methods of extraction.

The Tabowie, Taracol, and Chintui mines, all on different portions of one and the same fissure, require square-setting with medium heavy timber, due to large stoping width, soft walls, and much slipping of the back along the graphitic seams in the quartz.

As a rule, considerable quantities of waste and dike material are mixed with the ore, requiring systematic sorting and elimination of the largest boulders, before the ore can be dumped into the shaft-pockets. Most of the sorting is done in the stopes, and the discard used for filling.

The increased costs of inferior grades of timber and lagging caused the management to consider changes in methods of underground work, whereby the consumption might be reduced. The former practice of running long stopes concentrated together, requiring the changing of many manway and chute-sets, was changed to a more effective and economical method of carrying up as short

STOPES AND PILLARS IN KUK SAN DONG MINE

stope-length as practicable. While the former system enabled the gathering of larger crews and easier supervision, these factors were greatly offset by the high cost to keep them open and safe for the miners.

At present, most stopes do not exceed 40 ft. in length, with a chute and manway at each end. The upper portion of one chute is used to convey filling material into the stope from the above level. The results of this new method have been highly gratifying, and the change exemplified by two years of practice enables a stope to be finished in one-third of the former time with greater

THE CHITTABALBIE MINE, THE FIRST TO BE OPERATED BY THE ORIENTAL CONSOLIDATED

GENERAL VIEW SHOWING THE MAIN PORTION OF THE

Left: Mine timber and fuel yards. The inclined track connects with a narrow-gauge railway, 20 miles long, used to
Centre: General stores, Tabowie 80-stamp mill, sub-stations.
Right: The river follows the strike of the central fault. On the right bank of the river can be seen the Taracol mine head-frame.

economy. The average stoping width of these mines is about 12 ft., but often extends to 50 ft. or more.

Ore-breaking is done by hand-drilling, using 40% gelignite. All filling is obtained from the development headings—mostly the lower levels. Due to the comparatively low cost of labor, machine-drills have not proved economical for this company, except in shaft-sinking and development headings where rapid progress is desired. Development progresses slowly, requiring almost constant advance of all headings to maintain a moderate ore-reserve. Above is a table showing the footage of work done at each mine during the last fiscal year:

Kind of work	Tabowie	Taracol	Tongkol	Chintui	Charabowie	Maibong	Prospect	Total
Driving	7,675	7,246	2,601	1,473	452	353	204	20,004
Cross-cutting	1,834	1,393	268	516	214	37	16	4,278
Raising	2,597	3,643	918	666	218	130	7	8,179
Winzes	1,062	....	406	205	130	108	216	2,136
Shaft-sinking	80	526	60	104	...	...	...	770
Hoist and pump stations	239	86	26	33	...	...	...	....
Total of each mine	13,487	12,894	4,279	2,997	1,023	628	533	35,841

The various costs at the principal mines are shown in the following table:

Cost per Ton of Ore Mined During Fiscal Year 1918

	Tabowie	Taracol	Chintui	Tongkol	*Charabowie
Tons of ore	128,106	101,617	23,881	8,040	42,028
Miners and timbermen	$0.455	$0.371	$0.413	$1.222	$0.333
Shovelers and trammers	0.067	0.062	0.058	0.184	0.043
Explosives	0.226	0.189	0.163	0.929	0.157
Drill-steel and tools	0.044	0.078	0.035	0.146	0.003
Candles and carbide	0.078	0.062	0.159	0.216	0.049
Timber	0.433	0.374	0.465	0.325	0.092
Wood and coal	0.102	0.057	0.073	0.060	0.075
Shops and machinery	0.021	0.039	0.022	0.033	0.008
Power and light	0.112	0.146	0.286	0.192	0.506
Miscellaneous	0.069	0.043	0.050	0.133	0.034
Engineers, firemen, cage-tenders, etc.	0.044	0.053	0.089	0.202	0.086
Blacksmiths, carpenters, and surfacemen	0.102	0.066	0.159	0.195	0.134
Supervision	0.103	0.126	0.124	0.165	0.109
Total	$1.860	$1.666	$2.005	$4.002	$1.623

*Calculated for 11 months only.

All development and stoping of the ore is done by contract, and the method adopted has been satisfactory to both the company and miners. All the work of an entire level generally is given to one bidder, the contractor agreeing to break, sort, and tram the ore, and timber the various workings on the level for a fixed rate of payment. This system eliminates a great many trivial troubles and disorders. The total costs at the various mines are fairly uniform, except at Tongkol, where the finding of small erratic high-grade pockets increase the costs noticeably.

In the smaller mines the ore can be extracted without the use of much timber, but the other items make their operations expensive.

In accordance with standard mining practice a large reserve of broken ore is held in stopes as well as a month's supply kept on the surface in case of any interruption to the hoisting service.

The company employs 2000 men underground.

MILLING. The company is now operating three stamp-mills: Tabowie, 80 stamps; Taracol, 80 stamps; and Maibong, 40 stamps. The mines supplying ore to these mills are as below:

Mine	Monthly tonnage	Mill delivered to	Number of Stamps
Tabowie	11,000	Tabowie	80
Taracol	8,000	Taracol	
Chintui	2,400	"	80
Tongkol	800	"	
Charabowie	3,300		
Maibong	500	Maibong	40
Total	26,000		200

The design of the plants and process of treatment are similar at the three plants, hence the description will be general.

The ore before being dumped into the mine-pockets is sorted carefully, all waste and large boulders being eliminated, thus providing uniform feed to the crushers. The material is mostly quartz, medium hard, containing about 7% by weight of the sulphides of iron, zinc, and lead.

The ore is trammed to the mills in standard 1½-ton cars, weighed on Fairbanks scales, and dumped on grizzlies with 1¾-in. spacings, and set on a 45° slope. The oversize passes to 10 by 15-in. Blake crushers, which reduce the material to the same size as that passing through the grizzlies to the bin. The bin capacity is sufficient to supply the mills for 36 hours.

A modified Challenge feeder delivers the ore to 1050-

ORIENTAL CONSOLIDATED COMPANY'S PROPERTIES

convey timber to the mines from the forest. On the hillside are the explosives magazines, as outlined by the zig-zag road
mine hoisting plant, and lode-outcrop in the background.
and along the opposite hills, the car-line to Tongkol mine. The displacement of the lode along this fault-plane is about 3500 feet.

lb. stamps arranged in the usual unit of 10 stamps.

Mill Operations for Fiscal Year 1918

	Tabowie	Taracol	Malbung
Number of stamps	80	80	40
Ore crushed, tons	128,106	133,538	42,028
Stamp-duty, tons	4.70	4.87	3.28
Value of ore	$6.56	$5.07	$6.57
Recovery by amalgamation, per cent	44.79	40.01	71.01
Recovery by concentration, per cent	46.14	49.42	18.88
Value of tailing	$0.66	$0.60	$0.06

The stamps make 102 drops of 7½ in. per minute. The discharge is 4 in. Punched round hole screens of 26-mesh (diam. 0.038 in.) are used. The mortar-blocks are of concrete. A ½-in. sheet of rubber is placed between the block and the mortar. Two lines of main shafting are carried on the floor timber beneath the ore-bin. Each shaft is belt-driven by a 100-hp. motor; the batteries are driven in sets of 10 stamps each.

Amalgamation of the gold is done inside the batteries, upon apron-plates, and in Pierce amalgamators. The copper plates are 4 ft. 6 in. wide and 10 ft. long, with a slope of 1½ in. per foot. After leaving the plates the pulp passes through amalgam-traps, beneath which are set the Pierce amalgamators. These machines catch about 3½% of the total amalgam. The percentages of recovery by amalgamation are:

Place	%
Inside of batteries	4.50
Apron-plates	92.00
Pierce amalgamators	3.50

After passing the amalgamating plant the pulp flows to two sets of vanners. These machines are adjusted to make a concentrate containing a large portion of coarse sand to facilitate leaching at the cyanide works. The concentrate goes to the central cyanide plant at Taracol. The tailing is passed to cone classifiers. The coarse spigot material flows to waste, while the overflow passes over a double set of canvas-tables. These tables collect at little cost an additional small quantity of valuable sulphide slime which is treated by agitation.

These two 80-stamp mills are similar in design and

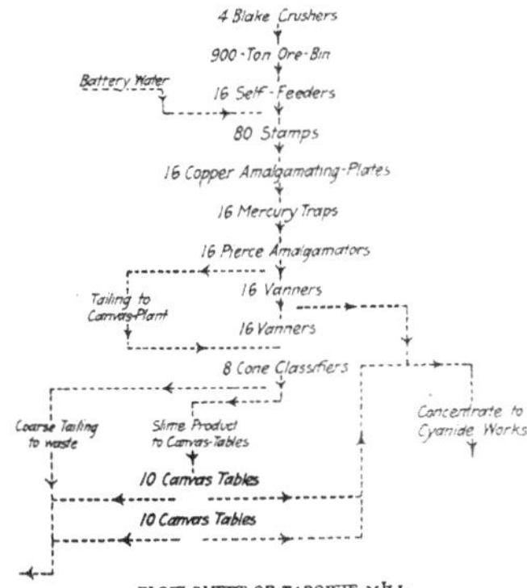

FLOW-SHEET OF TABOWIE MILL

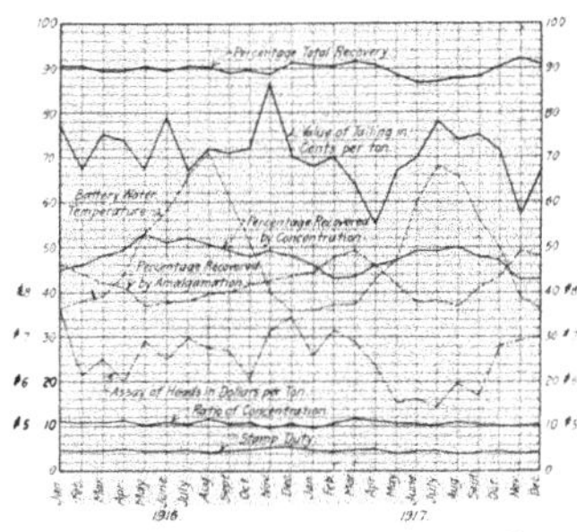

GRAPH OF OPERATING RESULTS AT TABOWIE MILL DURING TWO YEARS

operation, and both treat about the same monthly tonnage. In the Maibong mill, the crusher is housed in a separate building, and the concentrate is treated in a small auxiliary tube-mill plant.

The company has done much experimenting at the Tabowie and Taracol plants with a view to improve, if possible, the simple yet effective milling methods in vogue, but the increased extraction obtainable has never justified the change, due to the exceedingly high cost of operating the additional machinery.

Milling Costs per Ton for Fiscal Year 1918

Article	Tabowie 128,106 tons	Taracol 133,538 tons	Maibong 42,028 tons	Average cost per ton
Cordwood	$0.04992	$0.04565	$0.03460	$0.04592
Shoes	0.04273	0.04061	0.02803	0.03976
Dies	0.02376	0.02882	0.02200	0.02573
Bosses	0.00226	0.00064	......	0.00123
Tappets	0.00020	0.00083	......	0.00049
Cam-shafts	0.00375	0.01078	0.00148	0.00653
Extras	0.00123	0.00037	......	0.00069
Screens Crusher Crusher dies Crusher extras	0.00231	0.00465	0.00123	0.00319
Concentrator extras Concentrator belt	0.00440	0.02082	0.00787	0.01210
Belting	0.00044	0.00011	0.00133	0.00042
Pipe and fittings Valves Pumps and fittings	0.00022	0.00258	0.00034	0.00128
Iron, bar Iron, sheet Iron, other	0.00080	0.00266	......	0.00150
Steel Babbitt and solder Hardware Tools Packing Canvas Waste	0.00442	0.00800	0.00627	0.00625
Candles Oil, kerosene Oil, cylinder Oil, engine Oil, other Oil, lubricant	0.00102	0.00320	0.00381	0.00262
Quicksilver	0.00782	0.00750	0.01301	0.00840
Lumber Brooms Leather, lacing Bolts, nuts, washers Cement, lime, bricks Miscellaneous	0.00834	0.00756	0.01394	0.00878
Total supplies	0.15431	0.18478	0.13391	0.16489
Assays	0.00485	0.00650	0.01092	0.00642
Shop and power	0.15895	0.20640	0.22513	0.18897
Salaries and pay-roll	0.13604	0.13096	0.22109	0.14558
Total	$0.45415	$0.52864	$0.59105	$0.50586

TREATMENT OF CONCENTRATE. The central leaching-plant is at Taracol, and treats all the coarse concentrates and slimes from the Tabowie and Taracol mills. The capacity of the plant is 70 tons per day, with a 20-day treatment. The plant, originally designed by S. J. Speak, contains twenty 5 by 20-ft. leaching-vats, five steel zinc-boxes, solution and stock-tanks, pumps, and accessory apparatus.

The concentrate, after being weighed and sampled for assay and moisture, is dumped into the vat. The amount of lime needed for neutralization is also added during filling, thus being well mixed with the charge. After the vat is filled the charge is given a preliminary water-wash, which is run to waste. From this stage the treatment begins, one strength of solution being used during the entire treatment.

Grading Analysis of Tabowie and Taracol Concentrates

Screen (mesh)	Tabowie Weight, %	Tabowie Value, %	Taracol Weight, %	Taracol Value, %
Through 20 on 30	18	3	3	1
" 30 " 40	20	10	20	10
" 40 " 60	17	17	26	27
" 60 " 100	11	16	15	19
" 100 " 150	7	13	8	10
" 150 " 200	6	9	7	8
" 200 (slime)	21	32	21	25
Total	100	100	100	100

After five days of percolation and aeration in the first vat, the charge is removed to another, where it receives similar treatment, and so on until it has passed through four vats and consumed 20 days of time. The final solution is displaced by water, and the residue discharged onto the tailing stock-pile.

The pregnant solution passes through a small settling-tank to the precipitation-boxes. Zinc-shaving is used in steel boxes. These are 2 ft. high by 3 ft. wide by 18 ft. long, and have six compartments, the last having a canvas filter through which the solution ascends and passes to the stock-tank. The precipitate is collected and melted twice a month.

Formerly the precipitate was melted by charcoal in well furnaces, using the following flux:

Product	Parts
Precipitate	100
Sodium carbonate	10
Borax	40
Sand	20
Manganese di-oxide	10

The gold buttons were re-melted in the same crucibles and furnace. The bars averaged 1000 oz. each.

The high cost and scarcity of charcoal necessitated a change to the use of oil as fuel. At present one large well furnace holding six No. 80 crucibles, placed in two rows of three each, with the blast-flame passing through the centre, is being used. Cupellation is done in a separate furnace designed for the use of charcoal as fuel. The cupel 'test' is made of dry cement, pressed firmly by hand into an iron casing. This change of method of melting has not yet been completed, but experiments have proved that it will be much cheaper and more efficient than the old way of melting with charcoal.

Operating Table, Taracol and Tabowie Cyanide Plant, 1918

	Taracol mill	Tabowie mill
Ore treated, tons	13,907	13,555
Assay-value	$334,372	$387,779
Value, per ton	$24.04	$28.61
Bullion recovered	$277,668	$323,061
Recovery, per ton	$19.97	$23.84
Extraction, per cent	83.0	83.3
Cost, per ton	$1.95	$1.95

The slag is re-melted later, with sweepings from the refinery, in a small blast-furnace of local make. By this means most of the metallics, which adhere to the slag while pouring the meltings, is recovered.

The fineness of the bullion, as sent to the Imperial Japanese Mint at Osaka, Japan, is 950 or higher. The bars average 170 oz. in weight, and are shipped by parcel post direct from the mines.

The principal feature about this leaching-plant is the simplicity of treatment with a fairly satisfactory recovery at low cost. Due to the high cost of supplies during the War, operating expenses have increased from $1.40 per ton in 1912 to $1.95 in 1918.

Cyanide Treatment Costs at Taracol Plant, 1918

Item	Quantity, lb.	Cost per ton
Cyanide	[illegible]	[illegible]
Zinc	[illegible]	[illegible]
Lime	[illegible]	[illegible]
Charcoal		[illegible]
Cordwood		[illegible]
Crucibles		[illegible]
Borax	[illegible]	[illegible]
Assaying		[illegible]
Electric power		[illegible]
Other supplies		[illegible]
Miscellaneous		[illegible]
Transportation		[illegible]
Salaries and payroll		[illegible]
Total		[illegible]

The use of different strengths of solution is unnecessary, as well as sulphuric-acid treatment of the precipitate. The use of sodium carbonate and litharge in the melting-flux has been discontinued, results being as good without them. The cyanide strength is kept at 3½ lb., and the protective alkalinity at 5½ lb. per ton of ore treated. The extraction has been gradually increased from year to year, and now averages over 84%.

POWER. Previous to 1913 steam was used as power at all of the mines, and for part of each year in the mills and shops. All machinery except the larger hoists, which are driven by air or steam, was electrified during that year. About 650 hp., used chiefly for pumping and hoisting at the smaller mines, is procured from a hydro-electric plant belonging to the company. This plant constructed in 1906, consists of a 500-kw. turbine-driven generator, water for which is stored in a small reservoir 3 miles from the plant, and delivered through a box-flume with a head of 113 ft. Since 1913 the company has purchased 1200 hp. from a Japanese firm operating a steam-driven plant on the Anshu river, 60 miles from the mines. Electricity is used to compress air for hoisting and for rock-drills, pumping, ventilating, lighting, and for driving the mills, shops, and miscellaneous machinery.

As a rule, the mine water is lifted by stages of a few hundred feet, using centrifugal pumps on the upper levels and motor-driven vertical-triplex pumps at the bottom, where the heights of stages are often changed.

The motors used are of different types and sizes as deemed most suitable. Auxiliary generating units, connected with the old steam plants, are maintained in case of any interruption to the regular supply.

The company has just commenced construction of another hydro-electric project on the Kuron river, 25 miles from the mines. The work will consist of a 650-ft. diversion dam, a 955-ft. tunnel, power-station, and transmission-line to the mines. The water will be delivered to the generators under a 45-ft. head, producing an average of 1000 kw. This new source of supply will materially reduce power expenses.

VANNER-FLOOR, TARACOL 80-STAMP MILL

MECHANICAL. This department, always indispensable around mining plants, is doubly so on these mines because of their isolation from sources of supplies. The work that this department is called upon to do ranges from the making of nuts and bolts to the manufacture of complete machines. Considering the range and quantity of the work demanded of it, the equipment is simple, consisting of one 30 in. by 22-ft. lathe, one 24 in. by 9-ft. lathe, one 16 in. by 5-ft. lathe, one 3½ by 3½ by 8-ft. planer, one 22-in. shaper, one 4-ft. radial-drill, one upright drill, and pipe-threading machines.

The wood-working shop is equipped with the usual complement of lumber and timber-planers, rip and band-saws, turns out all manner of wood material, does the framing for all new construction, dresses the lumber for other departments, and furnishes patterns for the foundry.

The blacksmith-shop has all the machines and tools usually found in a good shop.

The small foundry operated by the department has a normal capacity, when using coke, of two tons per hour. However, coke being unattainable at present, charcoal is used and the capacity of the cupolas is considerably decreased. The foundry casts all liners, guides, and feeder-tables for the mills, in addition to the innumerable small jobs that turn up daily from the mines and metallurgical plants.

In the company shops are built the smaller hoists used at the various mines, also many of the electrically-operated pumps, of the vertical-triplex type, as well as much other machinery needed.

All machinery in the shops is electrically driven, power being supplied by the company's hydro-electric plant. Most of the machinists, blacksmiths, foundrymen, carpenters, and pattern-makers are Japanese; however, Koreans have been trained throughout the department and do satisfactory work. The wages in this department are higher than in any other, and materials are so hard to procure that a comparison of costs would not, at present, be fair to the plant; however, it serves its purpose well, and too much credit cannot be given it.

TIMBER SUPPLY. The comparative scarcity of timber, coupled with the high cost, makes it an important item in the local cost of mining. Below is given a table showing the cost of timber, cordwood, lumber, and charcoal used at all mines, showing the timber to be 25% of the total mining cost for the fiscal year 1918. Ore mined, 303,672 tons.

Material	Cost
Cordwood	$0.06972
Mining timber	0.30921
Lumber	0.05654
Charcoal	0.01047
Total timber cost	0.44594
Total mining cost	1.82979

The company's timber concession lies to the north of Unsan in the two adjoining districts, the boundary being a chain of rugged mountains rising 2000 ft. above the floor of the valley, wherein are situated the two largest mines—Tabowie and Taracol. These mountains, forming an effective barrier to all ordinary means of transportation, necessitated the construction and operation of a small railway and gravity planes. This is now an organization, separate from the mines, and its operation has proved satisfactory and economical. During the first 10 years of operation the company purchased all timber from native contractors cutting in Government forests, but the exclusive timber-right on the present concession, a mountainous region 300 square miles in area, was obtained from the Japanese Residency General during 1909. The bulk of the forest consists of oak, maple, birch, and ash; the maximum size averages 2 ft. diameter. In addition there are some fir, scrub pine, and other soft-wood trees. All cutting is done by contract, supervised by company rangers, who enforce compliance with the Government forest regulations regarding protection of young growth, and the leaving of certain varieties of trees.

The narrow-gauge railroad, started in 1906 at a pass two miles from Tabowie and at an elevation 1500 ft. above the mine, winds around the mountain sides into the timber-belt. The road has been extended yearly to a total length of 20 miles, and is used exclusively for transporting timber and lumber. Being built around the sides of the rugged mountains, it of necessity has many sharp curves and some steep grades. Many of the curves on the older sections of the road have only a 50-ft. radius. The railway is also a scenic wonder, and many visitors are unanimous in proclaiming it the "crookedest road existing." A yearly tax of $12,500 for re-forestation of this area is paid to the Government.

LABOR. One of the original, and which later proved to be one of the most important agreements between the

NATIVE DRILLING-CONTEST ON JULY FOURTH

Emperor and the concessionaire, was a condition that natives should be employed to as great an extent as possible in all branches of the company's business, and all due facilities given them to acquire a knowledge of modern mining methods as carried on abroad. This agreement seemed to be an anticipation to Mr. Perkins' policy of always using local labor. By the support of the manager and the sympathy of his staff at the mines the company has fulfilled this labor pledge so far as was found practicable.

The labor question here, however, has never offered any serious perplexities. About 90% of the men are Korean. The number of Chinese workers is on the increase; their work underground is confined to drilling in hard ground and as trammers, and on the surface as stone-masons and general rough workers. The more skilled laborers, such as carpenters, smiths, and machinists are mostly Japanese.

The Koreans' environment seems to lend them a special aptitude for underground work, and after a comparatively short training make excellent miners. They are fairly intelligent, docile, obedient, and easy to handle.

but careless and require strict supervision. They work intermittantly, due principally to a failing for alcoholic beverages, but remain at work on the mines for years, and not a few have been employed since the beginning of operations. The average native will perform about one-third the work of a white man under the same conditions. Their wages range between 25 and 40 cents per day.

The Chinese are more industrious and enterprising than the natives and physically much stronger, but as a general all-around mine workman the Korean has proved himself far superior and more efficient than his celestial rival. Aside from the few Chinese mentioned above, the Korean performs all the labor in the mines, on the surface and about the mills and cyanide works; as blacksmiths, machinists, carpenters, in the metallurgical plants, and even in the accounting and engineering departments they have shown their ability. In many departments they have replaced high-priced white employees to a large extent. Between 4000 and 5000 Koreans find employment with the company.

Safety and Welfare Work. Until a few years ago, the real value of safety work was not recognized; rather dangerous practices and conditions existed in the mines and the accident rate was high. By co-operative efforts the mine officials have brought about a marked change for the better. Excellent progress has been made in this work during the past three years, and today the accident rate among the native miners is little over that in many American metal mines.

A manifestation for the welfare and safety of their fellow-workmen is now shown by the natives, a characteristic entirely lacking a few years ago. Now all dangerous and unprotected working places are reported immediately to the shift-bosses, and accidents and fatalities are reported to the Police Department, which makes a thorough investigation of each case.

The increasing depth of the workings, great quantities of decaying timber, and high temperatures, coupled with the natives' natural carelessness, makes the danger from mine fires a constant worry to the management. The company keeps at each of the large mines a boss trained in first-aid work and the use of rescue apparatus.

The company donates considerable sums of money to the civil authorities for the promotion of welfare work among the miners. Among these things might be mentioned street improvements, establishment of a fire department, a large central free bath-house, support of a sanitation service, and donations to schools and numerous civic organizations and activities. Besides this the company also maintains a large and well-equipped hospital run under the direction of a competent physician and surgeon. All medical treatment is free to the company employees and their families.

Having large and proved resources the company has made all improvements of a permanent and substantial character. The foreign operating staff, numbering about forty-five, and their families, are well housed with all modern conveniences, everything being furnished by the company. A fine civic centre has also been established with a school-house, recreation grounds, tennis-courts, etc., and a large club-house for social gatherings and amusements. The company's welfare work is being promoted in a commendable manner and it has proved a good investment. The company's concession rights date to 1954.

General. Being so distant from the base of all supplies, the company has always made a practice of keeping on hand a large stock of mining materials and spare parts for machinery. The value of such a policy was

NATIVE MILL USED BY PROSPECTORS

demonstrated at the outbreak of war, when shipping facilities were so badly disorganized. The transportation department handles all supplies and freight from the various ports of entry. This department formerly conveyed all the bullion from and money to the mines, but these have been transported through the Imperial Japanese post-office since the attempted robbery by bandits in October 1916. The expense of transportation represents a considerable item on the supply cost-sheet.

Besides the mines now operating the company has a number of partly developed prospects, which later will be brought to the producing stage. The exploration department is continually seeking new prospects, and it is not improbable that more deposits may yet be found within the company's concession. Extensive alluvial deposits, the richer portions of which were worked early by the natives, extend through the area and cheap power may make them yield a profit by the use of dredges.

A large concentrate tailing dump at Taracol, the accumulation of years of leaching at the central cyanide plant, is expected to yield a good profit by re-treatment after fine grinding, as soon as a lower cost of chemicals and supplies will warrant construction of suitable plants.

The Oriental Consolidated Mining Co. has, since beginning operations in 1896, mined 4,766,270 tons of ore having a gross value of $29,423,235, from which $7,938,645 has been distributed among shareholders as dividends.

The writers acknowledge with thanks the suggestions and data given by the various department heads and plant foreman, as well as the interest and aid extended by the management. The company officers are: Henry C. Perkins, president; Alf Welhaven, general manager; Thomas W. Van Ess, assistant-general manager; and Joseph B. Lower, superintendent.

Mining in the Footsteps of Javan

It was D. C. Jackling who said that all the great porphyry copper mines of today had long been known as sources of that metal, although upon a far smaller scale. This is a broad generalization, but not so universally true as to act as a deterrent upon investigation of copper prospects that lack an industrial history. Nevertheless the feeling is strong among copper miners that the old sources of world supply are worthy of re-examination. Several years ago an expedition was sent through the Sinai peninsula where the Egyptians mined and smelted copper actively in the epoch of the Rameses. It is here that Moses is supposed to have gone before his exile, and to have had some connection, as a royal representative, with the cherished copper industry. Another group of American engineers was sent into the northern part of Asia Minor to study the deposits that were worked by Tubal Cain, the traditional and semi-historic father of iron and copper metallurgy, leading to an industry that was great for that age, and which made his descendants, the Tibareni, noted throughout the world. They were the early makers of brass instruments of music, which were shipped to all countries, and the steel which they produced served as the basis for the skilled workmen who turned out the famous Damascus blades. Except for the catastrophe of war these ancient mines by this time would have become active again, producing copper under the direction of American mining engineers and metallurgists.

Another early centre of copper production was the Island of Cyprus. The very name of this bit of land means 'copper', Κυπρος in the Greek, from which came the Latin name for copper, cuprum. In the Scriptures the island is known by an early form of the same word, that is, Kaphtor, and it is told that Javan, a brother of Tubal Cain, both being sons of Japhet, went there, and he is said to have become famous as a worker of copper on Mount Alasya, on the Cyprian island. The mines were long regarded as an important source of copper, and were worked by the Phoenicians and later by the Romans. The accompanying picture of a Mediterranean miner with an ore-bucket on a trolley was taken by Karl S. Twitchell, formerly engineer for the De Lamar mine in Idaho, in present-day exploratory workings on these same deposits that are supposed to have been operated in a primitive way by Javan and the tribe that sprung from him. This mono-rail haulage system is in use on the 915-ft. level of the Skouriotissa mine in Cyprus. Mr. Twitchell writes, "We cannot get any track, cars, or other mine supplies, so I rigged up this scheme, and it works very well. The rail is mostly $\frac{7}{8}$-in. octagonal drill-steel. The buckets are carbide drums. These buckets are run to the shafts, unhooked, and put on the hoist-rope." Mr. Twitchell has found that the peculiar knack of the pioneer in new fields has its value also in realizing the opportunities present in regions dominated by the remnants of worn-out civilizations. He was engaged in cutting timbers and in making lumber by primitive methods for the use of the British army in Egypt before going to Cyprus.

A MAKE-SHIFT

MILLS AND CYANIDE WORKS in the goldfields of Ontario have a total daily capacity of 6110 tons, says the 'Mining Review' of Cobalt. There are 20 plants, of which 16 were closed during the latter part of the War; but many are to resume soon. Porcupine mills can treat 5400 tons per day, the Hollinger leading with 2800, and Dome with 1350 tons. Kirkland Lake mills treat 490 tons; while the two at Boston Creek treat 80, two at Munro 90, and two at Larder Lake 50 tons.

The Colorado Pitchblende Company

*The following report was addressed, on February 18, 1919, to the President of the Colorado Manufacturers Association. It is signed by Richard A. Parker, as chairman, and George A. Stahl, as secretary:

The Mining Bureau of the Civic and Commercial Association which, at your solicitation in December last, named Mr. J. M. McClave as an engineer to be employed by the Colorado Pitchblende Co. to examine and report upon its property, received the final draft of Mr. McClave's report on February 13, 1919. We hand you herewith the McClave report, together with his bill for services. Please see that the bill for Mr. McClave's services is paid before delivering the report to the Colorado Pitchblende Company.

The following comment upon the company and its enterprise seems appropriate and proper.

The subject in hand naturally divides itself into three principal heads:

1. The company's promotion methods.
2. The engineer's report.
3. The commercial aspects.

1. The company's promotion methods. We feel that the advertising methods adopted by the company cannot be too strongly condemned. The advertisements which have appeared are hugely sensational and manifestly designed to induce small investments in the hope of securing large profits which we believe can never be realized. The company's advertisements contain certain misleading statements, for instance,

(a) "$3,290,400 a year potential profits," when such profits can be realized only if and when a 1000-ton mill is constructed and operated on the basis of anticipated success and assumed market conditions, neither of which we consider warranted from figures submitted.

(b) "It is estimated that less than $1,000,000 will be required to equip this company with production capacity equaling one thousand tons a day (or $3,290,400 profits a year). This would indicate that each dollar invested would earn $3.29 a year."

This statement leaves out of the calculation the 640,000 shares of outstanding stock which, of course, must participate equally in profits with the stock which the company is proposing to sell. On the basis of the company's own figures, each share of 1,140,000 shares of stock outstanding in a company earning $3,290,400 per annum would be entitled to $2.80, or, as the company is now offering stock for $2 per share, the profit on the price paid would be 140% per annum instead of 329%, as stated in the advertisements.

These advertisements are calculated to arouse an abnormal sympathy and interest in the general public by strongly intimating, in fact, charging in some instances, that those who do not believe in the wonderful future claimed for the enterprise and, therefore, conscientiously urge conservatism in respect to it, are actuated by ill-patriotic motives, when nothing could be further from the fact.

The advertisements emphasize the property as a radium property, thus exciting the popular conception that the enormous profits claimed are to come from the recovery and sale of that rare and mysterious mineral, when the reports show, as a matter of fact, that other products are expected to return more than one-half of the anticipated profits when operating on a 1000-ton basis.

We feel that the Colorado Pitchblende Co. is not justified in either the method or substance of its advertisements.

The Denver Civic and Commercial Association is, of course, always anxious to aid any meritorious Colorado enterprise which is conservatively managed and on a sound business footing, but the Mining Bureau feels that the advertisements of the Colorado Pitchblende Co. are of such a nature that it cannot be regarded as in the class entitled to any manner of commendation at the present time.

2. The engineers' report. The report of Mr. James M. McClave, who was designated by this Bureau to examine the Jamestown properties, at the expense of the Colorado Pitchblende Co., is attached hereto.

We cannot agree with the conclusion reached by Mr. McClave from the figures contained in his report. We accept Mr. McClave's conclusion that there is a large tonnage of ore in the properties examined, but we do not believe that there has been a sufficient measurement of technical ore to justify any determination of total available tonnage, and, upon the experience of many competent authorities, we believe his estimates of mining costs are low.

We also accept his conclusion of a probable 75% recovery in a suitable mill, notwithstanding the fact that the conclusion is based entirely on laboratory experiments and is not supported by mill-tests; we think, however, that there must be an additional loss of 10% in that portion of the mill-product which must be subjected to oil-flotation, and a further loss of 20% in the chemical treatment of the uraninite for the recovery of the radium.

3. Commercial aspects. From a commercial standpoint there are three products to be considered:

(a) The gohl-silver-lead concentrate.
(b) The fluorite.
(c) The uraninite.

(a) The gold-silver-lead concentrate. Upon the evidence of experienced producers of all classes of minerals we feel that Mr. McClave's estimate for freight and treat-

*Report of the Mining Bureau of the Civic and Commercial Association, of Denver.

ment charges is low. However, assuming his figures of $2.70 as the per ton value of gold, silver, and lead in the crude ore, and $3.50 as the per ton cost of operation, it is manifest that this product alone cannot make a profit.

(b) The fluorite. Our inquiry into the fluorite situation convinces us that no considerable market can be anticipated for this product in the future. Immense accumulated supplies in excess of the market requirements, produced as an incident in metal mining, have for years been available in England for immediate shipment. That this competition has been formidable is evidenced by the large tonnage imported in the past notwithstanding a duty of $1.50 per ton. This competition will undoubtedly return as ocean transportation returns to normal conditions. The domestic production has come mainly from the Illinois-Kentucky district where the pre-war prices obtained were fixed largely by the cost of production. That this district failed to furnish sufficient for our entire home consumption in the immediate past, appears to have been due to the labor shortage and not to any deficiency in the source of supply.

Fluorite was not shipped from Colorado until the abnormal conditions in the iron and steel industry, due to the War, had caused prices to advance sufficiently to overcome the heavy freight to Eastern points of consumption. Under these conditions several thousand tons of Colorado fluorite were sold, but it appears extremely doubtful if such sale could continue should the price recede to a level even considerably above that prevailing before the War.

Extensive inquiry among producers and consumers failed to develop any active demand at present, the only spar moving to market now, being such as is shipped under long-time war contracts. The proposed production of the Colorado Pitchblende Co. equals fully half the entire United States consumption in 1917 or 1918, and such an amount, if placed upon the market, would create a great over-supply. Under such conditions the Illinois-Kentucky field would probably be the one to survive, owing to low production cost and proximity to market. The higher price which the washed product is claimed to command would scarcely half offset the higher freight-rate to points of consumption.

(c) The uraninite. This subject divides itself naturally into two parts: (1) uranium oxide, and (2) radium.

1. Uranium oxide. At times small quantities of this commodity are marketed but consumption is so small that it cannot be regarded as a source of income.

2. Radium. After investigation of the possibilities of profit from the radium in the uraninite content of the ore, we submit the following figures as our estimate of the maximum profit available from an ore containing 1.08 pounds of pitchblende per ton, such as the ore under consideration:

Basis:

Uraninite content of ore, per ton	1.08
Value of radium, per mg	$100
Cost of chemical treatment, refining, and marketing, per mg	$ 40
Loss by table concentration, per cent	25
Loss by oil-flotation, per cent	10
Loss by chemical treatment and refining, per cent	20

Calculation:

Value of radium in 1.08 lb. uraninite	$ 13.82
Loss by table concentration, 25%	3.45
Value of radium in water concentrate	10.37
Loss by oil-flotation, 10%	1.03
Value of oil-flotation product	9.34
Loss by chemical treatment and refining, 20%	1.87
Value of final radium salt	7.47
Cost of chemical treatment and refining	5.00
Value of final product per ton of ore	2.47

These figures, however, are based upon the assumption that the entire overhead mining, operating, and milling costs of recovering the uraninite from the crude ore have been borne by other products. If such costs are to be charged to the radium product alone, the profit would disappear.

Conclusion: Our conclusion is that the business hazards of this enterprise, which we have touched upon briefly in this report, are such that its commercial success is a problem still insufficiently demonstrated, and that, upon present evidence, no such profits as advertised can be expected.

Mineral Production of Ontario

Preliminary figures for 1918, prepared by the Bureau of Mines at Toronto, have just been issued. The principal products are as under, compared with 1917:

Product	1918 Quantity	1918 Value	1917 Quantity	1917 Value
Cobalt, metal, pounds	404,348	$887,960	396,395	$589,290
Cobalt, oxide, pounds	476,053	725,105	418,703	533,489
Copper, tons	23,556	8,532,790	21,466	7,961,662
Fluorspar, tons	1,834	42,102	4,327	66,974
Gold, ounces	411,879	8,502,542	420,893	8,698,735
Gypsum, tons	38,214	151,564	48,493	130,138
Iron, pigs, tons	50,072	1,359,541	49,485	1,016,690
Iron pyrite, tons	267,786	1,152,027	286,049	1,111,264
Lead, tons	835	149,841	886	172,601
Molybdenite, pounds	47,014	59,067	77,517	47,614
Nickel, tons	44,297	26,578,200	41,887	20,943,500
Silver, ounces	17,409,264	17,364,918	19,479,692	16,183,208
Talc, tons	17,465	246,691	16,076	179,554

The total value of metallic products was $66,119,792, and non-metallic $14,045,928, against $56,831,857 and $15,261,975, respectively, in 1917.

The outlook for gold mining for 1919 is considered bright. Last year, Porcupine produced 816,037 tons of $9.60 ore, and Kirkland Lake 55,523 tons of $11.89 ore. The Hollinger led with 578,755 tons valued at $5,706,214, followed by the McIntyre with 176,976 tons and $1,561,735, Lake Shore with 16,749 tons and $415,230, Tough-Oakes with 22,000 tons and $136,828, Porcupine Crown with 10,907 tons and $123,563, and Dome Lake with 11,929 tons and $100,799. The Hollinger, McIntyre and Lake Shore distributed $1,873,042 in dividends.

The silver output was 17,409,263 oz., of which 16,558,420 oz. came from Cobalt and 774,403 oz. from Gowganda and other districts, a total of 17,332,804 oz. Of this, 9,506,017 were extracted at Cobalt, 5,014,469 oz. at refineries at Deloro, Thorold, and Welland, and 2,812,318 oz. at refineries in the United States.

Mines yielding over 1,000,000 oz. were: Coniagas, 1,006,104 oz.; Kerr Lake, 2,221,811 oz.; Mining Corporation, 1,994,061 oz.; Nipissing, 5,785,739 oz.; and O'Brien, 1,074,312 oz. Seven companies distributed $4,696,513 to shareholders, making $75,518,342 to date.

Tungsten

Of the $8,500,000 available for re-payment under the War Minerals Relief measure, it is estimated that tungsten producers will receive a large proportion.

The following notes, including the graphs, are from the February report of H. C. Morris of the U. S. Bureau of Mines:

The information obtained from various sources regarding tungsten and tungsten products during the month indicates clearly the extremely unsettled conditions of the industry in every branch. Estimates as to stocks of concentrates on hand in the East varied from 2500 to 7000 tons, and showed the desirability of some such assistance as the trade will receive from the compilation of reports or questionnaires. A moderate amount of concentrates of good grade have been disposed of during the past month at considerably under $10 per unit, and it is reported that England is offering first-grade material for 30 shillings [$7.20]. It is also said that a standard grade of English high-speed steel is being offered in New York at $1.70 per pound, and that some such steel may come on the market at a much lower price. The curves presented herewith show various interesting and pertinent facts regarding tungsten and tungsten products.

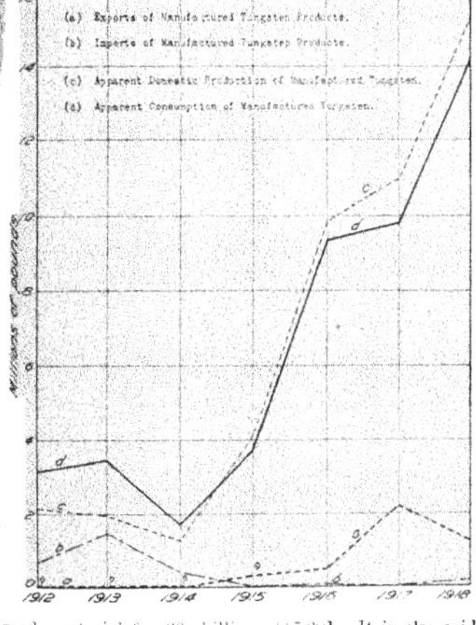

At a meeting of the Tungsten Committee held at New York on March 12, the following resolution was proposed and adopted, according to advice from Charles Hardy:

"It was moved that the chairman appoint a committee of three to present to James T. McCleary, secretary of the American Iron and Steel Institute, a resolution known as 'Resolution No. 1' in person, and to explain to

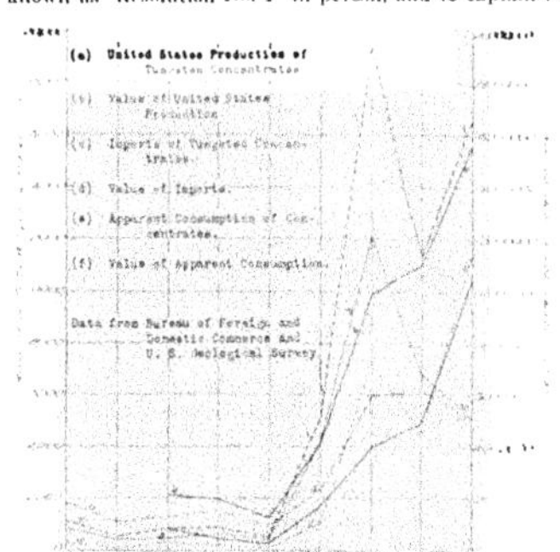

Mr. McCleary the personnel of the committee of nine, the method of election and our right to represent the industry, and that we also ask of the American Iron and Steel Institute that our committee of nine, known as the Tungsten Committee, receive consideration in the appointment of a chairman to represent the tungsten industry in presenting our case to the Redfield Peek Commission through their assistance."

Discussing the position of the tungsten industry of Sheffield, England, John M. Savage, U. S. Consul, said

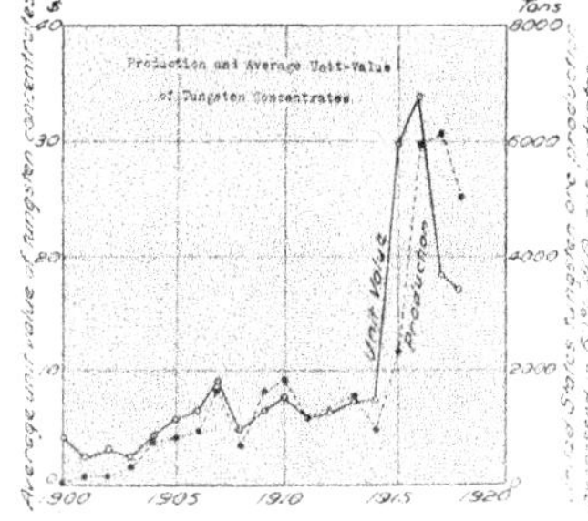

that the demand for high-speed steel has dropped to such an extent that one of the new tungsten plants at Sheffield alone is able to supply more of the alloy than is needed in that city, and grave apprehensions are felt as to future requirements. Meanwhile the Government has reduced the price of wolfram ore £1 10s. ($7.20) per unit, and the prices of ferro-tungsten and tungsten powder have fallen 2s. (48 cents) per pound.

Rapid Method for Determination of Tungstic Oxide

By F. A. RAPP

The following, a modification of Low's cinchonine sulphate analysis, is a quick method for tungstic acid in scheelite. By slightly changing the procedure, concentrate may also be tested. This system was used by the Tungsten Mines Co. at Bishop, California.

Grind 2 grammes of the sample to a fine powder. Weigh into a 600-cc. beaker. Digest slowly on the hot-plate with 40 cc. of aqua regia (10 cc. nitric and 30 cc. hydrochloric acid). Take down to 5 to 8 cc., stirring occasionally. Remove, add about 100 cc. of water and stir. After settling for half an hour, filter through an 11-cm. filter paper, retaining as much of the residue as possible, in the beaker. Add to the beaker about 5 cc. of the ammonia solution made from 80 cc. ammonium hydroxide, 4 cc. hydrochloric acid, and 400 cc. of water. Warm on the hot-plate and pour through the original filter. Repeat this operation. Wash beaker and filter three times with a 2% hot ammonia solution.

Remove filtrate from underneath the funnel, and add about 6 cc. of the cinchonine solution made from 50 gm. cinchonine sulphate, 200 cc. hydrochloric acid, and 200 cc. of water. In case the filtrate is not acid before adding the cinchonine solution, it should be made so by the addition of a little hydrochloric acid. Place the beaker on the hot-plate and heat for 1 hour, or until all the WO_3 is precipitated. Remove and filter, catching the precipitate on a 9-cm. ashless filter-paper. Wash 7 to 10 times with a dilute solution of the above cinchonine solution. Ignite the filter in platinum and weigh, subtracting the weight of the filter-ash. The difference in the weight will be WO_3. Divide by 200 to get the percentage.

Calcium Carbide Derivatives

By F. H. MASON

The exigencies of war have done much to awaken the genius of chemists all over the world. In the 'Press' of January 11, I gave an outline of the methods of preparing acetone from seaweed at the Hercules Powder Co.'s plant, near San Diego. As stated then, acetone came into great demand during the War for the blending of nitroglycerine and nitro-cellulose in the manufacture of cordite and other high explosives. At Shawinigan Falls, in the Province of Quebec, acetone was prepared on an extensive scale by quite a different method. There, acetylene, prepared from calcium carbide, is first subjected to treatment with sulphuric acid and a salt of mercury, which convert it into acetaldehyde. After purification by distillation, this compound is converted into acetic acid by a catalyst, and the acetic acid, after purification by distillation, is oxidized by the aid of a catalyst to acetone. Fortunately, there is no need for an obituary notice, as was the case with the San Diego plant, to the two plants at Shawinigan Falls, for, though there is no longer any great demand for acetone, such a high grade of acetic acid is produced that it is in considerable demand for the manufacture of dyes and for other industrial purposes. After distillation, the acid is over 99% pure, and is entirely free from tars and resins, so often associated with the acid when it is obtained from the destructive distillation of wood, and so detrimental in the manufacture of fine dyes. The two plants at Shawinigan Falls have been in operation since 1916, and each yielding from 700 to 800 tons of glacial acetic acid per month.

As long ago as 1907, calcium carbide was used for the manufacture of calcium cyanamide, from which ammonia has since been prepared, while the ammonia thus made has been oxidized by the aid of a catalyst to nitric acid. In fact, everything seems to point to the bulk of the nitrates of the future being made from the air by the aid of calcium carbide. Recently, carbide has come to the front as the starting point for the synthetic preparation of a number of chemicals, among which may be mentioned alcohol, acetylene, tetrachloride, chloral hydrate, chloroform, ethyle acetate, formaldehyde, and monochlor acetic acid. This seems likely to be only the beginning of a long list of chemicals that in future will be derived indirectly from calcium carbide. Thus, it will be seen, largely through the use of catalysts, calcium carbide, which originally was discovered accidentally during the attempt to reduce the metal calcium from lime by carbon in an electric furnace, seems likely to become a competitor with coal-tar as the nucleus for the synthetic preparation of many chemicals hitherto made by more costly methods.

Shaft-Sinking Record

By R. C. WARRINER

A new world's record in shaft-sinking was made during December 1918, at the Crown Mines, Johannesburg, of which I was consulting engineer to the end of 1918. The shaft in question is circular, having an outside diameter of 21½ ft., and 20 ft. inside the walling. During the period mentioned it was sunk 279 ft. from a depth of 655 to 934 ft., equal to an average of 9 ft. per 24 hours. The previous world's record was also held by this company, when 252 ft. were sunk in a 31-day month at No. 14 circular shaft of the Crown Mines. This was also a 20-ft. shaft. The cost of sinking, exclusive of walling, was between £13 and £14 ($62.40 and $67.20) per foot.

SULPHUR remains at the same price as during the War, namely, $22 per ton, f.o.b. mines. Little business is being done at that figure, but the Louisiana-Texas producers are not inclined to make any cut.—Sulphuric-acid production has been curtailed considerably, and 66°B. acid is offered at $20 per ton in the East. By-product acid, 50°, from zinc plants, is as low as $10 per ton at Chicago.—Pyrite stocks were large last November, and until these are absorbed, and markets and prices are re-adjusted, the demand is likely to remain uncertain.—R. R. Horner in charge of this division of the U. S. Bureau of Mines.

DIVIDE, NEVADA

The Tonopah Divide Opens Rich Ore at 465 Ft.; Official Assay Given.—What is Being Done by Others in the District.

A meeting of operators and claim-owners has adopted formally the name of Divide to designate the district, and the townsite will be known as Divide. Application will be made later for a post-office; mail is now received at Tonopah.

In the Tonopah Divide mine, the silver vein has been cut on the 465-ft. level. The shaft has been sunk below 550 ft., and another cross-cut will be driven to the vein at 565 ft. A. I. D'Arcy, the consulting engineer, has supplied the following information: The fourth level cross-cut penetrated the vein 140 ft. from the shaft, in low-grade material, over 25 ft. wide. The drift south-east near the foot-wall entered ore within a short distance. This drift, the main haulage-way for this level, is at least 5 ft. wide. A sample across the face, 30 ft. from the cross-cut, assayed $269.10, containing 1.26 oz. gold and 243.9 oz. silver. The second round following exposed a full face assaying $473 per ton. On the third, 365-ft. level, the ore-shoot has been developed for a length of 420 ft., and the south-east drift is still in shipping ore. The raise from this level, 250 ft. from the shaft cross-cut, is up 40 ft. Mine-car samples for this distance give an average of $70 per ton. This raise will connect with the second level at a point where ore assaying $58 has been opened for a width of 30 ft. The sill on the third level, at the fault intersection, is now 50 by 20 ft. and broken to a height of 10 ft. Ore broken in this area has averaged over $80 per ton. One day's output of 46 mine-cars sampled $95 per ton. Shipments of 35 tons daily go to the MacNamara mill at Tonopah. The treatment cost is $5 per ton and extraction is over 90%. Freight teams are used to haul the ore. Before April 1 the volume of output will be increased, but not in large measure. The milling contract provides for a minimum of 40 tons and maximum of 60 tons daily. When water-level is reached, the directors will consider building a mill at the property. The nearest present water-supply is at Tonopah.

On the 500-ft. level of the Brougher Divide, the south cross-cut from the shaft has penetrated the Divide vein 25 ft., the vein material assaying $6 to $7 per ton. Drifts are being started both ways in the vein. Two seams of ore, assaying $18.85 and $80, were cut in driving to the vein. No other work has been done below the 177-ft. level, where small seams of ore were found.

In the Gold Zone, a drift is being advanced south-east on the vein at the 500-ft. level. This has exposed some $16 and seams of high-grade ore. Similar ore was found at this depth near the Divide boundary, at the north-west. Cross-cuts are to be driven here to explore for parallel veins.

The Hasbrouck company's 900-ft. tunnel has cut the main lode of the mountain at great depth, and has exposed good ore, showing free gold. This point is over 600 ft. below the apex. The first vein, 400 ft. from the portal, produced 1000 tons of $15 ore when silver was at 50 cents per ounce, and the consulting engineer estimates 3000 tons of similar ore available for shipment. The product will be sent to a mill at Tonopah, beginning shortly. The 400-ft. shaft is being re-timbered and equipped with high-power hoist and compressor. The first vein will be cut within 80 ft. of the shaft, 460 ft. below the tunnel-level. The company has $35,000 cash. George A. Kornick is president and H. F. Bruce is manager.

On the Gold Reef Divide property, adjoining the Gold Zone on the south-east, the main shaft is being sunk with good machinery at a point nearly in line with the trend of the Divide silver vein. The property has been prospected by several shallow shafts, open-cuts, and a short tunnel, exposing ore in small quantity, and one shaft contains the only water in the district. 'Dick' Williams has held this group for 12 years. The directors are San Francisco men, identified with the Western Union company.

The High Divide company, controlled by Wingfield and Brougher, has started work on its large group, covering a high conical mountain north-east of the Divide mine.

The Divide Consolidated has one of the best surface plants in the district, and is sinking a two-compartment shaft on ground adjoining the Brougher Divide and in line with the Divide fissure. Vein breccia broken near the surface assayed $9 across the width of the shaft. The company is leased by J. H. Miller, and Richard Finn is superintendent.

The East Divide shaft is down 370 ft. and cross-cuts will be driven at 400 ft. The shaft is in the lower Divide breccia, so-called, which forms the casing of the Divide vein, and seams of quartz have appeared. A large compressor has been provided to supply the drills of the East Divide and adjoining Alto Divide.

Equipment on the Alto Divide, adjoining the Gold Zone and Gold Reef, is complete, and sinking is in progress near the large vein exposed on the East Divide.

The Divide Extension shaft is making good progress near the Divide boundary and near a vein parallel to the Divide fissure. Zeb Kendall is president and manager.

Machinery of the Sutherland Divide will be in operation shortly at the 400-ft. incline shaft, near the Tonopah road. The property has shipped high-grade ore in the past, from the deep shaft and from shallow workings farther east. The shaft will be sunk 200 ft. deeper and drifts will explore the vein on the 300 and 400-ft. levels.

The Tonopah Dividend shaft is being sunk below the 300-ft. level, where two veins were explored without finding pay ore other than in small seams. Quartz seams, yielding low assays, have been cut in the shaft.

The Florence Divide, adjoining the Sutherland, is preparing to sink a deep shaft.

On the Rosetta Divide the new shaft has been started near a large vein from which good assays are obtained.

The Gold Wedge Divide, in the south-eastern part of the district, is sinking with good equipment near the Rosetta vein.

The Allied Divide, with claims adjoining the Gold Reef and East Divide, has secured hoisting equipment and will begin sinking its shaft soon on the Marquette claim.

The Gold Wedge Homestake group, owned since 1901 by William Watters, superintendent of the Tonopah Divide mine, has been transferred to Hugh H. Brown, counsel for the Tonopah Mining Co., as trustee for men connected with that company.

GOLD HILL, OREGON

Status of Mining in Southern Oregon.

Chrome miners in this region, who all suspended work in November, are still inactive, not taking up the mining of other minerals. They were all heavy losers and are collecting proofs of their losses in hopes of recovering from the appropriation made recently by Congress. Many, if successful in obtaining repayment, will be able to resume gold mining, in which they were engaged before the War. But little gold mining will be done in this district under the present high prices for machinery, supplies, and labor. A few fully equipped properties will be operated in the coming season, but no new development will be undertaken. The manganese properties are closed. The Rainier Mercury Co. and several small properties in the Meadows district north of Gold Hill are still operating their furnaces at the reduced price for quicksilver, and claim that they can produce at a good profit with the metal at $50 per flask.

The Nellie Wright group, under lease to R. M. Wilson of Gold Hill, and the Ray & Haff group, under the management of J. G. Davies, of Sacramento, are the only gold properties being operated at present in this district. Several leases have been made recently for important gold properties based on future operations. Among them are the Alice quartz mine, an old producer, three miles south of Gold Hill, leased to H. F. McClellan, W. S. Webb, and C. C. Clark of Medford.

Benjamin Hays and Horten Beeman, experienced local miners, recently took a lease on the Lucky Bart gold mine six miles north, and after two months work extending an old drift, uncovered a large body of $35 ore, 100 ft. below an old pay-shoot which produced $150,000. This property is well equipped with a 10-stamp mill, and has yielded $250,000 since the early 'nineties.

BISBEE, ARIZONA

Fire Fighting in the Shattuck.—Good Ore in the Denn.—Calumet & Arizona's Operations.—Stripping at Sacramento Hill.

The fate of the Shattuck-Arizona mine is a matter of much interest in the Warren district, since the ground in which there is fire on the 800-ft. level has been flooded with water. Except for fire fighting and a small amount of surface work no operations of any kind are under way at this property, and the management holds out no hope for resumption at an early date. Only 50 men are employed. Fire was discovered on about February 15. A cursory examination, all that was possible, showed that No. 1 stope at 800 ft. was the seat of the fire. Work was started at once, and by March 8 the ground up to the 700-ft. level had been bulkheaded. Flooding then was started with water obtained from the town supply and from other companies. This operation was found to be difficult on account of the fact that the fire was in old ground, much broken; but at last reports the water in the shaft stood above the 800-ft. level. It is proposed to flood the mine to 700 ft. if the ground holds water. At least two weeks must pass before water can reach the burning area, according to calculations, and after the fire is extinguished several months will be necessary to pump out the water and prepare the mine for operation.

Although it is questionable whether the management of the Denn-Arizona will decide to continue production at the present rate of 400,000 lb. of copper per month, it is certain that development will be hurried, in view of the recent discovery on the 1600-ft. level. This ore is now a carbonate. Work at 1700 ft. has been speeded up, the station having just been completed and driving started. The shaft is down 1800 ft. It is intended to cut a station on that level soon and start driving to develop the ore-zone toward which the 1700-ft. level is heading. Two hundred men are employed at present.

The Calumet & Arizona company is shipping enough ore to its smelter at Douglas to make approximately 3,500,000 lb. of copper per month. As far as information is obtainable there is no intention at present of reducing this output. The force employed has been held constant since the closing of the Cole and Oliver shafts. The policy of returning former employees arriving from Army or Navy to the positions they held before enlisting continues, and for that reason there is a considerable turnover in labor, although the number employed remains about stationary. Development in the Junction mine, where driving toward the Denn-Arizona side-line is under way, continues unabated, though with no results of particular interest. The 1600-ft. drift is in porphyry, while the 1400-ft. level, on which carbonate ores were found several weeks ago, has passed through the mineralized zone and again is in barren country. Advantage is being taken of the present lull in operations to make small repairs and betterments in equipment both in mines and smelters. At the smelter at Douglas, plans are being prepared for a new system of direct overhead charging of the furnaces.

No curtailment in operations of the Copper Queen on Sacramento hill is to be made, it is learned from official sources. Despite the short month of February, 160,000 tons of overburden was removed by the steam-shovel operating there. Neither there nor in any other department has the Phelps Dodge Corporation curtailed its force to any appreciable extent. There have been numerous changes in personnel, it is true, but these have been brought about chiefly by the return of men from the Service. It is peculiar to see men in sailor or soldier uniforms going to work.

The labor situation at Bisbee is complicated by the arrival of many young men who have been discharged from the Army in the training camps of the South-West, but who never before the War worked here or in mines anywhere. As many of these as can be placed are being put to work.

CRIPPLE CREEK, COLORADO

General Notes from Small Properties.

The Reva company, operating the Rose Nicol mine on Battle mountain under a six years lease, commenced shipping this week, moving ore to the loading-station over the new aerial tram. Production from now on will be continuous. The company for two years has been engaged in development and has expended $105,000, but now has a mine. On two levels—the sixth at 800 ft. from surface, and seventh at 1000 ft.—two distinct shoots on the Fluorine vein are under development. One of these is 150 ft. long, the other has been opened 80 ft., so far. The ore in both is of good milling grade. Ore has also been opened on the Rose Nicol at the Roosevelt tunnel-level, 2100 ft. below the collar of the Rose Nicol shaft. This body will be developed later.

Gold production from leased properties of the United company in February showed an increase of 350 tons over the preceding month. The gross value is estimated at $22,700. The Trail mine was the largest producer.

Seven sets of lessees on the Mary McKinney on Raven and Gold hills produced close to 400 tons of milling ore in February.

The Granite company and its lessees are extracting 35 tons daily from its Battle mountain estate.

A 75-hp. electric hoist has been moved from the Katinka mine on Guyot hill to the Nichols shaft on the north end of the El Paso Consolidated's estate.

The Cresson's net return for January amounted to $75,-884. Cash in the bank on March 1 was $1,678,526. Shareholders of this company are not required to include the dividends paid during 1918 in their income-tax returns, as the distributions of that year were paid from the sale of ore-reserves acquired prior to March 1, 1913.— —Shareholders of the Portland are not so advised, as the directors consider dividends paid by the company in 1918 to be taxable.

The New Gold Dollar Mining Co. has been incorporated. It succeeds to the holdings of the Gold Dollar Consolidated Mining Co., recently dissolved, and is capitalized with 3,000,000 shares of 5 cents par value. The holdings comprise 62 acres on the western slope of Beacon hill. A. E. Carlton is one of the directors.

Inclusion of the United Gold Mines Co. in a list published by the current issue of 'World's Work' under the caption 'A Thousand Worthless Investments', the final of a series of articles entitled 'Pirates of Promotion' by Louis Guenther, owner of the 'Financial World' of New York, has aroused intense indignation on the part of local shareholders, also at Denver and Colorado Springs. The properties of this company are active, have produced approximately $3,890,000, and shareholders have received $521,800 in dividends. The last was paid in 1917. The February output by lessees was valued at $22,700. A retraction will be demanded.

SILVERTON, COLORADO

Snow Hampers Work in All Branches of Mining.

Severe snowstorms, causing numerous slides, have raised havoc with mining and general business in this district. The railroads were blocked, tramways carried away, power-lines cut, and bunkhouses were damaged. Fortunately the slides have run without loss of life, although many narrow escapes have been reported. The Silverton branch of the D. & R. G. was blocked by a huge slide at Elk Park, 9 miles south. Although large crews have been at work trying to move the slide, several days elapsed before traffic was resumed. The first heavy storm began on February 25, accompanied by high winds, and within 24 hours all railroads were blocked. The Silverton Northern had several slides, and after a delay of 4 days, the road was cleared as far as Eureka. The crew then commenced operations on the Gladstone branch, in order to permit the moving of a large quantity of machinery en route to the Gold King Extension mines. The D. & R. G. had difficulty in forcing a way through the heavy drifts on Cumbres pass, on the main line to the east, and 4 days were required to open the road, so that the entire south-western Colorado was cut off from outside communication for this period.

The Anvil Leasing Co. is now in a position to resume shipping from the Coming Wonder mine, on the Emerald lode, and operated under a lease. The entire year of 1918 was spent in development, principally in the driving of a tunnel to cut the main vein. This is now nearing completion, the operators reporting satisfactory results.

The Sunnyside M. & M. Co. is running three shifts at the mine and mill, but a shortage of power resulting from a shortage of water in the reservoirs of the Western Colorado Power Co. permits working of the mill at only half capacity. Snowslides carried out seven towers of the Sunnyside aerial tram, cutting 50 ft. of cable and tearing out the bull-wheel, thus cutting off the ore supply. The Sunnyside is now shipping a car of zinc and a car of lead concentrate daily. The numerous reports as to the purchase of the Silverton Northern lines by the Sunnyside company have not been confirmed so far, but there are many factors that give credence to the report.

The Gold King Extension Mines Co. reports a large enough quantity of good-grade ore on hand to run the mill one shift, but no immediate start is contemplated. The snow has interfered with the plans of the company to such an extent as to defer the opening of the mill to June 1, as a large quantity of milling machinery en route to the mine has been stalled, entailing a delay to construction work. About 70 men are now employed.

The Iowa-Tiger mill tram had two towers carried out by snowslides, causing a shortage of ore supply for the mill, and affecting the output of the Iowa-Tiger and Mayflower properties.

MAP FROM U. S. G. S. FOLIO SHOWING ELEVATION IN SILVERTON DISTRICT, COLORADO.

The general outlook for the next few weeks is not very favorable from a production standpoint, as slides are to be expected for the ensuing month, the snow is heavy and in a condition to run. The weather conditions therefore have a marked bearing on the mining problems of this district.

In Bulletin 685 of the U. S. Geological Survey, just issued, W. W. Atwood discusses the relation of landslides and glacial deposits to reservoir-sites in the San Juan mountains. Most of the reservoirs built and projected are in lakes, but as these lakes are held back by detritus, many of the dams leak and give trouble.

CANANEA, MEXICO

Condition of the Northern States.

Discussion of Mexican affairs occupied a great part of the program of the Arizona Bankers' Association concention, held last week at Nogales, according to Russell Lowry, vice-president of the American National Bank, of San Francisco. Mr. Lowry says that he came away from the convention impressed with the idea that the reports of disturbances in Mexico were greatly exaggerated. According to Nogales bankers and business-men, he said most of the trouble has been in Chihuahua, the States of Sonora and Sinaloa being quiet and peaceable, and, moreover, extremely anxious to be on friendly terms with the United States. The business-men of the border towns sympathize heartily with the people of México. Recently a party from the Chamber of Commerce of Nogales went through Sonora and Sinaloa and were everywhere welcomed. A return excursion is being organized by the Mexican business-men, who will come as far north as San Francisco and will probably be accompanied by border bankers, who are desirous of seeing uninterrupted business relations resumed. Mr. Lowry said further that, from reports of Nogales bankers, there are great possibilities in trade across the border.

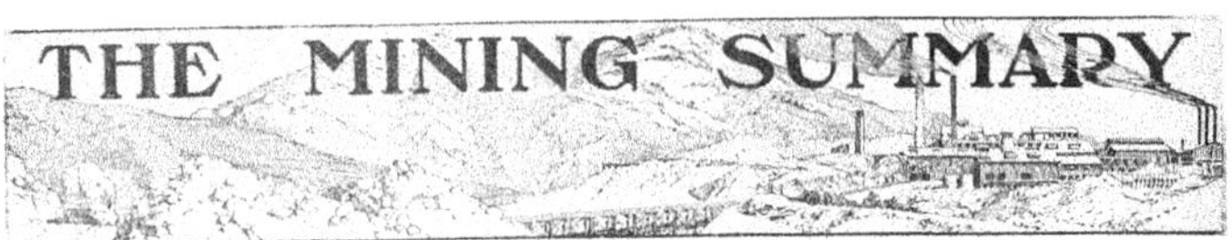

ARIZONA

Globe.—In the apex and water suits of the Arizona Commercial v. the Iron Cap, heard at Boston last week, the Court issued a preliminary injunction restraining the defendant from disposing of its assets, but reserved decision on the demurrer, and suggested that counsel confer. The contention of the Iron Cap that only Arizona courts should hear the case is being considered by the full bench.

Jerome.—The Jerome-Superior Copper Co. has been carrying on operations at its extensive property continuously. A mile north of Jerome, under the direction of George Mitchell and G. D. Case, and has not been inconvenienced by the strikes at the other properties. A complete equipment has been erected. The shaft is now over 600 ft. in depth, opening an encouraging showing of chalcocite and copper-iron sulphides. The west drift on the 500-ft. level is in 300 ft. through leached ore and gossan, and is making 40,000 gal. of water daily. An ample duplicate pumping system has been put in. A labor contract has recently been made providing for the sinking of the shaft 200 ft. deeper. This work is now being carried on.

During the shut-down of the United Verde Extension, extensive alterations to the smelting plant are being carried out. Work is continued in the shafts and haulage-tunnel.

The striking of high-grade ore in the Main Top workings of the Jerome Verde has caused a considerable advance in the price of shares. The cross-cut driven to determine the thickness of the orebody has shown it to be 17 ft. wide.

Kingman.—The Rural mine at Mineral Park has been taken over by M. B. Dudley and New York associates. A hoist has been erected and unwatering of the 200-ft. shaft is proceeding. This mine is said to have produced $100,000 in silver from shallow workings.

It is reported that the Record Lode mine has cut its vein at the 500-ft. level, where it is 20 ft. wide, 8 ft. of which assays as high as $28 gold per ton.

Oatman.—The Gold Dust mine is now operating with two shifts. This property, which was worked some years ago by A. L. White, is well equipped to carry on deep exploration. There is said to be a considerable quantity of milling ore above the 300-ft. level.

A. C. Werden, general manager of the Gold Ore Mining Co., announces that the finances of the company are so satisfactory that work is to be resumed soon.

CALIFORNIA

Bakersfield.—Oil production of all fields during February totaled 7,896,442 bbl., against 8,740,471 bbl. in January. The daily average was 65 bbl. ahead of the previous month. There were 8584 producing wells. Stocks on March 1 totaled 28,814,643 bbl., a gain of 77,061 barrels.

Eureka.—Bids were to be received on March 15 for construction of the highway from Orleans in Humboldt to Happy Camp in Siskiyou county. This will be of great benefit to mining.

Grass Valley.—The city council last week ordered the sale of mineral rights under the city cemetery to the North Star Mines for $300. The matter had been pending for several weeks.

Articles of incorporation of the Idaho Maryland Mines have been filed with the county clerk. The incorporators are Roy H. Elliott, Rufus Thayer, and A. B. Seybold, each of whom has subscribed $1000. The company is under the laws of Nevada with the principal place of business at Reno. The capital is fixed at 3,000,000 shares of $1 each.

Plymouth.—The Plymouth Consolidated in January treated 10,300 tons of ore, yielding $61,900 and a profit of $16,300. On the 2450-ft. level, the rise at 350 ft. north is up 113 ft., where 47 in. assays $7.50 per ton. The west drift at 308 ft. north was advanced 46 ft., assaying $8.95 across 24 in. The south drift, 616 ft. east, is out 26 ft. in $3.10 ore across 50 inches. At one point 635 ft. south on the 1600-ft. level, Plymouth Consolidated reports 5 ft. of $18 ore. The last 30 ft. assayed $13 across 55 inches.

Shawmut.—The Belmont Shawmut company expects to resume operations at its mine and mill early in April. The winze below the 2600-ft. level is down 180 ft, in good ore.

Sonora.—The old Dead Horse mine on the east belt above Tuolumne is being opened again, in charge of O. F. Heizer. The State Mining Bureau report on the property of the United Mines states that the Dead Horse has an 1800-ft. shaft, and the Grizzly one of 1000 ft., while the Lady Washington lower tunnel is a 2000-ft. cross-cut connecting with the Dead Horse shaft. The Dead Horse vein was extensively worked through the tunnel and shafts.

COLORADO

Georgetown.—The 300-ton flotation plant of the Colorado Central company is working full time concentrating dump material. The product—5 to 10 tons daily—assays 100 oz. silver per ton. Work is also under way in the old Marshall tunnel.

Idaho Springs.—The Randolph Gold M. M. & T. Co. has taken over the Empire T. & T. Co.'s property at Empire. W. A. Snyder is general manager. The Empire has been tied-up in litigation for some years. According to a recent report, there is estimated to be 1,773,000 tons of $6.25 ore available, which should yield $2 per ton net. A new mill is contemplated.

Leadville.—The Yak company has reduced wages by $1 per shift, effective April 15. This is considered to be the forerunner of a general cut in the district.

Norwood.—The Primos Chemical Co. has lost its blacksmith-shop by fire, adding to the heavy loss sustained three weeks ago when the mill was consumed. The cause has not been ascertained.

The Radium Company of Colorado operated continuously during the winter with a large force, and has been hauling ore from the mines in the Long Park district. At present, six 6-horse teams, two 4-horse teams, and three 2-ton motor-trucks are busy hauling ore.

Ouray.—The Camp Bird company office in London recently issued the following circular:

"In view of the very interesting work being carried out in the east drive from the tunnel at the Camp Bird mine, the directors think the shareholders will be glad to have the following summary in non-technical language of the recent cables which have been published, showing what has so far been accomplished. The cable information has been somewhat amplified by letters from the mine, and the directors are thus enabled to give additional general information to the shareholders.

"It may be useful to recall that the tunnel intersected the Camp Bird lode almost exactly at the point predicted by our engineers. At the point of intersection no value was encountered, which is what was to be expected from the conditions existing in the old workings above this point. Having thus proved the existence of the lode, its exploration was at once undertaken by a drift east. At about 1500 ft. from the point of intersection a run of high-grade ore was encountered, which seems to correspond with the body of ore extracted from workings on the old 9th level above it. Further driving on the tunnel level disclosed a small body of ore, the value consisting largely of silver. After passing through these two runs of ore, the east drift was continued in low value till at about 1950 ft. from the point of intersection another run of ore of good value was entered, and from this point to the present face appearances are very encouraging. This last-named run of ore probably corresponds with the important body of ore (which yielded a profit of some £500,000) which was extracted from the No. 3 shaft workings at and above the old 9th level, this being some 450 ft. above the present low-level tunnel. The manager has no hesitation in believing that the lode encountered—and driven upon for about 2000 ft.—from the tunnel is the true Camp Bird vein with known characteristics established in the old workings. The mineral hematite has made its appearance in the tunnel, and its presence seems to be an indicator of the existence of value in this section, as it always was in the upper workings.

"The directors conveyed to the manager their wish that connection should be made between the tunnel-level and the 9th level, by means of a raise (at the 1500-ft. point, where high value was found) simultaneously with pushing ahead of the east drift. He, however, has pointed out the difficulties, owing to insufficient ventilation, of doing this work on the two points at the same time, and further information is awaited hereon, with final decision of the manager as to the best policy. In the meantime exploratory work has been carried out by means of two raises about 30 ft. apart in the neighborhood of the two runs of ore at the 1500-ft. point. These raises have already passed through 13 ft. of good-grade ore, revealing a large vein, but the total width of the ore here is not yet determined. From the tunnel three cross-cuts also are being put in 50 ft. apart; notwithstanding this, the manager finds the results on the tunnel-level under the main No. 9 level ore-shoot (about the present end of the drift) so encouraging that he strongly recommends exploration at this point. In a letter just received from the manager describing existing conditions above the tunnel-level he says: '* * * vein conditions otherwise correspond with those on 9th level a little farther west, leading one to believe that probably the conditions existing in 9th level, at parallel 1450, are to be repeated in this level; and it was east of this point that we had the best stope in the 9th level'."

Rico.—The Hiawatha vein in the Group tunnel has been leased to Victor Lee. A large quantity of low-grade dump ore is being worked over.

The Syndicate M. & M. Co. has started to drive a cross-cut tunnel from the Group tunnel with the objective of cutting the Shouldn't Wonder, McKelvie, and Rider veins, opened by the main Group tunnel several years ago. The operators expect to cut these veins after they have passed through the large cross-veins known to exist in Newman hill. Rapid progress is being made in driving, 4½ ft. per shift; machine-drills are in use. Power is supplied at minimum cost, as the local power company is owned by the operators. An electric sinking-pump is being put in to handle the water that accumulates in the Smuggler south drift, in the Syndicate mine. A section of the company's holdings has been leased to A. Hay and A. S. Herron, who will drive a cross-cut to cut into a 'split' of the vein.

The Rico Wellington company has uncovered a good body of ore in the Mountain Spring tunnel. Copper ore has been opened in the Wellington tunnel. Large copper precipitation tanks are being erected in the 57-ft. level, in order to recover the copper that has formerly been lost in solution.

The Rico-Argentine, Marmatite lease, is again shipping ore, two cars having recently been hilled out. There are, however, no extensive operations under consideration at this time.

Telluride.—The Belmont Wagner company expects to resume operations at its mine and mill during April.

IDAHO

Burke.—The auxiliary power-plant of the Federal M. & S. Co. was burned on March 9. The loss is estimated at $20,000. Power is also supplied by the Montana Power Co., so work will not be interrupted.

Kellogg.—The Caledonia company pays 1 cent per share on April 5. This is $26,050 and makes a total of $3,777,250.

Wallace.—The Miners Trade School recently started here under the auspices of the University of Idaho is making good progress, according to F. A. Thomson, dean of the School of Mines of the University. The work is proceeding along entirely novel lines, the class-room being the 1400-ft. level of the Morning mine, where men just returned from army service are being taught practical mining. The work is being carried on by the State in co-operation with the Federal Board for Vocational Training, operating under the Smith-Hughes Act. The School has taken a contract to drive a drift at a price per foot, and the surplus, after paying for explosives, will be distributed pro rata among the pupils.

MISSOURI

Joplin.—Production of the Tri-State region last week was as under:

State	Blende, tons	Calamine, tons	Lead, tons	Value
Kansas	1,324	...	611	$91,557
Missouri	1,312	77	207	78,315
Oklahoma	5,440	...	1,293	302,218
Total	8,076	77	2,111	$472,090
Average value ...	$41	$27	$61	

The demand for ore is about normal.

The Badger M. & D. Co. has started its new 250-ton mill. In three shafts ore is found, at 96, 155, and 185 ft. depth, respectively. The 'run' of ore is 1280 ft. long. T. E. Forester is president.

MICHIGAN

Houghton.—Ahmeek pays $1 per share on March 31, equal to $100,000.——Osceola pays $1, or $100,000, on the same date. These are both reductions of $1 per quarter. During 1918 the Osceola produced 15,919,647 lb. of copper at a cost of 17.37 cents per pound. Ore yielded 13.3 lb. per ton. Dividends totaled $961,500. There was 1,194,967 tons of ore milled, a decrease of 42,838 tons.

Mohawk in February produced 1,146,493 lb. of copper, a trifle less than January, but much over the average for 1918.——Wolverine yielded 440,905 lb., larger than any month of last year.

Mass Consolidated Mining Co. in 1918 made a loss of $25,598, but the year ended with cash assets totaling $295,773. Receipts amounted to $796,638.

Comparison of results in the last three years is as follows:

	1918	1917	1916
Ore hoisted, tons.......	216,431	285,769	318,968
Ore stamped, tons.......	196,456	244,671	287,900
Refined copper, lb.......	3,403,827	3,984,616	4,752,588
Copper per ton, lb.......	17.33	16.29	16.51
Cost per pound, cents....	23.82	19.81	15.37

The approximate tonnage of ore from the three mines of the Copper Range Co. in February totaled 77,954 tons: the Champion 45,700, the Baltic 20,254, and the Trimountain over 12,000 tons.

MONTANA

Butte.—The Butte Copper & Zinc Co.'s report for 1918 (really for 13 months) shows that $669,328 was received from sales of ore. The net income, taxes not deducted, was $619,986. Current assets total $630,056, and liabilities $154,798. Dividend No. 1, on July 2, absorbed $300,000. Ore shipments were 32,293 tons of zinc and 71,364 tons of manganese. Mining of the latter was stopped in November, when the daily output was 375 tons. Much of this ore was sent to the ferro-manganese plant of Anaconda at Great Falls, now closed. Attention is now devoted to zinc ore.

Anaconda is extracting over 2000 tons of 15% zinc and 7-oz. silver, ore from its Emma mine, mostly from 800 ft. The manganese workings are being kept open, as the company believes that it may eventually be able to sell its Great Falls ferro-manganese as far east as Chicago.

NEVADA

Austin.—The main tunnel at the Austin Nevada has penetrated Lander hill for 600 ft., and is expected to reach the main vein within 350 ft. On the surface the body is 80 ft. wide, carrying silver and gold. At 600 ft. east of the main workings a tunnel is advancing to cut a vein showing a width of 58 ft. at the surface. At 800 ft. south-east of the main tunnel 12, parallel veins have been intersected by a cross-cut-tunnel, which is approaching a vein that assayed high in silver near the surface. One of the veins assays $35 per ton in gold. This tunnel is opening a number of small rich veins, and is being extended to intersect the main orebody 150 ft. below the main workings. The Hiawatha tunnel has been cleaned out and track laid preparatory to mining ore exposed in old workings. H. G. Richardson is manager.

High-grade silver-gold ore has been uncovered on the 200-ft. level of the Austin Dakota, and a winze from this point is down 50 ft. in ore. A small pump has been put in to handle water recently appearing in the shaft. Driving both ways is proceeding on the San Jose vein, and extraction of ore from it will be started soon. Charles E. Littrell is manager.

Re-opening of the Diana shaft of the Austin Manhattan has been delayed by a heavy flow of water on the bottom level. The shaft has been closed for 30 years, and is being repaired to facilitate mining of ore from old workings. William Marshall is superintendent.

The drift from the second level on the Warner, in Washington canyon, is exposing milling ore for the full width, with several shoots assaying 40 to 300 oz. of silver. A large tonnage of rich ore has been placed on dumps for shipment as soon as roads permit. From the third level, a drift is advancing to cut the orebody 150 ft. below the second level. The mine is owned by Mrs. Rose Warner and is in charge of W. M. Thacher.

Carson.—The biennial report of the State Assayer and Inspector, F. C. Lincoln, for 1917-1918, is to hand. Under the Nevada statutes of 1917 this officer was appointed. Upon request of any shipper to any Nevadan purchaser, it becomes the duty of the State Assayer to take charge of the shipment in the interest of the owner and see that it is properly sampled and assayed. The fee for this is 25 cents per ton on lots over 50 tons, and actual cost of sampling on smaller lots. From August 1, 1917, to December 1, 1918, this Department reported on 189 lots of ore. These were from 75 different operators in 28 districts, sent to three buyers. The total was 5308 tons. The Western Ore Purchasing Co. at Hazen received 187 lots, the others being one each to the Thompson plant of the Mason Valley Mines Co., and the West End Consolidated at Tonopah. Companies purchasing ore in Nevada during the period were the Elko Prince Leasing Co. at Midas, 680 tons; Goldfield Consolidated, 799 tons; Mason Valley, 275,625 tons; Nevada Consolidated, 413,719 tons; Silvermines Corporation, 4448 tons; Tonopah Belmont, 28,704 tons; Union Consolidated, 14,647 tons; West End Consolidated, 21,234 tons; and Western Ore Purchasing, 48,442 tons. The Department has 761 operators on its mailing-list, but only 10% have patronized it. Some of these are large shippers employing their own ore-checkers, while some attend to sampling themselves; but there must be many who might employ the State Assayer. In order to ascertain how the Department was viewed, a questionnaire was sent to 75 past patrons. Generally, the answers showed satisfaction, but that the facilities were not sufficiently advertised.

Goldfield.—It has been announced that, except minor details, an agreement has been made granting the Silver Pick Consolidated a sub-lease on the southern half of the Mohawk No. 1, north third of the Mohawk No. 2, and north fourth of the Combination claim of the Goldfield Consolidated, now under lease by the Goldfield Development Co. The leased territory includes over 20 acres adjoining the Silver Pick on the east and south-east. Work has been in progress for a long period on the 1250 and 1305-ft. levels of the Silver Pick, and recently the most promising formation found in the mine was opened at the latter depth in a seam, believed to indicate that the cross-cut is nearing a vein apexing far to the west of Silver Pick ground. Ore has not been found, but the ground is heavily mineralized. A cross-cut was started recently from the 700-ft. level. This will continue 120 ft. to the western boundary of the Mohawk No. 1, and into this claim to cut the Silver Pick vein in leased territory. There is also under consideration a plan to cross-cut on the 300-ft. level to explore the Combination vein north of the rich ore-shoot mined in the early days of Goldfield by the Kalfus, Begole, and Sheets-Ish lessees.

Goodsprings.—By an explosion at the Yellow Pine last week, the power-plant, hoist, and engine were badly damaged. The manager, M. P. Kirk, considers that little of the machinery is worth salvaging.

Mill City.—The tungsten mines and mills in this district are closed, due to the uncertain market. An immense quantity of ore has been developed.

Round Mountain.—The Round Mountain company expects to sluice 150,000 yards of $1 gravel this coming season. There has been a heavy snowfall, which has packed well, ensuring plenty of water.

Tonopah.—Production of the district last week was 7351 tons, valued at $124,967. Some February yields were as under:

Mine	Tons	Silver, oz.	Gold, oz.	Profit
Belmont ...	8,549	101,129	1,064	$50,061
Extension ..	8,628	111,384	1,094	45,957
Mining	4,500	76,775	845	39,465

The Belmont is to distribute 10 cents per share, $150,000, on April 1. The company is to resume operations at its Colorado and California properties in April.

NEW MEXICO

Santa Fe.—A substitute bill for the mining bills before the State Legislature has been consented to by all concerned. The operators agree during 1919 and 1920 to be taxed on average output for 1916, 1917, and 1918, regardless of what the future output may be, provided that if the coming output exceeds the old basis the tax is to be on the larger future output. The compromise may yield the State between $600,000 and $700,000 net increase in taxes in the next two years.

OKLAHOMA

Miami.—The Oklahoma Ore Storage Association has issued a booklet describing its organization and showing views of the ore-storage warehouse at Picher. The project was described by J. McNicholas in the 'Press' of March 1.

Picher.—One machine-man and a helper in the Cosmos mine near here broke 1159 cans (1000 lb. capacity each) of ore last week, according to the Joplin 'Globe'. W. Smith and F. Greishaber of the Blue Bird mine at Commerce considered that this record was beaten at the mine where they are in charge, as one driller and a helper, with Sullivan and Leyner machines, broke 2522 cans of ore, varying from 1250 to 1650 lb. each. For two months, 2000 cans per week was the average, with one machine. Four shovelers moved 414 cans in 6½ hours. [At an average of 1450 lb. per can, each man shoveled 75 tons per shift.]

MILLS AT CARDIN, OKLAHOMA.

OREGON

Sumpter.—The Continental Mining Co., 23 miles from here, has opened high-grade gold-silver ore. There is 4 to 16 in. of rich ore in a vein 18 to 36 in. wide. The ratio of the metals is 3:1. A 20-ton flotation plant is being erected. The elevation of the mine is 6940 ft. W. W. Robbins is president.

TEXAS

Austin.—The Governor has signed the new bill imposing a 1½% gross tax on oil production in this State. It is estimated that the annual income will amount to to $2,000,000.

Thousands of owners of Texan lands are relieved by the decision of the State Supreme Court that all minerals upon public lands sold by the State under the Act of 1883 went to the purchaser. What makes the case specially interesting is that several million acres, in the western part of the State, where exploration for oil is now going on, were sold under the law that was being contested. If the decision of the Court had upheld the contention of the relator in the case, oil and other minerals that are now being produced upon land sold under the law of 1883 would have passed to the ownership of the State of Texas.

The Dudley mining law bill was advanced in the House to the third reading, so it is expected to pass when finally considered. The Senate has already passed the measure. Its enactment is expected to aid development of mines. Oil, gas, and coal are not included.

UTAH

Bingham.—The Bingham Mines Co. in 1918 made a profit of $164,272, plus $167,458 from subsidiaries, a total of $331,730. Dividends totaled $375,000. Current assets amount to $158,248, mostly cash.

Utah Consolidated paid 25 cents per share, $75,000, on March 25.

Dugway.—The Metal State Mining Co., Henry Sellepers, manager, has decided to erect a 50-ton concentrating plant. The ore carries copper and silver.

The Metallic Hill and Lucky Star mines in this district of Tooele county are being worked continuously, the former having a carload of high-grade silver-lead-copper ore sacked.

Lark.—The Ohio Copper Co. closed its mine and mill on March 10. On hard ore, the flotation plant gave a high recovery; but on soft ore it was low.

Park City.—The Judge M. & S. Co. pays 12½ cents per share, $60,000, on April 1. The total is now $2,370,000.

The Daly West Mining Co. during 1918 sold ore, concentrate, and tailing, and received royalties from lessees totaling $184,592. Other income made a total of $217,564. The balance on January 1, 1919, was $23,623, against $30,208 a year ago. The treasury has now $163,000, including the new capital. All matters being cleared up, systematic exploration is to be carried on.

Salt Lake City.—In the prolonged argument in the Legislature over the Mine Tax Bill, on March 15, conferees of the House and Senate agreed to recommend that the assessment be fixed at three times the net proceeds of mines. This upheld the stand taken in the House, and the report was offered in the Senate on that date. The Senate finally passed the measure, but it is said that the Governor will veto it, as the bill did not contain the words "not to exceed" before "three times their net proceeds." This was the principal cause of the dispute between the House and Senate.

Governor Bamberger approved of the mine-tax law on March 21.

Tintic.—The Tintic Standard pays 8 cents per share on March 29, equal to $93,976. This makes $492,849 to date.

VIRGINIA

Midvale.—Advice from the Irish Creek Tin Mines company, which is prospecting a tin deposit in Rockbridge county, according to the U. S. Bureau of Mines, is to the effect that the orebodies, so far, are disappointing, both as to size and metal content. Of 19 samples taken, 14 gave blank returns, and the remainder an average of less than 1.5% tin.

WASHINGTON

Chewelah.—The United Copper Mining Co. during 1918

reduced its indebtedness of $74,919 to $39,879, but by April 1919 this would be wiped out. The revenue last year was $282,965, of which $46,674 was operating profit. Depreciation, taxes, etc., reduced this to $18,174. The output was $66,180 tons of ore, yielding 987,524 lb. of copper and 142,005 oz. of silver. When shipments of the new high-grade ore commences, profits are expected to be at least $30,000 monthly.

Northport.—The Electric Point company pays 3%, or $23,790, on April 1. The total will be $277,575.

Republic.—The Lone Pine-Surprise mines have been acquired by the Northport Smelting & Refining Company.

CANADA

British Columbia

Ainsworth.—The Florence Silver Mining Co. pays 1½ cents per share, $17,650, on April 20. The total is now $35,300. Monthly dividends are now to be paid. Two feet of galena, assaying 70% lead and 22 oz. silver, has been opened at a depth of 350 feet.

Anyox.—Granby Consolidated pays a dividend of 1½%, $187,500, on May 1.

Hedley.—The Hedley Gold Mining Co. paid 10 cents per share, $12,000, on March 31.

Nelson.—The Kootenay Gold Exploration Co., which operated the Granite-Poorman mine, is expected to resume operations shortly. Action has been taken toward paying off local creditors, and it is expected that the company named, which bonded the property from the old Kootenay Gold Co., will commence work without delay.

Victoria.—The sum of $207,523 has been expended by the Provincial government in construction of roads, trails, and bridges to mineral claims in British Columbia, since the present administration took charge late in 1916.

The development of a number of promising copper properties on Vancouver Island is to be continued this summer. Generally speaking, the policy of operators appears to be to proceed with the blocking out of ore to be ready for the readjustment of the market.

Ontario

Boston Creek.—The Miller Independence company is to sink a central vertical shaft to a depth of 600 ft. to intersect the vein, which dips at 50 to 60°. The encouraging results by diamond-drilling in the Cotter property adjoining are important to the Independence.

Kirkland Lake.—Lake Shore produced gold worth $45,162, from 1725 tons, in January. The estimated yield since the plant started in March 1918 is $515,000.

The U. S. Civil Service Commission, Washington, D. C., announces open competitive examinations by April 15 for junior metallurgist and junior mining engineer. At present there are two vacancies in the position of junior metallurgist at Seattle, each at $1500 per year, and two vacancies in the position of junior mining engineer, one at Seattle, at $1500, the other at Pittsburgh, at $1200. Competitors will not be required to report for examination at any place, but will be rated on education, training, and experience, 80; and publications, reports, or thesis (to be filed with application) 20. Under the first subject competitors will be rated upon the sworn statements in their applications and upon corroborative evidence adduced by the Commission.

The American Welding Society has been organized as a merger of the Welding Committee of the Emergency Fleet Corporation and the National Welding Council, also including several engineering societies. H. C. Forbes is secretary at 29 West 39th street, New York, the Engineering Societies building.

PERSONAL

Note. The Editor invites members of the profession to send particulars of their work and appointments The information is interesting to our readers.

D. P. Mitchell has arrived at Vladivostok.

B. C. Austin left for Teguchigalpa, Honduras, on March 22.

A. W. Stickney has moved from London to Galesburg, Illinois.

Thomas J. Jones is here on his way from London to Siberia.

E. M. Hamilton has returned to San Francisco from Parral, Mexico.

Denis Stairs, Captain in the B. E. F., was in Vancouver last week on his return from Siberia.

G. D. Delprat, manager of the Broken Hill Proprietary, has arrived from Australia on the 'Ventura'.

J. L. Zimmerman, of Columbus, Ohio, was in San Francisco on his return from Hermosillo, Mexico.

Drummond MacGavin, Captain in the Field Artillery, has returned from France to his home in San Francisco.

Fred. G. Farish is consulting engineer with the New England Exploration Co., with headquarters at Denver.

W. H. Blackburn, general manager for the Tonopah Mining Co., is in Nicaragua at the company's Eden mine.

John C. Greenway, Lieutenant-Colonel, has returned from Europe and is at Ajo, Arizona, recovering from the effects of gas.

Robert E. Montgomery, formerly in Denver, passed through San Francisco on his way from Victoria, B. C., to Texas.

Edward Steidle, well known from his mine-rescue work for the U. S. Bureau of Mines, lost an eye during the closing days of the War.

Harry Lee has retired from the superintendency of the Silver King Consolidated at Park City, Utah, and is succeeded by **Norman Blye.**

Courtenay De Kalb sailed by the 'Patria' for Spain on March 25. He goes on a special commission for the U. S. Department of Commerce.

G. W. Heintz, of the U. S. Smelting, Refining & Mining Co., is at Kennett, California, inspecting the properties of the Mammoth Copper Company.

Ira Joralemon, Major in the A. E. F., has returned from France to Berkeley and shortly will resume his duties as geologist to the Calumet & Arizona Copper Company.

J. Mackintosh Bell, Lieutenant-Colonel in the British Army, will resume his professional work as mining engineer. He has returned from Siberia and is now at Almonte, in Ontario, Canada.

F. R. Carroll, district manager (San Francisco) of the B. F. Goodrich Rubber Co., left on March 24 for the Orient on a special mission for that corporation. **W. T. Powell** will be acting manager in the interim.

John G. Kirchen, connected with many mining companies in Nevada, was unfortunate enough last week to have his foot crushed in the White Caps mill at Manhattan, rendering amputation necessary.

THE POSITION OF ASSOCIATE EDITOR ON THIS PAPER IS VACANT. APPLICATIONS FOR THE APPOINTMENT ARE INVITED.

Frederick Hobart, for more than twenty years on the editorial staff of our New York contemporary, died at Flushing, New York, on March 9. He was born in New York in 1842. He served in the Civil War and was a man of good sense, great kindness, and long-continued usefulness.

THE METAL MARKET

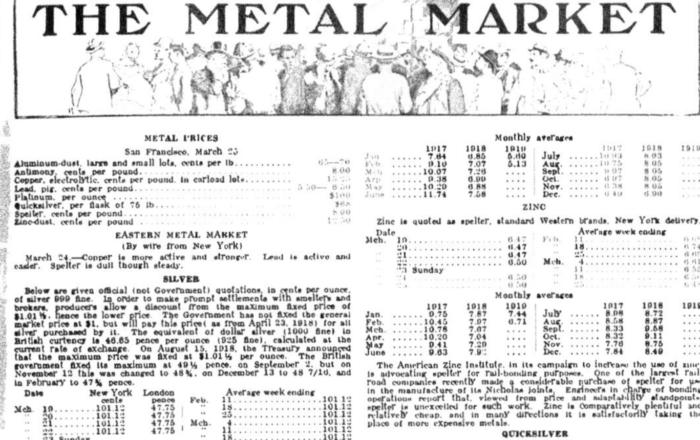

METAL PRICES

San Francisco, March 25

Aluminum-dust, large and small lots, cents per lb	65—70
Antimony, cents per pound	8.00
Copper, electrolytic, cents per pound, in carload lots	15.25
Lead, pig, cents per pound	5.50— 6.50
Platinum, per ounce	$100
Quicksilver, per flask of 75 lb	$68
Spelter, cents per pound	8.00
Zinc-dust, cents per pound	12.50

EASTERN METAL MARKET

(By wire from New York)

March 24.—Copper is more active and stronger. Lead is active and easier. Spelter is dull though steady.

SILVER

Below are given official (not Government) quotations, in cents per ounce, of silver 999 fine. In order to make prompt settlements with smelters and brokers, producers allow a discount from the maximum fixed price of $1.01½, hence the lower price. The Government has not fixed the general market price at $1, but will pay this price(as from April 23, 1918) for all silver purchased by it. The equivalent of dollar silver (1000 fine) in British currency is 46.65 pence per ounce (925 fine), calculated at the current rate of exchange. On August 15, 1918, the Treasury announced that the maximum price was fixed at $1.01½ per ounce. The British government fixed its maximum at 49½ pence, on September 2, but on November 12 this was changed to 48¾, on December 13 to 48 7/16, and in February to 47¾ pence.

Date		New York cents	London pence	Average week ending		
Mch.	19	101.12	47.75	Feb.	11	101.12
"	20	101.12	47.75	"	18	101.12
"	21	101.12	47.75	"	25	101.12
"	22	101.12	47.75	Mch.	4	101.12
"	23 Sunday			"	11	101.12
"	24	101.12	47.75	"	18	101.12
"	25	101.12	47.75	"	25	101.12

Monthly averages

	1917	1918	1919		1917	1918	1919
Jan.	75.14	88.72	101.12	July	78.92	99.62	....
Feb.	77.54	85.79	101.12	Aug.	85.40	100.31	....
Mch.	74.13	88.11	....	Sept.	100.73	101.12	....
Apr.	72.51	95.35	....	Oct.	87.38	101.12	....
May	74.61	99.50	....	Nov.	85.97	101.12	....
June	76.44	99.50	....	Dec.	85.97	101.12	....

Writing on March 6, Samuel Montagu & Co. of London said that the silver market continues quiet and steady in character. The Shanghai exchange fell to 4s.6½d. ($1.09) the tael. The Indian financial statement presented on March 1 reveals the inconvenience—to use no stronger word—caused by an insistence on metallic money. The word 'money' is used advisedly—and not currency—because the bulk of the silver coin is required for hoarding (notes being perishable) rather than currency. The circulation of one rupee notes (1 rupee = 32 cents) has risen to Rs. 90,000,000, but this amount—though encouraging—is slight, compared with the heavy absorption of coin recorded by the Indian currency returns, notwithstanding extremely large remittances of silver from America. Obviously the hoarding habit is still in full swing. The same conditions, though in a much less degree, obtain in West Africa, where an addition of £1,388,100 in silver coin was made in the year ended June 30 last. The fact is, that the natives of these populous countries are seeking to acquire possession of silver in excess of production and other sources of supply.

COPPER

Prices of electrolytic in New York, in cents per pound.

Date			Average week ending		
Mch.	19	14.87	Feb.	11	18.33
"	20	15.00	"	18	17.50
"	21	15.00	"	25	16.40
"	22	15.00	Mch.	4	15.25
"	23 Sunday		"	11	14.83
"	24	15.00	"	18	14.79
"	25	15.12	"	25	14.99

Monthly averages

	1917	1918	1919		1917	1918	1919
Jan.	29.53	23.50	20.43	July	29.67	26.00	....
Feb.	34.57	23.50	17.34	Aug.	27.42	26.00	....
Mch.	36.00	23.50	....	Sept.	25.11	26.00	....
Apr.	33.16	23.50	....	Oct.	23.50	26.00	....
May	31.69	23.50	....	Nov.	23.50	26.00	....
June	32.57	23.50	....	Dec.	23.50	26.00	....

Copper production of 18 of the largest mines in North and South America during February totaled 94,480,682 lb., a decline of 24% when compared with January, and 30% compared with November.

Rio Tinto in Spain paid 50 shillings ($12) per share during 1918, against 90s. in 1917, 95s. in 1916, 55s. in 1915, 35s. in 1914, and 75s. in 1913.

LEAD

Lead is quoted in cents per pound, New York delivery.

Date			Average week ending		
Mch.	19	5.25	Feb.	11	5.02
"	20	5.22	"	18	5.00
"	21	5.20	"	25	5.05
"	22	5.20	Mch.	4	5.25
"	23 Sunday		"	11	5.25
"	24	5.20	"	18	5.25
"	25	5.20	"	25	5.21

Monthly averages

	1917	1918	1919		1917	1918	1919
Jan.	7.64	6.85	5.60	July	10.93	8.03	....
Feb.	9.10	7.07	5.13	Aug.	10.75	8.05	....
Mch.	10.07	7.26	....	Sept.	9.07	8.05	....
Apr.	9.38	6.99	....	Oct.	6.97	8.05	....
May	10.29	6.88	....	Nov.	6.38	8.05	....
June	11.74	7.58	....	Dec.	6.40	6.90	....

ZINC

Zinc is quoted as spelter, standard Western brands, New York delivery.

Date			Average week ending		
Mch.	19	6.47	Feb.	11	6.68
"	20	6.47	"	18	6.74
"	21	6.47	"	25	6.69
"	22	6.50	Mch.	4	6.61
"	23 Sunday		"	11	6.55
"	24	6.50	"	18	6.50
"	25	6.50	"	25	6.48

Monthly averages

	1917	1918	1919		1917	1918	1919
Jan.	9.75	7.87	7.44	July	8.98	8.72	....
Feb.	10.45	7.97	6.71	Aug.	8.58	8.87	....
Mch.	10.78	7.67	....	Sept.	8.33	9.58	....
Apr.	10.20	7.04	....	Oct.	8.32	9.11	....
May	9.41	7.29	....	Nov.	7.76	8.75	....
June	9.63	7.92	....	Dec.	7.84	8.49	....

The American Zinc Institute, in its campaign to increase the use of zinc is advocating spelter for rail-bonding purposes. One of the largest railroad companies recently made a considerable purchase of spelter for use in the manufacture of its Nicholas joints. Engineers in charge of bonding operations report that, viewed from price and adaptability standpoints, spelter is unexcelled for such work. Zinc is comparatively plentiful and relatively cheap, and in many directions it is satisfactorily taking the place of more expensive metals.

QUICKSILVER

The primary market for quicksilver is San Francisco, California being the largest producer. The price is fixed in the open market, according to quantity. Prices, in dollars per flask of 75 pounds:

Date					
Feb.	25	85.00	Mch.	11	75.00
Mch.	4	85.00	"	18	68.00
			"	25	68.00

Monthly averages

	1917	1918	1919		1917	1918	1919
Jan.	81.00	128.06	103.75	July	102.00	120.00	....
Feb.	126.25	118.00	90.00	Aug.	115.00	120.00	....
Mch.	113.75	112.00	....	Sept.	112.00	120.00	....
Apr.	114.50	115.00	....	Oct.	102.00	120.00	....
May	104.00	110.00	....	Nov.	102.50	120.00	....
June	85.50	112.00	....	Dec.	117.42	115.00	....

TIN

Prices in New York, in cents per pound. The monthly averages in 1918 are nominal. On December 3 the War Industries Board fixed the price to consumers and jobbers at 72½c. f.o.b. Chicago and Eastern points, and 71¼c. on the Pacific Coast. This will continue until the U. S. Steel Products Co.'s stock is consumed.

Monthly averages

	1917	1918	1919		1917	1918	1919
Jan.	44.10	85.13	71.50	July	62.60	93.00	....
Feb.	51.47	85.00	72.44	Aug.	62.53	91.33	....
Mch.	54.27	85.00	....	Sept.	61.54	80.40	....
Apr.	55.63	88.53	....	Oct.	62.24	78.82	....
May	63.21	100.01	....	Nov.	74.18	73.67	....
June	61.93	91.00	....	Dec.	85.00	71.52	....

ORES (New York)

Manganese-Iron Alloys.—While most producers continue to quote $200 per ton, delivered, for 78 to 80% alloy, it is understood that this level will be reduced in the near future. They are taking no business at this price. It is stated that 80% ferro, re-sale material, has sold in carload lots as low as $130 per ton, delivered, and also that one producer has sold 75 to 77% alloy at the same figure. Spiegel, 16 to 18%, is quoted nominal at $40, furnace, with the higher percentage quoted at $45.

Molybdenum.—Quotations continue nominal at 80 to 85 cents per pound. The market is dead.

Tungsten.—There is little change and virtually no business reported. Quotations representing real values are impossible. This is also true of ferro-tungsten. Imports of ore into the United States in 1918 were 10,303 long tons, of which 1200 tons came from Japan, 500 tons from Argentina, 4000 to 5000 tons from China, and the remainder from Bolivia.

Regarding the War Minerals Relief Bill, the California State Mining Bureau says that all persons whose claims are judged worthy will receive questionnaires, and will be required to give exact date on which they began to produce or to prepare to produce chrome, manganese, pyrite, or tungsten. If they have had any correspondence in any form from the Department of Interior, War Industries Board, War Trade Board, Shipping Board, or Emergency Fleet Corporation, they will be required to submit proof. If their activities resulted from any oral statements of representatives, officers, or agents of any Government department, they will be required to state the circumstances and also offer proof. Whatever form of inducement was made to them or whatever circumstance lead them into the production of war minerals must be given in detail. They must be prepared to furnish affidavits if required.

Eastern Metal Market

New York, March 19.

Lack of buying is the chief characteristic of all the markets, but the price tendency may be regarded as fairly firm.

Antimony has declined slightly.

Copper prices have changed but slightly in the last week in spite of little buying.

Lead has become dormant, but prices are firm and unchanged.

Tin continues featureless and stagnant.

Zinc has a little better inquiry, but sales are small and the price tendency easy.

ANTIMONY

Wholesale lots of Asiatic metal for spot or early delivery are quoted at 6.62½ to 6.75c., New York, duty paid, with demand light. The jobbing market is about 7c., New York, duty paid.

ALUMINUM

There is no change in the situation. No. 1 virgin metal, 98 to 99% pure, is quoted at 29 to 31c. per lb. in wholesale lots for early delivery. Re-melt metal of the same analysis is about 2c. per lb. under this.

COPPER

The market is quite lifeless, demand from domestic or foreign sources being still very small. It is estimated that sales during the past week have been not over 12,000,000 lb., one authority placing those for the previous week at over 22,000,000 lb.—both insignificant figures when compared with normal markets. The past week has not witnessed any severe fluctuations in prices. These have ranged between 14.50 and 15c., depending on the seller and the quantity sold. The large producers claim that they are holding firmly at 15c. for electrolytic copper, but it is believed the smaller ones have sold at 14.50 to 14.75c. An attractive inquiry, it is believed, would bring a quotation as low as 14.75 to 14.87½c. from the larger makers. We quote the market for electrolytic copper at 14.87½c., New York, with Lake copper nominal at 15.25c., New York, demand for both being light. An interesting export inquiry comes from a British consumer asking for 2000 long tons of selected copper (99.75%) for which he offers £60 per ton, for delivery over the next 12 months. Considerable interest is directed toward the return in a week or so to this country of the committee of the Copper Export Association, which went to Europe to investigate the future European demand for copper. The quantity of copper salvaged from the battlefields of France is reported from British sources as so large that licenses for its exportation have been authorized.

IRON AND STEEL

Keen interest is manifested in the meeting in Washington today between steel makers and the Redfield Industrial Board regarding a lowering and stabilizing of prices. No one knows what is to be the result of this important meeting, and opinions vary as to what is best. Whatever price changes result, the week's market, scant as business has been, has further emphasized the downward tendency. There are widespread reports of sales of basic iron at $25, furnace, or a reduction of $5 per ton; one of these reports has been denied. The total involved was 15,000 tons. In semi-finished steel there is reported a sale of slabs to an Eastern mill at $40, while in heavy sheets there have been concessions of $6 per ton from prices early in the year. It is still true that the U. S. Steel Corporation's steel output is relatively larger than that of the independents, due to the carrying over of considerable tonnages that were put on the books in 1917. The total of the January and February steel bridge and building work put under contract was only 44,000 tons out of a two year's capacity of 2,160,000 tons, indicating the slump in building activity.

LEAD

After the demand of a week or two ago the market has turned extremely dull, but it is steady with little inquiry appearing. We quote both the outside (independents) and the other market (A. S. & R. Co.) firm at 5.25c., New York, or 5c., St. Louis, for early delivery. It is stated that an attractive firm offer would bring a concession from outside producers, but this has not been tested. One dealer said he would dislike to offer 5.15c., New York, unless he really wanted the metal. Production is generally estimated at a very low ebb, and this fact is cited as a prediction of a strong market some time. There is less expectation of an advance in quotations by the leading interest that hung over the market for some weeks.

TIN

It is the same old story—the market is stagnant and still under Government restrictions, and is featureless. The official price for the allocated metal still holds at 72.50c., New York, for Straits tin, and there is practically none available under this level. The fact is still emphasized that such tin could be purchased for future shipments from the Straits at around 52c., but this is impossible as imports are still prohibited except to the United States Steel Products Co., which organization is not buying at present, with the large stocks of allocated metal still on its hands. The only phase of interest is the fact that some consumers are paying more attention to the question of buying tin soon for future shipment, so as to have it nearer at hand as soon as the American import restrictions are removed. But this greater interest has not yet developed into any marked buying movement. General opinion is to the effect that all import restrictions will be removed by June 1, but this may be a mistake. The American Smelting & Refining Co.'s output of tin from Bolivian concentrates in 1918 is announced as having been 19,868,000 lb., compared with 12,130,000 lb. in 1917. Tin arrivals so far in March have been 1425 tons, all at Pacific ports. Spot Straits tin was quoted yesterday in London at £239 per ton, against £243 a week ago.

ZINC

Many consider that the zinc market has really touched bottom despite the apparent fact that production and stocks have not declined as much as the situation really has warranted. A better demand is reported thus far this week, but it has not developed into much buying. The feeling is that with an adjustment or stabilizing of steel prices next week will come a buying of steel sheet-bars by galvanizers, and as a result a buying also of spelter, as it is believed that galvanizers' stocks are low. The tone of the market is at least better than in the past few weeks. Prime Western for March, April, and May delivery is quoted at 6.12½ to 6.15c., St. Louis, or 6.47½ to 6.50c., New York.

Estimates of the production of portland cement in 1918 compiled under the direction of Ernest F. Burchard, of the U. S. Geological Survey, show a marked decrease in the total output; in fact, the output was the lowest since 1909. The estimated shipments in 1918 amounted to 71,645,000 bbl., valued at $113,910,000, compared with 90,703,474 bbl., valued at $122,775,088 in 1917, a decrease in quantity of 21% and in value of 7.2%.

Dividends From Mines, United States and Canada

UNITED STATES

Company and situation	Metal	Shares issued	Par value	Paid in 1919	Total	Latest dividends Date	Amount
Ahmeek, Michigan	copper	200,000	$25.00	200,000	11,150,000	Mch. 31, 1919	1.00
Allouez, Michigan	copper	100,000	25.00	100,000	2,850,000	Mch. 31, 1919	1.00
American S. & R., U. S. and Mex.	c.l.g.s.z.	650,000 (com.) 500,000 (pfd.)	100.00 100.00	6,500,000	....	Mch. 15, 1919	1.00
American Z. L. & S., United States	c.l.z.s.g.	96,500 (pfd.)	25.00	144,810	1,367,065	Mch. 1919	1.50
Anaconda, Montana	c.z.s.g.	2,331,250	50.00	5,828,125	15,485,625	Mch. 31, 1919	1.00
Argonaut, California	gold	200,000	5.00		1,800,000	Dec. 1918	0.05
Atolia, California	tungsten	100,000	1.00		5,204,500	Sept. 15, 1918	0.30
Arizona, Arizona	copper	1,519,896 £316,530 7% pfd.	1.20 ...		2,486,728 *1,432,161	Mch. 31, 1918 Aug. 21, 1918	 0.36
Arizona Commercial, Arizona	c.g.s.	175,000	5.00		1,219,000	Oct. 31, 1918	0.50
Barnes-King, Montana	gold	400,000	5.00	40,000	300,000	Feb. 15, 1919	0.10
Bingham Mines, Utah	l.s.g.	150,000	10.00	37,500	600,000	Mch. 1919	0.25
Bunker Hill & Sullivan, Idaho	l.s.	327,000	10.00	327,000	22,413,750	Mch. 1, 1919	0.25
Butte & Superior, Montana	z.s.l.	290,184	10.00	....	16,940,258	Sept. 1917	1.25
Butte Copper & Zinc, Montana	c.z.mn.	411,700	5.00	....	205,800	July 30, 1918	0.50
Caledonia, Idaho	l.s.	2,605,000	1.00	104,200	3,777,250	April 5, 1919	0.01
Calumet & Arizona, Arizona	copper	642,402	10.00	642,402	41,775,120	April 1, 1919	1.00
Calumet & Hecla, Michigan	copper	100,000	25.00		150,750,000	Dec. 31, 1918	15.00
Centennial, Michigan	copper	90,000	25.00	....	300,000	Dec. 31, 1918	1.00
Center Creek, Missouri	z.l.	100,000	10.00	....	655,000	April 1, 1918	0.50
Champion, Michigan	copper	100,000	25.00	....	23,374,540	Aug. 15, 1918	6.40
Chief Con., Utah	l.z.s.g.c.	884,223	1.00	110,529	1,345,399	Feb. 1, 1919	0.12½
Chino, New Mexico	copper	869,980	5.00	652,485	27,055,527	Mch. 31, 1919	0.75
Cerro Gordo, California	l.z.s.	975,000	1.00	....	209,375	Jan. 1917	0.05
Columbus-Rexall, Utah	c.s.g.	586,234	1.00	14,000	....	Jan. 15, 1919	0.02½
Copper Range, Michigan	copper	394,399	25.00	394,399	25,815,103	Mch. 15, 1919	1.00
Con. Arizona Smelting, Arizona	c.g.s.	1,063,000	5.00	....	498,000	Dec. 1918	0.05
Con. Interstate-Callahan, Idaho	z.l.s.	464,990	10.00	....	7,091,098	Oct. 21, 1918	0.75
Continental Zinc, Missouri	z.l.	22,000	5.00	....	638,000	Jan. 2, 1918	0.50
Cresson, Colorado	gold	1,220,000	1.00	366,000	7,515,163	Mch. 10, 1919	0.10
Daly, Utah	l.s.g.	150,000	20.00	....	3,030,000	Oct. 1, 1918	0.10
Davis-Daly, Montana	copper	600,000	10.00	....	450,000	Dec. 30, 1918	0.25
Dragon Con., Utah	c.l.s.g.	1,875,000	1.00	....	150,000	Oct. 1918	0.01
Ducktown, Tennessee	copper	198,000	4.80	....	2,078,702	May 1917	0.06
Eagle & Blue Bell, Utah	l.c.z.s.	893,146	1.00	44,657	1,205,747	Mch. 1919	0.05
East Butte, Montana	copper	411,000	10.00	....	1,402,828	Dec. 21, 1918	1.50
Electric Point, Washington	lead	793,500	1.00	23,790	277,575	April 1, 1919	0.03
Elko Prince, Nevada	gold	1,108,566	1.00	....	166,284	April 1918	0.05
Empire, Idaho	copper	1,000,000	1.00	....	880,000	July 1, 1918	0.05
Engels, California	copper	1,791,926	1.00	....	565,273	Oct. 1, 1918	0.01½
Federal M. & S., Idaho	l.z.s.	120,000	100.00	....	14,764,350	Dec. 15, 1918	1.75
First National, California	copper	600,000	5.00	90,000	660,000	Mch. 1919	0.15
General Development, U. S.	.....	120,000	25.00	....	4,913,917	Sept. 3, 1918	1.00
Golden Cycle, Colorado	gold	1,500,000	1.00	135,000	8,833,500	Mch. 10, 1919	0.03
Grand Central, Utah	l.s.	600,000	1.00	....	1,802,000	Dec. 21, 1918	0.03
Hecla, Idaho	l.s.	1,000,000	0.25	150,000	7,405,000	Mch. 28, 1919	0.15
Homestake, South Dakota	gold	251,160	100.00	376,740	41,704,444	Mch. 25, 1919	0.50
Inspiration, Arizona	copper	1,181,967	20.00	2,363,934	27,755,015	Jan. 27, 1919	2.00
Iron Blossom, Utah	l.s.g.	1,000,000	0.10	25,000	3,200,000	Jan. 25, 1919	0.02½
Iron Cap, Arizona	copper	144,872	10.00	....	887,823	Dec. 1918	0.25
Isle Royale, Michigan	copper	150,000	25.00	75,000	1,950,000	Mch. 31, 1919	0.50
Jim Butler, Nevada	s.g.	1,718,021	1.00	....	1,151,074	Aug. 1918	0.07
Judge M. & S., Utah	l.z.c.s.g.	480,000	1.00	60,000	2,320,000	April 1, 1919	0.12½
Kennecott, Alaska	copper	2,786,679	5.00	1,393,339	43,750,336	Mch. 31, 1919	0.50
Liberty Bell, Colorado	gold	133,560	5.00	....	2,594,181	Sept. 1918	0.05
Magma, Arizona	copper	240,000	5.00	120,000	1,784,000	Jan. 6, 1919	0.50
Mass Con., Michigan	copper	100,000	25.00	....	486,585	Nov. 1917	1.00
Miami, Arizona	copper	747,114	5.00	747,114	20,342,158	Feb. 15, 1919	1.00
Mohawk, Michigan	copper	100,000	25.00	200,000	8,825,000	Feb. 1, 1919	2.00
Nevada Con., Nevada	copper	1,999,457	5.00	749,796	43,019,633	Mch. 31, 1919	0.37½
Nevada Packard, Nevada	silver	1,164,502	1.00	....	87,351	Sept. 2, 1918	0.02½
Nevada Wonder, Nevada	s.g.	1,500,000	1.00	....	1,478,582	Nov. 21, 1918	0.10
New Cornelia, Arizona	copper	1,404,900	5.00	....	351,225	Nov. 25, 1918	0.25
New Idria, California	quicksilver	100,000	5.00	25,000	e.705,000	Jan. 1, 1919	0.25
New Jersey Zinc, New Jersey	zinc	350,000	100.00	1,400,000	....	Feb. 10, 1919	4.00
North Butte, Montana	c.s.g.	430,000	15.00	....	14,657,000	Oct. 28, 1918	0.25
North Star, California	gold	250,000	10.00	....	5,437,040	June 29, 1918	0.20
Old Dominion, Arizona	c.s.g.	203,353	25.00	....	13,774,244	Sept. 30, 1918	1.00
Ontario Silver, Utah	s.l.	150,000	100.00	75,000	15,187,000	Jan. 4, 1919	0.50
Oroville Dredging, Cal. and Colombia	gold	686,538	4.86	....	2,683,920	Sept. 1918	0.12
Osceola, Michigan	copper	96,150	25.00	96,150	17,467,925	Mch. 31, 1919	1.00
Phelps Dodge, Ariz., N. Mex., Mex.	c.s.g.	450,000	100.00	1,125,000	81,221,527	April 2, 1919	2.50
Plymouth Con., California	gold	240,000	4.80	86,400	696,080	Jan. 1, 1919	0.12
Portland, Colorado	gold	3,000,000	1.00	60,000	11,317,080	Jan. 20, 1919	0.02
Prince Con., Nevada	l.s.	1,000,000	2.00	....	575,000	Nov. 4, 1917	0.02
Quincy, Michigan	copper	110,000	25.00	....	26,452,500	Dec. 23, 1918	2.00
Ray Con., Arizona	copper	1,577,179	10.00	788,589	21,469,072	Mch. 31, 1919	0.50
Richmond, Idaho	copper	800,000	1.00	....	92,400	Oct. 1918	0.01
Rochester Mines, Nevada	s.g.	2,148,701	1.00	....	80,030	Oct. 1, 1918	0.02
Shannon, Arizona	copper	300,000	10.00	....	1,425,000	Nov. 15, 1917	0.25
Shattuck, Arizona	c.l.s.g.	350,000	10.00	262,500	7,348,000	April 19, 1919	0.25
Silver King Coalition, Utah	l.s.	1,250,000	5.00	....	15,108,560	Jan. 1918	0.15
Silver King Con., Utah	l.s.c.g.	700,000	1.00	....	1,502,705	April 1, 1918	0.10
St. Joe Lead, Missouri	lead	1,464,780	10.00	....	21,543,616	Dec. 20, 1918	0.50

Company and situation	Metal	Shares issued	Par Value	Paid in 1919	Total	Latest dividends Date	Amount
Tamarack & Custer, Idaho	l.s.	1,776,500	1.00	....	461,830	Aug. 27, 1918	0.06
Tennessee Copper, Tennessee	copper and acid	391,498	no par value	....	392,817	May 15, 1918	1.00
Tintic Standard, Utah	l.s.	1,175,000	0.10	93,976	492,849	Mch. 29, 1919	0.08
Tomboy, Colorado	g.s.	310,000	4.80	....	4,074,200	June 28, 1918	0.12
Tom Reed, Arizona	gold	909,555	1.00	....	2,620,000	Dec. 1918	0.02
Tonopah Belmont, Nevada	s.g.	1,500,000	1.00	300,000	9,868,063	April 1, 1919	0.10
Tonopah Extension, Nevada	s.g.	1,282,801	1.00	64,140	1,976,539	April 1, 1919	0.05
Tonopah Mining, Nevada	s.g.	1,000,000	1.00	....	14,525,000	Oct. 21, 1918	0.15
United Copper, Washington	copper	1,000,000	1.00	....	150,000	Oct. 15, 1917	0.01
United Eastern, Arizona	gold	1,363,000	1.00	231,710	1,485,670	Mch. 26, 1919	0.07
U. S. S. R. & M., U. S., Mexico	l.z.c.s.g.	pfd. 486,350	50.00	425,556	21,902,373	Jan. 15, 1919	0.87½
		com. 351,115	50.00	438,894	10,804,627	Jan. 15, 1919	1.25
United Verde Copper, Arizona	copper	300,000	no par value	450,000	51,047,000	Feb. 1919	1.50
United Verde Extension, Arizona	copper	1,050,000	0.50	1,312,500	7,083,000	 1919	0.50
Union Con., Nevada	s.g.	200,000	1.00	....	80,000	July 1918	0.05
Utah Apex, Utah	c.l.s.g.	528,200	5.00	....	1,122,425	Nov. 1918	0.25
Utah Con., Utah	c.l.s.g.	300,000	5.00	75,000	12,810,000	Mch. 25, 1919	0.25
Utah Copper, Utah	copper	1,624,490	10.00	2,436,735	94,452,517	Mch. 31, 1919	1.50
Utah Metal, Utah	l.c.g.s.	691,588	1.00	....	805,734	Dec. 10, 1917	0.30
Vindicator Con., Colorado	gold	1,500,000	1.00	15,000	3,787,500	Jan. 25, 1919	0.01
Wellington Mines, Colorado	l.z.	1,000,000	1.00	100,000	1,850,000	Jan. 1919	0.10
West End, Nevada	s.g.	1,788,486	5.00	89,424	1,162,516	Feb. 18, 1919	0.05
Wolverine, Michigan	copper	60,000	25.00	90,000	10,160,000	April 1, 1919	0.50
Yellow Aster, California	gold	1,064,310	1.00	....	1,245,789	July 20, 1917	0.05
Yellow Pine, Nevada	z.l.	1,000,000	1.00	....	2,310,000	Dec. 16, 1918	0.12
Yukon Gold, Alaska, Cal., Nev.	gold	3,500,000	5.00	....	9,858,110	June 1918	0.02½
CANADA							
Buffalo, Ontario	silver	1,000,000	1.00	....	3,287,000	Aug. 10, 1918	0.25
Coniagas, Ontario	silver	800,000	5.00	100,000	9,340,000	Feb. 1, 1919	0.02½
Con. M. & S., British Columbia	l.c.z.s.g.	419,098	25.00	523,872	5,779,912	April 1, 1919	0.62½
Florence, British Columbia	l.s.z.	1,100,000	1.00	17,650	35,300	April 20, 1919	0.01½
Granby Con. M. S. & P. B. C.	c.g.s.	150,004	100.00	562,467	10,339,352	May 1, 1919	1.25
Hedley, British Columbia	gold	120,000	10.00	12,000	2,424,000	Mch. 31, 1919	0.10
Hollinger, Ontario	gold	4,920,000	5.00	246,000	9,670,000	Feb. 25, 1919	0.05
Howe Sound, British Columbia	copper	1,984,150	1.00	99,207	295,621	Jan. 15, 1919	0.05
International Nickel, Ontario	n.c.	com. 1,673,384	25.00	....	52,276,984	Dec. 1918	1.00
		pfd. 89,126	100.00	133,689	7,085,403	Feb. 1, 1919	1.50
Kerr Lake, Ontario	silver	600,000	5.00	150,000	8,160,000	Mch. 15, 1919	0.25
Lake Shore, Ontario	gold	2,000,000	1.00	....	100,000	Dec. 10, 1918	0.02½
McKinley-Darragh, Ontario	silver	2,247,692	1.00	134,860	5,469,453	April 1, 1919	0.03
McIntyre, Ontario	gold	3,610,283	1.00	....	1,083,084	Nov. 30, 1918	0.05
Mining Corp., Ontario	silver	1,660,050	5.00	207,455	6,113,000	Mch. 31, 1919	0.62½
Nipissing, Ontario	silver	1,200,000	5.00	1,200,000	20,140,000	Mch. 31, 1919	0.50
Rambler-Cariboo, British Columbia	l.z.s.	1,750,000	1.00	17,500	560,000	Feb. 15, 1919	0.01
Standard, British Columbia	l.z.s.	2,000,000	1.00	....	2,700,000	Oct. 15, 1917	0.05
Temiskaming, Ontario	silver	2,500,000	1.00	....	2,125,000	Jan. 18, 1918	0.03
Tough-Oakes, Ontario	gold	531,500	5.00	....	398,625	Jan. 15, 1917	0.12½
Trethewey, Ontario	silver	1,000,000	1.00	50,000	1,211,999	Jan. 2, 1919	0.05

Abbreviations: g = gold, s = silver, c = copper, l = lead, z = zinc.

Note: Companies not included in the above list are requested to submit details. Changes in capitalization and new dividends will be entered on receipt of the information. This table will be published quarterly.

Company Reports

NATOMAS COMPANY OF CALIFORNIA

Property: 10 dredges, 2 machine-shops, and 2 rock-crushing plants at Natoma and Oroville, and extensive agricultural lands in Sacramento county, California, known as Reclamation Districts 1000 and 1001.

Operating Officials: Emery Oliver, general manager; L. D. Hopfield, in charge of dredges at Natoma; P. C. Knapp, secretary.

Financial Statement: to present this briefly for 1918 is impossible, owing to the complexities of the land business, but the following gives an idea of the position; the present report being mainly a retrospect or summary of operations since the reorganization:

Indebtedness at end of 1914, exclusive of bonds, interest, and stock of Natomas Consolidated	$3,098,751
Indebtedness at end of 1918	$460,943
Mortgage and bonded debt	10,869,485
Current liabilities	200,943
Capital assets	16,061,806
Securities at end of 1918	1,074,244
Current assets ($307,315 cash)	1,439,735
Total of last two items	$2,533,979

Dredging: during 1918 the boats dug 24,172,626 cu. yd., recovering gold worth $2,008,966, of which $746,119 was profit. In five years the total recovery was $11,517,170, giving a profit of $5,669,061. All of the dredging profits are absorbed in paying bond interest. In 1915 it was estimated that there was 216,000,000 cu. yd. of pay-gravel, but additions have been made, so that after 128,000,000 yd. of the original area have been dredged, there are 182,220,000 yd. still available, plus 40,000,000 yd. if pre-war costs prevail before this ground is reached. The apparatus placed on the boats to save fine gold has recovered $107,000 net, most of which would have been lost under previous methods. Four boats must be reconstructed during the next five years so as to complete the dredging operations.

Rock Crushing: in five years, the plant at Fair Oaks produced 1,733,944 tons of crushed rock, 198,944 tons of washed gravel, and 275,724 tons of screened gravel; and the plant at Oroville 451,364 tons of crushed rock, and 458,016 tons of screened gravel. The crusher products and field gravel are sold throughout the State.

Land Department: reclamation work has cost $4,480,500 to date, inclusive of accrued interest, etc. In district No. 1000, there have been sold 10,147 acres for $2,889,446; and in No. 1001, 1292 acres for $343,537. All of these properties are being irrigated, provided with roads, and generally prepared for sale.

DE BEERS CONSOLIDATED MINES

During the year ended June 30, 1918, this company sold diamonds amounting to £4,327,649 ($20,770,000). The profit was £2,771,515, of which £1,990,000 was distributed to shareholders. From 5,843,099 loads (1600 lb. each) of 'blue' ground, the average yield was 0.27 carats per load. Reserves are 22,000,000 loads.

REFERRING to the idea of establishing a Department of Mines in the national administration at Washington, a subject on which we published recently an interesting utterance by Mr. John F. Davis, we note that an agitation is afoot in England to organize a Mines Department for the United Kingdom.

FORMERLY, and for many years before the War, the prices of copper and lead showed a ratio of 3.4 to 1. Today that proportion does not obtain, because the price of copper was pushed to an extravagant figure during the first two years of the War, before the Government took a hand in price-fixing. It was our opinion then, as now, that the big copper producers showed lack of sagacity in encouraging an excessive price for the metal.

WE have received a few copies of the regulations prepared by the War Minerals Relief Commission, which has been appointed to adjust, liquidate, and pay claims arising out of losses suffered by persons, firms, or corporations producing, or preparing to produce, manganese, chrome, pyrite, or tungsten. We have also a few copies of the questionnaire to be used by claimants in filing claims for the consideration of the Commission. These can be obtained gratis from the Commission, whose address is Suite 2131, Department of the Interior Building, Washington, D. C.

STERLING exchange has dropped to $4.59 because the peg that fixed it at about $4.75 during the War has been removed. During three calendar years we sold Great Britain $5,956,000,000 worth of goods and imported only $733,000,000 worth, leaving a trade balance of $5,223,000,000. If sterling exchange had not been stabilized by purchases, through J. P. Morgan & Co., for the British government, it would have slumped long ago. Evidently the desire to restore normal conditions has prompted the step taken by the British government; also that of the French government, for the franc-dollar exchange likewise has been unpegged. The effect should be to curb imports into, and to stimulate exports from, Great Britain and France.

THE regular and early publication of an official statement dealing with the alloys and metallic minerals has long been desired by those engaged in mining. This need is now filled by the monthly excerpts from reports of the Minerals Investigation Committee of the U. S. Bureau of Mines, in charge of Mr. J. E. Spurr. Before us is the second number, that for February. Among the 43 pages the position of every metal and mineral of importance is discussed. In no way does this matter duplicate the valuable data published by the U. S. Geological Survey. Apart from a review of the production, imports, and exports of the principal base metals, those interested will find instructive information on antimony, chromite, graphite, magnesite, manganese, potash, pyrite, and zirconium. The market conditions for each metal or mineral are studied by officers of the Bureau detailed for this useful work.

THE 'Times' is not the paper it used to be, if it ever was quite the paper it was supposed to be, but it is still an authoritative exponent of British opinion; therefore we welcome the editorial statement made recently concerning the League of Nations and the international amity underlying any such agreement. The British people, says 'The Times', "without distinction of party, regards a better understanding with Americans as the crown of victory. . . . Our sole wish is to work with the American people in what we believe to be as much their ideals and interest as our own. Wishing that, with whom should we work but the President of the United States? That he is also leader of the Democratic party is a mere accident to our mind, and if the President had been a Republican we should have been at exactly the same pains to understand his point of view and work with him." That is frank and friendly. Undoubtedly Mr. Lloyd George is co-operating loyally with Mr. Wilson; the British premier is endeavoring, successfully, to reconcile the French and the American views on the war settlement.

WE are informed that the Chamber of Mines and Oil at Los Angeles has declined to support the Californian chapter of the American Mining Congress, preferring to work with the Oil Institute recently organized in this State. This we believe to be a mistake; it is merely a regrettable continuation of the lack of unified action marking the many elements in the mining industry. Obviously the various branches of mining acting separately cannot make such an effective presentation of a grievance or recommendation to those in authority at Washington as they could unitedly, through the agency established by the American Mining Congress. The oil industry of California has troubles that are peculiarly its own; they have become a subject of public controversy and they are less likely to be righted when treated as a matter that concerns a local industry than if they were treated as something injurious to the mining industry as a whole. Moreover, it is a blunder to assume, as is commonly done, that the winning of oil is not 'mining'; of course, it is; the fact that the product is liquid does not place the exploitation of petroleum deposits outside the scope of an ancient art. Salt and sulphur are recovered in liquid form; in placer mining the gold is won through the medium of water. United we stand; divided we fall. If the different branches of mining refuse to co-operate in their approach to the departments at Washington, they are sure to fail in obtaining proper recognition.

GOLD production in Australia continued to decrease in 1918. The official statistics show a diminution of 12% as compared with 1917 and of 60% as compared with ten years ago. Every State of the Commonwealth, except New South Wales, shows a decline, but Victoria is the most unfortunate, the drop being equal to 25%.

	1908, oz.	1917, oz.	1918, oz.
Victoria	670,910	201,044	158,827
Queensland	465,085	175,280	130,123
Western Australia	1,647,911	970,314	876,508
New South Wales	224,702	82,171	87,045
South Australia	8,542	7,647	7,160
Tasmania	37,085	14,237	11,286
	3,074,325	1,450,693	1,276,949

The output of New Zealand can only be estimated—at 210,000 ounces as compared with 260,000 estimated in 1917 and 506,281 in 1908—because the annual report of the Department of Mines of that State omits the statistics of gold production, for a curious reason. The official explanation is that "the Imperial authorities are of the opinion that during the period of the War it is inadvisable to give exact information regarding the import and export of gold and silver." The Imperial authorities seem not to have laid such an embargo on other colonies and dominions under the British flag, therefore this action on the part of the New Zealand authorities is difficult to understand; it looks like an over-zealous attempt to comply with a suggestion from London, because it would seem as if the only information to be withheld, for patriotic reasons, would be the destination of the gold exported.

CHAIRMAN HURLEY of the Shipping Board is seeking expressions of opinion on the future maritime policy of the United States. It is to be hoped that he will not be disappointed. It is one of the most momentous economic questions before the people of this country, and should be discussed in every civic club and chamber of commerce from the Atlantic to the Pacific. For a hundred years we have done nothing but blunder in our national shipping policies. We have cluttered the statute-books with legislation to make the building and operation of an American merchant marine as nearly hopeless as we could. We have tried subsidies, limited so as to favor a few and prevent a national response to such stimulus. We have then cut off the subsidies and allowed splendid fleets to be sold at junk prices; our registry laws have discriminated against American ships; and without international negotiation for an agreement, which incidentally we never could have reached, we enacted a seaman's law that was useful to every competitor who wished to drive our flag off the seas. Reports indicate that some new principles have been adopted at Paris likely to equalize our maritime position in the world of commerce, but the details have not come forward. Mr. Hurley should issue a synopsis of our existing shipping laws, as a basis for general discussion, and then the public should seriously accept his invitation to offer comment. We have now a fleet of really large proportions. It belongs to the Government, and it must either be operated, allowed to rust and decay, or be sold. If it is employed as an American fleet it must be run by the Government, or the shipping laws must be intelligently revised so that private individuals may be able to operate it without running into bankruptcy. If our foreign trade is to be developed as an outlet for increasing products of the factory and the mine, it is important that an American merchant marine be sustained.

THE financial results of a company whose mines, smelters, and refineries recovered 2,496,693 ounces of gold, 69,841,061 ounces of silver, 916,974,000 pounds of copper, 550,532,000 pounds of lead, 52,500,000 pounds of spelter, 33,087 tons of sulphuric acid, and large quantities of many other metals and by-products during 1918, should be a good criterion of the condition of the metal markets. In this we refer to the American Smelting & Refining Company, whose report for the past year is before us. During that period, sales of metals realized $360,060,487, compared with $405,616,167 in 1917, and $330,297,952 in 1916. The value of the manufactured products was $14,006,145, $22,785,294, and $16,304,914, respectively. The profit for the three years was $14,137,168, $25,035,-938, and $25,242,297. The total amount of dividends paid on both common and preferred shares during 1918 was 15% less than in 1917, itself a decrease of 2% from 1916. The company is carrying ore and products valued at $88,556,790, a trifle less than in 1917. Current assets total $35,530,676, and liabilities $30,654,731. Recently we referred to the retirement of the brothers Daniel, Murry, and S. R. Guggenheim from the directorate, after 18 years active participation in the company's varied operations. Since 1901, when these gentlemen became connected with the company, the annual turnover has increased from $82,000,000 to $390,000,000, and the profit and loss account from $2,900,000 to $27,000,000. The report, signed by Mr. Simon Guggenheim, states that the company has obtained no direct advantage from the increased value of the metals, and, on account of the complexities of the ore and metal markets, a conservative program must be maintained, so that dividends cannot be increased beyond 6%. The high costs of smelting and refining have been discouraging, but these items have lately been lowered; and although pre-war costs may never be realized again, the directors expect that pre-war profits per ton of ore smelted will be obtained as soon as normal business is resumed. Prospects in Mexico are considered to be encouraging. The smelters at Aguascalientes, Chihuahua, Matehuala, and Monterrey are in full blast: but Velardeña is not at work yet. The company is keen in its safety and welfare work, and reports a 28% reduction in the accident rate. The record is imposing, and we would like to be able to state that it synchronizes with an increase of public confidence in the methods employed by the 'smelter trust'. A business like this should have good-will in more senses than one. We would like to see the Senator, as Mr. Simon Guggenheim is still called by his friends, initiate a policy that would antagonize the ore-producers less and win public confidence more.

ACCORDING to Mr. S. R. Guggenheim, recently returned from Europe, it will be a long time before a large foreign outlet can be expected for American copper. Mr. D. C. Jackling stated at Salt Lake City recently that production costs are higher than the present market-price of the metal. To quote him, "There is no doubt whatever in my mind as to copper being stabilized, the same way as any other essential industry of the world. We are going through a hard winter in the copper industry. No one can say how long a hard winter will last, but there is an absolute certainty of spring; and, to carry out this simile, I believe we will have a bright and glowing summer." It was generally expected that at the conclusion of hostilities, Europe would need much metal of all kinds, but such is not the case as yet, for large stocks are lying in England, France, and Italy. These are a great factor in affecting the American markets, especially Great Britain, where, instead of stocks being consumed, they are actually increasing fast. For instance, the copper there on March 1 was nearly double the quantity at mid-December, lead was more than double, and spelter increased 40%; while aluminum, antimony, and nickel also had accumulated. To give an idea of normal supplies in England, we find that in 1913 those for copper totaled 11,500 tons, against 57,500 tons at present. A somewhat similar gain is shown by lead and spelter, of which there are respectively, 112,000 and 40,600 tons on hand. However, a few days ago Mr. C. F. Kelley of the Anaconda, on his return from Europe, stated that large accumulations of copper are in the hands of the Allied governments, but the copper-consuming industries are without stocks and the government supplies will be much reduced shortly by distribution among the consumers. Germany and her allies have no supply of copper and large quantities will be required when normal industrial activity is restored.

Bolshevism

Just a year ago we contrasted the conditions prevailing in Germany and Russia, under the heading 'Prussian or Bolshevist?' We said then: "On the one hand we see the concrete expression of highly organized and frankly autocratic militarism and on the other the disintegration of a nation plunging into the chaos of sentimental anarchy. To which of these extremes is the world drifting?" Twelve months have passed; the Germans did their best to distribute the propaganda of Bolshevism over eastern Europe before they themselves were beaten and held up their hands in abject surrender, but in their defeat they, like the Russians, succumbed to the poison of Bolshevism and fell into a riot of disorder, which in a few months has spread so fast over central Europe as to compel the Allies to face a further fight not with militarism, now cowed and dishonored, but with that foul fungus of anarchy which has sprung to life as if in a night upon the blood-soaked battlefields of Armageddon. What is this Bolshevism? The term Bolsheviki, now anglicized to Bolshevists, comes from the Russian word *bolsha*, meaning 'more'; they are the whole-hoggers; as is indicated more clearly by the synonym Maximalist, an abbreviation of Maximmmalist. The Bolshevists are the party of the *bolshinstvo*, or majority. It is a gross mistake to speak of Bolshevism as "the extreme phase of Socialism," because these two ideas differ as much as black from white, as chaos from order. Bolshevism is distinctly anti-social; it aims to destroy the organization of society that has been laboriously, painfully, and even bloodily evolved by man since he emerged from an ape and tiger existence. The basic notion of Bolshevism is class-control by the proletariat, that is, the people without property. The Bolshevists aim at industrial, as well as political, monopoly; they extirpate all minorities; they deal more ruthlessly with those differing from them in opinion than any czar or kaiser; they are the foes of democracy and the enemies of liberalism; their scheme of disorderly living is an attempt to return to the savage childhood of the race; it is a reversion to the jungle. In this country they are represented by the I. W. W.; in Russia they used to be called Nihilists, and it is a pity that this term, with its evident meaning of unmitigated destructiveness in politics and morals, has not been retained. The use of the new name, Bolshevist, suggests that a new idea has been brought forth by the Russian revolution: it is nothing of the kind, it is only a fresh breaking forth of the savagery latent in man, particularly if he be uneducated. Of the Russians, 90% are illiterate. It appears that illiteracy is favorable to Bolshevism, as it is to other manifestations of human ignorance, but a second factor must be taken into account. General Mangin said recently, 'Bolshevism is essentially a disease of conquered countries." That is patent. Bolshevism feeds on defeat; it is the product of national disintegration. This is logical, for the Bolshevist has no national spirit; he aims to destroy national boundaries and to reduce the world to an international mob, seeking food like a herd of cattle. The capitalist and the organizer of industry are anathema to him, for he fails to see, or does not care to see, that without the organization of industry the peoples of the earth could not live, but would be the prey of famine and pestilence as in days gone-by, before human beings united to fight the hostile forces of nature. Without promise of security no man will grow more corn than he needs himself, for to accumulate a store of grain is to invite depredation; without the protection of the community no man will be tempted to increase his flock or herd, for that also would bring the marauder upon him; without railways and ships, without highly organized methods of transport and distribution, there would be no market for a surplus and no way of expediting that play of supply and demand on which the teeming millions now depend for satisfying the needs of their daily life. As to the effects of Bolshevism in Russia, we do not know much accurately, but we do know that a brigand, a thief, and a liar, Nicolai Lenin, rules the roost for the moment. Attempts, such as that of the Overman Committee of the Senate, to elicit trustworthy information have been largely a failure, because the witnesses, such as Messrs. David R. Francis and Raymond Robins, contradicted each other and themselves; but the picture is lurid enough, ranging from the murder of men wearing clean linen to the legalized rape of women. The menace of the outlaw is felt by civilization; the recent outbreak of the Bolshevist disease in defeated Hungary has awakened the Allies to the danger of postponing the settlement of peace; even Germany, once so proud of her highly organized statehood, threatens to turn Bolshevist if we treat her justly for her crimes, not the least of which is the fact that Bolshevism in Russia was fed on the lies that the Germans manufactured. The propagandists of kultur, the very people that insolently purposed to force their idea of administration upon the whole world, now threaten to turn anarchist if we are not kind to them; in November they were whining, now they are truculent; they are like the small boy who refuses to play unless you play his kind of game. The world faces a crisis as great as that of a year ago when the German armies broke the Allied battle-front. The sentimental idea of peace without victory has been translated by the brutal logic of events into a victory without peace. In truth, our leaders have failed us; not one of them, but all collectively. The Great War will go down in history as one in which no superlative leader of men was produced. We are suffering from the maladministration of governments and the lack of cohesion among the constructive forces of society. The War was marked by colossal blunders on both sides; the Armistice has been followed by wrangling and indecision among both the vanquished and the victors. If only one of the leaders in Paris had risen to the occasion and by force of genius had dominated the position, we should have emerged long ago from this darkness of divided counsels into the daylight of intelligent decision. If, for example, Admiral Kolchak with his gallant Czecho-Slovaks and Siberians had been supported not half-heartedly, as happened, but whole-heartedly and vigorously, the condition of Russia, and of eastern Europe as a whole, would have been vastly different from what it is now. Civilization is on a lee shore, in a fierce storm, and only a bold navigator can save the ship. Meanwhile it behooves the crew to be active and the passengers to behave themselves. Those that fail to meet the test had best be thrown overboard, which means that the cure for Bolshevism in the United States is deportation.

Mine-Sampling Again

We are glad to re-open the discussion on mine-sampling by means of a contribution that we published in our issue of last week and that came to us from Mr. H. R. Sleeman, who writes from a remote corner of Western Australia. He goes over some old ground, but in a useful way, since it is never amiss to state first principles before elaborating new ideas; for instance, the question of the cleanness of the sample and its relation to the actual mining that it anticipates. Our own, more than local, experience would lead us to lay stress on this point, for we believe that much of the failure of sampling to function as a prophecy is due to the fact that the sampling done by a moil and hammer yields a product much cleaner—therefore smaller in tonnage and richer in contents—than the ensuing stoping with machine-drills. This is due frequently, as Mr. Morton Webber says, to the 'sloughing' of waste from the walls or 'horses' in the lode. The post-mortems of mines prove this. Take the report of any good engineer made ten years ago on a successful mine and compare his forecast of tonnage and grade with the output of the mine since the date of his report; usually the record shows a lower grade and a bigger tonnage, because the manager's business was not to verify the report but to make as much money as he could for the stockholders, and that he could do, in most cases, by stoping wider than the sampling and by avoiding the expense of sorting afterward. Moreover, the lowering of the milling cost, consequent upon a bigger scale of operations or improvements in the metallurgical treatment, incites a continually increasing rate of production, because, again, the lowering of cost is a feather in the manager's cap, and both he and his directors are likely to care more for the credit accruing therefrom than to consider too severely the need for amortizing the cost of the mill-extensions out of current revenue. Indeed this phase of the sampling problem is fundamental. As we have insisted before, the process of sampling is determinedly non-selective, the aim is to obtain an average; whereas the aim of mining is to select the ore so as to make the maximum profit. That profit should be the maximum as a whole for the entire life of the mine, but often it is the maximum during a period of high metal-prices or the period during which a particular management, representing a particular group of stockholders, is in control. The Alaska Gold was, as the 'Boston News Bureau' said the other day, "an honest failure," and it was so because a group of clever engineers, with special experience in big-scale copper mining, failed to recognize the greater erraticism of free-gold ores, and because, more particularly, they assumed that a first-rate mine-captain like the late John R. Mitchell would extract average ore from the old Perseverance mine. Under his management 375,000 tons of ore had been milled, and this was deemed an *average* 'sample'. It was nothing of the kind, as was discovered when the big mill clamored for ore. This point should be emphasized again and again: mining necessarily is selective; sampling essentially is non-selective.

DISCUSSION

The League of Nations

The Editor:

Sir—In your editorial article of March 15 you sanely say: "Before this country is committed to so basic a departure from established policy * * * it is imperative that full information be given to the people." Further, you seem to imply that neither the President nor such leaders as Mr. Taft have been quite candid. You are right. We are confronted not merely by the problem of settling the War, but by a proposal to change our form of government fundamentally; more than that, to institute a new government to be composed of elements conflicting not only in tradition and instinct, but also in interest and purpose. There never was greater necessity for dispassionate consideration after full information and ample opportunity for discussion.

We are not now dispassionate; we are not yet informed; and the indications are we are not going to be given much opportunity for discussion. In view of what is involved in the constitution of a League of Nations I greatly fear that, in these circumstances, your instinct was right when you thought of a 'scrap of paper': for, if the people do not understandingly and of the freest will accept the obligations imposed, there is grave danger that they may later repudiate the compact on the ground, valid to them, that there was no free meeting of minds.

I think we can all agree that there is no deeper degradation than that of a people who are not fully consulted as to the principle and plan of a new form of government to which they are to be subject. This is especially true when the Constitution under which they now live strictly limits the authority of their agent the President, and of their other agents the Senate. It seems to me that, at this moment of history, your article treats the American Constitution with too little gravity. It is no light thing when a people, even themselves, break with their traditions; when they cease to reverse the principles of conduct that have guided them along an orderly path of development; it is much more serious when their constituted authorities assume power to force the rupture.

The Romans had a concept of '*religio*' as the sum of the customs, traditions, and reverences that bind together in concord the otherwise discordant elements of society. In the sense that the Czardom was the '*religio*' of Russia, so is the Constitution the '*religio*' of America. Fortunately, the Constitution contains within itself the life-principle of growth. The President, the Senate, many of us, expressly, and all citizens implicitly, have taken the oath to defend the Constitution against enemies, foreign and internal. Let it not be thought that our Government is to be altered, or a new government instituted for us without orderly pursuit of the processes provided to that end. It is no longer a "group of men in the Senate;" it is no longer a question of Democrat or Republican, as already may be easily seen.

The chief danger to the United States lies, as always, in the hyphen—both the physical and the spiritual hyphen. Let us hope that the policy of America will not be determined by Irish-Americans, for whom strategical concessions are preparing; nor by German-Americans, who may be swayed by the already evident *rapprochement* of the governments, except France. Let us hope, too, that those who are spiritually French or spiritually British will not cease to remember that their first duty is to the United States. Above all let us not fail to "stand porter at the gate of thought" against the entry of ideas that are being sedulously propagated by the chancelleries of Europe for their own purposes, among the most insidious of which is the suggestion constantly reiterated that the League of Nations is an American concept, against which France and Great Britain are struggling, but struggling in vain.

C. IRVING WRIGHT.

Pebble Beach, Del Monte, Cal., March 17.

Duluth Engineers Club

The Editor:

Sir—I note in your editorial entitled 'The Institute Meeting', in your issue of March 8, that you refer to the Duluth Engineers' Club as though it might be considered a rival and endeavoring to assume the characteristics of a national society. The inference may not be intended, but it can easily be taken. If you will allow me some of your valuable space, I will endeavor to state the ideals we are seeking to realize.

The Duluth Engineers' Club is distinctly a local organization and has no intention nor desire to be anything but local. It does, however, desire to co-operate effectively with all other engineering organizations in promoting radical improvement in the technical, political, and economic status of the entire profession. We believe that the desired co-operation can best be obtained by a federation of local clubs. The two basic principles upon which it must be founded are, first, direct responsible representation of the local clubs as such, and second, standard qualifications for membership in the local clubs.

We do not say this cannot be brought about through a re-organization of the present United Engineering Societies and the Engineering Council, but we do believe a thorough re-organization conforming to the basic principles before-mentioned will be necessary before a satisfactory solution of organization problems will be found.

Here in Minnesota, we have the Minnesota Joint Engineering Board, which is composed of a delegate from each local club. It meets about ten times a year and considers matters of interest to the engineer and concerning which the engineer is best qualified to speak. Its advice and assistance are frequently sought and used by the Governor and Legislature. Its activities are State-wide, but confined to Minnesota. This is just the kind of a body we need for national affairs.

A national body should be so constructed that it could take over all the functions of the existing national societies. It is possible they could be absorbed almost intact and made subordinate technical sections or bureaus. Briefly, the machinery of the federation would be a body of delegates, a small executive council, and a chief executive. The executive council would be elected by and be responsible to the body of delegates and would direct and be responsible for the chief executive.

The profession is paying, in dues alone, close to a million dollars a year for results that are pitifully inadequate. The older national societies have gone to seed along technical lines. The technical matter produced is inferior in quality and badly digested and poorly presented. There is limitless room for improvement right in the field they now try to fill.

The American Association of Engineers now proposes to take up the long-neglected social problems and work for the economic betterment of the profession. We are in hearty sympathy with many of its objects, but feel that its organization is wrong in the same particulars that the other national societies are. They are organized from the top down instead of from the bottom up. Their branches are 'appendages' instead of strong independent organizations which exist because of the local determination to be and do something of value in the community. The American Association of Engineers has placed the purely economic question so strongly to the fore that it faces the danger of becoming little more than a labor-union. If the ideals for which it was founded and which still guide its present officials could be maintained, there might be some hope of its ultimate success as a social and professional organization. We believe its chances are small to accomplish much due to its faulty organization and the personnel of the majority of its members. We believe every effort should be made to retain the high plane and professional prestige of the older national societies and add to it the vigor and enterprise of the local clubs and the American Association of Engineers.

There will be much prejudice, selfishness, and inertia to overcome, but the goal is well worth the struggle. The engineer claims to be particularly capable of designing, organizing, and managing enterprises. If he is to be judged by the manner in which he has handled his own professional affairs, he receives about all the consideration he deserves.

We believe a General Engineering Congress should be called of delegates from all engineering organizations, national societies, local clubs, and local 'appendages'. The four founder societies now have the committees studying problems of organization and these committees should be able to present some suitable plans that could be considered and a united organization formed that would include every man in America who is engaged in technical engineering or engineering administration.

We are talking, writing, and working for engineering unity, and invite every engineer to join with us in our struggle for a united profession.

W. H. WOODBURY, Secretary,
Duluth Engineers' Club.

Duluth, March 14.

The Outlook for Copper

The Editor:

Sir—At the outbreak of the European war, it will be recalled, the copper mines reduced their production, and many of the large companies limited their output to 50% of the normal. This condition was induced by uncertainties contingent upon the European conflagration. There was at the time of this curtailment of copper production a need for the metal. It appears now, from a close analysis of the situation, that the uncertainties of what would be required by the new condition produced by the War, was instrumental in bringing about the curtailment. No one at the outbreak of the War appreciated what a great demand there would be for copper, and, if they did, they gave no evidence of confidence in their belief in such a demand. Many estimates have been made as to the amount of copper consumed for munitions, but exact figures have not yet been forthcoming. It is estimated from reliable sources that from 65 to 80% of the copper produced in this country went into the manufacture of munitions, up to the signing of the armistice. This left only 20 to 35% of the production available for domestic consumption. The normal consumption of the metal is about 1,300,000,000 lb., and for 1918 the production of the United States was 1,866,000,000 lb. In normal times the United States will consume about 73% of the copper coming from its own mines. From these figures it is evident that during the War the consumption of copper for the arts of peace was far below normal. During the period in which we were actively engaged in the European war there was great curtailment of the industries dependent upon copper. This curtailment in the manufacture of commodities needed in peace times has resulted in the depletion of stocks of copper goods. Likewise there was little extension of industry, the requirements of which in normal times would have increased the normal consumption of copper. In Europe there are only two countries which produce more copper than they consume, namely, Portugal and Spain. The production from Africa, Asia, and Australia does not increase, and they cannot be expected to furnish much toward the future demand, which is indicated. South America will add only a small quantity toward the total. It is evident that the United States will be called upon to furnish the major portion of the copper which will have to be mined to make up for the depleted stocks of copper manufactures. The Central Powers will require copper, and this will have to come from somewhere, and, even if it does not come from the United States directly, it is evident that this country will be called upon to make up the quantity consumed by them.

Should we graph the consumption of copper in this country over a period of 50 years, or even the last 15 years, it will be seen that it indicates a strong increase. This may be interrupted for a short time, but cannot be stopped because of the ever increasing industries that require the metal and are yet in their infancy. At the outbreak of the War many of the railroads were starting to electrify their lines. Inter-urban lines were greatly extended in the East as well as in the West. Water-power projects in the West were demanding greater quantities of copper every year. With the resumption of these projects there will be such a demand for copper as never before existed. There are large projects which contemplate the conversion of power at the mines in the East from coal to electric energy. This will require vast quantities of copper. The installation and extension of present electric transportation lines also will require large quantities. We are informed that buildings throughout the country are in great demand and that the general building program is far behind. This new construction will require no small amount of copper. In every industry we see depleted stocks and in every direction there appear new and large industries which require copper. The gravity of the situation, however, must not be underrated. During the days at the outbreak of the War in 1914 the copper market underwent a re-adjustment, born primarily of uncertainties. Despite the present surplus of copper now on hand, we find that for a long period the normal peace-demand for copper has not appeared. Not only will the lack of present stocks of finished copper products have to be replenished, but the onward march of new industries, with their ever greater demand for the metal, will have to be supplied.

Suppose we have in the United States 1,000,000,000 lb. of surplus copper on hand. The normal consumption is about 1,300,000,000 lb. for the United States. Of the two and a half billion pounds smelted in this country in 1918, approximately 75% has been converted into munitions or has gone into the destructive arts of war. This left 625,000,000 lb. for normal peace consumption. Therefore the constructive arts of peace have suffered to the extent of nearly 675,000,000 lb., which will eventually be made up. This will eat into the stocks on hand. The present condition is only temporary, and foresightedness under the present stringent conditions will place copper again to the fore. During the period of the War, copper production was increased at the expense of the most readily accessible ore-reserves. Development was either curtailed or kept at 'the irreducible minimum.' This has depleted the reserves of many of the large companies. To revert to a normal condition the development of ore-reserves will have to be pushed ahead of production. Advantage is being taken of this condition by some far-seeing mining companies who are at this time developing new properties and who intend to complete the development and equipment of their properties during the period while the market is unsettled. If the peace parley in Europe was finished the uncertainties would soon be removed, and with a clear vision ahead the copper industry would be advancing normally.

THEO. H. M. CRAMPTON.

Phoenix, Arizona, February 20.

Water Laws of Nevada

The Editor:

Sir—It is my understanding that the allotment of space to discussion in your publication is for the purpose of providing a forum for the discussion of current problems of general interest to the mining world—not an arena for the staging of personal controversies. It would appear that the discussion initiated some weeks ago by Mr. G. A. Duncan, regarding certain water litigation in the Eldorado Canyon district of southern Nevada is passing beyond the stage where it can be of interest or benefit to your readers.

The feature of general interest in Mr. Duncan's original contribution was his suggestion that the laws of Nevada, governing the disposition of surface-water, be applied to ground-water as well. In reply, I endeavored to point out the inherent difficulties of such an undertaking, and the danger to the mining community, already afflicted with an apex law, of further legislation of the same litigation-breeding species. The subsequent communications of Mr. Duncan and Mr. Brooks have been confined chiefly to a repetition of evidence introduced by them at the trial. To enter upon a refutation of their statements would be a further trespass upon the patience of your readers; but, in order not to let it appear, by default, that the complaint of Mr. Duncan is well founded, I desire to make a brief final statement in behalf of the mining company, which was the defendant of the water suit instituted by Mr. Duncan.

This defendant company, in accordance with laws and customs in effect since the inception of mining in the West, had been utilizing for milling purposes ground water, developed at its own expense by mining operations on its own claims. Mr. Duncan, by means of a freak water-right granted by the State Engineer, endeavored to appropriate this water. Had he been successful, it would have been possible for him, by carrying the matter to its logical conclusion, to have monopolized the entire water resources of Eldorado canyon, and by so doing to have compelled all the mines therein to close down or to pay him tribute. While the defendant company bore the brunt of the conflict, therefore, it had the material or moral support of practically all the other mining operators of the district. The trial of the case lasted a week; all the claims and contentions, which Mr. Duncan and Mr. Brooks have presented in their letters, were thoroughly threshed out; the defendant introduced abundant evidence in rebuttal; and the decision of the Court was to the effect that Mr. Duncan had failed to establish title to the water or to demonstrate that he had in any way been injured by the defendant company. That this decision was in accordance with the law and the evidence would appear to be sufficiently indicated by the significant fact that Mr. Duncan failed to appeal the case, as it was his privilege and duty to do if he believed otherwise.

Pioche, Nevada, March 8. R. T. WALKER.

[This discussion is now closed.—EDITOR.]

The Immutable Law of Self-Interest

The Editor:

Sir—There are at least two natural laws which have come down through the ages without change. Neither has been altered by the ravages of war or the pursuits of peace. The first is the law of gravity and the second the law of self-interest. The correct solution of any problem in the field of physics demands conformance to the immutable law of gravity. And likewise if we desire to determine the correctness of the practicability of a political doctrine, or the feasibility of a proposal of finance, whether it be domestic or international, the same must conform to the immutable law of self-interest. Failing to satisfy this test it may be assumed that the political doctrine or financial proposal will either not win endorsement, or if enforced as an artificial measure will soon become inoperative because it has failed to take into account the law of self-interest.

Under the caption 'An Internationalized Gold Reserve', published in your issue of March 1, you have by very sound logical deduction branded the unique proposal of the Federal Reserve Board for the establishment of an international gold fund as being Utopian and financially unsound. It is my purpose to analyze the same proposal to determine whether it satisfies the law of self-interest. The more enlightened self-interest an individual may possess the better citizen he becomes, the more he will be able to contribute to civilization, the more he will realize the necessity of becoming self-sustaining, morally, politically, and economically, and the less of a burden he will be to the commonwealth in which he lives. So it is with the Nation. The more enlightened self-interest a nation may develop the better member of the family of nations it becomes, the more that nation will be able to contribute to civilization, the more that nation will realize the necessity of becoming self-sustaining morally, politically, and economically, and the less of a burden that nation will become to the rest of the world. It must be recognized now that the enlightened self-interest of the Allied peoples has just won a decisive victory over the ignorant self-interest of autocracy and has yet to win a victory over the people who have no enlightened self-interest—the Bolshevists. It will be seen that the enlightened individual self-interest, to which I refer, is the mainspring of good government, and finds its freest expression in a democracy.

When the gold reserve of the United States had began to accumulate rapidly, after the European securities had been finally liquidated against the trade-balance in our favor, many of the smaller nations, including neutrals, were forced to part with their gold reserve in order to live. The gold reserves of these smaller nations as well as the larger ones are now below the pre-war trade standard and will necessarily have to be augmented to satisfy the exacting conditions of trade. In the past when exchange began to run against any one of these nations it was a challenge to its pride to build up its gold reserve to a point which would maintain its credit standard in international trade on a parity with other nations. Enlightened self-interest became the assertive force and financial independence was restored. Who will say that this incentive of self-interest did not improve this nation and the world at large? Who will say that this proposal of amalgamated gold reserves in an international pool will not eliminate the incentive of self-interest by which national initiative and independence are sustained? The answers to these questions are self-evident. The proposal is not only chimerical, but practically untenable, as it does not satisfy the immutable law of self-interest.

H. N. LAWRIE.

Portland, Oregon, March 10.

Explosives

The Editor:

Sir—In the excellent article on this subject by Mr. Robert S. Lewis, published in your issue of February 22, occurs the following: "Thawing should be done over steam-pipes at a temperature not above 122°F."

According to the best authorities, and also according to the rules of the Institute of Manufacturers of Explosives, this is not the proper way to thaw high explosives. Nitro-glycerine, an oil, loses its viscosity at high temperatures, and easily separates from the 'dope', or absorbent. Therefore, if cases of high explosives are stored over steam-pipes, and the dynamite should leak—which is not uncommon—nitro-glycerine might drop on the hot steam-pipes, causing an explosion. A drop of nitro-glycerine falling on a hot plate will explode.

Only exhaust-steam, hot air, or hot water should be used for thawing dynamite, and the radiator should be on one side of the thawing-house. The cases of high explosives should not be stored too near or *over* the radiator.

Mr. Lewis also states that a 60% low-freezing dynamite is not equal in strength to a 40% straight dynamite. This is not true of low-freezing 60% dynamite manufactured by the DuPont company. DuPont 60% Red Cross Dynamite (low freezing) and DuPont 60% Straight Dynamite are exactly of the same strength, both having a Triton value of 11, that is, 10 grammes of each of these dynamites is equivalent to 11 grammes of T.N.T. in the ballistic mortar.

S. R. RUSSELL.

Wilmington, Delaware, March 15.

Price-Levels and Readjustment

By RICHARD HOADLEY TINGLEY

The problems of post-war readjustment are proving more perplexing to the American business man than were those involved in adapting himself to war conditions four years ago. The War has been over several months, and business hasn't yet been able to figure out how to readjust itself. On the other hand, business had practically 'found itself' by December 1914. It had made up its mind, by that time, what war meant, and had its plans ready to meet it.

Business is still 'sitting tight' and waiting. It cannot make up its mind whether it is going to be good or bad; whether prices are going to advance or decline. This is the crux of the matter. As soon as business makes up its mind that commodity prices have reached a reasonably stable level, be it high or low, conditions cannot fail to improve.

There are two opposing theories regarding prices of the future. Let us examine them both.

Those who anticipate a radical decline in the near future base their conclusions on the fact that there is, and will be, a continuing volume of labor released from munition plants to resume the production of the goods of peace: that steel, copper, coal, shipping, and other essentials are being released from war needs again to contribute to the demands of peaceful pursuits; that millions of soldiers are returning to the farms, the factories, and other peaceful occupations, and that, in consequence, there will be an immense increase in the volume of goods available for civilian consumption. This condition, they say, should make for low price-levels and restricted business.

Those who entertain the opposite view maintain that war has produced a shortage in nearly all the essentials used by a civilian population. They maintain that almost every available factory that produces essentials has had a considerable proportion of its capacity engaged for the past few years in the manufacture of war goods of one kind or another, and that, in consequence, the stock of such goods available for civilian consumption has been reduced so far below normal that it will take a year, at least, to catch up with the demand. They cite the case of that prime essential to our bodily comfort, the cotton goods supply. During the year and a half in which this country was engaged in war the productive capacity of the factories of the cotton spinners has been engaged, on an average, about 60% on civilian goods and 40% on war supplies. The sudden disruption of plant organization has so reduced the efficiency of these plants that an output of hardly more than 80% of the 60% has been reached. It would appear, then, that in the manufacture of civilian goods, only about 50% of the normal use and demand has been produced during this period. A large proportion of this reduction in supply may now be called a shortage; a shortage of all kinds of cotton goods that amounts to upward of seven billion square yards of cloth! This shortage must, in part at least, be made up. We can deny ourselves these essentials for awhile and reasons of patriotism as well as of economy have influenced us in keeping down our purchases not absolutely needed. There comes a time, however, when we must 'stock up'. This time will come when we make up our minds that prices have sufficiently receded from war-levels and have reached something like a stable basis. Be that stable price high or low we will then be in the market for the purchase of those things that, for one reason or another, we have been doing without.

Much the same argument may be applied to the manufacture of almost every essential product and the effect, to my mind, is going to keep prices from a drastic drop till we have finished our operation of 'stocking up'.

Unless all previously accepted laws governing price-movements are to be violated there can be no drastic drop in commodity prices for some time to come, at least, no drop to anything like pre-war levels. We are taught that the presence of gold in abnormal quantities is sure to stimulate credits and that stimulated credits is sure to inflate prices. We are taught, too, that an inflated currency will surely make for high price-levels, and that high price-levels and good business always go hand in hand. Which is cause and which effect it is unnecessary to discuss here.

The exigencies of war have brought an abnormal supply of gold to our shores. More than a third of the stock of the gold of the world is at present in this country. Two-thirds of this is in the hands of the Federal Reserve banks. Our currency has been inflated from $34.56 per capita before the War, to approximately $55 at the present time, and we have had an unprecedented era of high prices. It would not be safe to argue that these abnormal monetary and credit conditions are solely responsible for the inflated prices we have had and that are still with us. The disrupting influences of war and the diversion of labor and capital from peaceful pursuits to those of destruction are, no doubt, more potent influences making for high price-levels than the monetary influences. The fact remains, however, that high prices are a sure accompanyment of an inflated currency and an abnormal supply of gold.

But what of the future? There is no indication that our stock of gold is likely to be reduced in the near future, nor the currency issue cut down. With an export business that is sure to be in excess of our imports; with interest money payments from European countries on our war loans to them coming in; with freight-charges accruing from earnings of our newly acquired merchant marine, there will be no compelling demand for our gold to leave us for other countries. On the other hand, more gold will be due us from abroad unless we adopt the broad policy of investing our surplus moneys due us from other nations in fostering their home industries.

All these conditions will continue to make, according to the theories of the economists, for high price-levels in this country till the conditions have changed. Will this theory be vindicated? Or, has the world-war created such different economic conditions that it will be upset and violated? Despite the fact of our abnormal gold and our inflated currency will prices drastically decline?

Let me quote another parallel from Dr. E. E. Pratt, Chief of the Bureau of Foreign and Domestic Commerce at Washington, on the effect of past wars on prices. He says that, taking the average prices in 1860 as 100, the index numbers show that during the eight years preceding the Crimean war, prices in England averaged 85, and during the ten years following this war they averaged 121.6 on a gold basis. Again, in Russia, prices averaged 102.8 during the period of ten years before the Russo-Japanese war, and 129.8 during the seven years following that war. In Japan the prices of food, clothing, and materials averaged 98.8 during the four years preceding, and 122.1 during the seven years following the war. Dr. Pratt concludes that Europe is now entering upon a period of high prices and thinks that this condition will continue for ten years or more. If this is true of Europe, much the same conditions may be expected in the United States.

In the light of all of the above the American business man must draw his own conclusions. It is the wise man, however, that correctly forecasts the business future. It was the wise man who, in 1914, realized what a state of war would mean to him in his business. It is the wise man who can see, a little in advance of others, what the readjustment of peace is going to mean to him, and, in the light of the evidence, there seems to be but one conclusion.

Ventilation and Fire Protection in the United Verde Extension Mine

By CHARLES A. MITKE

*VENTILATION. There are three shafts at the U. V. X.—the Little Daisy, Edith, and Audrey—and two raises to the surface, one for ventilation, the other for waste. The Audrey, when completed, will be the main hoisting shaft, the Edith, the supply shaft, while the Little Daisy is used entirely for ventilation. One suction-fan, having an air capacity of 40,000 cu. ft. per min. is placed at the top of the Little Daisy shaft; and another, of 135,000 cu. ft., will be erected at the top of the air-raise, which will become the main air-shaft. A connection will be made from the long tunnel directly to the large orebody on the 1300-ft. level. A raise will be driven from the 1400-ft. level, connecting at this point, so as to force all the fresh air entering the large tunnel down to the lower workings. Doors have been put in at the different shaft-stations on the 800, 1100, and 1200-ft. levels, in order to force all the air to pass through the different stopes.

*Abstract from Bulletin 147 of American Institute of Mining Engineers, February 1919.

Arrangements will be made for the proper coursing of the air through the Bonanza orebody, where it is most needed. Gangways, immediately beneath the capping and connecting old raises, have been preserved by building walls of waste-rock. These are maintained solely for ventilation purposes and will remain open for some time in order to afford a means of escape for the heated air from the old square-set sections.

While at present the temperature, humidity, and velocity of the air in the different working-places fall somewhat below the requirements for a good working atmosphere, when the necessary development work is completed, standard raises built, and the large mine-fan completed on the surface, the volume of air passing through the workings will amount to at least 400 cu. ft. of air per man per minute and the United Verde Extension will be one of the best ventilated mines in the South-West.

FIRE PROTECTION. A spraying-system has been fitted in the Edith shaft. In case of fire in this shaft, the fire-doors on the 1300 and 1400-ft. stations will be closed immediately by means of compressed air and the sprays, which are controlled from surface, put into operation. The doors on the 800, 1100, and 1200-ft. levels are ventilating-doors, and are always kept closed. The mine-fans would also be stopped at once, but not under any other circumstances.

The Little Daisy shaft, which is used entirely for ventilation, has a concrete connection from the fan to a depth of one set below the collar. From there down it is naturally so wet as to make a fire-protection system unnecessary. The new Audrey shaft is fire-proofed by its being concreted. The barriers of waste left by the Mitchell stoping method will serve as fire-breaks in that part of the Bonanza orebody in which this system is used.

A number of electric-blowers, and a sufficient supply of bulkheading material and fire-fighting equipment, are kept on hand so that the fire-area can immediately be put under pressure and steps taken to extinguish the fire. Should these measures fail, the general procedure will then be similar to that followed in mining out the fire-area in the small orebody, from which, for 1½ years, ore that was actually on fire was mined successfully under pressure without interfering with the production or the daily mining operations of the remainder of the mine. During this time not a single serious injury was reported.

PLATINUM production of Canada during 1918 totaled 39 crude ounces, a decrease of 18 ounces. This was all saved from placer mining in the Similkameen district of British Columbia.

CHROMITE imports in January were 12,263 tons, valued at $486,404; against 6858 tons and $318,293 in December. Neither New Caledonia nor Rhodesia are on the list yet.

The Yerington District, Nevada

By ADOLPH KNOPF

*The oldest geologic records of the district date back to the Triassic period. At this time 4000 ft. of andesitic and dacitic lavas, breccias, and tuffs were erupted, which were succeeded by a peculiar series of soda-rich felsite lavas and tuffs. Marine conditions then prevailed, and limestones mainly were laid down, interrupted, however, by occasional eruptions of felsite. At one time during the Triassic a bed of gypsum, as much as 450 ft. thick, was deposited.

These rocks were folded, probably in the beginning of Cretaceous time, and were intruded, probably early in the Cretaceous, by large masses of grano-diorite and quartz-monzonite. These intrusions were followed by others that brought in minor amounts of aplite and considerable amounts of quartz-monzonite porphyry. Faulting occurred during and immediately after this epoch of intrusion, and as a sequel to the intrusive activity the ore-bodies were formed.

A long period of erosion then ensued, during which the Triassic rocks were in places entirely removed and the granitic rocks were laid bare over wide areas. Volcanic eruptions followed, probably in the later part of the Miocene, and buried the fluvial deposits that had accumulated on the surface eroded upon the older rocks. The relief of this surface on which the Tertiary rocks accumulated appears to have been moderate, though on account of the small exposures and the profound faulting to which the rocks of the region have been subjected this conclusion is not firmly established. At any rate, the streams that flowed on this surface appear to have been powerful, as is indicated by the well-rounded boulders, six feet in diameter, occurring in their gravels.

The volcanic activity began with the effusion of a distinctive flow of black glass, a latite vitrophyre; this flow was succeeded by quartz-latites, which are especially characterized by their columnar structure; and upon these were piled about 4000 ft. of rhyolites and 1400 ft. of andesite-breccia. From time to time during the general period of eruptive activity fluvial and lacustral conditions prevailed; the most noteworthy of these interruptions led to the deposition of 430 ft. of lake-beds, which occur at the top of the rhyolites and underlie the andesite-breccia. This succession of rocks, beginning with the vitrophyre at the base of the section and including the andesite-breccia at the top, appears to correspond to the Esmeralda formation, which is now believed to be of late Miocene age.

After the deposition of these rocks a period of pronounced diastrophism set in, the most vigorous in this part of Nevada during Tertiary time. The rhyolites were tilted at angles of 25° to 65° and were greatly faulted, the rocks being displaced stratigraphically to the extent of thousands of feet. Erosion ensued, and subsequently andesites were erupted, now resting at low angles upon the worn edges of the rhyolites. This eruptive outburst was extremely moderate and is represented by only a few hundred feet of lava.

After the andesitic extrusion erosion again began,

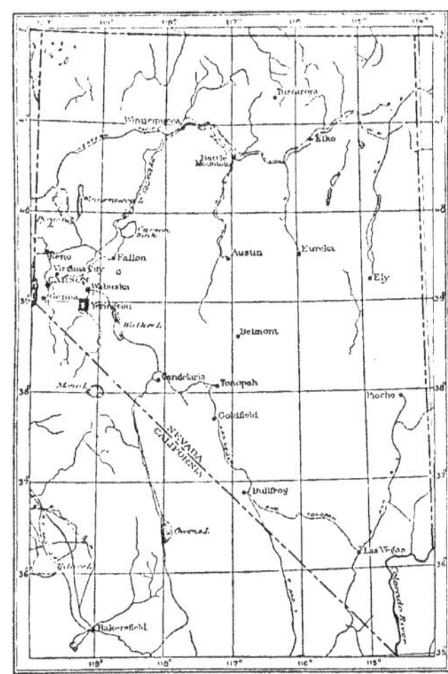

MAP OF NEVADA, SHOWING YERINGTON DISTRICT

rather extensive deposits of gravels accumulated, in places as much as 300 ft. thick; their unsorted, subangular character suggests that they are of fanglomerate origin. Eruptive forces, the final manifestation of volcanism in the district, once more became active, and a series of basalt flows was poured out. The basalts, although nearly horizontal, have been considerably faulted, and this period of vigorous diastrophism is held to mark the beginning of Quaternary time. The faulting that took place at that time blocked out the Singatse range largely as we see it now. Since this faulting the deep

*Abstracted from Professional Paper 114 of the U. S. Geological Survey.

canyons opening out upon Mason valley have been excavated, and the material thus derived has built up a series of alluvial cones fronting the range.

The main orebodies of the Yerington district are copper-bearing deposits characterized by a gangue of either pyroxene, garnet, or epidote, or a mixture of these minerals. Chalcopyrite is the chief copper-bearing mineral; pyrite is commonly associated with it, but no other primary sulphides occur in the district.

The deposits belong to the contact-metamorphic group. The primary ore is essentially unenriched by later sulphides, for supergene covellite and chalcocite, although occurring locally, are as a rule not abundant.

Orebodies of this kind have yielded the bulk of the metal output. The average tenor of the ore mined has ranged from 2.75 to 6% of copper, with gold and silver present in traces only. Among the representatives of this group are the orebodies of the Bluestone, Mason Valley, Ludwig, Douglas Hill, Casting Copper, and McConnell mines.

Other types of the copper deposits are sparingly represented in the district and as a whole are of minor economic importance. They are exemplified by the irregular bodies of rich cuprite ore in quartz-monzonite porphyry at the Empire-Nevada mine and by the fissure-veins in quartz-monzonite and quartz-monzonite porphyry.

The principal copper deposits of the district, characterized by their pyroxene, garnet, or epidote gangue, have, with one notable exception, been formed by the replacement of limestones. The Bluestone orebody, the exception alluded to, consists essentially of chalcopyrite in an epidote gangue and was produced by the replacement of brecciated garnetite and allied silicate rocks.

The limestone beds in which the orebodies developed are shown in the following paragraphs to have been relatively pure calcite-rocks. Their chemical composition is a matter of some theoretical interest. Lindgren and others have presented evidence to show that orebodies of this type have commonly formed in limestones of extreme purity. Leith and Mead,† however, consider the evidence thus adduced to be doubtful and inadequate, inasmuch as the specimens chosen for analysis represented only single strata, and they emphasize the fact that to obtain evidence of conclusive value samples must be taken across the full width of the ore-zones.

Analyses of the limestone in the ore-bearing zone of the Mason Valley mine of the Yerington district are available that in large measure meet Leith's requirement. The limestone was used as smelter flux and hence was carfully analyzed for lime and silica but less carefully for other constituents. A glory-hole 200 ft. long, 60 ft. wide, and 75 ft. deep was opened up. The limestone is mainly in beds ranging from 5 to 10 ft. in thickness but includes some thinly banded varieties. The beds strike north and dip 70° or more westward; the longer axis of the glory-hole is parallel to the strike of the strata. In column 1 of the subjoined table is given an average of seven analyses of limestone from the stope, and in column 2 an average of four analyses of limestone from the 'new stope' situated in the immediate hanging-wall country rock of the ore-bearing zone; from this stope limestone flux is now being obtained. The individual analyses do not vary widely from the average figures.

†Leith, C. K., and Mead, W. J., 'Metamorphic Geology', p. 148, 1915.

Analyses of Limestone From Mason Valley Mine

	1	2
CaO	46.9	48.5
MgO	2.3	0.6
SiO_2	9.1	5.7
Al_2O_3	4.0	2.2
Fe_2O_3	1.1	2.3
CO_2 (theoretic)	39.4	38.7
	102.8	98.0

In these analyses, according to the smelter manager, the lime and silica were carefully determined, as these are the constituents of importance in calculating the furnace charge, and the determinations of the other oxides are of nominal value only. The defective summations of the analyses are doubtless due to this imperfect determination of the minor constituents.

The analyses concur in showing that the limestones of the ore-bearing zone and of the hanging wall are relatively pure; they are slightly silicous but are low in magnesia, alumina, and iron.

Two specimens of limestone obtained from the south end of the ore-zone on the No. 3 level of the Mason Valley mine were analyzed in the laboratory of the U. S. Geological Survey. The great ore-lens on the south end of this level extends obliquely across strata of limestone of different colors, ranging from light bluish-white to dark-gray or black. These beds carry a few fibres of tremolite and sporadic cubes of pyrite. The limestone represented by column 1 of the subjoined table, taken 20 ft. from the edge of the orebody, is a dark-gray, almost black, crystalline limestone; under the microscope it proves to consist preponderantly of calcite grains, with accessory tremolite and pyrite. The limestone represented by column 2, taken from rock immediately adjoining the solid andradite of the periphery of the orebody, is a light-gray, rather dense, limestone; under the microscope it proves to consist essentially of calcite and a few scattered fibres of tremolite.

Analyses of Limestone From Mason Valley Mine
[W. C. Wheeler, analyst]

	1	2
CaO	52.12	51.63
MgO	0.84	3.17
SiO_2	3.04	1.80
Al_2O_3	1.30	0.14
Fe_2O_3 (total)	0.64	0.17
CO_2 (theoretic)	41.87	44.02
	99.90	100.93

These analyses show that the two specimens selected are somewhat purer than the average as found by the smelter determinations. The analyses are of the same general purport, however, and confirm the statements made as to the essentially non-magnesian character of the limestone of the ore-bearing zone and their low content of silica, alumina, and iron.

The orebodies at the other mines in the district have formed in coarse calcite-rocks, which without doubt are of the same general character as the limestones analyzed.

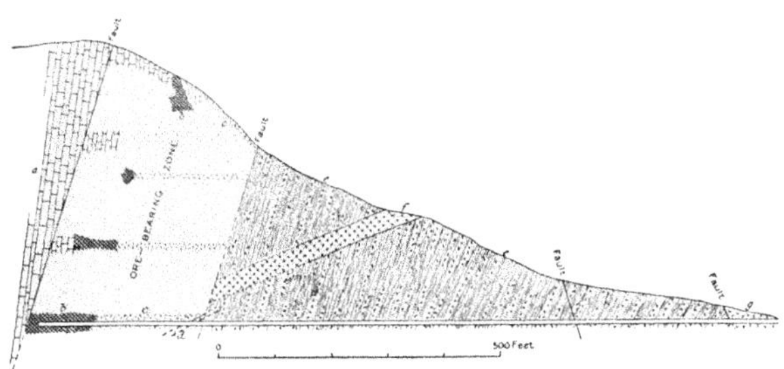

FIG. 2. SECTION THROUGH TUNNEL NO. 4 OF THE MASON VALLEY MINE

a, limestone; b, ore; c garnetiferous rock; d, basic dikes; e, lime-silicate rocks with intercalated felsites; f, quartz-monzonite porphyry; g, Tertiary rhyolite

The ore deposits are situated on or near fault-contacts. Commonly the faults separate dissimilar rocks, such as limestone from felsite, andesite, or stratified calc-silicate rocks. That the faulting occurred before the orebodies were formed is established by the following structural relations: (1) The faults displace the quartz-monzonite porphyry dikes, and the severed ends of the dikes and the fault drag from the dikes have been metamorphosed by the ore-forming solutions: the brecciated quartz-monzonite porphyry at the Bluestone orebody, which is an epidote-chalcopyrite deposit, is profoundly epidotized and pyritized; and the porphyry enclosed in the Ludwig lode is garnetized, silicified, and pyritized. (2) The calc-silicate rocks, such as the fine-grained grossularite rocks near the Douglas Hill mine, have been brecciated, and the shattered mass has been re-cemented by the coarsely granular andradite that was formed at the time the ore was deposited; at the Casting Copper mine a series of thin-bedded black garnetites and allied rocks abut at an angle of 45° upon a belt of crystalline limestone. The garnetites were broken along the contact, and the angular black fragments are enclosed in the yellow andradite that forms the gangue of the orebody. These significant structural relations, pointing to the considerable faulting that intervened between the time of intrusion of the quartz-monzonite and the deposition of the ores and proving the dependence of ore deposition on fissuring, will now be considered in some detail.

The relation of the ore deposits to faulting and brecciation is shown most strikingly at the Douglas Hill and Casting Copper mines; nor is elsewhere shown so clearly the distinctness of the ore-forming mineralization as a separate event that took place after the metamorphism accompanying the intrusion of the quartz monzonite. The mineralogically complex series of calc-silicate rocks on the west flank of Douglas Hill has been described: toward the top of the hill these rocks consist of exceedingly dense fine-grained garnetites, composed almost wholly of a nearly pure grossularite, as shown by its index of 1.75. The summit of the hill consists of an immense mass of andradite in which the ore occurs as irregular lenses. This great body of andradite resulted from the replacement of a massive limestone lying above the stratified series of aphanitic garnetites. The footwall of the ore-zone is a belt of remarkable breccia about 20 ft. thick. This breccia is composed of sharply angular fragments of the aphanitic garnetites enclosed in a

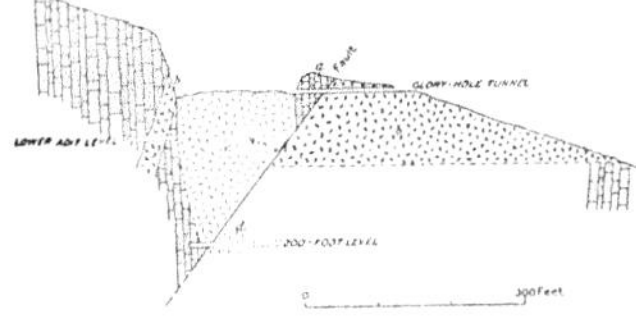

FIG. 1. SECTION THROUGH THE GLORY-HOLE TUNNEL OF THE McCONNELL MINE

a, limestone; b, basalt; c, garnet-rock and ore; d, Triassic andesite

cementing matrix of coarse euhedral yellow garnet. The index of this garnet proves to be 1.87 and determines the garnet to be a nearly pure andradite. The garnets of the two periods of metamorphism show, then, in this grossularite hornfels cemented by andradite their maximal possible contrast. The andradite cement carries a little interstitial quartz, apatite, and chalcopyrite.

The dependence of ore deposition on fissuring and the evidence of two distinct periods of garnetization are clearly shown at the Casting Copper mine. The ore-bearing zone lies along the fault-contact of a stratified series of black garnetites striking at an angle of 45° against massive limestone. The garnetites are dense, heavy, fine-grained rocks. Under the microscope they are seen to be composed wholly of garnet, which is clouded with carbonaceous inclusions, a feature that accounts for their black color. The massive limestone has been solidly replaced by coarsely granular resin-yellow andradite for over 400 ft. along its contact with the stratified garnetites. The garnetites were shattered along the contact, and the angular fragments of dense black rocks that resulted therefrom are now outlined by the thin veinlets of euhedral yellow andradite that traverse the breccia.

Some of the ore deposits, as the Bluestone, Mason Valley, and Western Nevada, are situated at the contact of the Triassic rocks with the quartz-monzonite or the grano-diorite. This contact, however, proves to be faulted; in fact, the grano-diorite at the Mason Valley mine is a narrow fault-wedge lying between the ore-zone and Tertiary rhyolites to the north. The time of the faulting, except that it is later than the intrusion of the quartz-monzonite porphyry dikes, is unknown, as is also the amount of displacement. The other garnetiferous ore deposits of the district are at some distance from the large intrusive bodies; that farthest distant—the Douglas Hill, which is characterized by its extraordinarily extensive mass of andradite—is 2500 ft. from the nearest surface exposure of quartz-monzonite.

The limestones adjoining the faults along which the ore-forming solutions rose were shattered, and there is some evidence that the shattering facilitated or governed the replacement of the limestone by the mineralizing solutions. In the Ludwig orebody, which is lode-like in form, the limestone was extremely broken and crushed by dynamic disturbance, forming breccias as much as 80 to 100 ft. thick. The garnetiferous quartz-pyrite ore, carrying coarse calcite as a minor component, forms a large low-grade shoot 50 to 100 ft. wide. Toward the foot-wall side of the orebody, where it grades into unreplaced limestone and where the mineralizing activity was presumably less intense, the result of the selective action of the solutions becomes apparent. Here the finely crushed limestone that formed the matrix of the larger angular fragments of the breccia was replaced by pyrite, and thus a limestone-breccia cemented by pyrite resulted. In the same way the brecciated condition of the quartz-monzonite porphyry occurring in the Bluestone orebody has been strikingly emphasized by the selective replacement of the more finely crushed portion of the breccia. It was further emphasized by the fact that the sulphides form margins around the larger fragments of the breccia.

The replacement of fractured and brecciated limestone by andradite and sulphides is recognizable along the periphery of the large ore-lens at the south end of the ore-zone of the Mason Valley mine. The andradite and sulphides have replaced a dark-gray fine-grained limestone; the junction between wholly replaced and unreplaced limestone is sharp; and the only change shown by the limestone is that where it adjoins the replaced rock it is bordered by a white band less than half an inch wide. The limestone has evidently been decarbonized in this band, but its grain has not been coarsened. At the McConnel mine, also, there is some evidence that the replacement by the mineralizing solutions progressed along fractures. See Fig. 1. However, it is difficult to obtain proof in many of the deposits in this district, as in others, that replacement by garnet, pyroxene, and allied silicates was governed by the fractured condition of the limestone in which they have developed. The conclusion to be drawn from this general lack of positive evidence is probably that the replacement of limestone by garnet and allied silicates is commonly so thorough that it has obliterated the evidence of the pre-mineral fracturing. There has consequently been a general tendency to regard ore deposits of this kind as having originated at high temperatures and pressures from solutions permeating the limestone by diffusion or through microscopic fractures.

From the preceding discussion it appears that the chief ore deposits were localized by the ascent of the ore-forming solutions along fault-fissures. The presence of limestone obviously appears to have favorably influenced the precipitation of ore. The main orebodies are in the limestone adjoining the faults, but concomitantly with the deposition of the ore large bodies of garnet and pyroxene were formed, which in amount greatly exceed the ore. To find the bodies of ore in this unprofitable envelope is one of the main problems of mining in the district. As a rule, not without important exceptions, however, the ore tends to occur in the marginal portion of the contact-silicate rock where this borders the limestone. This tendency shows most clearly in the orebodies of the Mason Valley (Fig. 2) and Casting Copper mines. That ore is most likely to occur on the limestone side of the contact-metamorphic copper deposits at Mackay, Idaho, has been recognized by Umpleby;[2] and in a later paper by the same writer[3] this rule is shown to apply to a considerable number of other contact-metamorphic deposits. The Yerington district broadly supports the rule.

Operating Data of the A. S. & R. Co.

The report of this company for 1918 gives the following summary:

	1917	1918
Number of men employed; excluding Mexico	24,698	21,765
Total wages and salaries, excluding Mexico	$24,497,836	$23,516,467
Average wages per 8-hour day	$3.31	$3.91
Charge smelted, tons	5,918,924	5,658,232
Bullion refined, tons	706,875	680,099
Coal used, tons	787,890	765,124
Coke used, tons	592,765	545,063
Fuel-oil used, barrels	1,560,535	1,659,337
Gas used, cubic feet	3,032,908,373	2,372,000,103
Ore mined, tons	2,318,925	2,325,280
Coal mined, tons	259,499	168,140
Coke produced, tons	186,107	171,245
Metal products:		
Gold, ounces	2,496,693	1,994,015
Silver, ounces	68,841,061	72,572,506
Platinum and palladium, ounces	1,597	1,516
Lead, tons	275,266	260,192
Copper, pounds	916,974,000	868,540,000
Spelter, pounds	52,522,000	41,238,000
Nickel, pounds	682,715	626,085
Tin, pounds (from Bolivian ore)	12,130,000	19,868,000
Sulphuric acid, tons	33,087	43,669
Arsenic, pounds	9,132,000	7,837,063
Copper sulphate, pounds	7,598,000	5,164,000
By-product metals, pounds	4,131,709	1,870,692

[2] Umpleby, J. B., 'The genesis of the Mackay copper deposits, Idaho': 'Econ. Geology', vol. 9, p. 321, 1914.

[3] Umpleby, J. B., 'The occurrence of ore on the limestone side of garnet zones': California Univ. Dept. Geology Bull., vol. 10, pp. 25-37, 1916.

Technical Writing: The Construction of Sentences

By T. A. RICKARD

*In order to write clearly—that is, so as to be understood beyond question—you should know not only what your words denote but how to build your sentences: you must not only choose your words carefully but you should construct your sentences properly. To achieve proper construction, you must obey the laws of syntax, because the meaning of clauses and sentences depends upon the order of words. A sentence is a combination of words that expresses thought: it says something about something. A clause is a subordinate sentence: it is part of a larger sentence. The Greeks call an editor a συντακτης (suntaktes), he who assembles the parts of a sentence. Hence our word 'syntax' for the branch of grammar that treats of the sentence and its construction. English is essentially a non-inflected language: and in that respect it is unlike not only Latin and Greek but its modern rivals, French and German. This lack of inflections, to indicate the relation of words, makes it supremely necessary that in English our words shall be placed in correct order, for we depend upon the order to indicate the sequence of thought. Any deviation from the logical sequence may endanger the meaning; for example:

When spies were feared in England at the beginning of the War, a local paper stated:

(1) "The authorities are now looking for a gray motor-car driven by a woman who is thought to have a wireless apparatus inside."

A technical journal announced:

(2) "We publish an article on errors latent in the sampling of mines by Mr. Blank." The mention of the author should have followed 'article'.

(3) "He blew out his brains after bidding his wife good-bye with a shotgun."

(4) "Mrs. Smith was killed on Wednesday morning while cooking her husband's breakfast in a shocking manner."

(5) "The owner of this property fishes and shoots himself."

(6) "The concentrating table was covered by the foreman with a new face of rubber."

(7) "The samples were preserved for analysis in a paraffin-sealed flask."

(8) "Care should be taken to see whether such wells are contaminated by frequent analyses."

The foregoing examples of incoherence break the rule that "the relation of each word and each clause to the context should be unmistakable." Another rule says: "Clauses that are grammatically connected should be kept as close together as possible." As a further warning I quote the following:

(9) "The expedition, which left Fairbanks March 13, expected to reach the summit of Mt. McKinley early in May, but was delayed three weeks cutting a passage three miles long through ice with hand-axes thrown across the ridge by an earthquake last summer."

That must have been a weird earthquake! it threw hand-axes across a ridge! Even if you place "with hand-axes" after "passage" you find yourself saying that the hand-axes were "three miles long." Note the slovenliness of style: the omission of 'on' before "March 13," of 'while' before "cutting," and of 'it' before "was delayed." The statement can be amended thus:

"The expedition . . . was delayed three weeks by having to cut with hand-axes a passage three miles long through ice, which had fallen across a ridge in consequence of an earthquake last summer."

Place clauses in their logical order; the inversion of ideas is confusing.

(10) "Combined with geological ability of an unusual degree, he was an all-around engineer."

No sensible man talks in this way; the phrasing is stilted and obscure. It is better to say:

"He was not only an all-around engineer, but also an excellent geologist."

(11) "Due to the richness of the new orebody on the tenth level, the mine has paid dividends." He means that:

"The mine has been able to pay dividends, thanks to the richness of the new orebody on the tenth level."

(12) "Compared with what I had seen in Nevada, Rhodesia is a poor goldfield." This may be changed to:

"I would consider Rhodesia a poor goldfield, as compared with Nevada."

Take care that your demonstrative pronouns are made to refer to the right thing.

(13) "A number of mines have adopted the use of cars to take the place of 'cans'. *These* hold from 1500 to 2000 lb. apiece."

The second sentence refers to the 'cars', not the 'cans'.

"A number of mines have substituted cars for cans. The cars hold from 1500 to 2000 lb. apiece" or

"In a number of mines the 'cans' have been replaced by cars, which hold from 1500 to 2000 lb. apiece."

(14) "Because a process is cheap does not prove it desirable."

(15) "It is because he was a scientific man that he insisted upon research."

*A chapter from a forthcoming book on 'Technical Writing', based on a series of lectures delivered at the University of California; to be published by John Wiley & Sons, New York.

In these two examples the causal clause is made substantive, thereby producing an awkward inversion. It would be better to write:

"A process is not desirable merely because it is cheap."

"He insisted upon research because he was a scientific man."

Kelley says:[1] "It should be insisted on again and again that if two forms of expression are both open to criticism, the chances are very large that something else could be better than either. Begin anew, and hammer out for yourself a sentence to which you can think of no reasonable objection. So a young writer learns his trade, and so a veteran keeps his style fresh and clean."

I should delete 'on' after 'insisted'; also the 'very' before 'large'; again, I should avoid the preposition-verb 'think of' and say "a sentence to which you can see no reasonable objection." However, the advice is admirable.

Do not compare things with qualities, the concrete with the abstract. Correspondence in form promotes lucidity and ease of statement.

(16) "He saw these issues more clearly than any [other] man."

(17) "No *other* man in the country has done more to advance the study of economic geology."

In the first quotation the 'other' is needed; in the second, it is out of place.

An intelligent interest in the rules of composition need not stiffen the writer's manner, nor make him pedantic.

Connectives should be placed carefully, and when used in couples they must correspond.

BOTH, AND;

(18) "I went both because I feared and because I hoped."

EITHER, OR;

(19) "The division of profits made by *either* governments, banks or industries."

Delete 'either' and insert a comma after banks.

NOT ONLY, BUT ALSO;

(20) "This was not only according to law, but also according to justice."

ON THE ONE HAND, ON THE OTHER HAND;

NEITHER HERE NOR THERE.

(21) Either in the city or in the country.

Do not omit to repeat the preposition.

(22) "Poets are either born in London or remote country places."

The 'either' is misplaced and 'in' is omitted before 'remote'.

"Poets are born either in London or in remote country places."

NEITHER, NOR:

(23) "I looked neither forward or back."

This likewise contains two errors:

"I neither looked forward nor back."

These seem small matters to the slovenly writer, but they are of the essence of clear writing. As Kelley says:

"No great difference? There is no great difference between lifting two pounds and lifting one pound; but I will not have my shoes weighted with lead. In the single and simple case, no great difference; but construct a complicated sentence in defiance of the laws of thought, or a long discourse with constant disregard of what is normal in structure and formally clear, and the reader will be wearied and repelled, unless your work is in other respects so good as to please him in spite of your slovenliness—and even if you please him, very likely you will have failed to make him understand you, and thereby to persuade or convince or instruct him as you would wish to do."

Young writers drift easily into long sentences, entangling their ideas in a wilderness of words. They shun the short sentence, preferring to link one thought to another by the aid of many 'ands', as an after-dinner speaker ekes out his lame remarks with a frequent 'urr' or 'err'. To err is human, to forgive divine; but it is hard to condone the unnecessary 'and'. Don't be afraid of short sentences or of using the full stop.

(24) "This quality of diffusion indicates molecular mobility; *and* a good example of this is furnished by etc."

"This quality of diffusion indicates molecular mobility, a good example of which is furnished by etc."

(25) "The methods employed in the underground work vary with the nature of the ore deposits *and* have been developed to suit the local conditions encountered in the various mines."

This is verbose and confused.

"Mining methods have been developed to suit local conditions, as modified by the varying structure of the ore deposits."

(26) "At the Zaaiplaats tin mine the cassiterite has mainly occurred in the Red granite; *and*, the author particularly notices that the color of granite round the pipes was often of a much deeper red; *and*, that a great deal of tourmalinization had taken place."

This requires several corrections: "At the Zaaiplaats tin mine, the cassiterite is found chiefly in the Red granite. The color of this granite is deeper in places around the pipes [ore-chimneys], where also tourmalinization is marked."

Such sentences are written by men that cannot claim lack of experience in writing. Here is a shocking example from the 'Times', of London:

(27) "The cities we remember from childhood, unvisited since, grow in our minds *and* become glorious *and* visionary. The memory itself is only a material which the mind uses, as in dreams it uses some fact of waking hours. There was a bridge, perhaps a mean iron bridge, *and* a few trees, *and* some decent houses beyond it. But all the mean details are forgotten, *and* the scale is so altered that the bridge seems to have spanned a deep valley with great arches, *and* to have been a causeway leading into a city of palaces *and* overshadowing trees. *And* along the causeway crowds were drawn into the city

[1] James P. Kelley, 'Workmanship in Words'.

and traffic coming from a great distance, as if to a festival. *And* there is a memory also of the sky itself as momentous—towering clouds flushed with the sunset, *and* the causeway shining after rain, *and* all the people in the streets enjoying the beautiful hours, with music [that was really a German band] adding a glory of sound to the glory of light *and* form *and* movement."

The excessive use of 'and' spoils an excellent piece of writing.

'And' is used as a feeble continuative by writers uncertain of the relation between their ideas.

(28) "Jackson went *and* examined the pump." That might be true; he might have gone toward the pump and then incidentally he might have examined it; but what the writer really meant was:

"Jackson went to examine the pump."

(29) "He told him to be sure *and* [to] attend to this matter."

(30) "When costs in California and Europe were compared—$75 here *and* [as against] Spanish mercury imported at $40 per flask—it became evident that an import duty was desirable."

(31) "It *is sometimes* [may be] found that the screening from one lot of ore is sufficiently rich to be shipped with the selected ore *and* [whereas] that from the next lot will be too poor."

(32) "Practically all the belts are 30 in. wide, 7-ply, *and* have $\frac{3}{16}$ in. rubber cover on the carrying side, *and* $\frac{1}{16}$ in. on the pulley side."

We see what he means, but it can be said more clearly:

"The belts are 7-ply and 30 in. wide; they have a $\frac{3}{16}$ in. cover of rubber on the carrying side and $\frac{1}{16}$ in. on the pulley side."

(33) "The mining world is indebted to the initiative of John Wiley & Sons for meeting so great a want, *and* they have been fortunate in securing the services of Mr. Peele as the guiding spirit to translate the conception into achievement."

Here the 'and' is introduced to correct a badly organized statement. When re-written it reads thus:

"John Wiley & Sons have placed the mining world under obligation through their initiative in meeting so great a want, and they have been fortunate in securing, etc."

(34) "Wet methods of treating the concentrate were not at all satisfactory, as there was a large amount of black residue in the concentrate that could not be decomposed by sulphuric acid and ferrous sulphate, *and which* carried high silver values."

If 'which' is replaced by 'that', the last clause would refer back to 'residue', but the chief fault lies in tying an important assertion to the end of the opening statement by means of the 'and'. He means:

"Wet methods of treating the concentrate proved unsatisfactory because it contained a large proportion of black residue, rich in silver, that could not be decomposed by sulphuric acid and ferrous sulphate."

(35) "It is obvious that the calculations can be shortened when one set of apparatus *and* conditions are used continuously for analyses."

He is connecting unlike ideas in a confusing manner.

"It is obvious that the calculations can be simplified by using the same apparatus under identical conditions during a series of analyses."

Sentences without logical connection should not be linked by a feeble 'and'. The reason for the connection should be made clear by using the proper connective or by inserting an explanatory clause.

(36) "For the retorting of lean shale, the Scottish retort gives fairly satisfactory results, but it is by no means perfect, *and* [although] it has been claimed that it is possible *to so* [so to] improve the retort as to make it less costly both to construct and to operate."

(37) "It is certainly not wise to construct small plants which are to be operated to recover both oil and nitrogen contents, *and* it will be especially poor business should it be also necessary to manufacture the acid required for the production of ammonium sulphate." I suggest:

"Certainly it is not wise to erect small plants that are to be operated to recover both the oil and the nitrogen contents, more particularly in a locality where it becomes necessary also to make the acid required in the production of ammonium sulphate."

Adjectives should follow each other in the order of thought.

(38) "The orebodies are easily mined and large."

The 'easy mining' is a consequence of 'largeness', and that is the order in which the adjectives should be given.

(39) "The ore is subjected to costly and prolonged treatment."

The idea of costliness follows upon the prolongation of the treatment.

Such inversion of adjectives is tiresome to the reader and detracts from the force of the statement.

Place subordinate words in obscure positions, so as to leave important words where they are clear and disentangled from other words that clog them. Avoid emphasis on words that do not "deserve distinction." Monosyllables usually make a feeble ending for a sentence. Lord Shaftesbury, in his 'Advice to an Author', says: "If, whilst they [writers] profess only to please, they secretly advise, and give instruction, they may now, perhaps, as well as formerly, be esteemed, with justice, the best and most honorable among authors."

That is a complex sentence so well arranged as to be perfectly clear.

Adverbs are commonly misplaced. Put the modifying word as near as possible to the word that it modifies. "The ore should properly be dried" does not mean that "the ore should be dried properly." The first refers to the need of a particular operation, the other to the need of conducting the operation in a particular way. "The words and groups of words that are near to one another in thought should be near in expression, and those that are separate in thought should be separate in expression."[2]

[2]A. S. Hill.

(40) "Such errors are frequent in the writings *even* of good authors."

The 'even' should follow 'frequent'.

'Only' and 'always' are commonly misplaced.

(41) "His exordium would have been admirable if *he only* had spoken; but Mr. Asquith's significant reference to future relations aroused speculation instead of stilling it." 'New Republic'.

'Only' should precede 'he'; the writer means that it would have been better for the purpose if Mr. Lloyd George had been the only speaker. As it is, the sentence expresses the wish that he had spoken.

(42) "The internal-combustion engine has been introduced on a large scale in refrigerating plants *only* in the last three years." This is correct, but it would be clearer if the 'only' came after 'years'; the statement might be taken to mean "in refrigerating plants only."

(43) "It is necessary to *always* roast the ore before chlorination" and "It is necessary to roast the ore *always* before chlorination" are both objectionable. In the first, 'always' splits the infinitive; in the second, it qualifies the wrong word. The sentence should read:

"Before chlorination, it is necessary *always* to roast the ore." This introduces 'chlorination' ahead of 'roasting' and is preferable to "It is necessary *always* to roast the ore before chlorination," because the necessity for roasting arises from the use of chlorination; therefore the ideas should be expressed in that order. As a grammarian would say, "Before chlorination" is the antecedent clause, and "it is necessary, etc." is the consequent clause.

Do not bring two verbs, belonging to different sentences, into close contact, as in the following quotation from the 'New Republic'.

(44) "What the more serious evils of that policy are *was* revealed by the election."

It were better to have written:

"The more serious evils of that policy were revealed by the election."

I shall not castigate the split infinitive; the use or non-use of it is a matter of taste. You should try not only to avoid splitting the infinitive but to keep your verbs intact. Thus do not say "The ore has never been so cheaply milled" but "The ore never has been milled so cheaply." In the first the verb 'has been milled' is dismembered into three parts by the intrusion of the adverbs.

The split infinitive, however, is more than a breach of good taste, despite the sanction of usage as cited by an eminent critic.[3] It suspends the sense. A similar error is that of interpolating words between the definite article and the noun, as in "the already deep shaft has been sunk another hundred feet." Those who write thus are also likely to say:

(45) "We today find nothing peculiar in this."

The emphasis is on 'today', which therefore should come first, instead of separating 'we' from 'find'. It is curious that such splittings, of the infinitive and of other verb phrases, are usually employed for emphasis, which can be obtained much better by other locutions. Such suspensions are "ugly in form as they are awkward in sense."[4]

Here is one from the 'New Republic':

(46) "Our men of wealth have accepted *profits and income taxation* with a better grace than those of any European nation, with the exception of England."

The reader wonders why it is necessary to say that rich men have accepted "profits and income", and is jarred by the statement, before he reaches the word 'taxation'. The quotation is an example of sloppy writing. 'Rich men' is better than "men of wealth"; 'except' is better than "with the exception of." The writer wallows in indirect reporter-like phraseology. He might have written:

"Our rich men have accepted the taxation of their profits and incomes with better grace than those in Europe, except England."

Similar suspensions are common in technical writing.

(47) "As between fine and coarse ore crushing, he recommended the Gilpin county type of deep-mortar long-drop stamps."

Here the interposition of 'fine and coarse ore' suspends the sense until 'crushing' is reached; similarly a long adjectival phrase intervenes between 'recommended' and 'stamps'.

"As between crushing fine or coarse, he recommended stamps of the Gilpin county type, that is, a deep mortar and a long drop."

(48) "In the hard ground at Miami it is advisable to use a *wide shrinkage stope and pillar* system."

Here the five words preceding "system" are used as an adjective, suspending the sense too long. It would be better to write "system of wide shrinkage-stopes and pillars."

(49) "In sending *in* orders it was *very* necessary to give *full shipping and marking* directions."

'In' and 'very' are redundant. The four words preceding 'directions' are an adjectival jumble. He might have written:

"In sending an order it was necessary to give full directions for shipping and marking."

Directness of statement is an aid to clearness. As Horn Tooke said: "The first aim of language was to communicate our thoughts; the second, to do so with dispatch."

(50) "So the new order strikes at the root of much of the difficulty that has disturbed the industrial world since the War began *by applying only to the unskilled.*"

The clause italicized should come after 'order', which it explains.

(51) "It might have been appropriate to have *developed* [provided that] these particular resources of manganese and platinum, so forcibly cited as an argument for shoving the Bill through the Senate, [should be developed] under the direct control and management of a Government bureau for the pecuniary benefit of the actual owners in law and equity."

Here the principal word 'developed' has been mis-

Lounsbury.

[4] Allbutt. Op. cit. Page 82.

placed, so as to mar the directness of statement.

(52) "What is regarded as a significant fact is that as yet the President has not yet officially announced the re-establishment of the present price as effective from June 1 to August 15, although the War Industries Board has so recommended."

It was the disregarding of the recommendation by the Board that was the significant fact, therefore the statement should be re-arranged thus:

"That the President, notwithstanding the recommendation of the War Industries Board, has not yet announced the official re-establishment of the present price, effective from June 1 to August 15, is considered significant."

(53) "An applicant had to file a copy of these regulations, to show that they had been complied with."

He means: "to show that he had complied with them."

(54) "Before a hole drilled in the manner described is blasted, the hole is sprung by exploding in the bottom of the hole several charges of dynamite."

The clause "drilled in the manner described" is interjected awkwardly; it is superfluous. The statement can then be corrected thus:

"Before the hole is blasted, it is 'sprung' by exploding several charges of dynamite in the bottom."

'Sprung' is treated as an unfamiliar term and is explained by the last clause; therefore the single quotation marks are desirable.

(55) "After a hole has been chambered sufficiently, the amount of which depends on the depth of the hole, the hardness and the tenacity and the volume of the rock to be broken, the hole is loaded for the final blast."

This statement contains several unnecessary inversions. The comma after the second 'hole' is not followed by a second comma after 'hardness', so that the continuity of the statement is broken. He might have written:

"The hole is loaded for the blast after it has been chambered sufficiently, this depending upon the depth of the hole, as well as upon the hardness, tenacity, and volume of the rock to be broken."

You will find it advantageous to place sundry adverbs, especially those of time or place, either at the end or at the beginning of a clause, gaining emphasis thereby. Thus:

(56) "Lately the ore has been crushed to 100-mesh" or

"The ore has been crushed to 100-mesh lately."

The first is preferable; either is better than

"The ore has lately been crushed to 100-mesh."

(57) "The vein is frequently faulted along the upper level."

Here the idea to be expressed is the repetition of faulting particularly on the upper level, therefore re-arrange thus:

"Along the upper level, the vein is faulted frequently."

So the most significant words are placed in the most prominent positions, at the beginning and at the end of the sentence. 'Along the upper level' and 'frequently' are emphasized. But 'frequently' carries the idea of time; substitute 'at many places'.

Aim at correct emphasis, but do not carry the effort to the extent of cultivating a mannerism. My purpose, in analyzing the foregoing examples, is to suggest the undesirability of separating the parts of a verb by an adverb or an adverbial clause. It has become common to say:

"It certainly is"

"It sure did"

and it is just such vulgarisms that mislead the student into illiteracies from which he finds it difficult to escape.

The habitual use of slang, including a decorative kind of profanity, is detrimental to the acquirement of skill in the correct expression of ideas. Slang beggars the vocabulary; profanity ignores it. The word 'damned' has to stand for a host of adjectives and things 'go to hell' in a thousand ways.

Chemicals Used and Costs at Benguet, Philippine Islands

The following figures were sent by C. M. Eye, superintendent for the Benguet Consolidated Mining Co., whose mill in 1918 treated 23,539 tons of ore assaying $21.35 gold per ton. Of this, 89% was extracted, using the following chemicals and costs:

Chemical	Pounds, per ton	Chemical	Pounds, per ton
Lime	10.00	Flint pebbles	3.77
Sodium cyanide	1.15	Mine rock, substitute for pebbles	6.70
Zinc shaving	0.72		

Cost	Centavos* per ton	Cost	Centavos* per ton
Lime	16	Lead acetate	3
Cyanide	83	Lubricants	4
Zinc	34	Fluxes and crucibles	24
Flint pebbles	27	Oil for melting	11
Mine rock	5	Acids	3
Battery renewals	12	Mine timber	87
Tube-mill liners	25	Lumber	17
Machinery renewals	17	Explosives	18
Piping and packing	10	Candles	16
Belting	13	Cars and track supplies	7
Mill tools	4	Mine tools	9

*100 centavos = 1 peso = 50 cents U. S.

The total cost of mining and milling was ₱11.89 per ton, of which superintendence was 44 centavos, labor ₱5.94, supplies ₱4.88, and general 63 centavos per ton treated. The direct cost of mining was ₱5.62, and of milling, ₱6.27 per ton.

Costs at the Falcon Mine, Rhodesia

Last year, this mine produced 37,701 oz. of gold, 80,528 oz. of silver, and 7,064,000 lb. of copper, from 170,074 tons of ore. Of this, 153,340 tons, assaying $5.10 gold and 2.19% copper, was concentrated by vanners and the Minerals Separation system of flotation, using eucalyptus oil. The ore was mined from a depth of 1000 ft. Departmental costs were as under:

	Per ton		Per ton
Development	$0.54	Sintering, smelting, converting	$3.[illegible]
Ore extraction	1.74	Royalty to Government	[illegible]
Transport, crushing, sorting	0.24	Realization charges	[illegible]
Stamp-milling	0.27	General	[illegible]
Tube-milling	0.22		
Concentrating and classifying	0.32	Total	$11.[illegible]
Minerals Separation flotation	0.62		

Antimony consumption in the United States is normally 1000 tons per month.

Unloading, Crushing, and Screening at the Arthur Mill of the Utah Copper Company

By F. G. JANNEY

DELIVERY OF ORE. The ore comes from the mine in trains of 40 cars, and at a point 15.3 miles from Bingham, or 2 miles above the Magna plant and 2.6 miles above the Arthur plant, the ore is diverted from the Bingham & Garfield main line to the Arthur high-line tracks. From here the train descends on a 0.4% grade over a 150-ton Strait scale, equipped with a Streeter-Amet automatic weighing and recording device, on which the ore is weighed in the train, while moving at the rate of two miles per hour. From the scale the train descends on an average 0.4% grade to the Arthur load-yard, which has a capacity of 102 cars. From here the loads are delivered by a switching crew to two dumper-load tracks, each having a capacity of 21 cars. These tracks are laid on a 1.5% descending grade, and the loads are fed one at a time by gravity to the car-dumped mule-pit. From the pit they are elevated 21 ft. up an 11.5% grade by means of an electric 'mule', and spotted on the car-dumper platen.

After the car has delivered its load it is bumped off the platen by the following load, and runs by gravity down a trestle track on a 5% grade, up a kick-back, and into either of the three empty-yard tracks, one of which is provided for cutting out all 'bad-order' cars. From the car-dumper empty-yard, the capacity of which is 90 cars, the empties are either switched to the general empty-yard, having a capacity of 136 cars, or picked up by the road-engines in making up their trains.

UNLOADING PLANT. The haulage and dumper mechanisms are electrically operated, and were designed, fabricated, and erected by the Wellman-Seaver-Morgan Co., in conjunction with the Utah Copper company's engineers, to handle the cars of ore delivered by the Bingham & Garfield railroad.

The haulage mechanism consists of one Esselius patented 'mule' car, with necessary haulage and tail ropes for operating it, upper and lower by-pass gates to allow the 'mule' to return to the pit when the car is standing between the mule-pit and the car-dumper. It is operated by a 300-kw. hoist, and the controlling mechanism is automatic. This mechanism is designed to handle cars having a total load of 215,000 pounds up an 11% grade at a rate of not less than 30 cars per hour, which is the rated capacity of the dumper. See Fig. 1, 2, and 3.

The car-dumper consists of a heavy steel framework supporting a rotating cradle upon which is mounted a movable platen, which carries the rails for the ore-cars. The cradle is supported from one side by heavy pivot-pins secured to the framework; the cradle-nose is rounded and provided with heavy wearing-plates. The 300-kw. hoisting mechanism for rotating the cradle is placed in a housing at the top of the framework. At the rear of the structure are the counter-guides and weights, with their cables passing over sheaves at the top of the framework, returning to the cradle and the three car-clamps. After the incoming car has been pushed onto the platen by the 'mule' and properly spotted on the platen by the car-rider, the cradle-hoisting machinery is started and the first motion of rotation releases the platen, which then moves sidewise toward the dumping side of the cradle until the side of the car rests against the cradle-blocking. Continued rotation of the cradle turns the car over so that it is tilted to an angle of 75° from the horizontal, thus discharging the contents of the car onto a grizzley. In winter when frozen ore is being unloaded and when a full load clings to the car, the cradle is not allowed to rotate beyond an angle of 45° from the horizontal. To take care of this extra weight additional counterweights are provided; they are readily attached at the will of the operator. During the motion of rotation the clamps which hold the car securely to the platen are automatically set by means of heavy counterweights which travel in guides at the rear of the main frame, these counterweights being operated by means of ropes so arranged that the pressure of the clamps is equally divided on the two sides of the car. This arrangement of clamps is a distinctive feature of the machine and causes less damage to cars than any other type constructed. The motion is entirely automatic, being controlled by counterweights and not dependent in any way on the operator. After the contents of the car have been discharged, the cradle returns to its original position, and the platen moves out so that its rails come into alignment with the approach and outgoing rails. The machine is now ready for another loaded car, which, on entering the cradle, displaces the empty car.

This entire unloading plant is operated by three car-riders, one car inspector, and one dumper operator, who, from his cab on the car-dumper, hauls the car up the incline and onto the dumper, where it is discharged.

As a reserve in case it becomes necessary to shut-down the car-dumper, the cars may be delivered over an auxiliary track to primary-storage bins of 10,000 tons capacity, where they are dumped from the bottom by hand. On top of these bins are grizzley-bars spaced 12 in. apart. Any pieces too large to pass are broken by sledge-hammers. Below these grizzlies are others, set at an angle of 40°, spaced 2¾ in. apart, the bars being made of special

Fig. 1. CAR ON PLATEN OF CAR-DUMPER AT BEGINNING OF ELEVATION; ALSO EMPTY CAR RETURNING THROUGH KICK-BACK TO EMPTY-YARD

Fig. 2. CAR BEING PUSHED UP 11.5% GRADE BY ELECTRIC MULE

FIG. 3. LOAD KICKING EMPTY CAR OFF THE CAR-DUMPER PLATEN

FIG. 4. STEEL PAN-CONVEYOR 48 INCHES WIDE

FIG. 5. GYRATORY CRUSHER, AND LOWER END OF GRIZZLEY

FIG. 6. MECHANISM OF DIRECT MOTOR-DRIVEN VIBRATING SCREEN

FIG. 7. TENSIONED SCREEN-CLOTH FOR RECEIVING VIBRATION

FIG. 8. ARRANGEMENT OF IMPACT-SCREENS WITH FEED-CHUTE

rolled steel. The oversize passes into pockets underneath and is drawn by steel apron-feeders, 48 in. wide, onto a steel pan-conveyor, also 48 in. wide. See Fig. 4. Tbis carries it to two No. 8 McCully gyratory crushers, each of which serves a unit, and is supplemented by a spare crusher of the same kind available for either unit whenever required. The undersize of the lower grizzlies is drawn from pockets by steel apron-feeders 48 in. wide onto a rubber belt of the same width, which in turn delivers it to the first sizing-screen set an an angle of 42°, the apertures of which vary from 1 to 3 in. by changing the screen according to the character and moisture of the ore. From this point on the handling of the ore is the same as that coming from the car-dumper.

This system of unloading is ideal for seven months of the year—from March to November—except for those cars which are loaded with extra large rocks, the size of which prevents them from passing through the bottom of the cats, requiring hand-breaking from the cars and through the 12-in. grizzlies. During the period from December to February the ore freezes in the railroad cars to a depth of from 6 to 12 in. on the top, sides, and bottom of the cars. When the ore is frozen, the hopper-shaped bottom of the cars prevents its free discharge when the bottoms are dropped; an unloading gang of approximately 30 men per shift is required to pick and bar the entire contents of the car through the openings. The ore also freezes in the primary bins, and it appears to break more coarsely at the mine in the winter than in the summer, requiring excessive breaking of ore by hand in order to dump it through the first grizzlies. For these months the loss of capacity is equal to 25%, as well as being costly. These troubles are overcome by the car-tipple and the No. 27 gyratory crusher.

Returning to the car-dumper, the contents of a car, after being tilted, discharges onto grizzlies set at an angle of 35°, made up of 12-in. 28½-lb. Bethlehem I-beams, 7¾ in. by 32 ft. long, capped with a special manganese-steel casting. These built-up grizzley-bars are so spaced that the openings at the top are 5 in. and at the bottom 6 in., the object of this differential spacing being to prevent wedging of the oversize. The oversize passes to a No. 27 Allis-Chalmers gyratory crusher, with a double discharge, which, at the present time, is the largest ever built, designed to handle 54-in. material and reduce it to an average of 4½ inches. See Fig. 5. At the time this photograph was taken the bed of ore had not formed in the crusher-pit. This crusher is driven by a 300-hp. squirrel-cage motor at 600 r.p.m., direct-connected through a set of Wuest cut herringbone gears reducing the speed to 275 r.p.m. To take care of repairs on this crusher, the shaft and mantle of which weigh 55 tons, there is a 60-ton (with 10-ton auxiliary) 4-motor electric traveling crane. This crane also serves the drives on the 60-in. conveyors. The undersize from the grizzlies is collected in storage-pockets designed to hold 1300 tons of free-feeding ore, and is fed with the crusher-product by means of two 72-in. pan-conveyors discharging toward each other, onto a short grizzley with openings of 2½ in., to a 60 in. rubber belt conveyor, the function of the short grizzley being to produce a bed of fine on the belt-conveyor before the larger material, which has passed the crusher and grizzlies, reaches the belt. The 60-in. conveyor is 224-ft. centres, set at an angle of 18°, and is operated by motors the speed of which may be varied at the option of the operator in the secondary crushing plant by means of a push-button control from a minimum speed of 115 ft. to a maximum speed of 350 ft. per minute. The flexibility of this control makes it possible for the secondary plant to be run at its greatest efficiency, owing to its finer grinding and smaller capacity as compared with the primary crushing plant. The 60-in. belt-conveyor discharges onto a second grizzley, the bats of which are specially bulb-shaped, 25 ft. long and inclined at an angle of 45°. The openings of this grizzley are changed to suit the character and moisture of the ore. The oversize from the grizzlies discharges into three No. 8 McCully gyratory crushers, and, as previously mentioned, two of the crushers, each of which serves a unit, are supplemented by a spare crusher of the same kind, available for either unit whenever required. It is at this point that the ore from the reserve crushing plant joins the circuit. The undersize from these grizzlies discharges onto two short rubber belt-conveyors, 36 in. wide, 20 ft. long, operating on an angle of 16°, at a speed of 400 ft. per minute. Serving each of these conveyors is a screen, 40 in. wide, 10 ft. long, and set at an angle of 45°. These screens take out the minus 1-inch material, which passes by means of a chute to rubber belt-conveyors delivering to the fine-crushing department. The oversize from this set of screens by-passes the McCully crushers but unites with their product.

This description is confined to one of the two units into which the car-dumper is divided, as each side of the crusher-discharge is an independent unit.

THE CRUSHED PRODUCT and screen-oversize are now divided into two parts, one going to the new roll installation and the other to the old. That portion going to the new is collected on a 60-in. rubber belt-conveyor, 25 ft. long, with a slope of 19°38′, and operating at a speed of 350 ft. per minute. The ore from this belt discharges to another conveyor running at right angles, also 60 in. wide, 150 ft. long, with a slope of 21°30′, traveling at the rate of 350 ft. per minute. This belt elevates and discharges into two 72 by 20-in. Garfield rolls of the moving pedestal type, operating at a speed of 125 r.p.m. The crushed product from each roll discharges on a separate rubber belt-conveyor, 42 in. wide, 118 ft. long, having a slope of 21°30′, and a belt-speed of 350 ft. per minute. At the terminus of each belt is a screen-tower, where the ore is delivered to four rotary feeders, each tower and set of feeders serving a roll. The feeders are 36 in. diameter, 64 in. long, and revolve at the rate of 2 r.p.m. Receiving the ore from each feeder is a 48 by 72-in. Mitchell vibratory screen. The oversize discharges onto a conveyor which runs horizontal at a speed of 250 ft. per minute. It is 42 in. wide, 25 ft. long, and discharges into a set of 72 by 20-in. Garfield rolls, operating at 125 r.p.m. The roll-product returns to the 60-in. conveyor feeding the first set of rolls. This puts the product in a closed circuit with one 60-in., two 42-in. conveyors, four sets of 72 by 20-in. rolls, and eight Mitchell vibratory screens, where it remains until it is all crushed to pass the screen-aperture. The undersize from the vibrating screens is conveyed by a 36-in. conveyor, 60 ft. long, operating at a speed of 340 ft. per minute, to the two conveyors, each of which are 36 in. wide, 150 ft. long, and traveling at a rate of 250 ft. per minute, which, in turn, discharge to similar conveyors 120 ft. long, which carry the ore to the secondary bins. The last two sets of conveyors serve both the old and the new coarse-crushing plants. That part of the feed passing to the old crushing plant is discharged to the boot of a 36-in. elevator equipped with staggered rows of buckets. This elevator travels at the rate of 350 ft. per minute and has a lift of 72 ft. From the elevator the ore is discharged into a chute having a screen-bottom 24 in. wide, 52 in. long, set at an angle of 45°, the aperture of the screen being one inch. The undersize passes by means of a chute to a 36-in. conveyor, which delivers to the 36-in. conveyors delivering to the secondary bins. The oversize is fed to a set of 72 by 20-in. rolls operated at a speed of 100 r.p.m. From the rolls this material flows down a chute, a portion of which has a screen-bottom 30 in. wide and 120 ft. long, placed at an angle of 40°. The screen has an aperture of one inch, the undersize to the conveyors delivering to the secondary bins. The oversize passes to a 30-in. elevator equipped with staggered buckets, the lift being 60 ft. The elevator discharges into a chute, a portion of the bottom being equipped with a screen 24 in. wide, 52 in. long, having an aperture of one inch and inclined at 40°. The undersize joins the belt-conveyors delivering to the secondary bins. The oversize returns to the last-mentioned elevator, which puts it in a closed circuit with the elevator screens and rolls, where it remains until crushed to pass the aperture of the screen.

THE VIBRATING SCREEN mentioned in the description of the secondary-crushing plant, has been developed by B. A. Mitchell, mechanical engineer to the Utah Copper company, during the last eighteen months and is now being placed in service. The principle is new and unique. The vibration is developed by a fractional horse-power motor which is totally enclosed with the vibration-producing mechanism, and, therefore, is absolutely dust-proof, fool-proof, and water-proof. This mechanism is underneath the screen-cloth (See Fig. 6) and in close contact with it at all times, transmitting its peculiar vibration to the tensioned (See Fig. 7) screen-cloth. This construction gives a free open screening surface for the material to be screened and for observation by the operator; it also permits rapid changing of worn-out screens. This type of screen requires fewer operators, less repairs and power (the power required being ¼ horse-power); it gives greater effective screening surface; therefore, greater screening efficiency than any other screening mechanism.

An idea of the character of ore mined and concentrated may be gained from the analysis which represents the ore milled for the month of November 1917:

	%		
Copper	1.27	Gold	0.0075 oz.
Iron	2.55	Silver	0.0675 oz.
Silica	68.80	Loss on ignition	1.85%
Aluminum oxide	14.56		
Sulphur	2.64		
Calcium oxide	0.22		
Potassium oxide	5.94		
Magnesium oxide	1.32		

The following is screen-analysis of the product as it left the crushing plant prior to the installation of the additional crushing machinery, and is therefore coarser than that which will eventually be obtained with the additional crushing arrangements.

Coarse-Crushing Product

	Mesh and opening	Per cent material	Accum. % material
Opening	1.050 in.	1.17	1.17
"	0.742 "	8.44	9.61
"	0.525 "	22.27	31.88
"	0.371 "	16.30	48.18
Mesh	3	12.11	60.29
"	4	7.24	67.53
"	6	4.07	71.60
"	8	4.27	75.87
"	10	3.61	79.48
"	14	2.82	82.30
"	20	2.31	84.61
"	28	1.92	86.53
"	35	1.74	88.27
"	48	1.55	89.82
"	65	1.53	91.35
"	100	1.27	92.62
"	150	0.82	93.44
"	200	1.07	94.51
Pass	200	5.49	100.00

From the bins the ore is drawn by steel apron-feeders adjustable to three rates of speed by step-pulleys, to which is attached a mechanical counter or tachometer, registering the number of revolutions of the head-pulley of the feeder, so that it is easy to adjust the proportion of tonnage passing into the thirteen sections into which the mill is divided.

The Transvaal in 1918

The Transvaal Chamber of Mines statement for December, just to hand, gives final figures for the past year, and comparing with the previous year, the following is the result:

	1918	1917
Ore hoisted (Rand only), tons	27,031,448	29,549,949
Waste sorted out (Rand only), per cent	7.80	7.73
Stamps dropping (Transvaal)	8,878	9,470
Days	278	301
Tube-mills grinding	338	332
Days	292	311
Ore treated (Transvaal), tons	25,267,302	27,868,851
Fine ounces	8,420,659	9,022,212
Total gold yield	£35,768,688 ($171,600,000)	£38,333,921 ($183,955,000)
Average per ton	28s. 1d. ($6.74)	27s. 3d. ($6.54)
Working costs per ton	21s. 8d. ($5.20)	19s. 4d. ($4.64)
Dividends paid	£5,273,033 ($25,315,000)	£6,718,604 ($32,251,000)

Operations in February were considerably affected by abnormal rain and floods; while September to December, inclusive, were severely affected by shortage of labor resulting from influenza. The outside districts contributed $4,540,000 to the total gold yield.

Prospecting at the Rooiberg tin mine in the Transvaal is done by hydraulicking, somewhat similar to the system at the Nipissing silver mine in Ontario.

Dredging and Re-Soiling

By M. W. von BERNEWITZ

Two of the eight dredges operated by the Natomas Company of California near Natoma, east of Sacramento, are leveling the dredged ground. They, No. 1 and 4, have dug about 250 acres each. The final condition of the ground is almost as level as before starting, especially where No. 4 is working. This area has been partly planted with figs and alfalfa. These two boats have 15-cubic foot buckets, and No. 1—on which I spent a day recently—digging to a depth of 25 feet, handles 400 yards per hour. The gravel is free from clay.

STERN VIEW OF NATOMAS No. 1
1. Discharge-sluices. 2. Pebble-stacker. 3. Cobble-stacker. 4. Cobble-chute.

The principal difference between an ordinary dredge and one that is re-soiling, is that the discharge of the tailing necessitates construction of four stacker-belts and two long double sluices for water (this is clearly shown in the stern view of the boat), in place of one stacker and one sluice. This is why a re-soiling dredge costs a little more to operate than the ordinary type. The stackers require more power, and another man is needed.

SIDE VIEW OF STERN OF NATOMAS No. 1
1. Discharge-sluices. 2. Pebble-stacker. 3. Cobble-stacker. 4. Cobble-chute.

From the revolving-screen the washed gravel moves as follows: the sand and water flow over the riffles, where the gold is caught, and then flow to the ends of the sluices; the pebbles, up to say 4 inches, fall onto two belts that carry them 20 feet behind the sluice discharges; cobbles from 4 to 12 inches fall onto two belts which are, say, 20 feet shorter than the others; and cobbles of this size also fall down two chutes directly behind the stern, near the spuds. Therefore, the big cobbles drop first, the pebbles next, and the sand and slime last—on top of all. By the old system, all stones were dropped on the sand, the tail-sluice being much shorter than the stacker, making the unsightly heaps of tailing.

According to L. D. Hopfield, in charge for the company at Natoma, uneven bedrock makes it difficult at times to level the ground as well as desired; however, it seems as if good work were being done, the land being returned to a cultivable condition.

RE-SOILED GROUND. BANK AT LEFT NOT DUG

Shoveling

By G. T. HARLEY

*Conclusions from a study of shoveling at the Burro Mountain copper mine at Tyrone, New Mexico, presented the following points:

Shoveling ore cost so much at Tyrone during 1917 that it was deemed advisable to conduct tests to see where the fault lay. The tests were in the nature of time-studies, and extended over a period of nearly a year.

To obtain a basis for comparison, it was necessary to determine the capacity of various types and sizes of shovels, so as to know whether the 21-lb. load was the best load underground as well as on the surface. A list of essential factors influencing shoveling was also made out during the course of a short series of preliminary time-studies, and the motions involved in shoveling were analyzed and subdivided for convenience in studying. The necessary forms and record-sheets were also decided upon at this time. A second short series of tests was then conducted on the surface, so as to be able to estimate the negative effects of underground work on the shovelers, and to minimize, as far as possible, the need for studying obviously poor types and sizes of shovels under the difficult local conditions in the mine.

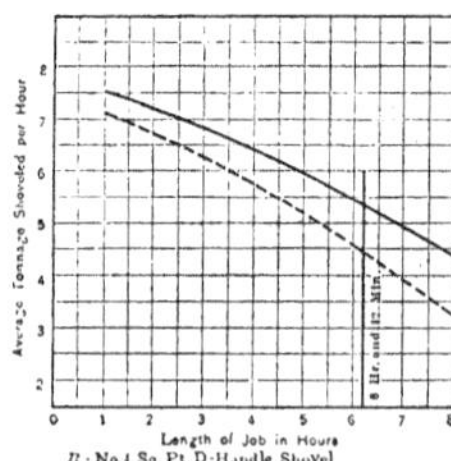

AVERAGE TONNAGE SHOVELED PER HOUR FOR ANY LENGTH OF JOB

The test work underground consumed most of the time and was divided into three series: shoveling directly into a chute, shoveling into a wheelbarrow and tramming to a chute, and shoveling into a car and tramming to a chute. In each series the following points were determined for various lengths of time worked: number of shovelfuls handled per minute, effect of distance thrown on shoveling speed, amount of rest required, amount of time consumed in tramming and dumping, proportion of working day occupied in shoveling, total tonnage handled during various working periods, effect of distance on tonnage handled during the day.

These tests showed that the design of the shovel has a marked effect on the shoveling efficiency, and that with the proper weight and size of tool the man's efficiency will be increased in spite of himself. It was shown that a man handling a total load of 26 lb. did the greatest day's work, other things being equal, and that this load is divided into a live load of 21 lb. and a shovel weight of 5½ lb. A shovel weighing 5½ lb., made out of the best alloy-steel, gives excellent service, and a lower cost per ton than a shovel having a lower first cost.

Further marked increases in shoveling efficiency are to be gained by instructing the shovelers in the proper methods of using a shovel, a thing that few laborers know, in spite of the fact that they may have been shoveling for years. Wages, the manner of paying the wage, and good-will are factors in efficiency work.

Scientific management systems applied to certain Eastern factories have proved conclusively that the efficiency of the average workman can be increased by from 50 to 250%, and at the same time the men will receive better wages, will remain in better health, and will be happy and contented, while the company will actually produce its products at a lower cost.

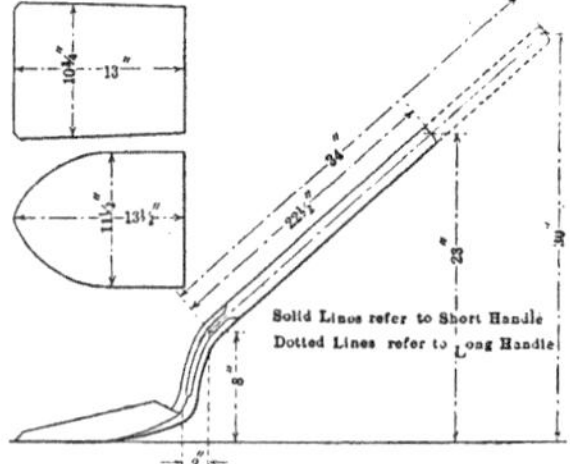

DESIGN OF SHOVEL BEST ADAPTED TO MINING WORK

F. W. Taylor, working at the Bethlehem Steel Co. plant several years ago, increased the capacity of the iron-ore shovelers from 16 to 59 tons per day per man, raised the men's wages from $1.15 to $1.88 per day, at the same time decreased the operating cost from 7.2 to 3.3 cents per ton shoveled. The increase in shoveling capacity amounted to 269%. Figures obtained at Tyrone indicate that the tonnage in at least one of the large stopes can be raised from 8.5 per man to 22.9 tons per man, an increase of 169%, the wages can be raised from $3.40 per day to $4, and the cost to the company reduced from 33 to 24 cents per ton, after taking care of all extra supervision needed. In addition to this actual saving in shoveling cost, the overhead and general mining charges will be reduced by mining a greater quantity per man; and the other classes of labor such as machine-miners and timber-men will be able to do more work, as they will not be hampered and delayed by the shovelers to such an extent as at present.

*Abstract from Bulletin 146 of American Institute of Mining Engineers, February 1919.

REVIEW OF MINING

JACKSON, CALIFORNIA

Serious Fire in Argonaut Mine.—Central Eureka Sinks.

Fire broke out on the 4000-ft. level of the Argonaut mine late on the afternoon of March 27. U. S. Bureau of Mines rescue-crews have arrived from Grass Valley and Berkeley. Up to the present, April 1, the fire is by no means under control. The fire-fighters have confined their efforts to bulkheading the shaft near the 3200-ft. level, and sealing the collar of the Muldoon shaft in an attempt to smother the flames. While the fire is believed to have started between 500 and 600 ft. back from the shaft, it is feared that it has burned close to the 3900-ft. station, on which is placed the immense underground hoist and valuable electric machinery: in fact, the woodwork in the station alone is said

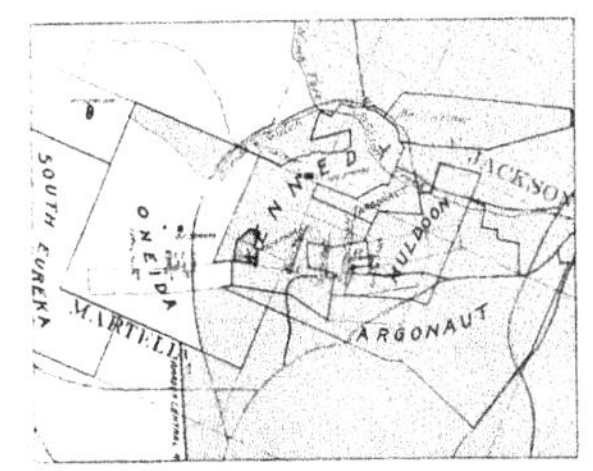

SKETCH SHOWING POSITION OF ARGONAUT MINE.

to be equal to the amount used in the construction of a good-sized dwelling. This station is equipped with a complete hoisting plant, practically a duplicate of the one on the surface, capable of hoisting from a depth of 7000 ft. Although the workings connecting the Argonaut and the Kennedy mine are closed, fumes and smoke have reached the north shaft of the adjoining property, and some fear is expressed as to the safety of men working in the Kennedy mine during the fire, the Kennedy's east or main working shaft being connected with the north shaft. Starting as it did during change of shift, the fire has so far entailed no loss of life. An engineer working at 3900 ft. was rescued after the fire was discovered, and two of the men working on the bulkhead on March 29 were overcome by fumes, but quickly resuscitated after reaching the surface. A gauge at the Muldoon shaft showed a slightly decreased air-pressure late that afternoon, indicating that the bulkheading of the shaft has had some effect. N. S. Kelsey, the company's superintendent, Edwin Higgins, safety and efficiency engineer, and W. F. Pyne, of the Industrial Accident Commission, and other prominent engineers are on the ground, and the neighboring mines are supplying all their trained men. It is hoped that the fire will be smothered before it reaches the shaft, but even if confined to the workings on the 4000-ft. level, the loss would be excessive, as the ground is heavy and the burning of the extensive timbering would cause serious caves. The Argonaut has a depth of over 5000 ft. on an incline of 60°. Including the men at the 60-stamp mill and surface employees, the cessation of work at this property throws over 200 men out of employment.

Telegraphic advice on April 1 stated that the fire was worse. A bulkhead was being built at 300 ft., as it was impossible to work much deeper in shaft. The Kennedy has been forced to close, as men are being gassed.

Sinking has been resumed at the Central Eureka mine, the intention being to put the shaft down 210 ft. farther, or to a point 280 ft. below the present lowest station—3500 ft. A winze sunk 100 ft. deep from 3500 ft. has opened some good ore, on which sufficient work has been done to warrant belief in its persistence. Contracts have been let for sinking, and two crews are working 8-hour shifts. During sinking, 20 or 25 stamps of the 40-stamp mill are profitably employed on ore from the stopes above the winze-level.

BISBEE, ARIZONA

Status of Employment.—Two New Mines of Promise.

Unemployment in the Warren district and at Douglas, the smelting centre for the ores mined here, while not alarming in its increase, has grown to such proportions as to demand public attention. The first real step toward relief was taken when a meeting of the Cochise County Community Labor Board, attended by the Board of County Supervisors and representatives of the mining companies, was held at the Y. M. C. A. building here on March 20. It was decided to issue a general call for attendance at a meeting of the supervisors to be held on April 8 at Tombstone. At that time, suggestions for relieving the situation will be asked for. The advisability of issuing bonds to cover road work in the country will be discussed. The way was paved by a bill recently signed by Thomas E. Campbell, Governor of Arizona, for county bond issues for road building during the emergency. In addition, the Community Labor Board adopted a resolution requesting that the Forestry Service, for which $9,000,000 was appropriated by the last Congress, expend a portion of the fund in improving roads leading into portions of the Coronado National Forest Reserve. The resolution recited the increase in the number of idle men in the State, but more particularly at Bisbee and vicinity, and the need for better roads. Reports of employment conditions in the district as given by representatives of the Phelps Dodge Corporation, Copper Queen Branch, and Calumet & Arizona company, indicated that both are maintaining their forces at the same level as earlier in March, with no additional curtailment considered at that time. Phelps Dodge has employed 164 soldiers and sailors in its mines here, while Calumet & Arizona has employed ninety.

Two new mines of importance will be added to the Warren district on the south side of the Mule range, at the extreme south-eastern edge of the hitherto recognized area of mineralization of the Bisbee circle. There are the Boras and Night Hawk leases, both of which are on Copper Queen ground, near the White Tail Deer mine of that property. Indications point to large orebodies in both leases, and their operators are hopeful. At the Boras, a shaft has been sunk to a depth of 250 ft., 100 ft. south of the incline shaft, in which ore originally was opened. A station was cut at 210 ft. and driving started to prospect the ground between the new shaft and the old incline. The chief work is being done in a northerly and north-easternly direction. Beneath the old incline, the same formation from which $25,000 worth of ore was shipped last year, was found. The ore was of practically the same width and carried the same average value, but the mineralized area was increased. More than 100 ft. of silicious ore carrying gold and silver was passed through before copper ore was opened. When the west drift had proved that at least two orebodies existed below the old incline, it was determined to sink an additional 100 ft. This work now is in progress. It is expected that the 300-ft. station will have been cut within the next two deeks, and the new drifts then will be started.——At the Night Hawk, the main shaft is more than 400 ft. deep. Some driving has been done, but in a winze 125 ft. deep, the first indications of ore in quantity were found. It has been decided to sink from 600 to 700 ft., and then prospect the ground overhead. The Night Hawk has shipped several carloads of ore to the Copper Queen smelter at Douglas, the returns aiding materially in paying for development.

Work at Sacramento Hill of the Copper Queen, where steam-shovels are removing the overburden from a great body of low-grade copper ore proved by diamond-drilling, is proceeding steadily.

TELLURIDE, COLORADO

What Snowslides are Doing in This Region.

The heavy storms that prevailed during the last days of February and the first week in March resulted in a number of slides, which blocked the Rio Grande Southern at a number of points, entirely stopping movement of ore. At Windy point, near Ophir, where there is a cut 500 ft. deep, the snow slid off the crest of the cut, filling the passage to a depth of 12 ft., and extending for a distance of 300 ft. This slide is the largest obstacle to clearing the road, being filled with trees and other debris, interferring with the operation of a rotary plow. A number of other slides resulted in loss and damage to the mines of the district, tramways being torn out, and boarding and bunk-houses smashed. Numerous narrow escapes are reported, but fortunately there is no loss of life nor severe injuries reported, rather remarkable considering the number and size of the slides. The Big Elephant Slide ran, damaging the electric surface tram that carries ore from the Tomboy mines to the mill, in addition to carrying off a section of the tram, taking out 100 ft. of snowsheds. A building was broken in, and part of the adit tramway carried out on the property of the Little Mary mine, when a slide ran down the gulch. The slide increased in depth and speed as it went down, striking the Humboldt tram of the Smuggler Union Mining Co. carrying away a section. Fortunately the tram has been idle since the closing down of the property a few weeks ago, and no one was injured. The Hanging Rock slide carried out a section of the Smuggler Union tram, and the power-line, interferring with movement of ore.

The Belmont Wagner company has completed the erection of the second Marey mill, and is now ready to resume milling, and shipping concentrate as soon after April 1 as snow conditions permit. The management estimates that it will be producing an average of 45 cars of lead concentrate weekly.

CANANEA, MEXICO

Curtailment of Copper Operations.

The mine and smelter of the Democrata Mining Co. here were closed on March 15. The property is owned by the Hoffman interests of Cincinnati, Ohio, and is managed by C. E. Hoffman. Notices had been posted early in March announcing the impending suspension, setting March 15 as the date. However, a serious breakage of machinery at the works, that probably would require ten days longer to repair, resulted in decision to close earlier. Only a sufficient force to keep the property in repair and guard its equipment was retained. Several hundred men, mostly Mexicans, were affected.

The Cananea Consolidated Copper Co. has made no decrease in force since the heavy cut of several weeks ago when approximately 1500 men, or about one-third of its total, were discharged, and the output reduced to about half of normal.

Hermosillo.—The Hermosillo Copper Co., of which J. L. Zimmerman of Columbus, Ohio, is president, in its 7000 ft. of workings has a large quantity of copper carbonate developed. As this ore contains considerable lime, and scrap iron for precipitation purposes is difficult to get, the ore cannot be leached. Therefore efforts are being directed to finding sulphides. If these are opened, a flotation plant will be erected, while the sulphidizing of carbonate ore will then be tried. New machinery recently passed through Nogales on its way to the property, where 25 men are employed. Mr. Zimmerman states that the mine has never been molested, and the general feeling of the Mexicans there is friendly toward Americans.

CRIPPLE CREEK, COLORADO

Rich Ore Found in Three Mines.—A Profitable Lease.

"The richest ever handled in the ore-house at No. 2 shaft of the Portland Gold Mining Co.," is being mined at a depth of 2131 ft. from two veins under development from the Roosevelt tunnel, according to G. M. Taylor the general manager. On No. 1 Portland, the ore as broken from 6 ft. width assays from 15 to 25 oz. per ton, while the eastern core of the vein, an 18-in. streak, samples 160 oz. A 4-in. streak on the western side samples 60 oz. The shoot on the Lee No. 5 vein has been proved for 200 ft. south, and has been carrying 5 and 6-oz. ore, but at a point 30 ft. distant from the junction of the Lee and the No. 1 Portland, a sample taken gave 284 oz. It is expected that the shoot at the junction will be the richest opened in the mine. The elevation at the collar of the Portland No. 2 shaft is 10,244 ft., and at the point of discovery 8113 feet.

Rich discoveries have been made on the American Eagles and Longfellow mines of the Stratton estate on Bull hill. At the first-named, Basket & Luce have sunk a winze 125 ft. on ore from the 1500-ft. level, and are mining 8 to 10-oz. ore from an 8-ft. vein, by drift from the bottom of the winze. The second discovery was made by winze from the 500-ft. level of the Llewellyn shaft on the Longfellow. This property is operated by the Excelsior M. L. & E. Co. of Denver, under long lease. The ore shipped is returning 5 oz. per ton.

H. Chapman, lessee of the Elkton Consolidated, operating south of the shaft in the Thompson claim, at a depth of 600 ft., has cut a new and rich shoot in virgin ground. Four cars shipped during the present week from the discovery have been sampled by the Eagle Ore Co. in transit to the Golden Cycle at Colorado Springs, and returned 2.10 to 2.50 oz. No work has been done in the Thompson claim above the Chapman shoot, and it is believed that the ore will extend to the surface.

Carnduff & Duncan, lessees at the Dead Pine mine of the Granite company, surrender their lease this week after operating the mine continuously for seven years. During this time they have mined 30,800 tons of ore, ranging in value from $8 to $112 per ton. The gross production of the lease has been in excess of $500,000, and both of the operators have accumulated a good-size fortune.

THE MINING SUMMARY

Mining companies will be pleased to know that on March 24, prices of explosives were reduced by the du Pont, Giant, and Hercules powder companies. A comparison of prices per 100 lb. for standard strength—40%—and two other grades follows:

	Quantity											
	Car lots				Ton lots				Less than ton lots			
Explosive	Mar. 24	Dec. 13	Nov.	Pre-war	Mar. 24	Dec. 13	Nov.	Pre-war	Mar. 24	Dec. 13	Nov.	Pre-war
Nitro-glycerine, 40%	$18.75	$20.75	$22.75	$11.50	$21.25	$23.25	$25.25	$13.00	$21.75	$23.75	$25.75	$13.50
Nitro-glycerine, low freezing, 40%	18.75	20.75	21.25	11.50	21.25	23.25	24.75	13.00	21.75	23.75	25.25	13.50
Gelatin, 40%	18.25	20.25	22.25	11.50	20.75	22.75	24.75	13.00	21.25	23.25	25.25	13.00
Extra low freezing, 40%	16.50	18.00	19.00	14.25	19.00	20.50	21.50	15.75	19.50	21.00	22.00	16.25
Railroad powder, 5%	10.75	10.75	11.75	6.50	13.25	13.25	13.25	8.00	13.75	13.75	13.75	8.50
Quarry powder, 27%	17.15	18.15	19.15	10.00	19.75	20.65	21.65	11.50	20.25	21.15	22.15	12.00

ALASKA

In an instructive lecture recently given at San Francisco, Vilhjalmur Stefansson, the Arctic explorer, gave a good description of the climate and resources of Alaska, particularly concerning the possibilities of the Territory in raising reindeer for meat. His experiences in the North on living on the country instead of carrying all the food required, his methods of hunting and use of clothes, and building of snow huts were practical and should be of value to Alaskans. In hunting, he averaged two tons of bear and seal meat for each pound of ammunition expended.

Anchorage.—Advice from Washington, on March 25, stated that a commission, consisting of three naval officers, a mining engineer, and a geologist, will be sent to Alaska to plan development of the Matanuska coalfield. The commission was expected to sail from the Bremerton navy yard about April 1. The naval members of the commission have not been selected, but Sumner Smith, superintendent of mining in Alaska, and Thedore Chapin, a geologist attached to the Alaskan Engineering Commission, are to be the civilian commissioners.

Juneau.—The February Bulletin of the Alaska Bureau of Publicity states that from present indications, general business activities will begin in this Territory nearly a month earlier than usual. Vance R. McDonald, United States commissioner at Long, on Ruby creek, reports that there are large tracts of low-grade placer ground in this district that could be profitably worked by dredges. This ground may be purchased on favorable terms. Labor for ordinary work costs $5 per day with board. There is also said to be good chances in hydraulicking at Eagle. Quartz mining is reported to be on the increase. The Bureau is also conducting a central labor department, and has a list awaiting employment.

Unalaska.—The Alaska Sulphur Co. is about to commence mining sulphur on Akum island, 45 miles from this place and the first island west of Unimak pass, on the way to Bering strait. On March 23 the steamer 'Horace X. Baxter' sailed from Seattle, loaded with 1750 tons of supplies and men for the enterprise. Udo Hesse is engineer, and the firm of Reitze, Storey & Duffey of Seattle examined the deposits. They estimate 560,000 tons of 50% sulphur ore available. A 2-mile aerial tram will convey ore from the mine to tidewater. The president of the company is W. W. Johnson of Seattle, and T. H. Landewick of Chicago is secretary.

ARIZONA

Bagdad.—The Hillside Development Co., which is operating the Copper King property, is employing two 6-ton trucks for hauling high-grade zinc ore. A large tonnage is claimed to be available.

Jerome.—After four months delay in waiting for a new high-pressure compressor cylinder, operations at the Pittsburgh-Jerome will be resumed. Two headings and a 500-ft. diamond-drill hole are to be started as soon as air is available.

Mayer.—The tailing dump at the Boggs mine of the Commercial Mining Co. at Arizona City has been purchased by E. E. Hill of Mayer. This material has been on the dump for 25 years.

Oatman.—The United Eastern Mining Co. in 1918 extracted $2,138,417 from 92,339 tons of ore. Operations cost $797,760. In January 1919 the output was $210,767 from 8835 tons, yielding a profit of $129,000.

The United Eastern has filed suit against the Tom Reed company, at the same time making application for an injunction to stop the Tom Reed from mining in the disputed area. The injunction has been granted.

Swansea.—The Swansea Consolidated Copper Co. has suspended operations, 300 men being thrown out of work.

Tucson.—A. F. Borrego and J. R. Hibbs of Bisbee have taken a bond and lease on the Matt Perry Mining & Milling Co., a gold property. The mill is to be overhauled.

The Magma Chief Copper Co., which is operating the Sombrero Butte mine, has signed a smelter contract and preparations are being completed to ship the 10 cars of 21% ore ready. This has been sorted from ore extracted during development.

CALIFORNIA

Alleghany.—In the suit of William Flynn versus the Twenty-One Mining Co. to recover $25,000, alleging that the mine he purchased for $250,000, of which the $25,000 was paid down, was salted, Judge T. F. Graham last week at San Francisco decided that it was not salted. Judge Graham gave a decision in favor of Flynn in 1916, but on appeal the mining company proved the mine had not been 'doctored' for Flynn's benefit before the sale. The Twenty-One company filed an appeal, but began to work the property itself. Within three months, more than $140,000 in gold was taken from the mine by the Twenty-One company. The Sixteen-to-One company, which owned adjoining property, brought suit in the Federal courts to enjoin the Twenty-One from working its claim, holding that the rich vein discovered in the Twenty-One was a continuation of the vein on the Sixteen-to-One. The injunction was issued. Because the $140,000 had been taken from the property after Flynn had given it up. Judge Graham decided the mine was not 'salted', and that Flynn is not entitled to get his money back on the ground he invested through false representation. In the 'Press' of March 22, in the Mining Decisions, we gave the text of the decision in the suit of the Twenty-One versus the Sixteen-to-One.

Castella.—The Trinity Asbestos Mining Co., which has done some work on claims 25 miles from this place, has filed a petition in bankruptcy. Liabilities are said to be $230,000. H. H. Schmidt is the principal creditor. H. T. and E. R. Mecum, with O. L. Goodhue of Oakland were the principal owners.

Downieville.—The working tunnel at the Wehe gravel mine, at St. Charles hill, has advanced 800 ft. and is expected to reach a point directly under the channel within six weeks. From this point a raise will be driven to open the main channel.

The Brown Bear gravel property has been cleared of water, and three shifts are driving the main drift toward the channel.

Grass Valley.—At a meeting of the trustees of the city of Grass Valley on March 22, acting upon the advice of city attorney C. A. Armstrong, that body decided to contest the application of the Golden Center Mining Co. to have the Roche quartz claim on Marshall street declared mineral land and subject to a Federal patent as such. This decision was reached at a special meeting of the board, after much local dissension. The view taken by the board was that to allow title to the claims to pass to claimant from the city would be to establish a dangerous precedent, in that any other portion of this townsite might be declared mineral and subject to filings for quartz and go to patent. The Golden Center is asserting ownership to a strip of land 300 ft. wide by 1500 ft. long, occupied by residences generally, with enough land for its surface plant. The company is operating extensively in the heart of the city and has worked for several years without hindrance or molestation from any source until now. The plant consists of a hoist and mill. The claim in question was likewise an early-day mine, but allowed to lapse. There was no contest whatever at the time the United States patent was issued for the townsite in 1869, and nothing done of any consequence on this early day claim until now. M. J. Brock of Grass Valley is interested in the forthcoming action, and gave the board his views and information concerning the past status of the land. The opinion was freely expressed that if the Department should allow a patent to issue there would be nothing to hinder almost any piece being taken, as it all was considered mineral land prior to 1869, and a great deal of placer work was done within the confines of the present city limits. A hearing has been set before the Sacramento Land Office on April 22, and many of the early-day residents will be called as witnesses.

Kennett.—The Shasta King mine near here, owned by the Trinity Copper Co., has been closed, the lease to the Mammoth Copper Co. having expired. For two or three years this mine has shipped ore steadily to the smelter at Kennett.

Placerville.—The old Church-Union property, which has produced many millions of gold, was recently examined by Albert Burch of San Francisco.——Operations at the Lotus mine are to be enlarged by N. K. Cooper and J. E. Staratt. ——The Burger mine is to be equipped with machinery.—— The Manzaneta mine is showing a strong vein of rich ore. —The Rising Hope deep-gravel mine is yielding gold regularly.

Sacramento.—The Senate Oil Committee voted on March 27 to report favorably Senator Ridgon's bill amending sections of the State Mining Bureau act relating to supervision over the petroleum industry of the State. The bill would add a paragraph to the section of the act authorizing the State Oil and Gas Supervisor to order tests or remedial work necessary to protect petroleum and gas deposits from damage by underground water, which would require the Supervisor or his representatives to deliver within five days to the operator a final written recommendation for the work in order that the owner may appeal to the district board of oil and gas commissioners which is elected by the companies. Another change in the bill would permit the State Mineralogist to appoint as supervisor a competent engineer or geologist experienced in petroleum development or an operator who has had five years experience in Californian oilfields.

COLORADO

Central City.—Mining is active in the Lake and Russell districts, there being 15 properties under development.

Lake City.—The Indiana-Colorado company contemplates erecting a 100-ton mill and aerial tram for its gold-silver property.

Ouray.—A six-mile railway between this place and Ironton will probably be surveyed this summer. This line will permit of the Sunnyside M. & M. Co. shipping concentrate throughout the year, instead of having the present outlet blocked by snow.

IDAHO

Mullan.—The National flotation mill was closed last week pending arrival of roll-shells, but it is not expected that the plant will resume until the copper market improves. On the 800-ft. level of the mine the ore recently cut out, but on raising to the east as good ore as previously mined was found.

The Old Hickory company has opened 2 to 4 ft. of ore for a distance of 300 ft. on the tunnel-level. The present depth is 600 ft. This is a new company, and is meeting with considerable encouragement.

Oakley.—The old Vipont silver mine, idle for 20 years, has recently been examined for Eastern and Utah capital. Phillips and Paddock are in charge at present.

MISSOURI

Joplin.—Production of the Tri-State region last week was as under:

State	Blende, tons	Calamine, tons	Lead, tons	Value
Kansas	1213	...	235	$62,855
Missouri	1704	410	111	86,377
Oklahoma	6122	...	781	292,521
Total	9039	410	1127	$441,753
Average price	$41	$27	$61	

The value was $31,000 less than in the previous week, but 1000 tons less lead and 1000 tons more blende was sold.

MONTANA

Butte.—The East Butte company's mining and smelting operations are now 70% of normal.

Clancy.—From the Free Coinage mine the Amalgamated Silver Mines Co. is shipping ore that settles for 129 oz. of silver per ton.

Troy.—The Liberty Montana Mining Co. has been organized by G. M. McKenna, J. T. Sugars, J. F. Powers, and others to operate 6 lead-silver-copper claims 5 miles south of this place. The main openings are by tunnels. A 50-ton mill, compressor, saw-mill, etc., are to be erected.

Wickes.—The Angelica Mining Co. is shipping 60 tons of $50 to $60 ore daily to Wickes. The tunnel is 4000 ft. long. A new strike is reported west of north-south fault, which threw the vein out of its course 400 ft. south. There is 5 ft. of galena at 900 ft. depth at breast of the 4000-ft. tunnel.

In the Lloyd-Crossley tunnel pay-ore has been opened in a drift west of the 3000-ft. tunnel. The ore is a gray copper, carrying silver.

NEVADA

Rand.— Shipments of highly silicious silver-gold ore are being made from the Nevada Rand mine in Mineral county to the smelter at Kennett, California. Two cars went forward in March, returns from the first assaying better than $42 per ton. On the 150-ft. level, in ground south of the main drift, a 4-ft. face is worth $39, while below this level in the 200-ft. stope, high-grade streaks are being prospected assaying from $397 to $1766 per ton. This ore is being taken out on canvas and sacked for future shipment. Laterals are being extended south from the main 250-ft. drift to pick up the extension of this rich material. West of this section, from the 250-ft. level, a raise showing 2 ft. of $69 ore is being extended east, and a shipment will shortly be made from this point. Ore is hauled by auto-trucks a distance of 17 miles from the mine to Nolan station on the Tonopah branch of the Southern Pacific, at which point a spacious ore platform has lately been erected by the company. W. H. Bray, superintendent, is in charge of the mine. The company is controlled by W. V. Rudderow of Reno. A complete assay-plant has been built, greatly facilitating work. Further extensive development of the mine is contemplated. The property is 5 miles south from the Jumbo Copper Mountain mine and 1½ miles west of the Golden Pen mine, both of which have produced considerable good ore. Ore tests and mill data are being prepared by local engineers.

Tonopah.—Production of the district last week, including 245 tons from Divide, was 7074 tons valued at $120,258.

In the Belmont, the south vein has been opened on the 1100-ft. level. This is of much importance to the company. Work is to be resumed on the 1200 and 1300-ft. levels in a short time.

In the Extension, the Murray vein at 1680 ft. averages 12 ft. in width, although in places it is up to 30 ft. The mill, in charge of Hugh Burk, is extracting 94% of the silver and gold content.

UTAH

Alta.—The Michigan-Utah company's aerial tram, 4 miles long, severely damaged by snowslides a few weeks ago, is being repaired, the underground force being utilized. This tram carries ore from other mines as well.

Alunite.—The Mineral Products Corporation, mining alunite and extracting potash therefrom, closed its works on March 27.

Bingham.—The apex suit of Utah Consolidated v. Utah Apex is to be heard by Judge T. D. Johnson of the U. S. District Court at Salt Lake City on June 2. A great array of legal and technical talent will appear for both sides.

Eureka.—The Eureka Lilly company's shaft is down 1660 ft., equal to 1400 ft. vertical. Some formation carrying copper and lead was passed through. Gas was troublesome at times. Lateral work is to be started at once. Grant Snyder is manager.

Gold Hill.— The Western Utah Copper Co. has resumed operations at its mines and mill. It has been decided to continue development on the 700-ft. level, which is 300 ft. below the point where shipments were made last year. The 50-ton mill, erected last year at Salt Springs on the Western Pacific line, 27 miles north of the mine, is to be moved to the property.

WASHINGTON

Chewelah.—According to James Allen, of the State Highway Commission at Spokane, there is $360,000 available for improving the road between the Spokane county line near Deer Park, and Chewelah. This will also improve the bad road from Colville to Spokane.

Republic.—Ore production has been resumed from the Quilp mine, closed for several years. The previous output was gold worth $492,843 from 39,653 tons. W. G. C. Lanskail is in charge of 25 men.

CANADA

Ontario

Cobalt. McKinley-Darragh is to start pumping tailing from Cobalt lake as soon as spring opens. The plant has a capacity of 350 tons daily. This material is to be treated in a flotation plant. On April 1 the company pays a dividend of 3%, equal to to $75,000.

The Nipissing company paid 5%, equal to $300,000, on March 31. The output in February was $243,176 from 125 tons of high and 6900 tons of low-grade ores.

Kirkland Lake.— It is officially announced that the Ontario government will build a branch line of the Temiskaming & Northern Ontario railway into this district.

Quebec

Quebec.— By the passing of a resolution in the Provincial Legislature on March 16, it has been decided to explore the territory of Ungava, or New Quebec.

MEXICO

The directors of the American Smelting & Refining Co. are at present making a personal examination of its properties in Mexico. The following table gives the names and positions of the mines:

State	Unit	Mine
		Mina Vieja
		Sin Nombre
	Santa Eulalia	Velardena
		San Antonio
		Santo Domingo
	Mayistral	Orizaba, La Union, etc.
Chihuahua	Calera	Prieta and Buena Vista
	Dolores	Jibosa
	Cordero	La Luz and Parcionera
	Parral	Guadalupe
	Santa Barbara	Tecolotes and Montezuma
		San Diego and Alfarena
	Veta Grande	Veta Grande, Veta Colorado, etc.
		San Jose
Coahuila	Sierra Mojada	Trinidad
		Volcan Dolores
		San Lorenzo
Durango	Velardeña	Santa Maria
		Copper Queen
		Santa Juana
Aguascalientes	Asientos	Santa Francisca
Michoacan	Angangueo	San Cristobal, Carmen, etc.
San Luis Potosi	Charcas	Tiro General
	Matehuala	Dolores
Zacatecas	Bonanza	Bonanza

With fully restored economic and political conditions in Mexico, these mines, it is believed, will produce fully 2,500,000 tons of ore per annum. The smelters of the company are at Chihuahua, Monterrey, Aguascalientes, Matehuala, and Velardeña. All of these are now operating except the last, and they are of sufficient capacity to reduce the product of the above mines, except copper ores at Chihuahua, together with large additional tonnages under contract. There are certainly many reasons at the present time for feeling encouraged with respect to political conditions in Mexico, according to the annual report of the A. S. & R. Company.

Mexico

El Oro.—Esperanza in January treated 15,685 tons of ore, yielding a profit of $11,000.

Mexico City.—The New York 'Tribune' gives the following figures showing the financial status of Mexico:

National debt up to 1913	₱427,000,000
Interest past due and pending	75,000,000
Cost of the Civil War	125,000,000
Total public debt in 1919	₱627,000,000
Estimated revenue for current year	₱149,000,000
Budget for fiscal year 1917-'18	187,000,000
Mexican exports to United States in 1918	$140,000,000
Mexican imports from United States in 1918	106,893,653

The Chamber of Commerce Mexican Trade Excursion left San Antonio, Texas, on March 28. There were over 70 who received passports. The convention is thoroughly representative of the principal industries, and returns to San Antonio on April 13, after visiting Nuevo Laredo, Monterrey, Tampico, Linares, Saltillo, San Luis Potosi, the City of Mexico, Queretaro, Celaya, Iripuato, Guadalajara, Aguascalientes, Zacatecas, Torreon, and Piedras Negras.

Instructions have been given for the investigation and revision of all mining claims now in existence in the republic. Since the year 1910 there have been granted 9516 such claims, distributed as follows: State of Aguascalientes, 57; Territory of Lower California, 287; State of Coahuila, 426; Colina, 13; Chiapas, 17; Chihuahua, 1052; Durango, 775; Guanajuato, 548; Guerrero, 386; Hidalgo, 371; Jalisco, 428; Mexico, 310; Michoacan, 320; Nuevo Leon, 596; Oaxaca, 445; Puebla, 122; Queretaro, 240; San Luis Potosi,

MAP OF MEXICO

444; Sinaloa, 632; Sonora, 1432; Tamaulipas, 69; Tepic, 92; Vera Cruz, 39; and Zacatecas, 539. Altogether, during the administration of ex-President Diaz, there were granted concessions of 56,000 mining claims, of which from 5000 to 6000 only were exploited.

According to Manuel Aguirre Berlanga, a member of the Government, there is 700 miles of railroad construction under way in the republic. The Federal and State governments are defraying the cost. All of the materials for building the lines are obtained in Mexico. The cross-ties come from the native lumber mills and the steel rails are manufactured at the plant of the Monterey Iron & Steel Co. at Monterrey. The railroads now under construction by the Government are to run between Cuatro Cienegas, in the State of Coahuila, to Chihuahua, via Sierra Mojada, a distance of about 450 miles; from Durango to the Pacific port of Mazatlan, a distance of about 135 miles, and from Durango to Canitas, a distance of about 130 miles. All of these lines are important. The building of a railroad from Durango to Mazatlan has been under consideration for 30 years or more. Many surveys were made to locate an easy route across the Sierra Madres. This has been finally accomplished, and the road will be finished in due time, thus establishing a new transcontinental line across Mexico. The Cuatro Cienegas-Chihuahua line will be the means of opening to development vast coalfields in northern Mexico, while the Durango-Cienegas road will shorten the rail distance between Durango and the capital about 200 miles and will give a shipping outlet to some rich mining districts.

San Luis Potosi

Matehuala.—The antimony mines and smelter of the Cia. Minera y Fundidora Internacional have been closed on account of the low price of the metal. During the War, when antimony rose to 40 cents, it was feared in the United States that the Mexican output would eventually depress prices.

PERSONAL

Note. The Editor invites members of the profession to send particulars of their work and appointments. The information is interesting to our readers.

F. L. Sizer is at Tonopah.

L. D. Ricketts and **John C. Greenway** are at Santa Barbara.

Howland Bancroft, of Denver, was in San Francisco, on his way to Mexico.

Percy E. Barbour is now assistant-secretary of the American Institute of Mining Engineers.

H. R. Wagner has gone from San Francisco to New York, where he will remain for several months.

Victor Ziegler has resigned from the Colorado School of Mines and will open an office as consulting geologist in the Empire building, Denver.

J. P. Montague has resigned his position with the Ray Con., at Hayden, Arizona, to take charge of the mining interests of C. F. Wittenberg at Manhattan, Nevada.

Roy H. Allen has received his discharge as Captain in the Air Service and will be connected with the Research Department of the National Aniline & Chemical Co., at Buffalo.

Dwight E. Woodbridge recently addressed the Tax Committee of the House of Representatives of Minnesota on the pending bills for tonnage tax on mining companies of that State.

F. A. Fahrenwald has returned from western Canada where he has been engaged for some months in the examination of industrial resources, especially mining, metallurgical, and chemical possibilities, in districts west from Winnipeg, along the route of the Grand Trunk Pacific railway to Prince Rupert.

G. Lavignino, so active formerly in the mining industry in Utah and at Cripple Creek, Colorado, died at Pasadena, California, on March 27, in his 70th year. He possessed various mining properties at the time of his death. He was a man of broad culture, a linguist, and a student. He leaves a wife, a daughter, and three sons, the older at West Point, the second just honorably discharged from the U. S. Army.

Obituary

W. H. Steinman, blast-furnace superintendent for the New Jersey Zinc Co., died recently at the age of 61.

G. McGregor, deputy supervisor of the Department of Petroleum and Gas of the State Mining Bureau for the First District (Los Angeles), died at San Francisco on March 21.

George W. Myers, for 18 years the Pacific Coast representative of the Chrome Steel Works, Chrome, N. J., died of heart failure on March 28. He was a native of New York; 56 years old. He leaves wife and family. His son was connected with him in business.

H. R. Hancock, inventor of the jig and rock-drill that bear his name, and for 22 years in charge of the Wallaroo and Moonta copper mines in South Australia, died on January 15, at the age of 83. He was born in Devon, England, going to Australia in 1859. His eldest son, H. Lipson Hancock, now manages the Wallaroo and Moonta mines.

Edward F. Freudenthal, mine operator and promoter of Pioche, Nevada, died on March 24 at the age of 55 years. He was a native of Pioche and had always made his home there, although spending much time in Salt Lake City and in the East. He is survived by his widow, two sons, and a brother.

THE METAL MARKET

METAL PRICES

San Francisco, April 1

Aluminum-dust, cents per lb	90.00
Antimony, cents per pound	8.00
Copper, electrolytic, cents per pound (in carload lots)	15.50
Lead, pig, cents per pound	5.50—6.50
Platinum, per ounce	$100
Quicksilver, per flask of 75 lb	$68
Spelter, cents per pound	8.00
Zinc-dust, cents per pound	12.50

EASTERN METAL MARKET

(By wire from New York)

April 1—Copper is quiet though strong. Lead is inactive but firm. Spelter is dull and easy.

SILVER

Below are given official (not Government) quotations, in cents per ounce, of silver 999 fine. In order to make prompt settlements with smelters and brokers, producers allow a discount from the maximum fixed price of $1.01½, hence the lower price. The Government has not fixed the general market price at $1, but will pay this price (as from April 23, 1918) for all silver purchased by it. The equivalent of dollar silver (1000 fine) in British currency is 46.65 pence per ounce (925 fine), calculated at the current rate of exchange. On August 15, 1918, the Treasury announced that the maximum price was fixed at $1.01½ per ounce. The British government fixed its maximum at 49½ pence, on September 2, but on November 12 this was changed to 48¾, on December 13 to 48 7/16, and in February to 47¾ pence. On March 23, on account of the low rate of exchange, the London price was adjusted accordingly, resulting in fluctuations to 50 pence.

Date		New York cents	London pence		Average week ending	
Mch.	26	101.12	49.31	Feb.	18	101.12
"	27	101.12	49.43	"	25	101.12
"	28	101.12	50.00	Mch.	4	101.12
"	29	101.12	49.75	"	11	101.12
"	30 Sunday			"	18	101.12
"	31	101.12	49.75	"	25	101.12
Apr.	1	101.12	49.56	Apr.	1	101.12

Monthly averages

	1917	1918	1919		1917	1918	1919
Jan.	75.14	88.72	101.12	July	78.92	99.62	....
Feb.	77.54	85.79	101.12	Aug.	85.40	100.31	....
Mch.	74.13	88.11	101.12	Sept.	100.73	101.12	....
Apr.	72.51	95.35	....	Oct.	87.38	101.12	....
May	74.61	99.50	....	Nov.	85.97	101.12	....
June	76.44	99.50	....	Dec.	85.97	101.12	....

COPPER

Prices of electrolytic in New York, in cents per pound.

Date				Average week ending	
Mch.	26	15.12	Feb.	18	17.50
"	27	15.25	"	25	16.40
"	28	15.25	Mch.	4	15.25
"	29	15.25	"	11	14.83
"	30 Sunday		"	18	14.79
"	31	15.37	"	25	14.99
Apr.	1	15.37	Apr.	1	15.27

Monthly averages

	1917	1918	1919		1917	1918	1919
Jan.	29.53	23.50	20.43	July	29.67	26.00	....
Feb.	34.57	23.50	17.34	Aug.	27.42	26.00	....
Mch.	36.00	23.50	15.05	Sept.	25.11	26.00	....
Apr.	33.16	23.50	....	Oct.	23.50	26.00	....
May	31.60	23.50	....	Nov.	23.50	26.00	....
June	32.57	23.50	....	Dec.	23.50	26.00	....

Copper stocks in this country are growing, and are now estimated at 1,300,000,000 lb., a gain of 300,000,000 lb. when compared with three months ago.

The members of the Copper Export Association are returning from Europe. They are reported to have no important orders for copper, but have a first-hand knowledge of conditions on the Continent.

TIN

Prices in New York, in cents per pound. The monthly averages in 1918 are nominal. On December 3 the War Industries Board fixed the price to consumers and jobbers at 72½c. f.o.b. Chicago and Eastern points, and 71¼c. on the Pacific Coast. This will continue until the U. S. Steel Products Co.'s stock is consumed.

Monthly averages

	1917	1918	1919		1917	1918	1919
Jan.	44.10	85.13	71.50	July	62.60	93.00	....
Feb.	51.47	85.00	72.44	Aug.	62.53	91.33	....
Mch.	54.27	85.00	72.50	Sept.	61.54	80.40	....
Apr.	55.63	88.53	....	Oct.	62.24	78.82	....
May	63.21	100.01	....	Nov.	74.18	73.07	....
June	61.93	91.00	....	Dec.	85.00	71.52	....

LEAD

Lead is quoted in cents per pound, New York delivery.

Date				Average week ending	
Mch.	26	5.25	Feb.	18	[illegible]
"	27	5.25	"	25	5.05
"	28	5.25	Mch.	4	5.25
"	29	5.25	"	11	5.25
"	30 Sunday		"	18	5.27
"	31	5.25	"	25	5.21
Apr.	1	5.25	Apr.	1	[illegible]

Monthly averages

	1917	1918	1919		1917	1918	1919
Jan.	7.64	6.85	5.60	July	10.93	8.03	....
Feb.	9.10	7.07	5.13	Aug.	10.75	8.05	....
Mch.	10.07	7.26	5.24	Sept.	9.07	8.05	....
Apr.	9.38	6.99	....	Oct.	6.97	8.05	....
May	10.29	6.88	....	Nov.	6.38	8.05	....
June	11.74	7.58	....	Dec.	6.49	6.90	....

The Spanish customs duty of one peseta per 100 kilos (20 cents per 220 lb.) on the export of argentiferous lead has been suspended until May 31.

ZINC

Zinc is quoted as spelter, standard Western brands, New York delivery, in cents per pound.

Date				Average week ending	
Mch.	26	6.52	Feb.	18	6.73
"	27	6.52	"	25	6.66
"	28	6.52	Mch.	4	6.61
"	29	6.52	"	11	6.55
"	30 Sunday		"	18	6.50
"	31	6.55	"	25	6.48
Apr.	1	6.55	Apr.	1	6.55

Monthly averages

	1917	1918	1919		1917	1918	1919
Jan.	9.75	7.87	7.44	July	8.98	8.72	....
Feb.	10.45	7.97	6.71	Aug.	8.58	8.87	....
Mch.	10.78	7.67	6.53	Sept.	8.33	9.58	....
Apr.	10.20	7.04	....	Oct.	8.32	9.11	....
May	9.41	7.29	....	Nov.	7.76	8.75	....
June	9.63	7.92	....	Dec.	7.84	8.49	....

QUICKSILVER

The primary market for quicksilver is San Francisco, California being the largest producer. The price is fixed in the open market, according to quantity. Prices, in dollars per flask of 75 pounds:

Date					
Mch.	4	85.00	Mch.	18	68.00
"	11	75.00	"	25	68.00
			Apr.	1	68.00

Monthly averages

	1917	1918	1919		1917	1918	1919
Jan.	81.00	128.06	103.75	July	102.00	120.00	....
Feb.	126.25	118.00	90.00	Aug.	115.00	120.00	....
Mch.	113.75	112.00	72.80	Sept.	112.00	120.00	....
Apr.	114.50	115.00	....	Oct.	102.00	120.00	....
May	104.00	110.00	....	Nov.	102.50	120.00	....
June	85.50	112.00	....	Dec.	117.42	115.00	....

PRICES OF OLD METALS

Business in New York is quiet, with the following prices in cents per pound:

Copper, heavy and crucible	13.00
Copper, heavy and wire	13.00
Copper, light and bottoms	10.50
Brass, heavy	7.50
Brass, light	6.00
Heavy machine composition	12.50
No. 1 yellow rod brass turnings	7.00
No. 1 red brass or composition turnings	10.00
Lead, heavy	4.25
Lead, tea	3.50
Zinc	4.50

Eastern Metal Market

New York, March 26.

There is a better tone in most of the markets, and in some of them prices have stiffened; but buying has not been of large proportions, when judged by normal standards.

Antimony has declined and is quiet.

Copper is much more active at advancing prices.

Lead is easier and slightly lower, with buying almost negligible.

Tin it yet at a standstill.

Zinc is quoted a little higher, but there has been little demand.

ANTIMONY

The market is lower with demand light. Spot delivery of Asiatic brands is quoted at 6.25 to 6.37½c., New York, duty paid, for wholesale lots.

COPPER

In the last few days the market has assumed an entirely different tone, and taken on a spurt of activity greater than has been witnessed since the signing of the armistice. Since last Friday, estimates place total sales at not less than 35,000,000 lb., which would be more than in either January or February. It is also figured that in the last 10 days about 175,000,000 lb. has been sold. Neither of these reports has been confirmed. As a result of these facts the market has advanced gradually until today, March 26, yesterday being a holiday in honor of the parade of the 27th Division, electrolytic copper is quoted at 15.25c., New York, with Lake copper nominal at 15.50. Most of the sales referred to as having been made in the last three or four days probably went at 14.87 to 15.12½c. There has been no pronounced demand from foreign consumers, and little is expected for a month or more. The return in a few days of the representatives of the Copper Export Association from Europe will throw interesting light on this. Some say that the imminence of this information is back of the present buying of copper, while others think that the activity is to be short lived. On March 31 next the New York Metal Exchange will commence trading in copper. To meet new conditions and to measure up to the demand of an active market, the rules have been revised by the authorities so as to make them virtually satisfactory to all interests. Announcement has been made of the details of the selling of the Government stocks of copper. The United Metal Selling Co., acting for the producers, will sell 5,000,000 lb. per month for 10 months, and then 10,000,000 lb. per month for 5 months at market prices.

IRON AND STEEL

The price reductions agreed upon last week at Washington range from $4.25 per ton on pig-iron and $5 on billets to $10 on standard rails, and amount to $7 per net ton on plates, shapes, bars, wrought pipe, sheets and tin-plate, and $5 on wire, wire nails, hoops, and light rails. Eastern bar-makers have met the reduction on steel-bars by dropping their price from 2.90c. to 2.35c., Pittsburgh. The opinion is general in the steel trade, says 'The Iron Age', that the reduced prices will bring out in the near future a moderate amount of new business, most of which buyers have held up since the stabilizing movement loomed up six weeks ago.

LEAD

The lack of interest and demand has continued during the entire week, and the market is dull with the outside market at slightly lower levels. The American Smelting & Refining Co. has not changed its quotation of 5.25c., New York, or 5c., St. Louis, but the outside sellers have shaded these proces to $5.20c., and 4.95c., respectively. Certain independents apparently have become restless, and attempted to attract consumers, but these have refused to be tempted. It is not believed that levels will fall much lower, not at least below 5c., New York, for the fundamental conditions of the market are sound. When buying in other raw materials commences, it is believed that there will be an active demand for lead. Stocks are low, and production has diminished to under 50% of capacity.

TIN

Another attempt has been made to force more quickly the allocated tin into consumer's hands by the rather drastic ruling that a leading American smelter of tin shall no longer sell 5-ton lots unrestrictedly, as has been possible up to now. This is regarded of course as a move to remove even this competition with the allocated metal which is fixed at 72.50c., the American tin having sold at a lower level right along to the detriment of the Government metal. It is said that if buyers will take the allocated metal, they will likely secure it at less than the fixed price when final adjustments are made. Spot Straits tin continues unchanged at the Government price of 72.50c., New York, with American 99% metal available at 68c., New York. No one seems able to fix a date as to when the allocated metal will be absorbed, and it is this on which the whole future of the market depends. According to the last estimates only 6000 tons of the original allocation of 10,000 tons has been booked. Arrivals so far in March have been 1425 tons of tin, all at Pacific ports—no more than a week ago. The London quotation for spot Straits tin is unchanged at $239 per ton.

ZINC

Producers generally have revised their ideas of market conditions and have slightly advanced their quotations to 6.17½ to 6.20c., St. Louis, or 6.52½ to 6.55c., New York, for prime Western for early delivery. To this extent the market may be regarded as firmer, but still quiet. The main reason back of this firmer tone is the expectation that galvanizers will purchase steel sheet-bars, now that a lower minimum price has been set, and hence will need more spelter.

ORES

Tungsten: There is little change, with still no testing of prices; therefore quotations are impossible. The buying of steel, expected to follow the fixing of prices, is expected to stimulate the tungsten market ultimately. The public auction of tungsten, scheduled for last Thursday, has been postponed until April 4. There are also no quotations for ferro.

Molybdenum: Outside of a possible demand from Great Britain, the market is without interest. Quotations are nominally unchanged at 80 to 85c., per lb. of MoS_2 in high-grade concentrate.

Manganese Alloys: Domestic producers of ferro have reduced their quotations of 80% alloy from $200 to $150, delivered, but there is no business. Consumers are well stocked apparently, and are buying only what they need as they need it, and mostly re-sale material at less than $150. Large quantities of British alloy are now coming in for delivery on old contracts, which call for some rather low prices ranging from under $50 to about $164 per ton, seaboard, but most of it is the higher-price material. It is stated that some of the lower-cost alloy is being re-sold at a profit.

Company Reports

BINGHAM MINES CO.

Property: the Dalton & Lark and Yosemite mines in the Bingham district, and the Eagle & Blue Bell and Victoria in the Tintic district, Utah.

Operating Official: Imer Pett, general manager.

Financial Statement: net receipts from all sources in 1918, including dividends from other companies, totaled $331,731. The surplus at the end of the year was $365,877.

Dividends: five of 50 cents each absorbed $375,000, making $562,500 to date.

Development: little development was done in the main workings of the Dalton & Lark, but new openings amounted to 2755 ft. A large tonnage should be developed on the Brooklyn, Lead Mine, and Lark veins below the Moscotte tunnel. Several lessees were at work.

Results on the Lead Mine vein in the Yosemite property were not satisfactory, but the ground is so favorably situated as to encourage further exploration.

In the Victoria there was performed 2313 ft. of work. The 1050-ft. level failed to reveal a downward continuation of the ore, but more success followed exploration of a probable upward extension to the main orebody. Recent favorable developments in the Eagle & Blue Bell at and below 1700 ft. emphasize the importance of the Victoria.

Prospecting and development—5519 ft.—in the Eagle & Blue Bell cost $52,589. Early in the year a considerable quantity of lead-silver ore was opened above 1550 ft., but la'er on this was more or less 'bunchy', requiring greater care and cost. In December, ore was found in a cross-cut driven east from the 1875 south drift, on a strong fissure. Nearly all levels above had been productive from orebodies found near this fissure, so the discovery is of importance. Much success and confidence has been obtained by carefully exploiting small showings:

Production:

	Dalton & Lark*	Yosemite	Victoria	Eagle & Blue Bell†
Ore, tons	31,070	2,010	6,791	40,370
Gold, ounces	1,606	80	1,048	2,605
Silver, ounces	172,504	10,189	139,304	579,075
Lead, pounds	1,320,636	314,258	176,019	9,380,376
Copper, pounds	875,000	21,034	165,508	10,012
Operating profit	$140,604	......	$44,319	$288,730

*Including lessees. †$267,944 paid in dividends, making $1,161,000 to end of 1918.

FALCON MINES, LIMITED

Property: extensive property and plant 60 miles west of Gwelo, Blinkwater district, Rhodesia.

Operating Official: C. E. Parsons, consulting engineer.

Financial Statement: sales of copper, gold and silver realized £485,406 ($2,320,000) during the year ended June 30, 1918. Operations cost £397,888 ($1,900,000). The profit was £88,449 ($420,000) plus £186,894 ($892,000) brought forward. After paying a dividend and allowing for taxes there remained a balance of £75,310 ($360,000).

Dividends: No. 1 of 20%, equal to £80,000 ($380,000) was paid.

Development: the main shaft was sunk 127 ft. to a depth of 1109 ft. All development covered 3808 ft., making over 5 miles of workings. A re-estimate of reserves shows 800,000 tons, averaging $5.40 gold and 2.32% copper, a decrease due to not including the recovery of certain broken and unbroken ore. On No. 10 level the orebody is 180 ft. long, 70 ft. less than on No. 9, but the width and value are similar.

Production: the mill concentrated 153,340 tons of $5.10 gold and 2.19% copper ore, producing 24,192 tons of vanner concentrate assaying $20.40 gold and 5.19% copper. This was smelted direct. The tailing from vanners, etc., was re-treated by flotation, which saved 18,010 tons of concentrate carrying $5.80 gold and 9.87% copper. This product was smelted. The total extraction was 81.9% gold and 87% copper. The smelter reduced direct 15,350 tons of $8.40 gold and 4.45% copper ore. The sintering-plant (16 pots) made 39,406 tons of product. The blast-furnace treated 80,559 tons of metal-bearing charge. The past four years yields are as under:

Year	Copper, tons	Gold, oz	Silver, oz
1918	3,542	37,701	80,528
1917	3,114	35,218	70,870
1916	3,108	36,577	65,537
1915	2,574	31,161	53,303

This was extracted from 722,482 tons of ore. All costs were 46/9 ($11.24) per ton in 1918.

SHATTUCK ARIZONA COPPER CO.

Property: mine and mill at Bisbee, Arizona.

Operating Officials: L. C. Shattuck, general manager; Arthur Houle, superintendent.

Financial Statement: the gross income in 1918 was $2,668,083. Operations cost $1,883,424, reserve for depletion $504,717, and depreciation $36,475, leaving a net profit of $243,467. The balance from 1917 was $1,003,129, and that carried to 1919 was $809,096, after deducting dividends and adding the profit for 1918. Current assets total $2,505,213, and liabilities $411,996.

Dividends: four absorbed $437,500, making $7,262,500 since 1910.

Development: to the 900-ft. level new work amounted to 15,125 ft., making 27 miles in all. Results were not favorable for copper ore, although between 800 and 900 ft. a large body of primary sulphides was exposed, carrying from 2 to 4% Cu. In the lead section good tonnages of 6% Pb, 8 oz. Ag, and $1.20 Au ore were developed.

Production: the lead mill, on which $294,902 has been spent, started in July, but electric power was short until November. This flotation plant dressed 27,851 tons of ore assaying 6.6% Pb, 8.1 oz. Ag, and 0.07 oz. Au. Results have not equaled experiments, and the loss of silver was excessive. The complete yields were:

Copper ore smelted, tons	91,002
Lead ore treated and smelted, tons	28,550
Copper, pounds	9,081,959
Lead, pounds	2,420,890
Gold, ounces	2,061
Silver, ounces	1,083,925
Operating cost per ton of ore	$14.125
Operating cost per pound of copper, cents	14.635
Price received for copper, cents	25.000

MOUNT ELLIOTT, LIMITED

Property: mines and smelter in the Cloncurry district, Queensland, Australia.

Operating Officials: A. E. Strick, mine superintendent; W. H. Corbould, consulting engineer.

Financial Statement: during the year ended June 30, 1918, a loss of £56,890 ($273,000) was made, after allowing for depreciation, etc., mainly due to the strike at mid-year.

Development: reserves in the seven mines total 1,861,000 tons. In Mt. Elliott is 600,000 tons of 3% and 10,000 tons of 10% ore, in Hampden Consols 450,000 tons of 4%, in Mt. Oxide 300,000 tons of 10%, in Argylla 200,000 tons of 4%, and in the limestone and jasper lodes of the Great Australia 203,000 tons of 2½ to 4% ore.

Production: 51,952 tons of ore smelted yielded 5,201,280 lb. of blister copper. Alterations to the plant were completed early in January 1918, since when it has worked well. The refinery produced 5,134,080 lb. of 'fire' refined metal.

Book Reviews

The Zinc Industry. By E. A. Smith. Pp. 223, ill., index. Longmans, Green & Co., London and New York, 1918. For sale by 'Mining and Scientific Press.' Price, $3.50.

It is several years since any new work has been written on zinc, during which time many new mines have been developed and advances made in the metallurgy, so this volume should fill the gap. Front a preliminary perusal we find the book contains the latest information, although statistics are only up to 1914, showing normal pre-war production. A map and a graph show clearly the principal zinc centres and the production of spelter in the world since 1845. In the chapter on rise and progress of production of the metal, the establishment of smelters in Europe, America, and especially in Great Britain, are traced. Europe reduced large quantities of Australian concentrates, while England depended mostly on imported ores to keep its industry going. Certain phases of the War resulted in the question of the Australian product being reduced in England, and the erection of more smelters for that purpose. The last chapter discusses the future of zinc in that country. The Belgian and German works are covered, also those in America, too well known by readers to need extended reference. The world's ores and sources of supply, including Japan and Siberia, find complete notice. Concentration and marketing of ores and the metal are considered; but 45 pages are devoted to roasting and distillation, including the production of zinc-dust and such by-products as sulphuric acid, blue powder, lead, silver, and cadmium. The notes on costs are instructive. Electric smelting and electrolytic exrtaction of zinc are fully discussed. Producers in America have been alive to the extended use of spelter, so the properties and industrial applications of the metal will be found of value herein; also the alloys and pigments. Our complete study of the book finds it to be up to date. The binding is poor, and advertisements before the title-page are out of place.

Compressed Air Plant. The production, transmission, and use of compressed air, with special reference to mine service. Third edition, largely re-written. By Robert Peele. Pp. 485, ill., index. John Wiley & Son, New York, 1919. For sale by 'Mining and Scientific Press'. Price, $4.25.

The author of this important work, who is professor of mining in Columbia School of Mines, is well known from the previous editions of this book and as being editor-in-chief of the valuable 'Mining Engineers' Handbook', published in 1918. This new edition should be on the shelves of every mechanical engineer, especially at mines. While compressed air, as a prime mover, is an expensive power, yet it cannot be dispensed with, and its use grows. The design of compressors and machines using air improves continually, likewise the efficiency of compressed air. Compressed air is now almost indispensible in expeditious development of mines, in hoisting, in underground haulage, in metallurgical plants, in machine-shops, in tamping railroad tracks, in sand-blasting, in shipbuilding, and in forcing concrete mix into forms. Mr. Peele has restricted his discussions to deal only with the production of air and its uses in mining and tunneling. The loss of compressed air in pipes is relatively small; there is no problem of disposal of the exhaust, as when steam is used; and the exhausted air is of some assistance in ventilating underground workings. Air is far more preferable than steam for machine-drills and hoists; while no electric drill can compete with an air drill. In an early issue of the 'Press' we are publishing a paper on compressing air efficiently, in which is discussed the design of compressors, their lay-out, piping, inter-coolers, etc., and in Peele we find these topics much elaborated, and illustrated by modern machines—steam, water, and electric driven. The factors entering into the compression of air are somewhat intricate, but here are shown by formulas and diagrams. Air inlet and discharge-valves and mechanically controlled valves are the subject of much study by designing engineers, so 38 pages are devoted to it. As so many mines are at high altitudes, compressors have to be designed accordingly, their effective capacity being much reduced. For instance, the volume of compressed air delivered at 60-lb. pressure, at 10,000-ft., elevation, is only 72.7% of the volume delivered at the same pressure by the same compressor at sea-level. Or, a machine that will drive 10 drills at sea-level will only furnish air for 7 drills at the height mentioned. So mining engineers must not forget this important factor. Explosions occur fairly frequently in compressors and receivers, and while generally credited to oil vapors, the reasons are rather obscure. This subject is fully discussed. Air may be compressed by the direct action of falling water, some notable examples being given. The second part of Peele is devoted to the conveyance of compressed air in pipes and its use in rock-drills, hoists, pumps, coal-cutting machinery, channeling machines, and locomotives in mines. Every modern type of machine under these heads is described and illustrated. Air-lifts—mine and mill—are also discussed. Frequent references are made to the technical press, and manufacturers of apparatus pertaining to compressed air; and the costs cited are recent and instructive. Anybody having problems involving compressed air will surely find the solution in this excellent volume.

Handbook of Mechanical and Electrical Cost Data. By Halbert P. Gillette and Richard T. Dana. Pp. 1716, ill., index. For sale by 'Mining and Scientific Press'. Price, $6.

As the preface states, this book is intended as a companion volume to Mr. Gillette's 'Handbook of Cost Data', and Mr. Dana's 'Handbook of Construction Plant'. The arrangement is similar to the former book, but there is little overlapping. In these days of abnormal prices, and of discussion as to whether or not large reductions will be made in the near future, some engineers and estimators may feel that a book of cost data, since its costs manifestly cannot be brought up to the minute, is of slight value. That this viewpoint is erroneous, provided the cost analysis is accurate and complete, is shown by the authors in the introductory chapter. The completeness of the book may be judged from the chapter-headings, which are as follows: General Economic Principles; Depreciation, Repairs, and Renewals; Buildings; Chimneys; Moving and Installing; Fuel and Coal Handling; Steam Power; Internal-Combustion Engines and Gas-Producers; Hydro-Electric Plants; First Cost and Operating Expenses of Electric Plants; Overhead and Underground Electric Transmission; Wiring; Drives; Compressed Air; Gas Plants; Pumps; Conveyors, Hoists, etc.; Heating, Cooking, Ventilating, Refrigerating; Electric Railways. The book is an excellent reference.

Western Canada Mining Directory. Edited by J. H. Hamilton. Pp. 110, index. Progress Publishing Co., Vancouver, B. C., 1919. For sale by 'Mining and Scientific Press'. Price, $3.

This useful reference comprises a complete directory of metalliferous and coal mines in British Columbia, Alberta, Saskatchewan, Manitoba, and the Yukon, including the names of owners, position, status of development, product, capital, and other data. In condensed form will be found the mining laws of the western provinces and those of the Dominion affecting those regions.

INDUSTRIAL PROGRESS

INFORMATION FURNISHED BY MANUFACTURERS

GASOLINE MINE LOCOMOTIVES

Within the last few years, gasoline locomotives have made considerable headway in mining operations for both surface and underground work.

The J. D. Fate Co., of Plymouth, Ohio, has devoted special attention to the development of a locomotive that is particularly well adapted to the requirements of mines—for both surface and underground use. Every detail has been perfected to make for the maximum of efficiency in construction and operation, as demonstrated by numerous mining companies who have been using Plymouth locomotives under all kinds of conditions for a number of years.

The Plymouth locomotive frame is of one solid casting, affording the best possible foundation for all the working parts, eliminating excessive vibration, and holding the bearings and shafting in correct alignment. Plenty of reinforcing webs have been provided to absorb the shocks and strain. It is built for any gauge of track from 18 to 56½ in. The regular height above the rail is 72 in., but locomotives can be supplied with a minimum height of 52 inches.

The three-ton locomotive is provided with a specially designed 'Continental' motor. A Bosch high-tension magneto is used, and a Stromberg carburetor. Combustion is so complete that no difficulty is experienced from fume in underground work where Plymouth locomotives are employed. A friction drive eliminates the clutch and differential, and the transmission is connected with the engine through an improved type of flexible coupling. Powerful brakes, with a leverage of 6000 lb. and sand-boxes for all four wheels, are provided. The machine is built throughout in a manner to assure a maximum of efficiency with a minimum of trouble. The material and workmanship is of the best. A 3-ton Plymouth gasoline locomotive exerts a 1200-lb. draw-bar pull at five miles per hour, and will haul from 30 to 50-ton load on the level, and an 8 to 10-ton load on a 4% grade. The 6-ton locomotive will handle from 60 to 100-ton load on the level, and 16 to 20-ton load on 5% grades.

The Eighty-Five Mining Co. of Lordsburg, New Mexico, is an example where Plymouth locomotives are used for both surface and underground work. This company has used two of the 3-ton locomotives in connection with its mining operations. The locomotive is operated on an 18-in. gauge track, and is equipped with a self-starter, electric lights, and electric horn. It is handling six 2½-ton cars on the track equipped with 36-lb. rails, and the manager reports that it would easily handle twice as many cars if necessary. The up-keep and cost of operations is reported to be extremely low, in fact, lower than any other locomotive with which the company had any experience. It is used in a 500-ft. tunnel, and the manager reports that there has never been

General View of Gasoline Locomotive

any trouble due to gases. The following performance data has been supplied by E. J. Inderrieden, general manager for the Eighty-Five company.

"From February 1, 1917, to February 1, 1918, one locomotive hauled 118,859 tons—20-cu. ft. cars—a distance of 1320 ft. and return, or two round trips per mile, or 59,429 car-miles.

Costs

Operating:		
Labor, 990 shifts at $3.50	$3,465	
Material, gasoline, 3240 gal. at 30c	972	
Lubricating oil, 60 gal. at 72c	43	
		$4,480
Maintenance:		
Labor, 20 shifts at $5	$100	
20 " " 3	60	
Material	296	
		456
Total cost for 59,429 car-miles		$4,936
Cost per car-mile	$0.083	

Conversation with drivers, also observation, indicate that

Gasoline Locomotive and Mine-Cars at Eighty-Five Mine, New Mexico the locomotive could easily have handled double the tonnage in the same time, as trips only averaged 7 cars. The locomotive has been an unusually satisfactory and reliable machine and has been operated by inexperienced men. The machine operates in a tunnel without sufficient clearance at switches, which accounts for knocking-off of grease-cups, and, in one case, caps of main roller-bearings. The fibre in the friction-wheel is replaced regularly, but only requires an hour's time."

Details as to construction and operation together with performance data and catalogues (No. 4-Bulletins A, B, G, and H) will be sent upon application by the J. D. Fate Co., Plymouth, Ohio.

CATERPILLAR MOTORS NOW AVAILABLE FOR ANY SERVICE

The Holt Manufacturing Co. of Stockton, California, announces that caterpillar tractor motors are now offered in two sizes—45 and 75 hp.—for stationary work. A number of these motors have been in use for pumping, hoisting, and

A Caterpillar Motor. These are made in three sizes—45, 55, and 75 hp.—for stationary work. The features are overhead-valve and a four-cylinder distillate-burning engine. They have had four years' war service and many years of agricultural service prior to that.

general stationary work at mines, contracting, and engineering work, but there has been no effort in the past to secure this business—the sales having been entirely unsolicited. These motors have given such splendid service in this sort of work that the Holt company is making a special effort in the stationary field. Tractor service is generally recognized as putting the gasoline motor under the most severe strain, the work always being under heavy load, dust, strain, and heat.

SEVERE TEST FOR A MOTOR-TRUCK

A remarkable test of a White heavy-duty motor-truck, equipped with double-reduction gear, the latest device of the White Company of Cleveland, Ohio, was reported in San Francisco last week. This machine made the grade (25%) from Union street to Broadway on Fillmore street with a five-ton load. The Fillmore-street hills make one of the steepest grades in the city, and are paved with rough basalt blocks, which makes the traction the poorest possible, according to Leon J. Pinkson. Another feat was the stopping of the truck on the grade and then starting again. This means that the motor and other parts were called upon to start a deadweight of 18,950 lb. on a 25% grade, a thing that will seldom happen in actual service. The gross weight of the loaded truck was 18,950 lb., the weight of the truck 9130 lb. There was also a demonstration of the braking power of the truck. This 10-ton weight was held on the hill, brought to a complete standstill on the slippery grass-covered slope without trouble. Bob Spiegel, factory expert of the White Company, drove the truck. He had tried the machine under all conditions at the factory at Cleveland, but had never tackled anything like this hill before. In order to prove that the gear ratio was standard 13.33 to 1, Spiegel marked a spot on the rear wheel and on the body, then moved the truck with the crank until the wheel made one complete revolution. The wheel turned in 13 revolutions of the crank. Standard Oil 'Red Crown' gasoline was used during this performance.

COMMERCIAL PARAGRAPHS

In Catalogue H-19, the **United Iron Works Co.** of Kansas City, Missouri, describes and illustrates its belt, steam, electric, horse, and hand-operated hoists for mines and works.

The Hydro-Electric Power Commission of Ontario has placed an order with the **Westinghouse Electric & Mfg. Co.** for two 45,000-kva. vertical water-wheel generators of 12,000 volts, 3 phase, 25 cycles, for its Queenstown development. These will be the largest water-wheel generators ever constructed, and indicate that the Commission thinks the present is a good period for construction work.

Mining machinery exported during January was valued at $956,874, plus $106,478 of oil-well appliances. South Africa took $157,788 of the former, followed by Canada with $142,639, Mexico with $112,224, Norway with $67,250, Chile with $64,852, and Australia with 58,181. Of oil-well machinery, Trinidad and Tobago took $28,741, Cuba $17,135, Dominica $15,605, Dutch East Indies $13,299, and Mexico $11,064.

Pumps and pumping machinery exported from the United States during January 1919 were valued at $572,445, according to the Division of Statistics of the U. S. Department of Commerce. Canada took $99,255 of the total, followed by Cuba with $86,088, Argentina with $59,744, Dutch East Indies with $43,993, England with $40,902, Mexico with $33,603, South Africa with $29,067, Japan with $20,811, Brazil with $19,650, and Australia with $14,662.

In its latest 144-page catalogue, the **Hercules Powder Co.** lists, describes, and illustrates the use of its high explosives, blasting and sporting powders, blasting supplies, and chemicals. Throughout the United States, including the large plant at Hercules, California, the works occupy 14,000 acres. Mining men and others will find in this publication a great deal of useful information. The photographs themselves are instructive in depicting the correct way in which to use explosives.

The Sullivan Machinery Co. desires to announce the establishment of a branch sales-office and warehouse for the convenience of its customers and friends in Mexico, at Edificio Oliver No. 3, Mexico City. Joseph F. Bennett, for a number of years sales engineer in Mexico, associated with the El Paso branch of this company, has been placed in charge of the Mexico City office. That office will serve customers and clients in central and southern Mexico, and in that part of the States of Sinaloa, Durango, Coahuila, and Tamaulipas, lying south of the 26th parallel.

The Chicago Pneumatic Tool Co. makes the following announcements: The Detroit office has been moved to 502 Farwell building.——An office and warehouse have been opened at Richards building, Tulsa, Oklahoma, and at El Dorado, Kansas.——The Boston office is now at 182 High street, with F. S. Eggleston in charge.——J. J. Edwards is now manager of the rock-drill sales division, succeeding E. Eklund, who has been appointed special representative, and who will leave shortly for Europe.——Fred H. Waldron, formerly Minneapolis representative, has been appointed manager of the pneumatic tool sales division, succeeding J. G. Osgood, resigned. Mr. Waldron's offices are now in the Fisher building, Chicago.——Nelson B. Gatch was recently appointed district manager of sales at Minneapolis, with offices at 301 Metropolitan Bank building.——J. K. Haigh has recently been appointed assistant district manager of sales in San Francisco, at 175 First street.

ON another page we publish a portion of a speech on current mining affairs in Mexico and elsewhere, delivered in London by Mr. R. T. Bayliss, who has many friends in this country, particularly in Montana, where he lived for several years as resident manager of the Drumlummon mine, owned by the Montana Mining Company, Ltd., at Marysville. As chairman of the old Exploration Company he occupies a position of importance in London and he uses his influence always on the side of good sense and high ideals of conduct in mining affairs.

COPPER dividends have been generally curtailed, without causing any collapse in the market-value of the shares of the companies producing the metal. This does credit to the good sense of everybody concerned. Even the dispirited return, from Europe, of the representatives of the Copper Export Association does not seem to have taken the heart out of the leaders of the industry; indeed, the sales of copper during March were encouraging rather than otherwise. In the light of subsequent events, if not in that of the facts as known at the time, the request—or command—of the War Industries Board for the continued full-scale production of copper after the signing of the Armistice and until the end of 1918, in order to maintain rates of wages, was a blunder.

SECRETARY LANE, of the Department of the Interior, has been attacked virulently by Mr. James Wickersham, the delegate to Congress from Alaska, in a letter that has been published in the daily press. Judge Wickersham demands the withdrawal of Mr. Lane from the official management of the Government railroad in Alaska, declaring that his administration is a failure caused by "incompetent and petty political partisanship." To any unprejudiced person, it is clear that the attack itself is written for political purposes; it is supported by wild conjectures and unsupported charges so reckless as to merit severe condemnation. The management of the Alaskan railroad may have defects, as is usual in any Government administration of any railroad, but in this case it is evident that Judge Wickersham has exceeded the limits of fair play.

CONVERSATION in the smoking-compartment of the train or steamer today occupies itself chiefly with the penance of prohibition. Wherever men congregate the incidence of prohibition is discussed. Means of evasion supplies a fruitful topic of conversation. What can be done with a raisin or a bit of yeast to elevate the alcoholism of feeble beverages; what home-made distillations will circumvent restrictive legislation; and whether the effort to discipline the citizen will be pushed so far as to prohibit smoking also; these are the topics of an idle hour. Are we to become a nation of law-breakers merely because the prohibitionists have succeeded in 'putting one over us'? We trust not; we believe not. This talk will pass, and the average citizen will accept the edict of constituted authority with as good a grace as he can, realizing that compliance with any particular law is of small importance as compared with obedience to the law, under which alone a democracy can be sustained in peaceful order.

ROMANCE still clings to mining, as is suggested by the story of the Bush mine in the Salmon River district of British Columbia. This prospect was under option, not long ago, to the Consolidated Mining & Smelting Company of Canada, whose engineer condemned it. Last year Mr. R. K. Neill, an experienced miner, happened to be inspecting some other claims in the district on a grubstake from some friends at Fernie, B. C. He found a tunnel showing no particular evidence of rich ore, but on cross-cutting a few feet he cut into a rich lode—no less than 25 feet of ore assaying 100 ounces of silver per ton. This lay alongside the drift, which therefore was practically in the casing of the lode and had just missed striking it! With barely a few hundred feet of development work he opened up ore to the value—it is said—of $11,000,000! This reminds us of the late Captain De Lamar's experience in the Terrible mine, near Silver Cliff, Colorado; he also had only to drive a few short cross-cuts into the wall of the relatively barren vein that the former owners had followed in their drift. Mr. Neill deserves his good luck; he was the man that exposed the placer hoax near Lander, in Wyoming, in which the late Thomas Greenough lost a quarter of a million dollars. Mr. Neill used to be millman for Finch & Campbell, of Spokane, and he found the Kendall mine for them. More power to his pick!

THE letter on 'The Engineer and Public Welfare', appearing in this issue, will be read sympathetically by many of our readers, even if they have not the added interest arising from a personal acquaintance with the writer, Mr. W. F. Staunton. We agree with him that the awakening interest in the welfare of the workers in the mining and metallurgical industries is one of the signs of the times, and the part played by members of our profession in steering that interest into beneficent activity is most gratifying, yet not without a realization of the comparative smallness of the effort and the relative paucity of the results. There is need, as Mr. Staunton insists, for a widespread teaching of the elementary principles of economics, lacking which idealists and visionaries are heard today when they propose schemes just as impossible as that of causing water to flow up-hill without mechanical aid or of making 2 and 2 into 5. We agree with our correspondent that individual freedom in a community is incompatible with lawlessness. For ourselves we would say that an honest policeman is the noblest work of man; to us he symbolizes the one thing that stands between us and the jungle; to us he, as the embodiment of law and order, is more deserving of respect than any king, potentate, and most presidents. The spectacle of the four representatives of the railroad brotherhoods sitting, watch in hand, to threaten the American Congress in a matter of legislation was intolerable: it was just as abominable as a British king sending grenadiers to overawe parliament or a French monarch placing his imperial guard at the doors of the legislative chamber. It was a hold-up, worthy of early days at Bodie or Tombstone. Yes, unionism and collective bargaining have come to stay, just as the collective enterprise of the corporation has become an established means of organizing capital for the purpose of business; but the trade-union should include all the men on the payroll, except the staff, of course; it should not exclude the quiet and more thoughtful men, the very ones most needed to give the right impulse to a legitimate effort at class betterment. In all this work the engineer should play his part; he stands between the predatory elements at both ends of society, the plutocracy and the proletariat; he has the mental training, and, let us hope, the character, fitting him to deal justly with the conflicting elements in a highly industrialized community. We thank Mr. Staunton for his thoughtful letter.

OUR State Legislature has been considering the enactment of a law that will restrict the tipping system by preventing the passing of the tip to a contractor or other employer. The idea is that the gratuity shall be personal and that the system shall not be exploited by employers. We approve of this as a step toward checking a miserable practice. When you redeem your hat for 10 cents at the restaurant your little fee does not go to the receiver, but to somebody back of him or her: somebody who has bought the privilege of preying upon you and the like of you. Under these conditions, the act of tipping, undemocratic as it is, is not justified by being a courtesy or kindness between two persons, it is merely a bit of graft—an imposition to which you succumb because you value your digestion too much to make a protest, either silent or noisy. indeed the whole tipping system is objectionable, unnecessary, and undemocratic. It is objectionable because it has become a bribe, implicit or understood, paid for service that should be included in the payment made by the purchaser. If you dine at a restaurant, you pay enough to cover good service; if you pay more, the proprietor deducts that much from the waiter's wages. The payer does not even get the benefit of a bribe, for, whether the service be good or bad, the force of custom impels him to leave a tip on the table. It is unnecessary because it has ceased to function as a means of obtaining good service; the victim is committed to the tip as soon as he sits down, and he will not withhold it even if he is badly served. On the Pullman dining-car the colored waiter will not say 'Thank you' unless you give him a tip equal to half the cost of your meal; the tip is merely a part of his regular pay, and, knowing it, you tip him however poor the attention he may have given you. Any traveler will have noted—as we have noted many times—the negro waiter's attitude to ladies giving a small order and likely to give a small tip; the present writer has seen a negro reject a 15-cent tip on a Boston-New York express train when offered by a gentlewoman of the school-teacher type. The system is undemocratic because it is based upon the idea of one man obtaining better service than another; it encourages the gross power of money. In clubs, tipping is prohibited, because it is inconsistent with the social spirit, that is, the desire to consider the rights of others. It is undemocratic because no democrat should ask another to do that which would demean him in his own eyes. If you bribe a man you demean him in your estimation; the fact that the bribe involves the payment of an insignificant amount does not alter the character of the transaction. In Europe tipping may have its place because there people are willing to demean themselves before those socially their superiors; the true democrat knows no superior, and no inferior.

Misinformation

Of late many of us have become keenly aware of difficulty in obtaining the correct information requisite for intelligent opinions. A great crisis in human history is evident; we want to know what is being done to meet it and to guide it for the benefit of our own country first and for that of the world in general; but we have not the data on which to proceed to an intelligent understanding of events, particularly those happening at Paris, where the leaders of the nations are now assembled in solemn conclave. For instance, we had concluded that Mr. Frank H. Simonds, of the New York 'Tribune', was a trustworthy informant; his articles during the War had been, in the main, both accurate and interesting; we read everything of his that we could, believing him to be one of the few writers whose hand was not only directed by talent but disciplined by conscience. Our confidence is now shattered. On April 4 we read in his dispatch dated April 2: "The League of Nations is dead. All chance of a real settlement of European problems is at an end." He proceeded to say that all the smaller nationalities are to be sacrificed to the placation of Germany; France is to be compelled to forego compensation, reparation, and defence against her old enemy. "We are sacrificing France on the west to the Germans. We are abandoning the small peoples of eastern Europe to the Bolshevists now, and to the Germans hereafter." This was calamitous news, if true; it would have meant eternal dishonour to England and to the United States; it would have stultified President Wilson. There was the clue to Mr. Simonds' aberration: political prejudice so bitter as to prevent him from seeing straight. A man's prejudices are his own, but he has no right to pose as a faithful chronicler and reviewer of current events if he is to surrender his good judgment to narrow partisanship. On April 6 the daily press published another dispatch also dated April 2 from Mr. Simonds, in which he discussed the fate of Poland, Czecho-Slovakia, Jugo-Slavia, and Rumania as if the Peace Conference were able and willing to protect each and all of them from German aggression. "It is seeking," he says, "to combine security with a recognition of the rights of the smaller races." How is the average citizen to reconcile these vagaries of a skilful reporter? Possibly he wrote the dispatch published on April 6 before he wrote the one published on April 4, in which case the public can complain against the stupidity of the editors of the papers in which the dispatches were printed without any explanation. Apart from the contradiction, it is clear that his announcement of the total failure of the Paris Conference was, like that of Mark Twain's death, "greatly exaggerated." At about the same time we learn that the article by Mr. Harold Begbie in the London 'Daily Chronicle' describing an interview with the Kaiser at Amerongen was fiction. On April 3 Mr. William Allen White, in the Hearst papers, asserted that "Lenine has displaced Wilson as director of the conference" at Paris; he suggested that Lenine "may sit actually at the peace table in the flesh, a stronger force than Wilson," and he coupled the name of Senator Lodge with that of the pirate of Petrograd as "the two unwelcome guests at the feast" of Versailles. This is sophomoric rot, yet it will have been read seriously by millions. On the same day the San Francisco 'Chronicle' printed a telegram from a special correspondent whose name we forget—it may have been fictitious—John Henry Tomkins or Charles Thomas Fernitny—saying that the royalist party is showing its head in Germany and there is talk of placing "the Kaiser's brother, Prince Henry of Battenburg" on the throne. This reminds us of a note, in the 'Bulletin', explaining that the Pyramids is a range of mountains between France and Spain, and one in the 'Call' saying that the British had landed a force on the Isle of Lemons. What is our friend the average citizen to do under these circumstances? The anonymous blunders of the daily press are bad enough, but when writers of reputation, men we have learned to respect as trustworthy, like Messrs. Simonds, Begbie, and White, send signed articles exhibiting the crudest partisanship and a plain lack of moral principle, have we not a right to protest? Journalism is a poor thing when it is without conscience and without honor; it is also a highly dangerous instrument in a democracy, in which it plays so large a part as a means of information and education. Why endow universities richly and lavishly by the score and then allow, for example, one non-moral citizen to distribute misinformation and miseducation by means of a dozen newspapers and magazines? Three or four years are spent at the university, thirty or forty years are spent under the teaching of the daily newspaper.

The World's Gold Production

The principal gold-producing countries have now published the statistics of last year's production, so that a comparison with 1917 is possible. As our readers are aware, the annual statistics of the world's yield of gold are always incomplete, because most of the minor contributors either publish no figures or announce them two or three years late. Fortunately much the larger part of the world's output comes from the English-speaking countries, which furnish prompt and trustworthy data on

	1918	1917	1916
Africa:			
*Congo, Madagascar, etc.	$3,200,000	$3,420,000	$3,673,700
Rhodesia	12,862,000	17,245,000	19,232,200
Transvaal	173,479,000	186,503,400	192,182,000
West Africa	6,467,900	7,445,600	7,860,100
Total	$196,008,900	$214,614,000	$222,948,000
Asia:			
*China, etc.	4,500,000	5,035,400	4,495,400
*East Indies	2,500,000	2,818,000	3,000,000
India	10,029,000	10,756,800	11,206,500
Japan and Korea	8,500,000	9,006,200	9,308,000
Total	$25,529,000	$27,606,400	$28,009,900
Australasia, total	29,800,000	35,945,400	40,475,800
*Central America, total	3,000,000	3,122,000	3,517,600
Europe:			
*France, etc.	1,000,000	1,717,000	2,019,900
*Russia and Siberia	10,000,000	18,000,000	22,500,000
Total	$11,000,000	$19,717,000	$24,519,900
North America:			
Canada	$14,687,000	$15,200,000	$19,235,000
*Mexico	10,000,000	9,000,000	7,690,700
United States	68,493,500	83,750,700	92,590,300
Total	$93,180,500	$107,950,700	$119,516,000
*South America, total	$14,000,000	$14,634,600	$15,188,400
Grand total	$372,518,400	$423,590,200	$454,176,500

the subject. We give a statement compiled from various sources, those that are estimated being marked with an asterisk. For 1916 and 1917 we quote the statistics published by the United States Mint. After making allowance for errors, especially in the figures for Russia and South America, the fact remains that the world's production of gold in 1918 decreased $51,000,000, equivalent to 12%, as compared with 1917, which, in turn, showed a decrease of $31,000,000, equivalent to 7%, as compared with 1916. In two years, therefore, the decline is measured by $82,000,000, or 18%. Revolution, war, and pestilence have played havoc with a basic industry. The full effects of the Mexican revolution are not evident in the figures for the last three years, because that factor came into play after 1911, when gold to the value of $31,000,000 was produced. The El Oro district used to contribute a quarter of this handsome total, but in recent years the gold-mining industry of Mexico has been stagnant, with flickering signs of revival during 1918. The revolution in Russia is accountable for the big decrease since 1916, the figures for last year being a guess. The Lenskoie, Orsk, and other important mines were not much affected by the Bolshevist outbreak. A great deal of gold is stolen from the Siberian mines and is taken into China, but whether minted there or in Russia, it becomes part of the world's stock of the standard metal. In Australasia the decline has been almost continuous during the last ten years: in 1903 the output was worth $89,206,000, and in that year Western Australia alone yielded $41,296,000. In the United States the peak of production was reached in 1915, when the output was worth $101,037,700. That was also the year of the world's maximum output, thanks largely to the Transvaal. The final figures for the United States are likely to be less than the latest estimate. The European production is small but interesting, because it comes from the oldest mining districts in the world, from Gaul, Dacia, and the Ural, chiefly the last. The War, of course, checked operations in these parts: it affected the production of gold everywhere, by decreasing the supply of labor, by increasing the cost of supplies, and by hindering the erection of plant. In the last quarter of 1918 the epidemic of influenza, decimated the labor supply, on the Rand especially, but in other districts as well. Besides these abnormal interruptions to gold mining we must reckon with the gradual impoverishment of mines, particularly in Alaska, Colorado, and Western Australia, but also in the Yukon, Victoria, West Africa, and, more especially, the Rand, which is still much the most productive of the world's goldfields, yielding 46% of the grand total. In truth, it is surprising, considering all the adverse conditions, that the world's output of gold has not suffered more, and this is due to the continued vitality of the industry, although no great discoveries have been made in the last two or three years, nothing comparable with those of Cripple Creek in 1893, of Kalgoorlie in 1896, of the Yukon in 1898, or of Goldfield in 1906. Nevertheless, single orebodies, enriching individual mines, have been discovered in many localities, and important finds and developments have been made, for example, in the East Rand, British Columbia, Ontario, Nevada, Arizona, Mexico, and Korea. The world produced less gold in 1918 than in any year since 1904, but we believe that the signs are propitious for an improvement. Of the total output in 1918, 18.4% came from the United States and 66% from the British dominions, so that over 84% came from the English-speaking countries. Another method of segregation may be based upon the alignment of the nations in the Great War. Mr. Hennen Jennings showed that in 1913 the Allies produced 91.3%, the Neutrals 8.1%, and the Central Powers only 0.6%. The comparison is complicated now by Russia's dubious standing, but it is noteworthy that the Germanic countries now depend almost entirely on Transylvania for their domestic gold, and that amounts to barely 0.5% of the world's production.

The War Minerals Relief Act

Rumor says that the Department of the Interior is likely to interpret the War Minerals Relief law to mean that claimants for compensation must demonstrate personal solicitation by Government agencies as a condition precedent to establishing a valid claim. It is a fact that an amendment to the Bill was offered in Congress providing for just that limitation, but it was insisted by the sponsors of the relief measure that the result would be to exclude a large number of honest claims, because the requests of the Government for the intensive production of war minerals were general, and did not constitute personal appeals. The limitation was removed, and the debates in Congress, as reported in the Congressional Record, will show that this restriction was duly considered and rejected. Therefore such an interpretation of the law is not in accord with the terms of the Act and suggests a breach of good faith such as calls for strong reprobation. It is said, by one not without authority, that these war demands for production were no different in principle from notices calling attention to opportunities for production to meet a market demand at any time, even before the War; but to this we demur unhesitatingly. The Department will incur just criticism unless it construes the Act liberally and in accord with its intent. If such a narrow interpretation is given to it, the question will certainly come before the courts and provoke bitter litigation. Although the Act affirms that the decision of the Secretary shall be conclusive and final, that proviso relates to his adjudication of "adjustments and payments in each case"; it has nothing to do with the interpretation of the Act, which is open to review in the courts, since such a right is secured to the people by the Constitution; it is not inhibited in this Act and cannot be inhibited by any act of Congress. The Act itself places a limitation upon the finality of the Secretary's decision in the matter, since the Government is specifically not barred from a review of any case arising under this law by any agency of the Government or by a Congressional committee. The rights of claimants are safeguarded in this measure and it will be most unfortunate if litigation is invited by a wrong interpretation of the Act. The one sharp limitation is that any claim to have standing before the Department must be filed within three months, that is, before June 2. On page 407 of our issue of March 22 we published the regulations and on page 445 of our issue of April 5 we stated that the requisite questionnaires can be obtained by writing to the War Minerals Relief Commission, whose address is Suite 2131, Department of the Interior building, Washington, D. C. The commission appointed to take charge of the payments due under the Act are Senator J. F. Shafroth of Colorado, Mr. Philip N. Moore of St. Louis, and Dr. M. D. Foster, formerly Representative from Illinois.

Flotation Patents

The Editor:

Sir—Sunday and waiting for a train is my excuse for making you my victim. I have just finished reading your interesting article in regard to the Wolf patent in your issue of the 22nd instant. Twenty-five years of experience as a lawyer before the Federal Courts have taught me not to assume that the Court is wholly devoid of intelligence, and that same experience leads me to the conclusion that little is to be expected from the Butte & Superior case. The courts are bound by the law, which includes the rules of practice. Such law, and it is the only one that can be safely admitted, requires the Court to act solely "upon the record before it"—and therefore the Court is not to be blamed for a decision based upon partial or erroneous information, if that is the record before it.

In the famous Hyde case, the "three errors" which constitute the support of the throne now graced by our Minerals Separation friends, namely, "agitation greater than," "froth so different from," and the "critical" quantity of oil were the points in controversy. The Butte & Superior was operating, or at least trying the case, on the theory that this 'trinity' was essential. Had the Court been shown that the 'agitation' and 'permanent froth' were non-essentials, and then had been invited to focus its attention on the alleged 'critical' quantity of oil, and had been advised that Wolf, Elmore, and others had patents covering froth produced by the 'critical' quantity of oil, the decision rendered might have been less obscure.

Coming back to the present appeal by the Minerals Separation v. Butte & Superior: as I recall the facts published by your magazine at the time, the appellee is bound by the 'law' as announced in the Hyde case—the parties being the same—and it admits that it used the sacred 'trinity', *plus*—that "plus" being oil above the 'critical' point, by reason of which (this plus) they asked to be held not to be violators of the rights of the Minerals Separation company.

Said record shows that two pounds of the 'emulsifying' and 'gathering' oils would do the work, and no good reason or excuse was given for the addition of 18 pounds more—and it can reasonably be said that such additional oil was less valuable than so much water, and that its presence was mere camouflage to get away from the 'critical' point in the Hyde case—however erroneous—the law as between parties. Now—giving the Court credit for having some intelligence and reasoning ability—what is it going to say? Taking the Butte & Superior position: The soused gentleman might say, "Yes, I get drunk on two drinks, but in this instance I took twenty; I, therefore, am not drunk."

Let a case be brought where the mining company does not use agitation, does not make a 'different' froth, and follows the methods within the claims of Wolf and Elmore, when the parties are not bound by 'the law of the case,' but are new-comers before the Court—not bound by the Hyde case—and give the Court a chance to hear and decide the matter on its merits, and you may get something understandable at least.

A. L. BEARDSLEY.

En Route, March 23.

The Engineer and Public Welfare

The Editor:

Sir—One of the striking lessons of the War has been a realization of the increasing dependence of civilization upon the engineer. Engineering genius, already appreciated as the mainspring of material progress, is seen also to have been absolutely necessary to the preservation of our ideals of democracy in the world. It has become apparent that the training in clear exact thought coming from technical education, constant contact and familiarity with the fundamental laws of Nature, and the diverse nature of engineering activities in all parts of the world, have given to the engineer a broad outlook upon the problems of society that makes his judgment particularly valuabe in questions of social organization. In the vital new problems everywhere pressing for solution, not alone in a physical sense but in the broad, economic, and humanitarian principles also involved, it is a welcome fact that the engineer is becoming increasingly active. The drift of thought toward social problems and the helpful spirit shown by giving such thought publicity in recent public utterances is reassuring; and engineers who, like J. Parke Channing in 'Man Power'; J. F. Kemp in 'The Human Side of Mining Engineering'; and T. A. Rickard in numerous editorials, have done a service of the greatest value. To these, we could all add the titles of many more articles brimming with uplifting thoughts on the great problems now before the world, showing that engineers as well as others must take an increasingly active part, and quickly, in the reconstruction and operation of the social machine if our country is to maintain its influential place in the world; perhaps one could go further and say, if it is to avoid disaster from trying working-scale experiments which an elementary knowledge of history and economics should prevent. But we listen, or read and agree, just as we do when we go to church, without doing anything practical, and it is feared that many of us slide back into our habitual grooves, leaving 'George' to do the rest; and yet we have before us problems compared with which going to war may prove to have been easy. There will be no flags, bands, and uniforms, as stimuli, nor the exuberant appropriation of billions to accomplish results regardless of cost. Economic laws, so lately suspended, will again be in full operation. Efficiency of labor, which, owing to the prodigious market that has existed, and the necessity of getting things quickly regardless of cost, has declined alarmingly here, but has, on the other hand, increased abroad; a production per man of ten times the pre-war rate having been reached in some lines according to eminent authority. A severe jolt to our complacent boast of superiority seems unavoidable when normal competition returns.

What, in a practical way, are we going to do about it? What is the solution of the problem? It is education; but not that sort that comes to the mind of the school-trained man when the word is used; not a vision of books and apparatus, but rather a knowledge of those simple, homely, historic, economic, ethic truths that man in his painful upward progress has again and again verified by the ghastly failure of experiments which this generation seems now about to repeat. Education is the key-note of Secretary Lane's 'Americanization'; but even in that masterly appeal one can wish for more emphasis on the elemental principles. The English language should be first, of course, for those ignorant of it, but after that, as between imparting the power given by the 'three R's', to be exercised in absorbing poisonous misinformation from the yellow press and reckless propaganda in general, and a knowledge of how to think clearly on the problems of everyday life, the latter is preferable; but there is no good reason for not having both.

It is a common experience that not many, even of the fairly enlightened people one meets, can give a clear and logical explanation of capital; what it really is, its origin, its benefit to all, laborers included; and why it is necessary for any material progress whether under individualism, socialism, or any other ism. So, in regard to what is possible in the long run in the payment of wages; that the market value of the things produced sets an absolute limit to them; that no legislation or strikes can change this condition, notwithstanding that an occasional professor arises to testify that the basis of minimum wages should be made by law the cost of a comfortable living, a condition we would surely all welcome, if true. But the place man is making for himself in the universe is an artificial one, and is maintained only by his successful struggle to re-direct forces tending otherwise, and it is success in this struggle, and consciousness of ability to succeed, that gives man's intelligence its god-like potentiality, that develops his strength, and supports the hope of progress. So the elementary idea should be taught that the things worth having, even those altruistic in character, are only the rewards of effort of muscle and of brain, and not within the power of legislatures or unions to bestow.

The conception of freedom, too, needs clarifying. The more we hear of it lately the less there seems to be. There is none when the laws guaranteeing a man protection from violence in the pursuit of his ordinary vocations are a dead letter, and when his head may be broken with impunity or approval if he fails to join a particular organization, which he does not want to join, for possibly very good reasons of his own. What unjust strike could succeed if unlawful violence were made impossible? The spectacle of four men forcing the American Congress to pass a law under direct threat of starvation to innocent millions by paralyzing the railroads, is not an indication of freedom regardless of the merits of the law. The unions and collective bargaining have come to stay; their justification is their undoubted improvement in the workers' economic status. As their potentiality for good is tremendous, so it may be also for harm, to the workers themselves and to society in general. The result of their unrestrained development needs no prediction. Fighting the abuse of their advancing arbitrary power and its inevitable train of needlessly repeated experimentation by the exercise of another arbitrary power is unintelligent, and enlightenment by education in the fundamentals of economics and ethics is the only way in which these agencies can be dealt with effectively; that is, by preserving the good and eliminating the evil. It is not too much to hope that some day membership in good standing in a trade union will be a guaranty of ability and integrity instead of a danger signal.

The practical wisdom (aside from any other cause) of a system of ethics should be made plain, and the fact that theists of all kinds, agnostics, atheists, even pagans, and probably Germans now, appreciate, and, in their hearts and minds, really believe in the essential truth of the broad principles of morality taught by Christ, and that the most rapid development of the human race, not alone in material things but also in the average of individual well-being and happiness, is coincident with the Christian era. A part at least of the unrest at the bottom of much of the present turmoil is doubtless due to the fading away of old religious beliefs without the substitution of other guides. With the disappearance of the blind acceptance of constituted authority, physical and moral, which we have seen everywhere, has come the dawn of an attempt to analyze the situation without the guide of historical or economic knowledge. We can imagine a new Russian thinking: "I find myself here on this planet wholly without my consent. I see others around me with far more of the things that might make life pleasant; indeed the sole occupation of many seems to be to devise new means of enjoyment, while I slave on a pittance. To be sure, they say that rules have been made permitting this condition, but I did not agree to these rules, and it even appears that they were made by people most of whom are now dead, and that they are perpetuated and revised by a small minority of those now here, the others not bothering to express themselves one way or another. I decline to recognize these rules, and I am going to get what I want in any way I can. The game has evidently been 'rigged' by a lot of people who happened to be here first, and I don't propose to stand for it.'' Perhaps not many have formulated the proposition in a manner so raw as this, but there is little doubt of the growth of some such feeling, and nothing but education can combat it. Fortunately, the kind of education needed is elementary in the extreme and not of a kind requiring much time or study. We can all be teachers in such a school; but in this as in other things in this world, the same old competitive system on which everything is planned is still in operation, and we have formidable competitors. Since the growth of conscious power from organization, which has come largely within the life-time of many of us, we have been forcibly reminded that great mental ability is quite compatible with moral obliquity, and that such mental ability can be hired for unworthy purposes. Many of the organizations we shall have to deal with are possessed of abundant financial means, and with their great numerical memberships can, and do, accumulate formidable sums from trifling individual payments, which sums constitute an irresistible temptation to brilliant but unscrupulous minds. Also, we have the venal yellow press, where control by one vicious mind permits feeding mental poison to millions. These are the worms at the root. Many people have acquired their whole education among the branches and twigs of the tree of knowledge, and know nothing about the roots and the trunk at which a busy little worm may be conducting operations, the effects of which they see among the leaves and try to combat with futile local treatment. J. R. Finlay has the happy faculty of going to the foundation of things and building thereon structures in which one cannot help feeling confidence. His 'Reorganization not Reconstruction' is a delight to one who believes in beginning at the beginning, in setting up as he does a row of axioms and building his argument firmly thereon. It is something like that which the enlightened people of the world must do to steady the structure of civilization. We must get down to the foundations and make them secure; patching the cracks afterward. Fixing foundations is pre-eminently an engineering job. It must be done by enlightening propaganda, elementary education, pounded into every crack and crevice that can be found, and, judging by the startling manifestations daily witnessed here, there, and everywhere throughout the world, there is no time to lose.

In olden times, ideas traveled slowly but today they are flashed to every corner of the world. That good ones can be spread quickly and that they will take effect with marvelous results, is shown by looking back at Mr. Hoover's work in food conservation, where a few simple, vital facts, spread like wildfire, found ready acceptance, accomplished the apparently impossible, and prevented the loss of the War, already privately conceded by Lord Rhondda on account of the supposed inevitable failure of the food-supply. Something like that can be done in back-firing against this social conflagration. This country is full of organizations. There are clubs and societies by the thousand, for this, that, and the other thing, but most of them in eager search for a really interesting object, notwithstanding their titles. They overlap and their members touch elbows constantly. They are mostly composed of rather enlightened people, employers of others in large and small degree, in the aggregate very numerous, their members move about so as to increase the points of contact to a degree that would make the spreading of propaganda well nigh perfect. They constitute a possible means of combating social heresies that could be of great value. At a recent meeting of one of the national engineering societies a letter from one of the members was read covering suggestions as to what subjects of discussion might assist in the necessary readjustments, and among his suggestions is "educating the workmen in economics." He said he believed that the society "should devote a large part of its discussions to the ascertainment of the best means of educating men along these and similar lines." This suggestion should be acted upon by all of us, but without waiting for discussion we should begin forthwith to preach the doctrines of social sanity as taught by history and common sense wherever an audience is found, with an eye particularly to getting similar missionary work done by the membership of such clubs and societies as we belong to, so that a beginning may be made, somewhat in chain-letter fashion, in furthering this important work, the most important by far before the world today. Let discussion follow by all means, and it is to be hoped that it will result in formulating something like a set of Mr. Finlay's axioms, with a superstructure of simple but definite conclusions on the vital economic questions, which can be used as propaganda in the way suggested or in some better way that may develop.

W. F. Staunton.

Los Angeles, California, February 12.

Cost of Mining Silver

The La Rose mine at Cobalt, Ontario, yielded 4,092,667 oz. of silver in 1911, but only 276,131 oz. in 1918, making a total of 24,484,053 oz. since 1907. Last year the mill treated 36,612 tons of ore, averaging 7.71 oz. per ton. The average price received was 99.83 cents per ounce, and the cost was 87.17 cents, details of which follow:

	Cents per oz.
Mine operation	47.61
Milling	32.49
Marketing	10.44
Depreciation	2.19
General	2.13
Total	94.86
Less sundry income	7.69
Net cost	87.17

The Prevention of Misfires

By GRANT H. TOD

From time to time articles appear in various technical journals concerning the causes of misfires, and many writers offer novel cure-alls for this old and annoying feature of blasting. The bulk of the blame is usually attributed to defective material, without serious thought being given to the careful selection, preparation, and use of explosives and accessories, and other important contributing factors. The cost of mining being a matter of the highest importance it appears well to investigate this subject from a practical standpoint, attempting to show the underlying causes and offering for approval some remedies that have already proved their value.

Unsuitable material is likely to be selected. Powders are used whose composition is entirely unsuited for the work. Caps too low in strength are chosen, and fuse is purchased for its price, without regard to its construction. A simple remedy for such conditions would be a letter to your powder company, giving an accurate description of the work to be performed. This would elicit reliable information, and, if circumstances warranted, a visit from one of their competent engineers.

All explosives demand dry storage. This means that, with few exceptions, underground storage is undesirable. It has been proved that powder, caps, or fuse sent into a mine a short time before use give the best results. The inconvenience and slight loss of time occasioned by using the haulage-motor or cage for this purpose is more than compensated in the decreased number of missed holes.

Probably the most fruitful source of misfires is the careless preparation of cap and fuse. The base of this trouble is at the mine or quarry, not at the factory. The remedy is as follows: Avoid any chance for wet fuse ends by cutting off a quarter of an inch from all fuse that has been exposed to air for any length of time. Cut the fuse squarely across, with a clean sharp instrument, insert it into the barrel of the cap until it comes in light contact with the fulminate, and, holding it firmly in this position, crimp with a broad-jawed crimper. It is well to remember that an unfilled air-space in a cap-barrel, after the fuse has been inserted, is an invitation for trouble. Of all operations where results justify a little extra care, none exceeds in importance the correct preparation of cap and fuse when forming them into a primer.

With electric exploders the most common cause of misfires is the practice of putting the exploder into the side of a cartridge and securing it by a half-hitch. This practice has a tendency to chafe the wire insulation and leave the wires in short circuit, or allowing water to get in and complete the short circuit. The rough handling of the tamping-bar will, at times, crush the sulphur plug and let water get to the cap.

The use of the following unsuitable materials to exclude water from a capped fuse should be avoided: axle-grease, engine-compound, oils of any kind, cable-dressing, electrical varnishes and paints containing solvents of the fuse-varnish. In place of these use P. & B. roofing paint, tar, paraffin-wax, or one of the preparations specially put on the market, by fuse manufacturers for this purpose.

Atmospheric conditions and systems of ventilation have a decided bearing on the subject. Where humidity is great and mine currents are sluggish there is a marked increase in missed holes where powder, caps, or fuse are stored in underground magazines or where these materials are allowed to remain in open containers, in the mine, for any length of time. A remedy is to cut and cap all the fuse at a central station, on the surface, and to send underground only sufficient quantities of capped fuse to last 72 hours, and likewise to limit the powder supply to practically immediate needs.

Exposed fuse-ends protruding from bore-holes must be protected from flying rock when blasting. This can be accomplished by coiling the fuse-end in the collar of the hole in such a manner that only enough remains in sight to ensure an easy 'spit'.

Where mine-pumps have to be lined with bronze to resist acid water the mine superintendent should realize that all fuse is not resistant to acid. It is suggested that a good tape-covered fuse will prevent many missed holes.

Failure to supply the miners with proper appliances to 'spit' the fuse is another cause of missed holes. Carbide lamps, now in common use, hot irons, and a newly marketed device, named the 'lead-spitter' are efficient. The lead-spitter is by a long way the best for the reason that water in any quantity cannot quench it.

The improper spacing of holes drilled in close proximity causes many a missed hole. Investigation underground disclosed that in wet ground the holes most frequently missing were 'lifters' in drifts and cross-cuts and in corner holes in shafts and winzes. It has been demonstrated that the reason for this was the small amount of ground left. As such holes are wet in nearly every instance it was found that the bursting of the hole immediately next them drove the water laterally through the fuse or delay-exploder in the hole that mis-fired, saturating them to a point that they could not perform their function of carrying fire to the cap. The remedy for this kind of misfires is closer attention to the spacing of the holes. The introduction of drills using water, in mines where the ground would be considered dry, necessitates precautions considered sensible in wet ground.

A cause of misfires not generally recognized is the sweep of air returning during blasting operations. This causes portions of the powder-charge in untamped holes to be thrown from the hole, including the primers. In wet holes the force of the returning air has, on occasion, been found great enough to displace the sulphur plug in an exploder and to saturate the powder and fuse with water, thereby destroying their usefulness.

Rough sharp rock when used for tamping may lead to misfires, and in instances where a steel-drill or a bar is used as a tamping-rod the hazard is likewise increased.

The League of Nations and the Covenant

By C. IRVING WRIGHT

The 'covenant' of the Paris Conference is not a treaty; if executed, it will constitute a new government of the world. Neither the President nor the Senate, nor both combined, have been given authority to represent the States, or the people of the United States, in the formation of a new government.

The attempt is made to persuade us that there is no real difference between the covenant and a treaty; it is said that many treaties impair, to a certain extent, the national independence of action, the sovereignty, of the high contracting parties. The analogy is specious; it captures the imagination even of intelligent men; but it is not true. Treaties, far from impairing sovereignty, involve the exercise of the highest right and power of a sovereign, the right and power to deal freely and on terms of equality with other sovereigns. Treaties are gentlemen's agreements, and derive their obligation, according to the universal understanding, solely from interest and good faith; in them is to be found no other compulsion, and they have no further sanction. Their terms are mutually interpreted by the parties and are performed only in accordance with the mutual interpretation; even when they are put to arbitration the award that may be made is enforceable only through free will and consent. No independent nation, it may be surely asserted, has ever seen in any treaty, executed by it, an obligation to submit its neck to the yoke. The very essence of sovereignty is unaccountability to a superior and immunity from control.

It is easy to determine whether the covenant is a treaty, or whether it constitutes a government to which the nations signing it will subject themselves. No nation in history has ever been troubled by difficulties of logic in distinguishing between the freedom that accompanies treaties and the control that follows subjection. With regard to this real and vital distinction, the common sense of the country, despite the propagandists, the gynagogues, and the special pleaders, is beginning to assert itself. Patriots like Mr. Taft, even though at first they may have misapprehended the nature of the document, are now calling for amendment. There is firm ground for faith that the truth can be made to appear before it is too late.

To reconcile the covenant with the Constitution, Mr. Taft is compelled to argue that future Congresses would still have authority to give it an American interpretation and to disregard any conflicting construction put upon it by the League. He says, however, that the exercise of this authority would be gravely dishonorable, and cases can easily be conceived of American interpretation and action that, under Art. XVI, would "*ipso facto* be deemed * * * an act of war against all the other members of the League." The foundations of our dishonor are being deeply laid, for in a war arising out of insistence upon our own views, we would be ostracized, outlawed, and treated, like the Hun, as having shocked the moral sense of mankind.

Already the differences of interpretation are bitter and momentous. Mr. Taft will not be the official interpreter of the instrument; nor will eminent Senators; nor the Senate; nor Congress; nor, indeed, the whole People. The document, once executed, creates irresponsible and uncontrollable super-national tribunals, which alone will have authority to determine its scope and meaning, and which are provided with well-nigh universal power to enforce decisions.

To attempt to forecast the decisions that will be made is futile, for the human mind is quite incapable of foreseeing the cases that will arise during even the next decade. We know, however, that the covenant, like other political instruments, will be construed more broadly year by year. This law, that power grows by exercise, is recognized by the official organ of the American Federation of Labor, which says that the League will inevitably grow in power, and will tend to treat every question from the international aspect, and that in this process national forces, such as labor and individual lives, are bound to be affected by its decisions. Indeed, as Mr. Wilson accurately says, "There is no subject that may touch the peace of the world that is exempt from inquiry and discussion."

"Inquiry and discussion?" Yes, and effectual action, too. By Art. XI, "the high contracting parties reserve the right to take *any* action that may be deemed wise and effectual to safeguard the peace of nations." "Any action," means action legislative, judicial, and executive; action without restraint or limit. Who would attempt to enumerate the categories of subjects which "any" action may rationally be deemed to include?

So, too, examine Art. XX by which the nations covenant "to endeavor to secure and maintain fair and humane conditions of labor for men, women, and children both in their own countries and in all countries to which their commercial and industrial relations extend." Equal wages throughout the world may be the League's interpretation of "fair" conditions of labor. Already the Commission on International Labor Legislation has issued a report, which, as the 'Christian Science Monitor' says (March 5), "is of a far-reaching nature and, if adopted by the Conference, will change, as is already being remarked, the whole aspect not only of the labor problem in the countries of the world, but will also relieve the export trade difficulties, which are dangerously and continually enhanced by higher wage and shorter hour demands." A code of labor legislation is proposed, with punishable offenses. Mr. Taft's argument that America has the right, under the covenant, to prohibit or to regulate Chinese or Japanese immigration, to discriminate against one nation and in favor of others, to insult the dignity and self-respect of a powerful race, is punctured, bubble that it is, by the provision in that code that no nation shall prohibit immigration or emigration except temporarily in periods of economic depression or for the protection of public health. It matters not what the Council may now do; the power to consider and decide now is the power to consider and decide otherwise in the future. Immigration is not, therefore, a "domestic" affair as Mr. Taft supposes; and the League is proving its power by acting.

What, then, is "domestic"? The tariff?

The super-national tribunal may decide, and there are many respectable thinkers in Europe now propagating the conviction that a chief cause of war is to be found in economic barriers. In Mr. Wilson's view, therefore, the import duties of the respective nations are open to "in-inquiry and discussion," and under Art. XI they are a proper subject of "effectual action." Free trade throughout the world may be decreed and enforced; and, since it is universally established that the power to accomplish a result carries with it all incidental powers deemed necessary or expedient as means to the end, the League may order destroyed all books that preach the peace-disturbing doctrine of protection: moreover, the arrest and imprisonment of men who speak or write in opposition to the edict may be commanded. This is only an example. Let there be no mistake, the powers that the League determines to exercise, it can, and will, in its own good time, exercise to the full; no restraints, verbal or of principle, are provided.

Eminent students of political science, and of the American Constitution, construe the covenant and hold that to ratify it, as it is now framed, would be to violate the most fundamental provisions of our institutions and organic law. Thus, it would not bind the United States (Geofroy v. Riggs, 133 U. S., 258). On the other hand, many of those who favor a league regardless of all things except their passionate hope that war will thereupon vanish from the earth, reply by themselves putting a contrary construction upon the instrument, or by saying that they do not think the fear is well-founded. With all respect to the eminence of the controversialists, it is submitted that the question of the constitutionality of the covenant probes much deeper than guesses as to what the document may ultimately be determined to mean. If its constitutionality depends upon the interpretation that may be given it by the League, then the President and the Senate cannot know whether they are exceeding their powers until after it has been ratified and has been interpreted in practice.

The very reason why the covenant is unconstitutional beyond the possibility of rational controversy is that it attempts to bind all succeeding Presidents, Senates, and Congresses, in a word, the United States, to accept whatever interpretation may be put upon it by a super-national tribunal constituted with power to enforce its decrees.

The League may not do one or another of a multitude of things, or the League may now, for strategic reasons, decide to do precisely what it will tomorrow undo. What will be done lies in the womb of fate, and, in any event, is quite beside the question. The loss of sovereignty of the United States, if this covenant be ratified, consists in our having parted with the effective right and power ourselves to resolve for ourselves from time to time, the vital problems that will present themselves for consideration throughout the future. The involved and subtle arguments of special pleaders are not needed to decide this simple question, which can easily be answered by any man who has the natural faculty of reason and who has learned to distinguish fact from fancy. For him there can be no doubt that by the covenant the United States would be parted from its sovereignty, and would henceforth, until a greater war, be bound a satellite of Europe, governed by every pull and push of her interests, and without rightful power to pursue an independent orbit.

Neither the American people, nor the States of the Union, have constituted any body, or delegated any authority, to barter or to give away the national independence. The President has no power to initiate, nor the Senate to ratify, any negotiations of such character. Insofar as the covenant conflicts with specific provisions thereof, the Constitution, if it be deemed expedient, may be amended by the processes provided to that end, but insofar as it is attempted to institute a new government, to create a new sovereign, there is no lawful power in three-quarters of the States, nor in nine-tenths of the States, to deprive an objecting State of its right to be represented in all matters concerning foreign relations or within the jurisdiction of the Senate under the present system. A revolution by force, a *coup d'etat*, may, of course, be effected, if at this juncture, and with the example of Europe before us, it is thought wise to unloose the now orderly forces of American society. But if regard be had to the organic development, and the continuity in history of our institutions, the League of Nations, as it is now framed, or if framed in anything like its present form, can be constituted only by the consent of every State of the Union. (See Geofroy v. Riggs, 133 U. S. 258; Fort Leavenworth R. R. Co. v. Lowe, 114 U. S. 525.) Is it proposed that coercion be employed and that our compact of union be disregarded?

Why, indeed, should New York State not have representation equal to that of Canada; or California equal to that of New Zealand? Unlike the British Dominions and Colonies, which are not now represented in foreign relations, our States, through their Senators, participate directly in foreign affairs; for our Government is federal. Not only in a legal and an historic, but also in a present, and a very real and practical sense, the States retain the right and power to make known and protect their interests, and they cannot be drawn into a new government against their will: neither can the Federal government abdicate its functions or secede.

The United States is of great territorial extent, and its various divisions have important differences of interest. Is Pennsylvania not specially interested in tariffs? Is California not vitally affected by immigration? On what theory can they be denied a hearing, while Canada, New Zealand, New South Wales, Australia, and South Africa gain important rights of representation not theirs before? Mr. Wilson says it is a wonderful thing, the trust that Europe has in America. Why, then, deny us the representation that is commensurate with our population, our wealth, and our extent of territory, and that is required by the structure of the institutions which we have developed in history?

To make "the supreme sacrifice" of our liberties, neither President nor Senate have mandate or authority; they were not elected with that in mind, nor were their offices created with such power. Already it is being propagated by chancelleries of Europe that the treaty of peace would have contained quite different terms had it not been thought that America would ratify the covenant. To this the answer is plain: Let the nations that deal with delegates look to their credentials, and let the words and acts of constituted authorities be compared with the Constitution that created them.

No country will be more prompt to fulfill obligations and to make sacrifices under the covenant than the United States, provided it shall freely and through orderly processes pledge its fealty. But our Sovereign does not reveal himself by intuition to those who feel inspired. He does not express himself by 'voices in the air' that cry out the changing emotions of the shifting mass. Only by diligent searching can his will be ascertained. We are hysterical—he is calm. We are deceived by propaganda—he sees reality. We love our friends and hate our enemies—he knows principles without respect of person. In a word, he is essentially wise and we are essentially foolish. This Sovereign is no other than our common and permanent right mind. Certainly, we cannot, at a given moment of history, completely discover him, but we can make the best humanly possible attempt. We can call into a Constitutional Assembly, to deal with the supreme problems that confront us, the best persons our common action can find, not merely in the Nation, but, as well, by States; for thus the regional divergences of interest will be reconciled, and the law of the structure of our institutions be fulfilled.

MANGANESE DEPOSITS are being worked near the town of San Antonio, Province of Pichincha, Ecuador. The principal orebody is a blanket deposit 3 to 9 ft. thick. The ore resembles gravel in appearance, and assays 46.36% Mn, with a little copper and phosphorus. Silica is only 6.4%. The altitude of the property is 7874 ft., and the district is wholly volcanic, partly covered by sand. Native laborers receive from 20 to 50 cents per 10-hour day. Quito is 28 miles distant. Mule carriage to rail at that place is 68 cents per 220 pounds.

A Device for Flotation Experiments

By WILL H. COGHILL

*In flotation experiments it is desirable to have a small hand-operated device correlating with the larger experimental and commercial machines. This phase of flotation has not been sufficiently developed. It is my purpose to describe a device which is intended to fill this gap.

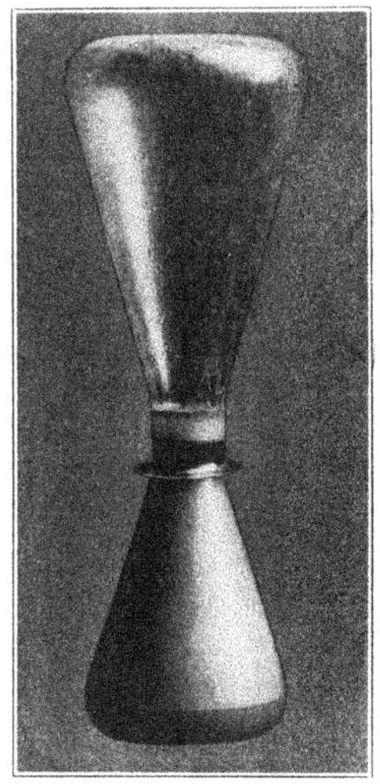

FLASKS USED FOR FLOTATION EXPERIMENTS

Success in designing a machine depends upon the principles selected to govern its detail. The selection of this device was based upon the two factors of pulp-density and ratio of solid to frothing surface. The importance of these factors can best be emphasized by quoting from Del Mar.‡

"Under manipulation may be included the shape or form of the collecting-chamber of the flotation machine, for the cells in any flotation system are used for two purposes, either to float a dirty concentrate, which must be cleaned before marketing, or to float a finished concen-

*Published by permission of the Director of the U. S. Bureau of Mines.

†Algernon Del Mar, 'Differential Flotation of Lead and Zinc Sulphides', M. & S. P., Nov. 23, 1918.

trate, which is ready for shipment. In the former case the collecting chamber of the machine should favor a quick discharge, that is, there should be a narrower chamber, but when we require a finished product the box must be sufficiently wide to allow the settlement of occluded waste or gangue. Manufacturers of flotation machines miss this point and therefore the same machine is often used for roughing and for cleaning, while the two operations require entirely different manipulation. This important structural feature in the flotation-chamber may make the difference between success and failure, for not only must a concentrate be produced, but it must attain a certain grade of metallic content to be fit for shipment."

On observing successful laboratory flotation machines of the mechanical-agitation type we find that when the pulp-density is 3:1, there is from 30 to 60 grammes of ore for every square inch of frothing surface. Let us see now if the test-tube, which was recommended a long while ago, has proportions that are consistent.

Take a test-tube of such a diameter that it gives a frothing area of 0.6 sq. in. The quantity of ore required is then, say, 30 grammes; and for a 3:1 pulp, 90 cc. of water must be added. But the ordinary test-tube of this diameter will hold only 85 cc. of water. It is eight inches long. We see that after making allowances for the volume of ore and air, the test-tube would have to be about a foot long. It is obvious that the adoption of these proportions in such a device would not be consistent. A loaded bubble that chanced to be at the bottom of the tube at the end of the agitation period would have to travel upward a distance of nearly 12 inches against a falling column of froth. Needless to say, it would be wrecked at the outset and buried beneath the column of ore.

Moreover, the test-tube has no facilities for discharging the froth.†

The device recommended here has been used at the North-West station of the U. S. Bureau of Mines at Seattle. It consists of two pyrex flasks, one of 250 cc and the other of 500 cc. capacity. A rubber nipple is placed on the neck of the smaller one, so that when the flaring portion is ground off it will fit snugly into the larger, as shown in the photograph. To prepare a test, the smaller flask is filled with a mixture of ore and water of the desired consistence and emptied into the larger one, after which about three cubic centimetres of water is added. After the desired flotation reagents have been added, a stopper is placed in the flasks and we are ready to proceed with the test.

The procedure of testing is by means of hand agitation for, say, five minutes. The stopper is removed, the flasks are united, and, after a brief agitation, they are placed in the position as shown. The extra three cubic centimetres of water elevates the lower level of the froth so that it will overflow into a collecting-pan when the larger flask is removed. The agitation may be repeated as often as desired by adding a little extra water each time.

The efficiency, of course, is low as compared with the mechanical devices, but the relative floatability of minerals and the relative effects of flotation reagents may be determined quickly. There are two reasons why the efficiency is low: first, there is no opportunity for the froth to build up during the agitation period; second, a small quantity of gangue lodges on the bench formed by the union of the inner and outer tubes, and by joining the overflow reduces the grade of the concentrate.

The quantity of modifying reagents must be determined by calibrated devices; otherwise impressions may be misleading. This is demonstrated by the following example. When four drops of oil was added from a medicine-dropper the pyrite floated so freely that the results were adverse. The dropper was then calibrated, and it was found that four pounds of oil per ton of ore had been used. The test was then repeated with one drop of oil and the results were encouraging.

This device then has three points of advantage over the test-tube: It has convenient discharging facilities; it provides for desirable pulp-densities and a consistent area of frothing surface.

†The separatory funnel recommended by 'A Special Correspondent,' M. & S. P., July 24, 1915, and by O. C. Ralston and Glenn L. Allen, M. & S. P., Jan. 8, 1916, is faulty because the proportions are not good and the froth has to stand until the tailing is removed.

Quebec in 1918

Mineral production of Quebec during 1918, according to Theo. C. Denis, superintendent of mines, was valued at $18,572,595, an increase of 14.72%. There was increased activity in the extraction of the war minerals, and the gain in these over 1913, a pre-war year, was 13.25%. The principal substances were as under:

Product	Quantity	Value
Asbestos, tons	142,375	$9,019,899
Chromite, tons	35,749	770,955
Graphite, pounds	200,583	17,760
Magnesite, tons	28,504	1,016,764
Mica, pounds	882,121	201,055
Molybdenite, pounds	342,298	383,252
Pyrite (including copper ore), tons	125,440	1,319,690

Chromite mining, it is feared, will decline considerably now that the urgency for it is past. An objection to the use of molybdenum is considered to be the irregular supply, but now that the industry is well established this should disappear. The graphite industry was unfortunate, and works were closed a great part of 1918. Good results are reported from flotation of this ore. There are 6125 men employed in the mining industry of Quebec.

Tin production of the Mount Bischoff company in Tasmania cost 7s.4d. ($1.76) per ton of ore mined during the last half of 1918. Mining is from open workings; the ore is carried by aerial trams and electric haulage; crushing is by stamps; concentration is by tables and jigs; and the black tin (oxide) is reduced to 99.87% metal in the company's own smelter. The output in the six months was 310,587 lb. Operations are highly profitable.

Selling: An Art

By CHARLES T. HUTCHINSON

that the War is over, all there is to do is to go out and sell everything we make. How simple it all sounds! What could be easier? Of course, it is generally deemed advisable to sell things at a price that will carry a profit to the seller, but even then, it is still simple. Just add whatever profit you would like to the cost, hire some salesmen, publish some catalogues, advertise, and, in the course of a short time, declare some dividends.

This is the idea that exists, in a more or less nebulous form, in the minds of a lot of people. The advertisements

of various institutions of learning known as 'correspondence schools' depict the science of selling in its simplest form. There is the illustration of our hero, in overalls, with sleeves rolled up over brawny arms, bursting through the front door of his humble dwelling with expressive countenance registering simultaneously joy, pride, and exultation. He is greeted by friend wife with outstretched arms, her expression a reflex of the ditto joy, pride, and exultation. She is clad in apron and the customary other details. She has been preparing the 'pork and', against the homecoming of her liege lord. Two or more, as the case might be, of their offspring are clinging to their mother's apron, gazing with rapt visage upon their dad. It is easy to learn by the illustration that dad has done something big. Then comes the dialogue.

He. Oh, Abigail, what do you suppose has done gone and happened. The Boss called me into his office today, and said "Hector, my boy, entirely without your knowledge, I have had my eye on you these past forty years, and when I saw the lessons from the R. S. V. P. Correspondence Schools sticking out of your trousers pocket, I said to myself, 'Ecce homo', which means that from now on you are no longer a boiler-makers helper, but General Manager of Sales at a salary of umpty-steen bright golden ducats per annum."

She. Hector, my king, my prince! Now I can have a new hat that will make that odious Mrs. Smith green with envy!

Joy, wassail, finis!

Finis, that is where the trouble comes in. It is not disclosed, now that Hector has got the job, whether or not he held the job, and for how long. These advertising stimuli end just like a popular novel, when the hero is married to the job, but whether they both lived together happily forever after is left to the imagination of the reader. Neither 'ad.' nor fiction writer sees romance or poetry in the divorce court.

Without being unduly cynical, we prophesy trouble ahead for Hector, unless his training has been much more varied and comprehensive than that offered by any correspondence school, excellent as many of them undoubtedly are. A correspondence course in selling, or any other course of study through books, is as the ABC's to a Doctor's degree in literature.

Selling involves not merely a mastery of the science of organization, but a profound knowledge of the Book of Life itself, a knowledge that can only be acquired by omnivorous reading, acute observation, and an analytical mind, by which apparently insignificant facts and tendencies of the human race may be dissected, ticketed, labeled, and made to reveal the ideas, desires, and longings of that impossible creature known as the average man, or woman.

Take all of the gainful occupations, compile a mass of statistics out of which may be determined the average compensation per individual for each, and it will be found that the profession of selling—or business of selling, if you like—is the most highly paid of all. Thus is proved by the reductio ad dollar method that selling is the most difficult of them all.

It is not the purpose of this article to enter into a discussion of the minutiae of selling, the methods of organization, the canvassing of the field, the compilation of statistics, the preparation of an advertising campaign, the territorial maps, or the hiring and firing of salesmen. These things constitute the machinery, the plant equipment, the inanimate forces of selling. What are much more interesting are the more delicate shades and factors that influence and often control sales; these are about to be brought under the microscope, so that those who read will understand and sympathize with the problems of the salesman, the difficulty in his making good, and his large and toothsome pay-check if he does.

Jones, the star salesman for the Alpha Beta Manufacturing Company, has just returned from New York. His entry into the office takes upon itself the nature of a triumphal procession. Everybody grins, the proletariat

in the outer office with envy, the Boss himself with congratulation tinged with relief. The strain has been a severe one, even those not in the confidence of the management knew that work in the shop was slack, and that a whole season's output hinged upon the success of Jones' mission, and Jones landed the contract. Now he is home, the contract itself, all signed up by Presidents and Secretaries and things, together with what was most important, a nice fat check for the first payment, are about to be extracted from the well-worn leather brief-case and spread on the mahogany table before the admiring gaze of the Boss.

Let us sneak into the private office before the door is closed and listen to Jones as he reports the intimate details of just how it all happened.

"Now Jonesy, old boy, have a cigar, and sit down and rest yourself for a while," said the Boss with a happy smile. The cigar was produced, from a special box covered with revenue stamps. That was some cigar. "Have a light, Jones. You will find that other chair more comfortable." Jones puffs away for a minute. It is his minute, and he is enjoying it hugely.

"Well, sir," replies our hero, after gazing rumina-

tively at the accumulating ash, "the real history of that interesting typed document which you see before you dates back a good long while. You remember the old yarn about the pig that started the war, and the cow that kicked over the lamp that set fire to Chicago? This par-

ticular job is very much the same sort of thing.

"When that Scotchman came in with the design for

the particular piece of apparatus which is now the backbone of the business, you may remember that the office-boy, like most office-boys, happened to have a grouch, and was just going to tell him that you were not in, or something, when you came out of the office-door and stopped long enough to look at what the Scotchman had, became interested, and the result was that he was given a job in the shop and is now our general superintendent. That little appliance was so good that it is now our best feature. So, you see, that is where this particular contract really started. In other words, if our stuff wasn't right, all the salesmen in the world wouldn't have done one bit of good in this case, or any other.

"Then another thing. You remember that habit of yours, pinning the envelopes on letters after they are opened instead of chucking them in the basket? That is another factor in getting this job. You will see why as the story unfolds.

"A third factor is a bit of elementary psychology, based upon the tendency of the human mind to want something immediately if told that it can't have it.

"The fourth factor is the efficiency of the modern telephone; the fifth lies in the fact that you made me fighting mad with those confounded telegrams of yours; and the sixth, and perhaps the most important one of all, lies in the element of luck, without which we might have been thoroughly licked in spite of ourselves.

"I landed in the big city on time, for a wonder, and, as soon as I had been wafted to my hall-bedroom at the Splitmore, after running the gauntlet of piratical taxi-drivers, door-men in general's uniforms, bell-hops, and other automatic coin-collectors, I sat me down to the writing-desk and wrote a line to the president of the company with whom we had been corresponding to let him know that I was in town and wanted to see him."

"Why didn't you go to see him, or call him on the phone?" asked the Boss.

"Because the only address I had was a post-office box number," replied Jones. "You remember that the property where the stuff is to be used is in Montana, and I hoped that they would have a regular office in the city. A diligent search through the telephone books, and also some sixteen directories didn't help me a bit, so there was only one thing to do, and that was to drop him a line: so I did.

"The next two days slipped by like nothing. I tried to round up some other prospects, but there was nothing doing. The weather was infernally hot, so all the natives who had the price were at the seashore, and those who hadn't didn't interest me at all.

"Then you started those confounded telegrams. How would you like to be sweltering away in a big city, thousands of miles away from home, and doing your darnedest, and then get something like this. 'If you don't land that job, this place will be shut down when you come back', or 'Make a noise like an order or stay in the East permanently'? Maybe you think I wasn't mad. I was determined to land that job or bust, and then wire you to go chase yourself forever, as far as I was concerned. I suppose all you really wanted was to arouse the fighting spirit; anyway, you certainly did."

"You will have to forgive me for the rough stuff, Jones," grinned the Boss. "Anyway, it was good medicine. It worked."

"All right," laughed Jones. "I am so darned good-natured now, that I don't care. But to resume. Two days, three days, and then four days passed, and I didn't hear a single word from him. I kept getting more and more nervous, until finally, one evening I was sitting in my room scratching my head in a vain effort to start an idea of some kind, when I went to my grip and absent-mindedly took out all the correspondence dealing with the case. Turning it over, I noticed a letter with an envelope pinned on. By Jingo: what do you think? The postmark was New Brunswick, New Jersey. That fellow must have been in New Jersey, in fact, must be staying there, perhaps with relatives.

"I grabbed the telephone, and soon was communing with the operator in my most honeyed tones, somewhat in this strain. 'Please, oh please, call New Brunswick, New Jersey. Then, ask the telephone operator if, by any happy chance she knows of a Montana mining man, who has planted his whereabouts in that beautiful suburb, and further, if said mining man perhaps is so situated as to be accessible to the telephone.' Then followed many objurgations as to the great and vital importance of this matter. After that down I sat, to possess my soul in patience, and wait, and fume.

"Half an hour passed to the great beyond. Then another half-hour. Then tinkle-tinkle went the bell. I jumped for the phone. Here is the way I got it.

TH' PARTY YOU WANT IS ATTA FARM 'BOUT FI' MILES OUT D'YOUWANTUM?

" 'Th' party you want is atta farm 'bout fi' miles out. D' you wantum?'

"Did I want him? I wonder. By the great horn spoon, he was on the wire in less than five minutes—so fast that, at first, I was almost tongue-tied. However, I soon got going, and told him what I wanted in good vigorous English too. He was most indifferent, in fact, he practically said he didn't care a hang whether he saw me or not, and wasn't ready to talk business anyway. Then he hung up the phone.

"I was sick, just sick over it. And the worst part of it was, that there didn't seem to be anything to do about it. Anyway, I turned in, and tried to get some sleep in the hope that some new hunch would appear in the morning.

"That was tough," remarked the Boss.

"You know it," returned Jones, with emphasis. "Well, next morning about seven, while I was dressing, my 'phone rang, and there he was again. To my surprise, and delight, he said that he didn't just get who I was over the 'phone the night before, and he had just received my note, and would try to get into town before I left. He explained further that his partner was in England trying to float bonds to raise the money needed, and that, until he came home, there would be nothing doing. We chatted pleasantly enough, and I hung up the 'phone with a heavy heart, and prepared to start for home in two days.

"I cleaned up the few odds and ends remaining, and, on the morning of the day I was to leave, I called him again, just for a spec. By jingo! he had received a wireless from his partner that day. The money was raised and the ship his partner was on would dock that day at noon. Well, you know about the drowning man and the straw. I stood up on my hind legs, and simply burned up that telephone wire. Told him that he must, MUST, MUST, meet me that afternoon, and finally I simply talked him into consenting. He was to show up at two o'clock, and bring his partner.

"At two, I was pacing the lobby. At three I was running around the lobby. At four, I was gasping for breath, my glazed eyes indicating that all was lost. At four fifteen, in they came. Do you know, I bet they don't know yet what happened to them. I had a head of steam on way above the safety mark, and, as soon as they got into my room I went after them. You see, I had to get this job signed up before they had a chance to see any of the other fellows, and I didn't let any grass grow under my feet.

"They bucked, and bucked. The book of a thousand excuses was completely used up, and the final clincher, was simply this: that the prices I had quoted were based upon that bargain-sale lot of brass you picked up, and if they didn't take advantage of the offer within an hour, all prices would be immediately withdrawn, and they would lose thousands of dollars by their procrastination.

"That was a clincher. Finally, he turned to his partner and said: 'Waal, Jimmy, what do you say? Shall we buy?' 'Might as well, Hank,' drawled the partner; and buy they did. The fountain pen was produced, everything was signed, sealed, and delivered, check and all; and, to cap the climax, when I suggested that it had been dry work for all of us, the partner looked at me sadly, and said: 'Me and Hank don't never touch a drop, and, young man, you would be a sight better off

if you didn't nuther.' They blew, and I collapsed in a chair."

Large organizations, international in their scope, go to great lengths in the compilation of individual statistical data on prospective buyers. Such matter is prepared carefully and painstakingly from a great many sources of information, and is elaborately card-indexed for ready reference in case of emergency. The methods are, in some cases, strikingly similar to those observed by criminal identification bureaus. Everything about the man, save his thumb-prints, photograph, and Bertillion measurements are available.

Here is the way it operates. Suppose the word is passed along that one Snodgrass, chief engineer for a great corporation, is about to collect data dealing with the proposed installation of a great plant-addition involving the purchase of vast quantities of apparatus and supplies. The scouts for the supply-houses and manufacturers know this long before any inkling appears in the daily press. Instantly the great general staff of the manufacturer clears decks for action. Interest centres on Snodgrass as the man who will in all probability be a big factor, if not perhaps the final factor, who will say yes or no as to who shall get the business.

Resort is first had to his dossier. There are disclosed all sorts of interesting facts. He is dissected, analyzed, and laid on the table under the microscope of the general staff, which is about to plan the campaign that will ultimately result in victory for their forces. Let us look over their shoulders and learn a thing or two about Snodgrass.

We find that Snodgrass is 49 years old, where he was born, full particulars as to his scholastic training, the name of his alma mater, the courses he took, and whether he went in for athletics or other forms of activity engaged in by the student body, whether he was a 'barb', or perhaps a member of the exclusive Alfalfa Delts, Eta Bita Pi's, or Moo Moo Cows. Then comes his professional record, the names of his former employers in chronological order, his engineering society affiliations, and his clubs. His professional fads are disclosed by his contributions to the engineering society proceedings or the technical journals, his social affiliations by his clubs. Then comes data as to his family, and hardly less important, the social activities, fads, and fancies of his wife. Under the heading of remarks, we learn that Snodgrass has a marked aversion to salesmen, likes to drive a high-powered car, suffers from indigestion, is a teetotaler, quick-tempered, plays golf for exercise, and hates like thunder to lose, is amenable to flattery if tactfully applied, in short is what is known in selling parlance as an all around hard case, but, to use another salesman's axiom, the higher they are, the harder they fall.

Pursuing the work of the general staff a little farther, Snodgrass' assistants are also smoked out with the same infinite care. Their influence and power of suggestion are not overlooked. Then various dignitaries are set to work on the job, each with a definite assignment, and the entire strength of the business Wilhelmstrasse is turned loose on the most interesting big-game hunt known to the commercial world. Of course, there are many of such campaigns under way continuously, but this, in brief, is the modus operandi. From the time of its inception to its consummation, one way or the other, the iron is kept hot at all times. Frequently the period of negotiation may represent years. Sometimes, there will be several flare-ups and die-downs before the deal is consummated, but it is a case of eternal vigilance, and Heaven help the salesman who is caught napping. His reputation and his job hang in the balance.

Competition is keen, and rivalries are intense. Out of it come many amusing contretemps, of which the following is an example:

A salesman, who had been following up a prospect on a big contract for some time, succeeded in establishing himself on such a firm personal footing with the buyer, that, when the buyer went to New York, the salesman met him at the station by prearranged plan, and accompanied him to his hotel. The buyer adjourned to the bath-room to remove the stains of travel, leaving the salesman to amuse himself in the bedroom meanwhile. The buyer safely in the tub, the telephone rang. "Answer that, Jimmy," came the orders from the tub. Jimmy did. It was the chief salesman of Jimmy's bitterest rival, and, then and there, over the phone that salesman, thinking that he was addressing the buyer, proceeded to rip Jimmy up the back, his concern up the back, and his goods up the same place. Then forthwith, when the salesman paused for breath, Jimmy took a hand, and, impersonating the buyer, proceeded to read the salesman a lecture on the fallacy of knocking one's competitor, decency in sales tactics, and other things in such plain, vigorous United States, that said salesman disappeared from human ken when the story got out, as such stories always do, and Jimmy got the job hands-down.

In the use to which such personal data on individuals is put, is involved the necessity of consummate skill and an infinite amount of tact. Many a good sale is lost, and a permanent prejudice established through a lack of appreciation of these facts. The amour propre of the buyer must be carefully observed, that it be not bruised or ruffled by overzealousness.

A buyer, who had the placing of a large amount of business every year, had occasion to go East at one time, and, of course, the scouts of a certain business concern duly apprised their principals of the fact, together with the usual data as to the time of his arrival in the big city, his favorite hotel, and the kind of hospitality which, they thought, would appeal to him. As this particular concern had fared rather ill at the hands of this buyer, they thought to grab this golden opportunity with both hands, and unfortunately overdid it badly.

When the buyer arrived, he was met by the genial type of spellbinder, who, willy-nilly whisked the buyer and his grips into a limousine de luxe and shunted him into his hotel, had a whole procession of bell-hops and things rush out to meet him and conduct him into a Louis Kansas suite which looked like $50 per day, filled his key-box with cards to clubs, kept the telephone tinkling constantly with theatre invitations while the poor buyer was trying to take a bath, and generally made an infernal nuisance of himself. As a result, the buyer, as soon as his entertainer vouchsafed to leave him for a minute, quietly sneaked out of the hotel and went to a friends' home and took with him a contempt and disgust for that particular concern which has lasted to this day.

Contrast this with the adventure of a certain well-know master salesman for a steel manufacturer. There was a big deal on for certain steel preducts with a foreign country. Millions were involved. After much scurrying around, the master salesman met the visiting foreign delegation at Sandy Hook, with the assistance of a sea-going tug, and, before the vessel docked, he was in possession of the whole circus. He had spent much time studying up the characteristics of the people with whom he was to deal, and, in consequence, his conduct to them was a model of suavity, diplomacy, and finesse. The visitors were charmed to find, in one supposed to belong to an uncouth race, the model of a gentleman of their own standards.

That night, the inevitable dinner was arranged in a private dining-room of a great hotel. The hostelry, given carte blanche in every particular, outdid itself. Rare exotics adorned the festal board. The silver and table appointments would have graced the table of the Czar himself, while spotless napery added the final touch to what was to be a gastronomic masterpiece.

Enter the visiting foreign delegation, resplendent in uniforms such as were only possible in the old world under the ancient regime. Gold lace, orders, decorations, medals, and monocles; fiercely waxed upturned mustaches and clanking sabres, there was the very breath of romance, the real Prisoner of Zenda atmosphere. Of course, there were toasts, drunk in hollow-stemmed glasses filled with rare vintages. The senior officer among those present proposed "His Imperial Majesty, the Czar." In a flash, all were on their feet. Heels clicked, sabres flashed aloft. "The Czar." Crash! Every glass went smash against the wall.

Then comes the master salesman. "Gentlemen," he said, "I long have admired the delightful custom of your country, that prevents the profanation of any glass after dedicating it to the sacred health of his Imperial Majesty. Now, I will show you how it is done in these United States. Gentlemen, his Excellency the President of the United States." All rose. Again the click of heels, the flash of sabres, and glasses aloft. No sooner drunk, than the master salesman seized the table-cloth, and with one sweep of his arm, one mighty crash, threw everything on the table to the floor.

Then pandemonium broke loose. Floor clerks, house detectives, bell-hops, and sundry other fauna that infest the halls and corridors of great hostelries, galvanized into action, rushed frantically about. Cheer upon cheer rose through the smoke-laden air and impinged upon the ceiling, scaring the life out of the old ladies on the next floor. Such magnificence, such lofty contempt for expense! Thousands of dollars worth of gorgeous cut-glass smashed to bits in honor of the President of the United States! This great man, this superb American, with his dramatic appeal to the imagination of the most temperamental people in the world, held the situation in the hollow of his hand. What chance did the poor plodder, the spectacled master of blueprints, specifications, and tests stand? Where, Oh where, were the efficiency engineer, the advertising manager, and the correspondence school-graduates? Who got the order? How can you ask?

Mineral Production of Canada in 1918

Preliminary figures for the past year, prepared by John McLeish, have just been published. The total value of all products was $210,204,970, an increase of 10.8% when compared with 1917, and 44.3% with 1913.

Metallic	Quantity	Value
Cobalt metal and oxide, at $2.50, pounds	1,347,544	$3,368,800
Copper, at 24.628c., pounds	118,415,829	29,163,450
Gold, ounces	710,526	14,687,875
Iron, pig, from Canadian ore, tons	47,444	1,204,703
Iron ore, sold for export, tons	112,886	469,352
Lead, at 9.25c., pounds	43,846,260	4,055,779
Molybdenite (MoS_2 content at $1.15), pounds	377,850	434,528
Nickel, at 40c., pounds	92,076,034	36,830,414
Platinum, ounces	39	2,500
Silver, at 96.772c., ounces	21,284,607	20,597,540
Zinc, at 8.150c., pounds	33,063,090	2,746,620
Total metallics		113,563,111
Non-metallic—	Tons	
Asbestos	141,462	$8,930,805
Chromite	21,994	807,122
Coal	14,979,213	55,752,671
Feldspar	20,232	117,379
Fluorspar	7,362	135,712
Graphite	3,051	270,054
Gypsum	152,287	823,006
Magnesite	39,365	1,016,765
Mica	....	268,375
Pyrite	413,698	1,688,991
Talc	18,190	112,727
Total non-metallics		78,230,195
Structural materials and clay products		18,411,664

Increases in quantities were: cobalt, 24.8%; copper, 8.4%; lead, 34.6%; molybdenite, 31.6%; nickel, 11.8%; zinc, 13.8%; and asbestos, 2.9%. Gold decreased 3.8%, and silver 4.2%.

Production of all minerals by Provinces was:

	1917	1918	Increase or decrease	%
Nova Scotia	$21,104,542	$22,754,780	+$1,650,238	7.82
New Brunswick	1,435,024	2,111,816	+ 676,792	47.16
Quebec	17,400,077	19,534,409	+ 2,134,332	12.26
Ontario	89,066,600	94,084,420	+ 5,017,820	5.63
Manitoba	2,628,264	3,197,697	+ 569,433	21.67
Saskatchewan	860,651	894,591	+ 33,940	3.94
Alberta	16,527,535	23,298,118	+ 6,770,583	40.97
British Columbia	36,141,926	42,080,741	+ 5,938,815	16.43
Yukon	4,482,202	2,248,398	— 2,233,804	49.83
Dominion	$189,646,821	$210,204,970	+$20,558,149	10.80

Ball-Mill Operation

By E. W. DAVIS

*From an elaborate series of tests, the following conclusions were deduced:

In the discussion, only the force of gravity and centrifugal force have been considered. In a mill containing water and ore, as well as balls, the force of adhesion ought to be considered. This force not only tends to hold the balls and ore together, but also tends to hold them against the lining of the mill. Just how important this force may be under ordinary operating conditions is difficult to say. It was shown, however, in a model mill, that adhesion tended to hold the particles together in their parabolic paths, and almost entirely eliminated the accidental particles that fall near the centre of the mass. It is impossible to apply the results secured in a small mill to a large mill in this respect, however, as adhesion varies inversely with the size of the particles considered. Adhesion also varies with the moisture, so the mill operator has a convenient means of controlling this force so as to produce the best results.

It is important to prevent slipping between the charge and the lining of the mill: the tendency to slip is much smaller with large charges than with small ones. If the friction between the charge and the lining of the mill is not great enough to carry the particles up high enough, the efficiency of the mill will be greatly reduced and the lining of the mill will be worn away rapidly. Flat sides will also appear on the balls, and the cycle of the charge will be slow and irregular. In an open trunnion-discharge mill, the pulp will not flow from the mill regularly, but will come in pulsations. Lifters or roughened liners are therefore desirable, as they ensure a greater coefficient of friction.

The following conclusions may be stated:

1. By use of formulas

$$K = -0.024 + 0.39\sqrt{7 - 10P} \text{ and}$$

$$N = \frac{48.948}{\sqrt{D}\sqrt[4]{1 + K^2}} \text{ in rev. per min.}$$

proper theoretical speed for operation may be computed.

2. This speed is correct only when there is no slipping between the charge and the lining of the mill, and when the pulp is not so thick as to produce strong adhesion between the particles.

3. In actual practice it may be found that more effective crushing can be done at some other speed, but it would appear that the variations above or below this theoretical speed should be small.

4. When operating at the speed shown by the second formula the crushing is done largely by impact.

5. At speeds lower than N (second equation) the proportion of the crushing done by attrition is increased.

6. At speeds higher than N (second equation) the proportion of the crushing done by impact is increased.

7. The amount of crushing done depends upon the number of blows struck and the work done at each blow.

8. The number of blows can be increased by adding to the number and decreasing the size of the balls.

9. The work done at each blow can be increased by adding to the weight of the ball and by increasing the diameter of the mill.

10. From this it follows that mills of larger diameter should be charged with smaller balls and mills of smaller diameter with larger balls, when working on the same feed.

11. The proper operating speed of a ball-mill varies inversely as the square root of the diameter.

12. The proper operating speed of a ball-mill increases as the size of the ball load increases.

13. Due to interference between the balls, the volume of the charge should not be over 60% of the volume of the mill.

14. Unless great care is exercised to prevent slippage, the volume of the ball charge should not be less than 20% of the volume of the mill.

15. It would then seem that a ball charge that occupies between 25 and 50% of the volume of the mill will give most satisfactory results.

16. In an 8-ft. mill, running at 22 r.p.m., with a 28,000-lb. charge of 2-in. balls, there will be an average of about 1,000,000 blows per minute; each of these blows will be equivalent to dropping a 2-in. ball 5 feet.

Conclusions as to ball wear were as follows:

1. In any mill, the rate at which the weight of any ball decreases is directly proportional to its weight.

2. In any mill, the rate at which the diameter of a ball decreases is directly proportional to its diameter.

3. In any mill, the rate at which the surface of any ball decreases is proportional to its surface.

4. Since the rate at which a ball loses weight varies as the work done upon it in the mill, it follows that the work done in wearing (or crushing) the ball, varies as the weight of the ball. This is seen to be Kick's law.

5. It then appears that Kick's law holds true for the ball wear in a rotating mill.

6. The natural tendency is for the small balls to accumulate in the mill charge.

7. Since these small balls do very little crushing, and exclude ore and larger balls from the mill, if allowed to accumulate too long, a marked decrease in crushing efficiency will result.

8. Since the large ball is just as likely to strike the small pieces of ore and the small ball is just as likely to strike the large pieces of ore as the reverse, it would seem that all the balls should be of a size to crush any of the particles of ore.

9. This means that the balls should be as nearly as possible of a uniform size.

10. Since spheres of uniform size provide the greatest amount of interstitial space, a mill charge composed of balls of uniform size will allow freer migration of the ore particles than a charge containing balls of different sizes.

*Abstract from Bull. 140, A. I. M. E., February 1919.

The Fourth Dimension

By JOHN ROGER

This is a fertile source of discussion among those interested in puzzles. No one has ever seen the fourth dimension or can tell us just what it is, but it is said that it must exist because we can write an equation for it.

The first question to consider in this connection is what is meant by dimensions; assuming these to be in an elementary way linear, superficial, and volumetric, that is, first, second, and third dimensions. Length, breadth, and thickness are not three dimensions, but are three measures of the first or linear dimension.

It seems to be customary to assume that the square of 12 inches (linear) is a square foot and that the cube of 12 inches (linear) is a cubic foot. It would be hard to conceive of any proposition more nonsensical than this. The definition of a line is something which has neither breadth nor thickness but only length. Length without breadth or thickness does not exist, except in theory, as it occupies no space. It, therefore, follows that it can make no difference how many times the length is squared or cubed, it can represent neither surface nor volume. Length without breadth or thickness materially is nothing, therefore the square of 12 linear inches is 144 linear inches and the cube of 12 linear inches is 1728 linear inches; it represents neither surface nor volume. The four 12-inch lines enclosing a square foot are no part of the enclosed area.

The same holds good as between superficial and volumetric dimensions. A surface without thickness represents no matter or displacement and does not represent quantity unless the third dimension is given, and these dimensions are not measurable one by the other. The square of 12 superficial inches is 144 superficial inches and the cube of 12 cubic inches is 1728 cubic inches. But to say that the cube of 12 linear inches is 1728 cubic inches is nonsense, as a linear inch has no volume and the cube of nothing is nothing. When we say 12 inches cube, it is only a simplified way of saying the cube of 12 cubic inches.

It must, therefore, be evident that there is only one measure of space and that is volumetric. Measures of length and surface are measures in space and not of space. No amount of surface can make a cubic inch and no amount of length can make a square inch. Volumes are, therefore, measured by units of volume, we may make the unit what we please and the multiples of it may be given as fourth, fifth, or sixth powers of any stated number of units, and these are measurable by such volumetric units—not by any linear measure. When we measure a rectangle 2 inches by 3 inches by 6 inches, we unconsciously assume through usage that 2 cubic inches by 3 cubic inches by 6 cubic inches equals 36 cubic inches. Three linear inches plus 3 linear inches plus 6 linear inches is necessarily 12 linear inches. In other words, we must determine beforehand whether we are calculating in the first, second, or third dimension; and in dealing with space there is only one dimension, namely, the third or volumetric. With lines we enclose surfaces and with surfaces we enclose volumes, but neither the lines nor the surfaces are any part of the volume. The so-called fourth dimension is, therefore, simply a multiple of the selected unit of volume and has no mathematical significance.

The Sweeney Mill at Kellogg, Idaho

By R. S. HANDY

*This plant was turned over to the Bunker Hill & Sullivan company by the Federal Mining & Smelting Co. on July 9, 1918. The work of sampling and estimating the contents of the tailing dump was started immediately, and 1000 tons of the material placed in the mill-bins for a working-test, in order to determine the possibilities of profitable treatment.

The fine jigs, which had been handling material below three millimetre in size, were taken out of the main building. Their feed was sent to two 20-mesh trommels. The oversize from these passed to the coarse Jigs. The undersize was spouted to the old slime-house, where it was classified and treated on tables and vanners.

The 1000-ton test indicated that treatment of the tailing was commercially practicable, so the plant was remodeled for convenient handling of the tailing as well as ore from lessees' operations in the old Last Chance mine workings. The changes consisted in the installation of 11 Wilfley tables on the floor that used to contain the fine jigs; a drag under the 3-mm. trommels to carry the undersize to the 20-mesh trommels; Calumet classifiers to classify the undersize of the 20-mesh trommels for table-feed; and a flotation plant on the west side of the coarse-jig floor. The flotation plant consists of three Bunker Hill and two Callow cells, it takes its feed from a 30 by 8-ft. Dorr thickener, which is on the ground west of the mill. The feed to the Dorr thickener is the overflow of the Calumet classifiers. Some of the rolls and the methods of feeding them have been somewhat changed. The coarse jigs, elevators, and Huntington mills were not materially altered.

The remodeled mill dresses 400 tons of tailing from the old dump in 16 hours, or it can concentrate 200 tons of lessees' ore in the same period. The old dump-tailing assays $1\frac{3}{4}\%$ lead. While operating on this tailing two valuable products are made. First, a middling that is taken off the jigs and tables assaying 10% lead, 4 oz. silver, and more than 20% excess of iron over silica, for which reason it is especially desired by the smelter for fluxing. The second product is the flotation concentrate, which assays 25% lead and 18 oz. of silver per ton.

A great deal of trouble has been faced in getting railroad transportation of the dump-tailing and lessees' ore to the mill, but the plant itself is working satisfactorily. Flotation, as was expected, presents a difficulty, on account of the high content of flocculent oxidized matter in the feed, and will require further study.

*Abstracted from 'Bunker Bullion', March 1919.

The Use and Abuse of Crucibles

By A. C. BOWLES

A few days ago, a local foundryman called me up and complained, in language more forceful than elegant, that the last batch of crucibles he had received 'was rotten' and that they fell to pieces before he was able to get even one heat out of them. He asked indignantly what we were going to do about it. Of course, I told him that I was sorry he had trouble and that we would make good any crucibles proved defective, but that I would like to see the crucibles to determine, if possible, the cause of their failure. To make a long story short, he had attempted to dry them in the moist atmosphere of the core-oven, with the inevitable result that they had scalped upon coming into contact with the fire.

Crucibles respond so readily to proper treatment, that it is worth while emphasizing again the few points that have to be observed if the maximum of service is to be obtained from graphite pots. There is nothing new about the right procedure. Most crucible users have known it, but probably on account of the stress of business during the past few years, have neglected to make use of their knowledge.

The manufacturer is not infallible and occasionally a bad batch of pots slips through, but the complete system under which he works, and the long years of practice in repeating the same operation, reduce the chances of mistakes on the part of the factory to the minimum. It is safe to say that 90% of the failures of crucibles are traceable directly to poor treatment on the part of the user.

The principal cause of the failure of crucibles is the lack of proper annealing. When the crucible comes from the kiln it contains but ½% of combined moisture, and in this condition it is impossible to scalp it. However, during transportation from manufacturer to user, it, like salt, absorbs moisture from the atmosphere, and once absorbed a temperature of not less than 250°F. is required to dispel this moisture.

Most crucible troubles occur in small shops. The large consumers have found it well worth while to equip their plants with drying-ovens especially to dry and anneal their crucibles before they are put into the furnaces. Whether annealing in a special oven or on top of the crucible furnace, there are four points that must be observed.

1. The temperature must go above 250°F.
2. This temperature should be reached gradually.
3. This temperature must be held a sufficient time to allow the moisture to thoroughly disappear.
4. The crucible must go into the fire with a temperature above 250°F.

It is a mistake to think that after the first three rules have been followed, the crucible has had its annealing and is impervious to moisture, for, if allowed to cool below 250°F. it will again take up moisture just as readily as the first time.

Another enemy of the crucible is mis-shapen tongs. When the crucible is hot, it is in a somewhat plastic condition and is easily squeezed out of shape or ruptured. The best tongs are the basket variety which grab the crucible both below and above the bilge and hold it firmly without squeezing. It has been found good practice to have an iron crucible cast, over which the tongs can be straightened and shaped at frequent intervals. This method is not only much quicker and simpler, but gives

CRUCIBLE BURST IN FIRE ON ACCOUNT OF MOISTURE

RESULT OF ALLOWING FLAME FROM OIL-BLAST TO TOUCH CRUCIBLE

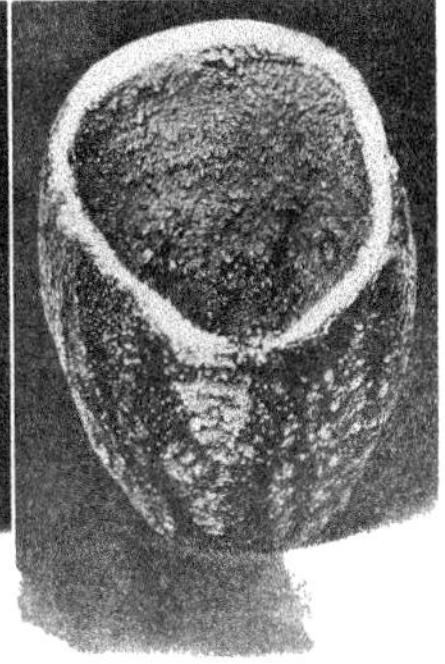

CRUCIBLE SQUEEZED AND RUPTURED BY BADLY-SHAPED TONGS

a better result than sending to a blacksmith. Some shops find it advisable to have tongs of two sizes; one for the new crucible and one for the old pot, which is considerably smaller.

In using an oil-furnace, the flames should never be allowed to play directly on the crucible, as scoring will follow, and the crucible will soon wear through on that side. In addition, one side will heat faster than the other, which is also bad practice. Oil-furnaces giving a rotary flame, seem to be the most satisfactory and to give the most even heat on all sides of the crucible.

The use of wet coke is also bad practice because steam comes in contact with the crucible and forms checks known as alligator-cracks. These will likewise form when a crucible is exposed to the moist gases on top of the furnace, while it is being annealed. Therefore care should be taken when annealing a crucible on top of the furnace, to see that it is kept away from direct contact with the flame.

The activities of the furnace-tender with his iron poker often shorten the life of the crucible. Many shops make a practice of keeping account of the number of melts each tender gets from a crucible so that the careless tender can be checked, and the average number of heats increased.

The number of heats obtainable from a crucible depends largely on the metal to be melted, and on the temperature required for the melt. A crucible that will last only three or four heats with nickel will last 25 heats with copper, or 40 or more with composition metal. If a flux is used, it lowers the life of the crucible by attacking the clay that holds the graphite together.

In general poor results are caused to a large extent by poor treatment. More attention to the details of storing and annealing the pots and to their treatment while in the furnace will pay large dividends in the increased service obtained.

Filter Litigation in Australia

*In the Supreme Court of Western Australia on December 23, Justice Burnside delivered his reserved judgment in the action brought by the Moore Filter Co. of Portland, Maine, against the Great Boulder Proprietary Gold Mines, Ltd., for alleged infringement of patent.

The hearing was started on September 2, and lasted for several weeks. Plaintiff alleged a breach by defendant of certain letters patent assigned to it by George Moore, the original grantee, in 1907, for an invention for improvements in filter processes for the extraction of gold from unleachable slimes, dated August 21, 1903. Plaintiff claimed an account of profits derived by the defendant from its alleged breach, or, at its discretion, an inquiry as to damages arising from the use of the processes between 1907 and the date of the issue of the writ. Defendant denied infringement of the patent, which it claimed did not possess the number of necessary elements of validity. It alleged that the patent was the amalgamation of four inventions patented in the United States. Plaintiff, it further contended, had brought the action without having complied with the provisions of part 8 of the Companies Act, 1893.

In the course of judgment, the delivery of which occupied an hour and a half, the Judge traced the history of the extraction of gold from slime, and exhaustively reviewed the various phases of the patent in question, touching upon the objections raised by the defense under the Companies Act. He held that while plaintiff had not complied with the provisions of the Act, its non-compliance, though rendering it liable to penalties, did not preclude it from bringing an action. Dealing with plaintiff's claims in the patent, he said that he found them far from clear and precise, but it was impossible to say that they were so bad as to leave a doubt in the mind of the worker skilled in the art of gold extraction as to the invention, which the patentee claimed as his monopoly. The question of novelty raised by the defense was determined by ascertaining whether the combinations claimed were novel for the most part. They were, in fact, novel. All the elements of which they were composed were old, but nobody had previously brought them together in the exact manner of the patentee. It was the novelty of the combination that made the claim. As to the issue whether the combination was useful, he had come to the conclusion that at the date of the grant the plaintiff had not invented what he now said he had. There were difficulties to be overcome that the plaintiff could not foresee, against which he had made no provision. Some of the combinations claimed might work, but all, the Judge was satisfied, would not. As to the element of invention, the evidence went to show that the problem still remained, though further improvements might have followed and that the ordinary worker skilled in the art, who was called in to operate the machine, with nothing more than the Western Australian patent and specifications, would not, without much experiment, arrive at a successful result. It was contended that the patent was a pioneer and a master patent. The patent was for the principle. In his view the claims disclosed no principle such as was or might be the subject matter of the patent. There was nothing to indicate the claim to the principle. The patent was for a mechanical combination, and it was not alleged that this had been infringed. In his opinion, the patent was not valued, and judgment should be entered for the defendant, with costs.

The Great Boulder mine has yielded $55,680,000 from 3,425,000 tons, and paid $26,250,000 in dividends.

[The filter apparatus used by the Great Boulder company at Kalgoorlie is known as the Ridgway. It consists of a 'basket' of leaves that are suspended at the end of an arm, which first lowers it into the slime-tank for formation of cakes, then lowers it into another tank for washing, finally raising the basket over a mixer for discharge. The machine is ingenious, simple, works rapidly, and gives good extraction at low cost.—EDITOR.]

*Abstract from Monthly Journal of Chamber of Mines of Western Australia, Dec. 1918.

Mr. Bayliss on Mining Conditions

Herewith we quote part of a speech made in London by R. T. Bayliss, as chairman of the Exploration Company, on the occasion of the recent annual meeting of shareholders:

You will expect me to say something with regard to Mexico. It certainly calls for our first consideration, as it represents our largest and, unfortunately, has been for some years our most troublesome investment. From the economic point of view conditions in that Republic are little, if at all, better than they were twelve months ago. From the political standpoint they are about the same. Except in the Federal District of Mexico, which includes Mexico City, the Government seems unable to check, or control, the activities of the various bands of rebels, whose sporadic raids keep the outlying portions of the Republic in a condition of insecurity and unrest, and render the peaceful and regular operation of all industries impossible. Now this makes matters very difficult for our engineers engaged in local management, and exasperating for those who, like my colleagues and myself, are responsible to their shareholders for the profitable operation of mining properties in Mexico. We are not discouraged, however. We believe that more stable conditions of government must ensue before long, and we confidently expect that, when other circumstances permit, the governments of England and the United States will see to it that these chaotic conditions are brought to an end.

In spite of all these difficulties, our subsidiary companies in Mexico, with the exception of the Santa Rosa Mining Co., which so far we have been unable to re-start, have been working during the past year with more success than seemed probable at its commencement. The El Oro company, under the circumstances, and notwithstanding the added disadvantage of a very serious epidemic of influenza, has done well; and the Suchi Timber Co., allied thereto, has had a successful year. The Buena Tierra mine has had greater difficulties to contend with. After an enforced shut-down it re-started in May last and for three months did very well. Then the inadequate facilities for transportation furnished by the local railway, over which the ore is transported to the smelter, caused interruption in shipments.

Our investment of next importance, having regard to the sum involved, is represented by debenture and shareholdings of the Chile Copper and Greene-Cananea companies. Of the former I think I may say that the claims made by its promoters with regard to its capacity for production have been fully justified in the past year's work. The output for that period was 100,000,000 lb., or 50,000 short tons of copper. The reduction plant has been working in excess of the capacity for which it was designed, and it is anticipated that by the 1st of June this year the proposed extensions thereto will have been completed to an extent that will render possible a production at the rate of 160,000,000 lb. per annum as from that date. Further additions to the plant, it is added, are in contemplation and will be made as conditions warrant. Considering the difficulties this company has had to contend with during the War, these results, I submit, must be regarded as very satisfactory. The Greene-Cananea, although hampered in its operations, like all mines in Mexico, is perhaps today in better physical condition than at any time in the past, and produced roundly 53,000,000 lb. of copper during 1918.

The outlook of the copper market at the moment is somewhat difficult to gauge, owing to the large supplies left in the hands of all the Allies on the termination of hostilities in November, and to the consequent abrupt curtailment in the consumption of copper for military purposes. Some time must necessarily elapse before electrical, engineering, and other industries dependent upon copper as raw material, but diverted during the War to the manufacture of munitions, resume their normal consumption. So many difficult problems surround the question of industrial reconstruction that it may take some time for the consumers of copper to resume their pre-war activities. The stability of the copper market depends very largely on the period of such reconstruction, and also on the wisdom displayed in the disposal of the large surplus stock which undoubtedly exists. In the meantime drastic steps are being taken in the United States to restrict production, and I am of the belief that an equilibrium will be reached in supply and demand more quickly, perhaps, than at the moment seems probable. There is, moreover, one practical feature with regard to this accumulation which should not be overlooked. In normal times the stocks of copper in the hands of manufacturers and consumers throughout the world would represent a very large proportion of the present surplus, which today is held in very few hands; and, as a believer in the ultimate and general revival of trade, I do not therefore regard the present accumulation with alarm, or feel any uneasiness with respect to our investments in copper-mining companies.

I should like to add a few remarks concerning the outlook for gold mining. I have on past occasions mentioned to you the increasing difficulty in purchasing good gold mines at reasonable prices. This is mainly due to the fact that the known goldfields have been thoroughly explored, and there is not any immediate prospect of new mining districts becoming available for development. Until recently it was believed that the next big development would take place in Russia and Siberia, but for the time being that expectation must be deferred. Mexico, I am still convinced, offers the best field for investigation. Even so, the high rate of taxation already imposed makes it difficult to purchase mines on terms which will yield a satisfactory rate of profit to the investor after the payment of taxes assessed in that country and the further provision for income-tax payable on this side. During the War, moreover, and apparently for some time to come, the gold miner has been and will be called upon to bear a very serious burden. In common with all other industries he has had to face largely increased costs; but, unlike such other industries, he has not been permitted to raise the selling price of his product, but has been compelled to dispose of it at the standard pre-war price of gold. Moreover, he has been obliged to accept payment therefor in a currency which has lost much of its purchasing value. Representations have been made by the producers of gold to the Treasury both in this country and in the United States, praying that they may receive some compensation for the exceptional hardship which has been imposed upon them, but there seems little encouragement for the hope that any relief will be granted. There is still another difficulty surrounding companies and individuals seeking mining enterprises abroad. The Treasury has announced its intention of maintaining the restrictions on new capital issues which prevailed during the War; and, while it may not absolutely prohibit all issues involving the investment of money abroad, the mere fact that the Treasury sanction must be obtained for this purpose adds to one's difficulty in negotiating the purchase of mines in alien countries. The outlook, therefore, for the gold-mine promoter and for companies such as this, which has rather specialized in gold mines, is not very encouraging, and it seems to us only the part of common sense and candor to recognize the fact.

While, therefore, we continue seeking for new mines, and are hopeful that we shall be successful in finding something we can confidently recommend to you, we feel it imperative to consider every or any description of business offered to us that may present favorable opportunities for investments of our funds. In pursuit of this policy we recently took an interest in the newly-formed British Metal Corporation, which undoubtedly starts with every prospect of becoming an important and successful institution, and, withal, will safeguard the non-ferrous metal industry within the British Empire. We have also acquired a substantial shareholding in the Burma Corporation. I feel very confident that the properties owned by that corporation will under its present exceptionally capable and prudent administration, prove to be one of the big and most successful enterprises of the world.

Labor Efficiency at Telluride, Colorado

The following notes are abstracted from the annual report of C. A. Chase, manager for the Liberty Bell Gold Mining Company:

The old productive areas in the mine [these had yielded 2,144,612 tons since 1899] were almost exhausted at the beginning of the financial year 1917-'18, but beyond the 4300-ft. east line there was a virgin area partly developed. Assays indicated ore of fair grade in a narrow vein. The section was completely equipped with hoisting, haulage, and air plant. Later on, the power supply failed, and much-needed skilled labor was lost from the mine.

Late in May a crisis was evident. More men could not be secured, and the competent men, long employed, were not working to capacity; in fact, an analysis showed that they were doing only as much per day as the shiftless wanderers. It is to be noted that on a day's pay basis of operating, both old men and new were paid equally. In this group of the skilled men, however, existed the capacity to make a production large enough to be profitable, and a study of individual records showed that, although they were doing no more per day, a few of them were doing a large part of the total work done because they were steady; for some reason they felt bound to work. This condition became a foundation stone, and the plan was devised to utilize their steadiness and then pay them on the contract system to work to capacity. The two classes of labor—mining and timbering—were consolidated in the contracts, doing away with interdependence. Beginning in June, the men were gradually weaned from distrust, and by August practically all work was on the new basis. The tabulation of special items for four months of approximately equal numbers of employees in mine illuminate the subject:

	Total mine shifts	Total tons stoped	Total square feet stoped
June	3,211	7,345	17,270
July	3,314	8,588	25,207
August	3,238	11,241	38,450
September	3,407	9,[illegible]	30,218

That area increased faster than tonnage, signifies a decrease in width of the vein and emphasizes the comparisons. Men working in adjacent and equal stopes, formerly paid alike, now earned severally, $3.50, $8, and $13 per day. The cost per ton fell, and the awste in the ore was less. Time to calculate precisely had been lacking and perhaps the contract rates were high, but too closely calculated rates would probably have found acceptance too slowly for the requirement. The number of men affected was about 15% of the total employees, but their work was the foundation on which profitable operation rested. The expedient was a reasonable success, and it was only regretted that other branches of the work could not be similarly benefited.

The great change in operating costs due to hardness of rock and narrow width of vein, in conjunction with high prices, is shown in the following comparative figures, per ton:

	Pre-war	1917	1918
Power	$0.092	$0.123	$0.220
Powder	0.100	0.175	0.520
Fuse and caps	0.014	0.042	0.077
Drill plant	0.055	0.075	0.334

THE mine-scale work of the U. S. Bureau of Standards is of special interest, in view of the need for maximum output of coal at the mines. Disputes over weighings cause strikes, loss of time, and reduced output. The Bureau experts were called upon, and they found conditions wholly unsatisfactory. In one case a 2-ton scale was 616 lb. in error against the miner. Improper installation, faulty methods of weighing and errors were corrected, and mines greatly improved. Indictments were found and fines imposed on the evidence. A general awakening and improvement resulted, and the prevention of strikes and the renewed satisfaction of the miner have gone far to maintain conditions favorable to a maximum output of coal.—Annual Report of Bureau of Standards.

TORONTO, ONTARIO

New Railways to Aid Mining.—Kirkland Lake, Boston Creek, and Porcupine Notes.

Mining exploration in northern Ontario will be enhanced by the latest project of the Temiskaming & Northern Ontario Railway Commission. Kirkland Lake, where work has been considerably retarded by transportation difficulties, is to be connected with the T. & N. O. line by a 7-mile branch from Swastika. This line will draw its revenue almost wholly from mining. A 3-mile spur will be built from Timmins in the Porcupine area to Metagami, which will tap a fertile area suitable for agriculture. The proposal to continue the T. & N. O. line to James bay is under consideration. Prior to the War, considerable exploration was done along the proposed route, and will this year be continued by a party of geologists and surveyors, whose report will be awaited before the Government decisively commits itself to the project.

Kirkland Lake.—H. H. Johnson, consulting engineer of the Kirkland Lake Proprietary, is at Kirkland Lake in connection with the proposed consolidation of the Tough-Oakes, Burnside, and Sylvanite properties, negotiations for which are stated to be making good progress.

The new 30-ton mill of the Burnside is now in regular operation.

A contract has been let for cross-cutting to cut the main vein of the Minaker-Kirkland at a depth of 125 ft., and for putting down the shaft to the 200-ft. level.

Boston Creek.—The plans of the Miller Independence have been altered. In place of driving an incline shaft on the vein to the 500-ft. level, a central vertical shaft will be sunk some distance south of the vein to a depth of 550 or 650 ft. and the vein reached by cross-cutting.

The first diamond-drill hole at the O'Donald has been completed, and results are officially stated to be highly encouraging.

At the Cullen-Renaud the shaft is being sunk to 150 ft. An electrically-driven plant will be installed.

Porcupine.—The Hollinger Consolidated has decided to erect additional and more powerful mining machinery at an outlay of $500,000.

The Davidson has contracted for extensive lateral work at the 500-ft. level. A cross-cut is being driven in the ore-body broken into by the shaft at the 460-ft. level to open a rich area indicated by diamond-drilling.

A syndicate from Butte, Montana, has taken over the Armstrong-Booth property and let a contract for extensive diamond-drilling.

CRIPPLE CREEK, COLORADO

Cresson Finds Rich Ore.—Three Good Discoveries in the Index Mine.—Strong Mine Leased.—Portland Shipments.—Dividends.

Gold production of the district in March was 74,643 tons of ore averaging $9.70 per ton.

A large body of ore has been entered in virgin ground at the 800-ft. level of the Cresson mine. A preliminary estimate gives a great value for the shoot. Mine samples have averaged $30 per ton as broken. The ore is believed to be the upward extension of the rich body opened at 1300 ft. two years ago, and later opened at 1000 ft. The management has planned a campaign of exploration of the area hitherto untouched.

Three important discoveries were made during March in the Index mine, on the south-western slope of Gold hill. The El Paso Extension company found ore at a depth of 1160 ft. at the junction of the main Index vein with a cross-vein. Samples at this point assay as high as 44.98 oz. gold. The ore is a basalt. On the fourth level, at a depth of 700 ft., the Beacon leasing company has opened ore on the Keystone vein, in the granite sill, extending south down Gold hill from the Midget mine. The vein, which is 3 ft. wide, is seamed with talc, itself almost filled with gold. Samples assayed up to 90 oz. Two cars—the first ore broken—one of coarse rock settled at $28, and a car of screenings at $57 per ton. None of the high-grade was included in this shipment. The third discovery was also made on No. 4, south on the Keystone vein by E. G. Fink, a lessee. The value here is as high as $67.

The Strong mine of the Strong Gold Mining Co., with a production exceeding $10,000,000, has been leased for the first time. Owen Roberts, well known in this district, is the lessee. He also was successful in a lease on the El Paso Gold King, in Poverty gulch, on the west side of the district.

Returns from the first 100 tons shipped from the recent discovery on the Roosevelt tunnel-level of the Portland settled at $58 per ton. This ore was mined at a depth of 2131 ft. In order to eliminate high freight and treatment rates on rich ore, this will be graded to 3 ounces.

The Modoc Consolidated has cut the upward extension of the new rich vein, first discovered north of the Last Dollar shaft, at a depth of 1200 ft., at the 1000-ft. level of the mine. The width and extent of the shoot at 1000 ft. has not been determined, but the gold content is 2 oz. The vein at 1200 ft. has widened to 20 ft. in about the centre of the shoot.

Production from the Nicholls shaft on the north end of the El Paso company's Beacon Hill estate will be resumed early in April. An electric hoist has been erected.

Dividends paid on the 10th of this month by the Cresson and Golden Cycle companies were $122,000 on $45,000, respectively. The Portland and Vindicator are also expected to pay quarterly dividends in April.

DURANGO, COLORADO

Power Shortage, Snowslides, and Railroads.

Silverton.—The outlook for ore production during the next two months is not promising. Owing to the dryness of last year, the Western Colorado Power Co. failed to secure sufficient water, with the result that reservoirs are getting low, and the local mines are not getting enough power. An early spring, causing rapid melting of the snow, may fill the reservoirs earlier than anticipated, which is during the latter part of April. This shortage affects operations of the Sunnyside M. & M. Co., most seriously, as the power now supplied is only sufficient to run the mine at two-thirds capacity, and the mill has been shut-down a week. If there is plenty of power at the time mentioned, the mill will resume operating about April 15, but the outlook is not very favorable. The Iowa-Tiger and Mayflower Leasing companies will also be obliged to curtail operations. The Gold King Leasing Co. will not be able to start a mill run until after June 1.

Snowslides are again causing trouble along the D. & R. G. branch from Durango to Silverton, and on the lines of the Silverton Northern. The former line was blocked for 6 days. All ore in transit has been stopped. Heavy sleet-storms accompanied the snow, resulting in added power troubles.

There is good foundation for the report that the Silverton Northern Railroad holdings have changed hands, and it should prove a great asset to the Sunnyside M. & M. Co., in view of the extensive developments in the Eureka district, to control this outlet for its ore. Reports from various sources indicate that the object of the U. S. S. R. & M. Co. in acquiring this property is to ensure an all-year round outlet for its product, by way of Ironton and Ouray to Salt Lake City. The distance from Ironton on the Silverton Northern to Ouray on the D. & R. G. is only eight miles, and would shorten the haul to Utah by 150 miles.

Telluride.—J. M. Belisle is mining and shipping carnotite ore, and has two carloads ready.

The power shortage mentioned will also affect operations in this district, although not as seriously as at Silverton, as the Smuggler Union company has its own power-plant, and is in a position to supply some power to the others in the district. Snowslides are recurring along the lines of the Rio Grande Southern, and ore is blocked at the present writing.

The heavy sleet resulted in the burning down of the transformer-house and the complete destruction of the transformer at the Iowa-Tiger. This will result in closing down the mill for at least a month, stopping concentration of not only the Iowa-Tiger ore, but also of the Mayflower, although the mines continue to operate and will probably ship some ore.

VICTORIA, BRITISH COLUMBIA

Ore-Testing Plants.—The Yukon.—Drilling in Kamloops.—New Development Contemplated in Scattered Regions.

The Dominion government is making provision in this year's estimates for the expenditure of $100,000 on one or more ore-testing laboratories in this Province. This is something for which British Columbian operators have been agitating for years. At present it is necessary to send ore for testing to Ottawa.

Klondike operators are preparing for extensive dredging and hydraulicking this year, according to reports from Dawson. Work will commence early in May. It is thought probable that the total gold output of $2,116,000 in 1918 will be considerably exceeded this season, as some of the larger companies, which have been tied-up by litigation and other matters, are planning to resume. It is estimated that 50 creeks of proved value remain in the Dawson district. The Canadian Klondyke Co.'s No. 4 dredge worked every day last winter and is going still, a remarkable feat under semi-Arctic conditions. The Mayo silver district is said to be opening encouragingly.

E. W. Parks, owner of a quicksilver mine in the Yukon, arrived from the north a few days ago and reported that a placer strike had been made above Marshall, a short distance beyond Holy Cross on the Yukon river. He states that he met a number of prospectors who have stampeded to the new diggings and that they report 50-cent pans as common. The creek on which these placer claims are situated, which ground is said already to be completely staked, runs into a slough of the Yukon river.

Four standard diamond-drill outfits have arrived at Thelia on the Kettle River Valley railroad, Kamloops district, and will be taken to the property of the Aspen Grove Amalgamated Mines, Ltd., for exploration purposes. Joseph Errington and associates are representing the bond-holders and extensive work is promised for the coming season. The property comprises 75 claims on which considerable work has been done.

Promising reports have been received from properties on Stone creek, 20 miles south of Prince George, where the Nechaco River Mines, a New York syndicate, has been carrying on development for two years. Its property is known as the Yellowjacket group. An assay from the quartz formation near the main lode returned $27 per ton in gold, silver, and lead. It is said that there are thousands of tons of similar formation on either side of the lode. The group lies four miles east of the Pacific Great Eastern railway grade and adjoins Stone Creek canyon. William West is in charge, but expects an engineer from New York to look over the ground and decide upon a plan of operations at an early date.

W. A. Phair, a pioneer placer miner of British Columbia, at present residing at Lillooet, offers a solution of unemployment for returned soldiers by their making a living from placer mining along the Fraser river.

The Echo Silver-Lead company, operating near Silverton, has entered the list of producers. Four cars of concentrate is produced monthly, containing 65% lead and 125 oz. silver, and 40 to 45% zinc and 60 oz. silver. The latter product is being stored at the mill on account of the market. The Echo mine is equipped with a two-bucket tram, connected with the Standard tram, by which ore is delivered to the latter's mill.

The manager of the Highland Valley Mining & Development Co., F. Keffer, states that its mine in the Ascroft district will be re-opened and probably placed on a producing basis this summer. The mine is well equipped, and has a concentrating mill.

The Committee of investigation into charges made by the Slocan lead-silver-zinc shippers against the Consolidated M. & S. Co.'s smelting rates at Trail is reported to be making good progress, but it is not expected that the report will be ready before two or three months.

The Nugget-Motherlode-Searchlight claims on Sheep creek have been acquired by a British Columbian syndicate, which has been incorporated as the Nugget Gold Mines Ltd. R. H. Stewart, well known in this Province, will supervise the work. A 10-stamp mill and cyanide plant is available.

The Portland Canal district, in the North-West, will be heard of more this summer, according to prospectors and others from that part. No one is more enthusiastic than R. W. Martin of Seattle, one of the owners of the Mineral Hill claims situated above the Bush mine, of which great things are expected this season.

The Mining Committee of the British Columbian Legislature has submitted a report declaring that the Taylor Engineering Co., which met with financial disaster during construction of a railway from the coast at Alice Arm to the Dolly Varden property, recently taken over by the Tomiskaming Mining Co. of Ontario, is justly entitled to payment in full for the cost of the work done, plus 10% contractor's profit. It is asserted that the evidence shows that the contracting company had assurances that its investment in the road, beyond the originally estimated cost, would be repaid and that, reposing confidence in these assurances, it went forward to the limit of its financial ability. Therefore the Committee takes the position that the contracting company and its creditors should be fully protected before the Provincial Legislature consents to the renewal of the railroad charter.

THE MINING SUMMARY

ARIZONA

Ajo.—The New Cornelia company has developed an ore-body on the southern claim, 400 ft. long by 260 ft. wide, carrying 4 to 9% copper. Underground work has been curtailed to two shifts per day with no Sunday work. Recent diamond-drilling done by the E. J. Longyear Co. has considerably increased the sulphide ore-reserve. The Regent and Silver Wing claims were recently acquired by the company from G. L. Ralston. In spite of decreased production and lowering of wages about 700 men are on the payroll

Hackberry.—A group of claims on the Hackberry lode has been taken over by W. W. Lewis, who has incorporated the Silver Bell Exploration Co. A tunnel is to be driven on the vein, which will pass at a considerable depth below the 100-ft. shaft.

The new 200-ton mill at the Hackberry mine is in operation. The recovery is about 85%. Sufficient ore has been opened for two years at full capacity of the mill.

Jerome.—The haulage-tunnel of the United Verde Extension has been holed through. Its length is 12,384 ft. In

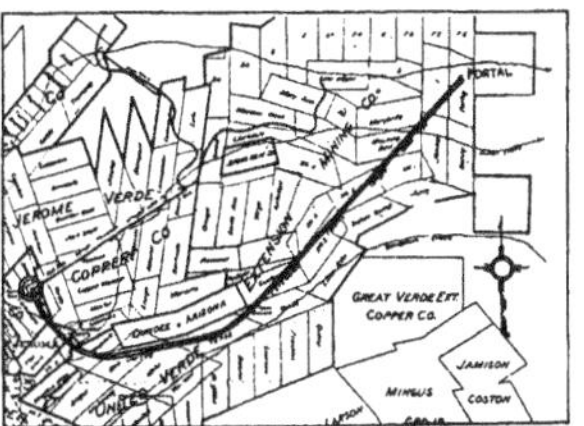

PLAN SHOWING U. V. X. HAULAGE TUNNEL.

order to drain water in the mine, the last 300 ft. of the tunnel was of normal drift size, so now this has to be enlarged to full size 11 by 10½ feet.

Kingman.—There is considerable activity at gold and silver properties around Chloride, Kingman, and Oatman. It is reported that the Amalgamated is to be in operation soon. The Adams company is unwatering its shaft. The Telluride M. & M. Co. has funds for further development. All of these companies are at Oatman. The Mossback mine, in the Silver Creek district, north of Oatman, is pushing development, and has recently opened a large quantity of milling ore. The company is to issue $400,000 of bonds to carry on work.

Patagonia.—Gross & Kennedy of Duluth, Minnesota, have taken an option on the American Boy and Hosey properties. A wagon-road is to be built to the former, and 300 ft. of shaft will be sunk in the latter.

Two shifts of miners are working at the El Paso mine of the Arizona Consolidated Copper Mines Co. The shaft has reached the 200-ft. level, and cross-cutting is being done at 150 ft. Development is also under way at the old Olive claim, which is yielding high-grade silver-lead ore.

Superior.—Magma Copper Co. produced 1,211,175 lb in February, an increase of 311,175 lb. over January.

Wickenburg.—The Empress Copper company, 18 miles from here, is doing nothing at present on account of the condition of the market. J. P. Hutchinson is manager.

CALIFORNIA

The Inyo range, the Mount Whitney region, and Owens valley, which lies between these two ranges, in eastern California, are described in a report just issued by the U. S. Geological Survey, as Professional Paper 110, by Adolph Knopf. This region is off the main lines of travel and is not so well known as other parts of the State, but when the roads and railway facilities are improved, Owens valley, which affords the easiest access to the region, will certainly become famous for its magnificent scenery. The Sierra Nevada, which reaches its highest point in Mount Whitney, forms the west wall of Owens valley, and as it rises abruptly above the valley without intervening foothills the range displays its majestic height far more imposingly here than anywhere else along its course. The top of the Sierra Nevada is readily accessible by trails that start from the pleasant towns of Lone Pine, Independence, Big Pine, and Bishop. Good roads extend into the heart of the range from Bishop, the chief town in Owens valley, so that an automobile trip of hardly more than an hour will take the traveler to the headwaters of Bishop creek, whose profoundly glaciated canyons and spacious ampitheatres are among the most impressive in the entire range. The country west of the crest of this part of the Sierra Nevada is included in the proposed Roosevelt National Park.

The region is rich in mineral resources—silver, lead, zinc, tungsten, gold, and marble—and the waters of Owens lake yield soda and other chemicals. The mines at Cerro Gordo, in the Inyo range, have produced more silver-lead ore than any other mine in California, their output of base bullion between 1869 and 1877 amounting to $7,000,000. After those early flush times the mines long lay idle, but in recent years they have been re-opened, and Cerro Gordo has again become California's foremost producer of lead ore.

In 1913, large bodies of tungsten ore were discovered in the Tungsten hills, west of Bishop. They remained practically unknown until the spring of 1916, when outside interests bought them and began to develop them energetically. By midsummer, two mills had been completed and were in active operation, and the district has since supplied a large quantity of tungsten. Geologic conditions similar to those in the Tungsten hills prevail over a wide extent of country along the east slope of the Sierra Nevada. The places of contact of the intrusive granites with other rock, shown in the geologic maps accompanying the paper, are the most likely places to prospect for other similar bodies of tungsten ore.

Grass Valley.—The electric tramline, connecting the Empire and Pennsylvania mines, both under the same management, is under construction and will shortly be completed.

The road is a quarter-mile long and will be used to transport ore exclusively.

The Idaho-Maryland company is unwatering its shaft so as to explore the workings of the Eureka mine, closed for 50 years, after producing a great deal of gold.

Ingot.—Once more the Afterthought company has started its flotation plant. The treatment of the complex copper-zinc ore involves many problems.

Jackson.—Six carloads of carbonic acid gas in containers has been used at the Argonaut mine in an endeavor to put out the fire. The gas was sent underground through pipes.

Oroville.—A. F. Vogelsang, the First Assistant Secretary of the interior, has reversed the Sacramento Land Office decision declaring mining land at Belden, on the north fork of the Feather river to be mineral bearing, and awarded the patent to Dr. and Mrs. P. F. Bullington of Chico. The action is based on the protest and contention of Gertrude Stewart that the land is agricultural and not mineral, and that she wants to make a homestead entry on the same. The order reversing the decision of the Land Office directs that a new hearing be conducted, to be confined, however, solely to the question of the character of the land. The case is of importance because of the fact that the Great Western Power Co., which proposes to construct a great hydro-electric plant in Butte valley, will need a right-of-way across the land in question for a railroad line to be built to the site of the power-plant. The right-of-way across these lands will be approximately a mile long.

San Francisco.—The State Mineralogist, Fletcher Hamilton, reports that the Secretary of the Interior announces that operators of chrome, manganese, pyrite, and tungsten mines may secure regulations and questionnaires for filing claims under the War Minerals Relief Act from the General Land Office, Customs House, San Francisco.

The attempted nullification of the present conservation law, providing for protection of Californian oil deposits, has been, in the main, rejected by the Senate Committee on oil. The State Mining Bureau, several months ago, called public attention to this attack. It was pointed out that the ultimate aim would be disguised under proposals that would leave merely the skeleton of an impotent law on the statute books; and would, furthermore, place its enforcement entirely in the hands of a few oil producers. The attack has already served a good purpose by bringing into public view a certain few large operators who have never recognized the interest of the public in the oil resources, and have obstructed reasonable enforcement of the law. The Senate Committee has reported the Rigdon bill out, minus some of its most destructive features, and has tabled the bill introduced by Senator J. R. Thompson of Santa Barbara, which proposed to make the present law thoroughly effective. As the Thompson bill is based upon correct governmental principles, it will continue to show the inadequacy of the present law. Due to its origin, the Rigdon bill (Senate Bill No. 199) still carries provisions that would, if enacted, lower the present standards of the State service and seriously interfere with and curtail constructive work, which the State officers are furnishing directly to the oil operators. A direct thrust at the foundation of successful supervision is contained in the proposal to remove the present legal requirements that the State officers—both Supervisor and Deputies—shall be technically trained as engineers or geologists. Past failures by both public and private concerns, aiming to develop and protect oil deposits, have hinged upon their ignoring the necessity for technical study and planning of underground work. All the large oil producers of California, with one single exception, now direct their field work by means of technically trained men. The standard of the State should be no lower than the highest found in private work. The return from the Army and Navy of young engineers, with oilfield experience, already ensures that there will be no scarcity of the necessary technical men.

The last weekly report of the California State Mining Bureau Department of Petroleum and Gas states that the Standard Oil Co., St. Helens Petroleum Co., General Petroleum Corporation, and Petroleum Midway Co. all filed notices this week to drill additional new wells in the Montebello field. Up to February 1, this field, which has occupied public attention for the past two years, has produced 8,700,-051 bbl. of oil. This production does not come from a single stratum of sand. There are at least two separate and distinct zones of productive strata in the field. This fact has been determined by engineers of the Department from data obtained during development by companies operating in that field. As the public has not yet been supplied any correct information as to the underground condition of the field, some facts may be interesting. The first or upper oil-zone, which an occasional improvident operator has not desired to protect from water, has yielded 1,876,121 bbl. of oil and 121,332 bbl. of water up to February 1, through 19 wells that are known to produce from this zone alone. These figures do not include a number of wells that produce from both first and second zones. It is noteworthy that two of the 19 wells mentioned, neither of which was drilled in a manner approved by the Department, produced 99,859 bbl. of water, or 82% of all the water produced to date from the first oil-zone. All operators are now beginning to realize that the production of this upper zone of oil formations is a valuable asset. Under the guidance of engineers of the State Mining Bureau it has been demonstrated that by properly drilling and casing wells, so as not only to exclude top waters but also the so-called intermediate waters, which appear to exist at depths slightly greater than 550 ft. below the top of the first oil-sand, all the oil measures will be protected from water and the greatest possible production obtained. The total production of oil from the second oil-zone to February 1, is 6,823,930 bbl. Three wells alone in the Montebello field produced 410,201 bbl. of water out of a total water production of 648,361 bbl. It is gratifying to note that the company operating the largest water producer, in this trio of offenders, is now taking steps to remedy this condition.

Sonora.—The If-I-Can gravel mine is reported to have been sold last week by O. B. Lefurgy of Oakland to L. R. Davis of Salt Lake City and R. Wallace of San Francisco, acting for others. The price was $25,000 cash. The property is 12 miles from Jamestown. It has been opened by a 1500-ft. bedrock tunnel. A disintegrating mill had a capacity of 130 tons per 24 hours.

COLORADO

Boulder.—Silver will be produced in large quantities from Boulder county this year, according to the 'Miner', as the Caribou, Congo Chief, Up-to-Date, Victoria, White Raven, and Yellow Tiger mines are all showing rich ore. While the tungsten industry here is practically at a standstill, the mining of silver will help make good the deficiency.

Breckenridge.—The Wellington Mines Co. in 1918 received $735,640 for lead-zinc ore sold. The profit was $386,319. Dividends absorbed $300,000, and now total $1,850,000. C. M. Henderson is in charge.

Leadville.—In spite of the high price of silver there are said to be a number of good mines idle in this district.

IDAHO

The U. S. Geological Survey has recently issued, as Bulletin 680, a report by A. R. Schultz, describing the coalfields of the Bighole mountains and other districts in Teton county, Idaho, and the adjacent part of Wyoming. The report also describes extensive phosphate deposits in the same general region. The existence of these deposits has been known for more than ten years, but their extent was not known until they were mapped in detail and sampled by Mr. Schultz.

Boise.— The governor, D. W. Davis, has signed House Bill No. 40, thereby creating a Bureau of Mines and Geology. The initial appropriation for two years is $30,000, plus $25,000 for co-operation with the U. S. Bureau of Mines and Geological Survey. The board of control is vested in the Governor, J. J. Day, D. C. Livingston, R. N. Bell, and F. A. Thomson.

Hailey.— The Mascot M. & M. Co. has been driving its lower tunnel all winter, and is in 148 ft. This will eventuall cut the veins at a depth of 700 ft. The ore carries lead and silver. A mill is contemplated. Charles Peter is general manager.

Mullan.— The Idaho-Carbonate Hill has $60,000 available and is to resume work in May, according to the president, W. D. Greenough. So far, $123,000 has been spent since the consolidation About 2000 ft. of driving and sinking from 450 to 800 ft. is contemplated. The ore carries lead and silver.

The Consolidated Interstate-Callahan reports a loss of $195,933 for 1918, this after paying $456,222 in dividends The operating profit was $291,938. Supplies advanced nearly 100% in cost.

Wallace.— The Hecla Mining Co. in 1918 shipped 15,133 tons of crude ore and milled 309,656 tons. This yielded 51,365,676 lb. of lead, 433,341 lb. of zinc, and 1,590,062 lb. of silver. The net profit was $2,054,716, of which $350,000 was paid in dividends. Ore-reserves total 1,584,115 tons.

MICHIGAN

Houghton.—Mohawk made a profit of $1,003,690 in 1918, compared with $1,971,601 in 1917. The output was 10,781,041 lb. of copper, a decrease of 1,500,000 lb. Costs totaled 14.641 cents, an increase of 2.58 cents.

Mohawk pays $1 per share on May 1. This is half of the previous quarterly distribution.

The Mohawk is to spend $40,000 for the tunnel under the Lake at the stamp-mill at Gay before it is completed. The work is ambitious, but is more than justified by the circumstances, and is more than warranted. The tunnel is now in 600 ft., going forward at the rate of 15 ft. per day. The shaft was sunk 125 ft., and the tunnel is 100 ft. under water all the way out. It is in sandstone most of the distance. It will go out 2200 ft., and from soundings at that point in the Lake there will be 30 ft. of water overhead and 50 ft. of rock. If conditions warrant, it is possible that the tunnel will go out 2600 ft., at which point there will be 44 ft. of rock and 33 ft. of water. The purpose of the tunnel is to provide water for the mill. Three electric pumps, each with a capacity of 7,000,000 gal. per day, operated by a 1250-kw. turbine, have been ordered. The excess electric power will be used for re-grinding, which may be part of the process at this mill. Experiments are now being conducted along these lines.

The Mayflower-Old Colony Copper Co. has levied an assessment of 50 cents per share, due on April 15. This is the second since the consolidation two years ago. The new shaft is down 1050 ft., and sinking continues with plenty of skilled men.

Calumet & Hecla in 1918 made a net profit of $4,349,196, after reserving $600,000 for federal taxes. This is about half of the profit for 1917. Dividends amounted to $55 per share. The output from 2,876,392 tons of ore was 58,722,969 lb., a decrease of 10,000,000 lb. Costs were 21.05 cents, an increase of 8.04 cents per pound.

The report of the Naumkeag Copper Company for 1918 shows that 997 ft. of driving and 617 ft. of sinking was accomplished. The incline shaft was deepened to 1027 ft. Work on the 400-ft. level was generally unsatisfactory, only a small 'local' shoot being found. The lode was passed by the shaft at 975 ft. About 500 ft. of work was done on the 1000-ft. level, but less satisfactory than at 400 ft., so work was stopped, and transferred to the south part of the adit-level, where it is now in progress. Cash on hand totals $28,126. J. H. Reeder is superintendent.

NEVADA

Carson.— The State Legislature has voted to divide Humboldt county, the new territory being named Pershing

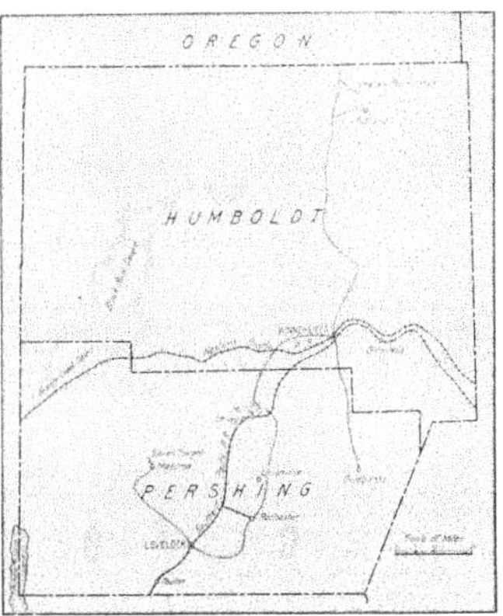

PART OF NEVADA SHOWING HOW THE ORIGINAL HUMBOLDT COUNTY WAS SUBDIVIDED.

county. The accompanying map shows the partition, also the principal mining centres therein.

On April 1, Governor Emmet D. Boyle vetoed A. B. No. 175 "an Act to amend an Act entitled 'An Act creating the Nevada State Bureau of Mines and prescribing it duties'."

Divide.—The Nye county commissioners have approved of the townsite, and town lots are on sale. A corner lot, 80 by 50 ft., sold for $250. The authorities at Washington have been asked to arrange for a post-office.

Jarbidge.—In 1916, I. W. Anderson of Tacoma obtained leases and options to purchase several groups of lode claims for Spokane capitalists. Later, there was organized the Jarbidge Mines Co., under the laws of the State of Washington, to operate La Veta group of 8 claims, which had been purchased for cash. This and the other claims are situated high up on the west slope of the Crater range or Jarbidge mountains, at an elevation of 8300 to 10,300 ft. The properties cover the mountain at the heads of Bonanza, Gorge, and Snowslide gulches. Work was started on the group and some money paid on the purchase-price. Some of the important veins of the Jarbidge district are found within these areas. The management of the Jarbidge Mines Co. is generally believed to have spent $30,000, when war suspended activities. The company is expected to resume as soon as financial conditions approach normal.

Thompson.—Mason Valley Copper Co. produced 947,336 lb in February, against 1,111,000 lb. in January.

MISSOURI

Joplin.—Mine-owners in the Tri-State region are to ask co-operation of retail dealers so that the cost of living may be reduced. Wages have been cut somewhat, but war prices for food still hold.

Production of the region last week was:

State	Blende, tons	Calamine, tons	Lead, tons	Value
Kansas	1,010	...	324	$74,899
Missouri	1,447	146	390	84,215
Oklahoma	7,651	...	1,248	366,866
Total	10,108	146	1,862	$525,980
Average value...	$37.50	$26	$60	......

The total value was $84,000 more than the previous week.

There are now 123 concentrating plants in operation in this region, six new ones being started last week. The total capacity is 10,000 tons of zinc-lead concentrate per week.

MONTANA

Butte.—Davis-Daly in February produced 291,624 lb. of copper and 10,848 oz. of silver, compared with 1,018,889 lb. and 39,093 oz. in January.

Anaconda has suspended work at the East Gray Rock, Silver Bow, and Butte-Alex Scott shafts. The last named mine will be operated through the West Colusa while the Scott shaft is being fire-proofed. The other two shafts are also to be fire-proofed. The daily tonnage of ore will be reduced by 900 thereby.

OKLAHOMA

Picher.—The Miami Wonder Mining Co., through its president, F. D. Whiting, has adopted a profit-sharing system for its employees.

At the Mahutska, controlled by the R. Y. Ramage interests, the mill dressed 1300 tons of 'dirt' in 70 hours last week, yielding 185 tons of lead and 99 tons of zinc concentrates. The ore averaged 10.77% lead and 6.07% blende recovered. W. L. Kepner is superintendent.

TEXAS

O'Donnell.—J. W. McRea and associates are constructing here the first unit of a plant for the separation of potash, epsom salt, and borax from material obtained from the beds of two large basins or lakes, eight miles west of O'Donnell. It is stated that the soil for a depth of 6½ ft. is highly impregnated with these products. Each lake is five miles in area. C. H. Doak, postmaster here, who has been making investigations of possible potash deposits in this section of western Texas for some time past, located the dry lakes and brought them to the attention of McRea.

Wichita Falls.—According to the 'Wichita Oil Reporter', the average daily output of oil in this State is 210,000 bbl. Of this, Wichita contributes 70,000 bbl., Ranger 70,000 bbl., and the remainder from southern Texas and the Gulf coast. It is said by some that labor is scarce in the Ranger field, while others report the reverse. Wages are from $4.50 to $12 per day.

UTAH

Eureka.—The new railway into the eastern end of the Tintic district is now being built by the Utah Construction Co. The length, including spurs, will be 11 miles, and the cost $300,000. Completion is expected by August.

Salt Lake City.—Dividends paid by companies in this State since January 1 total $2,995,398, as follows: Bingham Mines, $37,500; Chief Consolidated, $110,630; Daly, $37,000; Eagle & Blue Bell, $44,657; Iron Blossom, $25,000; Judge, $60,000; Ontario, $75,000; Tintic Standard, $93,976; Utah Consolidated, $75,000; and Utah Copper, $2,436,735.

Tintic.—The Tintic Milling Co., G. H. Dern, manager, is considering the erection of a cyanide plant to extract the gold from the ores offered for treatment. Regular shipments of bullion are made.

In Professional Paper 107 of the U. S. Geological Survey, the geology and ore deposits of the Tintic district are discussed in 282 pages by Waldemar Lindgren, G. F. Loughlin, and V. C. Heikes.

WASHINGTON

Boyds.—The Napoleon mine of the Canada Copper Corporation in Ferry county has been closed. The 5000-ft. Bleichert aerial tram has been moved to the Mountain Chief mine at Roneta.

Spokane.—Dividends paid by companies in the North-West during the first quarter of 1919 totaled $1,484,711, compared with $2,629,307 in that period of 1917. Idaho contributed $765,150, less than half of the previous amount; British Columbia, $695,711, nearly up to the mark; and Washington, $23,790, an increase of this sum.

CANADA

British Columbia

Ainsworth.—The Florence company is operating its mill 24 hours daily now. The monthly output of concentrate is expected to be 600 tons, assaying 70% lead and 24 oz. of silver. A Richards-Janney classifier and flotation plant recently added will recover an extra 10%.

Anyox.—The Granby Consolidated expected to blow-in its furnaces early in April.

Trail.—Ore received at the Consolidated M. & S. plant here during the third week in March totaled 8208 tons, an increase of 662 tons over the second week. The Centre Star at Rossland sent 2748 tons and the Sullivan 3970 tons.

Manitoba

The Pas.—According to R. C. Wallace, in the March Bulletin of the Canadian Mining Institute, the Mandy Mining Co. in 1918 shipped to Trail, B. C., 6000 tons of ore carrying 20% copper, 0.1 oz. gold, and 2.5 oz. silver, worth a total of $651,000. In 1917 the output was 3300 tons, valued at $274,560.

The late commissioner of northern Manitoba, J. A. Campbell, has had published a 52-page illustrated bulletin on Manitoba's Northland, including the Hudson Bay region and the Rice Lake gold area. The first article is 'Prospecting Areas in Manitoba', by E. L. Bruce of the Dominion Geological Survey. The accompanying map shows the known districts. 'The Northern Manitoba Mineral Belt' is the title of a report by Mr. Campbell, who also writes on 'Northern Copper Country Development'. M. C. Hendry of Winnipeg describes the 'Water-Power Resources of Manitoba', while C. A. Bramble covers 'The Rice Lake Gold Area', where several mines are being developed. The geologic features of Rice Lake are briefly discussed by R. C. Wallace and J. S. DeLury of the University of Manitoba. The natural resources of the region are great, including fish, fur, game, timber, and minerals. Those interested should secure a copy of this general review of northern Manitoba.

The manager of the Flin-Flon Syndicate, John Black, and John Hammel of the original owners, with R. C. Wallace and J. A. Campbell, of The Pas, formed a part of the Western delegation that recently waited upon the Government with reference to railway development in Manitoba. President Hanna, of the National Railways, received the delegates at Toronto, and after hearing their representations, he pledged to do the following railway construction:

Flin-Flon Railway—If the owners of the ore deposits there will guarantee to erect a smelter with a capacity of at least 2000 tons per day, the railway will be built from The Pas forthwith. The syndicate owning this ore has the matter in hand, and it is expected that it will agree to the erection of the works. It rests upon them whether the mineral fields of Manitoba will be opened this year.—— Melfort-The Pas railway—Mr. Hanna assured the delegates that this line would be partly constructed this year. Work would commence at Melfort, and up the Carrot valley for a distance of 30 or 40 miles. Grading only would be done this year.

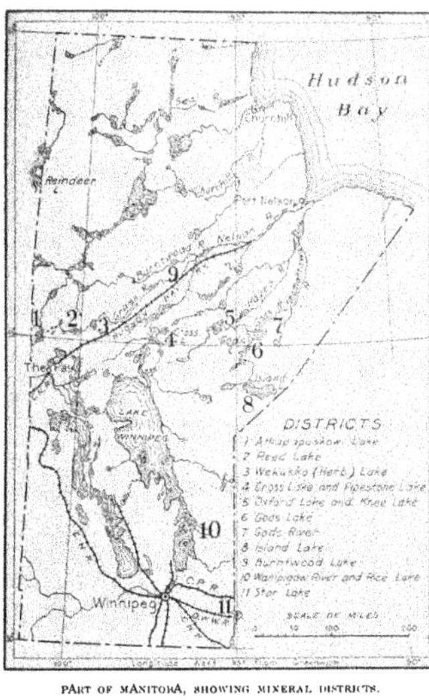

PART OF MANITOBA, SHOWING MINERAL DISTRICTS.

the rails laid down next year. The Vonda spur to Melfort will have 20 miles of steel laid this year. With the Carrot River line this will give direct connection with the Hudson Bay railway and The Pas. The Melfort-Saskatoon-Humboldt road from Breux to Humboldt will be completed this year. The Estevan and Souris delegates were told that a line was contemplated front west of Moose mountain to the Hudson Bay railway. The deputation also asked that Sturgis on the Thunder Hill line be connected up with the Hudson Bay railway. Assurance was given that half of this work would be done this year. All told, six lines projecting toward The Pas, to connect with the Hudson Bay railway, were favorably dealt with. Two more, one, the Flin-Flon road, are nearer realization than thought possible a week ago. The C. P. R. is reported to have surveyors out running a line west to The Pas, through the Carrot River valley toward Athapapuskow Lake region. These two bring the total up to eight railways pointing north.

Ontario

Porcupine.—The McIntyre-Porcupine company disburses 5%, or $180,514, on April 15. This makes $1,263,599 to date. The present monthly gold yield is $140,000.

PERSONAL

Note. The Editor invites members of the profession to send particulars of their work and appointments. The information is interesting to our readers.

F. W. Bunyan is in San Francisco.

J. B. Tyrrell was at Porcupine last week.

E. H. Nutter has returned from Washington.

H. N. Lawrie, of Portland, Oregon, is visiting San Francisco.

David T. Day, of the Geological Survey, was in San Francisco last week.

L. O. Howard has returned to Salt Lake City after a visit to El Paso, Texas.

T. M. Hamilton has left Santiago, Chile, and is now at Lewistown, Montana.

J. H. Mackenzie was at Divide, Nevada, last week, accompanied by **George Wingfield**.

P. R. Middleton, of Sydney, Australia, arrived in San Francisco on the 'Vertura', on his way to Salt Lake City.

Clyde Marsh, mechanical engineer at the Northport smelter, at Northport, Idaho, has been discharged from the Navy.

Thos. M. Miller, who served as First Lieutenant with the British Tank Corps for 13 months, in France, has returned to Berkeley.

E. P. Mathewson, director of the A. S. & R., passed through San Francisco on his way from El Paso to Tacoma, on a tour of inspection.

William W. Logan is leaving for Alaska this week to take charge of the cyanide plant of the Gold Bullion Mining Company, at Willow Creek.

W. J. Rose and **H. Warlow Davies**, of Broken Hill, Australia, are visiting Butte, Montana; they will also go to Trail, British Columbia.

J. E. Johnson, Jr. of New York, was killed in an automobile accident on April 5. Details will be published in our next issue.

The United States Potash Association was formed at Denver last week. T. W. Boyer of Salt Lake City was appointed president; A. C. Harrington of New York, vice-president and treasurer; and T. E. Evans of Omaha, second vice-president. Other members of the directorate are L. A. Cover of Baltimore, F. M. Edgell of Denver, W. E. Richardson of Central City, Nebraska, and T. J. Stewart of New York.

The fourth annual meeting of the American Association of Petroleum Geologists was held at Dallas, Texas, on March 13 to 15. More than 200 petroleum geologists and others were present. David White, of the U. S. Geological Survey, I. C. White, State Geologist of West Virginia, Ralph Arnold, valuation expert of the Internal Revenue Department of the U. S. Treasury, and Charles Schuchert, professor at Yale University, participated.

The U. S. Civil Service Commission announces an open competitive examination for mining engineer for metal and mineral investigations, on May 6, 1919. The register of eligibles will be divided into three grades, as follows: (1) $1800 to $2400; (2) $2400 to $3000; and (3) $3000 to $4000 per year. The entrance salary within the range stated for each grade will depend upon the qualifications of the appointee and the importance of the duty to which he is assigned. Competitors will not be required to report at any place, but will be rated on the following subjects, which will have the relative weights indicated: (1) education and experience, 80; and (2) publications, reports, or essay (to be filed with application), 20.

METAL PRICES

San Francisco, April 8

Aluminum-dust, cents per lb	60.00
Antimony, cents per pound	8.00
Copper, electrolytic, cents per pound, in carload lots	15.50
Lead, pig, cents per pound	5.50— 6.50
Platinum, per ounce	$100
Quicksilver, per flask of 75 lb	$67.50
Spelter, cents per pound	8.00
Zinc-dust, cents per pound	12.50

EASTERN METAL MARKET

(By wire from New York)

April 8.—Copper is dull though steady. Lead is quiet and firm. Spelter is inactive but steady.

SILVER

Below are given official (not Government) quotations, in cents per ounce, of silver 999 fine. In order to make prompt settlements with smelters and brokers, producers allow a discount from the maximum fixed price of $1.01½, hence the lower price. The Government has not fixed the general market price at $1, but will pay this price (as from April 23, 1918) for all silver purchased by it. The equivalent of dollar silver (1000 fine) in British currency is 46.65 pence per ounce (925 fine), calculated at the normal rate of exchange. On August 15, 1918, the Treasury announced that the maximum price was fixed at $1.01½ per ounce. The British government fixed it maximum at 49½ pence, on September 2, but on November 12 this was changed to 48¾, on December 13 to 48 7/16, and on February 20 to 47¾ pence. On March 25, on account of the low rate of exchange, the London price was adjusted, with a minimum of 95 cents, resulting in daily fluctuations.

Date		New York cents	London pence	Average week ending		Cents	Pence
Apr.	2	101.12	49.19	Feb.	25	101.12	47.75
"	3	101.12	48.87	Mch.	4	101.12	47.75
"	4	101.12	48.56	"	11	101.12	47.75
"	5	101.12	48.87	"	18	101.12	47.75
	6 Sunday			"	25	101.12	47.75
"	7	101.12	48.81	Apr.	1	101.12	49.63
"	8	101.12	48.87	"	8	101.12	48.86

Monthly averages

	1917	1918	1919		1917	1918	1919
Jan.	75.14	88.72	101.12	July	78.92	99.62	....
Feb.	77.54	85.79	101.12	Aug.	85.40	100.31	....
Mch.	74.13	88.11	101.12	Sept.	100.73	101.12	....
Apr.	72.51	95.35	....	Oct.	87.38	101.12	....
May	74.61	99.50	....	Nov.	85.97	101.12	....
June	76.44	99.50	....	Dec.	85.97	101.12	....

Writing from London on March 13, Samuel Montagu & Co. said that the absorption of sovereigns (gold) in India during the year 1917-'18 amounted to 1166 lacs of rupees ($37,312,000). The difficulties in providing sufficient silver to reinforce the silver balances, impelled the Government to release sovereigns for currency between April and August 1917, and in February and March 1918, principally in connection with Government purchases of wheat. The Government currency report, however, stated that the bulk of these sovereigns found their way shortly after issue to Bombay and Calcutta, where they were mostly turned into jewelry. According to the 'Times' of London on March 6, private advices suggest that India may be on the verge of a worse food famine than the visitation of 1900. There is also a grave fodder famine, which is said to be resulting in a wholesale loss of cattle, just as the herds of Gujerat were all but wiped out 18 years ago. Eastern banks do not appear to take so grave a view of the situation as outlined above, but should these forebodings be realized, the remarkable cumulative prosperity of India may be revealed by the putting into circulation of some of the vast number of silver rupees hoarded since the year of famine indicated above.

Silver produced by the U. S. S. R. & M. Co. in 1918 amounted to 15,337,465 oz., 2,337,000 oz. more than in 1917, and 3,700,000 oz. more than in 1916. Most of this comes from Mexico.

Silver sold by the Calumet & Hecla company in 1918 amounted to $238,308, a by-product of copper.

COPPER

Prices of electrolytic in New York, in cents per pound.

Date			Average week ending		
Apr.	2	15.12	Feb.	25	16.40
"	3	15.12	Mch.	4	15.25
"	4	15.50	"	11	14.83
"	5	15.50	"	18	14.70
	6 Sunday		"	25	14.99
"	7	15.12	Apr.	1	15.27
"	8	15.12	"	8	15.25

Monthly averages

	1917	1918	1919		1917	1918	1919
Jan.	29.53	23.50	20.43	July	29.67	26.00	....
Feb.	34.57	23.50	17.34	Aug.	27.42	26.00	....
Mch.	36.00	23.50	15.05	Sept.	25.11	26.00	....
Apr.	33.16	23.50	....	Oct.	23.50	26.00	....
May	31.00	23.50	....	Nov.	23.50	26.00	....
June	32.57	23.50	....	Dec.	23.50	26.00	....

Copper sales during the first three months of 1919 were only about 110,000,000 lb., compared with a refinery output of probably three times that quantity.

Brass companies, which normally consume the bulk of the copper output, are operating at 30% capacity with few orders on their books.

Dividends paid by copper companies during the first quarter of 1918 totaled $22,384,329, compared with $38,645,042, $45,341,307, and $29,537,100 in the same period of the previous years.

LEAD

Lead is quoted in cents per pound, New York delivery.

Date			Average week ending		
Apr.	2	5.25	Feb.	25	5.05
"	3	5.25	Mch.	4	5.25
"	4	5.25	"	11	5.25
"	5	5.25	"	18	5.25
"	6 Sunday		"	25	5.21
"	7	5.25	Apr.	1	5.25
"	8	5.25	"	8	5.25

Monthly averages

	1917	1918	1919		1917	1918	1919
Jan.	7.64	6.85	5.60	July	10.93	8.03	....
Feb.	9.10	7.07	5.13	Aug.	10.75	8.05	....
Mch.	10.07	7.26	5.24	Sept.	9.07	8.05	....
Apr.	9.38	6.99	....	Oct.	6.97	8.05	....
May	10.29	6.88	....	Nov.	6.38	8.05	....
June	11.74	7.58	....	Dec.	6.49	6.90	....

Lead on hand at the Trail, B. C., smelter, amounted to 8266 tons on March 1, against 9042 tons on February 1.

ZINC

Zinc is quoted as spelter, standard Western brands, New York delivery, in cents per pound:

Date			Average week ending		
Apr.	2	6.55	Feb.	25	6.69
"	3	6.55	Mch.	4	6.61
"	4	6.60	"	11	6.55
"	5	6.60	"	18	6.50
"	6 Sunday		"	25	6.48
"	7	6.65	Apr.	1	6.53
"	8	6.65	"	8	6.60

Monthly averages

	1917	1918	1919		1917	1918	1919
Jan.	9.75	7.78	7.44	July	8.98	8.72	....
Feb.	10.45	7.97	6.71	Aug.	8.58	8.87	....
Mch.	10.78	7.67	6.53	Sept.	8.33	9.58	....
Apr.	10.20	7.04	....	Oct.	8.32	9.11	....
May	9.41	7.29	....	Nov.	7.76	8.75	....
June	9.63	7.92	....	Dec.	7.84	8.49	....

Zinc ore prices slumped $2.50 per ton to $37.50, basis 60% metal at Joplin last week. The weak spelter market is the cause. It is said that it is costing $30 per ton to make concentrate at present.

The American Zinc, Lead & Smelting Co. in 1918 made a profit of only $911,415, one-half of that in 1917, and one-tenth of that in 1916. The average price of spelter in those three years was 7.89, 8.73, and 12.63 cents per pound.

QUICKSILVER

The primary market for quicksilver is San Francisco, California being the largest producer. The price is fixed in the open market, according to quantity. Prices, in dollars per flask of 75 pounds:

Date					
Mch.	11	75.00	Mch.	25	68.00
"	18	68.00	Apr.	1	68.00
			"	8	67.50

Monthly averages

	1917	1918	1919		1917	1918	1919
Jan.	81.00	128.06	103.75	July	102.00	120.00	....
Feb.	126.25	118.00	90.00	Aug.	115.00	120.00	....
Mch.	113.75	112.00	72.80	Sept.	112.00	120.00	....
Apr.	114.50	115.00	....	Oct.	102.00	120.00	....
May	104.00	110.00	....	Nov.	102.50	120.00	....
June	85.50	112.00	....	Dec.	117.42	115.00	....

TIN

Prices in New York, in cents per pound. The monthly averages in 1918 are nominal. On December 3 the War Industries Board fixed the price to consumers and jobbers at 72½c. f.o.b. Chicago and Eastern points, and 71¼c. on the Pacific Coast. This will continue until the U. S. Steel Products Co.'s stock is consumed.

Monthly averages

	1917	1918	1919		1917	1918	1919
Jan.	44.10	85.13	71.50	July	62.60	93.00	....
Feb.	51.47	85.00	72.44	Aug.	62.53	91.33	....
Mch.	54.27	85.00	72.50	Sept.	61.54	80.40	....
Apr.	55.63	88.53	....	Oct.	62.24	78.82	....
May	63.21	100.01	....	Nov.	74.18	73.67	....
June	61.93	91.00	....	Dec.	85.00	71.52	....

Eastern Metal Market

New York, April 2.

Firmness characterizes all the markets, with an optimistic tone in most cases.

Antimony is unchanged.

Copper sales have been fairly heavy, and prices have gradually advanced.

Lead is firm again with a better demand.

Tin is still stagnant and devoid of features.

Zinc is still lifeless, but the tone of the market is better with prices slightly firmer.

ANTIMONY

Quotations are nominally unchanged at 6.25 to 6.37½c., New York, duty paid, for Asiatic grades. Demand is light.

ALUMINUM

No. 1 virgin metal, 98 to 99%, is obtainable at the nominal quotation of 28 to 30c. per lb., New York, with re-melt metal of the same analysis 2c. per lb. under this.

COPPER

There is now no question but that the turn has come in the copper market. In March there was more buying than in any month since the armistice, and prices have gradually risen since the low point a few weeks ago. It is the opinion of many that those levels will not be reached again, even though a slight recession may be possible any time. As an indication of the position, one large producer told the writer yesterday that his company had done a splendid business in March, mostly all for April delivery, and that the volume was close to a normal turnover. Some estimates place the total sales in March at 75,000,000 lb., with nearly half of this sold last week. Demand continues good, and the market may be characterized as firm and steady, with the tendency upward. Electrolytic copper is quoted at 15.37½c., New York, for April delivery, with Lake copper largely nominal at 15.62½c., New York. Trading in copper on the New York Metal Exchange was started on Monday, March 31, and reports are that it was a successful and satisfactory inauguration of this new movement. A feature of it was the high prices bid, especially for future delivery, running up to 15.75c. for July shipment. No sales were reported on that day, but yesterday sales were made of 100 tons of electrolytic at 15.50c. for April delivery and 25 tons at 15.65c. for June. The report of the representatives of the Copper Export Association, who just returned from Europe, is not especially bullish, at least not so far as the immediate market is concerned. They say that stocks in the hands of the Allied governments are rapidly being depleted, and that consumers are not well supplied; also that Germany is bare of copper and buying from all these sources should be pronounced when peace is effected, or soon after. An unconfirmed rumor is to the effect that the export price of the Association is now 18c. per lb., New York, instead of 23 cents.

IRON AND STEEL

Little in the shape of a broadening demand has appeared in the second week of the new prices. Practically all the business offered is still recognized as having been held back awaiting the reduction in prices. The Railroad Administration's refusal to accept the new steel prices as arranged by the Industrial Board, or to be bound by those yet to be fixed on coal and other material, seriously threatens the whole program of stabilizing prices. The railroads would nominally buy over 25% of the country's output of coal and 20% of the steel production. The railroad authorities may yet be brought into line by Presidential pressure. Export inquiries are numerous, but so far little business has resulted. Heavy melting steel scrap, which last week fell so low that open-hearth steel plants started to use larger quantities, has advanced because of this and is now $2 or more per ton above the low point.

LEAD

All the cheaper lots of lead that were being offered a week or so ago have been apparently absorbed or withdrawn, and the market is firmer at 5.25c., New York, or 5c., St. Louis, for both the outside and the Trust. Inquiry is better than in the last two or three weeks, and the tone of the market is decidedly firm. There have been sales in fact of two fairly large quantities, and it is believed that the demand will improve from now on.

TIN

Instead of becoming less restricted the market has become more so. Those in authority have requested American tin smelters to cease selling their product until the allocated metal has been absorbed, or at least until further notice. This they have agreed to do, and American tin is practically unobtainable. Spot Straits tin is still obtainable only at the fixed price of 72.50c. per lb., New York. A Government statement is to the effect that stocks of tin in the United States on March 1 were about 20,000 tons, and that consumption was at the rate of about 3500 tons per month. Tin arrivals in March were 2070 tons, of which 1975 tons came in at Pacific ports. Stocks and landing on March 31 were 156 tons. Imports in the first quarter were 6341 tons, compared with 12,828 tons in the same quarter in 1918. The London market for spot Straits yesterday was £226 15s. per ton.

ZINC

Despite the fact that demand has not broadened, the market may be termed as firm and steady, with quotations slightly higher than a week ago. Prime Western for early or most any delivery is held at 6.20c., St. Louis, or 6.55c., New York. There has been some buying as well as inquiry front the galvanizing interests, but this has not been large. The hope is still strong that it will be larger as the weeks advance. There is almost no demand from brass-makers. There is little export demand. It is expected that the Government stocks of zinc, mostly high-grade, will be disposed of by a special arrangement similar to that of copper.

ORES

Manganese: Imports of high-grade ore in February are officially reported as 20,819 long tons. An interesting fact is that, of the January imports of ore 47,000 tons, over 14,000 tons came from Cuba.

Manganese Iron Alloys: Certain British producers are again offering their standard 80% alloy in the American market and are asking $150, seaboard. All import restrictions have just been removed. The British price compares with $150 delivered for the American 78 to 82% alloy, with $2 per unit deducted for each percentage under 78, making the 70% alloy $134 delivered. Spiegel is quoted at $40, freight allowed, for the 16 to 19% alloy, with $45 asked for the higher analysis.

Molybdenum: Prices continue nominal and unchanged at 80 to 85c. per pound. Exports of molybdenite are reported as good.

Tungsten: Only one mine is reported as operating in the United States. Foreign mines are also working on short time, if at all. These facts are regarded as the only hopeful phase of the situation, because stocks will soon be depleted.

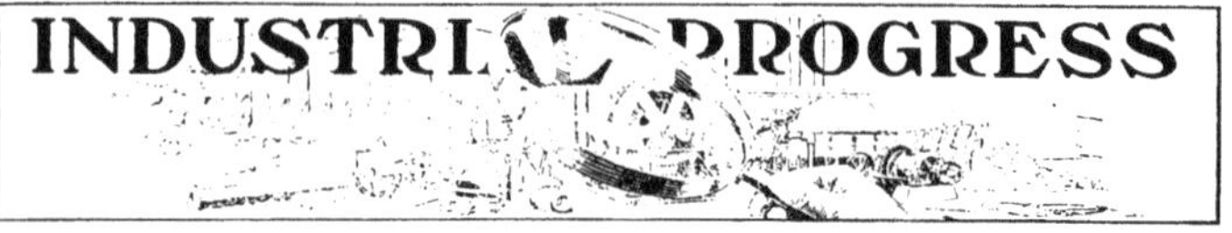

INFORMATION FURNISHED BY MANUFACTURERS

DISPOSAL OF MATERIAL BY AIRCRAFT BUREAU

Plans for the disposal of surplus material now in the possession of the U. S. Bureau of Aircraft Production, or which is being taken over by this Bureau upon settlement of contracts with manufacturers, have been completed, and the organization for carrying out the details is rapidly being perfected. The primary consideration in these plans, which have been matured under the general policies as laid down by the Director of Sales of the War Department, has been the prevention of any disruption of the market and as full and complete protection of the Nation's industries as possible, as the following outline will show:

There has been formed a Material Disposal Section of the Bureau, organized on a basis similar to that followed by large commercial houses that handle sales through branch offices. This Section will be under the direction of First-Lieutenant Charles S. Shotwell. Sales will be made under the supervision of a sales manager stationed at Washington. The Bureau will probably have for sale the following material, and as soon as this has been established as surplus and policy for the sale of same determined, the Bureau will issue bulletins covering the material for sale.

b-1	Machine tools and fixtures	b-8	Hardware
b-2	Electric machinery	b-9	buildings and lands
b-3	Dies, tools, jigs, and gauges	b-10	Fabrics
b-4	Chemicals, paints, and oils	b-11	Scrap
b-5	Metals	b-12	Shop equipment
b-6	Motor accessories	b-13	Office equipment
b-7	Lumber	b-14	Miscellaneous

Sales negotiations will be handled by salesmen in each of eight district branches, to be at Boston, Buffalo, Chicago, Dayton, Detroit, New York, Pittsburgh, and San Francisco. These salesmen will be authorized to make sales of property wherever located, after the same has been cleared by the Board of Sales Review of the office of the Director of Sales, so that the prospective buyers will communicate with the branch office in the city nearest them. This arrangement, it is expected, will make it possible for manufacturers needing machinery and supplies to purchase conveniently and at fair prices. The salesmen will have full authority to sell at the best offer made, provided that offer is at or above an appraised value arrived at independently, or at market-value in the case of raw material.

Bulletins containing full descriptions of material for sale will be issued from time to time, and be kept up to date. Those interested will be placed on the mailing-list upon request addressed to the Bureau of Aircraft Production, Material Disposal Section, Washington, D. C. To save delay requests should specify the commodities on which information is desired by reference to the sales classification.

INCREASE IN FILTER PRODUCTION

The following table, prepared by the Oliver Continuous Filter Co. of San Francisco, shows the growth of its export business during the last five years. In spite of export restrictions the Oliver output advanced each year. Prior to 1914 the business with Mexico was larger than in 1916, and from present indications it will advance again. A recent order was for $40,000 of cyanide equipment. Most of the Mexican business of late years was with the northern copper companies. The shipment to India was to the Burma Corporation, and that to Siberia to the Irtysh Corporation. Filters in Chile were principally for the nitrate industry, from which a big demand for the Oliver is expected.

Country	1914	1915	1916	1917	1918
Alaska	....	$6,334	$4,927	$1,544	$5,162
Australia	....	......	6,831	804	3,806
Bolivia	....	......	2,984	4,131	809
British Columbia	$53	3,829	9,152	16,389	3,190
Canada	464	2,528	11,287	17,707	25,967
Chile	....	......	....	19,379	14,752
Cuba	116	126	3,650	34	386
England	....	......	....	....	10,944
Egypt	....	......	....	....	39
Hawaii	....	......	....	....	151
Honduras	....	......	....	1,603	24
India	....	......	....	8,161	39,684
Italy	....	......	....	....	4,879
Japan	....	9,117	34,330	21,905	20,755
Mexico	8,433	2,318	20,951	15,007	26,180
Newfoundland	....	......	....	....	991
Nicaragua	....	2,142	....	....	358
Norway	....	......	....	800	12,407
Salvador	....	2,880	544	330	381
Peru	....	......	5,924	66	.....
France	....	......	....	2,025	.....
Siberia	....	......	....	13,330	.....
Korea	....	......	....	6,125	.....
Totals	$9,066	$29,274	$100,580	$132,205	$170,865

COMMERCIAL PARAGRAPHS

A handsome 64-page catalogue dealing with its chlorine control apparatus has been sent us by the **California Jewell** Filter Co., Merchants Exchange, San Francisco.

An 8-page leaflet of the Troy **Wagon Works Co.** of Troy, Ohio, gives a list of 209 users of its trailers with 86 makes of motor-trucks, used in congested cities and in country hauling.

Pratt-Gilbert Company, of Phoenix, Ariz., has just received an order for ITP carbide mine lamps from T. **Knight** **Bayne**, Victoria, B. C. This firm is building up a large trade in the West through the merits of the lamp and the quick service made possible by carrying a very large stock.

If you wish to fasten a step or handle to a concrete or brick wall, tighten a loose screw-driver handle, tighten the handle of a hammer, need a washer or lock-nut on a bolt, imbed expansion-sockets in cement, and a permanent lock-nut, the Smooth-On Manufacturing Co. of Jersey City, N. J., advises using Smooth-On iron cement No. 1.

The **Chicago Pneumatic Tool Co.** makes the following announcements:

F. V. Sargeant has been appointed district manager of sales at Boston, in place of F. S. Eggleston. The office at Wichita, Kansas, has been closed, an office and warehouse being established at Eldorado. A new office and warehouse have been opened at Tulsa, Oklahoma.

The **Sullivan Machinery Co.** of Chicago announces the establishment of a foreign trade department. Already this firm has branch offices at Salisbury House, London; Paris; Santiago, Chile; and Sydney, New South Wales; also there are engineering agencies of standing to handle Sullivan products at Christiania, Norway; Amsterdam, Holland; Gijon, Spain; Turin, Italy; Algiers, Tunis; Johannesburg, Transvaal; Durban, Natal; Shanghai, China; Tokyo, Japan; Lima, Peru; and Buenos Aires, Argentina.

EDITORIAL

POTASH from Lorraine is now for sale at New York; it comes from the mines formerly controlled by the Germans. This is an interesting development of our post-war trade relations with France, and although it is unfavorable to our domestic potash industry, we prefer it to the commercial invasion of the German Kali Syndicate.

BRAZIL, as a mining region, is likely to gain by the coming change of government, for the probable president, Sr. Ruy Barboza, is an enlightened and progressive man, with a proper desire to stimulate the development of the mineral resources of the country. He will enter into the duties of his office next June. We may add that the people of Brazil are eager to establish closer relations with the United States.

INFORMATION concerning the prospects of marketing copper in Europe is dribbling into print. It appears that England, France, and Italy together hold about 500,000,000 pounds of copper awaiting consumption. In France and in Italy the importation of copper is under governmental embargo, in order to permit the liquidation of existing supplies. In England manufacturers would be glad to buy American copper but they are deterred from doing so by reason of competition with the Government's stock of metal. It is asserted confidently that Germany will take at least 20 million pounds of copper just as soon as facilities for shipping and credit are available. Meanwhile international business waits for the gentlemen at Paris to conclude their labors.

EVIDENCE of improvement in Mexico is given in the annual report of the United States Smelting, Refining & Mining Company, from which it appears that the amount of silver produced by this company increased to 15,337,000 ounces, as compared with 13,000,000 in 1917 and 11,722,000 in 1916. This speaks well both for the company's mines at Pachuca and for the continuity of operations during Carranza's regime. Apropos of that we note Mr. Simon Guggenheim's remark at the recent annual meeting of the American Smelting & Refining Company; he said: "The Carranza government is daily growing in strength. We have received assurances that in three or four months the Villista bandits will be entirely driven out of northern Mexico." Since this was said the news has come that Emiliano Zapata, who has terrorized the State of Morelos for the past eight years, has been captured and killed, thereby removing a strong factor of unrest. Meanwhile Señor Rafael Nietto has failed in his effort to raise American money for the Mexican treasury, probably because the security was inadequate, and Señor Luis Cabrera succeeds him. This is inauspicious, but it may work for the best.

AMONG the excellent suggestions made at the New York meeting of the Institute—when we say "the Institute," our readers will need no further specification—was one made by Dr. A. R. Ledoux in his admirable little speech on international co-operation in North American mining affairs. He suggested the appointment of a permanent committee on co-operation to work with a similar committee representing the Canadian Mining Institute. Mr. Sidney Jennings gave his prompt endorsement to the suggestion. Perhaps a joint committee, of not more than five, representing the two institutes would serve the purpose. We have neither forts nor cannon on the international boundary, but there exist sundry barbed-wire entanglements that should be removed.

"ALL goes well," says Mr. Lloyd George; and indeed it seems as if good progress had been made by the Conference at Paris. The world waits impatiently for the conclusion of peace, not only to resume normal business but in order to prevent the further development alike of the reactionary and the revolutionary elements of society, both of which are lifting their heads aggressively in the war-scarred regions of Europe, threatening to reduce civilization to chaos. We note with satisfaction that France is to receive the Saar coalfield in compensation for the sabotage and other non-military destruction of the coal mines in the Valenciennes district, notably near Lens and Lille. This destruction was perpetrated with the deliberate purpose of crippling France industrially, and it is only just that reparation should be exacted in kind.

THE canards of the past week have included the assassination of the head of the Hungarian bolshevist government, the purchase of territory by the Japanese, the aeroplane accident to the king of the Belgians, the driving of the Murmansk expeditionary force into the sea, the vexation of the President to the point of calling for the 'George Washington' to ferry him homeward, and the mutiny of American troops on the Dvina. The last item of news may not have been without foundation, for evidently some of the men did demur to further fighting with the Russians, but it was made as sensational as possible, just as if a mutiny among soldiers was not lamentable, if not dishonorable. Every day we are told of things having happened that either did not happen at all or happened in a different way. The correction rarely overtakes the lie. As Dr. Raymond once said, what is printed in the newspapers is not the record of things that actually have been; it is the record of things that might as well have been as not.

GEOGRAPHY is a subject of which we have gained a better knowledge by reason of the War, particularly political geography. The various projects for aeroplane communication and for tunneling are serving the same purpose. When we read of the proposed transmarine flights between Europe and America we learn with surprise the shortness of the intervals of water separating various points of land. For instance, the crossing from Dakar in western Africa to Pernambuco in Brazil is only 1850 miles, and it can be divided by landing on the St. Paul islands, close to the line of the equator. Newfoundland is only 1860 miles from Ireland. Next we learn that the proposed completion of the Channel tunnel, 32 miles long, between England and France, is exciting talk of similar projects, such as the tunneling of the Bosphorus, the Strait of Gibraltar, and Bering Strait, the last about 50 miles wide. An enthusiastic scribbler writes an article headed 'London to New York by Train,' anticipating the accomplishment of these engineering feats, which, after all, are dependent more on policies and money than on physical difficulties. The scribbler just mentioned suggests that the tunnel will "open up the great coal deposits af Alaska," not knowing, apparently, that the Bering River coalfield is in south-eastern Alaska and about 850 miles from the strait of that name. He also speaks of a railway already existing on the Alaskan side of Bering Strait. Well, there is the Wild Goose narrow-gauge track from Nome to Lane's Landing, but that will not help the transcontinental traveler. The next nearest railway is the Government railroad now in course of construction between Seward and Fairbanks, which is 600 miles, as the crow—or the ptarmigan—flies, from Bering Strait. Even then the aid of a ship would be needed to reach any rail system pointing toward New York. On the Asiatic side there is a gap of 2400 miles of wilderness between the nearest rail-head, at Chita, on the Trans-Siberian line, and the eastern entry of the proposed tunnel; indeed, 5000-odd miles of railway through difficult country will be required both in north-eastern Asia and north-western Africa before the traveler can expect to go all the way from London to New York by rail.

MORE than two years ago, in reviewing the famous gold mines of various countries, we selected the New Modderfontein, in the Witwatersrand district of South Africa, as the premier gold mine of the world. This judgment appears to be confirmed by later evidence. Up to date it has paid £4,423,750, equal, at $4.85, to $21,455,177, in dividends, besides about $5,000,000 of capital expenditure. The proved reserve of ore consists of 9,000,000 tons of 8.6 dwt. ore averaging 65 inches in width, and there is probably 15,000,000 tons more to be developed in the ground not yet touched. Assuming a profit of $5 per ton on the whole 24 million tons, and a net divisible profit of 80%, the aggregate distribution, as foreshadowed by Sir Evelyn Wallers, the president of the Transvaal Chamber of Mines, will be $95,000,000 more, or about $125,000,000 altogether. Up to June last the New Modderfontein had yielded $62,500,000 in gold; the average recovery had been 36s.9d., or $9.19, per ton; it is estimated that the future yield will be 36s., or $9, per ton; therefore the gross production of gold, before the life of the mine is exhausted, should be fully $275,000,000. These are imposing figures. The Homestake has produced $159,677,849 in gold and paid $42,000,000 in dividends during 42 years. The ore now averages $4 per ton. We note that the Government Gold Mining Areas, a mine from which the Transvaal government draws a royalty ranging, on a sliding scale, between 10% and 50% of the net produce, is rated as coming next in productivity to the New Modderfontein. The Government property is contiguous to the Modderfontein; it has 8,000,000 tons of ore developed and is expected to yield at least $350,000,000 worth of gold from ore averaging 33s., or $8.25, per ton at a cost of 18s., or $4.50, per ton, yielding a profit of $190,000,000, of which the Government would receive $102,500,000 and the company $87,500,000. Keen rivalry between these two neighbors is anticipated; the Modderfontein will be crushing 100,000 tons per month as against a capacity of 135,000 tons in the Government Areas mill. It is possible that before long the latter will be expanded to a capacity of 2,000,000 tons per annum. This makes our Alaskan dreams look foolish.

Engineering Education

A revival of interest in education appears to be one of the consequences of the War, because that calamitous experience has given us a new datum-line from which to measure the value and effectiveness of mental training. A report upon engineering education has been issued recently by Mr. Charles R. Mann, of the University of Chicago, who has interpreted the mass of information collected by a joint committee on the subject representing the leading engineering societies. Professor Mann finds that the average student fails to gain a fundamental knowledge of science because he is swamped by special studies intended to apply directly to the industries. The sacrifice of the humanistic studies to those of technical interest has caused engineers to neglect literature, economics, and social philosophy; they cannot express themselves in good English nor can they handle men. A circular sent to 30,000 members of the four leading engineering societies elicited the opinion that character is the chief factor in engineering success, while technique was placed at the bottom of the list of qualities. The general agreement on these ratings is most interesting. Evidently the whole question of education is undergoing revision. We must make up our minds whether we intend to train a young man for leadership or for service; is he to be prepared to be a captain of industry or merely to be enabled to earn his bread and butter immediately upon graduation? We need different colleges for different purposes. We give engineering education to men wholly untitled, morally and physically, to perform the work of an engineer, who is a leader of men, a man that can do what nobody else can do. So we venture to give our own conclusions on the matter. Let us start with a definition: education means 'drawing out'; it signifies the development of the mental faculties, primarily for usefulness in life. Any process of training that exercises, invigorates, and disciplines the intellect is an 'education'; the process that supplies the brain with the memory of things and furnishes rules for doing them is 'instruction'. The best discipline for logical thinking is the study of mathematics. To "reason closely and in train" is the first step in science. A thorough schooling in mathematics, therefore, is essential. Then should follow physics, in which mathematical reasoning is given material form. Physics involves a knowledge of chemistry, as mathematics includes arithmetic. From inference and observation, we conclude that the most capable engineers have had a good training in mathematics, chemistry, and physics. Many clever men have failed in the crisis of their professional work because they lacked such a training. The success of the Columbia men, as we knew them in Colorado thirty years ago, is to be credited mainly to the severe grueling they received in mathematics. "Do ye ken Van Am?" The college song has a deeper meaning than most of its kind. To learn anything thoroughly is educative. To study Greek is a better preparation for mining engineering than to obtain a smattering of mechanics and geology. What is learned is less important than how it is learned. The thorough learning of a subject is discipline, the effects of which will endure. The smattering of a subject is a cerebral dissipation, enervating to the mind. A course of mining engineering should deal mainly with principles, not details of practice. Methods change; principles remain. The memorizing of facts is less important than the ability to understand their relation to one another. This is scientific; that is childish. The 'Principles of Copper Smelting' will help the student long after the same author's 'Practice of Copper Smelting' has become obsolete. The detailed description of ore-dressing soon becomes a matter of history, but the rationale of the process is never old. What is needed is a thorough grounding in the elements of science and the ability to reason logically on the operations of Nature; to learn how to learn; to know where to find knowledge. We venture to make another suggestion: that young engineers should be taught to use with precision their most important tool—the English language. Many members of the profession are handicapped throughout life by their inability to write well. Clear thinking and clear writing are two phases of the same mental process. They react mutually. It is a pity that among many of our young engineers in the West it is deemed effeminate to be refined in speech or graceful in writing. Such a notion is a sure sign of a defective education, for one of the best products of human culture is the ability to communicate thought and exchange ideas. It is well, therefore, to master the instrument of expression. Nor shall we close without reverting to the factor of character. Herbert Spencer long ago said that "of all the ends to be kept in view . . . all are unimportant compared to the end of character-making. This alone is national education." In the last resort mere cleverness will not take a man far; there is needed something more dependable, and dependability is character. A man of character will act the same way under the same conditions; he can be depended upon to do what is right, for 'character' stands for good character, a mental and moral endowment helping the individual man to become an exponent of ethical ideals. Whether that can be taught at college, by maxim or by association, is another problem. Is it inherited or is it the product of the right environment? We incline to the hopeful view that much can be done by precept from honored teachers and by contact with high-minded companions. The old world has its *noblesse oblige*, have we not a democratic ideal of conduct that will coerce to right ways?

Bolshevism Upstairs

Two topics are occupying the mind of the community: prohibition and bolshevism. Alike they have been assisted to a remarkable degree by a campaign of propaganda, itself a consequence of the facilities afforded to the products of the printing-press by a highly organized system of distribution, not only by means of rail and motor transport, but even, as happened in Europe when it was desired to reach enemy countries, by aid of the aeroplane. Prohibition and bolshevism are unlike in so far as the one aims to restrict and to discipline the habits of the citizen, whereas the other appears to remove all restraint and gives free rein to the bestial instincts of mankind. When, however, the eagerness to discipline members of the community goes so far as to disregard an implied contract between those in authority and citizens engaged in legalized industry, it would appear as if the intoxication of anarchy had taken possession of the protagonists of prohibition also. We venture to quote an interesting example, namely, the treatment of the grape-grower in California. The facts are as follows: The cultivation of the grape came to California with the Padres; wine was made first at the Missions and later by several Spanish land-owners. The Mission of San Gabriel was known in 1829 for the good wine it produced. In 1832 Don Louis Vigne, a Frenchman, living near Los Angeles, imported cuttings of choice varieties of the grape from the Bordeaux district; he was also the first to engage in

the growing of oranges on a commercial basis. The American immigrants drawn hither by the lure of gold were at first too excited for patient industry, but the wave of migration brought many Europeans to California, and among them were several versed in the making of wine. Some of these, having had their fill of mining, turned to viticulture. They succeeded so well that in 1855 the Legislature was asked to aid the industry, but nothing was done at that time except to award prizes at State Fairs for the best exhibits of the wine and brandy made by these pioneer vignerons. In 1861, however, the Legislature authorized a commission "to promote the improvement and culture of the grape-vine in California" and the Governor appointed Arpad Haraszthy, a Californian wine-grower, to make "an examination of the different varieties of grapes and the various modes of making wine in the vine-growing countries of Europe." This commissioner made a report of 420 pages, published by Harper & Brothers in 1862; he also purchased 100,000 grape-vines, representing 400 varieties, for importation from Europe to California, where they were planted successfully. During the two following decades not much was done by the State in this matter, but in 1880 an act was passed to promote "the viticultural interests of the State" and to provide a Board of Commissioners for the purpose. According to the Act it became the duty of the Board of Regents of the State University to give special instruction in the arts and sciences pertaining to viticulture. For this work the Legislature voted biennial appropriations, increasing until the Commission was receiving $17,500 per annum and the University $5000. This provision continued until 1894, when the Viticultural Commission was abolished and its effects transferred to the University, which proceeded with the study of viticulture with its own funds until, in 1913, the State organized a second Viticultural Commission, which it maintained until the present time at a cost of $7500 per annum. Thus the patronage and promotion of the State covered a period of about 40 years, with but slight interruption. The amount of money spent by the State was at least $300,000 and the stimulating literature resulting therefrom is voluminous. Nine-tenths of the work dealt with the wine-making phase of grape-growing; it was for the wine industry, not the production of raisins and table-grapes, that the State expended its money; for the establishment of this industry it made persistent effort. Thus blessed by Church and State the wine industry has grown until it uses 170,000 acres, apart from the 110,000 acres devoted to raisin-grapes and the 50,000 acres given to table-grapes. On a conservative valuation these vineyards are worth $200 per acre. The total investment in the 330,000 acres of vine-lands, together with plant and equipment, is estimated at $150,000,000. The value of the annual crop in 1918 was $46,220,250, as compared with $68,000,000 in 1917. The wine-grapes last year were worth $10,039,250, of which $5,950,000 represents the dry-wine grapes that are unsuitable for table use, for raisins, or for other purposes. The chief loss falls upon those whose grapes cannot be used for secondary purposes and whose vineyards have a soil unfitting them for any other cultivation except hay; for example, those of the foot-hill region in the counties of Napa, Sonoma, Mendocino, Contra Costa, Santa Clara, and Santa Cruz, who face a shrinkage in value from $175 or $200 to $25 or $30 per acre. The industry occupies 15,000 heads of families, that is, about 75,000 people are directly engaged in viticulture. It has claimed the education, energy, and devotion of many worthy citizens, who now face not only the extinction of their livelihood but the implied opprobrium of the community, due to confusing the saloon-keeper, who sells very little wine, with the wine-producer. The supposed affiliation of the liquor-dealers and the saloon-keepers with the grape-growers and wine-makers is due mainly to the fact that they were placed in the same class for purposes of internal revenue. That, however, is another story. We must treat this matter as an accomplished fact. The State encouraged its citizens to embark in the wine industry and the Federal Department of Agriculture also aided and abetted it to no inconsiderable degree. If an individual or a group had issued a glowing prospectus to induce the purchase and use of land with knowledge of impending confiscation of the industry to which the land was to be put, they would be placed under a criminal charge of using the mails to defraud; if they did it innocently, they would still be financially responsible to a purchaser who had depended upon their representations. Does the State escape a similar responsibility? Must these people, who have put their knowledge, energy, and capital into the wine-making business under the persuasion and guidance of the State, lose the major part of their property owing to a change of public opinion? Is this the square deal? It is no excuse for the State that prohibition against the making of wine is of Federal origin and contrary to the wish of the people of California as expressed by vote. The State is responsible because it promoted the industry more, and it benefited by the values and the trade created more than the Federal government. The position is comparable with the condemnation of private property for public use, which in this case is the change of public sentiment toward alcoholic beverages. The damage is manifest and the amount of it can be proved. It is not large, but whether large or small, it should be recognized as a matter of principle. We have condemned the German idea of the State because it claimed immunity from the morality it imposed upon its citizens; we condemn the Bolshevists because they disregard the rights of others and ride roughshod over the obligations created by the social code by virtue of which law and order are maintained in the community; shall we approve this apparent breach of good faith on the part of our own State? In all such matters not only should a good example be set by those in authority, but we go further and insist that unless municipalities, States, and the Federal government alike exhibit a consistent regard for their obligations to the citizen, individually and collectively, they undermine respect and sow the seed of anarchy.

Mining: An Investment, a Speculation, or a Gamble?

By T. A. RICKARD

*The Chairman of your Program Committee told me that the subject allotted to me was 'Mining as an Investment'. I assume that he meant the gainful use of money in mining, that is, the making of money through the exploitation of mineral deposits, not other people's pockets. However, I deem it well to start by defining the terms to be used in the present discussion, because definitions are essential to a correct understanding of any subject.

Money can be employed profitably in three ways: investment, speculation, gambling. An 'investment' looks to income; the use of the word assumes the comparative safety and stability of the principal. A 'speculation' looks to an increase of the principal; the use of this word suggests the minor importance of interest, income, or return on capital; it assumes not the stability, but the comparatively rapid appreciation of the principal. A 'gamble' involves a risk so large as to require the aid of luck; it ignores interest or income: it anticipates the alternative of a big winning or a total loss.

Obviously the definition is subjective; it is based upon the expectation of the individual making the purchase. To one man the use of money for a certain purpose is an investment; to another man the same use appears to be a speculation. Similarly, one man's speculation is another man's gamble. Six years ago Mr. Lloyd George and Lord Reading, then Sir Rufus Isaacs, were persuaded by Mr. Godfrey Isaacs, a brother of the present Ambassador and Lord Chief Justice, to buy a block of American Marconi shares as an 'investment', that is, as a steady dividend-payer. Three days after Mr. Lloyd George had bought his shares they rose so rapidly that he sold them, on the urgent advice of his broker, to whom he was disinclined to listen because his intention was to hold the stock "as an investment." He was then Chancellor of the Exchequer, therefore he was hauled over the coals for 'speculating': he was charged with a levity of conduct unbecoming the chief of the British treasury. He replied by saying that when he bought the shares it was his intention to hold them indefinitely and that the sudden and surprising rise justified him in selling. In short, his 'investment' had proved a 'speculation'. The distinction is in the mind of the purchaser. Similarly a Boston school-teacher may buy the shares of the Great Wildcat Extended as an 'investment', whereas a Wall Street broker recognizes that it is highly 'speculative', and a Nevadan mining engineer knows that it is a rank 'gamble'. These terms are relative; they connote a crescendo of risk: even an investment has a slight element of risk; a speculation has more; a gamble, most. Sometimes a stock is bought on the expectation of a rise: it remains steady for years; it proves to be what is called a 'forced' investment. The idea of expectation is implicit: the human factor is never absent; we are dealing not with lexicons but with human affairs.

The other significant word is 'mines'. A mine is an excavation in the earth's surface from which mineral is extracted. It is not a company nor the shares of a company owning that excavation. A flippant definition says that a mine is a hole in the ground with a liar sitting on top. A promoter is said to be a man who sells something he has not got to somebody who does not want it, or, if you prefer, a promoter tries to sell nothing for something to a man who expects something for nothing. However, these perversions of honest business do not concern us for the moment: my subject is the reasonable speculation that is based upon the legitimate exploitation of mines. Permit me to remind you that the word 'mine' was used in the arena of warfare before it entered the field of peaceful industry. It comes to us through the Latin *mina*, signifying an excavation to be used for killing the enemy. The original sense of the word survives in 'minatory', meaning threatening. During the War we have heard more of mines in the North Sea than of mines in Mexico, for example, and you will allow that those who sailed the seven seas had to deal much with speculation concerning mines, and the flotation of mines on water, reminding us of minatory performances on the stock exchanges during times of peace. Now, however, we hope soon to forget the derivation of the word and to interpret it, not in terms of maleficent activity, but of beneficent industry.

You will note that I have chosen 'speculation' in preference either to 'investment' or 'gambling' as the more appropriate to mining. The use of money in mining is seldom an 'investment'; usually when it is meant to be so it affords an example of the triumph of hope over experience. I admit that certain forms of iron and coal mining on a large scale are characterized by such security, continuity, and steadiness of income as to be 'investments', but the mining of the so-called base metals or of the precious metals, in which most of you are engaged, does not come within the category. In metal mining the chance of a considerable risk and of a correspondingly large gain is inherent. Some of you will demur, you will point at the Homestake, the Bunker Hill & Sullivan, or the Utah Copper as examples of an investment, as representing a type of security so safe as to be gilt-edged, but I venture to say that your opinion is *ex post facto*, you are writing last year's almanac, you

*An address delivered before the International Mining Convention at Vancouver, B. C., on March 17, 1919.

are wise after the event. The history of such persistently profitable mines causes you to regard them as safe because you can retrace their history for ten, twenty, or thirty years. You imagine yourself buying into such mines soon after they had undergone preliminary development and you know that if you had done so at an early date your purchase would have proved extremely remunerative; but I submit that in the early stages of development these splendid enterprises were speculative, as is suggested by the fact that these successful ones are a few of the survivors from the much larger number that were started at about the same time and proved disappointing. I may remind you, to make my point quite clear, that many of the famous mines of the world 'broke' those who first attempted to bring them to financial success. If today you were to advise a widow to put her savings in any one of the three magnificent mines that I have instanced, you would, in my opinion, be an unwise counselor, because looking forward, not backward, for ten or twenty years, they would represent a speculative use of the widow's savings. You might be sagacious in using your own money for such a purchase, because you could take the relatively small risk for the sake of the probably large gain, but the widow would be better advised to buy Liberty bonds.

At this stage of my argument I beg you not to be annoyed at my apparently over-cautious attitude; you will find that my conclusions will not depreciate the industry in which you and I alike are so deeply interested. I shall hammer my point home by one further suggestion. You would not be willing to lock up your mining stock in a safe for five or ten years, as you might do with first-class bonds; you know that in the course of five years the fluctuations in market-value are likely to be so wide as to compel you in your judgment either to cut a loss or take advantage of a market-profit. On the other hand, a mine is not a 'gamble', because the risk it involves is not unreasonable: it is diminished by knowledge and experience, it is lessened by the skill you can apply both to the finding and to the treatment of the ore. A miner always needs some luck, of course, but his luck is a friendly sprite, not the grinning devil that sits by the roulette-wheel. Every business involves one or more indeterminate factors and therefore contains an element of risk. Without risk there is no gain; but a large gain usually involves a large risk. There are people in mining, of course, that take big odds, that like a reckless bet: they are real gamblers, even if they are unaware of it; but the risks taken in legitimate mining are under some measure of control, they are met by scientific knowledge and by trained intelligence. A blend of pluck and judgment is required. You will recall a line in Kipling's poem, 'The Merry Gloster': "And I took the chances they wouldn't and now they're calling it luck." That is why I insist that mining, properly conducted, is not a gamble. On the other hand, no man of experience in these matters would expect to escape all the risk. The idea of eliminating risk from mining is both contrary to the spirit of the business and false to the history of it. To understand mining—to appreciate the principles guiding legitimate and successful speculation in mines—which is my subject—you must revert to the old Cornish word for shareholders; they were called 'adventurers', that is, men willing to make a venture.

Indeed the idea of avoiding risk in mining is a pathetic fallacy; a puerile endeavor to escape the inevitable. The attempt to find mines that would involve no risk to the capital sunk in them has tended to cripple the industry; the refusal of sundry so-called exploration companies to incur risk has stultified their operations and paralyzed development. And I may add that this policy has warped the judgment of some otherwise brilliant engineers. The story is told that Marcus Daly sent a mining engineer on a scouting expedition; he examined many prospects, without finding anything worth while. Daly became impatient; he slapped the engineer on the shoulder and exclaimed: "For God's sake, man, go out and spend some money." There is too much of a desire to play safe by buying mines with large blocks of proved ore, and to make money by means of an enlarged scale of operations, increased skill, or improved methods of metallurgy. The finding of ore, which is the real adventure, is relegated to the background; it is not only the chief attraction of mining, but the one that wins the greatest reward. When the ore-reserves of a mine are at a low ebb it may be the most speculatively attractive time to buy the property. There are those who say that the mining of the future will be the economic harvesting of known ore deposits of low grade, the beneficiation of masses of mineral already discovered, but heretofore regarded as too refractory for successful metallurgic treatment, that is, the utilization of the visible supply of skimmed milk instead of the finding of the metallic cream concentrated by the patient operations of Nature. I doubt that; the world is still young, and but half-explored, as is suggested by such discoveries as those of Nome, Cobalt, Porcupine, Tonopah, Goldfield, the United Verde Extension, the Bawdwin mines in Burma, and a host of other bonanzas during the last twenty years.

One does not need to be venerable in order to recall great changes in the philosophy of mining economics. In 1905 I published a book on this subject, in which was included a discussion upon various aspects of mining finance. Among those contributing, besides myself, were H. C. Hoover, J. H. Curle, and W. R. Ingalls. Mr. Curle, at that time the leading London authority on such matters, a man of wide travel and stalwart independence of mind, advised his countrymen to stick to gold mining as being the safest, because gold had a "fixed value." We know today, by unpleasant experience, how gold can so depreciate in terms of other commodities that the gold miner is placed at a decided disadvantage. Mr. Curle insisted that the only correct kind of gold mining was based upon a careful estimate of the ore in reserve, and that at least 60% of the price of the mine ought to be represented by net profit from the developed ore. He even went so far as to lay down the rule that gold mines should yield 10% of their market valuation. Later he put the interest at 15%. We have traveled far since then. Most of these *obiter dicta* served a purpose in their day, fifteen years ago, as a means of educating the British shareholder, who is a simple-minded person, because Mr. Curle accompanied them with much straight information and trenchant criticism, but all such attempts to compress mining into a formula are a failure. They were based largely on the experience—then incomplete—of the Rand, in South Africa, where continuous beds of gold-bearing conglomerate were being exploited on the largest scale known to the modern world. These beds of 'banket', as they were called, after the Boer name for almond-cake, were comparatively uniform in their gold contents and were mined and milled so cheaply as to yield handsome profits. Their uniformity of grade and persistence in depth caused them to be regarded as the basis for 'investments' of the safest kind, suitable for widows and orphans. Later experience has shown that they were neither so uniformly nor so persistently rich as had been expected, the result being to turn the 'investments' into 'speculations', out of which a comparatively few made a great deal of money and comparatively many lost more than they could afford. The Rand proved to be the greatest goldfield in the world, in extent and in yield, but I am making the point that it did not escape the vicissitudes latent in mining, and the successful effort to persuade the public that it would escape those vicissitudes led, in the end, to a tremendous and widespread loss of money, which passed from the pockets of the public to those of the promoters. Money was made honestly on the Rand during the development stage, when adventurous spirits risked a total loss of their stake in order to make a big gain; but when the operators and promoters turned to the man of small means and persuaded him that the latent risks were eliminated and that a gilt-edge investment was available to him in the stock of over-capitalized mines, they deceived him. Some of the operators and promoters knew no better; others were advised by good engineers, and simply victimized the unsuspecting by unloading their holdings upon them at a handsome premium. To illustrate how the public was victimized, I can state that the market-value of the shares in the three principal companies representing consolidations of groups of mines declined $203,931,610 between 1911 and 1918. That huge loss was due to ignoring the common experience that mines eventually become impoverished in depth, just as surely as men grow old, and also to the assumption that a 60% ore-reserve, that is, having 60% of the market-value 'in sight', furnished ample security. In the attempt to introduce one or two academic factors of safety the public was led to ignore the very essentials of the business, namely, that it involved no small risk, under the best conditions, and that the risk must be compensated by large dividends. Instead, the public accepted 6 or 7% as an adequate return and failed to recognize that they held a wasting asset. During the speculative—the frankly adventurous—stage of Rand mining it made money for nearly everybody engaged in it, but when the chicanery of the few was combined with the ignorance of the many into creating a false notion that the speculative phase had been transformed into one of secure investment, then it was that share-dealing on the Rand became a cause of great loss to the public and a blot on honest industry. From the moment when the change in sentiment was effected, and the fallacy was established, the mining of the gold became less profitable than the mining of the pockets of the public.

This investment idea, of minimizing risks and limiting possibilities, would soon cause mining to die for want of breath. Before a profitable outcome is assured every mining enterprise must pass through several stages of speculativeness as surely as a child must take the chance of bumps and bruises, of measles and mumps. The biggest fortunes are made during the early stages of development; on the whole, more money is made by selling than by buying mines, simply because the final or so-called investment stage of a first-class mine is likely to represent an over-valuation, caused by an erroneous supposition that the essential hazard is precluded. I would even say that more money has been lost by the over-valuation of the great rich mines of the world, like the Con. Virginia, Mount Morgan, Broken Hill, and Nipissing, than in a multitude of worthless prospects. Small men lose their money in big mines, and big men in small mines. The inference therefore is not to try to get rid of the essential risk—because it cannot be done—but to require a rate of profit proportionate to it. A much more intelligent policy is to engage in such mining as allows a liberal margin both ways, taking a larger risk for the sake of the larger gain, that is, to speculate with eyes wide open, and not to invest with eyes half-shut.

Fifteen years ago the careful sampling of ore as a means of valuing mines was becoming advanced to an art and the tendency was to place great reliance upon it, with the consequence that capitalists began to think themselves safe in buying ore. They thought to escape the essential risk by assuring themselves a return of their money, diminishing the speculative features of the business as much as possible. Exploration companies were organized in London, New York, and Boston to scout for promising mines on which to apply the newly developed methods of valuation. Most of these seekers after bonanzas were disappointed; they failed to repeat the successes of the pioneers in this type of mining finance—such as the Exploration Company of the Hamilton & Smith era—because they were too timid; they expected to have their money in sight when they bought a mine; they were looking for a bet on a sure thing, with all the profits of a speculation. They lacked the temperament needed for adventure and should have placed their money in a bank, where at 4% it would double itself in 15 years. Many directors of these exploration companies bluffed themselves into the idea that they were bold navigators, when as a matter of fact they were only fair-weather sailors.

As I remarked at that time, "ore-reserves are not everything; expansion and development are the essence of successful mining." The big successes have been made by developing prospects into mines, not by buying blocks of ore that have been exhaustively sampled by meticulous young men. The profit to be made must depend upon the further extension of the ore: the larger the proportion of ore already proved the smaller the possibilities beyond. As Mr. Hoover pointed out, the probable depth of extension is more critical than the proportion of profit in sight. He worked out a rough rule for the gold mines of Western Australia, namely, the minimum extension of an orebody in depth should be not less than one-half its length. He called it a 'yard-stick' for use in forming a judgment, but he laid stress on the need for investigating the characteristics of the individual orebody, more particularly its geologic structure and that of the district in which it lies. Such a rough and ready formula, however, would fit only the mines that are dependent on one or two large shoots; it would be of little service in the valuation of mines depending on a series of recurring ore-shoots, as, for example, the Goldfield Consolidated, in Nevada, the Nipissing, at Cobalt, the Yoquivo, in Mexico. Mr. Hoover made the shrewd observation that "the quantity of ore in reserve is a matter of management not necessarily dependent on the size of the mine." In 1912 Morton Webber protested against the use of formulas in mine valuation and showed that "the relative magnitude of the ore-reserve in any particular mine is largely a matter of administrative policy." I myself remember, when practising as a mining engineer, advising a client not to extract the ore in his mine if he hoped to sell it to advantage, as he wished to do. The extension of the orebody was menaced by a fault. He listened to a saw-mill engineer, enlarged his mill from 20 to 40 stamps, extracted all the ore, and barely made enough profit to pay for the enlargement of the plant, leaving a hole in the ground in which several later operators have buried their good money. This was a gold mine in Idaho. Another example occurs to me: a small silver mine in Colorado. The ore was only five inches wide, but high-grade. A careful sampling showed $150,000 worth of ore assured, which would yield a net profit of $110,000. The owners were willing to sell for that sum, half cash and half in six months. I advised my clients not to buy, because the winzes below the adit-level showed that the vein was poor and much faulted. The history of neighboring mines was not promising as to prospects in depth. I considered the business unattractive because the risk of the known ore yielding less than the amount of profit estimated seemed to outweigh the chances of finding more ore. The subsequent story of the mine justified my opinion. On the other hand, I advised the purchase of the Camp Bird, in Colorado, for $6,000,000 when the bottom workings looked poor, and gave no promise of the ore persisting, because I believed that horizontal exploration would lead to the uncovering of more orebodies, especially westward, where the rising surface gave virgin ground increasing to a height of 1200 ft. above the adit. The mine had reserves equal to $6,118,000 gross, but the value of it lay largely in the good prospect of the further finding of rich ore, without sinking, as the sequel proved, for the Camp Bird has produced $20,000,000 since then, although poor in depth. Please pardon these reminiscences of a time, 20 years ago, when I was a mining engineer, not a journalist; I give them because personal experience is direct evidence.

In 1911 M. H. Burnham contributed a series of articles on sundry principles underlying the finance of mining enterprise, more especially the 'risk-rate'. He insisted rightly that the buyer of mines or shares in mines should expect not only a bank-rate of interest on his capital, but as much more as will cover the additional risk inherent in the business of mining. If, as I suggested at that time, he bought into the Goldfield Consolidated, in Nevada, then the most productive gold mine in the world, but with a reserve of ore so small as compared with its annual production as to ensure the return of only a small part of its market-value, he, the sane speculator, ought to expect a dividend of 35% per annum, or 31% more than the 4% bank-rate, that is, the mine should be valued on the basis of a three years purchase. This famous mine is now in the hands of lessees; its story has been told, and you can ascertain how nearly right was my diagnosis of the position. However, it is only mentioned as an example. On the other hand, a mine like the New Modderfontein in South Africa or the Homestake in South Dakota might show a life and a standard of production justifying a low estimate of risk, thus warranting a much smaller return, say, 6% more than the bank-rate. It amounts to this, that after an engineer has examined a mine and measured its ore-reserves, he must determine the risk-rate at which his clients' capital may be used in the purchase of that particular property. This risk-rate will be based upon the past history, the present condition, and the future prospects of the mine.

The sampling of mines has been allowed to obscure the need for good judgment. It is also another phase of the attempt to make an investment out of a speculation. The ore in reserve in a mine should be regarded chiefly as an indicator of the probability of being able to find and develop more ore of the same grade. The expectation of a profitable venture should be based not upon the extraction of the known ore, but upon the chances of further intelligent search.

A so-called 5% investment in a metal mine is an unwise use of money because the interest is too small for the risk, whereas a 20 to 25% speculation in a metal mine is sagacious, if the probable risk is compensated by the probable gain. As Mr. Hoover says, "there is an inherent speculation in mining, and it is this speculation that attracts." It attracts those that understand. It is the spirit of adventure that stimulates the best kind of mining. For instance, the controllers of the Homestake mine have spent 15 million dollars in 15 years on the Cerro de Pasco; they have received their money back and 100% added thereto, equal to about 7% in the 15 years, and now they have proved ore sufficient to last for 20 years. That is what I call a fine adventure!

The speculative side of mining has an attractiveness that is at the bottom of the energy with which it is followed, and when you bring it to the dead level of a steady investment you will find that the man of ordinary shrewdness saves time by going straight to his broker and buying bonds or consols. This does not mean that one is justified in playing the fool and expecting miracles to happen. The risk of mining should not be increased needlessly by human aberrancy. Mining enterprises come to grief often not so much on account of the failure to attain an investment basis, but because they are not put on a business basis. Even if the occurrence of ore in nature be erratic, and mining as a consequence be hazardous, there is no justification for piling human foolishness on top of nature's vagaries.

A large part of the public participation in mining is done by means of share-buying; this is a secondary and a less desirable form of speculation, as compared with the ownership or part-ownership of mines by individuals, partnerships, or small syndicates. It is a legitimate means, however, of distributing risk and of applying collective capital to undertakings too burdensome for an individual or a syndicate. It produces a fluctuating ownership. In practice, whatever may be his theory, the American 'investor' does not buy mining stocks to keep. Whatever he calls such holdings, he treats them as 'speculations'; he does not put them away for the sake of their dividend yield; he is always ready to realize upon them at an enhanced price; he buys them to sell. It has been said that the ownership in an American mining company changes, on an average, every five years. Hence the mysteries of amortization do not interest most of our people. They are looking for a quick turn-over, not a long-time investment. The individual owner of a mine rarely keeps it when it grows to a size involving a large amount of capital; he spreads the risk and gathers his winnings by disposing of the mine to a public company. Long-continued private ownership of a profitable mine is rare. W. B. Bourn and his father before him have controlled the Empire mine at Grass Valley, California, for 50 years, and I may add that this mine has been worked uninterruptedly for 66 years! It has proved a real investment, although started, of course, as a speculation. I venture to say, however, that if anybody were to buy it today on Mr. Bourn's valuation, or on that of an equally competent appraiser, he would be compelled to take it as a 'speculation,' for the simple reason that the odds are largely against the Empire mine continuing to be worked profitably in the future for any such length of time as in the past.

Of well-conducted mining ventures it can be said that they meet with a measure of success as large as, if not larger than, an ordinary manufacturing enterprise. I make no apology for mining, it has been—and is still—a glorious adventure for the youth of the world, for those young in spirit as well as in body. To mining we owe the exploration of the far corners of the earth and the development of its waste places. From the days of the Argonauts to that of the beach-diggers of Nome the call of adventure has caused men to go forth into the wilderness and prepare the way for the establishment of industry, for the extension of civilization, for the making of homes, which is the best fruit of human toil. If we stifle that spirit of adventure between formulas, if we suppress it by the maxims of an unreasoning caution, we shall shrivel a great industry into a picayune trading which will commit suicide in due course. No; risk is the very essence of mining; it is its life, and the true miner faces the risk with the cheerful confidence of the men who made the world more spacious "in the times of great Elizabeth," of the Argonauts of the Golden Age in California, of the trappers and *coureurs de bois* who opened up the great North-West.

Dredging and Hydraulicking Results of the Yukon Gold Co.

This company in 1918 operated five dredges near Dawson in the Klondike, one at Iditarod in Alaska, one on Prichard creek in Idaho, and one each on the American, Butte, Feather, Trinity, and Yuba rivers in California. The total gold recovered by these boats was $1,884,957, compared with $3,460,668 in 1917, and $3,853,125 in 1916. A table of operating results for last year follows:

	Alaska	California	Idaho	Klondike
Yardage	644,125	4,444,404	*1,118,306	2,707,058
Yield per yard, cents	83.06	7.00	12.97	30.87
Cost per yard, cents	73.72	6.00	7.30	34.30

*Includes December 1917, when this new boat commenced work.

None of the above costs include depreciation.

The Iditarod dredge worked 198 days, 6 days longer than the previous season. Floods caused much trouble at the power station. Hard 'roofs' of bedrock and clayey material reduced the capacity. The percentage of frozen ground thawed and dug was 97.72%, 11.17% more than in 1917. This boat is to be dismantled, as it has worked out its ground.

In California, the American River boat only worked 31% of the possible time, due to low water, shallow ground, and shortage of power. The boat on the Yuba suspended work in December, in order to re-arrange the tailing discharge, to conform to government regulations.

The Klondike dredges worked 139 days, 12 days shorter than in 1917, but they operated 90.1% of the possible time. Of the ground dug, 80.5% was frozen and had to be thawed with steam. No. 2 dredge has completed its area, and is to be moved.

Hydraulicking near Dawson moved 2,054,390 cu. yd., yielding 16 cents per yard at a cost of 8.4 cents. Each miners' inch of water moved 4.34 yards, and 473,115 inches was used in 129 days. The water supply in June, July, and August was excellent, but in September it was unusually limited.

The total gold yield of the company last year was $2,283,862, including that from miscellaneous operations.

CEYLON EXPORTED 15,453 tons of graphite in 1918, against 27,047 tons in 1917. America took 55%, a decrease of 26%. Lump plumbago sells for 5 to 10 cents per pound.

HARVESTING THE SALT

The Recovery of Salt From Sea-Water

By F. H. MASON

Probably the most complete series of investigations of the composition of sea-water was that made by Dittmar during the 'Challenger' expedition in 1884, when 77 samples were taken from different parts of the ocean. Dittmar found that, while the total of the solids varied in different samples, their analysis was remarkably constant. They showed an average solid content of 35.976 parts per thousand, and had an average density of 1.0297. The solids gave the following average analysis:

	%		%
Sodium chloride	77.758	Calcium sulphate	3.600
Magnesium chloride	10.878	Potassium sulphate	2.465
Magnesium sulphate	4.737	Calcium carbonate	0.345

About ten years later, Thorpe and Morton made a more complete analysis of water taken from the Irish Sea. Their analysis follows:

	Parts per thousand		Parts per thousand
Sodium chloride	26.43918	Calcium carbonate	0.04754
Potassium chloride	0.71619	Lithium chloride	trace
Magnesium chloride	3.15083	Ferrous carbonate	0.00503
Magnesium bromide	0.07052	Ammonium chloride	0.00044
Magnesium sulphate	2.06608	Silica	trace
Magnesium nitrate	0.00207		
Magnesium carbonate	trace	Total	33.85916
Calcium sulphate	1.33158		

It will be noticed that Thorpe and Morton suggest a slightly different arrangement of the combinations between bases and acids. but this, of course, is a purely theoretical difference.

It will be evident, then, as there is only about 3½% of solids to obtain which 95.5% of water has to be evaporated, that in selecting a site for a salt-works the principal things to be considered are a light rain-fall and rapid evaporation, caused by high temperatures combined with wind and absence of excessive atmospheric humidity. The Western Salt Co. is fortunate in its site at Chula Vista on San Diego bay, eight miles from the city of San Diego. The evaporation at this point, which, of course, like the rain-fall, varies from year to year, averages 60 inches per annum, from which must be deducted the average rain-fall of 10 inches, leaving a net evaporation of 50 inches. The principal unit of the San Diego water-system is so situated that it impounds practically all the water from the mountains in this neighborhood, but little fresh water finding its way into the bay at this point. This, under ordinary circumstances, is a great advantage, as the south end of the bay is shallow and forms a huge evaporating basin, giving the water an appreciably higher salt-content than that of the Pacific Ocean outside, but it proved to be disastrous in January of 1916, when the phenomenal floods broke the Lower Otay dam of the city water-system and caused the practical annihilation of the salt gardens and the 'durostone' or 'woodstone' works connected with them. Since then the salt plant has been rehabilitated, though it has not yet reached its pre-flood capacity of 15,000 to 20,000 tons per year, and a substantial dam is being erected by the city, which guarantees the prevention of a like disaster.

The salt gardens cover an area of 600 acres, and consist of a number of shallow pools known as tide-ponds, secondary ponds, lime or pickle ponds, and crystallizing-vats, divided from each other by embankments on some of

DUMPING-HOPPERS AND CRYSTALLIZING-POOLS

GENERAL VIEW OF THE SALT WORKS

SALT DUMP, SHOWING TRESTLE AND BASKET-BELT

which are car-lines to facilitate the harvesting of the salt. Water from the bay, averaging 3°B. and in the height of summer running as high as 5°B., enters the lowest pool through a gate that is opened and closed automatically by the tide; from this pool it is raised by a pump, having a capacity of 14,000 gal. per minute, to the highest pool, from where it gravitates to all the other pools. Any pool can be cut off from the system for harvesting, repair, or other purposes. A series of well-planned ditches protects the crystallizing pools from dilution by fresh water other than that which actually falls upon them.

Concentration by evaporation proceeds during the whole year, and the salt is harvested in the autumn months. The first salts to fall out of solution are the carbonates of iron and lime, which commence to precipitate when the brine reaches 7°B.; sulphate of lime starts to precipitate at 15°B., sodium chloride at 25°B., and a slight precipitation of magnesium sulphate occurs at 29°B. At 34°B. a critical point seems to be reached, the liquid declining to 33° with the precipitation of large quantities of magnesium sulphate and small amounts of potassium chloride, magnesium bromide, and magnesium chloride, together with double chlorides and sulphates of magnesium and potassium. If the evaporation is continued to 37° practically only magnesium chloride remains in solution. It is considered good practice, therefore, when a pure sodium chloride is the objective, as at these works, to keep the concentration of the brine below 30°B. The magnesium salts accumulate in the solution until a point is reached when further concentration would cause the precipitation of magnesium salts with the sodium chloride, so, at this stage the brine is run off into the bittern water pools. This has to be done two or three times during the year. The following is an average analysis of the bittern water:

	%		%
Sodium chloride	7.53	Magnesium bromide	0.24
Potassium chloride	2.86	Magnesium sulphate	5.53
Magnesium chloride	13.03	Ferrous sulphate	0.06

Prior to the flood, the bittern water was further concentrated, magnesium sulphate and a low-grade common salt recovered, and the liquor, which contained mainly magnesium chloride, was mixed with magnesium oxide, sawdust, pigments, and sand, and, under the name of 'durostone' or 'woodstone', was used extensively for kitchen sink-boards, kitchen and bathroom floors, and other places where either waterproof or fire-proof flooring was required. A considerable amount of this material was used in the various buildings at the Panama-California International Exposition, and it gave excellent satisfaction. Since the flood, the works in which this material was made have not been re-built, and at present the bittern water is run into the bay. This seems to be a pity, as, apart from the oxy-chloride cements, at many other works the bromine content is economically recovered, and there seems to be no good reason why it should not be recovered at Chula Vista.

When the salt is ready for harvesting, the liquor is drawn off and the salt, much of which is in large cubic crystals, is broken by picks, shovelled into light side-dumping steel cars of one ton capacity, transferred to the washer and stacker by means of gasoline power, and dumped into a series of hoppers. The hoppers are then opened, letting the salt into a trough below, along which it is moved by a screw-conveyor to a chain-bucket elevator, which drops into a long washing-box filled with a 15°B. salt solution from one of the pickle ponds—thereby dissolving as little of the salt as possible in washing—thence to a basket belt that takes it up an incline to the top of a high trestle, where it is screened, sized, and dumped into separate heaps according to size. After the salt is lifted in the wire baskets from the washing-box it is deluged with strong brine and on the way up the incline it is sprayed by a series of fine jets of pure water, thus rinsing off the 'mother liquor', or strong brine, and facilitating the drying and curing of salt in the stack. All the washings, which besides magnesium salts contain a considerable amount of sodium chloride, run back into the evaporating-pools. The salt is taken from the heaps, sized again in a portable bumping-screen operated by a cam, and is then ready for the market. The company produces an exceedingly pure article: the analysis of the salt harvested last fall running:

	%		%
Sodium chloride	99.75	Magnesium chloride	0.07
Calcium sulphate	0.09	Insoluble matter	0.03

The company is planning to keep the salt from contamination during storing and shipping by laying a paved or cement base over the ground upon which it is stacked.

All the machinery is operated by electricity, supplied by the San Diego Consolidated Gas & Electric Co. A loop line of the San Diego & Arizona railroad runs through the property, and this, when the line is completed, will materially facilitate shipping to such interior points as Imperial Valley, southern Arizona, New Mexico, and western Texas. Within a year the company will be making all grades of table, dairy, and packer salts, and also bricks and blocks for stock, and it is endeavoring to arrange for a subsidiary company to handle the bittern water, in the same way that it did before the flood destroyed the 'durostone' works.

Mill Improvements at Calumet & Hecla

Six units of the Hecla mill, stamping conglomerate ore, have been re-modeled. The slime made is treated by flotation, replacing the round-table system. Re-modeling of the Calumet plant is under way. A flotation plant to treat slime from the re-grinding plants will be ready early this summer. On its completion, all conglomerate will be subjected to either flotation or leaching with ammonia as a final treatment. No. 1 re-grinding plant is finished and employs 24 Hardinge mills in place of 48 Chilean mills. Last year this plant treated 1,245,664 tons of 0.599 to 0.868% copper tailing, at a cost of 4.33 to 6.75c. per pound. The leaching works treated 1,005,015 tons of 0.535% tailing, recovering 76% at a cost of 7.71 cents.

Hemet Magnesite

By F. B. RONEY

The stoppage of magnesite shipments from Austria and Greece during the War stimulated the mining of Western magnesite, notably in Washington and California. One enterprise that has been running continuously is the magnesite mine seven miles from Hemet, in Riverside county, California; this was opened some twenty years ago and operated intermittently in a small way. Several years ago a calcining and grinding plant was built, and the ore was handled at the mine by steam-shovel and tram-cars. The latter proved too expensive and was abandoned by the company then in control.

The property is now operated by Innis, Speiden & Co., of New York, under the direction of the Wellman-Lewis Co. of Los Angeles, designing and constructing engineers. A glory-hole method of mining is used. The magnesite is found in narrow veins forming a stockwork in a mass of serpentine. A shaft has been sunk to meet a raise from an adit. The overburden and orebody are blasted into the shaft and removed through the adit on an 18-inch belt-conveyor, passing over grizzlies and revolving screens. The intermediate material containing most of the magnesite is discharged into a large ore-bin. From here it is run onto a 30-in. belt-conveyor, the magnesite being picked off by hand and the residue carried by belt-conveyors to the dump. From the picking-room the magnesite is conveyed by belt to the washing-plant, which consists of a perforated revolving cylinder on an incline by which the ore descends against a heavy stream of water, which removes sand and clay. It is then carried down the mountain by gravity tram-cars to a storage-bin, holding 300 tons, at the mill.

In the calcining-plant the ore passes through an 8 by 12-in. Wheeling crusher and is then fed into the kiln by an elevator and screw-conveyor. The kiln is of the usual rotary type, 6 ft. diam. by 60 ft. long, lined with fire-brick, and revolving once per minute. It is fired with oil of gravity 18° to 20°B. under an air-pressure of 50 to 60 lb., the oil being heated in coils to 180°-250°F. At present the magnesite is being burned to a weight of 800 grammes per litre on the barreled product. The temperature required to reach this result is a bright cherry-red. No pyrometer tests have been made. Samples are taken from the furnace once an hour, or oftener; they run somewhat higher in weight than samples from the other barrels after grinding. Allowance is made for this difference in the burning to reach a weight of 800 lb. per barrel. Taking the weight per litre is a quick test and is occasionally checked by determining in the laboratory the CO_2 remaining after the calcining. The real running-test, however, of the furnace-heat is the eye. It may be noted that the magnesite leaving the furnace is considerably finer than the raw ore entering it. The change that takes place in the furnace appears to be a purely mechanical one, the CO_2 bursting the pieces of ore and passing up the stack, leaving the MgO in a porous condition easily broken with the fingers, which, by the way, is a test for good magnesite.

From the furnace the calcined ore is carried by elevator and drag, to be distributed on an inclined concrete cooling-floor holding five carloads. Under this cooling-floor is a tunnel containing a long screw-conveyor. The material is shoveled through small openings controlled by slides into the trough-conveyor and passed by elevator and belt to a bin over the coarse grinder. As more or less iron is liable to get into the ore between the glory-hole and the grinding-machines, an electro-magnet controlled by a small dynamo is placed just over the last belt-conveyor, which picks off iron and saves damage to the machines.

The No. 1 is the New Process Grinder made at Pottersville, N. J., and is set to grind to the size of wheat. No. 2 is the Sturtevant Rock Emery Mill made at Boston, and is set for 98% of the product to pass a 100-mesh sieve. Two Howes Barreling Machines made at Silver Creek, N. Y., take care of the product. A sample is taken from each barrel. The character of this product is indicated by the average analysis of 10 burns, as follows:

Screen	Weight per litre	CO_2	MgO	SiO_2	CaO	Fe
98.03	801	1.35	83.08	14.46	0.36	0.25

The alumina was not determined. The product is especially low in lime and iron. Four cars per month of the finished product are shipped. Nine electric motors of the Westinghouse and Fairbanks-Morse types furnish power throughout the property. The dump is estimated to contain between 400,000 and 500,000 tons.

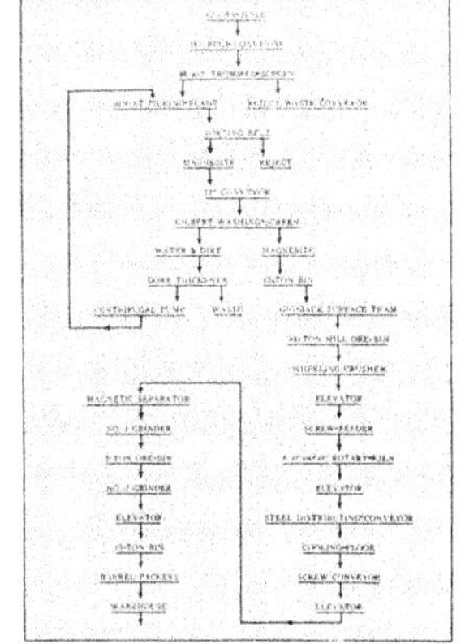

FLOW-SHEET OF MAGNESITE SORTING AND CALCINING-PLANT

The Gold-Quartz Lodes of Porcupine, Ontario

By ELLSWORTH Y. DOUGHERTY

INTRODUCTION. The Porcupine district is in the province of Ontario, Canada, about 100 miles north-west of the older silver district of Cobalt. Mining activity began with the discovery of the Dome lodes in 1909. During the stress of unfavorable economic conditions in the past few years such important mines as the Hollinger Consolidated and the McIntyre-Porcupine have maintained production and paid dividends. The shrinkage system of mining has been applied with success; timber consumption is relatively small; the mines are cool and comparatively dry; the ore is well adapted to cyanidation. Mining operations have been carried more than a thousand feet from the surface in several mines, and the diamond-drill has proved ore for many hundreds of feet below this horizon. The Hollinger property with reported reserves in excess of \$40,000,000[1] and others with smaller reserves will no doubt maintain Porcupine's position as the premier gold-producing district of Ontario for many years.

GENETIC FEATURES OF THE OREBODIES. The gold is won from pyritic gold-quartz lodes[2] in pre-Cambrian schists, and, since diabase dikes referred to Keweenawan[3] age cut the lodes, gold deposition itself undoubtedly took place in pre-Cambrian time. Enrichment or other alterations referable to descending meteoric waters are either insignificant or totally lacking. No secondary auriferous mineral masses are found cutting those of an earlier period. The occurrence of such diagnostic minerals as tourmaline and feldspar with abundant coarsely crystalline and fluid-enclosing ore-quartz has led to the classification of the orebodies as high-temperature deposits,[4] formed under great depth and pressure[5] through the agency of igneous activity.

THE LODE-FISSURES. Along the plane of the orebodies the country-rock is frequently sheeted, unusually fissile,[6] or separated by marked shear-planes. In places one of the latter may constitute a wall of the lode. In many occurrences it may be difficult to distinguish the structure controlling the disposition of the ore-minerals from the normal schistosity[7] of the rock.

A significant structural feature of the orebodies is the complexity and multiplicity of systems of adjacent discontinuous surfaces of dislocation marking the attitude of ore-minerals. These surfaces may vary from well-defined shear-planes traceable for 40 ft. or more along the strike and the dip to mere quartz-filled microscopic fissures.[8] A great capacity for differential movement was inherent in the rocks. This produced zones of intricate and closely-spaced surfaces of differential movement rather than single major breaks—an important point. If this phenomenon be considered carefully, it will be seen that it is related on the one hand to decided dislocation associated with faulting, and on the other to the close rock-mineral adjustments that produce schistosity; in other words, that it is a process intermediate in character between faulting and schist-forming adjustments.

THE LODES AND LODE-COMPONENTS. The more important properties occur along parallel zones, the longer axes of which strike east-northeast. One of these zones includes such mines as the Porcupine Crown, Vipond and North Thompson, Hollinger, McIntyre, Schumacher, and Newray; another embraces the Dome Lake, West Dome, Dome, and Dome Extension properties. These zones mark the major lode-systems, within which the minor lode-systems occur in parallel series. See Fig. 1 and 2. Within the lodes, parallel series of quartz lode-components characteristically occur. See Fig. 3, 4, 5, and 6. Each of the larger lode-components may itself be composed of smaller elements of quartz and schist.

SCHISTOSITY AND FAULTING. Fig. 1 illustrates in section the typical relations between the three main elements of structure, namely, the schistosity, the lodes, and the thrust-faults. The general rule is that the lodes truncate the schistosity though cases are found, as in Fig. 3, where

[1] 'M. & S. P.', March 1, 1919, p. 303.

[2] Following a distinction between veins and lodes defined by one of the earlier leaders of mining geology, S. F. Emmons, the term 'lode' is applied to the orebodies of Porcupine. Emmons wrote: "The term 'vein' should be confined as far as possible to a single mineralized fissure or the orebody formed along a single fissure, while the term 'lode' is applied to an assemblage of ore-bearing fissures so closely spaced that the ore that has been formed along and between them may in places be considered to form a single orebody. "Text of Folio 39, U. S. G. S., 1899." An assemblage of closely spaced quartz-bearing fissures separated by bands and masses of mineralized (usually pyritized) country-rock, the entire mixture constituting an orebody, is the typical feature of the Porcupine lodes.

[3] See 24th Annual Report, Ontario Bureau of Mines, 1915.

[4] W. Lindgren, 'Mineral Deposits', p. 636; 1913.

[5] W. H. Emmons, 'The Principles of Economic Geology', p. 424; 1918.

[6] That is, divided into very small, closely-spaced, discontinuous partings, as distinguished from the more pronounced surfaces of dislocation, designated as sheeted surfaces.

[7] Strictly defined, 'schistosity' is a structure by virtue of which the rock may be cleaved along parallel planes determined by the parallel arrangement of the constituent minerals.

[8] It is not improbable, as suggested by microscopic study, that stresses in the rocks directly responsible for the larger surfaces of shearing also produced chemical re-arrangements and 'flow-cleavage' in the wall-rocks.

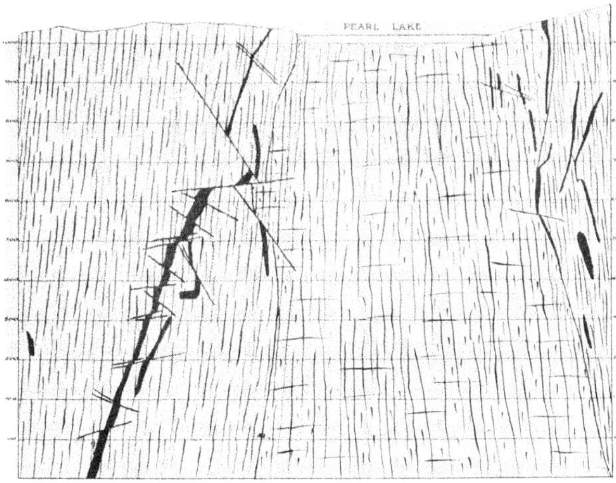

FIG. 1. CROSS-SECTION THROUGH McINTYRE MINE, LOOKING EAST

Regular broken lines: carbonate and chloritic schist. Long and short broken lines: Quartz-porphyry sericitic schist. Solid black: Lodes. Solid lines: Fault traces. Scale about 250 ft. to the inch.

FIG. 3. DETAILED SKETCH OF LODE IN FISSILE SCHIST, ON THE 300-FT. LEVEL OF THE McINTYRE-JUPITER MINE

The section is normal to the strikes of the lode-components and the lode. Solid black: Quartz and some carbonates. Fine lines: Fissile chloritic schist, in part pyritic. Heavy lines: Fault traces.

FIG. 4. DETAILED SKETCH OF LODE IN CONTORTED SCHIST, ON THE 1000-FT. LEVEL OF THE McINTYRE MINE

The section is normal to the strike of the lode-components and also roughly normal to the general strike of the lode. Solid black: Quartz. Curved lines: Contorted quartz-porphyry sericitic schist.

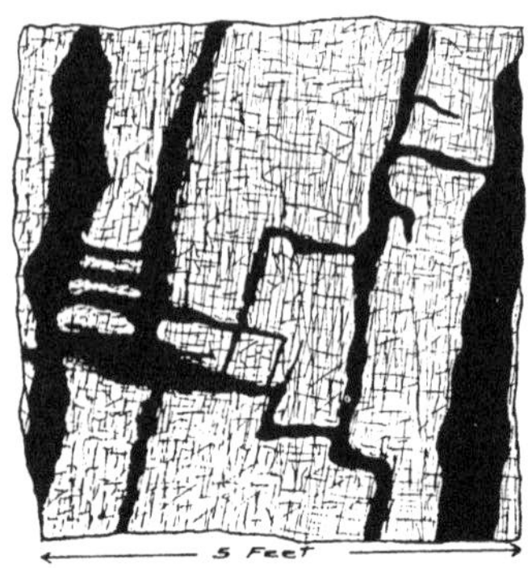

FIG. 5. DETAILED SKETCH OF LODE, ILLUSTRATING INTERSECTING THE LODE-COMPONENTS, ON THE 600-FT. LEVEL OF THE McINTYRE MINE.

Solid black: Quartz and some carbonates. Irregular fine lines: Chloritic schist, in part pyritic. The section is normal to the strikes of the lode-components and also roughly normal to the strike of the orebody.

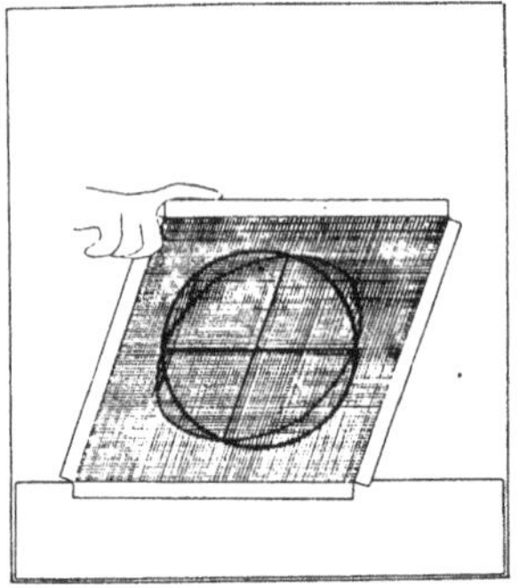

FIG. 8. EXPERIMENTAL DEMONSTRATION OF ROTATIONAL STRAIN OR SHEAR

(After C. K. Leith)

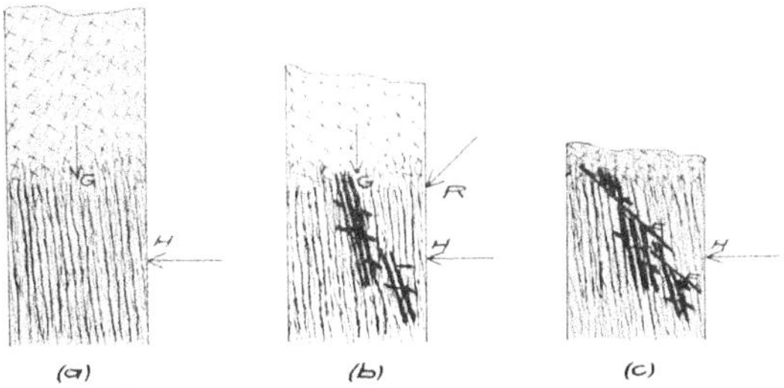

(a) (b) (c)

FIG. 7. DIAGRAMMATIC REPRESENTATION OF SUCCESSIVE DYNAMIC STAGES

(a) Schist forming stage. (b) Shearing stage. (c) Faulting stage.

the quartz lode-component appear to parallel the schistosity or a shearing parallel with the schistosity. Again, as shown in Fig. 4, the quartz lode-components partly parallel the schistosity and partly cut across it. It is clear, in the majority of instances, that the ore-solutions have been diverted along sheared surfaces which exerted a more efficacious control than the schistosity. It is clear also that this shearing was superimposed upon the schistosity, and therefore was developed subsequently.

The faults dislocate the lodes; they are therefore post-mineral. Of several hundreds studied by me, all are upthrust in character, that is, the segment of lode on the hanging-wall side of the fault has moved upward with respect to the segment on the foot-wall side of the fault. A nearly horizontal movement is not uncommon.

The lode-fissures therefore were developed later than the schistosity, and earlier than the faults. The agency that produced all three phenomena was clearly a recurrent or continuous compressive stress, namely, a tangential earth-thrust. A fundamental difference in the environment of the rocks at the times this stress was acting is indicated by the variations in the character of the deformations; the progressive decrease in the weight of the overlying rock-mass is suggested as the most generally applicable cause of these variations.

FIG. 6. CROSS-SECTION OF INTERSECTING LODE-COMPONENTS, ON THE 400-FT. LEVEL OF THE NEWRAY MINE

White is quartz. Country-rock is greenstone-schist. The pick-handle is 16 in. long

ORIGIN OF THE LODE-FISSURES. Fig. 7 represents diagrammatically the three stages of schist-forming, shearing, and faulting. H is a principal axis of horizontal (tangential) pressure; G, the weight of the superincumbent load above the particular rock-mass now exposed to view in the mines. The third principal axis of stress may be considered as acting normal to the plane of the paper. The relative force along the three principal axes of stress would be reflected in the attitudes of the resultant surfaces of dislocation.

In (a) G, the weight of the superincumbent rock-mass is greater than the breaking strength of the rock and H far exceeds G. Schistosity is therefore produced. In (b) is shown a condition in which, through erosion, G has been decreased, the zone of rock-flowage correspondingly descends with respect to the particular rock-mass under consideration; H and G do not entirely exceed the crushing strength of the rock, the resultant being represented by R and the rock-mass is thrust horizontally, presumably over a zone of flowage. The result is the formation of shear-surfaces dominantly developed along zones and surfaces of maximum capacity for differential movement. The traces of a frequently observed combination of shear-surfaces are represented by the solid lines. This is the interpretation of the principal operative process in the formation of the lode-fissures. In (c) the operation of thrust-faulting is shown. G has now become so reduced that the application of H results in the rise of the rock-mass above F, toward the relatively free surface of the earth, according to experimental evidence on the mechanism of thrust-faulting.[9]

Variations in the rigidity of the rocks and in other factors necessarily affect the character of deformation, even in rocks horizontally contiguous. The three processes are transitional and the lode-fissures form the connecting link between the extremes.

An experimental demonstration of the operation figured in (b) is given in the extremely useful little book, 'Structural Geology'.[10] Fig. 8 is a tracing of Fig. 7 of that book. The shearing of the top of the wire-net over the stationary bottom resting on the table produces traces of shear-planes represented by the lines connecting the intersections of the circle and the ellipse. The experiment illustrates rotational strain. The analogy between these traces and the cross-sectional view of the lode-components shown in Fig. 5 and 6 is striking. The wide-spread occurrence of steeply inclined, and horizontal or flatly inclined, intersecting lode-components suggests strongly that the stress-strain relations shown in Fig. 8 were probably closely paralleled even in the heterogenous medium of the earth's crust at Porcupine. Since the normal direction of weakness, due to schistosity, is steeply dipping, and since this weakness existed at the time the lode-fissures were formed, it is not surprising to find a dominance of steeply-dipping lodes and lode-components especially in the more schistose rock-terrains.

Copper and Gold in Manitoba

By R. C. WALLACE

*For the last four years prospecting has been active in the mineral belt north of The Pas, along the Hudson Bay railway line, and in some districts north-east of Lake Winnipeg. During the whole period, especially during the last two years, the number of prospectors has been small. Notwithstanding this fact, several orebodies, which admit of operation under present difficult transportation facilities, have been discovered; while others await the coming of the railway into the mineral belt. From a remarkably rich lens of copper sulphide, ore (9300 tons) has been transported to the Trail, B. C., smelter for two seasons. Other deposits of low-grade copper sulphide, in particular the large one at Flinflon lake, can only be developed when a railway has been built and a smelter erected at the mine. A reconnaissance survey is at present being made by the Canadian National Railway authorities from The Pas to Cranberry Portage, thence to the Flinflon property, a total distance of approximately 85 miles. A railway along this route would traverse part of the mineral belt, and assist in developing several other properties. A situation that demands serious attention in connection with the initiation of copper smelting in this district is the relatively high cost of fossil fuel. It would seem that circumstances demanded that the question of electric smelting of copper-sulphide ores on an industrial scale should be studied in the interests of the development of mining in this district. Experimental work would seem to have established fairly conclusively that electric smelting of this mineral is practicable on such a scale, and that it is economically preferable to reduction by coke, where coke prices are high and electric energy readily accessible. Investigations conducted by the Dominion Water Power Branch indicate that power may be developed at Sturgeon-Weir river 35 miles distant, or on the Churchill river 60 miles away, from the Flinflon property. There seems little reason to doubt that a copper industry of considerable importance will be established in this district, with probably large ore-reserves which it will be necessary to mine on a narrow margin of profit, if the price of copper should decline to pre-war quotations.

When conditions established by the War, and adverse to the gold-mining industry, are removed, several gold properties will be developed, more particularly in the Wekusko Lake area, which has fairly satisfactory service by the Hudson Bay railway and Government wagon-road. It is expected, however, that prospecting for gold will now be carried on over a much wider field, and that the Pipestone and Cross Lake areas and the belt on the south of the Hayes river, will, for the first time, receive the serious attention of prospectors. The first and greatest need is undoubtedly the trained prospector; for him the mining field is now an attractive one. The second is sufficient capital—and a large amount will be needed—to establish the copper industry on a secure basis. When both needs have been met, northern Manitoba will become an important factor in the mining industry of Canada.

DIVIDENDS paid by mining companies in Rhodesia last year amounted to £615,640 ($2,997,000). The total cash disbursements to the end of 1918 was £6,902,987 ($33,479,000). The Globe & Phoenix led last year with £165,614, followed by the Shamva with £90,000, Lonely Reef with £81,302, Falcon with £80,000, Eldorado Banket with £45,000, and Rhodesia Chrome with £6000.

ACETYLENE is now capable of making a 24-in. cut in an ingot. Beyond that it is necessary to use hydrogen.

---

[9]H. M. Caddell, 'Geological Structure of the Northwest Highlands of Scotland'. Memoir, Geol. Survey of Great Britain, 1907.

[10]By C. K. Leith.

*Abstract from Bulletin, Canadian Mining Institute, March 1919.

The Determination of Manganese: A Modification of Volhard's Method

By W. C. RIDDELL

*INTRODUCTION. The following modification of Volhard's well-known method[1] for the determination of manganese was adopted, after comparison with several other methods.[2] It has been used for some time by several analysts, for ores ranging from 10 to 60% manganese. The usual procedure recommended for Volhard's method is shortened by omission of the evaporation with sulphuric acid and the aliquoting of the solution after the addition of zinc-oxide emulsion. A number of the features of this method have been already suggested.[3]

One important advantage of the method as outlined is that the end-point is readily determined, thus shortening the time required for an analysis. The determination of manganese in an ore can be made by one operator in 15 to 20 minutes, and a series of 12 to 15 determinations in about two hours, exclusive of the time required for preparing the samples.

OUTLINE OF PROCEDURE. The weighed sample (using a 0.3296-gm. sample and 0.2 N. $KMnO_4$ solution, 1 cc. of solution = 1% Mn) is transferred to a 400-cc. beaker. 10 to 15 cc. HCl (sp. gr. 1.2) are added and the solution evaporated down to about one-half its volume. If the ore contains insoluble manganese silicate, which can usually be determined by the pinkish color of the insoluble residue, about 1 cc. of HF is added, and the evaporation is continued until decomposition is complete. The glass is only slightly attacked by the HF, and beakers used in this way will last for some time. If the solution should evaporate to dryness, a few cubic centimetres of HCl and hot H_2O are added and heated until the salts are in solution. Dilute to about 300 cc. with boiling water, add 5 to 6 grammes $ZnSO_4 \cdot 7H_2O$ and a small excess of ZnO emulsion. Run into the hot solution an excess of standard $KMnO_4$ solution, which may be added rapidly with no great care, and determine the excess by back titration with a solution of $MnSO_4$ that has been standardized against the $KMnO_4$.

*Published by permission of the Director of the U. S. Bureau of Mines. The writer is consulting chemical engineer to the Bureau.

[1] J. Volhard. Chem. New, Vol. XI, p. 207. A discussion of the Volhard method will be found in 'Sampling and Analyses of Iron and Steel', by Bauer and Deiss, translated by Hall and Williams. McGraw-Hill Book Co., New York. 1915.

[2] For a brief outline of these methods consult Circular No. 26, U. S. Bureau of Standards. 'Analysed Iron and Manganese Ores—Methods of Analysis'.

[3] See Brearley and Ibbotson. 'The Analysis of Steel-Work Materials—Bibliography of Analytical Methods for Manganese', p. 388. Published by Longmans-Green Co., 1902.

NOTES. The use of an excess of $KMnO_4$ effects a more nearly complete oxidation of the manganese in solution to MnO_2 than is accomplished by the original Volhard procedure. It enables one to add the standard $KMnO_4$ solution more rapidly than is possible where back titration is not utilized. It also causes the MnO_2 precipitate to settle rapidly and in a condition favoring the determination of the end-point. It is especially useful when a number of ores are being analyzed, the manganese content of which is entirely unknown and of wide variation. The method has also been used for slags and ferro-manganese. The addition of $ZnSO_4$ tends[4] to lessen the occlusion of MnO in the MnO_2 precipitate with consequent low results, as shown by the following experiments: 40 cc. $MnSO_4$ required 39.5 cc. 0.2 N. $KMnO_4$ when no $ZnSO_4$ was added; 40 cc. $MnSO_4$ required 40.1 cc. 0.2 N. $KMnO_4$ when 5 gm. $ZnSO_4 \cdot 7H_2O$ was added; 40 cc. $MnSO_4$ required 40.1 cc. 0.2 N. $KMnO_4$ when 10 gm. $ZnSO_4 \cdot 7H_2O$ was added.

Experiments to determine the effect of not removing HCl by evaporation with H_2SO_4 to SO_3 fume indicate that this procedure is unnecessary. Definite volumes of $MnSO_4$ solution were measured out and to the solution varying quantities of HCl (sp. gr. 1.2) were added. The solution was then neutralized with ZnO emulsion and titrated with standard $KMnO_4$.

Table I

Experiment number	$MnSO_4$, 0.2 N. cc.	ZnO	HCl 1.2 sp. gr. cc.	$ZnSO_4 \cdot 7H_2O$ gm.	$KMnO_4$, 0.2 N cc.
1	40.0	Slight excess	2	6	40.1
2	40.0	" "	5	5	40.1
3	40.0	" "	5	0	40.1
4	40.0	" "	0	0	39.4

The experiments indicate that the removal of HCl by evaporation with H_2SO_4 is not necessary but that it is essential to have zinc ions present. These may be introduced by the addition of zinc sulphate or, as in experiment No. 3, by neutralizing an excess of acid with zinc oxide.

The $MnSO_4$ solution can be prepared by mixing a bottle of C. P. manganese sulphate, weighing out 1 gramme, determining the manganese as outlined, and calculating the quantity required for any desired volume. The water of crystallization in manganese sulphate varies. Ordinarily about 12 gm. in one litre will give a solution of about the desired strength for use with 0.2 normal $KMnO_4$. 1 cc. of a 0.1 normal solution of $KMnO_4$

[4] Volhard. Fischer's modification of Volhard's method. Ztschr. anal. Chem., Vol. 48, 1909, p. 751; Cahen and Little. 'Analyst', Vol. 36, 1911, p. 52; Brearley and Ibbotson's bibliography.

=0.001648 gm. manganese. Using 0.2 normal $KMnO_4$ and a 0.3296 gm. sample. 1 cc. $KMnO_4$ = 1% manganese. (This applies only to the Volhard titration).

The following table gives some comparative results. The permanganate used was standardized with Bureau of Standards sodium oxalate:

Table II

Ore number	Analyst	Precipitated as MnO_2 with Br	Ford-Williams method	Modified Volhard method as outlined	Regular Volhard method no correction factor used
1	A	37.5	...	37.7	37.4
	B	37.5	...	37.6	...
	C	37.6	...	...	...
	A	47.9	47.8	47.8	47.6
		47.9	47.8	47.75	47.7
		...	...	48.0	...
3	A	57.9		58.3	57.8
	B	...		58.4	...
	A	22.5		22.5	22.3
	[illegible]	...		56.1	...
				56.1	55.7
				56.2	55.8
	D	...	...	56.0	55.5

Ore No. 5—Bureau of Standards manganese sample No. 25. The manganese value of this ore given by the Bureau of Standards is 56.4% Mn. Blum[5] later determined the manganese by the bismuthate method, and gives the value as 56.2-56.3% Mn.

One of the most convenient and accurate methods available for standardizing $KMnO_4$ is by the use of the Bureau of Standards' sodium oxalate. The value of the standard $KMnO_4$ may also be determined by analyzing a weighed sample of the Bureau of Standards' standard manganese sample No. 25 according to the procedure as outlined and calculating the value of the solution in terms of manganese.

Electrolytic Zinc Improvements

In the annual report of the Judge Mining & Smelting Co. of Park City, Utah, the superintendent of the zinc plant, J. T. Ellsworth, makes the following remarks:

The year 1918 was one of continuous alterations and improvements, particularly in the electrolytic department; as a result only one-third capacity was attained for practically the full twelve months. Inability to obtain necessary chemicals for purification of solutions made it necessary to carry on prolonged experimentation to find substitutes. This has now been done and operation will be practically free from the chemical market. On account of men going into the Army, the general effect on efficient operation of the plant was harmful, as experienced men are necessary.

The original form of electrolytic cells with rotating cathodes were found inefficient and expensive, and were therefore replaced during the year by stationary cells with rectangular anodes and cathodes—much simpler cells—and by which the trouble due to warping of plates and poor contact of cathode-plates are largely overcome. The stripping cost per pound of zinc is also considerably reduced.

[5]W. Blum. Determination of manganese as sulphate and by the sodium bismuthate method. Eighth International Congress of Applied Chemistry, Vol. I, p. 61.

PLATTEVILLE, WISCONSIN

Factors Affecting Zinc, Lead, and Pyrite Production.—Need for Making High-Grade Blende.

During March, markets were irregular and unsatisfactory, but fairly good weather and fair roads enabled many operators to make good yields and shipments. A comparison of prices paid to Missouri and Wisconsin zinc miners shows that the latter was given a slight advantage, by reason of their nearness to the smelters in Illinois. The fine outputs and deliveries last month are due to certain factors at work in the Wisconsin field, tending ultimately to centralize zinc mining here into a few hands. Independent ore producers of any size, determined to remain in the game, have arrived at the conclusion that existence depends on being able to convert the low-grade concentrate into one of high-grade ready for immediate reduction on arrival at the smelter. For this reason, producers lacking the facilities for making a high-grade product, have been shut-out; and the March record, during a rather off season, is credited to fewer mining corporations equipped with refining plants or associated directly with subsidiary organizations so provided. The initial cost of erecting refining plants at mines is so great at present that before long the large concerns operating in this field will absorb the smaller producer entirely, and shipments to smelters will in time be made up exclusively of high-grade blende, assaying 60% zinc or better.

Prices for high-grade refinery product held at the beginning of the month at $45 per ton, base. Some ore sold at above this figure. The price held steadily until the 22nd, when the first break in many months was registered, the price receding to $42.50, at which level it closed the month. On second-grade product more irregularity was shown, the price moving from $41.50 to $42, $41, and $40 per ton. Low-grade producers where unprotected on open-market offerings through lack of contract agreements, were shut-out of the market entirely, and several suspended production.

Lead-ore producers found offerings for their product steady and fair, but little ore reached market. $60 for 80% concentrate held most of the month, but such ore as did clear was sold at figures under the ruling quotation. The Flint Mill & Furnace Co., a new smelter at Wauwatosa, Wisconsin, using oil-fuel, entered the field as a buyer, but its presence failed to create much interest. It appears that the price is the thing that counts. Good weather enabled many miners out of employment to enter shallow and surface deposits, making a fair extraction of ore. The reserve in the field at the close of the month was over 1000 tons.

Pyrite shippers had a discouraging month, although shipments of acid from local plants were normal. Prices were unsatisfactory to ore refiners, from whom most of this class of ore is now obtained. The reserve in the field is conservatively estimated at 5000 tons.

Gains were made in production of zinc-carbonate ore. The price averaged $27 per ton, 40% zinc content. Independent producers shared but little in the continued high price for this product. Such carbonate as is mined here is used almost exclusively in the manufacture of zinc oxide, and the Mineral Point Zinc Co. is not finding as ready a market for it as formerly, and has large stocks.

Deliveries of concentrate in March, from mines to refining plants in the field, and from mines to smelters direct, were:

	Zinc, lb.	Lead, lb.
Benton	18,674,000	550,000
Galena	4,954,000	82,000
Mifflin	3,872,000	......
Highland	2,360,000	234,000
Hazel Green	2,232,000	68,000
Shullsburg	848,000	76,000
Cuba City	678,000	......
Platteville	192,000	......
Linden	50,000	......
Total	33,860,000	1,010,000

The gross recovery of crude concentrate, from mines, amounted to 17,624 short tons; net deliveries to smelters, out of the field, 10,084 tons.

TORREON, MEXICO

Notes on the Smelter at Torreon.

Ownership of the smelter of the Compania Metalurgica de Torreon has passed out of the hands of the Madero family to a syndicate of Mexican capitalists, according to a recent authoritative announcement. This plant, which is at Torreon, is said to be the largest independent smelter on the continent. The company was organized October 10, 1900, and the plant was finished and placed in operation two years later. It is equipped with nine blast-furnaces for reduction of lead-silver ore, each having a capacity of 115 tons daily. Besides these, there is a 250-ton copper-furnace and a copper-converter good for 15 tons per day. During the three years immediately preceding the beginning of the Madero revolution, the Torreon smelter treated 770,518 tons of ore, valued at ₱24,077,063. The smallest tonnage was recorded in 1909, due to the scarcity of silicious ore available. In 1907, 1908, and 1909 the value of exports in the form of silver-lead bars was ₱30,526,840. Originally the Torreon smelter company was capitalized at ₱1,250,000 and started operations with only four furnaces, establishing agencies at Parral, Chihuahua, and Guanacevi. From the first it provided comfortable homes, schools, and the conveniences of a modern hospital and drug-store for its employees. In 1903 the capital was increased to ₱1,750,000 and two furnaces were added to the plant. Though invited under flattering conditions to join the smelter trust, the company steadfastly declined and remained independent. The Torreon smelter treated in its second year of activity 140,495 tons of ore, making a profit of ₱701,049. In 1904 it increased its capital to ₱3,500,000, in that year adding two furnaces and treating 201,612 tons of ore at a profit of ₱629,370. In 1905 there was treated 238,326 tons at a profit of ₱700,944. Still another furnace was added to the plant in 1906, this for treatment of copper ore, and in that year there went through the plant 259,552 tons of ore, upon which the profit was ₱775,286. Later there was erected a 150-ton concentrator at the company's San Diego mine at Santa Barbara, Chihuahua, producing daily 50 tons of 40 to 50% zinc concentrate. The last increase in capitalization was made in 1907, when the total was raised to its present status, ₱5,000,000. Ernesto Madero was president of the company.

Dividends paid by the Torreon smelter were 20% in 1902, 18% in 1903, 14% in 1904, 12% in 1905, 12% in 1906, and 6% in 1909. Declining dividend percentages were due to the steadily increasing capitalization throughout this period. No dividends were declared in 1907 and 1908, because in those years a large reserve-fund was provided for, and early bonds of the company were redeemed.

CRIPPLE CREEK, COLORADO

General Notes on the District.

Labor conditions are about normal again, more miners seeking employment.

The Excelsior company, operating the Longfellows of the Stratton estate, is mining a high average grade of ore between the fifth and sixth levels. During March, nearly 200 tons sent to the Golden Cycle mill, mined from a vein 10 ft. wide, assayed better than 5 oz. gold per ton, the last settlement being $74.40.

The Modoc company in March shipped from the Last Dollar mine on Bull hill 350 tons of ore, worth from $18 to $38 per ton.

A sacked consignment of ore from the Mary McKinney mine on Raven hill was settled at $2367 per ton. The gold content was 88 oz. and silver 600 oz. A 35-ton lot shipped at the same time averaged 5 oz. gold.

The Chesapeake claim, adjoining the Portland on the eastern slope of Battle mountain, owned by the Cripple Creek & Chesapeake Gold Mining Co. of Boston, has been leased to John L. McLean of Victor. The property has lain idle for 15 years or more.

Lessees of the United Gold Mines in March shipped 1000 tons of over 2-oz. ore from the Trail and Bonanza mines.

JACKSON, CALIFORNIA

Argonaut Mine Fire Out, and Damage Nominal.—Road Construction in the County.

On April 12 the bulkheads closing the Argonaut and Muldoon shafts of the Argonaut company were removed, and men entered the mine. The fire discovered on the 4000-ft. level of the Argonaut shaft on March 27 is believed to be out, and men who went down as far as 3900 ft. say that the hoisting-station on that level appears to be uninjured and the fire did not reach the shaft. There is evidence of a cave about 80 ft. back from the 3900-ft. station, and doubtless the burning of timbers in the stopes above 4000 ft. has resulted in a great deal of caving. Fears were entertained that the shaft would be lost, and for a while there seemed small hope that the hoist at 3900 ft. could be saved, so the reports made on the 12th are most gratifying. The Muldoon mine is connected with the Argonaut shaft on the 2400-ft. level, and as soon as the blowers there could be started, the gases reached the surface through the Muldoon shaft. The condition of the shaft and levels below 3900 ft. has not yet been investigated, as the air is still bad. It is expected that the cessation of pumping after the bulkheads were placed has allowed the water to rise far enough to cause some damage on the lower levels of this deep mine, but the early resumption of work on the usual scale is contemplated. In order to extinguish any fire that might have been smoldering in the mine, carbonic acid gas was forced into the shaft before the bulkheads were removed. This alone is said to have cost the company not less than $12,000. The cost of catching up caves, unwatering the lower levels, and restoring the property to its former condition is difficult to estimate, but all interested are well pleased at the prospect of operations being resumed at this rich mine with so little loss of time. Great credit in the handling of the trying situation is due the general manager, N. S. Kelsey, the chief mine inspector, H. M. Wolflin, officers of the Industrial Accident Commission, and the U. S. Bureau of Mines rescue-teams. [On April 14 it was reported that smoke was again coming out of the Argonaut shaft.]

At the Kennedy mine adjoining the Argonaut the fume from the fire made work on the various levels unsafe, and all operations there ceased shortly after the Argonaut shaft was bulkheaded, with the exception of pumping and shaft repairs. The danger now appears past and miners returned to work there on Saturday last.

Road construction, which means much to the mines of Amador county, is now well under way, four trucks and a number of men being employed on the wagon-road from the cross-county highway at the summit of Sutter hill to the Ruggles saw-mill above Pine Grove. Ruggles, who has large timber interests in the eastern part of this county, as well as in Calaveras county, subscribed $10,000 for this work on condition that the County Supervisors would expend $5000. The opening of this road should ensure ample timber for the mine at reasonable price.

TORONTO, ONTARIO

Blue Sky Bill Withdrawn.—Re-Opening of Dome Mine.—Kirkland Lake Railway.

A serious menace to mining in Ontario has been averted by the withdrawal of the 'Sale of Shares Act', commonly known as the 'blue sky law', proposed by the Ontario government. It was a drastic measure intended to protect the public against fraud by the sale of worthless shares, but in the form in which it was drawn up would have greatly checked legitimate investment, and prevented expenditure of capital by men willing to take speculative chances on new and improved prospects. The main feature of the bill provided for the appointment of a commissioner, whose permission must be obtained before shares in a company were offered for sale. The announcement of the intended introduction of this measure was met by so strong an opposition from the mining industry that the Government presented the bill in a modified form, exempting mining companies from its operation, and intimating that it would probably not be passed this session.

Porcupine.—It is officially stated that the Dome Mines company will resume milling operations on April 1. Erection of the large underground crusher continues, and is expected to be completed in about a month. The working-staff has been largely reinforced.

The Porcupine Crown has been unwatered and mining operations resumed. There is enough $10 ore broken to supply the mill at capacity for six months.

Kirkland Lake.—The Temiskaming & Northern Ontario Railway Commission will begin construction of a branch line seven miles in length from Swastika to Kirkland Lake, at an early date.

DIVIDE, NEVADA

Brief Review of This New District.

Out of the dozens of companies organized to operate in this district, at least thirty are doing exploration work; but beyond the already rich developments in the Tonopah

Divide, to a depth of 465 ft., the opening of milling-ore at 500 ft. in the Brougher Divide, and the following of some good seams in the Gold Zone, Gold Wedge, and one or two others, nothing has been found, certainly nothing to justify the rapid rise and high prices of shares dealt in by the San Francisco Stock Exchange. Calculating on the number of shares issued and their present prices, in any of the Divide companies, none of the developments represent a net value equal to the market-value.

A full face of ore has been showing for over a week in the Brougher, at a distance of 135 ft. from the main cross-cut on the 500-ft. level.

The Tonopah Divide last week sent 420 tons of ore to the MacNamara mill at Tonopah. It is said that the mill-heads assay from $29 to $48 per ton, but an average of $35 is to be maintained for better treatment. A large compressor that was at the Goldfield Merger mine is being erected.

The Hasbrouck is re-opening workings done years ago on the 200-ft. level.

The Gold Zone, on the 500-ft. level, has driven south-east about 500 ft., with reported improved conditions. A 30-in. face on April 12 is said to have assayed $85.70 per ton. F. A. Burnham is manager.

Some of the other prospecting companies are the Emancipator, Hennessey, Keystone, Smuggler, Harmill, Reno, and Ben Hur, all with Divide attached to their names.

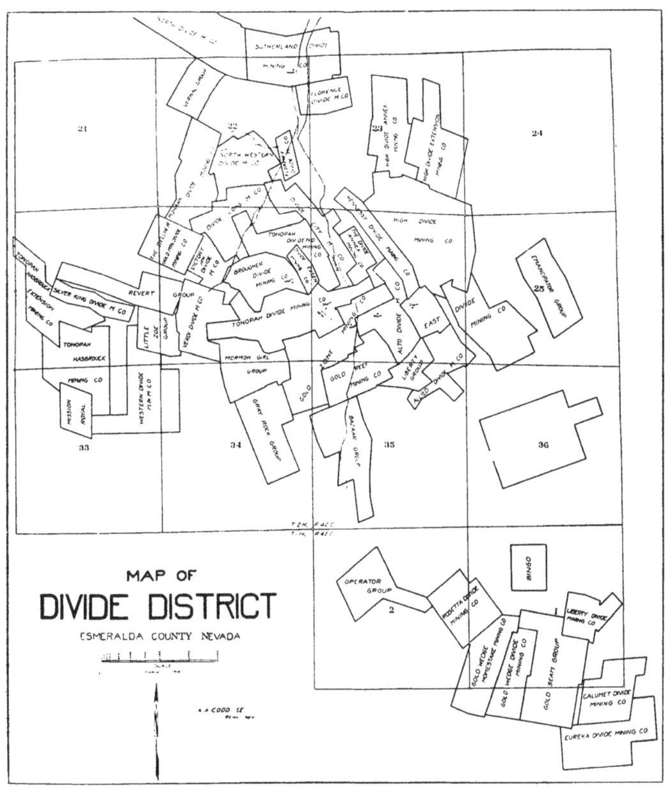

ALASKA

In Professional Paper 109 of the U. S. Geological Survey, the Canning River region (70° N. lat. and 146° long.), in northern Alaska is discussed in 251 pages by E. de K. Leffingwell. On page 178 the author gives brief notes on the mineral resources. From a prospector named Arey, who had lived in that country many years, Mr. Leffingwell gained a good idea of the possibilities. The general conditions of climate, isolation, and transportation are such that even if parts of the region are mineral bearing the chances for their development are not favorable, and it is not likely that they will attract prospectors. A few fine flakes of gold constitute the only definite evidence of any occurrence of valuable minerals. A seepage of oil and some coal outcrops were found in the western part of the Arctic Slope region. There are no trees or bushes, but there is ordinary tundra vegetation. In summer there is sufficient grass for a party with 6 horses. The barren-ground caribou is easily the most important animal, both for food and clothing. The reindeer has thrived in Arctic Alaska, but their number has not grown with the demands of the country. There is grazing ground enough for millions of reindeer. There are also foxes, mountain sheep, polar and other bear, whale, seal, ducks, ptarmigan, and fish. Useful hints on living and traveling in this region are given.

Juneau.—Alaska Gastineau in March treated 183,550 tons of 76.9-cent ore, recovering 76.3%. The first quarter of 1919 totals 497,465 tons, against 469,698 tons in 1918, the latter being over 15 cents higher grade.

Kennecott.—The Mother Lode Coalition Mines is to be incorporated in Delaware, with 2,500,000 shares of no par value. The Kennecott Copper Corporation will hold 51%. Shareholders can exchange their shares for those in the new company on the basis of one share ($10 par) of Mother Lode Copper Mines Co. The new company will pay off the old company's $500,000 bonds and provide a working capital of $1,000,000.

Valdez.—The Harmon Machinery Co. of Cordova, G. A. Harmon manager, has taken an option on the Big Four mine on Mineral creek. The new operators are called the Alaskan Hercules Mining Co. C. M. Anderson is to be in charge. A mill was purchased at Seattle recently.

The Cache Creek Mining Co. has increased its holdings, and will start hydraulicking as early as possible.——The Cache Creek Dredging Co. is to erect a hydro-electric plant for its boat

ARIZONA

Duncan.—The Ash Peak Mines Co., 9 miles west of this place, has opened a considerable quantity of silver-sulphide ore, and it is reported, contemplates the immediate erection of a 100-ton cyanide-plant.

Gunsight.—The Gunsight Gold & Tungsten Mining Co.'s mill is being overhauled, new and heavier stamps being erected. The mill is to be leased to L. Tiel to treat the Tiel & Sullivan ores. The plant will be able to treat custom ores from the district.

Oatman.—The United Eastern pays 7 cents per share, $95,140, on April 28. This makes $1,581,080 to date.

The Tom Reed company in March produced gold valued at about $77,000. Most of the ore is from the Aztec claim, mixed with a little from the Gray Eagle and Bald Eagle claims. Net profits are said to be about 3 cents per share monthly, say $27,000.

CALIFORNIA

Idria.—New Idria Quicksilver Mining Co. in 1918 produced 10,700 flasks of mercury, a decrease of 300. Sales of metal realized $1,311,394. Operations, depreciation, and depletion amounted to $1,101,205, and the net profit, subject to Federal taxation, was $167,540. Current assets total $398,743, and liabilities $256,684. The San Carlos and Idria mines are both in good condition. Five rotary-kilns, a plan of which was shown in the 'Press' of January 4, 1919, were completed by April 1, 1919. They have a total calcining capacity of 400 or 500 tons daily. Electric power is to be available in the spring. Twenty new dwellings and a 4000-bbl. oil reservoir were built. The report leaves much to be desired. As the average price for qicksilver in America last year was $118, the company must have sold about 11,100 flasks, taking some from stock. At $68 per flask for costs in 1917, as given by the manager, H. W. Gould, to the Federal Tariff Commission, there was a profit of about $50 per flask, or a total of $555,000. Even a cost of $75 per flask in 1918 would give a total of $477,000. From what source the large amount of construction work done was paid is not stated.

Plymouth.—The Plymouth Consolidated in February treated 10,200 tons of ore yielding $58,000. The profit was $16,000. On the 2450-ft. level the west drift at 380 ft. north is out 102 ft., the last 56 ft. assaying $8.50 per ton across 52 inches.

Winthrop.—The assay-office and administration office of the Bully Hill Mines were burned on April 7. The loss was $8000. The oil-flotation plant escaped damage. The offices will be re-built.

IDAHO

'A Preliminary Report on the Mining Districts of Idaho', Bulletin 166, by Thomas Varley, superintendent of the Salt Lake mining experiment station of the U. S. Bureau of Mines, and others, has just been issued. In 1917 the Bureau and the University of Idaho arranged to co-operate in an investigation looking to the improvement of mining and milling methods in the mining districts of that State, with a special view to the wider development of the mineral deposits and greater efficiency in the treatment of the low-grade ores. This work has been made possible largely through the generosity and active assistance of the mine operators, especially certain companies in the Coeur d'Alene region.

As the first step in the work under the co-operative agreement, it was decided to gather all data possible on the various mining districts throughout the State, both active and abandoned, in order to ascertain their potential possibilities, special attention being paid to methods of metallurgical treatment and to the solution of the many metallurgical problems in order to effect a greater commercial saving. With this plan in veiw, field work was begun in the

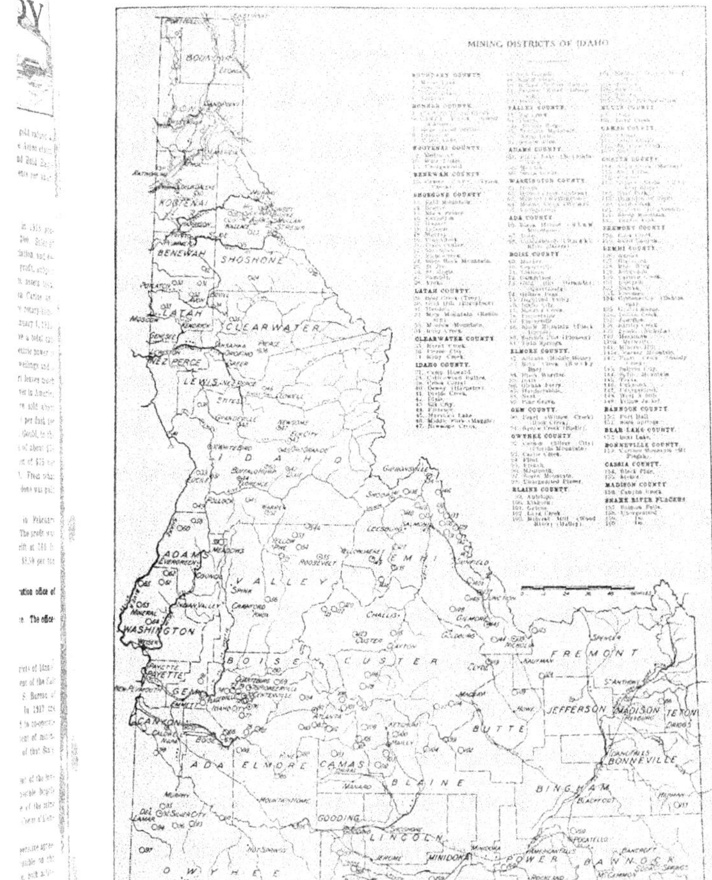
MINING DISTRICTS OF IDAHO
BOUNDARY COUNTY
BONNER COUNTY
KOOTENAI COUNTY
BENEWAH COUNTY
SHOSHONE COUNTY
LATAH COUNTY
CLEARWATER COUNTY
VALLEY COUNTY
ADAMS COUNTY
WASHINGTON COUNTY
ADA COUNTY
BOISE COUNTY
ELMORE COUNTY
BUTTE COUNTY
CAMAS COUNTY
CUSTER COUNTY
FREMONT COUNTY
LEMHI COUNTY
KOOTENAI
BENEWAH
SHOSHONE
LATAH
CLEARWATER
NEZ PERCE
LEWIS
IDAHO
ADAMS
VALLEY
WASHINGTON
PAYETTE
GEM
CANYON
BOISE
CUSTER
LEMHI
FREMONT
JEFFERSON
MADISON
TETON
BONNEVILLE
BUTTE
ADA
ELMORE
CAMAS
BLAINE
BINGHAM
GOODING
LINCOLN
MINIDOKA
POWER
BANNOCK
OWYHEE
TWIN FALLS
CASSIA
ONEIDA
FRANKLIN
BEAR LAKE

latter part of May 1917, and was continued during the summer. E. K. Soper, formerly professor of mining, University of Idaho, and now dean of the mining department of the Agricultural College at Corvallis, Oregon, visited the mining districts in central and south-western Idaho, also some of those in the northern part of the State. D. C. Livingston, professor of geology in the University of Idaho, at Moscow, also visited some of the mining districts in central Idaho during the summer; in addition, much valuable information he had gathered on former trips to many other districts is included in this report. Credit is also due Mr. Livingston for the maps covering the State, as well as the bibliography at the end of each chapter. Thomas Varley spent a short time in the field, principally in the mining districts in central and northern Idaho, and made a brief visit to the south-western districts with Mr. Soper. The field work of C. A. Wright, metallurgical engineer of the Bureau, in direct charge of the co-operative work, was chiefly in the Coeur d'Alene region. Mr. Wright visited nearly all of the districts in the region, and devoted most of his time to studying milling methods.

The bulletin aims to give the localities of the various mining districts, and the nature of the present operations and those that have been carried on in the past. The writers do not wish to imply that all districts mentioned in this bulletin were visited during the summer of 1917, for a great deal of the material has been gathered from other reports, especially from publications of the U. S. Geological Survey. However, it is hoped that this report will be of help to those who are interested in mining in the State of Idaho. The plan is to continue the field work and subsequently publish the results of the investigations in much more detail, with greater emphasis given the metallurgical treatment of the ores and the problems involved. Copies of this bulletin may be obtained by addressing the Director of the Bureau of Mines, Washington, D. C.

Adair.—The Richmond M. M. & R. Co. shipped 8 cars of 14% copper ore during February, and 5 cars in March. This output is defraying all expenses. B. N. Sharp is manager.

Elk City.—According to W. O. McNutt, secretary of the Elk City Good Roads Association, in a letter to the North-west Mining Association at Spokane, the acting-director of the U. S. Department of Agriculture, Bureau of Public Roads, states that it is hoped to begin the survey of the south fork of the Clearwater River road soon, and to follow with construction as soon thereafter as possible. This road will make accessible an important undeveloped gold belt.

Wallace.—According to the 'Miner', although several of the larger properties are closed, there are several development companies about to resume operations. Some of these are the Carbonate Hill, Copper King, Grant Ledge, Cedar Creek, Bullion, Lucky Swede, Columbus, and Chicago-Boston.

MISSOURI

Joplin.—Production of the Tri-State region last week was as under:

State	Blende, tons	Calamine, tons	Lead, tons	Value
Kansas	1,179	...	201	$53,321
Missouri	989	263	62	......
Oklahoma	5,981	...	1,466	321,219
Total	8,149	263	1,729	$423,491
Average price	$40	$27	$60	......

The total value was $103,000 less than the previous week.

MONTANA

Butte.—The March output of Butte & Superior was 7,250,000 lb. of zinc and 135,000 oz. of silver, about half of normal capacity.

Hassel.—The Iron Mask mine is to be developed by a long cross-cut tunnel, which will cut the vein at a depth of about 700 ft. The shaft is 350 ft. deep, and produces silver-lead ore. The mine is 9 miles from shipping point at Townsend.

Helena.—The Lebannon group of claims at Granite Butte, 40 miles north-west of this place, has been sold for $20,000. The gold ore is suitable for cyanidation.

Thompson Falls.—The Montana Power Co., which supplies power to many mining companies in this State, and in Idaho, also for over 400 miles of the Chicago, Milwaukee & St. Paul Railroad, reports gross earnings in 1918 amounting to $7,558,741. In 1917 and 1916 the respective totals were $6,905,256 and $6,219,148. Preferred shares received $677,026 and common $1,916,208. The hydro-electric plants generated 1,108,125,350 kw-hr., an increase of 17%. The connected load at the end of 1918 was 301,825 kw., a gain of 7%. New construction cost $750,000. Additions to the Thompson Falls and Holter plants call for the issuance of $2,836,000 bonds.

NEVADA

Goldfield.—The Goldfield Development Co. is proceeding with its plan to open and mill the large tonnage of $5.60 ore in the Combination mine. Among this is 100,000 tons of $7 ore, which may be treated first.

The Atlanta is still cross-cutting at 1900 ft.——The Kewanas is driving from the bottom of a winze from the 840-ft. level.——Grandma is driving north-west at 830 ft. to open a cross-vein in quartz formation.——Great Bend is prospecting at various points.——In the Merger, the cross-cut from the main south-east drift on the 910-ft. level of the Spearhead is well into the Merger.——The Spearhead has driven an incline raise over 100 ft. from the south-east drift on the 910-ft. level to reach the shale-latite contact.——Red Hill Florence is driving and raising at 600 ft.——On the 320-ft. level of Cracker Jack, 6 ft. across the winze gives low assays in gold.——The important work in the Silver Pick is at 700 ft.——The Lone Star is sinking to the contact, believed to occur at shallow depth at this point.

Jarbidge.—The Jarbidge Nevada Mines Co., of which O. B. Olson, of Tacoma, is president, has taken a lease and option to purchase the Alpha mine and stamp-mill. This property is on the south side of Bourne gulch, 2000 ft. east of the North Star mill. A good deal of Alpha ore was treated there. At depth the vein is wider, with an increase of sulphides. The silver content has increased, but the gold remains about the same. A Wilfley table was put in to concentrate the sulphide ore, and several tons of concentrate was sent to the smelter. The Jarbidge Nevada owns the Legitimate mine, adjoining the Alpha on the north. The two will be worked together and their ores treated at the Alpha mill. Miners are cleaning out the Legitimate tunnels. The lowest—Starlight tunnel—starts on Bourne creek, just above the quartzite dike. It is 1650 ft. long. At 1500 ft. it was expected to cut the Starlight vein, which is still missing. It is believed that a raise will be driven at the 1500 ft. point. There is an extensive fault in Starlight hill. The faulted block is 1600 ft. wide at right angles to the fault movement. The Legitimate fault-plane marks the south edge of the faulted block, and the foot-wall of the Flaxie vein marks the north edge of the block. The faulted block is not considered deep-seated. The Starlight tunnel cut the Legitimate fault-plane, giving much water. This drained the Legitimate mine, which is higher in elevation and 1500 ft. east. Carpenters are completing the aerial tram that is intended to carry the Starlight ore to the Longhike mill. Work is progressing on the lowest North Star tunnel, the portal of which is 250 ft. south of the North Star mill. Development work has been resumed on the Elmore 2 and 3 claims.

Pioche.—There is said to be some excitement over recent

discoveries of rich silver-lead ore in the Harvey mine, a mile east of this place. Donahue & Stindt are the lessees.

Goodsprings.—The mill at the Galena Canyon is to go into commission before the end of April. The mine has been developed under the management of John P. Broker. The five-mile pipe-line from a well in Sandy Valley to the mill is completed. Carl Schlutz of Los Angeles is president and Henry Gross, secretary of the company.

The old mill at the Yellow Pine has been dismantled and new machinery erected in the building. Debris from the recent fire at the mine is being cleared away, and the mine and mill will be operated with full crews shortly. It is stated that the new plant permits of treating larger amounts of ore with a higher recovery.

OREGON

Homestead.—According to D. M. Drumheller, Jr., recently returned to Spokane, the region between the Iron Dike mine and the Seven Devils country, 300 to 400 square miles in extent, in Baker county, has great possibilities as a copper producer. Lack of transportation is the main hindrance to exploitation. The Oregon Short Line enters from Huntington, in a northerly direction, but goes no farther into the belt. The town of Homestead is 135 miles from Lewiston, Idaho, and both being on the Snake river, Lewiston becomes a logical point in the route for the construction of a railroad to Portland by water grade. The railroad company is repairing its tunnel at Ox Bow, four miles from Homestead. Fire destroyed the timbers and released a large quantity of loose material that filled the tunnel, which is half a mile in length. Approximately $500,000 is being expended in the restoration. Concrete is being used. The Iron Dike is using trucks for hauling its concentrate to Ox Bow in the meantime. The big orebodies were formed along the mineralized sheer-zones and usually where intersected by an intrusion, such as a dike. The Iron Dike mine is of this form. Little high-grade veins are found all through the country. In addition to copper, Homestead contains a little silver and gold. The Iron Dike employs 60 men and is operating its mill at capacity, which is 125 tons daily. Operations have been proceeding for several years with highly profitable results, it has been stated. Other properties under development are the Copper Syndicate, McCarty, Copper Queen, Olympia, and Red Ledge. Spokane capital is considerably interested in the region.

TEXAS

Burkburnett.—A well is to be sunk here to a depth of 5000 ft. by Harry Byrens of Fort Worth.

UTAH

Salt Lake City.—The Utah Copper Co. has filed suit in the U. S. District Court to recover $158,520, alleging that tax assessments levied by the County Assessor and tax collector on tailing from reduction mills at Garfield were made without authority of the law.

Tintic.—Chief Consolidated pays 6½ cents per share on May 1. This amounts to $57,471, and makes $1,402,873 to date.

The North Standard company is equipping its mine with a new electric hoist, compressor, machine-drills, and other machinery. The new two-compartment shaft is down 85 ft., the rate of sinking being 4 ft. daily. This will continue to 500 ft. J. H. Manson is in charge.

MEXICO

Chihuahua

Batopilas.—The Lluvia de Oro Mining Co., operating south-west of this place, has suffered almost no interruption during the past three years. A stamp-mill and cyanide plant are treating the rich gold ore. L. Underwood is manager.

PERSONAL

Note. The Editor invites members of the profession to send particulars of their work and appointments. The information is interesting to our readers.

E. P. Matheson is visiting Anaconda.

N. H. Emmons, 2nd, is at New Orleans.

C. H. Hulbert sailed for Manila on April 10.

W. W. Mein has arrived here from Nicaragua.

Oliver E. Jager, temporarily residing at Corvallis, Oregon, has been in San Francisco.

Joseph T. Terry, Jr., has opened an office as consulting metallurgist at Salt Lake City.

John F. Coats, of Vancouver, B. C., has been examining mines at Placerville, California.

Arthur O. Gates, Lieutenant in the U. S. Navy R. F., arrived in San Francisco on the 'Marblehead'.

Carrol F. Reece, Lieutenant in the 102nd Infantry, has been awarded the D. S. C. for heroism in battle.

D. H. McDougall, president of the Nova Scotia Steel & Coal Co., has been elected president of the Canadian Mining Institute.

Jay A. Carpenter, recently in charge at Belmont for the Nevada Wonder company, is now superintendent of the Ben Hur mine at Divide.

L. Salazar, director of the Mexican Geological Institute, is visiting San Francisco to study the work of the California State Mining Bureau.

Harold Cogswell, formerly engineer and metallurgist at the Original Amador Consolidated mine, now Captain in the 316th Engineers, is on his way home.

F. V. Smitnoff, who is traveling for capitalists operating in Russia and Siberia, was at Salt Lake City last week. He inspected the Utah Copper Co.'s properties.

Charles W. De Witt has resigned as mine superintendent for the Chicksan Mining Co., in Korea, and is now at Omsk, Siberia, in the service of the U. S. Government.

E. H. Clausen has been discharged as Captain of Engineers in the U. S. Army, and is now associated with the Mine & Smelter Supply Co. at its New York office.

L. H. Rand and **H. H. Wadsworth**, of Oakland, members of the California Debris Commission, recently returned from an inspection of the Omega dam near Washington, Nevada county, California.

Edward W. Berry and **Joseph T. Singewald** have been appointed by Johns Hopkins University to study the geology and mineral resources of the Central Andes in Bolivia and Peru. Mr. Singewald's work 'Mineral Deposits of South America', written with **Benjamin L. Miller**, of Lehigh University, has just been published.

The **U. S. Civil Service Commission** at Washington, D. C., announces an open competitive examination for a coal-mining engineer at $2400 to $4000, and assistant at $1800 to $2400 per annum. Competitors will not be assembled for examination but will be rated on education, professional experience, and essay, publications, or reports (to be filed with application). Under the first two subjects competitors will be rated upon the sworn statements in their applications, and upon corroborative evidence adduced by the Commission.

The Utah section of the American Institute of Mining and Metallurgical Engineers gave a banquet at the Hotel Utah on April 7. The affair was attended by 150 members and guests. Informal addresses were delivered by **Horace V. Winchell**, of New York, president of the Institute, **C. K. Leith**, **James F. Kemp**, and Senator **Reed Smoot**.

THE METAL MARKET

METAL PRICES

San Francisco, April 15

Aluminum-dust, cents per pound	50—60
Antimony, cents per pound	8
Copper, electrolytic, cents per pound	15½
Lead, pig, cents per pound	5¼—6¼
Platinum, per ounce	$100
Quicksilver, per flask of 75 lb.	$75
Spelter, cents per pound	8
Zinc-dust, cents per pound	12½

EASTERN METAL MARKET

(By wire from New York)

April 15.—Copper is inactive and easier. Lead is dull and weaker. Spelter is lifeless and lower.

SILVER

Below are given official (not Government) quotations, in cents per ounce, of silver 999 fine. In order to make prompt settlements with smelters and brokers, producers allow a discount from the maximum fixed price of $1.01½, hence the lower price. The Government has not fixed the general market price at $1, but will pay this price (as from April 23, 1918) for all silver purchased by it. The equivalent of dollar silver (1000 fine) in British currency is 46.65 pence per ounce (925 fine), calculated at the normal rate of exchange. On August 15, 1918, the Treasury announced that the maximum price was fixed at $1.01½ per ounce. The British government fixed it maximum at 49½ pence, on September 2, but on November 12 this was changed to 48¾, on December 13 to 48 7/16, and on February 20 to 47¾ pence. On March 25, on account of the low rate of exchange, the London price was adjusted, with a minimum of 95 cents, resulting in daily fluctuations.

Date		New York cents	London pence	Average week ending		Cents	Pence
Apr.	9	101.12	48.86	Mch.	4	101.12	47.75
"	10	101.12	48.86	"	11	101.12	47.75
"	11	101.12	48.86	"	18	101.12	47.75
"	12	101.12	48.94	"	25	101.12	47.75
"	13 Sunday			Apr.	1	101.12	49.63
"	14	101.12	48.87	"	8	101.12	48.86
"	15	101.12	48.81	"	15	101.12	48.87

Monthly averages

	1917	1918	1919		1917	1918	1919
Jan.	75.14	88.72	101.12	July	78.92	99.62	....
Feb.	77.54	85.79	101.12	Aug.	85.40	100.31	....
Mch.	74.13	88.11	101.12	Sept.	100.73	101.12	....
Apr.	72.51	95.35	....	Oct.	87.38	101.12	....
May	74.61	99.50	....	Nov.	85.97	101.12	....
June	76.44	99.50	....	Dec.	85.97	101.12	....

The superintendent of the Mint at San Francisco, T. W. H. Shanahan, announces that the rule that was suspended during the War, giving the option to depositors to take payment in fine bars for silver deposits will be resumed on and after May 1.

COPPER

Prices of electrolytic in New York, in cents per pound.

Date			Average week ending		
Apr.	9	15.37	Mch.	4	15.25
"	10	15.37	"	11	14.83
"	11	15.37	"	18	14.79
"	12	15.37	"	25	14.09
	13 Sunday		Apr.	1	15.27
"	14	15.25	"	8	15.25
"	15	15.25	"	15	15.33

Monthly averages

	1917	1918	1919		1917	1918	1919
Jan.	29.53	23.50	20.43	July	29.67	26.00	....
Feb.	34.57	23.50	17.34	Aug.	27.42	26.00	....
Mch.	36.00	23.50	15.05	Sept.	25.11	26.00	....
Apr.	33.16	23.50	....	Oct.	23.50	26.00	....
May	31.69	23.50	....	Nov.	23.50	26.00	....
June	32.57	23.50	....	Dec.	23.50	26.00	....

Copper production of the large mines during March was as under:

Mine	Pounds	Mine	Pounds
Anaconda	13,900,000	Miami	4,551,115
Arizona Copper	2,800,000	New Cornelia	2,434,000
Calumet & Arizona	3,730,000	Old Dominion	2,574,000
East Butte	1,700,230	Phelps Dodge group	8,334,000
Greene-Cananea	3,200,000	Shattuck (mine closed by fire)	2,452
Inspiration	6,700,000		

Phelps Dodge net earnings in 1918 were $15,045,083, compared with $22,456,906 in 1917. Dividends were the same, $10,800,000.

QUICKSILVER

The primary market for quicksilver is San Francisco, California being the largest producer. The price is fixed in the open market, according to quantity. Prices, in dollars per flask of 75 pounds:

Date					
March	18	68.00	Apr.	1	68.00
	25	68.00	"	8	67.50
			"	15	75.00

Monthly averages

	1917	1918	1919		1917	1918	1919
Jan.	81.00	128.00	103.75	July	102.00	120.00	....
Feb.	126.25	118.00	90.00	Aug.	115.00	120.00	....
Mch.	113.75	112.00	72.80	Sept.	112.00	120.00	....
Apr.	114.50	115.00	....	Oct.	102.00	120.00	....
May	104.00	110.00	....	Nov.	102.50	120.00	....
June	85.50	112.00	....	Dec.	117.42	115.00	....

During February there was imported from Mexico 244 flasks of quicksilver. Exports amounted to 366 flasks, of which 265 went to Japan, and 50 to Hongkong. Most of the remainder went to Denmark and Norway.

In 'Quicksilver in 1917', advance chapter of 'Mineral Resources of the United States', by F. L. Ransome, will be found a good deal of useful information on this metal.

LEAD

Lead is quoted in cents per pound, New York delivery.

Date			Average week ending		
Apr.	9	5.25	Mch.	4	5.25
"	10	5.20	"	11	5.25
"	11	5.00	"	18	5.25
"	12	5.00	"	25	5.21
"	13 Sunday		Apr.	1	5.25
"	14	5.00	"	8	5.25
"	15	5.00	"	15	5.07

Monthly averages

	1917	1918	1919		1917	1918	1919
Jan.	7.64	6.85	5.60	July	10.93	8.03	....
Feb.	9.10	7.07	5.13	Aug.	10.75	8.05	....
Mch.	10.07	7.26	5.24	Sept.	9.07	8.05	....
Apr.	9.38	6.99	....	Oct.	6.97	8.05	....
May	10.29	6.88	....	Nov.	6.38	8.05	....
June	11.74	7.58	....	Dec.	6.49	6.90	....

The A. S. & R. Co. reduced its price of lead from 5¼ to 5 cents on April 9.

The National Lead Co., manufacturers of lead oxides, lead products, type metal, bearing metal, painters' materials, and chemicals, made a net profit of $4,692,815 during 1918. Dividends totaled $3,048,333. The surplus is $16,659,907, a decrease of $3,048,333. The company has 7286 shareholders, an increase of 134.

ZINC

Zinc is quoted as spelter, standard Western brands, New York delivery, in cents per pound:

Date			Average week ending		
Apr.	9	6.65	Mch.	4	6.61
"	10	6.60	"	11	6.55
"	11	6.55	"	18	6.50
"	12	6.55	"	25	6.48
"	13 Sunday		Apr.	1	6.53
"	14	6.55	"	8	6.60
"	15	6.50	"	15	6.57

Monthly averages

	1917	1918	1919		1917	1918	1919
Jan.	9.75	7.78	7.44	July	8.98	8.72	....
Feb.	10.45	7.97	6.71	Aug.	8.58	8.87	....
Mch.	10.78	7.67	6.53	Sept.	8.33	9.58	....
Apr.	10.20	7.04	....	Oct.	8.32	9.11	....
May	9.41	7.29	....	Nov.	7.76	8.75	....
June	9.63	7.92	....	Dec.	7.84	8.49	....

TIN

Prices in New York, in cents per pound. The monthly averages in 1918 are nominal. On December 3 the War Industries Board fixed the price to consumers and jobbers at 72½c. f.o.b. Chicago and Eastern points, and 71½c. on the Pacific Coast. This will continue until the U. S. Steel Products Co.'s stock is consumed.

Monthly averages

	1917	1918	1919		1917	1918	1919
Jan.	44.10	85.13	71.50	July	62.60	93.00	....
Feb.	51.47	85.00	72.44	Aug.	62.53	91.33	....
Mch.	54.27	85.00	72.50	Sept.	61.54	80.40	....
Apr.	55.63	88.53	....	Oct.	62.24	78.82	....
May	63.21	100.01	....	Nov.	74.18	73.67	....
June	61.93	91.00	....	Dec.	85.00	71.52	....

The tin smelters now in operation in this country and their approximate annual capacity are as follows, according to the U. S. Bureau of Mines March report:

	Metallic tin, tons
American Smelting & Refining Co., Perth Amboy, N. J.	10,000 to 12,000
Williams Harvey Corporation, Jamaica Bay, N. Y.	6,000
Eastern Metal Refining Co., Charleston, Mass.	700

The market for tungsten concentrates was further depressed during March, and some sales were made at considerably less than the prices quoted ($10 per unit) for February. Most, if not all, of the producers have closed down. At a meeting held in New York during March, a committee was appointed to represent the industry as a whole and to effect a working agreement among all the interests involved, for mutual protection. —R. C. Morris in March report of U. S. Bureau of Mines.

The price of American fertilizer potash varied during March from $3 to $3.75 per unit. Muriate, of 80% grade, in bags, averaged $260 per ton during the month; and sulphate, basis 90%, was $275 per ton, but fell to $225 toward the end of the month.

Eastern Metal Market

New York, April 9.

The markets are all quiet, with the tone in some of them easier than a week ago. Buying of all metals is light.

Antimony has advanced in a quiet market.

Copper demand has fallen, but prices are fairly firm and unchanged.

Lead is quiet with prices unchanged nominally.

Tin is still stagnant and without feature.

Zinc demand continues light, but prices have firmed because of economic conditions in the market.

ANTIMONY

The market is quiet and demand is light, but quotations are higher at 6.62½ to 6.75c., New York, duty paid, for wholesale lots for early delivery.

ALUMINUM

No. 1 virgin metal, 98 to 99% pure, is quoted at 29 to 31c., New York, for early delivery. The market is featureless.

COPPER

The activity in evidence most of last week and the week before has subsided, and demand has fallen off. There is still some inquiry with some business being done, and the recession is regarded as largely temporary. Prices are unchanged, with electrolytic quoted at 15.37½c., New York, and Lake copper at 15.62½ to 15.87½c. While export demand is not large, it is interesting. There have been fair sales of wire-bars in foreign countries during the past few weeks, mostly to England and at prices substantially above domestic levels. It is believed that there is no established export-price, but it is anything that anyone can get. An interesting development is the trading in copper on the New York Metal Exchange. Yesterday, 600 tons were sold for delivery in the next six months at 100 tons per month at the flat price of 15.75c. per lb. In fact, each day since this new procedure was adopted there has been a little business done, the results showing what dealers think of the future prospects. A good start is believed to have been made in copper trading on the Exchange, despite the fact that some has been disappointing so far.

LEAD

The market continues dull with prices unchanged at 5.25c., New York, or 5c., St. Louis, for early delivery. These are nominally correct, but there has been in the last few days a little under-selling by one or two interests, restive under the present inactivity. These sellers have offered early delivery metal at 5.20c., New York, and it is probable that a little business was done, but not much. The leading interest (A. S. & R. Co.), and the outside market continue to quote the same level. February exports of lead were 6847 tons. [On the 9th, the trust price was lowered to 5c.]

TIN

The tin market is the same old story—featureless, stagnant, and still held down by Government restrictions. The nominal price is still the one of 72.50c., New York, but there is almost no buying, and it is now practically impossible to purchase even American tin, the sales of this having been stopped about a week ago. The entire situation is one of 'watchful waiting', and little progress seems to be in process in disposing of allocated metal. There has been some buying of tin for future shipment for storage in England or in Canadian ports against the removal of import restrictions, but this has been small. Tin has been offered recently as low as 47.50c. for April-May shipment from the Straits. When Government restrictions are lifted an active market is expected—one that may become even wild until the situation adjusts itself. So far no arrivals have been reported in April. The London market yesterday for spot Straits was £226 10s. per ton.

Tin smelters now in operation in the United States have a yearly capacity of 18,700 tons of metallic tin. They are the American Smelting & Refining Co., 12,000 tons; the Williams Harvey Corporation, 6000 tons; and the Eastern Metal Refining Co., Charlestown, Massachusetts, 700 tons.

ZINC

Because of a reduction of $1 per day in the wages of employees at Western smelters and because of the prospect of strikes as a result of this, quotations have gradually stiffened until yesterday prime Western for early delivery was quoted at 6.30c., St. Louis, or 6.65c., New York. There have been less strikes and fewer shut-downs than expected, it is stated, and now there is a softening tendency until it is claimed that the metal can be bought at 6.27½c., St. Louis, for April or early delivery. Demand is not large and consumers continue to be shy, though dealers are more active. The unsettlement in the steel price situation is one cause, there being less immediate prospect of buying by galvanizers. It is stated that Government stocks of zinc, mostly high grade, will be disposed of in the same manner as the copper stocks, sales to be made over the next 15 months. This metal is said to be less than originally estimated, a press report today giving it as 93,346,000 pounds.

ORES

Antimony: Importations of ore from Chile in February were in quantities containing 3008 lb. of metal, with an amount from Peru in the first half of March having a metal content of 9276 lb. Quotations are not obtainable.

Manganese: Of the total February imports of 21,819 long tons, 11,619 tons came from Cuba and only 5450 tons from Brazil. It is interesting also that 2240 tons came from Japan and 1950 tons from Argentina.

Manganese-Iron Alloys: While the quotation of 80% ferro-manganese is still $150, delivered, re-sale alloy has sold as low as $115. Production in the United States in March was close to 20,000 tons, bringing the total for the first quarter to about 63,000 tons—a large output considering conditions. Added to this is the importation of British alloy, which has been nearly 7000 tons this year to March 15, with about twice as much yet to come. Spiegeleisen is quoted at $40 to $45 delivered. Demand for these alloys is hand-to-mouth.

Molybdenum: The market is quiet and inactive, with quotations nominal at about 80c. per pound of MoS_2 in the 90% concentrates. Imports of ore in February were 68,599 lb., valued at $48,255, most of it from Canada. There were no imports in the first half of March.

Tungsten: A leading broker reports that a fair quantity has changed hands during the past week. No quotations, however, are published or obtainable from other sources. The market is depressed and most, if not all, of the producers have closed down. In the first half of March, imports of tungsten-bearing ores were 393 tons, valued at $242,189. There were no ferro-tungsten imports. The mineral investigators of the U. S. Bureau of Mines state that as a result of a questionnaire the average loss of tungsten in making the ferro-alloy is about 14%. This is regarded as too low, as it is believed that this is nearer 25% actually. No quotations are available on ferro-tungsten.

High-speed tool-steel is quoted at $1.70 per pound.

Company Reports

GOLDFIELD CONSOLIDATED MINES CO.

As is well known now, the property of this company has been leased to the Goldfield Development Co., which is to sub-lease sections and work other parts of the mines itself. The twelfth annual report covers the year 1918, and the following notes are from the statements of the secretary, C. F. Burton, and general manager, E. A. Julian:

Financial Statement: the net income last year was $796,-410. Operations resulted in a loss of $7801, but on adding other items, and charging off $350,000 on the Montana Mines Co., the total loss was $324,381. Depreciation amounted to $193,380. Undivided profits on December 31, 1918, were $1,880,816, including $136,062 cash.

Dividends: none has been paid since October 30, 1915, so the total remains at $28,999,832.

Development: there was 4848 ft. of new work accomplished, compared with 16,477 ft. in 1917, and 28,333 ft. in 1916. This was nearly all in the upper levels. There is no measurable ore-reserve. Forty sets of lessees were operating on the split-check system. They mined 25,085 tons. Treatment of 2422 tons from mine dumps, averaging $2.98 per ton, resulted in a slight loss, and indicate no encouragement from the remaining 50,000 tons.

Production: the mill treated from all sources 94,654 tons of $11.25 ore, against 250,550 tons of $8.14 in 1917, and 338,680 tons of $7.52 in 1916. Extraction was 86%. In two years there was 240,715 tons of $1.27 tailing treated at a cost of 59 cents per ton, extraction being 57%. The output to date is $73,440,672 from 3,187,662 tons of ore, and $312,499 from 246,006 tons of tailing.

The Goldfield Development Co. now proposes to mine a large area in the Combination mine, and according to its general manager, A. I. D'Arcy, the following is the plan:

The vein from which the production of the Combination mine was made is an almost vertical fissure, having an average width of 50 ft. and extending from what is known as the January shaft to the boundary-line of the Florence mine, a distance of approximately 380 ft. The tonnage contained in a block of ground having the dimensions as given would be approximately 1,500,000 tons. The method formerly used in mining was by square-set stopes, and filling of the stopes with low-grade vein material known as 'gob'. A compilation of over 1000 samples taken from the filling of the stopes or 'gob' gave an average assay value of $5.60 per ton in gold. It is apparent that if a cheap mining method were put into effect upon this tonnage and grade of ore, a profitable operation would result. The Goldfield Development Co. proposes to adopt a method for the mining of this large tonnage of ore, which has been successfully used in other mines, and which has resulted in a mining cost of less than $1 per ton. Briefly, the method will consist of driving haulage-ways on a level below the 380-ft. level throughout the length of the ore-channel from the January shaft to the Florence line, and by a system of raises and chutes the ore will be drawn off and hoisted to the surface. As the Combination shaft is partly in the vein, it would be impossible to use this shaft, as when the drawing-off process was started the surface ground would cave and destroy it, so it is therefore proposed to use a shaft which was sunk in the early days and which is in good order with the exception of requiring new timbering. This shaft is approximately 600 ft. deep and 300 ft. distant from the vein. It would be necessary to drive a cross-cut from the shaft to the vein as part of the haulage-system, then extend the haulage-way for the entire length of the ore-channel. The cost of the necessary drifts, cross-cuts, raises, chutes, stations, and repairs to the shaft to adapt the Combination mine to this method of mining should not exceed $60,000, and this would be the total cost of the undertaking at the mine, as the property is equipped with hoists, air-compressors, underground electric-haulage locomotives, and in fact everything necessary for handling the large tonnage of ore. The success of the undertaking would depend on being able to handle from 500 to 1000 tons of ore per day. This could be accomplished with the equipment on hand at the mine, and as the Consolidated mill has a record for the treatment of ores in excess of 35,000 tons per month, there would be no difficulty in the treatment of the ore. As the ores of the Combination mine are particularly amenable to cyanidation, it is proposed to give the ore a simple cyanide treatment and do away with some of the processes in vogue at the Consolidated mill, such as concentrate treatment, etc., thus cutting the cost as low as possible. Before milling operations are started there will be some necessary changes and repairs at the plant, which will require an expenditure of $15,000, therefore the estimated expenditure to put the proposition on a paying basis would be $75,000. With the cheap mining method at the mine and a simple cyanide treatment at the mill, it will be profitable to handle ores of a value as low as $3 per ton, with a value in excess of $5 per ton and approximately 1,500,000 tons the undertaking should show a profit of $3,000,000, or a net profit of $1.20 per share for the entire capitalization of the company.

LIBERTY BELL GOLD MINING CO.

Property: mines and mill at Telluride, Colorado.

Operating Officials: C. A. Chase, manager; H. G. McClain, superintendent; M. L. Anderson, mine superintendent; A. J. Weinig, metallurgist; and E. J. Woodworth, accountant.

Financial Statement: the income during the year ended September 30, 1918, totaled $1,148,523 net. Operations, plus depletion $24,405, cost $837,858, leaving a surplus of $310,664. The balance on October 1, 1917, was $481,152, and after adding profit and reduction of capital, etc., and deducting depletion of ore for 1909 to 1917, and dividends, the balance carried to 1919 was $645,364. Investments are valued at $267,431.

Dividends: these amounted to $387,310, making a total of $2,594,181.

Development: the 3073 ft. of new work was a decrease of 1603 ft. All openings amount to 16 miles. The old productive areas were almost exhausted early in the year, but a partly developed area in the eastern part of the mine was further opened and equipped for motor haulage. The compressor plant had to be duplicated. As the efficiency of the men fell off considerably, it was decided to start the contract system, which improved matters greatly in costs and less waste among the ore. There has been extracted from this mine 2,144,612 tons of ore, and reserves now amount to 600,000 sq. ft., equal to 100,000 tons.

Production: the mill treated 90,700 tons, assaying 0.529 oz. gold and 2.565 oz. silver per ton, of which 98% and 85%, respectively, was extracted. Gold from cyanidation was $1,084,700, and from concentrate $68,343. The total since 1899 is $14,043,893. Underground work cost $8.83, and treatment $3.13 per ton.

EAST RAND PROPRIETARY MINES

This company has a property covering 5267 acres on the Rand, also a mill containing 820 stamps, 25 tube-mills, and cyanide plants. During 1918 there was treated 1,372,000 tons of ore averaging $5.58 per ton. The profit was 18 cents per ton. Ore-reserves are estimated at 2,200,000 tons, averaging $6.50 per ton. In 1917, 1,741,300 tons yielded a profit of 46 cents per ton. Reserves then were 4,200,000 tons of $6.10 ore.

BLUE-SKY legislation has been denied by the lawmakers of Ontario. A bill to regulate the sale of stocks and shares aroused successful opposition, largely, it appears, because the terms of enactment were so severe as to restrict legitimate financial activity. The wild-cats are purring.

IN our last issue we referred to a committee on co-operation to be appointed by the American and Canadian mining institutes. We note now with pleasure that the American Institute has appointed Messrs. E. P. Mathewson, Albert R. Ledoux, and L. K. Armstrong as representatives for the purpose, and that Messrs. D. H. McDougall, Willet G. Miller, and R. H. Stewart will represent the Canadian Mining Institute. This is an excellent selection and carries the promise of good work in furthering friendly relations between the two organizations and the two neighboring countries.

MEXICAN misrule comes again into unpleasant prominence owing to the sad news that Edward L. Dufourcq, of New York, assistant manager of the Teziutlan Copper Company, was killed on April 18 by a band of so-called Zapatistas, who waylaid him when engaged in professional duties near the plant. Mr. Dufourcq is known to many of our readers as an engineer of high character. Insult is added to injury by calling the murderers "Zapatistas." Zapata is dead; these are plain bandits. The effort to give a political color to marauding ruffians by calling them 'istas of any kind is damnable nonsense. We hope, in spite of the improbability, that the Department of State at Washington will make an immediate inquiry into this outrage and insist upon prompt punishment.

OLE HANSON has been in San Francisco. The mayor that made Seattle famous is a man after Theodore Roosevelt's own heart, and that means he is very much of a man indeed. With his family of eight children, his rise to useful prominence as a citizen, his fearless insistence on observance of the law, and a capacity to put his ideas of civic government into effect, this virile Norseman has proved himself 100% American. Most of us like men that know their own minds and follow the lead of courageous principle. There is too much of listening leadership in the world. We thank heaven, as Tennyson did, "for a man with heart, head, hand like some of the simple great ones gone"; for "one who can rule and dare not lie." Mr. Hanson recognizes that "a mass attack is being made against civilization" and that this is a time "to cast aside all prejudices, forget all party ties, and study the problems that confront us from the standpoint of American citizenship." He warned the labor-unions against the I. W. W. or Bolshevist groups, whose domination would cause Union Labor to "slip back 25 years and lose the wonderful advances it has made by honest struggle and hard work." This is good advice, and it comes from a friend of the working-man.

DELAY in starting the investigation of claims for compensation under the War Minerals Relief Act is causing anxious comment among the producers of chrome and manganese, because the mine workings, in some instances, will have caved before an examination can be made by the Government engineers. It is suggested therefore that the producers would save time and expedite a settlement of their claims by causing examinations to be made and reports to be written by mining engineers having such a standing as will command the confidence of the Government's representatives, namely, the Commission appointed for this purpose. The small expense incurred would represent less money than that entailed by the long wait likely before the Government inspectors arrive on the ground and make their estimate.

SIGNS of antagonism between Mr. Lloyd George and Lord Northcliffe are manifest. In his speech before Parliament on April 16 the British Premier made pointed reference to the publisher of many newspapers and imputed his attacks on the Peace Conference to injured vanity. In this respect, and in others more objectionable, Lord Northcliffe resembles Mr. Hearst, although he is a politer edition of that unblushing exponent of yellow journalism. Mr. George said that he would rather have "a good peace than a good press"; he described some of the difficulties under which the Conference labored, conducting its deliberations while stones fell on the roof and wild men screamed at the keyhole. The Northcliffe press is as much a curse to the democracy of Great Britain as the Hearst press is to the more advanced democracy of this country. We are glad to see Mr. George lock horns with the controller of the London 'Times', the influence of which is due largely to a tradition now exploded, and we hope that the result of this personal conflict will be to curb the sinister use of influential newspapers by an ambitious and irresponsible publisher. The freedom of the press is essential to the preservation of democratic institutions, but the license of the press ministers to a kind of unchartered power that is deadly to democracy. We look forward to the time when the President and his official family at Washington will exhibit a larger aloofness from Mr. Hearst's malignant influence.

BOLSHEVIST propaganda is said to be responsible for the emigration from this country of a large number of aliens. According to the Savings Bank section of the American Bankers Association an exodus of six million persons, taking with them four billion dollars, is probable, unless steps are taken to check the propaganda. The New York Customs House officials are said to have asserted that those now sailing from that port carry with them from $2000 to $15,000 apiece in United States currency. Also it is estimated that fully 1,300,000 persons cannot be stopped from departing and they will take four-fifths of the total currency in this country. As many as six million aliens may be lured, it is said, by the Bolshevist call. "This is very serious," says the New York dispatch issued by the Universal Service. Yes, it would be extremely serious if it were true. Our newspapers every day contain statements quite capable of robbing us of our sleep if we had to believe them. We doubt whether any such number will want to leave or could be permitted to leave for some time to come; we doubt their ability to carry away so much currency; and if they were really Bolshevists in spirit we would speed their departure with a swift kick, even if they went away with pockets bulging with money.

IN this issue we publish the first part of the Alien Property Custodian's report on the German metal octopus. We shall discuss the subject more fully at a later date; meanwhile we note that a sale of enemy holdings of American Metal Company stock was held at New York early in April and that 49% of the outstanding capital was acquired by Mr. Charles Hayden, of Hayden, Stone & Company, in behalf of a syndicate the membership of which is not disclosed. The transaction involves the payment of $4,850,160 for voting-trust certificates representing 34,644 shares out of the 70,000 issued. The sale took place under the auspices of the Alien Property Custodian, who, three years ago, seized the property of the three principal metal-dealing German firms. Mr. H. W. McAteer, representing another syndicate, bought 562 shares out of 25,000 shares of the Compania de Minerales y Metales, a Mexican subsidiary of the American Metal Company. This block of stock fetched $57,000. No change in the management or status of the American Metal Company, now in the safe hands of the Custodian, is to be made for the present. Members of the old management, still employed by the Custodian, own 27% of the stock, while the British Public Trustee, occupying a position analogous to that of our Alien Property Custodian, holds the 24% formerly owned by Henry R. Merton & Co., one of the tentacles of the German octopus.

Siberia

Dispatches from Paris state that the Omsk government in Siberia is to be recognized by the Peace Conference. This is important news and most gratifying. Amid the chaos of Russian misrule the establishment of order in Siberia has been the one hopeful sign. It will be remembered that early last year Admiral Koltchak, formerly commander of the ill-fated Black Sea fleet, seized the reins of administration and established a government, with the support of the Siberian and Czecho-Slovak troops. At a national conference held at Ufa, in the Ural, a program for the unification and regeneration of Russia was accepted. This program was upset by Admiral Koltchak's *coup d'état* and in its place a government was set up at Omsk. This obtained the support of the Allied troops in Siberia and succeeded in restoring some semblance of order throughout Asiatic Russia from Vladivostok to Orenburg. Theodore Roosevelt in his last hours advocated the sending of aid to the heroic Czecho-Slovaks in Siberia and of supporting the *de facto* Government of Siberia in its effort to hold back the tide of Bolshevism advancing from western Russia. The part played by the Czecho-Slovaks appealed keenly to his sympathy and the apparent political detachment of Siberia from European Russia seemed to him to furnish a base for checking Bolshevism. The recognition of the Siberian government will annoy some people because it may look like an encouragement of the reactionary element, but we take the view that the Government of Siberia can be liberalized with more prospect of success than a soviet pandemonium can be rationalized. The party of Admiral Koltchak stands for a national republican form of government, representing all the people, not the proletariat alone; it came into conflict with the social revolutionists led by Nicolai Avksentieff, who was driven from Omsk, but we understand that Avksentieff is now supporting Koltchak, who is also backed by the old Cadet party of constitutional reformers, including such worthy Russians as Professor Paul Miliukoff, Prince George Luov, Madame Breshkovskaya, Messrs. Sergius Sasanoff, the former Minister of Foreign Affairs, Nicolai Tchaikovsky, and Boris Bakhmetieff, the ambassador to the United States. This party stands for order, a constituent assembly, and the popular choice of a form of government through a general election. Those living in Siberia will be grateful for the restoration of order even if the political tint of the present administration is not quite as warm as some of them might wish. For ourselves, we realize that Allied support will regularize the *de facto* Government and give it a chance to bring Siberia out of the gloom of anarchy into the daylight of law. It will have an immediate effect upon the mining industry of a rich, vast, and most interesting country, not only stabilizing the operations already started at Kyshtim, Spassky, Ridder, Tanalyk, and the Lena, for example, but stimulating new enterprises, in which the American mining engineer should play a leading part.

he becomes, for example, the Smith that wrote on the structure of ore deposits in a manner commanding attention; Jones likewise is no longer merely one of a tribe but an individual of distinction when he explains the operations of a flotation process in a lucid and informing manner. When either Smith or Jones travels outside his bailiwick he is greeted by the well-informed as one who wrote something that has been appreciated by the members of the fraternity. One thought more: not much can be accomplished without co-operation; help others and they will help you; play a lone hand and you lose the game. The mining profession is not a mere collection of selfish adventurers or egotistic practitioners, it is a fraternity, a brotherhood of earnest and kindly men, hoping to achieve the worthy purpose of winning friends and of proving effective. Enduring achievement calls for co-operative effort; the engineer's first duty is to be helpful.

Who Will Hold the Sack?

One of the sure signs of a revival of speculative interest in mining is the appearance of prospectuses and circulars inviting the public to become rich suddenly. The wild-cat has issued from his lair and grins cheerfully on a greedy world. A typical invitation is that of the Homestake Gold Mining Company, incorporated in the State of Washington and controlling mining claims in Idaho. By using the name of a famous mine it starts under a flattering illusion, but one provoking suspicion immediately. It "offers the investor the greatest possible opportunity." Another false note, because a prospect is not an 'investment' under any circumstances. The advertisement fails to quote the report of a reputable engineer, therefore its assertion that "there is no question as to the great ultimate value this mining property will attain" is entirely unconvincing. Another interesting 'proposition' is the Ophir Silver Mining Company, the shares of which are offered to us in a circular just to hand from Toronto. We are told that "the vein averages three inches in width, and while there has naturally not been time for assays, my engineer informs me that the ore has every indication of values in excess of five thousand ounces to the ton." This is delightfully ingenuous. We are informed that "Ophir sold up to 11 cents on this news and closed in strong demand." Ophir is a good name, for is it not associated with Solomon and his glory, not to mention the Queen of Sheba; and Cobalt, where this prospect is situated, is a good name in itself; yet we would advise against the purchase of stock in a mine appraised by an engineer unable to find time for a few necessary assays. The circular concludes by asserting that "'the stock will double in value very shortly." It can be doubled by peddling it at twice the price at which it was previously offered, if the supply of shares is controlled by the promoters. That is simple. Next our attention has been called to an offer of treasury stock in the Big Chief Copper Company by means of an advertisement in which it is asserted that this stock "is entitled to be recognized and placed in the column of 'safe investments'." The promoters state that they "recommend it as such," and they proceed to explain that the property "has many exposures of ore carrying copper, gold, and silver, and it looks like a wonderful bonanza mine from the very surface," although as yet the proof of this awaits the "penetration of this ore-shoot" by a lower tunnel. It is acknowledged that other prospects near-by are "speculations, pure and simple, as the ore is yet to be found," but "the ore once found generally proves, under efficient management, to be a bonanza." We recognize that bad management may turn 'ore' into 'waste', but no management, however skillful, can put ore where nature has failed to do so. This is one of the fledglings hatched by the boom at Tonopah, the consequence of the big success scored by the Tonopah Divide mine, a genuine bonanza. Already 125 companies have been incorporated to operate in the same locality and thirty of them are actually engaged in exploratory work. Groups of claims with no showing of ore, not even the same rock formation as that enclosing the Divide orebody, are selling for large sums of money. The fact that the Divide shaft was sunk in a hungry-looking breccia in order to reach the extension of the gold ore previously found in the adjacent rhyolite is taken as an evidence of probability in favor of other barren outcrops. The superintendent of the Divide expected to find gold ore in rhyolite and discovered silver ore in breccia, therefore any other similar illogical result seems justifiable to the incubators of wild-cats. It would be natural to argue that as the Divide obviously was the result of accident, assisted by drill and pick, therefore a similarly fortuitous enterprise is more desirable than the 'safe investment'. As a matter of fact, the Divide orebody was found in November 1917, and the proof of an extension of the rich ore has been obtained by eighteen months of honest mining, not reckless conversation. Already the exuberance of a boom has carried share quotations to unjustifiable figures; for instance, the Tonopah Divide is owned by a company capitalized at 1,250,000 shares, which, at the current price of $11, represents $13,750,000. To return that amount of money together with 10% per annum for ten years, for example, will require a gross production probably of something like $40,000,000. The Goldfield Consolidated paid $29,000,000 in dividends out of a gross output of $73,000,000. Mines adjoining the Divide, and owned by companies whose shares are quoted at prices that give these prospects a market valuation of two or three million dollars, have only a few thousand tons of ore, plus glittering expectations, to show for the inflation. Of course, the wise ones do not expect to hold the shares for ten years, or even for ten months; they are expecting to find somebody more optimistic on whom they can unload. Perhaps they will; but that is not mining, it is what is vulgarly called the mining 'game', which has the same relation to legitimate mining as the vagaries of the turf have—or had, for they are now extinguished by law—to the breeding of thoroughbred horses. Mining is an industry, not a gamble.

An Engineer's Duty

In a letter received recently from a mining engineer abroad we found this remark: "You are entirely correct in your statement that the writing of an occasional article is a stimulus, and I often regret my neglect of that phase of what should really be considered a part of an engineer's duty." We think it is; an engineer has many duties to perform; this is one of them; it is one of the most useful, and it brings its own reward. The subject is worthy of consideration, particularly in a day and generation when we are realizing with increased bewilderment how little accurate knowledge is obtainable from amid the mass of misinformation that finds its way into print. Our profession, on the whole, is singularly inarticulate. The number of engineers who can write or speak with satisfaction to themselves and their audience is relatively small. The talking is done mostly by the lawyers and the writing by the professors. Yet the engineer is the man that does things, who travels and observes, who comes into personal contact alike with capital and with labor, and who applies himself to the manifold phases of industry with what we call the scientific spirit, namely, a consistent effort to ascertain the truth. The best way to do so is to start by giving away what small part is already acquired. To give is to receive. A humorist has said that the quickest method of obtaining knowledge of a subject is to write a book on it. Many a true word is said in jest. It is certain that the writing of a technical article, for example, is mentally more enriching to the writer than to any of his readers. While engaged in such work he discovers how much he does not know concerning the subject, he proceeds to correct the deficiency, to fill the holes and to bridge the gaps, and, above all, to correlate facts so that their real significance emerges in the form of logical statement. He seizes hold of the amorphous information he has been storing in the lumber-room of his mind and crystallizes it into a shape likely to prove useful to himself and to others. Card-indexes are excellent things in their way, but the habit of writing is a better aid to memory, for it causes the items of knowledge and of experience to be placed in a logical order rendering them memorable. An engineer who puts his ideas and observations into print soon acquires a storehouse of information, which is easily accessible to him, and it is indestructible. We recall the misfortune that befell a Californian family of mining engineers whose notes and data were being collected for their own use, not for publication, because that meant the giving away of trade secrets, as it were. The San Francisco fire turned this accumulation of special information into smoke. They lost it all; if they had put it in print, perhaps for the benefit of others incidentally, they would have derived advantage from the fact that publication involves such multiplication as to escape individual loss by fire or other catastrophe. We recall a mining engineer at Denver who had a hobby for collecting data of technical interest. He accumulated a great mass of valuable information, of which he himself made but little use, and when he died his notes were not in a condition rendering them useful to anybody else, so they also might as well have gone skyward in a pillar of fire or a cloud of smoke. No waste is so pitiful as the waste of experience. Furthermore, of the fund of knowledge that any one of us may possess, all but a small fraction has been given to us. The amount of first-hand knowledge accumulated by any individual is insignificant when compared with that which he has acquired either from his fellows gratuitously or from books at a price relatively negligible. Mean is the spirit of the man that would secrete the little original information he has gained, instead of giving it without reservation in unequal exchange for all that has come to him without cost. Narrow is the mind of him that would withhold information from others, and foolish too, because what he might give is small in comparison with what he might receive in generous reciprocity. Secret technology is an absurdity, in any event, because no process or practice in mine or mill can escape the intelligent curiosity of a man determined to know about it. No extraordinary detective skill is required to ascertain facts the knowledge of which must be shared with numerous operatives, or by a staff the personnel of which is liable to change. Managers notorious for inhospitality in such matters have often proved to be laggards in technical progress, whereas those remarkable for generosity in giving forth information concerning their operations have usually been distinguished for successful work. Engineers willing to help others have been more than recompensed by the friendly assistance offered to them in turn. Apart from such recompense, the engineer finds that his effort to describe his own methods gives him a better understanding of the principles involved and aids him in designing improvements. To write carefully on anything is to clarify one's notions concerning it. Writing becomes a mental stock-taking, a necessary preliminary to intellectual exchange. Two other phases of the subject should appeal to the professional man. The writing of an interesting and useful article—and to be either interesting or useful it must be written carefully and intelligibly, if not attractively—is one of the few ways of achieving honorable prominence. To have ability or experience is not of much avail unless others know that the engineer possesses them. He cannot assert the fact by vulgar advertisement, but he can prove it by occasionally opening the doors of his mind and sharing its valuable contents. Mining, like every profession, is over-crowded; it is well to emerge from the 'and others' for fear of being counted among the 'also rans'. The professional man to be successful in this workaday world must escape from the promiscuity of the mob; he must win individuality and distinction; and he can do it by an occasional writing good enough to give him honorable identity. Next we like to dwell on the pleasant thought that the publication of a signed article makes mental friends; it promotes an acquaintance wider than that of physical contact; it brings a man at once into the intellectual company of thousands. Smith ceases to be one of that numerous family;

Colorado Pitchblende Company

The Editor:

Sir—In your editorial of the 29th ult. in discussing the review of the committee appointed by me to consider the McClave report on the Colorado Pitchblende Company's property, you were good enough to give me more credit than possibly I am entitled to. The committee consisted of Messrs. Nye, Malm, and Lowden with Mr. Stahl as secretary, and they are the ones to receive not only your words of endorsement but also the thanks of this community for the care given and time spent upon it. I was out of the city while the review was being formulated and signed it as chairman as a matter of form on my return.

RICHARD A. PARKER.

Denver, April 3.

The Status of Gold

The Editor:

Sir—I have read, with much interest, Mr. John McPherson's letter in your issue of March 22 in reply to Mr. Van Dyck's letter in your issue of February 1, and I find it serves a double purpose because it, also, replies to Mr. Robbins' letter, published in the same issue, that of the 22nd ultimo.

With two or three exceptions, those of your correspondents who have contributed to the discussion on this subject do not seem to comprehend the basic principles of money, presumably because they have not studied political economy sufficiently. There is no royal road to knowledge, but I had hoped that in my article entitled 'What is a Dollar' (M. & S. P., Aug. 3, 1918) I had answered that query with reasonable completeness. Apparently, however, I did not; or else the above-mentioned correspondents did not read it understandingly or did not read it at all. Permit me, therefore, to add the following:

The 'dollar' of the United States of America is 23.22 gr. of fine or pure gold, no more and no less. Similarly the British sovereign or pound sterling is 113.+ gr. of fine or pure gold, no more and no less. Graphically, they may be represented by two cubes respectively 0.16833 in. and 0.2853 in. on each edge. A cube of pure gold of the smaller size will weigh 23.22 gr. and one of the larger size will weigh 113.+ gr.; and 113.+ gr. divided by 23.22 gr. equals 4.8665+, which means that there is 4.8665+ times as much pure gold in a 'sovereign' as there is in a 'dollar'.

Recently, I showed a sketch of the two cubes to a friend, who had given the subject of political economy some thought and study, and, after viewing them for a moment or two he remarked very positively, referring to the smaller cube, "That may represent correctly the size of a piece of gold that will weigh 23.22 gr. but it is not a 'dollar' till the Government stamp is put on it." I replied, with even greater positiveness, that he was wrong, for the simple reason that such stamps or designs are only the Government's assay-certificates, which certify to the fact that the coins, *when freshly minted*, contain the weight of pure gold indicated by the die or stamp. For if, because of abrasion from use, or of mutilation of one kind or another, the original weight of gold is materially diminished and such diminution of contents is discovered, even though the imprint of the stamp is still quite legible, such a coin will not be accepted at its face-value by the Government, by a bank, or even by an individual.

Furthermore, in settlement of balances between nations, the gold in the form of coin or bars or both is melted and assayed and weighed before full credit for their metallic contents is given, because such shipments might contain counterfeits, in addition to coins of light weight due to abrasion or mutilation. My friend admitted the soundness of my argument and confessed that he was wrong in insisting that the Government's stamp gave the 23.22 gr. of gold its value; and I hope any one who may be interested enough to read this will be similarly convinced, for it is a bare statement of fact. To lessen the amount of gold in our gold coins and to then call them by the same names as before would be debasing our money; and 'debasement' is an ugly word; for it simply means dishonesty and fraud, if the new coins are intended to be circulated at the same face-value as the old ones. Let anyone who is interested in this subject read 'A Treatise on the Coins of the Realm', by Lord Liverpool, if he would like to learn about the injury to trade and commerce in earlier times caused by debasing money.

Mr. McPherson's "gold-brass twin coin" is an apt illustration of our *silver* 'dollar', which passes current at its face-value. For, in reality, its currency value is duplex, because it consists of 77.34 cents bullion value, reckoning silver at $1 (23.22 gr. of gold) per oz. and 22.66 cents fiat, or Government credit value. The value of our gold coins is entirely bullion or commodity value, whereas the value of the silver 'dollar' is composite, being made up partly of bullion-value and partly of credit-value; and the value of our paper currency (gold certificates and silver certificates excepted) consists wholly of Government credit.

Much confusion of thought and meaning is occasioned by calling different things by the same name. The silver 'dollar' was made our unit of value when the Mint was established in 1792, and it consisted of 416 gr. of silver of the fineness of 892.4 thousandths. The gold coins of $10, $5, and $2.50 were called eagles, half-eagles, and quarter-eagles respectively. Now, however, all our currency, in common parlance, is a 'dollar' or multiples thereof, whether it consist of gold or silver or paper. In other words, the true meaning of the term 'dollar' is lost sight of because it is commonly used to designate 23.22 gr. of gold, 371.25 gr. of silver, and five different kinds of promises to pay gold.

Finally, and in spite of the foregoing, I would like very much indeed to meet Mr. Robbins and talk with him about the great Hollinger mine, with its multiplicity of veins; and, incidentally, to dine him at a certain club in this city, and, afterward, to select for his perusal a half-dozen books from the 800 or more volumes on economics that may be found in its library. It might take several days, perhaps a week or more, as well as sundry cigars and refreshments to convince him, but I am reasonably sure that, if he will avail himself of the opportunity, it will no longer seem to him "that re-coining at one-half or two-thirds of the present weights of gold coins is a matter which merits a continued discussion.

New York, April 2. W. DEL. BENEDICT.

International Control of Minerals

The Editor:

Sir—In your number of March 15 there appears an article by C. K. Leith on this subject. From the wording of your editorial, in reference to the same, it is to be presumed that you printed this matter rather to promote criticism and discussion than with any idea that it should be read as gospel. I note with surprise, however, that this same article is to be published in 'Mineral Resources' of 1917. In other words, being contributed by a mineral adviser to the War Industries and Shipping Boards, and approved by the U. S. Geological Survey, it is to be held out to the world as an official sample of American thought on the subject.

Mr. Leith says, "The efforts made to promote or hinder international mineral movement by tariffs, bonuses, embargoes, subsidies, transport control, patents, Government management, financial pressure, and other means have been incited mainly by national or imperial self-interest and have thus been to some extent inimical to an internationalization based on the principle of the greatest good to the greatest number."

In an editorial of the same issue as that containing Mr. Leith's article you correctly say: "Even the relinquishment of some part of the sovereignty of the United States is not terrifying, for every decision of international law involves some surrender of national rights; they are conceded just as the individual citizen forgoes some of his private rights for the sake of the community as a whole." Apparently Mr. Leith would surrender national rights of a nature that the individual citizen would not for a moment forego. The individual reserves to himself the right to buy whatever he chooses with his own money so long as he does not monopolize any market. Undoubtedly the statesmen of other nations will require that their countries shall reserve the same kind of freedom. An import tariff is a luxury paid for by the nation itself; it is no one else's business whether that nation buys of other nations or not. I do not believe any foreigner ever objected to the right of the United States to levy lead, zinc, and diamond tariffs, for example. Such a statesman as President Wilson could never have had a thought of binding the United States to any tariff policy, and no such shrewd politician as Senator Knox ever thought the President had such an idea.

If a nation pays a bonus, or a subsidy, or controls its own transport service, or governs its own patents, what business is it of any other nation? the oceans are public highways and not privately owned public utilities. Does not a merchant have a right to give bonuses or discounts to large or particularly desirable purchasers? Does he not have a right to deliver the goods he sells without extra charge or to manufacture his own patented goods? Certainly he does, because he pays the bill with his own money, and everyone else has the same right.

Mr. Leith makes the reservation that his purpose is "to state the problem of international control of minerals, rather than to present an argument for it." He then immediately indicates the nature of the control he advocates by saying, in the same sentence, "such control entails difficulties which are especially burdensome on the United States, and which at present may be insuperable." What minerals are there, produced in the United States, for which the foreign consumer has to pay more than the home consumer? I do not believe that there are normally any export-taxes, embargoes, Government managements, or financial pressures applying to exported raw materials or manufactured goods. Neither can it be said that the United States has any control over the minerals of other countries. Mr. Leith must therefore have in mind some scheme to make the United States a sort of charitable institution, dispensing aid to peoples who do not even ask it, much less think of making war for it.

There is, however, a legitimate field for international regulations concerning minerals, because some nations make the outsider pay, in excessive mineral prices, the accounts that really belong to its own inhabitants. For example, the government of Chile supports itself by making foreign consumers of nitrate pay all the taxes of the country instead of its own people. The South African war was brought about by conditions of a somewhat similar nature, and many costly civil wars have resulted in other parts of the world owing to disputes over the control of a revenue which the people as a whole have no interest in limiting.

"The proposals of the League of Free Nations Association of New York, quoted by Mr. Leith, wisely confines itself to monopolies, but fails to include the very important category mentioned above. Neither the evil nor the corrective for these monopolies would seem to have anything in common with the problem stated by Mr. Leith. It is easily understood that the artificial conditions created by the War cannot all be dispensed with in a moment, but the undue or indefinite continuation of such "Government management" is entirely opposed to a basic principle of our civilization, the equality of economic opportunity.

BLAMEY STEVENS.

Guanacevi, Mexico, March 29.

Investing in Oil Stock: A Caution

The Editor:

Sir—During recent months the country has been deluged with a flood of oil promotions, fostered by recent developments in the north-central Texas region. This hysterical fever for speculation which sweeps the country periodically always gives birth to a litter of wild-cats. The last epidemic of the sort centred in the Jerome district in 1916, and a particularly virulent form of the disease it was. Most of the companies organized at that time are now defunct, many without even having started to develop their properties, while a few of the more successfully financed are still spending their remaining funds in an attempt to find another United Verde Extension bonanza. It is a startling proof of the inherent and unthinking optimism of human nature that the very victims of the Jerome awakening are now eager to take a chance on the more distant and less familiar, and consequently more alluring, oilfields of Texas. The oil literature of today shows the same disregard for the truth, the same neglect to mention important facts and places, the same emphasis on valuable discoveries on properties in many cases miles away, as the copper prospectus of three years ago.

There are several important oilfields in north-central Texas, of which Ranger is the best known and most spectacular. It is a mistaken idea that this is an entirely new area, however. The first well at Ranger, the McCleskey, was drilled on October 25, 1917. It was not long before many of the large oil companies and independent producers had acquired leases on the most favorable acreage in an area 150 miles wide by 200 miles long, after careful and exhaustive geological surveys had been made. Six months ago, when the first of the new companies was formed and its stock floated, only areas that for some reason or other had been 'passed up' by the geologists of the big companies could be leased, and those were held at greatly inflated prices. It should be remembered that boring for oil even in a proved field is a decidedly risky undertaking. The reward of success should be, and often is, great enough to compensate for the risk of complete failure; but in buying shares in a new oil venture the prospective reward and the risk of failure should be carefully weighed so that the gambler will at least get 'a run for his money'. This he rarely finds in a company planned and organized as are those now scattering their stock broadcast. Many factors should be considered in this connection, and these factors are usually the very ones that are never mentioned in the average promotion literature. An analysis of the risk involved is far from the thoughts of the oil promoter.

Almost without exception the wells that have 'come in' have had a definite relation to either surface or underground structure. These structural features guide the experienced oil operator in making his locations but are given scant consideration by the wild-cat promoter. Even favorable structure has in many instances failed to yield oil because of local pinching of the oil-sand, a condition that cannot be foreseen. It is evident, then, that even with favorable structure there is a large chance of failure, but without structure almost a certainty of it. To keep the inherent risk-factor as low as possible a careful study of the ground should be made by an oil geologist and his advice followed.

Most of the companies of this nature fail to mention in their literature the large blocks of promotion stock that have been issued for services or leases of doubtful value. Control is usually vested in the few original organizers, who have made only a nominal contribution, while the public at large finances the whole proposition for only a minority interest in the possible profit. A statement of the promotion stock issued as well as of the total authorized amount should be made, so that a prospective purchaser can determine for himself what share in the future profits he will have if oil is found. To protect the stockholders the promotion stock should be placed in escrow until production is secured or the funds are exhausted. The Arizona 'blue sky' law is remiss in many particulars. The mere fact that an organization is permitted to sell stock does not mean that it has the tacit approval of the Corporation Commission; as a matter of fact, most of them are unincorporated and are merely selling shares in an association.

Another important consideration is the heavy expense of prospecting this field, where the most productive sand is in the neighborhood of 3500 ft. deep. Only a company with ample resources should attempt it. A single hole costs between $40,000 and $60,000, and many a hole is lost before reaching its objective. Sufficient funds for at least two or three tests should be available, for by the law of average the first, even if completed, is likely to be dry. It is furthermore necessary for the protection of a lease to be prepared to drill offset-holes to any producing wells on neighboring tracts near the boundary-line. Otherwise neighboring wells will drain oil which rightfully belongs to the lease. It should, therefore, be evident that a strong treasury is essential for successful prospecting.

The question of offsets is also important in connection with the size and shape of the lease. A small or a long narrow tract is undesirable because of the comparatively large number of offset-holes which would have to be drilled to protect it in the event that oil were found. Where holes are so deep and so costly this becomes a vital consideration for the small company.

Most important of all, perhaps, are the men who are behind the organization. The success of the undertaking depends upon them to no small degree, but even with able and trustworthy sponsors a company should lay all the essential facts on the table when it comes to the public for funds. And the public should insist upon getting the facts or refuse to subscribe. Drilling for oil in wild-cat, or undeveloped, territory is a perfectly legitimate speculation. It is only by taking a big risk in the hope of big profit that expansion and development of the natural resources of the country will proceed, but when the risk involved is entirely disproportionate to the possibility of profit the speculation should be avoided. The risk in oil prospecting is very great even when all possible precautions are taken. The chance of success, however, will be far greater if only those amply financed companies, controlled by able and reliable business men, which propose to drill ground recommended by a reputable geologist, are considered. The tracts must not be too small nor too narrow, nor should the company be overburdened with a great load of promotion stock. Those who after reading the lurid promises of the average prospectus 'invest' savings that might otherwise swell the Victory Loan, deserve the fate that is in store for them.

PHILIP D. WILSON.

Warren, Arizona, April 12.

Flotation Litigation

The Editor:

Sir—I have read with great interest the article appearing in your issue of March 22, under the above heading.

Allow me to call your attention to the fact that the trial of the suit referred to between Messrs. Sulman and Picard and myself took place in May 1905 and the judgment was rendered on May 20, 1905. The application for their British patent No. 7803 (corresponding to their United States patent No. 835,120) was filed on April 12, 1905, but I had no information that such application had been filed until after the issue of the patent in January 1906. The application for the United States patent No. 835,120 was filed on May 29, 1905, and the patent was issued on November 6, 1906. Neither the British nor the United States patent was involved in that litigation.

Allow me also to point out that the examination and cross-examination of Dr. Samuel P. Sadtler were had, not in the Hyde case, but in the case of Minerals Separation, Ltd., v. Butte & Superior Mining Company, as appears from the record in the Circuit Court of Appeals for the Ninth Circuit in that case.

In concluding, let me express my appreciation of your having called the attention of the mining world to facts with regard to my patent which were not brought out in the various litigations to which Minerals Separation was a party. As you well point out, the flotation issue will not necessarily be settled by the decision of the Supreme Court in the pending Butte & Superior case, and, as far as my patent is concerned, can only be settled in a litigation in which my patent is directly involved.

New York, April 7. J. D. WOLF.

Persistence of Ore in Depth at Cripple Creek

Recent correspondence from Cripple Creek, published in the Review of Mining, reports numerous discoveries of rich ore in the district. Some of these have been made by lessees, others by companies, at depths varying from 800 to 2130 ft. The Cresson company has found an extensive shoot at 800 ft., while the Portland is developing two rich veins from the Roosevelt drainage-tunnel, at a depth of 2130 ft. The elevation of the Portland's new workings is 8113 ft. above sea-level. On the other hand, the annual report of the Vindicator Consolidated contains the following:

"Early in 1918 development was discontinued on the 20th level, the bottom of the Golden Cycle shaft. On this level a total of 4240 ft. of work has been done, and no ore of a commercial grade exposed. This work has systematically explored the known ore-zones which at this level should possibly produce ore. The vein-systems were found in place and the fracturing was strong and well defined, and with a general physical appearance favorable to ore-deposition. However, the value necessary to make commercial ore was lacking. This level is at a depth of 2150 ft. from the collar of the shaft, and at an elevation of 7920 ft. above sea-level. The productive areas in the property maintained well with depth to an elevation of about 8300 ft. In sinking below this there was a gradual but marked decrease in the production of the areas, the ore-shoots being more broken up, and showing a decrease in the average grade of the ore produced. Extensive work has been done on the 20th level with the view of developing ore below a possible barren zone existing at the elevation of the 19th level, with negative results. There are possibly existing orebodies at a greater depth, but it is the opinion of the operating-staff, from a thorough study of the habits of the existing orebodies, that there will not in this property be sufficient ore opened at a greater depth than that to which exploration work has been carried to warrant the expenses of sinking and exploring. However, this does not mean that exploration should stop, as there is a considerable area on the upper levels of the property that has not been thoroughly prospected, and it is the intention of the management to explore this ground during 1919. Due to the intense labor shortage during the year 1918, this work was impossible."

FINAL FIGURES of the pig-iron output of the United States during 1918 show a total of 39,051,991 tons, compared with 38,621,216 tons in 1917, and 39,434,797 tons in 1916. The production last year was much below capacity.

VILLAGE OF IRON MOUNTAIN

A Metallurgical Journey to Shasta, California

By HERBERT LANG

Shasta county boasts a metal production valued at nearly $200,000,000. Gold, in placers and veins, was the first metal to be discovered. Then came the discovery of silver in the early 'eighties, and now copper, zinc, iron, lead, and chromium have been added to the list, proving the varied resources of this northern Californian mineral-bearing area.

The first metallurgical work in Shasta county was done with a frying-pan. Armed with this instrument, Major Pearson B. Reading, a rancher from Sutter's Fort, near Sacramento, tested the sand of Clear creek and found gold. Later, with the assistance of a few Indians and with the rudest extemporized apparatus, he made himself the possessor of $60,000, working, they say, within a space no greater than a horse-blanket. Others followed him, and still others; and for years Clear creek was the best known and most productive district in northern California. The rich gravel is now worked out; but placer mining is still carried on. The waters of the creek are turbid with the debris of many placers, where the progress of mining methods is marked step by step from the pan to the rocker, the long-tom, the ground-sluice, the hydraulic stream, and finally the floating dredge. At the lower end of Clear creek float the dredges of Gardella; at its headwaters important quartz mines have been exploited successfully. It was at the Washington quartz mine that the first stamp-mill in Shasta was erected. This was of six heads, and seems to have antedated most of the arrastras with which the county was sprinkled. The mill and mine, it is agreeable to relate, produced in all about a million dollars.

Instances of a similar character might be multiplied; the salient fact is that the course of events was like that of other Western regions: as the richer placers became exhausted the poorer gravels began to be worked in a larger way, whereas the quartz mines, which began operations a few years later than the placers, have kept up production ever since, with vicissitudes of depression and excitation. About 1880 the base-metal deposits began to receive attention. Regarded as silver mines pure and simple, they were worked on a small scale for several years, and a few mills were built. Within a comparatively short time the richer silver ores, which, following the general rule, were close to the surface and limited in quantity, were exhausted, and the mills without exception were shut down. This was prior to the fall in silver, which took place in the early 'nineties. A period of depression followed in 1895, while the West was staggering under the blow dealt to silver. Diminishing production marked those years, the annual output, which had been much greater, sinking to $800,000. The mining camps of Shasta assumed a seedy appearance, giving the impress of age to what were relatively new settlements. Old-time camps, such as Piety Hill, Horsetown, Whiskytown, and others, were in decadence. The town of Shasta itself, once the distributing point for the Northern mines, seemed to live only upon the reputation of its former usefulness, one of its principal claims to eminence being the fact that it was the former abode of James Keene, the celebrated financial juggler.

At this time, when the mines had fallen off in their yield and the best blood of the county was leaving, an event took place which was to have the most far-reaching effects upon the fortunes of the county, and in fact upon those of the entire State. This was the sale of the Iron Mountain copper mine to an English company.

The Iron Mountain mine was discovered in 1880, and was acquired by James Sallee, Charles Camden, and their associates. For a time it was regarded as a silver mine, the existence of copper not being suspected. The orebody, as is common in Shasta county, and indeed in many other regions, carried an 'iron hat' of portentous dimensions, easily seen from a distance of miles. Great quantities of this gossan are scattered on the surface and along the canyon of Slick Rock creek. It is a mystery how its content of gold and silver escaped detection for so many years, during which the region was combed by prospectors. But prospecting at that time was an adventure; now it is a business; some day it will become a science. James Sallee, who died, much lamented, about a year ago, was an assayer, and a practical kind of person, whose gifts of industry and enterprise proved valuable to the county in after-days. He it was who took hold of the Bully Hill mines after they had been practically abandoned for years. After some little development, he sold out to Capt. Joseph R. De Lamar. Of this transaction something remains to be said in these notes.

Having at hand no means of reducing the Iron Mountain ores, the new firm proceeded to ship a quantity of selected material to outside smelters, receiving therefor the handsome sum of $100,000. It should be mentioned that certain portions of the orebody had been surface-enriched to a great extent, assays of 100 or even 200 ounces of silver being not uncommon. The rich spots were soon exhausted, however, and the company turned its attention to constructing a mill, in which they were assisted by John O. Earl, an enterprising San Franciscan, who furnished the money for building the plant, the most complete reduction works at that time in northern California. A brief description of this somewhat celebrated silver-mill may not be out of place. The ore to be worked consisted of oxidized material, chiefly limonite, the familiar hydrated oxide of iron, rendered impure by the inclusion of aluminous derivatives of the country-rock, then known as granite, but now called 'alaskite', 'alaskite porphyry', or, more simply, 'quartz-porphyry'. This is the prevailing country-rock of the Shasta copper belt. It analyzes about 70% silica—a fact having a bearing on its employment as flux in the smelting processes subsequently introduced. The copper-sulphide zone had scarcely been reached, nor was its importance recognized for years afterward, as will be shown. Copper was disregarded. Gold existed to a trifling extent in the Iron Mountain ore, as in the other base-metal mines, except the Bully Hill, where it occurred rather abundantly at the very surface. For this reason, attention was given only to the silver. Thus the new mill was a silver-mill, pure and simple, which is not to say that such a mill could not save gold also, for on the Comstock lode, in Nevada, such mills were exclusively employed in treating the gold-silver ore, with reasonable success.

Tests with the mill were said to have shown that 80% of the silver could be saved by simple pan-milling without roasting; and that by roasting the ore before panning, 96% was recovered. This figure is probably an exaggeration, since it was only with exceptionally favorable ore and the greatest skill and care that such result could be attained, and it is certain that the Iron Mountain ores were not exceptional in this respect. Even today in Nevada, such high extraction is uncommon.

The pan process, which is now of little more than historic interest, was carried on in the following way at Iron Mountain:

The ore as it came from the mine was fed to rock-breakers, of which there were two, 7 by 10 in. When broken to egg size, the ore was delivered by gravity to the drying-furnace, a simple cylinder of sheet-iron, placed on a slight incline and fired at the lower end. The dried ore while still hot went next to the stamps, of which there were 20, each weighing 950 lb. and having a total capacity of 40 tons per day, crushing to 40-mesh. The pulverization was dry. Next, the pulp was conveyed to the roasting-furnace, a Brückner cylinder, and was roasted with the addition of 5% of common salt, by which the silver minerals were converted into chloride, susceptible to the attack of mercury. The chloridized pulp was then conveyed to amalgamation pans, of which there were 16, of the combination pattern much used at that day, ground wet with quicksilver, thus forming an amalgam, whose density and mechanical condition admitted of a complete separation from the worthless pulp. After prolonged treatment in pans more water was added and the mixture passed into the settlers, of which there were eight. In these the pulp was stirred gently, permitting the amalgam to settle and to be removed after filtering through canvas, after which it was retorted to separate the silver from the mercury. The silver was melted into bars, commonly of a purity above 95 or even 98%. This is the roasting-amalgamation, or Reese River process. The roasting was sometimes omitted, when the method became essentially that known as the Comstock process, which is effective upon silver ores containing but small quantities of the more difficult compounds, such as the arsenates and antimonates of silver. It was found that the roasting operation increased the cost of treatment from $9 per ton to $17, largely by reason of the expense of fuel and the lessened capacity of the plant. The fuel used was necessarily wood, which cost $4 per cord delivered, and of which a plentiful supply, pine and oak, was available. Eight cords of wood were burnt daily in the furnaces and four cords under the boilers, of which there were two, to provide for the 150-hp. Corliss engine. So much for the Iron Mountain mill, which in its time was regarded as the last word in metallurgical science.

Like most mines the Iron Mountain became poorer with depth, the surface ores of good grade became scarce, and in 1888 the plant was shut-down. This was five years before the disastrous fall in the price of silver. When the mill closed Mr. Earl left the company, relinquishing his rights to Sallee, Camden & Co. They had no trouble in getting rid of him; that gruff personage was said to have observed: "Take your damned old mill, which I have built, and go to hell." They took the mill, but never ran it again. After a period of idleness the property was taken under bond, about 1895, by Hugh McDonnell and Judge Cleary, promoters, who eventually sold it through the agency of Alexander Hill, to British investors, notably Jardine, Matheson & Co., great London merchants connected with the Rio Tinto copper mines in Spain. Then began a new era in Shasta county, during which copper took the place of gold and silver as the main object of exploitation. Whatever development the mines of Shasta have undergone is due largely to the initiative of the Mountain Copper Company, as the new organization came to be known. Mr. Hill was one of the first to recognize the great possibilities of the property as a copper producer, but not quite the first, since it lies in my recollection that W. Lawrence Austin, the inventor, or at least the improver, of the pyritic method of smelting, who had visited the mine prior to Mr. Hill, had spoken of it as an enormous sulphide body, and had recognized the amenability of its ore to the pyritic process. This was about the year 1891. It is also remembered that the mine was offered for sale to local people, including many Californian capitalists, who were unanimous in 'turning it down', the prevailing impression hereabouts having been that there could be no copper in that part of the State since "our people" had lost money after the copper boom of the 'sixties when, as will be recalled, copper took a decided drop.

IRON MOUNTAIN MINE

LOADING-BUNKERS, IRON MOUNTAIN MINE

It is pleasant to record that although the owners of the mine received but $75,000 for it, out of the $300,000 for which McDonnel and Cleary sold it, they were eminently satisfied, in particular Mr. Camden, who retired on his little fortune to Oakland, where all good miners eventually go, and observed the progress of operations with complacency until the mine under its new ownership began to make large profits. Having felicitated himself at first that he had the better of the British people, his tune changed afterward and he spent his days in complaining that he had been cheated. Mr. Camden, like his partner, Sallee, has gone over the range, while his mine, after an active existence of 20-odd years and the production of nearly $40,000,000, is still alive and profitable. It would be interesting, no doubt, to know who 'absorbed' the difference between the $300,000, which was paid the vendors for the mine, and the $1,000,000 for which it was turned over to the real purchasers, the Mathesons and the other Rio Tinto people who formed what ultimately became the Mountain Copper Co. But this is irrelevant: in fact it is nobody's business, and the question, in view of the present international amity, had better be left alone. It is certain that no American got it.

The methods of the new company differed in some respects from those usually employed in this country, in being more deliberate and more thorough. The opening of the mine is a case in point. Most American engineers would have seen in the great Iron Mountain deposit an opportunity for cheapening extraction by the use of the 'glory-hole' method, whereby timbering with its many drawbacks could have been avoided. The mine suffered from a number of cavings and was on fire for years. Oxidation in such great masses of sulphides is rapid when once the air has access to the interior, and the heat set up frequently proved sufficient to ignite the timbers. The mine was fairly wet, but this fact tended, if anything, to hasten combustion. The fact of rapid oxidation was sufficiently shown in the earlier years by the quality of the water draining from the lower openings, for this effluent water carried copper to such an extent that its recovery was attempted by the old-time method of precipitation on scrap-iron, and a motley array of tubs, tanks, sluices, and vats decorated the hillside for many years. It is likely that the greater part of the cupriferous liquid came from the gossan, the lower portions of which, just above the sulphide orebody, contained, here and there, some copper in the form of chalcanthite. This was moist and porous, facilitating contact with the air, thus forming additional sulphate. The orebody was opened up thoroughly and its limits determined under the direction of Alexander Hill, a most competent manager, who after a distinguished career in various parts of the world, died in 1912. Mr. Hill, at first consulting engineer to the new company, later succeeded Gilbert McM. Ross as manager, and was himself succeeded by Lewis T. Wright, and he by William F. Kett, who now administers the company's affairs. Over all these, and continuously since the inception of the enterprise, has been C. W. Fielding, managing director of the company, now, in consequence of his eminence in financial and, it is said, national, affairs, Sir Charles Fielding, as he was knighted last year.

It has often been remarked that the managers of the Mountain Copper Co. were thorough in their plans and methods. This is shown in the construction of the Iron Mountain railway which connects the mine with the smelter at Keswick and with the outer world. This road is an excellent piece of work, well laid out and well built, though passing through rough country. It was engineered and constructed under the supervision of M. M. O'Shaughnessy, now City Engineer of San Francisco. Its only fault is its steepness, the grade being excessive even for a mining railway, namely $3\frac{1}{2}\%$. With its numerous and sharp curves (it is one of the crookedest railroads in the world) it is extremely hard on rolling-stock. The wear and tear upon wheel-flanges and brake-shoes is appalling. Down the descent of 1700 ft. in 10 miles two million tons of ore have rolled and slid to the smelter, the brakes tightly set and everything screeching and groaning. Perhaps it would have been as well to have made the road a little longer and have it come out somewhere else; but smelter-sites are scarce in that part of the country, and Keswick was perhaps the best that could be reached by a road of reasonable length. Perhaps also it would have been as well to have built an aerial tramway. Between the two there was not much choice, as the experience of neighbors has demonstrated. Looking regretfully at the expense and trouble of the steam railroad, Mr. Kett, of the Mountain Copper Co., sighs for a tramway. Others, provided with trams, yearn for railways. Both are good. It is rather a pity that someone with an eye for the future, did not build a real mineral railway, taking in as many of the numerous copper and gold mines as possible, so as to bring their product to some common centre on the main line, thereby solving the problem of transport once for all. The amount of ore thus far handled on rails and wires has already reached seven or eight million tons, and the end is not yet. It has been said that there are, between the Iron Mountain mine on the south and the Golinsky on the north, more than 200 ore exposures that have been mined, and that there are at least 1000 on which locations have been made. None of the mines so far as known have been exhausted, though many are getting poorer. The matter of transport, therefore, continues to be of serious future import.

In order to appreciate the advances that have been made in the metallurgical treatment of local ores, it will be well to consider the character of the minerals composing them. The prevailing ores of Shasta county, excluding the auriferous gravel, may be divided into two classes, namely, gold-bearing quartz and the base-metal sulphides. The former, occurring in typical veins, is in no respect different from the ordinary millstuff of other gold-mining districts. It consists of quartz carrying a small proportion of sulphides—almost exclusively pyrite—with a little gold, free or enclosed in the sulphide mineral. Other sulphides, such as galena, blende, chalcopyrite, mispickel, and pyrrhotite, occur subordinately, as elsewhere. Calcite and dolomite are also found intermixed with the quartz, but generally in small quantity; and fluorite and barite are not unknown. Taken as a whole, the gold-bearing quartz deposits of Shasta are typical of their class, so that no special metallurgy has been needed, old methods sufficing.

Even such exceptional vein-matter as that of the Niagara mine, in the high divide above French gulch, which carried much calcite, and that of the Banghart mine, near Stella, which yielded large lumps of gold from its gouge-like ore, derived not from a quartz vein but a decomposed dike, required no more specialized treatment than ordinary mill-ore. The Banghart, indeed, obtained the major part of its yield from a plain little arrastra.

The stamp-milling practice could scarcely be called good. None of the mills were distinguished for their size, capacity, or excellence of design, and probably few of them did effective work, if one may judge by contemporary accounts or by the evidence of the tailing heaps. Notwithstanding that by the year 1895 the practice of concentrating the tailing had become general elsewhere, the mills of Shasta county were only in part provided with apparatus for this purpose, and it was common even at that date to allow the sand to escape into the stream. In that year the mills of the county contained 290 stamps, but possessed only 35 concentrators, of which the great majority were Frue vanners. Hence there was one machine to eight stamps—a ridiculous disproportion. One mill, the Uncle Sam, with 35 stamps, the largest of all, had 14 Frue vanners, or two to every battery of five stamps—a proportion usual in modern mills.

The lack of capital caused the early operators to resort to many makeshifts, in which respect they do not differ from those of today. Some have an interest, for example, in the miniature plant of a certain little mine at the foot of Iron mountain. Having for a part of the year the use of one of the small periodic streams so common in that region, the owners built a 16-ft. overshot wheel with 84-in. breast, driving a 9-ft. arrastra, with stone drags and pavement. The ore contained a small proportion of auriferous pyrite, necessitating some means of concentrating, so that the tailing was run over, first, a strip of carpet, 25 in. wide by 15 ft. long, and then over 12 ft. of canvas, 5 ft. wide. Thus one ton of concentrate was saved each month. The Little Maud claim, not far away, improved on this modest installation, putting in, instead of the arrastra, a Jones mill, so-called, which was one of the innumerable inventions of that day by which the apparent inconveniences of the stamp-battery were to be obviated. The Jones mill has, like most of its kind, passed into oblivion, and it is only recorded that it resembled the Huntington pulverizer in outward form, but instead of crushing by the pressure of the rollers upon the peripheral die, it had hammers. It had a pan 3.5 ft. diameter and its rate of crushing was 6 tons in 24 hours. Determined not to use any so-called standard methods, copper plates gave way to cone-shaped amalgam-traps.

The arrastra process, introduced to treat the silver-bearing ores of Spanish America, was modified when transplanted to the gold-mining regions of the United States. The arrastra is not a continuously working agent: it works by charges, and when applied to the reduction of gold-quartz is made to combine the functions of pulverizing and amalgamating. After introducing the ore, which is usually first broken by hand to egg-size or less, it is mixed with enough water to form a thick paste when the grinding is completed, in this respect resembling the ordinary pan treatment of silver ores. Unlike the latter, only a small quantity of mercury is added—just enough, in fact, to form an amalgam of the maximum density, which is in the neighborhood of 16, the proportion of gold being nearly 50%. In the silver process a large addition of mercury, sometimes amounting to 50 times the weight of the silver, is made for reasons connected with the specific gravity of the amalgam, which is comparatively low, and also on account of the solubility of the silver amalgam in mercury, which exercises a favorable influence on its separation from the pulp.

After the amalgamation of the metal, which is ascertained by panning, the charges in both cases are thinned by the addition of water, the speed of the grinding parts is increased, and the charge suffered to flow out. But in the arrastra, the amalgam, having subsided to the bottom, collects in the interstices of the rock composing the bed, and remains there to be removed at the clean-up, when the bed must be broken out.

This neat, though slow and laborious, process was much used in Shasta in former days and was highly esteemed. One notable attempt was there made to improve it. Almarin B. Paul, a noted Californian metallurgist, who had distinguished himself in connection with the mines of other localities, notably the Comstock, was a devotee of the arrastra, and made it an important feature of the Calumet mill, not far from Copley. This was a radical departure from ordinary design. Crushing was performed in two of Howland's circular batteries, which, on account of Mr. Paul's advocacy, came to be known as the Paul mill. The peculiarity of the Howland mill lies in the shape of the mortar, which is saucer-shaped instead of straight, the stamps being arranged on the circle. They were simple gravity-stamps, of the usual kind, 8 or 12 in number and of the usual weight. They were lifted by means of a cam fastened to a vertical revolving shaft in the centre, to which motion was communicated by means of gearing. This mill achieved some popularity, but was neither better nor worse than the ordinary type, its principal advantage lying in the less first cost, but particularly in the increased crushing area of the mortar.

Following the stamps came four of Paul's patent blanket concentrators, also a forgotten invention. Finally the pulp passed to four arrastras in which it was reground and again amalgamated. Some success was achieved and the works continued active for several years. In 1892 Mr. Paul added another invention of his to the mill in the form of an Americanized arrastra, of which he set up 24. Later he introduced the cyanide process, but having developed his dry amalgamation process and patented it, he gave his attention later exclusively to this method, which achieved no vogue.

In the effort to avoid stamp-milling a great many other devices for pulverizing and amalgamating came into use. Thus Shasta became, like Boulder county in Colorado, a refuge for the inventive process-man. Among the legion of 'improved' machines, the cannon-ball mill for a time held an exalted place. This mill, which became the progenitor of many better forms, proved faulty in several particulars. The balls followed each other around a circular raceway, which they were supposed to fit, grinding the ore beneath them. While they kept their size and shape they performed well; but as they wore away the useful effect diminished. When the balls became small the raceway became larger and their surfaces ceased to connect, so that the capacity of the mill decreased. Many of these machines, so beautiful in principle, were erected in California in early days, but it was rare that one ran longer than a month or two. It was only after men had learned to turn the balls loose in the ore and let them take their own path that success was achieved. To do this it was necessary to tip up the mill so that its vertical driving axis became horizontal, and to increase the number and diminish the size of the balls.

The New Price Revolution

By IRVING FISHER

At the present time there is a marked halt in production. Industry is slowing down. Unemployment of labor increases. Some industrial concerns are failing to earn profits, and others are suffering the dissipation of their accrued profits, because, even by shutting their plants down, they cannot save certain of their expenses or any of their fixed charges. The Government's revenues, dependent as they are upon the national income, may fall short at the very time we need them most. In brief, we are threatened with a widespread business depression and from peculiar causes, for the unsound conditions usually preceding a widespread business depression are absent.

The main reason why business is not going ahead better is that most people expect prices to drop. The merchant is selling, but not buying. The manufacturer holds up the purchase of his raw materials. People quote the disparity between present prices and those prevailing "before the War," and decide they will not buy much until present prices get down to "normal." This general conviction that prices are sure to drop is putting a brake upon the entire machinery of production and distribution. Readjustment waits because we keep on waiting for it. We have waited in vain for over three months. It is interesting to observe that many manufacturers think that prices must come down, including the price of labor; but they are ready to demonstrate to you that their own prices cannot come down, nor can they pay lower wages. Almost everything they buy somehow costs twice as much as before the War, and their labor is twice as dear. They cannot pay their labor less if labor is to meet the increased cost of living. Now, as a matter of fact, when we investigate almost any individual one of the so-called high prices for industrial products we are likely to find that individually it is not high; that is, it is not high relatively to the rest. Our quarrel is with the general level of prices.

Variations in the general price level may be compared to the tides of the sea, while individual prices may be compared to waves. Individual prices may vary from this general level of prices for specific reasons peculiar to individual industries, just as the height and depth of waves vary from the general level established by the tide. The causes controlling the general price-levels are as distinct from those controlling individual prices as the causes controlling the tides are distinct from those controlling individual waves.

All prices have risen, but some have risen more, some less, than the average for particular reasons affecting each industry. In some cases an improved organization of both employers and employees has enabled them to combine against the public and take full advantage of the price-advance. The War brought about an abnormal demand for certain products like copper and steel, and they advanced faster than the average. The abnormal demand having disappeared, these prices are being adjusted downward. Wheat is a case where demand increased and at the same time certain of the usual sources of supply—Russia, Australia, and Argentina—disappeared, with a resultant abnormal price increase. The closed sources of supply have opened again, and wheat prices in the world market have dropped. In some cases, as in many of the industries making building materials, the War meant a great slackening in demand, an enforced curtailment in use by Government order. In such instances we are likely to see an upward swing in prices as the suppressed demand again makes itself felt. To-day we are witnessing throughout the country such price readjustments, up and down, but the general price-level has shown little sign of falling, as is evidenced by price index-numbers. It is apparent to every thoughtful observer that some great force has affected all prices, creating a new standard to which they are all conforming.

The fundamental practical question confronting business men is whether the general level of prices is going to fall. In my opinion, it is not going to fall much, if at all. We are on a *permanently* higher price-level, and the sooner the business-men of the country take this view and adjust themselves to it the sooner will they save themselves and the Nation from the misfortune that will come if we persist in our present false hope.

The general level of prices is dependent upon the volume and rapidity of turnover of the circulating medium in relation to the business to be transacted thereby. If the number of dollars circulated by cash and by check doubles while the number of goods and services exchanged thereby remains constant, prices will about double.

The great price changes in history have come about in just this manner. The 'price revolution' of the 16th century came upon Europe as a result of the great influx of gold and silver from the mines of the New World. Europe was flooded with new money. More counters were used than before in effecting exchanges and prices became 'high'. People talked then of *temporary* 'inflation', just as they talk of it now. But it was not temporary; it was a new price-level.

A similar increase in prices all over the world occurred between 1896 and 1914, following the discovery of the rich goldfields of South Africa, Cripple Creek, and Alaska, the invention of the cyanide process in mining, and the vast extension of the use of bank-credit.

Circulating credit, that is, bank deposits subject to check and bank-notes, is a multiple of the banking reserve behind these deposits and notes; and the essence of this reserve is gold. Our present monetary system is an inverted pyramid, gold being the small base and bank-notes and deposits being the large superstructure. The superstructure grows even faster than the base. The deposits are the important elements. They are transferred by check from one individual to another; that is, the circulation of checks is really the circulation of deposits.

Thus any increase in the country's gold-supply has a multiplied effect. The possible extent of that effect is dependent upon (1) the amount of gold available, and (2) the gold-reserve requirements, determining the volume of credit that can be put into circulation based upon the gold. Over a billion dollars in gold has come into this country from abroad since 1914, and a large amount has disappeared from domestic circulation. The gold from both these sources has found its way into the United States Treasury and into bank reserves. On June 30, 1918, the portion of the *gold* reserve of the Federal Reserve banking system, which supported National Bank deposits and Federal Reserve notes, was more than three times as large as the gold reserves under the old national banking system on June 30, 1914—$1,786,000,000, compared to $592,000,000. During the same period credit instruments (demand deposits and notes) increased about twofold—from $6,100,000,000 to $11,700,000,000. This increase of credit instruments is typical of the banking situation for the country as a whole and largely explains the present high level of prices. The increase of gold has been so great, however, that the base has grown faster than the superstructure—which is contrary to the normal tendency. The ratio of gold to credit has risen from 9.6% to 15.3%. The legal reserve requirements of the present system are such that for 1918 there is an excess of gold above these requirements of more than $700,000,000. The reserve required by law to support the $11,700,000,000 of credit instruments of 1918 is $1,070,000,000. The $700,000,000 of free gold could support an additional superstructure 70% as large as the existing one, which indicates that for the banking of the country as a whole a potential future expansion of 50% is a conservative estimate.

Many people, referring to this inflation in the circulating medium, and assuming that it is temporary, are waiting for this inflation to subside. When we speak of *inflation* we mean more circulating medium than is needed to transact the business of the country on a given price-level. But what price-level? Some people mean the price-level of 1913-'14. Our currency is certainly inflated in terms of the prices of that period, just as the currency in 1914 was inflated with respect to the prices of 1896, but our currency is not inflated at the present time relative to the new level of prices in the world which the War has brought. The country's volume of money will have to be judged in terms of this new price-level, not in terms of a price-level that is past. To speak of the present 'inflation' as temporary is to assume the very thing about which we are contending—to assume that the normal prices are those of 1914.

Let us examine the factors upon which any future price movements must depend:

1. Gold will not return to circulation.—No great effect in the direction of falling prices can be expected from any return of gold and other lawful money into daily circulation. Such a reversion would be contrary to monetary experience everywhere. When people have learned to leave their gold and silver in the banks and use paper-money and checks instead they find the additional convenience so great that they will never fully return to the old practice.

2. No great outflow of gold through international trade.—It should be noted that many of the former reasons for a flow of gold from America abroad have disappeared. We used to owe Europe a huge balance of interest payments upon American securities she held. The situation is reversed today. Moreover, Europe must pay us money for the materials we will send her for reconstruction, or at least pay us interest on credit we will extend her. Thus our exports will probably exceed our imports during the reconstruction period. We used to pay ocean-freight money to foreign carriers; today the American merchant marine will keep in American hands tens of millions of dollars of ocean-freight money. The huge volume of American tourist-travel abroad, for whose expense we had to settle, has stopped and can not resume for a year at least. For all these reasons the lines are laid for a movement of gold from Europe here rather than a movement of gold from America to Europe.

"Yes, but," people say, "wait until trade is resumed between the United States and Europe, then surely 'low-priced European goods' will flow over here in such enormous volume that they will liquidate all annual obligations to us in goods." Ultimately Europe must pay her obligations to us in goods, but it will take many years. Meanwhile she needs our tools, machinery, and raw materials for immediate reconstruction.

At the present time European goods are not 'low priced' (however little the money-wages of European labor will buy). Prices in Europe since the War began have risen more than they have in the United States. The price-rise has been less the farther from the seat of hostilities. It was least in Australia and New Zealand. It was next least in the United States, Canada, and Japan. Then came neutral Europe; then our present allies; and finally Germany and Russia. Gold tends usually to flow from high-priced countries to low-priced countries, so that until 'inflated' European prices fall gold is not likely to flow thither. Prices are no more likely to fall there than here, and for the same reasons, which will be explained below.

3. Reduction of outstanding credit.—The chief dependence of those who predict lower prices is on a reduction of the superstructure of credit resting upon our gold rather than on any reduction in the volume of this gold itself. They look for a contraction of bank-credit,

a reduction in the volume of deposits subject to check, which circulate throughout the country.

But the main cause for the present extension of bank-credit is the Liberty Loan, and there is soon to be another. Subscribers for the new loan will not pay for their bonds in full any more than they did in the previous cases, but rather less. Many of them will deposit the bonds with the banks as security for loans to be re-paid later. The effect on our circulating medium will be the same as if the Government were to impose a levy of \$6,000,000,000 of credits upon the Federal Reserve banks, and then order them to apportion these credits out among the banks of the country. This process will certainly lead to an expansion of credits. The former issues of Liberty bonds are still carried by the banks to a considerable extent. It may be contended that the bank-credit expansion represented by the new Victory notes has already occurred in the form of Treasury certificates, which are merely to be funded by the Victory notes. The Victory note issued thus represents only a shifting of the obligation to pay credits advanced to the Government, a shifting from the shoulders of the banks to the shoulders of the Victory-note buyers. The volume of outstanding bank-credit remains the same. To a certain degree this contention is true. But a portion of the April Victory-note issue will go to pay future expenditures, not accrued expenditures. Then as soon as the Government needs additional money, it will issue new Treasury certificates, resulting in new extension of bank-credit. Moreover, there is little doubt that there will be at least one more Government bond-issue during the reconstruction period, and this will tend to further increase our present credit structure. [The Secretary of the Treasury says that there will be no more issues.—EDITOR.]

The banks must lend credit and create deposits to meet the expenditures not only of our own Government, but of foreign governments as well. The same thing results even if these governments are served directly by private investors here instead of through the United States Treasury. These investors pay for foreign Government bonds as they do for our Liberty bonds—on the installment plan—paying a small part down and borrowing the rest from the bank. This increased purchasing power will be mostly spent in this country for supplies to be sent abroad for rehabilitation. This continuance of vast loan-issues, connected with war and reconstruction throughout the world, is a factor which will maintain the high price-level temporarily, which means many months.

It is also worth keeping in mind that Liberty bonds and other Government securities held here do not wholly cease being a source of credit expansion when the individual subscribers have completed their payments on the bonds and really own them. These new bonds are unrivaled security for further borrowings from banks for commercial purposes, and they will continue to be so until the Government which issues them redeems them.

The availability of the vast issues of war-bonds as bases for future credit expansion, coupled with the fact that our banking system has still many unused reefs, sure to be taken out later, when business wishes to spread more sail, is the chief reason why prices will keep up permanently, that is, for many years.

Between the period of temporary and the period of permanent effects, there may be a slight dip in the price-level, say, a year from now. If so, it is the more incumbent upon business to proceed now; for it cannot wait a year. During the War the flotation of stocks and bonds of commercial concerns has been greatly diminished. During the period upon which we are now entering, the issue of such securities will increase greatly.

Against any considerable reduction in bank-credit and hence in the general level of prices, we shall find the whole business community in arms. Falling prices mean hard times for the individual and for the nation, and every one resists the tendency. At the end of the Civil War the Treasury started to reduce the quantity of greenbacks. A start had hardly been made, however, before the business depression of 1866 and 1867 caused Congress to forbid by law any further reduction. Should the Federal Reserve banks attempt, by raising their discount-rate or otherwise, to reduce the volume of bank-credit outstanding, they will meet with the same sort of opposition. Moreover, the hostile attitude of labor toward the lowering of wages will deter legislators and bankers from any organized policy of contraction.

Looking into the still more remote future, there will be in Europe, particularly on the Continent, a vast increase in deposit-banking. The need of the governments there for funds during war-times hastened the introduction of deposit-banking. Money went out of circulation into bank-vaults, and there became the basis for circulating credits. This means a new habit which will lead to a great currency expansion. Far-away countries, like India and China, are also learning to use deposit-banking. It is as if a new source of gold-supply had been discovered. What has been discovered is a new way of using the gold-supply. The world, during the course of the War, has thus started, or has hastened, an equivalent of the price revolution of the 16th century.

Business-men should face the facts. To talk reverently of 1913-'14 prices is to speak a dead language today. The buyers of the country, since the Armistice, have made an unexampled attack upon prices through their waiting attitude, and yet price recessions have been insignificant. The reason is that we are on a new high-price level, which will be found a stubborn reality. Business men are going to find out that the clever man is not the man who waits, but the one who finds out the new price-facts and acts accordingly.

ARRANGEMENTS have been made to continue the investigations on the manufacture of graphite crucibles at the U. S. Bureau of Mines' experiment station, at Columbus, Ohio, with particular reference to quality of crucibles that may be made of domestic graphite. Statistics of production and stocks of graphite are no longer collected monthly by the U. S. Geological Survey.—F. B. Hyder in March report of the Bureau of Mines.

The German Metal Octopus—I

ISSUED BY THE ALIEN PROPERTY CUSTODIAN

INTRODUCTION. To appreciate what has been accomplished in ridding the metal industry of the United States of the influences of the so-called German metal octopus, it is necessary to briefly sketch the growth of the German metal concerns on their native soil, and then to point out how these gradually invaded foreign markets and to what extent the American metal markets came under their domination. At the outset, however, it must be pointed out that however much justification there is for the assertion that the German metal combine controlled the metal markets of Europe and Australia—especially in zinc and lead—it is not the fact that they controlled the metal market of the United States. Their influence here was potent, no doubt, and it was growing, but it was far from sufficient to control either the production or the price of metals in the United States. The octopus was spreading his tentacles across the Atlantic, but he had not yet assumed the 'octopian' proportions.

The Alien Property Custodian has taken over the German-owned metal concerns in the United States, and, by disbanding some and Americanizing others, it is believed that the German influences in our metal market have been completely eliminated.

GROWTH OF THE GERMAN METAL TRADE. Germany has never been a great producer of metals. Her production of copper is but 3%* of the world's output, against about 60% produced by the United States. Her production of refined zinc is about 28% of the world's output, and of lead she produces 16% of the world's total production. Yet unquestionably Germany has for years controlled the zinc and lead metal markets of Europe and of the rest of the world except the United States. What is the secret of her power? It is not alone that she is a large consumer of metal. For though she consumes annually about 500,000,000 pounds of copper more than she produces, she consumes only 23% of the world's zinc against her own production of 28% of the world's output; and of lead she consumes only 20% of the world's output against her own production of about 16%. Yet she completely controls the zinc and lead markets of the world. The secret of her power lies in the fact that her great metal firms act in concert in the purchase of zinc and lead ores, co-operate in the control of smelters and refineries, and, by the free use of unlimited credit extended to them by the German banks, who themselves participate in these industrial enterprises, they are enabled to buy and sell huge quantities of metals, thereby influencing the market prices.

THE GERMAN METAL TRIUMVIRATE. There are but three great international metal concerns in Germany—the Metallgesellschaft of Frankfurt, Aron Hirsch & Sohn of Halberstadt, and Beer, Sondheimer & Co. of Frankfurt. These giant organizations, whose operations now circle the globe, are of comparatively recent development and are the growth of very small and humble beginnings.

*All figures herein regarding Germany are for 1913.

Around the year 1800 there were in Germany three small concerns or individuals devoting themselves to the metal business, namely, Jacob Raviné, Berlin; Philip Abram Cohn, Frankfurt; Aron Hirsch, Halberstadt. They traded in the products of the country—lead produced in the Hartz mountains or in Saxony or Silesia, copper produced by the Mansfield works and other small concerns, and they also brought in some copper from Sweden.

In the 19th century the three concerns developed on somewhat different lines: Raviné drifted more into the iron business, Cohn developed into a large metal merchant, and Hirsch developed into a combination of industrial manufacturer and metal merchant.

(1) *The Metallgesellschaft* is the largest of these concerns and is by far the most powerful metal concern in the world. It is a stock corporation with a capital of 18,000,000 marks. It is the outgrowth of the metal business founded by Philip Abram Cohn early in the 19th or late in the 18th century. In the early 'sixties of the last century, Henry Merton, whose real name was Moses and who was related to Philip Abram Cohn, founded a metal firm in London which later became the powerful house of Henry R. Merton & Co. The Metallgesellschaft and the Merton firm worked hand-in-hand for the advancement of German domination of the metal markets of the world.

(2) *Aron Hirsch & Sohn*, a co-partnership, is the business founded by Aron Hirsch and it has always been kept in the Hirsch family. This house has not confined itself strictly to metal trading but has also engaged in metal manufacturing. It has interests all over the world.

(3) *Beer, Sondheimer & Co.*, a co-partnership, was founded in the latter part of the 'seventies by Messrs. Beer and Sondheimer, two salesmen of the Metallgesellschaft, who broke away from the Metallgesellschaft and with the assistance of the Mitteldeutsche Credit Bank started in business for themselves under the name of Beer, Sondheimer & Co. This firm has confined its activities principally to the zinc-smelting business.

The Federal Trade Commission in its Report on Co-operation in American Export Trade issued in 1916 has included a very excellent chart showing the inter-relations between the German metal-houses. This has been used as a basis for the charts hereto annexed which have been brought to date according to the latest information available, and which show the ramifications of the German metal combine. We find in their control not only German metal and chemical companies, but also French, Belgian, English, Australian, American, Swiss, Austrian, Italian, Spanish, and Mexican. In addition, they control syndicates for the exploration of mines in South America, Hungary, Russia, and the African continent. In this vast combine we find charted 245 separate companies whose interests lie in almost every part of the globe and who produce every known form of mineral.

THE ZINC SYNDICATES. At the outbreak of the European war the zinc industry of the whole world, save only the United States (as to which comment will be made separately), was completely in the control of the German metal triumvirate—the Metallgesellschaft, Aron Hirsch & Sohn, and Beer, Sondheimer & Co. The control of the purchase of ores, principally Australian ores, was exercised by means of joint accounts among the three German firms, while the control of the smelters and the zinc spelter which they produced was exercised in Germany by the German Zinc Syndicate, and in the other European countries by an International Zinc Syndicate. But the Metallgesellschaft—and its English offshoot, Henry R. Merton & Co.—Aron Hirsch & Sohn, and Beer, Sondheimer & Co. were in absolute control of these syndicates.

(a) The Australian zinc-ore purchasing combine. When Australia, during the 'nineties of the last century, came to the fore as a large metal-producing country, principally zinc ore, the German metal triumvirate—the Metallgesellschaft, Aron Hirsch & Sohn, and Beer, Sondheimer & Co.—took hold of the situation and became the dominating influence in the purchase of the Australian zinc ores. This took the form not of a syndicate but of an arrangement for joint accounts, resulting in the elimination of nearly all competition both in the purchase of raw material and in the allocation of the ore among the smelters on the European continent. It is interesting to note the development of this combine:

The Broken Hill mines in Australia were prolific producers of zinc ore. The annual production was about 477,000 tons. The ore was refractory, and there was great difficulty in disposing of the huge production. England, apparently, was not in a position to handle the product, and a situation developed more or less similar to the situation which arose in the United States in the 'eighties when England, through her inability or unwillingness to treat the copper product coming from America, stimulated the erection of large smelting and refining plants in the United States. The three German metal concerns immediately invaded the field and sought to find a market for this tremendous output. Each of them opened an agency of its own in Australia. The Metallgesellschaft created for this purpose the Australian Metal Co. Aron Hirsch & Sohn formed a connection with Francis H. Snow of Adelaide. Beer, Sondheimer & Co. engaged the shipping firm of Elder Smith & Co. as their agents. At first these German firms were in keen competition with one another in the Australian field, and there were also in the field several English firms, as well as the great Belgian zinc smelting concern, Société Vielle Montagne. Competition was very keen and profits small. Production was increasing all the time. During the Boer war and the depression incidental to it the metal concerns suffered severely under their contracts with Australians and as a result of the losses which they suffered during that period they came to the conclusion that, being the largest buyers of products coming from Australia, a way should be found to eliminate the competition both in the purchase of raw material and its disposal to the various smelters on the European continent. About the year 1902 joint accounts were arranged—first between the Metallgesellschaft and Aron Hirsch & Sohn in which later on Beer, Sondheimer & Co. were included and a working arrangement was reached with the Société Vielle Montagne. These arrangements were nothing but loose joint-account arrangements changeable and changed from time to time, but, in effect, they resulted in a dominating influence as far as the purchaser of zinc ore was concerned, which continued to be exercised by the German metal triumvirate until the outbreak of the European war.

Having acquired what amounted to practically a monopoly of zinc ore, the German metal triumvirate next sought to obtain control of the smelters where the ore was treated and of the spelter, which is the finished product. And here they sought not only to control the output of the metal but also to fix the prices. They established zinc smelters in Germany, Belgium, France, Russia, Poland, and Austria, and they even acquired interests in British zinc smelters. Aron Hirsch & Sohn, for instance, practically owned a zinc smelter at Swansea Vale, in Wales. They succeeded completely in Germany, where they established the German Zinc Syndicate, which controlled the output of zinc in Germany and fixed the prices therefor. They also succeeded in establishing an international zinc syndicate, but through that they regulated only the output outside of Germany and not the prices.

(b) The German Zinc Syndicate (Zinkhüttenverband). This was organized in 1909 with a capital of 2,000,000 marks. The organizers were the same old triumvirate, the Metallgesellschaft, Aron Hirsch & Sohn, and Beer, Sondheimer & Co. All the large zinc concerns of Germany entered the syndicate, with the single exception of the firm of Giesche's Erben; but even this concern agreed to sell only at prices fixed by the syndicate. The triumvirate was appointed the exclusive selling agent of the syndicate and through a subsidiary of the syndicate, the Kolner Zinkhüttenverband, the syndicate regulated the prices of zinc in Germany. The syndicate is said to be absolute in its control of the German zinc output and in price-fixing. Through the German Zinc Syndicate the Germans have controlled one-half the zinc output and about one-third the world's output.

(c) The International Zinc Syndicate. With such a large control of the world's zinc output the German Zinc Syndicate became a menace to the English, French, and

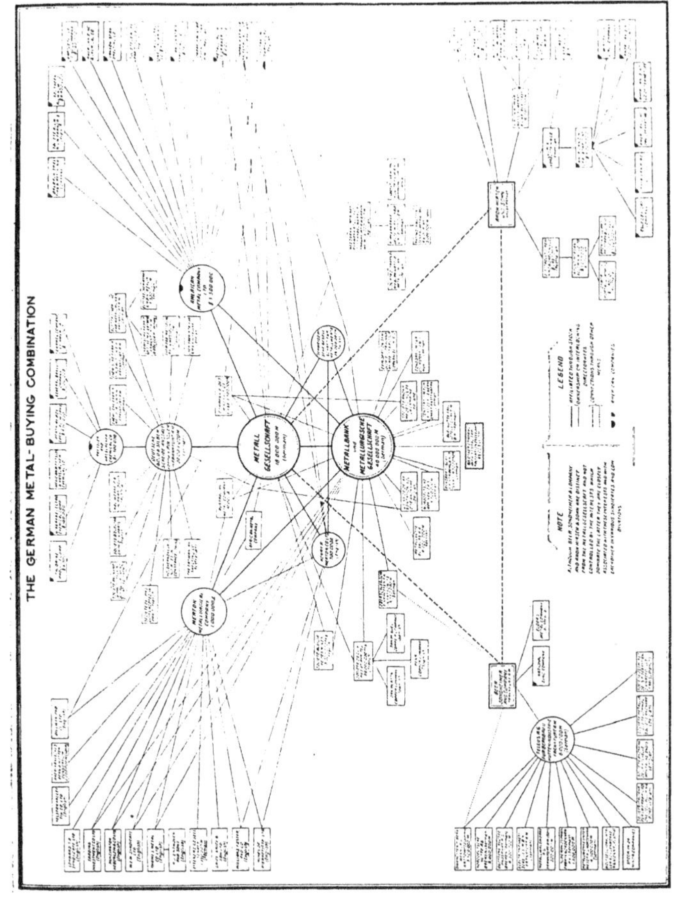

THIS CHART APPEARED IN A REPORT OF THE FEDERAL TRADE COMMISSION DATED JUNE 30, 1916

Belgian smelters. For their own protection, therefore, the English works formed a syndicate of their own, while the Belgian and French works formed a separate syndicate. The most important Belgian zinc concern, the Société Vielle Montagne, which had extensive works all over the world, had, however, entered into a working agreement with the German zinc syndicate, so that the German Zinc Syndicate's preponderance over all the others were so great that they were forced to join the Germans in the formation of the International Zinc Syndicate, which was formed in 1911. In the preamble to the contract creating the International Zinc Syndicate, the purpose of the syndicate is stated as follows:

"The undersigned German, Austrian, Belgian, French, Dutch, and English zinc smelters have agreed to combine for the purpose of curtailing the actual total production, if proof is available that consumption does not absorb the production."

The duration of this syndicate is fixed for five years beginning January 1, 1911. There are three groups, the first group representing the German zinc smelters, Belgian and French smelters controlled by German concerns; the second group represents Belgian zinc smelters owned by Belgians; the third group English smelters regardless of ownership. The arrangement states:

"A curtailment of production is to be effected whenever the stocks held by the various zinc smelters at the end of a quarter exceeds 50,000 tons, provided, however, that if the price of spelter in London should be £23 or more no curtailment of production is to take place."

Changes in the price for the metal were agreed upon from time to time at meetings held by the zinc smelters, according to the necessities of the market. For the purpose of distributing the product of the smelters and for the purpose of avoiding competition, the sale of the metal was placed in the hands of the three German metal concerns—the Metallgesellschaft, Aron Hirsch & Sohn, and Beer, Sondheimer & Co. and their branches. Not all the zinc smelters were bound; some of the more important ones retained their selling organizations, but they were bound to the price agreement as laid down by the zinc syndicate.

This syndicate absolutely controlled the world's output of spelter (except the United States), and though theoretically all the syndicate members except the German works were free to fix their own prices, in practice the German metal triumvirate fixed the prices, since the International Zinc Syndicate prices and those of the German Zinc Syndicate were always the same.

THE LEAD SYNDICATE. At the outbreak of the European war the lead output of the world was likewise centred in the hands of the Germans. The Metallgesellschaft had the exclusive sales agency of what was known as the International Lead Convention, which was formed in 1909 and continued thereafter for a number of years. It embraced the principal Australian lead-producers, as well as most of the German, and most of the Spanish and Belgian lead mines. At least two American firms, to wit, the American Smelting & Refining Co. and the American Metal Co., as far as their production of lead from ores imported in bond is concerned, and some of the Mexican mines, were likewise members of the syndicate which regulated output and fixed prices.

COPPER. In copper the Germans were never able to gain control of production, but they had a marked influence on the market price of the metal. Their inability to control the production was due to the fact that the mining industry of the United States, which produces more than 60% of the world's total output of copper, could not be brought under German domination. The large American producers have maintained their own agencies abroad and have through those agencies dealt directly with the foreign consumers. Important American producing concerns like Anaconda had branch-offices of their own in London and later on in Berlin and Paris. The American Smelting & Refining Co. had the same organization. The Calumet & Hecla Co. was represented at London and Paris, and at Bonn, in Germany. Phelps, Dodge & Co. were represented in London, Paris, and Frankfort on the Main. All these important American producers practically prohibited the sale of copper except to consumers, through their foreign branches. Nevertheless, the European metal merchants did buy copper from some of the large producing companies in America, but these purchases were negotiated in nearly every instance in New York between the seller and the respective agent of the European purchaser.

Outside the United States, and especially in Australia, the Germans did largely control the copper output. The Metallgesellschaft through its Australian Metal Co. at one time exercised a decided influence in the copper business of Australia. Aron Hirsch & Sohn, however, later became the most important copper interest in Australia. This firm had control, through refining and purchasing contracts, of the copper production of the three largest copper producers in Australia, to wit, the Mount Morgan Gold Mining Co., the Wallaroo & Moonta Mining & Smelting Co., and the Mount Lyell M. & R. Co., having a combined total output of about 15,000 tons as against 45,000 tons, which was Australia's total annual output of copper.

But though Germany has never controlled the output of the world's copper, she has exercised a powerful influence over the price of the metal. This was due to two causes: (1) Because Germany was a large consumer: (2) on account of the activities of the German metal triumvirate.

In 1913 the world's total production of copper was about 993,000 tons. Germany produced only about 30,000 tons, or a little over 3%. The world's consumption of copper in 1913 was about 1,000,000 tons and Germany alone consumed 256,500 tons, or more than 25% of the world's total consumption. Germany imported most of her copper from the United States. In 1913 she took from the United States about 200,000 tons. It is but natural that the huge buying power of German consumers would wield a marked influence on the price of copper. There is no direct proof, however, to show that the German consumers buy as a unit nor that the German metal triumvirate act in concert in making purchases of copper. In fact, Beer, Sondheimer & Co. play an unimportant part in the metal trade as far as copper is concerned. The most powerful group in the copper markets of the world, outside the large American producers, was the Merton-Metallgesellschaft-American Metal Co. group. Next to them the Hirsch-Vogelstein group. There is no evidence that these two groups co-operated in their copper business. Statistics show that the American Metal Co. controls by purchasing contracts and selling agreements about 250,000,000 lb. of American copper; Vogelstein controls in a similar way about 150,000,000 lb. of American copper. In addition to this the Hirsch group controls about 30,000,000 lb. of Australian copper, while the Merton-Metallgesellschaft group controls probably a similar quantity of copper of various origin. It might be assumed, therefore, that the two groups control together about 460,000,000 lb. of copper, or approximately 23% of the world's market. This in itself would not have given them the power which they exercised in the market. The underlying reason for that power must, therefore, be found elsewhere.

It is believed that the underlying reasons will be found primarily in the ability of the German metal concerns, by the use of their unlimited credits, to finance large purchases of copper over long periods of time, including periods of depression, and secondarily in their splendid organizations and ability to operate on metal exchanges abroad, thus taking immediate advantage of fluctuations which in a large measure they themselves create.

Since the days when Lewisohn Bros., in New York, were active trade manipulators and selling agents of copper—from 1890 to 1899—there was no important copper house in the world outside the two above-mentioned German firms. These firms took advantage of the psychology of the situation as well as of the facilities which the European markets offered to them and the high credit which was at their disposal. They operated on the metal exchanges of London, Hamburg, Berlin, and Havre, and, anticipating market movements, they either bought or sold on these exchanges, thereby creating sentiment, and, through a well-developed chain of agencies which they had established in all of the principal consuming centres of the world, they had a decisive influence on the policy of consumers. In America there was no open trading in copper and the business was done absolutely between selling agencies and consumers. In Europe the metal dealers, and there were many in addition to the three big German firms, acted, so to say, as a buffer between the producing interests and the consuming interests and helped to tide over changes in the markets so that the changes were much more gradual than in the United States. American consumers, and, as a matter of fact, all consumers, prefer to buy on a rising market and hesitate to buy in a falling market. When markets were lowest, when producers were tired out by a long period of business inactivity, when stocks were accumulating in the hands of producers, these large German metal firms entered into the market and bought large tonnages of copper at low prices. The purchases were often in quantities of 10,000 and 25,000 tons at a time. The effect of these purchases was, in the first place, to relieve the producer of his accumulating stock of copper and thereby remove pressure from the market; in the second place, after they had purchased these large quantities of copper, then by encouraging the buyers, by manipulating the metal-exchange markets, and by withholding offers from the market, they created an improved market sentiment and started the market on a boom of which they in turn took advantage by selling at higher prices quantities of copper that they had accumulated at low prices.

As pointed out recently by a prominent American producer, the manipulation of markets for futures and the power to buy huge quantities of copper at low prices have given to foreign consumers the advantage of having been able to buy American copper on an average of one cent less per pound than the domestic consumers had to pay for it.

While the German metal-houses largely speculate in futures of copper, the theory of the large American producers has been that speculation should be eliminated. The results of such a policy are rigid conditions and long periods of inactivity following periods of advances. It stands to reason that at the termination of a purchasing movement when consumers had bought at advancing prices and an increased impetus for forward delivery had run its course, a market had to be reached when purchases ceased and when consumers sat down to wait for weeks and months until they should resume purchases. These were the periods when the Germans came into the market and made purchases in large quantities.

Thus we see that Germany through her three large metal concerns absolutely controlled the zinc and lead markets of the world and exercised a powerful influence over the price of copper to the extent of being able to buy her copper from America at a lower price than the domestic American consumer had to pay for it. But of what significance is all this to the United States since the German and international zinc syndicates did not control the American output of zinc and only partially that of lead, and since they could not control our huge production of copper? This brings us to a consideration of the activities of the triumvirate.

(To be Continued)

Operating and developing costs at the North Star gold mine at Grass Valley, California, averaged $7.77 per ton from 1884 to the end of 1918. During that time, 1,898,584 tons of $11.47 ore was extracted and treated.

Vanadium ore imported from Peru during February amounted to 841,257 lb., valued at $2510, equal to about $6 per ton. Imports of ore from the same country in the first 15 days of March were 373,900 lb., worth $1106.

Piping that is used to carry acetylene or hydrogen should be painted a distinctive color so that it will not be possible to mistake the line for anything else.

Chromite in Wyoming, and Manufacture of Ferro-Chrome in Colorado

According to the annual report of the Vindicator Consolidated Gold Mining Co. of Cripple Creek, Colorado, three claims, 23 miles south-east of Glenrock on the C. B. & Q. railroad, were purchased from Wheeler and others in September 1918. The lease-rights were sold for $7500, and the bond called for a purchase-price of $25,000. The lease also called for a royalty of 12½% on cars at Glenrock, the amounts not to be deducted from purchase-price. In October, the owner accepted $8750 cash in lieu of the bond price of $25,000, due a year later, so the Vindicator became owner. The sellers had extracted 500 tons of 34% chromite. Some prospecting showed other lenses in the east end of the property, carrying 39% ore. During development, 610 tons were shipped, and there is available 2000 tons and over, according to the February 10, 1919, report of the Ferro Alloy Co., absorbed by the Vindicator company in September 1918. A good deal of road construction had to be done, also three surface trams—two of 500 and 1200 ft. on 36° incline, and one level of 500 ft. This work, buildings, and development cost $30,897. The purchase of lease and property cost $16,250, so the total outlay was $47,147. Chromite sold realized $9602, leaving $37,544 net expenditure to the end of 1918, reduced by February 10, 1919, to $33,602. Since January 1, $5469 has been received from ore sold. When the indicated ore is extracted, the mine will show a profit, after having paid the purchase-price of the property, development, and improvements. Californian, Oregon, and Washington chromite has a freight-rate $8.70 per ton higher than from Glenrock to Denver.

The electric smelting plant of the Ferro Alloy Co. at Utah Junction, Colorado, was purchased by the Vindicator Consolidated in September 1918 at a cost of $68,697. Up to the end of 1918 the plant resulted in an operating loss of $2270. S. B. Tyler is now in charge, and is producing ferro-chrome at low cost, considering the low capacity of 100 tons per month. When the additional 1500-kva. General Electric furnace is in operation the output will be doubled. The company has some contracts for delivery of the alloy during 1919, and is receiving orders frequently for spot delivery. Having its own chrome mine, a low freight-rate, and its own smelter the manager, Nelson Franklin, considers that the company is in a position to compete with others in the manufacture of ferro-chrome. A profitable year is expected during 1919.

Phosphate Rock

There was little change in the phosphate-rock market during March. Labor costs are one of the principal items in the mining and preparation of phosphate rock, and there has been no change in these charges; hence there has been no marked change in the price of this important fertilizer commodity. Florida land pebble, containing 68% bone phosphate, f.o.b. Tampa, Florida, was about $5 per ton; with 75%, the price was $7.50 to $8 per ton; high-grade Florida hard rock, containing 77%, f.o.b. Florida ports, was $9 to $10 per ton. Tennessee rock, guaranteed to contain 75% bone phosphate of lime, averaged $9.50 to $10. The Tennessee rock with 58 to 72%, ground so that it will pass through a 100-mesh screen, was priced at $7.25 to $7.50 per ton.—W. C. Phalen in March report of the U. S. Bureau of Mines.

Molybdenum

By H. C. MORRIS

*Persistent statements to the effect that the use of molybdenum is increasing with relative rapidity are being received from various sources, although it is not known to what extent these are based upon the war uses in parts of airplane engines, etc. It is clearly the presumption that if a molybdenum alloy was found satisfactory in these engines, it may also be desirable in automobile engines, unless the price or difficulty of working is too great. Molybdenum steel, once it is made, has many desirable qualities, but the chief difficulty with the metal seems to be in the making of the steel. The molybdenum volatilizes, is difficult to mix uniformly in the steel, and causes a red shortness responsible for a large scale loss.

Imports of molybdenum ore during February totaled 68,599 lb., valued at $48,255. The greater part came from Canada. There were no imports of molybdenum metal or ferro-molybdenum. There were no imports of ore in the first 15 days of March, none of metal or ferro.

Flotation at Cripple Creek

The annual report of the Vindicator Consolidated Gold Mining Co. contains the following data regarding its milling operations during 1918:

On company account there was hoisted 230,304 tons of crude ore, averaging $6.15 per ton. Of this quantity, 6.67% was sorted out and sent to the Golden Cycle mill at Colorado Springs. All rejects from ore-dressing operations and the Golden Cycle shaft ore-house are delivered to the flotation plant, where they are screened and all coarse waste rejected, and the residue sent to the flotation-plant crusher. During the year there were sent to the flotation plant from all sources 222,626 tons of ore, of an average assay-value of $2.13 per ton. Of this, 176,623 tons, assaying $1.42 per ton, was rejected by screening, and 46,003 tons valued at $4.18 sent to the flotation-plant crusher. There was shipped from the flotation plant 6209 tons of concentrate having a gross value of $206,255, equal to $34.21 per ton, and a net value after marketing charges of $171,038. After the deduction of all operating costs the net profit from this source amounted to $27,955. The royalty paid on flotation rights was $2578, equal to 5½ cents per ton on 46,003 tons so treated.

*Abstract from March report of U. S. Bureau of Mines.

PACHUCA, MEXICO

SANTA GERTRUDIS, EL BORDO, AND REAL DEL MONTE.

The Santa Gertrudis Company in London recently issued a circular, accompanied by reports on the properties by Hugh Rose and L. Chevrillon. These, in part, are as follows, with a property-map:

Mr. Rose stated that El Bordo, in which Santa Gertrudis acquired a 40% interest, is in the centre of the Pachuca district, surrounded by the most-highly productive mines thereof, and 3½ miles from the Santa Gertrudis mill, with which El Bordo is being connected by an aerial tram capable of transporting 100 tons of ore per hour. By reference to the attached sketch, it will be noted that there are four groups—El Bordo, Malinche, El Cristo, and La Zorro. The last-mentioned is on a vein of minor importance with no record of production, and is of no special interest at this time.

El Bordo mine has produced a large tonnage of ore in the past, and its present reserves are taken at 300,000 tons of ore averaging 1.60 dwt. gold and 17 oz. silver, with large development possibilities both in depth and laterally. Production at the beginning will be from this property alone.

The Malinche mine is practically a virgin property. The only development, done many years ago, consists of two shafts—Santa Tomas and Enseñanza—both sunk to a depth of 750 ft., where a limited amount of cross-cutting was done to the main Vizcaina vein. As this work was not at sufficient depth to reach the ore-zone as indicated in the mines to the west, these shafts are to be sunk another 250 or 300 ft., whereupon extensive development of both the Vizcaina and Maravillas veins is to be started. Particular attention is invited to the possibilities of this property.

Two strong vein-systems enter the ground at B and D (see map). On the Vizcaina to the west are located three great mines—Camelia, San Rafael, and El Bordo, as well as the smaller Santa Ana mine covering a succession of large orebodies from A to B, a distance of 8000 ft. on the strike of the vein. In the Camelia mine, 150 ft. west of the Malinche line, is an orebody 50 ft. in width, averaging 20 oz. silver per ton. The Maravillas vein, for a great many years, over a length of 8000 ft. from C to D has yielded a large quantity of ore to the Maravillas company. Near point D the vein enters the property of the Real del Monte company, where it was worked to the Malinche boundary-line, at which place the ore is reported to have averaged over 30 oz. silver for a width of 20 ft. Upon the foregoing record and information are based favorable expectations in Malinche.

El Cristo is an old mine, which has yielded a considerable tonnage of high-grade ore, and has in sight 125,000 tons of ore averaging 9.5 oz. silver, and probably capable of considerable expansion, and likely to prove a useful feeder of low-grade ore to the mill. No development will be undertaken on this group until El Bordo is in regular operation.

At the present price of silver, 101½ cents (U. S.) per fine ounce, and on the proposed basis of treating 500 tons of ore per day from El Bordo, the net mining profit is

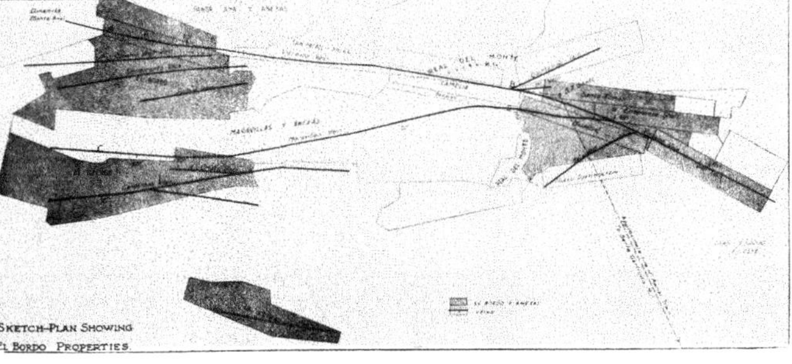

SKETCH-PLAN SHOWING EL BORDO PROPERTIES

estimated at an average of £30,000 ($145,000) per month, Santa Gertrudis 40% share amounting to £12,000 per month. For a time at first, owing to higher-grade ore, the monthly profit should be from £40,000 to £45,000, Santa Gertrudis share amounting to £16,000 to £18,000. It is expected, barring unforeseen delays, that El Bordo will commence production next July or August, with full-rate earnings probably reached a month or two later. Therefore it may be expected that combined profits from Santa Gertrudis and El Bordo mines will reach £35,000 to £40,000 by the coming late summer or early fall. Later on, as the grade of El Bordo ore is reduced to normal, these profits should total £30,000 to £35,000 monthly ($145,000 to $169,000).

Although not connected with El Bordo business, mention might be made of the several other properties that are being taken by Santa Gertrudis under option to purchase, after two years in which to develop. The most important of these is Espiritu Santo, which is believed to have the northerly extension of the Veta Nueva, the vein upon which within the past four years the Real del Monte company has discovered and developed a very large and rich orebody, said to contain £8,000,000 ($38,800,000) profit. At any rate, a good and strong vein has been surficially developed in Espiritu Santo ground, and it is proposed to sink the shaft a further 300 ft. and drive, on the supposition that sufficient depth to reach the main ore-zone has not been reached. Sinking will be done on a small exposure of pay-ore. Such work as the above, while entirely of a prospecting nature, is undoubtedly good business for Santa Gertrudis to undertake, having in view the great productivity of the Pachuca district and desirability of providing further sources of ore-supply for the mill.

Mr. Chevrillon said that he could only convey to the directors of Santa Gertrudis his full endorsement of Mr. Rose's report. The results obtained have so far borne out, in El Bordo proper, the expectations formed at the time of examination by the engineers; and it is gratifying to note that after a few months of development the tonnage and grade of ore available are sufficient to more than repay any past or future outlay connected with the equipment of El Bordo and the acquisition of the interest in the group. At the time of Mr. Chevrillon's visit in December last the principal orebody showed a decided tendency to persist both along the strike and in depth.

The annual report of the U. S. S. R. & M. Co., which controls Real del Monte, operating at Pachuca, contains the following:

With the exception of the high costs pertaining to supplies, operations in Mexico during 1918 may be considered to have run on a normal basis. The two mills treated 690,000 tons of ore, approximately 58,000 tons per month. Extraction of ore from the new vein was increased from month to month, and will before long reach the anticipated regular tonnage. This ore being of much higher grade than the average formerly supplied to the Guerrero mill, has had the effect of materially raising the mill-heads, resulting in a substantial increase in profits. No difficulty is anticipated in maintaining these results. A moderate tonnage of the highest-grade ore obtained from this vein is being shipped direct to smelter. The output from this vein and from other localities, both in the Real del Monte and Pachuca districts, is capable of an increase beyond the present capacity of the two mills. This situation will be met by the additions to the mills started last year, and are now approaching completion. It is expected that by the middle of 1919 the capacity will reach 80,000 tons per month. The erection of a third mill of 15,000 tons monthly capacity is still under consideration. Tests are not completed to determine the best process to be adopted, neither do costs and deliveries of materials favor construction at this time. In view of the more stable general conditions in Mexico, and the favorable results in opening ore-reserves, the prospects for earnings in these properties are more favorable than ever before.

GOLDFIELD, NEVADA

LESSEES' RICH ORE.—EXPLORATION IN THE CONTACT.

A carload of ore each week is being shipped from the Witt-Brandon-Taylor-Mechlin lease at the Florence Goldfield, which attracted attention several months ago by the opening of a seam showing free gold over a width of from 6 to 18 in. The grade has been much lower than was anticipated when shipments were started, carload lots assaying under $100 per ton. A stope 80 ft. long has been started from the 400-ft. level, and the material is being broken for a width of from 3 to 4 ft. When first opened, assays of $400 per ton were returned from a width of from 4 to 6 ft., but recent assays have proved that a short distance above the level practically the entire value of the vein is confined to the rich seam, so the lessees are planning to raise the value of shipments by breaking ore over the narrowest possible width. The ore was opened in a drift from the top of a 116-ft. raise, and the lessees have started to explore the vein 50 ft. below to determine if the rich seam extends to this depth. Nine other lessees are working, shipments of low-grade ore being made by them at irregular intervals.

The Spearhead, Merger, and Grandma are exploring at or near the shale-latite contact. The first is raising toward the contact from the 910-ft. level and the raise, after having, in the opinion of the management, paralleled the surface of the shale, dipping west at this point, for a distance of over 100 ft. has been turned at right angles, and is expected to break into the latite within a short distance. Owing to the numerous seams of good ore found on the 910-ft. level in an intrusion of the latite into the shale it is supposed that the opening of the contact on which a large mass of quartz is known to lie, will result in the discovery of an orebody of good size and grade. Small quantities of ore of shipping grade are being saved from work at other points on this level.—— The Merger, which recently secured permission from the Spearhead company to work through the latter's shaft, has advanced a cross-cut well into Merger ground. This cross-cut is being driven to open in the Merger, the contact of the quartz-mass with the shale.——The Grandma is working at a depth of 815 ft. in the Spearhead-Grandma vein, a vein distinct from the quartz-mass lying on the shale. Although at 815 ft. the Grandma shaft is in the shale, drifts and cross-cuts driven in all directions from the shaft have failed to expose this formation again. A number of promising cross-veins have been found. The claims of these three companies adjoin and their efforts to find ore on the shale-latite contact are of interest at this time.

YERINGTON, NEVADA

WORK AT THE MASON VALLEY, BLUESTONE, NEVADA-DOUGLAS, WESTERN NEVADA, WALKER RIVER COPPER COMPANY, BUCKSKIN, AND NORTHERN LIGHT.

The entire copper district of Lyon county is very quiet since the smelter at Thompson closed on March 1. All the small properties are closed, and nearly all lessees have stopped work. Locally it is thought that the smelter may not re-open until next year, although it is realized that this will depend on the foreign demand for copper. At present prices, with continued high cost of supplies and labor, it is not possible for the local mines to make profits.

The Mason Valley Copper Co. has 30 men working.

The Bluestone M. & S. Co. is reported to be making plans for increasing the size of its flotation plant, which was a big success. Concentrates were shipped to Utah smelters, as the Thompson plant is not equipped for handling such product. It is, however, thought that the smelter will be so improved before re-starting.

Nevada-Douglas development is giving good results; this is also true of the Western Nevada mine owned by the same company. Large bodies of sulphide ore have been opened in the latter, and a flotation plant is under consideration. This mine is near or at the southern extremity of the mineralized limestone belt, which is the ore-bearing zone of the district, and adjoins the McConnell mine on the south but at a lower elevation.

The Walker River Copper Co. continues drilling operations on its Empire Nevada group. Many engineers consider that this property has the brightest future of any in the district. Large tonnages of oxidized ore have been developed, and no doubt a leaching-plant will be built in the near future, as the ore is ideal for sulphuric-acid leaching process. The general formation is monzonite, and the valuable copper minerals at or near the surface are the carbonates and oxides. The ore is highly silicious, and has been in demand for converter lining, etc. Iron minerals are conspicuous by their absence. J. E. Gelder is in charge of operations.

The Northern Light, 15 miles east of Yerington, is the scene of the most recent strike in the district. This property has some of the characteristics of the Ludwig, but is not a vein. The limestone is not garnetized as in Mason Valley district proper, and the orebodies are irregular lenses in a rather narrow belt of limestone. This property has been worked almost entirely by lessees, and as the ore is usually of a grade better than 8% it has been profitable for them. The recent strike is a lens of sulphide ore reported to average over 15% copper, and more extensive than any deposits found in the past.

CHLORIDE, ARIZONA

CHANGES IN OWNERSHIP AND NEW DEVELOPMENTS.

The McCracken Silver-Lead Mining Co. has taken over the Otsega mine. Development done during the past few months has opened good ore on the 100-ft. level. It is expected that the workings will be ready for stoping and shipping within a short time.

McKesson & Marinez, lessees at the Gold Trails mine, have made a shipment of ore assaying over $400 gold per ton. The company owning the property proposes to do extensive development.

The Arizona Ore Reduction Co. has taken over the Diana mine at Chloride. Unwatering and cleaning out the old workings is under way. The shaft is 200 ft. deep. The late owners took out $10,000 worth of ore.

The Cerbat Silver Mining & Milling Co. has taken over the Elkhart property at Chloride. The company proposes to spend $250,000. The Elkhart is situated on the Tennessee lode to the north, and has been developed to a depth of 600 ft. The ore is refractory, but it is believed that it can be treated by flotation. A considerable tonnage of high-grade ore has been shipped in the past.

E. F. Campbell has taken a bond and lease on the old Distaff mine at Chloride. Large shipments of rich silver ore have been made from the property in the past.

F. E. Berry has completed arrangements for taking over the interests of the Washington-Arizona mine at Mineral Park. He has completed financing, and the mine and a 10-ton mill are to be operated at once.

The Lookout mine has been optioned by A. Fuller of Phoenix. A 10-ton mill is to be erected immediately.

DIVIDE, NEVADA

SOME RECENT UNDERGROUND PROGRESS.

On its 465-ft. level the Tonopah Divide company has driven the south-east drift over 200 ft. to get under the high-grade area of No. 3 level. A station is to be cut on No. 5 level as soon as the 1200-cu. ft. compressor is erected. Shipments last week were 420 tons. William Watters is superintendent.

The south-east drift at 500 ft. depth in the Brougher Divide is out 125 ft., for the greater part in milling ore, a good distance averaging $24 per ton. It was reported that the first lot of ore was to go to the West End mill at Tonopah early this week. Gust. Hanson is superintendent.

The Gold Zone Divide has opened a number of promising seams, but has so far no great quantity of pay-ore. The shaft is to be sunk 300 ft. below the 500-ft. level.

Divide Consolidated has erected its head-frame, sunk the shaft 50 ft., and is preparing to erect a 10-drill compressor, and a hoist. W. S. Norris is manager.

The Aztec Divide has purchased a hoist and other machinery, and has started sinking. Rudolph Burton is in charge.

THE MINING SUMMARY

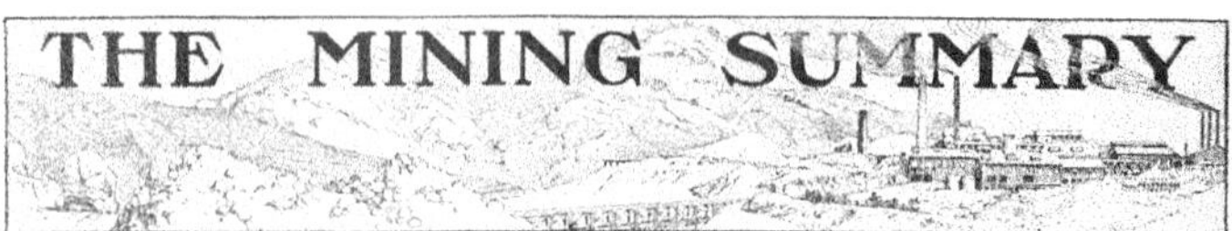

ARIZONA

Ajo.—New Cornelia during 1918 made a net profit of $2,527,806. This is the first full operating year. The mining profit was $4,791,180, depreciation, ore-depletion, and interest absorbing the balance. The output of copper was 46,950,139 pounds.

Duncan.—The Ash Peak Mines Co. has arranged to purchase part of the dismantled cyanide-plant of the Aurora Consolidated at Aurora, Nevada. The Ash Peak plant when completed will be of 100-ton capacity.

Miami.—The Miami Copper Co. pays 50 cents per share, $373,557, on May 15. This makes $1,120,771 for 1919, and $20,715,715 to date. The last distribution was $1.

Inspiration Consolidated during 1918 made a profit of $8,229,163, after paying taxes, compared with $11,086,732 in 1917, and $20,629,489 in 1916. Dividends totaled $9,455,736. Ore mined amounted to 5,139,132 tons, yielding 98,540,041 lb. of copper.

Phoenix.—The State Tax Commission announces that the total valuation of producing mines in Arizona, including machinery and equipment, increased from $153,385,383 in 1915 to $467,941,673 in 1918. In 1915 the valuation of mining property was 36½% of the assessed valuation of the State; in 1918 it had increased to 56%. The Commission says that the outstanding feature of the past two years' assessment of producing mines under the new method had been the large increase in valuation of this class of property brought about with comparatively little friction and a minimum amount of litigation.

Ray.—The Ray Hercules during the first 25 days of March treated 878 tons of 1.6% copper ore daily. The recovery is 80%.

CALIFORNIA

Bakersfield.—Oil shipment from Californian fields during March averaged 284,641 bbl. daily, an increase of 18,000 bbl. over February, but production was 278,665 bbl., almost similar to the previous month. Stocks declined 185,236 barrels.

Campo Seco.—The smelter of the Penn Chemical Co. near this place in Calaveras county was closed on April 1, and will probably remain idle for six or eight months, during which time extensive repairs are to be made in the mine.

Grass Valley.—Operations have been started on the proposed debris and power dam at Bullard's bar on the Yuba river, 28 miles west of Grass Valley. W. F. Mandry and associates will erect a saw-mill of a daily capacity of 20,000 ft. three miles from the site. He also has a contract for hauling machinery and supplies to the site. The dam will be 140 ft. long, and the first section 80 ft. high, backing the water 6½ miles. A double use will be made of the proposed reservoir; one for tailing from the Brandy City hydraulic mines, and the overflowing water converted into electrical energy. The mine-owners will be charged for debris storage, and the finished dam will permit of hydraulic operations on a large scale in that district.

The North Star company has commenced development of new ground on an extensive scale, following the reduced cost of steel and explosives.

There has been an exodus of miners from Grass Valley to Divide, Nevada, but as their places have been taken by newcomers the labor market has not been affected.

Nevada City.—The Monarch Consolidated quartz mine, in Sierra county, will be re-opened in the spring on an enlarged scale. The property is equipped with a 20-stamp mill and good mine plant. It was formerly a heavy gold producer.

Driving is progressing on a 4-ft. vein in the Argo quartz mine ,and a good showing is made of free gold. A new tunnel, 150 ft. below the present workings, is proposed, and if the value continues, a small mill is to be erected.

Jackson.—After the fire in the Argonaut mine revived on the 13th, drifts and the Muldoon shaft were quickly bulkheaded to confine the outbreak. Pumping and hoisting water is progressing steadily from the 4000-ft. level of the Argonaut shaft.

Redding.—All the mining equipment at the Tedoc chrome mine at Beegum, over the line in Tehama county, is being shipped to a gold mine in Arizona. The Tedoc company last season spent $40,000 building a wagon-road to haul its ore to rail, and 75 men were employed.

COLORADO

Breckenridge.—The state of the metal markets resulted in closing the Wellington zinc mine, the Climax molybdenum mine, and other base-metal producers, but increased activity in gold and silver help to keep Summit county going. Five dredges are ready for the season's work. Several gold and silver mines are reported to be yielding rich ore.

Durango.—The Lewis Mountain M. & M. Co., J. F. Warnecke, manager, has driven its tunnel 3400 ft. in the Ten Broeck property, finding vein formation in limestone at a depth of 2000 ft. The company proposes to erect a power-plant and mill. The owners of this property are Perini brothers of Denver.

On April 21, fire destroyed all buildings except the transformer-house at the Sunnyside mine at Eureka, the property of the U. S. S. R. & M. Co., causing a loss estimated at $250,000. A special train was sent from Durango to bring back 300 miners who lost all their personal effects by the destruction of the company boarding-house.

Idaho Springs.—Mining men here are optimistic as to the future price of silver, and expect a rise before long. The Randolph Gold M. M. & T. Co., composed of Denver and Cheyenne people, has acquired the Empire T. & T. Co.'s property at Empire. An examination shows 1,773,000 tons of $6.35 ore, on which a profit of $2 is expected.

Leadville.—A general strike was likely to start here on April 20 as a result of the cut in wages from $4.50 to $3.50 per day.

The threatened strike took place on the 20th. The men organized a local union. A committee will suggest $4 per day to the mine-owners, against the latters' $3.75.

During 1918 the Ibex (Little Johnny) employed 125 men, about half of normal, but the full complement is again at work. The property is leased to a number of different syndicates. Four shafts are in operation, the company looking after these. Gold ore is being extracted from the 300 to the 1200-ft. level. Some of this ore is in pockets, and is rich. One lease is yielding copper-silver-gold ore.

At the Fanny Rawlins new electric machinery has replaced the steam-plant burned last fall, and developments are reported as very encouraging. The New Monarch Mining Co. is to unwater its New Monarch shaft so as to develop the large gold-copper and silver-lead-zinc deposits worked by lessees in the upper levels. E. G. Kelly is in charge.

Rico.—The Rico Wellington, in charge of H. R. Trenholm, is sending three 100-ton lots of iron pyrite to Alabama, Florida, and Ohio acid and fertilizer-works. The ore carries 51% sulphur and 44% iron, and is free from impurities. An immense quantity is available. At a point 2500 ft. from the portal of the Mountain Spring tunnel of the Rico company, and 270 ft. below the Wellington level, a line body of copper ore is being opened.

IDAHO

Burke.—It is reported that the Hercules and Tamarack & Custer mines are to resume operations at an early date. These properties, and the smelter at Northport and Lone Pine-Surprise-Pearl mines at Republic, Washington, are all controlled by Day brothers. The smelter is expected to be blown-in 30 days after the Idaho group resumes. These properties will employ 600 men when in full operation.

Moscow.—The University of Idaho School of Mines Bulletin No. 2, for January 1919, contains detailed statements on tungsten, cinnabar, manganese, molybdenum, and tin deposits of Idaho, by D. C. Livingston, and notes on the antimony deposits, by F. A. Thomson. The examination of these deposits, save those of molybdenum, were undertaken during the summer of 1918. Those interested should secure copies of this useful reference.

Mullan.—Further exploration of the West Hunter claims, between the Morning and Gold Hunter mines, is to be started on May 1. T. B. Cosgrove is in charge for the new owners. The No. 2 tunnel, in 950 ft., is to be extended to cut the vein, estimated to be 150 ft. ahead.

Salmon.—The Pope Shenon Mining Co. is to issue bonds in order to hasten construction of a 50-ton mill. The ore carries copper. A. Boulais is superintendent. Utah capital controls the property.

MISSOURI

Joplin. Production of the Tri-State region last week was as under:

State	Blende, tons	Calamine, tons	Lead, tons	Value
Kansas	1,631	...	544	$97,880
Missouri	1,409	852	285	96,481
Oklahoma	4,576	...	747	223,294
Total	7,616	852	1,576	$417,555
Average per ton...	$39	$26	$60	.....

The stocks on hand have become about normal, 100,000 tons. Sales last week were equal to the present weekly production, which has been greatly curtailed by the mines closing down on account of unsatisfactory prices.

PILING ZINC CONCENTRATE ON THE DUMP, AT A MILL IN OKLAHOMA, SUGGESTING THE ABSENCE OF A FAVORABLE MARKET.

MONTANA

Butte.—The East Butte Copper Co. in 1918 made a profit of $765,469, a little less than in 1915, but compared with $1,021,962 in 1917 and $1,565,768 in 1916. The cost of production was 19.71 cents per pound, a rise of 2.03 cents, but 7.86 cents more than in 1915. There was mined 184,493 tons of 4.25% ore, yielding 24,599,890 lb. of copper, 776,818 oz. of silver, and 1419 oz. of gold.

The Butte & Superior company last year made a profit of $628,348, compared with $2,450,686 in 1917. Ore mined amounted to 462,744. A review of the recent apex suit will appear in the 'Press' at an early date.

Elliston.—The Monarch Mining & Power Co., operating on Bison mountain, in Powell county, 14 miles south of Elliston, has a large tonnage of silver-lead ore. A 200-ton concentrating mill and hydro-electric plant are to be erected as soon as possible. The sawmill on the ground cuts all lumber needed. A 15 drill air-compressor and 150-hp. boilers are in commission. The shipping-point is Elliston. Auto-trucks are to be used in transporting ore and material.

NEVADA

Rochester.—Under the management of Charles Mayer, the Preston & Mayer lease on the Buck & Charley is shipping sulphide ore averaging $67 gold and silver. The ore comes from a deposit opened in a winze 90 ft. below the tunnel. The richer part of the vein is 4 ft. wide. A gasoline hoist was recently erected.

Silver Peak.—The Allied Mining & Milling Co. has been incorporated at Lewiston, Montana, with a capital of $500,000, to develop the old McNamara mine in this district. A. Heinecke of Lewiston is president, D. M. Trepp of Butte vice-president, and E. G. Ivins secretary. The property was discovered in 1875 by Mathew MacNamara, who also located the mine of the same name at Tonopah. Some work has been done to a depth of 175 ft., but a hoist and other machinery are to be put in at once.

Tonopah.—Production of the district last week, including 420 tons from the Tonopah Divide, totaled 7099 tons, valued at $120,683. Some March outputs were as under:

Mines	Tons	Silver, oz.	Gold, oz.	Profit
Belmont	9800	113,571	1080	$58,802
Mining	4915	77,780	665	35,825
Extension	9000	104,975	999	36,190

Virginia City.—Somewhat of a boom has been started here by the finding of $165 silver-gold ore at 2500 ft. from the C. & C. shaft of the Consolidated Virginia. Recent shipments of 407 tons averaged $39.07 per ton, but not from this point.

The Gould and Curry, Savage, and Chollar properties have been consolidated, also a working agreement arranged with the Best and Belcher, so that the four mines will be explored together. H. L. Slosson, Jr., will be in charge. Drilling is to be undertaken below the 1640-ft. level, the depth of the Sutro tunnel. The first drill will start on the property line of the Gould and Curry and Best and Belcher mines. Water has always made exploration costly in the past. All of these mines produced many millions in the early days.

NEW MEXICO

Alamogordo.—The Alamorgordo Shale & Oil Co. is to diamond-drill a 5-in. hole to a depth of 2500 ft., after which the size will be 4 in. J. H. Hogan is in charge.

Pinos Altos.—The Calumet-New Mexico Mining Co.'s new mill is almost ready for work. Thirty-five men are employed in the Langston mine, which is producing a good deal of ore assaying 0.24 oz. gold, 6.94 oz. silver, 1.16% copper, 8.64% lead, and 18.2% zinc. Joseph Hunt is superintendent.

SOUTH DAKOTA

Hill City.—The National Tin Corporation, through J. Robinson-Duff & Co. of New York, has issued a prospectus. The company has leased the property and mill of the American Tin & Tungsten Co. The Cowboy mine has been opened to a depth of 250 ft., and 6000 tons of ore are said to be available in bins. A net return of 1.98% tin was given by assays made by the Denver Engineering Works and Henry E. Wood of Denver. A trial run of the mill yielded 50 tons of 61% concentrate.

TEXAS

Austin.—The Governor, W. P. Hobby, on April 4 vetoed the Dudley mining bill, which applied only to metals. In disapproving this measure, the Governor gave the following as his reasons: "This bill, S. B. No. 186, is disapproved because it limits the compensation allowed the State to $250 per acre for minerals other than oil, coal, gas, and lignite. There are circumstances which may arise that would cause the State to lost heavily. As the result of such a law, if it might be discovered that an acre of the land from which the mineral rights are sold contained a deposit of gold, silver, quicksilver, copper, or other minerals and the same might be taken therefrom over a period of years to the value of $1,000,000, yet when $250 is paid out as royalty, that would be the extent of what the State would receive for the mineral deposit. I am in favor of the purpose of this bill to provide a way for development of the mineral resources of the State's land, and so I will submit the subject to the called session, to the end of accomplishing this and at the same time fully protecting the State."

R. M. Dudley of El Paso, the senator who was responsible for the mining bill, was much surprised at the Governor's action, saying that he had only given an excuse, not a reason, for doing so. "The Governor just went wrong, that's all," said Senator Dudley. "Mining out in west Texas is not like it is in some parts of Arizona and New Mexico. It is a pretty blank prospect. It needs stimulation and encouragement. This bill was the result of hard work by some of the best mining men in the West and was modeled after the United States mining laws. It was passed by an almost unanimous vote, after thorough discussion in both Houses. The Governor seems to be using his own judgment where the representatives of the people were practically unanimous otherwise. I don't think the veto power was intended to be for the individual use of the Governor just because he did not agree with the Legislature, but the veto was to prevent hasty partisan legislation, and not to upset the deliberate and sober wish of the people as expressed through their representatives. He seems to have the deluded idea that the 'hard' metals should have the same laws as oil and gas. Oil and gas pay one-eighth of their gross production as a tax where produced from State lands, but 'hard' metals cannot do that. Such a law will absolutely prohibit the mineral development of west Texas."

Bay City.—The Texas Gulf Sulphur Co., which recently increased its capital from $1,000,000 to $3,000,000, is now operating its third well or shaft, increasing the daily output of raw sulphur to 1600 tons. Other wells are being sunk, and will be connected with the boiler-plant as rapidly as they are finished. The company is constructing storage and shipping facilities at Texas City, and will make that port its ocean shipping-point. It expects to handle not less than 200,000 tons of sulphur per year through Texas City, in addition to rail shipments.

Burkburnett.—The Burk-Waggoner well, 3½ miles west of town, came-in last week with a flow of 2000 bbl. of oil. The oil-sand was picked-up at 1630 ft., yielding oil soon after.

UTAH

Alta.—Rich lead carbonates and sulphides and silver ore has been opened in the Woodlawn mine. Some months ago, at a point 1245 ft. in the main tunnel, high-grade ore was found. This yielded a good deal of ore. Then further exploration opened the new orebody. Henry Gardner is in charge.

Marysvale.—It has been announced officially that the Armour company had purchased the full interest of H. F. Chappell and of the U. S. S. R. & M. Co. in the Mineral Products Corporation. The alunite mine and potash works were closed several weeks ago, but they are to resume within 60 days. C. F. Hagedorn is chief chemist for the Armours, and R. H. Knapp superintendent of the plant here.

Tintic.—Grand Central pays 4 cents per share on April 31. This is equal to $20,000, and makes $1,822,000 to date.

The Greeley M. & M. Co. is to sink a shaft on the old Empire fissure, expected to be found at a depth of 500 ft. Theo Nicholes is manager.

WASHINGTON

Chewelah.—The winze below 1100 ft. in the United Copper mine has reached a depth of 1400 ft. It followed rich silver ore for 70 ft. During March, 100 tons of crude ore and 450 tons of concentrate were sent to smelter.

Loon Lake.—The new concentrator for the Loon Lake

Copper Co. is over 60% complete, according to W. L. Ziegler, who is in charge. A 200-hp. semi-Diesel engine will drive the plant. Ball-mills will reduce the ore for treatment. A six-drill Ingersoll-Rand compressor is ready for the mine.

Nespelem.—Waste dumps left many years ago near this place by miners who could not be bothered with silver while searching for gold, are yielding good returns to the Great Metals Mining & Milling Co. This concern was formed by Big Bend wheat-farmers and old prospectors of Nespelem. A 100-ton mill was constructed last year at the falls on the Nespelem river, three miles from the townsite. Water concentration and flotation is the process, and the dumps treated to date have shown a recovery of 80%. Newly-mined ore has in many cases shown a recovery of 90%. A number of high-grade leases were worked out in the early times, but the bulk of the ore carries from 10 to 20 oz. silver per ton, with some gold and lead.

Seattle.—In Bulletin No. 4 (124 pages and map) of the Engineering Experiment Station of the University of Washington, 'A Summary of Mining in the State of Washington,' has been prepared by A. H. Fisher. The text is really a compilation, but one of much value. Part 1 is a summary of the more important metalliferous resources, together with the factors influencing their development. Part 2 is a list of mining districts, set under their principal economic metal. The other section of the book is in the nature of a bibliography, listing practically everything published concerning mining in the State. A peculiar but important omission, is the entire lack of mention of the great magnesite deposits in Stevens county. The bulletin is edited by Milnor Roberts.

MEXICO

According to the El Paso 'Herald', copies of two proposed mining laws to be submitted to the Mexican national congress when it convenes on May 1 were received at El Paso last week by American mining men having interests in Mexico. Of two bills, published in parallel columns in book form, one was prepared by the Department of Mines of the section of Industry, Commerce and Labor. The other was drafted by a commission appointed by the national congress of industries held at Mexico City last year. The one proposed by the Department is considered even more drastic than the present mining law. If passed, it would make difficult the operation of mining companies by foreigners, as it prohibits foreign companies from owning mining claims within 100 kilometers of the national boundaries, or 50 kilometers from the seacoast. Individual foreigners may own and operate claims within this zone by special permission, but companies are specifically barred unless they become Mexican corporations. The proposed bill also seeks to compel operations or forfeit the claims. In the past it has been possible to hold such claims by paying the pertenencia taxes.

Jalisco

El Favor.—At El Favor and Mololoa mines, the mills have been re-built, and 15 of 35 stamps are dropping. High-grade ore is being sent to smelters. Twenty-two cars had been shipped to the end of March, the last one being settled for $5043 net, expenses of $34.12 per ton deducted. The gross value was $217.38 per ton. Makeever brothers of New York, who control these properties, are sanguine over conditions in Mexico, and are preparing for another plant at their Candelaria mine.

El Oro.—The Mexico Mines of El Oro during the year ended June 30, 1918, made a profit of $1,272,000, and paid $960,000 in dividends. Ore-reserves decreased slightly to 416,200 tons, averaging $11.72 gold and 8.34 oz. silver per ton. The mill treated 121,793 tons, yielding $1,631,373 gold and 945,320 oz. silver.

Guadalajara.—Part of the railway to Chamela was opened last week.

PERSONAL

Note. The Editor invites members of the profession to send particulars of their work and appointments. The information is interesting to our readers.

Ralph W. Perry is at Tonopah.

P. K. Lucke, consulting mining engineer, is now in Mexico City.

Bulkeley Wells has arrived in San Francisco from Colorado.

Edmond N. Skinner has returned from Tonopah to New York.

Lawrence Addicks goes from New York to London on May 17.

Frederick Burbridge, of Wallace, Idaho, has been in Oklahoma.

Hennen Jennings and **W. W. Mein** are on their way to New York.

D'Arcy Weatherbe is at Toronto, he has not yet started for London.

Willet G. Miller sailed last week from New York on his way to London.

W. W. Mein is expected in San Francisco on his return from Nicaragua.

W. C. Ralston has moved from Reno, Nevada, to 25 Broad St., New York.

Joseph L. White is superintendent of the Bluebell mine, at Mayer, Arizona.

Frank H. Probert has returned from Europe to the University of California.

Harry M. Rockwell is with the International Smelting Co., at Tooele, Utah.

John W. Mercer, Major in the American Red Cross, is now at Berne, Switzerland.

W. J. Clifford, recently of the 27th Engineers, has returned to San Francisco.

C. C. Broadwater, now in London, will be returning to San Francisco early in May.

Hugh Rose, manager of the Santa Gertrudis, has returned from London to Mexico City.

G. B. Holderer recently returned to New York from an extended trip through Mexico.

I. J. Colo is making an examination of nitrate deposits near Yale, in Malheur county, Oregon.

Cecil A. Gorelangton, Captain of Engineers, has returned from Camp Humphreys to Pasadena, California.

Preston E. St. Clair Locke, head of the A. S. & R. Exploration Department, at Seattle, was in San Francisco this week.

Howland Bancroft and **B. L. Thane** have formed a partnership as consulting engineers with offices in the Crocker Bdg., San Francisco.

William Beaudry, director and manager of the Stewart Mining Co. and of the Nabob Consolidated Mining Co., at Kellogg, Idaho, has resigned.

J. R. Buchanan has been discharged from the Army as Captain of Engineers, and has resumed his position with the Homestead Iron Dyke Mines Co., at Homestead, Oregon.

C. K. Leith, professor of geology in the University of Wisconsin, has returned from Paris, where he served as mineral adviser to the economic section of the American Peace Commission.

W. B. Devereux, Jr., Major in the Air Service, has returned from overseas and received his discharge. He will resume his work with the firm of Wilkens & Devereux, in New York.

Theodore J. Hoover has been appointed Dean of the Mining Department of Stanford University, to take effect on

October 1. He will organize the department on the basis of graduate study.

George W. Blackinton, Major in the A. E. F., formerly office manager at Denver for the Sullivan Machinery Co., has been awarded the D. S. C. for extraordinary heroism at Xammes, France, on September 12, 1918.

Amor F. Keene has accepted the position as consulting engineer and a member of the New York advisory committee of the Gold Fields American Development Co., which is associated with the Consolidated Gold Fields of South Africa.

Claude Cooper, recently returned from overseas service as Captain in the U. S. Army, has been named as superintendent of the Calumet & Hecla electrolytic plant at Hubbell, Michigan, succeeding J. C. Bryant. Mr. Cooper was formerly assistant-superintendent of the C. & H. smelting-plant.

Obituary

George F. Becker, the veteran physicist and geologist, an officer of the U. S. Geological Survey, died at Washington on April 21. He was born in New York in 1847, the son of a Dane. He graduated successively from Harvard, Heidelberg, and the Royal School of Mines at Berlin. For four years, 1875-'79, he was instructor in mining and metallurgy at the University of California, leaving to join the U. S. Geological Survey. He wrote voluminously and well on many scientific subjects, notably the origin of the South African banket and the quicksilver deposits of the Pacific Coast.

C. S. McKenzie, two weeks ago, established an office with Jay A. Carpenter as mining engineers at Tonopah, Nevada, having charge of three of the new properties at Divide; but immediately after the partnership was formed McKenzie died, on April 18. He was discharged from the Chemical Warfare Service, as divisional gas-training officer at Camp Fremont, in January. Three days after returning to Tonopah he contracted pneumonic-influenza, resulting in his death. His wife died four years ago. He was born at Melones, California, in 1889. For several years he was on the Tonopah Belmont company's engineering staff.

Joseph Estey Johnson, Jr., had already achieved the essentials of a great career when death cut short his activities on April 4, 1919, in the 49th year of his age. He belonged to a family of iron blast-furnace men and mine managers. His father, Major J. E. Johnson, after serving with distinction in the Army of the North, identified himself with the iron mines and blast-furnace at Longdale, Virginia, with which he was connected during almost his entire business life. From him his son obtained not only a thorough training in blast-furnace practice and iron mining, but great personal courage and force of character. His mother, who survives both her husband and sons, possesses rare intellectuality, humor, and a tenderness and human sympathy which those who were privileged to know well J. E. Johnson, Jr., recognized beneath his exterior of aggressiveness and will power. His early education was obtained under a private tutor at Longdale, and this circumstance probably enhanced a natural tendency to independence of character and individuality, which, however, under the control of his straight thinking and clear analysis never allowed him to go far astray. If once he set his mind to a problem, however knotty, he scored a bull's-eye before the subject was dropped. His manner of attacking a subject involved first mastering the details of the available knowledge; then putting this acquired information to one side with an untrammeled mind blazing out a path of his own, so clear, so well-defined, and expressed in such simple terms that he illuminated the whole subject without distorting the original data or discussion. His two books on the iron blast-furnace together form the most comprehensive, the most enlightening, and the most useful treatise on the subject ever produced in any language. But his ability did not end with the mastery and elucidation of principles enunciated by his predecessors. His own discoveries and inventions in the metallurgy of iron have established his reputation. Many stories are told of Esrey Johnson's personal courage; probably the most spectacular is the prevention of an attempted lynching in Virginia in 1908. A young white girl had been murdered by a colored boy under those horrifying circumstances, with accounts of which we are all too familiar. Johnson was not only manager of the mines and the blast-furnace in that locality but was one of the officials of the county. He organized the search whereby the negro was captured, brought to Johnson's office and a confession of the crime wrung from him. The usual crowd collected quickly, thirsting for vengeance in the form of hanging or burning. Practically alone, Johnson held this crowd at bay for several hours, sometimes mixing with the crowd and pledging his honor that the colored boy should be tried and executed according to law, sometimes pleading for the good name of the community, and when necessary, 'showing his teeth' to those who can understand no other argument for the curbing of their personal inclinations or intentions. He has told me that he expressed himself in substantially these words: "I am going to see this nigger hung in accordance with law and order. If you fellows try to prevent me, you may get me, but I will get some of you first." I am sure that at this point in the argument he smiled, for he had an expressive smile which endeared his friends to him, and which he could make very convincing when he desired. Finally, the morning train arrived on the track just outside Johnson's office. He realized that this was the moment when a coup would be attempted, but he had already laid his plans with the sheriff over the long-distance telephone. The train stopped exactly where he had directed. He rushed the trembling culprit by the crowd of angry heavily-armed men into an empty railroad-car occupied only by the sheriff. The door was barricaded behind the three men and the train pulled out before a rush could be accomplished. Another crowd had to be over-awed at the entrance of the county courthouse, where the judge had called a special term of the court. To him Johnson delivered his prisoner and made good his promise that justice should be done. Johnson led a white life. There was no weak spot in his professional or personal armor of honor and sincerity. His home life was unusually happy and congenial. He married Margaret C. Hilles of Wilmington, Delaware; she was not only his friend and comrade, but an intellectual stimulus and helpmate in a busy life. Johnson always identified himself with the public work of his profession and community. He was for many years a member of the principal engineering societies, and especially of the American Society of Mechanical Engineers, the Mining and Metallurgical Society of America, and the American Institute of Mining and Metallurgical Engineers. H. S.

The annual meeting of the American Zinc Institute is to be held at St. Louis on May 12.

The Kansas City club of the American Association of Engineers at its meeting on March 21 elected the following officers: chairman, J. E. Jacoby; vice-chairman, W. B. Cast; secretary, R. N. Clark; and treasurer, S. M. Bate.

The Washington chapter of the American Association of Engineers at its Seattle meeting on March 25 elected the following officers: president, Harry Stevens; first vice-president, A. Y. Hess; second vice-president, Clegge Thomas; secretary, E. L. Howard; and treasurer, O. M. Sutherland.

THE METAL MARKET

METAL PRICES

San Francisco, April 22

Aluminum-dust, cents per pound	40—60
Antimony, cents per pound	8
Copper, electrolytic, cents per pound	15½
Lead, pig, cents per pound	5½—6½
Platinum, per ounce	$100
Quicksilver, per flask of 75 lb	$75
Spelter, cents per pound	8
Zinc-dust, cents per pound	12½

EASTERN METAL MARKET

(By wire from New York)

April 22.—Copper is inactive and easy. Lead is listless though steady. Spelter is dull and lower.

SILVER

Below are given official (not Government) quotations, in cents per ounce, of silver 999 fine. In order to make prompt settlements with smelters and brokers, producers allow a discount from the maximum fixed price of $1.01½, hence the lower price. The Government has not fixed the general market price at $1, but will pay this price (as from April 23, 1918) for all silver purchased by it. The equivalent of dollar silver (1000 fine) in British currency is 46.65 pence per ounce (925 fine), calculated at the normal rate of exchange. On August 15, 1918, the Treasury announced that the maximum price was fixed at $1.01½ per ounce. The British government fixed it maximum at 49½ pence, on September 2, but on November 12 this was changed to 48¾, on December 13 to 48 7/16, and on February 20 to 47¾ pence. On March 25, on account of the low rate of exchange, the London price was adjusted, with a minimum of 95 cents, resulting in daily fluctuations.

Date		New York cents	London pence	Average week ending		Cents	Pence
Apr.	16	101.12	48.94	Mch.	11	101.12	47.75
"	17	101.12	48.94	"	18	101.12	47.76
"	18	101.12	48.94	"	25	101.12	47.75
"	19	101.12	48.94	Apr.	1	101.12	49.63
"	20 Sunday			"	8	101.12	48.86
"	21	101.12	48.94	"	15	101.12	48.85
"	22	101.12	48.94	"	22	101.12	48.94

Monthly averages

	1917	1918	1919		1917	1918	1919
Jan.	75.14	88.72	101.12	July	78.92	99.62	....
Feb.	77.54	85.79	101.12	Aug.	85.40	100.31	....
Mch.	74.13	88.11	101.12	Sept.	100.73	101.12	....
Apr.	72.51	95.35	....	Oct.	87.38	101.12	....
May	74.61	99.50	....	Nov.	85.97	101.12	....
June	76.44	99.50	....	Dec.	85.97	101.12	....

Some silver authorities predict that silver will work higher after May 1, according to the 'Boston News Bureau'. On that date Government control over the metal ceases in the domestic market. At present the Government will not receive the metal for assay unless it is sold to it. After May 1, the Government will either buy metal or return it to producers. This, however, only applies to domestic silver. The embargo has not yet been lifted on shipments abroad.

An official statement was made in the Imperial Legislative Council of India that during the last four years, 1200 millions of rupees (1 rupee = 30 cents) have been drawn from the Mints. This quantity, vast as it is, represents less than one rupee per annum for each inhabitant of that Empire.

The stock of silver at Shanghai on March 8 consisted of 30,600,000 oz. in sycee and 16,800,000 dollars, compared with 30,500,000 oz. in sycee and 15,900,000 dollars on the 1st.

ZINC

Zinc is quoted as spelter, standard Western brands, New York delivery in cents per pound:

Date			Average week ending		
Apr.	16	6.50	Mch.	11	6.55
"	17	6.45	"	18	6.50
"	18	6.40	"	25	6.48
"	19	6.40	Apr.	1	6.53
"	20 Sunday		"	8	6.60
"	21	6.35	"	15	6.57
"	22	6.35	"	22	6.41

Monthly averages

	1917	1918	1919		1917	1918	1919
Jan.	9.75	7.78	7.44	July	8.98	8.72	....
Feb.	10.45	7.97	6.71	Aug.	8.58	8.87	....
Mch.	10.78	7.67	6.53	Sept.	8.33	9.58	....
Apr.	10.20	7.04	....	Oct.	8.32	9.11	....
May	9.41	7.29	....	Nov.	7.76	8.75	....
June	9.63	7.92	....	Dec.	7.84	8.49	....

COPPER

Prices of electrolytic in New York, in cents per pound.

Date			Average week ending		
Apr.	16	15.25	Mch.	11	14.83
"	17	15.25	"	18	14.70
"	18	15.25	"	25	14.09
"	19	15.12	Apr.	1	15.27
"	20 Sunday		"	8	15.25
"	21	15.12	"	15	15.33
"	22	15.12	"	22	15.18

Monthly averages

	1917	1918	1919		1917	1918	1919
Jan.	29.53	23.50	20.43	July	29.67	26.00	....
Feb.	34.57	23.50	17.34	Aug.	27.42	26.00	....
Mch.	36.00	23.50	15.05	Sept.	25.11	26.00	....
Apr.	33.16	23.50	....	Oct.	23.50	26.00	....
May	31.69	23.50	....	Nov.	23.50	26.00	....
June	32.57	23.50	....	Dec.	23.50	26.00	....

Copper production of the United States has been curtailed by 163,000,000 lb. per year by the complete shut-downs and over 200,000,000 by the general reduction.

Copper output of the A. S. & R. refinery in New Jersey is 70,000,000 lb. monthly at present.

LEAD

Lead is quoted in cents per pound, New York delivery.

Date			Average week ending		
Apr.	16	4.95	Mch.	11	5.25
"	17	4.95	"	18	5.25
"	18	4.95	"	25	5.21
"	19	4.95	Apr.	1	5.25
"	20 Sunday		"	8	5.25
"	21	4.90	"	15	5.07
"	22	4.90	"	22	4.93

Monthly averages

	1917	1918	1919		1917	1918	1919
Jan.	7.64	6.85	5.60	July	10.93	8.03	....
Feb.	9.10	7.07	5.13	Aug.	10.75	8.05	....
Mch.	10.07	7.26	5.24	Sept.	9.07	8.05	....
Apr.	9.38	6.99	....	Oct.	6.97	8.05	....
May	10.29	6.88	....	Nov.	6.38	8.05	....
June	11.74	7.58	....	Dec.	6.49	6.90	....

TIN

Prices in New York, in cents per pound. The monthly averages in 1918 are nominal. On December 3 the War Industries Board fixed the price to consumers and jobbers at 72½c. f.o.b. Chicago and Eastern points, and 71¼c. on the Pacific Coast. This will continue until the U. S. Steel Products Co.'s stock is consumed.

Monthly averages

	1917	1918	1919		1917	1918	1919
Jan.	44.10	85.13	71.50	July	62.60	93.00	....
Feb.	51.47	85.00	72.44	Aug.	62.53	91.33	....
Mch.	54.27	85.00	72.50	Sept.	61.54	80.40	....
Apr.	55.63	88.53	....	Oct.	62.24	78.82	....
May	63.21	100.01	....	Nov.	74.18	73.67	....
June	61.93	91.00	....	Dec.	85.00	71.52	....

QUICKSILVER

The primary market for quicksilver is San Francisco, California being the largest producer. The price is fixed in the open market, according to quantity. Prices, in dollars per flask of 75 pounds:

Date					
Mch.	25	68.00	Apr.	8	67.50
Apr.	1	68.00	"	15	75.00
			"	22	75.00

Monthly averages

	1917	1918	1919		1917	1918	1919
Jan.	81.00	128.08	103.75	July	102.00	120.00	....
Feb.	126.25	118.00	90.00	Aug.	115.00	120.00	....
Mch.	113.75	112.00	72.80	Sept.	112.00	120.00	....
Apr.	114.50	115.00	....	Oct.	102.00	120.00	....
May	104.00	110.00	....	Nov.	102.50	120.00	....
June	85.50	112.00	....	Dec.	117.42	115.00	....

Tungsten. An improvement in sentiment and in business done in the last week is reported. As high as $8 per unit is said to have been paid for concentrates. High-grade scheelite is obtainable at $10 per unit. One dealer states that tungsten metal has sold at $1.50 per lb. Another dealer says that unless he wanted ferro-tungsten badly he would not offer as much as $1.25 per lb. of contained tungsten.

The United States Steel Corporation during 1918 reported the following production: iron ore mined, 28,332,939 tons; limestone quarried, 5,141,365 tons; coal mined, 31,748,136 tons; coke made, 17,757,630 tons (by-product coke 43%); pig-iron and ferro-alloys, 15,940,954 tons; steel ingots, 19,583,493 tons; rolled and other finished products, 13,849,483 tons; spelter, 41,715 tons; sulphate of iron, 42,321 tons; fertilizer, 12,022 tons; and cement, 7,287,000 barrels.

Eastern Metal Market

New York, April 16.

A decidedly easier tone has developed in nearly all of the metals as the week progressed, resulting in lower prices.

Antimony has not changed.

Copper demand has decreased decidedly, but prices have not fallen much, and are fairly firm at slightly lower levels.

Lead has been reduced, with little increase in demand as a result.

Tin is still stagnant and under control.

Zinc is inactive, and prices have eased off on light demand.

ANTIMONY

The market is unchanged and is fairly firm at 6.62½ to 6.75c. per lb., New York, duty paid, for Asiatic grades.

ALUMINUM

Quotations are nominally unchanged at 29 to 31c., New York, for No. 1 virgin metal, 98 to 99% pure, with about 2c. per lb. less for re-melt metal of the same analysis.

COPPER

The market has turned quiet, and the demand and buying in evidence a few weeks ago has largely disappeared. This is attributed almost entirely to the probability that consumers have provided for their immediate wants, which could not be very large or expansive as to the future under present conditions. The market is fairly firm, however, and the drop in quotations has been small and mostly by small interests so far. Electrolytic copper is quoted at 15.25c., New York, for early delivery, with Lake at 15.50c., a decline in the week of only ¼c. The export situation is unchanged. There is some demand, mostly from England, with a little from neutral countries, mostly Scandanavian. A report is current that the British government plans to sell its copper at the market-price, and will thus be in a position to undersell any new offerings. British stocks of copper on April 1 are reported as 48,702 long tons, a slight decline from those a month before.

LEAD

The American Smelting & Refining Co. reduced its price for lead from 5.25 to 5c., New York, or 4.75c., St. Louis, on April 9, much to the surprise of the rest of the trade. It was entirely unexpected, because conditions were not regarded as bad, and it is believed that production cannot thrive at a price below 5c. The 5.25c. price was therefore considered as justified and sound. The real cause for the decline seems to have been the Mexican output, and the inability of its absorption by foreign interests, particularly the British. Mexican lead could be delivered at American ports, duty paid, in competition with the American product. Business in general has been small, and the reduction has not brought out purchasers. On Monday there was a substantial inquiry for future delivery, but sellers are not eager to negotiate this position. Yesterday, Tuesday, there was good inquiry, involving 500 tons, for prompt delivery. British Government stocks on April 1 were 96,456 tons, an increase of nearly 100% over those on hand at the middle of December. The outside American market is 4.95c., New York, or 4.75c., St. Louis.

IRON AND STEEL

Steel producers are booking but little new business, and do not seem worried about the future course of prices while they await the outcome of the price muddle at Washington as to Government aid to resumption in buying of steel. The scale of operations is gradually declining, with the U. S. Steel Corporation's plants in the Chicago district working at less than 74% capacity, against 80% a week ago. Most of the independent companies of the country are operating at 40 to 45% of capacity. Foreign trade in steel is insignificant, but prospects for locomotive orders are good, with every industrial country short of motive power. American rails for export are now quoted at $55 to $57 per ton, against $45 to $47 for domestic consumers. Pig-iron sellers, especially those making basic iron, see little prospect of an active market for several months. Revised figures of the 1918 steel ingot output makes the total 815,000 tons larger than earlier estimated, or 43,027,000 tons.

TIN

The market continues stagnant and devoid of interest from a market point of view. There is but one price, and that is the controlled one of 72.50c, New York. With American tin out of the market, there is nothing left but the allocated metal, all of which is said to have reached this country. An evidence of this is that there have been no arrivals at Atlantic or Pacific ports so far in April. The absorbing topic is the date on which a free open market will again prevail. As to this there are all sorts of guesses. Some give the date as May 1, others at June 1, and still others at July 1; while there is also a small number who contend that it will be months before import restrictions are removed. The majority of those best informed or qualified to express an opinion hold to June 1 as the probable date. It ought to be not later than this, they argue, so that the gap between the possible arrival of tin from the Far East and the absorption of the allocated metal may be as small as possible and thus prevent a wild or excited market. There are already offers of metal for shipment from the East as soon as restrictions are lifted. The London quotation yesterday for spot Straits was £223 per ton.

ZINC

The market has turned weak, due largely to a decided lack of demand from all classes of consumers, and to some pressure to sell by a few producers or dealers. Prime Western for early delivery is quoted at 6.15c., St. Louis, or 6.50c., New York, with the probability that this would be shaded to 6.10 to 6c., St. Louis. The uncertainty in the steel market, particularly as to prices for sheet-bars, is one cause of lack of demand from the galvanizers. Zinc stocks in Great Britain in the hands of the Government on April 1 were 27,676 tons of ordinary grades and 10,371 tons of high-grade metal.

ORES

Ferro-silicon: The 50% alloy is obtainable at $90 per ton, delivered, on contract or spot requirements. A 15%, guaranteed 14 to 16%, electric ferro is obtainable for $55 per ton, delivered. The maker of this alloy also offers a silico-manganese of 20 to 25% silicon and 50% manganese, low in carbon and phosphorus.

Manganese: Indian manganese ore is offered at 55c. per unit at the Atlantic seaboard, the lowest price in many months. No sales are reported yet.

Manganese-Iron Alloys: Domestic 80% ferro has sold as low as $110 per ton, delivered, but it was re-sale material. Producers continue to quote $150 delivered for 78 to 82% alloy, less $2 per unit under 78%. Spiegel is quoted at $40 to $45, delivered, depending on quantity and analysis. Business is very light in either alloy.

Molybdenum: The market is lifeless, with quotations nominally unchanged at 80 to 85c. per pound.

Company Reports

HECLA MINING CO.

Property: mine and mill at Burke, Idaho.

Operating Official: J. F. McCarthy, general manager

Financial Statement: the income in 1918 was $4,035,339, of which $2,054,717 was profit, taxes, etc., deducted. The surplus is $2,943,962.

Dividends: these amounted to $350,000, compared with $1,600,000 in 1917. The total to March 1919 is $7,405,000.

Development: new work covered 13,566 ft. The shaft was sunk to 2000 ft., station cut, and driving toward the ore started. Reserves are 1,180,058 tons in the Hecla, and 404,057 tons in the Ore-Or-No-Go.

Production: a comparison with previous years follows:

	1918	1917	1916	1915
Ore shipped, tons	379,703	374,213	250,559	146,675
Ore milled, tons..........	326,809	328,096	210,727	120,461
Lead, per cent	18.55	18.77	19.25	17.55
Silver, ounces	30.06	30.06	29.30	26.40
Zinc, per cent	4.50	7.65	....	....
Lead, pounds	51,635,676	44,363,559	40,217,573	24,917,807
Silver, ounces	1,590,062	1,366,960	1,195,841	692,444
Zinc, pounds	133,341	507,888	....	....

YUKON GOLD CO.

Property: gold-bearing gravels, dredges, hydraulicking plant, ditches, and power-plants in Alaska, California, Idaho, and the Klondike.

Financial Statement: the revenue in 1918 was $2,283,862. Working costs were $1,980,117, leaving an operating gain of $303,745. After paying royalty, interest, and general charges, the profit was $45,899. Depletion and depreciation totaled $921,420, so the year ended in a deficit of $875,521. Assets include $409,362 for supplies, $1,863,990 advances to Eikoro Mines Co. in Nevada, $259,525 for accounts collectable, $204,653 for bullion in transit, $938,630 cash, and $249,000 in U. S. Liberty and Canadian Victory bonds. Liabilities include $195,877 for accounts payable, and $5,000,000 to the Yukon-Alaska Trust. The excess of assets over liabilities, including all items, is $4,255,576. Note No. 2 for $625,000, due the Trust, due on February 1, 1918, was eventually extended to February 1, 1926. Note No. 3, of like amount, was liquidated.

Production: details will be given in another issue of this journal. In 1918, the dredges and other plant recovered gold worth $2,283,862.

JUDGE MINING & SMELTING CO.

Property: mine, mill, and electrolytic zinc plant at Park City, Utah.

Operating Officials: G. W. Lambourne, general manager; O. N. Friendly, general superintendent; J. T. Ellsworth, zinc plant superintendent.

Financial Statement: the revenue in 1918 totaled $1,090,342, plus the previous balance of $133,840. All expenditures were $912,002, and after paying dividends the balance remaining was $72,180.

Dividends: four—No. 31-34—absorbed $240,000, making $2,310,000 to the end of 1918.

Development: the year was a trying one for the mine, on account of abnormal conditions, and only half of the orebodies were worked, and these in the dry areas. If operations had been normal the output could have been doubled. On three veins on four levels—900 to 1400 ft.—there was 5761 ft. of work done.

Production: crude ore sold amounted to 9633 tons, and ore milled 40,622 tons. Metal production was 490 oz. gold, 508,434 oz. silver, 7,931,566 lb. lead, and 371,036 lb. copper, also 1310 tons of 99.9% spelter. These sold for $1,061,642, making $9,337,660 to date. There was on hand or in transit at the end of the year, 801 tons of high-grade spelter, 1000 tons of zinc concentrate, and 1200 tons of residue.

SILVER KING CONSOLIDATED MINING CO. OF UTAH

Property: mines and mills at Park City, Utah.

Operating Officials: Solon Spiro, general manager; H. A. Lee, assistant.

Financial Statement: the balance on January 1, 1918, was $239,086, and receipts during 1918, $570,241, (including $266,265 from sales of shares), making a total of $809,327. All disbursements were $762,619, leaving a balance of $46,708 for 1919.

Dividends: No. 19 absorbed $70,000, making $1,562,705 since 1913.

Development: the principal interest at the property lies in driving the Spiro tunnel, which was advanced 4001 ft last year, to a point 9001 ft. from the entrance. Most of the distance was in Woodside shale, but in October this formation gave place to limestone, alternating with bands of shale. The tunnel will eliminate shaft-sinking, hoisting, water troubles, and the surface transportation of ore and supplies.

Production: the California-Comstock mill was remodeled, and by December was at capacity of 150 tons daily. Crude ore sold—4032 tons—assayed 0.037 oz. gold, 38.63 oz silver, 22.10% lead, and 1.04% copper, worth $49.45 per ton. Concentrate—869 tons—contained 0.059 oz. gold, 58.23 oz. silver, 37.45% lead, and 1.35% copper, worth $88.14 per ton. Total sales were $275,971.

VINDICATOR CONSOLIDATED GOLD MINING CO.

Property: gold mines and works at Cripple Creek, Colorado; chrome mine in Wyoming, and ferro-chrome reduction plant in Colorado.

Operating Officials: G. A. Stahl, general manager; W. E. Ryan, general superintendent; S. B. Tyler, metallurgist at ferro-chrome plant.

Financial Statement: ore sales, lessees' royalties, and sundries during 1918 totaled $1,175,471. The operating profit was $538,951. Current assets total $574,928, and liabilities $32,724, giving a net working capital of $542,203. There was spent on a chrome mine in Wyoming $45,671, and in purchase of the Ferro Alloy Co.'s works in Colorado $68,897.

Dividends: two absorbed $60,000, making $3,772,500 to the end of 1918.

Development: new work in the Vindicator and Golden Cycle mines totaled 5113 ft., of which 2899 ft. was by lessees. Total openings are 50 miles. On No. 20 of the Golden Cycle, 4240 ft. has exposed no commercial ore, so work was discontinued. As it was only possible to do a moderate amount of development in the mines, reserves were greatly depleted, the total now being 104,230 tons.

Production: 230,304 tons of crude ore was hoisted, on company account, producing 21,392 tons of shipping ore valued at $1,166,295; and 53,463 tons of lessees' ore, yielding 24,320 tons, worth $463,514, making a total of $1,629,809. Further reference to development, flotation, and chrome will be found in other issues of this journal.

ARIZONA COMMERCIAL MINING CO.

Property: mine at Globe, Arizona.

Operating Official: R. R. Boyd, mine superintendent.

Financial Statement: during 1918 the operating profit was $270,158, less $156,912 for depletion, leaving $113,246. In 1917 the net total was $464,751.

Dividends: the total was $262,000.

Development: new work covered 6729 ft., nearly double that of 1917. Results in the east end of the mine were so favorable that a new shaft is being sunk and is now down over 240 ft. The upper portion has been concreted. On No. 15 level—the lowest developed—west of the fault a vein of more than normal width and value than ore in the eastern section of the mine, has been opened. Water pumped totaled 311,000,000 gal., a decrease of 56,000,000 gal. The maximum flow on November 1 was 1,202,500 gal., and minimum on October 13 was 692,500 gal. The apex litigation with the Iron Cap Copper Co. has already been referred to in this journal.

Production: the last two years compare as under:

	1918		1917	
		Copper		Copper
	Tons	%	Tons	%
Smelting ore	11,712	10.26	12.686	9.64
Concentrating ore	51,052	4.86	27,015	4.52

The totals were 62,796 tons of 5.8% and 39,702 tons of 6.15%.

Concentrating ore goes to the Old Dominion mill.

UTAH CONSOLIDATED MINING CO.

Property: mines at Bingham, Utah.

Operating Official: Fred Cowans, manager; A. S. Winther, mine superintendent.

Financial Statement: sales of metal in 1918 realized $3,067,919. Deducting all charges, and adding sundry receipts, the profit was $252,764. Litigation with the Utah Metal and Utah Apex companies cost $101,155. The former trouble has been settled. Current assets total $2,130,981, and liabilities $317,213.

Dividends: $450,000, making over $12,700,000 to date.

Development: new work covered 21,067 ft. The most important exploration was in opening 1400, 1500, and 1600-ft. levels off a vertical winze from 1300 ft. The copper orebodies improved in metal content as follows from 1200 to 1600 ft., inclusive: 1.90%, 2.30%, 2.36%, 2.37%, and 2.65%. These shoots are in limestone. The lead shoots at 1400 and 1500 ft. are maintaining their width and value. Reserves consist of 277,939 tons of 2.33% copper, 0.78 oz. silver, and 0.048 oz. gold ore; 29,591 tons of 15.93% lead, 5.23 oz. silver, 0.058 oz. gold, and 0.8% copper ore, an increase; and 526,000 tons of 1.63% copper, 0.55 oz. silver, and 0.042 oz. gold ore. Flotation tests are being made on the last class of ore. The Yampa mine was purchased for $100,000, and is developing satisfactorily. An option is held on the Utah Lead & Copper Co.'s claims.

Production: shipments to the International smelter at Tooele were 221,651 tons of copper and 31,725 tons of lead ores, yielding 8,476,197 lb. of copper, 7.812.653 lb. lead, 306.152 oz. silver, and 13,307 oz. of gold.

CONSOLIDATED INTERSTATE-CALLAHAN MINING CO.

Property: mines and mill at Interstate, Coeur d'Alene region, Idaho.

Operating Official: C. W. Newton, mine manager; L. J. Fogle, mill superintendent.

Financial Statement: the income in 1918 amounted to $1,228,616. Operations cost $936,678, leaving a profit of $291,938, less $31,650 for construction, etc. After paying dividends, the surplus of $556,992 at the end of 1917 was reduced to $254,552 by January 1919. For a greater part of 1918, operations were on half capacity.

Dividends: one of 50 and one of 75 cents per share, amounting to $456,222, were paid, making $6,966,082 since April 1915.

Development: new work amounted to 5389 ft., also 20,000 cu. ft. of station and skip-chutes. The three-compartment shaft was sunk to No. 9 level, a total depth of 1100 ft. below No. 4 level, the main working-tunnel. Development at this depth added considerably to the resources of the mine, proving that the lower levels maintain high-grade zinc-sulphide ore. The mine is in splendid condition for future heavy production. In the mine is 293,000 tons of ore of average grade, and on dump is 125,000 of 10% zinc tailing.

Production: this may be summarized as under:

Ore mined, tons	85,363
Crude ore shipped, tons (48.3% zinc, 3.46% lead)	2,757
Crude ore shipped, tons (54.7% lead, 19.91 oz. silver)	1,634
Ore concentrated, tons (6.51% lead, 19.64% zinc, 2.21 oz. silver)	69,002
Tailing concentrated, tons (2.11% lead, 11.02% 0.86 oz. silver)	84,065
Contents of all products:	
Zinc, pounds	40,891,881
Lead, pounds	12,098,429
Silver, ounces	202,850

The gross value, as sold to smelters, was $1,866,444, compared with $5,153,398 in 1918. The Graselli Chemical Co. takes the zinc until June 1, 1919; and the Ohio & Colorado S. & R. Co. at Salida takes the lead-silver ore until 1920.

NORTH STAR MINES CO.

Property: mines and mills in Grass Valley district, California.

Operating Officials: A. B. Foote, superintendent; R. H. Bedford, in charge of North Star mine; R. E. Tremoureux, in charge of Champion mine, Nevada City.

Financial Statement: gold realized $1,046,797 during 1918, and adding the previous balance of $989,408, plus sundries, there was available $2,072,536. Operations cost $989,128, and improvements, etc., $32,759. After paying two dividends the balance carried to 1919 was $950,648. This sum consists of cash, $127,352; investments, $671,430; bills receivable, $61,000; and supplies, $80,866.

Dividends: No. 54 and 55, equal to 4%, absorbed $100,000, making $5,437,040 since 1884.

Development: North Star mine—the 3400, 4000, 4400, 4700, and 5000-ft. levels produced most of the ore. The yield was $3.64 per ton less than in 1917, due to unfavorable conditions, and the poorer and less uniform quality below 4000 ft. Bunches of rich ore are noticeably absent. No development was done between March and September. A re-estimate of reserves reduces the positive ore by 100,000 tons, making them equal to two or three years for the mill. Prospects for additional ore, both on and above 4000 ft. and at the bottom of the mine—6300 ft. are very favorable. The X vein at 6300 ft. has been opened for 1000 ft. It is rather irregular in value, and difficult to separate from waste. The outlook for 1919 is considered encouraging.

Champion mines—for the first time this property gave a profit amounting to $8000. Nearly all of the ore came from the 2400 to 2700-ft. levels of the Providence mine. Apart from the 2700-ft. orebody, which is developing favorably, exploration revealed nothing of value, and the outlook is not promising. The Champion venture has been disappointing.

Production and Cost:

	North Star	Champion
Ore mined, tons	130,445	41,300
Waste discarded, per cent	7.6	.....
Ore treated, tons	99,550	41,300
Value per ton	$7.79	$6.56
Extraction, per cent	94	.....
Cost per ton mined	$7.29	.....

The cost of development was only 9 cents per ton, against 65 cents in 1917; so if the equivalent had been spent in 1918 the total cost would have been $7.85 per ton, compared with $7.19 in 1917, $5.43 in 1914, and $5.20 in 1913.

Book Reviews

Making the Small Shop Profitable. By John H. Van Deventer. Pp. 110, ill., index. The McGraw-Hill Book Co., Inc., New York. For sale by 'Mining and Scientific Press'. Price, $1.75.

This book comprises articles and other material from 'The American Machinist'. Machine-shop practice and allied subjects from pattern-making to painting the completed device are discussed, with particular reference to the small shop. About half the book is devoted to sketches of various 'shop kinks'.

Metal Statistics, 1919. Compiled by C. S. J. Trench and B. E. U. Luty. Pp. 384. American Metal Market Co., New York, 1919. For sale by 'Mining and Scientific Press'. Price, 50 cents.

This is one of the most useful of our desk references, especially as prices and production of metals are given for many years. The publishers of this annual issue what they term the 'steel and metal trio'—the 'American Metal Market', daily; the 'Steel and Metal Digest', monthly; and 'Metal Statistics', yearly. Any one wishing to learn anything about any of the metals will find it in this work, also a long list of manufacturers and dealers.

Oil, Paint and Drug Reporter Year-Book, 1918. Pp. 321, charts. May be obtained from Oil, Paint and Drug Reporter, Inc., 100 William street, New York.

Among our valued weekly contemporaries is the 'Reporter', published by the above firm. In it is given an immense amount of information on the state of the chemical, oil, and mineral markets, our only adverse comment being the alternation of reading matter with advertisements. The Year-Book is an all-the-year encyclopedia for desk use, from which we will abstract from time to time, and also keep right at hand. The comparison of prices from 1914 to 1919 is of great value; so is the matter on trade, patents, dye-stuffs, drugs, fertilizers, oils, paints, and the like. The editors' names are not given, which is rather an oversight.

Physics and Chemistry of Mining and Mine Ventilation. Second edition, revised and enlarged. By J. J. Walsh. Pp. 219, ill., index. D. Van Nostrand Co., New York, 1918. For sale by 'Mining and Scientific Press'. Price, $2.

The author is mines inspector at Wilkes-Barre, one of the coal centres of Pennsylvania, and this book is intended to be a practical handbook for vocational schools, and for those qualifying for mine foreman and mine-inspector certificates. We recently published some data on ventilation in the mines of the Coeur d'Alene, Idaho, and at the United Verde Extension mine in Arizona, so this subject is of much interest. Metal-mining companies will find herein much of value. The fundamental laws of matter, motion, liquids, heat, and gases, including one on the barometer, occupy the first ten chapters. No. XI, on the sampling and analysis of mine gases, is new matter. It includes the preparation of re-agents and description of apparatus. Sixty-four pages are devoted to mine-ventilation problems, which discuss air pressure, gages, friction, air-currents, fans, shafts, doors, and regulators. In view of the recent fire at the Argonaut mine in California, the chapter on mine fires is apropos and instructive. Air consists of 20.93% O and 79.04% N, plus 0.03% CO_2, and after a fire is sealed it will burn brightly until it has consumed 3 to 4% O, after which the flame diminishes, finally dying away when the O has fallen to 13%; then a smoldering fire exists, as is the case in several American metal mines today. After each chapter in this book are a number of questions and answers, and all the problems discussed are worked out in detail, leaving nothing to be understood. Mr. Walsh's presentation of the subject is well worth-while.

Mineral Deposits of South America. By H. L. Miller and J. T. Singewald. P. 589, ill., maps, index. McGraw-Hill Book Co., New York, 1919. For sale by 'Mining and Scientific Press'. Price, $5.

Most Americans, even mining men, when asked about the mineral deposits of the southern continent, show only a vague idea of that country, in spite of the fact that there are numbers of great copper, gold, iron, manganese, and nitrate properties in full production. The authors of this

much-wanted work made an extended trip through Bolivia, Brazil, Chile, and Peru, also rapid trips through some of the other republics, during 1915. In the 'Bulletin' of the Pan-American Union and our New York contemporary they published their observations. Additional to their own studies, the authors have been aided largely by many government departments, mining companies, and individuals in order to bring the subject-matter up to date. In the first chapter is a review of the economic geology of South America, in which it is said that the continent possesses both varied and rich deposits, and the mineral industry has not reached the state of development of that of Europe and the United States. Inadequate means of transportation, lack of exact information, and lack of capital are the causes that have hindered exploitation. Then follow 11 chapters covering a résumé of mineral production, topographic and geologic features, distribution of deposits, and details of each class of ore worked, in Argentina, Bolivia, Brazil, Chile, Colombia, Ecuador, the Guianas, Paraguay, Peru, Uruguay, and Venezuela. Each chapter has a small map showing positions of the mining districts, and each has a complete bibliography, Chile having 219 and Peru 218 references. It is impossible to review this complete work as it should be, but suffice it to say that the lack of knowledge of South America should be remedied thereby.

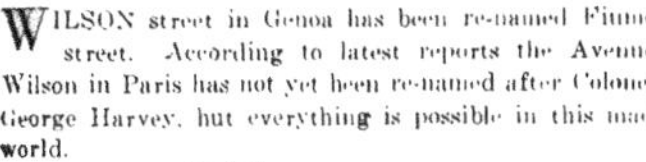

WILSON street in Genoa has been re-named Fiume street. According to latest reports the Avenue Wilson in Paris has not yet been re-named after Colonel George Harvey, but everything is possible in this mad world.

SO, the Germans have arrived in Paris at last! They expected to be there in September 1914 and they are there in April 1919; they expected to arrive as conquering heroes; they come now to ratify an abject surrender. Against the triumphal entry into Paris of which they vaingloriously dreamed, they can set the cowardly procession of their great warships into the Scapa Flow.

ESTIMATES of the cost of producing copper are the product not only of arithmetic but of emotion; they are largely subjective and vary with the feelings of those responsible for making them. According to the 'Boston News Bureau', officials of copper-mining companies consider 15½ cents per pound a correct average today; but this represents the direct operating expense, to which must be added allowances for the depletion of orebodies and the burden of taxation, which, with depreciation, bring the total cost, it is said, close to 20 cents per pound.

GREAT COBAR shares, says the 'Financial Times' of London, "curled up" recently, collapsing from the equivalent of a dollar to the "nimble bob", which we call "two bits", the price of a good cigar. A few years ago they stood at $22. Thus ends one of the worst fiascos in British mining enterprise, and one involving the reputations of several honorable engineers, whose names we forbear to mention. Irresponsible finance and reckless share-dealing were the undoing of this mining venture, which might have made profit and reputation for all concerned, but which now leaves a soiled page in the records of mineral exploitation. The mine was over-estimated and over-capitalized from the very beginning; it was burdened with excessive promotion profits and started with an entirely inadequate working capital. All these handicaps were caused by mixing engineering with financial participation, corrupting the judgment and undermining the conscience of men from whom an unbiased opinion and a trustworthy management were expected. The various efforts to put the mine on its feet and to establish a profitable production of copper during the last five or six years have been farcical, largely because the chairman and directors were without first-hand experience in mining and were embarrassed by undue attention to the share-market. Great Cobar's story is a sad warning to the British public against mixing promotion with engineering and management with share speculation.

IF denunciation, satire, and contempt could drive a Government official back into private life, then the Postmaster General would cable his resignation to the President. Mr. Burleson has been called many bad names and has awakened the hearty dislike of many kinds of people. He has shown himself narrow, vindictive, and intolerant. It seems a pity sometimes that cabinet ministers at Washington are not accountable to Congress, because by such accounting they could be compelled to defend or explain their official acts. Mr. Burleson has challenged the publishers to make good their attacks upon his administration. They will. We shall be disappointed if he is still a member of the President's cabinet when Mr. Wilson's term expires. As Mr. Samuel Gompers says, "he must walk the plank sooner or later." Let us hope that it will be sooner.

COMPARING the markets for steel and for copper, it has been noted that whereas the price of steel during the War advanced 233% as compared with the preceding decade, that of copper gained only 127%; again, when our Government fixed prices, steel retained an advance of 111%, while copper kept only 69%; it is noteworthy also that current quotations show a drop of only 14% from the former 'fixed' price of steel, as against a drop of 42% from the copper peg; finally, that the present price of copper is 2% below the pre-war quotation, whereas that of steel is 80% above the peace normal. All of this argues that copper is unduly depressed. However, it is to be remembered that much of the buying of copper before the War, especially the purchases made by Germany, was stimulated by the expectation of hostilities. In 1913 the United States exported 826,441,000 pounds, of which 307,151,000 pounds went to Germany. Exportation was checked by the War until the Allies began to clamor for the metal at the close of 1916. In January 1917 exports totaled 51,322 long tons and during that year exportation reached its maximum, of 493,156 tons, equivalent to 1,104,893,240 pounds. By December 1918 exports had declined to 19,379 tons, and in March this year to 9735 tons only. Europe used to take 40% of our production: that 40% now would be equivalent to about as much as our entire exportation of the metal in 1913. Europe is in greater need of copper than in the year preceding the War, and would import it if only industrial equilibrium were re-established across the Atlantic. The copper market waits on the declaration of peace.

AN official statement shows that on November 11, 1918—the day of the Armistice—the various belligerents had mobilized strengths as follows: Great Britain 5,680,000, France 5,075,000, United States 3,707,000, Italy 3,420,000, making a grand total of 17,882,000 in the Allied armies. On the other side Germany had 4,500,000, Austria-Hungary 2,230,000, Bulgaria 500,000, and Turkey 400,000, making 7,630,000. The figures for our enemies, except Germany, represent conditions at the end of October, for soon after that the process of demobilization and dispersion had begun in Austria, Bulgaria, and Turkey. The British total includes the Indian army and garrisons abroad not available for fighting the enemy. By February the Allied forces had been diminished, by demobilization, to a grand total of 13,360,000, whereas the Enemy forces had dwindled to 1,125,000, of whom 820,000 were in Germany.

IN order to give its readers a story about the Tonopah mining boom, the 'Examiner' sent Mr. Peter Clark MacFarlane into Nevada, and last Sunday it published a sophomoric article on the subject. Mr. MacFarlane is, we are told, "a war correspondent and trained observer." He may be all that, but whatever he may know about war, his geology is like "the Kingdom of Heaven, which cometh not by observation." He saw "a big fault-fissure which shows itself plainly on the surface, towering 40 ft. into the air." A fault or a fissure or the combination of the two that can "tower into the air" is a phenomenon beyond the ken of the oldest prospector. It reminds us of the mine manager in Australia who wrote to his company that the ore-shoot was looking well and all that was needed was a winze on the bottom level, whereupon the secretary of the company cabled to him authorizing him to procure a first-class winze without delay! Mr. MacFarlane has been informed that the ore in the Divide mine is estimated to be worth $5,000,000, whereupon he proceeds to tell us that it is "the greatest defined orebody of silver-bearing character since the days of the Consolidated Virginia." Shades of Broken Hill and Leadville, of Huanchaca and Nipissing! has no silver bonanza been uncovered since the days of the Comstock boom, 40 years ago, or have we been dreaming? In behalf of the wild-cats clustering around the Divide mine, he suggests that one point in their favor is that "they are all located within one or two miles of what is proven to be a great mine." Somebody ought to tell him that a mile from a bonanza is about as near to wealth as a drive into a bunker is to winning the hole. It can be done, but it is rarely done. The second point in their favor is analogy with Tonopah and Goldfield, both of which, according to him, but contrary to our recollection, had only a single successful strike "at first," meaning presumably during the first year or two, for the Divide orebody was cut a year and a half ago. The analogies suggested by a war correspondent are not likely to be safe guides for those who speculate in mines. In short, the 'Examiner' is as trustworthy as usual.

Finish the Job

The American people has participated, honorably and successfully, in a stupendous task, namely, the defence of the world against an onslaught of savagery, the restoration of civilization, and the assertion of the ideals underlying democracy. We met the Prussian threat by raising three and a half millions of soldiers and by subscribing 18½ billions of dollars in four Liberty loans; our soldiers and sailors did their duty so effectively that the War was brought to a victorious end many months earlier than we had hoped; but our work is not yet finished and it behooves us to see that it is finished properly. We owe a debt to those who died for us on land and sea, not only our own fighters but those of our Allies, whom we continue to assist by money and in other ways. A fifth Liberty loan is offered for popular subscription, it is for four and a half billion dollars, in four-year notes bearing 4¾%. The opportunity to subscribe expires on May 10. It is the duty of every citizen, more particularly those unable on account of age or other disability to serve in the Army or Navy, to subscribe his quota, that is, the largest sum within his means. No more advantageous use of money is possible; the loan is safe and it offers a high rate of interest; as a short-time investment the market can offer nothing better. It is called the Victory loan because it is to be used to set the seal on the work done by our victorious Army in comradeship with the victorious armies of England, France, Belgium, and Italy. They have done their share toward winning the great War of Liberation; it is for us to discharge the debt incurred in that effort. After a battle there is much 'mopping up' to be done, says the returned soldier. There are machine-gun nests to be bombed, there are stray units to be captured, there are wounded to be gathered and removed, there are munitions to be collected, and so forth. This is a 'mopping up' loan; the money is needed to clean up our accounts and finish the job. We still have two million men under arms, and we still have to bring them home; moreover, there is the subsidy on wheat, one of our most onerous obligations, still to be met; we still have a swollen organization in Washington and elsewhere; we are still finding food and money for our Allies in the great enterprise on which we started two years ago; let us complete these remaining tasks cheerfully and thoroughly. In order to do so the Victory loan must be supported loyally. Another point suggests itself: a new enemy is lifting his ugly head, Bolshevism, the spawn of defeat. We are proud of our domestic ideals and of the principle of 'live and let live' on which this nation is founded. Let us answer this menace as we did the Prussian, and prove that we are standing whole-heartedly behind our Government—no matter what our politics—in the great work to which the United States is committed. Buy your bonds before it is too late!

Alaska's Resources

In this issue we publish an unusual article, by Mr. F. Le Roi Thurmond, who describes the accidents and hazards of a journey into Alaska for the purpose of examining a prospect on which he had been engaged to report. He had all sorts of bad weather and worse luck, but in the end he achieved the purpose of his journey and returned safe and sound. The transcript from the diary will appeal to the reader as a genuine record of the sort of experience that the prospector undergoes in the North, but it must not be supposed for a moment that every mining engineer engaged in similar work has to undergo anything so unpleasant; on the contrary, most journeys of inspection in that great region are as devoid of danger as they are rich in all the pleasures of outdoor life; indeed, we believe that the day will come when the extraordinarily vitalizing air of the 'inside' of Alaska, that is, the country beyond the coast range, will attract the valetudinarian and the invalid. For the present, it attracts the most vigorous of the race: the hunter, the fisherman, and the prospector. The mineral resources of Alaska constitute only a part of its wealth, but they are remarkable. The output during 1918 suffered for lack of labor and shipping, due to the War; in fact, since 1914 the mining activities of the entire region have been crippled by the same cause. In 1917 the value of the gold produced was $17,950,000, of which $11,140,000 came from placers and $5,910,000 came from lode mining. Last year the total output was worth only $10,000,000. The grand total yielded by the Territory since it was bought from Russia is $302,000,000, and the reader will recall the fact that the Territory, which covers 590,884 square miles, was bought for the sum of $7,200,000 in 1867. Soon after William Seward, as Secretary of State, had concluded this transaction with the Russian envoy, Edward de Stoeckl, he was asked what he considered the most important event in his career. "The purchase of Alaska," he replied, "but it will take the people a generation to find it out." It did, for not until 1900 was the varied richness of the country fully appreciated. In 1916 the output of copper, namely, 114 million pounds, was worth $28,000,000, or nearly four times the price Seward paid. In 1918 a big decrease was caused by an unfavorable combination of circumstances, the output having been only 70 million pounds, worth $17,180,000. Of this total, four mines in the Chitina district yielded 52,585,000 pounds, which suggests the importance of the Kennecott mine. Alaska responded to the call of the War and contributed a considerable tonnage of chrome and tungsten, besides some antimony, lead, and tin. In 1916 the total mineral production was worth $50,900,000. Altogether, Alaska in 32 years has yielded fifty times the price at which the Territory was bought from Russia. But that is only a part of her production. In 1916 she produced 285,000,000 pounds of marketable fish, the value of which was $26,156,560. This included 4,900,627 cases of canned salmon, worth $23,269,430. A sum of $39,569,612 has been invested in the fisheries of Alaska. It is believed that this industry is still capable of expansion and that the fishing for herring and cod can be developed much beyond its present stage. On another page we show a photograph of a salmon cannery, set amid beautiful scenery. The waste from the canneries yielded 4,443,880 pounds of fertilizer, besides 1,040,376 gallons of fish-oil. The fur trade, which first brought the white man to Alaska and was the chief industry before gold was discovered, is declining. From 1880 to 1890 the annual winning of pelts was worth $3,500,000, but in 1916 it was valued at only $1,143,601, to which the skins of the fox contributed $482,469, the lynx $259,296, and the seal $211,830. Here we may make mention of a new resource, namely, the herds of reindeer, which have increased to a total of 170,000 animals, valued at about $5,200,000. In 1892 the first reindeer were introduced to provide profitable activity for the Eskimo and the Indian. Apart from their service for haulage, the reindeer give a meat as palatable and nourishing as mutton, and their milk compares well with that of the domestic cow. The herds are said to be multiplying rapidly under the favorable conditions in which they find themselves. There remains another asset to be considered, and it is most important, namely, agriculture. Most of us are so accustomed to thinking of the North as a land of snow and ice, wolves and auroras, that it surprises us to learn how far the cultivation of grains and vegetables has been advanced. We give a couple of photographs showing the crops of wheat and cabbages grown in the vicinity of Fairbanks, which is to be the terminus of the Government railroad now being built inland from the coast at Seward. In 1917 the potato yield of Central Alaska, of which Fairbanks is the chief community, sufficed for the local consumption, in addition to the demands of the northwestern region, that is, the Seward peninsula. It is anticipated that soon Alaska will be able to produce all the vegetables required by her people, besides wheat and other grains, the growing of which is as yet in an experimental stage. Much credit is due to the experiment stations established by the Government at Rampart, Fairbanks, Sitka, Copper River, and Kodiak. Rampart is in latitude 65° 40′, just inside the Arctic Circle, yet even there it has been found possible to mature barley and oats from year to year, besides rye and wheat three years out of four. The aim of those in charge of these stations is to develop varieties of grain that will mature even in the most unfavorable season. In the Tanana and Matanuska valleys, the ripening of wheat, oats, barley, and rye is as perfect as in the Mississippi valley; moreover a most promising start has been made in the growing of sugar beets in the Matanuska district, along the line of the Government railroad. In 1918 the first flour-mill was erected at Fairbanks. It is estimated that Alaska contains 90,000 square miles available for pasturage and agriculture, that is, an area equal to that of the two States of New York and Pennsylvania. For a comparison we can quote Finland, which is bounded on the south by latitude 60° and on the north by latitude 70°; it covers an area of 148,000 square miles, or about a quarter of Alaska; and one-third of Finland is lake or marsh, yet it supports a population of 3,000,000, which is about sixty times that of Alaska. What the Territory needs is population and transport—in other words, men and markets. Of the 5000 men that were enlisted in the Army and Navy fully 80% will return to Alaska, and we shall be surprised if the youth of the States does not hear 'the call of the wild' and go to the North now that the War is over. The building of the Government railroad promises some of the facilities of transport that the country needs for the distribution and exportation of its products, but the restoration of the shipping is even more important at this time. Coastal trade will be stimulated by the successful exploitation of the coal deposits of south-eastern Alaska, in the Bering River and Matanuska districts especially. We hope that the Chambers of Commerce at Portland, Seattle, and San Francisco will awaken to the importance of the subject and make a renewed effort to initiate activity in that direction. Alaska is a great American asset and it deserves the most friendly attention of our people, and of Congress.

The Italian Impasse

Whatever may be the final settlement of Italy's insistent demand for the possession of Fiume, it is evident that the dispute affords a premature test of the sincerity of the efforts to organize a league of nations for the settlement of international differences. It is a fact that the secret arrangement between France, England, and Italy, known as the Treaty of London, signed just before Italy became a militant Ally, did not give Fiume to Italy but to Croatia, at that time a province of Austria and now a part of the consolidated Jugo-Slavia, which includes all the Slavic elements in the Balkan-Adriatic area. If Italy stands by the pact of London, she must not pick the clauses that suit her; she must abide by all of them, and that would leave her without Fiume. To give possession of this port to Italy would be unjust to the new republic on the eastern shore of the Adriatic, for without it the Jugo-Slavs would have no gate to the sea. Italy has regained Trieste, which is near-by, and she has Venice, at the head of the Adriatic. That the population of Fiume is largely Italian may be true, but Alexandria and Smyrna are largely Greek in population, so likewise many other ports are populated by those of a race alien to their governments; it would be wholly impracticable to re-distribute sovereignty on such a basis without doing wrong to the peoples using these ports as their front doors. In adjusting conflicting claims it may be necessary to hurt the feelings or even to trespass on the rights of one of the opposing claimants in the effort to settle a difficulty and establish a stable government. If Italy refuses to play the game and prefers to sulk by herself at this great juncture, she will do herself grave discredit. The ardent desire of the Italian populace for this outpost of Italian commerce is not enough to upset the great plans to which her leaders have committed themselves at Paris. France does not receive all she wants, yet her delegates do not leave the council chamber in protest. The crisis has given President Wilson a great opportunity and he has risen to it superbly. We confess that many of his utterances leave us cold, but his statement, issued at Paris on April 23, was an appeal commanding the approval and sympathy of every good citizen, not only in this country but wherever men dream and hope for a peaceful adjustment of international affairs. In refusing to recognize the secret treaties made before the United States became a partner in the War and in emphasizing the impracticability of carrying out these secret agreements in the face of changed circumstances, more particularly the creation of a number of independent States, he will be justified by the good sense of mankind; moreover, his insistence on the principles upon which the Armistice was signed and to which Italy is a consenting party, the principles for which he has made himself the chief spokesman, is entirely logical, for without adherence to this definite basis of adjustment it is impossible to fulfill the purpose for which we and our Allies have fought. Italy is no longer threatened by the Austrian navy, for Austria-Hungary no longer exists, and the League of Nations will place such limitation on armaments as to render aggression impossible from the eastern side of the Adriatic. Italy, as the President says, has become a trustee for a new order of things, and it behooves her to play her part honorably, not to withdraw at the first suggestion of a sacrifice of a small part of her territorial ambitions. Without her Allies she would have been crushed and starved; if fortunately she chose to break away from the Central Powers and to throw in her lot with the Allies, she must join with them now in subordinating one of her many desires to the fulfillment of the great object for which the Allies fought, or else suffer the stigma of having played a supremely selfish part. The War has done great things for Italy; it has unified her people; it has restored to her the old frontiers; it has smashed her dangerous neighbors; it has given new warmth to her national life. The action of her delegates at this time is calamitous if it should be sustained by her Parliament, for it threatens to disrupt the League of Nations on the very eve of its formation; if the members of the league are going to refuse to play ball every time the referee gives an adverse decision it will be useless to continue the game. We hope Italy will re-consider her action. As the President has said, "it is within her choice to be surrounded by friends; to exhibit to the newly liberated peoples across the Adriatic that noblest quality of greatness, magnanimity, friendly generosity, the preference of justice over interest." In other words, to play the game like a sportsman.

The Internal Corrosion of Cables

By WM. FLEET ROBERTSON

This paper owes its origin to a fatal accident that occurred in the Protection Island shaft of the Canadian Western Fuel Co.'s colliery at Nanaimo, B. C., on September 10, 1918. By this accident 16 men were instantly killed through the hoisting-rope breaking, thus dropping the cage to the bottom of the shaft. A coroner's inquest was held at Nanaimo and a governmental investigation ordered to determine the cause of the failure of the rope. I was called upon to make this investigation.

To give an intelligible account of the accident it will be necessary to describe in brief outline the colliery itself:

The Nanaimo colliery was opened up about 1853 by the Vancouver Coal Co., an English corporation. Two circular shafts were sunk within a few feet of the shore of Nanaimo harbor to cut the Douglas seam of coal at a depth of about 603 ft. This shaft today is known as the No. 1 or Esplanade shaft.

The coal was found to be dipping to the east, that is, under the harbor at a low angle, about 10°. At the entrance to the harbor is an island, Protection island, under which the coal beds extend, and there later a shaft was sunk, to cut the Esplanade shaft seam at a depth of about 630 ft. This shaft was fully equipped and for years hoisted coal. Eventually the underground workings of the Esplanade shaft and the Protection Island shaft were connected, the direct distance between the two shafts being about 1½ miles.

For economic reasons the hoisting of coal was discontinued at the Protection Island shaft, the entire output being raised through the Esplanade shaft. The former shaft ceased to be used for hoisting in 1904 but it continued in use for the lowering and raising of men working in that part of the now extensive workings. A small amount of coal continued to be raised here but only enough to generate steam for a fan, air-compressor, pump, and the hoisting-engine, the records showing that this amounted to less than 1000 tons per month, in two cages, or about 500 tons per rope.

At the Esplanade shaft there was hoisted from 15,000 to 20,000 tons of coal per month on each rope, together with a greater number of men than at the Protection Island shaft and all the mine-timber, etc.

The hoisting-plant at Protection island was steam-driven, the hoisting-drum being cylindrical, 10 ft. diam., and the head-sheave likewise 10 ft. in diameter. The hoisting-cable was 1½ inches in diameter, Lang's lay of crucible steel wires, 6 strands of 16 wires each around a hemp centre about ⅞ in. diameter.

The shaft was vertical, each compartment fitted with four wooden guides of 4¾ by 4¾ in. lumber. The cage was provided with four pairs of safety-clutches, a pair on each guide, brought into operation by four pairs of tension spiral springs, three inches in diameter of ½-in. round steel. Each spring when new, as shown by subsequent tests, had a safe elongation within the elastic limit of 30%, when it had a pull of 1200 pounds.

Why these safety-clutches failed to work is an unanswered question, but they never touched the guides. Possibly it was on account of its being a descending trip, and, as the rope broke 179 ft. above the cage, the lash of the rope may have kept the clutches out of action.

The shaft was used as an intake-air shaft, being housed over the top and attached to a forcing fan, the air being used as an auxiliary to the general supply. It was a very wet shaft, but the water falling into it was free from acid, being somewhat alkaline as shown herewith:

	Gr. per gal.
Calcium sulphate	14
Calcium chloride	103
Magnesium chlorite	190
Alkali chlorides (soda and potash)	1262

The rope had been installed on March 6, 1915; it broke on September 10, 1918; so that the period of service was 1282 days or almost exactly 3½ years. It broke 179 ft. above its point of attachment to the cage, and, as nearly as can be ascertained, the break occurred about the time the point of break had just passed over the head-sheave on a descending trip.

The load on the rope was

	Lb.
Weight of car	4357
Weight of 179 ft. of rope	540
Weight of 16 men	2720
	7617 lb. say 4 tons

The evidence was that the cables were examined almost daily by a man appointed for the purpose, but his examination consisted of allowing the cable to pass slowly through his gloved hand, or holding a piece of stick against the moving cable, a practice that might detect broken or projecting wire-ends, but gave no indication as to internal corrosion of the cable.

The method of lubrication consisted of frequently applying cold ordinary black lubricating oil on waste or burlap to the cold cable, but the oil evidently did not penetrate the cable at all.

Three coils of the cable, of about 100 ft. each, were taken to Montreal and tested in the Physical Testing Laboratory of McGill University for tensile strength under the supervision of Professor H. M. Mackay, with S. D. McNab in charge of the laboratory. One coil of the cable was from the hoisting-drum and had always been under shelter and not exposed to the shaft conditions. This part of the cable stood up to a strain of 80 tons, which was 89.35% of the aggregate strength of the individual wires tested separately and was above the guarantee of the makers, T. & W. Smith, of Newcastle-on-Tyne, England, of 78 tons for the new rope, and represented a tensile strength of the steel wires equivalent to 208,000 lb. per square inch. The test indicated a cable well made and of first class material.

The accompanying sketch shows the positions from which test-pieces were taken and their respective breaking-strengths.

These tests showed conclusively that deterioration of the rope was 'spotty'; it followed no order of progression and apparently was unaccounted for by any local conditions in the shaft. They also illustrated the futility of putting any reliance upon a test for tensile strength made on a piece of cable cut from the portion next to the cage.

A close examination of the external surface of the cable failed to show any wire-ends broken, worn, or projecting, the usual danger-signals when the cable is failing from wear. The wear or the rusting of the externally visible wires was not such as to cause apprehension. Micro-photographs by Dr. Stansfield showed conclusively that no crystallization had taken place in the steel of the cable.

An examination of the fractured ends of the test-pieces settled so conclusively that the failure of the cable was entirely due to the corrosion of the internal wires that further search was unnecessary. The wires externally exposed had been subjected to frequent applications of an oily rag, which supplied a sufficiently superficial lubrication to protect the wires externally, but the interior of the cable had evidently been absolutely devoid of oil, or other protective agent, and the wires internally were badly rusted, many of them corroded to threads and others completely eaten through, in fact, in Test No. 5, in opening up the ends for attachment to the grip, 32 wires were picked out, completely severed.

It became evident that the strength surviving in the cable was approximately in proportion to the cross-sectional area of the wires remaining unoxidized, the quality of the steel remaining about the same as in the unrusted wires. This was so obvious that a visual examination of the broomed out end of a test-piece enabled a close estimate to be made in advance as to what the breaking-strength of the test would be. Conversely, the breaking-strength of the portions of the cable was a fair index of the amount of oxidation that had taken place in these respective portions.

The results of these tests have been to emphasize most strongly the fact that the external conditions of a cable is no criterion as to its remaining strength in cases similar to the one described. Of course, if a calte is subjected to heavy external wear it will deteriorate from that cause, possibly before internal corrosion could have become serious, but such deterioration, being visible, ceases to be dangerous. In the case under review, however, the external appearance of the cable would lead any rope inspector, such as is usually employed, to believe the cable to be perfectly safe, whereas it was a "whited sepulchre" and rotten inside.

That this case has a much wider application was brought to my notice by a piece of 1¼-in. cable from a Sudbury mine that came into the McGill laboratory to be tested during my stay there. This cable, from all outward appearances, was practically as good as new, but the tensile test and the broken ends showed it to be internally rotted with rust.

A subsequent critical examination of the interior of other cables made by the British Columbian Mines Inspection staff further indicates the disease to be only too prevalent. To my mind, the cause is the total lack of internal lubrication and the remedy must be continued—internal lubrication with suitable oils—beginning when the cable is new and renewed at short intervals; for, if the rust is allowed to start it is difficult if not impossible to stop it.

As to how this internal lubrication can best be effected is an open question, but I am convinced that, to be effective, the cable must be immersed in oil for an appreciable time and that both the oil and the rope must be heated above the boiling-point of water, and also that the immersion of the cable in the oil must be repeated at frequent intervals. Ben B. Thayer of the Anaconda Copper Mining Co. informed me that it was the practice of his company at Butte to pass the cables periodically through a bath of oil contained in a long trough heated with live steam. A mine manager to whom I suggested this, remarked, "If this is necessary, why do not the makers of the cable tell us to do it?" It may be news to the makers that they are supposed to supply such instructions with their commodities, but they might well take the hint.

Observation of the fact that the pieces of cables tested had tensile strengths approximately proportional to the sectional area of the wires remaining intact and unoxidized, brought back to me one of the few electrical principles remaining in my mind of the instruction I received many years ago at McGill, namely, that the conductivity of a wire is directly proportional to its cross-sectional area. This suggested the thought that if we could test the conductivity of any suspected part of a cable, this ratio would give us, approximately, the ratio between the tensile strength of the new and the suspected part of the cable.

To test this theory I appealed to W. D. Fowler of the electrical department of McGill University; I had with me a piece of the unused cable and a length of 65 ft. of the deteriorated cable, which extended between test-piece No. 3, with a tensile strength of 25 tons, and test-piece No. 4, with a tensile strength of 55 tons. Mr. Fowler tested the unused cable and also tested the 65 ft. of cable in sections of five feet each for electrical resistance, and his report is given in graphic form in the accompanying sketch showing the electrical resistance found in the successive 5-ft. sections of the 65 ft. of defective cable.

These tests were only approximate, as the method of attachment of the wires to the cable was imperfect, but they were close enough to show the theory to be substantially correct.

The tests showed the electrical resistance to be as follows:

No		Resistance in ohms per foot
1	Unused cable	0.000105
2	Defective cable in 5-ft. lengths immediately adjoining test No. 4 having a tensile strength of 55 tons	*0.000120
3	Defective cable in 5-ft. lengths immediately adjoining test No. 3, which had a tensile strength of 25 tons	†0.000231

*About 10% greater resistance than No. 1, the unused cable.
†About 120% greater resistance than No. 1, the unused cable.

These figures, while admittedly inconclusive, show such marked variations as to be sufficiently serviceable for detecting any dangerous internal destruction in a cable. The principle has a wide field of application to the stand-in cables of rope-tramways, suspension bridges, etc., and quite possibly it may be found applicable to test the amount of corrosion that has taken place in iron or steel members used in reinforced concrete structures where such are concealed from observation. That a simple and rapid method can be devised to test cables seems probable from observing the rapidity with which a man tests the condition of connections at the rail-joints on the electric street-railways with a small galvanometer wound in one direction for resistance in a given length of rail including joint, when, if the joint is as good as the rail, the galvanometer stands at zero. An enlargement of this appliance would be applicable for testing cables.

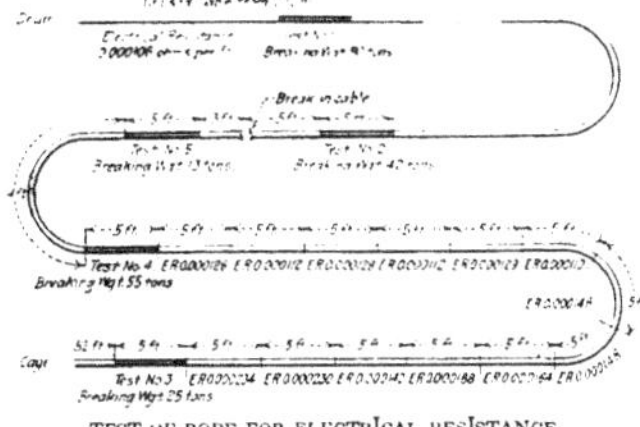

TEST OF ROPE FOR ELECTRICAL RESISTANCE

A BOILER that is to be out of commission for some time, say two weeks or longer, should be prepared for laying-up as follows: Shell or drums are opened, thoroughly cleaned, and all scale, dirt, or other foreign material removed. Plates should be wire-brushed where accessible. Then manhole and handhole-plates should be replaced firmly, the air-cock on top of boiler opened, and the boiler filled full of water, leaving no air-pockets in shell or drums. The air-cock should then be closed. This will exclude all air, and prevent rusting or corrosion of the interior of the boiler. In freezing weather this plan cannot be carried out, so another method is as follows: After the interior has been cleaned, and the boiler ready for closing-up, metal pans or trays, as large as can be passed through the manhole-plates, are placed inside the boiler. The pans are filled two-thirds full of unslaked lime, then the manhole-plates are secured, main steam, auxiliary steam, feed and blow-off stops are firmly closed, to exclude all moisture, the various lines being broken, and blank flanges put on if necessary. The lime will absorb all moisture from the air, and this will again prevent internal deterioration.—L. D. Miller, formerly with California Industrial Accident Commission, now in the Navy.

Inspiration Mill Statistics for 1918

The annual report contains the following data:

Ore milled, dry tons	5,110,101
Average per day of milling operations, tons	11,172
Number of sections running	11.8
Average rate per section, tons	956
Screen analysis of mill-feed to concentrating machine (on 48-mesh), per cent	3.4
Assay of mill-feed, per cent copper	1.301
Oxide copper in mill-feed, per cent	0.291
Assay of general mill tailing, per cent	0.380
Oxide copper in general mill tailing, per cent	0.253
Smelter assay of concentrates produced, per cent	30.398
Assay of flotation concentrates, per cent	35.26
Assay of table concentrates, per cent	10.31
Moisture in general concentrates, per cent	20.46
Ratio of concentration	32.5
Recovery:	
Recovery of copper in milling (smelter assays) calculated from assays only, per cent	72.99
Assays and weights of concentrates and ore, per cent	72.27
Assay and weights of concentrates and tailings, per cent	72.82
Assays and weights of ore and tailings, per cent	73.02
Recovery of copper sulphide in ore, per cent	88.51
Net water used per ton of ore (310 gal.), tons	1.29
Power used per ton of ore milled, kw.-hour:	
Coarse crushing	0.45
Fine grinding and concentrating	10.12
Blowers for flotation air	2.79
Filtering and reclaiming water	2.32
Lighting	0.12
Total	15.80
Steel ball consumption in fine grinding per ton of ore milled, pounds	1.82
Flotation oil consumption per ton of ore milled, pounds:	
Coal-tar	1.20
Sundry oils	0.15
Total	1.35

Tungsten Losses in Making Ferro-Tungsten

An interesting fact brought out by the U. S. Bureau of Mines questionnaire sent to tungsten manufactures, and compiled for the last six months of 1918, is that the average loss in tungsten, in the making of ferro-tungsten is about 14%. This figure is, however, doubtless considerably too low, as correspondence has brought out the fact that the tendency was to give the lowest figures realized rather than true averages; hence it is believed that about 25% would be nearer the true average of loss. These losses are largely mechanical, though in the chemical processes there is a loss due to incomplete reactions, incomplete precipitation, etc. The questionnaires for 1918 showed that in a monthly production of about a million pounds of contained tungsten, approximately 22% was tungsten powder, and the remainder was contained in ferro-tungsten.—H. C. Morris in Monthly Report of U. S. Bureau of Mines.

The German Metal Octopus—II

ISSUED BY THE ALIEN PROPERTY CUSTODIAN

THE GERMAN METAL TRIUMVIRATE IN THE UNITED STATES. At the outbreak of the European war each member of this triumvirate had a branch of its business in the United States. The Metallgesellschaft had the American Metal Co., Aron Hirsch & Sohn had L. Vogelstein & Co., and Beer, Sondheimer & Co. had a branch under its own name. All these branches were centred in New York City, and all developed vast and extensive interests in the United States, Mexico, and South America, including the control of mines, smelters, and refineries. We now proceed to point out somewhat in detail the ramifications of these three German-owned and German-controlled companies.

(a) *American Metal Co. (Ltd.).* In or about the year 1887 the Metallgesellschaft sent to the United States two of its representatives, to wit, Jacob Langeloth and Berthold Hochschild, to establish a branch of the Metallgesellschaft's business. At that time the present banking firm of Ladenburg, Thalmann & Co. were doing a metal business and had connections with the Metallgesellschaft. An arrangement was made resulting in the organization of a corporation called the American Metal Co., under the laws of the State of New York, with a capital of $200,000, divided into 2000 shares, to which corporation Ladenburg, Thalmann & Co. turned over their metal department. The stock of the corporation was issued as follows:

	Shares
Metallgesellschaft	600
Henry R. Merton & Co	595
Ladenburg, Thalmann & Co	710

The balance of the stock was allotted to various officers. It will be noted that from the very organization of the American Metal Co. the stock control thereof was in the hands of Henry R. Merton & Co. and the Metallgesellschaft. These German interests continued to retain that control through all the years of the development of the American Metal Co., and had the control at the outbreak of the European war. The capital stock of the American Metal Co. was increased from time to time, as follows:

1891, from $ 200,000 to $ 300,000
1897, from 300,000 to 600,000
1899, from 600,000 to 1,000,000
1902, from 1,000,000 to 1,500,000
1904, from 1,500,000 to 2,000,000
1906, from 2,000,000 to 3,000,000
1909, from 3,000,000 to 3,500,000
1917, from 3,500,000 to 7,000,000

That the Metallgesellschaft and Henry R. Merton & Co. at all times controlled more than a majority of the stock of the American Metal Co. will appear from the following tabulation:

Year	Total shares out	Metallgesellschaft and Henry R. Merton & Co. held
1891	3,000	1,892
1897	6,000	3,789
1899	10,000	5,795
1902	15,000	8,605
1904	20,000	11,460
1906	30,000	17,640
1909	35,000	23,312
1917	70,000	46,624

From the time of its organization and up to the outbreak of the European war the American Metal Co. did its business on the European continent through the Metallgesellschaft and in Great Britain through Henry R. Merton & Co. No sales were made by the American Metal Co. in Europe except through these two concerns. Prior to the European war it was the custom of the company to receive cable quotations for various metals daily, both from the Metallgesellschaft and from Merton & Co., and, based upon the advices thus received, daily they planned their business for the day.

At first the American Metal Co. confined its business to trading in metals both for export and import as well as in the domestic market, but, as will presently appear, it soon acquired interests in smelters and refineries, and became an extensive owner of mines in the United States, Mexico, and South America. Through the ownership of stock in other companies, it has gained the control of the output of copper, zinc, and lead mines, and it operates smelters in the United States and Mexico, producing copper, zinc, and lead. Annexed hereto is a chart prepared by the officers of the American Metal Co., showing in three groups (1) companies owned or controlled and operated by the American Metal Co., (2) companies in which American Metal Co. has a part-ownership and a board representation and with which it has important contractual relations, and (3) companies in which the American Metal Co. owns shares and bonds as investments.

In amplification of the chart, the company has furnished the following particulars regarding its most important subsidiaries:

Name	Capital stock	Per cent owned
In the United States:		
American Zinc & Chemical Co.	$2,500,000	100
Bartlesville Zinc Co.	500,000	100
American Metal Transport Co.	100,000	100
Metallurgical Co. of America	100,000	100
Langeloth Coal Co.	100,000	100
Langeloth Mercantile Co.	5,000	100
Langeloth Townsite Co.	5,000	100
Chanute Spelter Co.	5,000	100
Clarksburg Clinkering Co.	5,000	100
Ohio & Colorado Smelting & Refining Co.	3,000,000	65
In South America and Mexico:		
The South American Metal Co.	250,000	100
Compania de Minerales y Metales	1,250,000	97.7

The *American Zinc & Chemical Co.* owns a zinc smelting plant with a capacity for the treatment of from 7000 to 8000 tons of zinc ores per month, and the production of 3000 to 4000 tons of spelter. It also owns a sulphuric acid plant with a capacity of 7000 to 8000 tons of sulphuric acid monthly. This property represents an investment of over $4,000,000, and may be divided into the following subheads:

1. Zinc smelting plant. This plant consists of eight blocks of two furnaces each, each block containing 912 retorts, making a total retort capacity of 7296. Each block is equipped with waste-heat boilers; the furnaces are fired by Woods gas-producers, one producer to each block. The smelting plant has complete accessories, such as power-house, two steam-turbine generator units of 2000 kw. each, up-to-date machine-shop, carpenter-shop, and pottery plant.

2. Sulphuric acid works. This department has a chamber-capacity of from 8000 to 8500 tons of 60°B. sulphuric acid monthly, and also has a contacting plant for the conversion of about 3500 tons of 60° acid into 66° acid. The raw material used in the manufacture of sulphuric acid is zinc sulphide ore, for the roasting of which four Hegeler kilns with necessary accessories are available. These kilns have a capacity of about 5000 tons of ore monthly, which would correspond to approximately 5000 tons of 60° acid. For the handling of the crude ore the works are equipped with modern drying and sampling plants, and storage-bins with a capacity of about 18,000 tons, with overhead cranes. The sulphuric acid plant is one of the most modern in the country, and can be expanded for the production of other acid-products whenever desired.

3. Coal mine. The company owns coal-mining rights over an area of 2450 acres of the Pittsburgh and Rooster veins. It was estimated that there was a coal reserve in this tract of over 18,000,000 tons, from which only a little over 1,000,000 tons have been mined. Of the above acreage the company owns surface and coal-mining rights on 723 acres and coal-mining rights on the remainder. The mine is equipped to produce about 50,000 tons of coal monthly. The coal mine is subject to a mortgage of $476,000, against which there was on deposit with the Colonial Trust Co., of Pittsburgh, on December 31, 1918, a sinking-fund credit of $23,905.93.

4. The Langeloth Townsite Co. was incorporated for the purpose of taking over a block of real estate adjacent to the works of the American Zinc & Chemical Co., embracing about 400 acres, with the idea of developing it into a modern industrial town. The town-site has nearly 400 houses completed, some of which have been sold and others leased to the workmen on easy payments. Modern sewerage, complete sanitary water-supply, first-class schools, and playgrounds have been provided.

5. For the convenience of the workmen, the company operates a general store under the name of the Langeloth Mercantile Co. The store-building is owned by the American Zinc & Chemical Co., which leases it to the Mercantile Co. The latter company sells from $300 to $400 worth of merchandise per day, on which it attempts to make a profit only sufficient to cover operating expenses.

6. By-products plants. The company owns and operates:

(a) A zinc-oxide plant with a capacity of about 500 tons of zinc oxide monthly.

(b) A zinc-dust plant which produces from 150 to 200 tons of zinc-dust monthly.

(c) A zinc-sulphate plant which has been running only intermittently, owing to lack of demand for this material.

Bartlesville Zinc Co. owns and operates two zinc-smelting plants at Bartlesville and one at Blackwell, Oklahoma, representing a total investment of $2,500,000. One of the Bartlesville plants was formerly owned by the Lanyon Starr Smelting Co. (which latter company has now been consolidated with the Bartlesville Zinc Co.). This plant has six furnaces of 576 retorts each, making a total retort-capacity of 3456. The other Bartlesville plant has nine furnaces of 576 retorts each, making a total retort-capacity of 5184; it also has two re-distilling blocks on which high-grade spelter is made.

The Blackwell plant has 12 furnaces of 800 retorts each, a total retort capacity of 9600. At Bartlesville there is also a zinc-oxide plant, which produces about 350 tons of oxide monthly; also a zinc-dust plant, which produces from 100 to 150 tons monthly. Both Bartlesville and Blackwell smelters are equipped with clinkering-plants in which the residue-carrying precious metals are treated to make them available for blast-furnace treatment for the recovery of their remaining metal-values. This clinkering process is covered by patents owned by the American Metal Co. The total capacity of the Bartlesville, Lanyon Starr, and Blackwell plants in normal times is approximately 14,000 tons of ore per month, from which 5000 to 6000 tons of spelter are produced.

Clarksburg Clinkering Co. owns and operates a clinkering-plant at Bridgeport, West Virginia, under the patents mentioned above, for the treatment of value-bearing residues.

Chanute Spelter Co. owns in fee 628 acres and holds under lease about 17,000 acres of land, mostly in Cherokee county, Kansas, adjacent to the Joplin district of Missouri. This acreage was selected after careful study, of the geological conditions governing the ore occurrences in this district, and the Metal Co. has invested, through the Chanute Spelter Co., for the acquisition of fees and leases, as well as in development work, approximately $500,000. The leases provide for the payment of royalties varying from 5 to 12½% on the sales-value of the ore produced. It is the expectation of the company that during 1919 they will draw at least a portion of their zinc-ore requirements from their holdings in this district, and that the ore production from these properties will steadily increase in the future.

Metallurgical Co. of America was incorporated for the purpose of carrying on experiments in metallurgy, perfecting and improving metallurgical processes, and holding all metallurgical patents in which the American Metal Co. was interested. A few years ago all of its properties, patents, etc., were transferred to the American Metal Co. and the Metallurgical Co. became merely a department of the parent company. Today it owns nothing except $100,000 in cash, which is the equivalent of its outstanding capital stock.

American Metal Transport Co. was incorporated for the purpose of handling all the shipping of the parent corporation and its subsidiaries, primarily between the United States and South America. It is also engaged in the operation of steamers under charter and has likewise been employed by the United States Shipping Board in the operation of steamers owned or leased by the Government.

In addition to the foregoing properties in the United States, of which the American Metal Co. owns 100%, it has substantial stock interests in a number of other corporations in the United States and elsewhere, of which the following merit separate description:

Ohio & Colorado Smelting & Refining Co., of which the American Metal Co. owns 38,557 shares out of 50,000 shares issued. This company owns a lead smelter at Salida, Colorado, with a smelting capacity of about 12,000 tons of ore per month, from which it produces from 1000 to 1500 tons of lead bullion. The smelting company is indebted to the metal company for over $1,000,000 and is not considered a valuable investment.

Balbach Smelting & Refining Co., of which the American Metal Co. owns 1300 preferred shares and 1302 common, representing approximately a one-third interest, with a book value of $225,600. This company operates a copper and lead smelting and refining plant at Newark, New Jersey, with a capacity for the treatment and refining of about 4000 tons of lead and approximately 4,000,000 lb. of copper monthly. It also owns real estate in the city of Newark and on Newark Bay valued at approximately $500,000.

Nichols Copper Co. The American Metal Co. owns 1400 preferred and 9805 common shares in this company; also 450 bonds. The share interest is about 14%. The Nichols Copper Co. owns and operates a copper refinery at Laurel Hill, Long Island, with a capacity for the treatment of about 40,000,000 lb. of copper monthly. The American Metal Co. carries the common shares on its books at $100 and the preferred shares and the bonds at par, making a total investment of $1,570,500.

The South American Metal Co. This company was organized in June 1917, for the purpose of conducting a general trading business in South America, especially in Chile, in minerals, coal, coke, and wholesale merchandise generally. Although up to the present time, owing to the diversion of shipping tonnage to business most essential to the conduct of the War, trade between South America and the United States has been substantially reduced, the company has been carrying on a fairly active business, chiefly in coal and coke.

The South American Metal Co. controls the Guayacan copper smelter at Guayacan, in the Province of Coquimbo, Chile, which was incorporated in 1917 as the Fundicion de Guayacan, with 150,000 shares at £1 each, of which it (as agent of the American Metal Co.) owns 120,750 shares, the balance being owned by Chilean citizens. The smelter represents an investment of over $400,000, and includes in its holdings extensive water-fronts on the harbor of Guayacan as well as several small tributary mines, together with barges, boats, and miscellaneous smelter-equipment. The smelter is capable of producing from 350 to 500 tons of copper matte per month. It was shut-down in 1917 on account of war conditions, and has not yet re-commenced operations.

The South American Metal Co. also supervises mining explorations which the American Metal Co. carries on in South America.

MEXICAN HOLDINGS. The American Metal Co. also owns extensive properties in Mexico; these are handled through a Mexican holding corporation known as the Compania de Minerales y Metales. The latter is capitalized at 25,000 shares of the par value of ₱100 each, of which the American Metal Co. owns 24,423 shares. The original capital of the Minerales Co. was 1250 shares of the par value of ₱100 each, of which the Metal Co. owned originally 673 shares, the remaining 577 shares being owned by the Metallgesellschaft of Frankfurt, Germany. In 1917, finding itself in need of additional capital, the Minerales Co. increased its capitalization by the addition of 23,750 additional shares, which were offered pro rata to the stockholders, subject to subscription within 30 days, shares not subscribed by any stockholder to be offered to those subscribing for the remainder. The notices of the proposed increase were published as required by law in Mexico, and the American Metal Co. duly subscribed for its pro rata of the new shares, amounting to 12,887. The German shareholders failed to subscribe for their pro rata, namely, 10,863, and those were subsequently offered to and purchased by the Metal Co., thereby increasing its holdings of Minerales shares to 24,423, leaving the German interest 577 shares, representing their original holdings. Of these, 565 shares are in the possession of the Alien Property Custodian and will be offered for sale separately. The remaining 15 shares are in possession of the German stockholders or their agents in Mexico.

Compania de Minerales y Metales, S. A., owns outright the following properties:

1. Smelter and mines at Guadalupe, in Nuevo Leon.
2. Mines and smelter at Cerralvo, in Nuevo Leon.
3. Providencia mines, in Zacatecas.
4. Mines at Guanacevi, in Durango.
5. Mining leases at Santa Eulalia, in Chihuahua.
6. Oil leases in the State of Vera Cruz.
7. Railroad equipment and machine shops.
8. Real estate.

Compania de Minerales y Metales has the management or control of the following companies:

9. Agujita coal mines in Coahuila.
10. Fuel Sales Co.
11. Torreon smelter in Coahuila.
12. Parrena Mining Co., in Coahuila.
13. Paloma mines, in Coahuila.

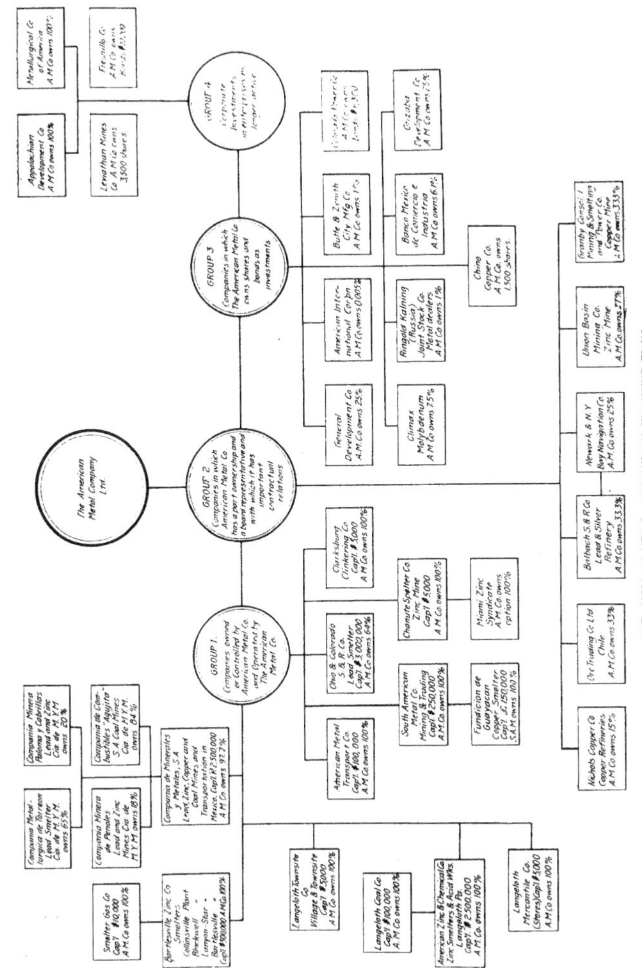

THE AMERICAN METAL COMPANY AND ITS CONNECTIONS

14 Penoles mines, in Durango.
15 Smelter and refinery at Monterrey.

1. Near Guadalupe the company owns mining-lands embracing 2270 acres, from which are produced lead and zinc ores that are sent over a narrow-gauge railway of 18 miles to the treatment plant at Guadalupe. This plant has one blast-furnace with a smelting capacity for 75,000 tons of lead ores, annually, from which may be produced 7000 to 8000 tons of bullion. There is also a calcining-plant at Guadalupe for the treatment of zinc-carbonate ores, capable of handling 7000 tons per month. This calcining-plant is used for the treatment not only of the ores from the mines near Guadalupe, but also from the company's other mines and such as may be purchased from outside parties. At Guadalupe there is also a modern power-plant, offices, workmen's houses, schools, hospitals, and other miscellaneous equipment for the operation of a modern smelting unit.

2. *Cerralvo.* This unit also consists of a mine and smelter. The mine covers 790 acres and produces a high-grade silver-lead ore which is treated at the concentrator and subsequently shipped out or treated at the smelter at Cerralvo. The mine is producing 1200 tons of 40% lead ore and is capable of furnishing 300 tons of zinc carbonate ores monthly. The smelter at Cerralvo has facilities for the treatment of 35,000 tons of lead ore per annum. Transportation between the mine and smelter and the railroad junction at Herreras is by means of five automobile-trucks.

3. *Providencia Mines.* These mines embrace an acreage of 788 and are capable of producing 4500 tons of lead-silver ores per month, of an average grade of 18% lead and 13 oz. of silver, and also 1500 tons of oxidized zinc ores running about 35% zinc. The ore is transported by an aerial tramway and narrow-gauge railway to the national railway at Saltillo. The zinc ores are sold in the United States and the lead-silver ores are treated at the various smelting-plants controlled by the company. A first-class power-plant is now under construction at these mines. The company has erected dwellings, hospitals, schools, and other modern conveniences for the workmen have been provided.

4. *Guanacevi.* In Guanacevi the company has recently acquired valuable silver properties with a total acreage of 415. As Guanacevi is far removed from the railway and in a district which has for the past two or three years been unsettled, the company has not yet begun operations there. Sufficient work has already been done on the properties to show that they are worth more than the amounts invested. As soon as conditions justify, the company anticipates active operations in this district.

5. *Santa Eulalia.* The Santa Eulalia properties cover 2935 acres, which are operated under lease, with an option to purchase. The leases run from 10 to 15 years and require the payment of a royalty. These properties are still in the development stage. Ores will be transported by aerial tram from Santa Eulalia to the main line of the national railway.

6. *Vera Cruz oil-lands.* Early in 1917, before the enactment of the new oil-land laws in Mexico, which have been the cause of so much dissension, the company acquired 6710 acres of oil-land under leases in the State of Vera Cruz. Some of these properties are adjacent to producing properties and are considered valuable, although no development work has been undertaken owing to high cost of operation and unsettled conditions.

7. *Railway equipment.* The company owns and operates about 30 locomotives and 900 cars, which equipment it was compelled to purchase in order to transport its product over the national lines. Operation is maintained under a contract with the Mexican government. The company has constructed extensive machine-shops at Monterrey, in order to keep its equipment in first-class condition. This equipment is used to haul the products of the company's mines to the smelter and from the mines to the border, and also to haul supplies from the States to the various plants, and has made it possible for the company to continue operation at a time when the service of the national railways could not be depended upon.

8. *Real estate.* The company owns office-buildings at Monterrey, Laredo, and Saltillo; also a recreation park in Monterrey.

9. *Compania de Combustibles Agujita, S. A.* This company was incorporated in 1917 with a captital stock of 65,000 shares of ₱100 each. Of these shares the Minerales Co. owns approximately 55,000, the rest being owned by Mexican citizens. The company owns coal-lands aggregating 2700 acres at Agujita and 1525 acres at Lampacitos. The developed tonnage is estimated at 18,000,000 tons, and the mines are capable of maintaining a production of 45,000 tons per month. A modern washery, recently completed, serves a coking-plant with a capacity of 12,000 tons at Agujita and 500 at Lampacitos. The largest proportion of the output of the Agujita Co., both coal and coke, goes to the Minerales Co. and the national railway lines. The excess is sold to domestic consumers through a fuel-selling company, which the Minerales Co. also controls.

10. *Fuel Sales Co. (Cia. de Combustible Nacional y Transportes, S. A.)* This company was incorporated with 1250 shares of ₱100 each, of which the Minerales owns 750, for the purpose of disposing of the excess production of coal and coke not required by Minerales and its subsidiaries or by the National Railway companies. This company has its own transportation equipment, consisting of three 90-ton locomotives and 60 standard-gauge cars, and maintains a retail-sales agency in Sabinas and Mexico City.

11. *Compania Metallurgica de Torreon.* This company has a capital stock of 50,000 shares of ₱80 par value, of which the Minerales Co. owns approximately 83%. The company owns 503 acres, including mines and a large smelting-plant near Torreon, which is a very central location, having good railway connections. The plant consists of nine lead blast-furnaces and one copper

blast-furnace, with an annual capacity of 400,000 tons. There is a copper converter to take care of the treatment of copper matte, and two Dwight-Lloyd roasting-machines, and all the necessary auxiliaries, such as power-plant, etc. The company has an extensive townsite, with dwellings suitable both for laborers and officials, offices, hospitals, schools, etc. This plant has been operated as a custom smelter for the past 15 years, and is well known throughout the northern mining districts of Mexico. The mining industry has not yet recovered from the effects of the Revolution, and the plant cannot be operated to full capacity at the present time. The normal production of this plant is 20,000 tons of silver-lead bullion per annum and 2500 tons of blister copper.

12. *Parrena Mining Co.* The capital stock of this company is ₱500,000, of which the Minerales Co. owns 50%. The company owns mining properties in the Sierra Nojada district, covering 475 acres, from which are produced lead-silver, copper, and zinc ores. The Parrena Co. also owns a 50% interest in the San Salvador mine in the same district, which has been producing for over 30 years. The Parrena Co.'s own properties are still in the development stage, although the value of the production up to date covers development expenses.

13. *Cia. Minera Paloma y Cabrillas, S. A.* This company has a capital stock of 72,000 shares of ₱50, which is distributed throughout the United States, Mexico, and foreign countries. The company owns 278 acres of mining properties near Higueras, in the State of Coahuila, and is connected with the National Railway lines at that point by an aerial tramway. It is capable of producing 5000 tons of iron-lead ores containing 15% lead and 3 oz. of silver, and 800 tons of zinc carbonate ores containing 32% zinc. The mine is equipped with adequate power-plant facilities as well as offices, workmen's houses, hospitals, schools, etc.

14. *Compania Minera de Penoles.* This company has a capital stock of 120,000 shares of ₱30 each. Its property, which is one of the best and longest known in Mexico, covers 7123 acres, from which 15,000 tons of lead-silver ores are being produced monthly, containing 14% of lead and 13 oz. of silver and 1 oz. of gold. The company also owns and operates a smelter at Mapimi, with five blast-furnaces and necessary roasting-plant for the treatment of 400,000 tons of charge per annum. The company also has an arsenic plant which produces arsenic as a by-product from smelting operations. One power-plant serves both mine and smelter, as well as the town. A narrow-gauge railway of about 25 miles connects both mine and smelter with the National Railway lines at Bermejillo. Both at the mine and smelter, which are about six miles apart, the company has provided adequate housing facilities for between 8000 and 10,000 persons; it also has erected first-class hospitals and schools, and has taken every possible precaution to protect the health and well-being of its employees. The normal production of the plant is 25,000 tons of silver-lead bullion and 5000 tons of white arsenic per annum.

15. *Smelter and refinery at Monterrey.* In 1918 Minerales perfected a leasing arrangement with the Compania Minera, Fundidora y Afinadora Monterrey, S. A., for the operation of its smelting and refining plant at Monterrey. This plant was recently modernized by its owners, and is now operating under the management of the Minerales staff. It has a capacity for smelting 200,000 tons of lead ores per annum and a refining capacity of 50,000 tons of lead bullion. It also has an electric silver parting plant for the separation of gold and silver, equivalent to a production of 10,000,000 oz. of silver. this plant is engaged primarily in treating ores and bullion controlled by Minerales, but it also handles custom business.

In addition to the above, the Minerales Co. has minority interests in several other companies which it does not operate, and also maintains a trading department for the purpose of facilitating the marketing of its own product as well as for the purchase and sale of the products of independent companies operating in the Republic. Owing to its facilities for transportation and its connection with the American Metal Co. in the States, it is always competitive for such outside purchases, which in the past have been principally of zinc ores.

The corporation, through its subsidiaries and allied companies, owns or controls the following products, the average annual quantities produced being as indicated below:

Electrolytic copper, pounds	100,000,000	to	125,000,000
Zinc (spelter), all grades, tons	75,000	"	100,000
Bonded (Mexican) lead, tons	60,000	"	75,000
Domestic lead, tons	12,000	"	15,000
Sulphuric acid, tons	80,000	"	100,000
White arsenic, tons	4,000	"	6,000
Coal in Pennsylvania, tons	350,000	"	400,000
Coal in Mexico, tons	500,000	"	600,000
Silver, ounces	12,000,000	"	15,000,000
Zinc oxide (Polar and Arctic brands), tons	7,000	"	10,000
Zinc dust (American Extra Pure and Zenith brands), tons	3,000	"	4,000
Antimonial lead, tons	1,000	"	1,500
Molybdenum concentrate, tons	500	"	1,000

In addition to its own production of metals, the company buys and sells metals in the open market, and also contracts to take the entire output of various mines, smelters, and refineries in the United States, Canada, Mexico, and South America, as follows:

Copper

For copper it has contracts with the following (contract calls for entire production):

	Lb. (estimated)
Granby Consolidated M. S. & P. Co., B. C.	50,000,000
Old Dominion Copper M. & S. Co., Arizona	30,000,000
East Butte Copper Mining Co., Montana	22,000,000
Central Chile Copper Co., Panulcillo, Chile	15,000,000
Ducktown Copper, Sulphur & Iron Co., Tennessee	12,000,000
Balbach Smelting & Refining Co., New Jersey	9,000,000
Shannon Copper Co., Arizona	8,000,000
Penn Mining Co., California	4,000,000
Democrata Copper Co., Cananea, Mexico	3,000,000
Ore Trading Co., Santiago, Chile	17,000

Copper Received During 1918

	Lb.
Central Chile Copper Co	2,856,048
Ducktown Sulphur, Copper & Iron Co	5,116,183
Beer, Sondheimer & Co	494,227
South American Metal Co	4,905,248
Old Dominion Copper Co	12,545,500
Granby Consolidated M. S. & P. Co	39,115,072
East Butte Copper Co	23,087,501
Democrata Copper Co	7,820,880

	Lb.
Shannon Copper Co.	6,805,520
Ore Trading Co.	13,445,643
Clarksburg Clinkering plant	33,781
Henry R. Merton & Co.	4,028,739
Nichols Copper Co.	9,500,000
Cia. de Minerales y Metales	2,399,748
Tintic Mining & Milling Co.	214,775
Penn Mining Co.	3,121,084
Tezuitlan Copper Co.	2,013,195
Balbach Smelting & Refining Co.	2,750,065
Ohio & Colorado Smelting Co.	1,145,164
Total	141,398,982

In addition therto the company trades in copper futures and also purchases copper in the open market. The copper is refined by the Balbach Smelting & Refining Co. of New Jersey and the Nichols Copper Co., in both of which American Metal Co. has a substantial interest.

The entire turnover of the company in copper is about 250,000,000 lb. per annum, which is about 15% of the country's total production of copper.

It obtains its zinc ores by contract from the following concerns:

Ores Received July 1916–June 1917

	Lb.
Consolidated Interstate Callahan Mining Co.	71,000,000
Butte & Superior Mining Co.	263,000,000
Linden Zinc Co.	3,219,000
Western Chemical Co.	10,000,000
Surprise Mines	1,700,000
Union Basin Mining Co.	57,000,000
Galena Farms Mining Co.	7,000,000
Cia. Minerales y Metales	134,000,000

These ores are treated by the smelters of the company's subsidiaries at Bartlesville, Oklahoma; Langloth, Pennsylvania; and Chanute, Kansas. The average monthly production is about 17,000,000 lb. In addition to this production the company buys and sells spelter on the open market.

The zinc ores purchased by the American Metal Co. and treated by the smelters of its domestic subsidiaries for the two years ended June 30, 1917, amounted to approximately 1,700,000,000 lb. In addition to that, the company purchased spelter during those two years in the open market amounting approximately to 585,000,000 pounds.

Spelter Received During 1918

	Lb.
Consolidated Interstate Callahan Mining Co.	22,873,579
Yellow Pine Mining Co.	1,063,546
Butte & Superior Mining Co.	58,364,324
Afterthought Copper Co.	636,669
Montana Mines	1,373,088
Yak Mining & Smelting Co.	82,828
Judge Mining & Smelting Co.	122,245
Joplin Ores	31,629,656
Wisconsin Ores	5,249,749
Cia. de Minerales y Metales	11,569,243
Western Chemical Co.	2,945,551
Union Basin Mining Co.	1,052,744
Surprise Mines	1,242,955
Galena Mining & Milling Co.	269,378
Downtown Mining Co.	247,075
Becker, Hanraty & Thomas	270,609
	138,903,230

The following are the concerns from whom the Metal company secures the bulk of its supply of lead:

Production for 1917

	Lb.
Cia. Minerales y Metales, Mexico	130,000,000
Ohio & Colorado Smelting & Refining Co., Colorado	30,000,000
Balbach Smelting & Refining Co., New Jersey	8,000,000

The company owns over 60% of the stock of the Ohio & Colorado and 97% of the Minerales companies, and 33⅓% of the stock of the Balbach Smelting & Refining Company.

The above figures, except those from Minerales Co., are of domestic lead purchases, but in addition the company buys bonded lead, which is the product of foreign mines and is smelted in bond.

The growth of the company is indicated by the following statistics:

Total sales and net earnings of the corporation after deducting all expenses, profit-sharing, taxes, fixed charges, etc., during the past ten years, have been as follows:

	Capital stock outstanding	Total sales	Net earnings
Year ending July 1, 1909	$3,120,000	$64,274,040.94	$854,719.78
Year ending July 1, 1910	3,500,000	84,402,083.11	685,334.86
Year ending July 1, 1911	3,500,000	68,519,484.06	842,780.75
Year ending July 1, 1912	3,500,000	57,060,048.26	1,365,816.12
Year ending July 1, 1913	3,500,000	79,243,602.96	1,001,895.12
Year ending July 1, 1914	3,500,000	68,835,488.65	1,088,770.94
Year ending July 1, 1915	3,500,000	68,468,179.67	2,498,639.83
Year ending July 1, 1916	3,500,000	153,796,848.31	7,638,336.85
Half year ending Dec. 31, 1916	3,500,000	82,015,281.86	4,899,750.50
Year ending Dec. 31, 1917	7,000,000	149,216,409.21	2,892,387.45
Year ending Dec. 31, 1918	7,000,000	106,166,089.07	*832,157.69

*Estimated.

(To be Continued)

Nitrates

An interesting event in the nitrate situation has been the effort of the Government to dispose of its large supplies of nitrate. Stocks amounted to 226,000 tons in the United States, and 120,000 tons in Chile, all acquired at high prices. It has been decided to offer this for sale through the trade with as small a loss as possible, and the first price set was $4.20 per 100 lb. ex vessel at Atlantic and Gulf ports. Early in March this price was cut to $4.07½, this to hold during March and April only. Though this reduction led to increased sales, the price is still high compared with pre-war prices, but the Government is not making any profit. It is thought that manufacturers of explosives also hold considerable stocks of nitrate. Imports of nitrate of soda during February amounted to 44,817 long tons, and during the first half of March were 11,751 tons.—W. C. Phalen in March report of the U. S. Bureau of Mines.

Costs at the North Star mine, at Grass Valley, California, were as follows during 1918:

Department	Per ton mined	Per ton milled
Mining	$3.870	$5.047
Milling	0.456	0.595
Cyaniding	0.363	0.473
Tailing disposal	0.037	0.048
Bullion charges	0.018	0.024
Miscellaneous	0.251	0.328
New York office	0.116	0.152
Taxes	0.305	0.397
Accident and benefit	0.115	0.150
Development	0.071	0.093
Total	$5.602	$7.307
Less sundry credits	0.010	0.014
Net cost	$5.592	$7.293

Of the ore mined, 8% was discarded as waste, accounting for the two sets of costs. Ore extraction was from the 3400 to the 5000-ft. levels, while development was done down to 6300 ft., on the incline. The ore is crushed by stamps and cyanided, treatment being simple.

Examining a Prospect in Alaska

By F. LE ROI THURMOND

I left Anchorage, in Alaska, on March 14, 1918, in company with 'Doc' McCallie, veteran prospector, dentist, and hard-boiled Westerner, and 'Slim' Neff, dog-musher[1] extraordinary. Our destination was the locality of some claims owned by the doctor near the head of the Ohio river, a small tributary of the Chulitna river and about 30 miles in a north-westerly direction from Mt. McKinley.

The Alaskan Engineering Commission ran an accommodation train to Houston, a station 60 miles from Anchorage, where a coal mine was being operated. All the mushers going north loaded their dogs and outfits into cattle-cars and stowed themselves in Pullmans for this part of the trip. The get-away from Anchorage in the gray winter morning was full of color and sound. Switching engines, bumping cars, hustling baggage-men, cursing, befurred, and mukluked dog-mushers, yelping, snarling, fighting malamutes, near-malamutes, far-malamutes, and non-malamutes, with strains of every canine breed which the fancy of man and exigencies of evolution have produced.[2]

The train finally got away at 8:30 and out onto the low rolling glacial-formed terrain that skirts Knik Arm. The country is thickly wooded with small spruce and several varieties of birch, the latter, extremely graceful in themselves, presented a most pleasing and fantastic appearance with their delicate and intricate boughs covered with a crystalline deposit of frost.

Knik Arm itself appeared when the railroad wound around the base of some bluffs forming the valley-wall. Huge masses of anchor-ice lay stranded at high tide, then miles of hummocky ice-strewn flats marking the upper limits of the tide merging with the overflow from the deltas of the Knik and Matanuska rivers. The road crossed both these rivers close to their deltas and struck north through rolling gravelly ground, strewn with innumerable small lakes and swamps, an ideal moose country.

[1]We shall abstain from editing the text severely because it is impossible to do so without spoiling its spirit and local color. Alaskans will like the author for using the terms with which they are familiar. A 'mukluk' is a moccasin; a 'malamute' is an Eskimo dog; a 'siwash camp' is a camp without bedding, tent, or other conveniences. 'Siwash' from the French 'sauvage,' is a name given to the Indians of the North-West. A 'sour-dough' is a seasoned frontiersman. These prospectors and woodmen, unable to procure yeast, carry a little can filled with sour dough-batter; with this and by the addition of a little baking-soda they start the leavening of the bread in the form of pancakes, or 'flap-jacks'.—Editor.

[2]The word 'musher' is Chinook and comes from the French 'marcher', to walk. It is one of many words brought to the North-West by the French trappers.—Editor.

Arriving at Houston at 1:30 p.m., men and dogs detrained and put up at the road-house till the following morning. Here we met a party of mushers who had come over the trail from Fairbanks and who entertained us

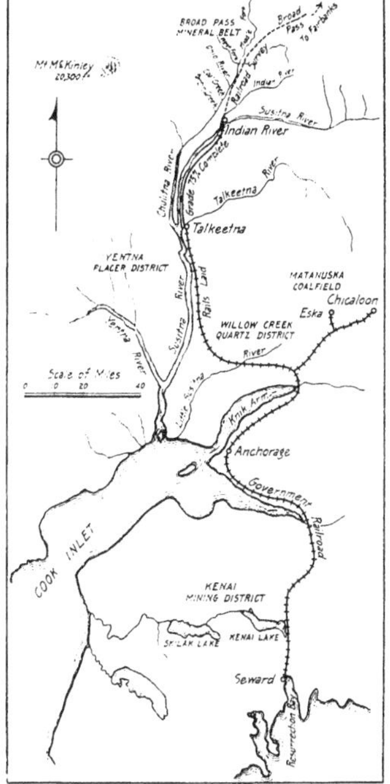

A PART OF ALASKA, SHOWING LOCALITIES MENTIONED IN THE NARRATIVE

with vivid accounts of the difficulties of the trail and the hardships that lay before us. The following morning, with a minus 28° temperature, we strung out our dogs and got away flying at 8 o'clock. The trail was well-beaten and the going good. We did 18 miles by 3 p.m. and were obliged to call it a 'day' if we wished to spend the night at a road-house. Next day a stiff wind blew from the north and with sore muscles we whipped our dogs into it and fought it all day, making 20 miles. We stopped for the night at a tie-camp on Sheep creek. In the morning the wind was blowing with such fury that traveling was impossible, so we laid up all day, glad of the chance to rest. The following morning the wind having subsided, we started for Talkeetna, 23 miles, which we made at 6:30 and stopped at the road-house kept by a Mrs. Small, where the musher's physical requirements were anticipated and well-provided for.

From Talkeetna the trail lay on the Susitna river, as affording the only feasible route of travel. Our next camp was Dead Horse, 23 miles, where the Alaskan Engineering Commission maintains a large summer camp. Here were mess-house, dormitories, offices, hospitals, barns, and warehouses built of cottonwood lumber sawn on the ground. A watchman and a storekeper were in charge of the camp and provided us accommodations for the night. An incident occurred that served as a warning of the thieving propensities of Alaskan dogs, which will steal and eat anything that has ever been even remotely connected with animal tissue, with a special liking for rawhide snowshoe-thongs. While we were at dinner a stray dog belonging to the camp had torn open the lashings and tarpaulin on our sled and succeeded in dragging out a piece of bacon weighing ten pounds, which constituted a part of our dog feed. He evidently was not very hungry, as he left several square inches of rind, and the gelatine and cloth coating that protected the bacon. His little dinner-party cost us just $4, but he appeared to think it worth the price as he licked his chops well out of the range of boot or other missile.

Another day's march brought us to Indian River at the head of navigation on the Susitna, and the following day we reached the Chulitna river and made camp late in the evening.

The following notes, in the third person, written by one of the members of the party, narrate the incidents of the next few days:

"The party struck bad weather from the start and had to outface old Boreas day after day. On the ninth day out from Anchorage, they left their camp on the Chulitna river in the morning and planned to reach a cache which was known to exist at Shot Gun creek eight miles up the Ohio river—which river is the same as designated "the unnamed river" by Belmore Brown in his account of the successful ascent[3] of Mt. McKinley by himself, Prof. Hershel Parker, and Merle La Voy in 1912.

There was no trail and the soft loose snow had to be packed with snow-shoes before the dogs and sled could negotiate it. The three men would mush on a couple of hundred yards and then back to the dogs. Then the sled would be brought up and left while another piece of trail was beaten down. In the afternoon the wind increased and it started to snow heavily, which added nothing to the gaiety of the occasion. When the mushers would get back to the sled after making a hundred yards ahead, there was no sign of trail, it being completely obliterated by falling and drifting snow. Night came on, the wind and snow increased, the men were exhausted and forced to make a 'siwash' camp for the night. As they did not expect to camp on the road, trusting to stop at caches made the previous summer, they had no cooking utensils or food that could be prepared without, so they spent the night supperless. But thanks to Prometheus or whoever it was that stole the heavenly flame from high Olympus, they had a fire; and if it was a choice between food and fire under such circumstances, the latter would win of necessity.

In the morning after breakfast—the hour, not the act—Slim started up the river to look for the cache, knowing that it must be near. Thurmond started an hour later, the storm was unabated and no sign of Slim's trail could be seen. Thurmond went about three miles up the river, and decided that he had passed the cache, owing to the storm, and turned back. Leaving the river in order to inspect a wooded bench where he suspected the cache might be, he caught a glimpse of a white tent-shaped canvas high up in the spruce tops. It proved to be the cache he was seeking, so he returned to the river and placed a note in a crotched stick and an arrow pointing to the cache for the benefit of Slim whenever he should return from his fruitless search up the river.

Returning to the cache, a tent left standing the previous summer was discovered as a slight unevenness in the expanse of snow. With a shovel from the cache, it was soon dug out. Inside were dry wood and shavings ready for the match, left the previous summer by some real member of the sourdough clan.

Within an hour, rice and biscuits, tea and bacon were ready and Slim came staggering in, having found the sign, too far spent to take off his snow-shoes. He had missed the cache, gone four miles up the river and was going back to the siwash camp for another night. The tea and food put heart and life into both men and they started back to get 'Doc' and the outfit. It was only two miles from the siwash camp to the cache, but two miles of adverse trail in the teeth of a blizzard with spent dogs can yield a sight of grief. All three men, with dogs and outfit, reached the cache at 7 o'clock and supper was gotten, with a feed of rice and bacon for the dogs.

That night a little 7 by 9-ft. tent in the heart of the Alaskan wilderness held more luxury than a king's palace. Ten days the storm continued, snow and wind. It was only four miles to where the party planned to make a permanent camp, but it might as well have been four hundred. Then when the storm had worn itself out they made the remaining distance and established permanent camp, just in time to escape another storm, which playfully hove in from the north and tarried 13 days. During this wind the hard-packed and frozen snow on the river and gravel flats which had been accumulating all winter to a depth of five feet was cut down to the ice and rock by the force of the blast."

[3]'The Conquest of Mt. McKinley', Putnams, 1913.

To continue my narrative in the first person: It was now the 21st of April. I had been out more than a month and had not seen the ground. My information was that as the outcrops had a southern exposure the ground could be examined in April. The unusually late storms and heavy snow had delayed the spring thaw fully two weeks. A trip was made to the ground, three miles farther up the canyon, but as there was no evidence of bare ground we returned to camp to wait until the weather warmed up. The first of May the snow was sufficiently melted to get into a couple of prospect-tunnels, and the next three days were spent in making a rough reconnaissance of the ground, very unsatisfactory, however, on account of lingering snow. As there were signs of the rivers breaking, rendering travel impossible, and my affairs needing my attention in Anchorage, I decided to start on the 5th, leaving the other men, who were going to stay till midsummer to prospect the ground.

ON THE TRAIL

It was now so warm during the day that the snow was mushy and travel impossible, so taking two of the dogs on a light Yukon sled, I started down the river as soon as the night frost had formed a crust sufficient to support dogs and sled, at about 1:30 a.m. At this time of the year the sun was so far north that it gave light enough to travel all night. It was a crisp morning when I left and as the sled went slipping down the river, a cock ptarmigan resplendent in his mating finery got up from under the leading dog's nose and flew sputtering and cackling a hundred yards down the river, where he strutted and fretted for the benefit of any lady ptarmigan who might be in the vicinity.

About 2:30 a splash of crimson in the north-east heralded the rising sun and for the next two hours a truly amazing kaleidescope of color fascinated and awed me. In all the catalogue of Nature's wonders there is nothing more sublime than a sunrise in the mountains of the North.

I had covered 20 miles by the time that the trail got soft, at 9 a.m., so I unhitched the dogs and tied them under a tree, rolled myself in a blanket and went to sleep. I awoke about six o'clock, gave the dogs each about a pound of bacon and ate a biscuit myself. Then I hitched up the dogs and hit the trail with snow-shoes, putting the dogs on a long lead and taking the gee-pole, as the crust would not support me on the sled at this hour in the evening. I had to cross a wooded summit of about six miles, between the Chulitna and the Indian river, and the going through brush and timber was extremely rough. To anyone interested in synchronized movements, I would recommend a study made on snow-shoes astraddle of a tow-line, with a gee-pole in hand, on a trail that seems bent on describing a straight line—by antithesis.

THE AUTHOR

By the time I reached Indian river and the snow was well crusted, I had gotten up a sweat that soaked my clothing. To have ridden on the sled in such condition would most certainly have been folly, so I built a snappy fire of the dry twigs and limbs that are found around the base of the spruce, and so dried and warmed myself, before going further.

An hour's run down the river brought me to a canyon where the river was open from wall to wall. Sounding it with a pole, I found I could wade it, so pulled off my socks to keep them dry, rolled up trousers, and with my 'packs'[4] on my feet to protect them from rocks and ice, I

[4]A 'pack' or 'shoe-pack' is a moccasin made of waxed hide. 'Cache' is a French word; it means a place for concealing or storing anything, especially provisions.—Editor.

waded across, carrying dogs and outfit, necessitating three trips. My feet were paralyzed from the icy water; but after getting my socks on, and stamping around to warm my feet, I started again, running behind the sled. A hundred yards farther, and I ran into another hole and had to repeat the performance.

Getting out of this, I continued down-river, running hard behind the sled to restore circulation in my feet. I was just leaving the river-trail to take a short cut through the woods when my dogs stopped and began to bark furiously. I got out my revolver, as I suspected that it might be a brown bear which had early crawled out of its winter quarters and might consider myself or dogs as suitable spring forage. Peering down the river, I saw a moving body and heard the voices of men and barking of dogs. They were going into the country I had just left and as 'Doc.' and Slim were short of sugar and I desired to send them some, I invited one of the men to accompany me back to Indian River station where I would get the sugar and give my dogs and sled to him if he would carry it to 'Doc.' This he agreed to do. Arriving at Indian River about 2:30 I procured the sugar and despatched him, while I got a cup of coffee and a bite to eat, and was off on foot down the Susitna river. The snow was hard-crusted and the going so splendid that I wished to put as much of the trail behind me as possible while the crust lasted. I carried my snow-shoes for an emergency, but snow-shoes in mushy snow are only a little better than none. I arrived at Dead Horse, 20 miles, at 2 p.m., having traveled 55 miles since the previous morning. I was worn and hungry, so, after a lunch, I lay down to sleep leaving instructions to call me at midnight, when, after a little breakfast, I again hit the trail, and arrived at Talkeetna, 23 miles, at 10:30. Here the river was breaking up and the snow almost gone. Resting another night I found the trail bare of snow and the following day I walked into Houston, from where we had started with our dogs, six weeks earlier, and boarded a train for the final lap to Anchorage.

My trip, while absorbing six weeks' time, was productive of such meager information that I was again commissioned to visit the property late in the summer. Accordingly, I left Anchorage on August 22 and traveled by train to Montana Creek, 35 miles farther than on the previous journey. Here, after waiting two days, I got passage up the river on a boat belonging to the Alaskan Engineering Commission, a fleet of these boats being engaged in distributing material and supplies for the railroad construction from Montana Creek to Indian River. The first day an incident occurred that disturbed the monotony of the lazy summer afternoon. I am moved to remark in passing that there are more ways of killing a bear than letting daylight through his innards with a vest-pocket siege-gun, but the following way, which came under my observation, is not one of them.

I was lying asleep in a berth in the pilot-house of the B. and B. No. 2, while the boat was rapidly steaming up-river at the rate of a mile an hour when I was startled by some one shouting "Bear!" I came to with camera in hand and got out on the bow before any considerable quantity of time had flown. Looking up-stream and toward the right bank I saw a big bear wade out into the stream and start to swim across. The current carried him down-stream and his attention being attracted by the movement of the boat, he turned and started to swim directly toward it. Standing on the bow, I pulled out the camera to a 100-ft. focus and set the shutter and diaphragm, after consulting my exposure metre, and waited for eventualities. They were not long in arriving. The boat was going up-stream, the bear down, each seemed bent on making the acquaintance of the other, and it looked like something ought to happen. The bear came up to within five feet of where I stood on the low flat deck, with one eye appraising the various points of vantage among the cargo, in case the bear decided to take passage on the boat, and the other steely gazing right into those of Mr.—or Mrs.—Bruin, I snapped the camera. About that time the action commenced. A deck-hand made a lunge at the bear with a pike-pole and caught him just abaft the shoulder. The pike would have gone through, had not the right-angle prong prevented. As it was, it gave bruin quite a shock and rolled him over in the water, when another deck-hand tried to fish him in with the hook of his pike. Just what he intended doing with the bear when he should get him on deck, I failed to comprehend. The bear, his feelings injured by the reception he had met, allowed the current to carry him past the boat, when the captain thought to take a hand in the chase, and put the wheel hard over, intending to turn and follow the bear down river. The boat had turned through about 140° and was going down-stream at a pace when the bottom of the river came up and hit the keel a wallop. The boat took the count on a sand-bar, while bruin swam across the river and crawled out, shook himself, and with a bare glance at the stranded boat, bade farewell to the scene. I turned to close my camera and noticed the focusing scale set at 100 ft.—and the bear was only five feet away when I snapped the shutter! Being handicapped in the matter of expression, speaking only two languages, American and profane, I forbore, and charged up the loss of a rare picture to buck fever, while I went to help the crew get the boat off the sand-bar.

Three days on the river and I arrived at Indian River station, where I was met by Jack Frisby, a guide with a pack-horse, and the following morning we proceeded, following the same trail I had traveled by dog-team in the winter, for about 20 miles, when instead of crossing the Chulitna river, we went up-stream to the forks, crossed the east fork and camped for the night on the west fork in an old cabin near the Golden Zone property of the Wells brothers, which was the scene of considerable excitement and activity in 1914 and 1915.

During the afternoon we passed a U. S. G. S. party in charge of D. C. Witherspoon, dean of topographers, and I made arrangements with J. E. Luttrell, one of the party, to meet me on the Ohio river in five days and conduct me to a property that he owned on Partin creek and which he was desirous that I examine. We also passed a big brown bear in a blueberry patch busily engaged in building up calories against the long hard winter.

In the cabin where we camped I found a note from a prospector whom I had met on the trail the previous winter. He had frozen his feet the night we siwashed on the Ohio river and had lived in the cabin several months while waiting for them to heal. His body was found several weeks later on a sand-bar of the west fork by Witherspoon's party. It appeared that he had lost his life while attempting to ford the river and had been dead several months when found.

The following morning we climbed out of the valley of the west fork and struck across the hills toward the Ohio river. We were in an open country above timber-line, with easy contours and pleasant traveling. The ground was cut up with caribou trails made in previous years, when great herds made their spring and fall migrations between their summer range on the flanks of Mt. McKinley and the northern slope of the Alaskan range, where the snow is less heavy in winter. We saw no caribou, as they are becoming very scarce in this region, but many bear, both black and brown; the rightly-respected *Ursus Gyas* of south-western Alaska, the largest member of the bear family, and judging from abundant evidence, the most ill-natured. Blueberries grew in great profusion and furnished a most appetizing lunch whenever it pleased our fancy. They were a welcome change from bacon and bannocks. Bears are very fond of blueberries and hardly a day but we passed one or more, busily devouring the sweet little fruit. We carried no guns, not wishing to be detained by hunting or killing of game.

We reached our destination in 11 days from Anchorage. I spent five days in examining the property and making a reconnaissance survey. We then packed up and started down the river, expecting to meet Luttrell at Pauley's cache on Shot Gun creek, as we had arranged. Arriving there at noon, we found no sign of him. After a meal I sent my guide and packer out with the samples I had taken while I started across the mountains alone to examine Luttrell's prospect, knowing that there was a prospector in there whom I could depend on for food if the meager supply I had gave out. I traveled all afternoon up a mountain slope, carrying about 40 pounds: camera, tripod, used with Brunton compass and camera, tape, note-book, biscuits, and chocolate. At night, I found I had followed the wrong fork of Shot Gun creek and was obliged to camp a long way above timber-line, near a glacier.

The following notes are taken from my diary from September 6 to 12.

"Sept. 6. I am writing this somewhere near the top of the world, left camp on Ohio river this a.m. 7:30. A beautiful day. The sun shone magnificently. We traveled to Pauley's cache, on Shot Gun creek, where we unpacked and lunched. I then sent Frisby out by the west fork. I took nine biscuits, a pound of bacon, 1½ lb. sweet chocolate, my 30-40 rifle, 12 shells, camera, Brunton compass, and tripod, and started over the mountain, following the north fork of Shot Gun creek. The first thousand feet of elevation was through heavy alders; then I came out on the open mountain. I was tired when starting and it became a task to force my legs and lungs to do the work of carrying me. I kept up all afternoon and estimate that I have traveled 10 miles and climbed [illegible] ft. Once on looking miles across the valley of the Ohio river I saw Frisby's horse outlined against the sky and then disappear down the opposite slope. A feeling of uneasiness attacked me. For all that I knew to the contrary, I was the only human being in the vast territory west of the Chulitna river, and with rations for only three or four days at the most.

All about me are bare and mighty mountains. I am on a summit and near a great ice-field in which the stream I have been following heads. The cold wind from the glacier is sending a chill into my bones, through sweat-soaked clothing. There is absolutely no fuel here, not a twig. I will have to go down into the valley where there are probably willows. It is 9:30. The sun has just set behind a great sawtooth range and the mountains stand out against a lambent sky, like barriers against the invasion of the mysterious region beyond. To the south-east, two hundred miles away, I can see the snow-clad summits of the south-eastern arm of the great crescent of the Alaska range, lavishly painted by the setting sun. A peculiar phenomenon is seen in the North. Great rays of pink, violet, and amethyst radiate from a point on the horizon near the magnetic pole. The phenomenon resembles the Northern Lights but, in the rarer tints of the evening sky, surpasses the Aurora in delicacy of coloring.

I am getting cold. I hear a noise on the slope below—a bear probably. I must descend into the valley and see if I can find some fuel. I shall freeze here.

Sept. 7—8 a.m. Went part way down the mountain last night. Found some small willows in a gulch, enough to keep a handful of fire all night. Found this morning I was in a glacial cirque with no way out except the way I came in. I am on the wrong fork of the creek, should have taken the first creek to the left and crossed this one. It is starting to rain. I will go back to Pauley's cache, stay there tonight and start again in the morning.

Sept. 8—7 a.m. Made Pauley's cache at two o'clock, slept three hours, feel much refreshed. No grub in cache except rice, no salt or sugar but some coffee. Boiled a piece of bacon which I had left in order to get some salty water to cook rice. It is raining hard today. Streams rising. I cannot get across the Ohio river to follow Frisby if I would, so I must make another try for Partin creek.

8 p.m. Tried to get over to Partin creek today; rained hard and snowed. Had to wade the creek through canyons, and fight alders. Got above timber five miles up-creek, drenched to the hide, cold wind cut to bone, sapped my strength. Decided it suicidal to continue—no fuel—turned and stumbled down-hill through drenched grass and dripping alders. Waded in creek, grasping overhanging alders to keep my feet, too numb with cold

and weakness to fight a way through the tangled alders. Nearly perished. Did not think I would get back to Pauley's cache. The cold had sunk into my bones and was paralyzing me. Got back to Pauley's cache about three o'clock, got a fire started, and wet clothes off while a pot of coffee was making. The coffee and fire set my blood to circulating and I sat naked by the fire, letting the warmth soak in.

Sept. 9. Yesterday's exposure affected my heart and lungs. Ate some rice without salt for breakfast and it sickened me. Have still got coffee. Rained all night, snow on summits. I cannot travel today and have no food. There is an old cache across Shot Gun creek which I am going to investigate if I can fall a tree so as bridge the creek.

Later. Got sugar, salt, beans, and flour in cache; have enough to eat for ten days; found an old mouth-organ in cache, gave it a sterilizing bath and tried to play on it, found it had but one tune, "Home Sweet Home", so I threw the damn thing away. Found a few disconnected leaves of a serial story in a fiction classic, 'Adventure' and am having a literary debauch. Have developed pleurisy from exposure yesterday, cannot travel until it gets better and storm quits. Wonder how the War goes. Fifteen days since I left Indian creek. The rivers are raging and could not cross them without a horse. May have to stay here until freeze-up and get out on ice.

Sept. 10. Rained all night, furiously. Ate no breakfast, but drank a cup of coffee. Have only coffee enough for two more days. Then I will be in bad. Prospected right bank of Shot Gun, got a few fine colors. Took rifle and went a distance up-creek, looking for a bear. Did not find him. Snow came down to about 3000 ft. last night; clearing up today. If sun shines tomorrow, will make another try for Partin creek.

Sept. 11. My stock went down last night. It was raining when I went to sleep. On waking this morning, not hearing the pelting on tent, thought it had stopped. Looking out, found it had—and then snowed a foot. Things look black. What now? I am too weak to travel. The sole has come off one shoe from continual wetting and climbing over rocks. It is 80 miles and five rivers to cross to get to Indian.

Sept. 12. Made Partin creek and found prospector's camp at 4:30. Heart-breaking trip over mountain through snow mid-leg deep. Saw and photographed tracks of big brown bear. Saw ptarmigan changing to winter coat. Rock formation sedimentary. Found vein in gulch near head of creek, 12 ft. wide. Took a small hasty sample. From summit saw two white objects in valley of Partin creek, thought they were tents, not sure, got down, found it so, crazy prospector named Partin in one of them."

Returning to my narrative. I rested a day with Partin and then the following morning had him guide me to the prospect that I was seeking, where I made a brief examination and returned to his camp in the evening. As it was nearly 100 miles to Indian River and four glacial streams to cross, to return by the way I came, I decided to attempt a crossing of the Chulitna river and thus save about 60 miles. As Partin wished to go out with me, we left his camp on the morning of the 15th and made a stop on the banks of the Chulitna that night. It rained steadily, so that we were obliged to stand up all night. The following day we built a raft. While getting out timbers, I was obliged to climb a birch to cut off a limb that had caught and held a dry spruce which we desired for our raft. When half-way through the limb, it suddenly snapped and pinned me in the crotch of the tree. Partin climbed the tree and with a hand-spike released my leg, which felt as if it had been broken, but after getting the circulation restored, found it uninjured.

Our raft was completed just before dark and as the river was rising and becoming more obstreperous, owing to the continual rain, I decided to make the crossing at once. We had built the raft just below a canyon where the current was confined to one channel, and which, immediately below, split into many channels where it traversed a wide gravel-bar. It was my plan to launch the raft where the current set toward the opposite bank and with the aid of a steering oar, so angle it that the current would force it across, before getting into the split channels.

A mile and a half below was a box canyon through which no raft could live and to enter which meant certain destruction. We had a pair of oars rigged to help in getting across. Partin manned the oars and I handled the tail-sweep. I pushed it out into the stream and when she began to throb, jumped on, and yelled to Partin to pull. Before I got control with the sweep, the current caught and whirled the raft around several times and threw it against a snag in mid-stream, which was just on the dividing line between safety and disaster. She swung around and went down the wrong split of the channel. We were in mid-stream and going fast. The opposite bank of the channel was the inner side of a curve and by angling the raft against the current I calculated to get close enough to jump. Partin was crazy with fear and was predicting disaster and wailing when I shut him up in a manner more effective than polite. "Pull! You blankety blank fool, or you'll have supper in hell and a gullet full of Chulitna mud!" He shut up and applied himself to the sweeps. We were nearing the point of the bend and I saw we would miss it, so I yelled to Partin to jump, and with knapsack in hand I followed. It was shallow enough to gain a footing and we climbed out while the raft went whirling down toward the canyon.

The problem that confronted us now was to get across the remaining channels. By cautiously fording at the widest places and using a stick between us, one upstream, the other down, we made the opposite bank after wading eleven channels.

It was now dark, and we built a big fire under a friendly spruce and proceeded to siwash it another night. We boiled a little rice and made some coffee, and spent the night drying our clothing. In the morning, after more coffee and rice, we started for Indian River. It

ON THE SUSITNA RIVER, AT TALKEETNA

ALASKAN ENGINEERING COMMISSION'S BOAT AT TALKEETNA, ALASKA

THE ERICKSON FARM, NEAR FAIRBANKS, ALASKA

A CABBAGE PATCH AT FAIRBANKS

THE SANTA ANNA SALMON CANNERY

THE HERD OF REINDEER OWNED BY THE AMERICAN MISSIONARY ASSOCIATION

FIELDS OF WILD COTTON ON THE EAGLE RIVER NEAR JUNEAU

AT THE HEAD OF NAVIGATION ON THE SUSITNA RIVER, ALASKA

started to snow as we left camp and continued to snow steadily all day.

We followed a blaze going in our general direction until noon when the blaze was lost in a swamp; we traveled by compass until we struck a survey where the brush was cut and traveling was easier. The snow was soft and wet and lay on one's shoulders until it melted and ran through and trickled down one's spine and oozed out of one s boots. Our way lay through a spruce swamp that had been surveyed and re-surveyed as a feasible route for the railroad, three parties having left blazes and slashings, intersecting the swamp. Travel by compass across the swamp was extremely difficult and irksome owing to a tangle of brush and the soft snow and tundra. So we followed several blazes and cuttings until we lost them in a bog, or in a labyrinth of criss-cross trails that marked the site of a survey-camp. We were seeking to intersect the main trail, the position of which I was fairly well aware.

There was a big tent on the trail used by horse-wranglers packing to the survey party which was now working on the east fork. Partin said he knew where the tent was and as he had been over the trail many times I trusted to his instinct to guide him aright. It was growing dark, we had been going all day, cold and wet and hungry, to say nothing of weariness after two nights of sleeping on our feet. Partin said we were near the tent and would make it in less than a mile. I was nearly ready to drop. We finally came to the track of two men in the fresh snow, not over an hour old. Partin yelled that we were saved. I examined the tracks, and shuffled off my pack—decided it was time to camp when one begins to walk around in circles. Partin, the damn fool, would not believe they were our own tracks.

We rustled a little dry wood from under the wet snow and with the aid of the dry twigs that I found around the butts of swamp spruce got a fire going. We cut down a green spruce about a foot in diameter to have fuel enough to last till morning. It rained and snowed all night. We could not lie down or even sit down. The ground was swimming; our clothing was saturated. We boiled and ate the last of our rice, about four ounces for each.

That was the most awful night I ever lived through, with every fibre of my body shrieking for rest—cold, wet, and hungry. Standing before the fire unable to relax, I was still able to jest. Partin, the demented, was morose and dispirited. Toward morning I lost consciousness long enough to fall forward into the dying fire. I broke the fall and prevented a burn by reaching instinctively and grasping the unburned end of the green log.

As soon as it was light we started again, I taking the lead and going entirely by compass, turning only for several small lakes. The going was desperately hard, over snow-covered tundra and through tangled snow-laden brush. Toward eleven o'clock, I felt myself growing weak and my legs frequently gave way under me. We were not making much progress, it still snowed and I knew that we were in a serious position. I was sure that another night out would do for us and leave our bones for the wolverines.

I took off my pack and threw away some samples which I had packed for three days, also my tripod for camera and compass. They would be no good to me or the wolverines, and I stood a better chance of getting out if I lightened my load. In half an hour I had found the trail and after following it for two miles came to the wranglers' tent.

It was in a mud-hole made by horses' hoofs; the snow had broken it down, there was several inches of mud and water in it and the rain ran through the roof in streams. There was a battered camp-stove on stilts, and the pipe had blown down. There was no wood cut, but there was one dry corner in the tent and some food in a box.

It was real salvation and if I ever get to Paradise. I know that I will not have more of joy than percolated through my blunted consciousness when it hove in sight. While Partin got wood, I started the fire and made a dive into the grub-box. I found a can of Van Camp's pork and beans, and with a benediction on old Van and an axe I cut it open and emptied it into a skillet with about a pound of bacon-drippings and then listened to the heavenly music while they sputtered in the pan. Then I found a tin of corned beef and sent it to join the beans and then made a gallon of coffee, specific gravity about 2.5, and then finding a box of macaroni, I boiled and drained a pot of it and slithered it in butter and it followed the beans and corned beef and coffee. Then, the edge of our appetite being somewhat blunted, we proceeded to dry our clothing. When the pack train pulled up, and started to unload, it was bringing out Secrists' locating party, which had just finished its season's work in Broad Pass. There were 15 horses and 10 men, including Lon Wells and Jack Coffee, old-time prospectors and guides, and J. L. McPherson, secretary of the Alaska Bureau of the Seattle Chamber of Commerce, who was on his way to the coast from Nenana, after having made his annual tour of Alaska. They carried a cook and a generous supply of food and after camp was established, a lean-to covered with a 'tarp' [tarpaulin] and a reflector of green logs for the fire in front, the tent repaired and carpeted with boughs, a supper was prepared in which we were invited to join.

McPherson shared his blankets with me under the lean-to, but the physical reaction was so severe that I could not sleep and suffered severely all night with muscular contortions and mental phantoms. The next morning after breakfast, we all continued the journey and arrived at Indian River in the middle of the afternoon. From there the following day we went down-stream on the 'Betty M.' to Montana Creek and thence to Anchorage over the railroad.

WATER-JACKETS in use since June 1913 at the blast-furnace plant of the Calumet & Arizona were replaced in 1918. The deterioration was confined almost entirely to the inside of the water space, the outside face showing little wear.

The Iron and Coal of France

Frank H. Probert, consulting engineer of the U. S. Bureau of Mines, and dean of the College of Mining, University of California, member of a special American Commission to investigate the damage done by the Germans during the War to the coal and iron and steel works of France and Belgium, after a personal investigation, has just returned to Washington with a first-hand story of the almost unbelievable atrocities of the Hun in the destruction and wreckage of the industrial life of France and Belgium. In a preliminary report, he says:

"Early in the War the German hordes swept southward through the iron basins of French Alsace and Lorraine, and for nearly four years this renowned mining area was held and exploited by the invaders. Many of the employees were made captives and compelled to work in the mines under German direction. The international boundary between France and Germany was drawn in 1871, to give the victor of the Franco-Prussian war control of the iron-fields, but since that time scientific development, guided by a better understanding of the local geology, exposed for France a greater ore-reserve at lower horizons than that of Lorraine Annexeé. With the return of Alsace and Lorraine to the mother land, France will become the dominant factor in the future steel industry of Europe. During the German occupation, the iron mines were not intensively exploited because of the necessity of recruiting into the Teuton army every able-bodied man and on account of the large accumulation of minerals in preparation for the War. The actual physical damage to the iron mines is relatively small when compared with the destruction of the coal-fields of northern France, which was as reprehensible as it was complete. Only in a few cases, where pillars have been robbed, is there any collapse of underground workings in the iron mines, but the equipment, both surface and underground, has been misused, and where ore has been mined, the lack of development will defer realization of capital until the exploratory work is sufficiently advanced to admit of daily output approximating pre-war conditions. The mines are not seriously crippled, but what of the steel plants in which the iron ores are smelted? No such atrocity was ever perpetrated against the industrial life of any country. Magnificent plants, comparing favorably with anything we have in the United States, are now but a tangled twisted mass of structural steel and broken stone. The wilful demolition was scientifically planned and systematically carried out. This after the removal of all such mechanical and electrical power units as could be used in Germany. The maliciousness and efficiency with which this crime against French industry was conducted is almost unbelievable.

In the coal districts of the Pas de Calais and the Nord, a sector fought over from the beginning to the end of the War, changing hands frequently, bombarded all the time, all surface structures whether of town, village, or mining enterprise have been razed. This may be legitimate warfare, but now that the guns are silenced and the frenzy of combat is past, it is horrible to look upon. Arras, Douai, Bethune, Bapaume, Lens, Loos, Courriere, centres of coal-mining activity but a few years ago and the mainspring of French industrial life, are gone, but the indomitable spirit of France survives and already plans are laid for the future. Bruay, at the western edge of the known coal-field, was not in the fighting zone and its output has been steadily maintained, but going eastward the frightfulness is more and more appalling, for the hate of the Hun left its mark on the mines during his forced retreat. The coal measures are overlain by water-bearing strata, necessitating special methods of shaft-sinking and support to keep the mines dry. The steel lining of the shafts was dynamited, letting in the quicksand and flooding the underground workings for many miles. In the entire Pas de Calais region it is estimated that 120 million cubic metres of water must be pumped before mining operations are resumed. Having flooded the mines, the head-frames and surface equipment were systematically dynamited, the twisted debris in many cases filling up the demolished shafts. It will probably be five years before this coal district can be rehabilitated and twelve to fifteen years before it gets back to normal pre-war output. The first great need is for buildings in which to house the workman.

The Saar coal-fields were visited by the Bureau of Mines officials. Here, in striking contrast to the mining districts of France and Belgium, the coal industry is at its height. German workmen and German engineers are still employed, but under the direction and supervision of French officers. A spirit of unrest is apparent everywhere, the suspense of the peace negotiations, uncertainty as to indemnity to be exacted, and lack of food, is telling on the already broken morale of the German workmen. Unfortunately the Saar coal does not give a desirable metallurgical coke to the French and the blast-furnaces now running are working inefficiently.

The French attitude toward her allies is an interesting psychological study. France has been hurt, really hurt by the long conflict. She has suffered perhaps more than any other nation, the battles have been fought mostly on her soil, her manhood has been drained of its best and most productive blood, her industries, her economic mainsprings have been ruthlessly destroyed. These two classes of French thought are desirous that France re-build herself, financed by German indemnity. They seek neither money nor advice from others; the irrespressible spirit will be all sustaining. Directors of industry, mine-owners, and employers of labor, possessed of the same love of country, look on the problem from another viewpoint. They claim that money borrowed from other countries at reasonable interest rates, new equipment for mines and plants purchased from America for early delivery, will admit of an earlier return to pre-war scale of operation and the higher immediate cost will be more than offset by the earlier realization of profits from natural resources and raw materials.

ALMA, COLORADO

SILVER MINING IN PARK COUNTY

Park county is experiencing more activity in mining than for many years, as the old silver properties, which have lain dormant for so many years, are now being re-opened, and are revealing large bodies of good milling and some rich ore already developed in the old workings.

The Moose mine, on Mt. Bross, has been purchased by the Louisiana-Colorado Mining Co. from the estate of Ludlow Patton of New York, and is to be re-opened. This company now owns 40 claims, equal to about 450 acres. It entered this field during 1917 and purchased the Dolly Varden property, which adjoins the Moose on the south, and immediately started erection of a 150-ton flotation plant and an 8000-ft. aerial tram from mine to mill. These were completed late last fall. A trial-run was made and two cars of concentrate was shipped to the smelter at Denver, which gave returns of 0.02 oz. gold, 177 oz. silver, and 4½% lead. The mill is now being equipped with a concentrate dryer and other machinery, and will be in full operation within a few weeks. E. A. Ritter, who is in charge, has succeeded in finding the fault that displaced the porphyry dike, along which the ore occurred in the old workings of the Dolly Varden, and is now driving a drift along the fault-plane to pick up the dike and the ore-shoot on their extension to the west. A discovery recently made in the workings known as the Drum Major tunnel bids fair to prove important. A flat contact deposit of from 8 to 10 ft. thick has been opened 200 ft., without coming to the limits of the ore. The whole orebody will average about 40 oz. of silver per ton just as the ore is broken, the first lot assorted for shipment returning 0.8 oz. gold, 388 oz. silver, 31% lead, and 3.65% copper.

The Louisiana-Colorado company was financed by southern capitalists, the officers consisting of A. J. Trone, president; E. A. Ritter, vice-president; and A. J. Brand, secretary-treasurer. These with Eugene Constantin, J. W. Lepine, W. H. Price, and Dr. Thomas Stark compose the board of directors.

The Reserve Mining Co., under the directorship of the State Treasurer, Harry E. Mulnix, Judge M. S. Bailey, and Senator James Moynahan, has acquired the Mineral Park property, which is directly under the Dolly Varden and covers the same mineral-bearing contact as the latter; and the Hoil group of 40 acres at the foot of Mt. Lincoln. The Hoil has produced the highest grade silver ore ever mined in the Alma district, and while the workings are in much the same condition as those of the Dolly Varden when that property was taken over, it bids fair to rival the latter in the quantity of developed ore. The work of re-opening the tunnels will be undertaken as soon as spring opens.

The Fanny Barret Mining & Leasing Co., under the directorship of A. D. Aitken, W. H. Spurgeon, and N. B. Cool, of Colorado Springs, has secured the Fanny Barret property on Mt. Loveland, and is erecting an aerial tram to facilitate movement of ore. This property has a substantial production of high-grade silver ore, and the tunnel now being driven will re-open the ore known to exist in the mineralized section adjacent to the old workings.

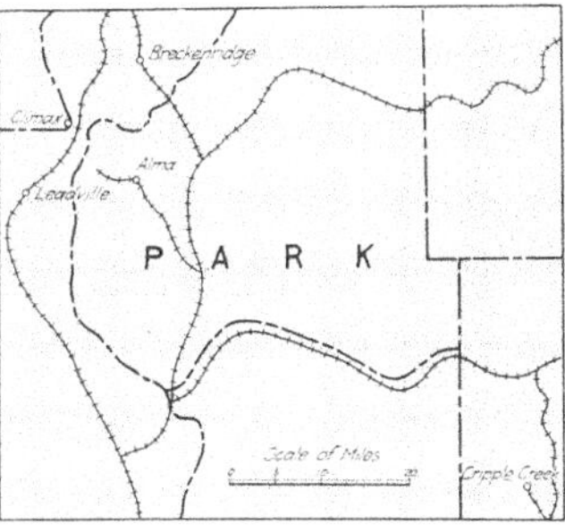

PART OF COLORADO, SHOWING PARK COUNTY

The Orphan Boy mine is being operated under lease and option by E. P. Young and associates. A few men are employed in cleaning-up the workings and getting ready for early operation.

G. W. Logan, manager for the Silver Tip Mining Co., states that work will be resumed on the Hock Hocking mine shortly. This property is equipped with a modern mill, and at the present price of silver should yield good profits from the ore now developed.

The London mine never looked better than at present. A steady production of ore assaying over 5 oz. is being sent out from the different leases in the upper workings. The London Mining & Milling Co., the owner, has erected a new compressor and will resume driving the lower tunnel, which will cut the vein 600 ft. deeper. The manager, C. P. Aicher, expects to have about 200 men employed before next fall.

The J. G. Blaine mine, under the management of J. E. Dollison, is being operated by Pittsburg people and shipments of grey copper ore, high in silver, are being made.

Development has been carried on with a small force at the Colorado Springs group for the past year, and it is now rumored that the transmission-line of the Colorado Power Co. is to be extended to this property and extensive development undertaken.

The Commonwealth Mining Co., with a large number of claims on North Star mountain, including the Magnolia and Lee Goss, will resume operations this spring, after an enforced idleness of a year, due to labor shortage. The aerial tram should be in running order by July 1. The ores will be treated in the Eddy mill, which has been remodeled for cyanidation.

The orebody cut in the workings of the Russia mine, while not as yet developed sufficiently to determine its size, promises to be extensive. The ore occurs in blanket form, is about 6 ft. thick, and averages 20 oz. silver per ton as mined. Negotiations are now pending that may result in the installation of machinery and extensive development.

The No End mine is being worked with a few men, by Warren F. Page and associates of Leadville. This property is situated in a highly-mineralized area, and adjoins the Great West mine, which made an output of rich gold and silver ore some years ago.

The Sun-Moon Leasing Co. has had 15 men employed on development for several months past. Several carloads of silver-lead ore have been shipped, and a steady output will be maintained during the summer. The property, known as the Hill Top, is in the Horse Shoe district, and has produced a large tonnage of silver, lead, and zinc carbonate ore.

BUTTE, MONTANA

ENGINEERS HOLD ANNUAL MEETING.—BUTTE & SUPERIOR INCREASES OUTPUT.—DAVIS-DALY TO IMPROVE EQUIPMENT.

The Montana Society of Engineers held its annual meeting at Great Falls on April 10 and 11. On the second day they inspected the new hydro-electric power-plant at Volta on the Missouri river, 13 miles from Great Falls. Current is generated at 100,000 volts by turbine-driven generators suspended on Armstrong bearings. The turbines are 155 ft. below the crest of the dam, which is 90 ft. high, and of solid concrete construction. On that afternoon the party also visited the new copper wire and rod plant at Great Falls. Here, the copper from the electrolytic refinery is melted, cast into wire billets, and rolled into the size of wire desired. At the present time the Chicago, Milwaukee & St. Paul Railroad is taking practically the entire output for the electrification of its road between Othello and Seattle. Next the electrolytic-zinc plant of the Anaconda was visited, where the process of leaching and precipitation was explained. On the 12th the party visited the filtration plant of the Great Falls water-works; and in the afternoon the annual meeting and banquet was held, at which the following officers were elected for the ensuing year: Samuel Barker, of Butte, president; C. A. Lemon, of Anaconda, first vice-president; George T. McGee, of Helena, second vice-president; C. H. Moore, of Butte, secretary; and H. H. Cochrane, of Butte, treasurer. After the business meeting the retiring president gave an address, and D. C. Bard, of Butte, gave a scheme for consolidation of the Montana Society of Engineers with the five national engineering societies as outlined by Mr. Rice, a member of the American Society of Mechanical Engineers.

The Butte & Superior Mining Co. has recently increased its output. Since November it has been operating at 50% capacity, but at present work is up to about 80%.

The Davis-Daly Copper Co.'s directors have been inspecting the property, and report that plans are under way for improvement of the surface equipment at the Colorado shaft, which will materially decrease costs. The party consisted of H. M. Burton, president; Charles G. Schrimer, secretary-treasurer; William Bloom, vice-president; Frank A. Schrimer, and Fred M. Kimball.

VICTORIA, BRITISH COLUMBIA

PRODUCTION OF IRON.—FOREIGN METALS.—OIL INVESTIGATION.—MINING ON INDIAN RESERVATIONS.—SMELTER SMOKE.—BELMONT SURF INLET DECLARES FIRST DIVIDEND. — NEW 8-HOUR LAW EFFECTIVE. — FRENCH PROCESS.

There was one fatality in the metal mines of British Columbia during the first quarter of the current year, compared with three in the same period of 1918. The death referred to was caused by a skip in the shaft of the Belmont Surf Inlet mine, Princess Royal island.

Experiments are soon to be started to determine the practicability of producing iron from British Columbian ores within the Province. The authority for this was given the Minister of Mines by an act passed at the recent session of the Provincial Legislature. Instructions have been given W. M. Brewer, district mining engineer, to take the necessary steps to obtain quantities of iron ore for shipment to those plants that have asked for it. Two smelters near Vancouver have undertaken to make the changes required for reduction of the magnetite ores. Under the terms of the act the Department of Mines can expend up to $50,000 in this work.

At a recent meeting of the Trail Reconstruction Board, objection was taken to the marketing in Canada of foreign metals, and representations were made to the Dominion government.

'The Coal and Petroleum Appropriation Act, 1919' is the title of a measure introduced by Hon. T. D. Pattullo, Minister of Mines, during the last session of the Legislature, and has become law. It provides authority for the expenditure of $50,000 in the investigation and exploration of potential oilfields in this Province. The work also will have in view the location and the obtaining of all possible information as to the possibility of developing on Crown lands new coal-producing areas. It is understood that attention first will be directed to the lands of the Peace River district, near the Albertau boundary.

Two measures passed at the last session of the Legislature affect the mining industry in an important manner. One of these provides for the amendment of the Placer Mining Act to permit every free miner, during the continuance of his certificate, to "enter, locate, prospect, and mine for gold and other precious metals and stones" upon Indian reservations. The other amends the Mineral Act to permit holders of free miners' certificates to "enter, locate, prospect, and mine" upon Indian reservations. These amendments do not come into effect until proclaimed law by the Lieutenant-Governor of British Columbia. The Dominion government, it should be explained, is the legally constituted guardian of the Indians, and it may take the position that the Province has no authority to permit miners and prospectors upon reservations. It will be necessary, therefore, before the said proclamation is issued for the Province to come to some understanding with the Federal authorities on the point and this matter already is being taken up by the British Columbian administration with Ottawa.

In the vicinity of the Trail smelter there is a considerable agricultural area, and the owners have been complaining of injury to their crops caused by the smoke from the plant. The petitions received from the farmers resulted in the enactment at the last session of the Legislature of the Industrial Operations Damage Compensation Act. The chief clause of this measure sets out that any company, owning or operating any reduction works or industrial plant, or proposing to acquire or operate any ore reduction works or industrial plant, "may make an agreement with the owner of any land for payment to the owner of compensation for any damage or injury resulting or likely to result to the land, or in respect of its present or future use, from the operation of the ore reduction works or industrial plant." If the company and the land-owner cannot come to an agreement, it is provided that application may be made to the Public Utilities Commission for the fixing of the amount of compensation rightfully due the latter. This, of course, constitutes a recognition of the claims of the farmer, and there is no doubt that it will result in a settlement of the issue between industrial companies and those agriculturists in the Province who have felt themselves aggrieved, but with no means of obtaining redress.

Considerable interest has been aroused by the recent declaration of an initial dividend of 5% by the Belmont Surf Inlet company, operating on Princess Royal island. The amount is $125,000.

The eight-hour working day for metalliferous miners came into force on April 1; 5500 men were affected. The law, which was passed at the session of 1918, provides for eight hours of work to metal miners from bank to bank, and for the same working day for those employed on the surface, the latter's time to commence from the moment they report for duty.

The French Complex Ore Reduction Co., which has a plant near Nelson, designed to experiment in the treatment of the complex ores from this Province, was granted $25,000 by the Provincial government in 1918, the same to be a charge on its assets. Of this amount the Government held back a sum to meet back interest on bonds previously guaranteed by the Province on behalf of the company. Thomas French, the manager, claimed that this seriously handicapped him in the work he has in hand and made such representations to the Mining Committee of the Legislature during the late session, that the Government will release to him $7906, representing the total of the aforesaid interest. Mr. French states that, providing this financial relief is forthcoming without delay, thus obviating unnecessary overhead expense, it would be sufficient to enable him to demonstrate the commercial feasibility of his method of treatment of complex zinc ores. Owing to past delays he states that his expenses have been excessive.

CRIPPLE CREEK, COLORADO

CRESSON RESERVES.—DIVIDENDS.—STRONG LEASES AND ROYALTY.—INCREASED ACTIVITY.

Roads for hauling ore have been cleared of melting snow, and shipments from properties not connected direct by rail are increasing. Dump operators are also returning to work, and the quantity of low-grade ore treated will be much heavier than during the long winter.

The monthly report of the Cresson gives an estimate of ore-reserves as worth $2,431,284. Details are given of two important discoveries: one, known as 812, has been developed a length of 55 ft., showing a width of 22 ft., with grab-samples averaging $29.60 per ton. The new orebody at the 11th level, while not fully developed, promises to be substantial, with grab-samples assaying $54.70 per ton. The ore shipped from the mine in February netted $90,002.

The Portland paid its regular quarterly dividend of 2 cents per share, $60,000, on April 20.——The Vindicator paid its quarterly of 1 cent, $15,000, on April 25.

Prospective lessees have been swarming to the Strong mine every day since it was announced that Owen Roberts, the lessee, would sub-lease, and every available block has been taken. The terms are severe: 25% royalty to the Strong G. M. Co., with 1% war-tax, leaving 74% of net returns to be divided 50-50 between the sub and original lessee. On ore returning $100 net, the sub-lessee therefore would receive but $37.

The Larson lease at the Six Points, and Basket and Luce lease at the American Eagles, mines of Stratton's Cripple Creek M. & D. Co., are shipping 2-oz. ore.

Two Ironclad Hill properties—the Jerry Johnson and Forest Queen—which have been under a snow blockade for three weeks, had teams employed the latter end of last week, loading out ore. The ore-houses at both properties are congested.

At the meeting of the Eagle Ore Co., held at the sampler in this district on April 12, the former officers, headed by G. S. Wood as president and G. A. Stuhl, secretary, were re-elected.

Properties in the district are now operated with full complements of men. Lessees are resuming at mines inactive during the winter, and others for more than a year. With further reduction in operating costs by lower prices for explosives and other supplies, the district would become more active than for a long time past.

DURANGO, COLORADO

POWER SHORTAGE.—GENERAL DEVELOPMENT NOTES.

TELLURIDE.—The shortage of power is noticeable in the number of men being laid-off. The Tomboy continues to operate; the Smuggler has its own power-plant, only buying power to operate hoists; the Liberty Bell has shut-down its mill, and will close the mine as soon as sufficient ore is in bins for re-starting the mill when power is again supplied; the Black Bear mine of the Smuggler Union will be the only holding of this company to cut down heavily, although, the Inamo and Perino lease, (Caruthers lease) will not be able to start as was originally intended. Warmer weather now prevails, but not warm enough to fill the reservoirs as rapidly as desired, yet the outlook is favorable for an early return to normal power conditions.

Snowslides still cause some damage, the Bob-Tail slide running and knocking a number of buckets from the Tomboy aerial tram. This slide is peculiar in that it has reformed and run several times this winter. No great damage was sustained. Snow and mudslides again blocked the Rio Grande Southern lines at intervals from March 31 to April 5, but the longest delay was only for one day. At this time of the year, with the rains mudslides are common, and cause numerous delays to ore in transit. The district is now passing through the dull period that precedes the opening of a new season, the usual occurrence. The power shortage has, of course, resulted in the postponement of many activities, the most important of which is that of the Belmont Wagner Mining Company.

SILVERTON.—Snowslides have caused another blockade, extending from March 31 to April 5. No ore moved on the D. & R. G. lines, and the Silverton Northern was also blocked. The district is quiet, and mining is at a low ebb. The shortage of power will have a more serious effect on Silverton than on other districts, as this is entirely dependent upon current furnished by the Western Colorado Power Co. Crude ore shipments are on the increase, particularly from the Dora, Champion, and Detroit & Colorado properties.

A number of examinations of the workings of the old One Hundred mine indicate a marked interest in the property by outside capital, and many believe that the litigation that has tied it up during the past eight years is nearing settlement, and that the famous producer of former years will be re-opened. The trouble is a contest between the original title-holders and the creditors of the lien-holders of the old One Hundred corporation, the former refusing to co-operate with the creditors. The mine contains large continuous veins of good ore, and shipped large tonnages prior to 1907, during which year operations ceased, owing to the financial panic. Just prior to closing, a mill and tram were erected.

The Highland Mary Leasing Co. has men employed getting ready to ship; the mill is also being overhauled, and it is proposed to work this property on a much larger scale than before. The Highland Mary carries veins of rich ore, especially high in silver.

The D. L. & W. M. & R. Co. suffered a set-back to operations when its blacksmith-shop, compressor-house, and mining machinery were destroyed by fire. The fire started from an overheated stove in the shop and spread rapidly. The damage is estimated at $7000, all of which was covered by insurance. There is no power to run the compressor and operations will be continued by hand-drilling.

The Iowa Tiger mine and mill have had serious set-backs during the past few weeks, owing to machinery troubles. The hoist at the mine broke-down, involving a delay of a few days; but the most important damage was that of the destruction of the mill transformer by lightning, causing a delay of ore treatment for a few weeks. The Iowa-Tiger was fortunate in securing the transformers at the Pride of the West, which are now being installed, and milling will probably be resumed in the near future.

RED MOUNTAIN.—This district has been actively developed during the past winter, and the outlook is favorable for continuous and heavy shipping during the coming season. Among the properties that expect to produce are the Guston, Yankee Girl, Robinson, Congress, Barstow, and Silver Bolt.

ANIMAS FORKS.—There is marked interest in development of this section, and as an early run-off of snow is expected, the district expects to be listed among the early shippers.

The Animas Forks Consolidated M. & M. Co., and the Gnome Mining Co. have leased their extensive holdings to W. M. Johnston of Animas Forks, with the option of purchase.

PLACERVILLE.—During 1918 radium extracted from the ores of Paradox valley totaled 22 grammes. The principal producer is the Standard Chemical Co., which will resume operations on a larger scale in the near future.

O. B. Willmarth, purchaser of radium-bearing ore, operating a reduction plant at Montrose, and who purchases most of the output of the small producers, is investigating the Long Park area with the view of developing several promising prospects.

Increased activities in such deposits is indicated by the purchase of two portable prospecting outfits by the Schlesinger company, and the Radium Luminous Metals Co., respectively.

SAWPIT.—The Colorado Vanadium Co. is shipping a car of ore daily to the Primos Chemical Co.

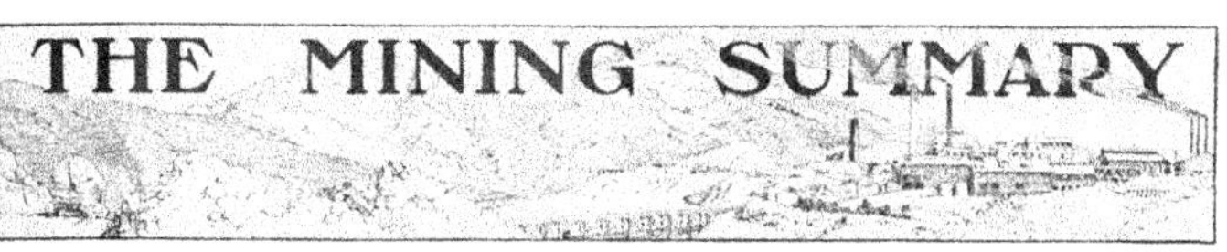

ALASKA

Anchorage.—In Bulletin 668 of the U. S. Geological Survey, just issued, the Nelchina—Susitna region is described by Theodore Chapin. Although the area is much more accesible than many parts of the Territory which are far better known, it had up to 1913 been visited relatively little. Little productive mining has been done, and the geology does not encourage the hope of finding extensive placers, yet the wide distribution of alluvial gold indicates considerable mineralization, according to Alfred Brooks in the preface to the publication. It may be that deeply-buried placers exist, but they would have to be rich to meet the operating costs. When the railway is finished to the Matanuska coalfield the region will be readily accessible.

PART OF ALASKA, SHOWING THE NELCHINA—SUSITNA REGION.

Juneau.—Alaska Gastineau in 1918 operated at a loss of $116,565, plus $219,685 for interest on bonds and notes, a total deficit of $336,250. In 1917 there was a surplus of $42,274. There was treated 1,285,445 tons of $1.09 ore, compared with 2,240,346 tons of $1.10 in 1917.

Skagway.—A gold strike that is attracting much attention is reported on the Morley river, 150 miles north-east of this town, and just a few miles south of the international boundary. Morley river runs into Teslin lake. The surface 'dirt' is said to yield 30 to 50 cents. Bedrock has not yet been struck.

ARIZONA

Humboldt.—Consolidated Arizona Smelting produced 720,000 lb. of copper during March, a decrease of 280,000 pounds.

Miami.—The Miami Copper Co.'s profit in 1918 was $5,262,419, of which $3,362,013 was distributed. The output from 2,132,941 tons of ore was 58,407,563 pounds.

Pearce.—High-grade silver ore has been found on the seventh level of the Middlemarch mine, 9 miles west of Pearce. This ore carries 4% copper and 12% zinc, with silver up to 50 oz. per ton. The ore is different from that on the levels above, and much higher grade. On the eighth level there is now 10 ft. of ore running from 2 to 16% copper, as shown in the cross-cut, with high-grade ore still in the face. This ore carries 2 oz. of silver also. The strike is considered important, as showing improved value at depth. The district has had very little development below 300 ft. in depth.

Prescott.—Frank L. Carlisle, of Pittsburgh, has purchased further interests in the Tip Top mine. It is said that he has now practically full ownership.

Concrete foundations for the new 50-ton mill at the Peck mine have been completed. A ball-mill, Wilfley tables, and cyanide-tanks are being erected to treat the 20,000 tons of silver-bearing tailing.

Ray.—During 1918 Ray Consolidated made a profit of $4,803,455, less than half that of 1917. Dividends totaled $5,275,831, a decrease of $1,300,000. The output was 86,919,270 lb., 1,600,000 lb. less than in the previous year. Costs rose from 12.65 to 17.19 cents per pound. There was 3,411,000 tons of 1.613% ore treated.

Superior.—Magma Copper produced 1,002,000 lb. during March, a reduction of 211,000 pounds.

CALIFORNIA

Auburn.—The Yukon Gold Co.'s dredge on the little fork of the American river was robbed of gold amalgam worth $2000 last week.

Downieville.—Good gravel has been found in the Old Miners' mine at Howland Flat in Sierra county. The pay is in two formations—gravel and pipe-clay. The gravel washes freely, but the clay presents difficulties which nothing but machinery will overcome. Miners are being engaged as fast as operations permit.

The Loftus Blue Lead Co. of Los Angeles is piping out the ground on which stands the old town of St. Louis in the northern part of the county. Five shafts were sunk last summer, and prospects warranted the present work. Woodwork of the buildings is being removed preparatory to washing away the stone walls. The tailings go to a restraining-dam.

Dr. H. H. Barrows of Oakland is in the county for the purpose of making an extensive examination of the placers in the northern part, and to investigate the feasibility of working the black sands from the abandoned hydraulic mines. The work will extend over several weeks.

Loeffler brothers of Sierra City have found the vein in a tunnel after spending much time and money. The ore prospects well in free gold and sulphides.

The El Dorado mine near Alleghany is expected to resume operations about May 1.

The Brush Creek mine near the Mountain House, idle for years, will be re-opened early in May.

Jackson.—The fire in the Argonaut has been confined to parts of the 3700 and 4300-ft. levels, and mining will be resumed at an early date. The Kennedy mine adjoining, closed for a time on account of fume, is again in operation.

Keswick.—The Mountain Copper Co. is surveying for a tram from its Iron Mountain and Hornet mines to a point on the Southern Pacific railroad, four miles north of Keswick Junction on the Iron Mountain line and the Southern Pacific. It is reported but not officially confirmed that the company will ship ore by this tram eventually and abandon the Iron Mountain road. It is also said that the tram would save enough in two years to pay for itself.

Melones.—The supervisors of Calaveras county on May 5 will open bids for construction of a new grade from the Melones bridge across the Stanislaus river to the top of the hill on the county road to Angels, a distance of 1½ miles. The county called for bids for the work some time ago, but the figures were too high, the lowest being about $20,000 per mile. The old road from Melones to the top of the hill on the Angels road is very bad and dangerous. The mines in this region will benefit considerably by any improvement to the roads.

Oroville.—In his suggestions for improvement of roads in Butte county, E. B. Wulff, Federal highway engineer, has a list of 25 roads, those that would benefit mining districts being as follows: Oroville-Honcut, 12.3 miles, $92,000; Oroville-Forbestown, 11.5 miles, $40,000; Oroville-Quincy, 30 miles, $178,000; and Pentz-Magalia-Powelton, 35.2 miles, $125,000.

Rutherford.—The White Rock magnesite mine of F. R. Sweasey, of San Francisco, 20 miles east of this place, has been re-opened after several months idleness. The ore is calcined at the mine, and is high in iron, desirable for refractory purposes.

Taylorsville.—The Trask & Coffer Mining Co. has erected a compressor at its mine in Moonlight canyon, adjoining the Engels mine. Developments with a large force will be resumed early in May. L. L. Coffer is manager and Gerald P. Roman superintendent.

COLORADO

Aspen.—The mining outlook for this district is rather discouraging, as the principal silver producer, the Smuggler, has been closed. The pumps have been stopped, and the lower workings are at present flooded with water.

Breckenridge.—The Summit County Metal Mining Association has arranged its headquarters in town here. J. R. Wood is president, and recently addressed the Association on the possibilities of the region.

Durango.—The Durango smelter was shut-down from March 1 to 31, partly owing to a shortage of ore, caused by snowslides on the railroads, also to permit of overhauling the plant. It is again operating three shifts, and receiving a fair supply of ore, although the power shortage in the tributary districts has had the effect of curtailing receipts. The sampling-mill is being remodeled and enlarged. A large crusher is being erected, which will probably double its capacity.

Leadville.—A compromise has been arranged over the wage dispute, miners receiving $4 per shift instead of $3.50 as first suggested by mine-owners.

IDAHO

Adair.—The Montana-Idaho Copper Co. is now working two shifts instead of one. The main tunnel has been driven 4265 ft., where it attained a depth of 1100 ft. A drift started at the 3865-ft. point has been driven 1050 ft. to a depth of 1300 ft. About $70,000 has been spent in operations, and a large sum in equipment, which includes a compressor, water and electric power, and drill-sharpener. The Monitor shaft is 3000 ft. ahead. It will be undercut by 1100 ft., and a depth of 1800 ft. attained from the surface.

Kellogg.—The Caledonia Mining Co. in 1918 had gross receipts amounting to $1,096,776, less $288,077 smelter charges. Mining and shipping cost $160,879 leaving a profit of $647,819. Dividends totaled $937,800. Production was 17,971 tons of ore, containing 6,038,784 lb. lead, 668,784 oz. silver, and 94,326 lb. copper. Mining cost $8.68 per ton. Cash assets exceed liabilities by $445,392. Caledonia pays 1 cent per share, $26,050, on May 5. This makes $130,250 for 1919 and $3,803,300 to date.

Wallace.—Lessees at the Success mine have accumulated 400 tons of ore in two weeks and are operating the mill. The lease is between the 700 and 200-ft. levels. The royalty is 20% on lead and silver and 15% on zinc contents of the ore, and $20 daily for the use of the plant.

There is reported to be a shortage of labor in the Coeur d'Alene region, so the Hercules and other companies that are resuming operations are unable to secure enough men.

Wardner.—Over 100 lessees and employees are extracting ore from the old upper workings of the Bunker Hill & Sullivan and Last Chance mines, which sections the company is not working. The ore is treated at the Co-operative or old Bunker Hill mills.

MICHIGAN

Houghton.—Mass Consolidated is re-timbering its B shaft throughout. This work has been postponed on account of lack of skilled men, now available. Copper production is curtailed 15%.

Copper production of the Calumet & Hecla group in March totaled 9,652,053 lb. Of this, C. & H. contributed 4,592,295; Ahmeek, 1,930,333 lb.; Isle Royale, 1,093,660 lb.; and Osceola, 1,038,204 pounds.

The Stanton properties—Mohawk and Wolverine—produced 1,229,772 and 485,234 lb. of copper, respectively, during March.

The Mohawk mine is estimated to have a life of 26 years, there being over 260,000,000 lb. of copper in ore available. The output so far has been over 169,000,000 lb. The profit on the future metal, based on a 15-cent market, is $13,000,000, equal to $130 per share. The ore averaged 23.7 lb. per ton in 1918, when costs were 14.64 cents.

MISSOURI

Joplin.—Concentrate production of the Tri-State region last week was as under:

State	Blende, tons	Calamine, tons	Lead, tons	Value
Kansas	1,078	...	89	$47,861
Missouri	1,223	252	52	......
Oklahoma	5,443	...	833	267,279
Total	7,744	252	974	$370,848
Previous week	7,616	852	1,576	417,555
Average per ton	$39	$27	$60	......
Previous average	39	26	60	......

The Joplin 'News Herald' of April 20 contains a special mining section covering operations in this region.

MONTANA

Great Falls.—The Anaconda company announced on April 18 that it is preparing to blow-in a furnace for the manufacture of calcium carbide, using one of the five furnaces built last year for ferro-manganese. The company is now operating a lime-kiln at its quarries at Albright. The first run will be to make 25 to 30 tons of calcium carbide to test its quality. If it is of good quality, an additional furnace will be blown-in, and the idea is to manufacture from 50 to 100 tons of carbide daily. The carbide will be pressed and sealed in cans, each of 100-lb. capacity. The company recently sold 125 tons of ferro-manganese made last year, when it produced 1000 tons, nearly all of which is now stored at the plant. It is stated that the outlook for marketing it is growing brighter, according to the Anaconda 'Standard'.

In Bulletin 691-E of the U. S. Geological Survey, just issued, oil and gas geology of the Burch Creek-Sun River area of north-western Montana are discussed by Eugene Stebinger. The area described lies adjacent to the front range of the Rocky Mountains, and is part of a large region

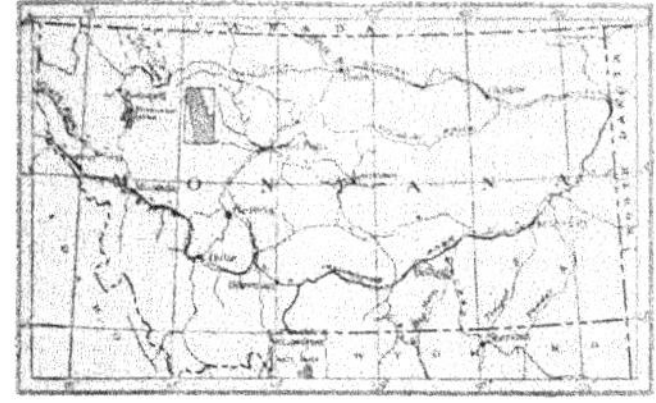

MONTANA, SHOWING POSITION OF BIRCH CREEK-SUN RIVER AREA.

in the Northern Great plains of the United States and Canada that seems to deserve consideration as prospective territory for oil and gas development. The outcrops of the Cretaceous formations afford unquestionable evidence of being petroliferous, so that drilling in places of favorable structure, such as on well-developed domes or anticlines, seems to offer a reasonable chance of success. Random drilling so far has been uniformly unsuccessful.

NEVADA

Austin.—Shipping ore has been opened by two tunnels in the Austin Nevada Consolidated, and a new orebody exposed in a deep gulch west of the main lateral. At point of discovery the vein assays $10 gold, with the drift showing no sign of the walls. The main tunnel is advancing rapidly to cut extensions of the Panamint, Frost, Curtis, and other famous veins. The general manager, H. G. Richardson, proposes to start shipments of high-grade gold-silver ore in a few weeks. A mill-site has been picked out near the portal of the main tunnel, which has been driven into Lander hill for approximately 750 feet.

Las Vegas.—The Eldorado Gold Mining Syndicate has been organized with a capital of 1,000,000, $1 shares by H. L. Powers and others, to supply water for all the mines in the Canyon district. It is proposed to erect a plant on the Colorado river, pump water 7 miles up the canyon, build a mill, and treat custom ores.

Rochester.—The Nevada Packard treated 2868 tons of ore during March. Extraction was 91.3%. Milling costs decreased 6%. A dividend of 2 cents per share was paid on April 20. This amounts to $23,292.

The Rochester Nevada Silver Mines Co. treated 168 tons daily of $11 ore in March.

Virginia City.—According to Whitman Symmes, the United Comstock Pumping Association has made an agreement with the Truckee River General Electric Co. whereby the debt of $398,000 owed the latter for power for pumping at the mines is practically nullified. The Pumping Association agrees to buy power in future in amount equal to its present indebtedness, this then to be entirely canceled without cost to it. Payments made each month for current power bills will be deducted from past indebtedness.

Willard.—It is said that this old boom gold camp of 1915 is showing signs of revival. It is 9 miles north-east of Lovelock in Pershing county. J. H. Borland, J. J. Garnier, J. Funt, W. Opperman, and several others are doing some work.

OREGON

Baker.—The White Swan gold mine, 12 miles east of here, has been acquired under bond from the Susan D. Mines Co. by H. B. Smalley and others of Spokane. The mine has been full of water since 1904.

UTAH

Alta. Mine-owners are complaining about the lack of assistance given for road building by the County Commissioners. The road is in such bad condition that ore can only be moved with difficulty.

Green River.—The Shale Products Co. is selecting a site near this place for a plant in which to treat its shale by the Jenson process. Willard Funk of Salt Lake City is largely interested.

The Homestake Gold Placer Mining Co. has been organized in Utah by W. B. Barker and others of McGill, Nevada, to develop placer ground along the Green river in the Uintah basin. The gold-bearing material is said to be black sands, 'extremely rich' in gold.

Park City.—The Silver King Consolidated has purchased the Haneter ranch of 75 acres at the mouth of the Spiro tunnel now in nearly 10,000 ft. This land will give the company plenty of space for dumps, ore-bins, railroad spurs, mill, and for residue disposal.

Tintic.—The Emerald Mining Co. reports encouraging indications on the 1000-ft. level, and it is considered that the quartz formation in which ore was mined at 600 ft. is nearby.

CANADA

British Columbia

Anyox.—The Granby Consolidated smelter resumed operations on April 4, having been idle since March 2. Men to take the places of those who left last month were obtained in Vancouver and elsewhere in the Province, those who received and accepted or rejected applications giving preference to returned soldiers. The latter, therefore, are largely represented at Anyox at present. F. M. Sylvester, managing director of the company, made the announcement that the new by-product coking-ovens at Anyox will be opened early in June.

Franklin.—The Maple Leaf mine in the Boundary district is to have a small smelter to treat its ore. The furnace is being made at Grand Forks, and will have a capacity of 50 tons per day. The furnace is 44 in. diameter and is of cupola type. A 35-hp. gasoline engine will be used to drive the blower. The ore contains copper and silver.

Kamloops.—A road between Princeton and the Aspen Grove mining camp is to be opened by the Provincial government this season. It is known as the One-Mile road, and will shorten the distance between Princeton and Merritt by 17 miles.

Princeton.—Construction of the branch railway to Cooper Mountain for the Canada Copper Corporation has received a temporary check, as 300 laborers employed by the contractors downed tools. They claim that they were asked to work 10 hours at the same wages as was given for 9 hours. Now they want an 8-hour day and a fixed wage of 50 cents per hour, or $4 per day. The strikers are orderly, no trouble having been experienced at Princeton or Allenby, the communities nearest to the mining camp.

Trail.—Ores and concentrates weighing 96,542 long tons have been received at the Consolidated M. & S. plant here during the first three months of the current year. A comparison is shown below. At present the management is not seeking ores of any kind, none being accepted from the

United-States. About 85% of the current receipts are from the company's own properties. To the present date only 60 outside properties have shipped to Trail this year.

Month	1917	1918	1919
January	36,570	27,404	35,283
February	40,967	33,989	30,450
March	42,949	41,725	30,809
Total tons	120,486	103,118	96,542

Ontario

Boston Creek.—Three claims of W. Arnold and J. A. Hughes, adjoining the Cotter, itself next to the Miller Independence, have been optioned to Mr. Savage of Buffalo.

Cobalt.—Kerr Lake pays 25 cents per share, $150,000, on June 16. This makes $300,000 for 1919. Kerr Lake produced 104,101 oz. of silver during March, equal to normal.

Nipissing yielded silver worth $261,158 during March, extracted from 208 tons of high-grade and 6962 tons of low-grade ores. The refinery shipped 802,698 oz., partly custom metal. Underground operations were satisfactory everywhere.

Good ore continues to be opened and bagged in the Advance, and 33-oz. ore is being put on the dumps. The company contemplates erection of a 75-ton mill.

It is rumored that there is friction between the Beaver and Temiskaming companies. There are several points in dispute, but the main one concerns ore extracted from the upper workings, containing about 50,000 oz. of silver. These companies both sank shafts to 1600 ft. through the diabase sill to the lower contact. The Beaver met with encouraging results, but the Temiskaming did not.

Kirkland Lake.—The Lake Shore company distributed $50,000 on May 1, bringing the total to $150,000.

The Teck-Hughes gold mine produced 2261 tons of $9.70 ore during March.

Porcupine.—Men are arriving in large numbers at all the goldfields in northern Ontario, and one by one the properties closed are being re-opened. It is expected that the Dome Mines company will require 500 men by summer.

Sudbury.—The Mond Nickel Co. has reduced operations at its Worthington and Levack mines, also at its smelter at Coniston, from three to one shifts per day. The International Nickel Co. is also at about third capacity. International pays a dividend of $1.50 per preferred share on May 1. This is equal to $133,689, and is the same as that paid on February 1.

MEXICO

Chihuahua

Parral.—On Sunday, April 20, Villa and his army fought their way into this centre. He announced that none of the mining properties would be molested, but is said to be renewing demands for taxes for protection offered.

Jalisco

Guadalajara.—During the last week in March, President Carranza attended the formal opening of the first section—25 miles—of the railroad from Guadalajara to the Pacific port of Chamela. This line starts from near Ameca on the Mexican Central, and runs west from Guadalajara to Cocutla.

Sonora

Cananea.—Greene Cananea has discharged 700 additional men. To help these to other points, the company chartered a special train.

El Tigre.—The Lucky Tiger-Combination Gold Mining Co. continues to pay dividends. The last was on March 20, 1919, when 10 cents per share was distributed. This amounted to $214,601, and makes $5,201,955 to date.

PERSONAL

Note. The Editor invites members of the profession to send particulars of their work and appointments. The information is interesting to our readers.

Morton Webber is here.

Oliver E. Jager is at Butte.

Henry M. Howe has gone to Europe.

F. G. Stevens has returned from Mexico to Toronto.

C. L. Beckwith, of Phoenix, is visiting northern California.

Arthur J. Hoskin, of Denver, was in the De Beque oil-shale district last week.

Frederick H. Minard has moved from 111 Broadway to 21 East 40th street, New York.

James F. Kemp, Horace V. Winchell, and **Charles K. Leith** are at Butte as experts in the Elm Orlu case.

F. W. Bradley has gone to Kellogg, Idaho, and from there to Juneau, Alaska, on a periodical inspection.

Raymond Brooks is in charge of the Benson mines, in St. Lawrence county, New York, succeeding **W. D. B. Motter, Jr.**

H. C. Dudley who held a commission in the 36th Engineers, in France, was here last week on his way from Arizona.

F. W. Sherman, who designed and constructed the Hackberry mill at Chloride, Arizona, has resigned as superintendent.

Charles W. Whitley, for many years general manager of the American Smelting & Refining Company's plants in Utah, has been promoted to the position of vice-president.

A. D. Brokaw, A. F. Dixon, L. G. Donnelly, A. H. Garner, and **H. H. McKee**, geologists and petroleum engineers, announce a partnership, with offices at 120 Broadway, New York.

A. B. Emery, general manager of the Messina copper mine, in the Transvaal, has left San Francisco and will go to Seattle, Butte, and Salt Lake City, on his return to London.

E. G. Banks, superintendent for the Waihi Gold Mining Co., New Zealand, is here on his way to London. He is visiting several American mining centres in order to study the flotation of gold and silver ores.

An Association of Members of American National Engineering Societies in Cuba has been formed "to foster the interests of the various national engineering societies represented on the island." **T. Carlile Ulbright** is secretary of the organization, which has its office at Havana.

Edwin C. Holden, general manager for the Davison Sulphur & Phosphate Co., having brought the Carlota mine, in the province of Santa Clara, Cuba, to a shipping stage, is moving to the headquarters of the company at Baltimore. **Chester A. Fulton**, superintendent, succeeds him as manager in Cuba.

The Pittsburgh chapter of the American Association of Engineers has a secretary. This is the first chapter outside of national headquarters at Chicago to have a secretary giving all of his time to the work of the Association. **F. B. N. Thatcher** has been selected for the position, and will have an office at 1312 Fulton Bdg., Pittsburgh.

'Business Law for Engineers', an evening lecture course, was started on April 21, at the San Francisco Public Library, under the direction of the Extension Division of the University of California. The series will include 30 lectures by Eugene G. McCann, a member of the California bar, who has had seven years' experience in engineering work in this State.

THE METAL MARKET

METAL PRICES

San Francisco, April 29

Aluminum-dust, cents per pound	50—60
Antimony, cents per pound	8
Copper, electrolytic, cents per pound	15½
Lead, pig, cents per pound	5¼—6¼
Platinum, per ounce	$100
Quicksilver, per flask of 75 lb.	$75
Spelter, cents per pound	8
Zinc-dust, cents per pound	12½

EASTERN METAL MARKET

(By wire from New York)

April 29.—Copper is inactive but steady. Lead is dull and unchanged. Spelter is stagnant though firm.

SILVER

Below are given official (not Government) quotations, in cents per ounce, of silver 999 fine. In order to make prompt settlements with smelters and brokers, producers allow a discount from the maximum fixed price of $1.01½, hence the lower price. The Government has not fixed the general market price at $1, but will pay this price (as from April 23, 1918) for all silver purchased by it. The equivalent of dollar silver (1000 fine) in British currency is 46.85 pence per ounce (925 fine), calculated at the normal rate of exchange. On August 15, 1918, the Treasury announced that the maximum price was fixed at $1.01½ per ounce. The British government fixed it maximum at 49½ pence, on September 2, but on November 12 this was changed to 48¾, on December 13 to 48 7/16, and on February 20 to 47¾ pence. On March 25, on account of the low rate of exchange, the London price was adjusted, with a minimum of 95 cents, resulting in daily fluctuations.

Date		New York cents	London pence	Average week ending		Cents	Pence
Apr.	23	101.12	48.87	Mch.	18	101.12	47.77
"	24	101.12	48.87	"	25	101.12	47.75
"	25	101.12	48.81	Apr.	1	101.12	49.63
"	26	101.12	48.87	"	8	101.12	48.86
	27 Sunday			"	15	101.12	48.85
"	28	101.12	48.62	"	22	101.12	48.94
"	29	101.12	48.62	"	29	101.12	48.78

Monthly averages

	1917	1918	1919		1917	1918	1919
Jan.	75.14	88.72	101.12	July	78.92	99.62	....
Feb.	77.54	85.79	101.12	Aug.	85.40	100.31	....
Mch.	74.13	88.11	101.12	Sept.	100.73	101.12	....
Apr.	72.51	95.35	....	Oct.	87.38	101.12	....
May	74.61	99.50	....	Nov.	85.97	101.12	....
June	76.44	99.50	....	Dec.	85.97	101.12	....

The silver coin and bullion in India is increasing, as on March 31 it totaled 3235 lacs of rupees ($103,520,000), against 2563 lacs ($82,016,000) on the 15th. At the same time the silver coin and bullion out of India decreased to 504 lacs ($16,128,000) from 1201 lacs ($38,432,000). The value of the gold in and out of that country remained stationary. The value of coins minted during the last week of March was 149 lacs ($4,768,000).

The stock of silver at Shanghai is increasing, the total at the end of March being 30,750,000 oz. and 17,900,000 dollars (50 cents).

Silver production of the principal mines at Cobalt, Ontario, in 1918, was as follows, with the cost:

Mine	Ounces	Cost per ounce
Beaver	385,042	....
Buffalo	767,740	....
Coniagas	974,264	33.87
La Rose	228,556	87.17
McKinley-Darragh-Savage	904,543	68.42
Mining Corporation	1,708,252	40.96
Nipissing	3,701,416	39.02
Trethewey	269,000	54.00

TIN

Prices in New York, in cents per pound. The monthly averages in 1918 are nominal. On December 3 the War Industries Board fixed the price to consumers and jobbers at 72½c. f.o.b. Chicago and Eastern points, and 71¼c. on the Pacific Coast. This will continue until the U. S. Steel Products Co.'s stock is consumed.

Monthly averages

	1917	1918	1919		1917	1918	1919
Jan.	44.10	85.13	71.50	July	62.60	93.00	....
Feb.	51.47	85.00	72.44	Aug.	62.53	91.33	....
Mch.	54.27	85.00	72.50	Sept.	61.54	80.40	....
Apr.	55.63	88.53	....	Oct.	62.24	78.82	....
May	63.21	100.01	....	Nov.	74.18	73.67	....
June	61.93	91.00	....	Dec.	85.00	71.52	....

COPPER

Prices of electrolytic in New York, in cents per pound.

Date			Average week ending		
Apr.	23	15.12	Mch.	18	14.79
"	24	15.12	"	25	14.99
"	25	15.12	Apr.	1	15.27
"	26	15.25	"	8	15.25
	27 Sunday		"	15	15.33
"	28	15.25	"	22	15.18
"	29	15.25	"	29	15.18

Monthly averages

	1917	1918	1919		1917	1918	1919
Jan.	29.53	23.50	20.43	July	29.07	26.00	....
Feb.	34.57	23.50	17.34	Aug.	27.42	26.00	....
Mch.	36.00	23.50	15.05	Sept.	25.11	26.00	....
Apr.	33.16	23.50	....	Oct.	23.50	26.00	....
May	31.69	23.50	....	Nov.	23.50	26.00	....
June	32.57	23.50	....	Dec.	23.50	26.00	....

Copper production of the 'porphyry' group during March was as follows, in pounds:

Mine	March	Normal
Chino	3,770,000	6,500,000
Nevada	3,650,000	7,000,000
Ray	3,792,000	7,500,000
Utah	8,360,000	18,000,000

QUICKSILVER

The primary market for quicksilver is San Francisco, California being the largest producer. The price is fixed in the open market, according to quantity. Prices, in dollars per flask of 75 pounds:

Date					
Apr.	1	68.00	Apr.	15	75.00
"	8	67.50	"	22	75.00
			"	29	75.00

Monthly averages

	1917	1918	1919		1917	1918	1919
Jan.	81.00	128.06	103.75	July	102.00	120.00	....
Feb.	126.25	118.00	90.00	Aug.	115.00	120.00	....
Mch.	113.75	112.00	72.80	Sept.	112.00	120.00	....
Apr.	114.50	115.00	....	Oct.	102.00	120.00	....
May	104.00	110.00	....	Nov.	102.50	120.00	....
June	85.50	112.00	....	Dec.	117.42	115.00	....

LEAD

Lead is quoted in cents per pound, New York delivery.

Date			Average week ending		
Apr.	23	4.95	Mch.	18	5.25
"	24	4.95	"	25	5.21
"	25	4.95	Apr.	1	5.25
"	26	4.95	"	8	5.25
"	27 Sunday		"	15	5.07
"	28	4.95	"	22	4.93
"	29	4.95	"	29	4.95

Monthly averages

	1917	1918	1919		1917	1918	1919
Jan.	7.64	6.85	5.60	July	10.93	8.03	....
Feb.	9.10	7.07	5.13	Aug.	10.75	8.05	....
Mch.	10.07	7.26	5.24	Sept.	9.07	8.05	....
Apr.	9.38	6.90	....	Oct.	6.97	8.05	....
May	10.29	6.88	....	Nov.	6.38	8.05	....
June	11.74	7.58	....	Dec.	6.49	6.90	....

ZINC

Zinc is quoted as spelter, standard Western brands, New York delivery, in cents per pound:

Date			Average week ending		
Apr.	23	6.35	Mch.	18	6.50
"	24	6.40	"	25	6.48
"	25	6.40	Apr.	1	6.53
"	26	6.40	"	8	6.60
"	27 Sunday		"	15	6.57
"	28	6.40	"	22	6.41
"	29	6.40	"	29	6.39

Monthly averages

	1917	1918	1919		1917	1918	1919
Jan.	9.75	7.78	7.44	July	8.98	8.72	....
Feb.	10.45	7.97	6.71	Aug.	8.58	8.87	....
Mch.	10.78	7.67	6.53	Sept.	8.33	9.58	....
Apr.	10.20	7.04	....	Oct.	8.32	9.11	....
May	9.41	7.29	....	Nov.	7.76	8.75	....
June	9.63	7.92	....	Dec.	7.84	8.49	....

Eastern Metal Market

New York, April 23.

All the non-ferrous metals are in poor demand, with sales few and small; prices, however, are just about holding their own. The general slump in these markets is attributed by many to the steel price muddle.

Antimony is quiet and slightly lower.

Copper is very quiet, with prices only slightly lower.

Lead is decidedly inactive, but prices are holding firm.

Tin has no market, and conditions are unchanged.

Zinc is in poor demand, and quotations have fallen moderately.

ANTIMONY

There is very little change in the market which is quoted at 6.50 to 6.62½c., New York, duty paid, for wholesale lots for early delivery. The market is quiet.

ALUMINUM

No. 1 virgin metal, 98 to 99% pure, is slightly higher at 30 to 32c. per lb. for prompt and early delivery. Re-melt metal of the same purity is about 2c. less per pound.

COPPER

The market continues in the quiet, inactive condition noted a week ago. Demand has fallen off decidedly, and sales have been few. This state of affairs is regarded as normal by some producers. They contend that the fairly heavy buying of a few weeks ago entirely satisfied consumers' needs for April and early May, therefore buying now would be light. There is little desire to purchase beyond immediate needs, and still less inclination by sellers to sell for extended future delivery. The price fiasco in the steel industry has had its effect on copper and other metals. It is a fact that one fairly large buyer of copper intended to place orders about the time that the Director General of Railroads declined to accept the steel prices, but because of this he refused to pursue his original intention and so far as known has not bought yet. Electrolytic copper is quoted at about 15.12½c., New York, for early delivery, with Lake copper nominal at 15.37½ to 15.50c. Large producers are asking 15.25 to 15.37½c., New York, for electrolytic copper, with small interests willing to shade this from ¼ to ½ cent.

IRON AND STEEL

It has not been generally recognized that an open market in steel really exists because widespread and sensational price-cutting has not been in evidence. The industry has been limiting operations to cover incoming business only, and there has been considerable shutting-down of steel plants and banking of blast-furnaces. A 50% operation is reported for independent companies with the U. S. Steel Corporation on about a 70% basis in the Chicago and 60% in the Pittsburgh district.

LEAD

There has been no demand in the past week and the market continues lifeless. It is believed, however, that despite the inactivity and lack of buying the metal cannot be bought below the present quotations of 4.70c., St. Louis, or 4.95c., New York, obtaining in the outside market. The American Smelting & Refining Co. continues its asking-price at 5c., New York, and 4.70c., St. Louis. The market is regarded by most sellers as firm. A revival in demand is not looked-for until buying in steel has been resumed.

TIN

The question as to how fast the U. S. Steel Products Co. is disposing of its allocated metal is the only interesting question before traders, but efforts to learn about the present stocks have all been unavailable. It is hoped that an open market will prevail after June 1, but there is no certainty regarding this. The market continues absolutely dead, with no transactions reported. The only metal changing hands is that passing from this company to consumers at 72.50c. per lb., the fixed Government price. American tin is unavailable, having been withdrawn from the market. The quotation for future shipment from the Far East is about 49c. per lb. for shipments to start after import restrictions have been removed. There has been a little buying under these conditions, but only a little. If restrictions should be removed on June 1, this would mean that such tin so purchased would not reach the Pacific Coast until about September 1.

ZINC

One large producer calls the market "sick". There is absolutely no demand of any consequence, and prices have again fallen slightly. Prime Western for early delivery is quoted at 6.05c., St. Louis, or 6.40c., New York, with futures slightly higher. A sale for June delivery is reported at 6.15c., St. Louis. About 100 tons has been sold for export to Australia, and Japan is today inquiring for some for export to that country. While the amounts involved are small, as affecting the market, the interesting fact is that both Australia and Japan are producers and exporters of the metal. The latter country is now sending zinc to England. Grade A zinc is offered at 6.75c, with brass special for prompt delivery held at about 6.15c., St. Louis.

ORES

Manganese: The Indian manganese ore, available at 55c. per unit seaboard last week, has not been sold.

Molybdenum: The market is quiet and prices are nominal at 80 to 85 cents per lb. of MoS_2 in regular concentrate.

Tungsten: There is no change in conditions and very little demand. There has also been no fair test of the market. Quotations are being made in some quarters at $10 to $12 per unit for best grades of scheelite, but these are probably nominal. There has been no fair test of the ferro market.

Book Review

Galvanizing and Tinning. By W. T. Flanders. Pp. 312, ill., index. David Williams Co., New York. For sale by 'Mining and Scientific Press', San Francisco. Price, $4.

This is a complete revision of the author's earlier work on the same subjects. In this he has had the assistance of several men that are authorities on certain special processes. The first chapter contains a general discussion of corrosion and its prevention, and then comes a description of hot-galvanizing plant and equipment, including pyrometers. The author then considers materials used in galvanizing, also preparing work for galvanizing, including pickling, water-rolling, tumbling, and sand-blasting. Then come several chapters devoted directly to the hot-galvanizing process. The Schoop 'metal-spray' process is then considered. Then come several chapters on tinning, and following that a discussion of electro-galvanizing. Sherardizing is then considered. The final chapter is devoted to galvanizing specifications and tests. The book is well-illustrated and will be of value to anyone interested in the subjects discussed, whether as a manufacturer or as a consumer of galvanized and tinned products.

GEOPHONE is the name of a most interesting device, a description of which will be found upon another page of this issue. It can be used to detect the position whence sound comes underground, so that it will be useful in mine accidents and fires. This is one of the devices invented during the War for use in sapping operations.

PROCEEDINGS against the Minerals Separation company before the Federal Trade Commission have been supplemented by the tiling of a brief on certain jurisdictional points by the American Mining Congress, through its counsel, Messrs. Pershing, Nye, Frye & Tallmadge, of Denver. This brief takes strong ground in support of the Commission in its charges, filed last November, against Minerals Separation, Ltd.

SENATOR PHELAN, in his apparent anxiety to keep in the public eye, is playing the Hearst game. First he tries to scare the people of California with his Japanese picture-bride story; then he concocts a weird tale of British efforts to control the entire oil industry of California. Hearst features these irresponsible yarns and repeats the oil story even after it has been categorically denied. In the same issue of his paper we find a cablegram stating that the British are making a $250 automobile out of "slag, clinker, and sawdust, and covered with a metal solution." The metal must resemble that famous alloy, Hearst brass.

PEACE is in sight. The rise in quotations on the Stock Exchange reflects the cheering prospect. The German delegates may fuss and fume; they may bluff and bluster; but they will sign. Germany's naval and military powers are shattered; her government knows that to refuse to come to a settlement is futile; the terms are more nearly just than she would have imposed in the event of herself emerging victorious in the War; the threat of a relapse to bolshevist chaos will not intimidate the Peace Conference. Italy's dispute with her Allies does not affect the settlement with Germany, for the Fiume controversy is part of the settlement to be made not with Germany but with Austria-Hungary. We are going to celebrate peace soon and thereby set the seal on the Armistice.

DISCUSSION this week includes a timely letter from Mr. Walter E. Gaby on the geology of the Yerington mining district, a subject on which he is particularly well qualified to speak. He joins with Mr. Adolph Knopf in emphasizing the importance of fissuring upon the distribution of the ore, and the consequent importance of a detailed study of the system of fissures. Mr. F. C. Brown is again a welcome contributor. He discusses 'Invention' and manages to infuse a dry subject with religious poetry. We know that his seriously thoughtful way of looking at things, even technical subjects, pleases many of our readers, as it does us. Mr. John Randall, like Mr. Brown, uses allegory to explain his ideas. His letter on 'The Status of Gold' comes as an appropriate sequel to the series of contributions published by us on this subject during the last three or four months.

PALE and almost fainting with emotion, we are told, was Count von Brockdorff-Rantzau, the head of the German delegation, when he presented the credentials of his party to M. Jules Cambon, the chairman of the Peace Commission at Paris. Life is full of compensations, if one but waits. M. Cambon was the French ambassador to Berlin at the time when the Prussian began his onslaught upon civilization and many of our readers will recall the scurvy manner in which the Germans treated him, threatening and insulting him and his staff while on their way out of Germany, refusing even to give them any food in the course of their journey by rail from Berlin to Copenhagen, and compelling them to pay in cold cash for the cost of the special train on which they traveled. That was on August 5, 1914. On May 2, 1919, the German representatives upon arrival in Paris, to sign a humiliating peace, appeared before M. Cambon "pale and almost fainting with emotion."

FURTHER installments of the Alien Property Custodian's report on the workings of the German metal combination are appearing in our pages. The last will be published next week, when we shall offer a few supplementary remarks. We allude to the subject now in order to warn the reader against the attempt, appearing on page 638, to explain the flotation process. Mr. A. Mitchell Palmer, or Mr. Francis P. Garvan, or whoever is directly responsible for the report issued from the office of the Alien Property Custodian, would have been wise to submit anything written on the technique of flotation to somebody versed in the subject or else abstain from all attempts to instruct the public on the matter. Only a thorough knowledge of a technical subject will enable one to explain it to the non-technical; a popular description when offered by an amateur is about as effective as the ointment that went down Aaron's beard, even unto the skirts of his garment; it only made a mess!

The Geology of the Divide District

In this issue we publish a short article, by Mr. Frank L. Sizer, on the Divide district and the boom that followed the uncovering of a large orebody in the Tonopah Divide mine. He is careful not to commit himself too deeply, in the absence of the necessary evidence, but he brings out clearly the fact that the distribution of ore, and of two kinds of ore, is dependent upon the relation of two distinct systems of fissuring. Apparently the extent and character of the zone of secondary enrichment, or intense concentration, has yet to be ascertained by further exploration. Our own experience permits us to hazard the suggestion that, in deciding upon the influence of subordinate ore-bearing fractures, it is important to discriminate between 'droppers' and 'robbers', between those that enrich and those that impoverish. While referring to this part of Nevada, we take the opportunity to correct a possible misapprehension caused by an erroneous paragraph in a recent issue of the San Francisco 'Chronicle', in which it was stated that the Divide, or Gold Mountain, district "has been unfavorably reported on by the U. S. Geological Survey." The Director of the Survey, Mr. George Otis Smith, informs us that Mr. J. E. Spurr visited the district in 1902 and made merely an incidental mention of Gold Mountain, in connection with his geological work at Tonopah. The paragraph runs as follows: "The Gold Mountain district lies nearly half-way between Tonopah and Klondike and is in the stage of development. Gold mountain is composed of rhyolite, both in solid flows and in consolidated tuffs and breccias. Through these rhyolites run strong and persistent veins of quarts and delicately colored chalcedony veins, sometimes containing pyrite. In some parts of these veins, especially in the oxidized portions, rich essays have been obtained. The mineralization is probably of a later date than that which has produced the ores at Tonopah, but may be of the same age as those at Klondike, although the ore deposits themselves are of a different character." In Bulletin No. 308, by S. H. Ball, published in 1907, the district now known as Divide is briefly mentioned. It is stated: "The Kanakee Mining Company has a 100-foot shaft, which passes through rhyolite, tuffs, and breccia. Dense quartz fills the interstices of breccia and also occurs in veins. The ore is free-milling and is said to run about $30 in gold and silver per ton, although assay-returns have reached $317." Then follows a quotation from Mr. Spurr's paragraph as cited above. In his report on the Tonopah district, published by the Survey in 1905, Mr. Spurr, in referring to a certain group of comparatively unproductive veins at Tonopah, states: "The mineralization is then probably the same in time, nature, and origin as that at Gold Mountain, four miles south of Tonopah, and very likely similar to that in the newly discovered camp of Goldfield, about 28 miles south of Tonopah." The foregoing are the only references to the Divide district that have appeared in the reports of the U. S. Geological Survey, and there is nothing in them to justify the sweeping assertion of the 'Chronicle' that the district "has been unfavorably reported on." The fact that the veins at Divide were compared or correlated by Mr. Spurr, in the passage just quoted, with a set of rather unproductive veins at Tonopah might perhaps in itself be interpreted by some readers as indicating little promise for Divide, but the inclusion of Goldfield in the comparison negatives this suggestion, and Mr. Spurr himself nowhere states that veins belonging to the same period as the later and less productive veins at Tonopah may not in other districts be rich. We are glad to say this much in fairness to the Geological Survey.

President of the University

Just now a very proper interest is being taken, not only in California but farther afield, in the selection of a president for the University of California. The present incumbent, Mr. Benjamin Ide Wheeler, retires in July, after twenty years of distinguished service, marred near its end by an irretrievable blunder. Mr. Wheeler was one of the exchange professors sent to Berlin, on the Kaiser's initiative, and unfortunately while in the precincts of Potsdam he was so overcome by the condescension of the great, including familiar converse with the All Highest, that he returned home an admirer of the Prussian king and a friend of Germany. When the War began in Europe he was outspoken in behalf of the country against which the United States declared war on April 6, 1917. In short, he made the biggest blunder that a clever man could make in the second decade of the 20th century. So his retirement is logical. It will be difficult, however, to replace him, for in scholarship, in administration, and in his public appearances as a spokesman for the University, he played his part well. The Regents have appointed a committee from among themselves to select a new president. Their task is one of much difficulty and heavy responsibility. The annual budget of the University of California calls for the sum of $3,500,000 and its student body numbers 8500. The presidency of our State University is the most influential position west of the Mississippi river; it is more important that the governorship or the senatorship in any State or all the States within that geographic limit; it represents the intellectual leadership of the Pacific Coast. Therefore the choice, soon to be made, is of great interest not only in academic circles but to the public. Our readers, many of whom are professional men and college graduates, are keenly aware of the importance of choosing the right man. What sort of a man should he be? First, he must be a scholar and a gentleman; he must be a man of vision; next he must be an executive and an administrator; he ought to possess tact and be a man of the world in order to deal successfully with the representatives of the community that supports the University, notably the State legislature, which apportions the funds needed for its work; he should be able to make a good speech and thereby interpret scholastic ideals to the public; if he be a man of fine presence—looking like 'presidential timber'—so much the better; finally, in order to do his work well and to continue to do it for a period long enough to establish an effective tradition, he ought to be physically vigorous and comparatively young. Indeed, he is assumed to resemble the Admirable Crichton. The abilities and the qualities, mental and physical, that are demanded are those of a splendid specimen of the *genus homo* and the *species sapiens*; he is expected to be a 100% man. It being unlikely that the perfect specimen can be found, which of the qualifications are essential and which are accessory? Among those mentioned for the appointment are a financial comptroller, a Cabinet minister, a paleontologist, and an economist with military experience. The University depends on the goodwill of the Legislature, therefore a man of engaging and persuasive manners is useful. The University is a big business institution, therefore financial acumen is an asset in its president. These factors cause stress to be laid upon abilities that are not common among scholars: indeed, many people insist that the president must be a business man, with some scholastic attainments, of course, but certainly much more of a man of the world than merely an inspiring teacher. It is true, universities have become business enterprises and public utilities requiring popular support, legislative approval, and organized publicity. There appears a danger that the more they approach the ideals of successful business the less they are likely to express the much higher ideals of mental and spiritual progress. At the present moment four important universities are seeking new chiefs. One would suppose that among the deans of faculties there would be found the necessary supply of college presidents, but it is not so, because the combination of the necessary qualities is rare. A tendency has developed, therefore, as between a scholar with little business training and an administrator not eminently a scholar, to select the man who can best represent a university in its relations with the public, and with the Legislature, if it be a State institution, or, if not, with such of the rich as have an inclination to play the part of benefactor. We venture to suggest that the begging for money can be done, in some measure, by the regents and that the lobbying is best done by the comptroller, not by the president. A university, especially a State university, should be a focus of intellectual activities, a centre of scientific research, a seat of true learning; it should be, as Huxley said, "a fortress of the higher life of the nation." Neither the number of the students nor the beauty of the buildings makes the university. Indeed, the generosity of Mrs. Hearst in providing money for the construction of white palaces at Berkeley has been negatived in large measure by the pestilential activity of the yellow journalist, her son, whose newspapers, in San Francisco and Los Angeles, have countermined the higher education of the University itself. As Huxley said, at the opening of Johns Hopkins University, 43 years ago, "administrators of educational funds have sometimes made a palace and called it a university." Not buildings, but men; not endowments, but teachers, make a university. It were better to spend less money on handsome structures and beautiful gardens, so that the real makers of the university, namely, the members of its faculty, were better paid; so that the least of them were paid better than a hod-carrier. Agassiz, it will be remembered, said that a university is a professor at one end of a log and a student at the other. The University is not a glorified department store of odds and ends of knowledge, it is "a place where moral worth and intellectual clearness are cherished." So said the great philosopher of the last century, himself an educator of the highest type and the widest usefulness. Therefore we venture to say for the mining profession, in which so many of the graduates from Berkeley now hold a distinguished position, that we hope the need for administrative or executive ability will not be permitted to override the supreme need for selecting as president of the University of California a man of high character and wide vision, an exponent of human aspirations and an interpreter of American ideals, a man of courage and of conviction, a scholar and a gentleman.

The Cost of High Living

Much of the high cost of living is the consequence of high living; it is the extravagance of the rich that makes life difficult for the average citizen. The industrial prosperity due to the War, the fortunes easily made by profiteering, and the successful winnings of stock-exchange gamblers have greatly increased the number of those with more money than sense and with more love for extravagance than for comfort. For these reasons we do not regret to note the incidence of the new luxury tax, which imposes a Federal tax of 10% on retail prices in excess of the amounts specified by law. The Retail Dry Goods Association in San Francisco is said to have collected 100,000 protests against this sumptuary enactment, and the reason is obvious; it will restrict the careless spending of money for high-priced articles. When, however, we read the list of retail prices in excess of which the tax is levied, we find ourselves within the limit except for a hat on which we paid a war price six months ago, and we do not expect to do it again, law or no law. On the other hand the taxation of women's hats in excess of $15 incites no violent objection on our part; being a high-minded patriot we accept it without demur. Indeed, this luxury tax may well provoke a smile from the professional man, from those who work for their living; it is no terrible imposition, but a reasonable check on those who, like drunken sailers, spend their money heedlessly. "Let the galled jade wince, our withers are unwrung." It is about time to call a halt on the orgy of extravagance that has disgraced our larger city communities during the very time when brave men were sacrificing everything in a great cause. The spread of education and the general interest in social economics are bound to bring about some serious thinking on the subject of unnecessary extravagance in living; and with serious thought will come organized opposition, such as the new law, to ways of living that make it hard for those unable to meet the artificial prices created by spend-thrifts. It is commonly said that it is none of our business how a man spends his money and it is also said that such spending stimulates trade and is therefore a good thing for the community. Such ideas are mistaken. The acts of a citizen in an organized community do concern the community if they interfere with the welfare of a large number of other citizens; the lavish spending of money does affect others injuriously in that it creates fictitious prices and thereby renders the cost of living more burdensome for others. The man that gives a big tip in a restaurant renders it difficult for his fellow, unable or unwilling to pay so much for servility, to obtain proper service. The people that buy the most expensive things without discrimination are making it hard for those whose purses are not illimitable. Today even the cost of most things is high largely because we have in this community, for example, so large a number of persons eager to obtain what they want regardless of its price. The luxury tax by its levy upon excessive prices will check the sale of unnecessarily costly articles, because no man or woman likes to pay a tax, whether large or small. The dry-goods establishments will soon adapt themselves to the new conditions and incidentally will be less able to foster a kind of sumptuary drunkenness that has been at least as injurious to the community as excessive alcoholism. We sympathize with teachers as a class, with the professors in the colleges and the instructors in the schools, because they not only are underpaid, having regard to the pre-eminently valuable character of their work, but because life has been made harder for them by reason of the reckless spending of a far less worthy type of men and women—the idle rich. The cost of everything, even in university communities, has been pushed to prohibitive prices by the careless spending of people without any serious purpose in life. Moreover, the drunken sailor's kind of spending, such as characterizes the successful stock-broker or the fortunate profiteer, breeds parasites innumerable, because every time money is given in excess of the service rendered it incites men to hang around the wild spenders in the hope of getting something for nothing, or next to nothing. Every city contains thousands of men, many of them young and vigorous, that are idle and vicious, simply because they can pick up a fairly good living by standing where the millionaire's money is being splashed about. Such extravagances and stupidity foster social unrest, naturally; a hard-working carpenter or a steady-going tailor, with a family to support, may be pardoned for feeling the injustice to him of a social convention that condones the spending of what to him is a month's wages by an idle man on a luncheon at a restaurant or the careless throwing of a tip to a lackey that would give food and medicine to a sick child for several weeks. The injustices of life are many, and many of them are inevitable; to these the sensible man reconciles himself; but there is much in our social system, notably its crass materialism, that calls for attention, not only for the sake of the less fortunate, who are the more numerous, but for the sake of the foolish minority of persons not sufficiently educated to know how to spend money decently. Unfortunately a bad example is set in the highest quarters. The extravagance of the Government has become Proverbial. We are asked to buy War Saving Stamps and thereby promote "wise buying, intelligent saving, and good citizenship"; yet every mail is loaded with printed matter issued from Government departments, much of it entirely wasted and often in duplicate. One Congressman, hoping to become a Governor of his State, spent $288,000 of public money in sending a parcel of books to each elector; he sent 640,000 parcels on one day, saving himself 45 cents of postage per package. In one year another Congressman sent out under frank one-fortieth of the entire mail matter of the country. It was stated recently in Congress that a Congressman caused attacks on preparedness to be printed at the Bureau of Printing, and then distributed them under frank, with franked envelopes enclosed, so that each recipient could re-mail them to other individuals. We are threatened with a flood of projects for giving a helping hand to everybody. The Government departments are sending commissions to Europe of which it need only be said that they will eat luncheons, make speeches, see the sights in the war-zone, and return safely. A commission organized by the U. S. Bureau of Mines, and including technical men brought all the way from California, was sent to Europe for the purpose of examining the iron districts of Lorraine when another commission of mining-engineer officers from the 27th Regiment was returning from the same region, having just finished a similar investigation. It is time to take to heart the truth stated by Mr. Martin Dies of Texas, as recorded in the Congressional Record, itself rich in evidence of the unnecessary printing of speeches that were never made. This Congressman from Texas reminded his hearers that "Government is not created to support the people but is a creature supported by the people." The Government asks us to save and yet affords the spectacle of spilling the revenue with a lavish hand in every direction, from sending a couple of hundred ensigns from New York to San Francisco, where they remained in idleness varied by dissipation for three months before being sent back whence they started, to handing out billions of dollars for unproductive experimentation in aeroplanes. While our Government and our people are wasting money in every direction, millions are in want or are actually starving in Europe and elsewhere, and the hideous bogey of bolshevism gibbers at us from amid the morasses of defeat and disorder. It is the cost of high living, not the high cost of living, that is a menace to this representative democracy we are proud to call the United States of America.

DISCUSSION

The Yerington District

The Editor:

Sir—The abstract from Professional Paper 114, U. S. G. S., on the geology of the Yerington district, in Nevada, could have been read by no one with more interest and appreciation than it aroused in me. I spent several months in this district last year working up data to guide the prospecting and exploratory work of one of the larger companies operating there, and more than once expressed the wish that the Survey might give us a complete report on the district as a whole. I had hoped, if the opportunity arrived, to contribute something in this direction, and it is gratifying to find my observations and hypotheses supported in so large a measure by such an experienced observer as Adolph Knopf.

My investigations led me into a detailed mapping of geologic structure in the Ludwig, Casting Copper, Douglas Hill, and Western Nevada mines, combined with what microscopic research I could do at Ludwig. I made a distinction between fault-fissures, which Mr. Knopf emphasizes as controlling ore deposition, and fissures along which little, if any, movement had occurred, which latter, if trending more or less nearly parallel with the axis of the Singatse range, I held to be, in general, the localizing agents of primary ore deposition in the metamorphosed limestone. My maps aimed to picture the occurrence of ore with relation to these structures, as well as to the igneous rocks, to the pure marmorized limestones, to the less highly metamorphosed portions of strata, and to the more highly metamorphosed portions marked by strong development of garnet and diopside.

It always seemed to me that the term 'contact-metamorphic' was misleading in its application to the Yerington ores, for none of the orebodies to my knowledge borders on an intrusive or shows any such close structural relationship. Igneous exposures are rare near mineralized ground in the mines named above, although intrusive masses of quartz-monzonite lie but short distances from any of the mines. But many of these latter exposures are profoundly affected by the metamorphism and some consist almost wholly of garnet. I believe the primary ores were deposited along fissured zones during the final stages of an aqueo-igneous process. It seems to me that shrinkage of the pure limestones, on metamorphism to garnet and pyroxene, caused the fissures to form, mainly along lines paralleling the igneous core of the range. We find ores of the type most common to the district traversed longitudinally by such fissures, strongly developed in the garnet-pyroxenite and dying out in the less altered limestone.

Of course, there has been movement on some of these older fissures, and some cross-fracturing has occurred, especially in the brittle, hence weaker, localities occupied by sulphide orebodies. These later fractures were of great importance in aiding subsequent enrichment by descending water, without which, I am sure, few ores of the district would be of smelting grade, say, 2½% and above. The garnet ores of the Western Nevada are an exception, having about 75% of their copper value in primary chalcopyrite as against 50% or less for ores from the Ludwig, Casting Copper, Douglas Hill, and McConnell mines; in fact, the Ludwig would never have been the mine it has been but for a large strike-fault traversing the mine; this so broke and crushed the country and the primary orebodies as to lay it open for active replacement by descending waters, and subjecting the sulphides to enrichment.

From the two geologic sections given in the abstract as well as from my own observations, I am inclined to regard the strong faulting and brecciation, so interesting to the miner, as decidedly later than the period of metamorphism and primary ore deposition. In the Casting Copper and Douglas Hill mines I have observed the network of enhedral yellow garnet veinlets in fractured fine-grained garnetite. This I believe to be incident to the fissuring that preceded the garnetization, but not to represent a breccia. The rock is fractured, but in place. I have some interesting thin sections showing this. Where yellow sulphides appear to form a filling around fragments of garnet ore the occurrence has been in an orebody much broken by minor slips of recent origin, also in the zone of sulphide enrichment, and with all possibility of the pyrite or chalcopyrite being a supergene mineral. Neither has recent exploration in the Casting Copper mine, along the boundary between the calcium silicate and pure lime carbonate areas, demonstrated a zone of brecciation, as some have inferred from the peculiar surface exposures above on the same "contact". I should also add that the primary ores, while probably favoring this transitional boundary, are garnet ores, even though they lie within a marmorized limestone. I wish I had space to describe the sort of outcrop that marks the mineralized fissures where exposed in the marmorized limestone.

If one is prospecting mines in this district, and others like it, careful analysis of structure is necessary; and I think too much emphasis cannot be given, as Mr. Knopf does, to the dependence of ore deposition on fissuring. My work was restricted to the business of outlining a scheme of exploration and the finding of ore; both these were accomplished in satisfactory degree, and if future developments prove as fortunate, a detailed account of the geology of these mines may be worthy of publication. The Yerington district has had drawbacks that cannot be laid to Mother Nature.

WALTER E. GABY.

Santa Rita, New Mexico, April 8.

Invention: What Is It?

The Editor:

Sir—Life in the mountains, at this time of the year, offers attractions and opportunities for observation and meditation that those who dwell in cities have but a faint conception of. The snow-fall has been heavy this winter; the huge drifts and the miles and miles of great pine-trees, each with a load of glistening snow on its branches, make an awe-inspiring sight, especially when one considers that the piling of the snow on the tops of the mountains is part of the system of the Great Master Hand, in providing food for those who toil and labor in the valleys below. "They (the waters) go up by the mountains; they go down by the valleys unto the place which thou hast founded for them;" and down in the valleys are great dams, one of which is over 350 ft. high, and vast irrigation systems, to impound the waters and distribute them over the former arid wastes, but which are now converted into the most fertile farming-lands.

The irrigation systems are the pride of man, and the engineers who conceived and constructed them are loaded with praise, and rightly so. But what, after all, is the feat of impounding the waters to that of lifting them from the seas, and piling them upon the tops of the mountains, and by a method, apparently so simple, that most of us pass it by as being merely Nature! Truly we can say to such, "Hast thou entered into the treasures of the snow?" and sought out Him "who bringeth forth the wind out of his treasury?" If not, there is an experience awaiting those who will but spend a winter in the glorious mountains, where storms seem to receive their birth, and the wind bowls with fury as it sweeps through the pines. "Oh that man would praise the Lord for his goodness, and for his wonderful works to the children of men!"

Some years ago I spent the winter at one of the old mining camps away back in the mountains, which had seen its palmy days back in the 'seventies, and which has now to eke out an existence on the memories of its past glories. Timber is scarce in such a camp, as the miners in the old days had not studied the principles applying to the conservation of natural resources; and the storms sweep unimpeded over the bare mountains, piling the snow in huge drifts that 'cone' over and provide fine opportunity for the boys to do 'stunts' on their skis.

Many of the old-timers are still there, each living in some venerable shack, left intact from the ruins around. Every evening they meet, with common consent (including that of the proprietor), around the huge stove in the lobby of the one hotel, and recount their experiences of bygone days. They tell of ore of wonderful richness left at the bottom of the shafts now filled with water; many an unwary visitor has been lured by these stories to raise money for re-opening an old prospect, only to find that the old-time miners knew the good ore about as well as we do now, and that what they left is not likely to make many of us rich. I have heard it hinted that these evening meetings around the hotel stove were to save fuel in the individual stoves at home—this may be so, but I would impute a different motive as the chief incentive, as I have often listened to the learned discussions into which these old solons invariably lapsed.

One evening, when the wind was "blowing great guns" and the snow drifting in blinding waves, I put forward the following question for discussion: "What is invention?" The first answer was, "Why, you get an idea, and make application to the Patent Office and get a patent." This, of course, is just a patent, and there may, or may not be, 'invention'. Another answer was, "You have an idea, and you work and work at it till it works, and then you get a patent." This seemed to me to fill the bill better, especially as Mr. Edison, who ought to be an authority on this subject, says that 90% of invention is hard work. I then asked where the idea comes from, and the general opinion was, "why, you just get it." The discussion about the "idea" continued till late in the evening, but we did not make much headway. I have often thought of the definition of 'invention' as being like that of the Irishman of salt—"it is the stuff that makes potatoes taste bad when you don't put it in"—as, in so many cases, an invention is that which makes men rich who didn't make it.

To illustrate the idea factor of invention, I will give an experience I had many years ago. I was in charge of a mine, and in order to eke out the handsome salary I was receiving, I went into a venture to re-treat a large deposit of tailing, and induced several friends to go in with me. A plant was erected, which cost considerably more than we had figured it would—not an unusual case, I believe; and after we got started all sorts of unlooked for difficulties arose, the chief of these being the absolute failure of some huge stirring devices put in at my suggestion. The things simply wouldn't work. Our limited capital was vanishing, because, if there is anything that eats up money quickly, it is a plant that does not run properly—I truly think we could add this to the four things which Auger, the son of Jakeh, in the Book of Proverbs, sets forth as being never satisfied. In desperation I cabled my company tendering my resignation, unless they could allow me two days each week to visit this plant. The permission was granted, and all my thought and endeavor was directed to the saving of the money my friends and I had risked in the undertaking. I pointed out to my partners that if the stirring device could not be made to work, we were done.

On one occasion I had been all day at the plant, and left late in the evening, with a long ride over the mountains in the pouring rain to reach home. I arrived at 2 a.m., drenched and chilled through, crept into bed, and after a while fell into a sort of slumber. Those who have made a study of the sub-conscious mind say that when a person goes to sleep, he commences to dream, and this continues all through his sleep, but the only dreams or portions of them that are impressed on the conscious mind are those that occur just before waking—the connection of the absent with the present, as it were. When I awoke it was daylight. In my dreams I had been talking to someone, and these words were left ringing in my ears, "Why not put a chimney in it?" I puzzled over the words all day, as I had an intuitive knowledge that they contained the key to the solution of my difficulty, and my wife and some visitors remarked how strange and preoccupied I was.

As soon as the assayer had finished his work for the day, I took possession of the laboratory and started experimenting, and I soon began to get on the right track. At about 10 o'clock, my wife came down, determined to find out what was the matter with me, and in answer to her enquiry as to what I was doing, I jokingly told her that I was on the eve of a great invention. In order to get compressed air for my experiments, I pumped the tank used for the gasoline full, and attached a rubber tube to the small pet-cock at the top of the tank. I was so eager to watch the operation of the apparatus I had constructed that I lit a match to get more light, and lo! the whole thing blew up—I had forgotten that I was using air mixed with gasoline vapor. I had to start all over again, but at 2 a.m. I had the thing perfected—it worked—and strange to say, the principles of it have never been altered.

In a few weeks we were over our stirring or agitation difficulties, but alas! our capital was exhausted, and anyone who understands mining will realize how hopeless the situation is without money. I went to London to try to raise capital, and incidentally, to try to get someone interested in my invention, as I had no money left to take out patents. I prepared drawings, thinking that engineers would jump at so simple a device, but, nothing of the sort, and I began to get some experience of the 'wet blanket'. Fortunately my company had faith in me, and they put up the money for the patents for an interest in the invention. One well-known engineer before whom I placed it, said in a condescending way, "Of course, it might work in a laboratory, but we could never use such a device for practical work." It was some satisfaction, a few years later, to have one of the mines with which this man was connected put in a large number of my stirring-machines.

In the meantime the plant was shut down and was the joke of the district, and often when I had to pass by it, while riding with my wife to a neighboring town, I would tell her to look the other way, so as not to see it, and we christened it "the nightmare". Eventually the whole concern was advantageously sold to a company organized to operate it, and for many years, from 400 to 500 tons per day were treated, the war conditions finally bringing about a cessation of operations. The invention brought in large royalties, some of which actually found their way to the inventor.

As the years roll by, I often ponder over these things; I am a great reader of the Bible, as I consider this the book of books, and I recall the time when young Daniel and his three friends were in deadly peril because no one could give the meaning of the dream which the great king had had, but had completely forgotten. Yet the secret was revealed to Daniel in a night vision, and in his prayer of thanks and praise, he blessed his God "who revealeth the deep and secret things."

There is one thing I have been impressed with in my 30 years of mining life, and it is that perseverance in honest endeavor will bring some good result, though often quite different to that expected or sought for. This might be termed the 'work' factor or aspect of invention. "Necessity is the mother of invention," which perhaps expresses the same thought as "Man's extremity is God's opportunity," and the God-given idea, followed by man's persevering effort, will "save him out of all his troubles."

Quartzburg, Idaho, April 10. F. C. BROWN.

The Status of Gold

The Editor:

Sir—Will you permit me to make a short contribution to a rather lengthy discussion on this subject by relating some things I have seen and heard rather than venturing an opinion, for I have learned not to value even my own opinions as highly as I once did.

Axiom: You can make two bites of a cherry, but you cannot make two cherries by biting one. Corollary: A bitten cherry is worth no more than a whole one. Scholium: Each man will for himself interpret this as an axiom, a theorem to be disproved or a foolish remark and his judgment will be final for there is no court of appeal.

Now, my brothers, if you will listen a moment I will tell you how I was in a few things as wise as the mountain lions and the foxes and the coneys that live among the rocks. Once upon a time a man who was then young arose in a Chicago convention and made mention of a crown of gold. His speech was so charged with something akin to magnetism that there went out many orators, likened to a swarm of grasshoppers, with speeches which they had learned by heart from a book called Coins' Financial School, saying: "We will take 16 ounces of silver now of the value of ten pieces of gold and we will split the silver into twenty pieces and when these pieces are stamped in a press they will be worth twenty pieces of gold." They said to the farmer that would make his dollar wheat worth two dollars, but the farmer replied, "I will in truth need two, for your new dollars look to me like fifty cents." Then they said, "The product of your toil is low because there is a money famine, but we have a plan whereby such famines will cease forever." But the farmer replied, "All you can do is to make the money into more pieces, but I work early and late and have no time to count such money." Then they showed the farmer how he could pay his debts at half-price, but, with some impatience, he said, "Go to; I will pay according to my promise." Some said it was hayseed in his hair but others said it was brains in his head and uprightness in his heart that caused the farmer to say these things, and I mention this to show how in important matters men are not always agreed. Then the orators told their story to the men who dig for silver and some fell for it, but others were not greatly impressed, for they said they did not want silver to use but only to sell to their Uncle Samuel. And so it fell out that after the November election the orators were heard no more.

But now prices are high, for in time of war men clamor loudly for all kinds of stuff and will brook no delay, valuing money but lightly, being content if it bring them only a little of what they most need and that quickly. One day while I was musing on these things a strange appearing man came before me dressed in a flowing robe on which were embroidered in gold various mathematical signs and formulas. He told me that the same cure proposed in former times for low prices would heal all the disorders of the present time, including even the low price of British consols, and the cure was simply to split our twenty-dollar gold-pieces in two parts, thus doubling the value of the metal. He said such marvelous cures were not unusual, for in times past was there not a liquor that would keep out the heat as well as the cold besides curing ills of the mind as well as of the body? But I told him I feared the people who believe in axioms would raise objection and say that even Consols will recover when the clamor for stuff is somewhat abated and men turn their attention to these securities and are content with the modest return therefrom, but if the increase on Consols is paid in pounds of light weight, as he proposed, these securities might go still lower; that many men have no faith in certain kinds of new schemes, and say that touching what they call basic principles there is no new thing under the sun; that even our ancient friend Euclid made no invention but taught us only things that had been from the beginning of time. For these men have been made tired by hearing much speaking and are become apt in laying snares for reformers. In this I saw that the man agreed with me, for he said, "I have a plan for overcoming the enemy by noiseless speech and if we cannot refrain from writing let us write upon the air and save both paper and ink. Let us discard the alphabet of 26 letters that represent so much noise and confusion and turn to the Arabic or decimal system whereby we can operate the rule of three, the slide-rule, or other like devices that emit no sound whatever. We remember that all the pictures of Coin show him making figures upon a blackboard whereby he started a wonderful crusade, but his followers talked, and in that they made the mistake of their lives. Let us then take to figures, which are both accurate and convincing, but eschew logic, which is a pitfall for the unwary and something that all do not understand. Some of us might express our burning thoughts upon the abacus, but I use the figures you see on my garment. However, a frock-coat would be sufficient for some men, for what logic could be more unanswerable than a wave of the coat-tail, writing as it were upon the air in dignified silence? They should also carry a piece of chalk, as Coin did. Do you say blackboards would be inconvenient? Ah! but they shall make figures; figures, yes, figures on their coat-tails and thus hurl our theorems into the very teeth of the foe.

I might have laughed at the strange proposal of the man had not my vanity been tickled by his agreeing with me in some things, and, as I fell under the spell of his eloquence, I looked out on the plain and saw his plan working, or rather playing, for the people had ceased to work and were joyfully splitting the dollars they already had instead of laboriously searching for more gold as I had been doing that day. I saw the earth transformed into a paradise while zephyrs from flowery fields wafted perfume to my nostrils and the rippling laughter of the four rivers made music in my ears. I saw one man in admirable pantomime demonstrate by mathematics that if a dollar were split once every minute there would still be metal left in it for a gold standard.

Then my head bumped against a rock and I arose quickly, but the man who had talked with me was gone. The only reminder of the perfume wafted from Elysian fields was the fragrance of the burning cedar with which I had kindled a fire a short time before to dry my clothes as I sat down in the shelter of a rock to refresh my body by chewing a piece of green bark from a near-by shrub, for I had nothing to eat. The crags above me frowned inhospitably, the keen wind made me shiver, my camp was miles away, and there were no winged horses standing ready to carry me thence. I did not even think of conjuring horses or chariots to my assistance, as one might have done after seeing such wonderful things, but started out over a broad expanse of rock with hardly a seam, for I was at the foundation of things, amid large-scale realities, on the very floor of the world, with no kindly soil to cushion my footfall and at every step my aching feet came in contact with a perfectly sound axiom. I did not even speculate on a plan for splitting the miles to make the way shorter, for when a man is traveling alone and night is coming on and a raindrop now and then falls in his face all his faculties become alert after the manner of the leopard when she hides her kittens from the fury of the hurricane while it is yet in the distance. Even fatigue will be forgotten and one will settle into a stride that will put the miles behind as rapidly as when setting out in the morning.

Now, whether it was the logic of my head or of my heels that should have the greater credit for causing me to come in out of the rain I care not, for I hold that a man is at his best when some emergency awakens all his faculties to equal action, for then he will clearly see the Things that Are. So it happened that in a few things I was as wise as the mountain lions and the foxes and the coyotes that live among the rocks.

JOHN RANDALL.

Mogollon, New Mexico, April 21.

The Elm Orlu Case

By ROBERT M. SEARLS

Whenever, after a judicial silence covering a period of several months, the mining world begins hopefully to conclude that probably the last word has been said on extra-lateral questions, a new case is sure to bob up and demand scrutiny. The latest contribution to the bewildering maze of decisions is the ruling of the Supreme Court of the United States in the case of Butte & Superior Copper Co. v. Clark-Montana Realty Co., more familiarly known as the Elm Orlu case. The opinion, written by Justice McKenna, decides an appeal taken by the Butte & Superior Copper Co. to review a decree of the Circuit Court of Appeals, Ninth Circuit, affirming a decree of the District Court for Montana in favor of the Clark-Montana company.

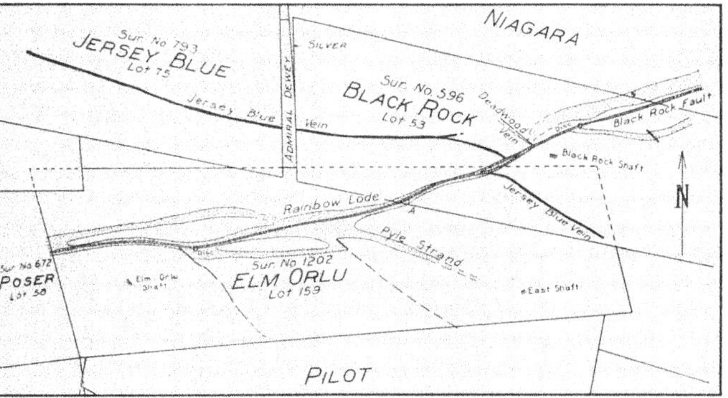

MAP OF THE GROUND IN DISPUTE AT BUTTE, MONTANA

The facts as found by the trial court, and upon which the opinion is based, will be made clearer by reference to the accompanying diagram, which is presented through the courtesy of John P. Gray, of Coeur d'Alene, Idaho, counsel for the appellees.

The Clark-Montana company owned the Elm Orlu claim and had leased it to the Elm Orlu Mining Co., which was also one of the appellees. The Butte & Superior Co., appellants, were owners of the Black Rock, Admiral Dewey, and Jersey Blue claims. The Elm Orlu was the prior location, but the Black Rock, Admiral Dewey, and Jersey Blue patents were granted first. Owing to the failure of the Elm Orlu owners to adverse, the Black Rock patent included the surface areas in conflict; and the same was true of the Admiral Dewey and Jersey Blue patents.

The main vein involved in the dispute was the Rainbow lode, which enters the Elm Orlu claim through its westerly end-line and passes out of the claim through the northerly side-line, dipping steeply to the north. Near the centre of the claim the Rainbow lode splits into two branches, the southerly one of which was termed the Pyle strand and extended easterly in the Elm Orlu claim for a disputed distance. The Pyle strand was considered as part of the main vein and not as a secondary vein. The Jersey Blue vein crosses the west end-line of the Black Rock claim and coursing easterly through the claim for a disputed distance crosses the Rainbow lode on both dip and strike. The Pyle strand, dipping north at a flatter angle than the main Rainbow lode and changing its strike almost due east as it dips, unites with the Rainbow at the 1100-ft. level beneath the Black Rock claim. The orebodies in dispute lie in the Rainbow lode under both claims, and vertically beneath the territory traversed by the common side-line.

Inasmuch as the owners of the Elm Orlu lost their right to that portion of the Rainbow apex lying northeasterly of the common side-line between the Elm Orlu and the Black Rock, owing to their failure to adverse the patent, their extra-lateral rights based on the main

Rainbow apex would be terminated by a plane passing through the point A parallel with the Elm Orlu west end-line. However, they could show an apex on the Pyle strand entirely within the Elm Orlu prior location; and this, as has been stated, dips to a junction with the main Rainbow lode at the 1100-ft. level. This Pyle apex did not outcrop at the surface and its easterly course beyond the terminus shown on the map was so far a matter of speculation that the trial court refused to make any finding beyond that point, and expressly left the case open to further determination when actual work should have developed its course and extent. Enough was shown, however, to justify the conclusion that the owners of the Pyle vein were entitled to the orebodies lying within its demonstrated extension. This, it will be seen by reference to the plat, would include the orebodies in dispute beneath the common side-line, because a plane passing through the terminus of the Pyle strand shown on the map parallel with the Elm Orlu west end-line would intersect the main Rainbow vein east of those orebodies. Such was evidently the conclusion of the Court in quieting the title to them in the Elm Orlu owners.

Both the Circuit Court of Appeals and the Supreme Court confirmed these findings on appeal. The Supreme Court also discusses several points of law that were raised. It appeared that the locators of the Elm Orlu did not comply fully with the local requirements of the laws of Montana in making their location, and the Black Rock owners therefore asserted that no claim could be based on the seniority of location. Several decisions of the Montana courts were cited to that end. In reply the Elm Orlu owners contended, first, that the Federal courts were not bound by the Montana rule; second, that the Elm Orlu people were at all times in possession of and working their claim, of which fact the Black Rock owners had due knowledge; third, that the defects in location were cured by patent. The Supreme Court upheld the latter two contentions of the appellees, observing that the first one also "had impressive strength and was conceded to have in Yosemite Gold Mining & Milling Co. v. Emerson," and that the Montana legislature had largely nullified the State court rulings to the contrary through curative statutes. The Supreme Court's reasoning seems to be that local rules designed to give constructive notice to other locators need not be strictly observed, providing the acts of the locator are such as to put such others on actual notice of his rights.

The Court then goes on to say that if the Elm Orlu location was senior to the Black Rock when patent was issued to the Elm Orlu, its senior rights were confirmed even though the date of the patent itself might be subsequent to that of the Black Rock. The rule in Lawson v. United States Mining Co. that in the absence from the patent record of an adverse suit, nothing is determined by the patent except surface conflicts is re-affirmed. The Black Rock owners by their prior patent thus gained title to all of the surface of the Elm Orlu lying northeasterly of the south Black Rock side-line, and the latter line became then the common side-line to both claims. But the Elm Orlu location being senior to the Black Rock, the owners of the former could still assert extra-lateral rights upon the Pyle strand, and, as the latter united with the Rainbow on the dip, could quiet title to the orebodies at and below the point of union.

There was some discussion also as to the effect of a quit-claim deed given by the Elm Orlu owners to the appellants, covering rights based on the Black Rock location which the Supreme Court held irrelevant, and finally the Court approved the action of the District Court in reserving for later determination the extent of the rights of the appellees in an easterly direction on the Pyle vein.

The case, as a whole, does not decide any particularly novel questions of law, although it embodies an interesting play of facts. If a corollary is to be derived from the decision, I might phrase it by saying "There is nothing like having several apexes to your vein." The opinion is of real value, however, in confirming the rule that a locator may not be foreclosed of his extra-lateral rights by failure to adverse the patent application of an adjacent claim, where he retains the apex and the existence of a sub-surface conflict is not known.

THE perfection and production on quantity basis of helium, the non-inflammable gas, by American chemists is one of the most amazing scientific achievements of the War. If Germany could have filled the gas-chambers of her huge zeppelins with it instead of hydrogen gas there would have been a different story written of their accomplishments in the War. But helium was one of the rare gases. Its cost ranged from $1500 to $6000 per cubic foot. When we entered the War the Allies told us that there was a crying need for a balloon-gas that would not burn. They suggested that our chemists pay some attention to helium. That the attention given was most thorough and adequate is shown by the fact that the cost of manufacture was brought down from $1500 to 10 cents per cubic foot, and even this figure may be lowered.

THE group of gold mines in the Kolar field of India—the Balaghat, Champion Reef, Mysore, Mundydroog, and Ooregum—having a total monthly output of $820,000, are all under the one general management, and combine for general purposes. For instance, the Cauvery River power-plant, 90 miles distant, the steam power-plant at the mines, the brickmaking works utilizing mill-slime, and the medical establishment, are all jointly operated.

EXPERIENCE has proved that wear on rope increases with speed; therefore, true economy results from increasing the load within the safety limit and diminishing the speed.

WASTE HEAT from four reverberatory furnaces at the Calumet & Arizona works at Douglas produces steam that generates 1000 kw. of electric power for the mine at Bisbee.

The Divide District

By FRANK L. SIZER

INTRODUCTION. The impetus given to prospecting by the recent favorable development of the Tonopah Divide mine can hardly fail to bring some good results to that part of Nevada which is tributary to Tonopah and Goldfield. The fact that the Gold Mountain mining district has been so late in 'coming into its own' is not at all strange, since the more attractive surface showings of the two big mining centres, above mentioned, more quickly claimed the attention of the miners. To a very few of the faithful ones, who showed their faith by 'good works' (and in one instance spent $25,000 in development) is due the present success of the Divide mine and the consequent 'boom' in surrounding properties, now well under way.

THE TONOPAH DIVIDE MINE

The situation of Gold mountain, only five miles from Tonopah and the ready access to the new district afforded by hundreds of automobiles, make it easy to visit. The accommodations, though crowded, will undoubtedly be enlarged, and visitors are fortunate in having the established settlement of Tonopah as a base to work from.

Tonopah is the nearest railroad station, but a spur from the main line between Tonopah and Goldfield is already under discussion and will be built if the present indicated importance of the new district is maintained.

GEOLOGICAL. The important geologic features are the pronounced fissuring of the area now under discussion, in which the Divide vein occupies a central position, and the volcanic uplift, which undoubtedly is responsible for this fissuring. The Divide mine is on the east flank of Gold mountain, which in this description is called the central intrusive mass. The High Divide and adjacent ground occupy the larger part of a mountain one mile east of the Divide mine; the Hasbrouck ridge is one and a half miles west of Divide.

The main lines of fracture have a north-west strike, the general parallelism of these fractures being particularly noticeable and significant. The fact that an important ore-shoot has been opened in the ground of the Tonopah Divide company naturally directs attention to this fissure system; but there is no good argument to be advanced against the probable discovery of ore in quantity on some portion of other veins, many of which are so prominently exposed in the immediate vicinity of Gold mountain.

The engineer who writes of this district six months from now will have the advantage of me, by reason of exposures made by the shafts and cross-cuts now in progress. My present diagnosis is offered as a tentative analysis of structural conditions, after ten days observation of all that can be seen on surface, as well as under-

Tonopah is Over the Ridge — Tonopah Divide Mine — GOLD

ground, in the district, and some omissions will doubtless be supplied after a subsequent visit.

The subsidiary fissuring, which has varying strikes from east-west to northeast-southwest has no known importance, although this minor fissuring was the basis of many of the older locations, upon which the prospecting of narrow widths of gold-bearing quartz has been carried on, in a somewhat desultory fashion, for the past sixteen years. The favorable development following the discovery, about eighteen months ago, at a depth of 165 ft., of the wide vein of silver-gold ore now constituting the Divide ore-zone, has completely reversed the previously expressed opinion of some of the best informed engineers, that the mineralization found in the Divide vein was erratic and undependable, lacking in silicification and not likely to persist to any great depth. This feature having been answered affirmatively, to a depth of 470 ft., it now remains for speculation as to prospects when the primary ore is reached.

Apparently some importance attaches to the ratio existing between silver and gold in the average ore of the Divide vein, which is in the proportion of 100 ounces of silver to one of gold; or, in other words, five times as much value in silver as in gold. This happens to be the ratio noted in a majority of the Tonopah ores, and agreement on this matter influences opinion as to the probable persistence of the ore at Divide.

As to the formation in which the most favorable conditions of deposition will obtain, it is a little early to make predictions; but it is generally conceded that the rhyolite cap, 80 to 400 ft. thick, must be penetrated before the ore-bearing rock, the Divide breccia, is reached. The mineralization, in dike or vein, within the limits of the Divide breccia is continuously favorable, if we are to judge by the result of the limited development already open to inspection. There is evidence, in places, that the Divide breccia is exposed on surface, by the erosion of the rhyolite cap; but so far as known to me, petrographic work on the rocks of the district has been limited and some of the opinions expressed are colored by the desire of the individual to see Divide breccia as soon as the first few shovelfuls of rock have been removed from the ground.

It is apparent that oxidation and subsequent leaching in the fissured zone has reduced the metal content near the surface and probably localized the richer ore in chimneys, bunches, or short shoots, so that speculation as to the effect of re-deposition, and the merging of oxidized into sulphide ore, will remain an open question, and an important one, until a considerably greater depth is attained, possibly 300 to 500 ft. deeper than the present bottom level of the Divide mine.

In Professional Paper No. 104, of the U. S. Geological Survey, Messrs. Bastin and Laney state: "The solutions that deposited the great bulk of the minerals of the Tonopah ores were exudations from cooling, buried bodies of igneous rock or magma. * * * In a region where there has been recurrent volcanic activity, it is possible, if not probable, that similar mineralization might take place at more than one period." These differing periods of mineralization will probably be identified in the Divide district, as work proceeds.

The important practical feature seems to be that the veins, to a considerable depth, are subject to the oxidizing influences that permitted a deposition of the gold near the surface in the minor fractures and a more liberal and important concentration of silver-gold ore in the major fissures that traverse at least one mile of the district from north-west to south-east. That some of the parallel veins may yield orebodies is highly probable, but their possible value, as compared with the Divide mine, is open to a wide range of guessing. The occurrence of gold in the ore of these veins at or near the surface is taken by some operators as a favorable sign, whereas others take pride in saying that their dikes, on surface, are just like the Divide dike, in that they show no assay-value whatever. Undoubtedly, the gold-value on the surface, in some of the fissure-fillings, is due to the removal of other constituents of the vein-matter, and yet the gold found in the larger veins has been almost negligible, with silver showing only at depths of 100 ft. or more.

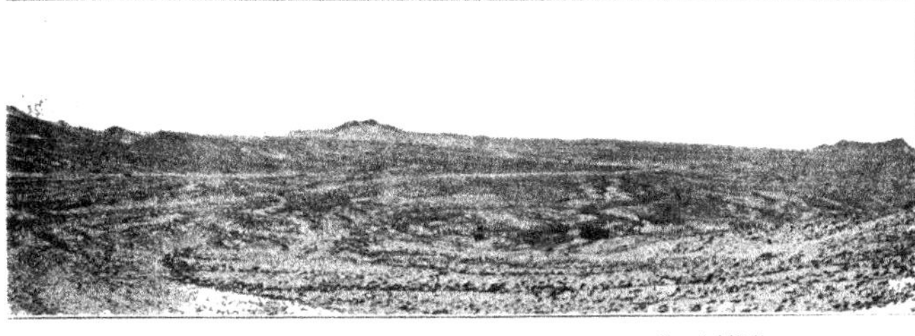

Toward Goldfield

MOUNTAIN

FINANCIAL. The companies that have been financed for exploratory work are all planning to sink shafts to a depth of 500 ft. or more, and in many instances they will not do any driving or cross-cutting until this depth is reached. Development now in progress will doubtless alter previously announced plans, by reason of changes of opinion which are quite likely to occur in a district as new as this. Any opinion as to depth at which the breccia will be reached is subject to early revision as the work progresses.

The Tonopah Divide mine has four levels 100 ft. apart, each exposing the orebody, and a fifth level, at a depth of 570 ft., from which a cross-cut to the vein is now being driven. The greatest length of ore so far developed on any level is 480 ft., and the width is from 30 to 50 ft. On the third level, a cross-cut into the hanging shows from 10 to 16 oz. silver per ton for a distance of 50 ft. beyond the assumed position of the hanging wall. A gouge separates the ore from the foot-wall rhyolite, but the hanging wall is not so clearly defined. On this gouge, and along similar seams interior to the mass, hornsilver can frequently be seen, accounting for some of the very high assays that have been given to the public. Estimates of visible ore in the Divide mine have varied from $5,000,000 to $9,000,000 gross, the latter figure, in my opinion, being justified only on the assumption that the fifth level will soon prove the vein no less in size and value than on the fourth level, the best showing in the mine.

The general geology, along the strike of the Divide vein, is depicted on the accompanying sketch, which is a compilation of the ideas of those best acquainted with the district and is here offered in a tentative way until further development work makes certain some of the doubtful points. The thickness of the rhyolite cap and the depth at which the Divide breccia merges into some other formation are points that will influence the speed at which development will proceed and the ultimate success or failure of some of the operations now under way.

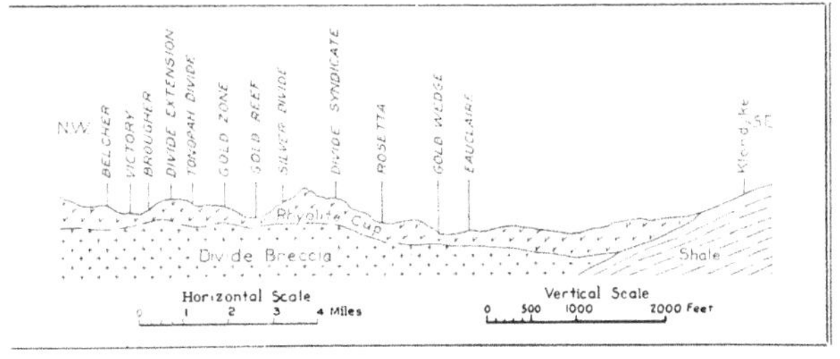

LONGITUDINAL SECTION ALONG THE STRIKE OF THE DIVIDE VEIN

The near neighbors of the Divide mine are those for whom expectations of early favorable results are reasonably assured; but this does not bar the strong probability of ore being found on some or all of the parallel fissures; it is this that constitutes the greatest hope of the district becoming an important silver-producing centre.

An Underground Trouble Detector

The geophone, a listening instrument invented by the French during the War to detect enemy sapping and underground mining operations, also for the position of artillery, is now being used by the U. S. Bureau of Mines as a possible aid in locating miners who have been entombed after a disaster. The instrument was developed by American engineers, and is now used by the Bureau according to plans drawn by these engineers. Alan Leighton, assistant chemist for the Bureau, who now has charge of these investigations, has given the following statement of general information regarding the geophone.

The instrument, though small, is essentially a seismograph, since it works on the same principle as the ponderous apparatus with which earthquake-tremors are recorded. It consists of an iron ring $3\frac{1}{2}$ in. diameter, within the centre of which is suspended a lead disc fastened by a single bolt through two mica discs, one of which covers the top and the other the bottom of the ring. Then there are two brass cap-pieces, the top one having an opening in its centre to which is fastened a rubber tube, leading to a stethoscopic ear-piece. These cap-pieces are fastened with bolts to the iron ring, and also serve to hold the mica discs in place.

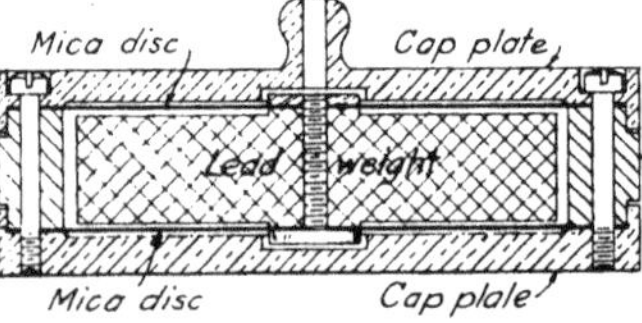

SECTION OF A GEOPHONE

The apparatus is really nothing but a lead weight suspended between two mica discs across a small air-tight box. If the instrument is placed on the ground, and anyone is pounding or digging in the vicinity, energy is transmitted as wave motion to the earth, and the earth-waves shake the geophone case. The lead weight, on account of its mass and because it is suspended between the mica, remains comparatively motionless. There then is produced a relative motion between the instrument case and the lead weight. The result is that a compression and refraction of the air in the instrument takes place. Since the rubber tube leading to the stethoscopic ear-piece is connected with this space in the geophone, this rarefication and compression is carried to the ear-drums. Usually two instruments are used, one for each ear.

When the two instruments are used, it has been found that the sound is apparently louder from the instrument nearer its source. It is evident that by moving the instruments properly, a point can be found when the sound will be of the same apparent intensity in both ears. The direction of the sound is then on a perpendicular to the line connecting the centres of the two instruments, either in front of or behind the observer. Further observation will show which side. Direction is accurately determined in this way. The sound is not actually louder in one ear than in the other, but the ear is capable of distinguishing the difference in time at which the sound arrives in the two instruments. Since this is the case, persons who are slightly deaf in one ear are said to still be able to determine direction with the instruments.

Trials showed that sounds were transmitted only about half as far in clay as in shale strata, and about a quarter as far in clay as in coal. Pounding with a pick on bituminous coal can be detected for a distance of 900 ft., and the direction determined; and pounding with a sledge can be heard as far as 1100 ft. The explosion of a one-ounce charge of dynamite was detected a distance of over 2000 ft. through shale. One interesting feature of the instruments is that the sound as transmitted to the ear is characteristic of the instrument producing the sound. To illustrate: 12 mining and carpentering operations were carried out on the coal rib. An engineer of the Bureau who had never used the geophones, and who did not know what tools were to be operated, was able to recognize and name nine of the instruments at a distance of several hundred feet through the strata. The other three sounds were accurately described, but the machines were not identified. Wind greatly interferes with the successful operation of the instruments.

In metal mines, expensive surveys have sometimes to be made in order that approaching tunnel headings may be brought accurately together. Since direction can be determined so well with the geophones, it is thought that they can be used to guide such work. It would simply be necessary to go into each heading and locate the direction from which pounding in the other heading was coming.

Observations were made recently of a mine fire burning from 20 to 40 ft. below the surface. A low rumbling noise could be heard as if air were being drawn-in along crevices, and occasionally sounds could be heard from the snapping and falling of pieces of coal or rock. As well as can be determined, the fire-area was accurately determined, but owing to the fact that the fire cannot be approached from the inside the data cannot be checked absolutely. It is interesting to note that similar sounds could be heard from only one point on the inside of the mine, and that point was the one nearest the area as detected on the surface.

LEAD LINING in sulphuric-acid leaching-vats, lead piping, and lead-lined pumps should be inspected every time opportunity offers.

ABSORPTION of sulphurous-acid gas in the reduction towers of the New Cornelia plant in Arizona was 90.5% last year.

The German Metal Octopus—III

ISSUED BY THE ALIEN PROPERTY CUSTODIAN

(b) L. Vogelstein & Co. (Inc.) Aron Hirsch & Sohn was ten years behind the Metallgesellschaft in establishing a branch in the United States. In 1897, Ludwig Vogelstein started an agency for Aron Hirsch & Sohn in New York. Soon thereafter Vogelstein formed the firm of L. Vogelstein & Co. and associated with himself one Ernest G. Hothorn. In this firm Aron Hirsch & Sohn had a direct interest. The business was conducted as a co-partnership until the end of 1916, when the present corporation, L. Vogelstein & Co. (Inc.), was formed. During these 19 years the Vogelstein business was conducted purely as an agency of Aaron Hirsch & Sohn. There were agreements between Vogelstein and the Hirsch concern for the division of profits upon the American business and upon some of the European business. The business of Vogelstein & Co. was purely that of trading in metals, both for export and in the domestic market, and they were very active in importing copper ores into the United States. They contracted for the entire output of the mines, principally copper; and they were practically the only metal concern in the United States that imported ores. These importations were mainly from South America, where they contracted for the output of several mines. They had an interest in a copper refinery at Chrome, New Jersey, and the imported copper was refined there. They also had contracts with this refinery and others, whereby they were appointed the exclusive selling agents of the product of those refineries, or they contracted to purchase on a sliding-scale basis for the entire product of mining, smelting, and refining companies.

BEER, SONDHEIMER & CO., AND CONNECTIONS

In July 1901, Vogelstein entered into an agreement with the late Capt. J. D. De Lamar for the erection of an electrolytic copper refinery at Chrome, with a capacity of 3,000,000 lb. per month. De Lamar was to contribute 75% and Vogelstein 25% of the required capital. Vogelstein agreed to finance the copper business of the refinery in return for the sole selling-agency for a period of years, for which financing he was to receive 1% commission. The plant commenced operation in 1902 under the name of De Lamar's Copper Refining Co. Since that time the capacity of this refining plant has been greatly increased and it is now capable of turning out 21,000,000 lb. per month. A smelter has also been added which has a capacity of 200,000 tons of ore per annum.

In 1905 Vogelstein bought De Lamar's entire interest in the refining company and sold a part thereof to the United States Mining Co., the predecessor of the present

United States Smelting, Refining & Mining Co. The name of the refinery has been changed and is now known as the United States Smelting & Refining Co. The capitalization of the refinery is $1,550,000 preferred and $1,550,000 common. Of both issues United States Smelting, Refining & Mining Co. own two-thirds and Vogelstein & Co. one-third. Vogelstein took a contract for a period of 10 years commencing January 1, 1906, for the exclusive selling agency of the refinery and for the financing of its operations. In order to facilitate these operations the International Metals Selling Co. was formed with an authorized capital of $250,000, Vogelstein & Co. and United States Mining Co. each taking half of the stock of the Metals Selling Co. The U. S. Mining Co. subsequently sold its interest in the International Metals Selling Co. to Vogelstein & Co., who now own all of it.

In 1916 the capital of the International Metals Selling Co. was increased to $500,000, Vogelstein & Co. paying into the treasury $250,000 cash. Vogelstein & Co. has used the International Metals Selling Co. as a buying and selling agency in South America, principally in Chile and Peru.

For ten years prior to October 1915, Vogelstein had the sole selling agency of the American Zinc, Lead & Smelting Co., and he financed its operations. When this agency terminated, a zinc-smelting plant was built in Arkansas and the Arkansas Zinc & Smelting Corporation was formed to operate it with a capital of $200,000 preferred and $400,000 common. L. Vogelstein & Co. took a five-year agreement with the corporation to finance its operations and act as its selling agent.

The following is a list of contracts for the purchase of the output of various mines which Vogelstein & Co. had during the years 1915, 1916, 1917, and 1918:

	Estimated output, tons
South American Syndicate, Tucacas, Venezuela copper ore	14,400
Sociedad Minera Backus y Johnston del Peru, Lima, Peru, copper bullion	12,000
Gatico Mining Co., Valparaiso, Chile, copper bullion	4,200
Chimborazo Mining Co., Lima, Peru, copper ore	3,600
E. A. Orbegoso, Lima, Peru, silver and gold ore	900
Bunker Hill Smelter, San Francisco, Cal., pig-lead	40,800
Arkansas Zinc & Smelting Corporation, Van Buren, zinc ore	24,000
Arkansas Zinc & Smelting Corporation, Van Buren, zinc metal	12,000
Butte & Superior Mining Co., New York, zinc ore	3,600

In addition, Vogelstein & Co. under contract with the United States Metals Refining Co., purchase about two-thirds of the entire production of the United States Metals Refining Co., amounting to about 96,000 tons refined copper per annum.

They had contracts whereby they were appointed exclusive selling agents for the following smelters and refineries: Arkansas Zinc & Smelting Corporation, Bunker Hill Smelter, and in part United States Metals Refining Company.

The business of Vogelstein & Co. developed very rapidly. The following tables show the annual turnover of the various metals for the past five years:

Turnover

	Quantity	
Copper:	Lb.	Value
1914	118,012,134	$16,285,370.21
1915	151,914,378	28,608,673.53
1916	195,457,773	55,265,255.06
1917	220,263,737	61,302,312.65
1918	185,253,715	45,725,120.92
	870,931,737	$207,196,741.36
Gold:	Oz.	Value
1914	150,768,251	$3,058,664.12
1915	152,104,969	3,131,917.93
1916	94,371,388	1,943,633.25
1917	94,095,091	1,944,544.88
1918	86,798,492	1,791,344.49
	578,138,191	$11,870,104.67
Silver:	Oz.	Value
1914	7,150,091.06	$3,976,791.34
1915	4,313,182.20	2,146,635.61
1916	3,808,045.48	2,370,764.14
1917	4,558,215.24	3,505,677.82
1918	5,290,599.28	5,166,244.54
	25,120,134.16	$17,166,113.45
Lead:	Lb.	Value
1914	76,762,030	$2,957,007.54
1915	106,884,777	4,847,903.33
1916	30,455,969	2,110,839.68
1917	31,676,373	2,696,337.08
1918	77,319,865	5,708,048.05
	323,099,014	$18,320,735.68
Spelter:	Lb.	Value
1914	64,746,906	$3,366,015.69
1915	116,363,256	16,611,610.14
1916	118,152,558	18,511,828.04
1917	50,983,574	5,256,087.55
1918	47,494,062	4,068,469.98
	397,740,356	$47,814,011.40
Tin:	Lb.	Value
1914	26,183,461	9,400,112.02
1915	19,130,577	6,738,442.01
1916	24,988,819	10,067,965.80
1917	17,332,524	8,688,107.65
1918	3,493,242	2,141,020.35
	91,128,623	$37,035,647.83
Miscellaneous:		Value
1914		$502,428.63
1915		829,808.64
1916		902,192.15
1917		579,846.61
1918		320,558.28
		$3,134,834.31

The total annual turnover during the last five years was as follows:

Copper (870,931,737 lb.)	$207,196,741.36
Gold (578,138,191 oz.)	11,870,104.67
Silver (25,120,134.16 oz.)	17,166,113.45
Lead (323,099,014 lb.)	18,320,735.68
Spelter (397,740,356 lb.)	47,814,011.40
Tin (91,128,623 lb.)	37,035,647.83
Miscellaneous	3,134,834.31
Total	$342,538,188.70

(c) *Beer, Sondheimer & Co. (Inc.)*.—Beer, Sondheimer & Co. of Frankfurt established a New York branch in 1906. Like the Metallgesellschaft, it sent over two young men, Benno Elkan and Otto Frohnknecht, who established the business here under the name of Beer, Sondheimer & Co., American Agency. The name was subsequently changed to Beer, Sondheimer & Co., American Branch, and the business was conducted under that name until August, 1915, when it was incorporated, under circumstances which will be hereinafter discussed. The New York business was owned at all times by the Frankfurt house, Elkan and Krohnknecht being only agents upon a salary and a profit-sharing basis.

Like the parent company, Beer, Sondheimer & Co., American Branch, confined its activities mainly to dealing in zinc. It made contracts with various zinc-ore producers for their entire output, and in 1907 acquired a controlling interest in the National Zinc Co., which owned a zinc smelter at Bartlesville, Oklahoma, and had under lease another zinc smelter in Springfield, Illinois, and an acid plant at Argentine, Kansas. In 1908, Beer, Sondheimer & Co. obtained control of the old El Cobre copper mine near Santiago, Cuba. It organized a corporation known as Cuba Copper Leasing Co. to operate the mine in Cuba. In 1908, Beer, Sondheimer & Co. took a long lease of a copper smelter at West Norfolk, Virginia, and

In recent years Beer, Sondheimer & Co. has also become interested in the development of zinc mines in the Butte district. It has taken options on various mining claims in that district and has done considerable prospecting therein. The following tables show copper, spelter, and lead turnover of Beer, Sondheimer & Co. for several years:

List of Contracts for Zinc Ore

Name of seller	Commodity covered by contract	Tonnage delivered during				
		1914	1915	1916	1917	1918
Federal Mining & Smelting Co., Wallace, Idaho	Total output of zinc concentrate for 3 years from date of first shipment	1,799		.....		
Silverton Mines (Ltd.), Silverton, B. C.	Total output of zinc concentrate for 3 years from July 1, 1914	2,203		.....	.....	
Elm Orlu Mining Co., Butte, Mont.	Total output of zinc concentrate for 5 years 6 months, extended to March 31, 1920, for 3000 tons monthly	10,270	10,577	51,581	31,157	13,123
Standard Silver Lead Mining Co., Spokane, Wash.	Total output of zinc concentrate to Nov. 11, 1914, delivered	4,440	.....	.....	.....	
Pingrey Mines, Leadville, Colo.	Total output of zinc concentrate to January 1915	570	.....	.....	.....	
Maxwell W. Atwater, Basin, Mont.	Total output of zinc concentrate amounting to about 8000 to 10,000 tons.	1,997	2,021	4,180	.....	.....
Rambler Carlbon Mining Co. (Ltd.), Spokane, Wash.	Total output for 1 year	1,715	.....	.....	.....	.....
American Metal Co. (Ltd.), New York.	50,000 tons clinkered residue from Clarksburg	....	7,761	6,561	9,993	9,074
Standard Silver Lead Mining Co., Spokane, Wash.	Accumulation of zinc concentrate to the end of 1915 and production from 1916 to 1920	....	2,837	8,656	5,384	1,305
Western Metals Co., Salt Lake City.	Output of zinc carbonate from Stanton mines to Dec. 31, 1917	1,100	.....	.....	.....	....
John F. Milliken, St. Louis, (Afterthought Copper Co.).	Output of zinc concentrate for 5 years	....	.....	.....	.....	1,801
Rambler Cariboo Mining Co. (Ltd.), Spokane, Wash.	Output of zinc concentrate for 1 year	....	.....	.....	.....	311

List of Contracts for Copper Ore and Copper Concentrate

Name of seller	Date of contract	Commodity covered by contract	Tonnage delivered during				
			1914	1915	1916	1917	1918
British Columbia Copper Co., New York	Mch. 21, 1911	36,000,000 lb. blister copper	2,992	475	2,470	127	.....
American Metal Co. (Ltd.), of New York	Feb. 5, 1914	18,000 tons Lebanon cinder	5,756	4,807	3,830	2,333	.....
American Smelting & Refining Co., New York	Apr. 6, 1914	4800 long tons Elect. Cu from May 1914 to April 1915	1,125	.....	.....	.....	...
Bingham New Haven Copper Gold Mining Co., New Haven	Jan. 22, 1913	Copper and lead resulting from ores shipped to International Smelting & Refining Co.:					
		Copper	721	750	1,618	.....	...
		Lead	3,019	3,164	1,764	.....	.....
United Metal Selling Co., New York	Mch. 24, 1914	1500 gross tons Elect. Copper, delivery May-October 1914	1,000	.....	.....	.....	.....
Quincy Mining Co., New York	June 12, 1914	75 tons monthly of Lake copper with 6 months notice of cancellation	285	.....	.....	.....	...
Cuba Copper Co., New York-Santiago	June 2, 1914	Total output of copper concentrate and crude ore from El Cobre mines:					
		Concentrate	10,892	17,552	22,370	26,957	31,100
		Crude ore	3,006	8,081	6,722	2,038	1,811
Manuel Luciano Diaz, Habana, through C. L. Constant Co.	July 8, 1914	9000 tons low-grade copper ore	1,760	7,380	.....	.....	.....
Do	.... do	9000 tons high-grade copper ore	6,319	3,066	.....	.....	.....
Virginia Smelting Co., Boston, Mass.	Jan. 8, 1916	Copper ore from Blanton Copper Mining Syndicate, San Domingo for 2 years	....	.....	348	233	.....
Eustis Mining Co., Boston	April 4, 1912	Lump cinder and fine cinder from Eustis pyrites	2,120	1,720	.....	.....	
Do	May 15, 1912	Lump cinder	2,552	2,965	.....	.....	
Do	Feb. 12, 1914	Fine cinder and lump cinder produced by Eustis Mining Co.	16,800	20,600	20,000	20,600	18,000

organized a corporation known as the Norfolk Smelting Co., through which it has been operating the copper smelter. The product of the El Cobre mine and such other copper ore as Beer, Sondheimer & Co. purchased was treated at the Norfolk plant.

Turnover

Spelter dealt in:	Lb.	Value
1915	73,143,943	$8,118,004.00
1916	75,563,802	10,342,882.00
1917	57,459,556	5,330,090.00
1918	49,814,465	4,131,826.00
Total	255,981,766	$27,922,802.00

Lead dealt in:	Lb.	Value
1915	6,210,758	278,710.00
1916	5,754,419	378,098.00
1917	6,230,411	527,232.00
1918	673,727	70,539.00
Total	18,869,315	$1,254,583.00
Copper dealt in:		
1915	17,071,632	$2,550,490.00
1916	24,295,095	5,530,191.00
1917	27,056,933	7,326,273.00
1918	10,450,315	2,627,004.00
Total	78,873,975	$18,032,958.00

Minerals Separation Agency

The history of Beer, Sondheimer & Co.'s activities in the United States would not be complete without mentioning its connection with the various Minerals Separation companies.

The various Minerals Separation companies have successively claimed to own patents covering an improved process of ore concentration. Ore concentration in metallurgical operations is the separation of the mineral or metallic part of the ore from the non-metallic or worthless material found associated with it in nature, in order that the valuable metallic particles may be in proper condition for the subsequent process of smelting.

Expressed in language that laymen can understand, this new process may be described as the addition of a very small quantity of oil to the ore-pulp (which is ore finely pulverized floating on water) followed by vigorous agitation of the pulp and the introduction of air-currents into the mixture resulting in the development and distribution throughout the mixture of small bubbles of air which attach to themselves the valuable metallic particles and with them rise to the surface forming a mineral froth of such coherence as to afford full opportunity for its removal from the surface for further treatment of the metallic particles, while the worthless material sinks to the bottom.

Prior to the invention of this new process, ore concentration, or the separation of the mineral from the useless parts in ore, was effected by the water or gravity process. In that process the ore was mixed with water forming the ore-pulp; the pulp was shaken, thereby separating the metallic particles from the worthless parts of the ore, and the metallic particles being heavier than the water, sank to the bottom, while the worthless particles being lighter than the metallic particles, though heavier than the water, were subjected to an up current of water which carried the worthless particles to the surface and over the container. The old process was commercially unsuccessful because it permitted a large percentage of the metal in the ore to be carried off with the worthless particles. The material thus rejected was called 'slime'. For years dumps consisting of millions of tons of such slime, which were known to contain a large percentage of metal, lay useless because there was no known process by which they could be treated and the metal extracted.

In 1906, H. L. Sulman, H. F. K. Picard, and John Ballot, all of London, England, claiming to be the inventors of the new process, obtained a patent thereon in the United States. In 1910, Sulman and H. H. Greenway and A. H. Higgins, all of London, obtained another patent in the United States, and in 1914, Greenway, then of Melbourne, Australia, obtained a third patent in the United States, the latter two patents involving the same process as the first one, but including improvements thereon. These patents run for a period of 17 years from their respective dates.

In 1905, and before the first United States patent was obtained, the patentees obtained a patent in England exactly similar to the first United States patent. The validity of the English patent was attacked in the English courts, but was sustained by the House of Lords. (Minerals Separation v. British Ore Concentration Syndicate, 27 R. P. C., 33.)

In 1903, Minerals Separation, Ltd., which will be hereafter designated as the parent company was formed under the English law. The three United States patents were assigned to this company. In 1910, the parent company having acquired the United States patents, and similar patents obtained in Canada and Mexico, conveyed these patents to a corporation called Minerals Separation Syndicate, for the purpose of enabling the American syndicate to exploit these patents in America. This, too, was an English corporation.

In 1911 the American syndicate made a contract with Beer, Sondheimer & Co., whereby it gave to that firm the exclusive agency to represent the syndicate in America. For reasons unimportant to the present inquiry, this first American syndicate was soon dissolved and a new syndicate was formed, called Minerals Separation American Syndicate (1913), Ltd. This, too, was a British company. The 1913 syndicate renewed the agency agreement of Beer, Sondheimer & Co., and appointed that firm sole agents to conduct all of the syndicate's commercial affairs in the United States, Canada, and Mexico, the agency to continue for a minimum period of 10 years with a provision for renewal for the rest of the life of the patents. Beer, Sondheimer & Co. were to receive a commission of 10% of all gross royalties received for the use of the patents and 10% on all profit-sharing business (the syndicate intending not only to give licenses, but also to buy up and treat ores), and also a percentage as a commission of the sale of products so treated by the syndicate.

When the agency agreement was made Beer, Sondheimer & Co. had an American branch of its business in New York City, which was in charge of Benno Elkan and Otto Frohnknecht, and was being conducted under the name of Beer, Sondheimer & Co., American branch. The parties entered into the performance of the agreement, and inasmuch as most if not all of the business was done in the United States the agent's end of the business was conducted by the American branch of Beer, Sondheimer & Co.

In addition to having the exclusive agency, Beer, Sondheimer & Co. were also stockholders of the 1913 syndicate, owning 32,615 shares of said stock. In 1916 the property of the 1913 syndicate was conveyed to an American corporation called Minerals Separation North American Corporation, and each stockholder became entitled to two shares of the American corporation's stock for each share of the 1913 syndicate stock.

The importance of the control by this German-owned branch of Beer, Sondheimer & Co. of the Minerals Separation process, and the power to grant or withhold from the United States metal industry licenses to use the flotation process, can hardly be over-estimated. The Custodian, as will be pointed out later, has taken over all of the Minerals Separation stock held by Beer, Sondheimer & Co., and the latter's control of the Minerals Separation process in the United States has broken.

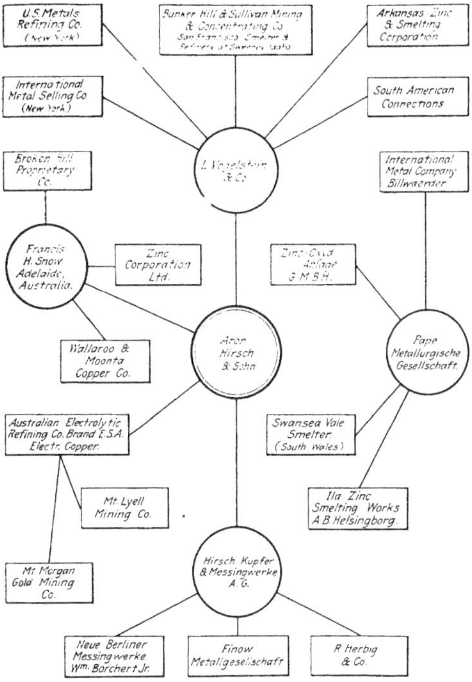

Who will say that these three powerful German-owned or German controlled companies were not a standing menace to the security of our domestic metal industry as well as to the development of our own commercial interests in Mexico and South America? It is no answer to the obvious potential power for evil which these companies possessed to point to the fact that since the European War the American Metals Co. has been entirely officered by Americans who have shaped the policy of that powerful organization, or to show that Vogelstein is a naturalized American citizen, or to remind us that Elkan and Frohnknecht, in control of Beer, Sondheimer & Co., are likewise American citizens—they were late converts to citizenship. The power lay in the hands of Hirsch & Sohn and Beer, Sondheimer & Co. and the Metallgesellschaft and its stepchild, Henry R. Merton & Co., at any time and all times to direct the policy of these American concerns. These outposts of German commercial aggression having gained a foothold in the United States, were gradually spreading into Mexico and South America, which are legitimate fields for our own commercial development. In Mexico today the American Metal Co. is second only to the American Smelting & Refining Co. in its control of the mineral wealth of that country. In Peru and Chile and in other parts of South America these companies not only control the output of mines and smelters, but the American Metal Co. also owns mining claims of great extent. With unlimited resources at their command, they bought up mines, financed and built smelters and refineries, bought and sold huge quantities of metals, organized and controlled their own transportation facilities, and even invaded the oil industry. With the controlling power of these great organizations centred in the hands of the Germans—knowing what we know about Germany and Germans—who will deny that they have been a menace to the country?

We are not alone in our fear of German commercial aggression, nor in our desire to eradicate the German influences. England has gone even further than we have. Finding that the Germans had practically complete control of the Australian metal output, the English courts

ARON HIRSCH & SOHN, AND CONNECTIONS

have declared void as against public policy all contracts between the Germans and the Australian mines, and the English have now completely supplanted the Germans in control of Australia's metal industry. In the meantime, in 1918, England passed an act for the purpose of controlling the non-ferrous metal industry and required that all persons engaged therein should first obtain a license from the Board of Trade. Henry R. Merton & Co. were refused such license, and in consequence thereof that company, together with its subsidiary, the Merton Metallurgical Co., Ltd., have gone into liquidation.

France and Belgium are re-building their smelters and building new ones. And it may safely be assumed that German ownership in the French and Belgian smelters and refineries will never be restored to them. Thus cut off from their control of the Australian zinc ores and from the control of Belgian and French smelters, their world domination of zinc and lead has been irreparably shattered.

This brings us to a consideration of what effect our participation in the War has had upon the German-controlled American companies, and how we have endeavored to deal with them.

When the European War broke out, these three American branches of the German metal triumvirate found themselves cut off from their German principals. Germany was in great need of metals, especially copper, and at first the American Metal Co., Vogelstein, and Beer, Sondheimer & Co., as well as other large American selling agencies, sought to supply that need by making shipments to neutral countries, but destined for Germany. The British blockade, however, soon tightened and after some consignments were seized by the British, an agreement was entered into between the six principal American selling concerns—Vogelstein & Co. and American Metal Co. included—and the British Admiralty whereby the American copper selling agencies agreed not to ship any copper to any country except those allied with England, without special permission from the British authorities. It is believed that after that agreement had been entered into, it was scrupulously observed by the American Metal Co. and Vogelstein & Co. The year 1916 was a very profitable year for all three of these German metal concerns. The American Metal Co. made a profit of $7,000,000 during 1916. Vogelstein & Co. showed a profit of $3,000,000, and Beer, Sondheimer & Co. showed a profit of $2,000,000.

(To be Continued)

CORRECTION. In our issue of March 22 it was stated that the quantity of graphite ore milled in Canada last year was 19,614 tons; this should have been in 1917. During 1918, the output of graphite was 3051 tons, valued at $270,054. There was treated a total of 9958 tons, which yielded 3162 tons of milled or refined graphite.

THE Tennessee Copper & Chemical Corporation in 1918 made 283,092 tons of 60° sulphuric acid.

Grinding-Pebbles and Tube-Mill Liners

A falling-off in the production of pebbles and liners for use in tube-mills, as shown by final figures for 1918, compiled by the U. S. Geological Survey, reflects both uncertainty of market and changes in grinding practice.

Natural pebbles for grinding rock, ores, minerals, cement-clinker, and many other materials, were obtained in 1918, as in preceding years, from the beaches between Oceanside and Encinitas, San Diego county, California. According to reports received by the Survey, the entire output was marketed by Robert Burns & Co., Oceanside; the Pacific Coast Pebble Co., Encinitas; and Thebo & Tingman, Encinitas. The output of these pebbles in 1918 was considerably smaller than in 1917, probably in large part because the growing use of steel balls is supplanting the use of pebbles; but the decrease was due in part to the uncertainty of the market, which deterred pickers from collecting and sorting stocks that they might have marketed.

The output of artificial pebbles in 1918 was considerably greater than in previous years. These so-called artificial pebbles are either roughly cubical or mechanically smoothed and rounded blocks of quartzite manufactured by the Jasper Stone Co., Sioux City, Iowa; or mechanically smoothed and rounded blocks of silicified or chalcedonized rhyolite, manufactured by Omer Maris, Manhattan, Nevada.

In 1918, the sales of pebbles and of cubes and artificially-rounded blocks for use in grinding amounted to 9734 tons, valued at $82,350. This was a decrease, roughly, of 2300 short tons, or nearly 20%, compared with the sales in 1917. The value, however, shows an increase of nearly $24,000, or about 30%, compared with that for 1917. Besides this marketed output, there was an indeterminable consumption, probably large, of substitutes for grinding-pebbles by mills that used local pebbles, boulders, lumps of ore, or native rocks.

Only estimates are available to show the quantities of flint pebbles imported. The records of the Bureau of Foreign and Domestic Commerce indicate that the quantity of pebbles imported in 1918 was probably a little over 10,000 tons, about 70% of which came from Denmark, the remainder from France.

The total new supply of grinding-pebbles contributed to domestic markets in 1918 appears thus to have been 20,000 tons, compared with 25,500 tons in 1917, 32,000 tons in 1916, and 31,000 tons in 1915. This diminishing supply is evidence of the growing use of steel balls or other substitutes for grinding-pebbles.

The domestic output of flint or quartzite tube-mill lining in 1918 was 2535 tons, valued at $46,634, compared with 3050 tons, valued at $59,250, in 1917. In 1918 there were only two producers—the American Flint Co., Tron City, Tennessee; and the Jasper Stone Co., Sioux City, Iowa.

POWDERED COAL is being tested as fuel in blast-furnaces of the Tennessee Copper & Chemical Corporation.

CANANEA, SONORA

PRESENT ACTIVITIES IN NORTHERN SONORA

Mexican (Sonora) ore shipments to the United States during March, through the 'port' of Agua Prieta, were 6238 tons, valued at $1,236,500. This is considered to be a little more than the average per month. Individual shipments were as follows, in tons: Moctezuma Copper Co., 5480; El Tigre, 459; San Pablo, 29; La Colorado, 13; La Caridad, 93; San Ygnacia, 63; La Escuadra, 10; San Nicolas, 39; Promontorio, 42; and Rosales, 10 tons. Much of the ore now being sent through this port is lead and silver-bearing. Reports from Nacozari and vicinity are to the effect that prospectors are crowding into the country in increasing numbers. While copper properties are not changing hands at present, there is a marked effort to get hold of silver mines, already developed or promising prospects.

At the property of the Nacozari Consolidated Copper Co., near Nacozari, the deep development tunnel had traversed the recently encountered copper zone for 73 ft. without apparent diminution in the amount or quality. Mining men who recently returned to Douglas state that a body of considerable magnitude is being developed. The management contends that as no pay-ore was expected before reaching the main vein, still several hundred feet away from the breast of the tunnel, the ore-zone is proving far more extensive than calculated. Machine-drills are in continuous operation, driving 8 ft. each 24 hours. The tunnel is now over 3000 ft. long. The copper minerals are chalcopyrite and bornite, similar to the higher grades of ore in the Pilares de Nacozari mine of the Moctezuma Copper Co., a Phelps Dodge holding. John G. Alexander, general manager for the Nacozari Consolidated, reports also that good progress is being made at the San Pablo, where work was recently recommenced. A new vein of high-grade silver ore was opened recently, adding considerably to the ore-reserves. The San Pablo is preparing to resume shipping silver ore to the El Paso smelter in the near future.

At Cananea, the only active copper producer at present is the Cananea Consolidated Copper Co., which is working most of its shafts on a small scale, having only watchmen and repair-gangs on duty at some of them. The smelter is working at quarter capacity. During the last month several hundred additional men were laid off. The company adopted the policy of supplying transportation to these men and their families to any point in northern Mexico they might wish to go. At least one special train carrying several hundred Mexicans left Cananea early in April for southern Sonora and Sinaloa points. Most of them chose the latter State, it being more largely devoted to agriculture, therefore affording a better opportunity to tide over the dull period in mining. By ridding Cananea of the unemployed surplus, the 'Four C' company has avoided repetition of political

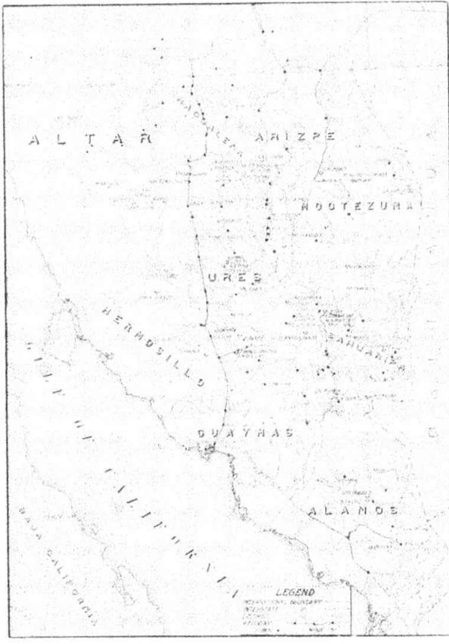

THE STATE OF SONORA, MEXICO

and social unrest. The copper output in March was 3,200,000 lb., about half of normal.

Operations in the northern districts of Sonora are showing considerable revival with the opening of spring. Several deals of importance are reported to be pending, while a number of properties have been re-opened, and there is a growing demand for silver mines. A leader in importance among the newer properties is the San Nicholas, a silver property being operated by Leo G. Cloud and associates under the name of the Compania Mexicana Dessaralladora de Minas (Mexican Development & Mining Co. under a lease from the Transvaal company. The property lies 15 miles west of Cumpas, centre of the Moctezuma mineral district. Fairly good roads lead from it to Nacozari, the nearest rail point. C. N. Knutsen is resident manager. While the underground force is extracting ore for the small mill on the property, machinery has been ordered for a 50-ton flotation plant. This includes a K & K machine, a Marcy mill, and a Dorr classifier. Altogether the property is considered to have exceptionally good prospects, the ore being readily amenable to flotation. Shipments have been started and it is intended to send one carload of concentrate monthly for the present.

The Tepacate group, an old property in the vicinity of Bonamachi, has been taken over by the Hosier brothers, representing Kansas City capital. A gasoline hoist has been erected, and the old workings are being re-timbered. When this has been done a considerable amount of ore will be within reach. Experiments are being made on the ore to ascertain the best method of treatment, after which a mill may be built.

The Bavicanora group, adjoining the famous Las Chispas mine near Arizpe, has been taken over by F. Oldfield Bostwick and associates. This is one of the most important properties in the Arizpe district, having been opened first in the days of Maximillian, but later abandoned on account of the hostility of the natives. Latterly the workings within reach of the surface were gutted by 'gambocinos' (Mexican high-graders), and so much of the old timbering removed or rotted away that many of the drifts caved-in. When Bostwick took hold of the property considerable timbering had to be done, but the result was to make available considerable bodies of silver-gold ore. A 10-stamp cyanide mill has been erected, and while mechanical troubles have been frequent, the plant now is being adjusted. Mr. Bostwick has made some shipments of concentrate recently, which are understood to have netted him excellent returns.

Las Chispas mine, owned by the Pedrazzini interests of Switzerland, and managed by Antonio Pedrazzini, nephew of the principal owner, also has returned to work after a considerable period during which the management was at loggerheads with the Sonora government and that of Mexico over taxes and local conditions. These differences were adjusted some time ago to the satisfaction of both sides. The 20-stamp mill is in regular operation and shipments are being made at the rate of a carload of high-grade concentrate each month.

El Carmen mine, near Chinapa in the Arizpe district, is being re-opened by Louis Burgonia. The old shafts and drifts are being re-timbered and being put in shape. El Carmen yielded several hundred thousand dollars of silver in the 'seventies, but has been closed down for a number of years.

El Canario Copper Co., whose properties adjoin those of the Moctezuma, is working the Lillie group, 8 miles from Nacozari, on a considerable scale. The company is concentrating on development in shafts, tunnels, and drifts, and has blocked out a considerable tonnage of a good ore. A large compressor, hoist, and other machinery has been installed, while good roads have been built to Nacozari. Several motor-trucks are used to haul supplies between the railroad at Nacozari and the mine. These later will be used to carry ore to rail. The same company is working the Canario group, adjoining La Caridad mine, 18 miles from Nacozari. Development is the only effort at present, large bodies of copper ore being ready when market conditions warrant. J. P. Harvey is the manager, maintaining his residence at Nacozari.

A custom mill to treat ores of the district surrounding the Cinco de Mayo property at Pilares de Terras, is being erected on the Roy property, which is owned by the First National Bank of Douglas. This will help the district considerably. The mill is not the property of the bank mentioned, but is being constructed by arrangement with the bank. In the meantime, the Roy mine staff is getting out ore and stacking it preparatory to putting it through the mill when it begins work within the next few weeks.

OATMAN, ARIZONA

OPERATIONS IN THE OATMAN AND GOLDROAD DISTRICTS.

In addition to the steady operation of the United Eastern and Tom Reed companies, the Oatman district is showing renewed activity, especially in prospecting. ——The Red Lyon has begun cross-cutting south from the 220-ft. level.——The Telluride is down 20 ft. in a new shaft. This company will also continue prospecting from the old shaft at the eastern end of the property. ——The Lexington is cross-cutting from the 250-ft. level. The latest report is that the vein has been reached.—— It is said that the Mushrush property, consisting of two well-located claims on the strike of proved orebodies, has changed hands, and will shortly be equipped and operations begun.——The United Oatman has reached a depth of 584 ft.——The Alcyone is driving on the 400-ft. level. ——The Lazy Boy is driving on the vein at 200 ft.—— On the Blue Bird (Big Jim Con.) the shaft has reached a depth of 300 ft. An 18-ft. vein of calcite, dipping to the south, was encountered at 265 ft. Systematic cross-cutting and driving is planned when the 400-ft. level is reached.

In the Goldroad district the Gold Road Bonanza continues work at a depth of 550 ft.—A few men are employed at the Gold Ore.—The Goldroad mine is still inactive, although there is sufficient ore blocked out to run several years. It is reported that this company (the U. S. S. R. & M. Co.) will not resume operations during the present range of high prices.

MISSOULA, MONTANA

POSSIBILITIES OF GOLD MINING IN THE EAST COEUR D'ALENE REGION.

This region lies between Fish creek in the east of Mineral county and Saltese to the west in the same county, on the north slope on Coeur d'Alene range and that part of Idaho drained by the St. Joe river. The area is essentially gold-bearing, although a few copper and lead deposits have been found. In the 'seventies a number of large producers of placer gold was in operation, but the Frazer river and Cariboo excitement depleted the district of miners. In the early days it was only the shallow and rich ground that was worked: what did not yield $1 to $1.50 per yard was hardly considered. With the hydraulic giant, hydraulic elevator, and other placer machinery, a revival has gradually taken place. A small dredge was erected on Cedar creek, but it had to be abandoned on account of hard 'reefs' of bedrock, and ground too deep for its capacity. Several small hydraulic plants have been put in, but have generally been failures, being too small to work economically.

In 1917 a modern hydraulic plant was installed on Windfall creek by the Windfall Placer Mining & Development Co. This company owns 600 acres, which has been found to average better than 30c. per yard. The plant consists of a sawmill, 1¼ mile of flume carrying water to the penstock, from where a 24-in. pipe leads to the pit, giving a head of 375 ft. at the giants. There are two of No. 3 size, fitted with Hoskins deflectors. A hydraulic derrick, having a capacity of 3 tons has been erected to handle boulders. The ground is well suited for hydraulicking, having a good water-supply, plenty of dumping-ground, and a uniform grade of 6%, and in some places more. The gold is coarse and easy to save; it is high-grade, running 984 fine. This company under proper management should make a handsome profit on its investment. The equipment has been financed by local capital.

On Trout creek, one of the larger streams, there is about to be erected a large hydraulic plant financed by Eastern capital. The estimated capacity will be 3000 in. of water under 250-ft. head, handling 4500 yd. per day. It is claimed by the owner of the ground that the value will average over $1.50 per yard.

Some of the equipment for the Niagara Mining Co.'s placer mine on Niagara creek is at the railway station awaiting transportation over the mountain to its property. It is doubtful if the pack-trail will be open before the later part of May.

There are a number of good placer prospects where money could be made if properly equipped. In some places hydraulic elevators would have to be installed in order to handle the gravel. At other places dredges could be worked profitably, but capital is required.

In gold-quartz mining the east Coeur d'Alene offers good opportunities for exploration. A number of promising prospects can be found all along the range. The veins generally have a strike parallel with the main range—NW to SE. Veins are found in slate, porphyry, quartzite, and granite. Several of them carry fair value, and are remarkably persistent both in strike and dip. There is an abundance of water for power for all purposes. The field is well worthy of consideration by mining men, and it should in the near future prove to be one of great activity.

GOLDFIELD, NEVADA

PREPARATORY WORK FOR MINING LOW-GRADE ORE.

The Goldfield Development Co. has started a cross-cut at a depth of 380 ft. to connect the main south-east drift in the Combination with the Combination Fraction shaft, which will be the main working shaft for the glory-holing operations in this area. The cross-cut will be extended 300 ft. to the Fraction shaft, which is in good condition and will require little re-timbering. After the cross-cut is complete, the main drift will be widened to accommodate double tracks, and raises will be driven into the stope-filling at 25-ft. intervals. It is estimated that 1,500,000 tons of material assaying $5.60 per ton will be drawn from the vein south-east of the Combination shaft and north-west to the January shaft, a total diistance of 1000 ft. A concrete foundation is being laid for a hoist at the Fraction shaft, and within a few days construction of ore-bins will be started. The hoisting-plant of the Mohawk mine will be used, as its shaft is now useless. After a complete sampling of the Red Top it is calculated that 200,000 tons of material there will assay between $6 and $7 per ton, with a large area not developed by the Goldfield Consolidated company holding important possibilities. This tonnage was not included in the original estimates of the manager, A. I. D'Arcy, on the possibility of mining low-grade ore in the Consolidated. No repairs have yet been made to the Consolidated mill, where the ore will be treated, and none will be made until the mines have been placed in condition for production, as it is considered that few alterations will be necessary, and these will occupy little time.

SILVERTON, COLORADO

SUNNYSIDE COMPANY HAS DISASTROUS FIRE.

On April 21 fire started in one of the buildings of the Sunnyside M. & M. Co. and spread with such rapidity that in two hours property valued at $200,000 was destroyed. The new bunk-houses and commissary buildings, construction of which was recently completed, were totally destroyed, all wearing apparel and other personal effects of the miners being lost. The bunk-houses were considered to be the best in this State in respect to comfort and sanitation, and two years was required for their construction. The 300 men employed were deprived of quarters and are being temporarily accommodated at Eureka and Silverton. The compressor-house was totally destroyed and all the machinery ruined, with the result that all mining operations were brought to a standstill. The transformers were saved, and the flames were also prevented from reaching the tramway. As several months will be required to replace the buildings destroyed with even temporary structures, there is not much possibility of work being resumed by the company for some time.

This disaster has resulted in a surplus of labor in the Silverton district. Fortunately, Telluride is in need of miners and will absorb a large number of them.

DIVIDE, NEVADA

WHAT IS BEING DONE IN THE NEW DISTRICT.

Large numbers of persons—miners, would-be mine-owners, engineers, and promoters—are arriving daily at Tonopah from the north and south, answering the call of a mining boom that is assuming proportions rivaling that of Goldfield. Buildings are being hauled to or erected at Divide, but the only accommodations at present are at Tonopah, six miles distant, where the hotels and lodging-houses are congested and guests are compelled to 'double-up' in inadequate quarters. Locations nominally in the Divide district cover an area five by eight miles, and have been made nearly continuous to a point far south of Klondyke, or 10 miles south of the Tonopah Divide mine. A new gold discovery, half-way between Klondyke and Goldfield, bids fair to extend this area another seven miles to the south. Claims have been selling from $500 to $5000 each, even at a great distance from the central properties, and more than 150 companies have applied for charters. At least 50 of these have sold treasury shares at prices ranging from 5 to 15 cents each in sufficient number to give them substantial funds for development, these sums varying from $15,000 to $100,000. Deposits in two banks at Tonopah have increased approximately $3,000,000 within the past two months, representing funds realized from the sale of shares in Divide corporations. In view of the fact that there is little other than position on the map to recommend one claim over another, and in the absence of any proof that company funds are employed for other purposes than mining, there is no evidence of wild-catting in the Divide district. There have been patent instances of 'market rigging', however, by procuring fictitious quotations on stocks the majority of which is in pool. The stock exchanges have shown no inclination to discourage this practice, which has brought discredit and suspicion upon legitimate mining in the past. An authoritative analysis of the geology of the Divide district is still lacking, and much misleading publicity has been given to so-called geological reports that apparently have been designed to aid individual promotion schemes. The consulting engineer for the Tonopah Divide company, A. I. D'Arcy, has prepared a brief statement covering the central part of the district, a summary of this report appearing in the Press of January 25, 1919. This report is accepted as authentic for the area covered. Many of the successful operators, mine managers, and superintendents of Goldfield's active period are among the leaders in the Divide activity.

The shaft of the Tonopah Divide mine has been sunk to a depth of 565 ft., and a station at this point has been cut and timbered. The superintendent, William Watters, has completed massive foundations for a 1200-cu. ft. compressor and for a double-drum hoist, to be used after opening the next level. This work has delayed the starting of the fifth level cross-cut, which will now be driven to the silver vein. On the fourth level the main south-east drift, following the hanging wall, has advanced 250 ft., and the face is nearly under the rich area opened on the third level. The drift has continued in good ore, with face assays at times as high as 2000 oz. of silver. The richest ore is seamed with kaolin, containing slabs and flakes of pure horn silver. No cross-cuts have been driven on the fourth level, as efforts here have been devoted to driving to reach the high-grade area below the third level sill. The latter has been broken 50 by 20 ft. in extent, 10 ft. high, and all ore taken from this area averaged above $80 per ton. Raises from the second and third levels have connected with the levels above, providing good air, and other raises are being driven from these levels. All these raises have continued in high-grade ore, the third-level raise averaging over $70. Two sills have been cut to supplement, if necessary, ore from development work, the source of all production to date. Shipments to the MacNamara mill at Tonopah are 60 tons daily, transported by motor-trucks which have replaced the 8 and 10-horse teams. Mr. D'Arcy says that in order to secure the best extraction and lowest cyanide consumption he has endeavored to keep the mill-heads at $30, but the output of two recent days had an assay-value of over $70 per ton.

On the 500-ft. level of the Brougher Divide, the south cross-cut penetrated the vein for 30 ft., and a drift south-east was started without continuing to the foot-wall. The vein material was low-grade, but within a short distance ore appeared on the foot-wall side, and the drift was turned farther south and has progressed 140 ft. Most of this ore has been of milling grade.

The Gold Zone is preparing to sink from the 500-ft. level to a depth of 800 ft. The south-east drift and north-east cross-cut on the 500-ft. level have exposed seams of rich ore, the latter development being regarded as highly significant in view of the extensive faulting between the Gold Zone and Tonopah Divide workings. It is held that the newly-opened fissure or fracture-zone may prove to be the true Divide fissure.

The Hasbrouck has started shipping ore to Tonopah from the vein cut 400 ft. in the lower tunnel. At 950 ft., this tunnel has penetrated the main lode of the mountain, showing free gold 600 ft. below the apex. The shaft, 360 ft. deep, is being re-timbered and the old workings on the 200-ft. level, 260 ft. below the tunnel-level, are being re-opened. A drift on this level, driven about the year 1902 by John McKane, is said to have exposed a large tonnage of ore assaying from $15 to $26 per ton, with silver at 50 cents per ounce.

THE MINING SUMMARY

ARIZONA

Globe.—The Arizona Asbestos Co. has resumed operations. Contracts have been let for haulage. The output of the mine is sold under contract with the Johns-Manseville company.

Jerome.—The United Verde Extension tunnel having drained the country around the Dundee-Arizona mine, the latter is to re-commence sinking immediately. This company has 50,000 tons of carbonate ore developed, and plans are being drawn for a leaching-plant to treat it.

Ray.—What appears to be the largest gold strike made in Arizona for some time is reported at Chelota, near Ray. The property on which the ore was found is being developed by New York capital. The vein is 24 in. wide, and specimens exhibited show large pieces of tree gold. E. R. Tufts is manager.

CALIFORNIA

Englemine.—The Engels Copper Mining Co. has issued its report for the first quarter of 1919. The income from sales of copper concentrate was $295,468, and operating expense $294,151, leaving a profit of $1317. The cost, excluding depreciation, was 16.68 cents per pound of metal; but in March this item was reduced to 15.19 cents. For 1918 the average was 19.58 cents. A reduction in power rates, from the Great Western Power Co., is probable. Storms in February cut off power for 5 days. Expenditure on No. 2 shaft, ore-bins, water-supply, mill, diamond-drilling, etc., totaled $34,693. Current assets are $401,864, and liabilities $244,023. Underground exploration was very satisfactory. On No. 6 level the last cross-cut passed through 70 ft. of solid bornite, averaging 5% copper. At least 500,000 tons were added to reserves, making them 2,775,000 tons. The metallurgical results were as under:

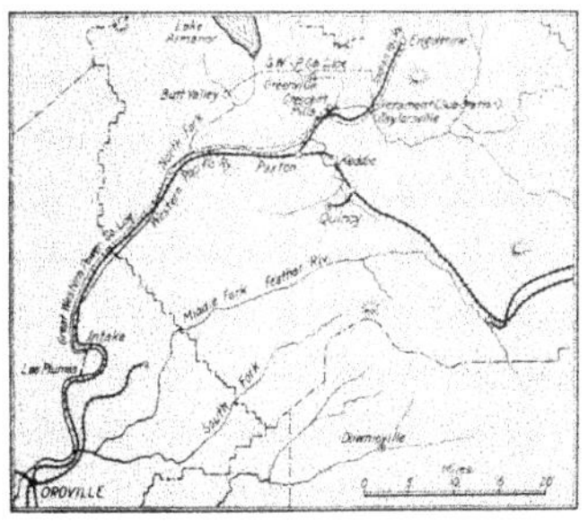

PART OF PLUMAS COUNTY, CALIFORNIA, SHOWING POSITION OF ENGELS MINE

	Engels mill	Superior mill	Total
Ore treated, tons	34,484	45,594	80,078
Copper content, per cent	2.38	1.95	2.17
Concentrate shipped, tons	1,789	2,701	4,490
Copper content, per cent	29.39	23.02	26.20
Recovery, per cent	66.90	81.19	74.35
Copper paid for, lb	1,023,141	1,352,290	2,375,431
Silver, ounces	10,966	23,515	34,481
Gold, ounces	129	147	276

The large quantity of carbonate ore treated in the Engels mill, coupled with power troubles, resulted in the lower recovery.

Grass Valley.—The ore in the Golden Center mine in the centre of this town continues to improve, but the revenue comes principally from assessments.

The North Star and Empire mines are operating at full capacity of about 400 men each, despite the fact that a constant stream of men are leaving for Divide, Nevada.——The Brunswick remains closed, but the Orleans is being developed.

Igo.—Three thousand feet of 9-in. galvanized iron pipe was laid during April in the long tunnel in the Silver Falls silver claims near Igo, and by using a blower the workings have been ventilated so that the mine may be examined. The mine was closed 25 years ago, when silver was at a low price, so now that the metal is $1 per ounce an examination is to be made to determine whether it can be operated profitably. The group includes the Pilchuck, Richmond, Chicago, Cold Springs, and Union claims. They belong to F. M. Archer of San Francisco. The main tunnel, over half a mile long, is in good condition, no caving having occurred in all these years. All that is needed is ventilation.

Nevada City.—Logs are ready for raising the dam at the Liberty hydraulic mine, 7 miles east of this place. A spillway is being cut out with a monitor and by blasting. The mine is idle pending completion of the dam and erection of derricks for handling boulders.

Oscar Ford of Riverside has secured the contract for erecting a large concrete dam at Bullard's Bar across the North Yuba river, 20 miles west of Nevada City, for impounding tailing from Brandy City mines.

Shawmut.—In the Belmont Shawmut Mining Co.'s report for the 10 months ended December 31, 1918, the following information appears, written on March 1, 1919:

In June, mining and milling of ore was commenced, but after five months of adverse conditions, all work was suspended save development on the lower levels, No. 18. The mill treated 29,336 tons of ore averaging $4.90 per ton. The concentrate—3229 tons—contained 6418 oz. The extraction was 92.18%. The ratio of concentration was 9.08:1. Construction and improvements during the period cost $94,962 and exploration $66,080. New openings totaled 2133 ft., 85% being below No. 16 level. Results were encouraging. Ore-reserves increased considerably to 424,733 tons. Wages for miners increased 26% and for mill-men and mechanics 38% over those of the previous year. These were not so serious as the decreased efficiency, namely, 65% of normal effort. The labor turnover underground was 280% in October. Mining supplies advanced 37.7%, water from 12½ to 37½ cents per inch, electric power 36%, and freight-rates 25%, also smelter charges. There is plenty of labor available now, and operations were expected to be resumed early in April. O. McCraney is superintendent and Albert Silver is in charge of the mill.

San Francisco.—The statistical division of the State Mining Bureau, under the direction of Fletcher Hamilton, State Mineralogist, has now received complete returns from operators on the output of a number of the mineral products for 1918. The data are given herein in advance of the main report, in order that those interested may receive the information at an early date. The date of publication of the final and complete bulletin on the mineral yield of the year is dependent upon the promptness of replies from operators. So far this season, most of the returns have come in earlier and in better form than in previous years; for which reason it is expected that the final bulletin will be issued earlier than usual. Some of the yields were as under:

	1918		1917	
Mineral	Tons	Value	Tons	Value
Asbestos	229	$9,903	136	$10,225
Borax	88,772	1,867,908	109,944	2,561,958
Cement, bbl.....	4,772,921	7,969,909	5,790,734	7,544,282
Magnesium salts.	1,008	29,955	1,064	34,973
Pyrite	131,029	425,012	111,325	323,704
Pumice	2,114	28,669	525	5,295

Most of the asbestos came from Nevada county. The pyrite came from two mines in Alameda, and one each in Eldorado and Shasta. The pumice was mined in Siskiyou and Imperial counties.

COLORADO

Boulder.—The Chamberlain sampler here, re-opened by the Boulder Ore Sampling Co. early in March, handled over 400 tons during the first month. The business is growing steadily.

Idaho Springs.—The Argo tunnel and mill are idle for the present.

Leadville.—The Derry Ranch Gold Dredging Co., in charge of Robert F. Lafferty, re-started its boat on April 20, after being closed for four months during the winter. This company finds it more profitable to stop work in the winter than try and operate. This is the fourth season of dredging, the previous three being highly profitable. A. C. Ludlum, president of the New York Engineering Co., is the principal owner.

Telluride.—The leading companies of this district have agreed to increase the price of board to $1.35, a 35-cent advance over the prevailing scale, to take effect May 1. The operators have been losing an average of 50 cents a day on the present basis, and the increase will, in a measure, offset the high cost of operating.

An important development is the change in the control of the Black Bear mines. These holdings of the Smuggler Union Mining Co. were formerly operated by a leasing company, but are now to be under the direct operation of the Smuggler Union. The Black Bear is across the range from the main workings of the Smuggler Union, and is believed to have a continuation of the main orebodies, although of a much lower grade and carrying more copper, it is generally similar to that of the main deposits. A tramway connects the Black Bear workings with the Smuggler Union mill. The property is well opened up by four levels, shafts, chutes, and manways. Extensive development was started early in May with the object of shipping larger tonnages this season.

IDAHO

Osburn.—While there is not much mining activity in this district at present, there are said to be silver deposits worth attention. The Silverado, Nellie, Mineral Point, and one or two other mines are working. The first-named has a mill.

MISSOURI

Joplin.—Production of the Tri-State region last week was as under:

State	Blende, tons	Calamine, tons	Lead, tons	Value
Kansas	1,476	...	384	$75,457
Missouri	997	415	116	......
Oklahoma	6,440	...	616	278,600
Total	8,913	415	1,116	$407,432
Previous week ...	7,744	252	974	370,848
Average per ton..	$37	$27	$55	......
Previous week ...	39	27	60	......

NEVADA

Ely.—Nevada Consolidated in 1918 made a profit of $3,402,070, about one-third of that of 1917. The mill concentrated 11,650 tons of ore daily, the concentrate containing 76,607,062 lb. of copper. Costs rose from 11.68 to 16.60 cents per pound.

Goldfield.—All shares offered by the Goldfield Development Co. have been subscribed, and the books are closed, according to the announcement of the secretary, H. G. McMahon. The offering of 1,500,000 shares was limited to Goldfield Consolidated and Goldfield Development holders.

A raise from the 910-ft. level of the Spearhead has cut the shale-latite contact at a height of nearly 150 ft. Ore was not found on the contact. Another raise has been advanced 30 ft. in a seam of ore of erratic value near where the 150-ft. raise was driven, and small quantities of ore of shipping grade are being saved at this point.

Jungo.—D. J. Sullivan of Lovelock has purchased the Black Diamond mine from Frank Carpenter for $10,000. The mine is in the Antelope range and has been undergoing development several years. Gold, silver, and some lead are the important metals.

Mina.—The Simon Lead Mines Co. has sunk its shaft to the 400-ft. level. A large tonnage of good ore is blocked out at 300 feet.

National.—The National Treasure Co. has resumed operations on gold-silver ore. A complete plant was erected at the property last summer by Utah people. J. A. McAllister is general manager.

Under management of Hon. W. J. Bell, the Buckskin National Co. is preparing for operations. The mine has been developed to a depth of over 400 ft. by a shaft, the orebodies have been opened for 3500 ft. by drifts and crosscuts, and 3000 ft. from the main workings the same vein-system has been opened by lessees. At the Halcyon lease, at the north end, development is to be resumed.

UTAH

Alta.—The Greater Consolidated Mines Co. has erected a motor-driven, 10 by 12-in. compressor. Three shifts, with a total of 25 men, are soon to be driving the tunnel a distance of 4 miles to cut several ore-bearing fissures. The portal is at an elevation of 7200 ft. A small tunnel is already in 100 ft., but this is to be enlarged to 8 by 9 ft. with a ditch.

Newhouse.—Operations of the Utah Leasing Co., which consisted in treating tailing from the old Cactus mill, has been completed. The venture was somewhat remarkable, as there was treated profitably 700,000 tons of material assaying slightly under 0.7% copper. The method of treatment employed was oil flotation, and the work extended over a period of 3½ years.

PERSONAL

Note. The Editor invites members of the profession to send particulars of their work and appointments. The information is interesting to our readers.

Abbot A. Hanks is in New York.

John W. Finch, of Denver, has returned to China.

Rensselaer Toll is in the Fresno district of California

Richard Roelofs was in San Francisco this week, oh a holiday.

E. C. Homersham has returned from Johannesburg to London.

Bancroft Gore has returned from South America, and is now at Boston.

Thos. H. Leggett was in San Francisco last week, on his way from New York to Oregon.

Harold Cogswell, Captain in the 316th Engineers, has returned front France to San Francisco.

C. W. Purington is at Shanghai. He will remain in China three months, returning to Vladivostok in September, and home by Christmas.

Robert E. Cranston has returned to San Francisco from Washington after serving with the U. S. Food Administration for seven months.

Ralph T. Mishler, resident manager for the Tigre Mining Co., in Sonora, Mexico, has returned to the mine after a short holiday in California.

James O. Greenan, Lieutenant in the 27th Engineers, formerly superintendent for the Olympic Mines Co. at Mina, Nevada, has returned from France.

Fred W. Denton, consulting engineer for the Copper Range properties in Michigan, now residing in Boston, has been at Houghton on a visit of inspection.

H. H. Adams, formerly with the Utah Leasing Co., at Newhouse, is spending a month in California, after which he goes to Arizona. His work in Utah is finished.

H. H. Burhans, formerly first lieutenant with the 316 Engineers, recently returned from France, and is superintendent for the Montana Yukon Mining Co., in the Yukon.

D. W. Shanks, Walter Parsons, and **E. F. Waldner** have gone to the Rio Plata mine in Chihuahua, Mexico, as manager, mine superintendent, and mill superintendent, respectively.

F. G. Lasier, Captain of Engineers, who has been stationed in Washington in the Office of the Chief of Engineers, has received his discharge and will resume his consulting work at Detroit.

A special meeting of the Montana Section of the A. I. M. E. was held at Butte on May 2. There were present **James F. Kemp** and **Charles K. Leith**. Mrs. J. F. Kemp spoke on the purposes and plans of the Woman's Auxiliary.

William H. Schact, general manager for the Copper Range Co., delivered a lecture to students at the Michigan College of Mines on the steam regenerating-system in use at the Champion copper mine. **James MacNaughton**, vice-president of the Calumet & Hecla delivered a lecture on practical improvements in underground haulage.

In co-operation with the U. S. Bureau of Mines and the Idaho Bureau of Mines and Geology, the University of Idaho at Moscow offers in the School of Mines a number of fellowships. These fellowships are open to college graduates who have had good training in mining, metallurgy, or chemistry, and who are qualified to undertake research work. The income of each fellowship is $720 per year for the twelve months beginning July.

Obituary

George Ferdinand Becker died in Washington on April 20, at the age of 72. He was born in New York City and was the son of Alexander Christian Becker, of Denmark, and Sarah Cary Tuckerman Becker, the daughter of the Rev. Joseph Tuckerman, of Boston. Dr. Becker was the last member of the group of distinguished geologists who in 1879 were associated with Clarence King at the time of the organization of the U. S. Geological Survey. He was a leader in mining geology and geophysics, and for many years had been the chief of the division of chemical and physical research in the Geological Survey. The investigations under his direction led to the establishment of the Geophysical Laboratory of the Carnegie Institution of Washington. Dr. Becker was a graduate of Harvard, he received the degree of Doctor of Philosophy at Heidelberg, and later graduated from the Royal School of Mines at Berlin. He was for four years an instructor of mining and metallurgy in the University of California, from which he came to the U. S. Geological Survey. He was one of the pioneers in governmental efforts to guide and encourage the development of the mineral resources of the West. In 1880, when the entire technical staff of the Geological Survey was utilized by the Bureau of the Census in taking the census of mineral production, the statistical work west of the Mississippi river was placed in Dr. Becker's charge. A little later his personal solicitations before a committe of Congress were largely responsible for the permanent establishment, under the auspices of the Geological Survey, of the annual statistical canvass of the mineral industry of the country now carried on by the Division of Mineral Resources. In 1880 he began the study of the geology of the famous Comstock silver lode, which, even at that time, had yielded $325,000,000 in bullion and is imperishably associated with some of the most romantic episodes in American mining. The results of this work were published in monographic form in 1882. The summers of 1883 to 1885 were spent by him in the study of the quicksilver deposits of California, and in connection with these studies a visit was made by him to the famous old Almaden mine in Spain. He was one of the pioneers in geological work in the coalfields and gold districts of southern Alaska, which he visited in 1895. His geological observations and studies were not, however, confined to the United States, for in 1896, under the auspices of an English company, he visited the Rand goldfield in South Africa, some of his observations there being later published by the Geological Survey. In 1898 he reported to the Military Governor of the Philippines as geologist and spent 14 months in the islands. Although prevented from accomplishing much in the way of active field-work because of the hostile attitude of the natives, he was able, during that period, to compile a useful review of the geology of the islands as known at that time. In connection with this Philippine service Dr. Becker prepared a special report for President Roosevelt on the desirability of scientific explorations in the Philippine Islands. He also rendered national service in the Canal Zone as a member of a special committee under the auspices of the National Academy of Sciences, for the purpose of investigating the geologic phases of the engineering problems of the Panama Canal.

Dr. Becker was a member of the National Academy of Sciences, the Washington Academy of Sciences, the American Institute of Mining Engineers, and the Metropolitan and Chevy Chase clubs. In 1914 he was elected president of the Geological Society of America. He was the author of more than a hundred scientific papers, and exercised a wide influence in the development of geological science, more particularly the interpretation of physical phenomena. G. O. S.

THE METAL MARKET

METAL PRICES

San Francisco, May 6

Aluminum-dust, cents per pound	50—60
Antimony, cents per pound	8
Copper, electrolytic, cents per pound	15½
Lead, pig, cents per pound	5¾—6¾
Platinum, per ounce	$100
Quicksilver, per flask of 75 lb.	$75
Spelter, cents per pound	8
Zinc-dust, cents per pound	12½

EASTERN METAL MARKET

(By wire from New York)

May 6.—Copper is inactive but firm. Lead is quiet and lower. Spelter is dull and weak.

SILVER

Below are given official or ticker quotations, in cents per ounce of silver 999 fine. From April 23, 1918, to May 5, 1919, the United States government paid $1 per ounce for all silver purchased by it, fixing a maximum of $1.01½ on August 15, 1918. On May 5, 1919, all restrictions on the metal were removed, resulting in fluctuations. During the restricted period, the British government fixed the maximum price five times, the last time being on March 23, 1919, on account of the low rate of sterling exchange, this resulting in daily fluctuation. The equivalent of dollar silver (1000 fine) in British currency is 46.65 pence per ounce (925 fine), calculated at the normal rate of exchange.

Date	New York cents	London pence	Average week ending	Cents	Pence
Apr. 30	101.12	48.68	Mch. 25	101.12	47.75
May 1	101.12	48.68	Apr. 1	101.12	49.63
" 2	101.12	48.68	" 8	101.12	48.86
" 3	101.12	48.81	" 15	101.12	48.85
" 4 Sunday			" 22	101.12	48.94
" 5	101.25	48.68	" 29	101.12	48.78
" 6 Holiday			May 6	101.14	48.71

Monthly averages

	1917	1918	1919		1917	1918	1919
Jan.	75.14	88.72	101.12	July	78.92	99.62	....
Feb.	77.54	85.79	101.12	Aug.	85.40	100.31	....
Mch.	74.13	88.11	101.12	Sept.	100.73	101.12	....
Apr.	72.51	95.35	101.12	Oct.	87.38	101.12	....
May	74.61	99.50	....	Nov.	85.97	101.12	....
June	76.44	99.50	....	Dec.	85.97	101.12	....

On May 5, restrictions on the export of silver and fixed price of $1.01½ per fine ounce were removed by the Federal Reserve Board, thus establishing a free market for silver in the United States and throughout the world. The secretary of the Treasury does not contemplate any further sales of silver under the Pittman Act, except to the Director of the Mint.

Silver valued at $8,424,000 was shipped from San Francisco to the Orient on the 'Venezuela' on May 3.

COPPER

Prices of electrolytic in New York, in cents per pound.

Date		Average week ending	
Apr. 30	15.25	Mch. 25	14.99
May 1	15.25	Apr. 1	15.27
" 2	15.25	" 8	15.25
" 3	15.25	" 15	15.33
" 4 Sunday		" 22	15.18
" 5	15.25	" 29	15.18
" 6	15.25	May 6	15.25

Monthly averages

	1917	1918	1919		1917	1918	1919
Jan.	29.53	23.50	20.43	July	29.67	26.00	....
Feb.	34.57	23.50	17.34	Aug.	27.42	26.00	....
Mch.	36.00	23.50	15.05	Sept.	25.11	26.00	....
Apr.	33.16	23.50	15.23	Oct.	23.50	26.00	....
May	31.60	23.50	....	Nov.	23.50	26.00	....
June	32.57	23.50	....	Dec.	23.50	26.00	....

TIN

Prices in New York, in cents per pound. The monthly averages in 1918 are nominal. On December 3 the War Industries Board fixed the price to consumers and jobbers at 72½c. f.o.b. Chicago and Eastern points, and 71¾c. on the Pacific Coast. This will continue until the U. S. Steel Products Co.'s stock is consumed.

Monthly averages

	1917	1918	1919		1917	1918	1919
Jan.	44.10	85.13	71.50	July	62.60	93.00	....
Feb.	51.47	85.00	72.44	Aug.	62.53	91.33	....
Mch.	54.27	85.00	72.50	Sept.	61.54	80.40	....
Apr.	55.63	88.53	72.50	Oct.	62.24	78.82	....
May	63.21	100.01	....	Nov.	74.18	73.67	....
June	61.93	91.00	....	Dec.	85.00	71.52	....

LEAD

Lead is quoted in cents per pound, New York delivery.

Date		Average week ending	
Apr. 30	4.95	Mch. 25	5.21
May 1	4.90	Apr. 1	5.25
" 2	4.90	" 8	5.25
" 3	4.85	" 15	5.07
" 4 Sunday		" 22	4.93
" 5	4.80	" 29	4.95
" 6	4.80	May 6	4.87

Monthly averages

	1917	1918	1919		1917	1918	1919
Jan.	7.64	6.85	5.60	July	10.93	8.03	....
Feb.	9.10	7.07	5.13	Aug.	10.75	8.05	....
Mch.	10.07	7.26	5.24	Sept.	9.07	8.05	....
Apr.	9.38	6.99	5.05	Oct.	6.97	8.35	....
May	10.29	6.88	....	Nov.	6.38	8.05	....
June	11.74	7.58	....	Dec.	6.49	6.90	....

QUICKSILVER

The primary market for quicksilver is San Francisco, California being the largest producer. The price is fixed in the open market, according to quantity. Prices, in dollars per flask of 75 pounds:

Date			
Apr. 8	67.50	Apr. 22	75.00
" 15	75.00	" 29	75.00
		May 6	75.00

Monthly averages

	1917	1918	1919		1917	1918	1919
Jan.	81.00	128.06	103.75	July	102.00	120.00	....
Feb.	126.25	118.00	90.00	Aug.	115.00	120.00	....
Mch.	113.75	112.00	72.80	Sept.	112.00	120.00	....
Apr.	114.50	115.00	73.12	Oct.	102.00	120.00	....
May	104.00	110.00	....	Nov.	102.50	120.00	....
June	85.50	112.00	....	Dec.	117.42	115.00	....

Quicksilver in New York is quoted at $77.50 per flask.

ZINC

Zinc is quoted as spelter, standard Western brands, New York delivery, in cents per pound:

Date		Average week ending	
Apr. 30	6.40	Mch. 25	6.48
May 1	6.35	Apr. 1	6.53
" 2	6.35	" 8	6.60
" 3	6.30	" 15	6.57
" 4 Sunday		" 22	6.41
" 5	6.27	" 29	6.39
" 6	6.27	May 6	6.32

Monthly averages

	1917	1918	1919		1917	1918	1919
Jan.	9.75	7.78	7.44	July	8.98	8.72	....
Feb.	10.45	7.97	6.71	Aug.	8.58	8.87	....
Mch.	10.78	7.67	6.53	Sept.	8.33	9.58	....
Apr.	10.20	7.04	6.49	Oct.	8.32	9.11	....
May	9.41	7.29	....	Nov.	7.76	8.75	....
June	9.83	7.92	....	Dec.	7.84	8.49	....

The zinc-ore market at Joplin, Missouri, is reported to be in a deplorable condition. The price of concentrate last week, basis of 60% metal, was $37 per ton, a drop of $2 in the week.

PRICES OF METAL PRODUCTS

Pig-iron, composite of 8 Eastern brands, per ton	$28.0350
Scrap machine castings, per ton	22.00—23.00
Scrap car-wheels, per ton	22.00—23.00
Scrap heavy melting steel, per ton	12.00—13.00
Steel plates, per lb.	0.0265
Steel pipe, ¾ to 3 in. black, per lb.	0.0415
Steel wire nails, per lb.	0.0325
Finished steel, composite of 7 products, per lb.	0.0325
Copper sheet, hot rolled, per lb.	0.2250
Copper rods, round, per lb.	0.1925
Brass rods, high and low, per lb.	0.1775—0.2125
Bronze rods, per lb.	0.2275
Lead sheets, mill, per lb.	0.0775
Zinc plates, per lb.	0.0900
Zinc sheets, per lb.	0.1000

Eastern Metal Market

New York, April 30.

All the markets are stagnant and generally inactive, but prices hold fairly well. The steel-price tangle is generally blamed for the poor demand for non-ferrous metals.

Antimony is quiet and firm.

Copper demand continues light, but quotations are steady

Lead is flat, with a tendency to softness

Tin continues under Government control, and there is almost no trading.

Zinc demand is absent, but prices have remained fairly firm.

ANTIMONY

There is little change, but it is for the better if anything. Prices are a shade firmer at 6.62¼ to 6.87½c., New York, duty paid, for Asiatic grades for wholesale lots for early shipment.

ALUMINUM

Prices as quoted are slightly higher at 31 to 33c. for No. 1 virgin metal, 98 to 99% for early delivery. Re-melt metal of the same purity is about 2c. per lb. lower. The market is quiet.

COPPER

Lack of demand continues to characterize the copper market. The past week witnessed no improvement over conditions reported in this letter a week ago, and consumers manifest no desire to enter the market except for immediate needs. The steel-price situation is blamed for the lack of interest in this market as well as in most of the other non-ferrous metals, but it is probable that consumers' needs have been largely provided for well into May, and there is no need for anxiety. Quotations are largely nominal at 15.25c., New York, for electrolytic copper for early delivery, with Lake at 15.50c., New York. Some Lake changed hands at this price during the last week. Production is still fairly heavy, it is believed, at least in excess of present consumption. Fundamental conditions are considered sound. Casting copper is ½c. below electrolytic.

LEAD

The market is flat and stale, with almost no transactions reported. Quotations are unchanged at 4.95c., New York, in the outside market and 4.70c, St. Louis. The American Smelting & Refining Co. still maintains its New York quotation at 5c., with St. Louis at 4.70c. The tendency is soft if anything, and it is believed that a slight cut in these prices is possible, though it has not transpired so far. Some sellers are impatient, but the concensus of opinion is that there is nothing to be gained by forcing the issue. It is generally admitted that production is still in excess of demand

IRON AND STEEL

Producers see little indication of good business in the next two months, and some expect little improvement before the fall, although business in several finished steel lines has picked up some in the past week. In the trade at large, disappointment rules because the country has not been notified decisively how the price matter stands or because some decision has not been reached. As to railroad buying, the Administration announces that it is not delaying purchases to force down prices, but is using up surplus material piled up during the War. This confirms steel producers in the belief that in any event such buying would not be large. Operations in the Chicago district average 60% of capacity, in the Youngstown district 45 to 50%, and in eastern Pennsylvania 40%.

TIN

The tin market is enjoying (?) the distinction of being the only Government controlled market, and it is laboring under a decided disadvantage. There is no certainty as to when import restrictions will be lifted, and now the rumor is revived that they will not be removed even after the U. S. Steel Products Co. itas distributed all its allocated metal. It is stated that restrictions will continue until the Government metal has been largely consumed. This state of affairs make for dissatisfaction and discontent, and the future position is demoralizing. It is stated that some consumers have large stocks of tin which they cannot sell because of the restrictions and cannot sell as tin-plate because of lack of demand; they are still compelled to take allocated metal. Opinion still prevails that June 1 or soon after will see an end of import restrictions. An interesting fact is that during the past week a sale has been made of Straits tin from abroad at 48.25c. per lb. for shipment when restrictions are removed. There have been no arrivals of tin reported at Atlantic or Pacific ports so far this month. Straits tin in London was quoted at £227 per ton yesterday.

ZINC

The situation shows no improvement, and consumers are still absenting themselves from the market, except for such small quantities as they need at once. The steel-price muddle is the restraining influence, particularly in this market, as galvanizers are nominally heavy buyers of spelter. Prices have held well in the last week, generally at 6.05c., St. Louis, but today quotations are made at 6.02½c., St. Louis, or 6.37½c., New York, for prime Western for early delivery, at which price at least one sale was made. Some think that 6c. St. Louis could be done. Production is still in excess of demand, it is said, and no marked improvement is looked for until steel prices are settled and buying sets in. There has been some speculative buying around 6 to 6.10c., St. Louis.

ORES

Ferro-chromium: This product, containing 60 to 70% chromium, is quoted at 34c. per lb. for 4 to 6% carbon and at 32c. per lb. for 6 to 8% carbon material in carload lots, with 2c. per lb. added for less than carloads.

Manganese: Imports in March are officially reported as 48,238 long tons, bringing the total for the first quarter to 115,321 tons, a large amount under present conditions in the ferro market. These imports contrast with 118,536 tons for the first quarter in 1918. Indian ore is offered at 55c. seaboard, but no sales of any ore are reported.

Manganese-Iron Alloys: Re-sale carload lots of ferro have gone at $110, delivered, in the last week, but domestic producers still quote $150, delivered, for 78 to 82% alloy, with $2 per unit deducted under 78%. Imports in March were 5741 tons, making the total for the first quarter 9211 tons, against 6022 tons for the first quarter of 1918. Spiegel is nominal at $37.50, delivered, with almost no business or inquiry.

Molybdenum: The market is dead, and prices are nominal with no interest manifested.

Tungsten: Some Chinese ore is reported to have changed hands at $7 per unit for spot delivery. High-grade scheelite and wolframite is quoted at $10 per unit. The future of the market is regarded as somewhat dependent on the settlement of steel prices. There are quotations of $1.50 per lb. of contained tungsten in ferro-tungsten, but it is likely that this could be substantially shaded.

Company Reports

UNITED STATES SMELTING, REFINING & MINING CO.

Property: mines and works in Arizona, California, Chicago, Colorado, Kansas, Mexico, New Jersey, Oklahoma, and Utah.

Operating Officials: Frederick Lyon, vice-president in charge of operation; S. J. Jennings, vice-president in charge of exploration and mining investment; G. W. Heintz, vice-president and general manager of western operations; D. S. Calland, vice-president and general manager of operations in Mexico; F. Y. Robertson, vice-president and manager of metal sales.

General Officials—A. P. Anderson, consulting mining engineer; C. F. Moore, consulting engineer; G. W. Cushing, traffic manager.

U. S. S. R. & M. Co.—C. E. Allen, manager of mines, Utah; G. W. Metcalfe, manager Mammoth plant; R. E. Hanley, general superintendent Mammoth mines; J. H. Kervin, superintendent Mammoth smelter, California; L. D. Anderson, manager Midvale smelter, Utah; O. J. Egleston, chief engineer; Ambrose Nord, cashier, Salt Lake City; D. R. Muir, manager Gold Road and Needles properties, Arizona; D. D. Muir, Jr., manager zinc mines and smelters; J. F. Barnard, superintendent, Bingham mines; and A. P. Mayherry, superintendent, Centennial Eureka mine, Utah.

Richmond-Eureka Mining and Niagara Mining Companies—G. W. Heintz, general manager; and C. E. Allan, manager.

Compania de Real del Monte y Pachuca—Salvador M. Cancino, president; and D. S. Calland, director.

U. S. Metals Refining Co.—F. Y. Robertson, vice-president and general manager; R. W. Deacon, superintendent copper refinery, Chrome, New Jersey; William Thum, superintendent lead refinery, East Chicago, Indiana.

United States Fuel Co.—R. M. McGraw, general superintendent.

Utah Railway Co.—G. S. Anderson, vice-president and general manager.

The Sunnyside Mining & Milling Co.—M. H. Kuryla, manager.

United States Stores Co.—J. H. Horlick, manager.

Financial Statement: the net earnings of all companies in 1918, after charging cost of production, selling expenses, repairs, interest, depreciation, and depletion, was $4,775,690. Adding the previous balance of $13,004,970, there was available $17,780,060. After paying dividends there remained a surplus of $14,322,260. Current assets, including cash, bonds, metals, and products, total $18,476,191, and liabilities $7,595,341, including $864,450 for the dividend on January 15, 1919.

Dividends: preferred stock received $1,702,225, equal to 7%; and common stock $1,755,575. At March 31, 1919, there were 9499 preferred and 26,344 common stockholders.

Production: metals from all sources were as follows: copper, 20,359,378 lb.; gold, 137,315 oz.; lead, 96,567,485 lb.; silver, 15,337,465 oz.; and zinc, 18,771,684 pounds.

The tonnage of ores produced from Centennial-Eureka, Mammoth, Naylor, Ritz, Sunnyside, and Bingham mines, also in Mexico, was 1,220,722, of which the value of the metal contents was in the proportion of 10% copper, 10% lead, 7% zinc, 61% silver, and 12% gold.

The coal output was 1,272,081 tons, a gain of 363,443 tons.

Mines in Arizona

The Gold Road mine near Oatman was shut-down on account of abnormal condition.

Mines in California

Ore-reserves were maintained at the Mammoth. The Friday Lowden orebody is developing into one of considerable importance. The Mammoth and Section 29 sent 77,695 tons of ore to the smelter at Kennett.——Exploration in the Stowell was not encouraging, so work was suspended.——The Keystone mine was purchased in November, owing to favorable drilling results. A 1004-ft. tunnel was driven and raising to the ore is progressing.——The smelter reduced 413,082 tons of charge from all sources, 236,142 tons of which was sulphides. At the electrolytic-zinc plant a new process is being tried.

Mines in Colorado

The Sunnyside property, at an elevation of 12,000 ft. in San Miguel county, is now prepared to produce 500 tons of ore daily for the new mill. [A disastrous fire at the mine on April 21, 1919, has delayed operations indefinitely.]

Mines in Kansas

At the Naylor zinc tract, developments were good, but prices for concentrate sold in the open market were low.

Mines in Mexico

At Real del Monte y Pachuca, the two mills will soon be ablé to treat 80,000 tons of silver ore monthly. A third one of 15,000 tons capacity for ore from the 'new' vein is under consideration. This orebody contains a large tonnage of high-grade and good milling ore.

Mines in Oklahoma

The Ritz zinc mine continued to open favorably, yielding good ore.

Mines in Utah

The Bingham mines shipped 41,661 tons of copper and 127,560 tons of lead ore. Reserves were materially enlarged.——The Centennial-Eureka yielded 29,558 tons of ore. While no large deposits were found, a moderate amount of new ore was opened.——The Richmond-Eureka remained closed.——The lime quarry supplied 90,526 tons for the Midvale smelter in Utah. Another blast-furnace was added to this plant, making seven.

Refineries

The lead refinery at Grasselli, Indiana, and the copper refinery at Chrome, New Jersey, operated to the full limit of their enlarged capacities under great handicaps.

Mining Decisions

Grant of Coal—Injury to Surface

Where a grant of coal underlying the surface provides that the grantee may enter upon the lands and mine and remove coal without any liability for damages from the exercise of such rights, he is not liable for injury to the surface by mining operations.

Weakland v. Cymbria Coal Co. (Pennsylvania), 105 Atlantic, 558.

Mining Agreement—Construction

A mining agreement contained an option to purchase, but also provided that the consummation of the purchase should not affect a certain lease in force between the parties. Held, that the lessee by exercising his option to purchase and depositing the full amount of the purchase price to the lessor's credit could not relieve himself of the obligation to pay the balance of the rent due up to the expiration of the term of the lease, but that the lessor's remedy lay in damages, and he could not evict the lessee by unlawful detainer proceedings for failure to pay the rentals, as the lessee was entitled to possession when he became a purchaser.

Rayburn v. Stewart-Calvert Co. (Washington), 178 Pacific, 454 and 455. February 14, 1919.

Prices of Chemicals for Five Years

The Year-Book of the 'Oil, Paint and Drug Reporter' of New York for 1918, a valuable reference of 321 pages, contains the following comparative figures, prices in cents per pound:

	1914 August	1915 January	1916 January	1917 January	1918 January	1918 December	1919 April 14
INDUSTRIAL CHEMICALS							
Alum, ground	1¾—2	2⅜—2¾	4¼—4⅝	4⅛—4½	4¾—5½	5½—6½	4½—5
Ammonia, aqua, anhydrous	25	25	25	25	30—32	33—46	30—35
Ammoniac, sal, gray	5¾—6¼	6¼—6½	6½—7	12—15	13—15	20—22	12¾—13¼
Antimony, needle	3¾—4	6½—7½	35	20	13—14	11—14	10½—13
Arsenic, white	2⅞—3	4—4½	3⅞—4½	8—8¼	15½—17½	9—12	9½—11
Barium chloride	1½—1⅝	2½—3	5½	4⅞—5⅛	3¼—4½	3½—5	3⅝—4
Bleaching powder, 35%	......	1⅜—1⅝	12—14	1⅜—6½	1½—3	2—3½	1½—2⅝
Cream tartar, powder	24	30—31	37—39	10	50—61	64½	52—58
Lead acetate, white	8⅝—9	8⅜—9	11¾—12¼	12¼	16½	16½—17	14—14½
Lead nitrate	7⅞—8	8	13¾—14	15½—16	Nominal	85—86	85—86
Litharge, powdered	5½—5¾	5—5¼	6½	9¾	9½—11¾	10⅝—11¼	11
Phosphorus, yellow	35—1.00	25—90	75—90	80	Nominal	50—1.10	45—55
Potassium carbonate, 80–85%	3—3⅛	5—6	45—50	38—40	55—60	28	15—17
Potassium caustic, 88–92%	4⅜—4⅝	8—9	45—50	90—95	83—84	67—70	50
Potassium cyanide	19—22	Nominal	Nominal	2.25—2.30	60—70	67—70	......
Potassium permanganate	9¾—10	14—15	1.75	2.75—3.00	Nominal	1.35—1.60	60—70
Pyrite, domestic concentrate, at mill per unit of sulphur	7—9½	7—9½	11—12	11—12	25—30	27—28	Nominal
Salt cake, unground, ton	8.00—9.00	8.00—9.00	8.00—9.00	......	25.00—26.00	23.00—28.00	16.00—18.00
Saltpeter, granulated	4¾—5	5½—6	32—33	......	28—28½	27—27½	20—20½
Soda ash, dense, 58%, cwt	67½—72½	67½—72½	1.85—2.10	4.00—4.50	3.50—4.00	2.00—4.00	2.00—2.70
Soda, bicarbonate	1—1⅛	1—1⅛	1¼—1⅝	1⅝—1⅞	2¼—2⅞	3⅛—4	2⅝—4
Soda, caustic, 76%, solid, drums, cwt	1⅝—1¾	1½—1⅝	3½—3¾	4⅝—4⅞	6½—7	3.70—4.00	2.60—3.00
Soda, cyanide	......	......	......	1.90—2.00	37—45	30—40	30—35
Soda, sulphide, 60%, fused	2¼—2½	2¼—2½	5⅝	3—3¼	4—4½	7—7⅝	4—5½
Sulphur, refined, cwt	1.85—2.00	1.85—2.00	1.85—2.60	1.95—2.70	3.70—4.60	3.20—4.25	2.50
Zinc-dust	5¾—6	9—10	35—38	20—33	16—17	13—15	10—12
OTHER CHEMICALS							
Acetone	10½—11½	17—20	35—40	21½—23	35—36	21—21½	15¼—16
Ammonia, carbonate	8—8¼	8¼—9	8½—9½	9½—10½	10⅝—11	13—13½	13—13½
Bismuth, sub-carbonate	2.10—2.15	2.80—2.85	3.10	3.40—3.45	3.25—3.30	3.50—3.55	3.50—3.55
Borax, powdered	4—4¼	4—4¼	6¼—6½	7¼—7½	7¾—8¾	7¾—8¾	7¾—8¾
Bromide, potassium	39—40	70—81	5.50—5.51	1.35—1.36	1.45—1.46	65—66	55—56
Bromine, bulk	30—35	40—45	5.00—6.50	1.40	75	50	55
Calcium phosphate	......	......	......	......	34—35	22—23	22—23
Carbon bisulphide, bulk	6½—8	7—8	9—15	5½—6½	7½—8	7½—9	7½—9
Hydrogen, peroxide, per gross, bottles	4.00—9.00	6.00—16.00	8.00—24.00	6.50—18.00	7.50—20.00	7.25—9.25	7.25—9.25
Magnesia, carbonate	5½—6	4¾—5¼	14—15	20—23	18—22	25—30	25—30
Mercury, chloride	51—61	81—86	1.53	1.29	1.71	1.79	1.36
Nitrate of silver, oz	33¾—35¾	31¼—33¼	34⅝—36⅝	46⅝—48⅝	53—55	65¼—66½	63¼—65¼
Phenolphthalein	......	......	......	......	9.50—10.50	5.00—5.50	4.50—5.00
ACIDS							
Acetic, glacial, 99%	7¾—8¼	7¾—8¼	30—35	30—40	33—38	19.50 cwt.*	13.50—14.50
Carbolic, crystals, drums	10—10½	50—52	1.35—1.40	55—55½	53—55	15—30	7¼—10
Citric, crystals	53—53½	55—55½	50—50½	65—65½	75	1.25—1.25½	1.25—1.25½
Hydrofluoric, 30%	3—3½	3—3½	3—3½	5—5½	6—6¼	8—8¼	8—8¼
Muriatic, 20°	1⅜—1⅝	1⅜—1⅝	2—2¼	1⅝—2	2	2.05—2.30†	1.60—1.90
Nitric, 40°	4½—4⅞	4½—4⅞	7—7½	6—6¼	7½—8	7.75 cwt.*	7.70—8.00
Oleum, 20%, bulk	1¼—1½	1¼—1½	2¼—3	2—2¼	2¾—3	28.00 ton*	20.00—25.00
Oxalic	7¼—7½	13—14	50—51	47—50	45—46	36—38	29—31
Sulphuric, 60°, bulk	¾—1	¾—1	1½—1¾	11—12	1½—2	16.00 ton*	10.00—16.00
COAL-TAR BASES							
Acid, cresylic, 95–97%, gal	......	......	......	......	1.10—1.15	1.20	90—1.00
Creosote oil, gal	......	......	......	......	35—40	45—55	40—45
Cresol, lb	......	......	......	......	18—20	18—20	17—19
Phenol, lb	......	......	......	......	54—57	15—30	7¼—10
ESSENTIAL AND OTHER OILS							
Castor, cases, lb	9—9½	9—9¼	15½—16	18¼—19	27½	31—32	25—26
Cod, Newfoundland, gal	36½—37½	36—38	63—65	80—82	1.00—1.02	1.51—1.55	1.15—1.20
Eucalyptus, Australian, lb	45—50	45—50	47½—50	70—75	60—65	55—60	60—62½
Eucalyptus in London	30	......	31	48	92	1.38	......
Pine-oil, gal	34—38	34—36	55	Nominal	57—58	60—63	56—60
Tar-oil, gal	18—20	18—20	20—22	21½	27	35—36	35—36
Tar, retort, 200 lb	6.50	6.00	6.00—6.50	9.25—9.50	14.00	14.00—14.50	13.50
Turpentine, wood, destructive distilled, gal	36—38	38	42	46½	40	58—60	61—64

*Fixed by Government. †Per cwt.

Book Review

Applied Mechanics. By Charles E. Fuller and William A. ohnsto n. Volume II—Strength of Materials. Pp. 538, ill, udex. John Wiley & Sons, Inc., New York. For sale by Mining and Scientific Press'. Price, $3.75.

This is a text-book prepared by two members of the faclty of the Massachusetts Institute of Technology. It is a ood text-book, and makes no claim to be anything else. he mathematical discussion of the various principles involved is complete, and it is illustrated at the end of nearly every chapter by a number of problems. The student may, however, be disappointed to find that few of them are worked out for him, neither are there any 'answers' in the back of the book. The scope may be judged from the chapter headings, which are Physical Properties of Materials, Analysis of Stress and Strain, Uniform Stress and Uniformly Varying Stress, Stresses in Beams, Deflection of Beams, Continuous Beams, Combined Stresses, General Theory of Flexure, Columns, Shafting and Springs, Curved Bars, and Reinforced Concrete Beams and Columns.

Company Reports

UNITED STATES SMELTING, REFINING & MINING CO.

Property: mines and works in Arizona, California, Chicago, Colorado, Kansas, Mexico, New Jersey, Oklahoma, and Utah.

Operating Officials: Frederick Lyon, vice-president in charge of operation; S. J. Jennings, vice-president in charge of exploration and mining investment; G. W. Heintz, vice-president and general manager of western operations; D. S. Calland, vice-president and general manager of operations in Mexico; F. Y. Robertson, vice-president and manager of metal sales.

General Officials—A. P. Anderson, consulting mining engineer; C. F. Moore, consulting engineer; G. W. Cushing, traffic manager.

U. S. S. R. & M. Co.—C. E. Allen, manager of mines, Utah; G. W. Metcalfe, manager Mammoth plant; R. E. Hanley, general superintendent Mammoth mines; J. H. Kervin, superintendent Mammoth smelter, California; L. D. Anderson, manager Midvale smelter, Utah; O. J. Egleston, chief engineer; Ambrose Nord, cashier, Salt Lake City; D. R. Muir, manager Gold Road and Needles properties, Arizona; D. D. Muir, Jr., manager zinc mines and smelters; J. F. Barnard, superintendent, Bingham mines; and A. P. Mayberry, superintendent, Centennial Eureka mine, Utah.

Richmond-Eureka Mining and Niagara Mining Companies—G. W. Heintz, general manager; and C. E. Allan, manager.

Compania de Real del Monte y Pachuca—Salvador M. Cancino, president; and D. S. Calland, director.

U. S. Metals Refining Co.—F. Y. Robertson, vice-president and general manager; R. W. Deacon, superintendent copper refinery, Chrome, New Jersey; William Thum, superintendent lead refinery, East Chicago, Indiana.

United States Fuel Co.—R. M. McGraw, general superintendent.

Utah Railway Co.—G. S. Anderson, vice-president and general manager.

The Sunnyside Mining & Milling Co.—M. H. Kuryla, manager.

United States Stores Co.—J. H. Horlick, manager.

Financial Statement: the net earnings of all companies in 1918, after charging cost of production, selling expenses, repairs, interest, depreciation, and depletion, was $4,775,090. Adding the previous balance of $13,004,970, there was available $17,780,060. After paying dividends there remained a surplus of $14,322,260. Current assets, including cash, bonds, metals, and products, total $18,476,191, and liabilities $7,995,341, including $864,450 for the dividend on January 15, 1919.

Dividends: preferred stock received $1,702,225, equal to 7%; and common stock $1,755,575. At March 31, 1919, there were 9499 preferred and 26,344 common stockholders.

Production: metals from all sources were as follows: copper, 20,359,378 lb.; gold, 137,315 oz.; lead, 96,567,485 lb.; silver, 15,337,465 oz.; and zinc, 18,771,684 pounds.

The tonnage of ores produced from Centennial-Eureka, Mammoth, Naylor, Ritz, Sunnyside, and Bingham mines, also in Mexico, was 1,220,722, of which the value of the metal contents was in the proportion of 10% copper, 10% lead, 7% zinc, 61% silver, and 12% gold.

The coal output was 1,272,081 tons, a gain of 363,443 tons.

Mines in Arizona

The Gold Road mine near Oatman was shut-down on account of abnormal conditions.

Mines in California

Ore-reserves were maintained at the Mammoth. The Friday Lowden orebody is developing into one of considerable importance. The Mammoth and Section 29 sent 77,695 tons of ore to the smelter at Kennett.——Exploration in the Stowell was not encouraging, so work was suspended.——The Keystone mine was purchased in November, owing to favorable drilling results. A 1004-ft. tunnel was driven and raising to the ore is progressing.——The smelter reduced 413,082 tons of charge from all sources, 236,142 tons of which was sulphides. At the electrolytic-zinc plant a new process is being tried.

Mines in Colorado

The Sunnyside property, at an elevation of 12,000 ft. in San Miguel county, is now prepared to produce 500 tons of ore daily for the new mill. [A disastrous fire at the mine on April 21, 1919, has delayed operations indefinitely.]

Mines in Kansas

At the Naylor zinc tract, developments were good, but prices for concentrate sold in the open market were low.

Mines in Mexico

At Real del Monte y Pachuca, the two mills will soon be ablé to treat 80,000 tons of silver ore monthly. A third one of 15,000 tons capacity for ore from the 'new' vein is under consideration. This orebody contains a large tonnage of high-grade and good milling ore.

Mines in Oklahoma

The Ritz zinc mine continued to open favorably, yielding good ore.

Mines in Utah

The Bingham mines shipped 41,661 tons of copper and 127,560 tons of lead ore. Reserves were materially enlarged.——The Centennial-Eureka yielded 29,558 tons of ore. While no large deposits were found, a moderate amount of new ore was opened.——The Richmond-Eureka remained closed.——The lime quarry supplied 90,526 tons for the Midvale smelter in Utah. Another blast-furnace was added to this plant, making seven.

Refineries

The lead refinery at Grasselli, Indiana, and the copper refinery at Chrome, New Jersey, operated to the full limit of their enlarged capacities under great handicaps.

Mining Decisions

Grant of Coal—Injury to Surface

Where a grant of coal underlying the surface provides that the grantee may enter upon the lands and mine and remove coal without any liability for damages from the exercise of such rights, he is not liable for injury to the surface by mining operations.

Weakland v. Cymbria Coal Co. (Pennsylvania), 105 Atlantic, 558.

Mining Agreement—Construction

A mining agreement contained an option to purchase, but also provided that the consummation of the purchase should not affect a certain lease in force between the parties. Held, that the lessee by exercising his option to purchase and depositing the full amount of the purchase price to the lessor's credit could not relieve himself of the obligation to pay the balance of the rent due up to the expiration of the term of the lease, but that the lessor's remedy lay in damages, and he could not evict the lessee by unlawful detainer proceedings for failure to pay the rentals, as the lessee was entitled to possession when he became a purchaser.

Rayburn v. Stewart-Calvert Co. (Washington), 178 Pacific, 454 and 455. February 14, 1919.

Prices of Chemicals for Five Years

The Year-Book of the 'Oil, Paint and Drug Reporter' of New York for 1918, a valuable reference of 321 pages, contains the following comparative figures, prices in cents per pound:

	1914 August	1915 January	1916 January	1917 January	1918 January	1918 December	1919 April 14
INDUSTRIAL CHEMICALS							
Alum, ground	1¾—2	2⅜—2¾	4½—4⅝	4½—4⅝	4¼—5¼	5¼—6¼	4½—5
Ammonia, aqua, anhydrous	25	25	25	25	30—32	33—46	30—35
Ammoniac, sal, gray	5¾—6¼	6¼—6½	6½—7	12—15	13—15	20—22	12¾—13¼
Antimony, needle	3¾—4	6½—7½	35	20	13—14	11—14	10½—13
Arsenic, white	2¾—3	4—4½	3¾—4½	8—8¼	15½—17½	9—12	9½—11
Barium chloride	1½—1⅝	2½—3	5½	1½—5¼	3¼—4½	3½—5	3¾—4
Bleaching powder, 35%	......	1⅜—1⅝	12—14	4⅜—6½	1½—3	2—3½	1½—2⅜
Cream tartar, powder	21	30—31	47—50	40	50—61	64½	52—58
Lead acetate, white	8⅝—9	8⅝—9	11½—12½	12½	16½	16½—17	14—14½
Lead nitrate	7¾—8	8	13¼—14	15½—16	Nominal	85—86	85—86
Litharge, powdered	5½—5¾	5—5¼	6½	9¾	9½—11¾	10¾—11½	11
Phosphorus, yellow	35—1.00	25—90	75—90	80	Nominal	50—1.10	45—55
Potassium carbonate, 80–85%	3—3¼	5—6	45—50	38—40	55—60	28	15—17
Potassium caustic, 88–92%	4⅜—4⅝	8—9	45—50	90—95	83—84	67—70	50
Potassium cyanide	19—22	Nominal	Nominal	2.25—2.30	60—70	67—70	......
Potassium permanganate	9¾—10	14—15	1.75	2.75—3.00	Nominal	1.35—1.60	60—70
Pyrite, domestic concentrate, at mill per unit of sulphur	7—9½	7—9½	11—12	11—12	25—30	27—28	Nominal
Salt cake, unground, ton	8.00—9.00	8.00—9.00	8.00—9.00	......	25.00—26.00	23.00—28.00	10.00—18.00
Saltpeter, granulated	4¾—5	5½—6	32—33	......	28—28½	27—27½	20—20½
Soda ash, dense, 58%, cwt	67½—72½	67½—72½	1.85—2.10	4.00—4.50	3.50—4.00	2.90—4.00	2.60—2.70
Soda, bicarbonate	1—1⅛	1—1⅛	1¼—1⅜	1⅝—1⅞	2¼—2⅞	3¼—4	2⅝—4
Soda, caustic, 76%, solid, drums, cwt	1⅜—1½	1½—1⅝	5½—5¾	4⅝—4¾	6½—7	3.70—4.00	2.00—3.00
Soda, cyanide	....	....	....	1.90—2.00	37—45	30—40	30—35
Soda, sulphide, 60%, fused	2¼—2½	2¼—2½	5¾	3—3¼	4—4½	7—7¾	4—5½
Sulphur, refined, cwt	1.85—2.00	1.85—2.00	1.85—2.00	1.95—2.70	3.70—4.60	3.20—4.25	2.50
Zinc-dust	5¾—6	9—10	35—38	20—33	16—17	13—15	10—12
OTHER CHEMICALS							
Acetone	10½—11½	17—20	35—40	21½—23	35—36	21—21½	15½—16
Ammonia, carbonate	8—8¼	8¼—9	8½—9½	9½—10½	10¾—11	13—13½	13—13½
Bismuth, sub-carbonate	2.10—2.15	2.80—2.85	3.10	3.40—3.45	3.25—3.30	3.50—3.55	3.50—3.55
Borax, powdered	4—4¼	4—4¼	6¼—6½	7¼—7½	7¾—8¾	7¾—8¾	7¾—8¾
Bromide, potassium	39—40	70—81	5.50—5.51	1.35—1.36	1.45—1.46	65—66	55—56
Bromine, bulk	30—35	40—45	5.00—6.50	1.40	75	50	55
Calcium phosphate	....	....	....	....	34—35	22—23	22—23
Carbon bisulphide, bulk	6½—8	7—8	6—15	5½—6½	7½—8	7½—9	7½—9
Hydrogen, peroxide, per gross, bottles	4.00—9.00	6.00—16.00	8.00—24.00	6.50—18.00	7.50—20.00	7.25—9.25	7.25—9.25
Magnesia, carbonate	5½—6	4¼—5¼	14—15	20—23	18—22	25—30	25—30
Mercury, chloride	51—61	81—86	1.53	1.29	1.71	1.79	1.36
Nitrate of silver, oz	33¾—35¾	31⅛—33⅛	34⅝—36⅝	40⅝—48⅝	53—55	65⅛—66⅛	63⅛—65⅛
Phenolphthalein	....	....	....	....	9.50—10.50	5.00—5.50	4.50—5.00
ACIDS							
Acetic, glacial, 99%	7¾—8¼	7¾—8¼	30—35	30—40	33—38	19.50 cwt.*	13.50—14.50
Carbolic, crystals, drums	10—10½	50—52	1.35—1.40	55—55½	53—55	15—30	7¼—10
Citric, crystals	53—53½	55—55½	59—59½	65—65½	75	1.25—1.25½	1.25—1.25½
Hydrofluoric, 30%	3—3½	3—3½	3—3½	5—5½	6—6¼	8—8¼	8—8¼
Muriatic, 20°	1⅜—1⅝	1⅜—1⅝	2—2¼	1¾—2	2	2.05—2.30†	1.60—1.90
Nitric, 40°	4½—4¾	4½—4¾	7—7½	6—6¼	7½—8	7.75 cwt.*	7.70—8.00
Oleum, 20%, bulk	1¼—1½	1¼—1½	2¼—3	2—2¼	2¾—3	28.00 ton*	20.00—25.00
Oxalic	7¼—7½	13—14	50—51	47—50	45—46	36—38	29—31
Sulphuric, 60°, bulk	¾—1	¾—1	1½—1¾	11—12	1½—2	16.00 ton*	10.00—16.00
COAL-TAR BASES							
Acid, cresylic, 95–97%, gal	....	....	....	....	1.10—1.15	1.20	90—1.00
Creosote oil, gal	....	....	....	....	35—40	45—55	40—45
Cresol, lb	....	....	....	....	18—20	18—20	17—19
Phenol, lb	....	....	....	....	54—55	15—30	7¼—10
ESSENTIAL AND OTHER OILS							
Castor, cases, lb	9—9¼	9—9¼	15½—16	18½—19	27½	31—32	25—26
Cod, Newfoundland, gal	36½—37½	36—38	63—65	80—82	1.00—1.02	1.51—1.55	1.15—1.20
Eucalyptus, Australian, lb	45—50	45—50	47½—50	70—75	60—65	55—60	60—62½
Eucalyptus in London	30	......	31	48	92	1.38	......
Pine-oil, gal	34—38	34—36	55	Nominal	57—58	60—63	56—60
Tar-oil, gal	18—20	18—20	20—22	21½	27	35—36	35—36
Tar, retort, 200 lb	6.50	6.00	6.00—6.50	9.25—9.50	14.00	14.00—14.50	13.50
Turpentine, wood, destructive distilled, gal	36—38	36	42	46½	40	58—60	61—64

*Fixed by Government. †Per cwt.

Book Review

Applied Mechanics. By Charles E. Fuller and William A. Johnston. Volume II—Strength of Materials. Pp. 538, ill., index. John Wiley & Sons, Inc., New York. For sale by 'Mining and Scientific Press'. Price, $3.75.

This is a text-book prepared by two members of the faculty of the Massachusetts Institute of Technology. It is a good text-book, and makes no claim to be anything else. The mathematical discussion of the various principles involved is complete, and it is illustrated at the end of nearly every chapter by a number of problems. The student may, however, be disappointed to find that few of them are worked out for him, neither are there any 'answers' in the back of the book. The scope may be judged from the chapter headings, which are Physical Properties of Materials, Analysis of Stress and Strain, Uniform Stress and Uniformly Varying Stress, Stresses in Beams, Deflection of Beams, Continuous Beams, Combined Stresses, General Theory of Flexure, Columns, Shafting and Springs, Curved Bars, and Reinforced Concrete Beams and Columns.

INFORMATION FURNISHED BY MANUFACTURERS

DETAILS OF A MODERN DREDGE

The dredge shown in the accompanying illustration was built and designed by the Union Iron Works, San Francisco, for the Marysville Dredging Co. in 1914. It has 16-cu. ft. buckets arranged to dig 70 ft. below water-level, also a 20-ft. bank above water.

The general dimensions of the hull are as follows: length, 155½ ft.; width, 55 ft.; and depth, 11½ feet.

The digging-ladder is of the solid-girder type, 133 ft. long and weighs 126 tons, without rollers, buckets, or tumbler.

THE MARYSVILLE DREDGING CO.'S BOAT ON THE YUBA

The stacker-ladder is 146 ft. long, and is of the lattice type. The upper deck of the stacker-ladder is made in the form of an inverted V, so that material spilling off the belt does not collect thereon, but drops into the pond.

The revolving-screen is 9 ft. diameter and 50 ft. long, with perforated holes varying from ¼ to 7/16 in. The weight of the screen is 70 tons, and is driven at the lower end by one roller, there being two guide-rollers to keep this central over the drive-roller; in other words, one roller carries a weight of approximately 35 tons plus the weight of the material being washed, which would easily amount to another 25 tons.

The buckets are of manganese steel throughout and weigh complete with lip 3880 lb. Theoretically, they hold 16½ cu. ft. The pins are 7½ in. diameter, and are of special alloy steel, properly heat treated. Each pin is tested for hardness with the Shore scleroscope.

The upper tumbler is six-sided, cast integral with the shaft, and of nickel-steel. Bearings are 18 in. diameter by 30 in. long. This casting weighs 22 tons before machining. The tread-plates are of special forged steel, as manganese flows too readily under this load. The upper tumbler is driven by two spur-gears, each 14 ft. diameter and 15-in. face, one on each side of the shaft. The intermediate gearing has herringbone teeth. There is an equalizing device so that the load on both bull-wheels is equally divided. All the main drive gearing is of cast steel with cut teeth.

The main motor is 400 hp., and is belted to the main drive pulley, which is 12 ft. diameter with a 36-in. face. This is of the solid type wood construction, the same as used for stamp-mills. The main drive motor also operates the main ladder-hoist, there being two V-type clutches permitting either, or both, to be operated at the same time. The brake bands on the ladder-hoist drum are compounded off the countershaft. The main winch has eight drums, all friction driven by means of internal expanded bands. There is a speed-change device so that the drum can be thrown into high or low gear without stopping the winch. No jaw-clutches are used on any portion of this winch. Further, the two forward drums that do 90% of the work of the dredge are made the full width of the winch, this increasing the life of the swinging-lines easily 90% as the rope fleets evenly.

The steel spuds for holding the boat to its work are 60 in. deep and 38 in. wide. Each spud weighs 45 tons and is made of four Bethlehem 30-in. 180 lb. per foot I-beams, with 1½ by 38-in. cover-plates, all bolted together with fitted bolts, no rivets being used in this work. The point is of cast steel and weighs 13 tons.

The water used for gold-saving purposes is supplied by two 14-in. pumps, one high pressure 72-ft. head, the other low pressure 40-ft. head, each pump delivering about 5500 gal. per min. There is also one jet-pump used for washing out the buckets, save-all, etc., which is a 6-in. two-stage pump and delivers 1000 gal. per min. The gold-saving tables are laid at a grade of 1 in. per foot and are lined with wooden riffles shod with iron. The total area of the tables is 8064 square feet.

The motors for the various parts of the dredge are as follows: main drive, 400 hp., 505 r.p.m.; main winch, 50 hp., 570 r.p.m.; high-pressure pump, 150 hp., 600 r.p.m.; low-pressure pump, 75 hp., 600 r.p.m.; jet-pump, 50 hp., 1200 r.p.m.; screen drive, 100 hp., 580 r.p.m.; and stacker drive, 60 hp., 695 revolutions per minute.

Power is brought aboard the dredge by means of 750 ft. of one 0 three-conductor stranded armoured cable, and is transformed by means of three 200-kw. with 4000 volts primary secondary. The boat cost approximately $450,000.

COMMERCIAL PARAGRAPHS

Root & Norton have opened a chemical laboratory and assay-office at Durango, Colorado, but will continue the operation of their office at Silverton.

Into Catalogue No. 35, vest-pocket size of 94 pages, the **A. Leschen & Sons Rope Co.** of St. Louis has condensed a great deal of useful data on ropes and accesories. Engineers at mines and works should secure a copy of this.

The April number of 'The Yellow Strand', a monthly of the **Broderick & Bascom Rope Co.** of St. Louis, contains interesting notes on the use of cables in tying log-rafts, in quarries, in logging, and a simple device for lubricating wire ropes.

In a recent leaflet, the **West Coast Gas Engine Co.** of San Diego, represented at Los Angeles by Collins & Webb, gives some details of its engines, especially mining and prospector's hoists. Collins & Webb are also agents for the Mansfield Engineering Co., of Indianapolis, makers of excavating machinery.

OIL development proceeds apace, particularly in Texas. There is need for this liquid mineral. A statement issued by the Department of Commerce shows that 682,226 barrels of oil were supplied during February to vessels engaged in foreign trade, as compared with 387,965 barrels similarly consumed in February 1918. For the eight months ending with February 1919 a total of 4,902,060 barrels was used thus, as against 3,787,690 barrels in the corresponding period of the previous year. The consumption in February is equivalent to 165,000 tons of bunker-coal.

EXPORTATION of gold from Australia is now in the hands of a Gold Producers Association, the mine-owners of the Commonwealth having obtained the Government's permission to sell their own production of the metal for three months as best they see fit, thereby securing a premium on the standard price. The Association deals only in Mint certificates, obtaining the gold from the Treasury as required, the output having been pooled and refined at the three mints, at Sydney, Melbourne, and Perth. The profit is shared pro rata among the producers. If successful, this arrangement will be continued.

THE American Institute of Mining and Metallurgical Engineers will hold its next convention at Chicago, on September 22 and the four following days. This meeting promises to be one of unusual importance, as subjects of vital concern to modern metallurgy will be under discussion. In addition to the technical discussions, an elaborate social program is being arranged and excursions by the Institute as a body are planned to many points of interest in the vicinity, including the steel mills at Gary, the oil-refineries at Whiting, metallurgical plants at East Chicago and North Chicago, and to the LaSalle district, where the cement, coal, and zinc industries are represented.

QUOTATIONS for silver have risen in a way to gladden the miner. For more than a year, that is, since the price was fixed by Anglo-American agreement at about $1 per ounce, the mining community has awaited the time when a free market for the metal would be established by removing the embargo upon export, feeling assured that the removal of the restriction would cause an immediate demand for the metal from other countries, particularly the Orient. On May 5 the United States government lifted the embargo and on May 10 the British government followed suit, the immediate consequence being a rise to $1.05¾ on May 9 and to $1.19¾ on May 12. On May 10 the steamer 'Nanking' took $14,000,000 worth of silver from San Francisco to India.

DISMISSAL of the appeal in the case of Amalgamated Properties of Rhodesia v. Globe & Phoenix Company is recorded by the 'Financial Times'. This suit has been long-drawn, for the first hearing started in October 1915. The cost of the litigation to the defendant is estimated at about a million dollars. Our London contemporary remarks: "It is to be hoped that, either as the result of a reform of the Rhodesian mining law or the self-control of those who hereafter feel themselves aggrieved, the question of extra-lateral rights will never have to be fought out again in the British courts." This will interest our readers because 'the law of the apex' was introduced into Rhodesia by American mining engineers.

THOSE compelled by the necessities of business to travel by rail are not enamored of the Government administration of this important public utility. It is more costly and less comfortable than it used to be, and the traveler has the annoying feeling that he is helpless to protest. Since the Government took hold of the railroads the increase in rates and fares has been $1,100,000,000 per annum, and only a few weeks ago a further $65,000,000 was added to the several increases in wages previously granted, making the average wages of all employees $1460 per annum as compared with $1004 in 1917. We miss the competition that provided redress for poor service. The bureau for complaints and suggestions affords no substitute for the discipline of healthy competition.

ON another page we publish an account of the meeting of the Montana section of the Institute; this was called mainly on account of the fortunate presence, at Butte, of Messrs. James F. Kemp and Charles K. Leith, both of whom delivered the thoughtful and interesting speeches that would be expected of them. Our readers will be glad to read the summary of their remarks as recorded by Mr. Oliver E. Jager, who was kind enough to act as our correspondent. We note, with pleasure, that Mrs. Kemp took part, making a persuasive speech in behalf of the women's work and laying stress on the importance of Americanizing the alien elements in our population. Mrs. Kemp is president of that branch of the Institute's activities known as the Women's Auxiliary, which now has 23 local sections. To Mr. E. B. Young, the secretary of the Montana section, is due the credit for the successful arrangement of this meeting.

AUSTRALIA, like other parts of the world, is going through a post-war crisis. With the exception of the Mount Morgan, Mount Lyell, and Wallaroo & Moonta mines, every copper producer is idle and 30,000 men have been thrown out of employment. The agreement between the Broken Hill mining companies and the British government for the marketing of lead is about to end, and anxiety exists as to the future disposal of this metal also. The arbitration award expires on June 30 and it is feared that the labor-unions will demand impracticable terms, such as 33 hours of work per week and a minimum wage of 16 shillings, as against the present minimum of 12 shillings. Australia is realizing the smallness of its domestic manufacturing industries and the large volume of imports in its trade.

PROHIBITION would not seem to be connected with the mining of copper; at least, nobody has suggested that the men mining that particular metal come especially under the embargo as to intoxicants; but we are informed that prohibition does affect copper mining in a curious way, namely, that there is a great demand for the copper tubing required to make stills. At Houghton it is reported that demand for copper is coming from every part of the country, notably from the States in which prohibition is the law. Two yards of copper tube is required for every kitchen plant used in the manufacture of beer or whiskey, so that each still is counted to use 150 pounds of copper. However, the producer of copper must not become unduly stimulated by this good news, for Uncle Sam has a way of enforcing his laws, among which are included severe penalties for the unlicensed use of stills.

AMONG the opportunities for becoming rich offered to the public we note an advertisement in the 'El Paso Herald' issued by a gentleman whose business address is given as the Paso del Norte hotel. He asks the readers of that newspaper to "take a flier" in Government lands having geologic features inviting the supposition that they are oil-bearing. He states that the land examined by him was made "within the last 1000 years," for it is a pre-Cambrian formation. Evidently his idea of geologic chronology is out of joint. The printer may be responsible for some of the errors in his statement that this Cambrian—he drops the "pre" as insignificant—"zone' is overlaid by the "Carboniferous formation of the jures toras age." Does he mean Jura-Trias? Perhaps he does, but even the typographic blunder does not greatly mar the significance of his information. The Devonian formation, coming next, "is undoubtedly of animal age." It is a queer menagerie, is it not? the delirious trimmings of geology. The limestone contains "fossiteles," monsters of the primeval slime, presumably, and "a great thickness of oysters"; hence the milk in the cocoa-nut.

REMEDIAL action against trade combinations in England has caused the suggestion to be made that syndicated newspaper concerns like the Northcliffe press should be made subject to discipline. With the suggestion comes a reminder of the baleful influence of the Hearst string of papers. Our readers will recall the fact that not long ago, in these columns, we advocated a restriction of newspaper mongers, because the control of a number of papers by any one man gave him, as it gives Northcliffe and Hearst, a power wholly out of proportion to his moral worth or intellectual character. Mr. J. L. Garvin, editor of the 'Observer' and one of the most notable of living journalists, asserts that Lord Northcliffe's personal press campaign against the British Premier, Mr. Lloyd George, "will mean the end of Lord Northcliffe as proprietor of the syndicated newspapers." We hope so. He proceeds to say: "Legislation would be introduced and carried putting an end to multiple proprietorship of the opinion-making powers of the press. It would be declared incompatible with the moral basis of representative government and with the unwarped play of democratic freedom." A true word, well spoken.

DISCUSSION, this week, starts with a letter from Mr. Oliver E. Jager, formerly smelter superintendent at Cerro de Pasco, and now at Butte, Montana, where he is collecting notes for a series of articles to be published by us. He discusses the foreign language question and the mental training obtained by the foreigner that learns to speak English, not without adverting to the failure of so many in our profession to obtain the educative effect of learning the languages of other peoples. Mr. P. A. Robbins, formerly the manager of the Hollinger mine, at Porcupine, returns to the charge and meets sundry criticisms offered lately by our friend Mr. W. DeL. Benedict of New York. Our recent editorial on wild-cat activities has elicited some pertinent remarks from Mr. W. D. Bohm, of Boise, Idaho. He has no particular sympathy for the simpletons that are worked by irresponsible promoters, taking the view that most of them expect to find somebody more gullible than themselves on whom to unload at a profit. Mr. J. H. Devereux, of New York, differs from Mr. Beardsley, who wrote, a month ago, demurring to some of our editorial comment on the flotation litigation. Mr. Devereux writes as a mining engineer keenly aware of the high-handed methods of the Minerals Separation company. It may be mentioned here, incidentally, that we have received copies of the briefs and arguments submitted before the U. S. Supreme Court, last March, in the final hearing of the Butte & Superior case, and we expect to publish excerpts from these records, knowing that they will interest many of our readers.

The Treaty of Peace

Citizens returning homeward on May 7 read their evening papers with faces set sternly, for most of them were reading the terms of the treaty presented that afternoon to the representatives of Germany at Versailles. If they thought the terms severe, they had but to recall the fact that the day was the anniversary of the sinking of the 'Lusitania', whereby 1154 non-combatants, including many women and children, were murdered. In truth, it would be a sloppy sentiment that would regret the severity of the punishment imposed upon the Enemy. Only a man whose memory failed him could feel sorry for the plight of those who broke into Belgium and there ravaged and destroyed life and property for four long years, for those who invaded France and exercised every devilish ingenuity in devastating a country engaged from the first in defending itself against remorseless aggression, for those who aimed by piracy to win command of the seas, for those who claimed that necessity knew no law and the will to power no compunction. They disregarded every covenant that hindered their ambitious purpose; they trampled the Hague convention in the dust and tore the Belgium treaty into scraps of paper; they flouted every rule devised by man for mitigating warfare; they scoffed at chivalry and sneered at sportsmanship; they deemed themselves above all international laws; they made themselves outlaws. Let those who now pity their plight imagine their own country treated as Belgium was; their own homes destroyed by scientific incendiarism, their wives and daughters debauched, their sons carried into slavery, soon to die of mistreatment or to be returned the mere wreckage of manhood; let them think of the beastliness and the horror that were the portion of the innocent people of Belgium and of the misery and sabotage inflicted upon the people of northern France; are their memories so poor that they have forgotten these damning facts already, are they callous to the sufferings of their own friends in order to cherish sympathy for a pitiless enemy, who would have done "so to them and more also," if he had broken the defense of the Allied line. Remember the fallen. Shall we hold the sacrifice of their life and happiness so cheaply as to forget for what they fought, and for what they died? Shall we compromise with the Enemy, whose insane ambition and bloody purpose called them from peaceful toil into a living hell, and from the sunshine of home into the darkness of a foreign grave? Keep faith with the dead! The terms are no more than sufficient to destroy Germany's power to start a military, naval, or economic offensive for a generation at least. We rejoice to think that the defender at the gate of western civilization, France, is assured of protection and will now be able in security to recover her vitality and her happiness. It was a great moment for M. Georges Clemenceau, The only survivor of the French deputies that signed the protest against the seizure of Alsace and Lorraine 48 years ago, he stood before the gathering of delegates from the four corners of the earth and in words of grim significance presented the account to the great marauder. The reference to the "second" treaty of Versailles recalled not the first treaty of that name, a compact signed in 1756 between Louis XV of France and Maria Theresa of Austria, but the meeting in 1871, at the end of the Franco-Prussian war, at which the German kings and princes constituted themselves into the German Empire and crowned William I, the grandfather of the fugitive at Amerongen. The performance of that ceremony in the palace of Louis XIV was a gratuitous insult to the French, but it is now compensated by the acceptance in the same palace by the Germans, no longer represented by kings and princes, but by citizen delegates, of the terms of their humiliating surrender, in the form of a penitential volume containing the numerous conditions deemed necessary to guarantee a durable peace. The German spokesman, Count von Brockdorff-Rantzau, made a haughty reply, but admitted the acceptance of defeat and the necessity of reparation; he acknowledged the wrong done to Belgium and demanded that Germany be admitted into the League of Nations. He did not rise to speak, but kept his seat without apology—as if to remind us of Junker manners. His speech was so truculent as to be considered insulting by some of those present. Retribution has come to the aggressor, but not regret. The German's attempt to win domination caused the loss of millions of lives and suffering that seared mankind, but his main regret is that he failed. The temper of the envoy's reply does not augur well for the performance of the drastic conditions imposed by the treaty or for those yet to be specified in completing the work of reparation, but justice is well prepared. The complete demobilization of the German armies and the surrender of her fleet, the demolition of all military defences within a zone 50 kilometres east of the Rhine, together with other precautions on the part of the Allies as specified in the Treaty, will render bad faith impotent if it should prompt an attempt to evade the conditions prescribed. The punishment befits the colossal crime of which an outraged civilization has found Germany guilty. What a contrast between this day and a year ago! If any man be tempted to be tender-hearted to the pitiful culprit, to the fighter that would not stay for the count, to the swashbuckler that yelled 'kamerad' as soon as he saw the fight was going against him, let him imagine what terms a victorious Germany would have imposed on Belgium, France, England, the United States, nay, upon the neutral countries also, because they had refused to play her game. Nor is much imagination needed, for do not the so-called treaties of Brest-Litovsk and Bucharest indicate what the vanquished were to expect? Remembering them, the treaty of Paris seems moderate in its exactions. But what terms of pacification could be so humiliating as the acts of the Germans themselves? Any man may be wrong, any man may be beaten in a fight, and yet preserve his self-respect; but to cease fighting at the first sign of defeat is contrary to all ideas of sport. The Germans sneer at our Anglo-Celtic notions of sport, of playing the game, and of taking a licking, if need be, manfully. They are welcome to their code. To us it seems that the climax of the German tragedy was not at Versailles, not on the Marne, neither at Verdun, nor the Argonne, but at Scapa Flow in the Orkney islands, when the German grand fleet came under its own steam to surrender to an enemy it had refused to fight. They planned to win the sovereignty of the seas, they built a splendid navy, they looked to the day of victory, they toasted *Der Tag*—and they took their navy under its own steam into prison, there to be scrapped. They might have fought and gone down in imperishable glory, defeated but not disgraced. Think of the Germans ever starting to build a new navy and of talking again about *Der Tag!* Echo would answer *Der Nacht*—from every cave on every coast of the seven seas; derisive laughter would shake the sides of every screaming sea-gull from the North Cape to Patagonia. There is the German defeat, not that her enemies encompassed her at last and brought here to her knees, broken, but that she was a quitter. And these were the people that had a heaven-sent mandate to rule the world! They will bluff and they will whine in order to escape the consequences of their crimes, they will use bolshevism as a blackmailing threat, they will appeal to the humane feelings that they themselves trampled underfoot, but the Peace Conference will stand firm in the consciousness of doing right. The Allies must support the Conference, which has endeavored to reconcile their conflicting interests. If most of them are dissatisfied, on selfish grounds, it only serves to prove the impossibility of pleasing everybody and the probability that where nobody is wholly satisfied, everybody's interest has been fairly considered. The Treaty of Peace is a sincere effort to adjust a vast disagreement equitably and justly.

Labor and the Treaty

Nine claims proposed by the Commission on International Labor Legislation for insertion in the treaty of peace, were adopted by the Peace Conference in plenary session at Paris on April 28. The effect of including this statement of economic principles in the Treaty will prove far-reaching, for it is stipulated that (1) labor shall no longer be regarded as an article of commerce, (2) the employee and the employer alike shall have the right of association or combination, (3) a rate of wages adequate to maintain a reasonable standard of living shall be established, together with (4) a standard eight-hour day, and (5) a weekly day of rest, (6) the abolition of child labor is stipulated, also (7) equality of payment to men and women performing work of equal value, and (8) a system of State inspection in which women shall participate. No fair-minded man will be inclined to regret the recognition of any of these principles, but it is to be hoped that they will be put into practice with equal fairness. A standard eight-hour day pre-supposes eight hours of honest labor; likewise a rate of wages enabling the workman to live decently carries with it the obligation to perform his share of the contract honorably. Agreements, contracts, and statements of high principles are of little use unless they are accepted as binding on both sides. We do not say that organized capital, in the form of companies, has not tried to evade its obligations here and there, but usually the possession of tangible property gives opportunity for legal punishment for such breaches of faith, whereas organized labor, in the form of unions, has too frequently welched, relying upon escape from legal punishment through the lack of possessions or of persistent identity. For example, the copper miners have accepted the sliding scale based upon the price of the metal and have been pleased to accept the bonus due to them monthly on account of the rise in copper quotations, but, as soon as the market relapsed and the sliding scale turned against them, they have not hesitated, in places, to revoke, without penalty. It is a poor rule that will not work both ways, and it is a futile agreement that is concocted for the benefit of one party. We hope—and the wish, of course, is father to the thought—as fair concessions are made, grudgingly by some, unselfishly by others, to the laboring men, that they will rise to the opportunity of making these concessions of the maximum value by living up to the spirit of them, so that they may be maintained in beneficent existence. It must be recognized that labor and capital are mutually dependent; only when employed intelligently together do they become valuable. The rate of wages will not create a comfortable way of life unless the cost of living is kept down, and that is impossible if labor is inefficient. In the last resort, it is the efficiency of labor that regulates the cost of production; but we do recognize the burden imposed by the middle-man and realize the growth of that parasite on the social economy. The distribution and marketing of staple commodities is done in an unnecessarily expensive manner even in a highly developed social organism such as ours. Most of us learned that by personal experience during the War. A higher standard of living is dependent not only upon wages but upon a higher standard of thinking, which is the product of education. Happiness does not come from idleness, although we can forgive the workmen for believing it, having regard to the example set by many of their employers. Neither rich nor poor, neither plutocrat nor proletariat, finds happiness in doing nothing; yet both alike make the pathetic blunder of thinking that happiness can be found in dissipation, a fallacy that is usually punctured by a funeral. It is noteworthy that the points scored by the Commission on International Labor appear to omit reference to the housing of laborers, to providing them with homes, without which no decent or self-respecting conditions of living can be maintained. We shall not be sorry if the Treaty of Peace includes stipulations helpful to the stabilizing of industrial conditions and the removing of grievances, and we hope that such inclusion of them will promote a more reasonable attitude on the part of the two elements necessary to economic prosperity.

English and Foreign Languages in Our Schools

The Editor:

Sir—In Mr. W. F. Staunton's excellent letter published in your issue of April 12, emphasis is placed on the necessity of an education designed to give a person the power to think rationally and logically, as distinguished from the German idea of 'training'. The German was 'trained', not 'educated'. Mr. Staunton says, "The English language should be first, of course, *for those ignorant of it.*" The italics are mine, but I wish to emphasize the phrase. At first glance it might seem to refer to newly-arrived immigrants, but let me enlarge its meaning to include all the rest of us. How many of us really know our own language? Why do we enjoy a speech by a university dean, or a sermon by a noted divine, or a classic play? Is it entirely because of the sentiments expressed? Not altogether. Notice the comments made afterward by the hearers, and you will find in nearly every case a tribute to the beautiful language used. That means that the speaker knows English. It is safe to say that our knowledge of the language is not what it should be. I would not say that our entire educational system is wrong, or that no attempt is made to teach our mother-tongue; but I do say that the system needs to be watched and improved, and that more importance should be attached to English in our schools. Look at the average newspaper; while some papers make praiseworthy efforts to maintain a high standard, it is not hard to find instances of the careless application of the rules of grammar and syntax. The plethora of magazines with which we are inundated month by month seems to indicate a desire for quantity production rather than for quality. Some of these publications apparently prefer a story to be liberally embellished with slang. Consider the average letter you receive—excepting purely business letters, which are a thing apart—and analyze the composition, the phraseology, and even the [illegible] You will see room for improvement and [illegible]bulary needs enlarging. We are also too [illegible]r daily speech. It is getting to a point [illegible]guage is considered merely as a vehicle for [illegible] ideas, regardless of the forms used. It is [illegible] to note that most of our important mining sch[illegible]ow giving more attention to English in the engi[illegible]ourses, so that the gradute may be an educate[illegible]ot a mere technician.

N[illegible] us consider the question of the foreign lang[illegible]n the school curriculum. This point has received considerable attention lately, owing to debates in some State legislatures, and elsewhere, as to the complete elimination of German in schools and colleges. This subject may be considered under three headings: (1) educational; (2) commercial; (3) patriotic or national.

The mental training acquired by the study of a foreign language is very great; and, further, it is not until you commence the study of a foreign language that you realize how little you know about your own. Translation does not consist in the mere ability to substitute the words of one language for those of another. There is a feeling—a spirit—that can only be properly caught when one has acquired the art of *thinking* in language other than his own. The enlarged horizon that comes from knowing another language is something worth striving for, and must be experienced in order to be appreciated. It opens up a new world to its possessor. The foreigner will tell you that the average American, unlike the European, does not learn a foreign language easily. One reason for this is our isolated position. Another is the narrow viewpoint of those who maintain that "English is good enough for me." This attitude is to be deprecated, as it tends to prevent a proper appreciation of other peoples. It is impossible to get close to a man when you talk to him only through an interpreter, as the personal element is missing. The real viewpoint, the real spirit, the active tendencies, and the true thoughts of a people can only be acquired by knowing their language. It may be urged against this that translation of books and newspaper articles are easily obtainable, but when one compares the large amount of publication with the small amount of translation, this argument fails. During the first two years of the War we had access to several German weekly papers, the perusal of which was instructive for this reason: it showed the kind of misinformation that was being served up to the German people. It was appalling to think that a supposedly intelligent people should be so systematically deceived, but it made clear many things that would otherwise have remained obscure, and we obtained first-hand information on what the German was thinking about. Was not such a thing worth while? Of course, I do not pretend to say that everyone should learn Spanish, in particular, or French or Italian, but I maintain that the study of some living foreign language is an important part of a good education. It is not necessary for everyone to learn German, but that is quite different from saying that nobody shall learn it, which is what its banishment from the schools practically amounts to. Another thing worth remembering is that to have studied any foreign language is of immense benefit in the study of some other foreign language, no matter how dissimilar the two may be, as one learns, in the first case, to think in some other man's way. That is to say, having studied French would make it easier to learn Norwegian than if no foreign tongue had ever been attempted.

Coming now to the commercial aspect of the case, it is almost needless to enlarge on the fact that one cannot do business with a man with whom it is impossible to converse. What chance has modern salesmanship by the medium of an interpreter? I have in mind, especially, South American trade, having heard a lot lately about capturing this trade. Some of the attempts to do this which I have witnessed were ludicrous in the extreme. One of the principal reasons why the German was getting so much of the Spanish-American trade was that the German is a born linguist. He gets close up to his prospective buyer by talking to him in his own language—at the same time handing him a catalogue printed in Spanish. To expect men who speak no Spanish to secure orders in South America is foolish on the face of it, but I have met many commercial travelers there who were trying to do it. When one considers that, with the exception of Brazil and the Guianas, the Spanish language covers the vast territory lying between the Rio Grande and Cape Horn, it must be admitted that Spanish has a commercial value. Within recent months there has been some discussion in the correspondence columns of the 'Engineering & Mining Journal' on Spanish for the mining man. The case for the 'Spanish-not-essential' side of the question seems very weak. A good knowledge of Spanish is necessary for the mining or metallurgical operator in Spanish countries. Inefficiency and accidents result from an inability to explain things properly to the native workmen, while the finer points of influencing officialdom—which has to be done quite often—are impossible without considerable fluency. The other languages of interest to mining men are German and French, on account of the technical and scientific publications, which are not often translated.

Under the patriotic heading I would enter a protest against the entire banishment of the German language. Let it be clearly understood that I am not advocating German for its own sake, but because the lack of knowledge of this tongue would give the German an advantage. No one will dispute the fact that the War has shown us that, even after the peace treaty is signed and sealed, the German will still need watching. How are we going to watch the German in our midst if he can talk without our understanding him? How are we to keep in touch with what the German in Germany is thinking about, if we cannot read his books and newspapers? It has been argued that the teaching of German in our schools gives an opportunity to a teacher of pro-German tendencies to instill into the youthful mind the pernicious ideas of militarism, or what not, by using certain books as school-readers. My answer to this is that there is something radically wrong with our school-boards if anything but good Americanism is allowed to get into the teaching. The idea of getting rid of everything that savors of Germany is all right, but, like all reforms, it is liable to go too far by eliminating something we could use to our own advantage.

After the excitement of the war and the peace has cooled down, and we again become capable of making calm decisions, let us hope that the question of languages, both English and foreign, will receive its proper consideration at the hands of our educators and legislators. At the same time let us retain a little good, honest hate, "lest we forget."

Oliver E. Jager.

Butte, Montana, April 27.

The Status of Gold

The Editor:

Sir—In the issue of March 22 appeared a letter from me on this subject, comparing the relative values of British consols and gold in the years 1812 and 1918. My figures were based upon an assumed present value of £80 for a consol of £100 denomination. You corrected this valuation to £59, but unfortunately did not extend the correction throughout the article. The corrected conclusions should have read:

"In 1812 one hundred sovereigns in gold were worth the future labor pledged in a consol bearing the inscription £100. In 1918, sixty sovereigns are worth the future labor pledged in a consol bearing the inscription £100. In other words, the investment value of an ounce of gold in 1918 was 50% greater than in 1812. Gold has enhanced 50% in its labor equivalent. . . . Therefore, for the purposes of hoarding, gold has an enhanced value over government securities, for today a man with 61 sovereigns will hoard them rather than hoard a British consol of £100 denomination."

In regard to the criticism by Mr. Benedict in your issue of April 26, I do not find much which calls for reply, for my argument is dismissed by the suggestion that I "do not seem to comprehend the basic principles of money, because I have not studied political economy sufficiently," and in his concluding paragraph my critic offers the use of 800 books upon the subject of economics. While admittedly the professional proof-reader has covered more ground than I, yet within the limits of my understanding, that which I have read, particularly in regard to money, has been digested and absorbed. Between the lines of Mr. Benedict's concluding paragraph, I read, "Shoemaker stick to thy last:" Ill-timed advice, else were Germany and Poland without their presidents, and the world without its food administrator. Has Mr. Benedict been so deeply immersed in his library of 800 books that he has failed to mark the present tendency to insist that the shoemaker shall lay aside his last—for a portion of each day at least? Adage and proverb for the unthinking past; today even a mining engineer must think beyond the confines of his profession if he would perform his full share of the world's work.

No proof is presented by Mr. Benedict that the financial world reached finality in its conceptions of 1812; indeed, did not the same masters of destiny who ascribed its weight to the gold sovereign also fix the boundaries of European countries so as to preserve peace? Mr. Benedict is not quite clear in his argument that it is not the Government stamp which fixes the value of the coin. The weight and fineness of the coin are fixed by statute, and the Government stamp upon the coin guarantees the legal weight and fineness at the time of minting. When we buy drill-steel we choose a brand known to possess the qualities that particular brand guarantees. But the manufacturer does not guarantee the brand against short weight in retail trade, nor against substitution of inferior steel by unscrupulous dealers, nor does the brand fix the price. Milk is bought by the quart, and by a system of inspections the Government tries to protect consumers against fraudulent measures, but the inspection stamp upon a measure or weight does not guarantee that these will not be tampered with after inspection. The coin is not redeemable; it is the final commodity in commercial settlements. The quantity of gold in a coin is fixed by statute in order that the receiver may know just what weight of gold he is entitled to receive. It is the statute and not the embossing stamp which fixes the "status of gold."

I cannot feel that Mr. Benedict and his array of 800 books, fortified by cigars and refreshments, would alter my opinions unless coupled with confuting evidence.

I have had some such experiences as he proposes, two of which produced the most valid reasons for protesting against an alteration in the weight of coins. One friend, a gold medallist in political economy at a leading university, whose youthful knowledge had been increased by 25 years of legal Practice, finally concluded a series of discussions (with cigars and refreshments) by exclaiming, "I have it, your plan means repudiation, repudiation of debts, an impossible step for any stable government to take;" to which I could only reply, "Repudiation, yes; but so is increased taxation repudiation; in order to pay for the War, we must repudiate the incomes and heritages which we have guaranteed to individuals."

Another friend, financial editor of a leading Canadian daily paper, voiced the opinion (after cigars and refreshments) "your talk sounds all right, but the plan is not workable, one reason being the great quantity of paper, commercial as well as governmental, which is redeemable in gold at its present value." A practical but not an insuperable objection.

I have not read Mr. Benedict's article upon 'What is a Dollar', and I presume that Mr. Benedict has not read some previous notes of my own, hence probably neither of us is conversant with the extreme depth of erudition of the other, but I grant, without discussion, that in those 800 books he marshals a crushing weight of argument. Referring to the article of Mr. McPherson, not, however, dismissing Mr. Benedict's criticism, but coupling the two together, there are some points to be considered.

In British consols, I find Mr. McPherson's 'twin-coin' idea exemplified. Great Britain issued her gold sovereigns of a legal weight and fineness, and then, doing exactly what Mr. McPherson suggests, she printed £100 on pieces of paper and issued these as running mates for the gold coins. Neither the gold coins nor the pieces of paper are redeemable; they are both money, the only difference being that the consol bears interest. Mr. McPherson says it can't be done, but the fact remains that Great Britain did it, and did it successfully on a large scale.

Mr. McPherson says "yet he (Mr. Van Dyke) would laugh in reasonable merriment at a Mexican leader or a Bolshevist ruler who should order the printing-presses to start as the nation was running short of money, to pay foreign debts, or any debts."

Yet during the past four years the printing-presses of France, Italy, Great Britain, Canada, and, in fact, all the Powers, have been doing this very thing, and if Mr. Van Dyke's figures are correct, from a total pre-War indebtedness of 28 billions a printing-press credit of 280 billions has been created by the belligerents.

Mr. McPherson says further: "If any nation or group of nations can double the figure on the face of a gold coin . . . that nation can as easily treble it or . . . multiply it by tens or hundreds. There is, however, one obstacle always in the way of this, and that is the intrinsic and social value of the metal itself." Just what is meant by "the intrinsic and social value" is not clear, but the facts are that there is no obstacle in the way of any nation doubling the figure upon the face of a gold coin. Possibly Mr. McPherson is not aware that Argentina had, long ago, done this; that it has provided a flexible internal credit and that no disaster has followed the innovation. It is only in international exchange that Argentina recognizes the international value of gold; internally gold has double the international value.

If by "intrinsic" value is meant the value in open markets, then it should be noted that in the Orient gold has for some time been selling at from 25 to 30% premium. If by "social value" is meant local selling-value, in the arts and trades, it is interesting to note that the value in London and Paris has been at a high premium, from 25 to 30%.

The statement "gold is called into active functioning as a monetary metal during war times" may be true in the time of small wars on account of increased commercial activity, but it has not been true during the present war. The balance of trade has been so overwhelmingly against Europe and Canada in reference to United States that gold ceased to perform its regulating functions. The statement "if gold coin itself were arbitrarily stamped with figures far above its intrinsic value it would not possess complete security as a means of value" is seemingly based upon the common misconception that gold has a standard intrinsic value. Gold has an arbitrary monetary value, but an intrinsic value is a matter of locality and existing conditions in that locality.

I have already pointed out that within Argentina the

purchasing power is doubled, and in my letter which appeared in your issue of March 22 I pointed out that under the conditions existing in England in 1812 gold was accepted at a less value than it is accepted at today under existing conditions. The adoption of gold as a standard of exchange did not give to it its value as an article of exchange any more than did the adoption by the medical profession of quinine as a drug give to that drug its medicinal value. Gold was adopted because it possessed facility of exchange, and quinine was adopted because it possessed medicinal value.

The fundamental human regard for gold seems to be atavistic, regardless of any decree of governments. All that governments can do is to standardize and stabilize the relationship between gold and the mass of other wealth. Great Britain tried to do this and her effort seemed successful, but time has shown a gradually accumulating error, and the present value of consols indicates that a considerable adjustment is necessary in the status of gold.

Manifestly, there is no hope of paying the balances of war-indebtedness by exchanges of gold, but ordinary trade-balances will have to be settled by the exchange of some commodity that is internationally acceptable. Previous to the War the exchange of gold was somewhere in the vicinity of 1% of the total trade, but what it will be in the future we cannot say; all we know is that the creditor nations will have to accept a balance of trade against themselves, otherwise the debtors will not be able to liquidate their indebtedness, and it is only reasonable to expect that the demand for gold for exchange purposes will be greater than before the War. As there is only a definite amount of gold in the world, either some substitute for gold will be necessary, or it would seem necessary to ascribe a greater exchange-value to an ounce of gold.

The dominating commercial position of Great Britain before the War was due to her gold resources; her gold was to a large extent placed with foreign and local institutions, subject to call, and it was her ability to call in gold from any part of the world that enabled her to regulate exchanges in her favor and thus maintain her position as the clearing-house of the world. Before the Franco-Prussian war, Paris shared with London a large part of the exchange business of the world, but after the war the gold resources of France were required to successfully maintain the value of the franc, and she gradually lost her profitable business of discounting foreign bills.

Differences in trade-balances might be (and during the War have been) settled by an exchange of securities. But securities are subject to 'bull' and 'bear' manipulation. Inside information that a government proposed to use securities as a means of settling its debt would inevitably lead to speculation in those securities, a fact which makes such exchanges dangerous to business done upon a small margin of profit. Hence gold, with an ascribed value, forms a stable exchange commodity, subject usually to only a small fractional variation due to difference in insurance and express charges, and fractional premiums caused by local shortages in reserve stocks.

Government stocks are the resting places of the bulk of the world's supply of gold, and by arrangement with domestic financial institutions the foreign credits of a country are bolstered up by the Government. If each Government possessed a surplus of gold over any demands likely to be made in the support of its commercial credits, then there would be little need of altering the ascribed monetary value of gold. There is, however, grave danger of a shortage of the commodity owing to the huge trade-balances that will have to be settled in the future, and to the enormous payments of interest on war bonds.

Financial institutions are becoming largely internationalized and a shortage of gold in the world's business would tend to form closer financial alliances for the purpose of manipulating exchanges. The result of such manipulation would, if not counteracted, cause a reduction in the costs of production of raw and manufactured commodities; it would react to re-establish British consols, and enhance the values of high interest-bearing war-bonds.

Reductions in costs could only be brought about by increased output of workmen or reduction of wages. There is small possibility that organized labor, backed by a newly created sympathetic public sentiment, will permit conditions to revert to pre-war standards, and if anything like present standards of output and wages are maintained then the need will increase for a revision of the status of gold.

If an actually higher value were to be ascribed to gold, the entire stock of metal would naturally be commandeered by the various governments and re-issued, all profits in the transaction accruing to the governments; if, however, the adjustment be made by reducing the costs of commodities and thus giving a relatively higher value to gold, then the profits would accrue largely to the holders of securities. In opposition to a reduction in the cost of commodities there is the proposal of international labor agreements, with limited hours, minimum wages, exclusion of child labor and other reforms. A strong public sentiment has grown in favor of these, and it is doubtful if labor will consent to speed up in the future as in the past, and it is quite certain that wages will not return to pre-war standards either in Europe or upon this continent. It, therefore, seems probable that sooner or later the status of gold will of necessity be adjusted.

The easier method of making the adjustment is to adjust the valuation of an ounce of gold. The benefits of such an action will be distributed to the entire population of the civilized world. If the adjustment be made by reducing the costs of commodities then the profit in the adjustment will accrue to the relatively small class of bond-holders. This will only aggravate the conditions that exist today by widening the gulf between those who have a surplus and those who have none.

The payment of war debts can only be made in the

products of future labor or by the exchange of such tokens of labor as gold, silver, and platinum, of which accumulated stocks exist in the world. It will, therefore, be understood that the payment of war debts merely means a re-adjustment of the wealth held by individuals.

The securities that cover the war debts are held by certain individuals. Other individuals must produce commodities with which to redeem those securities, and as the security-holders receive their incomes, portions of the incomes will be taken away from them to apply in reducing the war debts. Thus we have a recurrent cycle of operations which will eventually reduce the average of individual fortunes until the war debts are extinguished and the process will be long or short, depending upon how drastic taxation becomes.

The whole world is not going to speed up and produce more commodities than are required, thus piling up unused stocks and proclaiming the debts paid. Production is going to meet demands and only from a profitable exchange of commodities can the debts be extinguished. The only exception to this is in stocks of precious metals, which can be stored for use by future generations. The building of public utilities as a charge against future generations will not be above normal unless heavier taxation be resorted to. It seems to me that the maintenance of gold at its present value is going to increase the gravity of the present financial situation. The raising of gold to a higher valuation would ease present conditions and stimulate production of precious metals.

Increased production of precious metals would mean a certain storage of unused commodities which could be paid for by future generations. This phase of the subject is so complex that I have made no attempt to analyze it in the short space of this letter, but if what I have written causes thought upon the subject, I feel that others will at least see a reasonable argument in favor of recoining gold coins at one-half or two-thirds of their present weight.

P. A. Robbins.

San Francisco, May 1.

Who Will Hold the Sack?

The Editor:

Sir—That pertinent editorial in your issue of April 26 revives a perennial question. In my long experience, covering most of the known mining regions, I have found—whether it be in the U. S. A., Australasia, Africa, or anywhere, that the majority of the public—of whom somebody remarked something about 90 odd per cent fools—will persist in regarding mining as a "game" and a mighty low-down one at that.

I think, therefore, that we ought not to regard the promotion question too seriously, but take a more Gilbertian view of it. Let us, for instance, endeavor to permit "the punishment fit the crime"—and the criminal—and, instead of hounding the average promoter, arrange something pleasant "with boiling oil in it" for the rascals—expecting something for nothing, or hoping to 'pass the buck'—who buy wild-cat stuff.

Repeatedly have I been assured, in many instances undoubtedly in good faith, by broker-promoters that they heartily wished that the public would join them in the development of meritorious prospects on their face-value on equitable terms for all, but that attempts along such lines had always failed to meet with any response, while the highly spiced rubbish was quickly absorbed.

From the innumerable examinations that I have made for clients who 'groused' at being hooked by sharks, and who afterward had to admit that they really had hooked themselves in their craze for getting the edge on some other fellow, I am led to at least suspect that the responsibility rests about 50-50 with the promoter and the dear public.

When the public can be induced—if it ever can be—to realize that opening up mines is almost as risky as opening a new grocery store, it may take a tumble, and incur the risk intelligently and economically. The final analysis, to my mind, places the greatest onus on those looking for 'sure things', of which it must be said, in common honesty to all nature, that there can be no such animal. Hoping for the day when we can again mine like men, taking our chances open-eyed, and unafraid in legitimate development, I am

W. D. Bohm.

Boise, Idaho, May 3.

Flotation Patents

The Editor:

Sir—I cannot agree with Mr. Beardsley's conclusion, as stated in your issue of April 12. The Courts not only are required to act solely upon the record before them, as he states, but also the litigants are bound by their own testimony. Did not the Minerals Separation company claim that until it reduced the oil to a "critical point" it failed to get the separation? Did it not claim as its invention the ability to get with a small percentage of oil a result that it could not get with a larger percentage? Did it not state in court that with a larger quantity of oil the process would not work? If so, then the Butte & Superior has also made a discovery. The fact that it is trying to avoid the Minerals Separation patent and the claim that an increased quantity of oil is unnecessary cut no ice.

In 1893 to avoid the Edison Incandescent patents, the Westinghouse Lamp company used a lamp with a cemented plug. It was admitted, indeed it was advertised, that the object was to avoid a detailed specification of the Edison patent. If the Minerals Separation company tied itself to half of 1% of oil, it releases everyone using more, even if it is used for the purpose of avoiding a patent. If a patentee specifies a hexagonal nut as essential, he cannot prohibit another from using a square nut.

As I see it, the Minerals Separation claim is, "You can get drunk on two drinks but you cannot on twenty." Then if a man takes twenty drinks, they cannot charge him with being drunk.

J. H. Devereux.

New York, April 25.

Mine Development in China

By GILMOUR E. BROWN

China is a vast and comparatively unknown country, but it does not follow, as is apparently assumed by many non-technical writers, that its mineral resources are also vast and entirely unknown.

It is scarcely possible to form a reliable estimate of its mineral wealth from one's own comparatively insignificant travels, supplemented by a perusal of the somewhat scanty and unreliable literature available, but conversations with engineers who have visited other provinces has led me to agree with them that the mineral deposits of China are more disappointing than otherwise. It is generally conceded, however, that the coal resources of China are of the first magnitude.

During a prospecting trip undertaken several years ago along the China-Burma frontier I was impressed with the history of the conflicts between the Chinese and the Shans of Northern Burma for the possession of the huge silver-lead-zinc orebody now known to the world as the Bawdwin mines, the property of the Burma Corporation, the silver ultimately finding its way to Peking. That did not tend to corroborate the tales of the great undeveloped mineral wealth of China, and the impression formed then has gained in strength through subsequent travels in several provinces.

The areas most richly mineralized are, as a general rule, closed to the newcomer, either by previous agreements with foreigners or by being in the sphere of influence of a particular nation, or by being situated in a province such as Hunan, where the co-operation of foreigners is not desired; in fact, many American engineers attracted to China during recent years have thrown up their hands in disgust and taken an early opportunity of departing for more enticing lands. I could name a dozen prominent American mining engineers and geologists who have come and gone during the past three years without accomplishing a single stroke of business.

A good example of the locking up of the mineral wealth of the country is that of the Pritchard-Morgan agreement covering an area, 60,000 square miles greater than France, of what appears to be the most richly mineralized province of China and in which although the agreement dates from 1899 no mine has yet been developed under the terms of the agreement. Yunnan, perhaps the next best province from the mineral standpoint, is a French sphere of influence, while the Japanese stranglehold on Manchuria makes the American or European hesitate before venturing capital in that part of the country.

An engineer unacquainted with the history of the existing concessions is likely to pay for his lack of knowledge if he ventures into the arena. One example will suffice: An American concern in the early years of the War secured a contract to build from 1500 to 2000 miles of railway, which was hailed in America as a great success for American enterprise. After surveying parties had been formed and dispatched, no fewer than four nations protested, alleging infringement of spheres of influence, previous agreements, and the like, so that the contractors were left with only one route, which is at present in abeyance, nearly all the engineers having returned to the States.

The acquisition of mining rights over a particular area is so often a political matter that the engineer may be amazed at the results of what in another country would be a simple mining transaction attracting little or no attention. Formerly concessions were granted outright to foreigners, but that is no longer possible except by special agreement with the provincial authorities and the consent of the national parliament. A recent example of such special legislation was the agreement with the Standard Oil Co. for the exploitation of the oil resources of several provinces, from which, however, no benefit accrued to the company.

If foreigners desire to engage in mining they can do so by forming joint companies with the Chinese, 50% of the shares being held by Chinese. That is not usually acceptable to the foreign speculator. The liability of the shareholders in these Sino-foreign companies, as they are called, has not yet been clearly defined.

The present mining laws leave much to be desired. A perusal of a translation of the principal laws failed to reveal any reference to hydraulicking or dredging, forms of mining that are still unpractised in China. These laws have not received recognition by the Diplomatic Body of Peking, and most engineers would feel inclined to ask what the Diplomatic Body has to do with the application of the mining laws. In the non-recognition of the laws by the Diplomatic Body lies a pitfall for the unwary. A case with which I am thoroughly acquainted will illustrate this point.

A company with a foreign interest of —— nationality acquired by purchase a small coal concession from a company with a foreign interest of ——nationality, adjoining a concession of another company with a foreign interest of the same nationality as the newcomers. Work was commenced on the property and preparations made for shaft-sinking, the new-comers having received the verbal permission of the engineers of the Bureau of Mines to commence work while the transfer papers were passing through the necessary departments.

The already established company with the foreign interest of —— nationality approached its legation and urged the legation to prevent the advent of the new-comer on the grounds that damage would result to its property through its presence in the same valley, and besides it had rented the surface rights of the land acquired by the new-comers and under the old mining laws it was owner of the mining rights thereof. No notice was taken by the legation that the objecting company had received an extension of its area under the new mining laws and had paid its mine taxes under these laws, and had also neglected to pay the rents of the land it had rented since the new laws had come into force. The legation forthwith proceeded to demand that the officials of the Bureau of Mines stop the operations of the new-comers and eject them from the valley under the terms of the old laws. The new-comers were told by its legation that if they shouldered the debts of the objecting company, and amalgamated with it, the legation's opposition would be withdrawn.

The Chinese officials of the Bureau of Mines were entirely in favor of the new-comers and resented the demands of the —— legation, but as that legation was very powerful they dared not disregard its opposition. Then the legation of —— nationality, representing the vendor interest, appeared on the scene and its support was sufficient to give courage to the Chinese officials, although it was not sufficiently strong to effect a settlement. Finally, when all were tired, the Bureau of Mines appointed a commission to inquire into the dispute under the direction of the foreign advisor to the Bureau of Mines, the finding being entirely in favor of the new-comers. An opportunity was given to the legation of — nationality to climb down gracefully (at the expense of the new-comers) and the transfer papers were issued 20 months after the new-comers had commenced development operations.

The foregoing is a typical example of what one may expect under existing conditions in China and enables one to appreciate the humor of the definition of a diplomat as "one who lies abroad for the benefit of his country".

With his concession papers in order the engineer may think his troubles are over but, he is soon to be disillusioned. All over China the mineral deposits have been burrowed at their outcrops, the burrows being mostly close to the stream-beds, as affording the shortest distance to the deposit. When one burrow is flooded another is started, but in north China most of them are flooded during the heavy downpours of the wet season. When the burrows cannot be unwatered by hand-labor at the height of the dry season, they are abandoned altogether and constitute a menace to future operations. Ample pumping capacity has to be installed to drain them annually, by any foreign-controlled company operating below the outcrops.

These small mines are worked under permits from the local magistrate only; they necessitate constant watchfulness and an expensive organization in the capital of the province to prevent them re-starting work within the boundaries of the concession, for they know full-well that the foreign-controlled concern is going to install pumps and leave these old workings high and dry. It is of little use appealing to the local magistrate, for the ways of the Chinese official are numerous and all equally tedious. It is usual to put him on the pay-roll and avoid trouble.

Mining taxes are not heavy, but the engineer would not object to paying double the taxes if he was relieved thereby of the incubus of defending his concession against the holders of local permits. The Japanese Minister at Peking backed his nationals in 'mailed fist' style in a case against the holders of local permits, so that now the Government officials pay a little more heed to the protests of the people who pay taxes to them.

There is this to be said for the administration of the mining laws, that as long as the operations at the mines are conducted with reasonable care there is practically no interference with the management of the mine. There

PART OF CHINA

are none of those inquiries into fatal accidents which are a nuisance in more civilized countries.

A great drawback at the commencement of operations is the time necessary to secure a permit for the purchase of explosives. This usually takes four months, the application having to pass through four departments, while the permit has to pass through the same departments in the reverse order. The permit names the place at which the explosives can be purchased and if it is desired to purchase explosives at another place it takes four months to effect the necessary alteration.

During the first years of the War I held a permit for the purchase of explosives at the nearest port, where, at that time, there were no explosives or any prospect of a shipment from abroad. As the need was pressing, inquiries were made and a quantity owned by a Government railway, was found at an inland town. A request to hold the explosive for four months, until the permit could be changed, was acceded to, but, by the time the permit was altered, a clean sweep had been made of the directorate of the railway, and the explosive was no longer for sale. Another four months were consumed in having the permit re-altered and in answering the questions necessitated by the double change.

It took nearly half an hour on one occasion to convince a customs official that 20 cases of dynamite was a reasonable quantity for a mine to possess.

The railway companies are in a chronic state of shortage of cars due partly to the War but mostly to the wants of the military party in the campaign against the South. Railway cars are not only held up for weeks but several covered cars have been fitted with furniture as residences for officers. There is much to be said for such a dwelling when it is desired to make a speedy departure from the scene of military operations. The foreign-controlled concerns are the first to suffer in the matter of such shortage, which seriously affects the output of the coal mines.

The Chinese coolie is a noteworthy laborer, but, as often happens, cheap labor does not imply a low cost of production. the average coal mine in China showing a higher cost per ton than the corresponding mine in the United States. As far as I am aware, although attempts have been made by foreigners to operate metal mines, there is not one profitable metal mine in the hands of foreigners at the present time.

The coolies are docile and industrious but in the Chinese-owned mines his life is short, owing to the terribly unsanitary state of the workings. Coal is often carried out on men's backs for a distance of a mile underground, there being little or no ventilation possible through the one and only inclined shaft.

The coolie does not appreciate the hygienic conditions of the foreign-controlled mine, but he does appreciate a guarantee of a coffin if he dies or is killed in the mine. With the promise of a coffin he is the company's servant until he fills it. *Resquiescat in pace.*

Costs at the Homestake Mine

During 1918 there was treated a total of 1,628,630 tons of ore, yielding $3.633 per ton. The principal items of expense were the following:

Underground work and hoists	$1.52
Stamp-mills and amalgamation	0.31
Re-grinding	0.02
Cyanidation of sand and slime	0.24
General expenses	0.12
Compensation and sociological	0.08
Taxes	0.21

Some of the other large charges were $107,050 for the Ellison shaft coal plant, and $121,894 for the No. 2 Spearfish hydro-electric plant. Labor in the mine cost 77 cents per ton, and explosives 13 cents. Labor in the mills cost 12 cents, and quicksilver nearly 1 cent. Cyanidation of sand cost 15 cents.

INDICATORS used in acidimetry and alkalimetry are organic, but the direct cause of color change is not fully understood.

Cadmium Production and Its Use in Solders

The critical scarcity of tin in this country during the War, according to C. E. Siebenthal, of the U. S. Geological Survey, led to Government control of its distribution as well as to a campaign for its conservation. One method of saving tin is to substitute cadmium for it in solder. In the last year of the War the Government and certain large companies began experiments with cadmium solders as a means of saving tin. The results were promising, but the demand for tin decreased, and the armistice was signed before cadmium solders became widely used. The first of the belligerent nations to make large use of cadmium as a substitute for tin in solders was Germany, which from the beginning of the War was cut off by the blockade almost entirely from the world sources of tin. Solders containing 10% cadmium were used in Germany early in the War, and some were reported to contain as high as 30% of cadmium and only 2% of tin instead of the customary 40 to 50%.

About 600 tons of cadmium accumulates annually in America as dust and residue, by-products of the lead and zinc industries, and from these by-products about 100 tons of metallic cadmium is recovered. If all the cadmium dust and residue were treated, the output of metallic cadmium would be small in comparison to the 19,000 or 20,000 tons of tin annually used in this country in solder, even if due allowance is made for the fact that 1 lb. of cadmium can replace from 3 to 5 lb. of tin.

The output of metallic cadmium in the United States in 1918 was 127,164 lb., compared with 207,408 lb. in 1917, and the output of cadmium sulphide in 1918 was 51,702 lb. as against 50,169 lb. in 1917. The average value per pound for metal and for sulphide was $1.48 and $1.36 in 1918, against $1.47 and $1.41 in 1917. Exports of cadmium in 1918 were 62,320 lb., of which 30,440 lb. was sent to France and 20,000 lb. to Japan. The market for metallic cadmium was not strong in the first half of 1918, and considerable stocks accumulated. Production was somewhat curtailed before August and almost stopped during the remainder of the year.

DIAMOND PRODUCTION of the Union of South Africa in 1918 was 2,537,360 carats, valued at £7,114,867. The Cape (Kimberley mostly) contributed 1,418,440, the Transvaal (Premier mine) 896,039, and Orange Free State 222,881 carats. The output in the previous seven years was as follows:

Year	Carats	Value
1917	2,902,417	£7,713,810
1916	2,346,330	5,728,391
1915	103,386	390,810
1914	2,801,017	5,487,194
1913	5,163,547	11,380,807
1912	5,071,882	10,061,480
1911	4,891,909	8,746,724

One carat equals 205.3 milligrams, about 3.2 grains. £1 normally equals $4.85. Many thousands of natives and whites are employed in the mining and treatment of the 'blue' and 'yellow' diamondiferous ground.

The German Metal Octopus—IV

ISSUED BY THE ALIEN PROPERTY CUSTODIAN

DISCLOSURES BY INVESTIGATIONS CONDUCTED BY ALIEN PROPERTY CUSTODIAN

After the passage of the Trading with the Enemy Act in October, 1917, and the subsequent appointment of the Alien Property Custodian, he caused investigations to be made of the American Metal Co., Vogelstein & Co., and Beer, Sondheimer & Co., as a result of which he took over the entire business of Vogelstein & Co. and of Beer, Sondheimer & Co. and 49% of the stock of the American Metal Co. The investigations disclosed the following state of facts:

As to Beer, Sondheimer & Co.—In August, 1915, Benno Elkan and Otto Krohnknecht, who, as pointed out above, were simply the agents of the Frankfort firm of Beer, Sondheimer & Co. and were conducting, in the United States, a branch of the business of the Frankfort firm under the name of Beer, Sondheimer & Co., American Branch, without the knowledge or consent and against the express wish of the Frankfort firm formed a corporation under the laws of the State of New York called Beer, Sondheimer & Co., capitalized at $1,000,000, and transferred to that corporation all of the assets of the capital stock of the new corporation. Correspondence passing between the Frankfort firm and the American attorneys who advised Elkan and Krohnknecht in this situation and did the legal work in organizing the corporation, clearly shows that the corporation was organized and the assets were transferred to it for the express and only purpose of making it impossible for the United States government, in case of a war between the United States and Germany, to exercise its belligerent rights and take control of enemy property in the United States. One of these American lawyers, writing to Beer, Sondheimer & Co., of Frankfort, after the corporation had been organized and the assets transferred, explains the purpose of the organization as follows:

September 15, 1915.

Gentlemen: I thought it in line with my duty to you, both in my professional capacity and as an interested friend, that I should write you relative to the recent incorporation of the American branch.

Having discussed a similar proposition with you during my recent visit, and knowing your mind upon the subject, I naturally counseled Messrs. Elkan and Krohnknecht to consider the matter with extreme care before any decisive step was taken. Shortly after my arrival the situation here looked very grave, and the diplomatic complications were a source of apprehension to me. From the various opinions that I was able to secure, it was quite clear that the situation was very serious. Having these facts in mind, and also knowing that you were not inclined to favor the incorporation, Mr. Elkan believed that we should take counsel.

The firm of X. Y.,* which is, as you already know, one of our best firms here (being the same firm that rendered an opinion on the question of * * * †), was employed by Mr. Elkan. This firm of X. Y., after mature consideration, both as to law and the known facts of the diplomatic situation, advised without reservation, that it was necessary to incorporate; in these views I fully concurred.

The means of communicating with you were so meagre and the necessity of keeping the facts from our enemies so evident, that we were compelled to act with extreme caution. We sent you as many messages as possible, under the circumstances; but we received no answer to the cables and wireless messages sent you on the subject, yet we delayed taking action until we believed it was hazardous to wait longer, therefore we acted upon our best judgment.

As far as the incorporation is concerned, personally I looked upon it as the only practical means of protecting your interests here, so that your business could be carried on in spite of any difficulties that might arise between the Governments. The idea was executed with the sole and only purpose of guarding your interests, there being no other consideration present in the working out of the idea. Further than this, the whole matter under our laws here is at present in such position, that at any time, either now or after the conclusion of peace, the corporation can be dissolved and the entire business can be put back under the name of the American branch just as it was before the incorporation. In other words, your interests are the same now as they were before except as to form, but the legal status of the property here has been changed. The whole question is one for you to determine, whether you desire to have the business continue under the present company or not.

I might suggest for your guidance that for the present, and until the War is over that the incorporation stand as it is, because it not only makes a difference in the conduct of the business as a matter of law, but as you must realize, it makes a decided difference in the opinion of Americans. There is no denying the fact that the great preponderance of American sympathy is with the Allies, and this phase of the question you must bear in mind in considering the advisability of taking any immediate step to dissolve the corporation.

I also want you to know that in taking the step there was absolutely nothing that was done that was not thoroughly discussed and agreed upon by Messrs. Elkan and Krohnknecht, and we attorneys. The company is so organized that it is impossible at this time, or at any other time, except with your consent, that any separation of interests could be made. In other words, the whole business is absolutely in your control.

The matter of the indebtedness of the branch to you, although it is not expressed in any way in the incorporation papers, has, nevertheless, been taken care of satisfactorily. The accountings for interest upon the indebtedness and the various other details in connection therewith have been and will be carried on so that there can be no question arising as to these matters. The only difference will be that of form.

The statement in X. Y.'s opinion which reads "We pre-

---

*The use of initials is ours. †The omission is ours.

pared to meet your desire to secure to the corporation at least for a period of substantially three years the same personal management and direction which has been enjoyed by your American branch," needs a little explanation. Usually voting trust agreements are made for this purpose and under ordinary circumstances that reason is given for the execution of such voting trust agreements. The real reason in this incorporation for executing the agreement and the transfer of the stock to voting trustees was for the sole purpose of putting the stock in such legal form that in case any action was taken by the Government here that your interests could not in any way be legally jeopardized—that the business should go on without interruption. In other words, there is and was no intention of perpetuating anybody in the management or direction of the American branch.

I have gone into these matters in details because I realize that it is difficult for you at so great a distance, and with your known objection to corporate form, to understand the reasons underlying such a move. I can give you my personal assurances that the incorporation is the only solution open to us at the present time, and although we may disagree as to the conditions and as to the seriousness of the situation, nevertheless, in my judgment the step was not only wise and proper, but absolutely necessary. I should have deemed it a breach of duty to you to have subjected all of your assets in this country to the dangers that were apparent, and this fact alone was of sufficient weight to determine my agreement with the opinion of X. Y. Without trying in any way to seek justification for the action taken, as I do not deem that necessary, I think it will be all too apparent to you that the consummation of the proposition was but an honest fulfillment of a duty to you to protect your property, and in the last analysis the facts must be judged on this basis. The only misgivings that I have had were that we could not advise with you more fully before completing the work, but as I have already said, this was impossible in the nature of things, nevertheless such communications as were possible to send were sent.

To sum up the whole matter, I would say that we have given you an insurance policy upon your assets here, and, like all insurance policies, this one is subject to cancellation.

I hope that all of my good friends are in good health and that peace will soon be concluded so that we may all return to the normal business relations.

With my kindest and best respects and wish to you all, I am

Very sincerely yours,

(Signed) ——— ———.

The assets thus transferred to the corporation amounted to about $3,250,000, which did not include the profits made by the business in 1915, amounting to about $1,200,000, and the profits of 1916, amounting to $2,000,000. Between September, 1915, and February 3, 1917, Beer, Sondheimer & Co., of New York, transferred to Beer, Sondheimer & Co., of Frankfort, $2,047,000. The last remittance of $700,000 was made on February 3, 1917, the very day on which Count Von Bernstoff received his passports and was sent out of the country. When this happened and it became clear that the United States and Germany were on the brink of war, Elkan and Frohnknecht, to further make it impossible for the Government to seize the German property in their possession, caused to be transferred to the corporation 7000 out of the 10,000 shares of the stock of the corporation which had been issued to the Frankfort firm as consideration for the transfer of the assets to the corporation, and to effect this transfer, they did not hesitate to cause the name of the Frankfort firm to be indorsed upon the back of the stock certificate without any apparent authority. The other 3000 shares of stock they claimed to have bought from the Germans in 1916 at the rate of $80 per share, when the book-value thereof was in excess of $30 per share and in the face of a profit made by the business in that one year of $2,000,000. Thus the two individuals claimed to become the owners of all the business and assets formerly belonging to their German principals less the portion of profits sent to Germany as above stated.

Though they have been in this country since 1906 Elkan and Frohnknecht did not become citizens till 1917. One of them became a citizen after Von Bernstoff got his passports and the other was admitted to citizenship in May, 1917, after we were at war with Germany. There is evidence to indicate that their sudden desire to embrace our citizenship was only a 'war measure' after all and that they asked for and obtained the approval of the Frankfort firm to their action.

The foregoing is but a bare outline of what the investigation disclosed, but it is sufficient to indicate that the transfers were void as against public policy, and in consequence thereof the Alien Property Custodian demanded and took over the entire business and assets of Beer, Sondheimer & Co., as German property.

As to L. Vogelstein & Co.—It had been the custom for years for Vogelstein to make annual settlements with Aron Hirsch & Sohn and to send and receive annual accounts upon the basis of which respective shares in the profits were determined as between Aron Hirsch & Sohn and L. Vogelstein & Co. The last accounting was had as of the end of 1914. Owing to the War it has been impossible for accountings to be had since that time. At the end of 1916 Vogelstein bought out the interests in the firm of L. Vogelstein & Co. owned by Ernest G. Hothorn and he then formed a corporation under the laws of the State of New York under the name of L. Vogelstein & Co., capitalized at $5,000,000, and transferred to the corporation all of the assets of the firm of L. Vogelstein & Co. in consideration of the issue of the entire capital stock. At that time the books of L. Vogelstein & Co. showed that the firm was indebted to Aron Hirsch & Sohn for its share of the profits of the American business and balances due in the sum of about $3,900,000. But inasmuch as there was no way of determining what profits, if any, Vogelstein was entitled to receive from the European business of Aron Hirsch & Sohn, no accounts having been stated between the parties since the end of 1914, there was no way of determining what amount was really due to Aron Hirsch & Sohn. Under these circumstances Vogelstein placed the entire 50,000 shares of stock in escrow with his attorneys, setting aside 39,000 shares thereof to be held to await a final accounting between the two firms. The Alien Property Custodian made a demand upon the attorneys who held the stock in escrow for the surrender to him of the interest of Aron Hirsch & Sohn in said stock. The entire 50,000 shares of stock, being the total capitalization of the con-pany, were turned over to the Custodian and he took control of the business.

As to American Metal Co.—In 1917 on the last increase of the capital stock of the American Metal Co., the Metallgesellschaft and the other German interests allied with it (not including Henry R. Merton & Co.) who appeared as stockholders of the American Metal Co., held 34.644 shares out of the 70,000 shares of stock outstanding. the Henry R. Merton & Co. and the interests allied with it held 16.736 shares. and the balance of 18,620 shares were held by Americans. The Americans were at this time in control of the board of directors of the company and all the officers were American.

The Alien Property Custodian demanded and received all of said 34,644 shares of stock owned by Germans, and appointed 5 out of the 15 directors of the company to represent him in the conduct of the affairs of the corporation.

In dealing with the German interests in the American Metal Co., L. Vogelstein & Co., and Beer. Sondheimer & Co., the Alien Property Custodian sought, not only to take possession of all such alien property, but also to eliminate as far as possible for all time German interests and German influences which existed and had been exercised in this country through the control of these three companies. and it is believed that the disposition made by the Custodian of the German interests in these companies has been such as to effectually eliminate all present and, it is hoped, future German control in the metal market and the metal industry of this country.

The Disposition of Property by the Custodian

As to Beer, Sondheimer & Co.—The business of Beer. Sondheimer & Co. is in process of liquidation. This includes not only the corporation Beer. Sondheimer & Co.. but also its subsidiaries. the National Zinc Co.. the Norfolk Smelting Co.. and the Cuba Copper Leasing Company.

When the Custodian took over the business of Beer. Sondheimer & Co. he placed it in control of a board of directors designated by him. Elkan and Frohnknecht maintaining that they owned all the stock of the corporation, filed a claim therefor. and thereafter brought suits to recover the same. These suits. however. have been withdrawn. and the Custodian through said board of directors is proceeding to liquidate the company. and as soon as the business has been liquidated the corporation itself will be dissolved, and Beer. Sondheimer & Co. will entirely have disappeared as a factor in the zinc and copper situation both in the purchase and sale of ores and in the control of mines and smelters. As pointed out above, the Frankfort firm of Beer. Sondheimer & Co. was a stockholder in the Minerals Separation Companies. In 1913 the Frankfort firm transferred to its American branch its interest in this stock. and when the American Minerals Separation was formed in 1916 under the name of Minerals Separation North American Corporation the stockholders of the predecessor. British Minerals Separation Co.. became entitled to exchange their shares for the stock of the new company upon the basis of one share of the old stock for two of the new. Thus Beer. Sondheimer & Co. became entitled to receive 65,230 shares of the stock of Minerals Separation North American Corporation. In addition to this amount of stock. Beer. Sondheimer & Co. had received from Minerals Separation North American Corporation 35,000 shares of stock as a consideration for the cancellation of the exclusive agency of Beer. Sondheimer & Co. theretofore granted by the British Minerals Separation Co., thus giving to Beer. Sondheimer & Co. a total of over 100,000 shares of the stock of Minerals Separation North American Corporation out of a total issue of 500,000 shares. The Custodian took over all of said 100,000 shares (in form of voting trust certificates) as property of Beer. Sondheimer & Co.. of Frankfort. This stock will likewise be disposed of by the Custodian and will go into American hands. Beer, Sondheimer & Co.'s control over the important flotation process has been destroyed.

As to Vogelstein & Co.—As in the case of Beer, Sondheimer & Co., when the Custodian took over the business of L. Vogelstein & Co.. he placed in control thereof a board of directors designated by him. Subsequent investigation by the Custodian disclosed that Vogelstein. who was a naturalized American citizen, had a preponderating interest in the assets of the corporation, and inasmuch as it has as yet been impossible to obtain from Aron Hirsch & Sohn an accounting so as to determine that concern's exact interest in the assets of L. Vogelstein & Co.. an arrangement has been perfected between the Custodian and Vogelstein whereby all of the stock of the corporation has been put into a voting trust for a period of five years. the Custodian naming two of the three voting trustees. Thus the control of the corporation for the next five years will be in the hands of trustees appointed by the Alien Property Custodian. Vogelstein has agreed not to resume his relations with the Germans during this period of five years and to conduct the business of the corporation as a purely American concern. The voting trust certificates have been made assignable only to Americans. Vogelstein has agreed to pay to the Custodian $1,668,671.49. being the amount of the apparent indebtedness from him to the Hirsches as of April 30. 1916, and has agreed to pay to the Custodian all additional moneys that may be found to be due to the Hirsches upon a final accounting which is to be had within six months after the declaration of peace. Thus circumscribed and guarded. the control of the business has been turned back to Vogelstein. the Custodian retaining two out of the five places on the board of directors as long as the Custodian may have any interest in the business.

As to American Metal Co.—Soon after the trading-with-the-enemy Act became a law. the Americans in control of the American Metal Co.. not only promptly filed the report required by the act and disclosed therein the German ownership of about 49% of the stock of the company. but offered to co-operate with the Custodian in any direction looking to the elimination of the German

interests. An investigation of the affairs of the company was courted and at the instance of the War Trade Board, such an investigation was made and subsequently the Alien Property Custodian likewise made an investigation of his own. The officers of the company heartily co-operated with the Alien Property Custodian, which resulted in the first instance in the transfer to the Custodian of the stock belonging to the Germans. The Custodian was satisfied with the good faith of the management of the corporation and, therefore, designated but five out of the 15 directors of the company.

By agreement between the Alien Property Custodian and the American stockholders, together controlling 53,-264 shares (out of 70,000 shares outstanding) all of said stock has been placed in a voting trust for a period of five years. The Alien Property Custodian is entitled to receive voting trust certificates representing the 34,644 shares of stock formerly held by enemy-aliens. It is his purpose to offer these certificates for sale to the American public at public auction.

The voting-trust agreement provides that the Alien Property Custodian shall appoint all five of the voting trustees. He has already appointed three trustees, who are now in actual control of the management and policy of the company. The trustees are Joseph F. Guffey, Henry Morgenthau, and Berthold Hochschild. Mr. Hochschild is one of the founders of the company and has been chairman of the board of directors for several years. The Alien Property Custodian will appoint the other two trustees after he shall have sold the voting trust certificates held by him.

The policy of the Alien Property Custodian to sell only to Americans will be strictly adhered to in this instance and none of the voting trust certificates will be permitted to go into any but American ownership. The immediate result is that 76% of the stock of the company will be owned by American citizens. The Alien Property Custodian is in correspondence with the British authorities with a view to the deposit under the voting-trust agreement of the 16,736 shares held by Henry R. Merton & Co. and its allied interests. It is hoped that such action will be taken in the near future. When this has been done, the Alien Property Custodian believes that all German ownership and influence will be effectually eliminated from the company.

The Result

To summarize the result of the activities of the Alien Property Custodian in so far as they affect German interests and German influences in the American metal market, it may be said that finding those interests and influences centred in three well-defined corporations, American in name but all controlled by the German metal triumvirate, the activities of which three corporations were not confined solely to the United States but penetrated into Mexico and South America, owning mines, smelters, refineries, oil concessions, railways, dealing in every known metal, doing a business which annually ran into hundreds of millions of dollars, he has succeeded in thoroughly Americanizing two of these concerns and liquidating the third, thereby entirely eliminating German influences in our metal markets and our metal industry.

The German metal octopus had spread his tentacles across the ocean and over the United States into Mexico and South America, but for the present surely, and for all time it is hoped, he has been driven back and a wall of Americanism erected which, it is hoped, he will never be able again to scale.

Pyrite and Sulphuric Acid

By R. R. HORNOR and A. E. WELLS

*Pyrite. As a result of further curtailment in acid manufacture the demand for pyrite and sulphur is not active. Many of the large consumers still have sufficient stocks on hand to take care of their immediate needs, consequently they are not disposed to make contracts for new material, preferring to wait until conditions are more settled. The producer, therefore, is confronted by a restricted demand, and finds it difficult to dispose of his product unless he happens to hold long-term contracts, providing for his entire output. It is thought by those who have an intimate knowledge of the industry that conditions will improve speedily, and within the next two or three months there should be a brisk demand for both pyrite and sulphur. The outlook in some of the industries that use large quantities of sulphuric acid, particularly oil and steel, is encouraging.

Sulphuric Acid. There is little demand for acid, and in spite of the fact that production has been greatly curtailed, there are heavy stocks on hand. Consumers of acid, knowing that the stocks are heavy, are not coming into the market, preferring to wait till the acid is offered. Producers are striving to maintain the price to at least equal to the costs, and are curtailing production to prevent a larger surplus being made. In the Mississippi valley where there is a large production of by-product acid, the price of this is lower than in the East.

The recent sale of acid at the plant of the Aetna Explosives Co. by the French government had a rather disturbing effect on the market, even though the purchaser stated that the goods purchased would not be offered for sale. The average price of 66°B. acid in the New York district is $18 per ton.

Some export business, especially to South America, is being done, and it is hoped that this may help to relieve the congestion of acid in the domestic market. It was hoped that the congestion would be relieved to some extent by the exportation of super-phosphate to Europe, but owing to various reasons, the amount of this fertilizer shipped has been below expectations.

In the suit of the Union Sulphur Co. v. the Freeport Sulphur Co., the U. S. Circuit Court held that the Frasch patent lacked inventive substance.

---

*Abstract from March report of U. S. Bureau of Mines..

Leaching of Oxidized Copper Ores With Ferric Chloride

By R. W. PERRY

INTRODUCTION. Numerous attempts to leach both oxidized and sulphide ores of copper by use of a solution of ferric chloride have been made, with regeneration of the solution after precipitating the copper on iron, either by the oxidizing action of chlorine, oxygen, or electricity.

The only one that ever went beyond the experimental stage was the Doetch process, applied to heap-leaching at Rio Tinto, where the solution was regenerated by chlorine, formed by heating ferrous sulphate and salt in a reverberatory furnace. I am not aware of any serious attempt having been made to use oxygen to regenerate ferric chloride, but there should be no serious difficulty beyond the amount of air required, as shown in the regeneration of ferric sulphate at Cananea and the great loss of the solvent by the precipitation of basic chlorides and oxy-chlorides. As will be seen later, this regeneration is continuous if the pulp is agitated in a ferrous chloride solution, and the ultimate extraction will probably be the same with a ferrous chloride solution with agitation as with a ferric chloride solution.

Ferrous chloride was successfully used as a solvent at Ore Knob, in North Carolina. Under the conditions of applying the solvent there, more or less ferric chloride must have been formed, if only momentarily. The Slater process as practised at Winona, in Michigan, depended upon the oxidation of ferrous chloride, by chlorine produced by the electrolysis of salt carried in the same solution.

The Walker River Copper Co. of Yerington, Nevada, has been experimenting with a process in which the regeneration of ferric chloride is caused by the precipitation, by electricity, of part of the iron in a ferrous chloride solution, with a corresponding regeneration of ferric chloride. The information concerning this process, as here published, has been taken from the operation of this company's experimental mill at Yerington, and supplementary laboratory work and small-scale tests, made while I was chemist there.

CHEMISTRY. The process* is based on the following generally accepted chemical reaction:

1. $3CuO + 2FeCl_3 + 3H_2O = 3CuCl_2 + 2Fe(OH)_3$
2. $3CuCl_2 + 3Fe = 3Cu + 3FeCl_2$
3. $3FeCl_2 + \text{Electricity} = Fe + 2FeCl_3$

In the first equation, the solution of the copper is accompanied by the formation of varying amounts of ferrous chloride and basic chlorides in a neutral solution. Owing to the hydrolysis of the ferric chloride solution, there is no neutral solution of ferric chloride, and the term as used here means a solution containing no free acid beyond that formed by the hydrolysis of the ferric chloride itself. The reactions show a complete regeneration of the solvent and also a production of one-third the iron necessary to precipitate the dissolved copper. Two to three per cent of salt was carried in a solution to increase the resistance of the electrolyte and to hold the cuprous chloride in solution, but no cuprous chloride can be formed while ferric chloride is present.

THE ORE treated was completely oxidized, no sulphides being present, in an altered monzonite gangue. The copper was present principally as malachite, accompanied with about 0.3% of cuprite, and some silicate. An incomplete analysis of the ore gave the following composition:

	%		%
Insoluble	63.0	CaO	0.7
Alumina	10.5	MgO	1.3
Iron	6.0	Ag	0.1 oz

A very small amount of the lime is present as calcium carbonate, due to atmospheric action near the surface, but the greater part is a constituent of the feldspars and is not affected by either ferric chloride or dilute sulphuric acid.

THE MILL. The accompanying flow-sheet shows the arrangement of the mill. The ore was crushed to pass a 20-mesh screen and was agitated for seven hours in a weak ferric chloride solution, at a temperature of 70°C., there being a continuous overflow of slime from the first agitator to the thickener, the overflow from which went alternately to each of two settling-tanks, from which it was by-passed to the pregnant-solution vat, or drawn through the leaves of the Moore filter to clarify it when necessary. At the temperature employed, the slime and the ferric hydrate formed during the solution of the copper, settled readily, and it was necessary to filter only a small part of the solution. The underflow from the Dorr thickener went to the Moore filter, where it was washed and discharged, the resulting solution going from a montejus to the pregnant-solution vat.

The copper-bearing solution was pumped from the pregnant-solution vat, by a hard-rubber reciprocating pump, to two revolving drums with oak staves and mounted on trunnions, where the copper was precipitated on iron turnings and shavings, the copper being separated in two small cones, and the overflowing ferrous chloride solution, going to the catholyte-storage vat, from which it was circulated by an ordinary centrifugal pump through the electrolytic department.

The arms of the Dorr agitators were covered at the

*The patent rights of this process are owned by the Midland Ores & Patents Company.

ends, except for a narrow slat, and only a small proportion of the pulp in circulation was allowed to discharge there, most of it overflowing near the centre of the tank. The flow of pulp from one tank to another was regulated as shown in the sketch, by means of a segment of a launder inside of each agitator, occupying about one-fifth the perifery of the agitator and receiving the discharge from the ends of the arms. The discharge from the last agitator went to a Dorr three-stage classifier and washer, the overflow of slime returning by means of an air-lift to the first agitator, and the sand discharging into two 5 by 12-ft. tanks, with filter-bottoms, where the remaining soluble metal was removed with water-washes, the first wash being returned to the circulating system, the weak final washes being run to waste after precipitation on scrap-iron.

Fresh strong solution from the anolyte vat was added in a launder connecting the first and second agitators, and as its volume was small in proportion to the circulating solution and its action on the copper minerals very rapid at this point, the actual extraction was done in a weak solution. The average composition of the solution is shown in the accompanying table.

	$FeCl_2$ %	$FeCl_3$ %	
Overflow from 1st agitator	0.72	0.07	to thickener
"	0.76	0.26	
2nd "	0.81	0.15	
3rd "	0.76	0.17	
4th "	6.72	0.33	

Fresh solution was added in sufficient quantities to have enough ferric chloride for the solution of all the copper contained in the ore, according to the equation given above.

SOLUTION. It will be noted that there is more ferric chloride in the discharge from the last agitator than at any other point in the system. This is to be accounted for by the small amount of copper dissolved there, the destruction of ferric chloride being slower than its formation by the air used in agitating. In the first agitator the ferric chloride contents are reduced to a very small quantity through contact with fresh ore, the action on the larger quantity of copper present here being more rapid than the oxidizing effect of the air. The sample from the discharge of the first agitator was taken from the launder after the fresh strong solution had been added, showing the quick action of ferric chloride at this point. Table No. 2 shows the extractions obtained at different stages.

Table No. 2

Discharge from Agitator

	No. 1		No. 2		No. 3		No. 4	
Feed Copper %	Copper %	Extraction %	Copper %	Extraction %	Copper %	Extraction %	Copper %	Extraction %
4.6	1.15	75.0	0.70	83.3	0.40	91.3	0.4	91.3
3.2	0.90	71.8	0.60	81.2	0.50	84.3	0.5	84.3
3.6	1.60	55.5	1.08	70.0	0.66	81.6	0.47	81.3
3.4	1.60	52.9	1.20	64.7	0.80	76.4	0.50	85.3
2.3	0.92	60.0	0.70	69.8	0.55	76.0	0.45	80.4

The extractions in the last column were the total extractions, as there was no further action in the classifier or filter-tanks. No samples were taken regularly from the slime as the quantity produced was small. What samples were taken assayed from 0.25 to 0.3% copper, which was probably present as cuprite.

PRECIPITATION of the copper was effected on iron turnings, and the iron recovered from the electrolytic plant in two revolving drums. The solutions were heated by steam before going to the drums, and the copper precipitated in the upper drum was settled in a cone, after which the solution passed through the lower drum, where precipitation was completed. Iron was charged intermittently as required, and probably no more than 300 lb. was present in the drums at one time. Although the turnings and shavings used were rusty and covered with grease, the precipitation was complete and the total consumption of iron amounted to only 1.5 lb. per pound of copper recovered, including that from the electrolytic department.

The precipitate was very fine, but settled readily, and as first obtained assayed over 80% copper. It oxidized rapidly on drying and as shipped was of the following composition:

H_2O	1.8%	Ag	0.3 oz.
Cu	66.9%	Cl	1.8%
Fe	10.0%		

When using the copper cathodes referred to below, part of the solution was diverted from the first drum to a stripping-tank in which the cathodes with their deposit of iron were immersed and the iron removed by the action of the copper solution and some manual labor, with brushes and scrapers.

REGENERATION OF FERRIC CHLORIDE. The electrolytic regenerating plant consisted of a 25-kw. motor-generator set delivering 1000 amperes at 25 volts, driven by power from the Truckee River Power & Electric Co. with the necessary switch-boards, etc. It contained 10 cells 24 by 32 by 35 in. connected in series of five. Each cell contained 9 cathodes and 10 anodes, the anodes being carbon and enclosed in canvas diaphragms. Solution was drawn from the catholyte-vat to small distributing-tanks above the cells to which it flowed by gravity, the quantity going to the anode compartment being regulated according to the quantity of ferric chloride required by the ore undergoing treatment or the current available.

As first started, the electrolysis was completed in one cell; but it was found that the oxidation of the ferrous chloride was under better control if it was not carried to completion in the same cell, so in the latter part of the work, the anolyte flowed through the series of five cells, entering the first at the bottom of the diaphragm compartment and discharging at the top through rubber connections to the bottom of the next cell, and an incomplete oxidation allowed to occur in each cell. The catholyte circulated through each cell separately, entering at the bottom and discharging at the top to a launder returning to the catholyte-vat.

A copper screen was employed for the cathodes at the beginning, in order to get an adherent deposit of iron, with the expectation that this iron would be dissolved in the stripping-tank in contact with the copper solution. The iron deposit proved to be so adherent that, on contact with the copper solution, the surface only was affected, requiring continuous work with brushes and iron scrapers to remove it. The rough handling during this operation caused the rapid deterioration of the screens and the labor cost was excessive. Before the plant closed, cathodes of sheet-iron, both plain and galvanized, were tried, with much more satisfactory results, the iron being deposited in a soft spongy form that could be easily removed, and while the plant was not run long enough to determine the life of these cathodes, it was demonstrated that their use would be economical both as to labor and material, as they could be used in the drums for precipitating copper when too much worn to be of value as cathodes. More care would be needed to get a clean precipitation of copper before the solution was electrolyzed, and their deterioration would be caused principally by the trace of copper remaining in the electrolyte.

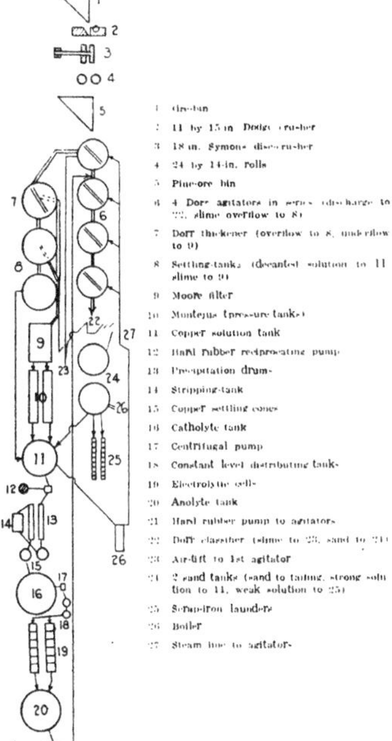

FIG. 3. FLOW-SHEET OF WALKER RIVER EXPERIMENTAL PLANT

It was found that 431 ampere-hours is required to precipitate one pound of iron, assuming a current-efficiency of 100%, of which 70% was attained in practice. In one run 2822 kw-hr. precipitated 1980 lb. of iron and regenerated the corresponding amount of ferric chloride. Since the plant was not run at full capacity at this time and there was more or less trouble with the circulation

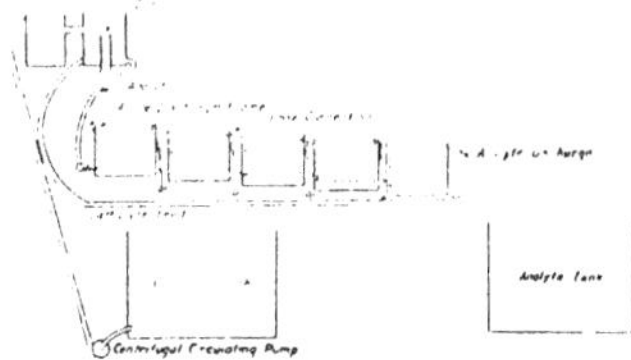

FIG. 1. DETAILS OF ELECTROLYTE CIRCULATION

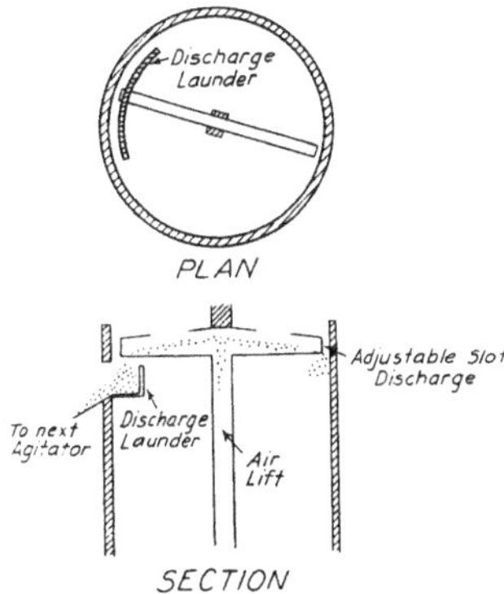

FIG. 2. SKETCH OF AGITATOR DISCHARGE

of the electrolyte, it should be easy to attain a current efficiency of 75%.

TROUBLES. At times much trouble was experienced with chlorine fume, which was apparently due to the poor circulation of the anolyte caused by the clogging of the connections to the cells. Unless hydrochloric acid to the extent of several hundred pounds per day was used in the catholyte, a slimy gelatinous precipitate of ferrous hydrate formed, becoming very troublesome in the small connections. The formation of this precipitate may have been caused by the decomposition of the salt with a production of sodium hydrate.

One of the principal troubles in operating was due to the bending of the thin cathodes, so that they touched the diaphragms in places and the iron deposit adhered to the canvas, not only causing a short circuit at this place, but also tearing the canvas when the cathode was removed. The life of the diaphragms was not determined, but the canvas showed little deterioration when the plant was operating normally. The trouble caused by the bending of the cathodes could have been easily remedied by increasing the distance between the electrodes to 2 or 2½ inches without causing any material loss of current-efficiency. The clogging of the connections could have been easily avoided by making some changes in them. At the time the plant closed, steps were being taken to make both these changes. There was no difficulty in securing a complete oxidation of the ferrous chloride in the anolyte, but on account of the danger of chlorine fume, when the oxidation was carried to completeness, owing to the irregularity of circulation, some ferrous chloride was generally allowed to remain unoxidized. Some typical analyses of the anolyte and catholyte are given.

	$FeCl_2$ %	$FeCl_3$ %	NaCl %
Anolyte	0.02	2.46	2.08
	0.80	1.60	2.00
	0.40	2.10	1.94
	0.50	1.90	1.90
Catholyte	2.48	0.08	2.24
"	2.49	0.10	2.32
	2.25	0.03	2.22
	2.60	0.02	2.31

The catholyte was circulated rapidly and, of course, in much greater volume than the anolyte.

PERCOLATION TESTS. A large number of tests were made on 10 kilogramme lots in the laboratory by percolation at different temperatures, and the results obtained are here tabulated.

Test	Mesh of ore between	Degrees C.	Hours	Head Copper %	Tail Copper %	Extraction %
1	-10 to +40	10	35	3.28	0.80	76
2	"	17	30	3.28	0.60	82
3	"	22	30	3.28	0.42	87
4	"	14	73	3.22	0.60	81
5	"	22	119	3.22	0.48	85
6	Proscreened	22	60	3.30	0.54	85
7	-4 to +20	49	44	2.70	2.02	25
8	"	16	242	2.70	0.54	80
9	-30 to +100	12	93	3.10	0.55	82
10	"	22	93	3.10	0.44	86
11	-20 to +80	15	158	3.05	0.38	87

A screen-analysis of tests No. 6 and 10, with copper contents of headings and tailings, are here given.

Mesh	No. 6 Head	Copper, %	No. 6 Tail	Copper, %	No. 10 Head	Copper, %	No. 10 Tail	Copper, %
+16	0.24	3.62	0.25	1.75	...	...	...	...
+20	12.50	2.70	12.25	0.72	...	...	...	...
+30	31.25	2.96	30.20	0.58	37.3	2.90	37.3	0.50
+40	13.76	3.04	15.05	0.65	27.0	3.05	25.0	0.36
+60			...	...	11.6	...	11.6	0.36
80	...	...	...	...			16.8	0.30
100	21.25	3.22	23.15	0.58	35.7	3.25	9.3	0.58
-100	21.25	4.16	18.50	0.52	...	...	...	...

The object in separating the different sizes in these tests was to avoid the possibility of the charge becoming clogged with the ferric hydrate precipitate, and it was also the intention to utilize the present experimental plant in connection with the leaching-plant if the experiments proved successful. Charge No. 6 run on unscreened ore proved that this clogging would take place on a charge of this character, because at the end of 60 hours, while a good extraction had been obtained, percolation had slowed down to an appreciable extent, and if this took place in a shallow charge, it was sure to be worse in a charge on any depth.

The variations in the extraction proved that as good work could be done with cold solutions as at higher temperatures, with a longer contact, and the loss of ferric chloride was considerably lower at the low temperatures.

The loss of ferric chloride in these tests was 8 to 12 pounds per ton as against a loss of 20 pounds at a temperature of 70°C. Treatment of the tailing from several of these tests with a strong solution of ferric chloride at just below the boiling-point reduced the copper contents to 0.3%, which was assumed to be the lowest obtainable on this ore with ferric chloride.

Solutions of three strengths were employed in these tests, as it was thought advisable to use a comparatively weak solution on the fresh ore in order to destroy the last trace of ferric chloride in the solution and finish with a strong solution to obtain the highest extraction. The use of a strong solution to increase the extraction was not found necessary, as a weak solution would do the same work.

Table No. 3 is a record of an average run, showing analyses of the solutions used at different times of contact.

Table No. 3

		Copper, %
Test No. 10. +30 mesh to +100.	Head	3.10
	Tail	0.44

10 kg. ore used.
14 litres solution of each strength used.

	$FeCl_2$, %	$FeCl_3$, %	Cu, %
1st solution	0.79	1.45	1.38
After 9 hours contact	0.77	0.15	2.08
" 13 " "	0.68	0.00	2.29
" 19 " "	0.66	0.00	2.41
" 22 " "	0.58	0.00	2.47
2nd solution	0.79	3.33	0.20
After 12 hours contact	0.65	2.05	1.05
" 36 " "	0.65	1.85	1.22
" 60 " "	0.76	1.65	1.38
" 76 " "	0.76	1.74	1.50
" 80 " "	0.76	1.74	1.52
3rd solution	0.60	4.12	0.20
After 24 hours contact	0.77	3.97	0.44
" 48 " "	0.79	3.97	0.52
" 96 " "	1.08	4.37	0.68

This test differs from regular test No. 10 in that each solution was allowed to act for a longer length of time than necessary, as the same extraction was obtained in test No. 10 in 93 hours total contact with the three solutions. The increase in copper contents of the solutions at the end being only apparent gains, due to the evaporation of the solution. It will be noted that there is considerable solution of copper by the ferrous chloride in the first solution after the ferric chloride is destroyed. There is also an apparent gain in ferric chloride in the last solution, due to the solution of ferric hydrate by strong ferric chloride. In some tests this increase was considerable.

Several tests were run with the addition of hydrochloric acid to prevent the precipitation of basic salts, but were not successful, unless sufficient acid was used to make the process an acid leaching one, as the acid was consumed by the copper minerals or dissolved the precipitate of ferric hydrate and became neutral.

Difficulty was experienced in determining the free acid in these solutions. The method used was to precipitate the iron and copper with mono-sodium phosphate and titrate the acid with sodium hydroxide solution, using methyl orange for the indicator. This gave good results on straight ferric chloride solutions, but was only accurate to 0.2% of the solutions in use. It was finally discovered that the copper in the tailing could be reduced to 0.1% by a subsequent treatment with hydrochloric acid if the ferric hydrate precipitate was removed by a preliminary wash and agitation. The use of 60 lb. of commercial hydrochloric acid per ton was sufficient for the solution of 8 to 10 lb. of copper in the tailing after removing the ferric hydrate. This was best added in one strong solution which was washed out after a few hours contact. If this same amount of acid was added without removing the ferric hydrate, the copper contents were reduced to 0.2%, or 4 lb. per ton. In this case the tailing in the upper part of the tank showed a much higher extraction than the lower part. As the removal of the ferric hydrate would require an extra handling and classification, it would probably not be desirable to do this in practice for the two pounds of copper that could be recovered. Since the addition of considerable quantities of hydrochloric acid is required to make up the loss of ferric chloride, incurred in treatment, it would be best to add it at this point on account of the extra recovery.

It has been estimated by manufacturers that commercial hydrochloric acid can be manufactured under local conditions, giving credit for the sodium hydroxide produced, at past prices for half a cent per pound, so the cost for solvents at these prices would only amount to 30 cents per ton of ore treated.

Loss of Ferric Chloride. This loss is caused in several ways. (1) There is some loss by volatilization at high temperatures. (2) $CaCO_3$ and $MgCO_3$ cause a loss of approximately four pounds in the treatment of this ore, and, of course, ores carrying any appreciable amount of these carbonates cannot be treated by this solvent, as it attacks them very energetically. (3) There is supposed to be some formation of oxychlorides by the action of air used in agitation on ferrous chloride. (4) The main cause of the loss is the formation of basic chlorides; while little is known concerning their formation, it has been noted by others. Sims and Ralston, in their article in 'Metallurgical and Chemical Engineering', October 1, 1916, entitled 'Electrolytic Recovery of Lead from Brines', offer this explanation of the non-accumulation of iron in the cyclic leaching of lead ores: "Iron builds up slowly in the solution with each cycle, until it reaches the neighborhood of 1½%, when it seems to approach equilibrium. As an amount of iron (one pound for three pounds of lead precipitated) equivalent to the amount of lead precipitated enters the solution during each electrolysis, then iron must also be thrown out of solution during each cycle. Analysis before and after a leach shows that it is left in the ore. As the leaching solution, although acid at the start, becomes neutral before the end of each agitation with the ore, the iron is probably hydrolyzed to either the hydroxide or to a basic chloride. When the electrolysis of the solution has been completed most of the iron is present as ferrous chloride, and it is obviously only the ferric iron that is precipitated. However it is possible in a neutral solution for the ferrous chloride to oxidize to a basic ferric chloride."

When ferrous and ferric chlorides are heated together in the same solution, some hydroxides or basic chloride separates, but the amount is not large, although the loss from this reaction might be considerable if continuous as in the operation of a plant. As explained above, the loss of iron by hydrolysis could not explain the loss of ferric chloride in this process, since the hydrochloric acid would become available for the solution of the copper and on completion of the cycle, would appear again as ferric chloride, and there would be no apparent loss of iron. Therefore the precipitation of basic chlorides would seem to be the only explanation for this loss. In the operation of the plant some 20 lb. of salt was lost per ton of ore.

Application of the Process. Further experimentation with the process was abandoned by the Walker River Copper Co. because the ore under consideration was so well adapted to leaching with sulphuric acid, which process could be used with a much simpler mill arrangement.

Any form of mill using the ferric chloride process would require the separation of the fine and coarse material and the treatment of the fine by agitation, since percolation of a fine charge would be stopped by the precipitation of ferric hydrate. Heat would also be required during agitation since the precipitate of ferric hydrate would impede filtration unless heated to 100°F. Of course, this extra expense would not be prohibitive on account of the small quantity of material agitated, but the actual operation of the plant would be more complicated and require greater attention.

This process, like the sulphuric acid process, cannot be employed on ores containing any amount of lime as carbonate on account of the consumption of the solvent. It would seem to be well adapted to the treatment of ores which show a high consumption of sulphuric acid due to the easy solubility of iron and aluminum minerals, and might prove valuable in treating mixed sulphide and oxide ores containing silver, as ferric sulphide in hot solutions is a good solvent of silver and copper sulphides.

In any case a supply of cheap hydrochloric acid would be a necessity, and on account of the difficulties of transportation and the small percentage of hydrochloric acid in the commercial acid, it would have to be manufactured at the plant. A fairly cheap supply of salt is available in many parts of the west, as at Salt Lake, and western Nevada or Kansas salt could be secured for Colorado and New Mexico at rates that would allow its use. With power at one cent per kilowatt-hour and making allowances for the sale of the sodium hydroxide produced, commercial acid should be produced for less than one cent per pound. However, anyone contemplating this method should proceed with caution, as the cost of the acid would depend primarily on the market for sodium hydroxide. With power at 1 cent per kw-hr. an acid at one cent per pound, the cost of solvents, regenerating solution, and iron for precipitating copper would amount to about $1 per ton on an ore carrying 2.5% copper and using 60 lb. of commercial acid to replace the ferric chloride lost.

Numerous petty annoyances would be encountered in the use of diaphragms, but I don't think they be serious, and the process could undoubtedly be made use of in localities where sulphuric acid was not available.

Items From the Annual Report of the Phelps Dodge Corporation

The 43-page report of the Phelps Dodge Corporation, covering the year 1918, contains the following notes:

The Copper Queen reduction works at Douglas treated a total of 1,311,742 tons of ores, concentrates, and other materials, yielding 192,063,212 lb. of copper, 32,709 oz. of gold, and 2,307,307 oz. of silver, a slight increase over the quantities in 1917. A copper-casting furnace was erected, also a new superheater and a coal-pulverizing plant for use on one reverberatory furnace. These works employed 1531 men.

The mill at the Detroit mine at Morenci treated 449,990 tons of ore assaying 1.91% copper. The concentrate —57,719 tons—carried 11.32% copper, and the ratio of concentration was 7.796 : 1. The saving, the average by four methods of calculations, was 76.22%. Additions were made to the flotation department, and by substituting electric motors for gas-engine drive a more dependable and economical power was obtained. This was done by erecting two Diesel engines to drive generators. The concentrator employed 112 men, and the smelter, where 154,216 tons of charge was reduced, 102 men.

At the Burro Mountain mine in New Mexico, the cost of ore extraction was reduced by the better condition of stopes and to increased drawing from the broken ore-reserves in the shrinkage-stopes. The caving system is employed successfully.

The mill treated 585,083 tons of 1.928% copper ore. This carried 3.094% moisture. The concentrate produced amounted to 53,146 tons, assaying 14.875% copper, and the ratio of concentration was 11.009 : 1. As the ore was of lower grade than in 1917, and in a more advanced stage of oxidation, the saving dropped from 72.301 to 70.065%. The daily tonnage was 1710, using 737 gallons of fresh water per ton, and 10.159 kw-hr. of power per ton milled. The single-unit flotation machines were replaced by those of three units, improving recovery. Experiments show that fine grinding in closed-circuit, more and improved flotation apparatus, and additional tables below the flotation units, will give a better saving, so plans for this object are in preparation. The leaching-beds at the mine were irrigated intermittently during 1918, dissolving 8.9% of the copper in the ore, making 33.8% in two years. This work has given valuable data as to the possibilities of the process.

Four Diesel engines are now available in the power-plant and give excellent service. The Diesel compressor was entirely satisfactory.

The Stag Cañon mine at Dawson, New Mexico, supplies the Phelps Dodge smelters with coke. Last Year's output was 281,916 tons of coke from 470,924 tons of coal, a yield of 64.8%. The percentage of ash is 18.09. Edison electric safety-lamps are used in the mines.

Many improvements were made at the Moctezuma copper mine at Nacozari, in Sonora, Mexico, and development of ore was very satisfactory. The hoist and compressor plants were increased, and doors and sprinkler-apparatus were installed for protection against mine fires.

More mechanical flotation apparatus was erected at the mill, and a large pneumatic unit was being put in during February 1919. The mill treated 762,089 tons of 3.392% ore, equal to 2320 tons daily (328.5 days). General concentrates amounted to 159,246 tons, containing 12.240%, and filter (flotation) concentrates 14,882 tons, averaging 16.913% copper. The ratio of concentration was 4.377%, and recovery, by four methods of figuring, 85.575%. Water used per ton of ore was 666 gallons, and power 12.535 kw-hr. Diesel engines are now being erected in the power-plant.

The Bunker Hill mine at Tombstone, Arizona, produced 19,312 tons of ores, yielding 1335 oz. of gold, 276,007 oz. of silver, 448,616 lb. of lead, 39,209 lb. of copper, and 417 tons of manganese. The last item represented shipments to the East, but 3952 tons of manganese tailing, carrying 34,971 oz. of silver, was sent to the smelter at Douglas.

The mercantile stores of the Corporation sold goods worth $10,408,913. The net profit was 7.98%, compared with 8.42% in 1917, and 10.38% in 1916. These stores employed 644 people. The balance-sheet shows that merchandise for sale is valued at $2,622,161.

The quantity of corundum and emery mined in the United States last year was 10,139 short tons. The quantity of crude emery and corundum marketed was 8702 tons, valued, f.o.b. mines, at $95,248. The output was 45% less than in 1916 and 52% less than that in 1917. The output in those two years, however, was abnormally large, and was stimulated by the demand due to the War, which required enormous quantities of abrasives for making munitions and other articles needed for military use, and prevented the importation of foreign corundum and emery, the former chief source of supply. Though the employment of substitutes and the increase of imports in 1918 reduced the demand for the domestic abrasives the output was many times that of normal years before the war.

Montana Section of the A. I. M. & M. E.

By OLIVER E. JAGER

The Montana section of the Institute took advantage of the presence of James F. Kemp and Charles K. Leith. who are on a professional visit to Butte, to hold a special meeting at the Silver Bow Club on the evening of May 2. The meeting was a representative gathering, numbering about 100, including many ladies. The proceedings opened with a dinner, after which the chairman. Frederick Laist, introduced Professor Kemp.

He said that, as the new president of the Institute was a prominent mining geologist, he hoped that more geology would appear in the Transactions. Butte was always well to the fore with contributions of this nature. He went on to show how geologic history resembled human history. There was a placid period followed by an upheaval, of which the last four years had furnished us a good example. We had now to face a period of reconstruction. The metal markets were dull, and yet men had to be got back to work. Such problems appeal to engineers, and the present one would give ample opportunity for constructive thinking. The army life was good for a man in some ways. It was healthy; it taught discipline and respect for authority; but it must be remembered that having everything arranged for a man was bad for his mentality and for his initiative. This fact must be kept in mind when handling returned soldiers. The soldier felt that he had made a sacrifice, and that the sacrifice demanded recognition in the shape of better conditions. On the other hand, there was still a lot of virtue in the old idea of "a good day's work for a good day's pay." The United States is less affected by the War than any other country, but we have an enormous debt. It was an engineer's war, and the reconstruction is even more a work for engineers. We have seen what Kultur meant—absolute selfishness on the part of one nation. This philosophy was now exploded. In the reconstruction we shall need the idealism of Josiah Royce, tempered by the pragmatism of William James. Even if we cannot evolve a perfect set of conditions at first, let us, at least, set up some ideals and see how they work, or why they don't work.

The next speaker was Mr. Leith. He showed how international relations were bound up with mineral problems. His speech was also instructive in showing how the lack of information was hampering the Peace Conference. It was not the fault of the Conference that it has moved so slowly; it could not move any faster on account of the magnitude of the problems involved, and of their far-reaching and interacting effects. Mr. Leith stated that one-third the world's minerals moved between international boundaries. The War had shown how little we really knew of mineral deposits, especially with respect to their geographic positions. The speaker had first realized the importance of minerals in international relations when he was employed on the Shipping Board, which was cutting down shipping space to make room for troops. This Board was working in conjunction with the War Industries Board and the War Trade Board. Information on many problems was hard to get, such as, for instance, on the complete movements of copper, including the final destination of the metal, especially with reference to Germany. Data of the kind required were non-existent, as they had never before been needed. Engineers from all parts were called in to help, and the big corporations assisted in every way. By the time the Armistice was signed a world balance-sheet had been prepared of all the great commodities, showing consumption, routes followed, tonnages, and other main facts. The result of this work was a shifting of interests in the mineral industry. The production of some minerals was stimulated, of others was discouraged. Mineral questions being expected at the Peace Conference, especially in reference to embargoes and indemnities, he went to Paris with his data. There he saw the mineral question in its international aspect. The American army had begun an independent appraisal of the war damages; 350 engineers were assembled to assess the amount of the devastations. The speaker helped to correlate the reports of these men on the damage to mineral industries. The damage to the coalfields of Northern France was as severe as had been reported, though a certain amount of coal will be produced in the near future. The methods of appraisal used by the French were different from those used by the Americans, but misunderstanding had given way to mutual appreciation. The destruction of the Belgian blast-furnaces and zinc-works developed an interesting problem. Supposing these zinc-works to be replaced, what about the ore-supply to operate them? Zinc ore from Broken Hill used to go to Belgium. It will now be deflected to England for some time to come. This fact was kept in mind when appraising the damage, and goes to show how complicated the whole affair was. Damage to the iron mines of Briey was not so great, as the Germans occupied them till the last moment, and did not have time to wreck them. The amount of ore extracted was not as great as was supposed. The open-pit mines of Lorraine were more energetically worked. In considering the indemnity that Germany should pay, many mineral questions came in. It was thought desirable to assess the value of the ore deposits in Alsace Lorraine, as it might be desired to allow this value to figure as part of the indemnity, a parallel case being in 1870, when Germany allowed France to subtract the value of the railroads taken from her. In Alsace there are potash deposits which were mined by the Germans. The French are making big plans to develop these deposits, so as to be independent of Stassfurt. In all this estimating, the values estimated by various engineers varied over a tremendous range—up to 3000% in some cases. The German colonies also have mineral deposits. These had to be valued in order to complete the information necessary to show whether these colonies should be considered as assets or as liabilities. Some were found to be in the latter class. Mineral problems also complicated the boundary questions. By moving a boundary a valuable mineral deposit might change its nationality, as in Poland. There was hardly a boundary question that did not involve a mineral deposit. Another group of questions involving minerals was that of embargoes, and how the excess of any mineral should be disposed of. Many embargoes have been established. The French have shut out practically all foreign materials, including minerals. England is not quite so drastic, but has developed a system of licenses to regulate imports. Many other nations had embargo problems. It was difficult to get the information necessary for solving such problems, as the information obtainable was of a local character only. These local information-sheets had to be combined to form data of international character. Till the world is readjusted to approximately normal trade conditions, these problems will come up. The Peace Conference is trying to settle things with the machinery at hand, but that machinery is inadequate. The far-reaching nature of the various problems calls for information of such gigantic scope as to be unobtainable under present conditions. More than half the time of the delegates in Paris was spent on these commercial problems. The French view the League of Nations plan from a material or commercial aspect, while England is partly ideal and partly practical. An international economic commission is in process of formation. This will consider general economic problems as they affect various countries. The degree of economic control that the Allied countries can exert will determine largely what indemnity Germany can pay. Minerals have been proposed as part of the indemnity; for example, Germany is to supply so many tons of coal per annum; but the problem has too many variables to be easily solved. The questions now before the Peace Conference are new and great, too great, in fact, for the present machinery to handle, so the men considering them are looking for guidance. He suggested that the engineers of this country should study the situation so as to be able to supply some of the information required. Some work is already being done to get this information. He thought that the technical journals could help.

Mrs. Kemp, who accompanied her husband in order to take the opportunity of urging on the Butte ladies the formation of a local section of the Woman' Auxiliary, was next introduced. She made a short but interesting speech in which she told how, when the United States entered the War, the women relatives of the members of the A. I. M. & M. E. got together to help the men who were going overseas. They raised money and clothing; they knitted; they adopted orphans, and did Red Cross work. She went on to describe the organization, and how it is governed. Now that there was no more need of war work, whither should their energies be directed? The answer was still the same: "help the men"; but help them at home, in the mines and in the smelters. There was plenty to do. Primarily they should combat ignorance. Till labor felt the need of capital as capital feels the need of labor, there would always be trouble. In this country eight and a half million persons over 10 years of age cannot read English, and five and a half million of these cannot read any language. Education must Americanize these illiterates, or they will some day be voting without knowing what they vote about. They must be taught to read a newspaper, and they must be taught our traditions, so that they eventually become part of us. The speaker thought that the women could get at the women-folk of these illiterates and so reach the children. She advocated the teaching of sewing and cookery as a means to this end. While these foreigners read a foreign language only, they may be molded to any form—mostly I. W. W.—by malcontents of their own race. Mrs. Kemp said that she hoped a Section of the Woman's Auxiliary would be formed at Butte, as there was a good field for such work. A meeting would be held on May 8 to consider the matter. There was already a Section at Anaconda. A local Section should be a valuable assistance to the men in their work. In regard to education, the night-school was doing well. She had visited the school that afternoon and was favorably impressed with what was being done.

W. E. Maddock, City Superintendent of Schools, was called on for a few words about the night-school. He said that it was organized last January to teach foreigners English, and the traditions and history of the United States. This had been attempted two years ago, but was postponed for legal reasons. This difficulty was now overcome, and the school was flourishing with an enrollment of 530, of whom 110 were women. Many had since left through unemployment, but very few—practically none—left the school for any other reason. The work was handled in three sessions, partly in the daytime and partly at night. The speaker described the work as fascinating, and stated that the pupils were earnest and enthusiastic. The movement could be written down a success. They had an exceedingly efficient corps of teachers, mostly from the public schools, who had been chosen on account of special qualifications for this work.

The Chairman made a few concluding remarks emphasizing the need of such education, and quoted an instance, that had lately come to his knowledge, of a letter in the Serbian language which was putting forward pernicious doctrines calculated to impress the ignorant.

The meeting was followed by informal conversation, the character of which indicated keen interest in the matters that had been discussed.

HOUGHTON, MICHIGAN

FURTHER CURTAILMENT.—MINE INSPECTORS MEET.

Depression in the copper industry is marked in the Lake Superior district. More companies contemplate suspension, and others on further curtailment. Such properties as the Mass Consolidated, Victoria, and White Pine in Ontonagon county, continue to operate. They are running at a loss, and while their total output of copper makes no great difference to the surplus on hand it does require a continuous and sustained drain on their treasuries, so that eventually they will have to shut-down.

Mine inspectors from every mining county in northern Michigan and safety-first experts representing every copper and iron property in the peninsula met at Houghton on April 23, 24, and 25. The meeting was arranged by B. C. Pickard of the U. S. Bureau of Mines and by F. W. Sperr, professor of mining in the Michigan College of Mines. This was the first meeting of mine inspectors ever held. The program was of great practical benefit.

LEAD, SOUTH DAKOTA

MINERAL PRODUCTION OF THE STATE DURING 1918.

According to the annual report of the State Mine Inspector, O. Ellermann, the production of gold and silver in the past year showed a decrease of $814,860 over the previous year's output. The total for 1918 was as follows:

Mine	Tons	Value
Homestake	1,628,630	$5,923,653
Trojan	107,373	530,642
Mogul-Ofer	33,750	169,975
Golden Reward	6,542	36,589
Bismarck	5,120	18,864
Miscellaneous	235	5,300
Placer	....	1,400
Total	1,781,650	$6,686,423

The shortage of labor was directly responsible for the decrease. The Golden Reward suspended operations in April. In addition to the above, the Homestake shipped tungsten ore (wolframite) valued at $281,475. The Bismarck received $2282 for ores of this class; and lessees and smaller producers received $3550, making a total tungsten production of $287,307. Of mica, 249 tons was shipped to market, valued at $10,464; 1500 tons of lithia ore, worth $82,500; 641 tons of copper ore, mostly from the Maloney Blue Lead Copper Co. near Keystone, valued at $9157; 159 tons of lead-silver ore and concentrate, valued at $6521; 916 tons of pyrite, worth $7200, from the Olaf Seim mine near Deadwood; gypsum, $45,160; coal, $39,237; kaolinite, $8000; beryl, $270; columbite, $280; and limestone and structural materials, $180,000; making the grand total for all mineral production of $7,362,520.

An average of 2049 persons was employed by the industry excluding coal mine and quarry employees. There were no fatalities.

DOUGLAS, ARIZONA

EPIDEMIC AT HILL TOP SUSPENDS WORK.—PATAGONIA AND COURTLAND DISTRICTS ACTIVITIES.—LABOR AND HIGHWAY CONSTRUCTION.

After a siege of several weeks, influenza has been routed at the Hill Top and Hill Top Extension mines in the Chiricahua mountains, and doctors and nurses who went from Douglas have returned here. Out of 50 cases at the Hill Top but two deaths occurred. However, the effect on the property was disastrous, as all work was suspended during the epidemic. R. O. Fife, the manager, decided that this was the best course. The clubhouse built recently by the company was transformed into a hospital and several miners were appointed orderlies. At the Extension, the manager, John Blumberg, was also forced to close the mine. No deaths have been reported from there. The Hill Top is a lead-silver mine, being developed by tunnels extending entirely through the mountains. A large body of ore has been opened. The owners are Kansas City people. About 75 men are employed.

One of the most important strikes known in the Patagonia district of Santa Cruz county was made recently at the Mowry mine, according to arrivals here. A new lens of high-grade silver ore has been cross-cut for more than 20 ft. and was still in rich ore when our informant left Patagonia. The ore occurs both as carbonates and sulphides. The latter is being shipped to El Paso. High-grade manganese is also being mined from a lease on the same property.

The labor surplus in the Warren district and at Douglas is said not to be showing any great increase, and steps are being taken promising to offer relief in the near future. The State Engineer, Tom Maddock, following an inspection of roadwork under way in Cochise county, stated that he intended recommending the expenditure of large sums of Federal aid funds on highways, spending dollar for dollar with the county on desiguated roads. At a meeting of prominent men from all parts of the county, held at Douglas on April 19, it was recommended that the Board of Supervisors call an election for a bond-issue of $1,000,000 to complete the highway system of the county. This is expected to be acted upon favorably by the Supervisors, who were instrumental in calling the meeting, as they desired to learn public sentiment in the matter.

Courtland, 45 miles north-west of Douglas, although a copper camp and somewhat neglected during the boom days of the industry, has shown increased activity with the fall in the price of the metal. The Great Western company, the largest operator, is developing a body of high-grade sulphide ore in its new shaft. The working-force is being increased gradually.

The lease of O. T. Smith, O. J. Smith, and Robert McKay of Johnson, on the Leadville Mining Co.'s property, includes the Freak claim and most of the original Leadville ground lying next to the Musso property. The lessees propose to sink a 200-ft. shaft, and then drive toward the Musso property to cut the extension of a high-grade orebody opened in the Musso. A 25-hp. gasoline engine has been installed. A 10 by 12-in. air-compressor is to be put in to drive drills and other machinery. Smith brothers and McKay also have leased No. 2 shaft of the Leadville company, including about 600 acres. On the 400-ft. level of this shaft considerable ore has been blocked out. Shipments are to be made at once to the Calumet & Arizona smelter at Douglas. Exploration will be the main endeavor for the present. By the fall it is believed that there will be 75 men employed. The lease operated by Peter Musso, also on part of the ground of the Leadville company, recently opened ore carrying over 8% copper, with gold and silver sufficient to pay transportation and smelting charges. Two carloads sent to Douglas recently are said to have netted more than $1000 each. Shipments are being made regularly.

TORONTO, ONTARIO

LEGISLATURE PASSES NEW MINING REGULATION.

An act amending the mining laws of the Province has been passed by the Ontario Legislature, making some important changes in the provisions to secure the safety and health of mine-workers. The extensive scale on which mining is now conducted, and the greater depth of mines, rendered the former rules as to precautions for safety entirely inadequate. The provisions now adopted are much more stringent and specific, especially regarding hoisting, providing for frequent inspections of the ropes and equipment, and the testing of the safety appliances under load conditions. The rules governing the use of electricity are based on those adopted by the U. S. Bureau of Standards. New and more detailed regulations regarding blast-furnaces are also embodied in the Act. Before it was placed on the statute book, both mine managers and labor organizations were consulted as to its provisions, which are understood to have been generally approved by all interested.

MONTERREY, MEXICO

METAL PRODUCTION AND MINES IN THE REPUBLIC.

Interesting statistics regarding the operation of mines in Mexico during 1918 are contained in a statement just issued by Leopoldo Lopez, chief of the Bureau of Mines of the Department of Industry and Commerce. The production figures cover only the first nine months of the year.

Metal	Kilogrammes	Value
Silver	1,001,331	₱65,654,571
Gold	6,185	3,244,881
Lead	70,335,620	23,800,689
Copper	55,080,286	66,096,344
Zinc	16,135,131	9,036,223
Antimony	2,208,121	2,471,147
Arsenic	901,512	....
Tin	13,537	24,638
Mercury	120,000	785,297
Tungsten	109,419	787,274
Graphite	4,178,686	668,580
Manganese	1,889,082	458,321
Molybdenite	23,761	36,038
Total		₱180,064,983

The total number of concessions in each State, and the additional number granted during 1918 follows:

State	Mines	Concessions in 1918
Aguascalientes	2,671	11
Lower California	827	28
Coahuila	814	74
Chihuahua	4,858	250
Durango	3,835	220
Guanajuato	1,233	155
Guerrero	1,024	34
Hidalgo	1,300	180
Jalisco	1,802	80
Mexico	853	4
Michoacan	632	37
Nuevo Leon	1,092	131
Oaxaca	1,610	63
Puebla	259	31
Queretaro	165	34
San Luis Potosi	707	79
Sinaloa	1,600	135
Sonora	5,090	489
Tamaulipas	147	11
Vera Cruz	67	7
Zacatecas	2,146	219
Miscellaneous	453	18
Total	33,186	2,289

The area of all claims is 1,183,437 acres, a gain of 53,357 during 1918.

TELLURIDE, COLORADO

MINING RARE MINERALS IN PARADOX VALLEY.

The comparatively newly discovered rare-mineral fields of Paradox valley are developing into an important mining region. The output of vanadium and carnotite ores has been considerable, and capital is now taking an interest in this part of the State. The only handicap to rapid development is the lack of good transportation, as the fields are at some distance from rail, and roads are in poor condition. The Primos Chemical Co. is building a larger mill to replace the 100-ton one lost by fire.

The Colorado Vanadium Co. is increasing production and is shipping ore at the rate of 30 tons per day.

The Standard Chemical Co. resumed milling on April 1 and is gradually working up to full capacity.

The W. L. Cummings Chemical Co. plans extensive development of its carnotite claims in lower San Miguel and Montrose counties. O. B. Willmarth, the rare-metal expert of Montrose, has been appointed local manager.

THE MINING SUMMARY

ALASKA

Juneau.—Alaska Gastineau in April treated 167,630 tons of ore averaging 81.3 cents per ton. The recovery was 78.47%. In March, 183,550 tons was treated. A year ago the quantity was 125,435 tons, assaying $1.148 per ton.

ARIZONA

Ajo.—New Cornelia had to suspend leaching ore last week on account of a fire at the pumping station at the main well of the water-supply system. Water was brought in by rail from Gila Bend for a while.

Kingman.—L. R. Myers and associates of Minneapolis have taken over the Middle Golconda mines and have consolidated it with the Golconda and O'Dea properties as the Highland Mining Co. A tunnel is to be driven from below Layne Springs in Todd basin to cut the veins of the Middle Golconda and Golconda at a depth of about 1000 ft. A mill is contemplated on completion of the tunnel, there being plenty of water available.

Morenci.—The old Stargo silver mine is to be re-opened by G. A. Stoneman, W. B. Harmony, C. B. Beach, and E. W. Baum of Phoenix. Previous work was to a depth of 1400 feet.

A syndicate of Arizonan men has taken over the 26 claims of the Stargo Silver Belt Mining Co. A large quantity of silver ore has been shipped from the property in the past.

Oatman.—The United Eastern company pays 7 cents per share, $95,410, on May 28. This brings the total to $1,676,-490, $422,530 of which was paid in 1919.

Prescott.—The 1600-ft. tunnel of the Black Canyon Mining Co. on Turkey creek has opened a 4-ft. vein assaying 25 oz. of silver per ton. The high-grade ore is being stacked in preparation for shipments. A mill is planned for the near future.

Tucson.—The Mineral Hill Consolidated Copper Co., in the San Xavier district, is to erect a large mill. Ore that was opened some time ago on the 340-ft. level has now been developed on the 600-ft. level. U. A. Fritschie is manager.

CALIFORNIA

Alleghany.—The El Dorado-Wisconsin Mining & Milling Co. has filed articles of incorporation with the Secretary of State at Carson, Nevada, with T. J. Flynn as president. The company has acquired the El Dorado, El Dorado Extension, and Gold Bullion claims in the Alleghany district of Sierra county. The property is equipped with a 10-stamp mill, compressor, and is operated by electric power. The mine has produced several hundred thousand dollars of gold above the present tunnel-level, from which a shaft is to be sunk.

Cerro Gordo.—The report of the Cerro Gordo Mines Co. operating in Inyo county, contains the following information: L. D. Gordon is general manager, J. C. Climo is superintendent, H. G. Rose is in charge of the mine office, and J. W. Reno is purchasing agent. Earnings in 1918 amounted to $126,794 from ore sold, plus settlements of $11,696 from 1917, sale of bonds, and cash $79,699, making a total revenue of $233,188. The cost of operation was $147,895, bonds $23,000, taxes $10,453, and No. 6 dividend $50,000, totaling $231,348. The cash balance at the end of December was $1840. Current assets total $138,005, and liabilities $8316. Development amounted to 4603 ft., costing $12.63 per foot. Production came mainly from the Newtown slope 1500 ft. north of the shaft. Driving on this vein at 700 ft. is under way, and while no ore-shoot has been found, pockets are, and possibilities are favorable. The Jefferson orebody was cut off by a fault above the 900-ft. level in 1917, and 500 ft. of exploration has failed to find it, and the search has been stopped. The output was 619 tons of zinc ore, carrying from 24.3 to 40.1%; 2166 tons of silver-lead ore, averaging 23.12 oz. silver, 21.4% lead, and 0.015 oz. gold; and 9389 tons of old slag, assaying 2.92 oz. silver and 12.27% lead. To treat the low-grade ores in the mine, an agreement was made with H. R. Layng of San Francisco to erect a mill on terms favorable to the company. A letter from Mr. Layng on April 5, 1919, states that he found concentration and flotation to give a recovery of 73% of the silver, 85% of the lead, and 28% of the zinc; but the concentrate was low-grade and excessive in zinc. A combination of concentration and volatilization is now being tried. On a basis of 50 tons daily of 7% lead and 8-oz. silver ore, the treatment cost would be $4.26 per ton, this including freight to market. If all goes well, a plant should be started at the Keeler by August, and be ready by November next.

Bishop.—The Nevada-California Electric Corporation, which has power-houses on Bishop creek, proposed plants on Baker creek, connections with lines to the extreme south

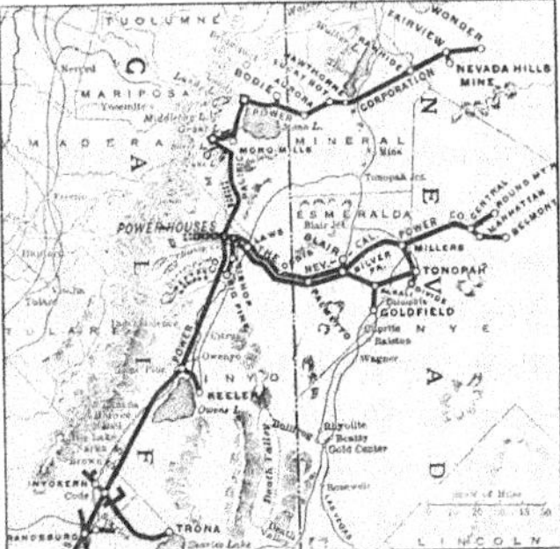

PART OF CALIFORNIA AND NEVADA, SHOWING MAIN TRANSMISSION-LINES OF THE NEVADA-CALIFORNIA ELECTRIC CORPORATION SUPPLYING MINING DISTRICTS

of California, and supplies current to the principal mining districts in Nevada, shows the following results for 1918, in comparison with the two previous years, according to the 'Commercial and Financial Chronicle' of New York:

	1918	1917	1916
Earnings from all sources	$2,158,706	$1,997,969	$1,550,775
Expenses	1,036,452	919,878	612,738
Operating profit	$1,122,254	$1,078,091	$938,037
Interest charge	635,011	549,775	463,585
Depreciation	118,553	121,318	95,370
Net earnings	$368,091	$406,998	$379,082
Adjustments to profit and loss	dr. 12,158	cr. 29,906	dr. 4,951
Discount on securities sold	dr. 50,199	dr. 17,334	dr. 9,407
Surplus	$305,734	$419,571	$364,724
Dividends	318,271	352,006	265,849
Net change in surplus	-$12,537	+$67,565	+$98,875

Crescent Mills.—The Crescent mine of the Philadelphia Exploration Co., closed since last August, has been re-opened. A. MacDonald of Boulder, Colorado, is the new superintendent; George Worthington, of the same place, is foreman; and Herbert Whiting of Quincy, California, is assayer.

Hutton.—At the Blue Ledge copper mine, in the Elliott district of Siskiyou county, near the Oregon border, the winter's accumulation of 1000 tons of sulphide ore is now being moved over the Rogue River Valley Railway and Southern Pacific at Medford, Oregon. The 34-mile haul by teams and trucks costs $10 per ton. Twenty-seven miles of standard crushed rock highway, extending to the California State line, is to be completed by the State of Oregon at a cost of $50,000. A moderate reduction in transportation costs will render available for shipment several hundred thousand tons of developed ore. Gold and silver are important metals in this ore. This district includes the Gray Eagle mines at Happy Camp, and is one of the most promising copper areas in California.

Kennett.—At the Mammoth smelter the boilermakers, machinists, electricians, and railroad men—30 in all—have demanded an increase of 50 cents per day, and a half-holiday each week. Wages at present are: machinists and boiler-makers, $5.72; electricians, $5.32; brakemen, $4.44; locomotive engineers, $5.72; firemen, $4.28; and conductors, $5.28 per 8-hour shift. According to the general manager, George Metcalf, the company is employing 600 men; but only development is being done in the Mammoth mine, while the works are smelting ore from the Balaklala mine. The mechanics went out on strike on May 12. The smelter will continue to work as long as possible.

Marigold.—The Marysville Dredging Co. lost a boat on May 10, fire starting in the transformers spreading all over the dredge. The hull was of wood, and had been operated for 8 years.

Plymouth.—The Plymouth mine in March produced 11,900 tons of ore yielding gold valued at $61,000. Operations cost $34,000, and development $10,000, leaving a profit of $17,000. On the 2450-ft. level a raise at 274 ft. north was driven 23 ft. in ore assaying $9.40 per ton across 48 inches.

San Francisco.—Details of every oilfield operation in California during the past fiscal year is briefly given in the third Annual Report of State Oil and Gas Supervisor, R. P. McLaughlin. The report has just been received from the State Printer, and copies may be obtained by addressing the State Mineralogist, Fletcher Hamilton, Ferry building, San Francisco; or by personal application to any of the branch offices of the Bureau. Besides the complete list giving the status of every well for which notice was filed with the Supervisor, the report sets forth the general conditions of all the oil-fields during the year ending June 30, 1918, such as distribution of ownership of proved oil-land and statistics of production by various fields.

COLORADO

Breckenridge.—The annual report of the Tonopah Mining Co. of Nevada, which controls the Tonopah Placers Co., operating three dredges near Breckenridge, contains the following: During 1918 the gross value of gold recovered was $282,974, but operations cost $332,902, leaving a loss of $49,928, reduced to $39,923 by sundry credits. The boats dug 3,267,307 cu. yd., averaging 8.6 cents per yard. The yield was 13,565 oz. of gold and 3345 oz. of silver.

Cripple Creek.—Gold output of this district in April was $674,715. Dividends totaled $242,000.

The Granite company is to put in a 175-hp. electric compressor at its Dillon shaft, which will become the main operating point. This shaft is 1700 ft. deep. The compressor is being moved from the Nicholls shaft of the El Paso.

The Vindicator's quarterly report states that 6781 tons of ore was shipped on company account and 4069 for lessees, from which net earnings were $100,000. There is a shortage of helpers underground.

Telluride.—In the Belmont Wagner Mining Co.'s report for the 10 months ended December 31, 1918, the following appears, written on March 1, 1919:

Preliminary work in the mine, a new crushing-plant at the St. Louis tunnel, a new aerial tram from this plant to the mill, remodeling of the old mill, a new compressor, quarters, shops, etc., were all completed and the mill started in July; but owing to labor conditions and influenza, work had to be suspended in November. During 121 days the plant operated only 22.3% of the possible time. Resumption was expected early in May of 1919. J. M. Fox is superintendent and H. F. Hillard is in charge of the mill.

MONTANA

Anaconda.—The new 525-ft. stack at the Washoe Reduction Works was connected with the furnaces on May 5. Ten of the Cottrell electric precipitators are in operation, and the remaining fifteen will be ready in six weeks. Until then the old stack will carry part of the smoke.

Butte.—The North Butte Mining Co. in 1918 made a profit of $278,545, compared with $641,126 in 1917, $2,479,595 in 1916, and $1,127,646 in 1915. Dividends were $430,000, against $1,075,000 in the previous year. The output was 20,680,695 lb. of copper, 891,157 oz. of silver, and 1375 oz. of gold, 6,000,000 lb. more than in 1917, but 4,000,000 lb. less than in 1916. The cost rose to 20.91 cents per pound from 17.35c., 15.57c., 13.12c., and 11.50c. for previous years.

The extensive development that has been carried on by the Anaconda company during the past year on the Bonanza group at the foot of Excelsior avenue has proved disappointing, and the company has decided to suspend further work, according to the Anaconda 'Standard'. John Berkin was superintendent. The pumps have been moved at the Bonanza from the 1000-ft. level, and the workings will be allowed to fill to 500-ft., where the east drift will be driven farther with the hope of picking up the Star West vein, which in the earlier days was a profitable ore producer. To date more than 5000 ft. of work has been done in the Bonanza, both the north vein and the Star West fissure having been cut and driven upon. The former is the 'north fork' of the Black Chief lode, which farther to the east in the Emma claim has been productive of both silver and manganese ores. The openings on both the 500 and 1000-ft. levels disclosed small streaks of silver-zinc ores with some pink manganese, but no deposits of commercial size or quality.

The south-eastern section has proved a disappointment to several large undertakings. The Butte & Superior company several months ago suspended work on a large group lying farther to the west on the Germania group of veins, after expending a large sum. Farther west and northerly, work on the Orphan Girl is reported to have resulted better and a deposit has recently started production for the Anaconda company. William Creden during the past year expended a large sum in development on a group lying between the Germania and the Bonanza groups, which also was disappointing. Both the Bonanza group and the Germania operations were carried on under working options, and the properties revert to the owners.

Three men were killed at the Rarus mine on May 2. The brakes refused to work, and before the hoist could be stopped the cages were drawn into the sheaves.

Troy.—Activity in this district is increasing, the present operators being the Snowstorm, producing 6000 tons of ore monthly, the Rambler, Iron Mask, Federal, and Liberty, all on silver-lead-zinc ore.

NEVADA

Divide.—The Belcher Divide, Belcher Extension, and Victory Divide properties have been optioned to George Wingfield and New York people.

Reserves in the Tonopah Divide mine are stated to be over 415,000 tons averaging $35 per ton.

Field.—From February 15 to April 1 the Goldfield Development Co. shipped 1030 tons of ore valued at $21,246, according to A. I. D'Arcy, the general manager. Shipments were made during this period by the company and lessees. Expenses were heavy, owing to preparations for mining on a large scale; but the returns were profitable. The report for April, which should be ready on May 15, will show a great increase in the gross value of ore shipped, as one carload worth $8600 was sent out during that month, and a number of other good lots were made. This ore was extracted by lessees in the Combination mine. Construction of a 500-ton ore-bin has been started at the shaft in Combination Fraction ground, which will be made the main working shaft of the Development company for hoisting ore from the Combination. The tonnage in the Red Top is estimated at 200,000, assaying from $7 to $8 per ton. The Red Top is being prepared for production, and sampling continues there and in the Combination.

The Florence Divide Mining Co., owning claims in the Divide district, has purchased the Witt-Brandon-Taylor-Mechlin lease on the Red King claim of the Florence Goldfield for $60,000, partly in cash and partly in shares of the Florence Divide. The lease will expire on January 1, 1920. The last four carloads of ore shipped averaged $60 per ton.

Klondyke.—The boom at Divide has spread to this old district, in that attention is being given to several deposits by newly-organized companies.

Pioche.—The Combined Metals Co. is to raise the sum of $300,000, to be spent on a treatment plant. According to the manager, E. S. Snyder of Salt Lake City, there is 150,000 tons of ore averaging 0.043 oz. gold, 8.26 oz. silver, 8.27% lead, and 18.15% zinc developed. Ore already marketed was worth $392,113, of which $142,803 was net from smelters. Workings in the mine total 4350 feet.

Tuscarora.—C. C. Griggs has been appointed general manager for the Holden Mining & Milling Co., owning mines in this district. Preparations are being made for resumption of work on a broad scale. Mr. Griggs is manager for the Stewart and Nabob Con. mines at Kellogg, Idaho.

Wonder.—The Nevada Wonder company pays 5 cents per share, $70,420, on May 21. The total is $1,549,002.

Yerington.—The Nevada-Douglas company's balance-sheet at January 31, 1919, shows current assets amounting to $478,987, of which $387,108 is copper in transit; while liabilities total $551,910, of which $151,554 is A. S. & R. Co. advances, $182,818 for Mason Valley company charges, and $134,923 for accounts and wages unpaid.

OKLAHOMA

Picher.—The Tri-State Safety and Sanitation Association will probably become the Tri-State chapter of the American Zinc Institute. Membership consists of mine operators and dealers in mine supplies. C. F. Dike is president and W. B. Shackelford is secretary.

SOUTH DAKOTA

Lead.—The roof of the old Ferris stope on the 100-ft. level of the Homestake mine collapsed last week, taking down with it two cars of drill-steel and a new drill-sharpening machine ready to be erected in the shop on the surface. The cave-in is 40 ft. across and 20 ft. deep.

The annual report of the Homestake Mining Co. for 1918 shows the following results, according to B. C. Yates, the superintendent:

A shortage of labor curtailed operations in every department. A total of 7354 ft. of development work was done. There are 1,716,418 tons of ore broken in stopes, and there is enough ore developed for many years of profitable operation. Two hoists and a 3000-cu. ft. compressor were changed to electric drive. One fan unit of the mine-ventilating system was erected, and another is being put in. A coal-storage bill of 7000-ton capacity was built. Wolframite sufficient to keep the special mill at work continually was mined, and a considerable tonnage remains.

The mills treated 1,628,630 tons of ore, yielding $3.633 per ton, a total of $5,916,890. Wolframite sold realized $167,468. With sundries, the total income was $6,121,347. Mining charges were $2,441,873; tramway operation, $46,793; milling, $510,113; re-grinding, $28,395; cyanidation, $387,982; Ellison coal plant, $107,050; Spearfish hydro-electric plant No. 2, $121,894; compensation and sociological, $141,774; general, office, salaries, legal, etc., $201,873; and taxes, $349,159. The total expenditure was $4,399,198, equal to $2.70 per ton. Dividends totaled $1,506,960. The net profit was $215,189. At the end of 1917 the excess of current assets over liabilities was $1,569,314, and at the end of 1918, $1,778,530.

TEXAS

Austin.—Two interesting bulletins have recently been issued by the University of Texas here: No. 1818 is on the geology of Dallas county, by E. W. Shuler; while No. 1822 discusses the anticlinal theory as applied to some quicksilver deposits in the Terlingua district, by J. A. Udden.

Wichita Falls.—A directory being prepared of oil com-

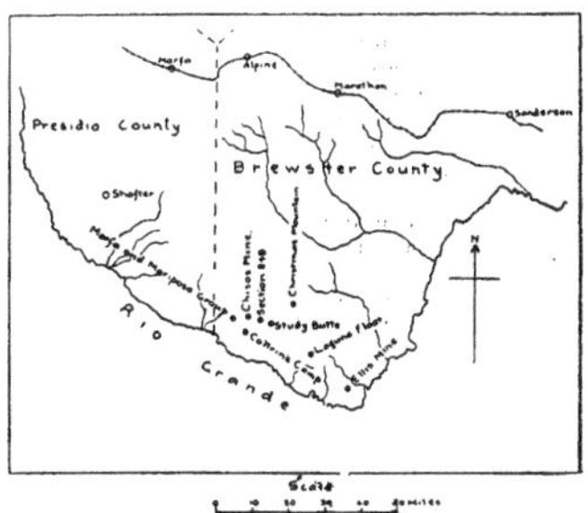

SKETCH-MAP OF QUICKSILVER DISTRICTS OF TEXAS

panies in this district so far contains the names of 762, with a capital of $38,100,000. Of these, only 70 have paid dividends, which total $5,468,659.

UTAH

Eureka.—The Ridge & Valley Mining Co. last Year produced ore sold for $141,721. The net profit was $4240.

On May 9, miners in this district decided to demand an increase of 75 cents per day, abolition of the rustling-card system, an 8-hour shift, and guarantees against discrimination by employers on account of organization affiliations of miners. These demands were decided upon at a meeting of 100 miners of the Tintic district held on the above date.

Park City.—All mines here were closed on May 6, the result of miners demanding $5.50 per day, a six-hour shift, and that two men be employed on all machine-drills. Wages were reduced by 75 cents on March 1, to the present rate of $4.50 for miners and $4 for helpers. About 1000 men are affected. The Judge company employs 400, Silver King Coalition 280, and Silver King Consolidated 90. One of the most serious results will be the flooding of the Ontario Silver mine. The Department of Labor has appointed Hywell Davies to investigate the trouble.

CANADA

British Columbia

Anyox.—In the Dolly Varden mines, railway, and Taylor Engineering Co. tangle, it is now stated that S. S. Taylor, on behalf of the creditors of the Taylor company, has offered $1,100,000 for the mines near Alice arm, there to be no commission. This price is $200,000 more than the sum offered the Dolly Varden Mines Co. by the Temiskaming Mining Co. of Cobalt, Ontario, its price of $900,000 including a commission of $50,000, provided the railway received a renewal of charter from the Provincial government.

Greenwood.—It is possible that the Greenwood smelter, recently closed by the Canada Copper Corporation, will be re-opened, as the company has offered the plant and contiguous properties to the citizens of Greenwood for the sum of $125,000. As the existence of the town depends upon the maintenance of mining, and as the company's proposal is considered reasonable, it is very probable that it will be accepted. At Boundary Falls is the New Dominion smelter, which has been idle for some years. This also has been offered to the Greenwood people, together with its mines, on favorable terms. The smelter at Greenwood is intact and ready to be blown-in at any time. Oscar Lachmund, metallurgical engineer, has been retained by the Greenwood committee in an advisory capacity.

Nelson.—Eastern British Columbia is to have an International Mining Convention here on June 19, 20, and 21. E. W. Widdowson, provincial assayer, is treasurer.

Phoenix.—There has been an immense cave-in in the workings of the Granby mine here. No serious damage, however, is reported, as the collapse was not altogether unexpected.

Trail.—The Consolidated Mining & Smelting Co. has reduced wages by 50 cents per day for copper miners and 25 cents for smelter-men. The minimum is $3.50 per shift. The company has reduced treatment charges on ore from $8.30 to $7.85 per ton, effective April 12.

Yukon

Dawson.—The ice on the river here broke on May 10. No damage was done, as was the case in 1918.

MEXICO

Cananea.—Bandits raided this place on May 9, robbing the bank of $20,000 and supplies from stores. They then headed south. Five were captured and executed.

PERSONAL

Note. The Editor invites members of the profession to send particulars of their work and appointments. The information is interesting to our readers.

C. N. Lakenan is in New York.

F. F. Sharpless is in Sonora, Mexico.

R. E. McConnell has returned from Germany to Los Angeles.

Charles A. Burdick has moved to 120 Broadway, New York.

Robert E. Kinzie has returned from the west coast of Mexico.

Robert Musgrave sailed from Victoria, B. C., for Shanghai on the 9th instant.

Deane P. Mitchell passed through San Francisco on his return from Siberia to London.

Edwin J. Collins of Duluth is in Arizona on a two weeks examination trip to the Ray district.

T. J. Jones sails from San Francisco for Vladivostok on his way to Kyshtim, Siberia, on May 29.

L. V. Bender, superintendent of the Washoe plant at Anaconda, is on a trip of inspection in the Southwest.

G. B. Holderer is in Cuba on professional business with headquarters in the Horter building, Habana.

A. H. Hubbell, of the editorial staff of the 'Engineering and Mining Journal', is visiting Western mining centres.

Charles Bocking, assistant manager of the Butte & Superior Mining Co., was in San Francisco during the past week.

H. C. Carlisle, superintendent for the Mandy Mining Co., operating a copper mine near Le Pas, Manitoba, is at New York.

F. W. McNair, president of the Michigan College of Mines, has been appointed consulting engineer to the U. S. Bureau of Standards.

George A. Chapman, of New York, consulting metallurgist to the Minerals Separation company, is in the Lake Superior district.

A. E. Drucker announces that he has organized the Drucker Smelting Corporation with an office at 30 Church street, New York.

Arthur S. Dwight, Major in the 11th Engineers, is expected at New York from France, where he performed distinguished service.

C. M. Weld has resigned as assistant executive to the War Minerals Investigation department of the U. S. Bureau of Mines, and will resume consulting practice in New York.

W. H. Blackburn, superintendent for the Tonopah Mining Co., returned to Nevada last week from the company's Eden gold mine in Nicaragua, where the new mill is working well.

A. W. Allen has resigned from the editorial staff of the 'Engineering and Mining Journal' to become chief engineer for the Penyon Syndicate. Mr. Allen expects to leave New York for Chile about the middle of June.

Sidney Stone, manager of the Butters' mill near Virginia City, Nevada, for nine years, died suddenly at Oakland, California, last week.

Edmundo Girault, for many years general manager for the Cia. Minera San Rafael y Anexas, Pachuca, Mexico, died on May 4. His widow and family are living at San Antonio, Texas.

The annual meeting of the American Zinc Institute will be held at St. Louis on June 9. This is a postponement from May 12. W. F. Rossman is chairman of the committee on arrangements, at the Fierce building, St. Louis.

METAL PRICES

San Francisco, May 13

Aluminum-dust, cents per pound	50—60
Antimony, cents per pound	8
Copper, electrolytic, cents per pound	15¾
Lead, pig, cents per pound	5¾—6¼
Platinum, per ounce	$100
Quicksilver, per flask of 75 lb	$80
Spelter, cents per pound	8
Zinc-dust, cents per pound	10—12

The report of the U. S. Bureau of Mines for April, covering the position of over 40 metals, minerals, and products, is now to hand. Excerpts will be made from this useful 54-page report. Summarizing, the report says:

"The mineral industry is still in a stage of readjustment. Markets are quiet and production is still largely curtailed. The various industries are gradually using up accumulated stocks, while the Government has been disposing of its supplies. Prices are reaching lower and more stable levels, and it is expected that conditions and production will improve. Building activity is being resumed. While prospects for foreign trade are improving and ocean rates are declining, the shortage of ocean bottoms is still acute. In the special mineral industries, such as manganese, potash, graphite, and pyrite, which have been developed during the War, activity is very limited, and many of the plants are closed. This condition will continue until it becomes evident as to what the movement and prices of foreign material will be."

EASTERN METAL MARKET

(By wire from New York)

May 13.—Copper is more active and higher. Lead is quiet but firm. Spelter is inactive but steady.

SILVER

Below are given official or ticker quotations, in cents per ounce of silver 999 fine. From April 23, 1918, to May 5, 1919, the United States government paid $1 per ounce for all silver purchased by it, fixing a maximum of $1.01½ on August 15, 1918. On May 5, 1919, all restrictions on the metal were removed, resulting in fluctuations. During the restricted period, the British government fixed the maximum price five times, the last time being on March 26, 1919, on account of the low rate of sterling exchange, but removed all restrictions on May 10. The equivalent of dollar silver (1000 fine) in British currency is 48.65 pence per ounce (925 fine), calculated at the normal rate of exchanage.

Date		New York cents	London pence	Average week ending		Cents	Pence
May	7	101.75	48.68	Apr.	1	101.12	49.63
"	8	103.00	48.68	"	8	101.12	48.86
"	9	105.75	53.50	"	15	101.12	48.85
"	10	111.00	53.50	"	22	101.12	48.94
"	11 Sunday			"	29	101.12	48.78
"	12	119.75	58.00	May	6	101.14	48.71
"	13	114.75	55.50	"	13	109.33	52.08

Monthly averages

	1917	1918	1919		1917	1918	1919
Jan.	75.14	88.72	101.12	July	78.92	99.62	....
Feb.	77.54	85.79	101.12	Aug.	85.40	100.31	....
Mch.	74.13	88.11	101.12	Sept.	100.73	101.12	....
Apr.	72.51	95.35	101.12	Oct.	87.38	101.12	....
May	74.61	99.50	....	Nov.	85.97	101.12	....
June	78.44	99.50	....	Dec.	85.97	101.12	....

The San Francisco Mint has suspended the melting of silver dollars.

Silver valued at about $14,000,000 was shipped from San Francisco to the Orient by the 'Nanking' on May 10.

COPPER

Prices of electrolytic in New York, in cents per pound.

Date			Average week ending		
May	7	15.25	Apr.	1	15.27
"	8	15.25	"	8	15.25
"	9	15.37	"	15	15.33
"	10	15.37	"	22	15.18
"	11 Sunday		"	29	15.18
"	12	15.50	May	6	15.25
"	13	15.50	"	13	15.37

Monthly averages

	1917	1918	1919		1917	1918	1919
Jan.	29.53	23.50	20.43	July	29.67	26.00	....
Feb.	34.57	23.50	17.34	Aug.	27.42	26.00	....
Mch.	36.00	23.50	15.05	Sept.	25.11	26.00	....
Apr.	33.16	23.50	15.23	Oct.	23.50	26.00	....
May	31.69	23.50	....	Nov.	23.50	26.00	....
June	32.57	23.50	....	Dec.	23.50	26.00	....

Copper production of some of the large mines in April was as under:

Mine	Pounds	Mine	Pounds
Anaconda	13,750,000	Miami	4,489,748
Arizona	2,400,000	Old Dominion	2,380,000
Cerro de Pasco	4,780,000	Phelps Dodge	8,262,176
East Butte	1,347,580		

Copper companies paid dividends totaling only $2,664,657 during April, compared with $4,361,644 in that month of 1917, and $7,875,834 in 1916. The first four months of each of the current and past three years show the following distribution: $25,048,080, $43,079,091, $53,252,471, and $35,020,058.

Copper surplus in this country is now estimated at 1,300,000,000 pounds

TIN

Prices in New York, in cents per pound. The monthly averages in 1918 are nominal. On December 3 the War Industries Board fixed the price to consumers and jobbers at 72½c. f.o.b. Chicago and Eastern points, and 71½c. on the Pacific Coast. This will continue until the U. S. Steel Products Co.'s stock is consumed.

Monthly averages

	1917	1918	1919		1917	1918	1919
Jan.	44.10	85.13	71.50	July	62.60	93.00	....
Feb.	51.47	85.00	72.44	Aug.	62.53	91.33	....
Mch.	54.27	85.00	72.50	Sept.	61.54	80.40	....
Apr.	55.63	88.53	72.50	Oct.	62.24	78.82	....
May	63.21	100.01	....	Nov.	74.18	73.07	....
June	61.93	91.00	....	Dec.	85.00	71.52	....

LEAD

Lead is quoted in cents per pound, New York delivery.

Date			Average week ending		
May	7	4.80	Apr.	1	5.25
"	8	4.80	"	8	5.25
"	9	4.85	"	15	5.07
"	10	4.85	"	22	4.93
"	11 Sunday		"	29	4.95
"	12	4.90	May	6	4.87
"	13	4.90	"	13	4.85

Monthly averages

	1917	1918	1919		1917	1918	1919
Jan.	7.64	6.85	5.60	July	10.93	8.03	....
Feb.	9.10	7.07	5.13	Aug.	10.75	8.05	....
Mch.	10.07	7.26	5.24	Sept.	9.07	8.05	....
Apr.	9.38	6.99	5.05	Oct.	6.97	8.05	....
May	10.29	6.88	....	Nov.	6.38	8.05	....
June	11.74	7.58	....	Dec.	6.49	6.90	....

Lead ore at Joplin, Missouri, last week averaged $57 per ton, basis 80% metal. The Tri-State output was 2189 tons of concentrate.

Cost of producing lead by the Bunker Hill & Sullivan company at Kellogg, Idaho, in 1918 was 5.340 cents per pound. The average price received was 7.375 cents, for 67,125,717 pounds.

The U. S. Bureau of Mines considers that the current rate of lead production is 450,000 tons per annum, equal to 83% of the output in 1918.

QUICKSILVER

The primary market for quicksilver is San Francisco, California being the largest producer. The price is fixed in the open market, according to quantity. Prices, in dollars per flask of 75 pounds:

Date					
Apr.	15	75.00	Apr.	29	75.00
"	22	75.00	May	6	75.00
			"	13	80.00

Monthly averages

	1917	1918	1919		1917	1918	1919
Jan.	81.00	128.06	103.75	July	102.00	120.00	....
Feb.	126.25	118.00	90.00	Aug.	115.00	120.00	....
Mch.	113.75	112.00	72.80	Sept.	112.00	120.00	....
Apr.	114.50	115.00	73.12	Oct.	102.00	120.00	....
May	104.00	110.00	....	Nov.	102.50	120.00	....
June	85.50	112.00	....	Dec.	117.42	115.00	....

ZINC

Zinc is quoted as spelter, standard Western brands, New York delivery, in cents per pound:

Date			Average week ending		
May	7	6.27	Apr.	1	6.53
"	8	6.27	"	8	6.60
"	9	6.30	"	15	6.57
"	10	6.30	"	22	6.41
"	11 Sunday		"	29	6.39
"	12	6.35	May	6	6.32
"	13	6.35	"	13	6.31

Monthly averages

	1917	1918	1919		1917	1918	1919
Jan.	9.75	7.78	7.44	July	8.98	8.72	....
Feb.	10.45	7.97	6.71	Aug.	8.58	8.87	....
Mch.	10.78	7.67	6.53	Sept.	8.33	9.58	....
Apr.	10.20	7.04	6.49	Oct.	8.32	9.11	....
May	9.41	7.29	....	Nov.	7.76	8.75	....
June	9.63	7.92	....	Dec.	7.84	8.49	....

Spelter in stock in this country approximates 40,000 tons.

Zinc ore at Joplin, Missouri, last week averaged $35 per ton, basis 60% metal. The Tri-State output was 7021 tons of blende.

Zinc in concentrate produced by Butte & Superior during April was 8,250,000 lb., also 150,000 oz. of silver.

The American Zinc, Lead & Smelting Co. reports a loss of $651 during the first quarter of 1919. The last quarter of 1918 gave a profit of $18,278, and the third period $287,207.

Zinc retorts in blast, according to the April report of the U. S. Bureau of Mines, number 90,000, compared with 165,000 at the end of 1918 and 220,000 in 1917. The greatest curtailment was in the natural-gas belt, where only 35,000 retorts are in use, against 125,000 in 1917.

Eastern Metal Market

New York, May 7.

There is little activity in any of the metals, and new features are scarce.

Antimony is firm and unchanged.

Copper demand continues light, with producers sitting tight. Quotations are virtually pegged and unchanged.

Lead is lower, and some metal has changed hands in the outside market.

Tin trading, in the market sense, is impossible.

Zinc is lifeless and prices have eased somewhat. The only buying is by dealers.

ALUMINUM

No. 1 virgin metal, 98 to 99% pure, is quoted at 31 to 33c. per pound for early delivery in wholesale lots.

ANTIMONY

The market remains unchanged at 6.62½ to 6.87½c., New York, duty paid, for wholesale lots for early delivery.

COPPER

There continues to be little domestic demand and nothing is heard about export business, except the hope that Germany and her allies will be a buyer soon after peace is signed. Present quotations are virtually pegged at 15.25c., New York, for electrolytic and 15.50c., New York, for Lake, both of which are largely nominal. Large producers hold at 15.25 to 15.37½c., with small ones at 15.12½ to 15.25c. for electrolytic for early delivery. Consumers are apparently fully covered well into May and have no incentive to enter the market, and producers see that nothing can be gained by lowering prices or pressing the market. The steel-price situation continues to act as a brake on the copper and other metal markets. That there is at least 1,500,000,000 lb. of copper above ground, with 600,000,000 lb. a normal amount, is the opinion of an authority and a leader in the industry. While present output is not over 50% of capacity, he asserts that further decided reduction is seriously needed.

IRON AND STEEL

Only mild interest is reported to be shown by steel-makers in the meeting this Thursday in New York of the Railroad Administration with the steel-makers' committee. It is hoped by some that this meeting will result in freeing the steel industry from deadly Government paltering, resulting in a probable market improvement in the end. Contraction in output and stocks is growing, and it is feared this may be overdone as in some other periods.

April pig-iron statistics of 'The Iron Age' show that 54 furnaces blew-out last month, leaving 212 active on May 1, against 372 on September 1 last year, when the peak of output was attained. The April output was 2,478,218 long tons or 82,607 tons per day, against 3,090,243 tons for the 31 days of March, or 99,685 tons per day. Production on May 1, estimating charcoal iron, was at the rate of only 28,000,000 tons per year, compared with an actual production of 39,052,000 tons in 1918.

LEAD

Because of a probable discounting by sellers of a possible reduction in the quotation of the leading interest, which is still 5c., New York, the local market experienced a decline in the past week and a part recovery. The outside market fell to 4.77½c. last Friday, with a report that 4.75c. was done. Since then the market has advanced again to 4.85c., New York, and 4.60c., St. Louis, yesterday. There is, however, little activity even at these low and probably attractive levels. Some business has been done on each day, but the prevailing feeling seems to be that while lead is cheap without doubt, buyers prefer to maintain their cash resources in a bank rather than enter the market and tie it up in lead.

At this writing the tone of the market is better. Some expect a reduction by the American Smelting & Refining Co., but there is no certainty about it.

TIN

Nothing has developed to change the situation, and the market is still under control by the Government with the price fixed at 72.50c., New York. Those who a few weeks ago felt that a free market would obtain by June 1, are now inclined to revise their guesses and say July 1. It is merely guessing, as nothing definite can be learned from those who know or should know what the future of the market is to be. It is rumored that the allocated stocks have fallen to 1500 or 2000 tons, but this is speculation also. Interest has subsided in purchases for shipment from the Far East when import restrictions are removed. Quotations for this range from 49c. for Far Eastern shipment to 49.50c. for shipment from London. There were no tin arrivals in April—the first time in many years that this has happened in any month. Spot Straits in London yesterday was quoted at £237 10s. per ton, an advance of 10s. for the week.

ZINC

Consumers still refrain from the market, although it was expected they would be interested when price-levels reached 6c., St. Louis, for prime Western, which they did the middle of last week. Yesterday this grade of metal was sold to dealers at 5.92½c., St. Louis, or 6.27½c., New York, which we quote as the market. Some express the opinion that the market will fall to 5.75c., St. Louis, at which level it is expected buying by galvanizers and perhaps brass-makers will appear. Production still continues in excess of demand, especially when Government stocks are taken into consideration. There have been further shut-downs of some smelters.

ORES

Tungsten: The best grades of scheelite are quoted at $10 to $12 per unit, and those of wolframite at $7 to $9 in 60% concentrate. Lower grades are all nominal. Demand is light, and quotations are not reliable nor even definitely nominal. There is no business in ferro and no quotations are heard of.

In high-speed steel, Government re-sale stock is selling at about $1 per pound, with regular producers quoting $1.50 to $1.60 per pound.

Molybdenum: The market is quiet and quotations are nominally unchanged at 80 to 90c. per pound of MoS_2 in 90% concentrate.

Manganese-Iron Alloys: Quotations for both ferro and spiegel are unchanged at $150 and $35 to $40 per ton, delivered, respectively. Sales of carload lots of the latter have been made, some of it re-sale material. The entire market is dead. Production of ferro in April was 14,500 long tons, against 21,000 tons per month in the first quarter, and over 28,750 tons per month in 1918. The April spiegel output was under 3000 tons.

Company Reports

ALASKA GASTINEAU MINING CO.

Property: mine and reduction works near Juneau, Alaska.

Operating Officials: G. T. Jackson, manager; D. J. Argall, superintendent of mine; Roy Hatch, superintendent of mill; W. T. Tolch, chief engineer.

Financial Statement: a comparison with previous years is necessary to show the results of this company:

	1918	1917	1916	1915
Revenue from gold	$1,130,223	$2,009,632	$1,837,201	$1,016,101
Operating charges	1,233,168	1,724,474	1,423,200	764,250
Operating profit or loss	−99,945	+285,158	+414,031	+251,848
Net profit or loss	−116,565	+270,827	+451,026	+278,771
Interest accrued or paid	219,685	228,552	217,747	......
Net income	−336,250	42,275	112,834	......
Current assets	692,470	806,082	911,027	695,315
Current liabilities	498,677	835,495	976,713	783,000
Reserves	642,605	325,045	......	......

The liabilities include for 1918 and 1917 notes payable, $400,000 and $500,000; and for 1916 and 1915, bond interest payable, $822,500 and $612,500.

Development: while it is impossible to re-survey the broken ore in stopes, owing to their caved condition, it is estimated roughly at 2,000,000 tons. The quantity in reserve—broken and unbroken—but prospected and prepared between No. 2 shaft and the west end of the property above No. 13 level, is 6,323,117 tons of $1.02 ore. No. 1 shaft, above No. 9 level, is to be abandoned in order to recover the shaft-pillar of 1,500,000 tons of $1.15 ore. The principal mining operations last year consisted in preparing stopes on No. 11 level.

Production: this might be tabulated as under:

	1918	1917	1916	1915
Ore treated, tons	1,285,445	2,240,346	1,892,788	1,115,204
Average value	$1.090	$1.110	$1.103	$1.157
Recovery, per cent	81.10	81.32	81.33	81.00
Cost of mining	$0.51	$0.42	$0.38	$0.31
Cost of milling	0.33	0.26	0.27	0.31
Total cost	0.96	0.77	0.75	0.71

An average of 452 men were employed in all departments, a decrease of 36%. The wage averaged $4.76, compared with $4.25 in 1917. The number of men now available, and their efficiency, is increasing in marked degree.

Considerable experimentation was done in the mill last year. A hearth furnace superseded the crucible furnace, used for reducing concentrate that carries most of the gold.

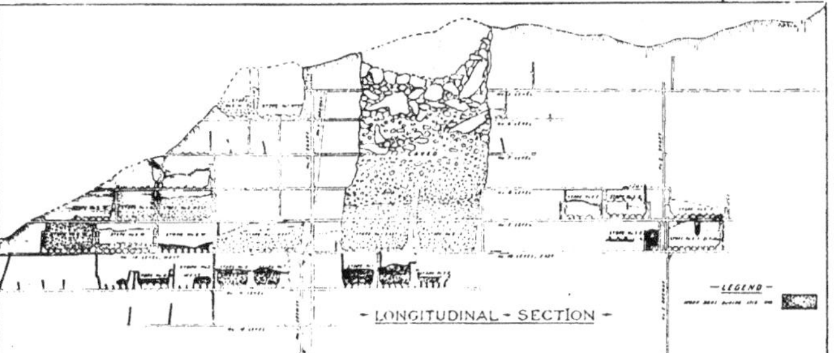

LONGITUDINAL SECTION OF PERSEVERANCE MINE OF THE ALASKA GASTINEAU COMPANY

HEDLEY GOLD MINING CO.

Property: gold mine, 40-stamp mill, and 1800-hp. power plant at Hedley, British Columbia.

Operating Officials: G. P. Jones, general superintendent.

Financial Statement: the net profit in 1918 was $132,578. Current assets total $27,930, and liabilities $10,155.

Dividends: three absorbed $108,000, making $2,412,000 to date.

Development: extensions amounted to 490 ft. Reserves are estimated at 263,000 tons of $9.40 and 87,650 tons of $6 ore, a little lower than at last calculations. The value has not decreased with depth, as the 900-ft. level shows the highest grade, which is going under foot.

Production: the mill treated 67,313 tons of $10.34 ore at a cost of about $8.30 per ton.

MODDERFONTEIN DEEP LEVELS, LIMITED

Property: 378 claims (1½ acres each), 70-stamp mill and cyanide plant in the Far East Rand, Transvaal.

Operating Official: H. R. Hill, general manager.

Financial Statement: during 1918 the gold yield was £1,035,473 ($5,019,000). Operations cost £441,622 ($2,143,000), plus £83,175 ($402,000) for taxes, etc., leaving a profit of £519,701 ($2,474,000). The year started with a balance of £126,475 ($611,000), and ended with £157,677 ($761,000), after paying dividends.

Dividends: No. 7 and 8 absorbed £487,500 ($2,362,000), making £1,425,000 ($6,911,000) todate (in 4 years).

Development: the total of new work was 5425 ft. Ore-reserves amount to 3,450,000 tons, averaging 8.8 dwt. per ton, across a stoping-width of 78 in. These figures are an increase above previous ones. Of the ore mined, 85.19% was broken by machines (2.41% by jackhammers) and 14.81% by hand. Water pumped was 29,123,800 gallons.

Production: the mill treated 506,100 tons of 9.945 dwt. ore. The duty per stamp-day was 23.7 tons (70 stamps and 8 tube-mills running 305 days). The total gold yield was 243,670 oz., and actual extraction 96.82%. In four years the mill has treated 1,844,500 tons, yielding £3,529,882 ($17,120,000).

Costs: on a basis of per ton milled—$2.38 for all underground work, 84 cents for treatment, and 96 cents for general charges, a total of $4.18 per ton.

There were 255 whites and 2310 natives employed.

PHELPS DODGE CORPORATION

Property: copper mines at Bisbee, Copper Basin, and Morenci; silver-gold mine at Tombstone, Arizona; copper mine at Tyrone, New Mexico; copper mine at Nacozari, Sonora, Mexico; coal mine at Dawson, New Mexico; smelters at Douglas and Morenci, Arizona; and mills at Morenci, Tyrone, and Nacozari; also mercantile stores at the various properties.

Operating Officials: Phelps Dodge Corporation—Gerald Sherman, mining engineer; H. K. Burch, concentrating engineer; C. F. Willis, department of industrial relations. Copper Queen Branch—G. H. Dowell, manager; W. H. Webster, assistant; Arthur Notman, mine superintendent; H. H. Stout, reduction works superintendent; P. B. Butler, assistant. Morenci Branch (Detroit mine)—J. P. Hodgson, manager; W. M. Saben, assistant. Burro Mountain Branch—E. M. Sawyer, manager; E. F. Pelton, mine superintendent. Copper Basin Branch—A. B. Peach, acting manager. Stag Cañon Branch—T. H. O'Brien, manager; J. B. Morrow, superintendent of coke department. Moctezuma Copper Co.—J. S. Williams, Jr., general manager; H. T. Hamilton, manager. Bunker Hill Mines Co.—J. H. Davis, superintendent. Phelps Dodge Mercantile Co.—W. A. Meyer, general manager.

Production: the past three years compare as under:

Metal	1918	1917	1916
Copper, pounds	169,035,687	153,974,692	152,263,729
Gold, ounces	30,434	24,423	28,873
Lead, pounds	1,683,113	8,136,356	10,404,341
Silver, ounces	1,772,119	1,524,632	1,642,055
Average price for copper, cents	24.58	26.67	24.48

Additional to the above for 1918, there was purchased or smelted on toll, ore yielding 43,348,592 lb. of copper, 973,-040 oz silver, and 6778 oz. of gold. Copper sold consisted of 279,995,770 lb. of C * Q electrolytic and 14,522,978 lb. of P. D. ingot.

Financial Statement: the total income last year was $59,-483,208. Expenses amounted to $43,537,525, including $903,630 for depreciation, $535,375 for Red Cross war funds, and $5,863,585 for all taxes. This left a profit of $15,945,683. Current assets total $39,223,793, and liabilities $15,463,003.

Dividends: these were $10,800,000, equal to 24%, and including that paid on April 2, 1919, the total is $81,221,527.

General: the report of A. T. Thomson, assistant to the president, Walter Douglas, is as follows:

Notwithstanding the general shortage of labor so prevalent throughout the country for the first 10 months of the year, the combined copper production of the various branches and subsidiaries exceeded that of any previous year. In order to keep the production at a maximum it was necessary to transfer men from development to stoping, and consequently the amount of development and exploratory work done was considerably below normal. In spite of this, the ore-reserves in nearly every case show an increase over those of a year ago.

The copper ore extracted from all properties amounted to 2,684,701 tons, of which 106,037 was mined and shipped by lessees. Of the total ores mined, 1,797,161 tons was given preliminary concentration and 887,184 tons was smelted direct. The total amount of copper-bearing material smelted by the company's plants, including ore, concentrates, old slag, scrap and cement copper, was 1,400,911 tons. The copper bullion contained 32,709 oz. of gold and 2,307,307 oz. of silver.

There was also mined and sold 5942 tons of manganese ores and concentrates from the Copper Queen and Bunker Hill mines and 7024 lb. of molybdenite from the Moctezuma Copper Co.'s La Fortuna and Bella Union mines.

Of the ores and concentrates smelted at the reduction works, 1,168,882 tons was developed from the company's properties, 188,074 tons was general custom ores, and 43,-955 tons was treated for the United Verde Extension Mining Company.

Unit costs in almost all operations show an increase in sympathy with the increased cost of labor and supplies, although, as a whole, they have not risen to the same degree. Three adjustments of wages in the form of advances were made during the year, so that the wages during the last quarter were paid on a basis of 32-cent copper when the market price was only 26 cents per pound. Up to November 11, 1918, maximum output was being well maintained, but since then the lack of demand for copper has called for a drastic curtailment and reduction in costs.

The total output of the Copper Queen reduction works was the largest in the history of the plant. Much valuable investigation work in connection with metallurgical problems was accomplished during the year, which will now be followed by large-scale tests to prove the results definitely.

At the Copper Queen Branch, credit is due to the mining department for maintaining production with, at times, less than 70% of the normal crew, as well as for keeping the major operating costs down in the face of increasing labor and supply costs. The ore-reserves at the end of the year showed a slight increase.

On Sacramento hill, stripping operations are sufficiently well advanced to estimate that, at the present rate of progress, a production of 4000 tons per day can be maintained after the middle of 1920.

At the Morenci Branch, the year 1918 represents the first full year of operations since 1914. Labor conditions have been normal, but efficiency has been poor. The power situation has been greatly improved by the addition of two new Diesel engines. The present ore-reserves are being completely re-sampled and re-estimated with a view to getting accurate data in connection with future operations.

At the Burro Mountain Branch the production exceeded that of the previous year, and the mining costs were substantially reduced. However, operations have been seriously affected by the drop in copper prices, the ore being of a uniformly low grade. The concentrator changes, when completed, will help here materially.

The Copper Basin Branch produced 1,907,205 lb. of copper from small-scale operations.

The Stag Cañon Branch mined 1,339,292 tons of coal, of which 470,924 tons was consumed in the production of 281,916 tons of coke. The mines and ovens operated continuously throughout the year, and although the output was slightly less than in 1917, due largely to labor shortage, the financial outcome obtained from this branch's operations was very satisfactory. Anticipating a heavy demand for both coal and coke, extensive development work and plant improvements were carried on and the mines put in shape for greatly increased output. After November 11, demand fell off immediately, as a consequence operations have been markedly curtailed. This sudden change in fuel market conditions has made a difficult situation for the coal company. Costs continue high and the Government control of wages still obtains.

The Moctezuma Copper Co. again broke all previous production records and ended the year with a very satisfactory increase in ore-reserves. The wreck of the turbine early in November forced an immediate reduction of output, as no reserve power was available. The armistice, however, followed shortly, so that the loss of production was not felt except as it affected the costs.

Operations of the Bunker Hill Mines Co. are at present confined to leasing on a small but profitable scale.

The average number of men working at the various major branches and subsidiaries in 1918 totaled 11,477. During the past year 647 employees left to enter the Service.

Book Reviews

Mineral Enterprise in China. By William F. Collins. Pp. 308, maps, index. The Macmillan Co., New York. 1918. For sale by 'Mining and Scientific Press'. Price $6.

The most noteworthy thing about this book is its price; but for an engineer who wishes to know about its subject the work is cheap. No similar book is known to the reviewer. In his first chapter the author shows that the ancient Chinese despised mining and regarded miners as the lowest class of citizens—worse even than soldiers. For 2000 years, imperial decrees have alternately permitted and prohibited mining. As late as 1744, gold and silver mines were closed because they attracted workers from the more useful copper and lead mines. Von Richthofen, writing in 1872, mentions the exactions of officials, robberies by workmen, brigandage of neighboring mining companies and, worse than all, the thievery of the soldiers, as causes depressing silver mining. Foreigners who have tried to open mines in China in recent years have been opposed by officials and gentry to such a degree that but few mines are now operated by Europeans. The second chapter is devoted to 'Feng-shui' (wind-water), that pseudo-science whose professors must be consulted every time that the ground is to be disturbed by excavations. Mining necessarily disturbs the beneficent dragon, turtle, or phoenix spirits that regulate the earth currents, and these injuries must be paid for. Disturbing graves is also a serious matter. Fortunately feng-shui is becoming less important. Pages 45 to 77 deal with what Lord Salisbury called the "Battle of the Concessions," an interesting bit of financial and diplomatic history. Five large concessions, granted in 1896 to 1902 by the Peking government are mentioned; every one of these met with fierce opposition— in 1900 the Shansi authorities went so far as to offer a reward for the head of the reviewer. Three of the concessions surrendered their rights to the Chinese for money payment. The Pekin Syndicate, which produced 500,000 tons of coal in 1915, is the only concession working mines. The remaining concession, the Eastern Pioneer, formed by Pritchard Morgan, is still pressing a claim for damages and for the right to work mines in Szechuan. Had Mr. Morgan's plan of forming a Mining Administration for China been carried out it would have resulted in great profits to both Chinese and foreigners, and probably would have checked the encroachments of foreign powers.

The Hanyang iron and steel enterprise, due to the scholar-viceroy, Chang-Chih-tung, is described. The works, with mines and collieries, employ 20,000 men, and turn out 250,000 tons of pig-iron annually. A financial failure from the start, the enterprise has been kept alive by large loans from the Government and from the Japanese; the amount due to the latter is probably not much short of $50,000,000 (Mex.). Iron mining throughout China is now restricted to Chinese. Standard Oil representatives spent $2,500,000 (Mex.) in sinking several wells 3000 ft. in Shensi, near the Yellow river; but finding nothing worth while abandoned the work. Antimony mines, practically monopolized by one Chinese company [the Wah Chang Mining & Smelting Co.] lead the world in production. Several pages are devoted to operations of the Germans in Shantung. The most important mining in China is done by the Chinese Engineering & Mining Co., now raising 70,000 tons of coal weekly. Japanese coal miners, at Fu Shun, near Mukden, produce 6000 tons of coal daily. Other large coal mines and iron furnaces, also near Mukden, at Pen-Hsi-hu, are operated by a Chinese-Japanese company. Near Urga—Outer Mongolia—a Russian company working 7000 men turned out 120 poods (say, 60,000 oz.) of alluvial gold in 1911. The Moho alluvial deposits, near the Amoor river, are the most celebrated in the Chinese republic. It is stated that they produced 100,000 oz. of gold monthly in recent times, but this seems incredible. General conditions affecting mining, legislation, and taxation occupy 50 pages, and eight are devoted to mining in Korea. Of the eight appendixes the most important is a translation of the Mining Enterprise Regulations, promulgated March 11, 1914. The chief mineral of China is coal, of which her stores are immense; iron, antimony, and tin are also important, but do not compare with coal. The fact that rich Chinese miners from the Malay States find it impossible to operate mines in China under present conditions plainly indicates that the chance for profitable investment of foreign capital is very slight. For the individual prospector and small capitalist China is the least promising of the mining countries. It is to be hoped that the sale of the book will warrant a second edition, in which case a few pages should be devoted to a mining bibliography, with notes on the principal works in the Chinese language. A most interesting chapter could be made of native mining methods, and a reproduction of Chinese mining maps with explanations would be entertaining. On the whole the mining profession should be grateful for this little work, which gives evidence of careful study.—W. H. S.

[On page 662 of this issue will be found an article on mining development in China, by Gilmour E. Brown, who fully corroborates the views of Mr. Collins, and the personal experiences of the reviewer.—Editor.]

Industrial Goodwill. By John R. Commons. Pp. 198, index. McGraw-Hill Book Co., Inc., New York. For sale by 'Mining and Scientific Press'. Price, $2.

Perhaps the most interesting thing about this book is the frank recognition by the author, himself an outsider, that an outsider cannot know as much about a given industrial dispute as the parties directly concerned. The fundamental idea of the book might be said to be that goodwill between employer and employee must be the foundation for any satisfactory industrial arrangement. The first chapter takes up the old idea that labor is a commodity to be treated like other commodities. Naturally, it does not take long to dispose of that theory. Next comes a discussion of the viewpoint that looks upon a workingman as a machine. While the good work accomplished by the efficiency engineers is recognized, their lack of appreciation of the human element is shown. The interest of the public in industrial relations is then discussed, this interest being the reason for legislation affecting certain industrial relations. However, the author, while in general favoring such measures as compulsory workmen's compensation and health insurance, he makes it clear that the general provisions of industrial legislation should preferably be agreed upon by the men directly concerned in the industry before being presented to the legislative body. In another chapter a strong plea is made for vocational education by the State. The author suggests a novel solution for the unemployment problem in the form of a basic day of eight or even less hours per day, thus providing work for practically everybody even during periods of depressions with the further advantage that the allowance for overtime would be the most satisfactory form for sharing the profits of prosperity. These are merely some of the 'high points' of a remarkable book. The last chapter is devoted to a brief review of industrial and social conditions since Karl Marx issued his Manifesto in 1848, showing how Marx and his followers guessed wrong and how industrial goodwill can be attained not through socialism but through the use of more rational methods. Reading and even study of this book will well repay both the employer and the labor leader. They will disagree with many of the conclusions expressed, but they will find considerable food for thought.

Office Administration. By J. W. Schulze. P. 290, ill., index. McGraw-Hill Book Co., Inc., New York. For sale by 'Mining and Scientfic Press', San Francisco. Price, $3.

Office managers and office clerks believing that scientific management would not affect them, that their work was 'different', have been living in a fool's paradise. The present volume is one of several appearing recently that discuss wastes in office operation and methods of promoting office efficiency. The principal subjects discussed are selection and training of office workers, office layout, establishment of routine processes, filing systems, order and billing systems, handling correspondence, and general office service. The discussion is illustrated by reference to methods actually used in many offices. While a number of these methods are suitable only for offices where hundreds or even thousands of clerks are employed, the manager of the small office will find many helpful suggestions. The weak point about the book is its almost total neglect of the human factor. The reader frequently pauses to wonder how some of the proposed systems would actually work when applied not to automatons, but to real live employees, who could quit if they wanted to do so, and get a job somewhere else. Some idea of this neglect of the human factor may be obtained from the fact that the chapter on the relationship between the employer and employee contains only six pages. Not that there is not plenty of space devoted to training and handling employees. There is, but the discussion is of exactly the same character as that regarding office furniture. Nevertheless, with these reservations, the book has a considerable value for the employer and the office manager.

Mining Manual and Year-Book, 1919. Compiled by W. R. Skinner. Pp. 766, maps, index. May be obtained by writing to W. R. Skinner, 11-12 Clements Lane, London, E. C. 4. Price, 21s. 6d. ($5.25 at normal exchange).

There is little new to be said regarding this useful annual, now in its 33rd year. The matter follows the regular arrangement of metal outputs of the mines of the world, a glossary of terms, full particulars of 1170 companies operating in all quarters, lists of directors, consulting engineers, an appendix of late information, and a supplementary index of 2470 names. A comparison with the previous edition shows that for 1919 to be 163 pages less, discusses 330 fewer companies, lists 220 more in the supplementary index, and the price has been raised from 19s. to 21s. 6d. (60 cents more). But these changes in no way detract from the value of the work.

Trautwine. Civil Engineer's Pocket-Book. 20th edition. Pp. 1528, ill., index. The Trautwine Company, Philadelphia. 1919. For sale by 'Mining and Scientific Press. Price, $6.

The new edition contains about 400 pages re-written since the 19th edition was printed in 1909. These cover mainly railroad engineering and allied subjects, the publishers apparently being under the impression that there has been no progress in any other branch of civil engineering during the past ten years. Furthermore, the pages that have been re-written have not been revised nearly enough. For instance they still contain the old cost data on earth work based on wages of $1 per day of 10 hours of common labor. What Trautwine's pocketbook really needs is a complete revision from cover to cover.

Iron and Steel. By Hugh P. Tiemann. Pp. 514, ill. McGraw-Hill Book Co., Inc., New York. For sale by 'Mining and Scientific Press'. Price, $4.

This is a pocket encyclopedia of the iron and steel industry. The more important terms, such as blast-furnace, heat treatment, and open-hearth process are described fully. The less important ones are either defined briefly, or else cross-referenced to the page of some one of the longer articles where a definition is given. No statement is given of the terms defined but the total must be several thousand.

Mining Decisions

Oil-Wells—Negligence in Keeping Oil Stored

Negligently allowing crude oil to escape from oil leasehold into a creek where it became ignited, was carried down stream and destroyed property, is grounds for recovery of damages by property-owner injured.

Northrup v. Oakes (Oklahoma), 178 Pacific, 266. February 11, 1919.

Oil-Lease—Unlawful Extension of Surface Possession

Where under an oil-lease granting to the lessee possession of so much of the surface as was necessary for sinking wells, the lessee proceeded to sublet sections of the surface to a third party for the erection of buildings and conduct of an oil-well supply business, held, that this use was not contemplated by lease, but that the lessor's remedy lay in suit for damages and not for a forfeiture of the lease and accounting.

Smith v. United Crude Oil Co. (California), 178 Pacific, 141. January 4, 1919.

Negligence of Mine-Owner in Not Informing of Danger

Where plaintiff was an entire stranger to defendant's mine, when taken into a stope and put to work as a miner, defendant owed him the duty of acquainting him with any dangerous conditions of which he had no knowledge, and which would not be apparent to him. The duty did not devolve upon the plaintiff to make the stope safe, and he had the right to assume that the defendant had used reasonable care to discover and remedy all dangerous defects.

Miller v. Utah Consolidated Mining Co. (Utah), 178 Pacific, 771. February 11, 1919.

Mineral Reservation in Deed—Construction

A deed reserved to the grantors the right to mine and remove all ores in and underneath the surface-area, provided certain buildings were not endangered by the operation. Thereafter the grantors in interest began to remove the ores by open-pit methods, which were in common use in mining copper ores in the vicinity. Held, that such mining was within the reserved rights under the deed, and the mining company was not limited to subterranean mining methods in extracting the minerals reserved.

Byron v. Utah Copper Co. (Utah), 178 Pacific, 53. December 28, 1918.

Lode Claim—Inchoate Possessory Rights

Until the actual discovery of mineral in place, all acts tending to consummate a valid lode location give the locator no right other than the right to continue a reasonable search for mineral. If the locator's right to possession of the claim be established, it carries with it the right to possession of the timber soil, country rock, percolating waters, natural springs, except certain mineral springs, and every appurtenant belonging to the realty. But if the locator fails to discover minerals within 90 days from the initiation of his location, under the laws of Arizona his right to exclusive possession terminates, although his actual possession cannot be disturbed until the Government intervenes or some qualified citizen initiates a better claim to the possession of the premises located.

McKenzie v. Moore (Arizona), 178 Pacific, 568. December 14, 1918.

INFORMATION FURNISHED BY MANUFACTURERS

NEW MOTOR-GENERATOR FOR MINE SUB-STATION

There are periods during the day when the electric load of a mine is very light, and then in an instant the demand for power may jump to several times the average. Such conditions occur with the starting or stopping of hoists and locomotives, and demand extra-good peak-load performance of the generating apparatus. This is especially true regarding synchronous motor-generator sets, for the generators are denied the relief afforded by the fall in speed of an engine-driven set, since they run at unvarying speed.

150-KW. SYNCHRONOUS MOTOR-GENERATOR SET

A new synchronous motor-generator set, which embodies the continuous power-factor correction common to such sets with every high overload and peak capacity, has recently been put on the market by the Westinghouse Electric & Mfg. Co. It consists of a type G, 3-phase, 60-cycle, synchronous motor, driving a type SK 150-volt 275-volt compound-generator. The machine has three bearings, the pedestals and field-frames being mounted on a common bed-plate. The full-load rating is based on continuous capacity with 35°C. rise on the generator; 45°C. on motor armature, and 50°C. rise on motor field with 80% power-factor. After a two-hours run at 50% overload, the generator temperature rise will not exceed 55°C., and the motor 55°C. On test, commutation was satisfactory at 250% load. The compound field is adjusted to give 10% increase in voltage from no load to full load.

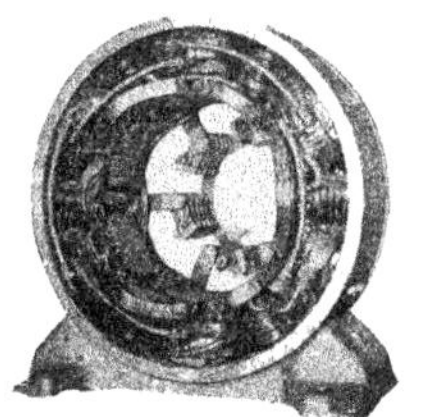

GENERATOR-FIELD UNIT COMPLETE, SHOWING POLE-FACE COMPENSATING WINDING

In addition to commutating poles of the generator, there is a compensating winding placed in slots in the faces of the main poles. This considerably improves the efficiency and gives extremely good commutating characteristics. As will be seen from the illustration, this winding consists of but one continuous coil per pole. Each coil is form-wound to exact dimensions, and is put into open slots in the pole-faces where it is held by wedges. This construction gives one joint per pole instead of two joints per conductor, as has been the custom in the past, where jumpers were used between bars. No difficulty is found in removing and replacing coils.

The motor is a 6-pole revolving-field machine, provided with squirrel-cage damper winding in the pole-faces. This permits of starting the set from the alternating-current side, and also ensures its stability under sudden variation of load. The field may be over-excited to draw 'leading' reactive current from the line, thus compensating for the 'lagging' current of induction-motors. This helps the voltage regulation, especially where a long transmission-line is used. A voltage-regulator may be employed, which will hold the alternating voltage constant within the range of the set.

The performance of this set is as follows: ½ load, efficiency 81.4%; ¾ load, 85%; full load, 86.5%, and 1½ load, 88%.

COMMERCIAL PARAGRAPHS

'Rails and Accessories' is the title of Bulletin 258 of W. A. Zelnicker & Co. of St. Louis. Copies are free to the trade.

Ben Sweetland, expert advertising agent, announces that his suite in the Singer Building annex, New York, has been doubled in size.

The Acme Motor Truck Co. of Cadillac, Michigan, issues an interesting 14-page monthly, that for March containing descriptions and illustrations of the uses of its motor-trucks.

Fuller & Smith of Cleveland, Ohio, announce that the Aspromet Company's name has been changed to the H. H. Robertson Company. The firm is manufacturer of asbestos products.

In a leaflet entitled 'A Little Talk About the Jordan', the O. F. Jordan Co., of East Chicago, Indiana, shows the ditching, shouldering, ballast-shaping, and carrying wing on its spreading-machine.

Bone-ash for assayers' cupels is the principal subject discussed in Bulletin 375 of the Denver Fire Clay Co., Denver, Colorado. A cupel machine, sieves, and laboratory crushers are also mentioned.

The Chicago Pneumatic Tool Co. has moved its Milwaukee office from room 1305 Majestic building to room 1418 in the same building, where more convenient quarters necessitated by the growing business of the company in this district have been obtained.

The former Lyons-Atlas Co. of Indianapolis and the former Hill Pump Co. of Anderson, Indiana, have come under a common control and a common management, and will henceforth be known as the **Midwest Engine Co.** The executive offices are in Indianapolis.

In a 79-page general catalogue, the **Fort Pitt Bedding Co.**, of Pittsburgh, Pa., illustrates and briefly describes its many types of beds, bunks, and accessories therefor. Mining companies that have bunk-houses, hospitals, and the like, should find much of interest herein.

Comments of the technical press upon the Crowe vacuum precipitation process, as used in cyanide plants, has been collected and published in pamphlet form by **The Merrill Company** of San Francisco. The system is used in 18 mills in North America, and two elsewhere.

A description and illustration of the **Link-Belt Company's**, of Chicago, Peck overlapping pivoted bucket-carrier for ore, coal, coke, ash, cement, stone, and other materials, will be found in Book No. 220. The buckets hold from 0.68 to 5.25 cu. ft., and are made of malleable iron.

Correction. In the March 1 issue it was stated in error that the **Denver Engineering Works**, Denver, Colorado, recently furnished ball-mills for the new mill at the U. S. S. R. & M. Co. at Eureka, Colorado. The principal grinding at the Sunnyside plant is done in Marcy mills.

The E. I. du Pont de Nemours & Co. announces that T. E. Doremus has been transferred to the company's export department as general Eastern manager, with headquarters at Shanghai, China. E. R. Galvin has been appointed manager of the sporting powder division to succeed Mr. Doremus.

The Marthon Mill Machinery Works, First National Bank Bdg., Chicago, is a new company that has been organized to take over the Marathon mill and other machinery formerly manufactured and sold by the Johnson Engineering Works. The latter will devote its attention to other lines of machinery.

D. Gleisen, chairman of the Board of Managers, industrial divisions, **General Motors Corporation**, and manager of the industrial bearings division **Hyatt Roller Bearing Co.**, announces the appointment of P. C. Funion as advertising manager for the industrial divisions, General Motors Corporation.

E. D. Bullard announces his new catalogue of carbide lamps, oxy-acetylene equipment, and safety supplies. Purchasing offices of mines, shipyards, manufacturers, welding-shops, etc., will probably be interested in this booklet, which will be supplied on application to 268 Market street, San Francisco.

'Mine and Quarry' for March, the monthly of the **Sullivan Machinery Co.** of Chicago, contains several readable articles, including 'Drill Sharpener Speeds Up Shipbuilding', 'Diamond-Drills Pick Dam Location', 'Heavy Drilling at Sacramento Hill, Bisbee', Sullivan Straight-Line Compressor with Plate-Valves', and 'Air-Lift Boosts Artesian Well Flow'.

The Huff Electrostatic Separator Co., having outgrown its plant at 60 India street, Boston, announces the opening of its new offices, laboratories, and works at Mystic and Summer streets, Arlington, Massachusetts, where it will maintain a fully-equipped modern laboratory and conduct investigations embracing all ore-dressing, metallurgical, and milling problems.

A splendid new building has just been completed for **Rosenberg & Co.**, machinery distributors of Los Angeles. This firm reports large sales of re-built machinery for Arizona and has also recently made a number of shipments to nearly every Western State. The company's recent large purchase of mining equipment has been attracting much attention, aand the stock is being rapidly sold.

The Dobbins Core Drill Co. of New York City announces the appointment of Harron, Rickard & McCone as its representatives in San Francisco, Los Angeles, and surrounding territory. The Salt Lake Hardware Co. has been appointed representative for the district contiguous to Salt Lake City. A new and interesting catalog has been issued by the Dobbins company describing its core-drills.

C. H. Ramsden, formerly chief engineer for the Western Pipe & Steel Co. of California; W. F. Focha, and Captain C. A. Duffie, who has just been discharged from the Army, have formed the **Steel Tank & Pipe Co. of California.** A modern plant for the fabrication of riveted-steel tanks and pipe is now under construction at Berkeley, California, and San Francisco offices have been opened at 241 Hansford building.

Smith, Emery & Co., chemical engineers and chemists of San Francisco and Los Angeles, have well under way the plans for a cement mill to be erected in an undisturbed part of Mexico. Materials to be used consist of limestone and natural pozzuolana. The preliminary burnings and engineering test have shown a sound, cheaply-produced portland cement. The capital, it is understood, is being furnished jointly by American and Mexican financiers.

Six **Oliver** filters, 12 by 16 ft., with complete vacuum-plant, have been ordered by the American Smelters Securities Co. for its Veta Grande mill at Parral, Chihuahua, Mexico. The Alvarado M. & M. Co. at Parral has one 12 by 18 and one 14 by 18-ft. Oliver filter. The vacuum equipment mentioned consists of a 23 by 12-in. duplex Imperial type XB-1 Ingersoll-Rand dry vacuum-pump, a 3-in. ball-bearing centrifugal pump, and Oliver vacuum receivers.

In Bulletin 34, the **Lidgerwood Manufacturing Co.**, whose works are at Brooklyn, N. Y., and Newark, N. J., describes and illustrates the operation of its coal-handling cableways. This device has proved successful on coal-storage work, where the ground available for storage could hardly be used with any other method. The firm has only recently looked into this field, and from investigation finds that there is little knowledge among engineers of the possibility of the cableway for this kind of work.

The Merrill Metallurgical Co. of San Francisco announces that the expansion of the business and professional work of the firm due to the increased use of its apparatus and processes and the acquisition of other processes, products, agencies, and devices, has necessitated the enlargement of its staff and facilities and made advisable incorporation of **The Merrill Co.** The new company takes over the patents and commercial business of its predecessor, and will continue to enlarge its scope as new devices and products become available, which it is justified in presenting to its clients as of unquestionable merit and efficiency. Charles W. Merrill is president.

A handsome 88-page loose-leaf catalogue is the novelty just sent us by the **Justrite Manufacturing Co., of Chicago.** As new goods are made or articles or prices changed, new leaves for insertion will be sent for addition or substitution. The company eight years ago developed and offered the Justrite miners' carbide lamp, but in this catalog illustrates and describes 42 distinct types of lamps and in many combinations manufactured by it. Mining companies will find this publication worth filing, as in it will be found the various lamps, their size, weight, charge of carbide, candle-power, burning capacity in hours, and prices; also data on repair parts.

WHEN the Germans, who managed to keep the war out of their own country and thereby, except for a part of East Prussia, escaped the horrors they visited on their neighbors, protest against the terms of peace, it is well to remember that the damage they did in France is estimated at 21 billion dollars, or about as much as the total war debt of the United States. They destroyed 22,999 factories, or about one-sixth of all the factories in France and about one-half the entire value of French property in factories. They destroyed 240,999 homes. Just imagine one of these homes to be your own.

UNDER the heading of 'Discussion' we publish a letter from Mr. Morton Webber in which he makes clear his professional connection with the Butte Copper Czar mine, which is the subject of a circular recently issued for the purpose of explaining the proposal to find fresh capital for this enterprise. We are glad at all times to give the use of our columns to members of the profession in the defence of their reputations. If a man stands right with the members of his profession, it matters little what the public thinks, because in the end the public must take its cue from those who are best informed.

IN this issue we publish the text of the oral argument made before the U. S. Supreme Court by counsel for the Minerals Separation company in the final hearing of the case against the Butte & Superior company, on appeal from the Ninth Circuit Court in San Francisco. The patentees, who are the petitioners, were represented by Messrs. Henry D. Williams and W. Houston Kenyon, both of whom made good arguments for their clients. Next week we shall give our readers an opportunity to read the argument on the other side, namely, the one made by Mr. J. Edgar Bull for the Butte & Superior company. The colloquies between counsel and members of the Court are particularly interesting to those who have followed this litigation.

CARRANZA'S government, it will be recalled, has refused to recognize the financial clause in the Armistice by which Germany pledged herself to the Allied governments not to dispose of her stocks in specie or any of her foreign title-deeds or bonds abroad, whether in possession of the Government, the savings-banks, private persons, or companies, without the previous consent of the Allies. In a note delivered to the French government on April 28, the Mexican government took the stand that these engagements made by Germany in the Armistice are contrary to the Mexican constitution and to the terms of the treaty between Germany and Mexico. This applies to the holdings of the American Metal Company and its subsidiaries in Mexico, all of which are detailed in the report of the Alien Property Custodian.

EXPORTS of copper during the last two months have fallen to 5966 and 4218 tons respectively in March and April, as compared with 31,188 and 23,811 tons in the corresponding months of last year. In January 1917 American exports of copper reached the maximum of 51,322 tons. If the present production be estimated at 125 million pounds per month, it is evident that the April exports represent 8% as against the normal 40% exportation from this country. As France and Italy are closed by governmental decree to the importation of American copper, and as England has on hand a tonnage nearly equal to that imported in 1913, it is evident that there will be no noteworthy improvement in the foreign demand until the signing of the Peace Treaty restores business communication with Germany and other parts of Central Europe.

IN April 1918 the Government, by authorization of the Pittman Act, began the melting of the 490,000,000 silver dollars hoarded in the Treasury. This was done to meet the urgent requirements of the British government of India. Within a year $250,000,000 worth of silver was shipped from the American mints, and of this 200,000,000 fine ounces were sold for the use of the Indian government. Concurrently the price of silver was fixed at $1.01½ per ounce and an embargo was placed upon private, as against governmental, exportation of silver. The lifting of this embargo caused the price of silver to rise promptly to a maximum of slightly over $1.20, followed by a recession during the last week to a low quotation of $1.10 per ounce. The prospects for a higher price are good, but the coinage ratio of $1.29, of course, will be the limit to which the quotation can go.

THE Institute bulletin for May contains a strange collection of reading-matter, including two pages of graphic diagrams showing the trend of the bond and stock markets, besides two other pages devoted to the annual dinner of the Rocky Mountain Club. Are these in their right place? Now that paper, printing, and postage are so expensive, is it well to incur the unnecessary expense of publishing irrelevant matter such as this? The Rocky Mountain Club has no connection with the profession or with the purposes of the Institute, nor are the antics of its members of more than ephemeral local interest to anybody. However, the bulletin does include, besides the text of the various papers contributed to the Transactions, a report of the symposium, held recently at New York, on 'The Engineer as a Citizen'. This is well worthy of inclusion.

OPTIMISM continues to characterize the mood of the American people. Their buying capacity appears to be hardly affected by conditions overseas, and the general trade of the country, in consequence, is lively and large. Undoubtedly the prosperity of the farmer, due to an abnormally good market and unusually big crops, is having its stimulating effect on business generally. Construction work is checked by the prevailing high prices of labor and materials, but the erection of houses, at least, cannot be much delayed, owing to the urgent demand created by the cessation of building during the active period of the War. The mining industry is suffering from the effects of an overstocked metal market and will not resume its normal expansion until the signing of the Treaty of Peace removes the barriers to international business that have arisen from a state of war; nevertheless there is a good deal of activity, especially in the search for the precious metals. The rise in the cost of labor has been corrected by the curtailment of operations at most of the copper and zinc mines, but no satisfactory adjustment of wages is likely until the output of food-stuffs in the belligerent countries is renewed in such volume as to restore the normal supply of the world and thereby reduce the cost of living.

RESUMPTION of work at the Argonaut and Kennedy mines is announced, and we are glad to record the fact. The fire underground, which was the cause of the interruption to the productive activities of these two important Californian mines, is under control, and will shortly be totally extinguished. References to the Argonaut as the deepest mine in the world, and so forth, have appeared in the local press. Therefore it may be well to state that the deepest metal mine in the world is the St. John del Rey, in Brazil. This famous old gold mine has reached a vertical depth of 6326 feet. On the Rand the Jupiter is 5040 feet, the Simmer Deep is 4780 feet, the Cinderella 4627 feet, and the Village Deep 4245 feet in vertical depth. The Brazilian and the South African mines are about three thousand feet deeper on the dip of the lodes than the figures quoted, but 'depth', of course, is the distance from surface. On the Kolar goldfield, in India, the Ooregum is 5250 feet and the Champion Reef 5380 feet deep. In the Lake Superior copper country the Tamarack No. 5 shaft is 5368 feet and the Tamarack No. 3 is 5281 feet. At Bendigo, in Australia, the Victoria Reef Quartz mine reached a depth of 4614 feet. The Argonaut is 4600 feet on the dip, or 3900 feet vertical, whereas the Kennedy is 4050 feet deep vertically. The world is a large place, therefore it is dangerous to make hasty generalizations. As a matter of fact the Argonaut and Kennedy mines are a thousand feet short of being remarkably deep, fortunately for their owners.

WE take pleasure in publishing a careful and comprehensive article on the oil-shale industry, with particular reference to Colorado, by Mr. Arthur J. Hoskin, of Denver. The subject is one well worthy the attention of the profession, even to those having no idea at present of becoming engaged in the exploitation of oil-shale, because it involves a number of interesting technical problems and it promises to be of increasing importance to the community. Long after our oil-wells cease to flow, either naturally or by mechanical means, the winning of oil from shale is likely to be engaging the activities of enterprising men. Mr. Hoskin, quite properly, does not give much space to the oil-shale industry as developed in foreign countries, in Scotland and Australia, for example, because the conditions abroad are so different from those with which we have to deal in our own country; indeed, American writings on this subject heretofore have been rich in details of foreign practice and poor in the information required more immediately for domestic exploitation. The technology of the subject offers several interesting phases, which Mr. Hoskin discusses usefully; but, after all, the commercial phase is the decisive factor, namely, the production of oil good enough and cheap enough to compete successfully with the wells from which we now obtain our supplies of liquid fuel.

The Metal Octopus

In our last issue we published the last of four instalments of the report issued by the Alien Property Custodian on the operations of the German metal octopus, namely, the group of metal-dealers headed by the Metallgesellschaft of Frankfort, in combination with Aron Hirsch & Sohn of Halberstadt, and Beer, Sondheimer & Company of Frankfort, together with their various associates and agents, including the American Metal Company, Henry R. Merton & Co., L. Vogelstein & Co., and their subsidiaries. We have thought it worth while to give so much space to this report because it contains information valuable to all those engaged in the production and selling of metals, and because the report emanates from a source in which we and our readers can have confidence. Mr. A. Mitchell Palmer was appointed Alien Property Custodian by the President as soon as the control and disposal of enemy business made such a Federal department necessary, and when, a few months ago, Mr. Palmer became U. S. Attorney General, he was succeeded by his first assistant, Mr. Francis P. Garvan. It is not stated who prepared the report on the German metal business, but we hazard the guess that Mr. Garvan, who was director of the Bureau of Investigation, deserves chief credit for it. It is unfortunate that the author of the report did not avail himself more of technical assistance, because some of the references to metallurgical processes are needlessly inaccurate. The Custodian has retained several of the former directors of the American Metal Company in office and it would appear reasonable to expect that from them, or through them, for example, he could have obtained the assistance required for the purpose of straightening the wrinkles in his metallurgy. However these minor blemishes do not affect the main purpose of the report, which is to disclose the ramifications of a combination that was threatening the mineral industry of the whole world. We have referred to the subject several times in these columns during the last four years, being first prompted to do so by the disclosures made in the Snow trial at Adelaide, in South Australia, at the end of 1914. The correspondence placed in evidence in that case showed how the various German firms aided each other in selling metals to Germany in disregard of the Australian law enacted at the commencement of hostilities. At the same time it was shown that 89% of the zinc output and 95% of the copper output of Australia was controlled by these German firms. The Custodian's report proves how the same commercial penetration had succeeded, before the War, in controlling a large part of the metal business of this country; it exposes the methods by which the members of these firms evaded war-time regulations by transferring their business to American agents or by going through the process of naturalization. Now, it appears to us quite clear that much of this pernicious activity, especially the industrial syndication, was objectionable in itself, not merely because it was German. The fact that it originated from an enemy country enabled the agents of our Government, and of the British government, to make a legal inquisition into its methods and manifestations, but it was destructive to business enterprise in the English-speaking countries not because it was German but because it was in restraint of trade. The Federal Trade Commission published its own report, to the same purpose, and we gave our readers the gist of it in our issue of January 19, 1918. The combination in restraint of trade, whereby these German syndicates were enabled to move the metal markets in their own interest was bad whether it was German, American, or British. Indeed, we go so far as to say that it was largely non-national in its spirit, it owed allegiance not to the kaiser but to the mark, the dollar, or the pound sterling, whichever was nearest; it was 'peeziness'; for it must be recognized that it was in the hands of Jews almost without exception. Even that eminently English name 'Merton' was mere camouflage, for the real name of the founder of Henry R. Merton & Co. was Moses, a cousin of the Cohen that founded the Metallgesellschaft. The fact is that the traffic in metals, with its intricacies and trickeries, suits the Jew so well that he has gradually acquired control of the world's trade. If the Australians allowed 80% of the products of their base-metal mines to be controlled by the German-Jew agencies, it was largely their own fault. If the British allowed the Australian zinc output, which was just equal to the British domestic consumption, to sail past their ports to Hamburg and Rotterdam, on consignment to German-Jew dealers, it was largely their fault also. If the American producers exercised so little sagacity as to permit themselves to be gathered within the tentacles of this octopus, they also have only themselves to blame. The members of this commercial cuttlefish wanted to do business, that is, to make money, and they used all the tricks of the trade to effect their purpose. They persuaded the German banks to finance them, they stood together against the producers, they assumed any nationality that suited them, even registering their German companies in London in order to obtain protection in their South American trade, and naturalizing themselves in the United States in order to evade the military embargo. In all this they were not working so much for Germany as for themselves, they were non-national in their aims, they were "after the stuff"—and they got it. It will be a blunder if in our anti-German enthusiasm we, that is, the American producers of metals, assume that the exposure of the German system and the seizure of their property in this country will put an end to the metal-brokers' control of the market. The Custodian, thanks to the exigencies of war, has released American and Mexican mining enterprises from "the dominance of Germany-owned corporations", as a Washington telegram says. The Custodian himself says, "it is believed that the German influences in our metal markets have been completely eliminated." This has been done by selling the German shareholdings in the American metal firms to American capitalists, and, concurrently, German shares in British firms have passed into English bands. So far, so good; but all danger has not been escaped, for many of the former directors are still on the boards of these companies and they are co-operating with the new directors, who were either nominated by the Custodian or are on the boards by reason of their purchase, by auction, of large blocks of shares. Business is non-moral and, except in times of national crisis, non-patriotic. It is quite on the cards that the new controllers of these concerns may get an oppressive grip on the metal market. During war a German control might be worse than an American or a British control, but in time of peace any control in restraint of trade will be obnoxious, no matter what the nationality of the combination. The producers should remain on their guard, and not lull themselves into a false sense of security. They must devise some means of protection. They suffer from the fact that the big custom-smelting companies both own mines and control metal-selling agencies. By owning mines they can ensure a part of their needed supply of ore and thereby apply the discipline of the sand-bag to recalcitrant customers; through their metal-selling agencies they hold an advantage over the ore-producer. It is against the law now for the anthracite coal companies to control the public railways used in their business because it was found that the interplay of ownership was detrimental to the welfare of the community. It might be well if custom smelters were debarred from owning mines or from engaging in metal-dealing outside their own production; indeed, the threat, made in Colorado, for example, of placing the smelters in the category of public utilities, thereby subjecting them to the State Commission created to supervise such business activities, is one that we would like to see put into force, if only we were sure that it would be used fairly. We know, of course, that the regulations for inter-State business are evaded by the smelters; they agree to cut their lawns on the same day or to look out of the window when politeness requires it; they do not compete unreservedly, and they enjoy sundry railroad freight-rates that are difficult to explain except on grounds similar to those that give 'inflooence' to O'Flaherty. Another escape from cuttlefishes is to organize an independent ore-producers selling agency for self-protection, that is, to meet collective buying with collective selling. It is an interesting problem and one to which we shall be glad to give space, if any of our readers care to express their views.

A Post-Mortem

In our issue of February 15 we discussed the record of the Camp Bird mining company and that of its Mexican subsidiary, the Santa Gertrudis. We have now been placed in possession of additional information, which is interesting, besides being corrective and supplementary. The Santa Gertrudis promotion was started by a syndicate, formed in 1909, consisting of Messrs. John Hays Hammond, Cortlandt E. Palmer, Hugh Rose, and Frank W. Royer, all well-known mining engineers. The first mine taken under option by this syndicate was the La Blanca at Pachuca. It was examined by Mr. Royer and a competent staff, the results being so favorable that it was decided to offer the property to the Camp Bird company, which accepted the option and sent Messrs. R. J. Frecheville, W. J. Cox, and E. E. Chase to examine the mine. Prior to the arrival of these engineers the promoters had induced the La Blanca company to start some winzes on the vein from the bottom level. At the time when the Camp Bird engineers arrived at Pachuca these winzes were giving evidence that the ore-shoot was shortening in depth. Meanwhile Mr. Royer had begun an examination of a neighboring mine, the Santa Gertrudis, with results so favorable that it was decided to offer the option, which had been obtained by the syndicate, to the Camp Bird company in lieu of the option on the La Blanca. Messrs. Frecheville, Cox, and Chase recommended the purchase of the Santa Gertrudis and the transaction was duly completed, on the terms quoted in our previous editorial. The appraisal of the Camp Bird engineers seemed justified by the evidence obtainable underground. The 17th level showed the ore-shoot at its best on that level, which was the deepest in the mine; the 18th level subsequently showed further improvement, the orebody being 1600 feet long, 15 feet wide, and averaging 39.3 ounces in silver, with $3.90 in gold per short ton. Every 100 feet of an orebody of this size and richness represented $3,750,000 net profit, the silver being taken at 50 cents per ounce. Competent engineers, of course, recognize the danger of estimating both the yield and the persistence of such high-grade ore-shoots, and they face a risk in recommending the purchase of such mines as the Santa Gertrudis, which are not purchasable at a price fully covered by the ore assured. The purchase is a sane speculotion based upon a reasonable expectation of the continuance of the ore below the bottom workings. In this case the expectation of continuance was based upon the record of other mines in the Pachuca district, and it seemed to them that the increasing strength of the Santa Gertrudis orebody down to the 17th level warranted the anticipation that it might continue to a further depth of 450 feet. Such did not prove to be the case. The 18th level more than fulfilled expectations, as already stated, but on the 19th the ore averaged only about one-third its assay-value on the 18th level, and the 20th level practically bottomed the ore-shoot. Although the country-rock did not change, nor were the structural conditions different, yet the mineralization seemed to end abruptly. On the other hand, whereas only 150,000 tons of fill in old stopes was included in the estimate of reserves, the former workings yielded more than a million tons of low-grade ore. Moreover, the Mexican revolution and the European war caused a loss of $1,500,000 in possible profit. Such is the post-mortem of the Santa Gertrudis. It confirms our previous autopsy. In fairness to three members of the syndicate it should be recorded—although we suggested nothing to the contrary—that Messrs. Palmer, Rose, and Royer had no professional connection with the Camp Bird company at the time of the purchase of the Santa Gertrudis; they simply examined the mine on their own account before offering it for sale. Mr. Hammond, consulting engineer to the Camp Bird company, had a quarter interest in the business; and as regards him it is fair to add that at first he advised against the purchase, being guided thereto by the adverse report of Mr. M. H. Burnham, whose opinion was set aside subsequently by a most painstaking inspection made by Mr. F. F. Sharpless. Mr. Rose became manager for the Camp Bird after the purchase had been completed. Largely on his initiative, the life of the enterprise has been lengthened profitably by the recent acquisition of the El Bordo property, another neighboring group of mines. All this does not palliate the extraordinary conduct of the directors in London, and of their consulting engineer, at the time of the flotation. They participated in the profits of the various underwritings and commissions—all except Mr. W. F. Fisher, who resigned from the board. An issue of preferred stock was guaranteed by the chairman and his friends for a commission of 10%, making $325,000. The total sum received by the consulting engineer and the directors altogether amounted to $775,000. These facts were disclosed at the time and the shareholders made no protest. Of course, the directors were serving as trustees for the shareholders and they should have done nothing of the kind so long as they occupied a fiduciary position. In the end Mr. Arthur M. Grenfell, the chairman, became badly involved in his dealings between the Camp Bird and other companies and went into bankruptcy just before the War, in which he did his duty as became the member of a family of gallant soldiers. The whole story is worthy of record. It carries its own moral, which we forbear further to emphasize.

Re-financing of the Butte Copper Czar

The Editor:

Sir—I beg to submit a circular which has been handed to me in respect to a proposal for re-financing the Butte Copper Czar Mining Co., the property of which is located at Butte, Montana. As I am the engineer mentioned in the circular, I feel, in the interest of the public, the facts should be known. I herewith quote part of the text of the circular.

"During the year of 1918, development work was carried on by a New York Company, with Mr. Morton Webber in charge. A station was cut on the 300-foot level, together with sump for water. There were 510 feet of cross-cut driven and after the vein was encountered 477 feet of drifting was done on the vein. The vein on this level varied from 4 feet to 8 feet wide, and is highly mineralized, proving an ore-chute continuous for more than 300 feet, carrying good values in silver and copper. Unfortunately, Mr. Webber did not come within 100 feet of the ore-chute where commercial ore shows above. On account of the high cost of labor and supplies the New York people decided to drop the option on the control of the Company and all stock not paid for has been turned back to the Treasurer of the Company, making a balance of 312,888 shares remaining in the treasury."

From the above it would appear by inuendo that the work entrusted to my charge had been performed in an incompetent manner. It would also appear that the whole basis for re-financing is that, owing to the incompetence exhibited in my management, the property did not get a fair trial. As for example: "Unfortunately, Mr. Webber did not come within 100 feet of the ore-chute where commercial ore shows above." This is a misrepresentation of fact. The ore-shoot shown in the surface workings constituted an attractive mining speculation. The development of the downward prolongation of this shoot was clearly the crux on which the future possibilities of the property would largely depend. I was thoroughly alive to the importance of this phase of the work. The drifting done under my direction clearly indicated that the ore-shoot did not persist in depth as my exploration would have caught the shoot, allowing for a rake of 45° either way from the vertical.

The circular also states: "The vein on this level varies from four to eight feet wide, and is highly mineralized, proving an ore-chute continuous for more than three hundred feet, carrying good values in silver and copper." I beg to state that this level was sampled under my direction and there were no values such as this statement might indicate; although the term "good values" is ambiguous. The highest assays that were ever obtained were less than 2% copper and two to three ounces in silver; and these were only in spots.

The circular also states, "On account of the high cost of labor and supplies, the New York people decided to drop the option on the control of the Company and all stock not paid for has been turned back to the Treasurer of the Company." There is no foundation for this statement. The corporation which I represented in this work has between three and four million dollars in liquid assets, and operations were terminated only on my advice that the development work we had done demonstrated that the prospects of the mine were very unfavorable; that further expenditure would mean further loss.

I write this letter in the interests of the public and also that I do not propose to sit calmly by and witness a re-financing the basis of which is evidently that I did not know my business. If there is any question as to who is right, I will suggest that the stockholders, before proceeding to re-financing, will first employ an independent engineer to report on the merit of the enterprise. A prime essential in his selection should be that his professional standing would carry the guarantee that he would be without prejudice.

MORTON WEBBER.

New York, May 14, 1919.

Mine Labor

The Editor:

Sir—The fourth paragraph on top of page 610 in the March Bulletin of the A. I. M. E., in Will L. Clark's vigorous discussion of Herbert M. Wilson's paper, 'Employment of Mine Labor', shows the American youth to have a hard future before him, because he is constitutionally hungry and opposed to steady work. The former characteristic reminds me of landing at the Bullion mine, in Idaho, some years ago, and my hostess asking if I were not hungry, when two little girls piped up, "I'se hungry, Mamma." Answer: "Oh you 'uns are always hungry." And another but recent scene in my own dining-room when my daughter had left a handsome piece of cake alone with her brother of sixteen, who, however, was six feet and weighed 165 lb. What became of it may be surmised from the conversation that floated from the room. There was probably an appeal for forgiveness. "Go away, don't touch me, you're a pig, and you have three brothers and they were pigs too, I know,

I was brought up with them." The same boy increased his age two years between the house and the recruiting stations and has been with the First Division for 17 months, and is with it now in Germany. His notes did not express any wish to be elsewhere than he was, perhaps he had not time to think about it, it was always "going day and night."

Possibly the "observer," mentioned in that paragraph, saw more of the rear camps than the front trenches. The same lad's eldest brother resigned his position to join the 25th Engineers, and he did seem to fret a little at only building supply-depots and railways in a non-combatant area, but going through the Argonne drive seems to have restored his spirits, and I do not hear any complaint from his long stay at Brest, although each month is a serious loss of time to him.

Regarding our men being broke, we might expect it from the most vigorous and ambitious youth of the land working in a strange country, on camp fare, for, say, $10 per month, after deductions are made from the $30. Since the wage question was settled by Congress I have had a sense of shame at the pittance, when we at home were prospering because of the War, and not the least those whose income was affected by the price of copper.

Referring to Californian garden work, it would be interesting to know the wages paid per hour, the amount this represents per pound of fruit, the ages of the Japanese, Chinese, etc., and whether the American youth have been idle while these were working. I remember my particular chum in old Californian days, who lived just outside San Jose, learning his lessons with the books hanging on the handle of the plow while attending the State Normal, and who would leave at 4:30 a.m. with a load of hay for town, returning in time to dress nicely for school. At Denver one of my own sons announced that during the high-school summer holiday he was going to Boulder to work on a ranch. I expected him back in a few days, but he only returned, with his pockets full of money from $20 per month, in time to buy a new suit of clothes and enter school. Afterward, returning from Mexico through Arizona, he stayed to work underground in a large copper mine, reducing his weight from 165 lb. to 135 lb. in 30 days, after which time he was discharged by a foreign shift-boss. However, he came north, and, through the kindness of the companies he has worked for, has not lost a day's wages in seven years.

Coming to foreigners and a mine employing 80% of them, I am reminded of the change from an Irish to a Cornish foreman of the mine. "And now the Irish are coming down the hill and the Cousin Jacks are going up." What do we mean by foreigners? Is it those who keep to themselves, usually getting a lower wage than the Anglo-Celtic or mixed nationalities? During the first year of the War I did tunnelling with a crew of one Canadian, who had two brothers in France, two Irishmen, two Germans, one Austrian, and two Americans. There was lots of chaffing, but no bitterness, for all were really Americans, and each was a splendid worker, well-informed and intelligent. I added ten dollars to the Austrian's check when he left, for "a good dinner in town on the company's account."

The worst time-killing laborers I have seen have been the real foreigner, from the Chinese in the old days in California to the south-eastern European of today. I have thought this slackness was accompanied by a lack of self-respect, repugnant to a man of better mentality.

I have often wondered, seeing criticisms by employers of their employees, in what country the employer could have secured happier results. At an Institute meeting, since we entered the War, one of the prominent managers in an important mining community stated what we have heard so often, that the work done per man had decreased as the wages increased. I was on the alert and sought him after adjournment; he said: "That is what the other managers tell me; in our case a bonus system was arranged which resulted in our getting more than the highest wages, while the work cost less than in pre-War times." This may have been extra exertion by the men and better arrangements by the management.

My opportunity for observation has not been varied during the War, but I judge that Americans are as appreciative of higher wages as the distinctly foreigners, that they stayed with their jobs pretty well, and there was no difference in the amount of work performed. Those leaving were mostly poor workmen and their move was a benefit to the employer. We are all in the same boat in this world, living from hand to mouth on the season's production, and we need a strong pull and a pull altogether.

Mr. Clark mentions the advantage of work about the copper plants; I think it offers excellent opportunity for earnest young men wishing to earn money for a college course. They could save enough in three years or less for a comfortable four years course and the summer vacations. During the three years the equivalent of two hours daily could be spent in study, besides time for general reading, equivalent to a solid year of six hours daily. Much thinking and actual assimilation can go on during working-hours, as the mind is largely free and often enough the hands.

JOHN B. HASTINGS.

Los Angeles, May 4.

THE GRAPHITE-MINING INDUSTRY is dependent directly upon the metal industries. The use of graphite in the manufacture of crucibles, of foundry facings, and of lubricants furnishes the link that ties the two industries. The steel business consumes 30 to 40% of the graphite crucibles manufactured. In October last, of the 39 mills in Alabama, 21 were operating; in April, only 11 were at work.—G. D. Dub in April report of U. S. Bureau of Mines.

SPELTER PRODUCTION per retort in the United States is slightly over four tons per annum. Elimination of much of the lower grades of ores has increased the output.

IRON in sand used for optical glass must be very little—from 0.004 to 0.02% Fe_2O_3.

LEDGE OF OIL-SHALE NEAR GRAND VALLEY, COLORADO

GREEN RIVER BEDS, NEAR DE BEQUE, COLORADO

OIL-SHALE IN UINTA BASIN, UTAH

SHALE BURNING, ON THE PROPERTY OF THE UTAH OIL-SHALE CO.

LEDGE OF RICH SHALE, BETWEEN DRAGON AND WATSON: THE PROPERTY OF THE UTAH OIL-SHALE CO.

OIL-SHALE NEAR GRAND JUNCTION, COLORADO

ANOTHER VIEW OF THE COLORADO SHALE

GENERAL VIEW OF OIL-SHALE BEDS ALONG ROAN CREEK, COLORADO

The Winning of Oil From Rocks

By ARTHUR J. HOSKIN

During the past two years considerable attention has been given to certain natural resources that may eventually prove the basis of one of America's greatest industries. The existence of combustible shale in several States has been known for many years. Here and there, in separate parts of our country, Indians, settlers, ranchmen, and surveyors long ago found rocks that would burn. Occasionally such a discovery was attended with disaster, as in the case of a Western school-house burning to the ground because its 'stone' fireplace proved combustible. A few relics of primitive attempts to utilize such rocks in the manufacture of 'coal-oil' may be found here and there, both in the East and in the West. Near Moab, in Utah, is a small retort said to have been built for this purpose by Mormon pioneers. A gulch in the hills near Dillon, in Montana, is known as Coal creek because a few early ranchmen here derived their fuel for domestic purposes from an outcropping ledge of shale, which they assumed to be a peculiar low-grade coal. A surveyor who, years ago, assisted in subdividing into sections a portion of the 'western slope' of Colorado told me it was common for his camping party to utilize the shale as fuel for cooking and heating.

So I conclude that we Americans have ignored for a long time a resource of significance, a resource that is perhaps even now coming in for serious recognition merely because of alarming statistics promulgated by our Federal bureaus regarding the diminishing sources of motor-fuel.

FOREIGN SHALE INDUSTRY. The authors of articles on this subject in American journals seem to think it necessary to review at length the oil-shale industry that has thrived abroad, especially in Scotland, France, and Germany for many years, and from such foreign data to draw conclusions as to what we may and should accomplish with similar shales in this country. The industry in France dates back 89 years, whereas that in Scotland has been active for about 60 years. I shall not gainsay a single statement concerning the established foreign oil-shale industries. I do, however, raise the point that there is so much dissimilarity between the American and the Scotch shales, for instance, that it is a mistake to draw close analogies as to what we may accomplish with our own deposits. Metallurgists know well that slight differences in the physical or chemical composition of ores of a single metal frequently call for different methods of treatment to recover that metal. Coal men know that very slight, often invisible, variations in coal from different neighboring mines have vital significance in coking qualities. So it is with regard to oil-shales, not only as to differences between such rocks in widely separated regions of the world, but, to a notable degree, between deposits in the same region and even as between contiguous strata. It is a fact that the majority of the American oil-shales differ radically from the Scotch shales in their geologic occurrence, their chemical composition, their texture, and especially in the products they will yield. Therefore, except by way of drawing vague comparisons, we should not base any plans for commercializing American oil-shales upon practices and successes in Scotland or elsewhere. For this reason, then, I shall restrict my discussion to conditions existing in the United States.

THE AMERICAN SHALE INDUSTRY. Although, as explained, there had long been some knowledge of such rocks in this country, it was not until about two years ago that general credence was given by the public to these resources. It was during the summer of 1916 that the first adventures were made into this new field of industry. A few men read the description of Scottish practice and erected experimental retorts copied from drawings in books. The experiments in general were disappointing. Undaunted by failure and spurred by the potentialities, these men became inventive, and we must credit them with whatever success has thus far been developed in this industry, which is really new so far as America is concerned.

THE OIL-SHALES. The term 'oil-shale' is a misnomer. A better name for rocks of this sort is 'bituminous shale'. An oil-sand carries native oil or petroleum, whereas an oil-shale contains no oil or, at most, only traces. There is no analogy between oil-sands and oil-shales, a fact not generally appreciated except by persons familiar with both types of rock. No oil is extractable from oil-shale by any mechanical or chemical process unless it be accompanied by the application of heat. There are, in oil-shale, microscopic substances residual from animal and plant life, and these when subjected to heat will create liquid hydro-carbons, which while nascent and under the influence of the same thermal conditions, will vaporize, the latter reaction being precisely the same as occurs when petroleum is refined in a still. The condensation of the vapor produces oil.

Oil-shales, like other shales, are sedimentary in origin. They were laid down as muddy deposits in shallow seas and the remains of organic life were disseminated in them. Such deposits were originally horizontal. In the Rocky Mountain region of Utah-Colorado-Wyoming, the shales have remained almost in this position, but in many regions they have been uptilted, warped, folded, and distorted just as have been rocks of all ages and modes of origin.

Beds of bituminous shale may range in thickness up to hundreds of feet. Bituminous and non-bituminous shales frequently intermingle and blend into one another along continuous strata. They also alternate in layers. The grade of shale depends wholly upon the amount of organic remains—the so-called 'kerogen' disseminated through it. A shale will vary in richness in this way from barren rock up to material of high value as gauged by the economically possible eduction of oil therefrom. It is the custom to speak of the grade of a shale in gallons per ton: a shale is of average grade if it can be made to yield one barrel, or 42 gallons, per ton. There are vast deposits that will yield this quantity of total oil upon ordinary distillation, whereas there are deposits of considerable size that will render twice this amount and even more. In the shale districts it is customary to plan the handling of rock that will produce at least one barrel of oil per ton.

Oil-shales are of several varieties, readily identified by persons familiar with such rocks. There are massive, papery paraffin, asphaltic, sandy, and limey. Each has its peculiar texture and behaves distinctively when subjected to heat or when undergoing pulverization. There is considerable range in the color of oil-shales, this ranging from deep black through all shades of brown and blue to a light gray. I know of at least one deposit the outcrop of which is a light yellow resembling ochre.

PROPERTY RIGHTS. In most of our Western States shale-land is public domain. Thus far it has been located as placer claims, although there have never been any legislative or Land-Office regulations specifically applicable to land of this character. Oil-placer locations do not strictly apply for the reason explained, namely, that the land is not technically oil-bearing. Nevertheless, lacking a more appropriate method of tiling, all claims have been located precisely as though they were on oil-land.

When, in 1916, it became certain that the public would soon take notice of oil-shale, prospectors filed upon tracts that would attract early attention from investors. The first official investigation of the Green River field (the principal district of the Utah-Colorado-Wyoming region) was made in 1913 by E. G. Woodruff and David T. Day of the U. S. Geological Survey. The bulletin covering the field work was published in 1914. The second investigation was by Dean Winchester, also of the U. S. Geological Survey, in 1916. By the end of 1917 practically all of the best land relatively close to a railroad had been located. This does not mean, by any means, that available land of good quality is scarce nor difficult to secure; this one field is of such vast extent that figures as to total acreage, even as to the number of square miles, mean but little. There is plenty of land for all comers. Land that has been carefully located is purchasable at reasonable prices.

Since the beginning of the movement to enact a Federal leasing bill for oil-lands, there has been uneasiness as to the validity of shale-land locations filed subsequent to December 3, 1917. Very few new claims were located last year. The bill failed to pass during the recent session of Congress and the status of oil-shale land remains doubtful. For that reason current transactions are restricted to such properties as were validly located prior to the end of 1917. Should a leasing bill be passed hereafter it will have little effect on the industry as land-rights would then be leaseholds from Uncle Sam at a nominal rental of 50 cents per acre per year. Single placer claims are of 160 acres each. Upon each such claim there must now be expended an annual assessment, in the nature of labor and improvements, amounting to $100. Under the leasing arrangement this annual expense would be only $80. All transfers of ownership thus far have been by the giving of miner's quit-claim deeds. Very few oil-shale properties in the West have been patented, that is, purchased from the Government.

MINING PROBLEMS. The future of this industry depends wholly upon success in recovering the valuable hydrocarbons. I have not dwelt upon the possibilities of manufacturing by-products from oil-shale. I believe that profits can be measurably augmented by making such products as ammonium sulphate and crude potash, but I feel that the chief attraction of these shales, in the immediate future, is their potential yield of oils and greases. I recommend the erection of simple plants at first and the recovery of a few simple products. When the manufacture of these products has been stabilized, it will be time to attempt the by-product end of the industry.

No doubt exists regarding vastness of resources. To date, the main problem has been to devise apparatus that will efficiently and systematically handle large amounts of shale. The matter is found to resolve itself into an industrial enterprise involving mining as the business that provides the raw material.

The mining of shale will introduce numerous interesting problems, no doubt. In a few instances it will be found practicable to excavate oil-shale by open-pit systems, but most of the shale beds must be mined underground by methods which will probably closely imitate those practiced in coal mining. Shale beds standing at steep dips will be excavated by overhead stoping methods. The Colorado-Utah-Wyoming oil-shale beds lie practically flat. When these beds cap the hills or constitute the uppermost formation in low districts, the shale may be handled with power-shovels. In many localities, however, the beds outcrop as steep cliffs and their excavation must be accomplished by driving entries and rooms. Engineers will probably evolve new methods of mining. It may be found, as underground workings are extended considerable distances, that mechanical means for ventilation will be required.

In the region around DeBeque and Grand Valley, in Colorado, it is proposed to exploit beds lying hundreds, even thousands, of feet above the sites for mills: therefore aerial tramways are planned for transporting the shale from mine to mill. One company will erect its plant several hundreds of feet below its thick ledge of shale. The mined material will be dropped over a perpendicular cliff for about half the distance and is expected to roll down a steep talus slope the remainder of the descent.

CRUSHING. Before being charged into retorts, raw shale must be crushed, the fineness differing according to the demands of the inventors of retorts. Some retorts are expected to work with shale broken into chunks roughly corresponding to 'egg' size in coal: other retorts are intended to handle the shale crushed to half-inch, quarter-inch, and 8-mesh; one or two processes require pulverization of the feed.

Some varieties of oil-shale may be crushed and ground as readily and with the same kinds of machines that are applied to brick-shales. However, massive shale that is unusually rich in oil-producing substances is refractory during grinding in the sense that it resists fracture because of its rather tough structure, and it becomes still tougher and even plastic under the influence of the heat generated in certain types of crushers. For this reason it is impossible to work certain oil-shales through jaw-crushers. In crushers that are completely housed or in which the grinding-chamber is itself a closed affair, the comminution of such rich shale creates sufficient heat to not only make the rock pasty but to cause vapors that form explosive mixtures with air. But, on the whole, the grinding of mine-run shale is not a serious problem, it being simply a matter of experimentation with various types of crushers, followed by intelligent selection.

The manufacture of shale-oil is not, as some persons have been led to believe, a formidable process, nor does it require an expensive plant. A typical shale-mill will have ample bins for mine-run storage, suitable crushing apparatus, a battery of retorts, simple air-cooled condensing pipes, means for separating the liquids from the non-condensible gases, a scrubber for such gases to recover ammonia and gas-tar, and tankage for all products. Additional apparatus for refining will be mentioned

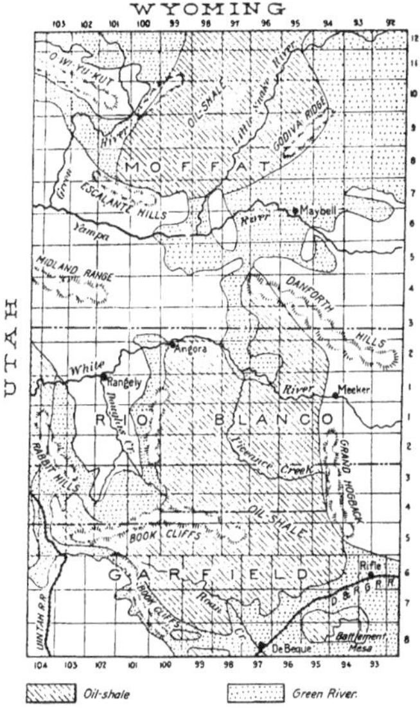

PART OF COLORADO, SHOWING POSITION OF SHALE DEPOSITS

later. The only step involving deviations from common practices in this country is the retorting.

AMERICAN RETORTS. The principles upon which American oil-shale retorts have been constructed are variant. It is not a simple matter to classify the retorting schemes except along broad lines. One might state that American retorts belong to the following two divisions: internally fired and externally fired.

Under this classification the majority of processes

would fall into the second class, for most inventors cling to the belief that the removal of the vapor should be performed in an atmosphere destitute of oxygen and gases of combustion. The Chew process is an example of internal firing. Shale is fed continuously into the top of a vertical cylindrical chamber the bottom of which is a slowly rotating grate upon which is maintained a fire of the lower 12 or more inches of the shale itself. The gases of combustion are drawn upward through the charge, imparting thermal units to the cooler fragments of shale and thereby generating an oil-vapor that passes from the retort at the top and thence through a water-cooled condensing apparatus.

The retorts that are fired externally may be subdivided as follows: those that distil vapor in their own atmosphere; those injecting live steam; and those introducing inert fixed gas from previous distillation. In the first type belong most of the recent retorts. They maintain a slight internal pressure caused by vaporization of water and nascent hydrocarbons, and this pressure causes the steady expulsion of vapor into the condensing system.

The introduction of steam has been proposed by some inventors to contribute thermal units to the shale charge, to increase the yield of ammonia, and to create a higher pressure in order to more vigorously expel the vapor. The opinion is advanced by a few authorities that the addition of live steam will prevent caking of the shale. All oil-shale carries natural moisture, as well as the water of physical structure, so that any retort will contain a relatively moist atmosphere. No matter how dry a charge of oil-shale may be apparently when charged into a retort, a considerable quantity of water will be recovered at the condenser.

The idea of returning non-condesible gases into the retort has merit. The Pritchard process will pre-heat such gas by conveying it through a coil of pipe in the waste-gas flue of the furnace. The gas will then enter the top of the retort and will filter its way down through the charge of shale. In this scheme there will be not only a conservation of fuel but the saved heat will be systematically distributed throughout the mass of shale within the retort. This added gas, blended with the newly-generated vapor and gas, is finally withdrawn from the bottom of the retort, the continually augmenting volume of fixed gas being accommodated by a gasometer.

Some retorts are designed to conduct their reactions in a rarified atmosphere maintained by a rapid withdrawal of the vapor into condensing apparatus under an incomplete vacuum. Others work under induced pressure, which may be produced by constriction of the vapor exits, by the introduction of live steam (as previously mentioned), or by the simple scheme of spraying water upon the heated charge of shale. Most processes, however, will create vapor at practically the atmospheric pressure, the exits being of ample area.

An obvious classification of oil-shale processes would separate them into those that operate intermittently and those that are charged and discharged continuously. Between these extremes we find schemes for an intermediate procedure. In the Fuller process this is accomplished by building the vertical retort in two sections. In the upper section the shale is heated sufficiently to distill its aqueous contents, when it is dropped through a trap-door or valve into the lower chamber to receive its ultimate distillation. When the upper chamber has been emptied it is immediately recharged with fresh shale, so that distillation is carried on practically continuously.

The Wallace retort, adopted by the Ute Oil Co. for operation in the Watson field, in Utah, is an upright cast-iron cylinder of 40 in. diameter and 10 ft. high. Placed centrally within this is a large vertical cast-iron tube having many perforations. The prepared raw shale is charged intermittently into the annular space between the two iron cylinders and heat is applied from without, the temperature being slowly raised to 1000°F. All vapors find egress through the central column and, blending together, are withdrawn from the retort to the condensing apparatus under slightly diminished pressure.

To satisfy the requirements of prospective purchasers of oil-shale equipment, numerous inventors have endeavored to obtain absolute continuity in the retorting process. This has led to adaptations of the mechanical principles involved in screw-conveyors, in raking and scraping types of ore-classifiers and in multiple-deck revolving ore-roasters. It is proposed to adapt coal-distillation schemes to the treatment of oil-shale. Among the processes devised to use scraping mechanisms may be mentioned the Beam and the Young. The Del Monte is one process that will force the shale continuously through an almost level retort by means of a spiral conveyor. The Green-Laucks will use the same mechanism in a vertical retort. The Wingett retort has multiple decks and plows somewhat similar to those in a MacDougal roaster. Alternating with the decks upon which the shale is heated are chambers within which heat is generated by jets for burning gaseous or liquid fuels.

Fractionation Processes. Shale processes may be classified into those that deliver a single oily product and those that deliver two or more fractions of the total oil. Perhaps the best known of the second sort is the new Galloupe, the mechanism of which is peculiar to itself. An outer, stationary, cast-iron vertical shell is provided with inwardly projecting narrow shelves arranged very much like winding stairways. Within this there slowly rotates a smaller cast-iron cylindrical shell outwardly provided with similar shelves so set as to pass between the shelves of the fixed shell. The shale, which is fed continuously into the top of this retort, works its way spirally down these shelves and is discharged at the bottom. Heated gases from the furnace pass upward through the inner shell as well as completely around the outer shell. As the shale descends from shelf to shelf it encounters successively hotter zones and simultaneously yields vapors of increasing density. These vapors promptly pass into condensing pipes, each such pipe delivering a distinct fraction.

LOOKING UP COON CREEK, IN GARFIELD COUNTY, COLORADO. CENTRAL MOUNTAIN IS THE PROPERTY OF THE AMERICAN SHALE & REFINING CO.

Practically the same theory is followed in all fractionating continuous processes. The shale is heated gradually and the resulting vapors are withdrawn before they can commingle with vapors of higher or lower densities. It is not expected that this sort of fractionation directly from the shale will be perfect, for it is inevitable that each such fraction will be more or less blended with vapors from adjacent higher and lower thermal zones of the retort. However, it is believed that, after any such retort has been in commission long enough to permit close adjustments of temperature and shale feed, the fraction delivered from each take-off will be fairly constant in quality.

TYPES OF RETORTS. Having now sketched a few salient features of recent shale retorts, we might wish to decide what description best fits each one of the many processes. Taking them up in this fashion, we shall find that almost no two of them may be similarly classified in all particulars. It would appear that all possible combinations have been contrived into individual retorts and one finds an interesting field before him in studying the technology of oil-shale distillation.

At least one process employs a principle in distillation that is unique, and is known as 'digestion'. The Ryan retort is partly filled with a heated hydrocarbon liquid of high density. This may be an oil, melted paraffine, or any other hydrocarbon with a relatively high temperature of vaporization. Into this liquid is charged pulverized shale, and the charge is constantly stirred. Heat reaches the shale through the bath of oil, the nascent oils thus generated dissolving or blending in the bath. The temperature maintained during the digestion is relatively low and this stage of the process is complete when the shale has become a muddy sludge. During digestion there is evaporation, from the surface of the bath, of the lighter volatiles, such as gasolene and naphtha, which are recovered at the condenser. The retort continuously discharges its sludge into a tall tank filled with gasolene or naphtha, which absorbs the oils while the earthy material is settling to the bottom. The wash-tank is steadily supplied with fresh light oil while the overflow goes to the refinery for fractionation.

It is claimed that this process will educe more than twice as much oil as does dry distillation, because no fixed gas is generated.

FUELS FOR RETORTING. Heat for the retorts will be secured by burning crude shale, spent shale, and the fixed gases. In this way the oil-shale distillation plant will require no fuel from outside sources. Raw shale, just as mined and crushed, may be used with complete success on any ordinary type of grate, but, owing to the high content of ash remaining from the burning of shale, the stoking of fires by hand offers objection. Automatic stokers and chain-grates will be used to obviate this difficulty.

After the removal of all volatile hydrocarbons from the shale, the residue, or spent shale, carries a considerable amount of fixed carbon or coke, which, as in French practice, can be advantageously used as fuel in the furnace, preferably discharging it, while hot, directly from the retort onto the grate. In most types of retort it is improbable that this fixed carbon will furnish sufficient fuel, so it is planned to burn the fixed gases, from the retort, as additional fuel. It is roughly estimated that the usual dry distillation of oil-shale of the one-barrel grade will produce 2000 cu. ft. of this gas, a rich hydrocarbon that burns freely. Sufficient experience has not as yet been gained to arrive at close estimates regarding the fuel consumption, but it is generally held that retorts will supply the requisite fuel in the two waste products, spent shale and fixed gas, possibly augmented by raw shale.

The condensation of vapors from retorts is accomplished by the ordinary air-cooling of pipes. Water-cooling often causes a congestion of the pipes by the rapid condensation of the heavy fractions.

REFINING OF SHALE-OIL will be as essential as refining of well-oil, that is, if the same uses are made of the products. There will be no special differences between procedures in the two cases. In general, the same marketable liquids will be recovered.

There are as great differences between the oils from different shales as there are between the petroleums from different oilfields. Most shale-oils are relatively lower in gasolene content, unless cracking is practised. Usually the content in lamp-oil or kerosene is sufficiently high to warrant the introduction of cracking. Shale-oils, as a rule, yield splendid grades of lubricating oils and greases.

A refinery will be more or less indispensable in every oil-shale plant. The use of fractionating retorts is recommended by their inventors upon the ground that at least some of the initial fractions will be immediately ready for market or, at any rate, they will be of such grades that they can be sold to custom refiners at much better prices than can be had for the total oil.

All shale-oils and their fractions are either dark in color at first or they take on continually darker tints as they age. This discoloration is probably due to traces of sulphur, although some persons believe it is caused by a natural dye. Shale-oil gasolene may be colorless as it comes from the still but it will be red the following day. To seal it from the atmosphere makes no difference. It appears that coloration may be hastened by sunlight. An automobile was driven several days with shale-gasolene as fuel and no deposit was left in the cylinders.

PRODUCTS AND BY-PRODUCTS. I have already stated that I believe early operations in oil-shale could well be restricted to the manufacture of a few staple liquids. The production of simple fractions from the total oil will prove profitable. Such products would include naphtha and gasolene as one product for motor-fuel; kerosene, an engine-fuel, or crackable into motor spirit; light and heavy lubricating oils; soft and hard greases; and a residuum heavy in paraffine or asphalt, or both, this last product varying with the character of the shale treated.

The average fractionation of shale-oils, as estimated from many tests, is: naphtha and gasolene, up to 150°C., 9%; kerosene, to 300°C., 37%; light lubricating oil, to 335°C., 20%; heavy lubricating oil, to 354°C., 23%. The average residuum from distilling shale-oil to 300°C. is a good agent for the flotation of minerals and one or two companies propose the standardization of blends to satisfy the requirements of flotation-oil consumers. With certain flotation machines and with certain minerals, the best results have been obtained with residuums at different temperatures of distillation, this simply meaning more or less of the lighter fractions in the blend. It is thought by some that approximately 50% of the total oil yield from shales could be standardized into products of this nature, saleable at around 50c. per gallon.

Potash exists in small amount in most oil-shales. It is claimed that the heat to which the shale is subjected during distillation converts the available potassium salts into readily soluble conditions. Attention may be given later to the commercial recovery of potash.

Some beds of oil-shale, such as those in Beaverhead county, Montana, are found to contain phosphoric acid. Samples taken and tested by C. F. Bowen of the U. S. Geological Survey show that the equivalent content in calcium phosphate varies from 5.7% to 33.96%. The phosphate is extractable from the spent shale.

Nitrogen occurs in all these shales and many operators anticipate the recovery of it in the form of ammonium sulphate. Dean Winchester, in Bulletin 691-B, U. S. Geological Survey, states that the average of 18 samples of the Green River oil-shale showed an average nitrogen content of 0.64% equivalent to 59.4 lb. of ammonium sulphate per ton. In commercial practice it will not prove economical to recover all the nitrogen. The manufacture of fertilizer will probably be one of the first by-product steps in the shale-oil industry.

A recent suggestion concerns the feasibility of manufacturing lamp-black from the heavy residue after removal of oils. It is believed that this residue might be burned directly and produce approximately 25% of its weight in commercial grades of lamp-black. If the residue be first rendered gaseous by additional apparatus and the gas then burned, approximately the same amount of soot may be made and this will be of a grade known in the trade as 'carbon black', which commands a higher price. In view of the increasing consumption of these substances in several trades, together with legislative prohibition in most States covering the manufacture of them from natural gases, it would seem that this proposal has merit.

There has been much talk about the manufacture of dyes from the heavy residue from shale-oil but it does not appear that this work offers particular attraction in the near future. It is improbable that any dyes not already being made from coal-tar would be discovered, and the research involved in working out methods would be extensive.

STATUS OF THE INDUSTRY. I am daily asked regarding the status of this oil-shale industry. There are many angles to the question and too many points to be discussed, so I shall not go into more than a few at this time. I have endeavored to show why progress has thus far been slow apparently. The progress to date has been largely along lines somewhat intangible to the public. I maintain that it has been appreciable, and that it portends big things commercially in the future. Processes have been developed to stages that satisfy prospective operators; I expect a few companies to erect relatively small plants this season and to be producing oil before next winter.

Interest in the industry is wide-spread. Projects are afoot in New Brunswick, Kentucky, Missouri, Colorado, Utah, Wyoming, Montana, Nevada, New Mexico, California, and Alberta. One hears most about the Utah-Colorado field because it is the largest and has been given most publicity in Federal publications. Equally good oil-shales are found in the other regions and in quantities warranting companies in starting commercial activities. The natural resources exist beyond doubt and efficient processes are becoming available. It is not supposed that perfection has been attained by any inventor, but I believe the time has arrived when projects may be started legitimately. As the handling of shale proceeds upon a large scale, operators will discover ways of improving efficiency, of lowering cost, and of increasing capacity. I have purposely avoided any discussion thus far of figures for costs of plants and for costs of operation, as likewise figures for values of products and for profits. Estimates in these directions vary tremendously in the opinions of different persons. They will vary with the process selected and with the scale of operations; however, I venture the remark that the public has been given exaggerated figures covering all of these points, especially with regard to the amount of capital that will be involved in erecting plants. I maintain that the expenditures required to establish and maintain oil-shale plants are no higher than those involved in other industrial projects of similar magnitude. When I run across persons who 'knock' this industry, I always find that they have been misinformed and that they base their criticisms upon unsound premises. I insist that success in this industry will be attained only when reliance is placed upon technical guidance. The treatment of oil-shale is a practical application of organic chemistry. Supervision of such work should not be assigned to men who lack qualification in this line nor to those who are deficient in plant-operating experience. The selection of a process should not be left to promoters. Stockholders in oil-shale companies would do well to insist that the first official appointed be a competent technologist, a man who knows enough about engineering and chemistry to take charge of all matters connected with the acquisition of land, the selection and erection of machinery, and the control of every phase of the operations.

Dredging Results of Canadian-Klondyke Company

The report of the receiver and manager, H. G. Blankman, for the Canadian Klondyke Mining Co.'s properties, near Dawson, shows that the operating profit in 1918 amounted to $216,963. This was reduced to $44.571 by extraordinary charges. The gold recovered by the dredges and sundry operations was $481.423. A comparison of gravel dug and costs is summarized below:

	1916			1917			1918		
Dredge	Yards	Yield, cents	Cost, cents	Yards	Yield, cents	Cost, cents	Yards	Yield, cents	Cost, cents
1	849,735	43.48	10.26	611,160	29.50	19.00	278,965	22.65	10.70
2	2,240,350	11.53	6.20	2,188,575	10.66	6.40	1,407,750	11.59	6.24
3	1,732,065	6.19	4.83	1,476,430	9.87	5.87	....	....	....
4	1,128,250	10.85	8.08	1,352,185	10.20	8.97	2,368,695	11.72	5.15
Last Chance...	143,060	20.06	15.66	20,000	7.45	5.22	245,500	11.72	2.16
Total	6,093,460	14.21	8.35	5,649,350	14.70	8.51	4,300,910	11.19	6.28

Upon adding administration, engineering, power, bond interest, and other extraordinary charges, the costs were increased to 14.22, 14.46, and 10.28 cents per yard, respectively. Thawing for No. 1 boat in 1918 cost $26.306, for No. 2, $6687, and for No. 4, $6497. The receiver places the total current assets of the company at $506,-901, and current liabilities $30,569.

SALES OF ELECTRIC POWER by the Pacific Gas & Electric Co. to consumers in California last year totaled $12,-384,499. Of this the mining industry paid $851,466, equal to nearly 7%. The output of electric energy was 922,037,604 kw-hr., so mining used 64,540,000 kw-hours.

Leaching Copper Ore in Utah

The leaching plant of the Utah Copper Co. during 1918 treated 434,143 tons of oxidized ore, an average of 1190 tons per day. The usual difficulties in starting a new plant were encountered. Shortage of labor and acid were also responsible for the small tonnage. Operations in the crushing and leaching departments were entirely satisfactory, but the capacity of the scrap-iron launders was insufficient, and cold weather interfered with precipitation during the winter. Basic iron phosphate, precipitated with the copper, rendered the drying of the product slow and difficult. Methods for handling the precipitate have been devised, and in future the plant should have a normal economical capacity of 3000 tons daily.

The ore averaged 0.822% copper, of which 0.665%, or 13.30 lb. per ton, was in soluble form. The recovery in leaching was 11.10 lb. per ton, corresponding to an extraction of 83.31% of the soluble copper. The recovery of the metal from the solution, in the form of a precipitate, was 0.5297%, or 10.594 lb. of copper per ton. The precipitate averaged 48.7727% copper, 9.6066% iron, and 2.74% insoluble. The consumption of 60°B. sulphuric acid averaged 55.7 lb. per ton, corresponding to 5 lb. of acid per pound of copper recovered in leaching.

The cost of milling, leaching, precipitating, handling tailing, and general expense at the leaching plant averaged $1.0568 per ton. This large figure is due principally to the higher cost of labor and supplies, but also to decreased efficiency and to the comparatively small quantity of ore treated.

The average cost per pound of net copper produced from the precipitate was 16.85 cents. In addition to the copper precipitated, there remained in solution 670,000 lb., of which 627,000 lb. is recoverable. Taking this into consideration, and allowing for the additional expense to cover precipitating, smelting, refining, and marketing of the 627,000 lb. of copper, the cost per net pound of all copper from leaching plant will average 15.089 cents. Operation of this plant was discontinued on December 31, 1918, on account of curtailment of production.

IRON COMPOUNDS IN ASBESTOS detract from its value for electrical insulation, and recently experiments have been made for the removal of such compounds. It has been found that treatment with a 2% aqueous solution of oxalic acid for 48 hours, followed by washing with water, increases the electrical resistance of such impure asbestos, while at the same time the strength of the asbestos is not affected. The second method is to heat the asbestos for 20 to 24 hours in a current of hydrogen or carbon monoxide at 390 to 400°C., followed by washing with very dilute hydrochloric or sulphuric acid, and afterward with water. In March, 9291 tons of asbestos was imported from Canada, worth $26 per ton.—O. Bowles in April report of U. S. Bureau of Mines.

Minerals Separation v. Butte & Superior

Hearing of the Case Before the U. S. Supreme Court. Arguments for the Petitioners, Minerals Separation, Ltd.

ARGUMENT OF HENRY D. WILLIAMS

MR. WILLIAMS: The patent here in suit was before this Court in the case of Minerals Separation, Limited, v Hyde. There the issue concerned the validity of the patent, as infringement was too clear to require argument if the patent were valid. In the instant case the issue is infringement, since validity is conceded.

As your Honors may recall, the defendant Hyde in that suit installed this air-froth flotation ore-concentration process for the Butte & Superior Mining Co., the defendant here. The defendant's participation in and continuation of that infringement are now before this Court.

In the Hyde case the District Court of Montana found that the patentees had discovered a new process, with a new result, and it was therefore patentable. The Circuit Court of Appeals of the Ninth Circuit reversed that finding and held that the process and the result were old, and that the only new thing which the patentees had discovered was that such an old process and old result could be achieved with a smaller amount of oil (which is one of the materials used in the process) and a smaller amount of oil than was used in any of the prior processes. That decision was reversed by this Court on *certiorari*, and this Court found, in agreement with the District Court, that the process and result were new and the invention was patentable.

The decision of this Court in the Hyde case was rendered on the 11th of December 1916. The defendant almost immediately began experimenting in its mill with a view to finding a way which, in its judgment, would enable it to avail itself of the benefits of the patented process and yet avoid the decision of this Court.

For two years prior to that time the defendant had used pine-oil as the only oil used, in a procedure which it admits infringed the patent. The defendant endeavored to avoid the continuance of the use of this pine-oil, and tried some 16 different mixtures of oils, without other alteration or procedure, but was unable to satisfactorily produce the result desired without continuing the use of the pine-oil which had formerly done the work, and had to content itself, finally, with adding to the pine-oil, which continued to do the work, kerosene oil and fuel-oil, or equivalents, which did not do the work. The use of such a mixture was continued from about the 7th of January, 1917, down to the time of the trial of this case in April, 1917. Prior to January 7, 1917, the defendant used a pound and a half of pine-oil to the ton of ore—7/100 of 1% on the ore. After January 7, 1917, and because it was using the kerosene and the fuel-oil above referred to in admixture with the pine-oil, defendant had to slightly increase the amount of pine-oil to overcome the deleterious effects of the make-weight oils which it added, but the increase did not average as much as one-tenth of 1%.

THE CHIEF JUSTICE: Do you mean eight-tenths were added?

MR. WILLIAMS: They added eight-tenths of these oils, which did not do the work of the process. The defendant, in his altered procedure, had to use as much as two-tenths of 1% of pine-oil instead of a little less than one-tenth of 1%, and added to that eight-tenths and a little bit more—just enough to go over 1%—of these oils that did not do the work.

MR. JUSTICE CLARK: I understood you to say that under the modified practice it was still less than one-tenth of 1% of pine-oil?

MR. WILLIAMS: Still less than two-tenths of 1% of the pine-oil.

All of those procedures were held by the District Court, after a five weeks' trial in open court, to be infringements of the patent in suit. The Circuit Court of Appeals, upon an appeal by the defendant, held that none of these procedures with more than one-half of 1% of total oils so used were infringements. The theory of the defendant and of the Circuit Court of Appeals was that this Court, in the Hyde case, construed the patent in such a way as to limit the language of each claim, whatever its natural meaning would otherwise be, to one-half of 1% of oil, and of any oil, whether it did the work of the process or not.

There are, therefore, two questions before this Court.

THE CHIEF JUSTICE: Did the Circuit Court of Appeals hold that they could add any percentage so as to make up the amount, although that added percentage was not a factor in what was done at all?

MR. WILLIAMS: That is what the Circuit Court of Appeals held, and, further than that, they put the limit at one-half of 1%.

THE CHIEF JUSTICE: I know that, but I was just thinking instead of adding, they didn't add anything. As a matter of fact they didn't add anything; they added nothing.

MR. WILLIAMS: That is our viewpoint.

The two points, as I have indicated them, are

FIRST: Shall the claims of this patent be read and construed in the light of the language used in the claims in the natural meaning of such language, or shall these claims, whatever their language, be so read as only to include, so far as oil is concerned, one-half of 1% as the maximum limit?

SECOND: In this process is the oil referred to in the

claim an oil which will produce the mineral-air-froth concentrate which is the object of the process, or shall all oils be counted as the oils of the process, whether or not they function in the process?

As to the first question, the Circuit Court of Appeals and the defendant here attribute to this Court the finding in the Hyde case that a mere matter of degree is patentable. Their viewpoint is that this Court agreed with the Circuit Court of Appeals in finding the process of the patent in suit had no new feature in it whatsoever except the novelty incident to the use of less oil, to operate in the same manner, to perform the same functions, and to produce the same result as the prior art processes.

Having attributed this remarkable finding to this Court, they next argue that since it appeared in the Hyde case that in practical operations it had not been found necessary to use more than two-tenths of 1% of oleic acid (which is the oily liquid described in the patent—of the example of the patent) or other equivalent oil to work the process and obtain the results called for, therefore they are free and everyone is free, if they choose to be uneconomical, to use more than one-half of 1% of oil and thereby to escape infringement.

Mr. Justice McReynolds: What sort of oil is this you say they use?

Mr. Williams: Pine-oil.

Mr. Justice McReynolds: Suppose they use more than 1% of that?

Mr. Williams: The evidence is that they could not get the result.

Mr. Justice McReynolds: It was definitely stated here before that if they used more than 1% of oil you had no objection.

Mr. Williams: No, your Honor.

Mr. Justice McReynolds: Yes. I asked that very particularly. My memory is very distinct. I understood you to say that until you reduced it to less than 1% you had no claim whatsoever.

Mr. Williams: Yes, but that was an operation under certain specific conditions with oleic acid and Broken Hill ore, and in that operation without any question the invention did not appear until you got down, in reducing the amount of oil, to one-half of 1%, and that operation cannot be carried on under those conditions and produce the process with more than one-half of 1%, and the defendant has demonstrated that in this case, because the defendant, in its mill, used this oleic acid for some two years, and the defendant did not use it well, and at one time he got up to a little more than nine pounds of oleic acid to the ton of ore (and ten pounds is one-half of 1%) and that is the greatest amount of oleic acid that has ever been used in concentrating ores by this process, and it is the greatest amount of any bubble-modifying oil mineral-froth-forming oil that has ever been used in this process, and the fact is now as it was then: but your Honors will remember in the other case there were certain prior art patents. The defendant carried on certain experiments. One of them—the one that was most important, we will say—used 3.6% of an oil, cotton-seed oil, which was a bubble-modifying mineral-froth-forming oil. We said: That is legerdemain of the laboratory. We proved that it could not be used in practical operations. That stands uncontradicted. We were not asked to say whether or not, if with that oil you could carry on the process, it would be within the patent. We were not asked that. But our witness in that case, Dr. Liebmann, when faced with that on the witness stand, said: If you can carry on this operation with 3.6% of cotton-seed oil, then it is the process of this patent. That was the evidence in the Hyde case, and that stands uncontradicted in this case.

Mr. Justice Day: What do you claim now is the particular merit of your invention recognized by this Court in the former case?

Mr. Williams: This Court recognized the merit of the invention as bringing about a new function of oil, a new operation, a new function of air, and a new froth concentrate, something that had never been produced before.

Mr. Justice Day: Oil in any quantity?

Mr. Williams: The element of oil quantity was an incident of the birth of the invention, and it appears to be an incident of the use of the invention. This Court did not express any opinion on the subject of oil quantity. This Court described the incidents of the birth of the invention, and this Court took into consideration—I was to take it up a little later in my argument on another matter.

Mr. Justice Day: I beg your pardon. Pursue your own course.

Mr. Williams: Four times in the decision of this Court the new froth-concentrate is described, and it is made quite clear that the prior art used oil-lift, and that the process in suit used chiefly air-lift; that it developed a new function of oil in combination with air bubbles producing a mineral-froth, in carrying on a process of concentrating ores.

The Chief Justice: I understood you to say, in answer to my question, and you say now, that the process of this patent could not be carried on with more than two-tenths of 1% of oil; is that it?

Mr. Williams: If the oil is an oil of that character which upon agitation produces a froth—

The Chief Justice: Your proposition now is that if the oil used is the character of oil you describe, what is called pine-oil, the process could not be accomplished if more than two-tenths of 1% is used, therefore the patent is limited to two-tenths of 1% of the character of oil that you describe. That is your proposition now, as I understand it.

Mr. Garrison: No.

Mr. Williams: I don't think that we ought to be bound by——

The Chief Justice: If you did not say that, all right, but I thought you had been saying it. I asked you what you have been saying. I want to know what you said. I only want to understand you right.

Mr. Williams: It is the fact——

The Chief Justice: You say that?

MR. WILLIAMS: Yes; it is the fact.

THE CHIEF JUSTICE: Now, then, what do you complain of? That they allowed something to be added, and set your patent aside? Because to allow oils to be added that did not produce the result adds nothing and looks like a fraud, if I may use a plain word——

MR. WILLIAMS: That is right, your Honor.

THE CHIEF JUSTICE: A mere scheme to beat your patent, because if they added something which did nothing, they added nothing, and they went on using their old process.

MR. WILLIAMS: Continued as they had before.

THE CHIEF JUSTICE: So your claim, as you now state it—and I want to follow it, if I can—your claim, as you now state it, is that the Court really treated your patent as referring to any oil, and allowing people to add any oil would thereby frustrate your patent?

MR. WILLIAMS: Yes, your Honor.

MR. JUSTICE PITNEY: Did you in your answer use the term "old process"?

MR. WILLIAMS: I may have.

MR. JUSTICE PITNEY: How old is it?

MR. WILLIAMS: If I said: "old process" I meant they continued to do what they had done before the decision of this Court. If I used the words "old process", I used them inadvisedly.

MR. JUSTICE PITNEY: What you say is that they are using an inefficacious, non-active oil, which does not contribute to the process at all?

MR. WILLIAMS: Yes; and not under any conditions are they going back to those things that were described in the written documents, in what we refer to as the prior art, or approaching anywhere near it.

Now in adding this fuel-oil and kerosene they did just one thing; they impaired the results of the process. Pouring in this material which did nothing to help the process, they injured it, and therefore they suffered a diminution of profit, and as a matter of fact they lost one-eighth of the profit which they would have otherwise made from their infringement by reason of the fact that they poured in these oils.

MR. JUSTICE BRANDEIS: That is, they retarded and obstructed the process?

MR. WILLIAMS: Yes; a mere obstruction.

THE CHIEF JUSTICE: More load to carry.

MR. WILLIAMS: They had to increase the pine-oil. And, more than that, they suffered a loss. Briefly, a million dollars a year was the loss. The profit for the year 1916, when they used the process at its best advantage, was $8,500,000; so they got down to $7,500,000 profit. That was the rate in this year in which they added these oils and injured the process. But certainly you cannot avoid a patent by using the process somewhat badly.

Now in the Hyde suit there was no occasion to consider any other oil than the identical example of the specification, oleic acid, a fatty acid—not an oil, but an oily liquid having the physical characteristics of an oil. The defendant used it, and the defendant used it at less than two-tenths of 1% on the ore. But in the Hyde decision this Court was called upon to pass upon the sufficiency of that disclosure of the specification which gave directions for discrimination as between oils and as to the quantity of oil to be used in any case in dealing with the infinite variety of ores with which the process was to be used. That part of the specification I will just take the time to read. It will be found at page 1, lines 61 to 69.

"The proportion of mineral which floats in the form of froth varies considerably with different ores and with different oily substances, and before utilizing the facts above mentioned"——

And that is the disclosure of the discovery of the invention.

"—and before utilizing the facts above mentioned in the concentration of any particular ore"——

MR. JUSTICE HOLMES: What are you reading from?

MR. WILLIAMS: Page 1 of the specification, lines 61 to 69, second column.

MR. JUSTICE HOLMES: I didn't understand what you were reading from.

MR. WILLIAMS: "A simple preliminary test is necessary to determine which oily substance yields the proportion of froth or scum desired."

This was the caution to the public. The patentees could not try the process with every one and every oil. That was altogether out of the question. As a matter of fact they tried it with oleic acid and the ore of Broken Hill, Australia, and they disclosed what they did under those circumstances, and then they said: Caution. You must make a preliminary test with every oil and every ore to find out what quantity of oil you need and what oil you need to carry out the process—what oil will do it.

So to that extent this Court in the Hyde case passed upon the question of discrimination between oils, and how the public was to be guided in following the disclosure of the patent in extending the use of the process to other ores with other oils.

Now in this case we have proved, as we contend, indubitably, that fuel-oil and kerosene, separately and together, are not mineral froth-forming oils with defendant's ore. That is the proposition that we set out to prove, and we do not need to carry it further. And there was no contradiction, no effort to show to the contrary. The defendant did not in its mill at any time make any effort to demonstrate that it could produce any results whatsoever by omitting the pine-oil, which did the work, but carried on in its mill these operations with this mixture, and produced the same froth-concentrate that it had produced before by the same means, and the same machines, practically—everything the same except the pouring in of these useless oils.

MR. JUSTICE BRANDEIS: Was there any effort made to show that they could use a smaller quantity of pine-oil by adding other oils in larger quantities?

MR. WILLIAMS: There was no experimentation at all except just that experimentation when they were trying to avoid the decision of this Court.

MR. JUSTICE HOLMES: When they poured in the others, they had to put in a little more pine-oil?

Mr. Williams: They had to use a little more pine-oil, yes.

Their operations for two years, successful operations, the best they ever did, with pine-oil alone, a pound and a half to the ton, demonstrated what could be done with pine-oil. Now to that they added these useless oils and a little more pine-oil to take care of it.

Mr. Justice Brandeis: They made no attempt, so far as appears, to do it with less pine-oil than they had used before?

Mr. Williams: Absolutely no.

ARGUMENT OF WILLIAM HOUSTON KENYON

Mr. Kenyon: May it please the Court, it will be my function to bring the discussion back to the one real issue—

Does the defendant infringe?

Has it respected the decision of this Court when it merely adds to a process otherwise admittedly infringing, and for the sole purpose of evading the patent, a mass of functionless oil—functionless to achieve or even to assist the process, and having no effect whatever except to harm it?

Is the substance of the invention taken by the defendant, as that invention has been defined by this Court in contrast with the prior art?

Mr. Justice Pitney: I gather from the argument of Mr. Bull that he does not claim it is a functionless oil; it is part of a functioning mixture.

Mr. Kenyon: I so understood it.

Mr. Justice Pitney: You are going to discuss that?

Mr. Kenyon: I shall discuss that.

First, as to the contrast, the prior art processes, as this Court defined them, does the defendant use any one of those processes? If it does, that is the end of this case.

This Court divided the prior arts processes into two classes, which it denominated "surface flotation process" and "metal-sinking process"—those two. What the defendant is doing is not the first. This Court defined what that was, saying that that *Surface Flotation Process* of the prior art operated by lifting the mineral particles chiefly by *the buoyancy of oil* and obtaining on the top of the pulp a resulting floating *"oil"*—and I quote the language of this Court—*"Impregnated or loaded with the metal* and metal-bearing particles."

No one really pretends that the defendant is using that process of the prior art. No one so argues. The buoyant lifting force in water of the total oil used by the defendant, even if it all went to the mineral, which it does not (for about half of it, according to the evidence, runs out with the tailing) would not account for the lifting of 1% of the mineral matter that is lifted.

Is the defendant's process, the "metal sinking process" of the prior art as defined by this Court, with its operation of *agglutinating*, sticking together, the mineral particles, and as a result, the forming of granules *which settle and sink* and are taken off at the bottom? No one in the record says that it is that process. No one here so argues. Although the Circuit Court of Appeals, in the instant case, says that defendant gets the same froth that Cattermole got. But Cattermole got no froth at all. What rose in Cattermole was lost. What sinks in defendant is lost.

That exhausted the prior art by definite finding of this Court, and the defendant's present process belongs neither to the one class of those two nor to the other.

It is a *glaring error of law* for the defendant to stand here and argue that it uses *prior art quantities*, that is to say, to compare mere quantities of oil *apart from functions and processes*, and yet that is what the Circuit Court of Appeals in the instant case has done, and what the defendant here argues. It is glaring error of law, unless this Court really defined the patentees' invention as a *mere saving of oil in an old* process, *a mere avoidance of waste*, which of course it did not do. And yet in defendant's brief from beginning to end that is the definition of the invention ascribed to this Court—*the mere avoidance of waste*.

In sharp contrast to this defendant's process *is* the patentees' process in all its essential features.

Let us see. First, it utilizes this novel *bubble modifying function of oil* referred to by this Court. No one denies that.

Second, it lifts the mineral particles through the pulp by the buoyancy of air bubbles in the way ascribed to this invention by this Court. No one denies that.

Third, it obtains as a result the froth-concentrate described by this Court as "consisting of air bubbles modified by the presence of the minute amount of oil used and holding in mechanical suspension 70 to 80%" of the mineral matter.

So far from denying this, defendant's expert witnesses asserted, and the District Court found, that these were the facts. The Circuit Court of Appeals did not find otherwise.

The defendant argues and the Circuit Court of Appeals found in the instant case that this Court had held that the invention has *no substance except mere avoidance of waste of oil in an old process*, and that defendant does not avoid that waste but courts it and so does not infringe, and defendant cites the damage that the fuel-oil and kerosene do to its process as evidence in support of its argument. And the defendant argues, and the Circuit Court of Appeals found in the instant case, that all oils function alike; that all oil processes are alike; that all produce froth and the froths are all alike; and that the only quality required of oil by the patent is preferential affinity for the mineral matter over the gangue.

Now that argument and those findings of the Circuit Court of Appeals misconceive the decision of this Court, misread the patent, and disregard the testimony of defendant's own witnesses and the facts.

First, as to the decision of this Court. This Court held that the patentees' process differed in kind from all prior oil processes; that it utilized a novel function of oil never known to exist before; that it proceeded by a novel air-lift never utilized before, and resulted in a froth-concentrate so different from the products of other processes, as this Court said, as to make it a patentable discovery.

Secondly, this Court also held, and I quote, "That it was well known that oil and oily substances had a selective affinity or attraction for, and would unite mechanically with, the minute particles of metal and metallic compounds found in crushed or powdered ores, but would not so unite with the quartz, or rocky non-metallic material, called 'gangue'."

So *that* was not the novel function of oil in the invention, although it is a necessary function.

Thirdly, this Court held that the patent must be confined to the results obtained as specified by it, namely, the novel froth-concentrate, and this necessarily and inevitably imported and implied the bubble-modifying function of oil that is necessary to obtain that result. An oil that does not have that power with a given ore, or has it in insufficient measure, and cannot obtain that result with that ore, is necessarily to that extent excluded by that decision.

Defendant's argument on this question of preferential affinity being the *only* function required in oil, for the accent is on the "only," misreads the patent. The preamble, in stating the object of the invention, gives the general class of reagents referred to, but does not distinguish within that class. Moreover, the words "which have a preferential affinity for mineral" etc. qualify not the word "oils" but the words that follow—"fatty acids and other substances', as if it said "oils, and fatty acids and other substances that, like oils, have a preferential affinity." The limitation "having preferential affinity" etc. cuts out some of the fatty acids, because there are gaseous fatty acids and there are soluble fatty acids; and it cuts out some of the other substances, but it does not cut out any of the oils. All oils have preferential affinity. This point is illustrated by the difference between the claims. The "oil" claims do not have that language in them—"preferential affinity," etc.—claims 9 to 12, inclusive. The "oily substance" claims do have that language in them—claims 1 to 3.

Defendant's argument really is, not that the oil must have the power of preferential affinity—there is no contest about that—but that *no other power of function is necessary*.

Now Cattermole oil must have the power of agglutinating, as well as the power of preferential affinity. Given both, the *mineral* will be agglutinated and not the gangue, and hence concentration at the bottom.

Similarly, why must not the oil, in the process in suit, have the power of frothing as well as the preferential affinity? Given both, the mineral is caused to form into a froth, and not the gangue, and hence concentration.

The specification of the invention in the patent, like the decision of this Court, *features the rising of the mineral in the form of a froth*. It is the keynote of the whole description.

And every claim is either in terms or by force of the disclaimer (that is, claims 9, 10, and 11), expressly limited to causing that result, that is, *causing the mineral to form a froth*.

And therefore the patent, like the decision, calls for, and requires, that power and function in the oil and excludes any oil that does not possess it.

And the specification warns that some oils may not answer with some ores, and prescribes a simple preliminary test to determine which oils will answer and in what quantity they should be used. This Court has decided that that is sufficient.

Finally, defendant's argument and the Circuit Court of Appeals' holding as to this matter overlooks the evidence and the facts. I will refer simply to one witness, an expert for the defendant, Prof. Taggart, of Yale, who tried to explain to us out there in Butte why this flotation process floated, and being asked what was the function of oil in it, said, "The oil in the agitation-froth process seems to have two functions; first, to aid in the formation of a stable froth; second, to act as a selective agent for the separation of the sulphide from the worthless rock."

The first it achieves by its bubble-modifying function. The second by its preferential affinity for the mineral matter. Both necessary. Both fundamental. But an oil that cannot achieve the first, the frothing function, cannot achieve the process, is not an oil of the process.

In any given case it is *a question of fact* whether a given oil with a given ore under all the conditions of its use has or has not the two functions referred to.

The question of fact arises here, not as to defendant's pine-oil, which admittedly has both functions, but as to its fuel-oil and kerosene, by which it boosts up its total oil quantity to a little above 1% to evade the decision of this Court, as it understands it.

Now what does the defendant's fuel-oil and kerosene in fact do in its process?

The District Court found that it does nothing, Mr. Bull to the contrary notwithstanding. The District Court found that it does nothing toward the operation of the patent, and worse than nothing. And since that is denied, just let me read from the opinion of the District Court a few words, at page 101 of the record:

"From the evidence it appears," says Judge Bourquin, "the larger part of the oil used by defendant"——

That is the fuel-oil and the kerosene, which is more that three-quarters——

MR. SHERIDAN: He does not say which oil, does he?

MR. KENYON: Which is more than three-quarters; it is nearly seven-eighths of the total oil used.

"——and all in excess of a fraction of 1% on the ore, if not inert is ineffective, wasted, and injurious to the process and results."

Then he explains that pine-oil so much, fuel-oil so much, kerosene so much, were used, and continues:

"As before stated many oils are ineffective to operate the process and that is because they have not the quality that contributes to bubble-making."

And also lower down on the page:

"The other factors the same, it is obvious the excess

petroleums in the mixture are responsible for the poorer results."

And a little lower down.

"The addition of the excess oil no more adds to or changes the process, no more avoids infringement, than would the addition of milk or other useless substance not a part of the process."

MR. JUSTICE MCKENNA: What did he find or decide they were used for?

MR. KENYON: No use.

MR. JUSTICE MCKENNA: What were they used for by the defendant?

MR. KENYON: To evade the patent.

MR. JUSTICE MCKENNA: Is that what the court said?

MR. KENYON: That is what the court said, and that is what the defendant's counsel said in argument there. "Like a burnt child we dread the fire." They say it here—that it is merely to evade the patent. They add 18 pounds of an oil without which their process is better than with it. For two years they had been using the pine-oil alone, about two pounds to the ton of ore. During the three months here in question they increased that two pounds to about three pounds and ran in about 18 pounds of this fuel-oil, etc., which they had never used before in any quantity. Mr. Bull was mistaken about that. Mr. Bull was mistaken in saying that in the time prior to January 7, 1917, the defendant used petroleum. It did not. It used nothing but pine-oil alone. (Mr. Bull dissents.)

Now the Circuit Court of Appeals seems to have reversed the District Court on this fact, and yet, as it seems to me—and I will come to that in a moment—its decision was really not based on that.

But the evidence overwhelmingly supports Judge Bourquin's finding of facts.

I will just touch upon three or four headings of that evidence.

FIRST. The defendant itself, for several years, had used pine-oil alone on the same ore and in the same quantity, about two pounds, and the work of the process was done and it was fully done. Its presence, therefore, in defendant's mixture sufficiently accounts for what happened.

Secondly, as to fuel-oil, etc. Fuel-oil and kerosene have never been used alone in the mills of the defendant; that is, without an oily frothing-agent—for example, pine-oil—or in the mills of any other company in attested and successful operation with any ore. When they tried they failed. Defendant's witness Engelmann, of the Ray Consolidated company, says, "We tried at different times to run on straight fuel-oil, but we could never maintain metallurgical results."

Thirdly, the practical effect of the adding of the 18 pounds of fuel-oil and kerosene per ton of ore was, not to increase the mineral frothing action or the ore concentration, but to diminish both, and to the extent of diminishing the profit from the whole operation by 12%. This is convincing evidence that the 18 pounds of fuel-oil, etc., does not take part in the fundamental operation of forming the mineral into a froth.

Fourthly, this testimony was confirmed by our presenting at the trial a test in open court by a witness who was cross-examined. We took the defendant's fuel-oil and kerosene in an amount equivalent to 18 pounds to the ton of ore; added it to the ore-pulp and agitated it. Nothing came. The result was not obtained. Then we added to that what corresponded to three or four pounds of pine-oil per ton of ore. We agitated again. Mineral-froth! That was the test, the simple preliminary test prescribed by our patent, and it showed, and would have shown to anybody, that that fuel-oil and that kerosene on that ore (it might be all right with some other ore) it is not an oil of this process.

Again, the defendant's witness, Prof. Bancroft, who also tried to explain this process to us out there, analyzed defendant's mixture, or characterized its components, this way: The fuel-oil, he said, is a "viscous non-frothing oil." The kerosene, he said, is "the typical non-frothing oil." And the pine-oil, he said, is the "frothing oil."

And these professors advanced what they called the "adsorption layer" theory as explaining this phenomenon—this process that has revolutionized the metallurgy of the world, and yet we do not know why it all happens. They went on the stand for defendant to present this adsorption layer theory, which had to do with layers so thin—we asked how thick is the adsorption layer you are talking about in the bubble. (There is one such layer on the outside of the water film of a bubble and one on the inside of the water film where the air contacts are.) Three one-hundred millionths of an inch, he said, would be about the thinnest. And another professor referred to the forces as "rather small forces." Indicating that only a microscopic amount of the oil anyway really is effective in the operation.

Now this addition of the 18 pounds of fuel-oil did not change the defendant's process one iota from the point of view of substance. The same operation proceeded by the same forces of nature in the same way to the same end after as before.

It is futile to cite the utility of minute amounts of fuel-oil with other ores when employed in connection with the oil-frothing agent of this patent. Many of our licensees do that. Why is it futile?

1. Because the evidence is clear and uncontradicted that a minute amount of that oil is sufficient for the purpose in question. One to three pounds of that fuel-oil is all that anybody uses anywhere for that purpose and the purpose is not to form a froth, but to cause a froth that something else forms to hold slightly larger particles of mineral. So they need not grind the ore quite so fine. They find that when they put in a little of this fuel-oil it makes, in a sense, a better kind of froth, a froth that will hold mineral particles a little larger, so that it is an improvement.

MR. JUSTICE PITNEY: By increasing the preferential affinity of the oil, or how does it do that?

MR. KENYON: I do not know how it does it. I won't speculate. There is no explanation of why it makes the froth more—some of the witnesses call it stabilizing the froth. Our witness, Mr. Higgins, who probably knows more about this flotation than any other man alive, says it enables the froth to hold slightly larger particles of the mineral than if not used. That does not account for the use of 18 pounds of fuel-oil per ton of ore. Nobody the world around uses that amount for that purpose.

MR. JUSTICE CLARK: Up to a certain point it improves the process?

MR. KENYON: Yes, up to a certain point. That is the testimony of our witnesses. It gives them a better kind of froth, a stiffer or more compact froth, or something.

MR. JUSTICE CLARK: What is the percentage?

MR. KENYON: From one to three pounds. The percentage of recovery is better.

MR. JUSTICE CLARK: Is better?

MR. KENYON: It is better. That is, the larger particles that might be lost are held, or you can save on your grinding, as I said, by having it all a little coarser.

MR. JUSTICE PITNEY: Is that true of all substances? Is it true of this particular material that we are dealing with at the Butte mines?

MR. KENYON: That is the next point I am going to make.

2. There is no evidence in the case at all that fuel-oil has any such effect upon the Butte & Superior ore. They never used it. They didn't use it. They did not use it before, during the years that they were using pine-oil in small quantity, although they knew of its use elsewhere. We may conclude from that that it has no such effect on that ore.

3. This is not a froth-forming operation anyway. It merely improves the froth. And yet that is the sole basis —what I have just explained is the sole basis for the repeated statements in defendant's brief that the fuel-oil and kerosene are not inert or inactive in defendant's process. The whole point is as immaterial on the issue of infringement as the use of sulphuric acid that is recommended in the specification of the patent as an improvement. Sulphuric acid does not create the preferential affinity of oil for mineral, but in some occult way it enhances that preferential affinity. That question and the patent for it was what was at issue before the British House of Lords. Sulphuric acid does not make froth: does not create the preferential affinity but it enhances both.

It is no answer to say that other documents than the patent in suit refer to other petroleum oils, and describe them as frothing agents. For this is not a question of law. It is a question of fact. What work does this fuel-oil, etc., do in the defendant's process?

It is no answer to say that the petitioners are estopped here from arguing infringement by what they said in the Hyde case. For there the things under discussion were not the things under discussion here. We talked there of the behavior of 36 pounds of oleic acid, 72 pounds of cotton-seed oil, both oils of the process, every one-tenth of 1% of which was capable of doing the whole frothing work. That was a different question. Here we have now a peculiar mixture that presents a brand new question.

Really the Circuit Court of Appeals reached its conclusion because of its erroneous view of the decision of this Court.

I must jump right to the matter of disclaimer.

MR. JUSTICE DAY: Before you get to that, is this pine-oil, as you call it, the only oil that will do this?

MR. KENYON: Oh, no. There are many others—eucalyptus oil. There is a whole range of oils that are excellent for that purpose. In Australia they use eucalyptus oil. Oleic acid is one oil. Cotton-seed oil is another.

THE CHIEF JUSTICE: You don't use petroleum? Petroleum may do it to some ores? You mention them in the patent.

MR. KENYON: Not in our patent, but in the British patent. With some ores they may do it.

MR. JUSTICE DAY: Your point is that with this particular ore it does no good?

MR. KENYON: It does no good.

MR. JUSTICE DAY: It is just bulk.

MR. KENYON: It is camouflage. The only question of fact that we have to consider is as to defendant's ore. We make no general proposition. We do not stand here and say that no petroleum will do it with any ore.

Now as to the disclaimer.

They say this Court said that claims 9, etc., were too broad because they included the use of any small quantity of oil. That was what Judge Bradford had said when he held claim 9 invalid a month or two before this Court did. He said it was invalid because it was not limited to the use of 1% of oil. This Court, with that before it, shifted the ground of criticism and said, as we judge from the context, that it was invalid because not limited, not confined, to the results obtained by the use of oil in these critical proportions.

So looking to the matter of results in the claims in question we find this to be the fact: Claims 9 to 11 differ from all the other claims of the patent in that they leave out the words "to cause the mineral matter" before the words "to form a froth", and the disclaimer practically reads that limitation "to cause *the mineral matter* to form a froth" into the claims.

THE CHIEF JUSTICE: We will have to stop here.

MR. KENYON: Thank you.

INDIA, during the 50 years ending with last year, has imported and retained £253,000,000 ($1,226,000,000) of gold—say one-ninth of the world's production during that period. As India has also imported and absorbed in this half-century the biggest share of the silver output, the amount of precious metal which it has assimilated, notwithstanding the exiguous individual wealth of its population, is really astonishing.—Weekly Report of Samuel Montagu & Co., London.

CHALK production of England is between 4,000,000 and 5,000,000 tons, with an approximate value of 10½ cents per ton. The output for 1913 was 4,458,126 tons, worth £213,479, of which 2,796,857 tons came from the county of Kent. Essex county was second with 835,769.
—R. B. Ladoo in April report of U. S. Bureau of Mines.

Treatment of Complex Ores in Idaho

*The treatment of Idaho ores involves several problems, but those that seem to be of greatest importance are (1) concentration of the complex lead-zinc-iron ores, and (2) treatment of gold-silver ores that are not amenable to straight amalgamation.

The first group is well represented in the Coeur d'Alene region, Shoshone county, and in the Wood River district, Blaine county. Under this group might be included, however, the deposits of the Lakeview and Blacktail districts in Bonner county, and those of the Clarke Fork district in Bannock county, as well as such lead-zinc-iron and lead-zinc-copper ores found in other parts of the State, as are separated with difficulty by the usual methods of gravity concentration.

Where the lead-zinc-iron ores are as finely disseminated as those in the mines of the Pine Creek, Nine Mile, and other districts of the Coeur d'Alene, to make clean products of lead and zinc by gravity methods is next to impossible. It has been found in examining material finer than 200-mesh under the microscope that some of the lead and zinc particles were still mechanically combined. Although at most mills a large percentage of both the lead and the zinc content is recovered in the concentrate from the jigs, fine grinding is essential to liberate the minerals and make a clean separation, with finely disseminated ores of this character. Owing to this fact, considerable amounts of zinc in lead concentrate, and no small amount of lead in zinc concentrate, is lost by the present methods of concentration. The question arises, therefore, as to whether a closer separation of the minerals is commercially feasible. Possible improvements in methods and equipment to effect a closer concentration are discussed in detail in the Bulletin under mill practice in the Coeur d'Alene region, such as finer grinding, larger flotation plants, fine grinding and differential flotation combined, preliminary roasting followed by flotation, or some hydro-metallurgical process.

To avoid radical changes in the mills, and in the local methods, it would seem advisable, if possible, to effect a better separation by differential flotation, with whatever changes in the existing methods of treatment this might necessitate. It is along these lines, therefore, that the U. S. Bureau of Mines, in co-operation with the University of Idaho and mine operators of the State, has been experimenting and will continue to do so.

Under the second group would come the gold ores of the Boise Basin region in Boise county, the Atlanta district in Elmore county, the Silver City and De Lamar districts in Owyhee county, the Seafoam and Greyhound districts in Custer county, and the central Idaho district, which is mainly in Idaho county.

The Boise Basin region, comprising the Quartzburg, Grimes Pass, Elk Horn, Idaho City, and other local districts, has many mines. In this region a large quantity of gold and silver ore in quartz or altered granite-gangue, said to average between $7 and $10 per ton, is available. The future of the region depends largely upon the successful solution of the serious milling and treatment problems which now confront the operators. The material worked in the earlier days in this region were principally free-milling gold ores, and all the plants were stamp-mills of the gravity type, with straight amalgamation. With depth, the ore gradually became more base, and table concentration and cyanidation were added to the process. Stamp-milling will now only save 50%, and much of the gold remaining in the ore is lost because of inadequate milling facilities. Thus far, only the concentrate has been subjected to cyanidation. The ore is still crushed in the original stamp-mills, and most of the mills are out of date and are making poor recoveries.

The history of the treatment of gold ore in the Silver City and De Lamar districts, Owyhee county, has been similar to those in the Boise Basin region. In the upper levels of the mines the ore was chiefly oxidized vein material, and included much material that was free-milling. Rich silver-chloride ore and lead-silver ore supplied much of the production from certain properties. As greater depth was attained the ore became more base, and could no longer be profitably amalgamated. This necessitated changes and alterations in the mills, especially the addition of cyanide-plants, and during the later years of activity in these districts practically all of the ore was cyanided. The costs of mining and treatment were always high in the Silver City district, largely because of the high cost of transportation and supplies. This resulted in a large quantity of ore of milling grade, partly oxidized, being left in some of the old stopes and on the old mine-dumps. Much of this material could probably be re-worked at a profit by proper milling methods. Considerable development is now under way in the district, tunnels being driven to intersect the orebodies at depths of 500 to 1000 ft. below the old workings. If ore in payable quantity is found at these greater depths there will be urgent need for metallurgical advice regarding proper methods of treatment. The problems involved will probably be confined to correct methods of grinding and cyanidation.

In the Seafoam and Greyhound districts, the ores comprise several distinct types, the principal ones being gold-bearing pyrite in quartz veins, associated with considerable arseno-pyrite and antimony sulphides, and complex ores containing mixtures of chalcopyrite, argen-

*Abstract from Bull. 166, 'A Preliminary Report on the Mining Districts of Idaho'. U. S. Bureau of Mines, 1919, by Thomas Varley, C. A. Wright, E. K. Soper, and D. C. Livingston.

liferous galena, and auriferous pyrite, associated with arsenical and antimonial sulphides. The hauling of concentrate from this district would not be practicable under present facilities, but experiments in cyaniding these ores would seem desirable, because the district contains some high-grade ore which could be mined at a profit if haulage costs were eliminated.

From these general statements it can be readily seen that the chief treatment problem for the complex and low-grade gold-silver ores is to determine the best method of milling, followed by cyanidation, or cyaniding direct, according to the metal content and character of the ore, in order to effect a high recovery and to produce bullion, thus eliminating the cost of haulage as much as possible. Many prospects and properties throughout the State await further development of their orebodies and the additional capital for making changes in the mills necessitated by the increase of sulphides in the ores, which are no longer free-milling. If the treatment problems of these ores were solved, many old properties might be re-opened and the production of gold increased.

There are other ore-dressing problems connected with the ores in this State that need attention, such as are encountered in the concentration of lead, zinc, and gold ores, also of molybdenite, tungsten, and manganese ores; but the main purpose of solving the many problems is to effect a higher recovery of the valuable mineral on a commercial scale, whether the ores are complex or low-grade.

Oxy-Acetylene and Electric Welding on Dredges

*The Canadian Klondyke Mining Co. operates three (the fourth is out of commission) large dredges near Dawson in the Klondike, and in its machine-shop has a good deal of repair work to undertake. A complete plant for the generation of oxygen and acetylene gas from chemicals was installed and in operation since last fall, together with a complete line of oxy-acetylene welding equipment and tools, including compressors for the purpose of storing gases under pressure in low-pressure cylinders constructed for that purpose. A valuable addition to this plant, and one which will largely decrease the cost of manufacturing oxygen gas, is now being completed by the installation of 10 Vulcan electrolytic cells for the manufacture of this gas from water by electric current. The present cost of oxygen gas approximates 15 cents per cubic foot. On completion of the new machinery this cost will be reduced to less than 1 cent. A valuable by-product from this process will be hydrogen gas, which can be stored at no additional expense, and which will be extremely valuable in connection with many uses in the welding and machine-shop. The installation, as an adjunct to this department, of an electric-arc welding-plant, consisting of a suitable direct-current generator, with a complete line of electric-arc welding-supplies, has also been made; and has been in operation for a number of months whenever the necessary power was available. In addition to repair work during the operating season, the above-mentioned equipment places the company in a position to operate throughout the entire winter with both electric-arc and oxy-acetylene torches on dredge-bucket reclamation work, and on all repairs where the welding and putting-on tools can be utilized to advantage. The total cost of this installation to date amounts to the sum of $12,757.

*Abstracted from report of the receiver, and manager, H. G. Blankman, for the Canadian Klondyke Mining Co. for 1918.

It is not too much to say that the value of the repairs and reclamation work accomplished by the welding department to date, if credited to that department, would already offset the major portion of the investment. With this equipment it will be possible to reclaim and place again in service over 120 dredge-buckets that have been cast aside as unfit for further service at an expense which will approximate less than $150 per bucket. As the landed cost of these buckets at the present time is almost $1500 each, the resultant possible saving can be appreciated more readily.

A campaign of dredge-bucket reclamation has been arranged for the winter months, in connection with which a course of investigation is being conducted by the receiver as to the practicability of erecting a one-ton unit electric furnace for the melting and re-manufacture of scrap steel into bucket-lips, bushings, etc. In view of the excessively high cost, unsatisfactory delivery, and heavy investment charges that the present market presents to the management in the matter of steel dredging repair-parts, such an installation is being taken under the most serious consideration. To give a small idea of the convenience and saving possible to be effected by the welding-plant installations, the following may prove of interest:

On June 6 last it was necessary to close down the Hunker pumping-station owing to a bad crack in the main controlling-valve. This part could not be replaced here, and to bring one in from the manufacturers would have meant the loss of many weeks and consequent decrease in production of many thousands of dollars. The repair was made by the company's oxy-acetylene welder at a total cost of $237, and the pump started, with total lost time of 34 hours and 4 minutes.

The de-plating and building-up of the faces of a lower tumbler of a dredge will serve as an illustration of the saving effected by this process:

	Former method	Welding
Cutting out countersunk rivets (labor)	$56	$14
Material for shims	180	80
Labor	155	50

The cost by the welding method would be reduced still further by using scrap steel for the building-up material.

EACH BARREL OF OIL burned under the New Cornelia power-plant boilers in Arizona yields 305.6 kw. net of alternating current to the switchboard.

TUCSON, ARIZONA

GEOLOGIC AND MINING INVESTIGATION IN SOUTH-EASTERN ARIZONA.

The University of Arizona, through the State Bureau of Mines, is offering an 8 weeks' summer course in field geology and mining in the Chiricahua and Dos Cabezas mountains, south-eastern Arizona. The class begins on July 1 and ends on August 18, and will be supervised by C. J. Sarle and M. Ehle, respectively, professors in the Departments of Geology and Mining Engineering, of the College of Mines and Engineering. It will be open to students of all universities and colleges who have had a course in physical and historical geology and mineralogy. The class is limited to sixteen and, if more apply, the selection will be made from those best qualified. The work will include geodetic and topographic surveying, mapping of areal geology, making of geologic cross-sections, studying mines or prospects and undeveloped ore deposits, and making mine examinations and reports. Maps and bulletins covering the area studied will be prepared by the professors in charge of the party, and will be published by the Bureau of Mines. Students sufficiently advanced may collaborate in the preparation of the reports, and data secured may be used in the preparation of theses. For the satisfactory completion of the entire course six university credits will be given.

The region chosen for the work lies in the Chiricahua and Dos Cabezas mountains in the south-eastern corner of Arizona. These ranges are connected fault-block structures situated in the Arizona Highlands region, an eastward extension of the Great Basin province. They are flanked on the east by the broad flat-bottomed San Simon valley and similarly on the west by the Sulphur Springs valley. They rise from fringing piedmont slopes at 4500 to 5000 ft. above sea-level, attaining over considerable areas, especially in the Chiricahua range, an elevation of between 7000 and 8000 ft. The upper reaches of the latter are heavily forested. The sharp relief of these mountains has favored rapid erosion and the carving of many deep and picturesque canyons, in which the formations and structures are splendidly revealed. The formations range in age from pre-Cambrian to Quaternary, and include a great diversity of igneous, sedimentary, and metamorphic rocks. Of the sedimentaries, the Paleozoics predominate. Several horizons are richly fossiliferous, and parts of the area are highly mineralized. The ore deposits are of several classes, and include some instructive examples of secondary enrichment. A few mines are being operated at present, although a larger number are idle on account of the metal situation. The Hill-Top mine in the California district, northern Chiricahuas, now operating, has been opened by seven tunnels at different levels, in all of which ore occurs; and a tunnel nearly a mile in length pierces the crest of the range, establishing communication with canyon roads approaching the mine from opposite sides. The King is another operating mine in this district. The so-called Gold Ridge in the Dos Cabezas district, southern Dos Cabezas, transects that range, and mining and

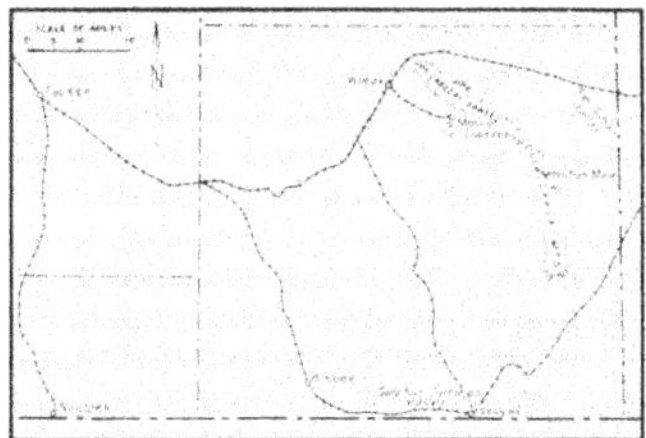

PART OF SOUTH-EASTERN ARIZONA

milling are being carried on from both sides. The Mascot is a well-known mine in this district. From the foregoing it readily may be seen that an opportunity for the study of all practical phases of geology, seldom realized within the compass of a single area, is presented here.

Although the inter-montane valleys of southern Arizona are very hot in the summer, the area selected, owing to its considerable elevation, affords almost ideal summer climatic conditions. The magnificent tree-shaded canyons, some with spring-fed streams, and the higher forested region furnish exceptionally fine camping-sites. Good roads traverse the valleys, and branch roads, passable for autos, developed mainly by the cattlemen and miners of the region, lead into all the more important canyons.

The University will furnish a full field equipment, including housing, camp cook, surveying instruments, and conveyances. Other field expenses will be met by charging each student a reasonable fee. The party will assemble at the University of Arizona on June 30 and will leave Tucson by train on the afternoon of July 1. A brief stop will be made at the copper centre of Bisbee. Here the students will have an opportunity to study some of the formations that will be encountered in their later work, and will examine mines and ore deposits in this important district. From Rodeo, New Mexico, the party will go by automobile to the first camp. Applications must be received by June 1. For further details address: The Director, Arizona Bureau of Mines, Tucson, Arizona.

BISBEE, ARIZONA

WORK AT THE SHATTUCK, DENVER, AND CALUMET & ARIZONA.—MANGANESE-SILVER ORE.

Fire-fighting in the Shattuck-Arizona's No. 1 stope on the 800-ft. level, started in February, is not yet complete, although it is hoped that during the next week or two the complete flooding of the lower workings up to the 700-ft. station will be reported. The loose nature of the ground has made flooding difficult, but at last reports the water in the shaft was about 25 ft. below the 700-ft. station. Thirty-eight bulkheads were built before water was turned in. The underground force consists of 50 men, most of whom are engaged on the fire, and in such repair work as the upper levels require.

The Denn-Arizona company is cutting a station on the 1800-ft. level. Recent developments on the 1600-ft. level, where carbonate ores were discovered, augur well for the 1700 and 1800-ft. levels. The 1700-ft. is being driven toward the ground.

The Calumet & Arizona company is raising the Campbell shaft at the present time. The head-frame, hoist, and surface buildings have been in place for several months. Ventilation underground is excellent. This was accomplished by raising an air-shaft from the 1400 to the 1300-ft. levels, alongside of the double-compartment working shaft. The draft thus created resulted in an unusually good air current. The main shaft now is above the 1300-ft. level and will be continued up to the 800-ft. level. Within the next few months it is expected that work will be started on the shaft at the surface to meet the raise. An underground hoist operates the cage that has been installed in the shaft to carry the workers up and down. The C. & A. is continuing to drive on the 1400 and 1600-ft. levels at the Junction shaft, and both drifts are reported to be in promising ground near the Denn-Arizona line.

The Boras lease, on the Don Luis side of the Mule mountains, is exploring on the 300-ft. level to get under the extensive orebodies opened at 210-ft. Beneath the old inclined shaft on that level was the same formation from which more than $25,000 of ore was shipped last year to the Copper Queen smelter at Douglas. More than 300 ft. of silicious rock, carrying small gold and silver was passed through before the copper ore was opened.——The A. B. C. company has resumed sinking its main shaft after being quiet during the War. It has small but good machinery. Both the A. B. C. and Boras are under the active management of the Hon. Harry Jennings.——The Wolverine-Arizona holdings, on the south side of the Mule mountains, also are being developed by shafts and tunnels with a few men.

The Black Eagle mine at Patagonia, owned and operated by Pearce and Gardner, is shipping regularly at the rate of 400 tons per month of a manganese-silver ore to the El Paso smelter. The ore is desirable as a flux. The average silver content is 50 oz. Costs, including mining, freight, and smelter charges, amount to $15 per ton.

CRIPPLE CREEK, COLORADO

GENERAL NOTES ON THE DISTRICT.

Dividends were paid on May 10 by the Cresson, $122,000, and the Golden Cycle, $45,000.

Prospecting by diamond-drill for the lost Farrel vein has been started on No. 7 level of the Mary McKinney mine by James Ahearn, the drilling expert, under contract with the company. Ahearn has been very successful in this work at the Cresson company's Raven Hill estate.

The Rocky Mountain Leasing Co., T. A. Auter superintendent, commenced shipping during the past week from the Deadwood mine of the United Gold Mines Co. on Bull hill.

Operations have been resumed on the property of the Blue Flag company, on the north-west slope of Raven hill. The shaft now 1100 ft. deep is to be sunk to 1400 ft. by the company.

ANYOX, BRITISH COLUMBIA

SILVER MINING IN THE ALICE ARM AND OTHER DISTRICTS.

According to D. J. Hancock, who operates the United Metals Co. on the Illience river, and the Independent Two, Three, and Four on the Kitsault river, development is progressing steadily with promising results in the Alice Arm district, although the railway difficulties that have interfered with operations at the Dolly Varden are much regretted. He expects renewed activity at that property when the tangle is straightened. At the time work ceased there, diamond-drilling in No. 2 tunnel had exposed 40 ft. of high-grade ore to a depth of 600 ft. In the main tunnel there was ore of good value, while in another and shorter tunnel ore had been extracted containing silver sulphides and native silver. The Wolf mine, Mr. Hancock stated, was recently sold for $50,000 cash. Diamond-drilling there has proved the existence of a large body of high-grade ore, and a lode has been traced 87½ ft. On the Vanguard there is a 20-ft. vein of chalcopyrite exposed for 300 ft. on the surface, and $180,000, which was offered the owners for the property, has been refused. The Last Chance and North Star, both in this district, are also said to be looking well. The La Rose mine recently shipped 35 tons of ore to the Trail smelter, and obtained an average of 38 oz. of silver per ton. At the United Metals during the past year development has been carried on to determine the extent of the orebody by open-cuts and small tunnels. Seventy-five tons of ore, which Mr. Hancock expects to go 300 oz. of silver per ton, has been sacked ready for shipment. In the Independent a tunnel has been driven

120 ft. This property is only 1500 ft. from tidewater, and contains silver. The ore is treated by the Granby company at its Anyox smelter free of charge because of its fluxing qualities.

Attention continues to be directed to the Premier mine, on the Salmon river, which shipped 205 tons to the Tacoma smelter, returning $67,484 gross. The Premier was formerly known as the Bush, and is owned by R. K. Neill of Spokane, and Woods and Trites of Fernie. Several important mining deals have taken place recently in which Portland Canal properties were the issue. New York men are said to have acquired a considerable interest in the Bush mine. The Forty-Nine and Yellowstone groups have been bonded to C. F. Caldwell for $125,000. The Silver King group, adjoining the Joker, has been bonded by O. B. Bush of Vancouver for $100,000. Mining properties now working in the Salmon River region are the Premier, Mineral Hill, and Joker. Work will commence by July on the Big Missouri, recently bonded to Sir Donald Mann, the Yellowstone, Bush mines, Forty Nine, and Silver Creek. With a considerable number of prospectors going into the country this summer, and with operations under way at the properties mentioned, not forgetting road and wharf construction planned by the Government, Salmon river should be the scene of much activity during the next few months. Mr. Caldwell, who is very enthusiastic about the district, expresses the hope that the Government will aid development by a railroad.

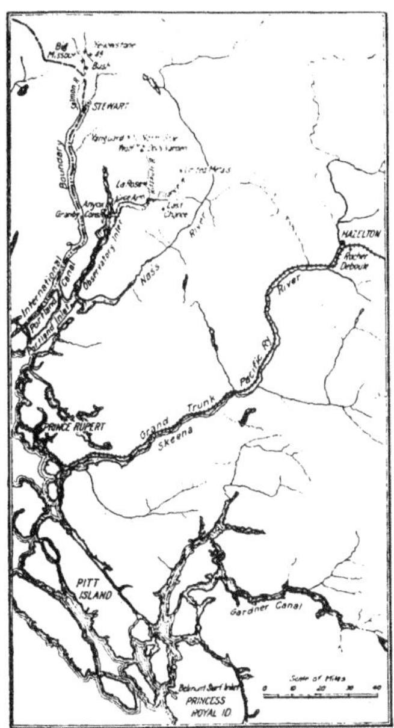

PART OF BRITISH COLUMBIA, SHOWING THE NEW SILVER AND OTHER DISTRICTS

HAZELTON.—The New Hazleton Gold-Cobalt Mines company, whose property is on Rocher de Boule mountain, has received the results of a test on 27 tons of ore sent to the testing-plant of the Department of Mines at Ottawa. An analysis gave 1.24 oz. gold, 1.12% cobalt, 1.40% molybdenite, 8.98% arsenic, 0.60% nickel. The arsenic, cobalt, nickel, and gold were intimately associated. The lot was divided into three parts, each of which was treated by a different method. The total actual recoveries were 77.6% of cobalt, 87.5% of nickel, 84.9% of arsenic, and 83.5% of gold, in table concentrates; and 54.4% of molybdenum in flotation products. The molybdenite is of secondary value compared with the other minerals. From the test work conducted, the Department reported, the procedure to follow on concentration of this ore would be as follows:

The crude ore broken in a jaw-crusher to 1½ or 1 in., ground in a wet ball-mill in circuit with a classifier to about 40-mesh, concentrated on tables of the Wilfley type, the table tailing re-ground in a ball or tube-mill to 100-mesh in circuit with a classifier, the molybdenite recovered in an oil flotation-unit, and the tailing from the flotation-unit concentrated on slime tables or vanners. Nicholas Thompson of Vancouver is president of the New Hazleton company.

SURF INLET.—In the report of the Belmont Surf Inlet Mines for the 10 months ended December 31, 1918, the following appears written on March 26, 1919:

F. W. Holler is superintendent, with H. J. O'Connell in charge of the mine, and F. H. Penn at the mill. Metals sold realized $744,432, of which $274,169 was net profit. Current assets total $422,811, and liabilities $67,-107. A dividend, the first, of 5 cents a share, $125,000, was paid in April 1919. Development amounted to 1887 ft., costing $15.12 per foot. The labor conditions prevented greater footage, but results were satisfactory for new ore. Reserves are calculated as 422,761 tons of all classes, an increase of 153,790 tons, plus 116,349 tons milled. The mill treated 273 tons daily, working 93.7% of the possible time. The total concentrated was 83,142 tons, averaging 0.481 oz. gold, 0.3114 oz. silver, and 0.2606% copper, equal to $11.12 per ton. Recoveries were 91.52%, 90.23%, about 100%, and 92.13%, respectively. Concentrate, 7498 tons, contained 36,606 oz. gold, 23,364 oz. silver, and 433,399 lb. copper. Operating costs were $4.83 per ton, plus 18 cents for sundries. The hydro-electric plant works well, delivering power at $0.002268 per kw-hour.

ALASKA

Kennecott.—The Kennecott Copper Corporation last year produced 60,994,757 lb. of copper and 684,779 oz. of silver. The most important development was the finding of a new orebody on the 600-ft. level of the Bonanza mine, and another at 900 ft. in the Jumbo mine. Operations now are at 30% of capacity.

Nome.—The Fairbanks station of the U. S. Bureau of Mines has completed concentration tests on the antimony ore from the Sliscovitch mine near Nome.

ARIZONA

Bisbee.—Calumet & Arizona produced 3,150,000 lb. of copper during April, somewhat more than half of full capacity.

Globe.—A special meeting of shareholders of the Barney Copper Co. is to be held on June 2 to effect a consolidation with the Porphyry Copper Co. The new company is to be called the Porphyry Consolidated Copper Co., having a capital of $500,000.

Oatman.—Shareholders of the Tom Reed Gold Mines Co. recently met at Kingman and elected directors for the ensuing year. During the past year there was milled 84,000 tons of ore, the average recovery being $9.36 per ton, and cost $5.58. This cost was considerably below that of previous years. Little of the ore treated came from the recently opened orebody in the Bald Eagle claim.

The Lexington cross-cut from the 250-ft. level has entered the vein for 6 ft., 2 ft. of which assays $15 gold per ton. The vein closely resembles that of the United Eastern and Tom Reed. It is reported that a contract is to be let to drive a 550-ft. drift east from the present workings, which will pass 100 ft. below the old 225-ft. shaft.

The United American Company, whose property is south of the Tom Reed, is preparing to sink to 500 feet.

Prescott.—The Boxer silver mine in the Black Canyon district has been sold to the Silver Zone Mining & Milling Co. for $10,000.

Yuma.—Water shortage for the King of Arizona Mining Co., operating in the Castle Dome mountains, has resulted in a dam being constructed in a near-by canyon.

CALIFORNIA

Bakersfield.—Oil production of the State during April averaged 279,154 bbl. daily from 8726 wells. This is about 500 bbl. more than in March. Stocks increased 57,322 bbl. to a total of 32,543,145 bbl. Forty new wells were brought-in with an initial yield of 10,920 bbl. per day.

Coram.—The Balaklala Consolidated Copper Co. is suing the Mammoth Copper company for settlement on ores shipped by it during part of November, December, and January. The tonnage was 18,000, and sum involved $40,000. A preliminary settlement was made on the basis of 15 cents per pound for copper, but the Balaklala wants the balance of a price of 18.39 cents.

The Balaklala company closed its mine completely on May 13. Normally, 200 men are employed, but latterly only 40 were on the payroll. Daily shipments to the Mammoth smelter at Kennett were 300 tons, but the Mammoth had asked that these be increased. There has been difficulty in securing enough laborers, as lumber and shipbuilding pay higher wages and so attract these men from the copper districts.

The Balaklala company has raised wages by 50 cents a day, restoring the scale effective to February 16. Miners will now receive $4.50; helpers, $4.25; shovelers, $4; and surface men, $3.75. Mechanics will also get the 50-cent increase. This news was given by the manager, S. A. Holman, on May 15, some days after it was announced that the mine would have to be closed.

Downieville.—The Gold Exploration Co. of Salt Lake City, has acquired the Alhambra, Sovereign, and Comet quartz mines, and is arranging for work on a large scale. The properties are in Jim Crow and Ladies canyons.

Hemet.—So far as the general situation in the magnesite industry is concerned, there has been no marked change from the quiet conditions prevailing during the past five or six months, according to W. C. Phalen in the April report of the U. S. Bureau of Mines. This industry is linked intimately with other large industries like those of steel and copper, in which magnesite is used in furnace linings, and to the building trade.

PLANT AT HEMET MAGNESITE MINE, RIVERSIDE COUNTY, CALIFORNIA

Kennett.—Locomotive crane-men downed tools on May 15, following the action of the mechanics last week. Without crane-men it is not possible to load ore. Two furnaces are in blast, but when the supply of ore runs out they will be stopped.

The smelter was closed on the 17th.

The Reid gold mine at Old Diggings will continue shipments of ore to the Kennett smelter, notwithstanding the shut-down. The ore, which is needed as a flux, will be put on stock-piles. The Reid employs 60 men.

Melones.—The Carson Hill Gold Mining Co., with a capital of 250,000 $1 shares, of which 185,914 have been issued, has been listed on the Boston Stock Exchange. The company is controlled by interests in the American Zinc, Lead

& Smelting Co., Pond Creek and Island Creek Coal companies. The board of directors consists of E. A. Clark, W. H. Coolidge, G. L. Stone, W. A. Ogg, and W. J. Loring. Through its subsidiary, the Carson Hill Gold Mines, Inc., the company owns 344 acres of land. The company has opened over 10,000 ft. underground. One shoot on the two lower levels is 160 ft. long and averages $24 per ton. On March 16, 1919, ore-reserves amounted to 201,830 tons, valued at $3,014,153, of which $1,999,933 would be profit.

Since the beginning of the year, the 20-stamp mill has treated the following:

	Tons	Value	Expenses	Profit
January	1,950	$30,084	$19,098	$10,985
February	3,450	41,948	20,592	21,356
March	5,400	70,781	30,476	40,304
April	8,000	.....	.....	47,500
Total	10,800	.....	.....	$120,145

A. D. Stevenot is superintendent.

Portola.—Surveys are being made for an aerial tram from the Walker copper mine to Spring Garden, a distance of 8 miles. At present, concentrates and supplies are trucked to Portola on the Western Pacific, which is 25 miles away.

San Francisco.—Owners and operators of chrome, manganese, pyrite, and tungsten mines who expect to file claims for reimbursement under the War Minerals Relief Act must see that such claims reach Washington, D. C., not later than June 2. The State mineralogist, Fletcher Hamilton, has just received a message from Senator John F. Shafroth, chairman of the Relief Commission, asking the co-operation of the Mining Bureau in giving further publicity to this fact. Blank questionnaires and full instructions may be obtained upon request by letter or telegram, from the Register, U. S. Land Office, Customs House, San Francisco. Immediate action is imperative by parties who consider that the Government should make good their losses, if they have not yet complied with the requirements of the Relief Act.

The State Mining Bureau, in order to aid development of the mining industry, is to establish permanent branch offices at Auburn, in Placer county, and at Redding, in Shasta county. C. A. Logan will be in charge of the former, which includes the Mother Lode and Sierra Nevada counties as far north as Plumas; while E. Huguenin will be in charge at Redding, for the eight counties north to the Oregon boundary.

IDAHO

Kellogg.—One furnace is in blast at the Bunker Hill & Sullivan smelter here, producing 90 tons of lead bullion daily.

Wallace.—Preliminary work preparatory to re-constructing the main highway across Shoshone county through the co-operation of the County, State, and Federal government, is progressing satisfactorily, according to the 'Miner'. The permanent location of the road from the Kootenai county line to Kellogg has been completed, the work being done by a party under the direction of G. I. Bassett, a State engineer. Under the agreement entered into between the Commissioners and the Highway Commission, Shoshone county will provide $100,000 for construction of the road during the next two years, and the State will contribute $50,000. With this amount secured, the Federal government, through the Forest Service, will contribute $150,000, making the total amount available for the construction of a standard road across the county $300,000. When this expenditure is made the county will be free from further expense in maintaining this highway, the State assuming responsibility for its maintenance. The most pressing improvement on the transcontinental highway across this county, an improvement that should have been made long ago, is changing the road to cross the Idaho-Montana divide at Lookout pass. This is regarded so by the State and Federal authorities, as well as by the Commissioners of this county.

MONTANA

Butte.—Anaconda pays $1 per share on May 26. This is equal to $2,331,250, and makes $8,159,375 for the current year, and $154,516,875 to date. Anaconda last year sold metals for $102,586,541. The profit from all sources was $20,802,870, $13,000,000 less than in 1917. Dividends totaled $17,484,372, a decrease of $24,000,000. The output was 293,603,726 lb. of copper, 10,967,905 oz. of silver, and 64,317 oz. of gold. The reduction works treated 4,350,446 tons of ore.

NEVADA

Battle Mountain.—Roads between Battle Mountain and the Maysville district have been opened after being blocked for five months. Heavy shipments of silver ore are arriving from the Kattenhorn and other mines.

Cherry Creek.—This old silver district is quite active again. From his lease on the Exchequer, J. W. Walker is shipping ore averaging $66 per ton.—F. W. Fletcher has resumed work on the Black Metal and will start shipping shortly.—Salt Lake City capital is developing the famous Tea Cup, and opening old workings.

Divide.—In the Tonopah Divide mine the drift south-east from the main cross-cut on the 475-ft. level is out 300 ft. Samples taken at 5-ft. intervals for the first 110 ft. average $148 per ton for the width of the drift, according to A. J. D'Arcy, the consulting engineer. The next 140 ft. is low-grade, as the drift left the hanging-wall and at one point went well into the foot-wall. The last 50 ft. assayed from $30 to $50 per ton. Two raises are being driven from the fourth level. The big air-compressor is being erected.

Since the boom started at Divide, men who have made the trip from Goldfield every week, have always passed from one to three Goldfield houses being moved to Divide; while every day for this period at least one house has been on the road. If such movement continues to the Cactus field, Goldfield will be soon de-housed.

Tonopah.—Production of the district last week, including 420 tons from the Divide, totaled 6738 tons, valued at $114,546.

The Tonopah Extension is to pay 10 cents per share, equal to $128,280. This makes $192,420 for the current year, and $2,104,819 to date.

Wonder.—The Nevada Wonder company has taken a 40-day option on the Spider and Wasp mine from Eli Cann and David Craig. The property comprises five claims, developed to a depth of 200 ft. Considerable lateral work has been done. Equipment includes a small hoist. Medium-grade ore is exposed.

UTAH

The State Road Commission has nearly $5,000,000 available for improvement of 1500 miles of roads, many of which are in mining counties.

Park City.—In the labor trouble here, a committee from the Ontario mine has conferred with the management. So far, the position is unchanged.

Tintic.—In the labor trouble in this district, the miners arranged that committees from each mine should confer with their respective managements.

The mine operators issued a statement, blaming the I. W. W. for an attempt to cause trouble here and throughout Utah.

CANADA

Ontario

Cobalt.—The sampling-plant of Campbell & Deyell, who were to retire from business recently, has been taken over by the Provincial government, to be under the supervision of Arthur A. Cole of the Temiskaming & Northern Ontario Railway Commission.

The Coniagas company paid 12½ cents per share, equal to $100,000 on May 1. This makes 236%, or $9,440,000 to date.

Kirkland Lake.—Companies operating in this area favor construction of a first-class highway for motor-trucks instead of a railway. The cost of the former is estimated at less than half that of the latter, which has been authorized by the Provincial government. It is pointed out that the motor road will be more flexible than the steam road, enabling everything to be delivered right at each property. A referendum on the question is being taken locally.

Acceding to this desire, the Government has decided to construct a highway instead of a railway.

The Ontario-Kirkland's shaft is down 320 ft., the last 120 ft. being sunk and timbered in 30 days.

Porcupine.—The Government is contributing $30,000 toward the cost of constructing a motor road from Timmins to South Porcupine and to the Dome mine. The total cost will be $60,000. The township of Tisdale is to furnish the balance.

The Hollinger Consolidated, in a quarterly report, states that there was treated 138,260 tons of $9.78 ore, at a cost of $5.38 per ton. The gold realized $1,368,980, of which $564,684 was profit. Dividends absorbed $246,000. Current assets total $2,534,865, and liabilities $185,872. The number of employees increased from 911 to 1311.

Yukon

Dawson.—According to the 'Daily News', lode claims are being developed in many parts of this Territory. At present there are 860 quartz claims held. There are some in the copper area at the head of the White river, 80 miles from Kennecott in Alaska; copper claims on Williams and Merritt creeks, at Whitehorse, and the lead deposits in the Mayo and other districts of southern Yukon. Near Dawson a great deal of exploration has been done and machinery erected. Among the lode properties of promise are those situated on Williams and Merritt creeks, on the left limit of the Yukon river, 215 miles south of Dawson. The owners are J. P. Guite, J. O. Lachapelle, and J. Viau, all residents of Dawson. The property is known as the Williams and Merritt group. The claims are located upon a contact between a coarse-grained metamorphic schist and schist of a gneissoid character. Shallow shafts have been sunk and a tunnel driven. In June 1917, about 7 tons of ore was sent to Anyox, B. C., averaging $178.75 per ton in copper, silver, and gold. The cost was $70.53 per ton. Owing to high cost of supplies, work was stopped in February 1919. Assays made in March of this year by the Territorial Assayer, W. C. Simes, yielded 8.09 to 12.74% copper, 1.34 to 1.60 oz. silver, and 0.06 to 0.05 oz. gold per ton. Local conditions are favorable for lode mining.

KOREA

Unsan.—The last four returns of the Oriental Consolidated are as below:

Month	Tons	Gold value	Profit
April	.....	$100,000	.....
March	21,322	103,200	.....
February	17,055	88,111	.....
January	22,212	101,771	$0,659

Good progress is being made with the Suribong hydroelectric project, the tunnel being holed through on February 23, and the river being turned through on March 12. The quantity of native labor is fairly satisfactory, but the quality is very inferior. Rice and millet prices are still unreasonably high, and there is an actual shortage of rice in Japan; but no means have as yet been devised by the authorities for relieving the situation. An arrangement has been made with the Tanaka Choten for the sale of gold and silver bullion, the rate for the former metal being a premium of 3.6% above the par value.

PERSONAL

Note. The Editor invites members of the profession to send particulars of their work and appointments. The information is interesting to our readers.

F. Le Roi Thurmond is returning to Anchorage, Alaska.

Arthur L. Pearse is expected in San Francisco, from London.

G. A. Overstrom, who is now living at Pasadena, was in San Francisco last week.

L. S. Noble, consulting engineer for the Cresson company of Cripple Creek, is in Mexico.

Joseph P. Ruth, of Denver, visited San Francisco on his way from Idaho and Washington.

William C. Phalen, Mineral Technologist to the U. S. Bureau of Mines, is here, from Washington, D. C.

James F. McCarthy, manager of the Hecla mine, in the Coeur d'Alene region, was in San Francisco last week.

C. R. Olson has been appointed mill-superintendent for the Como Consolidated Mines Co., near Dayton, Nevada.

C. W. Newton, manager and director for the Consolidated Interstate-Callahan Mining Co. at Wallace, Idaho, is in New York attending the annual meeting of the company.

Andrew Walz of New York last week completed examining the Victory, Belcher, and Belcher Extension properties at Divide for Aldrich-Jackling interests, which have taken them over.

Austin F. Rogers and **Cyrus F. Tolman, Jr.**, respectively, associate professors of mineralogy and economic geology in Stanford University, have been promoted to full professorships.

Burdette F. Grant, formerly general superintendent of the Swansea mines in Arizona, is now associated with **B. M. Snyder** in engineering practice in the Security Bdg., Los Angeles.

C. H. Clapp has been appointed director of the State Bureau of Mines at Butte, which is now being organized as a part of the School of Mines. He will be geologist for the Bureau; **H. B. Pulsifer** will be metallurgist; and **A. E. Adami** will be in charge of the department of mining engineering.

W. H. Nichols, president of the American Chemical Society, which has 13,000 members, addressed the San Francisco section at the Engineers' Club on May 19. There were 187 present. **H. W. Morse** gave an illustrated talk on the manufacture of potash and borax at Searles lake, California. **L. H. Duschak** was chairman for this interesting meeting.

John R. Brownell, superintendent of safety for the California Industrial Accident Commission, has resigned to take a position with the Equitable Life Assurance Society in San Francisco. Mr. Brownell will make a specialty of group and business insurance. He will be succeeded by **Hugh M. Wolflin**, chief mine inspector for the Commission. **G. Chester Brown** takes Mr. Wolflin's place. **T. W. Osgood** has been appointed superintendent of safety for the Los Angeles district.

The U. S. Civil Service Commission announces an open competitive examination for mining accountant on June 10. The salary for grade 1 is $2400 to $4200 per year, and for grade 2, $4200 to $6000. Appointments as a result of this examination will be made on a monthly basis, but the work may continue for a year or more. The duties of appointees to grade 1 positions will be to examine the accounts of producers of minerals in connection with claims made for losses growing out of the War. The duties of appointees to grade 2 positions will be to supervise the work of a number of accountants of grade 1.

THE METAL MARKET

METAL PRICES

San Francisco, May 20

Aluminum-dust, cents per pound	50—60
Antimony, cents per pound	8
Copper, electrolytic, cents per pound	18
Lead, pig, cents per pound	5½—6½
Platinum, pure, per ounce	$105
Platinum, 10% iridium, per ounce	$115
Quicksilver, per flask of 75 lb	$82
Spelter, cents per pound	7½
Zinc-dust, cents per pound	10—12

EASTERN METAL MARKET

(By wire from New York)

May 20.—Copper is active and stronger. Lead is in good demand and higher. Spelter is quiet and advancing.

SILVER

Below are given official or ticker quotations, in cents per ounce of silver 999 fine. From April 23, 1918, the United States government paid $1 per ounce for all silver purchased by it, fixing a maximum of $1.01½ on August 15, 1918, and will continue to pay $1 until the quantity specified under the Act is purchased, probably extending over several years. On May 5, 1919, all restrictions on the metal were removed, resulting in fluctuations. During the restricted period, the British government fixed the maximum price five times, the last being on March 25, 1919, on account of the low rate of sterling exchange, but removed all restrictions on May 10. The equivalent of dollar silver (1.000 fine) in British currency is 46.65 pence per ounce (925 fine), calculated at the normal rate of exchange.

Date		New York cents	London pence	Average week ending		Cents	Pence
May	14	111.00	54.00	Apr.	8	101.12	48.86
"	15	111.00	53.87	"	15	101.12	48.85
"	16	111.00	54.00	"	22	101.12	48.94
"	17	110.50	53.50	"	29	101.12	48.78
"	18 Sunday			May	6	101.14	48.71
"	19	109.50	53.12	"	13	109.33	52.98
"	20	109.00	52.87	"	20	110.33	53.50

Monthly averages

	1917	1918	1919		1917	1918	1919
Jan.	75.14	88.72	101.12	July	78.92	99.62	....
Feb.	77.54	85.79	101.12	Aug.	85.40	100.31	....
Mch.	74.13	88.11	101.12	Sept.	100.73	101.12	....
Apr.	72.51	95.35	101.12	Oct.	87.38	101.12	....
May	74.61	99.50	....	Nov.	85.97	101.12	....
June	76.44	99.50	....	Dec.	85.97	101.12	....

Raymond T. Baker, director of the Mint, is reported to have made the following remarks on silver: "At $1 an ounce silver mining is very profitable; even at 85 cents an ounce. Ordinarily the silver purchases for the Mint are much less than were made in 1918; in fact, the quantity handled during 1918 was 2 2/3 greater than the quantity handled in 1917. It is quite likely that the purchases of silver under the Act will extend over a period of 10 years, and also that these purchases will have the effect of keeping up the price of the metal during that period. There is still a tremendous demand for silver, from India and the Orient, and the European countries. The demand for silver will grow, I believe, with the expansion in world trade following upon reconstruction in Europe and revival of industry."

Opinions of brokers in New York and other Eastern financial centres differ as to what will be the future of silver, but they appear to agree that America must wait to see what happens in London and the Far East, both of which will be the determining factor. London prices will demonstrate the urgency of the world's silver demand.

P. D. Handy, of Handy & Harmon, says: "It is idle to speculate. I do not see any grounds for expecting, however, any fantastic price for silver." V. M. Bovie, superintendent of the New York Assay Office, says: "The decision, as I understand it, places silver on an entirely new basis and the market will be affected by any bidding that may arise. The decision can be taken at least as meaning no immediate reduction in price of silver." J. S. Scully, of Zimmermann & Forshay, is of the opinion that "We may look for a good deal higher price. But just where the movement will go it is too early to say. The Oriental demand is more than ever a factor. Anybody can ship silver to China, but imports into India are restricted by the Indian government through certain recognized channels."

COPPER

Prices of electrolytic in New York, in cents per pound.

Date			Average week ending		
May	14	15.75	Apr.	8	15.25
"	15	16.00	"	15	15.33
"	16	16.25	"	22	15.18
"	17	16.25	"	29	15.18
"	18 Sunday		May	6	15.25
"	19	16.37	"	13	15.37
"	20	16.50	"	20	16.24

Monthly averages

	1917	1918	1919		1917	1918	1919
Jan.	29.53	23.50	20.43	July	29.67	26.00	....
Feb.	34.57	23.50	17.34	Aug.	27.42	26.00	....
Mch.	36.00	23.50	15.05	Sept.	25.11	26.00	....
Apr.	33.16	23.50	15.23	Oct.	23.50	26.00	....
May	31.69	23.50	....	Nov.	23.50	26.00	....
June	32.57	23.50	....	Dec.	23.50	26.00	....

The reports of three porphyry companies for the first quarter of 1919 have been published, and show the following result:

	Nevada Con.	Ray Con.	Utah Copper
Operating deficit	$111,150	$244,067	$12,948
Deficit after dividends	800,955	940,887	1,955,410
Av. received for copper, cents	13.63	13.12	12.89
Cost, cents	14.85	15.15	13.72
Cost in previous quarter, cents	10.01	10.30	10.42

Copper production of some of the large mines in April was as under.

Mine	Pounds	Mine	Pounds
Calumet & Hecla and subsidiaries	8,054,113	Nevada Con.	3,703,000
Chino	3,498,000	Ray Con.	3,050,000
Greene-Cananea	3,000,000	Utah Copper	9,420,000

Copper output of 17 leading mines during April totaled 87,000,000 lb., a decrease of 3,000,000 lb. from March, and 48,000,000 lb. from last November.

LEAD

Lead is quoted in cents per pound, New York delivery.

Date			Average week ending		
May	14	4.95	Apr.	8	5.25
"	15	4.95	"	15	5.07
"	16	4.95	"	22	4.93
"	17	5.10	"	29	4.95
"	18 Sunday		May	6	4.87
"	19	5.10	"	13	4.85
"	20	5.25	"	20	5.05

Monthly averages

	1917	1918	1919		1917	1918	1919
Jan.	7.64	6.85	5.60	July	10.93	8.03	....
Feb.	9.10	7.07	5.13	Aug.	10.75	8.05	....
Mch.	10.07	7.26	5.24	Sept.	9.07	8.05	....
Apr.	9.38	6.99	5.05	Oct.	6.97	8.05	....
May	10.29	6.88	....	Nov.	6.38	8.05	....
June	11.74	7.58	....	Dec.	6.49	6.90	....

Lead ore at Joplin last week sold for $57 per ton, basis 80% metal. The Tri-State region produced 2180 tons.

The American Smelting & Refining Co. advanced the price of lead from 5 to 5.10 cents on May 16.

ZINC

Zinc is quoted as spelter, standard Western brands, New York delivery, in cents per pound:

Date			Average week ending		
May	14	6.40	Apr.	8	6.60
"	15	6.40	"	15	6.57
"	16	6.45	"	22	6.41
"	17	6.45	"	29	6.39
"	18 Sunday		May	6	6.32
"	19	6.50	"	13	6.31
"	20	6.55	"	20	6.46

Monthly averages

	1917	1918	1919		1917	1918	1919
Jan.	9.75	7.78	7.44	July	8.98	8.72	....
Feb.	10.45	7.97	6.71	Aug.	8.58	8.87	....
Mch.	10.78	7.07	6.53	Sept.	8.33	9.58	....
Apr.	10.20	7.04	6.40	Oct.	8.32	9.11	....
May	9.41	7.29	....	Nov.	7.76	8.75	....
June	9.63	7.92	....	Dec.	7.84	8.49	....

Zinc concentrate sold at Joplin last week averaged $35 per ton, basis 60% metal. The output of the Tri-State region was 7022 tons, but over 11,000 tons was shipped to smelters.

QUICKSILVER

The primary market for quicksilver is San Francisco, California being the largest producer. The price is fixed in the open market, according to quantity. Prices, in dollars per flask of 75 pounds:

Date					
Apr.	22	75.00	May	6	75.00
"	29	75.00	"	13	80.00
			"	20	82.00

Monthly averages

	1917	1918	1919		1917	1918	1919
Jan.	81.00	128.06	103.75	July	102.00	120.00	....
Feb.	126.25	118.00	90.00	Aug.	115.00	120.00	....
Mch.	113.75	112.00	72.80	Sept.	112.00	120.00	....
Apr.	114.50	115.00	73.12	Oct.	102.00	120.00	....
May	104.00	110.00	....	Nov.	102.50	120.00	....
June	85.50	112.00	....	Dec.	117.42	115.00	....

TIN

Prices in New York, in cents per pound. The monthly averages in 1918 are nominal. On December 3 the War Industries Board fixed the price to consumers and jobbers at 72½c. f.o.b. Chicago and Eastern points, and 71¼c. on the Pacific Coast. This will continue until the U. S. Steel Products Co.'s stock is consumed.

Monthly averages

	1917	1918	1919		1917	1918	1919
Jan.	44.10	85.13	71.50	July	62.60	93.00	....
Feb.	51.47	85.00	72.44	Aug.	62.53	91.33	....
Mch.	54.27	85.00	72.50	Sept.	61.54	80.40	....
Apr.	55.63	88.53	72.50	Oct.	62.24	78.82	....
May	63.21	100.01	....	Nov.	74.18	73.67	....
June	61.93	91.00	....	Dec.	85.00	71.52	....

Metal stocks in Great Britain on May 1 show a gain of 5,400,000 lb. of copper to 114,531,200 lb., 8,000,000 lb. of lead to 244,186,880 lb., 400,000 lb. of nickel to 5,750,080 lb., 200,000 lb. of antimony to 9,992,640 lb.; and a decrease of 9,000,000 lb. of spelter to 76,090,560 lb. When compared with stocks held in December, the present lot is much greater.

Eastern Metal Market

New York, May 14.

All the markets have a better tone, with demand in some of them active and prices higher.

Antimony is a little higher.

Copper is stronger and higher, with demand fairly good for all positions.

Lead is fair, with the market quiet but firm.

Tin interest in future shipment metal is stronger.

Zinc shows but little improvement, with quotations steady.

ANTIMONY

There has been little change, with demand light and the market firm at 6.75 to 6.92½c., New York, duty paid.

COPPER

The market has assumed an entirely different tone during the last week, and is much more active. To this time consumers had covered their requirements up to the middle of May, and are now apparently appearing for future needs. At any rate, demand has improved decidedly, but it finds producers firm in their quotations and ideas of values, and indisposed to book orders indiscriminately. Sales have been made of electrolytic copper at steadily advancing prices during the past week, both for early delivery and for shipment as far ahead as July, but the aggregate has not been very large. Quotations as a result of present conditions are about 15.75c., New York, for electrolytic copper for May and June delivery, with 16c. asked and obtained for July. Lake copper is held at 16c., New York, for early delivery. British Government stocks of copper on May 1 were 51,130 long tons, an increase of 2428 tons over April 1 and a gain of 23,600 tons over those of December 1, 1918.

IRON AND STEEL

The feeling is general that the result of the abandonment of any price-stabilization program is going to be beneficial to the entire trade. At a meeting in New York last Thursday, between the steel men and the Railroad Administration, the entire program of regulated prices was rescinded. The steel-makers told the railroad men that no further reductions on railroad steel would be made unless wages were reduced. One Eastern maker of large, wide plates, has advanced his price to 2.75c. per lb., or $2 per ton. Many think that prices in general will advance rather than otherwise.

LEAD

The market may be characterized as firm, quiet, and steady. The weakness apparent a week or 10 days ago has disappeared, due largely to the withdrawal of those sellers responsible for the lower prices at that time. Since then and as a natural result, other sellers found things coming their way until prices have risen to those quoted today, which are 4.95c., New York, in the outside market, with the St. Louis price unchanged at 4.60c. The American Smelting & Refining Co. did not in all this time lower its price which continues at 5c., New York, although a reduction was confidently expected at one time. At the figures mentioned some business has been done, but it has not been large. The situation is regarded as fundamentally sound, and there has been good buying by cable and pipe-makers. Stocks of lead in Great Britain on May 1 were 109,102 tons, an increase for the month of 12,556 tons. This contrasts with 49,111 tons on December 1.

TIN

The feature of an otherwise absolutely lifeless market is that more interest is being manifested by consumers in purchases of tin for shipment from either London or the Far East, after import restrictions are removed. Some business has resulted from this greater interest at prices varying from 49.25 to 50.25c. per lb. from the Far East and London respectively. Aside from this, conditions are unchanged, and the market is dull. It is stated, but unconfirmed, that American smelters refuse to quote for delivery after restrictions are removed, and the suggestion is made that some protection to these producers is involved. The London market is a little higher by about £10 per ton over last week, spot Straits having been quoted yesterday at £237 per ton. This is perhaps due to the possible nearness of the lifting of American import restrictions.

ZINC

There has been little change during the week. Quotations are slightly higher, due perhaps to a withdrawal of some small sellers or speculators, and to an appreciation of the probable fact that production has experienced a curtailment. Prime Western for early delivery is quoted at 6.05c., St. Louis, or 6.40c., New York, with July delivery held at 6.10c., St. Louis. Demand continues light with but little interest shown by galvanizers and brass makers. British Government stocks of spelter in May decreased, which is true only of this metal. As of May 1 the stocks of common zinc were 26,912 tons and of refined zinc, 7057 tons, a decrease from April 1 of 764 tons and 3314 tons, respectively.

ORES

Manganese-Iron Alloys: There is almost no business in ferro or spiegel except an occasional carload. Quotations are $150, delivered, for standard ferro, with spiegel obtainable at $33 to $35, furnace. The production of ferro during April, according to 'The Iron Age', was 16,325 long tons, and of spiegel only 2778 tons, the latter the lowest in many months.

Molybdenum: Prices are nominal at 80 to 90c. per pound.

Tungsten: The market is quiet with quotations largely nominal at $7 to $10 per unit for wolframite and scheelite in 60% concentrate. For ferro-tungsten, as high as $1.40 per lb. of contained tungsten is asked, but it is believed that a desirable firm inquiry would bring a lower price.

EXPORTATION OF GOLD AND MANUFACTURES THEREOF

The War Trade Board announced the following regulations governing the exportation of manufactures of gold, effective May 9:

All manufactures of gold, the bullion value of which does not exceed 65% of the total value, may be exported, without individual export licenses, under the special export licenses applicable to the exportation of commodities not on the Export Conservation List. The shipper must, however, state in his export declaration the bullion value of each item in the shipment and the total value of such item, and that no item in such shipment has a bullion value in excess of 65% of the total value of such item.

Every manufacturer of gold, the bullion value of which exceeds 65% of the total value, is now regarded, for the purpose of exportation, as gold bullion, the exportation of which is under the exclusive control of the Federal Reserve Board. All applications, therefore, to export manufactures of gold, the bullion value of which exceeds 65% of the total value, should be filed with the Federal Reserve Bank of the district from which the shipment is made. On such applications must be stated the value of the gold content of the articles proposed to be exported, as well as the total value of such articles.

Company Reports

Reports of the 'porphyry' companies for 1918:

CHINO COPPER CO.

Property: mine at Santa Rita and mill at Hurley, N. M.

Operating Officials: John M. Sully, general manager; H. G. S. Anderson, assistant; Horace Moses, superintendent of mines; O. F. Riser, assistant superintendent of mills; G. L. Webster, cashier.

Financial Statement: revenue from metals sold was $17,089,312. The net operating profit was $3,908,222, inclusive of sundries and less other charges. The surplus of current assets is $7,327,602, a decrease of $1,468,053.

Dividends: $4.50 per share, equal to $3,914,910, making $26,403,042 to date.

Development and Mining: churn-drilling on the South and South-west orebodies aggregated 15,020 ft., bringing the total to 264,748 ft. since commencement of operations. This work developed 114,528,178 tons of ore. Reserves were re-calculated, and are now 95,580,737 tons, averaging 1.63% copper; plus 882,824 tons of 1.86% on dumps; and 88,465 tons of 1.37% for experimental purposes. The steam-shovels moved 3,264,556 yards of overburden and 3,749,238 tons of ore. The cost of steam-shoveling was 69.55 cents per ton, an increase of 18.67 cents.

Production: the mill treated 3,836,400 tons, equal to 10,510 tons daily, 625 tons more than in 1917. The average copper content was 1.63%. The total ore concentrated is now 17,948,678 tons. The 278,413 tons of concentrate carried 14.25% metal. Recovery was 63.275%, a decrease of 6.041%, due to inclusion of oxide ore. Milling cost $1.37 per ton, a total gain of 33%, but only 6.08% for direct treatment, taxes accounting for the balance. The smelter output was 79,340,372 lb. of copper, a drop of 4,000,000 lb. Costs were 17.178 cents per pound, compared with 11.30 cents in 1917.

INSPIRATION CONSOLIDATED COPPER CO.

Property: mine and mill at Miami, Arizona.

Operating Officials: C. E. Mills, general manager; T. A. Donahue, general superintendent; H. W. Aldrich, assistant; Felix McDonald, mill superintendent.

Financial Statement: sale of copper realized $17,516,323. Expenses totaled $11,805,322. Depreciation written off was $750,000. Sundry receipts were $290,063. The balance at December 31, 1917, was $14,011,005. Copper on hand at end of 1918 was valued at $2,978,099. This, with the profit and balance made available $22,240,169. After paying dividends the balance forward was $12,784,433. Current assets total $19,372,943, and liabilities $3,125,161.

Dividends: No. 9, 10, 11, and 12 absorbed $9,455,736.

Development: a total of 14.88 miles were driven during 1918, making 127.85 miles to date; but 10.01 miles of workings were destroyed, making 63.90 miles, and leaving 63.95 miles open at the end of the year. No work was done for the purpose of increasing reserves. The average output of ore per man-shift was 21.5 tons.

Production: the mill concentrated 5,110,101 tons of 1.361% ore, recovering 73.02%. The copper output was 98,540,041 lb., including 1,063,464 lb. from 29,031 tons of oxide ore smelted direct. The cost per pound, exclusive of depreciation and income-tax, was 11.259 cents.

MIAMI COPPER CO.

Property: mine and works at Miami, Arizona.

Operating Officials: B. B. Gottsberger, general manager; F. W. Maclennan, assistant; F. W. Solomon, mill superintendent; R. B. Yerxa, assistant.

Financial Statement: sales of copper amounted to $14,446,704. Operations and taxes cost $8,727,534, leaving a profit of $5,719,170. The average received for copper was 24.65 cents, and cost 14.83 cents per pound. Current assets total $9,625,783, including $5,103,920 for investments and securities. Accounts payable amount to $2,479,894.

Dividends: No. 22-25 absorbed $3,362,013, bringing the total to $19,595,044.

Development and Mining: underground work consisted of 10,888 ft. of driving, 3102 ft. of raising, and 882 ft. of sinking. All the exploration was on and above 570-ft. depth.

MAP SHOWING POSITION OF THE PORPHYRY COPPERS AND THEIR SMELTERS

No. 5 shaft is 908 ft. deep, but will be sunk to 930 ft., to provide a haulage-level and ore-pocket for the deepest ore known to exist. The shaft is being concreted. Ore extraction is by top-slicing in the main and by caving in the Captain orebodies. Ventilation was improved by re-lining No. 3 shaft with concrete. Reserves are 12,570,000 tons of 2.38%, 36,000,000 tons of 1.06%, and 6,000,000 tons of 2% mixed ores. The cost of mining was $1.36 per ton.

Milling and Production: the plant treated 2,132,941 tons of 2.026% ore, recovering 71.15% in 76,750 tons of 40.147% concentrate. The cost of milling was 72.23 cents per ton. The total output of copper was 58,407,563 lb. The smelter returned to the company in refined form 95% of the copper in the concentrate.

NEVADA CONSOLIDATED COPPER CO.

Property: mines at Ely, railroad, and works at McGill, Nevada.

Operating Officials: C. B. Lakenan, general manager; W. S. Larsh, underground mine superintendent; F. E. Grant, shovel-pit superintendent; R. E. H. Pomeroy, smelter superintendent; G. C. Riser, concentrator superintendent.

Financial Statement: operating revenue during 1918 was $16,787,657; miscellaneous income, $1,051,694; operating expenses, $14,437,281, and profit, $3,402,071, the last item a decrease of $6,156,822. After paying dividends the balance at the end of the year was $9,934,361, compared with $13,180,526 at the beginning. The surplus of quick assets, including $6,809,668 for metals, was $11,436,904, a decline of $2,864,519.

Dividends: the total last year was $6,498,235, making $42,269,838 since the start of operations.

Development: efforts were confined entirely to production, although completion of some drilling was done at the Ruth mine. Twelve holes were drilled an average of 499 ft., and five were extended 154 ft., at a cost of $3.52 per foot. This churn-drilling cost $1.14 more than in 1917. Reserves at Copper Flat and in the Ruth are as under:

	Ruth		Copper Flat		Total	
	Tons	Copper, %	Tons	Copper, %	Tons	Copper, %
Developed to 12/31/'17	15,570,600	2.24	80,295,777	1.470	95,866,377	1.600
Added in 1918	119,168	...	2,404,680	1.360	2,523,848	1.280
Total, 1918	15,689,768	2.22	82,700,457	1.468	98,390,225	1.580
Milled, 1918	2,984,724	1.98	26,855,857	1.579	29,840,851	1.610
Ore remaining	12,705,044	2.24	55,844,600	1.414	68,549,644	1.570

Of the ore mined last year, 67% was obtained by steam-shovels and 33% from underground workings. Capping removed amounted to 2,617,771 cu. yd., making 27,280,088 yd. to date. Steam-shoveling ore cost 25.88 cents per ton of ore, against 18.9 cents in 1917, and 12.42 cents in 1916. Underground mining cost 98.08 cents, a gain of 16.56 cents.

Production: the mill concentrated 3,999,526 tons of 1.506% ore, recovering 67.28%; against 4,064,095 tons, 1.462%, and 73.08% in 1917. The drop was due to lower efficiency of the employees. Total milling charges were 93.1 cents per ton, an increase of 24.5%.

At the smelter the high moisture (15.25%) of the roaster charge reduced the tonnage per furnace-day from 72.5 to 67.2. Concentrate is to be further dewatered before roasting. Four to five reverberatories reduced 654,650 tons of charge. They are fired with pulverized coal, the new plant with a capacity of 600 tons of slack coal daily ground through 200-mesh, being started in May. The yield of copper was 76,607,062 lb., compared with 82,040,508 pounds.

NEW CORNELIA COPPER CO.

Property: mine and works at Ajo, Arizona.

Operating Officials: J. C. Greenway, general manager; M. Curley, general superintendent.

Financial Statement: the income for 1918, the first full year of operation, was $11,073,680, less $6,282,500 for expenditures, leaving a profit of $4,791,180. Current assets total $4,226,205, and liabilities $2,059,522.

Dividends: an initial distribution of 25 cents per share, $351,255, was made in November.

Development: as open-pit operations had been conducted near the south-west side-lines of the developed orebody, and exploratory work had not been completed at that point, two complete and two incomplete diamond-drill holes—1825 ft. total—exposed 916,980 tons of 1.573% ore. This is all sulphide ore, the carbonate capping carrying less than 0.6% copper. A three-compartment shaft, 16 ft. 4 in. by 6 ft. inside, was sunk 250 ft., and a 7 by 9-ft. cross-cut driven to the orebody in the Southern section. A total of 2227 ft. of work was done. This orebody yielded 81,417 tons of 3.39% ore, mostly from workings at 50-ft. depth. Ore-reserves now amount to 51,320,421 tons, 80% of which are sulphides.

Production: the crushing-plant, one No. 24 and four No. 8 gyratories, reduced 1,775,000 tons of 1.465% ore. The leaching-plant produced 31,264,642 lb. of electrolytic and 10,990,666 lb. of cement copper, while metal in ore shipped direct to the C. & A. smelter at Douglas was 4,694,831 lb. The total output therefore was 46,950,139 pounds.

RAY CONSOLIDATED COPPER CO.

Property: mine, railway, and mill at Ray and Hayden, Arizona.

Operating Officials: L. S. Cates, general manager; U. S. Boyd, assistant; C. A. Smith, superintendent of mines; D. D. Moffat, superintendent of mills; R. J. Ezell, cashier.

Financial Statement: the revenue from metals during 1918 was $19,209,311, of which $4,863,455 was profit, including sundries. After paying dividends, the balance of $16,890,196 at the end of 1917, was reduced to $16,417,819.

Dividends: with $150,000 for the Red Cross, etc., the total was $5,275,832, making $20,681,084 in all.

Development: new work consisted in extending the main haulage-ways on No. 3 level, also in preparing the orebody for stoping, a total of 61,711 ft., compared with 84,915 ft. in 1917. To the end of 1918 there were 134 miles of workings opened, and 69 miles destroyed, leaving 65 miles intact. As development approached the lower levels, the men could no longer walk to their places by adits and inclined shafts, so No. 4 main shaft was sunk 547 ft., concreted, and equipped with a 37-man hoist per trip. A brick change-house of 1200-man capacity was erected. Ore-reserves are 86,383,642 tons, averaging 2.061% copper. The cost of mining 3,476,749 tons was $1.695 per ton, plus 6.5 cents for coarse crushing and loading.

Production: the mill treated 3,411,000 tons of 1.613% ore, recovering 74.92%; compared with 3,560,900 tons, 1.635%, and 74.53% in 1917; 3,332,340 tons, 1.607%, and 70.20% in 1916; and 2,848,969 tons, 1.673%, and 64.11% in 1915. The recovery of copper sulphides was 83.68% last year, the oxides reducing the total to 74.92%. Including copper from direct smelting ore, the total output was 86,919,270 lb., about 5,000,000 lb. less than in 1917. The cost of milling was $1.01 per ton, an increase of 18 cents.

The average net cost of producing copper was 17.193 cents per pound, against 12.446 cents in 1917.

UTAH COPPER CO.

Property: mines at Bingham and works at Magna, Utah.

Operating Officials: R. C. Gemmell, general manager; J. D. Shilling, superintendent of mines; H. C. Goodrich, chief engineer of mines; F. G. Janney, general superintendent of mills; H. C. Smith at the Magna and T. A. Janney at the Arthur mill; J. M. Hayes, treasurer and assistant secretary; and C. F. Jennings, assistant purchasing agent.

Financial Statement: copper sold realized $43,029,021, gold $1,018,564, and silver $477,547, a total of $44,525,129. Operations cost $30,717,827. After adding $5,138,477 dividends from other properties, and deducting $500,000 for Red Cross and war work, the surplus was $18,445,780. The surplus of quick assets is $28,512,816, a decrease of $1,773,073. The face value of investments is $13,614,116.

Dividends: $10 per share, equal to $16,244,900, making $92,015,783 to date.

Development and Mining: churn-drilling at the Porphyry mine amounted to 7625 ft. In the Sulphide mine there are now 13,989 ft. of workings accessible. This mine produced 34,769 tons of copper-lead-zinc ore. The average thickness of the Porphyry orebody is now 556 ft., an increase of 18 ft. as proved by drilling. After 79,381,400 tons of ore had been extracted from the start of operations, reserves are still 374,040,000 tons, averaging 1.37% copper. Capping moved in 1918 amounted to 4,064,091 yards, making 48,042,824 yards in all, spread over 259 acres. The total cost of steam-shoveling was 53.7 cents per ton of ore.

Treatment and Production: the Magna mill treated 18,151 and the Arthur 15,166 tons daily, a total of 12,160,700 tons. The average grade was 1.2262% copper, and recoveries 65.11%—57.89% at the Magna and 73.39% at the Arthur. Improvements to the latter are complete, but those at the former are now under way. The cost of concentrating was 92.77 cents per ton. The leaching plant treated 1190 tons daily of oxide ore, at a cost of $1.0568 per ton.

Year	Tons	Copper, %	Copper, lb.	Cost per ton	Cost per lb., cents
1915	8,494,300	1.4340	156,207,376	$0.8624	6.612
1916	10,994,000	1.4350	197,417,480	0.9355	6.918
1917	12,542,000	1.3367	208,174,442	1.4170	12.708
1918	12,160,700	1.2262	197,978,557	1.7630	16.331

As the treatment plants have been described so fully in the 'Press' recently it is unnecessary here to note the many improvements.

The Bingham & Garfield railway carried 34,081 tons of ore daily, and a total of 617,749 passengers. The main line is 37 miles long, and other tracks 96 miles.

Book Reviews

Gasoline and Kerosene Carburetors. By Victor W. Page. Pp. 206, ill., index. Norman W. Henley Publishing Co., New York. For sale by 'Mining and Scientific Press'. Price, $1.50.

Where one man was interested in carburetors twenty years ago, there are probably one hundred today. Furthermore, the fact that gasoline production has failed to keep pace with consumption has increased interest in the development of carburetors for vaporizing the heavier constituents of petroleum. The present volume is non-technical, and within the province of anyone with enough intelligence to run an internal-combustion engine.

Introductory Mathematical Analysis. By W. Paul Webber and Louis Clark Plant. P. 299, ill., index. John Wiley & Sons, Inc., New York. For sale by 'Mining and Scientific Press', San Francisco. Price, $2.

This book was written for a college textbook, and this will constitute its principal field of usefulness, although the engineer that has forgotten his college mathematics may be able to use the book as a means of refreshing his memory. The first two chapters constitute a brief review of elementary algebra and geometry. The book then deals with co-ordinates, trigonometry, vectors, conic sections, series, and differential and integral calculus.

Handbook of Mechanical and Electrical Cost Data. By Halbert P. Gillette and Richard T. Dana. Pp. 1716, ill., index. McGraw-Hill Book Co., New York, 1919. For sale by 'Mining and Scientific Press'. Price, $6.

As the preface states, this book is intended as a companion volume to Mr. Gillette's 'Handbook of Cost Data', and Mr. Dana's 'Handbook of Construction Plant'. The arrangement is similar to the former book, but there is little overlapping. In these days of abnormal prices, and of discussion as to whether or not large reductions will be made in the near future, some engineers and estimators may feel that a book of cost data, since its costs manifestly cannot be brought up to the minute, is of slight value. That this viewpoint is erroneous, provided the cost analysis is accurate and complete is shown by the authors in the first chapter.

Essentials of Alternating Currents. By W. H. Timbie and H. H. Higbie. P. 360, ill. index. John Wiley & Sons, Inc., New York. For sale by 'Mining and Scientific Press', San Francisco. Price, $1.60.

This book is written with the needs of men having little training in higher mathematics in mind, and will be useful to them as a text and reference book rather than to college-trained engineers. The chapter-headings are as follows: Modern Systems of Power Transmission; Power Factor; Current and Voltage Relations in Series and in Parallel Circuits; Polyphase Circuits; Calculation of Wire Sizes; Motors, Starters, and Controllers. An appendix contains a number of useful electrical tables. The book is well illustrated. At the end of each chapter there is a brief summary of the important points discussed, which would be of great assistance to the student in reviewing.

Scrap Metals. By George H. Manlove and Charles Vickers. Pp. 278, index. The Penton Publishing Co., Cleveland. For sale by 'Mining and Scientific Press'. Price, $2.

The scrap-metal industry, like so many others, was unheralded and unsung until the War directed the public attention to its importance. The present volume is the first we have seen that is devoted entirely to this industry, which handles nearly one billion dollars worth of material each year. The first part of the book, by Mr. Manlove, is devoted almost entirely to iron and steel scrap, and discusses not only the scientific principles governing its use in blast-furnace, steel plant, and foundry, but also the principal sources and kinds of scrap and the methods of marketing and of financing the scrap industry. As the book was written while Government control of the industry was still in force, considerable space is devoted to this topic. The appendixes contain the principal classifications and specifications for scrap. The second part of the book, by Mr. Vickers, is devoted to the non-ferrous scrap metals, taking up each class of metal and alloy in turn, and showing how the various articles may be sorted in order to give the best results in the furnace.

The Turnover of Factory Labor. By Sumner H. Slichter. Pp. 442, index. D. Appleton & Co., New York. For sale by 'Mining and Scientific Press', San Francisco. Price, $3.

For centuries employers have been 'hiring and firing' and complaining of the cost of breaking in new employees without making any direct attempt to study labor turnover and the possibility of its reduction. In recent years, however, there has been considerable investigation and discussion of this subject. The present volume is probably the most complete that has appeared and presents the results of several years study. Most of the data given are for years preceding 1916, thus eliminating abnormal war conditions. The book first considers the various ways of expressing and measuring the turnover and then its classification under resignations, lay-offs, discharges, and miscellaneous causes. The effect of various factors on the size and rate of the turnover is then considered. Next comes the cost of turnover, both to the employer and employee. Turnover is then analyzed according to causes, the subdivisions being causes pertaining to the job, causes arising from relations between the men and the management, causes pertaining to the men, and causes pertaining to better opportunities elsewhere. The remainder of the book, about half, is devoted to methods of reducing turnover, based mainly on what certain firms have actually accomplished. While the book will appeal to the sociologist, it is thoroughly practical, and should be in the hands of employers of labor and superintendents.

Graphic Methods for Presenting Facts. By Willard C. Brinton. Pp. 363, ill., index. The Engineering Magazine Co., New York. For sale by 'Mining and Scientific Press'. Price, $5.

The man that said, "There are three kinds of lies, plain lies, damned lies, and statistics," probably had in mind, in part at least, the benumbing effect upon the brain of the average reader of a long line of figures with no means provided of properly correlating them. The fundamental idea of graphic methods is to assist the mind in visualizing the facts expressed in statistics. Yet, even here, as the author shows, care is needed, or the purpose of preparing the charts will be defeated. The book deals with the various kinds of graphic representations, including plain figures and diagrams, curves, maps, and combinations of these methods. The applications of the various methods to the domain of the engineer, the business man, the manufacturer, and the lawmaker are then discussed, particular attention being paid to the use of graphic methods for making company reports more intelligible to the average stockholder. The two final chapters are devoted to a discussion of the general methods of preparing graphical data and to the errors to be avoided in doing such work. The treatment of the subject throughout is non-technical, and makes no use of the higher mathematics. There are over two hundred illustrations showing various applications of graphic methods.

INFORMATION FURNISHED BY MANUFACTURERS

THE LATEST IN SMALL AIR-COMPRESSORS

In the emergency at the outbreak of war, there was a sudden call for a large number of small air-compressors for service where reliability was imperative, so the Ingersoll-Rand Co.'s offer to produce for immediate use the 'Imperial Fourteen Compressors,' which it had just completed testing and had adopted as the new standard small compressor type, was accepted. The field performance of these built-on-hurry-order machines was watched critically, but after a year's service their record was clear; they had proved themselves efficient, reliable, and inexpensive to operate.

Sectional View of the Imperial Fourteen Compressor

Types of the Imperial Fourteen Compressor

Now these little machines have been placed on the general market. There are four sizes, the capacity ranging from 3 to 45 cu. ft. per minute at pressures to 100 lb. per square inch. The small compressor's can, however, be used for pressure requirements up to 200 lb., the power needed being, of course, slightly increased. They are single-acting machines of the vertical type, built for belt-drive. Where driven from line-shaft, tight and loose pulleys are supplied; where the use of independent motor is planned they are ordinarily furnished as a unit complete with motor, endless belt, and short-drive attachment. In the latter case a hardwood base-plate is included with the standard equipments.

The machines are so well-balanced as to operate satisfactorily if bolted to any solid flooring, but where permanency of installation is desired, the building of a concrete foundation is advocated. The smallest size is built with ribbed cylinder for air-cooling where the service is intermittent, and with water-cooled cylinder of the reservoir type for continuous operation. Larger machines are water-cooled only, employing the reservoir-jacket system except that, in the case of the largest size, a closed jacket for connection to pressure-system is optional. In this connection it is worth noting that the reservoir-cylinder design affords unusually ample water-capacity, and that both cylinder-barrel and head are cooled. The manufacturer states that a single filling of the water-space will suffice for a 10-hour run.

In general design, the Imperial Fourteen reminds one strongly of an automobile engine. There is the same drop-forged crank-shaft and connecting-rod, the die-cast renewable bearings, the automatic splash-lubrication system, and general ruggedness and simplicity which have come to be recognized as guarantees of satisfactory service under all sorts of operating conditions. It is pointed out, however, that these little units were designed to meet exacting efficiency test and that, while simplicity was sought, efficiency was the outstanding requirement.

COMMERCIAL PARAGRAPHS

Mark R. Lamb's Paris office has secured an order from the Peñarroya company of Spain for two Hardinge conical mills, 6 ft. diameter, for fine grinding in the new flotation plant, which that company has erected.

Pioneer Rubber Mills is the name under which the Bowers Rubber Works of San Francisco is now operating. The change in name became effective April 1, but the management and policy of the company continue as under the old name. The Pioneer works will continue to make all the brands such as Skookum piston-rod packing, Copper Queen belting, and Victor fire-hose. G. N. Towne is vice-president and general manager, and D. D. Tripp is vice-president in charge of sales, at 68 Sacramento street, San Francisco.

The Chicago Pneumatic Tool Co. makes the following announcements: T. J. Hudson has been appointed acting manager of the pneumatic tool sales division, effective April 15, succeeding F. H. Waldron, who returns to Minneapolis, Minnesota, as district manager of sales for the Minneapolis territory.——Allan E. Goodhue has been elected managing director of its English subsidiary, the Consolidated Pneumatic Tool Co., Ltd., whose offices are at 170 Piccadilly, London, and whose plant is in Fraserburg, Scotland. Mr. Goodhue will also be in charge of European sales for the Chicago Pneumatic Tool Company.

INFLUENZA is a subject that came home to us not long ago; therefore it will interest our readers to learn that the Sanitary Commissioner of India estimates that five millions died of influenza in that country, besides a million more in the so-called Native States, making a total mortality of six millions. The worst period was in the last quarter of 1918, particularly in October and November.

HEADQUARTERS for field-assistants of the State Mining Bureau have been established at Auburn, in Placer county, and at Redding, in Shasta county, in charge, respectively, of Mr. C. A. Logan and Mr. E. Huguenin. The State Mineralogist, Mr. Fletcher Hamilton, has been moved to this new departure by a realization of the variety of minerals disclosed by the prospecting stimulated by the exigencies of the War; he appreciates the difficulties encountered in obtaining supplies of sundry industrial and structural mineral products, and hopes, by encouraging further investigation and prospecting, to develop our domestic resources.

OUR Canadian friends appear to appreciate the need for gold. The Minister of Finance is being importuned by the Vancouver Board of Trade, at the instance of Mr. Nicol Thompson and others, to extend the existing embargo on the export of gold bullion so as to include complex ores containing gold. Much of this kind of ore is smelted at Tacoma and other points outside Canada, therefore it is proposed, as an alternative to the total prohibition of exportation, to make it obligatory to return an amount of gold equivalent to that extracted from the ore exported outside the Province of British Columbia. The idea is to increase the reserve of gold in Canada and to encourage the refining of all metals within the Dominion.

CLAIMS for compensation to the producers of chrome, manganese, tungsten, and pyrite during the War are shortly to be adjudicated. The War Minerals Relief Commission, consisting of Messrs. John F. Shafroth, M. D. Foster, and P. N. Moore, with a competent staff, will be at Little Rock, Arkansas, on June 7 and there begin the first of a series of hearings to be distributed over the various mining districts. The itinerary of the Commission will cover, in the order named, the following cities: Tucson, Los Angeles, San Francisco, Medford, Portland, Baker City, Spokane, Butte, Salt Lake City, and Denver. The route indicated thereby is from Arkansas to Arizona, thence through California, Oregon, Washington, Montana, and Utah to Colorado. It is stated that 260 claims have been filed, calling for relief to the total amount of $6,000,000. The sum appropriated by Congress for this purpose was $8,500,000.

IN our last issue we gave the depth of the Ooregum mine, on the Kolar goldfield, in India, as 5380 feet. A later report, just to hand, states that two shafts, the Oakley and Bullen, have reached the 60th level, which is 5419 feet vertically below the surface. The Ooregum exploits an ore-shoot, or series of nearly parallel ore-shoots, on its pitch northward from the Mysore and Champion Reef mines. These properties, so successfully managed by the old and honorable engineering firm of John Taylor & Sons, have been highly productive since 1883. They were first explored by white men in 1871, when an Irish soldier, named Lavelle, began to prospect on the site of ancient workings, which were 300 feet deep in places, notably on the Mysore ground. Last year this group of four companies, all under the same capable management, produced $10,029,000 worth of gold.

STOCKS of metal held in England on May 1 show the highly congested condition of the market. The copper on hand is given at 114½ million pounds, as compared with 61¾ million pounds on December 19. Lead stocks have increased to 244 million pounds, as compared with 110 million pounds in December. A surfeit of lead is evident. At one time during the War the amount on hand is said to have been as high as 500 million pounds. Stocks of zinc and aluminum have increased from 56¾ and 22¾ million pounds, respectively, to 76 million and 25¾ millions, respectively. The spelter is of the highest grade, meant for making munitions, and is now saleable only on a par with 'prime western'. It is expected that these stocks of the base metals will now show progressive decrease, owing to increasing consumption, and it is evident that until they are liquidated the international market cannot regain its normal absorption.

TO assist the taxpayer engaged in the oil and gas industry in preparing his Federal tax-returns correctly and expeditiously, the Bureau of Internal Revenue has prepared a manual, which is based upon the information gathered last autumn by a corps of geologists, technologists, and engineers selected from all parts of the United States. This investigation was undertaken primarily to furnish a basis for valuing oil and gas properties and for estimating the deductions to be made under the headings of depletion and depreciation. Records of production all over the country were collected and tabulated, for subsequent classification and study with a view to establishing curves of production and standards of valuation. This has been done, and the manual is available to those needing such assistance. Copies, together with the necessary blanks to be filled by the taxpayer, can be obtained from the Commissioner of Internal Revenue at Washington or from the Internal Revenue Collector of the nearest district. Every oil operator and every professional man connected with the industry ought to have a copy of the manual in his hands. The curves and tabulations are intended to guide the taxpayer in computing his allowance for depletion, which, in turn, directly bears upon, and often controls, the amount of his tax. In the event of a sale of property the valuation deduced gives the basis on which the taxation of the profit is to be computed. The Treasury Department, however, declares itself in no way committed to the acceptance of estimates based on the curves it has supplied; every claim for deduction on account of depletion therefore must be inferred by the taxpayer from the facts covering his own operations, and it must be accompanied by a detailed statement of production. Hence the taxpayer will be well advised to seek competent technical assistance in the preparation of his returns, for experience has shown that unless this is done a demand for an excessive tax is likely to ensue from inadequate appraisement, that is, a demand may be made in excess of what the law intended the operator to pay. The Treasury officials declare frankly that every operator "must make his own case," which is a fair warning to all concerned.

The Flotation Issue

Our readers, we feel sure, will have shared our keen interest in reading the arguments presented to the U. S. Supreme Court in the final hearing of the case between Minerals Separation, Limited, and the Butte & Superior Mining Company. We would have liked to publish the briefs, but they are too long for our limited space, whereas the oral arguments are of a convenient length; moreover, the latter are the more interesting on account of the colloquies between counsel and the Justices on the bench. The first argument was that of the lawyers representing the petitioners, the Minerals Separation company. We can imagine the scene, having ourselves heard the appeal made in the Ninth Circuit Court here in San Francisco. Mr. Williams speaks with jaunty confidence and with a pleasantly smooth intonation. Mr. Kenyon has a staccato utterance and gesticulates nervously. The manner of the Minerals Separation senior counsel has the reinforcement of many successes in the long-drawn litigation, for Mr. Williams has guided his clients with notable skill through a variety of courts. Anybody reading his argument will be impressed by its cogency. The validity of the patent, No. 835,120, was conceded by the Supreme Court in the Hyde case, so the issue in this case is infringement of the patent as defined by the Court. The proportion of oil requisite for the working of the patented process is the crux of the conflict between the parties. The Butte & Superior had attempted to evade the Court's decision, so Mr. Williams argues, by camouflage, namely, by adding a large amount of ineffective mineral oil to the small amount of effective vegetal oil, thereby trying to prove that the so-called critical proportion of less than 1% was not essential to the success of the agitation-froth process of concentration. This addition of mineral oil is an immediate consequence of the Court's decision in the Hyde case, on December 11, 1916. The Butte & Superior interpreted that decision to mean that the patent was confined to one-half of 1% of the oil per ton of ore and that they could use any kind of oil they pleased. In this interpretation they were sustained by the Appellate Court of the Ninth Circuit. Note the colloquy between Mr. Justice McReynolds and Mr. Williams, in which the latter denies the possibility of getting the result with more than 1% of pine-oil; and then the one between him and the Chief Justice, in which the latter infers that the process cannot be performed with more than two-tenths of 1% of pine-oil. Mr. Williams asserts that the addition of the mineral oil decreases the efficiency of the process; he claims that the use of it caused a loss of $1,000,000 profit to the Butte & Superior company in 1917. By turning to the company's annual reports we find that the mill recovery in 1916 was 93.1% of the zinc, whereas in 1917 the recovery was 91.13%, and in 1918 it was 92.96%. Such slight difference as is shown may well have been due to the strike at Butte and the decreased efficiency of the labor available after the United States entered the War. The difference in profit is to be found in the decreased price of spelter, which averaged 12.63 cents per pound in 1916 and 8.57 cents in 1917. In the interchange with Mr. Justice Holmes it becomes evident, not for the first time, that the patent applies to conditions not anticipated at the time it was granted and that an effort is being made to stretch its specifications to a new metallurgy. The thick oily liquid called oleic acid as applied to Broken Hill ores is vastly different in its physical properties from the oils now in use, and that is why so many of the claims in the patent do not accord with actual practice in the United States. Then comes Mr. Kenyon, who asserts that the defendant is not using the process of the prior art; it seems evident to us that the flotation process of today is as different from the oleic acid and Broken Hill ore method of Minerals Separation as it is different from the prior art of Elmore, Kirby, and Delprat, for example. Flotation as now used in America has been evolved from a new experience and is in many essentials a new process related as much and as little to the prior art as to patent 835,120. One would suppose from Mr. Kenyon's statements that the prior art was represented by Cattermole's patent and no other. Cattermole's process was never even tried in this country; it was a rank failure even at Broken Hill. Any comparison with it is misleading. As we read Mr Kenyon's categorical denial of a frothing function to mineral oil we recall the experiment performed before the Court of Appeals in which the kerosene used at Butte without pine-oil yielded a splendid froth, although, according to the record, an identical experiment before the Supreme Court in the Hyde case produced only "three or four bubbles." To the onlooker it is apparent how incomplete is the evidence presented at these Court proceedings; it is always a lap behind. On the other hand, the testimony of Mr. E. W. Engleman, of the Ray Consolidated, denying the metallurgic efficacy of fuel-oil, is a noteworthy contradiction. As a matter of fact, the users of flotation know that some mineral oils produce a froth and some do not; also that the same mineral oil will undergo change so that it will function variably. What is not known about flotation greatly exceeds what is included within current technology. Mr. Kenyon concedes the fact that a little mineral oil is helpful; he does not know why; it improves the recovery, he says. Next we come to the counter-argument for the Butte & Superior. The senior counsel, Mr. Thomas F. Sheridan, did not take part; he left the presentation of his client's case to his associate Mr. Bull, a distinguished patent lawyer, who speaks quietly and clearly; his pose is that of a veteran. He started by reminding the Court that his client was using mineral oil, mixed with vegetal oil, before the decision in the Hyde case. Accepting that decision, and conforming to it, the Butte & Superior increased the proportion of oil so as not to infringe, that is, it used more than the critical proportion, "as described in the testimony and in the claims of the patent"—the words used in the Supreme Court's opinion. Mr. Bull traces the gradual decrease in the oil used, from 300% by the Elmores in 1898 to 1.2% by Cattermole in 1902 and less than 0.2% by Minerals Separation in 1905. What are the "critical proportions" as laid down by the Supreme Court in the Hyde case? On the answer to this question hinges the decision in this case. Minerals Separation has specified that the critical limits are between 0.05 and 0.02%, as quoted by Mr. Bull. He also cited their assertion that "if more oil is used, you do not operate the process, and you do not get the result." This refers primarily to vegetal oils, yet, even as regards other oils, "the process is dependent upon such definite minute amount of oil." The plain truth is that Minerals Separation did not know exactly how the oil functioned; they committed themselves to these positive statements in order to influence the decision of the Court and they are now inconvenienced by their previous tactics. Mr. Bull quoted the colloquy between Mr. Justice McReynolds and Mr. Kenyon in the Hyde case. This was cited in the Court of Appeals, on which occasion it was apparent how it made Mr. Kenyon squirm. In the course of that colloquy Mr. Kenyon gave away the case for Minerals Separation, and, it seems to us, furnished the Court ample reason for sustaining the adverse opinion of the Court of Appeals. He acknowledged that the use of more than half of 1% did not infringe. The patent specification made particular mention of a fatty acid, oleic, which is no longer used and does not enter into the comparison between vegetal and mineral oils. Again we say that the patent applied to metallurgical conditions that do not exist in current practice. Is not petroleum as much an "oily substance" as oleic acid? Has it not a "preferential affinity for metalliferous matter"? Mr. Bull pushed his argument home by showing that the first written description of the invention covered by patent 835,120 made mention of using petroleum residuum on Broken Hill ore and later the patentees used gasolene successfully. The most convincing evidence, however, is the fact that the Minerals Separation witnesses have acknowledged the use of mineral oils by their licensees, notably at Anaconda and Britannia; moreover, the proportion of vegetal to mineral oil in the mixture employed in the Butte & Superior mill is that adopted by two of the Minerals Separation licensees. That is the case for the Butte & Superior Mining Company and it seems to us a strong one. It remains impossible to predict the result; to us it appears that the Court of Appeals interpreted correctly the opinion of the Supreme Court, but the previous decisions of the various courts in the flotation litigation—the Hyde, Miami, and Butte & Superior cases—have been so discordant that no layman, and no lawyer, can forecast the judgment for which we are now waiting anxiously.

Lest We Forget

German protests against the severity of the peace terms exhibit a cynical forgetfulness of the threats they made when they expected to win the War they themselves provoked. Herr Scheidemann, for example, makes an appeal to the British people and says that he "cannot believe that fellow human beings, however much under the influence of wicked war, can really intend to reduce a kindred civilized people to slavery." The kinship did not count for much on June 20, 1915, when a representative group of German professors, diplomats, and superior government officials, posing as the spokesmen of kultur, assembled in the Künstlerhaus at Berlin, issued a manifesto in which they said: "If we found ourselves in a position to impose a war-indemnity upon England—England which has always been so niggardly in sacrificing the lives of its own citizens—no sum in money could be enough." They were predatory, those intellectuals of Berlin, but they were worse, they were cowards jibing at brave men. Let the spirits of the dead that lie in Flanders field, let the million British men that died in the effort to drive the Huns out of France and Belgium, answer the sneer that they joined to their anticipation of loot. The British were not "kindred" then! Whether they really intend to reduce the Germans to slavery, we have not been informed, but the fact is that the Germans "really" did reduce a people who would disdain to be called "kindred", but certainly were "civilized", to pitiless slavery. The pages of history for all time will damn the Germans for having kidnapped and enslaved the Belgians by tens of thousands, and all because they refused to allow their country to serve as a road into France. The less the Germans talk about slavery the better for them. Shall we so soon forget how young men were seized at night, placed in cattle-trucks, and deported to Germany, there to be forced to work under cruel conditions until they broke down physically, and either died or were returned the wrecks of manhood? A hundred thousand men underwent this treatment, such treatment as would hardly be given to cattle or swine. It was deeds such as this that turned the American neutrals of the Belgian Relief Commission, says Dr. Vernon Kellogg, "into a shocked, then bitter, and finally blazing band of men wishing to slay or be slain, if necessary, to prevent the repetition anywhere of the things they had to see done in these tortured lands." Shall we forget this now, when they whine about kindred races and civilization and throw up their hands à la kamerad? They cry out against the cession of the Saar coalfield and they call President Wilson all kinds of names because he approves the terms of reparation for their sabotage in France. What did they expect to do if they had won? In May 1915 six industrial associations, thoroughly representative of the agricultural, manufacturing, and trade interests of Germany, sent a petition to the German Chancellor, and to the governments of the various Federated States of the German Empire, in which they specified the terms of peace to be demanded. They insisted that Belgium "must be subjected to German Imperial legislation, both in military and tariff matters, and also in regard to currency, banking, and postal arrangements." .... "The government must be so managed that the inhabitants obtain no influence on the political fortunes of the German Empire .... and all economic and industrial undertakings and real estate, which are so vital for the government of the country, must be transferred into German hands." Would anything remain of Belgium by the time this program had been carried out? As to France, these German leaders said: "We should hold the French coastal districts from the Belgian frontier approximately as far as the Somme .... The hinterland, which must be acquired with them, must be so delimited as to secure to us the complete economic and strategic exploitation of those Channel-ports which we gain." That was not all. "The acquisition of the line of the Meuse and the French Channel-ports would carry with it the possession, not only of the iron-ore district of Briey mentioned above, but also the coal-country in the department of the Nord and the Pas-de-Calais"—in short, the industrial regions of northern France, together with the seaports through which their products passed. Here again the inhabitants were to have no political rights. The petition says that "these annexations must be so arranged that the populations of the annexed districts shall be precluded from exercising political influence on the fortunes of the German Empire, and all the economic resources of these districts, including both large and medium-sized estates, must be transferred to German hands." Oh yes, they were the mildest mannered gentlemen that ever cut a throat or scuttled a ship! They had their eye on the iron resources of France, having realized that when they seized Lorraine in 1871 they had overlooked a part of the spoils of war. So, on May 20, 1915, these representatives of German business urged their Chancellor to remedy Bismarck's oversight, in these words: "Hence the security of the German Empire in a future war imperatively demands the possession of the whole minette-bearing district of Luxemburg and Lorraine, together with the fortifications of Longwy and Verdun, without which this district cannot be held." 'Minette' is the name of the low-grade iron ore for which this region is famous. They summarized their demands thus: "The acquisition of territory suitable for agricultural settlement [referring to the Baltic provinces of Russia] and the appropriation of the iron-ore district of the Meurthe and Moselle, of the French coaling districts in the department of the Nord and the Pas-de-Calais, and also of the Belgian coalfields." These were captains of industry, and they naturally might be greedy, but what about the flower of German intellectuality, were they different? Not at all. We have quoted from their manifesto already. Here are some more of their high-minded demands. "We must have no mercy on France, however terrible the financial losses her own folly and British self-seeking have already brought upon her." .... "The German people consider it an absolutely unquestionable matter of honor [what a word to use in such a context!] to keep a firm hold on Belgium." .... "Russia is excessively rich in territory, and we demand that the territory which Russia is to surrender to us in lieu of war-indemnity shall be delivered to us for the most part free of private ownership." .... "We must look to other quarters of the globe also, if we are to secure adequate acquisitions." .... "Finally, as regards indemnity for the war, we naturally desire such an indemnity as will, so far as possible, cover the public cost of the war." Having outlined their modest demands, these intellectuals concluded their manifesto with a few remarks concerning "the German mind," which started the whole train of calamitous events and now bewails the consequences of its colossal crime. Recall the barbarities, cruelties, and atrocities perpetrated by German men, and women, during the War; recall the miserable mess they made of their great predatory campaign; recall the fact that they threw up their hands as soon as the fight went against them on land, and surrendered their proud navy because they feared to meet their enemy on the sea, and then read this insolent assertion of the 1341 German professors, diplomats, and officials: "The German mind is, in our opinion, beyond all doubt one supremely valuable asset. It is the one priceless possession amongst all our possessions. It alone justifies our people's existence and their impulse to maintain and assert themselves in the world; and to it we owe their superiority over all other peoples." The only reply that befits the occasion is that made by General Cambronne of the Old Guard at Waterloo; not the reply history records, "The guard dies, and never surrenders," but the one every Frenchman knows him to have made, too strong to appear in polite literature.

Justice to Our Native Young Men

The Editor:

Sir—The section of your magazine devoted to discussion has, for some time, been a deep source of interest to me, and I am, therefore, using it as a means to penetrate beneath the surface of my chosen subject and bring the matter under the close observation of the mine operators of the various districts, as I find, among the many manifestations of the spirit of intellectual anxiety which marks an important factor in the mining communities of today, is the failure, on the part of these gentlemen, to recognize the sons of the old residents of the mining districts, upon their graduation from college.

At every mining centre, both great and small, there are always a number of families who have met with sufficient success to enable them to send their sons to college to receive a professional training. After obtaining their degree, the old folks, hoping to have them near home, encourage a search for success in their home town, the place of their birth—hence very dear to their hearts. However, disappointment ensues. They find it almost impossible to obtain an opening at all worthy of their ability. By this I do not mean to imply that the mining settlements are devoid of responsible positions. Not so—there are many, the majority being held by technical men whom the operators have secured from afar, thus rendering it difficult for the native young men to return home with an expectation of progress or success at home.

Now why would it not be an honorable, as well as a just, scheme for the operators to keep a record of all the young men of their particular district, and materially aid in assisting those who have received their degrees and wish to return, by favoring them, in place of sending away for their technically trained men? Right here, we shall all agree that charity always begins at home, but whereas to some this might appear as such, I venture to state that it should simply be nothing more or less than a pledged duty on the part of the operators, as the parents, residents of the place for years, have spent both their time and money, through hardships and otherwise, in the upbuilding, as well as the uplifting of the mining community. So why should they not receive, at least, the small recompense of seeing their sons occupying the important positions at the mines and mills, thereby carrying on the good work in, possibly, a higher degree.

Then too it would be sensible to assume that these young men would prove of greater value to the mining companies than men from the outside, as naturally the entire interest of the company, as well as the district at large, is close to their heart, whereas, with the non-resident, it would be more likely to be simply a money proposition, and he would not seem so inclined to keep the "home fire burning," so to speak, or further the interests of the company or district. On the other hand, the native son, possessing a natural interest in the home district, would have at heart the best interest of the population, and where the people of a district are met with a sincere spirit they are pretty sure to practise a little reciprocity themselves, in return. So in this manner the native son would prove another ace, because he would help to promote a closer co-operation between the workmen and the managers, which is as essential to successful operation of mining companies as well as of other enterprises; so I think these suggestions might prove worthy of careful consideration, and if the fundamental values of the matter could be more clearly conceived and more directly pursued, it would drive home an affirmative conclusion with telling power.

In concluding, I might call to mind the statement so wisely made by Confucius, to the effect that the chief moral force in society is the example of the "superior man." Virtue in superiors will always call out virtue in common folks, for between man and man the rule of practice is reciprocity, which, needless to mention, is a worthy attitude toward one's fellowmen.

Warren, Arizona, May 9. M. Stockholm.

[The writer is a lady and probably the mother of sons; therefore we welcome her expression of opinion, which is reasonable and well worthy of sympathetic consideration.—Editor.]

Blue Sky Laws

The Editor:

Sir—The question of fraudulent promotions and the Blue Sky law has been brought rather strongly to our notice in Colorado during the past few months; first, because a Blue Sky law was proposed in the last Legislature, and (after many amendments were added) killed in committee for fear that it would interfere with the promotion of legitimate enterprises; and second, because of some promotions of large size that have not been looked upon with favor by competent engineers. In the last few months I have had the unpleasant task of disillusioning many investors in mining shares and of examining many stock certificates unearthed from the strong boxes of dead relatives. I have yet to find a valuable one, or to announce to some investor that he has a fortune. Most of the letters are pathetic. They are from people who could ill afford to lose the money the stock represents: many of them are illiterate, and not a few have given everything they own to some fraudulent promoter. A passage comes to my mind: "This man told us to mortgage our home and put the money in this company, and it would make us rich." That line is a tragedy in itself, and there are many of them. Of course the rejoinder to any complaint of this sort of thing is, "Well, they should have known better," which smacks not a little of a remark of Cain's.

Do the Blue Sky laws prevent this sort of thing? The experience with the sale of mining stocks in Kansas and Nebraska would lead me to believe that the Blue Sky law is worse than useless in dealing with mining frauds, however valuable it may be in other cases. Let me give an example. The X company (the State law prohibits my giving the company's name) organized to operate a mine in Grand county, Colorado, passed the Blue Sky law of Kansas, and I believe of Nebraska. This mine is an old one which has been long operated to the profit of its promoters. The first organization specialized on negroes, and apparently raised large sums of money in the upper Mississippi Valley. Wild statements pervade its literature, and its agents made still wilder ones. Every stockholder was a potential millionaire. The company was then re-organized, took a new name, and specialized in ministers; as soon as the harvest was reaped there, another re-organization was carried out, which is now said to be garnering the pennies of the country school-teachers. There is a mine back of the company, which does a little work. There is some ore, but, to my knowledge, none has ever been sold. In our office files there are at least a hundred letters on this one concern, upon which the good State of Kansas has set its official guarantee. There is in an old letter case of mine, the prospectus of a company with a mine at Ward, Colorado, showing steamboats ascending Left Hand creek, and receiving ore at the company's docks. Left Hand creek, by the way, has a fall of 200 ft. per mile, and is seldom more than a foot deep. This prospectus was issued for consumption in Michigan and Minnesota.

While I do not believe that the Blue Sky law is a preventive, I do believe that a law would be of great value if it would make the statute of fraud apply in the case of promoters or venders of stocks who wilfully make false statements, or conceal facts concerning mining stocks that they are offering the public.

The English Directors Liability Act of 1890 was based on this principle, and has been successful. One cannot speak too strongly of the need of some such reform. The continued promotion of fraudulent mining companies is a disgrace to the mining industry, and to those of us who are engaged in the direction of mining enterprises. Furthermore, for our own comfort, it must be said that a rigid law will increase the faith of the public in mining and mining men.

J. TERRY DUCE.

Secretary, State Bureau of Mines, Colorado.

Denver, May 7.

The Miner and Prohibition

The Editor:

Sir—The relation of prohibition to the miner and operator is of the greatest importance, more especially from the operator's point of view; and strange to relate, prohibition measures have been passed by many Western States chiefly through the votes of the miners themselves.

It is likewise true that a certain class of city workmen have heralded the slogan "no beer, no work!" in view of national prohibition, which it is believed will be a reality after July 1, 1919, but the miners of the West, as a class, appear to know the great danger occasioned by even one of their number under the influence of liquor—not only to himself but to the many innocent lives in contact with him—while working underground. Operators of large mines are constantly on the alert through competent foremen, shift-bosses, and time-keepers, in order to thus shield their men from the menace of this great foe.

It must be remembered that many thousands of men that enjoy an occasional glass of liquor, of varying degrees of strength or character, have gladly given up their desires in order that the man who cannot control this appetite may be cured and probably saved from a premature death, and in many cases, actually enable his pay-check to provide a living for himself and family, which otherwise frequently becomes dependent upon friends or the authorities. These are not the only classes that will be greatly benefitted, for it is most noticeable that the rich and well-to-do, from the most fashionable quarters of our large cities, and professional men of the highest standing, compose a great proportion of those that occupy the psycopathic wards of the county hospitals.

I was won over to total prohibition by witnessing the grand work it has performed in the State of Kansas, where may be seen families that have since grown up without a saloon or a drunk, or knowing or desiring the taste of liquor. Here is a new generation with brains unimpaired by alcohol. During its growth the insane asylums have been well-nigh emptied, the need of police protection largely diminished, and the work of the courts and its officers greatly lessened, thereby proportionately lessening taxes, much greater than when licenses were paid by the liquor interests, which alone created the large majority of criminals.

Hence, by analogy, we have learned that, if national prohibition becomes a reality, within the course of the next 10 years we will have lost the desire for liquor and in 30 years a new generation shall have taken our places; and they will carry on the business of these United States in a manner, I predict, so superior from that of today, that our action of today in giving up the long-established use of alcohol and in wiping out of the great liquor trust, which is putting up the greatest fight of its life, solely because of its enormous profits, would appear as nothing in the balance.

W. W. WISHON.

Searchlight, Nevada, May 10.

Oiling Mine-Cables in Place

By WM. FLEET ROBERTSON

*In a previous paper I have had occasion to draw attention to the destructive deterioration of certain wire cables, by reason of the excessive rusting of the wires in the interior portion of the cable, while the exterior wires remained comparatively intact.

The explanation of this condition seems, without doubt, to be that the external wires were protected from oxidation by such scant lubrication as the cables had received externally, which, applied cold, failed to penetrate the core or the strands of the cable, leaving these unprotected from the corroding action of water and damp air.

The need for oiling the interior of the cable is, first, to provide lubrication for the wires moving on one another, although my observations have not shown any excessive wear on the wires in its absence—and, secondly, and by far its most important function, to provide a protective covering for the wires to prevent oxidation.

My recent observations deal with cables of 1¼ in. and 1½ in. diameter composed of steel wires formed into strands, these strands again being wound around a hemp core, which seems to be the accepted practice in the manufacture of cables of this size.

The internal hemp core when it leaves the factory is usually saturated with grease, which thus acts as a reservoir of lubricant for the wires of the cable, and lasts for some time, for, as a strain is put upon the cable, it compresses the core, thus expelling the grease among the wires.

In a comparatively short time, this 'reservoir' becomes exhausted of lubricant, its place being taken by air and water. It seems to be the accepted and logical conclusion that before the reservoir is depleted it should be promptly renewed, if the cable is to be protected internally from oxidation, and thus such renewal must be re-

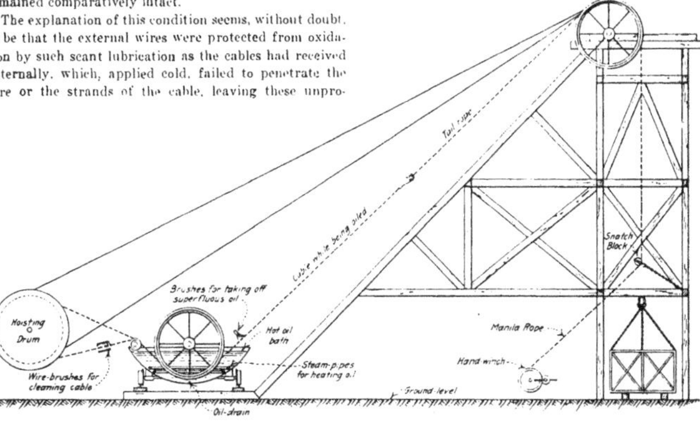

DEVICE FOR OILING MINE-CABLES

*A paper read before the recent meeting of the Canadian Mining Institute at Montreal. By courtesy of the author.

peated periodically. How frequently this should be done will depend upon the conditions under which the cable is being used and would probably have to be determined experimentally.

The danger lies in the false assumption that a cable once lubricated internally always remains so and in the only too prevalent practice of trusting to the outward application of a little grease or oil, usually applied cold. That this will not penetrate the strands is a foregone conclusion. It seems to be generally conceded that such penetration can most surely be obtained by the immersion of the cables for a certain time in the lubricant. As to how this can best and most easily be accomplished has elicited numerous suggestions, one of which is the placing of the cable, coiled up, either off or on a reel, in a tank of oil for some hours. Some argue that this would be sufficient to be effective, while others demand that the tank be closed and its contents be subjected to a pressure—175 lb. per square inch being suggested—a rather serious and costly procedure. A further suggestion is that the oil in the tank be also heated, and this last is, in my opinion, the only effective method.

The interstices in the core and the strands, under working conditions, become filled with air and water, which cannot be driven out by the oil through pressure applied equally on all sides. Consequently pressure alone would be ineffective, while as an adjunct to heat it is superfluous and would be very expensive. If the lubricant be heated to above 212°F. all water in the cable will be driven off as steam, while air would be so expanded as to be also expelled and into the vacuum thus formed the oil would be forced by atmospheric pressure.

This tank treatment would probably be effective and is all very well for cables as received and on reels, although not so necessary with new cables, as they are usually fairly well lubricated. If a renewal of the lubricating process is necessary, this would entail the removal of the cable from the shaft and from the drum, because coiling of it on a reel, together with its transportation to and from the tank, is a lengthy process during which the shaft must remain idle unless a spare cable is available. The whole procedure represents such an expenditure of time and money as to not be favorably considered by the mine manager.

To obviate this double expenditure and thereby ensure that cables will be oiled and re-oiled, I beg to present in the accompanying sketch an arrangement that can be cheaply constructed from materials already around most mines, whereby a hoisting cable may be efficiently oiled without removal from the drum, without delay of more than half a shift, and at a nominal expense.

The cage is brought to the surface, and there blocked on timbers; the cable is detached from the cage and attached to a manila tail-rope. The cable is then wound up on the hoisting-drum until the end of the cable and tail-rope come to the oil-bath. The end of the cable is then detached and passed through the bath and under the sheave-wheel; it is then attached again to the tail-rope by which, with the aid of a hand-winch, the cable is slowly pulled through the heated oil-bath and back to the cage, where it is re-attached and the empty cage slowly lowered to the bottom. The operation is then reversed, the whole cable passing twice through the oil-bath.

About 16 ft. of the cable would be in the bath at one time and if the cable is passed through at a rate of four feet per minute it would then have two immersions of four minutes each, which should be sufficient. The oil in the bath must be kept at a temperature of over 212°F. by the aid of live-steam pipes and it is suggested that vaseline with flake-graphite mixed through it will probably be found to be most effective and lasting.

It is essential that the cable, before entering the bath, should be as thoroughly cleaned as possible of all dirt by the use of wire-brushes. The horizontal travel of the cable in unwinding will automatically move the bath and carriage on rails and so keep it in line at all times.

The supporting shaft of the bath sheave-wheel must be anchored down sufficiently to hold the upward pull of the cable after the cage is attached.

Talc

By R. B. LADOO

*The talc business in this country is largely dependent upon the paper industry for existence, roughly 80% of the domestic talc being used in the manufacture of paper. The other 20% is divided among many different industries, some of which are paint, rubber, textile, lubricant, etc. The high-grades of talcum powder for toilet uses are made almost exclusively from imported Italian and French talc. In the paper trade, domestic talc has to compete with English clay. While in many cases it can successfully replace clay as a filler, it is not usually suitable as a coating for the best grades of paper.

During the War, domestic talc producers expected a curtailment of clay and talc imports, and anticipated a large demand for their product. But imports were not materially reduced, and an unusual demand for domestic talc was not felt. At the present time the demand for paper talc is light, and the outlook is not very promising. It is stated that all the talc mines in New York State are now shut-down. It is felt in some sections of the industry that domestic talc cannot compete with imported talc and English clay, unless protected by tariff or greatly improved methods of grinding, sorting, and screening are used.

Paper-makers differ radically in their opinions as to the suitability of talc as a filler, but talc men assert that domestic talc properly treated can in most cases be substituted for English clay and a large financial saving made. It is stated that where a 50% retention of clay in the paper is customary, there is a retention of 75 to 90% of talc. Much of the so-called grit is merely improperly screened oversize talc, and not silica.

American talc is quoted at $20 to $40 per ton.

*Abstract from Monthly Report of U. S. Bureau of Mines, March 1919.

Minerals Separation v. Butte & Superior

Hearing of the Case Before the U. S. Supreme Court. Argument for the Respondent, Butte & Superior Mining Company

ARGUMENT OF J. EDGAR BULL.

MR. BULL: May it please the Court, the acts complained of in this case are the following:

Before this Court handed down its decision in the Hyde case the defendant was using one-tenth, or about one-tenth, of 1% of oil. It was using not only straight oils, such as oleic acid and pine-oil, but for a considerable time it had been using this particular mixture which it is using now; that is to say, vegetable oil and petroleum. We admit that this use was an infringement of the patent as it has been construed by this Court. An injunction has been granted against the continuance of that use, and an accounting ordered; so that your Honors have nothing to do with the use by the defendant of oil in quantities of about one-tenth of 1% on the ore.

As soon as the opinion of this Court in the Hyde case was handed down the defendant changed its practice, and thereafter it always used more than one-half of 1% of oil on the ore, and for a large portion of the time it has used more than 1% of oil on the ore.

THE CHIEF JUSTICE: Now as to the experiments made, you are assuming that the oil had nothing to do with it, and the experiments were made afterward, but the effect was produced. Counsel on the other side, who has just taken his seat, said that is a mere combination to make something appear to be something which is not something, which does not accomplish the result.

MR. BULL: I understand, and I am going to deal with that question later. I am simply pointing out now that the oil that we used at the time the opinion of this Court was handed down in the Hyde case was the same mixture—that is to say, a mixture of vegetable oil and petroleum—that we are using today.

As I say, as soon as this Court's opinion in the Hyde case was handed down we changed our practice and used larger quantities of oil, over one-half of 1%, and most of the time over 1%, of the same mixture we had used before; that is to say, a mixture of vegetable oil and petroleum. These acts are the only ones which this Court has to consider at this time.

We are here merely to construe your Honor's opinion in the Hyde case. That is all we asked the Court of Appeals to do, and that is all the Court of Appeals did. We are not here to quarrel with your Honor's opinion in the Hyde case in any particular. In fact, we are here justifying under that opinion.

As soon as that opinion was rendered we changed our practice, and it is conceded that that change of practice is costing my client millions of dollars a year in its effort to conform with what we understand to be this Court's decision in the Hyde case.

Now I shall take up the discussion of this Court's opinion in the Hyde case.

In your opinion in that case you used the following language, reading from pages 4 and 5 of my brief:

"The prior processes which we have described required the use of so much oil that they were too expensive to be used on lean ores, to which they were intended to have their chief application and the efforts of investigators for several years prior to the discovery of the process in suit had been directed to the search for a means or method of reducing the amount of oil used, and it is clear from the record that approach was being made, slowly but more and more nearly to the result which was reached by the patentees of the process in suit in March, 1905.

"The present invention differs essentially from all previous results. It is true that oil is one of the substances used but it is used in quantities much smaller than was ever heard of, and it produces a result never obtained before."

In concluding the opinion, you said:

"While we thus find in favor of the validity of the patent, we cannot agree with the District Court in regarding it valid as to all of the claims in suit. As we have pointed out in this opinion there were many investigators at work in this field to which the process in suit relates when the patentees came into it, and it was while engaged in study of prior kindred processes that their discovery was made. While the evidence in the case makes it clear that they discovered the final step which converted experiment into solution, 'turned failure into success', yet the investigations preceding were so informing that this final step was not a long one and the patent must be confined to the results obtained by the use of oil within the proportions often described in the testimony and in the claims of the patent as 'critical proportions' 'amounting to a fraction of one per cent on the ore', and therefore the decree of this Court will be that the patent is valid as to claims No. 1, 2, 3, 5, 6, 7, and 12, and that the defendant infringed these claims, but that it is invalid as to claims 9, 10, and 11."

Now, your Honors will remember that the only difference between claims 9, 10, and 11, which were held invalid, and the claims which were held to be valid, is that the claims which were held to be valid were limited in terms to the use of a fraction of 1% of oil, while the claims which were condemned as being too broad did not specify the amount of oil, except that it should be a "small quantity". We have called those the "small-quantity" claims,—those that were condemned; and the claims that were approved we have called the "fraction-of-one-per-cent" claims.

The first question is, How can counsel assist a Court in interpreting its own opinion? I certainly cannot assist your Honors by any amount of argument. I know of only one way in which I can assist you, and that is by refreshing your recollection as to the facts which were before you at the time the opinion was written. That is what I am going to do; and that is all I am going to do on this branch of the case.

Now, what did this Court have in mind when it said "It is clear from the record that approach was being made, slowly but more and more nearly to the result which was reached by the patentees of the process in suit"? What did this Court have in mind when it said "The investigations preceding were so informing that this final step was not a long one"?

Let me refresh your Honors' recollection as to the prior art which was before you in the Hyde case on that point. I have summarized it at page 11 of my brief. You will remember that the Elmore process, which was known as the 'bulk-oil' process, used some 100 to 300% of oil on the ore. Kirby used as little as 25% of oil on the ore.

[I may say that the figures which I am giving are the figures which were given by plaintiffs' witnesses and not those given by defendant's witnesses; because in some cases the defendant's witness made a lower estimate than did the plaintiffs' witnesses; but the figures which I am giving you are the figures which were given by the plaintiff's witnesses.]

I say Kirby used as little as 25% on the ore.

Haynes used as little as 11% on the ore.

Everson used as little as 5% on the ore.

The Froment patent used as little as 5% on the ore—the same as Everson.

Cattermole used as little as 4% on the mineral contents. Cattermole proportions were not given on the ore; they were given on the mineral contents of the ore; and he used as little as 4% on the mineral contents. Now, 4% on the mineral contents of the Broken Hill tailing, which was the ore to which this Cattermole process was applied by the plaintiffs in this case—4% on the mineral contents of that ore, Professor Chandler, plaintiffs' expert, tells us, equals 1.2% on the ore. So Cattermole proportions applied to the Broken Hill ore, as they were by the Minerals Separation, was only 1.2% on the ore.

The same proportions (that is, 4% on the mineral contents) applied to defendant's ores in this case, which carries 22% mineral contents, amounts to 0.88% on the ore. That is, practically speaking, 9/10 of one per cent.

When we come to the patent in suit we find that the proportions are as little as 2/100 of 1% on the ore. We find that the largest quantity that is mentioned in the patent anywhere is one-half of 1% on the ore. We find that the preferred quantity is one-tenth of 1% on the ore.

Mr. Justice Pitney: Do you understand it was intended to be specified that the percentage of oil was to be constant with different ores and different materials, or that the percentage of oil was to vary with the material? The specifications say that the oil is to have a certain affinity for the ore and the process is to be thus and so.

Mr. Bull: Your Honor, I appreciate that, and I will read you in one moment what my adversaries said on that point. They said that the largest amount which had ever been found useful in practice was two-tenths of 1% on the ore. I will read that. They said that of all the oils that had been used, and with all the ores that ever had been used up to that time, two-tenths of 1% was the largest quantity that had ever been found useful. I will refer to that later in my argument.

What, then, was the "final step" which this Court said was "not a long one"? I submit that it was a step from a large fraction of 1% to a very small fraction of 1%. In another art it might seem as if this was no step at all, but in this art very little things may be very big things measured in dollars and cents. It is in evidence here that in one of the Jackling group of mines, the Utah Copper Company, a reduction in oil from nine-tenths of 1% to one-tenth of 1% would effect a yearly saving in the cost of oil alone of three and a half million dollars. So in this art we must learn to respect little things.

What did this Court have in mind when it said "The patent must be confined to the results obtained by the use of oil within the proportions often described in the "testimony as 'critical proportions' "? What were the "critical proportions" often described in the testimony? May it please your Honors, every witness for the plaintiffs said that the critical proportions were somewhere in the neighborhood of one-tenth of 1% on the ore, and in practice had never been found to exceed two-tenths of 1%.

Counsel said in their brief before this Court in the Hyde case on that point this:

"It is the astonishing fact that, so far as the record here shows, with every ore the world over to which the process has been applied and with all the varying conditions of use, the largest quantity ever used has been four pounds to the long ton (that is, less than 2/10ths of 1%), and that the smallest quantity has been 9/10ths of a pound per long ton of ore (that is, less than 1/2 of 1/10th of 1%)."

Mr. Justice Clark: What are your reading from?

Mr. Bull: I am reading from page 14 of my brief.

Mr. Justice McKenna: That is an extract from the brief of counsel in the Hyde case?

Mr. Bull: Yes, your Honor.

The Chief Justice: Just read that extract over.

Mr. Bull: "It is the astonishing fact that, so far as the record shows, with every ore the world over to which the process has been applied and with all the varying conditions of use, the largest quantity ever used has been four pounds to the long ton (that is, less than 2/10ths of 1%), and that the smallest quantity has been 9/10ths of a pound per long ton of ore (that is, less than 1/2 of 1/10 of 1%)."

Now what were the "proportions that have been described in the testimony as the 'critical proportions' ":

Counsel summarized the testimony of their witnesses on this point beginning on the very first page of their brief in this Court in the Hyde case in the following language. I am still reading from page 14 of my brief.

"The distinctive feature of the invention patented is the employment of air bubbles in co-action with a *minute and critical* amount of oil in a mixture of ground ore and water so as to produce upon the surface of the water a froth containing substantially all of the metallic particles which can be easily flowed off or removed. This process was never used before. This result was never obtained before. The process is dependent upon the use of oil in a *minute and critical* amount and thorough aeration. If *more* oil is used, you do not operate the process, and you do not get the result. So also if less oil is used the process is not operated and the result is not obtained."

MR. JUSTICE PITNEY: They meant the kind of oil that they were dealing with, the oil that had a peculiar affinity for the ore.

MR. BULL: I am coming to that. That is the second point in my argument. I shall answer fully what I know is in your Honor's mind. I am not trying to answer it now.

MR. JUSTICE PITNEY: All right.

MR. BULL (continued reading): "By using other and greater quantities of oil you operate a different process and you obtain wholly different results. That the *critical* amount of oil characterizing the process is a *minute* amount of oil (varying slightly with different ores and different oils) is merely a fortuitous circumstance. Nevertheless the process is dependent upon such *definite minute amount of oil.*"

And at page 10 of their brief they said:

"It is also known that the process is destroyed if the amount of oil is increased over the *minute* proportions characteristic of the process. This latter fact, namely, that the process is in each instance conditioned on the use of *definite and astonishingly minute* oil proportions (varying slightly with different ores and different oils), is one of the important facts that is clearly proved in the evidence in behalf both of complainants and of defendant which the Circuit Court of Appeals overlooked or disregarded."

Counsel in the Hyde case repeated those statements over and over again in their brief and in their oral argument: and they emphasized them in colloquy with the Court. I read from page 17 of my brief. Mr. Justice McReynolds asked Mr. Kenyon, who was then in argument:

"I would like to ask you when in this process of reducing oil your invention came into existence?

"MR. KENYON: At about one-half of 1% of oil.

"MR. JUSTICE MCREYNOLDS: Before you got to the one-half of 1% did you have any invention?

"MR. KENYON: We were passing from the region of Cattermole, which was a distinct——

"MR. JUSTICE MCREYNOLDS: I want to know when your invention came into existence?

MR. KENYON: This invention was not reached, I should say, from those figures, until about 0.5, that is, one-half of 1% of oil was reached.

"MR. JUSTICE MCREYNOLDS: At 1% you had no invention?

"MR. KENYON: No.

"MR. JUSTICE MCREYNOLDS: At one-half of 1% you did have invention?

"MR. KENYON: It began to come. Remote, but it began to come. At 0.3 of 1% the float vastly increased.

"MR. JUSTICE MCREYNOLDS: *When this float has more than one-half of 1% of oil it does not infringe?*

"MR. KENYON: *It does not infringe.*

"MR. JUSTICE PITNEY: What have you to say in answer to what Mr. Scott said the other day to the effect that 1.8%, or perhaps more, of oil, would give the same result with increased agitation?

"MR. WILLIAMS: Absolutely no.

"MR. KENYON: It would not.

"MR. JUSTICE PITNEY: I understood him to say so yesterday, and I suppose there was something in the record to justify it.

"MR. KENYON: Nothing. That will be a part of my argument."

MR. JUSTICE PITNEY: Can you refer me to the text? This refers to certain pages and also refers to a copy of the printed oral argument. What is that copy?

MR. KENYON: I think we have a copy here.

MR. WILLIAMS: A copy of the printed oral arguments was sent to this Court after the argument in the Hyde case. Counsel joined in printing it. It was sent to this Court. I do not know whether it was treated as a filed document. I do not think it was. But we can supply your Honors with other copies.

MR. JUSTICE PITNEY: I have an idea that this colloquy occurred in connection with experiments leading up to the discovery.

MR. BULL: It did.

Plaintiffs' expert witnesses testified on this point as follows: Professor Chandler said that he understood "*a* fraction of 1%" referred to in the claims as being *the* fraction of 1% which is described in the specifications. The specifications contained this statement, and the only statement, as to quantity:

"To this is added a very small proportion of oleic acid, say from 0.02% to 0.5% on the weight of ore."

And he continues, "that is, from 1/50th of 1% up to 1/2 of 1%."

Professor Chandler said, after reading the claims, "What *this* fraction of 1% is, they do not mention." [That is, the claims do not state. They say *a* fraction of 1%, but they do not say *what* fraction of 1%.] He says, "What *this* fraction of 1% is, they do not mention. The only way in which I can interpret *this* fraction of 1% is by referring to other portions of the specification, where *this* fraction of 1% is expressed in figures; for example, at line 81 on page 1 of the specification is the following statement.''—which statement I have just read.

In other words, he said that *the* fraction of 1% which is the subject of this patent is *that* fraction which is between 1/50th of 1% and 1/2 of 1%.

Mr. Ballantyne, the English expert for the plaintiffs, stated that he did not understand that *the fraction* of 1% of this patent was *all fractions* of 1%. He said 0.999% would not, in his opinion, be the fraction of 1% which is referred to in the patent in suit.

So when this Court said ''the patent must be confined to the results obtained by the use of oil within the proportions often described in the testimony as critical proportions,'' we submit that it must be confined to the use of something in the neighborhood of one-tenth or two-tenths of 1% of oil, and not above one-half of 1%, which is the largest quantity mentioned in the patent, and which was a larger quantity than the plaintiffs said had ever been found useful in the process.

That is precisely what the Court of Appeals in this case has held, and that is all the Court of Appeals in this case has held.

I shall take up the contention that petroleum oils are not among the ''oils or oily substances'' of the patent in suit.

The defendant has used different mixtures, but the mixture which has been taken as typical by both sides is a mixture of three parts petroleum oils—that is, fuel-oil and kerosene, three parts.

MR. JUSTICE CLARK: Please repeat that.

MR. BULL: I say the mixture which has been taken as typical by both sides is three parts of petroleum (partly fuel-oil and partly kerosene) and one part of vegetable oil.

Now, the plaintiffs contend that petroleums are not among the ''oils or oily substances'' of the patent in suit, and that the petroleum should be subtracted from the amount of oil which we use in order to determine what is the actual amount of what they call 'effective' oil used by the defendant.

Your Honors doubtless understand that crude petroleum, as it comes from the wells, is separated by what they call fractional distillation into its several parts. The lightest is known as 'gasolene', the next heavier is known as 'kerosene', and the next heavier is known as fuel-oil', and the next heavier is known as 'lubricating oil', and what remains is known as 'residuum. These different petroleums differ from each other only in their boiling-points. They are separated simply by fractional distillation. Gasolene is the lightest and residuum is the heaviest of the series. And the question is, are these petroleums among the ''oils or oily substances'' of this patent.

This is a pure question of fact, may it please your Honors. It is a question of fact on which the District Court in this case, as well as the Court of Appeals in this case, has found in favor of the defendant. In other words, neither of the courts below has found that petroleum oils are not among the ''oils'' of this patent. We have never asked any court to find that anything in our mixture which is inert and inoperative in the process is a part of the oil of the patent.

In the first place, we take up the specifications of the patent in suit. They describe the ''oils'' which are to be used in the process in these words:

''Oils, fatty acids or other substances which have a ''*preferential affinity for metalliferous matter.*''

And when we come to the claims, we find that they all define the ''oils'' to be used in these words:

''An oily liquid having a *preferential affinity for metalliferous matter.*''

So, the first question is, Do petroleum oils have a *preferential affinity for metalliferous matter*, which is the requirement of the specifications and of the claims?

May it please your Honors, even my adversaries admit that petroleum oils have a preferential affinity for metalliferous matter. As a matter of fact, they have a very high preferential affinity, even a higher preferential affinity for metalliferous matter than does oleic acid, or pine-oil, or other vegetable oils. It is admitted, therefore, that petroleum oils fall literally within the terms, and literally within the four corners of the ''oils'' of the patent in suit.

In the next place, at the very birth of this invention, on March 5, 1905, the patentees wrote a report of the invention to the Minerals Separation, describing the invention. It is the first written description of the invention which appeared, written by the patentees, and I quote from it at the bottom of page 65 of my brief. After describing experiments with oleic acid, they say this:

''We may here conveniently note that other oils besides oleic acid may be employed in this modified recovery process, but so far as Broken Hill is concerned oleic acid gives by far the best results. Petroleum residuum''——

THE CHIEF JUSTICE: What term is that? Petroleum what?

MR. BULL: Petroleum residuum. That is the heaviest of the petroleums.

''—added as emulsion, paraffine oil alone''——

Paraffine oil is the English name for kerosene, so we can read it ''kerosene alone.''

''Petroleum residuum added as emulsion, paraffine oil alone, R_3P_1 and R_1P_3''——

Those formulæ mean, as explained in the testimony, a mixture of 3 parts of residuum and 1 part of kerosene, and a mixture of one part residuum and three parts kerosene

''—have also been used''——

MR. WILLIAMS: As emulsions. You omitted that.

MR. BULL: Well, they are mixtures.

MR. WILLIAMS: As emulsions.

MR. BULL: Well, mixtures, or emulsions, or anything you please, but they are both petroleum.

''—have also been used, and all give small proportions of float, but do not act nearly so vigorously or efficiently on Broken Hill ores as plain oleic acid.''

Now, the patentees in this first description, the very first description, of the invention, say that petroleum may be used instead of oleic acid, but they say on Broken Hill ores petroleums do not give as much froth or as good results as oleic acid.

As a matter of fact, very shortly after that description was written, Mr. Higgins, pursuing his investigations for the Minerals Separation tried gasolene, which, in England, is known as 'petrol': and he found that that gave, on Broken Hill ores, as good a recovery as oleic acid. That is admitted.

MR. JUSTICE CLARK: You say that is admitted?

MR. BULL: Yes, your Honor. It is his, Mr. Higgins' testimony. I have it in my brief.

In the next place, the British patent in its complete specification—the British patent which corresponds with the patent here in suit—wherever it mentions oleic acid invariably includes "petrol" as its equivalent. The phrase is always "oleic acid, petrol, etc."

The fact is, these British complete specifications were written after Mr. Higgins had tried gasolene and found that it worked on Broken Hill ores. That complete specification is almost word-for-word like the patent here in suit, except that wherever it mentions oleic acid it also mentions "petrol"—a petroleum.

In the next place, prior-art patents which were before your Honors in the Hyde case, almost every one of them mention the use of petroleums in this ore-recovery process. I have not time to refer to them, but you will find them each referred to in my brief, and the particular kind of petroleum product which is mentioned in each of them.

In the next place, plaintiffs, in the Hyde case, put their expert, Professor Chandler, on the stand to state in his direct examination, affirmatively, that petroleums were among the "oils or oily substances" of the patent in suit.

I may say (I am practically only reading my head-notes, because my time is very short) for every statement I have made, or will make, you will find a reference, by chapter and verse, to the part of the record where it is supported, in my brief.

In the next place, the plaintiffs' engineers in the Hyde case stated over and over again that they had used petroleum alone, and in mixtures, in the commercial practice of this invention, when using only about one-tenth of 1% on the ore. For example, their engineer Higgins said that he has successfully used not only "petrol" but also, quoting him, "Certain portions of "the distillate of crude petroleum, such as Cosmos oil" (and explained that Cosmos oil was petroleum lubricating oil).

Engineer Chapman said that at Broken Hill they use a mixture of oleic acid and Karsam soap, and he added that Karsam soap was a petroleum soap.

The same witness said that in the Braden mine in Chile they used a mixture of three parts Texas fuel-oil and one part American wood-tar oil. That is three parts petroleum and one part vegetable oil—precisely the mixture which the defendant is using at the present time.

All this testimony was before your Honors in the Hyde case. In this case the plaintiffs' witnesses amplify this very greatly. Their engineer Greninger says that he has used various mineral oils, fuel oils, and so forth. Fuel-oil, as you will remember, is a petroleum. Also that at the Inspiration plant they use a mixture of wood-tar oil and certain "mineral oils", which is only another name for petroleum. He also says that at the Britannia mine they use a mixture composed of three parts petroleum and one part wood-tar oil, which is precisely the mixture which the defendant is using in this case.

Plaintiffs' engineer Chapman says, in this case, that at the Consolidated Arizona mill they use a mixture of one-half stove-oil, which is a petroleum, and one-half turpentine; also at the Anaconda mine they use both stove-oil and fuel-oil, both of which are petroleums.

Plaintiffs' witness Wiggin says as a result of many tests at the Anaconda mine they found that the best oil to be used was a mixture of kerosene, sludge acid, wood-creosote, and stove-oil. Kerosene and stove-oil are petroleum.

Plaintiffs' witness Atwater says that at the Basin mill he used a mixture of live oils, one of which was kerosene.

The simple fact is that the use of mixtures containing petroleum is practically universal the world over today by the licensees of the plaintiffs, by those who are only using in the neighborhood of one-tenth of 1% on the ore. I have not referred to the testimony——

MR. JUSTICE PITNEY: You say that the use of petroleum mixtures is universal among those who are using one-tenth of 1%?

MR. BULL: Yes, your Honor. Every example which I have given here is an example where they were using in the neighborhood of one-tenth of 1% on the ore.

MR. JUSTICE PITNEY: How much are you actually using?

MR. BULL: We are using always more than one-half of 1%, and a large portion of the time more than 1%.

MR. JUSTICE PITNEY: In using more than 1% of the mixture——

MR. BULL: Yes, your Honor.

MR. JUSTICE PITNEY: —do you get the same process as described in the patent? I mean air-flotation. I mean froth-flotation, as distinguished from oil-flotation.

MR. BULL: Your Honor, you are asking me now a question which calls for legal interpretation. You ask me if we are using substantially the same process. Your Honor will recall that in the Hyde case we said that in using more than 1% of oil the process and the results were substantially the same as when you use a small fraction of 1% of oil. Your Honor remembers that that was our contention, and that was the contention which was sustained by the Court of Appeals in the Hyde case; and therefore the Court of Appeals held that the patent was invalid. Now, in the Hyde case my adversaries said, No; when you use more than 1%, or more than the "critical quantity", you are not practising the same process and you do not get the same result, because they said by the use of the critical quantity you get a *dry* froth, which carries the *maximum* amount of values.

They said, if you use a greater quantity of oil than the "critical quantity" you get an *oily froth*, which carries a *less quantity* of values; and they said, that is not *our* froth. And that is the contention which your Honors, as I understand it, adopted. They said, These prior-art quantities do not give *our* froth and do not give *our* result.

MR. JUSTICE PITNEY: Is it your present suggestion that they were mistaken about that?

MR. BULL: No, your Honor. I am saying this: I am saying that in precisely the same sense we are not using *their* process and we are not getting *their* results, because it is admitted by everyone that our froth is more *oily*, as it must obviously be when we use ten times as much oil. It is not only admitted, but it is affirmed, that our froth does not carry the *maximum* ore-values, for my friends put a witness on the stand to testify from our records that our results, our recoveries, were not as high when using this large amount of oil. They figured that we were losing more than a million dollars a year in reduced recovery by using this larger amount of oil. So when you ask me if we are practising the "same process", you see I can only answer by giving a legal definition as to what the "same process" is.

MR. JUSTICE PITNEY: You say practically you are practising the same process aside from percentage?

MR. BULL: I say we are practising the prior-art process.

MR. JUSTICE PITNEY: You are in a difficult position.

MR. BULL: We are infringing if the prior-art anticipates. If the prior-art does not anticipate, we are not infringing.

Now, I wish to say that the defendant here is one of a group of mines which are commonly known as the Jackling mines, and we have testimony from all those various mines, and at all of them, before the decision of this Court was handed down in the Hyde case, they were using this same mixture of oil (petroleum and vegetable oils) that they are using today. After your Honors handed down your decision in that case they all changed their practice and increased the amount of oil above one-half of 1% (the largest amount mentioned in the patent) and, much of the time, above 1%.

MR. JUSTICE MCREYNOLDS: Are the proportions just the same as they were?

MR. BULL: They are in some cases, but not in others. The proportion we are using now, as I pointed out, is used by two of the plaintiffs' licensees, where they are using less than one-tenths of 1%—that is, three parts of petroleum oil and one part vegetable oil.

MR. JUSTICE MCREYNOLDS: The proportions that you use now are the same as they were when suit was brought for infringement?

MR. BULL: As I stated before, we have used various mixtures. The one which I have taken here is the one which has been accepted by both sides as typical, because we had to talk about something, and we have taken that one; but, as your Honor will see from the record, we have used all sorts of proportions.

Now I wish to take up the question of the alleged disclaimer.

As your Honors know, at common law a patent containing one bad claim was bad in whole. It was totally void. That is the law in England today. That was the law in this country down to 1837. In that year Congress passed the disclaimer sections of the statute, which were designed to mitigate the hardship of that situation in a case in which the only defect of a patent was that it contains an overclaim; that is to say, that it claimed too much. And those sections provide that if a patent contains an overclaim, and merely an overclaim, the patentee may file in the Patent Office a disclaimer, and that he may maintain suit on the patent while it is in that defective condition, provided that he does not "unreasonably neglect or delay to enter his disclaimer." The language of the section is as follows:

"Sec. 4917. Whenever, through inadvertence, accident or mistake, and without any fraudulent or deceptive intention, a patentee has claimed more than that of which he was the original or first inventor or discoverer, his patent shall be valid for all that part which is truly and justly his own, provided the same is a material or substantial part of the thing patented; and any such patentee, his heirs or assigns, whether of the whole or any sectional interest therein, may, on payment of the fee required by law, make disclaimer of such parts of the thing patented as he shall not choose to claim or to hold by virtue of the patent or assignment, stating therein the extent of his interest in such patent. Such disclaimer shall be in writing," and so forth.

Section 4922 reads:

"Whenever, through inadvertence, accident or mistake, and without any wilful default, or intent to defraud or mislead the public, a patentee has, in his specification, claimed to be the original and first inventor or discoverer of any material or substantial part of the thing patented, of which he was not the original and first inventor or discoverer, every such patentee, his executors, administrators and assigns, whether of the whole or any sectional interest in the patent, may maintain a suit at law or in equity, for the infringement of any part thereof, which was *bona fide* his own, if it is a material and substantial part of the thing patented, and definitely distinguishable from the parts claimed without right, notwithstanding the specifications may embrace more than that of which the patentee was the first inventor or discoverer. But in every such case in which a judgment or decree shall be rendered for the plaintiff, no costs shall be recovered unless the proper disclaimer has been entered at the Patent Office before the commencement of the suit. But no patentee shall be entitled to the benefits of this section if he has unreasonably neglected or delayed to enter a disclaimer."

What are the "benefits" of that section? The "benefits" of that section, may it please the Court, are that a patentee can maintain a suit on a patent while it is in a defective condition, something that he could not do before that section was enacted, and the condition of enjoying those "benefits" is that the patentee must not unreasonably neglect or delay to enter his disclaimer. If he unreasonably neglects or delays to enter the disclaimer then he cannot maintain a suit on his patent.

As soon as your Honors' decision in the Hyde case was handed down, in which you pointed out that three of the claims were too broad, that patent began to expire. It could only be saved by a prompt surgical operation; it could only be saved by either cutting out of the patent altogether those small-quantity claims, which were declared to be invalid, or by trimming those claims down so that they were limited to the results obtained by the use of a fraction of 1% of oil. Now, neither of these things was done. A paper called a disclaimer was promptly filed, but our contention is that that paper was not a disclaimer in fact or in law. Our contention is that that paper did not cut out anything at all. Our contention is that that paper, masquerading as a disclaimer, as a matter of fact was intended to and actually did broaden the condemned claims. If we are right the plaintiffs have no right at the present time to maintain a suit on their patent.

Now I shall read to your Honors the material part of the alleged disclaimer, which you will find quoted at the bottom of page 101 of my brief. The material part of the disclaimer reads as follows:

"Your petitioner does hereby disclaim from claims 9, 10 and 11 of said letters patent No. 835,120, any process of concentrating powdered ores excepting where the "*results obtained are the results obtained* by the use of oil in a quantity amounting to a fraction of one per cent on the ore."

Your Honors will observe there, at once, the curious repetition of the words "results obtained." What your Honors said in your opinion was that these claims must be confined to the results obtained by the use of a critical amount of oil. What this disclaimer says is that these claims are limited to a process in which the "results obtained are the results obtained" by the use of oil in a quantity amounting to a fraction of 1%. In other words, these claims are now for a process in which the results obtained are *like those obtained* by using a fraction of 1% on the ore. These claims now are claims avowedly for a result. The "small quantity" of these claims is now any quantity, however large, provided the results obtained are *like those* obtained by using the small critical quantities. In other words, the claims have now been changed to claims for a result, and broadened, because the "small quantity" of these claims now is any quantity, however large, which will produce the desired results—which will do the work. And that is not only the effect of the disclaimer, but counsel for plaintiffs have told the Court it was the purpose of the disclaimer. I shall read from page 102 of my brief. This was a colloquy between Mr. Kenyon and the district judge. The Court said:

"The patent here in suit has been rather narrowly construed?

"MR. KENYON: On the contrary I think the Supreme Court has construed this patent broadly as for the process if and whenever the results obtained are those that are obtained when you effectively used this small quantity of oil."

And I read from page 93 of his brief before that court, in which counsel said that these claims, as changed by disclaimer, read as follows: He is paraphrasing the claims as they now read, as amended by disclaimer. He says, for example, claim 9 reads:

"The process of concentrating powdered ores which consists in separating the mineral from the gangue by coating the mineral with oil in water containing a small quantity of oil, agitating the mixture to form a froth, and separating the froth, when the results obtained are *substantially those that are obtained by the same procedure when the oil effectively used is a fraction of one per cent on the ore.*"

He adds, "That is the legal effect of that disclaimer."

That will be found at pages 103 and 104 of my brief.

In his brief in this Court plaintiffs' counsel says, and I am quoting now from page 105 of my brief.

THE CHIEF JUSTICE: What page?

MR. BULL: Page 105 of my brief. Having stated that Judge Bourquin regarded the opinion of this Court as a narrowing opinion, he says in this Court now:

"Petitioners do not so interpret the decision of this Court and respectfully present their interpretation, viz., that this Court, although having no evidence before it that the process could be worked with one per cent or more of any oil, nevertheless, in confining the patent and thereby limiting its scope, did *not* confine it to the use of a fraction of one per cent of oil, but to a *process identifiable by its results*, wherein the 'results obtained' were the new results first obtained by the process of the patent in suit."

In other words, these claims have been changed and expanded by disclaimer. There is nothing better settled in law than that anything which does not limit a claim is not a disclaimer in law or in fact; it is a nullity; and we submit that no legal disclaimer has been filed up to the present time. We submit that the paper that has been filed in the name of a disclaimer is not a disclaimer in fact or in law, but is an attempt to broaden and change the claims of the patent. That is a function which a disclaimer cannot legally perform; and if no legal disclaimer has yet been filed, the plaintiff has no right to maintain this suit.

We submit that plaintiffs have not honorably complied with the conditions which were imposed upon them by your Honors' decision in the Hyde case, but have, by shifty practices, avoided complying with those conditions. They have used the exact words of your Honors' decision but, by a repetition of them, they have put an entirely different meaning upon them.

We submit that it is important, it is extremely important, that this Court at this time should lay down the rules as to what a patentee may, or may not, do under the guise of disclaimer.

Mechanical Charging of Silver-Lead Blast-Furnaces

By L. D. ANDERSON

*At the Midvale, Utah, smelter of the United States Smelting & Refining Co. there is in use a system of mak-

BELT-FEEDER FOR HOPPER-BOTTOM ORE-BINS

ing-up blast-furnace charges that is interesting by showing how largely hand labor can be eliminated by the employment of mechanical and electrical devices. The charges for silver-lead blast-furnaces are carefully proportioned according to the chemical composition of the various ores and fluxes entering into their make-up. The ordinary practice is to weigh the ingredients in hand-buggies, pull these up to and carefully distribute their contents in large charge-cars, which are run over the furnaces into which the proportioned charges are then dropped. This scheme worked well as long as operations were on a small scale, but as they increased in magnitude the bins required became extensive, necessitating long hauls for the buggies. The result was the development of a formidable crew of charge-wheelers, whose direction and management became a serious problem. Errors on their part were not infrequent, causing excessive metallurgical losses.

To overcome the difficulties constantly encountered, it was decided at Midvale to change the system completely. This was done by substituting for the charge-wheelers, electrically-driven gathering-cars, which run under two long rows of bins, stopping at designated points and drawing out proper quantities of the required materials at the respective points. The hoppers of these cars are suspended on scale-beams, whose leverage systems end in a pointer immediately in front of the operator. Just before this pointer is a scale beam-box supplied with a sufficient number of beams to enable the operator to make settings for each and every ingredient for the charges.

Ordinary bin-gates are out of the question when accurate weighing is necessary, so resort was made to electrically-operated mechanical gates or feeders. The necessity of utilizing an existing heavy bin construction made it compulsory to use two different types, an under-cut arc-gate for the row of flat-

UNDER-CUT ARC-GATES FOR FLAT-BOTTOM ORE-BINS

*Abstract from Monthly Journal of Utah Society of Engineers, Jan. 1919.

bottom bins, and a belt-feeder for the row of hopper-bottom bins. Both types are operated in the same manner, the power being a 7½-hp. motor on the scale car. By means of a swinging-gear on the car, this motor is put in mesh with the main gear driving each set of gates. This swinging-gear is thrown into mesh by simply pressing down a foot-treadle on the car. The belt-feeders move through the simple rotation of the large pulley at the rear, while the balanced arc-gates are actuated by a crank and connecting-rod mechanism.

For accurate weighing, the belt-feeders are found at the start to be more sensitive than the arc-gates; on the other hand, after a little skill has been acquired, a good operator can do about as well with either type. The under-cut arc-gate has one advantage in that it is seldom troubled by a preponderance of either coarse or fine material. The common bin-gate, wherein closing is effected from above, often catches on a large lump, permitting fine material to slide by. The under-cut arc-gate entirely overcomes this difficulty, getting a quick sharp cut-off. For the belt-feeders, heavy canvas belts, 36 in. wide, are used. Canvas has been found to have some advantages over the metal slat-type of belt or apron-feeders. It is considerably cheaper, and it does not have the tendency to jamb and stick, which sometimes happens when slats are bent by the shock of ore dumped upon them. The belts generally last from six to twelve months, according to the character of material handled. Some belts have given service several times as long as that.

ELECTRICALLY-DRIVEN GATHERING CAR WITH WEIGHING HOPPERS

Various metallurgical considerations had to be kept in mind in designing the several details, but space is too limited to discuss them here. It might be stated that the installation of the equipment thus briefly described, built by the Brown Hoisting Machinery Co., and patented by the Smelting company, has effected a saving of from 55 to 65 men formerly required to charge the blast-furnaces.

The smelter of the U. S. S. R. & M. Co. at Midvale, Utah, now contains seven blast-furnaces, one being added during 1918 to meet the large supply of ore.

THE WEST END CONSOLIDATED mill at Tonopah during 1918 treated 66,518 tons of company and custom ore averaging $24.06 per ton. The gold content was 14.316 oz. and silver content 1,334,010 oz., of which 94.30 and 91.95%, respectively, was extracted. The actual cost of treatment was $2.94 per ton of ore, equal to 14.5 cents per ounce of bullion; and the additional cost of sampling and marketing was 35.4 cents per ton or 1.8 cents per ounce. The consumption of sodium cyanide was 0.131 lb. per fine ounce, and that of zinc 0.053 lb. Two crucible melting-furnaces were replaced by a No. 3 double-chamber Rockwell furnace, a No. 3 Root blower, and a briquetting-machine, at a cost of $3303. This new equipment reduced 1,240,177 oz. of bullion, costing, including briquetting of the precipitate, $0.0035 per ounce. The saving over the cost in 1917 was a total of $1596, so that in about one year's operation the furnace saved nearly 50% of its first cost.

The Efficient Compression of Air

By CHARLES A. HIRSCHBERG

*Economical and efficient operation of air-compressors demands regular inspection. The compressor as a whole should be inspected at least once a month, making necessary adjustments, such as taking-up of packing-glands and replacement of worn parts. Air-valves should be examined and should show an oily surface free from carbon. Ports and passages also should be examined for carbon or other obstructions. Carbon deposit on valves prevents their seating properly, causes leakage and results in reduced compressor-capacity and low efficiency. Obstructions in air-passages reduce their area and cause loss in friction. A carbon deposit, in combination with high temperature, due to improper cylinder cooling, sticking of valves, or insufficient lubrication, may result in explosions, if allowed to persist. Remove any carbon deposited.

The use of packing is often misunderstood. Drawing up too tightly will cause heating, and scoring of the piston-rod. This means higher temperatures and increased mechanical friction, with transmitting of increased temperature to the air cylinder, causing trouble from moisture, lowering the air density, and thereby reducing the output.

In placing the packing in a stuffing-box, put the rings in so that the joints of the several rings stagger. Fill the box without crowding, and with new packing force in slightly with the gland until the compressor warms up; then draw up just enough to prevent blowing. Crowding the packing will squeeze-out the lubricant it contains, causing the packing to become hard and unyielding. If upon examination packing is found to be hard, it may be revived by removing, loosening up, and working in a mixture of graphite and grease. Asbestos-sheet packing is generally used between cylinder-heads and cylinders. If for any reason it becomes necessary to remove a head, care should be exercised not to injure this head-gasket. If necessary to replace it, be sure to use material of the same thickness as the original, so as to maintain the clearance established by the builder.

Do not have the air-intake open to the engine-room. Carry it outdoors and extend upward a sufficient height, with hood and screen, to prevent foreign substances from being drawn-in and to ensure cool intake air. Fig. 1 shows an ideal method of handling the air-intake. Take the air into the compressor as cool as possible is the rule without any exception. Cooling the intake air is a direct saving of power by reducing the volume to be compressed. The capacity of the air to hold moisture falls off rapidly as its temperature is reduced.

*Abstract from 'Power Plant Engineering' and 'Compressed Air Magazine'.

Pipe-lines should be of ample size, as small transmission-lines mean excessive loss of pressure due to friction. Large pipe-lines are especially desirable where the pipes are long or the supply has to meet the demands of a great many devices. Reduced pressure due to friction means inefficient operation of tools. The accompanying chart, Fig. 2, covering loss in pressure due to friction in pipe-lines, will serve to indicate the need for having the pipe-line of ample size. Take, for example, the following case:

The loss in pressure in transmitting 50 cu. ft. of free air per minute at 100 lb. pressure through 1000 ft. of 1-in. pipe is 11.89 lb., and only 0.27 lb. in transmitting the same volume of air the same distance through a 2-in. pipe.

Air-lines should receive monthly inspection for leaks. Assuming that 1 cu. ft. of air per minute at 100 lb. pressure costs $5 per year, this cost being computed from an estimated charge for electricity at 1c. per kw-hr., interest and depreciation at 10%, and a year as 300 eight-hour days, the following demonstrates the economy of regular pipe-line inspections:

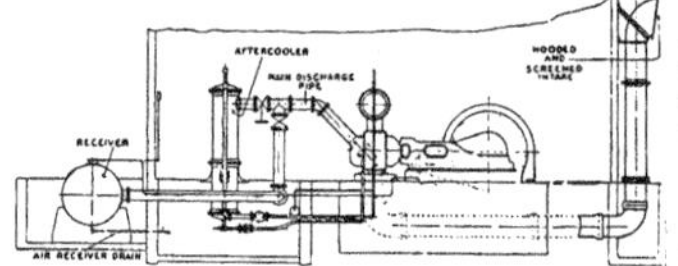

FIG. 1. PROPER ARRANGEMENT OF AIR-INTAKE AND PIPING

Amount of Leak in Cubic Feet

Diameter of hole, inches	Free air per minute	Cost per year
1/16	6.45	$32
1/32	1.61	8
1/64	0.40	2

Further calculations of possible loss through leaks may be quickly made by applying the above constant to the various discharge volumes shown in Fig. 3.

It is always advisable to provide numerous outlets in the transmission-line. This will have future reconstruction, and make it possible to use comparatively shorter lengths of hose. Where a number of supply-lines radiate from the main line, it is well to provide a gate-valve for cutting out any of these lines when they are to be idle for any considerable period of time.

Several methods are used of detecting air leaks: By the use of a lighted candle at all joints and connections, by swabbing soapy water around the joints, or by following the practice of one Illinois manufacturer, who, at regular intervals, put essence of peppermint into the air system and then has all the pipes inspected. Leaks are revealed by the odor.

Delivery in Cu. Ft. of Compressed Air per Min.	Equiv. Delivery in Cu. Ft. of Free Air per Min.	Size of Pipe, Inches																	
		1	1¼	1½	2	2½	3	3½	4	4½	5	6	7	8	9	10	12	14	16
		Loss of Pressure in Pounds by Friction in 1000 Feet Length of Pipe																	
At 60 Pounds Gauge																			
[illegible]	50	18.24	5.00	1.95	.47	.15	.05												
[illegible]	75	...	11.34	4.33	.95	[illegible]	[illegible]	.01											
[illegible]	100	...	20.16	7.79	1.69	.52	[illegible]	[illegible]	[illegible]										
[illegible]	125	...	...	12.23	2.65	[illegible]	[illegible]	[illegible]	[illegible]	[illegible]									
[illegible]	150	...	...	17.53	3.80	1.16	[illegible]	[illegible]	[illegible]	[illegible]	[illegible]								
[illegible]	175	...	...	...	5.17	[illegible]	[illegible]	[illegible]	[illegible]	[illegible]	[illegible]	.01							
[illegible]	200	...	...	...	6.75	2.09	[illegible]	[illegible]	[illegible]	[illegible]	[illegible]	[illegible]	.01						
[illegible]	250	...	...	...	10.61	3.26	[illegible]	[illegible]	[illegible]	[illegible]	[illegible]	[illegible]	.01						
[illegible]	300	...	...	...	15.20	4.65	[illegible]	[illegible]	[illegible]	[illegible]	[illegible]	[illegible]	[illegible]	.01					
[illegible]	350	...	...	...	...	6.35	[illegible]	[illegible]	[illegible]	[illegible]	[illegible]	[illegible]	[illegible]	.01					
[illegible]	400	...	...	...	...	8.28	[illegible]	[illegible]	[illegible]	[illegible]	[illegible]	[illegible]	[illegible]	[illegible]					
[illegible]	450	...	...	...	...	10.47	[illegible]	[illegible]	[illegible]	[illegible]	[illegible]	[illegible]	[illegible]	[illegible]	.01				
[illegible]	500	...	...	...	...	...	[illegible]	[illegible]	[illegible]	[illegible]	[illegible]	[illegible]	[illegible]	[illegible]	.01				
[illegible]	600	...	...	...	...	...	[illegible]	[illegible]	[illegible]	[illegible]	[illegible]	[illegible]	[illegible]	[illegible]	[illegible]	[illegible]			
[illegible]	700	...	...	...	...	...	[illegible]	[illegible]	[illegible]	[illegible]	[illegible]	[illegible]	[illegible]	[illegible]	[illegible]	[illegible]			
[illegible]	800	...	...	...	...	...	...	[illegible]	[illegible]	[illegible]	[illegible]	[illegible]	[illegible]	[illegible]	[illegible]	[illegible]	[illegible]		
[illegible]	900	...	...	...	...	...	...	[illegible]	[illegible]	[illegible]	[illegible]	[illegible]	[illegible]	[illegible]	[illegible]	[illegible]	[illegible]		
[illegible]	1000	...	...	...	...	...	...	[illegible]	[illegible]	[illegible]	[illegible]	[illegible]	[illegible]	[illegible]	[illegible]	[illegible]	[illegible]	.01	
[illegible]	1500	...	...	...	...	...	...	...	[illegible]	[illegible]	[illegible]	[illegible]	[illegible]	[illegible]	[illegible]	[illegible]	[illegible]	.01	
[illegible]	2000	...	...	...	...	...	...	...	...	[illegible]	[illegible]	[illegible]	[illegible]	[illegible]	[illegible]	[illegible]	[illegible]	[illegible]	[illegible]
[illegible]	2500	...	...	...	...	...	...	...	...	...	[illegible]	[illegible]	[illegible]	[illegible]	[illegible]	[illegible]	[illegible]	[illegible]	[illegible]
[illegible]	3000	...	...	...	...	...	...	...	...	...	...	[illegible]	[illegible]	[illegible]	[illegible]	[illegible]	[illegible]	[illegible]	[illegible]
[illegible]	3500	...	...	...	...	...	...	...	...	...	...	[illegible]	[illegible]	[illegible]	[illegible]	[illegible]	[illegible]	[illegible]	[illegible]
[illegible]	4000	...	...	...	...	...	...	...	...	...	...	...	[illegible]	[illegible]	[illegible]	[illegible]	[illegible]	[illegible]	[illegible]
[illegible]	4500	...	...	...	...	...	...	...	...	...	...	...	[illegible]	[illegible]	[illegible]	[illegible]	[illegible]	[illegible]	[illegible]
[illegible]	5000	...	...	...	...	...	...	...	...	...	...	...	[illegible]	[illegible]	[illegible]	[illegible]	[illegible]	[illegible]	[illegible]
At 80 Pounds Gauge																			
7.74	50	14.31	3.90	1.53	.35	.10	.05	.01											
[illegible]	75	...	8.40	3.26	.71	.21	.05	.01											
[illegible]	100	...	15.31	5.92	1.28	.39	.14	.06	[illegible]	[illegible]	.01								
[illegible]	125	...	...	9.64	2.09	.64	.24	.11	[illegible]	[illegible]	[illegible]								
[illegible]	150	...	...	13.79	2.99	.91	.34	.15	[illegible]	[illegible]	[illegible]	.01							
[illegible]	175	...	...	...	4.09	1.25	[illegible]	[illegible]	[illegible]	[illegible]	[illegible]	[illegible]							
[illegible]	200	...	...	...	[illegible]	1.65	[illegible]	[illegible]	[illegible]	[illegible]	[illegible]	[illegible]							
[illegible]	250	...	...	...	8.32	2.56	[illegible]	[illegible]	[illegible]	[illegible]	[illegible]	[illegible]	.01						
[illegible]	300	...	...	...	12.01	3.62	1.39	[illegible]	[illegible]	[illegible]	[illegible]	[illegible]	.01						
[illegible]	350	...	...	...	...	4.99	1.85	[illegible]	[illegible]	[illegible]	[illegible]	[illegible]	[illegible]	.01					
[illegible]	400	...	...	...	...	[illegible]	2.45	1.11	[illegible]	[illegible]	[illegible]	[illegible]	[illegible]	.01					
[illegible]	450	...	...	...	...	[illegible]	[illegible]	[illegible]	[illegible]	[illegible]	[illegible]	[illegible]	[illegible]	.01					
[illegible]	500	...	...	...	...	[illegible]	[illegible]	[illegible]	[illegible]	[illegible]	[illegible]	[illegible]	[illegible]	[illegible]					
[illegible]	600	...	...	...	...	...	[illegible]	[illegible]	[illegible]	[illegible]	[illegible]	[illegible]	[illegible]	[illegible]	[illegible]				
[illegible]	700	...	...	...	...	...	[illegible]	[illegible]	[illegible]	[illegible]	[illegible]	[illegible]	[illegible]	[illegible]	[illegible]	[illegible]			
[illegible]	800	...	...	...	...	...	[illegible]	[illegible]	[illegible]	[illegible]	[illegible]	[illegible]	[illegible]	[illegible]	[illegible]	[illegible]	[illegible]		
[illegible]	900	...	...	...	...	...	...	[illegible]	[illegible]	[illegible]	[illegible]	[illegible]	[illegible]	[illegible]	[illegible]	[illegible]	[illegible]		
[illegible]	1000	...	...	...	...	...	...	[illegible]	[illegible]	[illegible]	[illegible]	[illegible]	[illegible]	[illegible]	[illegible]	[illegible]	[illegible]	.01	
[illegible]	1500	...	...	...	...	...	...	...	[illegible]	[illegible]	[illegible]	[illegible]	[illegible]	[illegible]	[illegible]	[illegible]	[illegible]	[illegible]	.01
[illegible]	2000	...	...	...	...	...	...	...	[illegible]	[illegible]	[illegible]	[illegible]	[illegible]	[illegible]	[illegible]	[illegible]	[illegible]	[illegible]	[illegible]
[illegible]	2500	...	...	...	...	...	...	...	...	[illegible]	[illegible]	[illegible]	[illegible]	[illegible]	[illegible]	[illegible]	[illegible]	[illegible]	[illegible]
[illegible]	3000	...	...	...	...	...	...	...	...	...	[illegible]	[illegible]	[illegible]	[illegible]	[illegible]	[illegible]	[illegible]	[illegible]	[illegible]
[illegible]	3500	...	...	...	...	...	...	...	...	...	[illegible]	[illegible]	[illegible]	[illegible]	[illegible]	[illegible]	[illegible]	[illegible]	[illegible]
[illegible]	4000	...	...	...	...	...	...	...	...	...	[illegible]	[illegible]	[illegible]	[illegible]	[illegible]	[illegible]	[illegible]	[illegible]	[illegible]
[illegible]	4500	...	...	...	...	...	...	...	...	...	...	[illegible]	[illegible]	[illegible]	[illegible]	[illegible]	[illegible]	[illegible]	[illegible]
[illegible]	5000	...	...	...	...	...	...	...	...	...	...	[illegible]	[illegible]	[illegible]	[illegible]	[illegible]	[illegible]	[illegible]	[illegible]
At 100 Pounds Gauge																			
[illegible]	[illegible]	[illegible]	[illegible]	[illegible]	[illegible]	[illegible]	[illegible]	[illegible]	[illegible]	[illegible]	[illegible]	[illegible]	[illegible]	[illegible]	[illegible]	[illegible]	[illegible]	[illegible]	[illegible]
At 125 Pounds Gauge																			
[illegible]	[illegible]	[illegible]	[illegible]	[illegible]	[illegible]	[illegible]	[illegible]	[illegible]	[illegible]	[illegible]	[illegible]	[illegible]	[illegible]	[illegible]	[illegible]	[illegible]	[illegible]	[illegible]	[illegible]

FIG. 2. LOSS OF AIR-PRESSURE IN PIPE TRANSMISSION

Pipe-lines may be tested for loss of pressure due to friction in transmission or to leakage by placing an air-gauge at the point of use of the air, and comparing its reading with that of the gauge on the air-receiver. The remedies are increasing the size of the air-line and eliminating of leaks.

All air contains moisture. When compressed, the moisture becomes more evident, as in the compressed state there is more water in the air than it can contain. The excess moisture is deposited almost immediately as the air travels to the receiver; part of it travels with the air through the transmission-lines, being gradually deposited and draining to low spots in the pipes, reducing the available area. Some of the moisture will find its way into the ports and exhaust-passages of the machinery using the air, resulting in interference with proper operation by freezing at exhaust-ports as the air expands to atmosphere.

One of the most effective and cheapest methods for the elimination of moisture from pipe-lines is the placing of suitable traps at intervals in the transmission-line, into which the condensed moisture will precipitate and can be conveniently withdrawn. A simple moisture trap, Fig. 4, consists of an enlargement of the air-line. It is provided with baffles and blow-off, the former having holes or slots drilled in the bottom so that moisture can work through to the blow-off pipe. By reason of the pressure always present in the separator the water can be taken from the top. This trap may be made of wrought or cast-iron pipe, with flanged or screwed heads. A good proportion is separator diameter 3 times the air-line diameter and 4 to 6 ft. long. Another effective design is shown in Fig. 5. It consists of a long-sweep tee, three times the diameter of the pipe, with a pocket below to catch the condensed moisture. Both of these separators may be made locally from standard pipe-fittings; also, there are a number of standard-built moisture-traps that may be purchased from various manufacturers. Moisture-traps should be placed at low points in the air-line.

Re-heating the air is a simple process, and serves the double purpose of eliminating annoyance due to freezing as a result of the moisture that the air may contain, and at the some time increasing the air volume.

When the warm compressed air leaves the compressor, and passes through the receiver and the transmission-lines to the point of use, the temperature of the air is considerably reduced. This represents a loss in volume. If the air were used immediately adjacent to the point of production, this loss would not be experienced; but the latter condition seldom, if ever, prevails.

Re-heating the compressed air, at the point where it is to be utilized, a temperature of 250°F., which is usual, results in expanding it in volume from 30 to 35%, at a cost of about ⅙ of the heat-units required to produce the same volume by compression. This approximation is based on the use of effective form of re-heater, and the use of the air in the cylinder of the engine immediately after passing from the re-heater. In using the re-heater, therefore, it should be placed as closely as possible to the point of use of the air, to prevent loss from radiation of heat after the re-heating process. The re-heater may consist of a cast-iron chamber containing a coil of pipe exposed to a fire, or a current of hot gas or steam. Fig.

6 shows a cross-section view of one standard type of re-heater, which requires no explanation.

Two tables given in Fig. 7 show the horse-power required for compressing air in single-stage and two-stage compressors at various gauge-pressures. All the conditions of the calculations given are explained in the headings.

Receiver Gauge Pressure Pounds	Diameter of Orifice												
	1/64 inch	1/32 inch	1/16 inch	1/8 inch	1/4 inch	3/8 inch	1/2 inch	5/8 inch	3/4 inch	7/8 inch	1 inch	1 1/8 inch	1 1/4 inch
	Discharge in Cubic Feet of Free Air per Minute												
2	.038	.153	.647	2.435	9.74	21.95	39	61	87.60	119.50	156	242.	350
5	.0597	.242	.965	3.86	15.40	34.60	61.60	96.50	133.	189	247	384	550.
10	.0842	.342	1.36	5.45	21.8	49.	87.	136	196	267.	350	543	780
15	.103	.418	1.67	6.65	26.70	60.	107.	167	240	326.	427.	665	960.
20	.119	.485	1.93	7.7	30.8	69	123.	193	277	378.	494.	770	......
25	.133	.54	2.16	8.6	34.5	77	138.	216	310	422.	550	860.	......
30	.156	.632	2.52	10	40	90.	161.	252	362	493	645.	1000.	......
35	.173	.71	2.80	11.2	44.7	100	179.	280	400	550	715.	......	......
40	.19	.77	3.07	12.27	49.09	110.45	196.35	306.80	441.79	601.32	785.40	......	......
45	.208	.843	3.36	13.4	53.8	121	215	336	482	658	860.	......	......
50	.225	.914	3.64	14.50	58.2	130	232	364.	522	710.	930.	......	......
60	.26	1.05	4.2	16.8	67	151	268	420	604.	622	......	......	......
70	.295	1.19	4.76	19	76	171	304	476.	685.	930	......	......	......
80	.33	1.33	5.32	21.2	85	191	340	532.	765.	1004	......	......	......
90	.364	1.47	5.87	23.50	94	211	376	587.	843.	......	......	......	......
100	.40	1.61	6.45	25.8	103	231	412.	645	925.	......	......	......	......
125	.486	1.97	7.85	31.4	125	282	502	785		......	......	......	......

FIG. 3. DISCHARGE OF AIR FROM ROUND HOLE TO ATMOSPHERE.

Mechanical efficiency of an air-compressor is represented by the ratio of the indicated air horse-power to the indicated steam horse-power in the case of a steam-driven machine, and to the brake horse-power in the case of a power-driven machine. The difference between the two represents excess power required to overcome frictional resistance of the machine, which is largely dependent on the design, workmanship, and supervision received when

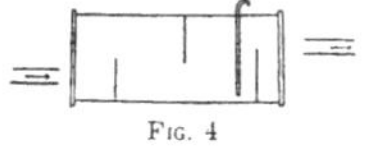

FIG. 4

in operation. Mechanical efficiency of a well-designed compressor ranges between 90 and 95%.

Let us assume a power-driven air-compressor of the

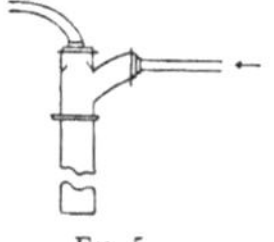

FIG. 5

following size and displacement, and determine its mechanical efficiency:

Diameter of low-pressure cylinder, 16 in.; diameter of high-pressure cylinder, 10 in.; stroke, 14 in.; r.p.m., 165; discharge-pressure, gauge, 100 lb.; piston displacement, cu. ft. per min., 534. From brake-test it was found that the brake horse-power is 93. The air indicator-cards give an indicated horse-power of 83.6. Therefore $83.6 \div 93 = 92\%$ mechanical efficiency.

As stated above, loss in mechanical efficiency is determined by frictional resistance. This is a factor that can be largely controlled by the supervising engineer. In general, it is desirable that attention be given to the lubrication system to ensure that all rubbing-parts are sufficiently lubricated at the following points: Bearings,

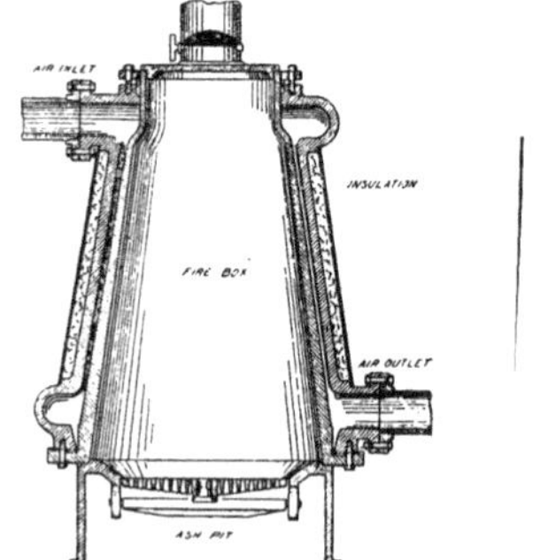

FIG. 6. STANDARD AIR RE-HEATER

cross-heads, stuffing-boxes, and cylinders, as they constitute the chief sources of loss due to friction. Bearings should be drawn up only enough to ensure smooth operation, without undue pressure. Instructions covering the packing of stuffing-boxes have already been given. Cross-head guides must be free enough to permit the cross-head to operate without undue pressure, and yet work without knocking.

Different measurements necessary for the calculation of efficiencies are given on the diagrams shown in Fig. 8 and 9. Following are stated the ratios of these measurements resulting in the respective efficiencies and performance measurements of an electrically-driven and a steam-driven compressor.

All compression efficiencies should be subject to correction to perfect inter-cooling, if the specified amount of water at specified temperature is not available.

The theory of compound or stage compression is very

Gauge Pressure Pounds	Absolute Pressure Pounds	Number of Atmospheres	Isothermal Compression: Mean Effective Pressure	Isothermal Compression: H. P.	Adiabatic Compression: Mean Effective Pressure Theoretical	Adiabatic Compression: Mean Eff. Pressure plus 15% Friction	Adiabatic Compression: H. P. Theoretical	Adiabatic Compression: H. P. plus 15% Friction
5	19.7	1.34	4.33	0.018	4.46	5.12	0.019	0.022
10	24.7	1.68	7.57	0.033	8.21	9.44	0.036	0.041
15	29.7	2.02	11.02	0.048	11.46	13.17	0.050	0.057
20	34.7	2.36	12.62	0.055	14.30	16.44	0.062	0.071
25	39.7	2.70	14.68	0.064	16.94	19.47	0.074	0.085
30	44.7	3.04	16.30	0.071	19.32	22.21	0.084	0.096
35	49.7	3.38	17.90	0.078	21.50	24.72	0.094	0.108
40	54.7	3.72	19.28	0.084	23.53	27.05	0.103	0.118
45	59.7	4.06	20.63	0.090	25.40	29.21	0.111	0.127
50	64.7	4.40	21.80	0.095	27.23	31.31	0.119	0.136
55	69.7	4.74	22.95	0.100	28.90	33.23	0.126	0.145
60	74.7	5.08	23.90	0.104	30.53	35.10	0.133	0.153
65	79.7	5.42	24.80	0.108	32.10	36.91	0.140	0.161
70	84.7	5.76	25.70	0.112	33.57	38.59	0.146	0.168
75	89.7	6.10	26.62	0.116	35.00	40.25	0.153	0.175
80	94.7	6.44	27.52	0.120	36.36	41.80	0.159	0.182
85	99.7	6.78	28.21	0.123	37.63	43.27	0.164	0.189
90	104.7	7.12	28.93	0.126	38.89	44.71	0.169	0.195
95	109.7	7.46	29.60	0.129	40.11	46.12	0.175	0.201
100	114.7	7.80	30.30	0.132	41.28	47.46	0.180	0.207
110	124.7	8.48	31.42	0.137	43.56	50.09	0.190	0.218
120	134.7	9.16	32.60	0.142	45.69	52.53	0.199	0.229
130	144.7	9.84	33.75	0.147	47.72	54.87	0.208	0.239
140	154.7	10.52	34.67	0.151	49.64	57.08	0.216	0.249
150	164.7	11.20	35.59	0.155	51.47	59.18	0.224	0.258
160	174.7	11.88	36.30	0.158	53.70	61.80	0.234	0.269
170	184.7	12.56	37.20	0.162	55.60	64.00	0.242	0.278
180	194.7	13.24	38.10	0.166	57.20	65.80	0.249	0.286
190	204.7	13.92	38.80	0.169	58.80	67.70	0.256	0.294
200	214.7	14.60	39.50	0.172	60.40	69.50	0.263	0.303

FIG. 7. SINGLE-STAGE COMPRESSION

Gauge Pressure Pounds	Absolute Pressure Pounds	No. of Atmospheres	Correct Ratio of Cylinder Volumes	Inter-cooler Gauge Pressure	Isothermal Compression: Mean Eff. Pressure	Isothermal Compression: H. P.	Adiabatic Compression: Mean Eff. Pressure Theoretical	Adiabatic Compression: Mean Eff. Pressure plus 15% Friction	Adiabatic Compression: H. P. Theoretical	Adiabatic Compression: H. P. plus 15% Friction	Percentage of Saving over One-stage Comp.
50	64.7	4.40	2.10	16.2	21.80	0.095	24.30	27.90	0.106	0.123	10.9
60	74.7	5.08	2.25	18.4	23.90	0.104	27.20	31.30	0.118	0.136	11.3
70	84.7	5.76	2.40	20.6	25.70	0.112	29.31	33.71	0.128	0.147	12.3
80	94.7	6.44	2.54	22.7	27.52	0.120	31.44	36.15	0.137	0.158	13.8
90	104.7	7.12	2.67	24.5	28.93	0.126	33.37	38.36	0.145	0.167	14.2
100	114.7	7.80	2.79	26.3	30.30	0.132	35.20	40.48	0.153	0.176	15.0
110	124.7	8.48	2.91	28.1	31.42	0.137	36.92	42.34	0.161	0.185	15.4
120	134.7	9.16	3.02	29.8	32.60	0.142	38.44	44.20	0.168	0.193	15.6
130	144.7	9.84	3.14	31.5	33.75	0.147	39.86	45.83	0.174	0.200	16.3
140	154.7	10.52	3.24	32.9	34.67	0.151	41.28	47.47	0.180	0.207	16.7
150	164.7	11.20	3.35	34.5	35.59	0.155	42.60	48.99	0.186	0.214	16.9
160	174.7	11.88	3.45	36.1	36.30	0.158	43.82	50.39	0.191	0.219	18.4
170	184.7	12.56	3.54	37.3	37.20	0.162	44.93	51.66	0.196	0.225	19.0
180	194.7	13.24	3.64	38.8	38.10	0.166	46.05	52.95	0.201	0.231	19.3
190	204.7	13.92	3.73	40.1	38.80	0.169	47.16	54.22	0.206	0.236	19.5
200	214.7	14.60	3.82	41.4	39.50	0.172	48.18	55.39	0.210	0.241	20.1
210	224.7	15.28	3.91	42.8	40.10	0.174	49.35	56.70	0.216	0.247	
220	234.7	15.96	3.99	44.0	40.70	0.177	50.30	57.70	0.220	0.252	
230	244.7	16.64	4.08	45.3	41.30	0.180	51.30	59.10	0.224	0.257	
240	254.7	17.32	4.17	46.6	41.90	0.183	52.25	60.10	0.228	0.262	
250	264.7	18.00	4.24	47.6	42.70	0.186	52.84	60.76	0.230	0.264	
260	274.7	18.68	4.32	48.8	43.00	0.188	53.85	62.05	0.235	0.270	
270	284.7	19.36	4.40	50.0	43.50	0.190	54.60	62.90	0.238	0.274	
280	294.7	20.04	4.48	51.1	44.00	0.192	55.50	63.85	0.242	0.278	
290	304.7	20.72	4.55	52.2	44.50	0.194	56.20	64.75	0.246	0.282	
300	314.7	21.40	4.63	53.4	45.30	0.197	56.70	65.20	0.247	0.283	
350	364.7	24.80	4.98	58.3	47.30	0.206	60.15	69.16	0.262	0.301	
400	414.7	28.20	5.31	63.3	49.20	0.214	63.19	72.65	0.276	0.317	
450	464.7	31.60	5.61	67.8	51.20	0.223	65.93	75.81	0.287	0.329	
500	514.7	35.01	5.91	72.1	51.70	0.229	68.46	78.72	0.298	0.342	

FIG. 7. TWO-STAGE COMPRESSION

readily understood. It is generally conceded that compound or stage compression should be employed (*a*) with small capacity machines when pressures range over 125 lb., (*b*) with large capacity machines when pressures range above 70 lb. The heat of compression increases with the pressure, therefore, the higher the pressure, the more difficult it is to reduce the temperature of the air to a point where efficient compression conditions and proper air-cylinder lubrication obtain. For instance, in compressing air to 100 lb. terminal gauge-pressure in a single cylinder, the final temperature would be about 485°F. Some of this heat would be absorbed by the cylinder-walls and water-jackets, but the final temperature would remain too high to ensure efficient compression conditions and proper lubrication.

For Electrically-Driven Compressors

$$\frac{\text{B.hp.}}{\text{E.hp.}} = \text{motor efficiency.}$$

$$\frac{\text{I.hp. air-cylinder}}{\text{B.hp. on shaft}} = \text{mechanical efficiency.}$$

$$\frac{\text{Free air actually delivered}}{\text{Piston displacement}} = \text{actual volumetric efficiency.}$$

$$\frac{\text{Length l.p. intake-line}}{\text{Length indicated diagram}} = \text{indicated volumetric efficiency.}$$

$$\frac{\text{Actual volumetric efficiency}}{\text{Indicated volumetric efficiency}} = \text{slippage efficiency.}$$

$$\frac{\text{I.hp. air-cylinder} \times 100}{\text{Cu. ft. actually delivered per min.}} = \text{I.hp. per 100 cu. ft. delivered per min.}$$

$$\frac{\text{E.hp. input at switchboard} \times 100}{\text{Cu. ft. actually delivered per min.}} = \text{E.hp. per 100 cu. ft. delivered per min.}$$

$$\frac{\text{Isothermal factor}}{\text{I.hp. per 100 cu. ft. delivered per min.}} = \text{isothermal compression efficiency.}$$

$$\frac{\text{Isothermal factor}}{\text{E.hp. per cu. ft. delivered per min.}} = \text{overall isothermal compression efficiency.}$$

For Steam-Driven Compressors

$$\frac{\text{I.hp. air-cylinders}}{\text{I.hp. steam-cylinders}} = \text{mechanical efficiency.}$$

$$\frac{\text{Free air actually delivered}}{\text{Piston displacement}} = \text{actual volumetric efficiency.}$$

$$\frac{\text{Length l.p. intake-line}}{\text{Length indicated diagram}} = \text{indicated volumetric efficiency.}$$

$$\frac{\text{Actual volumetric efficiency}}{\text{Indicated volumetric efficiency}} = \text{air I.hp. per 100 cu. ft. delivered per min.}$$

$$\frac{\text{Isothermal factor}}{\text{Air I.hp. per 100 cu. ft. delivered per min.}} = \text{isothermal compression efficiency.}$$

$$\frac{\text{Isothermal factor}}{\text{I.hp. steam-cylinder per 100 cu. ft. per min.}} = \text{overall isothermal compression efficiency.}$$

$$\frac{\text{Pounds steam per hour}}{\text{I.hp. steam-cylinder}} = \text{steam consumption per I.hp. hour.}$$

$$\frac{\text{Pounds steam per min.} \times 1000}{\text{Cu. ft. free air delivered per min.}} = \text{lb. steam per 1000 cu. ft. air delivered.}$$

In Fig. 10 is shown a theoretical combined indicator-diagram from a two-stage compressor. It is assumed that the compression follows the adiabatic curve in both cylinders, with perfect inter-cooling between. $AB =$ volume of low-pressure cylinder; $CD =$ volume of high-pressure cylinder, both drawn to the same scale. $ACF =$ pressure to some designated scale; BEK (adiabatic curve) $=$ relation between pressure and volume for any piston position, with no inter-cooling and no radiation through the cylinder-walls. In this curve the product $PV^{1.41}$ is constant (1.41 is the ratio between the specific heat of air at constant pressure and constant volume), where $P =$ pressure and $V =$ volume. BDH (isothermal curve) $=$ relation between pressure and volume, provided the temperature of the air under compression could be kept constant so that the product PV would also be constant. Air taken into the low-pressure cylinder at zero gauge-pressure, is compressed along the adiabatic curve BE until at E it attains a pressure of 26.3 lb., equal to that of the inter-cooler, allowing the discharge-valves to open and the air to pass into the cooler. In the inter-cooler, the volume of a definite weight of the air is reduced from CE to CD, so that the volume entering the high-pressure cylinder is less to the extent of DE, which is the same scale as CD and AB. This means that the given weight of air represented by the volume CE at a gauge-pressure of 26.3 lb., when cooled to the same temperature at which it was originally taken into the low-pressure air-cylinder, will be reduced in volume to CD provided the pressure of 26.3 lb. remains constant.

Air taken into the high-pressure air-cylinder at 26.3

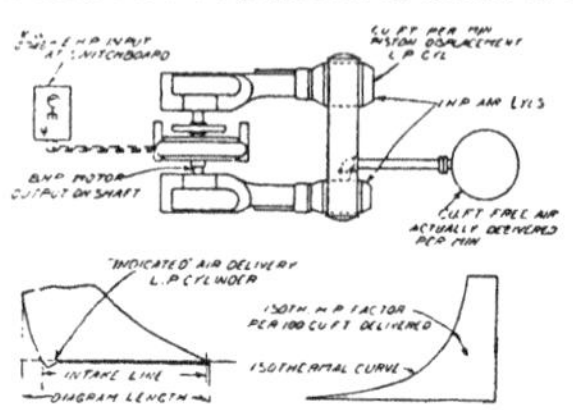

FIG. 8. ELECTRICALLY-DRIVEN COMPRESSOR

lb. is compressed along the adiabatic curve DG. At G the high-pressure discharge valves open and the air is discharged into the receiver at the desired gauge-pressure of 100 lb. The shaded portion represents the power saving effected by the inter-cooler.

The saving due to the reduction in temperature be-

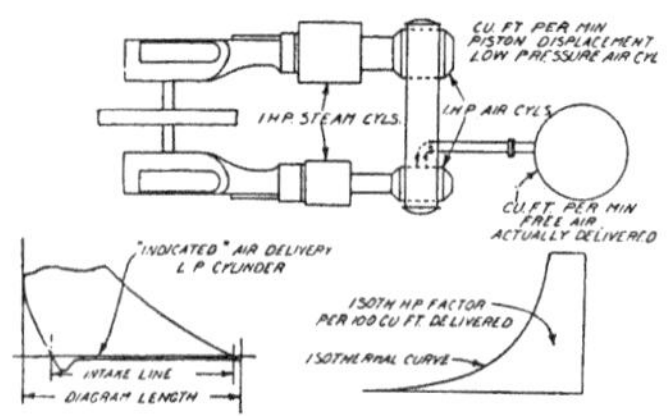

FIG. 9. STEAM-DRIVEN COMPRESSOR

tween stages is not the only advantage of stage compression. The maximum temperature in each cylinder is reduced to a point where the heat can be more thoroughly drawn off by the water-jackets surrounding the cylinder walls; also, the lower temperature in the cylinder is an insurance of good lubrication of piston and valves.

As already indicated, the theoretical function of the inter-cooler in stage compression is to reduce the temperature of the air after it leaves the low-pressure cylinder to the same point at which it was first taken into that cylinder, before it enters the next stage cylinder. Under practical working conditions, however, it will be found that the majority of coolers fail to accomplish this result, and a reduction to within 5 to 10° of the original temperature is considered a good accomplishment.

The inter-cooler consists of a shell containing a nest of tubes arranged in a series of groups through which water flows successively, entering the bottom row and finding an outlet through the top row. Surrounding the water-tubes is a series of baffle-plates, which direct the flow of the air so as to split it up into thin films and ensure intimate contact with the cold water-tube surfaces. By reducing the spacing of these baffles as the high-pressure cylinder is approached, the most efficient velocity of air in transit is attained. When the air comes in contact with the cold-tube surfaces, condensation of the moisture occurs, and it drips and flows down into the bottom of the

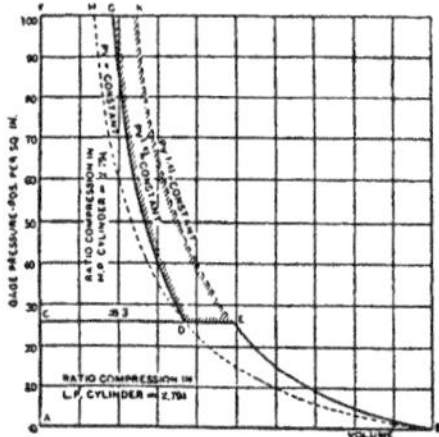

FIG. 10. COMBINED DIAGRAM

shell. In order to drain this condensed water the inter-cooler is usually placed at an incline, so that the water will flow into the pocket surrounding the water separator where a drain-cock is provided for the occasional removal of the water. Temperature changes in the inter-cooler cause the tubes to expand and contract, and in order to provide for this it is customary for the best of tubes to be fixed at one end only, while the other end, including the water-box, is left free to move with the tube-plate.

As for any other piece of machinery, the load-factor of an air-compressor is the average amount of work actually done, divided by the maximum capacity for work. The result represents the commercial efficiency of the machine, or in other words, the overall cost of production.

It is usual to install an air-compressor to take care of the maximum demand and depend upon some automatic means of regulation or unloading to vary the output of the machine to fluctuating needs. This varies the horse-power input with the load, and effects a saving in cost of operation. It is further usual where the load will vary materially, especially in electrically-driven plants of large capacity, to put in a number of small units and vary the number operating, keeping them at full load to comply with changes of load, to assist in maintaining the highest overall economy. In such cases, regulation depends upon automatic starting and stopping.

The reduction in horse-power input with power-driven air-compressors controlled by some form of part unloading device is not in direct ratio to the reduction in output. For instance, in Fig. 11 is shown a series of cards taken from 28 to 17½ by 21-in. electrically-driven two-stage air-compressor, operating at 185 r.p.m., and equipped with a four-step clearance regulator. It will be noted that at three-quarter load capacity, the horse-power input is 77.5%; at half-load, 55%; at quarter-load, 30%; and at no load 3.6%. The difference is accounted for by the fact that the mechanical efficiency drops off rapidly with a decrease in load; for example, in this particular case at full load the efficiency is 94%;

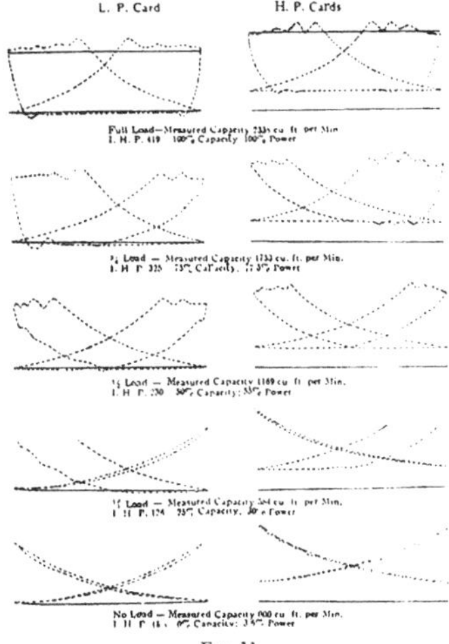

FIG. 11

three-quarter load, 92%; half-load, 87.5%; and at quarter-load, 80%.

Air-compressor control-devices are usually set by the manufacturer to meet the conditions imposed by the particular installation, and as the design of these devices varies with the different manufacturers, instructions of only a general nature can be given here. If the device fails to function properly, it is probably due to an obstruction in the way of dirt or other foreign substance, and not to a need for readjustment. It should be thoroughly cleaned and care taken in re-assembling to adhere to the adjustment existing prior to the overhaul.

THE BRADEN MILL in Chile last year produced 192,274 tons of concentrate carrying 21.20% copper, 21.94% insoluble, and 16.10% water as moisture. Seven Marcy mills were added, making sixteen. Thirty Hardinge mills were fitted with new drives and 150-hp. motors. Eight gear-driven M. S. machines of 20 cells each replaced similar belt-driven units.

Costs at the Bunker Hill & Sullivan

During 1918 the mines of this company in Idaho produced 389,027 tons of lead-silver ore. A comparison of mining and milling costs is as under:

Department	Per ton 1918	Per ton 1917	Department	Per ton 1918	Per ton 1917
Stoping	$1.828	$1.582	Screening	$0.018	$0.041
Electric tramming	0.078	0.058	Crushing, conveying	0.080	0.066
Hoisting	0.081	0.056	Jigging	0.089	0.078
Pumping	0.097	0.046	Grinding	0.073	0.071
General mine	0.802	0.500	Concentrating	0.108	0.101
			General mill	0.254	0.243

Economic Milling Data

Operation, days	326.6
Ore milled, tons	389,027.0
Assay of feed, lead, per cent	10.2234
Assay of feed, silver, ounces	3.8751
Contents of feed, lead, tons	39,771.855
Contents of feed, silver, ounces	1,507,530.84
Mill product, tons	84,169.74
Average assay of mill product, lead, per cent	39.8745
Average assay of mill product, silver, ounces	14.1605
Contents of mill product, lead, tons	33,562.858
Contents of mill product, silver, ounces	1,191,907.52
Extraction by mill product, lead, per cent	84.39
Extraction by mill product, silver, per cent	79.07
Mill Concentrates, tons	43,590.62
Average assay of mill concentrates, lead, per cent	66.5955
Assay of mill concentrates, silver, ounces	23.9463
Contents of mill Concentrates, lead, tons	29,029.416
Contents of mill concentrates, silver, ounces	1,043,837.27
Tons of middlings	40,579.12
Assay of middlings, lead, per cent	11.1713
Assay of middlings, silver, ounces	3.6487
Contents of middlings, lead, tons	4,533.442
Contents of middlings, silver, ounces	148,070.25
Value of feed	$7,301,985.18
Value of mill product	$3,949,878.07
Economic extraction, per cent	54.09

Summary

Actual run, days	326.6
Ore milled per 24 hours, tons	1,191.14
Mill product per 24 hours, tons	257.72
Silver produced per 24 hours, ounces	3,649.44
Lead produced per 24 hours, tons	102.76
Operating cost per ton milled	$0.712

The company shipped 85,165 tons of concentrates to the smelter at Kellogg at a cost of 31.1 cents per ton.

Approximate Cost and Selling Value of Year's Production

Cost

	Tons	Cost	Amount
Concentrates	84,169	$16.79	$1,413,599
Shipping	84,169	3.11	26,179
Cost on cars at Kellogg			$1,439,778
Loss by fire-assay			118,907
10% lead content			510,064
10% base price			71,515
50% advance over base price			255,859
Freight and treatment			1,084,489
Total lead charges			$2,050,434
5% silver discount			93,973
Total smelting cost			$2,144,407
Total cost			$3,584,185

Selling-Value

Production	Quantity	Average price, cents	Amount
Lead, pounds	67,125,717	7.3754	$4,951,847
Silver, ounces	1,191,907	95.8190	1,142,438
Total value			$6,094,285
Less cost			3,584,185
Profit			$2,510,100
Add refund from U. S. government—price concession adjustment			930
			$2,511,030
Kellogg cost per pound, lead, cents			2.14
Smelting cost per pound, lead, cents			3.20
Total cost per pound, lead, cents			5.34

THE DEEPEST SHAFT at Kalgoorlie, Western Australia, is at the Ivanhoe mine, which is bottomed at 3620 ft. Reserves are 1,000,209 tons of $8.16 ore.

Fire-Prevention in the Butte & Superior

In the annual report of the general manager, J. L. Bruce, the following appears relative to protection against fire in the mine:

Considerable improvements were made during 1918 in methods of supporting and protecting shaft-openings, shaft-stations, skip-pockets, permanent haulage-ways, and other underground openings. Part of these openings have been supported and protected by reinforced concrete; part by a light coating of sand-cement concrete placed directly on the rock or upon reinforcement of wire-netting attached to the timbers; and part by heavy 12 by 12-in. timbers placed face to face to form practically an air-tight timber lining, the latter in many cases being coated by gunnite cement for the purpose of giving additional fire protection and excluding the air. Each of these methods has been demonstrated to be very effective if suitably adapted to the conditions. Underground fire-protection has been greatly improved by the installation of sprinkling rings at intervals in the shafts, and by elimination of inter-communicating openings to other properties. One hundred and ten substantial fire-doors have been completed throughout the mine, and twenty more are under construction. Ten dead-end safety-stations, each isolated from the other mine-workings by fire-doors, have been constructed and equipped with connecting compressed air and water lines to supply air and water in case of emergency. Skip-pockets were completed on the 1600, 1700, 1800, and 1900-ft. levels; the latter, on account of exceptionally bad ground, being built of reinforced concrete in place of the 12 by 12-in. timber bricking used in the other pockets.

The Anaconda Smoke-Stack

On May 5 smoke was turned into the new smoke-stack at the Anaconda Reduction Works. The top of this chimney is 585 ft.* above the ground, making it the tallest in the world. The vertical flue measures 555 ft. by 60 ft. diameter at the top, and stands on a concrete base 30 ft. high. The accompanying photograph is the first to be made showing smoke issuing from the stack, and was taken 24 hours after the smoke was turned in. The old chimney is still working, as only a portion of the smoke can pass to the new stack pending the completion of the Cottrell installation. At the time the photograph was taken, there were no Cottrell treaters at work, but current has since been turned on at the bank of treaters to the left of the chimney.

1—Cottrell power-house
2—10 treaters
3—Cottrell plant
4—New chimney, 585 feet
5—10 treaters
6—Old chimney, 300 feet
7—Flue
8—Cold treater for arsenic
9—Reverberatory for smelting Cottrell dust
10—Flue
11—Hot treater for dust

THE NEW ANACONDA SMOKE-STACK, 585 FT. HIGH

*The 'M. & S. P.' of June 29, 1918, gives the height of this chimney as 525 ft. above the foundation. This original dimension was subsequently increased by 30 ft., making the chimney proper 555 ft. and its total height 585 feet.

KIRKLAND LAKE, ONTARIO

GOVERNMENT AID TO MINING.—KIRKLAND LAKE MINES.

The Minister of Mines for Ontario, the Hon. G. H. Ferguson during a trip to the mining districts last week, announced that the Government would undertake several public works in aid of the industry, as follows:

The ore-sampling plant of Campbell & Deyell at Cobalt, the owners of which announced their intention of discontinuing business, has been taken over, and its operation will be continued under the supervision of A. A. Cole, mining engineer for the Temiskaming & Northern Ontario Railway. This will be a great convenience to mining men and prospectors, who would have been seriously embarrassed by the closing of the plant.

In accordance with the wishes of the Kirkland Lake mining companies, who have expressed their preference for a good motor-road rather than a railroad, the Government has finally decided to build a tarvia macadam road from Swastika to the Lake, a distance of 7 miles, at a cost of $10,000 or $12,000 per mile. Another tarvia macadam road will be constructed from Elk Lake to Gowganda, estimated to cost $250,000.

The Government will also contribute a sum not over $30,000 for the construction of a first-class motor-road from the town of Timmins to South Porcupine, thence to the Dome mines, provided that the township of Tisdale contributes an equal amount toward the cost of the road, estimated at $60,000. A steel bridge will be built across the Mattagami river.

The Toronto Standard Stock and Mining Exchange has put in force one of the safeguards included in the blue-sky law, which failed to secure adoption during the last session of the Legislature. In order to prevent the marketing of worthless or doubtful shares, it has adopted a rule that before a company can be listed, the promoters must agree that at least 50% of the money realized by sales will be used for development work.

KIRKLAND LAKE.—Reports of two companies operating here have been issued for the past year:

The Beaver Consolidated Mines of Cobalt controls the Kirkland Lake Gold Mining Co., which owns 362 acres at Kirkland Lake. Development so far (5210 ft. to a depth of 700 ft.) has been confined to a vein that has been traced on the surface a distance of 1400 ft. Seven levels have been opened by No. 2 shaft, and the main shaft is to be sunk to connect with it at 600 and 700 ft. depth. About 8000 tons of ore has been raised to the surface for milling. The 150-ton plant consists of a crusher, 500-ton bin, Buchanan jaw-crusher, magnetic pulley, trommel, Telsmith crusher for trommel oversize, ore-bin, 8-ft. Hardinge ball-mill, Dorr classifier, tube-mill, and 15 solution tanks, pumps, presses, etc., for the counter-current decantation cyanide process. For the mine there are 4 and 10-drill Sullivan steam-driven compressors, a 12-drill electric-driven compressor, double-drum electric hoist, shop, bunk-houses, and all necessary buildings.

At the Lake Shore Mines at Kirkland Lake, R. C.

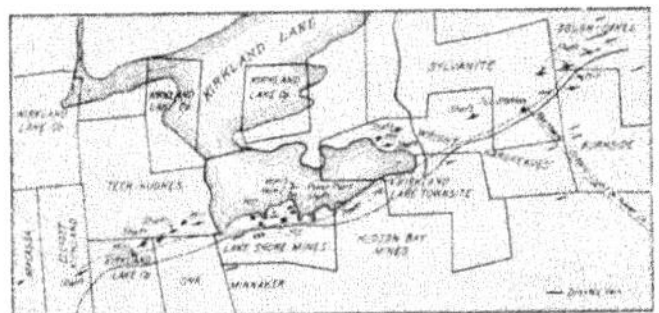

MAP OF THE KIRKLAND LAKE GOLD PROPERTIES

Coffey is mine manager. During the year ended November 30, 1918, receipts were $374,074, of which $144,978 was net profit, after allowing $90,000 for exhaustion. Current assets were $186,996, and liabilities $84,842. Payment of dividends and subscription to the Canadian Victory Loan totaled $150,000. No. 1 dividend, on August 20, and No. 2, on December 10, 1918, absorbed $100,000. A total of 2961 ft. of development was done on No. 1 and 2 veins; of the driving, 80% was in ore of milling grade. No. 1 vein was further opened on the 100, 200, 300, and 400-ft. levels, and No. 2 at 200 and 400 ft. The ore-lenses persist in size and value at the lowest level. The new mill commenced work in March 1918, and treated 14,948 tons of $24.76 ore. The operating cost of $158,176 is equal to $10.58 per ton. During April 1919, $44,782 was extracted from 1800 tons of ore. An assay-office, refinery, bunk-house, ice-house, bungalows, cottages, and other necessary buildings have been erected.

The Tough-Oakes company during April did 1016 ft. of exploration. Seven machines and 98 men were employed. A new vein of $20 gold ore was found. The mill is not in operation yet. The net working capital is now about $150,000. H. H. Johnston is in charge.

The Teck Hughes in April treated 2602 tons of $10.46 ore. D. L. Forbes is manager.

The Ontario-Kirkland has cut its vein at 300-ft. depth, there being 5 ft. of good ore with some visible gold.

HOUGHTON, MICHIGAN

LABOR AND ORE PRODUCTION.

The exodus of men from the Copper Country continues, 275 receiving settlements during the past week. Forty were laid off at Allouez, 50 at Osceola, and more at Centennial. Isle Royale continues to decrease its men, and ore shipments are only 60,000 tons per month. Ore from the Superior goes to the Tamarack mill. Centennial plans an extensive scheme of development, with further curtailment in copper output. Calumet & Hecla is erecting machinery for the additional flotation plant at the mills. Dismantling of No. 2 shaft rock-house is still under way. Pillars have been taken out to No. 7 level. There is plenty of rich ore above, but it cannot be moved as valuable surface plant is situated above. Hecla No. 12 shaft is now used exclusively for timber and supplies. It will be four months before the miners hole through for the lateral to permit transfer of Hecla ore to the Red Jacket shaft. No. 3 Tamarack shaft, now part of C. & H., is working but one shift.

During April the mines of the 'Copper Country' produced the following ore and metal:

Mine	Tons	Copper content, lb. per ton	Output, lb.
Ahmeek	64,700	...	1,490,311
Allouez	20,000	17.7	355,480
Baltic	22,000	34.0	748,000
Calumet & Hecla	218,082	20.0	4,361,645
Centennial	7,020	16.0	114,652
Champion	38,000	36.0	1,394,000
Franklin	25,135	10.0	251,350
Isle Royale	58,400	17.0	993,073
La Salle	850	20.0	17,000
Mass Consolidated	10,000	20.0	200,000
Michigan	5,240	30.0	157,000
Mohawk	49,000	24.0	1,176,000
Osceola	68,960	13.9	950,579
Quincy	100,000	17.0	1,700,000
Superior	3,700	20.0	74,000
Trimountain	15,000	26.0	390,000
White Pine	11,600	17.0	197,373
Wolverine	22,800	21.6	493,860

The White Pine mine, in Ontonagon county, a subsidiary of Calumet & Hecla, has suspended operations, not through any physical condition, but because the company had run out of cash. No. 2 shaft is down 1600 ft., of which 581 ft. is vertical, 392 ft. curved, and the remainder 45° underlay. All underground openings are generally better than before.

COBALT, ONTARIO

LABOR AND DEVELOPMENTS.

The number of men employed in the mines is considerably smaller than a year ago. The reason is that the standard of efficiency is much higher, and only competent workers are retained. This step was rendered necessary owing to the great increase in operating costs last year. This is being gradually reduced by higher labor efficiency and some decline in the price of supplies.

The recently installed electric-haulage system at the Crown Reserve is working satisfactorily. It is the first to be used at Cobalt, though the system has been adopted successfully by the Hollinger and McIntyre mines at Porcupine.

At the Adanac, high-grade ore is being taken from three veins. A vein 6 to 10 in. wide, with high-grade spots, is being opened in a winze below the 310-ft. level. A 2-in. high-grade vein has been cut on the Ophir at a depth of 600 feet.

An important strike has been made on the 600-ft. level of the Beaver, consisting of a 4-in. vein, said to carry between 2000 and 3000 oz. per ton.

GOLDFIELD, NEVADA

REVIVING THE CACTUS SILVER DISTRICT, ALSO THE TULE CANYON GOLD DISTRICT.

Joseph F. Nenzel of Rochester and associates have purchased seven claims in the Cactus district, owned by M. E. Bailey of Goldfield. Cactus is 24 miles east of Goldfield and, aside from work done by Bailey, there has been little development there for many years. Bailey sank two 100-ft. shafts and one 150-ft. shaft in a vein 2000 ft. long and from 2½ to 6 ft. wide, the average width being 4½ ft. John R. Magill, superintendent for a company organized to develop the claims, the Cactus Nevada Silver Mines Co., says that assays obtained on the surface show the entire outcrop to be good-grade milling ore. The average assay return is said by men interested in buying the claims to have been $25 per ton. From 90 to 95% of the value of the ore is in silver, the remainder in gold. The vein is in a contact of rhyolite and andesite, and the silver is in sulphide form. A fractured zone two miles long extends through the district, with a series of parallel veins, three of which strike almost due north through the group bought by Nenzel. All work done by Bailey is on one vein. Good assays have been obtained from another vein 600 ft. to the west, which is from 6 to 8 ft. wide. The new company has $30,000, and proposes to sink the 150-ft. shaft an additional 350 ft., and do 3000 ft. of lateral work at this depth. Since Nenzel entered the district a number of others have become interested in claims, and groups adjoining the Cactus Nevada will be opened. Buildings, machinery, and supplies are being hauled from Goldfield. The road from here to Cactus is in excellent condition, and Nye county is repairing the road from Tonopah, which is 29 miles north-west of Cactus.

The Ingalls mine in Tule canyon has been sold for $100,000 to Patsy Clark, a mining man of Seattle and Butte. The Borcherding-McDermitt-Hill lease on the entire mine and the 15-ton mill owned by the lessees have been sold to Clark for $75,000. The first payment of $25,000 has been made; the second installment is due in 60 days. According to Borcherding, who, with John Creighton of Elko county, negotiated the sale, there is 100,000 tons of $40 ore exposed in the mine, which, during the 30 years it was owned by Sheriff Ingalls of Esmeralda county, is said to have produced $200,000. The vein has been opened for a distance of 3000 ft. and to a depth of 100 ft. The average width is 6 feet.

The Goldfield-Tule Canyon Placer Mining Co. has started drift mining. This company owns 1½ miles of placer ground in the canyon, adjoining on the north the 6 miles of claims owned by a company of Goldfield men, in which A. I. D'Arcy is heavily interested.

SAN FRANCISCO, CALIFORNIA

STATISTICS OF OIL AND NATURAL GAS IN CALIFORNIA.

Compilation of the quantities of oil and gas produced throughout the State during 1918 has just been completed by the State Mining Bureau. The amounts are based on sworn statements from all producers. The total petroleum production is 99,459,177 bbl. This is an increase of 5,025,630 bbl. over 1917, and 12,395,982 bbl. more than the production of 1916. The yield for 1918 is second only to that of the year 1914, and demonstrates that the contention that regulation hinders development has no basis in fact.

The official totals are less than those published by private concerns such as the Independent Oil Producers' Agency and the Standard Oil Co. The latter, however, makes no allowance for water and other impurities in the oil when first produced and gauged. Aside from these differences, it should be noted that these private concerns have regularly supplied the public with accurate information.

There were no additions of importance during 1918, to the proved oil-lands determined by the State Mining Bureau for the assessment of 1917. The total proved acreage is 89,212, showing an increase of 1852 acres over the year 1918. The rate of assessment, levied to support the work of supervision of drilling operations so as to prevent the fields from damage by water and other causes, is based upon the quantities of oil and gas produced and the proved oil-land. The rate for the coming year amounts to $0.001076 per barrel of oil or 10,000 cu. ft. of gas produced, and $0.137 per acre of proved oil-land. The amount to be collected is $123,000, and is $6000 less than the total assessment for last year.

The figures in detail, showing comparative productions of oil and gas for 1917, are as follows:

Counties	Oil, bbl. 1918	Oil, bbl. 1917	Gas, 10-M cu. ft. 1918	Gas, 10-M cu. ft. 1917	Land acres	Wells No.
Fresno	16,068,919	16,146,707	80,300	50,180	13,319	1168
Kern	49,049,917	52,688,711	1,987,821	1,927,506	57,499	4926
Los Angeles	9,853,190	4,357,162	182,692	24,175	2,873	783
Orange	15,730,462	14,568,930	903,539	655,027	3,530	504
Ventura	1,339,342	989,720	10,484	......	1,776	374
Santa Barbara	7,334,104	5,589,223	71,313	60,157	9,363	412
San Luis Obispo	62,744	74,143	......	......	772	13
Santa Clara	20,499	18,855	......	......	80	8
Total	99,459,177	94,433,547	3,216,149	2,726,054	89,212	8188

Oil-field operations reported to the Bureau for the week ending May 10, show 17 wells ready to drill, making a total of 218 wells since the first of the year. Seven of the wells reported are to be drilled in the new Richfield field in Orange county.

TELLURIDE, COLORADO

POWER IN PLENTY AGAIN.—SNOWSLIDES A NUISANCE.—WORK RESUMED AT SEVERAL MINES.

The district is very active. The power supply is now abundant, permitting the Liberty Bell to resume operations, while the Belmont Wagner will start its mill earlier than expected. A shortage of labor still prevails, notwithstanding the high wages and the large number of miners released from the Sunnyside mines.

Snowslides were running again during the latter part of April and early in May, the result of warm weather. Such slides are known as 'wet slides', and are generally of mixed snow and mud. Such slides occurred at Antes, on the Rio Grande Southern railroad during the latter part of April, blocking all traffic for a few days. The great trouble and interference with traffic occasioned by the slides during the past winter has led to an investigation into some method of overcoming them, and through co-operation of railroad officials and mining companies of Telluride a plan is under consideration to drain the low marshy plateaus that lie at the head of the cuts, particularly at Ames, thus causing a drying out of the land. The general opinion is that were such places drained there would be no accumulation of water during the melting season, which is the principal factor in causing

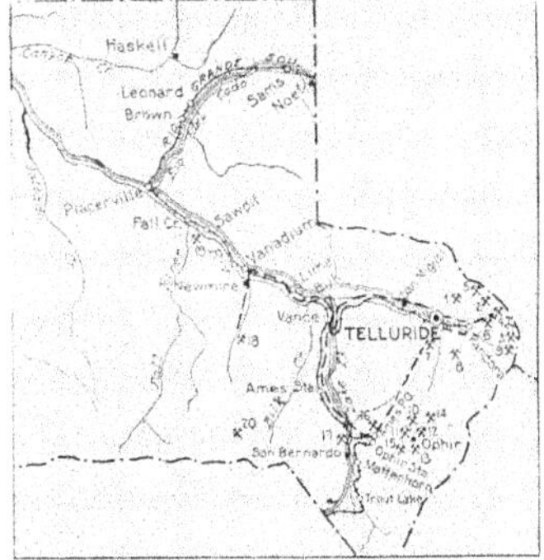

NUMBERS ON MAP REFER TO THE FOLLOWING MINES:

(1) Liberty Bell; (2) Smuggler Union; (3) Tomboy; (4) Japan; (5) Sheridan; (6) Bob Tail; (7) Contention; (8) Ballard; (9) Colorado Superior; (10) Alta; (11) Suffolk; (12) Highland Mary; (13) Favorite; (14) Carbonero; (15) Caribeau; (16) Silver Bell; (17) Butterfly; (18) Primos; (19) Primos; (20) Silver Pick.

THERE ARE 8 AERIAL TRAMS IN THE DISTRICT, WITH A TOTAL LENGTH OF 11 MILES.

the mud-slides. A large wet slide occurred at Pandora Park on April 18, damaging pipe-lines leading to the Pandora mill and stopping operations for a few days. On April 20 a slide ran from the Ophir tunnel of the Tomboy, carrying out 50 ft. of tram and smashing in the terminal building, but fortunately not damaging the machinery.

The higher price of silver has resulted in re-opening of the Humboldt workings by the Smuggler Union company. The men employed at the Black Bear will be diverted to the Humboldt. The cross-cut to the Bullion tunnel is now finished after 2 years' driving. Black Bear operations will be curtailed until the mill is enlarged, which has only sufficient capacity to treat the ore from the main Smuggler properties.

PLATTEVILLE, WISCONSIN

CONDITIONS IN THE ZINC FIELDS DURING APRIL.

The general status of zinc mining, heavy rains, interruption of power service, and a hesitancy to reduce wages, all tended to make April a poor month in the Wisconsin fields. A heavy reserve of zinc concentrate, carried over from the beginning of the month, was kept down by great effort and through important shut-downs. It now totals 10,000 tons. The Kennedy mine, at Hazel Green, owned and operated by the New Jersey Zinc Co., suspended operations after 30 years of consistent production. The Block-House mine at Platteville, for several years very profitable, suspended operations. Unsold zinc oxide, manufactured from raw carbonate ore, contributed further to a discouraging position. Of four blocks of furnaces usually operating at the works of the Mineral Point Zinc Co., only two blocks were kept hot during April, and every available space contained unsold oxide officially reported to your correspondent as amounting to nearly 10,000,000 lb. Acid plants were running at about half of normal capacity, three cars of commercial sulphuric going out weekly, whereas under better conditions shipments are from six to ten cars. Local electro-static zinc-ore separating-plants did their level best to make profits.

VICTORIA, BRITISH COLUMBIA

MINERAL AREAS OF ALBERNI CANAL.—COPPER AND BLACK SANDS.

Victor Dolmage, of the Canadian Geological Survey, to whom was assigned the work of a reconnaissance survey of the mineral areas of the northern portion of Vancouver Island during the season of 1918, after having gone over the district contiguous to Quatsino sound, cruised down the west coast of the Island and for three weeks examined as many mineral districts as possible. Owing to the lateness of the season and to the fact that local guides were not always available, many of the deposits, and in some cases the best, were not examined. Some prospecting was done during the trip, and such observations on the geology of the region made as would suffice to outline plans for future work.

One of the properties visited by Mr. Dolmage was the Indian Chief, situated on Sidney inlet. This is one of the only two claims in this portion that has reached the shipping stage—the other shipper being the Monitor, near the entrance to Alberni canal. The Indian Chief claims, now owned and operated by the Tidewater Cop. per Co., have been worked at many times and by many different companies since 1897, and have produced a lot of high-grade ore. At present it is equipped with a small oil-flotation concentrating-mill, which is on the beach, connected with the mine by aerial tram. The ore, consisting of bornite with small quantities of chalcopyrite and chalcocite, occurs in a garnetized limestone, capping a hill composed of grano-diorite. The limestone, except at the top of the mountain, is metamorphosed, and signs of mineralization are plentiful. Some rich lenses of bornite have been extracted from both the north and south sides of the hill, and some smaller ore-shoots have been discovered in the main tunnel on the south side. The mill, which was completed only a little over a year ago, was operated for a few months only and at a considerable loss. This was partly due to unsatisfactory machinery, and partly to an irregular supply of ore, often too low-grade. The mill was shut-down and a shipment of picked ore was made direct to smelter. At the time of the examination, a small force of miners was carrying on development work in the main tunnel.

The Monitor group of claims is on the north shore of Alberni canal, just at its entrance. The mineralized zone extends back from the shore several thousand feet. The property was discovered in 1898, and during 1900 and 1901 steadily produced ore, which was shipped to the Tacoma smelter. From 1902 it remained virtually idle until 1916. The present owner, Leonard Frank of Alberni, bought the property some years ago at a tax sale. Since 1916 it has been leased to James Skeen of Seattle, who has done considerable work on the various exposures that have been discovered since his taking charge, and has erected a good deal of expensive equipment. The ore consists of pyrrhotite and chalcopyrite, with small quantities of magnetite and pyrite. It occurs chiefly in the altered limestone, which consists of calcite, quartz, garnet, epidote, and actinolite. Some of the ore is found in the metamorphosed volcanic rocks, which are altered to epidote, chlorite, and hematite. Like all the deposits of this type found on the west coast of Vancouver Island, the ore is very irregular and the value of the mine, therefore, difficult to estimate. A considerable tonnage of ore averaging 8% copper has been blocked out, and in the new workings there are large lenses of concentrating ore of medium grade; but it is doubtful whether sufficient ore has been exposed to warrant the installation of a concentrating plant. At the time of the examination the mine was closed on account of financial difficulties. A visit was also paid to the Wreck Bay beach placers, lying between Kennedy lake and the West Coast of the Island, and extending from Ucluelet to Tofino inlet in a flat coastal plain composed of unconsolidated sands, fine gravels, and thin beds of blue clay. The plain is 60 ft. above sea-level, and is bounded along the coast by a perpendicular wave-cut cliff at the foot of which is a beautiful beach sloping gradually out to sea. These sediments contain a small quantity of black sand and fine gold which is being continually concentrated at the base of the cliff by the action of the waves. Prospectors and campers came periodically and cleaned-up the gold by panning the black sand found at the foot of the cliff. Several attempts have been made recently to use small concentrating machines operated by hand or by gasoline engines, but the amount of sand is too small for continuous operations and is soon worked out. A number of years ago some of the local settlers organized a company and built a flume and sluice-boxes, from which were obtained several thousand dollars worth of gold, this being the first time these wave-washed concentrates had been worked.

Gold producers in the United States should procure a copy of Bulletin 144 of the U. S. Bureau of Mines, which has just been issued, and is entitled 'Report of a Joint Committee Appointed from the Bureau of Mines and the U. S. Geological Survey by the Secretary of the Interior to Study the Gold Situation'. The committee consisted of Hennen Jennings, Charles Janin, J. H. Mackenzie, F. L. Ransome, and H. D. McCaskey. Their findings have been given in the 'Press', but this 76-page report is valuable in that it is replete with graphs and tables of production, costs, and wages.

ARIZONA

Ajo.—New Cornelia produced 2,674,000 lb. of copper during April, compared with 4,318,000 lb. in January.

The Ajo-Cornelia Copper Co. has been reorganized by Ajo business-men, who are now in control of the company. The offices are to be moved from Miami. This company owns 14 claims adjoining the New Cornelia on the east. There has been some shallow development work done and a diamond-drill hole put down 800 feet.

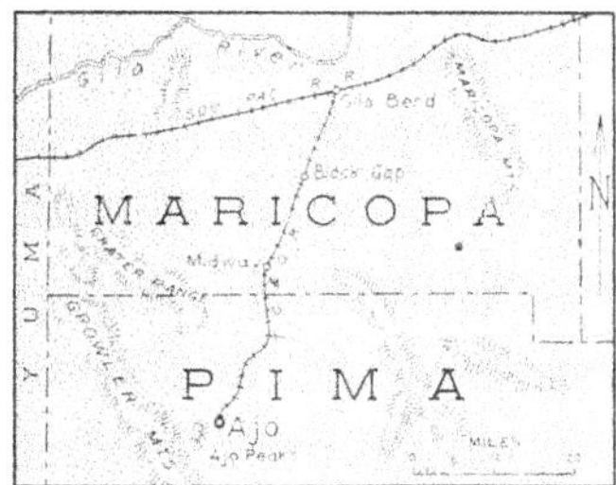

PART OF ARIZONA, SHOWING POSITION OF AJO

Chloride.—The Hackberry Consolidated Mines Co. is to increase its capital from 1,000,000 shares, $1 par, to double that amount. The money will be for further development and to bring the mill to the rated capacity of 250 tons daily. The plant is at present treating 80 tons in 10 hours, but another shift is to be put on shortly. The flotation plant is making a high recovery in charge of T. D. Walsh. William Neagle is general superintendent of this silver property.

The Rural and Buckeye gold-silver mines in the Mineral Park district have been taken over by M. B. Dudley and New York people. These mines yielded rich silver ore years ago. They were recently examined by W. W. Widdowson and G. W. Schilling. It is estimated that 22,000 tons of high-grade milling ore is available, plus 8000 tons of milling ore on the dump. The Rural shaft is 200 ft. deep, and from samples taken at the bottom there were high assays returned. The Buckeye has a 700-ft. tunnel, following the vein most of this distance, at least 500 ft. A large tonnage from this has been sent to smelters, and above this level is the milling ore. Tests are to be made on the ore, and a 100-ton mill is contemplated. The properties are favorably situated for power, roads, and rail, the last being only 5 miles away.

Jerome.—The United Verde and Extension Companies are to resume mining at about half capacity. The former is to raise its No. 6 shaft from 1650 to 430 feet.

CALIFORNIA

Downieville.—According to J. R. Hodges, in charge of the Hidden Nugget gravel claim on Kanaka creek, the company is to let a contract for driving the tunnel 300 feet.

Grass Valley.—The Empire Mines Co. is preparing to erect 20 additional stamps, to be ready early in the fall.

M. J. Brock has transferred all of his mining property within the city to the Grass Valley Boundary Mines Co., including the Oak Tree, New Idea, and Cabin Flat quartz claims, together with the mineral rights under several lots on Pleasant street. A complaint over mining ground that promises considerable interest and to be long drawn out, was filed in the Superior Court of Nevada county on May 21. The newly organized Grass Valley Boundary Mines Co. commenced an action against the Center of Grass Valley and the Golden Center of Grass Valley mining companies to quiet title to mineral rights to certain lots in the heart of Grass Valley, and claimed by defendants.

Sheridan.—The Rock Creek mine in Placer county is under option to W. B. Swears of San Francisco. The controlling interest was recently taken over by Buckeley Wells and associates. H. H. Ray is in charge of the mine, and has 15 men working.

COLORADO

Boulder.—The Colorado Pitchblende Co., according to the 'Salt Lake Tribune' of Utah, has opened an office in Salt Lake City, in charge of J. F. Brim. It is said that Utah capital is largely interested in this much-advertised company, and that the 100-ton mill will be increased to 500 tons capacity by adding a few tables.

The Colorado Pitchblende Co. has acquired a power-plant and water-rights in South St. Vrain canyon, including 160 acres of timber land.

The fiftieth anniversary of the discovery of the Caribou silver lode is to be celebrated here, and the Boulder County chapter of the Colorado Metal Mining Association has the matter in hand.

The Golden Cycle Mining & Reduction Co. of Colorado Springs has entered this district by issuing a schedule of freight and treatment rates for gold-bearing ore sent to its works.

Leadville.—The principal silver sections of this district—Iowa Gulch, St. Kevin, and Sugar Loaf—are to be exploited to a much greater degree than formerly, new work being in progress.

IDAHO

Kellogg.—The town has received $2806 from the Mine Owners' Association, being a reimbursement for money expended by the town during the floods of May 1917 and of

January 1918 in protecting property. A tailing dam of the Association at Osborne broke from the high waters of these floods and caused the river-bed to become filled with tailing and the river to spread out over its confines.

Talache.—The Armstead company on Pend Oreille lake in Bonner county has finished the 3-compartment raise from No. 3 to No. 2 tunnel, a height of 600 ft. The connection was perfect, as surveyed by Carl Wilson of Sandpoint. The raise is inclined. No injuries were reported during the work done in charge of W. A. Hackett. A mill is being designed by O. B. Hofstrand of Salt Lake City. There are 40 men employed in charge of D. G. McLachlan.

Wallace.—Wages in the Coeur d'Alene region were raised from $4.25 to $4.75 per day on May 20. During March there was a cut of $1.

Federal Mining & Smelting pays a dividend of 1%, $1 per share or $120,000, on June 14. This makes $14,884,-350 to date.

The net profits of mining companies operating in the Coeur d'Alene region in 1918 was $7,272,475, according to reports filed with the auditor of Shoshone county. First place is occupied by the Hecla with $1,984,920, second by the Hercules with $1,915,766, and third by the Bunker Hill & Sullivan with $1,379,318. The total value of the production by 14 companies was $24,093,203 and the total extraction by 13 companies was 4,447,120 tons. The only deficit is shown in the report of the Mace mine of the Federal company, which lost $5587. Several reports remain unfiled.

The Big Creek Mining Co., operating in the Evolution district, is to erect a 60-ton mill for its lead-silver ore. The property was recently examined by F. J. Davey of Wallace. G. S. Anderson is president.

MICHIGAN

Houghton.—The Franklin Mining Co. has levied an assessment of $1 per share, due on June 3. This will yield $166,000.

MISSOURI

Jefferson City.—A bill to impose a tax of 2% on the gross receipts of all zinc, lead, barite, and other mineral mines of the State failed to pass the Missouri Legislature.

MONTANA

Butte.—Davis-Daly has connected the 2500-ft. level of its Colorado mine with that of the Anaconda company's Belmont mine, resulting in proper ventilation of the lower levels of the former. Davis-Daly will soon be able to produce over 400 tons of copper ore daily. The Hibernia mine contains zinc ore high in silver, but on account of apex troubles no mining is being done there.

Butte & Superior is reported to have cut 8 ft. of rich zinc-silver ore on its 1900-ft. level.

Neihart.—The Cascade M. & M. Co. has cleared out the old Broadwater mine tunnel for 2000 ft., and exploration is under way. The old ore-shoot that yielded over 6,000,000 oz. of silver years ago is exposed for 1000 ft. in the lower tunnel-level, and it is estimated that there is 150,000 tons of 20-oz. ore above that point.

At the Moulton a winze is down to a depth of 585 ft. in the orebody. The mill is treating 135 tons daily, but additions will soon bring its capacity to 225 tons.

Philipsburg.—Lessees at the Scratch Awl property have opened a considerable quantity of rich silver ore. One car-load carried nearly 300 oz. per ton. George Nevling is largely interested.

Troy.—The Snowstorm Mines company is in need of 50 miners. A 150-men capacity dry-house is being erected, and a row of 6 to 8-men bunk-houses. The advance in price of silver has added $3 per ton to the value of the lead concentrate produced.

NEVADA

Divide.—Fifty-four operating companies have organized the Divide Mine Operators Association, with the following officers: A. H. D'Arcy, president; J. W. Hutchinson, vice-president; R. J. Davey, secretary and treasurer; E. J. Roberts, J. K. Turner, Allan Rives, L. R. Robins, H. F. Bruce, J. W. Hutchinson, and A. I. D'Arcy, executive committee.

There has been a considerable slump on the price of shares in this district, notably the Tonopah Divide, which fell from $11.50 to $7.60. Others show much lower prices.

The Tonopah Divide has its 1200-cu. ft. compressor in place and air-pipes laid to the working points. The important work in hand is opening the ore-channel on the No. 5 level and advancing the main south-east drift on No. 4. The output of ore last week was 420 tons.

The Gold Zone has finished installing electric motors in the hoist and compressor-house. Sinking to 800 from 500 ft. is to be started, and development of the encouraging exposures at 500 feet.

The south-east part of the Divide district is attracting attention. Here are the Ben Hur, Rosetta, Gold Wedge, Gold Team, Silver Divide, Belmont, and a score of others.

Eureka.—An air-compressor and machine-drills have been installed at the Silver Connor, on the west side of Prospect mountain. Re-timbering of 700 ft. of raises from the Prospect tunnel has been finished.

Goldfield.—Grandma Consolidated has issued a report covering 8 months ended February 28, 1919. Continuous development resulted in 443 ft. of new work. Shaft work cost $47.10 and cross-cuts $21.83 per foot. The shaft is 827 ft. deep. At 775 ft. the shaft entered the main Grandma-Spearhead formation, and continued in it until the shale was reached at 810 ft. Encouraging value was found to this point. A drift south on the 800-ft. level was driven 40 ft. in vein-matter of low value, so the formation was cross-cut, showing it to be 100 ft. wide. A north-westerly drift in the formation was out 155 ft. at the end of February. In the report of J. K. Turner, he considers that results are encouraging. A pump, compressor, motors, and other machinery were put in during the period.

Goodsprings.—The Yellow Pine Mining Co. is to resume work early in June, according to M. P. Kirk, the general manager.

Imlay.—Containing numerous veins assaying high in silver, gold, and lead, the Richland mining district, eight miles from Imlay, has been organized. It lies north of the Humboldt river, on the south slope of the Eugene mountains. Sampling of several claims shows assays ranging from $11 to $43 in gold and silver and 11 to 18% lead. Claims have been acquired by prominent Nevada men, including H. G. Humphreys, George B. Thatcher, and R. M. Preston of Reno, and T. J. D. Salter of Winnemucca. The Richland Mines Co. has been formed to develop several groups. J. R. Tullis of Imlay is president; J. W. Ferguson of Winnemucca is secretary; and C. T. Smith of Imlay is managing director.

Manhattan.—The White Caps company is stoping above No. 4, 5, and 6 levels, and is to sink a winze on the orebody from No. 6. With depth, the ore carries more sulphur, and roasting is now done practically without using any oil; in fact, last week the furnace worked one day without any fuel. The stack has been altered to eliminate fume and give better draft.

Mina.—The Copper Dome property, 25 miles east of Mina, has been taken under option by the Phelps Dodge Corporation, according to Louis Sirac, principal owner. The Copper Dome is three miles east of the Simon silver-lead mine, in the Cedar range, and comprises six claims. Large formations of copper-bearing ore traverse the claims, with the principal vein about 100 ft. wide. Prospecting indicates the copper is replaced at fair depth by silver-lead. A thorough test of the property is to be made with diamond-drills.

The Simon Silver Lead Mines Co. has decided on the erection of a 200-ton flotation plant at the property, 22 miles east of Mina. The orebody has been opened for a length of 300 ft. on the 300-ft. level, with the cross-cut showing the deposit to be 77 ft. wide. Between the 230 and 300-ft. levels there is estimated to be 140,000 tons of sulphide ore. The zinc content decreases with depth. The shaft is 400 ft. deep and water is flowing in at the rate of 20,000 gal. per day. The gasoline hoist, compressor, and pumping plant are to be replaced with heavy electrically-driven machinery. P. A. Simon is manager and O. E. Schiffner superintendent.

Virginia City.—Last week the Con. Virginia produced 322 tons of ore valued at over $8000, and the Ophir 296 tons worth nearly $9000. At 2050 ft. in the former, the ore assayed $46.27 per ton. The 2100 and 2150-ft. levels are also yielding rich ore. The Ophir is working at 1900 and 2000 ft. The Mexican mill treated last week 351 tons of $26.12 ore from the Con. Virginia, and 215 tons of $30.13 ore from the Ophir. Bullion worth $20,000 was sent to the San Francisco Mint.

NEW JERSEY

Franklin.—The New Jersey Zinc Co.'s income during the first quarter of 1919 was $2,855,427, compared with $5,338,796 in 1918. Federal taxes amounted to $570,000. After distributing $1,400,000 in dividends the surplus was $770,427, against $2,203,796 in that period of 1918.

SOUTH DAKOTA

Lead.—The Custer Peak Mining Co.'s new 100-ton dry concentrator at the Jungle mine is in operation. The ore averages 4% copper.

Rapid City.—The 'Pahasapa Quarterly' of the South Dakota School of Mines is a 'good roads number'. The State Legislature at Pierre, during the session ended March 9, 1919, appropriated $6,817,296 for road work. A new highway law was passed also. The Federal government has allotted $4,458,545 for highways. The mining counties of Lawrence, Pennington, and Custer will benefit thereby.

TENNESSEE

Copperhill.—The Tennessee Copper & Chemical Corporation is to raise $4,400,000 by the sale of 400,000 shares of new Tennessee stock to present holders on a share-for-share basis at $12.50 each. This money will be spent in developing a phosphate rock deposit, erecting plant, and making superphosphate, a fertilizer, using the acid made for this purpose.

Ducktown.—The School property here has recently been transferred to the Copper Pyrites Corporation of New York. Shipments of pyrite averaging 40% sulphur will probably begin about the middle of May. There is now available 50,000 tons of pyrite, besides large bodies of low-grade copper-bearing pyrrhotite, which will later be mined and treated by differential flotation for its copper content, according to R. R. Horner of the U. S. Bureau of Mines.

UTAH

The 'blue sky' law for this State went into effect on May 12. Brokers handling treasury or promotion stock after May 13, 1919, will be required by the State Securities Commission to file a bond of $5000 and secure a license from the Commission. Companies whose stock is listed on the Salt Lake Stock and Mining Exchange, and whose directors or agents are disposing of treasury stock through members of the Exchange, or any of whose directors or agents are disposing of promotion stocks through members of the Exchange, are required by the State Securities Commission to take out a license as an investment company.

PERSONAL

Note. The Editor invites members of the profession to send particulars of their work and appointments. The information is interesting to our readers.

John M. Boutwell is at Lima, Peru.

Arthur L. Pearse, of London, is at the Palace hotel.

G. R. Allen left San Francisco for the Orient on the 'Korea' on May 21.

Frank W. Oldfield, manager of the Cinco Minas, Jalisco, Mexico, is in New York.

Frederic R. Weekes has moved his office from 42 Broadway to 233 Broadway, New York.

Tomizo Sasabe, of the Mitsubishi Mining Co., is visiting the gold mines of Grass Valley, California.

George J. Bancroft, of Denver, is opening up the War Eagle copper mine, near Warren, in Idaho county.

Bailey Willis read a paper on the 'Structure of the Coast Ranges' before the Le Conte Club, in San Francisco, on May 23.

J. L. Rosenshine has succeeded H. A. Barker as manager for the Sociedad Explotadora de Caylloma Consolidada, at Arequipa, Peru.

Edwin S. Church, of the Wellman-Seaver-Morgan Co., delivered the commencement address to the Colorado School of Mines on May 23.

A. W. Stickney sailed for Siberia on the 'Empress of Russia', which left Vancouver on May 29. His address is care British Trade Commissioner at Vladivostok.

J. J. Shaw, for the past three years manager for the syndicate Mining Co. at Aroroy, has returned from the Philippine Islands and is registered at the Stewart hotel.

H. Foster Bain, who has been serving as Assistant Director of the U. S. Bureau of Mines, has resigned to resume exploration in the Far East. He sails for China from Seattle on June 12.

Thomas S. Chalmers, Major in the U. S. Engineers, has returned from France after being 21 months in the Army. He has returned to business as president of Chalmers & Williams, at Chicago.

William Neill, manager for the Cassel Cyanide Co., of Glasgow, Scotland, is touring North American mining districts. He was recently at Cobalt, Ontario. He has visited several Mexican mining districts.

William Frazier, superintendent for the Davis-Daly Copper Co. since 1907, and much respected at Butte, Montana, died on May 17, aged 44. He went to Butte in 1893, being connected with the late F. A. Heinze.

T. M. Owen, mill-superintendent for the Federal Mining & Smelting Co. at Wallace, Idaho, has gone to Australia to investigate the status of flotation in that country. He came from Broken Hill to the United States six years ago.

James Johnston, for many years mill-manager for the Nipissing Mining Co. at Cobalt, has resigned, and is on his way to England, where he will engage in consulting work with Charles Butters, with offices at 120 Bishopgate, London.

Victor C. Alderson, president of the State School of Mines at Golden, Colorado, with Harry J. Wolf, I. A. Palmer, F. M. Van Tuyl, and Samuel Z. Krumm, professor in that institution, are making an examination of the Cripple Creek district, including mining, metallurgical, and economic problems. The report will be available in a few months.

In order that engineers and mechanics trained by the State shall, upon discharge from the Army, receive the positions for which they are fit, the University of California Alumni Association has established a Bureau of Occupations. The secretary is Homer Havermale, and his address is 201 California Hall, Berkeley.

THE METAL MARKET

METAL PRICES

San Francisco, May 27

Aluminum-dust, cents per pound	50—60
Antimony, cents per pound	8
Copper, electrolytic, cents per pound	16.50
Lead, pig, cents per pound	5½—6½
Platinum, pure, per ounce	$105
Platinum, 10% iridium, per ounce	$115
Quicksilver, per flask of 75 lb	$92
Spelter, cents per pound	7½
Zinc-dust, cents per pound	10—12

EASTERN METAL MARKET

(By wire from New York)

May 27.—Copper is quiet and easy. Lead is inactive but firm. Spelter is sluggish though steady.

SILVER

Below are given official or ticker quotations, in cents per ounce of silver 999 fine. From April 23, 1918, the United States government paid $1 per ounce for all silver purchased by it, fixing a maximum of $1.01½ on August 15, 1918, and will continue to pay $1 until the quantity specified under the Act is purchased, probably extending over several years. On May, 5, 1919, all restrictions on the metal were removed, resulting in fluctuations. During the restricted period, the British government fixed the maximum price five times, the last being on March 25, 1919, on account of the low rate of sterling exchange, but removed all restrictions on May 10. The equivalent of dollar silver (1000 fine) in British currency is 46.65 pence per ounce (925 fine), calculated at the normal rate of exchange.

Date		New York cents	London pence	Average week ending		Cents	Pence
May	21	108.75	52.87	Apr.	15	101.12	48.85
〃	22	106.00	....	〃	22	101.12	48.94
〃	23	105.12	52.60	〃	29	101.12	48.78
〃	24	106.50	52.50	May	6	101.14	48.71
〃	25 Sunday			〃	13	109.33	52.98
〃	26	105.75	51.37	〃	20	110.33	53.56
〃	27	106.50	51.62	〃	27	106.44	52.17

Monthly averages

	1917	1918	1919		1917	1918	1919
Jan.	75.14	88.72	101.12	July	78.92	99.62	....
Feb.	77.54	85.79	101.12	Aug.	85.40	100.31	....
Mch.	74.13	88.11	101.12	Sept.	100.73	101.12	....
Apr.	72.51	95.35	101.12	Oct.	87.38	101.12	....
May	74.61	99.50	....	Nov.	85.97	101.12	....
June	76.44	99.50	....	Dec.	85.97	101.12	....

Silver production of the Nipissing mine at Cobalt last year was 4,117,389 oz., making 52,945,197 oz. since 1904. The cost in 1918 was 39.02 cents per ounce.

The process that has heretofore been used in the treatment of the high-grade ore, which gave satisfactory results for seven years, is an amalgamation process, using a large quantity of mercury. The price of this before the War was $33 to $39 per flask, but demand for war raised the price to $130. This so increased the cost of the process that it was decided to discontinue amalgamation and rely on cyaniding alone, after giving the ore a preliminary treatment with bleaching powder in the tube-mill. The necessary apparatus for this process was installed in the low-grade mill at a small cost and in August the old high-grade mill was shut-down. The new process is working smoothly and will be used as long as it shows a saving over amalgamation. The two plants treated during the year 430 tons of custom ore and bullion containing 1,668,350 oz., 938 tons of Nipissing ore assaying 1713 oz. per ton, and 513 tons of concentrate with an assay-value of 1609 oz. per ton, making a total of 1926 tons containing 4,178,510 oz. Of this, the old high-grade mill treated 1102 tons, containing 2,733,497 oz and the new plant 824 tons, containing 1,445,013 oz. The refinery also handled precipitate from the low-grade mill containing 816,737 oz. The bullion shipped averaged 998 fine, and amounted to 190 tons containing 5,632,881 oz. Residue shipments were 2157 tons, assaying 9.03% cobalt. The demand for this material is good, at much higher prices than ever received before. The present price of cobalt is $2.50 to $3.50 per pound.

COPPER

Prices of electrolytic in New York, in cents per pound.

Date			Average week ending		
May	21	16.50	Apr	15	15.33
〃	22	16.50	〃	22	15.18
〃	23	16.50	〃	29	15.18
〃	24	16.50	May	6	15.25
〃	25 Sunday		〃	13	15.37
〃	26	16.50	〃	20	16.24
〃	27	16.37	〃	27	16.16

Monthly averages

	1917	1918	1919		1917	1918	1919
Jan.	29.53	23.50	20.43	July	29.67	26.00	....
Feb.	34.57	23.50	17.34	Aug.	27.42	26.00	....
Mch.	36.00	23.50	15.05	Sept.	25.11	26.00	....
Apr.	33.16	23.50	15.23	Oct.	23.50	26.00	....
May	31.92	23.50	....	Nov.	23.50	26.00	....
June	32.57	23.50	....	Dec.	23.50	26.00	....

Cerro de Pasco, operating in Peru, during 1918, realized $22,807,807 from the sale of copper, gold, and silver. Mining, smelting, refining, and administration cost $9,659,536. Dividends totaled $4,393,353. Current assets total $16,818,731; and liabilities $3,608,439. A new smelter is to be erected near Oroya.

Chile Copper Co. in the last quarter of 1918 produced 29,305,514 lb. from 996,695 tons of 1.64% ore. The recovery by leaching was 84.3%. The operating profit was $817,590.

LEAD

Lead is quoted in cents per pound, New York delivery.

Date			Average week ending		
May	21	5.25	Apr.	15	5.07
〃	22	5.30	〃	22	4.93
〃	23	5.30	〃	29	4.95
〃	24	5.25	May	6	4.87
〃	25 Sunday		〃	13	4.85
〃	26	5.25	〃	20	5.05
〃	27	5.25	〃	27	5.27

Monthly averages

	1917	1918	1919		1917	1918	1919
Jan.	7.64	6.85	5.60	July	10.93	8.03	....
Feb.	9.10	7.07	5.13	Aug.	10.75	8.05	....
Mch.	10.07	7.26	5.24	Sept.	9.07	8.05	....
Apr.	9.38	6.99	5.05	Oct.	6.97	8.05	....
May	10.29	6.88	....	Nov.	6.38	8.05	....
June	11.74	7.58	....	Dec.	6.49	6.90	....

Lead ore at Joplin last week was $54 per ton, basis 80% metal, a drop of $3. Production of the Tri-State region was 932 tons.

ZINC

Zinc is quoted as spelter, standard Western brands, New York delivery, in cents per pound:

Date			Average week ending		
May	21	6.55	Apr.	15	6.57
〃	22	6.60	〃	22	6.41
〃	23	6.60	〃	29	6.39
〃	24	6.60	May	6	6.32
〃	25 Sunday		〃	13	6.31
〃	26	6.60	〃	20	6.46
〃	27	6.60	〃	27	6.59

Monthly averages

	1917	1918	1919		1917	1918	1919
Jan.	9.75	7.78	7.44	July	8.98	8.72	....
Feb.	10.45	7.97	6.71	Aug.	8.58	8.87	....
Mch.	10.78	7.67	6.53	Sept.	8.33	9.58	....
Apr.	10.20	7.04	6.49	Oct.	8.32	9.11	....
May	9.41	7.29	....	Nov.	7.76	8.75	....
June	9.63	7.92	....	Dec.	7.84	8.49	....

Zinc ore at Joplin last week averaged $35 per ton, basis 60% metal. On the 16th there was an advance of $1 per ton. The output of the Tri-State region was 8807 tons of blende.

QUICKSILVER

The primary market for quicksilver is San Francisco, California being the largest producer. The price is fixed in the open market, according to quantity. Prices, in dollars per flask of 75 pounds:

Date					
Apr.	29	75.00	May	13	80.00
May	6	75.00	〃	20	82.00
			〃	27	92.00

Monthly averages

	1917	1918	1919		1917	1918	1919
Jan.	81.00	128.06	103.75	July	102.00	120.00	....
Feb.	126.25	118.00	90.00	Aug.	115.00	120.00	....
Mch.	113.75	112.00	72.80	Sept.	112.00	120.00	....
Apr.	114.50	115.00	73.12	Oct.	102.00	120.00	....
May	104.00	110.00	....	Nov.	102.50	120.00	....
June	85.50	112.00	....	Dec.	117.42	115.00	....

TIN

Prices in New York, in cents per pound. The monthly averages in 1918 are nominal. On December 3 the War Industries Board fixed the price to consumers and jobbers at 72½c. f.o.b. Chicago and Eastern points, and 71¼c. on the Pacific Coast. This will continue until the U. S. Steel Products Co.'s stock is consumed.

Monthly averages

	1917	1918	1919		1917	1918	1919
Jan.	44.10	85.13	71.50	July	62.60	93.00	....
Feb.	51.47	85.00	72.44	Aug.	62.53	91.33	....
Mch.	54.27	85.00	72.50	Sept.	61.54	80.40	....
Apr.	55.63	88.53	72.50	Oct.	62.24	78.82	....
May	63.21	100.01	....	Nov.	74.18	73.67	....
June	61.93	91.00	....	Dec.	85.00	71.52	....

There is almost no inquiry or business in manganese-iron alloys and prices are nominally unchanged at $150 per ton, delivered, for standard ferro, and $33 to $35 per ton, furnace, for spiegel.

Eastern Metal Market

New York, May 21.

All the markets carry a better and stronger tone, and prices are generally higher.

Antimony is stronger.

Copper buying has been extensive and prices have advanced.

Lead prices have been advanced and buying has been heavy.

Tin purchases for shipment from the East, when restrictions are removed, is the feature.

Zinc is quiet but firm and steady with prices higher, largely in sympathy with other metals.

ANTIMONY

The market is stronger, with Asiatic grades in wholesale lots for early delivery quoted at 7.75 to 7.87½c., New York, duty paid.

ALUMINUM

There is no change and No. 1 virgin metal, 98 to 99% pure, is quoted at 31 to 33c. per lb. in wholesale lots for early delivery.

COPPER

Buying has been active and expansive almost daily for the last six days, but the amount sold is conjecture. Some say that for May, sales will exceed 100,000,000 lb. As a result of these conditions prices have advanced, also almost daily, until yesterday electrolytic copper was quoted and sold at 16.50c., New York, for May-June delivery with some producers asking 16.62½c. For July, 16.75c. is asked and obtained, but as a rule there is much disinclination to sell beyond this delivery. Lake copper for May-June is held at 16.75 to 17c., with demand good. The entire market is strong and in firm hands. Little export demand has yet appeared, but what business has been done has gone at about ¼c. per lb. higher than prevailing domestic prices. Production has been curtailed so that generally it is regarded as not more than 50% of capacity. The position of the producers generally is getting stronger and the market assuming a sellers' aspect.

IRON AND STEEL

The long-expected buying movement looked for as soon as price stabilizing was done away with has not appeared, although a measurable volume of business has developed. The conclusion is reached, however, from a survey of the position, that heavy buying cannot be delayed long. Concessions in prices are being made, but there is no general break. The most striking cut has been in steel plates for locomotives, but this involves a foreign order. A contract for 3000 tons has been split up among four companies at 2.50c., Pittsburgh, or $3 per ton below the domestic level. The Government has made no award of the 200,000 tons of rails recently inquired for, wide variations in quotations being reported. The leading interest is said to have named $45 on Bessemer and $47 on open-hearth rails, against four independent mills which are understood to have quoted higher, one as high as $55 and $57.

LEAD

Buying in lead was so large in volume late last week that the market was characterized by some to be almost booming or similar to the booming trade of months back. During the past week the American Smelting & Refining Co. advanced its price twice. On Friday, May 16, it raised its New York quotation from 5 to 5.10c. and on Monday, May 19, it pushed it to 5.25c., New York. Most of the buying referred to took place under the latter quotation, and it is stated that there has not been as much activity since the last lift in value. The outside market kept pace with the trust price. It is even stated that 5.30c., New York, had been done yesterday by outside sellers. In the last six or seven days or since the last report a large tonnage changed hands. In the opinion of one broker the lowest price for lead for some time has probably been seen, but he does not expect a decided expansion in prices.

TIN

This is the first time in many months that the tin market could be termed fairly active. In the latter part of last week a decided interest in future shipments from the Far East appeared, which resulted in sales in good volume for shipment as soon as restrictions are removed. The prices involved were from about 52 to 53.25c. per lb., an advance of 3c. per lb. over those realized for the small transactions in the week before last. If all sellers are taken into consideration it is stated that the total turnover in the last few days involves a fair tonnage, as the buying has extended into the present week. It is stated also that more tin could have been sold if more had been offered. Considerable English tin was also involved in the total movement at prices up to 52.50c. per lb. Buying has been more general than in a long time. The domestic price continues unchanged at the fixed level of 72.50c. for the allocated metal. There is no definite news as to when restrictions are to be removed, but July 1 is still generally expected as the approximate date. The London market continues strong and advancing, possibly on conditions supposed to exist when a free market in the United States obtains. Yesterday, spot Straits was quoted at £248 per ton, an advance of £8 in the week. In April, 3481 tons of tin arrived in England, but none in the United States.

ZINC

The zinc market seems to be the only one of the non-ferrous family that is not active, and yet quotations are a little higher. This is generally explained as due to the better tone in the other markets. At any rate prime Western for early delivery, May-June, is quoted today at 6.25c., St. Louis, or 6.60c., New York, with some small sales at this price. For July, 6.35c., St. Louis, is asked. The market is characterized as quiet, but strong and firm. Production has been curtailed somewhat in recent weeks, and some large producers are not operating at over 50% of capacity. Reports of considerable export business in the last few weeks are probably exaggerated, though there is some inquiry from England and there has been some little business done with Japan.

ORES

Antimony: High-grade ore is probably obtainable at 50 to 55c. per unit, Indian ore having already been offered at these levels. There is little demand and almost no sales.

Ferro-silicon: French 10 to 12% electric ferro is offered for American consumption at $77 French ports, which means over $100 per ton delivered in America. This contrasts with $45 to $55 per ton for the American product, and reveals the high cost conditions in France.

Molybdenum: Quotations range from 65 to 75c. per lb. of MoS_2 in 90% concentrates, with but little inquiry in evidence.

Tungsten: There is little activity or news. Prices are nominally unchanged at $7 to $10 per unit in 60% concentrates for high-grade ore. There are no developments in the ferro-tungsten market; prices are maintained as high as possible because of stocks of high-cost ores.

Company Reports

Reports of the companies at Tonopah, Nevada:

JIM BUTLER TONOPAH MINING CO.

Property: mine at Tonopah, Nevada; also interest with the Tonopah Belmont in the Shawmut mine in California and Wagner mine in Colorado.

Operating Officials: Frederick Bradshaw, general superintendent; L. R. Robins, mining engineer.

Financial Statement: the period of the report is for 15 months ended December 31, 1918. The net profit was $296,525, a decrease of $187,151. Cash and call loan at September 30, 1917, amounted to $485,982, while after paying dividends, etc., the balance at the end of 1918 was $69,075.

Dividends: No. 6 and 7 absorbed $292,064, making $1,151,074 in 6 years.

Development: exploration has failed to expose new veins of importance, and ore-reserves have been so depleted that only a small tonnage remains. The West End-McNamara vein, in the company's Eureka and Sunset claims, contains considerable ore, and as it can only be worked through the West End company's openings, a lease agreement will probably be made. In the extra-lateral right litigation the matter was settled in favor of the West End.

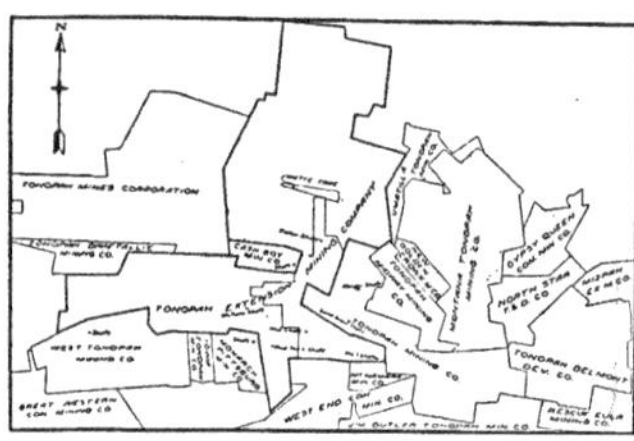

PROPERTY MAP OF TONOPAH DISTRICT

Production: a comparison with previous years follows:

Year	Tons	Silver, oz.	Gold, oz.	Cost	Profit
1918	27,688	663,141	6,821	$13.61	$296,525
1917	40,207	1,017,746	11,617	11.94	483,675
1916	46,489	1,125,268	12,370	10.80	359,387
1915	48,533	1,282,042	14,593	10.40	335,622
1914	34,722	942,257	10,500	12.18	247,502
1913	19,181	408,325	4,959	....	102,082

TONOPAH BELMONT DEVELOPMENT CO.

Property: mines and mill at Tonopah, Nevada; also control of the Shawmut mine in California, Surf Inlet in British Columbia, and Wagner in Colorado, all gold producers, in which a total of $2,317,799 has been invested. The Surf Inlet has repaid in full all money lent it.

Operating Officials: Frederick Bradshaw, general manager; L. R. Robins, mine superintendent; Herman Dauth, mining engineer; A. H. Jones, superintendent of milling; and W. H. Royston, mill superintendent.

Financial Statement: the net profit during the 10 months ended December 31, 1918, was $557,984, about half of that of 1917. Available assets total $643,097, and current liabilities $170,165. The balance of undivided profits on February 28, 1918 was $2,149,843, and after adding the 1918 profits and deducting depletion charges and dividends the surplus is $1,838,892.

Dividends: No. 35 and 36 totaled $337,505, making with the $150,000 paid on April 1, 1919, a total of $9,818,063 since 1906.

Development: there was completed a total of 9263 ft., at a cost of $1.069 per ton milled. Some small new veins were opened, and reserves were increased thereby, the total of positive ore being calculated at 82,798 tons. The total cost of mining was $5.118 per ton, a gain of 7.5 cents.

Production: the plant at Millers was idle during the period. The plant at Tonopah treated 60,361 tons of custom ore, as well as 87,089 tons of Belmont ore. The custom treatment gave a profit of $14,374. Total milling charges were $3.134 per ton, an increase of 5.3 cents. A comparison with previous years follows:

Year	Tons	Silver, oz.	Gold, oz.	Silver, oz.	Gold, oz.	Cost per oz. silver, cents
1918	87,089	15.30	0.162	1,076,944	10,974	20.67
1917-'18	130,991	15.88	0.162	1,946,757	19,953	20.02
1916-'17	145,024	....	....	2,629,465	27,831	14.92
1915-'16	164,972	19.60	0.196	2,908,564	31,112	16.23

TONOPAH EXTENSION MINING CO.

Property: mine and mill at Tonopah, Nevada.

Operating Officials: J. G. Kirchen, general manager, A. Case, general superintendent; J. L. Dynan, mine superintendent; E. M. Kirchen, mill superintendent; M. L. Davenport, purchasing agent.

Financial Statement: receipts last year (ended March 31, 1919) totaled $1,630,280, of which $515,509 was profit (more than double that in 1917), after deducting $104,366 for Federal taxes, and $44,886 for depreciation. Current assets at the end of 1918 were $2,393,421 in excess of liabilities.

Dividends: No. 23, 24, and 25 absorbed $192,407, making $1,912,399 to December 31, 1918.

Development and Mining: 3868 ft. of exploration was done at the No. 2 and 6454 ft. at the Victor shaft. Total workings measure 28.13 miles. At the former, the 1440-ft. level yielded most of the ore. Prospecting resulted in discovery of a number of good shoots, but chances for finding large orebodies are remote. At 1260 ft. a branch of the Murray vein yielded several thousand tons of unusually rich ore. At 1680 ft. in the Victor shaft, stopes on the Merger vein produced a large tonnage. The Murray vein ore-shoot is 600 ft. long, and from 3 to 30 ft. wide, of good grade. No definite calculations of reserves are possible. A new head-frame, Nordberg hoist, compressor, skips, ore-bins, and pumps are erected or are under erection at the Victor shaft.

Milling and Production: the mill treated 114,921 tons of ore, assaying 12.818 oz. of silver and 0.121 oz. of gold per ton, an increase of 1.047 oz. of the former and 0.004 oz. of the latter. Extraction was 93.05%, an increase of 2.54%, equal to 1,367,440 oz. of silver and 13,143 oz. of gold. Price for silver averaged $1.00944 per oz. The bullion realized $1,652,031, less $27,268 for freight and refining. Costs totaled $9.562 per ton, a decrease of 26.9 cents. Mining accounted for $4.804, and milling $3.447 per ton.

TONOPAH MINING CO. OF NEVADA

Property: mines at Tonopah, mill at Millers, Nevada; and control of dredging property at Breckenridge, Colorado; copper mine in Manitoba, and gold mines in Nicaragua.

Operating Officials: W. H. Blackburn, general superintendent; H. W. Stotesbury, mine superintendent; H. A. Johnson, mill superintendent.

Financial Statement: the report for 1918 shows that net earnings were $782,062. The surplus of $3,862,884 at the end of 1917 was increased to $4,199,444.

Dividends: No. 50-53 totaled $375,000.

Development: 4619 ft. of exploration from three shafts failed to disclose any new orebodies. Raises and cross-cuts from various veins opened parallel shoots near the Mizpah and Silver Top shafts. On the Mizpah Fault vein, at 500 ft. depth, a considerable quantity of ore is now being stoped.

No definite estimate of reserves is possible. Old pillars and blocks below old drifts were profitably mined.

Production: the plant at Millers treated 1499 tons of $26.73 ore, and 102,404 tons of $5.29 ore-house reject; while the Belmont company's mill treated 53,279 tons of $18.34 ore. Total costs were $5.245 per ton, a slight decrease owing to less development being done.

Nicaraguan Properties: the Eden Mining Co.'s new mill started in November. The Tonopah Nicaragua Company's property shows by drilling 1,482,088 tons of ore, averaging $0.91 gold, and 5.059% copper. A reduction plant is contemplated.

WEST END CONSOLIDATED MINING CO.

Property: mines and mill at Tonopah, Nevada; also property in Honduras, Central America; and at Searles Lake, California.

Operating Officials: J. W. Sherwin, general manager; H. D. Budelman, mine superintendent; W. D. Jenkin, mine foreman; F. C. Ninnis, mill superintendent.

Financial Statement: the revenue during 1918 totaled $2,030,897, including $1,478,488 from company and custom metals extracted, $68,017 from sundries, and approximately $316,375 from the money held in escrow during the dispute with the Jim Butler company. Expenses totaled $1,466,-949. The cash balance, after paying dividends, is $253,-907, against $47,656 at the end of 1917.

Dividends: $357,697, making a total of $1,073,092.

Development and Mining: the total of exploration was 7214 ft., costing $10.30 per foot for drifts, $9.70 for raises, $10.16 for cross-cuts, and $25.13 for winzes; while the cost per ton was $1.57, an increase of 12 cents. Work was continued aggressively in the West End section of the property, and while the orebodies cannot be measured satisfactorily, the future is very favorable. In the Ohio section, reserves are now 82,000 tons, nearly double those of a year ago, and with a gross value of over $2,000,000. Out of 2430 ft. of driving on the Ohio vein, 1410 ft. was in pay-ore, and of 225 ft. of raising, 198 ft. was in good ore. The cost of mining was $6.74 per ton, an increase of 69 cents. The direct proportion of this was $5.84 per ton.

Production: company ore treated amounted to 50,195 tons, assaying $19.73 per ton. The metal content was 835,-252 oz. of silver-gold bullion, of which 91.97% was extracted at a cost of $3.33 per ton, a rise of 6 cents. Custom ore treated was 16,323 tons.

MODDERFONTEIN B. GOLD MINES, LIMITED

Property: mine and mill in the Far East Rand, Transvaal.

Operating Officials: C. L. Butlin, manager.

Financial Statement: revenue from gold last year was £1,254,053 ($6,081,000), of which £658,587 ($3,196,000) was profit. Taxes amounted to £117,130 ($567,000). After paying dividends, the balance forward to 1919 was £198,-645 ($960,000).

Dividends: No. 12 of 42½% and No. 13 of 40% absorbed £577,500 ($2,798,000), making £3,027,500 ($14,683,000) to date.

Development and Mining: exploration amounted to 9894 ft. Of this footage, 62% was in pay-ore. The re-measured ore-reserves total 3,378,000 tons, averaging 9.2 dwt. across 62 in. This is a decrease of 150,000 tons. Of the total, 45% averages 12.7 dwt. per ton. To serve the deep sections of the mine a 20-ft. circular shaft is to be sunk.

Milling and Production: after sorting out 15% of the ore mined as waste, the 100 stamps and 7 tube-mills crushed 605,500 tons of ore. The stamp-duty was 17.2 tons per day. The ore contained 10.269 dwt. per ton. By amalgamation and cyanidation there was extracted 96.9%, equal to 301,-278 oz. of fine gold.

Costs totaled 19 8 ($4.72) per ton, an increase of 3d (6 cents).

The mine is now equal to a monthly output of 60,000 tons of ore. A new 65-drill air-compressor is to be erected.

CALUMET & ARIZONA MINING CO.

Property: mines at Bisbee and smelter at Douglas, Arizona.

Operating Officials: J. C. Greenway, general manager, W. B. Gohring, superintendent of mines; H. A. Clark, superintendent of reduction works; W. E. McKee, superintendent of machinery.

Financial Statement: the total revenue during 1918 was $15,528,530. Operations and taxes ($1,398,391) amounted to $9,905,176. Current assets total $16,443,220 and liabilities $2,086,881.

Dividends: No. 57-60 absorbed $5,140,062, making $41,-132,824 to date.

Development: including 16,281 ft. of diamond drilling, there was 99,355 ft. of work accomplished at the Briggs, Cole, Junction, and Oliver shafts. The Junction pumps lifted 1,664,518,511 gal. of water, a decrease of 100,000,060 gal. This shaft used 2,476,175,380 ft. of air, and the Oliver 952,189,000 ft. Reserves were increased somewhat. The output was 676,888 tons of dry ore. High sulphur-low copper ore sold to various smelters in Arizona totaled 98,948 tons, manganese ore to steel-makers 5793 tons, lead-zinc ore to paint-makers 254 tons, and 79 tons of lead ore to the smelter at El Paso.

At the Gadsen copper mine at Jerome, the shaft was sunk to 1230 ft. A cross-cut is now out 1100 ft. to find the Jerome fault, estimated to be from 1300 to 1600 ft. west on the 1200-ft. level.

Production: the reduction works handled the following:

	Roasters	Reverberatories	Blast-furnaces	Converters
Number working	18.4	4	2	....
Days		20.4, 337.6, 353.3, 344.7	335.3, 40.0	.....
Charge, tons ...	556,091	602,272	313,065	52,015
Blister copper output, tons		......	......	42,088

The roasters reduced the sulphur contents from 27.7 to 9.7%. The acid plant made 67,110 tons of 60 sulphuric, an increase of 16,885 tons.

OLD DOMINION COMPANY

Property: mines, mill and smelter at Globe, Arizona.

Financial Statement: sales of gold, silver, and copper in 1918 realized $5,731,082. Operations, plus $216,080 for taxes, totaled $5,125,125. Current assets are $3,307,336, and liabilities $2,677,768. With the balance of $4,974,324 from 1917, there was available $5,276,086. After paying dividends, the balance for 1919 was $4,087,802.

Dividends: No. 41-44 totaled $1,188,284, making $14,-405,260 since 1905.

Development: this covered 22,163 ft., a decrease of 2158 ft. On account of water, the A shaft was only sunk 5 ft., but when the electric centrifugal sinking-pump is put in sinking will be continued. Exploration on the No. 17 and 18 levels east was particularly encouraging, especially as the copper content persists. Results in the smelting ore-zone between No. 18 and 16 west have been disappointing for two years. The east side orebody produced most of the concentrating ore in 1918. The mine-pumps lifted an average of 3,730,000 gal. of water per 24 hours.

Production: ore of all classes totaled 230,451 tons, averaging 4.52% copper, compared with 199,888 tons and 4.97% in 1917. The metal output was 33,378,158 lb. of copper, 184,982 oz. of silver, and 5071 oz. of gold. Of the copper, 21,896,780 lb. was sold at 25.01 cents per pound.

Book Reviews

Chemical Calculations. By R. H. Ashley. Second edition, revised. Pp. 276, ill., index. D. Van Nostrand Co., New York, 1918. For sale by 'Mining and Scientific Press'. Price, $2.

We had just been reading a paper by P. A. Dean on chemical equations in the April Journal of Engineering of the University of Colorado when this new book came to hand. A beginner in chemistry may experience difficulty in writing chemical equations, even may advanced students, and the same might be said about chemical calculations. In order to solve any chemical equation or calculation, the formula for the reacting substances and the products formed must be known, the valence of the reacting substances, the direction and amount of the change of valence, and the atomic weights of the elements. The decomposition of mercuric oxide is a simple example. For instance, it is required to find the number of grams of oxygen that will be liberated by the decomposition of 1.7000 grams of mercuric oxide. The equation and calculation is:

$$2HgO = 2Hg + O_2$$
$$2(216.6) = 2(200.0) + 2(1.6)$$

and $\frac{2(16)}{2(216.6)} \times 1.7000 = 0.1256$ gram of O yielded by 1.7000 grams of HgO. In chemical calculations, ratios, approximate numbers, and interpolation should be thoroughly understood. Chapters 4 to 10 inclusive, give explanations, laws, and problems worked out on heat, specific gravity, gas, atomic weights, and gravimetric and volumetric analyses. There are 515 problems in all, with answers. An example in gas calculations is, calculate the composition of a gaseous mixture of carbon monoxide and acetylene, the volume of the mixture taken being 20 cc., the volume of oxygen added 50 cc., the volume of explosion 52 cc., and volume of oxygen left after KOH treatment 24 cc. The answer is 8 cc. of C_2H_2 and 12 cc. of CO. In acid calculations this one is typical: calculate the weight of 50° Baumé sulphuric acid equivalent to a shipment of 2160.61 cu. ft., measured at 120°F., a sample of which showed 56.14°B. at 80°F. The answer is 252,410 lb. We feel sure that metallurgical chemists will find this work of great aid in their calculations.

Quantitative Analysis. By E. G. Mahin. Second edition. Pp. 605, ill., index. McGraw-Hill Book Co., New York, 1919. For sale by 'Mining and Scientific Press'. Price, $3.50.

There were four impressions of the first edition of this work, and judging by the present one, which is 100 pages larger than the first, and has been revised, we would say that it fulfills its object in being a reference for students and semi-advanced chemists. In the book before us, improvements consist of bringing standard methods of analyses of industrial materials up to date, addition of analyses of certain alloy-steels, and soft-hearing metals, the re-writing of the discussion on metallography and treatment of steel, and a new system of chapter heading, particularly under the general caption of industrial products and raw materials. One of the outstanding features of Mahin are the excellent instructions on general principles and use of laboratory apparatus, whenever a new subject is started and the method is described. This is especially so in 72 pages, the chapter on gravimetric analysis. In the chapter on experimental gravimetric analysis will be found the determination of the chloride, sulphate, and phosphate radicals, and the chlorides, bromides and iodides of silver. In electro-analysis, it must be remembered that the principal reasons for failure to attain accuracy are (1) deposition may not occur upon passage of a current; (2) the deposit may be contaminated by other products of electrolysis; and (3) the deposit may not have the proper physical character so that it will not adhere to the electrode but crumbles off during electrolysis or washing. These factors are discussed. The short chapters on indicators and standardization of solutions are instructive in their conciseness; and that on oxidation and reduction fully explains these reactions. The 280 pages covering the analysis of industrial products and raw materials are divided into chapters dealing with rock analysis, fuels, oils, water, steels and alloys, and agricultural materials. Photo-micrographs show the structure of various steels. Students desiring a knowledge of the fundamentals of the fire-assay will find 20 pages on the subject.

Chemical Analyses of Rocks. By H. S. Washington. Third edition, revised and enlarged. Pp. 271, index. John Wiley & Sons, New York, 1919. For sale by 'Mining and Scientific Press'. Price, $2.50.

Briefly, this volume contains a selection of methods for the chemical analysis of silicate rocks, especially those of igneous origin. In the study of rocks and ore formations, petrological and chemical analysis are most essential; many mines have been unjustly condemned on account of their being no such investigation made. The main constituents of most rocks are SiO_2, Al_2O_3, Fe_2O_3, FeO, MgO, CaO, Na_2O, K_2O, and H_2O; these must be determined in every rock analysis. Of the minor constituents, TiO_2 and P_2O_5 are the most important, and should be determined also, otherwise they will affect the final results. When in the field, a sample of rock must be representative of the mass being examined, just as in sampling ore. After discussing the apparatus and reagents used in the laboratory, and the mode of operation, the methods are then described, including solution, separation, precipitation, ignition, and probable errors. The last four pages give detailed calculations in the analyses of a gray porphyritic basaltic lava from Mt. Etna, wherefor the reason for a peculiar looking frontispiece from an old woodcut. We think that the author could have easily selected some other rock masses for analysis and a good photograph to accompany it. Otherwise, the work is instructive, and the sequence of investigation continuous from sampling to reporting the result.

Broaches and Broaching. By Ethan Viall. Pp. 216, ill., index. McGraw-Hill Book Co., Inc., New York. For sale by 'Mining and Scientific Press'. Price, $2.

The author defines broaching as "the working out of holes or slots, or the machining of surfaces, by tools having a number of successive cutting teeth of increasing size, no matter whether these teeth are arranged singly or in multiple." The book discusses the special field and advantages of broaching work. The chapter-headings are: Broaching and Broaching Tools; Standard Types of Broaching Machines; Examples of Pull-Broaching Work and Practice; Examples of Push-Broaching Work and Practice; The Design of Pull-Broaches; The Design of Push-Broaches; Making Broaches. The book is well-illustrated with photographs of machines and of work done on them. It will be of value to machinists generally.

Analysis of Statistically Indeterminate Structures by the Slope Deflection Method. By W. M. Wisbon, F. E. Richart, and Camillo Weiss. Bulletin 108 of the Engineering Experiment Station, University of Illinois, Urbana, 1918. Pp. 214, illustrated.

The investigation was made to obtain a convenient method of analyzing the moments, stresses, and deflections for a number of typical structures. The explanations are in sufficient detail to enable a designing engineer to use them in his problems.

INFORMATION FURNISHED BY MANUFACTURERS

WATER-WHEELS FOR BRAKING AND INITIAL POWER

A unique use of water-wheels has been made in Plumas county, California, by the Spanish Peak Lumber Co. The equipment is on the company's timber lands, where water-power is available but access to the railroads is impossible. Two Pelton water-motors, set in opposition, have been adapted to an aerial tram control to furnish primary power and braking effort for the cableway.

The tram is essentially a gravity system, but due to the difference in elevation of loading and discharge-stations,

Type of Aerial Tram and Characteristic Country

power is required for braking when loaded carriages are hung on the cable. Power is also required for driving the haulage cable when unloaded. The tram has a total length of 27,200 ft., crossing a ridge of 4900-ft. elevation between the loading-station at the sawmill and the discharge-station at the railroad. The latter station is 890 ft. lower than the former, and a braking effort to absorb a maximum excess of 12 hp. is necessary when the cable is fully loaded. The system requires a torque of 20 hp. when the cable is not loaded.

Two 24-in. Pelton wheels, rigidly connected in opposition through a solid coupling, make up the driving and braking unit. They are controlled by a needle nozzle, actuated by oil governors, in regulating the cable speed, the regulation being to hold speed constant. The governors are so adjusted that when the cable slows below normal speed, due to a light load, water is admitted to the driving motor, and power is generated to maintain the normal speed. When the cable is loaded, speed tends to increase, and water is shut off the driving motors and admitted to the braking motor. The impact of the buckets of this wheel rotating against the jet develops the requisite braking effect and the speed is held at normal.

Water for this system is taken from an old mining ditch above the mill, with an effective head of 230 ft. Several smaller wheels are driven by water from the same supply, for driving small machines in the mill. Electricity for lighting the mill and other buildings is generated by a 15-kw. alternator, belt-driven from the flywheel of the cable-control unit. Fire protection is also provided by water from the ditch.

The handling costs for the cableway have been well under the contractor's guarantee of $2.40 per M board feet, and

The Driving and Braking Water-Wheels

operation has been so successful that the companies' entire stand of 200,000,000 ft. will be moved to the railroad at lower than that figure.

NEW TYPE OF STEAM ENGINE

The distinguished position that B. V. Nordberg has attained as a designer of steam engines lends special interest to the announcement by the Nordberg Manufacturing Co. of Milwaukee, Wisconsin, of a new type of Uniflow poppet-valve engine. The Nordberg company was the first to develop Uniflow engines in this country, and the advantages of this type in maintaining high economy at underloads and overloads is well known. The new Nordberg-Todd uniflow engine is built in sizes ranging from 200 to 2000 hp. for any available steam pressure, any available superheat, any available vacuum, and any available back pressure. The assertion is made that under any of these conditions these engines will operate with lower steam consumption per horse-power, over wider variations of load, than any steam prime-mover thus far developed. Of special interest is the fact that the engine can be changed from condensing to non-condensing operation, or the reverse, while running.

The Advance Machinery & Supply Co. of Denver, which is Western representative for the De Laval Steam Turbine Co., C. H. Wheeler, Uehling Instrument Co., Republic Flow Meters Co., Ohio Blower Co., Richardson-Phenix Co., Betson

Plastic Fire Brick Co., Heiney Chimney Co., Viking Pump Co., Yarnall-Waring Co., etc., announces that S. A. Koenig, first lieutenant in the Coast Artillery, has been discharged and joined the Advance company at Denver as sales manager.

A NEW ORE-TESTING PLANT

Since Sill and Sill of Los Angeles moved their plant and office to 1011 South Figueroa street, and added a great deal of new equipment, they now have a complete ore-testing works for both large lots and preliminary tests.

For concentration there is a gyratory crusher, a set of rolls, and shaking screens, for screening products, or an Overstrom hydraulic classifier where a hydraulically classified product is desired as a feed to the 6-ft. Wildey table.

Interior View of Part of Testing Plant

For crushing there is a 4-ft. Abbe tube-mill for cyanide, amalgamation, or flotation tests. The tube discharges to a pump, which raises the pulp to the distributing cone, where it is fed to a 3-ft. K & K oil flotation machine, or to the 4-ft. Senn batea amalgamator, or to the pachuca tanks, or the electro-cyanide-chlorination tank. This makes it possible to duplicate actual working conditions. For the final treatment of the pulp, from the pachuca tanks, or electro-cyanide, or flotation, there was added recently to the above equipment a 4-ft. single-leaf 32 sq. ft. area, American filter.

COMMERCIAL PARAGRAPHS

In an 8-page leaflet, the **Western Wheeled Scraper Co.** of Aurora, Illinois, shows its road-builder's dump-car, truck, service-car, track and switches; while useful diagrams illustrate the placing of industrial track and daily capacity of any given job.

The firm of **Collins & Webb**, Los Angeles, Cal., has opened a branch office at Tonopah, Nevada. D. W. Janney is the man in charge. A stock of compressors, motors, receivers, tanks, etc., will be carried in the warehouse there for immediate delivery.

The uses of the different kinds of Oronite paints are very varied, according to the **Standard Oil Co.** of California. Wherever a protective coating is needed—on metal, wood, brick, or concrete—everywhere conditions may be severe, these paints have shown their high quality and economy.

The Norwalk Iron Works Co., South Norwalk, Connecticut, recently issued a new bulletin on Norwalk air and gas compressors. It is attractively prepared, and gives specifications and descriptions of the entire line of compressors for all purposes of mining and metallurgy.

The United Filters Corporation, 65 Broadway, New York, announces the appointment of C. B. Oliver as manager of its Chicago office in the Peoples Gas Building. He has been identified with the company for several years, and has a wide and successful experience as a filtration engineer.

The Beckman & Linden Engineering Corporation is erecting a 100-kw. electric furnace in its research laboratories at 41 Minna street, San Francisco. This furnace is to be used for making investigations in the electric smelting of all kinds of ores for clients. The firm, within the near future, is to start an investigation of a nickel-copper ore, which, it is believed, can be reduced in the electric furnace, and a metal similar to Monel metal produced. This plant is the only one of its kind west of Niagara Falls. There are a number of problems in ore treatment that could be solved by the use of the electric furnace.

The Smooth-On Manufacturing Co. of Jersey City, New Jersey, has just issued a new and revised edition of 'Smooth-On Instruction Book No. 16'. This, like its predecessors, is made up of helpful and interesting descriptions of engine and boiler-room repairs of all kinds. These are described by the men who made them in such a way that similar problems can be quickly and economically solved by other engineers. The book is well illustrated by actual photographs and drawings. Among the subjects covered are engine repairs, pump repairs, boiler and tank repairs, pipe-line, maintenance, valve repairs, wheel pit and engine bed construction, etc. A copy of the book will be mailed free on request to the company.

The E. I. Du Pont de Nemours & Co., in discussing coverings for concentration tables, state that linoleum has generally been used for this purpose, but has not been entirely satisfactory because the cyanide solution used blisters it, thus making its life short. Recently a new material has been successfully tried, especially in gold recovery. It is a cotton-base fabric having a pyroxylin coating. It is thinner and decidedly more pliable than linoleum, but is as waterproof as rubber. The Portland mill at Victor, Colorado, has operated one of its tables, covered with this material, continuously for a year without change. It showed no blistering and little deterioration otherwise. The material was designed originally to be used for automobile and furniture upholstering—it is a leather substitute, in fact. Thomas B. Crow, of the Portland mill, and Luther Lennox, assistant, invite mining and concentrator men interested in this subject to write them for any additional information desired.

The American Malleable Castings Association of 1900 Euclid building, Cleveland, Ohio, through G. P. Blackiston, director of publicity, announces that at last an authentic treatise on malleable iron has been written, published, and is issued gratuitously by this Association. Although great progress has been made in this particular industry the last few years, little or no progress has been made in keeping the public informed regarding such activities. In fact there is but one book available at present treating on malleable iron, but it is so many years out of date that it is of little value. The latest booklet—'Malleable Iron'—although but a forerunner for a comprehensive volume to be issued later by the Association, is filled with valuable data. It is divided into three parts: I—What is Malleable Iron. II—The American Malleable Castings Association. III—The Use of the Malleable Iron Casting; Can Heavy Sections of Malleable Iron be Completely Annealed?; The Skin of a Malleable-Iron Casting; Malleable-Iron Castings Resist Rust. A copy of this book will be sent to anyone mentioning this paper if they address the Association at Cleveland, Ohio.

AS we go to press we hear that the Supreme Court's decision in the flotation case is against the Butte & Superior company in that it gives Minerals Separation patent rights to the use of oil up to 1%. We expect to publish the text of the decision in our next issue. This is a severe blow to the mining industry of the United States.

IN this issue we publish a timely article on the recovery of copper from flotation concentrate by leaching. It is written by Mr. Percy R. Middleton, now at Salt Lake City, but recently arrived from Australia, where he studied the subject in a practical way by means of experimentation on a working scale, notably at Mount Lyell. We know that what he says will be found interesting by those engaged in flotation and we hope that some of our readers will describe some of their own efforts to apply leaching to the products of flotation. By such exchange of ideas we may hope to conquer this metallurgic problem, which is one of the most insistent of the present day.

WE understand that the War Minerals Relief Commission has been unable to make extensive plans for a systematic examination of claims until recently on account of the irregularity with which the claims have been presented and the fact that many of them were forwarded without the questionnaire, which had to be completed before the claim could be considered as filed. On April 30, however, the Commission authorized general examinations in California and Oregon, and on May 17 gave a similar authorization to cover the rest of the United States. A corps of engineers and auditors is already in the field, including four engineers on the Pacific Coast, three of whom were with the Bureau of Mines during the War.

OIL of good quality and in considerable quantity has been struck in England for the first time. The discovery is due to the initiative of Lord Cowdray, formerly known as an engineer by his name of Sir Weetman Pearson. He built the Tehuantepec railroad across Mexico and is now identified with big oil interests in the Tampico field. On May 27 at a depth of 3000 feet in Derbyshire a well was 'brought in', the oil rising in the bore to 400 feet. This work, which is being backed by the British government, is the direct result of geologic deductions, supplemented by experience on other oil-fields. It is a highly interesting development, largely because it represents the application of scientific reasoning to industrial enterprise.

OUR country is prospering exceedingly. During April our exports had a total value of 715 million dollars and our imports 273 millions, leaving a balance of 442 millions. It is noteworthy that the so-called balance of trade in April was equal to the net aggregate balance accumulated in the same month of the 17 years prior to 1915. The annual average of exports in the ten years from 1904 to 1913 was only 147 million dollars, the imports 119 millions, and the difference 28 millions. During the first quarter of 1919 we have sold abroad products worth $2,350,000,000, which is more than was exported in any whole year prior to the War. That is why foreign exchange is so weak and the dollar so strong.

E. S. MARTIN has made 'Life' much more than a fountain of humor during recent years; he has made it a foremost organ of opinion. His editorial writings have made 'Life' influential during the War. In a recent issue, speaking of Germany's plight, he says: "The real thing for her to lament is not the loss of colonies or ships, or the Saar coal, or Danzig, but her loss of character." By losing the War she escaped, he says, "the complete spiritual downfall that would have come with victory." As The Book says: "What shall it profit a man if he gain the whole world and lose his own soul." Germany pawned her soul with the Devil for the sake of loot and the fiend gave her a Dead Sea apple, and the taste of Sodom is bitter.

PRESIDENT WILSON struck the right note in his Memorial Day address at the American cemetery of Suresnes. Although the number of our dead in France is small as compared with those of the Allies, the number seems more than big enough to those of us whose kinsmen are counted on the roll of honor. The sacrifice they made must not be in vain. Most of them went overseas because their country called upon them to go, and having accepted the duty they were determined to perform it up to the hilt, with the confident expectation of defeating the Germans and returning home as soon as the task was done. The false heroics that have been read into their fine performance only tend to belittle it. They attended to the matter in hand without bothering about the larger aspects of the question. But whether they foresaw the purpose of their deeds or only rejoiced in the opportunity of service for their flag, it is certain that they turned a page of history and saved civilization from a supreme outrage. "It is our privilege and our high duty to consecrate ourselves afresh on a day like this to the objects for which they fought." The President's words will find an echo in our hearts. Moreover, he is right in saying that these men will have died in vain if the result is not to make impossible another such war. The millions of dead on the battlefields of Europe and the thousands, many of them women and children, on the dark floor of the sea call upon the living to see to it that there shall never again be a war like this one from which we are now emerging. Whatever their politics or creed, the plain people of this country, as of every other civilized country, welcome any sincere effort to establish peace, and therefore will be willing to give a fair trial to the Covenant of the League of Nations.

HERBERT CASSON, in the 'Boston News Bureau,' tells us that the British are sick of bureaucracy, "the gigantic system of Government departments that was made necessary by the War; and which is now digging itself in and trying to become permanent." The "and which" is regrettable, but the interest of the statement survives. He adds: "The business man, like the soldier, has been carrying a heavy kit, and now he wants to throw it off," but officialdom is unwilling to free him from the burden. We in this country may not have been as tightly bound with red tape, but it must be confessed that to us also the halo-batted control of our amateurs in Washington is becoming irksome. War is destructive, business is constructive. Mr. George Creel and his press bureau, Mr. Bernard Baruch and his metals bureau, Mr. Harry Garfield and his coal bureau, together with a few others might be permitted to return to private life, with thanks.

CONDITIONS in Mexico have again reached the boiling-point. Carranza's government is menaced by revolt in many parts of the country, especially in the North, where Pancho Villa and Felipe Angeles have joined hands, with the support apparently of other subversive elements identified with Felix Diaz, Vasco Gomez, and Eulalio Gutierrez. It is said that a dozen distinct revolutionary movements are afoot in Mexico, ranging from mere banditry to real political protest. The *de facto* government of Carranza, having failed to raise a loan in New York, is in a bankrupt position and finds difficulty in placing any sort of army in the field. The request for permission to transport Carranza's troops across Texas, New Mexico, and Arizona was granted by two of the State governments but refused by Governor Hobby of Texas, because it might incite reprisals against Americans exposed to Villa's savagery. Some outrages have been committed recently and the position of Americans in northern Mexico is jeopardized for the moment. General Felipe Angeles is a man of education and unusual intelligence; he won distinction as an artillery officer in the Mexican revolution, and during the European war he represented the French government as inspector of munitions purchased in the United States. We understand that he is a graduate of the French school of artillery at Saint Cyr. It is said that he is held in high esteem by the French and that at the time of the Niagara Falls conference with the South American representatives in 1915 he was considered the best man for the Mexican presidency. His association with Villa, however, is against him. It may be necessary for conditions in Mexico to become worse before they become better. The present disorder is confined largely to the northern territory; on the west coast conditions are normal.

COSTS of producing copper appear to be declining from their war-time maximum, for the Utah Copper Company's latest quarterly report shows a cost of 13.72 cents per pound, as compared with 16.42 in the previous quarter; concurrently the Nevada Consolidated records a decrease from 19.01 in the preceding quarter to 16.85 cents per pound in the first quarter of this year. At the Ray the reduction has been even larger, from 19.3 to 15.1 cents, while at the Chino, with a 15c. cost, only 0.8 cent has been lopped off during the quarter. The fortunes of these big copper mines have been seriously affected by the drop in the price, as might readily be imagined. From a surplus of $1,248,786 on September 30 the Utah Copper has come down to a deficit on March 31, after paying its dividend, of $1,955,410. The four mines mentioned show an aggregate deficit of $4,583,178, as compared with an aggregate surplus of $574,721 six months earlier. During the first four months of 1919 the dividends paid by the copper mines of this country totaled $25,048,986, as compared with $53,252,471 two years ago.

RECOGNITION of Admiral Kolchak's *de facto* government in Siberia was anticipated by us in our issue of April 26. It is reported that the Council of Four at Paris has decided to recognize the anti-Bolshevik regimes of Admiral Kolchak and General Denikine on condition that they agree to convoke a genuine constitutional assembly and accept its verdict in determining the form of government to be established. This item of news is important to the mining profession because it warrants the anticipation that law and order will be established in Siberia, where are several important mines in which American mining engineers are interested as consulting engineers and managers. If once political stability is restored in that vast mineral region it may be expected that new enterprises will be set afoot. Alexander Vassilievich Kolchak [sometimes spelled Koltchak] came into power on November 12, 1918, when a group of officers, representing the Constitutional Democratic party in Russia, arrested the Social-Revolutionist members of the so-called Constituent Assembly, a loose aggregation of political units, while in session at Ufa, in the Ural province. These followers of the Admiral of the Black Sea Fleet even seized the president of the Assembly, Nicolai Avksentieff, and put him in prison together with a large part of the Assembly. By this *coup d'état* Admiral Kolchak sprang to power and became the leader of the anti-Bolshevik forces in Siberia

He won the support of the moderate parties and has established a strong administration at Omsk.

Prospecting in Canada

A short time ago we published an interview with Mr. Horace V. Winchell, a representative of the best type of American mining geologist; in this issue we give a similar interview with an equally worthy exponent of Canadian economic geology. Mr. Willet G. Miller is a stalwart Anglo-Celt, a big man physically and in character, a scion of the Viking breed, which has explored the far corners of the earth and carried the miner's pick in the vanguard of civilization. He is usually called Dr. Miller by reason of a double scholastic accolade, for he is a Doctor of Laws of Queen's University, where he taught, and also of Toronto University, his alma mater. He is one of those fortunate men whose services to the commonwealth have been recognized while they are still in the vigor of their manhood. Born in Canada of native-born parents, he typifies the traditions of a nation whose spirit was expressed with immortal eloquence during the War for Civilization. The interview tells the story of his life in a modest way. He would have said little if the interviewer had not cross-examined him with friendly persistence. His father had the tastes of a naturalist and from him he inherited the powers of observation which by academic training were developed into scientific research. While a student at college he early became a teacher also, the learning and the teaching being complementary and thereby fulfilling the true meaning of the word education—the drawing out of the mental faculties. His has been a fortunate career: early appreciated by his countrymen, he received an appointment, that of Provincial Geologist, for which he was well equipped, and then, by good luck, he had the chance of taking part in a mineral development of historic significance and industrial importance. Cobalt and Miller are names forever linked in honorable association. He appreciated the value of the discovery made in the course of cutting the grade for a railroad near Haileybury, in Ontario, and published a description of it almost immediately. The present writer, while editor of the 'Engineering & Mining Journal,' had the pleasure of printing that first account of the discovery at Cobalt in the issue of December 10, 1903. Although a cautious man—a trait inherited from his Scottish ancestors—Dr. Miller did not allow his scientific judgment to be stiffled; on the contrary, he came out boldly with the statement that "the ore is very rich, containing values in nickel, cobalt, silver, and arsenic; and a comparatively small vein could be worked at a handsome profit." In the 15 years since then Cobalt has produced 300 million ounces of silver. Dr. Miller has been amply justified in his forecast. He did more than that; he gave the miners in the Cobalt district a large measure of timely and practical geologic information; he did not wait until the mines were nearly worked out and then prepare a beautifully worded obituary notice or a highly scientific autopsy; he distributed technical data while he was collecting them in his official capacity and thereby gave to the exploration of the ore deposits an intelligent direction that ensured success. During the Cobalt boom, with its orgy of mine promotion and stock speculation, he did not lose his head nor endanger his integrity. While others became millionaires by following the advice he gave officially, he remained true to his duty. He might have enriched himself greatly, for he received many tempting offers to resign his appointment and accept both handsome retainers and profitable participation in attractive enterprises. It was all to no purpose; he loved his work and stuck to his post. His classification of the Cobalt rocks still holds good. From the start he expressed a preference for the silver veins in the conglomerate as distinguished from those in the schist and diabase; he also predicted that in passing from the Huronian conglomerate into the Keewatin schist the veins would probably become impoverished. These opinions have been confirmed by mining. Therefore our readers will note with keen interest his references to the unprospected regions of Canada. We publish a map in order to give additional point to his important statement. Experience, in Ontario particularly, has shown that the pre-Cambrian rocks constitute a terrain favorable to deposits not only of the precious metals but also of copper and nickel. There is an enormous area of such rocks in Canada, particularly in the north and north-east. We desire to draw special attention to Dr. Miller's observations concerning the Hudson's Bay territory, which will be rendered accessible shortly by means of the railroad now under construction from the main line of the Canadian Pacific railway to Port Nelson. In these spacious sub-Arctic regions there remains, as Dr. Miller says, the most attractive unprospected area in the world. It is comparatively free from brush or forest and therefore open to exploration. We shall publish further information on the subject at an early date. At present the Sudbury ore deposits dominate the nickel market, but the chance exists that somewhere in this pre-Cambrian shield of the North there may be found other nickel lodes of comparable richness. The part that the Canadian nickel resources played in the War is well known, and it is noteworthy that Dr. Miller was foremost in organizing those resources for the use of the Allies. He gives expression to the international goodwill now sealed by comradeship in arms; indeed the unfortified boundary separating Canada from the United States is an outward and visible sign of a peaceful policy more eloquent than any Hague convention or Paris conference. If the rest of the world were as amiably disposed as the members of the mining profession in the two English-speaking countries of North America there would be no anxiety as to the maintenance of international amity. They are exchanging knowledge and co-operating in beneficent industry with the most hearty accord, and in this respect such engineers as Dr. Miller and Mr. Winchell are typical. The joint committee appointed recently by the Canadian and American mining institutes should serve further to promote good feeling, by taking prompt steps to remove any minor points of disagreement arising more particularly from the barbed-wire entanglements of tariffs and custom laws. One thing is sure, any American engineer going to Ontario will find Dr. Miller, Mr. Thomas W. Gibson, Mr. Reginald W. Brock, and other men of their kind, only too glad to welcome them and to express their welcome by giving all the geologic information available. They may find the tall Doctor a bit reserved and non-commital at first, but when the crust of reserve has melted, they will find an inextinguishable warmth coming from a heart as big as his broad chest. Fertile in ideas, capable of wide generalizations, a good judge of human nature, shrewd but kindly, they will find a man neither easily deceived nor ever willing to deceive. His long legs are as much at home in the primeval bush as they are under the thwarts of a canoe: whether in the field or in the council-chamber, he is a born leader of men; and one whose leadership is accepted gladly. Alike as chief of an exploring party in the wilderness and as president of the Canadian Mining Institute in the city, he has won the confidence and affection of his fellows. Sentiment he has and the sense of humor, but most of all a willingness to help others. That characteristic has been evident throughout his life in Ontario, whether as student or teacher, geologist or official. He has trained a number of young men now honorably prominent in Canadian geology; he started them on careers of acknowledged usefulness. Honors have come to him, academic and professional, but no honor counts so greatly as the affectionate regard of the young men to whom he has given a helping hand. By his friends you shall judge him.

The Production of Silver

Herewith we give the statistics of the world's production of silver, in ounces. It will be noted that the total output, which declined in 1916 as compared with 1915, has increased slightly during the last two years. The maximum output was 226,000,000 ounces in 1911. Whereas the quantity produced in late years has varied but little, it will be seen that the value of the output has nearly doubled. The figures for last year are approximate. We note that the reports of the U. S. Mint confuse Burma with British India and that Australia is not credited with the silver in the lead and zinc concentrates exported, so that we have found it necessary to make sundry corrections. Broken Hill alone contributed 8,300,000 ounces in 1915, against the normal annual yield of 13,300,000, as in 1914. The increased output from Burma is due to the profitable activities of the Bawdwin mine of the Burma Corporation. Mexico shows a recovery, which will be accentuated this year by reason of recent favorable developments at Pachuca; likewise the mines of Nevada are likely to do better on account of the discoveries at Divide. The silver from India, Rhodesia, and the Transvaal is a by-product of gold mining. It is hardly to be expected that there will be a marked increase in the quantity of silver produced this year because the stimulus to the exploitation of the mines producing silver alone will not compensate for the decrease in the yield of silver as a by-product from the base-metal mines, notably those in which copper is the principal metal.

	1915	1916	1917	1918
United States	74,961,075	74,414,800	71,740,400	67,879,206
Canada	28,401,503	25,459,700	22,151,000	21,284,600
Mexico	39,570,151	22,838,400	31,214,000	40,000,000
Central America	2,920,496	2,602,500	2,369,500	2,300,000
South America	13,687,464	15,580,300	15,542,700	16,000,000
Total America	159,540,689	140,695,700	143,017,600	147,460,806
British India	284,875	280,000	275,000	270,000
Burma	285,112	977,121	1,793,659	1,970,503
Japan and Chosen	5,148,404	5,878,400	6,922,500	6,600,000
China and others	19,286	31,000	64,400	70,000
Dutch East Indies	450,000	450,000	450,000	450,000
Total Asia	6,187,777	7,616,521	9,505,550	9,360,503
Transvaal	996,379	968,900	950,000	900,000
Rhodesia	185,233	200,700	212,000	200,000
Congo and other Africa	6,427	33,400	32,000	32,000
Total Africa	1,188,039	1,203,000	1,194,000	1,132,000
Spain and other Europe	9,276,930	8,477,800	8,123,000	8,500,000
Australasia	9,250,000	10,700,000	10,800,000	11,000,000
Total output in ounces	185,443,335	168,693,021	172,640,159	177,453,309
Total value in dollars	92,138,249	110,763,837	138,934,217	171,721,567
Average price in cents	49.684	65.661	81.427	96.772

Recovery of Copper From Flotation by Leaching

By PERCY R. MIDDLETON

The use of the flotation process for the treatment of low-grade copper ores has introduced an additional problem in the form of smelting the finely divided concentrate resulting from the operation. The majority of Australian mining companies that adopted the flotation process were equipped with blast-furnaces and consequently some method of sintering had to be adopted before the concentrate could be successfully smelted. Under Australian conditions the cost of sintering is high, and considerable trouble has been experienced in obtaining a satisfactory product. The smelting and railroad facilities of the United States seem to have caused the American mining companies to overlook the fact that an increased profit could be made by treating the concentrate on the ground in preference to shipping it to the smelter.

It is well known that the sulphides of copper can be converted into the sulphate by roasting, and if the right conditions are maintained, from 85 to 90% of the copper may be turned into a water-soluble salt. Utley Wedge gives particulars of experiments on the sulphatizing roasting of copper ores and concentrates, in the Transactions of the A. I. M. E., Vol. XLIV (1912), and in view of his results it is hard to understand why more attention has not been given to this subject. Mr. Wedge conducted his experiments in a muffle-furnace, but I have found no difficulty in obtaining satisfactory results in the ordinary type of roasting-furnace. To obtain a satisfactory sulphatizing roast, skill and a thorough knowledge of furnace conditions are required; the cause of failure hitherto has been lack of the essential skill and knowledge of how the roast should be conducted. As in the majority of metallurgical operations, no fixed method can be applied to all ores. A wide variation in range of temperature will be found necessary to obtain the best results. I have made a special study of this subject and have roasted over one thousand tons of various ores and concentrates.

The recovery of the precious metals from the leached residues may appear at first to present insurmountable difficulties, but on investigation these disappear. Things that were impossible ten years ago, owing to the lack of apparatus, are now practicable. The improvement in mechanical appliances, for example, the vacuum-filter and the Dorr decantation system, has made commercially possible many processes that were formerly regarded as metallurgical curiosities. The extraction of copper after roasting and leaching is usually so complete that the cyanide process may be applied for the recovery of the gold and silver, without excessive consumption of cyanide, or the gold may be recovered by chlorination and the silver by either sodium hyposulphite or brine. Laboratory experiments have shown satisfactory results with cyanide; however, it is an open question whether the advantage of using one solution for the recovery of both gold and silver would off-set the danger of incomplete washing in a large plant. A good extraction of gold has been effected with chlorination in large-scale tests, but the ore on which the experiments were conducted carried practically no silver; on the other hand, laboratory experiments show that after chlorination the silver is in a condition suitable for extraction by either sodium hyposulphite or brine.

At the conclusion of some experimental work on the leaching of low-grade sulphide ores for the Mt. Lyell M. & R. Company, in Tasmania, I suggested the roasting and leaching of the flotation concentrate and was instructed by this company to carry out a complete investigation. Similar work was conducted for other Australian mining companies and in each case satisfactory results were obtained.

The following is a summary of some of the results of the above investigations:

CONCENTRATE No. 1. Assay: Cu 9.11%, Fe 26.7%, S 29%.

This sample was roasted at a temperature not exceeding 600°C., the product being leached with 5% sulphuric acid solution, with the following result:

Weight of sample before roasting, 1000 gm.; copper, 9.11%. Roasted product leached with two litres of 5% sulphuric acid solution. Resulting solution contained 45 gm. copper per litre.

Copper extracted, 90 gm., or 98.7%.

CONCENTRATE No. 2. Assay: Cu 20.52%, Fe 28.2%, Au 1.81 oz.

Roasted at a temperature not exceeding 650°C.

Weight of sample before roasting, 1000 gm.; copper, 20.5%. Roasted product leached with two litres of 5% sulphuric acid solution. Resulting solution contained 100.44 gm. copper per litre.

Copper extracted, 200.88 gm., or 97.9%.

CONCENTRATE No. 3. Assay: Cu 5.8%, Fe 35.0%, and Au 0.587 oz.

Roasted at a temperature not exceeding 650°C.

Weight of sample before roasting, 1000 gm.; copper, 5.8%. Roasted product leached with two litres of 5% sulphuric acid solution. Resulting solution contained 28.0 gm. copper per litre.

Copper extracted, 56 gm., or 96.5%.

Cyanide tests for the recovery of gold were conducted on the residue from the No. 2 and 3 leaching experiments. The residues were given a lime wash and then treated with cyanide solution. The copper present did not interfere with the gold extraction, no trace of troublesome cyanicides being detected. The average gold extraction over a number of tests was 90% and the consumption of cyanide about 1.5 lb. per ton of residue treated. Chlorination also gave satisfactory results when the acid-soluble iron in the roasted product was below 1%. In order to confirm the copper extraction obtained in these laboratory experiments, a bulk-test was conducted under actual working conditions in the Edwards metallurgical works, at Ballarat, Victoria. The roasting was performed in a 7-panel duplex Edwards furnace and the product was leached by percolation in vats fitted with filter-bottoms. Scrap-iron was used to precipitate the copper. The furnace was operated continuously at a temperature of about 650°C. The roasted material was dampened with water before being charged by hand into the leaching-vats, about 20 tons forming the charge, which was covered with a 5% solution of sulphuric acid; after 24 hours contact, this solution was drawn from the bottom of the vat into a launder connecting with the precipitation vats. The charge was then washed free from copper with water, which also went to the precipitation vats. In the above manner 110 tons of concentrate was roasted and leached with the following results: The tonnage treated was 110 tons of concentrate containing 7.6% copper, and the copper produced amounted to 19,856 lb. cement copper assaying 80% Cu, showing an extraction of 95%.

This bulk-test was conducted with the object of determining whether the concentrate could be roasted with satisfactory results on a working scale and did not include any experimental work on precipitation. The fact that copper can be commercially recovered from sulphate solutions by electrolysis has been established beyond dispute at Chuquicamata, in Chile, and at Ajo, in Arizona. The electrolytic deposition of copper from solutions resulting from the leaching of roasted ore is the ideal method of precipitation, as sufficient acid can be regenerated to carry on the process, thus obviating the need for an expensive acid plant, and the amount of acid-soluble iron in the roasted product is under control, being regulated by the furnace conditions; therefore the amount of 'bleeding' would not be as great as in the case of electrolyzing solutions resulting from the leaching of oxidized ores where there is no control over the amount of iron entering the electrolyte at each cycle.

In order to illustrate the possibilities of this process the following working-costs were compiled from figures obtained in working-scale tests: Assuming the concentrate to contain 12% copper, 9 oz. silver, and 0.25 oz. gold, and treating 100 tons per day, the items of cost would be:

Roasting	$0.30	
Leaching	0.15	
Gold and silver leach	0.75	
Handling residues	0.10	
		$1.30
Electrolytic deposition:		
Power, 240 kw-hr. @ 1c	$2.40	
Labor, etc.	0.70	
		3.10
Losses:		
5% of copper, 12 lb @ 15c	$1.80	
Silver, 1 oz. @ $1.01	1.01	
Gold	0.50	
		3.31
Capital account (retirement of $300,000 in five years):		
100 tons × 360 × 5 = 180,000 tons = $\frac{300}{180}$		1.66
Net cost		$9.37

The smelter returns from such a concentrate would be approximately as follows:

12% copper = 240 lb. less 15 lb. = 225 lb. @ 15c. less 3c	$27.00
9 oz. silver @ 95% of $1.01 = 96c. × 9c	8.64
0.25 oz. gold @ $19	4.75
Value of metals less smelter deductions	$40.39
Freight and treatment	12.00
Net daily returns per ton of concentrate	$28.39

Ratio of concentration, say, 3:1.

$\frac{\$2839}{100 \times 3}$ = $9.40 net return per ton of crude ore.

Summary of Costs of Both Processes

Smelting:		
100 tons @ 240 lb. copper per ton, 24,000 lb. at 15c		$3,600
100 tons @ 9 oz. silver per ton, 900 oz. silver @ $1.01		909
100 tons @ 0.25 oz. gold per ton, 25 oz. gold @ $19		475
Total value of all metals		$4,984
Returns from smelter = 100 × 28.39		2,839
Cost and losses by smelting		$2,145
Costs and losses per ton of concentrate	$21.45	
Costs and losses per ton of crude ore	7.15	
Net returns per ton of crude ore	9.46	
Roasting and leaching:		
Total value of metals as above		$4,984
Costs and losses, 100 tons @ $9.37		937
Net returns by leaching		$4,047
Costs and losses per ton of concentrate	$9.37	
Costs and losses per ton of crude ore	3.12	
Net returns per ton of crude ore	13.49	

Difference in favor of roasting and leaching, $4.03 per ton of crude ore.

If the working-costs and losses for roasting and leaching are raised to $12 per ton, instead of $9.37, the net return per ton of crude ore is changed to $12.61 per ton, the difference in favor of leaching being $3.25 per ton of crude ore.

A plant to treat 100 tons of concentrate per day would consist of two 13-panel duplex Edwards furnaces, five Dorr counter-current thickeners for copper leaching, four Dorr counter-current thickeners for gold extraction. If chlorination were employed a vacuum-filter and another series of Dorr thickeners would be required for silver extraction. In each case the thickeners would be 15 ft. diam. based on a settling-area of four square feet per ton of roasted product. In addition to the above plant, electrical equipment would be required for the precipitation of the copper.

PALAU is a trade name for an alloy containing about 80% gold and 20% platinum. The metal is somewhat darker in color than platinum, but resembles it otherwise. Its melting-point is 1370°; this is higher than that for gold, but 400° lower than that of platinum. The U. S. Bureau of Standards found that a crucible of this alloy was comparatively free from iron, and that its loss on heating to 1200° was less than that of a platinum crucible containing 2.4% of iridium. The resistance to acids and salts is comparable with that of platinum. The ware is suitable for fusions with sodium carbonate, but is decidedly attacked by fused pyro-sulphates. Crucibles of palau could not be used for work at high temperatures on account of its relatively low melting-point.

Use of Army Gas-Masks in Atmospheres Containing Sulphur Di-oxide

By A. C. FIELDNER and S. H. KATZ

*INTRODUCTION. The use of toxic gases in warfare has led to the development of an entirely new type of respiratory appliance, namely, the gas-mask, which promises to fill a long-felt want in the chemical and metallurgical industries. Heretofore workmen around plants using processes in which acid fumes are given off made shift to protect themselves, in a more or less inadequate manner, by wearing moistened handkerchiefs, or respirators containing wet sponges, over the mouth and nose. The close of the War now makes available the army type of gas-mask, which is admirably adapted to filtering out many chemical fumes and acid vapors from inspired air, provided the concentration of gas is low, less than 1 or 2%.

The possibility of using army masks around smelters and sulphide roasters for protecting the workmen from sulphur di-oxide fumes was suggested, almost a year ago, by George S. Rice, Chief Mining Engineer of the Bureau of Mines, and at his request several patterns of army masks were tested in various concentrations of sulphur di-oxide to determine the degree of protection afforded. Owing to the pressure of military work and the inability of obtaining masks for industrial use, this investigation was not completed until after the signing of the Armistice. The work is now completed, and the results are given in this publication.

FIG. 1. EARLY FRENCH TYPE OF MASK

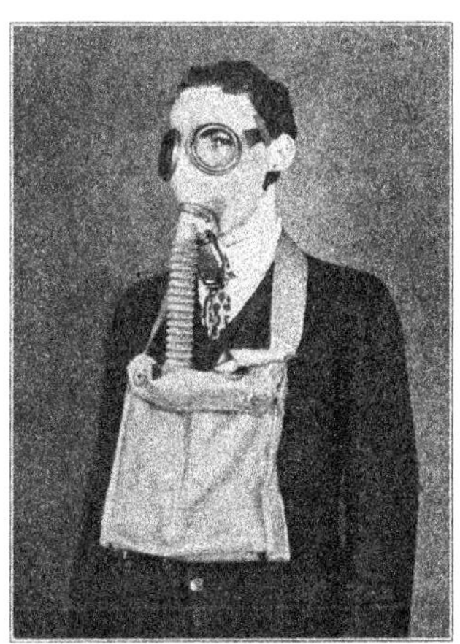

FIG. 2. THE TISSOT GAS-MASK

PHYSIOLOGICAL EFFECT OF THE GAS. Sulphur di-oxide is an irritating irrespirable gas, relatively non-toxic as compared with carbon monoxide or oxides of nitrogen. There is but little danger from sulphur di-oxide poisoning, as the fume is so irritating that the victim is compelled to seek air at once. In extreme cases[1] of high concentrations, when the victim cannot retire from the fume, death may result from respiratory spasms and asphyxia. Ordinarily, however, workmen exposed for some time to a mild degree of sulphur di-oxide poisoning complain of headache, anorexia, spasmodic cough, sneez-

*Published with the permission of the Director of the U. S. Bureau of Mines.

[1]Thompson, D. Gilman, M. D., 'The Occupational Diseases'. D. Appleton & Co., New York, 1914, p. 360.

ing, hernoptysis, bronchitis, constriction of chest, gastro-intestinal disorders, conjunctivitis, smarting of eyes, lachrymation, and anemia. For these symptoms workmen soon acquire toleration. The inhalation of large quantities of sulphur di-oxide produces ulceration of the mucuous membrane.

The Selby Smelter Commission[2] made a thorough investigation of the effect of various concentrations of sulphur di-oxide on the senses of a number of persons. The average results of these tests are tabulated below:

3 to 5 parts per million, by volume—Plainly or faintly detectable by smell or taste.

8 to 12 parts per million, by volume—Slight throat irritation and tendency to cough.

20 parts per million—Distinct throat irritation, coughing, constriction of chest, lachrymation, and smarting of eyes.

50 parts per million—More pronounced irritation of eyes, throat, and chest, but possible to breathe several minutes.

150 parts per million—Extremely disagreeable but could be endured for several minutes.

500 parts per million—So acutely pungent as to cause a sensation of suffocation, even with the first breath.

With no concentrations of less than 50 parts per million was there produced any feeling of nausea, and the tendency to nausea with the highest concentrations was only slight.

We repeated some of these experiments with substantially the same results: 370 parts per million (0.037%) could be endured for half a minute.

TESTS OF ARMY GAS-MASKS. The early French type of mask, shown in Fig. 1, consists of 40 thicknesses of cheese-cloth, fashioned to fit over the entire face, from neck over chin to the hair above the eyes from ear to ear. Suitable rubber-web bands held the mask closely to the face. Cellophane eye-pieces were built into the mask at the eyes. The 10 outside layers of cheese-cloth were impregnated with an unsaturated oil; the next 10 layers held an alkaline material; the next 10, hexamethylene tetramine; and the 10 next the face, nickel sulphate. The tests were made in a large air-tight gas-chamber, in which the sulphur di-oxide atmosphere was produced by burning sulphur. The air was well stirred by two electric fans, running continuously throughout the tests. The concentration of sulphur was determined by titration with iodine. After the required concentration was reached, two observers, wearing carefully adjusted masks, entered the room. The results are given in Table I.

Table I

Effects produced by atmospheres containing various proportions of sulphur di-oxide on persons wearing French patterned masks.

Test No.	Time	SO_2 by iodine, %	Effect on wearer of apparatus in atmosphere
1	2:15 2:31:00 to 2:31:45	0.57	Sulphur di-oxide penetrated masks. The eyes could feel it, but were not disturbed much. The biting was severe in the air-passages of the nose and throat. It could also be felt in the bronchial tubes and lungs. Observers could remain in this atmosphere only 45 seconds.
2	2:46 2:58:00 to 3:03:00	0.43	The observers could just bear the sulphur di-oxide that came through the masks. The biting in the air-passages extended all the way to the lungs. Coughing was caused. The eyes were not bothered. The breathing was deep and difficult. In case of necessity, one could probably travel ½ mile in this condition. It was thought best not to remain in this atmosphere longer than 5 minutes. After coming into the fresh air, all the sulphur di-oxide disappeared from the mask after three inhalations.
3.	3:24:00 to 3:27:00	0.24	At first one of the masks leaked at the sides, so that the eyes were bothered. After fixing this, the atmosphere was much better. The biting in the air-passages was not so severe, but coughing was caused. It is probable that one could stand this atmosphere one hour, in case of necessity.
4.	4:00	0.16	No difficulty was experienced in this atmosphere. The sulphur di-oxide was noticeable and the throat was slightly irritated, but work could be done with hardly more trouble than that due to the mask itself.

[2]Holmes, J. A., Franklin, E. C., and Gould, R. A., 'Report of the Selby Smelter Commission', Bureau of Mines Bull. 98, pp. 172-175.

From the experiments in Table I, it may be concluded that an atmosphere containing 0.16% of sulphur di-oxide may be safely entered and work performed by a person wearing a mask such as used in the experiments. Even though a mask were worn, it would be dangerous to attempt work in an atmosphere containing 0.2% of the gas, unless means of immediate exit were at hand and an observer watching from a place of safety to effect a rescue in case of necessity.

Prolonged exposure to the gas, even in moderate concentrations, is undoubtedly injurious. Five hours after the close of the above experiments, the observer who had been most exposed felt a soreness through the lungs and throat and the voice was slightly husky. The discharge from the nose was increased, and was slightly pink from blood. The next day he felt normal.

The French type mask is an unpleasant apparatus to wear at best, although it imposes no marked hardship on the wearer. The face is heated, and the atmosphere breathed necessarily contains much exhaled air, and is hot and close. To determine the composition of the atmosphere within a mask while worn by a person at rest, two samples of gas were taken from a point ½ inch above the nostrils—the first, during periods of exhalation, the second, during periods of inhalation. The results are given in Table II.

Table II

Composition of atmosphere within mask while worn in pure air.

No.	CO_2	O_2	N_2	
1.	2.90	17.41	79.69	Sample taken during exhalation
2.	1.37	19.15	79.48	Sample taken during inhalation

These tests show the bad effect of the large 'dead space' in this type of mask. Even while at rest the wearer has to inhale 1.37% of carbon di-oxide, which contributes to the oppressive feeling produced by this mask. Aside from the question of re-breathing a certain proportion of exhaled air, this type of mask furnished so little protection against sulphur di-oxide that it is of no practical value for use in the industries.

The standard U. S. Army gas-mask of the mouth-piece type is shown in Fig. 2 and 3. It consists essentially of a face-piece of rubberized fabric, impermeable to gas, connected to a canister containing the absorbents by a short length of flexible rubberized tubing. The wearer breathes through a rubber mouth-piece, the nose being closed by a spring-clip, mounted on the inside of the mask. Leakage through the face-piece will only affect the eyes of the wearer, as the gas cannot enter the lungs. The inhaled air enters the bottom of the canister through a disc-valve that closes on exhalation, the expired air passes out through a rubber flutter-valve, projecting downward from the metal elbow-tube just outside the face piece.

The type F standard army canisters shown in section in Fig. 1 is 5/12 in. high and contains 42 cu. in. of a mixture of coconut charcoal and 'purple' soda lime and two cotton-wadding filter-pads, placed at one-third and two-thirds distance from the bottom, respectively. One of us, wearing this outfit, entered the gas-chamber containing a concentration of 0.46% sulphur and remained one hour, without detecting any gas whatever, except on one occasion, when the mask was disarranged, and then

FIG. 3. U. S. ARMY GAS-MASK

sulphur di-oxide penetrated to and irritated the eyes. On adjusting the mask and clearing the face-piece, the gas disappeared, and no discomfort whatever was experienced thereafter from that source. During a part of the time, work was done on a bicycle dynamotor.

More sulphur was then burned, until a fog was produced in which objects could not be distinguished at distances beyond four feet. Analyses showed that the concentration was 1.17% sulphur di-oxide. No discomfort of any kind could be felt by the wearer, other than that due to the mask itself.

LIFE OF CANISTERS IN HIGH CONCENTRATIONS. Tests were made to determine the life of the standard type F Army canister in an atmosphere containing 5% sulphur di-oxide. The gas was put up in the chamber from a cylinder of liquid sulphur di-oxide, attached to the chamber. Analyses of the chamber-gas were made by drawing two litres of gas through a standard iodine solution and titrating back with standard sodium-thiosulphate solution. Twenty canisters were tested, in lots of 10 each. The men did not enter the chamber, but were seated outside, wearing the face pieces, which were connected to iron pipes that passed through the walls of the chamber. The canisters were attached to the other end of these pipes inside the chamber. As soon as a man detected gas coming through his canister, as shown by throat irritation, the time was taken, and the canister was considered exhausted.

Tested under these conditions, the 20 canisters served

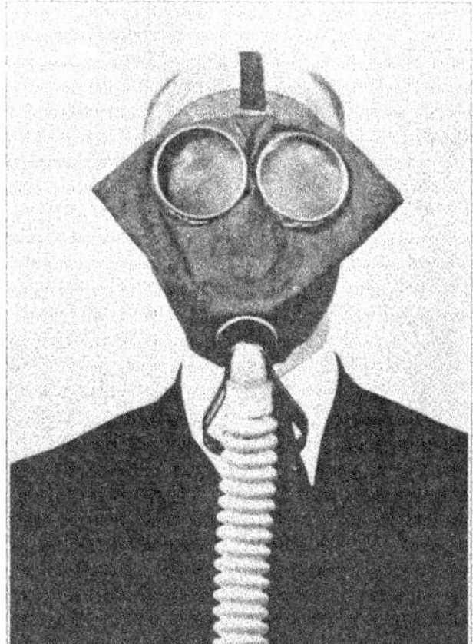

FIG. 4. U. S. ARMY GAS-MASK WITH MOUTH-PIECE

to remove all the gas for periods of time varying from 18 to 41 minutes. The average service time was 29 minutes. The large variation in service time for the individual canisters was due, in part, to differences in the canister fillings, but mostly to differences in the breathing rates of the men. Individuals breathe different amounts of air. A small man may breathe only 5 litres per minute when at rest, while a large individual may require 10 or 12 litres. The average rate of a number of men, when at rest, is about 8 litres per minute. Moderate exercise increases the rate to approximately 30 litres, and vigorous exercise causes a breathing rate of 60 to 70 litres. Hence, the efficient life of a gas-mask canister is proportionately less when the wearer is engaged on continuous work.

In making these tests with high percentages (5.07%) of sulphur di-oxide, the canisters became quite warm after 15 minutes use. A temperature of 80°C. was noted in some of the canisters. This elevated temperature made breathing rather uncomfortable toward the end of the test; however, all the men were able to continue breathing through the canisters until the gas finally penetrated the absorbent.

PRACTICAL TESTS. Several Army masks of the mouth-piece type (Fig. 1 and 2) fitted with standard type F canisters, containing soda-lime and charcoal mixture with two cotton-wadding filter-pads, were tested under practical conditions by James Kane Murphy, Assistant Superintendent of the Washoe reduction works of the Anaconda Copper Mining Co., at Anaconda, Montana. The following paragraphs are quoted from his report:

"On October 23, 24, and 25, we had considerable repair work to do on one of our Cottrell treaters; this treater takes one-quarter of the gas from roaster No. 2. During the repair-work on this treater, it was shut off as tight as possible, but there was such a leakage of SO_2 gas that it was impossible for a man to enter the treater to do any work. The iron-workers repairing this treater were able, two at a time, to put on these masks, and do their repair-work in the treater. The men stayed in about 20 minutes at one time; by that time, the heat and dust caused them to come out, but the masks were very satisfactory and work could be done with them by proceeding slowly. One test on these masks was performed in the No. 2 roaster ventilating-tunnels when flotation calcine was drawn into cars ahead of the man with the gas mask on. It is absolutely impossible for a man without a mask to even attempt to stay in this place. Most of the dust coming from the cars, which were being loaded ahead of the man with the gas-mask, will pass through 200-mesh, but none of the men wearing a mask in this place had any trouble with dust. A third mask was tested in a very high concentration of gas. The mask was carefully adjusted about the face and the person making the test was in an atmosphere containing about 5% SO_2. E. A. Bernard, Superintendent of Calcining, personally put the mask on in this atmosphere, besides two other men. All decided that the gas came through the canister. This test was made on gas from the top hearth of an Anaconda type of roaster-furnace. The hearths on this furnace are similar to a Wedge roasting-furnace. A steady wind was blowing against the east side of the furnace, so all doors on the top floor were opened, thus forcing a good part of the furnace gases out of the west doors. The testers stood as close as possible to the doors through which the gas came. This gas contains some SO_3, considerable moisture, dust, and some AS_2O_3, besides the SO_2. If possible, we would like to have two more canisters for further testing of these masks, as they have proved to be very valuable in certain places, from the industrial point of view."

This reports that the simple Army gas-mask is exceedingly valuable around sulphide roasters and, in fact, any industry in which sulphur di-oxide is given off. The third test in which gas penetrated the canister illustrates the limitation of this type of protective appliance. It must not be used in too high a concentration of gas. In this case, the percentage of SO_2 was probably higher than 5% as tests at the American University Experiment Station of the Chemical Warfare Service have shown that the standard Army canister will remove 5% of sulphur di-oxide for at least 15 minutes.

SPECIAL CANISTER FILLING. The standard Army canister contains 40% soda-lime and 60% charcoal. The charcoal is of less value in absorbing sulphur di-oxide than soda-lime. Hence, for use in sulphur di-oxide and dust an all soda-lime canister with cotton-wadding filter-pads will last from 50 to 100% longer than the standard canisters used in the Anaconda tests. This is shown in the comparative canister tests with different fillings against ½% SO_2.

Table III

Service times of canisters with standard and special fillings.
SO_2 concentration, 0.5% or 13.0 Mg per litre; relative humidity, 50%; average temperature, 26°C.

*Standard, 60% charcoal, 40% soda-lime...	32	36
Special, 100% charcoal..................	7	57
Special, 100% soda-lime	54	..

*Average of five canisters tested.

The life or service time of the canister is the time in minutes during which all traces of SO_2 are absorbed by the canister. The break-down of the canister is shown by the change in color of a sensitive potassium iodide-starch solution through which the effluent air from the canister is bubbling during the test.

ADVANTAGES OF LARGER CANISTER. The standard Army canister described in the foregoing tests contains 42 cu. in. of absorbent, weighs 1⅗ pounds and has a resistance to flow of 3½ to 4 in. water-column at 85 litres per minute flow. This high resistance obliges men to work rather slowly while wearing the mask. A second disadvantage to which Mr. Murphy has called special attention is the short service time of the absorbent.

Both of these defects can easily be remedied by increasing the cross-sectional area of the canister without increasing the height in proportion.

TYPE RECOMMENDED. Although the mouth-piece type of mask was found fairly satisfactory in practical use, it is believed that the later type of Tissot mask (Fig. 4) in combination with a 100 cu. in. soda-lime canister will prove the best outfit for exclusive use in sulphur di-oxide and acid gases. The elimination of mouth-piece and nose-clip increases the comfort, and enables the wearer to keep it on for hours at a time. The large eye-pieces held rigidly in proper position by the well-fitting substantial face-piece, afford a large angle of vision, thereby greatly increasing the efficiency of the workman wearing the mask. He should be able to do substantially the same amount of work as without the mask in a normal atmosphere.

OTHER USES OF RESPIRATORS. Aside from the many metallurgical operations in which sulphur di-oxide is given off, a respirator or mask designed for this purpose should be useful in sulphite-pulp and paper mills; in sulphuric acid plants and in fact for protection against any acid gas such as chlorine, phosgene, carbon di-oxide, hydrocyanic acid, oxides of nitrogen, and hydrochloric acid.

LIMITATIONS OF GAS MASKS. In closing this paper, we feel it necessary to issue a most emphatic warning against the indiscriminate use of gas-masks for any and all purposes. The soldiers in the Army have been taught that their mask will protect them absolutely against any gas the enemy may put up. These men, on returning to civil pursuits, carry this idea with them. They will not realize that the extremely poisonous gases used in warfare are chemically active, and, therefore, combine readily with the absorbents of the mask. Furthermore, outdoor gas concentrations seldom exceed a few hundredths of one

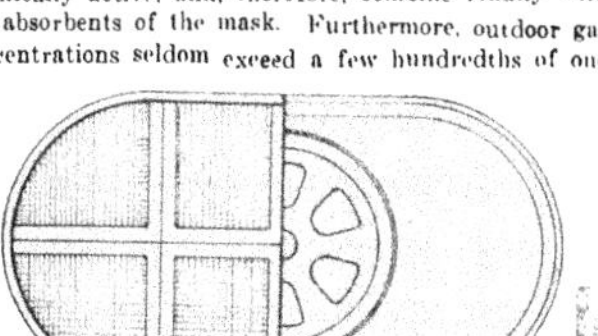

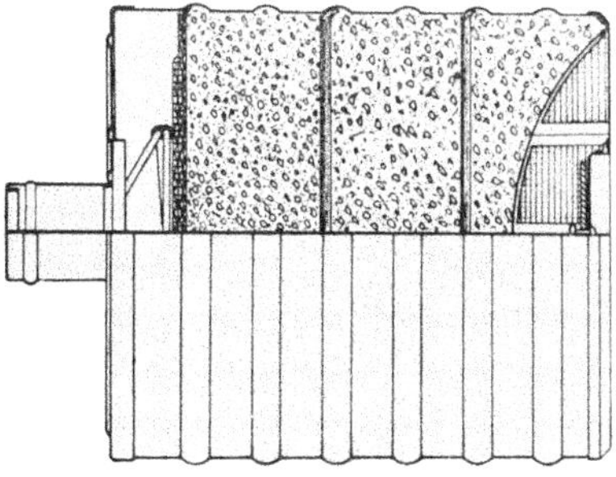

FIG. 5. AMERICAN CANISTER TYPE OF MASK

per cent. Some of the gases that are successfully absorbed by the mask at these battlefield concentrations will immediately penetrate it when present in quantities of 1 or 2%. In fact, the Army mask is useless against many of the most common industrial gases, as for example, carbon monoxide, ammonia, natural gas, producer and blast-furnace gas, mine-gases, coal and water gas, and probably any gas when occurring in concentrations exceeding 5%. In such cases the self-contained oxygen-breathing apparatus must be used, as the mask does not supply any oxygen whatever. In view of these serious limitations, the gas-mask should be used only with the advice of an expert who has a thorough understanding of the limitations of this apparatus.

Much of the charcoal used in Army masks was made by the Pacific Gas & Electric Co. at San Francisco.

Manganese

There is little change in the position of manganese ore from that of March. Reports from the various districts show that production of ore still continues, but operations are confined to high grade deposits, particularly in Arkansas, Arizona, Montana, and Virginia. It is very probable that mining will be resumed in Georgia and New Mexico, where chemical ores are known to occur in considerable quantities.

In Montana, the only producer of manganese ore at Butte is the Clark-Montana Realty Co. [Elm Orlu] which is operating on a contract with a Pittsburgh Steel Co. The contract calls for 1000 tons per month of crude ore and concentrates. The ore is treated at the plant of the New York-Montana Testing & Engineering Co. at Helena. The Ophir mill of the Butte-Detroit company closed in December, but is being kept in order for resumption of operations should occasion permit.

At Philipsburg the Philipsburg Mining Co. is the only miner and shipper; however, other operations were carried on until April 5. The Philipsburg Mining Co. is extracting 160 to 200 tons of ore per day, which assays 32.9% Mn and 37.7% SiO_2. This ore is treated in the company's mill, which has a daily capacity of 75 to 100 tons of concentrates, averaging 50.3% Mn and 10.4% SiO_2. No crude ore is shipped, but the concentrates are taken by Eastern concerns dealing in chemical ores. The concentrates are reported to contain 73.5% MnO_2.

Aside from the above-mentioned work and the small-scale operations in the Batesville district, Arkansas, manganese mining is practically at a standstill.

The market price of manganese ore has changed little during the past month, especially for the higher grades. Both domestic and foreign ores are quoted at 55 to 65 cents a unit f.o.b. South Chicago, and c.i.f. Atlantic ports. The domestic ore is, however, purchased on a long ton unit basis, while the foreign ore is on a short ton basis. Chemical ore is selling at $85 to $100 per gross ton, delivered, 80% basis. Powdered chemical ore is quoted at 7 to 8 cents per pound for 80% grade.

Imports during March totaled 48,238 tons, over double those in February. Brazil and Cuba contributed 44,000 tons.—W. R. Crane in April report of U. S. Bureau of Mines.

DURING the War, the lead smelter of the Broken Hill Associated Smelters, Proprietary, Ltd., at Port Pirie, South Australia, was enlarged and its capacity is now 165,000 short tons annually, making it the largest plant of its kind in the world. Most of the lead concentrates produced by the Broken Hill mines of New South Wales are reduced in this plant. Many improvements are in progress. Large quantities of refined silver are shipped.

Pyrite, Sulphur, and Sulphuric Acid

By R. R. HORNOR and A. E. WELLS

GENERAL. The pyrite and sulphur situation during April was about the same as in March, with probably somewhat greater demand for these materials. Producers are carefully watching developments in the sulphuric-acid industries and in other branches using these materials, and are prepared to bid for any business that may be offered. The outlook in the acid business is encouraging, and it is predicted that a few months will see the industry back to a normal basis. The same may be said of the industries using sulphur exclusively. Stocks of pyrite and sulphur in the hands of consumers are being diminished gradually, and it is expected that they will be in the market for new material in a short time. However, they prefer to hold off as long as possible before placing contracts, anticipating that much more favorable prices can be obtained than are now being quoted. Ore is quoted at 18 to 20 cents per unit.

PYRITE. In New York State, the St. Lawrence Pyrites Co. is now approaching a normal monthly output of 4000 tons of 42% concentrate. The New York Pyrites Co. is shipping over 1400 tons of 27 to 30% ore.

In the Mineral district of Virginia the Sulphur mine produced 3500 tons of lump ore and concentrate in April, and the Armenius mine from 1000 to 1200 tons. In the Dumfries district the Cabin Branch yielded 2500 to 3000 tons, one-third lump ore, the remainder concentrates.

The Spanish pyrite situation is greatly improving, and there is a growing demand in both the northern and the southern markets of the United States.

SULPHUR. The large sulphur companies of Louisiana and Texas continue to add to their reserve stocks of sulphur, and it is estimated they now have more than 1,250,000 tons above ground. The Texas Gulf Sulphur Co., since starting operation about the middle of March, has placed in production additional wells, and the present output is reported as 1000 to 1500 tons of sulphur per day.

It is rumored that the sulphur companies are preparing to invade the sulphuric-acid field in competition with pyrite, and that they have already made substantial reduction in price in the northern markets. A price of $22 per ton, f.o.b. New York and Boston, is said to have been made.

SULPHURIC ACID. As a result of an inquiry made of the acid manufacturers at the meeting in New York on April 2, it was evident that the rate of production of acid in the East during the first four months of 1919 was only about 330,000 tons per month, or about 60% of the rated capacity of all commercial plants in the East. However, distribution of this production is not the same in the South as in the North. In the South, that is, south of Virginia and Kentucky, most of the fertilizer plants are running at or near capacity, and the average rate of production of the plants is probably 90% of the rated capacity. In the North, however, production is only 50%. We have, therefore, a rate of production in the South of 120,000 tons per month, and an average in the North of 210,000 tons. These figures apply only to those plants east of the Mississippi. The output west of the Mississippi is estimated to be 30,000 tons. Adding these estimates of present production, we have a total for the United States of 360,000 tons per month, or 4,320,000 tons (basis of 50°B.) per year, which is approximately 320,000 tons more than the production of 1914, and this will undoubtedly increase as general business conditions throughout the country improve. Data compiled during the third quarter of 1918 showed that the general commercial business in the North during that period required 260,000 tons of acid. This is nearly 25% more than the rate during the first quarter of 1919. If stocks remained the same, this would indicate that the general commercial business had been reduced by 25%. However, as stocks have been increasing, and acid production at the same time has been decreasing, and is probably even less than 50% of the capacity of the plants at this time, the indications are that the general chemical business has been curtailed by more than 25%. The amount of acid owned or controlled by the Government, about 100,000 tons, is, therefore, somewhat greater than one-half of a month's supply for the demand in the North under present business conditions.

BLAST-FURNACES can economically use ores with an average content not much below 40% Mn and not much above 12% SiO_2. However, there are large quantities in the United States, particularly in the West, that contain a smaller proportion of manganese and a greater proportion of silica. There is a possibility of utilizing such ores by electric smelting. An electric-furnace can be constructed more rapidly than a blast-furnace. It can be operated economically in smaller units than a blast-furnace, and therefore can be placed wherever a suitable supply of ore and a suitable water-development are found near each other. An ore deposit inadequate to supply a modern blast-furnace would last a rather large electric-furnace for a considerable time. Hence the smaller electric unit can be so placed as to require smaller transportation charges than would be necessary for a more distant blast-furnace. The product that could be economically made at such an electric-furnace plant would be not ferro but silico, as this permits a much higher recovery of manganese. Silico is not used to any considerable extent in the United States, but it is in Europe. There is, however, a large quantity of steel made in this country in whose manufacture both ferro-manganese and ferro-silicon is used, and silico-manganese could just as well be used in this case. The utilization of ores low in manganese and high in silica is therefore dependent upon the education of the steel industry to use silico-manganese where a combination of ferro-manganese and ferro-silicon is now employed.—H. W. Gillett and C. E. Williams in U. S. Bureau of Mines bulletin 'Electric Smelting of Domestic Manganese Ores'.

MINING FOR NICKEL IN NEW CALEDONIA

Willet G. Miller, Canadian Geologist

AN INTERVIEW, By T. A. RICKARD

Dr. Miller, you are a Canadian?

Yes, I was born in Norfolk county, Ontario.

Was your father interested in mining?

No, he hadn't any technical training, but he was interested in natural history—trees, flowers, and rocks—and he brought home the first collection of fossils that I had ever seen, from Manitoulin island in Lake Huron.

So you acquired some taste for geology?

I didn't pay much attention to mineralogy and geology until I went to the University. I had never seen compact rock in place anywhere in my native county.

What was your schooling?

I went to country schools, and then to the Port Rowan high-school, and stayed there until I had completed the first year's work in the University of Toronto. Before completing my course I stayed out one year, and had the experience of teaching in the high-school. That was owing to the fact that our local high-school was short of a teacher and my old master wanted me to put in some time with him; and I am glad I did, because it gave me an opportunity of planning the course and appreciating more what it meant.

In what year did you graduate at Toronto?

In 1890.

At the time of graduation, had you any plans for a career?

No, during my university course I specialized in chemistry and took mineralogy and geology as well. After graduation I was appointed fellow in mineralogy and geology and held the fellowship for three years, until 1893. The fellowship was intended to give one an opportunity to do post-graduate work, but it required the holder of it to do some teaching—take part in the instruction. During the summers while I was a fellow I was a field-assistant on the Geological Survey of Canada, under Dr. Robert Bell, in the area along the north shore of Georgian Bay and Lake Huron, sometimes known as the classic Huronian area.

So you drifted into mining?

No; I chose mineralogy and geology as my subjects at college. It was fortunate for me that I was appointed a fellow. In 1893, at the termination of my fellowship, I was appointed lecturer in geology in the newly founded mining school of Queen's University, at Kingston, Ontario. Later I became a professor. Altogether I spent nine years at Queen's. During the time I was there I took short courses of post-graduate work at the universities of Chicago, Harvard, and Heidelberg, more with the object of becoming acquainted with the men and methods than of any particular study.

That brings us to 1902.

In 1902 I was appointed Provincial Geologist of Ontario. The term 'Provincial' is not always understood; it means 'State'. During part of the nine years I was at Queen's I had been doing special work for the Ontario Bureau of Mines. One of the most important studies that I had in hand in those days was in connection with the corundum industry of south-eastern Ontario.

That brings us close to one of the most interesting episodes in your life, I believe—the discovery of Cobalt.

I might say that when I became Provincial Geologist

I intended to hold the position for only about two years. I did not think that I would like Government work, but I thought it was a good opportunity.

To learn?

To get acquainted with the mineral resources of Ontario; in fact, I had leave of absence for only two years from Queen's University, but I had secured a good successor there in the person of Reginald W. Brock, who afterward became director of the Geological Survey of Canada, and by the time the two years had passed I was so interested in my duties that I stayed longer than I had intended.

You are still holding that position, are you not?

Yes.

Won't you proceed to describe the discovery of Cobalt, which, I believe, was the next important event in your life?

The Government of Ontario decided to build a railway from North Bay Junction, on the main line of the Canadian Pacific Railway, to Lake Temiskaming, to serve as an outlet for that agricultural region. During the construction of this railway, at a distance of 103 miles north of North Bay, some mineral deposits were discovered. There were no prospectors or miners in that region in those days.

Was there none in the crew working on the railway?

No, none. They were railroad men and nothing more. Late in the autumn of 1903 one of the men from that district brought a sample of ore to Toronto. He thought the sample was copper ore. It was the mineral niccolite, which resembles certain copper ores rather closely. When I saw the sample I knew that an interesting discovery had been made. I thought, of course, that it might indicate rich nickel deposits, as the well-known Sudbury area lies about 90 miles south-west of this locality, now known as Cobalt. As snow was likely to fall at any time in that latitude, it being late in the season—November—I hurried north, taking train to Mattawa, thence to the foot of Lake Temiskaming, and the steamer on to Haileybury, which is on the railway line, about five miles north of Cobalt. The steel had not been laid on the grade at that time, and the morning after our arrival I decided to go down to see the discovery. I walked along the grade, which was frozen, with a thin covering of snow, until I reached the place of discovery, which was on what came to be known as the La Rose mine.

Was there much ore showing in the railroad cutting, and what was the character of it?

No, it was on one side of the railroad, near the face of a cliff, at the bottom. A blacksmith employed on the right of way—named La Rose—had at one time worked in the phosphate deposits in Quebec and was more or less interested in minerals. He noticed this vein and when he had time he put a few shots in it. He evidently was after the 'copper', or niccolite, and was not taking much interest in the silver, for he blasted out some rich silver ore and threw it into the swamp.

Was there any native silver visible?

Yes, there was a lot of native silver; but the 'copper' was bright, and the silver was tarnished on the surface.

Did La Rose recognize the silver?

Apparently he knew it was silver, but he was not trying to save it, but was just blasting it out. Then there was a showing of silver in the bottom of a pit, the small opening that he had made. I got my pick under this and pried it up and got a piece about the size of my hand and about as thick. When I took that with me to Haileybury in the evening, the men there to whom I showed it began to get a little excited and decided to do some staking. Next day I went down to the discovery again, and I saw two or three other veins that had been found. One of these was a massive cobalt vein on what is now the Nipissing property. Another was on what afterward became known as the McKinley-Darragh, and the fourth was the most interesting vein discovered up to that time, or probably since. It was also on the Nipissing property, but the discoverer had not shown it to anyone. He was a Frenchman by the name of Hebert, who had been a professional strong man. The timber-cutters were at work on that area and Hebert was afraid that some of them might find his vein, so he took me to the place very cautiously. The vein was afterward called the Little Silver; it formed a fissure in the cliff, about 60 ft. high, and the face of the vein was weathered, leaving the silver exposed so that it was falling down the cliff. It was a real textbook vein.

Then the discoverers were not ordinary prospectors?

No; they were all employed in railway construction. La Rose was the blacksmith and Hebert was employed in some similar capacity, I don't know just what. He discovered some of these deposits by walking across to see a cousin, who, I think, was employed in cutting timber.

Then they had been in the employ of the railway construction company a few days before?

For some time; they were still employed. These discoveries were all within a few hundred yards of the railroad.

And all made within two or three days?

No; they had known of some of them for probably a month or two months, but hadn't paid much attention to them. I suppose they had never seen any ore before. La Rose had been working on phosphate, but I don't think he knew anything about metallic minerals.

Having made your inspection, what did you do?

I wrote to the Department, at Toronto, telling what I had seen.

Was that report published?

Yes. That letter was published with my subsequent report, I think. The result was that when I got out to the railway again the first thing I saw in the hotel was a large poster to the effect that the Government had withdrawn all the land for some distance along the railway, and for some distance on both sides—withdrawn

THE RAILWAY CUT IN WHICH THE MURRAY OREBODY WAS FOUND AT SUDBURY, ONTARIO

THE SHAFT-HOUSE OF THE CREIGHTON MINE, AT SUDBURY

it from prospecting and staking. A few months later the land was again thrown open to location.

And the locations were validated?

Yes; the locations on which the discoveries had been made were recognized from the beginning. The Government didn't try to take them away. It was difficult to get the public interested in these deposits. Not long before that we had had a mining boom, one of our periodical booms in Canada, in which many people had lost money. The public had lost interest in mineral deposits. I had a good exhibit of these cobalt-silver ores placed in the King Edward hotel at Toronto, for the benefit of the Canadian Mining Institute meeting in March 1904, but nobody took much interest in it. They were fine specimens, but that was about all! It took nearly eighteen months to arouse public interest.

Since then how much silver has the Cobalt district produced?

Over 292,000,000 ounces, besides cobalt, nickel, and arsenic.

Have you remained Provincial Geologist and continued your interest in the exploration of this Canadian hinterland? Did you have anything to do, officially, with Porcupine, in its early stage of development?

The result of the success of Cobalt was that we got many prospectors into the northern country and many men who were willing to give financial support to small syndicates of prospectors. Every year since then, almost every few months, some important discoveries have been made. Until the railway was completed north to Cochrane, the Porcupine country and other areas were rather inaccessible, requiring a roundabout canoe trip to get there. The important discoveries at Porcupine were made in 1908, but not much work was done until 1909, when we placed a party in the field, to map the area. We have had parties surveying and mapping the surrounding areas ever since, each year. Porcupine has become widely known and Kirkland Lake, a district farther south, is now becoming an important producer. Gold has been found in promising quantities over a wide extent of country. In so far as the geology is concerned, Cobalt has served as the key to a wide region. Any person having a good knowledge of the geology of Cobalt has little difficulty in mapping other areas in the region.

Do you consider that there is a likelihood of further important discoveries in that part of Canada?

Yes, Sir; I expect that many important discoveries will be made there.

I presume that some valuable outcrops may be covered by the lakes and swamps.

Yes; the most important vein at Cobalt, for instance, lay under a lake. The latest gold deposit developed in that northern country, namely, the Lake Shore mine, on Kirkland lake, is similarly situated. That, by the way, is an interesting mine. It is opened up to a depth of about 400 ft., and the ore from development work has given a recovery of over $24 per ton.

From gold in quartz?

Gold in quartz.

You have done a great deal of exploratory work in that part of Canada, and I should like to ask you to say something about the prospects generally, even outside Ontario, going so far as the Coppermine River district and Le Pas, in Manitoba. If you will be good enough to speak of the mining opportunities of this northern part of the continent I feel sure that what you say will be read with keen interest.

Canada has an area of about 3,750,000 square miles. About two-thirds of this area is occupied by pre-Cambrian rocks, and throughout these pre-Cambrian regions the conditions are much the same as they are in northern Ontario, where we have already proved that they contain important silver, gold, nickel, and copper deposits. We have great hopes therefore that many more Sudburies, Cobalts, and Porcupines will be discovered in these pre-Cambrian rocks. During the last three or four years important discoveries have been made in the provinces farther to the west, in Manitoba and Saskatchewan, for instance, the Flin Flon and Mandy lodes. The Canadian government has a railway nearly completed to Port Nelson, on Hudson's bay. The road is graded and I think only about 90 miles of steel remains to be laid. As soon as this railway is completed it will be possible for a prospector to take a boat on Hudson's bay and land on either the west or the east coast, where there are vast areas of promising mineral territory. I look on the regions around Hudson's bay, the pre-Cambrian shield, as it is sometimes called, as the most important prospecting ground, or unprospected territory, that remains anywhere in the world. While much of this big stretch of land is unprospected, the Canadian Geological Survey has had parties through these regions at various times, and we know what the character of the rock is. For instance, we know that the rocks in the Coppermine River region are much like those in the great copper belt of Michigan and we know that these Coppermine River rocks extend pretty close to the western shore of Hudson's bay. That country is, in many ways, easier to prospect than northern Ontario, because it has not such a growth of timber; it is more open. In some places, of course, it is low-lying, but elsewhere good exposures of rock are numerous. Then the east coast of Hudson's bay, which belongs to the Province of Quebec, is promising and has been prospected very little.

Why is that so?

Because this northern part of Quebec is difficult to reach by the St. Lawrence route. The rivers are rapid and difficult to navigate; but, as soon as we have some boats on Hudson's bay, the prospector will be able to get in and spend a good season there. The trouble with navigation there, of course, is in the straits; not in the bay itself. As you know, the Hudson Bay railway was built primarily to take grain from western Canada to Europe. I have always been in favor of building this road, not because I was particularly interested in grain,

COBALT IN 1911

THE CONGLOMERATE AT COBALT IN WHICH SILVER VEINS ARE FOUND

but because it seemed to me that such a vast region should easily support one railway. There are fisheries in Hudson's bay that have not been examined thoroughly, but the mineral possibilities are the more attractive to you and me.

You must have found your work as Provincial Geologist deeply interesting, having regard to the evident progress made by Ontario in mining.

Yes, our mineral industry has had a marvelous growth since 1902. Our annual output, for instance, at that time was valued at about $14,000,000, whereas for 1918 it is over $94,000,000, according to the estimate of the Mines Department at Ottawa. The work, in addition to being interesting, has been pleasant, as I have always felt that I have had the friendship and support of the Ministers of Mines under whom I have served, notably the Hon. Frank Cochrane, who was Minister during the development of Cobalt. And our Deputy Minister of Mines, T. W. Gibson, has always been my good friend. I have had opportunities to visit other countries during the period I have been Provincial Geologist, as the official representative of the Mines Department. I have made trips to many parts of the United States, and to old Mexico, to Cuba, to Great Britain, France, Scandinavia, Australia, and the South Pacific. Obviously, I was afforded unusual opportunities, for which I am grateful. Another thing that helped my work and made it pleasant was that I have had as my chief assistants former students of mine, from Queen's University, whom I knew thoroughly. Cyril W. Knight's work is well known in connection with Cobalt and other areas; so also that of A. G. Burrows. E. T. Corkill, one of my former students, was for a number of years Chief Inspector of Mines in Ontario, and is now superintendent of mines for the International Nickel Company, at Copper Cliff. Mr. Corkill was with us during the interesting developments at Cobalt.

Were any unusual difficulties settled during your time of service as Provincial Geologist? For instance, if I recall correctly, there was some complication over the Gillies Timber Limit.

When the Cobalt deposits were discovered the mining laws of Ontario were rather crude. The regulations had been devised more for taking up iron lands; they were not adapted to precious metal deposits. The result was that we had to spend much time in preparing the Mines Act and other legislative enactments. The regulations that we finally adopted included those for the discovery of the precious metals. As we officials had made the discoveries on the shore of Cobalt lake, I advised the Government to withdraw the lake from location. It also withdrew Kerr lake and afterward sold Cobalt lake for $1,085,000, deriving a large revenue from the Crown Reserve mine on Kerr lake. The Gillies Timber Limit adjoined the Cobalt area immediately to the south. It was withdrawn from staking in order to protect the timber. Finally, the Government itself decided to work this 'Limit'. I was put in charge. I did not believe that much would be discovered, however, as I had mapped the area in detail, but as the Government had decided on the policy I had to do the best I could. The Government was criticized a good deal by certain promoters, and prospectors kept constantly saying that if private individuals were working it a much greater success could be made of it. I quieted them to some extent by saying that I was "keeping a list of liars and lunatics who said they knew where there were rich veins on the Gillies limit." It is remarkable how many supposedly reputable citizens at that time solemnly affirmed that they had seen valuable deposits on the Limit! After working it for some time, I advised that we give these private individuals and companies an opportunity to work it. We then surveyed part of the Limit and put the claims up for sale by tender, the result being that the Government received a considerable sum of money; but no important discoveries have been made on it. I might add that, after the first sale, a discovery was made which created considerable excitement. Whereupon some of our newspapers said "I told you so" and "the Government did not handle this right," and so forth. I considered it quite a compliment to myself that when I immediately advised the Government to sell some more claims, it, despite the statements that were made in the press about the richness of the area, took my advice.

THE LAKE SHORE MINE ON KIRKLAND LAKE

You must have taken part in the efforts made to obtain the metals needed for the War? For instance, I might ask you to say something about the public feeling in Canada toward the American ownership of the nickel deposits at Sudbury and the friendly efforts made to adjust that difficulty.

Of course, when the War started our people naturally became a little nervous, or sensitive, as regards nickel, because, although we produced over 80% of the world's output, we were not refining any in Canada, and the public feared that some of our Canadian nickel might be getting to Germany.

There was considerable agitation on the subject, especially after the submarine 'Deutschland' was reported to have come to this side of the Atlantic to take back a cargo of nickel?

Yes; nickel has been a disturbing subject at different

times in the past; there has been a public demand for the erection of a refinery in Canada. The result of the agitation during the War was that the Ontario government decided to appoint a commission, known as the Royal Ontario Nickel Commission, which consisted of the late George T. Holloway, metallurgist, of London, England, McGregor Young, legal adviser, T. W. Gibson, Deputy Minister of Mines, and myself. We were given authority to investigate the nickel industry of the world thoroughly. We carried on work in Canada, the United States, and in Great Britain. Some of us went to France, Norway, Cuba, Australia, New Caledonia, and elsewhere. This work took a year and a half, our report being published in 1917. We now have a large new refining plant at Port Colborne. This belongs to our biggest nickel-mining company, the International Nickel Company. The Mond Nickel Co., an English corporation, which is also working at Sudbury, refines its matte near Swansea, in Wales. The British-America Corporation, in which the British government is a large stockholder, is erecting a refinery near the city of Ottawa; so that within a comparatively short time Canada will not only be the principal miner of nickel, but a large refiner of the metal as well.

Does any of the matte go, as it did previously, to New Jersey?

Yes, the International Nickel Co. refines a large part of its matte in New Jersey, at the Orford works, near Bayonne.

How much do they refine in Canada?

Their plant in Canada started about the first of July 1918. The capacity of the plant at Port Colborne is 10,000 tons of nickel per annum, but in time the efficiency of the Port Colborne Plant and double taxation may induce the company to do most of its refining in Canada. It is subject to taxation in both countries.

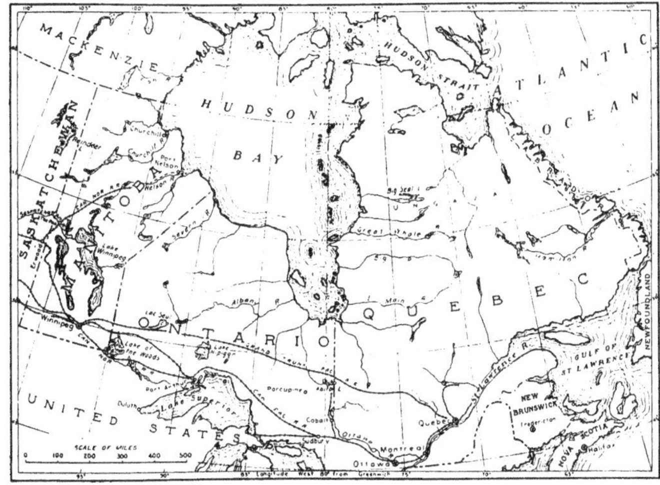

MAP SHOWING THE HUDSON'S BAY REGION

What are the prospects for the base-metal and precious-metal industries in Ontario at the present moment; that is, to what extent is the industry affected by the aftermath of war?

Our nickel output is not so large, but our gold output is expected to increase very much during the coming year. There has been a shortage of labor up to the present, but the mines are now getting all the men they need, I understand.

There is a confident feeling at Toronto, for example?

Yes, and I think this applies not only to Ontario, but to the more western provinces. British Columbia is optimistic. They have a large territory there to develop and their output has grown rapidly of late years. Then.

on the eastern seaboard we have an important iron and steel industry and vast coal deposits.

Dr. Miller, I understand, from my own limited acquaintance with conditions in Ontario and British Columbia, for instance, that many of the mines are owned by American capitalists. May I ask you to what extent the use of American capital in these Canadian mining regions is welcomed by the people of the Dominion?

It is always welcome. I might say that in Canada we have no restrictions on aliens from the Allied countries like you have in the United States. I understand that in the United States an alien cannot stake a claim. We have no such restrictions in Canada. Anybody but an enemy-alien can locate a claim, just the same as the native-born. We expect to get a great deal of capital from the United States, and we expect to have a large immigration from the United States, too, into the mining districts and into the agricultural districts of the West.

There is a duty on machinery, and I understand that there is even a duty on blueprints. Is there any prospect of a removal of some of these commercial barbed-wire entanglements?

I suppose that will depend not only on Canada, but on the United States. Of course, the feeling between the two countries could not be better than it is. We Canadians always feel at home in the United States, and we believe that citizens of the United States feel at home in Canada. We, in geology, for instance, in mining, chemistry, and in most of the other sciences, work very closely with our friends in the United States. For example, in pre-Cambrian geology I have been closely associated at times with C. R. Van Hise and C. K. Leith, and with other geologists in the United States. During my lifetime I have noted that the friendly feelings between Canadians and Americans have grown and increased constantly. Our peoples have become more friendly as the years have gone by, and, of course, the War has intensified this good feeling. We think that while we live under different flags we have the same aspirations, and nothing can interfere with these friendly relations in the future. Canada stands probably mid-way between the United States and Great Britain in many things.

Have you any signs of labor trouble in Ontario?

No; we do not think we shall have any trouble at all.

What is your labor chiefly?

It has been pretty well mixed in the past. Some of it is foreign, but a high percentage is English-speaking.

You have been a prominent member of the Canadian Mining Institute and of the American Institute of Mining Engineers. Would you say anything about the good work that either or both of them are doing?

I think it is recognized everywhere that the American Institute is doing wonderfully good work, not only for the industry, but also for the profession. Its growth during recent years has been wonderful. The Canadian Mining Institute is a much smaller organization, but it exercises a good influence in Canada. The governments of the Dominion and of the Provinces have always been willing to listen to recommendations made by the Canadian Mining Institute, and it has served a national purpose.

What are the prospects for an increase of production in nickel and of the discovery of new deposits, in your opinion, based on your recent investigation of the subject?

The quantity of ore proved in the Sudbury district has increased greatly during late years. When the Nickel Commission's report was published I estimated the proved ore—the ore blocked out—to be at least 75,000,000 tons. Since then there has been a considerable addition to this tonnage at Sudbury.

The other important source of ore is New Caledonia, I presume?

Yes, but there are no known deposits elsewhere in the world that can compete with Sudbury.

Are those of New Caledonia approaching exhaustion?

No; there is considerable ore there yet, but it occurs under conditions different from Sudbury. The New Caledonian ore occurs in lateritic deposits. Some of the deposits at Sudbury are probably unsurpassed in importance in the world among deposits of any kind, when you consider their size and the value of the ore. Of course, the War has encouraged the use of nickel-steel and other alloys. This means increased consumption of nickel in the future. Many people have used nickel-steel during the War that did not know anything about it before. Likewise the metal cobalt, for which there was little market, has come into prominence through the War. Cobalt is used with chromium and tungsten in the production of an alloy known as 'stellite', which is an important high-speed tool-steel. This use of stellite has increased the demand for cobalt very much.

Did you have any particular experience while in England that you might care to recall?

During my last visit in England, in 1918, I was the Canadian representative on the Imperial Mineral Resources Bureau. The Imperial War Conference of 1917 decided to have such a bureau organized. Its work is to size up the mineral resources of the British empire. When the War started it was found that, while the Empire could produce certain ores and minerals, refining facilities were inadequate or lacking within the Empire for such ores. It was decided that this condition should not continue. The aim now is to render the Empire as independent as possible, particularly to make it independent of the German reduction works. Arrangements have been made for smelting Australian zinc ores in England and also in Australia. During the summer there was an exhibition held in London called the 'Key Industries'. This showed what great developments had been made in smelting and refining since the War began. Great Britain is now self-contained to a much greater extent than she was in 1914.

GRASS VALLEY, CALIFORNIA

LAND TITLES IN DISPUTE - RE-WORKING OLD PROPERTY.

The case of the Golden Center Mining Co. of Grass Valley v. the city of Grass Valley was partly heard in the Sacramento Land Office on May 21. The contest was ordered by the Secretary of the Interior on petition, and the issue to be determined is whether the Roche Rock quartz claim, within the city limits, sought to be patented by the plaintiff, was mineral land at the time of the issuance of the townsite patent in 1869 or not. The company attempted to prove that the ground had always been considered mineral bearing, while the city contended that this claim had been abandoned for years and was therefore worthless for mining purposes. The principal witness for the company, John E. Carter, swore that the mine was worked in a general way for about eight months in the early days, but operations were not profitable. Later attempts also resulted in failure. The company exhibited records to show a clear title to the ground, although at one time eight persons were rival claimants. The ground in dispute was located in 1916, and adjoins the Golden Center mine. Recent discoveries of ore in the latter ground, pitching toward the Roche claim, are the real cause of the contention. The Golden Center, in spite of irregular operation, is generally looked upon as promising, although not as extensively developed as its neighbors. A network of gold-bearing veins underlie the city, and should the issue between the plaintiff company and the city be upheld by the Department of the Interior, the entire townsite area will be located, and parties now await a favorable outcome in order to locate. Some of these prospective locations are governed by the same conditions as the case at issue. The city and immediate vicinity have become famous as a gold-producing area. Another objection to the granting of a patent to the Röche Rock claim arises from civic pride at the behest of a few individuals who oppose mining within the residential district, and also to the precedent sought to be established, which may result in the upsetting of townsite titles. Aside from their own personal influence in opposing a patent, they prevailed upon the city trustees to oppose the granting of a patent. Compromise has been out of the question. Just where the city acquires the right to become a party in the adjudication of town titles is a problem, for the original patent was granted to the then judge of the County Court to be held in trust for the people and its successor, the present Superior Court. After the taking of testimony and hearing arguments the case was continued until June 20.

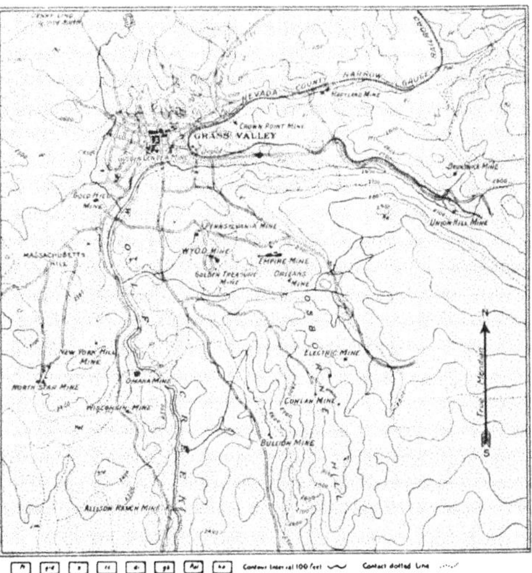

THE GRASS VALLEY DISTRICT, CALIFORNIA

A rich strike was made last week in the South Star mine in the Rough and Ready district four miles west of Grass Valley. A few men have been prospecting for several months under G. D. Freeborn.

A local co-partnership of 20 men, calling itself the State Highway Mining Co., until legally organized, has secured an option on the Morandi ranch of 200 acres a few miles south of town. Quartz veins were found in the early days and a small boom was in progress at one time. Revival of interest in that land was brought about by the recent discovery of specimen quartz by a member of a grading crew. Prospect holes from 30 to 40 ft. deep were sunk years ago, and some good ore extracted, yielding from a few dollars to $25 per ton, but no further interest was taken until recently. A gasoline hoist and pump have been installed on one shaft and two lots of men are at work preparatory to further operations. J. T. Blight is acting as manager and Fred Roehnert is secretary.

Dismantling of the machinery at the Idaho-Maryland is well advanced. The mill is gone, also the greater part of the plant around the hoist, all being shipped by rail to San Francisco.

The annual meeting of the Grass Valley Consolidated Mining Co., owner of the Allison Ranch mine, was held at Sacramento on May 24. Fair milling ore is coming from several upper levels and considerable prospecting is being done. A new board of directors was elected, namely: H. A. Heilbron, Sr., F. H. Buck, E. E. McMichael, A. E. Nelson, P. Huth. H. Kleisorge, Scott Ennis, and S. Jones. The board elected E. E. McMichael president, Scott Ennis vice-president, and H. A. Heilbron secretary-treasurer. C. A. Brockington will continue as superintendent.

HOUGHTON, MICHIGAN

IMPROVEMENTS AT THE QUINCY MINE AND MILL.

The Quincy company has completed the finest hoist-engine building in the Copper Country. Architecturally, it is admired by every visitor. It will house the most powerful hoist ever constructed—a new Nordberg engine that will pull a skip from a depth of 14,000 ft., the longest haul from any shaft in the world. The building was erected at a cost of $75,000. The interior finish is equal to the mine-office, yet the cost was not excessive, and includes the largest item, the concrete foundation for the engine. Erection of the hoist will require three, possibly four, months. It will serve No. 2 shaft, Quincy's deepest.

The Quincy mine is now yielding high-grade ore, the February production averaging 20 lb. (1%) per ton. This compares with 17.33 lb., the average for 1917. In March the yield was better than 19.5 lb. This includes a considerable quantity of mass copper. This is interesting, especially as the Quincy shafts all are very deep, and the yield of copper is higher than it has been at any time in ten years. It is indicative of the exclusion of the Pewabic lode from the general rule of the Lake Superior region that the copper content diminishes with depth. While mass and barrel copper continue to form an appreciable proportion of the Quincy output, the general run of ore at all of the newer openings is exceptionally good.

The company has instituted a scoop system to assist in stoping operations, which have become difficult in two of the shafts by reason of the flattening of the lode at great depth. This change in dip has prevented ore from dropping down the stope by gravity. A small 'puffer', operating a wide scoop, driven by an old wire hoisting-rope fixed along the roof of the stope, does the work successfully.

Quincy has the first stamp-mill with a plate-glass roof. Like the new hoisting-house at No. 2 shaft, the recent additions to the mill are very striking. The designs, in all cases, were made by engineering architects who knew nothing about stamp-mills or hoisting-plants. The glass roofs on the mill additions cost no more than the old style of roofing. They provide sunlight, saving electric light, and make the interior attractive for employees. The management contemplates the adoption of the glass-roof plan for the main sections of the mill, provided this experiment is successful, as seems likely. The additional mill capacity will probably increase the recovery from the milling ore by 4 or 5 lb. of copper, and reduce losses to a minimum.

An important source of copper was cut off by the Calumet & Hecla last week when the dredge that excavated sand from Torch lake went into dry dock for repairs. This shuts off 850,000 lb. per month. The boat has operated for five years. The plan to make extensive repairs was made more than a year ago, when the dock was built at Point Mills, five miles from the scene of dredge operations in Torch lake. The boat was towed through Torch lake and the canal into Big Portage to the specially constructed dry dock.

The exodus of workmen from the district has practically ended. No more men are being laid off by the C. & H., nor by its subsidiaries. The Quincy, Mohawk, Wolverine, and all three Copper Range mines—Baltic, Trimountain, and Champion—are working full time with full crews. Their copper output is not normal, but it has not been normal for more than a year. A limited number of the miners that were let out by the C. & H. and subsidiaries went to work at other mines in the district.

CHIHUAHUA, MEXICO

METAL PRODUCTION AND MINES IN OPERATION.

Fire recently destroyed most of the mining centre of Guadalupe y Calvo, near the border of Sinaloa, in southern Chihuahua. The nearest rail is at Parral.

For the first time since 1910 a complete statistical report of the mineral industry of Chihuahua has been compiled, giving the exact value of the mineral production for a whole year from all Chihuahua mines. The report was made by the State government.

The total value of metals from all mines in operation during 1918 amounted to ₱14,823,019. The value of the output in 1910 was ₱24,000,000. The principal companies that operated mines the past year were: The American Smelter & Refining Co., which produced P1,133,869; Potosi Mining, P5,629,605; Cusi Mining, P2,164,806; Buena Tierra Mining, P343,529; la Compania Minera de Lepanto, P95,951; Rio Plata Mining, P$80,013; Mines & Metals Security, P85,624; la Compania Rodriquez Ramos, P864; Erupcion Mining, P134,364; Moctezuma Lead, P112,309; Alvarado Mining, Florencio Villegas and others, of Parral, P1,000,000. All the companies whose names are not in Spanish are Amercan enterprises with the exception of the Lepanto, whose shareholders are Italians.

The location of the mines in operation in 1918 was at Sta. Eulalia, Villa Ahmada, Guazapares, Sta. Barbara, Parral, Almoloya (Jimenez) and Cusihuiriachic. The

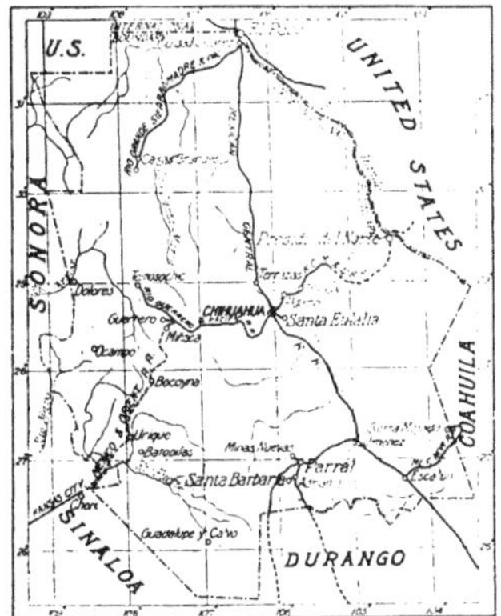

MAP OF STATE OF CHIHUAHUA

mines of Batopilas, Ocampo, Concheno, Dolores, Urique, Corralitos and Casas Grandes were not in operation during last year.

The following is a complete list of all the mining companies now working properties in Chihuahua, with the names of the mines and their location:

Dale Henos. y Co., the Inglaterra and the Emma at Sta. Eulalia.—Ing. Manuel Gameros, the Democracia, the Esmeralda, and the Plomosas. Sta. Eulalia.—San Toy Mining Co., the Galdiano, the Central and the Bustillos at Sta. Eulalia.—La Reina de Plata Ltd., the Las Contiguas de Sta. Fe, at Sta. Eulalia.—Buena Tierra Mining Co., the Buena Tierra, at Sta. Eulalia.—Potosi Mining Co., the Potosi and others at Sta. Eulalia.—American Smelting Co., the Sto. Domingo, at Sta. Eulalia.—Erupcion Mining Co., La Erupcion, at V. Gonzalez.—San Juan Mg. Co., the San Juan, at San Ignacio.—Rio de Plata Mg. Co., Sta. Barbara, the El Agua Novedad and the La Reina-Felipinas, at Rio Plata.—Moctezuma Lead Co. the Alejandria, at Sta. Barbara.—San. Fco. Mines of Mex. Ld. Co. Varias proprietades, at San. Fco. del Oro.—Comp. Metalurgica de Torreon, the San Diego, at Sta. Barbara.—Miguel Tinoco, El Calallo, at Sta. Barbara.—Florencio Villegas, the Clarines, at Sta. Barbara.—Carlos Villegas, La Cubana, at Sta. Barbara.—Alvarado Mng. Co., La Palomilla, at Parral.—Fco. Chavez (h), El Tajo, and the Ocho properties, at Parral.—Cia. Igno Rodriguez Ramos, at Allende.—F. F. Herrera, El Hundido, at Villa Lopez.—The Cusi Mining Co., the Promontorio, at Ciro, and y Anexas de Ciro, at Cusihuiriachic.—And the Cusi Mexicana Mng. Co., the San Miguel, at Cusihuiriachic.

DURANGO, COLORADO

SILVERTON, RED MOUNTAIN, RICO, AND OURAY DISTRICTS.

No great activity is expected in the Red Mountain district until later in the season, when market conditions may be better, and operating costs lower. The rising price for copper is encouraging development of the local mines.

The Radiant M. & M. Co. has started development, and expects to be ready to ship in the near future, probably as soon as the Red Mountain branch of the railroad is opened.

Driving by the Summit Copper Co. is completed, the Kohler tunnel and the second level of the Carbon Lake shaft are connected by a 150-ft. raise, improving ventilation and cutting handling costs from the various levels to the railroad.

The Red Mountain Mines Co., has started another important opening, a cross-cut from the Joker tunnel to the lower shaft workings of the Robinson.

Driving continues in the Meldrum tunnel. This is being driven from the Red Mountain side of the range, starting at a point near Ironton, the Silver Bell mine, with the objective of connecting with the Bridal Veil basin on the Telluride side, from where a similar tunnel has been started. The distance to be driven is four miles; 1000 ft. of this has been covered on the Red Mountain side, and one mile has been driven from the Bridal Veil Basin side. The tunnels are 12 by 12 ft., and are expected to cut the extension of the Tomboy lode at a depth of 2000 ft. lower than the present workings. Several lodes are reported to have been cut on the Telluride side, affording encouragement for further exploration.

The rising price of metals has had a marked effect upon the development of the Rico district, and the outlook for a busy season is excellent.

A demand for the iron sulphides of the Marmatite M. & M. Co. resulted in that property resuming operations upon an extensive scale, and a large force has been employed on the Rico Argentine properties. Ore is now being shipped at the rate of 2 cars per day, and production will be increased. A mud-slide carried out part of the tramway and temporarily interfered with operations. Development of the bodies of iron pyrite continues, and shipments are going regularly to Eastern points. A large quantity of zinc ore is being mined.

Preliminary work at the Resolute has encouraged the operating company to complete the purchase price. Bonds will be issued to the amount of $75,000, to be secured by mortgages on the Newman group. This sum will be devoted to paying off the balance of the price of the property, and to building a mill with a flotation unit.

The companies at Ouray have adopted the Telluride scale of pay, with the increase to $1.35 per day rate for board. With the increasing price for silver, the various mines yielding such ore are encouraged to ship.

The Camp Bird continues to develop along the tunnel-level east, and there is a good showing of ore. No immediate change in the plans of blocking out 40,000 tons of ore in the mine stopes before resuming milling is to be expected.

The Atlas Mining Co. will continue to develop its holdings, and intends to operate upon a much larger scale during the present season. A better grade of ore is being opened and the financial condition of the company is excellent.

During discussion of the proposed reduction in wages, mining operations fell to a low ebb here, adding to the depression caused by the fire at the Sunnyside mine, but the outlook is somewhat improved, as the men have agreed to a reduction in wages, the rate to be $4.25 per day, a cut of 50c.; $1.25 is to be for board. The early agreement was due largely to the local spirit of co-operation that prevails. In the present dispute all interests endeavored to arrive at a mutual understanding. There is no question but that operators have been working on a small margin, due to well-known causes, and this point was conceded by the miners. The principal objection raised by the Union was the prevailing high prices of goods at the local stores, and as many of the men were obliged to maintain their families in town, and to board themselves at the mines, they questioned the fairness of an increase in the rate for board, while merchants maintained their prices. The storekeepers thereupon cut prices somewhat, offsetting the increased rate for board, and facilitating the settlement of the trouble. The labor situation is now settled, although Telluride has attracted a large number of skilled miners, left idle by the Sunnyside fire. Some months will probably elapse before the district is operating on a large scale, but the rise in silver and the gradually rising price of copper is encouraging, and will no doubt result in an earlier return to normal than anticipated.

An interesting item is the re-opening of the Gold Fountain property. This was located 20 years ago by O. C. Hand; related to a Chicago man, John M. Smyth, who invested a large amount of money in it, largely in tunnels and shafts. Upon Smyth's death operations came to a standstill. Although many applications were made for a lease on the property, the heirs of the estate refused, and held out for too high a price for a sale, so that the property has lain idle for a number of years. A company has been organized recently to operate the property under bond and lease, composed of heirs of the estate, and other residents of Delta, Colorado. A purchaser of shares in the new company is to take in addition a 1/50 portion of the treasury shares, paying thereon an assessment of 3 mills a share each month. The fund from these assessments is to be used for prospecting and development. Should much pay-ore be opened, assessments cease and the treasury shares become worth par. Officers are O. C. Hand, president; Dr. O. W. McArthur, vice-president; and N. J. Bradley, secretary.

DIVIDE, NEVADA

LATEST DEVELOPMENTS.—NAMES OF SOME OF THE OUTSIDERS.

The Tonopah Divide last week sent 420 tons of ore to the MacNamara mill at Tonopah. Recent work includes driving raises for development of ore and improvement of ventilation, also cutting the station on the bottom level. On No. 3, the sill floor at 311 stope is in 45 ft., the ore averaging $85 per ton. No. 1 raise from No. 4 level is up 75 ft. in $60 ore. There are 38 men employed at the property.

The East Divide has cut a low-grade vein on the 400-ft. level. At latest advice the ore was 8 ft. wide, the other wall not being reached.

At the Gold Reef surface equipment is nearly complete. A motor-driven compressor and machine-drills have been put in. The shaft is down 115 feet.

The Dividend has replaced its gasoline machinery by electric motors. A station and pockets are to be cut at a depth of 500 ft., and the shaft sunk to 600 feet.

Other properties partly or fully equipped and at work include the Gold Reef Divide, Alto Divide, Sutherland Divide, Allied Divide, Rosetta, Gold Wedge, Ben Hur, Divide Annex, Verdi, Hennessy, Florence, Mohawk, East Divide Extension, Divide City Mining, High Divide, Victory, Crown, Western, Liberty, Calumet, Silver King, Syndicate, Trilby, Reno, Smuggler, Bevis, Pershing, Rand, Aztec, Old Timer, Hasbrouck Divide, Chariot, Kernick, Grimes, Silver Divide, Giant, Big Divide, Pyramid, Lookout, Goldsmith, Champion, Comstock, Wonder, Junior, Homestake, Mecca, Apex, Central, Doctor, Keystone, Western, Klondyke, Northwest, Portland, Charter, Ajax, Belmont, Bingo, Farrell, South, Telephone Girl, Ideal, Doughboy, Crescent, National, Sterling, Argentine, North, Wilson, Jim's, Mizpah, Kendall, Eureka, Treadwell, Gold Bank, Horseshoe, Marne, Sunbeam, Toggery, Mighty, Belcher, Operator, Midway, Rosalind, Emancipator, and many others.

The Emancipator is an enterprise of the Mudd, Webster, Wiseman syndicate, with W. C. Rannells, who managed the Hays-Monnette lease on the Goldfield Mohawk, in charge. The Kernick Divide, Giant Divide, Apex Divide, and Hercules Divide are Wingfield-Brougher companies; the Belcher and Victory are sponsored by officers of the Tonopah Belmont company; while the Argonne Divide, adjoining the Hercules and Rosetta, is headed by directors of the Tonopah Mining Company.

THE MINING SUMMARY

A bill to suspend all assessment work on mining claims during the War and for one year after peace is declared was introduced to Congress on May 31 by Representative Raker, and will be, it is reported, favorably considered by the House Mining Committee. The measure is important to veterans, inasmuch as many of the soldiers left their mining claims in California and other Western States to enter the Army, without performing their assessment work.

ALASKA

Anchorage.—The House Appropriation Committee at Washington decided on May 26 to include in the general deficiency bill an appropriation of $2,000,000 for immediate use in construction of the Government railroad in Alaska. Members of the Alaskan Engineering Commission said that construction would be interrupted unless money was provided soon by Congress. The Commission's request for an increase of the original $35,000,000 authorization for building the line, of which $31,000,000 has been spent, will be considered by the Committee in framing the new sundry civil appropriation bill.

Nome.—The ice on Bering Sea broke on May 27, a month earlier than last year, and the earliest since 1913.

ARIZONA

Bisbee.—Shattuck Arizona Copper Co. during the first quarter of 1919 made a loss of $163,988. Revenue from metals, etc., was $227,520. The output was 1,000,844 lb. of copper, 678,914 lb. of lead, 160 oz. of gold, and 44,129 oz. of silver, from 14,831 tons of copper and 3138 tons of lead ore. Development amounted to 1708 ft. On the 200-ft. level there was opened 12 ft. of 7.2% copper ore for a length of 76 ft. Good oxide ore was exposed at 500 and between 700 and 800 ft. As fire broke out in the sulphide zone between 700 and 800 ft., mining was stopped on February 22. The workings were flooded and the fire was expected to be extinguished early in May. Tests are being made to improve the reduction of lead ore in the mill.

Jerome.—The United Verde Extension Mining Co. has been awarded by the State Corporation Commission a railroad freight rebate amounting to $200,000 on shipments of ore from Clarkdale to Globe and Douglas. The companies that have to pay this are the Southern Pacific, Santa Fe, El Paso & Southwestern, Arizona Eastern, and S. F. P. & P. lines.

Phoenix.—The Arizona Corporation Commission is to aid the State's copper companies in their protest against excessive freight-rates on copper bullion sent to refineries in the East. Before the War, the rate from Douglas to New York by way of Galveston was $8.55 per ton. Then came a raise of 25%, and later another that brought the rate up to the present figure of $16.50. It is estimated that, on the basis of normal bullion production, this means an added exaction of nearly $4,000,000 a year, to be paid by the Arizona companies. There is to be a hearing in Chicago on June 2, the complaint including 47 separate rail and steamship lines. Complainants are the Phelps Dodge, Calumet & Arizona, Old Dominion, and United Verde Extension companies. The Ray Consolidated has a separate action of its own.

Quartzsite.—At the Goodman gold mine a new mill is being erected, as the mine developed so well during the past year.

The Copper bottom mine, which had an excellent record up to a few years ago, is being re-opened by Chicago capital. Those in charge evidently are competent and financially able to bring this property back to its former good standing.

The King Placer Co. is negotiating for a new and larger steam-shovel to replace the one laid up.

There are two concentrating plants working on silver-lead ore at Dome. One crushes wet, using Wilfley tables; the other crushes dry, using Stebbins concentrators. The dry process seems to give equal results with the wet tables on this ore.

Superior.—The Fortuna Consolidated Co. has been successfully financed, and sinking is to be started at once on the most favorable showing developed in the tunnel recently driven. A hoist and compressor are to be installed.

CALIFORNIA

Pala.—Lepidolite, a silicate of alumina and potash, is found in small quantities in many localities in this country, but the only known deposit of commercial size is at this place in San Diego county. A mine there is operated by the American Lithia & Chemical Co., of New York.

Portola.—The Anaconda Copper Mining Co., of Montana, which controls the International Smelting Co., has the following statement in its report for 1918, just issued:

Walker Mining Company—On October 1, 1918, the International Smelting Co. exercised its option on 630,000 out of a total of 1,250,000 shares of the Walker Mining Co.'s stock. This property is in Plumas county, California, 22 miles by wagon-road from Portola, a station on the Western Pacific railroad. The holdings of the Walker company consist of 38 patented lode claims and 2 placer claims, all forming a compact block of ground. The exploration of the property to the depth of 346 ft. has been accomplished by two shafts. Drifts from these shafts have opened an ore-body 800 ft. long averaging 16 ft. wide, and a grade of 4% copper. Recent developments by means of diamond-drill holes indicate an additional length of vein approximating 900 ft. There is still a considerable amount of unexplored ground. The following construction and development program is now in progress: (1) increasing capacity of concentrator to 200 tons per day; (2) construction of a new tailing dam; (3) erection of an aerial tram 8.2 miles long to carry concentrates to and supplies from the railroad; (4) driving a cross-cut tunnel from the concentrator site a distance of 3500 ft. to strike the extension of the vein, then following the vein to the shaft, a distance of 1200 (this tunnel will develop the property to a depth of 800 ft.) (5) additional housing facilities for employees; and (6) additional equipment in the form of electric hoist and small shops.

Washington.—R. E. Conrad, manager of the Sierra asbestos mine, a short distace from town, is preparing to resume work for the season. Mining was discontinued last fall because it was impossible to dress the rock except by the dry process. Mining is by open-cut.

John L. Whitney, superintendent of the Columbia mines

at Ormonde, has 10 men at work, and the 20-stamp mill will be started this week.

Thirty men are employed at the Gaston mine and ore is being extracted from the lower tunnel.

COLORADO

Boulder.—The City Bank & Trust Company's business at Denver was suspended on May 28, by order of the State Bank Examiner, Grant McFerson. According to W. J. Galligan, president of the institution, and George McLean, vice-president, a cashier named R. A. Brown and an assistant cashier named P. A. Simpson, and J. S. Barnhill, president of the Colorado Pitchblende Co., a depositor, figured in the transactions that caused the trouble. It is alleged that the cashiers mentioned accepted Barnhill's drafts on a bank at Burleigh, Idaho, and issued cashier's checks in return. The president of the bank had given orders that no money be loaned to Barnhill, but apparently the cashiers did so by irregular methods. Brown disappeared early in May, sending in his resignation. Simpson confessed what had been going on. Detectives were searching for Brown and Barnhill at the end of May. The secretary of the Colorado Pitchblende Co. said that all attempts to find Barnhill up to May 29 had been fruitless.

Cripple Creek.—According to D. C. Wannamaker, secretary of the Cripple Creek Mine Owners and Operators Association, while a number of miners have returned to the district and been given employment in the past three weeks, there is still need of 75 to 100 experienced machine-men and shovelers. Machine-men receive $4.50 and the shovelers $3.75 per day. Mr. Wannamaker states that there has been more demand for properties for leasing in the past month than for several years, and that a number of properties will start as soon as an ample supply of labor is

The Cripple Creek District Commercial and Auto Club has appointed a committee to wait on the mine-owners to see if they will make concessions on the rates of royalties and thereby encourage a lot of surface prospecting and other mine development, especially during the summer months.

The Vindicator has added four concentrators to its flotation plant.

IDAHO

Lenia.—The Idaho Gold & Ruby Mining Co. in Boundary county will have its 6-mile ditch completed in two months, according to the president, J. M. Schnatterly. Sluice-boxes are being built. Three 9-inch nozzles will be used to move the gravel.

Mullan.—The Federal Mining & Smelting Co., which operates the Morning mine and mill at Mullan, the Standard-Mammoth and Greenhill-Cleveland mines and mill at Mace, and the North Star-Triumph and Independence mines and mill at Hailey, reports gross sales of $2,405,867 during 1918. The profit was $545,876 plus $296,382 from other sources, a total of $824,258. Dividends amounted to $838,-854. After paying for miscellaneous charges there was a deficit of $108,917. Cash at the end of the year was $285,-440, against $1,601,157 on December 31, 1917. Settlement with the Minerals Separation company is placed at $142,536.

The Rex Consolidated is to resume work when prices are normal, and sink its shaft 400 ft. to 1100 ft. depth. The company has acquired an interest in a copper mine near Cima, California. Recently a good deal of its Idaho mine equipment was stolen.

MICHIGAN

Houghton.—Copper Range pays 50 cents per share on June 16. This is equal to $197,199 and makes $591,598 for the current year and $26,012,302 to date.

Wolverine pays 50 cents per share on July 1. This is equal to $30,000.

NEVADA

Elko.—The new Catlin 150-ton oil-shale plant is in operation, in charge of Walter Sheeler. There are 40 men employed at present.

Fallon.—The Travelers Oil & Development Co. has been organized by commercial travelers for the purpose of exploring the Linder oilfield in the Stillwater district, 20 miles east of Fallon. The field was recently examined by N. R. Garfims, who pronounced the geological indications indentical with those prevalent in the Coalinga, Fullerton, and Lost Hills fields of California. Preparations are being made to start a drill at the most promising point, where the shale yields traces of oil.

Jarbidge.—The Coeur d'Alene-Jarbidge Gold Mining Co. was organized under the laws of Idaho in 1910 to work the Victoria group of 11 claims. This property covered about half of the floor of Jack Creek crater, at an elevation of 8000 to 10,500 ft. Over $5000 was spent in development. Unfortunately, an empty treasury late in 1916 caused the company to forfeit its claims on January 4, 1917. The ground was immediately re-located, when 17 claims were staked, now known as the Bullion group. The new owners, A. L. Rinearson, V. M. and N. N. Vuckovich, have uncovered four new veins, the largest being 16 ft. between smooth walls. Hand samples show free gold. The old company had opened three veins, each 40 to 48 in. wide. Two of them contained ore that paid to sack. The intention was to pack the ore 4 miles down Jack creek to the wagon-road, then haul to Rogerson, Idaho, for shipment by rail to a smelter.

Isaac W. Anderson of Tacoma, Washington, was at Twin Falls, Idaho, recently when, it is said, he obtained a lease and option to purchase the Bluster mine and mill for Spokane capital.——It is also reported that George Wingfield has secured a lease and option to purchase the Success mine. The Success adjoins the Bluster on its north end. He had a previous option on the Success, but gave it up.

Reno.—The Star of the West Mining Co. has recently been incorporated and taken over the property formerly belonging to an English company, called the Nevada Mining Co. The mine is on the northern line of Nye county and consists of three patented claims and mill-sites. The property was tied up by litigation for years, preventing operations; but prior to that time it is stated that the owners produced more than a million dollars of gold and silver. More than a mile of underground development work has been done, and the deepest working is only 170 ft., with veins intact at that point, and the value ranging from $10 to $50 per ton. The old mills on the property are obsolete, and this company has purchased a mill from the Colorado Iron Works of Denver, one that will treat about 50 tons of ore per day, as a first unit of a larger plant. As soon as the weather permits, erection of the mill will be started.

Round Mountain.—The report of the Round Mountain Mining Co., Gibson Berry superintendent, for 1918, contains the following:

Placer gold realized $68,324, and sundry earnings brought the year's total to $98,889. Operations cost $74,-245, leaving a profit of $24,646. Current assets total $100,356 and liabilities $82,886. The cost statements are given in great detail. In the lode mine, lessees performed 2292 ft. of new work and restored 1033 ft. of levels, and resulted in the company getting $19,657 in royalties. They mined 2131 tons of ore averaging $36.70 per ton. This was reduced by Huntington and tube-mills in the company's own plant. In the placer mine, the season for water was poor, giving hydraulic head for only 1318 hours, against 2928 hours in 1917. Normally there is enough water for two giants, but last year there was not sufficient for one. The current season of 1919 had the greatest snowfall ever known in the district, and it is estimated that 200,000 yards of over $1 gravel will be moved, compared with 71,367 yards of 95.7-cent material in 1918. The operating cost was 68.35 cents per yard. The Star drilling-rig worked ahead of hydraulicking, and 600,000 cu. yd. has been sampled, averaging over $1 per yard.

UTAH

Alta.—Snow has been moved from the railway into the Cottonwood district, and ore is now being sent to market. In places, the snow was 15 ft. deep. Shay engines are used.

The Wasatch Mines Company's tunnel is in 4200 ft., and another 160 ft. is expected to reach the Rexall-Cardiff fault-plane, on which the Wasatch vein, in No. 5 stope, developed much rich ore above until the large volume of water prevented profitable extraction. When this objective is reached, the workings will be at a vertical depth of 575 ft. and the tunnel will permanently overcome all difficulties with water. During April the tunnel was advanced 222 ft. Progress is at the rate of from 7 to 10 ft. per day, with two shifts engaged.

American Fork.—Five mines are now at work in this district, the higher price for silver making the outlook more attractive.

Eureka.—The Chief Consolidated, Cecil Fitch superintendent, has issued a report covering the first quarter of 1918. The net profit was $125,304. Dividends—12½ and 6¼ cents—in February and May absorbed $168,004, making $1,402,875 to date. Current assets total $243,895, plus $505,504 in Liberty Bonds and $76,336 in cash. Liabilities amount to $82,456, plus $134,120 for taxes. New work in the mines covered 5070 ft., on the 1000, 1600, 1800, and 1900-ft. levels. The most important result was the discovery of ore on the 1052 drift, which has been prospecting ground 3000 ft. east from No. 1 mine. This is regarded as a new ore-channel. No. 2 shaft, being sunk, will serve as an outlet for this ore. Shipments were 15,170 tons of ore averaging 0.0406 oz. gold, 38.427 oz. silver, 9.23% lead in lead ore and 1.46% copper in copper ore. The gross value was $43.57 per ton. All costs were $35.30 per ton.

Morrissey.—The Utah Sulphur Co. in Beaver county has decided to construct furnaces for the subliming of sulphur, according to M. P. Morrissey, general manager. Improvements are estimated to cost $180,000. When the additions are complete the works will have a daily capacity of 600 tons of ore, yielding 150 to 200 tons of sublimed sulphur. Some sulphur disulphide will be made also. The two retorts in operation are making 40 tons of high-grade sulphur per day and the output has been sold for 60 days.

Park City.—The Silver King Coalition Mines Co. during 1918 received $797,181 from the sales of ore, etc. Of this, $97,651 was profit, less $51,602 for depreciation. Dividends absorbed $182,415, so the surplus was reduced by $136,365. In the mine, development covered 7143 ft. The output of crude ore was 8184 tons of first-class, assaying 32.72% lead, 28.42 oz. silver, 0.08 oz. gold, and 0.296% copper. Concentrate from 43,042 tons of ore carried 24.3%, 19.92 oz., 0.066 oz., and 0.235%, of these metals. The total output was 10,105,775 lb. of lead, 440,064 oz. of silver, 1375 oz. of gold, and 109,732 lb. of copper. During April, 1919, the 1300-ft. level is opening some important orebodies. S. A. Knowles is superintendent.

Silver City.—G. H. Dern has transfered his interest in the Tintic Milling Co. to Jesse Knight, who has been associated with him during the past four years. The daily capacity of the plant is 150 tons. T. P. Holt is superintendent.

Tintic.—On May 18, the miners on strike here decided to vote on the dispute on the 20th, but a meeting of 1200 men on the 19th voted to defer action until some later date.

The Tintic Bullion Mining Co. has been organized by J. M. Bestelmeyer and others to develop property adjoining the Eureka Bullion and other claims in the East Tintic district. The capital is 1,250,000 shares, 5 cents par.

WASHINGTON

Keller.—All of the machinery for the Addison Mining Co. has been delivered at the mine on Silver creek, near here. This is the largest plant and the most valuable addition to this district in many years.

Loon Lake.—The Loon Lake Copper Co.'s new mill has been started. Some high-grade bornite was recently opened on the 200-ft. level.

Oroville.—The Okanogan Power Co. is to construct a dam on the Similkameen river, also a 2000-hp. generator, 3½ miles from Oroville. While the primary consumption of power will be for irrigating purposes, the mines will have all they need.

Republic.—Lessees at the Ben Hur mine have driven an adit 45 ft. and cut a 2-ft. vein. Face samples assay from $10.50 to $25 per ton. They have built a tramway from the mine bin to deliver ore direct to railroad cars, and have shipped the first 50 tons of ore.

W. G. C. Lanskail, the lessee, has men extracting ore from the bottom level of the Quilp mine, at a depth of 800 ft. That level is 100 ft. deeper than where J. L. Harper stopped work on the same ore-shoot. The ore averages $16 per ton, mainly in gold. The first carload was shipped a week ago.

It is reported that a rich shoot was found in the bottom level of the Knob Hill mine a few days ago.

CANADA

British Columbia

Anyox.—The Granby Consolidated has announced another advance in wages. It amounts to 50 cents per day to miners and 25 cents to smeltermen and others; 1200 men are affected. This is in addition to a 25-cent raise for every 2-cent increase in the selling price of copper. Wages have been increased about $1 since April 1, when the plant was re-opened after being suspended for 30 days.

The Dolly Varden property, one of the most promising silver properties in the Alice Arm district, is expected to be taken over by the Taylor Engineering Co. This concern constructed a railway from the coast to the mine, which also serves a number of other good prospects. The Dolly Varden company failed to pay the Engineering company all that was claimed for this work and, by an act passed at the last session of the Provincial Legislature, the Dolly Varden and the Temiskaming Mining Co. of Ontario were given until May 19 to take care of claims amounting to $462,500. This they have not done apparently, and the Taylor company, therefore, has the power to take possession, its first responsibility on doing so being the discharge of wages due workmen amounting to about $150,000. This done, the same concern has authority to proceed with the operation of the mine.

According to reliable information, representatives of the Dolly Varden Mining Co. intend to appeal to the Dominion government for the disallowance of the Provincial legislation that gives the Taylor Engineering Co. power to take over the mine and other of the company's holdings in order to satisfy claims it has presented in respect of the construction of the railway from Alice Arm to the mine. It already has been reported that the time given the Dolly Varden company to meet the financial terms laid down by the Legislature has lapsed, and that the Taylor company is proceeding to take possession.

Hazelton.—Work was resumed at the Silver Standard property, Glen mountain, Omineca, on May 1. This is one of the largest producers of silver-lead-zinc ore in northern

British Columbia. Satisfactory arrangements have been made regarding freight-rates and treatment of concentrate at the smelter, etc. W. G. Norrie-Loewenthal is manager.

Nelson.—The properties in this mining division are mainly of the free-milling gold type. Many of them are idle, partly due to poor management in the past, and partly due to lack of capital and development. Those mines that the Consolidated M. & S. Co. of Trail acquired have been entirely satisfactory. It is certain that the idle mines could be purchased at low prices and on good terms.

A meeting of the Nelson, Slocan, and Eastern British Columbia Mining Associations was held here recently. Preliminary arrangements were made for the International Convention to take place on June 19, 20, and 21 at Nelson. An organization was appointed to prepare for the gathering, the personal of which is as follows: Hon. W. Slocan, Minister of Mines, honorary president; S. S. Fowler of Riondel, Sidney Norman of Spokane, Frank C. Bailey of Spokane, and A. B. Trite of Fernie, honorary vice-presidents; J. J. Malone of Nelson, president; W. A. Cameron of Rambler, A. N. Wallinger of Cranbrook, Fred J. Peters of Rossland, Alex. McCrea of Revelstoke, J. R. Hunter of Nelson, J. D. Blackwood of Nelson, and J. E. Thompson, vice-presidents; Fred A. Starkey of Nelson, secretary; J. A. Gilker of Nelson, treasurer; A. G. Larsen of Spokane, M. M. McCune, Sheep Creek, E. W. Widdowson, Nelson, I. G. Nelson, Nelson, and C. F. Caldwell, Kaslo, directors.

Salmo.—The Sheep Creek mining district was first opened in 1894, the date of staking the Yellowstone claim by Thomas Bennett of Ymir. The Aspen, Emerald, Hudson Bay, and Jersey contain silver, lead, and zinc; and the Ore Hill, Spokane, and Summit, gold, silver, and lead, the remainder of the groups yielding free-milling gold ore. The Mother Lode has a cyanide mill, 20 stamps are on the Queen-Yellowstone, and 4 stamps on the Nugget. There are some promising claims here held by prospectors, also some vacant land worth-while.

Silverton.—At a recent meeting of the Silverton Miners' Union it was decided to endeavor to obtain a six-hour shift as a day's work, at the rate of $1 an hour.

Stewart.—The revival and opening of silver mines in the Salmon River district, north of this place, has resulted in Stewart having a newspaper, the 'Cassiar News'. It is published in the interests of Salmon River, Portland Canal, Alice Arm, and the Anyox mining districts.

Ymir.—This district is in the Nelson mining division of west Kootenay. Its area is about 144 sq. miles. Eleven creeks flow into the Salmon river from different points. There are 300 claims staked, a good many held by prospectors, and a fair number of promise. The Yankee Girl is the only one at work. The ores mostly carry gold, although a few have silver, lead, and zinc. There is said to be lots of vacant ground for prospecting.

Ontario

Cobalt.—The Mining Corporation is to diamond-drill the contact that passes north-westerly through the south-eastern part of Buck township, two miles from Cobalt. The contact is assumed to be at a depth of 300 feet.

The Nipissing company in April produced silver worth $219,927 from 6512 tons of ore. The refinery shipped 301,458 oz. of silver. Developments generally were favorable. Vein 99 had been opened for 50 ft., showing 1 in. of 1000-oz. ore; and a winze down 50 ft. opened 1 in. of rich ore, alongside of which was a ½ in. of matted wire silver. On vein 109, over 130 ft. of driving showed 2 in. of 3000-oz. ore.

Porcupine.—The town of South Porcupine had a disastrous fire on the 15th whereby 20 buildings were destroyed.

PERSONAL

Note. The Editor invites members of the profession to send particulars of their work and appointments. The information is interesting to our readers.

H. C. Colburn, of Denver, is here.

Richard A. Parker is in New York.

E. W. Engelmann is now at Hayden, Arizona.

T. J. Jones sailed for Vladivostok on May 25.

T. H. Jenks, of Phoenix, Arizona, is at the Chancellor Hotel.

John A. Rice has returned to San Francisco from Cananea, Mexico.

Samuel H. Dolbear has gone to New York. He will be away for a month.

A. H. Richards has been promoted to superintendent of the Garfield smelter.

C. B. Brodigan has been appointed manager of the Brakpan mine in the Transvaal.

Clarence Woods is examining silver mines near Hermosillo, in Sonora, Mexico.

Edwin J. Collins, of Duluth, has been examining a copper property in the Ray district of Arizona.

Stewart L. Rawlings, general manager for the Cerro de Pasco, has arrived in New York from Peru.

J. T. Reeder has resigned after 30 years service as one of the Calumet & Hecla purchasing agents.

Ralph Arnold, who has been working for the U. S. Bureau of Internal Revenue, is returning to private practice.

A. J. Walton, manager of the Rose Deep, has been appointed manager of the Crown Mines, at Johannesburg.

Arthur S. Dwight, Major in the 11th Engineers, has been awarded the D. S. O. by the British military command.

L. C. Graton has taken charge of the copper division of the Industrial Unit of the U. S. Bureau of Internal Revenue.

A. H. Burroughs, Jr., has become associated, as mining engineer, with **H. H. Armstead**, and has gone to Talache, Idaho.

Charles McKinnis, manager for the National Copper Co., at Wallace, Idaho, has taken a lease in the Ranger oilfield in Texas.

Fred E. Carroll, State Commissioner of Mines for Colorado, has resigned to devote his time to mining interests in the Ouray district. He was Commissioner for four years.

Harry E. Nelson has opened an office in the Hollingsworth building, Los Angeles, where he will specialize in the design of treatment plants, particularly the crushing department.

L. H. Goodwin of 42 Broadway, New York, has left for an extended scouting trip through the principle silver-mining districts of the Western States and Canada, the work being undertaken for the firm of Rogers, Mayer & Ball.

R. S. Baverstock, of Baverstock & Payne, has returned from Trona, California, where he has completed the installation of a 30-ton Gibson mill and cyanide plant for the Stockwell Gold Mining Syndicate of Los Angeles.

William A. Daly, general superintendent of the mines of the Anaconda Copper Mining Co., has been promoted to assistant manager of mines, taking the post made vacant by the resignation of **B. H. Dunshee** last August. **Chauncey L. Berrien** has been advanced to general superintendent.

The Utah Society of Engineers held its annual banquet at Salt Lake City on May 21. The presidential address was given by Leonard Cahoon. The membership is now 211, an increase of 38 during the year 1918-'19. The net resources of the Society are $1729.

THE METAL MARKET

METAL PRICES

San Francisco, June 3

Aluminum-dust, cents per pound	50—60
Antimony, cents per pound	8.50
Copper, electrolytic, cents per pound	16.50
Lead, pig, cents per pound	5¾—6¾
Platinum, pure, per ounce	$105
Platinum 10% iridium, per ounce	$115
Quicksilver, per flask of 75 lb.	$95
Spelter, cents per pound	7¾
Zinc-dust, cents per pound	10—12

Nickel is 40 cents a pound. During 1918, the International Nickel Co. made a net profit of $5,022,830, after allowing for all charges. Dividends were $534,756 (6%) on preferred shares and $4,183,400 (10%) on common shares. Current assets are $12,900,580, and liabilities $3,708,902. There was $3,480,210 spent on new plant and property. Everything is in good physical condition.

EASTERN METAL MARKET

(By wire from New York)

June 3.—Copper is quiet but steady. Lead is dull and easier. Speller is inactive and lower.

SILVER

Below are given official or ticker quotations, in cents per ounce of silver 999 fine. From April 23, 1918, the United States government paid $1 per ounce for all silver purchased by it, fixing a maximum of $1.01½ on August 15, 1918, and will continue to pay $1 until the quantity specified under the Act is purchased, probably extending over several years. On May 5, 1919, all restrictions on the metal were removed, resulting in fluctuations. During the restricted period, the British government fixed the maximum price five times, the last being on March 25, 1919, on account of the low rate of sterling exchange, but removed all restrictions on May 10. The equivalent of dollar silver (1000 fine) in British currency is 48.65 pence per ounce (925 fine), calculated at the normal rate of exchange.

Date		New York cents	London pence	Average week ending		Cents	Pence
May	28	108.25	52.50	Apr.	22	101.12	48.94
"	29	108.25	52.50	"	29	101.12	[illegible]
"	30 Holiday			May	6	101.14	48.71
"	31	109.12	53.00	"	13	106.33	52.08
June	1 Sunday			"	20	110.33	53.50
"	2	109.37	53.12	"	27	109.44	52.17
"	3	109.50	53.37	June	3	108.90	52.90

Monthly averages

	1917	1918	1919		1917	1918	1919
Jan.	75.14	88.72	101.12	July	78.92	99.62	....
Feb.	77.54	85.79	101.12	Aug.	85.40	100.31	....
Mch.	74.13	88.11	101.12	Sept.	100.73	101.12	....
Apr.	72.51	95.35	101.12	Oct.	87.38	101.12	....
May	74.61	99.50	107.23	Nov.	85.97	101.12	....
June	76.44	99.50	...	Dec.	85.97	101.12	....

According to John D. Ryan, of the Anaconda company, which produced nearly 11,000,000 oz. last year, silver prices will remain high for several years and have not yet touched their highest level.

Writing on May 8, Samuel Montagu & Co., of London, say that although two days have elapsed since the United States removed restrictions on silver control, at the time of 'fixing', on that date, had not been removed from the London market. Business meanwhile is in absolute suspense, as the London quotations, calculated as they are upon the now fictitious basis of 101¼ cents, have no relation whatever to the actual value of silver. The Shanghai exchange has risen to 5s. ½d. ($1.21) the tael. Owing to activity of the Indian export trade, the Indian Council re-commenced offering remittances for tender. The amount thus dealt with on May 6 was 60 lacs ($1,920,000). A similar amount was to be put up for tender the next week. About a thousand more lacs of silver is held in the note reserves than on October 15, the last occasion when tenders were solicited.

COPPER

Prices of electrolytic in New York, in cents per pound.

Date			Average week ending		
May	28	16.37	Apr.	22	15.18
"	29	16.37	"	29	15.18
"	30 Holiday		May	6	15.25
"	31	16.37	"	13	15.37
June	1 Sunday		"	20	16.24
"	2	16.37	"	27	16.40
June	3	16.37	June	3	16.37

Monthly averages

	1917	1918	1919		1917	1918	1919
Jan.	29.53	23.50	20.43	July	29.67	26.00	....
Feb.	34.57	23.50	17.34	Aug.	27.42	26.00	....
Mch.	36.00	23.50	15.05	Sept.	25.11	26.00	....
Apr.	33.16	23.50	15.23	Oct.	23.50	26.00	....
May	31.69	23.50	15.91	Nov.	23.50	26.00	....
June	32.57	23.50		Dec.	23.50	26.00	....

According to John D. Ryan, of the Anaconda company, which produced 293,000,000 lb. last year, copper is in better position than for many months, but its future will depend on the restoration of European industry to pre-war prosperity. There can be no marked advance in the price of the metal until the European demand revives.

E. H. Gary, of the U. S. Steel Corporation, in commenting on the improving conditions in the iron and steel business, considered that 20-cent copper was probable.

The copper embargo on imports into France has been lifted.

LEAD

Lead is quoted in cents per pound, New York delivery.

Date			Average week ending		
May	28	5.25	Apr.	22	4.93
"	29	5.25	"	29	4.95
"	30 Holiday		May	6	4.87
"	31	5.20	"	13	4.85
June	1 Sunday		"	20	5.05
"	2	5.20	"	27	5.27
"	3	5.20	June	3	5.22

Monthly averages

	1917	1918	1919		1917	1918	1919
Jan.	7.64	6.85	5.60	July	10.93	8.03	....
Feb.	9.10	7.07	5.13	Aug.	10.75	8.05	....
Mch.	10.07	7.28	5.24	Sept.	9.07	8.05	....
Apr.	9.38	6.99	5.05	Oct.	6.97	8.05	....
May	10.29	6.88	5.04	Nov.	6.38	8.05	....
June	11.74	7.58	....	Dec.	6.49	6.90	....

Lead ore, basis 80% metal, averaged $50 per ton at Joplin, Missouri, last week. The Tri-State region produced 1085 tons.

ZINC

Zinc is quoted as spelter, standard Western brands, New York delivery, in cents per pound:

Date			Average week ending		
May	28	6.57	Apr.	22	6.41
"	29	6.55	"	29	6.40
"	30 Holiday		May	6	6.32
"	31	6.52	"	13	6.31
June	1 Sunday		"	20	6.46
"	2	6.50	"	27	6.50
"	3	6.50	June	3	6.53

Monthly averages

	1917	1918	1919		1917	1918	1919
Jan	9.75	7.78	7.44	July	8.98	8.72	....
Feb.	10.45	7.97	6.71	Aug.	8.58	8.87	....
Mch.	10.78	7.67	6.53	Sept.	8.33	9.58	....
Apr.	10.20	7.04	6.49	Oct.	8.32	9.11	....
May	9.41	7.92	6.43	Nov.	7.76	8.75	....
June	9.63	7.92	....	Dec.	7.84	8.49	....

Zinc ore, basis 60% metal, averaged $39 per ton at Joplin, Missouri, last week. There was an increase of $3 during the week, high-grade ore receiving $11, and second grades $10. The Tri-State region produced 10,000 tons.

QUICKSILVER

The primary market for quicksilver is San Francisco, California being the largest producer. The price is fixed in the open market, according to quantity. Prices, in dollars per flask of 75 pounds:

Date					
May	6	75.00	May	20	82.00
"	13	80.00	"	27	92.00
			June	3	95.00

Monthly averages

	1917	1918	1919		1917	1918	1919
Jan	81.00	128.00	103.75	July	102.00	120.00	...
Feb	126.25	118.00	90.00	Aug.	115.00	120.00	....
Mch.	113.75	112.00	72.80	Sept.	112.00	120.00	....
Apr.	114.50	115.00	73.12	Oct.	102.00	120.00	....
May	104.00	110.00	84.80	Nov.	102.50	120.00	....
June	85.50	112.00	....	Dec.	117.42	115.00	....

TIN

Prices in New York, in cents per pound. The monthly averages in 1918 are nominal. On December 3 the War Industries Board fixed the price to consumers and jobbers at 72½c. f.o.b. Chicago and Eastern points, and 71¼c. on the Pacific Coast. This will continue until the U. S. Steel Products Co.'s stock is consumed.

Monthly averages

	1917	1918	1919		1917	1918	1919
Jan	44.10	85.13	71.50	July	62.60	93.00	....
Feb	51.47	85.00	72.44	Aug.	62.53	91.33	....
Mch.	54.27	85.00	72.50	Sept.	61.54	80.40	....
Apr.	55.63	88.53	72.50	Oct.	62.24	78.82	....
May	63.21	100.01	72.50	Nov.	74.18	73.67	....
June	61.93	91.00	....	Dec.	85.00	71.52	....

Eastern Metal Market

New York, May 28.

There is less activity in all the markets, but price changes are absent and quotations firm.

Antimony prices are higher.

Copper demand has slackened decidedly, but prices are firm and unchanged.

Lead buying has declined, but the market is firm and strong.

Tin is stagnant and somewhat staggered by the report of the authorities on the tin supplies of the country.

Zinc market continues inactive, with prices steady.

ANTIMONY

The market is stronger and higher. Wholesale lots for early delivery, New York, duty paid, are quoted at 8.25 to 8.37½c. The metal is in strong hands.

ALUMINUM

For No. 1 virgin metal, 98 to 99% pure, the quotation is 32 to 33c. per pound for wholesale lots for early delivery.

COPPER

The activity that characterized the market for a week or 10 days has subsided. It gradually gave place to moderate buying about a week ago or late last week. Today the market is quiet but prices are firm, with electrolytic copper held at 16.50 to 16.75c., New York, for June-July delivery, with 17c. asked for August. A few producers are taking a little business at 16.37½c., New York. For delivery beyond July most of the large producers are extremely shy about selling, and are stiff in their ideas of prices, not less than 17c. being considered. The recent buying movement, which has subsided somewhat, represents a distributed consumption. Some producers are sold up for June delivery. The purchasing is distinctly analagous in its character to that which took place late in March or early in April. At that time consumers filled their needs well into May. On this movement they have satisfied their requirements possibly through July, and this is probably the reason for the quieter tone. The volume, however, was much larger this month than in the earlier period referred to. Export business is reported as better but not significant yet. Lake copper is quoted at 16.75 to 17c. for June-July delivery, with demand good.

IRON AND STEEL

Sentiment in the trade is generally better and demand for steel has improved. Predictions of lower prices are less frequent or confident; recent quotations are generally being maintained, and makers have generally been firmer than buyers expected. Ten large automobile companies have signed contracts for billets, sheets, wire tubes, all totaling over 300,000 tons. Another motor maker is in the market for a large tonnage. More buyers have come into the market in the past 10 days for contracts running for 60 to 90 days as against former hand-to-mouth buying. The rail order for 200,000 tons was distributed among six companies at $47 per ton for open-hearth. A decision is announced to reinstate on car-builder books some 20,000 cars for France, reinforcing the better tone.

LEAD

The market has turned quiet after the decidedly large volume of business done a week ago. Late last week a premium was realized in the outside market running as high as 5.37½c., New York, but these have disappeared and the market has settled down to the American Smelting & Refining Co.'s quotation of 5.25c., New York, or 5c., St. Louis, for early delivery. For business at these levels there are now plenty of sellers, but they all report demand light. The market, however, is quiet but firm.

TIN

Over the signature of George Ormsby, chief in charge of tin, a statement has been mailed to the trade setting forth the status of the market up to May 23. This shows that the supply of the metal in the hands of consumers, jobbers, dealers, and smelters on May 1 was 22,000 tons, including tin in ores and concentrates. It also states that the monthly consumption to May 1 has been only 3113 tons per month. The interesting revelation is the amount of allocated metal still on hand—of 10,169 tons originally apportioned to the United States, there was a balance on May 23 of 2199 tons. The effect of the report is difficult to gauge today, as it only reached the trade on Monday morning. Thus far, however, it has produced discouragement. It is figured that were consumption to increase to 4000 tons per month, it would take at least five months to use up present supplies in sight. An active market is not looked for soon on the strength of this report. Buying for future shipment when restrictions are removed has fallen off, but some has been done around 51c., with Banca tin offered at a fraction over 50c. per pound. The falling off in interest is attributed to the decline in London prices recently. There are two interesting unconfirmed reports, one to the effect that restrictions have already been removed on future shipments from the Straits, and another that those on Eastern shipments will be removed first, on English shipments second, and on Canadian last. The London market has turned stronger again with spot Straits quoted yesterday at £242 10s. per ton.

ZINC

Prime Western for early delivery is quoted at 6.25c., St. Louis, or 6.60c., New York, with demand light. This is nominal. For future delivery 6.30c., St. Louis, is asked for July and 6.35c. for August, at which levels some business has been done. As a whole there is no improvement. The market seems to be marking time, possibly awaiting developments in steel and other lines. There is a big void in galvanized sheets, and when building starts and steel begins to move a decidedly better spelter market is almost certain. In the meantime producers are sitting tight. The recent advance from the 6c., St. Louis, level is generally attributed now to fairly good export demand, largely from Japan.

For high-grade zinc about 6.62½ to 6.75c. is asked and obtained. The quoted price of sheet-zinc is $10 per 100 pounds.

ORES

Manganese: The best that can be done on Indian high-grade ore is about 68c. per unit, American seaboard. Some transactions are reported. South American ore is offered at about 60c. per unit, American seaboard.

Manganese-Iron Alloys: American producers of ferro are now quoting $125 delivered for 78 to 80% alloy, less $1.75 per unit under 78%. The former price was $150. No sales are recorded. Re-sale alloy has sold under $100 per ton in the last week. Spiegel, re-sale, has sold as low as $27 per ton, delivered; and one producer is offering alloy at $30, furnace. There has been a fair business in the last week.

Tungsten: There are reports to the effect that some business has been done, particularly in Bolivian ore at as high as $10.25 per unit. Prices are largely nominal for high-grade ore at $7 to $10 per unit in 60% concentrate. No testing of the ferro-tungsten market is reported. Prices for high-speed steel average about $1.60 per pound.

INDUSTRIAL PROGRESS

INFORMATION FURNISHED BY MANUFACTURERS

NEW TYPE OF STOPING-DRILLS

Drill engineers and manufacturers have been well aware of the fact that one type of drill could not be applied efficiently to all conditions of drilling. The old two-man piston machine is now used in relatively few places. One-man piston-drills, water hammer-drills for driving, rotating hand-feed hammer-drills for sinking, and air-feed stoping-drills for upper holes, are some of the developments of the past 15 years.

In each department of drilling, too, specialization has been found necessary with increasing competition and with the adaptation of new drills to work previously done by other means with less efficiency. The first air-feed stoping-drills were practically all of one type, consisting of the drill-cylinder proper, mounted on a reverse air-feed cylinder, in which the feed cylinder remained stationary and the air pressure carried the drill up to its work, supported on a piston rod between the drill proper and the feed-cylinder. The cylinder was clamped in a trunnion on a column-arm, or on a bar. These machines were offered for hard, medium, and soft ground, and for all conditions in drilling upper holes.

The Sullivan Machinery Co. was the first to introduce in this country that type of pneumatic feed in which the feed cylinder is attached directly to the pneumatic hammer, the feed piston-rod acting against an abutment. This type of pneumatic feed held supremacy for many years, in fact, is considered as the standard for non-rotating machines at the present time. Modifications of this pattern made by the Sullivan company included hard-hitting stopers for solid ground, light-hitting stopers for soft ground, and feed-cylinders of different diameters to provide a lighter or stronger holding power against the rock.

All of the earlier types of stoping-drills were rotated by hand. Demands of the past few years from the field for a successful stoping-drill include the following variety: (1) Light weight and small size to permit easy handling in high stopes; (2) automatic rotation to relieve the drill-runner of the incessant labor of turning the drill-bit by hand, particularly in hot stopes; (3) satisfactory regulation of the strength of the feed; (4) a water-jet for laying the dust when drilling in sulphide ores, or other formations in which dust is injurious to the health of the miner; and (5) automatic lubrication.

These are general outstanding features to which must be added in the design of a successful stoper, the usual features of convenience in handling, cutting-speed, air power, economy, simplicity of construction, accessibility for repairs, staunchness, and ability to resist wear and hard service. The first four of these elements need not necessarily all be combined in the same machine, but represent varying conditions called for by different fields. The last-mentioned features are essential to success in any satisfactory stoping-drills.

During the past three or four years the drill designers of the Sullivan company have been studying conditions and developing new features with the object of making stoping-drills more nearly meet these varying factors of the field. That their efforts have met with success in the types recently introduced may be judged from encouraging reports received from operators. Two of these new standard Sullivan stopers are shown in the accompanying illustrations. No. 1 shows class DT-44 light-weight hand-rotation machine, and No. 2 class DT-42 stoper with automatic rotation and water attachment.

The flexibility of the interchangeable part system, a vital element in all Sullivan drill design, permits the following combination and arrangements to suit different conditions (1) DT-44 light-weight stoper, hand rotation, direct feed, dry, solid steel; (2) DT-44 light-weight stoper, hand rotation, direct feed, with water attachment and hollow steel, (3) DT-44 light-weight stoper, hand rotation, with reverse feed, either dry or water type, for solid or hollow steel, (4) DT-42 rotating stoper with reverse feed and solid steel, dry; (5) DT-42 rotating stoper with reverse feed, hollow steel and water attachment; (6) DT-42 rotating stoper with direct feed and solid steel, dry; and (7) DT-42 rotating stoper with direct feed and water attachment, hollow steel

It will be seen that it is possible to furnish a stoper for practically any conditions. The light-weight stoper is a small, short machine, much lighter than any other stoper on the market. Its net weight is 66 lb., and with the feed piston drawn in, it is only 48 in. long over all.

The DT-42 self-rotating stoper is available for hot stopes or other places in which the demand is for a labor-saving machine. This is the first time that a self-rotating stoping-drill of satisfactory design has been placed on the market. The difficulty with rotating stopers has been of two kinds (1) To provide a compact positive means of rotation; and (2) to furnish some practical means of retarding the feed so that in starting a hole or in 'fitchery' ground the feed may be controlled positively and immediately. The difficulty with previously designed rotating stopers has been that in these two classes of work, the forward action of the feed, combined with the rotation of the steel, would throw the bit off the inclined surface of the rock, or into the seam or vug, so that a stuck steel or a crooked hole was almost sure to result, with equally sure results in loss of time and labor and frequent damage to the drill itself. In the Sullivan rotating stoper, the rotating mechanism is of the same type that has proved so successful in Sullivan DP-33 rotator hammer-drills and in the DR-6 mounted water hammer-drills. The parts comprising the rotation are all at the front end of the tool. There is no separate rifle-bar, and the piston is not weakened by a hole bored in the rear end to receive that part, as is necessary with rifle-bar rotation. Experience with these new stopers, as well as with the standard hammer-drills referred to has demonstrated that this form of rotation is substantial, positive, and reliable.

The builders state that in their experiments with independent rotating motors mounted at the front end of the machine, it was found that the increased weight at this point caused the machine to be very unwieldy, due to improper balance. While the present standard arrangement lengthens the machine, it permits a good balance to be maintained, enabling it to be handled a great deal easier than would be the case if the extreme front end were overweighted by a bulky mass of metal. The second element in the satisfactory rotating stoper, namely, control of the feed, has been the result of much study and experiment and is provided in these machines by means of a hand retarder or brake.

Among earlier unsuccessful developments were (1) pressure reducing-valves under hand control for varying the pressure of the air in the feed-cylinder. These failed, due to the unreliability of the valve, especially when wear took place, with resultant leakage; also to the fact that their control and operation is indefinite, as the operator has no means of knowing the extent to which the compressed air has been reduced in the feed-cylinder. (2) Feed-cylinders of various sizes were also experimented with, but these also were unpopular, due to the fact that a cylinder of any specified size is not sufficiently flexible to enable the operator to adopt the working pressure to varying ground conditions.

In the new Sullivan, the control is introduced by employing a reverse feed cylinder and piston, which is practically identical with the pneumatic feed mounting of the Sullivan 'pnufeed' rotator. A coil brake-band controlled by a handle is fitted at the front end of the feed-cylinder, the band surrounding or gripping the feed-piston in such a manner that the air pressure in the cylinder can be counteracted by a turn or two of the hand-grip, which is within easy reach of the operator. In spotting a hole with the bit held against the rock by the air pressure, the feed can be braked down to make practically an immovable mounting. When the drill has cut a satisfactory collar for the hole, the brake is released gradually, until full feeding strength is secured. The same method is employed for cutting through a seam, loose or broken ground, or a 'fitcher'. By tightening the brake, the rapidity of the feed is immediately reduced to the proper amount, so that the drill does not bury itself in soft ground, or drop out of line in crossing a vug or

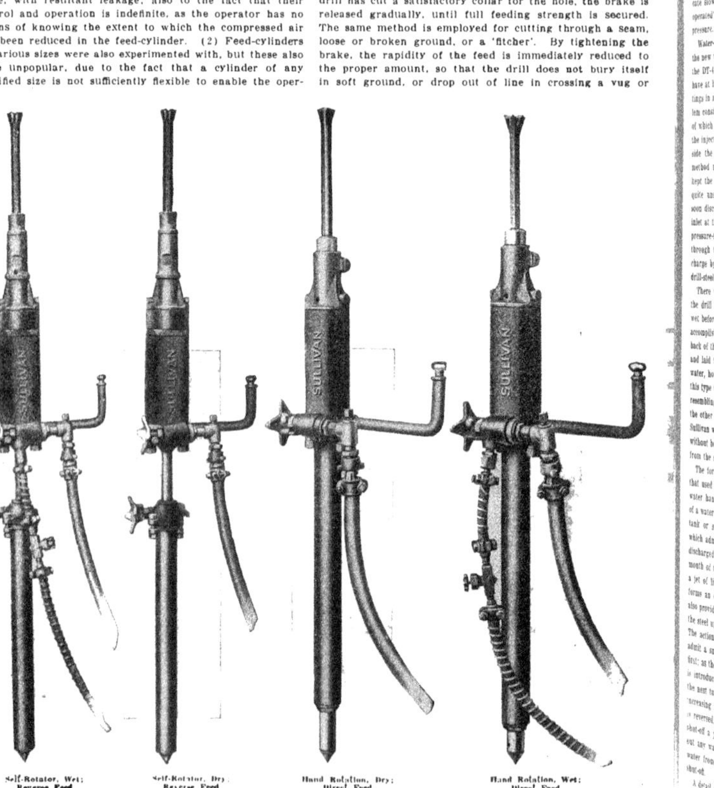

Self-Rotator, Wet; Reverse Feed — Self-Rotator, Dry; Reverse Feed — Hand Rotation, Dry; Direct Feed — Hand Rotation, Wet; Direct Feed

fitcher. This feature, as demonstrated in actual use in many parts of this country, gives complete adaptability for any ground conditions encountered from soft broken material to hard tough solid rock.

An important element in the success of the Sullivan rotating stoper with brake is the method of throttle control. This is the standard Sullivan stoper throttle, which is used on all types. With the hose valve turned to its wide-open position, the control of the drill and feed-cylinder is placed under the one throttle. Turning the throttle first admits air to the air-tubes and oil-pockets, and in the next position to the feed-cylinder, raising the drill to its work. Further turning of the valve causes the hammer to reciprocate slowly, and in the final open position, the machine is operated at full speed and the feed-cylinder receives full pressure.

Water-Stopers. The Sullivan drill designers feel that in the new water feature, which may be incorporated in either the DT-44 light-weight or the DT-42 rotating stoper, they have at last solved the problem of laying the dust and cuttings in a satisfactory manner. First attempts at this problem consisted in providing an outside water-spray by means of which water was drawn from a bucket through a hose on the injection principle and discharged by air pressure alongside the drill-steel, against the face of the rock. This method necessitated constant refilling of the bucket and kept the operator in a wet condition. In addition, it was quite unsatisfactory for drills rotated by hand, and was soon discarded. The next experiment consisted in a water-inlet at the front or nose of the drill, taking water from a pressure-tank or pipe-line. The water was then discharged through the hollow drill-steel, being assisted in this discharge by the air pressure, which found its way into the drill-steel from the front end of the cylinder.

There was considerable leakage, from the front end of the drill particularly, and the miner was apt to be fairly wet before the end of the shift. The object of the jet was accomplished, in that it discharged the water against the back of the hole while the drill cuttings were being formed, and laid the dust at that point. The constant leakage of water, however, proved a serious objection. A machine of this type was described by an unsympathetic drill-runner as resembling "a beautiful fountain playing in a park." On the other hand, it is customary for runners to operate the Sullivan water-stoper from one end of the shift to the other without becoming wet at all, except for an occasional splash from the sludge running from the drill-hole.

The form of water jet employed in the DT-42 stoper is that used with such success in the Sullivan DR-6 mounted water hammer-drill and in the water rotator. It consists of a water inlet to which a hose is attached from a pressure tank or supply-pipe, under control of the same throttle which admits air to the drill and feed-cylinder. Water is discharged through a central tube running well into the mouth of the drill-steel. This water-tube is surrounded by a jet of live air, taken from the back of the drill, which forms an effective seal against leakage at the chuck and also provides additional pressure to carry the water through the steel up against the back of the hole where it is needed. The action of the combined water and air throttle is to admit a small quantity of air to the tube or air-jet space first; as the throttle is turned to its next position, the water is introduced and brought to play in the drill-hole before the next turn of the throttle starts the piston moving with increasing rapidity. In stopping the machine, the process is reversed, so that the last thing before the air is finally shut-off a jet of live air blows through the steel, clearing out any water that may remain in it, and preventing this water from falling back into the chuck when the air is shut-off.

A detail of design that makes for the drill-runner's comfort, consists of a deflecting flange or cap, which forms a part of the drill-chuck. This contains downward-looking ports for the drill exhaust, as is the case in all Sullivan stopers, so that dust or cuttings falling from the hole are not blown into the operator's face or against the upper part of his body. With the water-stoper, these ports act to carry off, without inconvenience to the runner, any sludge or water that may run down the steel from the hole and find its way into the front end of the machine.

The great satisfaction reported by runners and mine superintendents alike, from many parts of the country, indicate that in this new machine a satisfactory self-rotating water stoper has at last been developed.

Automatic Lubrication. With each stroke of the piston a measured quantity of oil is drawn from a reservoir in the handle into the working parts of the drill. A supplementary oil-pocket in the throttle-valve casing is provided, which fills automatically with oil, when the machine is not in operation. On the opening of the throttle the entrapped oil is blown into the air-inlet passages of the cylinder, after which the automatic lubrication goes into effect. In the automatic rotation type the rotating mechanism is lubricated by an independent oiler in the throttle-valve, which blows oil into the ratchet chamber each time the drill starts working. In addition, the chuck-housing is furnished with a grease-chamber, from which the rotation parts are lubricated.

These new Sullivan stopers are both of the valveless pattern. The air-thrown piston is of the simplest possible design, and the cylinder is of one diameter throughout. In this design, the effort has been made to overcome previous detriments to valveless drills, consisting of high air consumption per unit of work done, and a rapid diminution of efficiency with increased wear. The Sullivan design embodies unusual simplicity in the number and shape of the working parts. The piston is equipped with ample bearing surface to insure it against wear and the design is such that when wear does occur, with inevitable increase in air consumption, the drilling speed will not be materially affected and the cushion which is provided at both ends of the piston travel is still retained in full effectiveness to protect the machine against undue jar and breakage.

As to drilling speed, results speak for themselves, reports from the field indicate that the machine measures fully up to the builder's expectations in this important particular. The principal factors that determine drilling speed are force and frequency of blow. Wearing parts of these machines have been made simple and easy to replace. All parts are made on the standard Sullivan interchangeable system, and every part of the machine is made from drop-forged steel billets of special alloy metal or from tool-steel bars.

COMMERCIAL PARAGRAPHS

A. E. Hitchner has been appointed manager of the mining section of the industrial sales department of the Westinghouse Electric & Manufacturing Co. with headquarters at East Pittsburgh, Pennsylvania.

If mine and works operators wish to learn something about blowers, collectors, exhausters, and fans, they should procure a copy of Section No. 400 of the **Buffalo Forge Co.**, Buffalo, New York. Tables give capacities with speed and power requirements.

The Hardinge Conical Mill Co. reports the honorable discharge from war service of J. C. Farrant, its London manager. Mr. Farrant for over four years was held a prisoner of war in Germany. 1st Lieut. J. J. Cadot, of Air Service, A. E. F., returns to take charge of the Denver office. Capt. Harlowe Hardinge, Signal Corps, Director Radio Schools in the A. E. F., will return to his duties as vice-president of the H. C. M. Co. in the New York office. The Hardinge Co.

anticipates the early return of three more of its staff and a consequent renewal of its pre-war service to its customers.

The spring number of 'The Yuba Bulletin' is an attractively prepared issue, showing the value of Yuba tractors in Californian agricultural operations. Besides pulling, a pulley attached to the tractor will drive stationary machines. Whether it goes through mud or is pulling stumps, the Yuba Manufacturing Co.'s Marysville, California, product does its work well.

The difference between the Allen sand cone and the slime cone is that the extent to which the spigot discharge is de-watered is under perfect control and is automatically maintained. The density of the discharge may be whatever is desired from the density of the feed to the density at which the dewatered product loses its fluidity. In No. 10 pamphlet, the Allen Cone Co. of El Paso, Texas, gives some interesting data on the use of its cone. To show how close is the regulation of density, samples taken every 15 minutes for 2½ hours only varied from 1.236 to 1.259, the average being 1.243.

Storage-battery driven locomotives, cranes, and cars are described and illustrated in Bulletin 1185 of the Atlas Car & Mfg. Co., Cleveland, Ohio. These are especially suitable for about mines. The storage-battery loco has passed the experimental stage, and continuous service in some of our largest and most modern mines has proven its economy and reliability. A battery loco will replace from three to six mules and drivers with the same tonnage hauled, it is easily operated, and is practically fool proof. Exclusive features found only in Atlas equipment are the drive unit with its compact design, hardened and heat-treated steel gears and pinions, and accessibility for oiling inspection.

What they term to be "the greatest advance in oil-engine construction since the Diesel engine first came into practical service" is meeting with tremendous success in engineering circles in all parts of the world, according to R. R. Sweitzer, general manager for the **Western Machinery Co.** of Los Angeles, manufacturers of the Western heavy-duty oil-engine.

This engine, it is claimed, embodies all of the desirable features of oil-engines of the heavy-duty type, but does not have the intricate construction complications such as high-pressure fuel-pumps, high-pressure air-compressors, spray-nozzles, hot heads, hot balls, hot plates, or other means of surface or electrical ignition common to the Diesel or so-called semi-Diesel type. It burns fuel oil of low gravity, producing more power per pound of this fuel, is fully as efficient and economical in operation and because of its simplicity, highly-skilled engineering ability is not required in its maintenance and operating. The Western is built in sizes from 25 b.h.p. per working cylinder in multiples up to 6 cylinders. The dimensions of the 6-cylinder unit is 15 by 6 by 8½ feet.

The **Allied Machinery Co. of America** has increased its capital to $5,000,000. This was made necessary by the decision of the American International Corporation to group all of its machinery export-selling subsidiaries under one head. This move contemplates the complete absorption of the Allied Construction Machinery Corporation by the Allied Machinery Co. The Allied Machinery Co. de France and the Allied Machinery Company d'Italia will retain their corporate entities, but their parent corporation will be the Allied Machinery Co. of America rather than the American International Corporation as before. This is also true of the Horne Company, Ltd., of Japan, which was purchased early in the year by the American International Corporation. All shares of the Allied Machinery Company of America will, as before, be owned by the American International Corporation. The Allied Machinery Co. was formed in 1911 by interests associated with the National City Bank of New York to sell machine-tools in Europe. In 1916 it was taken over by the American International Corporation, which immediately set about to expand and organize the business on a large scale. The business has increased rapidly and today the company is operating in 14 countries. J. W. Hook will continue as president of the Allied Machinery Co., in general charge of the business. F. A. Monroe, S. T. Henry, and T. G. Nee have been elected vice-presidents. The first is in charge of the administrative affairs; the second is in charge of sales and advertising; while the last is in Japan devoting his attention to the affairs of the Horne Company. R. P. Redler is general sales manager, with headquarters at Paris.

Stockholders of the **Joseph Dixon Crucible Co.** held their annual and regular meetings on April 21. The following were elected: Directors—George T. Smith, William G. Bumsted, J. H. Schermerhorn, George E. Long, Edward L. Young, Harry Dailey, and R. E. Jennings. Officers—George T. Smith, president; George E. Long, vice-president; J. H. Schermerhorn, vice-president; Harry Dailey, secretary; William Koester, treasurer; and Albert Norris, assistant secretary-treasurer. Of the 20,000 shares, 19,512 were voted. The American Graphite Co., incorporated in New York, is a subsidiary of the Dixon company. Its directorate is the same, and officers practically the same, as those of the Dixon company.

The Dixon company announces the removal of its Philadelphia sales office from 1020 Arch street to rooms 801 and 802 of the Finance building, South Penn Square, in that city. This sales district comprises Pennsylvania, southern New Jersey, Delaware, Maryland, District of Columbia, Virginia, and West Virginia.

Threaded joints that are gas-tight, permanent, and easy to open can be made by using **Dixon's graphite pipe-joint compound.** This is made in paste form from selected flake graphite and a carrier. The experience of many years of producing this and the use by many of the largest railroads and gas companies have carried it to a high state of development. Because of the graphite used in its manufacture, threads can be screwed up a little more than with any other compound and the fineness of the graphite allows it to fill up the little cracks in the threads, giving a very tight joint. As graphite is inert to all known reagents, such as acids and alkalies, the metals are protected thoroughly from all kinds of corrosion. To burn graphite requires a temperature of 1400 to 1500°F. and pure oxygen, which makes the likelihood of burning out very small. The compound is smeared on the threads, and then screwed into the fitting, thus giving a uniform coating throughout. The use of this compound on long sections of pipe keeps up the gas pressure by preventing the troublesome leaks found along the lines. In addition, the ease with which the joints can be unscrewed makes it vastly superior to either red lead or white lead, which depend for their effect on the hardening of the cement. For use around the retort-doors where heavy asbestos gaskets are used, the compound gives the necessary lubrication so that the doors open easily without tearing the gaskets apart or injuring them. Here also it acts as a preventive of corrosive action and keeps the asbestos packing in fine condition for a much longer time than is otherwise the case. The advantage this compound has over red or white lead and other cements are the tight joints possible, the ease of opening, and the greater bulk. This compound for an equal weight has fully three times the volume, which means three times the number of fittings can be put together. Flanges, ground connections, cylinder heads—in fact, wherever metal surfaces come together tightly—can have 'pipe-joint compound' used to good advantage. This material is put up in small tubes, 1 to 25 lb. cans, and kegs of 50 and 100 pounds.

FRANCE has lifted the embargo on the importation of lead and spelter, as well as of copper. Other Allied governments, we hope, will do likewise soon, so that the normal trade in metals may be restored.

CLAIMS made for compensation by producers of chrome, manganese, tungsten, and pyrite under the War Minerals Relief Act number 1287 and represent a total sum of eighteen million dollars. The last day for entering a claim was June 4. No further applications will be received.

FRIEDRICH STAMPFER, the editor of the 'Vorwärts', exclaims: "It would therefore be lunacy to believe that peace would be brought about by putting six German names on one piece of paper." It would; but signatures are considered desirable as a matter of record; they constitute part of the formality of a peace conference.

HENRY FORD, or his secretary, says a good thing occasionally. He referred recently to the use of alcohol for generating power and stated that even now he was getting 10% more power out of an engine by using alcohol instead of gasolene. Whereupon he concluded by asserting that "it is safer for an engine to be full of alcohol than for an engineer to be in a similar position." Another example of the right thing in the wrong place.

AS yet we have not received the text of the U. S. Supreme Court in the Butte & Superior flotation case, but we can add to what we said last week that the Supreme Court reversed the decree of the Court of Appeals in so far as it held that the patent was infringed only when using one-half of 1% or less than one-half of 1% of oil per ton of ore, but sustained the Appellate Court's decree in holding that the use of "petroleum products and pine-oil in excess of 1% on the ore did not constitute infringement." The case is remanded to the District Court of Montana for further proceedings in conformity with this opinion, so that Judge Bourquin will have the last say, as he had the first also, six years ago in the Hyde case.

FROM Dawson comes the tragic tale of the death of twelve men out of 36 participating in a dinner on May 22 at the Yukon Gold Company's plant on Hunker creek. The cause is given as ptomaine poisoning. Four more are dangerously ill. Among those who succumbed are William C. Lawson, assistant superintendent, and John Grant, honorably known in Colorado. Ptomaine is an enemy against which the miner, especially in the North, has ever to be on guard, because the circumstances of his frontier life compel him to depend largely upon preserved foods. We venture to recommend to the mining engineer the habit of always carrying in his valise a small bottle of castor-oil as a medicine to be taken immediately a suspicion of ptomaine poisoning arises. Capsules containing castor-oil are perhaps more convenient to take on a journey. The prompt use of an emetic or a purgative is essential to mitigating the effects of the poison. We speak from a disagreeable personal experience.

CONDITIONS in Germany as compared with those existing in the countries that the German armies ravaged and looted are so pleasant that more than one observer has been moved to bitter remark. An Australian prelate, Bishop Frodsham, writes as follows: "In some strange fashion it is like awakening from a bad dream to go into Germany from the war-zone. To retrace one's steps and to pass, within a few miles, from the white well-ordered towns of Aachen and Herbesthal to the squalid actualities of Pepinster—to proceed, in a crescendo of desolation, to Liège, to Huy, to Namur, to Mons, to Arras, and to those never-to-be-forgotten plains of France, is horrible. The transition fills one afresh with fiery indignation. Is it right, is it just, that Germany should not now be made to feel the true horrors of war—war as waged by Germans? Compared with the injuries they have done to others, the Germans are suffering nothing, and because they are suffering nothing they are neither sorry for the past nor desirous to amend in the future. It may be impossible in practice to alter this state of affairs, but it will be unutterably base and unjust if Germany is allowed to profit by the injuries it has wantonly and deliberately done to the French industries by getting away with the goods." Put this in your pipe when you think the terms of peace are too severe.

ECONOMISTS, even the more conservative of those devoted to the dismal science, are beginning to discuss bimetallism seriously in the light of recent events, more particularly the removal of Federal restrictions on the exportation of silver coin or bullion and the British declaration of a government monopoly on shipments of gold out of the United Kingdon. Despite their dislike of a resort to the bimetallic standard, they recognize the possibility of a reversion to it, in consequence of the stress of new circumstances. Paper currency has so generally replaced coin, and credit has been expanded so dangerously, that the wise ones doubt whether there is enough gold in the world to supply the necessary 'cover'. Even now the exportation of silver is controlled by licenses issued by the Federal Reserve Board, and the British Treasury exercises similar supervision over the outward movement of gold. In Canada the suggestion is being made that even shipments of gold ore to foreign smelters shall be compensated by the return of a quantity of gold equal to that taken out of the country in ores. It is evident that the need for husbanding the precious metals, as the foundation of paper money, is being considered by those in authority. The old argument, valid as it was, against the double standard, namely, that the adoption of it would involve the disappearance of the gold, has lost much of its force now that all the belligerent countries are really doing their business on a paper, not a gold, basis. In these matters, as in others, Great Britain and the United States are co-operating. What was impossible 25 years ago may be practicable now, because the exigencies of war have brought the principal nations together in such a way as to facilitate unity of action.

A CIRCULAR issued by the Eureka-Croesus Mining Company has come into our hands. The conjunction of 'Eureka' and 'Croesus' is a little like painting the lily or gilding refined gold, but we presume that it is the natural consequence of juxtaposition, not of what might be termed fiscal exuberance. The circular tries, not unsuccessfully, to do justice to the name. It is a mine at Eureka, Nevada, a district made famous as much by a great lawsuit as by its production of lead and silver forty years ago. It is said, in the circular, that "in many places in the old workings are breasts of high-grade ore left in place when the mine was closed." This is unlikely, although we are well aware how ore in an abandoned mine, especially if under water, has a way, in local gossip, of becoming richer the longer it remains untouched. In the old stopes, it is said in the circular, are "very large quantities of ore, too low-grade to be profitably mined and treated at that time, but of sufficient value to make them very high-grade milling ores when treated by the economical processes now in general use." Average samples are stated to "show values of better than $25 per ton." This again is unlikely; indeed we have heard of "average samples" that ran so much less as to make this estimate look careless. The writer of the circular, whose name is not significant, says that, allowing $5 per ton as a treatment charge, which, he says, would be "largely in excess of the actual cost," there would be "$20,000,000 left from the million tons of visible ore." How visible? Visible to the unaided eye or to the eye of an exuberant imagination? $15,000,000 net profit is a tidy sum even in these days of billion dollar affairs. It is no wonder that the capitalization of the Eureka-Croesus Company is said to be "only" $1,500,000, and that "it affords the safest and most profitable mining investment now known." If these statements were verified by the elaborate sampling of competent engineers, it might come within the category of at least an eminently sane speculation, but the circular gives no proof of an examination such as would warrant such a positive appraisal of the resources left so considerately by the former owners of the mine. Major Catlin's name is mentioned several times, but we decline to believe that he is a party to this flamboyant prospectus. It is too lacking in essentials and too much burdened with trumpery. For instance, Clarence King is quoted, not verbatim, as having "expressed the firm conviction that below water and in the property of the Eureka-Croesus Mining Company would be found the greatest gold mine ever discovered." The context suggests that King said this to Major Catlin; we doubt it; as also we doubt the statement that it is "his (Major Catlin's) belief that the property will become richer and the ore quantities greater as additional depth is gained." That is an old nursery tale, a pretty fantasy, on a par with the tale of the treasure at the rainbow's end. Such talk is out of date, but it goes well with the next assertion in the circular: "When this property shall be [will have been] developed as a whole there will be nothing comparable to it as a precious metal producing property in the Western hemisphere, either in richness or magnitude throughout." We appreciate the self-restraint of the broker or promoter, or whatever the writer may be, for he might as well have included the Eastern hemisphere, balancing "Eastern and Western" hemispheres with "richness and magnitude". He drags the Homestake and the New York & Honduras Rosario into his story, as if the yield of ore in these two mines, in South Dakota and Central America, had anything to do with the ease. His geographic amplitude does not stop there, he quotes the Alaska Treadwell, to prove that if $2.17 ore in that mine could be exploited profitably then the poorest ore in the Eureka-Croesus is a sure source of wealth; for, "in all the assays that Major Catlin has had made of the Eureka-Croesus ore, notwithstanding the fact that he diligently sought the leanest ores obtainable, he never has been able to get one running under $2 gold." Tell that to the horse-marines, my dear Sir. A miner does not "seek diligently for the leanest ore"; if he does, he needs the services of an alienist; and if, as a vagary, the Major sought lode-matter or veinstuff containing less than $2 in gold, he would have found it easily enough. There is lots of it at Eureka, even in a mine with $20,000,000 worth of phantom ore. The circular closes with a prediction that "the production of the company on a large scale will continue [but it has yet to begin!] without interruption for a long period, undoubtedly through several generations [most men outlive most mines, fortunately or unfortunately, as you look at it], and when the incontrovertible facts [he means 'cheerful expectations'] regarding the property become generally known among conservative investors [meaning venturesome simpletons], the stock will command a price warranted by the value [or otherwise] of the property,'' which (as amended) is true.

Copper in Arctic Canada

In this issue we publish an article on the deposits of native copper in Arctic Canada; it is written by Mr. J. J. O'Neill, of the Geological Survey of Canada. Last week, in commenting upon the remarks of Dr. Willet G. Miller concerning the scope for prospecting offered by the vast area of pre-Cambrian rocks in northern Canada, we dwelt upon the possibilities of mineral discovery in these outlying regions. We are glad therefore to print the information given by Mr. O'Neill concerning the distribution and mode of occurrence of native copper in the North, supplementing the suggestions of Dr. Miller concerning the resources of the north-eastern country between Hudson's Bay and the Labrador coast. Of all these far northern districts the Coppermine River is the one most conspicuous in the records of exploration. Mr. O'Neill summarizes the knowledge available concerning these deposits of native copper, the special interest of which lies in their analogy to the amygdaloid lodes of the Lake Superior region. Further information will be found in a paper by Mr. J. B. Tyrrell published in the Transactions of the Canadian Mining Institute in 1912. The copper deposits are near the mouth of the Coppermine river where it enters the Arctic Ocean at the head of Coronation Gulf, one of the most remote and least accessible places in the world. The existence of native copper on the banks of this river has been known for more than two centuries and its Indian name, Tzan dézé, meaning Metal river, shows that the natives were aware of the fact. They made use of the native copper in fashioning implements. The first white man to bring a description of these deposits was Richard Norton in 1717. It was the son of this Norton, who later became Governor of the Hudson's Bay Company, that sent Samuel Hearne to explore the Coppermine country in 1770. He knew nothing of mines or minerals, hence his report has no technical value. In 1822 Captain Franklin, afterward the celebrated Sir John Franklin, on his return from an Arctic voyage, made a survey of the lower part of the Coppermine river and recorded the finding of native copper in the valley-bottom, remarking that the Indians had ceased to search for copper as soon as they were able to buy ice-chisels and other instruments of iron at the trading-posts of the Hudson's Bay Company. In Franklin's party was Sir John Richardson, the naturalist, who described the native copper as being found in association with prehnite and calcite in an amygdaloid rock, and also in the reddish sandstone underneath. Richardson's account is most interesting. He says that the Indians obtained their copper from detritus in the valleys, not from lodes in place. In 1902 David Hanbury found native copper in basalt on Bathurst Inlet and Melville Sound, 175 miles east of the Coppermine river. In 1911 V. Stefansson reported rocks rich in native copper in the mountains north-east of Prince Albert Sound, on Victoria island, in latitude 70 N. The late James Douglas, half in jest, undertook to grubstake his kinsman Mr. George M. Douglas if he would examine and report upon ''the copper bearing rocks of Hearne's Coppermine river.'' He accepted the challenge, and organized a party consisting of Dr. August Sandberg, a Swedish geologist, Lionel D. Douglas, a lieutenant in the British navy, and himself. They started from Edmonton on May 11, 1911, and descended the Athabasca and Mackenzie rivers to Great Slave Lake, thence up the Bear river to Great Bear Lake, up the Dease river and the Dismal lakes, and then down the Kendall river to the Coppermine. They reached the object of their journey on August 17, and spent the winter in the Arctic, returning in October 1912. The story of this journey is told with great charm in a book entitled 'Lands Forlorn' written by Mr. George Douglas and published in 1914. Dr. Sandberg was able to examine only a small part of the region, but signs of copper were found over a distance of 300 miles. Dr. Douglas, in his preface to the book, suggests that ''the total area within which copper ore may possibly be found covers nearly ten thousand square miles.'' The Douglas expedition confirmed Richardson's identification of the copper-bearing rocks with the amygdaloid melaphyres and conglomerates of the Keweenaw series of Lake Superior, as was proved by a petrological examination of many specimens brought from the Coppermine country and examined by Mr. L. C. Graton. Such samples as were brought home assayed from traces up to 7%. Dr. Douglas concluded that ''the region may become one of the great copper producers of the world.'' He recognized its comparative inaccessibility, but he pointed to the fact that ''the easternmost exposure of these rocks, so far as known, is not more than 500 miles distant from navigable water in Hudson's Bay, over a possible railroad route.'' Now a railroad is nearly completed to Port Nelson, on the western shore of Hudson's Bay. Lignite is plentiful, and better coal is likely to be found nearer than is at present known, judging from analogy with other parts of the North-West. It seems a far cry from San Francisco or New York to the Coppermine river or Bathurst Inlet, but some of us will remember when Frederick Schwatka's description of his voyage down the Yukon in 1883 first made known that great river to the outside world and how his fascinating articles in the 'Century' magazine were followed fifteen years later by the romantic story of the Klondike rush. As Mr. O'Neill says, it is doubtful whether the copper-bearing rocks of Bathurst Inlet are a continuation of those in the Coppermine district. The numerous islands of the Inlet show native copper disseminated in basic flows of lava, but assays show only up to 0.25%, whereas the amygdaloid portion of the lava-flows yield assays of several percentages; so there is an opportunity for intelligent prospecting in this region also. The area is enormous and it remains for the engineer to make systematic search for those parts of the copper-bearing formation in which the copper is concentrated sufficiently to make ore. These Arctic and sub-Arctic regions are distant and rough, the summer is short and the winter severe, but Alaska and the Yukon have proved that enterprising men can overcome the handicaps of nature and live more healthily in the North than in the hot jungle of the tropics. Those who are accustomed to the winters of Lake Superior will find nothing more rigorous on this continent. We see no real obstacle to further exploration and eventual exploitation except the difficulties of transport, now to be lessened greatly by the building of the railroad to Hudson's Bay; so here is a field well worthy of the combined energies of the capitalist and the mining engineer.

Big Issues and Small Minds

When the Armistice was signed last November the warring peoples gave a deep sigh of relief, and some even jubilated hilariously, because they thought the War was over and peace would follow forthwith. Seven months have gone, no treaty has been signed, warfare is in progress on seven fronts, and recrimination on seven more. The Allied nations find that victory has created difficulties and burdens chilling to the warmth of their elation, whereas Germany and her dupes have begun to realize the consequences of defeat and the penalties of crime. The world is disillusioned, disappointed, even resentful. Nowhere is this state of mind more apparent than at Washington. There the rejoicing in victory, the happiness at the prospect of ending the great horror, the pride in American achievement, and the solidarity of patriotic purpose have given place to the feelings much less exalted, even to some that are mean. The national representatives at the Peace Conference are ridiculed; the President is the butt of envy, hatred, and all uncharitableness; even the Allies, our brothers in arms, are mentioned in terms hardly more appreciative than those applied to the Enemy. It is a sad world, and Washington cuts the sorriest figure in it just at this time. At a crisis in our national affairs calling for calm judgment and wise decision, we see the violent effervescence of the most narrow-minded partisanship and the play of the most petty politics. Senator Johnson attacks the President noisily, he protests that this country is being forced into an alliance with bankrupt nations, into "a league of armed nations in a gigantic war trust," and will be forced to "guarantee the bondage of every suffering people." Three days later he comes out as a candidate for the Presidency. Senator Lodge suggests that the President is responsible for letting Wall Street financiers get hold of advance copies of the treaty, for nefarious purposes, as if the alternative explanation of leakage through foreign agents were not obvious; Senator Borah charges the President with "a treacherous scheme for the betrayal of the American people," and Senator Reed splutters his usual inanities. We are not in politics; we are not sympathetic toward Mr. Wilson as an individual; but we do respect the office of President and we have also some sense of fair play; therefore we think it high time to protest against the campaign of vilification to which President Wilson is being subjected. If representative government is to be effective, we must show some respect for our foremost representative, duly elected by the people of the United States. Pitiful indeed is this sequel to a great and successful national effort. Our young men, and many times more young men from other countries, have died to defeat the piratic offensive of the Hun, to validate the sanctity of contracts, and to re-establish international law. Have these politicians at Washington so little regard for the honored dead that they must intrude their miserable little jealousies and their pothouse machinations into the settlement of the great affair for which the national flag was carried forward so gallantly to victory? As for the rest of us, we also are not without blame. Have we not shirked our proper interest and responsibility in the settlement now being concluded at Paris? We were keen on the news of battles and we hurrahed at the signing of the Armistice, but have we not overlooked the fact that all the effort of our two years of belligerency, and the four years spent by our Allies in bloody contest with the Enemy, are being consummated in this Treaty and in the covenant of the League of Nations? Too many of us are too easily annoyed by the delay; we want to have done with it; we care little about the details, particularly about the fate of sundry small nations about which we are spaciously ignorant, if only we can resume business along the old channels, even with the Enemy countries. We sneer at the ineptitude of our delegates at Paris and make sarcastic remarks about the whole conversazione at Versailles, as if we could bring such matters to a cut and dried conclusion in one-half the time. Let us show a little more sense and a larger measure of generosity. President Wilson and his assistants, Mr. Lloyd George and the British representatives, M. Georges Clemenceau and his aides, Signor Orlando and the Italian delegates, all of them, have been working themselves to death in the desire to bring the War legally to an end by arranging terms as nearly acceptable as practicable and as nearly just as possible. If the settlement had been given to a committee of lawyers and publicists of our own selection, would they not have found it enormously difficult to envisage all the problems and to adjudicate all the controversies? How much more difficult, how almost beyond the capability of mortal men, must be the framing of a plan that will commend itself to the representatives of a number of countries, alien in race and in speech, each of whom enters the council-chamber with ancient prejudices, national jealousies, and even a personal bias toward the interests involved. We think it remarkable that the Conference should have done so well and we are willing to accept the settlement, not without demur, but at least with the desire to give it a fair trial, believing that if it be rejected there will remain no alternative but the chaos of international strife and the probability of another calamity such as the one that darkened the sun for four long years.

The Status of Gold

The Editor:

Sir—I have been ruminating for a few days over Mr. Robbins' article anent the status of gold and his criticism of Mr. Van Dyck's letter appearing in your issue of February 1.

He says, "Great Britain issued her gold sovereigns of a legal weight and fineness and then . . . she printed £100 on pieces of paper and issued these as running mates for the gold coins. . . . and did it successfully on a large scale." In issuing her coins "the value," he says, "was arrived at by taking the value of an ounce of gold as expressed in terms of monetary nomenclature on the day that Act came into effect." If the British government of the present day were to take the monetary nomenclature of tomorrow or the day after as a basis on which to fix the figures on the face of the sovereign, where then does he derive his warrant to justify doubling the figures as expressed in the monetary nomenclature of today?

Mr. Robbins appears to be obsessed by the idea that a government by legislative action can infuse more labor-energy value into labor-energy value already existing in the shape of gold. In other words he assumes an Act of Parliament can take the material expression of one man's physical and mental labor for one day and immediately re-create it into the expression of two days' labor of the same degree of productiveness. Now, giving a new slant to Shakespeare's words, a rose by any other name would smell no sweeter, neither would an ounce of gold by any other name contain more labor-energy.

Mr. Robbins complains that I do not make clear what I mean by intrinsic and social value. I am glad to explain that I accept, as he himself does, Mr. Hennen Jennings' figure of the function of gold—"a storage-battery of human energy; its value representing a certain amount of labor at the command of the possessor of gold." I did not mean to imply that its value in the arts and trades and its value as a money metal constituted two distinct attributes or characteristics.

Mr. Robbins points out the case of Argentina. Argentina finds it feasible to use gold metal in domestic exchange in exactly the same way as the United States finds it feasible to use copper metal in domestic exchange; that is, as a token or promise to pay. He speaks of the domestic value of gold in Argentina being double its international value, yet he would hardly err so far as to speak of the domestic value of copper in the United States as opposed to its international value by reading that value from the face of a copper cent-piece. If Argentina should, in the course of possible commercial complications, be forced to engage in an exhausting war and suffer defeat, what then would become of the "value" which Mr. Robbins reads to us from the face of the gold coins of her realm? The moment of surrender to the opposing army would wipe out the fixed domestic standard and the gold coins would revert to the international standard value according to the weight of pure gold contained in each. This international standard value is not eternal and unchangeable, but is, however, the least variable of any commodity and the sum total of social labor necessary to wring gold from the stubborn earth, refine it, and place it in the channels of exchange is the determining factor in establishing its international standard value.

I cannot agree with him that the fundamental regard for gold seems to be atavistic. The human regard for gold is evolved from accumulated practical experience. Among the most primitive communities of humans, equally with the most highly civilized, it has been discovered that there exists a more or less latent conflict between the individual and the tribe or community. Modern civilization has accentuated this by revealing still other diversities of interest between the citizen and the nation, between nation and nation, and between the nation and the world. Gold being the commodity of least weight and bulk in relation to the amount of human toil and mental exertion embodied in it, the individual or the nation possessing it will cling to it with uncanny tenacity, being consciously or subconsciously aware that should the diversity of interest between him and his fellows, or between that nation and other nations, break at any time into open conflict the gold will always buy the needs of life, even from an enemy, if enough is offered.

Admitting, as Mr. Robbins contends, that gold has advanced 25% in the unrestricted markets of the world and therefore admitting it to be permissible to clip 20% off the sovereign and the dollar, the doing of this would not add one ounce of gold to the world's visible supply. The weight of metal to the labor consumed in its production would remain in the same ratio as before. Furthermore, the ratio existing between the labor expended in creating a given unit of any commodity and the labor expended in producing an ounce of gold would remain as before. What Mr. Robbins appears to be contending for is more value or purchasing power in gold rather than weight or visible supply. There is no obstacle, he says, in the way of ascribing value to gold coin. If a government or a league of governments can ascribe value to gold coin, it certainly would be illogical and a waste of energy for such governments in the same breath to pass any Act calculated to stimulate gold production, seeing that in Mr. Robbins' estimation they are already endowed with the power to ascribe value to gold already in existence by reducing the weights of coins—to ascribe value sufficient to cover existing deficiency. If he objects to this argument as a misinterpretation of the terms of his proposal, I must point out that he contends for a 20% cut in the weight of gold coins to cover the advanced cost of labor, and a further cut, presumably 25 or 30%, to narrow the gap which he says exists between gold and indebtedness. Now, if governments can at will raise the figures expressing value by reducing the weight of coins, it is evident these governments would have no incentive to ask for, or to assist in, any increase of production. Legislation could then arbitrarily ascribe the maximum of value to the minimum of weight, and Mr. Robbins does not state anywhere in his letter that there is any limit to the ascribing power possessed by governments.

He says, "if gold were demonetized, it would immediately rise in comparative value." It appears to me he is here confusing 'value' with 'price'. I will agree that the price would immediately rise, but I cannot agree that raising the figures on the faces of gold coins would give the possessor of gold more security in permanent value "at the present time," as he says, "when there is great unrest throughout the world." A parallel might be drawn from the fluctuation of prices of lots in a boom town. One might conceivably buy a lot at a temporarily high price and find himself the owner of a lot of future and permanently low value.

It is always safe to have the metal of the medium of exchange fixed at a comparatively low nominal figure in proportion to the cost of labor involved in its production. When the price of that metal becomes high in proportion to the cost of labor then it becomes dangerous as a medium of exchange owing to the fact that there is too wide a gap between its price and its value. Any political or social upheaval is likely then to bring financial distress. Of course, the fixing of a comparatively low nominal figure on coins is not a cure for all economic ills.

Mr. Robbins says that successfully and on a large scale Great Britain issued Consols and gold coins, and that both coin and Consols have no essential difference and are both money, and immediately points to the "grave financial situation"—caused by a paper currency he says. I would ask Mr. Robbins why did Great Britain ship those train-loads of gold to Canada to settle for war commodities purchased of the United States? If Consols are also money why did she not send this lighter money? Because Consols are but a promise to pay, while gold is payment itself.

The remedy for the "grave financial situation," which Mr. Robbins assures us exists, lies far remote from any altering in weight of gold coins or altering of the figures on their faces. A discussion of the application of such a remedy would be most interesting, but such a discussion would enter too far into the writhing intricacies of political economy and social relations to be immediately pertinent to the question of the status of gold.

Seattle, May 24. JOHN C. MCPHERSON.

The Flotation Issue

The Editor:

Sir—When I read some of your discourses on the evils and folly that enter into the affairs of the mining world I am thankful that there is an editor with brains and fearless enough to speak plainly and dispassionately regardless of consequences. When I read the court procedure in the Minerals Separation case, it seems as if immature minds were arguing, at the public expense, for their own enlightenment.

They did not invent anything; they simply experimented with, only, the elements that had been disclosed. Supposing a few weeks after the original patent was granted, over thirty years ago, some user of the process found that less than 1% of oil was preferable to a larger quantity, is it possible to conceive that our patent-office would give a patent that would be held valid, as a discovery and invention, when the inventor had opened gates into a field where not invention but intelligent use and experiment for economy and efficiency must arrive at or near the quantities to be used and the method of mixing, and prevent the original inventor from using the elements disclosed in the quantities and manner that would give the best results. Deferred action is immaterial; the submarine was left undeveloped over a hundred years!

It looks very suspicious that the M. S. company received a patent from Germany, whose patent system was to prevent anyone outside of Germany from getting protection; as the rejected claims in the offices of the patent attorneys in this country well show, they selfishly appropriated the brains of others after disclosure and rejection, possibly the kaiser or some of his satellites were interested in the future. All the brain atoms put into this world hold-up were put into scheming and now trying to befuddle the courts, for not a ray of brain-matter went into what they call an invention and discovery. There are souls so small that forty million can dance on the point of a needle. Files of patent applications, rejected, specially in German cases, should clearly disclose lack of invention by logical comparison.

Los Angeles, May 31. T. D. ROBINSON.

[Our correspondent is in error in speaking of the justices of the Supreme Court as "immature minds," although we quite appreciate how he feels about it. The various courts that have given such contradictory opinions did not lack intellectual force—quite the contrary, of course—but they were out of their element insofar as they had to deal with abstruse scientific principles and technical details outside their kin, and of this the litigants took advantage, with the result that the decisions are confusing and unconvincing to the detached onlooker.—EDITOR.]

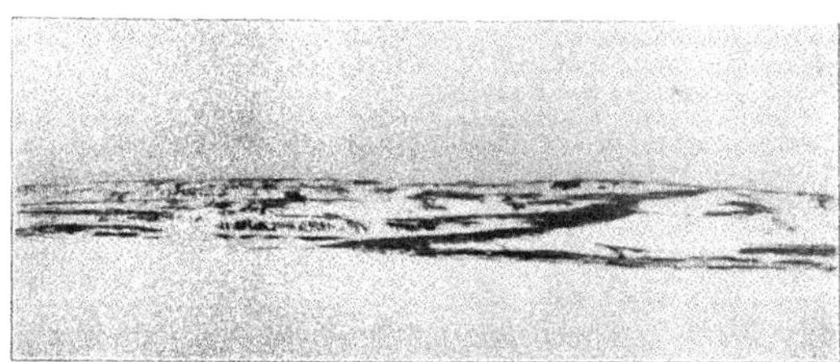

FIG. 2. EXPOSURE OF COPPER-BEARING AMYGDALOID ROCKS ON AN ISLAND IN BATHURST INLET

Deposits of Native Copper in Arctic Canada

By J. J. O'NEILL

*INTRODUCTION. The Government of Canada decided in December last to withdraw from staking for minerals all of Arctic Canada lying north of 65° North latitude, and between 105° and 116° West longitude, "in order that the deposit of native copper reported to exist in that region may be thoroughly examined." See map, Fig. 1, accompanying these notes.

The objects of the present paper are threefold:

(*A*) To indicate the distribution and general occurrence of the deposits of copper referred to in the Order in Council.

(*B*) To outline the general character of such an examination, and the conditions to be met in carrying it out, such as (1) means of access to the deposits, (2) amount of time available for actual work, together with the time consumed in travel and enforced idleness, (3) climate and general working conditions.

(*C*) To discuss the advisability of the use of aeroplanes for carrying out the work, and to indicate the most suitable bases from which such a scheme would be feasible.

HISTORICAL NOTES. It has been known for more than 200 years that native copper is to be found near the north-central coast of Arctic Canada; Samuel Hearne was the first white man actually to visit the deposits when, in 1771, he reached the Coppermine river, in com-

*Published by permission of the Geological Survey of Canada.

FIG. 5. TREE RIVER FALLS, SIX MILES FROM CORONATION GULF

pany with some Indians. His observations are of little value except as to the position of the deposit.

In 1821, Franklin reported that he found native copper along the Coppermine river, and also on the islands of Bathurst inlet; since that time Richardson, Rae, Dease, and Simpson, and Hanbury, have all confirmed both of Franklin's statements, but none of them had sufficient training to enable him to interpret correctly what he saw of these deposits. Most of these reports were exceedingly optimistic as to the amount and grade of copper ore to be found in those districts.

In 1835, Sir James Ross found trap-rocks on the east coast of Boothia in latitude 70° N. and notes copper ore from Agnew river.†

Large masses of native copper are found on the shores of Princess Royal islands, and large quantities of native copper on the shores of Prince of Wales island; according to DeRance‡ the copper at the first of these localities may have been carried there by the continental glaciers, but that on Prince of Wales island is not so easily accounted for, and may not be far from its source.

Copper in large masses is said to occur about 40 miles north-east of the head of Prince Albert sound, Victoria island; this was reported to Stefansson in 1910 by some Eskimos, and in 1915 many Eskimos testified to the Canadian Arctic Expedition concerning the same deposit; they produced some of the copper and said that masses much larger than a man protrude from the hillside, but whether they occur in solid rock or in drift could not be ascertained from them.

In 1917 a patrol of the Royal Northwest Mounted Police reported finding native copper in rocks about 60 miles east of Bathurst inlet, as shown on the map; the information from this locality is, like that from the others, very vague.

In summary, then, there are two large areas of copper-bearing rocks, namely, about the Coppermine river and in Bathurst inlet, which were first reported by Indians and Eskimos and later were visited and their occurrence confirmed by white men; two other areas of unknown extent have been reported by white men, one on Boothia peninsula, and one east of Bathurst inlet. Eskimos report that there are deposits of native copper in central Victoria island, on the Princess Royal islands, and on Prince of Wales island; the first and last of these reported occurrences seem worthy of some investigation.

Definite information has been obtained concerning the Coppermine river deposits by a party sent there in 1911 by the late James Douglas; the results of this investigation were presented at the annual meeting of the Canadian Mining Institute in 1913 in a paper by Dr. Douglas himself. The Bathurst inlet deposits were examined and mapped by me, in 1915 and 1916, while a member of the Canadian Arctic Expedition, and a summary of my results is printed in the bulletin of the Canadian Mining Institute for March 1917. Both these investigations were in the nature of reconnaissances, but a review of the data obtained will enable one to form some idea of the possibilities of the region.

THE COPPERMINE RIVER. These deposits are found in a series of superimposed flows of basaltic lava, with occasional interbedded conglomerates or sandstones, which occupy a belt 16 miles wide, and something more than 40 miles in length. This belt is known as the Copper mountains; it crosses the Coppermine river about 40 miles from the mouth, and runs in a direction a little north of west. The flows and sediments dip toward the north at about 12°, so that only the edges are exposed, the remainder passing under younger rocks to the north.

The Indians report finding copper in these mountains for 40 miles west of the Coppermine river, and Hearne's locality was about 25 miles east of the river; the deposits do not connect directly with those of Bathurst inlet, as was formerly thought, nor do they seem to swing out to the coast of Coronation gulf, so it is probable that they are entirely covered by younger formations somewhere within 75 miles east of the Coppermine, where they are cut off completely by the Laurentian granite.

The members of the Douglas party reported that they found native copper in place at Copper creek in an exposure of 30 ft. of basalt; the copper was in amygdules and as tiny shots or flakes in the massive portion of the rock. On Burnt creek they found copper similarly distributed through a total of 51 ft. of basalt, and in pebbles in 25 ft. of conglomerate. The assays ran from a trace up to one quarter of 1% of copper in the massive rock and up to 7.7% in the amygdaloidal portion. Copper stain was seen in many flows.

Just north of the Copper mountains the Eskimos find plates and masses of copper in large quantities in the drift.

Dr. Douglas considered that the information brought back by his party, although they only spent about one month in actual prospecting, was sufficient to warrant further extensive prospecting in that region.

BATHURST INLET. The copper-bearing rocks of Bathurst inlet are apparently distinct from those about the Coppermine river; they occupy an oval area which extends about 50 miles northwest-southeast and has a greatest width of about 25 miles. This area includes more than 150 islands ranging in size from a few hundred square yards to several square miles, also part of the western mainland, namely, Bank's peninsula, and a strip along the coast five or six miles broad extending from Arctic sound to Moore bay.

The formation is a series of basic lava-flows with a few thin beds of sediment; they are the youngest rocks in this region, and are exposed everywhere at the surface, since there is very little overburden of soil or drift. Prospecting would be an easy matter. The beds dip at about 6° (as shown in Fig. 2), so that they form a shallow basin, or basins in the area.

Native copper was seen on practically every island in this area as well as on the mainland. The distribution of the metal is remarkably uniform in the same flow

†'Narrative of second voyage in search of a North-West Passage', by Sir James Ross, 1835.

‡DeRance, in 'Nature', Vol. XI, p. 492.

FIG. 3. THINLY BEDDED DOLOMITE CONTAINING BORNITE ON BATHURST INLET

FIG. 4. SHATTER-PLANES STAINED WITH CARBONATE IN A SILL OF DIABASE CONTAINING DISSEMINATED CHALCOPYRITE. ON BATHURST INLET.

wherever found, for instance, one flow which was about 75 ft. thick, showed tiny shots or flakes of copper all through the groundmass; it was traced for more than two miles along Bank's peninsula and the copper content was apparently the same everywhere.

The native copper occurs in three forms:

1. As disseminated copper; minute flakes scattered throughout the dense groundmass of the basalts.

2. As amygdaloidal copper; irregular grains and small masses filling, or partly filling the branching gas-cavities near the surface of the basalts.

3. As vein-copper; in fissures and shatter-planes in any part of the basalts.

The disseminated copper may be said to be everywhere in this area, but the best to be expected from any of it is about 0.25%.

The amygdaloidal portion of the flows ranges from a few inches to several feet in thickness; in places this material will assay several percentages of copper, and in others the amygdules are entirely filled with chlorite, epidote, prehnite, opal, or agate. Where a flow is exposed at the surface this material is rather easily eroded, and the only broad surfaces now exposed are composed of the dense lower portions of the flows; the only place where the amygdaloidal portions may be seen is usually along the cliffs, and frequently there it is covered with talus. For these reasons it was not possible to judge of the relative extent and importance of this material during the reconnaissance mentioned.

The vein-copper assumes importance in some areas where the basalts have been considerably shattered, whether in cooling or otherwise, so that now they are traversed by a network of thin fissures containing plates of native copper, or vein-material containing native copper up to several percentages of the whole.

The problem to be faced in prospecting this area is to find the places where the amygdaloidal copper, or the vein-copper, or a combination of the two, is sufficiently concentrated to guarantee a large tonnage of profitable ore, and it may be possible to include considerable of the richer portions of the massive rock, to recover the relatively small content of copper.

I wish to emphasize the importance of investigating the deposits of sulphides in Bathurst inlet and to draw attention to the possibility that important deposits of sulphides may occur in the limestones of the Coppermine River region. In Bathurst inlet there is a series of dolomites immediately underlying the copper-bearing basalts, in the south and western portions of the region at least. See Fig. 3. This dolomite is exposed in several places in cliffs about the border of the area, and in three different deposits, a few miles apart, bornite was seen to have partly replaced the dolomite for several feet below the contact. Some of the thin layers were completely replaced, and others had masses of bornite scattered through them. The total amount of this material would probably have to be determined by drilling. An analysis of material from one layer six inches thick gave 49.87% copper.

Besides the bornite, which replaces the dolomites, there is a considerable amount of chalcopyrite disseminated through some of the large sills or dikes of diabase traversing the region. A grab-sample taken from one of these impregnations gave 1.18% of copper. See Fig. 4.

ACCESSIBILITY. The deposits in Bathurst inlet are situated on tide-water and could be reached by ship around Alaska and eastward along the north coast through Coronation gulf; in the average season the ship should reach there some time in August, but it would probably have to winter there.

Under present conditions the deposits in the Coppermine River region can be reached best by way of the Mackenzie river and across Great Bear lake; they could be reached by this route by the middle of August, and the explorer would have to winter in the country.

CLIMATE. The climate of the region under consideration is not extreme; in the winter the temperature seldom drops below -40°F., and seldom rises above 60°F. in the summer. The snowfall is about two feet; it is nearly all gone by the first part of June, and there is very little on the ground before the middle of October. The rivers open in the first part of June and do not freeze again until the end of September. Surface-work could be carried on from the middle of April until the middle of October without discomfort, and there should be little difficulty in carrying on underground work the year round.

POWER AND FUEL. Water-power in abundance for mining operations, and probably enough to take care of local transportation, is available from the Coppermine, Tree, and Hood rivers; the Coppermine river at Bloody Falls, is sometimes open all winter. See Fig. 5.

Coal, varying from lignite to bituminous, has been reported from the north shore of Bear lake, from the Horton river, from the north-east coast, and in central Banks island, and on the southern parts of the Parry islands.

Oil is known to occur in seepages in the Mackenzie valley as far north as Fort Norman, and the possibilities of production are being investigated by drilling.

There is plenty of spruce at the east end of Great Bear lake and in places between there and the Coppermine river; the tree-line is within 20 miles of the coast on the latter river.

TRANSPORTATION. The main difficulty in prospecting or opening up the deposits of copper in Arctic Canada is apparently one of transportation; the problem is simply this: there are two large areas of copper-bearing rocks that are to be tested to determine if there is a sufficient tonnage of commercial ore to warrant the expenditure of the large capital required to place the district on a producing basis.

To carry out this testing by aid of the present means of transportation, the explorers would have to spend at least one winter in the country whether they went in by boat or overland by way of the Mackenzie river route. The party could be placed on the ground in August at the earliest and have about three months for work the same year before having to settle down for the winter; the next spring they could start in May and work until the middle of August before returning. Thus it is seen that in 18 months they could accomplish six and a half months' work. They could double this working-time by remaining another 12 months, that is, for 30 months they would accomplish about 13 months' work in actual testing. These figures are assuming the best organization, management, and knowledge of the country. By using aeroplanes a party could spend between five and six months each year in actual testing, and it would not be necessary to keep the men in the North during the winter; since the cost of labor is the largest item, it will be readily seen that the saving in wages, not to speak of provisions and outfit, would be an important factor in figuring out the relative economy of the two methods of transportation. For the investigation of the deposits of native copper in Arctic Canada by aeroplanes or hydro-aeroplanes, the most suitable base which is easily accessible to railway lines is on Great Slave lake.

Fort Reliance at the east end of the lake would be the best base for operations in the Bathurst Inlet region, and Fort Rae, on the northern arm of the lake, would be best suited as a base for an investigation of the Coppermine River region; from either place the route would pass along rivers and chains of lakes for the major portion of the distance, and by the use of hydro-aeroplanes, intermediate bases could be established as desired.

The total distance from Fort Reliance to Bathurst inlet is only 260 miles, and by using Aylmer lake and Beechey lake as intermediate bases this would be split up into three parts, each of 100 miles in length, and practically the whole distance would be over water.

The total distance from Fort Rae to Dismal lake, which is in the centre of the Coppermine River district, is 315 miles, and this can be split up as desired by form-

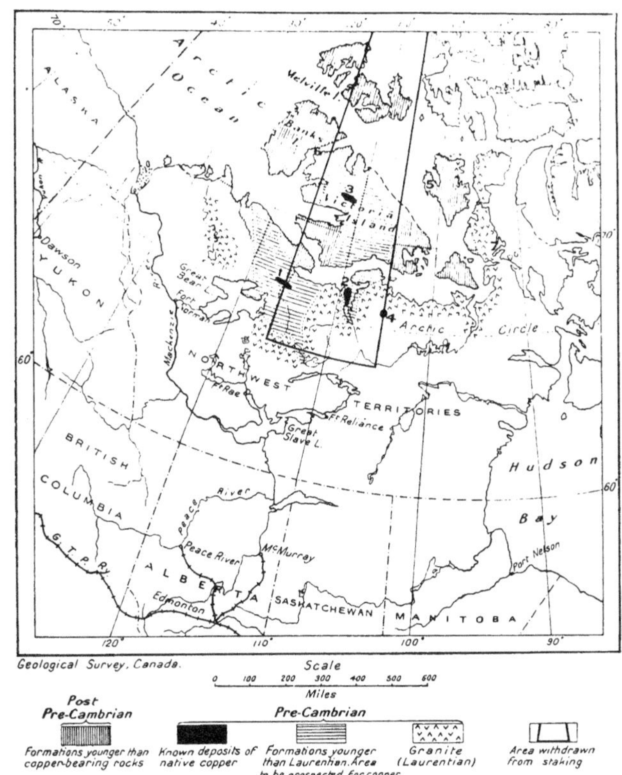

FIG. 1. MAP SHOWING THE GEOLOGY OF THE REGION ABOUT CORONATION GULF, IN ARCTIC CANADA, AND THE KNOWN COPPER-BEARING ROCKS

(1) Coppermine River area. (2) Bathurst Inlet area. (3) Victoria Island area. (4) Area reported by R. N. W. M. P. (5) Float copper on Prince of Wales island. (6) Float copper on Princess Royal islands. (7) Boothia peninsula area, reported by Sir J. Ross.

ing intermediate bases wherever desired along the chain of large lakes along this route.

Thus it will be seen that by using an air-service, the trip can be accomplished in a few hours; under present means of travel it would require two months with the expenditure of a great amount of energy, and many chances of delay or even failure.

[The reader is referred to an article on 'Prospecting in Canada' in our issue of June 7, and to the interview with Dr. Willet G. Miller in the same issue.—EDITOR.]

A Metallurgical Journey to Shasta, California—II

By HERBERT LANG

EARLY CYANIDATION. Almarin B. Paul's curious plant at the Calumet mine may be compared with the one erected to overcome the supposed eccentricities of the ore of the Tellurium mine on Middle creek. From a crusher the ore was fed to the hearth of a drying-furnace, 20 by 5 ft., under which the waste gases from a boiler were passed. The dried ore was then reduced to 30-mesh in a patent pulverizer, of a style now forgotten. It was then introduced into an agitator, where it was mixed with a solution, the composition of which has not been divulged, supposed to be competent to deal not only with the tellurium, which the ore may have contained, but with a large number even more deleterious substances, which it probably did not contain. After becoming sufficiently agitated, the mixture was passed to two rotating iron barrels. egg-shaped, measuring 3 by 4 ft. inside, and weighing 7000 lb. each, revolving on hollow trunnions like those of a tube-mill. With the pulp went 16 steel balls of 6 in. diameter. Rotation continued from 4 to 12 hours, according to the size of the particles of gold, the coarser ones requiring the longer time. Next came filtration; the filter, made of 10-oz. canvas reinforced by wire-gauze, was 4 ft. in diameter and took two tons of wet pulp. Pressure to the extent of 100 lb. per square inch was administered to the liquid, the filtrate going to a precipitating-tank 3 by 3 by 16 ft., lined with sheets of galvanized iron, in which the gold was abstracted from solution by plates of aluminum suspended in the tank. The gold, falling as a brown powder, was then gathered up and melted, while the residue from the filter was discharged over the dump. The saving claimed was 87%. Later it was ascertained that the 'secret' solution contained potassium cyanide. with some caustic soda. Herein we see an attempt at the cyanide process, a clumsy attempt. doing in a laborious and expensive way what by that time had been accomplished simply and in a rational manner. The dry crushing evidently was unnecessary, since the pulp was immediately wetted with the secret solution, and the double treatment. first in the agitator and next in the revolving vessels, could scarcely add to the efficiency of the process. Grinding in solution is indicated here for the first time, a practice that has been widely followed. The filtration under great pressure was a feature that further experience has shown to be unnecessary, but this fact was unknown at that time and for long afterward. Hence the excessive pressure employed was not so preposterous as would appear today. The extraction of 87% of the gold, if really achieved. was flattering, for it is not surpassed by current practice on ores of even moderate difficulty. If true, it proves that the ore of the Tellurium mine did not deserve its reputation for refractoriness; indeed, we may take it for granted that the ore was of no uncommon quality in any respect, and that no large proportion of the gold was combined with tellurium or with any other objectionable element.

It may seem to some that the treatment of the partly pulverized ore in a rotating barrel with the heavy steel balls foreshadowed modern practice with the ball or tube-mill; but one must go back farther to discover the germ of this inestimable invention. Some 15 years before the date of the Tellurium plant, Mr. Paul had built and was regularly using, at a mine in Butte county, California, a pulverizing appliance that was a close approach to the present forms of such mills. In connection with his noted dry amalgamation process. which he had installed in several mills, he used an apparatus described as follows:

"A revolving barrel, self-feeding and self-discharging, received the ore, already crushed coarsely under stamps, and revolved it together with pieces of quartz the size of the fist. The large fragments were used as a pulverizing material, the coarser pulverizing the finer. as well as being themselves worn down by attrition. The ore was thus brought to a fineness of 80 or 90 mesh. The internal arrangements of the barrel were such that the ore was passed through a series of sieves, only the first discharging outward into the hopper beneath, the remaining material returning to the centre of the barrel for further treatment."

This clearly antedates the modern style of pebble mill, which is often run with quartz masses instead of imported or other pebbles; and it is still doubtful which is the better. As for the use of balls within the rotating barrel. there is a bit of evidence still to be offered. The so-called Lundgren pulverizer, an apparatus in which cast-iron balls were employed as the comminuting agent, was used in the mills on the Mariposa Estate as early as 1864. as may be learned from the Government publication, 'Mineral Resources West of the Rocky Mountains'. This appliance consisted of a revolving barrel, 5 ft. long and of 3 ft. diameter. made of boiler-plate and lined with cast-iron plates one inch thick. It revolved 24 times per minute and required three horse-power to drive it. It worked dry, and took a charge of quartz weighing 800 lb., which had already been crushed under stamps to the size of wheat grains. With the quartz was introduced also 2400 lb. of iron balls. described as musket-balls. each weighing one ounce. In an hour. it was said. the ore was reduced to the finest flour; this was regarded as essential to the extraction of the gold by the subsequent amalgamation process, which, by the way, had a 'secret' about it, and was soon discarded. We note great divergencies between these methods, especially as to the weight of metal regarded as necessary for the pulverizing. In one case there was a very small number of very heavy balls; in the other a very large number of very light balls. The charges of ore weighed the same, namely, 800 lb.; whereas in the one case 2400 lb. of iron was used, amounting to three times the weight of ore, in the other only 512 lb. of steel was added, amounting to but five-eighths the weight of ore. In the one case there were but 16 balls, of the excessive weight of 32 lb. each; in the other there were no less than 38,400 balls (or pellets), or 2400 times as many. It is evident from this great divergence alone that no regular practice had developed, but that everything in connection with the comminution of ore was on an empirical basis. By going further into the 'dark backward and abysm of time' doubtless still more antique precursors of the tube, ball, or pebble mill might be discovered; but these instances may suffice.

CHLORINATION. When the chlorination process had become popular in California some 35 years ago, it was introduced into Shasta county, where the character of the ore and other circumstances seemed to favor it. The average run of the gold ores then being worked consisted of nearly pure quartz, intermixed with a small proportion, usually 2 or 3%, of sulphides, among which pyrite predominated; they were consequently precisely the material upon which that process had been found to work best. The ore itself was not, of course, subjected to chlorination, but only the concentrated sulphide—the essence of it, so to speak. The average run of such concentrate contained about 30% silica, the pyrite making up the remainder, with little gold, commonly not over 5 oz. per ton of concentrate. Nor is the process applied directly to the concentrate, which must be roasted so as to expel the sulphur to the utmost practicable extent before the chlorine can be made to combine with the gold and render it soluble. Whenever nature has thus expelled the sulphur, leaving oxidized iron compounds, the process can be applied directly, as was done at the great Mount Morgan mine in Australia, where the chlorination process was used on a big scale. Likewise an ore containing only quartz or some other gangue that is untouched by chlorine, and in which consequently the gold is in the native state, furnishes excellent material for the process provided the particles of gold are not too large; for chlorine attacks large fragments but slowly. However, although the process will work well on such a type of ore it is neither necessary nor advisable to use it, because amalgamation answers perfectly well on such material, and is much cheaper. Since chlorine is a powerful reagent, attacking many substances common to gold ores, its sphere of usefulness is contracted. In this respect chlorination is often compared with cyanidation, its successful rival. Chlorine is too strong; cyanogen is often too weak. The strength of chlorine is the weakness of the chlorination process: the weakness of cyanogen is the strength of that process.

Of the chlorination establishments built in California, numbering perhaps 50 in all, the average daily capacity was not more than two tons of concentrate. The average assay-value of the material treated was about $100 per ton, in gold. Usually it carried a few ounces of silver, up to 10 oz., as at Nevada City. While the extraction of gold was usually complete, reaching 90% or even more, the silver was lost, being left in the residue. It was frequently proposed to extract the silver from the tailing by leaching with hyposulphite—the old Patera process—but this was rarely done, although it would appear perfectly feasible, because the average concentrate contained too little silver to warrant a supplementary treatment.

Copper, which interferes with the chlorination process, rendering the dead roast more difficult, and absorbing a certain amount of chlorine during the lixiviation, is generally absent in gold ores. The concentrate from the Mother Lode mines carries, as a rule, only traces of that metal and gives no trouble. Should it occur more abundantly, its separation is not a difficult matter, requiring a separate lixiviation with or without dilute acid, according to the condition of the copper, which may exist in the menstruum as sulphate or chloride, or in the residue as undecomposed sulphide or as oxide, the product of the roasting. Should salt be used, the copper becomes soluble as a chloride, which is then easily precipitated on metallic iron, or as sulphide by means of hydrogen sulphide or sodium sulphide. These reactions were well understood by Deetken, who introduced the chlorination process into California, by Kustel, by Riotte, and others, among the earlier practitioners, but they were never put into commercial use.

Neither the ores nor the practice differed much from those of other mining regions, and the series of operations may be summarized briefly. The original Plattner vat process was generally preferred, as against the so-called barrel, or Mears, method, the latter being characterized by agitation of the pulp within enclosed receptacles and under pressure. The advantages of the Mears method for large operations were acknowledged. The difference between the two processes extends to the production of chlorine, which is accomplished in the original invention by the reaction of sulphuric acid upon a mixture of common salt and the di-oxide of manganese; in the later process by the use of chloride of lime (bleach), which is mixed with the acidulated ore. Notwithstanding the greater labor involved it was urged that with material so rich as to repay very careful work, the vats, in which the pulp remained quiescent, were preferable. The lower cost of installation was another point. Charles Butters who brought the process to the highest pitch of efficiency in Shasta county, is ranked among those who advocated the vat method. This method, as carried out at the Golden Gate works, in Tuolumne county, was typical. The concentrate, derived from the auriferous quartz of that mine, amounted to 4% of the total weight of ore, and assayed from 6 to 20 oz. gold, with 2 to 4 oz. silver per ton. The tailing assayed from 0.5 to 0.85 oz. gold, and 3 to 5 oz. silver. Great, but unascertained, losses occurred, amounting perhaps to 15 or 20% of the gold, besides the loss in the tailing. The concentrate, according to the invariable practice then, was roasted very slowly in a long-hearthed furnace rabbled by hand. This furnace was an excellent one in most respects, but it presented an example of bad construction because the arch was built too low, in obedience to the prevailing idea that the flame should be brought in contact with the charge, disregarding the principle of free-flame development. Three tons of material was in the furnace at one time, one ton being finished each day. A perfect roast cannot, of course, be expected, in the sense that all the sulphides are decomposed, and that all the sulphur is expelled, but the Golden Gate practice was good, regular tests showing but traces of soluble sulphates in the calcine. Three-quarters of a cord of pine wood was consumed to each ton of product, whence the fuel cost was $3.75 per ton. The total expense per ton was not far from $17, which was probably somewhat above the average of California chlorination plants. The reprehensible practice of adding salt to the charge, in imitation of the practice in silver mills, was followed, the addition being made when the woolly stage had been reached. At that time C. H. Aaron was just about to publish his observations on the volatilization of gold in salt roasting, the source of heavy and sometimes unexpected losses. These losses were no doubt heavy at the Golden Gate, but remissness in weighing and assaying had prevented their discovery. The late Professor Christy published the results of exhaustive experiments, which, had the process not been moribund would have had an important effect upon metallurgical practice. That it was possible, by long exposure to heat and the action of salt, to sublime and lose a fourth or even a half of the gold in a sample of pyritic material seemed incredible to even the most experienced operators; but so it was.

After withdrawing the roasted material from the furnace and allowing it to cool, it was then moistened slightly and placed carefully in a tank or vat made of wood, coated thickly inside and out with asphaltum paint, which is not attacked by chlorine gas. The calcine consisted approximately of one-third quartz grains, with two-thirds oxide of iron, partly ferric and partly magnetic. There were, of course, minor constituents, which, aside from the precious metals, need not be mentioned. The ore from which this material was derived was exceptionally simple in composition, showing upon analysis, scarcely any of the elements that we are wont to find in such a connection. There was, for example, no lead, no bismuth, no antimony, and but a trifle of arsenic. None of these play any part in chlorination provided the roast has been conducted properly.

It is necessary in the vat process to prepare the material so as to admit of the passage of the gaseous chlorine, through the charge, reaching all parts of it. It must be porous, in fact, but it cannot be wet. A little water is requisite, because the gold chloride must be dissolved as fast as formed, else the inside of the metallic particle will remain coated with the solid chloride and its decomposition prevented. Much water, by preventing the access of chlorine, spoils the operation in the vat, but does no harm in the barrel modification. It was generally supposed that chlorine was unable to attack gold in the absence of moisture; but this is a mistake. It attacks it dry and forms a chloride that is deliquescent, and the function of the moisture intentionally introduced is to dissolve immediately the newly formed auric chloride and get it in condition to be leached. The calcine is mixed at first with just enough water to enable the mass to hold together when squeezed in the hand. The moistened stuff is then shoveled, or, better, screened into the vat in a most careful way, avoiding a tendency to pack down, leaving it so that the gas can penetrate to all parts of the charge, which is about a foot and a half deep, and rests upon a canvas filter, which rests in turn upon a permeable layer of sand or gravel in the bottom of the vat. The operation goes on in the cold, and cold water is used to dissolve the new compound of gold and chlorine. It was regarded as a singular fact that a little of the gold in the Golden Gate calcine was soluble in water before the addition of chlorine; but this effect of undecomposed salt on metallic gold and silver is normal.

The precipitation of the gold from the very dilute solution resulting from leaching with repeated additions of water is easy up to a point, but to get all of it is another matter. A little remains persistently in the exhaust liquor, giving rise to not unimportant losses. The spent liquors were usually tested by the addition of ferrous sulphate and watching the color; but it is only by evaporating down an aliquot part and assaying the residue that an adequate idea can be obtained as to the extent of the loss. Many precipitants are known, but the general practice centred upon the use of copperas (ferrous sulphate) in preference to hydrogen, sodium sulphide, or charcoal. Most operators manufactured their copperas by acting on scrap-iron with sulphuric acid; for larger quantities, it would often be cheaper to make it from native pyrite by heap-roasting, after the manner in which the Mexicans make their magistral for use in the patio process.

Notwithstanding the certainty with which the reactions of the chlorination process take place and the simplicity of the operations and the apparatus, and the fact that 90% of the gold contents was habitually accounted for, it must be acknowledged that chlorination was a wasteful process. It can scarcely be doubted that millions of dollars have been lost in working the rich concentrate of the Californian mills, to prove which it is only necessary to consider the aggregate of the wealth contained in the tailing of the numerous chlorination plants scattered throughout the gold-mining regions. At one time there was over 40,000 tons of such tailing still preserved on the dumps of Amador county, which has always been regarded as the chosen home of chlorination, and where the art was carried on with unquestioned skill and intelligence. All this has been sold to smelters situated at great distances and treated at a profit. The Amador tailings averaged fully $10 per ton, a sum sufficient to pay both the cost of transport and the treatment charge, and yet leave a profit. Still larger quantities have been allowed to escape into the streams, to become a total loss.

A marked advance in metallurgy had been made early in the 'eighties by the introduction of the Plattner process of chlorination, which became popular throughout the quartz-mining regions of California, where, for many years, it fulfilled an important function. Previously the common practice in treating the gold-bearing pyrite, whether ore or concentrate, had been to grind in pans with quicksilver, trusting to fine comminution to render the gold amalgamable, or, in some cases, to subject it to a previous roasting. By this means a portion, only, of the gold was recovered, the remainder being allowed to run to waste with the tailing. This method was so wasteful that it was a question whether it paid to save the pyrite at all; accordingly, we find that in those years very few of the mills were provided with what would now be called an efficient concentrating plant. Progress was in the air, but nothing was more common than to find mills totally devoid of concentrators, while a small number had installed such makeshift contrivances as buddles and canvas plants, while the more progressive were just beginning to realize the effectiveness of the Frue belt-machine, which in time became the standard concentrator of the world. A great number of gold mills were provided with pans of the style common to silver-milling, and scarcely any other means was known of extracting the gold in the sulphides. Happily, through the skill and foresight of Deetken the chlorination process was brought over from Germany, and adapted to Western conditions. Wooden vats of considerable capacity took the place of the earthen jugs, and a suitable gas-generator was provided, capable of gassing a charge of a ton within two or three hours, which was considered a marvelous advance. It is rather curious that the process has remained substantially as Deetken left it 40 years ago; for the improvements suggested by later operators have never superseded former practice where close work is an object, although the capacity of the plants has been expanded.

In Shasta the ores adapted to chlorination were fairly abundant, consisting of the sulphides contained in the quartz treated in about 20 mills, aggregating 290 stamps. The stamps averaged about 850 lb. in weight. The largest mill was that of the Uncle Sam mine, west of Kennett, which had 35 stamps, and in 1896 had 14 Frue vanners, or two to each battery of five stamps. Previously, under the management of Daking & Co., it had 20 stamps with 4 Frue vanners and a canvas followed by a small chlorination works, probably the first erected in northern California. Eventually the 4-ft. vein was followed to a depth of 450 ft., which in those days seemed a great depth, and produced in all as much as a million dollars. It is worthy of remark that while the Uncle Sam had 14 vanners with its 35 stamps, all the other mills in the county, with 255 stamps, had only 19 concentrating machines between them, or one to every 13 stamps. The Murray mine, on Flat creek, not far from the Uncle Sam, had a cannon-ball mill and two concentrators. It worked a 2-ft. vein, the assay value of which is not recorded, but the 'sulphurets' were claimed to go $200 per ton. The Central mine, a more important property, on the east side of the Sacramento, used two Huntington mills, supplemented by 8 Frue vanners, producing, as the owners claimed, also a $200 concentrate. In the Old Diggings district, just north of Redding, there were the Utah & California, owned by the Walker Brothers, noted mine-operators of Salt Lake, and the Texas & Georgia, owned in part by R. G. Hart, another well-known and much-respected operator, now deceased. Both mills had concentrating apparatus, and became customers of the custom chlorination works established at Kennett in 1889.

As the superior advantages of smelting for such ore had not become fully appreciated, and as the enormous base-metal resources of the region were scarcely suspected, it might have been supposed that chlorination represented the final word in scientific metallurgy. This, no doubt, was the general impression, otherwise shrewd operators would scarcely have thought of establishing, either in Shasta or elsewhere, a plant designed to do business on a custom basis. The limitations of the process were fairly well understood, and this process, so scientific in its principles and so simple in its application, proved no better adapted to the ores of Shasta than of any other region. As before mentioned, chlorination is only perfectly applicable to material that, like the calcined concentrate of pyritiferous gold-quartz, contains only the oxide of iron mingled with a little quartz left by the imperfect dressing. Any substance upon which chlorine acts is invariably prejudicial to metallurgical success, and a great deal of the skill and ingenuity of its devotees have been mainly expended upon devices for overcoming the harmful effects of such impurities. The inability of the process to deal with silver is well known; when this metal is present a secondary process is necessary. These peculiarities detract from the value of chlorination, which is not a method of general utility. Nevertheless it has been used as a custom process to a considerable extent, especially in connection with the ores of Cripple Creek and the Black Hills, where, for a time, it was regarded as equal in value to cyanidation. It has long since been superseded, either by cyanidation or by smelting. Even the concentrate of the Mother Lode mines is no longer treated with chlorine; instead this product is shipped, unroasted, to the custom smelters, or, in one or two instances, it is cyanided, raw, with better results. Mount Morgan, in Australia, affords the best instance of direct chlorination. The gold ore of that mine contains its iron as ferric oxide, a substance, as before indicated, wholly unaffected by chlorine and consequently not wasteful of that reagent. The prodigious quantity of such ore at Mount Morgan and the scale on which the operations were carried out, made it the most remarkable of all such installations; but even at Mount Morgan the process has long since been superseded by smelting, largely owing to the discovery of copper-sulphide ore underneath the big gossan forming the crest of the mountain.

While the numerous chlorination plants of California almost without exception were technically successful, only two or three of those devoted to custom work seem to have proved financially profitable. Nor is it to be expected that any great profit can be won in operating on the small scale made necessary by the scarcity of suitable ores. There were, however, a few noteworthy exceptions. Probably the plants of Voorheis & Barney at Sutter Creek and Drytown, in Amador county, were the most successful, they having, in the course of some years, carried on a regular business in the purchase and treatment of the concentrates of the neighboring mines of the Mother Lode, during which some 25,000 tons of dressed material was put through the two plants, with an aggregate output of about $2,000,000, and aggregate gross earnings of one-fifth that amount. The regular charge for treating concentrate was $20 per ton. In this case, as in others, the smelters and railways conspired to take away the ore upon which the local establishments depended, bringing operations gradually to a close. It was not found practicable to do the close work required upon the material of such value for much less than $20 per ton, although private plants, that is, those operated on behalf of a single mine, published statements showing a cost as low in one case at least as $6 per ton.

The ordinary extraction by chlorination was about 90%. We may believe that in most cases it was less rather than more, because the residue of tailing generally showed a value of about $10 per ton when the concentrate itself carried $100 per ton. It should be noted, however, that the tailing weighs considerably less than the unroasted material. Pure iron pyrite, perfectly roasted, forms ferric oxide, which weighs only two-thirds as much. The roasting, however, produces some magnetic oxide of iron, which weighs still less; but some silica and other stony impurities are always left in concentrating, often amounting to one-third of the weight. On the whole, therefore, the tailing may weigh three-fourths as much as the original material, whence the loss might be 7.5%. But there are other losses, the amount of which it is impossible to tell with accuracy, largely because the chlorination operators with few exceptions (among whom we must number Messrs. Voorheis & Barney) were not careful in matters of weight and assays. The principal loss, no doubt, arose from the volatilization of gold, a matter not fully understood or appreciated.

The ordinary practice of chlorination as conducted in California is well illustrated by the operations at the Golden Gate plant, in Tuolumne county. The method here used was the original Plattner process as improved by Deetken, who used wooden vats for the reception of the roasted material. This plant, at which I studied the process some 40 years since, dealt only with the product of a single mine, the concentrate being, with the exception of the inevitable quartz grains and a trifle of arsenic, composed of pure pyrite and therefore presenting no obstacle to successful work. The chief difficulty was an inadequate supply, the output of concentrate amounting to only one ton per day. This, however, was uncommonly rich, containing from $150 to $400 per ton in gold. The concentrate was first dried upon the top of the furnace, which was of the type called by the Germans a fortschauffelungsofen, a hand-worked reverberatory about 50 ft. long by 10 ft. wide, with the usual arrangement of doors, fireplace, and chimney. The hearth was made of soapstone, quarried near-by, and well adapted to the purpose, since it was sufficiently refractory to withstand the moderate temperatures required, and particularly because the smoothness of the bed materially lightened the work of rabbling. The roasting, and indeed all the work of this plant, was carefully done, great pains being taken to ensure a perfect roast, perfect gassing, and perfect precipitation. Doubtless the work at this little plant might be compared in these respects with that done at the most noted German plants, which it resembled in the minute scale of its operations. A dead roast being the aim, the charge remained in the furnace, under constant rabbling, for 24 hours, the heat never being suffered to exceed a dull redness, except toward the end, when it was raised somewhat to ensure the complete decomposition of any remaining sulphates. Three charges, of about 1500 lb. each, covered the three divisions of the hearth, and were kept separate. At a certain stage, namely, the period of maximum formation of sulphate, common salt to the extent of 5% of the charge was added, an indiscreet and probably useless proceeding, but practised by nearly all chlorination managers. This practice, copied from silver metallurgy, is without justification, since the effect of salt is to decompose sulphates but not sulphides. There may be a glimmering of sense in it, though, since the persistence of ferrous sulphate in the chlorinating vats would induce the untimely precipitation of the gold. But to secure decomposition of any small residuum of ferrous sulphate would only require the addition of a mere trifle of salt, quite at the end of the roasting, before the charge was drawn from the furnace, or even after it had fallen into the 'cub' but still remained red-hot. A better expedient would be to add burnt lime or lime-water subsequently, by which the sulphate would be effectually broken up, without the possibility of causing a loss of gold. Further, the reaction between salt and ferrous sulphate gives rise to ferrous chloride and sodium sulphate, the former of which volatilizes at a moderate heat, with results that later experience has shown to be almost fatal to the process.

It was at this period that Charles H. Aaron published the results of his observations on the volatility of gold when roasted with salt, thereby rendering a great service to scientific metallurgy, but weakening public faith in the chlorination process itself. He showed the possibility, even the probability, of great losses on this account, and denounced in strong terms the practice of salt-roasting. His statements were received with incredulity, but they have been verified in full by various experimenters, among whom S. B. Christy was the most prominent. It may seem almost incredible that years had to elapse before the fact was discovered, and we can only lay it to the lack of systematic weighing and assaying by the operators, who were content for the most part to jog along in the old way, until the smelting fraternity entered the field and took away their business. The practice of weighing and assaying the charges never became general at chlorination plants, though some, as at Sutter Creek, adopted it, and consequently the operators never knew quite what they were doing. In this respect the practice of the Golden Gate mill was as bad as any, and the plant ran on for years without a suspicion that heavy losses were being incurred.

The procedure at the Golden Gate works was identical with that followed elsewhere, and we may safely assume that the losses there were not excessively greater. What these were never was known: but it is significant of the looseness with which accounts were kept that the manager remarked at the close of a long campaign that while he got $70,000, it cost $80,000 to get it, and that he didn't know where all the gold had gone. It was directly after that that Mr. Aaron made his announcement of the heavy volatilization of gold from the Murchie concentrate; this gave a pretty good idea where the gold had gone, and set the chlorination operators to thinking deeply. Christy published his quantitative determinations somewhat later, and the matter was settled once for all.

It will appear from the foregoing that the chlorination method is hardly applicable to large-scale work, although the proponents of the barrel system held to the contrary. We are the more convinced of the narrowness of its scope when it is considered in its relation to custom reduction of ores, as practised in a few plants. One of the most prominent of these was the establishment of Charles Butters, styled the Butters Ore Milling Works, at Kennett, in Shasta county. This was built in 1889, in a locality that then became and has since remained an important metallurgical centre. The Butters plant signalized itself by treating a variety of ores and products whose reduction by this method had not previously been attempted. Many of the expedients by which the difficulties of chlorinating complex or unsuitable ores were overcome are worthy of more extended description than space permits. Mr. Butters himself was surprised at the number and complexity of the operations that were sometimes required to be performed on a single vat of the chlorination plant. Here let it be said that he invented some ingenious operations, and mentioned them in a letter printed by him some 30 years ago, before his connection with the cyanidation process, which brought him fortune and reputation. Some extracts from the letter will throw light upon the expedients necessary in treating custom ores when competing with smelters, for at that time smelting had already become a powerful competitor. Mr. Butters brought auriferous material from points 200 miles away, "and came out," to use his own words, "more than even." The concentrate from the Idaho mine at Grass Valley gave much trouble; it contained lime and magnesia, together with manganese, zinc-blende, galena, and chalcopyrite, and assayed 4 oz. in gold, with 8 to 12 oz. of silver per ton. This material could not be roasted with salt, said Mr. Butters, "since

THE BUTTERS CHLORINATION PLANT IN 1890

the gold would go up the chimney.'' So it had to be roasted at a black heat, discharged, allowed to cool, wetted down, and screened rapidly, a little at a time, otherwise the pulp, being a natural cement, would consolidate. After the sulphates had absorbed all their water of crystallization, taking about two days, it had again to be screened carefully, put into a vat, and washed two or three days with cold water, then the carbonates and alkaline bases were neutralized with sulphuric acid, this taking from 60 to 100 lb. of 66°B. acid per ton. When the pulp had been acidified, 20 lb. of acid was added and circulated for 24 hours in order to dissolve the copper oxide. It was then washed for 48 hours with cold water, shoveled from the vat, the pulp was partly dried, screened, and transferred to a vat, where the chlorine gas was introduced. Mr. Butters said: ''When you have washed it out, precipitated, and got your clean spongy gold in elegant condition, you feel repaid for your trouble. The tailing, however, still contains from $4 to $6 per ton in gold and all the silver; and 'hypo' won't touch it, it having been roasted raw; and the acid does not dissolve out more than one ounce of silver to the ton. Now this has to be treated as a distinct ore; 5% salt is added to the wet pulp and it is put through the roaster just as fast as possible, when we get nearly all the balance. Gold is here united with the silver, and volatilization does not take place.''

Mr. Butters showed the inefficiency of ferrous sulphate as a precipitant, and in careful experiments found a temporary loss of 10% of the gold when the exhaust solution contained copper salts (chloride and sulphate). With less copper in the solution the loss in gold is naturally less; and he found on average, a loss of 2.2% on the value of gold and silver. As examples, he found in the copper water (the filtered solution from the precipitated gold) $3.06 per ton of ore treated; and in another case $2.22 in gold and 22c. in silver. In treating concentrate containing dolomite the copper water contained nearly 30c. worth of gold per ton of water. He concludes his remarks upon this point by saying that after the copper had been precipitated by metallic iron the liquid still contained, after standing for a week, 2.5 mg. gold and 10 mg. silver, per cubic foot of solution.

SODA-ASH production of the United States during 1918 was 1,390,628 short tons, valued at $35,635,520, compared with almost exactly the same quantity in 1917, valued at $38,028,000, according to R. C. Wells, of the U. S. Geological Survey. Sales in 1916 were 1,200,000 tons, valued at $18,000,000. These figures do not include sodium carbonate reported in the form of monohydrate and sesquicarbonate, for the production of which exact figures are not available, nor the soda-ash consumed by the manufacturers in their own plants in making caustic soda and other sodium compounds. The quantity of soda ash used for the latter purpose in 1918 is estimated at 664,000 short tons, against 482,000 short tons in 1917. Most of the soda ash is made from salt and limestone, but a small quantity is made in the West from natural sodium carbonate, chiefly that obtained from the water of Owens lake.

The Montana School of Mines

The establishment of the State Bureau of Mines and Metallurgy as a department of the Butte School of Mines, is further evidence of this institution's growing importance to the mining industry of Montana. The Act creating the Bureau was passed by the State legislature last February, and the sum of $20,000 was voted for the two years ending February 28, 1921. It was somewhat remarkable that, while 42 out of 48 States have their own Geological Survey or Bureau of Mines, the important mining State of Montana was not so equipped. The newly-created Bureau has already been called upon to make one or two investigations, and, with Charles H. Clapp, Ph. D., President of the Butte School of Mines as Director, it is safe to say that further useful work will be done. The objects and duties of the Bureau are similar to those of other such institutions, and will be found fully set forth in a Bulletin of the University of Montana, Bureau of Mines and Metallurgy, Series No. 1, which will appear in print in the near future. Suffice it to say that the Bureau is organized into four major departments: Administrative, Geology, Mining, and Metallurgy and Safety, for the purpose of aiding in the development of the mineral resources, and for the assistance and promotion of the mineral industry of the State. The Butte School of Mines is to be enlarged by the erection of new chemical and metallurgical laboratories, for which the sum of $100,000 has been voted by the State legislature and approved by the State Board of Examiners. This addition to the school buildings is in accordance with the plan originally laid out, and the architects are now engaged on the design. The total cost of two new structures will be nearly $200,000. The work of the school, like that of all such institutions, was greatly crippled by the War. The regular courses have now been resumed, however, and the registration of 92 is the largest in the history of the School, which enjoys the distinction of being situated in the world's greatest mining district. For purposes of instruction, the importance of having the Butte mines ''in the back yard'' cannot be over-estimated, while the metallurgical establishments of Anaconda and Great Falls are easily accessible. It goes without saying that, thanks to the liberal co-operation of the mining companies, full use is made of these facilities. During the past week the Junior class made a trip to study the geology and ore deposits of the Judith and Highwood mountains, the coal mines at Roundup, and the smelter and power-plants at Great Falls.

GOLD PRODUCTION of the Dutch East Indies during the past 8 years totaled 47,780,800 florins ($19,207,881). Of this, 80% came from the district of Benkolen on the island of Sumatra. In 1914 Sumatra yielded $2,700,000, and in 1918, $1,490,000. During this period the Celebes yield fell from $490,000 to $337,000.

Power Requirements of Rock-Crushing Plants

By MARK H. REASONER

At this time, where maintenance work is in demand, the question of requirements for rock-crushing is pertinent, and this depends primarily on the characteristics of the power employed. As most quarries are situated where electric power is available, it becomes primarily a question of motors. In the mining districts of the South-West and North this calls for the consumption of a large aggregate of kilowatt-hours supplied from large transmission systems, such as exist so opportunely in Washington, Montana, and California. Probably the largest individual groups of crushing machinery driven by electric motors are within the territories served by such systems.

But it is not alone among the large mining-plants that considerable opportunities exist for the use of electric power in driving crushing machinery. Scattered throughout the length and breadth of this country are thousands of quarries, gravel-pits, commercial rock-crushers, screening-plants, gypsum mills, phosphate and fertilizer plants that depend for their raw material on the rock formation in their vicinity. Nearly all of these are so situated as to secure energy to advantage.

Taking the country as a whole, it will be found that in many places direct-current systems are in use by numerous industries that involve crushing and in such cases they can be readily supplied with direct current, or, in some cases, with a trolley-line in the vicinity, or, in the case of an electrified railway, such as the Chicago, Milwaukee, & St. Paul, from its transmission line, or through a rotary convertor or motor-generator set at the plant where the energy is used. The application of the direct-current motor will not materially alter the horse-powers given in the table below, inasmuch as the latter are only approximate and will be governed by condition of service prevailing in the place where the power is used.

There are two general types of the induction motor that fulfill the usual requirements of rock-crushing plants, namely, the slip-ring and the squirrel-cage types. The former, when furnished with drum-type non-reversible controller and resistance, is suitable for service requiring frequent starting under load, or the starting of loads with high inertia. This motor has a phase-wound rotor and external resistance connected through slip-rings and it is due to this feature that it will start with a high torque and a comparatively small amount of current from the line. The resistance is gradually cut out as the motor comes up to speed, until short-circuited. When the motor reaches full speed the rotor resistance will be almost as low as that of the squirrel-cage type of motor and consequently good operating characteristics will obtain.

Approximate Power Requirements for Various Coarse Crushers

GYRATORY CRUSHER

No.	Hp.	No.	Hp.
1	6	8	100
2	10	9	140
3	15	10	175
4	20	12	200
5	26	18	250
6	40	21	300
7½	70		

BLAKE CRUSHER

Size	Hp.	Size	Hp.
4 by 10	4	10 by 20	20
7 by 10	7	15 by 24	25
9 by 15	12		

DODGE CRUSHER

Size	Hp.	Size	Hp.
4 by 6	4	8 by 12	12
7 by 9	8	10 by 16	18

CORNISH ROLLS

Size	Hp.	Size	Hp.
9 by 9	3	16 by 36	18
12 by 12	5	16 by 42	25
14 by 24	10	18 by 48	31
14 by 30	15		

Fine Crushers and Pulverizers

UNIVERSAL CRUSHERS

No.	Hp.	No.	Hp.
1	2–3	3M	12–15
1M	3–4	4	15–20
2	5–8	4M	20–25
2M	7–10	5	25–30
3	7–10	5M	30–35

SYMONS DISC CRUSHER

Size	Hp.	Size	Hp.
24-in.	18–25	48-in.	50–65
36-in.	30–40		

BRAINARD PULVERIZERS

No.	Hp.	No.	Hp.
0	8–12	2	20–25
1	12–16	3	40–50

STAMP-MILLS (for 10 stamps, 8-in. drop, 90 drops per min.)

Weight of stamps	Hp.	Weight of stamps	Hp.
750 lb.	15	1200 lb.	25
850 lb.	17	1600 lb.	32
1000 lb.	20		

HUNTINGTON MILLS

Size	Hp.	Size	Hp.
3.5 ft.	5	6-ft. standard	12
5 ft.	8	6-ft. heavy	17

CHILEAN MILLS

Size	Hp.	Size	Hp.
5 ft.	15	7 ft.	50
6 ft.	25		

GRIFFIN MILL

Size	Hp.
42 in.	50–60

STURTEVANT RING-ROLL

Size	Hp.
No. 2	70 to 80

FULLER MILLS

Size	Hp.	Size	Hp.
24 in.	10	42 in.	50
33 in.	35	57 in.	100

TUBE MILLS

Size	Starting hp.	Running hp.	Size	Starting hp.	Running hp.
5 by 22 ft.	125	50	6 by 22 ft.	150	100
5½ by 22 ft.	135	60			

BALL-MILL

Size	Hp.
7 by 7 ft.	60

The squirrel-cage motor, equipped with a compensator, is extremely simple and built to stand hard service. The absence of a commutator enables it to operate satisfactorily in positions where dust and dirt would prevent the employment of the slip-ring type; but its construction does not enable this type of motor to be started with a very high torque; consequently it is not adapted to certain loads, as for example ball-mills, tube-mills, etc. These mills require from 50 to 80% more power to start than is required for their normal operation.

Broadly speaking there are three conditions to be met with in rock-crushing and metallurgical plants, namely:

1. A complete installation containing no units requiring an abnormal starting torque.

2. An installation that includes one or more elements requiring a large starting torque, but that, for uniformity in operation, should be driven by a single motor.

3. Machines similar to (2) but such as to permit of the units being started or stopped independently.

It is obvious that the squirrel-cage type of motor should be specified in the first instance; the slip-ring type in the second, and a combination of both types in the third.

Ball-mills, tube-mills, and revolving drums (chlorination barrels or similar leaching-drums) are common representatives of the type of machines that require excessive starting torque. Hoisting machinery usually falls in this class also, but such machines as gyratory and jaw-type rock-crushers, rolls, hammer-mills, elevators and conveying machinery, dryers, jigs, concentrating tables, and many forms of roasting or calcining furnaces, can readily be put into motion with squirrel-cage motors. It is always doubtful economy to attempt to use a clutch-pulley to take the place of the proper type of motor, as the additional first cost and upkeep will in most cases show a decided balance in favor of the proper type of motor.

Great care should be exercised in locating motor-drives in dry-crushing plants owing to the presence of dust and grit. While there are some excellent designs of dust-proof motors being manufactured that meet such conditions, the most satisfactory solution of the dust problem where conditions will permit is to extend the drive-shaft to a point that will ensure safety from this evil.

In the foregoing tabulations is given the approximate horse-power required for various classes of crushing and pulverizing machinery. It is sufficiently accurate to serve as a basis for establishing the power requirements.

DEVELOPMENTS in design of internal-combustion engines reveal a peculiar condition, namely, the most efficient type, and one that can utilize the lowest-grade and cheapest of fuels, is only used in this country to the extent of little over 100,000 hp. This is the Diesel engine, which has developed a thermal efficiency of a little over 40% and a fuel economy of 0.45 lb. per brake horsepower. Another point that at first seems hard to realize is that the less efficient type of internal-combustion engine—the Otto cycle—is used extensively and there is possibly more horse-power of this type of engine in operation today than of any other prime-mover.—A. L. Taylor of Utah Society of Engineers.

Industrial Accidents in California

A report on special investigations of permanent injuries, composed largely of a survey of 700 cases where injury is so serious in character as to constitute at least an industrial and economic handicap, has been issued by the Industrial Accident Commission of California. Nearly all these cases are of sufficient duration for time and therapeutical efforts to have made whatever re-adjustments may be expected. At this time there is, therefore, chance to form a fair judgment of final consequences of the injuries. The findings are not the mere refinements of statistics gathered from reports; the facts included are not local; they are not gathered from a single community, from a particular line of industries, of a special class of workmen. They came from various communities in different parts of the State, and include almost every form of industry from street sweeping to banking. They were obtained at first hand by experienced investigators from the living sources themselves. The investigators met the injured in their homes, their places of employment, or in the offices of the Commission.

The percentage of injuries in the entire 700 cases were as follows: head and face, 4½; eye, 21; arm and hand, 36½; leg and foot, 23; trunk—including spine, 5½; and multiple injuries, 7.

In a classification by age, at the time of injury, there were 28 under 20, 580 over 20 but under 56, and 88 over 56 years.

In a classification by attitude toward injury and general outlook on life the following was found:

	Attitude	Outlook
Cheerful	503	..
Indifferent	75	..
Discouraged	122	..
Optimistic	...	19
Normal	...	606
Pessimistic	...	75

The general averages of all the classifications are:

Whole number under survey	700
Age at time of injury, years	37.8
Wage, before injury, weekly	$22.34
Wage, since injury, weekly	16.60
Disability rating, weeks	139
Compensation, weekly	$13.55
Time lost on account of injury, months	11.95
Number of dependents	2
Average age of children, years	9.5

While general averages often do not convey very definite and helpful information, there is still something about them that makes one wish to find what they are. This table will help very materially in forming a general conception of the conditions that obtain through permanent injury.

CONCENTRATE saved by the Waihi company in New Zealand last year amounted to 2676 tons from 188,998 tons of ore. It assayed 8.83 oz. of gold and 38.75 oz. of silver per ton. By grinding in tube-mills, agitating in pachuca tanks, and filtering in Dehne type presses the extraction was 98.4% of the gold and 95.2% of the silver. In the refinery, 46,758 lb. of precipitate yielded 561,348 oz. of doré bullion. This yielded gold 999.5 and silver 996 fine.

Employment-Management at the Eagle Mines

By ROBERT NYE

For a long time labor conditions at the Eagle mines of the Empire Zinc Co., at Gilman, Colorado, had been unsatisfactory. There had been no strikes and none were threatened, but the labor turn-over had been large and the average efficiency low, although probably no more so than in any other mining district in the Rocky Mountain region. It was recognized that this was primarily due to the great scarcity of labor and its attendant inefficiency. This did not seem, however, a sufficient reason for so many men leaving the company's employ to go to work soon afterward at other mines where the working and living conditions were no better and wages no higher.

The mines are dry, the ventilation much better than the average, and the wages as high as at any mine in the State. Board at the company's hotel was $1.10 per day, and as good as it could be made, at a loss of 45c. per day per man. Most of the single men had steam-heated rooms to themselves, rent-free. The married men lived in four-room houses with electric lights and modern plumbing, for which they paid $12 per month, including water. No restrictions were placed upon the men as to where they should board; some found accommodations in private families, while others lived in their own homes at Red Cliff, three miles away.

The company has a pension system, the benefits of which most of the men consider too remote to interest them. There is also in operation a bonus system by which every employee who has been with the company a full calendar year, receives a percentage of the wages earned during that year. This bonus depends upon the profit for the year, and has ranged from 5 to 15%. It is a highly prized feature with the men.

There is a good public-school at Gilman. The company has a sociological department, which maintains a free kindergarten, library, and reading-room. This department also conducts a club-house where 'soft' drinks, cigars, tobacco, and candy are sold, and pool and cards can be played at any time, and where moving pictures, community singing, dancing, and other social diversions are provided at regular intervals. There is a well-equipped hospital with a physician and trained nurse in regular attendance.

In short, the management felt that they had done about everything they could to make the working and living conditions as healthful and pleasant as the situation of the mines, at an elevation of 8900 ft. above sea-level, permitted.

After consulting the superintendent and foremen it was decided by the management to take the hiring and discharging of all men from the foremen and place it in the hands of an employment-manager. I was selected for this position and entered upon my new duties in January of this year.

Under the old system the foremen of the three mines each hired his own men. Most of it was done during the few minutes after the whistle blew for the shift to go to work at 8 a.m. and before the foreman followed his men underground. He then knew how many men had failed to show up for work. He was always in a hurry and seldom took the time to inquire closely into the past record or qualifications of the applicants for work. The first husky-looking individual who asked for a job usually got it. If he 'made good', all right; if he did not, he was fired and forgotten, often to go to work the next morning at one of the other shafts for another foreman. A man might work a day or two in each of the three mines in one week, and leave without any record being made as to what kind of work he had done.

Under the new system, each foreman telephones to the office, stating the number of men wanted and the kind of work for which they are wanted. When men apply to the foreman for work they are referred to the office and if the foreman is personally acquainted with any of them, or has any information about them, he sends it to the office by note or by telephone. The employment-manager gives each applicant a leisurely friendly interview, during which a large amount of information about the past experience and record of the man is usually brought out. An application card is made out upon which is recorded the man's full name, age, place of birth, if foreign born whether naturalized or not, whether married or single, dependents, name and address of nearest relative, two former employers and position with each, with reasons for leaving, kind of work wanted, experience in any other kind of work, and by whom recommended, if a recommendation is given. Sometimes former employers are written to, depending upon the position wanted. If the applicant has worked for too many different companies during the preceding year or two, he is seldom hired. If he is considered a promising man, he is sent to the company doctor for a thorough physical examination. It is always explained that this examination is for the protection, not only of the company, but of the man himself and the men that he will work with. So far there has not been a single protest against the physical examination. If the applicant passes the doctor's examination, and few fail to do so, he is given a note to the foreman that wants him and another to the steward of the hotel, who assigns him to a room. The date that he starts work, his position, and rate of pay are entered upon his application card. There are blank spaces on the card upon which to enter any transfers he is given, the date and reasons for leaving, when he is separated from his job, together with the degree of satisfaction he gave in each kind of work performed.

When a man quits, the foreman gives him a time-slip, which he takes to the employment-manager, who has a friendly talk with him and finds out his reasons for leaving. If it is found that he has been satisfied with conditions here, but is going to a better job or has other sufficient reasons for going, he is sent away with a blessing. If it develops that he is dissatisfied, and has some complaint to make, he is told to come around later for his cheek. In the meantime his complaint is investigated and if, as sometimes is the case, it is found to be justified, the cause of complaint is removed if possible and he is given a chance to go back, or he may be given a chance to go to work in a different part of the mine, as seems best in each individual case. In this way many good men have been retained that would otherwise have been lost, among them some of the best men we have. When a man proves unsatisfactory to a foreman much the same procedure follows; the man's story is heard; and if it seems that he has some grounds for complaint and there is a suspicion that a foreman or shift-boss has been giving him the worst of it, he is given a chance under some other boss, and often makes good. In this way the employment-manager becomes a sort of court of appeals. It has been found that foremen and shift-bosses are much more careful and reasonable in their treatment of the men under them since they know that they may be called upon to explain their conduct. They also realize that it is a reflection on their management of the men under them when a man they have turned down, makes good in another part of the mine under another boss.

As the force has only averaged about 250 men, it was seen that the employment-manager's time would not be fully occupied unless he had other duties. Accordingly, he was also made safety and efficiency engineer. This has proved to be a good combination as the two lines of work dovetail together nicely. The regular inspection trips through the mine and mill show under just what conditions each man is working and enables a useful acquaintance to be maintained. It is wonderful how far a few cheery words every few days go toward gaining the confidence of the men and how much easier they make it to decide justly when complaints are forthcoming.

During the three months in which the system has been in force the results have so fully justified the experiment that the management would not consider going back to the old method. In January the labor turn-over was 32.9%, in February 15.35%, and in March 11.58%. In March the turn-over would have been 6.84% if the hotel, with its average of ten employees, had been excluded, and the feeling has grown that kitchen and dining-room help are about as temperamental as opera singers. It is fully realized that labor conditions during the past three months have been abnormal and these figures might not have been duplicated in ordinary times. We are also getting more work per man, although our best men are not working any harder now than they did last year; in other words, we now have a much more efficient force, due to careful selection of new men, than we ever had before.

So far no records have been kept of each man's daily output, but it is hoped that a system for doing it can be evolved soon without adding to the expense or placing too much extra work upon the foremen and shift-bosses. Owing to the nature of the work such records cannot be made absolutely accurate, as, for instance, where a number of men are shoveling together in a stope, but it can be made accurate enough to be of great value to the management and a stimulus to the workers.

The maintenance of an employment department is a comparatively new thing among industrial organizations, but during the past few years the practice has been gaining in favor rapidly among the largest manufacturing and commercial companies. So far as known only a few of the largest mining companies have adopted this method of handling their labor. It is the belief of the management here that it will be advantageous for any mining company employing 150 or more men to have an employment department. Where the force is small the employment-manager can readily add to his duties that of safety and efficiency engineer, take care of camp sanitation, housing of employees, and general welfare work.

Blasting Old Concrete. Removal of old concrete or masonry is generally done by drilling holes with jumper steel and sledges by hand, then breaking off the material bit by bit with wedges. This is a slow and expensive way. The best, quickest, and cheapest method is by blasting. At first thought, most people would immediately say that explosives could not be used, as they would crack the walls of the building above or damage nearby machinery and be altogether too dangerous. As a matter of fact, explosives can be used with great economy in almost all cases, and with absolute safety. As a general rule, concrete is easily broken by blasting, and experience has shown that the better the concrete, the more easily it can be broken.

In doing this class of work, care must be exercised to see that the holes are properly placed—which, however, is true of all blasting—and that light charges are used. It requires no particular caution or ability to blast old walls of concrete, brick, etc., that are in open places, where there is little likelihood of damage to surrounding property. But it is in cases where the structures to be removed are close to and often are a part of valuable property, machinery, and buildings, that care and a good sense of judgment must be exercised. An explosive of relatively slow heaving action, like ammonia 30 to 40% strength, is best adapted for such work rather than a quick and shattering explosive. The drilling of holes is best done by self-rotating hammer-drills, but when the size of the work does not warrant such equipment, holes can be drilled by hand, using jumper steel or hand-drills and sledge. It is best to demolish the structure by gradual steps or benches, or a little at a time, especially inside or under a building. Six-foot holes are deep enough.

REVIEW OF MINING

COBALT, ONTARIO

RE-WORKING OLD MINES.—LABOR.—PORCUPINE AND MATACHEWAN GOLDFIELDS

Silver mining has been stimulated greatly by the recent large increase in the price for the metal, and operations are being resumed at many old mines and abandoned prospects, which had been closed. Labor is generally satisfactory. It was feared that the prevailing feeling of unrest might result in a strike, but investigations of the Industrial Relations Commission, which recently sat here, indicate that conditions in that respect are much less serious than was supposed. There is no difference between employers and employees on either wages or hours. The 8-hour day has been adopted, and the advance in the price of silver increases the bonus paid to miners, in addition to the regular wage-scale to $1.25 per day, so that the only point in dispute is the refusal of the mine managers to recognize the union. They are willing, however, to treat with committees representing their own employees, so that there appears to be no present danger of a walk-out.

At South Lorrain, operations will shortly be resumed at the Pittsburg-Lorrain and Wettlaufer mines, the former operating the Wettlaufer mill under lease. Horace Strong, recently of the Crown Reserve, will be in charge. The Keeley mine is also being re-opened.

At Gowganda, the Palmer-Paine, a new company, has acquired control of the property of the former T. C. 177 Mining Co. adjoining the Miller Lake O'Brien, on which considerable work has been done.

PORCUPINE. The mill of the Dome Mines is treating 600 tons of $7 ore daily, and gradually increasing its output as more men are being secured.

The cross-cut in Dome Extension has passed through the whole orebody, which is 99 ft. wide, and is stated to return assays of $5.50 per ton.

The mill of the Dome Lake is treating ore from the 600-ft. level extracted from a lens 200 ft. long, carrying $10 ore.

The orebody at the Davidson, which was 34 ft. wide where it was entered by the cross-cut, has widened considerably, and is improving in grade. The management contemplates adding to the mill to bring the capacity to 200 tons per day.

The McIntyre is employing 350 men and treating over 15,000 tons per month. The main shaft is being continued to a depth of 1375 ft., where another main haulage-level will be established. An intermediate level between the present one at 1000 ft. and the 1375-ft. level is under way. An ore-shoot 200 ft. long, worth $23 per ton, has been developed on the 8th level.

THE CONGLOMERATE IN WHICH MANY OF THE SILVER VEINS OF COBALT ARE FOUND

MATACHEWAN. The vertical shaft at the Matachewan

(formerly the Otisse) is down 100 ft., and has entered the orebody at a depth of 90 ft. It is over 50 ft. wide, and stated to carry high gold content.

GOLDFIELD, NEVADA

WORK BY THE GOLDFIELD DEVELOPMENT, LONE STAR, AND RED HILL FLORENCE.

A syndicate of New York men, headed by L. E. Whicher, has bought a large interest in the Goldfield Development Co., according to H. G. McMahon, secretary for the company. The sale was made in New York by McMahon, and followed an examination by Walter Harvey Weed of the plans of the Development company to extract a large tonnage of ore in Consolidated ground. More than $100,000 is in the treasury and preliminary underground work is well under way in the Combination, Mohawk, and Red Top mines. F. Dean Bradley, a metallurgist, is in Goldfield to prepare the Consolidated mill for treating this ore, and following his report on the alterations that will be necessary, re-modeling of the plant will be started. Little work will be necessary, and it is estimated that the plant will be ready to treat 1200 tons daily by July 1. The Red Top will be in condition to supply a full tonnage on that date. It may be several months before the Combination will be ready for making an output, but it will not be necessary to take ore from there for a long time. Mr. Weed will return to Goldfield in two weeks.

Assays of $8 and $9 are being obtained in the drift from the bottom of the 58-ft. shaft on the Examiner claim of the Lone Star. At the main workings in the eastern part of the ground the east cross-cut on the 252-ft. level of the Nelligan shaft has been extended 310 ft. The west cross-cut, out 240 ft., has been discontinued. Promising seams are being cut in the east cross-cut, but no driving has been done. This will be continued to cut a vein from which rich ore was shipped by early-day lessees, and if an orebody is not found it is believed that the Nelligan shaft will be abandoned and the shaft on the Examiner claim used for further development.

Following the resignation of J. B. Kendall from the management of the Red Hill Florence and the appointment of H. G. McMahon as his successor, work has been resumed in the 250-ft. south drift on the 500-ft. level. This work is considered important, because it is being done south of the great fault in the Rogers vein, beyond which an orebody has never been opened. Small quantities of ore assaying from $40 to $100 has been found in the drift. South of the fault the vein is 20 ft. wide at a depth of 500 ft. For the past year practically all work done by the Red Hill has been on the 600-ft. level, far to the north of the fault and nearly under the rich ore-shoot in the Florence Divide lease, formerly the Witt-Brandon. This was done in the Red King claim of the Florence Goldfield, leased by the Red Hill. All work at this depth has been stopped, as the entire territory has been explored without an orebody being found. The Red Hill also is exploiting the Rogers vein on the 150 and 329-ft. levels.

MEDFORD, OREGON

NOTES ON THE COPPER MINES.

The superintendent, Jerome A. Hilbert, of the Blue Ledge mine at Copper, California, was a visitor at Medford last week, and reports that everything is moving well at the mine, where they have 25 men employed mining and shipping 500 tons of ore per month, which is shipped to the Tacoma smelter, Washington. This ore averages 14.5% copper, 6 oz. silver, and $2 gold per ton. Copper at 15 cents and silver at $1 per ounce brings the value to $51.50 per ton. This is a good grade of ore, but the first 30 miles of its journey to smelter—mine to Jacksonville, Oregon, the rail head—it is conveyed by team 7 miles, auto-truck 23 miles, which costs $12 per ton, and runs into $6000 per month, that this mine alone pays out for freight on ore, besides the supplies and passenger traffic that is carried. This is an attractive item for any railroad to consider when it is remembered that it is claimed by those familiar with the district that there is a number of undeveloped properties with exposures fully as good as the Blue Ledge was at the same stage of development, but are handicapped by want of capital for development and wagon-roads. Among the good properties are the Bloomfield, Blue Canyon, Copper King, St. Albans, and Great Northern groups.

John Dixon and associates have met with good results at the Buck and Sullivan copper claims, which are situated on Squaw Lake creek, 6 miles north of the Blue Ledge mine.

O. F. Tainer and associates have just discovered and located a deposit of 9% copper ore, besides gold and silver. This is in the head of the Elliott Creek region north-east from the Blue Ledge mine.

E. W. Cooper of Sams valley, 15 miles north of Medford, is reported to be making good progress in driving the new tunnel on the Gold Wedge mine. This is intended to cut the vein at considerable depth, as milling ore of satisfactory grade in upper workings is all worked out.

The management of the Copper Lode Association announces its intention to resume work soon. They have an attractive copper prospect, equipped with a 30-hp. gasoline engine, air-compressor, and hoist. This property is 12 miles south of Jacksonville and is reached by a good auto-road.

The improving metal and mineral markets are shown by an increased amount of assaying, as reported by Campbell & Liljegran, of Medford.

SILVERTON, COLORADO

WAGE AGREEMENT.—GENERAL NOTES.

While this district is quiet, settlement of the wage-scale and the rising price of metal give encouragement to operators to continue development and get ready to ship ore. The outlook is favorable for a gradually increasing production. The Sunnyside M. & M. Co. has decided to re-build the structures destroyed by fire, this decision being reached after the wage agreement was made. While there has been some dissatisfaction over the new wage-scale, the general attitude is one of acceptance without complaint. Following is the agreement:

(1) Eight hours constitute a day's labor in and around mines, mills, tramways, and smelters.

(2) $4.25 shall constitute a day's wage with the exception of unskilled labor on the surface, which shall be $4.

(3) All classes of labor working in wet places, where rubber clothing is required, 50 cents additional.

(4) For sinking and raising, 50 cents additional.

(5) This scale shall be based upon $1.25 per day for board.

(6) Pay-day twice a month.

There is a mutual understanding that this will continue until the increase in metal prices permits a higher scale. The wages to be paid are as under:

Mine Men		Tramway Men	
Machine-men	$5.00	Oilers and linemen	$5.00
Machine-men helpers	4.50	Gripmen	4.50
Timber-men	4.75	Bucket-men	4.50
Timber-men helpers	4.25		
Engineers	5.00	**Mill-Men**	
Station tenders	4.25	Repairmen	$5.25
Blacksmiths	5.00	Oil-flotation operators	4.75
Blacksmith's helpers	4.25	All other operators	4.50
Blasters	4.50	Mud-pullers	4.25
Firemen	4.50	Crushermen	4.25
Mule-drivers	4.25	Roustabouts	4.25
Trammers	4.25		
Shovelers	4.25		

The Henrietta Copper Co. is getting its properties in condition for extraction of ore. During the close last season this mine yielded some high-grade ore, but the low market caused a stoppage of shipments.

The Radiant Mining Co. is starting men on development in Ruby basin. The road is now opened from the mines to Burro bridge, on the Silverton northern line, Red Mountain branch.

The Anvil Leasing Co. is developing and shipping from the Emerald lode, also known as the Coming Wonder mine. A new vein carrying good values in silver has been opened.

The Dora Consolidated has leased a portion of its workings, the Boston tunnel, to local men, and the lessees are shipping.

The Caledonian is to resume operations this season.

The Iowa Tiger has its mill operating again after a long delay due to a burned-out transformer, and Iowa Tiger and Mayflower ores are being treated. Snow slides recently broke down all of the towers on the Mayflower tram, but the damage has been repaired.

The Gladstone branch of the Silverton Northern is being opened. While the main object is to get in a large amount of machinery needed to complete the Gold King Extension Mining Co.'s mill, the early opening of the road will permit a number of smaller producers to ship earlier than usual.

CANANEA, MEXICO

TROUBLES AND TRIBULATIONS IN SONORA, MEXICO.

On account of raids by Yaqui Indians, the Villa element getting busy once more, and the numerous embarrassing State and national labor and mining laws in operation in Sonora, the lot of the mine operator is not particularly a happy one, no matter how rich or favored his property may be.

The Yaquis, supposedly in alliance with Villa, have been on the warpath in Sonora for several months, and lately have extended their activities to the southern part of the Moctezuma district of Sonora. Among recent outrages committed against mining men may be mentioned the attack of Indians upon a motor-truck train on the road between La Colorado and San Xavier while it was engaged in freighting ore from La Colorado mine to Hermosillo. H. S. White, an American chauffuer of one of the trucks, was killed, as were several of the Mexican freight-handlers riding on the trucks. The Indians attacked from ambush. The truck train was a comparatively new feature with La Colorado mine, having been in operation only a few months. La Colorado is owned and operated by W. C. Laughlin and E. C. Schroeter of New York, and it is reputed to be one of the richest silver mines in Sonora, but contains such complex ore that considerable technical skill is required. This was found out to their cost when State officials of Sonora during the course of a quarrel with the owners of the mine over taxes attempted to operate by 'hit or miss' methods. As a result, instead of showing a profit as it should, reports

PART OF SONORA AND CHIHUAHUA

from Hermosillo at the time said that the Mexicans were disgusted to find that there was a distinct loss.

On the same day that the attack on the truck train of La Colorado mine in the south-central part of Sonora took place, another band of 60 Yaquis entered the camp of the Monte Cristo mine, 30 miles south of Moctezuma, capital or county seat of the Moctezuma district, and after killing six Mexican inhabitants and driving the remainder into the hills, proceeded to rob the camp. Arms, explosives, food, and valuables of all kinds were stolen. James Lord, manager of the property, was robbed of the clothing he wore, but, as he had taken no part in the fight that marked the entry of the Indians, his life was spared. The Indians operated under a military system with officers in command instead of chiefs.

Earlier in the month, Cananea was the centre of trouble when a band of 22 Mexicans seized the town, killed five policemen, including the chief, liberated all prisoners in the two jails, forced the cashier of the Banco Mercantil to open the vaults, and thus obtained $40,000 in gold, looted four stores and rode out of town. Subsequent reports told of the death of seven of the band in fights with pursuing rural police, while one was captured at Agua Prieta, taken to Cananea and hanged to a telephone pole. The men declared themselves to be supporters of Villa, and several of them are said to have escaped into Chihuahua with their loot.

Another similar case, involving considerable suffering but allowing its victim to escape with his life, was that of Franklin B. Harding, chief consulting engineer for the Chicago Exploration & Development Co., who arrived at Douglas on May 31, from Helamer, on the Sonora-Chihuahua boundary, after a brush with bandits entailing enough excitement to last him a life time. Under the leadership of Arturo Lopez, a band of Villa followers raided the camp, intent upon getting hold of a cache of arms and ammunition they had been informed Harding had concealed. His protestation that there was nothing of the kind there resulted in nothing but maltreatment, he said. The appeals of the Mexican foreman and some of the Mexican miners, of which the company employs 75, resulted in no alleviation of his inquisition, while his life was threatened momentarily by the bandits. Looting the commissary and taking such moveable property as they wished to carry with them, the Villistas rode off with Harding as their prisoner. At the little pueblo of Mors, Chihuahua, Harding was liberated after being beaten and having almost all of his clothing and his shoes taken from him. The shoes, after the soles had been cut out, were returned to him and he was instructed to leave at once. He arrived in Agua Prieta after making a hike of more than 75 miles. From Agua Prieta, after resting a short time, Mr. Harding went to Hermosillo with the avowed intention of obtaining a military guard for the mine, then returning to Helamer and resuming operation of the silver property of which he is manager at the present time. Incidentally, after obtaining action of some sort from the Sonora government, he will lay his case before the State Department of the United States.

During 1918, the Greene Cananea Copper Co. sold metals worth $10,381,348, and had other revenue amounting to $520,418. The profit was $3,434,629, after deducting $1,139,853 for Mexican taxes and $528,734 for depreciation. Dividends amounted to $4,000,000. Current assets are $8,032,618, and liabilities $905,001. The surplus of $8,048,652 at the end of 1917 was reduced to $7,483,272. Development totaled 70,045 ft., and new ore exposed equaled that extracted. The mill concentrated 289,098 tons, and the smelter reduced 902,520 tons of copper-bearing material from all sources. The yield from company ores was 52,694,731 lb. of copper, 1,666,-993 oz. of silver, and 9846 oz. of gold, equal to an extraction of 2.42% copper, 1.502 oz. silver, and 0.008 oz. gold. Many improvements were made at the mines, mill, smelter, and railway. There were 170 Americans and 4015 Mexicans employed. The cost of production was 15.082 cents per pound of copper. T. Evans is general superintendent.

HOUGHTON, MICHIGAN

COPPER SALES AND OUTPUT.—GENERAL BUSINESS CONDITIONS.

Sales of copper produced in this region last week were equal to the current output, but not cutting into the surplus. The most encouraging feature is the fact that Calumet & Hecla has sold some metal at 17 cents per pound. The 50% curtailment in capacity of this group will be evident in the June outputs. The total for the current month will be lower than at any time since the strike in 1913, although this will not show in the figures from the Mohawk, Wolverine, Quincy, or Copper Range mines—Baltic, Champion, and Trimountain—as these properties are producing at approximately 85% of normal.

General business in the Copper Country is good, despite the departure of hundreds of miners and trammers, the result of closing many of the C. & H. subsidiaries and part operation at all of the C. & H. mines. Bank deposits are larger than ever before. This money is mainly the savings of employees of the copper mines. Michigan has been on the prohibition list for two years, this being a considerable factor in saving money.

BISBEE, ARIZONA

FIRE PREVENTION.—COPPER QUEEN PENSIONS.

As a result of several fires during the last year and a half, fire prevention is occupying considerable attention among the larger mining companies of Arizona. The Copper Queen recently installed an electric fire-alarm system, connected with the Bisbee city system. Signals are given by the big siren at the Czar shaft, which also gives city alarms. The Bisbee apparatus will respond.—The Arizona Copper Co. at Clifton recently retimbered its No. 6 shaft and put in a sprinkler system.

The Copper Queen annuity plan is being brought to the attention of employees through a recently established publicity department. Men who have been with the company for 15 years or more, or who are disqualified from active work by physical disability, are entitled to annuities of 2% of the average wage of the individual for the three years previous to retirement, multiplied by the number of years he was in service. The men make no contribution to this fund.

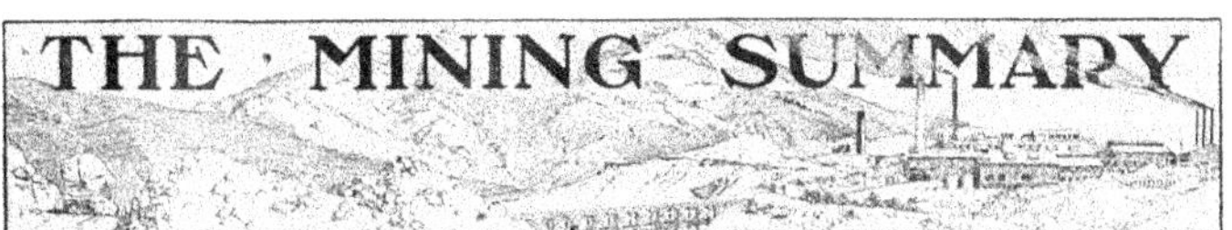

ALASKA

The U. S. Geological Survey has just issued two new bulletins on Alaska. No. 664, by G. C. Martin, discusses the Nenana coalfield; and No. 683, by G. L. Harrington, covers the Anvik-Andreafski region, including the Marshall district.

These publications are well illustrated, as usual.

The coal of Nenana occurs in many beds of different thickness, the thickest being perhaps 30 or 35 ft., which are distributed rather uniformly through the coal measures. At least 12 beds are of workable thickness, and six or more are over 20 ft. The coal is a lignite of good grade, the fixed carbon ranging from 27.83 to 41.71%, and ash 4.51 to 39.88%. The coal of this field can be brought to the present assured markets only over the Government railroad, now under construction.

The Anvik-Andreafski region embraces the territory west and north of the lower Yukon river between rivers of these names, and an extensive area of low-lying country immediately contiguous to the Yukon on its east and south sides. The first placer gold was produced in 1914, the output being $15,000 from two properties; then $25,000 in 1915; $270,000 in 1916, and $425,000 in 1917, the last from six claims on Willow creek. The first lode claims were staked in 1914.

Anchorage.—According to J. L. McPherson, engineer with the Alaskan Engineering Commission, who appeared before the House Appropriation Committee at Washington, the success of the Government railroad is dependent on its early completion to the navigable waters of the interior. This is necessary to make it possible for those pioneers in the interior to build homes and industries, and attract other pioneers to that region. So far, everybody has simply been 'creaming' the richer placer deposits at a great economic loss. The only way that condition can be righted is by the economic means of transportation, which will be afforded by the new railroad. Its major revenue for a number of years will be from the through traffic the road will carry: the longer the project is delayed in completion the less the traffic will be upon its completion. On the line, 252 of the 437 miles of new work has been done, and when joined with existing lines the connected mileage of the Territory would total 545. Large amounts of grading and other work also have been done on the unfinished part. In order that construction work may not be temporarily interrupted, the House approved an appropriation of $1,964,350 for the work in the general deficiency bill sent to the Senate last week. The present force of 1500 men will be doubled in June.

Juneau.—Alaska Gastineau during the first quarter of 1919 made a loss of $106,784, compared with $78,381 in the last period of 1918. The mill treated 497,469 tons of 79.6-cent ore, recovering 76.76%, at a cost of 83 cents per ton. The comparative figures for the previous term were 287,571 tons, 79.1 cents, 80.22%, and $1.06 per ton.

Alaska Gastineau during May treated 202,377 tons of 80.1 cent ore, recovering 77.65%. Tonnages since January, inclusive, have beer 151,515; 162,400; 183,550; 167,630; and 202,377.

Kennecott.—The Kennecott Copper Corporation distributed 50 cents a share on June 30. This amounts to $1,393,339, and makes $2,786,678 for 1919, and $45,143,675 to date.

ARIZONA

Chloride.—It is reported that rich gold ore has been struck 4 miles north of the Pilgrim mine and 12 miles west of Chloride. The strike is causing considerable local excitement.

Miami.—One of the four plants of the Salt River Valley Water Users' Association at the Roosevelt dam, which supply electric power energy to mines in this district and to the

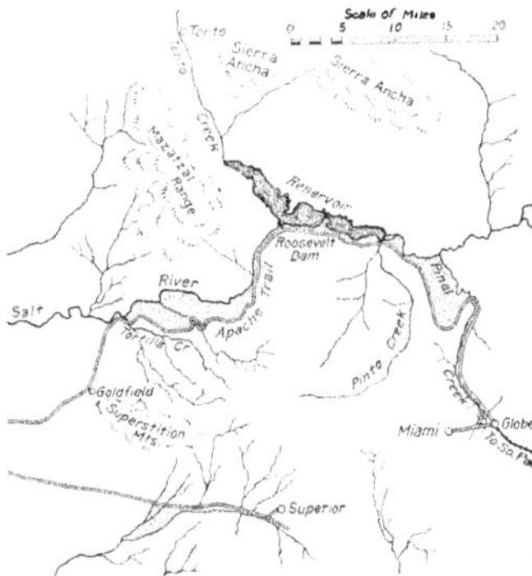

PART OF ARIZONA, SHOWING PART OF SOURCE OF POWER FOR THE MIAMI-GLOBE MINES.

city of Phoenix, was tied-up by a strike on June 7, when the Association refused a demand for a closed shop and increased wages.

Bisbee.—A new electric hoist is being put in the C & C shaft of the Copper Queen Branch of Phelps Dodge Corporation, in order to reduce sinking costs. Increased operations at Sacramento hill have necessitated additions of machinery at the machine-shops. In order to improve underground ventilation, plans and specifications are being drawn for the necessary equipment, which it is estimated will cost $30,000.

Phoenix.—For 1000,000 shares in the Kay Copper Co., S. J. Tribolet of this place received $166,000 cash last week. George Long, well known at Oatman, has taken an option on half of Tribolet's controlling interest. The mine is 40 miles north of Phoenix, near the Agua Fria river. Some rich shoots of ore have been developed to a depth of

600 ft., reserves being valued at several millions. Later on a concentrating plant and reverberatory furnace may be erected.

Superior.—The Magma Copper Co. has taken over the last of the Queen Copper Co.'s claims for $75,000.

Tucson.—The Lowell Gold M. & D. Co. has a mill in Horseshoe basin of the Quijatoas. The gold is said to be high-grade, and treatment is expected to commence within 60 days.

After sampling and testing the ore of the Banner, Olympic, and Hughs claims in the Sierrita mountains, they have been leased by F. Hereford and J. R. Hubbard. A mill has been constructed to treat the large quantity of low-grade silver ore that has been developed, as well as the dumps.

The Jimmie Lee property, one of the oldest patented properties in the State, has been bonded. It produced a lot of silver in the past.

Winkelman.—The Azlan Gold Syndicate, operating a property of 7 claims 7 miles from Winkelman, has recently opened some rich gold ore. Specimens are on exhibit at the Tucson Chamber of Commerce. Foundations for a mill on the Arizona Eastern Railroad are being constructed. An aerial tram from the mine to the mill, 4 miles away, is being planned. This property is controlled by H. A. Whitcomb and Eastern capitalists.

CALIFORNIA

Almaden.—Fire at the New Almaden quicksilver mines last week destroyed a great deal of the surface plant.

Caliente.—A. Trojanovich of Globe, Arizona, associated with George Kingdon, general manager for the United Verde Extension Mining Co., and several New York capitalists, have recently formed the Zenda Gold Mining Co. to operate the Zenda mine at Caliente, Kern county, California. It is the intention of Mr. Trojanovich to move the present mill up to the mine and erect a 150-ton cyanide mill, consisting of Marcy ball-mill, Dorr counter-current system of cyanidation, and other machinery, immediately. He now has men constructing a road to the mine.

The Cowboy mine at Caliente has been recently bonded by Walter X. Osborn, who will erect a small cyanide mill there and re-open and develop the mine.

Grass Valley.—The Norambagua mine, an old producer in the Forest Springs district, four miles west of this place, is to be re-opened at once. An entirely new plant is to be erected, including power lines, compressor, and hoist. The mine was closed because of war conditions, but a large body of ore had been opened. C. T. Green, the former manager, is in charge for Eastern capital.

Placerville.—The Gold Ridge district, 6 miles by road from this place, is attracting attention. Gold Ridge extends east and west for two miles or more between Rock Creek canyon on the east and Kelsey canyon (on which is Kelsey camp) on the west; and rises abruptly from the South Fork of the American river, which flows sinuously westward along its south base. The altitude of the river is 1100 ft. above mean sea-level. Down the south slope of the ridge there are three deep ravines known as Dark canyon, Ladies canyon, and Texas ravine; the last being farthest west and heads on the north side of and near the top of the ridge. Large quantities of gold were recovered from these ravines in the 'fifties by early-day miners; especially from the Texas ravine, as is evidenced by the extensive old-time placer workings along the head of the ravine. The Kelsey Gold & Silver Mining Co. owns several quartz claims north from the river across the west end of the Gold Ridge. It is reported that arrangements have been completed to erect a cyanide mill, air-drills, etc., to cost $25,000. E. N. Finn of New York recently inspected the property. Just east of the Kelsey is the Manzaneta mine, being developed by E. N. Fessler. He has a small mill and concentrator at work. Another group of lode claims is the Marshall, which has yielded a good deal of gold.

Sierra City.—The vein in the Cleveland mine is so promising that 10 stamps are being added to the mill, thus doubling its capacity. At the Monarch the output is satisfactory, and 25 men are at work. Both mines are owned by R. G. Gillespie, an oil operator of Pittsburgh, Pennsylvania, and managed by S. E. Montgomery.

Jackson.—The Gwin Mine Development Co. has decided to sell its entire surface plant preparatory to a complete abandonment of the property. The mine was bought from Wm. M. Gwin of San Francisco 20 years ago by the late F. F. Thomas, C. M. Belshaw, and others, who erected a complete 100-stamp mill, a large double-drum hoist, steel head-frame, compressor plant, etc. The property paid dividends for a few years, and it was during that period that a temporary hoist was replaced by a powerful one and 60 stamps added to the 40 then dropping. The large body of ore upon which the company's hopes had been based suddenly gave out, and assessments were levied regularly for a number of years. Shares fell from $11 to almost nothing. After a few years of extensive prospecting, which developed small and quickly worked out bunches of ore, the mine was closed, and for years has been in charge of a watchman. The disposition of the plant is in the hands of the Gwin Mine Sales Co., organized for that purpose.

Washington.—The 40-stamp mill, machine-shop, blacksmith-shop, compressor-building, and several other structures at the Gaston mine, 7 miles above Washington, were destroyed by fire on June 4. The loss is placed at $20,000, but the amount of insurance is not known. The Gaston has been a large gold producer, and re-opening of the mine commenced on May 1 in charge of W. L. Williamson. W. F. McCutcheon, an attorney of San Francisco, is the owner.

COLORADO

Cripple Creek.—Gold output of the district in May was $691,861 from 65,376 tons of ore.

Idaho Springs.—A number of mines are being re-opened in this district, especial attention being directed to silver properties.

Telluride.—The Radium Luminous Material Co. is trying a large tractor for hauling trucks loaded with ore from the Paradox valley to rail. If successful it will result in a large saving in haulage charges. This company and the Radium Company of Colorado are involved in litigation over the Phonograph lode in the East Paradox section. The district is active and the demand for men exceeds the supply.

The Mount Blaine Oil Shale Products Co. has one unit in operation and is at present treating the shale at De Beque.

MONTANA

Butte.—Davis-Daly has cut 6 ft. of 12.75% copper ore in a cross-cut north-west of the fault at 2500 ft. depth in its Colorado mine.

The report of Butte & Superior for the first quarter of 1919 shows a loss of $116,379, compared with $96,507 in the previous period. The average price for spelter was 6.189 cents per pound, compared with 7.893 cents in the preceding term. Only 71,298 tons of 15.436% zinc and 6.71 oz. silver ore was treated, a drop of nearly 40,000 tons. The 19,307 tons of concentrate averaged 54.5% zinc, this being 1.86% higher grade. The total zinc content was 22,044,540 lb., and silver, 424,000 oz. Costs were reduced from $11.86 to $10.77 per ton. Development did not reveal anything of particular importance. Reserves were slightly lower.

The Butte East Slope Mining Co. is preparing to resume

work at its property 8 miles east of Butte. Ore will be sent to smelter soon, as there is a 30-in. shoot opened. Where the vein was cut it assayed $8 in silver and gold across 23 ft. E. P. Lanas is in charge.

The Diamond mine of the Anaconda company was shut-down last week on account of a lack of skilled men. During the suspension the shaft will be fire-proofed with cement. The Badger State mine, which was closed through an accident to the hoist, has resumed work.

Anaconda produced 13,500,000 lb. of copper during May. This is a little less than half of normal. The company has reduced the compensation of salaried officers by 10%. Officials who were receiving $300 or less a month have had their salaries raised four times, equal to 30%, within the past few months.

Eddy.—The Jewel M. & M. Co. has opened No. 3 orebody in No. 2 tunnel. The first shoot was 80 ft. long, the second, 125 ft., and the third, so far, 85 ft. The ore carries silver and lead. A 200-hp. Pelton water-wheel has been ordered to drive a generator, and a Buffalo blower is being put in for ventilation. A. G. Amsbury is vice-president.

Elkhorn.—The Boston & Montana Development Co. has issued a 16-page booklet illustrating the work being done. The first trains over the Montana Southern line to Elkhorn are expected to run this month. Shipments of 100 tons daily will then commence. The mill contract has been let and it should be ready by November. Underground workings total 11,000 ft. on the 1000-ft. or main tunnel-level, and a large quantity of ore has been exposed. A test on 100 tons of ore made by the General Engineering Co. at Salt Lake City recovered 27.77 tons of concentrate, which assayed $8.20 gold, $48.21 silver, $7.25 lead, and $14.70 copper, a total of $78.36 per ton. A test by O. B. Hoffstrand checked this very closely.

Helena.—Representative mining men of Montana, particularly from districts contiguous to Helena, met here last week to discuss means by which the known and undeveloped areas might be aided and exploited. L. S. Ropes was chairman of the meeting. What most of the local mines require is a treatment plant on each property, instead of the expensive system of sending ore to smelters. Mr. Ropes contributed some general observations on the Helena district to the 'Montana Record-Herald'. Current production is negligible, due to past factors, such as the drop in silver in the 'nineties, failure of the First National bank at Helena, which tied up many properties in litigation, and subsequent abandonment of properties of merit. There is only one mine in the region that is 1500 ft. deep, and out of a list of 217 mines not six are down 1000 ft. Nobody can say whether these mines were worked out or 'knocked' out. A State geologist is required, and if there had been one this region would not have lain disregarded. A conservative estimate of production from 161 of the 217 mines listed is $162,815,000, and from 35 of the 83 placers $69,425,000, a total of $232,240,000. This is considered to be $40,000,000 low. Now that silver is high, the district should attract attention for this metal alone. Bulletin 527 of the U. S. Geological Survey, by Adolph Knopf, issued in 1913, covers the Helena region thoroughly.

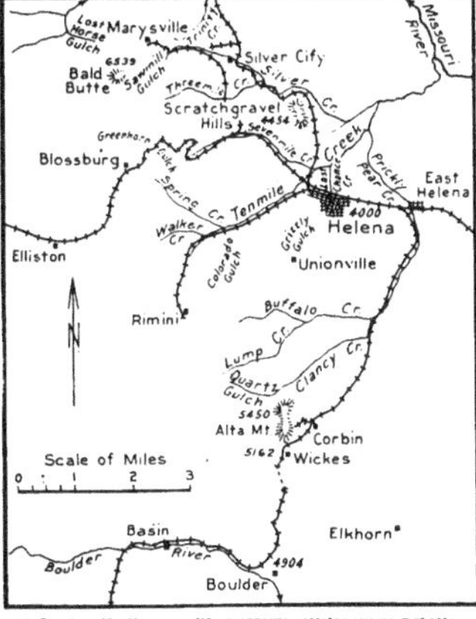

PART OF MONTANA, SHOWING DISTRICTS CONTIGUOUS TO BELENA.

Kendall.—The Barnes-King Development Co. made a profit of $23,647 during the first quarter of the current year. A dividend of 10 cents per share, $40,000, was paid on May 15. This makes $80,000 for 1919 and $340,000 to date. The balance of $131,037 at the end of 1918 was reduced to $92,010 at the end of March, plus $50,000 in Liberty Bonds. The mines yielded $179,050 of gold from 19,722 tons of ore. Development amounted to 4068 ft. An option was taken on the Silver Bullion claims in the Judith mountains, 10 miles from Kendall. The property is a prospect, but encouraging. The terms are $5000 in one year and $70,000 two years later, and a royalty of 15% on all ore treated during the interim. The April output was $59,000.

NEVADA

Ely.—The Nevada Consolidated mines and works are at about 50% capacity. There is said to be considerable activity at Cherry Creek and Ward.

Gold Circle.—It is reported that rich gold ore has been found in the Berry brothers property here, just over the Humboldt County line in Elko county, 5 miles north-east of Golconda.

Mina.—According to J. P. Hart, of the Tonopah Extension Mining Co., the Simon lead mine, 22 miles from Mina, was originally discovered 50 years ago. At various periods since that time it has been worked in a small way, and judging from the size of the old stopes, all of which are at shallow depth under the surface croppings, a considerable quantity of ore was taken out and shipped to smelters. The foot-wall is in limestone, with rhyolite formation in the hanging wall. The vein has been cross-cut at the 230 and 300-ft. levels, and the new cross-cut on the 405-ft. level is in ore 25 ft. showing a full face of solid sulphide ore. The 230 cross-cut shows the vein to be 70 ft. wide on that level, 30 ft. of which is carbonate and 40 ft. sulphide. The entire 70 ft. averages $20 per ton. Drifts have been driven 100 ft. in each direction on the hanging wall side, with the same grade of ore persisting. The crosscut shows the vein to have entered the real sulphide zone. The width on the 300 level is 77 ft., and this is a solid mass of glistening sulphides of lead and zinc, carrying in addition 7½ oz. of silver per ton. At no point across the 77 ft. is there a single indication of any waste.

Rochester.—The Nevada Packard is putting in a Marcy mill to replace the old ball-mill. The plant will then treat 130 tons of ore daily. Costs in April were reduced to $4.28 per ton.

Tonopah.—The Tonopah Belmont Development Co. pays a dividend of 10 cents a share, $150,000, on July 1. This makes $300,000 for 1919 and $10,018,063 to date. The Belmont has cut the downward extension of the South vein on the 1166-ft. level. This development is of great value to the life of the mine. So far there is 5 ft. of fair-grade ore. On the 1300-ft. level the drift shows 4½ ft. of good ore.

UTAH

Alta.—This district is now shipping a lot of ore, one day last week 160 tons was carried over the railway. The Michigan-Utah is mining 40 to 50 tons daily, while the Cardiff, Woodlawn, and others have a good deal awaiting transport.

Park City.—A meeting of 300 miners was held here on June 1, and 86 voted to call off the strike. Another general meeting of all concerned was to be held on the next day.

Tintic.—The Tintic Standard company may erect a mill to concentrate its silver-lead ore. Tests have been made on the ore recently.

CANADA.

British Columbia

Rossland.—The Le Roi No. 2 mine from September 30, 1918, to the end of February 1919, has shipped 7500 tons of ore, which realized $82,000. The expenditure was $56,000. In that part of the property known as No. 1 mine, orebodies of considerable promise have been found. On the south Rodney vein the winze is down to the 1950-ft. level, and is clear of the dike and into favorable mineralized ground.

Sandon.—The Silversmith company expected to resume milling early in May, treating from 80 to 100 tons of silver-zinc ore daily. Developments are reported to be very satisfactory.

Silverton.—The Standard Silver-Lead Mining Co. made a profit of $114,764 in 1918, compared with $377,494 in 1917. The surplus increased from $202,801 to $317,565. No dividends were paid, while $300,000 was distributed in 1917. Silver-lead ore sold realized $112,898, and zinc ore $227,338. The total in 1917 was $881,616.

Victoria.—It is reported by G. C. Mackenzie, late of the Canadian Geological Survey at Ottawa, that all available information relating to the manganese deposits of the Cowichan district, Vancouver Island, will be published shortly by the Canadian Munition Resources Commission.

The Bowena copper mine, on Bowena island, under lease to C. W. Tipping, is to have a concentrating plant, instructions having been given for its erection.

Ontario

Matachewan.—At the Otisee gold mine there are 30 men employed. A shaft is being sunk to 200 ft. Machinery taken to the property last year is ready for erection. During the coming summer the water route from Elk lake will be used to transport men and supplies to Matachewan.

Porcupine.—The West Dome mine, closed since the disastrous forest fire of July 11, 1911, whereby 25 people taking refuge in the shaft were asphyxiated, is to be re-opened.

Quebec

Amos.—The new mill at the Indian Peninsula Molybdenite mine in north-western Quebec is nearly ready. The flotation plant has a capacity of 50 tons daily. The property is operated by the Penn-Canadian Mines of Cobalt, Ontario.

MEXICO

Mexico

El Oro.—Esperanza in March treated 12,547 tons of ore and 11,540 tons of tailing for a profit of $17,000. The February profit was slightly under this sum.

KOREA

Unsan.—Oriental Consolidated extracted gold worth $90,530 during May. This is less than normal by $10,000.

PERSONAL

Note. The Editor invites members of the profession to send particulars of their work and appointments. The information is interesting to our readers.

W. J. Loring went to Boston on June 7.

Gelasio Caetani was in London recently.

Fred Searls, Jr., was in London recently, on leave from Germany.

Frank Cameron has returned to Salt Lake City from Rancagua, in Chile.

Morton Webber is at the Palace Hotel, on his return from Lower California.

George J. Bancroft passed through San Francisco on his way to Denver from Idaho.

Malcolm Roberts, manager of the Aramayo-Francke mines in Bolivia, is in England.

James M. Hyde has been appointed Professor of Metallurgy at Stanford University.

Bruno V. Nordberg has returned to Milwaukee after a visit to the Michigan copper region.

J. C. Ray, Captain commanding the 544th Engineers, has returned from France to Palo Alto, California.

Mark L. Requa has resigned as Federal Oil Administrator and returned from Washington to San Francisco.

Arthur W. Stevens has gone to Mohave, California, to take charge of the Quartz Hill silver mine in the Old Woman mountains.

Horace V. Winchell, President of the Institute, delivered an address before the Montana State School of Mines at Butte on June 4.

Heath M. Robinson has resigned from the U. S. Geological Survey and is now employed by F. Julius Fohs, consulting oil geologist, in New York.

Rush T. Sill, of Sill & Sill, is leaving Seattle on June 14 for the Willow Creek district, Alaska, where he will be engaged in professional work.

Walter X. Osborn has resigned from the Superior & Boston Copper Co. at Copper Hill, Arizona, to operate the Cowboy mine at Caliente, California, which he has recently purchased.

Calvert Townley, assistant to the president of the Westinghouse Electric & Manufacturing Co., was elected president of the American Institute of Electrical Engineers at New York.

On June 6 the Editor received a cablegram from Major **Ernest B. Lighthill** conveying the greetings of those attending the 42nd annual dinner of Royal School of Mines men in London to their fellow alumni in the United States.

Maxwell W. Atwater died on June 4 in the hospital of the Mayo brothers at Rochester, Minnesota. He was only 42 years of age and at the time of his death was manager for the Davis-Daly Copper Co. at Butte, Montana. He was a younger brother of R. M. Atwater, of New York. His untimely end will grieve many in the profession, of which he was an honored member.

The U. S. Bureau of Mines makes the following announcements:

F. B. Tough, petroleum technologist, left San Francisco on June 2 to take charge of co-operative work being carried on by the Bureau with the Midwest Refining Co. and the Ohio Oil Co. in Wyoming.——**C. P. Bowie**, petroleum engineer, has returned recently to San Francisco from a trip through the oilfields of Oklahoma and Texas.——**E. W. Wagy**, petroleum engineer, is in Illinois, studying the methods of production used by various oil operators in that region.

METAL PRICES

San Francisco, June 10

Aluminum-dust, cents per pound	50—60
Antimony, cents per pound	8.50
Copper, electrolytic, cents per pound	17.50
Lead, pig, cents per pound	5½—6½
Platinum, pure, per ounce	$105
Platinum, 10% iridium, per ounce	$115
Quicksilver, per flask of 75 lb.	$92
Spelter, cents per pound	7¾
Zinc-dust, cents per pound	10—12

EASTERN METAL MARKET

(By wire from New York)

June 10.—Copper is strong and higher. Lead is quiet but steady. Spelter is more active and advancing.

COPPER

Prices of electrolytic in New York, in cents per pound.

Date			Average week ending		
June	4	16.50	Apr.	29	15.18
"	5	16.62	May	6	15.25
"	6	16.75	"	13	15.37
"	7	16.87	"	20	16.24
"	8 Sunday		"	27	16.46
"	9	17.00	June	3	16.37
"	10	17.12	"	10	16.81

Monthly averages

	1917	1918	1919		1917	1918	1919
Jan.	20.53	23.50	20.43	July	29.67	26.00	....
Feb.	34.57	23.50	17.34	Aug.	27.42	26.00	....
Mch.	36.00	23.50	15.05	Sept.	25.11	26.00	....
Apr.	33.16	23.50	15.23	Oct.	23.50	26.00	....
May	31.69	23.50	15.91	Nov.	23.50	26.00	....
June	32.57	23.50	....	Dec.	23.50	26.00	....

SILVER

Below are given official or ticker quotations, in cents per ounce of silver 999 fine. From April 23, 1918, the United States government paid $1 per ounce for all silver purchased by it, fixing a maximum of $1.01½ on August 15, 1918, and will continue to pay $1 until the quantity specified under the Act is purchased, probably extending over several years. On May, 5, 1919, all restrictions on the metal were removed, resulting in fluctuations. During the restricted period, the British government fixed the maximum price five times, the last being on March 25, 1919, on account of the low rate of sterling exchange, but removed all restrictions on May 10. The equivalent of dollar silver (1000 fine) in British currency is 46.65 pence per ounce (925 fine), calculated at the normal rate of exchange.

Date		New York cents	London pence	Average week ending		Cents	Pence
June	4	109.37	53.25	Apr.	29	101.12	48.78
"	5	109.12	53.12	May	6	101.14	48.71
"	6	109.12	53.12	"	13	109.33	52.98
"	7	109.12	53.12	"	20	110.33	53.56
"	8 Sunday			"	27	106.44	52.17
"	9	109.50	53.37	June	3	108.00	52.90
"	10	110.37	53.62	"	10	109.43	53.27

Monthly averages

	1917	1918	1919		1917	1918	1919
Jan.	75.14	88.72	101.12	July	78.92	99.62	....
Feb.	77.54	85.79	101.12	Aug.	85.40	100.31	....
Mch.	74.13	88.11	101.12	Sept.	100.73	101.12	....
Apr.	72.51	95.35	101.12	Oct.	87.38	101.12	....
May	74.61	99.50	107.23	Nov.	85.97	101.12	....
June	76.44	99.50	....	Dec.	85.97	101.12	....

Samuel Montagu & Co. of London, writing on May 15, discusses the silver market since the lifting of all restrictions thus:

The immediate effect upon the market, which had been in a state of suspended animation for many months, was great. No available stock of silver existed from which the Continental [European] demands, which instantly set in, could be supplied, for the good reason that loyal adherence to the known wishes of the [British] authorities had eliminated the possibility of any stock composed of speculative holdings. As a consequence, the price moved at a speed absolutely without precedent. It leaped in one bound 4⅞d. on May 9 from 48⅝d. to 53½d., at which it was officially quoted 'buyers', both for cash and for forward delivery. On the 10th, 58d. for cash delivery and 57¾d. for forward delivery were reached. The quotation of 58d. is a record since January 1877.

The following prices, in pence, at any advance on which the principal silver coins (full weight-loco London) would show a profit when melted, are of interest, though it should be remembered that with the exception of India and the United Kingdom, the amount of such coins in circulation is comparatively small: Indian rupees (at 1s.8d.), 53.81 pence; United States dollar, 58.9; Dutch 2½ guilder, 60.45; French 5-franc piece and similar coin, 60.87; British sterling silver, 66; and German mark, 67.3 pence.

The great driving force operating in the market for the last few years was clearly indicated by the statement made in the House of Commons on May 12 by the Secretary of State for India, when he said that Indian net imports of silver during the War had amounted to 516,202,000 oz. (sufficient to coin about 1,500,000,000 rupees). In addition to this enormous amount of precious metal, net imports of gold totalling £21,400,000 were received during the same period.

On May 12 the forward rate eased to 57½ pence, while the cash quotation remained unaltered. On the next and succeeding days, supplies were forthcoming on a scale sufficient to meet the demand, and brought about lower rates. It is satisfactory that a substantial business has been done during the week on this market, and it has been easy both to buy and to sell large quantities.

The China exchanges have not moved in anything like the same proportion as the value of silver. The silver quotation on May 15 is equal to 5s. 3 5/16d. per tael (expenses of transmission excluded) as compared with the cabled rate of 5s. 2½d. per tael (a tael is 579.84 grains of silver).

LEAD

Lead is quoted in cents per pound, New York delivery.

Date			Average week ending		
June	4	5.20	Apr.	29	4.95
"	5	5.20	May	6	4.87
"	6	5.20	"	13	4.85
"	7	5.20	"	20	5.05
"	8 Sunday		"	27	5.27
"	9	5.20	June	3	5.22
"	10	5.20	"	10	5.20

Monthly averages

	1917	1918	1919		1917	1918	1919
Jan.	7.64	6.85	5.60	July	10.93	8.03	....
Feb.	9.10	7.07	5.13	Aug.	10.75	8.05	....
Mch.	10.07	7.26	5.24	Sept.	9.07	8.05	....
Apr.	9.38	6.99	5.05	Oct.	6.97	8.05	....
May	10.29	6.88	5.04	Nov.	6.38	8.05	....
June	11.74	7.58	....	Dec.	6.49	6.90	....

Lead ore, basis 80% metal, averaged $57 per ton at Joplin, Missouri, last week. The Tri-State region produced 1302 tons.

ZINC

Zinc is quoted as spelter, standard Western brands, New York delivery, in cents per pound:

Date			Average week ending		
June	4	6.50	Apr.	29	6.39
"	5	6.55	May	6	6.32
"	6	6.55	"	13	6.31
"	7	6.60	"	20	6.46
"	8 Sunday		"	27	6.59
"	9	6.60	June	3	6.53
"	10	6.65	"	10	6.58

Monthly averages

	1917	1918	1919		1917	1918	1919
Jan.	9.75	7.78	7.44	July	8.98	8.72	....
Feb.	10.45	7.97	6.71	Aug.	8.58	8.87	....
Mch.	10.78	7.67	6.53	Sept.	8.33	9.58	....
Apr.	10.20	7.04	6.49	Oct.	8.32	9.11	....
May	9.41	7.92	6.43	Nov.	7.76	8.75	....
June	9.63	7.92	....	Dec.	7.84	8.49	....

Zinc ore, basis 60% metal, averaged $41 per ton last week at Joplin, Missouri. The Tri-State region produced 9530 tons of blende.

QUICKSILVER

The primary market for quicksilver is San Francisco, California being the largest producer. The price is fixed in the open market, according to quantity. Prices, in dollars per flask of 75 pounds:

Date					
May	13	80.00	May	27	92.00
"	20	82.00	June	3	95.00
			"	10	92.00

Monthly averages

	1917	1918	1919		1917	1918	1919
Jan	81.00	128.06	103.75	July	102.00	120.00	....
Feb	126.25	118.00	90.00	Aug.	115.00	120.00	....
Mch.	113.75	112.00	72.80	Sept.	112.00	120.00	....
Apr.	114.50	115.00	73.12	Oct.	102.00	120.00	....
May	104.00	110.00	84.80	Nov.	102.50	120.00	....
June	85.50	112.00	....	Dec.	117.42	115.00	....

TIN

Prices in New York, in cents per pound. The monthly averages in 1918 are nominal. On December 3 the War Industries Board fixed the price to consumers and jobbers at 72½c. f.o.b. Chicago and Eastern points, and 71¼c. on the Pacific Coast. This will continue until the U. S. Steel Products Co.'s stock is consumed.

Monthly averages

	1917	1918	1919		1917	1918	1919
Jan.	44.10	85.13	71.50	July	62.60	93.00	....
Feb.	51.47	85.00	72.44	Aug.	62.53	91.33	....
Mch.	54.27	85.00	72.50	Sept.	61.54	80.40	....
Apr.	55.63	88.53	72.50	Oct.	62.24	78.82	....
May	63.21	100.01	72.50	Nov.	74.18	73.67	....
June	61.93	91.00	....	Dec.	85.00	71.52	....

Eastern Metal Market

New York, June 4.

There is no pronounced activity in any of the markets; some are strong and some are easy.

Antimony is strong.

Copper has broadened, with prices firm and the tendency upward, following a week of lighter demand.

Lead has become very quiet and prices are easier.

Tin is quiet, with developments of a minor nature.

Zinc is lifeless and prices are nominal.

ANTIMONY

The market is strong with wholesale lots for early delivery quoted at 8.37½ to 8.50c., New York, duty paid.

COPPER

The market is quiet, but there is a steady demand, which has increased somewhat after the subsidence in activity last week. Buying during May was of large proportions—much larger than at any time since the War ended. Some say it is about equal to production, but this is not known. Output is generally conceded to be not over 50% of capacity. Prices are distinctly firm, with some producers well sold for June or June-July delivery. In fact, some of the large interests are only selling for June-July or not for June, and are asking 16.50 to 17c. for electrolytic. There are one or two smaller interests, and speculators who have sold as low as 16.25c.; but the quantity involved has been very small. For August delivery most sellers are averse to committing themselves, but when necessary they demand at least 17 to 17.25c. for electrolytic copper. Most of the recent and present buying is for domestic consumption with very little heard about export business about which there appears to be some mystery, especially as to prices involved. The general tone of the market is strong and firm, with electrolytic copper for early delivery quoted at 16.50 to 16.75c., New York, and Lake at 16.75 to 17c., New York.

IRON AND STEEL

Activity in the steel market continues moderate, but it is of an encouraging nature. The schedule of March 20, made between the steel-makers' committee and the Industrial Board, continues as the market standard, though there are some price irregularities. Export demand grows, and the business is more dependable. There are signs that foreign buyers, who were waiting to get their cue from the attitude of domestic buyers, are now coming forward. Japan is in the market for another lot of 10,000 tons of rails. Early expansion in structural orders is indicated by inquiries.

The blowing out of blast-furnaces continues. The output in May was 2,108,056 tons, or 68,000 tons per day, against 2,478,218 tons in April, or 82,607 tons per day. The May rate was the lowest since March, 1915.

LEAD

The market has become very quiet. As a result of the extensive buying a short time ago, which was of large proportions, consumers are apparently filled up and the activity has subsided. There are a few sellers who are now slightly shading the A. S. & R. price of 5c., St. Louis, or 5.25c., New York. They have done some business at 5.20c., or 4.95c., St. Louis, but it has not been large. Some of this is probably speculative metal bought at lower levels. We quote the market at these lower outside levels.

TIN

During recent weeks the only activity has been in future shipment metal when restrictions are removed—in fact it is only such trading that has been possible in a market still under war rules. But even this has subsided again to small proportions although in the last week there has been a little buying at 51 to 51.50c. for shipment from the Straits. On Monday, George Armsby, chief in charge of tin of the War Trade Board, made public the stocks of allocated metal still on hand on June 1 as 1615 tons. This is a decline of about 50% for May, and is taken to forecast the absorption of all the original 10,000 tons by July 1. There is no definite news as to when the market will again be free. The London market fell on May 23, following the state of the American market, but has turned stronger again since then.

ZINC

Conditions and demand are worse than at any time since the armistice, says one large producer. No betterment is looked for until general conditions in steel and other lines are improved decidedly. Quotations for prime Western are nominal at 6.15c., St. Louis, or 6.50c., New York, for early delivery, with transactions limited to small allotments to cover necessities in isolated cases. For future delivery a premium is asked, but there is but little demand.

ORE

Manganese: Imports in April were 59,470 long tons, a large quantity, bringing the total for the four months to May 1 to 174,791 tons, or 43,698 tons per month. This rate compares with 40,942 tons per month in all of 1918.

Manganese-Iron Alloys: British makers of ferro have met the American product and are offering the alloy at $121, seaboard, as against $125, delivered, for the American alloy. Spiegel is obtainable at $30 to $35, furnace. Demand for both is light.

Molybdenum: This market is dead and prices are nominal at say 80 cents per pound.

Tungsten: Conditions are unchanged and demand is not large. No fair test of the market has been reported. High-grade ores continue nominal at $7 to $10 per unit in 60% concentrates. Ferro-tungsten has not been tested, and no definite quotations are available.

Book Review

Waterproofing Engineering. By Joseph Ross. Pp. 427, ill., index. John Wiley & Sons, Inc., New York. For sale by 'Mining and Scientific Press'. Price, $5.

As the author points out, the literature on waterproofing processes and practice is remarkable principally because there is so little of it. Not only has little investigation of the subject been done, but many of these who have made such studies have, for commercial reasons, kept the results of their work secret. The chapter-headings are as follows: Need and Function of Waterproofing; Systems of Waterproofing; Impervious Roofing; Waterproofing Expansion-Joints in Masonry; Waterproofing-Materials; Waterproofing Implements and Machinery; Technical and Practical Tests; Specifications; Recipes and Special Formulas; Application; Cost Data. Another chapter contains a number of tables of special use in this class of work. There are appendixes containing a discussion of mechanical analysis of concrete aggregates, concrete in sea-water, the American Society for Testing Materials report on waterproofing, a glossary, and a list of references. The book will be useful to anyone engaged in the erection of buildings or other structures that have to be waterproof, or at least moisture-resistive.

Company Reports

ANACONDA COPPER MINING CO.

Property: Copper and zinc mines at Butte, concentrating, flotation, and leaching plants for copper and zinc at Anaconda; copper smelter, acid, and power-plants at Anaconda; copper smelter and rod-mills, electrolytic copper refinery, zinc refinery, ferro-manganese, and calcium-carbide plants at Great Falls; also coal mines, lumber camps, and railroads, in Montana; also copper mines in Chile, and subsidiary smelting companies in Arizona, Indiana, and Utah.

Operating Officials: At Butte—Charles W. Goodale, chairman of safety-first committee; John Gillie, general manager of mines; Bertram H. Dunshee, assistant; William B. Daly, general superintendent of mines; John O'Neill, assistant; D. A. Welch, purchasing agent.

At Anaconda—Frederick Laist, manager of Washoe Reduction Works; Louis V. Bender, general superintendent; H. S. Ware, assistant; B. S. Morrow, superintendent of concentration; S. S. Rodgers and C. W. Morse, assistants; Pierce Barker, superintendent of blast-furnace department; R. W. Handley, superintendent of zinc concentrator; Wallace N. Tanner, chief mechanical engineer; Charles D. Demond, engineer of tests; L. E. Jones, chief electrical engineer; E. A. Barnard, chief chemist; F. W. C. Whyte, manager of coal mining department; H. A. Gallwey, manager of Butte, Anaconda & Pacific Railway; D. A. Welch, purchasing agent at Butte.

At Great Falls—James O'Grady, manager; Albert E. Wiggin, general superintendent; Milo W. Krejci, assistant; Earl S. Bardwell, metallurgist; Russell B. Caples, superintendent of electrolytic refinery; E. E. Brownson, chief chemist.

Financial Statement: the past four years compare as under:

	1918	1917	1916	1915
Sales of metals	$102,586,541	$109,035,593	$99,097,700	$81,473,677
Gross revenue, including metal on hand	147,618,801	156,203,157	148,190,046	87,273,886
Disbursements	122,902,728	118,706,777	91,647,708	67,806,191
Balance	24,716,073	37,496,380	56,542,338	19,467,695
Income from investments	2,867,514	2,749,083	2,350,641	112,922
Interest paid	676,532	526,275	951,144	984,233
Depreciation	6,104,185	5,387,437	7,113,463	1,900,578
Profit	20,802,870	34,333,751	50,828,372	16,695,806
Dividends	17,484,372	19,815,625	17,484,375	9,325,000
Surplus	3,318,498	14,518,126	33,343,997	7,370,806
Profit and loss surplus	66,232,486	62,913,988	48,395,862	15,051,865

Current liabilities total $71,979,453, including $27,865,266 for metals on hand, and liabilities $38,932,231.

Development and Mining: 41.85 miles of development, compared with 38.61 miles in 1917, was done. The shafts of the company were sunk additional depths aggregating 4991 ft. Results were quite satisfactory.

The Bonanza shaft was sunk an additional depth of 512 ft. to the 1000-ft. level. Cross-cuts were driven in both directions from both the 500 and 1000-ft. levels, and while several veins were cut, none of them were of value worthy of note. The shaft on the Orphan Girl claim was sunk to a depth of 525 ft. A cross-cut was driven in a southerly direction to cut the Orphan Girl vein. The vein was found, but was practically of no value. A north cross-cut was started to cut the veins known to apex on the Orphan Boy and Anglo-Saxon claims.

At the Never Sweat mine, one Ingersoll-Rogler compressor, having a capacity of 7500 cu. ft. of air per minute, was installed. At the Mountain Con. one Nordberg first-motion air-hoist was put in. There was erected at the Parnell shaft a plant for making concrete slabs for shaft-lining. At the Nettie mine, a new office and change-house were completed. At the Rarus shaft, installation was completed of a new 34 by 72-in. Nordberg hoisting engine, operated by air, together with new head-frame and complete shaft-collar equipment. There were erected five Sirocco double and single-inlet fans, having a capacity of 228,000 cu. ft. of air per minute. Experiments were carried on at the Parnell shaft endeavoring to improve the passage of the air-currents through the shaft by removing the resistance offered by exposed timbers. Concrete slabs were put in place between the timbers, and the results obtained were so satisfactory that it is the intention to equip all shafts in like manner. Several of the mines in which the new system of ventilation has been completed show markedly the good results obtained.

All of the stations and 3399 ft. of the High Ore shaft were fireproofed during the year. The Belmont shaft was

MAP OF WESTERN STATES SHOWING CENTRES OF OPERATIONS BY THE ANACONDA AND SUBSIDIARIES.

fireproofed from surface to the 2800-ft. level, including all stations. At the Rarus shaft, 1609 ft. was re-timbered and fireproofing placed upon the timbers from the surface to the 2100-ft. level, including all stations.

The mines of the company produced during the year 4,918,468 tons of ore, and 6553 tons of copper precipitates from water, a total of 4,925,021 tons.

Production: smelter output (including that from purchased ores) for a series of years follows:

	Copper, lb.	Silver, oz.	Gold, oz.
1918	293,603,720	10,967,965	64,317
1917	253,508,332	9,031,025	58,545
1916	331,893,273	11,837,790	92,090
1915	254,311,574	9,005,617	106,702
1914	223,720,202	8,314,116	96,651
1913	270,301,644	10,321,296	64,898
1912	294,474,161	11,014,737	61,314
1911	259,407,092	9,731,561	48,950
1910	266,608,461	9,534,888	57,260

The copper reduction works treated for all companies during the year 4,959,580 tons of ore and other cupriferous material at Anaconda, and 57,000 tons of ore and other cupriferous material at Great Falls. Of this amount, 4,350,446 tons of ore was produced by company mines, 618,256 tons of ore was either purchased from or treated for other companies, and 47,878 tons of precipitates and cleanings from the old works at Anaconda and Butte were treated.

At Anaconda there were produced 279,030,318 lb. of fine copper, 10,001,604 oz. of silver, and 59,403 oz. of gold. At Great Falls there were produced 14,573,408 lb. of fine copper, 966,300 oz. of silver, and 4914 oz. of gold. This makes a total of 293,603,726 lb. of fine copper, 10,967,905 oz. of silver, and 64,317 oz. of gold. Of the total production at these plants, 272,923,031 lb. of fine copper, 10,076,747 oz. of silver, and 64,317 oz. of gold were produced for the company.

The electrolytic copper refinery at Great Falls produced 191,404,125 lb. of cathodes, 189,067,167 lb. of which was melted into shapes at Great Falls.

The copper leaching-plant at Anaconda treated 500,688 tons of tailing and 64,978 tons of copper ore, from which was produced 6662 tons of cement copper.

The zinc plants at Anaconda and Great Falls treated 393,193 tons of ore and other zinciferous material, of which amount 255,057 tons of ore was produced by mines of the company, and 138,136 tons of ore and concentrates were purchased from other companies. At Great Falls there was produced 72,131,238 lb. of electrolytic zinc.

Reduction Works: The electrolytic zinc plant at Great Falls operated continuously with excellent results, as every effort was made to secure as great an output as possible in order to meet the requirements of the Government, as the zinc produced, on account of its purity, was used largely in munition work.

The rod and wire mill was completed during the summer, and the rod mill was put in operation on June 9, and both were in continuous operation during the latter part of the year.

As a result of experience gained in operating the various departments of the zinc plants of the company, it was found that by the expenditure of a proportionately small sum of money, the output of the electrolytic zinc plant at Great Falls could be increased from 100 to 150 tons per day, making it possible to secure a more complete utilization of all equipment at Anaconda and Great Falls, and also reduce the cost of production; accordingly, necessary construction was begun, equipment orders placed, and at the close of the year the increase in the plant had been almost completed.

At the solicitation of the United States government, five electric ferro-manganese furnaces were built at Great Falls, one of which was started in September, and two more went into commission in October and November. The furnaces had a capacity for treating 250 tons of manganese ore per day, and up to November 11 had produced upward of 1000 tons of ferro-manganese, made from ores purchased from Butte Copper & Zinc Co. As the demand for ferro-manganese ceased the furnaces were shut-down.

The mines at Diamondville, Wyoming, produced 625,600 tons of coal. Of this, 398,857 tons was shipped to other departments of the company, 180,409 tons was sold, and 46,334 tons was used at the coal mines. The mines at Washoe, Montana, produced 147,774 tons of coal; 72,513 tons was shipped to other departments, 65,258 tons was sold, and 10,002 tons was used at the coal mines. The mine at Sand Coulee, Montana, produced 292,366 tons of coal; 160,642 tons was shipped to other departments, 131,470 tons was sold, and 254 tons was used at the coal mines.

The sawmills at Hamilton, Hope, Bonner, and St. Regis cut 82,950,859 ft. of lumber, and purchased 41,219,939 ft.; of which 72,162,891 ft. was shipped to the mines, 35,765,541 ft. was sold, 1,415,915 ft. was used at the mills for repairs and construction, and 2,208,966 ft. was supplied to the factory for manufacturing; or a total disposition of 111,553,313 ft., increasing the stock of finished lumber on hand by 12,617,485 ft., leaving a balance on hand December 31, 1918, of 54,027,560 feet.

The subsidiary departments of the company realized a profit from the year's business of $354,187.

The Butte, Anaconda & Pacific Railway transported 5,630,451 tons of freight and ore, and 245,682 passengers. The gross earnings were $2,095,713; rental and miscellaneous receipts, $26,893; operating expenses, $1,535,724; taxes, interest, and rental of leased lines, $213,960; net income, $372,922.

The International Smelting Co. at Tooele, Utah, treated 262,772 tons of copper and 297,847 tons of lead ore, from which there were produced 21,821,657 lb. of fine copper, 62,034,920 lb. of fine lead, 5,827,134 oz. of silver, and 36,317 oz. of gold.

At the Andes Copper Mining Co., Chile, South America, additional churn-drilling was done, aggregating 11,800 ft., by which approximately 5,000,000 tons of ore was added to the reserves. Drifts and raises were driven totaling 2990 ft. It was decided to place the living quarters of the employees at the millsite, and at that point a townsite has been established. It is the intention of the company to make it as attractive as possible for the officials and other employees. One hundred and eighty-four houses are being constructed, varying from 30 to 100% toward completion. The grading of the railroad was completed to the millsite. Thirty-nine miles of track was laid to the west portal of tunnel No. 4, eight miles distant from the millsite.

THARSIS SULPHUR & COPPER CO., LIMITED

Property: mines and works in Spain, and works in Great Britain.

Financial Statement: profit for the year ended December 31, 1918, was £243,216 ($1,178,500), but after deducting taxes, general expenses, and depreciation, this was reduced to £154,035 ($746,900). The gross profit in 52 years totaled £14,891,985 ($72,226,000), of which £11,451,574 ($55,542,000) was net.

Dividends: £125,000 ($606,000) was paid in 1918, making £10,758,432 ($52,176,000) since 1866. Last year's rate was 10% on capital, and the total 948½%.

Production: the Calañas mine produced 328,601 tons of ore, a decrease of 78,618 tons. The yield of refined copper was 3246 long tons, compared with 4066, 3712, and 3970 tons in the previous three years.

At the Tharsis mine 215,000 cubic meters of overburden was removed. A large quantity of pyrite is now ready.

NORTH BROKEN HILL LIMITED

Property: mine and mill at Broken Hill, New South Wales, Australia.

Operating Official: G. Weir, general manager.

Financial Statement: during the half-year ended December 31, 1918, sales of concentrate and tailing realized £306,658 ($1,460,000). The profit was £176,609 ($840,000). The surplus of assets is £615,350 ($2,950,000).

Dividends: No. 49 and 50 absorbed £120,000 ($576,000).

Development: the main shaft was completed to a depth of 1778 ft. A ventilating shaft is being sunk to 800 ft. Total new work amounted to 861 ft. The quantity of ore available above the 1400-ft. level is calculated at 2,600,000 tons. Mining cost 21/8 ($5.20) per ton.

Production: the mill treated 74,385 tons, averaging 15.7% lead, 8.5 oz. silver, and 12.8% zinc. The recovery in concentrate was 82.5% of the lead and 62.7% of the silver, the 14,948 tons of concentrate assaying 64.6% lead, 26.6 oz. silver, and 7.4% zinc. The zincy tailing—40,683 tons carrying 15.3% zinc—was sent to the Amalgamated Zinc (De Bavay's) flotation plant for further treatment. Milling cost $2.08 per ton.

SILVER absorbed by India, that is, net imports, during the War, amounted to 516,202,000 ounces; and gold 5,030,000 ounces. The world's production during this period was 704,000,000 ounces of silver and 83,210,000 ounces of gold. Some interesting notes on silver were published on our metal page last week. The term 'Chinese tael' is frequently used in connection with silver movements, prices, and exchange in the Orient, and it might be explained here that the tael is not a coin but a weight equal to 579.84 grains.

COPPER is gaining in strength. The quotations of shares of the companies producing the metal are higher than at any time since the armistice was signed, although the price of the metal has declined six cents per pound during the intervening seven months. The buoyancy of the share-market reflects the general optimism of the country and of the mining public. France has lifted the embargo on imports of copper; other European countries, including those with whom peace is about to be concluded, will shortly become buyers. In May the sales of copper were larger than had been expected; they were even in excess of production during the month.

WE in this country hardly realize how we have escaped most of the effects of the War. We are optimistic and cheerful; in England they are anxious and gloomy. A metallurgist well known to our readers writes: "It all seems so strange. I cannot believe that people are five years older, that patents have five years less to run, or that generally five years have been taken out of my professional life." Another, a veteran formerly conspicuous in copper smelting, writes: "The whole world is in trouble. England particularly has labor pains, and what the issue will be, I don't know. It is at present full of gloomy forebodings."

AMONG methods of education we commend to the attention of our readers the lectures for shift-bosses organized by the Phelps Dodge Corporation at Bisbee. The Copper Queen branch of this public-spirited company is conducting a course of 43 lectures for shift-bosses. These lectures or talks are delivered for the most part by foremen, superintendents, and engineers on the company's staff. We note in addition that the manager, Mr. G. H. Dowell, will talk on 'Company Policies', Mr. R. B. von Kleinsmid, the President of the University of Arizona, will give a discourse on 'The Psychology of Handling Men', Mr. J. B. Tenney, the Chief Geologist, will explain 'The General Geology of the Warren District', and Mr. Gerald Sherman, the Consulting Engineer, will describe 'Caving Methods'. The list of subjects is most attractive, and we feel sure that the well-meant effort to give technical instruction to that worthy person the shift-boss will be successful. After all, there is the manager, and his assistant, and the engineer, and the geologist, but the real work of the mine is in the hands of the shift-boss. He is worthy of the most kindly and respectful consideration.

AT a recent meeting of the North Idaho Chamber of Commerce, while in session at Moscow, an address was delivered by Mr. J. B. Eldridge, vice-president of the Idaho Mining Association, and in the course of that address he made a plea for the building of roads to aid the development of the mineral resources of the State. We sympathize with that plea. As Mr. Eldridge said, barely one-tenth of Idaho's mineral area is open to profitable mining operations on account of the lack of transportation. In this matter we commend the State legislature to study the policy adopted by British Columbia, in which province the government builds a considerable mileage of roads every year and thereby stimulates the development of the country.

THE Canadian government has appointed a commission to inquire into the feasibility of introducing herds of reindeer and musk-oxen into parts of Arctic and near-Arctic Canada with a view to their forming a source of meat for the inhabitants of these remote regions. It would also be well to take strong measures for the protection of the few remaining musk-oxen and to pass a law forbidding the shooting of the female caribou. The natives in the far North are acquiring rifles and they are slaughtering these wild animals with great ease as compared to the time when they had only their bows and arrows. We make mention of this matter in the interest of the prospector, to whom the larger four-footed game affords a necessary source of food.

SUPPRESSION or curtailment of the foreign press in the United States is being advocated in Congress. This is due to the fact, it is reported, that evidence has accumulated to prove that the foreign press, in its effort to strengthen itself with the elements to which it appeals, has preached treason against our Government; it has tried to maintain the use of European languages and customs among our alien population and has endeavored to create a divided allegiance in the minds of their children. Much of this we believe to be true, but the total suppression of all papers and magazines not printed in the English language would be a step so illiberal as to warrant protest from those whose better judgment has not been swamped by violent prejudice. It seems to us that all that is desirable in the way of reform and discipline in this direction can be accomplished by passing a law to compel every foreign-language paper to print an English translation of its foreign text in the next column. This would serve, in the first place, as a tax on publication, increasing the cost sufficiently to diminish the number of foreign papers circulated; in the second place, such a regulation would, by furnishing an immediate English translation, help to teach our language to the immigrant and his children, thereby hastening the process of kindly assimilation.

IT is an interesting coincidence that at the time when the latest pronouncement of the U. S. Supreme Court in the flotation litigation is made known, it is announced that Mr. James M. Hyde has been appointed Professor of Metallurgy in Stanford University. We are glad of it, for Mr. Hyde has a logical mind and unusual power of exposition. He ought to prove an effective teacher, in co-operation with Mr. Theodore J. Hoover, who has been appointed Dean of the Mining Department at Stanford. Mr. Hoover, as our readers will recall, used to be metallurgical engineer to the Minerals Separation company and he wrote the first book on the flotation process. His world-wide experience of mining ought to stand him in good stead and his proved ability in the art of exposition likewise should serve him well as a professor. In early youth he had some training as a journalist on the Oakland 'Tribune' and since then his contributions to the technical press have enabled him further to develop his powers of expression. Here we may advert to the fact that Mr. Hugh F. Picard, the junior member of the firm of Sulman & Picard, the metallurgists to Minerals Separation and the recognized inventors of the basic patents, has been elected president of the Institution of Mining and Metallurgy in London. Mr. Picard is a brilliant technician and possessed of so many engaging qualities that his election has been received with pleasure both in London and in this country. We expect to publish his presidential address in a forthcoming issue of this paper.

IN these days of multitudinous newspapers and magazines it is remarkable how little really trustworthy information is available. For instance, note the extraordinary diversity of opinion concerning industrial conditions in the countries of Europe. The difficulty is due largely to personal bias and individual prejudice. A clever man like Mr. Vanderlip delivers a long and deeply interesting speech immediately after his arrival from Europe and one would suppose that his statements could be accepted unreservedly. Nothing of the kind. He said three or four things that any well-informed man knows to be incorrect, mainly by reason of exaggeration incidental to an effort to emphasize. The general effect of his speech was, we thing, misleading. Every great war is followed by a period of disorganization, poverty, and political unrest, but history tells us that in most cases the recovery and rehabilitation have been much more rapid than seemed possible while under the effects of the reaction inevitable from such a calamity. Mr. Hoover's speech, on the same topic, seems to us to be more sagacious and better balanced. His views concerning the feeding of the European peoples are nothing like so gloomy as Mr. Vanderlip's, but he recognizes the urgent necessity for allowing the European countries, especially Germany, to obtain the raw material that is essential to the life of manufacture. He makes the wise suggestion that we stop the lending of money by our Government to the European countries, because this invites extravagance, not thrift, but that the lending of capital be done by private persons and corporations to governments and individuals in Europe, in order to assist the restoration of industry and the re-establishment of a normal market for our products.

UNDER 'Discussion' we publish a letter from Mr. William Forstner, who is honorably known as a specialist in the mining of quicksilver. It is on this subject that he writes, making a plea for some measure of protection to the industry. As some of our readers are aware Mr. F. L. Ransome, of the U. S. Geological Survey, in a recent Bulletin, forecasted the decline of quicksilver mining in this country, because, among other reasons, it cannot compete with imports of cheaper metal from Spain. He expressed himself in opposition to the idea of stimulating the American production by tariff protection. As the industry is mainly centralized in California this official expression of opinion annoyed many of our friends in San Francisco, and one of them, Mr. Murray Innes, indited a vigorous protest to the Vice-Chairman of the Tariff Commission, taking strong exception to "this destructive attitude at Washington," which appeared to play into the hands of the Rothschilds. Mr. Fletcher Hamilton, the State Mineralogist of California, likewise made a protest, in the form of a letter to the Secretary of the Interior, in which he ascribed the depression in our domestic quicksilver industry to the "increasing importation of Mexican quicksilver, which is produced with the aid of peon labor." Now comes our friend Mr. Forstner with a temperate plea, to which our readers will, we think, give sympathetic attention. He says, most sensibly, that if the domestic producers of quicksilver desire to safeguard their industry they must co-operate with others similarly situated; it is useless to play a lone hand in any effort to influence legislative action. For ourselves, we think it highly desirable that this country should be independent of foreign supplies of metals and minerals if such supplies can be made available at home; the idea of being industrially self-contained is not one to be set aside lightly. Moreover, in respect of tin, antimony, chrome, manganese, tungsten, and quicksilver, we believe that if the mining of them is stimulated by some measure of protection, whether by an import-duty or a bonus, there is a chance of deposits being found and developed of such richness and size that an adequate supply will be forthcoming at a cost rendering the domestic industry strong enough to withstand foreign competition.

The Flotation Decision

On another page we publish the full text of the U. S. Supreme Court's opinion in the case of Minerals Separation, Limited, v. Butte & Superior Mining Company. The issue was the scope of patent No. 835,120, the validity of which had been established previously by the Court's decision in the Hyde case. In that decision the Court had limited the patent to a "critical proportion" of oil, "amounting to a fraction of 1% on the ore," but had not itself defined the fraction except by referring to the testimony in the case and to the patent itself. In consequence, the defendant company took the position that the critical proportion so described was one-half of 1% or less. This was tested by the starting of a new suit by the Minerals Separation company as soon as the Hyde case was concluded, this time against the company by whom Mr. J. M. Hyde was employed professionally and by whom he had been backed in his litigation with the Minerals Separation company. The District Court of Montana refused to accept "half of 1%" as a definition of the Supreme Court's "a fraction of 1%," but the Ninth Circuit Court of Appeals, sitting in San Francisco, decided in favor of that interpretation; whereupon the issue was referred again, on writ of certiorari, to the Supreme Court of the United States. This Court now holds that the appellate court, by limiting the scope of the patent to half of 1%, fell into error in interpreting the final decision in the Hyde case, and also holds that "the patent extends to and covers the use, in the process, of oils of the patent in amounts equal to *any* fraction of 1% on the ore." The italics are ours. The Supreme Court says that the patentees are entitled to claim "a reasonable degree of variation," in the proportion of oil used in the process, "within the terms of the claims" of the patent, and that "the restriction of the amount to a fraction of 1% was reasonable and lawful." Further, as to any conflict between two expressions used in the testimony and in the patent, "the language of the claims must rule in determining the rights of the patentees." Thus the importance of the admission made by Mr. Kenyon to Mr. Justice McReynolds, as quoted in the defendant's oral argument, which was printed in our issue of May 31, is lessened, although Mr. Justice Clarke, who delivered the opinion of the Supreme Court, says that it was "impressive and significant." Mr. Kenyon's admission and the evidence in the record have impelled the court of last resort to decide that the metallurgic results under the patent "could not be obtained with more than a fraction of 1%" of oil, therefore the appellate court's decree is sustained in so far as it held that the use of more than 1% does "not constitute infringement." As to the use of mineral-oil, the Court concludes that better results probably would have been obtained by the use of less than 1% of pine-oil alone, but since the mineral-oil has a "preferential affinity for metalliferous matter," as specified in the patent, the use of it is not an infringement if the aggregate amount of all oils is in excess of 1%. "The patent is on the process; it is not and cannot be on the result," says the Court. This is important; it may serve as a new point of departure. In short, the patent rights of the Minerals Separation company are upheld in respect of the use of any proportion of any oil up to 1%, but not beyond that point. This, even in the present state of the art, does not give them a monopoly of flotation, but it is a blow to the economical use of the process because, although it can be conducted successfully with more than 20 pounds of oil per ton of ore, it is a fact that the larger proportion of oil is a nuisance in the mill and entails an extra cost of about one cent per pound of additional oil. Nevertheless, even the extra cost and trouble will be preferred by the managements of some of the mining companies to paying a royalty to the Minerals Separation company and becoming subject to its inquisitorial methods. We are informed, for example, that the Butte & Superior company will continue to use more than 1% of oil, preferring to meet the additional cost of the extra proportion of cheap oils than to take a license from the Minerals Separation company and pay a royalty on its 'below 1%' process. It is also announced that the defendant in the recent suit is prepared to continue the use of the permissible proportion of oil until the expiration of the Minerals Separation patent in November 1923, "after which time," it is stated, "the use of the process with any quantity of oil will be free and open to the public." There remains also a reasonable expectation that before the expiration of patent 835,120, four years hence, a more economical and more efficient process of concentration will be devised, for a number of new ideas are in course of trial. Meanwhile the Minerals Separation people, presumably, will collect heavy damages for past infringements, not only from the Butte & Superior company but from the big copper-mining companies that have been using the same methods of flotation during the past three or four years. Whether they also will elect to use the 'over 1%' proportion of oil, rather than pay toll to the Minerals Separation company, we do not know, but as some of them are under the same direction as the Butte & Superior company, such a decision seems probable. What attitude the patent-owning company will assume toward the industry in the future is another matter of conjecture; in the past its tactics have been needlessly offensive and we have not hesitated to condemn them. Whether the legal weapon put into the hands of the Minerals Separation people will be used gently or fiercely, we cannot tell, but we venture to suggest that as the opinion of the Supreme Court affords a means of escape from their clutches, by the use of 20 pounds or more of oil, they will be wise in so arranging their scale of royalties that it will become advantageous to take a license from them, and besides abating their demand for excessive royalties they will show wisdom in adopting a more conciliatory policy in other respects. The entire controversy proves once again how undesirable it is to leave the decision of technical and scientific questions to courts composed of men without a special training for the understanding of such questions. With all respect to the Supreme Court, we venture to say that no unbiased metallurgist familiar with the operation of the flotation process will accept, even for a moment, the suggestion that the process that is successful when using half of 1% of oil is at all different from the process that works successfully when using 1% or 1.25% of oil. It is essentially the same process, and if the Minerals Separation people did anything for the advancement of the art it was in showing that so small a quantity as three or four pounds—0.15 or 0.2%—of oil sufficed with most ores to produce an effective metallurgic result; in other words, what they did was to show how oil could be economized and the process simplified thereby, for the more oil the more messy the operations. An issue involving an enormous amount of money and vital to the interests of a basic industry has gone for adjudication to jurists devoid of the special education required for the purpose, and without the time needed for the proper preparation of the requisite understanding of the technical problems involved. It is not the least remarkable feature of the latest opinion that it should have been delivered so soon, for the case was heard before the Court so recently as last March, less than three months ago. Of the eight decisions in the three flotation lawsuits (Hyde, Miami, and Butte & Superior) by the various courts, it can be said that they are as contradictory as they are diverse, and that each one has been vitiated by the incompleteness of the evidence in the record and by the lack, on the part of the courts, of the intimate knowledge of the subject that is necessary for a real understanding of it. We here repeat, what we have intimated more than once, that the story of the invention of the process as told in the courts is unconvincing and the explanations of its physical principles absurdly variable and contradictory. The essential features of the process as far as disclosed in the patent were known at Broken Hill some time before the supposed discovery in March 1905, and if the metallurgists at work in the Central mill at Broken Hill in 1903 and 1904 could have been subpoenaed before the American courts, it would have been possible, we believe, to throw a different light on the claims of the supposed inventors. Other patents remain and further litigation is assured, for some of the patents antedating No. 835,120 are held in this country by opponents of the Minerals Separation company. Therefore we deprecate any feeling of undue discouragement at this time and urge the leaders of the mining industry in the United States to consult with one another for the purpose of defensive co-operation immediately, since the District Court of Montana must forthwith amend its decision in conformity with the decree handed down by the Supreme Court.

Gold and Silver

The embargo on the exportation of gold and the control over foreign exchange were lifted by the Federal Reserve Board on June 9, thereby removing the prohibitions that went into effect on September 10, 1917. During the interval only small quantities of gold were allowed to go out of the country and only by special permission of the Federal Reserve Board, through whom the national control of gold is exercised. However, exportation of the standard metal is still denied to Russia and to the Enemy countries, although this remaining check may be removed as soon as peace has become a legal fact. Applications for both gold and silver exports must, however, continue to be made to the Federal Reserve Board, until such time as the President shall, by proclamation, formally bring to an end the present control. Now that the ban on the exportation of both the money metals has been lifted the restoration of foreign trade should be accelerated, without cutting into our supply of gold, because rates of exchange are generally below the point at which exportation is feasible; indeed, it is noteworthy that the first part of a shipment of $50,000,000 in gold has recently reached New York from Canada. We welcome the free movement of gold and silver as a means of restoring the precious metals to their normal function in commerce and of ascertaining the real status of the enormous volume of paper money created in the belligerent countries during the War. Meanwhile the resumption of silver exportation to the Orient has given that metal a market-value not far from its coinage-value and promises to maintain the price at the current high level, much to the advantage of the miner. Silver stands today at nearly double the average quotation during 1914. Production has declined all over the world, the total of 177,453,000 ounces in 1918 being 48,500,000 ounces less than in 1911. Of the 67,879,200 ounces of silver produced in the United States last year, 72,572,506 ounces came through the American Smelting & Refining Company and 10,700,000 ounces represented a by-product from the copper-mining operations of the Anaconda. In the same year the United States Smelting, Refining & Mining Company produced 15,337,465 ounces of silver, most of it however coming from its mines at Pachuca, Mexico. Of the total world's stock of gold the United States now holds one-third, as against one-quarter before the War. Of the total stock of gold money existing at the end of 1913, 63% was in government banks or treasuries and 37% in the hands of private banks and the public. A year ago the proportions had changed to 85% and 15% respectively. This is one of the momentous consequences of the War, which had the effect of withdrawing gold from circulation and of concentrating it in the hands of governmental institutions. Concurrently the production of gold has declined, in part owing to the world-wide inflation of labor, which has greatly increased the cost of producing the metal and discouraged the search for new ore deposits. It remains to be seen what will be the after-war effect on our monetary standard.

The Leaching of Flotation Concentrate

The Editor:

Sir—In regard to the interesting article by Percy R. Middleton in your issue of June 7 on the leaching of flotation concentrate, I think it would be instructive if he would give us a little more detail as to his proposed methods and flow-sheet.

1. I notice that in his tests at the Edwards metallurgical works he treated his roasted product by percolation but in his estimate for a 100-ton plant he evidently contemplates agitation treatment by means of Dorr counter-current thickeners: the question then arises, why does he abandon the idea of percolation, which presumably worked satisfactorily in his large-scale test? If it be possible to use percolation that method would seem much simpler than agitation and decantation.

2. He apparently proposes to use a sulphuric acid solution to dissolve the 5 or 10% of copper that has escaped sulphatization but he does not allow for any dissolving-tank or tanks preliminary to the Dorr counter-current system. Am I right in supposing that he intends to add his acid to the pulp as it flows into the first thickener? This would seem to involve a misplacement of acid, since the overflow of that thickener would normally go directly to precipitation: moreover, in order to obtain the maximum washing efficiency from the Dorr method dissolving should be as nearly as possible complete before washing begins.

3. I fail to grasp his meaning when he states that "it is an open question whether the advantage of using one solution for the recovery of both gold and silver would offset the danger of incomplete washing in a large plant." Is he referring to washing of the pulp between the copper extraction and the cyanide treatment for gold and silver, or to the final washing out of the gold and silver? If the latter, why worry, since this operation is being performed successfully every day in large as well as small plants?

4. He appears to assume that the silver could be extracted by cyanidation after roasting, without previous chlorination, but this is contrary to the usual experience. As a general rule the roasting of an ore which when raw is perfectly amenable to cyanidation renders it so refractory that only from 20 to 30% can be extracted by that method.

5. In his proposed flow-sheet he does not give any indication of the method he intends to adopt for chlorinating the pulp after it leaves the last washing-thickener of the copper-dissolving process.

6. He states that "laboratory experiments show that after chlorination the silver is in a condition suitable for extraction by either hyposulphite or brine." It would have been interesting if he had given some more data on this point, as, for instance, the methods used, and the extraction obtained, with original and residue assays.

7. In his profit-and-loss tables, comparing the wet treatment with smelting, he assumes an extraction of 90% of the gold and nearly 89% of the silver; has he any working data as a foundation for this estimate? And are the figures meant to apply to chlorination followed by water and 'hypo' treatment successively or to direct cyanidation?

I think that if he would make these various points clear the value of his article would be greatly enhanced.

E. M. HAMILTON.

San Francisco, June 9.

Protecting the Quicksilver Industry

The Editor:

Sir—The second annual report of the U. S. Tariff Commission contains a chapter discussing in detail the quicksilver industry. The conclusions of the Tariff Commission regarding the protection to be afforded to the quicksilver industry in the United States in the future, are as follows:

"In the case of quicksilver the question can be squarely raised as to whether the production of this metal can be considered an effective American industry, in as much as abundant cheaper sources of supply exist elsewhere. It is particularly an example of an industry whose products are placed on the market at high cost because of the relatively inferior natural resources of this country in the raw material. Quicksilver is an essential metal, however, of vital necessity in the conduct of war and widely used in the industries. It is stated that American resources, although low-grade, can furnish an adequate supply for many years if a stable and sufficient price be guaranteed. Without tariff protection the United States will be dependent in large part on outside sources for a vital commodity and a grave question of national expediency is involved."

From the above quotation it appears that the Tariff Commission considers the importance of quicksilver as a war material the main reason for advocating the protection of the quicksilver industry in the United States. Whether, in view of the very slight chance of this country again confronting war conditions within a large lapse of years, the importance of quicksilver as a war material would be a sufficient reason for Congress to protect this industry by a sufficiently high import-tax, is in my opinion very doubtful. The more so, as another Government department, the U. S. Geological Survey, is opposed* to any protection of the quicksilver industry, which would be sufficiently high to keep the price of the metal at a point reasonably remunerative to the producer.

There are no data at hand for the world production of quicksilver later than the year 1913; taking the years 1910 to 1913, the average contribution of the various producing countries was as follows:

	%		%
United States	18.7	Spain	34.1
Austria	19.7	Mexico, etc.	4.2
Italy	23.3		

The output of Spain and Italy being under the control of the Rothschilds, these control 57.5% of the world's output, leaving out of consideration the Austrian output, which it is claimed will also fall under their control. The contract between the Spanish government and the Rothschilds stipulates that the latter shall market the quicksilver on the London market for £7, or higher, and considering the cost of production in Spain and Italy, the Rothschilds can place the quicksilver on the market at that price, if they so desire, without incurring any loss. At the present costs for labor and materials no quicksilver can be produced in the United States at a figure enabling competition with such a price, and consequently, unless protected by a sufficiently high import-duty, the quicksilver industry in the United States finds itself entirely at the mercy of the Rothschilds in London, who, if they so desire, can close every quicksilver mine in the United States. It is useless to argue that such a proceeding is unlikely. Suppose even that the Austrian quicksilver production does not fall into their hands, as is generally believed will be the case, even then the Rothschilds after killing production in the United States, would control, taking the above given average for 1910 to 1913, a little over 70% of the world's production, and after having extinguished the quicksilver industry in the United States, they can put up the price at whatever figure they choose.

Leaving the war-time figures out of consideration, we find that for the period 1910 to 1915, both inclusive, the average yearly domestic production was 20,786 flasks, and the consumption 23,280 flasks; showing that prior to the War production was lower than consumption. Estimating the average cost of production during that period at $50 per flask, the total average yearly disbursement by the industry was $1,040,000.

While a tariff, high enough to prevent the extinction of the quicksilver industry in the United States, may for a time raise the cost of the metal to the consumer, it will, on the other hand, be a protection against extravagantly high prices in the future.

If the quicksilver producers in the United States, however, intend to protect the life of their industry they must come together, organize, and interest the other mineral producers in their case, so that they may be able to submit their contention to the powers that be, fortified by the support of interests large enough to command earnest consideration. They must realize that individual attempts to influence legislative action are of no avail, and only thoroughly organized efforts can possibly bring about the desired results.

WILLIAM FORSTNER.

San Francisco, June 7.

*See Bulletin, U. S. G. S. 666, F.F., p. 8.

The Status of Gold

The Editor:

Sir—Referring to Mr. Robbins' letter on this subject in your issue of May 17, permit me to offer the following quotations from his letter together with some comments thereon, which seem to me to be pertinent.

He says "No proof is presented by Mr. Benedict that the financial world reached finality in its conceptions of 1812."

The words of that paragraph seem to be somewhat involved, but if it is intended to mean that the adoption of the gold standard by Great Britain in 1812 (actually in 1816, as will be shown below) will forever prevent the adoption of any other standard by the financial world, I confess I have no proof to the contrary, nor do I feel called upon to present any, because there is nothing in my letter or in any of my previous contributions, that I am aware of, that even hinted at such an idea. But, in this connection let me quote from one of those 800 books on economics, for which he seems to have so little respect.

In 1774 "Parliament passed a law providing that the silver coins should not be legal tender for more than £25 in one payment, except by weight at the rate of 5s.2d. per ounce. It was enacted that gold coins deficient in weight should be called in and re-coined and thereafter such coins under a certain weight should not be legal tender at all. Light-weight coins were made unavailable in payments. After the experience of a quarter of a century Parliament and the people were convinced that the act of 1774, although adopted as a temporary measure, ought to be made permanent; accordingly it was made so in 1799. Yet it was not until 1816 that the true philosophy of the step was well enough understood to secure its enactment into a settled law."

In substance, that enactment required that 20 lb. troy of standard gold (eleven-twelfths fine) should be coined into 934½ parts or pieces each of which is called a sovereign or pound sterling. But whether that law will remain forever immutable is not for me to predict, as I am endeavoring only to point out a few well-known economic facts which have been "digested and absorbed" from standard works on the science of exchange, including a few of those 800 books.

Again, "Mr. Benedict is not quite clear in his argument that it is not the Government stamp which fixes the value of the coins."

Perhaps you are partly at fault for that, Mr. Editor, for you deleted the two little cubes whose sizes I had calculated so carefully and upon which so much of my argument was based. However, if Mr. Robbins will take the trouble to sketch two cubes of the sizes named in the text and then re-read the argument with the sketches before him it may seem clearer to him. At any rate the combination of the two cubes and the argument, as stated, thoroughly convinced my doubting friend and has since convinced others. Perhaps it might be added that it is perfectly well known to those who have mastered this branch of the science of exchange that it is the quantity of pure gold it contains and not the Government stamp that gives a gold coin its exchange-value or purchasing power.

Again. "In British consols I find Mr. McPherson's 'twin-coin' idea exemplified. Great Britain issued her gold sovereign of a legal weight and fineness and then, doing exactly what Mr. McPherson suggests, she printed £100 on pieces of paper and issued these as running mates for the gold coins. Neither the gold coins nor the pieces of paper are redeemable; they are both money (?), the only difference being that the consol bears interest." Also, in his letter in your issue of March 22, he says, "In 1812 Great Britain needed money for settling war bills and she set about raising these funds by issuing Consols or government bonds. Her proposition was this: To everyone who would give (lend?) her £100 in gold she would give a paper stamped £100."

With Mr. McPherson's permission, permit me to say that, after describing his combination of a $20 gold-piece having a disc of brass on which was stamped "20 dollars" coupled to it, he said, in continuation, "This gold-brass twin coin illustration is given to demonstrate more clearly the fact that one-half the coin is real money and the other half symbol money."

In the name of political economy, how in the world can Mr. Robbins reason out that a consol consists of one-half real money (gold) and the other half symbol money and how are the two coupled together in such a consol? It seems pertinent to add just here that Uncle Sam has just been borrowing the equivalent of gold from his nephews and nieces with which to pay his war-bills, issuing in exchange for such equivalent of gold certain obligations in the form of pieces of paper with various amounts of money printed on them. Some day these various kinds of obligations may be merged into 'American consols', but neither now nor then will they consist of one-half gold (real money) and one-half symbol money. Mr. Robbins did not seem to catch this point of Mr. McPherson's argument, that it is the quantity of gold it contains and not the Government stamp that gives exchange-value to a gold coin.

Again, "Mr. McPherson says further: 'If any nation or group of nations can double the figure on the face of a gold coin . . . that nation can easily treble it or . . multiply it by tens or hundreds. There is, however, one obstacle always in the way of this and that is the intrinsic and social value of the metal itself'. Just what is meant by "the intrinsic and social value" is not clear, but the facts are that there is no obstacle in the way of any nation doubling the figure on the face of a gold coin."

On the contrary, "the intrinsic and social value" *is* perfectly clear to anyone who comprehends what constitutes real money. (It was for the purpose of enabling Mr. Robbins to acquire this knowledge that I, in what was intended to be a kind and friendly way, offered to him the hospitality of a certain club, truly hoping he might visit this city in the near future and that I could meet him. I regret very much that my meaning should have been misinterpreted.)

To continue, there is, also, the obstacle of 'common honesty' in the way of doubling the figure on a gold coin, if such coin with the figure so doubled is to be made legal tender in payment for debts incurred before such change took place. It would be legalized robbery, pure and simple; excepting in cases of indebtedness where the contract specifically required the payment of a certain number of dollars in gold coin of the present weight and standard of fineness; which means that a certain weight of gold must be paid over in final settlement of the agreement. For example, $1000 in gold coin of the present weight and standard of fineness is 1000 times 25.8 grains, or 25,800 gr. of standard gold, equivalent to one hundred $10 gold-pieces fresh from the Mint. Mr. Robbins seems to think that if "20 dollars" is stamped on the face of such a $10 gold-piece it would be right and fair to use only fifty of such newly stamped pieces in cancelling an obligation to pay 25,800 gr. of standard gold; or, in other words, to pay 12,900 grains of standard gold in place of double that quantity, called for in the contract. Could anyone who has studied the money question in connection with the science of exchange be so foolish as to believe 232.2 grains of fine gold in the form of a coin with "20 dollars" stamped on its face will buy any more, in the marts of the world, than 232.2 gr. of gold in the form of a coin with "10 dollars" stamped on its face? Or, to put it in another form, as has been iterated and reiterated so often, a U. S. dollar is 23.22 gr. of fine gold, therefore 10 dollars must be 232.2 gr. of fine gold. But if a law is passed making 232.2 grains of fine gold '20 dollars' then one of such dollars would be 11.61 grains of fine gold or 12.9 gr. of standard gold, and as $1000 in gold coin of the present weight and standard of fineness is 25,800 gr. it would require 2000 of the new dollars to cancel an obligation to pay off the old (present) dollars. Could anything be clearer?

Again, "All that governments can do is to standardize and stabilize the relationship between gold and the mass of other wealth."

If Mr. Robbins would read understandingly (not after the manner of a "professional proof-reader") even parts of a very few of those 800 books and "digest and absorb" what he read, and if by "standardize and stabilize" he means to maintain a uniform ratio between gold and the mass of other wealth, he would learn that governments, so far, have been unable to accomplish any such thing. Instead, the ratio (relative-value) is determined by the exigencies of trade and commerce, wars, etc., as "exemplified" in Stock Exchanges, Boards of Trade, and similar institutions all over the world, to say nothing of what is termed retail trade.

Again. "As there is only a definite amount of gold in the world, some substitute for gold will be necessary, or it will be necessary to ascribe (give?) a greater exchange value to an ounce of gold" and "It seems to me that the maintaining of gold at its present value is going to increase the gravity of the present financial situation. The raising of gold to a higher valuation would ease present conditions and stimulate production of precious metals."

Here is that same, old, false notion cropping out again, namely that governments can fix ("ascribe") to an ounce or any other quantity of gold any old exchange-value they please. A suitable reference to even a particular one of those 800 books will refute ("confute") this notion, for it is shown therein that gold is a commodity and its exchange-value is "determined temporarily by supply and demand and permanently, on the average, by the cost of production." In round numbers, the world's production of gold for 30 years, 1866 to 1895 inclusive, has been estimated at 14,512,000 lb. troy, an average of 483,700 lb. per year: and from 1896 to 1917 inclusive, 22 years, 33,145,000 lb. or 1,506,000 lb. per year. In 1896, gold, as measured in supplies and commodities generally, has been estimated to have been worth nearly three times as much as it was in 1914. According to the foregoing figures, the average production for each of the 22 years was just about three times as much as it was per year for the previous 30 years, and during that 22 years its exchange-value steadily diminished. The state of war since 1914 has caused unnatural conditions, necessitating increased credit and an inflated currency, all of which have increased prices of other commodities abnormally, which means a corresponding reduction in the purchasing power of gold. Still, if the foregoing figures are substantially correct, the trebling of the yearly production of gold followed by an ultimate reduction of its exchange-value to one-third of its former worth may be something more than a mere coincidence. But it seems to prove conclusively that the Government stamp on a gold coin has nothing whatever to do with such a coin's purchasing power, excepting in so far as it indicates the weight of gold the coin ought to contain.

Again. "Within Argentina the purchasing power (of gold?) is doubled." Argentina has an inconvertible depreciated paper currency with an exchange-value (as measured in gold) of less than one-half of its face value (44% according to one reference) and it follows, as a matter of course, that the purchasing power of a gold peso is double that of a depreciated paper peso.

In conclusion, permit me to make two more quotations and comment thereon.

"Between the lines of Mr. Benedict's concluding paragraph I read 'Shoemaker stick to thy last'. Ill-timed advice," etc.

The paragraph meant precisely what it said, and, as before stated, it was intended in a kind and friendly way, for Mr. Robbins is a stranger to me: it contains no innuendo whatever, nothing to be read between the lines. I regret very much if it was so worded that it could be misconstrued into giving "Ill-timed advice."

Again, "I cannot feel that Mr. Benedict and his array of 800 books would alter my opinions unless coupled with confuting evidence."

It seems needless to say that ample "confuting evidence," sufficient to convince any reasonable person, is contained in that "array of 800 books," and it awaits Mr. Robbins' pleasure. Or, if there is no prospect of his coming here soon, perhaps he could find in San Francisco 'The Principles of Political Economy', by J. S. Mill; 'Money and Banking', by Horace White; 'A Treatise on the Coins of the Realm', by Lord Liverpool; 'A History of Currency in the U. S.', by A. B. Hepburn; 'The Evolution of Modern Money', by W. W. Carlile, and read at his leisure such chapters in them as treat upon the subject of money and currency.

W. deL. Benedict.

New York, May 24.

The Internal Corrosion of Cables

The Editor:

Sir—In his article on this subject, Mr. W. F. Robertson makes the statement that Mr. Ben. B. Thayer informed him that the cables used by his company periodically were given an oil-bath heated by steam. This I have never seen done at the Anaconda mines but I have helped to tar cables elsewhere at the mines of Butte. Mr. Thayer could have informed Mr. Robertson that at the Butte mines the cables are tarred with pine-tar and a substance called 'cable-dressing' once a week and at some mines twice a week. If this was not done a cable would not last a month, let alone a year. Mr. Thayer is a practical miner as well as a theoretical one and he will probably recollect that the cables used at the Bi-Metallic mine at Granite, Montana, were tarred when he was foreman of that mine some 30 years ago, although there is no copper water there as at Butte.

I have worked in many mines where flat or round cables were used and they were tarred. I have never seen oil used on cables.

A. N. C.

Miami, Arizona, May 7.

Phosphate rock marketed in 1918, according to R. W. Stone, of the U. S. Geological Survey, was 2,490,760 long tons, valued at $8,214,463, compared with 2,584,287 tons, valued at $7,771,084, in 1917. Florida land pebble constituted 80% of the total output. Tennessee accounted for 374,535 tons of rock.

Grindstones sold in the United States during 1918 totalled 56,554 tons, valued at $1,262,602. This is a gain of 4% in quantity and 56% in value. Over 85% of the material used in the manufacture of grindstones was sandstone quarried in Ohio; the remainder was sandstone quarried in Michigan and West Virginia.

Exit the Blast-Furnace

By OLIVER E. JAGER

While this article applies particularly to the Anaconda reduction works, it would cause no great surprise to see other large smelters follow the same course, and decrease, or even discard, their blast-furnace operation. The time-worn discussion of the respective merits of blast and reverberatory furnaces (except in particular cases) appears to be closed, as the trend of opinion for several years has been going steadily in favor of the reverberatory. In view of this, it is of interest to consider the conditions in general, and those at Anaconda in particular, that have led up to this radical change in smelting practice.

At Anaconda the intention is to use one or two small blast-furnaces as 'scavengers' only, doing practically all the ore-smelting in the reverberatories. This being so, the big Mathewson blast-furnaces will no longer be used, one of the 51-ft. units being already cut up into two 15-ft. furnaces from which it sprang, a remarkable instance of metallurgic atavism. The only reason for retaining these two furnaces is that the plant and equipment are already in existence, and it is cheaper to retain a portion of it than to build another reverberatory. The blast-furnace plant was scheduled to be shut-down over two years ago, but received a temporary lease of life through war conditions, which demanded the utmost possible production of copper. With the altered condition of the metal market a curtailment of output became necessary. The normal production at Anaconda is 26,000,000 pounds of copper per month; the present production is about 13,500,000 pounds. This reduction in output is accomplished by operating four reverberatories instead of seven, and at the same time shutting-down the blast-furnace plant entirely.

At the risk of recapitulation, there are herewith set out the principal disadvantages that have been urged against the two types of furnace under Anaconda conditions:

Blast-Furnace	Reverberatory
Unsuitable for fine ore.	Repairs are expensive.
Coke costs about twice as much as coal.	Coarse material must be crushed.
More labor and more water required than on roast-plus-reverberatory system.	Coal must be pulverized.
Higher cost of power.	Roasting is necessary; if much flotation concentrate is in the charge, dust losses must be combated.
No waste-heat credit.	Higher slag-assay, although less slag is made than in the blast-furnace.
Makes more slag, although of lower copper content than the reverberatory.	More capital is tied up in the bath of matte.

The case against the blast-furnace allows scarcely any argument. Even the last claim, of a lower slag-assay, is hardly tenable under present conditions at Anaconda. Formerly the regular ore-charge produced a slag carrying about 22% lime, but since the charge has become basic in character, silicious ores have to be added, and naturally the lime is held down as low as possible. The result of this is that the copper in the blast-furnace slag has increased to about 0.3%.

The objections against the reverberatory will now be considered. While repairs are expensive, the cost must be compared with the tonnage smelted before a repair is necessary. When it is considered that the first 40 ft. of a reverberatory roof will not need repairing until 140,000 tons of charge has been smelted in the furnace, the per-ton cost of the repair is reduced to a reasonable amount. The question of crushing must be viewed in conjunction with the scheme of concentration, although it is true that material is crushed that might otherwise be separated for smelting in the blast-furnace. The old system of sending Butte first-class ore and coarse concentrate to the blast-furnaces has been dropped, since the method of dividing ores into classes has been abandoned, and the largest size of concentrate now made is $\frac{3}{8}$ inch. With the adoption of flotation, calling for finer grinding, there is more fine concentrate made; in fact, it may be said that more tonnage is treated and more fine concentrate produced than ever before, all of which points to the reverberatory furnace as the logical appliance to be used in smelting. The cost of finer grinding at the concentrator is offset, in part, by the increased recovery made since that department was remodeled. The pulverizing of coal for firing, and the roasting of material to produce a suitable grade of calcine are two points about which there is little argument. They must be considered as necessary parts of the process, although the settling of the dust caused by roasting flotation-concentrate, while an important matter, can scarcely be held against the reverberatory furnace, being rather a consequence of the adoption of flotation. The two last objections on the list are largely overcome under present conditions of operation. The continuous-flow feature of the reverberatory furnace has reduced the slag-assay to a degree comparable with a blast-furnace slag, while the side-charging has diminished the matte-bath to a much smaller volume. These matters will be taken up at greater length in subsequent articles. The paramount question of cost is, of course, the main factor in the last analysis, and when the increased efficiency of the modern reverberatory using pulverized coal as fuel is considered, it is small wonder that the costs of crushing, coal-pulverizing, and roasting can be absorbed. In other words, reverberatory smelting, in spite of all the extra operations, is cheaper than blast-furnace smelting.

It is necessary only to make brief mention of the several stages of improvement through which the reverberatory has passed since it began to assume its present form. The original furnaces at the 'new works' at Anaconda in 1902 were 50 ft. by 19 ft. From 1903 to 1906 the length was increased, by stages, from 50 ft. to 115 ft. 10 in. The present reverberatories are 133 ft. 7 in. long by 22 ft. wide. Meanwhile calcine was being charged hot, and firing with fuel-oil had been developed; then came side-charging, and lastly, pulverized coal. Improvements in the manufacture of refractories have been of assistance in this development, and the addition of waste-heat boilers has furnished to the smelting operation a credit not to be despised. A ratio of at least 6.5:1 is obtained at Anaconda, and the present average daily total tonnage is 550, which gives 0.187 tons per square foot of hearth-area. With side-charging I am inclined to doubt the usefulness of this last figure for purposes of comparison, as it is practically impossible to determine the hearth-area, since some smelting undoubtedly takes place along the sides of the furnace. On the other hand, should the charge be sufficiently coarse to remain piled up at the sides of the furnace, the heap of material will project into the furnace and reduce the area by lessening the width. With the above tonnage and ratio, the efficiency of the reverberatory furnace is apparent, especially when the fuel question is considered. Firing with pulverized coal permits the use of coals whose ash content varies over a wide range. During a single month the ash has varied from 5 to 20%, which is worth the consideration of a smelter purchasing coal on a sliding scale according to its ash-content. The average ash in the coal now used is 13%, with a heating value of 11,000 B.t.u. per pound.

With no blast-furnaces in operation at Anaconda, it is of interest to consider the method of handling the coarse material that must be treated. The amount of this is small (about 200 tons per day); it consists of the following items: ladle-skulls and matte-runner cleanings: converter-floor cleanings: accretions from the hearths of roasting-furnaces; cleanings from the waste-heat boilers; Southern Cross ore and custom ore, all of which is crushed to pass a 4-in. opening. The Southern Cross ore and custom ore are further reduced to 2-in. size, and put through the roasters, which process, in the case of the first-named, is merely for the purpose of drying. Wet copper precipitates are also dried in this manner. Whatever material goes to the roasters, of course, reaches the reverberatories as part of the calcine. The matte-cleanings and other 'junk' are fed directly to the reverberatories in the usual manner, the only change that was necessary was the provision of a few charge-pipes of larger diameter: 12-in. pipes are being used for this, as against 6-in. for charging the finer material. It is planned to make all pipes of 10-in. diameter in future construction. The coarse charge is put into the furnace at a point about 15 ft. from the firing end; 40 tons per day is fed to each furnace, the large reverberatory that handles liquid converter-slag also taking its share. No difference has been noticed in the operation of the furnace on account of charging this coarse material, although it must be remembered that its introduction has a decided tendency to increase the copper in the slag, for the reason that it is high-grade, partly oxidized, and is not mixed with the other components of the charge.

When running at full capacity there would be double the amount of this coarse material, which, together with the silicious ore necessary to flux it, would provide sufficient charge for one 15-ft. blast-furnace all the time, and for two such furnaces part of the time, as provided for in the plan already mentioned.

So far as Anaconda is concerned, the blast-furnace has been definitely relegated to the 'scavenger' class. Its relative unimportance may be further realized from the fact that only 15.5% of the normal output of copper will be produced from material treated in blast-furnaces. Should any abnormal conditions again arise, it would, of course, be possible to produce extra copper by running more blast-furnaces, but the copper so produced would cost more than that credited to the reverberatory operations. With the general adoption of the flotation process, the copper smelter of today has to handle a greater quantity of fine material—a fact which certainly does not suggest more blast-furnaces—and when the increased efficiency and economy of the modern large reverberatory fired with pulverized coal or with oil is taken into account, there arises a set of conditions having an influence on present plant operation and future plant design that is incontestable.

THE WELL-KNOWN FIRM of British soap-makers, Iever Bros. (Ltd.), is preparing to introduce a new method of paying wages, which the chairman of the company outlined thus at the recent annual meeting of shareholders: "As to payment of wages, we want to introduce a different method. Instead of our men crowding round the wage-office and waiting their turn, each man should have a little private banking account in a bank near his own house—not the firm's bank, but one of his own selection. We would advise our bank to credit each man from the pay-sheet with the amount of money he is entitled to receive for his wages. Under this system a man will draw out of his bank what he wants for his household expenses and what he does not need will rest in the bank. The amount left as deposit with the bank will be supplemented by an addition from the firm—we are favorably considering this—and this will give a man 5% on his money left in the bank; so that, instead of the money lying at home earning no interest, by adopting this system it will earn interest. Further than that, the tendency will be always to leave a little more each week in the bank, and I feel confident that if we can get this system universally adopted it will not only raise the workingman's position but add to his dignity, because, instead of crowding round a little pay-office, he will be led to become a saver, having money to invest in the business he is engaged in, or other businesses." Such a system might well be tried by mining companies.

Minerals Separation v. Butte & Superior

Decision of the Supreme Court of the United States, on writ of certiorari to the United States Circuit Court of Appeals for the Ninth District

Decision of the Supreme Court of the United States, on writ of certiorari to the United States Circuit Court of Appeals for the Ninth Circuit.

On June 2 Mr. Justice Clarke delivered the opinion of the Court, as follows:

This is a suit by the Minerals Separation, Limited, et al, plaintiffs below and petitioners in this Court, against the Butte & Superior Mining Company, defendant below and respondent here, to recover for infringement of United States patent No. 835,120, applied for May 29, 1905, and issued November 6, 1906, the validity of which was sustained by this Court in *Minerals Separation, Limited, et al. v. Hyde*, 242 U. S. 261.

The patent has been so frequently described in court proceedings* that it will suffice to say of it here, in the terms of the specification, that it "relates to improvements in the concentration of ore, the object being to separate metalliferous material, graphite and the like, from gangue, by means of oils, fatty acids, or other substances, which have a preferential affinity for metalliferous matter over gangue."

The patent contains 13 claims, which, for the purposes of this opinion, may be conveniently grouped, as follows:

(1) Numbers 1, 2, 3, 4, and 12, as 'fraction of one per cent, claims', because they call for the use of that amount of oil on the ore; (2) Numbers 5, 6, 7, 8, and 13, as 'oleic acid claims', because they are limited to the use of oleic acid in a small fraction of 1% on the ore—0.02-0.5%; (3) Numbers 9, 10, and 11, as 'small quantity of oil claims', all three of which were held invalid by the former decision of this Court. Only the five 'fraction of 1% claims' are involved in this case.

The respondent denied the validity of the patent and the claim of infringement.

The lower courts followed the decision by this Court and sustained the patent except as to the three 'small quantity of oil claims'.

The new evidence introduced on the validity issue is meager in amount, and of a character so unsatisfying that we see no reason for modifying our former conclusion.

The chief controversy in the case centres about the claim of infringement based upon the use of oil by the respondent in excess of 1% on (of the weight of) the ore, after the decision of the former case by this Court.

The evidence shows, and counsel now admit, that prior to the decision by this Court in December 1916, the respondent used, in its ore concentration operations, various oils in quantities less than one-half of 1% on the ore, but that from January 9, 1917, to the time of trial, with the exception of two or three weeks, it used oils of a composition which we shall discuss later on, in quantities in excess of 1% on the ore. In other respects its methods were substantially those of the patent in suit.

On this showing, the District Court found the patent infringed by the respondent, when it used oil in quantities greater than, as well as when it used it in quantities less than 1% on the ore.

The Circuit Court of Appeals held the patent infringed only when the respondent used oil in quantities equal to or less than, one-half of 1% on the ore, and it therefore reversed both of the holdings of the District Court, but allowed recovery for the period when less than one-half of 1% of oil on the ore was used.

The Circuit Court of Appeals derived its authority to limit the claims to one-half of 1% on the ore from the construction which it placed upon the following clause of the opinion of this court in the former case:

"The patent must be confined to the results obtained by the use of oil within the proportions often described in the testimony and in the claims of the patent as 'critical proportions,' 'amounting to a fraction of 1% on the ore.'"

The reasoning which carried two members of the Court to their conclusion was, that, as shown by the evidence of the patentees and the argument of their counsel, the amount of oil which is "critical," in the sense of marking the point of transition from the processes of the prior art to the process and discovery of the patent, is one-half of 1% of oil on the ore, and that therefore this

*British Ore Concentration Syndicate, Ltd., v. Minerals Separation, Ltd., 25 R. P. C. 741.

Minerals Separation, Ltd. v. British Ore Concentration Syndicate, Ltd., 27 R. P. C. 33.

Ore Concentration Company, Ltd. v. Sulphide Corporation, Ltd., Supreme Court, New South Wales, 31 R. P. C. 216, 217.

Ore Concentration Company, Ltd. v. Sulphide Corporation, 31 R. P. C. 206, Privy Council British Empire.

Minerals Separation, Ltd. v. Hyde, 207 Fed. 956, (D. C. Montana).

Hyde v. Minerals Separation, Ltd., 214 Fed. 100, (C. C. A. 9th Circuit).

Minerals Separation, Ltd. v. Miami Copper Co., 237 Fed. 609 (D. C. Delaware).

Minerals Separation, Ltd. v. Miami Copper Co., 244 Fed. 752 (C. C. A. 3rd Circuit, including dissenting opinion of Judge Buffington, p. 775).

Court, by using the expression quoted, intended to limit the claims, not to a "fraction of 1%" but to a "fraction of one-half of 1% on the ore."

The specification of the patent points out that the proportion of mineral which floats in the form of froth varies with different ores and with different oily substances used and that simple preliminary tests are necessary to determine which oily substance will yield the best results with each ore. Of this feature of the patent this Court said:

"Such variation of treatment must be within the scope of the claims, and the certainty which the law requires in patents is not greater than is reasonable, having regard to their subject matter. . . . The process is one for dealing with a large class of substances and the range of treatment within the terms of the claims, while leaving something to the skill of persons applying the invention, is clearly sufficiently definite to guide those skilled in the art to its successful application, as the evidence abundantly shows. This satisfies the law."

Thus was it plainly held proper for the patentees to claim a reasonable degree of variation—"within the terms of the claims"—in the amount of oil to be used in the application of their discovery in practice, and that the restricting of the amount to a fraction of 1% on the ore was reasonable and lawful.

The two expressions "critical proportions" and "amounting to a fraction of 1% on the ore" being used, the former derived from the evidence and the latter from the claims of the patent, obviously, to the extent that they differ—if they differ at all—the language of the claims must rule in determining the rights of the patentees.

While in the former case this Court was not called upon, and in its opinion did not attempt, to define the scope of the claims, but was considering the patent only from the point of view of the invention and usefulness of the claimed discovery, nevertheless, the language quoted seems to indicate clearly enough that the opinion of the Court then was, as it is declared now to be, that as to the claims here involved the patent extends to and covers the use in the process of oils of the patent, in amounts equal to any fraction of 1% on the ore. The oleic acid claims are in terms limited to 0.02-0.5% on the ore. The Circuit Court of Appeals fell into error in the interpretation which it placed upon our opinion and its judgment in this respect is reversed.

Since the case must be re-tried, there remains to be considered the reversal by the Circuit Court of Appeals of the holding by the District Court that the use of oil by the respondent in excess of 1% on the ore constituted an infringement of the patent.

As we have said, prior to the former decision by this Court, the respondent used in its ore concentration process less than one-half of 1% of oil on the ore, and as to such practice infringement is clear, but from January 9, 1917, to the time of trial, with slight exceptions, it used in excess of 1% on the ore, and it is necessary to consider only the operations during this latter period.

The oil used during this period, was a compound, varying in composition from time to time, but we agree with the District Court in selecting as typical a mixture made up of 18% of pine-oil, and the remainder of petroleum products or derivatives—12% of kerosene oil, and 70% of fuel-oil. Of this compound there was used 30 pounds to the ton of ore, which would be 1.5% on the ore. As thus stated, without more, it is obvious that the use of such an amount of oil, would not infringe the claims of the patent which limit the oil to be used to a fraction of 1% on the ore.

But the contention of the petitioners, approved by the District Court, was, and now is, that kerosene and fuel-oil were inert and valueless, if not harmful, as used by the respondent in the process and rendered the recovery less than it would have been if the pine-oil only had been used; that they were added solely to carry the content of oil beyond the prescribed fraction of 1% on the ore, in the hope of technically avoiding infringement; and that essentially in its operations the respondent used the process of the patent with 0.27 of 1% of pine-oil on the ore, and therefore infringed it.

The respondent replied that it was not true that kerosene and fuel-oil were inert and useless, and asserted that they were oils of the patent, "having a preferential affinity for metalliferous matter;" that the patentees by the claims of their patent had limited their exclusive right to the use, in the process, of any oil or oily substance having such an affinity, but in an amount not greater than a fraction of 1% on the ore, and that, therefore, the process of the respondent, in which more than 1% of oil on the ore was used, did not infringe the patent.

The entire evidence in the Hyde case was introduced on the trial of this case, and whether the petroleum products or derivatives used by the respondent were oils within the scope of the patent must be determined from the record now before us.

It is admitted that petroleum products are "oils having a preferential affinity for metalliferous matter."

In each of the four claims of the "complete specification" of the British patent, filed by the same persons who were patentees of the patent in suit, on June 3, 1905, "petrol" is given as an equivalent of oleic acid in the process. This appears in the statement, repeated in each claim, that the ore and acidified water shall be mixed or agitated with "a small proportion of an oily substance such as oleic or petrol, amounting to a fraction of 1% on the ore." Petrol is the name used in England for gasoline.

The claims of the patent in suit which we are considering call for the use in the process of an "oily liquid," "an oily substance," and in the twelfth claim simply of an "oil." These expressions are said by Professor Chandler, an expert for the petitioners, much relied on in the Hyde case and in this, to include petroleum products.

Higgins, one of the experimenters who discovered the process in suit, and who is much relied upon by the petitioners as an expert witness in both cases, testified as follows in the Hyde case:

Q. Have you since found it possible to use other oils than oleic acid with the result of producing a froth?

A. Yes.

Q. What other oils?

A. I have obtained satisfactory results by the use of petrol and certain proportions of distillate of crude petroleum, such as Cosmos oil."

and he said "Cosmos oil" is "a petroleum distillate."

Chapman, an engineer and a witness for the petitioners in the Hyde case, testified that he had obtained good recoveries in the laboratory and in commercial practice, from the ore of the Braden mine, in Chile, using three pounds of Texas fuel-oil to one pound of American wood-tar oil per ton of ore. Texas fuel-oil is petroleum.

Graninger, an engineer employed by one of the petitioners in installing its flotation plants, testified in this case that in a mine in British Columbia he used a mixture of oil, 75% of which was derived from petroleum.

There is much more of the same character from witnesses for the petitioners and the evidence of the respondent is strongly to the effect that petroleum products are useful and efficient and have been widely used in the process in laboratory and commercial practice.

Without quoting more from the record before us, we must conclude that when the patent in suit was obtained, and even until the testimony in the Hyde case was closed in 1912, petroleum products were recognized by the petitioners, and that they are still used, as oils, efficient, and useful in the process of the patent in suit. Much of this evidence is especially impressive because the papers from which it is derived were written and the witnesses testified before the question as to petroleum, now made in this case, was raised or discussed.

While we thus conclude that petroleum and petroleum products are oils useful in this process of the patent, it is also clear that they are not as highly efficient as pine-oil and several other oils and combinations of oils, which, in the nomenclature of the record are called "frothing oils," and also that better results would probably have been obtained by the use of less than 1% on the ore, of pine-oil alone, than were obtained by the respondent with that oil in combination with the larger amounts of petroleum products. And this presents the further question necessary to a decision of the case, viz.:

Does the use of a more efficient, in combination with a less efficient, oil of the patent, constitute infringement, where the former is used in an amount within the limits of the claims but the combined amount is in excess of such limit, and when the amount of the more efficient oil used would probably produce better results from the process than are produced witth the combination of oils?

To answer this question requires a consideration of the state of the prior art as it was when the discovery of the patent was made, and of the scope of the claims which we are considering.

It is always difficult to recover the realities of a situation long past, such as we have here, but it is especially difficult when the importance of the discovery has led, as in this case, to extensive improvements in mechanical appliances for utilizing the invention and to large additions to the knowledge of the adaptability to the process of various oils, singly and in combination.

We held in the former case that the patentees came late into the field of ore concentration investigation and that their discovery rests upon a prior art so fully developed that it was "clear from the record that approach was being made slowly but more and more nearly to the result which was reached by the patentees of the process in suit in March 1905," and that their final step was not a long one.

Such a patent, in such a field of investigation, must be construed strictly, but candidly and fairly, to give to the patentees the full benefit, but not more, of the disclosure of their discovery which is to become a part of the public stock of knowledge upon the expiration of the patent period, and which was the consideration for the grant to them of a patent monopoly.

With the state of the prior art in mind, we come to consider the nature and extent of the disclosures of the patent in suit, but only with respect to the kinds and quantities of oil which may be used in the process.

The specification recites that the invention of the patent relates to an "improvement" upon prior processes employed in ore concentration "by means of oils, fatty acids, or other substances which have a preferential affinity for metalliferous matter over gangue."

Next come the specific disclosures required by the patent law (R. S. 4888), which are intended to describe the advance which the patentees claimed to have made from the prior art Cattermole agglomeration of metalliferous matter into granules, which separate from the gangue, and sink to the bottom of the pulp under treatment, to the discovery of the patent in suit, with its metal bearing froth, rising to the surface of the pulp. Here is the essence of the discovery and it is announced in these terms:

"We have found that if the proportion of oily substance be considerably reduced, say to a fraction of 1% on the ore, granulation ceases to take place, and after vigorous agitation there is a tendency for a part of the oil-coated metalliferous matter to rise to the surface of the pulp in the form of a froth or scum."

This is followed by the description of three "factors" on which "this tendency is dependent," viz: slight acidification, heat, and fine pulverization of the ore, and then the disclosure concludes with the statement that the proportion of mineral which floats in the form of froth varies with different ores and with different oily substances, and that a simple preliminary test is necessary to determine which oily substance yields the proportion of froth or scum desired.

The only additional statement contained in the specification, which is in the nature of a disclosure, is found in the description of the example of the application of the invention, in which it is stated that the "froth or scum" derives its power of flotation mainly from the inelusion of air-bubbles introduced into the mass by agitation, such bubbles or air-films adhering only to the mineral particles which are coated with oleic acid.

There remain the claims of the patent, in which the Act of Congress requires that the patentee shall "particularly point out and distinctly claim "the . . . improvement . . . which he claims as his invention or discovery." And of these this court has said in *Keystone Bridge Co. v. Phoenix Iron Co.*, 95 U. S. 274, 278:

"But the courts have no right to enlarge a patent beyond the scope of its claim as allowed by the Patent Office. . . . As patents are procured *ex parte*, the public is not bound by them, but the patentees are. And the latter cannot show that their invention is broader than the terms of their claim; or, if broader, they must be held to have surrendered the surplus to the public."

And in *White v. Dunbar*, 119 U. S. 47, 52:

"The claim is a statutory requirement, prescribed for the very purpose of making the patentee define precisely what his invention is; and it is unjust to the public, as well as an evasion of the law, to construe it in a manner different from the plain import of its terms."

And see *Motion Picture Patents* Co. v. *Universal Film* Co., 243 U. S. 502, 510.

Since we are concerned only with the five "fraction of 1% claims," and since the question we are discussing relates only to the use of petroleum products, we need consider them only with respect to the amount and character of the oil prescribed, and, as they are substantially identical, we quote the first as typical:

"The herein described process of concentrating ores which consists in mixing powdered ore with water, adding a small proportion of oily liquid having a preferential affinity for metalliferous matter (amounting to *a fraction* of 1% on the ore), agitating the mixture until the oil-coated mineral matter forms into a froth, and separating the froth from the remainder by flotation."

The first three claims declare that, so far as oil is concerned, the discovery resides or consists in "adding a small proportion of an oily liquid having a preferential affinity for metalliferous matter, amounting to a fraction of 1% on the ore;" the fourth claim differs only in substituting the word "substance" for "liquid" in the first three; and the twelfth claim provides for carrying out the process with "oil in water containing a fraction of 1% of oil on the ore."

From this consideration of the terms of the patent as written, it is apparent that it makes no differentiation whatever, either in the claims or in the specification, among the oils having a preferential affinity for metalliferous matter, and that its disclosure, to which the petitioners must be limited, is, that when a fraction of 1% on the ore of any such oil is used in the manner prescribed, there will be produced a metal-bearing froth, the result of the process. No notice is given to the public, and it is nowhere "particularly pointed out" in the claims, that some oils or combination of oils, having a preferential affinity for metalliferous matter, are more useful than others in the process, or that some may be used successfully and some not, or that some are "frothing oils," a designation not appearing in the patent, and that some are not. The patentees discovered the described process for producing the result or effect, the metal-bearing froth, but they did not invent that result or troth.—*their patent is on the process, it is not and cannot be on the result,*—and the scope of their rights is limited to the means they have devised and described as constituting the process. *Corning v. Burden*, 15 How. 252, 268; *LeRoy v. Tatham*, 14 How. 156, 175; *Fuller v. Yentzer*, 94 U. S. 288; *Robinson on Patents*, Section 149.

The patent in suit was applied for in this country on May 29, 1905, within a few weeks after the discovery which it embodies was made, and whether from haste or lack of investigation, from the necessity of meeting the exigencies imposed by the prior art or from a desire to make the claims as comprehensive as possible, this discussion of its terms makes it clear, that the only disclosure as to the kind and amount of oil which the patentees made to the public as necessary to the practising of their process is that it must be an oil or oily substance, or oily liquid having a "preferential affinity for metalliferous matter," and that it shall be limited in amount "to a fraction of 1% on the ore."

It is argued that the provision of the claims that the mixture prescribed, of oil, water, and ore, shall be agitated until the oil-coated mineral matter forms into a froth, serves to differentiate the "frothing oils" from others having the required preferential affinity for metalliferous matter but which, when agitated in the mixtures, may not produce the characteristic froth, if any such there are, and that a proper construction of the patent limits it to such "frothing oils" and renders the use of them in a fraction of 1% on the ore an infringement when used with "non-frothing oils" having the required affinity in amounts sufficient to make the combination exceed the quantity limit of the patent.

To give such a construction to the patent would subordinate the clear description contained in it of what are oils of the process, to an implied and vague description and classification which would leave the whole subject again at large, to become a field for further experimentation, without definition in the patent of what oils or froths would satisfy it. So interpreted the patent could not reasonably be said to contain a disclosure of the discovered process in the "full, clear, concise and exact terms" required by law (R. S. 4888) and the claims might conceivably be said to fall short of "particularly pointing out and distinctly claiming" any discovery at all within the meaning of the Act of Congress.

Thus when to our former conclusion that the respondent used an efficient oil of the patent, we add the further conclusions, derived from a study of its terms, that the patentees failed to differentiate among the oils described in the patent, we must conclude that it is impossible for the courts to distinguish among them, as more or less efficient in the process, without amending the claims of the patent and this they are powerless to do.

We are confirmed in the conclusion thus arrived at by

the evidence which the patentees in the *Hyde* case, petitioners in this, introduced to show that their discovered process could not be made operative when more than a fraction of 1% of oil on the ore was used, and that the use of a greater amount would not produce the typical froth which results from it—this without differentiation among the oils described in the patent, save as to their varying adaptability to different ores.

Thus, Ballantyne, a metallurgist and the patent agent who prepared the patent specifications for the petitioners, when called by them as an expert witness, testifies to intimate relations with the patentees and with their investigations before and since the patented discovery was made, and says:

"I have never seen the agitation-froth process successfully carried out by the use of an amount of oil equal to practically 1% by weight on the ore, and in my opinion 0.9999% of oil would not be a proper quantity (that is to say a suitable and economical quantity), as contemplated by the patent, and would not, therefore, be a suitable fraction of 1%, as contemplated by the patent."

Liebmann, an expert much relied upon by the petitioners, testified:

"Q. I understand from your answer . . . that you have never in your operations . . . obtained any floating mineral-bearing froth when using an amount of oil, or other selective agents, amounting to more than 1% of the weight on the ore. In order that there may be no misunderstanding, will you state whether I have understood you rightly?

"A. That is my recollection."

John Ballot, one of the patentees, testified that he had never seen a froth of the character produced by the patent in suit using a pulp containing more than 1% of oil.

There is much more of similar import in the record. This, however, will suffice, adding only the record of a remarkable incident which occurred in this Court during the argument of the *Hyde* case by Mr. Kenyon for the petitioners:

"Mr. Justice McReynolds: I would like to ask you when in this process of reducing oil your invention came into existence?

"Mr. Kenyon: At about one-half of 1% of oil.

"Mr. Justice McReynolds: Before you got to the one-half of 1% did you have any invention?

"Mr. Kenyon: We were passing from the region of Cattermole, which was a distant—

"Mr. Justice McReynolds: I want to know when your invention came into existence?

"Mr. Kenyon: This invention was not reached. I should say, from those figures, until about 0.5, that is one-half of 1% of oil was reached.

"Mr. Justice McReynolds: At 1% you had no invention?

"Mr. Kenyon: No.

"Mr. Justice McReynolds: At one-half of 1% you did have invention?

"Mr. Kenyon: It began to come. Remote, but it began to come. At 0.3 of 1% the float vastly increased. At 0.1 of 1% the float again vastly increased.

"Mr. Justice McReynolds: When this float has more than one-half of 1% of oil it does not infringe?

"Mr. Kenyon: It does not infringe.

"Mr. Justice Pitney: What have you to say in answer to what Mr. Scott said the other day to the effect that 1.8%, or perhaps more, of oil, would give the same result with increased agitation?

"Mr. Williams: Absolutely no.

"Mr. Kenyon: It would not."

While parties should not be held rigidly to statements made by their counsel in the stress of argument, even when replying to questions from members of the Court, nevertheless these statements from leading counsel in charge of the *Hyde* case and of this case, are impressive and significant.

This and much more of like character in the record brings us unhesitatingly to the conclusion that the scope we have given to the patent, based upon an interpretation of the language of the claims, is justified also by the evidence in the case and that it is, in fact, that which the petitioners and their counsel, until very recently, placed upon it in full confidence, that the essence of the discovery lay to such an extent in the use of a small amount of oil, such as is described in the patent, that the result could not be obtained with more than a fraction of 1% on the ore.

It must be added that the evidence is far from satisfying that the results of the respondent's process was, in fact, that peculiarly superior quality of metal-bearing froth characteristic of the patented process when worked with a fraction of 1% on the ore. The evidence, otherwise doubtful on the point, is rendered especially so by the testimony introduced by the petitioners, and not contradicted, that a computation on the basis of the tonnage of ore treated by the respondent shows that if the process as practiced by it after January 9, 1917, had been used through the year it would have involved a loss of over a million dollars in increased cost of oil and in diminished recoveries, as compared with what the results of operation would have been for the same time using the process of the patent as practiced by the petitioners. It is difficult to see how a process so wasteful and inefficient as that of the respondent is thus proved to be can be other than substantiallly different from that of the petitioners.

It is vaguely suggested in the testimony for the petitioners that there was some peculiarity in the composition of the ore of the respondent, or in the treatment of it, which resulted in the presence of "clayey gangue slimes" which absorbed an unusual quantity of oil and that this contributed to render it possible to produce the results of the patented process when more than the prescribed fraction of 1% of oil on the ore was used.

It is hard to see how this, if true, would be of value to the petitioners, but the evidence is quite too indefinite in character and meagre in extent to be accepted as the basis for the judicial determination of such a claim.

The respondent contends that the disclaimer filed by the petitioners with respect to the three claims held invalid by the decision of this Court in the former case, was so delayed and is so evasive in form that it is invalid and that, for this reason, the petitioners should not be permitted to further prosecute this suit, under the provisions of R. S. 4917, 9422.

The decision holding the three claims invalid was rendered on December 11, 1916, and the disclaimer was recorded on the 28th day of March, 1917. Having regard, to that fact that the owners of the patent in suit resided in a foreign country, and to the war-time conditions of communication then prevailing, the entry required by law was not "unreasonably neglected or delayed." While the wording of the disclaimer borders on finesse, we do not think it can be interpreted as giving any rights under the patent greater than may be legitimately obtained under the claims held valid, and we therefore deem it sufficient to meet the requirements of the statutes cited.

It results that the decree of the Circuit Court of Appeals that the respondent infringed the patent only when using one-half of 1% or less of oil on the ore must be reversed, but that its implied holding that the use made by respondent of petroleum products and pine oil in excess of 1% on the ore did not constitute infringement must be sustained. The cause is remanded to the District Court for further proceedings in conformity with this opinion.

Removal of Amalgam From Plates

By A. J. HERALD and A. KING

*USUAL METHOD AND ITS DISADVANTAGES. It is common practice in many mills to clean the amalgam from the steaming of plates, grinding it up with additional mercury, removing iron, pyrite, etc., in the ordinary way, and then press it into cakes ready for the retort. By this method a clean amalgam in a convenient form for the retort-pans and containing 27 to 30% fine gold is obtained, the amalgam in the process having taken up an additional 18 to 25% of mercury, practically all of which is ultimately recovered from the retort. Where large quantities of steam amalgam have to be handled this method has disadvantages obvious to those acquainted with the operation; several white men, including responsible officials, are tied to the amalgam-room continuously for a number of hours; other work and supervisory duties having to be neglected in the meantime, and the labor involved in carrying out the cleaning and pressing of this product is by no means light. There is always a certain amount of risk and danger in having several thousand ounces of amalgam exposed during the various stages of the process. The retorting and smelting of this cleaned amalgam present no difficulty however, bullion of 890 gold fineness being commonly obtained.

PROPOSED METHOD. The method which the authors have adopted, after slight variations, is as follows: The plates to be steamed are made reasonably clean by washing down and removing iron, etc. (by scraping lightly, if necessary), before steam is applied. After steaming and scraping the crude amalgam is introduced at once into the locked receptacle in which it is to be conveyed ultimately to the melting-room, no grinding with additional mercury being done. When charging the retort-pans a small quantity of oxidizer (such as manganese di-oxide) is sprinkled over the amalgam. The amount of oxidizer used is about 0.5% on the weight of amalgam, and is not enough to cause any ebullition or affect the bullion in any way except to oxidize the iron present in the amalgam so that it may be absorbed readily into the slag as a silicate during the subsequent melting of the retorted bullion. The retorted bullion will probably look impure on account of the iron oxide present, but will yield clean bars of 888 to 891 fineness without refining or skimming.

ADVANTAGES OF PROPOSED METHOD. These are obvious and important, particularly when a large quantity of amalgam has to be handled at a time. The amalgam has only to be weighed after it is taken off the plate, and can then be locked away immediately, risks of all kinds and danger of exposure being therefore reduced to a minimum. Labor is also reduced, no over-time being necessary even when 10,000 oz. of amalgam are steamed. It is also obvious that a smaller stock of mercury can be kept when steam amalgam does not require grinding and cleaning. Further, since the capacity of a retort for cleaned or uncleaned amalgam is practically the same, a greater weight of bullion is obtained from a retort full of the latter, as will be apparent from the figures already given.

If, for convenience of handling, it be desired to get the amalgam into a coherent cake this may be done by mixing the amalgam with water and then pressing. This involves more handling, exposure, and time, and does not seem necessary.

It will be noted that the method advocated is a simplified form of the older method, and in that respect might be taken as an example of an advance in practice by elimination of certain operations which were at one time considered essential rather than by further elaboration of the method. A parallel case is that of eliminating the risks involved in intimately mixing calcined gold-slime with fluxes preparatory to crucible-smelting by introducing the slime and flux into the crucible in separate layers.

*From the Journal of the Chemical, Metallurgical, and Mining Society of South Africa.

DOMESTIC CRYSTALLINE GRAPHITE marketed in 1918, as shown by the final figures compiled by H. G. Ferguson, of the U. S. Geological Survey, is indicated in the table below:

State	Pounds	Value
Alabama	7,705,475	$999,152
New York	3,206,518	273,188
Pennsylvania	1,016,000	112,050
California		
Montana	782,946	70,400
Texas		
	12,861,830	1,454,790
Sales in 1917	10,564,080	1,074,398

A Peculiar Experience in Shaft-Sinking

By ARTHUR JARMAN

INTRODUCTION. At the Waihi Grand Junction mine, in New Zealand, all the hoisting of rock, ore, and men is done through one shaft, which has four compartments besides the pump-and-ladder compartment. Early in 1912, the ore and rock hoisted per day averaged over 400 long tons and the lowest level was at 1098 ft. An air-shaft, 6 by 4 ft. in the clear, connected with the 494-ft. level and was used for ventilation only, being equipped with a Sirocco fan rated at 40,000 cu. ft. per minute. To facilitate the exploration and working of the eastern portion of the company's ground, it was decided to sink another shaft about 1150 ft. east of the main shaft, a suitable site being available, unencumbered by buildings and well situated with regard to the underground workings.

The first 80 ft. of sinking was made difficult by a pocket of mud encountered in the north-western corner of the shaft at a depth of 35 ft. An account of this work is given herewith.

PRELIMINARY WORK. Before excavating for foundations or erecting any gear, a trial pit, 5 by 5 ft., was sunk. This passed through firm clay, and at 22 ft. had bottomed in the so-called punice-rock of the district, which is really a much altered rhyolite with large porphyritic crystals.

The surface of the rhyolite dipped north-west about 15°, but at the proposed site of the engine-house it was exposed, as shown in plan on Fig. 1, and it is also seen at other places south and east of the shaft-site within a radius of 100 feet.

As everything appeared satisfactory, the shaft was started at full size, and was sunk and timbered for 11 ft., there being two compartments 3 ft. 9 in. by 6 ft. and one 6 ft. 6 in. by 6 ft. in the clear, the latter being for pump-and-ladder way. An old head-frame was erected, together with a hoisting-engine, boiler, economizer, and chimney, after which sinking was resumed.

THE RUSH OF MUD. When the fifth set of timber was put in, at a depth of 25 ft., the ground was firm with the exception of the north-western corner, in which the clay had given place to a soft white mud, the surface of the rhyolite having dipped almost vertically along the line *AB* as shown in the plan, Fig. 1. On prodding with a drill, the mud appeared to occupy a large cavity, and therefore particular attention was paid to this corner. Slabs were set closely behind the timber, and sacking packed behind them to stop the mud from running. The shaft-engineer inspected the corner every 45 minutes or so, and sinking and timbering proceeded very slowly, the mud being soft and troublesome. After sinking about 10 ft. in this way (total depth, 35 ft.) soft white mud entered and filled the shaft to a depth of 15 ft. in two or three seconds, the inrush being so sudden as to completely submerge one of the men. The others, however, sprang onto the ladder and timbers. On rising to the surface of the mud, the unlucky one was quickly pulled out, rather scared, but fortunately uninjured except for some bruises.

Simultaneously with this inrush of mud, the surface gave way under the north-western leg of the head-frame, the concrete foundation-block 5 by 4 by 6 ft. and surrounding ground falling six feet along the outline marked *C C C* on the plan, the concrete block disappearing under the subsoil.

The head-frame was thrown out of plumb, and the 'rub' of the falling ground dragged the shaft-timbers down 26 inches at the north-west corner and 19 inches

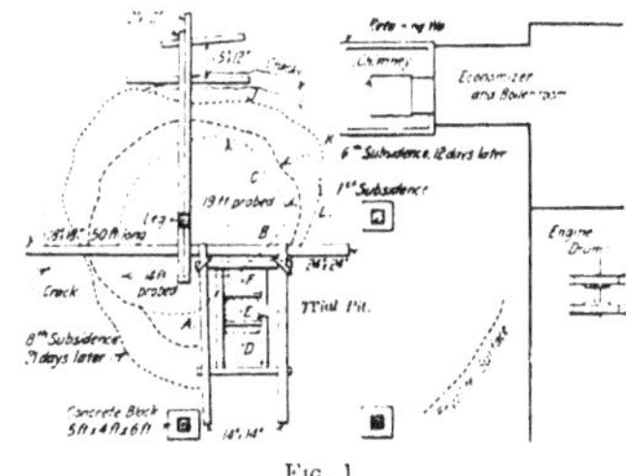

FIG. 1

at the north-east corner, the bearer under the collar-set being left without support at its western end. Fortunately, the leg affected was one on the side remote from the engine-house, so that stresses due to hoisting would have the effect of pulling the leg upward.

THE SUBSIDENCE. The hole at the surface was filled with subsoil as quickly as possible in order to support the walls of the cavity and prevent them from crumbling away. At the same time, slabs that had slipped down from behind the two top sets of shaft-timbers were renewed, so as to keep the soil from falling down the shaft. Support was then arranged for the shaft-timbers as shown in Fig. 3 and Fig. 4. An old leg of a head-frame was laid across the pit, or subsidence, to bridge the space. This timber was 50 ft. long and 24 by 24 inches, tapering to 18 by 18 inches at the smaller end. It was placed east and west at the north end of the shaft, and had more than 10 ft. of bearing surface at each end.

Upon this were laid 16-ft. baulks 14 by 14 inches, one along the eastern side and the other along the western side of the shaft, and from the northern ends of these the northern bearer of the collar set was suspended by straps and inch bolts; upon tightening these, the strain upon the shaft-timbering was relieved, the west end being raised 19 inches and the east end 7 inches. See plan, Fig. 1, and elevation, Fig. 3.

The suspended leg of the head-frame then came in for its share of attention. Two bearers, 12 by 12 inches and about 40 ft. long, were placed under it, resting on the 24 by 24-in. timber at one end, and at the other (north) end supported by timbers resting upon the ground. The ground here showed small cracks running parallel with the edges of the subsidence, hence the use of these timbers to obtain a bearing surface. The leg was then raised 15 inches by driving wedges under it, until the head-frame was straightened sufficiently to allow hoisting to proceed. The centre-line remained rather more than an inch out of plumb.

The slabbing of the shaft-timbers having had further attention, the mud was bailed out by hand. The trucks used for sinking were made without a door so that they were available for bailing.

Sinking Resumed. Mud flowed into the shaft at the corner on the slightest Provocation, but by excavating the rest of the shaft first, and forcing slabs into the soft mud at the north-western corner, by aid of jacks, it was possible to get a new set of timber into position and afterward slab the ground behind it. The mud was steadily on the move, oozing slowly nearly all the time, and had to be watched constantly by one of the party. It had the consistence of thick syrup. If its movement increased seriously, all hands retired 6 or 10 ft. up the timbers until it quieted down again. This movement was from the floor just inside the timbers in the north-western corner. Slowly, and with difficulty, a set would be placed in position and slabs secured behind it. Several rushes of mud occurred, and it was evident that the mud-hole was much larger than was at first thought. Over 100 cubic yards of filling had already been used.

Size of the Mud-hole. It therefore became necessary to find out what the extent of the hole was, as it might be necessary to abandon the shaft or seriously modify the procedure then being followed. The shaft was about 40 ft. down, and the expenditure upon it amounted to over $20,000, including equipment.

Probing by means of ¾-in. pipe, screwing lengths together as required, showed an almost vertical wall 32 ft. deep and a cavity approximately 15 by 20 ft. in width. See Fig. 1 and 2. The next step was to ascertain whether this cavity extended under the other compartment of the shaft. Three holes therefore were put down, using a 4-in. star-bit drill and a sludge-pump, one hole in the centre of each compartment, as shown in the vertical section, Fig. 1. The results were as follows:

D = pump and ladder-way compartment.

5 ft. of firm rock ('pumice').
14 ft. of softer rock, progress one inch per stroke.
7 ft. of firm rock.

26 ft. total.

E = south winding compartment.

10 ft. of firm rock.
8 ft. of soft rock, progress two inches per stroke.
22 ft. of firm rock.

40 ft. total.

F = north winding compartment.

10 ft. of firm rock.
8 ft. of soft 'pug', or gouge.
22 ft. of firm rock.

40 ft. total.

The walls of D and E stood well, and looked quite clean after clearing them with the sludge-pump. F did not stand well, the slime oozed out at the top from time to time, thus proving it to be directly connected with the mud-hole as shown in Fig. 1.

From the probing already made it appeared that the mud-hole would have a capacity of at least 414 cu. yd. (measurement of the filling used showed 409 cu. yd. excavated; allowing 10% increase, we get 450 cu. yd., but this measurement was only obtainable after all the difficulties were overcome and the filling material had stopped subsiding).

Procedure Adopted. From the size of the mud-hole and the fact that it would continue at the corner of the shaft for another 30 ft., it was evident that a large mass of mud had to be displaced and would come into the shaft from time to time. Sinking was continued slowly, filling the subsiding ground at the surface to support the sides of the hole and to thicken the mud by making it drier. The latter object was not attained, however, as the soil and mud rarely mixed, the mud that forced its way into the shaft being rarely discolored by the soil or the clay.

The northern end of the shaft was always left until the rest of the shaft was excavated and ready for timbering. If mud was troublesome, a dam or barrier of ground was left to keep the mud in check in the northern compartment while excavating the southern end; or a rough timber dam was rigged. The mud was baled out from behind this at intervals. When excavating the north end, slabs had to be forced into the mud to support it as far as possible; and, when placing timber in position, one man would shovel or scoop the mud out with his hand while another watched the mud coming up slowly from the floor. A mud-rush would be preceded by an increased movement from the floor, the mud squeezing up alongside the line AB in plan, Fig. 1, like a gigantic sausage, which was too soft to retain its shape when released. When this began to move at one to two inches per second, the whole party would take to the ladder-way and timbers. After expelling about 30 to 50 cu. ft. the mud would become more liquid, and with a 'flip-flop-flip-flop' the shaft would be filled to a depth of 5 to 10 ft. in two or three seconds, this representing

700 to 1400 cu. ft. of mud. The rustling of the earth against the slabs told of the subsidence of the filling overhead, and very soon the call would come "Below

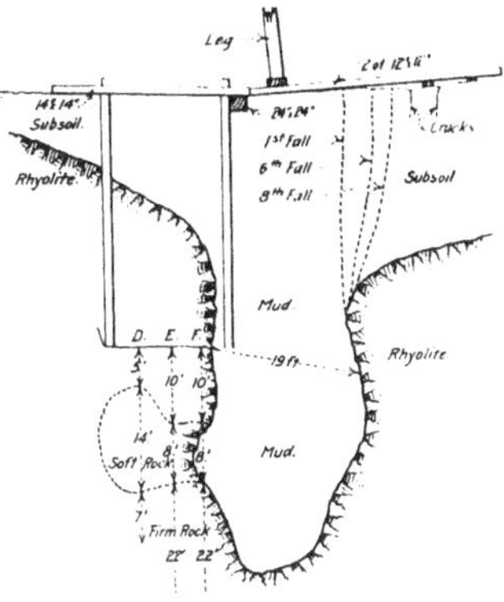

FIG. 2

there! the ground's sunk another 3 ft.," or whatever the amount might be.

As slabs were apt to be displaced and become dangerous to the workers below, panels were substituted for them, with good results, because these were very seldom displaced. After a 'rush', all hands commenced filling at the surface, bailing being postponed until the filling was in a forward state.

THE TIMBERING, shown in Fig. 3 and 4, illustrates the difficulty of supporting the north-western corner, the bearer breaking as shown in the drawing, Fig. 4, and the wall-plate on the western wall of the sixth set breaking also. The lowest set was therefore packed and wedged up from the floor of the shaft particularly along the western wall, thus relieving the strain upon the timbers higher up. The western side was cut last of all, and as soon as a new set had been put into position with its struts and packing-pieces the western side was again wedged up and jacked up from the floor.

Above the eighth set a central bearer 14 by 12 inches was placed having 18 inches of bearing at each end. No. 7 set was wedged up from this, the packing-pieces below were removed and No. 8 was then hung from No. 7 in the usual way. Pressure made it necessary to use 6 by 12-in. and 8 by 12-in. dividers, and insert them as soon as the set was in position. Hence a short cross-cut, or 'cuddy', was driven into the ground for 10 ft. south of the shaft to enable the 17-ft. wall-plates to be brought into position, otherwise they could not be lowered past the dividers. Later, another cross-cut was required for the same reason, after which the side pressure eased off.

Using a central bearer as above, the wall-plate or side-timber of each set on the western wall supported the downward pressure at the northern end by acting as a cantilever, the northern being the free end. The sixth set broke and the tenth also, later on, as shown in Fig. 4, and extra packing had to be used to support the northern end in each case.

This tenth set was supported by a 14 by 12-in. bearer with 4 ft. of bearing at each end, and the breaking of No. 10 wall-piece was due to a larger rush than usual, which caused the timber at the north-eastern corner to subside slightly, and the ground at the surface to subside two feet along the line *JKL*, which was uncomfortably near the foundations of the chimney. The roots and limbs of a white pine projected from the mud and had to be sawn away before the next set of timber could be placed in position.

After putting the twelfth set, at 50 ft. depth, a mud-rush occurred over-night, and it was then found that

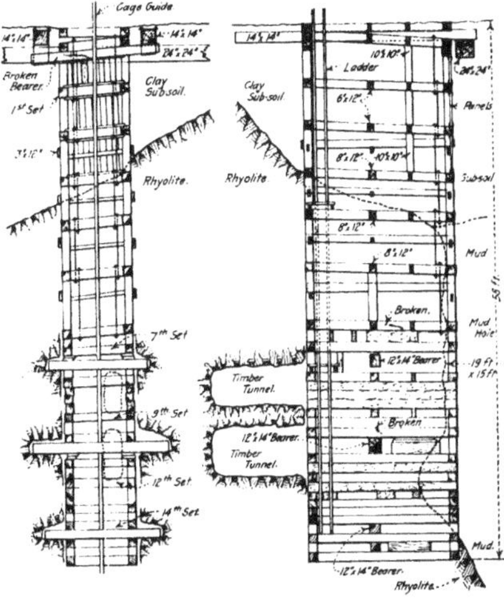

FIG. 3

FIG. 4

the bearers at the top of the shaft were free from strain, the nuts being loose on the suspension bolts from the temporary 14 by 14-in. bearers at the sides of the shaft at the northern end. From this we knew that the two special centre-bearers under the seventh and tenth sets had relieved the upper sets from the weight and drag of the north-western corner. Sets were placed two feet apart and a central bearer 14 by 12 in. was put under the fourteenth set.

Another run of liquid slime occurred, after which probing showed the depth of mud in the corner of the shaft to be only 4 ft. and the farthest distance out sideways only 8 ft. At 58 ft. deep, the sixteenth set was put in, the whole of the ground in the north-western corner now being firm rock. Sinking was continued down to 71 ft., when the northern corners were tested by drill-holes and found to be good firm rock, after which hitches were cut and bearers 14 by 18 in. by 14 ft. were put in at each end and the timbers supported upon these. The set at the top of the shaft was straightened, new posts inserted, and slabbing renewed where required. It was found that the north-western corner had to be raised a further 19 inches and the north-eastern corner 7 inches to bring them level, and the leg of the head-frame was set up a further 12 inches to line up. Filling material was spread over the area that subsided as shrinkage required it, and this ground became firm.

CONCLUSION. It had taken 11 weeks to sink the last 43 ft., and now, at 78 ft. deep, our mud troubles being over, a contract was let for sinking. Good progress was made, 46 ft. in the first 10 days, but when we reached a total depth of 183 ft. labor troubles stopped operations for over six months. Water accumulated in the shaft to 12 ft. from the collar, but when work was resumed and the water pumped out, half a dozen truck-loads of soil sufficed to make good the small depression at the surface, thus showing everything to be in good order.

The mud-hole was rather deep to be due to the river action alone, and no boulder or other hard object was detected when probing, so it was probably not a large pot-hole. It seems more likely that it was an old fumarole, of which there are many active examples in the adjoining thermal district of Rotorua. There have been no other mud-holes found when sinking shafts at Waihi.

W. McConachie and W. Johnson, mine-manager and shaft-engineer, respectively, were responsible for this work; and Matthew Paul, Inspector of Mines, approved of the methods taken to ensure safe working.

COMMENTS. If the shaft had been 10 ft. farther south, the mud-hole would not have been found. It is evidently much better to put down several boreholes, one for the shaft-centre and one for each leg of the head-frame, than to trust to a trial-pit, even though the rock of the district outcrops only 20 ft. away. The observed dip of the rock at the bottom of the trial pit, about 15°, did not suggest anything unusual. If the shaft be completed in the future, piles will have to be driven into the ground under the north-western leg of the head-frame in order to ensure safe foundation.

This Notice Appeals

In the psychology of persuasion, the first principle is that a person is most interested in that which directly

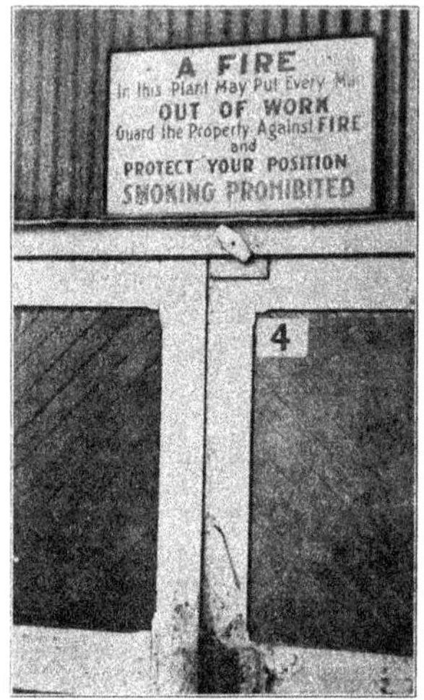

concerns himself, or in what comes within the range of his experience. This cleverly worded notice takes advantage of the above principle, making a direct appeal to the employee by subtly suggesting an empty pay-envelope. This notice is to be seen in the Anaconda plant, at Butte.

CRUDE GYPSUM mined in the United States in 1918 amounted to 2,056,462 short tons, a decrease of 639,764 tons, or 24% from the output of 1917, according to R. W. Stone, of the U. S. Geological Survey. The decrease was due to the reduction in building operations throughout the country required by the local and national Governments. New York led with an output of 606,268 tons, followed by Iowa with 461,864 tons, Michigan with 375,-803 tons, Texas with 257,328 tons, and California with 30,552 tons. The decrease in production was least in New York, where the output fell off only 12%; in Oklahoma, Michigan, and Ohio, the decrease was 20 to 26%, or about the average for the country. Texas suffered the greatest reduction in output, or about 39%. Utah was the only State that produced more gypsum in 1918 than in 1917.

KINGMAN, ARIZONA

RECENT DEVELOPMENTS IN MOHAVE COUNTY.

The Standard Minerals Co., operating a molybdenum property 24 miles east of Kingman, has opened a rich orebody in the Standard claim. The value across 30 inches of vein averaged $80 gold and 325 oz. silver per ton. A contract to sink to the 100-ft. level has been let and the work is under way. The company is operating a 40-ton flotation plant on the molybdenite-copper ore.

The Hackberry mill, at Hackberry, under the management of T. D. Walsh, is crushing 90 tons in 12 hours and making a high-grade concentrate. This is one of the first successful oil-flotation mills on lead-zinc ores in Mohave county. The lead and zinc products are high enough to meet smelter conditions, the lead carrying close to 200 oz. of silver. The mine stopes are being opened and will soon be able to meet the full requirements of the mill, when three shifts will be operated.

The Dorothy mine at Chloride is being equipped with a hoisting plant and other machinery, and the shaft sunk to the 300-ft. level. A tunnel has entered the Dorothy vein 125 ft. and a winze was sunk in 6 ft. of ore, which returned $40 net per ton in car lots. Water stopped sinking, a raise was driven to the surface, and a working shaft timbered. Sinking is under way.

The projected tunnel that is to serve the mines of Stockton hill, 11 miles north of Kingman, is soon to be in operation, Pittsburgh, Pennsylvania, people having completed the financing of the Arizona Butte company. The tunnel is to have a length of 10,000 ft., and will cut the vein near the summit of the Cerhat range at a depth of 1500 ft. Many of the important veins of that area will be cut at 1000 ft., and the whole mineralized area drained. A big vein—the Prince George—will be followed most of the length of the tunnel. The veins that will be cut by the tunnel have been heavy silver-lead producers for years.

The first mill-run by the Arizona Molybdenum Co., in the Cedar district, which recently put in new K & K machines, is reported to be a success. The new machines are making a good separation of the copper and molybdenite, the copper concentrate being clean and the molybdenite being rather free of copper and gangue.

The Twins mine, owned by the Daisell Mining Co., has at last picked up the vein beyond the fault on the 150-ft. level, and is now driving in 6 ft. of heavy sulphide ore. The vein faulted at the 80-ft. level, and although considerable effort was made to pick it up again failure has resulted. The shaft was carried to 300 ft., but no vein was found. The company now intends to start a cross-cut to cut the vein upon the lower level, and proceed with the further exploration of the property. From the surface to the 80-ft. level shipping ore was taken out, the principal metal being lead, with gold and silver.

M. B. Dudley has just returned from Los Angeles, where he purchased a 50-hp. electric hoist, an 80-kw. motor and a large compressor for the Rural mine, at

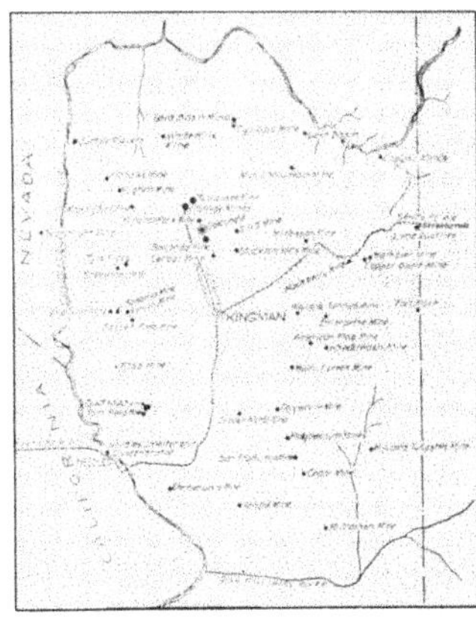

SOME OF THE MINING DISTRICTS OF MOHAVE COUNTY, ARIZONA

Mineral Park, which he and New York associates recently purchased. The machinery will be delivered immediately, and power is soon to be connected with the mine. A 100-ton mill is to be erected at once. It is estimated that there is sufficient ore on dumps of the Rural and Buckeye mines and in the stopes to keep a plant of that capacity in operation for the next year without further development. Streaks of rich silver ore have been found throughout the old workings.

A fine orebody has been found in the east drift of the Adams lode, at Oatman, after passing through a faulted zone. About 4 ft. of the 12-ft. vein assays nearly $40 in gold. A raise is also being driven in ore that carries as high as $90 per ton, although the orebody is narrower.

A cross-cut in the Tom Reed mine has passed through 6 ft of $15 ore in a new vein. This has been driven from a level in old workings at a depth of 400 ft. Virgin ground runs from this level to the surface, the strike being made in new ground. Tom Reed is also driving on a new vein found at 400 ft. in Bald Eagle ground, which is said to carry good milling ore. This property is the largest in the Oatman district and has many important veins that have not been thoroughly prospected.

HOUGHTON, MICHIGAN

COPPER STOCKS ON HAND AT SMELTERS AND DOCKS.

Copper on hand at Lake Superior smelting plants early in June did not aggregate 30,000,000 lb. Some of the mines have small quantities stored in New York warehouses, but practically none abroad. The total on hand is just one month's output of the Michigan mines, operating under normal conditions. Calumet & Hecla and subsidiaries have the largest amount, namely, 20,000,000 lb. This is at the plant at Hubbell and the Lake Superior Smelting Co.'s plant, a subsidiary, at Dollar Bay. This latter works was shut-down late in May, and all smelting hereafter will be done at Hubbell. A fair quantity of mass copper at Dollar Bay was re-shipped to Hubbell for reduction. Whether the Dollar Bay plant will be re-opened when conditions improve is not known now. Since the opening of navigation, shipments of metal have been heavy, and practically all of the copper has been sent out to fill urgent orders. There is practically no copper on the Copper Range docks at Houghton. The Michigan Smelting Co., which handles all of the Copper Range output, as well as the Mohawk, Wolverine, and other properties, has 4,000,000 lb. This is not embarrassing, although it is an accumulation that is not normal.

RENO, NEVADA

SAMPLING OF ORE SHIPMENTS AIDED IN NEVADA.

The State Ore Sampler, Francis Church Lincoln, has sent out copies of the State Ore Sampler Law, which superseded the State Assayer Law. The new regulations were approved March 27, 1919. The new law is broader in its scope than the old one, since it provides for the supervision of sampling of Nevada ores wherever they are purchased, and authorizes the Sampler to obtain rates for shippers, call for umpire assays, and fix reasonable charges. As ore producers, miners naturally wish to receive the greatest possible returns. The State Ore Sampler Department will be glad to assist in doing this by every legal means. It will advise concerning shipments free of charge; and will take charge of shipments at a reasonable rate—checking the weight, supervising the sampling, determining the moisture, assaying the pulp, calling for umpire when necessary, and mailing full reports. To secure this service it is only necessary to notify the State Ore Sampler at the State Mining Laboratory, Reno, Nevada, and to mark bills-of-lading "Care Nevada State Ore Sampler". At Hazen there is a minimum charge of $5 on small lots, and 25 cents per ton is charged on lots in excess of 20 tons. At the Selby Smelting Works and at the Nichols plant of the General Chemical Co., in California, there is a minimum rate of $7.50 on small lots and a charge of 25 cents per ton on lots in excess of 30 tons. At the Mammoth smelter in California and the Garfield and Murray smelters in Utah, the minimum rate is $6.25 on lots of less than 25 tons. Minimum rates at other points will be fixed as rapidly as possible, but at present rates at purchasing points not mentioned are actual costs of supervision for lots of less than 50 tons, and 25 cents per ton on lots of 50 tons or more. Special low rates may be made upon large lots to suit local conditions.

GOLD HILL, OREGON

COPPER, QUICKSILVER, AND GOLD MINING, AND CONTEMPLATED EXTENSIONS; ALSO ROAD CONSTRUCTION.

Gold mining companies in this region that took up the extraction of chrome, copper, manganese, and mercury during the War, and expected to resume the mining of gold afterward, are now fully convinced that the scarcity and high prices of labor and machinery will cause a prolonged suspension of a general resumption of gold mining in this region and in northern California.

The only copper property operating at present in southern Oregon is the Blue Ledge group on the Oregon-California boundary in the upper Applegate district. Its weekly output is three cars of ore carrying over 12%. The wagon haul to shipping at Jacksonville is 35 miles, at a cost of $11 per ton. The Tacoma, Washington, smelter, which is treating the ore, recently had officials at the mine and propose to double the output by handling lower-grade ore.

The Rainier Mercury Co., of Tacoma, has been operating two 12-pipe furnaces on rich cinnabar, with a daily output of three flasks during the past two years from the Utah group of 35 claims, north of Gold Hill. The new organization, the War Eagle Mining Co., recently organized at Medford, and composed principally of local men, has taken the property over, doing some development and operating the present plant. They propose to erect a 500-ton furnace during the coming season to calcine lower-grade ore, and claim that they can produce mercury at $55 per flask at a profit.

The original old channel or bed of the ancient river, recently uncovered in the Esterly placer mine in the Waldo district, west of Gold Hill, is being successfully developed, operating in gravel carrying coarse gold. After passing through a barren zone on the bed-rock sluiced off years ago, a pit to the depth of 25 ft. has been piped below the level of the former workings, at a point between two benches of bedrock. This pit opens a bed of gravel entirely different in character from clay banks that were so profitable during the past years. The depth of this gravel has not yet been determined, neither has any clean-up been made on which to show high gold content. Heretofore, the gold recovered at this mine has been fine and flour gold, and evenly distributed through the clay banks, which are from 10 to 40 ft. deep. This property, formerly known as the Logan mine, and the Simmons mine, has been worked at a large profit during the past 50 years, and consists of 4200 acres, practically all profitable placer ground. Water-right consists of 14,000 inches, and is supplied by a system of ditches 25 miles in length. It was purchased in 1916 at a cost of $140,000 by Seattle people, with George M. Esterly at the head as manager and superintendent, and has been yielding for some

CALIFORNIA-OREGON BOUNDARY REGION

years $40,000 in gold dust and $10,000 in platinum annually. The lack of grade for the dumping of tailing led to the erection of a hydraulic elevator system, the residue being lifted 73 ft. by two elevators. With the opening of the new pit an additional elevator has been erected, making a total lift of 89 ft. above the pit. All the standard placer gold-saving devices are in use, but due to the fineness of the gold much is lost and carried over in the tailing. It is proposed to dispense with this system this coming season at a cost estimated from $40,000 to $50,000, by opening a race through a 700-ft. tunnel through serpentine to the west fork of the Illinois river. The daily capacity of the mine at present is 1000 cu. yd., at an average cost of 6 cents per yard, but with the new system the capacity will be greatly increased, with a reduction of operating cost.

Yreka, California.—The San Francisco District Forester's office has notified the Yreka forest office of the awarding of two contracts for road construction on the proposed Happy Camp-Klamath River road, the section of 15 miles near Happy Camp being let to W. A. Bechtel of San Francisco for $215,000. This still leaves 26 miles to Orleans unaccounted for. Nearly all of this road will be cut out of rocky mountain sides. Another contract for 7½ miles between Orleans and Somes Bar in Humboldt county has been let to William B. Arndt, of San Francisco, for $150,000. The contracts for the construction of the balance of the road between Orleans and Happy Camp are expected to be let later in the season. All this road construction is being undertaken by the Department of Agriculture, Forestry Division.

GRASS VALLEY, CALIFORNIA

LABOR TROUBLES SUSPEND OPERATIONS.

At the time of changing shifts on June 13 a delegation from each department waited upon A. B. Foote, manager of the North Star mine, and demanded a 50-cent increase in pay per shift for each man underground. This was refused, and every man, 120 in all, left the property. The present scale is $4 for machine-men and $3.50 for shovelers, with bonuses for extra work. The causes are conjectured at this time. One report is that men received from the outside are getting more pay than the old hands, and another that such men receive their fare if they remain a month. The company denies the first charge, but a short time ago when men were leaving for Divide, Nevada, in such numbers as to seriously affect operations, the company advertised that the fare of men coming from the outside and remaining a month would be guaranteed them in addition to the usual mine wage. Everybody knew of that, and no dissatisfaction has openly appeared because of such guarantee. The day shift followed the night men at the North Star mine, and all underground work ceased. The strike then spread to the Empire where the men quit in a body, without consulting the management. A mass-meeting was held on the afternoon of the 14th, presided over by J. B. Bennetts. The position was discussed and committees appointed to present demands upon the management of the Allison Ranch, Champion, Empire, North Star, Orleans, and Pennsylvania. These are the large properties operating at present. The gist of the argument was to the effect that the miners could not support their families on the wages now paid, due to the increasing cost of living. Some alleged that local merchants were 30% and upward over Sacramento prices. Surface men present were requested to join the movement, but there was not a single response. The sense of the meeting was that all top men should demand a raise of 50 cents. Committees were appointed to encourage these men in that direction. Mr. Foote, of the North Star, is insistent upon closing indefinitely rather than accede to the demand. He states that under present conditions the mine is about holding its own and has not paid a dividend since the outbreak of the War. [One is to be paid on June 28.] A strike pledge was signed and a relief fund discussed. It seems that the bonus system has not been popular—the men want a flat rate of a 50-cent raise.

THE · MINING SUMMARY

ARIZONA

Ajo.—New Cornelia in May produced 1,866,000 lb. of copper, about half of normal.

Bisbee.—Calumet & Arizona pays 50 cents per share on June 26. This is equal to $321,231, and makes $1.50 ($963,693) for 1919, and $42,096,351 to date.

Calumet & Arizona in May produced 3,848,000 lb. of copper, compared with 4,768,000 lb. a year ago.

The Phelps Dodge properties in May yielded 8,355,900 lb. of copper, less than half of normal.

Clifton.—Arizona Copper Co. in May produced 2,400,000 lb. of copper, against 4,130,000 lb. a year ago.

Globe.—Old Dominion in May produced 2,564,000 lb. of copper, 700,000 lb. less than a year ago.

Jerome.—United Verde Copper Co. paid $1.50 per share to its 22 holders early in June. The amount was $450,000, making $900,000 for 1919 and $51,497,000 to date.

Operations are to be resumed at the Green Monster. The main shaft of the Silver Tip claim is to be unwatered and exploration carried on to develop the silver vein. The company is to sink a 200-ft. incline shaft on this claim.

Miami.—Inspiration Consolidated produced 6,200,000 lb. of copper in May, 5,000,000 lb. below capacity. Miami produced 4,989,580 lb., up to the average.

Oatman.—The United Eastern pays 7 cents per share on June 28. This is $95,410, making $517,940 for 1919 and $1,771,900 to date.

Driving on the 400-ft. level of the Bald Eagle claim of the Tom Reed mine has opened 6 ft. of gold ore said to average $15 per ton. This vein is believed to be a new one. It is expected that ore from this section of the Tom Reed property will be going to the mill within a month.

Patagonia.—The Three R M. & M. Co. has gone into the hands of a receiver due to the depression in the copper market. The company owes $200,000 and had been working the property under bond and lease from R. R. Richardson.

Prescott.—R. M. Merrill and Pacific Coast associates have acquired 560 acres of placer ground near Octave. Preliminary operations are now under way.

The property of the Swastika Mines Company, which has been working under lease, has been sold to the Swastika Silver & Copper Mining Co. The mine is to be equipped at once with a 50-ton mill and development is to continue. It is estimated that there is 70,000 tons of silver ore in the mine and on dumps.

Quartzsite.—The Meroquite Mining Co. started its Gold mill on May 28. A good deposit of high-grade free-milling ore was developed last winter.——The Ravina Scott mine has also opened a large quantity of high-grade gold ore, and the owners are arranging for a mill.——The Boyer Gold & Copper Co. has its machine-drills running and is opening stopes preparatory to shipping high-grade ore.——The Copper Chief shaft is down 600 ft. Driving on ore will soon begin.——The Perotche lead and silver mine, 7 miles east of Quartzsite, has men sorting ore for shipment.——The Cully copper mine, south of this place, has the richest copper ore found recently. Assays return up to $60 gold, $57 silver, and 26% copper.

Ray.—The Half Moon Mining Co. has been formed by local people to operate 10 claims at Red Hill, 12 miles from Florence. Some work has been done there, opening some high-grade copper-carbonate ore.

The controlling interest in the Little Bobbie Mining Co. has been obtained by the Ray-Broken Hill Mining Co. by the purchase of the shares of W. J. Graham, president of the former. Development is now being carried on by the Ray-Broken Hill, and it is expected that work will be extended into its new holdings.

On June 30 Ray Consolidated company pays 50 cents per share, equal to $788,589. This is similar to the previous dividend.

CALIFORNIA

Grass Valley.—The North Star Mines Co. has resumed paying dividends. On June 28, No. 56, of 40 cents per share, amounting to $100,000, will be distributed. The total is now $5,537,040.

David Whildin has sold the East Eureka claim to the Idaho-Maryland Mines Co. for $11,000. The claim lies between the Old Eureka and Idaho mines. Litigation several years ago resulted in Whildin having been awarded a clear title.

Jackson.—In the 'Press' last week some notes were given about the Gwin mine, closed since 1908. The large sums paid in dividends were not mentioned, and it is now stated that the last operations were not confined to "quickly worked-out bunches of ore." According to the State Mining Bureau's county report, issued in 1915, "the ore-shoots of the main vein are of great length, varying in width from a few inches to 20 feet."

La Porte.—This old placer-mining centre was partly destroyed by fire on June 14. The damage was confined to the business part of town. Some historic records are said to have been burned. Those documents and plans held by Surveyor Hendel were of great value to the State, especially concerning the exposed and buried gravel channels of Sierra county, and should be secured by the State Mining Bureau, as there is much gravel yet available.

Plymouth.—The Plymouth Consolidated during April treated 10,700 tons of ore for $60,000 of gold. The net profit was $14,000. On the 2450-ft. level, the raise at 274 ft. north was advanced 52 ft. to a total of 75 ft. The average value across 42 in. was $8.80 per ton. At 2600 ft. the shaft-station has been enlarged for an electric sinking-hoist. The report of the company for 1918 is to hand and contains the following:

After providing for depreciation there remained a net profit of $139,000. Adding the previous balance there was available $225,000. Two dividends absorbed $115,000. The balance carried to 1919 was $82,000. Current assets amount to $240,000, including $86,000 in cash; and current liabilities are $81,000. Development amounted to 6681 ft., on 12 levels to a depth of 2600 ft. Work on the north shoot at 2450 and 2600 ft. opened good ore, also south of the shaft at 1400 and 1500 ft. Reserves more than kept pace with extraction of ore. The mill treated 125,300 tons of \$6.19 ore, almost the same as in 1918. The yield was 33,382 oz. of gold and 8530 oz. of silver, 68% of the gold being saved by amalgamation and 32% by concentration. The extraction was 88.92%. Costs were 50 cents per ton for development, \$2.22 for mining, 48 cents for milling, 28 cents for bullion and concentrate charges, and 34 cents for general expenses, a total of \$3.82 per ton. J. F. Parks is superintendent.

Nevada City.—After an investigation by C. A. Logan—deputy in charge of the branch of the State Mining Bureau at Auburn—William Macguire located a deposit of barite at Liberty hill, a few miles east of Nevada City, and immediately put several men to determine its extent and quality. The outcrop is immense—60 ft. high and several hundred feet long. The deposit is six miles from Dutch Flat on the railroad, and should the quality meet market requirements, a local plant will be erected.

A suit of importace is being tried in the Superior Court, without a jury, involving title to valuable mining claims near Washington, 20 miles east of Nevada City. The plaintiff, Miss E. E. Hoeft, brought the action against Frank T. Smith and others to quiet title to the Lucky Strike and Lucky Strike Extension. Plaintiff acquired her title through purchase on a gold location; defendants located for gold and asbestos, claiming that plaintiff failed to perform the necessary assessment labor for 1916. At the same time defendants' locations are in doubt because of vagueness of description and uncertainty of position. The case has been complicated further from the fact that defendants bonded their locations, at the same time attempting to cover plaintiff's claims, to the Sierra Asbestos Co. of Oakland. The latter erected a mill and treated ore last year from an open-cut, and made one shipment of short fibre asbestos. The case is being contested bitterly. Defendants are each represented by counsel, five in all, with Thomas B. Dozier of San Francisco as senior counsel, while L. P. Larue and W. B. White of Grass Valley represent plaintiff's interest.

Melones.—The Carson Hill Gold Mining Co., directed by W. J. Loring, has been extracting some rich ore from its bottom level—675 ft. Some of the lots were as follows: 59 tons averaging \$249 per ton, 182 tons at \$87, 73 tons at \$70, 292 tons at \$34, and 530 tons at \$46.52. The profit for June will probably be \$70,000. The shaft is being sunk another 200 ft., and by August the 875-ft. level will be opened.

Sawyer's Bar.—The following notes will show what is being done in this part of Siskiyou county:

The Sauerkraut placer mine on Salmon river is being worked again with five men, opening old drifts and sawing lumber to build a new flume. Work will be carried on throughout the season. Charles Lilly is in charge.

The Nordhammer hydraulic claim is being tested by A. L. Fulton of Oakland, who is part owner. There are three men at work. If the tests are satisfactory a new flume will be built.

The Northern California Exploration Co., a Californian corporation, has taken over the Gilta and Knownothing quartz properties, and will prospect them thoroughly with diamond-drills. A driller and 5 men are there now. W. R. Beal is superintendent.

The Forks of the Salmon River Mining Co. is operating. This is the largest hydraulic mine to operate all the year around in America now, since Lagrange in Trinity county was closed. An 18-in. elevator has been erected. Three No. 5 giants, with 6-in. nozzles, under a 235-ft. head in the pit, are working. The main flume carries 3000 inches of water, and the lower flume about 2000 inches. A water-power derrick handles rocks up to 7 tons. During May, 30,000 cu. yd. of gravel was put through the main sluice. Nine men working. John D. Hubbard of San Francisco is in charge.

Trinity Center.—The new boat of the Estabrook Gold Dredging Co., the largest wooden dredge in the world, it is claimed, started work on June 9. The hull is 152 ft. long by 68 ft. wide. The craft cost over \$600,000. The buckets have a capacity of 20 cu. ft., there being 80 of them. One million feet of lumber, cut near the site, was used in construction. The hull was launched on November 26. The machinery was made in Milwaukee. The freight bill to Redding was \$50,000, and it cost as much more to haul the material by auto-trucks over the mountain roads for 54 miles to Trinity Center. The point of the spud weighs 8½ tons, and the spud complete 60 tons. The boat draws 10 ft. of water. The company has several hundred acres of ground along Trinity river. The new dredge supplants the old one built by the Alta llert company, which was in operation for several years, or until it sank.

COLORADO

Boulder.—None of the tungsten mines or the 11 concentrating plants erected in this district during 1916 are in operation. The only work is that of the Tungsten Products Co.'s refinery, making ferro-tungsten, and the Black Metals refinery, making tungstic acid. It is said that the acid is produced from ore imported from China, two carloads arriving last week.

Cripple Creek.—The Cresson's profit in May was only \$55,000, while monthly dividends of 10 cents per share amount to \$122,000. Ore-reserves are reported as containing large profits.

The Colorado Springs & Cripple Creek railroad—the Short Line—will probably resume running shortly. The road is in the hands of the bondholders.

The Portland company has announced a new schedule of treatment charges on low-grade mine and dump ores, as follows: Up to \$3 value, \$2.00 per ton; \$3.50 at \$2.25; \$4 at \$2.50; \$4.50 at \$2.65; \$5 at \$2.75 per ton.

Gateway.—A shortage of men continues in the Paradox valley. The importance of the new mining field is being recognized, and by the end of the year there will be improved transportation facilities, as the roads from Telluride will be repaired, and there is a survey under way from Gateway to the lower Paradox, with excellent prospects for its construction.

At the new mill of the Primos Chemical Co. construction is proceeding rapidly; the concrete foundations are laid, and the iron and steel for the structure is arriving, so the outlook is favorable for early completion.

The Radium Company of Colorado is confining operations to development, owing to the fact that there is a large quantity of ore on hand ready for shipment.

Georgetown.—The Georgetown Tunnel Transportation Co., C. G. Breitenbach president, is to build a mill near the mouth of the tunnel.

Leadville.—Before the end of August a number of idle properties will be at work. The Ibex and Garbutt are gradually getting back to normal production, while the Penrose and Dold properties are at full capacity. The Iron Silver company has moved pumps and water-columns from the Mikado to the Pyrenees shaft. Silver properties in the Sugar Loaf district are being worked by lessees and companies.

IDAHO

Bonners Ferry.—The Idaho Continental Mining Co., with properties at Klockmann, will resume operations at once, according to A. Klockmann, president and general manager. He stated that he would start with at least 100 men. Two shifts will be worked in the mine and three in the mill. Men are now overhauling the machinery.

Burke.—The Hecla Mining Co. is now employing 500 men at its mine here and the mill at Gem.

Mullan.—The National Copper company made a profit of $20,000 during May, from 7000 tons of ore. The new shoot on the 800-ft. level is responsible for this sum, which is a large increase. The orebody has widened from 4 in. to 25 ft. The shoot is 200 ft. long. Concentrate contains 16% copper and 47 oz. of silver per ton.

Wallace.—Since wages in the Coeur d'Alene were cut by $1 per day, and recently advanced by 50 cents, the national labor unions have been trying to unionize the men of this region. The local secretary, M. P. Villeneuve, at Burke, of the Coeur d'Alene District Miners' Union No. 14, International Union of Mine, Mill & Smelter Workers, formerly the Western Federation of Miners, circularized the managements of all the mines, asking them to confer on establishing an 8-hour day in all departments, an increase of 50 cents per day, and an agreement to form a basis of relationship between employers and employees, such as can be arranged in friendly conference. To this request the companies replied not to the Union, but "To all employees of the Coeur d'Alene mines." They stated that the 8-hour law has been adhered to strictly, that the present scale of wages is similar to that at Butte and higher than paid in California and Utah, and that the third proposal is recognition of the Union, which is refused on the grounds that the mines are on the open-shop basis. The reply is signed by the Bunker Hill & Sullivan, Caledonia, Consolidated Interstate-Callahan, Federal, Gold Hunter, Hecla, Hercules, Sierra Nevada, and Tamarack companies.

ILLINOIS

In Bulletin 169, Law Serial 15, J. W. Thompson of the U. S. Bureau of Mines has completed the Illinois mining statutes annotated, including all the mining laws of that State. Some of the principal subjects treated are the Engineering Department of the University at Urbana, the Geological Survey, mine fires, inspectors, mineral lands, miners wages, liens, and change-houses, corporations, mining rights, shot-firers, coal, and compensation acts.

MICHIGAN

Houghton.—Quincy pays $1 per share on June 30. This is equal to $150,000 and makes $300,000 for 1919. The company has purchased 125 acres of land from the Hancock for $235,000. In 1915 Quincy bought 80 acres from Hancock.

NEVADA

Ely.—Nevada Consolidated pays 37½ cents per share on June 30. This is equal to $749,796, and is the same as paid three months ago.

Goldfield.—The Original Klondyke, consisting of 200 acres in the Klondyke district, north of Goldfield, has been sold by Harry McNamara to the Original Klondyke Divide Mining Co., financed by New York interests. McNamara retains a controlling interest. The sale was made by Tim Connolly and J. W. Dunfee of Goldfield. The Original is one of the oldest mines in southern Nevada, having been worked 25 years ago, when the ore was hauled to Sodaville. The company that has taken it over is to sink a 1000-ft. shaft. The vein has been developed for a distance of 3000 ft., and has been exposed on the surface for widths of from 2 to 20 ft. None of the shafts is over 200 ft. deep. Until 1913 the mine was worked by James Golden, who is reported to have shipped ore valued at $290,000 gross. On the death of Golden, in 1913, McNamara took over operation of the mine and, according to smelter records investigated when the sale was made, shipped 123 carloads of ore averaging $28 per ton.

Sale of the Parker and Lockhart shares in the Florence Goldfield has been consummated, according to a telegram received from L. E. Whicher, head of the New York syndicate that bought control of the mine. The closing of the sale was reported in March, but according to information reaching Goldfield, Whicher had difficulty in securing delivery of the Parker shares. When the definite closing of the deal was announced, it was also made public that the Goldfield Development Co. had secured a lease on the northern part of the Florence, where, according to Development company's officials, there is 500,000 tons of low-grade ore in the extension into Florence ground of the Combination vein. This, according to estimates of A. I. D'Arcy, general manager for the Development company, will provide the company with from 2,150,000 to 2,200,000 tons of ore for treatment in the Consolidated mill. The estimate includes ore in the Combination, January, and Red Top.

Mina.—More than a dozen companies have been incorporated on the strength of developments in the Simon lead

MAP OF CENTRAL NEVADA

mine, 23 miles east of this place, and efforts are being made to boom the district. Engineers familiar with local conditions state that treatment of the ore presents difficulties, and that shipments to custom smelters will bring penalties for the zinc content, which runs from 10 to 14%. It is officially stated that a process has been devised for separation of the zinc from the silver-lead-gold ore, followed by treatment of the material by flotation at the Simon. Freight from the Simon to Mina costs $6 per ton.

The cross-cut on the 400-ft. level of the Simon mine has penetrated the orebody for a width of 145 ft. The last 10 ft. is said to assay 34 oz. silver, 38% lead, and 24% zinc. An electric power-line is to be extended to the property from Mina.

Pioche.—Lincoln county produced 104,146 tons of ore valued at $1,123,488 during 1918, according to tax statements filed here. This is a decrease of 40,850 tons, mostly due to troubles on the railway from the Prince mine.

Round Mountain.—The Fairview Round Mountain Mines Co., managed by Gibson Berry, with E. Michal as mill superintendent, and R. J. Ledwick as mine superintendent, made an operating profit of $115,986 during 1918. Two dividends of 1 cent per share each absorbed $19,049. Development amounted to 1546 ft. at $9.04 per foot. The mine is opened to a depth of 250 ft., and the general outlook is good. The mill treated 8808 tons of $21.79 ore, of which 93.1% was extracted. Costs totaled $7.164 per ton. On June 25 the company distributes 2 cents per share, amounting to $19.049.

MEXICO

Chihuahua

Parral.—Telegraphic advice from El Paso, Texas, on June 17, stated that the American Smelting & Refining Co. had ordered its American employees to leave Parral and outlying districts of this State and go to the border immediately. The Cusi Mining Co. also ordered its men to go to the border from Cusihuiriachic.

NEW MEXICO

Hanover.—The Republic Mining & Milling Co. last year made a net profit of $51,911. Current assets were $44,681, and liabilities $7594. New work amounted to 616 ft., making a total of 1586 ft. An estimate of ore-reserves gives 50,000 tons, averaging 20% zinc. Fully 25,000 tons should be exposed this year. When finances permit, a 50-ton mill is to be erected. A water-supply has yet to be found. Shipments during 1918 were 2925 tons, realizing $108,868.

Santa Rita.—Chino Copper Co. pays 75 cents per share on June 30. This amounts to $652,485, and is similar to that of the previous quarter.

Tyrone.—The Burro Mountain of Phelps Dodge Corporation is to suspend operations, according to an announcement made at Bisbee on June 6 from the office of A. T. Thomson, assistant to the president of the Corporation. At the present time only tests on concentrates are being made at Tyrone. When these have been completed the mill is to be closed until such time as it is determined the copper market justifies a resumption. Development will continue.

UTAH

The State Board of Equalization at Salt Lake City has calculated the assessed valuation of all mines in Utah at just under $100,000,000. This is an increase of $54,000,000, fixed under the old law.

Bingham.—Utah Copper Co. pays $1.50 per share, equal to $2,436,735. Three months ago the same distribution was made.

Tintic.—The Tintic Standard pays 8 cents per share, $93,976, on June 27. This makes $187,952 for 1919 and $588,386 to date. The daily output is 150 tons, netting $30 per ton. E. J. Raddatz is general manager.

CANADA

Ontario

Cobalt.—The McKinley-Darragh-Savage paid 3%, $67,428, on June 7, making $202,284 for the current year, and $5,551,879 to date.

The Nipissing pays 50 cents per share on June 21. This is equal to $600,000, and makes $1,200,000 for 1919 and $20,340,000 to date.

It is stated that the Gillies Limit, described by Willet G. Miller in the 'Press' of June 7, will not be thrown open for prospecting this year. The reason for this is that the Government wishes to allow the lumbermen to remove what timber is left standing before miners are given permission to locate claims.

Porcupine.—The West Dome mine, closed since the disastrous forest fire of July 11, 1911, whereby 25 people taking refuge in the shaft were asphyxiated, is to be re-opened.

Yukon

Whitehorse.—The first steamers for Dawson and Fairbanks left here on June 9.

PERSONAL

Note. The Editor invites members of the profession to send particulars of their work and appointments. The information is interesting to our readers.

Herbert H. Itoc has gone to Boston.

Walter Hovey Hill is opening up a silver mine at Pearl, Idaho.

Arthur **Jarman** has arrived from New Zealand and expects to reside at Berkeley.

H. S. Munroe is manager for the Consolidated Coppermines Co. at Kimberly, Nevada.

Gelasio Caetani is serving as an Italian Food Administrator, working under Mr. Hoover.

Thomas N. **Stanton** has returned from Morococha, in Peru, and expects to go to Arizona.

James S. Wroth, of 42 Broadway, New York, has just returned from professional work in Portugal.

Percy R. Middleton is doing experimental work for the Chief Consolidated Mining Co., at Eureka, Utah.

Marshall D. Draper sails from New York for the Orient on July 1, where he will engage in exploration work.

Donald F. Irvin is making a professional journey to Bolivia and Peru. He is now at Antofagasta, in Chile.

Fred Searls, Lieutenant of Engineers in the A. E. F., has returned to San Francisco and resumed practice as mining geologist.

Francis L. Bosqui has gone from London to New York, where he will establish himself as metallurgical engineer at 90 West street.

Lionel Lindsay, at one time News Editor on the M. & S. P., is an attaché on the Military Section of the British Delegation at Paris.

John L. Siboney and **K. T. Parks**, of the Federal Bureau of Mines, spent several days in the Grass Valley district during the past week.

Rensselaer Toll, who has been appointed War Minerals Relief engineer, is investigating claims in Santa Clara county, California.

Horace F. **Lunt** has been appointed Commissioner of Mines for the State of Colorado, in succession to Fred Carroll, who resigned.

H. C. Carlisle has been appointed general superintendent for the Nevada Wonder Mining Co., at Wonder, Nevada, to succeed **E. E. Carpenter**, who resigned.

R. G. Hall, resident manager for the Burma Mines Limited, has left Namtu, Northern Shan States, Burma, for London, on business for the corporation.

John D. Hubbard, recently Captain in the Army, is superintendent of the Forks of Salmon River Mining Co., near Sawyer's Bar, Siskiyou county, California.

The Deputy Minister of Mines, **R.** T. Tolmie, of British Columbia, who has been ill for some time, has been granted an extended sick-leave, and **W. Fleet Robertson**, the Provincial Mineralogist, by an order-in-council, has been made acting deputy.

W. A. Sloan and **E. Leland** have taken over the assaying and engineering office of Kempton & O'Neill at Nogales, Arizona. Both have been connected with the Shannon Copper Co., the one as mining engineer and the other as chemist for 8 and 10 years, respectively.

C. M. Eye, for many years superintendent in charge of the mines of the Benguet Consolidated Mining Co., Benguet, Philippine Islands, is returning to the United States in July. He expects to be in or near San Francisco, and mail may be addressed care of Wells Fargo Nevada National Bank.

METAL PRICES

San Francisco June 17

Aluminum-dust, cents per pound	50—60
Antimony, cents per pound	8.50
Copper, electrolytic, cents per pound	17.75
Lead, pig, cents per pound	5.65—6.65
Platinum, pure, per ounce	$105
Platinum, 10% iridium, per ounce	$115
Quicksilver, per flask of 75 lb	$95
Spelter, cents per pound	8
Zinc-dust, cents per pound	10—12

EASTERN METAL MARKET

(By wire from New York)

June 17.—Copper is quiet but steady. Lead is active and strong. Spelter is quiet though firm.

COPPER

Prices of electrolytic in New York, in cents per pound.

Date			Average week ending		
June	11	17.25	May	6	15.25
"	12	17.50	"	13	15.37
"	13	17.50	"	20	16.24
"	14	17.75	"	27	16.46
"	15 Sunday		June	3	16.37
"	16	17.75	"	10	16.81
"	17	17.75	"	17	17.58

Monthly averages

	1917	1918	1919		1917	1918	1919
Jan	29.53	23.50	20.43	July	29.67	26.00	....
Feb	34.57	23.50	17.34	Aug.	27.42	26.00	....
Mch	36.00	23.50	15.05	Sept.	25.11	26.00	....
Apr	33.16	23.50	15.23	Oct.	23.50	26.00	....
May	31.69	23.50	15.91	Nov.	23.50	26.00	....
June	32.57	23.50	....	Dec.	23.50	26.00	....

SILVER

Below are given official or ticker quotations, in cents per ounce of silver 999 fine. From April 23, 1918, the United States government paid $1 per ounce for all silver purchased by it, fixing a maximum of $1.01½ on August 15, 1918, and will continue to pay $1 until the quantity specified under the Act is purchased, probably extending over several years. On May 5, 1919, all restrictions on the metal were removed, resulting in fluctuations. During the restricted period, the British government fixed the maximum price five times, the last being on March 25, 1919, on account of the low rate of sterling exchange, but removed all restrictions on May 10. The equivalent of dollar silver (1000 fine) in British currency is 46.65 pence per ounce (925 fine), calculated at the normal rate of exchange.

Date		New York cents	London pence	Average week ending		Cents	Pence
June	11	111.50	54.25	May	6	101.14	48.71
"	12	112.25	54.75	"	13	109.33	52.08
"	13	110.75	54.00	"	20	110.33	53.58
"	14	111.12	54.25	"	27	106.44	52.17
"	15 Sunday			June	3	108.90	52.90
"	16	112.25	54.75	"	10	109.43	53.27
"	17	114.00	54.87	"	17	111.08	54.48

Monthly averages

	1917	1918	1919		1917	1918	1919
Jan	75.14	88.72	101.12	July	78.92	99.62	....
Feb.	77.54	85.79	101.12	Aug.	85.40	100.31	....
Mch.	74.13	88.11	101.12	Sept.	100.73	101.12	....
Apr.	72.51	95.35	101.12	Oct.	87.38	101.12	....
May	74.61	99.50	107.23	Nov.	85.97	101.12	....
June	76.44	99.50	....	Dec.	85.97	101.12	....

The American Smelting & Refining Co., the U. S. Smelting & Refining Co., and the Anaconda Copper Mining Co. are to form a silver export company to endeavor to alter the silver situation, particularly as regards price-fixing in Great Britain. These three companies in 1918 handled over 94,000,000 oz. of silver, equal to 55% of the world's output in that year.

On May 29, J. W. Rowe, U. S. vice-consul at Mexico City, cabled that a treasury circular published on the above date announces that the silver bars may be exported from Mexico during June without an export license, and without the necessity of importing any percentage of gold in substitution.

Discussing silver on May 22, Samuel Montagu & Co. of London said that the restoration of freedom to the London market has been accompanied by a healthy return of business. Supplies have been plentiful, and have so far anticipated the Continental demand, which is surely though slowly being resumed. As a matter of fact, the markets in the neighboring Allied and neutral countries hardly yet realize the fact that London is quite prepared to supply raw material for industries and for coinage, which has been suspended during the period that export of silver from the United Kingdom was restricted and the price officially regulated. The War Trade Department is giving the most cordial assistance in facilitating the provision of export licenses, which are granted freely. The abundance of supplies from America suggests that producers had laid in stocks for a rise, and, this not being forthcoming and there being a good profit on the original stocking price, are realizing with some freedom. When this special source of supply is taken off the market and the Continent has waked up, prices may perhaps be more robust, and buyers for forward delivery, who have been lately in considerable evidence, would then be able to justify their purchases. The Shanghai exchange eased slightly to 5s.1½d. the tael, equal to 52⅜d. ($1.04¾) per ounce standard (expenses of transmission excluded). There was the usual demand for the India Council allotments on the basis of 1s.8d. (40 cents) a rupee, the limit to which they were raised on May 13. It was officially stated on May 20 that 194,961,672 fine ounces had been delivered in India up to May 1 under the Pittman Act.

LEAD

Lead is quoted in cents per pound, New York delivery.

Date			Average week ending		
June	11	5.25	May	6	4.87
"	12	5.40	"	13	4.85
"	13	5.40	"	20	5.05
"	14	5.40	"	27	5.27
"	15 Sunday		June	3	5.22
"	16	5.40	"	10	5.20
"	17	5.40	"	17	5.38

Monthly averages

	1917	1918	1919		1917	1918	1919
Jan.	7.64	6.85	5.60	July	10.93	8.03	....
Feb.	9.10	7.07	5.13	Aug.	10.75	8.05	....
Mch.	10.07	7.26	5.24	Sept.	9.07	8.05	....
Apr.	9.38	6.99	5.05	Oct.	6.97	8.05	....
May	10.29	6.88	5.04	Nov.	6.38	8.05	....
June	11.74	7.58	....	Dec.	6.49	6.90	....

Lead ore at Joplin, Missouri, last week averaged $57 per ton, basis of 80% metal. The Tri-State output was 1066 tons.

ZINC

Zinc is quoted as spelter, standard Western brands, New York delivery, in cents per pound:

Date			Average week ending		
June	11	6.75	May	6	6.32
"	12	6.85	"	13	6.31
"	13	6.90	"	20	6.46
"	14	6.90	"	27	6.59
"	15 Sunday		June	3	6.53
"	16	6.90	"	10	6.58
"	17	6.85	"	17	6.88

Monthly averages

	1917	1918	1919		1917	1918	1919
Jan.	9.75	7.78	7.44	July	8.98	8.72	....
Feb.	10.45	7.97	6.71	Aug.	8.58	8.87	....
Mch.	10.78	7.67	6.53	Sept.	8.33	9.58	....
Apr.	10.20	7.04	6.49	Oct.	8.32	9.11	....
May	9.41	7.92	6.43	Nov.	7.76	8.75	....
June	9.63	7.92	....	Dec.	7.84	8.49	....

Zinc ore at Joplin, Missouri, averaged $41 per ton last week, basis of 60% metal. The Tri-State output was 7737 tons of blende.

QUICKSILVER

The primary market for quicksilver is San Francisco, California being the largest producer. The price is fixed in the open market, according to quantity. Prices, in dollars per flask of 75 pounds:

Date					
May	20	82.00	June	3	95.00
"	27	92.00	"	10	92.00
			"	17	95.00

Monthly averages

	1917	1918	1919		1917	1918	1919
Jan	81.00	128.06	103.75	July	102.00	120.00	....
Feb	126.25	118.00	90.00	Aug.	115.00	120.00	....
Mch	113.75	112.00	72.80	Sept.	112.00	120.00	....
Apr	114.50	115.00	73.12	Oct.	102.00	120.00	....
May	104.00	110.00	84.80	Nov.	102.50	120.00	....
June	85.50	112.00	....	Dec.	117.42	115.00	....

The quicksilver market is bare of supplies and the demand is good. New York quotes $92 per flask; and London about £18 ($85). Exports during May amounted to 1230 flasks, chiefly to Hongkong and Japan. This is an increase of 105 flasks over March, and 800 over February.

TIN

Prices in New York, in cents per pound. The monthly averages in 1918 are nominal. On December 3 the War Industries Board fixed the price to consumers and jobbers at 72¼c. f.o.b. Chicago and Eastern points, and 71¾c. on the Pacific Coast. This will continue until the U. S. Steel Products Co.'s stock is consumed.

Monthly averages

	1917	1918	1919		1917	1918	1919
Jan	44.10	85.13	71.50	July	62.60	93.00	....
Feb	51.47	85.00	72.44	Aug	62.53	91.33	....
Mch	54.27	85.00	72.50	Sept.	61.54	80.40	....
Apr	55.63	88.53	72.50	Oct	62.24	78.82	....
May	63.21	100.01	72.50	Nov.	74.18	73.67	....
June	61.93	91.00	....	Dec.	85.00	71.52	....

The Cassel Cyanide Co. of Glasgow, Scotland, paid a dividend of 6 pence (12 cents) per share, equal to £17,625 ($84,000), on June 2.

Eastern Metal Market

New York, June 11.

All the markets except that of tin are more active and stronger, and the price tendency is upward.

Antimony is steady and strong.

Copper buying has again developed heavily, resulting in advancing prices.

Lead is stronger in sympathy with copper.

Tin is dead and devoid of interest.

Zinc demand has increased, and prices are advancing gradually.

ANTIMONY

The market is quiet but strong at 8.37½ to 8.50c., New York, duty paid, for Asiatic grades.

COPPER

The market continues to improve, and the tone is strong with the price tendency upward. In the last few days demand and buying has been renewed with vigor and purchases have been heavy, particularly for August delivery. Some producers are well sold up for August. The price advance has been gradual almost each day, until today electrolytic copper for early or June delivery is quoted at 17.50c., with July and August held and sold at 17.75 to 18c., New York. Demand for Lake copper is good, with quotations ranging from ⅛ to ¼c. above electrolytic, early delivery being quoted at 17.75c., New York. The heavy buying referred to has been largely for domestic account, and both wire-makers and brass-makers have been involved. It is believed that demand is equal to or in excess of present output, but not enough yet to liquidate present stocks.

IRON AND STEEL

There appears to be generally less expectation of a decline in steel prices, though the volume of new business and rate of production have undergone little change in June. The improvement noted three weeks ago has been maintained. Outstanding features are new manufacturing capacity in the Middle West, and repairs and new construction work planned by a number of steel companies. Heavy demand for alloy-steel has come from automobile makers.

LEAD

The strong copper market has had its effect on lead. Both demand and prices have firmed as a result. Some business has been done since last Friday, which is reported to have been of fair proportions. The market is today quoted at 5.25c., New York, or 5c., St. Louis, with nothing lower obtainable. The cheap lots around 5.15c., New York, said to be available last week, are found upon investigation to have been impossible to secure. The market tone is strong and healthy.

TIN

Another statement from George Armsby, chief in charge of tin, appeared yesterday. It showed that stocks of the allocated metal had declined to 1907 tons on June 9, from 1615 tons on the 1st. Nothing definite is yet known as to when restrictions will be removed. It is, however, now established that imports of tin from Canada will not be permitted until shipments from the Far East have arrived, thus preventing any undue advantage to those who have collected tin for storage in that country. Such a procedure will thus protect the present buyers of allocated metal as well as the American smelters. It is announced that freight-rates from the Pacific Coast on tin to Eastern points has been reduced from $1.25 to 75c. per 100 lb., effective May 29. The market is stale and stagnant. Buying for shipment from the East or from England when restrictions are removed has tapered off to nothing, and prices for such shipments are nominal at 50 to 51c. The allocated metal is still held at 72.50c., New York, the fixed price.

ZINC

A much better inquiry than in some weeks has developed, which has resulted in some business, and the tone of the market is considerably better. Some feel that the final turn has come. Prime Western for early delivery is quoted at 6.30c., St. Louis, or 6.65c., New York, with July held at 6.35c., St. Louis, and 6.70c., New York. For still further positions producers are generally shy about committing themselves. The new demand has been mostly from brass makers and special interests.

ORES

Manganese-Iron Alloys: Domestic ferro is in better demand, and most re-sale material seems to have been absorbed. What little remains is higher at $110 to $115, delivered. Producers are asking $125, delivered, and the British alloy is quoted at $121, seaboard. Spiegel is quiet at $27 to $30, furnace, depending on the analyses and the delivery.

Molybdenum: No business has been reported. Quotations are nominally low, about 80 to 95c. per pound of MoS, in 90% concentrates, but inquiries are better and more encouraging.

Tungsten: The following bill by Charles B. Timberlake, Congressman from Colorado, according to the report of the American Mining Congress, has been referred to the Committee on Ways and Means (H. R. 2949):

"A bill to provide revenue for the Government and to promote the production of tungsten ores and manufactures thereof in the United States.

"Be it enacted by the Senate and House of Representatives of the United States of America in Congress assembled, that on and after the day following the passage of this Act there shall be levied, collected and paid upon the articles named herein when imported from any foreign country into the United States or into any of its possessions, except the Philippine Islands and the Island of Guam and Tutuila, the rates of duties which are herein prescribed, namely:

"First—crude tungsten, ores and concentrates, $10 per unit of tungsten trioxide therein contained, a unit being herein defined as 1% of tungstic acid in a short ton of 2000 pounds.

"Second—ferro-tungsten, powder, tungstic acid, calcium, tungsten steel salts, and compounds of tungsten, and all other manufactured materials containing tungsten, not especially provided for in this section, $1.25 per pound of tungsten contained therein.

"Sec. 2. That so much of any heretofore existing law or parts of law as may be inconsistent with this act is hereby repealed."

During the week the market for tungsten has been fairly active again. An excess of 100 tons of ore has changed hands, and while it shows a certain amount of business, the quantities ought to be much bigger in order to really make for higher prices. The sentiment, however, is much in favor of higher prices, as no material can be bought, according to advice received on June 9, from China at anywhere near the prices ruling heretofore. Bolivia also is reporting a much firmer market, and business under $10 for Bolivian scheelite and wolframite has been refused by the sellers. These prices refer only to the highest grade of ore.

Company Reports

WAIHI GOLD MINING CO.

Property: mine, mills, tramways, and power-plants in New Zealand.

Operating Officials: E. G. Banks, general superintendent; W. P. Gauvain, assistant; J. L. Gilmour, mine manager.

Financial Statement: gold and silver sold during 1918 realized £387,065 ($1,850,000), plus £27,773 ($129,000) for interest, etc. All operating expenditures totaled £215,564 ($1,030,000), leaving a profit of £199,274 ($949,000). From this, £42,851 ($201,000) was deducted for income-tax in New Zealand and London, and £16,724 ($76,000) for depreciation.

The market-value of investments at the end of the year was £538,125 ($2,580,000); also £49,845 ($235,000) cash at bankers, £30,400 ($144,000) for bullion in transit, and £55,357 ($264,000) stores on hand.

Dividends: four were paid—No. 99-102—of 24 cents per share each, making a total of £99,181 ($475,000). Since 1893 there has been distributed £4,974,446 ($23,875,000), and £551,314 ($2,640,000) paid as income-tax.

Development and Mining: new work covered 7366 ft., of which 3975 ft. was in 'suspense ore', that is, ore being extracted from arches and other workings. Reserves total about 610,000 tons. Eighty-five rock-drills were used. Ventilation was improved by more air-jets for induced currents. The electric plunger pumps lifted 413,492,100 gal. of water. A new turbine pump is being put in. The Cornish pump did not work. Two hoists are now driven by compressed air, generated by electric power. Electric heaters are used in the change-houses. Seventeen lodes contributed to the output of ore, the Martha accounting for 31% and the Empire 24%.

Milling and Production: the Victoria mill of 200 stamps and 11 tube-mills worked 298.6 days, an average of 120.4 stamps and 6.89 tube-mills running. They averaged 5.255 tons per stamp-day. The tonnage crushed was 188,998, assaying $7.50 gold and 2.75 oz. silver per ton. The proportions of ore-pulp treated were 21.77% as sand, 76.81% as slime, and 1.42% as concentrate, and the total extracted value was 91.7%. On the concentrate the extraction was 98.1%. During five years the extraction on the ore averaged 91.2%. The electrolytic refinery treated 561,348 oz. of doré bullion. The output since 1890 is valued at £12,265,771 ($58,870,000).

The hydro-electric plant, 51 miles from the mine, operated without trouble, and generated 17,107,550 units. The pressure is 50,000 and 11,000 volts.

Costs, including all office charges, totaled £1 2s.10d. ($5.48) per ton.

ALASKA JUNEAU GOLD MINING CO.

Property: mines and works near Juneau, Alaska.

Operating Officials: P. R. Bradley, general superintendent; John Richards, mine superintendent.

Financial Statement: the revenue during 1918 totaled $460,323, from gold bullion and concentrate. Operations cost $785,823, including $71,547 for interest and $26,920 for damages by storm. On April 1, 1919, the company's indebtedness, less cash assets totaled $1,580,000, which includes $943,000 of bonds sold of the new $3,500,000 issue. There has been spent to date $1,552,946 on mine development and $2,945,856 on construction and equipment.

Development: new work amounted to 5501 ft., mostly on No. 3 and 4 levels, preparing No. 410 stope. The assay-value of all development and preparatory mining work 'muck' samples (6921) taken between January 1913 and December 1918 averaged $1.041 per ton. Including 409 moiled samples taken since 1912 the average becomes $1.075.

Milling and Production: an endeavor was made to force the mill to its rated capacity during January and February, but the best daily average was 3832 tons, less than half of that expected. As wholesale mining and treatment was unprofitable at that time, sorting of the ore was done in March, April, and May; but because the 400 stope produced a lower grade and sorting was on so small a scale, there was no resultant economic advantage, therefore this work was stopped. The daily average during these three months was 1828 tons of 70.5-cent ore. During the next five months, when better ore was available, milling was reduced to the quantity of this material that could be mined with the labor available. The average daily run was 747 tons of $1.414 ore. The 50-stamp mill was incorporated into the flow-sheet, doing the work of the ball-mills. The stamps produced a ½-inch product, which went to the tube-mills. Many improvements were made during this period. In the last three months of the year, when the 410 stope was yielding more ore, 1094 tons of $1.08 ore was treated daily. On December 4 the mill resumed work with three shifts. Alterations to the plant are to cost $500,000; these are expected to bring the daily capacity to 8000 tons. During 1918 there was spent $104,675 on the new mill, $30,508 on the power-plant, and $10,806 on the stamp-mill.

The mill treated 574,285 tons of ore averaging 87.5 cents per ton. Of this, 51.89 cents was recovered by amalgamation and 16.82 cents in galena concentrates. From 1914 to 1918, inclusive, the mill treated 1,666,740 tons of ore averaging 98.44 cents per ton. Operations last year cost $1.1329 per ton.

BUNKER HILL & SULLIVAN MINING & CONCENTRATING CO.

Property: lead-silver mines, mills, and smelter in the Coeur d'Alene, Idaho.

Operating Officials: Stanly A. Easton, manager; William McDougal, mine superintendent; R. S. Handy, mill superintendent; M. H. Sullivan, smelter superintendent; R. A. Brockman, chief engineer; W. C. Clark, electrical engineer; E. P. Dudley, constructing engineer; F. P. Porter, master mechanic; C. W. Simmons, purchasing agent.

Financial Statement: the revenue during 1918 totaled $6,969,555, of which $6,128,667 was from metal sold, and $567,238 from the Caledonia and Sierra Nevada companies' dividends. Operations cost $3,769,138, which left a profit of $3,200,417.

Dividends: $1,553,250 was distributed, compared with $2,043,750 in 1917, bringing the total to $22,086,750.

Development and Mining: exploration consisted of 1740 ft. of drifts and cross-cuts, costing $13.739 per foot. The shortage of labor was especially noticeable in the second half of the year. Development on No. 15, or bottom level, was particularly successful, while the physical condition of the mines was fully maintained. Ore-reserves consist of 4,210,111 tons in the Bunker Hill, 135,479 tons in the Sullivan, and 16,434 tons in the Stemwinder. Stoping cost $1.582 per ton, and all underground work $2.385 per ton. Tramming by electric locomotive cost 7.8 cents, an increase of 2 cents; hoisting 8.1 cents, against 5.6 cents; and pumping 9.7 cents, more than double that in 1917.

Milling and Production: the mills concentrated 389,027 tons of ore, averaging 10.2234% lead and 3.8751 oz. silver per ton. The smelter produced 67,125,717 lb. of lead and 1,191,908 oz. of silver. The total cost of milling was 71.2 cents per ton, a gain of 11.2 cents. Since 1886, the output has been 8,275,913 tons of ore, valued at $86,341,659. Net smelter returns were $50,925,287, of which $28,771,132 was profit, plus $4,105,624 from other sources.

Book Reviews

Pumping Machinery. The history, design, construction, and operation of various forms of pumps. Second edition, revised. By A. M. Greene, Jr. Pp. 703, ill., index. John Wiley & Sons, Inc., New York, 1919. For sale by 'Mining and Scientific Press'. Price, $4.

Pumps and pumping machinery exported from the United States during February 1919 were valued at $711,450. During 1918 the total was $6,008,000. This machinery went to all parts of the world to be used in mining, oil, treatment works, and agriculture. The subject is one of great importance. In the book before us, which may be said to cover steam pumps, particularly, the first 130 pages on the historical development of pumps, from the time of the Egyptians to the present, will be found of value, as it shows the weakness of certain types and the improvements in design. A little more space might have been given to the Humphrey gas-pump, which has a big future in moving large volumes of water through low lifts. In the chapter on modern reciprocating pumps, consideration is given to boiler-feed pumps, fire pumps, a few well-known types of mine pumps, and deep-well pumps. A discussion of the dynamics of the water end of pumps, including the plunger and valves, occupies 70 pages; the design of pump parts 65 pages, and the dynamics of the steam end and steam-end details another 85 pages. Those chapters are for designing engineers. Among the high-duty pumps and water-works stations are shown a number of large installations, but one of the greatest of the high-duty types is that in Western Australia, where water is pumped 353 miles; this is not mentioned. Special pumping machinery, such as that for condensers, sewage, and hydraulic pressure, is described, including the ram. Injectors, pulsometers, and air-lifts come within the category of pumping apparatus, and are herein discussed, including calculations. Centrifugal pumps, especially those of the stage or turbine types for high lifts, are being used more and more, so the author devotes 130 pages to them. Many problems arise in their design and operation. The last chapter, of 19 pages, deals with mine pumps, but will be found rather short, as electric plunger pumps receive little attention and the 'shoe-string' centrifugal sinking type none at all. The millman will find nothing about acid, diaphragm, slime, or sand pumps. The descriptions and illustrations of modern pumps have been drawn largely from manufacturers' bulletins and from technical publications. It would seem that the book would be of value to designing engineers and to those who operate pumping plants of large units, more especially at water-works and in manufacturing industries. A good bibliography is available for all interested in pumping.

Applications of Electrolysis in Chemical Industry. By A. J. Hale. Pp. 148, ill., index. Longmans, Green & Co., London, 1918. For sale by 'Mining and Scientific Press'. Price, $2.50.

Electrolysis in the laboratory and refinery is expanding all the time, so the chemist and metallurgist must study what is published. This book will be found to contain a good deal of useful information. The introduction deals with the fundamentals of electrolysis. Suitable current may be generated by cells, thermopiles, dynamos, rotary-converters, and motor-generators. In giving costs of generating, British money might have been given in American also. The chapter on refining of metals includes American copper practice at Great Falls, and in New Jersey, lead at Trail, tin at Perth Amboy, and gold and silver at the Philadelphia Mint. It is said, under the heading of Cyanide Process, that the Siemens and Halske electrolytic process of recovering gold from solutions is much used in South Africa; this is not so now. Electrolysis is used in extracting metals from ores and chemicals, such as aluminum, calcium, sodium, and zinc. This treatment of copper and lead ores is not successful yet. Gases, such as hydrogen and oxygen, are used in large volume for welding, and they are made by electrolysis; the systems are explained. The electrolysis of alkali chlorides is an important industry, resulting in caustic soda, chlorine, bleaching liquor, hypochlorites, chlorates, and perchlorates, using aqueous solutions of sodium and potassium chloride. The various types of cells are fully considered. The last two chapters discuss the production of inorganic and organic compounds. Generally, a useful reference.

Irrigation Engineering. By Arthur P. Davis and Herbert M. Wilson. Pp. 617, ill., index. John Wiley & Sons, Inc., New York. For sale by 'Mining and Scientific Press'. Price, $4.50.

Wilson's 'Irrigation Engineering' has been a standard treatise and book of reference for over 20 years. In this seventh edition, the co-operation of Mr. Davis has been enlisted, and the result has been a complete revision, with the addition of much new matter. The principal changes include a fuller treatment of subjects connected with the operation and management of irrigation systems, such as soils, plant-food, preparation of land for irrigation, duty of water, applying water to land, and maintenance of canals. The principal chapter-headings are Soils, Soil-Moisture, Plant-Food, Water Supply, Evaporation, Pumping for Irrigation, Irrigable Lands, Application of Water to the Land, Duty of Water, Measurement of Water, Drainage, Canals and Laterals, Canal Structures, Storage Reservoirs, Sedimentation of Reservoirs, Dams, Water Rights, Operation and Maintenance, Investigation of a Project, and Specifications. The final chapter contains some hydraulic tables. The book is well illustrated and will be useful to irrigation engineers, and to others engaged in the construction or operation of irrigation systems.

Punches and Dies. By Frank A. Stanley. Pp. 425, ill., index. McGraw-Hill Book Co., Inc., New York. For sale by 'Mining and Scientific Press'. Price, $4.

This is probably the most complete and up-to-date book on the subject that has appeared. The author has had much practical experience along these lines, and, at the same time, writes about his subject clearly. The first chapter is devoted to a general discussion of press-tools, and then dies of various kinds are taken up in detail, including dies for blanking, piercing, cutting-off, shaving, trimming, drawing, bending, forming, embossing, marking, riveting, swaging, and indexing, as well as combinations of two or more of these operations. The last few chapters are devoted to design, layout, construction, and heat treatment of dies. The book is well illustrated with both photographs and line-drawings. It will be of value to machinists, shop superintendents and foremen, and, in fact, to anyone interested in punch-and-die work.

Steam-Engine Troubles. By H. Hamkens. Pp. 267, ill., index. The Norman W. Henley Publishing Co., New York. For sale by 'Mining and Scientific Press'. Price, $2.50.

This is a practical book for the operating engineer written in non-technical language so that anyone with enough intelligence and experience to run a steam-engine can understand it. Chapters are devoted to the various parts of the steam-engine and the possible troubles that may develop, also to such special subjects as foundations, erecting, valve-setting, and operation. The book is illustrated with nearly 300 small line-drawings. It will be of value to anyone who runs a steam-engine or has one run for him.

INFORMATION FURNISHED BY MANUFACTURERS

NEW REMCO CATALOGUE

The Redwood Manufacturers Co., 1611 Hobart building, San Francisco, has just issued a revised and up-to-date edition of its Remco redwood pipe catalog. This book is well printed and handsomely illustrated throughout. The various forms of Remco machine-banded and continuous-stave pipe are shown, and illustrations of typical installations are given. However, this book is more than a mere

catalog of the company's product. It contains much valuable data of all sorts compiled from long experience. In fact, it is a complete engineering text-book on wood-pipe construction. Tables are given showing the allowable curvature in wood pipe-lines, relative capacities between wood and metal pipe, water-wheel requirements, pump speed and capacities, friction losses, flow-tables for various sizes of pipe, and other tables.

The Redwood Manufacturers Co., it will be remembered, supplied the United States government with over two million feet of Remco pipe, which was used at cantonments and Government work in this and foreign countries. Every foot of this pipe passed Government inspection, both at the factory and at destination, and not one foot was rejected. The same is true of Remco tanks, over 800 of which were furnished the Government.

Engineers will find this Remeo redwood pipe catalog a handy adjunct to their library of technical information. It is not intended for free distribution except to men actively interested in pipe installations. The great expense necessary in its preparation prevents its being sent except where it can be used as intended. When writing for this catalog, note the work in which you are engaged and it will be sent without charge.

The Alaska Juneau Gold Mining Co., operating at Juneau, Alaska, with head offices at 1022 Crocker building, San Francisco, has sold $943,000 of its $3,500,000 bond issue, much of which is for improvements to the works. The annual report, just to hand, gives the following program for re-modeling:

Provision for sorting waste from Blake crusher feed, including stoneboats, gravity tramways, unloading-derricks, motors, track at west end of mill, 12-in. grizzlies over Blake crushers, water-supply for spraying, etc.

Substitution of the No. 9 by No. 6 gyratories.

Better speed adjustment of apron-feeders.

Construction of grizzlies at end of inclined conveyors.

Conversion of ball-mills into closed-circuit overflow type.

Installation of bucket-elevators for each two ball-mills.

Installation of double grizzlies at end of traveling conveyor over main ore-bins.

Installation of sorting and rejecting conveyor-belt over stamp-mill bin.

Installation of waste-disposal system for waste from stamp-mill picking-belt.

Construction of bins to receive and store pebbles from ball-mills at tube-mill floor.

Installation of shaking-screens in 50-stamp mill.

Extension of heating system into 50-stamp mill.

Re-locating mill and city salt-water pipe-line.

Purchase of additional ball-mill shells.

Extension of ball-mill crane and the working-door.

Installation of additional salt-water pumping equipment.

Purchase of additional haulage equipment consisting of five 18-ton locomotives, 250 ten-ton cars, and construction of additional sidings.

Passenger elevator in mill.

Reconstruction of mill-roof covering.

Suitable barriers erected at critical points to prevent damage from possible storms and slides.

The estimated cost of the above is $500,000.

The St. Louis Daily 'Globe-Democrat' has been printing a series entitled 'Romances of St. Louis Business', and in the issue of May 18 is a full page under the heading of 'The Yellow Strand'. This refers to the Broderick & Bascom Rope Co. In 1875, John J. Broderick and J. D. Bascom started the business, and were the first wire-rope manufacturers west of the Alleghany mountains. Now the firm makes enough rope each month to tie together its works and warehouses at St. Louis, New York, and Seattle. The rope made is used for street railways, aerial tramways, shaft hoists, drilling wells, and many other purposes, and 'The Yellow Strand' is the trade mark for these products.

Rogers, Mayer & Ball, 42 Broadway, New York, regretfully announce the death of Leighton Stewart, of pneumonia, at the Mount Zion hospital, San Francisco, on May 21, 1919.

IN the third week of September the Exposition of Chemical Industries will serve to attract a succession of conventions to Chicago. The American Institute of Mining & Metallurgical Engineers will assemble on September 22 and the American Electrochemical Society on the 25th.

GERMANY'S importation of copper from this country in 1914 amounted to 311,107,962 pounds; in 1913 it was 280,930,086 pounds; and in 1912 it was 217,869,953 pounds, the value in 1912 being $29,741,716 and in 1914 no less than $45,960,362. It was the War and preparation for the War, not peaceful industry, that caused the Germans to buy copper so freely.

CARRANZA'S government is in a bad way when his northern commander, General Manuel Dieguez, has to warn the peaceable, law-abiding, and tax-paying residents in the Mormon settlements of western Chihuahua to leave their homes and cross into the United States for self-protection. The first function of government is to maintain order and by that test the *de facto* government of Mexico has failed.

HEARST'S recent attack on the President, by means of one of his bombastic signed editorials, is of good augury; as is Lord Northcliffe's offensive against the British Premier. When yellow journalism supports high authority it is time for honest citizens to become anxious. Both Mr. Wilson and Mr. George will be strengthened by the withdrawal of support from such quarters. The development of democracy suffers by the prostitution of journalism to the personal vanity of irresponsible publishers.

CLEMENCEAU, speaking as president of the Peace Conference to the German delegation, in final reply to their request for modification of the conditions, said: "In the view of the Allied and Associated Powers the war which began on August 1, 1914, was the greatest crime against humanity and freedom of the people that any nation calling itself civilized has ever consciously committed. . . . The conduct of Germany is almost unexampled in human history. The terrible responsibility which lies at her doors can be seen by the fact that not less than 7,000,000 dead lie buried in Europe, while more than 20,000,000 others carry upon them the evidence of wounds and suffering because Germany saw fit to gratify her lust for tyranny by resort to war." Before signing the treaty Germany was reminded thus that she was not only a defeated enemy but a frustrated criminal.

UNDER 'Discussion', Mr. William E. Greenawalt gives us an interesting letter on the hydrometallurgy of copper, with special reference to Mr. Percy R. Middleton's recent article on the treatment of flotation concentrate. He demurs to the assumption that the success of the electrolytic method of collecting the copper in low-grade ores at Ajo and at Chuquicamata is such as to furnish an assured basis of departure for metallurgists in other districts. There is reason in what he says. According to the annual report the Chuquicamata plant, of the Chile Copper Company, made a recovery of only 82% in 1918, while at the Ajo plant, of the New Cornelia Copper Company, for the year ending May 1917 the recovery was 74%, but since then it has been improved to nearly 80%. Not that Mr. Greenawalt would depreciate the work done either in Chile or in Arizona, for he has long been an advocate of the wet metallurgical treatment of such copper ores, as our readers will recall.

AMONG the indiscretions provoked by the boom in the Divide district of Nevada we note a report by "an eminent mining engineer" whose geologic fantasies play havoc alike with the English language and the principles of a serious science. He avers that "the lithological structure of the Kickapah property is not difficult of fundamental determination." That remains to be proved. "The primary formation of the district essentially consists of a past carboniferous muscovite granite being the constituency of the core of Lone Mountain, some few thousand feet south and west of the property." The type-setter of the local newspaper from which we quote may have done his share in these "delirious trimmings" of geology, but even the proverbial printer's devil is not all to blame. Mr. Eminent Engineer finds a "silicified schistose zone" uplifted by "pyroxene diorite intrusives": therefore he concludes that "these intrusives are the primary genesis of deep-seated hydrothermal solutions depositing present enriched mineralization of value." That last phrase is precious; it appears to be pseudomorphic after flapdoodle. It is curious how some otherwise sensible men love to talk in terms they do not understand and try hard to be impressive by using the abstract instead of the concrete, with the wholly mistaken idea that they are making a hit. They fool a very few people for a very short time, and expose their ignorance to those whose good opinion would help them most. Meanwhile the story goes that one boomster was telling another: "I was looking over the southern edge of Divide today." Whereupon the other said: "Did you see Carranza?"

BY the time this appears in print the Treaty of Peace will have been signed. The Germans tried to delay the capitulation, they bluffed and they whined, but, as was confidently expected, they threw up their hands at the last moment, not without suggesting that the signing did not bind them to carry out the contract in good faith. The War has ended in what oarsmen call a dirty finish; at the moment when the German government decided to accept the terms, the German crews on the surrendered battleships at Scapa Flow scuttled all the vessels, thereby breaking the conditions of the armistice to which the Germans had subscribed. The German admiral, Von Reuter, assumed responsibility for the act, stating: "I ordered the sinking in the belief that the Armistice was terminated and following the German naval tradition which knows no surrender." What a sense of humor! Of honor it is not worth while to speak. The fleet was surrendered and brought into captivity last November under its own steam and by its own crews; why did they not sink it when they decided to avoid the test of battle, instead of scuttling it when they were on their honor to behave themselves. The tradition of the German navy, of which the Admiral boasted, has gone down, scuttled forever, under the waters of infamy. What an end to the grand dreams of William II, Von Hindenburg, and Von Tirpitz!

FORMATION of a silver export combination, that is, of a group of silver-producing companies, is announced. This combination, legalized by the Webb Act, is to include the Anaconda Copper Mining Company, the American Smelting & Refining Company, and the United States Smelting, Refining & Mining Company, but it is to be open to all producers of silver, after the style of the similar organization created to control the exportation of copper. The New York 'Times' says that "an endeavor to control the world price is the objective behind plans for the formation of a silver export company by the three largest producers in this country. . . . More than half the world's supply of silver is produced in this country, but for more than thirty years the price has been regulated by an arbitrary fixing of values by a committee of three, the Silver Triumvirate, which holds forth in London." Well, we for one would like to see "a check to the domination of the silver market by the English committee" or by anybody else, including any one of the three smelting and refining companies mentioned above, but we confess to surprise in seeing the old yarn about the wicked three revamped in so good a paper as the New York 'Times'. If we remember correctly the bold bad men used to number four and they met every morning at 11 o'clock in order to fix the price of silver for the world. The fact is that the principal dealers in silver in London meet daily at the same hour in order to compare reports upon the dealings in silver and therefrom ascertain the average price for the day. The brokers in London no more fix the price of silver than our worthy contemporary in New York, or we in San Francisco, by reporting the average price of copper sales, "fix" the price of copper.

ON another page we reproduce an address on 'The English-Speaking Peoples', with the hope of promoting goodwill among some at least of the 547 millions living in the Britannic and American commonwealths, including a vast majority of men and women not of the same birth or ancestry. We hold with Theodore Roosevelt that the American has long ceased to be a cousin of the British and that the United States is not to be regarded any longer as an independent and overgrown colony of English origin. The American has become individual and the American people has developed its own entirely separate identity in the society of nations, but, while recognizing this fact clearly, we venture to plead for the establishment of cordial friendship between peoples speaking the same language and striving after the same ideals of fair play, justice, and government. Roosevelt himself, shortly before his death, wrote to a friend, saying: "I agree absolutely with you that this war has brought home to the great majority of thinking men in this country that we, the English-speaking peoples of the United States and the British Empire, possess both ideals and interests in common. We can best do our duty, as members of the family of nations, to maintain peace and justice throughout the world by first rendering it impossible that the peace between ourselves can ever be broken." The address on which we are commenting appeared in a bulletin of the Canadian Mining Institute, and, much to our surprise, elicited a long and indignant letter from a mining engineer, who charged the author with being grossly unfair to the part the Canadians had played in North American history and entirely misleading in his partisanship of the American point of view. Our correspondent exhibited an anti-American feeling that was, to say the least, disconcerting to the optimist and surprising to one fairly familiar with Canadian sentiment. Ancient prejudices have an unhappy way of lurking in unexpected corners. Our Canadian friend can be matched with those who still hark back to 1812 or those who on each January 30 place a wreath at the foot of the statue of Charles I. There are too many Bourbons in the world, forgetting nothing and learning nothing. Let the dead past bury its dead and let us face the present with unjaundiced mind, striving to widen our sympathy and enlarge our understanding with all those who speak the language of Shakespeare. That way lies the hope of an even wider mutuality of goodwill, which in time shall be extended to all the peoples of the earth. Whatever we may hope from Hague conventions or Paris conferences, it is certain that the best augury of general peace lies in the 3500 miles of unfortified frontier between Canada and the United States.

Industrial Co-operation

We take pleasure in publishing, in this issue, the text of an address delivered by Mr. W. R. Ingalls on this subject. We have given considerable space to this address because Mr. Ingalls was for 14 years and until three months ago the editor of our contemporary in New York, he is an honored member of the mining profession, and holds views on economic questions that are all the more interesting because they differ from our own. His utterance, moreover, suggests the awakening of the mining engineer to his duties as a citizen and the broader outlook that the exigencies of the War have forced upon men not usually politically minded. The dismal science of political economy has become quite an engaging study since the average citizen has begun to realize the impact of its application on his personal affairs; and the unending quarrel between capital and labor has become vital to the professional man now that he has learned to appreciate the danger of his position mid-way between the opposing forces. Mr. Ingalls launches forth by stating sundry fundamental principles and soon steers—he does not drift—into a glorification of capitalism and a reprobation of labor that leaves us cold. Even when he waxes furious and labels industrial democracy as "clap-trap" and "jargon," we feel no warmth of resentment against his reactionary sentiment because we believe that the mining profession is well able to think for itself and will accept the good thought in his address without being misdirected by a prejudice so undisguised. Mr. Ingalls appears to respond to his propinquity too much, the economic laws that he recapitulates as if they came from Mount Sinai are but the deductions of fallible men and some of them were predicated on conditions different from those now obtaining. The former editor of the 'Engineering and Mining Journal', and now its consulting editor, we understand, seems to show an adaptation to his environment when he charges the miners with "rapacity" because they tried to get a share of the profit accruing to the smelters from the high prices paid for metals during the War. On another occasion, it will be remembered, our contemporary charged the producers of chrome and manganese with profiteering under the disguise of patriotism, thereby wantonly insulting hundreds of worthy men whose motives were entitled to some respect. Now Mr. Ingalls seeks to chloroform the quicksilver industry of California, labeling it a "useless industry." He takes a good deal upon himself when he undertakes to do that. Even the fact that our domestic supply of mercury proved so eminently useful during the War would not deter him from shutting down the quicksilver mines of California, Nevada, and Texas, rather than give them the protection of a tariff as against imports from the mines in Spain. He would buy the cheaper Spanish quicksilver and store it as a reserve against the day when the next war interrupts overseas trade. Well, we think this is poor political economy. It seems to us wholly desirable that this country should be as nearly self-contained as possible, as little dependent on foreign sources of supply as our mineral resources will permit, and that it is worth while to prevent the extinction of a domestic industry that has served us so well in a great emergency and may serve again under like circumstances. We leave other controversial points in this interesting address, suggesting only that no great measure of industrial co-operation will be attained so long as the mental attitude of one side is expressed by the last five words of Mr. Ingalls' address "the authority of the super-capable few."

Mining Operations in the War

On another page we publish Sir Douglas Haig's farewell to the American Expeditionary Force and his special message to the engineers. General Pershing in his dispatches and his generals in their divisional orders have taken occasion more than once to express a similar appreciation of the Engineer Corps of the Army. It will be remembered also that on March 21, 1918, when the British Fifth Army at La Fère was suddenly overwhelmed by the concentrated attack of the Germans under Von der Marwitz, the advance of the Enemy was checked by the hasty organization of an instant line of defence under the command of General Sandiman Carey. He collected every man available in the vicinity, among them being three companies of American engineers, who thus had the first opportunity of proving the quality of the troops that were destined to play so decisive a part in the eventual defeat of the German onslaught. Indeed, the engineer 'made good' in the great emergency; and in that branch of the service not the least was the mining engineer, and the Tunnelling Companies whom he commanded. In a special order Sir Douglas Haig conveyed his "very keen appreciation of the fine work" which they had done during the four years. "In their own special work, mine warfare," he said, "they have demonstrated their complete superiority over the Germans." Whether in defensive mining or in offensive, "they have shown," he added, "the highest qualities both as military engineers and as fighting troops." We can take pride in this tribute to our fellow-miners and fellow-professionals on the other side; if our own engineer units did not have the chance to engage in similar underground warfare it was only because the American Expeditionary Force arrived at a time when a war of movement, started by the last German offensive and ended by their final retreat, had superseded the long period of stationary fronts. So the British had more experience in mine warfare than we did. A recent meeting of the Institution of Mining & Metallurgy in London was devoted to the work of the miner on the Western Front, an excellent paper on the subject being presented by Major H. Standish Ball. He stated that by the end of June 1916 a force of 25,000 men was employed wholly in mining operations, the officers being engineers with an experience of mining in all parts of the world. It was discovered during the War that the ordinary soldier had a deep-rooted objection to going underground, say, below 12 or 15 feet, whereas the miner was used to it and was willing to engage in the subterranean warfare that became an important feature of the campaign, in Flanders particularly. Listening for enemy operations was aided by instruments invented for the purpose. Fortunately the Hun was given to shouting, as well as talking, thereby allowing our side 'to keep tabs' on him. The range of sound in various rock formations was determined and the audibility of the various noises made in the course of mining was compared. Mine-rescue equipment was used to enable men to work in gassed ground. Canaries were used to ascertain the presence of an excessive proportion of carbon monoxide gas, formed by the explosions in the chalk. When the canary dropped dead, it was time for the men to get out, or wear a mine-rescue mask. It was related how the Tunnellers, as they were called, fought the Germans at a depth of 600 metres in one of the coal mines near Lens and how a guard of them was killed to the last man by the Germans, who took advantage of the down-cast air-current of a shaft to admit concentrated mustard gas into the underground workings. In the end the Enemy was circumvented in this locality by the construction of a concrete 'stopping'. In a paper read before the Canadian Mining Institute it is recorded by Capt. L. B. Reynolds that the Germans took the initiative in mining and they had all the best of it until the Tunnelling Companies were organized by the British and French in the summer of 1915. Miners were recruited hastily and rushed to the front, where they proved that "a man with the sporting instinct, engaged in a game into which he puts the hardest work of his life, is in every way the superior of the machine-made German soldier." We quote Capt. Reynolds. Just before the battle of the Somme the shafts in the chalk had reached a depth of 146 feet, and the Germans were working in an incline several hundred feet long that had attained a depth of 212 feet. The explosive generally used was ammonal, a combination of aluminum dust and ammonium nitrate. The aluminum dust was made, among others, by Mr. Charles Butters, at Oakland, as his neighbors learned to their discomfort, for this chemical readily undergoes combustion, causing minor explosions disagreeable to suburban dwellers. Here we may mention that the famous explosion, or 'blow', at Messines on June 6, 1916, heard by Mr. Lloyd George at his house near Reigate, in England, was carried out under the direction of Major Ralph Stokes, now a Lieutenant-Colonel on the Murmansk front in northern Russia. Colonel Stokes was then 'Controller of Mines', a post for which his experience in peaceful mining had fitted him admirably. He used to be our regular correspondent at Johannesburg ten years ago and volunteered for military service from New York, enlisting as a private in the Royal Engineers, during the first month of the War. We note also with keen interest that Major-General E. D. Swinton, who developed the tank into a potent instrument of war and contributed thereby so largely to the victorious result, acknowledged at a dinner of the Institution in London that he obtained the idea of an armored tractor from a mining engineer, Mr. H. F. Marriott, who was president of the Institution last year. General Swinton stated that in July 1914 Mr. Marriott wrote to him from Antwerp about an American caterpillar tractor that could go over rough country and climb "like hell." The machine was the Holt tractor, made at Stockton, California, and from the suggestion offered by Mr. Marriott the General, then much lower in rank, set to work to devise a bullet-proof machine that could overcome the German machine-guns; and how well he did it, we all know. One of the most spectacular, and most effective, bits of mining warfare was done on the mountainous Italian front by Capt. Gelasio Caetani, an Italian of noble birth and an American metallurgist of recognized distinction. On April 17, 1916, on the Col di Lana, at an altitude of 8110 feet, a drift 300 feet long had been extended under the Austrians, who were counter-mining; five tons of gelatine and nitro-glycerine were exploded, 15,000 tons of rock was lifted, 80 of the enemy were destroyed, and 179 survivors, including 9 officers, were captured. However, despite such brilliant exploits on several fronts, the mining phase of warfare proved less important than had been expected at one time. It must be remembered that at the beginning of the War it was thought that forts fifteen or twenty miles apart would suffice for the defensive; when the German onslaught exposed the weakness of this plan, the idea of 'digging in', of a continuous trench system parallel with the front, came into play. It was to break through the trenches that mining operations were started, but this proved ineffective, because the Germans countered it by a series of small forts, in the form of machine-gun turrets, at intervals less than their range, so as to constitute a continuous line of defence. Then came the tanks, which were the chief invention of the British and helped to end the War, as poison-gas had been a deadly trick adopted by the Germans in the early days of the Flanders campaign. Underground warfare, by means of mines, was romantic and spectacular, but it played little part in the final result; it was a failure except in a few uncommon instances as at Vimy and Messines, and on the Italian front; its real value was in undermining the morale, rather than the defensive works, of the Enemy, because the uncertainty of not knowing what was going on underfoot was intimidating and unnerving to his infantry. The aeroplane checked successful mining because it made it difficult to camouflage the waste-rock taken out of the underground excavations; moreover, the closeness of the water-level to the surface in some localities and the hardness of the rock in others made mining impracticable. Such work took time, any change in the Enemy's front frustrated it, and, as we have said, to the engineers of the American armies the use of mining, if otherwise desirable, was denied by the fact that the Germans were on the move, forward and then backward, by the time the American Expeditionary Force got into action. The mining engineer, however, wrote a thrilling chapter in the Great Fight for Civilization, and it should be recorded in the archives of the profession.

DISCUSSION

A Union of Technical Men

The Editor:

Sir—A union of technical men has been formed in British Columbia with the following objects: "(1) To obtain adequate recognition of technical work; (2) to establish scales of standard fees for consultations, and obtain recognition for the same; (3) to obtain equitable remuneration for salaried technical men and their assistants; (4) to secure consultation and employment for local members of the technical profession for work in British Columbia and to discourage the employment of outside men for technical work when duly qualified men are available within the Province; (5) to protect members when handicapped by extraneous influences in the execution of their profession; (6) to co-operate with existing professional societies in the furtherance of the above objects, and, while not interfering with their usual activities, to assist them in every legitimate manner that will tend to maintain or improve the efficiency, status, and remuneration of the technical profession; (7) to protect the public by encouraging the employment of qualified technical men." The secretary is Charles T. Hamilton, 570 Hastings St. West, Vancouver, British Columbia.

The idea of a union of technical men seems altogether at variance with one's ideas of what is right and proper, and yet, when one considers conditions as they exist to-day, the wonder is, not at the formation of a technical men's union now, but rather that such a union should not have been formed long ago.

The man who decides on a technical profession, after leaving school, has to spend four or five years at a college or a university to fit himself for his life's work, and then he is drafted into some industrial work and for the next five or six years, and not infrequently longer, he is employed at a salary which is less than that received by many a common laborer today. After a time, these technical men become superintendents of departments, and, ultimately, if they are fortunate, intelligent, and industrious, general managers of big industrial concerns, and it is in the hope of filling such positions, together with the pure love of their work, that has enabled them to carry on, often through long hours, at the mere pittance they receive. Have the employers in the past been dealing quite a fair hand to these men, or have they stacked the cards to their own advantage? The employer has demanded loyalty from his technical assistants, and usually he has received it, but has he, in his turn, been loyal to his technical assistants? Has he given a fair return for what he has received? I think he has not, and I think the formation of the technical union demonstrates that he has not. The average man, especially the educated man, dislikes to have to beg for an increase in salary. Ranged on the side of his employer against organized labor, he has seen what labor has been able to accomplish for itself by organization and combination. The high cost of living in recent years has made it almost impossible for him to live on the pittance doled out to him. Is it any wonder, then, that he, too, has decided to organize?

F. H. Mason.

Victoria, B. C., June 6.

The Leaching of Flotation Concentrate

The Editor:

Sir—I read Mr. Middleton's article, on the leaching of copper concentrate, in your issue of June 7, with a great deal of interest. His ideas of the chemical treatment of flotation concentrates have much to commend them. However, the possibilities of leaching flotation or other concentrates, in the United States, has not been overlooked. Indeed, more attention is being given to it at the present time than ever before. The problem of the chemical treatment of flotation or of table concentrate is not an easy one. Much, if not most, depends upon the recovery of the copper from the leach solutions. Chemical precipitation, as so far developed, is out of the question, especially in the treatment of a concentrate. Even in the treatment of low-grade ores, chemical precipitation does not offer alluring possibilities. The chemical precipitate, which will usually be cement copper or copper sulphide, simply represents a higher-grade material, which, in turn, has to be smelted and refined much the same as an original ore. With iron precipitation, both the acid and the iron are irrecoverably lost. Even if sulphurous acid is used as the solvent, chemical precipitation appears to be inferior to electrolysis.

Manifestly, the hope lies in the electrolytic precipitation of the copper with the simultaneous regeneration of the solvent. It is doubtful whether any of the electrolytic methods so far made public will adequately solve the problem. They are not generally applicable. It is a question, even, whether much progress has been made in overcoming the real difficulty, and that is the neutralizing of the deleterious effects of the ferric salts in the electrolyte. Until that point has been adequately taken care of, the general application of leaching to copper ores and concentrates is not probable. When it has been adequately taken care of, it is reasonably certain that leaching will, to a very large extent, supplant smelting. The general application of leaching, to copper ores, must be attacked, not so much from the point of view of the extraction of the copper from the ore as from the view-point of the electrolytic deposition of the copper and the regeneration of the solvent. This is true whether the solvent be a chloride, a sulphate, sulphuric acid, or sulphurous acid. The greatest possibilities with either sulphuric or sulphurous acid are along the lines of electrolytic deposition of the copper and the application of the electric current to the regeneration of the solvent.

The phenomenally successful commercial results obtained at Ajo and at Chuquicamata do not affect the real issue, and, as a matter of fact, the vital point has not, even in those plants, been adequately met. At Chuquicamata the ore contains only a very small amount of iron, and it contains enough soluble copper to make the process practically self-sustaining in acid with electrolytic regeneration. Even at that it is necessary or desirable to discard large quantities of solution to keep down the ferric iron in the electrolyte. At Chuquicamata this discarding of large quantities of solution makes little difference, because the ore practically furnishes its own solvent for the copper. It would be unwise to attempt to duplicate the results obtained at Chuquicamata, as some have found out who have tried it, because the conditions there are exceptional and do not represent the ordinary leaching problem, either with a low-grade ore or a concentrate. At Ajo, a large proportion of the copper—approximately 25%—is precipitated with iron to reduce the effect of the ferric salts in the electrolyte. This copper precipitate is smelted much the same as a high-grade ore, or concentrate, with the regular furnace-charges. Iron precipitation of 25% of the copper also means a corresponding loss of acid. It is intended to maintain the ferric iron in the issuing electrolyte at about 0.5%, and only one-sixth of the copper is deposited in each cycle of the electrolyte through the cells. Even as small an amount as 0.5% ferric iron in the electrolyte is capable of doing a great deal of harm, and at Ajo it apparently does not take long to accumulate 0.5% ferric iron in the electrolyte, when 1.75 lb. of ferric iron is formed per pound of copper precipitated.*

Ferrous iron in the electrolyte is not particularly harmful; it may be decidedly beneficial. It is possible to get as large, or larger, efficiency with an electrolyte high in iron as from pure solutions, provided the iron is maintained in the ferrous condition. Ferric iron is harmful in proportion to its presence in the electrolyte. Many have tried, in a small way, to duplicate the success attained at Ajo and at Chuquicamata, without taking into account the elaborate precautions taken at those plants to overcome the deleterious effects of the ferric salts.

The real difficulty of copper leaching with electrolytic deposition and regeneration will not be overcome until the harmful effects of the iron in the electrolyte are adequately disposed of. It is fair to predict that when this difficulty is overcome, it will not be along the lines of purifying the solvent or of eliminating large quantities of solution to get rid of the ferric iron, but, rather, in making the iron work with the process and not against it. It would be much the same as in the ordinary concentration of ores. Before flotation was a success, high tailing-losses resulted from the tendency of certain minerals, such as chalcocite and chalcopyrite, to float away with the gangue. Numerous schemes were tried to make such minerals sink. The true solution of the difficulty came in helping the minerals to float, and not in trying to make them sink. And so it will be found in the electrolytic deposition of copper from impure solutions. The problem is not an easy one, but still, I am inclined to think, is quite capable of being solved.

In the treatment of concentrate the iron is an important factor. My own experience would indicate that it is quite impossible to make a large percentage of the copper soluble in water, without at the same time making also a considerable amount of the iron soluble either in water or in dilute acid. The difficulties, which are side-stepped at Ajo and Chuquicamata, where there is only a small amount of iron, are greatly magnified in the treatment of concentrates, which usually contain a high percentage of iron. If an attempt is made to roast so as to make the iron insoluble, the copper is also made insoluble, at least to such an extent as to make the extraction impracticable. The difference in the decomposition temperatures between the soluble salts of iron and the soluble salts of copper is too small to admit of close regulation in practical work on a large scale.

In conclusion, I might recall the statement made in the closing paragraph of my book on the 'Hydrometallurgy of Copper', published in 1912, before there was a single electrolytic copper extraction plant in successful operation:

"Copper is one of the most readily soluble of all the metals, and one of the most readily precipitated either chemically or electrolytically. Theoretically, the solvent processes, especially the electrolytic processes, offer all that could be desired, on ores chemically adapted; close extraction, cheap deposition, copper in its metallic form, saving of the precious metals, the installation of plants at the mines which may be operated in any unit and without admixture of other ores or fluxes. With these theoretical advantages it is reasonable to suppose that the chemical methods will ultimately be in as general use for the extraction of copper as the cyanide and chlorination processes now are for the extraction of gold and silver."

I see no reason now why this prediction will not be fulfilled. I am convinced now, as I was then, that the general application of leaching methods, especially to copper concentrates and high-grade ores, will depend largely, if not entirely, on the successful elimination of the harmful effects of the ferric salts in the electrolyte. I am convinced now, as I was then, that the solving of the problem of the ferric salts will be along the lines of

*See M. & S. P., Feb. 8, 1918.

making the iron work with the process, and not in eliminating it to such a degree as to restrict its capacity for doing harm.

WILLIAM E. GREENAWALT

Denver, June 9

Blue Sky Laws

The Editor:

Sir—The question, 'Do Blue Sky laws protect the people against fraud?' is much discussed. This law in Nebraska has not been a protective measure, but, on the contrary, it has afforded an inducement to commit fraud; many industrial corporations were floated which proved worthless. While proclaiming to protect the investor from fraud, operating under the permit plan, it is nothing more than license to take money from the investor without a guarantee of honesty or soundness.

The law as administered is a joke, a snare, and a delusion; it protects none but stock and bond brokers, trust companies, and other Wall Street interests who are seeking to control all the industry of the United States, which cannot be done by any other method or scheme. The mining industry of this nation is hit the hardest by these laws and they violate the constitutional rights of every citizen in the country by refusing him the privilege to dispose of his personal or real property as he may desire.

The Nebraska legislature, after investigation, found that the Blue Sky law offered opportunity for the strong financial organizations representing Wall Street to monopolize the sales of securities within the State, thereby retarding the development of the natural resources of the State; that it afforded no protection to the citizens against the sale of fraudulent securities, but on the contrary was highly injurious to the business interests of the State, and a menace to legitimate development and industry; and that it deprived persons of liberty and property rights, all tending to injure and ruin the credit and operation of legitimate business concerns; and that it permitted the sale of stocks and securities that do not offer a fair return on the investment, while permits were granted to corporations to sell 6 and 7% preferred stock with no assets other than the money received from the sale of such stock.

The old law was repealed and a new one substituted granting the Governor and Attorney General authority to administer the same, leaving these officials to use whatever means they may decide upon to investigate the proposed industry at its expense, which in the opinion of many of the people is more autocratic than the original Blue Sky law and unconstitutional.

Every State in the Union has a law against fraud, and if these laws were enforced no person would be permitted to deal in fraudulent securities; but the Wall Street interests, realizing the enormous losses incurred by the sale of fraudulent securities, are seeking to blindfold the public by making it appear the Blue Sky laws protect them from fraud. I have read the Blue Sky laws of the various States, and have yet to find one that protects the investor against fraud, but on the contrary it permits a monopoly of the sales of all securities as well as exempting the stock and bond brokers, trust companies, and other Wall Street interests, allowing these hogs of finance to feed on the people. Blue Sky laws have done mole to retard the development of the mining industry than any other act of our Government.

Mining is more or less a speculative proposition which involves some risk, but no person should be denied his lawful right to buy mining stock if he sees fit, but the mandate of the Blue Sky law says it cannot be done without its consent. Thus this industry is made to suffer for the reason that these officials are not competent to judge its value, nor will they do so from an unbiased standpoint.

These pirates of stock promotion are now clamoring for a national Blue Sky law, which should be fought tooth and toenail by every man interested in the mining industry for the reason that Blue Sky laws are autocratic laws, and are aimed directly at the man or corporation who seeks to develop our national resources. It is the worst form of tyranny, and it embodies and represents "taxation without representation." What we need today is not laws to restrict and destroy the mining industry, but laws that will encourage the development of our national resources, increase the opportunities for labor, and furnish this nation with gold and silver with which to pay off our National Debt, thereby increasing our prosperity.

ROY M. HARROP.

Omaha, June 1.

[In our issue of May 31 we published a letter on 'Justice to Our Native Young Men', signed "M. Stockholm." This was a typographical error, for the lady is named 'Stockham' and she is the wife of Mr. J. W. Stockham, of Warren, Arizona.—EDITOR.]

ZINC REDUCTION WORKS in Belgium consist of 14 smelters with a total of 50,696 retorts, 10 rolling-mills, with a combined capacity of 52,000 tons, and 10 chemical plants for roasting ores. About 60% of the smelting capacity can be said to be of modern construction. A plant at Rothem, with 3360 retorts, was completed just before the War, and one at Corphalie, with 2200 retorts, was built during the War. The tendency in the newer plants has been to increase to a considerable extent the mechanical handling of ores, also the mechanical charging and discharging of the furnaces. Belgian engineers have never looked with favor on the use of the large furnaces so common in the United States. The furnace generally used is one that has not over 200 retorts to the side, and it is only in the recently built plants that one finds the separate producers used, and in only a limited number have mechanical producers been used. The working floors of the furnace-rooms are well ventilated, and the hoods over the furnaces are connected with stacks for carrying away the zinc fume from the furnaces. For 10 years prior to 1914, 21.67% of the world's supply of spelter was produced in Belgium, but most of the ore was from foreign sources.—M. F. Chase in May report of the U. S. Bureau of Mines.

American Engineers in the War

On the eve of the departure of General O'Ryan with his troops from Brest, Sir Douglas Haig wrote him as follows:

"You are returning in victory from the first campaign in which American troops have fought on European soil, secure in the strength and limitless resources of your own great country on the other side of the Atlantic. The call of outraged humanity, which from the outset of the War sounded so loudly and closely in British ears, was heard from afar by the manhood of our sister nation.

"A people less far-sighted, less imbued with the lofty ideals of liberty, might never have heeded that call. You heard it; you gave heed; and when the time was ripe and every city, township, village, hamlet, and farm in your mighty land knew the full meaning of the desperate conflict raging beyond the seas, you flung yourselves into the fray, ardent and impetuous on the side of the right.

"You who now return to the homes that sent you forth in faith and hope to make, if need be, the supreme sacrifice for the belief that is in you, can say to those who greet you that in that triumph you have had your share. You can point to a proud record of achievement, to the months of patient, earnest training; to the incessant strain and watchfulness of the trenches; to the fury of great battles.

"You can point also to your sacrifices made with courage and devotion unsurpassed in all the dread story of the War, abundant in heroism, sacrifices which were the price of world liberty and peace, which you have helped so powerfully to build up anew.

"Returning, you and all ranks of the American Expeditionary Force carry back with you the pride, effection, and esteem of all who fought beside you, and not least of those with whom you share a common language and a common outlook upon life. The memory of our great attack upon the Hindenburg line on the 29th of September, 1918, in which the 27th American Division, along with the troops from all parts of the British Empire, took so gallant and glorious part, will never die, and the service then rendered by American troops will be recalled with gratitude and admiration throughout the British Empire.

"I rejoice to think that in the greater knowledge and understanding born of perils and hardships shared together we have learned at last to look beyond old jealousies and petty quarrels to the essential qualities which unite the great English-speaking nations.

"In bidding godspeed to you, whom for a time I was privileged to have under my command, I feel confident that the new era opened out before us by the appearance of American troops on the battlefields of the Old World will see the sympathy and friendship now established between our two nations constantly deepened and strengthened, to the lasting advantage of both peoples."

In Sir Douglas Haig's Official Dispatch he writes as follows:

"Other hostile attacks on both banks of the Somme were repulsed with heavy loss to the enemy by the 1st Cavalry Division, and the 3rd Australian Division, a battalion of United States Engineers rendering gallant service south of the river."

He concludes his dispatch by stating:

"Finally, I am glad to acknowledge the ready manner in which American Engineer Units have been placed at my disposal from time to time, and the great value of the assistaance they have rendered. In the battles referred to in this dispatch, American and British troops have fought shoulder to shoulder in the same trenches, and have shared together in the satisfaction of beating off German attacks. All ranks of the British Army look forward to the day when the rapidly growing strength of the American Army will allow American and British soldiers to co-operate in offensive action." [We refer to the subject on an editorial page.—EDITOR.]

Use of Manganese Di-Oxide Ore

By W. C. PHALEN

The quantity of manganese ore used in industries other than metallurgical vary from 25,000 to 50,000 tons per annum. The latter figure is probably more nearly correct. Most of the ore so used is the highest grade of pyrolusite (MnO_2) obtainable, and commands a much higher price than metallurgical ore. The manganese di-oxide ore is generally spoken of as chemical manganese ore.

The principal use of manganese ore, aside from its applications in the steel industry in the form of ferro-manganese and spiegeleisen, is as an oxidizing agent. It is so used principally in the manufacture of dry cells, as a decolorizer in certain kinds of glass, and as a drier in oils, paints, and varnishes. The ore is also used directly or indirectly in the manufacture of various manganese chemicals. Many of the textbooks describe its reaction with hydrochloric acid as a source of chlorine. It is no longer used commercially in making chlorine gas, as the latter is an abundant by-product in the manufacture of caustic soda and potash. Some chlorine may be made by this method when the object is the production, not of chlorine, but of manganese chloride. It has been mentioned as a soil stimulant, but its value in the fertilizer industry has not been established, and so far as known it is not a constituent of any commercial fertilizer.

The gasoline engine gave the development and production of the present type of dry cell great stimulus. Its use in ignition systems demanded a cheap portable cell able to recuperate after comparatively heavy current drains. In 1897, its manufacture attained considerable volume. The present normal yearly requirements of this production include 25,000 tons of high-grade manganese di-oxide ore, an equal amount of carbon (petroleum coke and graphite) and 8000 to 10,000 tons of sheet-zinc, together with corresponding quantities of zinc chloride, ammonium chloride, paper, carbon electrodes, pitch, and sundry other substances.—Abstract from Minerals Investigation Series, No. 16, of U. S. Bureau of Mines.

Continuous Overflow and Its Effect on the Slag Loss of Reverberatory Furnaces

By OLIVER E. JAGER

Any noticeable reduction in the copper content of a reverberatory slag is an achievement worthy of comment, and calls for some inquiry into the causes effecting it. The present article refers to the practice at the Anaconda reduction works, and I am indebted to Frederick Laist, the manager, for bringing the subject to my notice. It will be shown that there was a large decrease in the reverberatory slag-loss after the introduction of coal-dust firing and the continuous flow. That this improvement has not altogether been maintained is due to the altered nature of the furnace-charge. The saving at present effected, however, is sufficient to merit consideration of the various changes that have taken place in the reverberatory practice. One of the most important of these is the elimination of skimming by the adoption of the continuous overflow of slag. To my knowledge, the adaptation of continuous flow to the reverberatory furnace had been suggested as far back as 1904, but it was not until the introduction of the very large furnace, fired with pulverized fuel, that the feature was introduced. The details of the continuous overflow of slag are as follows:

The reverberatory furnaces at Anaconda are 133 ft. 7 in. long by 22 ft. wide, fired with pulverized coal, and using side-charging. Each furnace smelts on an average 550 tons of charge per 24 hours, which will mean a slag production of about 369 tons, equivalent to a flow of about 15.5 tons per hour. It is this large quantity, of course, that makes a continuous flow possible, though it would be interesting to know on just how small a furnace it could be used, taking into consideration at the same time the heat in the slag and its silicate degree. The front of the furnace is protected by a large water-cooled cast-iron plate, 10 ft. 6 in. long by 2 ft. 3 in. wide by 4½ in. thick, set flush with the outside face of the brickwork. It passes beneath the skinning-door, the skin-plate being set above it. One or two openings suitable for tapping matte are left in it, and cleats are provided to hold the taphole-plates in position, matte being tapped from the end of the furnace. The door formerly used for skinning is bricked up, except for a suitable slot through which the slag escapes. The slag flows out of the furnace, over the skin-plate in the usual way, and into a curved launder of cast-iron, an inch thick, made in three sections bolted together. The launder is of semi-circular section, 24 in. wide at the top, with a flange 2 in. wide along the edges to retain the brick lining. This launder curves in an easy bend, changing the direction of the slag stream about 135°, and discharging it over the granulating jet. The slag travels about 12 ft. in going from the furnace front to the granulator. For a couple of feet outside the skimming-door, the launder is kept covered by a few large lumps of coal and one or two brick slabs, with fettling thrown on top. Over the remainder of the launder a crust of slag soon forms, the molten slag flowing under this crust. This arrangement requires little attention, sometimes running for a couple of days without being touched, unless the matte rises in the furnace to a point where it starts to come over. The shooting calls the attention of the furnace-man, who shuts off the flow at the skinning-door till the matte is tapped, when the slag stream is started again. When slag is removed from a furnace by skinning, there is always an admission of cold air to the uptake. This is avoided by using continuous flow. The furnace work is easier on the men, and there are fewer cleanings, etc., to be re-smelted. Continuous flow uses more water than the intermittent skinning method.

Coming now to the question of the copper content in the reverberatory slag, the first point that suggests itself is the amount of copper saved. Cutting down the slag-assay a few one-hundredths of one per cent does not appear an important achievement at first glance, and makes no appeal to the imagination of some furnace superintendents. But when this modest difference is applied to the tons of slag produced, and the calculation is carried on to show money saved, it demonstrates the value of making an effort to produce cleaner slags.

For the six-monthly period ending June 30, 1914, which was just prior to the installation of pulverized coal-firing and continuous flow, the slag contained 0.41% copper. Taking the last six months of 1915, during which all furnaces were operating under the new system, the figure is 0.32% copper. While this decrease of nearly 0.1% was possible under the conditions prevailing at that time, it has not been attained with the present character of reverberatory charge, so that 0.35% copper is now a good average figure. The change in the charge is due to the large quantity of flotation concentrate now treated. This extremely fine material does not smelt as easily as the coarser quality formerly treated, and has a marked tendency, while being charged, to produce dust that gets into the slag. Owing to the fact that the blast-furnaces are not in operation at present, there is some high-grade partly oxidized material going to the reverberatories, and unmixed with the remainder of the charge.* This also has an adverse effect on the slag-assay, though the actual effect cannot be very great, as

*Oliver E. Jager, 'Exit the Blast Furnace', M. & S. P., June 21, 1919.

the tonnage of this material amounts to less than 8% of the total charge. Under normal conditions at Anaconda, seven furnaces are operated in the reverberatory building, smelting a total of 3850 tons of charge per 24 hours. Of this tonnage, 67% goes into the slag, giving 2580 tons of slag. Therefore, a decrease of 0.06% copper in the slag-assay means an annual saving of 565 tons of copper. Assuming the recovery of 98% of this copper, and that it sells for 16 cents per pound, there would be an annual saving of $177,000. Comparing the slag-analyses for the two above-mentioned periods with that of the present slag, no difference is to be found in their silicate degree. A calculation of oxygen ratios shows the slags to be extremely uniform, corresponding closely to sesqui-silicates, so that no question arises as to any difference in their fusibility.

It appears to be well established that the lower copper-assay is due to the continuous flow, though it might be argued by a meticulous person that it is really due to the introduction of coal-dust firing, as it was the latter process that brought about the adoption of continuous flow. When this method of firing was first installed, the furnace was skimmed in the usual way. It was soon found, however, that the ash from the coal formed a blanket of slag on top of the molten charge, and that this slag blanket was evidently holding up dust from the charge, thus increasing the copper loss in the slag, as samples of the slag blanket showed an abnormally high copper content. With a continuous flow, the slag-blanket is held back in the furnace, where the resulting condition of tranquillity allows a better separation of entrained metal. This is also assisted by the introduction of fine lime-rock through doors provided on either side of the skimming-door, as any tendency of the slag to thicken is overcome by the action of the flux.

In addition to the effects of the continuous flow, a significant factor in the reduced slag loss is the introduction of a proper system of mixing the charges going to the roasters.† Considerable care is now taken to produce a self-fluxing calcine, since it has been proved that sudden variations in the composition of the charge will produce similar variations in the slag-assay. For instance, a sudden excess of silicious material will upset the furnace operation by interfering with the proper fluxing of the charge, leaving a certain unfluxed portion to be taken care of by a subsequent charge. In other words, a 'floater' is formed. This condition was more often encountered in the old practice of dropping large charges into the centre of the furnace, than with the present system of side-charging, where the feed is introduced more gradually.

Another factor, due to the practice of side charging, is that there is no longer a large bath of matte in the furnace. With this lack of storage space for matte inside the furnace, there is more liability of the matte rising and getting out with the slag.

Summing up, the continuous flow is the most important factor in the reduction of the slag-loss (particularly when using pulverized coal as fuel), as there is a better opportunity for any entrained metal to settle out of the slag blanket, the quiet, steady flow being more conducive to this than the sudden rush of the large slag stream produced when skimming. There is no doubt that, under present conditions of operation, were skimming in vogue the slags would carry more copper than they do with continuous flow. The proper preparation of the charge also plays a considerable part in the production of slags of lower copper content, provided its effect be not nullified by the addition of large quantities of flue-dust, or other material not figured when making up the roaster charges. Firing with pulverized coal gives a slightly better combustion of fuel and more regular furnace conditions than grate-firing, as the former system produces the conditions necessary for proper combustion and heat radiation inside the furnace, though it has not been shown that any higher temperature is obtained. Side-charging favors the production of cleaner slags, though the diminished matte-space has a tendency to offset this. In conclusion, it may be said that, considering the general composition of the present reverberatory slag, it is as clean as a blast-furnace slag would be, if the latter were produced under prevailing conditions at Anaconda.

†C. D. Demond. 'Economy and Efficiency in Reverberatory Smelting'. Trans. A. I. M. E., August, 1914.

THE IRON INDUSTRY in Shansi province, China, is the oldest in the world. The ore is, unfortunately, in irregular lenses, the average thickness being about 1 ft. Mining this ore by modern large-scale methods is therefore impossible, although much of it can and is mined by native methods. The estimated quantity in Shansi is 300,000,000 tons, although this quantity is necessarily approximate. In other parts of China there is approximately 300,000,000 tons more, of which at least half can be worked by modern methods. In 1915 the total production of pig-iron was about 300,000 tons. Of this amount, 136,541 tons came from the Hanyang Iron Works and 29,529 tons from the Sino-Japanese Coal Co. at Penshihu. The rest came from small native furnaces in various parts of China. Besides supplying the Hanyang works, the Tayeh mine exported 298,350 tons of ore to Japan. The estimated total production of pig-iron in 1918 is 500,000 tons. The iron-ore deposits are now controlled by either Chinese or Japanese interests, the Chinese government making efforts to obtain control of deposits not already mortgaged to the Japanese.

MANGANESE MINING costs $9.50 per ton in the Erickson district of Utah, $8.25 in the Cartersville district of Georgia, $5 to $8 in Cuba, and $5 in Brazil. The Utah ore is from deep workings, the others from surface operations. The estimated average cost per long ton of manganese ore delivered to the consumer during 1918 was $29.70 per ton for domestic, 41% oxide and 36.5% carbonate, and $30 and $23.50 for Brazilian and Cuban 45 and 38% ores, respectively. The future cost will be about $24.65, $14.75, $18.50, and $16.50, respectively.—C. M. Weld and W. R. Crane of U. S. Bureau of Mines.

Industrial Co-operation

By W. R. INGALLS

*A few weeks ago in delivering an address before the Mining and Metallurgical Society of America, I took as my theme the 'Economic Duties of the Engineer'. In the address to which I have referred I expressed the fundamental idea that the civilized world has experienced such great losses of capital and man-power through the War that it is confronted by grave prospects unless the losses be off-set by great increase in efficiency in production, which will likely require an industrial reorganization. We, and especially we engineers, must strive for that and we may achieve it, but as an ominous counter-agent I see the spread of Bolshevism and many economic fallacies. I urged it therefore as one of the essential duties of the engineer that he saturate himself with sound economic doctrine and prepare himself to spread the gospel. I pointed out, that labor as the residual claimant upon the produce of industry already gets about 80% of the whole, leaving to capital only what comes to about 4% on the total investment, and that if labor should attempt to seize that moderate share and should succeed in doing so, it would meet with the disappointment of the child who grasps a soap-bubble; that the grievances of labor refer in the main to inequalities in distribution among its own classes; and finally that the only way of maintaining or improving the welfare of labor is to enable it to produce more. In order to enable it to do so, we must contemplate industrial reorganization and must accustom ourselves to think in terms of industries as a whole.

What I am going to say will be, perhaps, different from what you expect. I am not going to tell you that we must prepare for a new social order, or that the day of industrial democracy has come, or that henceforth the workers—meaning those who labor mainly with their hands—are going to run things. There has been a lot of talk of that sort, which has been sentimental, fallacious, and mischievous. On the contrary, I shall tell you that economic law is going to prevail and determine what people will do, and the less attempted interference with it there is, the better will everything be. I am going to tell you that labor instead of holding the gains that it made during the War is in danger of falling below the scale of living before the War. When I say labor, substitute people, for in the main the laborers are the people. We do not want to see any such downfall. It can be averted only by industrial co-operation. As I proceed you will see that what I mean by industrial co-operation is nothing like what some people mean by industrial democracy. There is great unrest among workers all over the world. This is mainly economic, and is based on ideas ranging from the moderate thought that labor does not get its fair share of the produce of industry to the extreme thought that it ought to recover what it thinks has been stolen from it in the past. Before entering upon constructive considerations, let us pause to examine if there be anything essentially wrong in the arrangements the industrial world has already worked out for itself, not merely in one country, but in all civilized countries, for the system is everywhere about the same.

In my previous paper I argued that there is nothing essentially wrong, for the reason that labor is the residual claimant upon the produce of industry, taking all that remains after the deductions of the shares of the landlord, the capitalist, the entrepreneur, and the State; that even if those deductions were not made labor would not get any more; that such inequalities in distribution that exist are not between capital and labor, but are among classes of labor itself. The expression that labor is the residual claimant upon the produce of industry is one of the things that I have been asked to explain. It is in no way a new thought, but rather is it classic economic doctrine, advanced by Jevons and developed by General Walker. I can offer no explanation so good as to quote freely from General Walker, without however using his exact words or confining myself simply to his statements.

On the lowest grades of land there is no rent. The cost of producing from them so much as must be produced to supply the needs of the people determines the price of agricultural produce. The rent of better lands is the excess of their produce after the cost of cultivating the no-rent lands has been paid. This rent does not affect the price of agricultural produce and does not come out of the remuneration of the agricultural laborer. The laborer cannot get it, or any part of it, by any economic means. It must go to the landlord unless it be confiscated by the State, or ravished away by violence, and in either of those events it will soon cease and no longer accrue for anybody.

The remuneration for the use of capital must be high enough to induce those who have produced wealth to save it, instead of consuming it. Manifestly what is paid as interest for the use of capital is no loss to labor, for it makes more produce out of which labor benefits. Indeed, the higher the rate of interest the more is the benefit of labor. The worst thing that could happen to labor would be such a curtailment of the rate of interest, either from economic or arbitrary causes, as would diminish the incentive of people to save and induce them rather to gratify personal appetites and tastes as consumers.

Profits economically partake of the nature of rents.

*An address prepared for presentation at the annual general meeting of the Canadian Mining Institute.

Just as there is a class of no-rent lands so is there a class of no-profit employers, the need for whose produce determines the market-price. From the point of no-profit production, profits range upward through the degrees of moderate profits, liberal profits, grand profits, monumental profits, but these consist wholly of wealth created by the entrepreneurs themselves and no economic means would carry any portion of them permanently to wages. To be sure, they may be taken by the State as taxes, and by the State paid out in extravagant wages, but this destroys the economic balance and produces conditions whereof the result is that nobody makes any profit, industry languishes and labor suffers. We are now witnessing just such a condition.

The matter of profits is one of the most complicated of economic questions, or, perhaps I should say, one that is a subject of much popular misconception. Capitalists themselves are responsible for much of this through the common desire to make a good showing, and disinclination ever to allow sufficient for the depreciation and obsolescence of plant. In the metallurgical industry we see repeatedly how plants have to be discarded and rebuilt entirely. How others have to be abandoned owing to failure of the mining districts that once supported them. How industries become over-built in order to supply temporary needs with the eventuality of surplus capacity that has to be thrown away. Thus the American zinc industry in 1915-'17 realized fabulous profits on paper, but a large part of them was re-invested in plant that subsequently ceased to have any earning capacity. Sometimes special conditions preclude a venture unless an extraordinary apparent profit can be expected. Thus, I once arranged for the purchase of a zinc smelter on the basis of an annual profit of 50%, for I could not estimate the endurance of natural-gas supply for but little more than two years. The purchasers merely got their money back plus an annual interest that really did not justify their risk. The exaggeration of profits contributes to the dissatisfaction of laborers who reason that their wages are pitifully small while the earnings of their employers are extravagant, and fail to appreciate that much of those earnings is merely replacement of principal or reward of extraordinary risks, without the prospect of which industrial progress would be checked. But after all, this is going into details and losing sight of the economic situation in its entirety, which is a common fault and source of misconception.

Rents, interest, profits, and taxes being deducted from the produce of industry all the rest goes to the laborers. "So far as, by their energy in work, their economy in the use of materials, or their care in dealing with the finished product, the value of that product is increased," says General Walker, "that increase goes to them by purely natural laws, provided only competition be full and free. Every invention in mechanics, every discovery in the chemical art, inures directly and immediately to their benefit, except so far as a limited monopoly may be created by law for the encouragement of invention and discovery."

General Walker illustrated this by supposing a community to be engaged in a certain production, which is divided among rent, interest, profits, and wages. Let it be supposed that over-night a higher class of population be substituted, and that it produces 5% more of goods. To whom does the gain go? Not to the landlord, for the material used makes no larger draft upon the land than formerly, and hence calls no lower grade of land into cultivation. Not to the capital class, for no more tools are required than formerly. Not to the employing class, for the substitution of intelligent workmen for those of a poorer quality has no tendency to drive production down to a less efficient grade of entrepreneurs. On the contrary the effect would be to raise the line of no-profit employers from which the profits of successful employers are measured upward. Hence the gain must go to labor, for it cannot go to anyone else, and this, says General Walker, is what is meant by the laboring class being the residual claimant upon the product of industry, which upon the assumption of perfect competition is both profoundly true and of illimitable importance in economics.

This is an expression of a great economic truth in the abstract, but it may be put in a definite statistical way. We know it to be the truth not only from scientific deduction, but also from examination of the income of nations and the distribution thereof. Numerous studies of the income of both Great Britain and the United States show that of the whole produce 60 to 80% goes to labor and that the remainder is but a relatively small return on the capital used.† But we are able to show and to say a good deal more than that, to wit, that during the last hundred years of great industrial development the major part of the benefit has accrued to labor.

It was the theory of Karl Marx, from whose teachings are derived so many of the fallacies of the present time, that labor, in its narrowest sense, produces everything, and therefore that labor should have all that it produces. That idea is frequently expressed now, all over the world. We have already seen that labor gets almost all as it is, and what remains it would not get, for if profits for example are the reward of intelligence—the removal of intelligence would remove profits also. So long as the world was dependent upon mere man-power there was no very great advance in the wealth of nations beyond what was due to increase in population. There is no good reason to believe that an Englishman in the reign of George IV could carry any more weight per hour or for any more hours, or could exhibit any other superiority of physical power, than an Englishman in the time of William the Conqueror. The great increase in pro-

†In my January address I indicated labor's share of the produce of industry of the United States as having been approximately 80% in 1916. Since then I have seen Dr. Bowley's excellent paper on the division of income in Great Britain, in which he arrives at the conclusion that labor's share in that country in some years immediately preceding the War was slightly more than 60%. There is some reason to suppose that labor's residual share in the United States is larger than it is in Great Britain. However, I am giving these figures only as rough indications.

duction has happened during the last century and a quarter and has not been because men have grown any stronger; but because mind has taught labor how to become more effective and has provided it with machines and with organization. It is the minds of the captains that have produced the great increase in wealth and to those captains might reasonably have accrued all that they earned, but the economic principle that labor is the residual claimant prevented any such result, even if it were desired. The income of England in 1801 was about £180,000,000. The income of the United Kingdom at the same rate, but allowing for the increase in population, in 1907, would have been about £900,000,000. Actually it was about £1,950,000,000, excluding the revenue from foreign investments. In the words of Mallock, "the mind of the larger employers was the primary producer of an income of some £1,050,600,000 added to an income that would otherwise have been £900,000,000 only." Then he shows conclusively that of this increment the representatives of Mind got only about £250,000,000 for themselves, including both profits and the interest on industrial capital.

I have shown, I hope, that there cannot be anything essentially wrong in the existing system of the distribution of the produce of industry as between labor and capital. Labor cannot divide among itself any more than there is to divide, that is, the total of what is produced. That is self-evident. It may attempt to seize the modest share of capital, but if it succeeds in doing so, that share dries up. If it confiscates capital itself it does not gain anything, for capital, without the directing minds to use it productively ceases to be of advantage to anybody. The experiences in Mexico and Russia have shown what happens. The Bolshevists of other countries will lead to the same end if they have their way. Why is it that while socialists are shouting from soap-boxes, inflaming the populace with irritant poisons, while doctrinaires who hold professorial chairs are issuing fallacies, while a motley crowd in Russia is performing the most cruel and disastrous experiment ever known, we cannot drive into the heads of people that even as things are under the capitalistic system they get all they can, that they can get no more than they produce, and that it is not the power of the mass, but rather the minds of the few that have uplifted them to the stage of comfort that they enjoy today, which is vastly superior to what it was a century ago. If the Marxian doctrine had been true labor would be paid now what it was 100 years ago, no more.

It is of profound importance to make the millions of workers see things correctly, for they are blindly approaching a time when adverse economic conditions are going to drive them, and no socialistic ranting or paternalistic policies by the governments are going to help them. The world has become so much poorer by the squandering of wealth and man-power during the War that no advance in the scale of living is to be expected from it. The prospect is just the reverse. The farmer does not lose his cattle and install improvements in his house because of his loss. The people of a city do not become profligate buyers of automobiles after a conflagration has swept away their houses. No more do nations become prosperous because war has consumed their substance. Instead of labor holding what it has gained during the War it is probable that it will suffer a relapse to a condition inferior to what it held just before the War, although the unions will struggle bravely against it. Fortunately we shall not see a loss of economic improvements, such as safety measures in industry, the provision of proper working quarters and conditions, because they are economic; but labor is in danger of losing the eight-hour day for the simple reason that it will have to work nine to ten hours in order to produce enough on which to live.

The inevitable will be violently but impotently resisted by the workers, who will not understand the compelling forces, and therein is something very pitiful, for the workers could do so much to help themselves if they would. "When men take twice as long as they ought in building their own houses," said Sir Charles Allom recently, "they increase their rents and thereby increase their cost of living before they increase their wages." He estimated that the workmen in the United States waste time to the value of over $8,000,000,000 per annum, an estimate that is only rough and requires a good deal of explanation, but nevertheless conveys an idea of the magnitude of this economic loss. He adds correctly, however, that capital "is the mainspring of enterprise and advancement and labor's profit. Rich men are rich not because they have robbed the workingman, but in spite of the workingman having robbed himself." But, alas! we cannot make the workingmen see this and try to help themselves, and therefore we are obliged to try to make good the losses of the world, avert backsliding and lay the foundations for further progress without their aid and even in spite of them. And thus, after this long preface I come to my thesis of industrial co-operation as one of the means of economic improvement that in this juncture is essential.

Now, economic improvement may be defined as the avoidance of waste. I can think of no better definition. I do not mean merely the elimination of obvious wastes, such as were features of many gospels that were usefully preached during the War, but rather the major things that we do not yet regard as wastes, or if so, do not yet know how to eliminate them. The diversion of unnecessary men, the prevention of misdirected effort, the increase in the foot-pounds of the man-day of work are all forms of cutting out the waste. If the railways of the United States could by virtue of improvements in organization, invention of automatic devices, etc., be operated with only one million men instead of two million there would manifestly be an enormous saving of labor, which could be diverted to the production of something else. The avoidance of waste is therefore fundamentally the avoidance of the waste of labor.

I must now pause to refer to another economic obstacle. I have already described the discouraging impediment that exists in the fallacies of the workmen. We have also to contend with something quite similar and equally serious in the minds of a large part of the employing class. This is the idea among thousands of them that they too do not get their due, that something is somehow stolen from them, in short, that they can get more than they produce. This idea finds expression in agrarian movements among the farmers to contest what they deem to be robbery by the millers and railways. It finds expression in the never-ending grievance of miners against the smelters. During the War the attitude of these people assumed the form of a rapacity that was only a little less extortionate than that of some classes of labor and which has a very ugly and dangerous aspect now. During the War governments could take billions of dollars from some classes of people and scatter it among others without thinking of anything but the immediate object of winning the war. There developed the pestilential idea of price-fixing, which it is going to take a long time to eradicate. I do not intend to discuss that intricate subject, which would require much more time than is at my disposal now, but I am going to point out some of the mischievous things that are inspired. An example is this: In the United States we had very high prices for sheet-zinc, due to deficiency in rolling capacity. The Government fixed a restrictive maximum, which was still high and the market-price stuck to that maximum owing to the shortage in supply. Ore-producers in certain districts claimed a participation in the profits of the rollers, who were also smelters, and through the agency of the Government obtained a grant of an ore-price far above the market-price. The ore of this grade being more than the smelter-rollers could take, the demand was allocated among themselves by the miners, who sold their surplus at the market-price. Thus instead of letting the rollers make monumental profits and recovering them through taxation, the profits were divided among numerous ore-producers, who frittered them away.

But to finish this story. Although the production of zinc required no stimulation, there being on the contrary over-production, the miners deemed the time ripe to compel the smelters to pay them the prices they would like to have, and the Government bowed to them and arranged things. This killed the goose that laid the golden egg. The smelters assented to the scale and then did not buy any ore at all, drawing upon their stocks and diverting their buying to other districts that were eager to sell at the market-price.

There was a great effort made to have the Government guarantee minimum prices for some ores. The legislation was not enacted until about a month before the Armistice, and then not in the form desired by its promoters, but as a result of concerted action, there is now to be an indemnification of mining losses incurred, it is alleged, in anticipation of the legislation, although in fact the bottom had begun to drop out of the markets two months previously.

The cotton-growers were immune against any price-fixing, and had a very sporting and highly profitable time, but now that the price of cotton is declining in company with that of other commodities they are demanding a guaranteed minimum.

These instances illustrate one form of industrial co-operation, a form of co-operation in dipping into the treasury of the public, but it is not the kind that I mean, and it is a kind that will infallibly make everybody poorer, the co-operators included. On the contrary, one of the first essentials now is for every country to rid itself of its useless industries. If anybody is trying to raise bananas in Canada (I suppose it might be done under glass) he is not adding anything to the wealth of the country. He is subtracting from it. Instead of encouraging him, he ought to be suppressed as a national waster. However, I will give a less extravagant example of my meaning. We have in the United States a considerable quicksilver industry, but owing to the poverty of our ores the metal is costly to produce. We can buy quicksilver much more cheaply from Spain where there are rich ores. Our domestic industry can be kept alive only by a high protective tariff. That would be a very costly tax upon all the people, a national loss of money, in order to afford a precarious existence to a few people who would better be doing something else. I shall immediately hear the suggestion of the necessity of military preparedness. Very good. Quicksilver is a highly essential article and last year our munitions requirements took a large part of the domestic output, but a little figuring will show that it would be far cheaper for our Government to buy from abroad the supply for several years, and pay storage and interest charges than to keep our own mines going.

There are not a few industries of this class in the United States, and in Canada you have them, too. I am not depreciating the principle of a protective tariff, or even of a bounty, in all cases. A country may have national resources, or opportunities, for the development of which a temporary stimulus may be helpful. In such a way was the manufacture of tin-plate in the United States established as a great industry. But the maintenance of production out of the poor hopeless ore deposits by means of donations at the expense of all the people is an economic crime. I repeat therefore that one of the first things in the way of industrial co-operation that should be done is the elimination of useless industries. I think that it is a great function of professional organizations like this to study and determine what are useless industries. Governments, subject as they are to political influences, cannot in time of peace, whatever they may have done in time of war, form so impartial an opinion. Indeed, the suppression of non-essential industries by the war-boards was generally of useful industries for the sake of those that under peaceful conditions would be useless.

Probably there are rather few absolutely useless industries. If the number of them were large a country would soon become bankrupt. Most industries are useful and profitable to a more or less degree, and assuming that national resources afford the proper foundation their economic position is probably in proportion to the co-operation that exists in them. I shall confine my illustrations to the metal industries, feeling a certain confidence that what lessons may be deduced from them and what opportunities for improvement in them may be discerned, may be extended to almost all other industries.

It seems to me that of all our great metal industries copper is the best organized industrially and affords the best example of industrial co-operation, which is the more remarkable in that there is no formal association, nor indeed is there any need for one. The satisfactory situation in this industry has resulted from the transparency that has been produced in it. By transparency I mean the excellent knowledge about all its affairs that is possessed by everybody, resulting from the withdrawal of all veils so that everybody can see through everything. The production is in the hands of a relatively small number of companies, and even the smaller of them are relatively large concerns. The controlling interests are fewer than the producing companies, but not so few that there is not sharp competition among them in the market. There is a perfect exchange of technical information, both through the medium of the technical press, the transactions of the societies, and inter-works visits. If at one works some new improvement is developed, such as coal-dust firing, no effort is made to keep it a secret, but rather is there an *esprit de corps* which leads to the prompt spreading of the details and the adoption of the new method wherever advisable. There is a similar publicity as to the methods of accounting, operating costs, and financial positions. The industry has learned the value of prompt statistical information and now co-operates as a matter of course in furnishing the data for it. Producing a metal that is generally in demand and for which there is no substitute, with conditions that have forced producers to resort to poorer and poorer deposits and to devise improved means permitting their profitable exploitation, the copper industry has escaped the burden of over-capitalization. The industrial co-operation in the copper industry, developed naturally as it has, and both tempered and stimulated by commercial competition as it is and should be, is so excellent that I am unable to suggest anything that should be done to improve it, except even better statistical information.

Among American mining and metallurgical industries I am inclined to put iron and steel next to copper in industrial co-operation and therefore in general efficiency, but I am not so familiar with it and therefore hesitate either to commend or criticize. The metallurgy of iron and steel certainly does not figure in current technical literature to anything like the extent that does the metallurgy of copper and data of cost of production and other things are far less easy to ascertain. The industry is well provided with statistics of production and some other rudimentary data. It is chronically overbuilt and subject to the alternate conditions of feast and famine. I feel convinced that there is much less transparency in this industry than in copper and that the state of what is only translucency, or perhaps I should say semi-obscurity, is an obstacle that might advantageously be overcome by the right kind of industrial co-operation, and I say this although there is an industrial organization for just that purpose.

Passing to the lead and zinc industries, we find less satisfactory conditions. Both the smelting of galena ore and of miscellaneous silver-lead ores, which result in producing the pig-lead of commerce, have been brought to high degrees of perfection to be sure, but the industry as a whole exhibits very little co-operation. Thus, until within a few years the mining companies of the south-eastern Missouri district, one of the major sources of lead supply, had very little to do with each other, although the exchange of information respecting the ore deposits would have been of great value to all. In the marketing of pig-lead all of the producers were hostile and secretive. There were no statistics available except the annual figures as to production. There was always mystery respecting unsold stocks. Amid this obscurity as to commercial conditions, the market was subject to sharp ups and downs, affording a lucrative hunting ground for speculators. In silver-lead smelting a large part of the works had passed into the hands of one great company, whose relations with its clients—the sundry ore-producers—were neither of the happiest nor conducive to the best interests of both parties. In British Columbia, where there is only one smelter, a similar condition of affairs has existed and still exists.

I do not intend to digress into any lengthy discussion of the chronic controversy between miners and smelters. The clearing-house among Colorado smelters, immediately preceding the general consolidation of American smelters about 20 years ago, was an excellent example of effective industrial co-operation. Previously no smelter could work to the best advantage; for needing ferruginous ore, calcareous ore, silicious ore, plumbiferous ore, and argentiferous ore in certain definite proportions, he might be short of one or two classes and consequently unable to compound the most economical smelting charge. The clearing-house became a reservoir and equalizer, which improved economic conditions to the advantage of everybody, miners as well as smelters. The consolidation perfected this idea and in the course of time improved greatly its technical practice. While the company out of this derived large profits for itself, as it should have done, without any doubt the ore-producers benefitted even more. A large part of them would not be able to operate at all today were it not for the economies of the big company, whose margin per ton of ore treated is, on the average, no more than reasonable, and indeed I might say, modest. In my own study of the affairs of this company about 10 years ago I showed that its profit on all ore smelted was only about \$2 per ton, while in some important districts it was only \$1. Nevertheless, it is undeniable that on the part of the miners, not only in this industry but also in others, zinc for example, there survived undisguised feeling of suspicion and hostility toward the smelters, instead of which there should be frankness, friendship, and co-operation. Who will gainsay that if such a relationship could be inspired it would fail to be of great advantage in improving the efficiency of the industry as a whole? In the commercial end, the marketing of the product, and in general matters of administration and introspection I am sure that the leaders of the lead-producing companies profited greatly from their association during the War. They learned something of what it means to think in terms of the industry, and not merely as individuals.

I can illustrate best what I mean by thinking in terms of an industry by referring to an address that I made to the zinc-producers of the United States last July. The American zinc industry at that time was already in a dangerous state owing to the aftermath of the feverish stimulation in 1915 and 1916. The fabulous prices for spelter during that period had the natural effect of increasing producing capacity enormously, primarily owing to more production being needed irrespective of cost; but from the outset it could be safely prophesied that the day would come when there would be a surplus of capacity and ecstasy would be followed by depression. I shall not spare the time to trace these interesting experiences in commercial economics. Suffice to say that the early part of 1918 saw the extinguishment of the ephemeral plants, while of the substantial concerns remaining, three-eighths of their capacity was idle at the mid-year, with fair prospects that it, representing a capital of $10,000,000, would be idle indefinitely. Besides this the industry was threatened with serious alterations in economic conditions. In this juncture I advised the industry to co-operate in a propaganda to increase the use of zinc, with the aim of substituting it for dearer metals, and to take steps to increase efficiency in production and selling, among which would be a well-developed statistical service, and the organization of a good system of uniform accounting. The desirability of increasing the uses of this metal, from the standpoint of the producers of it, is of course self-evident. But with respect to increasing the efficiency in selling and producing, the expression of the means in general terms will perhaps fail to convey clearly the ideas, wherefore some elaboration may be welcome.

The foundation of successful marketing is knowledge of conditions, both as to consumption and production. If everybody could see these conditions at all times the markets would be comparatively stable, just as are those for aluminum and nickel, which are controlled, on the producing side, by monopolies. Now, I do not intend to argue in support of the monopoly idea, my argument will be quite the reverse, but it is clear that the director of a monopoly, having full information respecting conditions of production and good information as to consumption, can eliminate minor fluctuations in price and needs conform only to broad swings of economic conditions. I do not think that monopoly, not even beneficent monopoly, is a good thing, but certainly it arrives at the result of relatively stable prices, and the nearer the same result can be attained under conditions of free competition the better it is for everybody except speculators. Manifestly the only means of accomplishing anything of that sort is knowledge, and fundamentally statistical knowledge. I think that it can be shown that in industries that have acquired such knowledge the fluctuation in their markets have moderated, but in no case is the statistical service yet as good as it ought to be.

I need scarcely point out the incalculable benefit both to capital and labor if it were possible to determine the state of economic conditions more promptly and more accurately than is possible at present, enabling both producers and consumers to cut their cloth accordingly, and incidentally eliminating the speculator, who in our present organization is simply a person who is more gifted for seeing in the dark than are most. There would be less waste of capital in over-building means of production, there would be fewer periods of over-stocked markets, and the lot of the workingman, assured of more regular employment, would be infinitely better. Of course, the last is just one of the things that socialists talk about effecting, and that is one of the expressions of a justifiable discontent, but the cure for it is not state control of industry, nor industrial democracy, but merely industrial co-operation in a sound and simple manner.

The improvement of efficiency in production is neither so simple nor so easy. I put this under the head of organization of a good system of uniform accounting, for until that is accomplished nobody can know just how the component parts of an industry stand, and what ought to be done to improve things generally. No man can know whether his business is being conducted efficiently or not unless he knows not only his own costs, but also has some standard with which to compare them. By such comparison he may ascertain that his costs are too high, and then upon analysis he may find that he is employing a wasteful type of furnace which it would be economical to discard, even at the expense of a new one of greater first cost. By this time the services of the engineer have been called in, which services are never invoked soon enough or often enough, or extensively enough. In some districts where the mines are small it would be advantageous for their owners to co-operate in retaining the services of one or more engineers for general advice. A general industrial association should have experts to aid the district and local groups. Manifestly, there would be no reason, whatever, why a company sufficiently strong and enlightened to do its own engineering and its own research work should not continue to do so. However, that should not cause the big company to hold aloof from the general co-operation.

The strong must help the weak, and in most cases it is the weak who know the least about their own business. Moreover, I conceive that it is in the interest of the strong to help the weak, and certainly it is never to their loss. The Anaconda Copper Mining Co., which has been a leader in developing the practice in copper metallurgy, has been generous in communicating information to other producers, and so far as I know has not lost anything by its generosity; rather has it gained something for itself. I have an idea that no one concern in any business can be very prosperous unless its industry as a whole is fairly prosperous. Let us suppose for example, that in Detroit, which has become a great centre for the manufacture of automobiles, there were one or two concerns, which by reason of excellence in design and construction of their cars, good business management, etc., stood head and shoulders above all the rest as commercial successes. The fact that Detroit had become such a centre inspired many kinds of accessory and elemental manufactures, even to the rolling of sheet-copper and the production of pig-iron. Suppose now that a general blight overtook automobile manufacturing, compelling many makers to suspend and consequentially many of the industries that supplied them with necessary things; but that the one or two conspicuous concerns escaped the blight. Certainly they would not escape the consequences, if the local rolling-mills and manufacturers of rough parts ceased production and if the population of skilled labor dispersed. The connection between one concern and all of the rest in its industry may not always be so clear as this, but that there is a connection is sure, and it is a reason why the strong should help the weak.

Now, labor has a direct interest in this branch of industrial co-operation, just as it has in the statistical service. Earlier in this paper I have pointed out how labor's residual claim on the produce of industry is determined by the deduction of the landlord for rent determined by the no-rent lands and by the profit of the employer as determined by the no-profit class. Obviously, therefore, everything that increases the produce of agricultural lands and contracts the circle of no-rents lands; or that increases the produce of the mines and factories and reduces the ranks of the no-profit class of employers is directly in the interest of labor. Although it would diminish the profits of some very successful employers at some times, they too would gain on the whole, for they would utilize their plants more fully and more steadily and while making smaller profits per unit of production would make more in the aggregate. In brief this is simply another expression of the gospel that it is to the interest of everybody to produce the most goods that can be produced. It is not money, or money-wages, that people want, although unfortunately that is what most of them erroneously think they want; but what they really want is the goods for which money can be exchanged.

If I should extend my remarks under the title of 'Industrial Co-operation', which, of course, is broad enough, to include co-operation by labor itself, I should put that at the head of everything, but while the eradication of its unfortunate delusions is not hopeless they are undoubtedly so deep-seated that any conversion to sound thinking will necessarily be slow. The laborer must be shown, and of course they can be, that by sound economic theory labor is the residual claimant upon the produce of industry; that its residual claim in America is 70 to 80% of the whole; that statistics prove that it gets it; that they show that when mind increases the produce of mere manual labor the latter gets the major part of the increment; that of the part of the produce of industry that they do not get they cannot get by any economic means; that in trying to get it by confiscatory means they not only do not get it, but also lose more or less of what they were previously getting as their residual share; that the only way they can get any more than they do now is to produce more; that slacking in any form, either by working full time at only partial efficiency, or by working only part of the time of the week is directly opposed to their own interest, and that they are greater sufferers thereby than anybody else. "The day when labor exerts its full energy," says Sir Charles Allom, "it will inherit the greatest dividend in the world," and he adds, "Never did laborers exhibit less judgment in disturbing employers than in their selection of this moment. If they are left workless it will be their just desert."

But to instill these truths, while the minds are filled with fallacies of Karl Marx, which are so gross that they have been dismissed by the intellectual socialists themselves, will be slow, and the crisis into which the world has entered will not await an educational movement among the masses. Therefore must we appeal to the directive factors in industry and urge upon them the exertion of new effort to produce more, and as a means toward that end I advocate industrial co-operation, and thinking in terms of industries as a whole. In the program that I have outlined herein it will be perceived that the arrangement of cartels or commercial agreements other than what are based on sound economic grounds plays no part. Anything that is founded on the idea of restricting production or interfering with the free play of competition would be the antithesis of my thought. Nor does my program comprise the co-operation of labor, not that it would be unwelcome, but rather that it is not foreseen that it can be won. The only co-operation by labor that would be worth anything is the common-sense kind. The talk about industrial democracy is clap-trap and does a lot of harm. It is mischievous when one of our leading newspapers writes editorially like the following:

"Let us recognize the truth that the autocracy of capital is coming to an end. Nobody more clearly recognizes this than the autocratic capitalists themselves. At least, the more intelligent among them have their eyes wide open to what is going on. They have fully made up their minds that a larger share of the new wealth produced is to go to the men and women who contribute the labor that enters into its production. They have also made up their minds that heavier taxation of rich men has come to stay. More important than this, they have come to see that plans for developing industry are hollow which do not provide for the willing co-operation and interest of workingmen. No one is more eager to accept and apply sensible schemes of that sort than the fully wide-awake among the employing capitalists."

What is, or ever was, the "autocracy of capital?" It sounds bad, but it does not mean anything. Substitute the "authority of the directing minds" and we shall come nearer to the truth. Diminish that authority in any way and production also will diminish, and the men and women who labor will not be thankful. No larger share of the new wealth is to go to them unless they themselves make it larger by their own efforts, or what is more likely, unless it be made larger by new efforts of the directing minds whose authority it is sought to curtail. Heavier taxation of rich men may have come to stay, but that in itself is going to be to the detriment of the men and women who contribute the labor that enters into production.

If industrial democracy means merely the improvement of working conditions, and listening for advice about it from the men and women who work, by all means let us have it; but who has that simple conception of the meaning of the phrase? Employers ought to provide proper working-places, they ought to make them safe and light and sanitary for the sound reason that thereby they will increase efficiency. For the same reason they ought to provide compensation for sickness and accidents, old-age pensions, and in general should take care of their people. But the more enlightened employers already do this to a more or less degree, perhaps not enough, but nevertheless progress in this direction has been steady. All of this falls, however, under the head of industrial co-operation, which may be urged in every possible direction that is economically sound. The jargon "industrial democracy" is simply an expression of the discredited theory of Karl Marx, repudiated by socialists themselves, who recognize in the words of Mallock, that "in any complex system of industry, such as that which prevails today, the efficiency of the workers as a whole is the average efficiencies of the many multiplied by the efficiencies of the few," the Few being "the natural monopolists of ability," whose function is to issue orders, while that of the Many is to execute them with strict obedience. I may well conclude this paper with Mallock's own concluding words in his great book on 'The Limits of Pure Democracy', to wit: "In any great and civilized State *Democracy only knows itself through the co-operation of oligarchy*, or that the many can prosper only through the participation in benefits which, in the way alike of material comfort, opportunity, culture, and social freedom, would be possible for no one unless the many submitted themselves to the influence or authority of the super-capable few."

Economies in Hand Drill-Steel

This subject was discussed by H. A. Read, of the Rand Mines Limited, before the Chemical, Metallurgical and Mining Society of South Africa.

During the five years ended with 1917 the issues of steel per native had a value of £310,250 ($1,480,000), or an average of 86 lb., and $6.60 in value per native per annum. Consideration of the large sums involved in these issues of steel led to examination of the losses in detail. It appeared that one of the principal losses was due to the shanking of the steel under the blows of the hammer; this in turn led to the conclusion that if shanking losses could be prevented by means of a permanent drill-head, an appreciable economy would be effected. After some experimenting, the problem was solved. It was ascertained that by heating the end of the drill and staying it up (either by means of a die and dolly in a Leyner press or by hand) so as to give the head of the drill a bulbous or pear shape and subsequently tempering it, the drill would be provided with a head capable of resisting hammer blows without shanking. The question will be asked why the new form of drill-head stands up to the work. The explanation appears to be that the head is so stayed-up that the least possible disturbance is created in the molecular formation of the steel. Correct draw tempering then clothes the bulbous-shaped head with a fine coating of hard-tempered steel—probably not much more than $\frac{1}{16}$ in. thick, below which is a body of low-tempered steel. This latter metal (increased as it is beyond the original section of the drill) provides a reinforcement that prevents the disturbance and disintegration of the molecules of metal, which otherwise take place under impact of the hammer. The advantages of the new form of drill-head are as follows: (1) The saving of steel by preventing crushing or 'mushrooming' of the shank end; (2) elimination of danger to miners, as there are no splinters or jagged ends; (3) improved drilling, as the natives have a uniform tempered surface to strike, and the energy hitherto absorbed in shanking is diverted to the work of drilling; (4) improved control of steel; (5) the drill, instead of being a ragged-ended piece of steel becomes a tool well suited for the job; (6) the cost of trimming up and periodic re-tempering of the old form of drill by lead bath or other method (where such is the practice) is saved. The drill-heads are practically permanent, and, as the starter becomes too short, they may be welded onto other steel.

Mr. Read gave results of experiments carried out with this new type of drill at the East Rand Proprietary and Ferreira Deep mines. The conclusions derived were briefly: (1) The loss of steel hitherto sustained by the mines through mushrooming or crushing can be entirely prevented by the new permanent head; (2) a simple system of steel control can be introduced which will eliminate the heavy losses of hand drill-steel from causes other than fair and proper wear and tear; (3) the consumption of hand drill-steel can then be reduced to the amount of steel actually used in the processes of drilling and sharpening; (4) accidents and lost shifts hitherto caused by splintering of drills can be practically eliminated by the use of the permanent head; (5) there is evidence of an appreciable improvement in efficiency when using the permanent drill-head, as the energy hitherto absorbed in the crushing up or mushrooming of the shank is available for drilling; (6) the importance of the foregoing to the mining industry lies in the fact that the work of a large number of natives (averaging 45,000 per annum) is beneficially affected; (7) there is a field for further investigation in losses during sharpening and designing a suitable hammer.

The English-Speaking Peoples

By T. A. RICKARD

*We rejoice that the world-war is ended. We are proud of the part played by the English-speaking peoples —all doing equal honor to the traditions they share in common. One of the compensations for the calamity of the past four years is the fact that the Briton and the American, striving together in the cause of human liberty, have learned to understand and to respect each other. The mother country entered the fight resolutely at the beginning, while yet unready to meet the carefully prepared onslaught of the enemy; then the sons from the overseas dominions rallied to the old battle-cry eagerly and effectively; and last, but not least, the stepsons came from across the Atlantic, speaking the same speech, playing the same game, and fighting in the same clean way.

It was a great foregathering of those that use the language of Shakespeare and idealize the principles of liberty for which the friends and associates of Shakespeare stood sponsor three centuries ago.[1] At a time like this it is pleasant to dwell upon the fact that the liberal Englishmen who organized the Virginia Company were the pioneers of self-government on the American continent. The Virginia Assembly, convoked in 1619, was the first example of a domestic parliament to regulate internal affairs on this side of the Atlantic.[2] The Governor of Virginia, Sir Edwin Sandys, had been a pupil of Richard Hooker at Oxford and from that political teacher he and his friends had imbibed the idea of combining civil liberty with constitutional order. To this group of large-minded Englishmen the American colonists owed their liberal charters and their successive triumphs over the royal prerogative. Let it be noted that the American colonists had to deal with James II and George III, the two smallest minds in the list of British kings. Another historical note, more pleasant to record, is the connection between the two principal groups of American settlers. In 1608 when the Pilgrim fathers, William Brewster and John Robinson, led their Separatist congregation to Holland and there prepared the expedition to America, they were assisted by Sandys and the Virginia Council, who were willing to share their privileges with them. When the Pilgrims set sail in 1620 they had the promise, obtained by Sandys from King James, that they should have freedom of worship, equality before the law, and the right to participate in the government of themselves. Thus the men whom we may regard as the friends of Shakespeare aided the founders of New England. Together they resisted the King's arbitrary dictation. "The political principles that inspired . . that noble company never died out of Virginia, never died out of the northern colony, called New England. These were the principles first logically developed and clearly formulated by the tutor of Sir Edwin Sandys, Richard Hooker. Disciples of Hooker, associates of Shakespeare, were the founders of the first republics in the New World."[3] These political doctrines of Hooker not only inspired the founders of the first English settlements in America, but found an echo in the minds of the men who led the Revolution and subscribed to the Declaration of Independence. Hooker's ideas passed to John Locke, and through him to Benjamin Franklin, Patrick Henry, and Thomas Jefferson.

It seems worth while to make this point insistently. The old Fourth of July talk is out of date, because it is historically untrue. George III was born of German parents and married a German woman. He spoke Shakespeare's language with a guttural accent. His government failed to impose its tyrannic orders on the British colonists in America because it was not supported by the British people. Unable to conscript a British army, he hired the Hessians. It was against the forces of a reactionary German king that a great Englishman, George Washington, led his men to the winning of their independence. Lafayette and Rochambeau brought French aid to the revolutionists, but their help was prompted less by love of the colonists than by the desire to hit at England, which was then at war with France. It was the despotism of Louis XVI that sent Rochambeau and his 6000 Frenchmen "to deal England a blow where she would feel it." That was in 1780. Permit me to remind you that only 18 years afterward, in 1798, the young United States was at war with France. This is not mentioned out of ill-will, but as a historic fact of some significance. We need not belittle the romance of the Lafayette episode, even though it has been highly colored, because it is helping today to stimulate cordiality between the United States and France, but we may demur to the twisting of history in order to represent the English people as reactionary and the French people as liberal at the time of the American revolution. As one who holds that "every man has two countries, his own and France," as one that held this view even in the days of Fashoda, I venture to say that the friendship now existing between the United States and France is all to the

*An address delivered before the joint session of the American Institute of Mining Engineers and the Canadian Mining Institute at New York on February 17, 1919.

[1]'Shakespeare and the Founders of Liberty in America', by Charles Mills Gayley; 1917.

[2]Alexander Brown, in 'English Politics in Early Virginia History'.

[3]Gayley, Op. cit., page 93.

good, because England and France likewise are firm friends. Their *entente cordiale* joins with French-American sympathy in establishing a mutuality of goodwill between the three great democracies of the world.

It remains to emphasize another fact, to which allusion has been made already, namely, that the English striving for political freedom prepared the way alike for American and for French democracy. Locke, whose doctrines fed the fires of the English revolution of 1688 and those of the American revolution of 1775, derived his ideas of constitutional liberty from his fellow-countryman, Hooker. It was Locke's theory that was embodied in the American Declaration of Independence in 1776 and that rationalized the French Declaration of the Rights of Man in 1789. Rousseau exercised no influence on the America of 1776; on the contrary, it was from English philosophers and from Anglo-American reformers that the French revolution took its cue. English liberalism, disciplined by centuries of conflict, from the Magna Charta to the Bill of Rights, was the political mother of democratic institutions in the free commonwealths of the world.

Much of the prejudice against England inherited by children in the United States is due to the unfriendly tradition perpetuated in their school-books. Great Britain did treat the colonists shabbily after they had broken away from the old country, and, as the history of this nation is concerned chiefly with those early events, it is not surprising that the young American should be impressed much more by the overbearing attitude of Lord North's government, which was not so very different from that of most governments in those days, than by the shabby treatment given, in turn, to the loyalists in the American colonies. The so-called War of 1812 was bound to loom large in the school-histories, because it was the first contest following the achievement of American independence; but it was a tempest in a teapot; on land it was badly fought on both sides, although at sea the young American proved himself a chip of the old block; it was a side-show started in the midst of England's great contest with Napoleonic France. At that time England had a navy many times bigger than the American, and Wellington had just returned home from his victorious Peninsular campaign at the head of 100,000 veterans—a big army in those days. In 1814 Napoleon had been defeated, yet it was Wellington that made himself responsible for an honorable peace with the United States. It must be remembered that to the United States the Revolution was the very beginning of things; to England it was only one incident in a long and eventful history. "The game was played, and she had lost. North America, in the eyes of her statesmen, was a strip of eastern seaboard; the great lakes were but dimly understood; the continent beyond the Mississippi was ignored."[4] Therefore the Revolution and the little war of 1812 left no such sting in the minds of the British as the memories that were cherished on this side of the Atlantic. It is worth noting that in 1788 the first English settlement was made in Australia, at Paramatta, in New South Wales. Thus Australia was added to the British dominions at the time of the American secession.

Another thought follows: looking back, it is probable that if England had been minded to recover the American colonies during the early period of their independence, she could have done so; but she had no mind to do so, and any Hanoverian king or government that had tried it would have had to face a revolution at home. Moreover, it is quite certain that the United States would have seceded sooner or later, because no government in Europe could have hoped to retain control over the growing giant of the West. I am frank to add that the idea of filling the United States with Englishmen is as unwelcome to my taste as the idea of peopling the British Isles with Americans. Variety is the spice of life.

> "Our dearest bond is this,
> Not like to like, but like in difference,
> Distinct in individualities."

Let us hope that the school-room histories in America will be re-written in a spirit less unfriendly to the mother country. It may be more than a coincidence that the names of some of the publishers should be, for example, Kruger, Koch, and Lemp. When a New Englander or a son of Old England hears Germans, Irish, and Finns talking loudly about the time when "We licked the British in 1812," he may be pardoned for smiling. There were more Germans and Irish on the reactionary side in 1812 than on the liberal side. An acquaintance of mine, an Austrian Jew, the editor of a Jewish paper in San Francisco, began to tell me about the time when "*We* licked the British," whereupon I called a halt and asked him *qu'allait-il faire dans cette galère?* I informed him that I had ancestors on both sides of that affair, at a time when his progenitors were wandering in the morasses of Eastern Europe without even a knowledge of the fact that the British were having a family quarrel. The foregoing story is capped by the statement appearing in a pamphlet prepared by the Sinn Feiners and intended for propaganda among the American soldiers stationed in Ireland. "We helped to win your independence," they assert.[5] The forefathers of this Republic may have had some outside help, but it is a little hard on them that they should be called upon at this late date to divide the honors with such as the Sinn Feiners. The people *they* helped were the Germans, not in 1776, but in 1917.

A couple of stories will illustrate this point further. During the Spanish war of 1898 I had as neighbors a man and his wife of British birth, but of American citizenship. One day the man, in the presence of his son, a boy 12 years old, remarked that the United States would defeat Spain. Whereupon the boy exclaimed: "Lick Spain, well I guess we will! Why we licked *you* twice!" That boy and his two brothers have fought side by side with the British in France, one of them wearing the uniform of his father's native land, because he could not wait until his own country entered the war.

[4]F. S. Oliver in 'Alexander Hamilton'. Page 115.

[5]As recorded in despatches published on January 11, 1918.

Another boy's historical knowledge concerning the relations between the United States and Great Britain consisted of three items:

(1) Major Pitcairn spoke contemptuously of the revolutionists while he stirred his punch at Lexington.

(2) Andrew Jackson refused to black the dirty boots of a British tyrant.

(3) The Americans licked the English twice, and would do it again for two cents.

Yet it is recorded that this same boy knocked down a perfectly well-behaved Bavarian in a barber-shop for expressing the opinion that England would be invaded. You could tell that boy all you pleased about the battle of Bunker Hill and the villainy of Lord North, but he would not forego his share of ownership in the Black Watch at Waterloo, of Nelson at Trafalgar, of Wolfe on the heights of Quebec, of Drake and the 'Golden Hind', or of the archers at Agincourt.

The tale of an ancient wrong should now be laid aside on a shelf beyond the reach of any but the most inquisitive student. The memory of Bunker Hill is overlaid by that of Manila Bay. Let me recall the story as recorded by Dewey himself.

When Commodore Dewey drew the attention of Vice-Admiral von Diedrichs to the disproportion between the German naval force at Manila and the German interests in the Philippines,[6] he was met with: "I am here by order of the Kaiser, sir." The German admiral made trouble for the Americans continually, while maintaining the most cordial terms with the Spaniards; this also, it is to be presumed, by order of the Kaiser. He repeatedly ignored the blockade that Dewey had established after the battle of Manila Bay, sending his warships into the harbor without allowing them to be boarded, as was necessary in order that they might be identified and assigned an anchorage. Dewey, in his autobiography, says: "Vice-Admiral von Diedrichs, in denial of the right, had notified us that he would submit the point to a conference of all the senior officers of the men-of-war in the harbor. But only one officer appeared, Captain Chichester, of the British 'Immortalité.' He informed the German commander that I was acting entirely within my right; that he had instructions from his government to comply with even more rigorous restrictions than I had laid down; and, moreover, that as senior British officer present he had passed the word that all British men-of-war upon entering the harbor should first report to me and fully satisfy any inquiries on my part before proceeding to the anchorage of the foreign fleet."[7]

It is related by General Younghusband, of the British army, who was at Manila at the time, that when Von Diedrichs asked Chichester what he intended to do, the Englishman replied: "Just what Admiral Dewey and I have agreed upon."

A more significant incident occurred later, just before the town of Manila was captured, on May 13. I quote Dewey again: "As we got under way the officers and men of the British ship 'Immortalité' crowded on the deck, her guard was paraded, and her band played 'Under the Double Eagle,' which was known to be my favorite march. Then, as we drew away from the anchorage from which for over three months we had watched the city and bay, Captain Chichester got under way also, and with the 'Immortalité' and the 'Iphigenia' steamed over toward the city and took up a position which placed his vessels between ours and those of the foreign fleet."[8] Thus the British warships were differentiated from the "foreign" fleet; they stood between Dewey and the Germans.

This was no mere idiosyncrasy of Chichester; it expressed the policy of the British government. In March 1898 Germany asked England to join her and France in putting their fleets between Cuba and the American fleet. The British Foreign Secretary promptly refused. Great Britain was the one power that prevented the formation of a European coalition against the United States at the time of the war with Spain. It was then that the Kaiser exclaimed: "If I had a larger fleet I would take Uncle Sam by the scruff of the neck." More recently that part of his own anatomy his been in acute danger. On May 11, 1898, while the Spanish-American war was in progress, Joseph Chamberlain, the Secretary of State for the Colonies, said in a speech at Birmingham:

"What is our next duty? It is to establish and to maintain bonds of permanent amity with our kinsmen across the Atlantic. There is a powerful and a generous nation. They speak our language. They are bred of our race. Their laws, their literature, their standpoint upon every question are the same as ours. Their feelings, their interests in the cause of humanity and the peaceful development of the world are identical with ours. I don't know what the future has in store for us; I don't know what arrangements may be possible with us; but this I do know and feel, that the closer, the more cordial, the fuller, and the more definite these arrangements are, with the consent of both peoples, the better it will be for both and for the world—and I even go so far as to say that, terrible as war may be, even war itself would be cheaply purchased if, in a great and noble cause, the Stars and Stripes and the Union Jack should wave together over an Anglo-Saxon alliance."

Therein Chamberlain exhibited not only a brotherly spirit, but also the highest quality of statesmanship—foresight. His hope was fulfilled in 1918.

The echoes of Yorktown and Saratoga are smothered by the glad shouts that come from Belleau Wood, Cambrai, Lille, and other recent battlefields on which the Union Jack and Old Glory were carried forward to victory. Then was fulfilled Jefferson's hope, as expressed in a letter to President Monroe, in 1824, advising him to accept the policy, now known as the Monroe doctrine, which had been suggested by George Canning, Secretary of Foreign Affairs for Great Britain. Thomas Jefferson

[6]'Autobiography of George Dewey, Admiral of the Navy', 1913. Page 257.

[7]Op. cit. Page 266.

[8]Op. cit. Page 277.

wrote: "Great Britain is the one nation which can do us the most harm of anyone, or all on earth; and with her on our side we need not fear the whole world. With her then, we should sedulously cherish a cordial friendship, and nothing would tend more to knit our affections than to be fighting once more, side by side, in the same cause." That pious wish, so like Chamberlain's, has been splendidly fulfilled. Do you remember one of the flashes of history that we found in the day's news last October? It ran something like this:

Somewhere on the Western front an assault was launched at dawn under cover of a creeping curtain of shell-fire. An American division advanced shouting 'Lusitania.' With them went a squadron of tanks. While this attack was progressing favorably, a British division on the left swam the canal and pushed forward, in the face of scores of German machine-guns, to the village of Bellеglise. By nine o'clock prisoners were being sent to the rear in droves. A pause followed this first phase of the battle. The Americans, tired, but elated, stood in the trenches they had captured, while an Australian regiment, moving to their support, passed over them, or 'leap-frogged,' to form the first wave of a new advance. The storm of cheering that greeted this manœuvre rose high above the din of battle.

We echo those cheers today. The word 'Lusitania' made those English-speaking soldiers a unit against

"A people with the heart of beasts
Made wise concerning men."

One fateful consequence of the War is the suicide of the German tradition. Before 1914 the Germans had a growing hold upon American business, they were grafting their kultur upon the American people, chiefly through the scheme of exchange-professors, whereby German propagandists were given a free hand at American universities, and, what was worse, sundry American professors went to Berlin, where they succumbed to the hospitality of the Kaiser and became sycophants to his purpose. The Germans were even obtaining success in imposing their language upon a large number of native-born Americans; and in doing this, they were undermining the English tradition, inherited legitimately from the founders of the United States. They were assisted in their propaganda by the fact that many Germans of the highest character migrated to the United States at the time of the War of Liberation in 1848. These proved excellent American citizens because they came mostly from the South German States and brought with them none of the Prussian idea. They were followed in later years by other Germans, not so liberal-minded, but of undoubted capacity in business. Clannish always, they co-operated, they became pioneers of the German idea, which had made considerable headway when William of Hohenzollern and his military caste, supported by the German people, began their onslaught upon Western civilization. During the time the German tradition waxed in the United States that of the mother country waned; for many reasons, some large, others small. The American alienation from the people of "the sceptred isle" has been due in part to sympathy for those of "the emerald isle." Undoubtedly the blundering policy of the British government in handling the Irish question has tended to perpetuate the prejudice against England; the Irish are born politicians; in the big cities of this country they exert an influence far out of proportion to their numbers or their character; they have played into the hands of the Germans and together they have fostered a sentiment that has tended continually to hinder the development of goodwill between our peoples. By "our peoples" I mean those represented by the Canadian Mining Institute and the American Institute of Mining Engineers. For generations it has been the popular thing in the United States "to twist the lion's tail"; it pleased both Irish and American prejudice; it was the regular stock-in-trade of frothy orators and Jingo editors.

The English-speaking peoples have so many proud and happy memories in common that it is about time to balance the account. England did treat the colonists arbitrarily, and they treated the loyalists meanly; the young United States soon after achieving independence did have a further fuss with the mother country, which withdrew from the quarrel voluntarily. So much for that. From her independent sons in America, England learned a lesson she has never forgotten, as is proved by the record of her relations with Canada, Australia, India, and Egypt, and her other territories, particularly her treatment of the Boers. She holds her overseas dominions by the silken thread of goodwill, by that and nothing more. The American people shares with the English people the glorious traditions derived from the men that helped to develop constitutional liberty before the Declaration of Independence, which was a logical sequel to the Magna Charta and the Bill of Rights. Many Americans, even those of British descent, may choose to forego the privilege of sharing those ancient glories, but they will not refuse to claim the inheritance of Chaucer and Spenser, of Shakespeare and Milton, of the King James version of the Bible and the Book of Common Prayer, of the English common law and the unwritten rules whereby both alike 'play the game' in war and peace. For those traditions we are joint trustees. To them we add now the vivid, the searing, the proud memories of the Great War, in which at last our men stood shoulder to shoulder to assert the principles of freedom on earth. Abraham Lincoln closed his first inaugural address by an appeal for reconciliation with the South: "The mystic chords of memory, stretching from every battlefield and patriot grave to every living heart and hearthstone all over this broad land, will yet swell the chorus of the Union, when again touched, as they surely will be, by the better angels of our nature." Does not this find an echo in our hearts today; do not the chords of our memory vibrate to the stories that have come from the battlefields in France, and will not the better angels of our nature play on those mystic chords a song to which we can pull together in unison for liberty, justice, and peace?

The visit of President Wilson to England, following our comradeship in arms during the War, is one of the great events of history. The intensely cordial greeting that he received during his visit, not only from King George, but from the crowd, augurs well for the friendship between the English-speaking peoples. One of our miserable San Francisco papers spoke of the reception accorded to the President as the most enthusiastic ever given to "a foreign citizen," as if a man who found himself in a country where his native tongue is spoken, where his mother was born, and from which his paternal grandfather came, could feel himself a 'foreigner.' Legally he may be, but setting aside the legal fiction, Mr. Wilson found himself among his own kinsmen. There are three kinds of people in the world: Americans, Britons, and foreigners. Does any one of us feel like a foreigner when he is either in Canada, England, or the United States? I trow not. However, I have lived so long in the United States that I venture to warn Britons against over-playing the 'kinsman' note. Mr. Wilson's ancestry brings him within the category, but most Americans do not like to be dubbed 'kinsmen' or 'cousins,' because they are strongly assertive of their nationality, and of their own identity as a people; moreover, the influx of alien blood from the other countries of Europe is so considerable that it is incorrect to regard the American as a cousin of the Briton. Indeed, this assumption was at the bottom of much of the chagrin felt in Great Britain and in Canada when the Government of the United States deliberately adopted an attitude of neutrality during the early part of the War. Impatient as most of us may have been at the aloofness of the United States during that period, we should have reminded ourselves that the American people includes a large proportion of citizens of other than British descent, about one half, of whom ten millions were born in Germany or born of German parents, and perhaps twice as many more have German ancestry. We ought to have reminded ourselves that even those who are of British descent feel their separateness strongly, partly on account of old revolutionary prejudice, and partly because there is that constant urge to emphasize the individuality of the American nation. That is why I deem it more tactful, and also more in accord with the facts, to lay stress on our common notions of fair play and our common insistence on the right to live and let live—the right that the Prussian and his cohorts undertook to suppress. The Briton must accept the fact that the American, especially those Americans who have no English blood in their veins, dislike an excess of emphasis on kinship. For instance, Theodore Roosevelt objected to it, and he was a typical American if ever there was one. He had Dutch blood, English blood, French blood, even German blood, in his veins, but there is no mistaking the fact that in him it was no mere mechanical mixture, but an ethnical compound, called 'American', because it is entirely different from any of the ingredients of which it is composed. As he himself said: "We are a new and distinct nationality. We are developing our own distinctive culture and civilization, and the worth of this civilization will largely depend upon our determination to keep it distinctively our own." That undoubtedly is the voice of young America, the expression of the virile nationalism that Roosevelt typified so splendidly. If the call of the blood were to be taken literally, the cries from America to Europe would be as confused as those which arose from the Tower of Babel. President Poincare at the opening of the Peace Conference said appropriately: "America, the daughter of *Europe*, crossed the ocean to rescue her mother from thraldom and to save civilization." Therefore it is wiser to base our international friendship upon the other factors: language, literature, law, sports, ideas, and ideals, themselves largely a consequence of our common ancestry.

Our peoples differ in their traditions and also in their outlook, or, to be more nearly correct, the Briton cares more for tradition than the American, who, on the other hand, cares more for outlook. The one feels his background, the other his foreground. The Englishman accepts his social environment; he is proud that his father and grandfather did as he is doing; he loves the continuity of custom. The aim of the American is social extrication; he sees no reason for following in the footsteps of his forbears; he blazes a fresh trail, and rejoices in breaking into a new environment. Britain is politically a democracy, but socially she still preserves many of the traditions of feudal days. These make for the amenities of life, but they, and the social manners derived from them, are distasteful to the unconventional men and women of a country that has broken definitely with all that such customs imply. To us, "the rank is but the guinea-stamp; the man's the gold for all that." In freeing ourselves from such trappings we may have gone to the other extreme; the lack of respect for authority is not the most desirable trait of the democrat.

Life is full of compensations; every loss has some gain. The engaging frankness of the American contrasts with the starving of emotion in the Englishman. He thinks it good form to suppress any expression of enthusiasm to the point of making himself appear cold or supercilious. It is an unlovely trait and destroys the natural grace of an intelligent human being. In England the religion of 'good form' is a disease among well-bred men, making spontaneity a mark of the socially uneducated. An American officer says to a British officer: "Well, I guess we'll have to clean up the Boches together!" The English officer, adjusting his eye-glass, says, "Really." That reply was not meant to be insulting, but it chilled any *rapprochement*. We are reminded thereby of "a certain condescension among foreigners," on which an American essayist expatiated. May I suggest that some of the British superciliousness is due to shyness, not to impertinence; it is what our French friends call *mauvaise honte*: it springs from the Englishman's inbred fear of making himself ridiculous. On the other hand, the autobiographical garrulity of an opposite kind of American and the boyish inquisitiveness with which he will dive into the affairs of a comparative stranger bear the marks of a crudity that may sometimes be repellant. Again, an Englishman will be severely critical of his own country, because to him to speak well of her is like speaking well of himself, which is taboo, whereas the American will sail in boyishly to praise his native country, and to assert how superior it is to every other. Such small national differences should be taken with good humor. The social code of a small island 3000 miles away does not fit the less formal, more spontaneous, life of a younger people sprawling across a continent more than 3000 miles wide. The American ought to understand the Briton if anybody is to do so, and, conversely, the Briton ought to meet the American half-way quicker than anybody else. Our mannerisms may be different, but our ideals are much the same. I am reminded of the story told of the judges who were preparing a congratulatory address for presentation to Queen Victoria, on the occasion of her jubilee. They were discussing the phrase "conscious as we are of our many infirmities," whereupon Bowen, the Master of the Rolls, suggested that the wording should be changed to "conscious as we are of each other's many infirmities." That, I regret to think, is what we do internationally. We are too much like the old man who said to his wife: "Everybody is queer except thee and me, and sometimes I think thee's a bit off." We need more tolerance—a more tolerant humor—remembering that a friend is a man whom you know well and still like. Britons and Americans can risk the closer acquaintance that leads to friendship, because they have fewer divergencies than common aims; and their friendship will be on a safer footing if they take each other as they are and determine to make the best of their interesting differences.

Let us look forward instead of backward. Whatever our differences in the past, let us realize the similarity of our aims, the identity of our political ideals, and endeavor so to act and speak that the harvest of this calamitous war shall be not the barren thistle of discord but the wholesome wheat of goodwill. The great sacrifices entailed by the War will be inadequately compensated if the result is not to establish closer relations of friendship between Britain and America. Indeed, it would be an immeasurable loss if the peace settlement should provoke any discord between the two English-speaking peoples. If we cannot agree to keep the peace, nay more, to work for human progress together, then no league of nations is conceivable that will do so. On the contrary, if there be any hope that mankind will advance not only from a jungle existence but from the organized vendetta of a semi-civilized state of society, if there be any hope of improvement in national relations, then that hope lies in one fact—a fact of which we have common reason for being intensely proud—and that is the 3500 miles of unfortified frontier between Canada and the United States. If we can live on such terms, with a willingness not only to arbitrate international differences but with a constant desire not to provoke them, then other nations—in time, all the nations of the world—will find it desirable, will find it imperative, to do the same. Let that physical frontier, without the menace of a fort, without the provocation of a single cannon, be the symbol of unaggressive neighborliness, of a mutual goodwill, of a promise of that "far off divine event"—of universal peace and amity—"to which the whole creation moves."

Flotation of Native Sulphur Ores

By JAMES M. HYDE

*The object of this investigation was not to work out the best practice for any particular ore, but to determine how generally concentration by flotation may be applied to sulphur ores, and what may be expected from its use.

A summary of results follows:

1. All sulphur ores so far tested by flotation yielded promising results.

2. The ores from several districts can be treated successfully if suitable water is available. Under favorable conditions, better than 80% of the sulphur should be recoverable as concentrate containing more than 80% sulphur. Much higher results may be obtained.

3. It is possible to make high-grade brimstone direct by flotation on at least one ore, and also by refining concentrate.

4. The concentrate appears to be suitable for many purposes for which high-grade sulphur is now used.

5. In addition to the demand for sulphur that previously existed, an ever-increasing demand for sulphur as a soil-dressing may be expected, and this should eventually consume a large quantity. Flotation concentrate will be especially suitable for this purpose.

6. Raw sulphur and raw phosphate rock may be used for the commercial manufacture of acid-phosphate fertilizer. Flotation concentrate should be especially suitable for this purpose.

The flotative agents so far used included pine oils, or creosotes, No. 80 and 350, from the Pensacola Tar & Turpentine Co., wood creosotes, No. 17 and 18, from the General Naval Stores Co., ore separation oil No. 1, from the Standard Oil Co., kerosene from the laboratory supply, cresylic acid No. 206, carbolic creosote No. 158, coal-tar creosote No. 118, and coal-tar No. 300 from the Hunter-Johnson Co. of San Francisco, wood creosote No. 1 and 2 from the Cleveland Cliffs Co., and mixtures of the above, amyl-alcohol, glycerin, and crude pyroligneous acid and sulphuric acid. All of these have been used with air in agitation and pneumatic flotation-test machines designed by me for my own use. Air without any other reagent save water has been used in both agitation and pneumatic flotation-test machines. With the exception of crude pyroligneous acid and glycerin, all of the reagents used facilitated the flotation of sulphur; but the results attained in the earlier tests led to the use of carbolic creosote No. 158, or a mixture of equal parts of kerosene and Pensacola No. 80, in most tests. These all gave satisfactory results.

*Abstract from Minerals Investigation Series, No. 15, U. S. Bureau of Mines, 1919.

JOPLIN, MISSOURI

STATUS OF ZINC MINING IN THE TRI-STATE REGION

A study of the zinc industry of Missouri, Arkansas, Kansas, and Oklahoma during the past ten months: an address delivered by Otto Ruhl before the American Zinc Institute at St. Louis:

A review covering the last 10 months mining operation in the Joplin-Miami district is but a repetition of that given a year ago, with the exception that the lights have been fading, and the shades are deeper, so to speak.

Hard hit last year, the zinc-mining industry of the four States today is in even a worse state than then. In Missouri one can count the active milling plants practically on the fingers of two hands; Arkansas has but a negligible output of zinc ore today; Oklahoma and Kansas are supplying the bulk of the output. Singularly enough we find the efforts of the field to curtail its output but partly successful, a fact due to the gradual but inevitable fruition of prospecting efforts begun two years ago. It has been said, and truthfully so, that 10 years prospecting was done in the Oklahoma field in two years time. The results have been the development of a large number of mines whose output has been thrown on the market, and kept up the output of this district in the face of untoward price conditions to an unusual level. Much of this output is not the result of studied operation, but incidental to prospecting and development, and in most cases produced at a staggering loss. Yet the tonnage of these mines in the aggregate has maintained the output of the district at close to 10,000 tons per week. It is difficult to reconcile this heavy production with the fact generally known as to prices for ores, and with the fact that so many mills are closed down. A census taken of the mills of the field within the past month showed out of 208, a total of but 58 operating, or approximately 28% of the potential producers. With these 58, however, the bulk of the tried operators and the low cost mills are found, a synonym for either high-class operation or extremely rich properties.

The following tables of shipments and prices for corresponding months of 1918 and 1919 show a consistent decline in prices received, but no such decline in output.

Comparative production all grades zinc ore 1918-'19, tons:

Month	1918	1919
January	32,995	27,102
February	22,250	40,228
March	47,955	50,851
April	45,810	30,899
May	44,315	47,579
	194,325	202,659
Surplus on hand	27,500	16,000
	221,825	218,050

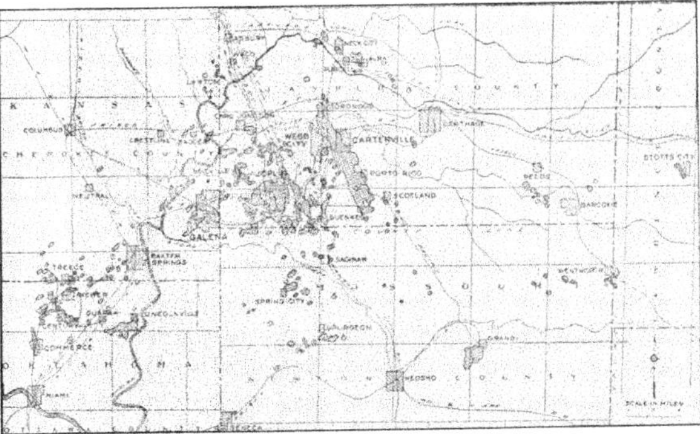

MAP OF AREAS THAT HAVE PRODUCED ZINC AND LEAD IN THE TRI-STATE REGION

Comparative zinc-ore prices 1918-'19, per ton:

Month	1918 Blende	1918 Calamine	1919 Blende	1919 Calamine
January	$57.02	$32.07	$43.41	$35.01
February	55.00	33.00	41.78	26.27
March	50.14	34.73	41.54	27.74
April	42.03	32.03	38.87	26.61
May	47.70	31.00	37.80	24.80

Compared with 1918, the 1919 period shows an average reduction of $11.89 for blende ore and $3.06 for calamine ore.

One would naturally anticipate that the reason for this condition must be explained by greatly reduced cost of operation. While there have been some reductions in costs, they have not been commensurate with the reduction in prices received for the product. The reductions in the former have been approximately 10% in labor and a small reduction in hard iron and powder. Other costs either have been maintained or actually advanced as in the case of power and lubricants. A reduction in one class of supplies is practically balanced by advances in others. It therefore becomes increasingly apparent that much of the output being maintained is produced at a loss. Recently, when the price of ore dropped to a $35 base, some of the very strongest operators in the field shut-down some of the best and richest properties, while weaker concerns and poorer properties can still be found desperately trying to keep going.

Under these conditions production of the field is approximately 9000 to 10,000 tons, and its potential production on a $45 to $55 market can be readily determined at 50 to 60% more. From this situation it is evident that Joplin operators are hoping for a hurried revival of zinc consumption and a greatly increased use for this metal.

The end of the War brought with it the end of all price agreements, and the co-operation between smelters and ore producers. The whole market situation reverted to the old open system where "everyone for himself and the devil take the hindmost." The co-operative action between the sheet-zinc manufacturers and the high-grade zinc ore producers, which was so satisfactory during the War, today is almost forgotten history and a similar movement to take care of all classes of ores and with all the smelters met a like fate before it was more than suggested. Certainly the industry needs such co-operation today as much if not more than during the War. But so far as one can now see, the inevitable law of the survival of the fittest must take its course, and only those with unusually rich deposits can survive the squeezing process of high production costs and low ore prices. How long this process must continue to bring about the extermination of the output, which will again balance local supply and demand, is difficult to answer.

It was pointed out at last years' meeting (of the Zinc Institute) that the "souls of operators were born, kissed by the enthralling rapture of eternal optimism." The past year's history is confirming evidence that they will endure impossible conditions and yet live. If they cannot produce ore for a profit they do it for philanthropy, and the world gets its zinc metal mined for less than cost.

The salient features of the year's history as reflected in the zinc-mining industry of Missouri, Kansas, Oklahoma, and Arkansas are:

1. That the production in Missouri and Arkansas has grown smaller since last year.

2. Output of Oklahoma and Kansas holds strongly at 9000 to 10,000 tons.

3. Production is maintained at a high level in spite of large numbers of mills closed down.

4. Only the richest ore deposits can be worked and the best organized companies can operate, and much of the ore is being produced at a loss.

5. Ore prices declined $11.89 per ton over last year, but this did not greatly reduce the output of ore.

6. Cost of production remains high, and changes in some items while lower have been balanced by others that have advanced.

7. End of war brought all price agreements to an end and no co-operative efforts since have been successful.

BISBEE, ARIZONA

PROGRESS AT SACRAMENTO HILL.—TOMBSTONE MARBLE DEPOSITS.

Removal of overburden from the Copper Queen's Sacramento hill in April was 176,000 cu. yd. This is a record. Although a little more than 2,000000 yd. of capping waste has been removed so far, exposure of the ore for steam-shovels is only 40% complete. This work is one of the largest mining operations in Arizona at present. Eighty trainloads of waste are removed daily, and used in filling ravines and gulches throughout the Warren district. The Dallas shaft of the Copper Queen is to be enlarged from two to five compartments in the near future. The Calumet & Cochise is undergoing development, it being intended to sink below the 1500-ft. level.

What is expected to be one of the largest marble quarries in the United States is being opened by Bisbee and Los Angeles capital 15 miles from Tombstone in the Dragoon mountains, 4 miles from Dragoon station on the Southern Pacific railroad. The Dragoon Marble & Mining Co., as it is known, has 1600 acres. A. T. Kolb is president; J. S. McNeish is secretary; Robert Hennessy of Bisbee, L. H. Turner of Pasadena, and George Weifenbaugh of Los Angeles are directors. The last named owns a large finishing plant in Los Angeles and will handle the finished product for the company. Mr. Kolb, an experienced marble man, states that marble of almost every variety is to be found on the property. There are 20 varieties that can be used for building purposes.

D. C. Sweet and John Falley of Hollywood have been at Tombstone to inspect mining property owned by Californian capital, which they represent. They have been examining the Brandt claims, known as the Free Coinage group, situated near the old State of Maine mine, in its day one of the largest producers of the district. A large vein of high-grade ore was opened recently, and development was to be started early in June.

JACKSON, CALIFORNIA

THE ARGONAUT, KENNEDY, OLD EUREKA, AND CENTRAL EUREKA.

Milling operations were resumed at the Argonaut mine on June 1, after a cessation of about two months. The fire discovered on the 4000-ft. level on March 27 is known to be burning still, but it is well under control, and strong bulkheads confine the fire to one level; this, fortunately, is not one on which the mill depends for ore. Mining and development are now under way both above and below the bulkheaded level. The odor of gas is plainly evident at all times in the vicinity of the Muldoon shaft, notwithstanding its being bulkheaded; the fire is known to be entirely on the Muldoon portion of the property, which accounts for miners working in safety in the Argonaut proper. About two weeks ago, one of the bulkheads failed and revived the fire, but this caused only a few days' delay, and 40 or more employees returned to work as soon as the bulkhead could be made tight; only a short time will elapse before the usual crew will be employed. The early return of this great mine to normal conditions means much to Amador county, as the Argonaut ordinarily employed over 200 men, and until the fire broke out, was one of the largest gold producers in the State. N. S. Kelsey is general manager of the property, which is equipped with a new 60-stamp mill and high-class electrically-driven machinery.

Aside from a cessation of mining for a few days when fumes from the Argonaut mine penetrated the Kennedy workings, adjoining the Argonaut on the north, the Kennedy continued in full operation with its 100-stamp mill. Webb Smith is still in charge of this mine.

A station has been cut on the 3000-ft. level of the Old Eureka mine at Sutter Creek and shaft-sinking from a point nearly 100 ft. below this station will be resumed shortly. A large amount of development will be done from the 3000-ft. station, both north and south, to prove the existence on that level of the veins worked so profitably in the early days on levels nearer the surface. Low-grade ore in large quantities is exposed on the 1200, 1600, and 2100-ft. levels, ore that could be worked far more profitably by modern methods than was possible when the mine was last worked over 30 years ago. This factor and the opening of high-grade ore found since re-opening the mine ensure the future success of the Old Eureka, and the discoveries at greater depth in the Central Eureka promise good things at similar depth for its neighbor. In addition to the expense incurred in equipping and unwatering the old mine to 2190 ft., formerly the deepest point, the new owners have enlarged the old shaft from one to three compartments from the 1600-ft. level down, and sunk the shaft nearly 1000 ft. additional. A great future is predicted for this old-time producer, after it has been sufficiently opened to warrant the erection of a mill. T. C. Gorrie is general manager, and Timothy Donovan is foreman. It is of interest to know that many of the enterprising men who have staked their money in the Old Eureka are also heavily interested in the Lincoln Gold Mining Co., which recently acquired the Wildman, Mahoney, and Lincoln mines, so that practically the same people own the mineral rights to a long stretch of the Mother Lode underlying the city of Sutter Creek.

Sinking at the rate of about 17 ft. per week continues at the Central Eureka mine, where the shaft has now reached a depth of 3720 ft. For 100 ft. or more, the shaft has been sunk in hard greenstone, but the contact slates have been reached. Progress will doubtless be better in this softer ground, until the point desired is reached. The present contractors are sinking the shaft 210 ft. at $31 per foot, this to cover cost of labor and explosives. The closing of this contract will mean a depth of nearly 275 ft. below the 3500-ft. station. The intention is to cut a large station at 3700 ft., and prospect from that point the good ore now being mined on the 3500-ft. level and the 3600-ft. or whize-level, on which more than half of the mill is constantly employed while development work proceeds. A. S. Howe is superintendent and H. Warrington is assistant.

DULUTH, MINNESOTA

MEETING OF SAFETY ENGINEERS.

Managers, superintendents, and safety engineers numbering 100, according to the estimate of B. O. Pickard of the U. S. Bureau of Mines, were to gather at Duluth on June 19 and 20 for the first important district safety conference for metal mine officials ever held in the United States. Mr. Pickard, who is district mining engineer for the Bureau in the mining States adjoining Lake Superior, arranged this conference after observing the results of a similar meeting at Houghton a month ago, the latter being for upper Michigan peninsula safety-men only. The Duluth conference is for a discussion of safety problems affecting the copper mines of Michigan, iron mines of Michigan and Minnesota, and zinc mines of Wisconsin. A committee consisting of George Martinson of Gilbert, Minnesota; William Conibear of Ishpeming, Michigan; and Stephen Quayle of Virginia, Minnesota, had the program in hand. C. E. Julian, of the U. S. Bureau of Mines experiment station at the University of Minnesota, Minneapolis, will give a welfare talk. Other speakers and papers will be as follows:

'Statistics and Practical Forms for Accident Records', A. H. Fay, Bureau of Mines, Washington, D. C. 'Safety in Mining Stopes', M. E. Richards, general manager, Judson Mining Co., Crystal Falls, Michigan. 'Care and Welfare of Labor', C. K. Quinn, president Quinn mining interests, Minnesota. 'The True Meaning of 'Safety First',' A. K. Krogdahl, Virginia, Minnesota. 'Problems in the Work of Accident Prevention', William Cinibear, chief safety engineer, Cleveland Cliffs Iron Mining Co., Ishpeming, Michigan. 'Mine Fire and Accident Signals', B. O. Pickard. Other speakers were to discuss safety in open-pit mines, vocational schools for miners, safety organizations for mining companies, rehabilitation of injured miners, and kindred subjects.

PORCUPINE, ONTARIO

LABOR TROUBLES.—NEW POWER SCHEME.

The mining fields of northern Ontario are affected by the general unrest and dissatisfaction prevailing in nearly all industries, and demands for recognition of the union, increased pay, and shorter hours have been made by the miners of Cobalt, Porcupine, and Kirkland Lake. These have been coupled by threats of a walk-out; Cobalt miners are reported to have voted in favor of a strike. It is considered hardly likely that any serious trouble will result, as it appears that the movement will not be financially supported by the international union; moreover, the local union is by no means a strong body, as only about half of the mine employees are members. The Porcupine miners have declared against a strike, and the position at Kirkland Lake is still undecided.

MATACHEWAN.—It is proposed to generate electric power for the field at Matachewan falls six miles north. Sutcliffe and Neelands, of New Liskeard, who have obtained permission from the Ontario government to develop the falls, have sold a half-interest to F. C. Sutherland & Co. of Toronto. The falls have a nearly vertical drop of 41 ft., rendering development a comparatively easy matter. At the Matachewan mine (formerly the Otisse) a rich lens of ore has been opened between the 50 and 100-ft. levels, showing much free gold.

WEST SHINING TREE.—An option on the Foisey claims, which include ¾ mile of the Ribble vein, has been given to E. J. Longyear Co., of Minneapolis and Sudbury. The same firm recently took over the Bennett claim. Their entrance into this field is regarded as assuring that its value will be thoroughly tested.

GOLDFIELD, NEVADA

PREPARATORY WORK BY THE DEVELOPMENT COMPANY.—GRANDMA AND ATLANTA.

Enlarging and repairing of what will be made the main haulage-way in the Combination mine has been started by the Goldfield Development Co. The main drift used during operations by the Consolidated will be used for this purpose. The cross-cut from this drift to the shaft, through which all ore in the Combination will be hoisted, has been advanced 150 ft. or half-way to the shaft. The drift and cross-cut will not be double-tracked as at first planned, as the electric locomotive to be used will haul over 20 tons on each trip from the chutes, which is considered ample. Raises are being driven at 50 instead of 25-ft. intervals, as was at first planned, it being considered that there will be less inconvenience from timbers blocking the raises than was at first thought. The first half of each raise above the haulage-way will be vertical. At the top will be a grizzley and space for shovelers to move the material as it comes from the upper or inclined half of the raise, which will be driven into the vein-filling. The incline raises will be made of sufficient size for the timbers that will be drawn with the ore to pass through, and it is believed that little blasting will be necessary to ensure a continuous flow. The timbers will be lowered through a compartment in the vertical raise to the haulage-way. The hoisting plant formerly in use at the Mohawk has been erected at the shaft, and grading is being done for ore-bins and railroad track, 900 ft. of which will have to be moved a short distance, so as to have it extend parallel to the bins. The Red Top is being prepared so the ore to be mined there can all be hoisted from the first level of the Laguna shaft. The shrinkage system can be used in the Red Top, but it has been determined that in the Mohawk, where the vein is flatter, the handling of the material will be left to lessees for the present. The mining of stope-filling and low-grade ore in place in the Mohawk is believed to hold great possibilities, but owing to the flat dip of the vein, the cost would be heavy because of the number of levels from which it would be necessary to work. The Development company's production during April was 922 dry tons having a gross value of $33,907, or an average value per ton of $36.77. The ore came from all mines, from the operations of both the company and lessees.

The Grandma has started a cross-cut west from the north-east drift on the 815-ft. level. The drift was driven in a cross-vein without opening pay-ore, and a cross-cut will be extended to the foot-wall of the vein in what may be the last work on this level before sinking of the shaft is resumed. It is estimated that the wall will be reached within 100 ft. from the drift.

The Atlanta is driving south-east on the 1900-ft. level, in an 8-ft. shoot of unpayable ore in the main Atlanta vein. This shoot is regarded as the most promising opened by the main east cross-cut in penetrating the vein.

HOUGHTON, MICHIGAN

OPERATIONS AT THE CALUMET & HECLA.

Calumet & Hecla's tailing reclamation dredge is again in commission, after having been in drydock at Point Mills. The revolving screen has been removed. The grinding and leaching plants are at full capacity, and the oil-flotation plant connected therewith will be in operation in three months. The C. & H. output is down to a 50% basis. Thirteen stamps out of twenty-eight are dropping at the mills, crushing conglomerate ore only. A small quantity from the Osceola amygdaloid lode comes from necessary shipments of ore extracted during development. Fourteen furnaces are working at the smelter. The only construction work that C. & H. is doing is erection of steel for the flotation plant. When this plant is working all of the conglomerate slime will receive either treatment by flotation or leaching.

DIVIDE, NEVADA

CHAMBER OF COMMERCE FORMED.—LATEST DEVELOPMENTS.

Mine-owners and business-men of Divide and Tonopah have organized the Divide-Tonopah Chamber of Commerce. The following general council was elected: George Wingfield, H. C. Brougher, John H. Miller, George H. Garry, Thomas J. Lynch, E. J. Erickson, A. C.

Raycraft, E. H. McMurray, J. Grant Crumley, M. M. Detch, James Grimes, J. M. Gilfoyle, Thomas Lindsay, Herman Albert, E. R. Kelly, J. K. Turner, John G. Kirchen, A. L. D'Arcy, Joseph H. Hutchinson, J. W. Hutchinson, and William Forman.

The Tonopah Divide company continues development, the main work being the cross-cut toward the vein at 585 ft. depth. Two raises have been driven from 480 to 370 ft., both in good ore. They were put up for ventilation and development purposes.

The Divide Extension, which opened rich ore at a depth of 45 ft. two weeks ago, in a new shaft sunk 450 ft. north of the old shaft, has proved the vein to be 55 ft. wide. A 6-in. streak on the hanging wall assays $1500 in silver and $100 in gold. Four feet next to this averages $90 per ton. The drift on the other side of the vein yields $100 across the face, and between the two drifts the ore averages $26. The old shaft is now 425 ft. deep. Machinery is being erected.

The Gold Reef Divide has a compressor and machine-drills, and sinking is under way below 135 ft. Present indications are reported to be favorable.

Among the many outside properties, prospecting for best sites for shafts is under way.

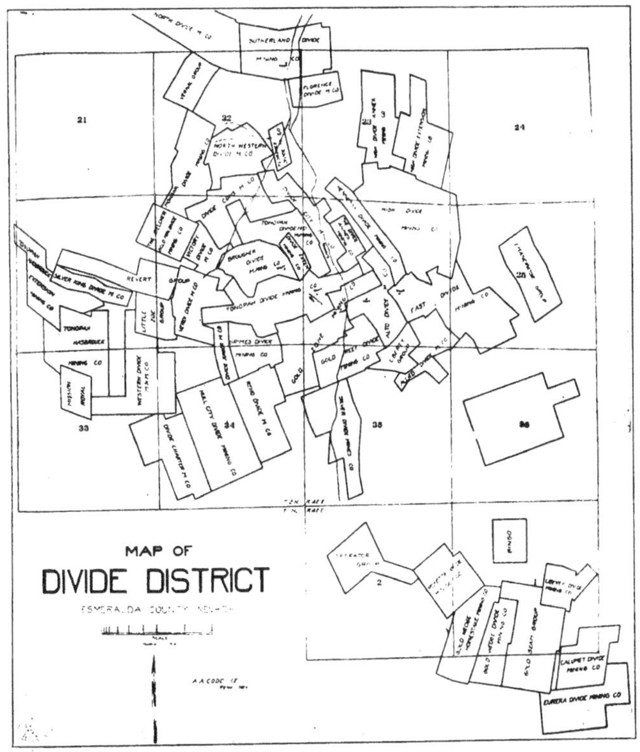

The War Minerals Relief Commission will be in San Francisco during July, the date not being fixed yet. According to an announcement made on the 23rd, claimants must file a brief upon the findings made by the Commission within 20 days. The claim will then be submitted to the Department of the Interior.

ALASKA

Fairbanks.—Boundaries of the Nenana recording precinct have been changed by order of court, giving that precinct more territory. The change is considered advantageous to miners, who will not be compelled to make the long journey to Fairbanks to record their papers.

Juneau.—All quartz mining companies in Alaska are complaining about the scarcity of labor. While all are working full time, more men are needed to obtain the disired results. The pay offered, from $4.50 to $6 per day, is sure, the accommodations are first class, and the work is steady, according to the May Monthly Bulletin of the Alaska Bureau of Publicity, of which E. J. White is chief. One trouble is that many of the men who went away during the War have not returned, and no others have come back to replace them.

CALIFORNIA

Bishop.—The Wilshire Consolidated Co. has added flotation equipment to its gold mine on Bishop creek and begun treatment of dumps. Unwatering of the mine has been started, and it is proposed to extract ore at capacity. With the improved mill the management hopes to treat the refractory ore without further trouble.

Darwin.—From its Lucky Jim mine, the Darwin Development Co. is shipping silver-lead ore to smelters in Utah. Operations were recently increased, and the property is being prepared for a larger output. Shipments of silver-lead ore are going out from the Rip Van Winkle, Wonder, Fernando, and other mines in this part. Numerous properties have been re-opened since silver passed the dollar mark.

Fresno.—Chrome miners in this county—about 40 in all—were to organize on June 28 to aid the War Minerals Relief Commission, which is to sit at Los Angeles and San Francisco early in July. Estimated losses in this region amount to $35,000. The chrome deposits are over 30 miles east and north-east of Fresno, near Piedra and Academy.

At the meeting of chrome men here last week it was decided to demand that the War Minerals Relief Commission hold a sitting at Fresno.

Grass Valley.—The cycle of events in the strike may be summarized as under:

Nine hundred men are out. At a meeting held on the 16th it was voted unanimously to strike for a wage increase of 50 cents. This decision was reached after a long discussion between the superintendents of the Empire, North Star, and Allison Ranch mines and the men. The managers were formally notified of the action on the 17th. During the conference, the following communication from the Empire Mines Co. was read: "We will be glad to welcome the return of our employees to their work. If we could raise the price of our product we would gladly increase wages. We sincerely hope that our employees will realize our position and return to their work." F. C. Nobs of the Empire, A. B. Foote of the North Star, and C. A. Brockington of the Golden Center each made a statement of considerable length. Mr. Foote said that the North Star had been run on a narrow margin for two years past, and continued operations because of a dislike to discharge men who had been with the company for many years. In his opinion it would have been a financial advantage to have closed the mine until the time was more favorable for gold mining. Mr. Brockington represented a promotion company, leasing, tributing, and contracting, in an effort to find ore. Increased wages would come from more assessments. Mr. Nobs stated that his mine was privately owned and he was not authorized to make a statement.

A former statement, and one of the points brought out in the controversy, that men from the Federal Employment Bureau at San Francisco were paid $4.50 per day at the North Star mine, was charged to a clerk's error, and Mr. Foote denied that his company placed an advertisement in the 'Chronicle' offering that rate.

Many surface men have signed the agreement, but there has been no enthusiasm to join. No attempt has been made by the engineers and pumpmen to leave their posts. The North Star men have not yet called for their checks. The Champion mine, near Nevada City, owned by the North Star, has not been affected; but if the men go out, pumps will be removed. A clean-up of the mill and cyanide plant was made on the 16th. At the Champion, a secret vote was taken on the 17th, but before voting, the superintendent, Roy Tremeroux, stated that they were either to close the property or keep it running. The vote resulted in 65 for operation and 9 against. Ten men quit but work was resumed.

The miners held another meeting on the 17th, at which the different committees appointed to interview the managers reported that the position remained as on the 13th. Mr. Ingram, State Senator, appealed to the men to consider the matter of inviting the State Labor Commissioner to come here and settle the trouble. Many favored the plan, but it was voted down by a large majority. The mine superintendents have not receded from the stand already taken. A motion was adopted to call out the pumpmen and enginemen on 48 hours' notice, and a committee was appointed to serve notice upon the superintendents on the 18th.

At the Pennsylvania and Empire mines, at Grass Valley, 19 underground mules were taken out.

On the 19th the pumps were being taken out of the North Star mine.

A conference was held on the 19th between a committee of citizens and miners, who later met the superintendents; but there was no result therefrom. The miners' organization on that night voted to extend the ultimatum given to withdraw the engine and pump-men in 24 hours. A committee of 12 citizens and 12 striking miners met in accordance with previous arrangement. A free discussion followed to devise some way out of the difficulty. There being no result, the same citizen committee invited the mine operators to confer, and a large part of the afternoon was spent in discussion. Nearly all the mines were represented;

nothing definite came of it. G. W. Starr, of the Empire, urged the men to return to work and help him carry out the plans under way at the mine to bring it to a condition whereby higher wages may be paid. The question of living costs came up, and he promised to assist in every way possible.

While the pumps are being removed from the North Star and Empire mines, both managements stated that this is but a precautionary measure, and did not necessarily mean an indefinite closing. Mr. Starr stated that the mines would be operated the moment the men returned.

On the 22nd, John S. Blair, deputy State Labor Commissioner, arrived at Grass Valley to investigate the dispute.

The engine and pumpmen at all mines quit work at 11 a.m. on Sunday.

C. A. Brockington of the Allison Ranch mine has stated that his company will accede to the new wage-schedule demanded by the miners for all men employed in those departments that have been affected by the strike, but only for a limited number so employed. At the same time he made it understood that only a few men would be affected, and that the remainder of the force was under the contract and tributing system, and in no way affected by the strike.

The miners decided that picketing should be enforced at once; this is to be confined to public streets and highways only. A peace committee was formed and members were to be on duty continuously to guard against possible violence or overt acts.

Porterville.—The new plant of the McKnight Fire Brick Co. commenced work on June 19. Chrome, magnesite, and silica from Californian deposits are used.

Trona.—In the Slate range of Inyo county, 8 miles northeast from this place, the Slate Range Minerals Co., whose head office is at Bakersfield, is operating. The number of men employed is from 20 to 40. Production in 1918 was 1,331,440 lb. of lead, 1786 oz. of gold, 64,389 oz. of silver, and 90,124 lb. of copper. The gross receipts were $142,822. The ore is mainly a lead carbonate with oxides, sulphates, and sulphides. The company is erecting a 50-ton concentrating mill, employing gravity and flotation. It has erected an 8-mile electric power-line. The mill is to treat low-grade ore, valued from $15 to $20 per ton. It is expected to be in operation by about July 15. There are three years supply blocked out. High-grade ore is shipped to the U. S. S. & R. Co. at Midvale, Utah. Morris B. Parker is superintendent.

Weaverville.—The contractor, F. Rolandi of San Francisco, for construction of 11 miles of highway in this county is preparing camps at Big Bar and North Fork, on the Trinity river. This road connects with and is part of the State highway from Eureka to Redding.

COLORADO

Bonanza.—The Rawley mine in Saguache county has been sold to Eastern people for a large sum. The main tunnel is 6235 ft. long, cutting orebodies at a depth of 1200 ft. Total workings amount to over 15,000 ft. Ore exposed is estimated at 200,000 tons, worth $25 per ton in silver, gold, copper, and lead. An aerial tram, 7 miles long, will connect with the proposed mill at Shirley on a branch of the D. & R. G. railroad.

Cripple Creek.—According to G. M. Taylor, the receiver, the Short Line will be in operation again by July 20. The roadbed is being repaired and a bridge re-built. One freight and one passenger train will be run for a start.

The United Gold Mines in May produced 1450 tons of ore worth $60,000. The Anderson & Benkelman lease at the Trail mine yielded 1250 tons of the total. Monthly royalties from lessees amount to $10,000. The company's cash balance is about $105,000.

A specimen from the 2100-ft. level of the Portland mine is on view at Colorado Springs. It assays 574 oz. of gold and 357 oz. of silver per ton. The ore was found on a waste pile on the tunnel-level. Water from the Portland flowing into the Roosevelt drainage-tunnel is only 50 gallons per minute.

La Plata.—There is a marked contrast between the beginning of this season and that of last year, and the present outlook is favorable for heavy production. The principal incentive to mining here is the higher price of silver, although the ores are principally gold-bearing with moderate silver content.

Red Mountain.—An important development is reported from the Barstow, being developed under lease by C. R. Wilfley & Co. A vein carrying numerous pockets of rich gold-silver ore has been found. The high-grade ore is in narrow streaks.

IDAHO

Leadore.—The Sunset M. & M. Co. has started its new 100-ton mill. The ore carries 14% lead and 12 oz. silver per ton. The concentration ratio is 4 into 1. W. Van Wagenen is superintendent.

Murray.—The Yukon Gold Co.'s dredge on Prichard creek is being overhauled. The principal repair is to be an 18-ton spud, several steel plates being cracked. The hull is also to be riveted at the stern, while the revolving-screen and driving gear are receiving attention. The 6600-volt transformers are to be fireproofed.

Wallace.—The Idaho-Nevada Exploration Co.'s property near here was sold at forced sale on June 9 for $60,000. The mortgage and interest totaled $73,916. The original owners bid in for the mine.

The labor question in the Coeur d'Alene region is unchanged from last week, but it is believed that therh will be no strike. R. M. McWade, U. S. Conciliation Commissioner from the Federal Department of Labor, arrived last week and is making a personal investigation from all concerned.

MICHIGAN

Houghton.—Copper production from this region during May was the lowest on record for any single month in 16 years, excepting the worst months of the strike period of 1913. The metal output was 13,106,220 lb., recovered from 555,550 tons of ore.

The Seneca has purchased the Gratiot property adjoining, for $25,000 cash and terms. The Lewisohn's arranged the deal. The Seneca is soon to start a cross-cut on its 1700-ft. level.

MONTANA

Anaconda.—The new 575-ft. stack at the Anaconda reduction works is in full working order, the second half of the furnaces being connected on June 9.

Basin.—This old district is to be revived by the financing of the Jib Mining Co. by Salt Lake and Montana people. A. E. Spriggs and Marcus Hewett are largely interested. The mines to be re-opened are the Hope and Katie, the former having been a large producer of silver ore, so has the latter. The district has produced many millions in silver. A new electric hoist is to be erected, and probably a mill.

NEVADA

Mason.—It is proposed to consolidate the Bluestone, Mason Valley, and Nevada Douglas properties in Lyon county. This will include the smelter at Thompson and the Nevada Copper Belt railway.

McGill.—Gold has been found in Rattlesnake canyon, and a small stampede set in last week.

Tonopah.—The West End and Jim Butler companies have made an agreement whereby the former is to lease a large block of the latter's ground directly south of the West End original claim. The West End will extract the ore and treat it, the profits to be its until the sum of $33,000 is reached, after which the profits will be divided between the two companies. This ground is part of that in dispute, and so settles the trouble.

The Tonopah Extension is driving a raise from the 1440-ft. level, and is in 10 ft. of milling ore, an important development.

Virginia City.—Both the Con. Virginia and Ophir mines are yielding rich ore, the former from 2100 ft., the latter from 1800 ft. depth. During the last three months they have produced $102,260 and $84,681, respectively.

UTAH

Bingham.—The Bingham Mines Co. pays 25 cents per share, equal to $37,500, on June 30. This is the second for 1919, and makes $637,500 to date.

Eureka.—The Chief Consolidated is busy putting in the new pumps at 1800, 1200, and 600 ft., where there are already small pumps at work. The new units have a capacity of 1000 g.p.m., compared with 260 for the present equipment.

Park City.—Miners on strike held a meeting on June 17 to decide whether they return to work or not. The resident class of men rather favored calling off the dispute, and in the end the strike was called off and the companies notified to that effect.

CANADA

British Columbia

Fernie.—A ludicrous situation has arisen from the strike here. S. Whitehouse, president of the local miner's union, has wired to the Hon. John Oliver, Premier of British Columbia, informing him that it was stated in a local paper that the Crow's Nest Pass Coal Co. intended to close its mine permanently. Mr. Whitehouse wanted to know what the Government would do, in the event of the company carrying out its threat, as such a course would mean the enforced idleness of a large number of men. Mr. Whitehouse is the president of the union that called the present strike. The Premier has replied, stating that he understands the company is taking such measures as it deems necessary under the circumstances to protect its property.

Grand Forks.—The Granby Consolidated smelter here was forced to suspend operations on the 21st on account of shortage of coke from Crows Nest Pass, where the coal mines are closed by a strike. The copper mines at Phoenix and the smelter here may be stopped for good.

Ontario

Kirkland Lake.—Preliminary work has been started on the new 7-mile motor road from Swastika to this place.

The Miner's Union has asked operators for a minimum of $4.50 per shift underground and $4 in the mills and on the surface, half time on Saturdays with full pay, time and a half for overtime and double time for Sundays, and recognition of the branch of the Union.

The strike that started is proving a 'boomerang', according to 'The Northern Miner' of Cobalt. Instead of getting demands, the Union has lost over half its members. About 300 men have left, and, despite the by-laws passed by the Union against leaving, 100 left by the morning train on the 13th. Ninety per cent of those leaving were foreigners, showing the high proportion of this class of labor employed and its instability. The situation is worrying Union officials, as the only ones remaining are a few single men living at the Union hall, and married men whom companies are allowing to stay in mine cottages. The strike threatens to smash the Union completely, as the exodus shows signs of continuing. Officials seem to have lost control of the men. All the mines are closed.

PERSONAL

Note. The Editor invites members of the profession to send particulars of their work and appointments. The information is interesting to our readers.

John D. Kearns, of Vancouver, is here.

J. R. Finlay is at Bear Valley, California.

F. L. Sizer has returned from Tonopah, Nevada.

R. B. Lamb, of New York, is in Colorado on professional work.

Richard S. McIntyre has returned to Berkeley from Burma.

Leslie Webb, of the Wedge Mechanical Furnace Co. of Philadelphia, is here.

H. D. G. Reynolds is returning to the mines of the Irtysh Corporation in Siberia.

James F. Kemp has been re-appointed Professor of Geology in Columbia University.

Donald G. Campbell, of Seattle, has gone on a journey of exploration to Lost River, Alaska.

C. W. Adams has gone from the Murray plant to the East Helena plant of the A. S. & R. Co.

Karl Eilers, a vice-president of the A. S. & R. Co., was in San Francisco last week, on a tour of inspection.

Hallet R. Robbins, Captain in the Military Intelligence Division, has returned from Peking and is now at Washington.

Oliver E. Jager has been appointed metallurgist to the British-America Nickel Corporation at Nickelton, in Ontario, Canada.

H. K. Masters, of W. R. Grace & Co., has been elected a member of the Board of Managers of the New York Metal Exchange.

J. A. Burgess has been promoted from superintendent to general manager of the United Eastern Mining Co., at Oatman, Arizona.

Ben B. Lawrence, who recently underwent a serious operation, is sojourning in California, spending a few days at the Bohemian grove.

Forbes Rickard, of Denver, has been examining the old Cashin copper mine, in the Paradox district, Colorado, for the Michigan Securities Corporation.

Charles E. Newton has been appointed Dean of the Oregon School of Mines, Corvallis, Oregon. He was formerly Associate Professor of Metallurgy at that institution.

G. K. Williams, in charge of the mechanical engineering department of the Chile Exploration Co.'s property at Chuquicamata, Chile, was at Salt Lake City on June 14.

J. F. McClelland has resigned as professor at Yale University and is now connected with the Industrial Department of the Liberty National Bank of New York, at 120 Broadway.

V. H. Hughes, petroleum and mining geologist, announces that he has severed his connection with the firm of Valerius, McNutt & Hughes, and has opened offices at 326 Mayo Bdg., Tulsa, Oklahoma.

Scott Turner was married on June 25 to Miss Amy Prudden of Lansing, Michigan. He has succeeded **D'Arcy Weatherbe** as consulting engineer to the Mining Corporation of Canada, and will reside at Toronto.

Arthur C. Terrill, for the last four years head of the department of Mining Engineering at the University of Kansas, Lawrence, Kansas, has resigned and accepted an appointment with the Kansas State Geological Survey. On July 1 he will move to Baxter Springs to take charge of lead and zinc investigations in south-eastern Kansas.

John J. Broderick, of the Broderick & Bascom Rope Co., died on June 7 at St. Louis.

THE METAL MARKET

METAL PRICES

San Francisco, June 24

Aluminum-dust, cents per pound	50—60
Antimony, cents per pound	8.50
Copper, electrolytic, cents per pound	18.25
Lead, pig, cents per pound	5.65—6.65
Platinum, pure, per ounce	$105
Platinum, 10% iridium, per ounce	$115
Quicksilver, per flask of 75 lb	$95
Spelter, cents per pound	8.25
Zinc-dust, cents per pound	9—12

EASTERN METAL MARKET

(By wire from New York)

June 24.—Copper is strong and advancing. Lead is active and firm. Spelter is active and higher.

SILVER

Below are given official or ticker quotations, in cents per ounce of silver 999 fine. From April 23, 1918, the United States government paid $1 per ounce for all silver purchased by it, fixing a maximum of $1.01½ on August 15, 1918, and will continue to pay $1 until the quantity specified under the Act is purchased, probably extending over several years. On May 5, 1919, all restrictions on the metal were removed, resulting in fluctuations. During the restricted period, the British government fixed the maximum price five times, the last being on March 25, 1919, on account of the low rate of sterling exchange, but removed all restrictions on May 10. The equivalent of dollar silver (1000 fine) in British currency is 46.65 pence per ounce (925 fine), calculated at the normal rate of exchange.

Date		New York Cents	London pence	Average week ending		Cents	Pence
June	18	112.60	54.87	May	13	109.33	52.98
"	19	112.37	54.75	"	20	110.33	53.50
"	20	111.75	54.50	"	27	106.41	52.17
"	21	111.25	54.25	June	3	108.90	52.90
"	22 Sunday			"	10	109.43	53.27
"	23	110.12	53.75	"	17	111.98	54.48
"	24	111.12	54.31	"	24	111.52	54.40

Monthly averages

	1917	1918	1919		1917	1918	1919
Jan.	75.14	88.72	101.12	July	78.92	99.62	....
Feb.	77.54	85.79	101.12	Aug.	85.40	100.31	....
Mch.	74.13	88.11	101.12	Sept.	100.73	101.12	....
Apr.	72.51	95.35	101.12	Oct.	87.38	101.12	....
May	74.61	99.50	107.23	Nov.	85.97	101.12	....
June	76.44	99.50	....	Dec.	85.97	101.12	....

The Director of the Mint, Raymond T. Baker, is reported to have said at Reno on June 20 that the price of silver will not fall below one dollar per ounce in less than seven years, and probably not for several years later than that time. He said that the probability of Congress repealing the Pittman silver bill was remote, and continued: "If the Government were to purchase the entire silver production of the United States for the next five years, the silver to be melted and sold to the allies under the terms of the Pittman bill would not be replaced. It would be impossible to purchase the entire output of the mines of the United States, hence it will be a somewhat longer period than five years, I should say not less than seven years, before the replacement would be completed. The Government has melted under the Pittman bill, 270,000,000 oz., and 200,000,000 oz. has been sent abroad."

COPPER

Price of electrolytic in New York, in cents per pound.

Date			Average week ending		
June	18	17.87	May	13	15.37
"	19	17.75	"	20	16.24
"	20	17.75	"	27	16.16
"	21	17.87	June	3	16.37
"	22 Sunday		"	10	16.81
"	23	18.00	"	17	17.58
"	24	18.12	"	24	17.89

Monthly averages

	1917	1918	1919		1917	1918	1919
Jan.	29.53	23.50	20.43	July	29.67	26.00	....
Feb.	34.57	23.50	17.34	Aug.	27.42	26.00	....
Mch.	36.00	23.50	15.05	Sept.	25.11	26.00	....
Apr.	33.16	23.50	15.23	Oct.	23.50	26.00	....
May	31.69	23.50	15.91	Nov.	23.50	26.00	....
June	32.57	23.50	....	Dec.	23.50	26.00	....

Copper production of 17 of the large mines in North and South America during May totaled 83,352,555 lb., a gain of 1,350,000 lb. over April. The output from all sources was estimated at 115,000,000 pounds.

ZINC

Zinc is quoted as spelter, standard Western brands, New York delivery, in cents per pound:

Date			Average week ending		
June	18	6.90	May	13	6.31
"	19	6.95	"	20	6.46
"	20	6.95	"	27	6.59
"	21	7.00	June	3	6.53
"	22 Sunday		"	10	6.58
"	23	7.15	"	17	6.88
"	24	7.20	"	24	7.02

Monthly averages

	1917	1918	1919		1917	1918	1919
Jan.	9.75	7.78	7.44	July	8.98	8.72	....
Feb.	10.45	7.97	6.71	Aug.	8.58	8.87	....
Mch.	10.78	7.97	6.53	Sept.	8.33	9.58	....
Apr.	10.20	7.04	6.40	Oct.	8.32	9.11	....
May	9.41	7.92	6.43	Nov.	7.70	8.75	....
June	9.63	7.92	....	Dec.	7.84	8.49	....

Zinc ore, basis 60% metal, averaged $41 per ton at Joplin last week. The Tri-State output was 8794 tons. Prices gained $1, due to better demand.

Spelter produced in the United States during 1918, according to C. E. Siebenthal of the U. S. Geological Survey, totaled 492,405 short tons from domestic sources, compared with 584,597 tons in 1917. Metal from foreign ore decreased from 84,970 to 25,522 tons, and re-distilled secondary from 16,835 to 9597 tons. The grades and prices were:

Grade	1917 Tons	1917 Cents	1918 Tons	1918 Cents
A	97,707	14.0	120,073	11.1
B	69,189	12.7	98,087	10.7
C	148,749	9.4	98,584	8.0
D	370,763	9.0	230,930	7.9
Total and average	686,408	10.2	527,524	9.1
Total value	$140,027,000		$96,000,000	

Before the Ways and Means Committee of the House of Representatives at Washington last week, Paul Edwards, representing Joplin zinc operators, asked for a duty of 2¢ on metal content of imported zinc ore instead of the existing duty of 10% ad valorem. He explained it cost $90 per ton to get American zinc ore to smelters, while it cost only $24 per ton to get foreign zinc ore to smelters. Chairman Fordney suggested that tariff valuation on imported ores be made on American basis, instead of foreign basis of price.

LEAD

Lead is quoted in cents per pound, New York delivery.

Date			Average week ending		
June	18	5.35	May	13	4.85
"	19	5.35	"	20	5.05
"	20	5.35	"	27	5.27
"	21	5.35	June	3	5.22
"	22 Sunday		"	10	5.20
"	23	5.35	"	17	5.38
"	24	5.40	"	24	5.36

Monthly averages

	1917	1918	1919		1917	1918	1919
Jan.	7.64	6.85	5.60	July	10.93	8.03	....
Feb.	9.10	7.07	5.13	Aug.	10.75	8.05	....
Mch.	10.07	7.26	5.24	Sept.	9.07	8.05	....
Apr.	9.38	6.99	5.05	Oct.	6.97	8.05	....
May	10.29	6.88	5.04	Nov.	6.38	8.05	....
June	11.74	7.59	....	Dec.	6.40	6.90	....

Lead ore, basis 80% metal, averaged $90 per ton at Joplin last week. The Tri-State output was 1308 tons. The gain was $2.50 per ton.

QUICKSILVER

The primary market for quicksilver is San Francisco, California being the largest producer. The price is fixed in the open market, according to quantity. Prices, in dollars per flask of 75 pounds:

Date					
May	27	92.00	June	10	92.00
June	3	95.00	"	17	95.00
			"	24	95.00

Monthly averages

	1917	1918	1919		1917	1918	1919
Jan.	81.00	128.00	103.75	July	102.00	120.00	....
Feb.	126.25	118.00	90.00	Aug.	115.00	120.00	....
Mch.	113.75	112.00	72.80	Sept.	112.00	120.00	....
Apr.	114.50	115.00	73.12	Oct.	102.00	120.00	....
May	104.00	110.00	81.80	Nov.	102.50	120.00	....
June	85.50	112.00	....	Dec.	117.42	115.00	....

TIN

Prices in New York, in cents per pound. The monthly averages in 1918 are nominal. On December 3 the War Industries Board fixed the price to consumers and jobbers at 72½c. f.o.b. Chicago and Eastern points, and 71½c. on the Pacific Coast. This will continue until the U. S. Steel Products Co.'s stock is consumed.

Monthly averages

	1917	1918	1919		1917	1918	1919
Jan.	44.10	85.13	71.50	July	62.60	93.00	....
Feb.	51.47	85.00	72.44	Aug.	62.53	91.33	....
Mch.	54.27	85.00	72.50	Sept.	61.54	80.40	....
Apr.	55.63	88.53	72.50	Oct.	62.24	78.82	....
May	63.21	100.01	72.50	Nov.	74.18	73.67	....
June	61.93	91.00	....	Dec.	85.00	71.52	....

The War Trade Board announces that applications will now be considered for licenses to import pig tin and all metal alloys containing tin, including tin drosses, tin oxides, solder drosses, type metals, anti-friction metals, waste metals, and other metals containing tin; subject, however, to the following conditions and limitations: (1) that such licenses will permit the importation only of shipments made from points of origin on or after June 30, 1919; and (2) that such import licenses will not be valid for entry until August 1, 1919.

Eastern Metal Market

New York, June 18.

The markets are all moderately active and prices are generally steady to firm, with a slight easing in some cases.

Copper demand is reported to have revived again, and prices are advancing.

Lead has advanced, but is again quiet after a short buying movement.

Tin is very quiet, but prospects appear to be better for an open market.

Zinc rose suddenly last week with a sharp advance, but prices and demand have eased off again to some extent.

COPPER

The market today reached the 18c. level for electrolytic, and the tone is strong and firm. Demand has again appeared in increased volume this week, after three or four days of relative quietness. The movement a week ago resulted in an advance for electrolytic to 17.50 to 17.75c., New York, at which level the market turned quiet. The cause of the movement a week ago is now rather freely acknowledged as due, in part at least, to buying by Japanese consumers. The present advance proceeds largely from domestic consumers. Lake copper is quoted today at 18.12½ to 18.25c., New York. There is also some export demand, but as yet it is not heavy when compared with normal times. For August delivery many producers are well sold, some to a larger extent than desired and for far future shipment they are generally reluctant to commit themselves, although demand is fair.

Japan's buying is said to have been put through because it is cheaper for them to buy in America than it is to produce in their own country. It is no longer profitable for them to work some of their old mines, and others were gouged in taking advantage of the high war prices to such an extent that they are now out of business. Japan is now branching out for a share of the world's trade in manufactured copper and brass, and can be counted on as a regular buyer of American copper, having increased facilities for manufacturing during the War.

IRON AND STEEL

Assertions as to the improvement in steel are in stronger terms this week. In a number of finished lines, orders are larger, and some assert that the May output will be the lowest for the year. Steel-mill operations of one large interest in the Pittsburgh district have advanced to a 75% rate. One or two blast-furnaces may be blown-in there; blowing-out of furnaces has been the rule lately. The leading producer has been booking sheets for export at the rate of 1000 tons per day, with wire products an important item in the export demand. Italy has bought 1000 tons of heavy rails. Ocean-freight rates have been reduced, making British markets more accessible to American steel. The special heralded drive for the organization of steel works labor is not a new departure. For many months, with the help of the War Labor Board, the campaign to unionize the industry has gone on. The pig-iron market is still active, but buying is less spirited than two weeks ago.

LEAD

The market has again become quiet after a fair amount of purchasing during the past week. On June 11, the American Smelting & Refining Co. advanced its price from 5.25c. to 5.40c., New York, which resulted in a considerable amount of business; but after this, demand slowed down. The outside market immediately came abreast that of the leading interest. At present, some outside lots are available at slightly under the Trust price, and we quote the market at 5.35c., New York, or 5.10c., St. Louis, with the tone steady.

TIN

An open tin market is surely nearer. So far as the confines of the United States are concerned there may be open trading in the metal in less than two weeks. George Armsby, on June 16, announced that on that date only 577 tons of the allocated metal remains unsold, and that all restrictions in the United States will be removed as soon as the remainder is disposed of, with a definite announcement of the removal of restrictions promised in due course. Of equal interest and importance is the announcement of the War Trade Board that licenses will be permitted for the importation of tin and tin ore shipments from points of origin on and after June 30, and that such licenses will not be valid for entry until August 1. One interpretation of these interesting news items is to the effect that they mean that shipments from the Straits and from England can be made in July, valid for entry into the United States, however, only after August 1. A free and open world market is looked for early in August at the latest, and some interesting developments are likely even in July, when a free market is probable within the United States. At present the market is quiet. During the last week there have been sales of July shipment from the East at 52.25c., but the interest is not active in this position. Buying for shipment when restrictions are removed, has been spasmodic over the last two months, but the volume has been fairly large amounting to 4000 to 5000 tons, it is estimated. The onl[illegible] tin available continues to be quoted at 72.50c., New Yor[illegible] the fixed price.

ZINC

About the middle of last week the zinc market took a sudden spurt, and rose to higher levels as a result of [illegible]creased demand. The revival of interest came both f[illegible] dealers and from export buyers. So insistent was the [illegible]ying that prices for prime Western rose to 6.62½c., St. L[illegible]is, or 6.97½c., New York, on Wednesday, at which levels t[illegible]re was a good turnover. One producer reports sales at 6.[illegible] St. Louis. Since then demand has subsided and values [illegible] fallen slightly until today quotations for prime Wester[illegible] early delivery are 6.50c., St. Louis, or 6.85c., New [illegible] There is some export inquiry reported with sales m[illegible]e Japan and other countries.

ORES

Manganese: Indian ore is firmer at 70c. per u[illegible] board. Demand is light and supplies plentiful.

Manganese-Iron Alloys: There are inquiries f[illegible] tons of ferro before the market. Prices are firm [illegible] delivered, for the American alloy, and $121, seabo[illegible] the British. Most re-sale material has disappea[illegible] what is left is higher at a minimum of $115 [illegible] Spiegel is quiet at $27 to $30, furnace, with sales [illegible]ing 500 tons last week, most of it at $30, furnace.

Molybdenum: Buying is hand-to-mouth, with [illegible] nominal at 65 to 75c. per pound of MoS_2 in regul[illegible]trates.

Tungsten: Some business has been done in th[illegible] weeks, but less this last week than a week ago. [illegible]ment is to the effect that the ore available at $[illegible] has been absorbed, while $10 is asked for ot[illegible]r grad[illegible] such as high-grade and Bolivian ore. Some Cal[illegible]rnian ore is quoted as high as $17, delivered, Eastern [illegible]ints. No test of the ferro-tungsten market has been rep[illegible]ed, but it is believed that values are around $1 per pound [illegible] contained tungsten.

CPSIA information can be obtained
at www.ICGtesting.com
Printed in the USA
BVHW04*1114270818
525723BV00008B/212/P